January 25–27, 2012
Philadelphia, PA, USA

Association for Computing Machinery

Advancing Computing as a Science & Profession

POPL'12

Proceedings of the 39th Annual ACM SIGPLAN-SIGACT Symposium on

Principles of Programming Languages

Sponsored by:

ACM SIGPLAN

In cooperation with:

ACM SIGACT

Supported by:

Microsoft Research, ARM,
Committee on the Status of Women in Computing Research,
The Coalition to Diversify Computing, Intel, Jane Street Capital,
Mozilla, Oracle Labs, National Science Foundation, Google,
IBM Research, Amgen, & NEC

Association for
Computing Machinery

Advancing Computing as a Science & Profession

The Association for Computing Machinery
2 Penn Plaza, Suite 701
New York, New York 10121-0701

ISBN: 978-1-4503-1083-3

Additional copies may be ordered prepaid from:

ACM Order Department
PO Box 30777
New York, NY 10087-0777, USA

Phone: 1-800-342-6626 (USA and Canada)
+1-212-626-0500 (Global)
Fax: +1-212-944-1318
E-mail: acmhelp@acm.org
Hours of Operation: 8:30 am – 4:30 pm ET

ACM Order Number: 549121

Printed in the USA

Welcome

Welcome to Philadelphia and POPL 2012, the thirty-ninth edition of the ACM SIGPLAN-SIGACT Symposium on Principles of Programming Languages.

Philadelphia is a fitting locale for POPL. Not only was ENIAC, the first programmable electronic computer developed here, but Philadelphia has a long history of fostering scientific advancement through such venerable institutions as the Academy of Natural Sciences, the American Philosophical Society, the College of Physicians, the Franklin Institute, the Library Company of Philadelphia, the Wagner Free Institute of Science, and numerous colleges and universities.

POPL'12 features the following co-located events:

- The Workshop on Declarative Aspects and Applications of Multicore Programming (DAMP)
- The Workshop on Languages for Distributed Algorithms (LADA)
- Off the Beaten Track: The Workshop on Underrepresented Problems for Programming Language Researchers (OBT)
- The International Symposium on Practical Aspects of Declarative Languages (PADL)
- The Workshop on Partial Evaluation and Program Manipulation (PEPM)
- The Programming Languages Mentoring Workshop (PLMW)
- The Workshop on Programming Languages meets Program Verification (PLPV)
- The Workshop on Types in Language Design and Implementation (TLDI)
- The International Conference on Verification, Model Checking, and Abstract Interpretation (VMCAI)
- The International Conference on Verified Software: Theories, Tools, and Experiments (VSTTE)
- TutorialFest!

LADA, OBT, PLMW and TutorialFest! are entirely new events, and VSTTE is co-located with POPL for the first time this year.

Support from corporate sponsors helps keep POPL's registration fees modest, and in particular, enables low cost access by student registrants to all conference events. The generosity of the POPL '12 sponsors has enabled us to maintain this tradition.

A great deal of work behind the scenes is required to make POPL happen. Much of this work was carried out by the terrific group of volunteers from the programming languages community that worked with me on the POPL'12 Organizing Committee. I am lucky to have had the benefit of their talents, time, and advice. The POPL'11 General and PC chairs, Tom Ball and Mooly Sagiv, along with the other members of the POPL Steering Committee, provided sound counsel throughout the organizing process. The following professionals contributed conscientious and diligent support for the conference: John Lateulere of Integrated Management Solutions; MIchael Moshell and Carole, David, and Mandy Mann of Registration Systems Labs; Lisa Tolles of Sheridan Printing, and Ashley Cozzi, Adrienne Griscti, Ginger Ignatoff, Maritza Nichols, and Stephanie Sabal of ACM SIG services. Finally, I am grateful to IBM Research and my current employer, Google, for granting me the time and resources I needed to organize POPL, to my wife Elise and daughter Lydia for their steadfast support, and to the POPL Steering Committee for the privilege of serving the POPL community.

John Field
POPL '12 General Chair
Google, New York, USA

Foreword

It has been my great pleasure and privilege to serve as the Program Chair of the 39th POPL. This section of the proceedings gives me the opportunity to tell you about the process we used to select this year's excellent program, and to thank those who played an important role in that process.

Following the recent history of SIGPLAN conferences such as PLDI and ASPLOS, we used both a program committee (PC) and extended review committee (ERC) to assess submitted papers. The PC of 26 researchers reviewed 20–22 papers each, while the ERC of 60 members reviewed an average of 3–4 papers each, with a maximum of 6. Both PC and ERC members could submit papers, but only the ERC reviewed PC papers, thus avoiding potential conflicts that could otherwise arise at the in-person meeting. At the end of the main review period (10 weeks total), authors were given four days to respond to their reviews, and the reviewers then discussed papers electronically for two weeks. The PC met in person over two days at the University of Maryland, College Park, USA, to decide the majority of the program. Out of 205 submissions, 44 were accepted; three of seventeen PC submissions were accepted following on-line discussion among the ERC.

This year we employed a form of double-blind reviewing (DBR), a first for POPL. In a double-blind process, the reviewers do not learn the identity of the authors (nor do authors learn reviewer identities, as usual). The intention of DBR is to increase the fairness of reviewing and the quality of the accepted papers by avoiding initial, perhaps unconscious bias for or against a paper based on its authorship. A reviewer who picks up a paper known to be written by a famous author and/or institution may grant more to it ("Joe wrote it so I'm sure it must be good") than to a paper by unknown authors from an obscure institution ("I've never heard of this place – do they even have reasonable PL researchers there?"). If this bias is strong enough, lesser papers may be accepted over ones of higher quality and certain population segments may be underrepresented. After consulting with the POPL Steering Committee and past Chairs of other conferences, and reading some relevant literature, I decided that DBR could have a positive effect and thus it was worth trying for POPL.

While DBR aims to improve fairness and quality, it complicates the process of writing and reviewing papers. To mitigate its disadvantages, we employed a "light" form of DBR. Authors needed to make only a few identity-masking changes to their paper: they redacted their names from the front page and cited their own work in the third person. More draconian changes to obscure likely authorship, such as altering the names of well-known systems, were not required, and most forms of post-submission dissemination were permitted. A paper's authors were hidden from a reviewer only until his or her review was submitted to the conference management system. The idea was that by the time a review is submitted, initial bias has been mitigated, so revealing author identity should not negatively impact fairness. This relaxed identity rule allowed me to call upon the PC to help find additional expert reviewers when needed without worry of unintended conflicts. I did this primarily by assigning a guardian to each paper. The guardian was responsible for submitting a review mid-way through the review period and if his or her own review was not expert-level (most were), he or she could request an additional review, either from the ERC or PC, or from an outside reviewer. In total, we received reviews or feedback from 50 outside reviewers, and we occasionally shuffled ERC and PC assignments to better take advantage of available expertise.

I believe this review process worked well. In a survey conducted after paper decisions were announced, a significant majority of authors and reviewers favored the process we used, with most reviewers very strongly in favor of using an ERC and using guardians (even if DBR is not employed). I plan to publish an analysis of the survey data in a forthcoming essay. Most compelling to me were anecdotes from PC members who confessed that in several cases they spent more time reviewing a paper than they would have if they had known the authors, and sometimes were very surprised when the actual authorship contradicted their expectations ("If I had known the paper was by Joe I would have reviewed it differently").

On the other hand, even the diminished costs of light DBR were troublesome to some authors and reviewers, and its benefits are not so easy to quantitatively assess, so we are not at the end of the story. Therefore I hope the community will continue to carefully consider the review processes we use. Peer review is the foundation of the scientific process – it is a gateway for new ideas and the foundation of our trust in published results. It is essential that we have the most effective process possible.

My heartfelt thanks goes to the PC, ERC, and outside reviewers. Ultimately they produced 852 reviews, and having read most of these reviews myself, I continue to believe that POPL reviewers are the best around. I must also thank the general chair, John Field, and the POPL Steering Committee for their excellent advice and guidance throughout. Eddie Kohler provided and supported the HotCRP software we used to manage reviewing, and Jamie Salts helped program some important extensions to it. Greta Yorsh provided expert help in organizing the program. Finally, thanks goes foremost to the authors of submitted and accepted papers, who provided the material for the excellent program we present to you this year. I hope you enjoy learning about their work as much as we have!

Michael Hicks
POPL'12 Program Chair
University of Maryland, College Park, USA

Table of Contents

Session 5.A: Concurrency

Session Chair: Matthew Parkinson *(Microsoft Research)*

Session 5.B: Type Theory

Session Chair: Stephanie Weirich *(University of Pennsylvania)*

Session 6.A: Dynamic Analysis

Session Chair: Aarti Gupta *(NEC Labs America)*

Session 6.B: Names and Binders

Session Chair: Zhong Shao *(Yale University)*

Invited Talk: J. Strother Moore

Session Chair: John Field *(Google)*

Session 7.A: Verified Transformations

Session Chair: Chris Hawblitzel *(Microsoft Research)*

POPL 2012 Organization

General Chair: John Field *(Google, USA)*

Program Chair: Michael Hicks *(University of Maryland, College Park, USA)*

Treasurer: Bor-Yuh Evan Chang *(University of Colorado, Boulder, USA)*

Publicity Chair: Swarat Chaudhuri *(Rice University, USA)*

Co-Located Events Chair: Matthew Might *(University of Utah, USA)*

Student Activities Chair: Tobias Wrigstad *(Uppsala University, Sweden)*

Steering Committee Chair: Thomas Ball *(Microsoft Research, USA)*

Steering Committee:
John Field *(Google, USA)*
Kathleen Fisher *(Tufts University, USA)*
Manuel Hermenegildo *(IMDEA Software, Spain)*
Michael Hicks *(University of Maryland, College Park, USA)*
Graham Hutton *(University of Nottingham, UK)*
Chandra Krintz *(University of California, Santa Barbara, USA)*
Jens Palsberg *(University of California, Los Angeles, USA)*
Mooly Sagiv *(Tel Aviv University, Israel)*
Philip Wadler *(University of Edinburgh, UK)*

Program Committee:
Swarat Chaudhuri *(Rice University, USA)*
Adam Chlipala *(MIT, USA)*
Dan R. Ghica *(University of Birmingham, UK)*
Aarti Gupta *(NEC Labs America, USA)*
Chris Hawblitzel *(Microsoft Research, Redmond, USA)*
Suresh Jagannathan *(Purdue University, USA)*
Ranjit Jhala *(University of California, San Diego, USA)*
Sorin Lerner *(University of California, San Diego, USA)*
Ondrej Lhotak *(University of Waterloo, Canada)*
P. Madhusudan *(University of Illinois at Urbana-Champaign, USA)*
Rupak Majumdar *(MPI-SWS, Germany)*
Matthew Might *(University of Utah, USA)*
Todd Millstein *(University of California, Los Angeles, USA)*
Greg Morrisett *(Harvard University, USA)*
Andrew Myers *(Cornell University, USA)*
Matthew Parkinson *(Microsoft Research, Cambridge, UK)*
Frank Piessens *(K.U. Leuven, Belgium)*
Andrew Pitts *(University of Cambridge, UK)*
Andreas Podelski *(University of Freiburg, Germany)*
François Pottier *(INRIA, France)*
Norman Ramsey *(Tufts University, USA)*
Tachio Terauchi *(Nagoya University, Japan)*
Mandana Vaziri *(IBM T.J. Watson Research Center, USA)*

Program Committee (continued):

Dimitrios Vytiniotis *(Microsoft Research, Cambridge, UK)*
Nobuko Yoshida *(Imperial College, London, UK)*
Francesco Zappa Nardelli *(INRIA, France)*

External Review Committee:

Umut Acar *(MPI-SWS, Germany)*
Rajeev Alur *(University of Pennsylvania, USA)*
Josh Berdine *(Microsoft Research, Cambridge, UK)*
Emery Berger *(University of Massachusetts, Amherst, USA)*
Hans Boehm *(HP Labs, USA)*
Ahmed Bouajjani *(University Paris Diderot, France)*
David Brumley *(Carnegie-Mellon University, USA)*
Bor-Yuh Evan Chang *(University of Colorado, Boulder, USA)*
James Cheney *(University of Edinburgh, UK)*
Koen Claessen *(Chalmers University of Technology, Sweden)*
William Cook *(University of Texas at Austin, USA)*
Derek Dreyer *(MPI-SWS, Germany)*
John Field *(Google, USA)*
Robby Findler *(Northwestern University, USA)*
Cormac Flanagan *(University of California, Santa Cruz, USA)*
Jeff Foster *(University of Maryland, College Park, USA)*
Nate Foster *(Cornell University, USA)*
Patrice Godefroid *(Microsoft Research, Redmond, USA)*
Andrew D. Gordon *(Microsoft Research and University of Edinburgh, UK)*
Dan Grossman *(University of Washington, USA)*
Rajiv Gupta *(University of California, Riverside, USA)*
Kohei Honda *(Queen Mary, University of London, UK)*
Joxan Jaffar *(National University of Singapore, Singapore)*
Somesh Jha *(University of Wisconsin, Madison, USA)*
Patricia Johann *(University of Strathclyde, UK)*
Neel Krishnaswami *(Microsoft Research, Cambridge, UK)*
Viktor Kuncak *(École Polytechnique Fédérale de Lausanne, Switzerland)*
Paul Levy *(University of Birmingham, UK)*
Yitzhak Mandelbaum *(AT&T Labs Research, USA)*
Roman Manevich *(University of Texas at Austin, USA)*
Ken McMillan *(Microsoft Research, Redmond, USA)*
Mayur Naik *(Georgia Institute of Technology, USA)*
Aditya Nori *(Microsoft Research, Bangalore, India)*
Luke Ong *(University of Oxford, UK)*
Erez Petrank *(Technion, Israel)*
Simon Peyton Jones *(Microsoft Research, Cambridge, UK)*
Brigitte Pientka *(McGill University, Canada)*
Mark Ryan *(University of Birmingham, UK)*
Andrey Rybalchenko *(Technical University of Munich, Germany)*
Vijay Saraswat *(IBM T.J. Watson Research Center, USA)*
Helmut Seidl *(Technical University of Munich, Germany)*
Peter Sewell *(University of Cambridge, UK)*
Chung-chieh Shan *(Cornell University, USA)*

External Review Committee (continued):

Zhong Shao *(Yale University, USA)*
Satnam Singh *(Microsoft Research, Cambridge, UK)*
Yannis Smaragdakis *(U. of Athens, Greece, and UMass, Amherst, USA)*
Manu Sridharan *(IBM T.J. Watson Research Center, USA)*
Sam Staton *(University of Cambridge, UK)*
Zhendong Su *(University of California, Davis, USA)*
Nikhil Swamy *(Microsoft Research, Redmond, USA)*
Ashish Tiwari *(SRI International, USA)*
Stavros Tripakis *(VERIMAG, France)*
Jean-Baptiste Tristan *(Harvard University, USA)*
Martin Vechev *(ETH Zurich, Switzerland)*
David Walker *(Princeton University, USA)*
Stephanie Weirich *(University of Pennsylvania, USA)*
Adam Welc *(Adobe Advanced Technology Labs, USA)*
Kwangkeun Yi *(Seoul National University, Korea)*
Steve Zdancewic *(University of Pennsylvania, USA)*
Noam Zeilberger *(University of Paris 7, France)*

Additional Reviewers:

Thorsten Altenkirch
Peter Baumgartner
Jean-Philippe Bernardy
Stephen Brookes
James Brotherston
Avik Chaudhuri
Ugo de'Liguoro
Romain Demangeon
Pierre-Malo Deniélou
Matthew Flatt
Luca Fossati
Blaise Genest
Michael Gordon
Michael Greenberg
Robert Harper
Masahito Hasegawa
Maurice Herlihy
Ralf Hinze
Raymond Hu
Alan Jeffrey
Mark P. Jones
Scott Kilpatrick
Dexter Kozen
Alexander Krauss
Marta Kwiatkowska
Wonchan Lee
Akash Lal
Percy Liang
Stephen Magill
Frank McSherry
Adam Megacz
Roland Meyer
Nick Mitchell
David Monniaux
Michael Norrish
Rodric Rabbah
Julian Rathke
Andreas Rossberg
Andrei Sabelfeld
Amr Sabry
Adrian Sampson
Jan Smans
Adam Smith
Matthieu Sozeau
Bas Spitters
Aaron Turon
Bill Wadge
David Wetherall
Hongwei Xi
Eran Yahav

Sponsors

Sponsor: ACM SIGPLAN

In cooperation with: SIGACT

Supporters

Microsoft Research

ARM

Computing Research Association CRA-W Women

The Coalition to Diversify Computing

intel

Jane Street

mozilla.org

ORACLE

NSF

Google

IBM Research

AMGEN

NEC

Presentation of the SIGPLAN Distinguished Achievement Award to Sir Charles Antony Richard Hoare, FRS, FREng, FBCS and Interview

Andrew P. Black
Portland State University

Peter W. O'Hearn
Queen Mary University of London

Categories and Subject Descriptors D.2.4 [*Software Engineering*]: Software/Program Verification; D.3.1 [*Formal Definitions and Theory*]; F.3.1 [*Logics and Meanings of Programs*]: Specifying and Verifying and Reasoning about Programs; F.3.2 [*Logics and Meanings of Programs*]: Semantics of Programming Languages

General Terms Verification, Reliability, Languages, Theory, Security

Award Citation

Tony Hoare's long career in computing is studded with seminal engineering and scientific contributions to Programming Languages; his views on programming language design have been recognized as profound even by those who declined to follow his advice.

Two contributions stand out as fundamental: the development of what is now known as Hoare logic, and Communicating Sequential Processes. Hoare logic is a system for reasoning about imperative programs. It was introduced in the 1969 article "An Axiomatic Basic for Computer Programming", which is perhaps the most influential 6-page paper ever published in CACM. Drawing on earlier work of Robert Floyd, an entire sub-area of computer science has developed from Hoare's initial ideas; many modern verification systems build on Hoare logic.

Only 9 years later, CACM published Hoare's paper on Communicating Sequential Processes (CSP). Contemporary with Milner's CCS, but pursuing complementary goals, CSP has been enormously influential. It provided the basis for the occam programming language and its realization in the Transputer; it has been used for modeling and verifying the concurrency properties of critical software systems; and it inspired a flowering of subsequent concurrency research.

Although either of these contributions would alone justify the achievement award, Hoare is doing more with his Unifying Theories research, which aims to unify theories of programming across paradigm, abstraction level and semantic style. Beyond all of this, Tony is renowned for his unfailing courtesy, his inspiration, and his dedication to his chosen calling. He is the epitome of a scholar and a gentleman.

A Note from Peter O'Hearn

As the POPL program was being planned, following a suggestion from Andy Gordon, the POPL PC, ERC, and organizing committees came up with the novel idea of accompanying the presentation of the SIGPLAN award with an interview of Tony. When the POPL chairs, John Field and Michael Hicks, approached me with this idea and asked if I would consider conducting the interview, I was filled with delight.

Obviously, Tony's ideas have influenced me enormously. At the beginning of my career I read essentially all of his papers covering a wide range of topics including language design, programming methodology, and theory. The significance and depth of his contributions is plain to see, but in reading his papers something else grabbed ahold of me time and again: their marvellous simplicity. Many of Hoare's contributions – including his work on Hoare logic, data types, data abstraction, structured programming, refinement, monitors, CSP and unifying theories – seem so natural as to be inevitable, almost obvious ... in retrospect.

How did he do it? How did he produce so many beautiful, simple ideas? Even though in recent years I have gotten to know Tony as a colleague and friend, and learnt a tremendous amount from him, I confess that I still don't know. During the interview we will go into Tony's relentless drive towards simplicity, his recollections and his hopes, and perhaps a few questions that I don't want him or you to know about just yet!

POPL'12, January 25–27, 2012, Philadelphia, PA, USA.
ACM 978-1-4503-1083-3/12/01.

Message of Thanks

On the receipt of the 2011 ACM SIGPLAN Distinguished Achievement Award

Tony Hoare

Principal Researcher, Microsoft Research Ltd.,
Hon. Mem. Cambridge University Computer Laboratory.

Categories and Subject Descriptors D.2.1 [*Programming Languages*]: Formal Definitions and Theory; D.2.4 [*Software Engineering*]: Software/Program Verification; F.3.1 [*Logics and Meanings of Programs*]: Specifying and Verifying and Reasoning about Programs; F.3.2 [*Logics and Meanings of Programs*]: Semantics of Programming Languages

General Terms Verification, Reliability, Languages, Theory, Security

Even to one who has lived long enough to receive many awards, the recognition of distinguished achievement from the scientific community in one's own research field is surprisingly welcome. I particularly treasure the SIGPLAN citation for my award, which singles out exactly the modest achievements of which I am most proud. I have known nearly all the previous winners of this award, and they number among my professional colleagues, rivals, and friends. I have derived inspiration from them all, and I am pleased to be regarded in their company.

The award prompts me to reflect again on the origins and progress of my professional career: how did I select the topics for my research? What methods did I consider appropriate for an academic researcher to pursue such research? What is the current level of maturity of research on these topics? What does the future hold for it? Why do I regard my renewed interest in unifying theories as a contribution to that future?

Computer programs

I have always regarded the computer program as a worthy topic for scientific study. Indeed, programs must surely be a central topic in computer science, both pure and applied. Having chosen this topic, I addressed myself to the fundamental questions that excite the curiosity of all scientists, no matter what their chosen topic of research.

What does it do? To answer this question, we need a conceptual framework and language for describing the externally observable properties and behaviour the program. Equally important is a description of the environment in which the program is executed, including its users. In many branches of science, separate branches of mathematics have been developed to provide effective descriptive frameworks for the topics relevant to that branch. Fortunately, logicians from around the beginning of the last century have shown that all branches of mathematics rest on a common foundation. To preserve the greatest generality in describing the behaviour of a general-purpose computer, we should exploit this common foundation. From it we get Boolean algebra, predicate calculus, and the theory of sets. When required, it is easy to define from these foundations the structures manipulated by our programs, for example functions, sums, products, types, relations, sequences, bags, etc. Experiments in application have shown that these concepts give concise and intuitive descriptions of computer systems, while preserving a level of abstraction that is appropriate for humanly comprehensible specifications.

How does it work? For this we need to look inside the program, to identify its internal components and the ways that they are connected. Again, the foundations of mathematics provide a language for defining the behaviour of each component, and the interfaces between them. In an idealised vision of rational software engineering, these interface specifications will be written in advance of the design. They will serve as a contract between the implementers of the various program components. This is an ideal that has inspired much excellent pure research in the field, aimed at the design of theories that exploit modularity (compositionality) of designs, even if it has to be sacrificed later to efficiency of the eventually executed program.

Why does it work? The answer to this deeper question must appeal to general principles, which apply not just to a particular program, but to a general range of similar programs, actual or hypothetical. The principles should support a proof that the joint working of all the components of a program will necessarily lead to the correct operation of the whole program, as described by its specification. Then we will really know both why and how the program works.

The principles of programming are often codified as a set of rules defining the semantics of the programming language in which the program is (or can be) expressed. Several forms of semantics have been developed to serve different purposes. An operational semantics provides a guide for an implementation of the programming language, and serves the programmer as a basis for diagnosing errors discovered in test. A deductive semantics gives the pattern for proving correctness of programs, which is a more difficult but more certain way of ensuring that no errors will detected in service. A denotational semantics constructs a mathematical model of the programming language, so that standard mathematical reasoning can be applied directly to it. Each of these styles of semantics

POPL'12, January 25–27, 2012, Philadelphia, PA, USA.
ACM 978-1-4503-1083-3/12/01.

has a clearly defined role. The last section of this message expresses the hope that a full theory of programming will eventually unify semantics expressed in all the styles, and so ensure their mutual consistency.

How do we know the theory applies to the real world? This is the question of greatest concern to the scientist. It is answered by conducting a series of varied experiments, with collection and interpretation of their observed results. Every claim of discovery of a new theory, and every extension/correction to an old theory, must be supported by appeal to experiment – even a thought experiment will do. Further and larger experiments are needed to explore the limits of applicability even of already well-supported theories. For objectivity, these experiments should be conducted by scientists independent of the proposers of the theory. Often the theory needs modification or extension to extend the range of its application. A unifying theory is one whose range of application is the widest of all.

How are the results of the research transferred to engineering practice? Modern engineering depends utterly on automation of the design process. It is the computer that works out in detail the implications of every engineering design decision, and checks the serviceability and safety of a product before it comes into service. An established design automation toolset provides a rapid means of world-wide transfer of new scientific results into every-day engineering practice. When scientists agree about the strength of the evidence of a new theory, or an amendment or extension of an old theory, the implementers and suppliers of the tools will compete to incorporate any consequential improvements in the next release of the toolset for which they have developed a market share.

Current state of the art

In mature branches of science, it is the natural world that supplies the experimental observations that support, refute, or refine the theories of pure scientists. Astronomers and physicists (and most recently geneticists) have collaborated on long-term international projects to build the telescopes and reactors to conduct experiments, whose results populate the enormous data bases of the world's computers. For an engineering science, the experiments are performed on the products made by man. In computer science, the programs developed by the open source movement already give cheap and public access to experimental material, on a scale that is fortunately more than adequate for our current research needs.

The main task for modern data-based science is to interpret the enormous volumes of experimental material, by relating it to the natural laws which are believed to explain them. Scientists write computer significant computer programs to analyse the mass of data automatically in the light of current theories. This is now the only way to extract scientifically illuminating information from the data, and so to refine, extend, and even unify existing theories. Analogous tools for scientific analysis of programs are used by the software industry to help in the engineering of critical parts of widely used software. They are often used to support the experimental side of research into the principles of programming.

The last decade has seen an enormous increase in the power of these programming tools. Moore's law predicts every decade a roughly a thousand fold increase in the space-time performance of commodity computer chips, often accompanied by a reduction in price. This rate of progress has been compounded by a comparable increase in the algorithmic efficiency of SAT and SMT solvers and model checkers. The advance in software tools has been driven by regular scientific competitions. These are regularly organised and refereed by independent scientists, and the whole experimental community collaborates in the assembly of realistic challenge material for conduct of the competitions.

A second fillip for program analysis has been the totally unexpected phenomenon of the computer virus. Viruses or other malware exploit a programming error to damage or even take control of (perhaps millions of) computers which run the erroneous program. That is why leading software manufacturers are continuing to invest heavily in the development of program analysis tools. These are based on the best available current theories of programming, and the best available SMT solvers and model checkers. The tools are now applied routinely to many millions of lines of commercial software before release.

The future?

I therefore predict an exciting future for further academic research on the principles of programming, and for further exploitation of its research results. The research will take advantage of the most advanced available industrial program analysis tools to perform experiments, at ever increasing scales, on real and realistic software. The tools themselves will evolve by exploiting experience of their use, both by scientists and by software developers. Continuous interaction of theorists, tool-builders and experimentalists will lead to an exponential increase in the rate of scientific progress; perhaps computer science will match the recent spurt in the progress of physics, astronomy, and more recently biology, which has been achieved by integrating computerised tools into the scientific method and culture.

Much of this progress will be made by collaboration between academic researchers and industrial software developers, who already welcome the opportunity of using program analysis tools to reduce the costs and the risks of programming error. At the same time, industry will continue to pour their resources into more immediately applicable tools, which concentrate on test case generation of early detection of programming errors.

Academic research should not be confined to competing with the better funded research of industrial users. It should also continue to pursue higher and longer term ideals, because this is the only way of ensuring a continued stream of new ideas and even breakthroughs to advance the state of the art. Ideals such as accuracy of measurement or purity of materials are the driving force of science. Even if the theory itself says that they can only be approximated, the approximations can be indefinitely refined. In computer science, the relevant scientific ideal is total correctness of computer programs, guaranteed by proofs conducted with the assistance of computers during their design and implementation. It is for the engineer to decide later in each case how far the ideals must be compromised to meet engineering constraints of cost and timescale.

Unification

My own personal research has recently reverted to pursuit of a scientific ideal, namely the unification of theories of programming. Since this is mentioned in my citation for the distinguished achievement award, I will devote this last section of my message of thanks to explaining why I believe that unification will make a contribution to the future described in the previous section.

In the natural sciences, the quest for a unifying theory is an integral part of the scientific culture. The aim is to show that a single theory applies to a wide range of highly disparate phenomena. For example, the gravitational theory of Isaac Newton applies very accurately both to apples falling towards the earth and to planets falling towards the sun. In many cases, a more homogeneous subset of the phenomena is already covered by a more specialised scientific theory. In these cases, the specialised theory must be derived mathematically from the claimed unified theory. For example, Newton's theory of gravitation unifies the elegant planetary theory of Kepler, as well as the less elegant Ptolemaic theories of astronomy.

The scientific benefit of a unified theory is that it is supported by all the evidence that has already been accumulated for all of the previous theories separately. Furthermore, each of the previous theories then inherits the support given by the total sum of evidence contributed by all the other theories.

The practicing engineer has different concerns from the scientist, including deadlines and budgets for the current project. The engineer will therefore continue to use familiar more specialised theories that have been found from experience to be well adapted to the particular features of the current project, or the needs of the current client. Indeed, the innovative engineer will often specialise the theory even further, adapting it so closely to current needs that there will never be an opportunity for repeated use. That is why the separate theories that are subsumed by a unifying theory often retain all their practical value, and they are in no way belittled or superseded by the unification.

The real practical value of unification lies in its contribution to the transfer of the results of scientific research into engineering practice. One of the main factors that inhibit the engineer (and the sensible manager) from adopting a scientific theory is that the scientists do not yet agree what that theory should be. Fortunately, there is an agreed method of resolving a scientific dispute. An experiment is designed whose result is predicted differently by all the theories that are party to the dispute. The engineer can then have increased confidence in the winner.

But sometimes, no such decisive experiment can be discovered. This may be because, in spite of differences in their presentation, the theories are in fact entirely consistent. In this case, the only way of resolving the issue is to find a theory that unifies them all. Quantum theory provides an example. Three separate mathematical presentations of quantum theory were put forward by Heisenberg, Schroedinger and Dirac. Then Dirac showed that they were all derivable from a single unified theory. This is what enabled the award of a Nobel prize to all three of them. And quantum theory is now accepted as the nearest to a theory of everything that physics has to offer.

A second contribution of a unified theory to the practicing engineer is in the design and use of a suite of software tools that assist in automation of the design process. Since every major engineering enterprise today combines a range of technologies, it is important that all the specialised members of the tool suite should be based on a common theory, so that they can communicate consistently among each other on standard interfaces which are based upon the unification. The standards also facilitate competition among the tools, and permit independent evolution of separate tools for joint use in a design automation toolset.

Finally, the education of the general scientist and engineer will surely be facilitated by reducing the number of independently developed theories to a single theory, presented in a single coherent framework and notation. That in itself is sufficient justification for conduct by academics of research into unification of theories.

Freefinement

Stephan van Staden
ETH Zurich
Stephan.vanStaden@inf.ethz.ch

Cristiano Calcagno
ETH Zurich, Imperial College London
and Monoidics Ltd
c.calcagno@imperial.ac.uk

Bertrand Meyer
ETH Zurich
Bertrand.Meyer@inf.ethz.ch

Abstract

Freefinement is an algorithm that constructs a sound refinement calculus from a verification system under certain conditions. In this paper, a verification system is any formal system for establishing whether an inductively defined term, typically a program, satisfies a specification. Examples of verification systems include Hoare logics and type systems. Freefinement first extends the term language to include specification terms, and builds a verification system for the extended language that is a sound and conservative extension of the original system. The extended system is then transformed into a sound refinement calculus. The resulting refinement calculus can interoperate closely with the verification system – it is even possible to reuse and translate proofs between them. Freefinement gives a semantics to refinement at an abstract level: it associates each term of the extended language with a set of terms from the original language, and refinement simply reduces this set. The paper applies freefinement to a simple type system for the lambda calculus and also to a Hoare logic.

Categories and Subject Descriptors D.2.4 [*Software Engineering*]: Software/Program Verification; D.3.1 [*Programming Languages*]: Formal Definitions and Theory; F.3.1 [*Logics and Meanings of Programs*]: Specifying and Verifying and Reasoning about Programs

General Terms Languages, Theory, Verification

Keywords Formal Systems, Proof Theory, Refinement

1. Introduction

Many theories in computer science are presented, or approximated, by compositional *verification systems*. In this paper, a verification system is any formal system for establishing whether an inductively defined term, typically a program, satisfies a specification. For example, Hoare logics and type systems can be viewed as verification systems. In the case of Hoare logics, the system proves that a statement satisfies certain specifications given as preconditions and postconditions. In the case of type systems, the system proves that a term has a certain type in a type context.

Refinement systems play a similar role to verification systems, the main difference being that they relate terms to other terms, instead of terms and specifications. Another difference is that they typically include so-called specification terms. Intuitively, a term refines another if it is 'better', i.e. if it satisfies more specifications. *Refinement calculi* are formal systems for establishing refinements. For example, the calculus of Morgan [9] derives refinements between statements based on total correctness specifications. Starting from an appropriate specification statement, one can derive a correct algorithm for computing the factorial of a number by applying Morgan's refinement rules.

This paper originates from the observation that a Hoare logic and a refinement calculus for a command language do not have to be independent entities: once the Hoare logic is extended with specification statements, the two systems can be accommodated in a single theory. Moreover, there is a strong relation between the two systems. The paper explains that this relation is not a coincidence: it is possible to analyze the structure of the inference rules defining a verification system, and automatically generate a related refinement calculus. Freefinement is an algorithm that implements this transformation. Surprisingly, freefinement is not limited to Hoare logics, but can be applied to any verification system whose inference rules satisfy certain conditions. Several refinement rules proposed in the literature in different contexts arise in this way.

The freefinement algorithm works as follows. Given a term language and an accompanying verification system V_1 that satisfies certain conditions, freefinement extends the term language with specification terms and builds a verification system V_2 for extended terms. The conditions on V_1 ensure that it is possible to extend the terms without breaking the inference rules; V_2 is consequently a sound and conservative extension of V_1. Moreover, freefinement proposes a sound refinement system R that is in harmony with V_2. Harmony means that the two formal systems can interoperate smoothly. It entails, for example, that a term satisfies a specification according to V_2 if and only if it is possible to refine the specification into the term with R. In fact, proof translation between V_2 and R becomes possible because harmony is demonstrated constructively. Freefinement internally constructs the refinement calculus by 'linearizing' V_2 in a series of steps. The conditions on V_1 ensure that successful linearization is possible. According to the presentation below, at most six steps are needed for this 'refinement of refinement systems'. The situation is summarized as follows:

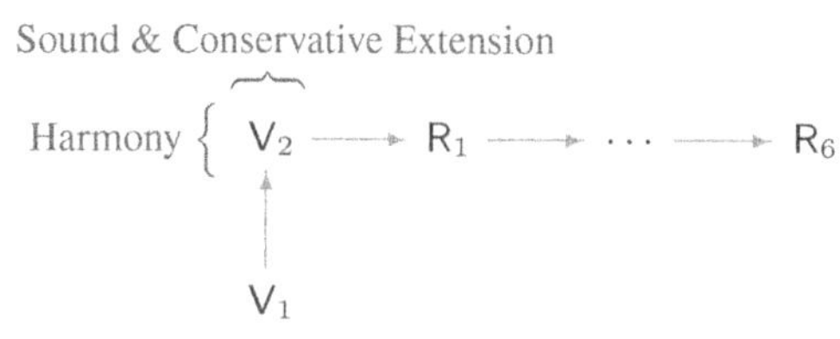

Freefinement requires no human intervention. The conditions it imposes are fulfilled by many program logics and type systems: examples include Hoare logic, separation logic, the simply-typed

POPL'12, January 25–27, 2012, Philadelphia, PA, USA.

lambda calculus and System F. Freefinement defines the semantics of refinement at an abstract level: it associates each term of the extended language with a set of terms from the original language, and refinement simply reduces this set.

With freefinement, tools that are based on verification systems can readily include refinement as a complementary or alternative development style. Freefinement provides correctness by construction for free.

Outline. Section 2 describes the freefinement algorithm, which is applied in Section 3 to a simple type system for the lambda calculus and also to Hoare logic. Section 4 concludes with related work.

2. Freefinement

2.1 The Inputs

Freefinement requires four things as input:

1. A set of constructors $\mathbb{K}$. The constructors give rise to a term language T, where an arbitrary term t of T is defined by the grammar:

$$t ::= C(t_1, \ldots, t_n)$$

where $C \in \mathbb{K}$.

2. A set of specifications $\mathbb{S}$.
3. A binary relation $\models_{V_1} \_ \, Sat \, \_$ between terms and specifications. Intuitively, $\models_{V_1} t \, Sat \, S$ denotes that term $t \in T$ satisfies specification $S \in \mathbb{S}$.
4. A formal system $V_1(\mathbb{K}, \mathbb{S}, \models_{V_1} \_ \, Sat \, \_)$, which consists of a set of inference rules for proving sentences of the form t *Sat* S. Each rule of V_1 must have the form A_1 or B_1:

$$A_1 \; \frac{t_1 \; Sat \; S_1 \qquad \ldots \qquad t_n \; Sat \; S_n}{C(t_1, \ldots, t_n) \; Sat \; S}$$
provided $Pred(C, S_1, \ldots, S_n, S)$.

$$B_1 \; \frac{t \; Sat \; S_1 \qquad \ldots \qquad t \; Sat \; S_m}{t \; Sat \; S}$$
provided $Pred(S_1, \ldots, S_m, S)$.

The t's, S's and C in the rule forms indicate where the rules of V_1 must use metavariables. Thus a rule of form A_1 has only the freedom to choose a concrete n and a definition for its proviso predicate Pred; the proviso predicate implements the side condition of the rule based on the arguments $C, S_1, \ldots, S_n$ and S. A rule of form B_1 is also a pair: a concrete m and a definition of a predicate with arguments $S_1, \ldots, S_m$ and S. Freefinement requires that the rules must be sound with respect to the following semantics:

Definition 1 (Semantics of the Inference Rules).

1.1 For rules of the form A_1:
$Pred(C, S_1, \ldots, S_n, S) \Rightarrow [\forall t_1, \ldots, t_n \in T \cdot \models_{V_1} t_1 \; Sat \; S_1 \wedge \ldots \wedge \models_{V_1} t_n \; Sat \; S_n \Rightarrow \models_{V_1} C(t_1, \ldots, t_n) \; Sat \; S]$

1.2 For rules of the form B_1:
$Pred(S_1, \ldots, S_m, S) \Rightarrow [\forall t \in T \cdot \models_{V_1} t \; Sat \; S_1 \wedge \ldots \wedge \models_{V_1} t \; Sat \; S_m \Rightarrow \models_{V_1} t \; Sat \; S]$

The rule forms stipulate that the rules of V_1 must be highly compositional – a requirement that freefinement will exploit. For example, rules cannot inspect or constrain the t's that appear in premises. This will allow freefinement to reuse the rules after specification terms are added to the term language.

Consider the following three rules over $\mathbb{K} = \{0, succ, pred\}$ and $\mathbb{S} = \{\mathbb{N}\}$, where n is a metavariable:

$$1 \; \frac{n : \mathbb{N}}{succ(n) : \mathbb{N}} \qquad 2 \; \frac{succ(n) : \mathbb{N}}{pred(succ(n)) : \mathbb{N}} \qquad 3 \; \frac{n : \mathbb{N}}{pred(n) : \mathbb{N}}$$
provided positive(n).

Rule 1 can be written in form A_1 with $n = 1$ by defining the proviso $Pred(C, S_1, S)$ as $C = succ \wedge S_1 = S = \mathbb{N}$. Rule 2 is unacceptable, because its premise inspects the term and requires it to match succ(n). Rule 3 is also unacceptable, because it constrains the term in its proviso.

It will become clear later that the 'structural' rules of Hoare logic, such as the rule of consequence, are examples of rules of form B_1. Other rules of Hoare logic, such as the assignment axiom and rule for sequential composition, have the form A_1.

Let $\vdash_{V_1} t \; Sat \; S$ denote that t *Sat* S is derivable with V_1. The soundness of the rules with respect to the semantics of Definition 1 implies the soundness of V_1:

Theorem 1 (Soundness of V_1). $\vdash_{V_1} t \; Sat \; S \Rightarrow \models_{V_1} t \; Sat \; S$

Proof. By induction on the derivation of t *Sat* S:

- A rule of the form A_1 was last applied. Assume $Pred(C, S_1, \ldots, S_n, S)$ and the induction hypothesis $\models_{V_1} t_1 \; Sat \; S_1 \wedge \ldots \wedge \models_{V_1} t_n \; Sat \; S_n$. Then $\models_{V_1} C(t_1, \ldots, t_n) \; Sat \; S$ by Definition 1.1.
- A rule of the form B_1 was last applied. Assume $Pred(S_1, \ldots, S_m, S)$ and also the induction hypothesis $\models_{V_1} t \; Sat \; S_1 \wedge \ldots \wedge \models_{V_1} t \; Sat \; S_m$. From Definition 1.2 follows $\models_{V_1} t \; Sat \; S$. □

Freefinement does not assume the completeness of V_1, i.e. it never assumes $\models_{V_1} t \; Sat \; S \Rightarrow \vdash_{V_1} t \; Sat \; S$.

2.2 The Extended Language and Formal System

This section extends the language T with specification terms that are useful for refinement. It gives a semantics to the resulting language U, and extends V_1 in a sound and conservative way to prove sentences of the form u *Sat* S where $u \in U$.

2.2.1 The Extended Language U

Suppose $\mathbb{K}$ and $\mathbb{S}$ are disjoint (if they are not, then they can always be decorated to become disjoint) and do not contain a symbol $\bigsqcup$. The extended set of constructors

$$\mathbb{K}' = \mathbb{K} \cup \mathbb{S} \cup \{\bigsqcup \text{ with arity } n \mid n \in \mathbb{N}\}$$

gives rise to an extended language U, which can also be written as:

$$u ::= C(u_1, \ldots, u_n) \mid S \mid \bigsqcup(u_1, \ldots, u_n)$$

A term of the form S is called a *spec* term, and a term of the form $\bigsqcup(u_1, \ldots, u_n)$ is called the *join* of $u_1, \ldots, u_n$. Intuitively, S is a generic term that satisfies S, and $\bigsqcup(u_1, \ldots, u_n)$ is a generic term that satisfies any S that any of the $u_1, \ldots, u_n$ satisfy. Although the details will become clear later, the reasons for adding these terms are simple: the refinement system should be able to refine spec terms into other terms for top-down development, and join terms will be important for simplifying rules of the form B_1 where $m > 1$. If there are no rules of the form B_1 where $m > 1$, then join terms and their consequent treatment can be omitted.

A couple of constructs are used for giving a semantics to U. Let X denote a subset of T, and let Y denote a subset of $\mathbb{S}$. Specs(X) is the set of all specifications that all the terms in X satisfy, and Terms(Y) is the set of terms of T that satisfy all the specifications in Y:

Definition 2 (Specs and Terms).

- $Specs(X) \stackrel{\text{def}}{=} \{S \mid \forall t \in X \cdot \models_{V_1} t \; Sat \; S\}$
- $Terms(Y) \stackrel{\text{def}}{=} \{t \mid \forall S \in Y \cdot \models_{V_1} t \; Sat \; S\}$

An antitone Galois connection[1] exists between Specs and Terms:

Lemma 1. $X \subseteq Terms(Y) \Leftrightarrow Y \subseteq Specs(X)$

Proof.
$$\begin{array}{ll} & X \subseteq Terms(Y) \\ \Leftrightarrow & \{\text{definition of Terms and } \subseteq\} \\ & \forall t \in X \cdot \forall S \in Y \cdot \models_{V_1} t\ Sat\ S \\ \Leftrightarrow & \{\text{predicate calculus}\} \\ & \forall S \in Y \cdot \forall t \in X \cdot \models_{V_1} t\ Sat\ S \\ \Leftrightarrow & \{\text{definition of Specs and } \subseteq\} \\ & Y \subseteq Specs(X) \end{array}$$
□

Antitone Galois connections have several well-known properties. For instance, ($Terms \circ Specs$) and ($Specs \circ Terms$) are extensive, increasing and idempotent and therefore closure operators. Freefinement relies on the following properties (their proofs appear in the Appendix):

Corollary 1.

1.1 $X \subseteq Terms(Specs(X))$
1.2 $Terms(Specs(Terms(Y))) = Terms(Y)$
1.3 $Specs(X) \subseteq Specs(X')$
$\Leftrightarrow Terms(Specs(X)) \supseteq Terms(Specs(X'))$
1.4 $Terms(Y \cup Y') = Terms(Y) \cap Terms(Y')$

The following auxiliary definition provides a shorthand for the set of all terms of the form $C(t_1, \ldots, t_n)$ where $t_1 \in X_1, \ldots, t_n \in X_n$:

$$C(X_1, \ldots, X_n) \stackrel{\text{def}}{=} \{C(t_1, \ldots, t_n) \mid \textstyle\bigwedge_{i \in 1..n} t_i \in X_i\}$$

For example, it yields a singleton set for nullary constructors:

$$\{C() \mid \textstyle\bigwedge_{i \in 1..0} t_i \in X_i\} = \{C() \mid True\} = \{C()\}$$

The semantics of U is given by the function $[\![\_]\!]$ of type $U \rightarrow \mathcal{P}(T)$, i.e. every term in U denotes a set of terms from T:

Definition 3 (Semantics of U).

$$\begin{array}{rcl} [\![C(u_1, \ldots, u_n)]\!] & \stackrel{\text{def}}{=} & Terms(Specs(C([\![u_1]\!], \ldots, [\![u_n]\!]))) \\ [\![S]\!] & \stackrel{\text{def}}{=} & Terms(\{S\}) \\ [\![\bigsqcup(u_1, \ldots, u_n)]\!] & \stackrel{\text{def}}{=} & \bigcap_{i \in 1..n} [\![u_i]\!] \end{array}$$

If the relation $\models_{V_1} \_\ Sat\ \_$ is well-behaved in a sense that will be made precise later, then $[\![u]\!]$ has a simple intuitive explanation: it denotes the set of all primitive terms, i.e. terms from T, that refine u. For a term $C(u_1, \ldots, u_n)$, first consider $C([\![u_1]\!], \ldots, [\![u_n]\!])$ – the set of terms of the form $C(t_1, \ldots, t_n)$ where $t_1 \in [\![u_1]\!]$ (i.e. t_1 refines u_1) and … and $t_n \in [\![u_n]\!]$. All the specifications that all these terms implement are then collected, and any primitive term that satisfies all such specifications refines $C(u_1, \ldots, u_n)$. The primitive terms that refine S are exactly those that satisfy S. Finally, $\bigsqcup(u_1, \ldots, u_n)$ is refined by any primitive term that refines all $u_1, \ldots, u_n$.

For all u, the set $[\![u]\!]$ is a fixpoint of $Terms \circ Specs$ and hence a closed element:

Lemma 2. $Terms(Specs([\![u]\!])) = [\![u]\!]$

Proof. By induction on the structure of u:

- If u has the form $C(u_1, \ldots, u_n)$ or S, then $[\![u]\!] = Terms(Y)$ for some Y and the result follows by Corollary 1.2.
- If u has the form $\bigsqcup(u_1, \ldots, u_n)$, assume $[\![u_i]\!] = Terms(Specs([\![u_i]\!]))$ for all $i \in 1..n$. So $[\![\bigsqcup(u_1, \ldots, u_n)]\!] = \bigcap_{i \in 1..n} Terms(Specs([\![u_i]\!]))$ $= Terms(\bigcup_{i \in 1..n} Specs([\![u_i]\!]))$ by Corollary 1.4, and Corollary 1.2 concludes the proof. □

[1] Also known as an *order-reversing* or *contravariant* Galois connection.

The rest of the paper introduces further properties of the semantics as needed.

2.2.2 Extending V_1: Preliminaries

The next section will extend V_1 to obtain a formal system V_2 for proving sentences of the form u *Sat* S. The aim is to construct a sound and conservative extension of V_1. Informally, a sound extension of V_1 must have equal or more power:

Definition 4 (Sound Extension). $V_2(\mathbb{K}', \mathbb{S}', \models_{V_2} \_\ Sat\ \_)$ is a sound extension of $V_1(\mathbb{K}, \mathbb{S}, \models_{V_1} \_\ Sat\ \_)$ if and only if

1. V_2 uses richer terms and specifications:
$\mathbb{K} \subseteq \mathbb{K}'$ and $\mathbb{S} \subseteq \mathbb{S}'$
2. V_2 can prove everything that V_1 can prove:
$\forall t \in T, S \in \mathbb{S} \cdot \vdash_{V_1} t\ Sat\ S \Rightarrow \vdash_{V_2} t\ Sat\ S$
3. V_2 uses a richer semantics:
$\forall t \in T, S \in \mathbb{S} \cdot \models_{V_2} t\ Sat\ S \Rightarrow \models_{V_1} t\ Sat\ S$
4. V_2 is sound:
$\forall u \in U, S' \in \mathbb{S}' \cdot \vdash_{V_2} u\ Sat\ S' \Rightarrow \models_{V_2} u\ Sat\ S'$

As a consequence, $\forall t \in T, S \in \mathbb{S} \cdot \vdash_{V_2} t\ Sat\ S \Rightarrow \models_{V_1} t\ Sat\ S$, which intuitively means that V_2 restricted to $\mathbb{K}$ and $\mathbb{S}$ is sound with respect to the semantics of V_1.

In a sound and conservative extension, the converse of requirement 2 also holds:

Definition 5 (Sound and Conservative Extension). A formal system $V_2(\mathbb{K}', \mathbb{S}', \models_{V_2} \_\ Sat\ \_)$ is a sound and conservative extension of $V_1(\mathbb{K}, \mathbb{S}, \models_{V_1} \_\ Sat\ \_)$ if and only if

1. V_2 is a sound extension of V_1.
2. V_1 and V_2 restricted to $\mathbb{K}$ and $\mathbb{S}$ have equal derivability:
$\forall t \in T, S \in \mathbb{S} \cdot \vdash_{V_1} t\ Sat\ S \Leftrightarrow \vdash_{V_2} t\ Sat\ S$

Although a sound and conservative extension cannot prove more sentences of the form t *Sat* S, it is still useful for extending the term language and installing a richer semantics. It can also extend the specifications, but the V_2 of the next section will simply use $\mathbb{S}$.

2.2.3 The Extended Formal System V_2

The construction of V_2 starts with the empty set of rules and proceeds in two steps:

1. For each rule of V_1, replace t's by u's and add the resulting rule. This change of metavariables yields the rule forms A_2 and B_2 in V_2:

$$A_2\ \frac{u_1\ Sat\ S_1 \quad \ldots \quad u_n\ Sat\ S_n}{C(u_1, \ldots, u_n)\ Sat\ S}$$
provided $Pred(C, S_1, \ldots, S_n, S)$.

$$B_2\ \frac{u\ Sat\ S_1 \quad \ldots \quad u\ Sat\ S_m}{u\ Sat\ S}$$
provided $Pred(S_1, \ldots, S_m, S)$.

2. Add the following rules for spec terms and joins:

$$\text{SPEC}\ \frac{}{S\ Sat\ S}$$

$$\text{JOIN}\ \frac{u\ Sat\ S}{\bigsqcup(\ldots, u, \ldots)\ Sat\ S}$$

By induction on the derivation, V_1 and V_2 are equivalent with respect to derivability on T, i.e. $\vdash_{V_1} t\ Sat\ S \Leftrightarrow \vdash_{V_2} t\ Sat\ S$. So for V_2 to be a sound and conservative extension of V_1, it will suffice to equip V_2 with a richer semantics and to prove it sound.

The *Sat* relation between U and $\mathbb{S}$ is defined as follows:

Definition 6 (Extended Satisfaction).
$\models_{V_2} u \; Sat \; S \overset{\text{def}}{=} \forall t \in [\![u]\!] \cdot \models_{V_1} t \; Sat \; S$

Furthermore, the U-semantics of t contains t as an element:

Lemma 3 (Term Embedding). $\forall t \in T \cdot t \in [\![t]\!]$

Proof. By induction on the structure of t. Suppose $t = C(t_1, \ldots, t_n)$ and assume $t_1 \in [\![t_1]\!], \ldots, t_n \in [\![t_n]\!]$. So $t \in C([\![t_1]\!], \ldots, [\![t_n]\!])$, which is a subset of $Terms(Specs(C([\![t_1]\!], \ldots, [\![t_n]\!])))$ by Corollary 1.1. □

Therefore $\models_{V_2} t \; Sat \; S \Rightarrow \models_{V_1} t \; Sat \; S$ holds, and the soundness proof of V_2 establishes that V_2 is a sound and conservative extension of V_1:

Theorem 2 (Soundness of V_2). $\vdash_{V_2} u \; Sat \; S \Rightarrow \models_{V_2} u \; Sat \; S$

Proof. By induction on the structure of the derivation:

- For each rule of the form A_2, assume $Pred(C, S_1, \ldots, S_n, S)$ and assume
$$\forall t_1 \in [\![u_1]\!] \cdot \models_{V_1} t_1 \; Sat \; S_1$$
$$\vdots$$
$$\forall t_n \in [\![u_n]\!] \cdot \models_{V_1} t_n \; Sat \; S_n$$
So $\forall t_1 \in [\![u_1]\!], \ldots, t_n \in [\![u_n]\!] \cdot \models_{V_1} C(t_1, \ldots, t_n) \; Sat \; S$ because the corresponding rule of the form A_1 in V_1 is sound with respect to Definition 1.1. So $S \in Specs(C([\![u_1]\!], \ldots, [\![u_n]\!]))$ and hence $\forall t \in Terms(Specs(C([\![u_1]\!], \ldots, [\![u_n]\!]))) \cdot \models_{V_1} t \; Sat \; S$.
- For each rule of the form B_2, assume $Pred(S_1, \ldots, S_m, S)$ and assume $\forall t \in [\![u]\!] \cdot \models_{V_1} t \; Sat \; S_1 \; \wedge \; \ldots \; \wedge \; \models_{V_1} t \; Sat \; S_m$.
Now $\forall t \in [\![u]\!] \cdot \models_{V_1} t \; Sat \; S$ because the corresponding rule of the form B_1 in V_1 is sound with respect to Definition 1.2.
- SPEC: $\forall t \in Terms(\{S\}) \cdot \models_{V_1} t \; Sat \; S$ by definition.
- JOIN: Assume $\forall t \in [\![u]\!] \cdot \models_{V_1} t \; Sat \; S$. If $t \in [\![\bigsqcup(\ldots, u, \ldots)]\!]$ then $t \in [\![u]\!]$ and hence $\models_{V_1} t \; Sat \; S$. □

Extended satisfaction has an alternative characterization that freefinement will also use:

Lemma 4. $\models_{V_2} u \; Sat \; S \;\Leftrightarrow\; S \in Specs([\![u]\!])$

Proof.
$$\begin{aligned} & \models_{V_2} u \; Sat \; S \\ \Leftrightarrow \; & \{\text{definition}\} \\ & \forall t \in [\![u]\!] \cdot \models_{V_1} t \; Sat \; S \\ \Leftrightarrow \; & \{\text{definition of Specs}\} \\ & S \in Specs([\![u]\!]) \end{aligned}$$
□

2.3 System V_2 and Refinement

The next section will construct several refinement systems, or calculi, that are based on V_2. These refinement systems are formal systems for proving sentences of the form $u \sqsubseteq u'$. The definition of the refinement relation makes the semantics of refinement precise:

Definition 7 (Refinement). $\models u \sqsubseteq u' \overset{\text{def}}{=} [\![u]\!] \supseteq [\![u']\!]$

This definition leads to simple proofs, and is equivalent to several other formulations. The following theorem states one such alternative, and its proof mentions others:

Lemma 5 (Equivalent Characterization of Refinement).
$\models u \sqsubseteq u' \;\Leftrightarrow\; \forall S \cdot \models_{V_2} u \; Sat \; S \Rightarrow \models_{V_2} u' \; Sat \; S$

Proof.
$$\begin{aligned} & [\![u]\!] \supseteq [\![u']\!] \\ \Leftrightarrow \; & \{\text{Lemma 2}\} \\ & Terms(Specs([\![u]\!])) \supseteq Terms(Specs([\![u']\!])) \\ \Leftrightarrow \; & \{\text{Corollary 1.3}\} \\ & Specs([\![u]\!]) \subseteq Specs([\![u']\!]) \\ \Leftrightarrow \; & \{\text{definition of } \subseteq\} \\ & \forall S \cdot S \in Specs([\![u]\!]) \Rightarrow S \in Specs([\![u']\!]) \\ \Leftrightarrow \; & \{\text{Lemma 4}\} \\ & \forall S \cdot \models_{V_2} u \; Sat \; S \Rightarrow \models_{V_2} u' \; Sat \; S \end{aligned}$$
□

If $\models_{V_1} \_ \; Sat \; \_$ is well-behaved, then there is also another explanation for defining $\models u \sqsubseteq u'$ as $[\![u]\!] \supseteq [\![u']\!]$: u′ refines u iff every primitive term that refines u′ also refines u. Put differently, u′ refines u iff u′ constrains the set of eventual primitive terms that refinement can produce to the same or higher degree compared to u. So u can be seen as a placeholder for any of the primitive terms in $[\![u]\!]$, and the role of refinement is to reduce the uncertainty.

Many examples of refinements will follow later, so here is a small one: a join term implements the least upper bound (join) of its immediate subterms with respect to $\sqsubseteq$, hence the name. In particular:

1. $\forall i \in 1..n \cdot \models u_i \sqsubseteq \bigsqcup(u_1, \ldots, u_n)$
2. If $(\forall i \in 1..n \cdot \models u_i \sqsubseteq u)$, then $\models \bigsqcup(u_1, \ldots, u_n) \sqsubseteq u$.

The notation $u \equiv u'$ is a shorthand for $[\![u]\!] = [\![u']\!]$, which is equivalent to $\models u \sqsubseteq u' \wedge \models u' \sqsubseteq u$.

A refinement system R will be sound if and only if $\vdash_R u \sqsubseteq u'$ implies $\models u \sqsubseteq u'$. In the next section, freefinement will construct several sound refinement systems where each system R is related to V_2 by the properties Harmony 1 and 2 below.

Harmony 1. If $\vdash_{V_2} u \; Sat \; S$ and $\vdash_R u \sqsubseteq u'$, then $\vdash_{V_2} u' \; Sat \; S$.

Intuitively, Harmony 1 says that V_2 contains sufficient machinery to prove the same properties about u′ that it could prove about u. In other words, R is not too powerful for V_2.

Harmony 2. If $\vdash_{V_2} u \; Sat \; S$, then $\vdash_R S \sqsubseteq u$.

Intuitively, Harmony 2 means that the refinement system R contains sufficient machinery to refine a specification into any term that satisfies it according to V_2. In other words, V_2 is embedded in R and hence R is not too weak.

Harmony 1 is stronger than the converse of Harmony 2:

Theorem 3. If V_2 and a refinement system R are related by Harmony 1, then $\vdash_R S \sqsubseteq u \;\Rightarrow\; \vdash_{V_2} u \; Sat \; S$.

Proof. Assume $\vdash_R S \sqsubseteq u$. Since $\vdash_{V_2} S \; Sat \; S$ by SPEC, it follows from Harmony 1 that $\vdash_{V_2} u \; Sat \; S$. □

A refinement system R is called *harmonic* iff it satisfies Harmony 1 and 2. Harmonic refinement systems interoperate nicely with V_2. In fact, the proofs of Harmony 1 and 2 in the next section are constructive in the sense that they enable proof translation. Given a V_2-proof of u *Sat* S and an R-proof of $u \sqsubseteq u'$, they describe a V_2-proof of u′ *Sat* S. Based on a V_2-proof of u *Sat* S, they show how to build an R-proof for $S \sqsubseteq u$. Since Harmony 1 is established constructively, given an R-proof of $S \sqsubseteq u$, the proof of Theorem 3 shows how to build a V_2-proof for u *Sat* S.

The final refinement system that freefinement produces will also have a specific desired form. This form guarantees that refinement proofs are 'linear' developments where terms can be refined in-place. Formally, a refinement system has the desired form if the rules with premises describe either the transitivity or the monotonicity of refinement. All the other rules must be axioms, i.e. without any premise.

2.4 The Refinement of Refinement Systems

V_2 can be linearized in a series of steps to obtain a sound and harmonic refinement system of the desired form. At most six steps are necessary according to this presentation – the exact number depends on V_1. The steps make it easy to prove and maintain soundness and harmony, which would otherwise be more complex to establish for the final refinement calculus.

Many of the steps take a previously constructed refinement system and add or remove rules to obtain a new system. If a sound and harmonic refinement system is extended with a rule that is sound and respects Harmony 1, then the resulting system will be sound and harmonic. There is no need to prove Harmony 2 again, because the new refinement system can still derive all sentences that the old one could derive. If a rule is removed from a sound and harmonic refinement system, then the resulting system remains sound and will also be harmonic if it satisfies Harmony 2. A simple way of showing that Harmony 2 still holds is to show that any application of the old rule can be achieved by a combination of rules that remain in the system.

2.4.1 Getting Started: R_1

The first refinement system R_1 is obtained from V_2 by a simple syntactic transformation: each sentence u *Sat* S becomes $S \sqsubseteq u$. R_1 has rules of the form A_3 and B_3, a SPEC rule and also a JOIN rule if join terms were needed:

$$A_3\ \frac{S_1 \sqsubseteq u_1 \quad \ldots \quad S_n \sqsubseteq u_n}{S \sqsubseteq C(u_1, \ldots, u_n)}$$
provided $\mathrm{Pred}(C, S_1, \ldots, S_n, S)$.

$$B_3\ \frac{S_1 \sqsubseteq u \quad \ldots \quad S_m \sqsubseteq u}{S \sqsubseteq u}$$
provided $\mathrm{Pred}(S_1, \ldots, S_m, S)$.

$$\textsc{Spec}\ \frac{}{S \sqsubseteq S}$$

$$\textsc{Join}\ \frac{S \sqsubseteq u}{S \sqsubseteq \bigsqcup(\ldots, u, \ldots)}$$

V_2 and R_1 are isomorphic: a proof of u *Sat* S in V_2 corresponds to a proof of $S \sqsubseteq u$ in R_1 and vice versa, so $\vdash_{V_2} u\ \mathit{Sat}\ S \Leftrightarrow \vdash_{R_1} S \sqsubseteq u$. The soundness proof of R_1 relies on the following equivalence:

Lemma 6. $\models_{V_2} u\ \mathit{Sat}\ S \Leftrightarrow \models S \sqsubseteq u$

Proof.
$\models_{V_2} u\ \mathit{Sat}\ S$
$\Leftrightarrow$ {Lemma 4}
$\{S\} \subseteq \mathrm{Specs}([\![u]\!])$
$\Leftrightarrow$ {Lemma 1}
$[\![u]\!] \subseteq \mathrm{Terms}(\{S\})$ □

Theorem 4 (Soundness of R_1). $\vdash_{R_1} u \sqsubseteq u' \Rightarrow \models u \sqsubseteq u'$

Proof. If $\vdash_{R_1} u \sqsubseteq u'$, then u has the form S and $\vdash_{V_2} u'\ \mathit{Sat}\ S$. The soundness of V_2 implies $\models_{V_2} u'\ \mathit{Sat}\ S$, and Lemma 6 in turn implies $\models S \sqsubseteq u'$. □

Theorem 5. R_1 is harmonic.

Proof. Harmony 2 holds by construction. For Harmony 1, assume $\vdash_{R_1} u \sqsubseteq u'$. Then u has the form S″ and $\vdash_{V_2} u'\ \mathit{Sat}\ S''$ by construction. That $\vdash_{V_2} u\ \mathit{Sat}\ S'$ (i.e. $\vdash_{V_2} S''\ \mathit{Sat}\ S'$) implies $\vdash_{V_2} u'\ \mathit{Sat}\ S'$ for all S′ follows by induction on the derivation of $S''\ \mathit{Sat}\ S'$:

- SPEC: S′ and S″ are the same. Since $\vdash_{V_2} u'\ \mathit{Sat}\ S''$, it holds that $\vdash_{V_2} u'\ \mathit{Sat}\ S'$.
- For each rule of the form B_2: S and S′ are the same. Assume $\mathrm{Pred}(S_1, \ldots, S_m, S)$, $\vdash_{V_2} u\ \mathit{Sat}\ S_1, \ldots, \vdash_{V_2} u\ \mathit{Sat}\ S_m$, and by the induction hypothesis also $\vdash_{V_2} u'\ \mathit{Sat}\ S_1, \ldots, \vdash_{V_2} u'\ \mathit{Sat}\ S_m$. So the rule being considered is applicable and $\vdash_{V_2} u'\ \mathit{Sat}\ S$. Hence $\vdash_{V_2} u'\ \mathit{Sat}\ S'$. □

Note: if V_2 has only rules of the form A_2 where $n = 0$ and/or rules of the form B_2 where $m = 0$, then R_1 is a refinement system of the desired form and freefinement stops.

2.4.2 Adding Transitivity: R_2

The refinement system R_2 extends R_1 with the rule TRANS which states that refinement is transitive:

$$\textsc{Trans}\ \frac{u_1 \sqsubseteq u_2 \qquad u_2 \sqsubseteq u_3}{u_1 \sqsubseteq u_3}$$

TRANS is sound because $\supseteq$ is transitive, and it maintains Harmony 1 since implication is transitive. So R_2 is sound and harmonic.

2.4.3 Simplification: R_3

The presence of SPEC and TRANS in R_2 allows the simplification of rules of the form B_3 with $m = 1$:

$$B_3\ \frac{S_1 \sqsubseteq u}{S \sqsubseteq u}$$
provided $\mathrm{Pred}(S_1, S)$.

For an arbitrary rule of this form, consider the derivation

$$B_3\ \frac{\textsc{Spec}\ \frac{}{S_1 \sqsubseteq S_1}}{S \sqsubseteq S_1}$$
provided $\mathrm{Pred}(S_1, S)$.

By virtue of having been derived, the new rule

$$B_3\ \frac{}{S \sqsubseteq S_1}$$
provided $\mathrm{Pred}(S_1, S)$.

is sound and maintains Harmony 1, and can therefore be added to R_2 to obtain a sound and harmonic refinement system. In fact, it can replace the old version without breaking Harmony 2, since removing the old version will not decrease the derivable set of sentences: every application of the old B_3 can be changed into:

$$\textsc{Trans}\ \frac{B_3\ \frac{}{S \sqsubseteq S_1} \qquad S_1 \sqsubseteq u}{S \sqsubseteq u}$$

since $\mathrm{Pred}(S_1, S)$ is guaranteed.

The refinement system R_3 is the same as R_2, except that the rules of the form B_3 with $m = 1$ are replaced by their simplified versions. R_3 is sound and harmonic.

Note: if V_2 has only rules of the form A_2 where $n = 0$ and rules of the form B_2 where $m \leq 1$, then R_3 is a refinement system of the desired form and freefinement stops.

2.4.4 Adding Monotonicity: R_4

All the constructors of U are monotone with respect to $\sqsubseteq$, i.e. the following rules are sound:

$$\textsc{C-}i\ \frac{u_i \sqsubseteq u_i'}{C(u_1, \ldots, u_i, \ldots, u_n) \sqsubseteq C(u_1, \ldots, u_i', \ldots, u_n)}$$

$$\textsc{Join-}i\ \frac{u_i \sqsubseteq u_i'}{\bigsqcup(u_1, \ldots, u_i, \ldots, u_n) \sqsubseteq \bigsqcup(u_1, \ldots, u_i', \ldots, u_n)}$$

Moreover, these rules maintain harmony:

Lemma 7. C-i maintains Harmony 1.

Proof. Assume $\forall S' \cdot \vdash_{V_2} u_i\ \mathit{Sat}\ S' \Rightarrow \vdash_{V_2} u_i'\ \mathit{Sat}\ S'$. That $\forall S \cdot \vdash_{V_2} C(u_1, \ldots, u_i, \ldots, u_n)\ \mathit{Sat}\ S \Rightarrow \vdash_{V_2} C(u_1, \ldots, u_i', \ldots, u_n)\ \mathit{Sat}\ S$ follows by induction on the derivation of $C(u_1, \ldots, u_i, \ldots, u_n)\ \mathit{Sat}\ S$:

- A_2: Suppose $\vdash_{V_2} u_j\ \mathit{Sat}\ S_j$ for $j \in 1..n$, and also suppose $\mathrm{Pred}(C, S_1, \ldots, S_n, S)$ holds. Since $\vdash_{V_2} u_i'\ \mathit{Sat}\ S_i$, the same rule A_2 can be applied to derive $C(u_1, \ldots, u_i', \ldots, u_n)\ \mathit{Sat}\ S$.

- B_2: Suppose $\vdash_{V_2} C(u_1, \ldots, u_i, \ldots, u_n)$ *Sat* S_j for $j \in 1..m$, and suppose $Pred(S_1, \ldots, S_m, S)$. The induction hypothesis is the assumption $\vdash_{V_2} C(u_1, \ldots, u_i', \ldots, u_n)$ *Sat* S_j for $j \in 1..m$. Since $Pred(S_1, \ldots, S_m, S)$, the same rule B_2 is applicable and hence $\vdash_{V_2} C(u_1, \ldots, u_i', \ldots, u_n)$ *Sat* S. □

Lemma 8. JOIN-i maintains Harmony 1.

Proof. Assume $\forall S' \cdot \vdash_{V_2} u_i$ *Sat* $S' \Rightarrow \vdash_{V_2} u_i'$ *Sat* S'. That $\forall S \cdot \vdash_{V_2} \bigsqcup(u_1, \ldots, u_i, \ldots, u_n)$ *Sat* $S \Rightarrow \vdash_{V_2} \bigsqcup(u_1, \ldots, u_i', \ldots, u_n)$ *Sat* S follows by induction on the derivation of $\bigsqcup(u_1, \ldots, u_i, \ldots, u_n)$ *Sat* S:

- JOIN: Suppose u_j *Sat* S was the premise for some $j \in 1..n$. If $j \neq i$, then apply JOIN to the premise u_j *Sat* S to derive the required $\bigsqcup(u_1, \ldots, u_i', \ldots, u_n)$ *Sat* S. If $j = i$, then by assumption $\vdash_{V_2} u_i'$ *Sat* S holds, and the result follows by JOIN.
- B_2: Suppose $\vdash_{V_2} \bigsqcup(u_1, \ldots, u_i, \ldots, u_n)$ *Sat* S_j for $j \in 1..m$, and suppose $Pred(S_1, \ldots, S_m, S)$. The induction hypothesis is the assumption $\vdash_{V_2} \bigsqcup(u_1, \ldots, u_i', \ldots, u_n)$ *Sat* S_j for $j \in 1..m$. Since $Pred(S_1, \ldots, S_m, S)$, the same rule B_2 is applicable and hence $\vdash_{V_2} \bigsqcup(u_1, \ldots, u_i', \ldots, u_n)$ *Sat* S. □

Let the notation v[u] denote a term in U whose parse tree is factored into two parts: a core tree v with a 'hole' where the subtree for u fits. The rule MONO packages C-i and JOIN-i in a single convenient form:

$$\text{MONO}\ \frac{u \sqsubseteq u'}{v[u] \sqsubseteq v[u']}$$

Informally, the rule MONO allows in-place refinement: if u_0 can be factored as v[u], and u′ refines u, then v[u′] refines u_0.

MONO is sound and maintains harmony because C-i and JOIN-i are sound and maintain harmony. The refinement system R_4 extends R_3 with MONO. It is sound and harmonic.

2.4.5 Simplification: R_5

The rule MONO makes it possible to simplify:

- The JOIN rule:

$$\text{JOIN}\ \frac{S \sqsubseteq u}{S \sqsubseteq \bigsqcup(\ldots, u, \ldots)}$$

- Rules of the form A_3 with $n \geq 1$:

$$A_3\ \frac{S_1 \sqsubseteq u_1 \quad \ldots \quad S_n \sqsubseteq u_n}{S \sqsubseteq C(u_1, \ldots, u_n)}$$
provided $Pred(C, S_1, \ldots, S_n, S)$.

Consider the derivation:

$$\text{JOIN}\ \frac{\text{SPEC}\ \dfrac{}{S \sqsubseteq S}}{S \sqsubseteq \bigsqcup(\ldots, S, \ldots)}$$

By virtue of having been derived, the simplified rule

$$\text{JOIN}\ \frac{}{S \sqsubseteq \bigsqcup(\ldots, S, \ldots)}$$

is sound and respects Harmony 1. It can replace the old version of JOIN without decreasing derivability, because any application of the old version can be achieved by:

$$\text{TRANS}\ \frac{\text{JOIN}\ \dfrac{}{S \sqsubseteq \bigsqcup(\ldots, S, \ldots)} \qquad \text{MONO}\ \dfrac{S \sqsubseteq u}{\bigsqcup(\ldots, S, \ldots) \sqsubseteq \bigsqcup(\ldots, u, \ldots)}}{S \sqsubseteq \bigsqcup(\ldots, u, \ldots)}$$

Likewise, for each rule of the form A_3, the derived rule

$$A_3\ \frac{}{S \sqsubseteq C(S_1, \ldots, S_n)}$$
provided $Pred(C, S_1, \ldots, S_n, S)$.

is sound and respects harmony. It makes the old version redundant, since any application of the old rule can be replaced by:

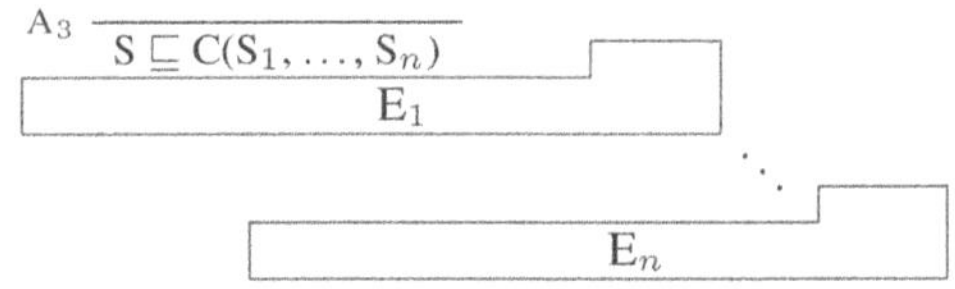

where E_i is given by:

$$\text{TRANS}\ \frac{S \sqsubseteq C(u_1, \ldots, u_{i-1}, S_i, \ldots, S_n) \qquad P_i}{S \sqsubseteq C(u_1, \ldots, u_i, S_{i+1}, \ldots, S_n)}$$

and P_i is the proof tree:

$$\text{MONO}\ \frac{S_i \sqsubseteq u_i}{C(u_1, \ldots, u_{i-1}, S_i, \ldots, S_n) \sqsubseteq C(u_1, \ldots, u_i, S_{i+1}, \ldots, S_n)}$$

Apart from these simplifications, the refinement system R_5 is the same as R_4. It is sound and harmonic.

Note: if V_2 does not include rules of the form B_2 where $m > 1$, then R_5 has the desired form and freefinement stops.

2.4.6 Wrapping Up: R_6

It remains to simplify rules of the form B_3 with $m > 1$:

$$B_3\ \frac{S_1 \sqsubseteq u \quad \ldots \quad S_m \sqsubseteq u}{S \sqsubseteq u}$$
provided $Pred(S_1, \ldots, S_m, S)$.

If $Pred(S_1, \ldots, S_m, S)$, then R_5 can derive:

$$B_3\ \frac{\text{JOIN}\ \dfrac{}{S_1 \sqsubseteq \bigsqcup(S_1, \ldots, S_m)} \quad \ldots \quad \text{JOIN}\ \dfrac{}{S_m \sqsubseteq \bigsqcup(S_1, \ldots, S_m)}}{S \sqsubseteq \bigsqcup(S_1, \ldots, S_m)}$$

The derived rule

$$B_3\ \frac{}{S \sqsubseteq \bigsqcup(S_1, \ldots, S_m)}$$
provided $Pred(S_1, \ldots, S_m, S)$.

is therefore sound and respects Harmony 1. Together with the rule:

$$\text{UNJOIN}\ \frac{}{\bigsqcup(u, \ldots, u) \sqsubseteq u}$$

which is trivially sound and respects Harmony 1, it can replace the old B_3 because any application of the old rule can be rewritten as:

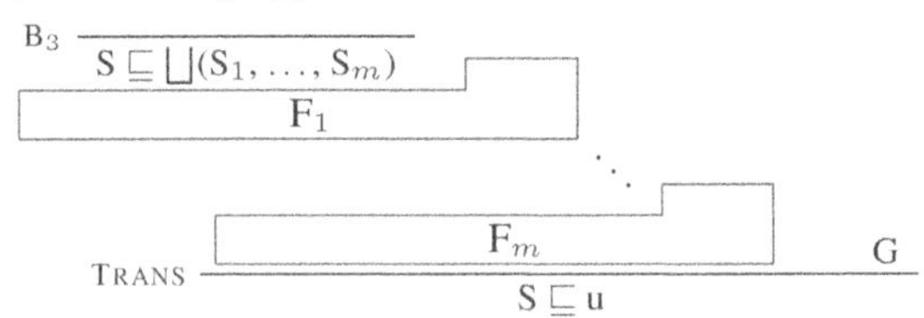

where G is UNJOIN, F_i is given by:

$$\text{TRANS}\ \frac{S \sqsubseteq \bigsqcup(\overbrace{u, \ldots, u}^{i-1}, S_i, \ldots, S_m) \qquad Q_i}{S \sqsubseteq \bigsqcup(u, \ldots, u, S_{i+1}, \ldots, S_m)}$$

and Q_i is the proof tree:

$$\text{MONO}\ \frac{S_i \sqsubseteq u}{\bigsqcup(u, \ldots, u, S_i, \ldots, S_m) \sqsubseteq \bigsqcup(\underbrace{u, \ldots, u}_{i}, S_{i+1}, \ldots, S_m)}$$

R_6 is the same as R_5, except that it includes UNJOIN and replaces rules of the form B_3 where $m > 1$ with their simplified versions. R_6 is sound, harmonic and of the desired form.

2.5 Discussion

R_6 can be made more powerful in several ways. For example, the following generalization of JOIN is sound and preserves Harmony 1:

$$\text{JOIN}' \; \frac{}{u \sqsubseteq \bigsqcup(\ldots, u, \ldots)}$$

The same holds for the reflexivity of refinement, which generalizes SPEC, and other rules such as UNNEST:

$$\text{UNNEST} \; \frac{}{\bigsqcup(u_1, \ldots, u_n) \sqsubseteq \bigsqcup(u_1, \ldots, u_{i-1}, u'_1, \ldots, u'_m, u_{i+1}, \ldots, u_n)}$$

provided $1 \le i \le n$ and $u_i = \bigsqcup(u'_1, \ldots, u'_m)$.

In specific applications of freefinement, it might also be useful to add derived rules to R_6. Examples of this will follow later.

Freefinement assumes as little as possible about $\models_{V_1} \_\ \mathit{Sat}\ \_$ and is consequently very generic. As one might expect, additional assumptions can help to construct more powerful refinement systems. For example, suppose 'plus' is a constructor that is commutative in the sense that

$$\forall t_1, t_2 \in T, S \in \mathbb{S} \cdot \models_{V_1} \mathrm{plus}(t_1, t_2)\ \mathit{Sat}\ S \;\Leftrightarrow\; \models_{V_1} \mathrm{plus}(t_2, t_1)\ \mathit{Sat}\ S$$

Then $\mathrm{Specs}(\mathrm{plus}(\llbracket u_1 \rrbracket, \llbracket u_2 \rrbracket)) = \mathrm{Specs}(\mathrm{plus}(\llbracket u_2 \rrbracket, \llbracket u_1 \rrbracket))$ because

$$\begin{array}{ll} & S \in \mathrm{Specs}(\mathrm{plus}(\llbracket u_1 \rrbracket, \llbracket u_2 \rrbracket)) \\ \Leftrightarrow & \forall t_1 \in \llbracket u_1 \rrbracket, t_2 \in \llbracket u_2 \rrbracket \cdot \models_{V_1} \mathrm{plus}(t_1, t_2)\ \mathit{Sat}\ S \\ \Leftrightarrow & \forall t_1 \in \llbracket u_1 \rrbracket, t_2 \in \llbracket u_2 \rrbracket \cdot \models_{V_1} \mathrm{plus}(t_2, t_1)\ \mathit{Sat}\ S \\ \Leftrightarrow & S \in \mathrm{Specs}(\mathrm{plus}(\llbracket u_2 \rrbracket, \llbracket u_1 \rrbracket)) \end{array}$$

So $\llbracket \mathrm{plus}(u_1, u_2) \rrbracket = \llbracket \mathrm{plus}(u_2, u_1) \rrbracket$ and therefore the refinement rule $\mathrm{plus}(u_1, u_2) \equiv \mathrm{plus}(u_2, u_1)$ is sound. Depending on the rules of V_1, it might also preserve harmony.

As mentioned before, the semantic function $\llbracket \_ \rrbracket$ and the refinement order $\sqsubseteq$ have nice interpretations when $\models_{V_1} \_\ \mathit{Sat}\ \_$ is well-behaved. Here is the definition:

Definition 8 (Well-behavedness)**.** $\models_{V_1} \_\ \mathit{Sat}\ \_$ is well-behaved iff
$\forall C \in \mathbb{K}, t_1, \ldots, t_n \in T, S \in \mathbb{S} \cdot \models_{V_1} C(t_1, \ldots, t_n)\ \mathit{Sat}\ S \Rightarrow$
$\forall t \in C(\mathrm{Terms}(\mathrm{Specs}(\{t_1\})), \ldots, \mathrm{Terms}(\mathrm{Specs}(\{t_n\}))) \cdot \models_{V_1} t\ \mathit{Sat}\ S$

There is also an alternative characterization of well-behavedness:

Lemma 9. $\models_{V_1} \_\ \mathit{Sat}\ \_$ is well-behaved iff
$\forall C \in \mathbb{K}, t_1, \ldots, t_n \in T \cdot \mathrm{Terms}(\mathrm{Specs}(\{C(t_1, \ldots, t_n)\})) =$
$\mathrm{Terms}(\mathrm{Specs}(C(\mathrm{Terms}(\mathrm{Specs}(\{t_1\})), \ldots, \mathrm{Terms}(\mathrm{Specs}(\{t_n\})))))$

Proof. $t_i \in \mathrm{Terms}(\mathrm{Specs}(\{t_i\}))$ for $i \in 1..n$ by Corollary 1.1, so $\{C(t_1, \ldots, t_n)\} \subseteq C(\mathrm{Terms}(\mathrm{Specs}(\{t_1\})), \ldots, \mathrm{Terms}(\mathrm{Specs}(\{t_n\})))$. Hence by Corollary 2.3 in the Appendix, $\mathrm{Specs}(\{C(t_1, \ldots, t_n)\}) \supseteq \mathrm{Specs}(C(\mathrm{Terms}(\mathrm{Specs}(\{t_1\})), \ldots, \mathrm{Terms}(\mathrm{Specs}(\{t_n\}))))$.

Therefore:

$\models_{V_1} \_\ \mathit{Sat}\ \_$ is well-behaved

$\Leftrightarrow$

$\forall C \in \mathbb{K}, t_1, \ldots, t_n \in T, S \in \mathbb{S} \cdot \models_{V_1} C(t_1, \ldots, t_n)\ \mathit{Sat}\ S \Rightarrow$
$\forall t \in C(\mathrm{Terms}(\mathrm{Specs}(\{t_1\})), \ldots, \mathrm{Terms}(\mathrm{Specs}(\{t_n\}))) \cdot \models_{V_1} t\ \mathit{Sat}\ S$

$\Leftrightarrow$

$\forall C \in \mathbb{K}, t_1, \ldots, t_n \in T, S \in \mathbb{S} \cdot S \in \mathrm{Specs}(\{C(t_1, \ldots, t_n)\}) \Rightarrow$
$S \in \mathrm{Specs}(C(\mathrm{Terms}(\mathrm{Specs}(\{t_1\})), \ldots, \mathrm{Terms}(\mathrm{Specs}(\{t_n\}))))$

$\Leftrightarrow$

$\forall C \in \mathbb{K}, t_1, \ldots, t_n \in T \cdot \mathrm{Specs}(\{C(t_1, \ldots, t_n)\}) \subseteq$
$\mathrm{Specs}(C(\mathrm{Terms}(\mathrm{Specs}(\{t_1\})), \ldots, \mathrm{Terms}(\mathrm{Specs}(\{t_n\}))))$

$\Leftrightarrow$ {by the reasoning above}

$\forall C \in \mathbb{K}, t_1, \ldots, t_n \in T \cdot \mathrm{Specs}(\{C(t_1, \ldots, t_n)\}) =$
$\mathrm{Specs}(C(\mathrm{Terms}(\mathrm{Specs}(\{t_1\})), \ldots, \mathrm{Terms}(\mathrm{Specs}(\{t_n\}))))$

The result then follows by Corollary 1.3. □

Freefinement does not require well-behavedness of $\models_{V_1} \_\ \mathit{Sat}\ \_$, but the next theorem shows that the intuitions behind the definitions are simple when $\models_{V_1} \_\ \mathit{Sat}\ \_$ is well-behaved. For example, Theorem 6.3 says that $\llbracket u \rrbracket$ is the set of all primitive terms that refine u.

Theorem 6. If $\models_{V_1} \_\ \mathit{Sat}\ \_$ is well-behaved, then

6.1 $\forall t \in T \cdot \llbracket t \rrbracket = \mathrm{Terms}(\mathrm{Specs}(\{t\}))$
6.2 $\forall t \in T, S \in \mathbb{S} \cdot \models_{V_1} t\ \mathit{Sat}\ S \;\Leftrightarrow\; \models_{V_2} t\ \mathit{Sat}\ S$
6.3 $\forall t \in T, u \in U \cdot t \in \llbracket u \rrbracket \;\Leftrightarrow\; \models u \sqsubseteq t$

Proof.

6.1 By induction on the structure of t. Suppose $t = C(t_1, \ldots, t_n)$ and assume $\llbracket t_i \rrbracket = \mathrm{Terms}(\mathrm{Specs}(\{t_i\}))$ for $i \in 1..n$. Then:
$\llbracket t \rrbracket = \mathrm{Terms}(\mathrm{Specs}(C(\llbracket t_1 \rrbracket, \ldots, \llbracket t_n \rrbracket)))$
$=$ {induction hypothesis}
$\mathrm{Terms}(\mathrm{Specs}(C(\mathrm{Terms}(\mathrm{Specs}(\{t_1\})), \ldots, \mathrm{Terms}(\mathrm{Specs}(\{t_n\})))))$
$=$ {Lemma 9}
$\mathrm{Terms}(\mathrm{Specs}(\{C(t_1, \ldots, t_n)\})) = \mathrm{Terms}(\mathrm{Specs}(\{t\}))$.

6.2 $\models_{V_1} t\ \mathit{Sat}\ S$
$\Leftrightarrow$ {definition of Specs}
$S \in \mathrm{Specs}(\{t\})$
$\Leftrightarrow$ {Corollary 2.7 in the Appendix}
$S \in \mathrm{Specs}(\mathrm{Terms}(\mathrm{Specs}(\{t\})))$
$\Leftrightarrow$ {Theorem 6.1}
$S \in \mathrm{Specs}(\llbracket t \rrbracket)$
$\Leftrightarrow$ {Lemma 4}
$\models_{V_2} t\ \mathit{Sat}\ S$

6.3 The $\Leftarrow$ proof is trivial since $t \in \llbracket t \rrbracket$. For $\Rightarrow$, assume $\{t\} \subseteq \llbracket u \rrbracket$. Then $\mathrm{Terms}(\mathrm{Specs}(\{t\})) \subseteq \mathrm{Terms}(\mathrm{Specs}(\llbracket u \rrbracket))$ by Corollary 2.5 in the Appendix, and $\llbracket t \rrbracket \subseteq \llbracket u \rrbracket$ by Theorem 6.1 and Lemma 2. □

Whether $\models_{V_1} \_\ \mathit{Sat}\ \_$ is well-behaved depends partly on the expressivity of specifications. For example, suppose

$$\mathbb{K} = \{x := e \mid e \text{ is an arithmetic expression}\} \cup \{\_ \fatsemi \_\}$$

i.e. there is a nullary constructor $x := e$ for all arithmetic expressions e, and a binary constructor for sequential composition. Suppose $\mathbb{S} = \{\mathrm{Even\_x}\}$, and $\models_{V_1} t\ \mathit{Sat}\ \mathrm{Even\_x}$ holds iff, if t is executed in any state where x is even, then x is even in every resulting state. So $\models_{V_1} x := x + 1 \fatsemi x := x + 1\ \mathit{Sat}\ \mathrm{Even\_x}$, but it is not the case that $\models_{V_1} x := x + 1\ \mathit{Sat}\ \mathrm{Even\_x}$. In fact, $x := x + 1$ does not satisfy any specification. This implies that $\mathrm{Terms}(\mathrm{Specs}(\{x := x + 1\})) = T$, so $x := 1 \fatsemi x := 1 \in \mathrm{Terms}(\mathrm{Specs}(\{x := x + 1\})) \fatsemi \mathrm{Terms}(\mathrm{Specs}(\{x := x + 1\}))$. But $\models_{V_1} x := 1 \fatsemi x := 1\ \mathit{Sat}\ \mathrm{Even\_x}$ does not hold, hence $\models_{V_1} \_\ \mathit{Sat}\ \_$ is not well-behaved.

Even though $\models_{V_1} \_\ \mathit{Sat}\ \_$ is not well-behaved, it is still possible to have inference rules that are amenable to freefinement, for example:

$$1\; \frac{}{x := e\ \mathit{Sat}\ \mathrm{Even\_x}} \qquad 2\; \frac{t\ \mathit{Sat}\ \mathrm{Even\_x} \qquad t'\ \mathit{Sat}\ \mathrm{Even\_x}}{t \fatsemi t'\ \mathit{Sat}\ \mathrm{Even\_x}}$$

provided $e \in \{\ldots, \text{-}2, 0, 2, \ldots\}$.

If $\mathbb{S}$ is instead a set of specifications of the form $[P, Q]$, where P is a precondition and Q a postcondition, and

$$\models_{V_1} t \fatsemi t'\ \mathit{Sat}\ [P, Q] \;\Leftrightarrow\; \exists R \cdot \models_{V_1} t\ \mathit{Sat}\ [P, R] \wedge \models_{V_1} t'\ \mathit{Sat}\ [R, Q]$$

then it is easy to show that this $\models_{V_1} \_\ \mathit{Sat}\ \_$ is well-behaved.

The completeness of V_1 is a sufficient condition for the well-behavedness of $\models_{V_1} \_\ \mathit{Sat}\ \_$:

Theorem 7. If V_1 is complete, then $\models_{V_1} \_\ \mathit{Sat}\ \_$ is well-behaved.

Proof. If V_1 is complete, then $\models_{V_1} C(t_1, \ldots, t_n)\ \mathit{Sat}\ S \Leftrightarrow \vdash_{V_1} C(t_1, \ldots, t_n)\ \mathit{Sat}\ S$. The well-behavedness of $\models_{V_1} \_\ \mathit{Sat}\ \_$ follows by induction on the derivation of $C(t_1, \ldots, t_n)\ \mathit{Sat}\ S$:

- For each rule of the form A_1, assume $\mathrm{Pred}(C, S_1, \ldots, S_n, S)$ and $S_i \in \mathrm{Specs}(\{t_i\})$ for all $i \in 1..n$. So $\forall t'_i \in \mathrm{Terms}(\mathrm{Specs}(\{t_i\}))\cdot \models_{V_1} t'_i \ \mathit{Sat}\ S_i$ for all $i \in 1..n$. The rule is sound with respect to Definition 1.1, hence $\forall t \in C(\mathrm{Terms}(\mathrm{Specs}(\{t_1\})), \ldots, \mathrm{Terms}(\mathrm{Specs}(\{t_n\})))\cdot \models_{V_1} t\ \mathit{Sat}\ S$.
- For each rule of the form B_1, assume $\mathrm{Pred}(S_1, \ldots, S_m, S)$ and $\forall t \in C(\mathrm{Terms}(\mathrm{Specs}(\{t_1\})), \ldots, \mathrm{Terms}(\mathrm{Specs}(\{t_n\})))\cdot \models_{V_1} t\ \mathit{Sat}\ S_i$ for all $i \in 1..m$. The rule is sound w.r.t. Definition 1.2, so $\forall t \in C(\mathrm{Terms}(\mathrm{Specs}(\{t_1\})), \ldots, \mathrm{Terms}(\mathrm{Specs}(\{t_n\})))\cdot \models_{V_1} t\ \mathit{Sat}\ S$. □

3. Applications

3.1 Lambda Calculus

The top left corner of Figure 1 contains a type system λ_1 for the lambda calculus. By considering pairs of the form (typing context, type) as specifications, it is possible to apply freefinement and obtain a refinement calculus for (extended) lambda terms in the spirit of Denney [4]. The inputs to freefinement are as follows:

1. $\mathbb{K} = \mathrm{Var} \cup \{\lambda x.\, \_ \mid x \in \mathrm{Var}\} \cup \{\_\ \_\}$
   Note that $\mathbb{K}$ defines the language T of lambda terms:
   $$e ::= x \mid \lambda x.\, e \mid e\ e'$$
   Here and in the following, x ranges over the set of variables Var, and e ranges over T.
2. $\mathbb{S} = \{[\Gamma; \tau] \mid \Gamma \in \mathrm{Context} \wedge \tau \in \mathrm{Type}\}$, where Context is the set of typing contexts and Type is the set of types that contains the type constructor $\_ \rightarrow \_$. The intended representation of a typing context Γ is a list of variable names paired with types. Variables may appear more than once in Γ, and variable lookup uses the rightmost occurrence. In the following, σ and τ range over Type, and Γ ranges over Context.
3. $\models_{V_1} \_\ \mathit{Sat}\ \_$ is defined by:
   - $\models_{V_1} x\ \mathit{Sat}\ [\Gamma; \tau] \Leftrightarrow x : \tau \in \Gamma$
   - $\models_{V_1} \lambda x.\, e\ \mathit{Sat}\ [\Gamma; \tau] \Leftrightarrow \exists \sigma, \tau' \cdot \tau = \sigma \rightarrow \tau' \wedge \models_{V_1} e\ \mathit{Sat}\ [\Gamma, x : \sigma; \tau']$
   - $\models_{V_1} e\ e'\ \mathit{Sat}\ [\Gamma; \tau] \Leftrightarrow \exists \sigma \cdot \models_{V_1} e\ \mathit{Sat}\ [\Gamma; \sigma \rightarrow \tau] \wedge \models_{V_1} e'\ \mathit{Sat}\ [\Gamma; \sigma]$
4. V_1, shown in the top right corner of Figure 1, is obtained from λ_1 by replacing $\Gamma \vdash e : \tau$ with $e\ \mathit{Sat}\ [\Gamma; \tau]$. The rules VAR, ABS and APP are all of the form A_1 with $n = 0, 1$ and 2 respectively. For example, in the case of ABS, $\mathrm{Pred}(C, S_1, S)$ is defined as $\exists x, \Gamma, \sigma, \tau \cdot C = \lambda x.\, \_ \wedge S_1 = [\Gamma, x : \sigma; \tau] \wedge S = [\Gamma; \sigma \rightarrow \tau]$.

Since V_1 does not contain rules of the form B_1 where $m > 1$, freefinement does not add join terms to the lambda calculus. The system λ_2 in Figure 1 is V_2 where $f\ \mathit{Sat}\ [\Gamma; \tau]$ is written instead as $\Gamma \vdash f : \tau$. The system R_5, shown in the bottom right of Figure 1, is the final harmonic refinement calculus that freefinement produces.

Here is an example top-down typing derivation with R_5:

$$\begin{array}{ll} & [\Gamma; (\sigma \rightarrow \tau) \rightarrow (\sigma \rightarrow \tau)] \\ \sqsubseteq & \text{“ABS”} \\ & \lambda x.\, [\Gamma, x : \sigma \rightarrow \tau; \sigma \rightarrow \tau] \\ \sqsubseteq & \text{“MONO with ABS”} \\ & \lambda x.\, \lambda y.\, [\Gamma, x : \sigma \rightarrow \tau, y : \sigma; \tau] \\ \sqsubseteq & \text{“MONO with APP”} \\ & \lambda x.\, \lambda y.\, ([\Gamma, x : \sigma \rightarrow \tau, y : \sigma; \sigma \rightarrow \tau]\ [\Gamma, x : \sigma \rightarrow \tau, y : \sigma; \sigma]) \\ \sqsubseteq & \text{“Twice MONO with VAR”} \\ & \lambda x.\, \lambda y.\, (x\ y) \end{array}$$

λ_1	V_1
VAR $\dfrac{x : \tau \in \Gamma}{\Gamma \vdash x : \tau}$	VAR $\dfrac{}{x\ \mathit{Sat}\ [\Gamma; \tau]}$ provided $x : \tau \in \Gamma$.
ABS $\dfrac{\Gamma, x : \sigma \vdash e : \tau}{\Gamma \vdash \lambda x.\, e : \sigma \rightarrow \tau}$	ABS $\dfrac{e\ \mathit{Sat}\ [\Gamma, x : \sigma; \tau]}{\lambda x.\, e\ \mathit{Sat}\ [\Gamma; \sigma \rightarrow \tau]}$
APP $\dfrac{\Gamma \vdash e : \sigma \rightarrow \tau \quad \Gamma \vdash e' : \sigma}{\Gamma \vdash e\ e' : \tau}$	APP $\dfrac{e\ \mathit{Sat}\ [\Gamma; \sigma \rightarrow \tau] \quad e'\ \mathit{Sat}\ [\Gamma; \sigma]}{e\ e'\ \mathit{Sat}\ [\Gamma; \tau]}$
λ_2	R_5
VAR $\dfrac{x : \tau \in \Gamma}{\Gamma \vdash x : \tau}$	VAR $\dfrac{}{[\Gamma; \tau] \sqsubseteq x}$ provided $x : \tau \in \Gamma$.
ABS $\dfrac{\Gamma, x : \sigma \vdash f : \tau}{\Gamma \vdash \lambda x.\, f : \sigma \rightarrow \tau}$	ABS $\dfrac{}{[\Gamma; \sigma \rightarrow \tau] \sqsubseteq \lambda x.\, [\Gamma, x : \sigma; \tau]}$
APP $\dfrac{\Gamma \vdash f : \sigma \rightarrow \tau \quad \Gamma \vdash f' : \sigma}{\Gamma \vdash f\ f' : \tau}$	APP $\dfrac{}{[\Gamma; \tau] \sqsubseteq [\Gamma; \sigma \rightarrow \tau]\ [\Gamma; \sigma]}$
SPEC $\dfrac{}{\Gamma \vdash [\Gamma; \sigma] : \sigma}$	SPEC $\dfrac{}{[\Gamma; \sigma] \sqsubseteq [\Gamma; \sigma]}$
	TRANS $\dfrac{f_1 \sqsubseteq f_2 \quad f_2 \sqsubseteq f_3}{f_1 \sqsubseteq f_3}$
	MONO $\dfrac{f \sqsubseteq f'}{g[f] \sqsubseteq g[f']}$

Figure 1. Freefinement and a typed lambda calculus

Since R_5 is harmonic and V_2 is a sound and conservative extension of V_1, it holds that $\vdash_{\lambda_1} \Gamma \vdash \lambda x.\, \lambda y.\, (x\ y) : (\sigma \rightarrow \tau) \rightarrow (\sigma \rightarrow \tau)$.

One might wish to extend R_5 using knowledge particular to lambda calculus typing. It is simple to show that V_1 is complete, so

$$\vdash_{\lambda_1} \Gamma \vdash e : \tau \Leftrightarrow \vdash_{V_1} e\ \mathit{Sat}\ [\Gamma; \tau] \Leftrightarrow \models_{V_1} e\ \mathit{Sat}\ [\Gamma; \tau]$$

Furthermore, by Theorems 7 and 6.2,

$$\models_{V_1} e\ \mathit{Sat}\ [\Gamma; \tau] \Leftrightarrow \models_{V_2} e\ \mathit{Sat}\ [\Gamma; \tau]$$

and because V_2 is a sound and conservative extension of V_1,

$$\vdash_{V_1} e\ \mathit{Sat}\ [\Gamma; \tau] \Leftrightarrow \vdash_{V_2} e\ \mathit{Sat}\ [\Gamma; \tau]$$

Consider the property of *preservation*:

Definition 9. A relation $\rightsquigarrow \subseteq T \times T$ satisfies preservation $\stackrel{\text{def}}{=}$ $\forall \Gamma, \tau, e, e' \cdot$ if $\vdash_{\lambda_1} \Gamma \vdash e : \tau$ and $e \rightsquigarrow e'$, then $\vdash_{\lambda_1} \Gamma \vdash e' : \tau$.

Theorem 8. If $\rightsquigarrow$ satisfies preservation, then:

8.1 If $e \rightsquigarrow e'$, then $\models e \sqsubseteq e'$.
8.2 If $\vdash_{V_2} e$ Sat $[\Gamma; \tau]$ and $e \rightsquigarrow e'$, then $\vdash_{V_2} e'\ \mathit{Sat}\ [\Gamma; \tau]$.

Proof. The proof of 8.2 is trivial. For 8.1:

$$\begin{array}{l} \forall \Gamma, \tau, e, e' \cdot \vdash_{\lambda_1} \Gamma \vdash e : \tau \ \wedge\ e \rightsquigarrow e' \Rightarrow \vdash_{\lambda_1} \Gamma \vdash e' : \tau \\ \quad \Leftrightarrow \quad \{\text{predicate logic}\} \\ \forall e, e' \cdot e \rightsquigarrow e' \Rightarrow (\forall \Gamma, \tau \cdot \vdash_{\lambda_1} \Gamma \vdash e : \tau \Rightarrow \vdash_{\lambda_1} \Gamma \vdash e' : \tau) \\ \quad \Leftrightarrow \\ \forall e, e' \cdot e \rightsquigarrow e' \Rightarrow (\forall S \in \mathbb{S} \cdot \models_{V_2} e\ \mathit{Sat}\ S \Rightarrow \models_{V_2} e'\ \mathit{Sat}\ S) \\ \quad \Leftrightarrow \quad \{\text{Lemma 5}\} \\ \forall e, e' \cdot e \rightsquigarrow e' \Rightarrow \models e \sqsubseteq e' \end{array}$$

□

So any relation that satisfies preservation contains only sound refinements that satisfy Harmony 1, and can augment R_5 to yield a sound and harmonic refinement system. Examples of relations that satisfy preservation include:

- The α-conversion relation.
- The β-reduction relation.
- The η-contraction relation. So $\lambda x.\,(e\ \ x) \sqsubseteq e$, provided x does not appear free in e.
- The relation $\leq$ on closed terms, where $e \leq e'$ exactly when e has fewer types than e'.

Here is a small example that uses the η-contraction extension:

$$\begin{array}{ll} & \lambda x.\,\lambda y.\,\lambda z.\,((x\ \ y)\ \ z) \\ \sqsubseteq & \{\textsc{Mono}\text{ with }\eta\text{-contraction}\} \\ & \lambda x.\,\lambda y.\,(x\ \ y) \\ \sqsubseteq & \{\textsc{Mono}\text{ with }\eta\text{-contraction}\} \\ & \lambda x.\,x \end{array}$$

3.2 Hoare Logic

The top left corner of Figure 2 contains system H, a Hoare logic for simple imperative programs. P is a precondition, Q a postcondition, and c a command in the Hoare triple $\{P\}c\{Q\}$, and $\models_H \{P\}c\{Q\}$ is the usual partial correctness interpretation of $\{P\}c\{Q\}$. By interpreting a specification as a pre-post pair, the rules of H do not fit the rule forms A_1 and B_1, since the proviso of AUXVARELIM inspects the command c to determine the variables that it writes and reads. However, if specifications also keep track of written and read variables, then it becomes possible to apply freefinement to obtain a refinement calculus in the spirit of Morgan [9]. Here are the inputs:

1. There are constructors for assignments, sequential composition, conditionals and loops:

$$\begin{array}{rcl} \mathbb{K} & = & \{x := e \mid x \in \text{Var} \ \wedge\ e \in \text{IntExp}\} \\ & & \cup\, \{\_\,\fatsemi\,\_\} \\ & & \cup\, \{\textbf{if}\ b\ \textbf{then}\ \_\ \textbf{else}\ \_ \mid b \in \text{BoolExp}\} \\ & & \cup\, \{\textbf{while}\ b\ \textbf{do}\ \_ \mid b \in \text{BoolExp}\} \end{array}$$

2. A specification consists of two sets of variables and two assertions, written in a notation resembling Morgan's specification statement [8]:

$$\mathbb{S} = \{\overline{x}; \overline{y} : \{P, Q\} \mid \overline{x}, \overline{y} \in \mathcal{P}(\text{Var}) \ \wedge\ P, Q \in \text{Assertion}\}$$

3. In the specification $\overline{x}; \overline{y} : \{P, Q\}$, the $\overline{x}$ and $\overline{y}$ are upper bounds on the sets of variables written and read by the command respectively, the P is a precondition and the Q a postcondition:

$$\models_{V_1} c\ \textit{Sat}\ \overline{x}; \overline{y} : \{P, Q\} \stackrel{\text{def}}{=} \textit{writes}(c) \subseteq \overline{x} \ \wedge\ \textit{reads}(c) \subseteq \overline{y} \ \wedge\ \models_H \{P\}c\{Q\}$$

4. V_1, shown in the top right corner of Figure 2, has the following relationship with H:

$$\vdash_{V_1} c\ \textit{Sat}\ \overline{x}; \overline{y} : \{P, Q\} \Leftrightarrow \textit{writes}(c) \subseteq \overline{x} \ \wedge\ \textit{reads}(c) \subseteq \overline{y} \ \wedge\ \vdash_H \{P\}c\{Q\}$$

   Note that:

   - The non-structural rules of H have counterparts in V_1 that embody the definitions of *writes* and *reads*. For example, the conclusion of COND reflects that

$$\textit{writes}(\textbf{if}\ b\ \textbf{then}\ c\ \textbf{else}\ c') \stackrel{\text{def}}{=} \textit{writes}(c) \cup \textit{writes}(c') \text{ and}$$
$$\textit{reads}(\textbf{if}\ b\ \textbf{then}\ c\ \textbf{else}\ c') \stackrel{\text{def}}{=} \textit{reads}(c) \cup \textit{reads}(c') \cup \textit{FV}(b).$$

   - The structural rules of H that inspect c for its write and/or read sets have counterparts in V_1 that consult the specification instead. See for example the proviso of AUXVARELIM.
   - CONSEQUENCE in V_1 allows the enlargement of write and read sets. This loosening of the bounds is useful in refinement developments, because then the resulting code is not forced to write and read all the variables that were originally available for writing and reading.

The V_1-counterparts of the structural rules of H are all of the form B_1. For example, $m = 1$ in the case of CONSTANCY, and $m = 2$ for DISJ. The other rules are of the form A_1. For example, $n = 2$ in the case of COND, and $n = 1$ for LOOP.

The systems V_2 and R_6 that freefinement produces appear at the bottom of Figure 2. R_6 yields several derived rules that may be useful in practical refinement developments. For example, the rule:

$$\textsc{DerivedVarAssign}\ \frac{}{\overline{x}; \overline{y} : \{P, Q\} \sqsubseteq z := e}$$
provided $z \in \overline{x}$ and $\textit{FV}(e) \subseteq \overline{y}$ and $P \Rightarrow Q[e/z]$.

can replace VARASSIGN, and is similar to the assignment law of Morgan (Law 1.3 on p. 8 of [9]). Likewise, the derived rule:

$$\textsc{FollowingVarAssign}\ \frac{}{\overline{x}; \overline{y} : \{P, Q\} \sqsubseteq \overline{x}; \overline{y} : \{P, Q[e/z]\} \fatsemi z := e}$$
provided $z \in \overline{x}$ and $\textit{FV}(e) \subseteq \overline{y}$.

is similar to the *following assignment* law of Morgan (Law 3.5 on p. 32 of [9]).

Here is an example showing that R_6 can derive a correct factorial algorithm starting with its specification:

$$\begin{array}{ll} & y,z;\, x,y,z : \{\text{true},\ y = x!\} \\ \sqsubseteq & \text{“}\textsc{SeqComp}\text{”} \\ & y,z;\, \emptyset : \{\text{true},\ y = 1 \wedge z = 0\} \fatsemi y,z;\, x,y,z : \{y = 1 \wedge z = 0,\ y = x!\} \end{array}$$

The first spec statement is refined as follows:

$$\begin{array}{ll} & y,z;\, \emptyset : \{\text{true},\ y = 1 \wedge z = 0\} \\ \sqsubseteq & \text{“}\textsc{SeqComp}\text{”} \\ & y;\, \emptyset : \{\text{true},\ y = 1\} \fatsemi z;\, \emptyset : \{y = 1,\ y = 1 \wedge z = 0\} \\ \sqsubseteq & \text{“Twice }\textsc{Mono}\text{ with }\textsc{Consequence}\text{”} \\ & y;\, \emptyset : \{1 = 1,\ y = 1\} \fatsemi z;\, \emptyset : \{y = 1 \wedge 0 = 0,\ y = 1 \wedge z = 0\} \\ \sqsubseteq & \text{“Twice }\textsc{Mono}\text{ with }\textsc{VarAssign}\text{”} \\ & y := 1 \fatsemi z := 0 \end{array}$$

And for the second spec statement:

$$\begin{array}{ll} & y,z;\, x,y,z : \{y = 1 \wedge z = 0,\ y = x!\} \\ \sqsubseteq & \text{“}\textsc{Consequence}\text{”} \\ & y,z;\, x,y,z : \{y = z!,\ y = z! \wedge \neg z{\neq}x\} \\ \sqsubseteq & \text{“}\textsc{Loop}\text{”} \\ & \textbf{while}\ z{\neq}x\ \textbf{do}\ y,z;\, y,z : \{y = z! \wedge z{\neq}x,\ y = z!\} \\ \sqsubseteq & \text{“}\textsc{Mono}\text{ with }\textsc{SeqComp}\text{”} \\ & \textbf{while}\ z{\neq}x\ \textbf{do}\ z;\, z : \{y = z! \wedge z{\neq}x,\ y{\cdot}z = z!\} \fatsemi y;\, y,z : \{y{\cdot}z = z!,\ y = z!\} \end{array}$$

H	V_1
$\textsc{AuxVarElim}\ \dfrac{\{P\}c\{Q\}}{\{\exists v\cdot P\}c\{\exists v\cdot Q\}}$ provided $v \notin \mathit{writes}(c) \cup \mathit{reads}(c)$. $\textsc{Consequence}\ \dfrac{\{P'\}c\{Q'\}}{\{P\}c\{Q\}}$ provided $P \Rightarrow P'$ and $Q' \Rightarrow Q$. $\textsc{Constancy}\ \dfrac{\{P\}c\{Q\}}{\{P \wedge R\}c\{Q \wedge R\}}$ provided $FV(R) \cap \mathit{writes}(c) = \emptyset$. $\textsc{Disj}\ \dfrac{\{P\}c\{Q\} \qquad \{P'\}c\{Q'\}}{\{P \vee P'\}c\{Q \vee Q'\}}$ $\textsc{VarAssign}\ \dfrac{}{\{P[e/x]\}x := e\{P\}}$ $\textsc{SeqComp}\ \dfrac{\{P\}c\{Q\} \qquad \{Q\}c'\{R\}}{\{P\}c \mathbin{;} c'\{R\}}$ $\textsc{Cond}\ \dfrac{\{P \wedge b\}c\{Q\} \qquad \{P \wedge \neg b\}c'\{Q\}}{\{P\}\textbf{if } b \textbf{ then } c \textbf{ else } c'\{Q\}}$ $\textsc{Loop}\ \dfrac{\{I \wedge b\}c\{I\}}{\{I\}\textbf{while } b \textbf{ do } c\{I \wedge \neg b\}}$	$\textsc{AuxVarElim}\ \dfrac{c\ \mathit{Sat}\ \ \overline{x};\overline{y}:\{P,Q\}}{c\ \mathit{Sat}\ \ \overline{x};\overline{y}:\{\exists v\cdot P, \exists v\cdot Q\}}$ provided $v \notin \overline{x} \cup \overline{y}$. $\textsc{Consequence}\ \dfrac{c\ \mathit{Sat}\ \ \overline{x'};\overline{y'}:\{P',Q'\}}{c\ \mathit{Sat}\ \ \overline{x};\overline{y}:\{P,Q\}}$ provided $\overline{x} \supseteq \overline{x'}$ and $\overline{y} \supseteq \overline{y'}$ and $P \Rightarrow P'$ and $Q' \Rightarrow Q$. $\textsc{Constancy}\ \dfrac{c\ \mathit{Sat}\ \ \overline{x};\overline{y}:\{P,Q\}}{c\ \mathit{Sat}\ \ \overline{x};\overline{y}:\{P \wedge R, Q \wedge R\}}$ provided $FV(R) \cap \overline{x} = \emptyset$. $\textsc{Disj}\ \dfrac{c\ \mathit{Sat}\ \ \overline{x};\overline{y}:\{P,Q\} \qquad c\ \mathit{Sat}\ \ \overline{x};\overline{y}:\{P',Q'\}}{c\ \mathit{Sat}\ \ \overline{x};\overline{y}:\{P \vee P', Q \vee Q'\}}$ $\textsc{VarAssign}\ \dfrac{}{x := e\ \ \mathit{Sat}\ \ x; FV(e):\{P[e/x], P\}}$ $\textsc{SeqComp}\ \dfrac{c\ \mathit{Sat}\ \ \overline{x};\overline{y}:\{P,Q\} \qquad c'\ \mathit{Sat}\ \ \overline{x'};\overline{y'}:\{Q,R\}}{c \mathbin{;} c'\ \ \mathit{Sat}\ \ \overline{x} \cup \overline{x'}; \overline{x} \cup \overline{x'}:\{P,R\}}$ $\textsc{Cond}\ \dfrac{c\ \mathit{Sat}\ \ \overline{x};\overline{y}:\{P \wedge b, Q\} \qquad c'\ \mathit{Sat}\ \ \overline{x'};\overline{y'}:\{P \wedge \neg b, Q\}}{\textbf{if } b \textbf{ then } c \textbf{ else } c'\ \ \mathit{Sat}\ \ \overline{x} \cup \overline{x'}; \overline{y} \cup \overline{y'} \cup FV(b):\{P,Q\}}$ $\textsc{Loop}\ \dfrac{c\ \mathit{Sat}\ \ \overline{x};\overline{y}:\{I \wedge b, I\}}{\textbf{while } b \textbf{ do } c\ \ \mathit{Sat}\ \ \overline{x};\overline{y} \cup FV(b):\{I, I \wedge \neg b\}}$
V_2	R_6
$\textsc{AuxVarElim}\ \dfrac{s\ \mathit{Sat}\ \ \overline{x};\overline{y}:\{P,Q\}}{s\ \mathit{Sat}\ \ \overline{x};\overline{y}:\{\exists v\cdot P, \exists v\cdot Q\}}$ provided $v \notin \overline{x} \cup \overline{y}$. $\textsc{Consequence}\ \dfrac{s\ \mathit{Sat}\ \ \overline{x'};\overline{y'}:\{P',Q'\}}{s\ \mathit{Sat}\ \ \overline{x};\overline{y}:\{P,Q\}}$ provided $\overline{x} \supseteq \overline{x'}$ and $\overline{y} \supseteq \overline{y'}$ and $P \Rightarrow P'$ and $Q' \Rightarrow Q$. $\textsc{Constancy}\ \dfrac{s\ \mathit{Sat}\ \ \overline{x};\overline{y}:\{P,Q\}}{s\ \mathit{Sat}\ \ \overline{x};\overline{y}:\{P \wedge R, Q \wedge R\}}$ provided $FV(R) \cap \overline{x} = \emptyset$. $\textsc{Disj}\ \dfrac{s\ \mathit{Sat}\ \ \overline{x};\overline{y}:\{P,Q\} \qquad s\ \mathit{Sat}\ \ \overline{x};\overline{y}:\{P',Q'\}}{s\ \mathit{Sat}\ \ \overline{x};\overline{y}:\{P \vee P', Q \vee Q'\}}$ $\textsc{VarAssign}\ \dfrac{}{x := e\ \ \mathit{Sat}\ \ x; FV(e):\{P[e/x], P\}}$ $\textsc{SeqComp}\ \dfrac{s\ \mathit{Sat}\ \ \overline{x};\overline{y}:\{P,Q\} \qquad s'\ \mathit{Sat}\ \ \overline{x'};\overline{y'}:\{Q,R\}}{s \mathbin{;} s'\ \ \mathit{Sat}\ \ \overline{x} \cup \overline{x'}; \overline{x} \cup \overline{x'}:\{P,R\}}$ $\textsc{Cond}\ \dfrac{s\ \mathit{Sat}\ \ \overline{x};\overline{y}:\{P \wedge b, Q\} \qquad s'\ \mathit{Sat}\ \ \overline{x'};\overline{y'}:\{P \wedge \neg b, Q\}}{\textbf{if } b \textbf{ then } s \textbf{ else } s'\ \ \mathit{Sat}\ \ \overline{x} \cup \overline{x'}; \overline{y} \cup \overline{y'} \cup FV(b):\{P,Q\}}$ $\textsc{Loop}\ \dfrac{s\ \mathit{Sat}\ \ \overline{x};\overline{y}:\{I \wedge b, I\}}{\textbf{while } b \textbf{ do } s\ \ \mathit{Sat}\ \ \overline{x};\overline{y} \cup FV(b):\{I, I \wedge \neg b\}}$ $\textsc{Spec}\ \dfrac{}{\overline{x};\overline{y}:\{P,Q\}\ \ \mathit{Sat}\ \ \overline{x};\overline{y}:\{P,Q\}}$ $\textsc{Join}\ \dfrac{s\ \mathit{Sat}\ \ \overline{x};\overline{y}:\{P,Q\}}{\bigsqcup(\ldots, s, \ldots)\ \ \mathit{Sat}\ \ \overline{x};\overline{y}:\{P,Q\}}$	$\textsc{AuxVarElim}\ \dfrac{}{\overline{x};\overline{y}:\{\exists v\cdot P, \exists v\cdot Q\} \sqsubseteq \overline{x};\overline{y}:\{P,Q\}}$ provided $v \notin \overline{x} \cup \overline{y}$. $\textsc{Consequence}\ \dfrac{}{\overline{x};\overline{y}:\{P,Q\} \sqsubseteq \overline{x'};\overline{y'}:\{P',Q'\}}$ provided $\overline{x} \supseteq \overline{x'}$ and $\overline{y} \supseteq \overline{y'}$ and $P \Rightarrow P'$ and $Q' \Rightarrow Q$. $\textsc{Constancy}\ \dfrac{}{\overline{x};\overline{y}:\{P \wedge R, Q \wedge R\} \sqsubseteq \overline{x};\overline{y}:\{P,Q\}}$ provided $FV(R) \cap \overline{x} = \emptyset$. $\textsc{Disj}\ \dfrac{}{\overline{x};\overline{y}:\{P \vee P', Q \vee Q'\} \sqsubseteq \bigsqcup(\overline{x};\overline{y}:\{P,Q\}, \overline{x};\overline{y}:\{P',Q'\})}$ $\textsc{VarAssign}\ \dfrac{}{x; FV(e):\{P[e/x], P\} \sqsubseteq x := e}$ $\textsc{SeqComp}\ \dfrac{}{\overline{x} \cup \overline{x'}; \overline{x} \cup \overline{x'}:\{P,R\} \sqsubseteq \overline{x};\overline{y}:\{P,Q\} \mathbin{;} \overline{x'};\overline{y'}:\{Q,R\}}$ $\textsc{Cond}\ \dfrac{}{\overline{x} \cup \overline{x'}; \overline{y} \cup \overline{y'} \cup FV(b):\{P,Q\} \sqsubseteq \textbf{if } b \textbf{ then } \overline{x};\overline{y}:\{P \wedge b, Q\} \textbf{ else } \overline{x'};\overline{y'}:\{P \wedge \neg b, Q\}}$ $\textsc{Loop}\ \dfrac{}{\overline{x};\overline{y} \cup FV(b):\{I, I \wedge \neg b\} \sqsubseteq \textbf{while } b \textbf{ do } \overline{x};\overline{y}:\{I \wedge b, I\}}$ $\textsc{Spec}\ \dfrac{}{\overline{x};\overline{y}:\{P,Q\} \sqsubseteq \overline{x};\overline{y}:\{P,Q\}}$ $\textsc{Join}\ \dfrac{}{\overline{x};\overline{y}:\{P,Q\} \sqsubseteq \bigsqcup(\ldots, \overline{x};\overline{y}:\{P,Q\}, \ldots)}$ $\textsc{Trans}\ \dfrac{s_1 \sqsubseteq s_2 \qquad s_2 \sqsubseteq s_3}{s_1 \sqsubseteq s_3}$ $\textsc{Mono}\ \dfrac{s \sqsubseteq s'}{t[s] \sqsubseteq t[s']}$ $\textsc{Unjoin}\ \dfrac{}{\bigsqcup(s, \ldots, s) \sqsubseteq s}$

Figure 2. Freefinement and Hoare logic

$\sqsubseteq$ "MONO with VARASSIGN"

while $z{\neq}x$ **do** $z; z : \{y = z! \wedge z{\neq}x, y{\cdot}z = z!\}$ ⨟ $y := y{\cdot}z$

$\sqsubseteq$ "MONO with CONSEQUENCE"

while $z{\neq}x$ **do** $z; z : \{y{\cdot}(z{+}1) = (z{+}1)!, y{\cdot}z = z!\}$ ⨟ $y := y{\cdot}z$

$\sqsubseteq$ "MONO with VARASSIGN"

while $z{\neq}x$ **do** $z := z{+}1$ ⨟ $y := y{\cdot}z$

Since $\vdash_{R_6}$ y,z; x,y,z : {true, y = x!} $\sqsubseteq$ y := 1 ⨟ z := 0 ⨟ **while** z≠x **do** z := z+1 ⨟ y := y·z, it is the case that $\vdash_{V_1}$ y := 1 ⨟ z := 0 ⨟ **while** z≠x **do** z := z+1 ⨟ y := y·z *Sat* y,z; x,y,z : {true, y = x!} and hence also $\vdash_H$ {true}y := 1 ⨟ z := 0 ⨟ **while** z≠x **do** z := z+1 ⨟ y := y·z{y = x!}.

Here is another example of using R_6; it involves join statements. The statement $\bigsqcup(\overline{x}; \overline{y} : \{P_1, Q_1\}, \overline{x}; \overline{y} : \{P_2, Q_2\})$ is the join of the specification statements $\overline{x}; \overline{y} : \{P_1, Q_1\}$ and $\overline{x}; \overline{y} : \{P_2, Q_2\}$. Expressing it as a spec statement is simple because

$$\bigsqcup(\overline{x}; \overline{y} : \{P_1, Q_1\}, \overline{x}; \overline{y} : \{P_2, Q_2\}) \equiv \overline{x}; \overline{y} : \{P_1, Q_1\} \textbf{ also } \{P_2, Q_2\}$$

where the definition of $\{P_1, Q_1\}$ **also** $\{P_2, Q_2\}$, taken from [11], is: $\{(P_1 \wedge z{=}1) \vee (P_2 \wedge z{\neq}1), (Q_1 \wedge z{=}1) \vee (Q_2 \wedge z{\neq}1)\}$ where z is fresh. R_6 can derive both directions of refinement. Firstly:

$\bigsqcup(\overline{x}; \overline{y} : \{P_1, Q_1\}, \overline{x}; \overline{y} : \{P_2, Q_2\})$

$\sqsubseteq$ "Twice MONO with CONSEQUENCE"

$\bigsqcup(\overline{x}; \overline{y} : \{\exists z{\cdot}\, (P_1{\wedge}z{=}1 \vee P_2{\wedge}z{\neq}1) \wedge z{=}1, \exists z{\cdot}\, (Q_1{\wedge}z{=}1 \vee Q_2{\wedge}z{\neq}1) \wedge z{=}1\},$

$\overline{x}; \overline{y} : \{\exists z{\cdot}\, (P_1{\wedge}z{=}1 \vee P_2{\wedge}z{\neq}1) \wedge z{\neq}1, \exists z{\cdot}\, (Q_1{\wedge}z{=}1 \vee Q_2{\wedge}z{\neq}1) \wedge z{\neq}1\})$

$\sqsubseteq$ "Twice MONO with AUXVARELIM"

$\bigsqcup(\overline{x}; \overline{y} : \{(P_1{\wedge}z{=}1 \vee P_2{\wedge}z{\neq}1) \wedge z{=}1, (Q_1{\wedge}z{=}1 \vee Q_2{\wedge}z{\neq}1) \wedge z{=}1\},$

$\overline{x}; \overline{y} : \{(P_1{\wedge}z{=}1 \vee P_2{\wedge}z{\neq}1) \wedge z{\neq}1, (Q_1{\wedge}z{=}1 \vee Q_2{\wedge}z{\neq}1) \wedge z{\neq}1\})$

$\sqsubseteq$ "Twice MONO with CONSTANCY"

$\bigsqcup(\overline{x}; \overline{y} : \{P_1{\wedge}z{=}1 \vee P_2{\wedge}z{\neq}1, Q_1{\wedge}z{=}1 \vee Q_2{\wedge}z{\neq}1\},$

$\overline{x}; \overline{y} : \{P_1{\wedge}z{=}1 \vee P_2{\wedge}z{\neq}1, Q_1{\wedge}z{=}1 \vee Q_2{\wedge}z{\neq}1\})$

$\sqsubseteq$ "UNJOIN"

$\overline{x}; \overline{y} : \{P_1, Q_1\}$ **also** $\{P_2, Q_2\}$

Secondly:

$\overline{x}; \overline{y} : \{(P_1 \wedge z{=}1) \vee (P_2 \wedge z{\neq}1), (Q_1 \wedge z{=}1) \vee (Q_2 \wedge z{\neq}1)\}$

$\sqsubseteq$ "DISJ"

$\bigsqcup(\overline{x}; \overline{y} : \{P_1 \wedge z{=}1, Q_1 \wedge z{=}1\}, \overline{x}; \overline{y} : \{P_2 \wedge z{\neq}1, Q_2 \wedge z{\neq}1\})$

$\sqsubseteq$ "Twice MONO with CONSTANCY"

$\bigsqcup(\overline{x}; \overline{y} : \{P_1, Q_1\}, \overline{x}; \overline{y} : \{P_2, Q_2\})$

Leino and Manohar [7] mention several uses of the join of spec-like statements.

3.3 Discussion

The type system λ_1 considered above is very simple. Freefinement also applies to System F and other more sophisticated type systems.

Although λ_1 had only rules of the form A_1, typing rules of the form B_1 are quite common – examples include rules for subtyping and intersection types:

$$\text{SUB}\ \frac{\Gamma \vdash e : \tau}{\Gamma \vdash e : \tau'} \text{ provided } \tau <: \tau'. \qquad \text{INTER}\ \frac{\Gamma \vdash e : \tau \qquad \Gamma \vdash e : \tau'}{\Gamma \vdash e : \tau \wedge \tau'}$$

There is no golden recipe for adapting proof systems to make them amenable to freefinement. However, enriching specifications and/or terms might help. The Hoare logic example used enriched specifications to keep track of write and read sets. Consider again the two problematic rules from before:

$$2\ \frac{\text{succ}(n) : \mathbb{N}}{\text{pred}(\text{succ}(n)) : \mathbb{N}} \qquad 3\ \frac{n : \mathbb{N}}{\text{pred}(n) : \mathbb{N}} \text{ provided positive}(n).$$

Rule 2 can be accommodated by choosing $\mathbb{S} = \{\text{‘z’}, \text{‘s’}, \text{‘p’}\} \times \{\mathbb{N}\}$. Intuitively, the specification $(\text{‘s’}, \mathbb{N})$ tracks the fact that the outermost constructor is ‘succ’. The rule then becomes:

$$2\ \frac{n : (\text{‘s’}, \mathbb{N})}{\text{pred}(n) : (\text{‘p’}, \mathbb{N})}$$

Rule 3 can be accommodated by choosing $\mathbb{S} = \mathbb{N} \times \{\mathbb{N}\}$. Then the sentence $n : (i, \mathbb{N})$ tracks the fact that term n denotes the natural number i. The adapted rule is of the form A_1 with $n = 1$:

$$3\ \frac{n : (i, \mathbb{N})}{\text{pred}(n) : (i-1, \mathbb{N})} \text{ provided } i > 0.$$

In some cases it might be useful to enrich the term language. For example, consider the rule of concurrent separation logic [3] that removes auxiliary commands (ghost assignments):

$$\text{AUXILIARY}\ \frac{\Gamma \vdash \{P\}c\{Q\}}{\Gamma \vdash \{P\}c\backslash a\{Q\}}$$
provided $a \in aux(c)$ and $a \cap (FV(P) \cup FV(Q)) = \emptyset$.

This rule is not of the form A_1 or B_1, because it contains a meta-operation in the conclusion. However, if the meta-operation is turned into an explicit constructor (and specifications track auxiliaries), then the rule is of the form B_1 with $m = 1$ and freefinement can handle it.

To get an approximate idea of what will happen when freefinement is applied to a separation logic, consider the frame and concurrency rules:

$$\text{FRAME}\ \frac{\{P\}c\{Q\}}{\{P * R\}c\{Q * R\}}$$

$$\text{CONCURRENCY}\ \frac{\{P_1\}c_1\{Q_1\} \qquad \{P_2\}c_2\{Q_2\}}{\{P_1 * P_2\}c_1||c_2\{Q_1 * Q_2\}}$$

A concrete setting and system will typically make syntactic restrictions on the commands in the triples. So the specification statement {P, Q} might contain more components, but freefinement will yield refinement versions of the rules that look roughly as follows:

$$\text{FRAME}\ \frac{}{\{P * R, Q * R\} \sqsubseteq \{P, Q\}}$$

$$\text{CONCURRENCY}\ \frac{}{\{P_1 * P_2, Q_1 * Q_2\} \sqsubseteq \{P_1, Q_1\} \,||\, \{P_2, Q_2\}}$$

4. Related Work

In his work on refinement for the lambda calculus, Denney [4] treats types as rudimentary specifications and introduces a specification construct $?_\tau$ for each type τ. Conceptually, $?_\tau$ corresponds to $[\Gamma; \tau]$ where the context Γ is left implicit. For example, consider the term $\lambda x : \sigma. ?_\tau$ in the context Γ. The $?_\tau$ inside the term corresponds to $[\Gamma, x : \sigma; \tau]$. Denney also considers richer specifications for lambda terms in his PhD thesis [5]. This results in a more powerful refinement calculus in which specification constructs can contain logical assumptions.

The specification statement $\overline{x} : [P, Q]$ of Morgan [8] is analogous to $\overline{x}$; Var : $\{P, Q\}$, since there is no restriction on the variables that the statement may read. However, his specification statement is a total correctness specification, and the accompanying refinement calculus [9] establishes total correctness. Similar refinement calculi for total correctness were proposed by Back [1, 2], Morris [10] and Hehner [6]. The books [2, 6, 9] contain many examples of how correct algorithms can be constructed from their specifications via refinement.

Leino and Manohar [7] consider the join of Morgan's specification statements $\overline{x} : [P_1, Q_1]$ and $\overline{x} : [P_2, Q_2]$, and mention several of its uses. Freefinement adds explicit constructors for joins, and relies on the ability to join arbitrary terms from U in order to establish harmony.

There is a relationship between observational equivalence of terms and the function Specs, because $\models_{V_1} \_ \; Sat \; \_$ gives rise to a notion of observability from the specification point of view. In particular, two terms t and t′ are observationally equivalent in this sense iff $t \sim t'$, where

$$t \sim t' \stackrel{\text{def}}{=} \text{Specs}(\{t\}) = \text{Specs}(\{t'\})$$

It is trivial to check that $\sim$ is an equivalence relation. If $\models_{V_1} \_ \; Sat \; \_$ is well-behaved, then $t \sim t' \Leftrightarrow [\![t]\!] = [\![t']\!]$ (i.e. $t \sim t' \Leftrightarrow t \equiv t'$) by Corollary 2.9 in the Appendix and Theorem 6.1.

Acknowledgments

Van Staden was supported by ETH Research Grant ETH-15 10-1. Calcagno was partially funded by EPSRC.

References

[1] R.-J. Back. Correctness preserving program refinements: Proof theory and applications. *Mathematical Centre Tracts*, 131, 1980.

[2] R.-J. Back and J. von Wright. *Refinement Calculus: A Systematic Introduction*. Springer-Verlag, 1998. Graduate Texts in Computer Science.

[3] S. Brookes. A semantics for concurrent separation logic. *Theor. Comput. Sci.*, 375:227–270, April 2007.

[4] E. Denney. Simply-typed underdeterminism. *Journal of Computer Science and Technology*, 13:491–508, 1998.

[5] E. Denney. A theory of program refinement. Technical Report ECS-LFCS-99-412, University of Edinburgh, 1999.

[6] E. C. R. Hehner. *A practical theory of programming*. Springer-Verlag New York, Inc., New York, NY, USA, 1993.

[7] K. R. M. Leino and R. Manohar. Joining specification statements. *Theor. Comput. Sci.*, 216(1-2):375–394, 1999.

[8] C. Morgan. The specification statement. *ACM Trans. Program. Lang. Syst.*, 10:403–419, July 1988.

[9] C. Morgan. *Programming from specifications (2nd ed.)*. Prentice Hall International (UK) Ltd., Hertfordshire, UK, 1994.

[10] J. M. Morris. A theoretical basis for stepwise refinement and the programming calculus. *Sci. Comput. Program.*, 9:287–306, December 1987.

[11] M. J. Parkinson and G. M. Bierman. Separation logic, abstraction and inheritance. In *POPL '08*, pages 75–86, New York, NY, USA, 2008. ACM.

A. Antitone Galois Connections

Lemma 1 established that an antitone Galois connection exists between the functions Specs and Terms:

$$X \subseteq \text{Terms}(Y) \Leftrightarrow Y \subseteq \text{Specs}(X) \qquad (*)$$

Theorems derived from this equivalence come in pairs because of the symmetry between Specs and Terms. Here are a few well-known ones together with their proofs:

Corollary 2.

2.1 $X \subseteq \text{Terms}(\text{Specs}(X))$
2.2 $Y \subseteq \text{Specs}(\text{Terms}(Y))$
2.3 $X \subseteq X' \Rightarrow \text{Specs}(X) \supseteq \text{Specs}(X')$
2.4 $Y \subseteq Y' \Rightarrow \text{Terms}(Y) \supseteq \text{Terms}(Y')$
2.5 $X \subseteq X' \Rightarrow \text{Terms}(\text{Specs}(X)) \subseteq \text{Terms}(\text{Specs}(X'))$
2.6 $Y \subseteq Y' \Rightarrow \text{Specs}(\text{Terms}(Y)) \subseteq \text{Specs}(\text{Terms}(Y'))$
2.7 $\text{Specs}(\text{Terms}(\text{Specs}(X))) = \text{Specs}(X)$
2.8 $\text{Terms}(\text{Specs}(\text{Terms}(Y))) = \text{Terms}(Y)$
2.9 $\text{Specs}(X) \subseteq \text{Specs}(X') \Leftrightarrow \text{Terms}(\text{Specs}(X)) \supseteq \text{Terms}(\text{Specs}(X'))$
2.10 $\text{Terms}(Y) \subseteq \text{Terms}(Y') \Leftrightarrow \text{Specs}(\text{Terms}(Y)) \supseteq \text{Specs}(\text{Terms}(Y'))$
2.11 $\text{Specs}(X \cup X') = \text{Specs}(X) \cap \text{Specs}(X')$
2.12 $\text{Terms}(Y \cup Y') = \text{Terms}(Y) \cap \text{Terms}(Y')$

Proof.

2.1 In (∗), instantiate Y with Specs(X).

2.3 $X \subseteq$ "Assumption" $X' \subseteq$ "2.1" $\text{Terms}(\text{Specs}(X'))$. In (∗), instantiate Y with Specs(X′).

2.5 If $X \subseteq X'$, then $\text{Specs}(X) \supseteq \text{Specs}(X')$ holds by 2.3. The result follows from 2.4.

2.7 From 2.1 and 2.3 follows $\text{Specs}(X) \supseteq \text{Specs}(\text{Terms}(\text{Specs}(X)))$. Instantiating Y with Specs(X) in 2.2 yields $\text{Specs}(X) \subseteq \text{Specs}(\text{Terms}(\text{Specs}(X)))$.

2.9 $\Rightarrow$ holds by 2.4. From $\text{Terms}(\text{Specs}(X)) \supseteq \text{Terms}(\text{Specs}(X'))$ and 2.3, $\text{Specs}(\text{Terms}(\text{Specs}(X))) \subseteq \text{Specs}(\text{Terms}(\text{Specs}(X')))$. $\text{Specs}(X) \subseteq \text{Specs}(X')$ by 2.7.

2.11 Proof by indirect equality. For arbitrary Y:

$$\begin{aligned}
& Y \subseteq \text{Specs}(X \cup X') \\
\Leftrightarrow\ & \{\text{By } (*)\} \\
& X \cup X' \subseteq \text{Terms}(Y) \\
\Leftrightarrow\ & \{\text{Set theory}\} \\
& X \subseteq \text{Terms}(Y) \ \wedge \ X' \subseteq \text{Terms}(Y) \\
\Leftrightarrow\ & \{\text{By } (*)\} \\
& Y \subseteq \text{Specs}(X) \ \wedge \ Y \subseteq \text{Specs}(X') \\
\Leftrightarrow\ & \{\text{Set theory}\} \\
& Y \subseteq \text{Specs}(X) \cap \text{Specs}(X')
\end{aligned}$$

□

Underspecified Harnesses and Interleaved Bugs

Saurabh Joshi
IIT Kanpur, Kanpur, India
sbjoshi@cse.iitk.ac.in

Shuvendu K. Lahiri
Microsoft Research, Redmond, WA, USA
shuvendu@microsoft.com

Akash Lal
Microsoft Research, Bangalore, India
akashl@microsoft.com

Abstract

Static assertion checking of open programs requires setting up a precise *harness* to capture the environment assumptions. For instance, a library may require a file handle to be properly initialized before it is passed into it. A harness is used to set up or specify the appropriate preconditions before invoking methods from the program. In the absence of a precise harness, even the most precise automated static checkers are bound to report numerous false alarms. This often limits the adoption of static assertion checking in the hands of a user.

In this work, we explore the possibility of automatically filtering away (or prioritizing) warnings that result from imprecision in the harness. We limit our attention to the scenario when one is interested in finding bugs due to concurrency. We define a warning to be an *interleaved bug* when it manifests on an input for which no sequential interleaving produces a warning. As we argue in the paper, limiting a static analysis to only consider interleaved bugs greatly reduces false positives during static concurrency analysis in the presence of an imprecise harness.

We formalize interleaved bugs as a *differential* analysis between the original program and its sequential version and provide various techniques for finding them. Our implementation CBugs demonstrates that the scheme of finding interleaved bugs can alleviate the need to construct precise harnesses while checking real-life concurrent programs.

Categories and Subject Descriptors D.2.4 [*Software Engineering*]: Software/Program Verification

General Terms Verification, Reliability

Keywords Concurrency verification, differential analysis, static analysis, false alarms

1. Introduction

Static analysis is concerned with the problem of finding bugs (or proving their absence) in code without actually running the code. In this paper, we apply static analysis to *open* programs or libraries (i.e., programs that do not have a main procedure, but instead expose a set of API methods). In such a setting, the user of static analysis has to provide a *harness* that invokes appropriate methods from the library.

POPL'12, January 25–27, 2012, Philadelphia, PA, USA.

Often times, the exercise of writing a correct harness is difficult and error prone when done manually. One reason for this difficulty is that the libraries usually have undocumented *preconditions* that must be satisfied before invoking particular methods. For instance, before invoking a `read` operation on a file, the library may assume that file handle is properly initialized. If one applies static analysis to such a library without the precondition, the `read` operation can fail, and the static analysis will report a bug. However, this does not reveal any bug in the implementation of the library; instead, it only reveals a problem with the harness that was used to invoke the library. Thus, no matter how precise the static analysis is, it is bound to report false alarms while using *underspecified* harnesses. In our experience, the problem of false alarms (including those due to underspecified harness) severely limits the adoption of static analysis tools that aim at checking user-defined assertions in programs.

The problem of spurious warnings due to underspecified harness does not get better while checking concurrent programs. However, there is a very natural option for prioritizing false alarms in order to look for the more *interesting* warnings:

> Find violations to assertions *assuming* that the sequential executions of the concurrent program (under a correct harness) do not violate any assertion.

This assumption about the sequential executions being "safe" may be justified because a program is more likely to be thoroughly tested for interesting inputs rather than for different interleavings (as it is beyond the control of a tester).

This assumption immediately leads to pruning of the set of inputs to the program: if an input i fails an assertion in the program in a sequential interleaving, then it has to be an *illegal* input (that should have been filtered by a missing precondition in the harness). Hence, we are left to search for over the space of inputs for which no sequential execution violates an assertion. If an input in this space violates an assertion, it has to manifest in a complex interleaving of threads. We term bugs that manifest on such inputs as *interleaved bugs*. The static analysis problem then becomes that of finding interleaved bugs instead of finding all bugs.

Formally, a concurrent program P has an *interleaved bug* if some assertion in the program fails for an input i for which no sequential interleaving of threads in P result in an assertion failure.[1] Interleaved bugs might still be spurious. However, we make the following conjecture based on looking at a large number of spurious warnings:

> If an illegal input (due to an underspecified harness) violates an assertion, then it does so in a fairly simple execution.

More precisely, whenever an illegal input leads to an assertion failure, there would be a sequential interleaving witnessing this failure.

[1] We formally define the notion of sequential interleavings in §4 as one in which threads do not *interfere* with each other.

(It may be possible that a concurrent execution on an illegal input fails; we are only claiming that in such a case, there would also be some sequential execution that fails.) Under this conjecture, most interleaved bugs would correspond to real errors. Our experiments (§5) support this conjecture: all interleaved bugs that we found were actual bugs in the program. Although this result might not hold for all programs, it gives us greater confidence that our approach retains actual concurrency bugs. Note that our technique does not provide help when one is looking for sequential bugs. We are only addressing the scenario when one is interested in finding concurrency bugs, but static analysis results in many false alarms.

Let us contrast the approach of looking for interleaved bugs against two other incomparable approaches for filtering warnings. One possibility is to find (a) the set S of warning locations (failing asserts) that manifest in sequential executions, and (b) the set C of warning locations that manifest in concurrent executions, and only report the locations in the difference of C and S. This approach does not provide any guarantee on the absence of bugs when the program has been sequentially verified (unlike our approach). This is because the presence of a single illegal input that can fail an assertion sequentially suppresses that assert, even when a legal input could fail the same assert.

Another approach is to suppress all the sequential traces that violate an assertion, and only report those traces that have interleaving between threads. This may still report too many false alarms — it may report *trivial* interleavings that still transform the shared state in manner similar to some sequential interleaving. An example of such a program is given in §2.2. We believe that interleaved bugs achieves a good trade-off for suppressing false alarms due to underspecified environment assumptions while not supressing true concurrency bugs.

In this paper, we devise algorithms for finding interleaved bugs. We formalize the problem as a *differential* analysis of two programs. For two programs P_1 and P_2, DIFFERROR(P_1, P_2) is the problem of finding an input i such that P_2 can fail when started with i but P_1 cannot. In some sense, P_1 acts as a *filter* for P_2: run P_2 on an input only when P_1 doesn't fail on it.

Let P be the concurrent program under test. Let P_s be the same as P but executions of P_s are restricted to be sequential, i.e., P_s can have multiple threads, but it does not interleave them. We formally describe how to capture P_s as a program in §4. Then, finding interleaved bugs is the same as solving DIFFERROR(P_s, P). Although solving all instances of DIFFERROR is infeasible (it is undecidable), we provide techniques (§3) that allow us to find interleaved bugs in many real-world programs.

We also show that one can choose various interesting *underapproximations* of P_s for the purpose of proving the absence of interleaved bugs; the various choices have impact on the performance of the analysis.

One technical complication is that DIFFERROR(P_1, P_2) is harder when the programs are non-deterministic, i.e., when they have multiple possible executions for a given input. As with any static-analysis tool, non-determinism is unavoidable — it comes comes from modeling of external calls as well as the thread scheduler. We give techniques to handle this difficulty.

We have implemented our algorithms for finding interleaved bugs in a tool called CBUGS that uses POIROT [17], an SMT-based bug finder, as the static analysis tool. We evaluated CBUGS on (real and concurrent) Windows device drivers. Examples of false alarms and real bugs in these drivers can be found in §2.

This paper makes the following contributions:

1. We define *interleaved bugs* for assertion checking of concurrent programs (§4), and illustrate its role in reducing false alarms due to underspecified harnesses.
2. We describe the problem of finding interleaved bugs as an instance of the DIFFERROR problem for comparing two non-deterministic programs with respect to a set of assertions, and various techniques for solving it (§3).
3. Our experiments (§5) show that CBUGS is able to remove all of the false alarms due to missing preconditions, and retain true concurrency bugs.

The rest of the paper is organized as follows. In §2, we present real-world examples to justify our observation on underspecified harnesses for concurrent programs. In §3, we formalize the more abstract problem DIFFERROR and present algorithms for solving it. In §4, we apply DIFFERROR for finding interleaved bugs, and discuss specific filters and optimizations. In §5, we evaluate our approach experimentally. In §6, we mention related work.

2. Motivation

We motivate our work with a few real-world examples of checking properties of concurrent programs, where (a) missing environment assumptions result in spurious warnings, (b) the spurious warnings often manifest in sequential traces, and (c) our technique only reports true concurrency bugs without requiring the user to specify environment assumptions.

2.1 Example 1

Figure 1 illustrates a simplified version of a bug found by the STORM [15] tool in a Microsoft Windows device driver `usbsamp` [22]. This particular bug is an instance of "use-after-free" class of bugs where an object is accessed after it has been destroyed. The method `UsbSamp_EvtIoRead` is a dispatch routine that handles *read* requests sent to this driver — denoted by the `Request` parameter. Among other things, the method makes a call to `WdfRequestMarkCancelable` with the request and a *cancel* method `UsbSamp_EvtRequestCancel`; one of the side-effects of the call is to set a field `Request->cancelRoutine` to `UsbSamp_EvtRequestCancel`. After this call, the cancel method may be called asynchronously on `Request` by the device driver to cancel the request by invoking the `Cancel` routine. Similarly, the method `WdfRequestUnmarkCancelable` sets the `Request->cancelRoutine` to `NULL`, disabling the cancel routine from being invoked. The request is *completed* (or destroyed) by a call to `WdfRequestComplete` method. The cancel method `UsbSamp_EvtRequestCancel` accesses fields in the request by a call to `GetRequestContext`. It is the responsibility of the driver developer to ensure that a request is not accessed after being completed. Several guidelines such as the following are provided for driver writers — "If a driver has called `WdfRequestMarkCancelable`, and if the driver's `EvtRequestCancel` callback function has not executed and called `WdfRequestComplete`, the driver must call `WdfRequestUnmarkCancelable` before it calls `WdfRequestComplete` outside of the `EvtRequestCancel` callback function."[2]

The use-after-free property can be modeled by (a) introducing a ghost field `completed` for each request; it is set to `true` by a call to `WdfRequestComplete`, and (b) guarding every access to a request `Request` by the assertion `assert(!completed(Request))`. These assertions are implicitly present in this program before the calls to the methods `WdfRequestMarkCancelable`, `WdfRequestComplete` and `GetRequestContext` that access fields in `Request`.

The routine `Test` is the *harness* (or the test driver); it invokes a set of procedure calls (in `BODY:`). Some of these procedures may

[2] http://msdn.microsoft.com/en-us/library/ff549983(v=VS.85).aspx

```
1 // Thread T1
2 VOID UsbSamp_EvtIoRead(
3     ...,
4     WDFREQUEST Request
5   ) {
6   ...
7   WdfRequestMarkCancelable(
8     Request,
9     UsbSamp_EvtRequestCancel);
10  ...
11  WdfRequestUnmarkCancelable(
12    Request);
13  ...
14  WdfRequestComplete(Request,
15                     status);
16  ...
17 }
```

```
1 // Thread T2
2 VOID UsbSamp_EvtRequestCancel(
3     WDFREQUEST Request
4   ) {
5   PREQUEST_CONTEXT rwContext;
6   ...
7   rwContext =
8     GetRequestContext(Request);
9   ...
10 }
11
12 VOID Cancel(WDFREQUEST Request) {
13   f = Request->cancelRoutine;
14   Request->cancelRoutine = NULL;
15   if (f) f(Request);
16 }
```

```
1 //Harness
2 VOID Test(
3     ...,
4     WDFREQUEST Request
5   ) {
6 INIT:
7   //assume(!completed(Request));
8 BODY:
9   async UsbSamp_EvtIoRead(..., Request);
10  async Cancel(Request);
11 }
```

Figure 1. Stripped down version of a bug found by STORM [15] in the `usbsamp` device driver. The three columns show the two threads and the test driver (harness).

be executed asynchronously by spawning new threads (using the `async` keyword). In addition to the method calls, the user has to additionally constrain the inputs to the methods. This can be done by either constructing objects that are passed on to the methods, or specifying some constraints on the inputs. The (commented out) "assume" statement in the test is one such constraint that has to be manually specified to model the environment assumptions for the open program. Let us understand the need for these assume statements by looking at the warnings reported by a precise analysis for this program.

We describe an interleaved trace by a sequence of events $\langle \ldots, (tid_i, l_i), \ldots \rangle$, where $tid_i \in \{1, 2, \ldots\}$ is a thread identifier and l_i is the line number of event. We sometimes avoid specifying all the events in the trace and specify only the end points of an uninterrupted context in each thread.

1. The trace $\langle (1,\ 2), (1,\ 7) \rangle$ would cause an assertion failure for the access to `Request` in `WdfRequestMarkCancelable`. However, this is a spurious warning because the read routine is called with incomplete requests in any legal execution.
2. The trace $\langle (2,\ 13), (2,\ 15), (2,\ 7) \rangle$ is another spurious warning that may happen if `Request->cancelRoutine` is set to `UsbSamp_EvtRequestCancel`, and `Request` is completed in the input to `Test`.
3. The trace $\langle (1,\ \ 2), (1,\ \ 7), (2,\ \ 13), (2,\ \ 15), (1,\ \ 11), (1,\ 14), (2,\ 7) \rangle$ denotes a feasible trace that may cause the device driver to access a completed request in line 7 in the second thread. This was the bug reported by STORM [15] and has been fixed in future versions of the device driver. Note that the bug manifests in a small window — the instruction $(2,\ 13)$ has to be executed between $(1,\ 7)$ and $(1,\ 11)$.

It is easy to observe the only the third warning is an interleaved bug, i.e. it cannot manifest on any sequential interleaving of the threads. On the other hand, the first two manifest in a sequential interleaving. Our method only reports the third alarm (without the need for environment assumption in line 7 in `Test` that rules out the first two warnings), thereby reducing false alarms automatically. On the other hand, if we use a strategy to suppress any error location that can fail sequentially, we will be unable to discover this bug.

2.2 Example 2

Figure 2 shows another example where failure to specify environment assumptions may cause large set of false alarms. The example is a simplified version of the `serial` device driver [22]. The example consists of two threads running two dispatch routines for write (`SerialWrite`) and read (`SerialRead`) respectively. The `PIRP` structure denotes a pointer to an *interrupt request packet* (IRP) or a request, and we check a similar use-after-free property. The main differences in this example are (1) the driver explicitly manipulates nested pointer fields in the IRP (e.g. `Tail.Overlay.CurrStckLoc` in line 21 of `SerialWrite`), (2) the completion routine `SerialCompleteRequest` may destroy all pointers reachable from a `PIRP` pointer that it completes. Unlike the `usbsamp` driver in §2.1, the `serial` driver (an older driver) does not use much data abstraction mechanisms and often manipulates deeply nested fields — making it more challenging for analysis. We have explicitly added the various assertions to model the use-after-free property.

Ideally, a tool that analyzes the `Test` harness should report that there are no assertion violations in this example. This is because for any concrete execution, the device driver ensures the following precondition to `Test`: (a) the pointers reachable from each request are not completed, and (b) the two requests `Irp1` and `Irp2` are *disjoint*, i.e., the set of pointers reachable from `Irp1` and `Irp2` do not overlap. It is not hard to see that in the absence of such assumptions, any tool will yield false alarms. For example, the sequential warning traces $\langle (1,\ 9), (1,\ 14) \rangle$ and $\langle (2,\ 9), \ldots, (2,\ 23) \rangle$ require a precondition that pointers reachable from `Irp1` and `Irp2` are not completed. Similarly, the trace $\langle (1,\ 9), (1,\ 29), (2,\ 9), (2,\ 23) \rangle$ requires that two requests have disjoint set of reachable pointers.

One approach taken in practice is to create *fresh* objects by invoking constructors; this ensures that the set of pointers in two requests are disjoint and not completed. However, this approach is not always desirable for several reasons. First, a freshly created request packet may not represent the *most general* request packet and thereby provide poor coverage of the code it exercises. Secondly, in our case the routines that create a request resides in the kernel and may not be invoked from the driver. Therefore, a user of a tool is forced to write the environment assumptions as a non-trivial set of precondition constraints in the `INIT` block (not shown here). Among the various preconditions, constraining the two requests to be disjoint is quite cumbersome to express.

Instead, our tool is able to automatically rule out all warnings because `UsbSam_EvtIoRead` and `UsbSam_EvtIoWrite` do not have any interleaved bugs. An interesting fact about this example is that the false alarms manifest in both sequential orderings of threads: `SerialWrite;SerialRead` as well as `SerialRead;SerialWrite`. This observation motivated our definition of interleaved bugs given in §4.

```
1 // Thread T1
2 VOID
3 SerialWrite(
4     PDEVICE_OBJECT DO,
5     PIRP Irp
6     )
7 {
8
9   PSERIAL_DEVICE_EXTENSION Extn =
10          DO->DevExtn;
11  struct _IO_STACK_LOCATION *csl;
12
13  ...
14  assert(!completed(Irp));
15  Irp->IoStatus.Status =
16      STATUS_SUCCESS;
17
18  ...
19  assert(!completed(Irp));
20  csl =
21    Irp->Tail.Overlay.CurrStckLoc;
22
23  assert(!completed(csl));
24  if (csl->Parameters.Write.Length){
25    //put the write into a queue
26  } else {
27     ...
28     assert(!completed(Irp));
29     SerialCompleteRequest(.., Irp, 0);
30  }
31 }
```

```
1 // Thread T2
2 VOID
3 SerialRead(
4     PDEVICE_OBJECT DO,
5     PIRP Irp
6     )
7 {
8
9   PSERIAL_DEVICE_EXTENSION Extn =
10          DO->DevExtn;
11  struct _IO_STACK_LOCATION *csl;
12
13  ...
14  assert(!completed(Irp));
15  Irp->IoStatus.Status =
16      STATUS_SUCCESS;
17
18  ...
19  assert(!completed(Irp));
20  csl =
21    Irp->Tail.Overlay.CurrStckLoc;
22
23  assert(!completed(csl));
24  if (csl->Parameters.Read.Length){
25    //put the read into a queue
26  } else {
27     ...
28     assert(!completed(Irp));
29     SerialCompleteRequest(.., Irp, 0);
30  }
31 }
```

```
1 //Harness
2 VOID Test(
3     PDEVICE_OBJECT DO,
4     PIRP Irp1,
5     PIRP Irp2
6   ){
7 INIT:
8
9 BODY:
10  async SerialWrite(DO,Irp1);
11  async SerialRead(DO,Irp2);
12 }
```

Figure 2. Simplified example (from `serial` device driver) illustrating the need for aliasing preconditions.

The reader might argue that we are only looking for buggy traces that require an "interleaving" of actions from different threads. However, such a scheme will report numerous warnings for this example. For instance, the assertion in line 23 can fail on many interleavings between the two threads (e.g. $\langle(1,\ 9),(2,\ 9),(2,\ 14),\ldots,(1,\ 23)\rangle$).

This example may seem trivial from the perspective of concurrency analysis, but that is because we have omitted the synchronization protocol that guards a request among different threads. We use this example only to show the difficulty of understanding false alarms and writing preconditions to rule them out manually.

2.3 Non-deterministic filters

As noted earlier, we find interleaved bugs using sequential interleavings as filters. However, the program that captures these interleavings may be *non-deterministic*, i.e., it may have multiple behaviors for the same input state. There are two main reasons for non-determinism in the filter programs:

- *Data non-determinism*: The concurrent program may have calls to external libraries that are modeled non-deterministically. For example, in order to model `GetTimeOfDay`, one would write a model (or *stub*) that returns any non-deterministically chosen time (possibly, in an increasing sequence). The sequential program inherits these sources of non-determinism.
- *Control non-determinism*: As we illustrate in §4, the program representing the sequential interleavings may have a limited amount of non-determinism in scheduling. For example, the filter used in §2.2 has to capture scheduling either of the two threads first.

One of the main technical challenges in this work is to deal with these non-deterministic filters. Therefore, we start by considering the problem of comparing two non-deterministic programs in the next section (§3).

3. Differential error checking

In this section, we study the more abstract problem DiffError of comparing two (possibly non-deterministic) programs with respect to a set of assertions. In §4, we apply the results of this section towards finding interleaved bugs.

3.1 Programs

We consider a simplified syntax for imperative programs with shared-memory concurrency. We assume that there is a single global variable g of type T. We intentionally leave T undefined.[3] We only require the presence of certain predicates over T. Let *Failed* be a predicate of type T $\rightarrow$ *Bool*.

A program is a list of procedure declarations. Each procedure takes a single variable of type T as input, returns a single variable of type T as output, and has a single statement. A program statement st has the syntax:

st	::=	st; st	(Sequence)
	|	if (e) st else st	(if-then-else)
	|	while (e) do st	(loop)
	|	x := e	(Assignment)
	|	assume e	(Assume)
	|	assert e	(Assert)
	|	havoc x	(Non-deterministic assignment)
	|	call x := foo(e)	(Procedure call)
	|	return x	(Procedure return)
	|	async call foo(e)	(Thread spawn)

[3] One can encode programs with multiple global variables into our syntax by simply considering T to be a vector of types.

Here e is an expression over variables in scope, using some operators that we leave undefined. Semantics of our language is standard. The havoc x statement assigns a non-deterministically-chosen value to a variable x. An assume e statement blocks in a state when e does not hold, and has no effect otherwise. An assert e statement fails in a state when e does not hold, in which case the control jumps to the end of the program and the global variable g is modified such that *Failed*(g) holds. (There is no other way for *Failed*(g) to hold.) An async call foo(e) statement spawns a new thread that executes procedure `foo` with argument e.

Even though we have defined a compact syntax, we will still use C-like syntax for easy writing of example programs. We will sometimes write `x = *` in place of havoc x

Non-determinism in this language arises from two sources: the havoc statement induces *data* non-determinism, whereas concurrency (via threads spawned by async statements) induces *control* non-determinism. For the rest of this section, we do not distinguish between these two sources of non-determinism.

We identify a program with the name of its main procedure. At any point in a program's execution, we refer to the value of variables in scope as the program's *state*. In particular, the *input* and *output* state of a program is the value of global variable g at beginning and end of the main procedure of the program, respectively. Given a program P, let F_P be its *input-output relation*: We say that $(s, t) \in F_P$ if there is some execution of the program from input s that ends in a state t. A program has a buggy execution on input s if $(s, t) \in F_P$ for some t and *Failed*(t) holds.

3.2 Problem formulation

In this section, we describe the problem of *differential error* (DIFFERROR) in more detail, along with different algorithms to solve it. We aim to solve DIFFERROR over two programs that expect the same input. Also, we assume that we are always given programs with assertions that capture the property of interest. The DIFFERROR problem can be formally defined as follows.

DEFINITION 3.1 (DIFFERROR). *Given two programs P_1 and P_2,* DIFFERROR(P_1, P_2) *holds if there exists an input state s such that (1) there is some execution of P_2 starting at s that violates an assertion and (2) no execution of P_1 on s can violate an assertion. We say that P_1 acts as an* input-filter *for P_2.*

Note that DIFFERROR is harder than standard verification. Let $\phi(x, y)$ be a formula in a decidable fragment of logic, say quantifier-free first-order logic with equality. Then we can reduce the satisfiability check of $\exists x.\forall y.\phi(x, y)$ to the DIFFERROR problem as follows. Construct two programs P_1 and P_2 with a global variable x and local variable y in P_1:

$$P_1()\ \{\text{havoc y; assert } \phi(\text{x}, \text{y});\}$$
$$P_2()\ \{\text{assert false;}\}$$

Then DIFFERROR(P_1, P_2) holds if and only if $\exists x.\forall y.\phi(x, y)$ is true. Thus, even though verifying P_1 and P_2 individually is decidable, DIFFERROR(P_1, P_2) is not (because checking the satisfiability of quantified first-order logic with function symbols and equality is undecidable [3]).

The next few subsections describe a few algorithms for solving the DIFFERROR problem. In §3.3, we consider the case when the filter program is deterministic and terminating. In §3.4, we consider a method for non-deterministic filter programs; the method may not terminate for all programs. Both these approaches (§3.3 and §3.4) use quantifier-free reasoning of theorem provers.

3.3 Deterministic filters

When the program P_1 is deterministic (i.e., given a fixed input, it has exactly one execution) and terminating (i.e., given any input, the program either terminates or fails an assertion in finite amount of time) then we have an easy way of solving DIFFERROR by reducing it to standard verification. Let `P1Assume` be a program obtained from P_1 by replacing all assert e statements with assume e statements. Consider the program P, shown in Fig. 3, that executes `P1Assume` and P_2 on the same input.

```
var g: T;

Program P() {
   var g0 := g;
   call P1Assume();
   g := g0;
   call P2();
}
```

Figure 3. A program P constructed from two programs P_1 and P_2.

Because we have replaced asserts by assumes in P_1, the program `P1Assume` will block on all inputs that cause P_1 to fail. Consequently, an execution of P on that input will not even reach the call to P_2. Thus, P can only fail on some input i provided P_1 does not fail on i and P_2 fails on i, which exactly solves DIFFERROR.

THEOREM 3.2. *For a deterministic program P_1, the following statements are true: (a) if the program P in Fig. 3 fails on some input, then* DIFFERROR(P_1, P_2) *holds, and (b) if P_1 is also terminating and P does not fail any assertion, then* DIFFERROR(P_1, P_2) *does not hold.*

This theorem states that checking DIFFERROR can be reduced to checking assertions in a program and we can leverage standard verification techniques. Note that the requirement that P_1 is deterministic and terminating is important for this theorem as the next example shows.

Consider the example in Fig. 4. P_1 and P_2 are two programs that take a pointer `p` as input. The final assert in `foo` can fail because the programmer made a mistake: the operation in the `else` branch should be subtraction, not addition. We assume that both programs have implicit assertions for pointer dereferences, i.e., there is an `assert (p != null)` before any statement that dereferences `p`. The intention is to find a bug in P_2 that reveals that the assertion in the last line can fail. Static analysis of P_2 can get distracted and report that the initial dereference `p->x` can fail when `p == null`. However, solving DIFFERROR(P_1, P_2) correctly guides us to the desired bug. P_1 will filter out the input `p == null` because it can fail on that input.

Note that Thm. 3.2 doesn't apply for this example because P_1 is non-deterministic. If we were to construct the program P as in Fig. 3, then P can still fail on input `p == null`. A similar argument holds when P_1 is non-terminating. For example, consider a program P_1 with a single statement assume false. This program never fails, and should not filter any input for P_2. However, for the program P of Fig. 3, it will block all input from reaching P_2.

3.4 Non-deterministic Filters

We now describe a technique for solving DIFFERROR(P_1, P_2) that can handle non-deterministic filter programs. However, the technique may fail to terminate on all programs, even when both P_1 and P_2 are bounded-length programs.

First, note that the construction of Fig. 3 is useful even when the filter program P_1 is not deterministic (but terminating) because then P necessarily fails less often than P_2. More specifically, P does not fail on those inputs on which P_1 deterministically fails (i.e., every execution of P_1 fails). Hence, we can always replace P_2 by P.

P_1

```
struct ST *p;

void bar() {
   int t; havoc t;
   if(t) {
      p->x = 0;
   }
}
```

P_2

```
struct ST *p;

void foo() {
  int x;
  p->x = 0;
  if(p->y > p->x) {
     t = p->y - p->x;
  } else {
     t = p->x + p->y;
  }
  assert(t >= 0);
}
```

Figure 4. A non-deterministic filter program.

Algorithm 1 Algorithm for solving DIFFERROR

Require: Programs P_1 and P_2

1: **loop**
2: $r_1 :=$ FINDBUG(P_2)
3: **if** $r_1 =$ NOBUG **then**
4: **return** NOBUG
5: **end if**
6: Let TRACE$(t, i) = r_1$
7: $r_2 :=$ FINDBUG(P_1, i)
8: **if** $r_2 :=$ NOBUG **then**
9: **return** r_1
10: **end if**
11: Let TRACE$(t', i) = r_2$
12: $\phi := pre(Determinize(t'), \text{true})$
13: $P_2 :=$ assume $\neg\phi; P_2$
14: **end loop**

Our algorithm is shown in Alg. 1. It uses a static-analysis tool, which we call FINDBUG. We assume that FINDBUG, given a program with assertions, either returns NOBUG (meaning that the program has no bugs) or returns TRACE(t, i), meaning that the program can fail on input i and t is the execution trace witnessing that failure. A trace consists of a sequence of program statements (in the order in which they got executed), along with values of variables at each point in the trace. FINDBUG can also be supplied with an input, in which case it only checks the program under that input. Alg. 1 returns its output in the same format as FINDBUG: it returns NOBUG if there is no input for which DIFFERROR(P_1, P_2) holds; or returns TRACE(t, i) such that DIFFERROR(P_1, P_2) holds and t is an execution of P_2 that fails on input i (but P_1 does not fail on input i).

The algorithm works by iteratively filtering away more and more inputs. If it finds a bug in P_2 (line 2), then it checks to see if P_1 has a bug on the same input i (line 7). If P_1 doesn't, then it returns this input (line 9). If P_1 does have a bug, then i needs to be filtered. For this, it uses a modification of the trace t' itself to create a deterministic filter f (line 12) that filters out i as well as other inputs that cause P_1 to fail along the trace t'. In some sense, f acts as a *sub-filter* that filters out some of the input that causes P_1 to fail.

The procedure *Determinize*(t') takes a trace t' and performs the following modification to it — it replaces the havoc x statements with x $:= c$, where c is the concrete value assigned to x in the trace. The predicate transformer $pre(t, \psi)$ takes a trace t (a sequence of statements) and a formula ψ and returns a formula representing the *path condition* in terms of the inputs to the trace. It is defined inductively on the structure of the trace as follows (note that *Determinize* removes havoc statements from the trace):

$$\begin{array}{lcl} pre(\mathsf{skip}, \psi) & = & \psi \\ pre(\mathsf{assume}\ \phi, \psi) & = & \phi \wedge \psi \\ pre(\mathsf{assert}\ \phi, \psi) & = & \neg\phi \wedge \psi \\ pre(\mathtt{x} := e, \psi) & = & \psi[e/\mathtt{x}] \\ pre(s; t, \psi) & = & pre(s, pre(t, \psi)) \end{array}$$

Fig. 5 (a) shows an example of a trace that fails the assertion in P_1 in Fig. 4. For the statement `havoc t`, we indicate the value (say, 5) assigned to `t` in the trace. Fig. 5 (b) shows the formula ϕ constructed in line 12, which is equivalent to `p == null`.

(a)	(b)

`havoc t; // 5`
`assume t != 0;`
`assert p != null;`
	`(5 != 0 && p == null)`

Figure 5. (a) A trace through P_1 from Fig. 4 and (b) the corresponding formula.

The most expensive parts in Alg. 1's loop are the calls to FINDBUG. One can optimize these calls in cases when FINDBUG is *incremental*. For instance, the calls on line 2 always contains the same program pre-pended with an increasing list of assume statements. The calls on line 7 are to the same program but with different inputs. Thus, any information that FINDBUG infers about P_1 or P_2 can be retained across iterations.

THEOREM 3.3. *The following statements are true. (a) If Alg. 1 returns* NOBUG, *then* DIFFERROR(P_1, P_2) *does not hold, and (b) if Alg. 1 returns* TRACE(t, i) *then* DIFFERROR(P_1, P_2) *holds and input i and trace t are the witnesses.*

Alg. 1 is not guaranteed to terminate (even for bounded-length programs), which is expected because DIFFERROR is undecidable in general. However, it does terminate for bounded-length programs with *bounded* non-determinism. Formally, non-determinism in a program is *bounded* if for any non-deterministic choice value v in the program, v only appears in expressions of the form $v \bowtie c$, where $\bowtie \in \{=, \leq, <\}$ and c is a constant. This subsumes the case when v is Boolean, i.e., $v \in \{\mathsf{true}, \mathsf{false}\}$. We did not come across unbounded non-determinism in our experiments.

Consider the example in Fig. 6, where the `hashFunc` is a procedure with complex operations to compute the hash value of an input. It is not hard to see that DIFFERROR(P_1, P_2) does not hold for this example. However, Alg. 1 will diverge by enumerating all the possible values of the non-deterministic choice of `i` in P_1. (The variable `j` in P_1 is not necessary for the divergence.)

There are several ways to extend our approach to deal with such cases, at the cost of predictability. A natural extension is to set a bound k on the number of times a source of non-deterministic values participates in *Determinize* during the execution of Alg. 1. After this threshold is exceeded, we perform $pre(,)$ on the trace t' directly instead of determinizing it. We extend $pre(,)$ for havoc statements:

$$pre(\mathsf{havoc}\ \mathtt{x}, \psi) \quad = \quad \exists x.\ \psi$$

This results in quantified filters in line 13 of Alg. 1. For the above example with $k = 0$, we will generate the filter:

$$\neg(\exists i, j :: j \neq 0 \wedge \neg \mathsf{a}[i] \geq 0)$$

If FINDBUG is able to reason about such quantifiers, then we will be able to prove that DIFFERROR(P_1, P_2) does not hold for this example. However, if FINDBUG is unable to reason precisely about these quantifiers, then Alg. 1 may diverge enumerating the same path in P_1. For example, if FINDBUG is an SMT-based theorem prover, the quantified verification condition generated may not be

```
void P1(int a[], int b){
    int i = *;
    int j = *;
    if (j != 0)
       assert a[i] >= 0;
}
```

```
void P2(int a[], int b){
    int i = hashFunc(b);
    assert a[i] >= 0;
}
```

Figure 6. Example where Alg. 1 diverges.

amenable to the *trigger-based* schemes for instantiating quantifiers in most SMT solvers [7] — there is no good trigger for the bound variable j in the formula above (this is the reason why j is present in P_1). The above formula would need some simplifications (e.g. quantifier elimination) in conjunction with quantifier instantiations. We also present a variant of this idea in Appendix A that instead produces a quantified formula to precisely describe whether DIFFERROR(P_1, P_2) holds for bounded programs, and then hands it off to a theorem prover. The main difference is that it pushes the divergence from within Alg. 1 to within the theorem prover.

4. Interleaved bugs

We now return to the topic of finding *interleaved bugs* for concurrent programs in the presence of underspecified harnesses. We start by defining the problem formally, show how it can be cast as a DIFFERROR problem, and then describe a few optimizations specific to our setting.

Let P be a concurrent program with dynamic thread creation (using async statements). We define a *non-interleaved program execution* to be one that has a single-thread of execution. Formally, a non-interleaved execution, while executing thread T_1, follows one of two possibilities at an async statement that spawns thread T_2:

- T_1 waits for T_2: The spawned thread T_2 executes immediately and T_1 waits until T_2 and any thread spawned by T_2 completes. Additionally, while T_2 is executing, any async call must follow this same option. In some sense, the async call acts like a synchronous procedure call.
- T_2 waits for T_1: The spawned thread T_2 does not execute until T_1 finishes. When T_1 finishes, any of the threads spawned by it can start executing.

Let F_P^{seq} be a subset of F_P such that $(s, t) \in F_P^{seq}$ if and only if $(s, t) \in F_P$ and there is some non-interleaved execution of P from input s that ends in state t. Our intuition is that assertion violations resulting from illegal inputs will often manifest in non-interleaved executions. Thus, they will be captured in F_P^{seq}.

DEFINITION 4.1 (Interleaved bug). *A program P has an interleaved bug if there is a pair of states $(s, t) \in F_P$ such that Failed(t) holds and for all $(s, t') \in F_P^{seq}$, Failed(t') does not hold.*

We find interleaved bugs using DIFFERROR.

THEOREM 4.2. *Given two concurrent programs P and Q the following statements are true. (i) If $F_Q \subseteq F_P^{seq}$ and* DIFFERROR(Q, P) *does not hold, then P has no interleaved bugs. (ii) If $F_P^{seq} \subseteq F_Q$ and* DIFFERROR(Q, P) *holds, then P has an interleaved bug.*

Thm. 4.2 suggests that it suffices to work with *underapproximations* of F_P^{seq} while proving the absence of interleaved bugs and *overapproximations* of F_P^{seq} while proving the presence of interleaved bugs. In §4.1 and §4.2, we define under-approximate filters as programs. In §4.3, we define the program that captures F_P^{seq} precisely. In each case, we define the filter using a syntactic program transformation, and the resultant filter is a sequential program.

```
void AsyncAsEventsOrGeneral(args) {
  EventSet = new MultiSet<Event>();
  EventSet.Add(new Event(main, args));
  while(!EventSet.empty()) {
    let (f,e) = EventSet.GetAny();
    f(e);
  }
}
```

Figure 7. Entry procedure for $AsyncAsEvents$ and $AsyncGeneral$.

4.1 Filter: $AsyncAsSync$

The filter program $AsyncAsSync$ always chooses the behavior where the async statement is treated as a synchronous procedure call that executes immediately. This corresponds to the first option in the definition of non-interleaved executions. The use of this filter is desirable as it can lead to a deterministic filter if the program does not make use of data non-determinism (or the non-determinism does not influence the assertions).

This filter can be obtained from P simply by replacing all async calls with normal procedure calls. The program shown in Fig. 1 uses this filter to remove all non-interleaved bugs.

4.2 Filter: $AsyncAsEvents$

The filter program $AsyncAsEvents$ explores all behaviors in which spawned threads are delayed until the parent thread finishes. This corresponds to the second option in the definition of non-interleaved executions.

We capture this filter as an *event-driven* program. Note that an async call, in this case, is like posting an event that has to be processed when the current event finishes. This behavior is typical of event-driven programs.

Let `main` be the entry procedure of P. Let `EventSet` be a multiset of *events*, where each event is a function pointer along with its arguments. The filter has the entry procedure shown in Fig. 7. It initializes the set of events with the `main` procedure and then executes an arbitrary event from `EventSet` in a loop. Events are added to the set by executing a async statement; the following transformation is applied to each async statement:

`async foo(e)` $\mapsto$ `EventSet.Add(new Event(foo, e))`

It is easy to see that a spawned thread does not execute until the parent thread finishes.

There are several existing analyses of event-driven programs. The work by Sen and Viswanathan [18] discusses the complexity of analyzing such programs. Jhala and Majumdar [13] present a software-model-checking approach, and Emmi et al. [10] present an underapproximate SMT-based analysis. A real-world example where this filter is required is described in §5.1.2. In our experiments, we use a tool based on the approach of Emmi et al. [10].

Remark. When the concurrent program P has synchronization (e.g., thread join operations) then it is possible that $AsyncAsEvents$ may deadlock. This is acceptable in our setting because we do not consider deadlocks to be bugs.

4.3 Filter: $AsyncGeneral$

The $AsyncGeneral$ filter program explores all non-interleaved executions. Such a program can have strictly more behaviors than both previous options put together. This is because it allows an execution to follow the first option (in the definition of non-interleaved executions) in some places and to follow the second option in other places.

```
NTSTATUS
IoCreateDevice(...,
              OUT PDEVICE_OBJECT *DeviceObject)
{
  PDEVICE_OBJECT deviceObject;

  int x = nondet();
  if (x == 0) {
    // Allocate device
    deviceObject = (PDEVICE_OBJECT)
                   malloc(sizeof(DEVICE_OBJECT));
    ...
    *DeviceObject = deviceObject;
    return STATUS_SUCCESS;
  } else if (x == 1) {
    // Fail
    return STATUS_INSUFFICIENT_RESOURCES;
  } else if (x == 2) {
    // Fail
    return STATUS_OBJECT_NAME_EXISTS;
  } else ...
}
```

Figure 8. Stub for `IoCreateDevice`.

Let `main` be the entry procedure of P. Let `EventSet` be as defined in §4.2. The $AsyncGeneral$ filter has the same entry procedure as $AsyncAsEvents$. The difference is in the transformation of async statements. We add a Boolean variable `First` to $AsyncGeneral$, initialize it to `false`, and then carry out the following transformation:

```
async foo(e)  ↦
  if(First) {
      foo(e);
  } else if(nondet()) {
      First = true; foo(e); First = false;
  } else {
     EventSet.Add(new Event(foo, e));
  }
```

The variable `First` is `true` when we have decided to execute a spawned thread immediately. In this case, any recursively spawned thread must also be executed immediately. When `First` is `false`, we non-deterministically decide between two options: execute the thread immediately or delay it until the current thread finishes.

4.4 Non-determinism

The filters defined in previous sections have multiple sources of non-determinism (which justifies our interest in non-deterministic filters). The main source of non-determinism is from the environment. As for any static analysis tool, one has to close the program by writing *stubs* for the environment (such as the operation system). These stubs over-approximate the environment and are inherently non-deterministic. For instance, in order to model `IoCreateDevice` system call in Windows[4], we used the stub shown in Fig. 8. It can non-deterministically choose to allocate the device object or fail and return one of a fixed number of error codes. These stubs were created for an earlier study on static analysis; we did not modify them.

Another source of non-determinism is in modeling the filters themselves. Both $AsyncAsEvents$ and $AsyncGeneral$ have non-determinism in the order in which they pick events. The filter $AsyncAsSync$ does not add any extra non-determinism.

The stub in Fig. 8 and the filter structure both induce a bounded amount of non-determinism, which is suitable for our lazy algorithm (§3.4). However, some stubs have unbounded-nondeterminism. For instance, the stub that we use for `malloc` is one that can return any address which has not been previously allocated. However, such unboundedness has never been a problem in our experiments. One reason could be that programs (and, consequently, bugs) do not rely on the actual address values.

[4] http://msdn.microsoft.com/en-us/library/ff548397(v=vs.85).aspx

```
int x;                        void bar(int *p) {
void main(int *p) {           L1:
  x = 0;                        if(nondet()) {
  async foo();                    if(x == 1) x = 2;
  async bar(p);                   if(x == 3)
}                             L2:     *p = 10;
void foo() {                    } else {
  if(x == 0) x = 1;           L3:     *p = 5;
  if(x == 2) x = 3;             }
}                             }
```

Figure 9. Example to show incompleteness of the optimization.

4.5 Optimizations

For the purpose of finding interleaved bugs, we have a special instance of DIFFERROR(P_1, P_2), namely one in which $F_{P_1} \subseteq F_{P_2}$. In this setting, we can optimize Alg. 1 by avoiding a few calls to FINDBUG.

More concretely, let (t, i) be as defined on line 6 of Alg. 1. Then t is a concurrent execution, possibly with many threads. We can permute statements in t such that the resulting trace conforms to the filter in use, and then check the feasibility of the resulting trace. For example, let t have two threads T_1 and T_2, and consists of statements executed in the following order:

$$t = (a_1; a_2; a_3; b_1; b_2; a_4; a_5; b_3; b_4; a_6;)$$

where the a_is refer to statements fired by T_1, and the b_is refer to statements fired by T_2. Further, let a_3 be the statement that spawns thread T_2. Let t_1 and t_2 be the following permutations of statements in t:
$t_1 = (a_1; a_2; a_3; b_1; b_2; b_3; b_4; a_4; a_5; a_6;)$
$t_2 = (a_1; a_2; a_3; a_4; a_5; a_6; b_1; b_2; b_3; b_4;)$
Then t_1 conforms to $AsyncAsSync$, t_2 conforms to $AsyncAsEvents$, and both conform to $AsyncGeneral$. Suppose we are using $AsyncAsSync$ as the filter, and t_1 happens to be feasible on input i (i.e., i satisfies $pre(t_1, \mathsf{true})$), then we can let r_2 be TRACE(t', i) and jump to line 11, thereby avoiding the call to FINDBUG on line 7. In general, there are many ways to permute a given concurrent trace to make it correspond to a filter. In our implementation we try a few permutations. If any of these work, then we can avoid a call to FINDBUG.

Note that this optimization does not work the other way. Consider the example shown in Fig. 9, where every dereference is implicitly protected by a null-pointer assertion. It has an execution that fails on line L2 that requires four context switches and no sequential permutation of this execution is feasible. However, we cannot conclude that the execution is an interleaved bug because there is a sequential execution on the same input (but takes a different path due to the non-determinism at L1) that fails at label L3.

5. Evaluation

We implemented Alg. 1 (mentioned in §3) on concurrent programs in a tool called CBUGS. It first uses the *AsyncAsSync* filter. If it does not find bugs in the presence of this filter, then it stops. Otherwise, it uses the *AsyncGeneral* filter and reports resulting bugs as interleaved bugs. The use of *AsyncAsSync* is an optimization because it is easier to analyze than *AsyncGeneral*. CBUGS uses POIROT as the tool for finding bugs in concurrent programs, i.e., POIROT acts as FINDBUG in Alg. 1. POIROT is one of the bug-finding tools for concurrent programs that uses iterative context-bounding to look for bugs [6, 15, 17].

We conducted experiments to evaluate CBUGS on two goals. First, can CBUGS rule out bugs caused by illegal input, while retaining the true bugs? Second, we compare CBUGS against a different filtering strategy, namely one that filters based on asserts. In this strategy, if a sequential trace leads to an assertion violation, then we remove that assertion and repeat until no more warnings are produced.

5.1 Results

We chose a collection of Windows device drivers from the WinDDK suite [22] for conducting experiments. Some of these drivers were manually seeded with bugs by others in an independent study. To the best of our knowledge, these are the only bugs present in the code. We suffix the driver name with "_bug" when it has a (single) seeded bug. This allows us to conduct a controlled study. None of the drivers have a precise harness.

We checked the "Cancel" property (mentioned in §2) as well as for null-pointer dereferences ("NullDeref"). The results are reported in Fig. 10. Each row of this table has: the name of the driver (Name); the number of non-empty non-assert lines of code exercised by tool (LOC) along with the number of assertions shown in parenthesis; the property being checked (Prop.); and the type of bug present in the code (either "none" or "interleaved" or "sequential"). The next column (#LF) is the number of iterations of Alg. 1, i.e., the number of lazy filters generated by CBUGS. The rest of the columns show the number of false positives (#FP) and false negatives (#FN) of the two approaches and the total time taken to generate all the warnings (barring the manual effort of classifying a warning as a true or false positive). Whenever CBUGS used *AsyncGeneral* for generating a lazy filter, we mention it in the (#LF) column with "AG".

For instance, the first row is for the `daytona` driver with the cancel property. The driver does not have any actual bugs, however, when we run static analysis (FINDBUG), it reports a warning (false positive) because of the imprecise harness. CBUGS, on the other hand, suppresses this warning automatically (it generates one lazy filter).

Our experiments show: (1) CBUGS does not report any false positives, whereas the assert suppression technique reported 63 false positives; (2) CBUGS did not miss any of the interleaved bugs, whereas assert suppression missed one in `mouclass_bug2`; (3) the use of *AsyncAsSync* is a useful optimization and is enough to rule out false warnings in most cases. As expected, CBUGS also ends up suppressing true sequential bugs, however, it demonstrates good results for catching concurrency bugs.

We now explain some of the results in more detail, to illustrate the need for *AsyncGeneral* and the kinds of preconditions that these drivers required.

5.1.1 Cancel Property on `ndisprot`

The existing harness for the `ndisprot` device driver (for the Cancel property) added two preconditions: (1) a particular lock must be initialized, and (2) a doubly-linked list (of requests) is empty. Although the first is a valid precondition, the second one is the simplest way to establish the actual preconditions: (a) the incoming request does not belong to the list, and (b) the list is well-formed doubly linked list that respects the relationships between the forward and the backwards links. Unless the latter is enforced, the pointer manipulations performed to insert or delete an element of the list does not have the desired effects. Both these preconditions are very hard to express for low-level C programs, even for bounded lists. However, by limiting the input to contain an empty list, most of the interesting logic related to list traversal in the code does not get exercised.

There are three versions of this driver, depending on which dispatch routine is chosen (`read`, `write`, or `ioctl`). In the absence of preconditions, we get false alarms in each of the three versions, whereas CBUGS does not report any false alarms. For `read`, CBUGS requires the use of *AsyncGeneral* filter. With *AsyncAsSync* alone, it reports a false alarm where the input list is not well-formed. This example shows that in the presence of complicated preconditions, one needs *AsyncGeneral*, although at the expense of more runtime.

```
void ReadFn(PIRP irp) {
   if(irp->b) {
     *irp->ptr = 10;
   }
   if(irp->cancel) {
     Foo(irp);
   }
}
void Foo(PIRP irp) {
    *irp->ptr = 10;
}
```

```
void CancelFn(PIRP irp) {
   irp->cancel = true;
}

void Test(PIRP irp) {
   async ReadFn(irp);
   async CancelFn(irp);
}
```

Figure 11. Example of null-dereference checking on `daytona` driver. Every dereference of a pointer has an implicit non-null check preceding it.

5.1.2 Null-Dereference Checking

We also checked several drivers for the absence of null-dereferences. Each pointer dereference was preceded with a non-null assertion. As shown in Fig. 10, this property introduced a large number of assertions in the program.

Fig. 11 shows an example (motivated by `daytona`) that requires the $AsyncGeneral$ filter to remove the false alarms. The harness `Test` needs the preconditions that both `irp` and `irp->ptr` are non-null, to ensure that the concurrent program does not fail any assertions. It is easy to observe that the illegal inputs where `irp` is null fails by executing `ReadFn(irp)` sequentially, and is, thus, filtered away by $AsyncAsSync$.

Consider the non-null check for the dereference `*irp->ptr`. If we restrict the executions of `Test` to only consider $AsyncAsSync$, the `*irp->ptr` is dereferenced only when either `irp->b` or `irp->cancel` is set in the input. This implies that using the $AsyncAsSync$ filter will generate failure traces where the body of `CancelFn` is executed before the test on `irp->cancel` inside `ReadFn`. However, using the $AsyncGeneral$ filter, we can defer `ReadFn` to execute after `CancelFn` has executed, thereby failing the assertion on any input. A similar situation requires the use of $AsyncGeneral$ for the example in §2.2.

6. Related work

In this paper, we presented an approach for reducing *false alarms* due to underspecified *environments* during static assertion checking in concurrent programs, by using the *sequential behaviors* as an oracle. We position our work in the context of previous work in each of the italicized areas in the next few subsections.

6.1 Filtering static analysis alarms

Engler et al. [11] propose a method of discovering bugs by observing *inconsistent behavior* in source code. Dillig et al. [9] provide a semantic basis for finding such inconsistent behaviors by posing the problem as a type-inference problem. Both these approaches have been applied to find null dereference errors in large sequential

Name	LOC	Prop.	Buggy?	CBUGS				Assert Supression		
	(Asserts)			#LF	#FP	#FN	Time	#FP	#FN	Time
daytona	485 (10)	Cancel	No	1	0	0	122	1	0	17
daytona_bug1	484 (10)	Cancel	Seq.	2	0	1	136	1	0	21
daytona_bug2	485 (10)	Cancel	Int.	1	0	0	110	1	0	34
daytona_bug3	484 (10)	Cancel	Seq.	2	0	1	161	3	0	41
daytona_bug4	485 (10)	Cancel	Seq.	2	0	1	162	1	0	19
daytona_bug5	485 (10)	Cancel	Int.	1	0	0	126	1	0	29
ndisprot_read	588 (35)	Cancel	No	10 (AG)	0	0	2894	3	0	38
ndisprot_write	588 (35)	Cancel	No	4	0	0	217	1	0	15
ndisprot_ioctl	588 (35)	Cancel	No	7	0	0	424	1	0	32
mouclass_bug1	582 (19)	Cancel	Seq.	10	0	1	905	4	0	131
mouclass_bug2	582 (19)	Cancel	Int.	10	0	0	944	3	1	186
daytona	485 (223)	NullDeref	No	13 (AG)	0	0	459	3	0	43
kbdclass_read	695 (346)	NullDeref	No	1	0	0	227	11	0	846
kbdclass_ioctl	695 (346)	NullDeref	No	1	0	0	229	10	0	737
mouclass_read	582 (271)	NullDeref	No	1	0	0	98	10	0	965
mouclass_ioctl	582 (271)	NullDeref	No	1	0	0	91	9	0	918

Figure 10. Results obtained from running CBUGS on Windows device drivers. Times are in seconds.

codebases. These work can also be seen as filtering false alarms if usage is consistent with some (unknown) protocol; e.g., if all dereferences of a variable x is not protected by a null-check, the accesses to the variable is most likely safe due to some invariant in the program. One can think of interleaved bugs as discovering inconsistencies (with respect to a given set of assertions), where the sequential behaviors describe an implicit protocol. On the other hand, unlike these approaches, we do not require a separate analysis for different patterns and provide a formal guarantee of relative correctness if there are no interleaved bugs.

Approaches for suppressing or ranking warnings have ranged from statistical techniques (such as *Z-ranking* [14]) to more domain specific methods (such as suppressing data-race warnings [21]). Although these approaches are applied to the results of static analyses that scale to large modules, they do not provide any formal guarantees of the bugs that are suppressed. Besides, most of these approaches are aimed at combating the imprecision of static analysis, as opposed to the environment problem.

6.2 Sequential filters

The idea of using sequential behaviors as *oracle* for concurrent implementations has been studied in the context of checking *linearizability* [12], which provides a natural specification in many settings for checking concurrent programs. Various static and dynamic tools have been built to check concurrent behaviors against sequential ones. LINEUP is a dynamic analysis tool that flags a concurrent behavior when it outputs a value that no sequential execution produced [4]. Burnim et al. [5] provide runtime techniques to check parallel implementations against non-deterministic sequential specifications. Siegel et al. [19] employ symbolic execution along with enumeration of interleavings to check against the sequential behaviors for numerical programs. Unlike these approaches, we consider the dual problem when specifications are present in the program but the environment is imprecise. Because we check for user-specified assertions, we can apply the technique to any concurrent program even if it is not linearizable.

6.3 Environment synthesis

Generating environments for model checking of open systems is a well-studied problem. Tkachuk et al. [20] generate environment models from user-specified assumptions and by analyzing environment implementations. Alur et al. [1] address the problem of synthesizing the most liberal environment using a combination of predicate abstraction and automata learning. One can view our approach as inferring the most liberal environment that does not induce failures on sequential executions, and using it to check the concurrent program. As demonstrated in §5, inferring legal environment preconditions may involve inferring complex aliasing relationships on the input data that may not be amenable to finite-state approaches. Nonetheless, it would be interesting to combine synthesis techniques with our algorithm.

7. Conclusion

In this paper, we highlight the problem of false alarms in static analysis due to missing environment assumptions and present a solution when checking assertions in concurrent programs. We define a class of warnings as interleaved bugs when they are retained by a filter that attributes all warnings in the sequential interleavings to the underspecified harness (or to missing preconditions). We believe this can be an effective way to prioritize high quality warnings when looking at warnings generated by a static analyzer for concurrent programs. Our preliminary experience with a simple implementation to find interleaved bugs is encouraging, although we expect more work to deal with unbounded non-determinism in the filter programs.

More generally, the paper makes one of the first contributions to the area of using *semantic* techniques for prioritizing alarms from static analysis. Sequential filters are natural filters when prioritizing alarms for concurrency analysis. We believe that one can extend this idea to use artifacts other than sequential executions in the source code to automatically define filter programs for other domains as well.

Acknowledgments

We thank Tom Ball, Sriram Rajamani and the anonymous reviewers for their feedback on an earlier draft. We thank Madan Musuvathi for pointing us to similarities with work on using sequential executions as oracles for concurrent modules. Finally, we thank Zvonimir Rakamaric and Shaz Qadeer who wrote many of the concurrent harnesses for the device drivers, which served as a starting point for our experiments.

References

[1] R. Alur, P. Cerný, P. Madhusudan, and W. Nam. Synthesis of interface specifications for java classes. In *Principles of Programming Languages (POPL '05)*, pages 98–109, 2005.

[2] M. Barnett and K. R. M. Leino. Weakest-precondition of unstructured programs. In *Program Analysis For Software Tools and Engineering (PASTE '05)*, pages 82–87, 2005.

[3] E. Börger, E. Grädel, and Y. Gurevich. *The Classical Decision Problem.* Springer-Verlag, 1997.

[4] S. Burckhardt, C. Dern, M. Musuvathi, and R. Tan. Line-up: a complete and automatic linearizability checker. In *Programming Language Design and Implementation (PLDI '10)*, pages 330–340, 2010.

[5] J. Burnim, T. Elmas, G. C. Necula, and K. Sen. Ndseq: runtime checking for nondeterministic sequential specifications of parallel correctness. In *Programming Language Design and Implementation (PLDI '11)*, pages 401–414, 2011.

[6] L. Cordeiro and B. Fischer. Verifying multi-threaded software using smt-based context-bounded model checking. In *International Conference on Software Engineering (ICSE '11)*, pages 331–340, 2011.

[7] D. Detlefs, G. Nelson, and J. B. Saxe. Simplify: a theorem prover for program checking. *J. ACM*, 52(3):365–473, 2005.

[8] E. W. Dijkstra. Guarded commands, nondeterminacy and formal derivation of programs. *Communications of the ACM*, 18:453–457, 1975.

[9] I. Dillig, T. Dillig, and A. Aiken. Static error detection using semantic inconsistency inference. In *Programming Language Design and Implementation (PLDI '07)*, pages 435–445, 2007.

[10] M. Emmi, S. Qadeer, and Z. Rakamaric. Delay-bounded scheduling. In *Principles of Programming Languages*, pages 411–422, 2011.

[11] D. R. Engler, D. Y. Chen, and A. Chou. Bugs as inconsistent behavior: A general approach to inferring errors in systems code. In *Symposium on Operating Systems Principles (SOSP '01)*, pages 57–72, 2001.

[12] M. Herlihy and J. M. Wing. Linearizability: A correctness condition for concurrent objects. *ACM Trans. Program. Lang. Syst.*, 12(3):463–492, 1990.

[13] R. Jhala and R. Majumdar. Interprocedural analysis of asynchronous programs. In *Principles of Programming Languages*, pages 339–350, 2007.

[14] T. Kremenek and D. R. Engler. Z-ranking: Using statistical analysis to counter the impact of static analysis approximations. In *Static Analysis Symposium (SAS '03)*, LNCS 2694, pages 295–315, 2003.

[15] S. Lahiri, S. Qadeer, and Z. Rakamaric. Static and precise detection of concurrency errors in systems code using SMT solvers. In *Computer Aided Verification*, 2009.

[16] K. R. M. Leino, T. D. Millstein, and J. B. Saxe. Generating error traces from verification-condition counterexamples. *Sci. Comput. Program.*, 55(1-3):209–226, 2005.

[17] Poirot: The Concurrency Sleuth. `http://research.microsoft.com/en-us/projects/poirot/`.

[18] K. Sen and M. Viswanathan. Model checking multithreaded programs with asynchronous atomic methods. In *Computer Aided Verification*, pages 300–314, 2006.

[19] S. F. Siegel, A. Mironova, G. S. Avrunin, and L. A. Clarke. Using model checking with symbolic execution to verify parallel numerical programs. In *International Symposium on Software Testing and Analysis (ISSTA '06)*, pages 157–168, 2006.

[20] O. Tkachuk, M. B. Dwyer, and C. S. Pasareanu. Automated environment generation for software model checking. In *Automated Software Engineering (ASE '03)*, pages 116–129, 2003.

[21] J. W. Voung, R. Jhala, and S. Lerner. Relay: static race detection on millions of lines of code. In *Symposium on Foundations of Software Engineering (ESEC/SIGSOFT FSE '07)*, pages 205–214, 2007.

[22] Microsoft windows driver kit (WDK). `http://www.microsoft.com/whdc/devtools/ddk/default.mspx`.

A. Quantified VC generation

In this section, we describe a method for generating a (quantified) verification condition (for bounded-length programs) in the presence of non-deterministic and possibly non-terminating filter programs.

Recall that the goal of DIFFERROR(P_1, P_2) is to filter any input i, such that there is *some* choice of the non-deterministic values in P_1 that fails P_1. This implies that the non-determinism in P_1 is *angelic* (in contrast to the *demonic* nondeterminism in P_2). One option is to extend our language (in §3.1) to introduce a statement choose x (in addition to havoc x), to model the angelic non-determinism. And then create a program similar to one described in Fig. 3, where we replace the havoc x statements in P_1 with choose x statements, in addition to the transformation of the assert e statements.

However, we are not aware of any efficient verification condition (VC) generation algorithm in the presence of such non-determinism. Let us highlight one of the main difficulties of extending VC generation algorithms with choose statements. Most efficient VC generation algorithms (see [2]) generate a formula whose size is at most quadratic in the size of the program. This is achieved by using a variant of static single assignment, where auxiliary variables are introduced to hold different incarnations of a program variable after an assignment, a havoc statement, or at merge points. These variables are implicitly universally quantified in the resultant VC (when checking for validity). The presence of choose statements introduces an existential quantifier (e.g. $wlp(\text{choose x}, \phi) = \exists x.\phi$, whereas $wlp(\text{havoc x}, \phi) = \forall x.\phi$, where $wlp(.,.)$ refers to *weakest liberal precondition* predicate transformer [8]). This interacts badly with the use of auxiliary variables in the VC, as determining quantification (∀ vs. ∃) of a particular variable and the nesting can be challenging.

Instead, we present (in Alg. 2) a VC generation mechanism for DIFFERROR that leverages off-the-shelf VC generation along with symbolic execution along error paths, to lazily add the quantifier alternation. The idea is simple: we enumerate all the program paths in P_1 that lead to an assertion violation, and create an expression (purely in terms of the inputs to P_2) that characterizes all the conditions under which P_1 fails. We generate a VC for P_2 using any off-the-shelf VC generation technique after blocking all these inputs.

The formula ϕ represents the set of inputs for which there is a choice of the non-deterministic values such that an assertion in P_1 fails. Similarly, the set A represents a set of paths in P_1 that lead to an assertion violation. These variables are initialized to false and $\{\}$ respectively (line 1 and line 2). The loop from line 3 to line 11 enumerates different paths in P_1 that fail an assertion. We use an oracle FINDBUG (in line 4) that takes as arguments (i) a program and a (ii) set of paths and finds an error trace that avoids the set of paths specified, or NOBUG therwise (indicating that there are no bugs). FINDBUG can be implemented by augmenting VC generation to avoid a set of paths while checking assertions [16]. Once all the error paths have been explored, the algorithm computes the VC for P_2 after "blocking" all the inputs in ϕ using assume $\neg\phi$ (line 6). Otherwise, for a given error r, we extract the error trace t and the input i and update A and ϕ respecively (line 9 and line 10).

The predicate transformer $wlp(.,.)$ is extended for havoc statements:

$$pre(\text{havoc x}, \psi) \quad = \quad \exists x.\ \psi$$

Observe that $pre(t, \text{true})$ is a formula whose free variables are inputs to P_1, and can be massaged to a formula of the form $\exists x_1, \ldots, x_k.\phi'$, where ϕ' is a ground formula, after renaming the bound variables introduced due to havoc to avoid variable capture.

Algorithm 2 Algorithm for generating a VC for DIFFERROR

Require: Programs P_1 and P_2

Ensure: A formula representing the VC for $\text{DIFFERROR}(P_1, P_2)$

$\phi :=$ false
$A := \{\}$
loop
  $r := \text{FINDBUG}(P_1, A)$
  if $r = \text{NOBUG}$ **then**
    return VC(assume $\neg\phi$; $P_2.body$)
  end if
  Let $\text{TRACE}(t, i) = r$
  $A := A \cup \{t\}$
  $\phi := \phi \vee pre(t, \text{true})$
end loop

THEOREM A.1. *Given programs P_1 and P_2, if ψ be the formula returned by Alg. 2, then $\text{DIFFERROR}(P_1, P_2)$ holds if and only if ψ is satisfiable.*

It is interesting to note that the theorem above holds even when the filter program P_1 does not terminate on some inputs — this is because we only enumerate paths in P_1 that lead to an assertion violation. For instance, if we consider the non-terminating example from §3.3, where P_1 was simply assume false, then we will not find any bugs in P_1, and Alg. 2 will simply return the VC of P_2.

Consider the example in Fig. 6, where the `hashFunc` is a procedure with complex operations to compute the hash value of an input. It is not hard to see that $\text{DIFFERROR}(P_1, P_2)$ does not hold for this example. However, Alg. 1 will diverge by enumerating all the possible values of the non-deterministic choice of `i` in P_1. Instead, Alg. 2 generates the following precondition to P_2 by capturing all the inputs that fail P_1:

$$\neg(\exists i, j :: j \neq 0 \wedge \neg \mathsf{a}[i] \geq 0)$$

which is equivalent to $\forall i :: \mathsf{a}[i] \geq 0$, and sufficient to prove the assertion in P_2 for any implementation of `hashFunc`.

Although the algorithm presented here generates a precise VC for the DIFFERROR problem, the undecidable nature of the DIFFERROR problem precludes any algorithm to solve all instances of the problem. The algorithm presented here may not be complete due to the incompleteness of automatic theorem provers to deal with quantifiers in the resulting VC. For example, the quantified VC generated may not be amenable to the *trigger-based* schemes for instantiating quantifiers in most SMT solvers [7] — there is no good trigger for the bound variable j above. The above formula would need some simplifications (e.g. quantifier elimination) in conjunction with quantifier instantiations. Nevertheless, by translating the $\text{DIFFERROR}(P_1, P_2)$ to a logical formula, we can hope to leverage advances in automated theorem provers to obtain more precise and efficient solution for $\text{DIFFERROR}(P_1, P_2)$.

Towards a Program Logic for JavaScript

Philippa Gardner
Imperial College London
pg@doc.ic.ac.uk

Sergio Maffeis
Imperial College London
maffeis@doc.ic.ac.uk

Gareth Smith
Imperial College London
gds@doc.ic.ac.uk

Abstract

JavaScript has become the most widely used language for client-side web programming. The dynamic nature of JavaScript makes understanding its code notoriously difficult, leading to buggy programs and a lack of adequate static-analysis tools. We believe that logical reasoning has much to offer JavaScript: a simple description of program behaviour, a clear understanding of module boundaries, and the ability to verify security contracts.

We introduce a program logic for reasoning about a broad subset of JavaScript, including challenging features such as prototype inheritance and `with`. We adapt ideas from separation logic to provide tractable reasoning about JavaScript code: reasoning about easy programs is easy; reasoning about hard programs is possible. We prove a strong soundness result. All libraries written in our subset and proved correct with respect to their specifications will be well-behaved, even when called by arbitrary JavaScript code.

Categories and Subject Descriptors F.3.1 [*Theory of Computation*]: Logics and Meanings of Programs—Specifying and Verifying and Reasoning about Programs

General Terms Reliability, Theory, Verification

Keywords JavaScript, Separation Logic, Web

1. Introduction

JavaScript has become the de-facto language for client-side web programming. Ajax web applications, used in e.g. Google Docs, are based on a combination of JavaScript and server-side programming. JavaScript has become an international standard called ECMAScript [14]. Adobe Flash, used in e.g. YouTube, features ActionScript, a programming language based on ECMAScript. Even web applications written in e.g. Java, F♯ or purpose-designed languages such as Flapjax or Milescript are either compiled to JavaScript, or they lack browser integration or cross-platform compatibility. JavaScript is currently the assembly language of the Web, and this seems unlikely to change.

JavaScript was initially created for small web-programming tasks, which benefited from the flexibility of the language and tight browser integration. Nowadays, the modern demands placed on JavaScript are huge. Although this flexibility and browser integration are still key advantages, the inherent dynamic nature of the language makes current web code based on ECMAScript 3 notoriously difficult to write and use [12, 18, 28]. The expectation is that ECMAScript 5 and future standards will improve the situation. However, although the main browsers now support ECMAScript 5, the majority of code being written today is in ECMAScript 3. Even if there is a wide acceptance of ECMAScript 5, which is certainly not clear from the current blogs, it is inevitable that ECMAScript 5 libraries will have to interface properly with ECMAScript 3 code. We therefore believe that there is a growing need for general-purpose, expressive analysis tools for both ECMAScript 3 and 5, which provide simple, correct descriptions of program behaviour and a clear understanding of module boundaries.

We introduce a program logic for reasoning about ECMAScript 3. While it is tempting to ignore the 'ugly' parts of the language, and reason only about 'well-written' code, in practice JavaScript programs have to interface with arbitrary web code. We therefore use a model of the language that does not shun the most challenging JavaScript features. For example, the behaviour of prototype inheritance, and the interplay between scoping rules and the `with` statement, is complex. This means that our basic reasoning rules must also be complex. We overcome this complexity by establishing natural layers of abstraction on top of our basic reasoning. With principled code, we can stay within these layers of abstraction and the reasoning is straightforward. With arbitrary code, we must break open the appropriate abstraction layers until we can re-establish the invariants of the abstraction. In this way, we are able to provide clean specifications of a wide variety of JavaScript programs.

Our reasoning is based on separation logic. Separation logic has proven to be invaluable for reasoning about programs which directly manipulate the heap, such as C and Java programs [2, 3, 8, 20, 36]. A key characteristic of JavaScript is that the entire state of the language resides in the object heap, in a structure that imperfectly emulates the variable store of many other programming languages. It is therefore natural to investigate the use of separation logic to verify JavaScript programs. In fact, we had to fundamentally adapt separation logic, both to present an accurate account of JavaScript's emulated variable store (see Section 2: Motivating Examples) and also to establish soundness. For soundness, it is usual to require that all the program commands are 'local', according to a definition first given in [20]. Many JavaScript statements are not local by this definition: for example, even a simple variable read is non-local because its result may depend on the *absence* of certain fields in the emulated variable store. We instead prove soundness using a concept of *weak locality*, recently introduced by Smith [30].

In this paper, we reason about a substantial subset of JavaScript, including prototype inheritance, `with`, simple functions (no recursive or higher-order functions) and simple `eval`. Our treatment of functions and `eval` is precisely enough to expose fully the complexity of the emulated variable store. Building on the work of Charlton and Reus [6, 29], we will extend our reasoning to higher-order functions and complex `eval` in future. We prove soundness of our reasoning with respect to a faithful subset of the formal

POPL'12, January 25–27, 2012, Philadelphia, PA, USA.

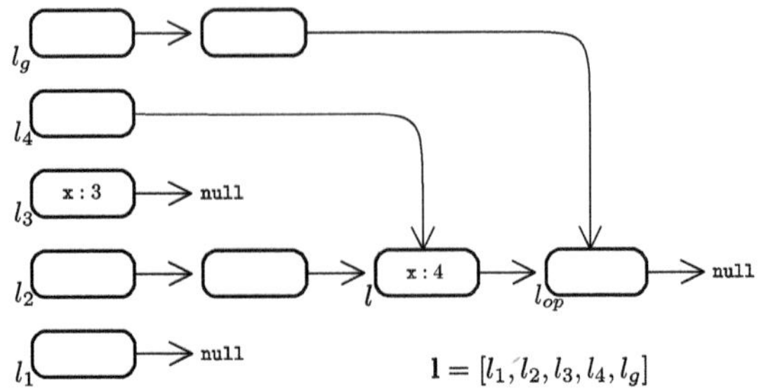

Figure 1. A JavaScript emulated variable store

operational semantics of Maffeis *et al.* [18]. Our soundness result has powerful implications. Library code written in our subset and proved correct with respect to their specifications will be well-behaved, even when called by arbitrary JavaScript code. Our result is constructed in such a way that it will be simple to extend to reasoning about higher-order functions and complex `eval` in due course.

2. Motivating Examples

As convincingly argued in [12, 18, 27, 28], there are many reasons why the behaviour of JavaScript programs is complex. For a start, JavaScript is a dynamically typed, prototype-oriented language, which does not have a standard notion of variable store. Instead, JavaScript variables are best regarded as being stored in the heap, in a structure which imperfectly emulates the variable store. This structure consists of an abstract list of scope objects, called the *scope chain*, analogous to stack frames in other languages. Every scope object has a pointer to a linked list of prototypes, providing prototype-based inheritance. Since scope objects inherit data from their prototypes, the value of a variable cannot be resolved by a simple list traversal. Variable resolution is further complicated by the fact that JavaScript objects may share a common prototype.

JavaScript's behaviour can make apparently simple programs deceptively counter-intuitive. Consider the code C defined below:

```
x = null; y = null; z = null;
f = function(w){x = v; v = 4; var v; y = v;};
v = 5; f(null); z = v;
```

What values should the variables x, y and z store at the end of the program? The correct answer is `undefined`, 4 and 5 respectively. We explain how this occurs as we walk through our reasoning.

In Section 6.2 we prove the following triple of this code:

$$\{\ \mathsf{store}_{\mathrm{LS}}(\mathtt{x},\mathtt{y},\mathtt{z},\mathtt{f},\mathtt{v}|) * \mathbf{l} \doteq \mathrm{LS}\ \}$$
$$\mathtt{C}$$
$$\left\{\begin{array}{l}\exists \mathrm{L}.\,\mathsf{store}_{\mathrm{LS}}(|\mathtt{x}:\mathtt{undefined},\mathtt{y}:4,\mathtt{z}:5,\mathtt{f}:\mathrm{L},\mathtt{v}:5)\\ * \mathbf{l} \doteq \mathrm{LS} * \mathrm{true}\end{array}\right\}$$

We distinguish a global logical expression $\mathbf{l}$ with value LS denoting the scope chain. The store predicate $\mathsf{store}_{\mathrm{LS}}(\mathtt{x},\mathtt{y},\mathtt{z},\mathtt{f},\mathtt{v}|)$ states that the store-like structure referred to by LS contains *none* of the program variables mentioned; the variables occur to the left of the bar. The store predicate $\mathsf{store}_{\mathrm{LS}}(|\mathtt{x}:\mathtt{undefined},\mathtt{y}:4,\mathtt{z}:5,\mathtt{f}:\mathrm{L},\mathtt{v}:5)$ denotes the final values for all the variables; the variables occur to the right of the bar with assigned values.

To understand the complexity of the heap structures described by store predicates, consider the example heap given in Figure 1. This diagram illustrates a typical shape of a JavaScript variable store. Each object is denoted by a box. In this example, the current list of scope objects is given by $\mathbf{l} = [l_1, l_2, l_3, l_4, l_g]$, where the l_i are object addresses and l_g is a distinguished object containing the global variables which must occur at the end of the current list of scope objects. Each scope object has a pointer to a list of prototypes, with the arrows representing prototype relationships. These prototype lists can be shared, but cannot form cycles. In ECMAScript 3, prototype lists must either end with the distinguished object l_{op} or be empty. However, many implementations (SpiderMonkey, V8 and WebKit) allow the programmer to directly access and change the prototype pointers, allowing incomplete prototype chains ending in `null` but not allowing the creation of cycles. We work with incomplete prototype chains, since we want ECMAScript 3 library code to work well with such implementations.

To look up the value of a variable x in our example heap, we check each object for a field with name x, starting with l_1, checking the prototype list from l_1 then moving along the list of scope objects. In our example, the x in object l will be found first, since the whole prototype chain of l_2 will be visited before l_3. When reading the value stored in x, this is all we need to know. If we write to the same variable x, the effect will be to create a new field x at l_2. This new field will override the x field in object l in the usual prototype-oriented way.

All of this messy detail is abstracted away by the store predicate. The formation of this predicate is subtle and requires some adaptation of separation logic. As well as the separating conjunction $*$ for reasoning about disjoint heaps, we introduce the *sepish* connective $\uplus$ for reasoning about partially separated heaps. It is used, for example, to account for the sharing of prototype lists illustrated in Figure 1. We also use the assertion $(l, \mathtt{x}) \mapsto \varnothing$, which states that the field x is *not* present at object address l. This predicate is reminiscent of the 'out' predicate in [7] stating that values are not present in a concurrent list. It is necessary to identify the first x in the structure: in our example, the x at l is the first x, since it does not occur in the prototype list of l_1 nor in the prototype list of l_2 until l.

Our store predicate allows us to make simple inferences about variable assignments, without breaking our store abstraction:

$$\{\ \mathsf{store}_{\mathrm{LS}}(\mathtt{x},\mathtt{y},\mathtt{z},\mathtt{f},\mathtt{v}|) * \mathbf{l} \doteq \mathrm{LS}\ \}$$
$$\mathtt{x = null;}$$
$$\left\{\begin{array}{l}\mathsf{store}_{\mathrm{LS}}(\mathtt{y},\mathtt{z},\mathtt{f},\mathtt{v}|\mathtt{x}:\mathtt{null})\\ * \mathbf{l} \doteq \mathrm{LS} * \mathrm{true}\end{array}\right\}$$

where the assertion true hides potentially garbage-collected prototype lists.

The evaluation of the function expression `function(w) {...}` has the effect of creating a new function object and returning the address L of that object. The object contains a number of internal housekeeping fields, including @*body* which contains the body of the function and @*scope* which stores the function closure LS. Our inference for the function definition is approximately:

$$\{\ \mathsf{store}_{\mathrm{LS}}(\mathtt{f},\mathtt{v}|\mathtt{x}:\mathtt{null},\mathtt{y}:\mathtt{null},\mathtt{z}:\mathtt{null}) * \mathbf{l} \doteq \mathrm{LS}\ \}$$
$$\mathtt{f = function(w)\ \{...\}}$$
$$\left\{\begin{array}{l}\exists \mathrm{L}.\,\mathsf{store}_{\mathrm{LS}}(\mathtt{v}|\mathtt{x}:\mathtt{null},\mathtt{y}:\mathtt{null},\mathtt{z}:\mathtt{null},\mathtt{f}:\mathrm{L}) *\\ (\mathrm{L}, @body) \mapsto \lambda w.\{\ldots\} * (\mathrm{L}, @scope) \mapsto \mathrm{LS} *\\ \mathbf{l} \doteq \mathrm{LS} * \mathrm{true}\end{array}\right\}$$

As well as the store predicate, we assert that the state also contains object cells such as $(\mathrm{L}, @scope) \mapsto \mathrm{LS}$. This assertion means that there is an object with address L in the heap, and it definitely contains at least the field @*scope* which has value LS. The assertion says nothing about any other field of L. We assert that our function object has fields @*body* and @*scope*. The full specification, given in Section 6.2, is actually a little more complicated than this. For now, we hide additional housekeeping fields in the assertion true.

We know that this program example is challenging, because the final values of the variables are counter-intuitive. All the complexity of the example occurs within the function call. When JavaScript calls a function, it performs two passes on the body: in the first pass, it creates a new scope object and initialises local variables to `undefined`; in the second pass, it runs the code in the newly constructed local scope. Our reasoning reflects this complexity. The Hoare triple for the function call has the following shape:

$$\left\{\begin{array}{l} \mathsf{store}_{\mathrm{LS}}(|\mathtt{x}:\mathtt{null},\mathtt{y}:\mathtt{null},\mathtt{z}:\mathtt{null},\mathtt{f}:\mathrm{L},\mathtt{v}:5) * \\ (\mathrm{L},@body) \mapsto \lambda w.\{\ldots\} * (\mathrm{L},@scope) \mapsto \mathrm{LS} * \\ \mathbf{l} \doteq \mathrm{LS} * \mathrm{true} \end{array}\right\}$$

```
f(null);
```

$$\{\ ???\ \}$$

To find a suitable postcondition, we must reason about the function body. The precondition of the function-body triple given below is constructed from the first pass of the function call. As well as containing the precondition of the function call, it contains a new scope object L' with fields given by the parameter of the function and the local variables discovered by the first pass. For our example, it contains the assertions $(\mathrm{L}',\mathtt{w}) \mapsto \mathtt{null}$ for the parameter declaration and $(\mathrm{L}',\mathtt{v}) \mapsto \mathtt{undefined}$ for the local variable declaration. The object L' also has a $@proto$ field, which points to `null` since scope objects do not inherit any behaviour, and a $@this$ field, which can only be read. We also have the predicate $\mathsf{newobj}(\mathrm{L}',@proto,@this,\mathtt{w},\mathtt{v})$, which asserts the absence from L' of all the fields we have not mentioned as parameters. Knowing this absence of fields is essential if, in the function body, we wish to write to variables, such as the `x` and `y`, which do not appear in the local scope object. Finally, the new scope object L' is prepended to the scope list $\mathbf{l}$.

Using this precondition, we are now able to give the triple obtained by the second pass of the function call:

$$\left\{\begin{array}{l} \exists \mathrm{L}'.\,\mathbf{l} \doteq \mathrm{L}' : \mathrm{LS} * \\ \mathsf{store}_{\mathrm{LS}}(|\mathtt{x}:\mathtt{null},\mathtt{y}:\mathtt{null},\mathtt{z}:\mathtt{null},\mathtt{f}:\mathrm{L},\mathtt{v}:5) * \\ (\mathrm{L},@body) \mapsto \lambda w.\{\ldots\} * (\mathrm{L},@scope) \mapsto \mathrm{LS} * \\ \mathsf{newobj}(\mathrm{L}',@proto,@this,\mathtt{w},\mathtt{v}) * \\ (\mathrm{L}',\mathtt{w}) \mapsto \mathtt{null} * (\mathrm{L}',\mathtt{v}) \mapsto \mathtt{undefined} * \\ (\mathrm{L}',@proto) \mapsto \mathtt{null} * (\mathrm{L}',@this) \mapsto \mathrm{L}'' * \mathrm{true} \end{array}\right\}$$

```
x = v ; v = 4 ; var v ; y = v;
```

$$\left\{\begin{array}{l} \exists \mathrm{L}'.\,\mathbf{l} \doteq \mathrm{L}' : \mathrm{LS} * \\ \mathsf{store}_{\mathrm{LS}}(|\mathtt{x}:\mathtt{undefined},\mathtt{y}:4,\mathtt{z}:\mathtt{null},\mathtt{f}:\mathrm{L},\mathtt{v}:5) * \\ (\mathrm{L},@body) \mapsto \lambda w.\{\ldots\} * (\mathrm{L},@scope) \mapsto \mathrm{LS} * \\ \mathsf{newobj}(\mathrm{L}',@proto,@this,\mathtt{w},\mathtt{v}) * \\ (\mathrm{L}',\mathtt{w}) \mapsto \mathtt{null} * (\mathrm{L}',\mathtt{v}) \mapsto 4 * \\ (\mathrm{L}',@proto) \mapsto \mathtt{null} * (\mathrm{L}',@this) \mapsto \mathrm{L}'' * \mathrm{true} \end{array}\right\}$$

The postcondition follows simply from the three assignments in the function body: first, variable `x` gets the value `undefined`, since this is the current value of the local `v`; then the local `v` is assigned 4; and, finally, the global variable `y` is assigned the value of the local variable `v`. The `var v` statement has no effect in the second pass of the function call.

The postcondition of the function call is the postcondition of the function body, with local scope object L' popped off the current scope list $\mathbf{l}$:

$$\left\{\begin{array}{l} \exists \mathrm{L}'.\,\mathsf{store}_{\mathrm{LS}}(|\mathtt{x}:\mathtt{undefined},\mathtt{y}:4,\mathtt{z}:\mathtt{null},\mathtt{f}:\mathrm{L},\mathtt{v}:5) * \\ (\mathrm{L},@body) \mapsto \lambda w.\{\ldots\} * (\mathrm{L},@scope) \mapsto \mathrm{LS} * \\ \mathsf{newobj}(\mathrm{L}',@proto,@this,\mathtt{w},\mathtt{v}) * \\ (\mathrm{L}',\mathtt{w}) \mapsto \mathtt{null} * (\mathrm{L}',\mathtt{v}) \mapsto 4 * (\mathrm{L}',@proto) \mapsto \mathtt{null} * \\ (\mathrm{L}',@this) \mapsto L'' * \mathbf{l} \doteq \mathrm{LS} * \mathrm{true} \end{array}\right\}$$

Reasoning about the final assignment is straightforward, with `z` assigned the value of the global variable `v`. The final postcondition is obtained using the consequence rule to hide the function object and local scope object behind the assertion true, since they are surplus to requirements, and existentially quantifying function object L:

$$\left\{\begin{array}{l} \exists \mathrm{L}.\,\mathsf{store}_{\mathrm{LS}}(|\mathtt{x}:\mathtt{undefined},\mathtt{y}:4,\mathtt{z}:5,\mathtt{f}:\mathrm{L},\mathtt{v}:5) * \\ \mathbf{l} \doteq \mathrm{LS} * \mathrm{true} \end{array}\right\}$$

Part of the challenge of understanding this example is knowing the scope of local variable `v`. In JavaScript, variables can only be declared local to functions, not other blocks such as `if` and `while`. This can lead to undesirable behaviour, especially when a local variable overloads the name of a global variable. One controversial technique for solving this problem is to use the `with` statement and a literal object to declare local variable blocks precisely where they are needed. Using `with` is often considered bad practice, and it is deprecated in ECMAScript 5. However, it is widely used in practice [22, 28] and can certainly be used to improve the program readability. We are able to reason about even extremely confusing uses of `with`. Consider the program `C'`:

```
a = {b:1}; with (a){f=function(c){return b}};
a = {b:2}; f(null)
```

Armed with an operational understanding of JavaScript's emulated variable store, it is not so difficult to understand that this program returns the value 1, even though the value of `a.b` at the end of the program is 2. It may not be quite so clear that this program can fault. It may also execute arbitrary code from elsewhere in the emulated variable store, leading to a possible security violation.

We only understood this example properly by doing the verification. In Section 6.2, we prove the triple:

$$\{\mathsf{store}_{\mathbf{l}}(\mathtt{a},\mathtt{f}|) \uplus (l_{op},\mathtt{f}) \mapsto \varnothing \uplus (l_{op},@proto) \mapsto \mathtt{null}\}$$

```
C'
```

$$\{\mathbf{r} \doteq 1 * \mathrm{true}\}$$

A similar proof is possible for a precondition where `a` and `f` are in the store with arbitrary values. Either precondition ensures the program returns the value 1 as expected. The obvious first try was to have e.g. just $\mathsf{store}_{\mathbf{l}}(\mathtt{a},\mathtt{f}|)$ as the precondition. This does not work as, when reasoning about the assignment to the variable `f`, we cannot assert that the variable `f` is not in the local scope. As discussed earlier, we work with incomplete prototype chains in the emulated variable store. With some web code, it is possible for programmers to directly access and change the prototype pointers, resulting in the distinguished object l_{op} not being a part of the emulated variable store. This means that l_{op} may contain the field `f` without violating our proposed precondition. The statement `a = {b:1}` then results in the creation of a new object L, with no field `f` as expected, but with field $@proto$ pointing to l_{op} which may contain f:

$$\exists \mathrm{L}.\,(\mathrm{L},\mathtt{b}) \mapsto 1 * (\mathrm{L},\mathtt{f}) \mapsto \varnothing * (\mathrm{L},@proto) \mapsto l_{op}$$

The `with` statement makes this new object L the most local cell in our emulated variable store. But because `f` is an inherited property of L, the meaning of the assignment to `f` has now changed – it has become an overriding assignment of a local variable. We write the new function `f` into the most local object L. When the program returns from the `with` statement, the function call to `f(null)` will fault, since there is no `f` in scope to call. In many web browsers (including Chrome, Firefox, and Safari), this behaviour can be induced by running the program `Object.prototype.f = 4 ; window.__proto__ = null ; C'` in the default starting state[1]. The `__proto__` notation allows the programmer to directly access and change the internal $@proto$

[1] In web browsers, `Object.prototype` usually contains a pointer to the object l_{op} and `window` usually contains a pointer to the object l_g.

fields, resulting in a program state which causes the program C′ to fault. Non-standard features such as this are widely used in practice, and so it is important that our reasoning be robust to the states they produce. In this example, it is possible to induce a similarly tricky starting state without the use of any non-standard features, which results in the call to `f()` executing arbitrary code not mentioned in our program. Consider running the program `Object.prototype.f = function(c) {C″};C′` where C″ is suspicious code. This could result in a security breach if `f` is passed sensitive data.

3. Operational Semantics

We define a big-step operational semantics for a large subset of JavaScript that represents faithfully the inheritance, prototyping and scoping mechanisms described in the ECMAScript 3 standard. Our semantics follows closely the full small-step JavaScript semantics of Maffeis, Mitchell and Taly [18], except that we make some simplifications as discussed in Section 3.5. We work with a big-step semantics because it connects better to our reasoning.

3.1 Heaps

The JavaScript heap is a partial function $H:\mathcal{R} \rightharpoonup \mathcal{V}$ that maps *references*, $r \in \mathcal{R} = \mathcal{L} \times \mathcal{X}$, which are pairs of memory locations and field names, to values. This structure emphasises the important role that references play in the semantics of the language. Values $v \in \mathcal{V}$ can be basic values $\mathtt{v}$, locations l and lambda abstractions $\lambda\mathtt{x.e}$. The set of locations $\mathcal{L}$ is lifted to a set $\mathcal{L}_{\mathtt{null}}$ containing the special location `null`, analogous to a null-pointer in C, which cannot be in the domain of any heap. We denote the empty heap by `emp`, a heap cell by $(l, x) \mapsto v$, the union of two disjoint heaps by $H_1 * H_2$, and a read operation by $H(l, x)$.

An object is represented by a set of heap cells addressed by the same location but with different field names. For ease of notation, we use $l \mapsto \{x_1\!: v_1, \dots, x_n\!: v_n\}$ as a shorthand for the object $(l, x_1) \mapsto v_1 * \dots * (l, x_n) \mapsto v_n$.

As discussed, JavaScript has no variable store. Instead, variables are resolved with respect to a scope object implicitly known at run time. Scope objects are just objects whose locations are recorded in the *scope chain* (we use a standard notation $[\,], e{:}L, L \mathbin{+\!\!+} L$ for lists). Each scope object has a pointer to a *prototype list* (which need not point to l_{op}). A variable x is resolved as the property named "x" of the first object in the scope chain whose prototype list defines "x". Scoping constructs, such as function calls and `with`, cause sub-expressions to be evaluated with respect to a local scope object, by putting the local scope object at the beginning of the scope chain and then removing it after the sub-expressions have been evaluated. All user programs are evaluated starting from the default scope chain $[l_g]$, where l_g is the location of the global JavaScript object, described below. The final object in any scope chain is always l_g, but duplicates in a scope chain *are* allowed. For example, the JavaScript program `with(window){C}` is perfectly valid, and (usually) results in the subprogram C being evaluated in a state in which l_g is both the most global *and* the most local object.

The auxiliary scope function σ, defined below, returns the location of the first object in the scope chain to define a given variable. It depends on the prototype function π, which returns the location of the first object in the prototype chain to define the variable.

Scope and prototype resolution: $\sigma(H, l, x)$ **and** $\pi(H, l, x)$**.**

$$\sigma(H, [\,], x) \triangleq \mathtt{null}$$

$$\frac{\pi(H, l, x) \neq \mathtt{null}}{\sigma(H, l{:}L, x) \triangleq l} \qquad \frac{\pi(H, l, x) = \mathtt{null}}{\sigma(H, l{:}L, x) \triangleq \sigma(H, L, x)}$$

$$\pi(H, \mathtt{null}, x) \triangleq \mathtt{null}$$

$$\frac{(l, x) \in \mathsf{dom}(H)}{\pi(H, l, x) \triangleq l} \qquad \frac{(l, x) \notin \mathsf{dom}(H) \quad H(l, @proto) = l'}{\pi(H, l, x) \triangleq \pi(H, l', x)}$$

The set of variable names $\mathcal{X}$ is partitioned in two disjoint sets: the *internal* variable names $\mathcal{X}^{\mathrm{I}}$ and the *user* variable names $\mathcal{X}^{\mathrm{U}}$. The internal names $\mathcal{X}^{\mathrm{I}} \triangleq \{@scope, @body, @proto, @this\}$ are not directly accessible by user-defined ECMAScript 3 code, but are used by the semantics. As noted in Section 2, some implementations do give programmers direct access to some of these internal variables, but we do not model those implementation-dependant programs. We do model all the program states that such programs might create, and take care not to make strong assumptions about the types or values of those suspect internal variables. In this way, libraries verified using our techniques are robust in the presence of unverified real-world code. User names are denoted by $\mathtt{x}, \mathtt{y}, \mathtt{z} \in \mathcal{X}^{\mathrm{U}}$ and are considered a subset of strings; keywords such as `var` are not valid variable names. It is worth anticipating at this point a subtlety of the JavaScript semantics. The evaluation of a user variable `x` does not return its value, but rather the reference $l'{\cdot}\mathtt{x}$ where such value can be found (l' is obtained using the σ predicate). In general, the values $r \in \mathcal{V}^{\mathrm{R}}$ returned by JavaScript expressions can be normal values $\mathcal{V}$ or references $\mathcal{R}$. When a user variable `x` needs to be dereferenced in an expression, the semantics implicitly calls the dereferencing function γ, defined below, which returns the value denoted by the reference.

Dereferencing values: $\gamma(H, r)$**.**

$$\frac{r \neq l{\cdot}\mathtt{x}}{\gamma(H, r) \triangleq r} \qquad \frac{\pi(H, l, \mathtt{x}) = \mathtt{null} \quad l \neq \mathtt{null}}{\gamma(H, l{\cdot}\mathtt{x}) \triangleq \mathtt{undefined}} \qquad \frac{\pi(H, l, \mathtt{x}) = l' \quad l' \neq \mathtt{null}}{\gamma(H, l{\cdot}\mathtt{x}) \triangleq H(l', \mathtt{x})}$$

We introduce the definition of a well-formed JavaScript heap. A JavaScript expression can only be evaluated in a sub-heap of a well-formed heap, with respect to a valid scope chain. All JavaScript expressions maintain the well-formedness of heaps. A heap H is *well-formed* (denoted by $H \vdash \diamond$) if its objects and prototype chains are well-formed (prototype chains must be acyclic, they can end with `null` rather than l_{op}), and if it contains the global scope object l_g and the distinguished objects l_{op} and l_{fp}, which we will see later serve as the default prototypes for new objects and functions. A scope chain L is *valid* with respect to heap H, denoted by $\mathsf{schain}(H, L)$, if all the locations in the chain correspond to objects allocated in H, and if it ends with the global object l_g. Formal definitions are given in [11].

The default initial state $H^{\emptyset}$ is the smallest well-formed heap that also contains the special function object l_e (the `eval` function) and its prototype l_{ep}:

$$H^{\emptyset} \triangleq \left(\begin{array}{c} \mathsf{obj}(l_g, l_{op}) * \mathsf{obj}(l_{op}, \mathtt{null}) \\ * \,\mathsf{obj}(l_{fp}, l_{op}) * \mathsf{obj}(l_e, l_{ep}) * \mathsf{obj}(l_{ep}, l_{op}) \end{array} \right)$$

where $\mathsf{obj}(l, l')$ denotes an object at location l which is empty except for the prototype l':

$$\mathsf{obj}(l, l') \triangleq (l, @proto) \mapsto l'$$

We conclude this section by defining the heap update $-[-]$ operation which will be used by the semantics. Many JavaScript expressions update a heap cell if it is present, or create it if it is not present. We reflect this form of update in our heap update operation.

Update $H[(l, \mathtt{x}) \mapsto v]$**.**

$$\frac{(l, \mathtt{x}) \notin dom(H) \quad l \neq \mathtt{null}}{H[(l, \mathtt{x}) \mapsto v] \triangleq H * (l, x) \mapsto v}$$

$$(H * (l, \mathtt{x}) \mapsto v)[(l, \mathtt{x}) \mapsto v'] \triangleq H * (l, \mathtt{x}) \mapsto v'$$

$$H[(\mathtt{null}, \mathtt{x}) \mapsto v] \triangleq H[(l_g, \mathtt{x}) \mapsto v]$$

The last rule says that an update to a non-allocated reference (whose location is `null`) has the effect of allocating and updating a new global variable, which mimics JavaScript's behaviour of implicitly creating global variables when a variable name is first used.

3.2 Values and Expressions

To aid our presentation, we introduce the syntax of all JavaScript programs, statements and expressions simply as expressions. Our operational semantics will only describe the behaviour of well-formed programs, as defined by [18].

Syntax of terms: values v and expressions e.

$$
\begin{array}{lll}
\mathtt{v} & ::= & \mathtt{n} \mid \mathtt{m} \mid \mathtt{undefined} \mid \mathtt{null} \\
\mathtt{e} & ::= & \mathtt{e;e} \mid \mathtt{x} \mid \mathtt{v} \mid \mathtt{if(e)\{e\}\{e\}} \mid \mathtt{while(e)\{e\}} \mid \mathtt{var\ x} \\
 & & \mid \mathtt{this} \mid \mathtt{delete\ e} \mid \mathtt{e} \oplus \mathtt{e} \mid \mathtt{e.x} \mid \mathtt{e(e)} \mid \mathtt{e\ =\ e} \\
 & & \mid \mathtt{function\ (x)\{e\}} \mid \mathtt{function\, x(x)\{e\}} \mid \mathtt{new\ e(e)} \\
 & & \mid \{\mathtt{x}_1 : \mathtt{e}_1 \ldots \mathtt{x}_n : \mathtt{e}_n\} \mid \mathtt{e[e]} \mid \mathtt{with(e)\{e\}}
\end{array}
$$

where $\oplus \in \{+, -, *, /, \&\&, ||, ==, .\}$

A basic value `v` can be a number `n`, a string `m` (including the user variable names), the special constant `undefined` or the `null` location. The operator $\oplus$ denotes a standard number and boolean operator, or string concatenation. Expressions `e` include sequential composition, variable lookup, literal values, conditional expressions, loops, local variable declaration, `this`, deletion, arithmetic and string concatenation, object property lookup, function call and eval, assignment, function declaration, recursive functions, constructors, literal objects, computed access and the `with` statement.

3.3 Evaluation Rules

An expression `e` is evaluated in a heap H, with respect to a scope chain L. If it successfully terminates, it returns a modified heap H' and a final value r. Selected evaluation rules are given below and then discussed. See [11] for the full definition. Recall that the set of variables is a subset of the set of strings, that a heap value v can be a basic value `v`, a memory location l or a function closure $\lambda\mathtt{x}.\mathtt{e}$, and that a return value r can also be a reference $l{\cdot}\mathtt{x}$.

Operational semantics: $H, L, \mathtt{e} \longrightarrow H', r$.

Notation: $H, L, \mathtt{e} \xrightarrow{\gamma} H', v \triangleq \exists r.(H, L, \mathtt{e} \longrightarrow H', r \wedge \gamma(H', r) = v)$.

(Definition)
$$\frac{H, L, \mathtt{e} \longrightarrow H', v}{H, L, \mathtt{var\ e} \longrightarrow H', \mathtt{undefined}}$$

(Value)
$$H, L, \mathtt{v} \longrightarrow H, \mathtt{v}$$

(Member Access)
$$\frac{H, L, \mathtt{e} \xrightarrow{\gamma} H', l \quad l \neq \mathtt{null}}{H, L, \mathtt{e.x} \longrightarrow H', l{\cdot}\mathtt{x}}$$

(Computed Access)
$$\frac{H, L, \mathtt{e1} \xrightarrow{\gamma} H_1, l \quad l \neq \mathtt{null} \quad H_1, L, \mathtt{e2} \xrightarrow{\gamma} H', \mathtt{x}}{H, L, \mathtt{e1[e2]} \longrightarrow H', l{\cdot}\mathtt{x}}$$

(Variable)
$$\frac{\sigma(H, L, \mathtt{x}) = l}{H, L, \mathtt{x} \longrightarrow H, l{\cdot}\mathtt{x}}$$

(Object)
$$\frac{H_0 = H * \mathsf{obj}(l, l_{op}) \quad \forall i \in 1..n. \begin{pmatrix} H_{i-1}, L, \mathtt{ei} \xrightarrow{\gamma} H_i', v_i \\ H_i = H_i'[(l, \mathtt{xi}) \mapsto v_i] \end{pmatrix}}{H, L, \{\mathtt{x1{:}e1}, \ldots, \mathtt{xn{:}en}\} \longrightarrow H_n, l}$$

(Binary Operators)
$$\frac{H, L, \mathtt{e1} \xrightarrow{\gamma} H'', \mathtt{v1} \quad H'', L, \mathtt{e2} \xrightarrow{\gamma} H', \mathtt{v2} \quad \mathtt{v1}\, \overline{\oplus}\, \mathtt{v2} = \mathtt{v}}{H, L, \mathtt{e1} \oplus \mathtt{e2} \longrightarrow H', \mathtt{v}}$$

(Assignment)
$$\frac{H, L, \mathtt{e1} \longrightarrow H_1, l{\cdot}\mathtt{x} \quad H_1, L, \mathtt{e2} \xrightarrow{\gamma} H_2, v \quad H' = H_2[(l, \mathtt{x}) \mapsto v]}{H, L, \mathtt{e1{=}e2} \longrightarrow H', v}$$

(This)
$$\frac{\sigma(H, L, @\mathit{this}) = l_1 \quad \pi(H, l_1, @\mathit{this}) = l_2 \quad H(l_2, @\mathit{this}) = l'}{H, L, \mathtt{this} \longrightarrow H, l'}$$

(Function)
$$\frac{H' = H * \mathsf{obj}(l, l_{op}) * \mathsf{fun}(l', L, \mathtt{x}, \mathtt{e}, l)}{H, L, \mathtt{function\ (x)\{e\}} \longrightarrow H', l'}$$

(Function Call)
$$\frac{\begin{array}{lll} H, L, \mathtt{e1} \longrightarrow H_1, r_1 & \mathsf{This}(H_1, r_1) = l_2 & \gamma(H_1, r_1) = l_1 \\ l_1 \neq l_e & H_1(l_1, @\mathit{body}) = \lambda\mathtt{x}.\mathtt{e3} & H_1(l_1, @\mathit{scope}) = L' \\ H_1, L, \mathtt{e2} \xrightarrow{\gamma} H_2, v & & \\ H_3 = H_2 * \mathsf{act}(l, \mathtt{x}, v, \mathtt{e3}, l_2) & H_3, l{:}L', \mathtt{e3} \xrightarrow{\gamma} H', v' & \end{array}}{H, L, \mathtt{e1(e2)} \longrightarrow H', v'}$$

(Eval)
$$\frac{H, L, \mathtt{e1} \xrightarrow{\gamma} H_1, l_e \quad H_1, L, \mathtt{e2} \xrightarrow{\gamma} H_2, \mathtt{m} \quad \mathsf{parse}(\mathtt{m}) = \mathtt{e} \quad H_2, L, \mathtt{e} \xrightarrow{\gamma} H', v'}{H, L, \mathtt{e1(e2)} \longrightarrow H', v'}$$

(With)
$$\frac{H, L, \mathtt{e1} \xrightarrow{\gamma} H_1, l \quad H_1, l{:}L, \mathtt{e2} \longrightarrow H', r}{H, L, \mathtt{with(e1)\{e2\}} \longrightarrow H', r}$$

σ, π, γ, obj defined earlier
fun, `this`, act defined below

We briefly discuss some of the evaluation rules that show non-standard features typical of JavaScript. Rule (Definition) for `var e` simply executes `e` and throws away the return value. The `var` declaration is only used by defs (defined below) to identify function local variables. Rule (Variable) uses σ to determine the scope object where a given variable can be found, without de-referencing the variable. Rules (Member/Computed Access) return a reference to the object field denoted by the corresponding expressions. Rule (Object) uses the obj notation introduced in Section 3.1 to introduce a fresh, empty object at location l, and then initialises its fields accordingly. Freshness is ensured by well-formedness of H and disjointness of $*$. Rule (Binary Operators) assumes the existence of a semantic version $\overline{\oplus}$ for each syntactic operator $\oplus$. Each $\overline{\oplus}$ is a partial function, defined only on arguments of a basic type (in this case numbers or strings) and returning results of some other (possibly the same) basic type, corresponding to the intended meaning of the operation. Rule (Assignment) is quite subtle. Suppose we have the expression `x=4`. Now consider Figure 1 of Section 2. If `x` were defined as a field of the object l_1 then `x=4` would be an *overwriting* assignment. The value of the field `x` in the object l_1 would be overwritten with the value 4. If `x` were not found anywhere, then it would be created as a global variable – a field of the object l_g. Finally, consider the actual case in this figure: `x` is found to be a field of object l, which is a prototype of l_2, which is in the scope chain. In this case, `x=4` is an *overriding* assignment, with the effect of creating a new field `x` in the object l_2 to override the existing `x` in l. This complexity is handled in two places. Firstly, the variable rule uses the σ function (defined in Section 3.1) to return a reference $l_2{\cdot}\mathtt{x}$. Note that the σ function does not return a reference to $l{\cdot}\mathtt{x}$ precisely because we wish to model this behaviour. Secondly, the heap update operation $H_2[\ldots]$ manages the business of either overwriting an existing field or, in this case, creating a new field. Rule (This) resolves the `this` identifier. As we will see, when executing a method of an object, we use the internal variable $@\mathit{this}$ to store the location of that object. When executing a function call, $@\mathit{this}$ points to the global object l_g. The (This) rule uses σ and π to retrieve the value of $@\mathit{this}$ which is then returned by the `this` statement. Rule (Function) introduces the notation $\mathsf{fun}(l', L, \mathtt{x}, \mathtt{e}, l) \triangleq$

$$l' \mapsto \{@\mathit{proto}{:}\, l_{fp}, \mathtt{prototype}{:}\, l, @\mathit{scope}{:}\, L, @\mathit{body}{:}\, \lambda\mathtt{x}.\mathtt{e}\}$$

to allocate a fresh function object at location l'. The internal prototype of the new function object points to the standard function prototype object l_{fp}. The rule also creates a new empty object at l and stores a pointer to it in the `prototype` field of the new function. If the function is ever used as a constructor (using the `new` keyword) then the object pointed to by this `prototype` field will serve as the prototype of the newly constructed object. Note that the field is mutable, and so may be used by a programmer to emulate a class-like inheritance structure.

Recall from Section 2 that JavaScript function calls can be surprisingly complex. We now describe rule (Function Call), which uses two auxiliary functions This and act. Recall also that the rule (This) uses internal @*this* fields to determine the semantics of the `this` keyword. The values of the @*this* fields are determined by the (Function Call) rule using the auxiliary function This:

$$\begin{array}{lll} \mathsf{This}(H, l\cdot\mathtt{x}) & \triangleq & l \quad [(l, @this) \notin dom(H)] \\ \mathsf{This}(H, r) & \triangleq & l_g \quad [\text{otherwise}] \end{array}$$

To understand This, first notice that every newly created local scope object has a @*this* field, while no other objects ever will[2]. The (Function Call) rule finds a pointer to a function in the location $l\cdot\mathtt{x}$. If l is a regular object (which has no @*this* field), then the function must be a method of that object, and so the @*this* field of our new local scope object should point to l. On the other hand, if l is a special local scope object (which has a @*this* field), then the function must be a regular function (and not a method), and so the @*this* of our new local scope object should point to l_g. This unique behaviour precisely captures the behaviour of the ECMAScript 3 `this` keyword. The auxiliary function act describes the allocation of a new local scope object: $\mathsf{act}(l, \mathtt{x}, v, \mathtt{e}, l'') \triangleq$

$$l \mapsto \{\mathtt{x}{:}\, v, @this{:}\, l'', @proto{:}\, \mathtt{null}\} * \mathsf{defs}(\mathtt{x}, l, \mathtt{e})$$

The object is allocated at address l, and contains a function parameter `x` with value v, the internal fields @*this*, @*proto* and the local variables declared in an expression `e`. The auxiliary function defs, defined in [11], searches the function body `e` for instances of the `var` keyword, and sets all the appropriate fields of our new local scope object to the value `undefined`, as discussed in Section 2. Rule (Eval) looks like an ordinary function call, but the function being called is not an ordinary function object. It is the special built-in object l_e. It assumes a partial function parse that parses a string `m` into a JavaScript expression `e`, only if there are no syntax errors.

The control expressions are mostly standard (see [11]), except for the unusual (With) rule that evaluates `e2` in a scope-chain starting with the object obtained by evaluating `e1`.

3.4 Safety

An important sanity property of the evaluation relation is that it preserves well-formedness of the heap, for any valid scope chain.

Theorem 1 (Well-Formedness). *Let H, L be such that $H \vdash \diamond$ and* $\mathsf{schain}(H, L)$. *If $H, L, \mathtt{e} \longrightarrow H', r$ then $H' \vdash \diamond$.*

Although the theorem is about end-to-end well-formedness, its proof (reported in [11]) shows that starting from a well-formed state and scope chain, all the intermediate states and scope chains visited during the computation are also well-formed, and all the locations occurring in intermediate return values correspond to objects effectively allocated on the heap.

3.5 JavaScript Subset

We work with a subset of JavaScript, in order to limit the size and complexity of our semantics for this paper. Our subset is substantial and, despite some minor omissions and simplifying assumptions discussed below, faithful to the ECMAScript 3 standard. A significant property of our semantics is that our programs will run reliably in states generated by any valid JavaScript program (including those reached by programs using non-standard features that we do not model, such as `__proto__`), or getters and setters. Our reasoning of Section 5 will therefore interface well with real-world JavaScript programs.

We do not model implicit type-coercion functions. Adding them is straightforward but would add significantly to the length of our presentation. We have no boolean type. Instead, where control structures (`if` and `while`) require a boolean, we use other types whose behaviour is equivalent to the type conversion that occurs in JavaScript. Values such as 0 and `null` behave like `false` and values such as 1 and `"string"` behave like `true`. For simplicity, we use an implicit return statement for functions. Moreover, our functions take only one parameter, rather than the arbitrary list of parameters usual in JavaScript, and do not have the `arguments` object or the `constructor` property. As mentioned in Section 3.2, we simplify our presentation of JavaScript programs, statements and expressions, into a single class of expressions. We also omit several JavaScript constructs such as labels, `switch` and `for`, as they do not contribute significantly to the problem of program reasoning. In this presentation we only consider the core language ECMAScript 3, and do not model the many standard libraries which browsers make available to programmers. Instead of exceptions, we have a single error condition denoted fault. Our reasoning conservatively avoids faults. This means that programs which are proved using our fault-avoiding local Hoare reasoning will run without throwing exceptions in JavaScript interpreters.

[2] l_g has @*this* in some, not all, implementations; [14] is silent on the issue.

4. Assertion Language

Our assertion language follows that of Parkinson and Bierman [4, 23, 24], in their work on reasoning about Java. They use assertions of the form $(\mathrm{l}, \mathrm{x}) \mapsto \mathrm{v}$ to denote that a partial heap contains the object l with field x which has value v. Using the separating conjunction $*$ [20], the assertion $((\mathrm{l}, \mathrm{x}) \mapsto \mathrm{v}) * ((\mathrm{l}, \mathrm{y}) \mapsto \mathrm{w})$ declares that a heap contains an object l which must have two separate fields x, y with the appropriate values. The assertion $(\mathrm{l}, \mathrm{x}) \mapsto \mathrm{v} * (\mathrm{l}, \mathrm{x}) \mapsto \mathrm{w}$ is unsatisfiable since it declares two fields x for l.

This style of reasoning is not enough for JavaScript. We must also assert negative information about fields not being in the heap, and extend the structural assertions of separation logic to account for partial separation due to shared prototype chains. Recall the example of a JavaScript emulated variable store in Figure 1. To find the value of x in the store, we must not only determine that the object l has a field x but also determine that no fields named x occur earlier in the emulated store. We use assertions $(\mathrm{l}, \mathrm{x}) \mapsto \varnothing$ to declare that a heap contains an object l which *does not* have a field x. The assertion $(\mathrm{l}, \mathrm{x}) \mapsto \varnothing * (\mathrm{l}, \mathrm{y}) \mapsto \mathrm{w}$ declares that the heap contains an object l which does not have field x but does have field y. The assertions $(\mathrm{l}, \mathrm{x}) \mapsto \mathrm{v} * (\mathrm{l}, \mathrm{x}) \mapsto \varnothing$ and $(\mathrm{l}, \mathrm{x}) \mapsto \varnothing * (\mathrm{l}, \mathrm{x}) \mapsto \varnothing$ are unsatisfiable. Thus, the assertion $(\mathrm{l}, \mathrm{x}) \mapsto \varnothing$ states the full knowledge that field x is not in object l.

Now consider what happens when we want to describe the state of more than one variable at a time. In Section 5 we introduce a predicate σ which allows us to assert, for example, "The variable x is found in the store in object l_2": $\sigma(\_, \mathbf{l}, \mathtt{x}, l_2)$ or "The variable y is not in the store": $\sigma(\_, \mathbf{l}, \mathtt{y}, \mathtt{null})$. Both of these assertions must make use of the @*proto* fields in order to navigate the variable store, so we cannot separate them using $*$. But the first assertion does not mention any `y` field, and the second assertion does not mention any `x` field, so we cannot join them with $\wedge$. In order to make both assertions about the same variable store, we need a way for them to share their common parts. To do this, we introduce the *sepish connective* $P \uplus Q$ which allows *partial* separation between heaps. We can use $\uplus$ to describe the state of more than one variable in a given store: $\sigma(\_, \mathbf{l}, \mathtt{x}, l_2) \uplus \sigma(\_, \mathbf{l}, \mathtt{y}, \mathtt{null})$, and we shall see in Section 5 that it is also invaluable when defining the σ predicate.

An assertion may be satisfied by a triple (h, L, ϵ) consisting of an abstract heap h, a scope chain L, and a logical environment ϵ. An *abstract JavaScript heap* is a partial function $H{:}\, \mathcal{R} \rightharpoonup \mathcal{V} \cup \{\varnothing\}$ that maps references, $r \in \mathcal{R} = \mathcal{L} \times \mathcal{X}$ to values $v \in \mathcal{V}$ or $\varnothing$. Abstract heaps thus declare information about fields not being present in an object, as well as the fields that are present. We also define an evaluation function $\lfloor \_ \rfloor$ which takes an abstract heap to a concrete heap:

$$\lfloor h \rfloor(l, x) \triangleq h(l, x) \text{ iff } (l, x) \in \mathsf{dom}(h) \wedge h(l, x) \neq \varnothing$$

We use this function in Section 5 to define the relationship between our reasoning using Hoare triples and our operational semantics.

We define a logical environment ϵ, which is a partial function from logical variables $\mathrm{X} \in \mathcal{X}^{\mathrm{L}}$ to logical values $\mathcal{V}^{\mathrm{L}}$, which may be a return value r, any expression $\mathtt{e}$, $\varnothing$ or a list Ls of logical values. We also define logical expressions E, which are different from program expressions in that they can not read or alter the heap. Expressions E are evaluated in a logical environment ϵ with respect to a current scope chain L.

Logical expressions and evaluation: $[\![E]\!]^L_\epsilon$.

$$\mathrm{v} \in \mathcal{V}^{\mathrm{L}} ::= e \mid v \mid \varnothing \mid Ls \qquad \epsilon : \mathcal{X}^{\mathrm{L}} \rightharpoonup \mathcal{V}^{\mathrm{L}}$$

$E ::=$	X	Logical variables
	$\mid \mathbf{l}$	Scope list
	$\mid \mathrm{v}$	Logical values
	$\mid E \oplus E$	Binary Operators
	$\mid E{:}E$	List cons
	$\mid E \cdot E$	Reference construction
	$\mid \lambda E.E$	Lambda values

$$[\![\mathrm{v}]\!]^L_\epsilon \triangleq \mathrm{v} \qquad [\![\mathbf{l}]\!]^L_\epsilon \triangleq L \qquad [\![\mathrm{X}]\!]^L_\epsilon \triangleq \epsilon(\mathrm{X})$$

$$[\![E_1{:}E_2]\!]^L_\epsilon \triangleq [\![E_1]\!]^L_\epsilon{:}Ls \text{ if } [\![E_2]\!]^L_\epsilon = Ls$$

$$[\![E_1 \cdot E_2]\!]^L_\epsilon \triangleq l \cdot \mathrm{x} \text{ if } [\![E_1]\!]^L_\epsilon = l \wedge [\![E_2]\!]^L_\epsilon = \mathrm{x}$$

$$[\![E_1 \oplus E_2]\!]^L_\epsilon \triangleq v \,\overline{\oplus}\, v' \text{ if } [\![E_1]\!]^L_\epsilon = v \wedge [\![E_2]\!]^L_\epsilon = v'$$

$$[\![\lambda E_1 . E_2]\!]^L_\epsilon \triangleq \lambda \mathrm{x}.[\![E_2]\!]^L_\epsilon \text{ if } [\![E_1]\!]^L_\epsilon = \mathrm{x}$$

Assertions include the boolean assertions, structural assertions of separation logic and our new sepish connective, basic assertions for describing cells in a JavaScript heap, expression equality, set and list assertions, and quantification over logical variables.

Assertions.

$P ::=$	$P \wedge P \mid P \vee P \mid \neg P \mid \mathrm{true} \mid \mathrm{false}$	Boolean assertions
	$\mid P * P \mid P \mathrel{-\!\!*} P \mid P \boxast P$	Structural assertions
	$\mid (E, E) \mapsto E \mid \oslash$	JavaScript heap assertions
	$\mid E = E$	Expression equality
	$\mid E \in \mathrm{SET}$	Set membership
	$\mid E \in E$	List element
	$\mid \exists \mathrm{X}.\, P \mid \forall \mathrm{X}.\, P$	Quantification

Notation: $E \not\circ E \triangleq \neg(E \circ E)$ for $\circ \in \{=, \in\}$

$E_1 \dot{\circ} E_2 \triangleq E_1 \circ E_2 \wedge \oslash$ for $\circ \in \{=, \neq, \in, \notin\}$.

The logical operators bind in order: $\neg, \boxast, *, \wedge, \vee, \mathrel{-\!\!*}$.

The structural assertions $*$ and $\mathrel{-\!\!*}$ are standard separation logic assertions. The separating conjunction $P * Q$ says that the heap may be split into two disjoint heaps, one satisfying P and the other Q. The right adjoint $P \mathrel{-\!\!*} Q$ says that, whenever the heap is extended by a heap satisfying P, then the resulting heap satisfies Q. It is useful in proving the soundness of some of our layers of abstraction in Section 6, as given in [11]. The sepish connective $P \boxast Q$ is novel. It says that the heap may be split into two heaps, one satisfying P and the other Q, but these two heaps need not be disjoint. They may share zero or more common cells. We shall see in Section 5 that this is particularly useful when reasoning about the emulated variable store. It is possible to define $\mathrel{-\!\!\boxast}$ analogously with $\mathrel{-\!\!*}$, but since this is not useful for JavaScript reasoning we omit it here. Note that $P \wedge Q \Rightarrow P \boxast Q$ and $P * Q \Rightarrow P \boxast Q$, but neither of the reverse implications hold. The assertion $(E_1, E_2) \mapsto E_3$ declares information about a cell, including the information that field E_2 does not occur in object E_1. Assertion $\oslash$ says that the heap is empty. The notation SET denotes a literal set, or a named set such as $\mathcal{X}$, the set of JavaScript field names. Note that since there are sets for numbers, strings and locations, we can use set inclusion to assert the type of a particular JavaScript value.

The satisfaction relation $h, L, \epsilon \models P$ is defined below. The cases for the boolean assertions are not given as they are standard.

Satisfaction of assertions: $h, L, \epsilon \models P$.

$$
\begin{array}{lcl}
h, L, \epsilon \models P * Q & \iff & \exists h_1, h_2.\, h \equiv h_1 * h_2 \wedge \\
& & (h_1, L, \epsilon \models P) \wedge (h_2, L, \epsilon \models Q) \\
h, L, \epsilon \models P \mathrel{-\!\!*} Q & \iff & \forall h_1.\, (h_1, L, \epsilon \models P) \wedge h \# h_1 \\
& & \implies ((h * h_1), L, \epsilon \models Q) \\
h, L, \epsilon \models P \boxast Q & \iff & \exists h_1, h_2, h_3. \\
\multicolumn{3}{l}{\quad h \equiv h_1 * h_2 * h_3 \wedge (h_1 * h_3, L, \epsilon \models P) \wedge (h_2 * h_3, L, \epsilon \models Q)} \\
h, L, \epsilon \models (E_1, E_2) \mapsto E_3 & \iff & h \equiv ([\![E_1]\!]^L_\epsilon, [\![E_2]\!]^L_\epsilon) \mapsto [\![E_3]\!]^L_\epsilon \\
h, L, \epsilon \models \oslash & \iff & h = \mathtt{emp} \\
h, L, \epsilon \models E_1 = E_2 & \iff & [\![E_1]\!]^L_\epsilon = [\![E_2]\!]^L_\epsilon \\
h, L, \epsilon \models E \in \mathrm{SET} & \iff & [\![E]\!]^L_\epsilon \in \mathrm{SET} \\
h, L, \epsilon \models E_1 \in E_2 & \iff & [\![E_1]\!]^L_\epsilon \text{ is in the list } [\![E_2]\!]^L_\epsilon \\
h, L, \epsilon \models \exists \mathrm{X}.\, P & \iff & \exists \mathrm{v}.\, h, L, [\epsilon | \mathrm{X} \leftarrow \mathrm{v}] \models P \\
h, L, \epsilon \models \forall \mathrm{X}.\, P & \iff & \forall \mathrm{v}.\, h, L, [\epsilon | \mathrm{X} \leftarrow \mathrm{v}] \models P
\end{array}
$$

We have given a direct definition of the sepish connective. When logical variables range over heaps, it can be derived: $P \boxast Q \Leftrightarrow \exists \mathrm{R}.\, (\mathrm{R} \mathrel{-\!\!*} P) * (\mathrm{R} \mathrel{-\!\!*} Q) * \mathrm{R}$. It remains to be seen what natural logical properties are satisfied by this connective.

5. Program Reasoning

In the spirit of separation logic, we give small axioms and inference rules which precisely capture the behaviour of all JavaScript expressions, except for the usual approximation for `while` and conservative approximations of function call and `eval`. Reasoning about function call and eval is interesting and complex, and will be the focus of future work as outlined in Section 8. Because our reasoning captures the full complexity of JavaScript semantics, particularly with respect to the emulated variable store and the `with` command, it is possible to prove properties about extremely subtle programs. Unfortunately, proving any program at this level of abstraction involves a level of detail which most programmers would understandably rather avoid. We therefore provide several *layers of abstraction* which make it possible to reason at a natural high level about well-behaved JavaScript programs. We discuss these abstractions in Section 6.

Our fault-avoiding Hoare triples take the form: $\{P\}\mathtt{e}\{Q\}$, which means "if $\mathtt{e}$ is executed in a state satisfying P, then it will not fault, and if it terminates it will do so in a state satisfying Q". The postcondition Q may refer to the special variable $\mathbf{r}$, which is equal to the return value of $\mathtt{e}$.

5.1 Auxiliary Predicates

For our reasoning rules, we require predicates that correspond to functions, such as σ, π and γ, used by the operational semantics in Section 3.3. These predicates present us with two distinct challenges: sharing and precision. To consider sharing, recall the scope function σ from Section 3.1 when searching for a variable `y` in the example emulated store given in Figure 1. Since `y` is not present in the emulated store, σ will check the entire structure before returning `null` to indicate that `y` cannot be found. What is of interest to us is the order in which the cells in the store will be checked. Notice that the cell l will be checked twice, and the cell l_{op} will be checked three times. This is because the cells l and l_{op} are shared between the prototype chain of the object l_2 and the object l_4. In addition, l_{op} is shared by these prototype chains and the prototype chain of l_g. As we shall see below, we can describe these partially shared structures using our sepish connective $\boxast$. To consider precision, recall the function σ when this time searching for a variable `x` either in the emulated store of Figure 1, or in the identical store but for the omission of a single object such that the prototype of l_2 would be l. In each of these stores, the σ function will return the same value – the location l_2. In our program reasoning, our σ predicate (which will correspond to the σ function of the operational semantics) must be more precise as we need to distinguish between these two possible cases. With the challenges of sharing and precision in mind, we first give, then explain, the logical predicates σ, π and γ.

Logical predicates: σ, π, γ.

$$\sigma([], [], \_, \mathtt{null}) \triangleq \emptyset$$
$$\sigma([Ls], L' : Ls', X, L') \triangleq \exists \mathrm{L}.\, \pi(Ls, L', X, \mathrm{L}) * \mathrm{L} \not\doteq \mathtt{null}$$
$$\sigma((Ls_1 : Ls_2), L' : Ls', X, L) \triangleq \pi(Ls_1, L', X, \mathtt{null}) \uplus \sigma(Ls_2, Ls', X, L)$$

$$\pi([], \mathtt{null}, \_, \mathtt{null}) \triangleq \emptyset$$
$$\pi([L], L, X, L) \triangleq \exists \mathrm{V}.\, (L, X) \mapsto \mathrm{V} * \mathrm{V} \not\doteq \varnothing$$
$$\pi((L' : Ls), L', X, L) \triangleq \exists \mathrm{N}.\, (L', X) \mapsto \varnothing * (L', @proto) \mapsto \mathrm{N} * \pi(Ls, \mathrm{N}, X, L)$$

$$\gamma([], Val, Val) \triangleq Val \not\mathrel{\dot\in} \mathcal{R}$$
$$\gamma(Ls, L\cdot X, \mathtt{undefined}) \triangleq \pi(Ls, L, X, \mathtt{null}) * L \not\doteq \mathtt{null}$$
$$\gamma(Ls, L_1\cdot X, Val) \triangleq \exists \mathrm{L}_2.\, \pi(Ls, L_1, X, \mathrm{L}_2) \uplus (\mathrm{L}_2, X) \mapsto Val * Val \not\doteq \varnothing$$

These predicates closely follow the structure of the functions defined in 3.1, using $\uplus$ to manage the challenge of sharing prototype chains mentioned earlier. The predicate $\sigma(\_, L, \mathtt{x}, l)$ holds only for abstract heaps h such that the function from Section 3.1 gives us $\sigma(\lfloor h \rfloor, L, \mathtt{x}) = l$, meaning that the value of the variable $\mathtt{x}$ in the emulated variable store given by the list L can be found in the object (or a prototype of the object) at address l. However, recall the challenge of precision mentioned earlier. In order to distinguish between all the possible heaps which satisfy the predicate $\sigma(\_, L, \mathtt{x}, l)$, we work with an additional first argument. The predicate $\sigma(Ls, L, \mathtt{x}, l)$ is "precise" in the sense that, for any abstract heap h, it holds for at most one subheap of h. The first argument Ls is a list of lists, which specifies the exact cells which must be visited (and the order in which they must be checked) in order to determine which object in the emulated variable store defines the variable $\mathtt{x}$. For example, recall the heap illustrated in Figure 1. If the prototype of the cell l_2 has address l', then the predicate $\sigma([[l_1], [l_2, l', l]], \mathbf{l}, \mathtt{x}, l_2)$ is satisfied by the abstract heap consisting of the $\mathtt{x}$ and $@proto$ fields of the four objects in the lower left corner of that diagram. Notice that we do not need to visit every object in the variable store in order to discover the location of the variable $\mathtt{x}$. In the spirit of the small axioms of separation logic, our predicate holds for the smallest possible heap in which we can be sure of discovering the variable we are interested in.

The predicates π and γ are similar in that they mirror their operational counterparts, with the addition of one extra argument to make them precise. In the case of π and γ, the first argument Ls is simply a list of addresses, rather than a list of lists of addresses, because each predicate only walks down at most one prototype chain.

The inference rules also require logical predicates corresponding to a number of other auxiliary functions given in Section 3. Below, we define newobj and fun predicates, which assert the existence of a fresh object and function object, and decls that returns the local variables of an expression. In order to reason about function call, we also use a defs predicate which we define in [11].

Auxiliary predicates

$$\mathsf{This}(L\cdot\_, L) \triangleq (L, @this) \mapsto \varnothing \quad \text{where } L \neq l_g$$
$$\mathsf{This}(L\cdot\_, l_g) \triangleq \exists \mathrm{V}.\, (L, @this) \mapsto \mathrm{V} * \mathrm{V} \not\doteq \varnothing$$

$$\mathsf{True}(E) \triangleq E \not\mathrel{\dot\in} \{0, \text{``''}, \mathtt{null}, \mathtt{undefined}\}$$
$$\mathsf{False}(E) \triangleq E \mathrel{\dot\in} \{0, \text{``''}, \mathtt{null}, \mathtt{undefined}\}$$
$$\mathsf{newobj}(L, V_1, \ldots, V_n) \triangleq \circledast_{V \in \mathcal{X} \setminus \{V_1 \ldots V_n\}} (L, V) \mapsto \varnothing$$

$$\mathsf{fun}(F, Env, X, Body, Proto) \triangleq (F, @scope) \mapsto Env * (F, @body) \mapsto \lambda X.Body * (F, \mathtt{prototype}) \mapsto Proto * (F, @proto) \mapsto l_{fp}$$

$$\mathsf{decls}(X, L, \mathtt{e}) \triangleq \mathtt{x1}, \ldots, \mathtt{xn} \quad \text{where } (L, \mathtt{xi}) \in \mathsf{dom}(\mathsf{defs}(X, L, \mathtt{e}))$$

5.2 Inference Rules

We define below some inference rules $\{P\}\mathtt{e}\{Q\}$ for reasoning about JavaScript expressions. The full list can be found in [11].

Inference rules: $\{P\}\mathtt{e}\{Q\}$.

(Definition)
$$\frac{\{P\}\mathtt{e}\{Q\} \qquad \mathbf{r} \notin \mathsf{fv}(Q)}{\{P\}\mathtt{var\ e}\{Q * \mathbf{r} \doteq \mathtt{undefined}\}}$$

(Value)
$$\{\emptyset\}\mathtt{v}\{\mathbf{r} \doteq \mathtt{v}\}$$

(Variable)
$$\frac{P = \sigma(Ls_1, \mathbf{l}, \mathtt{x}, L) \uplus \gamma(Ls_2, L\cdot\mathtt{x}, V)}{\{P\}\mathtt{x}\{P * \mathbf{r} \doteq L\cdot\mathtt{x}\}}$$

(Variable Null)
$$\frac{P = \sigma(Ls, \mathbf{l}, \mathtt{x}, \mathtt{null})}{\{P\}\mathtt{x}\{P * \mathbf{r} \doteq \mathtt{null}\cdot\mathtt{x}\}}$$

(Member Access)
$$\frac{\{P\}\mathtt{e}\{Q * \mathbf{r} \doteq V\} \qquad Q = R * \gamma(Ls, V, L) * L \not\doteq \mathtt{null}}{\{P\}\mathtt{e.x}\{Q * \mathbf{r} \doteq L\cdot\mathtt{x}\}}$$

(Computed Access)
$$\frac{\begin{array}{ll}\{P\}\mathtt{e1}\{R * \mathbf{r} \doteq V_1\} & R = S_1 * \gamma(Ls_1, V_1, L) * L \not\doteq \mathtt{null} \\ \{R\}\mathtt{e2}\{Q * X \mathrel{\dot\in} \mathcal{X}^{\mathrm{U}} * \mathbf{r} \doteq V_2\} & Q = S_2 * \gamma(Ls_2, V_2, X)\end{array}}{\{P\}\mathtt{e1[e2]}\{Q * \mathbf{r} \doteq L\cdot X\}}$$

(Object)
$$\frac{\begin{array}{l}\forall i \in 1..n.\ (P_i = R_i * \gamma(Ls_i, Y_i, X_i) \quad \{P_{i-1}\}\mathtt{ei}\{P_i * \mathbf{r} \doteq Y_i\}) \\ Q = \left(P_n * \exists \mathrm{L}. \left(\begin{array}{l}\mathsf{newobj}(\mathrm{L}, @proto, \mathtt{x1}, \ldots, \mathtt{xn}) * \\ (\mathrm{L}, \mathtt{x1}) \mapsto X_1 * \ldots * (\mathrm{L}, \mathtt{xn}) \mapsto X_n * \\ (\mathrm{L}, @proto) \mapsto l_{op} * \mathbf{r} \doteq \mathrm{L}\end{array}\right)\right) \\ \mathtt{x1} \neq \cdots \neq \mathtt{xn} \qquad \mathbf{r} \notin \mathsf{fv}(P_n)\end{array}}{\{P_0\}\{\mathtt{x1:e1}, \ldots, \mathtt{xn:en}\}\{Q\}}$$

(Binary Operators)
$$\frac{\begin{array}{ll}\{P\}\mathtt{e1}\{R * \mathbf{r} \doteq V_1\} & R = S_1 * \gamma(Ls_1, V_1, V_3) \\ \{R\}\mathtt{e2}\{Q * \mathbf{r} \doteq V_2\} & Q = S_2 * \gamma(Ls_2, V_2, V_4) \\ V = V_3 \,\bar{\oplus}\, V_4 & \end{array}}{\{P\}\mathtt{e1} \oplus \mathtt{e2}\{Q * \mathbf{r} \doteq V\}}$$

(Assign Global)
$$\frac{\begin{array}{ll}\{P\}\mathtt{e1}\{R * \mathbf{r} \doteq \mathtt{null}\cdot X\} & \\ \{R\}\mathtt{e2}\{Q * (l_g, X) \mapsto \varnothing * \mathbf{r} \doteq V_1\} & Q = S * \gamma(Ls, V_1, V_2)\end{array}}{\{P\}\mathtt{e1\ =\ e2}\{Q * (l_g, X) \mapsto V_2 * \mathbf{r} \doteq V_2\}}$$

(Assign Local)
$$\frac{\begin{array}{ll}\{P\}\mathtt{e1}\{R * \mathbf{r} \doteq L\cdot X\} & \\ \{R\}\mathtt{e2}\{Q * (L, X) \mapsto V_3 * \mathbf{r} \doteq V_1\} & Q = S * \gamma(Ls, V_1, V_2)\end{array}}{\{P\}\mathtt{e1\ =\ e2}\{Q * (L, X) \mapsto V_2 * \mathbf{r} \doteq V_2\}}$$

(Function)
$$\frac{Q = \left(\begin{array}{l}\exists \mathrm{L}_1, \mathrm{L}_2.\, \mathsf{newobj}(\mathrm{L}_1, @proto) * (\mathrm{L}_1, @proto) \mapsto l_{op} * \\ \mathsf{newobj}(\mathrm{L}_2, @proto, \mathtt{prototype}, @scope, @body) * \\ \mathsf{fun}(\mathrm{L}_2, \mathbf{l}, \mathtt{x}, \mathtt{e}, \mathrm{L}_1) * \mathbf{r} \doteq \mathrm{L}_2\end{array}\right)}{\{\emptyset\}\mathtt{function\ (x)\{e\}}\{Q\}}$$

(While)
$$\frac{\begin{array}{ll}\{P\}\mathtt{e1}\{S * \mathbf{r} \doteq V_1\} & S = R * \gamma(Ls, V_1, V_2) \\ \{S * \mathsf{True}(V_2)\}\mathtt{e2}\{P\} & \\ Q = S * \mathsf{False}(V_2) * \mathbf{r} \doteq \mathtt{undefined} & \mathbf{r} \notin \mathsf{fv}(R)\end{array}}{\{P\}\mathtt{while(e1)\{e2\}}\{Q\}}$$

(With)
$$\frac{\begin{array}{ll}\{P * \mathbf{l} \doteq L\}\mathtt{e1}\{S * \mathbf{l} \doteq L * \mathbf{r} \doteq V_1\} & S = R * \gamma(Ls, V_1, L_1) \\ \{S * \mathbf{l} \doteq L_1{:}L\}\mathtt{e2}\{Q * \mathbf{l} \doteq L_1{:}L\} & \mathbf{l} \notin \mathsf{fv}(P, Q, R)\end{array}}{\{P * \mathbf{l} \doteq L\}\mathtt{with(e1)\{e2\}}\{Q * \mathbf{l} \doteq L\}}$$

(Function Call)

$$\frac{\begin{array}{l}\{P\}\texttt{e1}\{R_1 * \mathbf{r} \doteq F_1\} \\ R_1 = \left(\begin{array}{l} S_1 \uplus \mathsf{This}(F_1, T) \uplus \gamma(Ls_1, F_1, F_2) * \\ (F_2, @body) \mapsto \lambda X.\mathsf{e3} * (F_2, @scope) \mapsto Ls_2 \end{array}\right) \\ \{R_1\}\texttt{e2}\{R_2 * \mathbf{l} \doteq Ls_3 * \mathbf{r} \doteq V_1\} \quad R_2 = S_2 * \gamma(Ls_4, V_1, V_2) \\ R_3 = \left(\begin{array}{l} R_2 * \exists \mathrm{L}. \mathbf{l} \doteq \mathrm{L}{:}Ls_2 * (\mathrm{L}, X) \mapsto V_2 * \\ (\mathrm{L}, @this) \mapsto T * \\ (\mathrm{L}, @proto) \mapsto \mathtt{null} * \mathsf{defs}(X, \mathrm{L}, \mathsf{e3}) * \\ \mathsf{newobj}(\mathrm{L}, @proto, @this, X, \mathsf{decls}(X, \mathrm{L}, \mathsf{e3})) \end{array}\right) \\ \{R_3\}\texttt{e3}\{\exists \mathrm{L}.\, Q * \mathbf{l} \doteq \mathrm{L}{:}Ls_2\} \qquad \mathbf{l} \notin \mathsf{fv}(Q, R_2) \end{array}}{\{P\}\texttt{e1(e2)}\{\exists \mathrm{L}.\, Q * \mathbf{l} \doteq Ls_3\}}$$

(Frame)

$$\frac{\{P\}\mathsf{e}\{Q\}}{\{P * R\}\mathsf{e}\{Q * R\}}$$

(Consequence)

$$\frac{\{P_1\}\mathsf{e}\{Q_1\} \quad P \implies P_1 \quad Q_1 \implies Q}{\{P\}\mathsf{e}\{Q\}}$$

(Elimination)

$$\frac{\{P\}\mathsf{e}\{Q\}}{\{\exists \mathrm{X}.\, P\}\mathsf{e}\{\exists \mathrm{X}.\, Q\}}$$

(Disjunction)

$$\frac{\{P_1\}\mathsf{e}\{Q_1\} \qquad \{P_2\}\mathsf{e}\{Q_2\}}{\{P_1 \vee P_2\}\mathsf{e}\{Q_1 \vee Q_2\}}$$

Although most of the rules correspond closely to their operational counterparts, some rules deserve further comment. Rule (Definition) shows the use of the reserved variable **r** to record the result of an expression. Rule (Variable) shows the use of $\uplus$ to express the overlapping footprints of predicates σ and γ. Rule (Assign Global) shows the use of $\varnothing$ to assert that certain known memory cells are available for allocation. Rule (Function Call) describes JavaScript's dynamic functions but does not support higher order reasoning. Rule (Frame) does not have the usual side condition because JavaScript stores all its program variables on the heap, so any variable modified by an expression is necessarily contained entirely within the footprint of the expression. Rules (Consequence), (Elimination) and (Disjunction) are standard.

5.3 Soundness

We show that our inference rules are sound with respect to the operational semantics of Section 3.3. When proving the soundness of any system involving the frame rule, it is usual to first show the locality of the programming language, and use that property to show the soundness of the frame rule [20]. Unfortunately, many JavaScript statements are not local according to this standard definition. We therefore use the recently introduced notion of weak locality from Smith's thesis [30].

Definition 2 (Soundness of a Hoare triple). A Hoare triple $\{P\}\mathsf{e}\{Q\}$ is sound if, for all abstract heaps h, scope chains L and environments ϵ, it satisfies the following two properties:

$$\textit{Fault Avoidance} : h, L, (\epsilon \setminus \mathbf{r}) \models P \implies \lfloor h \rfloor, L, \mathsf{e} \not\longrightarrow \mathsf{fault}$$

$$\textit{Safety} : \forall H, r.\ h, L, (\epsilon \setminus \mathbf{r}) \models P \wedge \lfloor h \rfloor, L, \mathsf{e} \longrightarrow H, r \implies \exists h'.\, H = \lfloor h' \rfloor \wedge h', L, [\epsilon | \mathbf{r} \leftarrow r] \models Q.$$

Theorem 3 (Soundness). *All derivable Hoare triples* $\{P\}\mathsf{e}\{Q\}$ *are sound according to Definition 2.*

The proof (reported in [11]) involves showing that the predicates used by the Hoare rules correspond to the auxiliary functions used by the semantics, showing that all JavaScript expressions are weakly local with respect to their preconditions, and finally showing that all our inference rules are sound.

6. Layers of Abstraction

As mentioned in Section 5, using the rules given so far, reasoning about JavaScript program involves detail that most programmers need never consider. Most of the time, programmers will work at a higher level of abstraction, for example, treating the emulated variable store as if it were a regular variable store. This is a good practice as long as the abstraction holds. However, if the program happens to come across a corner case that breaks the abstraction, its resulting behaviour can appear almost inexplicable. This may be a particular problem when writing library code, since the programmer has no control over the programming discipline of the client who uses the library. In this section, we introduce several explicit abstraction formalisms. Many alternatives are possible, but those presented here are enough to demonstrate the concept and reason about some interesting programs. We are able to use these formalisms to reason at a comfortable, high-level way about many well-behaved programs. Crucially, we know exactly what the boundaries of these layers of abstraction are, so we can ensure that our programs remain safely within the abstraction. If we wish, we can even choose to temporarily break an abstraction, execute some particularly subtle low-level code, re-establish the abstraction and then continue to work at the high level.

6.1 Layer 1: Exploring the Scope List

Central to reasoning about JavaScript variables are the σ and π predicates. The first abstraction layer consists of alternative versions of these predicates which make reasoning about certain common cases simpler. The $\overline{\sigma}$ predicate unrolls from the end (the most global end) of the scope rather than from the beginning (the local end) which makes modifying a variable easier to specify. It makes use of $\not\sigma$ which says that a variable does not exist in a particular partial scope. The $\not\sigma^{l_g}$ predicate does the same, but excludes l_g from its specification, in order to make reasoning about global variable instantiation simpler. We give several useful triples about variable assignment. In [11], we prove these triples by using $\overline{\sigma}$ and showing the equivalence of σ and $\overline{\sigma}$.

Layer 1 Predicates.

$$\overline{\sigma}(Ls, Ls', Var, \mathtt{null}) \triangleq \not\sigma(Ls, Ls', Var, \mathtt{null})$$
$$\overline{\sigma}(Ls_1 +\!\!+ (Ls_2 : [\,]), Ls', Var, L) \triangleq$$
$$\quad \not\sigma(Ls_1, Ls', Var, L) * \exists \mathrm{L2}.\, \pi(Ls_2, L, Var, L2) * \mathrm{L2} \not\doteq \mathtt{null}$$

$$\not\sigma([\,], L' : Ls', \_, L') \triangleq \emptyset$$
$$\not\sigma(Ls_2 : Ls, L' : Ls', Var, End) \triangleq$$
$$\quad \pi(Ls_2, L', Var, \mathtt{null}) \uplus \not\sigma(Ls, Ls', Var, End)$$

$$\not\sigma^{l_g}([\,], L' : Ls', \_, L') \triangleq \emptyset$$
$$\not\sigma^{l_g}(Ls_2 : Ls, L' : Ls', Var, End) \triangleq$$
$$\quad \pi^{l_g}(Ls_2, L', Var, \mathtt{null}) \uplus \not\sigma^{l_g}(Ls, Ls', Var, End)$$

$$\pi^{l_g}([\,], \mathtt{null}, \_, \mathtt{null}) \triangleq \emptyset$$
$$\pi^{l_g}([\,], l_g, \_, \mathtt{null}) \triangleq \emptyset$$
$$\pi^{l_g}([L'], L', Var, L') \triangleq \exists \mathrm{V}.\, (L', Var) \mapsto \mathrm{V} * \mathrm{V} \not\doteq \varnothing * L' \not\doteq l_g$$
$$\pi^{l_g}((L' : Ls), L', Var, L) \triangleq \exists \mathrm{N}.\, (L', Var) \mapsto \varnothing *$$
$$\quad (L', @proto) \mapsto \mathrm{N} * \pi^{l_g}(Ls, \mathrm{N}, Var, L) * L' \not\doteq l_g$$

These predicates give us much more flexibility to reason about JavaScript variables found in various places in the emulated variable store. Even at this quite low level, it is possible to prove general specifications about programs with many corner cases. A good example of this sort of reasoning is simple assignment statements. We prove the following general triples about simple assignments. The first three triples deal with the assignment of a constant to a variable, in the cases of variable initialisation, variable override, and variable overwrite respectively. The fourth triple deals with assigning the value of one variable to another. All four are proved sound in [11].

Simple assignments.

$$\frac{\begin{array}{l} P = \sigma(L_1 +\!\!+ ((l_g{:}L_2){:}L_3), \mathbf{l}, \mathrm{x}, \mathtt{null}) \\ Q = \left(\begin{array}{c} \exists \mathrm{L}_1', \mathrm{L}_3', \mathrm{Ls}', \mathrm{G}.\quad \not\sigma^{l_g}(\mathrm{L}_1', \mathbf{l}, \mathrm{x}, l_g) \uplus \\ \pi(L_2, \mathrm{G}, \mathrm{x}, \mathtt{null}) \uplus \not\sigma^{l_g}(\mathrm{L}_3', \mathrm{Ls}', \mathrm{x}, \mathtt{null}) * (l_g, \mathrm{x}) \mapsto \mathrm{v} * \\ (l_g, @proto) \mapsto \mathrm{G} * \mathbf{l} \doteq \_ +\!\!+ (l_g{:}\mathrm{Ls}') * \mathbf{r} \doteq \mathrm{v} \end{array}\right) \end{array}}{\{P\}\texttt{x = v}\{Q\}}$$

$$P = \sigma(L_1 +\!\!+ [L{:}L_2]), \mathbf{l}, \mathrm{x}, L) \boxast (L, \mathrm{x}) \mapsto \varnothing \boxast \gamma(L{:}L_2, L\cdot\mathrm{x}, V)$$

$$\dfrac{Q = \left(\begin{array}{l} \exists \mathrm{L}'.\ \not\sigma(L_1, \mathbf{l}, \mathrm{x}, L) * (L, \mathrm{x}) \mapsto \mathrm{v} * (L, @\mathit{proto}) \mapsto Pr * \\ \pi(L_2, Pr, \mathrm{x}, \mathrm{L}') \boxast (\mathrm{L}', \mathrm{x}) \mapsto V * \mathbf{r} \doteq \mathrm{v} \end{array} \right)}{\{P\}\texttt{x = v}\{Q\}}$$

$$\dfrac{\begin{array}{l} P = \sigma(L_1 +\!\!+ [[L]], \mathbf{l}, \mathrm{x}, L) \boxast (L, \mathrm{x}) \mapsto V * V \not\doteq \varnothing \\ Q = \not\sigma(L_1, \mathbf{l}, \mathrm{x}, L) * (L, \mathrm{x}) \mapsto \mathrm{v} * \mathbf{r} \doteq \mathrm{v} \end{array}}{\{P\}\texttt{x = v}\{Q\}}$$

$$P = \left(\begin{array}{l} \sigma(Ls_1, \mathbf{l}, \mathrm{y}, L_y) \boxast \gamma(Ls_2, L_y\cdot\mathrm{y}, V_y) \boxast \\ \sigma(L_1 +\!\!+ [[L]], \mathbf{l}, \mathrm{x}, L) \boxast (L, \mathrm{x}) \mapsto V * V \not\doteq \varnothing \end{array} \right)$$

$$\dfrac{Q = \sigma(Ls_1, \mathbf{l}, \mathrm{y}, L_y) \boxast \not\sigma(L_1, \mathbf{l}, \mathrm{x}, L) * (L, \mathrm{x}) \mapsto V_y * \mathbf{r} \doteq V_y}{\{P\}\texttt{x = y}\{Q\}}$$

Compared to the (Assign Global) and (Assign Local) inference rules, these triples provide an explicit account of the footprint of the assignment, and more clearly describe the destructive effects of assignment. Yet, they are still quite complex and are difficult to compose. It would be useful to ignore some information about the exact structure of the variable store, while retaining the information about the mappings of variable names to values. To do this, we introduce a new store predicate.

6.2 Layer 2: a Simple Abstract Variable Store

The predicates below provide a convenient abstraction for an emulated variable store.

The store **Predicate.**

$$\begin{array}{l} \mathsf{store}_L(X_1 \ldots X_n | X'_1{:}V_1 \ldots X'_m{:}V_m) \triangleq \\ \quad \exists Ls_1 \ldots, Ls_n, Ls'_1, \ldots, Ls'_m, Ls''_1, \ldots, Ls''_m.\ \mathsf{thischain}(L) \boxast \\ \quad \boxast_{i \in 1..n} \not\sigma(Ls_i, L, X_i, \mathtt{null}) \quad \boxast (l_g, X_i) \mapsto \varnothing \\ \quad \boxast_{j \in 1..m} \sigma(Ls'_j, L, X'_j, L_j) \quad \boxast_{k \in 1..m} \gamma(Ls''_k, L_k\cdot X'_k, V_k) \end{array}$$

$$\begin{array}{lll} \mathsf{thischain}([\,]) & \triangleq & \emptyset \\ \mathsf{thischain}(L : Ls') & \triangleq & (L, @\mathit{this}) \mapsto \_ * \mathsf{thischain}(Ls') \end{array}$$

The assertion $\mathsf{store}_{\mathrm{LS}}(\mathsf{a}, \mathsf{b} | \mathtt{x} : 1, \mathtt{y} : 2)$ describes a heap emulating a variable store given by scope chain LS, in which the variables a and b are *not* present and the variables x and y take the values 1 and 2 respectively. The body of the predicate uses the $\not\sigma$ predicate to assert the absence of a and b, and the σ and γ predicates to assert the presence and values of x and y. This information about the exact structure of the emulated store and the locations of x and y is hidden from the programmer, since at this level of abstraction it should be of no concern. The thischain part of the body of the predicate ensures that the store predicate always encompasses enough resource to call any function that is stored in the emulated variable store. The variables a and b can be re-ordered, as can the variables x and y. To facilitate program reasoning at this level of abstraction we provide several inference rules, all of which are derived (using previous levels of abstraction) in [11]. We start by giving rules for initialising, overwriting and overriding a variable with a constant and with another variable.

Writing to a store**.**

Let $Q_1 = \mathsf{store}_{\mathbf{l}}(\mathrm{X}_1 \ldots \mathrm{X}_n | \mathrm{x}{:}v, \mathrm{X}'_1{:}\mathrm{V}_1 \ldots \mathrm{X}'_m{:}\mathrm{V}_m)$.
Let $Q_2 = \mathsf{store}_{\mathbf{l}}(\mathrm{X}_1 \ldots \mathrm{X}_n | \mathrm{x}{:}\mathrm{V}, \mathrm{y}{:}\mathrm{V}, \mathrm{X}'_1{:}\mathrm{V}_1 \ldots \mathrm{X}'_m{:}\mathrm{V}_m)$.

$$\dfrac{\begin{array}{l} \mathrm{x} \neq \mathrm{X}_1 \neq \cdots \neq \mathrm{X}_n \neq \mathrm{X}'_1 \neq \cdots \neq \mathrm{X}'_m \\ P = \mathsf{store}_{\mathbf{l}}(\mathrm{x}, \mathrm{X}_1 \ldots \mathrm{X}_n | \mathrm{X}'_1{:}\mathrm{V}_1 \ldots \mathrm{X}'_m{:}\mathrm{V}_m) \end{array}}{\{P\}\texttt{x = v}\{Q_1 * \mathrm{true} * \mathbf{r} \doteq v\}}$$

$$\dfrac{\begin{array}{l} \mathrm{x} \neq \mathrm{X}_1 \neq \cdots \neq \mathrm{X}_n \neq \mathrm{X}'_1 \neq \cdots \neq \mathrm{X}'_m \\ P = \mathsf{store}_{\mathbf{l}}(\mathrm{X}_1 \ldots \mathrm{X}_n | \mathrm{x}{:}\mathrm{V}, \mathrm{X}'_1{:}\mathrm{V}_1 \ldots \mathrm{X}'_m{:}\mathrm{V}_m) \end{array}}{\{P\}\texttt{x = v}\{Q_1 * \mathrm{true} * \mathbf{r} \doteq v\}}$$

$$\dfrac{\begin{array}{l} \mathrm{x} \neq \mathrm{y} \neq \mathrm{X}_1 \neq \cdots \neq \mathrm{X}_n \neq \mathrm{X}'_1 \neq \cdots \neq \mathrm{X}'_m \\ P = \mathsf{store}_{\mathbf{l}}(\mathrm{x}, \mathrm{X}_1 \ldots \mathrm{X}_n | \mathrm{y}{:}\mathrm{V}, \mathrm{X}'_1{:}\mathrm{V}_1 \ldots \mathrm{X}'_m{:}\mathrm{V}_m) \end{array}}{\{P\}\texttt{x = y}\{Q_2 * \mathrm{true} * \mathbf{r} \doteq \mathrm{V}\}}$$

$$\dfrac{\begin{array}{l} \mathrm{x} \neq \mathrm{y} \neq \mathrm{X}_1 \neq \cdots \neq \mathrm{X}_n \neq \mathrm{X}'_1 \neq \cdots \neq \mathrm{X}'_m \\ P = \mathsf{store}_{\mathbf{l}}(\mathrm{X}_1 \ldots \mathrm{X}_n | \mathrm{x}{:}\mathrm{V}', \mathrm{y}{:}\mathrm{V}, \mathrm{X}'_1{:}\mathrm{V}_1 \ldots \mathrm{X}'_m{:}\mathrm{V}_m) \end{array}}{\{P\}\texttt{x = y}\{Q_2 * \mathrm{true} * \mathbf{r} \doteq \mathrm{V}\}}$$

Notice that each of these rules has a postcondition which includes true. This is because initialising or overriding a variable may render a portion of the emulated variable store superfluous. For example, consider the overriding assignment `x = 1` in the store given in Figure 1. In this case the cell (l, x) has become surplus to requirements. In separation logic it is not sound to simply forget about these cells, so we hide them in the general assertion true.

One limitation of this level of abstraction is that the abstraction only covers a static (and unknown) scope chain. If we call a function which adds a new cell to the scope chain, then the rules above are insufficient to reason about our program. The following rules allow us to reason at this level of abstraction about a program which alters a global variable from within a new local scope frame.

Writing to a store **from a deeper scope.**

Let $Q = \mathsf{store}_{\mathrm{LS}}(\ \mathrm{X}_1, \ldots, \mathrm{X}_n | \mathrm{x} : \mathrm{V}', \mathrm{X}'_1 : \mathrm{V}'_1, \ldots, \mathrm{X}'_m : \mathrm{V}'_m\ )$ and $S = (\mathrm{L}, @\mathit{proto}) \mapsto \mathtt{null} * (\mathrm{L}, \mathrm{x}) \mapsto \varnothing * (\mathrm{L}, \mathrm{y}) \mapsto \mathrm{V}' * \mathbf{l} \doteq \mathrm{L} : \mathrm{LS}$.

$$\dfrac{\begin{array}{l} \mathrm{x} \neq \mathrm{y} \neq \mathrm{X}_1 \neq \cdots \neq \mathrm{X}_n \neq \mathrm{X}'_1 \neq \cdots \neq \mathrm{X}'_m \\ P_1 = \mathsf{store}_{\mathrm{LS}}(\ \mathrm{x}, \mathrm{X}_1, \ldots, \mathrm{X}_n | \mathrm{X}'_1 : \mathrm{V}'_1, \ldots, \mathrm{X}'_m : \mathrm{V}'_m\ ) \end{array}}{\{P_1 * S\}\texttt{x=y}\{Q * S * \mathrm{true}\}}$$

$$\dfrac{\begin{array}{l} \mathrm{x} \neq \mathrm{y} \neq \mathrm{X}_1 \neq \cdots \neq \mathrm{X}_n \neq \mathrm{X}'_1 \neq \cdots \neq \mathrm{X}'_m \\ P_2 = \mathsf{store}_{\mathrm{LS}}(\ \mathrm{X}_1, \ldots, \mathrm{X}_n | \mathrm{x} : \mathrm{V}, \mathrm{X}'_1 : \mathrm{V}'_1, \ldots, \mathrm{X}'_m : \mathrm{V}'_m\ ) \end{array}}{\{P_2 * S\}\texttt{x=y}\{Q * S * \mathrm{true}\}}$$

Finally, we provide two rules for a more general case of store interaction. In these cases, the value which is to be written to the variable is the result of computing some arbitrary expression. These specifications are therefore necessarily more complicated, since they must incorporate some features of sequential composition. We insist that whatever the expression does, it must not alter the variable store in a way that changes the visible values of the variables.

Destructive store **Initialisation.**

$$\dfrac{\begin{array}{l} \mathrm{x} \neq \mathrm{X}_1 \neq \cdots \neq \mathrm{X}_n \neq \mathrm{X}'_1 \neq \cdots \neq \mathrm{X}'_m \\ R = \mathsf{store}_{\mathbf{l}}(\mathrm{x}, \mathrm{X}_1 \ldots \mathrm{X}_n | \mathrm{X}'_1{:}\mathrm{V}_1 \ldots \mathrm{X}'_m{:}\mathrm{V}_m) \\ \{R * P\}\mathsf{e}\{R \boxast \gamma(LS, \mathrm{V}', \mathrm{V}) * Q * \mathbf{r} \doteq \mathrm{V}'\} \qquad \mathbf{r} \notin \mathsf{fv}(Q) \\ S = \left(\begin{array}{l} \mathsf{store}_{\mathbf{l}}(\ \mathrm{X}_1 \ldots \mathrm{X}_n | \mathrm{x}{:}\mathrm{V}, \mathrm{X}'_1{:}\mathrm{V}_1 \ldots \mathrm{X}'_m{:}\mathrm{V}_m\ ) \\ \boxast \gamma(LS, \mathrm{V}', \mathrm{V}) * Q * \mathrm{true} * \mathbf{r} \doteq \mathrm{V} \end{array} \right) \end{array}}{\{R * P\}\texttt{x = e}\{S\}}$$

$$\dfrac{\begin{array}{l} \mathrm{x} \neq \mathrm{X}_1 \neq \cdots \neq \mathrm{X}_n \neq \mathrm{X}'_1 \neq \cdots \neq \mathrm{X}'_m \\ R = \mathsf{store}_{L:SLS}(\mathrm{x}, \mathrm{X}_1 \ldots \mathrm{X}_n | \mathrm{X}'_1{:}\mathrm{V}_1 \ldots \mathrm{X}'_m{:}\mathrm{V}_m) \boxast \not\sigma(Nsls, \mathbf{l}, \mathrm{x}, L) \\ \{R\}\mathsf{e}\{R \boxast \gamma(LS, \mathrm{V}', \mathrm{V}) * Q * \mathbf{r} \doteq \mathrm{V}'\} \qquad \mathbf{r} \notin \mathsf{fv}(Q) \\ S = \left(\begin{array}{l} \mathsf{store}_{L:SLS}(\ \mathrm{X}_1 \ldots \mathrm{X}_n | \mathrm{x}{:}\mathrm{V}, \mathrm{X}'_1{:}\mathrm{V}_1 \ldots \mathrm{X}'_m{:}\mathrm{V}_m\ ) \boxast \\ \not\sigma(Nsls, \mathbf{l}, \mathrm{x}, L) \boxast \gamma(LS, \mathrm{V}', \mathrm{V}) * Q * \mathrm{true} * \mathbf{r} \doteq \mathrm{V} \end{array} \right) \end{array}}{\{R * P\}\texttt{x = e}\{S\}}$$

It may seem surprising that we only provide derived rules for destructive variable initialisation, and not for destructive variable *update*. This is because such an update rule would be unsound. The destructive expression might have the side effect of overriding the variable we wish to update. This serves to further demonstrate the need for the low-level reasoning introduced earlier in this paper. We can use high-level abstractions such as the store predicate where they are sound, but if we wish to reason about programs with side-effecting expressions, we will sometimes be forced to reason at a lower level.

The scope of a variable. The store abstraction gives us the tools we need to easily reason about programs with large numbers of variables. For example, consider the program from Section 2:

$\{\ \mathsf{store_l}(\mathtt{x},\mathtt{y},\mathtt{z},\mathtt{f},\mathtt{v}|)\ \}$

`x = null;y = null;z = null;`

$\{\ \mathsf{store_l}(\mathtt{f},\mathtt{v}|\mathtt{x}:\mathtt{null},\mathtt{y}:\mathtt{null},\mathtt{z}:\mathtt{null}) * \mathrm{true}\ \}$

`f = function(w){x=v ; v=4 ; var v ; y=v};`

$\left\{\begin{array}{l}\exists \mathrm{L}.\ \mathsf{store_l}(\mathtt{v}|\mathtt{x}:\mathtt{null},\mathtt{y}:\mathtt{null},\mathtt{z}:\mathtt{null},\mathtt{f}:\mathrm{L}) * \\ (\mathrm{L},@body) \mapsto \lambda\mathtt{w}.\{\ldots\} * \\ (\mathrm{L},@scope) \mapsto \mathsf{l} * \mathrm{true}\end{array}\right\}$

`v = 5;`

$\left\{\begin{array}{l}\mathsf{store_l}(|\mathtt{x}:\mathtt{null},\mathtt{y}:\mathtt{null},\mathtt{z}:\mathtt{null},\mathtt{f}:\mathrm{L},\mathtt{v}:5) * \\ (\mathrm{L},@body) \mapsto \lambda\mathtt{w}.\{\ldots\} * \\ (\mathrm{L},@scope) \mapsto \mathsf{l} * \mathrm{true}\end{array}\right\}$

`f(null);`

$\left\{\begin{array}{l}\exists \mathrm{L}'.\ \mathsf{store_l}(|\mathtt{x}:\mathtt{undefined},\mathtt{y}:4,\mathtt{z}:\mathtt{null},\mathtt{f}:\mathrm{L},\mathtt{v}:5) * \\ \mathsf{newobj}(\mathrm{L}',@proto,@this,\mathtt{w},\mathtt{v}) * (\mathrm{L}',@proto) \mapsto \mathtt{null} * \\ (\mathrm{L}',\mathtt{w}) \mapsto \mathtt{null} * (\mathrm{L}',\mathtt{v}) \mapsto 4 * \mathrm{true}\end{array}\right\}$

[Frame]

$\{\ \mathsf{store_l}(|\mathtt{x}:\mathtt{undefined},\mathtt{y}:4,\mathtt{z}:\mathtt{null},\mathtt{f}:\mathrm{L},\mathtt{v}:5)\ \}$

`z = v;`

$\{\ \mathsf{store_l}(|\mathtt{x}:\mathtt{undefined},\mathtt{y}:4,\mathtt{z}:5,\mathtt{f}:\mathrm{L},\mathtt{v}:5) * \mathrm{true}\ \}$

[Frame]

$\left\{\begin{array}{l}\mathsf{store_l}(|\mathtt{x}:\mathtt{undefined},\mathtt{y}:4,\mathtt{z}:5,\mathtt{f}:\mathrm{L},\mathtt{v}:5) * \\ \mathsf{newobj}(\mathrm{L}',@proto,@this,\mathtt{w},\mathtt{v}) * (\mathrm{L}',@proto) \mapsto \mathtt{null} * \\ (\mathrm{L}',\mathtt{w}) \mapsto \mathtt{null} * (\mathrm{L}',\mathtt{v}) \mapsto 4 * \mathrm{true}\end{array}\right\}$

[Cons/Var Elim]

$\{\ \exists \mathrm{L}.\ \mathsf{store_l}(|\mathtt{x}:\mathtt{undefined},\mathtt{y}:4,\mathtt{z}:5,\mathtt{f}:\mathrm{L},\mathtt{v}:5) * \mathrm{true}\ \}$

$\left\{\begin{array}{l}\exists \mathrm{L}',\mathrm{LS}.\ \mathsf{l} \doteq \mathrm{L}':\mathrm{LS} * \\ \mathsf{store_{LS}}(|\mathtt{x}:\mathtt{null},\mathtt{y}:\mathtt{null},\mathtt{z}:\mathtt{null},\mathtt{f}:\mathrm{L},\mathtt{v}:5) * \\ (\mathrm{L},@body) \mapsto \lambda\mathtt{w}.\{\ldots\} * (\mathrm{L},@scope) \mapsto \mathrm{LS} * \\ \mathsf{newobj}(\mathrm{L}',@proto,@this,\mathtt{w},\mathtt{v}) * (\mathrm{L}',@proto) \mapsto \mathtt{null} * \\ (\mathrm{L}',\mathtt{w}) \mapsto \mathtt{null} * (\mathrm{L}',\mathtt{v}) \mapsto \mathtt{undefined} * (\mathrm{L}',@this) \mapsto \_ * \mathrm{true}\end{array}\right\}$

`x=v;v=4;var v;y=v;`

$\left\{\begin{array}{l}\exists \mathrm{L}',\mathrm{LS}.\ \mathsf{l} \doteq \mathrm{L}':\mathrm{LS} * \\ \mathsf{store_{LS}}(|\mathtt{x}:\mathtt{undefined},\mathtt{y}:4,\mathtt{z}:\mathtt{null},\mathtt{f}:\mathrm{L},\mathtt{v}:5) * \\ \mathsf{newobj}(\mathrm{L}',@proto,@this,\mathtt{w},\mathtt{v}) * (\mathrm{L}',@proto) \mapsto \mathtt{null} * \\ (\mathrm{L}',\mathtt{w}) \mapsto \mathtt{null} * (\mathrm{L}',\mathtt{v}) \mapsto 4 * \mathrm{true}\end{array}\right\}$

Figure 2. Reasoning about variable scopes.

```
x = null; y = null; z = null;
f = function(w){x=v;v=4;var v;y=v;};
v = 5; f(null); z = v;
```

With the store predicate and the results given above, reasoning about this program is simple. A proof of the main program is shown in Figure 2. It relies on a simple proof of the function body summarised here and given in full in [11].

Reasoning about `with`. This level of abstraction also leads itself to reasoning about the notorious `with` statement. Consider the `with` example from Section 2 (where `f` implicitly returns `b`):

```
a = {b:1}; with (a){f=function(c){b}};
a = {b:2}; f(null)
```

This program demonstrates the importance of modelling `with` correctly. Recall that when correctly modelled, the closure of the function `f` will refer to the object `{b:1}`, which was pointed to by the variable `a` at the time that `f` was defined. However, even though the variable `a` is changed to point to a different object before `f(null)` is called, the closure continues to point to the object `{b:1}`. Thus the program normally returns the value 1, not 2. Recall also that we must be careful with the `f` field of the object l_{op}.

We can reason about this program using the store predicate. The proof is in Figure 3. This proof relies on a sub-proof for the invocation of the function `f(null)`, which culminates with the judgement $\{P\}\mathtt{b}\{P * \mathbf{r} \doteq 1\}$, where P is

Let $P = (\mathrm{L},\mathtt{b}) \mapsto 1 * (\mathrm{L},@proto) \mapsto l_{op} * \mathrm{true}$

$\{\ \mathsf{store_l}(\mathtt{a},\mathtt{f}|) \uplus (l_{op},\mathtt{f}) \mapsto \varnothing \uplus (l_{op},@proto) \mapsto \mathtt{null}\ \}$

`a = {b:1};`

$\left\{\begin{array}{l}\exists \mathrm{L}.\ \mathsf{store_l}(\mathtt{f}|\mathtt{a}:\mathrm{L}) \uplus (l_{op},\mathtt{f}) \mapsto \varnothing \uplus \\ (l_{op},@proto) \mapsto \mathtt{null} * (\mathrm{L},\mathtt{f}) \mapsto \varnothing * P\end{array}\right\}$

`with (a){`

$\left\{\begin{array}{l}\exists \mathrm{LS},\mathrm{L}.\ \mathsf{l} \doteq \mathrm{L}:\mathrm{LS} * \\ \mathsf{store_{LS}}(\mathtt{f}|\mathtt{a}:\mathrm{L}) \uplus (l_{op},\mathtt{f}) \mapsto \varnothing \uplus \\ (l_{op},@proto) \mapsto \mathtt{null} * (\mathrm{L},\mathtt{f}) \mapsto \varnothing * P\end{array}\right\}$

`f=function(c){b}`

$\left\{\begin{array}{l}\exists \mathrm{LS},\mathrm{L},\mathrm{F}.\ \mathsf{l} \doteq \mathrm{L}:\mathrm{LS} * \\ \mathsf{store_{LS}}(|\mathtt{a}:\mathrm{L},\mathtt{f}:\mathrm{F}) \uplus (l_{op},\mathtt{f}) \mapsto \varnothing \uplus \\ (l_{op},@proto) \mapsto \mathtt{null} * (\mathrm{L},\mathtt{f}) \mapsto \varnothing * \\ (\mathrm{F},@body) \mapsto \lambda\mathtt{c}.\{\mathtt{b}\} * (\mathrm{F},@scope) \mapsto \mathrm{L}:\mathrm{LS} * P\end{array}\right\}$

`};`

$\left\{\begin{array}{l}\exists \mathrm{LS},\mathrm{L},\mathrm{F}.\ \mathsf{l} \doteq \mathrm{LS} * \\ \mathsf{store_{LS}}(|\mathtt{a}:\mathrm{L},\mathtt{f}:\mathrm{F}) \uplus (l_{op},\mathtt{f}) \mapsto \varnothing \uplus (l_{op},@proto) \mapsto \mathtt{null} * \\ (\mathrm{L},\mathtt{f}) \mapsto \varnothing * (\mathrm{F},@body) \mapsto \lambda\mathtt{c}.\{\mathtt{b}\} * (\mathrm{F},@scope) \mapsto \mathrm{L}:\mathrm{LS} * P\end{array}\right\}$

`a = {b:2};`

$\left\{\begin{array}{l}\exists \mathrm{LS},\mathrm{L},\mathrm{F},\mathrm{L}'.\ \mathsf{l} \doteq \mathrm{LS} * \\ \mathsf{store_{LS}}(|\mathtt{a}:\mathrm{L}',\mathtt{f}:\mathrm{F}) \uplus (l_{op},\mathtt{f}) \mapsto \varnothing \uplus (l_{op},@proto) \mapsto \mathtt{null} * \\ (\mathrm{L},\mathtt{f}) \mapsto \varnothing * (\mathrm{L}',\mathtt{b}) \mapsto 2 * (\mathrm{L}',\mathtt{f}) \mapsto \varnothing * (\mathrm{L}',@proto) \mapsto l_{op} * \\ (\mathrm{F},@body) \mapsto \lambda\mathtt{c}.\{\mathtt{b}\} * (\mathrm{F},@scope) \mapsto \mathrm{L}:\mathrm{LS} * P\end{array}\right\}$

`f(null)`

$\left\{\begin{array}{l}\exists \mathrm{LS},\mathrm{L},\mathrm{F},\mathrm{L}',\mathrm{LOC}.\ \mathsf{l} \doteq \mathrm{LS} * \\ \mathsf{store_{LS}}(|\mathtt{a}:\mathrm{L}',\mathtt{f}:\mathrm{F}) \uplus (l_{op},\mathtt{f}) \mapsto \varnothing \uplus (l_{op},@proto) \mapsto \mathtt{null} * \\ (\mathrm{L},\mathtt{f}) \mapsto \varnothing * (\mathrm{L}',\mathtt{b}) \mapsto 2 * (\mathrm{L}',\mathtt{f}) \mapsto \varnothing * (\mathrm{L}',@proto) \mapsto l_{op} * \\ (\mathrm{F},@body) \mapsto \lambda\mathtt{c}.\{\mathtt{b}\} * (\mathrm{F},@scope) \mapsto \mathrm{L}:\mathrm{LS} * \\ (\mathrm{LOC},\mathtt{b}) \mapsto \varnothing * (\mathrm{LOC},@proto) \mapsto \mathtt{null} * P * \mathbf{r} \doteq 1\end{array}\right\}$

$\{\mathbf{r} \doteq 1 * \mathrm{true}\}$

Figure 3. Reasoning about `with`.

$$\left(\begin{array}{l}\exists \mathrm{LS},\mathrm{L},\mathrm{F},\mathrm{L}',\mathrm{LOC}.\ \mathsf{l} \doteq \mathrm{LOC}:\mathrm{L}:\mathrm{LS} * \\ \mathsf{store_{LS}}(|\mathtt{a}:\mathrm{L}',\mathtt{f}:\mathrm{F}) \uplus (l_{op},\mathtt{f}) \mapsto \varnothing \uplus \\ (l_{op},@proto) \mapsto \mathtt{null} * \mathrm{true} * \\ (\mathrm{L},\mathtt{b}) \mapsto 1 * (\mathrm{L},\mathtt{f}) \mapsto \varnothing * (\mathrm{L},@proto) \mapsto l_{op} * \\ (\mathrm{L}',\mathtt{b}) \mapsto 2 * (\mathrm{L}',\mathtt{f}) \mapsto \varnothing * (\mathrm{L}',@proto) \mapsto l_{op} * \\ (\mathrm{F},@body) \mapsto \lambda\mathtt{c}.\{\mathtt{b}\} * (\mathrm{F},@scope) \mapsto \mathrm{L}:\mathrm{LS} * \\ (\mathrm{LOC},\mathtt{b}) \mapsto \varnothing * (\mathrm{LOC},@proto) \mapsto \mathtt{null}\end{array}\right)$$

For space reasons, we only give the reasoning for the case in which neither `a` nor `f` are in the variable store. The same techniques in tandem with the disjunction rule can be used to prove the general precondition.

In both the simple and the general case, we must constrain our precondition with the assertion $(l_{op},\mathtt{f}) \mapsto \varnothing \uplus (l_{op},@proto) \mapsto \mathtt{null}$. The requirement for this term may seem surprising. Consider running the above program in a state satisfying $\mathsf{store_l}(\mathtt{a},\mathtt{f}|) \uplus (l_{op},\mathtt{f}) \mapsto 4$. In this case, when the assignment to `f` is made, the function pointer will be written to the cell $(\mathrm{L},\mathtt{f})$, rather than into the global variable store. Since the variable store does not contain a function value for the variable `f`, the call to `f(null)` will cause the program to fault. The problem is potentially even worse if $(l_{op},\mathtt{f})$ contains a function pointer. In this case, the call to `f(null)` will not fault, but rather will execute whatever code it finds. This kind of unpredictability could lead to very confusing bugs. In the case of a system like Facebook which attempts to isolate user-application code from host-page code, it could even lead to a security flaw.

6.3 Layer 3: a Recursive Abstract Variable Store

While reasoning using the store predicate, it is possible to handle large numbers of assignments and small numbers of function calls. However, for large numbers of function calls, another abstraction is helpful. Consider an *abstract* variable store as a list of lists of variable-value pairs, with the most local scope frame at the head of the outer list. The list $[[x = 4], [y = 5], [x = 6, z = 7]]$ represents a store in which the global scope contains the variables x and z, an intermediate scope adds the variable y, and the most local scope overrides the variable x. The list elements of variable-value pairs can be represented in our logical expression language as lists containing two elements. For readability, we use the notation $x = v$ above. We define the recursive store predicate $\mathsf{recstore}_L(\mathit{NoVars}, \mathit{Store})$ which describes an abstract variable store Store, which does not contain the variables in the list NoVars.

The Recursive recstore **predicate.**

$$\mathsf{recstore}_L([\mathtt{x1}', \cdots \mathtt{xm}'], [[\mathtt{x1} = V_1, \cdots, \mathtt{xn} = V_n]]) \triangleq \mathsf{store}_L(\mathtt{x1}', \cdots \mathtt{xm}' | \mathtt{x1} : V_1, \cdots, \mathtt{xn} : V_n)$$

$$\begin{array}{l} \mathsf{recstore}_{L:LS}([\mathtt{x1}', \cdots \mathtt{xm}'], ([\mathtt{x1} = V_1, \cdots, \mathtt{xn} = V_n] : Ls')) \triangleq \\ \quad \mathsf{recstore}_{LS}([\mathtt{x1}', \cdots \mathtt{xm}'], Ls') * (L, @proto) \mapsto \mathtt{null} * L \dot{\neq} l_g * \\ \quad *_{i \in 1..m} \ (L, \mathtt{xi}') \mapsto \varnothing *_{j \in 1..n} \ (L, \mathtt{xj}) \mapsto V_j * \\ \quad \mathsf{nones}_L([\mathtt{x1}, \cdots, \mathtt{xn}], Ls') \end{array}$$

$$\mathsf{nones}_L(\_, [\,]) \triangleq \oslash$$

$$\begin{array}{l} \mathsf{nones}_L(Ls, ([\mathtt{x1} = V_1, \cdots, \mathtt{xn} = V_n] : Ls')) \triangleq \\ \quad *_{i \in 1..n}((\mathtt{xi} \dot{\in} Ls) \vee (\mathtt{xi} \dot{\notin} Ls \wedge (L, \mathtt{xi}) \mapsto \varnothing)) * \\ \quad \mathsf{nones}_L((\mathtt{x1} : \cdots : \mathtt{xn} : Ls), Ls') \end{array}$$

Notice that recstore uses the store predicate to constrain the most global scope frame in the abstract scope list, while being rather more restrictive about more local scope frames. Local scope frames must be emulated by JavaScript objects which contain fields for each variable defined at that scope level. Furthermore, they must assert the absence of fields which are not in the store (the NoVars), or which would otherwise shadow a variable declared in a more global position in the store. This is handled by the nones predicate. Notice that local scope frames have a `null` prototype, and may not be the l_g object. These criteria are met by the emulated scope frames created by a normal function call, and are not normally met by `with` calls. This makes this abstraction ideal for reasoning about programs with many function calls and no internal uses of the `with` statement. Notice, however, that we do not outlaw `with` calls in the enclosing scope, represented here by a top-level use of the store predicate. This means that this abstraction will facilitate reasoning about libraries which are written in a principled way, and which may be called by unprincipled clients.

We provide several rules for reasoning at this level of abstraction in [11], the most interesting of which are destructive variable initialisation and update.

Destructive recstore **update.**

$$\frac{\begin{array}{l} R = \mathsf{recstore}_{\mathsf{l}}((\mathtt{x} : \mathit{EmpVars}), (\mathit{Locals} +\!\!+ [\mathit{Globals}])) \\ \{R * P\}\mathsf{e}\{R * Q * \mathbf{r} \doteq \mathit{Var}\} \\ \mathbf{r} \notin \mathsf{fv}(Q) \\ S = \mathsf{recstore}_{\mathsf{l}}((\mathit{EmpVars}), (\mathit{Locals} +\!\!+ [\mathtt{x} = \mathit{Var} : \mathit{Globals}])) \end{array}}{\{R * P\}\mathtt{x} \ \texttt{=} \ \mathsf{e}\{S * Q * \mathrm{true}\}}$$

$$\frac{\begin{array}{l} R = \mathsf{recstore}_{\mathsf{l}}((\mathit{Emps}), (\mathit{Ls} +\!\!+ ((\mathtt{x} = \mathit{Var}) : \mathit{Curr}) +\!\!+ \mathit{Globs})) \\ \{R * \mathit{Globs} \dot{\neq} [\,] * P\}\mathsf{e}\{R * \mathit{Globs} \dot{\neq} [\,] * Q * \mathbf{r} \doteq \mathit{Var}'\} \\ \mathbf{r} \notin \mathsf{fv}(Q) \\ \forall \mathrm{LS} \in \mathit{Ls}.\,(\mathtt{x} = \_) \dot{\notin} \mathrm{LS} \\ S = \mathsf{recstore}_{\mathsf{l}}((\mathit{Emps}), (\mathit{Ls} +\!\!+ ((\mathtt{x} = \mathit{Var}') : \mathit{Curr}) +\!\!+ \mathit{Globs})) \end{array}}{\{R * \mathit{Globs} \dot{\neq} [\,] * P\}\mathtt{x} \ \texttt{=} \ \mathsf{e}\{S * \mathit{Globs} \dot{\neq} [\,] * Q * \mathbf{r} \doteq \mathit{Var}'\}}$$

Notice that we may not safely update variables in the global portion of the abstract variable store with the results of potentially destructive expressions. This is for the same reason as the corresponding restriction on the store predicate in Section 6.2; there is a corner case which would lead to very unexpected behaviour. At this level of abstraction however, we have an advantage. We can be sure that the local abstract scope frames were constructed in a more principled way, and so we are able to reason about updating them with destructive expressions using the second rule above.

$$\left\{ \begin{array}{l} \mathsf{recstore}_{\mathsf{l}}\left([], \left[\begin{bmatrix} \mathtt{data} = \mathrm{L}, \\ \mathtt{checkField} = \mathtt{\&undefined}, \\ \mathtt{i} = \mathtt{\&undefined} \end{bmatrix}, []\right]\right) * \\ (\mathrm{L}, \mathtt{numEntries}) \mapsto \mathrm{N} * (\mathrm{L}, \mathtt{buttonDisabled}) \mapsto \_ * \\ (\mathrm{L}, 0) \mapsto \mathrm{TXT_0} * \ldots * (\mathrm{L}, \mathrm{N}) \mapsto \mathrm{TXT_N} \end{array} \right\}$$

$$\ldots \mathtt{checkForm} \ldots$$

$$\left\{ \begin{array}{l} \exists \mathrm{L}'.\,\mathsf{recstore}_{\mathsf{l}}([\,], [[\mathtt{data} = \mathrm{L}, \mathtt{checkField} = \mathrm{L}', \mathtt{i} = \mathrm{N}], [\,]]) * \\ (\mathrm{L}, \mathtt{numEntries}) \mapsto \mathrm{N} * \\ (\mathrm{L}, 0) \mapsto \mathrm{TXT_0} * \ldots * (\mathrm{L}, \mathrm{N}) \mapsto \mathrm{TXT_N} * \\ \left(\begin{array}{l} \left(\begin{array}{l} \mathrm{TXT_0} \dot{\neq} \text{""} * \ldots * \mathrm{TXT_N} \dot{\neq} \text{""} * \\ (\mathrm{L}, \mathtt{buttonDisabled}) \mapsto 0 \end{array} \right) \\ \vee (\mathrm{L}, \mathtt{buttonDisabled}) \mapsto 1 \end{array} \right) \end{array} \right\}$$

Figure 4. The specification of `checkForm`.

Form validation. Consider a web form with a number of mandatory text fields and a submit button. If the button is "disabled" when the page loads, then an event handler on the form can be used to regularly check if valid data has been entered in all the fields before enabling the button. Let us assume that the programmer has separated the concerns of parsing the web page and of validating the data. The data validation function will be called with a single parameter: an object with one field for each text value to check, a count of those text values, and boolean toggle corresponding to whether the submit button should be disabled. An example function which might perform the validation check is:

```
checkForm = function(data) {
    data.buttonDisabled = 0;
    var checkField = function(text) {
        if(text == "") {data.buttonDisabled = 1;}}
    var i = 0;
    while(i < data.numEntries) {
        checkField(data[i]); i = i+1;}}
```

Notice that this code deals with variables in a principled way. It makes use of no global variables, preferring instead to use function parameters and local variables. The repeated work of the loop body is factored into a function which could be expanded to provide extra functionality or used elsewhere with little cost in readability. Using the recstore abstraction it is straightforward to show that the function body satisfies the specification given in Figure 4.

7. Related Work

We believe this paper is the first to propose a program logic for reasoning about JavaScript. Our program logic adapts ideas from separation logic, and proves soundness with respect to a big-step operational semantics. In this section, we discuss related work on separation logic and the semantics of JavaScript.

We build on the seminal work of O'Hearn, Reynolds and Yang [20], who introduced separation logic for reasoning about C-programs, and on the work of Parkinson and Bierman [4, 23, 24], who adapted separation logic to reason about Java. We made several adaptations to their work in order to reason about JavaScript. As in [4, 23, 24], we use assertions of the form $(\mathtt{1}, \mathtt{x}) \mapsto 5$ to denote that a field `x` in object `1` has value 5. We extend these assertions by $(\mathtt{1}, \mathtt{x}) \mapsto \varnothing$, which denotes that the field is *not* in `1`. This is inspired by Dinsdale-Young *et al.*'s use of the 'out' predicate to state that values are not present in a concurrent set [7]. We introduce the sepish connective ⋈ to account for partially-shared data structures. We have not seen this connective before, which is surprising since shared data structures are common for example in Linux. There has been much work on various forms of concurrent separation logic with sharing [9, 21, 35], but they all seem to take a different approach to our ⋈ connective.

We prove the soundness of our frame rule using a new technique developed in Smith's PhD thesis [30]. There are several approaches to proving soundness of the separation-logic frame rule, and we list the key developments here. The first and most commonly used approach by O'Hearn, Reynolds and Yang involves first proving that the commands of the programming language under consideration are *local*, and then using that property to prove the frame rule [20]. Later, Birkedal and Yang devised a method "baking in" the soundness of the frame rule into their definition of Hoare triples [5]. This made it possible to prove the frame rule without reference to locality, but did not extend well to concurrent programs. Vafeiadis solved the concurrency problem in [34], where he proves soundness of concurrent separation logic without reference to locality. Smith's thesis was written at the same time as [34], and takes a different approach. Rather than removing all reference to locality from the soundness proof, Smith uses a generalised *weak locality* property, which allows us to handle some non-local behaviour.

We prove our soundness result with respect to a big-step operational semantics of JavaScript, faithfully following the small-step semantics of Maffeis *et al.* [18] except where discussed in Section 3.5. Their semantics captures the complete ECMAScript 3 language, at the same level of abstraction to where a JavaScript programmer reasons. In contrast,Herman and Flanagan [13] provide a definitional interpreter of JavaScript written in ML, which has the advantage of being directly executable, but includes implementation details that obscure the semantic meaning. 'Elsewhere, Guha *et al.* [12] compile JavaScript to an intermediate Scheme-like language, in order to provide type-based analyses on the object language. They justify their translation in a novel way, by checking that it satisfies an established test suite of JavaScript programs. However, the translation is complicated and it is not immediately apparent that it is sound. In fact, many approaches translate JavaScript programs using troublesome features such as the `with` construct into programs which do not. For example, Park, Lee and Ryu show that this is often feasible [22], but do not handle interactions between `with` and `eval`. There are a number of more abstract models of JavaScript, which have proven useful to study selected language features [1, 32, 37], but which are not sufficiently concrete for our purpose. Overall, we have chosen the semantics in [18] because it appears to be the most faithful to the actual JavaScript semantics. As Richards *et al.* argue in [28], all the unusual features of JavaScript are well-used in the wild, and cannot be easily abstracted away.

8. Conclusions and Future Work

We have defined a program logic for reasoning about JavaScript, based on an operational semantics which is essentially faithful to ECMAScript 3. We have adapted separation logic to reason about a JavaScript subset, modelling many complex features such as prototype inheritance and `with`. We reason about the full dynamic nature of JavaScript's functions, but do not provide higher-order reasoning. We also provide only conservative reasoning about `eval`. Full reasoning about these features will be technically challenging, although we believe that we can build on the recent work of [6, 10, 29]. We do not currently reason about implicit type coercion. JavaScript allows the programmer to define functions to convert values between different types. Adding this feature to our operational semantics is simple. The complexity in handling it with our program reasoning will be in reasoning about higher-order functions, as discussed above.

Due to our choice of operational semantics, we have been able to prove a strong soundness result. Any library, formally specified using our reasoning, will behave well, even when called by arbitrary JavaScript code. In Section 2, we illustrated this property by demonstrating that our `with` example behaves according to its specification even when embedded in a program which maliciously uses the non-standard `__proto__` feature. Finally, our soundness result can be extended compositionally to include more sophisticated reasoning about higher-order functions and `eval`.

We have given several examples of our reasoning, demonstrating with small code examples that JavaScript is fiendish to understand and our reasoning can help. In particular, our `with` example shows a potential bug that could easily go unnoticed for some time, and perhaps lead to security holes in sanitised mashup environments. Despite the complexity of the language and the subtlety of the bug, reasoning about this and other examples is made surprisingly simple by our example abstraction layers.

We hope that this work will form the core of a larger body of work on client-side web programming. For example, Thiemann [33] has defined a type-safe DOM API, and Smith [30] has developed context-logic reasoning about DOM Core Level 1. It would be valuable to integrate these approaches to DOM modelling with the JavaScript reasoning presented here.

Maffeis et al. [16, 17, 19] have developed techniques for building secure JavaScript mashups out of untrusted code. They prove security properties of their enforcement mechanisms, but do not study their functional correctness. Our reasoning makes such an analysis possible. We also intend to develop reasoning for high-level libraries such as jQuery, Prototype.js and Slidy [15, 25, 26]. We will make each of these libraries the focus of its own layer of abstraction, following the examples in Section 6, to make reasoning about idiomatic uses of those libraries very natural. As with our existing layers of abstraction, it will be possible to safely break these abstractions where necessary in order to code and reason at a lower level.

While this paper deals with ECMAScript 3, the newer ECMAScript 5 and the ongoing ECMAScript Harmony both provide enticing targets. Taly and others have recently given a small-step operational semantics of ECMAScript 5 [31]. It would certainly be interesting to reason about ECMAScript 5 code, and to formalise the connections with our reasoning presented here about ECMAScript 3. We are particularly interested in understanding the behaviour of libraries written in ECMAScript 5 when called by code written in ECMAScript 3.

To make this program reasoning genuinely useful for JavaScript programmers, it is essential that we provide tool support. We intend to produce analysis tools capable of spotting bugs such as the one described in the `with` example in Section 6.2, and integrate our tools with IDEs such as Eclipse or Visual Studio.

Acknowledgements.
Gardner and Smith are supported by EPSRC grant COTFM_P21654.
Maffeis is supported by EPSRC grant EP/I004246/1.
We thank Charlton, Dinsdale-Young, Ntzik, O'Hearn, da Rocha Pinto, Wheelhouse, and Wright for insightful discussions.
We especially thank Daiva Naudziuniene for her impressive eye for detail.

References

[1] C. Anderson, P. Giannini, and S. Drossopoulou. Towards type inference for JavaScript. In *Proc. of ECOOP'05*, 2005. 7

[2] J. Berdine, C. Calcagno, and P. O'Hearn. Smallfoot: Modular automatic assertion checking with separation logic. In *FMCO*, 2005. 1

[3] J. Berdine, B. Cook, and S. Ishtiaq. Slayer: Memory safety for systems-level code. In *CAV*, 2011. 1

[4] G.M. Bierman, M.J. Parkinson, and A. M. Pitts. MJ: An imperative core calculus for java and java with effects. Technical report, Cambridge, 2003. 4, 7

[5] L. Birkedal and H. Yang. Relational parametricity and separation logic. In *FoSSaCS*, pages 93–107, 2007. 7

[6] N. Charlton. Hoare logic for higher order store using simple semantics. In *Proc. of WOLLIC 2011*, 2011. 1, 8

[7] T. Dinsdale-Young, M. Dodds, P. Gardner, M. Parkinson, and V. Vafeiadis. Concurrent abstract predicates. *ECOOP*, 2010. 2, 7

[8] D. Distefano and M. Parkinson. jStar: towards practical verification for Java. In *OOPSLA '08*, pages 213–226. ACM, 2008. 1

[9] M. Dodds, X. Feng, M.J. Parkinson, and V. Vafeiadis. Deny-guarantee reasoning, 2009. 7

[10] D. Dreyer, G. Neis, and L. Birkedal. The impact of higher-order state and control effects on local relational reasoning. In *ICFP*, pages 143–156, 2010. 8

[11] P. Gardner, S. Maffeis, and G. Smith. Towards a program logic for JavaScript. Imperial College London Technical Report number DTR11-11, November 2011. 3.1, 3.3, 3.3, 3.4, 4, 5.1, 5.2, 5.3, 6.1, 6.2, 6.3

[12] A. Guha, C. Saftoiu, and S. Krishnamurthi. The Essence of JavaScript. *ECOOP 2010*, pages 126–150, 2010. 1, 2, 7

[13] D. Herman and C. Flanagan. Status report: specifying JavaScript with ML. In *Proc. of ML'07*, pages 47–52, 2007. 7

[14] ECMA International. ECMAScript language specification. stardard ECMA-262, 3rd Edition, 1999. 1, 2

[15] jQuery: The write less, do more, JavaScript library. `http://jquery.com`. 8

[16] S. Maffeis, J. C. Mitchell, and A. Taly. Isolating javascript with filters, rewriting, and wrappers. In *ESORICS*, pages 505–522, 2009. 8

[17] S. Maffeis, J. C. Mitchell, and A. Taly. Object capabilities and isolation of untrusted web applications. In *IEEE Symposium on Security and Privacy*, pages 125–140, 2010. 8

[18] S. Maffeis, J.C. Mitchell, and A. Taly. An operational semantics for JavaScript. In *Proc. of APLAS'08*, LNCS, 2008. 1, 2, 3, 3.2, 7

[19] S. Maffeis and A. Taly. Language-based isolation of untrusted javascript. In *CSF*, pages 77–91, 2009. 8

[20] P. O'Hearn, J. C. Reynolds, and H. Yang. Local reasoning about programs that alter data structures. In *CSL*, 2001. 1, 4, 5.3, 7

[21] P. W. OHearn. Resources, concurrency, and local reasoning. *Theor. Comput. Sci.*, 375(1-3):271–307, 2007. 7

[22] Changhee Park, Hongki Lee, and Sukyoung Ryu. An empirical study on the rewritability of the with statement in javascript. In *FOOL*, 2011.

[23] M. J. Parkinson and G. M. Bierman. Separation logic, abstraction and inheritance. In *POPL*, 2008. 2, 7

[24] M. J. Parkinson. Local reasoning for Java. Technical Report 654, Univ. of Cambridge Computer Laboratory, 2005. Ph.D. dissertation. 4, 7

[25] Prototype Core Team. Prototype JavaScript framework: Easy Ajax and DOM manipulation for dynamic web applications. `http://www.prototypejs.org`. 4, 7

[26] Dave Raggett. W3C Slidy. `http://www.w3.org/Talks/Tools/Slidy2/`, 2005. 8

[27] G. Richards, C. Hammer, B. Burg, and J. Vitek. The Eval that men do A large-scale study of the use of Eval in JavaScript applications. Accepted for publication at ECOOP 2011. 8

[28] G. Richards, S. Lebresne, B. Burg, and J. Vitek. An analysis of the dynamic behavior of JavaScript programs. In *PLDI*, 2010. 2

[29] J. Schwinghammer, L. Birkedal, B. Reus, and H. Yang. Nested hoare triples and frame rules for higher-order store. In *In Proc. of CSL'09*, 2009. 1, 2, 2, 7

[30] G. D. Smith. Local reasoning about web programs. PhD Thesis, Dep. of Computing, Imperial College London, 2011. 1, 8

[31] A. Taly, U. Erlingsson, M. S. Miller, J. C. Mitchell, and J. Nagra. Automated analysis of security-critical javascript apis. In *Proc. of IEEE Security and Privacy'11*. IEEE, 2011. 1, 5.3, 7, 8

[32] P. Thiemann. Towards a type system for analyzing javascript programs. In *Proc. of ESOP'05*, volume 3444 of *LNCS*, 2005. 8

[33] P. Thiemann. A type safe DOM API. In *Proc. of DBPL*, pages 169–183, 2005. 7

[34] V. Vafeiadis. Concurrent separation logic and operational semantics. In *MFPS11*, 2011. 8

[35] Viktor Vafeiadis and M. Parkinson. A marriage of rely/guarantee and separation logic. In *IN 18TH CONCUR*. Springer, 2007. 7

[36] H. Yang, O. Lee, J. Berdine, C. Calcagno, B. Cook, D. Distefano, and P. O'Hearn. Scalable shape analysis for systems code. In *CAV*, 2008. 7

[37] D. Yu, A. Chander, N. Islam, and I. Serikov. JavaScript instrumentation for browser security. In *Proc. of POPL'07*, 2007. 1

7

Higher-Order Functional Reactive Programming in Bounded Space

Neelakantan R. Krishnaswami
MPI-SWS
neelk@mpi-sws.org

Nick Benton
Microsoft Research
nick@microsoft.com

Jan Hoffmann
Yale University
jan.hoffmann@yale.edu

Abstract

Functional reactive programming (FRP) is an elegant and successful approach to programming reactive systems declaratively. The high levels of abstraction and expressivity that make FRP attractive as a programming model do, however, often lead to programs whose resource usage is excessive and hard to predict.

In this paper, we address the problem of space leaks in discrete-time functional reactive programs. We present a functional reactive programming language that statically bounds the size of the dataflow graph a reactive program creates, while still permitting use of higher-order functions and higher-type streams such as streams of streams. We achieve this with a novel linear type theory that both controls allocation and ensures that all recursive definitions are well-founded.

We also give a denotational semantics for our language by combining recent work on metric spaces for the interpretation of higher-order causal functions with length-space models of space-bounded computation. The resulting category is doubly closed and hence forms a model of the logic of bunched implications.

Categories and Subject Descriptors D.3.2 [*Dataflow Languages*]

General Terms languages, design, theory

Keywords functional reactive programming, dataflow, space-bounded computation, linear logic, bunched implications

1. Introduction

Reactive systems engage in an ongoing interaction with their environment, consuming input events and producing corresponding output events. Examples of such systems range from embedded controllers and sensor networks up to complex graphical user interfaces, web applications, games and simulations. Programming reactive systems in a general-purpose imperative language can be unpleasant, as different parts of the program interact not by structured control flow, but by dynamically registering state-manipulating callback functions with one another. The complexity of writing and reasoning about programs written in such a higher-order imperative style, as well as the critical nature and resource requirements of many reactive systems, has inspired extensive research into domain-specific languages (DSL), libraries and analysis techniques for reactive programming.

Synchronous dataflow languages, such as Esterel [3], Lustre [4], and Lucid Synchrone [21], implement a domain-specific computational model deriving from Kahn networks. A program corresponds to a fixed network of stream-processing nodes that communicate with one another, each consuming and producing a statically-known number of primitive values at every clock tick. Synchronous languages have precise, analysable semantics, provide strong guarantees about bounded usage of space and time, and are widely used in applications such as hardware synthesis and embedded control software.

Functional reactive programming (FRP), as introduced by Elliott and Hudak [8], also works with time-varying values (rather than mutable state) as a primitive abstraction, but provides a much richer model than the synchronous languages: signals (behaviours) can vary continuously as well as discretely, values can be higher-order (including both first-class functions and signal-valued signals), and the overall structure of the system can change dynamically. FRP has been applied in problem domains including robotics, animation, games, web applications and GUIs. However, the expressivity and apparently simple semantics of the classic FRP model come at a price. Firstly, the intuitively appealing idea of modelling A-valued signals as elements of the stream type A^ω (or, in the continuous case, $A^\mathbb{R}$) and reactive systems as stream functions $\text{Input}^\omega \to \text{Output}^\omega$ does not rule out systems that violate causality (the output today can depend upon the input tomorrow) or reactivity (ill-founded feedback can lead to undefined behaviour). Secondly, as the model is highly expressive and abstracts entirely from resource usage, the time and space behaviour of FRP programs is hard to predict and, even with sophisticated implementation techniques, can often be poor. It is all too easy to write FRP programs with significant space leaks, caused by, for example, inadvertently accumulating the entire history of a signal.[1]

Subsequent research has attempted to reduce 'junk' and alleviate performance problems by imposing restrictions on the classic FRP model. The Yale Haskell Group's Yampa [11, 19], for example, is an embedded DSL for FRP that constructs signal processing networks using Hughes's arrow abstraction [12]. Signals are no longer first-class, and signal-processing functions must be built from well-behaved casual primitives by causality-preserving combinators. Arrowized FRP allows signals to carry complex values but is essentially first-order (there is no exponential at the level of signal functions), though certain forms of dynamism are allowed via built in 'switching' combinators. Yampa does not enforce reactiv-

[1] Closely related are 'time leaks', which occur when sampling a time-dependent value can invoke an arbitrarily lengthy computation to 'catch up' with the current time.

POPL '12 January 25–27, 2012, Philadelphia, PA, USA.

ity or provide resource guarantees but, empirically at least, makes certain kinds of leaks less likely.

Krishnaswami and Benton [13] recently described a semantic model for higher-order, discrete-time functional reactive programs based on ultrametric spaces, identifying causal functions with non-expansive maps and interpreting well-founded feedback via Banach's fixpoint theorem. They gave an associated language, featuring a Nakano-style [18] temporal modality for well-founded recursion, and showed the correctness of an implementation using an imperatively-updated dataflow graph. This implementation is much more efficient than directly running the functional semantics, but nothing prevents the dataflow graph from growing unboundedly as a program executes, leading to undesirable space leaks. In this paper, we solve the problem of such leaks by extending the ultrametric approach to FRP with linearly-typed resources that represent the permission to perform heap-allocation, following the pattern of Hofmann's work [9, 10] on non-size-increasing computation.

We give a denotational model for bounded higher-order reactive programming in terms of 'complete ultrametric length spaces', which carry both an ultrametric distance measure and a size function. Maps between such spaces must be non-expansive and non-size-increasing. Intuitively, the metric is used to enforce good temporal behaviour (causality and productivity of recursive definitions), whilst the size measure enforces good spatial behaviour, bounding the number of cells in the dataflow graph. The category of complete ultrametric length spaces is doubly-closed, forming a model of the logic of bunched implications [20] and exposing a (perhaps) surprising connection between the type theory of stream programming and separation logic.

We define a term language, with a rather novel type theory, that corresponds to our model and allows us to write bounded reactive programs. Judgements are all time-indexed, with the successor operation on times internalized in a modality $\bullet A$. Terms are typed in three contexts, one carrying linear (actually affine) resources of type $\diamond$, giving permission to allocate; one binding pure, resource-free variables; and one binding potentially resourceful variables. Resource-freedom is internalized via a $!A$ modality, in the style of linear logic. We give the language an interesting staged operational semantics, which separates the normalizing reduction that takes place within each time step from the transitions that take place when the clock advances, and show that this is soundly modelled in the denotational semantics. The operational semantics uses terms of the language itself to encode the heap context within which evaluation takes place.

We also give a number of examples in our language that illustrate properties of the model and the applicability of our approach, showing that one can work with recursively-defined higher-order functions and streams in a natural way while still ensuring causality, productivity and bounded space usage.

To improve readability, we invert the 'logical' order of presentation: Section 2 gives an informal account of the language that suffices for presenting some of the motivating examples. Section 3 formally defines the language and the type system. We then, in Section 4, define the operational semantics and, in Section 5 and 6, present the details of the denotational model. Finally, in Section 7, we discuss our work and relate it to existing research.

2. Programming Language

The language is essentially a simply-typed λ-calculus with a type constructor $\mathsf{S}(-)$ for infinite streams, extended with three non-standard notions: delay types, resource types, and pure types. We treat streams as much as possible as mathematical sequences, but want to ensure that we can also interpret them as the successive values of signals generated by implementable clocked systems. Thus a definition (in a generic functional syntax for now)

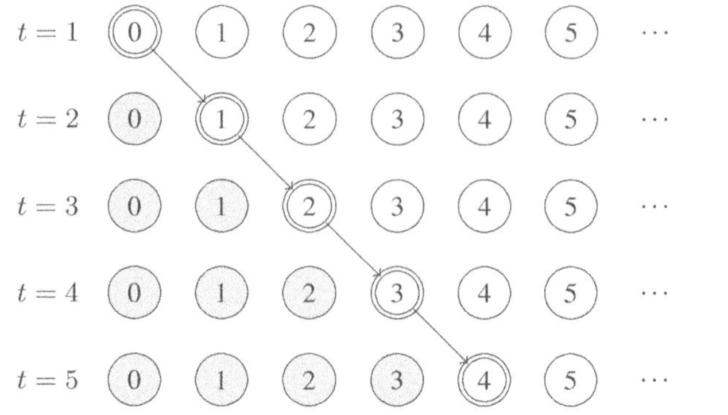

Figure 1. Memory Usage of Streams

$$nats : \mathbb{N} \to \mathsf{S}(\mathbb{N})$$
$$nats\ n = \mathsf{cons}(n,\ nats(n{+}1))$$

denotes a parameterised infinite stream but can also be understood as a stateful process ticking out successive natural numbers as time advances. It is necessary to restrict recursive definitions to ensure that signals are well-defined at all times. The recursion above is clearly *guarded*: the recursive call to $nats$ only occurs underneath a cons constructor, so successively unfolding the stream at each clock tick is productive. That is, we always discover at least one new cons constructor which we can examine to find the head and the tail of the stream at the current time.

However, simple syntactic guardedness checks (used by languages as varied as Lucid Synchrone, Agda and Coq) do not integrate well with higher-order. For example, one might want a stream functional that abstracts over the constructor:

$$higher\_order\ f\ v = f(v,\ higher\_order\ f\ (v + 1))$$

The guardedness of $higher\_order$ now depends on the definition of f, which is an unknown parameter. As in our earlier work [13], we instead use a *next-step* modality $\bullet A$ to track the times at which values are available in their types.

A value of type $\bullet A$ is a computation that will yield a value of type A when executed on the *next* clock tick. The tail function has type $tail : S(A) \to \bullet S(A)$, expressing that the tail of a stream only becomes available in the future. Similarly the type of $cons$ is refined to $cons : A \times \bullet S(A) \to S(A)$, capturing that streams are constructed from a value today and a stream tomorrow. By giving the fixed point combinator the type $fix : (\bullet A \to A) \to A$, we ensure that all recursive definitions are well-founded without restricting their syntactic form.

If we care about space usage, however, this use of types to track guardedness still admits too many programs. The problem is to limit the amount of data that must be buffered to carry it from one time tick to the next. In the case of $nats$ above, it is clear that the current state of the counting process can always be held in a single natural number. But consider a similar definition at a higher type:

$$constantly\_leak : \mathsf{S}(A) \to \mathsf{S}(\mathsf{S}(A))$$
$$constantly\_leak\ xs = \mathsf{cons}(xs,\ constantly\_leak\ xs)$$

The call $constantly\_leak\ xs$ yields a stream of streams which is constantly xs. This is a perfectly well-founded functional definition but, as a stateful process, requires the whole accumulated history of xs to be buffered so it can be pushed forward on each time step.

Figure 1 shows the evolution of a stream as time passes. The gray nodes denote the nodes already produced, the doubly-circled nodes show the current value of the head of the stream, and the white nodes mark the elements yet to be produced. At each time step, one node moves into the past (becomes gray), and the current head advances one step farther into the stream.

As *constantly_leak xs* retains a reference to its argument, it needs to buffer all of the gray nodes to correctly enumerate the elements of the streams to be produced in future. Running *constantly_leak xs* for n time steps thus requires $O(n)$ space, which is unreasonable. To see this more clearly, consider the following function:

```
f : S(A) → S(S(A)) → ℕ → ℕ → S(A)
f xs yss n m =
  let (x, xs') = (head xs, tail xs) in
  let (ys, yss') = (head yss, tail yss) in
  if n = 0 then cons(x, f (head yss') yss' m (m+1))
          else cons(x, f xs' yss' (n−1) m)

diag : S(A) → S(A)
diag xs = f xs ( constantly_leak xs) 0 1
```

Now, *diag* (*nats* 0) yields $(0, 0, 1, 0, 1, 2, 0, 1, 2, 3, \ldots)$, enumerating the prefixes of *nats* 0. As each prefix appears infinitely often, the whole history of the initial stream must be saved as the program executes. There are definitions with the same type as *constantly_leak* that *can* be implemented in constant space:

```
tails :: S(A) → S(S(A))
tails xs = cons(xs, tails ( tail xs))
```

Since *tails* returns the successive tails of its stream argument, we do not need to remember gray nodes (see Figure 1), and hence can implement the function without any buffering. Substituting *tails* for *constantly_leak* turns *diag* into the (space-efficient) identity.

To account for the memory usage associated with creating and buffering stream data, we adapt a variant of the linear (affine) *resource types* of Hofmann's LFPL [9, 10]. The type $\Diamond$ represents a permission to create one new stream; the tensor product $R \otimes S$ is the permission to do both R and S; and the linear function space $R \multimap A$ builds an A, consuming the resources in R. We further refine the construction of streams of type $S(A)$ to take *three* arguments using the syntactic form $\mathsf{cons}(u, e, u'.\ e')$. The term $u : \Diamond$ is a permission to allocate a cons cell and the term $e : A$ is the head of the stream. The tail, $e' : \bullet S(A)$, is defined in scope of the variable u', which re-binds the allocation permission that will be freed up on the next time step.

We still permit sharing of stream values without restriction since dataflow programs gain efficiency precisely from the ability to share. Therefore, we also support a context of unrestricted variables and an intuitionistic[2] function space $A \to B$. (Hofmann's original language featured a strictly linear type discipline.) Function closures can also need buffering if they capture streams in their environment, so it is useful to introduce the type constructor $!A$, which classifies those A-values that need no buffering and may be freely carried forward in time.

2.1 Examples

Our language makes the intuition of bounded resource consumption explicit, while remaining close to standard functional programming style. We begin with the definition of two classic stream functions, *nats* and *fib*, in our language:

```
nats : !ℕ → ◊ ⊸ S(!ℕ)
nats = fix loop : !ℕ → ◊ ⊸ S(!ℕ)
         λ x u. let !n = x in cons(u, !n, u'. loop !(n+1) u')

fibs : !ℕ → !ℕ → ◊ ⊸ S(!ℕ)
fibs = fix loop : !ℕ → !ℕ → ◊ ⊸ S(!ℕ).
         λ x y u.
           let !n = x in
           let !m = y in
           cons(u, !n, u'. loop !m !(n+m) u')
```

[2] We do *not* decompose the intuitionistic function space as $!A \multimap B$.

The function *nats* differs from the standard definition in two ways. First, we include an extra resource argument of type $\Diamond$, which contains a permission used as the extra argument to the cons operator. Furthermore, we require the argument of the function to be of the modal type $!\mathbb{N}$. Since the variable n is used in both the head and the tail of the cons-expression, we need to know that n can be used at different times without requiring additional space usage. This is exactly what the type $!A$ allows: an expression let $!a = a'$ in ... binds the modal value a' to a variable a which can be used at any current or future time. The introduction form $!e$ for $!A$ constructs a value of type A, which may only mention resource-free variables. The definition of the function *fibs* is similar.

Similarly, we give the definition of the *constant* function, which returns a constant stream of values.

```
constant : !A → ◊ ⊸ S(!A)
constant = fix loop : !A → ◊ ⊸ S(!A).
             λ a' u. let !a = a' in cons(u, a', v. loop !a v)
```

The modal type $!A$ in the typing of *constant* prevents one defining *constantly_leak* in terms of *constant*, since stream values are never resource-free (as cons-expressions include a resource argument).

However, we can still define functions constructing higher-order streams, so long as space usage is bounded. In this, we improve upon much previous work on efficient implementations of FRP. An example is the *tails* function that we described earlier; in our language, this is programmed as follows:

```
tails : S(A) → ◊ ⊸ S(S(A))
tails =
  fix tails : S(A) → ◊ ⊸ S(S(A)).
    λ xs u.
      let xs' = tail(xs) in
      cons(u, xs, u'. tails xs' u')
```

Higher type streams also let us *define* many of the switching combinators of FRP libraries, without having to build them in as primitive operations. For example:

```
switch : S(bool) → S(S(A)) → ◊ ⊸ S(A)
switch =
  let loop =
    fix loop : S(bool) → S(S(A)) → S(A) → ◊ ⊸ S(A).
      λ bs xss current u.
        let yss = tail(xss) in
        let bs' = tail(bs) in
        if head(bs) then
          let zs = tail(head xss) in
          cons(u, head(head xss), u'. loop bs' yss zs u')
        else
          let zs = tail(current) in
          cons(u, head(current), u'. loop bs' yss zs u')
  in λ bs xss u. loop bs xss (head xss) u
```

The function *switch* takes a stream of boolean events and a stream of streams. It then yields the elements of the head of the stream of streams until the boolean stream yields true, at which point it starts generating the elements of the current stream from the stream of streams. In this way, it is easy to go beyond simple static dataflow programs, without having to contort programs to fit a fixed set of combinators.

However, with the full resources of a higher-order programming language available, it is often convenient to define programs in terms of familiar stream functionals such as *map*.

```
map : !(A → B) → S(A) → ◊ ⊸ S(B)
map h =
  let !f = h in
  fix loop : S(A) → ◊ ⊸ S(B).
    λ xs u.
      let ys = tail xs in
      cons(u, f (head xs), u'. loop ys u')
```

This function illustrates a common pattern of higher-order programming in our language. We often wish to use functional arguments at many different times: in this case, we want to apply the argument to each element of the input stream. Therefore, the functional arguments in higher-order functions often need to be under the time-independence modality $!(A \to B)$.

The *unfold* function provides another nice example of higher-order programming:

```
unfold : !(X → A × •X) → X → ◊ ⊸ S(A) =
unfold h =
  let !f = h in
  fix loop : X → ◊ ⊸ S(A).
    λ x u.
      let (a, d) = f(x) in
      let •x' = d in
      cons(u, a, v. loop x' v)
```

Using *unfold*, one can directly translate deterministic state machines into stream programs, passing in the state transformer function and the initial state as the arguments. This function is also the first example with the delay modality — our state transformer takes a state, and returns a value and the state to use on the *next* timestep. The elimination form let $\bullet y = e$ in ... takes an expression of type $\bullet A$ and binds it to a variable y of type A, one tick in the future. This lets us use it in the third argument to cons, since the tail of a stream is also an expression one tick in the future.

Next, we illustrate the importance of being able to use streams intuitionistically, even as we track resources linearly.

```
zip : S(A) × S(B) → ◊ ⊸ S(A × B)
zip =
  fix zip : S(A) × S(B) → ◊ ⊸ S(A × B).
    λ (xs, ys) u.
      let xs' = tail(xs) in
      let ys' = tail(ys) in
      cons(u, (head xs, head ys), v. zip (xs', ys') v)

sum : S(ℕ) × S(ℕ) → (◊ ⊗ ◊) ⊸ S(ℕ) =
  λ (xs, ys) (u, v). map !+ (zip (xs,ys) u) v

double : S(ℕ) → (◊ ⊗ ◊) ⊸ S(ℕ)
double ns (u, v) = sum(ns, ns) (u, v)
```

We first define the function *zip*, which takes two streams and returns a stream of pairs, and the function *sum*, which takes two streams of natural numbers and pointwise sums their elements. These two functions are then used to define *double*, which takes a stream of numbers and returns a new stream of elements each of which is twice the size of the input. Note that *double* works by passing the *sum* function the *same* stream in both arguments, decisively violating linearity.

The *map* and *zip* functions (together with *unzip*, which we do not define here) witness that $S(\cdot)$ is a Cartesian functor. We can also define maps illustrating other semantic properties of streams.

```
cokleisli : !(S(A) → B) → S(A) → ◊ ⊸ S(B)
cokleisli g =
  let !f = g in
  fix loop : S(A) → ◊ ⊸ S(B).
    λ xs u.
      let ys = tail(xs) in cons(u, f xs, u'. loop ys u')

flip : S(•A) → •(◊ ⊸ S(A))
flip =
  fix flip : S(•A) → •(◊ ⊸ S(A))
    λ xs.
      let •x' = head(xs) in
      let xs' = tail(xs) in
      •(let •f = flip xs' in
          λ u. cons(u, x', u'. f u'))

unflip : •S(A) → ◊ ⊸ S(•A)
unflip =
  fix unflip : •S(A) → ◊ ⊸ S(•A).
    λ xs' u.
      let •ys = xs' in
      cons(u, •(head(ys)), u'.
             let ys' = tail(ys) in
             unflip (• ys') u')
```

The *cokleisli* function lifts a function from streams $S(A)$ to a type B to a function from streams of A to streams of B, giving a comonad structure [24] to the $S(\cdot)$ functor. The *flip* and *unflip* functions define an isomorphism between streams of delayed values and delayed streams of values. These operations make use of the ability to explicitly delay expressions e until the next tick with the $\bullet e$ introduction form for $\bullet A$.

In our earlier work, we had general delay operators $\delta_A : A \to \bullet A$, which shifted values of any type forward one tick into the future. However, a given piece of data may represent different values as time passes, and so we do *not* want delay maps of type $\delta_A : S(A) \to \bullet S(A)$, since this type does not capture the additional storage needed to move the argument forward one step in the future. However, it is possible in our system to *define* delay operators with types such as $S(!\mathbb{N}) \to \Diamond \multimap \bullet S(!\mathbb{N})$, which explicitly represent the buffering in the type:

```
buffer : !ℕ → S(!ℕ) → ◊ ⊸ S(!ℕ)
buffer b xs u =
  let !y = head(xs) in             // let head of y be usable later
  let ys = tail(xs) in             // ys at time 1
  cons(u, b, v. buffer !y ys v)    // now call buffer at time 1
```

The *buffer* function prepends a number to the front of a stream and can be used to construct a delay operator:

```
delaynats : S(!ℕ) → ◊ ⊸ •S(!ℕ)
delaynats xs u =
  let !y = head(xs) in     // let head of y be usable later
  let ys = tail(xs) in     // tail ys is at time 1
  •(buffer !y ys u)        // now call buffer at time 1 with y, ys
```

This gives a delay operator for streams, but additionally asks for a resource with which to construct the delayed stream. The definition illustrates our design philosophy that expensive crosstime operations should be programmed explicitly.

We conclude with a traditional example of stream programming, the sieve of Eratosthenes:

```
sieve : !(ℕ → bool) → S(!ℕ) → ◊ ⊸ S(!(option ℕ))
sieve p xs u =
  let !n = head xs in
  let ns = tail(xs) in
  let !pred = p in
  if pred n then
    let q = !(λ j. pred j ∧ j mod n ≠0) in
    cons(u, !(Some n), v. sieve q ns v)
  else
    cons(u, !None, v. sieve p ns v)

primes : ◊ ⊗ ◊ ⊸ S(ℕ)
primes (u,v) = sieve !(is_odd) (nats 2 u) v
```

The *sieve* function incrementally constructs a filter predicate that tests each element of the stream for divisibility by all the primes seen so far. Since the number of primes is infinite, the size of the sieve predicate's lambda-term grows without bound, but is nevertheless accepted by our language's type system. By design, we allow all ordinary call-by-value functional programs (which have reasonable compositional cost semantics [23]), and only use typing to track the unusual memory leaks of FRP. Hence our types only track the size of the dataflow graph (i.e., the number of live cons cells).

3. Syntax and Typing

We give the types and syntax of the programming language in Figure 2. The types include base types P, stream types $S(A)$, the next-step modality $\bullet A$, ordinary functions $A \to B$, the purity modality $!A$, and the linear function space $R \multimap A$. Resources R include the allocation permission $\diamond$, and the tensor product $R \otimes S$. For space reasons, we do not include products $A \times B$ or sums $A + B$ here. (Since we require coproducts to define switching combinators, we emphasise that this is purely for space reasons: there are no technical complications associated with sum types.)

The typing rules are defined in Figure 3. The two type judgements of our type theory are $\Theta \vdash t :_i R$ and $\Theta; \Pi; \Gamma \vdash e :_i A$. Both judgements are time-indexed, in the sense that the type system judges a term to have a type at a particular time i. Furthermore, each hypothesis in each context is indexed by the time at which they can be used. (As usual, we take contexts to be unordered, and implicitly assume alpha-renaming to ensure that all variables are distinct.)

The judgement $\Theta \vdash t :_i R$ states that in the context of affine resource variables Θ, the term t has resource type R, at time i. The resource terms are built from affine pairs of the ground type $\diamond$ and are permissions to allocate one or more cons cells.

The judgement $\Theta; \Pi; \Gamma \vdash e :_i A$ has three contexts: the affine resource context Θ contains again permissions to allocate cons cells; the intuitionistic context Π contains pure hypotheses (i.e., variables in Π bind non-state-dependent values); and the intuitionistic context Γ binds arbitrary value types, and permits unrestricted sharing and reuse of variables. Under these three contexts, we judge a term e to be an expression of type A at time i.

There are only two rules for the affine resource term calculus in Figure 3. The RHYP rule allows a resource to be used at any time after the context says it is available. The tensor rule R$\otimes$I lets one form an affine pair $\langle t, t' \rangle$, dividing the resources in the context between the two components. Observe that these rules allow weakening but not contraction.

The rule PHYP lets us use a pure hypothesis at any time after the time index in the variable context. In contrast, the rule EHYP only permits using a variable x at *exactly* its time index in Γ. This difference is one of the keys to accurately tracking space usage: we may substitute values which require buffering for variables in Γ, and by disallowing implicit transport of values across time, we ensure that the programmer uses explicit buffering whenever needed.

The rules $\to$I and $\to$E introduce and eliminate intuitionistic functions. The introduction rule does not permit the body to use any resources, since we can call functions multiple times. (The presence of Θ in the conclusion of $\to$I and the other value forms builds in weakening, so that we do not have to give a separate structural rule.) The elimination rule does allow expressions to use resources, since we will use a call-by-value evaluation strategy that will evaluate the two terms (using up their resource permissions) before substituting a value into a lambda-term.

The rules $\multimap$I and $\multimap$E introduce and eliminate linear functions. The introduction rule only permits the body to use the resources it receives in the argument, since we need to ensure that the function can be safely called multiple times. As a result, our typing rules do not permit currying of linear functions ($R \multimap S \multimap A \not\simeq R \otimes S \multimap A$), even though our underlying semantic model does permit it. If our type theory had the tree-structured contexts of the logic of bunched implications [20], then currying linear functions would be syntactically expressible. However, type checking for bunched calculi is still a difficult problem, and so in this work we restrict our attention to a linear fragment.

The rules SI, SE-HEAD and SE-TAIL are the introduction and elimination rules for streams. The syntactic form $\mathsf{cons}(t, e, u.\ e')$ takes three arguments: the expression t is a permission to create a cons cell, the expression e is the head of the stream, and e' is the tail of the stream. The tail subterm e' occurs underneath a binder for the resource variable u'. The intuition is that each stream takes up one unit of space at each successive time step, and u' names the permission t, after one time step has elapsed. This lets us pass the permission to use t to functions on subsequent time steps in the body of e'.

The rule SE-HEAD is straightforward: given a stream of type $S(A)$, we get a value of type A, at the same time. The rule SE-TAIL uses the form $\mathsf{let}\ x = \mathsf{tail}(e)\ \mathsf{in}\ e'$ to bind the tail of e to the variable x in e'. The tail of a stream at time i lives at time $i+1$ and we choose a binding elimination form to maintain the invariant that no term of time i contains any subterms at any earlier time.

The rules $\bullet$I and $\bullet$E introduce and eliminate delay terms. The rule $\bullet$I says that if e is a term of type A at time $i+1$, then $\bullet e$ is a term of type $\bullet A$ at time i. Like the other value introduction forms, it prevents e from using any resources, so that e can be substituted freely. The rule $\bullet$E gives a binding elimination $\mathsf{let}\ \bullet x = e\ \mathsf{in}\ e'$ for the next-step modality. We use a binding elimination for the same reason as in the rule SE-TAIL — we do not want terms of time i to contain subterms of time $< i$.

The rule !I introduces a term of pure type $!A$. It does so by typing the body of a term $!A$ at type A with an empty resource and shared context. Since e can only refer to hypotheses in Π, which are pure, it follows that e itself must be pure. The rule !E types the elimination form $\mathsf{let}\ !x = e\ \mathsf{in}\ e'$, which binds the value e to the variable x in the pure context Π.

The rule $\otimes$E is the elimination form for the tensor. Given a term t of type $R \otimes S$, the expression $\mathsf{let}\ \langle u, v \rangle = t\ \mathsf{in}\ e$ binds the components to the variables u and v for the scope of e.

The rule LET introduces local let-bindings. The introduced binding $x = e$ must be at the same time i as the overall expression.

The rule FIX types fixed points $\mathsf{fix}\ x : A.\ e$. The body e is typed at time i with the recursive hypothesis $x :_{i+1} A$ one tick later. The one-step delay ensures the guardedness of recursive definitions. Furthermore, the typing of the expression e is derived under an empty resource context and with an empty shared context. Since e may unfold multiple times, giving e resources would violate linearity. Furthermore, the unrollings can happen at different times, which means that using any variables in the shared context might require buffering.

We now state the structural and substitution principles.

Lemma 1. *(Admissibility of Weakening and Contraction)*

1. *If* $\Theta \vdash t :_i R$ *then* $\Theta, \Theta' \vdash t :_i R$.
2. *If* $\Theta; \Pi; \Gamma \vdash e :_i A$ *then* $\Theta, \Theta'; \Pi, \Pi'; \Gamma, \Gamma' \vdash e :_i A$.
3. *If* $\Theta; \Pi; \Gamma, x :_i A, y :_i A \vdash e :_i B$ *then* $\Theta; \Pi; \Gamma, x :_i A \vdash [x/y]e :_i A$.
4. *If* $\Theta; \Pi, x :_i A, y :_j A; \Gamma \vdash e :_i B$ *and* $i \leq j$ *then* $\Theta; \Pi; \Gamma, x :_i A \vdash [x/y]e :_i A$.

Theorem 1. *(Substitution) We have that:*

1. *If* $\Theta \vdash t :_i R$ *and* $\Theta', u :_i R \vdash t' :_j R'$, *then* $\Theta, \Theta' \vdash [t/u]t' :_j R'$.
2. *If* $\Theta \vdash t :_i R$ *and* $\Theta, u :_i R; \Pi; \Gamma \vdash e :_j A$, *then* $\Theta, \Theta'; \Pi; \Gamma \vdash [t/u]e :_j A$.
3. *If* $\cdot; \Pi; \cdot \vdash e :_i A$ *and* $\Theta; \Pi, x :_j A; \Gamma \vdash e' :_k B$ *and* $i \leq j$, *then* $\Theta; \Pi; \Gamma \vdash [e/x]e' :_k B$.
4. *If* $\cdot; \Pi; \Gamma \vdash e :_i A$ *and* $\Theta; \Pi; \Gamma, x :_i A \vdash e' :_j B$, *then* $\Theta; \Pi; \Gamma \vdash [e/x]e' :_j B$.

Lemma 1 and Theorem 1 can be proved by structural inductions on the type derivations in the respective premises.

Types

General	A	$::=$	$P \mid A \to A \mid S(A) \mid \bullet A$
		$\mid$	$!A \mid R \multimap A$
Resource	R	$::=$	$\Diamond \mid R \otimes R$

Terms

General	e	$::=$	$x \mid \lambda x : A.\ e \mid e\ e' \mid \lambda u : R.\ e \mid e\ t$
		$\mid$	$\mathsf{cons}(t, e, u.\ e') \mid \mathsf{head}(e)$
		$\mid$	$\mathsf{let}\ x = \mathsf{tail}(e)\ \mathsf{in}\ e'$
		$\mid$	$\bullet e \mid \mathsf{let}\ \bullet x = e\ \mathsf{in}\ e'$
		$\mid$	$!e \mid \mathsf{let}\ !x = e\ \mathsf{in}\ e'$
		$\mid$	$\mathsf{let}\ \langle u, v\rangle = t\ \mathsf{in}\ e \mid \mathsf{fix}\ x : A.\ e$
		$\mid$	$\mathsf{let}\ x = e\ \mathsf{in}\ e'$
Resource	t	$::=$	$u \mid \langle t, t'\rangle$
Values	v	$::=$	$\lambda x : A.\ e \mid \lambda u : R.\ e \mid\ !v \mid \bullet e \mid x$

Contexts

General	Γ	$::=$	$\cdot \mid \Gamma, x :_i A$
Pure	Π	$::=$	$\cdot \mid \Pi, x :_i A$
Resource	Θ	$::=$	$\cdot \mid \Theta, u :_i R$

Evaluation Contexts	C	$::=$	$\square \mid \mathsf{let}\ x = \mathsf{tail}(y)\ \mathsf{in}\ C$
		$\mid$	$\mathsf{let}\ x = \mathsf{cons}(u, v, u'.\ e)\ \mathsf{in}\ C$

Figure 2. Syntax

4. Operational Semantics

Theorem 1 formulates the substitution principles so that a general expression e that replaces a variables has to be typed without resource variables. That is, the substitution $[e/x]e'$ is only sound if the substituted term e uses no resource variables. On the other hand, the typing rule for cons cells demands the use of a resource, raising the question: what is the operational semantics of cons cells?

A purely substitution-based operational semantics cannot be correct, because it does not account for the sharing of cons cells. Consider the following expression that is well-typed in our system.

```
let xs = cons(u, ...) in // u is the linear allocation permission
sum (xs, xs) v
```

Here, we construct xs once, but use it twice in the call to sum. We cannot simply substitute the cons into the body of the let in our system, as that would duplicate the linear variable u.

One approach for managing permissions is to introduce a heap for cons cells, and refer to streams indirectly by reference. However, adding a heap moves us away from our functional intuitions and makes it more difficult to connect to our denotational model. Instead, we retain the idea of referring to streams by reference, but use *variables* for the indirect reference, by defining evaluation to put terms into let-normal form, such as:

```
let xs = cons(u1, e1, v1. e1') in
let ys = cons(u2, e2, v2. e2') in
let xs' = tail(xs) in
...
let zs = cons(u3, e3, v2. e3') in
let ys' = tail(ys) in
v
```

Now, the nested let-bindings act as our heap. The value v may contain many references to individual streams (such as xs), but since each stream is bound only once, we can respect the linearity constraint on the allocation permissions u_i. (Taking the tail of streams, as in the definition xs' and ys', also needs to be in let-normal form, since we cannot cut out the tail of a cons cell until

$$\boxed{\Theta \vdash t :_i R} \qquad \boxed{\Theta; \Pi; \Gamma \vdash e :_i A}$$

$$\frac{u :_i R \in \Theta \qquad i \le j}{\Theta \vdash u :_j R}\ \text{RHyp}$$

$$\frac{\Theta \vdash t :_i R \qquad \Theta' \vdash t' :_i R'}{\Theta, \Theta' \vdash \langle t, t'\rangle :_i R \otimes R'}\ \text{R}\otimes\text{I}$$

$$\frac{x :_i A \in \Pi \qquad i \le j}{\Theta; \Pi; \Gamma \vdash x :_j A}\ \text{PHyp} \qquad \frac{x :_i A \in \Gamma}{\Theta; \Pi; \Gamma \vdash x :_i A}\ \text{EHyp}$$

$$\frac{\cdot; \Pi; \Gamma, x :_i A \vdash e :_i B}{\Theta; \Pi; \Gamma \vdash \lambda x : A.\ e :_i A \to B}\ \to\text{I}$$

$$\frac{\Theta; \Pi; \Gamma \vdash e :_i A \to B \qquad \Theta'; \Pi; \Gamma \vdash e' :_i A}{\Theta, \Theta'; \Pi; \Gamma \vdash e\ e' :_i B}\ \to\text{E}$$

$$\frac{u :_i R; \Pi; \Gamma \vdash e :_i A}{\Theta; \Pi; \Gamma \vdash \lambda u : R.\ e :_i R \multimap A}\ \multimap\text{I}$$

$$\frac{\Theta; \Pi; \Gamma \vdash e :_i R \multimap A \qquad \Theta' \vdash t :_i R}{\Theta, \Theta'; \Pi; \Gamma \vdash e\ t :_i A}\ \multimap\text{E}$$

$$\frac{\Theta \vdash t :_i \Diamond \qquad \Theta'; \Pi; \Gamma \vdash e :_i A \qquad \Theta'', u :_{i+1} \Diamond; \Pi; \Gamma \vdash e' :_{i+1} S(A)}{\Theta, \Theta', \Theta''; \Pi; \Gamma \vdash \mathsf{cons}(t, e, u.\ e') :_i S(A)}\ \text{SI}$$

$$\frac{\Theta; \Pi; \Gamma \vdash e :_i S(A)}{\Theta; \Pi; \Gamma \vdash \mathsf{head}(e) :_i A}\ \text{SE-head}$$

$$\frac{\Theta; \Pi; \Gamma \vdash e :_i S(A) \qquad \Theta'; \Pi; \Gamma, y :_{i+1} S(A) \vdash e' :_i B}{\Theta, \Theta'; \Pi; \Gamma \vdash \mathsf{let}\ y = \mathsf{tail}(e)\ \mathsf{in}\ e' :_i B}\ \text{SE-tail}$$

$$\frac{\cdot; \Pi; \Gamma \vdash e :_{i+1} A}{\Theta; \Pi; \Gamma \vdash \bullet e :_i \bullet A}\ \bullet\text{I}$$

$$\frac{\Theta; \Pi; \Gamma \vdash e :_i \bullet A \qquad \Theta'; \Pi; \Gamma, x :_{i+1} A \vdash e' :_i B}{\Theta, \Theta'; \Pi; \Gamma \vdash \mathsf{let}\ \bullet x = e\ \mathsf{in}\ e' :_i B}\ \bullet\text{E}$$

$$\frac{\cdot; \Pi; \cdot \vdash e :_i A}{\Theta; \Pi; \Gamma \vdash\ !e :_i\ !A}\ !\text{I}$$

$$\frac{\Theta; \Pi; \Gamma \vdash e :_i\ !A \qquad \Theta'; \Pi, x :_i A; \Gamma \vdash e' :_i B}{\Theta, \Theta'; \Pi; \Gamma \vdash \mathsf{let}\ !x = e\ \mathsf{in}\ e' :_i B}\ !\text{E}$$

$$\frac{\Theta \vdash t :_i R \otimes S \qquad \Theta', u :_i R, v :_i S; \Pi; \Gamma \vdash e :_i C}{\Theta, \Theta' \vdash \mathsf{let}\ \langle u, v\rangle = t\ \mathsf{in}\ e :_i C}\ \otimes\text{E}$$

$$\frac{\cdot; \Pi, x :_{i+1} A; \cdot \vdash e :_i A}{\Theta; \Pi; \Gamma \vdash \mathsf{fix}\ x : A.\ e :_i A}\ \text{Fix}$$

$$\frac{\Theta; \Pi; \Gamma \vdash e :_i A \qquad \Theta'; \Pi; \Gamma, x :_i A \vdash e' :_i B}{\Theta, \Theta'; \Pi; \Gamma \vdash \mathsf{let}\ x = e\ \mathsf{in}\ e' :_i B}\ \text{Let}$$

Figure 3. Typing Rules

the next tick.) Using bindings to represent sharing will make it easier to continue using our denotational model to interpret the resulting terms. The scoping rules for let-binding also restrict us to a DAG dependency structure, an invariant that imperative reactive programming implementations based on dependency graphs must go to some lengths to implement and maintain.

Let-normalizing cons cells has a second benefit: we can advance the global clock by taking the tails of each cons cell in the context.

```
let xs = [u1/v1]e1' in
let ys = [u2/v2]e2' in
let xs' = xs in
...
let zs = [u3/v3]e3' in
let ys' = ys in
v
```

Since we know where all of the cons cells are, we can rewrite them to model the passage of time. Advancing the clock for tail expressions simply drops the tail. Intuitively, yesterday they promised a tail stream today, and after the step the binding they refer to contains that tail stream.

Our operational semantics has two phases: the within-step operational semantics, which puts an expression into let-normal form, and the step semantics, which advances the clock by one tick by rewriting the cons cells to be their tails.

4.1 Within-Step Operational Semantics

The syntax of values and evaluation contexts is given in Figure 2 and the typing and auxilliary operations are given in Figure 5. We define the reduction relation in Figure 6, in big-step style. We write $\Sigma \rhd_i \Omega_i \vdash C \dashv \Omega_i'$ for the evaluation-context typing judgement. The context Σ is a resource context Θ that consists only of $\Diamond$ hypotheses. Similar, the contexts Ω_i are restricted forms of general contexts Γ consisting only of stream variables at time i or $i+1$. Both are defined in Figure 4. The judgement $\Sigma \rhd_i \Omega_i \vdash C \dashv \Omega_i'$ reads as "the evaluation context C creates the bindings in Ω_i', uses the resources in Σ to do so, and may refer to the bindings in Ω_i".

The context-concatenation operation $C \circ C'$ appends two evaluation contexts C and C'. It is defined in Figure 5 and satisfies the following properties.

Lemma 2. *(Context Concatenation) We have that:*

- *$\circ$ is associative with unit $\Box$.*
- *If $\Sigma \rhd_i \Omega_i \vdash C \dashv \Omega_i'$ and $\Sigma' \rhd_i \Omega_i, \Omega_i' \vdash C' \dashv \Omega_i''$, then $\Sigma, \Sigma' \rhd_i \Omega \vdash C \circ C' \dashv \Omega_i', \Omega_i''$.*
- *If $\Sigma \rhd_i \Omega_i \vdash C_1 \circ C_2 \dashv \Omega_i'$, then there exist Σ_1, Σ_2 and Ω_i^1, Ω_i^2 such that $\Sigma = \Sigma_1, \Sigma_2$ and $\Omega_i' = \Omega_i^1, \Omega_i^2$ and $\Sigma_1 \rhd_i \Omega_i \vdash C_1 \dashv \Omega_i^1$ and $\Sigma_2 \rhd_i \Omega_i, \Omega_i^1 \vdash C_2 \dashv \Omega_i^2$.*

These properties all follow from routine inductions.

In Figure 6, we give the context semantics, evaluating an expression in a context into a value in a larger context. Note that the value forms for streams are variables, since we need to preserve sharing for them, and we can use variable names as pointers into the evaluation context. For most expression forms, the context semantics works as expected; it evaluates each subexpression in context, building a value in a larger context.

The rule CONSE is one of the two rules that extend the context. It evaluates a cons cell, creates a binding to a fresh variable, and returns the fresh variable as the value for that stream. The other rule that extends the context is TAILE. It adds a binding to the context naming the tail it constructs. The rule HEADE, on the other hand, uses the $C@x \Rightarrow v$ relation that is defined in Figure 5 to find the head of the cons cell bound to the variable x.

The rule FIXE looks entirely conventional. We simply unfold the fixed point and continue. We are nevertheless able to prove a normalization result for the within-step operational semantics since the fixed point substitutes for a variable at a future time.

We begin the metatheory with a type preservation proof.

Theorem 2. *(Type Preservation) If we have that*

$$\Sigma \rhd_i \cdot \vdash C \dashv \Omega_i, \quad \Sigma'; \cdot; \Omega_i \vdash e :_i A, \quad \textit{and} \quad C[e] \Downarrow C''[v],$$

then there is an Ω_i' and C' such that

$$C'' = C \circ C', \;\; \Sigma' \rhd_i \Omega_i \vdash C' \dashv \Omega_i', \;\; \textit{and} \;\; \cdot; \cdot; \Omega_i, \Omega_i' \vdash v :_i A.$$

This theorem follows from a routine structural induction.

To show soundness, we will prove termination via a Kripke logical relations argument. Since we evaluate terms e in contexts C, and return a value v in some larger context C', we take our Kripke worlds to be the closed contexts. That is, worlds are those C such that $\Sigma \rhd_i \cdot \vdash C \dashv \Omega_i$. We define the ordering $C' \sqsubseteq C$ on worlds so that there should be some C_1 such that $C' \equiv C \circ C_1$. Thus, a future world is one in which more bindings are available.

In Figure 4, we define the logical relation by induction on types. There is one clause $\mathcal{V}_A(C)$ for each type A, defining a subset of the well-typed expressions of type A, closed save for the variables bound by C. The expression relation $\mathcal{E}_A(\Sigma; C)$ consists of the expressions that use resources in Σ and evaluate to a value in $\mathcal{V}_A(C)$ in the context C.

The definition of the logical relation for streams states that a variable x is in $\mathcal{V}_{S(A)}(C)$ if x binds a cons cell with v in its head, and v is in the A-relation. As expected, the relation for functions consists of lambdas such that in any future world, applying a value in the A-relation should result in a term in the expression relation at type B. In the case of the delay modality we allow any well-typed value, since the within-step evaluation relation does not evaluate any terms at time i, and the body of a delay is at time $i+1$. The $!A$ relation consists of values $!v$ such that v is in the A-relation in the empty world $\Box$, since we want values of type $!A$ to not depend on the stream values C binds. Last, the relation at $R \multimap A$ consists of those lambda-terms $\lambda u : R.\ e$ such that for any resource t of type R in context Σ, the expression $[t/u]e$ is in the expression relation for A with resources Σ.

To prove the fundamental property, we define some auxilliary predicates in Figure 4. The predicate $Good(\Omega_i)$ picks out those contexts in which all of the bindings in Ω_i at time i contain true streams, according to the stream relation. The $\mathcal{V}(\Gamma_{\geq i}; C)$ and $\mathcal{V}!(\Pi_{\geq i})$ sets extend the value relation to substitutions rather than single values, and $\Sigma \vdash \vartheta : \Theta$ defines linear substitutions. The notations $\Pi_{\geq i}$ and $\Gamma_{\geq i}$ mean contexts where every variable is at time i or later. In these substitutions, we only require substitutands for variables at time i to lie in the logical relation, and require only well-typedness for other variables, since within-step evaluation only affects the current tick.

Theorem 3. *(Fundamental Property of Logical Relations) Suppose $\Theta; \Pi_{\geq i}; \Omega_i, \Gamma_{\geq i} \vdash e :_i A$. Furthermore, suppose that $C \in Good(\Omega)$ and $\Sigma \vdash \vartheta : \Theta$ and $\pi \in \mathcal{V}!(\Pi_{\geq i})$ and $\gamma \in \mathcal{V}(\Gamma_{\geq i}; C)$. Then $(\vartheta \circ \pi \circ \gamma)(e) \in \mathcal{E}_A(\Sigma; C)$.*

As is usual for logical relations, this theorem follows from a structural induction on the derivation of $e : A$.

The fundamental property suffices to prove normalization, once we observe that typing derivations satisfy the following history independence property:

Lemma 3. *(History Independence)*

- *If $\Theta; \Pi; \Gamma, x :_i A \vdash e :_j B$ and $i < j$, then $\Theta; \Pi; \Gamma \vdash e :_j B$.*
- *If $\Theta; \Pi, x :_i A; \Gamma \vdash e :_j B$ and $i < j$, then $\Theta; \Pi, x :_j A; \Gamma \vdash e :_j B$.*
- *If $\Theta, u :_i R; \Pi; \Gamma \vdash e :_j B$ and $i < j$, then $\Theta, u :_j R; \Pi; \Gamma \vdash e :_j B$.*

Parameter of the logical relation: i

$$\text{Base Contexts}\quad \begin{array}{rcl} \Sigma & ::= & \cdot \mid \Sigma, u :_0 \Diamond \\ \Omega_i & ::= & \cdot \mid \Omega_i, x :_i S(A) \mid \Omega_i, x :_{i+1} S(A) \end{array}$$

$$\boxed{\mathcal{V}_A(\Sigma \rhd_i \cdot \vdash C \dashv \Omega_i) \subseteq \{v \mid \cdot;\cdot;\Omega_i \vdash v :_i A\}}$$

$$\boxed{\mathcal{E}_A(\Sigma;\Sigma' \rhd_i \cdot \vdash C \dashv \Omega_i) \subseteq \{e \mid \Sigma;\cdot;\Omega_i \vdash e :_i A\}}$$

$$\begin{array}{l}
\mathcal{V}_{S(A)}(C) = \{x \mid \exists v.\ C@x \Rightarrow v \wedge v \in \mathcal{V}_A(C)\} \\
\mathcal{V}_{A \to B}(C) = \\
\quad \{\lambda x : A.\ e \mid \forall C', v \in \mathcal{V}_A(C \circ C').\ [v/x]e \in \mathcal{E}_B(\cdot; C \circ C')\} \\
\mathcal{V}_{\bullet A}(\Sigma \rhd_i \cdot \vdash C \dashv \Omega_i) = \\
\qquad \{\bullet e \mid \cdot;\cdot;\Omega_i \vdash \bullet e :_i \bullet A\} \\
\mathcal{V}_{!A}(C) = \\
\qquad \{!v \mid v \in \mathcal{V}_A(\Box)\} \\
\mathcal{V}_{R \multimap A}(C) = \\
\quad \{\lambda u{:}R.\ e \mid \forall C', \Sigma, t.\ \Sigma \vdash t :_i R \Rightarrow [t/u]e \in \mathcal{E}_A(\Sigma; C \circ C')\}
\end{array}$$

$$\begin{array}{l}
\mathcal{E}_A(\Sigma; C) = \\
\qquad \{e : A \mid \exists C', v.\ C[e] \Downarrow (C \circ C')[v] \wedge v \in \mathcal{V}_A(C \circ C')\}
\end{array}$$

$$Good(\Omega_i) = \{C \mid \forall x :_i S(A) \in \Omega_i.\ x \in \mathcal{V}_{S(A)}(C)\}$$

$$\begin{array}{l}
\mathcal{V}(\cdot; C) = \{\cdot\} \\
\mathcal{V}(\Gamma, x :_i A; C) = \\
\qquad \{(\gamma, [v/x]) \mid \gamma \in \mathcal{V}(\Gamma; C) \wedge v \in \mathcal{V}_A(C)\} \\
\mathcal{V}(\Gamma, x :_{j>i} A; \Sigma \rhd_i \cdot \vdash C \dashv \Omega_i) = \\
\qquad \{(\gamma, [e/x]) \mid \gamma \in \mathcal{V}(\Gamma; C) \wedge \cdot;\cdot;\Omega_i \vdash e :_j A\}
\end{array}$$

$$\begin{array}{l}
\mathcal{V}!(\cdot) = \{\cdot\} \\
\mathcal{V}!(\Pi, x :_i A) = \{(\gamma, [v/x]) \mid \gamma \in \mathcal{V}!(\Gamma) \wedge v \in \mathcal{V}_A(\Box)\} \\
\mathcal{V}!(\Pi, x :_{j>i} A) = \{(\gamma, [e/x]) \mid \gamma \in \mathcal{V}!(\Gamma) \wedge \cdot;\cdot;\cdot \vdash e :_j A\}
\end{array}$$

$$\boxed{\Sigma \vdash \vartheta : \Theta}$$

$$\frac{}{\cdot \vdash \cdot : \cdot} \qquad \frac{\Sigma \vdash t :_i R \qquad \Sigma' \vdash \vartheta : \Theta}{\Sigma, \Sigma' \vdash (\vartheta, [t/u]) : (\Theta, u :_i R)}$$

Figure 4. Logical Relation for Termination

These properties are all proved by structural induction.

The syntax ensures expressions at time $j > i$ do not depend on a variable of time i. As a result, we only need to consider contexts in which Π and Γ contain variables no younger than the current time. Normalization immediately follows:

Corollary 1. *(Normalization) Suppose* $\Sigma;\cdot;\cdot \vdash e :_i A$*. Then* $\Box[e] \Downarrow C[v]$.

Finally note that we are considering normalization of open terms, since we have no constants of type $\Diamond$. The non-existence of such constants is, of course, what ensures that the language respects space bounds.

Theorem 4. *(Space Bounded Evaluation) Suppose* $\Sigma;\cdot;\cdot \vdash e :_i A$ *and* $\Box[e] \Downarrow C[v]$*. Then the size of* C *— the number of cons cells it binds — is bounded by the size of* Σ*.*

Given type preservation, this theorem is straightforward. Each cons cell in the context needs a distinct resource variable, so the number of cons cells in C is clearly bounded by the size of Σ.

4.2 Next-Step Operational Semantics

Recall that when we advance time, we want to replace the tails of stream variables with just the variable. We define the necessary operations in Figure 7. To tick the clock, we define the relation $C[x] \leadsto e$, which takes a stream in context $C[x]$ and constructs a new expression e by cutting the tails of the streams in C, and sending each tail expressions $\mathsf{tail}(y)$ in C to y. This models the effect of advancing time by one tick, so that all the streams in the expression context become their tails, and all references to tails become references to the updated stream variable.

To show the type-correctness of this operation, we introduce the $\mathsf{Step}(\Omega_i)$ operation, which tells us how the typing changes: it sends all streams at time i to time $i+1$ (and leaves streams at time $i+1$ alone). Now, we can prove the following type soundness theorem.

Theorem 5. *(Ticking the Clock) If* $\Sigma;\cdot;\Omega_i \vdash C[x] :_i S(A)$ *and* $C[x] \leadsto e$*, then* $\Sigma;\cdot;\mathsf{Step}(\Omega_i) \vdash e :_{i+1} S(A)$.

This theorem follows from a routine structural induction, and establishes that our semantics is space-bounded. Since Σ is the same before and after the tick from $C[x] \leadsto e$, it follows that evaluating e will never construct more streams than Σ permits. Together with the within-step type preservation property, our clock-ticking theorem gives a (purely syntactic) proof of the space-boundedness of our language.

However, while our definition of advancing the clock is intuitively plausible, and even makes proving memory safety easy, it is still unclear in what sense it is *correct*. To illustrate the issues involved, observe that our language contains lambda-expressions (which may contain free variable references), and that the tick operator essentially imperatively updates stream values. It is important to prove that ticking the clock cannot change the meaning of a lambda-term in a way which violates the purely functional character of functional reactive programming.

To show this, we will first give a denotational semantics of stream programs. Then we will show that if $C[x] \leadsto e$, then the meaning of e does in fact equal the tail of the denotational meaning of $C[x]$, showing that ticking the clock really does advance the clock in the way we expect. This is morally a standard adequacy proof, applied to an unusual operational semantics.

5. Semantic Intuitions

5.1 Causality and Ultrametric Spaces

The intuition underpinning reactive programming is the *stream transformer*, a function which takes a stream of inputs and generates a stream of outputs. But not all functions on streams are implementable reactive programs — in order to be implementable at all, reactive programs must respect the *causality* condition. That is, the first n outputs of a stream function may depend on at most its first n inputs. Writing $\lfloor xs \rfloor_n$ for the n-element prefix of the stream xs, we formalize causality as follows:

Definition 1. *(Causality) A stream function* $f : A^\omega \to B^\omega$ *is* causal, *when for all* n *and all streams* as *and* as'*, we have that if* $\lfloor as \rfloor_n = \lfloor as' \rfloor_n$ *then* $\lfloor f\ as \rfloor_n = \lfloor f\ as' \rfloor_n$.

Furthermore, reactive programs often define streams by feedback. If a stream transformer can produce the first value of its output without looking at its input, then we can constructing a fixed point via feedback, taking the n-th output and supplying it as the input at time $n+1$. So as long as we can generate *more* than n outputs from the first n inputs, we can find a fixed point. Formalizing this gives us a definition of guardedness for defining fixed points:

Definition 2. *(Guardedness) A function* $f : A^\omega \to B^\omega$ *is* guarded, *when there exists* $k > 0$ *such that for all* n *and all streams* as *and* as'*, if* $\lfloor as \rfloor_n = \lfloor as' \rfloor_n$ *then* $\lfloor f\ as \rfloor_{n+k} = \lfloor f\ as' \rfloor_{n+k}$.

$$\boxed{\Sigma \rhd_i \Omega_i \vdash C \dashv \Omega_i'}$$

$$\frac{}{\Sigma \rhd_i \Omega_i \vdash \Box \dashv \Omega_i} \text{ EXTNIL}$$

$$\frac{\cdot;\cdot;\Omega_i \vdash v :_i A \qquad \Sigma', u' :_{i+1} \Diamond; \cdot; \Omega_i \vdash e :_{i+1} S(A) \qquad \Sigma \rhd_i \Omega_i, x :_i S(A) \vdash C \dashv \Omega_i'}{\Sigma, u :_i \Diamond, \Sigma' \rhd_i \Omega_i \vdash \text{let } x = \text{cons}(u, v, u'.\ e) \text{ in } C \dashv \Omega_i', x :_i S(A)} \text{ EXTCONS}$$

$$\frac{y :_i S(A) \in \Omega_i \qquad \Sigma \rhd_i \Omega_i, x :_{i+1} S(A) \vdash C \dashv \Omega_i'}{\Sigma \rhd_i \Omega_i \vdash \text{let } x = \text{tail}(y) \text{ in } C \dashv \Omega_i', x :_{i+1} S(A)} \text{ EXTTAIL}$$

$$\boxed{C \circ C'}$$

$$\begin{array}{l}\Box \circ C' \triangleq C' \\ (\text{let } x = \text{tail}(y) \text{ in } C) \circ C' \triangleq \text{let } x = \text{tail}(y) \text{ in } (C \circ C') \\ (\text{let } x = \text{cons}(u, v, u'.\ e) \text{ in } C) \circ C' \\ \quad \triangleq \text{let } x = \text{cons}(u, v, u'.\ e) \text{ in } (C \circ C')\end{array}$$

$$\boxed{C@x \Rightarrow v}$$

$$\frac{C \equiv C' \circ \text{let } y = \text{tail}(z) \text{ in } \Box \qquad C'@x \Rightarrow v}{C@x \Rightarrow v} \text{ LOOKUPTAIL}$$

$$\frac{C \equiv C' \circ \text{let } y = \text{cons}(u, v', u'.\ e) \text{ in } \Box \qquad C'@x \Rightarrow v}{C@x \Rightarrow v} \text{ LOOKUPNEXT}$$

$$\frac{C \equiv C' \circ \text{let } x = \text{cons}(u, v, u'.\ e) \text{ in } \Box}{C@x \Rightarrow v} \text{ LOOKUPCURR}$$

Figure 5. Context Typing and Operations

$$\boxed{C[e] \Downarrow C'[v]}$$

$$\frac{}{C[v] \Downarrow C[v]} \text{ VALE}$$

$$\frac{C[e] \Downarrow C'[\lambda x : A.\ e''] \qquad C'[e'] \Downarrow C''[v] \qquad C''[[v/x]e''] \Downarrow C'''[v']}{C[e\ e'] \Downarrow C'''[v']} \text{ APPE}$$

$$\frac{C[e] \Downarrow C'[\lambda u : R.\ e'] \qquad C'[[t/u]e'] \Downarrow C''[v]}{C[e\ t] \Downarrow C''[v]} \text{ LAPPE}$$

$$\frac{C[e] \Downarrow C'[v] \qquad x \text{ fresh} \qquad C'' = C' \circ \text{let } x = \text{cons}(t, v, u.\ e') \text{ in } \Box}{C[\text{cons}(t, e, u.\ e')] \Downarrow C''[x]} \text{ CONSE}$$

$$\frac{C[e] \Downarrow C'[x] \qquad C'@x \Rightarrow \text{cons}(t, v, u.\ e)}{C[\text{head}(e)] \Downarrow C'[v]} \text{ HEADE}$$

$$\frac{C[e] \Downarrow C'[y] \qquad (C' \circ \text{let } x = \text{tail}(y) \text{ in } \Box)[e'] \Downarrow C''[v]}{C[\text{let } x = \text{tail}(e) \text{ in } e'] \Downarrow C''[v]} \text{ TAILE}$$

$$\frac{C[e] \Downarrow C'[\bullet e_1] \qquad C'[[e_1/x]e'] \Downarrow C''[v'']}{C[\text{let } \bullet x = e \text{ in } e'] \Downarrow C''[v'']} \bullet\text{E}$$

$$\frac{C[[\text{fix } x : A.\ e/x]e] \Downarrow C'[v]}{C[\text{fix } x : A.\ e] \Downarrow C'[v]} \text{ FIXE}$$

$$\frac{C[e] \Downarrow C'[v] \qquad C'[[v/x]e'] \Downarrow C''[v'']}{C[\text{let } x = e \text{ in } e'] \Downarrow C''[v'']} \text{ LETE}$$

$$\frac{C[[t_1/u, t_2/v]e'] \Downarrow C'[v']}{C[\text{let } \langle u, v \rangle = \langle t_1, t_2 \rangle \text{ in } e'] \Downarrow C'[v']} \otimes\text{E} \qquad \frac{C[e] \Downarrow C'[v]}{C[!e] \Downarrow C'[!v]} \text{ !I}$$

$$\frac{C[e] \Downarrow C'[!v] \qquad C'[[v/x]e'] \Downarrow C''[v'']}{C[\text{let } !x = e \text{ in } e'] \Downarrow C''[v'']} \text{ !E}$$

Figure 6. Within-Step Operational Semantics

However, these definitions apply only to stream functions, and real programs need more types than just the stream type. So we need generalisations of causality which work at other types such as streams of streams and higher-order functions. To generalize these definitions, we follow our earlier work [13] by moving to a category of metric spaces. A *complete 1-bounded bisected ultrametric space* A (which we will simply call "ultrametric space") is a pair $(|A|, d)$, where $|A|$ is a set and $d \in |A| \times |A| \to [0, 1]$ is a distance function satisfying the following properties:

1. $d(x, y) = 0$ iff $x = y$
2. $d(x, y) = d(y, x)$
3. $d(x, z) \leq \max(d(x, y), d(y, z))$
4. $d(x, y) = 0$ or 2^{-n} for some n
5. All Cauchy sequences have limits

We take the morphisms between ultrametric spaces to be the *non-expansive maps* $f : A \to B$. These are the set-theoretic functions $f \in |A| \to |B|$ such that:

For all $a, a' \in |A|$, we have $d_B(f\ a, f\ a') \leq d_A(a, a')$

That is, a morphism between A and B is a function f such that it takes any two points in A to two points in B that are at least as close — it is a non-distance-increasing function.

The category of ultrametric spaces is useful for two reasons. First, the causal stream functions are *exactly* the nonexpansive maps between spaces of streams with the Cantor metric (i.e., the distance between two streams is 2^{-n}, where n is the first position at which they disagree). Since the category of 1-bounded complete ultrametric spaces is Cartesian closed, we have our higher-type generalisation of causality — one which would be very difficult to find from purely operational considerations. Second, nonempty metric spaces satisfy Banach's theorem, which lets us define fixed points at arbitrary types:

Proposition 1. *(Banach's Contraction Map Theorem) If A is a nonempty complete metric space, and $f : A \to A$ is a strictly contractive function, then f has a unique fixed point.*

5.2 Modeling Space Bounds with Length Spaces

As noted earlier, simple casuality still allows undesirable functions. Requiring a stream function to depend only on its history does not prevent it from depending on its *whole* history.

$$\boxed{C[z] \rightsquigarrow e}$$

$$\frac{}{\square[z] \rightsquigarrow x}$$

$$\frac{C[z] \rightsquigarrow e}{\mathsf{let}\ x = \mathsf{tail}(y)\ \mathsf{in}\ C[z] \rightsquigarrow \mathsf{let}\ x = y\ \mathsf{in}\ e}$$

$$\frac{C[z] \rightsquigarrow e}{\mathsf{let}\ x = \mathsf{cons}(u, v, u'.\, e')\ \mathsf{in}\ C[z] \rightsquigarrow \mathsf{let}\ x = [u/u']e'\ \mathsf{in}\ e}$$

$$\boxed{\mathsf{Step}(\Omega_i)}$$

$$\begin{array}{lcl} \mathsf{Step}(\cdot) & = & \cdot \\ \mathsf{Step}(\Omega_i, x :_i S(A)) & = & \mathsf{Step}(\Omega_i), x :_{i+1} S(A) \\ \mathsf{Step}(\Omega_i, x :_{i+1} S(A)) & = & \mathsf{Step}(\Omega_i), x :_{i+1} S(A) \end{array}$$

$$\boxed{\mathsf{Step}_{\Omega_i}(\omega) \in [\![\Omega_i]\!]_i \to [\![\mathsf{Step}(\Omega_i)]\!]_i}$$

$$\begin{array}{lcl} \mathsf{Step}_{\cdot}(\langle\rangle) & = & \langle\rangle \\ \mathsf{Step}_{\Omega_i, x:_i S(A)}(\omega, vs) & = & (\mathsf{Step}_{\Omega_i}(\omega), \mathit{tail}(vs)) \\ \mathsf{Step}_{\Omega_i, x:_{i+1} S(A)}(\omega, vs) & = & (\mathsf{Step}_{\Omega_i}(\omega), vs) \end{array}$$

Figure 7. The Next Step Operator

To deal with this issue, we adapt the *length spaces* of Hofmann [10], which give a model of space-bounded computation. The idea behind this model is to start with a partially ordered resource monoid R representing space resources ($\mathbb{N}$ in the original work). One then constructs the category of length spaces as follows.

A *length space* A is a pair $(|A|, \sigma_A : |A| \to R)$, consisting of a set of elements $|A|$ and a *size function* σ which assigns a size $\sigma_A(a)$ to each element $a \in |A|$. A morphism of length spaces $f : A \to B$ is a *non-size-increasing function*. That is, it is a set-theoretic function $f \in |A| \to |B|$ with the property that:

$$\forall a \in |A|.\ \sigma_B(f\ a) \leq \sigma_A(a)$$

The programming language intuition is that a morphism $A \to B$ is a term of type B with a free variable in A, and so a term cannot use more memory than it receives from its environment.

To model the permission to allocate, we can define a length space of type $\Diamond \triangleq (1, \lambda\langle\rangle.\ 1)$. The space $\Diamond$ is uninteresting computationally (its set only has the unit in it), but it brings a permission to allocate with it. So we can model computations which do allocation by giving them permission elements, thereby controlling the allocation performed.

6. The Denotational Semantics

6.1 The Resource Model

In the synchronous dataflow model, there is a global, ambient notion of time. Furthermore, higher-order reactive programs can create a dataflow graph dynamically, by waiting for an event before choosing to build cons cells to do some computation. So we need a resource structure capable of modelling space usage over time.

Therefore we take resources to be the monoidal lattice $R = (\text{Time} \to \text{Space}, \bot, \max, \top, \min, 0, \oplus, \leq)$, where $\text{Time} = \mathbb{N}$, and $\text{Space} = \mathbb{N} \uplus \{\infty\}$ (the vertical natural numbers with a topmost element). Intuitively, time is discrete, and measured in ticks. Space counts the number of cons cells used in the program, and may be infinite (obviously, we cannot implement such programs). We define the lattice operations as follows:

1. $\bot = \lambda k.\ 0$
2. $\top = \lambda k.\ \infty$
3. $0 = \lambda k.\ 0$
4. $\max(c, d) = \lambda k.\ \max(c_k, d_k)$
5. $\min(c, d) = \lambda k.\ \min(c_k, d_k)$
6. $c \oplus d = \lambda k.\ c_k + d_k$
7. $c \leq d$ iff $\forall k \in \text{Time}$, we have $c_k \leq d_k$

Essentially, we lift the lattice structure of the vertical natural numbers pointwise across time (with $(0, +)$ as the monoidal structure), so that a resource $c \in R$ describes the number of cons cells that are used at each time step.

We then turn R into an ultrametric space by equipping it with the Cantor metric:

$$d_R(c, d) = 2^{-n} \text{ where } n = \min\{k \in \text{Time} \mid c_k \neq d_k\}$$

6.2 The Category of Complete Ultrametric Length Spaces

A *complete 1-bounded bisected ultrametric length space* A (which we will gloss as "metric length space") is a tuple $(|A|, d, \sigma)$, where $(|A|, d)$ is a complete 1-bounded bisected ultrametric space, and $\sigma_A : |A| \to R$ is a size function giving each element of $|A|$ a size drawn from R.

Furthermore, the size function $\sigma : |A| \to R$ must be a nonexpansive map between $(|A|, d)$ and (R, d_R). Nonexpansiveness ensures that we cannot tell if the memory usage requirements of two elements of $|A|$ differs until we know that the elements themselves differ. In addition to being intuitively reasonable, this requirement ensures that limits of Cauchy sequences will be well-behaved with respect to size, which we need to ensure the completeness of the size-0 subspace of A that we use to interpret $!A$.

The morphisms of this category are the *nonexpansive size-preserving maps* $f : A \to B$, which are the set-theoretic functions $f \in |A| \to |B|$ such that:

- For all $a, a' \in |A|$, we have $d_B(f\ a, f\ a') \leq d_A(a, a')$
- For all $a \in |A|$, we have $\sigma_B(f\ a) \leq \sigma_A(a)$

That is, the morphisms we consider are the functions which are both causal and space-bounded.

6.3 Categorical Structure

Metric length spaces and nonexpansive size-preserving maps form a category that we use to interpret our programming language. First, it forms an intuitionistic bicartesian BI category, which is a doubly-closed category with both cartesian and monoidal closed structure, as well as supporting coproduct structure. Second, this category also models the resource types $\Diamond$ of Hofmann [10], as well as a resource-freedom modality $!A$, which is comonadic in the usual fashion of linear logic. Third, it supports a version of the delay modality of our earlier work [13], which lets us interpret guarded recursion via Banach's fixed point theorem.

We give the definitions of all of these objects below. In Figure 9, we define the distance and size functions, and in Figure 8, we give the natural transformations associated with the objects.

- $1 = (\{*\}, d_1, \sigma_1)$
- $A + B = (|A| + |B|, d_{A+B}, \sigma_{A+B})$
- $A \times B = (|A| \times |B|, d_{A\times B}, \sigma_{A\times B})$
- $A \Rightarrow B = (|A| \to |B|, d_{A\to B}, \sigma_{A\to B})$
- $A + B = (|A| + |B|, d_{A+B}, \sigma_{A+B}$

- $A \star B = (|A| \times |B|, d_{A \star B}, \sigma_{A \star B})$
- $A \mathrel{-\!\!\star} B = (|A| \to |B|, d_{A \mathrel{-\!\!\star} B}, \sigma_{A \mathrel{-\!\!\star} B})$
- $\bullet A = (|A|, d_{\bullet A}, \sigma_{\bullet A})$
- $S(A) = (|A|^{\omega}, d_{S(A)}, \sigma_{S(A)})$
- $!A = (\{a \in A \mid \sigma_A(a) = 0\}, \sigma_{!A})$
- $\Diamond = (\{*\}, d_1, \sigma_{\Diamond})$
- $\diamond = (\{*\}, d_1, \sigma_{\diamond})$

The construction of Cartesian and monoidal products closely follows that of Hofmann [10]. The Cartesian product is a "sharing product", in which the associated resources are available to both components (this explains the use of max), and the monoidal product is a "disjoint product", in which the resources are divided between the two components (explaining the use of $\oplus$ in the size function). The best intuition for the closed structure comes from implementing first-class functions as closures: the monoidal exponential $A \mathrel{-\!\!\star} B$ takes an argument which does not share with the captured environment, and the Cartesian exponential $A \Rightarrow B$ which does.

A difference between our work and earlier work on length spaces is our heavy use of the category's Cartesian closed structure. Indeed, dal Lago and Hofmann [15] use a realizability model to remove the Cartesian closed structure from their semantics — they wished to prevent duplicated variables in lambda-terms from enabling large increases in the size of a lambda-term under reduction, since this makes establishing strict resource bounds more difficult. As we only want to track the allocation of cells, but wish to allow free sharing otherwise, the CCC structure takes on a central role in our model.

Our next-step modality's metric $d_{\bullet A}$ is the same as in Krishnaswami and Benton [13], but the size function $\sigma_{\bullet A}$ (which shifts all sizes 1 timestep into the future relative to σ_A), means that $\bullet(A \to B) \not\simeq \bullet A \to \bullet B$. This breaks with Krishnaswami and Benton [13] and Nakano [18], significantly changing the elimination rules.

As mentioned earlier, this limitation is intentional: we do not want delay operators at types for which delay would be expensive. Our semantics rules out such maps with the size function for streams plus the requirement that morphisms are non-size-increasing. The size function for streams gives a size for the stream as 1 to account for the size of the stream itself, plus the maximum space usage of all the values the stream takes on. Intuitively, a stream can seen as taking the space for an infinitary Cartesian product $A \times \bullet A \times \bullet^2 A \times \ldots$, plus a constant for the stream cell itself. This is the only place where we increment the size of a value relative to its components, which justifies the idea that sizes measure the number of cons cells. Since delaying a stream shifts its time usage by one step, we have no *a priori* reason to expect that a delay map will exist at all types.

However, for types such as $\mathbb{N}$, $!A$, and $\Diamond$, there do exist maps $A \to \bullet A$, which is why time subsumption is justified for the linear and pure contexts. Furthermore, all types whose values are all of size zero have maps $A \to !A$. As a result, we can introduce constants corresponding to such maps for these types, allowing types such as numbers and booleans be promoted to the pure fragment. (In fact, our implementation applies these coercions implicitly, providing a slightly friendlier syntax than presented here.)

Our semantic model contains a space $\Diamond$ to interpret the resource type $\Diamond$, which gives 1 unit of space at every time tick. Our model uses the additional metric length space $\diamond$, which gives 1 unit of space at time 0, and no units of space at any other time. This lets us give a nice type to *cons* : $\diamond \star (A \times \bullet S(A)) \to S(A)$. Note that the type $A \times \bullet S(A)$ lacks the space to form a stream — we need 1 unit of space at time 0, which neither the A nor the $\bullet S(A)$ provide.

1	$: A \to I$	$=$	$\lambda a.\ *$
π_1	$: A \times B \to A$	$=$	$\lambda(a,b).\ a$
π_2	$: A \times B \to B$	$=$	$\lambda(a,b).\ b$
$\langle f, g\rangle$	$: A \to B \times C$	$=$	$\lambda a.\ (f\ a, g\ a)$
	where $f : A \to B, g : A \to C$		
$\lambda\langle f\rangle$	$: A \to B \Rightarrow C$	$=$	$\lambda a.\ \lambda b.\ f(a,b)$
	where $f : A \times B \to C$		
eval	$: (A \Rightarrow B) \times A \to B$	$=$	$\lambda(f,a).\ f\ a$
$f \star g$	$: A \star B \to C \star D$	$=$	$\lambda(a,b).\ (f\ a, g\ b)$
	where $f : A \to C, g : B \to D$		
α	$: (A \star B) \star C \to A \star (B \star C)$	$=$	$\lambda((a,b),c).(a,(b,c))$
α^{-1}	$: A \star (B \star C) \to (A \star B) \star C$	$=$	$\lambda(a,(b,c)).((a,b),c)$
γ	$: A \star B \to B \star A$	$=$	$\lambda(a,b).\ (b,a)$
ρ	$: A \star I \to A$	$=$	$\lambda(a,*).\ a$
ρ^{-1}	$: A \star I \to A$	$=$	$\lambda a.\ (a,*)$
$\hat{\lambda}\langle f\rangle$	$: A \to B \mathrel{-\!\!\star} C$	$=$	$\lambda a.\ \lambda b.\ f(a,b)$
	where $f : A \star B \to C$		
$eval_{\mathrel{-\!\!\star}}$	$: (A \mathrel{-\!\!\star} B) \star A \to B$	$=$	$\lambda(f,a).\ f\ a$
ϵ	$: !A \to A$	$=$	$\lambda a.\ a$
$f^{\dagger}$	$: !A \to !B$	$=$	$\lambda a.\ f\ a$
	where $f : !A \to B$		
$!f$	$: !A \to !B$	$=$	$\lambda a.\ f\ a$
	where $f : A \to B$		
δ	$: !A \to \bullet !A$	$=$	$\lambda a.\ a$
$\bullet f$	$: \bullet A \to \bullet B$	$=$	$\lambda a.\ f\ a$
	where $f : A \to B$		
η	$: !\bullet A \to \bullet !A$	$=$	$\lambda a.\ a$
η^{-1}	$: \bullet !A \to \bullet A$	$=$	$\lambda a.\ a$
head	$: S(A) \to A$	$=$	$\lambda(x \cdot xs).\ x$
tail	$: S(A) \to \bullet S(A)$	$=$	$\lambda(x \cdot xs).\ xs$
cons	$: \diamond \star (A \times \bullet S(A)) \to S(A)$	$=$	$\lambda(*,(x,xs)).\ x \cdot xs$
split	$: \Diamond \to \diamond \star \bullet \Diamond$	$=$	$\lambda *.\ (*,*)$
$split^{-1}$	$: \diamond \star \bullet \Diamond \to \Diamond$	$=$	$\lambda(*,*).\ *$
fix	$: !(\bullet !A \Rightarrow !A) \to !A$	$=$	$\lambda f.\ \mu(f)$
ι	$: \bullet A \times \bullet B \to \bullet(A \times B)$	$=$	$\lambda(a,b).\ (a,b)$
ι^{-1}	$: \bullet(A \times B) \to \bullet A \times \bullet B$	$=$	$\lambda(a,b).\ (a,b)$
$\iota_{\star}$	$: \bullet A \star \bullet B \to \bullet(A \star B)$	$=$	$\lambda(a,b).\ (a,b)$
$\iota_{\star}^{-1}$	$: \bullet(A \star B) \to \bullet A \star \bullet B$	$=$	$\lambda(a,b).\ (a,b)$
ξ	$: A \star B \to A \times B$	$=$	$\lambda(a,b).\ (a,b)$
σ	$: A \times !B \to A \star !B$	$=$	$\lambda(a,b).\ (a,b)$
ψ	$: !(A \times B) \to !A \star !B$	$=$	$\lambda(a,b).\ (a,b)$
ψ^{-1}	$: !A \star !B \to !(A \times B)$	$=$	$\lambda(a,b).\ (a,b)$

Figure 8. Categorical Combinators

6.4 Denotational Interpretation

We give the interpretation of types and contexts in Figure 10. The interpretation of types offers no surprises, but the interpretation of contexts is relative to the current time. The interpretations of Θ and Δ keeps hypotheses at times earlier than the current time, but Γ simply drops all earlier hypotheses. This corresponds to the difference between the type rules RHYP and PHYP on the one hand, and the rule EHYP on the other. In all three cases, future hypotheses are interpreted with the delay modality.

In Figure 11, we give a time-indexed interpretation function for expressions, $[\![\Theta;\Pi;\Gamma \vdash e :_i A]\!]_i$ which has the type $[\![\Theta]\!]_i \star ![\![\Pi]\!]_i \star [\![\Gamma]\!]_i \to [\![A]\!]$. The interpretation of $\bullet$I makes use of the functoriality of $\bullet A$ to interpret the body of the delay in the future, and then bring it back to the past, with the necessary action on contexts defined in Figure 10. The other rules are as expected, with the resource context managed in a single-threaded way and the other contexts duplicated freely. We can then show that this semantics is sound with respect to substitution.

$$
\begin{array}{lcl}
d_{A+B} & = & \lambda(v, v').\left\{\begin{array}{ll} d_A(x, x') & \text{if } v = \mathsf{inl}\ x \wedge v' = \mathsf{inl}\ x' \\ d_B(y, y') & \text{if } v = \mathsf{inr}\ y \wedge v' = \mathsf{inr}\ y' \\ 1 & \text{otherwise} \end{array}\right. \\
d_1 & = & \lambda(\langle\rangle, \langle\rangle).\ 0 \\
d_{A\times B} & = & \lambda((a,b),(a',b')).\ \max(d_A(a,a'), d_B(b,b')) \\
d_{A\star B} & = & \lambda((a,b),(a',b')).\ \max(d_A(a,a'), d_B(b,b')) \\
d_{A\Rightarrow B} & = & \lambda(f,g).\ \max\{d_B(f\ a, g\ a) \mid a \in |A|\} \\
d_{A\multimap B} & = & \lambda(f,g).\ \max\{d_B(f\ a, g\ a) \mid a \in |A|\} \\
d_{\bullet A} & = & \lambda(a,a').\ \frac{1}{2} d_A(a,a') \\
d_{S(A)} & = & \lambda(xs, ys).\ \max\{2^{-n} \cdot d_A(xs_n, ys_n) \mid n \in \mathbb{N}\} \\
d_{!A} & = & \lambda(a,a').\ d_A(a,a') \\
d_{\Diamond} & = & \lambda(\langle\rangle, \langle\rangle).\ 0 \\
d_{\diamond} & = & \lambda(\langle\rangle, \langle\rangle).\ 0
\end{array}
$$

$$
\begin{array}{lcl}
\sigma_{A+B} & = & \lambda v.\left\{\begin{array}{ll} \sigma_A(a) & \text{if } v = \mathsf{inl}\ a \\ \sigma_B(b) & \text{if } v = \mathsf{inr}\ b \end{array}\right. \\
\sigma_1 & = & \lambda\langle\rangle.\ 0 \\
\sigma_{A\times B} & = & \lambda(a,b).\ \max(\sigma_A(a), \sigma_B(b)) \\
\sigma_{A\star B} & = & \lambda(a,b).\ \sigma_A(a) \oplus \sigma_B(b) \\
\sigma_{A\Rightarrow B} & = & \lambda f.\ \min\{k \in R \mid \forall a \in |A|.\ \sigma_B(f\ a) \le \max(k, \sigma_A(a))\} \\
\sigma_{A\multimap B} & = & \lambda f.\ \min\{k \in R \mid \forall a \in |A|.\ \sigma_B(f\ a) \le k \oplus \sigma_A(a)\} \\
\sigma_{\bullet A} & = & \bullet\sigma_A \\
\sigma_{S(A)} & = & \lambda xs.\ \lambda k.\ 1 \oplus \max\{(\bullet^i \sigma_A)(xs_i) \mid i \in \text{Time}\} \\
\sigma_{\Diamond} & = & \lambda\langle\rangle.\ \lambda k.\ 1 \\
\sigma_{\diamond} & = & \lambda\langle\rangle.\ \lambda k.\ \text{if } k = 0 \text{ then } 1 \text{ else } 0 \\
\sigma_{!A} & = & \lambda a.\ 0 \\
\bullet\sigma & = & \lambda a.\ \lambda k.\ \text{if } k = 0 \text{ then } 0 \text{ else } \sigma(a)(k-1)
\end{array}
$$

Figure 9. The Distance and Size Functions

Theorem 6. *(Semantic Substitution) Suppose* $\theta \in [\![\Theta]\!]_i$, $\theta' \in [\![\Theta']\!]_i$, $\pi \in [\![\Pi]\!]_i$ *and* $\gamma \in [\![\Gamma]\!]_i$. *Then*

1. *If* $\Theta \vdash t :_i R$ *and* $\Theta', u :_i R \vdash t' :_j R'$, *then* $[\![\Theta, \Theta' \vdash [t/u]t' :_j R']\!]\ (\theta, \theta')$ *is equal to* $[\![\Theta', u :_i R \vdash t' :_j R']\!]\ (\theta', [\![\Theta \vdash t :_i R]\!]\ \theta)$.
2. *If* $\Theta \vdash t :_i R$ *and* $\Theta', u :_i R; \Pi; \Gamma \vdash e :_j A$, *then* $[\![\Theta, \Theta'; \Pi; \Gamma \vdash [t/u]e :_j A]\!]\ ((\theta, \theta'), \pi, \gamma)$ *equals* $[\![\Theta', u :_i R; \Pi; \Gamma \vdash e :_j A]\!]\ ((\theta', [\![\Theta \vdash t :_i R]\!]\ \theta), \pi, \gamma)$
3. *If* $\cdot; \Pi; \cdot \vdash e :_i A$ *and* $\Theta; \Pi, x :_j A; \Gamma \vdash e' :_k B$ *and* $i \le j$, *then* $[\![\Theta; \Pi; \Gamma \vdash [e/x]e' :_k B]\!]\ (\theta, \pi, \gamma)$ *equals* $[\![\Theta; \Pi, x :_j A; \Gamma \vdash e' :_k B]\!]\ (\theta, (\pi, [\![\cdot; \Pi; \cdot \vdash e :_i A]\!]\ (\langle\rangle, \pi, \langle\rangle)), \gamma)$
4. *If* $\cdot; \Pi; \Gamma \vdash e :_i A$ *and* $\Theta; \Pi; \Gamma, x :_i A \vdash e' :_j B$, *then* $\Theta; \Pi; \Gamma \vdash [e/x]e' :_j B$ *equals* $[\![\Theta; \Pi; \Gamma, x :_i A \vdash e' :_j B]\!]\ (\theta, \pi, (\gamma, [\![\cdot; \Pi; \Gamma \vdash e :_i A]\!]\ (\langle\rangle, \pi, \gamma)))$

These theorems follow from structural induction on the typing derivation of the term being substituted into.

Figure 12, gives the interpretation of contexts, using the expression semantics to define the meaning of each stream bound by the context. This interpretation is sound with respect to the "hole-filling" of terms in contexts:

Theorem 7. *(Context Soundness) If* $\Sigma \rhd_i \Omega_i \vdash C \dashv \Omega'_i$ *and* $\Sigma'; \cdot; \Omega_i, \Omega'_i \vdash e :_i A$ *and* $\sigma \in [\![\Sigma]\!]_i$ *and* $\sigma' \in [\![\Sigma']\!]_i$ *and* $\omega \in [\![\Omega_i]\!]_i$, *then* $[\![\Sigma, \Sigma'; \cdot; \Omega_i \vdash C[e] :_i A]\!]\ ((\sigma, \sigma'), \omega)$ *is equal to* $[\![\Sigma'; \cdot; \Omega_i, \Omega'_i \vdash e :_i A]\!]\ (\sigma', \langle\rangle, (\omega, [\![\Sigma \rhd_i \Omega_i \vdash C \dashv \Omega'_i]\!]\ (\sigma, \omega))$.

Now we can show that the within-step operational semantics is sound with respect to the denotational model:

Theorem 8. *(Soundness of Within-Step Semantics) Let* $\Sigma; \cdot; \cdot \vdash C[e] :_i A$ *and* $C[e] \Downarrow C'[v]$. *Then* $[\![\Sigma; \cdot; \cdot \vdash C[e] :_i A]\!]$ *equals* $[\![\Sigma; \cdot; \cdot \vdash C'[v] :_i A]\!]$.

Finally, we can show that advancing the clock has the expected semantics:

Theorem 9. *(Soundness of Advancing the Clock) Let* $\Sigma; \cdot; \Omega_i \vdash C[x] :_i S(A)$, *and* $\sigma \in [\![\Sigma]\!]_i$ *and* $\omega \in [\![\Omega_i]\!]_i$, *and suppose* $C[x] \leadsto e$. *Then we have that*

$$\mathsf{tail}([\![\Sigma; \cdot; \Omega_i \vdash C[x] :_i S(A)]\!]\ (\sigma, \langle\rangle, \omega))$$

is equal to $\bullet[\![\Sigma; \cdot; \mathsf{Step}(\Omega_i) \vdash e :_{i+1} S(A)]\!](\sigma', \langle\rangle, \omega'))$ *where* $\sigma' = \mathrm{Next}^i_\Sigma\ \sigma$ *and* $\omega' = \mathsf{Step}_{\Omega_i}(\omega)$.

This theorem connects the operation of stepping the heap with the denotational interpretation — each time we advance the clock, each stream in a closed context C will become its tail. So advancing the clock successively enumerates the elements of the stream.

7. Discussion

In this paper, we have introduced an expressive type system for writing stream programs, and given an operational semantics respecting the space-efficiency claims of the type system. Our semantic model is one of the primary contributions of this paper, since it lets us reason about space usage without surrendering the sets-and-functions view of FRP. Also, our model contains many operations which are not currently expressible in our language: for example, in the future we might want richer types in the affine context and function space, so that operations like in-place map can be typed $!(A \to B) \to S(A) \multimap\star S(B)$.

Our language contains an explicit delay modality (as in logical presentations of step-indexing [2, 7, 18]) and an update-based operational semantics. The reader may find it surprising that, although our operational semantics does make use of a form of mutable higher-order store, the logical relation we give is not step-indexed. The reason this is possible is essentially that FRP is a *synchronous* model of computation, in which all the updates happen in a separate phase from ordinary functional evaluation. This explains why we were able to present a two-phase semantics, and since no heap modifications take place during ticks, there is no need for step-indexing.

Wan et al. [25] introduced real-time FRP; a restricted subset of FRP sharing many of the same design choices of synchronous dataflow languages. It is essentially first-order (streams can carry general values of the host language, but these values can not themselves refer to streams), and makes use of a novel continuation typing to ensure that all recursive signals are tail-recursive. As a result, the language requires only constant-stack and constant-time FRP reductions. Event-driven FRP [26] is similar, but relaxes FRP's timing constraints by dropping the global clock.

None of our examples using higher-order functions or nested streams can be programmed in real-time FRP, which is carefully engineered to avoid exposing a first-class behaviour type, and so cannot express higher-order operations on streams. All productive real-time FRP programs can be written in our language, since we can define all of real-time FRP's stream operators (switching, delays, multimodal recursion) as ordinary user-level programs.

Liu et al.'s causal commutative arrows [17] are another attempt to control the memory and space usage of reactive programs. This work takes advantage of the fact that pure arrowized FRP (i.e., without switching) builds fixed dataflow graphs, allowing programs to be optimized into single-loop code via a transformation reminiscent of the Bohm-Jacopini theorem. Our language does not seem to support such an elegant normal form, because of the presence

$$
\begin{array}{lcl}
\llbracket A \to B \rrbracket & = & \llbracket A \rrbracket \Rightarrow \llbracket B \rrbracket \\
\llbracket S(A) \rrbracket & = & S(\llbracket A \rrbracket) \\
\llbracket \bullet A \rrbracket & = & \bullet \llbracket A \rrbracket \\
\llbracket !A \rrbracket & = & !\llbracket A \rrbracket \\
\llbracket R \multimap A \rrbracket & = & \llbracket R \rrbracket \multimap\!\star \llbracket A \rrbracket \\
\llbracket \Diamond \rrbracket & = & \Diamond \\
\llbracket R \otimes S \rrbracket & = & \llbracket R \rrbracket \star \llbracket S \rrbracket
\end{array}
$$

$$\boxed{\llbracket \Theta \rrbracket_i} \qquad \boxed{\llbracket \Pi \rrbracket_i} \qquad \boxed{\llbracket \Gamma \rrbracket_i}$$

$$
\begin{array}{lcll}
\llbracket \Theta \rrbracket_i & \in & \mathrm{Obj} & \\
\llbracket \cdot \rrbracket_i & = & I & \\
\llbracket \Theta, x :_n R \rrbracket_i & = & \llbracket \Theta \rrbracket_i \star \bullet^{n-i} \llbracket R \rrbracket & \text{when } n \geq i \\
\llbracket \Theta, x :_n R \rrbracket_i & = & \llbracket \Theta \rrbracket_i \star \llbracket R \rrbracket & \text{when } n < i
\end{array}
$$

$$
\begin{array}{lcll}
\llbracket \Pi \rrbracket_i & \in & \mathrm{Obj} & \\
\llbracket \cdot \rrbracket_i & = & I & \\
\llbracket \Pi, x :_n A \rrbracket_i & = & \llbracket \Pi \rrbracket_i \times \bullet^{n-i} \llbracket A \rrbracket & \text{when } n \geq i \\
\llbracket \Pi, x :_n A \rrbracket_i & = & \llbracket \Pi \rrbracket_i \times \llbracket A \rrbracket & \text{when } n < i
\end{array}
$$

$$
\begin{array}{lcll}
\llbracket \Gamma \rrbracket_i & \in & \mathrm{Obj} & \\
\llbracket \cdot \rrbracket_i & = & I & \\
\llbracket \Gamma, x :_n A \rrbracket_i & = & \llbracket \Gamma \rrbracket_i \times \bullet^{n-i} \llbracket A \rrbracket & \text{when } n \geq i \\
\llbracket \Gamma, x :_n A \rrbracket_i & = & \llbracket \Gamma \rrbracket_i & \text{when } n < i
\end{array}
$$

$$\boxed{\mathrm{Next}^i_\Theta \in \llbracket \Theta \rrbracket_i \to \bullet \llbracket \Theta \rrbracket_{i+1}} \qquad \boxed{\mathrm{Next}^i_\Pi \in \llbracket \Pi \rrbracket_i \to \bullet \llbracket \Pi \rrbracket_{i+1}}$$

$$\boxed{\mathrm{Next}^i_\Gamma \in \llbracket \Gamma \rrbracket_i \to \bullet \llbracket \Gamma \rrbracket_{i+1}}$$

$$
\begin{array}{lcll}
\mathrm{Next}^i_\cdot \ \langle\rangle & = & \langle\rangle & \\
\mathrm{Next}^i_{\Theta, x:_n R}\ (\theta, r) & = & (\mathrm{Next}^i_\Theta\ \theta, \delta(r)) & \text{if } n \leq i \\
\mathrm{Next}^i_{\Theta, x:_n R}\ (\theta, r) & = & (\mathrm{Next}^i_\Theta\ \theta, r) & \text{if } n > i
\end{array}
$$

$$
\begin{array}{lcll}
\mathrm{Next}^i_\cdot \ \langle\rangle & = & \langle\rangle & \\
\mathrm{Next}^i_{\Pi, x:_n A}(\pi, v) & = & (\mathrm{Next}^i_\Pi\ \pi, \delta(v)) & \text{if } n \leq i \\
\mathrm{Next}^i_{\Pi, x:_n A}(\pi, v) & = & (\mathrm{Next}^i_\Pi\ \pi, v) & \text{if } n > i
\end{array}
$$

$$
\begin{array}{lcll}
\mathrm{Next}^i_\cdot \ \langle\rangle & = & \langle\rangle & \\
\mathrm{Next}^i_{\Gamma, x:_n A}(\gamma, v) & = & \mathrm{Next}^i_\Gamma & \text{if } n \leq i \\
\mathrm{Next}^i_{\Gamma, x:_n A}(\gamma, v) & = & (\mathrm{Next}^i_\Gamma\ \gamma, v) & \text{if } n > i
\end{array}
$$

Figure 10. Interpretation of Types and Contexts

of higher-order streams and functions, but it would nonetheless be interesting to investigate related optimizations in our setting.

Sculthorpe and Nilsson's work [22] on safe functional programming uses Agda's types to ensure productivity, by having dependent types track whether signal processors have delays before permitting feedback. Our guardedness modality is simpler but less flexible, since it cannot depend on the *values* a signal produces. However, the advantage of our modality is that it works smoothly at higher-order.

Cooper and Krishnamurthi [6] described the FrTime system, which embeds FRP into the PLT Scheme (now Racket) implementation. One commonality between FrTime and our work is that switching does not come from special primitives, but from ordinary conditionals and case statements. Unlike our denotational model, Cooper's operational semantics [5] exemplifies the "imperative FRP" tradition, in which reactivity is modelled explicitly as

$$\boxed{\llbracket \Theta \vdash t :_i R \rrbracket_i \in \llbracket \Theta \rrbracket_i \to \llbracket R \rrbracket}$$

$$\boxed{\llbracket \Theta; \Pi; \Gamma \vdash e :_i A \rrbracket_i \in \llbracket \Theta \rrbracket_i \star ! \llbracket \Pi \rrbracket_i \star \llbracket \Gamma \rrbracket_i \to \llbracket A \rrbracket}$$

$$\llbracket \Theta \vdash u :_j R \rrbracket_i\ \theta = \theta(u)$$
$$\llbracket \Theta, \Theta' \vdash (t, t') :_j R \otimes S \rrbracket_i\ (\theta, \theta') = (\llbracket t \rrbracket\ \theta, \llbracket t' \rrbracket\ \theta')$$

$$\llbracket \Theta; \Pi; \Gamma \vdash x :_j A \rrbracket_i\ (\theta, \pi, \gamma) = \pi(x) \quad (\text{if } x :_i A \in \Pi)$$

$$\llbracket \Theta; \Pi; \Gamma \vdash x :_i A \rrbracket_i\ (\theta, \pi, \gamma) = \gamma(x) \quad (\text{if } x :_i A \in \Gamma)$$

$$
\begin{array}{l}
\llbracket \Theta; \Pi; \Gamma \vdash \lambda x : A.\ e :_i A \to B \rrbracket_i\ (\theta, \pi, \gamma) = \\
\quad \lambda v.\ \llbracket \cdot; \Pi; \Gamma, x :_i A \vdash e :_i B \rrbracket_i\ (\langle\rangle, \pi, (\gamma, v))
\end{array}
$$

$$
\begin{array}{l}
\llbracket \Theta, \Theta'; \Pi; \Gamma \vdash e\ e' :_i B \rrbracket_i\ ((\theta, \theta'), \pi, \gamma) = \\
\quad \text{let } f = \llbracket e : A \to B \rrbracket_i\ (\theta, \pi, \gamma) \text{ in} \\
\quad \text{let } v = \llbracket e' : A \rrbracket_i\ (\theta', \pi, \gamma) \text{ in} \\
\quad \mathit{eval}(f, v)
\end{array}
$$

$$\llbracket \Theta; \Pi; \Gamma \vdash !e :_i !A \rrbracket_i\ (\theta, \pi, \gamma) = \llbracket \cdot; \Pi; \cdot \vdash e :_i A \rrbracket_i^\dagger\ (\langle\rangle, \pi, \langle\rangle)$$

$$
\begin{array}{l}
\llbracket \Theta, \Theta'; \Pi; \Gamma \vdash \mathsf{let}\ !x = e\ \mathsf{in}\ e' :_i B \rrbracket_i\ (\theta, \pi, \gamma) = \\
\quad \llbracket e' \rrbracket_i\ (\theta', \psi^{-1}(\pi, \llbracket e \rrbracket_i\ (\theta', \pi, \gamma)), \gamma)
\end{array}
$$

$$
\begin{array}{l}
\llbracket \Theta, \Theta', \Theta''; \Pi; \Gamma \vdash \mathsf{cons}(t, e, u'.e') :_i S(A) \rrbracket_i\ ((\theta, \theta', \theta''), \pi, \gamma) = \\
\quad \text{let } (d, r) = \mathit{split}(\llbracket t \rrbracket_i\ \theta) \text{ in} \\
\quad \text{let } h = \llbracket e \rrbracket_i\ (\theta', \pi, \gamma) \text{ in} \\
\quad \text{let } t = \bullet \llbracket e' \rrbracket_{i+1}\ ((\mathrm{Next}^i_{\Theta''}\ \theta'', r), \mathrm{Next}^i_\Pi\ \pi, \mathrm{Next}^i_\Gamma\ \gamma) \text{ in} \\
\quad \mathit{cons}(d, (h, t))
\end{array}
$$

$$
\begin{array}{l}
\llbracket \Theta; \Pi; \Gamma \vdash \mathsf{head}(e) :_i A \rrbracket_i\ (\theta, \pi, \gamma) = \\
\quad \mathit{head}(\llbracket \Theta; \Pi; \Gamma \vdash e :_i S(A) \rrbracket_i\ (\theta, \pi, \gamma))
\end{array}
$$

$$
\begin{array}{l}
\llbracket \Theta, \Theta'; \Pi; \Gamma \vdash \mathsf{let}\ x = \mathsf{tail}(e)\ \mathsf{in}\ e' :_i B \rrbracket_i\ ((\theta, \theta'), \pi, \gamma) = \\
\quad \text{let } vs = \llbracket \Theta \rrbracket_i \Pi \Gamma e S(A) i \text{ in } (\theta, \pi, \gamma) \\
\quad \llbracket \Theta'; \Pi; \Gamma, x :_{i+1} S(A) \vdash e' :_i B \rrbracket_i\ (\theta', \pi, (\gamma, \mathit{tail}(vs)))
\end{array}
$$

$$
\begin{array}{l}
\llbracket \Theta; \Pi; \Gamma \vdash \bullet e :_i \bullet A \rrbracket_i\ (\theta, \pi, \gamma) = \\
\quad \bullet \llbracket \cdot; \Pi; \Gamma \vdash e :_{i+1} A \rrbracket_{i+1}\ (\langle\rangle, \mathrm{Next}^i_\Pi\ \pi, \mathrm{Next}^i_\Gamma\ \gamma)
\end{array}
$$

$$
\begin{array}{l}
\llbracket \Theta, \Theta'; \Pi; \Gamma \vdash \mathsf{let}\ \bullet x = e\ \mathsf{in}\ e' :_i B \rrbracket_i\ ((\theta, \theta'), \pi, \gamma) = \\
\quad \text{let } v = \llbracket \Theta; \Pi; \Gamma \vdash e :_i \bullet A \rrbracket_i\ (\theta, \pi, \gamma) \text{ in} \\
\quad \llbracket \Theta'; \Pi; \Gamma, x :_{i+1} A \vdash e' :_i B \rrbracket_i\ (\theta', \pi, (\gamma, v))
\end{array}
$$

$$
\begin{array}{l}
\llbracket \Theta; \Pi; \Gamma \vdash \lambda u : R.\ e :_i R \multimap A \rrbracket_i\ (\theta, \pi, \gamma) = \\
\quad \lambda r.\ \llbracket u :_i R; \Pi; \Gamma \vdash e :_i A \rrbracket\ (r, \pi, \gamma)
\end{array}
$$

$$
\begin{array}{l}
\llbracket \Theta, \Theta'; \Pi; \Gamma \vdash e\ t :_i A \rrbracket_i\ ((\theta, \theta'), \pi, \gamma) = \\
\quad \mathit{eval}_{\multimap\star}(\llbracket e \rrbracket\ (\theta, \pi, \gamma), \llbracket t \rrbracket\ \theta')
\end{array}
$$

$$
\begin{array}{l}
\llbracket \Theta, \Theta'; \Pi; \Gamma \vdash \mathsf{let}\ (u, v) = t\ \mathsf{in}\ e :_i A \rrbracket_i\ ((\theta, \theta'), \pi, \gamma) = \\
\quad \text{let } (r, s) = \llbracket \Theta \vdash t :_i R \otimes S \rrbracket\ \theta \text{ in} \\
\quad \llbracket \Theta', u :_i R, v :_i S; \Pi; \Gamma \vdash e :_i A \rrbracket\ ((\theta', r, s), \pi, \gamma)
\end{array}
$$

$$
\begin{array}{l}
\llbracket \Theta; \Pi; \Gamma \vdash \mathsf{fix}\ x : A.\ e :_i A \rrbracket_i\ (\theta, \pi, \gamma) = \\
\quad \text{let } f = \lambda v. \left(\begin{array}{l} \text{let } \pi' = \psi^{-1}(\pi, \eta^{-1}\ v) \text{ in} \\ \llbracket \cdot; \Pi, x :_{i+1} A; \cdot \vdash e :_i A \rrbracket_i\ (\langle\rangle, \pi', \langle\rangle) \end{array} \right) \text{ in} \\
\quad \mathit{fix}(f)
\end{array}
$$

$$
\begin{array}{l}
\llbracket \Theta, \Theta'; \Pi; \Gamma \vdash \mathsf{let}\ x = e\ \mathsf{in}\ e' :_i B \rrbracket_i\ ((\theta, \theta'), \pi, \gamma) = \\
\quad \text{let } v = \llbracket \Theta; \Pi; \Gamma \vdash e :_i A \rrbracket_i\ (\theta, \pi, \gamma) \text{ in} \\
\quad \llbracket \Theta'; \Pi; \Gamma, x :_i A \vdash e' :_i B \rrbracket_i\ (\theta', (\pi, v), \gamma)
\end{array}
$$

Figure 11. Denotational Semantics of Terms

$$\boxed{[\![\Sigma \rhd_i \Omega_i \vdash C \dashv \Omega'_i]\!] \in [\![\Sigma]\!]_i \star [\![\Omega_i]\!] \to [\![\Omega'_i]\!]}$$

$$
\begin{array}{l}
[\![\Sigma \rhd_i \Omega_i \vdash \Box \dashv \cdot]\!]\ (\theta, \gamma) = \langle\rangle \\
[\![\Sigma \rhd_i \Omega_i \vdash \mathsf{let}\ y = \mathsf{tail}(x)\ \mathsf{in}\ C \dashv y :_{i+1} S(A), \Omega'_i]\!]\ (\theta, \gamma) = \\
\quad \text{let } v = \mathit{tail}(\gamma(x)) \text{ in} \\
\quad \text{let } \gamma' = [\![\Sigma \rhd_i \Omega_i, y :_{i+1} S(A) \vdash C \dashv \Omega'_i]\!]\ (\theta, (\gamma, v)) \text{ in} \\
\quad (\gamma', v) \\
[\![\Sigma, \Sigma', \Sigma'' \rhd_i \Omega_i \vdash \mathsf{let}\ x = \mathsf{cons}(u, v, u'.\, e)\ \mathsf{in}\ C \dashv \Omega'_i, x :_{i+1} S(A)]\!] \\
((\theta, \theta', \theta''), \gamma) = \\
\quad \text{let } (r, d) = [\![\Sigma' \vdash u :_i \Diamond]\!]\ \theta' \text{ in} \\
\quad \text{let } h = [\![\cdot; \cdot; \Omega_i \vdash v :_i A]\!]\ (\langle\rangle, \langle\rangle, \gamma) \text{ in} \\
\quad \text{let } \theta''_1 = (\mathrm{Next}^i_{\Sigma''}\ \theta'', d) \text{ in} \\
\quad \text{let } \gamma_1 = \mathrm{Next}^{\Omega_i}_\gamma \text{ in} \\
\quad \text{let } t = \bullet[\![\Sigma'', u' :_{i+1} \Diamond; \cdot; \Omega_i \vdash e :_{i+1} S(A)]\!]\ (\theta''_1, \langle\rangle, \gamma'_1) \text{ in} \\
\quad \text{let } vs = \mathit{cons}(r, (h, t)) \text{ in} \\
\quad \text{let } \gamma' = [\![\Sigma \rhd_i \Omega_i, x :_i S(A) \vdash C \dashv \Omega'_i]\!]\ (\theta, (\gamma, vs)) \text{ in} \\
\quad (\gamma', vs)
\end{array}
$$

Figure 12. Interpretation of Contexts

a kind of heap update in the operational semantics. We think the operational semantics in this paper, which is quasi-imperative in flavour, is close enough to both a denotational model and Cooper's semantics that it makes sense to study how to reunify the pure and the imperative flavours of FRP.

Krishnaswami and Benton [14] have also presented a language for writing reactive GUI programs. This language also makes use of linear types, but in this case they are used to track the allocation of new GUI widgets. It is not yet clear to us how one might combine space-boundedness with this kind of dynamism: we may need to add a dynamic allocation monad to our model to integrate the two lines of work.

Supporting other dynamic data structures (not necessarily streams) suggests looking at the work of Acar et al. [1], who have studied adding user-controlled incrementalization to self-adjusting computation, which shares many implementation issues with FRP. Conversely, it will be worth investigating whether our denotational semantics can be adapted to provide a useful categorical cost semantics for self-adjusting computation[16].

References

[1] U. A. Acar, G. E. Blelloch, R. Ley-Wild, K. Tangwongsan, and D. Türkoglu. Traceable data types for self-adjusting computation. In *PLDI*, pages 483–496, 2010.

[2] A. W. Appel, P.-A. Melliès, C. D. Richards, and J. Vouillon. A very modal model of a modern, major, general type system. In M. Hofmann and M. Felleisen, editors, *POPL*, pages 109–122. ACM, 2007. ISBN 1-59593-575-4.

[3] G. Berry and L. Cosserat. The ESTEREL synchronous programming language and its mathematical semantics. In *Seminar on Concurrency*, pages 389–448. Springer, 1985.

[4] P. Caspi, D. Pilaud, N. Halbwachs, and J. Plaice. LUSTRE: A declarative language for real-time programming. In *POPL*, 1987.

[5] G. Cooper. *Integrating dataflow evaluation into a practical higher-order call-by-value language.* PhD thesis, Brown University, 2008.

[6] G. Cooper and S. Krishnamurthi. Embedding dynamic dataflow in a call-by-value language. *Programming Languages and Systems*, pages 294–308, 2006.

[7] D. Dreyer, A. Ahmed, and L. Birkedal. Logical step-indexed logical relations. In *LICS*, pages 71–80. IEEE, 2009.

[8] C. Elliott and P. Hudak. Functional reactive animation. In *ICFP*, 1997.

[9] M. Hofmann. A type system for bounded space and functional in-place update. *Nordic Journal of Computing*, 7(4), 2000.

[10] M. Hofmann. Linear types and non-size-increasing polynomial time computation. *Information and Computation*, 183(1), 2003.

[11] P. Hudak, A. Courtney, H. Nilsson, and J. Peterson. Arrows, robots and functional reactive programming. In *Advanced Functional Programming*, volume 2638 of *LNCS*. Springer, 2003.

[12] J. Hughes. Generalizing monads to arrows. *Sci. Comput. Program.*, 37(1-3), 2000.

[13] N. Krishnaswami and N. Benton. Ultrametric semantics of reactive programs. In *LICS*. IEEE, 2011.

[14] N. Krishnaswami and N. Benton. A semantic model of graphical user interfaces. In *ICFP*, 2011.

[15] U. D. Lago and M. Hofmann. Realizability models and implicit complexity. *Theor. Comput. Sci.*, 412(20):2029–2047, 2011.

[16] R. Ley-Wild, U. A. Acar, and M. Fluet. A cost semantics for self-adjusting computation. In Z. Shao and B. C. Pierce, editors, *POPL*, pages 186–199. ACM, 2009. ISBN 978-1-60558-379-2.

[17] H. Liu, E. Cheng, and P. Hudak. Causal commutative arrows and their optimization. In *ICFP*, 2009.

[18] H. Nakano. A modality for recursion. In *LICS*, pages 255–266, 2000.

[19] H. Nilsson, A. Courtney, and J. Peterson. Functional reactive programming, continued. In *ACM Haskell Workshop*, pages 51–64. ACM, 2002.

[20] P. W. O'Hearn and D. J. Pym. The logic of bunched implications. *Bulletin of Symbolic Logic*, 5(2), 1999.

[21] M. Pouzet. *Lucid Synchrone, version 3. Tutorial and reference manual.* Université Paris-Sud, LRI, 2006.

[22] N. Sculthorpe and H. Nilsson. Safe functional reactive programming through dependent types. In *ICFP*, 2009.

[23] D. Spoonhower, G. E. Blelloch, R. Harper, and P. B. Gibbons. Space profiling for parallel functional programs. In J. Hook and P. Thiemann, editors, *ICFP*, pages 253–264. ACM, 2008. ISBN 978-1-59593-919-7.

[24] T. Uustalu and V. Vene. The essence of dataflow programming. In K. Yi, editor, *APLAS*, volume 3780 of *Lecture Notes in Computer Science*, pages 2–18. Springer, 2005. ISBN 3-540-29735-9.

[25] Z. Wan, W. Taha, and P. Hudak. Real-time FRP. In *ICFP*, pages 146–156, 2001.

[26] Z. Wan, W. Taha, and P. Hudak. Event-driven FRP. In *PADL*, pages 155–172, 2002.

The Marriage of Bisimulations and Kripke Logical Relations

Chung-Kil Hur Derek Dreyer Georg Neis Viktor Vafeiadis
Max Planck Institute for Software Systems (MPI-SWS)
{gil,dreyer,neis,viktor}@mpi-sws.org

Abstract

There has been great progress in recent years on developing effective techniques for reasoning about program equivalence in ML-like languages—that is, languages that combine features like higher-order functions, recursive types, abstract types, and general mutable references. Two of the most prominent types of techniques to have emerged are *bisimulations* and *Kripke logical relations (KLRs)*. While both approaches are powerful, their complementary advantages have led us and other researchers to wonder whether there is an essential tradeoff between them. Furthermore, both approaches seem to suffer from fundamental limitations if one is interested in scaling them to inter-language reasoning.

In this paper, we propose *relation transition systems (RTSs)*, which marry together some of the most appealing aspects of KLRs and bisimulations. In particular, RTSs show how bisimulations' support for reasoning about recursive features via *coinduction* can be synthesized with KLRs' support for reasoning about local state via *state transition systems*. Moreover, we have designed RTSs to avoid the limitations of KLRs and bisimulations that preclude their generalization to inter-language reasoning. Notably, unlike KLRs, RTSs are transitively composable.

Categories and Subject Descriptors D.3.1 [*Programming Languages*]: Formal Definitions and Theory; D.3.3 [*Programming Languages*]: Language Constructs and Features; F.3.1 [*Logics and Meanings of Programs*]: Specifying and Verifying and Reasoning about Programs

General Terms Languages, Theory, Verification

Keywords Kripke logical relations, bisimulations, relation transition systems, contextual equivalence, higher-order state, recursive types, abstract types, transitivity, global vs. local knowledge

1. Introduction

One of the grand challenges in programming language semantics is to find scalable techniques for reasoning about the observational equivalence of programs. Even when the intuitive principles of local reasoning suggest that a change to some program module should not be observable to any client, it can be fiendishly difficult to establish that formally. Denotational semantics offers a tractable way of proving equivalence of programs by showing that they *mean* the same thing in some adequate model of their language. However, traditional denotational methods do not scale well to general-purpose languages like ML that combine support for functional, *value-oriented* programming (*e.g.,* higher-order functions, polymorphism, abstract data types, recursive types) with support for imperative, *effect-oriented* programming (*e.g.,* mutable state and control effects, among other things).

Fortunately, in recent years, there has been a groundswell of interest in the problem of developing effective methods for reasoning about program equivalence in ML-like languages. A variety of promising techniques have emerged [29, 36, 19, 20, 34, 33, 23, 5, 35, 12, 25], and while some of these methods are denotational, most support direct reasoning about the operational semantics of programs. In particular, there has been a healthy rivalry between techniques based on **Kripke logical relations (KLRs)** [29, 5, 26, 13, 12, 17, 37] and **bisimulations** [36, 19, 34, 33, 23, 35].

This paper is motivated by two high-level concerns:

(1) KLRs and bisimulations offer complementary advantages, which we would like to synthesize in a single proof method.

(2) There is a specific sense in which both KLRs and bisimulations appear to be fundamentally limited, and some fresh idea seems necessary to circumvent this limitation.

Concerning motivation (1): The latest KLR techniques [5, 12] use *state transition systems* to provide more flexible principles for reasoning about local state than bisimulations do. However, in order to account for the presence of recursive features, such as recursive types and higher-order state, KLRs require tedious manipulation of tricky "step-indexed" constructions [6, 2].[1] In contrast, bisimulation techniques use *coinduction* to model such recursive features very elegantly, but their support for reasoning about local state is weaker than KLRs' (see Section 9). These complementary strengths have led us and other researchers to wonder whether there is some fundamental tradeoff between KLRs and bisimulations.

Concerning motivation (2): We are interested in scaling equational reasoning techniques to the setting of *inter-language reasoning, i.e.,* reasoning about equivalences between programs in different languages. Inter-language reasoning is essential to the development of *compositional certified compilers* [7, 17], and may also have applications to the verification of multi-language (inter-operating) programs [4]. Unfortunately, both KLR and bisimulation methods rely on technical devices that prevent them (it seems) from scaling to the inter-language setting. Specifically, in order to deal with higher-order functions, bisimulation methods employ various "syntactic" devices that restrict the applicability of the methods to single-language reasoning (see Section 3 for details). KLRs, in contrast, *have* been shown to generalize to inter-language reasoning [17], but there remains a key problem: KLR proofs are in general *not transitively composable*, at least in part due to the use of step-indexed constructions as mentioned above. In order to prove compositional correctness of *multi-phase* compilers for ML-like

[1] This has led to a series of papers—some written by authors of the present paper—on how to hide the "ugliness" of step-indices [11, 13, 8].

POPL'12, January 25–27, 2012, Philadelphia, PA, USA.

languages, it is crucial to be able to prove the correctness of each phase individually and then compose them transitively, so KLRs' lack of transitivity is a showstopper for that application.

1.1 Contributions

In this paper, we present a new technique for reasoning about program equivalence, called **Relation Transition Systems (RTSs)**. RTSs marry together some of the most appealing features of KLRs and bisimulations, while circumventing their limitations.

In particular, RTSs show how the use of state transition systems (from KLRs) can be synthesized with the coinductive, step-index-free style of reasoning (from bisimulations), thereby enabling clean and elegant proofs about local state *and* recursive features simultaneously. Thus, concerning the long-standing open question of whether there is a fundamental tradeoff between KLRs and bisimulations, we provide a definitive answer: no, there is not.

We explore RTSs here in the setting of $\mathsf{F}^{\mu!}$—a CBV λ-calculus with general recursive types, products, sums, universals, existentials, and general references [5]—as this provides a clear point of comparison with recent work on both KLRs [12] and bisimulations [35]. With one notable exception (see Section 9), we believe RTSs are capable of reasoning effectively about all the challenging $\mathsf{F}^{\mu!}$ equivalences studied in the aforementioned papers, and we demonstrate RTSs' effectiveness on several such equivalences.

Although we do not study inter-language reasoning in this paper, we have designed RTSs so as to avoid the use of any technical devices that would preclude a future generalization to the inter-language setting. To achieve this goal, we had to come up with a novel way of accounting for higher-order functions in the context of a coinductive bisimulation-like proof method, without relying on the "syntactic" devices that previous bisimulation methods use. Our solution—a new technique we call **global vs. local knowledge**—is one of the major contributions of this paper. Relying heavily on this new technique, we have proven that RTS equivalence proofs *are* transitively composable, which suggests they may serve as a superior foundation to KLRs for inter-language reasoning.

The remainder of this paper is structured as follows. In Section 2, we define $\mathsf{F}^{\mu!}$, the language under consideration. In Section 3, we motivate our key novel technical idea of global vs. local knowledge. We then present the formal development of RTSs. For pedagogical reasons, we begin in Section 4 with the presentation of a relational model for λ^{μ} (a pure subset of $\mathsf{F}^{\mu!}$ with recursive types), and then proceed in Sections 5 and 6 to extend that model to handle the full language $\mathsf{F}^{\mu!}$. In Section 7, we demonstrate the expressive power of our method by proving several challenging equivalences from the literature. In Section 8, we briefly sketch our proof of transitivity for the λ^{μ} model. (The transitivity proof for full $\mathsf{F}^{\mu!}$ is complex and sophisticated, meriting a detailed discussion that is beyond the scope of the present paper. We will present it in a follow-on paper.) Finally, in Sections 9 and 10, we discuss related and future work, and conclude.

Our online appendix provides detailed proofs of the metatheory of RTSs, both on paper and machine-checked in Coq.

2. The Language $\mathsf{F}^{\mu!}$

In Figure 1, we present the syntax and the operational semantics of $\mathsf{F}^{\mu!}$, a completely standard PCF-like language extended with products, sums, universals, existentials, general recursive types, and general reference types. Formally, we distinguish between "static" *programs* p, which are explicitly typed and do not include memory locations ℓ (since the programmer cannot write them), and "dynamic" *expressions* (or *terms*) e, which include memory locations and in which all type information is erased. The static semantics of $\mathsf{F}^{\mu!}$ (see the online appendix) defines the program typing judgment $\Delta; \Gamma \vdash p : \tau$, wherein $\Delta ::= \cdot \mid \Delta, \alpha$ and $\Gamma ::= \cdot \mid \Gamma, x : \tau$, while

$$
\begin{array}{lll}
\tau_{\text{base}} & ::= & \mathsf{unit} \mid \mathsf{int} \mid \mathsf{bool} \\
\tau \in \text{Typ} & ::= & \alpha \mid \tau_{\text{base}} \mid \tau_1 \times \tau_2 \mid \tau_1 + \tau_2 \mid \tau_1 \to \tau_2 \mid \mu\alpha.\,\tau \mid \\
& & \forall\alpha.\,\tau \mid \exists\alpha.\,\tau \mid \mathsf{ref}\,\tau \\
p \in \text{Prog} & ::= & x \mid \langle\rangle \mid n \mid \mathsf{tt} \mid \mathsf{ff} \mid \mathsf{if}\ p_0\ \mathsf{then}\ p_1\ \mathsf{else}\ p_2 \mid \\
& & \langle p_1, p_2\rangle \mid p.1 \mid p.2 \mid \mathsf{inj}^1_\tau\, p \mid \mathsf{inj}^2_\tau\, p \mid \\
& & (\mathsf{case}\, p\, \mathsf{of}\, \mathsf{inj}^1\, x \Rightarrow p_1 \mid \mathsf{inj}^2\, x \Rightarrow p_2) \mid \mathsf{roll}_\tau\ p \mid \\
& & \mathsf{unroll}\ p \mid \mathsf{fix}\, f(x{:}\tau_1){:}\tau_2.\, p \mid p_1\ p_2 \mid \Lambda\alpha.\, p \mid p[\tau] \mid \\
& & \mathsf{pack}\ \langle\tau, p\rangle\ \mathsf{as}\ \exists\alpha.\,\tau' \mid \mathsf{unpack}\ p_1\ \mathsf{as}\ \langle\alpha, x\rangle\ \mathsf{in}\ p_2 \mid \\
& & \mathsf{ref}\ p \mid {!p} \mid p_1 := p_2 \mid p_1 == p_2 \\
v \in \text{Val} & ::= & x \mid \langle\rangle \mid n \mid \mathsf{tt} \mid \mathsf{ff} \mid \langle v_1, v_2\rangle \mid \mathsf{inj}^1\, v \mid \mathsf{inj}^2\, v \mid \mathsf{roll}\ v \mid \\
& & \mathsf{fix}\, f(x).\, e \mid \Lambda.\, e \mid \mathsf{pack}\ v \mid \ell \\
e \in \text{Exp} & ::= & v \mid \mathsf{if}\ e_0\ \mathsf{then}\ e_1\ \mathsf{else}\ e_2 \mid \\
& & \langle e_1, e_2\rangle \mid e.1 \mid e.2 \mid \mathsf{inj}^1\, e \mid \mathsf{inj}^2\, e \mid \\
& & (\mathsf{case}\, e\, \mathsf{of}\, \mathsf{inj}^1\, x \Rightarrow e_1 \mid \mathsf{inj}^2\, x \Rightarrow e_2) \mid \mathsf{roll}\ e \mid \mathsf{unroll}\ e \mid \\
& & e_1\ e_2 \mid e[] \mid \mathsf{pack}\ e \mid \mathsf{unpack}\ e_1\ \mathsf{as}\ x\ \mathsf{in}\ e_2 \mid \\
& & \mathsf{ref}\ e \mid {!e} \mid e_1 := e_2 \mid e_1 == e_2 \\
K \in \text{Cont} & ::= & \bullet \mid \mathsf{if}\ K\ \mathsf{then}\ e_1\ \mathsf{else}\ e_2 \mid \langle K, e\rangle \mid \langle v, K\rangle \mid K.1 \mid K.2 \mid \\
& & \mathsf{inj}^1\, K \mid \mathsf{inj}^2\, K \mid \mathsf{case}\, K\, \mathsf{of} [\mathsf{inj}^i\, x \Rightarrow e_i] \mid \\
& & \mathsf{roll}\ K \mid \mathsf{unroll}\ K \mid K\ e \mid v\ K \mid K[] \mid \\
& & \mathsf{pack}\ K \mid \mathsf{unpack}\ K\ \mathsf{as}\ x\ \mathsf{in}\ e \mid \\
& & \mathsf{ref}\ K \mid {!K} \mid K := e \mid v := K \mid K == e \mid v == K \\
h \in \text{Heap} & ::= & \text{Loc} \overset{\text{fin}}{\rightharpoonup} \text{CVal} \qquad \text{Loc} = \{\ell_1, \ell_2, \ldots\}
\end{array}
$$

$$
\begin{array}{rcll}
h, \mathsf{if}\ \mathsf{tt}\ \mathsf{then}\ e_1\ \mathsf{else}\ e_2 & \hookrightarrow & h, e_1 & \\
h, \mathsf{if}\ \mathsf{ff}\ \mathsf{then}\ e_1\ \mathsf{else}\ e_2 & \hookrightarrow & h, e_2 & \\
h, \langle v_1, v_2\rangle.i & \hookrightarrow & h, v_i & \\
h, \mathsf{case}\, \mathsf{inj}^j\, v\, \mathsf{of} [\mathsf{inj}^i\, x \Rightarrow e_i] & \hookrightarrow & h, e_j[v/x] & \\
h, (\mathsf{fix}\, f(x).\, e)\ v & \hookrightarrow & h, e[(\mathsf{fix}\, f(x).\, e)/f, v/x] & \\
h, (\Lambda.\, e)[] & \hookrightarrow & h, e & \\
h, \mathsf{unpack}\ (\mathsf{pack}\ v)\ \mathsf{as}\ x\ \mathsf{in}\ e & \hookrightarrow & h, e[v/x] & \\
h, \mathsf{unroll}\ (\mathsf{roll}\ v) & \hookrightarrow & h, v & \\
h, \mathsf{ref}\ v & \hookrightarrow & h \uplus [\ell \mapsto v], \ell & \text{where } \ell \notin \text{dom}(h) \\
h \uplus [\ell \mapsto v], {!\ell} & \hookrightarrow & h \uplus [\ell \mapsto v], v & \\
h \uplus [\ell \mapsto v], \ell := v' & \hookrightarrow & h \uplus [\ell \mapsto v'], \langle\rangle & \\
h, \ell == \ell & \hookrightarrow & h, \mathsf{tt} & \\
h, \ell == \ell' & \hookrightarrow & h, \mathsf{ff} & \text{where } \ell \neq \ell' \\
h, K[e] & \hookrightarrow & h', K[e'] & \text{where } h, e \hookrightarrow h', e'
\end{array}
$$

Figure 1. The syntax and semantics of $\mathsf{F}^{\mu!}$.

the dynamic semantics says how to execute expressions e. There is a straightforward erasure of programs p into expressions, written $|p|$; and when discussing equivalence informally, we will often gloss over the program/expression distinction.

Using evaluation contexts (aka continuations) K, we define the small-step reduction relation, $\hookrightarrow$, between configurations consisting of a heap and an expression. The reduction rules shown in Figure 1 are deterministic except for the rule for allocating reference cells, which is completely non-deterministic. For technical reasons, we find it convenient to assume that allocation is in fact deterministic, but we do not care which deterministic allocator is used. Thus, we will assume that $\hookrightarrow$ is some unknown determinization of the rules shown in the figure, and our model will be parametric w.r.t. that determinization. It is easy to show that if two $\mathsf{F}^{\mu!}$ programs are contextually equivalent under all deterministic allocators, then they are contextually equivalent under a non-deterministic allocator, so nothing is lost by this assumption.

In the following, we write $\hookrightarrow^*$ for the reflexive, transitive closure of $\hookrightarrow$. We also say that a configuration diverges, denoted $h, e\!\uparrow$, if it can perform an infinite sequence of $\hookrightarrow$-reductions.

Two programs are contextually equivalent if, under any well-typed closing context C (as defined in the appendix), they either both terminate or both diverge.

Definition 1 (Contextual equivalence).
Let $\Delta; \Gamma \vdash p_1 : \tau$ and $\Delta; \Gamma \vdash p_2 : \tau$. Then:

$$\Delta; \Gamma \vdash p_1 \sim_{\text{ctx}} p_2 : \tau \overset{\text{def}}{=} \forall C, h, \tau'.$$
$$\vdash C : (\Delta; \Gamma; \tau) \rightsquigarrow (\cdot; \cdot; \tau') \Longrightarrow (h, |C[p_1]|\!\uparrow \iff h, |C[p_2]|\!\uparrow)$$

3. Global vs. Local Knowledge

Our new method of relation transition systems (RTSs) is essentially *coinductive*, following the style of existing bisimulation techniques in many respects. As explained in the introduction, coinductive reasoning makes it easy to deal with recursive features (such as recursive types and higher-order state) without requiring the use of step-indexed constructions.

The two main ways in which RTSs differ from existing bisimulation techniques are in their treatment of:

Local state. From recent work on KLRs [5, 12], we borrow the idea of using *state transition systems (STSs)* to establish invariants on how a module's local state may evolve over time. STSs enable one to encode more flexible state invariants than are expressible using "environmental" bisimulations [33, 35].

Higher-order functions. In order to reason about higher-order functions in a coinductive style, but without confining ourselves to single-language reasoning, we employ a novel technical idea: *global vs. local knowledge*.

The treatment of local state using state transition systems follows prior work very closely, so we postpone further discussion of that idea until Section 5 and focus attention here instead on motivating our new idea of global vs. local knowledge.

Coinductive Reasoning One way of formulating contextual equivalence is as the *largest adequate congruence relation* [28]. Being adequate means that if two terms of base type are related, then either they both diverge (run forever) or they both evaluate to the same value (*e.g.*, if one term evaluates to 3, then the other must evaluate to 3 as well). Being a congruence means the relation is closed under all the constructs of the language (*e.g.*, if f_1 and f_2 are related at $\tau' \to \tau$, and e_1 and e_2 are related at τ', then $f_1\, e_1$ and $f_2\, e_2$ are related at τ).

To prove using coinduction that two terms e_1 and e_2 are contextually equivalent at type τ, one must exhibit a (type-indexed) term relation L that contains (τ, e_1, e_2) and then prove that L is an adequate congruence. The relation L serves as a "generalized coinduction hypothesis", by which one proves equivalence for all pairs of terms related by L simultaneously. However, while it is possible for one to employ this kind of "brute-force" coinductive proof, it is typically not very pleasant, because proving a relation to be a congruence directly can be incredibly tedious.

Bisimulation techniques help make coinductive proofs manageable by lightening the congruence proof burden. Typically, this is achieved by only requiring one to show that L is closed under type-directed *uses* (*i.e.*, evaluation or deconstruction) of the terms it relates. This results in proof obligations that look like the following:

(1) If $(\tau, e_1, e_2) \in L$, then either $e_1 \uparrow$ and $e_2 \uparrow$, or $\exists v_1, v_2.\ e_1 \hookrightarrow^* v_1$ and $e_2 \hookrightarrow^* v_2$ and $(\tau, v_1, v_2) \in L$.

(2) If $(\mathsf{int}, v_1, v_2) \in L$, then $\exists n.\ v_1 = v_2 = n$.

(3) If $(\tau' \times \tau'', v_1, v_2) \in L$, then $\exists v_1', v_1'', v_2', v_2''.\ v_i = \langle v_i', v_i'' \rangle$ and $(\tau', v_1', v_2') \in L$ and $(\tau'', v_1'', v_2'') \in L$.

(4) If $(\mu\alpha.\tau, v_1, v_2) \in L$, then $\exists v_1', v_2'.\ v_i = \mathsf{roll}\ v_i'$ and $(\tau[\mu\alpha.\tau/\alpha], v_1', v_2') \in L$.

The most problematic proof obligation is the one for function values. It usually looks something like this (simplifying fix to λ):

(5) If $(\tau' \to \tau, v_1, v_2) \in L$, then $\exists x, e_1, e_2.\ v_i = \lambda x.e_i$ and $\forall v_1', v_2'.\ (\tau', v_1', v_2') \in \boxed{G} \Rightarrow (\tau, e_1[v_1'/x], e_2[v_2'/x]) \in L$.

In other words, if L relates function values v_1 and v_2, then applying them to any "equivalent arguments" v_1' and v_2' should produce results that are also related by L. The big question is: what is this relation G from which the arguments v_1' and v_2' are drawn?

Global vs. Local Knowledge First, some (non-standard) terminology: There are many equivalent terms in the world, but when we do a bisimulation proof, we only make a claim about some of them. So let us make a distinction between "local" and "global" knowledge about term equivalence. The relation L describes our *local knowledge*: these are the terms whose equivalence we aim to validate in our proof. The relation G, on the other hand, embodies the *global knowledge* about all terms that are equivalent in the world. In proof obligation (5), we draw equivalent function arguments from G (rather than L) since they might indeed originate from "somewhere else" in the program (some unknown client code), and thus our local knowledge L may not be sufficient to justify their equivalence. This leaves us with the question of how to define G.

Whence Global Knowledge? Coming up with a sound (and practically usable) choice for G is far from obvious, and existing bisimulation methods make a variety of different choices. For example:

- *Applicative* bisimulations [1] define G to be the syntactic identity relation on closed values.

This is a nice, simple choice, which works well for pure λ-calculus. Unfortunately, for higher-order stateful languages like $\mathsf{F}^{\mu!}$, it is unsound [18], so more advanced approaches are needed:

- *Environmental* bisimulations [36, 19, 33, 35] take G to be the "context closure" of L, *i.e.*, the relation that extends the syntactic identity relation on closed values by including closures of open values v with pairs of values (w_1, w_2) that are related by L (formally: $\{(\sigma, v[\overline{w_1/y}], v[\overline{w_2/y}]) \mid \{\overline{(\sigma', w_1, w_2)}\} \subseteq L\}$).[2]
- *Normal form* (or *open*) bisimulations [21, 34, 22, 23] sidestep the whole question by choosing a fresh variable name x and representing equivalent arguments by the same x. As a result, these bisimulations are built over open terms, and proof obligation (1) above must be updated to account for the possibility that the evaluations of e_1 and e_2 get stuck trying to deconstruct the same free variable x (more about that below).

All of these methods define global knowledge in a very "syntactic" way that is well suited to proving contextual equivalences. However, as explained in the introduction, we wish to develop a method that will be capable of generalizing to the setting of inter-language reasoning, where G may relate different languages. We therefore seek an account of global knowledge that is more "semantic".

Parameterizing Over Global Knowledge The essential difficulty in choosing G has to do with higher-order functions: if the argument type τ' is (or contains) a function type, then equivalence at τ' is very hard to characterize directly.[3] Our solution is simple: we don't try to define the global knowledge at all; instead, we take G to be a *parameter* of our model!

Our key observation is that it is not necessary to pin down exactly what G is, so long as we make our coinductive proof for L as parametric as possible with respect to it. (We will clarify what "as parametric as possible" means in Section 4.) This parametricity makes our proofs quite robust by allowing G to be instantiated in a variety of different ways. In particular, we make no assumptions whatsoever about the values that G relates at function type. For all we know, G might even include "garbage" like $(\mathsf{int} \to \mathsf{int}, 4, \mathsf{tt})$.[4]

Our approach can be viewed as a more semantic account of the idea behind normal form bisimulations (see above), which is

[2] We are glossing over a lot of details here. To be precise, environmental bisimulations are actually *sets* of L's. For more details, see Section 9.

[3] Conversely, if τ' were arrow-free (*e.g.*, in a first-order language), it would be easy to characterize equivalence at τ' directly.

[4] The ability to instantiate G with a "trashy" relation is surprisingly useful. We will make critical use of it in our transitivity proof in Section 8.

to model "equivalent arguments" as black boxes about which nothing is known. Consequently, just as for normal form bisimulations, we need to adapt proof obligation (1) above to account for the possibility that e_1 and e_2 get stuck. For normal form bisimulations, e_1 and e_2 may get stuck if they try to deconstruct a free variable x, and so normal form bisimulations loosen proof obligation (1) to allow e_1 and e_2 to reduce to terms of the form $K_1[x\ v_1]$ and $K_2[x\ v_2]$, where K_1 and K_2 are equivalent continuations and v_1 and v_2 are equivalent values. In our case, e_1 and e_2 may get stuck if they try to apply some bogus functions that are equivalent according to the global knowledge but that turn out (like 4 and tt) to not even be functions. Hence, we will allow e_1 and e_2 to reduce to terms of the form $K_1[f_1\ v_1]$ and $K_2[f_2\ v_2]$, where K_1 and K_2 are equivalent continuations, and where $\{(\tau' \to \tau, f_1, f_2), (\tau', v_1, v_2)\} \subseteq G$. In this way, the parameter G serves as a semantic analogue of free variables in normal form bisimulations.

Intuitively, although the idea of parameterizing over the global knowledge may seem surprising at first, we find it to be comfortingly reminiscent of Girard's method for modeling System F [14]. In Girard's method, a potential cycle in the definition of the logical relation for impredicative universal types $\forall\alpha.\tau$ is avoided by parameterizing over an arbitrary relational interpretation of the abstract type α. In our scenario, the problem of how to define the global knowledge is avoided by parameterizing over an arbitrary relational interpretation of *function types*. In essence, we are treating a function type $\tau_1 \to \tau_2$ as an unusual kind of abstract type: the coinductive proofs about different "modules" in a program all treat the global interpretation of $\tau_1 \to \tau_2$ abstractly, while simultaneously they each contribute to defining it.

Parameterizing over the global knowledge turns out to be *very* useful. First and foremost, it makes it easy to soundly compose our coinductive proofs for different "modules" together (and hence prove soundness of our method w.r.t. contextual equivalence). Second, it enables us to reason about open terms (Section 4) and higher-order state invariants (Section 6), replacing the use of context closure or free variables for those purposes in environmental and normal form bisimulations, respectively. Finally, it is the key to establishing transitivity for our proof method (Section 8).

4. Warmup: A Relational Model for λ^μ

To ease the presentation of relation transition systems (RTSs), we begin in this section by using the idea of global vs. local knowledge, motivated in the previous section, to define a relational model for λ^μ, a sub-language of $\mathsf{F}^{\mu!}$ containing base, function, product, sum, and recursive types, but not universal, existential, or reference types. This model cannot properly be called an RTS model, since it does not include any transition systems! The transition systems will come into play when dealing with state in Sections 5 and 6. However, by ignoring the transition-systems aspect of RTSs for the time being, we can focus attention on other aspects of the model.

Figure 2 lists the various semantic domains we will be using. Here, Type denotes the types of λ^μ, and CType denotes closed types (*i.e.*, types with no free type variables α). The next four are standard: relations on closed values, closed expressions, closed continuations, and heaps, indexed by the relevant types (in case of KRel, input and output types).

Next, we define what we call the *flexible* types, CTypeF, along with the *flexible relations*, VRelF, which are just relations on closed values indexed by such flexible types. Whereas bisimulation methods typically allow terms of arbitrary type to be included in the bisimulation, we find it useful to restrict local and global knowledges to relate only values of "flexible" types. Intuitively, these are the types at which value equivalence may depend on module-specific knowledge. In $\mathsf{F}^{\mu!}$, there will be several kinds of flexible types, but in λ^μ, the only flexible types are function types.

$$
\begin{array}{lcl}
\tau \in \mathrm{Type} & ::= & \alpha \mid \tau_{\mathrm{base}} \mid \tau_1 \to \tau_2 \mid \tau_1 \times \tau_2 \mid \tau_1 + \tau_2 \mid \mu\alpha.\,\tau \\
\mathrm{VRel} & := & \mathrm{CType} \to \mathbb{P}(\mathrm{CVal} \times \mathrm{CVal}) \\
\mathrm{ERel} & := & \mathrm{CType} \to \mathbb{P}(\mathrm{CExp} \times \mathrm{CExp}) \\
\mathrm{KRel} & := & \mathrm{CType} \times \mathrm{CType} \to \mathbb{P}(\mathrm{CCont} \times \mathrm{CCont}) \\
\mathrm{HRel} & := & \mathbb{P}(\mathrm{Heap} \times \mathrm{Heap}) \\
\mathrm{CTypeF} & := & \{ (\tau_1 \to \tau_2) \in \mathrm{CType} \} \\
\mathrm{VRelF} & := & \mathrm{CTypeF} \to \mathbb{P}(\mathrm{CVal} \times \mathrm{CVal})
\end{array}
$$

Figure 2. Semantic domains for λ^μ.

$$
\begin{array}{lcl}
\overline{R}(\tau) & := & R(\tau) \qquad \text{if } \tau \in \mathrm{CTypeF} \\
\overline{R}(\tau_{\mathrm{base}}) & := & \mathrm{ID}_{\tau_{\mathrm{base}}} \\
\overline{R}(\tau_1 \times \tau_2) & := & \{ ((v_1, v_1'), (v_2, v_2')) \mid \\
& & \quad (v_1, v_2) \in \overline{R}(\tau_1) \wedge (v_1', v_2') \in \overline{R}(\tau_2) \} \\
\overline{R}(\tau_1 + \tau_2) & := & \{ (\mathsf{inj}^1\, v_1, \mathsf{inj}^1\, v_2) \mid (v_1, v_2) \in \overline{R}(\tau_1) \} \cup \\
& & \{ (\mathsf{inj}^2\, v_1, \mathsf{inj}^2\, v_2) \mid (v_1, v_2) \in \overline{R}(\tau_2) \} \\
\overline{R}(\mu\alpha.\,\tau) & := & \{ (\mathsf{roll}\, v_1, \mathsf{roll}\, v_2) \mid (v_1, v_2) \in \overline{R}(\tau[\mu\alpha.\,\tau/\alpha]) \}
\end{array}
$$

Figure 3. Value closure for λ^μ (if $R \in \mathrm{VRelF}$, then $\overline{R} \in \mathrm{VRel}$).

$$
\begin{array}{lcl}
\mathit{beta}(e) & := & \begin{cases} e' & \text{if } e \hookrightarrow e' \\ \text{undef} & \text{otherwise} \end{cases} \\
\mathrm{FunVal} & := & \{ f \in \mathrm{CVal} \mid \forall v.\ \mathit{beta}(f\ v) \text{ defined} \} \\
R' \supseteq R & := & \forall \tau.\ R'(\tau) \supseteq R(\tau) \\
\mathrm{LK} & := & \{ L \in \mathrm{VRelF} \to \mathrm{VRelF} \mid L \text{ is monotone w.r.t. } \subseteq \wedge \\
& & \quad \forall G.\, \forall (f_1, f_2) \in L(G)(\tau_1 \to \tau_2).\ f_1, f_2 \in \mathrm{FunVal} \} \\
\mathrm{GK}(L) & := & \{ G \in \mathrm{VRelF} \mid G \supseteq L(G) \}
\end{array}
$$

Figure 4. Definition of local and global knowledge for λ^μ.

In contrast, value equivalence at the remaining types—base, product, sum, and recursive types, which we call *rigid*—is fixed and agreed upon by all modules once the meaning of the flexible types is defined. This is achieved by a closure operation that takes a relation $R \in \mathrm{VRelF}$ and returns its closure $\overline{R} \in \mathrm{VRel}$. It is defined as the least fixed-point of the set of equations in Figure 3. Note that R only occurs covariantly, so $\overline{R}$ is inductively well defined, even though the type gets bigger on the r.h.s. in the case of $\mu\alpha.\,\tau$.

Local and Global Knowledge In λ^μ, a local knowledge $L \in \mathrm{LK}$ is essentially a flexible relation, except that, as shown in Figure 4, this relation is actually parameterized by the global knowledge, G. In effect, $L(G)$ describes the values that we wish to prove are equivalent, assuming that G correctly represents the global knowledge. This parameterization is necessary in order to reason about open terms, and we will see its utility below in the proof of compatibility for fix. We require that L is monotone w.r.t. G: intuitively, passing in a larger global knowledge should never result in fewer terms being related by L.

We also require that the values related by the local knowledge at function type are indeed functions, in the sense that their application to an arbitrary value should not be a stuck configuration, but should reduce at least for one step. This is a technical requirement that is used in our transitivity proof in Section 8.

We want to restrict attention to global knowledges that are closed w.r.t. the local knowledge in question: For a particular L, we define $\mathrm{GK}(L)$ to be the set of flexible relations G s.t. $G \supseteq L(G)$. This requirement makes sense since the global knowledge must by definition be a superset of any local knowledge. Observe, however, that we do not restrict what other values G relates. Indeed, G may relate values at function type that are not actually functions, or that are obviously inequivalent (*e.g.*, 4 and tt, cf. Section 3).

Relating Expressions and Continuations Figure 5 shows how equivalence is defined for expressions, e, and continuations, K.

$$
\begin{array}{lll}
\mathbf{E}(G)(\tau) & := & \{ (e_1, e_2) \mid (e_1\!\uparrow \wedge\, e_2\!\uparrow) \vee (\exists v_1, v_2.\, e_1 \hookrightarrow^* v_1 \wedge e_2 \hookrightarrow^* v_2 \wedge (v_1, v_2) \in \overline{G}(\tau)) \\
& & \vee\, (\exists \tau', K_1, K_2, e_1', e_2'.\, e_1 \hookrightarrow^* K_1[e_1'] \wedge e_2 \hookrightarrow^* K_2[e_2'] \wedge (e_1', e_2') \in \mathbf{S}(G, G)(\tau') \wedge (K_1, K_2) \in \mathbf{K}(G)(\tau', \tau)) \} \\
\mathbf{K}(G)(\tau_1, \tau_2) & := & \{ (K_1, K_2) \mid \forall (v_1, v_2) \in \overline{G}(\tau_1).\, (K_1[v_1], K_2[v_2]) \in \mathbf{E}(G)(\tau_2) \} \\
\mathbf{S}(R_f, R_v)(\tau) & := & \{ (f_1\, v_1, f_2\, v_2) \mid \exists \tau'.\, (f_1, f_2) \in R_f(\tau' \to \tau) \wedge (v_1, v_2) \in \overline{R_v}(\tau') \} \\
\mathit{consistent}(L) & := & \forall G \in \mathrm{GK}(L).\, \forall (e_1, e_2) \in \mathbf{S}(L(G), G)(\tau).\, (\mathit{beta}(e_1), \mathit{beta}(e_2)) \in \mathbf{E}(G)(\tau) \\
\Gamma \vdash e_1 \sim_L e_2 : \tau & := & \mathit{consistent}(L) \wedge \forall G \in \mathrm{GK}(L).\, \forall \gamma_1, \gamma_2 \in \mathrm{dom}(\Gamma) \to \mathrm{CVal}. \\
& & (\forall x{:}\tau' \in \Gamma.\, (\gamma_1(x), \gamma_2(x)) \in \overline{G}(\tau')) \implies (\gamma_1 e_1, \gamma_2 e_2) \in \mathbf{E}(G)(\tau) \\
\Gamma \vdash e_1 \sim e_2 : \tau & := & \exists L.\, \Gamma \vdash e_1 \sim_L e_2 : \tau
\end{array}
$$

Figure 5. Mutually coinductive definitions of (closed) expression equivalence, $\mathbf{E} \in \mathrm{VRelF} \to \mathrm{ERel}$, and continuation equivalence, $\mathbf{K} \in \mathrm{VRelF} \to \mathrm{KRel}$, and definitions of consistency and program equivalence for λ^μ.

Specifically, we introduce two new relations, $\mathbf{E} \in \mathrm{VRelF} \to \mathrm{ERel}$ and $\mathbf{K} \in \mathrm{VRelF} \to \mathrm{KRel}$, which are defined coinductively.

Given a type τ, a local knowledge $L \in \mathrm{LK}$, and a global knowledge $G \in \mathrm{GK}(L)$, we say that two expressions are "locally" equivalent, written $(e_1, e_2) \in \mathbf{E}(G)(\tau)$, if they either both diverge or both terminate producing related values. Along the way, however, they may make calls to "external" functions, that is, functions that are related by G, but not necessarily by the local knowledge $L(G)$. More precisely, we say two closed expressions are equivalent if and only if one of the following three cases holds:

1. Both expressions diverge (run forever).
2. Both expressions run successfully to completion, producing related values.
3. Both expressions reduce after some number of steps to some expressions of the form $K_i[f_i\, v_i]$, where both the f_i and v_i are related by the global knowledge G at the appropriate types, and the continuations, K_1 and K_2, are equivalent. We say that two continuations are equivalent if instantiating them with equivalent values (according to the global knowledge G) yields equivalent expressions.

As $\mathbf{E}$ and $\mathbf{K}$ are defined mutually dependent over a complete lattice and all operations involved are monotone, we can take the meaning of these definitions to be either the least or the greatest fixed-point. We choose the greatest fixed-point, corresponding to coinduction, because this can in principle relate more terms and is somewhat easier to work with.[5]

Consistency and Program Equivalence We say that a local knowledge L is *consistent* (in Figure 5) if and only if any two functions that it declares equivalent do in fact beta-reduce to equivalent expressions when applied to equivalent arguments. In the formal definition, we parameterize over an arbitrary global knowledge $G \in \mathrm{GK}(L)$; the functions being tested for equivalence are drawn from the local knowledge, $L(G)$, while the arguments to which they are applied are drawn from the global knowledge, G.

We say that two expressions are equivalent at type τ in the context Γ, written $\Gamma \vdash e_1 \sim e_2 : \tau$, if and only if there exists a consistent local knowledge, L, that shows that $\gamma_1 e_1$ and $\gamma_2 e_2$ are equivalent at type τ for arbitrary value substitutions γ_1 and γ_2 that are related at Γ by an arbitrary global knowledge G extending L.

Two programs are equivalent simply if their type-erased versions are equivalent expressions: $\Gamma \vdash |p_1| \sim |p_2| : \tau$.

4.1 Properties of Program Equivalence and Soundness

We move on to some properties of our constructions.

[5] In particular, were we to extend the language with other forms of recursion (such as while loops or primitive recursion), the coinductive interpretation would be essential for proving congruence of expression equivalence.

$$\frac{\Gamma, f{:}\tau' \to \tau, x{:}\tau' \vdash e_1 \sim e_2 : \tau}{\Gamma \vdash \mathsf{fix}\, f(x).\, e_1 \sim \mathsf{fix}\, f(x).\, e_2 : \tau' \to \tau}\ \textsc{Fix}$$

$$\frac{\Gamma \vdash e_1 \sim e_2 : \tau' \to \tau \qquad \Gamma \vdash e_1' \sim e_2' : \tau'}{\Gamma \vdash e_1\, e_1' \sim e_2\, e_2' : \tau}\ \textsc{App}$$

$$\frac{\Gamma \vdash p : \tau}{\Gamma \vdash |p| \sim |p| : \tau}\ \textsc{Refl} \qquad \frac{\Gamma \vdash e_2 \sim e_1 : \tau}{\Gamma \vdash e_1 \sim e_2 : \tau}\ \textsc{Symm}$$

$$\frac{\Gamma \vdash e_1 \sim e_2 : \tau \qquad \vdash C : (\Gamma; \tau) \rightsquigarrow (\Gamma'; \tau')}{\Gamma' \vdash C[e_1] \sim C[e_2] : \tau'}\ \textsc{Cong}$$

$$\frac{\Gamma, x{:}\tau' \vdash e_1 \sim e_2 : \tau \qquad \Gamma \vdash v_1 \sim v_2 : \tau'}{\Gamma \vdash e_1[v_1/x] \sim e_2[v_2/x] : \tau}\ \textsc{Subst}$$

$$\frac{\Gamma \vdash e_1' \sim e_2' : \tau \qquad \forall \gamma.\, \gamma e_1 \hookrightarrow^* \gamma e_1' \qquad \forall \gamma.\, \gamma e_2 \hookrightarrow^* \gamma e_2'}{\Gamma \vdash e_1 \sim e_2 : \tau}\ \textsc{Expand}$$

$$\frac{\Gamma, x{:}\tau' \vdash e_1 \sim e_2 : \tau \qquad \Gamma \vdash v_1 \sim v_2 : \tau'}{\Gamma \vdash (\lambda x.\, e_1)\, v_1 \sim e_2[v_2/x] : \tau}\ \textsc{Beta}$$

Figure 6. Some basic properties of our equational model.

The following lemma states that consistency of local knowledges is preserved under (pointwise) union. This is important for ensuring that equivalence proofs for different subterms, which rely on different local knowledges, can be soundly composed.

Lemma 1.
If $\mathit{consistent}(L)$ and $\mathit{consistent}(L')$, then $\mathit{consistent}(L \cup L')$.

Figure 6 shows some of the basic properties of our program equivalence relation. First, we have a set of rules stating that equivalence is compatible with all the language constructs. These rules state that if two terms start with the same term constructor and their immediate subterms are component-wise equivalent, then so are the composite terms. For brevity, we just present the rules for recursive function definition (Fix) and function application (App), whose proofs are the most interesting.

We briefly sketch the proof of the Fix rule. From the premise, there exists L such that $\Gamma, f{:}\tau' \to \tau, x{:}\tau' \vdash e_1 \sim_L e_2 : \tau$. Define

$$
\begin{aligned}
L'(G) := \{ (\tau' \to \tau, \gamma_1 \mathsf{fix}\, f(x).\, e_1, \gamma_2 \mathsf{fix}\, f(x).\, e_2) \mid \\
\gamma_i \in \mathrm{dom}(\Gamma) \to \mathrm{CVal} \wedge \\
\forall y{:}\tau'' \in \Gamma.\, (\gamma_1(y), \gamma_2(y)) \in \overline{G}(\tau'') \}.
\end{aligned}
$$

Note here how the parameterization of L' over G provides it with a source from which to draw the closing substitutions γ_1 and γ_2.

The goal now is to prove

$$\Gamma \vdash \mathsf{fix}\, f(x).\, e_1 \sim \mathsf{fix}\, f(x).\, e_2 : \tau' \to \tau.$$

Showing that L' (and thus $L \cup L'$) relates any appropriately closed instances of these two values is simply a matter of unfolding definitions. It therefore remains to establish $consistent(L \cup L')$. By Lemma 1, this boils down to showing

$$(\gamma'_1 e_1, \gamma'_2 e_2) \in \mathbf{E}(G)(\tau)$$

for any $G \in \mathrm{GK}(L \cup L')$, where

- $\gamma_i \in \mathrm{dom}(\Gamma) \to \mathrm{CVal}$,
- $\forall y{:}\tau' \in \Gamma.\ (\gamma_1(y), \gamma_2(y)) \in \overline{G}(\tau')$,
- $(v_1, v_2) \in \overline{G}(\tau')$,
- $\gamma'_i = \gamma_i, f \mapsto (\gamma_i \mathsf{fix}\, f(x).\, e_i), x \mapsto v_i$.

Finally, as $(\gamma_1 \mathsf{fix}\, f(x).\, e_1, \gamma_2 \mathsf{fix}\, f(x).\, e_2) \in L'(G)(\tau' \to \tau) \subseteq \overline{G}(\tau' \to \tau)$, we can instantiate $\Gamma, f{:}\tau' \to \tau, x{:}\tau' \vdash e_1 \sim_L e_2 : \tau$ with γ'_i and are done.

The proof of rule APP relies on Lemma 1 as well, in order to show that the consistent local knowledges for its two premises combine to form a consistent local knowledge for the conclusion. In addition, the proof relies on the following lemma about plugging equivalent expressions or continuations into equivalent continuations, proved by mutual coinduction and case analysis.

Lemma 2. If $(K_1, K_2) \in \mathbf{K}(G)(\tau', \tau)$, then:

1. $(e_1, e_2) \in \mathbf{E}(G)(\tau')$
   $\implies (K_1[e_1], K_2[e_2]) \in \mathbf{E}(G)(\tau)$.
2. $(K'_1, K'_2) \in \mathbf{K}(G)(\tau'', \tau')$
   $\implies (K_1[K'_1], K_2[K'_2]) \in \mathbf{K}(G)(\tau'', \tau)$.

To prove APP, we apply the first case of this lemma with $e_i := \gamma_i\, e_i$ and $K_i := \bullet\ \gamma_i e'_i$, which leaves us to prove K_1 and K_2 to be equivalent according to $\mathbf{K}$. Unfolding the definition of $\mathbf{K}$, we have to show that for arbitrary equivalent values v_1 and v_2, $(v_1\ \gamma_1 e'_1, v_2\ \gamma_2 e'_2)$ is in $\mathbf{E}$, for which we apply Lemma 2 again with $e_i := \gamma_i\, e'_i$ and $K_i := v_i\ \bullet$. Then we are left to prove $v_1\ \bullet$ and $v_2\ \bullet$ equivalent, *i.e.*, that $(v_1\ v'_1, v_2\ v'_2)$ is in $\mathbf{E}$ for arbitrary equivalent values v'_1 and v'_2, which follows from the third disjunct of the $\mathbf{E}$ definition.

As a consequence of these "compatibility" rules, by a straightforward induction on the typing derivation, we can show that equivalence is reflexive on well-typed programs (rule REFL). This corresponds to the "fundamental property" of logical relations. Equivalence is also symmetric: this follows trivially from the symmetric nature of our definition. Likewise, by induction on the typing derivation of contexts, we can show that our equivalence is a congruence: if two equivalent terms are placed in the same contexts, the resulting compositions are equivalent.

Next, we have a substitutivity property for values, an expansion law for pure execution steps, and finally a direct corollary of these two, namely β-equivalence (on value arguments).

We move to a key lemma about $\mathbf{E}$. Given a consistent local knowledge L, if the global knowledge extends L with some additional external knowledge $\mathcal{R}$, then the third case in the definition of $\mathbf{E}$ can be restricted so that it applies only to external function calls (*i.e.*, calls to functions related by $\mathcal{R}$, not by L).

Lemma 3 (External call)**.** For any $consistent(L)$, any $G \in \mathrm{GK}(L)$ and $\mathcal{R} \in \mathrm{VRelF}$, we have:

$$G = L(G) \cup \mathcal{R} \implies \mathbf{E}(G) = \mathbf{E}^{\mathcal{R}}(G)$$

where the definition of $\mathbf{E}^{\mathcal{R}}$ is the same as $\mathbf{E}$ except that, in the third disjunct, $\mathbf{S}(G, G)$ is replaced by $\mathbf{S}(\mathcal{R}, G)$.

The $\supseteq$ follows directly from the observation that $\mathcal{R} \subseteq G$. To prove the other direction, we essentially have to eliminate all uses of the third disjunct of $\mathbf{E}$ where the functions being invoked are related by $G \setminus \mathcal{R}$. Since all such functions are by definition in $L(G)$, and since we know $consistent(L)$, we can in fact always "inline" the equivalence proofs for all such function calls.

A corollary of Lemma 3 (for $G = \mu R.L(R)$ and $\mathcal{R} = \emptyset$) is adequacy, which says that equivalent closed terms either both diverge or both terminate returning proper values. In particular, they never get stuck during evaluation.

Lemma 4 (Adequacy)**.** If $\vdash e_1 \sim e_2 : \tau$, then:

$$(e_1 \uparrow \wedge\, e_2 \uparrow) \vee (\exists v_1, v_2.\, e_1 \hookrightarrow^* v_1 \wedge e_2 \hookrightarrow^* v_2)$$

Finally, combining adequacy and congruence, we show our main soundness theorem: for well-typed programs, our equivalence relation is included in contextual equivalence.

Theorem 5 (Soundness)**.** Let $\Gamma \vdash p_1 : \tau$ and $\Gamma \vdash p_2 : \tau$. If $\Gamma \vdash |p_1| \sim |p_2| : \tau$, then $\Gamma \vdash p_1 \sim_{\mathrm{ctx}} p_2 : \tau$.

4.2 Example

Consider the following example concerning streams as functions (taken from Sumii and Pierce [36]):

$$\begin{array}{rcl} \tau & := & \mu\alpha.\, \mathsf{unit} \to \mathsf{int} \times \alpha \\ \mathsf{ones} : \mathsf{unit} \to \mathsf{int} \times \tau & := & \mathsf{fix}\, f(x).\, \langle 1, \mathsf{roll}\ f \rangle \\ \mathsf{twos} : \mathsf{unit} \to \mathsf{int} \times \tau & := & \mathsf{fix}\, f(x).\, \langle 2, \mathsf{roll}\ f \rangle \\ \mathsf{succ} : \tau \to \tau & := & \mathsf{fix}\, f(s).\, \mathsf{let}\ \langle n, s' \rangle = \mathsf{unroll}\ s\ \langle\rangle\ \mathsf{in} \\ & & \quad \mathsf{roll}\ \lambda x.\, \langle n{+}1, f\ s' \rangle \end{array}$$

The goal is to show $\vdash \mathsf{roll\ twos} \sim \mathsf{succ\ (roll\ ones)} : \tau$.

Constructing a Suitable Local Knowledge Note that we have

$$\mathsf{succ\ (roll\ ones)} \hookrightarrow^* \mathsf{roll\ twos'}$$

for $\mathsf{twos'} := \lambda x.\, \langle 1 + 1, \mathsf{succ\ \ (roll\ \ ones)} \rangle$. We define a local knowledge L that relates exactly twos and twos′:

$$L(G) := \{\, (\mathsf{unit} \to \mathsf{int} \times \tau, \mathsf{twos}, \mathsf{twos'})\, \}$$

Proving Its Consistency For $G \in \mathrm{GK}(L)$ we must show:

$$(\langle 2, \mathsf{roll\ twos} \rangle, \langle 1{+}1, \mathsf{succ\ (roll\ ones)} \rangle) \in \mathbf{E}(G)(\mathsf{int} \times \tau)$$

Using the second case in $\mathbf{E}$ and the definition of $\overline{G}$, this reduces to showing $(2, 2) \in \overline{G}(\mathsf{int})$ and $(\mathsf{roll\ twos}, \mathsf{roll\ twos'}) \in \overline{G}(\tau)$. The former is trivial. The latter is equivalent to $(\mathsf{twos}, \mathsf{twos'}) \in \overline{G}(\mathsf{unit} \to \mathsf{int} \times \tau)$, which holds by construction because G extends $L(G)$.

Showing the Programs Related By It It remains to show:

$$\forall G \in \mathrm{GK}(L).\, (\mathsf{roll\ twos}, \mathsf{succ\ (roll\ ones)}) \in \mathbf{E}(G)(\tau)$$

Again using the second case in $\mathbf{E}$ we end up having to show $(\mathsf{roll\ twos}, \mathsf{roll\ twos'}) \in \overline{G}(\tau)$, which we have already done above.

5. Local State Transition Systems: A Review

In the next section, we will extend our model to account for abstract types and state. The key extension there will be to incorporate support for *state transition systems (STSs)* in the style of Dreyer *et al.*'s recent work on KLRs [5, 12]. We use this section to review the basic idea behind that work by means of a concrete example.

Perhaps the simplest example that demonstrates the utility of STSs for reasoning about local state is the "well-bracketed state change" example, due originally to Jacob Thamsborg (which is itself a variant of Pitts and Stark's "awkward" example) [5, 29]:

$$\begin{array}{rcl} \tau & := & (\mathsf{unit} \to \mathsf{unit}) \to \mathsf{int} \\ v_1 & := & \lambda f.\, (f\ \langle\rangle; f\ \langle\rangle; 1) \\ e_2 & := & \mathsf{let}\ x = \mathsf{ref}\ 0\ \mathsf{in}\ \lambda f.\, (x := 0; f\ \langle\rangle; x := 1; f\ \langle\rangle; !x) \end{array}$$

(Here and in later examples we write $\lambda x.\, e$ for $\mathsf{fix}\, f(x).\, e$ when f is not free in e.) The goal is to show that v_1 and e_2 are contextually equivalent (at the type τ). To see intuitively why they are equivalent, observe that e_2 allocates a fresh (local) location x, which initially points to 0, and then returns a function value—call it v_2. When v_1 and v_2 are applied (at any point in the future) to some callback function f, they both call f twice. Before the first and second calls, v_2 will set x to 0 and 1, respectively. Thus, even if the second call to f internally applies v_2 again, the last thing x will get set to (before it is dereferenced) is always 1. Note that this reasoning assumes that control flow in the language is "well-bracketed"—in the sense that the call to f cannot escape its current continuation—and also that the language lacks exceptions (both are true for $\mathsf{F}^{\mu!}$).

In order to prove this example, we need to be able to establish an invariant concerning the local state of v_2. However, we really need more than just a simple fixed invariant because the only such invariant that holds here is the one stating that x points to *either* 0 or 1, and that is not strong enough. This is where STSs come in. Dreyer *et al.* [12] prove this example using the following STS:

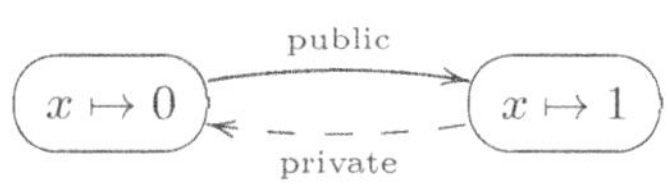

The states of this STS represent the possible "abstract" states in which the functions we are proving equivalent may find themselves, and associated with each abstract state is a "physical" relation on heaps. In the left state, the heap of the second program must contain $[x \mapsto 0]$, and in the right state, it must contain $[x \mapsto 1]$. (No restrictions are placed on the heap of the first program, since v_1 does not manipulate any local state.)

The accessibility relation between these abstract states is governed by two transition relations (preorders on the state space): a *private* and a *public* one. The rough intuition is that the private (or "full") transition relation includes all legal state transitions, while the smaller, public transition relation governs the legal transitions that *function calls* can make (when their behavior is viewed extensionally). For proving equivalence of v_1 and v_2, we require transitions of some kind from each of these states to the other because repeated applications of v_2 will indeed result in x flip-flopping back and forth between 0 and 1. However, the transition from $x \mapsto 1$ to $x \mapsto 0$ may be considered private, not public, because when the behavior of v_1 is viewed end-to-end, it will never start with $x \mapsto 1$ and end with $x \mapsto 0$. Moreover, restricting the public transition relation in this way is essential to making the proof go through: since the second call to f starts with $x \mapsto 1$ and is required (by definition) to make a public transition, we know that, when it returns, x must still point to 1, and thus $!x$ will evaluate to 1.

What we have described here is the high-level idea of the equivalence proof of v_1 and e_2, which is essentially the same when using our RTSs as it is when using STS-indexed KLRs. One difference is that, with KLRs, the proof is driven by the need to show that (v_1, e_2)—and thus also (v_1, v_2)—are in the logical relation at the type τ. With RTSs, there is no logical relation defining what it means for functions to be related at type τ. Instead, in typical coinductive style, we need to enter v_1 and v_2 into the "local knowledge" of our RTS, which in turn generates a proof obligation to show that these function values do in fact behave equivalently when passed arguments that are related by the global knowledge. Fundamentally, this ends up being only a minor change to the structure of the proof. (We will see the formal RTS proof of this example in Section 7.1.)

6. Relation Transition Systems for $\mathsf{F}^{\mu!}$

In this section, we present our full-blown relation transition system (RTS) model for $\mathsf{F}^{\mu!}$. This RTS model generalizes the model from Section 4 in a superficially very simple way: whereas previously we proved two terms equivalent by exhibiting a consistent local knowledge L, we now do so by exhibiting a consistent *world* W.

$$
\begin{aligned}
\tau \in \text{Type} &::= \ldots \mid \forall\alpha.\,\tau \mid \exists\alpha.\,\tau \mid \mathsf{ref}\,\tau \mid \mathbf{n} \\
\text{CTypeF} &:= \ldots \cup \{ (\forall\alpha.\,\tau) \in \text{CType} \} \cup \{ \mathsf{ref}\,\tau \in \text{CType} \} \\
&\quad\; \cup \{ \mathbf{n} \in \text{TypeName} \}
\end{aligned}
$$

Figure 7. Semantic domains for $\mathsf{F}^{\mu!}$.

$$
\begin{aligned}
\overline{R}(\tau) &:= R(\tau) \qquad \text{if } \tau \in \text{CTypeF} \\
&\;\;\vdots \\
\overline{R}(\exists\alpha.\,\tau) &:= \{ (\mathsf{pack}\,v_1, \mathsf{pack}\,v_2) \mid \exists\tau'.\,(v_1, v_2) \in \overline{R}(\tau[\tau'/\alpha]) \}
\end{aligned}
$$

Figure 8. Value closure for $\mathsf{F}^{\mu!}$ (if $R \in \text{VRelF}$, then $\overline{R} \in \text{VRel}$).

$$
\begin{aligned}
&\text{DepWorld}(P) \;:=\; \{ (\mathsf{S}, \sqsubseteq, \sqsubseteq_{\text{pub}}, \mathsf{N}, \mathsf{L}, \mathsf{H}) \in \\
&\quad \text{Set} \times \mathbb{P}(\mathsf{S} \times \mathsf{S}) \times \mathbb{P}(\mathsf{S} \times \mathsf{S}) \times \mathbb{P}(\text{TypeName}) \times \\
&\quad (\mathsf{S}_P \to \mathsf{S} \to \text{VRelF} \to \text{VRelF}) \times (\mathsf{S}_P \to \mathsf{S} \to \text{VRelF} \to \text{HRel}) \mid \\
&\;\; \sqsubseteq, \sqsubseteq_{\text{pub}} \text{ are preorders} \wedge \sqsubseteq_{\text{pub}} \text{ is a subset of } \sqsubseteq \wedge \\
&\;\; \mathsf{L} \text{ monotone in 1st arg w.r.t. } \sqsubseteq_P, \text{ in 2nd w.r.t. } \sqsubseteq, \text{ in 3rd w.r.t. } \subseteq \wedge \\
&\;\; \mathsf{H} \text{ monotone in 3rd arg w.r.t. } \subseteq \wedge \\
&\;\; \forall s_{\mathrm{P}}, s, G. \\
&\quad (\forall \mathbf{n} \notin \mathsf{N}.\, \mathsf{L}(s_{\mathrm{P}})(s)(G)(\mathbf{n}) = \emptyset) \wedge \\
&\quad (\forall \tau_1, \tau_2.\, \forall (f_1, f_2) \in \mathsf{L}(s_{\mathrm{P}})(s)(G)(\tau_1 \to \tau_2).\, f_1, f_2 \in \text{FunVal}) \wedge \\
&\quad (\forall \alpha, \tau.\, \forall (v_1, v_2) \in \mathsf{L}(s_{\mathrm{P}})(s)(G)(\forall\alpha.\,\tau).\, v_1, v_2 \in \text{TyFunVal}) \}
\end{aligned}
$$

where

$$
\begin{aligned}
\text{FunVal} &:= \{ f \in \text{CVal} \mid \forall v.\, \mathit{beta}(f\ v) \text{ defined} \} \\
\text{TyFunVal} &:= \{ v \in \text{CVal} \mid \mathit{beta}(v[\,]) \text{ defined} \} \\
\mathit{beta}(e) &:= \begin{cases} e' & \text{if } \forall h.\, h, e \hookrightarrow h, e' \\ \text{undef} & \text{otherwise} \end{cases}
\end{aligned}
$$

$$
\begin{aligned}
\text{World} &:= \{ W \in \text{DepWorld}(\{*\}, \{(*, *)\}) \} \\
\text{LWorld} &:= \{ w \in \text{DepWorld}(W_{\text{ref}}.\mathsf{S}, W_{\text{ref}}.\sqsubseteq) \mid \\
&\qquad \forall s_{\text{ref}}, s, G, \tau.\, w.\mathsf{L}(s_{\text{ref}})(s)(G)(\mathsf{ref}\,\tau) = \emptyset \}
\end{aligned}
$$

Figure 9. Definition of worlds (relation transition systems) and auxiliary RTS definitions.

Worlds Worlds are state transition systems (equipped with "public" and "private" transitions, just as described in Section 5) that control how the local knowledge of a module and the properties of its local state may evolve over time. Formally (Figure 9), a world consists of: the transition system's (possibly infinite) state space (S); the private (or full) transition relation ($\sqsubseteq$) and a smaller public transition relation ($\sqsubseteq_{\text{pub}}$), both preorders; a set of type names that are used to represent abstract types (N); a mapping from states to local knowledges (L); and a mapping from states to heap relations (H). For now, ignore the distinction between different kinds of worlds as well as the S_P, s_P, and $\sqsubseteq_P$ objects in that figure.

As before, the local knowledge (at each state) is parameterized by—and must be monotone in—the global knowledge G. The same applies to the heap relation, which describes pairs of subheaps that are "owned" by the RTS. The parameter G here provides a way of referring to the global equivalence on values when establishing invariants on the contents of local heaps; this is especially critical in dealing with higher-order state. While the local knowledge mapping must be monotone in its state index (w.r.t. $\sqsubseteq$), the heap relation mapping need not be. Indeed, since a module's local state is hidden from the environment, there is no reason to require that heaps related in one state will continue to be related in future states (*e.g.*, in the example in Section 5, $x \mapsto 0$ or $x \mapsto 1$ but not both).

We have seen in the previous section section how a local knowledge and its closure relate values at λ^{μ} types. This carries over to the full setting. But how do we deal with the additional types of $\mathsf{F}^{\mu!}$, *i.e.*, with universal, existential, and reference types?

$$
\begin{aligned}
W_{\text{ref}}.\mathsf{S} \quad &:= \{\, s_{\text{ref}} \in \mathbb{P}_{\text{fin}}(\text{CType} \times \text{Loc} \times \text{Loc}) \mid \\
&\quad \forall(\tau,\ell_1,\ell_2) \in s_{\text{ref}}.\ \forall(\tau',\ell_1',\ell_2') \in s_{\text{ref}}. \\
&\quad (\ell_1 = \ell_1' \implies \tau = \tau' \wedge \ell_2 = \ell_2') \wedge \\
&\quad (\ell_2 = \ell_2' \implies \tau = \tau' \wedge \ell_1 = \ell_1') \,\} \\
W_{\text{ref}}.\sqsubseteq \quad &:= \subseteq \\
W_{\text{ref}}.\sqsubseteq_{\text{pub}} &:= \subseteq \\
W_{\text{ref}}.\mathsf{N} \quad &:= \emptyset \\
W_{\text{ref}}.\mathsf{L}(s_{\text{ref}})(G)(\mathsf{ref}\,\tau) &:= \{\, (\ell_1,\ell_2) \mid (\tau,\ell_1,\ell_2) \in s_{\text{ref}} \,\} \\
W_{\text{ref}}.\mathsf{H}(s_{\text{ref}})(G) \quad &:= \{\, (h_1,h_2) \mid \\
&\quad \text{dom}(h_1) = \{\, \ell_1 \mid \exists \tau,\ell_2.\ (\tau,\ell_1,\ell_2) \in s_{\text{ref}} \,\} \\
&\quad \wedge\ \text{dom}(h_2) = \{\, \ell_2 \mid \exists \tau,\ell_1.\ (\tau,\ell_1,\ell_2) \in s_{\text{ref}} \,\} \\
&\quad \wedge\ \forall(\tau,\ell_1,\ell_2) \in s_{\text{ref}}.\ (h_1(\ell_1),h_2(\ell_2)) \in \overline{G}(\tau) \,\}
\end{aligned}
$$

Figure 10. W_{ref} provides the meaning of reference types.

Treatment of Universal and Existential Types Universal types, like function types, are considered flexible. That is, the local knowledge can relate any values at any closed type $\forall\alpha.\tau$, as long as, when instantiated, those values can run for at least one step.

Existential types, like product types, are considered rigid, and thus their interpretation is given by the value closure (Figure 8). Note that the witness of related packages must be the *same* type τ'. How, then, do we support reasoning about parametricity?

The key is that the witness type τ' may be an abstract *type name*. We extend the syntax of types in our RTS model with type names $\mathbf{n}$ (Figure 7), and the local knowledge of a world can pick a subset of these names and interpret them however it wants. To avoid conflicts with other worlds, the choice of names must be recorded in the N component of the world (no other names may be interpreted).

Treatment of Reference Types Reference types are considered flexible, but they really are a special case. Intuitively, the collection of all reference types can be seen as a separate module that is used by all other modules. Consequently, we construct a designated world W_{ref} (explained below) that interprets $\mathsf{ref}\,\tau$, and bar ordinary worlds from relating anything at such types. We therefore distinguish between two kinds of worlds: *local worlds* and *full worlds*. For conciseness, both are defined in terms of the same underlying structure of *dependent worlds*.

A dependent world is a world as described above, except that it is parameterized by a preorder $P = (\mathsf{S}_P, \sqsubseteq_P)$ that its local knowledge and heap relation may depend on (via the $s_P \in \mathsf{S}_P$ argument of L and H in Figure 9). Intuitively, P is the state transition system of some other world and s_P is that world's current state. Thus, a full world $W \in$ World is simply a world depending on nothing (a singleton set). In contrast, a local world $w \in$ LWorld is a world that depends on—will later be "linked" with—W_{ref} and does not itself relate any values at reference types.

As a matter of notational convenience: if $W \in$ World and $s \in W.\mathsf{S}$, then we will often just write $W.\mathsf{L}(s)$ for $W.\mathsf{L}(*)(s)$, and similarly for the H component. (We use the dot notation to project components out of a world.)

The World for Reference Types Figure 10 defines $W_{\text{ref}} \in$ World, the world that provides the meaning of reference types. Its states are finite ternary relations (between a type τ and two locations ℓ_1, ℓ_2) that are functional in the location arguments. They associate each allocated location on the left with the corresponding one on the right and the type of values stored. The relations are finite because only a finite number of locations can ever be allocated. And, as dictated by the language, they can only grow over time.

Its local knowledge $W_{\text{ref}}.\mathsf{L}(s_{\text{ref}})$ relates precisely the locations related by the current state s_{ref}, at the corresponding reference types. The heap relation $W_{\text{ref}}.\mathsf{H}(s_{\text{ref}})$ relates heaps that contain exactly the locations related by the current state s_{ref} and that store (globally) related values at those locations. Note the critical use of the global knowledge parameter G in defining $W_{\text{ref}}.\mathsf{H}$.

$$
H_1 \otimes H_2 := \{ (h_1 \uplus h_1', h_2 \uplus h_2') \mid (h_1,h_2) \in H_1 \wedge (h_1',h_2') \in H_2 \}
$$

$$
\begin{aligned}
w\!\uparrow\!.\mathsf{S} &:= W_{\text{ref}}.\mathsf{S} \times w.\mathsf{S} \\
w\!\uparrow\!.\sqsubseteq &:= \{\, (p,p') \mid p.1 \sqsubseteq p'.1 \wedge p.2 \sqsubseteq p'.2 \,\} \\
w\!\uparrow\!.\sqsubseteq_{\text{pub}} &:= \{\, (p,p') \mid p.1 \sqsubseteq_{\text{pub}} p'.1 \wedge p.2 \sqsubseteq_{\text{pub}} p'.2 \,\} \\
w\!\uparrow\!.\mathsf{N} &:= w.\mathsf{N} \\
w\!\uparrow\!.\mathsf{L}(s_{\text{ref}},s)(G) &:= W_{\text{ref}}.\mathsf{L}(s_{\text{ref}})(G) \cup w.\mathsf{L}(s_{\text{ref}})(s)(G) \\
w\!\uparrow\!.\mathsf{H}(s_{\text{ref}},s)(G) &:= W_{\text{ref}}.\mathsf{H}(s_{\text{ref}})(G) \otimes w.\mathsf{H}(s_{\text{ref}})(s)(G)
\end{aligned}
$$

$$
\begin{aligned}
(w_1 \otimes w_2).\mathsf{S} &:= w_1.\mathsf{S} \times w_2.\mathsf{S} \\
(w_1 \otimes w_2).\sqsubseteq &:= \{\, (p,p') \mid p.1 \sqsubseteq p'.1 \wedge p.2 \sqsubseteq p'.2 \,\} \\
(w_1 \otimes w_2).\sqsubseteq_{\text{pub}} &:= \{\, (p,p') \mid p.1 \sqsubseteq_{\text{pub}} p'.1 \wedge p.2 \sqsubseteq_{\text{pub}} p'.2 \,\} \\
(w_1 \otimes w_2).\mathsf{N} &:= w_1.\mathsf{N} \uplus w_2.\mathsf{N} \\
(w_1 \otimes w_2).\mathsf{L}(s_{\text{ref}})(s_1,s_2)(G) &:= w_1.\mathsf{L}(s_{\text{ref}})(s_1)(G) \\
&\quad \cup\ w_2.\mathsf{L}(s_{\text{ref}})(s_2)(G) \\
(w_1 \otimes w_2).\mathsf{H}(s_{\text{ref}})(s_1,s_2)(G) &:= w_1.\mathsf{H}(s_{\text{ref}})(s_1)(G) \\
&\quad \otimes\ w_2.\mathsf{H}(s_{\text{ref}})(s_2)(G)
\end{aligned}
$$

Figure 11. Lifting ($\uparrow\ \in$ LWorld $\rightarrow$ World) and separating conjunction ($\otimes \in$ LWorld $\times$ LWorld $\rightarrow$ LWorld) of worlds.

Lifting and Separating Conjunction of Local Worlds Now, if we have a local world $w \in$ LWorld, then we can link it with W_{ref}, thereby *lifting* it to a full world $w\!\uparrow\ \in$ World. This operation is defined in Figure 11. The full world's transition system is the synchronous product of W_{ref}'s and w's. Its local knowledge relates values iff they are related by either component's local knowledge, and its heap relation relates heaps iff they can be split into disjoint parts that are related by $W_{\text{ref}}.\mathsf{H}$ and $w.\mathsf{H}$, respectively. Note how the state s_{ref} of the reference world W_{ref} is passed to $w.\mathsf{L}$ and $w.\mathsf{H}$ along with the state of w itself.

Similarly, given two local worlds $w_1, w_2 \in$ LWorld that own disjoint sets of abstract types (*i.e.*, $w_1.\mathsf{N} \cap w_2.\mathsf{N} = \emptyset$), we can construct their separating conjunction $w_1 \otimes w_2 \in$ LWorld. The definition is given in Figure 11. Note how the same shared state s_{ref} is passed to the L and H components of both w_1 and w_2. Separating conjunction of worlds is a generalization of the union operation on local knowledges, which we have seen in Section 4 to be critical for composing proofs (cf. Lemma 1).

Program Equivalence With these constructions in hand, we can now describe the definition of program equivalence in Figure 12.

We say that two expressions are equivalent ($\sim$) iff there exists a local world w that (1) does not depend on a particular choice of names to represent its abstract types; (2) is *stable*; and (3) when lifted, relates the expressions. Stability means that the local world's heap relation in some sense tolerates "environmental" changes: whenever the shared world W_{ref} is advanced to a future state, s_{ref}', then w should be able to respond to that change by moving to a public future state, s', such that any local heaps that were related previously by $w.\mathsf{H}$ are still related at s'. This is a very technical condition that is required for soundness but is satisfied trivially in the common case that $w.\mathsf{H}$ does not actually depend on its s_{ref} parameter. See the end of this section for further discussion.

A world W (such as $w\!\uparrow$) relates two expressions ($\sim_W$) iff (3a) it is *inhabited*; (3b) it is *consistent*; and (3c) the expressions, when closed using related substitutions, are related by the expression relation (see below). Inhabitance says there exists a state at which $W.\mathsf{H}$ relates the empty heaps. Consistency is essentially the same as for λ^{μ}, but extended straightforwardly to universal types. In all these definitions, the global knowledge G is drawn from $\text{GK}(W)$. As before, this enforces that G must *contain* the local knowledge. At reference types, and at abstract type names owned by W, however, $\text{GK}(W)$ also enforces that G must *not extend* the local knowledge. Intuitively, this is because W should completely control the meaning of those types. Furthermore, since G is state-indexed, it must, like the local knowledge of W, be monotone w.r.t. $\sqsubseteq$.

$$
\begin{array}{lcl}
R' \geq^{\mathcal{N}}_{\mathrm{ref}} R & := & R' \supseteq R \wedge \forall \tau.\, R'(\mathsf{ref}\,\tau) = R(\mathsf{ref}\,\tau) \wedge \forall \mathbf{n} \in \mathcal{N}.\, R'(\mathbf{n}) = R(\mathbf{n}) \\
\mathrm{GK}(W) & := & \{\, G \in W.\mathsf{S} \to \mathrm{VRelF} \mid G \text{ is monotone w.r.t. } \sqsubseteq \wedge \forall s.\, G(s) \geq^{W.\mathsf{N}}_{\mathrm{ref}} W.\mathsf{L}(s)(G(s)) \,\} \\
\mathbf{E}_W(G)(s_0, s)(\tau) & := & \{\, (e_1, e_2) \mid \forall (h_1, h_2) \in W.\mathsf{H}(s)(G(s)).\, \forall h_1^{\mathrm{F}}, h_2^{\mathrm{F}}.\, h_1 \uplus h_1^{\mathrm{F}} \text{ defined} \wedge h_2 \uplus h_2^{\mathrm{F}} \text{ defined} \implies \\
& & \quad ((h_1 \uplus h_1^{\mathrm{F}}, e_1)\uparrow \wedge (h_2 \uplus h_2^{\mathrm{F}}, e_2)\uparrow) \\
& & \quad \vee (\exists h_1', h_2', v_1, v_2.\, (h_1 \uplus h_1^{\mathrm{F}}, e_1) \hookrightarrow^* (h_1' \uplus h_1^{\mathrm{F}}, v_1) \wedge (h_2 \uplus h_2^{\mathrm{F}}, e_2) \hookrightarrow^* (h_2' \uplus h_2^{\mathrm{F}}, v_2) \wedge \\
& & \qquad \exists s'.\, s' \sqsupseteq s \wedge s' \sqsupseteq_{\mathrm{pub}} s_0.\, (h_1', h_2') \in W.\mathsf{H}(s')(G(s')) \wedge (v_1, v_2) \in \overline{G(s')}(\tau)) \\
& & \quad \vee (\exists h_1', h_2', \tau', K_1, K_2, e_1', e_2'. \\
& & \qquad (h_1 \uplus h_1^{\mathrm{F}}, e_1) \hookrightarrow^* (h_1' \uplus h_1^{\mathrm{F}}, K_1[e_1']) \wedge (h_2 \uplus h_2^{\mathrm{F}}, e_2) \hookrightarrow^* (h_2' \uplus h_2^{\mathrm{F}}, K_2[e_2']) \wedge \\
& & \qquad \exists s' \sqsupseteq s.\, (h_1', h_2') \in W.\mathsf{H}(s')(G(s')) \wedge (e_1', e_2') \in \mathbf{S}(G(s'), G(s'))(\tau') \wedge \\
& & \qquad\qquad \forall s'' \sqsupseteq_{\mathrm{pub}} s'.\, \forall G' \supseteq G.\, (K_1, K_2) \in \mathbf{K}_W(G')(s_0, s'')(\tau', \tau)) \,\} \\
\mathbf{K}_W(G)(s_0, s)(\tau_1, \tau_2) & := & \{\, (K_1, K_2) \mid \forall (v_1, v_2) \in \overline{G(s)}(\tau_1).\, (K_1[v_1], K_2[v_2]) \in \mathbf{E}_W(G)(s_0, s)(\tau_2) \,\} \\
\mathbf{S}(R_f, R_v)(\tau) & := & \{\, (f_1\ v_1, f_2\ v_2) \mid \exists \tau'.\, (f_1, f_2) \in R_f(\tau' \to \tau) \wedge (v_1, v_2) \in \overline{R_v}(\tau') \,\} \\
& \cup & \{\, (f_1[], f_2[]) \mid \exists \tau_1, \tau_2.\, \tau = \tau_1[\tau_2/\alpha] \wedge (f_1, f_2) \in R_f(\forall \alpha.\, \tau_1) \,\} \\
\mathit{inhabited}(W) & := & \forall G \in \mathrm{GK}(W).\, \exists s_0.\, (\emptyset, \emptyset) \in W.\mathsf{H}(s_0)(G(s_0)) \\
\mathit{consistent}(W) & := & \forall G \in \mathrm{GK}(W).\, \forall s.\, \forall \tau.\, \forall (e_1, e_2) \in \mathbf{S}(W.\mathsf{L}(s)(G(s)), G(s))(\tau).\, (\mathit{beta}(e_1), \mathit{beta}(e_2)) \in \mathbf{E}_W(G)(s, s)(\tau) \\
\mathit{stable}(w) & := & \forall G \in \mathrm{GK}(w\!\uparrow).\, \forall s_{\mathrm{ref}}, s.\, \forall (h_1, h_2) \in w.\mathsf{H}(s_{\mathrm{ref}})(s)(G(s_{\mathrm{ref}}, s)). \\
& & \forall s_{\mathrm{ref}}' \sqsupseteq s_{\mathrm{ref}}.\, \forall (h_{\mathrm{ref}}^1, h_{\mathrm{ref}}^2) \in W_{\mathrm{ref}}.\mathsf{H}(s_{\mathrm{ref}}')(G(s_{\mathrm{ref}}', s)).\, h_{\mathrm{ref}}^1 \uplus h_1 \text{ defined} \wedge h_{\mathrm{ref}}^2 \uplus h_2 \text{ defined} \implies \\
& & \exists s' \sqsupseteq_{\mathrm{pub}} s.\, (h_1, h_2) \in w.\mathsf{H}(s_{\mathrm{ref}}')(s')(G(s_{\mathrm{ref}}', s')) \\
\Delta; \Gamma \vdash e_1 \sim_W e_2 : \tau & := & \mathit{inhabited}(W) \wedge \mathit{consistent}(W) \wedge \forall G \in \mathrm{GK}(W).\, \forall s.\, \forall \delta \in \Delta \to \mathrm{CType}.\, \forall \gamma_1, \gamma_2 \in \mathrm{dom}(\Gamma) \to \mathrm{CVal}. \\
& & \quad (\forall x{:}\tau' \in \Gamma.\, (\gamma_1(x), \gamma_2(x)) \in \overline{G(s)}(\delta\tau')) \implies (\delta\tau, \gamma_1 e_1, \gamma_2 e_2) \in \mathbf{E}_W(G)(s, s) \\
\Delta; \Gamma \vdash e_1 \sim e_2 : \tau & := & \forall \mathcal{N} \in \mathbb{P}(\mathrm{TypeName}).\, \mathcal{N} \text{ countably infinite} \implies \exists w.\, w.\mathsf{N} \subseteq \mathcal{N} \wedge \mathit{stable}(w) \wedge \Delta; \Gamma \vdash e_1 \sim_{w\uparrow} e_2 : \tau
\end{array}
$$

Figure 12. Mutually coinductive definitions of expression equivalence, $\mathbf{E}_W \in \mathrm{GK}(W) \to W.\mathsf{S} \times W.\mathsf{S} \to \mathrm{ERel}$, and continuation equivalence, $\mathbf{K}_W \in \mathrm{GK}(W) \to W.\mathsf{S} \times W.\mathsf{S} \to \mathrm{KRel}$, and definitions of world consistency and program equivalence for $\mathsf{F}^{\mu!}$.

Expression and Continuation Equivalence The new definitions of $\mathbf{E}$ and $\mathbf{K}$ are also given in Figure 12. Notice that they are now defined relative to a world W (as $\mathbf{E}_W$ and $\mathbf{K}_W$) and that their types have changed to $\mathrm{GK}(W) \to W.\mathsf{S} \times W.\mathsf{S} \to \mathrm{ERel}$ and $\mathrm{GK}(W) \to W.\mathsf{S} \times W.\mathsf{S} \to \mathrm{KRel}$, respectively: they take both an "initial" state, s_0, and a "current" state, s, as arguments.

Given a world W, a global knowledge $G \in \mathrm{GK}(W)$, states $s_0, s \in W.\mathsf{S}$, and a type τ, we say that two expressions are "locally" equivalent, written $(e_1, e_2) \in \mathbf{E}_W(G)(s_0, s)(\tau)$, iff, when executed starting in heaps that satisfy the heap relation of W at the current state s, then (as before) one of three cases holds:

1. Both expressions diverge (run forever).
2. Both expressions run successfully to completion, producing related values. In this case, the values need not be related in the current state s, but rather in some future state, $s' \sqsupseteq s$, which, however, must also be a public future state of the initial state of the expression: $s' \sqsupseteq_{\mathrm{pub}} s_0$. Moreover, this future state must be consistent with the resulting heaps: $(h_1', h_2') \in W.\mathsf{H}(s')(G(s'))$.
3. Both expressions reduce after some number of steps to some expressions of the form $K_i[e_i']$, where e_i' are either both applications or both instantiations that are related at some future state $s' \sqsupseteq s$. This state must be consistent with the corresponding heaps. Finally, the continuations, K_1 and K_2, are equivalent under any public future state, $s'' \sqsupseteq_{\mathrm{pub}} s'$, and any (pointwise) larger global knowledge, $G' \supseteq G$.

   We restrict s'' to be a public future state of s' rather than an arbitrary future state because the end-to-end effect of a function call (or universal instantiation) is assumed to always be a public transition. For this assumption to be sound, in return we will have to ensure that the end-to-end behaviors of equivalent function bodies indeed change the state only into public future states. This is why we thread the s_0 argument through the coinduction and check that the final RTS state in the previous case (2) is a public future state of s_0.

   The intuitive reason for quantifying over a larger global knowledge G' is this: At the point when the continuations are run, not only might W's state s' have changed to a future state s'', but also the states of all other "modules", which is reflected by the growth of the global knowledge.

In all three cases, the definition quantifies over frame heaps, h_1^{F} and h_2^{F}: the execution of e_1 and e_2 should not update any disjoint part of the heap that they do not own according to the heap relation of the current state. This framing aspect of our definition is a semantic version of the frame rule of separation logic and allows us to concentrate the reasoning about the heaps only on the parts of the heaps accessed by the program. (Baking the frame rule into the semantic model is quite common in more recent models of separation logic [9, 39], essentially because it allows one to avoid proving any "safety monotonicity" or "frame" properties of the operational semantics itself.)

Properties of Program Equivalence and Soundness The properties presented in Section 4 for λ^{μ}, as well as the corresponding soundness proofs, extend naturally to the full model, but we omit further details here due to space considerations. We plan to present them in an expanded version of this paper. Meanwhile, we refer the reader to our online appendix (see the link at the end of the paper).

A Word on Dependency In the examples in the next section, we will not actually rely on the ability of local knowledges and heap relations to depend on the state of the reference world W_{ref}. Consequently, the stability property in the definition of program equivalence will be trivially satisfied (by choosing $s' := s$). However, dependent worlds are of critical importance in the RTS transitivity proof for full $\mathsf{F}^{\mu!}$. We will report on this issue in a future paper.

7. Examples

In this section, we present several example RTS equivalence proofs. For convenience, we drop the s_{ref} argument from the L and H components of local worlds since we do not use it in our examples.

7.1 Well-Bracketed State Change

Recall the example from Section 5 and its high-level proof-sketch using an STS. We will now show in some formal detail how this proof is done using our method. Concretely, we prove $\vdash v_1 \sim e_2 : \tau$, where:

$$\begin{array}{lll} \tau & := & (\mathsf{unit} \to \mathsf{unit}) \to \mathsf{int} \\ v_1 & := & \lambda f.\,(f\,\langle\rangle; f\,\langle\rangle; 1) \\ v_2 & := & \lambda f.\,(x := 0; f\,\langle\rangle; x := 1; f\,\langle\rangle; !x) \\ e_2 & := & \mathsf{let}\ x = \mathsf{ref}\ 0\ \mathsf{in}\ v_2 \end{array}$$

Constructing a Suitable RTS We construct an RTS w that we will then show to be consistent and to relate v_1 and e_2.

Since the programs don't involve abstract types, we can define $w.\mathsf{N}$ to be empty. The STS that we build into w is essentially the one from Section 5. A state $s \in w.\mathsf{S}$ is to be understood as follows: for each running instance of e_2, identified by the location ℓ that that instance initially allocated, $s(\ell)$ says whether it is in the (pictorially) left state (ℓ points to 0) or in the right one (ℓ points to 1). Accordingly, the heap relation $w.\mathsf{H}$ at state s is just $\{(\emptyset, s)\}$. Finally, the local knowledge $w.\mathsf{L}$ at state s relates v_1 with $v_2[\ell/x]$ for any location ℓ belonging to an instance.

$$\begin{array}{ll} w.\mathsf{S} & := \mathrm{Loc} \xrightarrow{\mathrm{fin}} \{0,1\} \subseteq \mathrm{Heap} \\ w.\sqsubseteq & := \{(s,s') \mid \mathrm{dom}(s) \subseteq \mathrm{dom}(s')\} \\ w.\sqsubseteq_{\mathrm{pub}} & := \{(s,s') \in w.\sqsubseteq \mid \forall(\ell,1) \in s.\ (\ell,1) \in s'\} \\ w.\mathsf{N} & := \emptyset \\ w.\mathsf{L}(s)(G)(\tau) & := \{(v_1, v_2[\ell/x]) \mid \ell \in \mathrm{dom}(s)\} \\ w.\mathsf{H}(s)(G) & := \{(\emptyset, s)\} \end{array}$$

It is easy to see that $w \in \mathrm{LWorld}$. In particular, $w.\mathsf{L}$ and $w.\mathsf{H}$ are monotone as required. Note that $\mathit{stable}(w)$ (the dependency is vacuous) and that $\mathit{inhabited}(w\!\uparrow)$ for $s_0 = (\emptyset, \emptyset)$. To show $\vdash v_1 \sim_{w\uparrow} e_2 : \tau$, two parts remain.

Proving Its Consistency Establishing $\mathit{consistent}(w\!\uparrow)$ is the real meat of the proof. Consider two functions related by $w\!\uparrow\!.\mathsf{L}$ at a state $(s^1_{\mathrm{ref}}, s_1)$. Clearly, one is v_1 and the other is $v_2[\ell/x]$ for some $\ell \in \mathrm{dom}(s_1)$. Now suppose we are given related arguments $(v_1', v_2') \in \overline{G_1(s^1_{\mathrm{ref}}, s_1)}(\mathsf{unit} \to \mathsf{unit})$. We need to show:

$$\begin{array}{l} ((v_1'\,\langle\rangle; v_1'\,\langle\rangle; 1), (\ell := 0; v_2'\,\langle\rangle; \ell := 1; v_2'\,\langle\rangle; !\ell)) \\ \qquad \in \mathbf{E}_{w\uparrow}(G_1)((s^1_{\mathrm{ref}}, s_1), (s^1_{\mathrm{ref}}, s_1))(\mathsf{int}) \end{array}$$

Note that for $(h_1, h_2) \in w.\mathsf{H}(s_1)(G(s^1_{\mathrm{ref}}, s_1))$ we know by construction that $h_1 = \emptyset$ and $h_2 = s_1$. Consequently, for any frame heaps $h_1^{\mathrm{F}}, h_2^{\mathrm{F}}$, we have

$$\begin{array}{l} h_2 \uplus h_2^{\mathrm{F}}, (\ell := 0; v_2'\,\langle\rangle; \ell := 1; v_2'\,\langle\rangle; !\ell) \hookrightarrow^* \\ (s_1 \backslash \ell) \uplus [\ell \mapsto 0] \uplus h_2^{\mathrm{F}}, (v_2'\,\langle\rangle; \ell := 1; v_2'\,\langle\rangle; !\ell) \end{array}$$

where $s_1 \backslash \ell$ denotes the restriction of s_1 to domain $\mathrm{dom}(s_1) \setminus \{\ell\}$. Since $h_1 \uplus h_1^{\mathrm{F}}, (v_1'\,\langle\rangle; v_1'\,\langle\rangle; 1) \hookrightarrow^* h_1 \uplus h_1^{\mathrm{F}}, (v_1'\,\langle\rangle; v_1'\,\langle\rangle; 1)$, it suffices, by the third disjunct in the definition of $\mathbf{E}_{w\uparrow}$, to find $s_1' \sqsupseteq s_1$ such that:

1. $(\emptyset, (s_1 \backslash \ell) \uplus [\ell \mapsto 0]) \in w.\mathsf{H}(s_1')(G_1(s^1_{\mathrm{ref}}, s_1'))$
2. $\forall (s^2_{\mathrm{ref}}, s_2) \sqsupseteq_{\mathrm{pub}} (s^1_{\mathrm{ref}}, s_1').\forall G_2 \supseteq G_1.$ $((\bullet; v_1'\,\langle\rangle; 1), (\bullet; \ell := 1; v_2'\,\langle\rangle; !\ell)) \in$ $\mathbf{K}_{w\uparrow}(G_2)((s^1_{\mathrm{ref}}, s_1), (s^2_{\mathrm{ref}}, s_2))(\mathsf{unit}, \mathsf{int})$

Naturally, we pick $s_1' = (s_1 \backslash \ell) \uplus [\ell \mapsto 0] \sqsupseteq s_1$. Then (1) holds by construction of w and it remains to show (2).

After repeating the whole procedure one more time, we arrive at the goal of finding $s_2' \sqsupseteq s_2$ such that:

3. $(\emptyset, (s_2 \backslash \ell) \uplus [\ell \mapsto 1]) \in w.\mathsf{H}(s_2')(G_2(s^2_{\mathrm{ref}}, s_2'))$
4. $\forall (s^3_{\mathrm{ref}}, s_3) \sqsupseteq_{\mathrm{pub}} (s^2_{\mathrm{ref}}, s_2').\forall G_3 \supseteq G_2.$ $((\bullet; 1), (\bullet; !\ell)) \in$ $\mathbf{K}_{w\uparrow}(G_3)((s^1_{\mathrm{ref}}, s_1), (s^3_{\mathrm{ref}}, s_3))(\mathsf{unit}, \mathsf{int})$

Naturally, we pick $s_2' = (s_2 \backslash \ell) \uplus [\ell \mapsto 1] \sqsupseteq s_2$. Then (3) holds by construction of w and it remains to show (4).

We observe that, for any $s_3 \sqsupseteq_{\mathrm{pub}} s_2'$, it must be that $s_3(\ell) = 1$ since $s_2'(\ell) = 1$. Hence for $(h_1', h_2') \in w.\mathsf{H}(s_3)(G(s^3_{\mathrm{ref}}, s_3))$ we know by construction $h_2'(\ell) = 1$. Consequently, for any frame heaps $h_1^{\mathrm{F}\prime}, h_2^{\mathrm{F}\prime}$, we have:

$$h_2' \uplus h_2^{\mathrm{F}\prime}, (\langle\rangle; !\ell) \hookrightarrow^* h_2' \uplus h_2^{\mathrm{F}\prime}, 1$$

Since of course $h_1' \uplus h_1^{\mathrm{F}\prime}, (\langle\rangle; 1) \hookrightarrow^* h_1' \uplus h_1^{\mathrm{F}\prime}, 1$ and $(1,1) \in \overline{G_3(s^3_{\mathrm{ref}}, s_3)}(\mathsf{int})$ by definition, we are done if we can show $(s^3_{\mathrm{ref}}, s_3) \sqsupseteq_{\mathrm{pub}} (s^1_{\mathrm{ref}}, s_1)$. Indeed, this is easy to verify.

Showing the Programs Related By It Given how we constructed our RTS, this final goal is fairly easy to accomplish. Formally, we must show

$$(v_1, e_2) \in \mathbf{E}_{w\uparrow}(G)((s_{\mathrm{ref}}, s), (s_{\mathrm{ref}}, s))(\tau)$$

for any G, s_{ref}, s. Note that if $(h_1, h_2) \in w.\mathsf{H}(s)(G(s_{\mathrm{ref}}, s))$, then for some fresh ℓ we have $h_2, e_2 \hookrightarrow h_2 \uplus [\ell \mapsto 0], v_2[\ell/x]$ and, of course, $h_1, v_1 \hookrightarrow^* h_1, v_1$. It therefore suffices to find $s' \sqsupseteq_{\mathrm{pub}} s$ such that the following hold:

5. $(h_1, h_2 \uplus [\ell \mapsto 0]) \in w.\mathsf{H}(s')(G(s_{\mathrm{ref}}, s'))$
6. $(v_1, v_2[\ell/x]) \in \overline{G(s_{\mathrm{ref}}, s')}(\tau)$

We pick $s' = s \uplus [\ell \mapsto 0]$. Note that s' is well-defined because ℓ is fresh (so $\ell \notin \mathrm{dom}(s)$), and that $s' \sqsupseteq_{\mathrm{pub}} s$ as required. To show (6), it suffices by definition of GK to show $(v_1, v_2[\ell/x]) \in w.\mathsf{L}(s')(G(s_{\mathrm{ref}}, s'))(\tau)$. This holds by construction of w and s', and so does (5).

7.2 A Free Theorem

The next example demonstrates the treatment of universal types, and the fact that our method may be used to prove at least some simple so-called "free theorems" [40]. Suppose $\vdash p : \forall\alpha.\alpha$ and $|p| = v$. We want to prove that $h, v[]\!\uparrow$ for any h.

We start by applying REFL to obtain $\vdash v \sim v : \forall\alpha.\alpha$. This gives us w with $\vdash v \sim_{w\uparrow} v : \forall\alpha.\alpha$ and $w.\mathsf{N} \subseteq \mathrm{TypeName}\backslash\{\mathbf{n}\}$ for some arbitrary $\mathbf{n}$ of our choosing. We now instantiate $G \in \mathrm{GK}(w\!\uparrow)$ to be the least solution of $\forall s.\ G(s) = w\!\uparrow\!.\mathsf{L}(s)(G(s))$. From $\vdash v \sim_{w\uparrow} v : \forall\alpha.\alpha$ we then get

$$(v, v) \in \mathbf{E}_{w\uparrow}(G)(s_0, s_0)(\forall\alpha.\alpha)$$

where s_0 is the state witnessing $\mathit{inhabited}(w\!\uparrow)$. Consequently, we get $s \sqsupseteq_{\mathrm{pub}} s_0$ such that:

1. $(v, v) \in \overline{G(s)}(\forall\alpha.\alpha) = G(s)(\forall\alpha.\alpha)$
2. $(\emptyset, \emptyset) \in (w\!\uparrow).\mathsf{H}(s)(G(s))$

From (1), the construction of G, and $\mathit{consistent}(w\!\uparrow)$, we derive

$$(\mathit{beta}(v[]), \mathit{beta}(v[])) \in \mathbf{E}_{w\uparrow}(G)(s, s)(\tau)$$

for any τ. So, in particular, we have

$$(\mathit{beta}(v[]), \mathit{beta}(v[])) \in \mathbf{E}_{w\uparrow}(G)(s, s)(\mathbf{n}).$$

In fact, due to the construction of G, Lemma 3 tells us

$$(\mathit{beta}(v[]), \mathit{beta}(v[])) \in \mathbf{E}^{\mathcal{R}}_{w\uparrow}(G)(s, s)(\mathbf{n})$$

for $\mathcal{R} = \lambda s.\emptyset$. Together with (2), this allows only two cases for any heap h: either $h, \mathit{beta}(v[])$ diverges (then we are done), or it terminates and the resulting values are related by $\overline{G(s')}(\mathbf{n})$ for some $s' \sqsupseteq_{\mathrm{pub}} s$. However, because $W_{\mathrm{ref}}.\mathsf{N} = \emptyset$ and $w.\mathsf{N} \subseteq \mathrm{TypeName}\backslash\{\mathbf{n}\}$, we know $\overline{G(s')}(\mathbf{n}) = w\!\uparrow\!.\mathsf{L}(s')(G(s'))(\mathbf{n}) = \emptyset$, which rules out that second case.

7.3 Twin Abstraction

This final example (originally due to Ahmed *et al.* [5]) demonstrates the interaction of local state with abstract types.

$$\begin{array}{lll}
\tau & := & \exists\alpha.\,\exists\beta.\,(\mathsf{unit} \to \alpha) \times (\mathsf{unit} \to \beta) \times (\alpha \times \beta \to \mathsf{bool}) \\
e_1 & := & \mathsf{let}\ x = \mathsf{ref}\ 0\ \mathsf{in} \\
 & & \mathsf{pack}\ \langle \mathsf{int}, \mathsf{pack}\ \langle \mathsf{int}, \lambda_.\, x := !x + 1; !x, \\
 & & \qquad \lambda_.\, x := !x + 1; !x, \\
 & & \qquad \lambda p.\, p.1 = p.2 \rangle\rangle \\
e_2 & := & \mathsf{let}\ x = \mathsf{ref}\ 0\ \mathsf{in} \\
 & & \mathsf{pack}\ \langle \mathsf{int}, \mathsf{pack}\ \langle \mathsf{int}, \lambda_.\, x := !x + 1; !x, \\
 & & \qquad \lambda_.\, x := !x + 1; !x, \\
 & & \qquad \lambda p.\, \mathsf{ff} \rangle\rangle
\end{array}$$

Both e_1 and e_2 return a name generator ADT consisting of two abstract types α and β, together with a function for generating a fresh name of type α, a function for generating a fresh name of type β, and a function for comparing an α name and a β name for equality. Both implementations represent names as integers, and in e_1, the comparison operation really tests the names for equality. In e_2, however, the comparison just always returns false right away. Nevertheless, the two programs are contextually equivalent because the α names and the β names are generated by the *same* underlying integer counter, and thus no value can be both an α name and a β name at the same time.

We now show the construction of an RTS w that can be used to prove $\vdash e_1 \sim e_2 : \tau$. Let a countably infinite $\mathcal{N} \in \mathbb{P}(\mathrm{TypeName})$ be given. Since Loc is also countably infinite, we can think of $\mathcal{N}$ as being split into $\{\mathbf{n}^\alpha_\ell \mid \ell \in \mathrm{Loc}\} \uplus \{\mathbf{n}^\beta_\ell \mid \ell \in \mathrm{Loc}\}$. We define w as follows:

$$\begin{array}{ll}
w.\mathsf{S} & := \{s \in \mathrm{Loc} \times \mathrm{Loc} \xrightarrow{\mathrm{fin}} \mathbb{P}(\mathbb{N}_{>0}) \times \mathbb{P}(\mathbb{N}_{>0}) \mid \\
 & \qquad \mathrm{dom}(s)\ \text{partial bijection} \wedge \\
 & \qquad \forall(\ell_1,\ell_2,S_1,S_2) \in s.\ S_1 \cap S_2 = \emptyset\} \\
w.\sqsubseteq & := w.\sqsubseteq_{\mathrm{pub}} \\
w.\sqsubseteq_{\mathrm{pub}} & := \{(s,s') \in w.\mathsf{S} \times w.\mathsf{S} \mid \forall(\ell_1,\ell_2,S_1,S_2) \in s. \\
 & \qquad \exists S_1' \supseteq S_1, S_2' \supseteq S_2.\ (\ell_1,\ell_2,S_1',S_2') \in s'\} \\
w.\mathsf{N} & := \mathcal{N} \\
w.\mathsf{L}(s)(G) & := \\
 & \quad \{(\mathbf{n}^\alpha_{\ell_1}, n, n) \mid \exists \ell_2, S_1, S_2.\ (\ell_1,\ell_2,S_1,S_2) \in s \wedge n \in S_1\} \\
 & \uplus \{(\mathbf{n}^\beta_{\ell_1}, n, n) \mid \exists \ell_2, S_1, S_2.\ (\ell_1,\ell_2,S_1,S_2) \in s \wedge n \in S_2\} \\
 & \uplus \{((\mathsf{unit} \to \mathbf{n}^\alpha_{\ell_1}), {+\!\!+}\ell_1, {+\!\!+}\ell_2) \mid (\ell_1,\ell_2) \in \mathrm{dom}(s)\} \\
 & \uplus \{((\mathsf{unit} \to \mathbf{n}^\beta_{\ell_1}), {+\!\!+}\ell_1, {+\!\!+}\ell_2) \mid (\ell_1,\ell_2) \in \mathrm{dom}(s)\} \\
 & \uplus \{((\mathbf{n}^\alpha_{\ell_1} \times \mathbf{n}^\beta_{\ell_1} \to \mathsf{bool}), (\lambda p.\, p.1 = p.2), (\lambda p.\, \mathsf{ff})) \mid \\
 & \qquad \exists \ell_2.\ (\ell_1,\ell_2) \in \mathrm{dom}(s)\} \\
w.\mathsf{H}(s)(G) & := \{(h_1,h_2) \mid \mathrm{dom}(h_1) = \Pi_1(\mathrm{dom}(s)) \wedge \\
 & \qquad \mathrm{dom}(h_2) = \Pi_2(\mathrm{dom}(s)) \wedge \\
 & \qquad \forall(\ell_1,\ell_2,S_1,S_2) \in s. \\
 & \qquad\quad h_1(\ell_1) = h_2(\ell_2) = \max(\{0\} \uplus S_1 \uplus S_2)\}
\end{array}$$

Here, ${+\!\!+}\ell$ is short for $\lambda\_.\,\ell := !\ell{+}1; !\ell$; and $\Pi_i : \mathbb{P}(\mathrm{Loc}\times\mathrm{Loc}) \to \mathbb{P}(\mathrm{Loc})$ for the appropriate projection function.

Similar to the world construction in Section 7.1, states $s \in w.\mathsf{S}$ are functions defined for those locations (ℓ_1, ℓ_2) that, intuitively, were allocated in an instance of e_1 and e_2, respectively. They are mapped to sets S_1 and S_2 of positive integers, representing[6] the current inhabitants of the abstract types α and β, respectively, for that instance. The crucial invariant here is that S_1 and S_2 are always disjoint. The local knowledge $w.\mathsf{L}$ declares e_1's functions equivalent to those of e_2; it also defines the meaning of type $\mathbf{n}^\alpha_{\ell_1}$ as the identity relation restricted to those numbers that inhabit α in the instance pair identified by ℓ_1 (and similarly for $\mathbf{n}^\beta_{\ell_1}$ and β).

[6] To keep the definitions as simple as possible, the state space includes some states that actual program behaviour cannot result in (but that nevertheless are consistent with the property we want to prove).

According to this interpretation, the transition relation only allows S_1 and S_2 to grow (the distinction between public and private transitions is not needed for this example). Finally, $w.H$ says that the related heaps at state s are any (h_1, h_2) where h_i contains exactly those locations allocated in instances of e_i, and each such location stores the largest value handed out so far (no matter if at α or β). This latter condition is critical to ensure that S_1 and S_2 stay disjoint in each instance.

Using this world, it is straightforward to finish the proof. Details can be found in the online appendix.

7.4 World Generators

As one may observe from the examples in Sections 7.1 and 7.3, worlds must often describe "n-ary" state spaces, where each state consists of n copies of states drawn from some simpler state space, one copy for each dynamic instance of the object or ADT. Thus, it would be convenient if one were able to reason about program equivalence under the degenerate case of a single copy (*i.e.*, $n = 1$). Fortunately, it is not hard to (i) define a *world generator* that, given a single-instance world, automatically performs the multiplexing; and (ii) show that program equivalence in a single-instance world implies equivalence in the automatically multiplexed world. For space reasons, we do not present the details here but refer the interested reader to our online appendix, where the proofs of the examples from Sections 7.1 and 7.3 are simplified greatly with the help of such a world generator.

8. Transitivity

In this section, we briefly sketch our proof of transitivity of RTS equivalence in the pure, simplified setting of λ^μ (as defined in Section 4). Transitivity also holds for the full RTS model described in Section 6, but the proof of that result is much more complex (involving a notion of weak isomorphism between worlds), so we leave its presentation to a future paper.

The main lemma we would like to prove is the following:

Lemma 6. If $\Gamma \vdash e_1 \sim_{L_1} e_2 : \tau$ and $\Gamma \vdash e_2 \sim_{L_2} e_3 : \tau$, then there exists L such that $\Gamma \vdash e_1 \sim_L e_3 : \tau$.

Naturally, we can expect L to be some sort of composition of the given local knowledges L_1 and L_2. Defining this composition is, however, quite subtle. The problem is that the local knowledge takes the global knowledge G as a parameter, but then what global knowledges G_{L_1} and G_{L_2} should be passed on to L_1 and L_2 in constructing L? Assuming we somehow pick G_{L_1} and G_{L_2} appropriately, L can be defined as follows:

$$L(G)(\tau) := L_1(G_{L_1})(\tau) \circ L_2(G_{L_2})(\tau)$$

where $\circ$ stands for ordinary relation composition.

The key part of the proof is showing transitivity of $\mathbf{E}$:

$$\begin{array}{l}
\forall G \in \mathrm{GK}(L).\ (e_1', e_2') \in \mathbf{E}(G_{L_1})(\tau) \wedge \\
\qquad (e_2', e_3') \in \mathbf{E}(G_{L_2})(\tau) \implies (e_1', e_3') \in \mathbf{E}(G)(\tau)
\end{array}$$

In order to prove this, we want the disjunct of $\mathbf{E}$ by which e_1' and e_2' are related to match the disjunct of $\mathbf{E}$ by which e_2' and e_3' are related (recall the three disjuncts in the definition of $\mathbf{E}$). To illustrate, say e_1' and e_2' are related because they reduce to related values (second disjunct). Now consider the three cases regarding e_2' and e_3':

(1) They both diverge. Fortunately, this contradicts our assumption about e_2', so this case cannot arise.

(2) They are related for the same reason as e_1' and e_2' are—*i.e.*, e_2' and e_3' reduce to related values. This is the "good" case. Relying on determinacy of reduction, we are done if we can show transitivity of the value relation. Formally, we need to show that $\overline{G_{L_1}}(\tau) \circ \overline{G_{L_2}}(\tau) \subseteq \overline{G}(\tau)$.

(3) They reduce to related function calls with related continuations. It is unclear how to make sense of this situation, so we want to rule it out!

In order to make case (2) straightforward to show, while simultaneously ruling out case (3) from consideration, we will need to define G_{L_1} and G_{L_2} carefully.

The key idea is as follows: for each pair of function values $(f_1, f_3) \in G$, come up with a value, v_2, that (1) uniquely identifies f_1 and f_3, and that (2) is not a normal function, but rather a "bad" value that gets stuck when applied to an argument. The first requirement allows us to ensure $G_{L_1}(\tau) \circ G_{L_2}(\tau) = G(\tau)$, as needed in proving transitivity of the value relation, by relating $(f_1, v_2) \in G_{L_1}$ and $(v_2, f_3) \in G_{L_2}$. The second requirement, together with Lemma 3, rules out the "bad" case (3) above.

Formally, since Type and CVal are countable sets, there exists an injective function $\mathbf{I} \in \text{Type} \times \text{Type} \times \text{CVal} \times \text{CVal} \rightarrow \mathbb{N}$. Using this function, one can decompose $G \in \text{VRelF}$ as follows:

$$G_{(1)}(\tau_1 \rightarrow \tau_2) := \{ (f_1, \mathbf{I}(\tau_1, \tau_2, f_1, f_3)) \mid (f_1, f_3) \in G(\tau_1 \rightarrow \tau_2) \}$$
$$G_{(2)}(\tau_1 \rightarrow \tau_2) := \{ (\mathbf{I}(\tau_1, \tau_2, f_1, f_3), f_3) \mid (f_1, f_3) \in G(\tau_1 \rightarrow \tau_2) \}$$

Taking G_{L_1} to be $G_{(1)}$ is, however, incorrect because if L_1 relates any values at function type, then the global knowledge will not be closed w.r.t. it (*i.e.*, $G_{(1)} \notin \text{GK}(L_1)$). To address this problem, we simply close $G_{(1)}$ accordingly, *i.e.*, we take G_{L_1} to be the least solution to the fixed-point equation $G_{L_1} = L_1(G_{L_1}) \cup G_{(1)}$ (and similarly for G_{L_2}).

With these definitions, we can show $\overline{G_{L_1}}(\tau) \circ \overline{G_{L_2}}(\tau) = \overline{G}(\tau)$ (if $G \in \text{GK}(L)$). Moreover, if we are in case (3) above, then Lemma 3 tells us that the functions being called—say, (f_1, f_2)—are *really* external, meaning that they are related by $G_{(2)}$. But by construction, this means that f_2 is an integer and thus e_2' gets stuck, contradicting the prior assumption that e_1' and e_2' reduce to values.

For further details, we refer the interested reader to our online appendix.

9. Related Work and Discussion

Our method of relation transition systems builds closely on ideas from several prior techniques. We compare here only to the most immediately related work.

Kripke Logical Relations The method of *logical relations* is an old and fundamentally important technique for proving a variety of deep properties in *higher-typed* languages, such as strong normalization [14] and parametricity [31]. Although they were originally geared toward reasoning about pure λ-calculi, logical relations have been successfully generalized to reason about state. In Pitts and Stark's seminal work on *Kripke logical relations (KLRs)* [29], logical relations are indexed by *possible worlds*, which characterize the runtime environment (*e.g.*, the assumptions about heaps) under which two programs are considered to be equivalent.

In the most recent work on KLRs, Dreyer *et al.* [5, 12] showed how to generalize Pitts and Stark's technique to reason about (1) modules whose correctness proofs require fine-grained control over how local state evolves over time, and (2) ML-like languages with higher-order state. W.r.t. point (1), they model possible worlds as *state transition systems (STSs)*, as we have described in Section 5. RTSs adopt Dreyer *et al.*'s STS technique directly, and thus it is relatively straightforward to port all the $\mathsf{F}^{\mu!}$ equivalence proofs given in their papers from using KLRs to using RTSs.

W.r.t. point (2), the challenge of supporting higher-order state in Kripke logical relations is that a naive attempt to construct a model of general reference types leads to a circularity. Intuitively, ℓ_1 and ℓ_2 are related at $\mathsf{ref}\,\tau$ under a possible world W iff W encodes the invariant that the heaps of the two programs map ℓ_1 and ℓ_2 to values v_1 and v_2 that are logically related at type τ. But how can the logical relation be indexed by a possible world W, which itself is defined in terms of the logical relation? If τ is restricted to base type (*e.g.*, int), there's no issue because the logical relation at int is simply the identity relation, but at higher type we have a problem.

Dreyer *et al.* handle higher-order state by means of Appel, McAllester, and Ahmed's technique of *step-indexed logical relations (SILRs)* [6, 2]. That is, they cut the aforementioned semantic circularity by indexing the model by a natural number ("step index") k, which represents the number of steps left on "the clock" and which gets decremented every time around the cycle between logical relations and possible worlds.

While step-indexing is a powerful weapon, it can be somewhat annoying to work with, due to the tedious threading of step counting throughout proofs [11]. More importantly, it seems fundamentally difficult to compose SILR proofs transitively. Ahmed studied the transitivity problem in her first paper on binary SILRs [3]. There, she observed a serious problem in naively proving that Appel and McAllester's original binary SILRs formed a PER. She proposed a way of regaining transitivity of SILRs for a pure language with recursive types [3], but her approach relies on baking syntactic typing assumptions into the model. Such an approach is unlikely to scale to reasoning about the intermediate and low-level languages of a certified compiler (one of our ultimate goals), which in general may be untyped. Moreover, we are not aware of any successful attempts to generalize her technique to SILRs for richer languages.

RTSs employ the idea of global knowledge in order to avoid the need for step-indexing in modeling higher-order state. Specifically, by parameterizing the heap relations in our worlds over the global knowledge G, we give heap invariants a way of referring to the global value equivalence, which is essentially what the step-indexed stratification of Kripke worlds is trying to achieve as well. In contrast to SILRs, we already have a proof that RTS equivalence for $\mathsf{F}^{\mu!}$ is transitive, and our method does not bake in any syntactic typing assumptions. In fact, our transitivity proof *depends* on instantiating global knowledge parameters with "trashy" (syntactically ill-typed) relations.

Bisimulations Aside from their general coinductive flavor, RTSs are closely related to two different bisimulation techniques.

From *normal form* (or *open*) bisimulations [32, 21, 34, 22, 23], we take the idea of treating unknown equivalent functions as black boxes. In particular, our expression equivalence relation $\mathbf{E}$, which deals explicitly with the possibility (in its third disjunct) that related terms may get stuck by calling unknown functions, is *highly* reminiscent of the formulation of normal form bisimulations. The main difference is that we express the notion of "stuckness" semantically, via the global knowledge parameter G, whereas normal form bisimulations express it syntactically by requiring related stuck terms to share a common head variable.

Normal form bisimulations draw much inspiration from game-semantics models [25], and our distinction between global and local knowledge has a seemingly gamey flavor as well. We leave a deeper study of the connection to game semantics to future work.

Sumii *et al.*'s *environmental* bisimulations (aka "relation-sets bisimulations") are perhaps the most powerful form of bisimulation yet developed for ML-like languages [27, 36, 19, 33, 35]. As the latter name suggests, these bisimulations are not term relations, but *sets* $\mathcal{X}$ whose elements are themselves term relations R (possibly paired with some additional environmental information, such as knowledge about the state of the heap). In essence, each $R \in \mathcal{X}$ defines some piece of "local knowledge" (following our terminology) about program equivalence. In order to show $\mathcal{X}$ to be a bisimulation, one must check that for all $R \in \mathcal{X}$, uses of terms related by R will never result in observably different outcomes and will always produce values that are related by some $R' \in \mathcal{X}$ s.t. $R' \supseteq R$.

Viewed in terms of RTSs, one can understand an environmental bisimulation $\mathcal{X}$ as effectively defining an abstract state space, with each $R \in \mathcal{X}$ as a distinct state. However, the accessibility (transition) relation between these states is essentially baked in: roughly speaking, a term relation R' is (publicly) accessible from another term relation R if $R' \supseteq R$. Thus, environmental bisimulations provide less control over the structure of the transition system than RTSs do, and they do not support anything directly analogous to the distinction between public and private transitions.

As a consequence, environmental bisimulations are most effective at proving equivalences that require transition systems with only public transitions (*e.g.*, the twin abstraction example), and their proofs for examples where private transitions are required (*e.g.*, the well-bracketed state change example) are comparatively "brute-force". It is an open question whether environmental bisimulations can be generalized to support the full power of RTSs with both public and private transitions.

Our approach to reasoning about parametricity of ADTs, by populating the local knowledge of a world with relations at abstract *type names*, is inspired directly by Sumii and Pierce [36].

Large vs. Small Worlds While RTSs build very closely on the state transition systems in Dreyer *et al.*'s KLRs [5, 12], there is a big difference between them, which we like to think of in terms of *large* vs. *small* worlds.

Under Dreyer *et al.*'s approach, in order to demonstrate the equivalence of functions f_1 and f_2 under a "possible world" W, one proves that they behave the same when passed arguments that are related under any "future world" W' of W, which may contain arbitrary new invariants concerning the local state of other modules in the program. One can really think of the "future world" relation (*i.e.*, the Kripke structure) as defining its own transition system (or *large* world), with the possible worlds W as its states.

In contrast, our RTSs rely only on *small* worlds. For us, worlds W are static entities that contain only the local invariants relevant to the module we are reasoning about, and nothing about any invariants for other parts of the program. In proving equivalence of functions f_1 and f_2 under W, we never quantify over any future worlds that extend W. Of course, in order to support compositional reasoning—*i.e.*, in order to show that consistency of worlds is preserved under separating conjunction—we must show that f_1 and f_2 behave the same when applied to arguments drawn from some larger relation than just W's local knowledge; but for that purpose we quantify over the global knowledge G, which is not a world, but rather an arbitrary extension of W's local knowledge.

These different accounts of worlds are strongly reminiscent of the different techniques that have been proposed for modeling resource invariants in logics of storable locks. Gotsman *et al.* [15] and Hobor *et al.* [16] presented, roughly contemporaneously, two different models of a concurrent separation logic for local reasoning about programs that dynamically allocate locks and store them in the heap. The central challenge in developing such a model is in dealing with the semantic circularity that arises when accounting for locks whose resource invariants are essentially recursive.

Gotsman *et al.* deal with this circularity syntactically, by assuming a static set of named "sorts" of resource invariants, which includes not all possible invariants, but only those needed for reasoning about a particular program. In contrast, Hobor *et al.* (and more recently, Buisse *et al.* [10]) deal with the circularity head-on, defining once and for all what recursive resource invariants *mean* using step-indexing. The latter is analogous to Dreyer *et al.*'s "large worlds" approach, which defines the space of all possible heap invariants, while the former is analogous to our "small world" approach of defining only the heap invariants needed within the module we are reasoning about.

Which is better? It is hard to say. Our small-world relations seem easier to compose transitively, precisely because we make no assumption whatsoever about the relatedness of functions defined outside of whatever module we are reasoning about. That is, the global knowledge G that we quantify over (*e.g.*, when proving world consistency) could include complete garbage, and the transitivity proof sketched in Section 8 relies in a fundamental way on the surgical insertion of contentful garbage into the global knowledge. On the other hand, it is also possible that this approach is what leads our model not to validate η-equivalence.

The Trouble with η-Equivalence One limitation of RTSs is that they do not validate the η-equivalence rules for function and universal types. To see why, suppose the η rule for functions were true (a similar argument applies to universals):

$$f : \tau_1 \rightarrow \tau_2 \vdash f \sim \lambda x.\, f\ x : \tau_1 \rightarrow \tau_2$$

Then, by definition, there would exist a consistent world W s.t. for all $G \in \mathrm{GK}(W)$, and for all functions f_1 and f_2 related by G, we would have f_1 and $\lambda x.\, f_2\ x$ related by G as well. (We're glossing over the role of states and transitions here because they're orthogonal.) The problem is that it is easy to construct an "uncivilized" G that contains (f_1, f_2) but not $(f_1, \lambda x.\, f_2\ x)$. Ironically, the same uncivilized G's that make our proof of transitivity (Section 8) possible also cause η to fail.

As a result, there are certain examples that have appeared in the literature on relational reasoning for ML-like languages [36, 22, 11], which our method cannot handle, precisely because they depend fundamentally on η-equivalence. The best-known one is the *syntactic minimal invariance* example [30], which demonstrates that the "infinite η-expansion" at a general recursive type (*e.g.*, $\mu\alpha.\mathsf{unit} + (\alpha \rightarrow \alpha)$) is equivalent to the identity function.

The lack of η in our model makes a lot of sense because our proofs make no assumptions about whether unknown functions are even λ-expressions, let alone whether they obey η. In this respect, RTSs are again similar to normal form bisimulations [21, 34], which are sometimes easier to prove congruent in their non-η-supporting formulations. There are known ways to close normal form bisimulations over η-equivalence by complicating the definition of consistency, and it is possible that we could adapt such techniques to work for RTSs.

However, our concern, based at this point solely on intuition, is that there may be a fundamental tradeoff between supporting η and supporting transitive composition of RTS equivalence proofs. In that case, we would consider transitivity a more important desideratum, at least in the context of reasoning about multi-phase compiler correctness. Moreover, our lack of support for η may in fact render our method applicable to reasoning about higher-order languages with more restricted equational theories (*e.g.*, OCaml with its equality tests on function pointers). We leave this matter to be explored further in future work.

10. Conclusion and Future Work

We have developed a novel method—*relation transition systems*—for proving equivalence of ML-like programs, combining some of the best aspects of Kripke logical relations, environmental bisimulations, and normal form bisimulations. In addition to providing a useful synthesis of the complementary advantages of its ancestors, our method shows promise as a way of reasoning about equivalences between different languages, thanks to (1) our avoidance of "syntactic" devices that would preclude inter-language reasoning, and (2) the transitive composability of RTS equivalence proofs. We have briefly sketched the proof of transitivity here in a simplified setting, and we intend to report on the full transitivity result in a forthcoming paper. We have mechanized the metatheory of RTSs in Coq and made the proofs available at the link below.

There are several exciting directions for future work. First and foremost, we aim to concretely demonstrate the suitability of RTSs for inter-language reasoning. For example, we would like to take Hur and Dreyer's recent work on Kripke logical relations between ML and assembly [17], replace the logical relations with RTSs, and then apply the technique to reasoning about compositional correctness of multi-phase compilation.

Second, following Dreyer *et al.*'s work on Kripke logical relations [12], we would like to explore how well our account of RTSs can be adapted to handle the introduction of control effects (call/cc, exceptions) into the language and/or the restriction of the language to first-order state. In principle, we believe it should be possible to employ techniques similar to theirs, but we have not yet tried.

Lastly, we have recently discovered what appears to be a deep connection between our technique of global vs. local knowledge and *Mendler-style recursion* [24, 38], in particular the notion of a *robustly postfixed-point (rpofp)*. L is defined to be a rpofp of an endofunction F if $\forall G \geq L.\ L \leq F(G)$. This bears a striking resemblance to our definition of consistency for local knowledges L, at least in the pure setting of Section 4. One interesting feature of rpofps is that they enjoy a "robust" version of Tarski's fixed-point theorem, which applies even when the endofunction F is not monotone. Indeed, in our scenario, F is *not* monotone, due to the quantification over related function arguments, and this is precisely what motivated our parameterization over G. We intend to explore this connection further in future work.

Online Appendix

Details of the RTS metatheory (in PDF and Coq) are available at:

`http://www.mpi-sws.org/~dreyer/papers/marriage`

Acknowledgments

We thank Deepak Garg, Eijiro Sumii, and the anonymous reviewers for very helpful feedback on the paper, as well as Andrew Pitts for alerting us to the connection with Mendler-style recursion.

References

[1] S. Abramsky. The lazy lambda calculus. In D. A. Turner, editor, *Research Topics in Functional Programming*, pages 65–117. 1990.

[2] A. Ahmed. *Semantics of Types for Mutable State*. PhD thesis, Princeton University, 2004.

[3] A. Ahmed. Step-indexed syntactic logical relations for recursive and quantified types. In *ESOP*, 2006.

[4] A. Ahmed and M. Blume. An equivalence-preserving CPS translation via multi-language semantics. In *ICFP*, 2011.

[5] A. Ahmed, D. Dreyer, and A. Rossberg. State-dependent representation independence. In *POPL*, 2009.

[6] A. Appel and D. McAllester. An indexed model of recursive types for foundational proof-carrying code. *TOPLAS*, 23(5):657–683, 2001.

[7] N. Benton and C.-K. Hur. Biorthogonality, step-indexing and compiler correctness. In *ICFP*, 2009.

[8] L. Birkedal, R. E. Møgelberg, J. Schwinghammer, and K. Støvring. First steps in synthetic guarded domain theory: step-indexing in the topos of trees. In *LICS*, 2011.

[9] L. Birkedal, N. Torp-Smith, and H. Yang. Semantics of separation-logic typing and higher-order frame rules for Algol-like languages. *LMCS*, 2(5:1), 2006.

[10] A. Buisse, L. Birkedal, and K. Støvring. A step-indexed Kripke model of separation logic for storable locks. In *MFPS*, 2011.

[11] D. Dreyer, A. Ahmed, and L. Birkedal. Logical step-indexed logical relations. *LMCS*, 7(2:16):1–37, June 2011.

[12] D. Dreyer, G. Neis, and L. Birkedal. The impact of higher-order state and control effects on local relational reasoning. In *ICFP*, 2010.

[13] D. Dreyer, G. Neis, A. Rossberg, and L. Birkedal. A relational modal logic for higher-order stateful ADTs. In *POPL*, 2010.

[14] J.-Y. Girard, Y. Lafont, and P. Taylor. *Proofs and Types*, volume 7 of *Cambridge Tracts in Theoretical Computer Science*. Cambridge University Press, 1989.

[15] A. Gotsman, J. Berdine, B. Cook, N. Rinetzky, and M. Sagiv. Local reasoning about storable locks and threads. In *APLAS*, 2007.

[16] A. Hobor, A. Appel, and F. Zappa Nardelli. Oracle semantics for concurrent separation logic. In *ESOP*, 2008.

[17] C.-K. Hur and D. Dreyer. A Kripke logical relation between ML and assembly. In *POPL*, 2011.

[18] V. Koutavas, P. B. Levy, and E. Sumii. From applicative to environmental bisimulation. In *MFPS*, 2011.

[19] V. Koutavas and M. Wand. Small bisimulations for reasoning about higher-order imperative programs. In *POPL*, 2006.

[20] J. Laird. A fully abstract trace semantics for general references. In *ICALP*, 2007.

[21] S. Lassen. Eager normal form bisimulation. In *LICS*, 2005.

[22] S. B. Lassen and P. B. Levy. Typed normal form bisimulation. In *CSL*, 2007.

[23] S. B. Lassen and P. B. Levy. Typed normal form bisimulation for parametric polymorphism. In *LICS*, 2008.

[24] N. P. Mendler. Inductive types and type constraints in the second-order lambda-calculus. *Annals of Pure and Applied Logic*, 51(1–2):159–172, 1991.

[25] A. S. Murawski and N. Tzevelekos. Game semantics for good general references. In *LICS*, 2011.

[26] G. Neis, D. Dreyer, and A. Rossberg. Non-parametric parametricity. *JFP*, 21(4&5):497–562, 2011.

[27] B. C. Pierce and D. Sangiorgi. Behavioral equivalence in the polymorphic pi-calculus. *Journal of the ACM*, 47(3):531–586, 2000.

[28] A. Pitts. Typed operational reasoning. In B. C. Pierce, editor, *Advanced Topics in Types and Programming Languages*, chapter 7. MIT Press, 2005.

[29] A. Pitts and I. Stark. Operational reasoning for functions with local state. In *HOOTS*, 1998.

[30] A. M. Pitts. Relational properties of domains. *Information and Computation*, 127:66–90, 1996.

[31] J. C. Reynolds. Types, abstraction and parametric polymorphism. In *Information Processing*, 1983.

[32] D. Sangiorgi. The lazy lambda calculus in a concurrency scenario. *Information and Computation*, 111(1):120–153, 1994.

[33] D. Sangiorgi, N. Kobayashi, and E. Sumii. Environmental bisimulations for higher-order languages. In *LICS*, 2007.

[34] K. Støvring and S. Lassen. A complete, co-inductive syntactic theory of sequential control and state. In *POPL*, 2007.

[35] E. Sumii. A complete characterization of observational equivalence in polymorphic λ-calculus with general references. In *CSL*, 2009.

[36] E. Sumii and B. Pierce. A bisimulation for type abstraction and recursion. *Journal of the ACM*, 54(5):1–43, 2007.

[37] J. Thamsborg and L. Birkedal. A Kripke logical relation for effect-based program transformations. In *ICFP*, 2011.

[38] T. Uustalu and V. Vene. Mendler-style inductive types, categorically. *Nordic Journal of Computing*, 6(3):343–361, 1999.

[39] V. Vafeiadis. Concurrent separation logic and operational semantics. In *MFPS*, 2011.

[40] P. Wadler. Theorems for free! In *FPCA*, 1989.

Information Effects

Roshan P. James
Indiana University
rpjames@indiana.edu

Amr Sabry
Indiana University
sabry@indiana.edu

Abstract

Computation is a physical process which, like all other physical processes, is fundamentally reversible. From the notion of type isomorphisms, we derive a typed, universal, and reversible computational model in which information is treated as a linear resource that can neither be duplicated nor erased. We use this model as a semantic foundation for computation and show that the "gap" between conventional irreversible computation and logically reversible computation can be captured by a type-and-effect system. Our type-and-effect system is structured as an arrow metalanguage that exposes creation and erasure of information as explicit effect operations. Irreversible computations arise from interactions with an implicit information environment, thus making them a derived notion, much like open systems in Physics. We sketch several applications which can benefit from an explicit treatment of information effects, such as quantitative information-flow security and differential privacy.

Categories and Subject Descriptors D.3.1 [*Formal Definitions and Theory*]; F.3.2 [*Semantics of Programming Languages*]; F.3.3 [*Studies of Program Constructs*]: Type structure

General Terms Languages, Theory

Keywords Arrows, Linear logic, Quantum computing, Reversible logic.

1. Introduction

> "Turing hoped that his abstracted-paper-tape model was so simple, so transparent and well defined, that it would not depend on any assumptions about physics that could conceivably be falsified, and therefore that it could become the basis of an abstract theory of computation that was independent of the underlying physics. 'He thought,' as Feynman once put it, 'that he understood paper.' But he was mistaken. Real, quantum-mechanical paper is wildly different from the abstract stuff that the Turing machine uses. The Turing machine is entirely classical, and does not allow for the possibility the paper might have different symbols written on it in different universes, and that those might interfere with one another." [11, p.252]

The above quote by David Deutsch, originally stated in the context of quantum computing, stems from the observation that *even the most abstract models of computation embody some laws of Physics*. Indeed, conventional classical models of computation, including boolean logic, the Turing machine, and the λ-calculus, are founded on primitives which correspond to *irreversible* physical processes. For example, a *nand* gate is an irreversible logical operation in the sense that its inputs cannot generally be recovered from observing its output, and so is the operation of overriding a cell on a Turing machine tape with a new symbol, and so is a β-reduction which typically erases or duplicates values in a way that is destructive and irreversible.

Our main thesis is that by embodying irreversible physical primitives, conventional abstract models of computation have also inadvertently included some *implicit* computational effects, which we call *information effects*. As a consequence of this approach, many applications in which information manipulation is computationally significant are put beyond the reach of our conceptual model of computation. Such applications include quantitative information-flow security [42], differential privacy [14], energy-aware computing [29, 48], VLSI design [30], and biochemical models of computation [9].

In more detail, in Physics, the fundamental laws describe processes in closed systems where every action is reversible. Open systems, which allow irreversible processes, are a derived notion — they can be considered as a subsystem of a closed system which treats the rest of the system as a *global environment*. Pushing the analogy to computation, and as the remainder of the paper formalizes, an irreversible computation can therefore be considered as one that interacts with some global environment via implicit computational effects. Put differently, irreversible computational models like the λ-calculus embody some implicit computational effects which, following the tradition of programming language research, we find useful to expose and study as first-class entities.

Structure and Main Results.

- We develop a pure reversible model of computation that, unlike many other models, does not pre-suppose an existing irreversible model. Our model is obtained from the type isomorphisms and categorical structures that underlie models of linear logic and quantum computing. Technically, the model treats *information* as a linear resource that can neither be erased nor duplicated in a way that is reminiscent of forbidding contraction and weakening in linear logic and the no-cloning and no-deleting theorems of quantum mechanics.[1]
- We develop an *arrow metalanguage* that layers effects on top of the pure reversible model above using an arrow abstract type [24]. These arrow effects consist of an explicit `erase` operation that can be used to discard values and an explicit `create` operation which can be used to introduce and duplicate

[1] An embedding of our reversible programming model in Haskell along with several examples can be downloaded from `http://www.cs.indiana.edu/~sabry/papers/Pi.hs`.

POPL'12, January 25–27, 2012, Philadelphia, PA, USA.

values. This construction has the immediate benefit that the information effects are exposed and tracked by the type system.

- We show how to translate a Turing-complete first-order functional language with loops to our reversible model. The translation exposes the implicit erasure and duplication of information in the source language as explicit computational effects. The translation and its associated correctness proof constitute the main technical contribution of the paper.
- We establish connections to, and explore how, the explicit treatment of information effects can benefit applications such as quantitative information-flow security and differential privacy.

2. Logical Reversibility and Information

We review the notion of logical reversibility and its connection to information.

2.1 Reversible Logic

Toffoli's pioneering work on reversible models of computation [44] established the following fundamental theorem.

THEOREM 2.1 (Toffoli). *For every finite function* $\phi : bool^m \rightarrow bool^n$ *there exists an invertible finite function* $\phi^R : bool^{r+m} \rightarrow bool^{r+m}$, *with* $r \leq n$, *such that* $\phi(x_1, \ldots, x_m) = (y_1, \ldots, y_n)$ *iff*

$$\phi^R(x_1, \ldots, x_m, \overbrace{false, \ldots, false}^{r}) = (\overbrace{\cdots}^{m+r-n}, y_1, \ldots, y_n)$$

The proof of the theorem is constructive. Intuitively, the function ϕ is "compiled" to a reversible function ϕ^R which takes extra arguments and produces extra results. When the extra arguments are each fixed to the constant value *false* and the extra results are ignored, the reversible function behaves exactly like the original function. For example, the function $and : bool^2 \rightarrow bool$ can be compiled to the function $toffoli : bool^3 \rightarrow bool^3$ which behaves as follows:

$toffoli(v_1, v_2, v_3) =$
  if $(v_1$ *and* $v_2)$ **then** $(v_1, v_2, not(v_3))$ **else** (v_1, v_2, v_3)

A quick examination of the truth table of the *toffoli* function shows that it is reversible. Moreover, we can check that:

$toffoli(v_1, v_2, false) =$
  if $(v_1$ *and* $v_2)$ **then** $(v_1, v_2, true)$ **else** $(v_1, v_2, false)$

which confirms that we can recover *and* if we ignore the first two outputs.

Toffoli's fundamental theorem already includes some of the basic ingredients of our results. Specifically, it establishes that:

- it is possible to base the computation of finite functions on reversible functions;
- irreversible functions are special cases of reversible functions which interact with a global heap (which supplies the fixed constant values) and a global garbage dump (which absorbs the undesired results); and
- it is possible to translate irreversible functions to reversible functions to expose the heap and garbage.

In this context, our results can be seen as extending Toffoli's in the following ways:

- Instead of working with truth tables, we work with a rich type structure and use (partial) bijections between the types;
- We introduce term languages for irreversible and reversible computations and develop a type-directed compositional translation;
- We extend the entire framework to deal with infinite functions, e.g., on the natural numbers.
- We establish that the manipulations of the heap and the garbage constitute computational effects that can be tracked by the type system.

2.2 Thermodynamics of Computation and Information

Toffoli's work was performed in the context of the work of Landauer [28] and Bennett [7] that established the remarkable result, known as the *Landauer principle*, relating irreversible computations to increase in information uncertainty (entropy).

DEFINITION 2.2 (Entropy of a variable). *Let 'b' be a (not necessarily finite) type whose values are labeled* $b^1, b^2, \ldots$. *Let* ξ *be a random variable of type b that is equal to* b^i *with probability* p_i. *The entropy of* ξ *is defined as* $-\sum p_i \log p_i$.

DEFINITION 2.3 (Output entropy of a function). *Consider a function* $f : b_1 \rightarrow b_2$ *where* b_2 *is a (not necessarily finite) type whose values are labeled* $b_2^1, b_2^2, \ldots$. *The output entropy of the function is given by* $-\sum q_j \log q_j$ *where* q_j *indicates the probability of the output of the function to have value* ${b_2}^j$.

DEFINITION 2.4. *We say a function is* information-preserving *if its output entropy is equal to the entropy of its input.*

For example, consider a variable ξ of type $bool \times bool$. The information content of this variable depends on the probability distribution of the four possible $bool \times bool$ values. If we have a computational situation in which the pair $(false, false)$ could occur with probability $1/2$, the pairs $(false, true)$ and $(true, false)$ can each occur with probability $1/4$, and the pair $(true, true)$ cannot occur, the information content of ξ would be:

$$1/2 \log 2 + 1/4 \log 4 + 1/4 \log 4 + 0 \log 0$$

which equals 1.5 bits of information. If, however, the four possible pairs had an equal probability, the same formula would calculate the information content to be 2 bits, which is the maximal amount for a variable of type $bool \times bool$. The minimum entropy 0 corresponds to a variable that happens to be constant with no uncertainty.

Now consider the $bool \rightarrow bool$ function *not*. Let p_F and p_T be the probabilities that the input is *false* or *true* respectively. The outputs occur with the reverse probabilities, i.e., p_T is the probability that the output is *false* and p_F is the probability that the output is *true*. Hence the output entropy of the function is $-p_F \log p_F - p_T \log p_T$ which is the same as the input entropy and the function is information-preserving. As another example, consider the $bool \rightarrow bool$ function $constT(x) = true$ which discards its input. The output of the function is always *true* with no uncertainty, which means that the output entropy is 0, and that the function is not information-preserving. As a third example, consider the function *and* and let the inputs occur with equal probabilities, i.e., let the entropy of the input be 2. The output is *false* with probability $3/4$ and *true* with probability $1/4$, which means that the output entropy is about 0.8 and the function is not information-preserving. As a final example, consider the $bool \rightarrow bool \times bool$ function $fanout\ (x) = (x, x)$ which duplicates its input. Let the input be *false* with probability p_F and *true* be probability p_T. The output is $(false, false)$ with probability p_F and $(true, true)$ with probability p_T which means that the output entropy is the same as the input entropy and the function is information-preserving.

2.3 Logical Reversibility

We are now ready to formalize the connection between reversibility and entropy, once we define logical reversibility of computations.

DEFINITION 2.5 (Logical reversibility [49]). *A function* $f : b_1 \rightarrow b_2$ *is logically reversible if there exists an inverse function* g :

$b_2 \rightarrow b_1$ *such that for all values* $v_1 \in b_1$ *and* $v_2 \in b_2$, *we have:* $f(v_1) = v_2$ *iff* $g(v_2) = v_1$.

The main proposition that motivates and justifies our approach is that logically reversible functions are information-preserving.

PROPOSITION 2.6. *A function is logically reversible iff it is information-preserving.*

Looking at the examples above, we argued that $constT$, and are not information-preserving and that not, $fanout$ are information-preserving. As expected, neither $constT$ nor and are logically reversible and not is logically reversible. The situation with $fanout$ is however subtle and deserves some explanation. First, note that the definition of logical reversibility does not require the functions to be total, and hence it is possible to define a *partial* function $fanin$ that is the logical inverse of $fanout$. The function $fanin$ maps $(false, false)$ to $false$, $(true, true)$ to $true$ and is undefined otherwise. Arguing that partial functions like $fanin$ are information-preserving requires some care. Let the inputs to $fanin$ occur with equal probabilities, i.e., let the entropy of the input be 2. Disregarding the partiality of $fanin$, one might reason that the output is $false$ with probability $1/4$ and $true$ with probability $1/4$ and hence that the output entropy is 1 which contradicts the fact that $fanin$ is logically reversible. The subtlety is that entropy is defined with respect to observing some probabilistic event: an infinite loop is not an event that can be observed and hence the entropy analysis, just like the definition of logical reversibility, only applies to the pairs of inputs and outputs on which the function is defined. In the case of $fanin$ this means that the only inputs that can be considered are $(false, false)$ and $(true, true)$ and in this case it is clear that the function is information-preserving as expected.

Intermezzo. Linear logic [18] is often used as a framework for controlling resource use. Linearity however must not be confused with the criterion of information preservation presented here. Consider $constT'(x) = \textbf{if } x \textbf{ then } true \textbf{ else } true$ which is extensionally equivalent to the constant function $constT(x) = true$ above. In a linear type system that tracks the *syntactic* occurrences of variables, $constT'$ would be deemed acceptable because x is linearly used. However as shown above the function $constT$ is not information-preserving. Despite this difference, there does however appear to be some deep connections between linear logic and the physical notions of reversible and quantum computing. Indeed as Girard explains [18, pp. 6,17], linear logic embodies a simple and radical change of viewpoint from other logics and this change has a physical flavor.

3. Bijections: Π

Building on the insights of Toffoli, we now turn our attention to defining a logically reversible language with a type structure and a term language. A natural starting point for such a language is the notion of type isomorphisms. In this section, we restrict ourselves to isomorphisms between finite types and show that they naturally lead to a simple programming language which we call Π. In addition to presenting the syntax, type system, and semantics of Π, we establish that Π is universal for reversible combinational circuits.

3.1 Types

The set of finite types b is constructed using sums and products of the primitive type 1. We have the following syntax for types and values:

$$\begin{array}{rcl} value\ types, b & ::= & 1 \mid b + b \mid b \times b \\ values, v & ::= & () \mid left\ v \mid right\ v \mid (v, v) \end{array}$$

The type 1 has exactly one inhabitant called (). Sums allow us to create values that we can distinguish using *left* and *right* constructors and pairs allow the encoding of tuples. Thus we have the type judgements:

$$\frac{}{\vdash () : 1} \qquad \frac{\vdash v_1 : b_1 \quad \vdash v_2 : b_2}{\vdash (v_1, v_2) : b_1 \times b_2}$$

$$\frac{\vdash v : b_1}{\vdash left\ v : b_1 + b_2} \qquad \frac{\vdash v : b_2}{\vdash right\ v : b_1 + b_2}$$

Two types b_1 and b_2 are isomorphic if we can construct a bijective map between their values. The set of sound and complete isomorphisms for finite types is the *congruence closure* of the following primitive isomorphisms [15]:

$$\begin{array}{rcl} b_1 + b_2 & \leftrightarrow & b_2 + b_1 \\ b_1 + (b_2 + b_3) & \leftrightarrow & (b_1 + b_2) + b_3 \\ \\ 1 \times b & \leftrightarrow & b \\ b_1 \times b_2 & \leftrightarrow & b_2 \times b_1 \\ b_1 \times (b_2 \times b_3) & \leftrightarrow & (b_1 \times b_2) \times b_3 \\ \\ (b_1 + b_2) \times b_3 & \leftrightarrow & (b_1 \times b_3) + (b_2 \times b_3) \end{array}$$

These isomorphisms are already familiar to us from arithmetic or logic (reading 1 as $true$, $\times$ as conjunction, and $+$ as disjunction). Note however that the isomorphisms do not include some familiar logical tautologies, in particular:

$$\begin{array}{rcl} b \times b & \not\leftrightarrow & b \\ b_1 + (b_2 \times b_3) & \not\leftrightarrow & (b_1 + b_2) \times (b_1 + b_3) \end{array}$$

Even though these identities are expected in propositional logic, they are not satisfied in standard arithmetic nor in any logic that accounts for resources like linear logic.

3.2 Syntax and Semantics

We turn the above isomorphisms into a programming language by associating primitive operators corresponding to the left-to-right and right-to-left reading of each isomorphism. We gather these operators into the table below:

$$\begin{array}{rcl} swap^+ : & b_1 + b_2 \leftrightarrow b_2 + b_1 & : swap^+ \\ assocl^+ : & b_1 + (b_2 + b_3) \leftrightarrow (b_1 + b_2) + b_3 & : assocr^+ \\ unite : & 1 \times b \leftrightarrow b & : uniti \\ swap^\times : & b_1 \times b_2 \leftrightarrow b_2 \times b_1 & : swap^\times \\ assocl^\times : & b_1 \times (b_2 \times b_3) \leftrightarrow (b_1 \times b_2) \times b_3 & : assocr^\times \\ distrib : & (b_1 + b_2) \times b_3 \leftrightarrow (b_1 \times b_3) + (b_2 \times b_3) & : factor \end{array}$$

Each line of this table is to be read as the definition of one or two operators. For example, the third line declares the two operators $unite : 1 \times b \leftrightarrow b$ and $uniti : b \leftrightarrow 1 \times b$. Each of the two cases of commutativity defines one operator that is its own inverse.

Now that we have primitive operators we need some means of composing them. We construct the composition combinators out of the closure conditions for isomorphisms. Thus we have program constructs that witness reflexivity id, symmetry sym, and transitivity $⨾$, and two parallel composition combinators, one for sums and one for pairs.

$$\frac{}{id : b \leftrightarrow b} \qquad \frac{c : b_1 \leftrightarrow b_2}{sym\ c : b_2 \leftrightarrow b_1} \qquad \frac{c_1 : b_1 \leftrightarrow b_2 \quad c_2 : b_2 \leftrightarrow b_3}{c_1 ⨾ c_2 : b_1 \leftrightarrow b_3}$$

$$\frac{c_1 : b_1 \leftrightarrow b_3 \quad c_2 : b_2 \leftrightarrow b_4}{c_1 + c_2 : b_1 + b_2 \leftrightarrow b_3 + b_4} \qquad \frac{c_1 : b_1 \leftrightarrow b_3 \quad c_2 : b_2 \leftrightarrow b_4}{c_1 \times c_2 : b_1 \times b_2 \leftrightarrow b_3 \times b_4}$$

DEFINITION 3.1. *(Syntax of Π) We collect our types, values, and combinators, to get the full language definition.*

$$\begin{array}{rcl}
\textit{value types}, b & ::= & 1 \mid b+b \mid b \times b \\
\textit{values}, v & ::= & () \mid \textit{left}\ v \mid \textit{right}\ v \mid (v, v) \\
\\
\textit{comb. types}, t & ::= & b \leftrightarrow b \\
\textit{iso} & ::= & \textit{swap}^{+} \mid \textit{assocl}^{+} \mid \textit{assocr}^{+} \\
& \mid & \textit{unite} \mid \textit{uniti} \\
& \mid & \textit{swap}^{\times} \mid \textit{assocl}^{\times} \mid \textit{assocr}^{\times} \\
& \mid & \textit{distrib} \mid \textit{factor} \\
\textit{comb.}, c & ::= & \textit{iso} \mid \textit{id} \mid \textit{sym}\ c \mid c \fatsemi c \mid c+c \mid c \times c
\end{array}$$

By design, every program construct $c : b_1 \leftrightarrow b_2$ has an adjoint $c^{\dagger} : b_2 \leftrightarrow b_1$ that works in the other direction. Given a program $c : b_1 \leftrightarrow b_2$ in Π, we can run it by supplying it with a value $v_1 : b_1$. The evaluation rules $c\ v_1 \mapsto v_2$ for the primitive isomorphisms are given below:

$$\begin{array}{rlcl}
\textit{swap}^{+} & (\textit{left}\ v) & \mapsto & \textit{right}\ v \\
\textit{swap}^{+} & (\textit{right}\ v) & \mapsto & \textit{left}\ v \\
\textit{assocl}^{+} & (\textit{left}\ v_1) & \mapsto & \textit{left}\ (\textit{left}\ v_1) \\
\textit{assocl}^{+} & (\textit{right}\ (\textit{left}\ v_2)) & \mapsto & \textit{left}\ (\textit{right}\ v_2) \\
\textit{assocl}^{+} & (\textit{right}\ (\textit{right}\ v_3)) & \mapsto & \textit{right}\ v_3 \\
\textit{assocr}^{+} & (\textit{left}\ (\textit{left}\ v_1)) & \mapsto & \textit{left}\ v_1 \\
\textit{assocr}^{+} & (\textit{left}\ (\textit{right}\ v_2)) & \mapsto & \textit{right}\ (\textit{left}\ v_2) \\
\textit{assocr}^{+} & (\textit{right}\ v_3) & \mapsto & \textit{right}\ (\textit{right}\ v_3) \\
\textit{unite} & ((), v) & \mapsto & v \\
\textit{uniti} & v & \mapsto & ((), v) \\
\textit{swap}^{\times} & (v_1, v_2) & \mapsto & (v_2, v_1) \\
\textit{assocl}^{\times} & (v_1, (v_2, v_3)) & \mapsto & ((v_1, v_2), v_3) \\
\textit{assocr}^{\times} & ((v_1, v_2), v_3) & \mapsto & (v_1, (v_2, v_3)) \\
\textit{distrib} & (\textit{left}\ v_1, v_3) & \mapsto & \textit{left}\ (v_1, v_3) \\
\textit{distrib} & (\textit{right}\ v_2, v_3) & \mapsto & \textit{right}\ (v_2, v_3) \\
\textit{factor} & (\textit{left}\ (v_1, v_3)) & \mapsto & (\textit{left}\ v_1, v_3) \\
\textit{factor} & (\textit{right}\ (v_2, v_3)) & \mapsto & (\textit{right}\ v_2, v_3)
\end{array}$$

The semantics of composition combinators is:

$$\frac{}{\textit{id}\ v \mapsto v} \qquad \frac{c^{\dagger}\ v_1 \mapsto v_2}{(\textit{sym}\ c)\ v_1 \mapsto v_2} \qquad \frac{c_1\ v_1 \mapsto v \quad c_2\ v \mapsto v_2}{(c_1 \fatsemi c_2)\ v_1 \mapsto v_2}$$

$$\frac{c_1\ v_1 \mapsto v_2}{(c_1 + c_2)\ (\textit{left}\ v_1) \mapsto \textit{left}\ v_2} \qquad \frac{c_2\ v_1 \mapsto v_2}{(c_1 + c_2)\ (\textit{right}\ v_1) \mapsto \textit{right}\ v_2}$$

$$\frac{c_1\ v_1 \mapsto v_3 \quad c_2\ v_2 \mapsto v_4}{(c_1 \times c_2)\ (v_1, v_2) \mapsto (v_3, v_4)}$$

The use of the *sym* constructor uses the adjoint to reverse the program. We can now verify that the adjoint of each construct c is its inverse in the sense that the evaluation of the adjoint maps the output of c to its input. This property is a strong version of logical reversibility in which the inverse of a program is simply obtained by the adjoint operation.

PROPOSITION 3.2 (Logical Reversibility). $c\ v \mapsto v'$ *iff* $c^{\dagger} v' \mapsto v$.

3.3 Expressiveness

There are several universal primitives for conventional (irreversible) hardware circuits (for example, *nand* and *fanout*). In the case of reversible hardware circuits, the canonical universal primitive is the *toffoli* gate (mentioned in Sec. 2.1) which we can express in Π as shown below. Let us start with encoding booleans. The type $1+1$ is the type of booleans with *left* () representing *true* and *right* () representing *false*. Boolean negation *not* is simply $\textit{swap}^{+}$. The Toffoli gate takes three boolean inputs: if the first two inputs are *true* then the third bit is negated. Even though Π lacks conditional expressions, they are expressible using the distributivity laws as we demonstrate. Given any combinator $c : b \leftrightarrow b$ we can construct a combinator called $\mathbf{if}_c : \textit{bool} \times b \leftrightarrow \textit{bool} \times b$ in terms of c, where $\mathbf{if}_c$ behaves like a one-armed *if*-expression. If the supplied boolean is *true* then the combinator c is used to transform the value of type b. If the boolean is *false*, then the value of type b remains unchanged. We can write down the combinator for $\mathbf{if}_c$ in terms of c as $\textit{distrib} \fatsemi ((\textit{id} \times c) + \textit{id}) \fatsemi \textit{factor}$.

Let us look at the combinator pictorially as if it were a circuit and values are like particles that flow through this circuit. The diagram below shows the input value of type $(1+1) \times b$ processed by the distribute operator *distrib*, which converts it into a value of type $(1 \times b) + (1 \times b)$. In the *left* branch, which corresponds to the case when the boolean is *true* (i.e. the value was *left* ()), the combinator c is applied to the value of type b. The right branch which corresponds to the boolean being *false* passes along the value of type b unchanged.

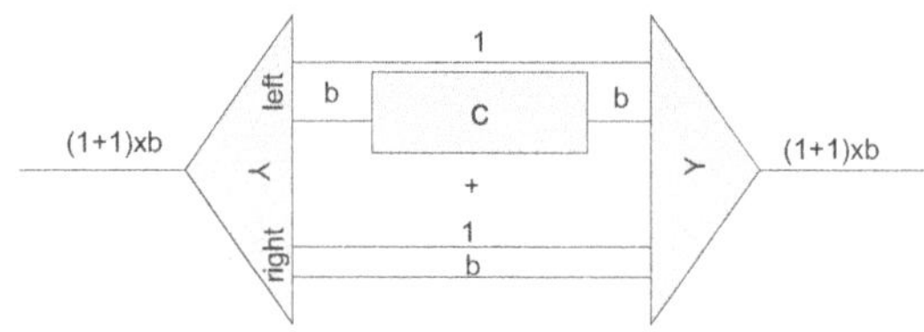

We will be seeing many more such wiring diagrams in this paper and it is useful to note some conventions about them. Wires indicate a value that can exist in the program. Each wire, whenever possible, is annotated with its type and sometimes additional information to help clarify its role. When multiple wires run in parallel, it means that those values exist in the system at the same time, indicating pair types. When there is a disjunction, we put a + between the wires. Combinators for distribution *distrib* and factoring *factor* are represented as triangles. Other triangles may be used and, in each case, types or labels will be used to clarify their roles. Finally, we don't draw boxes for combinators such as *id*, commutativity, and associativity, but instead just shuffle the wires as appropriate.

The combinator $\mathbf{if}_{not}$ has type $\textit{bool} \times \textit{bool} \leftrightarrow \textit{bool} \times \textit{bool}$ and negates its second argument if the first argument is *true*. This gate $\mathbf{if}_{not}$ is often referred to as the *cnot* gate. If we iterate this construction once more, the resulting combinator $\mathbf{if}_{cnot}$ has type $\textit{bool} \times (\textit{bool} \times \textit{bool}) \leftrightarrow \textit{bool} \times (\textit{bool} \times \textit{bool})$. The resulting gate checks the first argument and if it is *true*, proceeds to check the second argument. If that is also *true* then it will negate the third argument. Thus $\mathbf{if}_{cnot}$ is the required Toffoli gate.

4. Partial Bijections: Π^o

We extend Π with recursive types and a family of looping operators. The resulting language, Π^o, is still a language of bijections but, because it can express infinite loops, the bijections may be partial. Despite this extension, the strong version of logical reversibility (Prop. 3.2) still holds for Π^o.

4.1 Isorecursive Types and Trace Operators

We extend Π in two dimensions: (i) by adding recursive types and (ii) by adding looping constructs. The combination of the two extensions makes the extended language, Π^o, expressive enough to write arbitrary looping programs, including non-terminating ones.

DEFINITION 4.1. *(Syntax of Π^o) We extend Def. 3.1 as follows:*

$$\begin{array}{rcl}
\textit{value types}, b & ::= & \ldots \mid \mu x.b \mid x \\
\textit{values}, v & ::= & \ldots \mid \langle v \rangle \\
\\
\textit{combinator types}, t & ::= & b \rightleftharpoons b \\
\textit{isomorphisms}, \textit{iso} & ::= & \ldots \mid \textit{fold} \mid \textit{unfold} \\
\textit{combinators}, c & ::= & \ldots \mid \textit{trace}\ c
\end{array}$$

The remainder of this section explains the new additions in detail. First, as we illustrate below, it is possible to write infinite loops in Π^o and hence the combinators may correspond to *partial* bijections. We distinguish the type of partial bijections from the previous type of total bijections by using the symbol $\rightleftharpoons$ instead of $\leftrightarrow$.

Isorecursive Types. The finite types are extended with isorecursive types $\mu x.b$. These types fit naturally within the framework of a reversible language as they come equipped with two isomorphisms *fold* and *unfold* that witness the equivalence of a value of a recursive type with all its "unrollings:"

$$fold : \quad b[\mu x.b/x] \rightleftharpoons \mu x.b \quad : unfold$$

To create recursive values, we introduce the notation $\langle v \rangle$ with the following type rule:

$$\frac{\vdash v : b[\mu x.b/x]}{\vdash \langle v \rangle : \mu x.b}$$

In other words, to construct a value of type $\mu x.b$, we must first have a value of type $b[\mu x.b/x]$. Depending on the structure of b, this may or not be possible. For example, if the recursive type is $\mu x.x$ then to construct a value of that type, we need to have a value of the same type, ad infinitum. In contrast, if the recursive type is $\mu x.1 + x$, then we can create the initial value *left* () of type $1 + (\mu x.1 + x)$ which leads to the value $\langle$*left* ()$\rangle$ of type $\mu x.1 + x$ and then $\langle$*right* $\langle$*left* ()$\rangle\rangle$, $\langle$*right* $\langle$*right* $\langle$*left* ()$\rangle\rangle\rangle$ and so on. In fact, the type $\mu x.1 + x$ represents the natural numbers in unary format. The semantics of *fold* and *unfold* is simply $fold\ v \mapsto \langle v \rangle$ and $unfold\ \langle v \rangle \mapsto v$.

Trace Operators. Traced categories [25] have proved useful for modeling recursion [21]. In the context of Π, the fundamental idea is to add a trace operator with this typing rule:

$$\frac{c : b_1 + b_2 \rightleftharpoons b_1 + b_3}{trace\ c : b_2 \rightleftharpoons b_3}$$

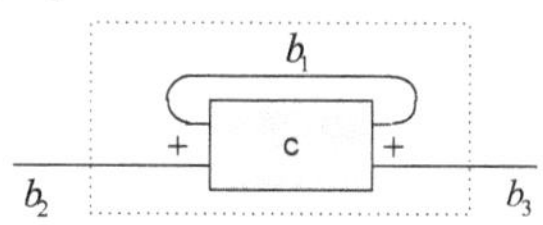

Intuitively, we are given a computation c that accepts a value of type $b_1 + b_2$ and we build a looping version *trace c* that only takes a value of type b_2. As the diagram illustrates, the value of type b_2 is injected into the sum type $b_1 + b_2$ by tagging it with the *right* constructor. The tagged value is passed to c. As long as c returns a value that is tagged with *left*, that tagged value is fed back to c. As soon as a value tagged with *right* is returned, that value is returned as the final answer of the *trace c* computation. Formally, we can express this semantics as follows:

$$\frac{(c \fatsemi loop_c)\ (right\ v_1) \mapsto v_2}{(trace\ c)\ v_1 \mapsto v_2} \quad \frac{(c \fatsemi loop_c)\ (left\ v_1) \mapsto v_2}{loop_c\ (left\ v_1) \mapsto v_2}$$

$$\frac{}{loop_c\ (right\ v) \mapsto v}$$

where for each c, $loop_c$ is an internal cyclic version of c.

As before, each combinator has an adjoint and the language is reversible.

PROPOSITION 4.2 (Logical Reversibility). $c\ v \mapsto v'$ *iff* $c^\dagger\ v' \mapsto v$.

Proof. The operators *fold* and and *unfold* are adjoint to each other. The adjoint of *trace c* is *trace* $c^\dagger$.

4.2 Expressiveness

We now present several programming examples that illustrate the expressiveness of Π^o. These examples are interesting in their own right and are further developed in the accompanying Haskell code which includes implementations of various recursive functions on numbers and lists. Of more immediate relevance however is that these examples establish idiomatic constructions used to compile conventional source language constructs to Π^o as explained in the next sections.

In the code below we use *bool* as abbreviation for $1 + 1$ and *nat* as abbreviation for $\mu x.1 + x$. In most cases, we present the examples using diagrams — the full details are included in the accompanying Haskell code.

Bounded Iteration. The simplest class of examples takes a number n and iterates a particular combinator n times. For example, it is possible to write a function $even? : nat \times bool \rightleftharpoons nat \times bool$ which, given inputs (n, b), reveals whether n is even or odd by iterating *not* n-times starting with b. The iteration is realized using *trace* as shown in the diagram below (where we have omitted the boxes for *fold* and *unfold*):

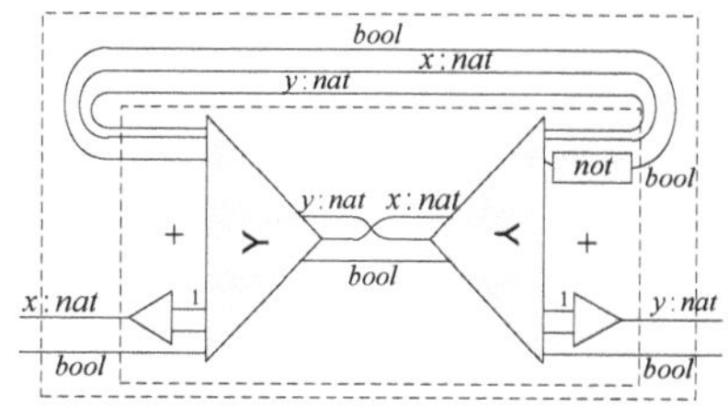

Partiality. The combinator $just : b \rightleftharpoons 1 + b$ below injects a value into a larger type. This combinator is significant because it shows that Π^o admits non-terminating computations as the adjoint of *just* diverges on *left* ():

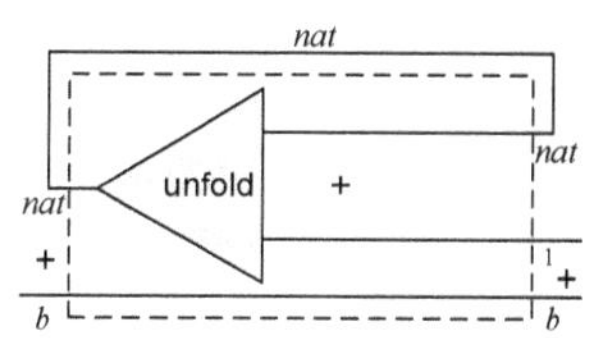

Using *just*, we can conveniently write add_1 and sub_1 as $add_1 = just \fatsemi fold$ and $sub_1 = sym\ add_1$. (The definition implies that sub_1 0 diverges.) We can also create, for any particular value v, a constant function returning v. For example, we can trivially write functions that introduce the values *false* and *true* as:

$introF, introT : 1 \rightleftharpoons bool$
$introF = just$
$introT = just \fatsemi not$

Given these functions, we can inject a value into a left or right summand. For example,

$injectR : a \rightleftharpoons a + a$
$injectR = uniti \fatsemi (introF \times id) \fatsemi distrib \fatsemi (unite + unite)$

We can introduce 0 as follows:

$introZ : 1 \rightleftharpoons nat$
$introZ = trace\ (swap^+ \fatsemi fold \fatsemi injectR)$

Similarly, we can also introduce an empty list of any type. More precisely, let the encoding of lists be $[b] \equiv \mu x.1 + b \times x$. Given a type b and a combinator $introConst_b$ to introduce a constant of type b, we can write $introNil : 1 \rightleftharpoons [b]$ which introduces an empty list of type $[b]$. Adding an element to a list can be achieved using a construction that is similar to add_1; accessing the head and tail of a list can be realized using constructions that are similar to sub_1.

5. Source Language

Having designed Π^o as a language that embodies the physical idea of reversibility, we now wish to demonstrate how irreversible programming language constructs correspond to open systems which implicitly communicate with a global heap and garbage dump. To make this idea concrete, we need a canonical irreversible language.

We use for that purpose a simply-typed, first-order functional language with sums and pairs and **for** loops. The language is fairly conventional and is presented without much discussion.

We present this language as two fragments: the first of these, LET, is strongly normalizing, and the second, LET^o, includes natural numbers and **for** loops for iteration.

The syntax of LET is given below:

$$\begin{array}{rcl} \mathit{Base\ types}, b & = & 1 \mid b+b \mid b \times b \\ \mathit{Values}, v & = & () \mid \mathit{left}\ v \mid \mathit{right}\ v \mid (v,v) \\ \mathit{Expressions}, e & = & () \mid x \mid \mathit{let}\ x = e_1\ \mathit{in}\ e_2 \\ & \mid & \mathit{left}\ e \mid \mathit{right}\ e \\ & \mid & \mathit{case}\ e\ x.e_1\ x.e_2 \\ & \mid & \mathit{fst}\ e \mid \mathit{snd}\ e \mid (e,e) \\ \mathit{Type\ environments}, \Gamma & = & \epsilon \mid \Gamma, x : b \\ \mathit{Environments}, \rho & = & \epsilon \mid \rho; x = v \end{array}$$

The most interesting aspect of LET is that expressions may freely erase and duplicate data in irreversible ways.

The extended language, LET^o, includes additionally $nats$, operations on $nats$ and a **for** loop:

$$\begin{array}{rcl} \mathit{Base\ types}, b & = & \ldots \mid \mathit{nat} \\ \mathit{Values}, v & = & \ldots \mid n \\ \mathit{Expressions}, e & = & \ldots \mid n \mid \mathit{add}_1\ e \mid \mathit{sub}_1\ e \mid \mathit{iszero?}\ e \\ & \mid & \mathbf{for}\ x = e_1\ \mathbf{if}\ e_2\ \mathbf{do}\ e_3 \end{array}$$

The most interesting aspect of the extended language LET^o is that it admits partial functions. Its type system is entirely conventional except for the rule below:

$$\frac{\Gamma \vdash e_1 : b \quad \Gamma, x : b \vdash e_2 : \mathit{bool} \quad \Gamma, x : b \vdash e_3 : b}{\Gamma \vdash \mathbf{for}\ x = e_1\ \mathbf{if}\ e_2\ \mathbf{do}\ e_3 : b}$$

Here is an example of iterative addition of two numbers n and m in this syntax:

$$\begin{array}{l} \mathit{snd}\ (\mathbf{for}\ x = (n,m)\ \mathbf{if}\ \mathit{not}\ (\mathit{iszero?}\ (\mathit{fst}\ x)) \\ \quad \mathbf{do}\ (\mathit{sub}_1\ (\mathit{fst}\ x), \mathit{add}_1\ (\mathit{snd}\ x))) \end{array}$$

The not operator over the type $\mathit{bool} = 1+1$ can be macro encoded as $\mathit{not}\ x = \mathit{case}\ x\ [y.\mathit{right}\ ()]\ [y.\mathit{left}\ ()]$.

For the semantics, we say $\mathit{eval}_{let}(e) = v$ if $\langle e, \epsilon \rangle \mapsto^*_{let} v$ according to a conventional big-step relation mapping closed expressions and environments to values, of which we show a few representative cases below:

$$\frac{\rho(x) = v}{\langle x, \rho \rangle \mapsto_{let} v} \qquad \frac{\langle e_1, \rho \rangle \mapsto_{let} v_1 \quad \langle e_2, \rho; x = v_1 \rangle \mapsto_{let} v_2}{\langle \mathit{let}\ x = e_1\ \mathit{in}\ e_2, \rho \rangle \mapsto_{let} v_2}$$

$$\frac{\langle e, \rho \rangle \mapsto_{let} \mathit{left}\ v_1 \quad \langle e_1, \rho; x = v_1 \rangle \mapsto_{let} v}{\langle \mathit{case}\ e\ x.e_1\ x.e_2, \rho \rangle \mapsto_{let} v}$$

$$\frac{\begin{array}{c}\langle e_1, \rho \rangle \mapsto_{let} v_1 \\ \langle e_2, \rho \rangle \mapsto_{let} v_2\end{array}}{\langle (e_1, e_2), \rho \rangle \mapsto_{let} (v_1, v_2)} \qquad \frac{\begin{array}{c}\langle e_1, \rho \rangle \mapsto_{let} v \\ \langle e_2, \rho; x = v \rangle \mapsto_{let} \mathit{false}\end{array}}{\langle \mathbf{for}\ x = e_1\ \mathbf{if}\ e_2\ \mathbf{do}\ e_3, \rho \rangle \mapsto_{let} v}$$

$$\frac{\begin{array}{c}\langle e_1, \rho \rangle \mapsto_{let} v \quad \langle e_2, \rho; x = v \rangle \mapsto_{let} \mathit{true} \\ \langle \mathbf{for}\ x = e_3\ \mathbf{if}\ e_2\ \mathbf{do}\ e_3, \rho; x = v \rangle \mapsto_{let} v'\end{array}}{\langle \mathbf{for}\ x = e_1\ \mathbf{if}\ e_2\ \mathbf{do}\ e_3, \rho \rangle \mapsto_{let} v'}$$

6. Metalanguages and Translations: An Overview

The technical goal of the next four sections (Secs. 7 to 10) is to translate the source language LET^o with irreversible primitives to the target information-preserving language Π^o.

Arrow Metalanguage. The first important point is that the translation is defined via a metalanguage for information effects. This metalanguage isolates the typing and semantics of the effects from the remainder of the language, thus playing a role similar to Moggi's monadic metalanguage [36] in the translation of conventional computational effects (e.g., control operators [22]). Our metalanguage is defined, not by extending the λ-calculus with monadic combinators, but by extending Π^o with arrow combinators. Starting with Π^o instead of the λ-calculus is expected since Π^o plays the role of the pure effect-free language in our setting, just like the λ-calculus plays the role of the pure effect-free language in the conventional setting. The choice of using the arrow combinators rather than the monadic combinators is because the notion of information effects does not appear to be expressible as a monad. For the purposes of presentation, the metalanguage is defined in two stages: ML_Π in Sec. 7 which is used to compile the strongly-normalizing subset of the source language using two effect combinators `create` and `erase`, and ML_{Π^o} in Sec. 10.1 which is used to compile the full source language using an additional effect combinator `traceA`. Thus, Secs. 7, 8 and 9 focus on the translation from LET to Π and Sec. 10 handles the translation from LET^o to Π^o.

Translation from Source to Metalanguage. The translation from the source language to the metalanguage essentially exposes the implicit erasure and duplication of environment bindings. For example, the evaluation rule of a pair (see Sec. 5) duplicates the environment which can only be done in the metalanguage using explicit occurrences of the `create` effect combinator. Similarly, the evaluation of a variable projects one value out of the environment, implicitly erasing the rest of the environment, which again can only be done using explicit occurrences of the `erase` effect combinator. Technically, we define two translations $\mathcal{T}_1 : \mathsf{LET} \Longrightarrow \mathsf{ML}_\Pi$ and $\mathcal{T}_1^o : \mathsf{LET}^o \Longrightarrow \mathsf{ML}_{\Pi^o}$. The first maps the strongly-normalizing subset of the source to ML_Π (Sec. 8) and the second is an extension that handles the full source and targets ML_{Π^o} (Sec. 10.2).

Translation from Metalanguage to Target. This translation essentially needs to compile the effect combinators to the target language. The basic scheme is based on Toffoli's idea described in Sec. 2.1: an irreversible function of type $a \to b$ is translated to a bijection $(h,a) \leftrightarrow (g,b)$ where h is the type of the heap that supplies the constant values and g is the type of the garbage that absorbs the un-interesting and un-observable outputs. Once the primitive effect combinators have been translated, the arrow combinators then thread the heap and garbage through more complex computations. Technically, we again have two translations: one for the strongly-normalizing subset of the source language and one for the full source language. The first translation $\mathcal{T}_2 :: \mathsf{ML}_\Pi \Longrightarrow \Pi$ (Sec. 9) selects particular values for the heap and garbage to embed the irreversible effects into bijections.[2] The second translation $\mathcal{T}_2^o :: \mathsf{ML}_{\Pi^o} \Longrightarrow \Pi^o$ (Sec. 10.3) works for the full language. It has an important difference which arises from the fact that there is an inherent asymmetry between `create` and `erase`: the operator `create` is always used to create a known constant while `erase` is used to erase information that is only known at run time. This inherent asymmetry of the operators is a consequence of the fact that the source language is (forward) deterministic, but lacks backward determinism. As we saw in Sec. 4.2, Π^o can express the creation and erasure of constants and we leverage this to completely eliminate the heap in favor of using `traceA`.[3]

7. Arrow Metalanguage ML_Π

To construct our arrow metalanguage ML_Π, we simply add the generic arrow combinators to Π and add the particular operators that model the information effects we wish to model. In particular,

[2] This idea has been the basis of translations similar to ours [5]. The literature also includes translations for other languages [2, 12, 19, 23, 26, 41, 49] that share some of the intuition of the translation we present but differ significantly in the technical details.

[3] If LET^o had an operation that introduced values unknown at compile time, such as an input operation or a random number generator, we would have to re-introduce the heap.

we add two operators `create` and `erase` which correspond to the creation and erasure of information that is implicit in the semantics of LET. These operators are not isomorphisms and hence cannot have $\leftrightarrow$ types. They can only have arrow types.

DEFINITION 7.1. *(Syntax of ML_Π) The sets of value types, values, and isomorphisms are identical to the corresponding sets in Π (see Def. 3.1). The extended combinator types and arrow computations are defined as follows:*

$$\begin{array}{rcl} \mathit{types}, t & ::= & b \leftrightarrow b \mid b \rightsquigarrow b \\ \mathit{arrow\ comp.}, a & ::= & \mathit{iso} \mid a + a \mid a \times a \mid a \fatsemi a \\ & \mid & \mathtt{arr}\ a \mid a \ggg a \mid \mathtt{first}\ a \mid \mathtt{left}\ a \\ & \mid & \mathtt{create}_b \mid \mathtt{erase} \end{array}$$

The type $b_1 \rightsquigarrow b_2$ is our notion of arrows. The three operations `arr`, $\ggg$, *and* `first` *are essential for any notion of arrows. The operation* `left` *is needed for arrows that also implement some form of choice. The two operators* $\mathtt{create}_b$ *and* `erase` *model the particular effects in the information metalanguage.*

The types of the arrow combinators in ML_Π are similar to their original types in the traditional arrow calculus except that `arr` lifts $\leftrightarrow$ types to the abstract arrow type $\rightsquigarrow$ instead of lifting regular function types to the abstract arrow type:

$$\frac{a : b_1 \leftrightarrow b_2}{\mathtt{arr}\ a : b_1 \rightsquigarrow b_2} \qquad \frac{a_1 : b_1 \rightsquigarrow b_2 \quad a_2 : b_2 \rightsquigarrow b_3}{a_1 \ggg a_2 : b_1 \rightsquigarrow b_3}$$

$$\frac{a : b_1 \rightsquigarrow b_2}{\mathtt{first}\ a : b_1 \times b_3 \rightsquigarrow b_2 \times b_3} \qquad \frac{a : b_1 \rightsquigarrow b_2}{\mathtt{left}\ a : b_1 + b_3 \rightsquigarrow b_2 + b_3}$$

$$\frac{}{\mathtt{create}_b : 1 \rightsquigarrow b} \qquad \frac{}{\mathtt{erase} : b \rightsquigarrow 1}$$

The semantics is specified using the relation $\mapsto_{ML}$ which refers to the reduction relation $\mapsto$ for Π. We only present the reductions for the arrow constructs:

$$\frac{a\ v_1 \mapsto v_2}{(\mathtt{arr}\ a)\ v_1 \mapsto_{ML} v_2} \qquad \frac{a_1\ v_1 \mapsto_{ML} v_2 \quad a_2\ v_2 \mapsto_{ML} v_3}{(a_1 \ggg a_2)\ v_1 \mapsto_{ML} v_3}$$

$$\frac{a\ v_1 \mapsto_{ML} v_2}{(\mathtt{left}\ a)\ (\mathit{left}\ v_1) \mapsto_{ML} \mathit{left}\ v_2} \qquad \frac{}{(\mathtt{left}\ a)\ (\mathit{right}\ v) \mapsto_{ML} \mathit{right}\ v}$$

$$\frac{a\ v_1 \mapsto_{ML} v_2}{(\mathtt{first}\ a)\ (v_1, v_3) \mapsto_{ML} (v_2, v_3)} \qquad \frac{}{\mathtt{erase}\ v \mapsto_{ML} ()} \qquad \frac{}{\mathtt{create}_b() \mapsto_{ML} \phi(b)}$$

The operator `erase` at type b takes any value of type b and returns () which contains no information. For any type b, $\mathtt{create}_b$ returns a fixed (but arbitrary) value of type b which we call $\phi(b)$ and which is defined as:

$$\phi(1) = () \qquad \phi(b_1 \times b_2) = (\phi(b_1), \phi(b_2)) \qquad \phi(b_1 + b_2) = \mathit{left}\ (\phi(b_1))$$

The two operators $\mathtt{create}_b$ and `erase`, along with the structure provided by the arrow metalanguage, are expressive enough to implement a number of interesting idioms. In particular, it is possible to erase a part of a data structure (as shown using `fstA` below); it is possible to inject a value in a sum type (as shown using `leftA` below); it is possible to forget about choices (as shown using *join* below); and it is possible to make a copy of any value (as shown using *clone* below).

***Erasing part of a data structure* (`fstA`).** The combinator `fstA` of type $b_1 \times b_2 \rightsquigarrow b_1$ takes a pair and erases the second component. We apply `erase` to the second component of the pair and then appeal to $(\mathtt{arr}\ \mathit{unite}) : 1 \times b \rightsquigarrow b$ to absorb the (). Thus we have:

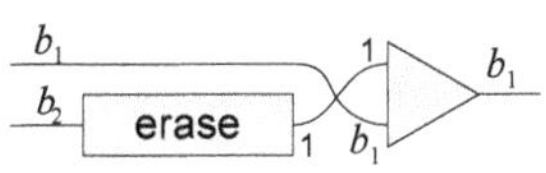

$\mathtt{fstA} : b_1 \times b_2 \rightsquigarrow b_2$
$\mathtt{fstA} = \mathtt{second\ erase} \ggg \mathtt{arr}\ (\mathit{swap}^\times \fatsemi \mathit{unite})$
where $\mathtt{second}\ a = (\mathtt{arr}\ \mathit{swap}^\times) \ggg \mathtt{first}\ a \ggg (\mathtt{arr}\ \mathit{swap}^\times)$. The combinator `sndA` that deletes the first component of a pair is defined symmetrically.

***Injecting a value in a larger type* (`leftA`).** The combinator $\mathtt{leftA} : b_1 \rightsquigarrow b_1 + b_2$ takes a value and injects it in a larger sum type. Its definition is involved so we begin by defining the following combinator in Π:

$\mathit{leftSwap} : (b_1 + b_2) \times b_1 \leftrightarrow (b_1 + b_2) \times b_1$
$\mathit{leftSwap} = (\mathit{distrib} \fatsemi (\mathit{swap}^\times + \mathit{id}) \fatsemi \mathit{factor})$

Given values v_1 and v_1' both of type b_1, the application of *leftSwap* to $(\mathit{left}\ v_1, v_1')$ produces $(\mathit{left}\ v_1', v_1)$, which moves the *left* constructor from v_1 to v_1'. We use this combinator to implement `leftA` as follows. Let us give the input to `leftA` the name v_1'. We first create a default value *left* v_1 of type $b_1 + b_2$, use *leftSwap* to produce $(\mathit{left}\ v_1', v_1)$, and complete the definition by using `fstA` to erase the default value v_1. Thus `leftA` is:

$$(\mathtt{arr}\ \mathit{uniti}) \ggg (\mathtt{first}\ \mathtt{create}_{b_1+b_2}) \ggg (\mathtt{arr}\ \mathit{leftSwap}) \ggg \mathtt{fstA}$$

or pictorially:

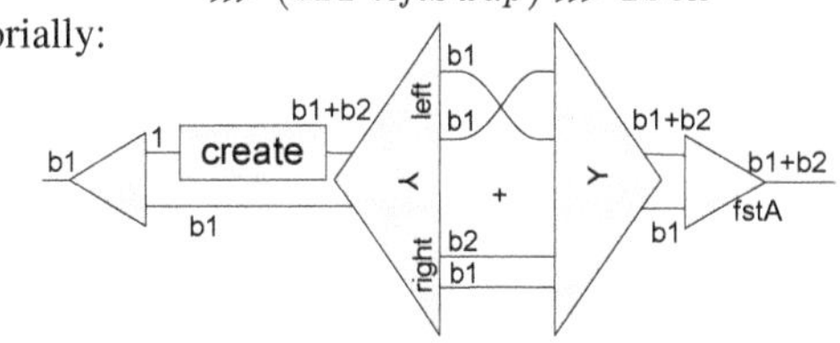

The symmetric combinator `rightA` can be defined similarly.

***Forgetting about choices* (*join*).** We define an operator $\mathit{join} : b + b \rightsquigarrow b$ that takes a value of type b tagged by either *left* and *right* and removes the tag. The definition converts the input $b + b$ to $(1 + 1) \times b$ and then erases the first component:

$$((\mathtt{arr}\ \mathit{uniti}) \oplus (\mathtt{arr}\ \mathit{uniti})) \ggg (\mathtt{arr}\ \mathit{factor}) \ggg \mathtt{sndA}$$

***Copying values* (clone_b).** As the following lemma shows, it is possible, for any type b, to define an operator clone_b that can be used to copy values of that type.

LEMMA 7.2 (Cloning). *For any type b, we can construct an operator clone of type $b \rightsquigarrow b \times b$ such that: clone $v \mapsto_{ML} (v, v)$*

Proof. We proceed by induction on the type b:

- Case 1: We need to exhibit a combinator $a : 1 \rightsquigarrow 1 \times 1$ and this is given by $a = \mathtt{arr}\ \mathit{uniti}$
- Case $b_1 \times b_2$: By induction we have combinators $a_1 : b_1 \rightsquigarrow b_1 \times b_1$ and $a_2 : b_2 \rightsquigarrow b_2 \times b_2$ and we have to construct $a : (b_1 \times b_2) \rightsquigarrow (b_1 \times b_2) \times (b_1 \times b_2)$. The required combinator a uses a_1 and a_2 to clone the components and then shuffles the pairs into place:

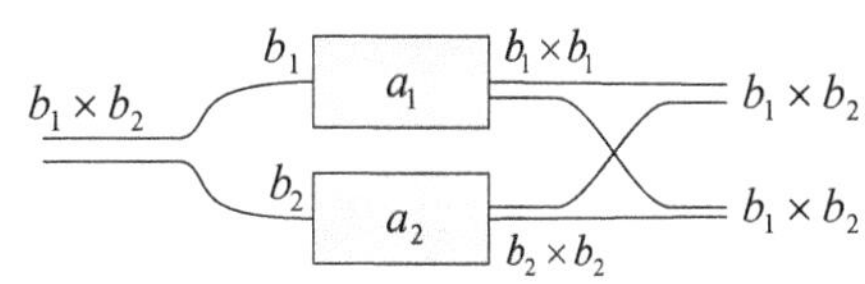

Thus we can write $a = (a_1 \otimes a_2) \ggg \mathit{shuffle}$ where *shuffle* is the operator which rearranges the pairs as pictured.

- Case $b_1 + b_2$: By induction we have combinators $a_1 : b_1 \rightsquigarrow b_1 \times b_1$ and $a_2 : b_2 \rightsquigarrow b_2 \times b_2$ we have to construct $a : (b_1 + b_2) \rightsquigarrow (b_1 + b_2) \times (b_1 + b_2)$. Consider the diagram below which has the type $b_1 \rightsquigarrow b_1 \times (b_1 + b_2)$:

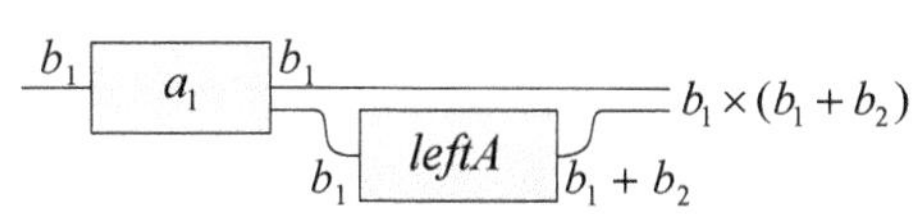

This combinator clones b_1 and then applies `leftA` to one of the copies. Let us call this combinator $a_1' : b_1 \rightsquigarrow b_1 \times (b_1 + b_2)$. We can do the same with b_2, except that we apply `rightA`, resulting in combinator $a_2' : b_2 \rightsquigarrow b_2 \times (b_1 + b_2)$. The required combinator a can be constructed by applying these in parallel and factoring out the results, i.e., $a = (a_1' \oplus a_2') \ggg (\texttt{arr}\ \mathit{factor})$

8. Translation from LET to ML_Π

The translation $\mathcal{T}_1$ maps a closed term of type b in LET to an ML_Π combinator $c : 1 \rightsquigarrow b$. As the translation is type-directed, it must also handle terms with free variables that are supplied by an environment.

8.1 Environments

A LET type environment Γ is translated to an ML_Π type as follows:

$[\epsilon]^\times = 1$

$[\Gamma, x : b]^\times = [\Gamma]^\times \times b$

A value environment $\rho : \Gamma$ is translated to a value $v_\rho : \Gamma^\times$:

$[\epsilon]^\times = ()$

$[\rho, x = v]^\times = ([\rho]^\times, v)$

LEMMA 8.1 (Lookup). *If $\Gamma \vdash x : b$ and $\Gamma^\times$ is the encoding of Γ, then there exists a combinator $a_{lookup(x)} : \Gamma^\times \rightsquigarrow b$ that looks up x in $\Gamma^\times$.*

Proof. The required combinator a depends on the structure of Γ:

- Case ϵ: This cannot arise because Γ must contain x.
- Case $\Gamma', x' : b'$ and $x' = x$: Then $a = \texttt{sndA}$
- Case $\Gamma', x' : b'$ and $x' \neq x$: Then we know that the required x must be bound in Γ', i.e. $\Gamma' \vdash x : b$. Thus by induction there exists $a' : [\Gamma']^\times \rightsquigarrow b$. So the required combinator is $a = (a' \otimes id) \ggg \texttt{fstA}$.

8.2 The Translation $\mathcal{T}_1$

We translate a LET judgment of the form $\Gamma \vdash e : b$ to an ML_Π combinator $a : \Gamma^\times \rightsquigarrow b$ in such a way that the execution of the resulting ML_Π term simulates the execution of the original term. Because the evaluation of LET expressions requires an environment ρ, the evaluation of the translated combinator must be given a value v_ρ of type $\Gamma^\times$ denoting the value of the environment.

LEMMA 8.2 ($\mathcal{T}_1$ and its correctness). *For any well typed LET expression $\Gamma \vdash e : b$, $\mathcal{T}_1[\Gamma \vdash e : b]$ gives us a combinator 'a' and a type $\Gamma^\times$ in ML_Π such that:*

1. $a : \Gamma^\times \rightsquigarrow b$
2. $\forall\, (\rho : \Gamma), \exists\, (v : b).$ *if* $\langle e, \rho \rangle \mapsto^*_{let} v$ *then* $a\ [\rho]^\times \mapsto^*_{ML} v$.

We simultaneously present the translation and prove its correctness:

- Case $()$:

$$\frac{}{\Gamma \vdash () : 1 \dashrightarrow \texttt{erase} : \Gamma^\times \rightsquigarrow 1}$$

We have that $\texttt{erase}\ v_\rho \mapsto_{ML} ()$.

- Case x:

$$\frac{\Gamma(x) = b}{\Gamma \vdash x : b \dashrightarrow a_{lookup(x)} : \Gamma^\times \rightsquigarrow b}$$

- Case $let\ x = e_1\ in\ e_2$:

$$\frac{\Gamma \vdash e_1 : b_1 \dashrightarrow a_1 : \Gamma^\times \rightsquigarrow b_1 \qquad \Gamma, x : b_1 \vdash e_2 : b_2 \dashrightarrow a_2 : \Gamma^\times \times b_1 \rightsquigarrow b_2}{\Gamma \vdash let\ x = e_1\ in\ e_2 : b_2 \dashrightarrow a : \Gamma^\times \rightsquigarrow b_2}$$

To construct the required a we first clone $\Gamma^\times$. We can apply a_1 to one of the copies to get b_1. The resulting value of type $\Gamma^\times \times b_1$ is the input required by a_2 which returns the result of type b_2:

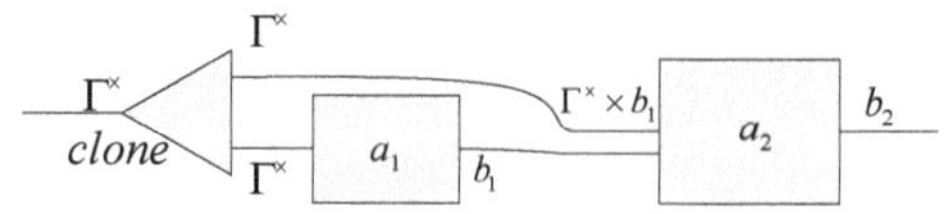

Thus the required combinator is:

$a = clone_{\Gamma^\times} \ggg (\texttt{second}\ a_1) \ggg a_2$

- Case (e_1, e_2):

$$\frac{\Gamma \vdash e_1 : b_1 \dashrightarrow a_1 : \Gamma^\times \rightsquigarrow b_1 \qquad \Gamma \vdash e_2 : b_2 \dashrightarrow a_2 : \Gamma^\times \rightsquigarrow b_2}{\Gamma \vdash (e_1, e_2) : b_1 \times b_2 \dashrightarrow a : \Gamma^\times \rightsquigarrow b_1 \times b_2}$$

As with *let*, we clone $\Gamma^\times$ and use each copy to create one component of the pair. Thus we have:

$a = clone_{\Gamma^\times} \ggg (a_1 \otimes a_2)$

- Cases *fst e*, *snd e*:

$$\frac{\Gamma \vdash e : b_1 \times b_2 \dashrightarrow a_1 : \Gamma^\times \rightsquigarrow b_1 \times b_2}{\Gamma \vdash fst\ e : b_1 \dashrightarrow a : \Gamma^\times \rightsquigarrow b_1}$$

We have $a = a_1 \ggg \texttt{fstA}$. And similarly for $snd\ e$ we have $a = a_1 \ggg \texttt{sndA}$.

- Cases *left e*, *right e*:

$$\frac{\Gamma \vdash e : b_1 \dashrightarrow a_1 : \Gamma^\times \rightsquigarrow b_1}{\Gamma \vdash left\ e : b_1 + b_2 \dashrightarrow a : \Gamma^\times \rightsquigarrow b_1 + b_2}$$

We have $a = a_1 \ggg \texttt{leftA}$ and similarly for $right\ e$ we have $a = a_1 \ggg \texttt{rightA}$.

- Case $case\ e\ x.e_1\ x.e_2$:

$$\frac{\Gamma \vdash e_1 : b_1 + b_2 \dashrightarrow a_1 : \Gamma^\times \rightsquigarrow b_1 + b_2 \qquad \Gamma, x : b_1 \vdash e_2 : b_3 \dashrightarrow a_2 : \Gamma^\times \times b_1 \rightsquigarrow b_3 \qquad \Gamma, x : b_2 \vdash e_3 : b_3 \dashrightarrow a_3 : \Gamma^\times \times b_2 \rightsquigarrow b_3}{\Gamma \vdash case\ e_1\ x.e_2\ x.e_3 : b_3 \dashrightarrow a : \Gamma^\times \rightsquigarrow b_3}$$

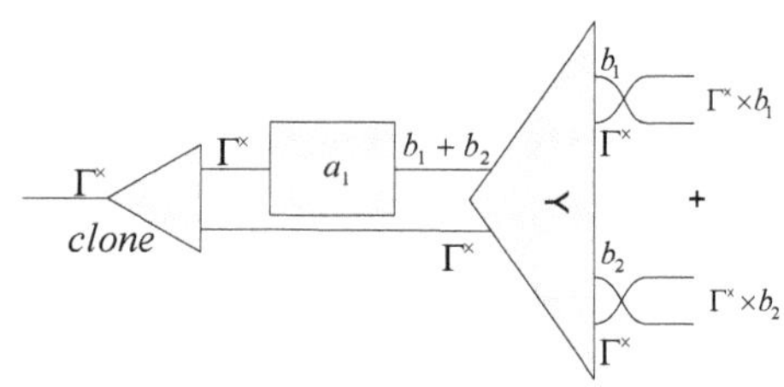

Here we have cloned $\Gamma^\times$ and constructed $b_1 + b_2$ using one copy of $\Gamma^\times$ and a_1. We then distributed $\Gamma^\times$ over $b_1 + b_2$ and resulting in two possible environments $\Gamma^\times \times b_1$ or $\Gamma^\times \times b_2$. At this point, we can apply a_2 and a_3 to these environments resulting in $b_3 + b_3$ which we can *join* to get the desired result b_3. Thus we have:

$a = clone_{\Gamma^\times} \ggg (\texttt{left}\ c_1) \ggg (\texttt{arr}\ distrib) \ggg$
$\quad ((\texttt{arr}\ swap^\times) \oplus (\texttt{arr}\ swap^\times)) \ggg (a_2 \oplus a_3) \ggg join$

9. Translation from ML_Π to Π

The translation $\mathcal{T}_2$ maps an ML_Π combinator $a : b_1 \rightsquigarrow b_2$ to an isomorphism $h \times b_1 \leftrightarrow g \times b_2$. The types h and g are determined based on the structure of the combinator a and are fixed by the translation $\mathcal{T}_2$. The translation is set up such that when we supply $\phi(h)$ for the heap along with the given input value of type b_1, the compiled combinator produces some unspecified value for g and the value for b_2 that the original arrow combinator would have produced.

LEMMA 9.1 ($\mathcal{T}_2$ and its correctness). *For any* ML_Π *combinator* $a : b_1 \rightsquigarrow b_2$, $\mathcal{T}_2[a : b_1 \rightsquigarrow b_2]$ *gives us c, h and g in* Π *such that:*

- $c : h \times b_1 \leftrightarrow g \times b_2$
- $\forall\ (v_1\ :\ b_1), \exists\ (v_g\ :\ g), (v_2\ :\ b_2)$ *if* $a\ v_1 \mapsto^*_{ML} v_2$ *then* $c\ (\phi(h), v_1) \mapsto^* (v_g, v_2)$.

As before, we present the translation along with the proof of correctness.

- **arr** a:

$$\frac{a : b_1 \leftrightarrow b_2}{\mathbf{arr}\ a : b_1 \rightsquigarrow b_2 \dashrightarrow c : h \times b_1 \leftrightarrow g \times b_2}$$

To construct the required c we choose $h = g = 1$ and thus we have $c = id \times a$. It is easy to verify that $c\ ((), v_1) \mapsto ((), v_2)$ assuming $a\ v_1 \mapsto v_2$.

- $a_1 \ggg a_2$:

$$\frac{\begin{array}{l} a_1 : b_1 \rightsquigarrow b_2 \dashrightarrow c_1 : h_1 \times b_1 \leftrightarrow g_1 \times b_2 \\ a_2 : b_2 \rightsquigarrow b_3 \dashrightarrow c_2 : h_2 \times b_2 \leftrightarrow g_2 \times b_3 \end{array}}{a_1 \ggg a_2 : b_1 \rightsquigarrow b_3 \dashrightarrow c : h \times b_1 \leftrightarrow g \times b_3}$$

We choose $h = h_1 \times h_2$ and $g = g_1 \times g_2$ and we have

$$c = assocr^\times \fatsemi (id \times c_1) \fatsemi shuffle \fatsemi (id \times c_2) \fatsemi assocl^\times$$

where $shuffle = (assocl^\times \fatsemi (swap^\times \times id) \fatsemi assocr^\times)$.

- **first** a: Given that $a : b_1 \rightsquigarrow b_2$ translates to $c_1 : h_1 \times b_1 \leftrightarrow g_1 \times b_2$, we translate **first** $a\ :\ b_1 \times b_3 \rightsquigarrow b_2 \times b_3$ to $c : h \times (b_1 \times b_3) \leftrightarrow g \times (b_2 \times b_3)$ where $h = h_1, g = g_1$, and $c = assocl^\times \fatsemi (c_1 \times id) \fatsemi assocr^\times$
- **left** a: Given that $a : b_1 \rightsquigarrow b_2$ translates to $c_1 : h_1 \times b_1 \leftrightarrow g_1 \times b_2$, we translate **left** $a\ :\ b_1 + b_3 \rightsquigarrow b_2 + b_3$ to $c : h \times (b_1 + b_3) \leftrightarrow g \times (b_2 + b_3)$ as explained next. Assume $c_1\ (\phi(h_1), v_1) \mapsto (v_{g_1}, v_2)$, we need to prove:

$$c\ (\phi(h), left\ v_1) \mapsto (v_{g'}, left\ v_2)$$
$$c\ (\phi(h), right\ v_3) \mapsto (v_{g''}, right\ v_3)$$

Here $v_{g'}$ and $v_{g''}$ have the type g and $v_1\ :\ b_1,\ v_2\ :\ b_2$ and $v_3 : b_3$. We define the required types h and g as shown below.

$$h = (h_1 \times ((b_2 + b_3) \times (b_3 + b_2)))$$
$$g = g' + g''$$

where:

$$g' = (g_1 \times (b_2 \times (b_3 + b_2)))$$
$$g'' = (h_1 \times ((b_2 + b_3) \times b_3))$$

We construct the required c in terms of two combinators c' and c'' that handle the *left* and *right* cases of the input $b_1 + b_2$. We first construct the combinator c' that has the following type and semantics:

$$c' : b_1 \times h \leftrightarrow g' \times (b_2 + b_3)$$
$$c'(v_1, \phi(h)) \mapsto (v_{g_1}, left\ v_2)$$

To construct c', we need the *leftSwap* combinator that was defined in Sec. 7. We can draw a wiring diagram for c' as follows:

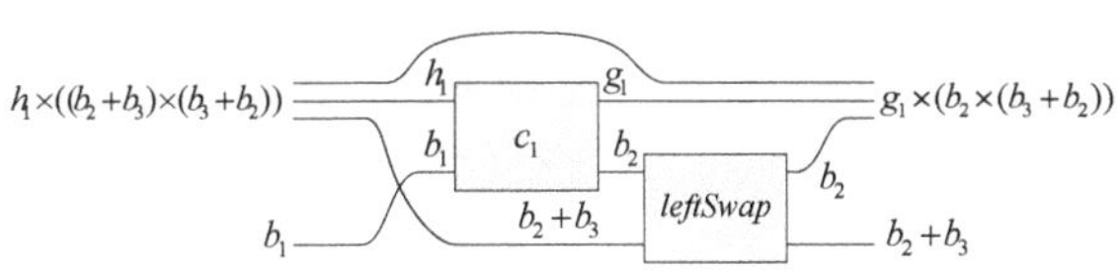

The combinator c' uses c_1 to obtain a value of type b_2 and then uses *leftSwap* to construct a value of type $b_2 + b_3$. We can now define c'' that works on the *right* branch to be:

$$c'' : b_3 \times h \leftrightarrow g'' \times (b_2 + b_3)$$
$$c''(v_3, \phi(h)) \mapsto (v_{g_2}, right\ v_3)$$

As before we need the *leftSwap* combinator, but this time at the type $b_3 \times (b_3 + b_2)$. The wiring diagram for c'' is shown:

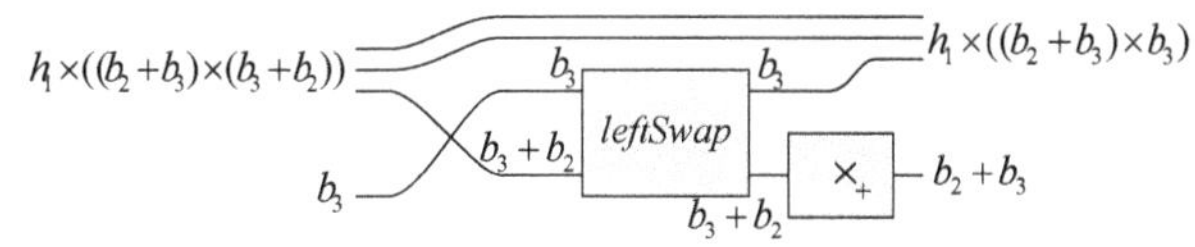

The definition of c'' takes the value of type b_3 and constructs a value of type $b_2 + b_3$ using *leftSwap* and $swap^+$. Given the construction of c' and c'' we can construct the required c as:

$$c : h \times (b_1 + b_3) \leftrightarrow g \times (b_2 + b_3)$$
$$c = swap^\times \fatsemi distrib \fatsemi (c' \times c'') \fatsemi factor$$

- **create**:

$$\frac{}{\mathbf{create} : 1 \rightsquigarrow b \dashrightarrow c : h \times 1 \leftrightarrow g \times b}$$

We choose $h = b$ and $g = 1$ and we have $c = swap^\times$. The definition of **create** is simple because we have taken care to correctly thread a value of type h and **create** simply reifies this value.

- **erase**:

$$\frac{}{\mathbf{erase} : b \rightsquigarrow 1 \dashrightarrow e : h \times b \leftrightarrow g \times 1}$$

We choose $h = 1$ and $g = b$ and we have $c = swap^\times$. Note that this is operationally the same as **create**. The difference is in the types. Since we have set up the rest of the computation to thread the value of type g through and never expose it, to erase a value we simply have to move it to the garbage.

10. Translation from LET^o to Π^o

The required translation $\mathcal{T}^o$ is factored into $\mathcal{T}_1^o : \mathsf{LET}^o \Longrightarrow \mathsf{ML}_{\Pi^o}$ and $\mathcal{T}_2^o : \mathsf{ML}_{\Pi^o} \Longrightarrow \Pi^o$ where the intermediate language ML_{Π^o} extends ML_Π.

10.1 Arrow Metalanguage : ML_{Π^o}

The arrow metalanguage, ML_{Π^o}, extends ML_Π with natural numbers and loops.

DEFINITION 10.1 (Syntax of ML_{Π^o}).

$$\begin{array}{rcl} base\ types, b & = & 1 \mid b \times b \mid b + b \mid nat \\ values, v & = & () \mid (v, v) \mid left\ v \mid right\ v \mid n \\ types, t & ::= & b \rightleftharpoons b \mid b \rightharpoonup b \\ arrow\ comp., a & ::= & iso \mid a + a \mid a \times a \mid a \fatsemi a \mid trace\ a \\ & \mid & \mathbf{arr}\ a \mid a \ggg a \mid \mathbf{first}\ a \mid \mathbf{left}\ a \\ & \mid & \mathbf{traceA}\ a \mid \mathbf{create}_b \mid \mathbf{erase} \end{array}$$

The types extend the finite types with nat which is an abbreviation for $\mu x.1 + x$. In addition to the usual finite values, we also include natural numbers n which are abbreviations for sequences of *right*-applications that end with *left* (). The arrow type $\rightharpoonup$ is analogous to $\rightsquigarrow$ of ML_Π: we use a different symbol to emphasize that the underlying bijections are partial. The set of underlying isomorphisms extends the ones for finite types with $unfold : nat \rightleftharpoons 1 + nat : fold$. We define $\phi(nat) = 0$ and hence $\mathbf{create}_{nat} = 0$. Finally, the language includes one additional arrow combinator **traceA** with the typing rule:

$$\frac{a : b_1 + b_2 \rightharpoonup b_1 + b_3}{\texttt{traceA}\ a : b_2 \rightharpoonup b_3}$$

In contrast to *trace* which defines looping computations whose bodies are (partial) bijections, `traceA` can be used to define looping computations whose bodies may create and erase information. The semantics of `traceA` is similar to that of *trace* but with an important technical difference. The body of the `traceA`-loop may produce garbage values which `traceA` collects in a list as the iteration progresses. (See the last case of the translation $\mathcal{T}_2^o$ below.) As before we can clone any particular value.

LEMMA 10.2 (Cloning). *For any type b, we can construct an operator clone of type* $b \rightharpoonup b \times b$ *such that: clone* $v \mapsto_{ML} (v, v)$

Proof. This is an extension of Lemma 7.2. The only new datatype is nat. We `create` a 0 and use the loop of Sec. 4.2 to iteratively add_1.

10.2 Translation $\mathcal{T}_1^o$ from LET^o to ML$_{\Pi^o}$

The translation $\mathcal{T}_1^o$ extends the translation $\mathcal{T}_1$ from LET to ML$_\Pi$.

LEMMA 10.3 ($\mathcal{T}_1^o$ and its correctness). *For any well typed LET^o expression* $\Gamma \vdash e : b$, $\mathcal{T}_1^o[\Gamma \vdash e : b]$ *gives us a combinator 'a' and a type* $\Gamma^\times$ *in ML$_{\Pi^o}$ such that:*

1. $a : \Gamma^\times \rightharpoonup b$
2. $\forall\,(\rho : \Gamma), \exists\,(v : b).$ *if* $\langle e, \rho\rangle \mapsto^*_{let} v$ *then* $a\ [\rho]^\times \mapsto^*_{ML} v$.

- Cases $add_1\ e$, $sub_1\ e$: These follow from simply lifting the add_1 construction and its adjoint from Sec. 4.2.

$$\frac{\Gamma \vdash e : nat \dashrightarrow a : \Gamma^\times \rightharpoonup nat}{\Gamma \vdash add_1\ e : nat \dashrightarrow a \fatsemi (\texttt{arr}\ add_1) : \Gamma^\times \rightharpoonup nat}$$

- Case iszero? e:

$$\frac{\Gamma \vdash e : nat \dashrightarrow a_1 : \Gamma^\times \rightharpoonup nat}{\Gamma \vdash iszero?\ e : nat \dashrightarrow a : \Gamma^\times \rightharpoonup bool}$$

where $a = a_1 \fatsemi \texttt{arr}\ unfold \fatsemi \texttt{first erase} \fatsemi \texttt{arr}\,unite$

- Case n: The required combinator of type $\Gamma \rightharpoonup nat$ is given by $\texttt{erase} \fatsemi \texttt{create}_{nat} \fatsemi add_1^n$ (where add_1^n is n iterations of add_1).
- Case **for** $x = e_1$ **if** e_2 **do** e_3:

$$\frac{\Gamma \vdash e_1 : b \dashrightarrow a_1 : \Gamma^\times \rightharpoonup b \quad \Gamma, x : b \vdash e_2 : bool \dashrightarrow a_2 : \Gamma^\times \times b \rightharpoonup bool \quad \Gamma, x : b \vdash e_3 : b \dashrightarrow a_3 : \Gamma^\times \times b \rightharpoonup b}{\Gamma \vdash \textbf{for}\ x = e_1\ \textbf{if}\ e_2\ \textbf{do}\ e_3 : b \dashrightarrow a : \Gamma^\times \rightharpoonup b}$$

The construction is illustrated in the diagram below, in which wires of type 1 used for `erase`, *distrib* etc. have been dropped for the sake of clarity.

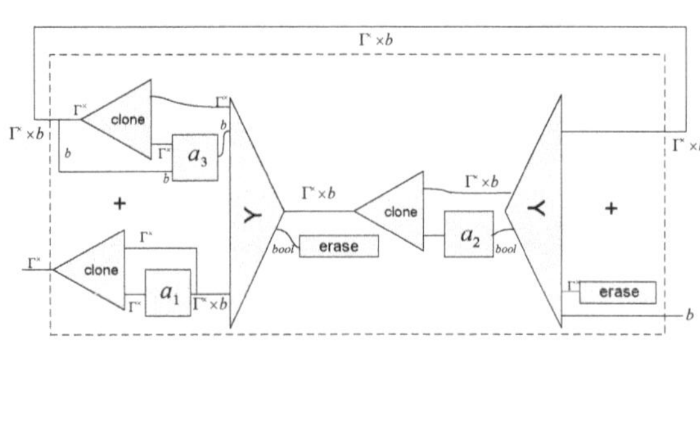

Conceptually, each iteration of the `traceA` is determined by the result of a_2. If the conditional is true then the iteration causes a_3 to be executed.

10.3 Translation $\mathcal{T}_2^o$ from ML$_{\Pi^o}$ to Π^o

Translation $\mathcal{T}_2^o$ is similar to $\mathcal{T}_2$. As discussed in the overview (Sec. 6) the significant difference comes from the fact that Π^o can create constants hence eliminating the need for an input heap type. The translation only needs to track the garbage produced by combinators.

PROPOSITION 10.4. *For any type b of ML$_{\Pi^o}$ we can construct* $createConst_b : 1 \rightleftharpoons b$ *such that* $createConst_b\ () \mapsto_{ML} \phi_b$.

LEMMA 10.5 ($\mathcal{T}_2^o$ and its correctness)). *For any ML$_{\Pi^o}$ combinator* $a : b_1 \rightharpoonup b_2$, $\mathcal{T}_2^o[a : b_1 \rightharpoonup b_2]$ *gives us c and g in* Π^o *such that:*

- $c : b_1 \rightleftharpoons g \times b_2$
- $\forall\,(v_1 : b_1), \exists\,(v_g : g), (v_2 : b_2).$ *if* $a\ v \mapsto^*_{ML} v_2$ *then* $c\ v_1 \mapsto^* (v_g, v_2)$.

The interesting cases to consider are:

- Case `arr` c: The required combinator is $c \fatsemi uniti : b_1 \rightleftharpoons 1 \times b_2$ where the garbage is 1.
- Case $\texttt{create}_b$: The required combinator is $createConst_b \fatsemi uniti : 1 \rightleftharpoons 1 \times b$ with $g = 1$.
- Case `erase`: The required combinator is $uniti \fatsemi swap^\times : 1 \rightleftharpoons b \times 1$ with $g = b$.
- Case `traceA` a:

$$\frac{a : b_1 + b_2 \rightharpoonup b_1 + b_3 \dashrightarrow c : b_1 + b_2 \rightleftharpoons g \times (b_1 + b_3)}{\texttt{traceA}\ a : b_2 \rightharpoonup b_3 \dashrightarrow c_1 : b_2 \rightleftharpoons g' \times b_3}$$

As shown in Sec. 4.2, we can create and manipulate empty lists of any given type in Π^o. The diagram below is the required combinator c_1 with $g' = [g]$, i.e., the resulting garbage is the list of garbage values produced at each step in the iteration, of type g.

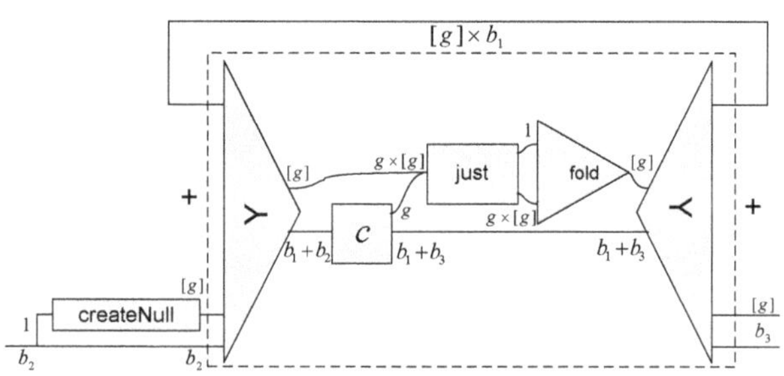

11. Applications

The technical contribution of the paper was devoted to designing a semantic foundation of computation which treats information as a computational resource. We now briefly explore the application of such a framework to security and privacy.

11.1 Quantitative Information Flow

Research in the domain of quantitative information-flow security is aimed at tracking the amount of information leakage through a computation [10, 32, 33]. Instead of devising *ad hoc* analyses, one can in our framework simply observe the program's types and see how much information has been erased.

As an example, consider a password checker, $check : bool \times bool \to bool$, which takes a 2-bit user input and has access to a 2-bit secret password. The type $bool \times bool$ has 4 inhabitants. With probability $1/4$ an attacker guesses the real password ($\log 4$ bits learned) and with probability $3/4$ guesses wrong thus eliminating one candidate password ($\log 4 - \log 3$ bits learned), making the average information gained $1/4 \log 4 + 3/4(\log 4 - \log 3) = 0.8$. One call to the password checker has thus hidden 1.2 bits of information from the attacker.

The Landauer principle implies that the 1.2 bits dissipated by $check$ must be accounted for by some logically irreversible erasure of 1.2 bits. And indeed, the minimum any Π^o implementation of $check$ must `erase` is 2 bits which would manifest itself by a use of `erase` at type $bool \times bool$. The fact that ML_{Π^o} types indicate a lower bound on a program's intrinsic secrecy deserves further investigation. Further, a finer analysis allowing us to capture the exact erasure of fractional bits, may be achieved by enriching the type system of ML_{Π^o} to track the probability of disjunctive branches, such as in the probabilistic λ-calculus [39].

11.2 Orthogonality and Differential Privacy

Physical processes operate on physical representations of values which exist in space and have associated costs (e.g. amount of energy). Physical processes must not only be reversible but they must do so in a way that respects this additional structure. Toffoli and Fredkin [16] captured this additional restriction on physical processes using what they called "Conservative Logic" in which values can only be shuffled around by computation. This guarantees that processes maintain whatever cost is associated with the values they operate on. In quantum mechanics, this additional restriction is modeled in a different way using the mathematical structure of Hilbert spaces. Specifically, the fundamental building blocks of quantum computation are that (i) quantum states are equipped with an inner product that induces a norm (i.e., a metric), and that (ii) quantum transformations must be *unitary*, i.e., must be reversible transformations that preserve the norm induced by the inner product. They key definition is the following.

DEFINITION 11.1 (Isometry). *Given a metric d_τ on values of type τ, a function $f : \tau_1 \to \tau_2$ is said to be an isometry iff $d_{\tau_2}(f(x), f(y)) = d_{\tau_1}(x, y)$ for all $x, y \in \tau_1$.*

In an apparently unrelated development, Reed and Pierce [40] introduce a calculus for differential privacy. The fundamental building blocks of their calculus are (i) that types are equipped with a metric that defines what it means for values to be "close," and that (ii) functions must preserve distances between the values. They key definition is the following.

DEFINITION 11.2 (c-sensitive function). *Given a metric d_τ on values of type τ, a function $f : \tau_1 \to \tau_2$ is said to be* c-sensitive *iff $d_{\tau_2}(f(x), f(y)) \leq c \cdot d_{\tau_1}(x, y)$ for all $x, y \in \tau_1$.*

In other words, the distance between the values x and y in the domain of the function cannot be magnified by more than a factor c. Clearly quantum evolution is restricted to the special case of 1-sensitive functions.

To further investigate this connection would require us to extend our model by associating a metric with each type. However, unlike previous work, the introduction of the metric in our case would be justified by additional physical considerations.

12. Conclusions and Future Work

Starting with the notion that closed physical systems are the "purest," we have developed a pure language in which computations preserve information. We show that even what are often called "pure functional languages" exhibit computational effects related to the creation and deletion of information. This development reasserts the fact that information is a significant computational resource that should, in many situations, be exposed to programmers and static analysis tools. One of our main contributions therefore is in bridging the information theoretic analysis of computations (for example in the domain of quantitative information flow security) and the traditional world of type and effect systems.

The main thesis of the paper is that the study of programming languages, their typing, their semantics, their computational effects, and even their security properties can tremendously benefit from taking the physical aspect of computation seriously. Our paper provides the conceptual foundation for such investigations.

Reversible Computing. Our pure language is logically reversible and hence shares some common features with previously developed reversible languages [6, 34, 37, 47] although none are based on the simple notion of isomorphisms between types [8]. The practice of programming languages is replete with *ad hoc* instances of reversible computations such as database transactions, mechanisms for data provenance, checkpoints, stack and exception traces, logs, backups, rollback recoveries, version control systems, reverse engineering, software transactional memories, continuations, backtracking search, and multiple-level "undo" features in commercial applications. A possible application of our work is that, in principle, such reversible programs could be automatically derived from common irreversible programs (which are typically easier to write) by translations similar to the one we presented. Similarly, our wiring diagrams could be directly realized as hardware circuits and pave the way for speculative execution and backtracking infrastructure in CPUs that are inherently reversible and use minimal bookkeeping resources [20].

Quantum Computing. Many programming models of quantum computing start with the λ-calculus as the underlying classical language and add quantum features on top of it [5, 13, 43, 45]. This strategy is natural given that the λ-calculus is the canonical classical computational model. However, since quantum evolution is reversible, this strategy complicates the development of quantum languages as it forces the languages to devise complicated ways to restrict their implicit information effects. A simpler strategy that loses no generality is to build the quantum features on top of a reversible classical language.

Optimality and Equivalence Preservation. For our purpose of establishing a semantic connection, we have made no attempt to optimize the types h and g generated by the translation to the reversible target language. For applications concerned with the implementation of Π^o circuits, optimizations like in Toffoli's original paper will need to be developed.

Also, equivalent source terms may be translated to terms of *different types*, as the types h and g are chosen by the translation based on the *syntax* of the input terms. The situation is similar to the closure conversion translation of a compiler which exposes the type of the environment and the fix should follow the same general strategy [4, 35].

Higher-Order Functions. As the development of lambda calculi with linear [27, 46] and bunched types [38] shows, controlling the creation, duplication, and sharing of resources is largely orthogonal to higher-order functions. Furthermore, existing work suggests that adding higher-order functions to a language like Π^o can be done in a systematic way as shown for example by the 'Int construction' of Joyal, Street and Verity in the context of traced monoidal categories [25], or by Abramsky [1, 3] and Mackie [31] in the context of the geometry of interaction and Ghica [17] in the context of the geometry of synthesis. These constructions need to explored in the context of Π^o.

Acknowledgments

We thank Amal Ahmed, Esfandiar Haghverdi, and Erik Wennstrom for helpful discussions. We also thank the anonymous reviewers for their helpful comments and suggestions. This project was partially funded by Indiana University's Office of the Vice President for Research and the Office of the Vice Provost for Research through its Faculty Research Support Program. We also acknowledge support from Indiana University's Institute for Advanced Study.

References

[1] S. Abramsky. Retracing some paths in process algebra. In U. Montanari and V. Sassone, editors, *CONCUR*, volume 1119 of *Lecture Notes in Computer Science*, pages 1–17. Springer, 1996.

[2] S. Abramsky. A structural approach to reversible computation. *Theor. Comput. Sci.*, 347:441–464, December 2005.

[3] S. Abramsky and R. Jagadeesan. New foundations for the geometry of interaction. *Inf. Comput.*, 111:53–119, May 1994.

[4] A. Ahmed and M. Blume. Typed closure conversion preserves observational equivalence. In *ICFP*, pages 157–168. ACM, 2008.

[5] T. Altenkirch and J. Grattage. A functional quantum programming language. In P. Panangaden, editor, *LICS*, pages 249–258. IEEE Computer Society Press, June 2005.

[6] H. G. Baker. NREVERSAL of fortune - the thermodynamics of garbage collection. In *Proceedings of the International Workshop on Memory Management*, pages 507–524. Springer-Verlag, 1992.

[7] C. H. Bennett. Logical reversibility of computation. *IBM J. Res. Dev.*, 17:525–532, November 1973.

[8] W. J. Bowman, R. P. James, and A. Sabry. Dagger Traced Symmetric Monoidal Categories and Reversible Programming. In *Workshop on Reversible Computation*, 2011.

[9] L. Cardelli and G. Zavattaro. On the computational power of biochemistry. In *Third International Conference on Algebraic Biology*, 2008.

[10] D. Clark, S. Hunt, and P. Malacaria. A static analysis for quantifying information flow in a simple imperative language. *J. Comput. Secur.*, 15:321–371, August 2007.

[11] D. Deutsch. *The Fabric of Reality*. Penguin, 1997.

[12] A. Di Pierro, C. Hankin, and H. Wiklicky. Reversible combinatory logic. *MSCS*, 16:621–637, August 2006.

[13] R. Duncan. *Types for quantum computation*. PhD thesis, Oxford University, 2006.

[14] C. Dwork. Differential privacy. In *ICALP (2)'06*, pages 1–12, 2006.

[15] M. Fiore. Isomorphisms of generic recursive polynomial types. In *POPL*, pages 77–88. ACM, 2004.

[16] E. Fredkin and T. Toffoli. Conservative logic. *International Journal of Theoretical Physics*, 21(3):219–253, 1982.

[17] D. R. Ghica. Geometry of synthesis: a structured approach to VLSI design. In *POPL*, pages 363–375. ACM, 2007.

[18] J.-Y. Girard. Linear logic. *Theor. Comput. Sci.*, 50:1–102, 1987.

[19] R. Glück and M. Kawabe. Revisiting an automatic program inverter for Lisp. *SIGPLAN Not.*, 40:8–17, May 2005.

[20] L. Hammond, M. Willey, and K. Olukotun. Data speculation support for a chip multiprocessor. In *ASPLOS*, pages 58–69, New York, NY, USA, 1998. ACM.

[21] M. Hasegawa. Recursion from cyclic sharing: Traced monoidal categories and models of cyclic lambda calculi. In *TLCA*, pages 196–213. Springer-Verlag, 1997.

[22] J. Hatcliff and O. Danvy. A generic account of continuation-passing styles. In *POPL*, pages 458–471. ACM, 1994.

[23] L. Huelsbergen. A logically reversible evaluator for the call-by-name lambda calculus. *InterJournal Complex Systems*, 46, 1996.

[24] J. Hughes. Generalising monads to arrows. *Sci. Comput. Program.*, 37(1-3):67–111, 2000.

[25] A. Joyal, R. Street, and D. Verity. Traced monoidal categories. *Math. Proc. Camb. Philos. Soc.*, 119(3):447–468, 1996.

[26] W. E. Kluge. A reversible SE(M)CD machine. In *International Workshop on Implementation of Functional Languages*, pages 95–113. Springer-Verlag, 2000.

[27] Y. Lafont. The linear abstract machine. *Theor. Comput. Sci.*, 59:157–180, July 1988. ISSN 0304-3975.

[28] R. Landauer. Irreversibility and heat generation in the computing process. *IBM J. Res. Dev.*, 5:183–191, July 1961.

[29] X. Ma, J. Huang, and F. Lombardi. A model for computing and energy dissipation of molecular QCA devices and circuits. *J. Emerg. Technol. Comput. Syst.*, 3(4):1–30, 2008.

[30] E. Macii and M. Poncino. Exact computation of the entropy of a logic circuit. In *Proceedings of the 6th Great Lakes Symposium on VLSI*, Washington, DC, USA, 1996. IEEE Computer Society.

[31] I. Mackie. Reversible higher-order computations. In *Workshop on Reversible Computation*, 2011.

[32] P. Malacaria. Assessing security threats of looping constructs. In *POPL*, pages 225–235. ACM, 2007.

[33] J. L. Massey. Guessing and entropy. In *Proceedings of the IEEE International Symposium on Information Theory*, page 204, 1994.

[34] A. B. Matos. Linear programs in a simple reversible language. *Theor. Comput. Sci.*, 290:2063–2074, January 2003.

[35] Y. Minamide, G. Morrisett, and R. Harper. Typed closure conversion. In *POPL*, pages 271–283, New York, NY, USA, 1996. ACM.

[36] E. Moggi. Notions of computation and monads. *Inf. Comput.*, 93: 55–92, July 1991.

[37] S.-C. Mu, Z. Hu, and M. Takeichi. An injective language for reversible computation. In *International Conference on Mathematics of Program Construction*, pages 289–313, 2004.

[38] P. O'hearn. On bunched typing. *J. Funct. Program.*, 13:747–796, July 2003.

[39] A. D. Pierro, C. Hankin, and H. Wiklicky. Probabilistic lambda-calculus and quantitative program analysis. *J. Log. Comput.*, 15(2), 2005.

[40] J. Reed and B. C. Pierce. Distance makes the types grow stronger: a calculus for differential privacy. In *ICFP*, pages 157–168. ACM, 2010.

[41] B. J. Ross. Running programs backwards: The logical inversion of imperative computation. *Formal Aspects of Computing*, 9:331–348, 1997.

[42] A. Sabelfeld and A. Myers. Language-based information-flow security. *IEEE Journal on Selected Areas in Communications*, 21(1):5–19, 2003.

[43] P. Selinger and B. Valiron. A lambda calculus for quantum computation with classical control. *MSCS*, 16(3):527–552, 2006.

[44] T. Toffoli. Reversible computing. In *Proceedings of the Colloquium on Automata, Languages and Programming*, pages 632–644. Springer-Verlag, 1980.

[45] A. van Tonder. A lambda calculus for quantum computation. *SIAM Journal on Computing*, 33(5):1109–1135, 2004.

[46] P. Wadler. Linear types can change the world! In M. Broy and C. Jones, editors, *IFIP TC 2 Working Conference on Programming Concepts and Methods*, pages 347–359. North Holland, 1990.

[47] T. Yokoyama, H. B. Axelsen, and R. Glück. Principles of a reversible programming language. In *Conference on Computing Frontiers*, pages 43–54. ACM, 2008.

[48] H. Zeng, C. S. Ellis, A. R. Lebeck, and A. Vahdat. Ecosystem: managing energy as a first class operating system resource. *SIGPLAN Not.*, 37(10):123–132, 2002.

[49] P. Zuliani. Logical reversibility. *IBM J. Res. Dev.*, 45:807–818, November 2001.

A Language for Automatically Enforcing Privacy Policies

Jean Yang Kuat Yessenov Armando Solar-Lezama
MIT CSAIL
{jeanyang, kuat, asolar} @csail.mit.edu

Abstract

It is becoming increasingly important for applications to protect sensitive data. With current techniques, the programmer bears the burden of ensuring that the application's behavior adheres to policies about where sensitive values may flow. Unfortunately, privacy policies are difficult to manage because their global nature requires coordinated reasoning and enforcement. To address this problem, we describe a programming model that makes the system responsible for ensuring adherence to privacy policies. The programming model has two components: 1) core programs describing functionality independent of privacy concerns and 2) declarative, decentralized policies controlling how sensitive values are disclosed. Each sensitive value encapsulates multiple views; policies describe which views are allowed based on the output context. The system is responsible for automatically ensuring that outputs are consistent with the policies. We have implemented this programming model in a new functional constraint language named Jeeves. In Jeeves, sensitive values are introduced as symbolic variables and policies correspond to constraints that are resolved at output channels. We have implemented Jeeves as a Scala library using an SMT solver as a model finder. In this paper we describe the dynamic and static semantics of Jeeves and the properties about policy enforcement that the semantics guarantees. We also describe our experience implementing a conference management system and a social network.

Categories and Subject Descriptors D.3.3 [*PROGRAMMING LANGUAGES*]: Language Constructs and Features

General Terms Languages, security

Keywords Language design, run-time system, privacy, security

1. Introduction

As users share more personal data online, it becomes increasingly important for applications to protect confidentiality. This places the burden on programmers to ensure compliance even when both the application and the policies may be evolving rapidly.

Ensuring compliance with privacy policies requires reasoning globally about both the flow of information and the interaction of different policies affecting this information. A number of tools have been developed to check code against privacy policies statically [4, 19] and dynamically [27]. While these checking tools can help avoid data leaks, the programmer is still responsible for implementing applications that display enough information to satisfy the user's needs without violating privacy policies. The programming model that we propose goes beyond checking to simplify the process of writing the code that preserves confidentiality.

The main contribution of this paper is a new programming model that makes the system responsible for automatically producing outputs consistent with programmer-specified policies. This automation makes it easier for programmers to enforce policies specifying how each sensitive value should be displayed in a given context. The programming model has two components: a core program representing policy-agnostic functionality and privacy policies controlling the disclosure of sensitive values. This separation of policies from core functionality allows the programmer to express policies explicitly in association with sensitive data rather than implicitly across the code base. The declarative nature of policies allows the system to ensure compliance even when these policies interact in non-trivial ways.

We have implemented this programming model in a new functional constraint language named Jeeves. Jeeves introduces three main concepts: *sensitive values*, *policies*, and *contexts*. *Sensitive values* are introduced as pairs $\langle v_\bot | v_\top \rangle_\ell$, where $v_\bot$ is the low-confidentiality value, $v_\top$ is the high-confidentiality value, and ℓ is a level variable that can take on the values $\{ \bot, \top \}$ and determines which view of the value should be shown. *Policies* correspond to constraints on the values of level variables. The language of policies is a decidable logic of quantifier-free arithmetic constraints, boolean constraints, and equality constraints over records and record fields. A policy may refer to a *context* value characterizing the output channel and containing relevant information about how the data is viewed.

For example, in a small social networking application we implemented as a case study, we included a policy that allows users to restrict the disclosure of their location to users in their geographic vicinity. Because the location is a sensitive value, a function such as **print** that tries to output a value derived from a location will need to be passed a context containing the location of the user to whom this value is about to be displayed. Using this context, the runtime system can then derive an output that is consistent with the policy.

We formally specify Jeeves to show that the high-confidentiality component of a sensitive value can only affect program output if the policies allow it. We define Jeeves in terms of λ_J, a constraint functional language that describes the propagation and enforcement of policies in Jeeves. λ_J is different from existing constraint functional languages [9, 10, 15, 18, 25] in the restrictions it places on the logical model and its use of default logic to provide determinism in program behavior. These restrictions make it possible for λ_J to have an efficient execution model without sacrificing too much expressiveness. There is a straightforward translation from Jeeves

This work was funded in part by the U.S. Government under the DARPA UHPC and NSF Graduate Research Fellowship programs. The views and conclusions contained herein are those of the authors and should not be interpreted as representing the official policies, either expressed or implied, of the U.S. Government.

POPL'12, January 25–27, 2012, Philadelphia, PA, USA.

Level	::=	$\bot \mid \top$	levels
Exp	::=	$\upsilon \mid Exp_1$ (op) Exp_2	expressions
	|	**if** Exp_1 **then** Exp_t **else** Exp_f	
	|	$Exp_1\ Exp_2$	
	|	$\langle Exp_\bot \mid Exp_\top \rangle(\ell)$	
	|	**level** ℓ **in** Exp	
	|	**policy** ℓ: Exp_p **then** *Level* **in** Exp	
Stmt	::=	**let** $x : \tau = Exp$	
	|	**print** $\{Exp_c\}$ Exp	

Figure 1: Jeeves syntax.

to λ_J: Jeeves level variables for sensitive values are logic variables, policies are assertions, and all values depending on logic variables are evaluated symbolically. The symbolic evaluation and constraint propagation in λ_J allow Jeeves to automatically enforce policies about information flow.

We implemented Jeeves as a domain-specific language embedded in Scala [20] using the Z3 SMT solver [17] to resolve constraints as a way to demonstrate the feasibility of the Jeeves programming model. To evaluate the expressiveness of Jeeves, we have used our Scala embedding to implement a small conference management system and a small social network. The case studies show that Jeeves allows the separate implementation of functionality and policies. For example, in the conference management example the code makes no attempt to differentiate between users, or even the general public, yet the policies ensure that the system displays the right level of information to each user through every phase of the review process.

In summary, we make the following contributions in this paper:

- We present a programming model and language, Jeeves, that allows programmers to separate privacy concerns from core program functionality.
- We formalize the dynamic and static semantics of Jeeves in terms of a λ_J, a new constraint functional language. We prove that Jeeves executions satisfy a non-interference property between low and high components of sensitive values.
- We describe the implementation of Jeeves as an embedded domain-specific language in Scala using the Z3 SMT solver.
- We describe small case studies that show that Jeeves supports the desired policies and allows the programmer to separately develop core functionality and policies.

2. Delegating Privacy to Jeeves

Jeeves allows the programmer to specify policies explicitly and upon data creation rather than implicitly across the code base. The Jeeves system trusts the programmer to correctly specify policies describing high- and low-confidentiality views of sensitive values and to correctly provide context values characterizing output channels. The runtime system is responsible for producing outputs consistent with the policies given the contexts. Jeeves guarantees that the system will not leak information about a high-confidentiality value unless the policies allow this value to be shown.

In this section, we introduce a simple conference management example to explain the main ideas in Jeeves: introducing sensitive values, writing policies, providing contexts, and implementing the core program logic. Conference management systems have simple information flow policies that are difficult to implement given the interaction of features. Being able to separately specify the policies allows the core functionality to be quite concise. In fact, we can write a single program that allows all viewers to access the list of papers directly for searching and viewing. The program relies on the Jeeves runtime system to display the appropriately anonymized information for reviewers vs. the general public.

For the sake of brevity, we present Jeeves using an ML-like concrete syntax, shown in Figure 1.

2.1 Introduction to Jeeves

We first describe how to introduce sensitive values, use them to compute result values, and display the results in different output contexts. Suppose we have the policy that a sensitive value name should be seen as "Alice" by users with a high confidentiality level and as "Anonymous" by anybody else. A Jeeves program can use the name value as follows:

```
let msg = "Author is " + name
print { alice } msg   (* Output: "Author is Alice" *)
print { bob } msg     (* Output: "Author is Anonymous" *)
```

To achieve the different outputs for alice and bob, we associate a policy with name by declaring it through the following Jeeves code:

```
let name =
  level a in
  policy a: ! (context = alice) then ⊥ in
    <"Anonymous" | "Alice">(a)
```

This code introduces a level variable a and associates with it a policy that if the **context** value is not alice, then the value is $\bot$. The context value represents a viewer in the output channel. The code then attaches this policy to the sensitive value <"Anonymous" | "Alice">(a), which defines the low-confidentiality view as the string "Anonymous" and the high-confidentiality view as "Alice". When this code is executed, the Jeeves runtime ensures that only the user alice can see her name appearing as the author in the string msg. User bob sees the string "Author is Anonymous".

Each sensitive value defines a low-confidentiality and high-confidentiality view for a value. The Jeeves programmer defines sensitive values by introducing a tuple $\langle v_\bot | v_\top \rangle_\ell$ where $v_\bot$ is the low-confidentiality value, $v_\top$ is the high confidentiality value, and ℓ is a level variable associated with a set of policies determining which of the two values to show. An expression containing n sensitive values can evaluate to one of 2^n possible views. Level variables provide the means of abstraction to specify policies incrementally and independently of the sensitive value declaration. Level variables can be constrained directly (by explicitly passing around a level variable) or indirectly (by constraining another level variable when there is a dependency). It is possible to encode more than two privacy levels, but for the sake of simplicity the paper assumes only two.

Policies, introduced through **policy** expressions, provide declarative rules describing when to set a level variable to $\top$ or $\bot$. Notice that the policy above forces a to be $\bot$ when the user is not alice; other policies could further restrict the level variable to be $\bot$ even for alice, but no amount of policy interactions can allow a different user to see the $v_\top$ value in contradiction with the policy. Policies may mention variables in scope and also the **context** variable, which corresponds to an implicit parameter characterizing the output channel.

The **context** construct relieves the programmer of the burden of structuring code to propagate values from the output context to the policies. Statements such as **print** that release information to the viewer require a context parameter. The Jeeves runtime system propagates policies associated with sensitive values so that when a value is about to be displayed though an output channel, the right context can be inserted into the policy and the appropriate result can be produced. In addition to **print** shown above, other output channels include sending e-mail and writing to file.

2.2 Declarative and Decentralized Policies

We now describe how to write policies in Jeeves using fragments of our conference management example. The paper record is defined below; it assumes single author papers to simplify the presentation.

```
type paper { title : string
           ; author: user
           ; reviews: review list
           ; accepted: bool option }
```

The idiomatic way of attaching policies to values is to create sensitive values for each field and then attach policies:

```
let mkPaper
  ( title : string) (author: string)
  (reviews: review list ) (accepted: bool option): paper =
  level tp, authp, rp, accp in
  let p = { title  = < "" | title >(tp)
          ; author = < "Anonymized" | author>(authp)
          ; reviews = < [] | reviews>(rp)
          ; accepted = < none | some accepted >(accp) } in
  addTitlePolicy p tp; addAuthorPolicy p authp;
  addReviewsPolicy p rp; addAcceptedPolicy p accp;
    p
```

This function introduces level variables for each of the fields, creates sensitive values for each of the fields, attaches policies to the level variables, and returns the resulting paper record.

The Jeeves programmer associates policies with sensitive values by introducing level variables, attaching policies to them, and using them to create sensitive values. Consider the policy that the title of a paper should be visible to the authors of the paper, reviewers, and PC members and only visible to the general public after it is public that the paper has been accepted. We can define addTitlePolicy as follows:

```
let addTitlePolicy (p: paper) (a: level ): unit =
  policy a: ! (context.viewer = p.author
    || context.viewer. role = Reviewer
    || context.viewer. role = PC
    || (context.stage = Public && isAccepted p)) then ⊥
```

This function attaches to level variable a a policy that sets the level to $\bot$ unless the viewer has a right to see the paper title.

Policies may refer to values corresponding to the output channel through the **context** variable. The condition for the policy in function addTitlePolicy uses the viewer and stage fields of the **context** variable, which have types confView and confStage types, respectively:

```
type confView { viewer: user; stage: confStage }
type confStage = Submission | Review | Decision | Public
```

A context value of type confView must be produced in order for an output channel to access a sensitive value produced by the addTitlePolicy function. With type inference, it is not necessary for the programmer to provide the context type annotation. In the Scala implementation, the programmer does not need to provide context annotations.

2.2.1 Policy Interactions

The Jeeves model helps prevent the programmer from inadvertently leaking information about one value through the enforcement of a policy for another value. We show how Jeeves can prevent the programmer from writing code where the policy for paper titles leaks information about a paper record's accepted field.

Consider the following situation in which the policy for one sensitive field (paper titles) depends on another sensitive field (whether the paper has been accepted). In the addTitlePolicy function, the predicate isAccepted p depends on the accepted field of the paper p, which is **some** accepted if a decision has been made (and the decision is known) or **none** otherwise. The accepted field needs its own policy to prevent its status from being leaked early. The following function adds the appropriate policy:

```
let addAcceptedPolicy (p: paper) (a: level ): unit =
  policy a: ! (context.viewer. role = Reviewer
    || context.viewer. role = PC
    || context.stage = Public) then ⊥
```

This policy allows reviewers and program committee members to always see whether a paper has been accepted and for others to see this field only if the stage is Public. With this policy in place, the title field cannot leak information about the accepted tag. Even if the policy for paper titles were to drop the **context**.stage = Public requirement, the policy for accepted would prevent the titles of accepted papers from being leaked before the Public stage.

2.2.2 Circular Dependencies and Defaults

The Jeeves system can also enforce policies when there are circular dependencies between sensitive values, as could happen when a context value depends on a sensitive value. Consider the following function that associates a policy with the authors of a paper:

```
let addAuthorPolicy (p: paper)(n: level ) : unit =
  policy n:
    !( isAuthor p context.user ||
      (context.stage = Public && isAccepted p)) then ⊥
```

This policy says that to see the author of a paper, the user must be an author or the paper must be a publicly accepted paper. Now consider functionality that sends messages to authors of papers:

```
let sendMsg (author: user) =
  let msg = "Dear " + author.name + ... in
  sendmail { user = author; stage = Review } msg
```

The policy for level variable n depends on **context**.user. Here, **context**.user is a sensitive value, as the value of the author variable depends on the viewer.

This leads to a circular dependency that makes the solution underconstrained: the value of the message recipient on the context value, which contains the message recipient. Either sending mail to the empty user or sending mail to the author is correct under the policy. The latter behavior is preferred, as it ensures that user *a* can communicate with user *b* without knowing private information about user *b*. The Jeeves runtime ensures this maximally functional behavior by setting level variables to $\top$ by default: if the policies allow a level variable to be $\top$ or $\bot$, the value will be $\top$.

3. The λ_J Language and Semantics

To more formally describe the guarantees, we define the semantics of Jeeves in two steps; first, we introduce λ_J, a simple constraint functional language based on the λ-calculus, and then we show how to translate Jeeves to λ_J. λ_J differs from existing constraint functional languages [9, 10, 15, 25] in two key ways: 1) λ_J restricts its constraint language to quantifier-free constraints involving boolean and arithmetic expressions over primitive values and records and 2) λ_J supports *default values* for logic variables to facilitate reasoning about nondeterminism. λ_J's restrictions on the constraint language allow execution to rely on an off-the-shelf SMT solver.

In this section, we introduce the λ_J language, the dynamic semantics, the static semantics, and the translation from Jeeves. The λ_J language extends the λ-calculus with **defer** and **assert** for introducing and constraining logic variables, as well as a **concretize** construct to produce concrete values from them. The dynamic semantics describe the lazy evaluation of expressions with logic variables and the interaction with the constraint environment. The static semantics describe how the system guarantees evaluation progress and enforces restrictions on symbolic values and recursion. The translation from Jeeves to λ_J illustrates how Jeeves uses λ_J's lazy evaluation and constraint propagation, combined with Jeeves restrictions on how logic variables are used, to provide privacy guarantees.

c	::=	$n \mid b \mid \lambda x:\tau.e \mid$ record $\overline{x:v}$	
	$\mid$	**error** $\mid$ ()	concrete primitives
σ	::=	$x \mid$ **context** τ	symbolic values
	$\mid$	c_1 (op) $\sigma_2 \mid \sigma_1$ (op) c_2	
	$\mid$	σ_1 (op) σ_2	
	$\mid$	**if** σ **then** υ_t **else** υ_f	
υ	::=	$c \mid \sigma$	values
e	::=	$\upsilon \mid e_1$ (op) e_2	expressions
	$\mid$	**if** e_1 **then** e_t **else** $e_f \mid e_1\ e_2$	
	$\mid$	**let** $x:\tau = e_1$ **in** e_2	
	$\mid$	**let rec** $f:\tau = e_1$ **in** e_2	
	$\mid$	**defer** $x:\tau\ \{e\}$ **default** υ_d	
	$\mid$	**assert** e	
	$\mid$	**concretize** e **with** υ_c	

Figure 2: The λ_J abstract syntax.

3.1 The λ_J Language

λ_J is the λ-calculus extended with logic variables. Figure 2 shows the abstract syntax of λ_J. Expressions (e) include the standard λ expressions extended with the **defer** construct for introducing logic variables, the **assert** construct for introducing constraints, and the **concretize** construct for producing concrete values consistent with the constraints. λ_J evaluation produces irreducible values (υ), which are either concrete (c) or symbolic (σ). Concrete values are what one would expect from λ-calculus, while symbolic values are values that cannot be reduced further due to the presence of logic variables. Symbolic values also include the **context** construct which allows constraints to refer to a value supplied at concretization time. The **context** variable is an implicit parameter [14] provided in the **concretize** expression. In the semantics we model the behavior of the **context** variable as a symbolic value that is constrained during evaluation of **concretize**. λ_J contains a **let rec** construct that handles recursive functions in the standard way using **fix**.

A novel feature of λ_J is that logic variables are also associated with a *default value* that serves as a default assumption: this is the assigned value for the logic variable unless it is inconsistent with the constraints. The purpose of default values is to provide some determinism when logic variables are underconstrained.

3.2 Dynamic Semantics

The λ_J evaluation rules extend λ-calculus evaluation with constraint propagation and symbolic evaluation of logic variables. Evaluation involves keeping track of constraints which are required to be true (hard constraints) and the set of constraints we use for guidance if consistent with our hard constraints (default assumptions). To correctly evaluate conditionals with symbolic conditions, we also need to keep track of the (possibly symbolic) path condition. Evaluation happens in the context of a path condition $\mathcal{G}$, an environment $\Sigma = \emptyset \mid \{\sigma\} \mid \Sigma \cup \Sigma'$ storing the current set of constraints, and an environment $\Delta = \emptyset \mid \{\sigma\} \mid \Delta \cup \Delta'$ storing the set of constraints on default values for logic variables. Evaluation rules take the form

$$\mathcal{G} \vdash \langle \Sigma, \Delta, e \rangle \rightarrow \langle \Sigma', \Delta', e' \rangle.$$

Evaluation produces a tuple $\langle \Sigma', \Delta', e' \rangle$ of a resulting expression e' along with modified constraint and default environments. In Figure 3 we show the small-step dynamic λ_J semantics.

3.2.1 Evaluation with Logic Variables

λ_J has the expected semantics for function application and arithmetic and boolean operations. The E-APP1, E-APP2, and E-APPLAMBDA rules describe a call-by-value semantics. The E-OP1 and E-OP2 rules for operations show that the arguments are evaluated to irreducible expressions and then, if both arguments become concrete, the E-OP rule can be applied to produce a concrete result.

Conditionals whose conditions evaluate to concrete values evaluate according to the E-CONDTRUE, and E-CONDFALSE rules as one would expect. When the condition evaluates to a symbolic value, the whole conditional evaluates to a symbolic **if-then-else** value by evaluating both branches as described by the E-CONDSYMT and E-CONDSYMF rules. Note that λ_J expressions are pure (effects are only in Jeeves statements) so side effects cannot occur in conditional branches.

Evaluating under symbolic conditions is potentially dangerous because evaluation of such conditionals with a recursive function application in a branch could lead to infinite recursion when the condition is symbolic. Our system prevents this anomalous behavior by using the type system to enforce that recursive calls are not made under symbolic conditions (Section 3.3).

3.2.2 Introduction and Elimination of Logic Variables

In λ_J, logic variables are introduced through the **defer** keyword. To illustrate the semantics of **defer** consider the example below.

```
let x: int = defer x': int { x' > 0 } default 42
```

As we show in the E-DEFER evaluation rule, the right-hand side of the assignment evaluates to an α-renamed version of the logic variable x'. Evaluation adds the constraint $\mathcal{G} \Rightarrow$ x' > 0 to the constraint environment and the constraint $\mathcal{G} \Rightarrow$ x' $= 42$ to the default constraint environment. The constraint $\mathcal{G} \Rightarrow$ x' > 0 is a hard constraint that must hold for all derived outputs, while $\mathcal{G} \Rightarrow$ x' $= 42$ is a constraint that is only used if it is consistent with the resulting logical environment. Hard constraints are introduced within the braces ({ }) of **defer** expressions and through **assert** expressions; soft constraints are introduced through the **default** clause of **defer** expressions.

In addition to the constraints in **defer**, the program can introduce constraints on logic variables through **assert** expressions. The E-ASSERT rule describes how the constraint is added to the constraint environment, taking into account the path condition $\mathcal{G}$. For instance, consider the following code:

```
if (x > 0) then assert (x = 42) else assert (x = -42).
```

Evaluation adds to the constraint environment the constraints x $> 0 \Rightarrow$ x $= 42$ and $\neg$(x $> 0) \Rightarrow$ x $= -42$.

Symbolic expressions can be made concrete through the **concretize** construct. Evaluation of **concretize** expressions either produces a concrete value or an error. A **concretize** expression includes the expression to concretize and a context:

```
let result : int = concretize x with 42.
```

As we describe in the E-CONCRETIZESAT rule, concretization adds the constraint **context** $= 42$ to the constraint environment and finds an assignment to x consistent with the constraint and default environments. An important observation is that the context itself may be symbolic, in which case the system will also be finding a concrete context consistent with the hard constraints. The MODEL function takes the constraint and default environments, computes a satisfying assignment to free variables, and produces a substitution $\mathcal{M} : \upsilon \rightarrow c$ that is used to produce a concrete value, as shown in the E-CONCRETIZESAT rule.

The CONCRETIZE-UNSAT rule describes what happens if there is no satisfiable expression consistent with the constraint environment. In this case, evaluation of the **concretize** expression produces the **error** value.

3.2.3 Interaction with the Constraint Environment

Valid constraint expressions consist of λ_J expressions that do not contain λ-expressions. This constraint language corresponds to constraints that can be solved by off-the-shelf SMT solvers. The

$$\boxed{\mathcal{G} \vdash \langle \Sigma, \Delta, e \rangle \rightarrow \langle \Sigma', \Delta', e' \rangle}$$

$$\frac{\mathcal{G} \vdash \langle \Sigma, \Delta, e_1 \rangle \rightarrow \langle \Sigma', \Delta', e_1' \rangle}{\mathcal{G} \vdash \langle \Sigma, \Delta, e_1\ e_2 \rangle \rightarrow \langle \Sigma', \Delta', e_1'\ e_2 \rangle}\ \textsc{E-App1} \qquad \frac{\mathcal{G} \vdash \langle \Sigma, \Delta, e_2 \rangle \rightarrow \langle \Sigma', \Delta', e_2' \rangle}{\mathcal{G} \vdash \langle \Sigma, \Delta, \upsilon\ e_2 \rangle \rightarrow \langle \Sigma', \Delta', \upsilon\ e_2' \rangle}\ \textsc{E-App2}$$

$$\frac{}{\mathcal{G} \vdash \langle \Sigma, \Delta, \lambda x.e\ \upsilon \rangle \rightarrow \langle \Sigma, \Delta, e[x \mapsto \upsilon] \rangle}\ \textsc{E-AppLambda} \qquad \frac{c' = c_1\ (\mathrm{op})\ c_2}{\mathcal{G} \vdash \langle \Sigma, \Delta, c_1\ (\mathrm{op})\ c_2 \rangle \rightarrow \langle \Sigma, \Delta, c' \rangle}\ \textsc{E-Op}$$

$$\frac{\mathcal{G} \vdash \langle \Sigma, \Delta, e_1 \rangle \rightarrow \langle \Sigma', \Delta', e_1' \rangle}{\mathcal{G} \vdash \langle \Sigma, \Delta, e_1\ (\mathrm{op})\ e_2 \rangle \rightarrow \langle \Sigma', \Delta', e_1'\ (\mathrm{op})\ e_2 \rangle}\ \textsc{E-Op1} \qquad \frac{\mathcal{G} \vdash \langle \Sigma, \Delta, e_2 \rangle \rightarrow \langle \Sigma', \Delta', e_2' \rangle}{\mathcal{G} \vdash \langle \Sigma, \Delta, \upsilon\ (\mathrm{op})\ e_2 \rangle \rightarrow \langle \Sigma', \Delta', \upsilon\ (\mathrm{op})\ e_2' \rangle}\ \textsc{E-Op2}$$

$$\frac{\mathcal{G} \vdash \langle \Sigma, \Delta, e_c \rangle \rightarrow \langle \Sigma', \Delta', e_c' \rangle}{\mathcal{G} \vdash \langle \Sigma, \Delta, \textbf{if}\ e_c\ \textbf{then}\ e_t\ \textbf{else}\ e_f \rangle \rightarrow \langle \Sigma', \Delta', \textbf{if}\ e_c'\ \textbf{then}\ e_t\ \textbf{else}\ e_f \rangle}\ \textsc{E-Cond}$$

$$\frac{\mathcal{G} \vdash \langle \Sigma, \Delta, e_t \rangle \rightarrow \langle \Sigma', \Delta', e_t' \rangle}{\mathcal{G} \vdash \langle \Sigma, \Delta, \textbf{if true then}\ e_t\ \textbf{else}\ e_f \rangle \rightarrow \langle \Sigma', \Delta', e_t' \rangle}\ \textsc{E-CondTrue} \qquad \frac{\mathcal{G} \vdash \langle \Sigma, \Delta, e_f \rangle \rightarrow \langle \Sigma', \Delta', e_f' \rangle}{\mathcal{G} \vdash \langle \Sigma, \Delta, \textbf{if false then}\ e_t\ \textbf{else}\ e_f \rangle \rightarrow \langle \Sigma', \Delta', e_f' \rangle}\ \textsc{E-CondFalse}$$

$$\frac{\sigma \wedge \mathcal{G} \vdash \langle \Sigma, \Delta, e_t \rangle \rightarrow \langle \Sigma', \Delta', e_t' \rangle}{\mathcal{G} \vdash \langle \Sigma, \Delta, \textbf{if}\ \sigma\ \textbf{then}\ e_t\ \textbf{else}\ e_f \rangle \rightarrow \langle \Sigma', \Delta', \textbf{if}\ \sigma\ \textbf{then}\ e_t'\ \textbf{else}\ e_f \rangle}\ \textsc{E-CondSymT}$$

$$\frac{\neg\sigma \wedge \mathcal{G} \vdash \langle \Sigma, \Delta, e_f \rangle \rightarrow \langle \Sigma', \Delta', e_f' \rangle}{\mathcal{G} \vdash \langle \Sigma, \Delta, \textbf{if}\ \sigma\ \textbf{then}\ \upsilon_t\ \textbf{else}\ e_f \rangle \rightarrow \langle \Sigma', \Delta', \textbf{if}\ \sigma\ \textbf{then}\ \upsilon_t\ \textbf{else}\ e_f' \rangle}\ \textsc{E-CondSymF}$$

$$\frac{\mathcal{G} \vdash \langle \Sigma, \Delta, e \rangle \rightarrow \langle \Sigma', \Delta', e' \rangle}{\mathcal{G} \vdash \langle \Sigma, \Delta, \textbf{defer}\ x : \tau\ \{e\}\ \textbf{default}\ \upsilon_d \rangle \rightarrow \langle \Sigma', \Delta', \textbf{defer}\ x : \tau\ \{e'\}\ \textbf{default}\ \upsilon_d \rangle}\ \textsc{E-DeferConstraint}$$

$$\frac{\textsf{fresh}\ x'}{\mathcal{G} \vdash \langle \Sigma, \Delta, \textbf{defer}\ x : \tau\ \{\upsilon_c\}\ \textbf{default}\ \upsilon_d \rangle \rightarrow \langle \Sigma \cup \{\mathcal{G} \Rightarrow \upsilon_c[x \mapsto x']\}, \Delta \cup \{\mathcal{G} \Rightarrow x' = \upsilon_d\}, x' \rangle}\ \textsc{E-Defer}$$

$$\frac{\mathcal{G} \vdash \langle \Sigma, \Delta, e \rangle \rightarrow \langle \Sigma', \Delta', e' \rangle}{\mathcal{G} \vdash \langle \Sigma, \Delta, \textbf{assert}\ e \rangle \rightarrow \langle \Sigma', \Delta', \textbf{assert}\ e' \rangle}\ \textsc{E-AssertConstraint} \qquad \frac{}{\mathcal{G} \vdash \langle \Sigma, \Delta, \textbf{assert}\ \upsilon \rangle \rightarrow \langle \Sigma \cup \{\mathcal{G} \Rightarrow \upsilon\}, \Delta, () \rangle}\ \textsc{E-Assert}$$

$$\frac{\mathcal{G} \vdash \langle \Sigma, \Delta, e \rangle \rightarrow \langle \Sigma', \Delta', e' \rangle}{\mathcal{G} \vdash \langle \Sigma, \Delta, \textbf{concretize}\ e\ \textbf{with}\ \upsilon_c \rangle \rightarrow \langle \Sigma', \Delta', \textbf{concretize}\ e'\ \textbf{with}\ \upsilon_c \rangle}\ \textsc{E-ConcretizeExp}$$

$$\frac{\textsc{Model}(\Delta, \Sigma \cup \{\mathcal{G} \wedge \textbf{context} = \upsilon_c\}) = \mathcal{M} \quad c = \mathcal{M}[\![\upsilon_v]\!]}{\mathcal{G} \vdash \langle \Sigma, \Delta, \textbf{concretize}\ \upsilon_v\ \textbf{with}\ \upsilon_c \rangle \rightarrow \langle \Sigma, \Delta, c \rangle}\ \textsc{E-ConcretizeSat}$$

$$\frac{\textsc{Model}(\Delta, \Sigma \cup \{\mathcal{G} \wedge \textbf{context} = \upsilon_c\}) = \textsc{Unsat}}{\mathcal{G} \vdash \langle \Sigma, \Delta, \textbf{concretize}\ \upsilon_v\ \textbf{with}\ \upsilon_c \rangle \rightarrow \langle \Sigma, \Delta, \textbf{error} \rangle}\ \textsc{E-ConcretizeUnsat}$$

Figure 3: Dynamic semantics for λ_J.

MODEL procedure in the E-CONCRETIZE rule is the model finding procedure for default logic [1]. The default environment Δ and constraint environment Σ specify a supernormal default theory (Δ, Σ) where each default judgement $\sigma \in \Delta$ has the form

$$\frac{\textbf{true} : \sigma}{\sigma}\ .$$

The MODEL procedure produces either a model $\mathcal{M}$ for the theory if it is consistent, or UNSAT. We use a fixed-point algorithm for MODEL that uses classical SMT model-generating decision procedures and iteratively saturates the logical context with default judgements in a non-deterministic order.

3.3 λ_J Static Semantics

The λ_J static semantics ensures that evaluation produces either a concrete expression or a well-formed symbolic expression. Recall that symbolic expressions must be valid constraints, which include arithmetic, boolean, and conditional expressions but not functions. (In the λ_J semantics we do not explicitly address data structures such as lists. Data structures are also required to be concrete but may have symbolic elements.) Thus the static semantics guarantee that 1) concrete values are supplied when concrete values are expected, 2) symbolic values are well-formed, 3) evaluation under symbolic conditions does not cause unexpected infinite recursion, and 4)

δ	::=	**concrete** | **sym**	determinism tag
β	::=	$\textbf{int}_c$ | $\textbf{bool}_c$ | **unit**	base type
	|	**int** | **bool**	
τ	::=	$\beta \mid \tau_1 \xrightarrow{nr} \tau_2 \mid \tau_1 \rightarrow \tau_2$	type

Figure 4: λ_J types.

context values have the appropriate types. The type system therefore ensures that the logical state will always be well formed, although it cannot guarantee that it will be logically consistent.

To guarantee properties 1-3, the λ_J type system tracks the flow of symbolic values, ruling out symbolic functions and *reentrant applications* under symbolic conditions. Reentrant applications are function applications that may recursively call the current function; we prevent such applications under symbolic conditions to prevent non-termination that may arise from evaluating both sides of a conditional branch with a symbolic condition. Property 4, on the other hand, is enforced by ensuring that the type of the context used at concretization is an upper bound for the types of contexts required by all the relevant policies.

We show the λ_J types in Figure 4 and the subtyping, type well-formedness, and typing rules in Figure 5. Base types β are the standard λ-calculus types extended with the $\textbf{int}_c$ and $\textbf{bool}_c$ types to indicate values that are necessarily concrete. (Expressions of function type are not permitted to be symbolic.) There are two function types: $\overset{nr}{\to}$ for functions whose application cannot be reentrant and $\to$ for functions whose application can be reentrant. We will use the term *reentrant function* to refer to a function whose application can be reentrant.

Typing judgments have the form $\Gamma;\gamma \vdash e:\tau$. A judgment says that in the type environment Γ under a path of type γ (**sym** or **concrete**), the expression e has type τ. Γ is defined $\Gamma ::= \cdot \mid x:\tau \mid \Gamma,\Gamma'$. The typing rules keep track of whether a value may be symbolic (**int** or **bool** type) or must be concrete ($\textbf{int}_c$, $\textbf{bool}_c$, and functions). This information is used to determine the value of the γ tag in the T-CONDC and T-CONDSYM rules. Information about whether the condition is symbolic is used in 1) ruling out symbolic functions and 2) ruling out self-calls under symbolic branches.

Symbolic functions are prevented by the T-DEFER and T-CONDSYM rules, which restrict the production of symbolic functions. The T-DEFER rule restricts the explicit introduction of symbolic values to have base type β, while the T-CONDSYM rule restricts the implicit introduction of symbolic values to base type β.

The T-LETREC rule shows that recursive functions must be considered reentrant (have $\to$ type) within their own definitions, since applying the function will cause a recursive call to the current function. Outside their declaration, on the other hand, they can have $\overset{nr}{\to}$ type. A second restriction on reentrant functions is imposed by the type well-formedness predicate **rep**, which requires that functions taking arguments that may be reentrant ($\to$) be themselves labeled as reentrant. This prevents high-order functions from being used to circumvent the restrictions on reentrant calls.

According to the rules, a reentrant call cannot occur under a symbolic condition. The T-CONDSYM rule sets $\gamma = \textbf{sym}$ when the condition is symbolic. The T-APPCURREC rule allows applications of recursive functions only under concrete paths. This implies that canonical recursive functions such as factorial can only type-check if they require a concrete argument. This restriction does not prevent recursive sort or other recursive structure-traversing functions because data structures are necessarily concrete, so conditions involving their structure are also concrete.

The subtyping relationship $<:$ allows values that are necessarily concrete to be used as potentially symbolic values. This way, functions that require concrete values can only be applied when concrete arguments are supplied, but a concrete value can be used as a symbolic value (for instance, $\textbf{int}_c$ as **int**). The subtyping rules allow non-reentrant functions ($\overset{nr}{\to}$) to be used as reentrant functions ($\to$).

3.3.1 Contexts

We also have typing rules (not shown in Figure 5) ensuring that contexts of the appropriate type are provided in **concretize** expressions. In the T-CONCRETIZE rule, the context typing judgment $\vdash^c$ enforces that the context type supplied is the context type expected. The context typing judgement is $\Gamma \vdash^c x:\tau_c$, where τ_c is the *context* type of an expression. The rules propagate the context type, enforce that matching contexts are provided for sub-expressions, and enforce that the correct context type is supplied at concretization.

We define a lattice describing when different context types may be combined. The bottom of the lattice is $\bot$ and for all types τ, we have the relationship $\bot <:_c \tau$. Contexts support width subtyping on record types:

$$\text{record } \vec{m} <:_c \text{record } \vec{n}, \forall n_i.(\exists m_i | m_i = n_i).$$

A record with fields $\vec{m}$ can be used as a context whenever a record with fields $\vec{n}$ expected as long as the labelled fields of m_i are a superset of the labelled fields of $\vec{n}$.

3.4 Translation from Jeeves

There is a straightforward translation from Jeeves to λ_J. Sensitive values and level variables in Jeeves correspond to λ_J logic variables, level policies correspond to λ_J assertions, and contextual enforcement corresponds to producing concrete values consistent with the logical environment. Default values provide determinism in handling policy dependencies.

We show the translation of levels and sensitive values from Jeeves to λ_J in Figure 6. We have the $Exp \hookrightarrow e$ rule to describe how a Jeeves expression translates to a λ_J expression e. The translation has the following properties: 1) level variables are the only logic variables, 2) expressions containing sensitive values yield symbolic results, 3) only Jeeves policies introduce assertions, and 4) the **concretize** construct can only appear at the outermost level and is associated with an effectful computation.

3.4.1 Sensitive Values

A Jeeves sensitive value `<v1 | v2>(a)` is translated to a symbolic value equal to either `v1` or `v2` depending on the value of level variable `a`. Because sensitive values are symbolic, all expressions computed from this sensitive value are subject to policies depending on the value of level variable `a`.

3.4.2 Level Variables

Jeeves level variables are translated to λ_J expressions binding a new logic variable of **level** type equal to either $\bot$ or $\top$. The default value of level variables is $\top$: the constraint solving oracle first resolves the constraint environment with the assumption that each level is $\top$ and only adjusts this belief if the variable must be equal to $\bot$. This provides the programmer with some guarantees about program behavior when level variables are underconstrained. Underconstraint can arise, for instance, if values in the context depend on sensitive values.

Besides being useful in handling circular dependencies, having the default value of level variables as $\top$ prevents the programmer from leaking a value as a result of an underspecified value. If a level variable is underconstrained, policies on a subsequent variable can affect the value it can take:

```
1 let x = level a in <0 | 1>(a)
2 let y = level b in
3   policy b: true then ⊤ in
4   policy b: x = 1 then ⊥ in
5   <0 | 1>(b)
```

If the value of x were fixed, this would yield a contradiction, but instead these policies indirectly fix the value of x and a:

true

$\therefore$ (1) $\mathsf{b} = \top$ (line 3)	$\therefore$ (2) $\mathsf{x} \neq 1$ (line 4)
$\therefore$ (3) $\mathsf{x} = 0$ (line 1)	$\therefore$ (4) $\mathsf{a} = \bot$ (line 1)

Making underconstrained level variables $\top$ by default forces programmers to explicitly introduce policies setting level variables to $\bot$. For this reason, underspecification will only cause level variables to be set to $\bot$ instead of $\top$.

3.4.3 Declarative Constraint Policies

As we show in Table 6, level policies are translated to λ_J **assert** expressions. Level policies can be introduced on any logic variables in scope and are added to the environment based on possible path assumptions made up to that point. The policy that a Jeeves expression (Exp) enforces consists of the constraint environment produced when evaluating Exp as a λ_J expression. More specifically, we are talking about Σ', Δ' where $Exp \hookrightarrow e$ and $\vdash \langle \emptyset, \emptyset, e \rangle \to^* \langle \Sigma', \Delta', \upsilon \rangle$. This policy contains constraints determining whether level variables can be $\bot$ or $\top$.

$$\boxed{\tau_1 <: \tau_2}$$

$$\frac{}{\tau <: \tau}\ \textsc{S-Reflexive} \qquad \frac{}{\textbf{int}_c <: \textbf{int}}\ \textsc{S-Int} \qquad \frac{}{\textbf{bool}_c <: \textbf{bool}}\ \textsc{S-Bool} \qquad \frac{}{\tau_1 \xrightarrow{nr} \tau_2 <: \tau_1 \rightarrow \tau_2}\ \textsc{S-RecFun} \qquad \frac{\tau_1' <: \tau_1 \quad \tau_2 <: \tau_2'}{\tau_1 \rightarrow \tau_2 <: \tau_1' \rightarrow \tau_2'}\ \textsc{S-Fun}$$

$$\boxed{\textbf{rep}\ \tau}$$

$$\frac{\textbf{rep}\ \tau' \quad \tau' <: \tau}{\textbf{rep}\ \tau}\ \textsc{Ok-SubType} \qquad \frac{}{\textbf{rep}\ \beta}\ \textsc{Ok-BaseType} \qquad \frac{\textbf{rep}\ \tau_2}{\textbf{rep}\ \beta_1 \rightarrow \tau_2}\ \textsc{Ok-BaseFunction}$$

$$\frac{\textbf{rep}\ (\tau_1 \xrightarrow{nr} \tau') \quad \textbf{rep}\ \tau_2}{\textbf{rep}\ (\tau_1 \xrightarrow{nr} \tau') \xrightarrow{nr} \tau_2}\ \textsc{Ok-HOFunction} \qquad \frac{\textbf{rep}\ \tau_1 \rightarrow \tau_2}{\textbf{rep}\ (\tau_1 \rightarrow \tau_2) \rightarrow \beta}\ \textsc{Ok-RecFunctionBase} \qquad \frac{\textbf{rep}\ \tau_1 \rightarrow \tau_2 \quad \textbf{rep}\ \tau_1' \rightarrow \tau_2'}{\textbf{rep}\ (\tau_1 \rightarrow \tau_2) \rightarrow (\tau_1' \rightarrow \tau_2')}\ \textsc{Ok-RecFunction}$$

$$\boxed{\Gamma;\gamma \vdash e : \langle \tau, \delta \rangle}$$

$$\frac{x \in \Gamma}{\Gamma;\gamma \vdash x : \Gamma(x)}\ \textsc{T-Var} \qquad \frac{}{\Gamma;\gamma \vdash n : \textbf{int}_c}\ \textsc{T-Int} \qquad \frac{}{\Gamma;\gamma \vdash b : \textbf{bool}_c}\ \textsc{T-Bool} \qquad \frac{}{\Gamma;\gamma \vdash () : \textbf{unit}}\ \textsc{T-Unit} \qquad \frac{\textbf{rep}\ \tau}{\Gamma;\gamma \vdash \textbf{context}\ \tau : \tau}\ \textsc{T-Context}$$

$$\frac{\Gamma;\gamma \vdash e_1 : \tau_1 \quad \Gamma;\gamma \vdash e_2 : \tau_2 \quad \tau_1, \tau_2 <: \tau \quad \textbf{rep}\ \tau}{\Gamma;\gamma \vdash e_1\ (\mathrm{op})\ e_2 : \tau}\ \textsc{T-Op} \qquad \frac{\Gamma;\gamma \vdash e : \textbf{bool}_c \quad \Gamma;\gamma \vdash e_t : \tau_1 \quad \Gamma;\gamma \vdash e_f : \tau_2 \quad \tau_1, \tau_2 <: \tau \quad \textbf{rep}\ \tau}{\Gamma;\gamma \vdash \textbf{if}\ e\ \textbf{then}\ e_t\ \textbf{else}\ e_f : \tau}\ \textsc{T-CondC}$$

$$\frac{\Gamma;\gamma \vdash e : \textbf{bool} \quad \Gamma;\textbf{sym} \vdash e_t : \beta_1 \quad \Gamma;\textbf{sym} \vdash e_f : \beta_2 \quad \beta_1, \beta_2 <: \beta_c \quad \textbf{rep}\ \beta_c}{\Gamma;\gamma \vdash \textbf{if}\ e\ \textbf{then}\ e_t\ \textbf{else}\ e_f : \beta_c}\ \textsc{T-CondSym}$$

$$\frac{\Gamma, x : \tau_d;\gamma \vdash e : \tau' \quad \textbf{rep}\ \tau \quad \textbf{rep}\ \tau'}{\Gamma;\gamma \vdash (\lambda x : \tau_d.e) : \tau_d \rightarrow \tau'}\ \textsc{T-Lambda} \qquad \frac{\Gamma;\gamma \vdash e_1 : \tau_1 \xrightarrow{nr} \tau_2 \quad \Gamma;\gamma \vdash e_2 : \tau_1' \quad \tau_1' <: \tau_1 \quad \textbf{rep}\ \tau_1 \quad \textbf{rep}\ \tau_2}{\Gamma;\gamma \vdash (e_1\ e_2) : \tau_2}\ \textsc{T-App}$$

$$\frac{\Gamma, f : \tau_1 \rightarrow \tau_2;\gamma \vdash e_1 : \tau_1 \rightarrow \tau_2 \quad \Gamma, f : \tau_1 \xrightarrow{nr} \tau_2;\gamma \vdash e_2 : \tau_2 \quad \textbf{rep}\ \tau \quad \textbf{rep}\ \tau_2}{\Gamma;\gamma \vdash \textbf{let rec}\ f : \tau_1 \xrightarrow{nr} \tau_2 = e_1\ \textbf{in}\ e_2 : \tau_2}\ \textsc{T-LetRec}$$

$$\frac{\gamma = \textbf{concrete} \quad \Gamma;\gamma \vdash e_1 : \tau_1 \rightarrow \tau_2 \quad \Gamma;\gamma \vdash e_2 : \tau_1' \quad \tau_1' <: \tau_1 \quad \textbf{rep}\ \tau_1 \quad \textbf{rep}\ \tau_2}{\Gamma;\gamma \vdash (e_1\ e_2) : \tau_2}\ \textsc{T-AppCurRec}$$

$$\frac{\Gamma, x : \beta;\gamma \vdash e_c : \textbf{bool} \quad \Gamma;\gamma \vdash \upsilon : \beta}{\Gamma;\gamma \vdash (\textbf{defer}\ x : \beta\{\, e_c \}\ \textbf{default}\ \upsilon) : \beta}\ \textsc{T-Defer} \qquad \frac{\Gamma;\gamma \vdash e_c : \textbf{bool}}{\Gamma;\gamma \vdash (\textbf{assert}\ e_c) : \textbf{unit}}\ \textsc{T-Assert}$$

$$\frac{\Gamma;\gamma \vdash e_1 : \beta \quad \Gamma;\gamma \vdash^c e_1 : \beta' \quad \Gamma;\gamma \vdash \upsilon : \beta'}{\Gamma;\gamma \vdash (\textbf{concretize}\ e_1\ \textbf{with}\ \upsilon) : \beta_c}\ \textsc{T-Concretize}$$

Figure 5: Static semantics for λ_J describing simple type-checking and enforcing restrictions on scope of nondeterminism and recursion. Recall that β refers to base (non-function) types.

$$\frac{}{\bot \hookrightarrow \textbf{false}} \qquad \frac{}{\top \hookrightarrow \textbf{true}} \qquad \frac{Exp_l \hookrightarrow e_l \quad Exp_h \hookrightarrow e_h}{\langle Exp_l \mid Exp_h \rangle(\ell) \hookrightarrow \textbf{if}\ \ell\ \textbf{then}\ e_h\ \textbf{else}\ e_l}\ \textsc{Tr-SValue}$$

$$\frac{Exp \hookrightarrow e}{\textbf{level}\ \ell\ \textbf{in}\ Exp \hookrightarrow \textbf{let}\ \ell = \textbf{defer}\ \ell' : \textbf{bool default true in}\ e}\ \textsc{Tr-Level}$$

$$\frac{Exp_p \hookrightarrow e_p \quad Exp \hookrightarrow e \quad Lvl \hookrightarrow b}{\textbf{policy}\ \ell : Exp_p\ \textbf{then}\ Lvl\ \textbf{in}\ Exp \hookrightarrow \textbf{assert}\ (e_p \Rightarrow (\ell = b))\ \textbf{in}\ e}\ \textsc{Tr-Policy}$$

$$\frac{Exp_c \hookrightarrow e_c \quad Exp \hookrightarrow e}{\textbf{print}\ \{Exp_c\}\ Exp \hookrightarrow \textbf{print}\ (\textbf{concretize}\ e\ \textbf{with}\ e_c)}\ \textsc{Tr-Print}$$

Figure 6: Translation from Jeeves to λ_J

3.4.4 Contextual Enforcement at Output Channels

Effectful computations such as **print** in Jeeves require contexts corresponding to the viewer to whom the result is displayed. As we show by the TR-PRINT rule, **concretize** is inserted in the translation. Because sensitive values can only produce concrete values consistent with the policies, this ensures enforcement of policies at output channels.

4. Properties

We describe more formally the guarantees that Jeeves provides. We prove progress and preservation properties for λ_J. We show that the only way the value for the high component of a sensitive value to affect the output of the computation is if the policies permit it.

4.1 Progress and Preservation

We first show the correctness of evaluation. We can prove progress and preservation properties for λ_J: evaluation of an expression e always results in a value υ and preserves the type of e, including the internal nondeterminism tag δ.

There are two interesting parts to the proof: showing that all function applications can be reduced and showing that all **defer** and **assert** expressions can be evaluated to produce appropriate constraint expressions. We can first show that the λ_J type system guarantees that all functions are concrete.

Lemma 1 (Concrete Functions). *If υ is a value of type $\tau_1 \to \tau_2$, then $\upsilon = \lambda x : \tau_1.e$, where e has type τ_2.*

Theorem 4.1 (Progress). *Suppose e is a closed, well-typed expression. Then e is either a value υ or there is some e' such that $\vdash \langle \emptyset, \emptyset, e\rangle \to \langle \Sigma', \Delta', e'\rangle$.*

Proof. The proof mostly involves induction on the typing derivations. One interesting case is ensuring that MODEL will either return a valid model $\mathcal{M}$ or UNSAT for the E-CONCRETIZESAT and E-CONCRETIZEUNSAT rules. Since the λ_J type system rules out symbolic functions, only well-formed constraints can be added. The other interesting case is function applications $e = e_1\ e_2$, where e_1 and e_2 are well-typed with types $\tau_1 \to \tau_2$ and τ_1. We can rule out the cases when e_1 and e_2 are not values by applying the induction hypothesis. For the case when e_1 and e_2 are both values, we can apply the Concrete Functions Lemma to deduce that e_1 must have the form $\lambda x : \tau_1 : e$, where $e : \tau_1$. In this case, we can apply the E-APPABS rule. □

We can also prove a preservation theorem that evaluation does not change the type of a λ_J expression.

Theorem 4.2 (Preservation). *If $\Gamma \vdash e : \tau\delta$ and $e \to e'$, then $\Gamma \vdash e' : \tau\delta$.*

Proof. We can show the preservation of both τ and δ by induction on the typing derivation. The δ value for all evaluation rules except for the E-CONCRETIZE rules is the same for both sides. □

4.2 Confidentiality Theorem

We show that level variables enforce the confidentiality of values: once the policy sets a level variable $\ell = \bot$, where we have some $\langle Exp_l | Exp_h\rangle_\ell$, the output will be derived as if Exp_h was not involved in evaluation at all. Because we have $\ell = \bot$ if and only if we have policies that require $\ell = \bot$, Jeeves programmers can rely on policies to enforce confidentiality.

We first prove that the high-confidentiality views of the sensitive values are protected by level variables. We can show that for a sensitive value $v = \langle Exp_l | Exp_h\rangle_\ell$, the only way the value for the high component Exp_h may affect the output of the computation is when $\ell = \top$ is consistent with the policies. It is impossible for an observer to distinguish between $v = \langle Exp_l | Exp_h\rangle$ and $v' = \langle Exp_l | Exp'_h\rangle$ if the policy requires $\ell = \bot$.

Theorem 4.3 (View Non-Interference). *Consider a sensitive value $V = \langle E_l | H\rangle_\ell$ in a Jeeves expression E. Assume:*

$$E[H \mapsto E_h] \hookrightarrow e \qquad \vdash \langle \emptyset, \emptyset, e\rangle \to^* \langle \Sigma, \Delta, \sigma\rangle$$
$$E[H \mapsto E'_h] \hookrightarrow e' \qquad \vdash \langle \emptyset, \emptyset, e'\rangle \to^* \langle \Sigma', \Delta', \sigma'\rangle$$

For any context value v, if

$$\Sigma \cup \{\textbf{context} = v\} \vdash \ell = \bot$$
$$\Sigma' \cup \{\textbf{context} = v\} \vdash \ell = \bot$$

then

$$\{c \mid\ \vdash \langle \Sigma, \Delta, \textbf{concretize}\ \sigma\ \textbf{with}\ v\rangle \to \langle \Sigma_0, \Delta_0, c\rangle\} =$$
$$\{c' \mid\ \vdash \langle \Sigma', \Delta', \textbf{concretize}\ \sigma'\ \textbf{with}\ v\rangle \to \langle \Sigma'_0, \Delta'_0, c'\rangle\}$$

Proof. From the rules of Jeeves translation, V maps to an irreducible symbolic expression **if** ℓ **then** e_h **else** e_l in e where $E_l \hookrightarrow e_l$ and $E_h \hookrightarrow e_h$. Thus, we can say that e' is e with the expression e_h replaced by e'_h where $E'_h \hookrightarrow e'_h$. In addition, we also know that both e and e' are λ_J expressions with no **concretize** sub-expressions. This makes evaluation of e and e' deterministic and allows us to put their derivation trees in correspondence. There are two places where evaluation differs: (1) reduction of e_h and e'_h (rule E-CONDSYMT) and (2) substitution of the reduced sensitive value (rule E-APPLAMBDA.) Let us understand how they affect the logical environment and the resulting symbolic value.

The values σ and σ' may differ only in the subexpressions e_h and e'_h reduce to. These subexpressions are guarded by the level variable ℓ. Since the logical environments entail that $\ell = \bot$ under context v, any model chosen at concretization sets ℓ to $\bot$. Therefore, under such models σ and σ' evaluate to the same value. Then to show that the set of concrete values is the same, it suffices to show the models of (Δ, Σ) are models of (Δ', Σ') and vice versa.

The dynamic semantics populates Σ and Σ' with the same constraints (modulo substitution of the sensitive variable) except during reduction of e_h and e'_h. The constraints added at rule E-CONDSYMT are all guarded by the level variable ℓ. Since Σ and Σ' both entail $\neg\ell$, and these guarded constraints are implied by $\neg\ell$, we can safely eliminate them from both Σ and Σ'. That leaves us with the same set of hard constraints introduced through **defer** and **assert** expressions.

The default judgements in Jeeves all have the form $\ell_0 = \textbf{true}$. Therefore, for the shared level variables Δ and Δ' use the same default value **true**. The remaining level variables do not affect evaluation of σ and σ'. □

Our non-interference theorem allows programmers rely on policies to enforce confidentiality. In Jeeves, policies have the form $\phi \Rightarrow (\ell = \top)$ or $\phi \Rightarrow (\ell = \bot)$. By the theorem, once the policy setting ℓ to $\bot$ is guaranteed to be added to the constraint environment, the output is going to be the same as if the high view component of the sensitive value was not involved in evaluation at all. If policies permit both $\bot$ and $\top$ levels, then the default logic model finder will guide evaluation to a model maximizing levels set to $\top$.

Note that if policies are contradictory and the set of constraints is unsatisfiable, the evaluation halts with an error and no value is exposed. The theorem still holds and this behavior is safe.

5. Scala Embedding

We have implemented Jeeves as an embedded domain-specific language in Scala programming language [20]. Scala's overloading capabilities offer us the necessary flexibility in designing a domain specific language for λ_J with the benefit of interoperability with existing Java technology.

In this section we discuss our Scala embedding of λ_J and our implementation of the Jeeves library on top of that. We describe how we used features of Scala to implement λ_J's lazy evaluation of symbolic expressions, how we collect constraints, and how we interact with the Z3 SMT solver. On top of the functional model we have presented, we also handle objects and mutation.[1]

5.1 ScalaSMT: Scala Embedding of λ_J

Every kind of symbolic expression in λ_J has a corresponding Scala case class, for instance IntExpr corresponding to symbolic integer expressions. Arithmetic and boolean operators are defined as methods constructing new expressions. We use *implicit type conversions* to lift concrete Scala values to symbolic constants. Scala's type inference resolves x+1 to x.+(Constant(1)) which in turn evaluates to Plus(x, Constant(1)), where x is a symbolic integer variable. Implicit type conversion allows us to use concrete expressions in place of symbolic ones but requires type annotations where a symbolic expression is expected to be used.

The three core language extensions **defer**, **assert**, and **concretize** are implemented as library calls. We implement the library as a Scala trait that maintains the logical and default constraint environments as lists of symbolic boolean expressions. Calls to **concretize** invoke an off-the-shelf SMT solver [17] for the satisfiability query MODEL. We translate λ_J constraints to the QF_LIA logic of SMT-LIB2 [2] and use incremental scripting to implement the default logic decision procedure. Concretization in ScalaSMT differs from λ_J in two ways. First, **concretize** accepts an arbitrary boolean expression rather than a **context** equality predicate. Second, **concretize** is not allowed to be a part of a symbolic expression in ScalaSMT. Since concretization generally happens as part of **print** routine, this restriction does not affect our case studies.

In addition to boolean and linear integer constraints, the Scala embedding supports symbolic expressions for objects corresponding to λ_J records with equality theory. Objects are modeled as a finite algebraic data type in Z3 [17]. The set of available objects is maintained by ScalaSMT using registration of instances of a special trait Atom. Object fields are modeled as total functions interpreted at the time of concretization. Fields are (sort-)typed with values that are arbitrary ScalaSMT expressions and constants. ScalaSMT does not check types of symbolic object expressions: we rely on Scala's support for dynamic invocaton to resolve field dereferences. We use special zero values (null, 0, or false) to represent undefined fields in SMT.

ScalaSMT does not support symbolic collections. Instead, we use implicit type conversions to extend the standard Scala collection library with filter and has methods that take symbolic arguments. The argument to filter is a function f from an element to a symbolic boolean. It maps every element o to conditional expression IF (f(o)) o ELSE NULL. Method has takes a symbolic object o and produces a disjunction of equalities between elements of the collection and o.

5.2 Jeeves as a Library in Scala

We have implemented Jeeves as a library on top of ScalaSMT. Our library has function calls corresponding to Jeeves's sensitive values, **level** construct, **policy** construct, and contextual output functions (see Figure 7.)

Levels are introduced using mkLevel method that returns a logical level variable which can be either $\top$ or $\bot$. Sensitive values are created with mkSensitive methods that take a level variable together with high and low values. Context is a logical object variable CONTEXT. To introduce a level policy, the programmer calls policy method and supplies a level variable, the desired level, and a boolean condition. The boolean condition is passed by name to delay its evaluation until concretization. This way policies that refer to mutable parts of the heap will produce correct constraints for the snapshot of the system at concretization.

[1] The code is publicly available at
http://code.google.com/p/scalasmt/.

```
trait JeevesLib extends ScalaSMT {
  trait JeevesRecord extends Atom {register( this )}
  val CONTEXT: Symbolic // Context variable.

  def mkLevel(): LevelVar
  def policy( lvar : LevelVar, f: ⇒ Formula, l: Level)

  def mkSensitiveInt( lvar : LevelVar,
    high: IntExpr, low: IntExpr): IntExpr
  def mkSensitive( lvar : LevelVar,
    high: Symbolic, low: Symbolic): Symbolic

  def concretize [T](ctx: Symbolic, e: Expr[T]): T
}
```

Figure 7: Jeeves library in Scala

The Jeeves library supports mutation in variables and object fields by treating the mutable state as part of the context in **concretize** call to ScalaSMT. Mutable fields are interpreted at the time of **concretize**. Policies that depend on mutable state are evaluated to boolean conditions during concretization. The set of allocated JeevesRecords is supplied at concretization. These conditions together with the equality predicate CONTEXT = ctx are used to concretize expressions in ScalaSMT.

6. Experience

We have implemented a conference management system and a social network. Our experience suggests that Jeeves allows the programmer to separate the "core," non-privacy-related functionality from the privacy policies, allowing the programmer to separately test policies and functionality.

6.1 Conference Management System

We have implemented a simple conference management system backend, JConf, to demonstrate how a well-known system with privacy concerns looks in Jeeves. This system is similar to the example we described in Section 2. Our implementation demonstrates that Jeeves allows us to implement all JConf functionality, including search and display over final paper versions, with a core functionality that is separate from the policies.

JConf supports the following subset of the functionality mentioned on the website for the HotCRP conference management system [12]: smart paper search (by ID, by reviewer, etc.), paper tagging (for instance, "Accepted" and "Reviewed by: ...") and search by tags, managing reviews (assigning, collecting responses, and displaying), and managing final paper versions. JConf does not implement functionality for which confidentiality is less key: for instance, the process of bidding for papers.

All JConf core functionality adheres to the privacy policies. JConf implements the following information flow policies:

- *Paper titles* are visible to the authors of the paper, reviewers, and PC members during all stages. Paper titles are visible to everyone during the public stage.
- *Author names* are visible to the authors on the paper during all stages, to reviewers and PC members during and after the rebuttal stage, and to everyone during the public stage if the paper has been accepted.

File	Total LOC	Policy LOC
ConfUser.scala	11	0
PaperRecord.scala	103	37
PaperReview.scala	21	6
ConfContext.scala	6	0
JConfBackend.scala	56	0
Total	195	42

Table 1. Breakdown of lines of code across the JConf source.

```
class PaperReview(id: Int, reviewerV: ConfUser, var body:
    String, var score: Int) extends JeevesRecord {
  val reviewer = {
    val level = mkLevel();
    val vrole = CONTEXT.viewer.role;
    val isInternal = (vrole == ReviewerStatus) ||
      (vrole == PCStatus)
    policy(level, isInternal, ⊤);
    policy(level, ! isInternal, ⊥);
    mkSensitive[ConfUser](level, reviewerV, NULL)
  }
}
```

Figure 8:

- *Reviewer identities* are revealed only to PC members.
- *Reviews* and *scores* are revealed to authors of the paper, reviewers, and PC members after the review phase. During the review phase, reviewers must have submitted a review for a paper p before they can see p's reviews.

Our JConf implementation allows us to separate the declaration of policies and code: we show the breakdown of code and policies in Table 1. The policies are concentrated in the data classes PaperRecord.scala and PaperReview.scala, which describe the attributes and policies associated with maintaining data associate with papers and paper reviews. The other files, including JConfBackend.scala, do not contain policies. This allows the core functionality to be concise: the implementation of our back-end functionality as specified is only 56 lines.

The implementation of the core functionality of JConf is agnostic to the policies. The JConf back end stores a list of PaperRecord objects and supports adding papers, updating components of papers, and searching over papers by ID, name, and tags. We show the function to search papers by tag below:

```
def searchByTag(tag: PaperTag) =
  papers.filter(_.getTags().has(tag))
```

This function produces a list of symbolic PaperRecord objects which are equal to objects containing paper data if the paper tag tag is present and null otherwise. The core program can be concise because it does not have to be concerned with policies.

We implement policies specified in terms of program variables such as a paper's list of tags and values from the output context. To provide an example of a data class definition, we show the definition of the PaperReview class in Figure 8. A PaperReview object has the fields reviewer, body, and score. The PaperReview class defines a policy that the identity of the reviewer as stored in the reviewer field is visible only to other reviewers and PC members. The code introduces a new level variable level, adds a policy that the context viewer must be a reviewer or PC member to see the object. The policies on allowed contexts for seeing the entire PaperReview object are defined in the PaperRecord class representing data associated with papers.

Localizing the policies with respect to data facilitates policy updates. To change at what stage of the conference when reviewers are allowed to see names of authors, we can simply change the few lines of code corresponding to the author list policy. The programmer does not have to make coordinated changes across the code base to update policies.

6.2 Social Network

For social networks it is important to rapidly develop code that implements information flow policies. Privacy issues have put the social network website Facebook under the scrutiny of the American Federal Trade Commission [26], making it crucial that they do not leak sensitive data. On the other side, one of Facebook's key values is to "move fast:" rapidly develop innovative features [28]. Separation of policies and core program functionality can help developers rapidly develop privacy-aware features.

To investigate this hypothesis, we have implemented Jeeves Social Net, a toy social network that uses Jeeves policies to control confidentiality of user-shared data. Jeeves Social Net core functionality involves storing and allowing queries over user attributes such as names, e-mails, and networks, a friendship relation between users, and dynamically changing properties such as user location. Jeeves Social Net allows a user u to define policies about who can see which versions of these attributes based on the relationship of the viewer to the u. The system allows the user to define different versions of their information to be shown to viewers given which level they satisfy. These policies are stateful: for instance, a policy on the visibility of user u's location refers to the location of u and the location of output viewer v.

Jeeves allows the programmer to develop policies and core functionality separately. In our source, all policies reside in UserRecord class representing a user, while the query code in SocialNetBackend is left intact. The programmer can extend the SocialNetBackend arbitrarily and rely on the Jeeves system to enforce information policies. The programmer can also easily change the policies enforced across the program by changing the policy code in UserRecord.

In the rest of this section, we walk through how we implement interesting policies in Jeeves Social Net: support for user-defined policies that may depend on the friendship relation, stateful location-data policies, and policies that have mutual dependencies as a result of a symbolic context.

Defining Viewer Levels. Each sensitive field in a UserRecord object is defined in terms of the level of the output viewer. We use Jeeves level variables to define three levels: Anyone is most permissive and allows public access, Friends allows access only to friends, and Self is most restrictive and disallows access to everyone except the user herself. The following function creates level variables associated with user-defined viewer levels:

```
def level(ul: UserLevel) = {
  val a = mkLevel();
  val me = CONTEXT == this;
  ul match {
    case Anyone =>
    case Self => policy(l, ! me, ⊥)
    case Friends =>
      policy(l, ! (me || friends.has(CONTEXT)), ⊥);
  };
  a
}
```

The CONTEXT variable refers to the user at the other end of the output channel. The mutable set of friends is encapsulated in a private field friends of UserRecord.

We use this function to create sensitive values for user fields based on user-specified viewer levels. The constructor for the

UserRecord class takes parameters nameL: UserLevel and friendL : UserLevel to specify who can see the name and friends fields. To create a sensitive property for the name of a user, passed to the constructor as nameV: string, we declare an observer field:

```
val name = mkSensitive(level(nameL), nameV, NULL)
```

We can create a friends list that is visible based on the friends level friendsL as follows:

```
def getFriends() = {
  val l = level(friendsL);
  friends.map(mkSensitive(l, _))
}
```

When these fields are accessed, the results will only be displayed to viewers who have an appropriate level of access.

Policies become implicitly combined when different sensitive values interact. To get names of friends of a user, we simply call:

```
user.getFriends().map(_.name)
```

Although the code looks the same as if without Jeeves, the context user here must simultaneously be able to access the list of friends and the name property to see the name of a friend.

Location Policy. The location mash-up website PleaseRobMe [3] demonstrates that if disclosure of geographic location information is not carefully managed, people can easily use this information for harm, for instance in determining candidates for apartment robberies. Jeeves allows programmers to easily express policies protecting location data based on not just "friend" relationships, but also on policies involving dynamically-changing user locations.

A user may choose to share her location with friends, with users nearby, or only to friends who are nearby. To write the policy that only a nearby user can see the location, we create sensitive values for coordinates in the setter method guarded by DISTANCE policy:

```
1  var X: IntExpr = 1000
2  var Y: IntExpr = 1000
3
4  def setLocation(x: BigInt, y: BigInt) {
5    val l = mkLevel();
6    policy(l, DISTANCE(CONTEXT, this) ≥ 10, ⊥);
7    this.X = mkSensitiveInt(l, x, 1000);
8    this.Y = mkSensitiveInt(l, y, 1000);
9  }
10
11 def DISTANCE(a: Symbolic, b: Symbolic) =
12   ABS(a.X − b.X) + ABS(a.Y − b.Y)
```

The policy uses sensitive values for X and Y to guard the values themselves. We can do this because whenever there are such circular dependencies, the Jeeves runtime will choose a safe but locally-maximal assignment to levels. For example, if all users in the network are nearby, it is safe to return low values for everyone. However, Jeeves would output the actual values, since that maximizes the number of $\top$ levels without sacrificing safety.

Since policies and query code are separated, to change the location policy, we only need to modify the setter. A stronger policy that permits only *friends* nearby to see the location requires one change to line 5 to replace mkLevel() with level(Friends).

Symbolic Context. Jeeves also allows the context to contain sensitive values. As an example, consider the following function, which sends a user's name to her friends:

```
def announceName(u: UserRecord) =
  for (f ← u.getFriends())
    yield email(f, u.name)
```

The email function sends to f a concretizated version of u.name with CONTEXT = f. Since the friends list is symbolic, f is symbolic as well. This means that f will take high value only if the corresponding friend of u is allowed to see the list of friends of u. The name of u is revealed only if its policies permit f to see. Because Jeeves handles circular dependencies by finding a safe but locally-maximal assignment, the Jeeves runtime system will send the name to each friend if the friend is permitted to see the name. Such reasoning about symbolic contexts is hard to simulate in runtime systems such as Resin [27] that do not use symbolic constraints.

6.3 Jeeves Limitations

Jeeves currently provides only a limited amount of static checking. The implementation of Jeeves as a domain-specific embedded library in Scala relies on Scala type-checking to enforce static properties. At present, Jeeves does not provide static feedback about more complex program properties. For instance, neither the Jeeves design nor the implementation provide support for statically determining whether policies are consistent or total. We anticipate being able to detect properties such as underspecification and inconsistency using enhanced static analysis that we can implement as a Scala compiler extension.

There are many open questions regarding the usability of Jeeves. Symbolic evaluation and SMT are technologies that have been improving in performance, but it is not clear they can handle the demands of real-world applications. One direction for future exploration includes scalability of Jeeves programs, how to efficiently handle data persistence, and development of lighter-weight execution models. Another direction for exploration involves the ease of programming and testability of Jeeves programs.

7. Related Work

Jeeves privacy policies yield comparable expressiveness to state-of-the-art languages for verifying system security such as Jif [19], Fine [4], and Ur/Web [5]. These are static approaches that have no dynamic overhead. Rather than providing support for verifying properties, the Jeeves execution model handles policy enforcement, guaranteeing that programs adhere to the desired properties by construction, but with dynamic overhead.

The Jeeves runtime is similar to the system-level data flow framework Resin [27], which allows the programmer to insert checking code to be executed at output channels. Jeeves's declarative policies allow the programmer to specify policies at a higher level and allow automatic handling of dependencies between policies.

There are also parallels with dynamic approaches to security. Devriese and Piessens's secure multi-execution approach executes multiple copies of the program, providing defaults to copies that should not get access to secret inputs [7]. Jeeves's symbolic evaluation obviates the need to execute multiple program copies and Jeeves allows more complex policies, for instance ones that may depend on sensitive values. In this space is also Kashyap *et al.*'s scheduling-based dynamic approach, which partitions a program into sub-programs for each security level for ensuring timing and termination non-interference. The focus of this is different from our work, which does not address timing or termination.

Jeeves can also be compared to aspect-oriented programming (AOP) [11]. Existing frameworks for AOP provide hooks for explicit annotations at join points. Jeeves differs from AOP because Jeeves's constraint-based execution model supports more a more powerful interaction with the core program. The most similar work in AOP is Smith's logical invariants [24] and method for generating aspect code for behavior such as error logging automatically [23]. Smith's method is static and involves reconstructing values such as the runtime call stack in order to insert the correct code at fixed control flow points. Jeeves allows policies to affect control flow decisions.

The way Jeeves handles privacy is inspired by angelic nondeterminism [8]. Jeeves most directly borrows from CFLP-L, a constraint functional programming calculus presented by Mück *et al.* [18]; similar functional logic models have also been implemented in languages such as Mercury [25], Escher [15], and Curry [9, 10]. Our system differs in the restrictions we place on nondeterminism and the execution model. λ_J leaves functions and the theory of lists out of the logical model. λ_J execution also supports default logic [1] to facilitate reasoning when programming with constraints.

Our work is also related to work in executing specifications and dynamic synthesis. Jeeves differs from existing work in executing specifications [16, 21] in our goal of propagating nondeterminism alongside the core program rather than executing isolated nondeterministic sub-procedures. Program repair approaches such as Demsky's data structure repair [6], the Plan B [22] system for dynamic contract checking, and Kuncak *et al.*'s synthesis approach [13] also target local program expressions.

8. Conclusions

Our main contribution is a programming model that allows programmers to separate privacy concerns from core program functionality. We present the Jeeves programming language, formally define the underlying constraint functional language λ_J, and prove that Jeeves executions satisfy a non-interference property between low and high components of sensitive values. We describe our implementation as an embedded domain-specific language in Scala. We also describe our case studies, which illustrate how the programmer can separately develop core functionality and privacy policies while relying on the system to produce outputs consistent with the policies.

Acknowledgments

We would like to thank Saman Amarasinghe, Arvind, Michael Carbin, Gregory Malecha, Sasa Misailovic, Andrew Myers, Joseph Near, Martin Rinard, and Joe Zimmerman for their input and feedback.

References

[1] G. Antoniou. A tutorial on default logics. *ACM Computing Surveys (CSUR)*, 31(4):337–359, 1999.

[2] C. Barrett, A. Stump, and C. Tinelli. The smt-lib standard: Version 2.0. In *SMT Workshop*, 2010.

[3] B. Borsboom, B. v. Amstel, and F. Groeneveld. PleaseRobMe. `http://pleaserobme.com`, July 2011.

[4] J. Chen, R. Chugh, and N. Swamy. Type-preserving compilation of end-to-end verification of security enforcement. *SIGPLAN Not.*, 45 (6):412–423, 2010. ISSN 0362-1340. doi: http://doi.acm.org/10.1145/1809028.1806643.

[5] A. Chlipala. Static checking of dynamically-varying security policies in database-backed applications. In *Proceedings of the 9th USENIX conference on Operating systems design and implementation*, OSDI'10, pages 1–, Berkeley, CA, USA, 2010. USENIX Association. URL `http://portal.acm.org/citation.cfm?id=1924943.1924951`.

[6] B. Demsky and M. Rinard. Data structure repair using goal-directed reasoning. In *ICSE '05: Proceedings of the 27th international conference on Software engineering*, pages 176–185, New York, NY, USA, 2005. ACM. ISBN 1-59593-963-2. doi: http://doi.acm.org/10.1145/1062455.1062499.

[7] D. Devriese and F. Piessens. Noninterference through secure multi-execution. *Security and Privacy, IEEE Symposium on*, 0:109–124, 2010. ISSN 1081-6011. doi: http://doi.ieeecomputersociety.org/10.1109/SP.2010.15.

[8] R. W. Floyd. Nondeterministic algorithms. *J. ACM*, 14:636–644, October 1967. ISSN 0004-5411. doi: http://doi.acm.org/10.1145/321420.321422. URL `http://doi.acm.org/10.1145/321420.321422`.

[9] M. Hanus. Improving control of logic programs by using functional logic languages. In *Proc. of the 4th International Symposium on Programming Language Implementation and Logic Programming*, pages 1–23. Springer LNCS 631, 1992.

[10] M. Hanus, H. Kuchen, J. J. Moreno-Navarro, R. Aachen, and I. Ii. Curry: A truly functional logic language, 1995.

[11] G. Kiczales, J. Lamping, A. Mendhekar, C. Maeda, C. V. Lopes, J.-M. Loingtier, and J. Irwin. Aspect-Oriented Programming. In *ECOOP*, pages 220–242, 1997.

[12] E. Kohler. HotCRP. `http://www.cs.ucla.edu/~kohler/hotcrp/`.

[13] V. Kuncak, M. Mayer, R. Piskac, and P. Suter. Complete functional synthesis. In *PLDI*, pages 316–329, 2010.

[14] J. R. Lewis, J. Launchbury, E. Meijer, and M. B. Shields. Implicit parameters: dynamic scoping with static types. In *Proceedings of the 27th ACM SIGPLAN-SIGACT symposium on Principles of programming languages*, POPL '00, pages 108–118, New York, NY, USA, 2000. ACM. ISBN 1-58113-125-9. doi: http://doi.acm.org/10.1145/325694.325708. URL `http://doi.acm.org/10.1145/325694.325708`.

[15] J. W. Lloyd. Programming in an integrated functional and logic language. *Journal of Functional and Logic Programming*, 3, 1999.

[16] C. Morgan. The specification statement. *ACM Trans. Program. Lang. Syst.*, 10(3):403–419, 1988. ISSN 0164-0925. doi: http://doi.acm.org/10.1145/44501.44503.

[17] L. D. Moura and N. Björner. Z3: An efficient SMT solver. In *In Conference on Tools and Algorithms for the Construction and Analysis of Systems (TACAS)*, 2008.

[18] A. Mück and T. Streicher. A tiny constraint functional logic language and its continuation semantics. In *ESOP '94: Proceedings of the 5th European Symposium on Programming*, pages 439–453, London, UK, 1994. Springer-Verlag. ISBN 3-540-57880-3.

[19] A. C. Myers. JFlow: Practical mostly-static information flow control. In *In Proc. 26th ACM Symp. on Principles of Programming Languages (POPL)*, pages 228–241, 1999.

[20] M. Odersky, P. Altherr, V. Cremet, B. Emir, S. Maneth, S. Micheloud, N. Mihaylov, M. Schinz, E. Stenman, and M. Zenger. An overview of the scala programming language. Technical report, Citeseer, 2004.

[21] D. Rayside, A. Milicevic, K. Yessenov, G. Dennis, and D. Jackson. Agile specifications. In *OOPSLA Companion*, pages 999–1006, 2009.

[22] H. Samimi, E. D. Aung, and T. D. Millstein. Falling back on executable specifications. In *ECOOP*, pages 552–576, 2010.

[23] D. R. Smith. A generative approach to aspect-oriented programming. In G. Karsai and E. Visser, editors, *GPCE*, volume 3286 of *Lecture Notes in Computer Science*, pages 39–54. Springer, 2004. ISBN 3-540-23580-9.

[24] D. R. Smith. Aspects as invariants. In O. Danvy, H. Mairson, F. Henglein, and A. Pettorossi, editors, *Automatic Program Development: A Tribute to Robert Paige*, pages 270–286, 2008.

[25] Z. Somogyi, F. J. Henderson, and T. C. Conway. Mercury, an efficient purely declarative logic programming language. In *In Proceedings of the Australian Computer Science Conference*, pages 499–512, 1995.

[26] J. E. Vascellaro. Facebook grapples with privacy issues. In *The Wall Street Journal*. May 19 2010.

[27] A. Yip, X. Wang, N. Zeldovich, and M. F. Kaashoek. Improving application security with data flow assertions. In *Proceedings of the 22th ACM Symposium on Operating Systems Principles (SOSP '09)*, Big Sky, Montana, October 2009.

[28] H. Zhao. Hiphop for PHP: Move fast. `http://developers.facebook.com/blog/post/358/`, February 2010.

Probabilistic Relational Reasoning for Differential Privacy

Gilles Barthe Boris Köpf Federico Olmedo Santiago Zanella Béguelin
IMDEA Software Institute, Madrid, Spain
{gilles.barthe,boris.koepf,federico.olmedo,santiago.zanella}@imdea.org

Abstract

Differential privacy is a notion of confidentiality that protects the privacy of individuals while allowing useful computations on their private data. Deriving differential privacy guarantees for real programs is a difficult and error-prone task that calls for principled approaches and tool support. Approaches based on linear types and static analysis have recently emerged; however, an increasing number of programs achieve privacy using techniques that cannot be analyzed by these approaches. Examples include programs that aim for weaker, approximate differential privacy guarantees, programs that use the Exponential mechanism, and randomized programs that achieve differential privacy without using any standard mechanism. Providing support for reasoning about the privacy of such programs has been an open problem.

We report on CertiPriv, a machine-checked framework for reasoning about differential privacy built on top of the Coq proof assistant. The central component of CertiPriv is a quantitative extension of a probabilistic relational Hoare logic that enables one to derive differential privacy guarantees for programs from first principles. We demonstrate the expressiveness of CertiPriv using a number of examples whose formal analysis is out of the reach of previous techniques. In particular, we provide the first machine-checked proofs of correctness of the Laplacian and Exponential mechanisms and of the privacy of randomized and streaming algorithms from the recent literature.

Categories and Subject Descriptors D.3.1 [*Programming Languages*]: Formal Definitions and Theory; F.3.1 [*Logics and Meanings of Programs*]: Specifying and Verifying and Reasoning about Programs; F.3.2 [*Logics and Meanings of Programs*]: Semantics of Programming Languages—Operational semantics, Denotational semantics, Program analysis.

General Terms Languages, Security, Theory, Verification

Keywords Coq proof assistant, differential privacy, relational Hoare logic

1. Introduction

When dealing with private data one is faced with conflicting requirements: on the one hand, it is fundamental to protect the privacy of individuals; on the other hand, the desire is to maximize the utility of the data by mining and releasing partial or aggregate information, e.g. for medical statistics, market research, or targeted advertising. Differential privacy [17] is a quantitative notion of privacy that achieves an attractive trade-off between these two conflicting requirements: it provides strong confidentiality guarantees, yet it is permissive enough to allow for useful computations on private data. The key advantages of differential privacy over alternative definitions of privacy are its good behavior under composition and its weak assumptions about the prior knowledge of adversaries. For a discussion of the guarantees provided by differential privacy and their limitations, see [21, 22].

As the theoretical foundations of differential privacy become well-understood, there is momentum to prove privacy guarantees for real systems. Several authors have recently proposed methods for reasoning about differential privacy on the basis of different languages and models of computation, e.g. SQL-like languages [24], higher-order functional languages [29], imperative languages [9], the MapReduce framework [30], and I/O automata [35]. The unifying basis of these approaches are two key results: (i) the observation that one can achieve privacy by perturbing the output of a deterministic program by a suitable amount of noise [17] and (ii) theorems that establish privacy bounds for sequential and parallel composition of differentially private programs [24]. In combination, both results form the basis for creating and analyzing programs by composing differentially private building blocks.

While approaches relying on composing building blocks apply to an interesting range of examples, they fall short of covering the expanding frontiers of differentially private mechanisms and algorithms. Examples that cannot be handled by previous techniques include mechanisms that aim for weaker guarantees, such as approximate differential privacy [16], or randomized algorithms that achieve differential privacy without using any standard mechanism [18]. Dealing with such examples requires fine-grained reasoning about the complex mathematical and probabilistic computations that programs perform on private input data. Such reasoning is particularly intricate and error-prone, and calls for principled approaches and tool support.

In this paper we revisit the foundations of differential privacy and provide a framework for fine-grained reasoning about an expressive class of confidentiality policies, including (approximate) differential privacy and probabilistic non-interference. Our framework, coined CertiPriv, is built on top of CertiCrypt [3], a machine-checked framework to verify cryptographic proofs in the Coq proof assistant [34]. CertiPriv goes beyond the state-of-the-art in three fundamental aspects. First, CertiPriv takes a foundational approach that allows reasoning directly about the outcome of probabilistic computations. This is key to its flexibility: rather than being limited to a fixed set of building blocks, one can define and use arbitrary blocks. Second, CertiPriv allows to construct proofs from first principles. This is key to its precision: proofs in CertiPriv can rely on sophisticated machinery, without any limitation other than being elaborated from first principles. Third, CertiPriv inherits the generality of the Coq proof assistant and allows modeling

POPL'12, January 25–27, 2012, Philadelphia, PA, USA.

and reasoning about arbitrary domains and datatypes. This is key to its expressiveness: instead of being confined to a fixed set of datatypes, CertiPriv can be extended on demand (e.g. with types and operators for graphs). Accessorily, CertiPriv requires that all intermediate reasoning steps are justified formally, so that proofs can be verified independently and automatically by the Coq type checker.

In order to illustrate the applicability of CertiPriv, we present the first machine-checked proofs of three representative examples: (i) we prove the correctness of the Laplacian and Exponential mechanisms, (ii) we prove the privacy of a randomized approximation algorithm for the Minimum Vertex Cover problem [18], and (iii) we prove the privacy of randomized algorithms for continual release of aggregate statistics of data streams [8]. Taken together, these examples demonstrate the generality and versatility of our approach.

The starting point of our technical development is the observation that differential privacy can be construed as a quantitative 2-property [11, 33]. Informally, a probabilistic computation c is (ϵ, δ)-differentially private iff, given two initial memories m and m' that are sufficiently close, the output distributions generated by c are related up to a multiplicative factor $\exp(\epsilon)$ and an additive term δ. More formally, a computation c satisfies (ϵ, δ)-differential privacy with respect to a relation Ψ on memories iff for every pair of memories m, m' related by Ψ and for every event E:

$$\Pr\left[c, m : E\right] \leq \exp(\epsilon) \Pr\left[c, m' : E\right] + \delta$$

where $\Pr\left[c, m : E\right]$ denotes the probability of event E in the distribution obtained by running c on initial memory m. This formulation of differential privacy is slightly more general than the standard definition; however, the latter is recovered by letting the precondition Ψ capture adjacency of memories, i.e. letting Ψ relate memories at distance at most 1 for some adequate notion of distance.

Our definition of differential privacy has two natural readings. The first reading is as an information flow property. Indeed, if Ψ is an equivalence relation and $\epsilon = \delta = 0$, the definition states that the output distributions obtained by executing c in two related memories m and m' coincide, entailing that an adversary who can only observe the final distributions cannot distinguish between the two executions. The second reading of the definition is as a continuity property: in case Ψ models adjacency between initial memories, the definition states that c is a continuous mapping between metric spaces, with the understanding that the universally quantified inequality above provides a measure of closeness of the two output distributions. In this paper, we leverage on both readings to provide a fresh foundation for reasoning about differentially private computations.

As a first step in our formalization, we introduce the notion of α-distance. α-distance generalizes statistical distance with a skew parameter α and enables us to cast (ϵ, δ)-differential privacy as a continuity property. In particular, we show that a computation c is (ϵ, δ)-differentially private w.r.t. a pre-condition Ψ iff δ is an upper bound of the $\exp(\epsilon)$-distance between the output distributions obtained by running c on two memories m and m' satisfying Ψ.

As a second step, we define an approximate probabilistic Relational Hoare Logic (apRHL), following Benton's seminal use of relational logics to reason about information flow [7]. Judgments in apRHL have the form

$$c_1 \sim_{\alpha,\delta} c_2 : \Psi \Rightarrow \Phi$$

and capture that δ is an upper bound on the α-distance of the probability distributions generated by two probabilistic programs c_1 and c_2, modulo relational pre- and post-conditions Ψ and Φ on program states. For the special case where Φ is the identity on states, $c_1 = c_2 = c$, and $\alpha = \exp(\epsilon)$, the above judgment entails that the output distributions obtained by executing c starting from two initial memories related by Ψ are at α-distance at most δ, and hence that c is (ϵ, δ)-differentially private w.r.t. Ψ.

As further detailed in Section 5.2, this intuitive understanding of apRHL judgments extends to the important case where Φ is an equivalence relation; such judgments generalize simultaneously differential privacy and information flow and can be used to model confidentiality for a large class of adversaries, under the view that the equivalence relation captures their observational capabilities. For the general case, the interpretation of apRHL judgments is based on the novel notion of (α, δ)-lifting of relations on states to relations on distributions. The definition crisply generalizes existing notions from probabilistic process algebra [12, 20, 32] and enjoys good closure properties from which we derive the soundness of the apRHL logic.

Summary of contributions Our contributions are twofold. On the theoretical side, we lay the foundations for reasoning formally about an important and general class of approximate relational properties of probabilistic programs. Specifically, we introduce the notions of α-distance and (α, δ)-lifting, and an approximate probabilistic relational Hoare logic. On the practical side, we demonstrate the applicability of our approach by providing the first machine-checked proofs of differential privacy properties of fundamental mechanisms and complex approximation algorithms from the recent literature.

Organization of the paper The remainder of this paper is structured as follows. In Section 2 we illustrate the application of our approach to an example algorithm; Section 3 introduces the representation of distributions and basic definitions used in the remainder. Section 4 presents the semantic foundations of apRHL, while Section 5 presents the core proof rules of the logic. Section 6 reports on case studies. We survey prior art and conclude in Sections 7 and 8. The Coq development containing machine-checked proofs of the results and examples presented here, and an extended version of this paper with pencil-and-paper proofs of the key results can be obtained from

`http://certicrypt.gforge.inria.fr/certipriv/`

2. Illustrative Example

In this section we illustrate the applicability of our results by analyzing a differentially private approximation algorithm for the Minimum (Unweighted) Vertex Cover problem [18].

A *vertex cover* of an undirected graph $G = (V, E)$ is a set of vertices $S \subseteq V$ such that for any edge $(v, w) \in E$, either $v \in S$ or $w \in S$. The Minimum Vertex Cover problem is the problem of finding a vertex cover S of minimal size. In the privacy-preserving version of the problem the goal is to output a good approximation of a minimum cover while concealing the presence or absence of edges in the graph. Contrary to other optimization algorithms where the private data only determines the objective function (i.e. the size of a minimum cover), in the case of the Minimum Vertex Cover problem the edges in the graph determine the feasible solutions. This means that no privacy-preserving algorithm can explicitly output a vertex cover of size less than $n-1$ for a graph with n vertices, for otherwise any pair of vertices absent from the output reveals the absence of an edge connecting them. To overcome this limitation, the algorithm that we analyze outputs an implicit representation of a cover as a permutation of the vertices in the graph. This output permutation determines an orientation of the edges in the graph by considering each edge as pointing towards the endpoint appearing last in the permutation. A vertex cover can then be

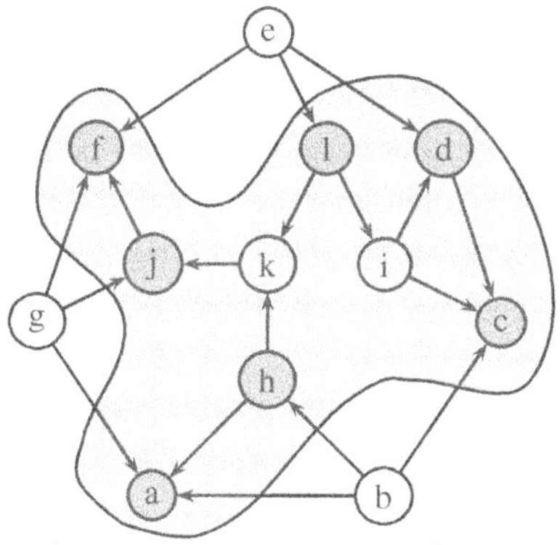

$\pi = [b, g, e, h, l, k, j, i, f, d, c, a]$

Figure 1. A minimum vertex cover (vertices in gray) and the cover given by a permutation π of the vertices in the graph (vertices inside the shaded area). The orientation of the edges is determined by π.

recovered (presumably in a privacy-preserving distributed manner) by taking for each edge the vertex it points to (Fig. 1).

The algorithm that we study, shown in Fig. 2, is based on a randomized, albeit not privacy-preserving, approximation algorithm from [27] that achieves a constant approximation factor of 2. (It is conjectured that no efficient approximation algorithm for the Minimum Vertex Cover problem can achieve a constant approximation factor better than 2.) The idea behind this algorithm is to iteratively pick a random uncovered edge and add one of its endpoints to the cover set, both the edge and the endpoint being chosen with uniform probability. Equivalently, this iterative process can be seen as selecting a vertex at random with probability proportional to its uncovered degree. The privacy-preserving algorithm in Fig. 2 is obtained from this base algorithm by perturbing the distribution according to which vertices are sampled by a carefully calibrated weight factor that grows as more vertices are appended to the output permutation. In the algorithm in the figure, at each iteration the instruction $v \xleftarrow{\$} \mathsf{choose}(V, E, \epsilon, n, i)$ chooses a vertex v from V with probability proportional to $d_E(v) + w_i$, where $d_E(v)$ denotes the degree of v in E and

$$w_i = \frac{4}{\epsilon}\sqrt{\frac{n}{n-i}}$$

Put otherwise, the expression $\mathsf{choose}(V, E, \epsilon, n, i)$ denotes the discrete distribution over V whose density function at x is

$$\frac{d_E(x) + w_i}{\sum_{y \in V} d_E(y) + w_i}$$

Consider two graphs $G_1 = (V, E)$ and $G_2 = (V, E \cup \{(t, u)\})$ with the same set of vertices but differing in exactly one edge. To prove that the above algorithm is ϵ-differentially private it is sufficient to show that the probability of obtaining a permutation π of the vertices in the graph when the input is G_1 differs at most by a multiplicative factor $\exp(\epsilon)$ from the probability of obtaining π when the input is G_2. We show this using the approximate relational Hoare logic that we present in Section 5. We highlight here the key steps in the proof; a more detailed account appears in Section 6.3.

To establish the ϵ-differential privacy of algorithm VERTEXCOVER it suffices to prove the validity of the following judgment:

$$\models \text{VERTEXCOVER}(V, E, \epsilon) \sim_{e^\epsilon, 0} \text{VERTEXCOVER}(V, E, \epsilon) : \Psi \Rightarrow \Phi$$

```
function VERTEXCOVER(V, E, ε)
  n ← |V|; π ← nil; i ← 0;
  while i < n do
    v ←$ choose(V, E, ε, n, i);
    π ← v :: π;
    V ← V \ {v}; E ← E \ ({v} × V);
    i ← i + 1
  end
```

Figure 2. A differentially private approximation algorithm for the Minimum Unweighted Vertex Cover problem

where

$$\Psi \overset{\text{def}}{=} V\langle 1\rangle = V\langle 2\rangle \wedge E\langle 2\rangle = E\langle 1\rangle \cup \{(t, u)\}$$
$$\Phi \overset{\text{def}}{=} \pi\langle 1\rangle = \pi\langle 2\rangle$$

Assertions appearing in apRHL judgments, like Ψ and Φ above, are binary relations on program memories. We usually define assertions using predicate logic formulas involving program expressions. When defining an assertion $m_1 \ \Phi \ m_2$, we denote by $e\langle 1\rangle$ (resp. $e\langle 2\rangle$) the value that the expression e takes in memory m_1 (resp. m_2). For example, the post-condition Φ above denotes the relation $\{(m_1, m_2) : m_1(\pi) = m_2(\pi)\}$.

To prove the judgment above, we show privacy bounds for each iteration of the loop in the algorithm. Proving a bound for the i-th iteration boils down to proving a bound for the ratio between the probability of choosing a particular vertex in the left-hand side program and the right-hand side program, and its reciprocal. We distinguish three different cases, and use the fact that for a graph (V, E), $\sum_{y \in V} d_E(y) = 2|E|$ and the inequality $1 + x \leq \exp(x)$ to derive upper bounds in each case:

(a) the chosen vertex is not one of t, u and neither t nor u are in π.

$$\frac{\Pr[v\langle 1\rangle = x]}{\Pr[v\langle 2\rangle = x]} = \frac{(d_{E\langle 1\rangle}(x) + w_i)\sum_{y \in V}(d_{E\langle 2\rangle}(y) + w_i)}{(d_{E\langle 2\rangle}(x) + w_i)\sum_{y \in V}(d_{E\langle 1\rangle}(y) + w_i)}$$
$$= \frac{(d_{E\langle 1\rangle}(x) + w_i)(2|E\langle 1\rangle| + (n-i)w_i + 2)}{(d_{E\langle 1\rangle}(x) + w_i)(2|E\langle 1\rangle| + (n-i)w_i)}$$
$$\leq 1 + \frac{2}{(n-i)w_i} \leq \exp\left(\frac{2}{(n-i)w_i}\right)$$

$$\frac{\Pr[v\langle 2\rangle = x]}{\Pr[v\langle 1\rangle = x]} \leq 1$$

(b) the vertex v chosen in the iteration is one of t, u. We analyze the case where $v = t$, the other case is similar.

$$\frac{\Pr[v\langle 1\rangle = t]}{\Pr[v\langle 2\rangle = t]} \leq 1$$

$$\frac{\Pr[v\langle 2\rangle = t]}{\Pr[v\langle 1\rangle = t]} = \frac{(w_i + d_{E\langle 1\rangle}(t) + 1)(2|E\langle 1\rangle| + (n-i)w_i)}{(w_i + d_{E\langle 1\rangle}(t))(2|E\langle 1\rangle| + (n-i)w_i + 2)}$$
$$\leq 1 + w_i^{-1} \leq 1 + w_0^{-1} \leq \exp(\epsilon/4)$$

(c) either t or u is already in π, in which case both executions are observationally equivalent and do not add to the privacy bound.

$$\frac{\Pr[v\langle 1\rangle = x]}{\Pr[v\langle 2\rangle = x]} = \frac{\Pr[v\langle 2\rangle = x]}{\Pr[v\langle 1\rangle = x]} = 1$$

Case (a) can occur at most $(n-2)$ times, while case (b) occurs exactly once. Thus, multiplying the bounds over all n iterations,

$$\frac{\Pr[\textsc{VertexCover}(G_1,\epsilon) : \pi = \vec{v}]}{\Pr[\textsc{VertexCover}(G_2,\epsilon) : \pi = \vec{v}]} \leq \exp\left(\sum_{i=0}^{n-3} \frac{2}{(n-i)w_i}\right) \leq \exp(\epsilon)$$

$$\frac{\Pr[\textsc{VertexCover}(G_2,\epsilon) : \pi = \vec{v}]}{\Pr[\textsc{VertexCover}(G_1,\epsilon) : \pi = \vec{v}]} \leq \exp(\epsilon/4) \leq \exp(\epsilon)$$

The above informal reasoning is captured by a proof rule for loops parameterized by an invariant and a stable property of the product state of both executions (i.e. a relation that once established remains true). We use the following invariant (note that if pre-condition Ψ above holds, the invariant is established by the initialization code appearing before the loop):

$$\begin{array}{l}(t \in \pi\langle 1\rangle \vee u \in \pi\langle 1\rangle \implies E\langle 1\rangle = E\langle 2\rangle) \wedge \\ (t \notin \pi\langle 1\rangle \wedge u \notin \pi\langle 1\rangle \implies E\langle 2\rangle = E\langle 1\rangle \cup \{(t,u)\}) \wedge \\ V\langle 1\rangle = V\langle 2\rangle \wedge \pi\langle 1\rangle = \pi\langle 2\rangle\end{array}$$

and the following stable property:

$$t \in \pi\langle 1\rangle \vee u \in \pi\langle 1\rangle$$

The application of this proof rule requires to prove three judgments as premises, corresponding to each one of the cases detailed above; we detail them in Section 6.3.

3. Preliminaries

3.1 Probabilities and Reals

In the course of our Coq formalization, we have found it convenient to reason about probabilities using the axiomatization of the unit interval [0, 1] provided by the ALEA library of Audebaud and Paulin [1]. Their formalization supports as primitive operations addition, inversion, multiplication, and division, and proves that the unit interval [0, 1] can be given the structure of a ω-cpo by taking as order the usual $\leq$ relation and by defining an operator sup that computes the least upper bound of monotonic [0, 1]-valued sequences.

In order to manage the interplay between the formalizations of the unit interval and of the reals, we have axiomatized an embedding/retraction pair between them and built an extensive library of results about the relationship between arithmetic operations in the two types, e.g.:

Addition: $x +_{[0,1]} y = \min_{\mathbb{R}}(x +_{\mathbb{R}} y, 1)$;

Inversion: $-_{[0,1]}x = 1 -_{\mathbb{R}} x$;

Multiplication: $x \times_{[0,1]} y = x \times_{\mathbb{R}} y$;

Division: if $y \neq 0$, then $x/_{[0,1]}y = \min_{\mathbb{R}}(x/_{\mathbb{R}}y, 1)$.

3.2 Distributions

We view a distribution μ over a set A as a function that maps a unit-valued random variable (a function in $A \to [0,1]$) to its expected value [1, 28]: when applied to an event $E \subseteq A$ represented by its characteristic function $\mathbb{1}_E : A \to [0,1]$, $\mu(\mathbb{1}_E)$ corresponds to the probability of E. When applied to an arbitrary function $f : A \to [0,1]$, $\mu(f)$ gives the expectation of f w.r.t. μ. For discrete distributions μ, $\mu(\mathbb{1}_a)$ corresponds to the probability density of μ at a, and we denote it using the shorthand $\mu(a)$. The connection between density and expectation is given by the following equation.

$$\mu(f) = \sum_{a \in A} \mu(a)\ f(a)$$

Formally, a distribution over A is a function μ of type

$$(A \to [0,1]) \to [0,1]$$

together with proofs of the (universally quantified) properties:

Monotonicity: $f \leq g \implies \mu\ f \leq \mu\ g$;

Compatibility with inverse: $\mu\ (\mathbb{1} - f) \leq 1 - \mu\ f$, where $\mathbb{1}$ is the constant function 1;

Additive linearity: $f \leq \mathbb{1} - g \implies \mu\ (f+g) = \mu\ f + \mu\ g$;

Multiplicative linearity: $\mu\ (k \times f) = k \times \mu\ f$;

Continuity: if $F : \mathbb{N} \to (A \to [0,1])$ is monotonic, then $\mu\ (\sup\ F) \leq \sup\ (\mu \circ F)$

Note that we do not require that $\mu\ \mathbb{1} = 1$, and thus, strictly speaking, our definition corresponds to sub-probability distributions. This provides an elegant means of giving semantics to runtime assertions and programs that do not terminate with probability one. We let $\mathcal{D}(A)$ denote the set of distributions over A and μ_0 denote the null distribution.

Distributions can be given the structure of a monad; this monadic view eliminates the need of cluttered definitions and proofs involving summations, and allows to give a continuation-passing style semantics to probabilistic programs. Formally, we define the unit and bind operators as follows:

$$\begin{array}{rl}\mathsf{unit} & : A \to \mathcal{D}(A) \stackrel{\text{def}}{=} \lambda x.\ \lambda f.\ f\ x \\ \mathsf{bind} & : \mathcal{D}(A) \to (A \to \mathcal{D}(B)) \to \mathcal{D}(B) \\ & \stackrel{\text{def}}{=} \lambda \mu.\ \lambda M.\ \lambda f.\ \mu\ (\lambda\, x.\ M\ x\ f)\end{array}$$

The unit operator maps $x \in A$ to the Dirac distribution that assigns probability 1 to x and 0 to all other elements of A, while bind takes a distribution on A and a conditional distribution on B given A, and returns the corresponding marginal distribution on B.

In the remainder we use the following operations and relations:

$$\begin{array}{rl}\mathsf{range}\ P\ \mu & \stackrel{\text{def}}{=} \forall f.\ (\forall a.\ P\ a \implies f\ a = 0) \implies \mu\ f = 0 \\ \pi_1(\mu) & \stackrel{\text{def}}{=} \mathsf{bind}\ \mu\ (\lambda(x,y).\ \mathsf{unit}\ x) \\ \pi_2(\mu) & \stackrel{\text{def}}{=} \mathsf{bind}\ \mu\ (\lambda(x,y).\ \mathsf{unit}\ y) \\ \mu \leq \mu' & \stackrel{\text{def}}{=} \forall f.\ \mu\ f \leq \mu'\ f\end{array}$$

The formula range $P\ \mu$ states that elements of A with a non-null probability w.r.t. μ satisfy predicate P. For a distribution μ over a product type $A \times B$, $\pi_1(\mu)$ (resp. $\pi_2(\mu)$) defines its projection on the first (resp. second) component. Finally, $\leq$ defines a natural order on $\mathcal{D}(A)$.

4. First Principles

4.1 Skewed Distance of Distributions

In this section we define the notion of α-distance, a parameterized distance between distributions. We show how this notion can be used to express ϵ-differential privacy, (ϵ,δ)-differential privacy, and statistical distance.

We begin by augmenting the standard distance between two real numbers a and b (defined as $|a-b| = \max\{a-b, b-a\}$) with a skew parameter $\alpha \geq 1$. Namely, we define the α-distance $\Delta_\alpha(a,b)$ between a and b by

$$\Delta_\alpha(a,b) \stackrel{\text{def}}{=} \max\{a - \alpha b, b - \alpha a, 0\}$$

Note that Δ_α is non-negative by definition and that Δ_1 coincides with the standard distance between reals. We extend Δ_α to a distance between distributions as follows.

Definition 1 (α-distance). *The α-distance $\Delta_\alpha(\mu_1,\mu_2)$ between two distributions μ_1 and μ_2 in $\mathcal{D}(A)$ is defined as:*

$$\Delta_\alpha(\mu_1,\mu_2) \stackrel{\text{def}}{=} \max_{f:A\to[0,1]} \Delta_\alpha(\mu_1\ f, \mu_2\ f)$$

The definition of α-distance quantifies universally over all unit-valued functions. The next lemma shows that for discrete distributions this definition is equivalent to an alternative definition in which quantification ranges only over Boolean-valued functions, i.e. those corresponding to characteristic functions of events.

Lemma 1. *For all distributions μ_1 and μ_2 over a discrete set A,*

$$\Delta_\alpha(\mu_1, \mu_2) = \max_{E \subseteq A} \Delta_\alpha(\mu_1\, \mathbb{1}_E, \mu_2\, \mathbb{1}_E)$$

An immediate consequence of Lemma 1 is that Δ_1 coincides with the standard notion of statistical distance, i.e.,

$$\Delta_1(\mu_1, \mu_2) = \max_{E \subseteq A} |\mu_1\, \mathbb{1}_E - \mu_2\, \mathbb{1}_E|$$

Differential privacy is a condition on the distance between the output distributions produced by a randomized algorithm. Namely, for a given metric on the input space, differential privacy requires that for any pair of inputs at distance at most 1, the probability that an algorithm outputs a particular value differs at most by a multiplicative factor $\exp(\epsilon)$. *Approximate* differential privacy relaxes this requirement by additionally allowing for an additive slack δ. The following definition captures these requirements in terms of α-distance; Lemma 1 establishes the equivalence to the original definition [16].

Definition 2 (Approximate differential privacy). *Let d be a metric on A. A randomized algorithm $M : A \to \mathcal{D}(B)$ is (ϵ, δ)-differentially private (with respect to d) iff*

$$\forall a, a' \in A.\ d(a, a') \leq 1 \implies \Delta_{\exp(\epsilon)}(M\ a, M\ a') \leq \delta$$

Notice that $(\epsilon, 0)$-differential privacy corresponds to vanilla ϵ-differential privacy [13].

It is folklore that for discrete domains the definition of differential privacy is equivalent to its pointwise variant where one quantifies over characteristic functions of singleton sets rather than those of arbitrary sets; however, this equivalence breaks when considering approximate differential privacy [16]. The following lemma provides a way to establish bounds for α-distance (and hence for approximate differential privacy) in terms of characteristic functions of singleton sets. Note that the inequality is strict in general.

Lemma 2. *For all distributions μ_1 and μ_2 over a discrete set A,*

$$\Delta_\alpha(\mu_1, \mu_2) \leq \sum_{a \in A} \Delta_\alpha(\mu_1(a), \mu_2(a))$$

We conclude this section by stating some important properties of α-distance; these properties are used for reasoning about approximate lifting and proving the soundness of our logic. All properties are implicitly universally quantified.

Lemma 3 (Properties of α-distance).

1. $0 \leq \Delta_\alpha(\mu_1, \mu_2) \leq 1$
2. $\Delta_\alpha(\mu, \mu) = 0$
3. $\Delta_\alpha(\mu_1, \mu_2) = \Delta_\alpha(\mu_2, \mu_1)$
4. $\Delta_{\alpha\alpha'}(\mu_1, \mu_3) \leq \alpha' \Delta_\alpha(\mu_1, \mu_2) + \Delta_{\alpha'}(\mu_2, \mu_3)$, *or else* $\Delta_{\alpha\alpha'}(\mu_1, \mu_3) \leq \Delta_\alpha(\mu_1, \mu_2) + \alpha\, \Delta_{\alpha'}(\mu_2, \mu_3)$
5. $\alpha \leq \alpha' \implies \Delta_{\alpha'}(\mu_1, \mu_2) \leq \Delta_\alpha(\mu_1, \mu_2)$
6. $\Delta_\alpha(\mathsf{bind}\ \mu_1\ M, \mathsf{bind}\ \mu_2\ M) \leq \Delta_\alpha(\mu_1, \mu_2)$

Most of the above properties are self-explanatory; we briefly highlight the most important ones. Property (4) generalizes the triangle inequality with appropriate skew factors; (5) states that α-distance is anti-monotonic with respect to α; (6) states that probabilistic computation does not increase the distance (which is a well-known fact for statistical distance).

4.2 Approximate Lifting of Relations to Distributions

The logic we present in the next section can be used to establish assertions about probabilistic programs w.r.t. pre- and post-conditions on states. In order to give meaning to these judgments, we need to interpret post-conditions as relations between distributions over states rather than as relations between states. To this end, we define the (α, δ)-lifting of a relation to distributions. Intuitively, two distributions $\mu_1 \in \mathcal{D}(A)$ and $\mu_2 \in \mathcal{D}(B)$ are related by the (α, δ)-lifting of $R \subseteq A \times B$, whenever there exists a distribution over $A \times B$ whose support is contained in R and whose first and second projections are at most at α-distance δ of μ_1 and μ_2, respectively.

Definition 3 (Lifting). *Let $\alpha \in \mathbb{R}^{\geq 1}$ and $\delta \in [0, 1]$. The (α, δ)-lifting of a relation $R \subseteq A \times B$ is a relation over $\mathcal{D}(A) \times \mathcal{D}(B)$ defined as follows:*

$$\mu_1 \sim_R^{\alpha,\delta} \mu_2 \stackrel{def}{=} \exists \mu. \begin{cases} \mathsf{range}\ R\ \mu \\ \pi_1\ \mu \leq \mu_1\ \wedge\ \pi_2\ \mu \leq \mu_2 \\ \Delta_\alpha(\pi_1\ \mu, \mu_1) \leq \delta \wedge \Delta_\alpha(\pi_2\ \mu, \mu_2) \leq \delta \end{cases}$$

We say that a distribution μ satisfying the above conditions is a witness *for the lifting.*

The notion of (α, δ)-lifting generalizes previous notions of liftings, such as the lifting from [20] which is obtained by taking $\alpha = 1$ and $\delta = 0$, and δ-lifting [12, 32] which is obtained by taking $\alpha = 1$. The next lemma shows that (α, δ)-lifting is monotonic w.r.t. the slack δ, the skew factor α, and the relation R. An immediate consequence is that for $\alpha > 1$, (α, δ)-lifting is more permissive than the previously proposed notions of lifting.

Lemma 4. *For all $1 \leq \alpha \leq \alpha'$ and $\delta \leq \delta'$, and relations $R \subseteq S$,*

$$\mu_1 \sim_R^{\alpha,\delta} \mu_2 \implies \mu_1 \sim_S^{\alpha',\delta'} \mu_2$$

We next present a fundamental property of (α, δ)-lifting, which is central to the applicability of apRHL to reason about α-distance (and hence differential privacy). Namely, two distributions related by the (α, δ)-lifting of R yield probabilities that are within α-distance δ when applied to R-related functions. We say that two functions $f : A \to [0, 1]$ and $g : B \to [0, 1]$ are related by a relation $R \subseteq A \times B$, and write $f =_R g$, iff for every $a \in A$ and $b \in B$, $R\ a\ b$ implies $f\ a = g\ b$.

Theorem 1 (Fundamental Property of Lifting). *Let $\mu_1 \in \mathcal{D}(A)$, $\mu_2 \in \mathcal{D}(B)$, and $R \subseteq A \times B$. Then, for any two functions $f_1 : A \to [0, 1]$ and $f_2 : B \to [0, 1]$,*

$$\mu_1 \sim_R^{\alpha,\delta} \mu_2 \wedge f_1 =_R f_2 \implies \Delta_\alpha(\mu_1\ f_1, \mu_2\ f_2) \leq \delta$$

In particular, if $A = B$ and R is the identity relation ($\equiv$),

$$\mu_1 \sim_\equiv^{\alpha,\delta} \mu_2 \implies \Delta_\alpha(\mu_1, \mu_2) \leq \delta$$

Theorem 1 provides an interpretation of (α, δ)-lifting in terms of α-distance. Next we present two results that enable us to actually construct such liftings.

The first result is the converse of Theorem 1 for the special case of R being the identity relation: we prove that two distributions are related by the (α, δ)-lifting of the identity relation if their α-distance is smaller than δ. This result is used to prove the soundness of the logic rule for random assignments given in the next section.

Theorem 2. *Let μ_1 and μ_2 be distributions over a discrete set A. If $\Delta_\alpha(\mu_1, \mu_2) \leq \delta$, then $\mu_1 \sim_\equiv^{\alpha,\delta} \mu_2$.*

The proof is immediate by considering as a witness for the lifting the distribution with the following density function:

$$\mu(a, a') = \begin{cases} \min(\mu_1(a), \mu_2(a)) & \text{if } a = a' \\ 0 & \text{if } a \neq a' \end{cases}$$

The second result shows that (α,δ)-liftings compose. This result allows to derive a judgment relating two programs c_1 and c_2 by introducing an intermediate program c and proving the validity of judgments relating c_1 and c on one hand, and c and c_2 on the other. This approach is used in the examples of Section 6.2, and more extensively in cryptographic proofs, see e.g. [3].

Theorem 3. *Let μ_1, μ_2 and μ_3 be distributions over discrete sets A, B, and C, respectively. Let $R \subseteq A \times B$ and $S \subseteq B \times C$. For all $\alpha, \alpha' \in \mathbb{R}^{\geq 1}$ and $\delta, \delta' \in [0,1]$,*

$$\mu_1 \sim_R^{\alpha,\delta} \mu_2 \wedge \mu_2 \sim_S^{\alpha',\delta'} \mu_3 \implies \mu_1 \sim_{R \circ S}^{\alpha\alpha',\delta''} \mu_3$$

where $\delta'' \stackrel{\text{def}}{=} \max(\delta + \alpha\,\delta', \delta' + \alpha'\,\delta)$ and $\circ$ denotes relation composition.

For the proof, let μ_R and μ_S be witnesses for the judgments on the left-hand side of the implication. Then, the distribution μ defined by the following density function is a witness for the lifting on the right-hand side:

$$\mu(a,c) = \sum_{\{b \in B \mid \mu_2(b) \neq 0\}} \frac{\mu_R(a,b)\,\mu_S(b,c)}{\mu_2(b)}$$

We conclude this section with an observation on (α,δ)-lifting for equivalence relations. Jonsson, Yi, and Larsen [20] show that for equivalence relations, their definition of lifting coincides with the more intuitive notion that requires the two distributions to yield equal probabilities on all equivalence classes. Formally, if R is an equivalence relation over a discrete set A, then

$$\mu_1 \sim_R^{1,0} \mu_2 \iff \forall a \in A.\ \mu_1\, \mathbb{1}_{[a]} = \mu_2\, \mathbb{1}_{[a]}$$

where $[a]$ denotes the R-equivalence class of $a \in A$. This characterization extends naturally to arbitrary α and $\delta = 0$:

$$\mu_1 \sim_R^{\alpha,0} \mu_2 \iff \forall a \in A.\ \Delta_\alpha(\mu_1\, \mathbb{1}_{[a]}, \mu_2\, \mathbb{1}_{[a]}) = 0$$

The characterization for arbitrary δ is more involved and is presented in the extended version.

5. Approximate Relational Hoare Logic

This section introduces the central component of CertiPriv, namely an approximate probabilistic relational Hoare logic that is used to establish privacy guarantees of programs. We first present the programming language and its semantics. We then define relational judgments and show that they generalize differential privacy. Finally, we define a proof system for deriving valid judgments.

5.1 Programming Language

CertiPriv supports reasoning about programs that are written in the typed, procedural, probabilistic imperative language pWHILE. Formally, the set of commands is defined inductively by the following clauses:

$\mathcal{I}$	::=	$\mathcal{V} \leftarrow \mathcal{E}$	assignment
	|	$\mathcal{V} \overset{\$}{\leftarrow} \mathcal{DE}$	random sampling
	|	if $\mathcal{E}$ then $\mathcal{C}$ else $\mathcal{C}$	conditional
	|	while $\mathcal{E}$ do $\mathcal{C}$	while loop
	|	$\mathcal{V} \leftarrow \mathcal{P}(\mathcal{E},\ldots,\mathcal{E})$	procedure call
	|	assert $\mathcal{E}$	runtime assertion
$\mathcal{C}$	::=	skip	nop
	|	$\mathcal{I};\ \mathcal{C}$	sequence

Here, $\mathcal{V}$ is a set of variable identifiers, $\mathcal{P}$ is a set of procedure names[1], $\mathcal{E}$ is a set of expressions, and $\mathcal{DE}$ is a set of distribution expressions. The significant novelty of CertiPriv (compared to CertiCrypt), besides the addition of runtime assertions, is that the interpretation of distribution expressions may depend on the program state. This allows to express programs that sample from dynamically evolving probability distributions, such as the one presented in Section 2.

[1] For the sake of readability, we omit procedure calls from most of the exposition; we keep them in the description of the language because we use them to describe the algorithm SMARTSUM in Fig. 9 and modularize its analysis.

$$\begin{array}{ll}
[\![\mathsf{skip}]\!]\ m & = \mathsf{unit}\ m \\
[\![i;\ c]\!]\ m & = \mathsf{bind}\ ([\![i]\!]\ m)\ [\![c]\!] \\
[\![x \leftarrow e]\!]\ m & = \mathsf{unit}\ (m\,\{[\![e]\!]\ m/x\}) \\
[\![\mathsf{assert}\ e]\!]\ m & = \mathsf{if}\ [\![e]\!]\ m = \mathsf{true\ then}\ (\mathsf{unit}\ m)\ \mathsf{else}\ \mu_0 \\
[\![x \overset{\$}{\leftarrow} \mu]\!]\ m & = \mathsf{bind}\ ([\![\mu]\!]\ m)\ (\lambda v.\ \mathsf{unit}\ (m\,\{v/x\})) \\
[\![\mathsf{if}\ e\ \mathsf{then}\ c_1\ \mathsf{else}\ c_2]\!]\ m & = \begin{cases} [\![c_1]\!]\ m & \mathsf{if}\ [\![e]\!]\ m = \mathsf{true} \\ [\![c_2]\!]\ m & \mathsf{if}\ [\![e]\!]\ m = \mathsf{false} \end{cases} \\
[\![\mathsf{while}\ e\ \mathsf{do}\ c]\!]\ m & = \lambda f.\sup\,(\lambda n.\ [\![[\mathsf{while}\ e\ \mathsf{do}\ c]_n]\!]\ m\ f)
\end{array}$$

$$\text{where}\quad \begin{array}{lcl} [\mathsf{while}\ e\ \mathsf{do}\ c]_0 & = & \mathsf{skip} \\ [\mathsf{while}\ e\ \mathsf{do}\ c]_{n+1} & = & \mathsf{if}\ e\ \mathsf{then}\ c;\ [\mathsf{while}\ e\ \mathsf{do}\ c]_n \end{array}$$

Figure 3. Semantics of pWHILE programs

The semantics of programs is defined in two steps. First, we give an interpretation $[\![T]\!]$ to all object types T—these are types that are declared in CertiPriv programs, such as the graph type in the example in Section 2—and we define the set $\mathcal{M}$ of memories as the set of mappings from variables to values. Then, we implement dependently typed evaluators that give the semantics of an expression e of type T, a distribution expression μ of type T, and a command c, respectively, as functions of the following types:

$$[\![e]\!] : \mathcal{M} \to [\![T]\!] \qquad [\![\mu]\!] : \mathcal{M} \to \mathcal{D}([\![T]\!]) \qquad [\![c]\!] : \mathcal{M} \to \mathcal{D}(\mathcal{M})$$

Informally, the semantics of an expression e takes a memory and returns a value in $[\![T]\!]$, the semantics of a distribution expression μ takes a memory and returns a distribution over $[\![T]\!]$, and the semantics of a program c takes an initial memory and returns a distribution over final memories. The semantics of programs complies with the expected equations; Figure 3 provides an excerpt.

5.2 Validity and Privacy

apRHL is an approximate probabilistic relational Hoare logic that supports reasoning about differentially private computations. Judgments in apRHL are of the form

$$c_1 \sim_{\alpha,\delta} c_2 : \Psi \Rightarrow \Phi$$

where c_1 and c_2 are programs, Ψ and Φ are relations over memories, $\alpha \in \mathbb{R}^{\geq 1}$ is the skew, and $\delta \in [0,1]$ is the slack. In our formalization we use a shallow embedding for logical assertions, allowing us to inherit the expressiveness of the Coq language when writing pre- and post-conditions.

An apRHL judgment is valid if for every pair of memories related by the pre-condition Ψ, the corresponding pair of output distributions is related by the (α,δ)-lifting of the post-condition Φ.

Definition 4 (Validity). *A judgment $c_1 \sim_{\alpha,\delta} c_2 : \Psi \Rightarrow \Phi$ is valid, written $\models c_1 \sim_{\alpha,\delta} c_2 : \Psi \Rightarrow \Phi$, iff*

$$\forall m_1\, m_2.\ m_1\ \Psi\ m_2 \implies ([\![c_1]\!]\ m_1) \sim_\Phi^{\alpha,\delta} ([\![c_2]\!]\ m_2)$$

The following lemma is a direct consequence of the fundamental property of lifting (Theorem 1) applied to Definition 4. It shows that statements about programs derived using apRHL imply bounds on the α-distance of their output distributions.

Lemma 5. *If* $\models c_1 \sim_{\alpha,\delta} c_2 : \Psi \Rightarrow \Phi$*, then for all memories* m_1, m_2 *and unit-valued functions* $f_1, f_2 : \mathcal{M} \to [0,1]$,

$$m_1 \,\Psi\, m_2 \wedge f_1 =_\Phi f_2 \implies \Delta_\alpha(\llbracket c_1 \rrbracket\, m_1\, f_1, \llbracket c_2 \rrbracket\, m_2\, f_2) \leq \delta$$

The statement of Lemma 5 can be specialized to a statement about the differential privacy of programs.

Corollary 1. *Let* d *be a metric on* $\mathcal{M}$ *and* Ψ *an assertion expressing that* $d(m_1, m_2) \leq 1$*. If* $\models c \sim_{\exp(\epsilon),\delta} c : \Psi \Rightarrow \equiv$*, then* c *satisfies* (ϵ, δ)*-differential privacy.*

Corollary 1 is the central result for deriving differential privacy guarantees in apRHL. Using Theorem 2, one can prove the converse to Corollary 1, yielding a characterization of approximate differential privacy.

The logic apRHL can also be used to reason about more traditional information-flow properties, such as probabilistic noninterference. To see this, let Ψ be an arbitrary equivalence relation on initial states and let $\equiv$ be the identity relation on final states. A judgment $\models c \sim_{1,0} c : \Psi \Rightarrow \equiv$ entails that two initial states induce the same distribution of final states whenever they are related by Ψ. In particular, this implies that an adversary who can observe (or even repeatedly sample) the output of c will only be able to determine the initial state up to its Ψ-equivalence class. In this way, Ψ can be used for expressing fine-grained notions of confidentiality, including probabilistic noninterference [31]. Our interpretation of apRHL judgments generalizes to arbitrary equivalence relations as post-conditions. In this way, one can capture adversaries that have only partial views on the system, as required for distributed differential privacy [5].

We finally show how apRHL can also be used for deriving generalized Lipschitz-conditions of probabilistic programs. As a first step, we show that valid apRHL judgments imply statements for input distributions that are related by (α, δ)-lifting.

Lemma 6. *If* $\models c_1 \sim_{\alpha,\delta} c_2 : \Psi \Rightarrow \Phi$*, then for all distributions* μ_1 *and* μ_2 *of initial memories we have:*

$$\mu_1 \sim_{\Psi}^{\alpha',\delta'} \mu_2 \implies (\mathsf{bind}\ \mu_1\ \llbracket c_1 \rrbracket\ ) \sim_{\Phi}^{\alpha\alpha',\delta+\delta'} (\mathsf{bind}\ \mu_2\ \llbracket c_2 \rrbracket)$$

By instantiating pre- and post-conditions in Lemma 6 to the identity relation on memories $\equiv$ and applying Theorems 1 and 2, one obtains the following generalized Lipschitz-condition for probabilistic programs on random inputs.

Corollary 2. *If* $\models c_1 \sim_{\alpha,\delta} c_2 : \equiv \Rightarrow \equiv$*, then*

$$\Delta_{\alpha'}(\mu_1, \mu_2) \leq \delta' \implies \Delta_{\alpha\alpha'}(\mathsf{bind}\ \mu_1\ \llbracket c_1 \rrbracket, \mathsf{bind}\ \mu_2\ \llbracket c_2 \rrbracket) \leq \delta + \delta'$$

5.3 Logic

This section introduces a set of proof rules to support reasoning about the validity of apRHL judgments. In order to maximize flexibility and to allow the application of proof rules to be interleaved with other forms of reasoning, the soundness of each proof rule is proved individually as a Coq lemma. Nevertheless, we retain the usual presentation of the rules as a proof system.

We present the core apRHL rules in Figure 4; all rules generalize their pRHL counterpart, which can be recovered by setting $\alpha = 1$ and $\delta = 0$. (Any valid pRHL derivation admits an immediate translation into apRHL.) We begin by describing the rules corresponding to language constructs.

The [skip], [assert] and [assn] rules are direct transpositions of the pRHL rules. Rule [rand] states that for any two distribution expressions μ_1 and μ_2 of type A, the random assignments $x_1 \xleftarrow{\$} \mu_1$ and $x_2 \xleftarrow{\$} \mu_2$ are (α, δ)-related w.r.t. pre-condition Ψ and post-condition $x_1\langle 1 \rangle = x_2\langle 2 \rangle$, provided the α-distance between the distributions $\llbracket \mu_1 \rrbracket\, m_1$ and $\llbracket \mu_2 \rrbracket\, m_2$ is smaller than δ whenever m_1 and m_2 are related by Ψ. The soundness of rule [rand] follows from Theorem 2.

Rule [seq] has tight connections to composition theorems for differentially private algorithms, as further developed in Section 5.4.

Rule [cond] states that branching statements are (α, δ)-related w.r.t. pre-condition Ψ and post-condition Φ, provided that the pre-condition Ψ ensures that the guards of both statements are equivalent, and that the true and false branches are (α, δ)-related w.r.t. pre-conditions $\Psi \wedge b\langle 1 \rangle$ and $\Psi \wedge \neg b\langle 1 \rangle$, respectively.

The rule for loops may be best understood by taking $\delta = 0$. In this case, the rule [while] states that two bounded loops that execute in lockstep are $n \ln(\alpha)$-differentially private when their bodies at each iteration are $\ln(\alpha)$-differentially private and n is an upper bound for the number of iterations. The rule [while] is sufficient for proving differential privacy of examples like the k-median from [18], where the skew remains unchanged at each iteration. Other examples, like the ones discussed in the next section, require applying more sophisticated rules in which the skew and the slack may vary across iterations. For instance, the rule [gwhile] shown in Figure 5 allows for a finer-grained case analysis depending on a predicate P on program memories whose validity is preserved across iterations. Assume that when P does not hold, the iterations of each loop can be related with a privacy factor of $\alpha_1(i)$ in case P does not hold after their execution, and with a privacy factor of α_2 in case it does. Furthermore, assume that the iterations are observationally equivalent when P holds initially. Then, the two loops are related with a privacy factor of $(\prod_{i=1..n} \alpha_1(i))\ \alpha_2$. Intuitively, as long as P does not hold, the iterations of each loop are $\ln(\alpha_1(i))$-differentially private, while the single iteration where the validity of P may be established (this occurs necessarily at the same time in both loops) incurs an $\ln(\alpha_2)$ privacy penalty; the remaining iterations preserve P and do not add to the privacy bound.

We continue by explaining the structural rules given in Figure 4. The rule [case] allows one to perform a case analysis in the pre-condition of a judgment. The weakening rule [weak] generalizes the rule of consequence of (relational) Hoare logic by allowing to increase the skew and slack; its soundness follows from Lemma 4. The composition rule [comp] permits to structure proofs by introducing intermediate programs (as in the game-playing technique for cryptographic proofs [3]); its soundness follows from Theorem 3. Together with rule [transp], it yields a rule for the case when Ψ and Φ are partial equivalence relations which, specialized to $\alpha = \alpha' = 1$, reads:

$$\frac{\models c_1 \sim_{1,\delta} c_2 : \Psi \Rightarrow \Phi \qquad \models c_2 \sim_{1,\delta'} c_3 : \Psi \Rightarrow \Phi}{\models c_1 \sim_{1,\delta+\delta'} c_3 : \Psi \Rightarrow \Phi}$$

Finally, the [frame] rule allows one to strengthen the pre- and post-condition with an assertion Θ whose validity is preserved by executing the commands of the judgment. (In the figure, the notation $\times$ is used to denote the product of two distributions.)

5.4 Sequential and Parallel Composition Theorems

Composition theorems play an important role in the construction and analysis of differentially private mechanisms. A central result states that an ϵ-differentially private query followed by an ϵ'-differentially private query to the same dataset corresponds to a single $(\epsilon + \epsilon')$-differentially private query [24]. An important variant of this result deals with the case in which both queries access disjoint parts of the dataset. This so-called parallel composition of queries leads to a stronger, $\max\{\epsilon, \epsilon'\}$-privacy bound [24]. Both composition results admit a natural interpretation in apRHL, which we present below.

We begin by introducing additional notation that allows us to express independence of computations and observational capabilities of adversaries. For a set of variables $Z \subseteq \mathcal{V}$, we define the

$$\frac{m_1\ \Psi\ m_2 \stackrel{\text{def}}{=} (m_1\{[\![e_1]\!]\ m_1/x_1\})\ \Phi\ (m_2\{[\![e_2]\!]\ m_2/x_2\})}{\models x_1 \leftarrow e_1 \sim_{1,0} x_2 \leftarrow e_2 : \Psi \Rightarrow \Phi}\,[\mathsf{assn}] \qquad \frac{\forall m_1\, m_2.\ m_1\ \Psi\ m_2 \implies \Delta_\alpha([\![\mu_1]\!]\ m_1, [\![\mu_2]\!]\ m_2) \leq \delta}{\models x_1 \stackrel{\$}{\leftarrow} \mu_1 \sim_{\alpha,\delta} x_2 \stackrel{\$}{\leftarrow} \mu_2 : \Psi \Rightarrow x_1\langle 1\rangle = x_2\langle 2\rangle}\,[\mathsf{rand}]$$

$$\frac{\Psi \implies b\langle 1\rangle \equiv b'\langle 2\rangle}{\models \mathsf{assert}\ b \sim_{1,0} \mathsf{assert}\ b' : \Psi \Rightarrow \Psi \wedge b\langle 1\rangle}\,[\mathsf{assert}] \qquad \frac{\models c_1 \sim_{\alpha,\delta} c_2 : \Psi \Rightarrow \Phi' \qquad \models c_1' \sim_{\alpha',\delta'} c_2' : \Phi' \Rightarrow \Phi}{\models c_1; c_1' \sim_{\alpha\alpha',\delta+\delta'} c_2; c_2' : \Psi \Rightarrow \Phi}\,[\mathsf{seq}]$$

$$\frac{}{\models \mathsf{skip} \sim_{1,0} \mathsf{skip} : \Psi \Rightarrow \Psi}\,[\mathsf{skip}] \qquad \frac{\models c_1 \sim_{\alpha,\delta} c_1' : \Psi \wedge b\langle 1\rangle \Rightarrow \Phi \qquad \models c_2 \sim_{\alpha,\delta} c_2' : \Psi \wedge \neg b\langle 1\rangle \Rightarrow \Phi \qquad \Psi \implies b\langle 1\rangle \equiv b'\langle 2\rangle}{\models \mathsf{if}\ b\ \mathsf{then}\ c_1\ \mathsf{else}\ c_2 \sim_{\alpha,\delta} \mathsf{if}\ b'\ \mathsf{then}\ c_1'\ \mathsf{else}\ c_2' : \Psi \Rightarrow \Phi}\,[\mathsf{cond}]$$

$$\frac{\models c \sim_{\alpha,\delta} c' : \Psi \wedge b\langle 1\rangle \wedge b'\langle 2\rangle \Rightarrow \Psi \wedge b\langle 1\rangle \equiv b'\langle 2\rangle \qquad \forall m_1\, m_2.\ m_1\ \Psi\ m_2 \implies [\![\mathsf{while}\ b\ \mathsf{do}\ c]\!]\ m_1 = [\![[\mathsf{while}\ b\ \mathsf{do}\ c]_n]\!]\ m_1}{\models \mathsf{while}\ b\ \mathsf{do}\ c \sim_{\alpha^n,n\delta} \mathsf{while}\ b'\ \mathsf{do}\ c' : \Psi \wedge b\langle 1\rangle \equiv b'\langle 2\rangle \Rightarrow \Psi \wedge \neg b\langle 1\rangle \wedge \neg b'\langle 2\rangle}\,[\mathsf{while}]$$

$$\frac{\models c_1 \sim_{\alpha,\delta} c_2 : \Psi \wedge \Theta \Rightarrow \Phi \qquad \models c_1 \sim_{\alpha,\delta} c_2 : \Psi \wedge \neg\Theta \Rightarrow \Phi}{\models c_1 \sim_{\alpha,\delta} c_2 : \Psi \Rightarrow \Phi}\,[\mathsf{case}] \qquad \frac{\models c_1 \sim_{\alpha,\delta} c_2 : \Psi \Rightarrow \Phi \qquad \models c_2 \sim_{\alpha',\delta'} c_3 : \Psi' \Rightarrow \Phi'}{\models c_1 \sim_{\alpha\alpha',\max(\delta+\alpha\,\delta',\delta'+\alpha'\,\delta)} c_3 : \Psi \circ \Psi' \Rightarrow \Phi \circ \Phi'}\,[\mathsf{comp}]$$

$$\frac{\models c_1 \sim_{\alpha',\delta'} c_2 : \Psi' \Rightarrow \Phi' \qquad \Psi \Rightarrow \Psi' \qquad \Phi' \Rightarrow \Phi \qquad \alpha' \leq \alpha \qquad \delta' \leq \delta}{\models c_1 \sim_{\alpha,\delta} c_2 : \Psi \Rightarrow \Phi}\,[\mathsf{weak}] \qquad \frac{\models c_2 \sim_{\alpha,\delta} c_1 : \Psi^{-1} \Rightarrow \Phi^{-1}}{\models c_1 \sim_{\alpha,\delta} c_2 : \Psi \Rightarrow \Phi}\,[\mathsf{transp}]$$

$$\frac{\models c_1 \sim_{\alpha,\delta} c_2 : \Psi \Rightarrow \Phi \qquad \forall m_1\, m_2.\ m_1\ \Theta\ m_2 \implies \mathsf{range}\ \Theta\ ([\![c_1]\!]\ m_1 \times [\![c_2]\!]\ m_2)}{\models c_1 \sim_{\alpha,\delta} c_2 : \Psi \wedge \Theta \Rightarrow \Phi \wedge \Theta}\,[\mathsf{frame}]$$

Figure 4. Core proof rules of the approximate relational Hoare logic

$$\frac{\begin{array}{c} \Phi \implies (b_1\langle 1\rangle \equiv b_2\langle 2\rangle \wedge P_1\langle 1\rangle \equiv P_2\langle 2\rangle \wedge i\langle 1\rangle = i\langle 2\rangle) \\ \forall m_1\, m_2.\ m_1\ \Phi\ m_2 \implies [\![\mathsf{while}\ b_1\ \mathsf{do}\ c_1]\!]\ m_1 = [\![[\mathsf{while}\ b_1\ \mathsf{do}\ c_1]_n]\!]\ m_1 \\ \models c_1;\ \mathsf{assert}\ (\neg P_1) \sim_{\alpha_1(j),0} c_2;\ \mathsf{assert}\ (\neg P_2) : \Phi \wedge b_1\langle 1\rangle \wedge i\langle 1\rangle = j\ \wedge \neg P_1\langle 1\rangle \Rightarrow \Phi \wedge i\langle 1\rangle = j+1 \\ \models c_1;\ \mathsf{assert}\ (P_1) \sim_{\alpha_2,0} c_2;\ \mathsf{assert}\ (P_2) : \Phi \wedge b_1\langle 1\rangle \wedge i\langle 1\rangle = j \wedge \neg P_1\langle 1\rangle \Rightarrow \Phi \wedge i\langle 1\rangle = j+1 \\ \models c_1 \sim_{1,0} c_2 : \Phi \wedge b_1\langle 1\rangle \wedge i\langle 1\rangle = j \wedge P_1\langle 1\rangle \Rightarrow \Phi \wedge i\langle 1\rangle = j+1 \wedge P_1\langle 1\rangle \end{array}}{\models \mathsf{while}\ b_1\ \mathsf{do}\ c_1 \sim_{(\prod_{i=a}^{a+n} \alpha_1(i))\times\alpha_2,0} \mathsf{while}\ b_2\ \mathsf{do}\ c_2 : \Phi \wedge i\langle 1\rangle = a \Rightarrow \Phi \wedge \neg b_1\langle 1\rangle}\,[\mathsf{gwhile}]$$

Figure 5. Generalized rule for loops

relations $\doteq_Z$ and $=_Z$ as follows:

$$\begin{array}{rcl} m =_Z m' & \stackrel{\text{def}}{=} & \forall y \in Z.\ m\ y = m'\ y \\ m \doteq_Z m' & \stackrel{\text{def}}{=} & \exists z \in Z.\ m =_{(Z\setminus\{z\})} m' \end{array}$$

Note that $m \doteq_Z m'$ corresponds to $d_Z(m, m') \leq 1$, where d_Z measures the number of variables in Z in which two memories differ, i.e. their Hamming distance. Using this notation, we can interpret judgments of the form

$$\models c \sim_{\exp(\epsilon),0} c : \doteq_X \Rightarrow =_Y$$

as a definition of a computation c on variables in X that is ϵ-differentially private w.r.t. adversaries that can only observe variables in Y. Similarly, we can interpret judgments of the form

$$\models c \sim_{\exp(\epsilon),0} c : \doteq_X \wedge =_{X'} \Rightarrow =_Y$$

as a definition of a family (indexed by X') of computations c on variables in X that are ϵ-differentially private w.r.t. adversaries that can only observe variables in Y. To emphasize the roles of the sets X, Y, and Y' we say that c is a computation from X to Y that is parameterized by Y'. Finally, we interpret premises of the form

$$\models c \sim_{1,0} c : =_X \Rightarrow =_X \qquad \models c \sim_{1,0} c : \doteq_X \Rightarrow \doteq_X$$

as a statement that c does not modify variables in X. Note that this reading of premises is sound, but stronger than the actual semantics.

The sequential composition theorem is a direct application of rule [seq] and is captured by the rule:

$$\frac{\begin{array}{c} \models c \sim_{\exp(\epsilon),0} c : \doteq_X \Rightarrow (=_Y \wedge \doteq_X) \\ \models c' \sim_{\exp(\epsilon'),0} c' : (=_Y \wedge \doteq_X) \Rightarrow =_{(Y\cup Y')} \end{array}}{\models c; c' \sim_{\exp(\epsilon+\epsilon'),0} c; c' : \doteq_X \Rightarrow =_{(Y\cup Y')}}$$

With the intuitive reading introduced above, the rule states that the composition of an ϵ-differentially private computation c from X to Y, with a parameterized ϵ-differentially private computation c' from X to Y' is an $(\epsilon+\epsilon')$-differentially private computation $c; c'$ from X to $Y \cup Y'$, provided that c' does not modify variables in Y, and c does not modify variables in X.

The parallel composition theorem is captured by the rule:

$$\frac{\begin{array}{l} \models c \sim_{\exp(\epsilon),0} c : (\doteq_X \wedge =_{X'}) \Rightarrow =_{(Y\cup X')} \\ \models c \sim_{1,0} c : (=_X \wedge \doteq_{X'}) \Rightarrow (=_Y \wedge \doteq_{X'}) \\ \models c' \sim_{\exp(\epsilon'),0} c' : (=_Y \wedge \doteq_{X'}) \Rightarrow =_{(Y\cup Y')} \\ \models c' \sim_{1,0} c' : =_{(Y\cup X')} \Rightarrow =_{(Y\cup Y')} \qquad X \cap X' = \emptyset \end{array}}{\models c; c' \sim_{\exp(\max(\epsilon,\epsilon')),0} c; c' : \doteq_{X\cup X'} \Rightarrow =_{(Y\cup Y')}}$$

With the intuitive reading introduced above, the rule states that the composition of an ϵ-differentially private computation c from X to Y, with a parameterized ϵ-differentially private computation c' from X' to Y', where X' is disjoint from X, is a $\max(\epsilon, \epsilon')$-differentially private computation $c; c'$ from $X \cup X'$ to $Y \cup Y'$. As a prerequisite we require that c does not modify variables in X' and is non-interfering w.r.t. input variables X and output variables Y, and that c' does not modify variables in Y and is non-interfering w.r.t. input variables X' and output variables Y'.

6. Case Studies

We illustrate the versatility of our framework by formalizing two prominent mechanisms, namely the Laplacian and the Exponential mechanisms, and proving their correctness from first principles. We then apply these mechanisms to prove differential privacy for several streaming algorithms. Finally, we detail the proof of differential privacy of the Minimum Vertex Cover algorithm introduced in Section 2.

6.1 Exponential and Laplacian Mechanisms

Many algorithms for statistics and data mining are numeric, i.e. they return (approximations of) real numbers. The Laplacian mechanism of Dwork et al. [17] is a fundamental tool for making such computations differentially private. This is achieved by perturbing the algorithm's true output with noise drawn from a Laplace distribution. The density function at x of the Laplace distribution centered around r with scale factor σ is proportional to

$$\exp\left(-\frac{|x-r|}{\sigma}\right)$$

To transform a deterministic computation $f\colon A \to \mathbb{R}$ into a differentially private computation, one needs to set r to the true output of the computation and choose σ (i.e. the amount of noise) according to the *sensitivity* of f. Informally, the sensitivity is a Lipschitz-parameter that captures how far apart f maps nearby inputs. Formally, the sensitivity $\mathbf{S}_f$ is defined relative to a metric d on A as follows:

$$\mathbf{S}_f \stackrel{\text{def}}{=} \max_{a,a' \mid d(a,a') \leq 1} |f\ a - f\ a'|$$

The justification for the Laplacian mechanism is a result that states that for a function $f : A \to \mathbb{R}$, the randomized algorithm that on input a returns a value sampled from the Laplacian distribution centered around $f(a)$ with scale factor $\sigma = \mathbf{S}_f/\epsilon$ is ϵ-differentially private [17].

One limitation of the Laplacian mechanism is that it is confined to numerical algorithms. The Exponential mechanism [23] is a general mechanism for building differentially private algorithms with arbitrary (but discrete) output domains. The Exponential mechanism takes as input a base distribution μ on a set B, and a scoring function $s : A \times B \to \mathbb{R}^{\geq 0}$; intuitively, values b maximizing $s(a, b)$ are the most appealing output for an input a. The Exponential mechanism is a randomized algorithm that takes a value $a \in A$ and returns a value $b \in B$ that approximately maximizes the score $s(a, b)$, where the quality of the approximation is determined by a parameter $\epsilon > 0$. Formally, the Exponential mechanism $\mathcal{E}^{\epsilon}_{s,\mu}$ maps every element in A to a distribution in B whose density function at b is given by:

$$\mathcal{E}^{\epsilon}_{s,\mu}(a)\ b = \frac{\exp(\epsilon\ s(a,b))\ (\mu\ b)}{\sum_{b \in B} \exp(\epsilon\ s(a,b))\ (\mu\ b)}$$

The definition implicitly assumes that the sum in the denominator is bounded for all $a \in A$. McSherry and Talwar [23] show that $\mathcal{E}^{\epsilon}_{s,\mu}$ is $2\epsilon\mathbf{S}_s$-differentially private, where $\mathbf{S}_s$ is the maximum sensitivity of s w.r.t. a, for all b.

In our proofs, the Exponential and Laplacian mechanisms are defined as instances of a general construction $(\cdot)^\sharp$ that takes as input a function $f : A \to B \to \mathbb{R}^{\geq 0}$ and returns a function $f^\sharp : A \to \mathcal{D}(B)$ such that for every $a \in A$ the density function of $f^\sharp\ a$ at b is given by:

$$f^\sharp\ a\ b = \frac{f\ a\ b}{\sum_{b \in B} f\ a\ b}$$

We derive the correctness of the Laplacian and Exponential mechanisms as a consequence of the following lemma.

Lemma 7. *Let B be a discrete set and consider a function $f : A \to B \to \mathbb{R}^{\geq 0}$ such that $f^\sharp$ is well defined. Let $a, a' \in A$, $\gamma \geq 0$ be such for all b, $f(a, b) \leq \gamma\ f(a', b)$ and $f(a', b) \leq \gamma\ f(a, b)$. Then,*

$$\Delta_{\gamma^2}(f^\sharp\ a, f^\sharp\ a') = 0$$

If moreover $\sum_{b \in B} f\ a\ b = \sum_{b \in B} f\ a'\ b$, then

$$\Delta_{\gamma}(f^\sharp\ a, f^\sharp\ a') = 0$$

Using the construction $(\cdot)^\sharp$ defined above, the Exponential mechanism for a scoring function s, base distribution μ and scale factor ϵ is defined as

$$\mathcal{E}^{\epsilon}_{s,\mu} \stackrel{\text{def}}{=} (\lambda a\ b.\ \exp(\epsilon\ s(a,b))\ (\mu\ b))^\sharp$$

whereas the Laplacian mechanism with mean value r and scale factor σ is defined as

$$\mathcal{L}(r,\sigma) \stackrel{\text{def}}{=} \left(\lambda a\ b.\ \exp\left(-\frac{|b-a|}{\sigma}\right)\right)^\sharp r$$

The privacy guarantees for the Exponential and the Laplacian mechanisms are stated as the rules [lap] and [exp] in Figure 6; their soundness is a corollary of Lemma 7 above.

Observe that the premise of rule [lap] requires to prove that the values around which the mechanism is centered are within distance k. This is the case when these values are computed by a k-sensitive function starting from adjacent inputs, which corresponds to the usual interpretation of the guarantees provided by the Laplacian mechanism [17].

As a further illustration of the expressive power of CertiPriv, we have also defined a Laplacian mechanism $\mathcal{L}^n$ for lists; given $\sigma \in \mathbb{R}^+$ and a vector $a \in \mathbb{R}^n$, the mechanism $\mathcal{L}^n$ outputs a vector in $\mathbb{R}^n$ whose i-th component is drawn from distribution $\mathcal{L}(a[i], \sigma)$. More formally, we have proved the soundness of the following rule

$$\frac{m_1\ \Psi\ m_2 \implies \sum_{1 \leq i \leq n} |[\![a[i]]\!]\ m_1 - [\![a[i]]\!]\ m_2| \leq k}{\models x \xleftarrow{\$} \mathcal{L}^n(a, \frac{k}{\epsilon}) \sim_{\exp(\epsilon),0} y \xleftarrow{\$} \mathcal{L}^n(a, \frac{k}{\epsilon}) : \Psi \Rightarrow x\langle 1\rangle = y\langle 2\rangle}$$

which we refer to as [lap*].

6.2 Statistics over Streams

In this section we present an analysis of algorithms for computing private and continual statistics in a data stream [8]. As in [8], we focus on algorithms for private summing and counting. More sophisticated algorithms, e.g. computing heavy hitters in a data stream, can be built using sums and counters as primitive operations and inherit their privacy and utility guarantees.

We consider streams of elements in a bounded subset $D \subseteq \mathbb{R}$, i.e. with $|x - y| \leq b$ for all $x, y \in D$. This setting is slightly more general than the one considered by Chan et al. [8], where only streams over $\{0, 1\}$ are considered. On the algorithmic side, the generalization to bounded domains is immediate; for the privacy analysis, however, one needs to take the bound b into account because it conditions the sensitivity of computations. This requires a careful definition of metrics and propagation of bounds, which is supported by CertiPriv.

Although in our implementation we formalize streams as finite lists, we use array-notation in the exposition for the sake of

$$\frac{m_1\,\Psi\,m_2 \implies |[\![r]\!]\,m_1 - [\![r]\!]\,m_2| \le k \qquad \exp(\epsilon) \le \alpha}{\models x \xleftarrow{\$} \mathcal{L}(r, \frac{k}{\epsilon}) \sim_{\alpha,0} y \xleftarrow{\$} \mathcal{L}(r, \frac{k}{\epsilon}) : \Psi \Rightarrow x\langle 1\rangle = y\langle 2\rangle}\,[\mathsf{lap}] \qquad \frac{m_1\,\Psi\,m_2 \implies d([\![a]\!]\,m_1, [\![a]\!]\,m_2) \le k \qquad \exp(2k\mathbf{S}_s\epsilon) \le \alpha}{\models x \xleftarrow{\$} \mathcal{E}^{\epsilon}_{s,\mu}(a) \sim_{\alpha,0} y \xleftarrow{\$} \mathcal{E}^{\epsilon}_{s,\mu}(a) : \Psi \Rightarrow x\langle 1\rangle = y\langle 2\rangle}\,[\mathsf{exp}]$$

Figure 6. Rules for the Laplacian and Exponential mechanisms

readability. Given an array a of n elements in D, the goal is to release, for every point in time $0 \le j < n$ the aggregate sum $c[j] = \sum_{i=0}^{j} a[i]$ in a privacy-preserving manner. As observed in [8], there are two immediate solutions to the problem. The first is to maintain an exact aggregate sum $c[j]$ and output at each iteration a curated version $\overline{c}[j] \xleftarrow{\$} \mathcal{L}(c[j], b/\epsilon)$ of that sum. The second solution is to maintain and output a noisy aggregate sum $\tilde{c}[j]$, which is updated at iteration $j+1$ according to

$$\overline{a}[j+1] \xleftarrow{\$} \mathcal{L}(a[j+1], b/\epsilon);\ \tilde{c}[j+1] \leftarrow \tilde{c}[j] + \overline{a}[j+1]$$

The stream $\overline{c}[0] \cdots \overline{c}[n-1]$ offers weak, $n\epsilon$-differential privacy, because every element of a may appear in n different elements of $\overline{c}$, each with independent noise. However, each $\overline{c}[j]$ offers good accuracy because noise is added only once. In contrast, the stream $\tilde{c}[0] \cdots \tilde{c}[n-1]$ offers improved, ϵ-differential privacy, because each element of a appears only in one ϵ-differentially private query. However, as shown in [8], the sum $\tilde{c}[j]$ yields poor accuracy because noise is added j times during its computation.

One solution proposed by Chan et al. [8] is a combination of both basic methods of releasing partial sums that achieves a good compromise between privacy and accuracy. The idea is to split the stream a into chunks of length q, where the less accurate (but more private) method is used to compute the sum within the current chunk, and the more accurate (but less private) method is used to compute summaries of previous chunks. Formally, let $s_t = \sum_{i=0}^{q-1} a[t\ q + i]$ be the sum over the t-th chunk of a and let $\overline{s}_t \xleftarrow{\$} \mathcal{L}(s_t, b/\epsilon)$ be the corresponding noisy version. Then, for each $j = qr + k$, with $k < q$, we compute

$$\hat{c}[j] = \sum_{t=0}^{r-1} \overline{s}_t + \sum_{i=0}^{k} \overline{a}[qr + i]$$

The sequence $\hat{c}[0] \cdots \hat{c}[n-1]$ offers 2ϵ-differential privacy, intuitively because each element of a is accessed twice during computation. Moreover, $\hat{c}[j]$ also offers improved accuracy over $\tilde{c}[j]$ because noise is added only $r + k$ times rather than $j = qr + k$ times.

We will now turn the above informal security analysis into a formal analysis of program code. The code for computing $\overline{s}_t$ is given as the function PARTIALSUM in Figure 7, the code for computing $\overline{c}$ is given as the function PARTIALSUM' in Figure 8, and the code for computing $\hat{c}$ is given as the function SMARTSUM in Figure 9 (we omit the code for computing $\tilde{c}$ and the proof of its privacy bound). We next sketch the key steps in our proofs of differential privacy bounds for each of these algorithms. For all of our examples, we use the pre-condition

$$\begin{aligned}\Psi \stackrel{\text{def}}{=}\ & \mathsf{length}(a\langle 1\rangle) = \mathsf{length}(a\langle 2\rangle) \wedge a\langle 1\rangle \doteq a\langle 2\rangle \wedge \\ & \forall i.\ 0 \le i < \mathsf{length}(a\langle 1\rangle) \implies |a[i]\langle 1\rangle - a[i]\langle 2\rangle| \le b\end{aligned}$$

which relates two lists $a\langle 1\rangle$ and $a\langle 2\rangle$ whenever they have the same length, differ in at most one element, and the distance between the elements at the same position at each array is upper-bounded by b.

PARTIALSUM The proof of differential privacy of PARTIALSUM proceeds in two key steps. First, we prove (using the pRHL fragment of apRHL) that

$$\models c_{1-5} \sim_{1,0} c_{1-5} : \Psi \Rightarrow |s\langle 1\rangle - s\langle 2\rangle| \le b$$

```
function PartialSum(a)
1  s ← 0; i ← 0;
2  while i < length(a) do
3    s ← s + a[i];
4    i ← i + 1;
5  end;
6  s ← L(s, b/ε)
```

Figure 7. A simple ϵ-differentially private algorithm for summing over lists

where c_{1-5} corresponds to the code in lines 1-5 in Figure 7, i.e. the initialization and the loop. We apply the rule [lap] that gives a bound for the privacy guarantee achieved by the Laplacian mechanism (see Figure 6) to $c_6 = s \xleftarrow{\$} \mathcal{L}(s, b/\epsilon)$ (the instruction in line 6) and derive

$$\models c_6 \sim_{\exp(\epsilon),0} c_6 : |s\langle 1\rangle - s\langle 2\rangle| \le b \Rightarrow s\langle 1\rangle = s\langle 2\rangle$$

Using the rule for sequential composition, applied to c_{1-5} and c_6, we derive the following statement about PARTIALSUM, which implies that its output s is ϵ-differentially private.

$$\models \textsc{PartialSum}(a) \sim_{\exp(\epsilon),0} \textsc{PartialSum}(a) : \Psi \Rightarrow s\langle 1\rangle = s\langle 2\rangle$$

PARTIALSUM' Our implementation of PARTIALSUM' in Figure 7 differs slightly from the description given above in that we first add noise to the entire stream (line 1), before computing the partial sums of the noisy stream (lines 2-6). This modification allows us to take advantage of the proof rule for the Laplacian mechanism on lists. By merging the addition of noise into the loop, our two-pass implementation can be turned into an observationally equivalent one-pass implementation suitable for processing streams of data.

The proof of privacy for PARTIALSUM' proceeds in the following basic steps. First, we apply the rule [lap*] to the random assignment in line 1 (noted as c_1) of PARTIALSUM'. We obtain

$$\models c_1 \sim_{\exp(\epsilon),0} c_1 : \Psi \Rightarrow \overline{a}\langle 1\rangle = \overline{a}\langle 2\rangle$$

i.e. the output $\overline{a}$ is ϵ-differentially private at this point. For lines 2-6 (denoted by c_{2-6}), we prove (using the pRHL fragment of apRHL) that

$$\models c_{2-6} \sim_{1,0} c_{2-6} : \overline{a}\langle 1\rangle = \overline{a}\langle 2\rangle \Rightarrow s\langle 1\rangle = s\langle 2\rangle$$

This is straightforward because of the equality appearing in the precondition; this result can be derived using the apRHL rules, but is also an immediate consequence of the preservation of α-distance by probabilistic computations (see Lemma 3).

Finally, we apply the rule for sequential composition to c_1 and c_{2-6} and obtain

$$\models \textsc{PartialSum'}(a) \sim_{\exp(\epsilon),0} \textsc{PartialSum'}(a) : \Psi \Rightarrow s\langle 1\rangle = s\langle 2\rangle$$

which implies that the output s of PARTIALSUM' is ϵ-differentially private.

SMARTSUM Our implementation of the smart private sum in Figure 9 makes use of PARTIALSUM and PARTIALSUM' as building blocks, which enables us to reuse the above proofs.

In addition, our implementation makes use of a procedure OFFSETCOPY that given two lists s and x, a constant c and non-negative integers i, q, returns a list which is identical to s, but where

```
function PartialSum'(a)
  ā ←$ L^n(a, b/ϵ);
  s[0] ← ā[0]; i ← 1;
  while i < length(a) do
    s[i] ← s[i − 1] + ā[i];
    i ← i + 1;
  end
```

Figure 8. An ϵ-differentially private algorithm for partial sums over lists

```
function SmartSum(a, q)
1  i ← 0; c ← 0;
2  while i < length(a)/q do
3    b ← PartialSum(a[iq..i(q + 1) − 1]);
4    x ← PartialSum'(a[iq..i(q + 1) − 1]);
5    s ← OffsetCopy(s, x, c, iq, q);
6    c ← c + b;
7    i ← i + 1;
8  end
```

Figure 9. A smart 2ϵ-differentially private algorithm for partial sums over lists

the entries $s[i] \cdots s[i+(q-1)]$ are replaced by the first q elements of x, plus a constant offset c, i.e. $s[i+j] = x[j]+c$ for $0 <= i < q$. We obtain

$$\models s \leftarrow \text{OffsetCopy}(s, x, c, i, q) \sim_{1,0} s \leftarrow \text{OffsetCopy}(s, x, c, i, q) : =_{\{s,x,c,i,q\}} \Rightarrow s\langle 1\rangle = s\langle 2\rangle$$

We combine this result with the judgments derived for PartialSum and PartialSum' using the rule for sequential composition, obtaining

$$\models c_{4-7} \sim_{\exp(2\epsilon),0} c_{4-7} : \Psi \Rightarrow s\langle 1\rangle = s\langle 2\rangle$$

where c_{4-7} denotes the body of the loop in lines 4-7. To conclude, we apply the rule for while loops in Fig. 5 with $\alpha_1(i) = 1$ and $\alpha_2 = \exp(2\epsilon)$. This instantiation of the rule states that a loop that is non-interfering in all but one iteration is 2ϵ-differentially private, if the interfering loop iteration is 2ϵ-differentially private. More technically, the existence of a single interfering iteration is built into the rule using a pair of stable events for each command. In our case, the critical iteration corresponds to the one in which the chunk contains the position in which the two lists differ.

6.3 Minimum Vertex Cover

We conclude this section with a more detailed account of the proof of differential privacy of the Minimum Vertex Cover approximation algorithm of Section 2. The main step of the proof is an application of the rule for loops in Fig. 5 with parameters

$$\alpha_1(i) = \exp\left(\frac{2}{(n-i)w_i}\right) \qquad \alpha_2 = \exp\left(\frac{\epsilon}{4}\right),$$

the following invariant Φ

$$\begin{array}{l}(t \in \pi\langle 1\rangle \vee u \in \pi\langle 1\rangle \implies E\langle 1\rangle = E\langle 2\rangle) \wedge \\ (t \notin \pi\langle 1\rangle \wedge u \notin \pi\langle 1\rangle \implies E\langle 2\rangle = E\langle 1\rangle \cup \{(t,u)\}) \wedge \\ V\langle 1\rangle = V\langle 2\rangle \wedge \pi\langle 1\rangle = \pi\langle 2\rangle,\end{array}$$

and stable properties $P_1 = P_2 = t \in \pi \vee u \in \pi$.

The first and second equivalences appearing in the premises of the rule are of the form:

$$\models c_1; \text{assert } P \sim_{\alpha,0} c_2; \text{assert } P : \Psi \Rightarrow \Phi$$

For each of them, we first hoist the assertion immediately after the random assignment. At this point the expression in the assertions becomes $(t, u \notin (v :: \pi))$ in the case of the first premise and $(t \in (v :: \pi) \vee u \in (v :: \pi))$ in the case of the second. We then compute the weakest pre-condition of the assignments that now follow the assertions. The resulting judgments simplify, after applying the [weak] and [frame] rules, to judgments of the form

$$\models c \sim_{\alpha,0} c : \Psi \Rightarrow v\langle 1\rangle = v\langle 2\rangle$$

where

$$\Psi \stackrel{\text{def}}{=} E\langle 2\rangle = E\langle 1\rangle \cup \{(t,u)\} \wedge V\langle 1\rangle = V\langle 2\rangle \wedge t, u \notin \pi \wedge i\langle 1\rangle = i\langle 2\rangle = j \wedge \pi\langle 1\rangle = \pi\langle 2\rangle$$

For the first premise we have $\alpha = \alpha_1(j)$ and

$$c = v \xleftarrow{\$} \text{choose}(V, E, \epsilon, n, i);\ \text{assert } (t, u \notin (v :: \pi))$$

whereas for the second premise we have $\alpha = \alpha_2$ and

$$c = v \xleftarrow{\$} \text{choose}(V, E, \epsilon, n, i);\ \text{assert } (t \in (v :: \pi) \vee u \in (v :: \pi))$$

To establish the validity of both judgments, we cast the code for c as a random assignment where v is sampled from the interpretation of choose(V, E, ϵ, n, i) restricted to v satisfying the condition on the assertion. In the first case, the restriction amounts to $v \neq u, t$ whereas in the second it amounts to $v = t \vee v = u$. For each one of these cases, we apply the rule for random assignments and are thus left to prove that the α-distance of the corresponding distributions is null. In view of Lemma 2, this in turn amounts to verifying for each element x in the support of the distribution that the ratio between the probability of v being equal to x in the left-hand side (resp. right-hand side) program and the right-hand side (resp. left-hand side) program is bounded by α, which directly translates into the inequalities appearing in Section 2. Technically, these inequalities are proved by appealing to a variant of Lemma 7.

The proof in apRHL yields a bound of $5\epsilon/4$ rather than the ϵ bound from [18]. This difference is due to the symmetric nature of our logic. We believe that the optimal bound can be proved in apRHL at the cost of a more complicated proof by using rule [comp] to introduce intermediate programs or, more elegantly, by using an asymmetric version of apRHL. See the appendix for a discussion on what it would take to build an asymmetric logic and how it could be used to improve the privacy bound from $5\epsilon/4$ to just ϵ.

7. Related Work

Our work builds upon program verification techniques, and in particular (probabilistic and relational) program logics, to reason about differential privacy. We briefly review relevant work in these areas.

Differential privacy There is a vast body of work on differential privacy. We refer to recent overviews, see e.g. [14, 15], for an account of some of the latest developments in the field, and focus on language-based approaches to differential privacy. The Privacy Integrated Queries (PINQ) platform [24] supports reasoning about the privacy guarantees of programs in a simple SQL-like language. The reasoning is based on the sensitivity of basic queries such as `Select` and `GroupBy`, the differential privacy of building blocks such as `NoisySum` and `NoisyAvg`, and meta-theorems for their sequential and parallel composition. AIRAVAT [30] leverages these building blocks for distributed computations based on MapReduce.

The linear type system of [29] extends sensitivity analysis to a higher-order functional language. By using a suitable choice of metric and probability monads, the type system also supports reasoning about probabilistic, differentially private computations. As in PINQ, the soundness of the type system makes use of known composition theorems and relies on assumptions about the sensitivity/differential privacy of nontrivial building blocks, such as arithmetic operations, conditional swap operations, or the Laplacian mechanism. While the type system can handle functional data structures, it does not allow for analyzing programs with conditional branching. Work on the automatic derivation of sensitivity properties of imperative programs [9] addresses this problem and can (in conjunction with the Laplacian mechanism) be used to derive differential privacy guarantees of programs with control flow. Although this approach supports reasoning about probabilistic computations, the reasoning is restricted to Lipschitz-conditions.

In contrast to [9, 24, 29], CertiPriv supports reasoning about differential privacy guarantees from first principles. In particular, CertiPriv enabled us to prove (rather than to assume) the correctness of Laplacian and Exponential mechanisms, and the differential privacy of complex interleavings of (not necessarily differentially private) probabilistic computations.

A recent approach considers the verification of privacy properties based on I/O-automata [35]. There, the focus lies on the verification of the correct use of differentially private sanitization mechanisms within interactive systems, where the effect of a sanitization mechanism is soundly abstracted using a single, idealized transition.

An early approach to quantitative confidentiality analysis [26] uses the distance of output distributions to quantify information flow. Their measure is closely related to $(0, \delta)$-approximate differential privacy, which can be reasoned about in CertiPriv. More recent approaches to quantitative information-flow focus on measures of confidentiality based on information-theoretic entropy. Techniques for code-based structural reasoning about these measures are developed in [10]. For an overview and a discussion of the relationship between entropy-based measures of confidentiality and differential privacy, see [2].

Probabilistic and relational program verification Program logics have a long tradition and have been used effectively to reason about functional correctness of programs. In contrast, privacy is a 2-safety property [11, 33], that is, a (universally quantified) property about two runs of a program. There have been several proposals for applying program logics to 2-safety, but these proposals are confined to deterministic programs and impractical.

A seminal paper [7] develops a relational Hoare logic (RHL) for a core imperative programming language and shows how it can be used to reason about information flow properties of programs. This line of work has been generalized to a probabilistic setting by CertiCrypt [3], which formalizes an extension of RHL for probabilistic programs. CertiPriv builds upon and significantly extends CertiCrypt [3]. The most outstanding difference between the two frameworks is that CertiPriv supports reasoning about a wide range of quantitative relational properties, whereas CertiCrypt is confined to baseline information flow properties. Although we make a modest use of this feature, CertiPriv supports (for a richer language) the certified program transformations that are implemented in CertiCrypt. Thanks to a recent development, the construction of game-playing proofs [6] in CertiCrypt can be achieved efficiently using EasyCrypt [4], a front-end that generates automatically probabilistic RHL derivations using SMT solvers and a verification condition generator. There are exciting opportunities to exploit the synergies between CertiPriv, CertiCrypt and EasyCrypt, as further discussed in Section 8.

There is also a growing body of work that uses proof assistants for reasoning about properties of probabilistic algorithms. For instance, Hurd and co-workers [19] formalized in the HOL system a theory for reasoning about a probabilistic extension of Dijkstra's guarded command language, and used it to prove the correctness of the Miller-Rabin primality test.

8. Future Work and Conclusions

CertiPriv is a machine-checked framework that supports fine-grained reasoning about an expressive class of privacy policies in the Coq proof assistant. In contrast to previous language-based approaches to differential privacy, CertiPriv allows to reason directly about probabilistic computations and to build proofs from first principles. As a result, CertiPriv achieves flexibility, expressiveness, and reliability, and appears as a plausible starting point for capturing and analyzing formally new developments in the field of differential privacy.

An immediate objective for future work is to use the game-playing technique from [3] for verifying in CertiPriv the privacy of multi-party computation algorithms, where one is concerned with ensuring privacy against (computationally bounded) adversaries that only have a partial view of the state, concretely the local state of corrupt participants [5, 25]. This objective is within reach, since CertiPriv inherits from CertiCrypt a formalization of probabilistic polynomial-time algorithms, and can already capture this variant of differential privacy.

Another exciting avenue for further research is to automate the verification of differentially private computations. There are three facets to this work: building an automated checker for apRHL derivations, automatically inferring relational loop invariants, and implementing a precise dependency analysis for an optimal usage of existing composition theorems. EasyCrypt [4] provides an excellent starting point for these tasks.

9. Acknowledgments

This work was partially funded by European Projects FP7-256980 NESSoS and FP7-229599 AMAROUT, Spanish project TIN2009-14599 DESAFIOS 10, Madrid Regional project S2009TIC-1465 PROMETIDOS and French project ANR SESUR-012 SCALP.

References

[1] P. Audebaud and C. Paulin-Mohring. Proofs of randomized algorithms in Coq. *Sci. Comput. Program.*, 74(8):568–589, 2009.

[2] G. Barthe and B. Köpf. Information-theoretic bounds for differentially private mechanisms. In *24rd IEEE Computer Security Foundations Symposium, CSF 2011*, pages 191–204, Los Alamitos, 2011. IEEE Computer Society.

[3] G. Barthe, B. Grégoire, and S. Zanella Béguelin. Formal certification of code-based cryptographic proofs. In *36th ACM SIGPLAN-SIGACT symposium on Principles of Programming Languages, POPL 2009*, pages 90–101, New York, 2009. ACM.

[4] G. Barthe, B. Grégoire, S. Heraud, and S. Zanella Béguelin. Computer-aided security proofs for the working cryptographer. In *Advances in Cryptology – CRYPTO 2011*, volume 6841 of *Lecture Notes in Computer Science*, pages 71–90, Heidelberg, 2011. Springer.

[5] A. Beimel, K. Nissim, and E. Omri. Distributed private data analysis: Simultaneously solving how and what. In *Advances in Cryptology – CRYPTO 2008*, volume 5157 of *Lecture Notes in Computer Science*, pages 451–468, Heidelberg, 2008. Springer.

[6] M. Bellare and P. Rogaway. The security of triple encryption and a framework for code-based game-playing proofs. In *Advances in Cryptology – EUROCRYPT 2006*, volume 4004 of *Lecture Notes in Computer Science*, pages 409–426, Heidelberg, 2006. Springer.

[7] N. Benton. Simple relational correctness proofs for static analyses and program transformations. In *31st ACM SIGPLAN-SIGACT symposium on Principles of Programming Languages, POPL 2004*, pages 14–25, New York, 2004. ACM.

[8] T.-H. H. Chan, E. Shi, and D. Song. Private and continual release of statistics. In *37th International colloquium on Automata, Languages and Programming, ICALP 2010*, volume 6199 of *Lecture Notes in Computer Science*, pages 405–417, Heidelberg, 2010. Springer.

[9] S. Chaudhuri, S. Gulwani, R. Lublinerman, and S. Navidpour. Proving programs robust. In *8th joint meeting of the European Software Engineering Conference and the ACM SIGSOFT International Symposium on Foundations of Software Engineering, ESEC/FSE '11*. ACM, 2011.

[10] D. Clark, S. Hunt, and P. Malacaria. A static analysis for quantifying information flow in a simple imperative language. *Journal of Computer Security*, 15(3):321–371, 2007.

[11] M. R. Clarkson and F. B. Schneider. Hyperproperties. *Journal of Computer Security*, 18(6):1157–1210, 2010.

[12] J. Desharnais, F. Laviolette, and M. Tracol. Approximate analysis of probabilistic processes: Logic, simulation and games. In *5th International Conference on Quantitative Evaluation of Systems, QEST 2008*, pages 264–273. IEEE Computer Society, 2008.

[13] C. Dwork. Differential privacy. In *33rd International Colloquium on Automata, Languages and Programming, ICALP 2006*, volume 4052 of *Lecture Notes in Computer Science*, pages 1–12, Heidelberg, 2006. Springer.

[14] C. Dwork. Differential privacy: A survey of results. In *Theory and Applications of Models of Computation*, volume 4978 of *Lecture Notes in Computer Science*, pages 1–19, Heidelberg, 2008. Springer.

[15] C. Dwork. A firm foundation for private data analysis. *Commun. ACM*, 54(1):86–95, January 2011.

[16] C. Dwork, K. Kenthapadi, F. McSherry, I. Mironov, and M. Naor. Our data, ourselves: Privacy via distributed noise generation. In *Advances in Cryptology – EUROCRYPT 2006*, volume 4004 of *Lecture Notes in Computer Science*, pages 486–503, Heidelberg, 2006. Springer.

[17] C. Dwork, F. McSherry, K. Nissim, and A. Smith. Calibrating noise to sensitivity in private data analysis. In *3rd Theory of Cryptography Conference, TCC 2006*, volume 3876 of *Lecture Notes in Computer Science*, pages 265–284, Heidelberg, 2006. Springer.

[18] A. Gupta, K. Ligett, F. McSherry, A. Roth, and K. Talwar. Differentially private combinatorial optimization. In *21st Annual ACM-SIAM Symposium on Discrete Algorithms, SODA 2010*, pages 1106–1125. SIAM, 2010.

[19] J. Hurd, A. McIver, and C. Morgan. Probabilistic guarded commands mechanized in HOL. *Theor. Comput. Sci.*, 346(1):96–112, 2005.

[20] B. Jonsson, W. Yi, and K. G. Larsen. Probabilistic extensions of process algebras. In J. Bergstra, A. Ponse, and S. Smolka, editors, *Handbook of Process Algebra*, pages 685–710. Elsevier, Amsterdam, 2001.

[21] S. P. Kasiviswanathan and A. Smith. A note on differential privacy: Defining resistance to arbitrary side information. Cryptology ePrint Archive, Report 2008/144, 2008.

[22] D. Kifer and A. Machanavajjhala. No free lunch in data privacy. In *2011 International conference on Management of Data, SIGMOD '11*, pages 193–204. ACM Press, 2011.

[23] F. McSherry and K. Talwar. Mechanism design via differential privacy. In *48th Annual IEEE Symposium on Foundations of Computer Science, FOCS 2007*, pages 94–103, Washington, 2007. IEEE Computer Society.

[24] F. D. McSherry. Privacy integrated queries: an extensible platform for privacy-preserving data analysis. In *35th SIGMOD international conference on Management of Data, SIGMOD 2009*, pages 19–30, New York, 2009. ACM.

[25] I. Mironov, O. Pandey, O. Reingold, and S. Vadhan. Computational differential privacy. In *Advances in Cryptology – CRYPTO 2009*, volume 5677 of *Lecture Notes in Computer Science*, pages 126–142, Heidelberg, 2009. Springer.

[26] A. D. Pierro, C. Hankin, and H. Wiklicky. Approximate non-interference. *Journal of Computer Security*, 12(1):37–82, 2004.

[27] L. Pitt. A simple probabilistic approximation algorithm for vertex cover. Technical Report TR-404, Yale University, 1985.

[28] N. Ramsey and A. Pfeffer. Stochastic lambda calculus and monads of probability distributions. In *29th ACM SIGPLAN-SIGACT symposium on Principles of Programming Languages, POPL 2002*, pages 154–165, New York, 2002. ACM.

[29] J. Reed and B. C. Pierce. Distance makes the types grow stronger: a calculus for differential privacy. In *15th ACM SIGPLAN international conference on Functional programming, ICFP 2010*, pages 157–168, New York, 2010. ACM.

[30] I. Roy, S. T. V. Setty, A. Kilzer, V. Shmatikov, and E. Witchel. Airavat: security and privacy for MapReduce. In *7th USENIX conference on Networked Systems Design and Implementation, NSDI 2010*, pages 297–312, Berkeley, 2010. USENIX Association.

[31] A. Sabelfeld and D. Sands. Probabilistic noninterference for multi-threaded programs. In *13th IEEE workshop on Computer Security Foundations, CSFW 2000*, pages 200–215, Los Alamitos, 2000. IEEE Computer Society.

[32] R. Segala and A. Turrini. Approximated computationally bounded simulation relations for probabilistic automata. In *20th IEEE Computer Security Foundations symposium, CSF 2007*, pages 140–156, 2007.

[33] T. Terauchi and A. Aiken. Secure information flow as a safety problem. In *12th International Symposium on Static Analysis, SAS 2005*, volume 3672 of *Lecture Notes in Computer Science*, pages 352–367, Heidelberg, 2005. Springer.

[34] The Coq development team. The Coq Proof Assistant Reference Manual Version 8.3. Online – `http://coq.inria.fr`, 2010.

[35] M. C. Tschantz, D. Kaynar, and A. Datta. Formal verification of differential privacy for interactive systems. *Electronic Notes in Theoretical Computer Science*, 276:61–79, 2011.

A. Asymmetric Logic

Asymmetric versions of apRHL can be obtained by re-defining α-distance as

$$\Delta_\alpha(a, b) \stackrel{\text{def}}{=} \max(b - \alpha a, 0)$$

and dropping in Definition 3 either of the inequalities

$$\Delta_\alpha(\pi_1\ \mu, \mu_1) \leq \delta$$
$$\Delta_\alpha(\pi_2\ \mu, \mu_2) \leq \delta$$

Dropping the second inequality yields a logic for which the validity of a judgment

$$c_1 \sim_{\alpha,\delta} c_2 : \Psi \Rightarrow \Phi$$

implies only that for m_1, m_2 s.t. $m_1 \Psi m_2$ and f_1, f_2 s.t. $f_1 \leq_\Phi f_2$,

$$[\![c_1]\!]\ m_1\ f_1 \leq \alpha([\![c_2]\!]\ m_2\ f_2) + \delta$$

Application to the Minimum Vertex Cover Problem An asymmetric version of the logic would allow to prove in an independent way that for any permutation $\vec{v}$, $\exp(\epsilon)$ is a bound for both, the ratio

$$\frac{\Pr\left[\text{VERTEXCOVER}(G_1, \epsilon) : \pi = \vec{v}\right]}{\Pr\left[\text{VERTEXCOVER}(G_2, \epsilon) : \pi = \vec{v}\right]} \tag{1}$$

and its reciprocal. Each ratio could be bounded by applying an asymmetric version of the rule for while loops shown in Figure 5, and each application would in turn require to independently bound for each iteration the ratios

$$\frac{\Pr[v\langle 2\rangle = x]}{\Pr[v\langle 1\rangle = x]} \quad \text{and} \quad \frac{\Pr[v\langle 1\rangle = x]}{\Pr[v\langle 2\rangle = x]}$$

This would allow to choose tighter values for the parameters α_1 and α_2 in each case. E.g., when bounding (1), one could take $\alpha_1(i) = \exp(2/(n-i)w_i)$ and $\alpha_2 = 1$, whereas when bounding its reciprocal one could take $\alpha_1(i) = 1$ and $\alpha_2 = \exp(\epsilon/4)$.

Access Permission Contracts for Scripting Languages

Phillip Heidegger
University of Freiburg, Germany
heidegger@informatik.uni-freiburg.de

Annette Bieniusa *
INRIA Paris-Rocquencourt and LIP6
Annette.Bieniusa@inria.fr

Peter Thiemann
University of Freiburg, Germany
thiemann@informatik.uni-freiburg.de

Abstract

The ideal software contract fully specifies the behavior of an operation. Often, in particular in the context of scripting languages, a full specification may be cumbersome to state and may not even be desired. In such cases, a partial specification, which describes selected aspects of the behavior, may be used to raise the confidence in an implementation of the operation to a reasonable level.

We propose a novel kind of contract for object-based languages that specifies the side effects of an operation with *access permissions*. An access permission contract uses sets of access paths to express read and write permissions for the properties of the objects accessible from the operation.

We specify a monitoring semantics for access permission contracts and implement this semantics in a contract system for JavaScript. We prove soundness and stability of violation under increasing aliasing for our semantics.

Applications of access permission contracts include enforcing modularity, test-driven development, program understanding, and regression testing. With respect to testing and understanding, we find that adding access permissions to contracts increases the effectiveness of error detection through contract monitoring by 6-13%.

Categories and Subject Descriptors D.2.4 [*SOFTWARE ENGINEERING*]: Software/Program Verification: Assertion Checkers, Programming by Contract; D.3.1 [*PROGRAMMING LANGUAGES*]: Formal Definitions and Theory: Semantics

General Terms Algorithms, Design, Experimentation, Languages, Reliability, Theory, Verification

Keywords scripting languages, contracts, JavaScript

1. Introduction

Design by contract is a methodology for software development based on specifications (contracts) of operations [35, 36]. The correctness of an implementation with respect to a contract may be statically guaranteed by program verification or it may be dynamically checked via contract monitoring. As the latter variant permits more expressive specifications and puts less demands on the theorem proving skills of the programmer, it is widely used in practice as evidenced by implementations of contract checking in various forms and for many languages [1, 14–17, 25, 27, 29, 45].

* Research was done while at University of Freiburg.

POPL'12, January 25–27, 2012, Philadelphia, PA, USA.

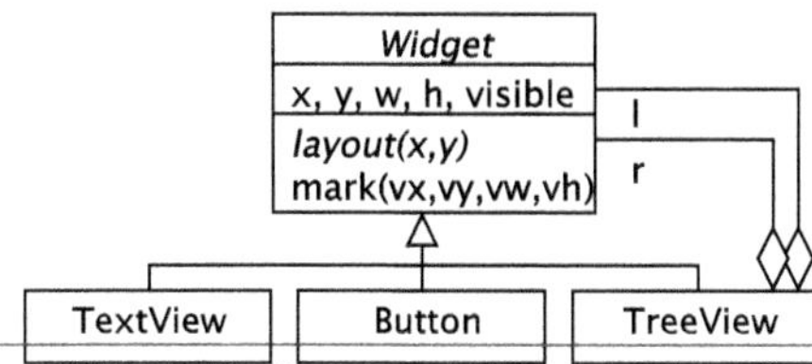

Figure 1. Example widget hierarchy.

Originally, contracts were meant to provide full specifications. However, contracts for partial specifications, which only fix certain aspects of an operation, also have their uses. For example, in a dynamically-typed language, like Scheme or JavaScript, a contract could have the form of an expressive type signature and impose restrictions similar to a type system [2, 25, 44]. Contract monitoring for such type contracts detects type errors at operation boundaries.

A type contract has one important drawback. It only imposes restrictions on the values passed to an operation and returned from it. In an imperative language like Scheme or JavaScript, many operations have an effect on the heap, which is not captured by a type contract. For those operations, a contract that also specifies the effect would be more appropriate.

In the past, this drawback has driven the evolution of type systems towards effect systems that enable the specification and inference of side effects (e.g., [19, 43]). In analogy, we propose to extend type contracts with a language-dependent notion of effects and to check them with an application-dependent notion of monitoring. In this paper, we develop a notion of effect suitable for scripting languages and for JavaScript in particular. The application scenarios that we have in mind are enforcing modularity, test-driven development, program understanding, and regression testing.

1.1 Effects for Scripting Languages

Like other scripting languages, JavaScript implements an object as a reference to a map from properties to values where some of the values may be objects again. Every read or write access to the resulting object graph can be described by a *base object*, a *path* (a sequence of property names), and a *classifier* indicating the operation on the last step of the path (read or write).

This observation has lead us to define effects by *access permissions* that specify a set of paths that an operation may read or write relative to some base object in scope. The base object may be `this`, an argument of the operation, or a global variable.

As an example, consider a JavaScript implementation of the widget class hierarchy described by the class diagram in Fig. 1. The `layout` operation computes the screen position of each widget. It accepts a pair of absolute starting coordinates and returns the width and height of the rendered widget. As a side effect, it stores the bounding box of each subwidget in its representation. A programmer working on the code of this operation might like to ascertain that the layout computation only ever changes the bounding box properties of a widget by attaching the following contract to the layout operation:

```
(int, int) → {w: int, h: int} with [this.*./x|y|w|h/]
```

This contract specifies an operation that accepts two integers, returns an object with two integer properties named w and h, and modifies at most the x, y, w, and h properties of objects reachable through this. Furthermore, the contract allows the operation to read *all* properties reachable through this: a write path has to match the entire access permission, whereas a read path is accepted if it matches a prefix of the permission. More precisely, this specifies the base object, "." separates the path components, * matches any sequence of property names, and /x|y|w|h/ is a regular expression that matches the names of the properties with write permission.

Here are some further conventions for reading access paths. Parameters can be specified as base objects for a path by name or using a positional notation $1, $2, ... The symbol ? is short for the regular expression /.*/ that matches any property name. A path ending in @ indicates a read-only path.

1.2 Application Scenarios

Regarding the application scenarios, contract monitoring for the layout contract is useful during the initial **test-driven development** of the code because any violation of the access permission triggers an exception as part of a test run. It is also useful for **program understanding**. A programmer who would like to confirm that the layout operation works in the outlined way would impose the contract and watch for failing test cases. The access permissions also indicate what operations are independent of one another. For example, an operation that marks those widgets which are visible in a given viewport might have a contract like this:

```
({vx: int, vy: int, vw: int, vh: int}) → any
    with [$1.?.@, this./l|r/*./x|y|w|h/.@, this./l|r/*.visible]
```

The path, $1.?.@, grants read access to any property of the first parameter, but no write permission; only the bounding box of a widget may be read; and only its visible property may be written. Only l and r properties may be traversed recursively along the last two paths. In **regression testing**, changes to the code that violate the contract are detected early in a run of a test suite, assuming sufficient coverage.

Last, but not least, **modularity**: JavaScript programs often rely on a number of libraries and freely include third-party code (mashups) that may change arbitrarily between different program runs. Programmers do not want this code to corrupt their global variables or to inflict arbitrary changes on their object structures. Wrapping a monitored contract around the third-party code confines these effects and guarantees the integrity of the program's state.

1.3 Monitoring of Effects

There are two approaches to defining a semantics of monitoring for an access permission. The *location-based semantics* attaches permissions to each object location. It traverses the object graph starting from the base object according to the access paths and registers a read or write permission (according to the path's classification) for each object property along the path. In contrast, the *path-based semantics* pairs each object reference with an access path and computes the permission at a read/write access based on the path through which the object has been reached.

In the absence of aliasing, the location-based semantics is equivalent to the path-based semantics. In general, however, the semantics differ, which indicates that they serve different purposes. The following example highlights the differences. It is further elaborated in Sec. 2.1.

Suppose an object is reachable from the base object via two different paths, where one path grants write permission for property p, but a second path only grants read permission to p. With the path-based semantics, the path used to access the object determines the permission, but which permission should be granted by the location-based semantics? If p gets write permission, then an execution that arrives at the object via the read path can write. If p only gets read permission, then an execution that arrives at the object via the write path cannot write. To prevent this counterintuitive behavior in the second scenario, the location-based semantics must assign the least restrictive permission of **all paths** reaching p. A similar dilemma may arise between "no permission" and "permission to read."

Both location- and path-based semantics are non-trivial to implement efficiently. With the location-based semantics, the installation of a contract requires that the locations of all objects reachable through the contract's access paths must be marked with access rights. This marking cannot be delayed because aliasing may provide a shortcut into a data structure on which the contract grants read or write permission. In the worst case, the time needed to install a contract is bounded only by the size of the entire object graph. A read or write operation can be implemented in almost constant time.

In contrast, the path-based semantics requires time linear in the number of installed contracts for each read and write operation, whereas the installation of a contract takes constant time. Read operations are a bit tricky because they have to juggle access paths in the right way (see Sec. 3.2).

This paper explores the path-based semantics because it is the semantics of choice for our intended application scenarios as explained in Sec. 2. The location-based semantics most likely has a role to play in monitoring access control in a security scenario, but it is based on a different set of assumptions and a separate investigation is required to explore it [24].

Contributions

1. Design of a contract framework with access permissions.
2. Specification of a path-based formal semantics of access permissions and their dynamic enforcement.
3. Formal proof that the semantics guarantees stability of access violations under addition of aliasing, subject to mild conditions.
4. Prototype implementation of access permissions with monitoring in a contract and testing framework for JavaScript based on program transformation.
5. Assessment of the effectiveness of access permission contracts by observing the impact of random code modifications on hand-annotated case studies.
6. Practical evaluation of the approach on different code bases.

A technical report [24] extends this paper by an appendix with further examples, proofs of all theorems, a definition of the location-based semantics, a sketch of its application to the security scenario, and additional information regarding the case studies.

Outline

In Sec.2, we explain the design choices underlying our contract framework with examples and explore some of the alternatives. Section 3 presents a formal framework for reasoning about access permissions. It presents an operational semantics of contract monitoring and formally defines and proves two properties that are consequences of the design choices. Section 4 explains the basic approach taken by the implementation. The evaluation in Sec. 5 explores the effectiveness of access permission for detecting programming errors using mutation testing.

2. Design Choices

For each programmer, an access permission has an intuitive meaning that coincides with the intuition of other programmers in the vast majority of cases. These intuitions differ when aliasing comes into play, because each programmer has different application scenarios in mind, each with its own requirements to the semantics.

As already indicated in the introduction, our intention is to employ access permissions as partial specifications of a program's effect. We regard it as a dynamic counterpart to previous work on static effect systems [19, 22]. This intention motivates the four major design choices we have taken for the monitoring semantics for access permissions.

Path-Dependent Access An access permission grants the right to read or modify a property of an object depending on the path through which the object has been reached.

Dynamic Extent An access permission for a function is in force for the duration of a function activation.

Pre-State Snapshot An access permission only applies to objects and paths in the heap at the time when the contract is installed.

Sticky Update A property assignment keeps the access paths of the value on its right-hand side.

The rest of this section explains the choices in depth, gives a critical overview of the alternatives, and thus provides a rationale for the design of our framework.

2.1 Path-Dependent Access

> An access permission grants the right to read or modify a property of an object depending on the path through which the object has been reached.

This choice has two consequences.

Reference Attachment Permissions are attached to individual references, not to heap locations. That is, if two variables or properties hold a reference to the same object, then accesses through each variable may have different access rights.

Stability of Violation An access violation is preserved under increased aliasing. See Sec. 3.5 for a formal statement.

Section 1.3 already argues in favor of the path-based semantics. Here, we give a concrete example where the location-based semantics behaves different from a static analysis.

```
1 /*c (obj, obj) → any with [x.b,y.a] */
2 function h(x, y) {
3   y.a = 1;
4   y.b = 2; // violation?
5 }
6 function h1() {
7   var o = { a: −1, b: −2 };
8   h(o, o);
9 }
```

Any modular attempt to verify h's access permissions statically (for example, using the dynamic frame rule of Smans and coworkers[41]) cannot assume that x=y. Without this assumption the analysis would fail because the contract disallows the access to y.b in line 4.

The *path-based semantics* is consistent with such an analysis: Any invocation of h —in particular the call from h1— triggers a contract violation regardless of the aliasing among the arguments. We call this behavior **stability of violation**.

With the *location-based semantics*, h1 would *not* trigger a violation. As x and y are aliased, their underlying location would obtain permission to write properties a and b and the two assignments would go through without violation. Furthermore, the location-based semantics breaks stability of violation. Calling h *without aliasing* as in h2 detects a violation.

```
function h2() {
  h({ a: −1, b: −2 }, { a: −1, b: −2 });
}
```

In a security setting, the location-based semantics appears better suited because a permission like window./^((?!location$).)/ seems to rule out any access to the location property of the window object, even if this object has been reached via some alias. However, the following example demonstrates that this appearance is deceptive:

```
/*c (obj, any) → any with [x.?,window./^((?!location$).)/] */
function k(x, y) {
  x.location = y; // violation?
}
function k1() {
  k(window, "http://www.evil.com/");
}
```

As x and window are aliases of one another, the permission x.? grants write permission for all properties of window and the permission window./^((?!location$).)/ grants write permission for all properties of window, except location. Hence, the location-based semantics permits writing to window.location in the body of k.

For the record, the path-based semantics does not trigger a violation, either: for all x, any property of x may be read and written; for window, all properties except location may be read and written. The body of k does not exceed these permissions, so no violation can happen.

2.2 Dynamic Extent

> An access permission for a function is in force for the duration of a function activation.

If a permission is attached to a function, then each invocation of the function installs an instance of the permission and this same instance is withdrawn at the matching function return.

As a consequence, permissions get refined in a chain of function calls. Because an access permission expresses the promise that the contracted function does not exceed its permissions, each additional function call can only restrict the accessible properties further. For example, consider these functions:

```
20 /*c (obj) → any with [x.a] */
21 function d1(x) {
22   return x.a; // violation if called from d2
23 }
24 /*c (obj) → any with [] */
25 function d2(x) {
26   return d1(x);
27 }
```

The contract of function d2 disallows *any* access to its argument. Invoking d2 with any object triggers a violation of d2's contract when trying to execute line 22, although this line is in d1, which has a more permissive contract.

As another consequence, a closure returned from a function is not restricted by the access permission of the function. For example, consider the permission of f in this code fragment:

```
/*c (obj) → (() → any) with [x.b] */
function f(x) {
  return function() { return x.a + " " + x.b; };
}
function f1() {
  var r = f({ a: "secret", b: "revealed" });
  r();
}
```

Running the function f1, which is unrestricted (because there is no contract associated with f1), returns "secret revealed". It does not violate the contract of f because the access to x.a happens outside the dynamic extent of the call to f in line 33.

The choice for dynamic extent is inspired by the distinction between direct and latent effects in static effect systems. Evaluation of the function expression in line 30 does not cause an access to x.a or x.b. For this reason, a static effect system categorizes this effect as a *latent effect* and places it on top of the function arrow in its type. When the function is applied, the effect is exercised. However, at that point, there is no contract in force that would restrict the effect.

On the other hand, the following variant of the program fragment leads to a violation.

```
36 function g(x) {
37   return function() { return x.a + x.b; };
38 }
39 /*c (obj) → any with [x.b] */
40 function g1(x) {
41   var r = g(x);
42   r(); // violation
43 }
```

As the invocation of r() happens in the extent of the invocation of g1, its permission **with** [x.b] is in force and the violation by accessing x.a is detected. In contrast, the function g by itself does not impose any restriction on accesses to x, so that a direct call to g does not lead to a violation.

An alternative design would consider access permissions as contagious (having static extent determined by lexical scope) and have closures capture the permissions in force at their definition site. This design seems more appropriate in a security setting and it would report violations for the examples involving functions f and g.

2.3 Pre-State Snapshot

> An access permission only applies to objects and paths in the heap at the time when the contract is installed.

One immediate implication of this choice is that the program can access and modify newly allocated objects without restriction. As these objects are not present in the heap snapshot at installation time (the pre-state), the contract does not restrict access to them. This behavior is analogous to the treatment of the assignable clause and newly allocated objects in JML [32, 38].

We see two alternatives to this design but consider neither viable: to choose a different reference heap or to choose a different interpretation of access paths.

The only other reference heap for a contract would be the post-state of a function, that is, the heap at the time the contract is withdrawn. However, the final heap is not a sensible choice because the programmer expects the paths in a contract to refer to the situation at the time a function is invoked. The final heap may exhibit very different paths.

Another interpretation of access paths might consider the permissions as symbolic paths that may be traversed regardless of the changes in the underlying heap. This interpretation violates the programmer's intuition and it is inconsistent with static verification as the following example shows.

```
44 /*c (obj, obj) → any with [x.a, y.a, y.a.b] */
45 function b(x, y) {
46   y.a = x.a;
47   y.a.b = 42; // allowed?
48 }
```

Reading just the contract, a programmer expects that x.a.b does not change. However, the symbolic interpretation of paths would not flag the assignment in line 47, which changes x.a.b, counter to the expectation of the programmer. In contrast, a static verification of access permissions [41] keeps track that y.a is really x.a in line 47 and rejects the function. The pre-state snapshot interpretation is consistent to static verification and reports a violation.

2.4 Sticky Update

> A property assignment keeps the access paths of the value on its right-hand side.

A property assignment of the form x.p = y, where y refers to an object, creates a new path through x.p to the object graph reachable from y. Sticky update means that the access information for y is kept along with the reference so that a subsequent access through x.p is considered an access through y. This choice is compliant with the Hoare-calculus rule for assignment:

$$\{P[\mathsf{y}/\mathsf{x.p}]\}\ \mathsf{x.p} = \mathsf{y}\ \{P\}$$

For suppose that $P[\mathsf{y}/\mathsf{x.p}]$ is the predicate "location ℓ' is reachable from location ℓ via some path γ and y= ℓ'". Then a suitable candidate for P is "location ℓ' is reachable from location ℓ via some path γ and x.p= y = ℓ'".

Here is an example.

```
49 /*c (obj) → any with [x.a,x.b.a] */
50 function l(x) {
51   x.a = x.b;
52   x.a.a = 42;
53 }
54 function l1() {
55   var x = { a: {}, b: {}};
56   l(x);
57 }
```

In this code fragment, line 51 is clearly permitted as x.a may be assigned to and x.b may be read. The following read access to x.a in line 52 returns the reference to the object that was accessible through x.b when the permission was installed. As this object is the one that was reachable via x.b in the pre-state, the access permission for x.b counts so that the assignment to x.a.a is sanctioned by the path x.b.a. Thus, function l1() runs without violation!

Things look different in a slightly modified version of the example that creates the alias **before** installing the permission.

```
58 /*c (obj) → any with [x.a,x.b.a] */
59 function m(x) {
60   var y = x.a;
61   y.a = 42; // violation
62 }
63 function m1() {
64   var x = { a: {}, b: {}};
65   x.a = x.b;
66   m(x);
67 }
```

In this case, running m1() yields a violation. While the first read access to x.a in line 60 is sanctioned by x.a, the write access to property a of this object is not. Indeed, this behavior is consistent with invoking m on an object without any aliasing, which reports a violation under any semantics.[1]

3. Formalization

A formal semantics of monitoring for access permissions is needed as the basis of an implementation that adheres to the design choices. For that reason, we define the calculus λ_{obj}^{AP} as a call-by-value lambda calculus extended with objects and access permissions. For

[1] The location-based semantics runs both examples, l1 and m1, without triggering a violation.

variable	x	$\in$	*Var*
property name	p	$\in$	*Prop*
access path	π	$\in$	$Path = Prop^*$
path language	L	$\in$	$PLang = \wp(Path)$
expression	e	$\in$	$Expr$
		$::=$	$x \mid \lambda x.e \mid e(e)$
		$\mid$	$\texttt{new} \mid e.p \mid e.p := e$
		$\mid$	$\texttt{permit}\, x : L_r, L_w\, \texttt{in}\, e$

Figure 2. Syntax.

this calculus, we specify the semantics, including monitoring, and prove that it adheres to the properties stated in Sec. 2, in particular, pre-state snapshot and stability of violation.

Let's fix some notation before we start. Given sets A and B, we write $\wp(A)$ for the power set of A, $A + B$ for the disjoint union of A and B, and $A \times B$ for their Cartesian product. $A \rightharpoonup B$ denotes the set of finite (partial) functions from A to B with $\emptyset$ standing for the empty mapping and if $f \in A \rightharpoonup B$, then $dom(f) \subseteq A$ denotes the domain of f and $f{\downarrow_{A'}}$ denotes the restriction of f to $A' \subseteq A$. The updated function $f' = f[a \mapsto b]$ is defined by $f'(a) = b$ and $f'(a') = f(a')$, for all $a' \neq a$. We also write $[a \mapsto b] = \emptyset[a \mapsto b]$ for the singleton map with domain $\{a\}$. If we write $f(a)$ as part of a premise, this use implies the additional premise $a \in dom(f)$.

3.1 Syntax

Figure 2 specifies the syntax of λ^{AP}_{obj}. The calculus extends a call-by-value lambda calculus with object construction (`new` creates a fresh object devoid of properties), reading of an object's property, and writing/defining an object's property. The syntax is close to that of existing JavaScript core languages [23, 26].

The novel construct of the calculus is the access permission expression $\texttt{permit}\, x : L_r, L_w\, \texttt{in}\, e$ that restricts accesses through variable x during evaluation of e governed by the two languages L_r and L_w. Both languages specify a set of access paths (sequences of properties) starting from the object bound to x (which must be in scope). Read accesses to descendants of x are limited to paths in L_r whereas write accesses are limited to paths in L_w. Evaluation of e stops if it tries to perform any access that is not permitted.

The read language L_r should be prefix closed, because it does not make sense to permit reading of $x.a.b$ without permitting to read $x.a$, too. Similarly, writing to $x.a.b$ is not possible without reading $x.a$, first. So, each path in the write language L_w should extend a path in the read language by one property, that is, $L_w \subseteq \{\pi.p \mid \pi \in L_r, p \in Prop\}$.

Our implementation restricts L_r and L_w to regular languages so that the word problem is decidable for them. Furthermore, contracts with access permissions can only be attached to functions and a contract can state multiple `permit`s in one go.

3.2 Semantics

Figure 3 defines the semantic domains and the inference rules for a big-step evaluation judgment of the form

$$\rho, \mathcal{R}, \mathcal{W} \vdash H; u; e \hookrightarrow H'; u'; v$$

This judgment declares that given a variable environment ρ and indexed collections $\mathcal{R}$ and $\mathcal{W}$ of read and write permissions, the expression e transforms the initial heap H to the final heap H' and returns value v. Furthermore, it threads a time stamp $u, u' \in Stamp$ that is incremented at each property write operation and at each `permit` expression. The permission collections $\mathcal{R}$ and $\mathcal{W}$ are indexed by the time stamps of the heaps for which the permissions were granted. The time stamp of a permission uniquely identifies different executions of permit expressions and determines their relative order with respect to heap modifications.

Semantic domains

$$\begin{array}{rcl}
\ell \in Loc & & \text{infinite set of locations} \\
u \in Stamp & = & Integer \\
H \in Heap & = & Loc \rightharpoonup Obj \\
Obj & = & Prop \rightharpoonup (Stamp \times Val) \\
\mathcal{P}, \mathcal{R}, \mathcal{W} \in & & Stamp \rightharpoonup PLang \\
\mathcal{M}, \mathcal{N} \in PMap & = & Stamp \rightharpoonup Path \\
(\ell, \mathcal{M}) \in Ref & = & Loc \times PMap \\
v \in Val & = & Ref + (Env \times Expr) \\
\rho \in Env & = & Var \rightharpoonup Val
\end{array}$$

Checking permissions

CHECK PERMISSION
$$\frac{\forall u \in \mathrm{dom}(\mathcal{P}) \cap \mathrm{dom}(\mathcal{M}) : \mathcal{M}(u) \in \mathcal{P}(u)}{\mathcal{P} \vdash_{\text{chk}} \mathcal{M}}$$

Evaluation rules

VAR
$$\rho, \mathcal{R}, \mathcal{W} \vdash H; u; x \hookrightarrow H; u; \rho(x)$$

LAM
$$\rho, \mathcal{R}, \mathcal{W} \vdash H; u; \lambda x.e \hookrightarrow H; u; (\rho{\downarrow_{FV(\lambda x.e)}}, \lambda x.e)$$

APP
$$\frac{\begin{array}{c}\rho, \mathcal{R}, \mathcal{W} \vdash H; u; e_0 \hookrightarrow H'; u'; (\rho', \lambda x.e) \\ \rho, \mathcal{R}, \mathcal{W} \vdash H'; u'; e_1 \hookrightarrow H''; u''; v_1 \\ \rho'[x \mapsto v_1], \mathcal{R}, \mathcal{W} \vdash H''; u''; e \hookrightarrow H'''; u'''; v\end{array}}{\rho, \mathcal{R}, \mathcal{W} \vdash H; u; e_0(e_1) \hookrightarrow H'''; u'''; v}$$

NEW
$$\frac{\ell \notin dom(H)}{\rho, \mathcal{R}, \mathcal{W} \vdash H; u; \texttt{new} \hookrightarrow H[\ell \mapsto \emptyset]; u; (\ell, \emptyset)}$$

PUT
$$\frac{\begin{array}{c}\rho, \mathcal{R}, \mathcal{W} \vdash H; u; e_1 \hookrightarrow H'; u'; (\ell, \mathcal{M}) \\ \rho, \mathcal{R}, \mathcal{W} \vdash H'; u'; e_2 \hookrightarrow H''; u''; v \\ \mathcal{W} \vdash_{\text{chk}} \mathcal{M}.p \qquad H''' = H''[\ell \mapsto H''(\ell)[p \mapsto (u'', v)]]\end{array}}{\rho, \mathcal{R}, \mathcal{W} \vdash H; u; e_1.p := e_2 \hookrightarrow H'''; u'' + 1; v}$$

GET
$$\frac{\rho, \mathcal{R}, \mathcal{W} \vdash H; u; e \hookrightarrow H'; u'; (\ell, \mathcal{M}) \qquad \mathcal{R} \vdash_{\text{chk}} \mathcal{M}.p}{\rho, \mathcal{R}, \mathcal{W} \vdash H; u; e.p \hookrightarrow H'; u'; \mathcal{M}.p \circledcirc H'(\ell)(p)}$$

PERMIT
$$\frac{\begin{array}{c}\rho', \mathcal{R}[u \mapsto L_r], \mathcal{W}[u \mapsto L_w] \vdash H; u+1; e \hookrightarrow H'; u'; v \\ \rho' = \rho[x \mapsto \rho(x) \lhd [u \mapsto \varepsilon]]\end{array}}{\rho, \mathcal{R}, \mathcal{W} \vdash H; u; \texttt{permit}\, x : L_r, L_w\, \texttt{in}\, e \hookrightarrow H'; u'; v}$$

Figure 3. Semantics.

A value $v \in Val$ is either a reference or a closure consisting of an environment and a lambda expression. The representation of a reference is a pair of a heap address ℓ and a collection $\mathcal{M}$ of access paths, indexed by time stamps. The collection $\mathcal{M}$ records all permitted access paths that have been traversed during evaluation so far to obtain this reference value. The indexing is again used for marking modifications with time stamps. This representation is dictated by the design choice of path dependency (see Sec. 2.1).

A heap maps a location to an object and an object maps a property name to a pair of a time stamp and a value. The time stamp indicates the time of the write operation that last assigned the property. It is required to implement the "sticky update" from Sec. 2.4.

The evaluation rules VAR, LAM, and APP for variable, lambda abstraction, and function application expressions are standard. They

$$\mathcal{M}' \circledcirc (u, v) := \begin{cases} (\ell', \mathcal{M}' \circledcirc_u \mathcal{N}) & \text{if } v = (\ell', \mathcal{N}) \\ v & \text{if } v \notin \mathit{Ref} \end{cases}$$

$$(\mathcal{M} \circledcirc_u \mathcal{N})(u') := \begin{cases} \mathcal{N}(u') & \text{if } u' \in \mathit{dom}(\mathcal{N}) \\ \mathcal{M}(u') & \text{if } u' \in \mathit{dom}(\mathcal{M}) \backslash \mathit{dom}(\mathcal{N}) \land u < u' \\ \text{undefined} & \text{if } u' \in \mathit{dom}(\mathcal{M}) \backslash \mathit{dom}(\mathcal{N}) \land u \geq u' \\ \text{undefined} & \text{if } u' \notin \mathit{dom}(\mathcal{M}) \cup \mathit{dom}(\mathcal{N}) \end{cases}$$

$$(\mathcal{M}.p)(u) := \begin{cases} \mathcal{M}(u).p & \text{if } u \in \mathit{dom}(\mathcal{M}) \\ \text{undefined} & \text{if } u \notin \mathit{dom}(\mathcal{M}) \end{cases}$$

$$v \lhd \mathcal{M} := \begin{cases} (\ell, \mathcal{N} \lhd \mathcal{M}) & \text{if } v = (\ell, \mathcal{N}) \\ v & \text{if } v \notin \mathit{Ref} \end{cases}$$

$$(\mathcal{N} \lhd \mathcal{M})(u) := \begin{cases} \mathcal{M}(u) & \text{if } u \in \mathit{dom}(\mathcal{M}) \\ \mathcal{N}(u) & \text{if } u \notin \mathit{dom}(\mathcal{M}) \end{cases}$$

Figure 4. Auxiliary definitions.

thread the time stamp and propagate the permissions $\mathcal{R}$ and $\mathcal{W}$ unchanged to their sub-evaluations, if any.

The evaluation rule NEW creates a new object in the heap. The new object has no properties and its collection of access paths is empty. The latter indicates that the newly created object is completely unrestricted (following Sec. 2.3). Any of its properties may be read or written. The time stamp does not change when allocating a new object because no object in the current heap is modified.

The PUT rule specifies the operation that writes and (if necessary) defines a property. It first computes the location ℓ and the collection $\mathcal{M}$ of access paths of the object and then checks the write permission to the object with the premise $\mathcal{W} \vdash_{\text{chk}} \mathcal{M}.p$. It overwrites the object's property with the new value and assigns it a new, incremented time stamp to implement the "sticky update" (Sec. 2.4). Hence, the time stamp of a property is always the time of its last update.

The rule GET defines the read operation of object properties. It relies on some auxiliary operations defined in Figure 4. It first expects e to evaluate to a reference $(\ell, \mathcal{M})$, which denotes the base object for the property read. In this reference, ℓ is the heap address of the object and $\mathcal{M}$ contains a collection of access paths for the object corresponding to heap traversals reaching this object, one path for each active access permission. The other premise $\mathcal{R} \vdash_{\text{chk}} \mathcal{M}.p$ checks the read permission for these paths extended with property p. This check is specified by rule CHECK PERMISSION which requires that, for each active access permission with time stamp u, the current access path for u is an element of the set of permitted access paths for u, i.e., $\mathcal{P}(u)$.

If the read operation is permitted, then there are two possibilities. If the property contains a closure, then this closure is the result of $e.p$. However, if the property contains an object reference, say $(\ell', \mathcal{N})$, then this read operation has discovered that the paths in $\mathcal{M}.p$ are also access paths for object ℓ'. The reference value returned from the read operation must somehow merge the different ways to reach ℓ': via $\mathcal{N}$ and via $\mathcal{M}.p$. Computing the desired collection of access paths depends on the last time u when the property $\ell.p$ was updated. This complication is required to adhere to the pre-state snapshot property (Sec. 2.3).

The operator $\circledcirc$ in Fig. 4 implements the required merger operation. Its right-hand argument comprises the contents of an object's property: (u, v) where u is the time stamp of the last update and v the stored value. Its left-hand argument is the collection $\mathcal{M}' = \mathcal{M}.p$ of newly discovered paths to the property. If v is not a reference, then $\circledcirc$ just returns v as already discussed. Otherwise, $v = (\ell', \mathcal{N})$ in which case it returns the location ℓ' paired with the collection of paths computed by the operator $\circledcirc_u$ applied to the new paths $\mathcal{M}'$ and the old paths $\mathcal{N}$.

In an application $\mathcal{M} \circledcirc_u \mathcal{N}$, the first argument $\mathcal{M}$ contains the access paths that were detected when checking the read access. The second argument $\mathcal{N}$ contains the access paths as they are stored in the heap at location ℓ'. The subscript u is the time stamp of the last write to the property. The definition in Figure 4 distinguishes three cases depending on when the property has been written last and what access paths were given to the written value. Let u' be the time stamp of an execution of a permit expression.

1. The object's property value already has an access path for index u' (in $\mathcal{N}$). Thus, the property has been overwritten after the installation of u'. In this case, a potential new access path for u' in $\mathcal{M}$ is ignored. Instead, the existing access path is returned according to the pre-state snapshot property (Sec. 2.3) as it reflects an access path at the time when the permission attached to u' has been installed.
2. The object's property value has no access path for index u' (in $\mathcal{N}$) and it had been written *before* the permission with index u' has been installed as can be seen from $u < u'$. In this case, we attach the new u'-path to the value. This path is realizable in the pre-state snapshot at time u' because the property has been written at $u < u'$, that is, before u'.
3. There is no access path for index u' (in $\mathcal{N}$) and the property has been written *after* the contract with index u' has been installed (viz. $u \geq u'$). In this case, no u'-path is attached because this property was not linked to the data structure in the pre-state snapshot at time u'.

The examples in Section 3.3 illustrate these three cases.

The rule PERMIT installs an access permission contract. Each such permission is bound to the time stamp u of the heap in which the permission is installed. It increments the time stamp to avoid clashes with the next permission. Then, evaluation proceeds with the body of the permit-expression, but with an updated variable binding for x, which records the time stamp u for the heap reachable from the object bound to x (if any) by attaching $[u \mapsto \varepsilon]$ to it, and updated read and write permissions, which record the stated permission set L_r and L_w for the object network reachable from x.

An access permission has dynamic extent (Sec. 2.2) because the access permissions are propagated with the flow of execution and the rule CHECK PERMISSION only considers the entry points in the domain of the current access permission $\mathcal{P}$. In particular, access permission contracts are not captured by closures created while they are in force: Closure creation (rule LAM) ignores the access permissions and function application (rule APP) continues to use the current permissions with the body of the invoked function. Hence, after evaluation of the body of an access permission is complete, the information associated with its index u could be garbage collected both from the value and from the heap.

3.3 Examples

The code fragments in Fig. 5 illustrate the different cases of the $\circledcirc_u$ operator. The fragments (a) and (b) correspond to the examples l1 and m1 in Sec. 2.4. They differ only in the placement of the permit expression. The code fragment (a) installs the permission *before* creating an alias with the assignment `x.a = x.b` whereas version (b) installs the permission afterwards. In both cases, let the permit expression be associated with time stamp u'.

In fragment (a), the expression `x.b` in line 6 returns the location ℓ_b paired with the map $[u' \mapsto b]$ (case 2 of $\circledcirc_u$: $u < u'$ because it was generated by the preceding assignment `x.b = new`). This value

```
1 let x = new in
2   x.a = new;
3   x.b = new;
4   permit x :
5     {a,b,b.a},{a,b.a} in
6     x.a = x.b;
7     x.a.a = 42
```

(a) Valid access

```
1 let x = new in
2   x.a = new;
3   x.b = new;
4   x.a = x.b;
5   permit x :
6     {a,b,b.a},{a,b.a} in
7     x.a.a = 42
```

(b) Invalid access

```
1 let x = new in
2 let y = new in
3   x.a = new;
4   permit y : {a}, {a} in
5   permit x : {a}, {a} in
6     x.a = y;
7     x.a.a = 42
```

(c) Nested permissions

Figure 5. Exercising the definition of $\olessthan$.

PERMIT'

$$\frac{\begin{array}{c}\rho', \mathcal{R}[u \mapsto L_r], \mathcal{W}[u \mapsto L_w], \mathcal{F}' \vdash' H; u+1; e \hookrightarrow H'; u'; v \\ \rho' = \rho[x \mapsto \rho(x) \lhd [u \mapsto \varepsilon]] \\ \mathcal{F}' = \text{ if } \rho(x) = (\ell, \mathcal{M}) \text{ then } \mathcal{F}[u \mapsto (\ell, H)] \text{ else } \mathcal{F}\end{array}}{\rho, \mathcal{R}, \mathcal{W}, \mathcal{F} \vdash' H; u; \mathtt{permit}\, x : L_r, L_w \,\mathtt{in}\, e \hookrightarrow H'; u'; v}$$

Figure 6. Gathering foretime information.

is written to x.a. The following access to x.a returns $(\ell_b, [u' \mapsto b])$ according to case 1 of $\olessthan_u$ which governs that the paths stored in the object take precedence over the actual path taken. For the final write access, the extended access map $[u' \mapsto b.a]$ is checked against the set of write permissions and succeeds.

In fragment (b), x.a = x.b is executed before the permit expression. Hence, x.a contains $(\ell_b, \emptyset)$ and the GET rule makes it return $(\ell_b, [u' \mapsto a])$ according to case 2 of $\olessthan_u$. For the write operation, the extended access map $[u' \mapsto a.a]$ is checked against the set of write permissions and fails.

The code in Figure 5(c) exercises case 3 of the definition of $\olessthan_u$. After establishing the two permissions, the environment ρ is: $[x \mapsto (\ell_x, [u_3 \mapsto \varepsilon]), y \mapsto (\ell_y, [u_2 \mapsto \varepsilon])]$ where the u_i are sorted according to their indexes i. After the assignment x.a = y (with time stamp u_4) the object in location ℓ_x is: $\{a : (u_4, (\ell_y, [u_2 \mapsto \varepsilon]))\}$. In line 7, x.a evaluates to

$$\begin{array}{rl} & [u_3 \mapsto a] \olessthan (u_4, (\ell_y, [u_2 \mapsto \varepsilon])) \\ = & (\ell_y, [u_3 \mapsto a] \olessthan_{u_4} [u_2 \mapsto \varepsilon]) \\ = & (\ell_y, [u_2 \mapsto \varepsilon]) \end{array}$$

Observe that case 3 of $\olessthan_u$ applies because $u_4 \geq u_3$. In consequence, u_3 vanishes from the domain of the map because the object that was reachable via x.a before line 6 has become garbage. With this reasoning the update of x.a.a is permitted because it is equivalent to y.a and realizable in the heap after line 5.

3.4 Pre-state Snapshot

Our first technical result is a soundness results that underlines that our semantics adheres to the pre-state snapshot property (Sec. 2.3). It ensures that any value produced during evaluation contains correct path information with respect to all relevant pre-states in the following sense. Consider a reference value of the form $v = (\ell, \mathcal{M})$ where $\mathcal{M}$ is a map from time stamps to access paths. For each time stamp $u \in \mathit{dom}(\mathcal{M})$ there is an access permission installed at time u for heap H_u with base object ℓ_u that affects the value v. The information contained in $\mathcal{M}$ is correct with respect to u if there is a path from the base object ℓ_u to ℓ along the properties of $\mathcal{M}(u)$ in the pre-state heap H_u.

To formally define this notion, suppose the information about the pre-states and the base objects of all contract installations is gathered in a time-stamp indexed *foretime map* $\mathcal{F} : \mathit{Stamp} \rightharpoonup (\mathit{Loc} \times \mathit{Heap})$. It maps the time stamp u of the installation of an access permission to a pair (ℓ_u, H_u), where ℓ_u is the location of the base object and H_u is the heap snapshot at that time.

Definition 3.1 *Let $\mathcal{F}$ be a foretime map.*
A value v is $\mathcal{F}$ path consistent *if*

- *$v = (\rho, \lambda x.e)$ and ρ is $\mathcal{F}$ path consistent or*
- *$v = (\ell, \mathcal{M})$ and, for all $u \in \mathit{dom}(\mathcal{M})$, if $\mathcal{F}(u) = (\ell_u, H_u)$, then there is a path from ℓ_u to ℓ along $\mathcal{M}(u)$ in H_u.*

An environment ρ is $\mathcal{F}$ path consistent *if, for all $x \in \mathit{dom}(\rho)$, $\rho(x)$ is $\mathcal{F}$ path consistent.*

A heap H is $\mathcal{F}$ path consistent if all values stored in all object properties are $\mathcal{F}$ path consistent. That is, for all $\ell \in \mathit{dom}(H)$ and for all $p \in \mathit{dom}(H(\ell))$, if $H(\ell)(p) = (u, v)$, then v is $\mathcal{F}$ path consistent.

To gather the foretime map, a suitably extended evaluation judgment $\rho, \mathcal{R}, \mathcal{W}, \mathcal{F} \vdash' H; u; e \hookrightarrow H'; u'; v$ is required. It records the base object and the heap snapshot at each successful contract installation in the foretime map $\mathcal{F}$. Fig. 6 contains the correspondingly modified PERMIT' rule. The remaining rules for the extended judgment extend the ones for the original judgment in Fig. 3 by passing the foretime map in exactly the same way as $\mathcal{R}$ and $\mathcal{W}$.

Showing adherence to the pre-state snapshot property amounts to proving that an evaluation that starts on a path consistent heap and environment produces a path consistent heap and value.

Theorem 3.1 *Suppose that $\rho, \mathcal{R}, \mathcal{W}, \mathcal{F} \vdash' H; u; e \hookrightarrow H'; u'; v$.*
If ρ and H are $\mathcal{F}$ path consistent, then so are H' and v.

There is also an accompanying completeness result that guarantees that the $\mathcal{M}$ component of a reference value is non-empty if it has been accessed via a pre-state path [24].

3.5 Stability of Violation

Stability of violation is a property linked to the reference attachment property (Sec. 2.1). It states that a violation of an access permission is preserved (in a precisely defined sense) when performing the same computation on a heap with more aliasing.

Let's first fix what we mean with "more aliasing." If H_1 and H_2 are heaps, then H_2 has more aliasing if it identifies locations that are distinct in H_1 and merges the contents of the objects in these locations. That is, if o' and o'' are distinct objects in H_1 which are merged to object o in H_2, then o has all properties from o' and o''. Properties present in o' and o'' must have suitably related values that map into the same value in H_2. We call H_1 a *refinement* of H_2 because it makes more distinctions between objects.

Definition 3.2 *A heap H_1 is a γ-*refinement *of heap H_2, written as $H_1 \succcurlyeq_\gamma H_2$, if $\gamma : \mathit{dom}(H_1) \to \mathit{dom}(H_2)$ is a surjective mapping between heap locations and $\forall \ell_1 \in \mathit{dom}(H_1)$, $o_1 = H_1(\ell_1)$, $o_2 = H_2(\gamma(\ell_1))$:*

RH1 *$\mathit{dom}(o_1) \subseteq \mathit{dom}(o_2)$ (objects in the refined heap have fewer properties) and*

RH2 *$(\forall p \in \mathit{dom}(o_1))\ o_1(p) = (u_1, v_1) \wedge o_2(p) = (u_2, v_2) \wedge u_1 = u_2 \Rightarrow v_1 \succcurlyeq_\gamma v_2$*

A value is a γ-refinement of another, $v_1 \succcurlyeq_\gamma v_2$ iff

GET-CRASH2

$$\frac{\rho, \mathcal{R}, \mathcal{W} \vdash H; u; e \hookrightarrow H'; u'; (\ell, \mathcal{M}) \qquad \mathcal{R} \not\vdash_{\mathsf{chk}} \mathcal{M}.p}{\rho, \mathcal{R}, \mathcal{W} \vdash H; u; e.p \Uparrow^{R}}$$

GET-CRASH3

$$\frac{\rho, \mathcal{R}, \mathcal{W} \vdash H; u; e \hookrightarrow H'; u'; (\ell, \mathcal{M}) \qquad \mathcal{R} \vdash_{\mathsf{chk}} \mathcal{M}.p}{\rho, \mathcal{R}, \mathcal{W} \vdash H; u; e.p \Uparrow^{O}}$$

PUT-CRASH3

$$\frac{\begin{array}{c}\rho, \mathcal{R}, \mathcal{W} \vdash H; u; e_1 \hookrightarrow H'; u'; (\ell, \mathcal{M}) \\ \rho, \mathcal{R}, \mathcal{W} \vdash H'; u'; e_2 \hookrightarrow H''; u''; v \qquad \mathcal{W} \not\vdash_{\mathsf{chk}} \mathcal{M}.p\end{array}}{\rho, \mathcal{R}, \mathcal{W} \vdash H; u; e_1.p := e_2 \Uparrow^{W}}$$

Figure 7. Essential crashing rules.

RV1 $v_1 = (\ell_1, \mathcal{M}_1)$ *and* $v_2 = (\ell_2, \mathcal{M}_2)$ *and* $\ell_2 = \gamma(\ell_1)$ *and* $\mathcal{M}_1 = \mathcal{M}_2$*, or*

RV2 $v_1 = (\rho_1, e_1)$ *and* $v_2 = (\rho_2, e_2)$ *and* $\rho_1 \succcurlyeq_\gamma \rho_2$ *and* $e_1 = e_2$.

An environment is a γ*-refinement of another,* $\rho_1 \succcurlyeq_\gamma \rho_2$ *iff*

RE1 $dom(\rho_1) = dom(\rho_2)$ *and*

RE2 $(\forall x \in dom(\rho_1))\ \rho_1(x) \succcurlyeq_\gamma \rho_2(x)$.

The reader might wonder about the implication in **RH2**. This choice allows the coarser heap H_2 to contain a value which does not refine to all corresponding values in heap H_1: for each object in H_2, there may be any number of γ-preimages of this object in H_1. **RH2** says that such an object need not be consistent with all its preimages. This case can be detected by the condition $u_1 < u_2$: the shared version of the object has been updated after one of its unshared preimages. The remaining case $u_1 > u_2$ can never arise.

We allow such inconsistencies in a heap refinement because they only influence the semantics of a program if there is a subsequent read operation that observes the inconsistency. In this case, the criterion $u_1 < u_2$ detects the inconsistency.

Having established the notion of heap refinement, it remains to formalize running the same program on two heaps and compare the outcomes. To this end, it is not sufficient to consider successful, terminating evaluations, but also evaluations ending in a contract violation and interrupted evaluations. Figure 7 specifies the key rules of three judgments of the form $\rho, \mathcal{R}, \mathcal{W} \vdash H; u; e \Uparrow^{i}$ where $i \in \{R, W, O\}$. Each judgment formalizes an interrupted evaluation. The superscript R indicates violation of a read permission (rule GET-CRASH2), superscript W indicates violation of a write permission (rule PUT-CRASH3), and superscript O indicates nondeterministically giving up on a read operation (rule GET-CRASH3). The remaining rules(see [24]) are straightforward variants of the evaluation rules in Fig. 3 that propagate an error condition like an exception.

Our theorem says that crashes due to violated read or write permissions are preserved when more aliasing is added. The main complication is that an inconsistent read operation (in the sense discussed after Definition 3.2) in the version with additional aliasing may lead to arbitrary behavior of the program, including nontermination. Therefore, the theorem constructs a related execution up to the first inconsistent read. Its proof along with auxiliary definitions may be found in our technical report [24].

Theorem 3.2 *If* $H_1 \succcurlyeq_\gamma H_2$ *and* $\rho_1 \succcurlyeq_\gamma \rho_2$ *and*

$$\rho_1, \mathcal{R}, \mathcal{W} \vdash H_1; u; e \Uparrow^{i} \tag{1}$$

(for $i \in \{R, W\}$*) then*

$$\rho_2, \mathcal{R}, \mathcal{W} \vdash H_2; u; e \Uparrow^{j} \tag{2}$$

such that either $i = j$ *or* $j = O$ *and the derivation of* (2) *ends in an inconsistent read operation with respect to* (1).

Informally, the proof constructs a derivation of (2) by induction on a derivation of (1). As $H_1 \succcurlyeq_\gamma H_2$, it is either the case that (2) always reads the same values from the heap as (1). In this case, the derivation of (2) is isomorphic to the derivation of (1) and $i = j$. Otherwise, there is an instance of a GET rule in the derivation of (1) such that applying this rule as part of (2) would return a different value. A sufficient criterion for this case is to check if $u_1 < u_2$ when reading the property as shown in **RH2**. In this case, we give up, emit a GET-CRASH3 rule instead of GET, and complete the derivation with propagation rules for $\Uparrow^{O}$.

The theorem also holds in a language with conditionals as they can be simulated in the lambda calculus. If the language were extended with pointer equality, then a condition might turn out differently on H_2 than on H_1. However, Theorem 3.2 would still hold if a rule analogous to GET-CRASH3 were introduced that allowed us to derive a $\Uparrow^{O}$ judgment in (2) instead of executing an inconsistent pointer equality.

⟦ $e_1[e_2]$ ⟧	=	pRead(⟦e_1⟧,⟦e_2⟧)
⟦ $e_1[e_2] = e_3$ ⟧	=	pAssign(⟦e_1⟧,⟦e_2⟧,⟦e_3⟧)
⟦ $e(e_1,\ldots,e_n)$ ⟧	=	fCall(⟦e⟧,[⟦e_1⟧,...,⟦e_n⟧])
⟦ e.m($e_1,\ldots,e_n$) ⟧	=	mCall(⟦e⟧,m,[⟦e_1⟧,...,⟦e_n⟧])
⟦ **new** $e(e_1,\ldots,e_n)$ ⟧	=	cCall(⟦e⟧,[⟦e_1⟧,...,⟦e_n⟧])
⟦ **for** (**var** i **in** e) {s} ⟧	=	**var** o=⟦e⟧; **for** (**var** i **in** o}) { **if** (mCall(o,"hoP",[i])) {⟦s⟧}}
⟦ **function** $f(x,\ldots)$ {s} ⟧	=	**var** f = enableWrapper(**function** $(x,\ldots)$ {⟦s⟧})

Figure 8. Transformation rules (simplified excerpt).

```
/** (any) → any
    with
  [ $1.a.b.@ ] */
function f(x) {
  var z = x.a;
  return z.b;
};
```

⇝

```
TESTS.c1 = ... // contract
var f = enableWrapper(
  function f'(x) {
    var z = pRead(x,"a");
    return pRead(z,"b");
  }, [TESTS.c1]);
```

Figure 9. Example of a transformation.

4. Implementation

The implementation of the framework for monitoring access permissions is available on the Web [2]. It consists of two parts. The first part is an off-line JavaScript-to-JavaScript compiler written in OCaml. The second part is a JavaScript library that handles the dynamic aspects of enforcing access permissions.

The implementation supports the JavaScript language according to the standard [11] except for prototypes and the **with** statement. As demonstrated in Sec. 2, contracts can be attached to a function or method in a special kind of comment /*c ... */.

The compiler transforms the annotated code such that it monitors access permissions at run time. Figure 8 illustrates some of the transformation steps in a simplified form. All operations that involve heap accesses, like reading and writing of properties, are redirected to library functions that dynamically manage access permissions. These library functions introduce wrappers for references that remember the access paths of the wrapped reference.

[2] http://proglang.informatik.uni-freiburg.de/jscontest/

Figure 9 shows an example of a transformed function definition. The library function enableWrapper creates a wrapper for f that generates a fresh time stamp each time a function is called and marks the parameters with the corresponding access path information at run time such that pRead can check if it has permission to read $1.a. The library call to pRead returns a wrapper with the access path $1.a for z. Reading the property b of z uses the access path stored in the wrapper of z, extends it to $1.a.b, and checks if reading this path is permitted. The permission is granted because the access permission attached to f is $1.a.b.@.

Calls to native or non-transformed code would fail if wrapped objects were passed. Because it is not possible to statically decide which function is applied at a call site, the framework strips the access meta data from parameter objects before passing them to the function. It stores the meta data on a global stack that is used to re-wrap the objects if the callee itself is a transformed function. This approach is compatible with uses of eval: code generated by eval can execute, but its read and write operations are not monitored.

For interoperability with non-transformed code, it is also necessary to remove wrappers when storing object properties. To this end, an additional map (__infos__) is attached to each object. This map stores the wrappers for each of the properties. The function pRead uses this map to reconstruct wrapped objects if necessary.

As the library stores the access path information in the __infos__ property of the objects, this property must not become accessible to user code. Therefore, we provide a substitute for hasOwnProperty (hoP) that masks out the __infos__ property. We also transform the statement **for** (**var** i **in** e) { s } to ensure that internal properties used by the implementation do not leak out to the program. Technically, this protection is achieved by changing the body s to **if** (hoP(o,i)) { s }. The functions pRead and pAssign also safeguard the special property __infos__.

If native code or non-transformed code iterates over all properties of an object, then it is not possible to hide the __infos__ property. We are not aware of any way to reliably hide this property short of modifying the underlying JavaScript engine. However, in the case studies that we performed the special property caused no problem.

Some features of JavaScript are not covered by the core calculus from Sec. 3, most notably prototypes and the **with** statement. In both cases, it turns out that write operations are not a problem: a property write never gets propagated to a prototype object and the **with** statement only changes the meaning of property reads.

A proper semantics of property reads in the presence of prototypes would first check the permission on the original object, check the presence of the property, and then recursively continue with the prototype object, until the property is not found or there is no further prototype. Our present implementation does not implement this semantics. It only checks the top-level permissions and relies on the built-in prototype resolution to do the actual read operation. Thus, it ignores restrictions imposed on a prototype object.

A proper semantics of **with** statements would have to proceed similarly, but traversing the stack of objects associated with currently open **with** statements for each access to a local variable. Our implementation does not support **with** at all because our case studies do not require it.

While an extension of the transformation to support prototypes and the **with** statement is possible, it does not appear sensible because it would require mimicking yet more details of the underlying execution engine (possibly introducing mismatches). Hence, we are working on an implementation inside a JavaScript engine, where it should be simple to overcome the restrictions of our transformation-based implementation with only a moderate impact on performance. For example, hiding the metadata and ensuring that it does not affect program execution is straightforward. Similarly, it is possible to monitor property reads and writes of native functions to fully support prototypes, eval, and dynamically loaded code. Due to the direct access to the scope chain the support for **with** statements is also simple inside a JavaScript engine.

	type		type+effect	
fulfilled contracts	1011	18.0 %	711	12.7 %
rejected contracts	4607	82.0 %	4907	87.3 %
reason for rejection (a mutant may be counted multiple times)				
type contract failure	2020	43.9 %	1643	33.5 %
signaled error	2034	44.1 %	2136	43.5 %
browser timeout	553	12.0 %	243	5.0 %
read violation	-	0.0 %	1018	20.7 %
write violation	-	0.0 %	1606	32.7 %
read/write violation	-	0.0 %	1842	37.5 %

Table 1. Testing random mutations for singly-linked lists.

5. Evaluation

How effective are access permissions for detecting programming errors? To answer this question, we hand-annotated the code of several libraries and applications with contracts and ran it with monitoring enabled. We applied random code modifications [7] to check to what extent the enforcement of access permissions detects changes in the program's behavior.

5.1 Case Study: Singly- and Doubly-Linked Lists and Trees

The first case study examines a collection of libraries implementing data structures like singly- and doubly-linked lists and search trees.[3] The code sizes range from 200-400 LOC per library. As the results are similar for all libraries, we discuss the singly-linked list implementation as a representative example.

The list interface comprises one constructor for list nodes and six methods to operate on a list: add, remove, item, size, toArray, and toString. For each method we developed contracts with access permissions. Annotating the code and implementing a custom contract to drive the input generation took about one hour. The code with all contracts is available on our webpage.

From the implementation we derived about 5600 random mutations and tested each mutant against the original contracts. The mutations affected operators, constants, and variable names. Each of the six functions was tested with 1000 randomly generated test cases and was run in two configurations:

type contracts for integer lists without effects: only violations of the type contracts are detected,

type+effect contracts for integer lists with effects: type and access path violations are detected.

Table 1 shows the results of the test runs. The "fulfilled" row counts mutations that are not detected because the mutant fulfills all six contracts. The "rejected" row registers mutants that fail at least one contract. These two rows indicate the effectiveness of effect monitoring. Adding access permissions to type contracts improves the detection rate for mutations from 82% to 87.3%, an improvement of 6.4%. The remaining rows break down the reasons for the failure of a mutant. As there are multiple functions in a mutant, there are multiple reasons why a single mutant may fail so that the percentages do not add to 100%.

We manually inspected the cases where the contract system did not detect a mutation. In many cases the mutated code is semantically equivalent to the original version, for instance, when x.p was changed to x.q, where both properties p and q were always

[3] https://github.com/nzakas/computer-science-in-javascript

	type		type + effect	
fulfilled contracts	1148	38.9%	911	30.8%
rejected contracts	1807	61.1%	2044	69.2%
reason for rejection (a mutant may be counted multiple times)				
type contract failure	872	48.3%	866	42.4%
signaled error	1052	58.2%	1037	50.7%
browser timeout	28	1.5%	30	1.5%
read violation	0	0.0%	202	9.9%
write violation	0	0.0%	149	7.4%
read/write violation	0	0.0%	349	17.1%

Table 2. Testing random mutations of the Richards case study.

undefined. In other cases, the contract was fulfilled by a mutant because the modification did not change any property access or return value from a type perspective, for instance, **return** true is changed to **return** false. While these mutations change the semantics, a type or access permission contract cannot detect such changes.

We also manually inspected ten randomly selected mutants that timed out. In all cases, the mutation caused an infinite loop.

5.2 Case Study: Richards and Deltablue Benchmarks

A second case study was performed on the Richards and Deltablue benchmarks from the Google V8 benchmark suite.[4] The Richards benchmark simulates the task dispatcher of an operating system. The code comprises 29 functions in 650 LOC. A person without prior knowledge of the code under test provided the contracts and implemented custom generators in about four hours. It took another two hours to develop the access permissions.

Table 2 shows the result of testing about 2950 mutated versions. These test runs executed 50 tests per function for each mutant to test for effect and contract violations. We chose to run a smaller number of tests to reduce the overall run time and to check if a small number of test cases is sufficient to obtain a high detection rate of mutants.

Adding access permissions increases the detection rate from 61.1% to 69.2%, which amounts to a 13% improvement. This increase is quite surprising as the percentages of detected read or write violations are much smaller than in the linked-list case study.

In the Deltablue application (59 contracts in 670 LOC), the access permissions led to an increase in error detection from 75.6% to 84.2%, an improvement by 11.4%. In contrast to the other studies, Deltablue does not permit unit testing on a per function basis as it relies heavily on global state. Further details may be found in the technical report [24].

5.3 Performance Evaluation

All case studies and benchmarks were executed on a Lenovo Thinkpad X61s notebook with a Core 2 Duo processor with 1.60 GHz and 2GB Ram running the Google-Chrome browser (7.0.517.44) on top of Linux version 2.6.35-23-generic. In this setting, a test run of a mutant is about four times slower with monitoring enabled than without monitoring (in both case studies).

To give ballpark numbers, running 1000 tests for each of the six functions of the linked-list test suite takes about 6 seconds with monitoring compared to 1.5 seconds without. For Richards, running 50 tests for each of the 29 functions takes 1.85 seconds with monitoring compared to 0.5 seconds without.

For the Richards benchmark we timed the original code (without mutation) once with monitoring and once without to measure the slowdown for code that never violates the effect annotations. This experiment masks out the effects of contract violations, which

[4] `http://v8.googlecode.com/svn/data/benchmarks/v6/`

```
/*c ... with [this._root./left|right/*.value.@, this._root,
          this._root./left|right/*./left|right/] */
BinaryTree.add = function(elem) { ... }
```

Figure 10. Contract of a binary search tree.

cause the program to stop earlier on faulty mutants than on correct code. However, the slowdown is similar: running 1000 test cases for each of the 29 functions took 32.4 seconds with monitoring enabled versus 7.4 seconds without, a slowdown factor of 4.4.

5.4 Example Contracts for Case Studies

Figure 10 contains a representative contract for an add method that inserts an element in a binary search tree. The method adds new elements by creating a new node object that is inserted into the tree at the appropriate place. Its contract reveals that the method only reads and modifies objects reachable via this._root and then following left or right properties. It does not change the value property of any node that is already part of the tree, but it reads this data to find the place for the new node.

6. Related Work

Access permissions are closely related to effect systems. Effect systems have been conceived for functional languages [19] to describe and infer the scope of side effects, with the goal of detecting parallelizable code fragments and improving memory management.

There are too many papers on effect systems to do them all justice here. Greenhouse and Boyland [22] introduce effect annotations for Java which closely resemble our contracts. In contrast to our system, effects are collected for regions which comprise a set of objects. Their approach aims to track data dependencies of software components. The main differences to our work are that most effect systems are integrated in type systems and thus geared towards static analysis (whereas ours performs dynamic analysis) and that our prime motivation lies in the detection of software defects.

The effect system proposed by Bocchino and coworkers [28] for deterministic parallel Java relies on a very similar notion of effect, based on paths over regions (sets of instance variables). They use the effect system to statically prove the absence of data races. Our system might be extended to check this property at run time.

The static verification system of Smans and coworkers [41] has a special **acc** predicate that helps simplifying proof obligations for the frame problem in method calls. The argument to **acc** is an access path similar to, but more restricted than the notion put forward in our work. A preliminary investigation suggests that their static semantics agrees with our monitoring semantics, but further work is needed to work out the exact connection.

Similarly related is work on ownership and aliasing control. Again, with the exception of the dynamic ownership system of Boyland and coworkers [6], most ownership systems statically impose tree-like ownership structures on object graphs [3, 10, 39, 46]. The main difference to ownership types is that our system is entirely access path-based whereas ownership types are context-based. Furthermore, some ownership systems forbid the mere existence of references, whereas access permissions forbid the traversal of certain paths. Effective ownership [33] does not restrict referencing of objects, but enforces the encapsulation of an object's representation by confining modifications to the owner.

Bierhoff and Aldrich [5] define a static checker for access permissions in Java. It combines typestate and object aliasing information to design and verify protocols for safe object access. They also focus on the correct usage of single resources. Their access permissions are statically verified.

Deutsch's [8] analysis for sharing and aliasing is also entirely based on access paths. It is a static analysis phrased as an abstract interpretation of a storeless semantics.

Run-time monitoring is an approach to providing safety and security guarantees. Erlingsson [13] provides an overview of such applications. As a notable difference, security monitoring is mostly geared towards eliminating (sequences of) uses of undesired operations and can often be implemented by finite automata, whereas access path monitoring rules out undesired accesses and requires more specific implementation techniques to deal with aliasing.

BrowserShield [40] provides run-time monitoring of JavaScript. BrowserShield rewrites code to redirect critical operations according to user-specified policies. The Google Caja project [20] employs an online compilation process of JavaScript code to a safe subset named Cajita which enforces certain security policies.

Maffeis and coworkers [34] combine several isolation techniques for restricting heap accesses of third-party code. They disallow `eval`, **`function`**, and `constructor` within untrusted code and also rewrite property accesses with wrappers to enable run-time checks.

These systems operate within the browser during interactive user sessions and provide complete interposition. In contrast, our tool is focused on development and testing of applications.

Finifter and coworkers [18] design a JavaScript heap analysis framework to detect information leaks. To prevent exploits, third-party code is restricted to a name space by prefixing properties with a unique identifier. In contrast, we restrict accesses via path conditions.

ConScript [37] enforces fine-grained application-specific security policies at run time by modifying a JavaScript execution engine. Compared to our approach, they have different goals and less overhead.

Further related research deals with dynamic contract checking. Findler and Felleisen [16] develop dynamically checked type contracts for Scheme. In a similar way, JSConTest [25] extends JavaScript with type contracts that are monitored dynamically and can be used to automatically generate random test cases for contracted functions. Our paper extends their work with access permissions to check side effects of a contracted function.

Program specification frameworks like Spec# [4] or Eiffel [12] permit the formulation of access permissions as FOL-formulas in Hoare-style pre- and postconditions. Because specialized syntax is missing, the annotation process is rather heavy-weight. Besides, these frameworks are geared towards full specifications, whereas we are targeting partial specifications.

JML [31] features an `assignable` clause to specify which object fields may be modified during a method call, similar to our write permissions (read accesses cannot be restricted). In contrast to our work, JML is mostly geared towards (static) program verification. Of the approaches that employ JML for run-time checks (that is, contract monitoring) only a few fully support `assignable`. Lehner and Müller [32] provide such an implementation of run-time checks. Their implementation relies on code rewriting, but the main contribution of their work is an efficient check of `assignable` clauses for dynamic data groups. The semantics of these checks is reminiscent of the location-based semantics discussed in Sec. 1.3.

Spoto and Poll [42] define a static analysis for object-local `assignable` specifications. They include alias information in their system by tracking what aliases are introduced when a field is modified. Their analysis also seems to implement the location-based semantics.

7. Conclusion

We proposed a novel extension of software contracts with access permissions that specify the side effects of an operation in terms of access paths. We implemented monitoring for access permissions in JavaScript by a program transformation and demonstrated that this implementation has an acceptable overhead. As a theoretical basis for the implementation, we developed a formalization that enabled us to cleanly specify the interaction of monitoring and aliasing, to prove soundness of monitoring, and to prove stability of violation.

Our case studies showed that the specification of contracts with access permissions on an unfamiliar code base takes about 30-40 minutes per 100 LOC and that in return the number of bugs detected by contract monitoring increases between 6% and 13%, which is a remarkable improvement on type contracts. In each case, the access permissions provided valuable insights in the behavior of the program. Hence, access permissions could be a worthwhile extension of testing frameworks.

A major design choice was the adoption of the path-based semantics because it behaves consistently with respect to static verification, it guarantees stability of violation, and it is reasonably efficient. Although single read and write accesses are more expensive than for the location-based semantics, we believe that the potentially unbounded time for installing a location-based permission is not amortized by the subsequent exploration of the object graph: We conjecture that only a small fragment of the objects affected by a contract is actually explored, but we have yet to conduct an empirical evaluation with realistic implementations of both semantics.

In future work, we want to pursue various directions. We believe that our approach is more widely applicable to any object-based language, not just to scripting languages, but also to nominally typed languages like Java and C#. In the latter cases, to avoid breaking encapsulation, it is likely necessary to introduce concepts like regions or data groups analogously to other work in this area [22, 28, 31]. In this context, it would also be interesting to investigate a mix of static checking and dynamic enforcement as has been done in work on manifest contracts [21].

Another obvious extension would be a special treatment for effects on the DOM [30]. Because DOM structures are guaranteed to be trees (no aliasing!), many of the complications of general object graphs do not arise in the case of DOM structures.

We further plan to investigate the location-based variant of the monitoring semantics in the context of security and access control. For this application, it appears that many of our design choices have to be reverted: for reliable monitoring of access control policies the location-based semantics with lexical scoping of permissions along with a notion of path exclusions (negative permissions) seems to be a superior approach. However, the path-based semantics can also be extended to reliably forbid access to certain objects, as shown in our technical report [24]. In any case, a browser-based implementation of access permission monitoring is required to further validate claims in this direction.

References

[1] P. Abercrombie and M. Karaorman. jContractor: Design by contract for Java. `http://jcontractor.sourceforge.net/`, 2003.

[2] A. Ahmed, R. B. Findler, J. G. Siek, and P. Wadler. Blame for all. In *Proc. 38th ACM Symp. POPL*, pages 201–214, Austin, USA, Jan. 2011. ACM Press.

[3] J. Aldrich and C. Chambers. Ownership domains: Separating aliasing policy from mechanism. In M. Odersky, editor, *18th ECOOP*, volume 3086 of *LNCS*, pages 1–25, Oslo, Norway, June 2004. Springer.

[4] M. Barnett, K. R. M. Leino, and W. Schulte. The Spec# Programming System: An Overview. In *CASSIS 2004: Construction and Analysis of Safe, Secure and Interoperable Smart devices*, pages 49–69. Springer, 2004.

[5] K. Bierhoff and J. Aldrich. Modular typestate checking of aliased objects. In *Proc. 22nd ACM Conf. OOPSLA*, pages 301–320, Montreal, QC, CA, 2007. ACM Press, New York.

[6] J. Boyland, J. Noble, and W. Retert. Capabilities for sharing: A generalisation of uniqueness and read-only. In J. L. Knudsen, editor, *15th ECOOP*, volume 2072 of *LNCS*, pages 2–27, Budapest, Hungary, June 2001. Springer.

[7] R. A. DeMillo, R. J. Lipton, and F. G. Sayward. Hints on test data selection: Help for the practicing programmer. *Computer*, 11:34–41, April 1978.

[8] A. Deutsch. A storeless model of aliasing and its abstractions using finite representations of right-regular equivalence relations. In *Proc. IEEE International Conference on Computer Languages 1992*, pages 2–13, Oakland, CA, Apr. 1992. IEEE.

[9] T. D'Hondt, editor. *24th ECOOP*, volume 6183 of *LNCS*, Maribor, Slovenia, 2010. Springer.

[10] W. Dietl and P. Müller. Universes: Lightweight ownership for JML. *Journal of Object Technology (JOT)*, 4(8):5–32, Oct. 2005.

[11] ECMAScript Language Specification, Dec. 2009. ECMA International, ECMA-262, 5th edition.

[12] Eiffel: Analysis, design and programming language, June 2006. ECMA International, ECMA-367, 2nd edition.

[13] Ú. Erlingsson and F. B. Schneider. SASI enforcement of security policies: A retrospective. In *Proceedings of the 1999 New Security Paradigms Workshop*, Caledon Hills, Ontario, Canada, Sept. 1999.

[14] M. Fähndrich, M. Barnett, and F. Logozzo. Embedded contract languages. In S. Y. Shin, S. Ossowski, M. Schumacher, M. J. Palakal, and C.-C. Hung, editors, *SAC*, pages 2103–2110, Sierre, Switzerland, 2010. ACM.

[15] R. B. Findler and M. Felleisen. Contract soundness for object-oriented languages. In *Proc. 16th ACM Conf. OOPSLA*, pages 1–15, Tampa Bay, FL, USA, 2001. ACM Press, New York.

[16] R. B. Findler and M. Felleisen. Contracts for higher-order functions. In S. Peyton-Jones, editor, *Proc. ICFP 2002*, pages 48–59, Pittsburgh, PA, USA, Oct. 2002. ACM Press, New York.

[17] R. B. Findler, S. Guo, and A. Rogers. Lazy contract checking for immutable data structures. In O. Chitil, Z. Horváth, and V. Zsók, editors, *Implementation and Application of Functional Languages, 19th International Workshop, IFL 2007*, number 5083 in Lecture Notes in Computer Science, pages 111–128. Springer, 2008.

[18] M. Finifter, J. Weinberger, and A. Barth. Preventing Capability Leaks in Secure JavaScript Subsets. In *Proceedings of Network and Distributed System Security Symposium*, pages 375–388. Internet Society, 2010.

[19] D. Gifford and J. Lucassen. Integrating functional and imperative programming. In *Proc. 1986 ACM Conf. on Lisp and Functional Programming*, pages 28–38, 1986.

[20] google-caja: A source-to-source translator for securing JavaScript-based web content. `http://code.google.com/p/google-caja/`.

[21] M. Greenberg, B. C. Pierce, and S. Weirich. Contracts made manifest. In J. Palsberg, editor, *Proc. 37th ACM Symp. POPL*, pages 353–364, Madrid, Spain, Jan. 2010. ACM Press.

[22] A. Greenhouse and J. Boyland. An object-oriented effects system. In R. Guerraoui, editor, *13th ECOOP*, volume 1628 of *LNCS*, pages 205–229, Lisbon, Portugal, June 1999. Springer.

[23] A. Guha, C. Saftoiu, and S. Krishnamurthi. The essence of JavaScript. In D'Hondt [9].

[24] P. Heidegger, A. Bieniusa, and P. Thiemann. Access permission contracts for scripting languages (extended version). Technical Report 264, Universität Freiburg, July 2011. `http://proglang.informatik.uni-freiburg.de/jscontest/`.

[25] P. Heidegger and P. Thiemann. Contract-driven testing of JavaScript code. In *Proceedings of the 48th International Conference on Objects, Models, Components, Patterns*, TOOLS'10, pages 154–172, Malaga, Spain, June 2010. Springer.

[26] P. Heidegger and P. Thiemann. Recency types for analyzing scripting languages. In D'Hondt [9].

[27] R. Hinze, J. Jeuring, and A. Löh. Typed contracts for functional programming. In P. Wadler and M. Hagiya, editors, *Proceedings of the 8th International Symposium on Functional and Logic Programming FLOPS 2006*, pages 208–225, Fuji Susono, Japan, Apr. 2006. Springer.

[28] R. L. B. Jr., V. S. Adve, D. Dig, S. V. Adve, S. Heumann, R. Komuravelli, J. Overbey, P. Simmons, H. Sung, and M. Vakilian. A type and effect system for deterministic parallel Java. In S. Arora and G. T. Leavens, editors, *Proc. 24th ACM Conf. OOPSLA*, pages 97–116, Orlando, Florida, USA, 2009. ACM Press, New York.

[29] R. Kramer. iContract — the Java design by contract tool. In *Proceedings of the Technology of Object-Oriented Languages and Systems*, pages 295–307, Santa Barbara, CA, USA, 1998.

[30] P. Le Hégaret, R. Whitmer, and L. Wood. W3C document object model. `http://www.w3.org/DOM/`, Aug. 2003.

[31] G. T. Leavens, A. L. Baker, and C. Ruby. JML: A Notation for Detailed Design. In H. Kilov, B. Rumpe, and I. Simmonds, editors, *Behavioral Specifications of Businesses and Systems*, pages 175–188. Kluwer, 1999.

[32] H. Lehner and P. Müller. Efficient runtime assertion checking of assignable clauses with datagroups. In D. S. Rosenblum and G. Taentzer, editors, *FASE*, volume 6013 of *Lecture Notes in Computer Science*, pages 338–352. Springer, 2010.

[33] Y. Lu and J. Potter. Protecting representation with effect encapsulation. In S. Peyton Jones, editor, *Proc. 33rd ACM Symp. POPL*, pages 359–371, New York, NY, USA, Jan. 2006. ACM.

[34] S. Maffeis, J. C. Mitchell, and A. Taly. Isolating JavaScript with filters, rewriting, and wrappers. In *ESORICS'09: Proceedings of the 14th European Conference on Research in Computer Security*, pages 505–522, Saint-Malo, France, 2009. Springer-Verlag.

[35] B. Meyer. Applying "Design by Contract". *IEEE Computer*, 25(10):40–51, Oct. 1992.

[36] B. Meyer. *Object-Oriented Software Construction*. Prentice-Hall, 2nd edition, 1997.

[37] L. A. Meyerovich and B. Livshits. ConScript: Specifying and enforcing fine-grained security policies for Javascript in the browser. In *IEEE Symposium on Security and Privacy*, May 2010.

[38] P. Müller, A. Poetzsch-Heffter, and G. T. Leavens. Modular specification of frame properties in JML. *Concurrency and Computation: Practice and Experience*, 15(2):117–154, 2003.

[39] J. Noble, J. Vitek, and J. Potter. Flexible alias protection. In E. Jul, editor, *ECOOP*, volume 1445 of *LNCS*, pages 158–185, Brussels, Belgium, July 1998. Springer.

[40] C. Reis, J. Dunagan, H. J. Wang, O. Dubrovsky, and S. Esmeir. BrowserShield: Vulnerability-driven filtering of dynamic HTML. *ACM Trans. Web*, 1(3):11, 2007.

[41] J. Smans, B. Jacobs, and F. Piessens. Implicit dynamic frames: Combining dynamic frames and separation logic. In S. Drossopoulou, editor, *23th ECOOP*, volume 5653 of *LNCS*, pages 148–172, Genova, Italy, 2009. Springer.

[42] F. Spoto and E. Poll. Static Analysis of JML's assignable Clauses. *International Workshop on Foundations of Object-Oriented Languages*, Jan. 2003.

[43] J.-P. Talpin and P. Jouvelot. The type and effect discipline. *Information and Computation*, 111(2):245–296, 1994.

[44] P. Wadler and R. B. Findler. Well-typed programs can't be blamed. In G. Castagna, editor, *Proc. 18th ESOP*, volume 5502 of *LNCS*, pages 1–16, York, UK, Mar. 2009. Springer-Verlag.

[45] D. N. Xu, S. Peyton Jones, and K. Claessen. Static contract checking for Haskell. In B. Pierce, editor, *Proc. 36th ACM Symp. POPL*, pages 41–52, Savannah, GA, USA, Jan. 2009. ACM Press.

[46] T. Zhao, J. Palsberg, and J. Vitek. Lightweight confinement for Featherweight Java. In *Proc. 18th ACM Conf. OOPSLA*, pages 135–148, Anaheim, CA, USA, 2003. ACM Press, New York.

Recursive Proofs for Inductive Tree Data-Structures

P. Madhusudan Xiaokang Qiu Andrei Stefanescu
University of Illinois at Urbana-Champaign, USA
{madhu, qiu2, stefane1}@illinois.edu

Abstract

We develop logical mechanisms and procedures to facilitate the verification of full functional properties of inductive tree data-structures using recursion that are sound, incomplete, but terminating. Our contribution rests in a new extension of first-order logic with recursive definitions called DRYAD, a syntactical restriction on pre- and post-conditions of recursive imperative programs using DRYAD, and a systematic methodology for accurately unfolding the footprint on the heap uncovered by the program that leads to finding simple recursive proofs using formula abstraction and calls to SMT solvers. We evaluate our methodology empirically and show that several complex tree data-structure algorithms can be checked against full functional specifications automatically, given pre- and post-conditions. This results in the first automatic terminating methodology for proving a wide variety of annotated algorithms on tree data-structures correct, including max-heaps, treaps, red-black trees, AVL trees, binomial heaps, and B-trees.

Categories and Subject Descriptors F.3.1 [*Logics and Meanings of Programs*]: Specifying and Verifying and Reasoning about Programs: Mechanical verification; D.2.4 [*Software Engineering*]: Software/Program Verification: Assertion checkers

General Terms Algorithms, Reliability, Theory, Verification

Keywords heap analysis, recursive program, tree, SMT solver

1. Introduction

The area of program verification using theorem provers, utilizing manually provided proof annotations (pre- and post-conditions for functions, loop-invariants, etc.) has been a focus of intense research in the field of programming languages. Automatic theory solvers (SMT solvers) that handle a variety of quantifier-free theories including arithmetic, uninterpreted functions, Boolean logic, etc., serve as effective tools that automatically discharge the validity checking of many verification conditions [7].

A key area that has eluded the above paradigm of specification and verification is heap analysis: the verification of programs that dynamically allocate memory and manipulate them using pointers, maintaining structural invariants (e.g. "the nodes form a tree"), aliasing invariants, and invariants on the data stored in the locations (e.g. "the keys of a list are sorted"). The classical examples of these are the basic *data-structures* taught in undergraduate computer science courses, and include linked lists, queues, binary search trees, max-heaps, balanced AVL trees, partially-balanced tree structures like red-black trees, etc. [10]. Object-oriented programs are rich with heap structures as well, and structures are often found in the form of records or lists of pointers pointing to other hierarchically arranged data-structures.

Dynamically allocated heaps are difficult to reason with for several reasons. First, the specification of proof annotations itself is hard, as the annotation needs to talk about several intricate properties of an unbounded heap, often requiring quantification and reachability predicates, and needs to specify aliasing as well as structural properties of the heap. Also, in experiences with manual verification, it has been observed that pre- and post-conditions get unduly complex, including large formulas that say how the frame of the heap that is *not* touched by the program remains the same across a function. Separation logic [19, 23] has emerged as a way to address this problem, mainly the frame problem mentioned above, and gives a logic that permits us to compositionally reason with the footprint touched by the program and the frame it resides in.

Most research on program logics for functional verification of heap-manipulating programs can be roughly divided into two classes:[1]

- **Logics for manual/semi-automatic reasoning:** The most popular of these are the class of *separation logics*[19, 23], but several others exist (see *matching logic* [24], for example). Complex structural properties of heaps are expressed using *inductive algebraic definitions*, the logic combines several other theories like arithmetic, etc., and uses a special separation operator ($*$) to compositionally reason with a footprint and the frame. The analysis is either manual or semi-automatic, the latter being usually sound, incomplete, and non-terminating, and proceeds by heuristically searching for proofs using a proof system, unrolling recursive definitions arbitrarily. Typically, such tools can find simple proofs if they exist, but are unpredictable, and cannot robustly produce counter-examples.
- **Logics for completely automated reasoning:** These logics stem from the SMT (Satisfiability Modulo Theories) and automata theory literature, where the goal is to develop fast, terminating, sound and complete decision procedures, but where the logics are often constrained heavily on expressivity in order to reach these goals. Examples include several logics that extend first-order logic with reachability, the logics LISBQ [14] and CSL [6], and the logic STRAND_{dec} [16] that combines tree theories with integer theories. The problem with these logics, in general, is that they are often not sufficiently expressive to state complex properties of the heap (e.g. the balancedness of

[1] We do not discuss abstraction-based approaches such as shape analysis here as such approaches are geared towards less complex specifications, and often are completely automatic, not even requiring proof annotations such as loop invariants; see Section 6.

POPL'12, January 25–27, 2012, Philadelphia, PA, USA.

an AVL tree, or that the set of keys stored in a heap do not change across a program).

We prefer an approach that combines the two methodologies above. We propose a strategy that (a) identifies a class of *simple and natural* proofs for proving verification conditions for heap-based programs, founded on how people prove these conditions manually, and (b) builds terminating procedures that efficiently and thoroughly search this class of proofs. This results in a sound, incomplete, but terminating procedure that finds natural proofs automatically and efficiently. Many correct programs have simple proofs of correctness, and a terminating procedure that searches for these simple proofs efficiently can be a very useful tool in program verification. Incompleteness is, of course, a necessary trade-off to keep the logics expressive while having a terminating procedure, and a terminating automatic procedure is useful as it does not need manual help. Furthermore, as we shall see in this paper, such decision algorithms are particularly desirable when they can be made to work very efficiently, especially using the fast-growing class of efficient SMT solvers for quantifier-free theories.

The idea of searching for only simple and natural proofs is not new; after all, *type systems* that prove properties of programs are essentially simple (and often scalable) proof mechanisms. The class of simple and natural proofs that we identify in this paper is, however, quite different from those found by type systems.

In this paper, we develop logical mechanisms to identify a simple class of proofs based on a deterministic proof tactic that (a) unfolds recursive terms *precisely* across the footprint, (b) uses *formula abstractions* (that replace recursively defined terms with *uninterpreted terms*) to restate the verification condition in a quantifier-free decidable theory, and (c) checks the resulting formula using an automatic decision procedure. We deploy this technique for the specialized domain of *imperative programs manipulating tree data-structures*, developing an extension of first-order logic with recursion on trees called DRYAD to state properties of programs, and building procedures based on precise unfoldings and formula abstractions.

Motivating formula abstractions

When reasoning with formulas that have recursively defined terms, which can be unrolled forever, a key idea is to use *formula abstraction* that makes the terms *uninterpreted*. Intuitively, the idea is to replace recursively defined predicates, sets, etc. by uninterpreted Boolean values, uninterpreted sets, etc.

The idea of formula abstraction is extremely natural, and utilized very often in manual proofs. For instance, let us consider a binary search tree (BST) search routine searching for a key k on the root node x. The verification condition of a path of this program, typically, would require checking:

$$(bst(x) \wedge k \in keys(x) \wedge k < x.key) \Rightarrow (k \in keys(x.left))$$

where $bst()$ is a recursive predicate defined on trees that identifies binary search trees, and $keys()$ is a recursively defined set that collects the multiset of keys under a node. Unrolling the definition of $keys()$ and $bst()$ gives the following formula (below, $i < S$ means that i is less than every element in S):

$$bst(x.left) \wedge bst(x.right) \wedge keys(x.left){<}x.key \wedge keys(x.right){>}x.key \wedge k{\in}(keys(x.left){\cup}keys(x.right){\cup}\{x.key\}) \wedge k{<}x.key) \Rightarrow (k{\in}keys(x.left))$$

Now, while the above formula is quite complex, involving recursive definitions that can be unrolled *ad infinitum*, we can prove its validity soundly by viewing $bst()$ and $keys()$ as *uninterpreted* functions that map locations to Booleans and sets, respectively. Doing this gives (modulo some renaming and modulo theory of equality):

$$(b_1 \wedge b_2 \wedge K_1{\leq}xkey \wedge K_2{>}xkey \wedge k \in (K_1 \cup K_2 \cup \{xkey\}) \wedge k{<}xkey) \Rightarrow (k{\in}K_1)$$

Note that the above formula is a quantifier-free formula over integers and multisets of integers, and furthermore is valid (since $k{<}xkey$ and $K_2{>}xkey$, k must be in K_1). Validity of quantifier-free formulas over sets/multisets of integers with addition is *decidable* (they can be translated to quantifier-free formulas over integers and uninterpreted functions), and can be solved using SMT solvers efficiently. Consequently, we can prove that the verification condition is valid, completely automatically. Note that formula abstraction is *sound* but incomplete.

This idea has been explored in the literature. For example, Suter et al. [25] have proposed abstraction schemes for algebraic data-types that soundly (but incompletely) transform logical validity into much simpler decidable problems using formula abstractions, and developed mechanisms for proving *functional programs* correct.

Reasoning with DRYAD

In order to build the procedures for reasoning with programs manipulating trees, using precise unfolding and abstraction, we develop a new recursive extension of first-order logic, called DRYAD that allows stating complex properties of heaps without recourse to explicit quantification. DRYAD combines quantifier-free first-order logic with recursive definitions, and these recursive definitions, themselves expressed in DRYAD, can capture several interesting properties of trees, including their height, the multiset of keys stored in them, whether they correspond to a binary search tree (or an AVL tree), etc.

The main technical contribution of this paper is to show how a Hoare-triple corresponding to a basic path in a recursive imperative program (we disallow while-loops and demand all recursion be through recursive function calls) with proof annotations written in DRYAD, can be expressed as a pair consisting of a finite footprint and a DRYAD formula. The finite footprint is a *symbolic heap* that captures the heap explored by the basic block of the program precisely. The construction of this footprint and formula calls for a careful handling of the mutating footprint defined by a recursive imperative program, calls for a disciplined approach to unrolling recursion, and involves capturing aliasing and separation by exploiting the fact that the manipulated structures are trees. In particular, the procedure keeps track of locations in the footprint corresponding to trees and precisely computes the value of recursive terms on the these. Furthermore, the verification condition is accurately described by unfolding the pre-condition so that it is expressed purely on the *frontier* of the footprint, so as to enable effective use of the formula abstraction mechanism. In order to be accurate, we place several key restrictions on the logical syntax of pre- and post-conditions expressed for functions.

We then consider the problem of solving the validity problem for the verification condition expressed as a footprint and a DRYAD formula. We first show a small syntactic fragment of verification conditions that is entirely decidable (without formula abstraction) by a reduction to the decidable logic STRAND_{dec} [16]. Although this fragment of DRYAD is powerful enough to express certain restricted structural properties of simple tree data-structures like binary search trees, max-heaps, and treaps, it is completely inadequate in verifying more complex properties of the above structures as well as properties of more complex tree data-structures such as red-black trees, binomial heaps, etc.

We turn next to abstraction schemes for DRYAD, and show how to abstract DRYAD formulas into quantifier-free theories of sets/multisets of integers; the latter can then be translated into formulas in the standard quantifier-free theory of integers with uninterpreted functions. The final formula's validity can be proved using standard SMT solvers, and its validity implies the validity of the DRYAD formula.

$$
\begin{array}{llll}
dir \in Dir & i^* : Loc \rightarrow Int & x \in Loc \text{ Variables} & S \in \mathcal{S}(Int) \text{ Variables} \\
f \in DF & si^* : Loc \rightarrow \mathcal{S}(Int) & j \in Int \text{ Variables} & MS \in \mathcal{MS}(Int) \text{ Variables} \\
p^* : Loc \rightarrow \{\texttt{true}, \texttt{false}\} & msi^* : Loc \rightarrow \mathcal{MS}(Int) & q \in Boolean \text{ Variables} & c : Int \text{ Constant}
\end{array}
$$

$$
\begin{array}{rcl}
Loc \text{ Term: } lt, lt_1, lt_2 \ldots & ::= & x \mid \texttt{nil} \mid lt.dir \\
Int \text{ Term: } it, it_1, it_2, \ldots & ::= & c \mid j \mid lt.f \mid i^*(lt) \mid it_1 + it_2 \mid it_1 - it_2 \mid \texttt{ite}(\varphi, it_1, it_2) \\
\mathcal{S}(Int) \text{ Term: } sit, sit_1, sit_2, \ldots & ::= & \emptyset \mid S \mid \{it\} \mid si^*(lt) \mid sit_1 \cup sit_2 \mid sit_1 \cap sit_2 \mid sit_1 \setminus sit_2 \mid \texttt{ite}(\varphi, sit_1, sit_2) \\
\mathcal{MS}(Int) \text{ Term: } msit, msit_1, msit_2, \ldots & ::= & \emptyset_m \mid MS \mid \{it\}_m \mid msi^*(lt) \mid msit_1 \cup msit_2 \mid msit_1 \cap msit_2 \mid msit_1 \setminus msit_2 \mid \texttt{ite}(\varphi, msit_1, msit_2)
\end{array}
$$

$$
\begin{array}{rcl}
\text{Formula: } \varphi, \varphi_1, \varphi_2, \ldots & ::= & \texttt{true} \mid q \mid p^*(lt) \mid lt_1 = lt_2 \mid it_1 \leq it_2 \mid sit_1 \subseteq sit_2 \mid msit_1 \subseteq msit_2 \mid \\
 & & sit_1 \leq sit_2 \mid msit_1 \leq msit_2 \mid it \in sit \mid it \in msit \mid \neg\varphi \mid \varphi_1 \vee \varphi_2
\end{array}
$$

$$
\begin{array}{rcl}
\text{Recursively-defined integer : } i^*(x) & \stackrel{def}{=} & \texttt{ite}(x = \texttt{nil},\ i_{base},\ i_{ind}) \\
\text{Recursively-defined set-of-integers : } si^*(x) & \stackrel{def}{=} & \texttt{ite}(x = \texttt{nil},\ si_{base},\ si_{ind}) \\
\text{Recursively-defined multiset-of-integers : } msi^*(x) & \stackrel{def}{=} & \texttt{ite}(x = \texttt{nil},\ msi_{base},\ msi_{ind}) \\
\text{Recursively-defined predicate : } p^*(x) & \stackrel{def}{=} & \texttt{ite}(x = \texttt{nil},\ p_{base},\ p_{ind})
\end{array}
$$

Figure 1. Syntax of DRYAD

Finally, we evaluate our logical mechanisms and procedures, by writing several tree data-structure algorithms using pure recursive imperative programs, annotating them using DRYAD in order to state their complete functional correctness, derive the verification conditions expressed as footprints and DRYAD formulae, and prove them valid using the formula abstraction scheme. Much to our surprise, all verification conditions in all the programs were proved valid automatically and efficiently by our procedure.

We have verified full functional correctness of data-structures ranging from sorted linked lists, binary search trees, max-heaps, treaps (which are binary search trees on the first key and max-heaps on the second), AVL trees and red-black trees (semi-balanced search trees), B-trees, and binomial heaps. This set of benchmarks is an almost exhaustive list of algorithms on tree-based data-structures covered in a first undergraduate course on data-structures [10]. To the best of our knowledge, the work presented here is the first methodology that can prove such a wide variety of algorithms on tree data-structures written in an imperative language fully functionally correct using a sound and terminating procedure.

2. The DRYAD Logic for Heaps

The recursive logic over trees, DRYAD, is essentially a *quantifier-free* first-order logic over heaps augmented with recursive definitions of various types (e.g., integers, sets/multisets of integers, etc.) defined for locations that have a tree under them. While first-order logic gives the necessary power to talk precisely about locations that are near neighbors, the recursive definitions allow expressing properties that require quantifiers, including reachability, collecting the set/multiset of keys in a tree, and defining natural metrics, like the height of a tree, that are typically useful in defining properties of trees.

Given a finite set of *directions* Dir, let us define Dir-trees as finite trees where every location has either $|Dir|$ children, or is the `nil` location, which has no children (we assume there is a single `nil` location). Binary trees have two directions: $Dir = \{l, r\}$.

The logic DRYAD is parameterized by a finite set of *directions* Dir and also by a finite set of *data-fields* DF. Let us fix these sets.

Let $Bool = \{\texttt{true}, \texttt{false}\}$ stand for the set of Boolean values, Int stand for the set of integers and Loc stand for the universe of locations. For any set A, let $\mathcal{S}(A)$ denote the set of subsets of A, and let $\mathcal{MS}(A)$ denote the set of all multisets with elements in A.

The DRYAD logic allows four kinds of recursively defined notions for a location that is the root of a Dir-tree: recursively defined integer functions ($Loc \rightarrow Int$), recursively defined set-of-keys/integers functions ($Loc \rightarrow \mathcal{S}(Int)$), recursively defined multiset-of-keys/integers functions ($Loc \rightarrow \mathcal{MS}(Int)$), and recursively defined Boolean predicates ($Loc \rightarrow Bool$). Let us fix disjoint sets of countable names for such functions. We will refer to these recursive functions as recursively defined integers, recursively defined sets/multisets of integers, and recursively defined predicates, respectively. Typical examples of these include the height of a tree or the height of black-nodes in the tree rooted at a node (recursively defined integers), the set/multiset of keys stored at a particular data-field under nodes (recursively defined set/multiset of integers), and the property that the tree rooted at a node is a binary search tree or a balanced tree (recursively defined predicates).

A DRYAD formula consists of a pair (Def, φ), where Def is a set of recursive definitions and φ is a formula. The syntax of DRYAD logic is given in Figure 1, where the syntax of the formulas is followed by the syntax for recursive definitions. We require that every recursive function/predicate used in the formula φ has a unique definition in Def. The figure does not define the syntax of the base and inductive formulas in recursive definitions (e.g. i_{base}, i_{ind}, etc.); we give that in the text below.

Location terms are formed using pointer fields from location variables, and include a special location called `nil`. Integer terms are obtained from integer constants, data-fields of locations, and from recursively defined integers, and combined using basic arithmetic operations of addition and subtraction and conditionals (`ite` stands for if-then-else terms that evaluate to the second argument if the first argument evaluates to `true` and evaluate to the third argument otherwise).

Terms that evaluate to a set/multiset of integers are obtained from recursively defined sets/multisets of integers corresponding to a location term, and are combined using set/multiset operations as well as conditional choices. Formulas are obtained by Boolean combinations of Boolean variables, recursively defined predicates on a location term, and using various relations between set and multiset terms. The relations on sets and multisets include the subset relation as well as the relation $\leq$ which is interpreted as follows: for two sets (or multisets) of integers S_1 and S_2, $S_1 \leq S_2$ holds whenever for every $i \in S_1, j \in S_2, i \leq j$.

The recursively defined functions (or predicates) are defined using the syntax: $f^*(x) = \texttt{ite}(x = \texttt{nil},\ f_{base},\ f_{ind})$, where f_{base} and f_{ind} are themselves terms (or formulas) that stand for what f evaluates to when $x = \texttt{nil}$ (the base-case) and when $x \neq \texttt{nil}$ (the inductive step), respectively. There are several restrictions on these terms/formulas:

- f_{base} has no free variables and hence evaluates to a fixed value (for integers, it is a fixed integer; for sets/multisets of integers, it is a fixed set; for Boolean predicates, it evaluates to `true` or `false`).
- f_{ind} only has x as a free variable. Furthermore, the location terms in it can only be x and $x.dir$ (further dereferences are disallowed). Moreover, integer terms $x.dir.f$ are disallowed.

Intuitively, the above conditions demand that when x is `nil`, the function evaluates to a constant of the appropriate type, and when $x \neq$ `nil`, it evaluates to a function that is defined recursively using properties of the location x, which may include properties of the children of x, and these properties may in turn involve other recursively defined functions.

We assume that the inductive definitions are not *circular*. Formally, let *Def* be a set of definitions and consider a recursive definition of a function f^* in *Def*. Define the sequence $\psi_0, \psi_1, \ldots$ as follows. Set $\psi_0 = f^*(x)$. Obtain ψ_{i+1} by replacing every occurrence of $g^*(x)$ in ψ_i by $g_{ind}(x)$, where g is any recursively defined function in *Def*. We require that this sequence eventually stabilizes (i.e. there is a k such that $\psi_k = \psi_{k+1}$). Intuitively, we require that the definition of $f^*(x)$ be rewritable into a formula that does not refer to a recursive definition of x (by getting rewritten to properties of its descendants). We require that every definition in *Def* have the above property.

Example: Red Black Trees Red black trees are semi-balanced binary search trees with nodes colored red and black, with all the leaves colored black, satisfying the condition that the left and right children of a red node are black, and the condition that the number of black nodes on paths from the root to any leaf is the same. This ensures that the longest path from root to a leaf is at most twice the shortest path from root to a leaf, making the tree roughly balanced.

We have two directions $Dir = \{l, r\}$, and two data fields, *key*, and *color*. We model the color of nodes using an integer data-field *color*, which can be 0 (black) or 1 (red). We define four recursive functions/predicates: a predicate $black^*(x)$ that checks whether the root of the tree under x is colored black (this is defined as a recursive predicate for technical reasons), the black height of a tree, $bh^*(x)$, the multiset of keys stored in a tree, $keys^*(x)$, and a recursive predicate that identifies red-black trees, $rbt^*(x)$.

$$\begin{aligned}
black^*(x) &\stackrel{def}{=} \mathtt{ite}(\ x = \mathtt{nil},\ \mathtt{true},\ x.color = 0\ )\\
bh^*(x) &\stackrel{def}{=} \mathtt{ite}(\ x = \mathtt{nil},\ 1,\ \mathtt{ite}(\ x.color = 0,\ 1,\ 0\ ) +\\
&\qquad \mathtt{ite}(bh^*(x.l) \geq bh^*(x.r), bh^*(x.l), bh^*(x.r)\ )\\
keys^*(x) &\stackrel{def}{=} \mathtt{ite}(\ x = \mathtt{nil}, \emptyset, \{x.key\} \cup keys^*(x.l) \cup keys^*(x.r)\ )\\
rbt^*(x) &\stackrel{def}{=} \mathtt{ite}(\ x = \mathtt{nil},\ \mathtt{true},\\
&\qquad rbt^*(x.l) \wedge rbt^*(x.r) \wedge\\
&\qquad keys^*(x.l) \leq \{x.key\} \wedge \{x.key\} \leq keys^*(x.r) \wedge\\
&\qquad (x.color = 1 \rightarrow (black^*(x.l) \wedge black^*(x.r)))\wedge\\
&\qquad bh^*(x.l) = bh^*(x.r)\ )
\end{aligned}$$

The $bh^*(t)$ function definition says that the black height of a tree is 1 for a `nil` node (`nil` nodes are assumed to be `black`), and, otherwise, the maximum of the black heights of the left and right subtree if the node x is *red*, and the maximum of the black heights of the left and right subtree plus one, if x is `black`. The $keys^*(t)$ function says that the multiset of keys stored in a tree is $\emptyset$ for a `nil`-node, and the union of the key stored in the node, and the keys of the left and right subtrees. Finally, the $rbt^*(t)$ holds if: (1) the left and right subtrees are valid red black trees; (2) the keys of the left subtree are no greater than the key in the node, and the keys of the right subtree are no less than the key in the node; (3) if the node is `red`, both its children are `black`; and (4) the black heights of the left and the right subtrees are equal.

We can also express, in our logic, various properties of red black trees, by including the above definitions and a formula like:

$$(rbt^*(t) \wedge \neg black^*(t) \wedge t.key = 20) \rightarrow 10 \notin keys^*(t.r)$$

and using the procedures outlined in this paper, check the validity of the above statement.

Semantics

The Dryad logic is interpreted on (concrete) heaps. Let us fix a finite set of *program variables PV*. Concrete heaps are defined as follows ($f : A \rightharpoonup B$ denotes a partial function from A to B):

Definition 2.1. *A concrete heap over a set of directions Dir, a set of data-fields DF, and a set of program variables PV is a tuple*

$$(N, nil, pf, df, pv)$$

where:

- *N is a finite or infinite set of locations;*
- *$nil \in N$ is a special location representing the null pointer;*
- *$pf : (N \setminus \{nil\}) \times Dir \rightarrow N$ is a function defining the direction fields;*
- *$df : (N \setminus \{nil\}) \times DF \rightarrow \mathbb{Z}$ is a function defining the data-fields;*
- *$pv : PV \rightharpoonup N \cup \mathbb{Z}$ is a partial function mapping program variables to locations or integers, depending on the type of the variable.* □

A concrete heap consists of a finite/infinite set of locations, with a pointer-field function *pf* that maps locations to locations for each direction $dir \in Dir$, a data-field function *df* mapping locations to integers for each data-field *DF*, along with a unique constant location representing `nil` that has no data-fields or pointer-fields from it. Moreover, the function *pv* is a partial function that maps program variables to locations and integers.

A Dryad formula with free variables F is interpreted by interpreting the program variables in F according to the function *pv* and the other variables being given an interpretation (hence, for validity, these other variables are universally quantified, and for satisfiability, they are existentially quantified).

Each term evaluates to either a normal value of the corresponding type, or to `undef`. A location term is evaluated by dereferencing pointers in the heap. If a dereference is undefined, the term evaluates to `undef`. The set of locations that are roots of *Dir*-trees are special in that they are the only ones over which recursive definitions are properly defined. A term of the form $i^*(lt)$, $si^*(lt)$ or $msi^*(lt)$ will evaluate to `undef` if lt evaluates to `undef` or is not a root of a tree in the heap; otherwise it will be evaluated inductively using its recursive definition. Other aspects of the logic are interpreted with the usual semantics of first-order logic, unless they contain some subterm evaluating to `undef`, in which case they also evaluate to `undef`.

Each Dryad formula evaluates to either `true` or `false`. To evaluate a formula φ, we first convert φ to its *negation normal form (NNF)*, and evaluate each atomic formula of the form $p^*(lt)$ first. If lt is not undefined, $p^*(lt)$ will be evaluated inductively using the recursive definition of p^*; if lt evaluates to `undef`, $p^*(lt)$ will evaluate to `false` if $p^*(lt)$ appears positively, and will evaluate to `true` otherwise. Intuitively, undefined recursive predicates cannot help in making the formula true over a model. Similarly, atomic formulas involving terms that evaluate to `undef` are set to false or true depending on whether the atomic formula occurs within an even or odd number of negations, respectively. All other relations between integers, sets, and multisets are interpreted in the natural way, and we skip defining their semantics.

We assume that the DRYAD formulas always include a recursively defined predicate *tree* that is defined as:

$$tree^*(x) \stackrel{def}{=} (x = \texttt{nil}, \texttt{true}, \texttt{true})$$

Note that since recursively defined predicates can hold only on trees and since the above formula vacuously holds on any tree, $tree^*(x)$ holds iff x is a root of a *Dir*-tree.

Programs and basic blocks

We consider imperative programs manipulating heap structures and the data contained in the heap. In this paper, we assume that programs do not contain *while* loops and all recursion is captured using recursive function calls. Consequently, proof annotations only involve pre- and post-conditions of functions, and there are no loop-invariants.

The imperative programs we analyze will consist of integer operations, heap operations, conditionals and recursion. In order to verify programs with appropriate proof annotations, we need to verify linear blocks of code, called *basic blocks*, which do not have conditionals (conditionals are replaced with *assume* statements). Basic blocks always start from the *beginning* of a function and either end at an assertion in the program (checking an intermediate assertion), or end at a function call to check whether the precondition to calling the function holds, or ends at the end of the program in order to check whether the post-condition holds. Basic blocks can involve recursive and non-recursive function calls.

We define basic blocks using the following grammar, parameterized by a set of directions *Dir* and a set of data-fields *DF*:

$$\begin{array}{lll} bb & :- & bb'; \mid bb'; \texttt{ return } u; \mid bb'; \texttt{ return } j; \\ bb' & :- & bb'; bb' \mid u := v \mid u := \texttt{nil} \mid u := v.dir \mid u.dir := v \mid \\ & & j := u.f \mid u.f := j \mid u := \texttt{new} \mid j := aexpr \mid \\ & & \texttt{assume}\ (bexpr) \mid u := f(v, z_1, \ldots, z_n) \mid j := g(v, z_1, \ldots, z_n) \\ aexpr & :- & j \mid aexpr + aexpr \mid aexpr - aexpr \\ bexpr & :- & u = v \mid u = \texttt{nil} \mid aexpr \leq aexpr \mid \neg bexpr \mid bexpr \vee bexpr \end{array}$$

Since we deal with tree data-structure manipulating programs, which often involve functions that take as input a tree and return a tree, we make certain crucial assumptions. One crucial restriction we assume for the technical exposition is that all functions take in at most *one* location parameter as input (the rest have to be integers). Basic blocks hence have function calls of the form $f(v, z_1, \ldots z_n)$, where v is the only location parameter. This restriction greatly simplifies the proofs as it is much easier to track one tree. We can relax this assumption, but when several trees are passed as parameters, our decision procedures will implicitly assume a precondition that the trees are all disjoint. This is crucial; our decision procedures cannot track trees that "collide"; they track only equal trees and disjoint trees. This turns out to be a natural property of most data-structure manipulating programs.

Pre- and Post-conditions of functions

We place stringent restrictions on annotations pre- and post-functions that we allow in our framework, and these are important for our technique and is the price we pay for automation. Recall that we allow only two kinds of functions, one returning a location $f(v, z_1, \ldots, z_n)$ and one returning an integer $g(v, z_1, \ldots, z_n)$ (v is a location parameter, $z_1, \ldots, z_n$ are integer parameters). We require that v is the root of a *Dir*-tree at the point when the function is called, and this is an implicit pre-condition of the function called.

Each function is annotated with its pre- and post-conditions using *annotating formulas*. Annotating terms and formulas are DRYAD terms and formulas that do not refer to any child or any data field, do not allow any equality between locations and do not allow `ite`-expressions. We denote the pre-condition as a *pre-annotating formula* $\psi(v, z_1, \ldots, z_n)$.

The post-condition annotation is more complex, as it can talk about properties of the heap at the pre-state as well as the post-state. We allow combining terms and formulas obtained from the pre-heap and the post-heap to express the post-condition. Terms and formulas over the post-heap are obtained using DRYAD annotating terms and formulas that are allowed to refer to a variable old_v which points to the location v pointed to in the pre-heap. These terms and formulas can also refer to the variable ret_loc or ret_int to refer to the location or integer being returned. Terms and formulas over the pre-heap are obtained using DRYAD annotating terms and formulas referring to old_v and old_z_i's, except that all recursive definitions are renamed to have the prefix $old\_$. Then a *post-annotating formula* combines terms and formulas expressed over the pre-heap and the post-heap (using the standard operations).

For a function $f(v, z_1, \ldots z_n)$ that returns a location, we assume that the returned location always has a *Dir*-tree under it (and this is implicitly assumed to be part of the post-condition). The post-condition for f is either of the form

$$\texttt{havoc}(old\_v) \wedge \psi(old\_v, old\_z_1, \ldots, old\_z_n, ret\_loc)$$

or of the form

$$old\_v \# ret\_loc \wedge \psi(old\_v, old\_z_1, \ldots, old\_z_n, ret\_loc)$$

where ψ is a post-annotating formula. In the first kind, $\texttt{havoc}(old\_v)$ means that the function guarantees nothing about the location pointed to in the pre-state by the input parameter v (and nothing about the locations accessible from that location) and hence the caller of f cannot assume anything about the location it passed to f after the call returns. In that case, we restrict ψ from referring to $r^*(old_v)$, where r^* is a recursive predicate/function on the post-heap. In the latter kind $old\_v \# ret\_loc$ means that f, at the point of return, assures that the location passed as parameter v now points to a *Dir*-tree and this tree is disjoint from the tree rooted at ret_loc.

In either case, the formula ψ can relate complex properties of the returned location and the input parameter, including recursive definitions on the old parameter and the new ones. For example, a post-condition of the form $\texttt{havoc}(old\_v) \wedge keys^*(old\_v) = keys^*(ret\_loc)$ says that the keys under the returned location are precisely the same as the keys under the location passed to the function.

For a function g returning an integer, the post-condition is of the form

$$\texttt{tree}(old\_v) \wedge \psi(old\_v, old\_z_1, \ldots, old\_z_n, ret\_int)$$

or of the form

$$\texttt{havoc}(old\_v) \wedge \psi(old\_v, old\_z_1, \ldots, old\_z_n, ret\_int)$$

The former says that the location passed as input continues to point to a tree, while the latter says that no property is assured about the location passed as input (same restriction on ψ applies).

The above restriction that the input tree and the returned tree either point to completely disjoint trees or that the input pointer (and nodes accessible from it) are entirely havoc-ed and the returned node is some tree are the only separation and aliasing properties that the post-condition can assert. Our logical mechanism is incapable, for example, of saying the the returned node is a reachable node from the location passed to the function. We have carefully chosen such restrictions in order to simplify tracking tree-ness and separation in the footprint. In practice, most data-structure algorithms fall into these categories (for example, an insert routine would havoc the input tree and return a new tree whose keys are related to the keys of the input tree, while a tree-copying program will return a tree disjoint from the input tree).

3. Describing the Verification Condition in DRYAD

We now present the main technical contribution of this paper: given a set of recursive definitions, and a Hoare-triple $(\varphi_{pre}, bb, \varphi_{post})$, where bb is a basic block, we show how to systematically define the verification condition corresponding to it. Note that since we do not have while-loops, basic blocks always start at the beginning of a function and go either till the end of the function (spanning calls to other functions) or go up to a function call (in order to check if the pre-condition for that call holds). In the former case, the post-condition is a post-condition annotation. In the latter case, we need another form:

$$\texttt{tree}(y) \wedge \psi(\bar{x})$$

where $\bar{x}$ is a subset of program variables. The pre-condition of the called function implicitly assumes that the input location is a tree (which is expressed using $\texttt{tree}(y)$ above), and the pre-condition itself is adapted (after substituting formal parameters with actual terms passed to the function) and written as the formula ψ.

This verification condition is expressed as a combination of (a) quantifier-free formulas that define properties of the footprint the basic block uncovers on the heap, combined with (b) recursive formulas expressed only on the frontier of the footprint.

This verification condition is formed by unrolling recursive definitions appropriately as the basic block increases its footprint so that recursive properties are translated to properties of the frontier. This allows us to write the (strongest) post-condition of φ_{pre} on precisely the same nodes as φ_{post} refers to, which then allows us to apply *formula abstractions* to prove the verification condition. Also, recursive calls to functions that process the data-structure recursively are naturally called on the frontier of the footprint, which allows us to summarize the call to the function on the frontier.

We define the verification condition using two steps. In the first step, we inductively define a *footprint structure*, composed of a *symbolic heap* and a DRYAD formula, which captures the state of the program that results when the basic block executes from a configuration satisfying the pre-condition. We then incorporate the post-condition and derive the verification condition.

A symbolic heap is defined as follows:

Definition 3.1. *A* symbolic heap *over a set of directions Dir, a set of data-fields DF, and a set of program variables PV is a tuple*

$$(C, S, I, c_{nil}, pf, df, pv)$$

where:

- *C is a finite set of* concrete nodes*;*
- *S is a finite set of* symbolic tree nodes *with $C \cap S = \emptyset$;*
- *I is a set of integer variables;*
- *$c_{nil} \in C$ is a special concrete node representing nil;*
- *$pf : (C \setminus \{c_{nil}\}) \times Dir \rightharpoonup C \cup S$ is a partial function mapping every pair of a concrete node and a direction to nodes (concrete or symbolic);*
- *$df : (C \setminus \{c_{nil}\}) \times DF \rightharpoonup I$ is a partial function mapping concrete nodes and data-fields pairs to integer variables;*
- *$pv : PV \rightharpoonup C \cup S \cup I$ is a partial function mapping program variables to nodes or integer variables (location variables are mapped to $C \cup S$ and integer variables to I).* □

Intuitively, a symbolic heap $(C, S, I, c_{nil}, pf, df, pv)$ has two finite sets of nodes: concrete nodes C and symbolic tree nodes S, with the understanding that each $s \in S$ stands for a node that may have an arbitrary *Dir*-tree under it, and furthermore the separation constraint that for any two symbolic tree nodes s, $s' \in S$, the trees under it would not intersect with each other, nor with the nodes in C. The tree under a symbolic node is not represented in the symbolic heap at all. One of the concrete nodes (c_{nil}) represents the `nil` location.

The function *pf* captures the pointer-field *dir* in the heap that is within the footprint, and maps the set of concrete nodes to concrete and symbolic nodes. The pointer fields of symbolic nodes are not modeled, as they are part of the tree below the node that is not represented in the footprint. The functions *df* and *pv* capture the data-fields (mapping to integer variables) and program variables restricted to the nodes in the symbolic heap.

A symbolic heap hence represents a (typically infinite) set of concrete heaps, namely those in which it can be embedded. We define this formally using the notion of *correspondence* that captures when a concrete heap is represented by a symbolic heap.

Definition 3.2. *Let $SH = (C, S, I, c_{nil}, pf, df, pv)$ be a symbolic heap and let $CH = (N, nil, pf', df', pv')$ be a concrete heap. Then CH is said to* correspond *to SH if there are two function $h : C \cup S \to N$ such that the following conditions hold:*

- *$h(c_{nil}) = nil$;*
- *for any $n, n' \in C$, if $n \neq n'$, then $h(n) \neq h(n')$;*
- *for any two nodes $n \in C \setminus \{c_{nil}\}$, $n' \in C \cup S$, and for any $dir \in Dir$, if $pf(n, dir) = n'$, then $pf'(h(n), dir)) = h(n')$;*
- *for any $s \in S$, $h(s)$ is the root of a Dir-tree in CH, and there is no concrete node $c \in C \setminus \{c_{nil}\}$ such that $h(c)$ belongs to this tree;*
- *for any $s, s' \in S$, $s \neq s'$, the Dir-trees rooted at $h(s)$ and $h(s')$ (in CH) are disjoint except for the nil node;*
- *for any location variable $v \in PV$, if $pv(v)$ is defined, then $pv'(v) = h(pv(v))$;* □

Intuitively, h above defines a restricted kind of homomorphism between the nodes of the symbolic heap *SH* and a portion of the concrete heap *CH*. Distinct concrete non-nil nodes are required to map to distinct locations in the concrete heap. Symbolic nodes are required to map to trees that are disjoint (save the *nil* location); they can map to the *nil* location as well. The trees rooted at locations corresponding to symbolic nodes must be disjoint from the locations corresponding to concrete nodes. Note that there is no requirement on the integer variables I and the map pv' on integer variables and the maps *df* and *df'*. Note also that for a concrete node in the symbolic heap n, the fields defined from n in the symbolic heap must occur in the concrete heap as well from the corresponding location $h(n)$; however, the fields not defined for n may or may not be defined on $h(n)$.

A *footprint* is a pair $(SH; \varphi)$ where *SH* is a symbolic heap and φ is a DRYAD formula. The semantics of such a footprint is that it represents all concrete heaps that both correspond to *SH* and satisfy φ.

Tree-ness of nodes in symbolic heaps

The key property of a symbolic heap is that we can determine that certain nodes have *Dir*-trees rooted under them (i.e. in *any* concrete heap corresponding to the symbolic heap, the corresponding locations will have a *Dir*-tree under them).

For a symbolic heap $SH = (C, S, I, c_{nil}, pf, df, pv)$, let the set of *graph nodes* of *SH* be the smallest set of nodes $V \subseteq C \cup S$ such that:

- $c_{nil} \in V$ and $S \subseteq V$
- For any node $n \in C$, if for every $dir \in Dir$, $pf(n, dir)$ is defined and belongs to V, then $n \in V$.

Now define *Graph*(*SH*) to be the directed graph (V, E), where V is as above, and E is the set of edges (u, v) such that $pf(u, dir) = v$ for some $dir \in Dir$. Note that, by definition, there are no edges out of u if $u \in S$, as symbolic nodes do not have outgoing fields.

We say that a node u in V is the root of a tree in *Graph(SH)* if the set of all nodes reachable from u forms a tree (in the usual graph-theoretic sense).

The following claim follows and is the crux of using the symbolic heap to determine tree-ness of nodes:

Lemma 3.3. *Let SH be a symbolic heap and let CH be a corresponding concrete heap, defined by a function h. If a node u is the root of a tree in Graph(SH), then h(u) also subtends a tree in CH.*

A proof gist is as follows. First, note that symbolic nodes and the node c_{nil} are always roots of trees in *Graph(SH)* and the locations in the concrete heap corresponding to them subtend trees (in fact, disjoint trees save the *nil* location). Turning to concrete nodes, we need to argue that if c is a concrete node in *Graph(SH)*, then $h(c)$ is the root of a *Dir*-tree in *CH*. This follows by induction on the height of the tree under c in *Graph(SH)*, since each of the *Dir* children of c in *Graph(SH)* must either be the c_{nil} node or a summary node or a concrete node that is a the root of a tree of less height. The corresponding locations in *CH*, by induction hypothesis or by the above observations, have *Dir*-trees suspended from them. In fact, by the definition of correspondence, these trees are all disjoint except for the *nil* location (since trees corresponding to summary nodes are all disjoint and disjoint from locations corresponding to concrete nodes, and since concrete nodes in the symbolic heap denote).

The location corresponding to a concrete node in *Graph(SH)* that does not have all *Dir*-fields defined in *SH* may or may not have a *Dir*-tree subtended from it; this is because the notion of correspondence allows the corresponding location to have more fields defined. In the sequel, when we use symbolic heaps for tracking footprints, such concrete nodes with partially defined *Dir* fields will occur only when processing function calls (where all information about a node may not be known).

Initial footprint

Let the pre-condition be $\varphi_{pre}(u, j_1, \ldots, j_m)$, where u is the only location program variable, there is a *Dir*-tree rooted at u, and $j_1, \ldots, j_m$ are integer program variables. Then we define the initial symbolic heap:

$$(C_0, S_0, I_0, c_{nil}, pf_0, df_0, pv_0)$$

where $C_0 = \{c_{nil}\}$, $S_0 = \{n_0\}$, $I = \{i_1, \ldots i_m\}$, pf_0 and df_0 are empty functions (i.e. functions with an empty domain), and pv_0 maps u to n_0 and $j_1, ..., j_m$ to $i_1, ..., i_m$, respectively. The initial formula φ_0 is obtained from $\varphi_{pre}(u, j_1, \ldots, j_m)$ by replacing u by n_0 and $j_1, ..., j_m$ by $i_1, ..., i_m$, and by adding the conjunct $p^*(c_{nil}) \leftrightarrow p_{base}$ or $f^*(c_{nil}) = f_{base}$ for all recursive predicates and functions. Note that the formula is defined over the variables $S_0 \cup I_0$. Intuitively, we start at the beginning of the function with a single symbolic node that stands for the input parameter, which is a tree, and a concrete node that stands for `nil`. All integer parameters are assigned to distinct variables in I.

Expanding the footprint

A basic operation on a pair, $(SH; \varphi)$, consisting of a symbolic heap, and a formula is expansion. Let *SH* be

$$(C, S, I, c_{nil}, pf, df, pv)$$

and $n \in C \cup S$ be a node. We define $expand((SH; \varphi), n) = (SH'; \varphi')$, where SH' is the tuple

$$(C', S', I', c_{nil}, pf', df', pv')$$

as follows: if $n \in C$ (the node is already expanded), then do nothing by setting $(SH'; \varphi')$ to $(SH; \varphi)$; otherwise:

- $C' = C \cup \{n\}$, where n is the node being expanded
- $S' = S \uplus \{n_{dir} \mid dir \in Dir\} \setminus \{n\}$, where each n_{dir} is a fresh new node different from the nodes in $C \cup S$
- $I' = I \uplus \{i_f \mid f \in DF\}$, where each i_f is a fresh new integer variable
- $pf' |_{C \setminus \{c_{nil}\} \times Dir} = pf$, and $pf'(n, dir) = n_{dir}$ for all $dir \in Dir$
- $df' |_{C \setminus \{c_{nil}\} \times DF} = df$, and $df'(n, f) = i_f$ for all $f \in DF$
- $pv' = pv$;

The formula φ' is obtained from the formula φ as follows:

$$\begin{array}{rcl}
\varphi' & = & \varphi[\bar{p}_n, \bar{f}_n / \bar{p}^*(n), \bar{f}^*(n)] \\
 & \wedge & \bigwedge_{p^*} \left(p_n \leftrightarrow \hat{p}_{ind}(n)\right) \wedge \bigwedge_{f^*} \left(f_n = \hat{f}_{ind}(n)\right) \\
 & \wedge & n \neq c_{nil} \wedge \bigwedge_{n' \in C' \setminus \{c_{nil}\}, dir \in Dir} \left(n' \neq n_{dir}\right) \\
 & \wedge & \bigwedge_{dir \in Dir, s \in S} \left(n_{dir} = s \rightarrow n_{dir} = c_{nil}\right) \\
 & \wedge & \bigwedge_{dir_1, dir_2 \in Dir, dir_1 \neq dir_2} \left(n_{dir_1} = n_{dir_2} \rightarrow n_{dir_1} = c_{nil}\right)
\end{array}$$

where $\bar{p}_n$ are fresh Boolean variables, $\bar{f}_n$ are fresh term (integer, set, ...) variables, $p^*(x) \stackrel{def}{=} \texttt{ite}(x = \texttt{nil}, p_{base}, p_{ind}(x))$ ranges over all the recursive predicates, and $f^*(x) \stackrel{def}{=} \texttt{ite}(x = \texttt{nil}, f_{base}, f_{ind}(x))$ ranges over all the recursive functions. Intuitively, The variables $\bar{p}_n$ and $\bar{f}_n$ capture the values of the predicates and functions for the node n in the current symbolic heap. This is possible because the values of the recursive predicates and functions for concrete non-*nil* nodes are determined by the values of the functions and predicates for symbolic nodes and the *nil* node. The formula $\hat{p}_{ind}(n)$ is obtained from $p_{ind}(n)$, by substituting every location term of the form $n.dir$ with n_{dir} for every $dir \in Dir$, and substituting every integer term of the form $n.f$ with i_f for every $f \in DF$. The term $\hat{f}_{ind}(n)$ is obtained by the same substitutions.

Evolving the footprint on basic blocks

Given a symbolic heap *SH* along with a formula φ, and a basic block *bb*. We compute the symbolic execution of *bb* using the transformation function $st((SH; \varphi), bb) = (SH'; \varphi')$. The transformation function *st* is computed transitively; i.e., if *bb* is of the form $(stmt; bb')$ where *stmt* is an atomic statement and bb' is a basic block, then

$$st((SH; \varphi), bb) = st(st((SH; \varphi), stmt), bb')$$

Therefore, it is enough to define the transformation for the various atomic statements. Given $SH = (C, S, I, c_{nil}, pf, df, pv)$, φ and an atomic statement *stmt*, we define $st((SH; \varphi), stmt)$ as follows by cases of *stmt*. Unless some assumptions fail (in which case the transformation is undefined), we describe $st((SH; \varphi), stmt)$ as $(SH'; \varphi')$.

As per our convention, function updates are denoted in the form of $[arg \leftarrow new\_val]$. For example, $pv[u \leftarrow n]$ denotes the function pv except that $pv(u)$ maps to n. Formula substitutions are denoted in the form of $[new/old]$. For example, $\varphi[df'/df]$ denotes the formula obtained from the formula φ by substituting every occurrence of df with df'.

The following defines how the footprint evolves across all possible statements *except* function calls:

(a) $stmt : u := v$

If $pv(v)$ is undefined, the transformation is undefined; otherwise

$$\begin{array}{rcl}
SH' & = & (C, S, I, c_{nil}, pf, df, pv[u \leftarrow pv(v)]) \\
\varphi' & \equiv & \varphi
\end{array}$$

(b) *stmt* : u := `nil`

$$SH' = (C, S, I, c_{nil}, pf, df, pv[u \leftarrow c_{nil}])$$
$$\varphi' \equiv \varphi$$

(c) *stmt* : $u := v.dir$
If $pv(v)$ is undefined, or $pv(v) \in C$ and $pf(pv(v), dir)$ is undefined, the transformation is undefined. Otherwise we expand the symbolic heap:

$$((C'', S'', I'', c_{nil}, pf'', df'', pv''); \varphi'') = expand((SH; \varphi), pv(v))$$

Now $pv''(v)$ must be in $C'' \setminus \{c_{nil}\}$, and we set

$$SH' = (C'', S'', I'', c_{nil}, pf'', df'', pv''[u \leftarrow pf''(pv''(v), dir)])$$
$$\varphi' \equiv \varphi''$$

(d) *stmt* : $j := v.f$
If $pv(v)$ is undefined, or $pv(v) \in C$ and $pf(pv(v), f)$ is undefined, the transformation is undefined. Otherwise we expand the symbolic heap:

$$((C'', S'', I'', c_{nil}, pf'', df'', pv''); \varphi'') = expand((SH; \varphi), pv(v))$$

Now $pv''(v)$ must be in $C'' \setminus \{c_{nil}\}$, and we set

$$SH' = (C'', S'', I'' \uplus \{i\}, c_{nil}, pf'', df'', pv''[j \leftarrow i])$$
$$\varphi' \equiv \varphi'' \wedge i = df''(pv''(v), f)$$

(e) *stmt* : $u.dir := v$
If $pv(u)$ or $pv(v)$ is undefined, or $pv(u) = c_{nil}$, the transformation is undefined. Otherwise we expand the symbolic heap:

$$((C'', S'', I'', c_{nil}, pf'', df'', pv''); \varphi'') = expand((SH; \varphi), pv(u))$$

Now $pv''(u)$ must be in $C'' \setminus \{c_{nil}\}$, and we set

$$SH' = (C'', S'', I'', c_{nil}, pf''[(pv''(u), dir) \leftarrow pv''(v)], df'', pv'')$$
$$\varphi' \equiv \varphi''$$

(f) *stmt* : $u.f := j$
If $pv(u)$ or $pv(j)$ is undefined, or $pv(u) = c_{nil}$, the transformation is undefined. Otherwise we expand the symbolic heap:

$$((C'', S'', I'', c_{nil}, pf'', df'', pv''); \varphi'') = expand((SH; \varphi), pv(u))$$

Now $pv''(u)$ must be in $C'' \setminus \{c_{nil}\}$, and we set

$$SH' = (C'', S'', I'' \uplus \{i\}, c_{nil}, pf'', df''[(pv''(u), f) \leftarrow i], pv'')$$
$$\varphi' \equiv \varphi'' \wedge i = pv''(j)$$

(g) *stmt* : u := `new`
We assume that, for the new location, every pointer initially points to `nil` and every data field initially evaluates to 0.

$$SH' = (C \uplus \{n\}, S, I \uplus \{i_f \mid f \in DF\}, c_{nil}, pf', df', pv[u \leftarrow n])$$
$$\varphi' \equiv \varphi \wedge \bigwedge_{f \in DF} \left(i_f = 0\right) \wedge \bigwedge_{n' \in C \cup S} \left(n \neq n'\right)$$

where pf' and df' are defined as follows:

- $pf' \mid_{C \setminus \{c_{nil}\} \times Dir} = pf$, and $pf'(n, dir) = c_{nil}$ for all $dir \in Dir$
- $df' \mid_{C \setminus \{c_{nil}\} \times DF} = df$, and $df'(n, f) = i_f$ for all $f \in DF$

(h) *stmt* : $j := aexpr(\bar{k})$
If pv is undefined on any variable in $\bar{k}$, then the transformation is undefined; otherwise

$$SH' = (C, S, I \uplus \{i\}, c_{nil}, pf, df, pv[j \leftarrow i])$$
$$\varphi' \equiv \varphi \wedge i = aexpr[pv(\bar{k})/\bar{k}]$$

(i) *stmt* : `assume` $bexpr(\bar{v}, \bar{j})$
If pv is undefined on any variable in $pv(\bar{v})$ or in $pv(\bar{j})$, then the transformation is undefined; otherwise

$$SH' = SH$$
$$\varphi' \equiv \varphi \wedge bexpr[pv(\bar{v}), pv(\bar{j})/\bar{v}, \bar{j}]$$

(j) *stmt* : `return` u
If $pv(u)$ is undefined, the transformation is undefined; otherwise

$$SH' = (C, S, I, c_{nil}, pf, df, pv[ret\_loc \leftarrow pv(u)])$$
$$\varphi' \equiv \varphi$$

(k) *stmt* : `return` j
If $pv(j)$ is undefined, the transformation is undefined; otherwise

$$SH' = (C, S, I \uplus \{i\}, c_{nil}, pf, df, pv[ret\_int \leftarrow i])$$
$$\varphi' \equiv \varphi \wedge i = pv(j)$$

We can show that for any atomic statement that is not a function call, the above computes the strongest post of the footprint:

Theorem 3.4. *Let $(SH; \varphi)$ be a footprint and let* `stmt` *be any statement that is not a function call. Let $(SH'; \varphi')$ be the footprint obtained from $(SH; \varphi)$ across the statement* `stmt`*, as defined above. Let C denote the set of all concrete heaps that correspond to SH and satisfy φ, and let C' be the set of all heaps that result from executing* `stmt` *from any concrete heap in C. Then C' is the precise set of concrete heaps that correspond to SH' and satisfy φ'.* □

Handling function calls

Let us consider the statement $u := f(v, \bar{j})$ on the pair $(SH; \varphi)$. Let $f(w, \bar{k})$ be the function prototype and φ_{post} its post-condition. If $pv(v)$ or any element of $pv(\bar{j})$ is undefined, the transformation is undefined. We also assume that the checking of the pre-condition for f is successful; in particular, $pv(v)$ and all the nodes reachable from it are roots of trees.

Recall that certain nodes of the symbolic heap can be determined to point to trees (as discussed earlier). For any node $n \in C \cup S$, let us define $reach\_nodes(SH, n)$ to be the subset of $C \cup S$ that is reachable from n in $Graph(SH)$. Let

$$N_C = (reach\_nodes(SH, pv(v)) \cap C) \setminus \{c_{nil}\}$$
$$N_S = reach\_nodes(SH, pv(v)) \cap S$$

Intuitively, N_C and N_S are the concrete non-*nil* and the symbolic nodes affected by the call. Let n_{ret_loc} be the node returned by f. Let N' be the set of nodes generated by the call: $N' = \{n_{ret\_loc}, pv(v)\}$ if φ_{post} does not havoc old_w, and $N' = \{n_{ret\_loc}\}$ otherwise. The resulting symbolic heap is $(C', S', I', c_{nil}, pf', df', pv')$, where:

- $C' = C \setminus N_C$
- $S' = (S \setminus N_S) \cup N'$
- $I' = I$
- $pf' \mid_D = pf \mid_D$, and $pf'(n, dir)$ is undefined for all the pairs $(n, dir) \in (C' \setminus \{nil\} \times Dir) \setminus D$, where $D \subseteq (C' \setminus \{nil\}) \times Dir$ is the set of pairs (n', dir') such that $pf(n', dir') \in C' \cup S'$
- $df' = df \mid_{C' \setminus \{c_{nil}\} \times DF}$
- $pv' = pv[u \leftarrow n_{ret\_loc}]$

Intuitively, the concrete and symbolic nodes affected by the call are removed from the footprint (and get quantified in the Dryad formula), with the possible exception of $pv(v)$ (if φ_{post} does not havoc old_w, $pv(v)$ becomes a symbolic node). The returned node is added to S. The pf and df functions are restricted to the new set of concrete nodes, and all the directions and program variables pointing to quantified nodes become undefined.

Let ψ_{post} be the post-annotating formula in φ_{post}, we define the following formulas

$$\varphi_1 \equiv \varphi[\overline{pre\_call\_r_n / r^*(n)}] \wedge \bigwedge_{n \in N_C, r^*} \left(pre\_call\_r_n = \hat{r}_{ind}(n)\right)$$
$$\varphi_2 \equiv \psi_{post}[pv(v)/old\_w][\overline{pv(j)/old\_k}][n_{ret\_loc}/ret\_loc][\overline{pre\_call\_r_{pv(v)}/old\_r^*(pv(v))}]$$

where n ranges over $N_C \cup N_S$, r^* ranges over all the recursive predicates and functions; $pre\_call\_r_n$ are fresh logical variables; $\hat{r}_{ind}(n)$ is obtained from $r_{ind}(n)$ by replacing $n.dir$ with $pf(n, dir)$ and $n.f$ with $df(n, f)$ for all $dir \in Dir, f \in DF$, and then by replacing $r^*(n')$ with $pre\_call\_r_{n'}$ for all $n' \in N_C \cup N_S$; $\overline{r^*(n)}$ is the vector of all the recursive predicates and functions on all $n \in N_C \cup N_S$. Intuitively, in φ_1 we add logical variables that capture the values of the recursive predicates and functions for the nodes affected by the call. In φ_2 we replace the program variables in the ψ_{post} with the actual nodes and integer variables, and we replace the old version of the predicates and functions on old_w with the variables capturing those values. Then the resulting formula is

$$\varphi' \equiv \varphi_1 \wedge \varphi_2$$

The case of $j := g(v, \bar{k})$ is similar.

Example: Search in AVL trees To illustrate the above procedure expands the symbolic heap and generates formulas, we present it working on the search routine of an AVL tree. Figure 2 shows the `find` routine, which searches in an AVL tree t and returns `true` if a key v is found. The pre-condition φ_{pre}, post-condition φ_{post}, and user-defined recursive sets and predicates are also shown in Figure 2. In Figure 3, we present graphically how the symbolic heap evolves for a particular execution path of the routine. At each point of the basic block, we also formally show the updated symbolic heap SH and the corresponding formula φ.

Incorporating the post-condition

Finally, after capturing the program state after execution bb by a pair $(SH; \varphi)$, we incorporate the post-condition φ_{post}, which contains the annotating formula ψ, and generate a verification condition. We compute the set of tree-nodes in the footprint SH and compute the recursively defined predicates and functions on them. Let

$$\begin{aligned} SH &= (C, S, I, c_{nil}, pf, df, pv) \\ N &= (tree\_nodes(SH) \cap C) \setminus \{c_{nil}\} \\ \varphi_{vc} &\equiv \varphi \wedge \bigwedge_{n \in N, r^*} \big(vc\_r_n = \hat{r}_{ind}(n)\big) \end{aligned}$$

where vc_r_n is fresh logical variables; and $\hat{r}_{ind}(n)$ are obtained from $r_{ind}(n)$ by replacing $n.dir$ with $pf(n, dir)$ and $n.f$ with $df(n, f)$ for all $dir \in Dir, f \in DF$, and then by replacing $r^*(n')$ with $vc\_r_{n'}$ for all $n' \in N$. Intuitively, N are the non-*nil* concrete nodes that are tree roots, while φ_{vc} introduces variables that capture the values of the recursive predicates and functions on non-*nil* concrete nodes.

Let u and $\bar{k}$ be the original program variables of bb. Let v and $\bar{j}$ be the new program variables appearing in ψ (only when bb ends before a function call). Let N' be the set of nodes that should be the roots of disjoint trees, as required by φ_{post}: $N' = \{pv(v)\}$ if φ_{post} mentions $\texttt{tree}(v)$; $N' = \{n_0, pv(ret\_loc)\}$ if φ_{post} mentions $old\_u\#ret\_loc$; $N' = \{n_0\}$ if φ_{post} mentions $\texttt{tree}(old\_u)$; if φ_{post} mentions $\texttt{havoc}(old\_u)$, $N' = \{pv(ret\_loc)\}$ or $N' = \emptyset$ depending on the basic block is within a function returning a location or an integer. Let

$$\begin{aligned} \psi_{vc} \equiv\ & \psi[pv(v)/v][pv(\bar{j})/\bar{j}][pv(ret\_loc)/ret\_loc][pv(ret\_int)/ret\_int] \\ & [\overline{vc\_r_{pv(v)}}/\overline{r^*(pv(v))}][\overline{vc\_r_{pv(ret\_loc)}}/\overline{r^*(pv(ret\_loc))}] \\ & [n_0/old\_u][\bar{i}/old\_\bar{k}][oldest\_r_{n_0}/old\_r^*(n_0)][\overline{vc\_r_{n_0}}/\overline{r^*(n_0)}] \end{aligned}$$

where r^* ranges over all the recursive predicates and functions, n_0 and $\bar{i}$ are the initial node and integer variables, and $oldest\_r_{n_0}$ is the variable capturing the value of $r^*(n_0)$ in the pre-heap. The substitution of $r^*(n)$ with vc_r_n is only performed for nodes in N.

We should verify that:

(1) $N' \subseteq N \cup S \cup \{c_{nil}\}$, that is, the nodes required by φ_{post} to be tree roots are indeed tree roots;

(2) $reach\_nodes(SH, n_1) \cap reach\_nodes(SH, n_2) \subseteq \{c_{nil}\}$, for all $n_1, n_2 \in N'$, such that $n_1 \neq n_2$;

(3) $(SH; \varphi_{vc}) \rightarrow \psi_{vc}$, that is, the constraints on the current states imply the constraints required by ψ.

The first two are readily checkable. The last one asserts that any concrete heap that corresponds to the symbolic heap SH and satisfies φ_{vc} must also satisfy ψ_{vc}. Checking the validity of this claim is non-trivial (undecidable) and we examine procedures that can soundly establish this in the next section.

4. Proving the Verification Condition

In this section we consider the problem of checking the verification condition $(SH; \varphi_{vc}) \rightarrow \psi_{vc}$ generated in Section 3. We first show a small syntactic fragment of Dryad that is entirely decidable (without formula abstraction) by a reduction to the powerful decidable logic Strand$_{dec}$. We then turn to the abstraction schemes for unrestricted verification conditions, and show how to soundly reduce verification conditions to a validity problem of quantifier-free theories of sets/multisets of integers, which is decidable using state-of-the-art SMT solvers.

4.1 A Decidable Fragment of Dryad

Given verification conditions of the form $(SH; \varphi_{vc}) \rightarrow \psi_{vc}$, where SH is a symbolic heap and φ_{vc} and ψ_{vc} are Dryad formulas, the validity problem is in general undecidable. However, decision procedures for fragments are desirable, as when a program does not satisfy its specification, the decision procedure would *disprove* the program, and confirm it with a counterexample, which helps programmers debug the code. In this subsection, we identify a small decidable fragment, that is very restricted and practically useful for only a small class of specifications, called Dryad$_{dec}$. We omit the proof of decidability, in interest of space.

Let us fix a set of directions Dir and a set of data-fields DF. Dryad$_{dec}$ does not only restrict the syntax of Dryad, but also restricts the recursive integers/sets/multisets/predicates that can be defined. We first describe the ways allowed in Dryad$_{dec}$ to define recursions as follows:

- Recursive integers are disallowed;
- For each data field $f \in DF$, a recursive set of integers fs^* can be defined as

$$fs^*(x) = \texttt{ite}\Big(x = \texttt{nil},\ \emptyset,\ \{x.f\} \cup \bigcup_{dir \in Dir} fs^*(x.dir)\Big)$$

- For each data field $f \in DF$, a recursive multiset of integers fms^* can be defined as

$$fms^*(x) = \texttt{ite}\Big(x = \texttt{nil},\ \emptyset_m,\ \{x.f\}_m \cup \bigcup_{dir \in Dir} fms^*(x.dir)\Big)$$

- Recursive predicates can be defined in the form of

$$p^*(x) = \texttt{ite}\Big(x = \texttt{nil},\ \texttt{true},\ \varphi_p(x) \wedge \bigwedge_{dir \in Dir} p^*(x.dir)\Big)$$

where $\varphi_p(x)$ is a *local formula* with x as the only free variable. Local formulas are Dryad formulas disallowing set/multiset minus, `ite`, subset, equality between locations, positive appearance of belongs-to and and negative appearance of $\leq$ between sets/multisets. Intuitively, $p^*(x)$ is evaluated to true if and only if every node y in the subtree of x satisfies the local formula $\varphi_p(y)$, which can be determined by simply accessing the data fields of y and evaluating the recursive sets/multisets for the children of y.

The exclusion of recursive integers prevents us from expressing heights/cardinalities (which are required in many specifications).

There are however interesting algorithms on inductive data structures, like binary heaps, binary search trees and treaps, whose verification can be expressed in DRYAD$_{dec}$.

On the syntax of DRYAD, DRYAD$_{dec}$ does not allow to refer to any child or any data field, for any location, i.e., terms of the form *lt.dir* or *lt.f* are disallowed. Difference operations and subset relations between sets/multisets are also disallowed.

Overall, DRYAD$_{dec}$ is the most powerful fragment of DRYAD that we could find that embeds into a known decidable logic, like STRAND$_{dec}$. However, it is not powerful enough for the heap verification questions that we would like to solve. This motivates formula abstractions that we describe in the next section.

4.2 Proving DRYAD using formula abstractions

In typical data-structure algorithms, a recursive algorithm manipulates the data-structure for a few bounded number of steps, and then recursively calls itself to process the rest of the inductive data-structure, and finally fixes the structure before returning.

As argued in Section 1, in recursive proofs of such algorithms, it is very often sufficient to assume that the recursively defined predicates, integers, sets of keys, etc. are *arbitrary*, or uninterpreted,

```
int find(node t, int v)
{
  if (t = NULL) return false;
  tv := t.value;
  if (v = tv) return true;
  else if (v < tv) { w := t.left;
      r := find(w, v); }
  else { w := t.right;
      r := find(w, v); }
  return r;
}
```

$$\varphi_{pre} \equiv avl^*(\texttt{t})$$
$$\varphi_{post} \equiv avl^*(\texttt{t}) \wedge keys^*(\texttt{t}) = keys^*(\texttt{old\_t}) \wedge h^*(\texttt{t}) = h^*(\texttt{old\_t}) \wedge ret\_loc \neq 0 \leftrightarrow \texttt{v} \in keys^*(\texttt{t})$$
$$avl^*(x) \stackrel{def}{=} \texttt{ite}(\, x = \texttt{nil},\ \texttt{true},\ avl_{ind}(x)\,)$$
$$avl_{ind}(x) \stackrel{def}{=} avl^*(x.left) \wedge avl^*(x.right) \wedge keys^*(x.left) \le \{v.value\} \wedge \{v.value\} \le keys^*(x.right) \wedge x.hight = h^*(x) \wedge -1 \le h^*(x.left) - h^*(x.right) \wedge h^*(x.left) - h^*(x.right) \le 1$$
$$keys^*(x) \stackrel{def}{=} \texttt{ite}(\, x = \texttt{nil},\ \emptyset,\ keys_{ind}(x)\,)$$
$$keys_{ind}(x) \stackrel{def}{=} keys^*(x.left) \cup \{x.value\} \cup keys^*(x.right)$$
$$h^*(x) \stackrel{def}{=} \texttt{ite}(\, x = \texttt{nil},\ 0,\ h_{ind}(x)\,)$$
$$h_{ind}(x) \stackrel{def}{=} 1 + max(h^*(x.left),\ h^*(x.right))$$

Figure 2. AVL find routine (left); pre/post conditions and recursive definition of avl^*, $keys^*$, and h^* (right).

<table>
<tr><th>Graphical representation of SH</th><th>Formal representation of SH</th><th>Formula φ</th></tr>
<tr><td></td><td>$C = \{c_{nil}\}, S = \{n_0\}, I = \{i_1\}$
$dir = \emptyset, df = \emptyset$
$pv = \{\texttt{t} \mapsto n_0,\ \texttt{v} \mapsto i_1\}$</td><td>$avl^*(n_0)$</td></tr>
<tr><td colspan="3">assume(t ≠ nil)</td></tr>
<tr><td></td><td>$C = \{c_{nil}\}, S = \{n_0\}, I = \{i_1\}$
$dir = \emptyset, df = \emptyset$
$pv = \{\texttt{t} \mapsto n_0,\ \texttt{v} \mapsto i_1\}$</td><td>$avl^*(n_0) \wedge n_0 \neq c_{nil}$</td></tr>
<tr><td colspan="3">tv := t.value;</td></tr>
<tr><td>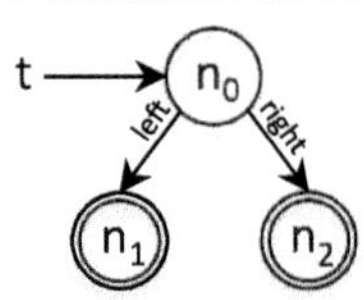</td><td>$C = \{c_{nil}, n_0\}, S = \{n_1, n_2\}, I = \{i_1, i_2, i_3, i_4\}$
$dir = \{(n_0, left) \mapsto n_1, (n_0, right) \mapsto n_2\}$
$df = \{(n_0, value) \mapsto i_2, (n_0, height) \mapsto i_3\}$
$pv = \{\texttt{t} \mapsto n_0,\ \texttt{v} \mapsto i_1,\ \texttt{tv} \mapsto i_4\}$</td><td>$avl_{n_0} \ \wedge\ n_0 \neq c_{nil} \wedge$
$avl_{n_0} \leftrightarrow \big(avl^*(n_1) \wedge avl^*(n_2) \wedge i_3 = h_{n_0} \wedge keys^*(n_1) \le \{i_2\} \wedge$
$\{i_2\} \le keys^*(n_2) \wedge -1 \le h^*(n_1) - h^*(n_2) \wedge h^*(n_1) - h^*(n_2) \le 1\big) \wedge$
$keys_{n_0} = keys^*(n_1) \cup \{v\} \cup keys^*(n_2) \wedge$
$h_{n_0} = 1 + max(h^*(n_1),\ h^*(n_2)) \wedge$
$n_0 \neq c_{nil} \ \wedge\ n_0 \neq n_1 \ \wedge\ n_0 \neq n_2 \ \wedge\ (n_1 = n_2 \rightarrow n_1 = c_{nil}) \ \wedge\ i_4 = i_2$</td></tr>
<tr><td colspan="3">assume(tv ≠ v)
assume(tv < v)
w := t.left;</td></tr>
<tr><td>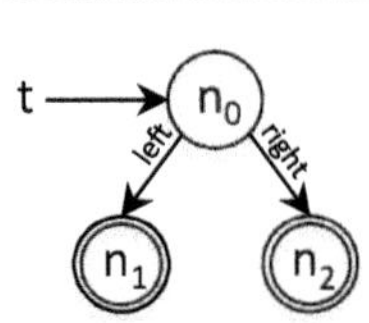</td><td>$C = \{c_{nil}, n_0\}, S = \{n_1, n_2\}, I = \{i_1, i_2, i_3, i_4\}$
$dir = \{(n_0, left) \mapsto n_1, (n_0, right) \mapsto n_2\}$
$df = \{(n_0, value) \mapsto i_2, (n_0, height) \mapsto i_3\}$
$pv = \{\texttt{t} \mapsto n_0,\ \texttt{v} \mapsto i_1,\ \texttt{tv} \mapsto i_4,$
$\texttt{w} \mapsto n_1\}$</td><td>$avl_{n_0} \ \wedge\ n_0 \neq c_{nil} \wedge$
$avl_{n_0} \leftrightarrow \big(avl^*(n_1) \wedge avl^*(n_2) \wedge i_3 = h_{n_0} \wedge keys^*(n_1) \le \{i_2\} \wedge$
$\{i_2\} \le keys^*(n_2) \wedge -1 \le h^*(n_1) - h^*(n_2) \wedge h^*(n_1) - h^*(n_2) \le 1\big) \wedge$
$keys_{n_0} = keys^*(n_1) \cup \{v\} \cup keys^*(n_2) \wedge$
$h_{n_0} = 1 + max(h^*(n_1),\ h^*(n_2)) \wedge$
$n_0 \neq c_{nil} \ \wedge\ n_0 \neq n_1 \ \wedge\ n_0 \neq n_2 \ \wedge\ (n_1 = n_2 \rightarrow n_1 = c_{nil}) \ \wedge\ i_4 = i_2$
$\wedge\ i_4 \neq i_1 \ \wedge\ i_4 < i_1$</td></tr>
<tr><td colspan="3">r := find(w, v);
return r;</td></tr>
<tr><td>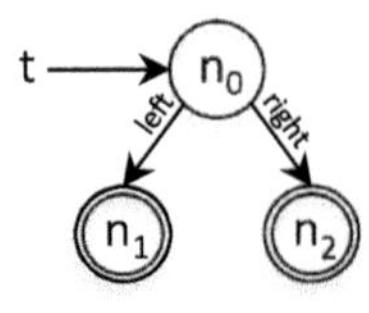</td><td>$C = \{c_{nil}, n_0\}, S = \{n_1, n_2\}$
$I = \{i_1, i_2, i_3, i_4, i_5, i_6\}$
$dir = \{(n_0, left) \mapsto n_1, (n_0, right) \mapsto n_2\}$
$df = \{(n_0, value) \mapsto i_2, (n_0, height) \mapsto i_3\}$
$pv = \{\texttt{t} \mapsto n_0,\ \texttt{v} \mapsto i_1,\ \texttt{tv} \mapsto i_4,$
$\texttt{w} \mapsto n_1,\ \texttt{r} \mapsto i_5,\ \texttt{ret\_loc} \mapsto i_6\}$</td><td>$avl_{n_0} \ \wedge\ n_0 \neq c_{nil} \wedge$
$avl_{n_0} \leftrightarrow \big(pre\_call\_avl_{n_1} \wedge avl^*(n_2) \wedge i_3 = h_{n_0} \wedge$
$pre\_call\_keys_{n_1} \le \{i_2\} \wedge \{i_2\} \le keys^*(n_2) \wedge$
$-1 \le pre\_call\_h_{n_1} - h^*(n_2) \wedge pre\_call\_h_{n_1} - h^*(n_2) \le 1\big) \wedge$
$keys_{n_0} = pre\_call\_keys_{n_1} \cup \{v\} \cup keys^*(n_2) \wedge$
$h_{n_0} = 1 + max(pre\_call\_h_{n_1},\ h^*(n_2)) \wedge$
$n_0 \neq c_{nil} \ \wedge\ n_0 \neq n_1 \ \wedge\ n_0 \neq n_2 \ \wedge\ (n_1 = n_2 \rightarrow n_1 = c_{nil}) \ \wedge\ i_4 = i_2$
$i_4 \neq i_1 \ \wedge\ i_4 < i_1 \ \wedge\ avl^*(n_1) \ \wedge\ keys^*(n_1) = pre\_call\_keys_{n_1} \ \wedge$
$h^*(n_1) = pre\_call\_h_{n_1} \ \wedge\ i_5 \neq 0 \leftrightarrow i_1 \in keys^*(n_1) \ \wedge\ i_6 = i_5$</td></tr>
</table>

Figure 3. Expanding the symbolic heap and generating the formulas

when applied to the inductive hypothesis that the algorithm works correctly on the smaller tree that it calls itself on. This is very common in manual verification of these algorithms, and the footprint formula obtained in Section 3 rewords the recursive properties expressed directly in terms of recursive properties on the locations that the program makes recursive calls. Hence, in order to find a simple proof, we can replace recursive definitions on symbolic nodes as uninterpreted functions that map the symbolic trees to arbitrary integers, sets of integers, multisets of integers, etc., which we call formula abstraction (see [25–27] where such abstractions have been used).

To prove a verification condition $(SH; \varphi) \rightarrow \psi$ using formula abstraction, we drop SH, and we replace recursive predicates on symbolic nodes by uninterpreted Boolean functions, replace recursive integer functions as uninterpreted functions that map nodes to integers, and replace recursive set/multiset functions with functions that map nodes to arbitrary sets and multisets. Notice that the constraints regarding the concrete and symbolic nodes in SH were already added to φ, during the construction of the verification condition. The formula resulting via abstraction is a formula $\varphi_{abs} \rightarrow \psi_{abs}$ such that: (1) if $\varphi_{abs} \rightarrow \psi_{abs}$ is valid, then so is $(SH; \varphi) \rightarrow \psi$ (the converse may not necessarily be true); (2) checking $\varphi_{abs} \rightarrow \psi_{abs}$ is decidable, and in fact can be reduced to QF_UFLIA, the quantifier-free theory of uninterpreted functions and arithmetic.

The validity of the abstracted formula $\varphi_{abs} \rightarrow \psi_{abs}$ over the theory of uninterpreted function, linear arithmetic, and sets and multisets of integers, is decidable. The fact that the quantifier free theory of ordered sets is decidable is well known. In fact, Kuncak et al. [13] showed that the quantifier-free theory of sets with cardinality constraints is NP-complete. Since we do not need cardinality constraints, we use a slightly simplified decision procedure that reduces formulas with sets/multisets using uninterpreted functions that capture the characteristic functions associated with these sets/multisets. We omit these details in the interest of space.

5. Experimental Evaluation

In this section, we demonstrate the effectiveness and practicality of the DRYAD logic and the verification procedures developed in this paper by verifying standard operations on several inductive data structures. Each routine was written using recursive functions and annotated with a pre-condition and a post-condition, specifying a set of partial correctness properties including both structural and data requirements. For each basic block of each routine, we manually generated the verification condition $(SH; \varphi)$ following the procedure described in Section 3. Then we examined the validity of φ using the procedure described in Section 4.2. We employ Z3 [11], a state-of-the-art SMT solver, to check validity of the generated formula $\varphi_{\mathcal{D}}$ formula in the quantifier-free theory of integers and uninterpreted functions QF_UFLIA. The experimental results are tabulated in Figure 4.

The data-structures, routines, and verified properties: Lists are trees with a singleton direction set. *Sorted lists* can be expressed in DRYAD. The routines `insert` and `delete` insert and delete a node with key k in a sorted list, respectively, in a recursive fashion. The routine `insertion-sort` takes a singly-linked list and sorts it by recursively sorting the tail of the list, and inserting the key of the head into the sorted list by calling `insert`. We check if all these routines return a sorted list with the multiset of keys as expected.

A *binary heap* is recursively defined as either an empty tree, or a binary tree such that the root is of the greatest key and both its left and right subtrees are binary heaps. The routine `max-heapify` is given a binary tree with both its left and right trees are binary heaps. If the binary-heap property is violated by the root, it swaps the root with its greater child, and then recursively max-heapifies that subtree. We check if the routine returns a binary heap with same keys as that of the input tree.

The *treap* data-structure is a class of binary trees with two data fields for each node: *key* and *priority*. We assume that all priorities are distinct and all keys are distinct. Treaps can also be recursively defined in DRYAD. The `remove-root` routine deletes the root of the input treap, and joins the two subtrees descending from the left and right children of the deleted node into a single treap. If the left or right subtree of the node to be deleted is empty, the join operation is trivial; otherwise, the left or right child of the deleted node is selected as the new root, and the deletion proceeds recursively. The `delete` routine simply searches the node to be deleted recursively, and deletes it by calling `remove-root`. The `insert` routine recursively inserts the new node into an appropriate subtree to keep the binary-search-tree property, then performs rotations to restore the min-heap order property, if necessary. We check if all these routines return a treap with the set of keys and the set of priorities as expected.

An *AVL tree* is a binary search tree that is balanced: for each node, the absolute difference between the height of the left subtree and the height of the right subtree is at most 1. The main routines for AVL are `insert` and `delete`. The `insert` routine recursively inserts a key into an AVL tree (similar to a binary search tree), and as it returns from recursion it checks the balancedness and performs one or two rotations to restore balance. The `delete` routine recursively deletes a key from an AVL tree (again, similar to a binary search tree), and as it returns from the recursion ensures that the tree is indeed balanced. For both routines, we prove that they return an AVL tree, that the multiset of keys is as expected, and that the height increases by at most 1 (for `insert`), can decrease by at most 1 (for `delete`), or stays the same.

Red-black trees are binary search trees that are more loosely balanced than the AVL trees, and were described in Section 3. We consider the `insert` and `delete` routines. The `insert` routine recursively inserts a key into a red-black subtree, and colors the new node red, possibly violating the red-black tree property. As it returns from recursion, it performs several rotations to fix the property. If the root of the whole tree is red, it is recolored black, and all the properties are restored. The `delete` routine recursively deletes a key from a red-black tree, possibly violating the red-black tree property. As it returns from recursion, it again performs several rotations to fix it. For both routines, we prove that they return a red-black tree, that the multiset of keys is as expected, and the black height increases by at most 1 (for `insert`), decreases by at most 1 (for `delete`), or does not change.

The *B-tree* is a data structure that generalizes the binary search tree in that for each non-leaf node the number of children is one more than the number of keys stored in that node. The keys are stored in increasing order, and if the node is not a leaf, the key with index i is no less than any key stored in the child with index i and no more then all the keys stored in the child with index $i + 1$. For each node except the root, the number of keys is in some range (typically between $T - 1$ and $2T - 1$). A B-tree is balanced in that for each node, the heights of all the children are equal. To describe the B-tree in our logic, we need three mutually recursive predicates: one that describes a B-subtree, and two that describe a list of keys and children. The $b\text{-}subtree^*(t)$ states that the number of keys stored in the node is in the required range, and that keys and children list satisfies either the $key\text{-}child\text{-}list^*(l)$ predicate (if the node is not a leaf) or the $key\text{-}list^*(l)$ predicate (if the node is a leaf). The $key\text{-}child\text{-}list^*(l)$ states that either the list has only one element, and the child satisfies the $b\text{-}subtree^*(t)$ predicate, or the list has at least two elements, the key in the head of the list is no less than all the keys stored in the child and no greater than the keys stored in the tail of the list, the child satisfies $b\text{-}subtree^*(t)$,

Data Structure	#Ints	#Sets	#MSets	#Preds	Routine	#BB	Max. #Nodes in Footprint	Total Time (s)	Avg. Time (s) per VC	VC proved valid?
Sorted List	0	0	1	1	`insert`	4	3	0.24	0.06	Yes
					`delete`	3	3	0.17	0.06	Yes
					`insertion-sort`	3	4	0.11	0.04	Yes
Binary Heap	0	0	1	1	`max-heapify`	5	8	1.89	0.38	Yes
Treap	0	2	0	1	`insert`	7	6	4.06	0.58	Yes
					`delete`	6	4	0.81	0.14	Yes
					`remove-root`	7	8	2.96	0.42	Yes
AVL Tree	1	0	1	1	`insert`	11	8	1.45	0.13	Yes
					`delete`	18	7	2.13	0.19	Yes
Red-Black Tree	1	0	1	1	`insert`	19	8	1.93	0.11	Yes
					`delete`	24	7	3.22	0.14	Yes
B-Tree	2	0	1	2	`insert`	12	6	0.40	0.03	Yes
					`find`	8	3	0.12	0.02	Yes
Binomial Heap	1	0	1	3	`delete-minimum`	3	7	0.29	0.10	Yes
					`find-minimum`	4	6	1.81	0.45	Yes
					`merge`	13	7	17.38	1.37	Yes
Total						147				

Figure 4. Results of program verification (see details at `http://www.cs.illinois.edu/~madhu/dryad`)

and the height of the child is equal to the height of the tail (the height of a list is defined as the maximum height of a child). The predicate *key-list**(*l*) is similarly defined. We consider the `find` and `insert` routines. The `find` routine iterates over the list of keys, and recurses into the appropriate child, until it finds the key or it arrives to a leaf. The `insert` procedure is more complex, as it assumes that the node it is inserting into is non-full, and prior to recursion it might need to split the child. For both routines, we check that the tree after the call is a B-tree, that the multiset of keys has the expected value, and that the height of the tree stays the same, or increases by at most 1 (for `insert`).

As an advanced data structure, the *binomial heap* is described by a set of predicates defined mutually recursively: *binomial-tree**, *binomial-heap** and *full-list**. Briefly, a binomial-heap of order k consists of a binary-tree of order k and a binary-heap of order less than k. A binomial-tree of order k is an ordered tree defined recursively: the root contains the minimum key, and its children compose a binomial-heap of order $k - 1$, satisfying the full-list property. A full-list of order k consists of a tree of order k and a full-list of order $k - 1$. The left-child, right-sibling scheme represents each binomial tree within a binomial heap. Each node contains its key; pointers to its leftmost child and to the sibling immediately to its right; and its degree. The roots of a binomial heap form a singly-linked list (also connected by the sibling pointer). We access the binomial heap by a pointer to the first node on the root list.

The `find-minimum` routine expects a nonempty binomial heap, and moves the tree containing the minimum key to the head of the list. It returns the original heap if it is a single tree. Otherwise, it calls `find-minimum` on its tail list, and appends the returned list to the head tree; then if keys of the roots of the first two trees are unordered, swaps the two trees. We check that `find-minimum` returns a binomial tree followed by a binomial heap, such that the root of the tree contains the minimum key, and the head of the binomial heap is either the first or the second root of the original heap. The `merge` routine merges two binomial heaps `x` and `y` into one. If one of the two heaps is empty, it simply returns the other one. Otherwise, if the heads of the two heaps are of the same order, it merges the two head trees into one, merges the two tail lists recursively, and returns the new tree followed by the new heap; if not, say, `x.order > y.order`, then it merges `x.sibling` and `y`, concatenates the head tree of `x` and the new heap in an appropriate way satisfying the binomial-heap property. We check that `merge` returns a binomial heap such that the keys are the union of the two input binomial heaps, and the order increases up to 1. The `delete-minimum` routine is non-recursive. It simply moves the minimum tree `m` to the head by calling `find-minimum`, and obtains two binomial heaps: a list of the siblings of `m`, and a list of the children of `m`. Finally it merges the two heaps by `merge`. We check that `delete-minimum` returns a binomial heap with the multiset of keys as expected.

Figure 4 summarizes our experiments, showing the results of verifying 147 basic blocks across these algorithms. For each data structure, we report the number of integers, sets, multisets and predicates defined recursively. For each routine, we report the number of basic blocks, the number of nodes in the footprint, the time taken by Z3 to determine validity of all generated formulas, and the validity result proved by Z3.

Note that only the first three data-structures (sorted list, binary heap and treap) fit in the decidable fragment described in Section 4.1 as they do not require recursively defined integers. Furthermore, since the difference operations between sets/multisets are disallowed, we can check all functional properties for these data-structures except checking that the set of keys/priorities at the end of the each routine is as expected.

We are encouraged by the fact that all these verification conditions that were deterministically generated by the methodology set forth in this paper were proved by Z3 efficiently; this proved all these algorithms correct. To the best of our knowledge, this is the first terminating automatic mechanism that can prove such a wide variety of data-structure algorithms written using imperative programming correct (in particular, binomial heaps and the B-trees presented here have not been proven automatically correct).

The experimental results show that Dryad is a very expressive logic that allows us to express natural and recursive properties of several complex inductive tree data structures. Moreover, our sound procedure tends to be able to prove many complex verification conditions.

6. Related Work

There is a rich literature on program logics for heaps. We discuss the work that is closest to ours. In particular, we omit the rich literature on general interactive theorem provers (like Coq [12]) as well as general software verification tools (like Boogie [2]) that are not particularly adapted for heap verification.

Separation logic [4, 19, 23] is one of the most popular logics for verification of heap structures. Many dialects of separation logic combine separation logic with inductively defined data-structures. While separation logic gives mechanisms to compositionally reason with the footprint and the frame it resides in, proof assistants for separation logic are often heuristic and incomplete [4], though a couple of small decidable fragments are known [3, 17]. A work that comes very close to ours is a paper by Chin et al. [8], where the authors allow user-defined recursive predicates (similar to ours) and build a terminating procedure that reduces the verification condition to standard logical theories. While their procedure is more general than ours (they can handle structures beyond trees), the resulting formulas are quantified, and result in less efficient procedures. Bedrock [9] is a Coq library that aims at mostly automated (but not completely automated) procedures that requires some proof tactics to be given by the user to prove verification conditions.

In manual and semi-automatic approaches to verification of heap manipulating programs [4, 23, 24], the inductive definitions of algebraic data-types is extremely common, and proof tactics unroll these inductive definitions, do extensive unification to try to match terms, and find simple proofs. Our work in this paper is very much inspired by the kinds of manual heap reasoning that we have seen in the literature.

The work by Zee et al. [26, 27] is one of the first attempts at full functional verification of linked data structures, which includes the development of the JAHOB system that uses higher-order logics to specify correctness properties, and puts together several theorem provers ranging from first-order provers, SMT solvers, and interactive theorem provers to prove properties of algorithms manipulating data-structures. While many proofs required manual guidance, this work showed that proofs can often be derived using simple tactics like unrolling of inductive definitions, unification, abstraction, and employing decision procedures for decidable theories. This work was also an inspiration for our work, but we chose to concentrate on deriving proofs using *completely automatic and terminating procedures*, where unification, unrolling, abstraction, and decidable theories are systematically exploited.

One work that is very close to ours is that of Suter et al. [25] where decision procedures for algebraic data-types are presented with abstraction as the key to obtaining proofs. However, this work focuses on sound and complete decision procedures, and is limited in its ability to prove several complex data structures correct. Moreover, the work limits itself to functional program correctness; in our opinion, functional programs are very similar to algebraic inductive specifications, leading to much simpler proof procedures.

There is a rich and growing literature on completely automatic sound, complete, and terminating decision procedures for restricted heap logics. The logic LISBQ [14] offers such reasoning with restricted reachability predicates and quantification. While the logic has extremely efficient decision procedures, its expressivity in stating properties of inductive data-structures (even trees) is very limited. There are several other logics in this genre, being less expressive but decidable [1, 5, 6, 18, 20–22]. STRAND is a recent logic that can handle some data-structure properties (at least binary search trees) and admits decidable fragments [15, 16] by combining decidable theories of trees with the theory of arithmetic, but is again extremely restricted in expressiveness. None of these logics can express the verification conditions for full functional verification of the data-structures explored in this paper.

Acknowledgements This work is partially funded by NSF CAREER award #0747041 and NSA contract H98230-10-C-0294.

References

[1] I. Balaban, A. Pnueli, and L. D. Zuck. Shape analysis by predicate abstraction. In *VMCAI'05*, volume 3385 of *LNCS*, pages 164–180. Springer, 2005.

[2] M. Barnett, B.-Y. E. Chang, R. DeLine, B. Jacobs, and K. R. M. Leino. Boogie: A modular reusable verifier for object-oriented programs. In *FMCO'05*, volume 4111 of *LNCS*, pages 364–387. Springer, 2005.

[3] J. Berdine, C. Calcagno, and P. W. O'Hearn. A decidable fragment of separation logic. In *FSTTCS'04*, volume 3328 of *LNCS*, pages 97–109. Springer, 2004.

[4] J. Berdine, C. Calcagno, and P. W. O'Hearn. Symbolic execution with separation logic. In *APLAS'05*, volume 3780 of *LNCS*, pages 52–68. Springer, 2005.

[5] N. Bjørner and J. Hendrix. Linear functional fixed-points. In *CAV'09*, volume 5643 of *LNCS*, pages 124–139. Springer, 2009.

[6] A. Bouajjani, C. Dragoi, C. Enea, and M. Sighireanu. A logic-based framework for reasoning about composite data structures. In *CONCUR'09*, volume 5710 of *LNCS*, pages 178–195. Springer, 2009.

[7] A. R. Bradley and Z. Manna. *The Calculus of Computation*. Springer, 2007.

[8] W.-N. Chin, C. David, H. H. Nguyen, and S. Qin. Automated verification of shape, size and bag properties via user-defined predicates in separation logic. *Science of Computer Programming*, in press, 2010.

[9] A. Chlipala. Mostly-automated verification of low-level programs in computational separation logic. In *PLDI'11*, pages 234–245. ACM, 2011.

[10] T. H. Cormen, C. E. Leiserson, R. L. Rivest, and C. Stein. *Introduction to Algorithms*. MIT Press, third edition, 2009.

[11] L. M. de Moura and N. Bjørner. Z3: An efficient SMT solver. In *TACAS'08*, volume 4963 of *LNCS*, pages 337–340. Springer, 2008.

[12] INRIA. The coq proof assistant. URL `http://coq.inria.fr/`.

[13] V. Kuncak, R. Piskac, and P. Suter. Ordered sets in the calculus of data structures. In *CSL'10*, volume 6247 of *LNCS*, pages 34–48. Springer, 2010.

[14] S. Lahiri and S. Qadeer. Back to the future: revisiting precise program verification using SMT solvers. In *POPL'08*, pages 171–182. ACM, 2008.

[15] P. Madhusudan and X. Qiu. Efficient decision procedures for heaps using STRAND. In *SAS'11*, volume 6887 of *LNCS*, pages 43–59. Springer, 2011.

[16] P. Madhusudan, G. Parlato, and X. Qiu. Decidable logics combining heap structures and data. In *POPL'11*, pages 611–622. ACM, 2011.

[17] S. Magill, M.-H. Tsai, P. Lee, and Y.-K. Tsay. THOR: A tool for reasoning about shape and arithmetic. In *CAV'08*, volume 5123 of *LNCS*, pages 428–432. Springer, 2008.

[18] G. Nelson. Verifying reachability invariants of linked structures. In *POPL'83*, pages 38–47. ACM, 1983.

[19] P. W. O'Hearn, J. C. Reynolds, and H. Yang. Local reasoning about programs that alter data structures. In *CSL'01*, volume 2142 of *LNCS*, pages 1–19. Springer, 2001.

[20] Z. Rakamarić, J. D. Bingham, and A. J. Hu. An inference-rule-based decision procedure for verification of heap-manipulating programs with mutable data and cyclic data structures. In *VMCAI'07*, volume 4349 of *LNCS*, pages 106–121. Springer, 2007.

[21] Z. Rakamarić, R. Bruttomesso, A. J. Hu, and A. Cimatti. Verifying heap-manipulating programs in an SMT framework. In *ATVA'07*, volume 4762 of *LNCS*, pages 237–252. Springer, 2007.

[22] S. Ranise and C. Zarba. A theory of singly-linked lists and its extensible decision procedure. In *SEFM'06*, pages 206–215. IEEE-CS, 2006.

[23] J. Reynolds. Separation logic: a logic for shared mutable data structures. In *LICS'02*, pages 55–74. IEEE-CS, 2002.

[24] G. Rosu, C. Ellison, and W. Schulte. Matching logic: An alternative to Hoare/Floyd logic. In *AMAST'10*, volume 6486 of *LNCS*, pages 142–162. Springer, 2010.

[25] P. Suter, M. Dotta, and V. Kuncak. Decision procedures for algebraic data types with abstractions. In *POPL'10*, pages 199–210. ACM, 2010.

[26] K. Zee, V. Kuncak, and M. C. Rinard. Full functional verification of linked data structures. In *PLDI'08*, pages 349–361. ACM, 2008.

[27] K. Zee, V. Kuncak, and M. C. Rinard. An integrated proof language for imperative programs. In *PLDI'09*, pages 338–351. ACM, 2009.

Symbolic Finite State Transducers: Algorithms and Applications

Margus Veanes
Microsoft Research
margus@microsoft.com

Pieter Hooimeijer *
University of Virginia
pieter@cs.virginia.edu

Benjamin Livshits
Microsoft Research
livshits@microsoft.com

David Molnar
Microsoft Research
dmolnar@microsoft.com

Nikolaj Bjørner
Microsoft Research
nbjorner@microsoft.com

Abstract

Finite automata and finite transducers are used in a wide range of applications in software engineering, from regular expressions to specification languages. We extend these classic objects with symbolic alphabets represented as parametric theories. Admitting potentially infinite alphabets makes this representation strictly more general and succinct than classical finite transducers and automata over strings. Despite this, the main operations, including composition, checking that a transducer is single-valued, and equivalence checking for single-valued symbolic finite transducers are effective given a decision procedure for the background theory. We provide novel algorithms for these operations and extend composition to symbolic transducers augmented with registers. Our base algorithms are unusual in that they are nonconstructive, therefore, we also supply a separate model generation algorithm that can quickly find counterexamples in the case two symbolic finite transducers are not equivalent. The algorithms give rise to a complete decidable algebra of symbolic transducers. Unlike previous work, we do not need any syntactic restriction of the formulas on the transitions, only a decision procedure. In practice we leverage recent advances in satisfiability modulo theory (SMT) solvers. We demonstrate our techniques on four case studies, covering a wide range of applications. Our techniques can synthesize string pre-images in excess of 8,000 bytes in roughly a minute, and we find that our new encodings significantly outperform previous techniques in succinctness and speed of analysis.

Categories and Subject Descriptors D.2.4 [*Software Engineering*]: Software/Program Verification; F.4.1 [*Mathematical Logic and Formal Languages*]: Mathematical Logic

* Work done while the author visited Microsoft Research.

POPL'12, January 25–27, 2012, Philadelphia, PA, USA.

General Terms Algorithms, Theory, Verification

Keywords Automata, Composition, Equivalence, SMT

1. Introduction

Finite automata are used in a wide range of applications in software engineering, from regular expressions to specification languages. Nearly every programmer has used a regular expression at one point or another to parse logs or manipulate text. Finite transducers are an extension of finite automata to model functions on lists of elements, which in turn have uses in fields as diverse as computational linguistics and model-based testing. While this formalism is of immense practical use, it suffers from certain drawbacks: in the presence of large alphabets, they can "blow up" in the number of transitions, as each transition can encode only one choice of element from the alphabet. Furthermore, the most common forms cannot handle infinite alphabets.

Symbolic finite transducers (SFTs) are an extension of traditional transducers that attempt to solve these problems by allowing transitions to be labeled with arbitrary formulas in a specified theory. While the concept is straightforward, traditional algorithms for deciding composition, equivalence, and other properties of finite transducers *do not* immediately generalize to the symbolic case. In particular, previous work on symbolic finite transducers have needed to impose restrictions on character theories to achieve decidable analysis [1, 38]. Our work breaks this barrier and allows for arbitrary formulas from *any decidable background theory*. In practice, we leverage the recent progress in satisfiability modulo theory (SMT) solvers to provide this decision procedure. We find that our algorithms are fast when used with Z3, a state of the art SMT solver.

The restriction we do make on SFTs is a semantic one: that the SFT is *single-valued*. This restriction is needed because equivalence is undecidable even for standard finite transducers. The single-valuedness property is decidable for symbolic finite transducers. This gives us a way to check transducers arising from practical applications before applying our algorithms.

While it was previously known that equivalence was decidable for single-valued finite transducers, again it does not immediately follow that equivalence should be decidable for single-valued *symbolic* finite transducers because typically

	Effective closure under composition	Equivalence	Alphabet
Finite State Transducers	closed	undecidable in general [23], decidable for single-valued case [43] and finite-valued case [12, 50]	finite set of elements, comparable with equality
Streaming Transducers [1]	closed (for finite alphabets)	decidable	total orders (infinite)
Symbolic Finite Transducers	closed (Proposition 1)	decidable for single-valued case (Theorem 2)	**any decidable theory**
Symbolic Transducers	closed (extension of Proposition 1)	undecidable (already for the single-valued case, through direct encoding of 2-counter machines)	**any decidable theory**

Figure 1. Summary of decidability results. The bottom two rows summarize our contributions.

Case study	Section	Feature
HTMLDecode	4.1	ST representation compactness, integer-linear arithmetic
Malware fingerprinting	4.2	SFT composition for program analysis
Image blurring	4.3	non-string module theory
Location privacy	4.4	stream manipulating programs

Figure 2. Summary of case studies.

even very restricted extensions of finite automata and finite transducers lead to undecidability of the core decision problems. In fact, our proof requires a delicate separation between the "automata theoretic" parts of our algorithms and the use of the decision procedure. Unusually, our algorithm for deciding equivalence is *nonconstructive*: while we can determine that two symbolic finite automata are not equivalent, our proof does not provide a way to find a counterexample. Fortunately, we provide a separate *model generation* semi-decision procedure that can find counterexamples once it is known that two automata are not equivalent.

Figure 1 summarizes known results about finite state transducers (over sequences) and extensions thereof, focusing on the key properties studied in this paper, namely functional *compositionality*, decidability of *equivalence*, and the role of the *alphabet*, in order to place our contributions in a clear context. In Section 3.2 we compare our main techniques to closely related techniques used for *streaming transducers* [1]. Section 5 describes further related work, including work on extending automata to trees.

1.1 Applications

Section 4 presents four comprehensive case studies in different areas. Our first case study extends previous work in using symbolic finite transducers to model web "sanitization functions" [4]. Our techniques allow the addition of *register variables*, which enable encoding a sanitizer that could not be handled efficiently by previous symbolic approaches. Our second case study shows an application to analysis of Javascript malware found on the Web. Our third and fourth case studies showcase additional theories beyond strings. Figure 2 summarizes how each case study reflects a novel feature of our work. In addition to these case studies, finite transducers have been employed in other areas such as analysis of web sanitization frameworks, host-based intrusion detection, and natural language processing. Our work immediately applies to these application domains.

1.2 Contributions

Our contributions are the following:

- We present novel algorithms for *composition* and *equivalence checking* of symbolic finite transducers. Our algorithms, unlike previous work, make no restrictions on the formulae used in the transducers: we require only a decision procedure for the background theory.
- We show that the single-valuedness property of symbolic transducers is decidable. This gives rise to a decidable complete algebra of symbolic transducers. The impact is that single-valued symbolic transducers can now be "first class" objects for constructing program analyses.
- We present four case studies that demonstrate how our new algorithms enable new applications. We demonstrate experimentally that our algorithms not only terminate, but that they run quickly in practice for problem instances of interest.

1.3 Paper Organization

The rest of this paper is structured as follows. In Section 2 we provide an introduction to symbolic finite state transducers. Section 3 describes the core transducer-based algorithms. Section 4 provides four detailed case studies of transducer use. Finally, we discuss closely related work in Section 5 and conclude in Section 6.

2. Symbolic Finite Transducers

We now formally define symbolic finite transducers, we give examples of how these objects model program behavior, and we define analyses that may be conducted on such transducers. We assume a *background structure* that has an effectively enumerable (countable) multi-typed carrier set or *background universe* $\mathcal{U}$, and is equipped with a language of function and relation symbols with fixed interpretations. We use τ, σ and γ to denote types, and we write $\mathcal{U}^\tau$ for the corresponding sub-universe of elements of type τ. As a convention, we abbreviate $\mathcal{U}^\sigma$ by Σ and $\mathcal{U}^\gamma$ by Γ, because these symbols are used frequently. The Boolean type is $\mathbb{B}$, with $\mathcal{U}^\mathbb{B} = \{\mathsf{t}, \mathsf{f}\}$ and the integer type is $\mathbb{Z}$. Terms and formulas are defined by induction over the background language and are assumed to be well-typed. The type τ of a term t is indicated by $t:\tau$. Terms of type $\mathbb{B}$, or Boolean terms, are treated as formulas, i.e., no distinction is made between formulas and Boolean terms. All elements in $\mathcal{U}$ are also assumed to have corresponding constants in the background language and we use elements in $\mathcal{U}$ also as constants. The set of free variables in a term t is denoted by $FV(t)$, t is *closed* when $FV(t) = \emptyset$, and closed terms t have Tarski semantics $[\![t]\!]$ over the background structure.

Substitution of a variable $x:\tau$ in t by a term $u:\tau$ is denoted by $t[x/u]$.

A *λ-term* f is an expression of the form $\lambda x.t$, where $x:\sigma$ is a variable, and $t:\gamma$ is a term such that $FV(t) \subseteq \{x\}$; the type of f is $\sigma \to \gamma$; $[\![f]\!]$ denotes the function that maps $a \in \Sigma$ to $[\![t[x/a]]\!] \in \Gamma$. As a convention, we use f and g to stand for λ-terms. A λ-term of type $\sigma \to \mathbb{B}$ is called a *σ-predicate*. We write φ and ψ for σ-predicates and, for $a \in \Sigma$, we write $a \in [\![\varphi]\!]$ for $[\![\varphi]\!](a) = \mathrm{t}$. We often treat $[\![\varphi]\!]$ as a *subset* of Σ. Given a λ-term $f = (\lambda x.t):\sigma \to \gamma$ and a term $u:\sigma$, $f(u)$ stands for $t[x/u]$ (i.e., we assume implicit β-reduction). A predicate φ is *unsatisfiable* when $[\![\varphi]\!] = \emptyset$; *satisfiable*, otherwise.

The following is a key notion in the paper. Two λ-terms $f, g:\sigma \to \gamma$ are *equivalent relative to a σ-predicate* φ, denoted $f \equiv_\varphi g$, when $f \not\equiv_\varphi g$ is unsatisfiable, where

$$f \not\equiv_\varphi g \quad \stackrel{\text{def}}{=} \quad \lambda x.\varphi(x) \wedge f(x) \neq g(x)$$

is called the *difference predicate of f and g relative to φ*.

Definition 1: A *label theory for* $\sigma \to \gamma$ is associated with an effectively enumerable set of λ-terms of type $\sigma \to \gamma$ and an effectively enumerable set of σ-predicates that is effectively closed under Boolean operations and relative difference. ⊠

Effective closure under Boolean operations in Definition 1 means that $[\![\varphi \wedge \psi]\!] = [\![\varphi]\!] \cap [\![\psi]\!]$ and $[\![\neg\varphi]\!] = \Sigma \setminus [\![\varphi]\!]$. An important and direct consequence is the following:

$$[\![\neg(f \not\equiv_\varphi g)]\!] \quad = \quad [\![\lambda x.\neg(\varphi(x) \wedge f(x) \neq g(x))]\!].$$

In particular, it is not possible to express relative equivalence of λ-terms directly, other than through unsatisfiability of a difference predicate. This is important in order to maintain our decidability results while making minimal assumptions about the label theory. In our use of label theories below, difference predicates play a central role and are always used in a positive context (i.e., not negated as above).

A label theory Ψ is *decidable* when satisfiability for $\varphi \in \Psi$, $IsSat(\varphi)$, is decidable. We assume an effective *witness* function for a σ-predicate φ such that, if $IsSat(\varphi)$ then $witness(\varphi) \in [\![\varphi]\!]$.

Example 1: As an example of a decidable label theory for $(\mathbb{Z} \times \mathbb{Z}) \to \mathbb{Z}$, consider the combined theory of pairs and quantifier-free integer linear arithmetic. Suppose π_1 and π_2 are the projection functions from pairs. Let f be $\lambda x.(2 * \pi_1(x))$, let g be $\lambda x.(\pi_1(x) + \pi_2(x))$, and let φ be $\lambda x.(\pi_1(x) = \pi_2(x))$. Then f and g are equivalent relative to φ, because $f \not\equiv_\varphi g$ is unsatisfiable, i.e.,

$$\lambda x.(\pi_1(x) = \pi_2(x) \wedge 2 * \pi_1(x) \neq \pi_1(x) + \pi_2(x))$$

is unsatisfiable. ⊠

Given a set X, we write X^* for the *Kleene closure* of X. Similarly, τ^* is the type of sequences over τ. A sequence of length $k \geq 0$ is denoted either by $[x_0, \dots, x_{k-1}]$ or $\boldsymbol{x}$ with $\boldsymbol{x}_i$ as the i'th element of $\boldsymbol{x}$ for $0 \leq i < |\boldsymbol{x}|$.

Next, we describe an extension of finite state transducers through a symbolic representation of labels. The advantage of the extension is succinctness and modularity with respect to any given label theory. It naturally separates the finite state transition graph from the label theory.

Definition 2: A *Symbolic Finite Transducer (SFT)* over $\sigma \to \gamma$ is a tuple (Q, q^0, F, R), where Q is a finite set of *states*, $q^0 \in Q$ is the *initial state*, $F \subseteq Q$ is the set of *final states*, and R is a set of *rules* $(p, \varphi, \boldsymbol{f}, q)$, where $p, q \in Q$, φ is a σ-predicate and, $\boldsymbol{f}$, is a a sequence of λ-terms, over a given label theory for $\sigma \to \gamma$. ⊠

We use the more intuitive notation $p \xrightarrow{\varphi/\boldsymbol{f}}_A q$ for a rule $(p, \varphi, \boldsymbol{f}, q) \in R_A$ and call φ its *guard*. We omit the index A when A is clear from the context. We treat $\boldsymbol{f} : (\sigma \to \gamma)^*$ as a function $\lambda x\ .\ [\boldsymbol{f}_0(x), \dots, \boldsymbol{f}_k(x)]$ where $k = |\boldsymbol{f}| - 1$. We lift the definition of relative equivalence of λ-terms to sequences $\boldsymbol{f}$ and $\boldsymbol{g}$ of λ-terms: $\boldsymbol{f} \equiv_\varphi \boldsymbol{g}$ iff $|\boldsymbol{f}| = |\boldsymbol{g}|$ and for all i, $0 \leq i < |\boldsymbol{f}|$, $\boldsymbol{f}_i \equiv_\varphi \boldsymbol{g}_i$. We use the notation of rules to also denote concrete transitions when the intension is clear. For $p, q \in Q_A$, $a \in \Sigma$ and $\boldsymbol{b} \in \Gamma^*$:

$$p \xrightarrow{a/\boldsymbol{b}}_A q \text{ if for some } p \xrightarrow{\varphi/\boldsymbol{f}}_A q \in R\text{: } a \in [\![\varphi]\!],\ \boldsymbol{b} = [\![\boldsymbol{f}]\!](a)$$

i.e., the transition $p \xrightarrow{a/\boldsymbol{b}} q$ is an *instance* of a rule. Concatenation of two sequences seq_1 and seq_2 is denoted $seq_1 \cdot seq_2$.

Definition 3: For $\boldsymbol{a} \in \Sigma^*$ and $\boldsymbol{b} \in \Gamma^*$, $p \xrightarrow{\boldsymbol{a}/\boldsymbol{b}}\!\!\!\!\rightarrow_A q$ denotes the *reachability relation*: there exists a path of transitions from p to q in A with input sequence $\boldsymbol{a}$ and output sequence $\boldsymbol{b}$: let $n = |\boldsymbol{a}| - 1$, when there exist subsequences $\boldsymbol{b}^i$, such that $\boldsymbol{b} = \boldsymbol{b}^0 \cdot \boldsymbol{b}^1 \cdots \boldsymbol{b}^n$ and

$$p = p_0 \xrightarrow{a_0/\boldsymbol{b}^0} p_1 \xrightarrow{a_1/\boldsymbol{b}^1} p_2 \cdots p_n \xrightarrow{a_n/\boldsymbol{b}^n} p_{n+1} = q$$

We let $p \xrightarrow{\epsilon/\epsilon}\!\!\!\!\rightarrow_A p$ for all $p \in Q_A$. ⊠

Definition 4: The *transduction* of A, denoted $\mathscr{T}_A$, is the following function from Σ^* to 2^{Γ^*}:

$$\mathscr{T}_A(\boldsymbol{a}) \stackrel{\text{def}}{=} \{\boldsymbol{b} \in \Gamma^* \mid \exists q \in F_A\, (q_A^0 \xrightarrow{\boldsymbol{a}/\boldsymbol{b}}\!\!\!\!\rightarrow q)\}.$$

Equivalently, $\mathscr{T}_A$ is viewed as the binary relation, or subset of $\Sigma^* \times \Gamma^*$, such that $\mathscr{T}_A(\boldsymbol{a}, \boldsymbol{b})$ iff $\boldsymbol{b} \in \mathscr{T}_A(\boldsymbol{a})$. The *domain* of A is $\mathscr{D}(A) \stackrel{\text{def}}{=} \{\boldsymbol{a} \in \Sigma^* \mid \mathscr{T}_A(\boldsymbol{a}) \neq \emptyset\}$. ⊠

The following subclass of SFTs captures transductions that behave as partial functions from Σ^* to Γ^*.

Definition 5: A is *single-valued* when $|\mathscr{T}_A(\boldsymbol{a})| \leq 1$ for all $\boldsymbol{a} \in \Sigma^*$. ⊠

A sufficient condition for single-valuedness is determinism.

Definition 6: A is *deterministic* when, for all $p \xrightarrow{\varphi/\boldsymbol{f}}_A q$ and $p \xrightarrow{\psi/\boldsymbol{g}}_A r$, if $IsSat(\varphi \wedge \psi)$ then $q = r$ and $\boldsymbol{f} \equiv_{\varphi \wedge \psi} \boldsymbol{g}$. ⊠

In terms of concrete transitions, determinism of A means that if $p \xrightarrow{a/\boldsymbol{b}}_A q$ and $p \xrightarrow{a/\boldsymbol{b}'}_A q'$ then $(\boldsymbol{b}, q) = (\boldsymbol{b}', q')$. It follows by induction over $|\boldsymbol{a}|$ for $\boldsymbol{a} \in \Sigma^*$ that, if $p \xrightarrow{\boldsymbol{a}/\boldsymbol{b}}\!\!\!\!\rightarrow_A q$ then $(\boldsymbol{b}, q)$ is unique for the given p and $\boldsymbol{a}$, in particular when $p = q_A^0$ and $q \in F_A$, and thus A is single-valued. Determinism is, however, not a necessary condition for single-valuedness, as is illustrated below. In the following examples, all SFTs are single-valued. The first example illustrates a few simple functional list transformations, expressed as deterministic SFTs that illustrate how global properties of SFTs depend on the theory of labels.

Example 2: Let the input type and the output type be $\mathbb{Z}$. All SFTs have a single state here. Predicates and terms are terms in integer linear arithmetic. *Negate* multiplies all elements by -1. *Increment* adds 1 to each element. *DeleteZeros* deletes all zeros from the input.

$$R_{Negate} = \{p \xrightarrow{\lambda x.\mathrm{t}/[\lambda x.(-x)]} p\}$$

$$R_{Increment} = \{q \xrightarrow{\lambda x.\mathrm{t}/[\lambda x.(1+x)]} q\}$$

$$R_{DeleteZeros} = \{r \xrightarrow{\lambda x.(x=0)/[]} r,\quad r \xrightarrow{\lambda x.(x\neq 0)/[\lambda x.x]} r\}$$

Properties such as commutativity and idempotence of SFTs depend on the theory of labels. For example, whether *Negate* and *DeleteZeros* commute or whether *DeleteZeros* is idempotent depend on properties of integer addition and multiplication. None of the examples can be expressed as traditional finite state transducers over a finite alphabet. Our results about composition and equivalence checking, discussed below, allow us to effectively establish such properties modulo decidability of a given label theory. ⊠

The following example illustrates a common string transformation where the use of nondeterministic SFTs is essential.

Example 3: Suppose that the following C# code is intended to implement a function `GetTags` that extracts from a given input stream of characters all substreams of the form $[\text{'<'}, x, \text{'>'}]$, where $x \neq \text{'<'}$. For example

```
GetTags("<<s><<>><f><t") = "<s><>><f>"
```

```
int q = 0; char c = (char)0;
foreach (char x in input) {
  if (q == 0) { if (x == '<') q = 1; else q = 0;}
  else if (q == 1) { if (x == '<') q = 1; else q = 2;}
  else if (q == 2) { if (x == '>') { yield return '<';
                                     yield return c;
                                     yield return '>';}
                     q = 0; }
  c = x; }
```

Note that the variable `q` keeps track of the relative position in the pattern $[\text{'<'}, x, \text{'>'}]$ and `c` records the previous character. The corresponding single-valued SFT is:[1]

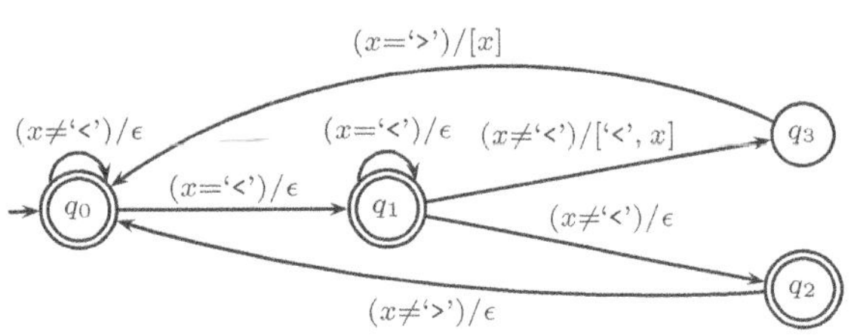

GetTags is nondeterministic because there are two rules from q_1 to q_2 and q_3, respectively, yielding different outputs for the same input. If the characters are represented as integers, then a deterministic version of *GetTags* does not exists, and if the characters are represented as 16-bit bitvectors (that corresponds precisely to the standard UTF-16 encoding of characters in C#) then the size of the equivalent deterministic SFT is 2^{16} times larger. (Example 7 below explains how *GetTags* is constructed from the C# code.) ⊠

3. SFT Algorithms

In this section we study algorithms for *composition* and *equivalence* of SFTs. First, we show that SFTs are effectively closed under composition. Next, we provide an efficient algorithm for *single-valued equality* of SFTs modulo a decidable theory of labels. Finally we introduce an algebra of SFTs that enables a variety of practically useful decision problems, such as deciding single-valuedness, and deciding commutativity and idempotence of single-valued SFTs.

[1] We omit λ's in figures for a more compact view.

3.1 Composition of SFTs

Given two transductions $\mathscr{T}_1$ and $\mathscr{T}_2$, $\mathscr{T}_1 \circ \mathscr{T}_2$ denotes the following function:

$$\mathscr{T}_1 \circ \mathscr{T}_2 \stackrel{\text{def}}{=} \lambda \boldsymbol{b}. \bigcup_{\boldsymbol{a} \in \mathscr{T}_1(\boldsymbol{b})} \mathscr{T}_2(\boldsymbol{a}).$$

This definition follows the convention in [21]. Notice that $\circ$ applies first $\mathscr{T}_1$, then $\mathscr{T}_2$, contrary to how $\circ$ is used for standard function composition. Note also that single-valuedness is trivially preserved by composition.

We say that label theories for $\sigma \to \tau$ and $\tau \to \gamma$ are *composable* if there is a label theory Ψ for $\sigma \to \gamma$ such that

- if $f : \sigma \to \tau$ and $g : \tau \to \gamma$ are a λ-terms then $\lambda x.g(f(x))$ is a valid λ-term in Ψ.
- if φ is a τ-predicate and $f : \sigma \to \tau$ is a λ-term, then $\lambda x.\varphi(f(x))$ is a valid σ-predicate in Ψ.

Proposition 1: Let A and B be SFTs over composable label theories. Then there exists an SFT $A \circ B$ that is obtained effectively from A and B such that $\mathscr{T}_{A \circ B} = \mathscr{T}_A \circ \mathscr{T}_B$.

The algorithm for $A \circ B$ can be implemented with a DFS procedure that, by assuming decidability of the label theory, eliminates incrementally all composed rules that have unsatisfiable guards and finally eliminates all *deadends* (*deadlock states*: states from which no final state is reachable).

3.2 Equivalence of SFTs

We introduce an algorithm for deciding equivalence of *single-valued* SFTs. While general equivalence of finite state transducers is undecidable [23] the undecidability is caused by allowing unboundedly many different outputs for a given input. Single-valued transducers, furthermore, correspond closely to functional transformations over lists computed by concrete programs. As illustrated above, this does not (in general) rule out nondeterministic SFTs.

SFTs A and B are *equivalent*, $A \equiv B$, when $\mathscr{T}_A = \mathscr{T}_B$. Deciding $A \equiv B$ reduces to two independent tasks:

Domain equivalence : $\mathscr{D}(A) = \mathscr{D}(B)$.

Partial equivalence : $(\forall \boldsymbol{a} \in \mathscr{D}(A) \cap \mathscr{D}(B))\ \mathscr{T}_A(\boldsymbol{a}) = \mathscr{T}_B(\boldsymbol{a})$

A *symbolic finite automaton* or *SFA* is an SFT all of whose outputs are empty. Let $\mathbf{d}(A)$ denote the SFA obtained from the SFT A by replacing all outputs by ϵ. Then $\mathscr{D}(A) = \mathscr{D}(B)$ iff $\mathbf{d}(A) \equiv \mathbf{d}(B)$. Equivalence of SFAs is decidable over decidable label theories [48]. The decidability of SFA equivalence depends on the assumption that the label theory is closed under *complementation*, this assumption is not needed for partial equivalence.

For developing a decision procedure for partial equivalence of single-valued SFTs we use the following weak form of partial equivalence.

Single-valued equality (or 1-equality $A \stackrel{1}{=} B$**)** :
$\forall \boldsymbol{a}\,\boldsymbol{b}\,\boldsymbol{c}((\boldsymbol{b} \in \mathscr{T}_A(\boldsymbol{a}) \wedge \boldsymbol{c} \in \mathscr{T}_B(\boldsymbol{a})) \Rightarrow \boldsymbol{b} = \boldsymbol{c})$

Proposition 2: A is single-valued iff $A \stackrel{1}{=} A$. If A and B are single-valued then $A \stackrel{1}{=} B$ iff A and B are partially equivalent.

Single-valued equality of two SFTs A and B may fail for two reasons. There is an input $\boldsymbol{a} \in \mathscr{D}(A) \cap \mathscr{D}(B)$ and outputs $\boldsymbol{b} \in \mathscr{T}_A(\boldsymbol{b})$ and $\boldsymbol{c} \in \mathscr{T}_B(\boldsymbol{a})$ such that:

1. A has a *length-conflict* with B: $|\boldsymbol{b}| \neq |\boldsymbol{c}|$.

2. A has a *position-conflict* with B: $|\boldsymbol{b}| = |\boldsymbol{c}|$ and, for some position i, $0 \leq i < |\boldsymbol{b}|$, $\boldsymbol{b}_i \neq \boldsymbol{c}_i$.

We introduce the following basic product construction of SFTs as a generalization of the product of SFAs [48]. The product construction is most effectively realized by using a DFS procedure. Note that the product of SFTs is a "2-output-SFT" (SFTs are not closed under product).

Definition 7: The *product* of SFTs A and B, denoted $A \times B$, is defined as the least fixpoint of pair states $Q \subseteq Q_A \times Q_B$ and rules under the following conditions:

- $(q_A^0, q_B^0) \in Q$,
- if $(p_1, p_2) \in Q$, $p_1 \xrightarrow{\varphi/\boldsymbol{f}}_A q_1$, and $p_2 \xrightarrow{\psi/\boldsymbol{g}}_B q_2$, then
  - $(q_1, q_2) \in Q$ and
  - $(p_1, p_2) \xrightarrow{\varphi\wedge\psi/(\boldsymbol{f},\boldsymbol{g})}_{A\times B} (q_1, q_2)$,

  provided that $IsSat(\varphi \wedge \psi)$.

All *deadends*, noninitial states from which $F_A \times F_B$ is not reachable, are eliminated from $A \times B$. ⊠

Example 4: Consider the SFT *GetTags* in Example 3. Then the product *GetTags*× *GetTags* has rules $(p,p) \xrightarrow{\varphi/(\boldsymbol{f},\boldsymbol{f})} (q,q)$ for all rules $p \xrightarrow{\varphi/\boldsymbol{f}}_{GetTags} q$ and no other rules due to elimination of deadends, e.g., (q_3, q_2) is a deadend because the guard of (the only possible rule)

$$(q_3, q_2) \xrightarrow{\lambda x.(x=\text{'>'} \wedge x \neq \text{'>'})/([\lambda x.x],\epsilon)} (q_0, q_0)$$

from (q_3, q_2) is unsatisfiable. ⊠

Let $\mathscr{D}(A \times B)$ denote the set of inputs that are accepted by the product. It follows from the product construction that:

$$\mathscr{D}(A \times B) = \mathscr{D}(A) \cap \mathscr{D}(B). \quad (1)$$

The reachability relation is lifted to $A \times B$ and the following holds for $p = (p_1, p_2), q = (q_1, q_2) \in Q_{A\times B}$:

$$p \xrightarrow{\boldsymbol{a}/(\boldsymbol{b},\boldsymbol{c})}\!\!\!\!\rightarrow_{A\times B} q \quad \Leftrightarrow \quad p_1 \xrightarrow{\boldsymbol{a}/\boldsymbol{b}}\!\!\!\!\rightarrow_A q_1 \wedge p_2 \xrightarrow{\boldsymbol{a}/\boldsymbol{c}}\!\!\!\!\rightarrow_B q_2. \quad (2)$$

We omit the index $A \times B$ when it is clear from the context. For $q \in Q_{A\times B}$, and $k \geq 0$, define the *offset relation*,

$$q \vartriangle k \stackrel{\text{def}}{=} \exists \boldsymbol{a}\,\boldsymbol{b}\,\boldsymbol{c}\,(q_{A\times B}^0 \xrightarrow{\boldsymbol{a}/(\boldsymbol{b},\boldsymbol{c})}\!\!\!\!\rightarrow q \wedge k = |\boldsymbol{b}| - |\boldsymbol{c}|) \quad (3)$$

The intuition behind $q \vartriangle k$ is that, for some common input $\boldsymbol{a}$, there exists an output $\boldsymbol{b}$ from A that is either ahead of an output $\boldsymbol{c}$ from B with k-positions at product state q when $k > 0$, or behind when $k < 0$. The following lemma is used to detect length-conflicts.

Lemma 1: If there exists $q \in Q_{A\times B}$ and $m \neq n$ such that $q \vartriangle m$ and $q \vartriangle n$ then A has a length-conflict with B. Moreover, A has a length-conflict with B iff there exists $q \in F_{A\times B}$ and $m \neq 0$ such that $q \vartriangle m$.

Lemma 1 suggests an efficient DFS algorithm to detect if a length-conflict exists and otherwise computes the fixed offset $\mathit{offs}(p)$ such that $p \vartriangle \mathit{offs}(p)$. In order to decide if a position-conflict exists between A and B, we first assume that A and B have no length-conflicts and assume that $\mathit{offs}(p)$ is defined and $\mathit{offs}(p) = 0$ for $p \in F_{A\times B}$. We say that $(\alpha, \beta) \in \Gamma^* \times \Gamma^*$ is a *promise* of a product state $p \in Q_{A\times B}$ when the following holds:

$$(\alpha = \epsilon \vee \beta = \epsilon) \wedge \exists \boldsymbol{a}\,\boldsymbol{b}\,\boldsymbol{c}\,(|\boldsymbol{b}| = |\boldsymbol{c}| \wedge q_{A\times B}^0 \xrightarrow{\boldsymbol{a}/(\boldsymbol{b}\cdot\alpha,\boldsymbol{c}\cdot\beta)}\!\!\!\!\rightarrow p)$$

It follows that

$$(|\alpha|, |\beta|) = \begin{cases} (\mathit{offs}(p), 0), & \text{if } \mathit{offs}(p) \geq 0; \\ (0, -\mathit{offs}(p)), & \text{otherwise.} \end{cases}$$

Lemma 2: If $A \stackrel{1}{=} B$ then each product state in $Q_{A\times B}$ has a fixed promise.

Proof. Assume $A \stackrel{1}{=} B$. Suppose, by way of contradiction, that there exists $p \in Q_{A\times B}$ with two distinct promises (α, β) and (α', β'). By Lemma 1 we know that $|\alpha| = |\alpha'|$ and $|\beta| = |\beta'|$ and either $\alpha = \epsilon$ or $\beta = \epsilon$. Suppose $\beta = \epsilon$ (the case $\alpha = \epsilon$ is symmetrical). Thus $\alpha \neq \alpha'$ (or else the promises are identical). By definition of promises there exist $\boldsymbol{a}, \boldsymbol{b}, \boldsymbol{c}, \boldsymbol{a}', \boldsymbol{b}', \boldsymbol{c}'$ such that, $|\boldsymbol{b}| = |\boldsymbol{c}|$, $|\boldsymbol{b}'| = |\boldsymbol{c}'|$,

$$q_{A\times B}^0 \xrightarrow{\boldsymbol{a}/(\boldsymbol{b}\cdot\alpha,\boldsymbol{c})}\!\!\!\!\rightarrow p, \quad q_{A\times B}^0 \xrightarrow{\boldsymbol{a}'/(\boldsymbol{b}'\cdot\alpha',\boldsymbol{c}')}\!\!\!\!\rightarrow p.$$

Since p is not a deadend, there exist $\boldsymbol{a}'', \boldsymbol{b}'', \boldsymbol{c}''$ and $q^f \in F_{A\times B}$ such that

$$p \xrightarrow{\boldsymbol{a}''/(\boldsymbol{b}'',\boldsymbol{c}'')}\!\!\!\!\rightarrow q^f.$$

It follows from $A \stackrel{1}{=} B$ that

$$\left.\begin{array}{l} \boldsymbol{b}\cdot\alpha\cdot\boldsymbol{b}'' \in \mathscr{T}_A(\boldsymbol{b}\cdot\boldsymbol{b}'') \\ \boldsymbol{c}\cdot\boldsymbol{c}'' \in \mathscr{T}_B(\boldsymbol{a}\cdot\boldsymbol{a}'') \end{array}\right\} \Rightarrow \boldsymbol{b}\cdot\alpha\cdot\boldsymbol{b}'' = \boldsymbol{c}\cdot\boldsymbol{c}''$$

$$\left.\begin{array}{l} \boldsymbol{b}'\cdot\alpha'\cdot\boldsymbol{b}'' \in \mathscr{T}_A(\boldsymbol{a}'\cdot\boldsymbol{a}'') \\ \boldsymbol{c}'\cdot\boldsymbol{c}'' \in \mathscr{T}_B(\boldsymbol{a}'\cdot\boldsymbol{a}'') \end{array}\right\} \Rightarrow \boldsymbol{b}'\cdot\alpha'\cdot\boldsymbol{b}'' = \boldsymbol{c}'\cdot\boldsymbol{c}''$$

and, since $|\boldsymbol{b}| = |\boldsymbol{c}|$ and $|\boldsymbol{b}'| = |\boldsymbol{c}'|$, it follows that $\alpha\cdot\boldsymbol{b}'' = \boldsymbol{c}''$ and $\alpha'\cdot\boldsymbol{b}'' = \boldsymbol{c}''$, contradicting that $\alpha \neq \alpha'$. □

Lemma 2 can be used to check for non-1-equality as follows: In a depth-first manner compute for every state in the product $Q_{A\times B}$ the current promise (α, β). If the state gets revisited with a different promise, then $A \stackrel{1}{\neq} B$.

Example 5: The product *GetTags*× *GetTags* in Example 4 has trivially no length-conflicts because offsets of all product states are 0 and thus promises of all product states are (ϵ, ϵ). ⊠

Finally, assuming $A \times B$ has no length-conflicts and each product state $p \in Q_{A\times B}$ has a fixed promise $\mathit{prom}(p) = (\alpha, \beta)$, then p is *conflict-free*, when, for all rules $p \xrightarrow{\varphi/(\boldsymbol{f},\boldsymbol{g})} q$, the maximal prefixes of $\alpha\cdot\boldsymbol{f}$ and $\beta\cdot\boldsymbol{g}$ are equivalent relative to φ. (Note, when concatenating $\alpha \in \Gamma^*$ with a sequence $\boldsymbol{f}$ of λ-terms of type $\sigma \to \gamma$ we assume an implicit conversion of α to $\lambda x.\alpha$.) Let $k = \min(|\alpha\cdot\boldsymbol{f}|, |\beta\cdot\boldsymbol{g}|) - 1$,

$$\bigwedge_{j=0}^{k} (\forall a (a \in [\![\varphi]\!] \Rightarrow [\![(\alpha\cdot\boldsymbol{f})_j]\!](a) = [\![(\beta\cdot\boldsymbol{g})_j]\!](a))). \quad (4)$$

We say that p is a *conflict-state* if p is not conflict-free. Verifying absence of conflict-states is a linear search over rules in $A \times B$ that verifies the condition (4) for each rule.

Lemma 3: If $A \times B$ has fixed promises and no length-conflicts then $A \stackrel{1}{\neq} B \Leftrightarrow Q_{A\times B}$ contains a conflict-state.

Proof. Assume that $A \times B$ is as stated.

($\Leftarrow$): existence of a conflict-state p implies, by definition, that there exists a position-conflict, since p is both reachable and not a deadend.

($\Rightarrow$): Assume $A \stackrel{1}{\neq} B$. We show that there exists a conflict-state. Since A and B have no length-conflicts there exist $\boldsymbol{a}, \boldsymbol{b}, \boldsymbol{c}$ such that $\boldsymbol{b} \in \mathscr{T}_A(\boldsymbol{a})$, $\boldsymbol{c} \in \mathscr{T}_B(\boldsymbol{a})$, $|\boldsymbol{b}| = |\boldsymbol{c}|$, and there exists a position i, $0 \leq i < |\boldsymbol{b}|$, such that $\boldsymbol{b}_i \neq \boldsymbol{c}_i$. Fix i to be the smallest such position. So there exists $\boldsymbol{a}^1, a, \boldsymbol{b}^1, \boldsymbol{b}^2, \boldsymbol{c}^2, \alpha, \beta, p, q$ such that $\boldsymbol{a}^1 \cdot a$ is a prefix of $\boldsymbol{a}$, $\boldsymbol{b}^1\cdot\alpha\cdot\boldsymbol{b}^2$ is a prefix of $\boldsymbol{b}$, $\boldsymbol{b}^1\cdot\beta\cdot\boldsymbol{c}^2$ is a prefix of $\boldsymbol{c}$, and

$$q_{A\times B}^0 \xrightarrow{\boldsymbol{a}^1/(\boldsymbol{b}^1\cdot\alpha,\boldsymbol{b}^1\cdot\beta)}\!\!\!\!\rightarrow p \xrightarrow{a/(\boldsymbol{b}^2,\boldsymbol{c}^2)} q$$

where $prom(p) = (\alpha, \beta)$ and $(\alpha \cdot \boldsymbol{b}^2)_j \neq (\beta \cdot \boldsymbol{c}^2)_j$ with $j = i - |\boldsymbol{b}^1|$. So there exists a rule $p \xrightarrow{\varphi/(\boldsymbol{f},\boldsymbol{g})} q$ such that $a \in [\![\varphi]\!]$ but $[\![(\alpha \cdot \boldsymbol{f})_j]\!](a) \neq [\![(\beta \cdot \boldsymbol{g})_j]\!](a)$. Thus, p is a conflict-state because (4) does not hold. □

The following theorem describes precisely the assumptions under which 1-equality of SFTs is decidable.

Theorem 1 (SFT-1-equality)**:** If A and B are SFTs over a decidable label theory then $A \stackrel{1}{=} B$ is decidable. Moreover, if the complexity of the label theory for instances of size m is $f(m)$ then the complexity of $A \stackrel{1}{=} B$ is $O(n^2 \cdot f(m))$ where n is the number of rules and m the size of the rules.

Proof. By using Lemmas 1, 2 and 3. Deciding satisfiability of φ is needed in the construction of $A \times B$. Deciding $f \equiv_\varphi g$ is needed for deciding validity of the formula (4). In Lemma 2, we need to decide if f is constant relative to a satisfiable formula φ: decide if $f \equiv_\varphi [\![f]\!](witness(\varphi))$.

Lemmas 1, 2 and 3 are combined into a single DFS algorithm, shown in Figure 3, that decides 1-equality of SFTs over a decidable label theory. Line 6 corresponds

Decide1equality$(A, B) \stackrel{\text{def}}{=}$
1 $C := A \times B$; $Q := \{q_C^0 \mapsto (\epsilon, \epsilon)\}$; $S := stack(q_C^0)$;
2 **while** $S \neq \emptyset$
3 $\quad p :=$ pop(S); $(\alpha, \beta) := Q(p)$;
4 $\quad$ **foreach** $(p, \varphi, (\boldsymbol{f}, \boldsymbol{g}), q) \in R_C(p)$
5 $\qquad (u, v) := (\alpha \cdot \boldsymbol{f}, \beta \cdot \boldsymbol{g})$;
6 $\qquad$ **if** $q \in F_C \wedge |u| \neq |v|$ **return** f;
7 $\qquad$ **if** $|u| \geq |v|$
8 $\qquad\quad$ **if** $\bigvee_{i=0}^{|v|-1} u_i \not\equiv_\varphi v_i$ **return** f;
9 $\qquad\quad w := [u_{|v|}, \ldots, u_{|u|-1}]$; $\mathbf{c} := [\![w]\!](witness(\varphi))$;
10 $\qquad\quad$ **if** $w \not\equiv_\varphi \mathbf{c} \vee (q \in Dom(Q) \wedge Q(q) \neq (\mathbf{c}, \epsilon))$ **return** f;
11 $\qquad\quad$ **if** $q \notin Dom(Q)$ push(q, S); $Q(q) := (\mathbf{c}, \epsilon)$;
12 $\qquad$ **if** $|u| < |v|$ ... (symmetrical to the case $|u| \geq |v|$)
13 **return** t;

Figure 3. 1-equality algorithm for SFTs.

to detection of a final state with non-zero offset by using Lemma 1. Line 8 corresponds to use of Lemma 3($\Leftarrow$). Line 10 corresponds to use of Lemma 2. Line 13 corresponds to use of contraposition of Lemma 3($\Rightarrow$).

The number of iterations of the loop as well as in the product construction is bounded by $|R_A| \cdot |R_B|$. The algorithm uses satisfiability checks during product construction in line 1, and in the loop in lines 8 and 10. In line 8 the number of checks is linear in the length of the output sequence v: decide if there exists i, $0 \leq i < |v|$, and $\varphi(x) \wedge u_i(x) \neq v_i(x)$ is satisfiable. Similarly for line 10. The complexity follows. □

Theorem 1 shows that complexity of 1-equality of SFTs depends on the complexity of the label theory. For example, if we use linear arithmetic with one free variable as the label theory, and guards are represented in normalized form as conjunctions of linear inequalities, then the Fourier-Motzkin elimination procedure [14] implies a polynomial worst-case complexity of 1-equality.

The algorithm for partial-equivalence of classical single-valued finite transducers, has complexity $O((|T|+|Q|)^2)$ [16], where T is the set of transitions. With a symbolic encoding we can replace $|T|$ by the decision complexity for the alphabet theory. Symbolic encodings also make expressing dependencies between input-output characters succinct. To

$$
\begin{array}{lcl}
\sigma, \tau, \gamma & ::= & \text{types} \\
sfa^\sigma & ::= & \text{explicit dfn of an SFA over } \sigma \\
sft^{\sigma/\gamma} & ::= & \text{explicit dfn of an SFT over } \sigma \to \gamma \\
A^\sigma & ::= & sfa^\sigma \mid A^\sigma - A^\sigma \mid A^\sigma \times A^\sigma \mid B^{\sigma/\gamma} \circ A^\gamma \\
B^{\sigma/\gamma} & ::= & sft^{\sigma/\gamma} \mid B^{\sigma/\tau} \circ B^{\tau/\gamma} \mid B^{\sigma/\gamma} \restriction A^\sigma \\
F & ::= & A^\sigma \subseteq A^\sigma \mid B^{\sigma/\gamma} \stackrel{1}{=} B^{\sigma/\gamma} \mid F \wedge F \mid \neg F
\end{array}
$$

Figure 4. Algebra of SFTs; A is a valid SFA expression; B is a valid SFT expression; F is a valid formula; label theories are assumed composable.

give the flavor, in a UTF-16 to UTF-8 encoder, we use transitions of the form

$$p \xrightarrow{\lambda x.\texttt{0xD800} \leq x \leq \texttt{0xDBFF}/[\lambda x.enc_1(x), \lambda x.enc_2(x), \lambda x.enc_3(x)]} q.$$

It succinctly represents 1024 transitions required by explicit finite transducer representations. Overall, the full SFT (over 16-bit bit-vector arithmetic) for the encoder uses 5 states and 16 rules, compared to 2^{16} concrete transitions required by an equivalent classical finite transducer. We also evaluate the benefits of SFAs in [24]. SFA equivalence is required for the domain equivalence check of SFTs.

Relation to One-Counter Automata. In closely related work, Alur et.al. [1] present *streaming transducers*, an extension of classical finite state transducers that is largely orthogonal to SFTs presented here. For example, streaming transducers allow reversing the input, which is not possible with SFTs, but require the character theory to be a total order, so that equivalence remains decidable. The authors prove the decidability of equivalence of streaming transducers by reducing it to reachability of *one-counter automata.* At a high level, the automaton is constructed so that it simulates the execution of the two given transducers in parallel, synchronized on the input tape, while using the counter to represent the length offset between outputs. If the one-counter automaton can reach a final state on a zero count, then the simulated transducers must have different output on some input.

While our main algorithm (1-equality algorithm in Figure 3) is similar in spirit, we do not make explicit use of the one-counter automaton construction. To do so would impose two restrictions on our approach: (1) the one-counter automaton construction would require satisfiability checking of conjunctions of formulae in the background theory; and (2) it would require special handling to deal with the fact that we allow elements in output sequences to be functions of the input symbols. While we are confident that the first requirement (1) can be readily accommodated, we are unaware of any way to circumvent the second restriction (2) without imposing additional limitations on the types of allowable output functions, and by adding a symbolic component to the one-counter automaton itself. Instead, we focus on a more ad-hoc construction that does not impose additional restrictions. With respect to the algorithm in Figure 3, (2) is reflected in the use of *witness or model generation* modulo the input condition and the output transformation functions, (2) is essentially the implementation of Lemma 2.

3.3 Algebra of SFTs

We introduce an algebra of SFTs, in Figure 4, that allows us to express several useful decision problems involving SFTs and SFAs. Note that $B \circ A$ of an SFT B with an SFA A is again an SFA because all the outputs of $B \circ A$ are empty. We call $B \circ A$ the *inverse image of B under A*. The definition of $B \upharpoonright A$ in our algebra is as follows.

Definition 8: Let B be an SFT and A an SFA. The *domain restriction of B for A*, denoted $B \upharpoonright A$, is the SFT obtained from $B \times A$ by eliminating the second output component ϵ from all the rules. ⊠

The following property follows from (1) and (2).

$$\mathscr{T}_{B \upharpoonright A}(\boldsymbol{b}) = \begin{cases} \mathscr{T}_B(\boldsymbol{b}), & \text{if } \boldsymbol{b} \in \mathscr{D}(A); \\ \emptyset, & \text{otherwise.} \end{cases} \tag{5}$$

We say that the SFT algebra in Figure 4 is *decidable* if validity of all the formulas F in the algebra is decidable.

Theorem 2 (SFT-algebra)**:** The algebra of SFTs is decidable if the label theories are decidable.

Proof. The SFA operations are effectively closed under intersection an complement and equivalence is decidable if satisfiability of the guards is decidable [48]. Decidability of 1-equality of SFTs is Theorem 1. Closure under composition is Proposition 1. Domain restriction is given in (5). □

The following corollary identifies a collection of practically relevant decision problems that follow from Theorem 2. *Subsumption* of SFTs, $A \sqsubseteq B$, is the problem of deciding if $\mathscr{T}_A(\boldsymbol{b}) \subseteq \mathscr{T}_B(\boldsymbol{b})$ for all $\boldsymbol{b}$. *Reachability* is the problem of existence of an input that is transformed to an output accepted by an SFA.

Corollary 1: The following decision problems over single-valued SFTs over a decidable label theory are decidable: Subsumption; Equivalence; Idempotence; Commutativity; Reachability.

Proof. Assume A and B are single-valued SFTs and recall Proposition 2. Subsumption, $A \sqsubseteq B$, is $\mathbf{d}(A) \subseteq \mathbf{d}(B) \wedge A \stackrel{1}{=} B$. Equivalence, $A \equiv B$, is $A \sqsubseteq B \wedge B \sqsubseteq A$. Idempotence is $A \equiv A \circ A$. Commutativity is $A \circ B \equiv B \circ A$. Reachability of a given output SFA D is $A \circ D \neq \emptyset$. □

The following example illustrates a use of the SFT algebra for reachability analysis of SFTs. The example is a digest behind security analysis of string sanitizers with respect to known XSS attack vectors.

Example 6: Consider the SFT $B = \mathit{GetTags}$ from Example 3. Is it possible that B does not detect all tags? In other words, does there exist an input $\boldsymbol{b}$ that matches the regex $P =$ ".*<[^<]>.*" but $\mathscr{T}_B(\boldsymbol{b}) = \{\epsilon\}$?

Let A_ϵ and $A_\emptyset$ be the SFAs such that $\mathscr{D}(A_\epsilon) = \{\epsilon\}$ and $\mathscr{D}(A_\emptyset) = \emptyset$. Let A_P be the SFA that accepts all strings that match the regex P.

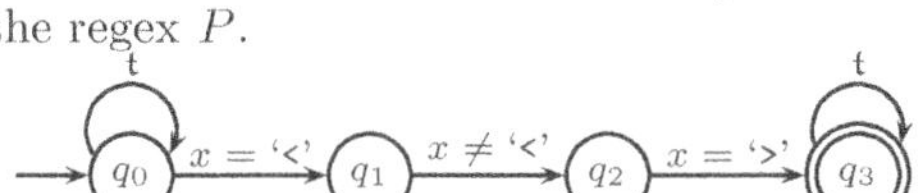

The question is equivalent to deciding if (6) fails,

$$\underbrace{(B \upharpoonright A_P) \circ A_\epsilon}_{D} \equiv A_\emptyset \tag{6}$$

because, for $\boldsymbol{b} \in \Sigma^*$,

$$\begin{aligned} \boldsymbol{b} \in \mathscr{D}(D) &\Leftrightarrow \exists \boldsymbol{a} \, (\mathscr{T}_{B \upharpoonright A_P}(\boldsymbol{b}) = \{\boldsymbol{a}\} \wedge \boldsymbol{a} \in \mathscr{D}(A_\epsilon)) \\ &\Leftrightarrow \mathscr{T}_{B \upharpoonright A_P}(\boldsymbol{b}) = \{\epsilon\} \\ &\Leftrightarrow \mathscr{T}_B(\boldsymbol{b}) = \{\epsilon\} \wedge \boldsymbol{b} \in \mathscr{D}(A_P) \end{aligned}$$

It turns out that D (when minimized) is an SFA with 8 states, e.g., "<a<a>" $\in \mathscr{D}(D)$. (What is remarkable is that D can be effectively converted back to a regex that describes *all* inputs where tags are not detected.) By considering the witness, it can easily be traced back to the missing case in the **GetTags** program: line 8 of the C# code should be q = (x == '<' ? 1 : 0);. By verifying (6) for the SFT corresponding to the fixed code, we can verify the new code indeed detects all tags. ⊠

It also follows from Theorem 1 and Proposition 2, that we can decide single-valuedness of SFTs. This is a practically valuable result that lifts the burden of the semantic assumption of single-valuedness in decision problems that assume single-valuedness.

Corollary 2: Single-valuedness of SFTs over a decidable label theory is decidable.

3.4 Extension with Registers

We extend SFTs to symbolic transducers or STs by allowing the use of registers. This will provide a more succinct representation, and enable more efficient symbolic analysis methods to be used, by taking advantage of recent advances is SMT technology [15]. An ST uses a set of variables called *registers* as a symbolic representation of states. The rules of an ST are guarded commands with a symbolic input and output component. Since the finite state component of an SFT can be represented with a particular register of finite type, the explicit state component is omitted from STs. Moreover, by using Cartesian product types, we represent multiple registers with a single (compound) register.

Definition 9: A *Symbolic Transducer* or *ST* with input type σ, output type γ and register type τ is a tuple (q^0, ϑ, R), where $q^0 \in \mathcal{U}^\tau$ is the *initial state*, ϑ is a τ-predicate called the *final state condition*, and R is a finite set of *rules* $(\varphi, \boldsymbol{f}, g)$ where φ is a $(\sigma{\times}\tau)$-predicate, $\boldsymbol{f}$ is a sequence of λ-terms of type $(\sigma{\times}\tau) \to \gamma$, and g is a λ-term of type $(\sigma{\times}\tau) \to \tau$. ⊠

We write $A^{\sigma/\gamma;\tau}$ to indicate the input/output element type σ/γ and the register type τ of an ST A. When we write $A^{\sigma/\gamma}$, we assume τ to be implicit. A rule $(\varphi, \boldsymbol{f}, g) \in R_A$ denotes the following set of concrete transitions:

$$[\![(\varphi, \boldsymbol{f}, g)]\!] \stackrel{\text{def}}{=} \{q \xrightarrow{a/[\![\boldsymbol{f}]\!](a,q)} [\![g]\!](a,q) \mid (a,q) \in [\![\varphi]\!]\}$$

Although the formal definition omits finite states, it is often useful to explicitly include a separate finite state component, we do this in the examples below. Moreover, it is technically convenient to extend final states with *final outputs* by extending ϑ to be a finite set of *final output rules* $(\psi, \boldsymbol{g})$ where ψ is a τ-predicate and $\boldsymbol{g}$ is a sequence of λ-terms of type $\tau \to \gamma$. Intuitively, a final output is the output produced when the end of the input has been reached, often this is ϵ, but it need not be. When all final outputs are ϵ then ϑ is equivalent to being a τ-predicate as in Definition 9, i.e., $q \in [\![\vartheta_A]\!]$ then means that $q \xrightarrow{/\epsilon}_A$. Final outputs correspond to a restricted use of input-epsilon rules as used in classical finite transducers.

The reachability relation $p \xrightarrow{\boldsymbol{a}/\boldsymbol{b}}\!\!\!\!\rightarrow_A q$ for $\boldsymbol{a} \in \Sigma^*$, $\boldsymbol{b} \in \Gamma^*$, and $p, q \in \mathcal{U}^\tau$ is defined analogously to SFTs. The definition of $\mathscr{T}_A$ is lifted similarly, for $\boldsymbol{a} \in \Sigma^*$:

$$\mathscr{T}_A(\boldsymbol{a}) \stackrel{\text{def}}{=} \{\boldsymbol{b} \cdot \boldsymbol{c} \mid \exists q \, (q^0_A \xrightarrow{\boldsymbol{a}/\boldsymbol{b}}\!\!\!\!\rightarrow_A q \wedge q \xrightarrow{/\boldsymbol{c}}_A)\}$$

Example 7: Consider the C# code in Example 3. There is a direct mapping of the code to an ST A that uses the compound register $\langle q, c \rangle$. The initial state of A is $\langle 0, 0 \rangle$, the final state condition is $\mathfrak{t}$ and the rules are (we omit λ's):

$$\begin{array}{ll}(q{=}0 \wedge x{=}\text{'<'}, \epsilon, \langle 1, x\rangle), & (q{=}0 \wedge x{\neq}\text{'<'}, \epsilon, \langle 0, x\rangle),\\ (q{=}1 \wedge x{=}\text{'<'}, \epsilon, \langle 1, x\rangle), & (q{=}1 \wedge x{\neq}\text{'<'}, \epsilon, \langle 2, x\rangle),\\ (q{=}2 \wedge x{=}\text{'>'}, [\text{'<'}, c, \text{'>'}], \langle 0, x\rangle), & (q{=}2 \wedge x{\neq}\text{'>'}, \epsilon, \langle 0, x\rangle)\end{array}$$

The register update $\langle r_q, r_c\rangle$ of a rule corresponds to the assignments $q := r_q$ and $c := r_c$. Since all assignments to c have the form $c := x$, c corresponds to the *previous* input character. A can be automatically transformed to the equivalent *GetTags* SFT; the register c is eliminated by using a new state and nondeterminism. ⊠

One can effectively construct a well-founded axiomatic theory $Th(A)$ of an ST $A^{\sigma/\gamma}$ over a background of *lists*, similarly to symbolic automata in [47]. $Th(A)$ defines a symbol T_A that provides a sound and complete axiomatization of $\mathscr{T}_A$, i.e., for any model $\mathfrak{A} \models_{\mathcal{U}} Th(A)$, $T_A^{\mathfrak{A}} = \mathscr{T}_A$.

Moreover, $Th(A)$ can be directly asserted as an *auxiliary theory* of any state-of-the-art SMT solver that supports lists. By deploying $Th(A)$ in this way, we obtain an *integrated decision procedure* for satisfiability and model generation for quantifier free formulas that may arbitrarily combine formulas over the background $\mathcal{U}$ with *transduction atoms* $T_A(u, v)$ where $u : \mathbb{L}\langle\sigma\rangle$ and $v : \mathbb{L}\langle\gamma\rangle$ are arbitrary list terms. A direct application, outlined in Figure 5, is a semi-decision procedure for *1-disequality* of STs, where the auxiliary theories are asserted to the solver in line 1, and successively longer input-lists are used to invoke the solver to decide 1-disequality of the instance in line 4. The semi-decision procedure computes a shortest-input witness of 1-disequality.

Witness1disequality$(A^{\sigma/\gamma}, B^{\sigma/\gamma}) \stackrel{\text{def}}{=}$

1 **assert** $Th(A) \cup Th(B)$;
2 $(u, v, w) := (\mathit{nil}, \mathit{NewVariable}(\mathbb{L}\langle\gamma\rangle), \mathit{NewVariable}(\mathbb{L}\langle\gamma\rangle))$;
3 **while** $\mathfrak{t}$
4   **if** $\exists\mathfrak{A}\,(\mathfrak{A} \models_{\mathcal{U}} T_A(u, v) \wedge T_B(u, w) \wedge v{\neq}w)$ **return** $(u^{\mathfrak{A}}, v^{\mathfrak{A}}, w^{\mathfrak{A}})$;
5   **else** $u := \mathit{cons}(\mathit{NewVariable}(\sigma), u)$;

Figure 5. Given STs $A \not\stackrel{1}{\equiv} B$, generates a witness $(\boldsymbol{a}, \boldsymbol{b}, \boldsymbol{c})$ such that $\boldsymbol{b} \in \mathscr{T}_A(\boldsymbol{a})$, $\boldsymbol{c} \in \mathscr{T}_B(\boldsymbol{a})$, and $\boldsymbol{b} \neq \boldsymbol{c}$.

4. Case Studies

We present four case studies for applications of SFTs. The first case study focuses on sophisticated string manipulation, that goes beyond our first case study of sanitizer analysis with BEK [4] (that is discussed further in Section 5), we want to emphasize that the utility of SFTs goes well beyond reasoning about string sanitizer processing. Figure 2 summarizes the essential features of each case study.

4.1 Representing HTMLDecode

To prevent injection attacks such as cross-site scripting (XSS) and SQL injection, Web applications employ *sanitizers*, which are string manipulation routines that remove or encode dangerous input characters. Many applications include their own sanitizer implementations. Recent work by Hooimeijer et al. [4] examines several such sanitizers, demonstrating that a subset of popular sanitizers can be modeled using transducers. Furthermore, they show that safety properties of Web sanitizers can be checked using transducer analyses.

We focus on the sanitizer `HTMLDecode` to evaluate the practical utility of the ST representation. Figure 6 outlines a

```
public String HTMLDecode( String input ) {
  StringBuffer sb = new StringBuffer();
  PushbackString pbs = new PushbackString( input );
  while ( pbs.hasNext() ) {
    Character c = decodeCharacter( pbs );
    if ( c != null ) { sb.append( c ); }
    else { sb.append( pbs.next() ); } }
  return sb.toString();
}

public Character decodeCharacter( PushbackString input ) {
  input.mark();
  Character first = input.next();
  if ( first == null ) { input.reset(); return null; }
  if ( first.charValue() != '&' ) {
    input.reset(); return null; }
  Character second = input.next(); if ( second == null ) {
    input.reset(); return null; }
  if ( second.charValue() == '#' ) {
    Character c = getNumericEntity( input );
    if ( c != null ) return c; }
  else if ( Character.isLetter( second.charValue() ) ) {
    input.pushback( second );
    Character c = getNamedEntity( input );
    if ( c != null ) return c; }
  input.reset();
  return null;
}

private Character getNumericEntity( PushbackString input ) {
  ...
  return parseNumber( input );
}

private Character parseNumber( PushbackString input ) {
  StringBuffer sb = new StringBuffer();
  while( input.hasNext() ) {
    Character c = input.peek();
    if ( Character.isDigit( c.charValue() ) ) {
      sb.append( c );
      input.next(); }
    else if ( c.charValue() == ';' ) {
      input.next();
      break; }
    else break; }
  try {
    int i = Integer.parseInt(sb.toString());
    return new Character( (char)i ); }
  catch( NumberFormatException e ) return null;
}
```

Figure 6. Excerpt `HTMLDecode` in Java (from OWASP 1.4.0). The code shown converts named entities (e.g., `<` to `<`) and numeric entities (e.g., `4` to `4`). The numeric entity conversion is difficult to model efficiently using previous approaches.

real-world implementation, taken from the OWASP library. `HTMLDecode` transforms HTML *entities* back to the symbol they represent. Entities can be named (e.g., `<` maps to `<`), or numeric in decimal or hexadecimal representation (e.g., decimal entity `0` maps to symbol `0`). For simplicity, we will restrict our attention to decimal entities.

Intuitively, `HTMLDecode` is difficult to cast as a transducer because it requires *lookahead*: a single output symbol may depend on a specific sequence of several characters. The full Unicode set consists of more than one million symbols. To decode a decimal entity, therefore, we need to inspect up to six digits. While that is possible using either SFTs or traditional transducers, it requires a large state space.

In contrast, the corresponding ST is quite succinct. Figure 7 shows a ST $\mathit{Decode}^{\mathbb{Z}/\mathbb{Z};Q\times(\mathbb{Z}\times\mathbb{Z})}$, that uses two registers to handle numeric entities with exactly two digits. The compound register is $\langle q, \langle y, z\rangle\rangle$ We illustrate explicitly the finite

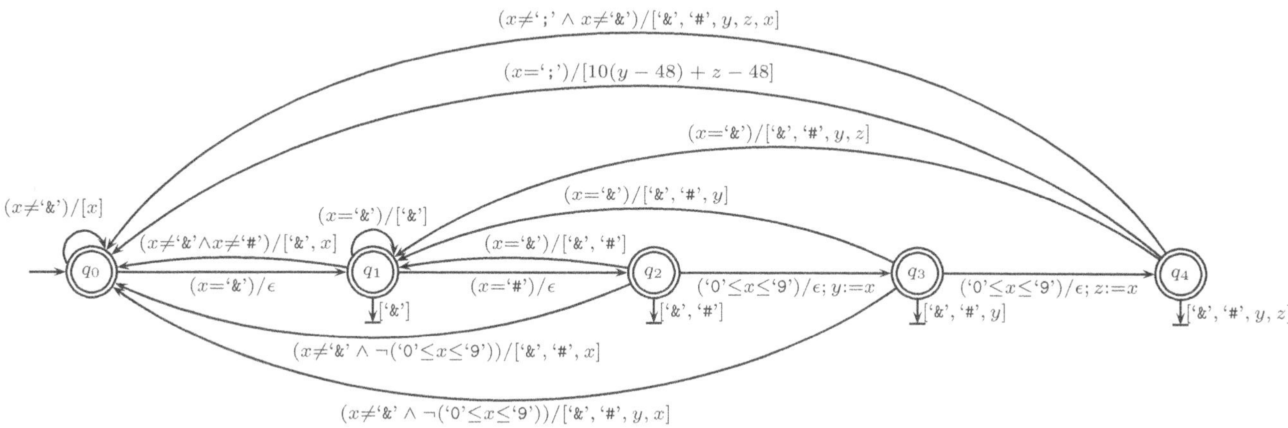

Figure 7. ST representation of the `HTMLdecode` code in Figure 6, restricted to decimal numeric entities of the form `&#[0-9][0-9];`. This ST uses two registers to remember one digit each, and uses integer-linear arithmetic to compute the corresponding code point. The λ-terms are implicit in the labels, e.g., the output $10(y-48)+z-48$ is short for $\lambda(x,(y,z)).10(y-48)+z-48$, where x is the input and (y,z) the register.

state component (that is the value of q). Final outputs, unless they are ϵ, are shown by labels on outgoing ⇥ arcs from final states. Characters correspond to their Unicode code points, e.g., '0' = 48. The actual decoding happens in the rule from state q_4 to q_0 with guard x = ';', where the output $10 \cdot (y-48) + z - 48$ corresponds to invocation of `parseInt` in Figure 6. The states q_i roughly correspond to the control flow of the code in Figure 6.

Evaluation: We compare the ST representation to the equivalent SFTs, in terms of size and analysis speed. Let $\mathsf{DecodeST}_n$ denote an ST that models `HTMLDecode` for entities of the form `&#[0-9]{1,n};` (i.e., up to n decimals, inclusive). For each $i \in [2;6]$, we compute an SFT that is equivalent to $\mathsf{DecodeST}_i$ by concretizing the possible register values at each state. Figure 8(a) shows the number of both states and edges on the y-axis, for both representations; the x-axis denotes the number of digits modeled. The most prominent take-away is that the ST representation is drastically smaller. For example, for the 6-digit encoding, the SFT encoding has over $10,000\times$ as many states, and $135,000\times$ as many edges, as the equivalent ST encoding.

We consider the speed of two algorithms: composition and equivalence checking. The experimental task is to find a witness (i.e., an input string) w that demonstrates that $\mathsf{DecodeST}_i(w) \neq \mathsf{DecodeST}_i(\mathsf{DecodeST}_i(w))$, for some number of self-compositions. We consider three different algorithms for performing this task: ST.E uses an in-memory representation and conducts an *eager* search (computing entire transducers); ST.L uses a *lazy* approach by encoding the entire ST into the underlying SMT solver; and SFT represents an eager SFT-based approach.

Figure 8(b) shows the speed results. Compositions represents the number of times we compose each class of transducer with itself. Composition refers to the time taken to perform the composition; for the lazy ST.L this time is negligible (since the composition is simply asserted to the underlying solver). IdempotenceChecking refers to the time taken to find the actual witness, after the composition. Each column represents a single experimental run; we employed a 2-hour timeout per run. The label OM marks runs that ran out of memory, while TO marks cases that hit the 2-hour timeout.

These results show that STs, in particular using the lazy representation, are significantly more scalable for this task than SFTs. The SFT representation either exhausts memory or passes the timeout in the majority of cases. The eager ST representation outperforms the lazy representation only for the smallest two testcases. For larger runs (i.e., more compositions and more digits), the lazy SFT representation scales much more reliably, ranging from 1 to 20 seconds over the 2-composition range (compared to several minutes for the eager representation).

4.2 Malware Fingerprinting Code

Millions of web pages today contain malicious JavaScript that attempts to take over a victim's web browser. An active research literature has proposed static and dynamic methods for detecting these attacks [9, 11, 13, 41]. A key finding of this work is that malware authors use *fingerprinting* techniques [17, 36] to decide which malware to deliver to the victim user.

Figure 9 shows an example of client-side browser fingerprinting. [2] The code iterates over the list of plugins installed in the browser and queries their version numbers. In some cases, version numbers are padded by optionally adding leading 0s to them. Finally, variables `quicktime_plugin` and `adobe_plugin` are combined to produce the final `fingerprint` value. This fingerprint value is then used to select a specific attack to run against the user.

Figure 12 list several concrete fingerprint values from real browser setups. Note that QuickTime 7.6.6 has at least one known vulnerability, and may thus be of special interest to an attacker.

We consider a scenario in which we have acquired these fingerprints (e.g., through network sniffing), and want to find out the corresponding plugin names. At a higher level, the question is: "Can we find out interesting properties by com-

[2] This code is simplified for illustrative purposes: the original considers more plugin types, including Flash, etc.

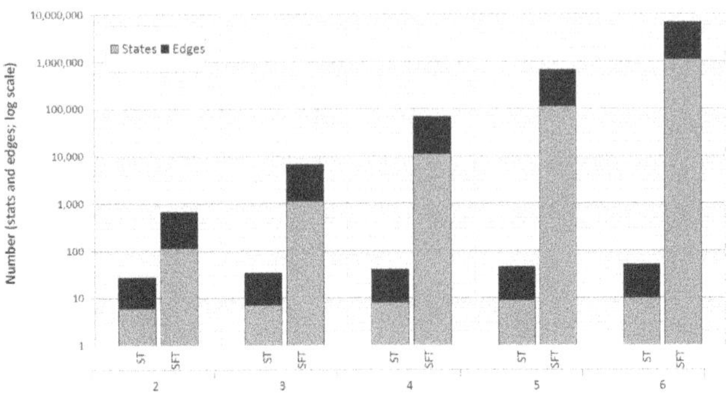

(a) Initial transducer sizes.

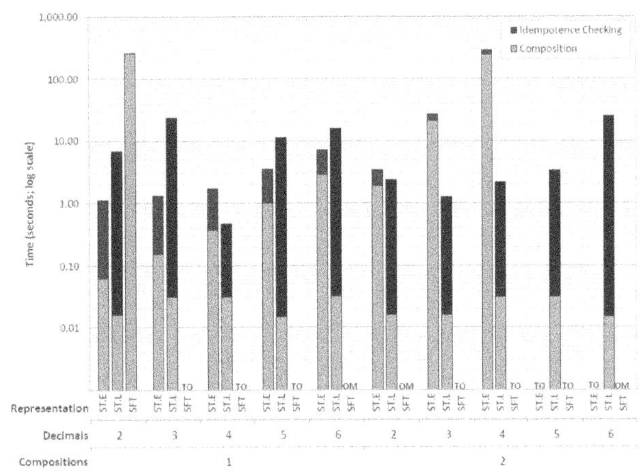

(b) Running times.

Figure 8. `HTMLDecode` results. The task is to prove that `HTMLDecode` does not commute with itself, and to provide a witness that demonstrates this for a given number of Compositions. We evaluate three representations: ST.E (eager ST composition), ST.L (lazy ST composition using Z3), and SFT (SFT composition). We consider five distinct models (indicated by Decimals, based on how many digits the ST or SFT can handle.

puting string-related pre-conditions based on a postcondition?"

Our techniques can answer this question in the affirmative by modeling the code of Figure 9 using multiple SFTs. The key idea is conditional assignment translates into nondeterministic case splits inside the SFT. At a high level, each transducer corresponds to a split or a merge in the control flow of the fingerprinting code, relative to a single variable of interest. This is illustrated in Figure 10, which shows the transducer `QuicktimeSplitter` together with the path predicates modeled by each of its three main branches. The transducer reads both `quicktime_plugin` and `plugin_name`, separated by a special `#` symbol. Its output is guaranteed to start with `#` if and only if the branch `if(quicktime_plugin == 0&&...` was taken.

For the sake of brevity, we do not display the remaining SFTs. Figure 11 lists the full set of SFTs and their statistics. `QuicktimeMerger` takes the output of `QuicktimeSplitter` and models the control flow join at the end of the first `if` statement. `QuickTimePadder` models the final while loop in Figure9. The manipulation of variable `adobe_plugin` is analogous.

```
var quicktime_plugin = "0", adobe_plugin = "00";

for(var i = 0; i < navigator.plugins.length; i++)
{
  var plugin_name = navigator.plugins[i].name;
  if (quicktime_plugin == 0 &&
    plugin_name.indexOf("QuickTime") != -1)
  {
     var helper = parseInt(plugin_name.replace(/\D/g,""));
     if (helper > 0) // not base 16
       quicktime_plugin = helper.toString(10)
  }
  if (adobe_plugin == "00" &&
    plugin_name.indexOf("Adobe Acrobat") != -1)
  {
    plugin_name = navigator.plugins[i].description;
    if(plugin_name.indexOf(" 5") != -1) adobe_plugin = "05";
    else if(plugin_name.indexOf(" 6") != -1) adobe_plugin = "06";
    else if(plugin_name.indexOf(" 7") != -1) adobe_plugin = "07";
    else adobe_plugin = "01"
  } else {
    // flash, java...
  }
}

while(quicktime_plugin.length < 8)
  quicktime_plugin = "0" + quicktime_plugin;

var fingerprint = "Q" + quicktime_plugin + "8" + adobe_plugin;
// ...
fetch_exploit(fingerprint);
```

Figure 9. Browser and plugin fingerprinting code found in JavaScript malware.

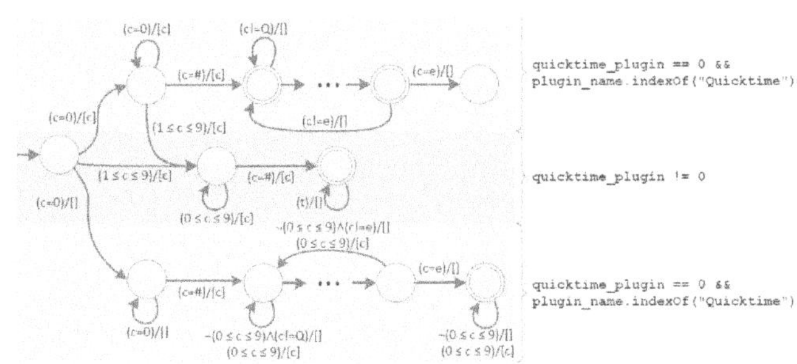

Figure 10. SFT `QuicktimeSplitter` with corresponding path predicates for the fingerprinting code.

Evaluation: We compute the pre-image of the composition transducers discussed above as follows. For each fingerprint w, we construct an SFA that accepts $\{w\}$ and corresponds to the postcondition `fingerprint == ` w. The pre-images of *QuicktimeComposed* and *AdobeComp* correspond to preconditions for a single iteration of the `for` loop in Figure 9. For example, for w = `Q00000769801`, we find a precondition that relates values of `quicktime_plugin` to values of `plugin_name`, as follows: (1) `quicktime_plugin` already had value `769`, possibly padded with up to five zeroes, or (2) `quicktime_plugin` consisted entirely of zeroes and `plugin_name` contained the substring Quicktime together with digits `7`, `6`, and `9` in that relative order. Condition (1) represents the case where `quicktime_plugin` had a previously-assigned version number, while condition (2) represents the case in which a version number was extracted inside the `for` loop. For all real fingerprints we tried, our analysis took less than one second per fingerprint.

Next, we evaluate whether inverse image generation, as used above, scales to relatively large output values. Unlike most previous string constraint solvers [26, 30, 42], SFT-

SFT	States	Edges
Quicktime (variable quicktime_plugin)		
QuicktimeSplitter	25	60
QuicktimeMerger	6	9
QuicktimePadder	37	37
Composed	534	1,425
Adobe (variable adobe_plugin)		
AdobeSplitter	36	81
AdobeMerger	21	40
Composed	203	797

Figure 11. SFTs used for the malware fingerprinting example. Statistics for the Quicktime and Adobe components are shown. The composition SFTs take approximately one second to compute.

Browser/plugin combination	Fingerprint
FF: Acrobat 9.4.5.236; no quicktime	Q00000000801
FF: Acrobat 9.4.5.236; Quicktime 7.6.9	Q00000769801
IE: no plugins of interest installed	Q00000000800
FF: Acrobat 9.4.5.236; Quicktime 7.5.5	Q00000755801
FF: Acrobat 9.4.5.236; Quicktime 7.6.6	Q00000766801

Figure 12. Browser fingerpints. Using an SFT model, computing input values for `quicktime_plugin` and `adobe_plugin` takes less than one second per fingerprint.

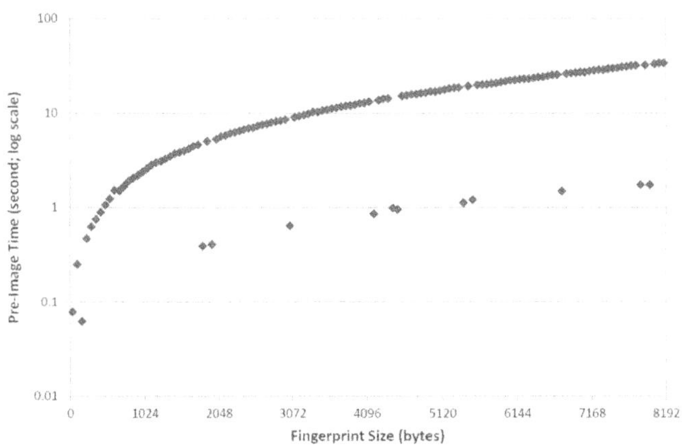

Figure 13. Inverse image generation time in seconds for fingerprint outputs up to 8192 bytes. The outputs were randomly generated from the language `Q[0-9]{n}801` over 16 bit characters.

based analysis does not impose length bounds on the strings under consideration. This is only beneficial if the approach actually scales to large strings. We show the approach *does* scale by generating random fingerprints of the form `Q[0-9]{n}801`, and measuring the time it takes to compute the inverse images for both the QuickTime and Adobe variables. Figure 13 shows encouraging results: in general, our approach takes less than half a minute to generate pre-images for up to *eight kilobytes* worth of output. In contrast, the Hampi solver was limited to finding pre-images up to fifty bytes worth of output.

Our malware case study demonstrates several important points. First, SFTs are well-suited for describing code by making use of non-determinism. The transducers needed can be large (on the order of hundreds of states and edges), but we can construct them from much smaller transducers (tens of states and edges) through composition. The pre-image computation reveals interesting relations among mutually dependent variables. Finally, the pre-image computation is efficient: it can generate valid string inputs for outputs that measure several kilobytes in size, while we are unaware of any previous string constraint solver that can handle this order of magnitude.

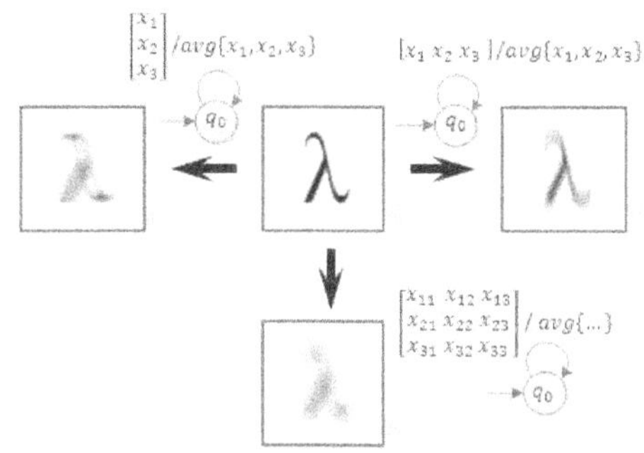

Figure 14. Blurring transformation illustrated.

Takeaways: From our first two case studies, we have the following key takeaways

- STs can be radically more succinct in representation than SFTs: we saw in our HTMLDecode example that our ST representation had 10,000 times fewer states and 150,000 times fewer edges than our SFT representation.
- Lazy ST encoding scales best for our `HTMLDecode` example, taking between 1 to 20 seconds for six characters and two compositions. Eager ST encoding is slower, and eager SFT encoding times out above two characters.
- SFTs can accurately model real examples of malicious Javascript fingerprinting code. Our analysis requires less than one second to recover plug-in versions from real examples of fingerprints generated by malicious code found "in the wild."
- Previous work in string constraint solving has focused almost exclusively on constraints that require fewer than 50 bytes; for example, the majority of Hampi experiments were conducted with length bounds of 15 bytes or fewer [30]. In contrast, our techniques can synthesize pre-images in excess of 8,000 bytes in roughly a minute.

4.3 Image Blurring

To illustrate the generality of SFTs, we look at image transformations. A clear advantage of representing image transformations in the form of transducers is the ability to do composition on transducers it gives us. In fact, image editors such as Google Picasa represent image contents as the original image as well as a series of image transformations, such as blurring, sharpening, black and white conversion, contrast enhancement, and the like.

In many cases, of course, editing a large-scale image that includes millions of 32-bit pixes before high-quality printing might involve a dozen of such transformations. Applying them one after another, in a sequence is often too time-consuming to be practical. A better alternative consists of composing the transformations together and applying them to the input image only a single time.

We focus on *image blurring*, which is a prototypical "textbook" image transformation [40]. Figure 14 illustrates the two transducers for *horizontal* and *vertical* blurring of an image.

Measuring privacy via entropy: A fascinating feature of our analysis is that we can estimate a *privacy* metric for image blurring using our techniques. Our starting point is the observation that if an image has a *unique* pre-image given blurring, then the blurring does not hide the original image at all. Just consider a black square: no matter how many times we might attempt to blur it, the image will remain unchanged. On the other hand, after blurring a face, there may be multiple original images that yield the same blurred face.

Put another way, a blurred face image defines a set of potential candidate original images. If we assume that all candidate original images are equally likely, then we can define the *entropy* H of the original face after a blurring transformation β as follows: $H = -log(|\beta(\beta^{-1})|)$, in other words, we use the reverse mapping β^{-1} given to us by the inverse transducer, and take the negated logarithm of the size of its preimage. For the entirely black image example, $H = 0$ because there is only one element in the preimage. To increase privacy, our goal is to maximize the entropy. Note that given for images of a given rectangular size, we can always exhaustively check if two images result in the same image after blurring.

Our techniques allow us to write down a SMT formula where the number of solutions is equal to the number of preimages of β on a specific image. This is the first connection to our knowledge between SMT techniques and probabilistic definitions of privacy. Of course computing the exact number of solutions is $\#P$-complete, but we can employ approximation techniques to estimate this quantity. Then we can programmatically compare different methods of blurring by the entropy induced. We leave exploration of the impact of different approximation techniques as future work.

4.4 Location Privacy

GPS sensors located in most mobile devices constantly track our location [2, 32]. While the popularity of applications such as Foursquares, Gowalla, and Facebook check-ins show user demand for sharing this information, this also raises privacy concerns.

As a reaction to privacy concerns, Google's Latitude location sharing service started allowing users to only release the *city* they are in, not their precise location, so that a trace of a user's day might look like

```
Menlo Park, CA; Palo Alto, CA; Los Gatos, CA;
Mountain View, CA; Los Gatos, CA.
```

Clearly, given the sizes of these cities, tracking the user precisely might present some difficulty. To generalize, one approach that has emerged is context sensitive choice of granularity; intuitively, if I am located in a densely-populated location such as midtown Manhattan, block-level location is fine to reveal. If I am in a sparsely-populated area such as the Death Valley, we should only reveal a coarse location approximation. This can be encoded with a transducer that works on a stream of recorded location measurements. To summarize, given GPS coordinates ⟨latitude/longitude⟩:

1. Use a lookup list of world cities and their latitude and longitude values and nearset point calculation to compute the nearest city to the current location;
2. Determine the city population via a lookup table;
3. Map the population to a high or low density area (`H` or `L`).
4. Based on the last five GPS readings, enter a high- or low-density output state. Depending on that, the ⟨latitude,longitude⟩ pair is approximated with different precision.

This can be captured by a transducer with different output actions depending on the current state. For instance, for high-density areas, we can drop GPS location seconds, and for low-density areas we can drop GPS location minutes. Krumm et al consider additional trace obfuscation techniques such as adding noise or quantizing traces, which can also be represented using our SFT framework [8].

5. Related Work

In an applied setting [27] we introduced and applied SFTs to analysis of security sanitizers in the Bek project. This work relied on semi-decision procedures for SFT analysis and did not state or prove any algorithmic results on SFT decision procedures. In comparison, the current paper provides the missing formal foundation for Bek program analysis. It further develops new and more general algorithms, including the more general 1-equality algorithm that factors out the decision problem for single-valuedness. The new support for registers enable new, previously infeasible, application areas. These include HtmlDecode, even Example 7 and most of the case study section. Furthermore, the new support for nondeterminism allows elimination of registers, as illustrated in Example 7, without violating single-valuedness.

General equivalence of finite state transducers is undecidable [23], and already so for very restricted fragments [28]. Equivalence of decidability of single-valued GSMs was shown in [43], and extended to the finite-valued case (there exists k such that, for all v, $|\mathscr{T}_A(v)| \leq k$) in [12, 50]. The decidability of equivalence of the finite-valued case does not follow from the single-valued case. Corresponding decidability result of equivalence of finite-valued SFTs is shown in [6]. Unlike for the single-valued case that has a practical algorithm (Figure 3), the finite-valued case is substantially harder, the 1-equality algorithm does not generalize to this case because the satisfiability checks cannot be made locally: Lemma 2 does not imply violation of partial-equivalence in the finite-valued case.

In recent years there has been considerable interest in automata over infinite languages [44], starting with the work on *finite memory automata* [29], also called *register automata*. Finite words over an infinite alphabet are often called *data words* in the literature. Other automata models over data words are *pebble automata* [37] and *data automata* [7]. Several characterizations of logics with respect to different models of data word automata are studied in [5]. This line of work focuses on fundamental questions about definability, decidability, complexity, and expressiveness on classes of automata on one hand and fragments of logic on the other hand. A different line of work on automata with infinite alphabets introduces *lattice automata* [22] that are finite state automata whose transitions are labeled by elements of an atomic lattice with motivation coming from verification of symbolic communicating machines.

Streaming transducers [1] provide another recent symbolic extension of finite transducers where the label theories are restricted to be total orders, in order to maintain decidability of equivalence, e.g., full linear arithmetic is not allowed.

Finite state automata with arbitrary predicates over labels, called *predicate-augmented finite state recognizers*, or *symbolic finite automata* (SFAs) in the current paper, were first studied in the context of natural language processing [38]. While the work [38] views symbolic automata as a "fairly trivial" extension, the fundamental algorithmic questions are far from trivial. For example, it is shown in [24] that symbolic complementation by a combinatorial optimization problem called *minterm generation* leads to significant speedups compared to state-of-the-art automata algorithm implementations. The work in [38] introduces a different symbolic extension to finite state transducers called *predicate-augmented finite state transducers*. This extension is not expressive enough for describing SFTs. Besides identities, it is not possible to establish functional dependencies from input to output that are needed for example to encode transformations such as `HtmlEncode`.

We use the SMT solver Z3 [15] for solving label constraints that arise during composition and equivalence checking algorithms, as well as for witness search by model generation using auxiliary SFT axioms.

Finite state transducers have been used for dynamic and static analysis to validate sanitization functions in web applications in [3], by an over-approximation of the strings accepted by the sanitizer using static analysis of existing PHP code. Other security analysis of PHP code, e.g., SQL injection attacks, use string analyzers to obtain over-approximations (in form of context free grammars) of the HTML output by a server [35, 49]. Yu et al. show how multiple automata can be composed to model looping code [51].

Our work is complementary to previous efforts in using SMT solvers to solve problems related to list transformations. The tools HAMPI [30] and Kaluza [42] extend the STP solver to handle equations over strings and equations with multiple variables. The work in [25] shows how to solve subset constraints on regular languages. In contrast, we show how to combine any of these solvers with SFTs whose edges can take symbolic values in the theories understood by the solver.

Top-down tree transducers [21] provide another extension of finite state transducers: a finite state transducer is a top-down tree transducer over a *monadic* ranked alphabet. Similar to finite state transducers, decidability of equivalence of top-down tree transducers is known for the single-valued case [18, 20], including a specialized method for the *deterministic* case [10], and also for the finite-valued case [45]. Several non-symbolic extensions of top-down tree transducers have been studied, e.g., [19, 21, 31, 33, 34, 39]. Symbolic top-down tree transducers are studied in [46] where partial equivalence is shown to be decidable for the linear single-valued case.

6. Conclusion

We introduced a symbolic extension of the theory of classical finite transducers, where transitions are represented by terms modulo a given background theory. Our approach enables a range of analyses in combination with state-of-the-art constraint solving techniques. The core algorithms we presented are composition and equivalence checking of single-valued symbolic finite transducers, and we showed how to decide whether arbitrary symbolic transducers have the single-valuedness property. We demonstrated how our work directly applies to analysis of web string sanitizers, malware detection, image manipulation, and location privacy, and we expect more applications to follow. Our techniques can synthesize string pre-images in excess of 8,000 bytes in roughly a minute, our ST representation had 10,000 times fewer states than previous approaches, and we found lazy ST encoding for our `HTMLDecode` example took at most 20 seconds even in the most extreme cases. These algorithms make it possible to work with symbolic representations of transducers, just as traditionally done with finite state transducers, as first class citizens in designing new analyses and program transformation techniques by leveraging the continuous advances and improvements in constraint solvers and satisfiability modulo theories solvers.

References

[1] R. Alur and P. Cerný. Streaming transducers for algorithmic verification of single-pass list-processing programs. In *POPL'11*, pages 599–610. ACM, 2011.

[2] D. E. Bakke, R. Parameswaran, D. M. Blough, A. A. Franz, and T. J. Palmer. Data obfuscation: Anonymity and desensitization of usable data sets. *IEEE Security and Privacy*, Apr. 2004.

[3] D. Balzarotti, M. Cova, V. Felmetsger, N. Jovanovic, E. Kirda, C. Kruegel, and G. Vigna. Saner: Composing static and dynamic analysis to validate sanitization in web applications. In *IEEE Oakland Security and Privacy*, 2008.

[4] Bek. http://research.microsoft.com/bek.

[5] M. Benedikt, C. Ley, and G. Puppis. Automata vs. logics on data words. In *CSL*, volume 6247 of *LNCS*, pages 110–124. Springer, 2010.

[6] N. Bjørner and M. Veanes. Symbolic transducers. Technical Report MSR-TR-2011-3, Microsoft Research, January 2011.

[7] M. Bojańczyk, A. Muscholl, T. Schwentick, L. Segoufin, and C. David. Two-variable logic on words with data. In *LICS*, pages 7–16. IEEE, 06.

[8] A. Brush, J. Krumm, and J. Scott. Exploring end user preferences for location obfuscation, location-based services, and the value of location. In *UbiComp*, September 2010.

[9] K. Z. Chen, G. Gu, J. Nazario, X. Han, and J. Zhuge. WebPatrol: Automated collection and replay of web-based malware scenarios. In *ASIACCS*, March 2011.

[10] B. Courcelle and P. Franchi-Zannettacchi. Attribute grammars and recursive program schemes. *Theoretical Computer Science*, 17:163–191, 1982.

[11] M. Cova, C. Kruegel, and G. Vigna. Detection and analysis of drive-by-download attacks and malicious JavaScript code. In *WWW Conference*, Raleigh, NC, April 2010.

[12] K. Culic and J. Karhumäki. The equivalence of finite-valued transducers (on HDTOL languages) is decidable. *Theoretical Computer Science*, 47:71–84, 1986.

[13] C. Curtsinger, B. Livshits, B. Zorn, and C. Seifert. Zozzle: Low-overhead mostly static javascript malware detection. In *Proceedings of the Usenix Security Symposium*, Aug. 2011.

[14] G. B. Dantzig and B. C. Eaves. Fourier-Motzkin elimination and its dual. *Journal of Combinatorial Theory (A)*, 14:288–297, 1973.

[15] L. de Moura and N. Bjørner. Z3: An Efficient SMT Solver. In *TACAS'08*, LNCS, 2008.

[16] A. J. Demers, C. Keleman, and B. Reusch. On some decidable properties of finite state translations. *Acta Informatica*, 17: 349–364, 1982.

[17] P. Eckersley. How unique is your web browser? In *Privacy Enhancing Technologies*, pages 1–18, 2010.

[18] J. Engelfriet. Some open questions and recent results on tree transducers and tree languages. In R. V. Book, editor, *Formal Language Theory*, pages 241–286. Academic Press, 1980.

[19] J. Engelfriet and S. Maneth. A comparison of pebble tree transducers with macro tree transducers. *Acta Informatica*, 39:2003, 2003.

[20] Z. Esik. Decidability results concerning tree transducers. *Acta Cybernetica*, 5:1–20, 1980.

[21] Z. Fülöp and H. Vogler. *Syntax-Directed Semantics: Formal Models Based on Tree Transducers*. EATCS. Springer, 1998.

[22] T. L. Gall and B. Jeannet. Lattice automata: A representation for languages on infinite alphabets, and some applications to verification. In *SAS 2007*, volume 4634 of *LNCS*, pages 52–68, 2007.

[23] T. Griffiths. The unsolvability of the equivalence problem for Λ-free nondeterministic generalized machines. *J. ACM*, 15: 409–413, 1968.

[24] P. Hooimeijer and M. Veanes. An evaluation of automata algorithms for string analysis. In *VMCAI'11*, LNCS. Springer, 2011.

[25] P. Hooimeijer and W. Weimer. A decision procedure for subset constraints over regular languages. In *Proceedings of the Conference on Programming Language Design and Implementation*, pages 188–198, New York, NY, USA, 2009. ACM. ISBN 978-1-60558-392-1.

[26] P. Hooimeijer and W. Weimer. Solving string constraints lazily. In *ASE*, 2010.

[27] P. Hooimeijer, B. Livshits, D. Molnar, P. Saxena, and M. Veanes. Fast and precise sanitizer analysis with bek. In *Proceedings of the USENIX Security Symposium*, August 2011.

[28] O. Ibarra. The unsolvability of the equivalence problem for Efree NGSM's with unary input (output) alphabet and applications. *SIAM Journal on Computing*, 4:524–532, 1978.

[29] M. Kaminski and N. Francez. Finite-memory automata. In *31st Annual Symposium on Foundations of Computer Science (FOCS 1990)*, volume 2, pages 683–688. IEEE, 1990.

[30] A. Kiezun, V. Ganesh, P. J. Guo, P. Hooimeijer, and M. D. Ernst. HAMPI: a solver for string constraints. In *ISSTA*, 2009.

[31] N. Kobayashi, N. Tabuchi, and H. Unno. Higher-order multiparameter tree transducers and recursion schemes for program verification. In *POPL*, pages 495–508. ACM, 2010.

[32] J. Krumm. A survey of computational location privacy. *Personal Ubiquitous Comput.*, 13:391–399, August 2009.

[33] A. Maletti, J. Graehl, M. Hopkins, and K. Knight. The power of extended top-down tree transducers. *SIAM J. Comput.*, 39:410–430, June 2009.

[34] T. Milo, D. Suciu, and V. Vianu. Typechecking for XML transformers. In *Proc. 19th ACM Symposium on Principles of Database Systems (PODS'2000)*, pages 11–22. ACM, 2000.

[35] Y. Minamide. Static approximation of dynamically generated web pages. In *WWW '05: Proceedings of the 14th International Conference on the World Wide Web*, pages 432–441, 2005. ISBN 1-59593-046-9.

[36] K. Mowery, D. Bogenreif, S. Yilek, and H. Shacham. Fingerprinting information in javascript implementations. In *Proceedings of Web 2.0 Security and Privacy 2011 (W2SP)*, May 2011.

[37] F. Neven, T. Schwentick, and V. Vianu. Finite state machines for strings over infinite alphabets. *ACM Trans. CL*, 5:403–435, 2004.

[38] G. V. Noord and D. Gerdemann. Finite state transducers with predicates and identities. *Grammars*, 4:263–286, 2001.

[39] C.-H. L. Ong and S. J. Ramsay. Verifying higher-order functional programs with pattern-matching algebraic data types. In *POPL'11*, pages 587–598. ACM, 2011.

[40] J. R. Parker. *Algorithms for Image Processing and Computer Vision*. Wiley and Sons, 2006.

[41] P. Ratanaworabhan, B. Livshits, and B. Zorn. Nozzle: A defense against heap-spraying code injection attacks. In *Proceedings of the Usenix Security Symposium*, Aug. 2009.

[42] P. Saxena, D. Akhawe, S. Hanna, S. McCamant, F. Mao, and D. Song. A symbolic execution framework for javascript. In *IEEE Security and Privacy*, 2010.

[43] M. P. Schützenberger. Sur les relations rationnelles. In *GI Conference on Automata Theory and Formal Languages*, volume 33 of *LNCS*, pages 209–213, 1975.

[44] L. Segoufin. Automata and logics for words and trees over an infinite alphabet. In Z. Ésik, editor, *CSL*, volume 4207 of *LNCS*, pages 41–57, 2006.

[45] H. Seidl. Equivalence of finite-valued tree transducers is decidable. *Math. Systems Theory*, 27:285–346, 1994.

[46] M. Veanes and N. Bjørner. Symbolic tree transducers. In *Perspectives of System Informatics (PSI'11)*, 2011.

[47] M. Veanes, N. Bjørner, and L. de Moura. Symbolic automata constraint solving. In C. Fermüller and A. Voronkov, editors, *LPAR-17*, volume 6397 of *LNCS*, pages 640–654, 2010.

[48] M. Veanes, P. de Halleux, and N. Tillmann. Rex: Symbolic Regular Expression Explorer. In *ICST'10*. IEEE, 2010.

[49] G. Wassermann, D. Yu, A. Chander, D. Dhurjati, H. Inamura, and Z. Su. Dynamic test input generation for web applications. In *ISSTA*, 2008.

[50] A. Weber. Decomposing finite-valued transducers and deciding their equivalence. *SIAM Journal on Computing*, 22(1): 175–202, February 1993.

[51] F. Yu, T. Bultan, and O. H. Ibarra. Relational string verification using multi-track automata. In *Proceedings of the 15th international conference on Implementation and application of automata*, CIAA'10, pages 290–299, 2011.

Constraints as Control

Ali Sinan Köksal Viktor Kuncak Philippe Suter *

School of Computer and Communication Sciences (I&C) - Swiss Federal Institute of Technology (EPFL), Switzerland

{firstname.lastname}@epfl.ch

Abstract

We present an extension of Scala that supports constraint programming over bounded and unbounded domains. The resulting language, Kaplan, provides the benefits of constraint programming while preserving the existing features of Scala. Kaplan integrates constraint and imperative programming by using constraints as an advanced control structure; the developers use the monadic 'for' construct to iterate over the solutions of constraints or branch on the existence of a solution. The constructs we introduce have simple semantics that can be understood as explicit enumeration of values, but are implemented more efficiently using symbolic reasoning.

Kaplan programs can manipulate constraints at run-time, with the combined benefits of type-safe syntax trees and first-class functions. The language of constraints is a functional subset of Scala, supporting arbitrary recursive function definitions over algebraic data types, sets, maps, and integers.

Our implementation runs on a platform combining a constraint solver with a standard virtual machine. For constraint solving we use an algorithm that handles recursive function definitions through fair function unrolling and builds upon the state-of-the art SMT solver Z3. We evaluate Kaplan on examples ranging from enumeration of data structures to execution of declarative specifications. We found Kaplan promising because it is expressive, supporting a range of problem domains, while enabling full-speed execution of programs that do not rely on constraint programming.

Categories and Subject Descriptors D.3.3 [*Programming Languages*]: Language Constructs and Features

General Terms Design, Languages

Keywords Constraint Programming, Satisfiability Modulo Theories, Executable Specifications, Scala, Embedded Domain-Specific Languages, Non-determinism

1. Introduction

Modern mainstream programming languages incorporate advances in memory safety, type systems, meta-programming and modularity. However, the sequential control in widely used systems remains largely unchanged compared to some of the earliest imperative and functional language designs. Although this simplicity has advantages in terms of predictable compilation, it prevents languages from approaching the abstraction level used in software design. In design we often encounter a conjunction of multiple orthogonal requirements that we need to meet simultaneously [29]. When conjoining multiple requirements, each of them needs to be a *partial* specification of possible executions, otherwise the conjunction would be contradictory. The desire to use partial constraints leads to non-deterministic specification constructs. Examples include guarded commands [18], wide-spectrum languages [6, 43], intermediate verification languages [15], Temporal Logic of Actions [36], Alloy [30], as well as models in proof assistants Coq [62] and Isabelle [52]. In contrast to specification languages, most mainstream executable languages have difficulty in implementing a conjunction of programs; their sequential commands tightly specify the set of possible behaviors.

The idea of Logic Programming [14, 34] is to allow programs that are non-deterministic and specify relations (predicates) between values. The original inspiration came from a restricted form of resolution as the execution mechanisms, which uses unification of logical variables ranging over finite trees. Functional logic programming extends logic programming with the narrowing technique and with benefits of functional programming [3]. Constraint Logic Programming, CLP [31] and later generations of Prolog [14] extend logic programming with the ability to perform constraint solving not only over trees but also over numerical domains. These paradigms hold great promise to raise the abstraction level of software. They are related to program synthesis research [26, 35, 39, 53, 58], which can be viewed as a compilation mechanism for declarative specifications.

We believe that key obstacles preventing broader use of non-deterministic declarative programming constructs include:

- the difficulty of solving declarative constraints and
- the difficulty of incorporating these constructs into existing languages and platforms.

We next briefly outline the approach that our system uses to meet these challenges.

Efficient interoperability with existing platforms. In this paper we present Kaplan, a system that supports Constraint Programming on top of the Scala language [50]. We address the difficulty of incorporating into existing platforms by choosing not to modify the semantics of the core Scala language, but instead use the flexibility of for-comprehensions in Scala. Because for-comprehensions present a syntax for monads in Scala, this aspect of our approach is related to using non-determinism monads in Haskell [21]. An important difference is that our starting language is not purely functional, but can have side effects.

Our solution is therefore to identify a functional Turing-complete sublanguage for constraints, and use it locally for declarative programming within the full Scala language (which has features of

* Philippe Suter was supported by the Swiss National Science Foundation Grant 200021_120433.

POPL'12, January 25–27, 2012, Philadelphia, PA, USA.

object-oriented, imperative and functional languages). The declarative control that we explore is based on describing iterations as a search process. The iteration ranges are specified as the set of solutions to constraints. Our constraints are declared using first-class functions and familiar combinators, such as &&. From a language point of view the integration is appealing because users hardly need to learn any new notation.

One approach to implementation of non-deterministic languages is to implement a virtual machine that supports backtracking, such as Warren's Abstract Machine for Prolog [1] or the Java Pathfinder model checker and its extensions [24]. Unfortunately, such an approach is costly in terms of both performance and engineering effort. We propose instead to encapsulate any need for backtracking into a for-comprehension that iterates over solution spaces. In addition, we allow constraint programming in code outside of loops. In such cases, logical variables and a constraint store help ensure that a program can find a solution without backtracking over the host imperative program, keeping backtracking within a specialized constraint solver.

Efficient solving of declarative constraints. The first implementations of declarative paradigms predate algorithmic advances of modern SAT solvers [57, 66]. The advances in SAT led to a paradigm shift in solving combinatorial problems, where it became often profitable to outsource constraint solving tasks to dedicated implementations, instead of relying on a programmer to hard-code a search strategy.

Fueled by the developments of SAT solvers, a more expressive technology emerged as the field of Satisfiability Modulo Theories (SMT), with a number of efficient implementations available today [8, 19, 44]. SMT techniques combine SAT solvers with decision procedures and their combination methods [17, 22, 46] that were and remain motivated by program verification tasks [32, 45].

Our aim is to leverage the remarkable progress in dedicated constraint solvers by deploying an SMT solver as a part of the run-time of a programming language. Whereas the developers of Prolog were influenced by the state-of-the-art theorem proving technology of their time (resolution for first-order logic), we aim to explore the potential of SMT. The fact that SMT solvers were developed to model programming language constructs makes them a particularly appropriate choice. However, the original motivation for SMT solvers was program verification, whereas we aim to use them as an execution mechanism for declarative constraints.

Many logical theories are natively supported by modern solvers, including algebraic data types, uninterpreted functions, linear arithmetic, and arrays. Nonetheless, we believe that constraint solving can reach its full potential only if users can define their own classes of constraints. We therefore choose to work with a solver for a rich logic in which users can define their own recursive functions and recursive data types [60]. We thus trade performance and decidability for greater expressive power and flexibility.

Contributions. This paper makes a concrete and implemented proposal for incorporating constraint programming into an underlying stateful language through several individual contributions:

- first-class constraints, which can be generated at run-time and which carry type and free-variable information; the constraints can use unrestricted operations on booleans (including negation), as well as built-in and user-defined recursive operations on integers, sets, maps, and trees;
- a programming model for constraint programming based on creating and iterating over a stream of solutions of a constraint using explicit control constructs; our programming model (unlike most solutions with backtrackable virtual machines) has no penalty for the code that does not use constraint solving;
- logical variables of numeric and symbolic types that postpone constraint solving steps, often substantially reducing the size of the search space;
- the use of fair function unrolling and SMT solving technology to provide expressive power, predictability, and efficiency of solving in many domains of interest;
- implementation of the system (Kaplan is publicly available from `http://lara.epfl.ch`);
- evaluation of the system on examples from several domains, such as executing declaratively specified data structure operations, software testing, and counterexample-driven construction of functions of a given template and a given specification.

Paper outline. The rest of this paper is organized as follows. The next section presents features of Kaplan through an extensive set of examples. Section 3 presents in more detail the Turing-complete language that we use to describe constraints. Section 4 gives the semantics of key Kaplan constructs. Section 5 outlines main implementation aspects of Kaplan. We present further evaluation and illustrate use cases of Kaplan in Section 6. We finally review the remaining related work and conclude.

2. Examples and Features

We present some of the features of Kaplan through examples. The simpler examples can be tried out directly in a Scala shell, provided that it is launched with the Kaplan plugin. Throughout the paper, we assume basic familiarity with Scala, but explain more advanced concepts and constructs as needed.

2.1 First-class Constraints

```
val c1: Constraint2[Int,Int] =
  ((x: Int, y: Int) ⇒ 2*x + 3*y == 10 && x ≥ 0 && y ≥ 0)
```

This first command declares a constraint with two free variables. Note that the representation of the constraint is a lambda term. The only difference between a declaration of a constraint and an anonymous function is the type of the expression. As an alternative to explicitly declaring the value to be of a constraint type, one can also append to the function literal a method call .c, so the following declaration is identical to the previous one:

```
val c1 =
  ((x: Int, y: Int) ⇒ 2*x + 3*y == 10 && x ≥ 0 && y ≥ 0).c
```

The type of `c1` is in this case determined by type inference, and this second way is generally shorter. In Kaplan, constraints are in fact extensions (in the object-oriented sense) of functions, and can thus be evaluated, given some values for their argument variables:

```
scala> c1(2,1)
result: false
scala> c1(5,0)
result: true
```

As is common in lambda calculus, the names given to the bound variables play no role; the constraint ((x: Int) ⇒ x ≥ 0) is equivalent to the constraint ((y: Int) ⇒ y ≥ 0). One should think of constraints being defined over (typed) De Bruijn indices rather than named variables.

Constraints can be queried for a single solution or for a stream of solutions by calling appropriate methods:

```
scala> c1.solve
result: (5,0)
scala> c1.findAll
result: non−empty iterator
```

The solve method computes a single solution to the constraint, while findAll returns an iterator over all solutions. The iterator computes and returns solutions on demand. (As a result of displaying the iterator in the console, a search for the first solution is triggered.) When the set of solutions is finite, one can compute it for instance as follows:

```
scala> c1.findAll.toList
result: List((5,0),(2,2))
```

The most general way to iterate over solutions is using a for-comprehension:

```
for(s ← c1.findAll) {
  println(s)
}
```

Constraints are first-class members of Kaplan, and can be created and manipulated as such. The following function, for instance, generates constraints describing an integer within bounds; if the second argument is true, the bounds are given by $[-m; m]$, else by $[0; m]$.

```
def bounded(m: Int, neg: Boolean = true) = {
  val basis: Constraint1[Int] = ((x: Int) ⇒ x ≤ m)
  basis && (if(neg)
    ((x: Int) ⇒ x ≥ −m)
  else
    ((x: Int) ⇒ x ≥ 0))
}
```

In this example, && is a call to a method defined as part of constraint classes, and which expects as argument a constraint of the same arity and with the same types of parameters as the receiver. This ensures that constraints can only be combined when the number and the types of their De Bruijn indices are compatible. Note that, thanks to type inference, we need not explicitly state that the two anonymous functions represent constraints. We can now use the function bounded to produce constraints:

```
scala> bounded(3, true).findAll.toList
result: List(0, −1, −2, −3, 1, 2, 3)
scala> bounded(3, false).findAll.toList
result: List(0, 1, 2, 3)
```

Another convenient constraint combinator is the product method, which combines two constraints into a new one whose solution set is the Cartesian product of the original two:

```
scala> (bounded(1, true) product bounded(1,false)).findAll.toList
result: List((−1,0),(0,0),(1,1),(−1,1),(1,0),(0,1))
```

Constructing constraints using combinators is a very concise way to solve general problems. For instance, consider the problem of solving a CNF SAT instance defined in a way similar to the standard DIMACS format, where the input

```
val p1 = Seq(Seq(1,−2,−3), Seq(2,3,4), Seq(−1,−4))
```

represents the problem

$$(x_1 \vee \neg x_2 \vee \neg x_3) \wedge (x_2 \vee x_3 \vee x_4) \wedge (\neg x_1 \vee \neg x_4)$$

The following function defines a solver for such problems:

```
def satSolve(problem : Seq[Seq[Int]]) : Option[Map[Int,Boolean]] =
  problem.map(l ⇒ l.map(i ⇒ {
    val id = scala.math.abs(i)
    val isPos = i > 0
    ((m : Map[Int,Boolean]) ⇒ m(id) == isPos).c
  }).reduceLeft(_ || _)).reduceLeft(_ && _).find
}
```

Note that in this case we used the find method on the final constraint rather than solve. They provide the same functionality, but find returns its result in an Option[_] type, where None corresponds to an unsolvable constraint, while solve throws an exception if the constraint has no solution. Another observation is that we use here a constraint over a single variable of Map type to encode a constraint over an unknown number of boolean variables. We found this to be a convenient pattern when the more rigid syntax of anonymous functions with explicit variable naming does not apply. Because all variables are of the same type, the approach works in our type-safe framework. We can now solve SAT problems:

```
scala> satSolve(p1)
result: Some(Map(2 → true, 3 → false, 1 → false, 4 → false)))
scala> satSolve(Seq(Seq(1,2), Seq(−1), Seq(−2)))
result: None
```

2.2 Ordering Solutions

As illustrated by some of the previous examples, the findAll method generates solutions in no particular order. This corresponds to the intuition that it enumerates the unordered set of solutions to a constraint. Similarly, the semantics of calls to solve or find are simply that if a value is produced, then it is an element of that solution set. Two invocations of solve on the same constraint may or may not result in the same solution.

It is sometimes desirable, though, to enumerate solutions in a defined order. To this end, Kaplan constraints support two methods; minimizing and maximizing. These methods take as argument an objective function. Just like constraints, objective functions are represented using an anonymous function, in this case one that returns an integer. The minimizing and maximizing methods ensure that the De Bruijn indices' types match those of the constraint. From the user's point of view, these functions are typed as IntTerms.[1]

Consider the knapsack problem: given a maximum weight and a set of items, each with an associated value and weight, find a subset of the items for which the sum of values is maximal while the sum of weights is less or equal to the maximum. The following code produces and solves an instance of the problem, where the solution is represented as a map from the item indices to booleans indicating which should be picked.

```
def solveKnapsack(vals : List[Int], weights : List[Int], max : Int) = {
  def conditionalSumTerm(vs : List[Int]) = {
    vs.zipWithIndex.map(pair ⇒ {
      val (v,i) = pair
      ((m : Map[Int,Boolean]) ⇒ (if(m(i)) v else 0)).i
    }).reduceLeft(_ + _)
  }
  val valueTerm = conditionalSumTerm(vals)
  val weightTerm = conditionalSumTerm(weights)
  val answer = ((x : Int) ⇒ x ≤ max).compose0(weightTerm)
    .maximizing(valueTerm)
    .solve
}
```

We briefly explain the code. A solution to a knapsack instance is a map indicating a choice of which objects should be picked. The conditionalSumTerm function builds, from a list of integers, an integer term parameterized by a choice map and representing a sum of values. The map defines whether each element in the list participates or not to the sum. We use this function twice, to produce the two terms that, given a choice of items, encode the total value and the weight respectively. Observe that we build the final constraint using a function composition: we start the construction of the constraint as (x : Int) ⇒ x ≤ max and compose it with the weight term to produce the constraint that the weight should not exceed the maximum. Function composition is a general and type-safe way to build constraints from smaller terms, as demonstrated

[1] The relationship from an implementation point of view between constraints and terms is explained in more details in Section 5.

in this example. We can now find optimal choices for instances of the knapsack problem:

```
scala> val vals : List[Int] = List(4, 2, 2, 1, 10)
scala> val weights : List[Int] = List(12, 1, 2, 1, 4)
scala> val max : Int = 15
scala> solveKnapsack(vals, weights, max)
result: Map(0 → false, 1 → true, 2 → true, 3 → true, 4 → true)
```

2.3 User-defined Functions and Datatypes

An important feature of Kaplan is the ability to perform constraint solving in the presence of user-defined functions and data types. Consider the following functions which compute, for a 2×2 matrix $\left[\begin{smallmatrix} a & b \\ c & d \end{smallmatrix}\right]$ represented as a tuple(a, b, c, d), its determinant and whether it is unimodular, respectively:

```
@spec def det(a: Int, b: Int, c: Int, d: Int): Int = a*d − b*c
@spec def unimodular(a: Int, b: Int, c: Int, d: Int): Boolean = {
  val dt = det(a, b, c, d)
  dt == 1 || dt == −1
}
```

The @spec annotation indicates that the user wishes to use the functions as part of constraints, and the Kaplan compiler enforces that such functions are written in the subset of Scala supported within constraints (see Section 3). We can now characterize unimodular matrices with small elements as

```
def boundedUnimodular(m: Int) = {
  val b = bounded(m, false)
  (b product b product b product b) && (unimodular _)
}
```

(The underscore after unimodular indicates to the Scala compiler that it should apply an η-conversion to produce an anonymous function, and ultimately a constraint, from the definition.) We can use these new definitions to generate unimodular matrices:

```
scala> boundedUnimodular(2).findAll.take(4).toList
result: List((0,1,1,0), (0,1,1,2), (0,1,1,1), (1,1,2,1))
```

Perhaps more interestingly, the @spec functions can be mutually recursive. As an example, consider the following declarative definition of prime numbers:

```
@spec def noneDivides(from : Int, j : Int) : Boolean = {
  from == j || (j % from != 0 && noneDivides(from+1, j))
}
@spec def isPrime(i : Int) : Boolean = (i ≥ 2 && noneDivides(2, i))
val primes = ((isPrime(_:Int)) minimizing ((x:Int) ⇒ x)).findAll
```

which we can subsequently enumerate:

```
scala> primes.take(10).toList
result: List(2, 3, 5, 7, 11, 13, 17, 19, 23, 29)
```

Kaplan users can also define their own recursive data types (also known as algebraic data types). The following code declares two such types for red-black trees:

```
@spec sealed abstract class Color
@spec case class Black() extends Color
@spec case class Red() extends Color
@spec sealed abstract class Tree
@spec case class Node(c : Color, l : Tree, v : Int, r : Tree) extends Tree
@spec case class Leaf() extends Tree
```

Algebraic data types are best manipulated using recursive functions and pattern-matching. Kaplan supports such function definitions:

```
@spec def size(tree : Tree) : Int = (tree match {
  case Leaf() ⇒ 0
  case Node(_, l, _, r) ⇒ 1 + size(l) + size(r)
}) ensuring(result ⇒ result ≥ 0)
```

This function also illustrates the use of *post-conditions*, written in Scala as anonymous functions in an **ensuring** clause [49]. In this case, the post-condition states that the result of size can never be negative. Such annotations can help the constraint solver discard parts of the search space. Kaplan uses the Leon verification system [60] to prove, at compile time, that the annotations are valid, so that it can then rely on them at run-time for constraint solving. We can similarly define recursive functions that compute whether a red-black tree contains sorted keys or has the right coloring properties. In the interest of space, we omit the complete definitions.

```
@spec def orderedKeys(t : Tree) : Boolean = ...
@spec def validColoring(t : Tree) : Boolean = ...
@spec def validTree(t : Tree) = orderedKeys(t) && validColoring(t)
@spec def valsWithin(t : Tree, min : Int, max : Int) : Boolean = ...
```

We expect that what these functions compute is clear from their name. With them, we can for instance count the number of red-black trees with a given number of elements:

```
scala> (for(i ← (0 to 7)) yield ((t : Tree) ⇒ validTree(t) &&
    valsWithin(t, 0, i) && size(t) == i ).findAll.size).toList
result: List(1, 1, 2, 2, 4, 8, 16, 33)
```

More advanced applications of data structure enumeration are presented in Section 6, including testcase generation for sorted list and tree manipulations.

2.4 Timeouts

The language of constraints supported in Kaplan is very expressive. For that reason, one cannot expect that any constraint will be solvable. As an example, given the definition (valid in Kaplan)

```
@spec def pow(x : Int, y : Int) : Int =
  if(y == 0) 1 else x * pow(x, y − 1)
```

it would be unreasonable to expect the system to find a solution to the constraint

```
val fermat = ((x : Int, y : Int, z : Int, b : Int) ⇒ b > 2 &&
  pow(x,b) + pow(y,b) == pow(z,b)).c
```

The search algorithm at the core of Kaplan is a semi-decision procedure: if a solution exists, then that solution will be found eventually. If there are no solutions, the procedure can discover this fact and stop [59, 60], or loop forever. The solve, find and findAll methods all take a parameter describing the timeout strategy. That parameter is optional, so by default no timeout is used. Because it is also implicit, a timeout strategy can be defined for an entire scope by a single definition that the Scala compiler then automatically inserts at each call site:

```
implicit val timeoutStrategy = Timeout(1.0)
```

Given the above declarations, the following attempt to confirm Fermat's last theorem results in an exception after 1 second:

```
scala> fermat.find
result: TimeoutReachedException: No solution after 1.0 second(s)
  at .solve(<console>)
  at .<init>(<console>)
  ...
```

2.5 Logical Variables

All the examples so far have illustrated *eager* solution enumeration, where solving constraints immediately produces concrete values. While this by itself is a convenient facility, much of the power of constraint programming in general and of Kaplan in our case comes from the ability to produce logical variables, which represent the *promise* of a solution. Logical variables in turn can be used to control the execution flow of the program in novel ways. We start by describing some of their basic properties. More advanced examples of programming with logical variables follow.

In Kaplan, logical variables are always produced as the result of *lazily* solving a constraint. This is done by calling lazySolve, lazyFind or lazyFindAll instead of solve, find or findAll respectively. Consider the constraint we defined earlier:

```
val c1 =
  ((x: Int, y: Int) ⇒ 2*x + 3*y == 10 && x ≥ 0 && y ≥ 0).c
```

We produce logical variables representing a solution as follows:

```
scala> val (x,y) = c1.lazySolve; println((x,y))
result: (L(?),L(?))
```

Notice that the result is not a pair of integers, as in the case of solve, but a pair of objects of type L[Int] representing the promise of integers. The question mark indicates that the value has not yet been fixed.

Logical variables in Kaplan have *singular* semantics [54], meaning that a given logical variable will always represent the same concrete value, even when it is copied or passed as an argument to a function. The identity of a logical variable is determined by the identity of the instance of the L[_] class. The value of a logical variable is fixed as soon as it is queried, which can be done with the .value method:

```
scala> x.value
result: 5
scala> println((x,y))
result: (L(5),L(?))
```

(Note that even though the y can at this point only hold the value 0, the solver has not necessarily detected that the solution is unique and thus still considers the value not to be fixed.) Fixing a value needs not always be done explicitly. The Kaplan library defines two implicit conversions between concrete and logical values:

```
implicit def concretize[T](l : L[T]) : T = l.value
implicit def lift[T](v : T) : L[T] = new FixedL[T](v)
```

The first one simply fixes the value whenever a function expects a concrete value and receives a logical variable. The second one converts a concrete value into a specialized representation of a logical variable. It is used to provide a common representation for concrete and logical values: because Kaplan is built as a thin layer over Scala and most code must execute as usual, we cannot afford to treat every value as logical. Instead, users decide which function can handle logical values by using L[_] types in their signature. Because concrete values can be lifted to logical status, such functions work indifferently with standard and logical variables. Logical variables created through this lifting mechanism are treated specially and do not add any complexity to the solving process.

2.6 Imperative Constraint Programming

Scala being a multi-paradigm language, users can alternate between different programming styles depending on their preferences and on the task at hand. The same is true for Kaplan; while eager solution enumeration is best used within functional style for-comprehensions, logical variables can be used rather naturally in an imperative style, thanks to novel control constructs. The Kaplan library defines the **assuming-otherwise** branching construct. It is similar in nature to if-then-else, except for an important difference: rather than strictly evaluating the branching condition, assuming-otherwise blocks check whether the condition is *feasible* and, if so, constrain the logical variables in the environment so that their values satisfy the branching constraint. If the condition contains no logical variable (or only logical variables that have already been fixed), then assuming-otherwise behaves exactly like if-then-else.

As an example, consider the classical puzzle that consists in finding distinct values for the letters representing digits in the following addition such that the sum is valid:

```
          s  e  n  d
  +       m  o  r  e
  =    m  o  n  e  y
```

We now present a solution in Kaplan written in an imperative style.

```
val anyInt = ((x : Int) ⇒ true).c
val letters @ Seq(s,e,n,d,m,o,r,y) = Seq.fill(8)(anyInt.lazySolve)
```

This second line uses pattern-matching syntax to achieve two things at once: 1) the eight letter variables are bound to eight independent (lazy) representations of a solution to the trivial anyInt constraint and 2) the variable letters is bound to the sequence of all letter variables. At this point, we have 8 unconstrained integer logical variables. We can imperatively add constraints:

```
for(l ← letters) asserting(l ≥ 0 && l ≤ 9)
```

If this loop terminates without any error, then at the end of it, the 8 variables each represent a number between 0 and 9. (Calling **asserting**(cond) is equivalent to **assuming**(cond) {} **otherwise** { **error** }, just like **assert**(cond) is (conceptually at least) equivalent to **if**(cond) {} **else** { **error** }. More details are given in Section 5.1.) We further constrain the letters representing most-significant digits:

```
asserting(s > 0 && m > 0)
```

We can now perform symbolic arithmetic using the existing and new logical variables. We define a new variable for the sum of each line and constrain it to the expected value:

```
val fstLine = anyInt.lazySolve
asserting(fstLine == 1000*s + 100*e + 10*n + d)
val sndLine = anyInt.lazySolve
asserting(sndLine == 1000*m + 100*o + 10*r + e)
val total = anyInt.lazySolve
asserting(total == 10000*m + 1000*o + 100*n + 10*e + y)
```

At this point, the value of the letters is still not fixed, however Kaplan ensures that all variables admit solutions satisfying the asserted constraints. Finally, we check for a solution to the puzzle using one last assuming-otherwise block:

```
scala> assuming(
  distinct(s,e,n,d,m,o,r,y) && fstLine + sndLine == total) {
    println("Solution: " + letters.map(_.value))
  } otherwise {
    println("The puzzle has no solution.")
  }
result: Solution: List(9, 5, 6, 7, 1, 0, 8, 2)
```

We mentioned that assuming-otherwise is conceptually close to if-then-else, and in fact equivalent in the absence of logical variables. One important difference is that the construct is asymmetrical; while

```
if(cond) thenExpr else elseExpr
```

is equivalent to

```
if(!cond) elseExpr else thenExpr
```

the same transformation cannot be applied to assuming-otherwise blocks; indeed, the semantics are that the control will attempt to satisfy the branching condition, so whether the positive or negative condition is tested has an impact on the rest of the execution. Section 5.1 discusses the implementation of assuming-otherwise blocks in terms of lazyFind.

$$\textsf{Int} \in \mathcal{T} \qquad \textsf{Boolean} \in \mathcal{T} \qquad \frac{T \in \mathcal{T}}{\textsf{Set}[T] \in \mathcal{T}}$$

$$\frac{T_1 \in \mathcal{T} \quad T_2 \in \mathcal{T}}{\textsf{Map}[T_1, T_2] \in \mathcal{T}} \qquad \frac{T_1 \in \mathcal{T} \quad T_2 \in \mathcal{T}}{T_1 \Rightarrow T_2 \in \mathcal{T}}$$

$$\frac{\textbf{sealed abstract class } C}{C \in \mathcal{T}}$$

$$\frac{\textbf{case class } C(\overline{n} : \overline{D}) \textbf{ extends } E \quad \overline{D} \in \mathcal{T} \quad E \in \mathcal{T}}{C \in \mathcal{T}}$$

Figure 1. Inductive definition of PureScala types, where Set and Map are the types defined in the package `scala.collection.immutable`.

3. Constraint Sublanguage

In this section, we describe the subset of Scala in which we can specify constraints in Kaplan, and which we call PureScala. PureScala is an extension of the language supported by the publicly available Leon verification system [60]. Since it is a subset of Scala, the language is executable and deterministic.

3.1 Language

Data types. Figure 1 presents an inductive definition of the data types supported in PureScala. An important feature is the ability to define (recursive) algebraic data types. In Scala, these types are defined using a hierarchy of special case classes. Algebraic data types are typically manipulated with pattern-matching, as shown in some of the examples in Section 2. A current limitation is that these user-defined types cannot take type parameters. The Map type represents finite, immutable maps, which can thus be viewed as partial functions. Because it supports unbounded data types and arbitrary recursive functions, the constraint language is itself Turing-complete. This can be viewed both as an advantage and an inconvenience: on one hand, this expressive power guarantees that just about any constraint is expressible, but on the other hand, standard incompleteness theorems predict that some constraints cannot be shown to have no solutions. In practice, we have found that constraints that come up in programming tasks such as the ones presented in this paper and in the context of functional software verification [60] (as opposed to theoretically hard ones) are handled well.

Expressions and function definitions. PureScala expressions can contain all standard arithmetic operators, map applications and updates, set operators and membership tests, function applications (of user-defined or anonymous functions), and constructor and selectors from user-defined data types. Expression can also contain **val**s to factor out common subexpressions. Indeed, a Scala block

```
{ val x1 = e2
  ...
  val xn = en
  e }
```

is to be understood as **let** x1 = e2 **in** ... **in let** xn = en **in** e. Expressions can contain pattern-matching on user-defined data types. Any sub-pattern can be bound to a variable and used accordingly on the right-hand side of patterns. Furthermore, patterns can contain arbitrary guards. At compile-time, Kaplan relies on Leon to prove that pattern-matching expressions are *exhaustive*, and thus rules out any possibility of a run-time match error in @spec functions. This exhaustiveness check goes beyond the capabilities of the standard Scala compiler, in that it takes into account the path conditions leading to the match expression.

A PureScala function body is defined by a single expression whose free variables are the arguments of the function. Functions can optionally be annotated with a post-condition, which can in some cases help the run-time constraint solver. These post-conditions are proved at compile-time, just like the pattern-matching expressions. Kaplan can thus be used purely as a verification system, and therefore strictly subsumes Leon.

3.2 Solver

Kaplan invokes Leon's core solving procedure both at compile-time, to validate post-conditions and prove that pattern-matching expressions are exhaustive, and at run-time, to find solutions to constraints. The procedure is based on a refinement loop that expands function definitions in a fair way, to guarantee that no valid solution is ever ignored. One can think of this search procedure as a form of bounded model-checking for functional programs. We have found that in practice it is fast in finding counter-examples. The details of the procedure are presented in [60].

Conceptually, Leon is the only solver used in the implementation of Kaplan. Because it is built as a layer on top of Z3, though, we will sometimes refer to Z3 directly when we discuss implementation details in Section 5. In particular, in the absence of user-defined recursive functions, Leon behaves exactly as Z3.

4. Semantics

In this section, we present an overview of the semantic aspects of Kaplan through operational semantic rules, shown in Figure 2. All features of Kaplan can be implemented in terms of the two constructs find and lazyFind, as well as conversions between concrete values and logical variables (denoted by l). Section 5 describes how to use the host language (Scala) to reduce other constructs (including solve, findAll, lazyFindAll) to this core.

A state consists of a triple $\textsf{expr}|\langle\mu,\kappa\rangle$, where expr is the expression under evaluation, μ encodes the part of the state that is proper to Scala, and κ is a *constraint store.* A constraint store is conceptually a formula whose free variables correspond to all logical variables used since the beginning of the computation.

The HOST rule captures the intuition that in the absence of invocations to the constraint solver, Kaplan behaves exactly like Scala: we assume the existence of a transition relation $\rightarrow_H$ describing the execution of normal Scala code, and which is lifted to Kaplan through the HOST rule. As one would expect, applying such transitions leaves the constraint store unchanged.

The rules S-SAT and S-UNSAT describe the possible results of an invocation of find, the simplest form of constraint solving. We use $(\lambda\overline{x}.\phi(\overline{x}))$ to denote a constraint that ranges over the variables $\overline{x}$ and that does not refer to logical variables. By $\mathcal{M}$ we denote a map from variables to constants. The condition $\mathcal{M} \models \phi$ denotes that $\mathcal{M}$ is a valid model of ϕ, i.e., a mapping of variables $\overline{x}$ of ϕ to constants such that $\phi[\overline{x} \mapsto \mathcal{M}(\overline{x})]$ holds. Examining the rules for find, S-SAT and S-UNSAT, we note that find has no impact and no dependency on the constraint store, which is consistent with its eager semantics.

The rules L-SAT and L-UNSAT for lazyFind are analogous, but with crucial differences: 1) logical variables can be present in the constraints to solve, which we therefore denote $(\lambda\overline{x}.\phi(\overline{x},\overline{l}))$, and 2) the L-SAT rule does not produce concrete values, but rather fresh logical variables.

The LIFT rule applies whenever a constant value needs to be used in place of a logical variable. Conceptually, it adds to the constraint store a new logical variable whose value is immediately constrained to be the constant. Finally, the VALUE rule specifies how concrete values can be extracted from a satisfying assignment

$$\text{HOST}\ \frac{t_1 \mid \mu_1 \rightarrow_H t_2 \mid \mu_2}{t_1 \mid \langle \mu_1, \kappa \rangle \ \rightarrow\ t_2 \mid \langle \mu_2, \kappa \rangle}$$

$$\text{S-SAT}\ \frac{\mathcal{M} \models \phi}{(\lambda\overline{x}.\phi(\overline{x})).\mathsf{find} \mid \langle \mu, \kappa \rangle \ \rightarrow\ \mathsf{Some}(\mathcal{M}(\overline{x})) \mid \langle \mu, \kappa \rangle} \qquad \text{S-UNSAT}\ \frac{\neg\exists\mathcal{M}\ .\ \mathcal{M} \models \phi}{(\lambda\overline{x}.\phi(\overline{x})).\mathsf{find} \mid \langle \mu, \kappa \rangle \ \rightarrow\ \mathsf{None} \mid \langle \mu, \kappa \rangle}$$

$$\text{L-SAT}\ \frac{\mathcal{M} \models \kappa \wedge \phi[\overline{x} \mapsto \overline{l}_f] \qquad \overline{l}_f \text{ fresh in } \kappa}{(\lambda\overline{x}.\phi(\overline{x}, \overline{l})).\mathsf{lazyFind} \mid \langle \mu, \kappa \rangle \ \rightarrow\ \mathsf{Some}(\overline{l}_f) \mid \langle \mu, \kappa \wedge \phi[\overline{x} \mapsto \overline{l}_f] \rangle}$$

$$\text{L-UNSAT}\ \frac{\neg\exists\mathcal{M}\ .\ \mathcal{M} \models \kappa \wedge \phi[\overline{x} \mapsto \overline{l}_f] \qquad \overline{l}_f \text{ fresh in } \kappa}{(\lambda\overline{x}.\phi(\overline{x}, \overline{l})).\mathsf{lazyFind} \mid \langle \mu, \kappa \rangle \ \rightarrow\ \mathsf{None} \mid \langle \mu, \kappa \rangle}$$

$$\text{VALUE}\ \frac{\mathcal{M} \models \kappa}{l.\mathsf{value} \mid \langle \mu, \kappa \rangle \ \rightarrow\ \mathcal{M}(l) \mid \langle \mu, \kappa \wedge (l = \mathcal{M}(l)) \rangle} \qquad \text{LIFT}\ \frac{c \text{ is a constant} \qquad l_f \text{ fresh in } \kappa}{c.\mathsf{lift} \mid \langle \mu, \kappa \rangle \ \rightarrow\ l_f \mid \langle \mu, \kappa \wedge (l_f = c) \rangle}$$

Figure 2. Small-step semantics of Kaplan-specific constructs.

(model) for the constraint store. Observe that when the rule applies, the value of the logical variable is then fixed for the rest of the program execution by the added equality to κ. This ensures singular semantics [54]: in any execution trace, all applications of the VALUE rule for a given logical variable l will produce the same value; a different value would contradict the premise that $\mathcal{M}$ is a valid model for the store.

We now show that execution never gets stuck in one of the Kaplan-specific rules. Because we are examining the behavior of our constructs taking a constraint solver as a parameter, we deliberately ignore termination properties of the constraint solver and assume that the outcome of the constraint solver call, denoted $\models$, becomes immediately available to test the applicability of a rule.

Theorem. *Suppose the constraint store is satisfiable in the initial state and that the $\rightarrow_H$ relation is total. Then the transition relation given by Figure 2 is also total.*

Proof. The case of HOST is clear from the hypothesis that $\rightarrow_H$ is total. For evaluations of find, we observe that the rules S-SAT and S-UNSAT have complementary premises, and therefore one of them necessarily applies. Similarly for lazyFind, L-SAT and L-UNSAT are complementary, regardless of the value of κ. LIFT has no precondition, so it remains to show that VALUE cannot get stuck, i.e. that it cannot be the case that there is no model $\mathcal{M}$ for the constraint store κ.

Using the assumption that in the initial state the constraint store is satisfiable, it is sufficient to show that no transition will make it unsatisfiable. Observe that only three rules affect the constraint store; VALUE, LIFT, and L-SAT. The addition of the equality $(l_f = c)$ in LIFT clearly does not affect satisfiability, because l_f is fresh. Similarly, the addition of $(l = \mathcal{M}(l))$ in VALUE preserves the model $\mathcal{M}$ by definition. Finally, L-SAT is guarded by a satisfiability check on precisely the next state of the store, so the model obtained in the premise is a valid model for the next state. ■

The proof suggests an implementation strategy: preserve at all times, alongside the constraint store, a satisfying assignment. When L-SAT is applied, cache the model $\mathcal{M}$ obtained from the satisfiability check. When LIFT applies, augment the cached model with the appropriate value for l_f. Finally, to apply VALUE, use $\mathcal{M}$ from the cache.

It is not hard to see that this strategy is a valid refinement of the presented rules, and it is, in fact, the strategy we have implemented in Kaplan, as explained in the next section.

5. Implementation

We implemented our extension to Scala as a combination of a runtime library and a compiler plugin, both implemented in Scala. In this section, we present the implementation aspect of these parts, along with the interaction with the underlying SMT solver Z3.

5.1 Run-Time Library

First-class constraints. In Kaplan, first-class constraints are implemented as a hierarchy of Term classes, as shown in Figure 3. The base Term class represents a lambda expression and is parameterized by its argument types and return type. A constraint is simply a Term instance where the return type is instantiated as boolean. We define subclasses of Term for each arity, generating them automatically, as it is the case for the tuple and function definitions in the Scala library. The base class defines methods common to terms of all arities, such as the solve, find and findAll methods for querying constraints. We ensure that these methods are only applicable when the return type is boolean by constraining it using an implicit parameter asBool. We use the same technique to guarantee that term instances are combined in a fully type safe way. We use the c method to trigger an implicit conversion from lambda expressions to Term instances.

Each term subclass extends the corresponding function class in Scala, and uses the original Scala code for the lambda expression to define function application. These classes define optimization methods (minimizing and maximizing) to obtain optimization constraints. The implementation of the optimization procedures is discussed later in this section.

The creation of terms from Scala lambda expressions relies on compile-time transformations. The transformations are implemented in a plugin for the official Scala compiler. We describe how the compile-time transformations work in Section 5.2.

Logical variables. In Kaplan, logical variables are instances of the L class, which is parameterized by the type of the symbolic value that it encapsulates. We define LIterator classes that extend the Iterator trait of Scala and that enumerate tuples of L values. We discuss the implementation of logical variables in Section 5.3.

The assuming-otherwise construct. We can define the assuming-otherwise construct naturally at the library level in Kaplan: it boils down to checking the satisfiability of a constraint of arity 0, and can therefore be implemented in terms of lazyFind. Figure 4 shows the code for this construct in Kaplan. The assuming block creates an Assuming instance. We rely on the implicit conversion mechanism

```
abstract class Term[T,R] { self ⇒
  def find(implicit isBool: R =:= Boolean): Option[T] = ...
  def solve(implicit isBool: R =:= Boolean): T =
    this.find.getOrElse(throw new UnsatException)
  def findAll(implicit isBool: R =:= Boolean) : Iterator[T] = ...
  def c(implicit isBool: R =:= Boolean): self.type = this
  ...
}

class Term0[R] extends Term[Unit,R] with Function0[R] {
  ...
}
class Term1[T1,R] extends Term[T1,R] with Function1[T1,R] {
  ...
}
class Term2[T1,T2,R] extends Term[(T1,T2),R]
    with Function2[T1,T2,R] {
  def ||(other: Term2[T1,T2,Boolean])
    (implicit isBool: R =:= Boolean): Term2[T1,T2,Boolean] = ...
  def &&(other: Term2[T1,T2,Boolean])
    (implicit isBool: R =:= Boolean): Term2[T1,T2,Boolean] = ...
  def unary_!(implicit isBool: R =:= Boolean):
    Term2[T1,T2,Boolean] = ...

  def compose0[A1](other: Term1[A1,T1]): Term2[A1,T2,R] = ...
  def compose1[A1](other: Term1[A1,T2]): Term2[T1,A1,R] = ...
  def compose0[A1,A2](other: Term2[A1,A2,T1]):
    Term3[A1,A2,T2,R] = ...
  def compose1[A1,A2](other: Term2[A1,A2,T2]):
    Term3[T1,A1,A2,R] = ...
  ...
  def product1[A1](other: Term1[A1,Boolean])
    (implicit isBool: R =:= Boolean):
      Term3[T1,T2,A1,Boolean] = ...
  def product2[A1,A2](other: Term2[A1,A2,Boolean])
    (implicit isBool: R =:= Boolean):
      Term4[T1,T2,A1,A2,Boolean] = ...

  def minimizing(objective: Term2[T1,T2,Int])
    (implicit asBool : R =:= Boolean):
      MinConstraint2[T1,T2] = ...
  ...
}
...
type Constraint[T] = Term[T,Boolean]
type Constraint0 = Term0[Boolean]
type Constraint1[T1] = Term1[T1,Boolean]
...
```

Figure 3. Term class hierarchy.

of Scala for implementing the construct: if the optional otherwise block is not defined, the type checking phase will insert a call to assuming2value, which will trigger a conversion from the Assuming instance to the value it encapsulates.

There exists a difference in the treatment of the optional second part of the built-in if-then-else construct and our library extension for assuming-otherwise: without an optional else block, an if(...) { ... } block is always type-checked as Unit. This is built in in the Scala compiler. We cannot achieve the same effect with assuming-otherwise without making deep changes to the compiler, so in our case, an assuming(...) { ... } block will throw an exception at run-time if the following three conditions occur: 1) the assuming test fails, 2) no otherwise block is defined, and 3) an expression of a type different from Unit is required.

5.2 Scala Compiler Plugin

The compile-time transformations of Kaplan programs include the following:

```
def assuming[A](cond: Constraint0)(block: ⇒ A): Assuming[A] = {
  val v: Option[A] = cond.lazyFind match {
    case Some(_) ⇒ Some(block)
    case None ⇒ None
  }
  new Assuming(v)
}

final class Assuming[A](val thenResult: Option[A]) {
  def otherwise(elseBlock: ⇒ A): A = thenResult match {
    case None ⇒ elseBlock
    case Some(tr) ⇒ tr
  }
}

implicit def assuming2value[A](a: Assuming[A]): A = {
  a.thenResult match {
    case Some(tr) ⇒ tr
    case None ⇒
      throw new Exception("otherwise block not defined")
  }
}
```

Figure 4. Implementation of assuming-otherwise in terms of lazyFind.

1. extracting user-defined specification functions and algebraic data types;
2. generating methods to allow conversion between values of these data types and their representation in our solver Leon;
3. transforming implicit calls to conversion methods in order to instantiate Term instances.

These transformations are implemented as a compiler plugin that constitutes a compiler phase that follows the type checking phase. Functions and classes that carry the @spec annotation are expected to be in the PureScala constraint sublanguage, presented in Section 3. Alternatively, developers can group these specification functions and data types in annotated Scala objects, instead of annotating each of them. These specifications are extracted during compilation to obtain a representation that we use in solving. In addition, method definitions are generated and inserted into the code in order to convert between these types and their representation.

We rely on the Scala compiler to signal to us the locations where a function literal needs to be lifted to a constraint literal. The type checking phase, which runs before ours, does so by surrounding such function literals by a call to an implicit function2term conversion function. These functions are defined in the Kaplan library but have no implementation: they simply serve as a guide to indicate to the type checker that the conversion is legal. (The effect of compiling code written for Kaplan without the Kaplan plugin is thus that all constraint manipulation operations result in a run-time NotImplemented exception.)

5.3 Implementation of the Core Solving Algorithms

Our implementation leverages the SMT solver Z3 through its extension, Leon [60]. In the following we refer simply to Z3, as the algorithms we cover in this section would remain the same if we used Z3 alone; what we gain by using Leon is the additional expressive power of recursive functions within constraints. We now describe the interactions with the solver that allow us to put into practice features such as enumeration, minimization, and logical variables.

Solution enumeration. find and lazyFind are used to implement findAll and lazyFindAll, respectively, through the use of an iterator.

```
def solveMinimizing(φ, t_m) {
  solve(φ) match {
    case ("SAT", m) ⇒
      model = m
      v = modelValue(m, t_m)
      pivot = v − 1
      lo = null
      hi = v + 1
      while (lo == null ∨ hi − lo > 2) {
        solve(φ ∧ t_m ≤ pivot) match {
          case ("SAT", m) ⇒
            model = m
            if (lo == null) {
              pivot = pivot ≥ 0 ? −1 : pivot × 2
              hi = pivot + 1
            } else {
              l_v = modelValue(m, t_m)
              pivot = l_v + (pivot + 1 − lv)/2
              hi = pivot + 1
            }
          case ("UNSAT", _) ⇒
            pivot = pivot + (hi − pivot)/2
            lo = pivot
        }
      }
      return ("SAT", model)
    case ("UNSAT", _) ⇒ return ("UNSAT", null)
  }
}
```

Figure 5. Pseudo-code of the solving algorithm with minimization. We invoke our base satisfiability procedure via calls to solve.

The iterator maintains a constraint at all times, starting with the original one. Each time a new solution is required, the iterator destructively updates the constraint by adding to it the negation of the previous solution, thus ensuring that all following solutions will be different. To make this process efficient, Kaplan relies on the incremental reasoning capabilities of Z3 (and thus Leon) to avoid solving the entire constraint each time. The implementation of lazyFindAll is conceptually identical, with the difference that it returns logical variables instead of concrete values. These logical variables are constrained in the store to be all-different. For an enumeration using lazyFindAll to terminate, Leon must therefore prove that the constraint has finitely many solutions.

Optimization constraints. Our procedure for optimizing a constraint with respect to an objective function can be seen as a generalization of binary search over the range of values that the objective can take. Let us consider the case of minimization (the maximization procedure is analogous). The pseudo-code for the algorithm can be seen in Figure 5.[2] It starts by attempting to find a satisfying assignment for the constraint. It then repeatedly looks for a model in which the objective is smaller than the last satisfying value, by exponentially increasing the difference until a lower bound is found. It further reduces the interval until the optimal value for the objective is found. The procedure maintains the invariants that: 1) lo is always less than any satisfying assignment to t_m; and 2) there always exists a satisfying assignment to t_m which is less than hi.

Ordered enumeration. Having defined the solving procedure that minimizes a given term, we can now compose it with solution enumeration to obtain ordered enumeration. We present in Figure 6,

```
def orderedEnum(φ, t_m) {
  solveMinimizing(φ) match {
    case ("SAT", m) ⇒
      v_m = modelValue(m, t_m)
      findAll(φ ∧ t_m = v_m) ++ orderedEnum(φ ∧ t_m > v_m, t_m)
    case ("UNSAT", _) ⇒ return Iterator.empty
  }
}
```

Figure 6. Pseudo-code of the ordered enumeration algorithm.

a recursive algorithm that will enumerate solutions to ϕ, ordered by the value of t_m, which should be minimized.

In this pseudo-code, we use findAll to get an iterator of all values satisfying the given predicate, and ++ to concatenate iterators.

Handling logical variables. We use a global context to keep track of the constraints associated with logical variables. Given a logical variable l and the constraint c_l associated with it, we create a guard (a boolean literal) g_l, denoting the *liveness* of the logical variable, i.e. whether its value has not been fixed yet. Throughout the execution, we maintain in the global context the set of guards that are still alive. Upon creation of the variable l, we add g_l to the set of alive variables and we assert c_l, guarded by the disjunction of all the guards in the set G, defined as the set containing g_l and the guards associated with all the logical variables that appear in c_l:

$$\bigvee_{g \in G} g \Rightarrow c_l$$

The reason for considering the guards associated with the other logical variables is to ensure the single value semantics of these. Consider the following simple example that illustrates the situation:

```
for (x ← ((x: Int) ⇒ x ≥ 0 && x < 4).lazyFindAll) {
  val y = ((y : Int) ⇒ y == x).lazyFind
  assuming (x ≥ 2) {
    ... // first block
  }
  assuming (y < 2) {
    ... // second block
  }
}
```

In each iteration of the outer for-comprehension, if the first block is entered, we do not want to enter the second one, as this would violate the single value semantics for the variable x. Since the constraint y == x will be enforced as long as either x or y has not been fixed, the conflicting situation is correctly avoided.

In the terminology of Section 4, g_l denotes whether the VALUE rule has been used for l (true means it has not), c_l is the constraint on which L-SAT was applied to introduce l into κ (as part of $\bar{l}_f$) and the logical variables represented by the set of guards G are those that contributed to the constraint (the $\bar{l}$ variables in L-SAT). Note that using individual guards for logical variables is not required by the semantics, but rather is an optimization that allows us to reduce the size of the constraint store when some values become known. When the value v_l of the variable l is set, we remove g_l from the set of alive guards, and we assert the following:

$$\neg g_l \wedge l = v_l$$

When all of the literals guarding a constraint c_l are removed from the alive set, the formula $\bigvee_{g \in G} g \Rightarrow c_l$ that was asserted becomes trivially true, and the constraint can be discarded by Z3. Another source of optimization is that we override the finalize method of the L instances such that, even if their value is never fixed, their guard is removed from the set of alive variables when they are being considered for garbage collection by the JVM. This

[2] We use pseudo-code for clarity, but it is not hard to see that it can be implemented using only standard Scala along with find or lazyFind.

example	time (s)
first examples	0.16
unimodular matrices	0.76
sat solving	0.05
knapsack	0.18
prime numbers	0.80
all red-black trees up to 7 nodes	27.45
send+more=money	1.17

Figure 7. Evaluation results for the examples presented in Section 2.

is again not strictly speaking required by the semantics, but helps reducing the overhead of tracking all logical variables.

Invocations of the solver. We summarize this section by presenting a list of all the places where an invocation of the solver occurs:

- calls to find, as they search for a solution eagerly,
- calls to lazyFind, as they check whether a satisfying assignment exists for logical variables,
- calls to the hasNext method of the iterators returned by calls to findAll and lazyFindAll, which are then translated into calls to find and lazyFind respectively, and
- evaluation of the constraint of assuming blocks, as they indirectly invoke the solver by invoking lazyFind on the constraint.

Note that, as the proof in Section 4 suggested, calls to the value method of logical variables do not trigger a solver invocation.

6. Advanced Usage Scenarios and Evaluation

In this section, we present an experimental evaluation of our constraint programming system by considering a number of examples.

As a first overview of the performance of our implementation, we present the running times for the examples that were introduced in Section 2. The results of our evaluation can be seen in Figure 7. We observe that most problems are solved almost instantly, with the exception of the red-black tree enumeration. We discuss the difficulty of enumerating data structures satisfying an invariant in the subsequent examples.

6.1 Enumerating Data Structures for Testing

One use of the findAll construct consists in enumerating data structures that satisfy given invariants. This is a problem that has been studied previously, and was motivated by [11]. Subsequent work [24] presents a Java-based language with non-deterministic choice operators that can be used for enumerating linked data structures.

We describe our experience in using Kaplan to enumerate functional data structures to find input values that violate function contracts. We consider a functional specification of red-black trees. We enumerate solutions to function preconditions and check whether the postconditions hold. As in [11, 24], we enumerate the data structures while bounding the range of values than can be stored in nodes. A red-black tree is a binary search tree characterized by the following additional properties: 1) each node is either red or black; 2) all leaves are black; 3) both children of every red node are black; and 4) every simple path from the root to any leaf contains the same number of black nodes.

The first method we consider is balance, which defines one of the cases erroneously to duplicate one of the subtrees and forgetting another while rebalancing the tree. This results in violating the post-condition of the add method as the result tree does not have the expected content. In this case, an example violating the post-condition is found after enumerating twelve trees. Our test harness

list size	20	40	60	80	100
time (s)	0.24	0.45	0.56	0.72	0.98

Figure 8. Evaluation results for declarative last method.

consists of enumerating trees that satisfy the precondition of add and calling the method in the body of the loop.

We then consider the case where the add method has a missing precondition, namely that the tree must be black-balanced. In this case, the precondition to a method that is called within add fails, and we find a bug-producing value using a similar harness after enumerating four trees, in 0.187 seconds. We argue that a random test-case generation approach would be insufficient in enumerating such data structures that satisfy complex invariants. While the results using constraint solving is not as fast as the specialized solving in UDITA [24], we should keep in mind that this is an experiment in using a general-purpose constraint solving engine. The generality of Kaplan is in contrast to previously proposed solutions for data structure enumeration, which rely on specialized techniques for linked heap data structures, or even techniques specialized to a particular data structure [7]. In the light of the generality of our technique and the overall difficulty of the problem, we consider these to be good results.

6.2 Executable Specifications

As another application of implicit computation, we now explore examples that consist of the "execution" of declarative specifications instead of explicit computation. Execution of specifications is the approach taken in Plan B [55], in which specifications are used as a fallback mechanism upon contract violations.

Consider, for instance, a function that computes the last element of a given list. We can define this function declaratively, by stating that the input list is equal to some list concatenated with the list that has only the element that we are looking for:

```
def last(list : List) : Int = {
  val (elem, _) = ((e: Int, zs: List) ⇒
                   concat(zs, Cons(e, Nil())) == list).solve
  elem }
```

As a more elaborate example, consider adding an element to (or removing an element from) a red-black tree. The explicit insertion and removal have to consider multiple cases in order to keep the invariants that red-black trees should satisfy, and are known to be tricky to implement. On the other hand, these methods can be stated succinctly in a declarative manner, using functions that check if a given tree is indeed a red-black tree, along with functions computing the content of the tree as a set:

```
def addDeclarative(x: Int, tree: Tree) : Tree =
  ((t: Tree) ⇒ isRedBlackTree(t) &&
    content(t) == content(tree) ++ Set(x)).solve
def removeDeclarative(x: Int, tree: Tree) : Tree =
  ((t: Tree) ⇒ isRedBlackTree(t) &&
    content(t) == content(tree) -- Set(x)).solve
```

The performance of the above methods is presented in Figure 9. We also show the results for the similar case of inserting into and removing from a sorted list. Note that we encounter essentially the same running times for the problem of declaratively sorting a list, by asking for a sorted list of the same content as a given list.

The above examples show that it is possible to replace the explicit computation for a method by its purely declarative specification, even for sophisticated contracts such as the ones on red-black trees. The declarative variants are notably slower than the imperative implementations, but it is likely preferable to rely on these executable specifications instead of simply crashing when the imperative version violates the contract.

size	list add	list remove	RBT add	RBT remove
0	0.07	0.02	0.03	0.02
1	0.08	0.02	0.10	0.05
2	0.12	0.05	0.14	0.09
3	0.16	0.10	0.55	0.41
4	0.24	0.18	0.66	0.76
5	0.39	0.38	1.07	0.91
6	0.55	0.45	1.51	1.56
7	0.97	0.67	9.32	13.09
8	1.48	1.09	11.13	18.80
9	2.27	1.80	24.49	25.79
10	3.32	2.22	11.51	20.55

Figure 9. Evaluation results for declarative add and remove, for red-black trees and for sorted lists. "size" is the size of the structure without the element. All times are in seconds.

As a final example, let us consider the implicit computation that gives the integer square root $\lfloor\sqrt{i}\rfloor$ of a positive integer i. This is concisely stated as following:

```
def sqrt(i : Int) : Int =
  ((res: Int) ⇒ res > 0 &&
                res * res ≤ i &&
                (res + 1) * (res + 1) > i).solve
```

Our implementation can handle numbers as large as hundreds of thousands, performing under 0.3 seconds in all cases.

6.3 Counter-example Guided Inductive Synthesis

Counter-example guided inductive synthesis (CEGIS) is a method for effectively solving $\exists\forall$ constraints using SMT solvers. Such constraints are particularly important for program synthesis, identified as the class of $\forall\exists$ synthesis problems in [53]. The counter-example guided approach for this problem was successfully applied to software synthesis in the algorithm for combinatorial sketching using SAT solvers [58]. This technique was later applied with an SMT solver as the satisfiability engine to synthesize loop-free bit-vector code fragments [26].

The technique starts by choosing some initial set of values for the universally quantified variables, then solving the constraint for the existentially quantified variables. If the values for the existentially quantified variables work for all values of the universally quantified variables, a solution has been found. Otherwise, there is a counterexample which is some valuation of the universally quantified variables. This counterexample is added to the set of values for universally quantified variables and the procedure is repeated until a solution is found.

This synthesis loop can be expressed in our system succinctly, using first-class constraints. As an example we consider the following: *Are there integers a and b such that, for every integer x, $a \cdot (x-1) < b \cdot x$?* In Kaplan we can describe the CEGIS approach as in Figure 10. When executed, the program finds correct values for a and b in two iterations of the loop. The output of the program is:

```
Initial x: 0
candidate parameters a = 1, b = 0
counterexample for x: 1
candidate parameters a = 1, b = 1
proved!
```

The example generalizes to arbitrary constraints (which, in this example, are cnstrGivenX and cnstrGivenParams), keeping the same simple structure. Note that we here explicitly constructed increasingly stronger first-class constraints; we can instead use logical variables and incrementally augment the constraint store.

```
var continue = true
val initialX = ((x: Int) ⇒ true).solve
def cnstrGivenX(x0: Int): Constraint2[Int,Int] =
  ((a: Int, b: Int) ⇒ a * (x0 − 1) < b * x0)
def cnstrGivenParams(a0: Int, b0: Int): Constraint1[Int] =
  ((x: Int) ⇒ a0 * (x − 1) < b0 * x)
var currentCnstr = cnstrGivenX(initialX)
while (continue) {
  currentCnstr.find match {
    case Some((a, b)) ⇒ {
      println("candidate parameters a = " + a + ", b = " + b)
      (! cnstrGivenParams(a, b)).find match {
        case None ⇒
          println("proved!")
          continue = false
        case Some(ce) ⇒
          println("counterexample for x: " + ce)
          currentCnstr = currentCnstr && cnstrGivenX(ce)
      }
    }
    case None ⇒
      println("cannot prove property!")
      continue = false
  }
}
```

Figure 10. Counter-example guided inductive synthesis in Kaplan

list size	time in Kaplan (s)	time in Curry (s)
10000	< 0.01	0.21
100000	< 0.01	2.41
1000000	< 0.01	23.88

Figure 11. Evaluation results for functional last method.

6.4 Comparison to Other Systems

Providing a fair comparison of running times of Kaplan against competing systems is difficult because Kaplan covers many areas for which specialized tools have been developed. We do not expect to match performance of each of these specialized systems. At the same time, there is no single system that subsumes Kaplan. This section illustrates how other tools can solve some of the problems we presented in this paper and solved using Kaplan. The running times should not be taken as a definitive statement of the relative merits of the systems, but rather as a guide to understanding key differences of the underlying constraint solving techniques.

Last element of the list. We first compare the performance of Kaplan and Curry on computing the last element of a list, both in a declarative way as presented in Section 6.2, and as a tail-recursive functional method. In Curry, the declarative version can be expressed as:

```
last xs | concat ys [x] =:= xs
    = x where x,ys free
```

The performance of the Curry implementation surpasses the performance of Kaplan that we reported in Figure 8, running under 0.01 seconds in lists of size up to 100. However, in Kaplan we also have the freedom of writing the constraint directly as a functional program. In such style, Curry performs at about the same speed as for a constraint-based definition, so Kaplan outperforms Curry on longer lists. Figure 11 shows the evaluation results for this case. It is of course the Scala compiler and the Java Virtual Machine that take credit for the good performance of the functional implementation; to the credit of Kaplan is simply that it does not lose any of this underlying efficiency. This basic consequence of Kaplan design is very important from a practical point of view. In principle, a static analysis could be used to recognize among logical constraints special classes that do not require constraint solving (consider, for example, mode analysis of Mercury [51]). However, this approach clearly requires significant compilation effort to merely recover the baseline performance of a functional or imperative code, whereas in Kaplan it follows by construction.

Generating data structures with complex invariants. We now report on our experience in comparing Kaplan with ScalaCheck [48] for generating red-black trees (results were similar for sorted lists). ScalaCheck is a tool for producing test cases using random test generation, similar to QuickCheck [13] for Haskell. We implemented basic generators for lists and trees using generator combinators in ScalaCheck. The problem with random generation is that, for many classes of properties, the probability of a random structure satisfying it may tend to zero as the structure size grows [10], making test cases vacuous for larger structures. To see this in practice, consider first our own performance: Figure 7 shows that Kaplan takes 27.45 seconds in total to generate *all* red-black trees of size n containing elements 1 to n, for all n from 0 to 7. We therefore defined a basic ScalaCheck generator that, with equal probability, generates an empty or a non-empty tree. We ran it for 29.1 seconds, generating 200'000 trees. Although 62% of all of them were red-black, that is because 104'544 were, in fact, empty. Of the rest, 18'191 had size one, 934 size two, and there were no red-black trees of larger size. In this experiment, we gave both Kaplan and ScalaCheck only the constraints, without any additional insight, which makes the comparison fair. Experienced users could write better ScalaCheck generators, but they could similarly write better Kaplan checkers. Like UDITA [24], Kaplan supports a full spectrum of intermediate approaches, where one puts more attention into either writing better generators, to increase the ratio of valid testcases, or into manually decomposing the implicit computation to reduce the search space.

Constraint satisfaction problems. Tools for constraint solving and optimization over finite domains have developed somewhat independently of SMT and the related technologies [4, 23, 47, 61]. Our anecdotal experience suggests that, for problems of moderate size over finite domains, the two technologies yield comparable results. A full experimental comparison between the state of the art of these two communities is beyond the scope of this paper. Note that we could incorporate into Kaplan solvers from either class, as long as they support our domains of interest (including, for example, algebraic data types).

7. Related Work

Existing languages. Functional logic programming [3] amalgamates the functional programming and logic programming paradigms into a single language. Functional logic languages, such as Curry [41], benefit from efficient demand-driven term reduction strategies proper to functional languages, as well as non-deterministic operations of logic languages, by using a technique called *narrowing*, a combination of term reduction and variable instantiation. Instantiation of unbound logic variables occur in constructive guessing steps, only to sustain computation when a reduction needs their values. The performance of non-deterministic computations depends on the evaluation strategy, which are formalized using definitional trees [2]. Applications using functional logic languages include programming of graphical and web user interfaces [27, 28] as well as providing high-level APIs for accessing and manipulating databases [12]. Our work can be seen as the practical experiment of building from existing components a system close in functionality to Curry: we proceeded by extending an existing language while preserving its execution model, rather than starting from scratch. As such, we lose the luxury of a total integration of paradigms; for instance, users of Kaplan need to specify which functions can handle logical variables. On the other hand, such a separation of features comes with benefits: we can readily use the full power of Z3 and the Leon verification system for constraint solving, and the execution efficiency of the Java virtual machine for regular code. Implementations of functional logic languages, on the other hand, must typically focus on efficiently executing either the logical or the functional components of the code.

The Oz language and the associated Mozart Programming System is another admirable combination of multiple paradigms [64], with applications in functional, concurrent, and logic programming. In particular, Oz supports a form of logical variables, and logic programming is enabled through unification. One limitation is that one cannot perform arithmetic operations with logical variables (which we have demonstrated in several of our examples), because unification only applies to constructor terms.

Some of the earlier efforts to integrate constraint and imperative programming resulted in the languages Kaleidoscope [37], Alma-0 [5] and Turtle [25]. This line of research put emphasis on designing novel ways to define constraints, ideally to resemble imperative-style programming. Kaleidoscope, for instance, promotes the integration of constraints with objects; programmers can define instance constraints that relate various members of an object, and constraints can be reassigned, just like mutable variables. Constraints are also associated to a *duration* (*once* or *always*), specifying intuitively the scope in which they can affect variables. Kaplan currently does not support constraints over mutable data types and could benefit from the integration of such features.

The integration of constraints as first-class members of the language is tighter in Kaplan than in any of the languages discussed above. For example, in Curry programmers can define constraints as functions that return the special type Success (which is *not* identical to Boolean). However, such functions (or rather predicates) in Curry can only be built from equality predicates and cannot be combined freely: while conjunction and disjunction are valid combinators, negation, for instance, is not. In Kaplan, on the other hand, any predicate expressed in PureScala can be used as a constraint, and terms of other types can also be manipulated and composed freely.

Another distinguishing feature of Kaplan is the native support for many theories (integers, sets, maps, data types) that comes from using Leon [60] and Z3 as the underlying constraint solver.

Language design. Monadic constraint programming [56] integrates constraint programming into purely functional languages by using monads to define solvers. The authors define monadic search trees, corresponding to a base search, that can be transformed by the use of *search transformers* in a composable fashion to increase performance. Our system differs from this work in its use of SMT solvers for search, and a more flexible way of mixing constraints with imperative programming.

Localized code synthesis techniques have been proposed to turn implicit declarations into explicit code [35]. The main limitation of that approach is the requirement that the theory should be decidable. We have shown that using a powerful, undecidable, logic for constraints can be beneficial. Ideally, compile-time techniques such as [35] should be combined with the run-time approach of constraint solving.

The work on uniform reduction to bit-vector arithmetic [40] (URBIVA) proposes a C-like language for specifying constraints. It uses symbolic execution to encode problems into bit-vector arithmetic and invokes one of the underlying bit-vector and SAT solvers. The system allows for the comparison of different solvers on examples involving solution enumeration and functional equivalence checking. The use of symbolic values in conditional statements and array indexing is not permitted. Because it uses native enumeration capability of solvers such as CLASP, it can be faster than our system on some of the benchmarks. URBIVA does not support unbounded domains; we are aware of no techniques to enumerate solutions for unbounded domains more efficiently than in Kaplan.

SMT as a programming platform. The Dminor language [9] introduces the idea of using an SMT solver to check subtyping relations between refinement types; in Dminor, all types are defined as logical predicates, and subtyping thus consists of proving an implication between two such predicates. The authors show that an impressive number of common types (including for instance algebraic data types) can be encoded using this formalism. In this context, generating values satisfying a predicate is framed as the *type inhabitation* problem, and the authors introduce the expression elementof T to that end. It is evaluated by invoking Z3 at run-time and is thus conceptually comparable to our find construct but without support for recursive function unfolding. We have previously found that recursive function unfolding works better as a mechanism for satisfiability checking than using quantified axiomatization of recursive functions [60]. In general, we believe that our examples are substantially more complex than the experiences with elementof in the context of Dminor.

The Scala^{Z3} library [33] is our earlier effort to integrate invocations to Z3 into a programming language. Because it is implemented purely as a library, we were then not able to integrate user-defined recursive functions and data types into constraints, so the main application is to provide an embedded domain-specific language to access the constraint language of Z3 (but not to extend it). A similar approach has been taken by others to invoke the Yices SMT solver [19] from Haskell.[3]

Applications of declarative programming. One approach in using specifications for software reliability is data structure repair [16, 20], where the goal is to recover from corrupted data structures by transforming states that are erroneous with respect to integrity constraints into valid ones, performing local heuristic search. [65] uses method contracts instead of data structure integrity constraints to be able to support rich behavioral specifications. While the primary goal is to perform run-time recovery of data structures, recent work [38] extends the technique for debugging purposes, by abstracting concrete repair actions to program statements performing the same actions. Data structure repair differs from our system in that it can perform local search to modify existing states, while we do not currently do so. We do not expect that a general-purpose constraint solving such as ours can immediately compare with these dedicated techniques.

The idea to use specifications as a fall-back mechanism, as in one of our application examples, was adopted in [55]. Similarly to our setting, dynamic contract checking is applied and, upon violations, specifications can be *executed*. The technique ignores the erroneous state and computes output values for methods given concrete input values and the method contract. The implementation uses a relational logic similar to Alloy [30] for specifications, and deploys the Kodkod model finder [63]. A related tight integration between Java and the Kodkod engine is presented in [42]. In both cases, due to the finite bound on the search space, a satisfying answer may not always be found, which makes the techniques incomplete. We have shown that executing declarative specifications is possible in our setting. We expect that a constraint solver such as the one deployed in Leon will ultimately be better suited than an approach based on KodKod, due to the presence of unbounded or large data types such as integers and recursive structures.

[3] http://hackage.haskell.org/package/yices-easy

8. Conclusion

We presented Kaplan, an extension of the multi-paradigm Scala language that integrates constraint programming while preserving the existing functional and object-oriented features of Scala. The behavior and performance of Kaplan is identical to Scala in the absence of declarative constraint solving. Kaplan integrates constraints as first-class objects in Scala, and logical variables for solving constraints lazily. It allows for solving optimization problems, as well as enumerating solutions in a user-specified order. Kaplan is implemented as a combination of a compiler plugin and a runtime library, and allows users to express constraints in a powerful and expressive logic. Kaplan relies on a procedure for satisfiability modulo recursive functions [59, 60] to solve these constraints.

We evaluated our system by considering applications such as solution enumeration, execution of declarative specifications, test-case generation for bug-finding and counterexample guided inductive synthesis, as well as numerous smaller, yet expressive, snippets. We observed that our model for introducing non-determinism using for-comprehensions integrates well with Scala.

Based on our experience with the Z3 SMT solver and the Leon verification system in constraint programming, we found that a number of features, if natively supported by solvers, could directly bring benefits to constraint programming. These include 1) support for enumeration of theory models and 2) solving constraints while minimizing/maximizing a given term. Overall, we believe there is great potential in extending standard programming languages with constraint solving capabilities. Many interesting problems are left open, both in language design and in constraint solving; a system such as Kaplan that integrates state-of-the-art tools from both domains is likely to benefit from progress made in each of them.

Acknowledgments

We thank Sergio Antoy for an interesting discussion on the status of the Curry programming language. We thank Nikolaj Bjørner and Leonardo de Moura for their help in using Z3, and Adriaan Moors for his help with the Scala compiler. We thank Swen Jacobs, Eva Darulová, and the anonymous reviewers for their feedback.

References

[1] H. Aït-Kaci. *Warren's Abstract Machine: A Tutorial Reconstruction*. MIT Press, 1991.

[2] S. Antoy. Definitional trees. In *ALP*, pages 143–157, 1992.

[3] S. Antoy and M. Hanus. Functional logic programming. *CACM*, 53 (4):74–85, 2010.

[4] K. R. Apt and M. Wallace. *Constraint logic programming using Eclipse*. Cambridge University Press, 2007.

[5] K. R. Apt, J. Brunekreef, V. Partington, and A. Schaerf. Alma-O: An imperative language that supports declarative programming. *TOPLAS*, 20(5):1014–1066, 1998.

[6] R.-J. Back and J. von Wright. *Refinement Calculus*. Springer-Verlag, 1998.

[7] T. Ball, D. Hoffman, F. Ruskey, R. Webber, and L. J. White. State generation and automated class testing. *Softw. Test., Verif. Reliab.*, 10 (3), 2000.

[8] C. Barrett and C. Tinelli. CVC3. In *CAV*, volume 4590 of *LNCS*, 2007.

[9] G. M. Bierman, A. D. Gordon, C. Hritcu, and D. E. Langworthy. Semantic subtyping with an SMT solver. In *ICFP*, pages 105–116, 2010.

[10] A. Blass, Y. Gurevich, and D. Kozen. A zero-one law for logic with a fixed-point operator. *Inf. Control*, 67, October 1986.

[11] C. Boyapati, S. Khurshid, and D. Marinov. Korat: Automated testing based on Java predicates. In *Proc. International Symposium on Software Testing and Analysis*, pages 123–133, July 2002.

[12] B. Braßel, M. Hanus, and M. Müller. High-level database programming in Curry. In *PADL*, pages 316–332, 2008.

[13] K. Claessen and J. Hughes. Quickcheck: a lightweight tool for random testing of haskell programs. In *ICFP*, pages 268–279, 2000.

[14] A. Colmerauer, H. Kanoui, and M. V. Caneghem. Last steps towards an ultimate PROLOG. In *IJCAI*, pages 947–948, 1981.

[15] R. DeLine and K. R. M. Leino. BoogiePL: A typed procedural language for checking object-oriented programs. Technical Report MSR-TR-2005-70, Microsoft Research, March 2005.

[16] B. Demsky and M. C. Rinard. Automatic detection and repair of errors in data structures. In *OOPSLA*, pages 78–95, 2003.

[17] D. Detlefs, G. Nelson, and J. B. Saxe. Simplify: a theorem prover for program checking. *J. ACM*, 52(3):365–473, 2005.

[18] E. W. Dijkstra. Guarded commands, nondeterminacy and formal derivation of programs. *Commun. ACM*, 18(8):453–457, 1975.

[19] B. Dutertre and L. de Moura. The Yices SMT solver, 2006. `http://yices.csl.sri.com/tool-paper.pdf`.

[20] B. Elkarablieh and S. Khurshid. Juzi: a tool for repairing complex data structures. In *ICSE*, pages 855–858, 2008.

[21] S. Fischer, O. Kiselyov, and C. Shan. Purely functional lazy non-deterministic programming. In *ICFP*, volume 44, pages 11–22, 2009.

[22] H. Ganzinger, G. Hagen, R. Nieuwenhuis, A. Oliveras, and C. Tinelli. DPLL(T): Fast decision procedures. In *CAV*, pages 175–188, 2004.

[23] I. P. Gent, C. Jefferson, and I. Miguel. MINION: A fast, scalable, constraint solver. In *European Conference on Artificial Intelligence*, pages 98–102. IOS Press, 2006.

[24] M. Gligoric, T. Gvero, V. Jagannath, S. Khurshid, V. Kuncak, and D. Marinov. Test generation through programming in udita. In *ICSE (1)*, pages 225–234, 2010.

[25] M. Grabmüller and P. Hofstedt. Turtle: A constraint imperative programming language. In *Innovative Techniques and Applications of Artificial Intelligence*, 2003.

[26] S. Gulwani, S. Jha, A. Tiwari, and R. Venkatesan. Synthesis of loop-free programs. In *PLDI*, pages 62–73, 2011.

[27] M. Hanus. Type-oriented construction of web user interfaces. In *PPDP*, pages 27–38, 2006.

[28] M. Hanus and C. Kluß. Declarative programming of user interfaces. In *PADL*, pages 16–30, 2009.

[29] D. Jackson. Structuring Z specifications with views. *ACM Transactions on Software Engineering and Methodology*, 4(4), October 1995.

[30] D. Jackson. Alloy: a lightweight object modelling notation. *ACM Trans. Softw. Eng. Methodol.*, 11(2):256–290, 2002.

[31] J. Jaffar and J.-L. Lassez. Constraint logic programming. In *POPL*, 1987.

[32] J. C. King. *A Program Verifier*. PhD thesis, CMU, 1970.

[33] A. S. Köksal, V. Kuncak, and P. Suter. Scala to the power of Z3: Integrating SMT and programming (system description). In *CADE*, pages 400–406, 2011.

[34] R. A. Kowalski and D. Kuehner. Linear resolution with selection function. *Artif. Intell.*, 2(3/4):227–260, 1971.

[35] V. Kuncak, M. Mayer, R. Piskac, and P. Suter. Complete functional synthesis. In *PLDI*, pages 316–329, 2010.

[36] L. Lamport. *Specifying Systems: The TLA+ Language and Tools for Hardware and Software Engineers*. Addison-Wessley, 2002.

[37] G. Lopez, B. Freeman-Benson, and A. Borning. Kaleidoscope: A constraint imperative programming language. In *Constraint Programming*, pages 313–329. Springer-Verlag, 1994.

[38] M. Z. Malik, J. H. Siddiqui, and S. Khurshid. Constraint-based program debugging using data structure repair. In *ICST*, pages 190–199, 2011.

[39] Z. Manna and R. Waldinger. A deductive approach to program synthesis. *ACM Trans. Program. Lang. Syst.*, 2(1):90–121, 1980. ISSN 0164-0925. doi: http://doi.acm.org/10.1145/357084.357090.

[40] F. Maric and P. Janicic. Urbiva: Uniform reduction to bit-vector arithmetic. In *IJCAR*, pages 346–352, 2010.

[41] E. Michael Hanus. Curry: An integrated functional logic language. `http://www.curry-language.org`, 2006. vers. 0.8.2.

[42] A. Milicevic, D. Rayside, K. Yessenov, and D. Jackson. Unifying execution of imperative and declarative code. In *ICSE*, pages 511–520, 2011.

[43] C. Morgan. *Programming from Specifications (2nd ed.)*. Prentice-Hall, Inc., 1994.

[44] L. de Moura and N. Bjørner. Z3: An efficient SMT solver. In *TACAS*, 2008.

[45] G. Nelson. Techniques for program verification. Technical report, XEROX Palo Alto Research Center, 1981.

[46] G. Nelson and D. C. Oppen. Fast decision procedures based on congruence closure. *Journal of the ACM (JACM)*, 27(2):356–364, 1980. ISSN 0004-5411. doi: http://doi.acm.org/10.1145/322186.322198.

[47] N. Nethercote, P. Stuckey, R. Becket, S. Brand, G. Duck, and G. Tack. MiniZinc: Towards a standard CP modelling language. *Principles and Practice of Constraint Programming*, pages 529–543, 2007.

[48] R. Nilsson. Scalacheck user guide. `http://code.google.com/p/scalacheck/wiki/UserGuide`, 2011.

[49] M. Odersky. Contracts in Scala. In *International Conference on Runtime Verification*. Springer LNCS, 2010.

[50] M. Odersky, L. Spoon, and B. Venners. *Programming in Scala: a comprehensive step-by-step guide*. Artima Press, 2008.

[51] D. Overton, Z. Somogyi, and P. J. Stuckey. Constraint-based mode analysis of Mercury. In *ACM SIGPLAN Workshop on Principles and practice of declarative programming (PPDI)*, 2002.

[52] L. C. Paulson, T. Nipkow, et al. Isabelle theorem prover - official website. `http://www.cl.cam.ac.uk/Research/HVG/Isabelle`.

[53] A. Pnueli and R. Rosner. On the synthesis of a reactive module. In *POPL*, 1989.

[54] A. Riesco and J. Rodríguez-Hortalá. Programming with singular and plural non-deterministic functions. In *PEPM*, pages 83–92, 2010.

[55] H. Samimi, E. D. Aung, and T. D. Millstein. Falling back on executable specifications. In *ECOOP*, pages 552–576, 2010.

[56] T. Schrijvers, P. J. Stuckey, and P. Wadler. Monadic constraint programming. *J. Funct. Program.*, 19(6):663–697, 2009.

[57] J. P. M. Silva and K. A. Sakallah. GRASP - a new search algorithm for satisfiability. In *ICCAD*, pages 220–227, 1996.

[58] A. Solar-Lezama, L. Tancau, R. Bodík, S. A. Seshia, and V. A. Saraswat. Combinatorial sketching for finite programs. In *ASPLOS*, 2006.

[59] P. Suter, M. Dotta, and V. Kuncak. Decision procedures for algebraic data types with abstractions. In *ACM SIGPLAN POPL*, 2010.

[60] P. Suter, A. S. Köksal, and V. Kuncak. Satisfiability modulo recursive programs. In *Static Analysis Symposium (SAS)*, 2011.

[61] G. Tack. *Constraint Propagation - Models, Techniques, Implementation*. PhD thesis, Saarland University, 2009.

[62] The Coq Development Team; INRIA LogiCal Project. The Coq proof assistant - official website. `http://coq.inria.fr`.

[63] E. Torlak and D. Jackson. Kodkod: A relational model finder. In *Tools and Algorithms for Construction and Analysis of Systems (TACAS)*, 2007.

[64] P. Van Roy. Logic programming in Oz with Mozart. In *ICLP*, 1999.

[65] R. N. Zaeem and S. Khurshid. Contract-based data structure repair using Alloy. In *ECOOP*, pages 577–598, 2010.

[66] L. Zhang, C. F. Madigan, M. W. Moskewicz, and S. Malik. Efficient conflict driven learning in boolean satisfiability solver. In *ICCAD*, pages 279–285, 2001.

Multiple Facets for Dynamic Information Flow

Thomas H. Austin   Cormac Flanagan

taustin@uscs.edu   cormac@ucsc.edu

University of California, Santa Cruz

Abstract

JavaScript has become a central technology of the web, but it is also the source of many security problems, including cross-site scripting attacks and malicious advertising code. Central to these problems is the fact that code from untrusted sources runs with full privileges. We implement *information flow controls* in Firefox to help prevent violations of data confidentiality and integrity.

Most previous information flow techniques have primarily relied on either static type systems, which are a poor fit for JavaScript, or on dynamic analyses that sometimes get stuck due to problematic implicit flows, even in situations where the target web application correctly satisfies the desired security policy.

We introduce *faceted values*, a new mechanism for providing information flow security in a dynamic manner that overcomes these limitations. Taking inspiration from secure multi-execution, we use faceted values to simultaneously and efficiently simulate multiple executions for different security levels, thus providing non-interference with minimal overhead, and without the reliance on the stuck executions of prior dynamic approaches.

Categories and Subject Descriptors D.3.3 [*Programming Languages*]: Language Constructs and Features; D.4.6 [*Operating Systems*]: Security and Protection—Information flow controls

General Terms Languages, Security

Keywords Information flow control, dynamic analysis, JavaScript, web security

1. Introduction

JavaScript has helped to usher in a new age of richly interactive web applications. Often times, developers build these sites by including JavaScript code from a number of different sources. With minimal effort, a web developer can build an impressive site by composing code from multiple sources.

Unfortunately, there are few restrictions on the included code, and it operates with the same authority as the web developer's own code. Advertising has been a particular source of malicious JavaScript. There are a wide array of security measures used to defend against these problems, but the bulk of them tend to rely on competent web developers. Given the mercurial nature of security challenges, even a conscientious web developer has difficulty keeping up with the latest trends and best practices.

POPL'12, January 25–27, 2012, Philadelphia, PA, USA.

Another option is to bake security controls into the browser itself. This strategy has been part of browser design since nearly the beginning, but the controls have tended to be fairly minimal.

Information flow analysis offers the promise of a systematic solution to many of these security challenges, but to date it has not achieved its potential, largely because much research on static information flow type systems is an awkward fit for dynamically typed JavaScript code. Additionally, there has been a folklore that dynamic information flow analysis is not sound in the presence of implicit flows.

This folklore is not true, however, and proposed mechanisms for dealing with implicit flows include the *no-sensitive-upgrade* semantics [39, 5] and the *permissive-upgrade* semantics [6]. Both semantics guarantee the key correctness property of termination-insensitive non-interference (TINI), which states that private inputs do not influence public outputs. (Private information can influence termination, but this channel is limited to a brute force attack [1]).

Despite this correctness guarantee, neither semantics provides an ideal foundation for JavaScript security since both suffer from the same weakness: in the presence of subtle implicit flows that are hard to track, the semantics halts execution in order to avoid any (potential) information leak. Note that this fail-stop is not caused by the web application violating a security policy; instead it is a *mechanism failure* caused by the *inability of the dynamic information flow analysis to track implicit flows*. Thus, these dynamic analyses reject valid programs that conform to the security policy.

An interesting solution to these mechanism failures is to simultaneously execute two copies of the target program: a high-confidentiality (H) process that has access to secret data, and a low-confidentiality (L) process that sees dummy default values instead of the actual secret data [9, 13]. This *multi-process execution* cleanly guarantees non-interference since no information flow is permitted between the two processes, and it also avoids mechanism failures. Unfortunately, for a web page with n principals (roughly, URL domains), we may require up to 2^n processes, one for each element in the powerset lattice for these principals.

In this paper, we combine the benefits of multi-process execution with the efficiency of single-process execution. The key technical novelty is the introduction of a *faceted value*, which is a pair of two raw values that contain low and high confidentiality information, respectively. By appropriately manipulating these faceted values, a single process can *simulate* the two processes (L and H) of the multi-execution approach. The primary benefit of this approach is that, for most data, the two raw values in a faceted value are identical, in which case we collapse the two simulated executions on identical data into a single execution, drastically reducing the overhead. In the presence of multiple principals and a complex security lattice, a faceted value can contain many raw values, rather than just two. In this situation, the semantics of tracking information flow is a little more complex, costing some run-time performance overhead. However, our experimental results suggest that faceted evaluation outperforms multi-process execution as the number of principals increases.

This paper includes a formal description of the faceted value approach to dynamic information flow analysis, and a proof that it achieves termination-insensitive non-interference. We also present a *projection theorem* showing that a computation over faceted values simulates 2^n non-faceted computations, one for each element in the powerset security lattice. We have implemented this mechanism inside the Firefox browser (using the Zaphod plug-in [26]) in order to validate its utility in a web browsing context. Additionally, we have used this implementation to compare the performance of faceted values against multi-process execution. Finally, we discuss declassification and how it relates to faceted values, noting this feature as an additional point of distinction with multi-process execution.

1.1 Overview of Faceted Evaluation

To motivate the need for faceted values in dynamic information flow, we start by considering the classic problem of *implicit flows*, such as those caused by a conditional assignment:

```
if (x) y = true
```

The central insight of this paper is that the correct value for y after this assignment depends on the authority of the observer. For example, suppose initially that $\texttt{x} = \texttt{true}$ and $\texttt{y} = \texttt{false}$, and that x is secret whereas y is public. Then after this assignment:

- A *private observer* that can read x should see $\texttt{y} = \texttt{true}$.
- A *public observer* that cannot read x should see $\texttt{y} = \texttt{false}$, since it should not see any influence from this conditional assignment.

Faceted values represent exactly this dual nature of y, which should simultaneously appear as true and false to different observers.

In more detail, a *faceted value* is a triple consisting of a principal k and two values V_H and V_L, which we write as:

$$\langle k ~?~ V_H : V_L \rangle$$

Intuitively, this faceted value appears as V_H to private observers that can view k's private data, and as V_L to other public observers. We refer to V_H and V_L as private and public facets, respectively.

This faceted value representation naturally generalizes the traditional public and private security labels used by prior analyses. A public value V is represented in our setting simply as V itself, since V appears the same to both public and private observers and so no facets are needed. A private value V is represented as the faceted value

$$\langle k ~?~ V : \bot \rangle$$

where only private observers can see V, and where public or unauthorized observers instead see $\bot$ (roughly meaning undefined).

Although the notions of public and private data have been well explored by earlier dynamic information flow analyses, these two security labels are insufficient to avoid stuck executions in the presence of implicit flows. As illustrated by the conditional assignment considered above, correct handling of implicit flows requires the introduction of more general notion of faceted values $\langle k ~?~ V_H : V_L \rangle$, in which the public facet V_L is a real value and not simply $\bot$. In particular, the post-assignment value for y is cleanly represented as the faceted value $\langle k ~?~ \texttt{true} : \texttt{false} \rangle$ that captures y's appearance to both public and private observers.

Based on this faceted value representation, this paper develops a dynamic analysis that tracks information flow in a sound manner at runtime. Our analysis is formulated as an evaluation semantics for the target program, where the semantics uses faceted values to track security and dependency information.

This evaluation semantics is designed to avoid leaking information between public and private facets. In particular, if $C[\bullet]$ is any program context, then the computation $C[\langle k ~?~ V_H : V_L \rangle]$ appears to behave exactly like $C[V_H]$ from the perspective of a private observer, and behaves exactly like $C[V_L]$ to a public observer (under a termination-insensitive notion of equivalence). This *projection property* means that a single faceted computation simulates multiple non-faceted computations, one for each element in the security lattice. This projection property also enables an elegant proof of termination-insensitive non-interference, shown in Section 3.2.

Faceted values may be nested. Nested faceted values naturally arise during computations with multiple principals. For example, if k_1 and k_2 denote different principals, then the expression

$$\langle k_1 ~?~ \texttt{true} : \bot \rangle ~\texttt{\&\&}~ \langle k_2 ~?~ \texttt{false} : \bot \rangle$$

evaluates to the nested faceted value

$$\langle k_1 ~?~ \langle k_2 ~?~ \texttt{false} : \bot \rangle : \bot \rangle$$

since the result false is visible only to observers authorized to see private data from both k_1 and k_2; any other observer instead sees the dummy value $\bot$.

As a second example, the expression

$$\langle k_1 ~?~ 2 : 0 \rangle ~\texttt{+}~ \langle k_2 ~?~ 1 : 0 \rangle$$

evaluates to the result

$$\langle k_1 ~?~ \langle k_2 ~?~ 3 : 2 \rangle : \langle k_2 ~?~ 1 : 0 \rangle \rangle$$

Thus, faceted values form binary trees with principals at interior nodes and raw (non-faceted) values at the leaves. The part of this faceted value tree that is actually seen by a particular observer depends on whose private data the observer can read. In particular, we define the *view* of an observer as the set of principals whose private data that observer can read. Thus, an observer with view $\{k_1, k_2\}$ would see the result of 3 from this addition, whereas an observer with view $\{k_2\}$ would see the result 1.

When a faceted value influences the control flow, in general we may need to explore the behavior of the program under both facets[1]. For example, the evaluation of the conditional expression:

$$\texttt{if (} \langle k ~?~ \texttt{true} : \texttt{false} \rangle \texttt{) then } e_1 \texttt{ else } e_2$$

evaluates both e_1 and e_2, and carefully tracks the dependency of these computations on the principal k. In particular, assignments performed during e_1 are visible only to views that include k, while assignments performed during e_2 are visible to views that exclude k. After the evaluations of e_1 and e_2 complete, their two results are combined into a single faceted value that is returned to the continuation of this conditional expression. That is, the execution is split only for the duration of this conditional expression, rather than for the remainder of the entire program.

1.2 Handling Implicit Flows

The key challenge in dynamic information flow analysis lies in handling implicit flows. To illustrate this difficulty, consider the code in the first column of Figure 1, which is adapted from an example by Fenton [16]. Here, the function f(x) returns the value of its boolean argument x, but it first attempts to "launder" this value by encoding it in the program counter.

We consider the evaluation of f on the two secret arguments $\langle k ~?~ \texttt{false} : \bot \rangle$ and $\langle k ~?~ \texttt{true} : \bot \rangle$ (analogous to the more traditional $\texttt{false}^H$ and $\texttt{true}^H$) to determine if the argument in any way influences any public component of the function's result.

For the argument $\langle k ~?~ \texttt{false} : \bot \rangle$ shown in column 2, the local variables y and z are initialized to true. The conditional

[1] The semantics is optimized to avoid such *split executions* where possible.

Figure 1: A JavaScript Function with Implicit Flows

	x = $\langle k\ ?$ `false` $: \bot\rangle$	x = $\langle k\ ?$ `true` $: \bot\rangle$			
Function `f(x)`	*All strategies*	*Naive*	*NSU*	*Permissive-Upgrade*	*Faceted Evaluation*
`y = true;`	y = `true`	y = `true`	y = `true`	y = `true`	y = `true`
`z = true;`	z = `true`	z = `true`	z = `true`	z = `true`	z = `true`
`if (x)`	—	$pc = \{k\}$	$pc = \{k\}$	$pc = \{k\}$	$pc = \{k\}$
`    y = false;`	—	y = $\langle k\ ?$ `false` $: \bot\rangle$	*stuck*	y = $\langle k\ ?$ `false` $: *\rangle$	y = $\langle k\ ?$ `false` : `true`$\rangle$
`if (y)`	$pc = \{\}$	—		*stuck*	$pc = \{\overline{k}\}$
`    z = false;`	z = `false`	—			z = $\langle k\ ?$ `true` : `false`$\rangle$
`return z;`	—	—			—
Return Value:	`false`	`true`			$\langle k\ ?$ `true` : `false`$\rangle$

branch on `x` when `x` = $\langle k\ ?$ `false` $: \bot\rangle$ is split into separate branches on `false` and $\bot$. The first test `if(false) ...` is clearly a no-op, and so is the second test `if(`$\bot$`) ...` since `if` is strict in $\bot$. Since `y` remains `true`, the branch on `y` is taken and so `z` is set to `false`. Thus, the function call `f(`$\langle k\ ?$ `false` $: \bot\rangle$`)` returns `false`.

We now consider the evaluation of `f(`$\langle k\ ?$ `true` $: \bot\rangle$`)` under different dynamic information flow semantics. While the prior semantics that we discuss here have no notion of facets, explaining them in terms of faceted values is illuminating.

Naive An intuitive strategy for handling the assignment `y=false` that is conditional on the private input `x` is to simply set `y` to $\langle k\ ?$ `false` $: \bot\rangle$ to reflect that this value depends on private inputs. Unfortunately, this approach is not sound, since it loses the critical information that a public observer should still see `y` = `true`. The next conditional branch on `y` exploits this confusion. Since `y` is $\langle k\ ?$ `false` $: \bot\rangle$, the branch is not executed, so `z` remains `true`, and so `f(`$\langle k\ ?$ `true` $: \bot\rangle$`)` returns `true`, as illustrated in column 3. Thus, this naive strategy fails to ensure TINI, since the public output of `f` leaks the contents of its private input.

Various prior approaches attempt to close this information leak without introducing full faceted values, with mixed results.

No-Sensitive-Upgrade With the *no-sensitive-upgrade* check [39, 5], execution halts on any attempt to update public variables in code conditional on private data. Under this strategy, the assignment to the public variable `y` from code conditional on a private variable `x` would get stuck, as shown in the *NSU* column of Figure 1. This strategy guarantees TINI, but only at the expense of getting stuck on some implicit flows.

Permissive-Upgrade A more flexible approach is to permit the implicit flow caused by the conditional assignment to `y`, but to record that the analysis has lost track of the correct (original) public facet for `y`. The *Permissive-Upgrade* represents this lost information by setting `y` to the faceted value $\langle k\ ?$ `false` $: *\rangle$, where "$*$" denotes that the public facet is an unknown, non-$\bot$ value.[2]

This permissive upgrade strategy accepts strictly more program executions than the no-sensitive-upgrade approach, but it still resorts to stuck executions in some cases; if the execution ever depends on that missing public facet, then the permissive upgrade strategy halts execution in order to avoid information leaks. In particular, when `y` is used in the second conditional of Figure 1, the execution gets stuck.

[2] The original paper [6] used the $\texttt{false}^P$ to represent $\langle k\ ?$ `false` $: *\rangle$, where the superscript P denotes "partially leaked".

Faceted Evaluation As shown in the last column of Figure 1, faceted values cleanly handle problematic implicit flows. At the conditional assignment to `y`, the faceted value $\langle k\ ?$ `false` : `true`$\rangle$ simultaneously represents the dual nature of `y`, which appears `false` to private observers but `true` to public observers. Thus, the conditional branch `if (y) ...` is taken only for public observers, and we record this information by setting the program counter label pc to $\{\overline{k}\}$. Consequently, the assignment `z=false` updates `z` from `true` to $\langle k\ ?$ `true` : `false`$\rangle$. Critically, this assignment updates *only* the public facet of `z`, not its private facet, which stays as `true`. The final result of the function call is then $\langle k\ ?$ `true` : `false`$\rangle$.

Comparing the behavior of `f` on the arguments $\langle k\ ?$ `false` $: \bot\rangle$ and $\langle k\ ?$ `true` $: \bot\rangle$, we see that, from the perspective of a public observer, `f` always returns `false`, correctly reflecting that `f(`$\bot$`)` returns `false`, and so there is no information leak on this example, despite its problematic implicit flows. Conversely, from the perspective of a private observer authorized to view `f`'s actual output, `f` exhibits the correct behavior of returning its private boolean argument.

2. A Programming Language with Facets

We formalize faceted evaluation for dynamic information flow in terms of the idealized language λ^{facet} shown in Figure 2. This language extends the λ-calculus with mutable reference cells, reactive I/O, a special value $\bot$, and a mechanism for creating faceted values. Despite its intentional minimality, this language captures the essential complexities of dynamic information flow in more realistic languages, since it includes key challenges such as heap allocation, mutation, implicit flows, and higher-order function calls. In particular, conditional tests can be Church-encoded in the usual fashion.

Expressions in λ^{facet} include the standard features of the λ-calculus, namely variables (x), constants (c), functions ($\lambda x.e$), and function application ($e_1\ e_2$). The language also supports mutable reference cells, with operations to create (`ref` e), dereference (`!`e), and update (e_1 `:=` e_2) a reference cell. To model JavaScript's interactive nature, λ^{facet} also supports reading from (`read`(f)) and writing to (`write`(f, e)) external resources such as files.

The expression $\langle k\ ?\ e_1 : e_2\rangle$ creates a faceted values where the value of e_1 is considered secret to principal k; observers that cannot see k's private data will instead see the public facet produced by e_2. We initially use the terms *label* and *principals* as synonyms and focus primarily on confidentiality—Section 5 later introduces integrity labels in the context of robust declassification.

The $\bot$ value is used to represent "nothing", mirroring Smalltalk's `nil` and JavaScript's `undefined`. It is primarily used as the public facet in a faceted value $\langle k\ ?\ V : \bot\rangle$, which denotes a value V that is private to principal k, with no corresponding public value.

Figure 2: The source language λ^{facet}

Syntax:

$e ::=$		*Term*
	x	variable
	c	constant
	$\lambda x.e$	abstraction
	$e_1\ e_2$	application
	$\texttt{ref}\ e$	reference allocation
	$!e$	dereference
	$e := e$	assignment
	$\texttt{read}(f)$	file read
	$\texttt{write}(f, e)$	file write
	$\langle k\ ?\ e_1 : e_2 \rangle$	faceted expression
	$\perp$	bottom
x, y, z		*Variable*
c		*Constant*
k, l		*Label (aka Principal)*
f		*File handle*

Standard encodings:

$$\begin{array}{rcl}
\texttt{true} & \stackrel{\text{def}}{=} & \lambda x.\lambda y.x \\
\texttt{false} & \stackrel{\text{def}}{=} & \lambda x.\lambda y.y \\
\texttt{if}\ e_1\ \texttt{then}\ e_2\ \texttt{else}\ e_3 & \stackrel{\text{def}}{=} & (e_1\ (\lambda d.e_2)\ (\lambda d.e_3))\ (\lambda x.x) \\
\texttt{if}\ e_1\ \texttt{then}\ e_2 & \stackrel{\text{def}}{=} & \texttt{if}\ e_1\ \texttt{then}\ e_2\ \texttt{else}\ 0 \\
\texttt{let}\ x = e_1\ \texttt{in}\ e_2 & \stackrel{\text{def}}{=} & (\lambda x.e_2)\ e_1 \\
e_1\ ;\ e_2 & \stackrel{\text{def}}{=} & \texttt{let}\ x = e_1\ \texttt{in}\ e_2, x \notin FV(e_2)
\end{array}$$

2.1 Standard Semantics of λ^{facet}

As a point of comparison for our later development, we first present a standard semantics for λ^{facet} that does not handle faceted expressions. In this semantics, values include constants, addresses, closures, and $\perp$, as shown in Figure 3. A closure $(\lambda x.e, \theta)$ is a pair of a λ-expression and a substitution θ that maps variables to values. Each reference cell is allocated at an address a, and the store σ maps addresses to values. The store also maps each file f to a sequence of values w. We use the syntax $v.w$ and $w.v$ to indicate a list of values with v as the first or last value, respectively, and use $\emptyset$ to denote both the empty store and the empty substitution.

We formalize the standard semantics via a big-step relation

$$\sigma, \theta, e \downarrow \sigma', v$$

that evaluates an expression e in the context of a store σ and a substitution θ, and which returns the resulting value v and the (possibly modified) store σ'. This relation is defined via the evaluation rules shown in Figure 3, which are mostly straightforward. For example, the rule [S-APP] evaluates the body of the called function, where the notation $\theta[x := v]$ denotes the substitution that is identical to θ except that it maps x to v.

The only unusual aspect of this semantics concern the value $\perp$, which essentially means "nothing" or "no information". Operations such as function application, dereference, and assignment are strict in $\perp$; if given a $\perp$ argument they simply return $\perp$ via the various [S-*-BOT] rules. This semantics for $\perp$ facilitates our later use of $\perp$ in faceted values, since, for example, dereferencing a faceted address $\langle k\ ?\ a : \perp \rangle$ operates pointwise on the two facets to return a faceted result $\langle k\ ?\ v : \perp \rangle$ where $v = \sigma(a)$.

Figure 3: Standard Semantics

Runtime Syntax

$$\begin{array}{llllll}
a & \in & Address & & \\
\sigma & \in & store & = & (Address \rightarrow_p value \\
 & & & & \cup\ File \rightarrow value^*) \\
\theta & \in & subst & = & Var \rightarrow_p value \\
v & \in & value & ::= & c \mid a \mid (\lambda x.e, \theta) \mid \perp \\
w & \in & value^* & &
\end{array}$$

Evaluation Rules: $\boxed{\sigma, \theta, e \downarrow \sigma', v}$

$$\frac{}{\sigma, \theta, c \downarrow \sigma, c} \quad \text{[S-CONST]}$$

$$\frac{}{\sigma, \theta, x \downarrow \sigma, \theta(x)} \quad \text{[S-VAR]}$$

$$\frac{}{\sigma, \theta, (\lambda x.e) \downarrow \sigma, (\lambda x.e, \theta)} \quad \text{[S-FUN]}$$

$$\frac{\begin{array}{c}\sigma, \theta, e_1 \downarrow \sigma_1, (\lambda x.e, \theta') \\ \sigma_1, \theta, e_2 \downarrow \sigma_2, v' \\ \sigma, \theta'[x := v'], e \downarrow \sigma', v\end{array}}{\sigma, \theta, (e_1\ e_2) \downarrow \sigma', v} \quad \text{[S-APP]}$$

$$\frac{\begin{array}{c}\sigma, \theta, e_1 \downarrow \sigma_1, \perp \\ \sigma_1, \theta, e_2 \downarrow \sigma', v\end{array}}{\sigma, \theta, (e_1\ e_2) \downarrow \sigma', \perp} \quad \text{[S-APP-BOT]}$$

$$\frac{\begin{array}{c}\sigma, \theta, e \downarrow \sigma', v \\ a \notin dom(\sigma')\end{array}}{\sigma, \theta, (\texttt{ref}\ e) \downarrow \sigma'[a := v], a} \quad \text{[S-REF]}$$

$$\frac{\sigma, \theta, e \downarrow \sigma', a}{\sigma, \theta, !e \downarrow \sigma', \sigma'(a)} \quad \text{[S-DEREF]}$$

$$\frac{\sigma, \theta, e \downarrow \sigma', \perp}{\sigma, \theta, !e \downarrow \sigma', \perp} \quad \text{[S-DEREF-BOT]}$$

$$\frac{\begin{array}{c}\sigma, \theta, e_1 \downarrow \sigma_1, a \\ \sigma_1, \theta, e_2 \downarrow \sigma_2, v\end{array}}{\sigma, \theta, e_1 := e_2 \downarrow \sigma_2[a := v], v} \quad \text{[S-ASSIGN]}$$

$$\frac{\begin{array}{c}\sigma, \theta, e_1 \downarrow \sigma_1, \perp \\ \sigma_1, \theta, e_2 \downarrow \sigma_2, v\end{array}}{\sigma, \theta, e_1 := e_2 \downarrow \sigma_2, v} \quad \text{[S-ASSIGN-BOT]}$$

$$\frac{\sigma(f) = v.w}{\sigma, \theta, \texttt{read}(f) \downarrow \sigma[f := w], v} \quad \text{[S-READ]}$$

$$\frac{\sigma, \theta, e \downarrow \sigma', v}{\sigma, \theta, \texttt{write}(f, e) \downarrow \sigma'[f := \sigma'(f).v], v} \quad \text{[S-WRITE]}$$

$$\frac{}{\sigma, \theta, \perp \downarrow \sigma, \perp} \quad \text{[S-BOT]}$$

3. Faceted Evaluation

Having defined the standard semantics of the language, we now extend that semantics with faceted values that dynamically track information flow and which provide noninterference guarantees.

Figure 4 shows the additional runtime syntax needed to support faceted values. We use Initial Capitals to distinguish the new metavariable and domains of the faceted semantics ($V \in \mathit{Value}$, $\Sigma \in \mathit{Store}$, $\Theta \in \mathit{Subst}$) from those of the standard semantics ($v \in \mathit{value}$, $\sigma \in \mathit{store}$, $\theta \in \mathit{subst}$).

Values V now contain *faceted values* of the form

$$\langle k \mathrel{?} V_{\rm H} : V_{\rm L} \rangle$$

which contain both a private facet $V_{\rm H}$ and a public facet $V_{\rm L}$. For instance, the value $\langle k \mathrel{?} 42 : 0\rangle$ indicates that 42 is confidential to the principal k, and unauthorized viewers instead see the value 0. Often, the public facet is set to $\perp$ to denote that there is no intended publicly visible facet. Implicit flows introduce public facets other than $\perp$.

We introduce a *program counter label* called pc that records when the program counter has been influenced by public or private facets. For example, consider the conditional test

$$\texttt{if } (\langle k \mathrel{?} \texttt{true} : \texttt{false}\rangle) \texttt{ then } e_1 \texttt{ else } e_2$$

for which our semantics needs to evaluate both e_1 and e_2. During the evaluation of e_1, we add k to pc to record that this computation depends on data private to k. Conversely, during the evaluation of e_2, we add $\overline{k}$ to pc to record that this computation is dependent on the corresponding public facet. Formalizing this idea, we say that a *branch* h is either a principal k or its negation $\overline{k}$, and that pc is a set of branches. Note that pc can never include both k and $\overline{k}$, since that would reflect a computation dependent on both private and public facets.

The following operation $\langle\!\langle\, pc \mathrel{?} V_1 : V_2 \,\rangle\!\rangle$ creates new faceted values, where the resulting value appears like V_1 to observers that can see the computation corresponding to pc, and appears like V_2 to all other observers.

$$\begin{array}{lcl}
\langle\!\langle\, \emptyset \mathrel{?} V_n : V_o \,\rangle\!\rangle & \stackrel{\rm def}{=} & V_n \\
\langle\!\langle\, \{k\} \cup \mathit{rest} \mathrel{?} V_n : V_o \,\rangle\!\rangle & \stackrel{\rm def}{=} & \langle k \mathrel{?} \langle\!\langle\, \mathit{rest} \mathrel{?} V_n : V_o \,\rangle\!\rangle : V_o \rangle \\
\langle\!\langle\, \{\overline{k}\} \cup \mathit{rest} \mathrel{?} V_n : V_o \,\rangle\!\rangle & \stackrel{\rm def}{=} & \langle k \mathrel{?} V_o : \langle\!\langle\, \mathit{rest} \mathrel{?} V_n : V_o \,\rangle\!\rangle \rangle
\end{array}$$

For example, $\langle\!\langle\, \{k\} \mathrel{?} V_{\rm H} : V_{\rm L} \,\rangle\!\rangle$ returns $\langle k \mathrel{?} V_{\rm H} : V_{\rm L}\rangle$, and this operation generalizes to more complex program counter labels. We sometimes abbreviate $\langle\!\langle\, \{k\} \mathrel{?} V_{\rm H} : V_{\rm L} \,\rangle\!\rangle$ as $\langle\!\langle\, k \mathrel{?} V_{\rm H} : V_{\rm L} \,\rangle\!\rangle$.

We define the faceted value semantics via the big-step evaluation relation:

$$\Sigma, \Theta, e \Downarrow_{pc} \Sigma', V$$

that evaluates an expression e in the context of a store Σ, a substitution Θ, and a program counter label pc, and which returns the resulting value V and the (possibly modified) store Σ'.

Rule [F-SPLIT] shows how evaluation of a faceted expression $\langle k \mathrel{?} e_1 : e_2\rangle$ evaluates both e_1 and e_2 to values V_1 and V_2, with pc updated appropriately with k and $\overline{k}$ during these two evaluations. The two values are then combined via the operation $\langle\!\langle\, k \mathrel{?} V_1 : V_2 \,\rangle\!\rangle$. As an optimization, if the current computation already depends on k-private data (i.e., $k \in pc$), then rule [F-LEFT] evaluates only e_1, thus preserving the invariant that pc never contains both k and $\overline{k}$. Conversely, if $\overline{k} \in pc$ then [F-RIGHT] evaluates only e_2.

Function application $(e_1\ e_2)$ is somewhat tricky, since e_1 may evaluate to a faceted value tree with closures (or $\perp$) at the leaves. To handle this situation, the rule [F-APP] evaluates each e_i to a value V_i and then delegates to the auxiliary judgement:

$$\Sigma, (V_1\ V_2) \Downarrow_{pc} \Sigma', V'$$

This auxiliary judgement recursively traverses through any faceted values in V_1 to perform the actual function applications. If V_1 is a closure, then rule [FA-FUN] proceeds as normal. If V_1 is a facet $\langle k \mathrel{?} V_{\rm H} : V_{\rm L}\rangle$, then the rule [FA-SPLIT] applies *both* $V_{\rm H}$ and $V_{\rm L}$ to the argument V_2, in a manner similar to the rule [F-SPLIT] discussed above. Rules [FA-LEFT] and [FA-RIGHT] are optimized versions of [FA-SPLIT] for cases where k or $\overline{k}$ are already in pc. Finally, the "undefined" value $\perp$ can be applied as a function and returns $\perp$ via [FA-BOT] (much like the earlier [S-APP-BOT] rule).

As an example, consider the function application $(f\ 4)$ where f is a private function represented as $\langle k \mathrel{?} (\lambda x.e) : \perp\rangle$. The rules [F-APP] and [FA-SPLIT] decompose the application $(f\ 4)$ into two separate applications: $((\lambda x.e)\ 4)$ and $(\perp\ 4)$. The first application evaluates normally via [FA-FUN] to a result, say V, and the second application evaluates to $\perp$ via [FA-BOT], so the result of the call is $\langle k \mathrel{?} V : \perp\rangle$, thus marking the result of the call as private.

The operand of a dereference operation $(\texttt{!}e)$ may also be a faceted value tree. In this case, the rule [F-REF] uses the helper function $\texttt{deref}(\Sigma, V_a, pc)$ to decompose V_a into appropriate addresses, retrieve the corresponding values from the store Σ, and to combine these store values into a new faceted value. As an optimization, any facets in the address V_a that are not consistent with pc are ignored.

In a similar manner, the rule [F-ASSIGN] uses the helper function $\mathit{assign}(\Sigma, pc, V_a, V)$ to decompose V_a into appropriate addresses and to update the store Σ at those locations with V, while ensuring that each update is only visible to appropriate principals that are consistent with pc, to avoid information leaks via implicit flows.

The faceted semantics of I/O operations introduces some additional complexities since it involves communication with external, non-faceted files. Each file f has an associated view $\mathit{view}(f) = \{k_1, \ldots, k_n\}$ describing which observers may see the contents of that file. The following section defines when a computation with program counter label pc is *visible* to a view L, and also interprets L to *project* a faceted value V to a non-faceted value $v = L(V)$. We use these two concepts to map between faceted computations and external non-faceted values in files.

A read operation $\texttt{read}(f)$ may be executed multiple times with different pc labels. Of these multiple executions, only the single execution where pc is visible to $\mathit{view}(f)$ actually reads from the file via [F-READ]; all other executions are no-ops via [F-READ-IGNORE]. The non-faceted value v read from the file is converted to a faceted value $\langle\!\langle\, pc' \mathrel{?} v : \perp \,\rangle\!\rangle$ that is only visible to $\mathit{view}(f)$, where pc' is the program counter representation of that view.

An output $\texttt{write}(f, e)$ behaves in a similar manner, so only one execution writes to the file via the rule [F-WRITE]. This rule uses the projection operation $v = L(V)$ where $L = \mathit{view}(f)$ to project the faceted value V produced by e into a corresponding non-faceted value v that is actually written to the file.

For simplicity, we Church-encode conditional branches as function calls, and so the implicit flows caused by conditional branches are a special case of those caused by function calls and are appropriately handled by the various rules in Figure 4. To provide helpful intuition, however, Figure 5 sketches alternative direct rules for evaluating a conditional test $\texttt{if } e_1 \texttt{ then } e_2 \texttt{ else } e_3$. In particular, if e_1 evaluates to a faceted value $\langle k \mathrel{?} V_H : V_L\rangle$, the if statement is evaluated potentially twice, using facets V_H and V_L as the conditional test by the [F-IF-SPLIT] rule.

3.1 The Projection Property

Recall that a view is a set of principals $L = \{k_1, \ldots, k_n\}$. This view defines what values a particular observer is authorized to see. In particular, an observer with view L sees the private facet $V_{\rm H}$ in a value $\langle k \mathrel{?} V_{\rm H} : V_{\rm L}\rangle$ only when $k \in L$, and sees $V_{\rm L}$ otherwise. Thus, each view L serves as a projection function that maps each faceted value $V \in \mathit{Value}$ into a corresponding non-faceted value

Figure 4: Faceted Evaluation Semantics

Runtime Syntax

$$
\begin{array}{rclcl}
\Sigma & \in & \mathit{Store} & = & (\mathit{Address} \rightarrow_p \mathit{Value}) \cup (\mathit{File} \rightarrow \mathit{Value}^*) \\
\Theta & \in & \mathit{Subst} & = & \mathit{Var} \rightarrow_p \mathit{Value} \\
R & \in & \mathit{RawValue} & ::= & c \mid a \mid (\lambda x.e, \Theta) \mid \bot \\
V & \in & \mathit{Value} & ::= & R \mid \langle k \;?\; V_1 : V_2 \rangle \\
h & \in & \mathit{Branch} & ::= & k \mid \overline{k} \\
pc & \in & \mathit{PC} & = & 2^{\mathit{Branch}}
\end{array}
$$

Evaluation Rules: $\boxed{\Sigma, \Theta, e \Downarrow_{pc} \Sigma', v}$

$$\frac{}{\Sigma, \Theta, c \Downarrow_{pc} \Sigma, c} \quad \text{[F-CONST]}$$

$$\frac{}{\Sigma, \Theta, x \Downarrow_{pc} \Sigma, \Theta(x)} \quad \text{[F-VAR]}$$

$$\frac{}{\Sigma, \Theta, (\lambda x.e) \Downarrow_{pc} \Sigma, (\lambda x.e, \Theta)} \quad \text{[F-FUN]}$$

$$\frac{\Sigma, \Theta, e_1 \Downarrow_{pc} \Sigma_1, V_1 \qquad \Sigma_1, \Theta, e_2 \Downarrow_{pc} \Sigma_2, V_2 \qquad \Sigma_2, (V_1\ V_2) \Downarrow_{pc} \Sigma', V'}{\Sigma, \Theta, (e_1\ e_2) \Downarrow_{pc} \Sigma', V'} \quad \text{[F-APP]}$$

$$\frac{k \notin pc \quad \Sigma, \Theta, e_1 \Downarrow_{pc \cup \{k\}} \Sigma_1, V_1 \qquad \overline{k} \notin pc \quad \Sigma_1, \Theta, e_2 \Downarrow_{pc \cup \{\overline{k}\}} \Sigma_2, V_2}{\Sigma, \Theta, \langle k \;?\; e_1 : e_2 \rangle \Downarrow_{pc} \Sigma_2, \langle\!\langle\, k \;?\; V_1 : V_2 \,\rangle\!\rangle} \quad \text{[F-SPLIT]}$$

$$\frac{k \in pc \qquad \Sigma, \Theta, e_1 \Downarrow_{pc} \Sigma', V}{\Sigma, \Theta, \langle k \;?\; e_1 : e_2 \rangle \Downarrow_{pc} \Sigma', V} \quad \text{[F-LEFT]}$$

$$\frac{\overline{k} \in pc \qquad \Sigma, \Theta, e_2 \Downarrow_{pc} \Sigma', V}{\Sigma, \Theta, \langle k \;?\; e_1 : e_2 \rangle \Downarrow_{pc} \Sigma', V} \quad \text{[F-RIGHT]}$$

$$\frac{}{\Sigma, \Theta, \bot \Downarrow_{pc} \Sigma, \bot} \quad \text{[F-BOT]}$$

$$\frac{\Sigma, \Theta, e \Downarrow_{pc} \Sigma', V' \qquad a \notin dom(\Sigma') \qquad V = \langle\!\langle\, pc \;?\; V' : \bot \,\rangle\!\rangle}{\Sigma, \Theta, (\mathtt{ref}\ e) \Downarrow_{pc} \Sigma'[a := V], a} \quad \text{[F-REF]}$$

$$\frac{\Sigma, \Theta, e \Downarrow_{pc} \Sigma', V \qquad V' = \mathit{deref}(\Sigma', V, pc)}{\Sigma, \Theta, \mathtt{!}e \Downarrow_{pc} \Sigma', V'} \quad \text{[F-DEREF]}$$

$$\frac{\Sigma, \Theta, e_1 \Downarrow_{pc} \Sigma_1, V_1 \qquad \Sigma_1, \Theta, e_2 \Downarrow_{pc} \Sigma_2, V' \qquad \Sigma' = \mathit{assign}(\Sigma_2, pc, V_1, V')}{\Sigma, \Theta, e_1 \mathtt{:=} e_2 \Downarrow_{pc} \Sigma', V'} \quad \text{[F-ASSIGN]}$$

$$\frac{\Sigma(f) = v.w \qquad L = \mathit{view}(f) \qquad pc \text{ visible to } L \qquad pc' = L \cup \{\overline{k} \mid k \notin L\}}{\Sigma, \Theta, \mathtt{read}(f) \Downarrow_{pc} \Sigma[f := w], \langle\!\langle\, pc' \;?\; v : \bot \,\rangle\!\rangle} \quad \text{[F-READ]}$$

$$\frac{pc \text{ not visible to } \mathit{view}(f)}{\Sigma, \Theta, \mathtt{read}(f) \Downarrow_{pc} \Sigma, \bot} \quad \text{[F-READ-IGNORE]}$$

$$\frac{\Sigma, \Theta, e \Downarrow_{pc} \Sigma', V \qquad pc \text{ visible to } \mathit{view}(f) \qquad L = \mathit{view}(f) \qquad v = L(V)}{\Sigma, \Theta, \mathtt{write}(f, e) \Downarrow_{pc} \Sigma'[f := \Sigma'(f).v], V} \quad \text{[F-WRITE]}$$

$$\frac{\Sigma, \Theta, e \Downarrow_{pc} \Sigma', V \qquad pc \text{ not visible to } \mathit{view}(f)}{\Sigma, \Theta, \mathtt{write}(f, e) \Downarrow_{pc} \Sigma', V} \quad \text{[F-WRITE-IGNORE]}$$

Application Rules $\boxed{\Sigma, (V_1\ V_2) \Downarrow_{pc} \Sigma', V'}$

$$\frac{\Sigma, \Theta[x := V], e \Downarrow_{pc} \Sigma', V'}{\Sigma, ((\lambda x.e, \Theta)\ V) \Downarrow_{pc} \Sigma', V'} \quad \text{[FA-FUN]}$$

$$\frac{k \notin pc \quad \Sigma, (V_H\ V_2) \Downarrow_{pc \cup \{k\}} \Sigma_1, V_H' \qquad \overline{k} \notin pc \quad \Sigma_1, (V_L\ V_2) \Downarrow_{pc \cup \{\overline{k}\}} \Sigma', V_L'}{\Sigma, (\langle k \;?\; V_H : V_L \rangle\ V_2) \Downarrow_{pc} \Sigma', \langle\!\langle\, k \;?\; V_H' : V_L' \,\rangle\!\rangle} \quad \text{[FA-SPLIT]}$$

$$\frac{k \in pc \qquad \Sigma, (V_H\ V_2) \Downarrow_{pc} \Sigma', V}{\Sigma, (\langle k \;?\; V_H : V_L \rangle\ V_2) \Downarrow_{pc} \Sigma', V} \quad \text{[FA-LEFT]}$$

$$\frac{\overline{k} \in pc \qquad \Sigma, (V_L\ V_2) \Downarrow_{pc} \Sigma', V}{\Sigma, (\langle k \;?\; V_H : V_L \rangle\ V_2) \Downarrow_{pc} \Sigma', V} \quad \text{[FA-RIGHT]}$$

$$\frac{}{\Sigma, (\bot\ V) \Downarrow_{pc} \Sigma, \bot} \quad \text{[FA-BOT]}$$

Auxiliary Functions

$$
\begin{array}{lcl}
\mathit{deref} : \mathit{Store} \times \mathit{Value} \times \mathit{PC} & \rightarrow & \mathit{Value} \\
\mathit{deref}(\Sigma, a, pc) & = & \Sigma(a) \\
\mathit{deref}(\Sigma, \bot, pc) & = & \bot \\
\mathit{deref}(\Sigma, \langle k \;?\; V_H : V_L \rangle, pc) & = & \begin{cases} \mathit{deref}(\Sigma, V_H) & \text{if } k \in pc \\ \mathit{deref}(\Sigma, V_L) & \text{if } \overline{k} \in pc \\ \langle\!\langle\, k \;?\; \mathit{deref}(\Sigma, V_H) : \mathit{deref}(\Sigma, V_L) \,\rangle\!\rangle & \text{otherwise} \end{cases}
\end{array}
$$

$$
\begin{array}{lcl}
\mathit{assign} : \mathit{Store} \times \mathit{PC} \times \mathit{Value} \times \mathit{Value} & \rightarrow & \mathit{Store} \\
\mathit{assign}(\Sigma, pc, a, V) & = & \Sigma[a := \langle\!\langle\, pc \;?\; V : \Sigma(a) \,\rangle\!\rangle] \\
\mathit{assign}(\Sigma, pc, \bot, V) & = & \Sigma \\
\mathit{assign}(\Sigma, pc, \langle k \;?\; V_H : V_L \rangle, V) & = & \Sigma' \quad \text{where } \Sigma_1 = \mathit{assign}(\Sigma, pc \cup \{k\}, V_H, V) \\
 & & \qquad \text{and } \Sigma' = \mathit{assign}(\Sigma_1, pc \cup \{\overline{k}\}, V_L, V)
\end{array}
$$

Figure 5: Faceted Evaluation Semantics for Derived Encodings

$$\frac{\Sigma, \Theta, e_1 \Downarrow_{pc} \Sigma_1, \texttt{true} \qquad \Sigma_1, \Theta, e_2 \Downarrow_{pc} \Sigma', V}{\Sigma, \Theta, \texttt{if } e_1 \texttt{ then } e_2 \texttt{ else } e_3 \Downarrow_{pc} \Sigma', V} \quad \text{[F-IF-TRUE]}$$

$$\frac{\Sigma, \Theta, e_1 \Downarrow_{pc} \Sigma_1, \texttt{false} \qquad \Sigma_1, \Theta, e_3 \Downarrow_{pc} \Sigma', V}{\Sigma, \Theta, \texttt{if } e_1 \texttt{ then } e_2 \texttt{ else } e_3 \Downarrow_{pc} \Sigma', V} \quad \text{[F-IF-FALSE]}$$

$$\frac{\Sigma, \Theta, e_1 \Downarrow_{pc} \Sigma', \bot}{\Sigma, \Theta, \texttt{if } \bot \texttt{ then } e_2 \texttt{ else } e_3 \Downarrow_{pc} \Sigma', \bot} \quad \text{[F-IF-BOT]}$$

$$\frac{\begin{array}{c} \Sigma, \Theta, e_1 \Downarrow_{pc} \Sigma_1, \langle k \; ? \; V_H : V_L \rangle \\ e_H = \texttt{if } V_H \texttt{ then } e_2 \texttt{ else } e_3 \\ e_L = \texttt{if } V_L \texttt{ then } e_2 \texttt{ else } e_3 \\ \Sigma_1, \Theta, \langle k \; ? \; e_H : e_L \rangle \Downarrow_{pc} \Sigma', V \end{array}}{\Sigma, \Theta, \texttt{if } e_1 \texttt{ then } e_2 \texttt{ else } e_3 \Downarrow_{pc} \Sigma', V} \quad \text{[F-IF-SPLIT]}$$

of the standard semantics:

$$\begin{array}{rcl} L : \mathit{Value} & \rightarrow & \mathit{value} \\ L(\langle k \; ? \; V_1 : V_2 \rangle) & = & \left\{ \begin{array}{ll} L(V_1) & \text{if } k \in L \\ L(V_2) & \text{if } k \notin L \end{array} \right. \\ L(c) & = & c \\ L(a) & = & a \\ L(\bot) & = & \bot \\ L((\lambda x.e, \Theta)) & = & (\lambda x.L(e), L(\Theta)) \end{array}$$

We extend L to also project faceted substitutions $\Theta \in \mathit{Subst}$ and stores $\Sigma \in \mathit{Store}$ into non-faceted substitutions and stores of the standard semantics. A file f is visible only to $\mathit{view}(f)$, and appears empty (ϵ) to all other views.

$$\begin{array}{rcl} L : \mathit{Subst} & \rightarrow & \mathit{subst} \\ L(\Theta) & = & \lambda x.\, L(\Theta(x)) \end{array}$$

$$\begin{array}{rcl} L : \mathit{Store} & \rightarrow & \mathit{store} \\ L(\Sigma) & = & \lambda a.\, L(\Sigma(a)) \\ & \cup & \lambda f. \left\{ \begin{array}{ll} \Sigma(f) & \text{if } L = \mathit{view}(f) \\ \epsilon & \text{otherwise} \end{array} \right. \end{array}$$

We also use a view L to operate on expressions, where this operation eliminates faceted expressions and also performs access control on I/O operations by eliminating accesses to files that are not authorized under that view:

$$\begin{array}{rcl} L : \mathit{Expr} \text{ (with facets)} & \rightarrow & \mathit{Expr} \text{ (without facets)} \\ L(\langle k \; ? \; e_1 : e_2 \rangle) & = & \left\{ \begin{array}{ll} L(e_1) & \text{if } k \in L \\ L(e_2) & \text{if } k \notin L \end{array} \right. \\ L(\texttt{read}(f)) & = & \left\{ \begin{array}{ll} \texttt{read}(f) & \text{if } L = \mathit{view}(f) \\ \bot & \text{otherwise} \end{array} \right. \\ L(\texttt{write}(f, e)) & = & \left\{ \begin{array}{ll} \texttt{write}(f, L(e)) & \text{if } L = \mathit{view}(f) \\ L(e) & \text{otherwise} \end{array} \right. \\ L(\dots) & = & \text{compatible closure} \end{array}$$

Thus, views naturally serve as a projection from each domain of the faceted semantics into a corresponding domain of the standard semantics. We now use these views-as-projections to formalize the relationship between these two semantics.

A computation with program counter label pc is considered *visible to a view* L only when the principals mentioned in pc are consistent with L, in the sense that:

$$\begin{array}{l} \forall k \in pc, k \in L \\ \forall \overline{k} \in pc, k \notin L \end{array}$$

We first show that the operation $\langle\!\langle\, pc \; ? \; V_1 : V_2 \,\rangle\!\rangle$ has the expected behavior, in that from the perspective of a view L, it appears to return V_1 only when pc is visible to L, and appears to return V_2 otherwise.

Lemma 1. *If* $V = \langle\!\langle\, pc \; ? \; V_1 : V_2 \,\rangle\!\rangle$ *then*

$$L(V) = \left\{ \begin{array}{ll} V_1 & \textit{if pc is visible to } L \\ V_2 & \textit{otherwise} \end{array} \right.$$

We next show that the auxiliary functions deref and assign exhibit the expected behavior when projected under a view L. First, if $\mathit{deref}(\Sigma, V)$ returns V', then the projected result $L(V')$ is a non-faceted value that is identical to first projecting the store $L(\Sigma)$, projecting the target address $L(V)$, and then dereferencing the projected store at the projected address $L(\Sigma)(L(V))$.

Lemma 2. *If* $V' = \mathit{deref}(\Sigma, V, pc)$ *then* $L(V') = L(\Sigma)(L(V))$.

Next, from the perspective of any view L, if pc is visible to L then the operation $\mathit{assign}(\Sigma, pc, V_1, V_2)$ appears to update the address $L(V_1)$ appropriately. Conversely, if pc is not visible to L, then this operation has no observable effect.

Lemma 3. *If* $\Sigma' = \mathit{assign}(\Sigma, pc, V_1, V_2)$ *then*

$$L(\Sigma') = \left\{ \begin{array}{ll} L(\Sigma)[L(V_1) := L(V_2)] & \textit{if pc is visible to } L \\ L(\Sigma) & \textit{otherwise} \end{array} \right.$$

A consequence of Lemma 3 is that evaluation with a pc that is not visible to a view L produces no observable change in the store.

Lemma 4. *Suppose pc is not visible to L and that*

$$\Sigma, \Theta, e \Downarrow_{pc} \Sigma', V$$

Then $L(\Sigma) = L(\Sigma')$.

Proof. In the auxiliary material for this paper.

We now prove our central projection theorem showing that an evaluation under the faceted semantics is equivalent to many evaluations under the standard semantics, one for each possible view for which pc is visible.

Theorem 1 (Projection Theorem)**.** *Suppose*

$$\Sigma, \Theta, e \Downarrow_{pc} \Sigma', V$$

Then for any view L for which pc is visible,

$$L(\Sigma), L(\Theta), L(e) \downarrow L(\Sigma'), L(V)$$

Proof. In the auxiliary material for this paper.

Consequently, if pc is initially empty, then faceted evaluation simulates 2^n standard evaluations, where n is the number of principals.

3.2 Termination-Insensitive Non-Interference

The projection property enables a very simple proof of non-interference; it already captures the idea that information from one view does not leak into an incompatible view, since the projected computations are independent. To formalize this argument, we start by defining two faceted values to be *L-equivalent* if they have identical standard values for view L. This notion of L-equivalence naturally extends to substitutions ($\Theta_1 \sim_L \Theta_2$) and stores ($\Sigma_1 \sim_L \Sigma_2$):

$$\begin{array}{lcl} (V_1 \sim_L V_2) & \text{iff} & L(V_1) = L(V_2) \\ (\Theta_1 \sim_L \Theta_2) & \text{iff} & L(\Theta_1) = L(\Theta_2) \\ (\Sigma_1 \sim_L \Sigma_2) & \text{iff} & L(\Sigma_1) = L(\Sigma_2) \end{array}$$

Together with the Projection Theorem, this notion of L-equivalence enables us to conveniently state and prove the standard correctness property of termination-insensitive non-interference.

Figure 6: Efficient Construction of Faceted Values

$$
\begin{array}{lcl}
\langle\!\langle \bullet ? \bullet : \bullet \rangle\!\rangle : \mathit{PC} \times \mathit{Value} \times \mathit{Value} & \rightarrow & \mathit{Value} \\
\langle\!\langle\ \emptyset\ ?\ V_n : V_o \rangle\!\rangle & = & V_n \\
\\
\langle\!\langle \{k\} \cup \mathit{rest}\ ?\ \langle k ? V_a : V_b \rangle : \langle k ? V_c : V_d \rangle \rangle\!\rangle & = & \langle\ k\ ?\ \langle\!\langle \mathit{rest} ? V_a : V_c \rangle\!\rangle : V_d \ \rangle \\
\langle\!\langle \{\overline{k}\} \cup \mathit{rest}\ ?\ \langle k ? V_a : V_b \rangle : \langle k ? V_c : V_d \rangle \rangle\!\rangle & = & \langle\ k\ ?\ V_c : \langle\!\langle \mathit{rest} ? V_b : V_d \rangle\!\rangle \ \rangle \\
\\
\langle\!\langle\ pc\ ?\ \langle k ? V_a : V_b \rangle : \langle k ? V_c : V_d \rangle \rangle\!\rangle & = & \langle\ k\ ?\ \langle\!\langle pc ? V_a : V_c \rangle\!\rangle : \langle\!\langle pc ? V_b : V_d \rangle\!\rangle \ \rangle \quad \text{where } k < \mathit{head}(pc) \\
\langle\!\langle \{k\} \cup \mathit{rest}\ ?\ \langle k ? V_a : V_b \rangle : V_o \rangle\!\rangle & = & \langle\ k\ ?\ \langle\!\langle \mathit{rest} ? V_a : V_o \rangle\!\rangle : V_o \ \rangle \quad \text{where } k < \mathit{head}(V_o) \\
\langle\!\langle \{\overline{k}\} \cup \mathit{rest}\ ?\ \langle k ? V_a : V_b \rangle : V_o \rangle\!\rangle & = & \langle\ k\ ?\ V_o : \langle\!\langle \mathit{rest} ? V_b : V_o \rangle\!\rangle \ \rangle \quad \text{where } k < \mathit{head}(V_o) \\
\langle\!\langle \{k\} \cup \mathit{rest}\ ?\ V_n : \langle k ? V_a : V_b \rangle \rangle\!\rangle & = & \langle\ k\ ?\ \langle\!\langle \mathit{rest} ? V_n : V_a \rangle\!\rangle : V_b \ \rangle \quad \text{where } k < \mathit{head}(V_n) \\
\langle\!\langle \{\overline{k}\} \cup \mathit{rest}\ ?\ V_n : \langle k ? V_a : V_b \rangle \rangle\!\rangle & = & \langle\ k\ ?\ V_a : \langle\!\langle \mathit{rest} ? V_n : V_b \rangle\!\rangle \ \rangle \quad \text{where } k < \mathit{head}(V_n) \\
\\
\langle\!\langle \{k\} \cup \mathit{rest}\ ?\ V_n : V_o \rangle\!\rangle & = & \langle\ k\ ?\ \langle\!\langle \mathit{rest} ? V_n : V_o \rangle\!\rangle : V_o \ \rangle \quad \text{where } k < \mathit{head}(V_n) \text{ and } k < \mathit{head}(V_o) \\
\langle\!\langle \{\overline{k}\} \cup \mathit{rest}\ ?\ V_n : V_o \rangle\!\rangle & = & \langle\ k\ ?\ V_o : \langle\!\langle \mathit{rest} ? V_n : V_o \rangle\!\rangle \ \rangle \quad \text{where } k < \mathit{head}(V_n) \text{ and } k < \mathit{head}(V_o) \\
\langle\!\langle\ pc\ ?\ \langle k ? V_a : V_b \rangle : V_o \rangle\!\rangle & = & \langle\ k\ ?\ \langle\!\langle pc ? V_a : V_o \rangle\!\rangle : \langle\!\langle pc ? V_b : V_o \rangle\!\rangle \ \rangle \quad \text{where } k < \mathit{head}(V_o) \text{ and } k < \mathit{head}(pc) \\
\langle\!\langle\ pc\ ?\ V_n : \langle k ? V_a : V_b \rangle \rangle\!\rangle & = & \langle\ k\ ?\ \langle\!\langle pc ? V_n : V_a \rangle\!\rangle : \langle\!\langle pc ? V_n : V_b \rangle\!\rangle \ \rangle \quad \text{where } k < \mathit{head}(V_n) \text{ and } k < \mathit{head}(pc)
\end{array}
$$

Theorem 2 (Termination-Insensitive Non-Interference). *Let L be any view. Suppose*

$$
\begin{array}{ll}
\Sigma_1 \sim_L \Sigma_2 & \Sigma_1, \Theta_1, e \Downarrow_\emptyset \Sigma'_1, V_1 \\
\Theta_1 \sim_L \Theta_2 & \Sigma_2, \Theta_2, e \Downarrow_\emptyset \Sigma'_2, V_2
\end{array}
$$

Then:

$$
\Sigma'_1 \sim_L \Sigma'_2 \qquad V_1 \sim_L V_2
$$

Proof. By the Projection Theorem:

$$
\begin{array}{l}
L(\Sigma_1), L(\Theta_1), L(e) \downarrow L(\Sigma'_1), L(V_1) \\
L(\Sigma_2), L(\Theta_2), L(e) \downarrow L(\Sigma'_2), L(V_2)
\end{array}
$$

The L-equivalence assumptions imply that $L(\Theta_1) = L(\Theta_2)$ and $L(\Sigma_1) = L(\Sigma_2)$. Hence $L(\Sigma'_1) = L(\Sigma'_2)$ and $L(V_1) = L(V_2)$ since the standard semantics is deterministic. □

This theorem can be generalized to computations with arbitrary program counter labels, but then non-interference holds only for views for which that pc is visible.

3.3 Efficient Construction of Faceted Values

The definition of the operation $\langle\!\langle\, pc ? V_1 : V_2 \,\rangle\!\rangle$ presented above is optimized for clarity, but may result in a suboptimal representation for faceted values. For instance, the operation $\langle\!\langle\, \{k\} ? \langle k ? 1 : 0 \rangle : 2 \,\rangle\!\rangle$ returns the faceted value tree $\langle k ? \langle k ? 1 : 0 \rangle : 2 \rangle$ containing a dead facet 0 that is not visible in any view. We now present an optimized version of this operation that avoids introducing dead facets.

The essential idea is to introduce a fixed total ordering on principals and to ensure that in any faceted value tree, the path from the root to any leaf only mentions principals in a strictly increasing order. In order to maintain this ordering, we introduce a *head* function that returns the lowest label in a value or program counter, or a result ∞ that is considered higher than any label.

$$
\begin{array}{rcl}
\mathit{head} : \mathit{Value} & \rightarrow & \mathit{Label} \cup \{\infty\} \\
\mathit{head}(\langle k ? V_1 : V_2 \rangle) & = & k \\
\mathit{head}(R) & = & \infty
\end{array}
$$

$$
\begin{array}{rcll}
\mathit{head} : \mathit{PC} & \rightarrow & \mathit{Label} \cup \{\infty\} & \\
\mathit{head}(\{k\} \cup \mathit{rest}) & = & k & \text{if } \forall k' \text{ or } \overline{k'} \in \mathit{rest}.\ k < k' \\
\mathit{head}(\{\overline{k}\} \cup \mathit{rest}) & = & k & \text{if } \forall k' \text{ or } \overline{k'} \in \mathit{rest}.\ k < k' \\
\mathit{head}(\{\}) & = & \infty &
\end{array}
$$

Figure 6 redefines the facet-construction operation to build values respecting the ordering of labels. The definition is verbose but straightforward; it performs a case analysis to identify the smallest possible label k to put at the root of the newly created value. The revised definition still satisfies the specification provided by Lemma 1.

4. Comparison to Prior Semantics

Prior work presented the *no-sensitive-upgrade* (NSU) semantics [39, 5] and the *permissive-upgrade* (PU) semantics [6] for dynamic information flow. In this section, we adapt both of these semantics to our notation to illustrate how faceted evaluation extends both of these prior techniques. For clarity, in this section we assume that there is only a single principal k and omit I/O operations, since the two prior semantics were formalized under these assumptions. Finally, we use the optimized facet-construction operation from Figure 6 in order to avoid reasoning about dead facets.

4.1 Comparison to No-Sensitive-Upgrade Semantics

We formalize the NSU semantics via the evaluation relation

$$
\Sigma, \Theta, e \Downarrow_{pc} \Sigma', V
$$

defined by the [NSU-*] rules in Figure 7. These rules are somewhat analogous to the faceted evaluation rules of Figure 4, but with some noticeable limitations and restrictions. In particular, the NSU semantics marks each raw value R as being either public or private:

$$
\begin{array}{rcll}
V & ::= & R & \text{public values} \\
& | & \langle k ? R : \bot \rangle & \text{private values}
\end{array}
$$

The NSU semantics cannot record any public facet other than $\bot$. The faceted value $\langle k ? R : \bot \rangle$ is traditionally written simply as R^k in prior semantics, denoting that R is private to principal k, with no representation for a corresponding public facet. This restriction on values means that the NSU semantics never needs to split the computation in the manner performed by the earlier [F-SPLIT] and [FA-SPLIT] rules. Instead, applications of a private closure $\langle k ? (\lambda x.e, \Theta') : \bot \rangle$ extends the program counter pc with the label k during the call, reflecting that this computation is dependent on k-private data. Thus, under the NSU semantics, the program counter label is simply a set of principals, and never contains negated principals $\overline{k}$.

$$
pc \in PC = 2^{\mathit{Label}}
$$

After the callee returns a result V, the following operation $\langle k \rangle^{pc} V$ creates a faceted value semantically equivalent to $\langle k ? V : \bot \rangle$, with

Figure 7: No Sensitive Upgrade Semantics

NSU Evaluation Rules: $\boxed{\Sigma, \Theta, e \Downarrow_{pc} \Sigma', V}$

$$\frac{}{\Sigma, \Theta, c \Downarrow_{pc} \Sigma, c} \quad \text{[NSU-CONST]}$$

$$\frac{}{\Sigma, \Theta, x \Downarrow_{pc} \Sigma, \Theta(x)} \quad \text{[NSU-VAR]}$$

$$\frac{}{\Sigma, \Theta, (\lambda x.e) \Downarrow_{pc} \Sigma, (\lambda x.e, \Theta)} \quad \text{[NSU-FUN]}$$

$$\frac{}{\Sigma, \Theta, \bot \Downarrow_{pc} \Sigma, \bot} \quad \text{[NSU-BOT]}$$

$$\frac{\Sigma, \Theta, e \Downarrow_{pc\cup\{k\}} \Sigma', V}{\Sigma, \Theta, \langle k \mathbin{?} e : \bot\rangle \Downarrow_{pc} \Sigma', \langle k\rangle^{pc} V} \quad \text{[NSU-LABEL]}$$

$$\frac{\begin{array}{c}\Sigma, \Theta, e_1 \Downarrow_{pc} \Sigma_1, (\lambda x.e, \Theta') \\ \Sigma_1, \Theta, e_2 \Downarrow_{pc} \Sigma_2, V' \\ \Sigma, \Theta'[x := V'], e \Downarrow_{pc} \Sigma', V\end{array}}{\Sigma, \Theta, (e_1\ e_2) \Downarrow_{pc} \Sigma', V} \quad \text{[NSU-APP]}$$

$$\frac{\begin{array}{c}\Sigma, \Theta, e_1 \Downarrow_{pc} \Sigma_1, \bot \\ \Sigma_1, \Theta, e_2 \Downarrow_{pc} \Sigma_2, V'\end{array}}{\Sigma, \Theta, (e_1\ e_2) \Downarrow_{pc} \Sigma', \bot} \quad \text{[NSU-APP-BOT]}$$

$$\frac{\begin{array}{c}\Sigma, \Theta, e_1 \Downarrow_{pc} \Sigma_1, \langle k \mathbin{?} (\lambda x.e, \Theta') : \bot\rangle \\ \Sigma_1, \Theta, e_2 \Downarrow_{pc} \Sigma_2, V' \\ \Sigma, \Theta'[x := V'], e \Downarrow_{pc\cup\{k\}} \Sigma', V\end{array}}{\Sigma, \Theta, (e_1\ e_2) \Downarrow_{pc} \Sigma', \langle k\rangle^{pc} V} \quad \text{[NSU-APP-K]}$$

$$\frac{\begin{array}{c}\Sigma, \Theta, e \Downarrow_{pc} \Sigma', V' \\ a \notin dom(\Sigma') \\ V = \langle\!\langle\, pc \mathbin{?} V' : \bot \,\rangle\!\rangle\end{array}}{\Sigma, \Theta, (\texttt{ref}\ e) \Downarrow_{pc} \Sigma'[a := V], a} \quad \text{[NSU-REF]}$$

$$\frac{\begin{array}{c}\Sigma, \Theta, e \Downarrow_{pc} \Sigma', V_a \\ V = deref(\Sigma', V_a, pc)\end{array}}{\Sigma, \Theta, !e \Downarrow_{pc} \Sigma', V} \quad \text{[NSU-DEREF]}$$

$$\frac{\begin{array}{c}\Sigma, \Theta, e_1 \Downarrow_{pc} \Sigma_1, \bot \\ \Sigma_1, \Theta, e_2 \Downarrow_{pc} \Sigma_2, V\end{array}}{\Sigma, \Theta, e_1 := e_2 \Downarrow_{pc} \Sigma_2, V} \quad \text{[NSU-ASSIGN-BOT]}$$

$$\frac{\begin{array}{c}\Sigma, \Theta, e_1 \Downarrow_{pc} \Sigma_1, a \\ \Sigma_1, \Theta, e_2 \Downarrow_{pc} \Sigma', V \\ pc = \texttt{label}(\Sigma'(a)) \\ V' = \langle\!\langle\, pc \mathbin{?} V : \bot \,\rangle\!\rangle\end{array}}{\Sigma, \Theta, e_1 := e_2 \Downarrow_{pc} \Sigma'[a := V'], V} \quad \text{[NSU-ASSIGN]}$$

$$\frac{\begin{array}{c}\Sigma, \theta, e_1 \Downarrow_{pc} \Sigma_1, \langle k \mathbin{?} a : \bot\rangle \\ \Sigma_1, \Theta, e_2 \Downarrow_{pc} \Sigma', V \\ pc \cup \{k\} \subseteq label(\Sigma'(a)) \\ V' = \langle\!\langle\, pc \mathbin{?} V : \bot \,\rangle\!\rangle\end{array}}{\Sigma, \Theta, e_1 := e_2 \Downarrow_{pc} \Sigma'[a := V'], V} \quad \text{[NSU-ASSIGN-K]}$$

Figure 8: Permissive Upgrade Semantics (extends Figure 7)

PU Evaluation Rules: $\boxed{\Sigma, \Theta, e \Downarrow_{pc} \Sigma', V}$

$$\frac{\begin{array}{c}\Sigma, \Theta, e_1 \Downarrow_{pc} \Sigma_1, a \\ \Sigma_1, \Theta, e_2 \Downarrow_{pc} \Sigma', V \\ V' = \langle\!\langle\, pc \mathbin{?} V : * \,\rangle\!\rangle\end{array}}{\Sigma, \Theta, e_1 := e_2 \Downarrow_{pc} \Sigma'[a := V'], V} \quad \text{[PU-ASSIGN]}$$

$$\frac{\begin{array}{c}\Sigma, \theta, e_1 \Downarrow_{pc} \Sigma_1, \langle k \mathbin{?} a : \bot\rangle \\ \Sigma_1, \Theta, e_2 \Downarrow_{pc} \Sigma', V \\ V' = \langle\!\langle\, pc \mathbin{?} V : * \,\rangle\!\rangle\end{array}}{\Sigma, \Theta, e_1 := e_2 \Downarrow_{pc} \Sigma'[a := V'], V} \quad \text{[PU-ASSIGN-K]}$$

the optimization that the label k is unnecessary if it is subsumed by pc or if it is already in V:

$$\begin{array}{lcl}\langle k\rangle^{\{k\}}\ V & = & V \\ \langle k\rangle^{\{\}}\ R & = & \langle k \mathbin{?} R : \bot\rangle \\ \langle k\rangle^{pc}\ \langle k \mathbin{?} R : \bot\rangle & = & \langle k \mathbin{?} R : \bot\rangle\end{array}$$

(This optimization corresponds to the [FA-LEFT] and [FA-RIGHT] rules of the faceted semantics.)

In order to preserve the NSU restriction on values, the NSU semantics needs to carefully restrict assignment statements. Essentially, the NSU evaluation rules for assignment statements halt execution in exactly those situations where the faceted semantics would introduce a non-trivial public facet. These rules use the following function to extract the principals in a value:

$$\begin{array}{lcl}\texttt{label} : \mathit{Value} & \rightarrow & PC \\ \texttt{label}(\langle k \mathbin{?} R : \bot\rangle) & = & \{k\} \\ \texttt{label}(R) & = & \emptyset\end{array}$$

The rule [NSU-ASSIGN] checks that pc is equal to the label on the original value $\Sigma'(a)$ of the target location a. If this condition holds, then the value $\langle\!\langle\, pc \mathbin{?} V : \bot \,\rangle\!\rangle$ stored by [NSU-ASSIGN] is actually equal to the value $\langle\!\langle\, pc \mathbin{?} V : \Sigma'(a) \,\rangle\!\rangle$ that the faceted semantics would store. Thus, this no-sensitive-upgrade check detects situations where the NSU semantics can avoid information leaks without introducing non-$\bot$ public facets. The rule [NSU-ASSIGN-K] handles assignments where the target address is private $\langle k \mathbin{?} a : \bot\rangle$ in a similar manner to [NSU-ASSIGN].

Because of these no-sensitive-upgrade checks, the NSU semantics will get stuck at precisely the points where the faceted value semantics will create non-$\bot$ public facets. An example of this stuck execution is shown in the *NSU* column of Figure 1. When the value for `y` is updated in a context dependent on the confidential value of `x`, execution gets stuck to prevent loss of information.

If the NSU semantics runs to completion on a given program, then the faceted semantics will produce the same results.

Theorem 3 (Faceted evaluation generalizes NSU evaluation)**.** *If* $\Sigma, \Theta, e \Downarrow_{pc} \Sigma', V$ *then* $\Sigma, \Theta, e \Downarrow\!\!\Downarrow_{pc} \Sigma', V$.

Proof. In the auxiliary material for this paper.

4.2 Permissive Upgrades

The limitations of the NSU semantics motivated the development of a more expressive *permissive upgrade* (PU) semantics, which reduced (but did not eliminate) stuck executions [6]. Essentially, the PU semantics works by tracking *partially leaked* data, which

Figure 9: Declassification of Faceted Values

Declassification Rule

$$\frac{\Sigma, \Theta, e \Downarrow_{pc} \Sigma', V \qquad \mathtt{U}^P \notin pc \qquad V' = \mathtt{downgrade}_P(V)}{\Sigma, \Theta, \mathtt{declassify}_P\ e \Downarrow_{pc} \Sigma', V'} \quad \text{[F-DECLASSIFY]}$$

Downgrade Function

$$\begin{array}{lcl}
\mathtt{downgrade}_P : \mathit{Value} & \rightarrow & \mathit{Value} \\
\mathtt{downgrade}_P(R) & = & R \\
\mathtt{downgrade}_P(\langle \mathtt{S}^P \ ?\ V_1 : V_2 \rangle) & = & \langle \mathtt{U}^P \ ?\ \langle \mathtt{S}^P \ ?\ V_1 : V_2 \rangle : V_1 \rangle \\
\mathtt{downgrade}_P(\langle \mathtt{U}^P \ ?\ V_1 : V_2 \rangle) & = & \langle\!\langle \mathtt{U}^P \ ?\ V_1 : \mathtt{downgrade}_P(V_2) \rangle\!\rangle \\
\mathtt{downgrade}_P(\langle l \ ?\ V_1 : V_2 \rangle) & = & \\
 & & \langle l \ ?\ \mathtt{downgrade}_P(V_1) : \mathtt{downgrade}_P(V_2) \rangle
\end{array}$$

we represent here as a faceted value $\langle k \ ?\ R : * \rangle$.[3]

$$\begin{array}{rclll}
V & ::= & R & & \text{public values} \\
 & | & \langle k \ ?\ R : \bot \rangle & & \text{private values} \\
 & | & \langle k \ ?\ R : * \rangle & & \text{partially leaked values}
\end{array}$$

Since the public facet is not actually stored, the PU semantics can never use partially leaked values in situations where the public facet is needed, and so partially leaked values cannot be assigned, invoked, or used as a conditional test. In particular, PU computations never need to "split" executions, and so avoid the complexities and expressiveness of faceted evaluation.

We formalize the PU semantics by extending the NSU evaluation relation $\Sigma, \Theta, e \Downarrow_{pc} \Sigma', V$ with the two additional rules shown in Figure 8. The new assignment rules leverage faceted values to handle the complexity involved in tracking partially leaked data. Specifically, if values are stored to a public reference cell in a high-security context, the data is partially leaked, and a new faceted value with a non-$\bot$ public facet is created.

Critically, there are no rules for applying partially leaked functions or assigning to partially leaked addresses, and consequently execution gets stuck at these points, corresponding to the explicit checks for partially leaked labels in the original PU semantics [6].

Faceted values subsume the permissive upgrade strategy. The permissive upgrade strategy gets stuck at the points where a faceted value with a non-$\bot$ facet is either applied or used in assignment.

Theorem 4 (Faceted evaluation generalizes PU evaluation)**.** *If* $\Sigma, \Theta, e \Downarrow_{pc} \Sigma', V$, *then* $\Sigma, \Theta, e \Downarrow_{pc} \Sigma', V$.

Proof. In the auxiliary material for this paper.

Again, the converse to this theorem does not hold, since Figure 1 shows an execution that gets stuck under the permissive upgrade semantics but not under the faceted semantics.

5. Facet Declassification

For many real systems, non-interference is too strong of a restriction. Often a certain amount of information leakage is acceptable, and even desirable. Password checking is the canonical example; while one bit of information about the password may leak, the system may still be deemed secure. *Declassification* is this process of making confidential data public in a controlled manner.

[3] In [6], these partially leaked values were represented as R^P, with a superscript P denoting partially leaked.

In the context of multi-process execution [13], declassification is rather challenging. The L and H processes must be coordinated in a careful manner, with all of the attendant problems involved in sharing data between multiple processes. Additionally, allowing declassification may re-introduce timing channels and the termination channel, losing major benefits of the multi-execution approach. In contrast, faceted evaluation makes declassification fairly straightforward. The public and confidential facets are tied together in a single faceted value during execution, so declassification simply requires restructuring the faceted value to migrate information from one facet to another.

Providing a declassification operation with no restrictions invalidates most security guarantees. For instance, an attacker could declassify a user's password, or overwrite data that would be declassified later by legitimate code. In this manner, valid code intending to declassify the result of a password check might instead be duped into declassifying the password itself.

To provide more reliable security guarantees in the presence of declassification with faceted values, we show how to perform *robust declassification* [40], which guarantees that an active attacker, able to introduce code, is no more powerful than a passive attacker, who can only observe the results. (We use robust declassification as an illustrative example, but faceted values could also support other approaches to declassification.)

Robust declassification depends on a notion of *integrity*, which in turn requires that we distinguish between the terms *label* and *principal*. In particular, we introduce a separate notion of principals (P) into our formalism. A label k then marks data as being secret ($\mathtt{S}^P$) or as being low-integrity or untrusted ($\mathtt{U}^P$), both from the perspective of a particular principal P [4].

$$\begin{array}{lllll}
P & \in & \mathit{Principal} & & \\
k & \in & \mathit{Label} & ::= \ \mathtt{S}^P & \text{secret to } P \\
 & & & \ \ \ |\ \ \mathtt{U}^P & \text{untrusted by } P
\end{array}$$

In the context of a principal P, we now have four possible views or projections of a computation, ordered by the subset relation.

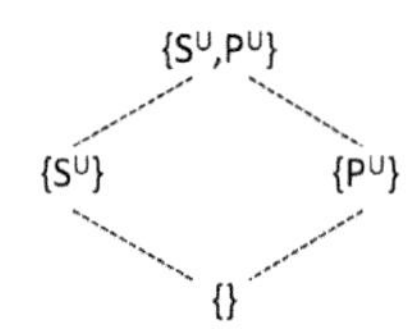

To help reason about multiple principals, we introduce the notation L_P to abbreviate $L \cap \{\mathtt{S}^P, \mathtt{U}^P\}$, so that L_P is one of the four views from the above combined confidentiality/integrity lattice. Note that in the absence of declassification, the projection theorem guarantees that each of these views of the computation are independent; there is no way for values produced in one view's computation to influence another view's computation.

We introduce an additional expression form $\mathtt{declassify}_P\ e$ for declassifying values with respect to a principal P. The rule [F-DECLASSIFY] in Figure 9 performs the appropriate robust declassification. Declassification cannot be performed by arbitrary unauthorized code, or else attackers could declassify all confidential data. Moreover, it is insufficient to allow code "owned" by P to perform declassification, since attackers could leverage that code to declassify data on their behalf. Hence, the rule [F-DECLASSIFY] checks that the control path to this declassification operation has not been influenced by untrusted data, via the check $\mathtt{U}^P \notin pc$.

Robust declassification allows data to move from the $\{\mathtt{S}^P\}$ view to the $\{\}$ view, but never from the $\{\mathtt{S}^P, \mathtt{U}^P\}$ view to the $\{\mathtt{U}^P\}$ view.

[4] This security lattice could be further refined to indicate which other principal was distrusted by P, which would permit more fine-grained decisions.

That is, secret data can be declassified only if it is trusted. The $\texttt{downgrade}_P$ function shown in Figure 9 performs the appropriate manipulation to declassify values. The following lemma clarifies that this function migrates values from the trusted secret view $\{\mathtt{S}^P\}$ to the trusted public view $\{\}$, but not into any other view.

Lemma 5. *For any value V and view L:*

$$L(\texttt{downgrade}_P(V)) = \begin{cases} L(V) & \text{if } L_P \neq \{\} \\ L'(V) & \text{if } L_P = \{\}, \text{ where } L' = L \cup \{\mathtt{S}^P\} \end{cases}$$

Proof. In the auxiliary material for this paper.

In the presence of declassification, the projection theorem does not hold for the public trusted view $\{\}$ since that view's computation may be influenced by declassified data. However, the projection theorem still holds for other views. To prove this relaxed version of the projection theorem, we extend the standard semantics to treat declassification as the identity operation:

$$\text{[S-DECLASSIFY]} \quad \frac{\sigma, \theta, e \downarrow \sigma', V}{\sigma, \theta, \texttt{declassify}_P\ e \downarrow \sigma', V}$$

Theorem 5 (Projection Theorem with Declassification). *Suppose*

$$\Sigma, \Theta, e \Downarrow_{pc} \Sigma', V$$

For any view L for which pc is visible, and where $L_P \neq \{\}$ for each P used in a declassification operation, we have:

$$L(\Sigma), L(\Theta), L(e) \downarrow L(\Sigma'), L(V)$$

Proof. In the auxiliary material for this paper.

As a result, non-interference also holds for these same views.

Theorem 6 (Termination Insensitive Non-Interference with Declassification). *Suppose $L_P \neq \{\}$ for each P used in a declassification operation and*

$$\begin{array}{ll} \Sigma_1 \sim_L \Sigma_2 & \Sigma_1, \Theta_1, e \Downarrow_\emptyset \Sigma_1', V_1 \\ \Theta_1 \sim_L \Theta_2 & \Sigma_2, \Theta_2, e \Downarrow_\emptyset \Sigma_2', V_2 \end{array}$$

Then:

$$\begin{array}{ll} \Sigma_1' \sim_L \Sigma_2' & V_1 \sim_L V_2 \end{array}$$

Proof. Follows from Theorem 5 via a proof similar to Theorem 2.

6. JavaScript Implementation in Firefox

We incorporate our ideas for faceted evaluation into Firefox through the Narcissus [15] JavaScript engine and the Zaphod [26] Firefox plugin. The ZaphodFacets implementation [4] extends the faceted semantics to handle the additional complexities of JavaScript. Exceptions are particularly tricky, and we halt execution if an exception may leak information.

We added two new primitives to the language. The `makePrivate` function turns a value into a faceted value with a public facet of `undefined` [5]. This approach allows developers to specify a different public value through the JavaScript idiom for specifying default values. The following code sets `x` to a faceted value of $\langle k \,?\, 42 : 0 \rangle$. The high value of x is set to 42, since `(42 || 0) === 42`; the low value will be 0, since `(undefined || 0) === 0`.

```
var x = makePrivate(42) || 0;
```

The second primitive is a `getPublic` function that extracts the public value of its input. For example, with the above code defining `x`, `getPublic(x)` would return `0`. Generally, the browser's security policy should use these two functions (or variants) on all input/output boundaries of the system in order to appropriately label data as it comes in and to appropriately monitor data as it goes out.

[5] A string specifying the principal can be given as the second argument if multiple principals are required.

To track information flow through the Document Object Model (DOM), our implementation uses the `dom.js` DOM implementation written in JavaScript [17], to preventing the attacker from sanitizing data by writing it to the DOM and later rereading it. Our implementation is available online with some examples [4], including the code from Figure 1.

6.1 Cross-Site Scripting (XSS) Example

To illustrate how our controls can be useful for enforcing practical defenses, we consider an example of a webpage with an XSS vulnerability. Our controls do not prevent XSS attacks. Rather, they provide an additional layer of defense, reducing an attack's power.

We specify a simple policy that the value of all password elements should be treated as confidential. Furthermore, any attempts to load files from a different origin should use the public facet; the server hosting the website, however, should see the true value.

In our example, the web developer is making use of a library for hashing passwords on the client side. The library is benign, but an attacker uses an XSS vulnerability in the page to wrap the hashing library and export the password to `evil.com`, a site under the attacker's control. The injected code is given below:

```
var oldHex = hex_md5;
hex_md5 = function(secret) {
  var baseURL = "http://evil.com/";
  var img = document.getElementById("spock");
  var title1 = document.getElementById("title1");
  title1.setAttribute("class", secret);
  var newVal = document.getElementsByTagName("h1")[0]
        .getAttribute("class");
  img.setAttribute("src", baseURL + newVal + ".jpg");
  return oldHex(secret);
}
```

The attack attempts to leak the password by loading an image from `evil.com`, incorporating the password into the name of the requested image. However, in an attempt to evade our controls, it first writes the password to the `class` attribute of the `title1` element and then rereads it from the first `h1` element. Without knowledge of the DOM structure of the page, it is not possible to know whether this code leaks information. However, with dom.js we persist the different facets of `secret` to the DOM so that no security information is lost. While the page can only render a single facet, it is critical that we maintain other views of the document.

With this example, `evil.com` sees only the public facet of `secret`, not the true password. Trusted same-origin sources *do* see the true value, and therefore work correctly with the page.

While our example policy is far from complete, we use it to illustrate how our mechanism can enforce different information flow policies. A richer policy could specify a variety of fields and potential output channels. Furthermore, we imagine that browsers would wish to allow web developers to specify application-specific sensitive fields, such as credit card numbers, and allow users to protect information that they considered confidential (for instance, restricting the release of geolocation information).

6.2 Performance Results

Our approach is similar to Devriese and Piessens's work on secure multi-execution [13]. To understand the performance tradeoff between these two approaches we also implemented both sequential and concurrent versions of secure multi-execution in Narcissus, and compared their performance to faceted execution.

Our tests were performed on a MacBook Pro running OS X version 10.6.8. The machine had a 2.3 GHz Intel Core i7 processor with 4 cores and 8 GB of memory. For our benchmark, we used

Figure 10: Faceted Evaluation vs. Secure Multi-Execution

	Times in ms		
	Secure multi-execution		Faceted
# principals	sequential	concurrent	execution
0	273,774	283,450	310,561
1	513,561	283,503	348,725
2	961,357	332,303	387,121
3	1,783,609	597,595	421,566
4	3,324,480	1,093,951	461,543
5	*	1,981,927	503,364
6	*	*	540,618
7	*	*	575,100
8	*	*	614,150

A result of "*" indicates a test that ran for more than one hour.

the crypto-md5 test from the SunSpider [38] benchmark suite. We modified this program to include 8 hashing operations with some inputs marked as confidential. Our test cases involve 0 through 8 principals. In each case, every principal marks one element as private; additional hash inputs are public. For example, test 1 hashes 1 confidential input and 7 public inputs. Test 8 hashes 8 confidential inputs, each marked as confidential by a distinct principal, and has no public hash inputs. Our results are summarized in Figure 10.

Our results highlight the tradeoffs between the different approaches. The sequential variant of secure multi-execution had the most lightweight infrastructure of the three approaches, reflected in its good performance when there are 0 principals. However, it can neither take advantage of multiple processors nor avoid unnecessary work. As a result, once even a single principal was involved, it was the worst performer. The time required roughly doubles with each additional principal.

Concurrent secure multi-execution outperforms our faceted evaluation implementation when the number of principals is small. However, as the number of principals increases, faceted evaluation quickly becomes the more efficient approach, since under secure multi-execution the number of processes increases exponentially compared to the number of principals. With three principals, faceted evaluation outperforms concurrent secure multi-execution in our tests. Beyond this point execution time for concurrent secure multi-execution roughly doubles with each added principal, as the elements in the lattice now outnumber the available cores.

7. Related Work

A few publications have discussed performing multiple executions to guarantee security properties. Capizzi et al.'s *shadow executions* [9] develop an approach similar to faceted values for use in securing information for desktop applications; they run both a public and a private copy of the application. The public copy can communicate with the outside world, but has no access to private data. The private copy has access to all private information but does not transmit any information over the network. With this elegant solution, confidentiality is maintained. Devriese and Piessens [13] extend this idea to JavaScript code with their *secure multi-execution* strategy, using a high and a low process to protect confidentiality in a similar manner. Our approach is similar in spirit, though we avoid overhead when code does not depend on confidential data. Kashyap et al. [23] clarify some properties of secure multi-execution.

Our semantics are closely related to work by Pottier and Simonet [28]. While they prove non-interference statically for *Core ML*, their proof approach involves a Core ML^2 language that has expression pairs and value pairs, analogous to our faceted expressions and faceted values. Our work departs from theirs in that we evaluate labeled expressions and values to dynamically guarantee non-interference, rather than using them to make static guarantees.

Kolbitsch et al. [25] use a similar technique in *Rozzle*, a JavaScript virtual machine for symbolic execution designed to detect malware. Rozzle uses *multi-execution* (not to be confused with secure multi-execution) to explore multiple paths in a single execution, similar to faceted evaluation. Their technique treats environment-specific data as symbolic, and explores both paths whenever a value branches on a symbolic value. The principal difference, besides the application, is that faceted values represent a lattice of different views of data, while Rozzle's symbolic heap values represent a range of possible values for different environments.

Other research has previously studied information-flow analysis for JavaScript. Vogt et al. [36] track information flow in Firefox to defend against XSS attacks. Russo and Sabelfeld [30] study timeout mechanisms. Russo et al. [32] discuss dynamic tree structures, with obvious applications to the DOM. Bohannon et al. [8] consider non-interference in JavaScript's reactive environment. Chugh et al. [11] create a framework for information flow analysis with "holes" for analyzing dynamically evaluated code. Dhawan and Ganapathy [14] discuss JavaScript-based browser extensions (JSEs). Jang et al. [21] give an excellent overview of how JavaScript is used to circumvent privacy defenses.

Information flow analysis largely traces its roots back to Denning [12]. Volpano et al. [37] codify Denning's approach as a type system, and also offer a proof of its soundness. Heintze and Riecke [19] design a type system for their purely functional SLam Calculus, which they extend to include mutable reference cells, concurrency, and integrity guarantees. Sabelfeld and Myers [33] offer an extensive survey of other research on information flow.

Myers [27] discusses JFlow, a variant of Java with security types to provide strong information flow guarantees. JFlow was the basis for Jif [22], a production-worthy language with information flow controls. Birgisson et al. [7] show how capabilities can guarantee information flow policies. Hunt and Sands [20] describe a flow-sensitive type system. Russo and Sabelfeld [31] discuss the tradeoffs between static and dynamic analyses in some depth. Le Guernic et al. [18] examine code from branches not taken, increasing precision at the expense of run-time performance overhead. Shroff et al. [34] use a purely-dynamic analysis to track variable dependencies and reject more insecure programs over time.

Zdancewic [40] uses integrity labels to provide *robust declassification*. Askarov and Myers [2] consider *checked endorsements*. Chong and Myers [10] use a framework for application-specific declassification policies. Askarov and Sabelfeld [3] study a declassification framework specifying what and where data is released. Vaughan and Chong [35] infer declassification policies for Java programs. Askarov et al. [1] highlight complications of *intermediary output channels*. Rafnsson et al. [29] buffer output to reduce data lost from intermediary output channels and termination behavior. King et al. [24] study false alarms caused by implicit flows.

8. Discussion

Information flow non-interference is a tricky security property to enforce via dynamic monitoring, since it is a *2-safety property*: non-interference can be refuted only by observing two executions (cmp. Theorem 2). Conversely, a *1-safety property* can be refuted by observing a single execution, and so 1-safety properties are more amenable to dynamic enforcement. From this perspective, various prior techniques dynamically enforce a 1-safety property that conservatively approximates the desired 2-safety property of non-interference, but this conservative approximation introduces false alarms on implicit flows. Interestingly, our projection property (Theorem 1) is a 1-safety property that suffices to prove non-interference (Theorem 2) without introducing false alarms.

Acknowledgements We thank the anonymous POPL reviewers for their constructive feedback on this paper. We would also like to thank Brendan Eich, Andreas Gal, and Dave Herman for valuable discussions on information flow analysis, and David Flanagan and Donovan Preston for their help working with the dom.js project. This work was supported by NSF grant CNS-0905650.

References

[1] Aslan Askarov, Sebastian Hunt, Andrei Sabelfeld, and David Sands. Termination-insensitive noninterference leaks more than just a bit. In *ESORICS '08*, pages 333–348. Springer-Verlag, 2008.

[2] Aslan Askarov and Andrew Myers. A semantic framework for declassification and endorsement. In *ESOP*, pages 64–84, 2010.

[3] Aslan Askarov and Andrei Sabelfeld. Tight enforcement of information-release policies for dynamic languages. In *IEEE Computer Security Foundations Symposium*, pages 43–59, Washington, DC, USA, 2009. IEEE Computer Society.

[4] Thomas H. Austin. ZaphodFacetes github page. `https://github.com/taustin/ZaphodFacets`, 2011.

[5] Thomas H. Austin and Cormac Flanagan. Efficient purely-dynamic information flow analysis. In *PLAS '09: Proceedings of the ACM SIGPLAN Fourth Workshop on Programming Languages and Analysis for Security*, pages 113–124, New York, NY, USA, 2009. ACM.

[6] Thomas H. Austin and Cormac Flanagan. Permissive dynamic information flow analysis. In *Proceedings of the 5th ACM SIGPLAN Workshop on Programming Languages and Analysis for Security*, pages 1–12. ACM, 2010.

[7] Arnar Birgisson, Alejandro Russo, and Andrei Sabelfeld. Capabilities for information flow. In *PLAS '11: Proceedings of the ACM SIGPLAN Fourth Workshop on Programming Languages and Analysis for Security*. ACM, 2011.

[8] Aaron Bohannon, Benjamin C. Pierce, Vilhelm Sjöberg, Stephanie Weirich, and Steve Zdancewic. Reactive noninterference. In *ACM Conference on Computer and Communications Security*, pages 79–90, 2009.

[9] R. Capizzi, A. Longo, V.N. Venkatakrishnan, and A.P. Sistla. Preventing information leaks through shadow executions. In *ACSAC*, pages 322 –331, dec 2008.

[10] Stephen Chong and Andrew C. Myers. Security policies for downgrading. In *CCS '04: Proceedings of the 11th ACM conference on Computer and communications security*, pages 198–209, New York, NY, USA, 2004. ACM.

[11] Ravi Chugh, Jeffrey A. Meister, Ranjit Jhala, and Sorin Lerner. Staged information flow for javascript. In *PLDI*, pages 50–62, 2009.

[12] Dorothy E. Denning. A lattice model of secure information flow. *Communications of the ACM*, 19(5):236–243, 1976.

[13] Dominique Devriese and Frank Piessens. Noninterference through secure multi-execution. *Security and Privacy, IEEE Symposium on*, 0:109–124, 2010.

[14] Mohan Dhawan and Vinod Ganapathy. Analyzing information flow in javascript-based browser extensions. In *ACSAC*, pages 382–391, 2009.

[15] Brendan Eich. Narcissus–JS implemented in JS. Available on the web at `https://github.com/mozilla/narcissus/`.

[16] J. S. Fenton. Memoryless subsystems. *The Computer Journal*, 17(2):143–147, 1974.

[17] Andreas Gal, David Flanagan, and Donovon Preston. dom.js github page. `https://github.com/andreasgal/dom.js`, accessed October 2011, 2011.

[18] Gurvan Le Guernic, Anindya Banerjee, Thomas P. Jensen, and David A. Schmidt. Automata-based confidentiality monitoring. In *ASIAN*, pages 75–89, 2006.

[19] Nevin Heintze and Jon G. Riecke. The SLam calculus: Programming with secrecy and integrity. In *Symposium on Principles of Programming Languages*, pages 365–377, 1998.

[20] Sebastian Hunt and David Sands. On flow-sensitive security types. In *POPL*, pages 79–90, 2006.

[21] Dongseok Jang, Ranjit Jhala, Sorin Lerner, and Hovav Shacham. An empirical study of privacy-violating information flows in javascript web applications. In *ACM Conference on Computer and Communications Security*, pages 270–283, 2010.

[22] Jif homepage. http://www.cs.cornell.edu/jif/, accessed October 2010.

[23] Vineeth Kashyap, Ben Wiedermann, and Ben Hardekopf. Timing- and termination-sensitive secure information flow: Exploring a new approach. In *IEEE Security and Privacy*, 2011.

[24] Dave King, Boniface Hicks, Michael Hicks, and Trent Jaeger. Implicit flows: Can't live with 'em, can't live without 'em. In *International Conference on Information Systems Security*, pages 56–70, 2008.

[25] Clemens Kolbitsch, Benjamin Livshits, Benjamin Zorn, and Christian Seifert. Rozzle: De-cloaking internet malware. Technical Report MSR-TR-2011-94, Microsoft Research Technical Report, 20011.

[26] Mozilla labs: Zaphod add-on for the firefox browser. `http://mozillalabs.com/zaphod`, accessed October 2010.

[27] Andrew C. Myers. JFlow: Practical mostly-static information flow control. In *Symposium on Principles of Programming Languages*, pages 228–241, 1999.

[28] François Pottier and Vincent Simonet. Information flow inference for ML. *Transactions on Programming Languages and Systems*, 25(1):117–158, 2003.

[29] Willard Rafnsson and Andrei Sabelfeld. Limiting information leakage in event-based communication. In *PLAS '11: Proceedings of the ACM SIGPLAN Fourth Workshop on Programming Languages and Analysis for Security*. ACM, 2011.

[30] Alejandro Russo and Andrei Sabelfeld. Securing timeout instructions in web applications. In *IEEE Computer Security Foundations Symposium*, 2009.

[31] Alejandro Russo and Andrei Sabelfeld. Dynamic vs. static flow-sensitive security analysis. In *IEEE Computer Security Foundations Symposium*. IEEE Computer Society, 2010.

[32] Alejandro Russo, Andrei Sabelfeld, and Andrey Chudnov. Tracking information flow in dynamic tree structures. In *ESORICS*, pages 86–103, 2009.

[33] Andrei Sabelfeld and Andrew C. Myers. Language-based information-flow security. *Selected Areas in Communications, IEEE Journal on*, 21(1):5–19, Jan 2003.

[34] Paritosh Shroff, Scott F. Smith, and Mark Thober. Dynamic dependency monitoring to secure information flow. In *CSF*, pages 203–217, 2007.

[35] Jeffrey Vaughan and Stephen Chong. Inference of expressive declassification policies. In *IEEE Security and Privacy*, 2011.

[36] Philipp Vogt, Florian Nentwich, Nenad Jovanovic, Engin Kirda, Christopher Krügel, and Giovanni Vigna. Cross site scripting prevention with dynamic data tainting and static analysis. In *NDSS*, 2007.

[37] Dennis Volpano, Cynthia Irvine, and Geoffrey Smith. A sound type system for secure flow analysis. *Journal of Computer Security*, 4(2-3):167–187, 1996.

[38] Webkit.org. SunSpider JavaScript benchmark. `http://www.webkit.org/perf/sunspider/sunspider.html`, accessed October 2011.

[39] Stephan Arthur Zdancewic. *Programming languages for information security*. PhD thesis, Cornell University, 2002.

[40] Steve Zdancewic. A type system for robust declassification. In *19th Mathematical Foundations of Programming Semantics Conference*, 2003.

Defining Code-injection Attacks

Donald Ray Jay Ligatti

Department of Computer Science and Engineering
University of South Florida
{dray3,ligatti}@cse.usf.edu

Abstract

This paper shows that existing definitions of code-injection attacks (e.g., SQL-injection attacks) are flawed. The flaws make it possible for attackers to circumvent existing mechanisms, by supplying code-injecting inputs that are not recognized as such. The flaws also make it possible for benign inputs to be treated as attacks. After describing these flaws in conventional definitions of code-injection attacks, this paper proposes a new definition, which is based on whether the symbols input to an application get used as (normal-form) values in the application's output. Because values are already fully evaluated, they cannot be considered "code" when injected. This simple new definition of code-injection attacks avoids the problems of existing definitions, improves our understanding of how and when such attacks occur, and enables us to evaluate the effectiveness of mechanisms for mitigating such attacks.

Categories and Subject Descriptors C.2.0 [*Computer Communication Networks*]: General—Security and protection; D.3.1 [*Programming Languages*]: Formal Definitions and Theory—Syntax

General Terms Security, languages, algorithms

1. Introduction

As the popularity of web applications has increased, so have reports of attacks against them [20–22]. The most commonly reported type of attack involves injecting code into a program output by an application, as in SQL-injection attacks [22].

Standard examples of code-injection attacks include an attacker entering the following strings as input to an application:

- `' OR 1=1 --`, to make the application output the program `SELECT balance FROM acct WHERE password='' OR 1=1 --'` (underlined symbols are those the attacker has injected into the output program). This SQL program always returns the balance(s) from the `acct` table, even though an empty-string password is supplied, because: (1) the `1=1` subexpression is true, making the entire `WHERE` clause true, and (2) the `--` command comments out the final apostrophe to make the program syntactically valid. In this case, the attacker has injected the code symbols `OR`, `=`, and `--` into the output program.
- `exit()`, to make the application output the program `SELECT balance FROM acct WHERE pin=exit()`. In this case, the attacker has injected the code symbols `exit()` into the output program to mount a denial-of-service attack against the remote database.

These attacks are commonly referred to as "code-injection attacks" or "command-injection attacks" (CIAs, or just IAs), but here we use the more specific term "code-injection attacks on outputs" (CIAOs) to distinguish these attacks, which require code to be injected into an application's *output*, from more general notions of CIAs, which require code to be injected only into *memory used by* an application (e.g., [39]).

Much research has focused on mechanisms for mitigating CIAOs, and a few efforts have been made to define CIAOs rigorously [3, 34, 37]. However, as Section 2 discusses, existing definitions are based on the flawed belief that CIAOs occur whenever an application's input alters the syntactic structure of its output program. Incorrectly conflating CIAOs with changes to syntactic structures causes existing definitions to be neither sound nor complete: some CIAOs are not recognized as CIAOs (false negatives), and some non-CIAOs are recognized as CIAOs (false positives). The false negatives allow attackers to circumvent existing mechanisms for preventing CIAOs.

Without a satisfactory definition of CIAOs, we can't effectively develop or analyze mechanisms for mitigating them; preventing CIAOs in general requires understanding exactly how and when they succeed. As Sun Tzu's *The Art of War* famously expresses it, "If you know yourself but not the enemy, for every victory gained you will also suffer a defeat" [36].

This is a paper about "knowing the enemy"; it defines precise circumstances under which CIAOs can be said to occur. Defining CIAOs requires two subdefinitions: first we must define which symbols in applications' output programs constitute *code*; second we must define when symbols have been *injected* into output programs. The primary contribution and novelty of this paper lies in the first of these subdefinitions; the second subdefinition can be approached with well-known (but difficult-to-implement) techniques of taint tracking. For the first subdefinition, this paper defines "code" significantly differently from previous work—instead of code being parse-tree-changing symbols, code here refers to symbols that do not form *values* (i.e., fully evaluated terms). This paper argues that CIAOs occur when at least one symbol injected into an output program is used outside of a value.

To keep the definitions general, this paper tries to abstract as much as possible from underlying languages, programs, and system architectures. Although the definitions will require a few technical assumptions about the languages of applications' output programs (such as that they have a well-defined set of normal-form values), this paper's definitions are not limited to SQL or other popular programming languages; the new definition of CIAOs applies equally well to other code-injection attacks (e.g., LDAP-injection, HTML/script-injection (XSS), and shell-injection attacks). Similarly, the only assumption we make of applications is that tainted inputs can be correctly tracked through them, so we know which symbols in their outputs have been injected.

POPL'12, January 25–27, 2012, Philadelphia, PA, USA.

1.1 Summary of Contributions and Roadmap

This paper demonstrates problems in the conventional definition of CIAOs (in Section 2). The problems make existing CIAO-mitigating mechanisms neither sound nor complete—some CIAOs are considered benign, while some non-CIAOs are considered attacks. After discussing previous work, the paper presents (in Sections 3–4) a new definition of CIAOs that avoids these problems.

Ultimately, a definition of CIAOs has two important high-level uses. First, a definition of CIAOs enables us to precisely determine whether applications exhibit CIAOs. We put the new definition to this first use by illustrating the new definition's improved ability to determine whether applications exhibit CIAOs (primarily in Section 3.3). Second, a definition of CIAOs enables us to analyze the effectiveness of mechanisms at mitigating CIAOs. We put the new definition to this second use by analyzing the effectiveness of several classes of mechanisms for detecting CIAOs (in Section 5).

More specifically, several properties of CIAOs become apparent by considering the new definitions:

- Defining CIAOs as occurring when nonvalue symbols get injected into output programs improves our ability to recognize attacks. We illustrate the improvements in an idealized version of SQL called SQL°, "SQL Diminished" (Sections 3–4.1).
- CIAOs can be classified as copy-based or data-dependency-based, depending on how applications propagate untrusted (tainted) inputs into output programs (Section 4.2.1).
- A class of attacks related to CIAOs exists, which we call code-*interference* attacks. The definition of these attacks takes into account control dependencies ignored by taint-tracking mechanisms (Section 4.2.2).
- Surprisingly, every application that always copies some untrusted input verbatim into an (SQL°) output program is vulnerable to CIAOs (Section 5.1). This result implies that sound static mechanisms for detecting CIAOs must disallow all such applications, conservatively ruling out a large class of applications in practice. The proof of this result (in Section 5.1) is constructive; the proof defines inputs that will successfully attack any application that verbatim copies some untrusted input into the output program. Although the proof is tailored to SQL°, the proof techniques are general and applicable to other languages.
- Similarly, applications that always copy some untrusted input verbatim into an (SQL°) output program are vulnerable to code-interference attacks (Section 5.1).
- Neither static nor black-box analysis of applications can precisely detect CIAOs. (Section 5.2)
- Precisely detecting CIAOs requires white-box, runtime-monitoring mechanisms. Under reasonable assumptions, such mechanisms can detect CIAOs in output programs of size n in $O(n)$ time and space. However, there are obstacles that make it difficult to implement such mechanisms in practice. (Sections 5.3–5.4).

After presenting these results in Sections 2–5, Section 6 concludes.

2. Related Work

Conventionally, CIAOs are considered to occur whenever an application's input alters the intended syntactic structure of its output program. Bisht, Madhusudan, and Venkatakrishnan call this "a well-agreed principle in other works on detecting SQL injection" [3]. Indeed, this definition has appeared in many documents: [2–5, 9, 10, 13, 17, 27, 31, 34, 37]. Although a few papers define CIAOs in other ways (e.g., CIAOs occur exactly when keywords or operators get injected, including apostrophes used to form string values in SQL [8, 25], or when injected strings span multiple tokens [38]), the conventional definition dominates the literature.

However, the conventional definition of CIAOs has inherent problems: some CIAOs do not alter the syntactic structures of output programs, while some non-CIAOs do. To illustrate these problems, Sections 2.1 and 2.2 discuss the conventional definitions of CIAOs used by SQLCHECK [34, 37] and CANDID [2, 3]. As far as we're aware, these are the only existing formal definitions of CIAOs.

2.1 CIAOs in SqlCheck

SQLCHECK considers the intended syntactic structure of an output program to be any parse tree in which each injected input is the complete derivation of one terminal or nonterminal. For example, parsing the output program `SELECT balance FROM acct WHERE password='' OR 1=1 --'` produces a parse tree in which the injected symbols `' OR 1=1 --` are not the complete sequence of leaves for a single terminal or nonterminal ancestor; SQLCHECK therefore recognizes this CIAO.

However, some of what SQLCHECK considers intended (i.e., non-attack) structures are actually attacks. For example, parsing the output program `SELECT balance FROM acct WHERE pin=exit()` produces a tree in which the input symbols `exit()` are the complete sequence of leaves for a single nonterminal (function-call[1]) ancestor. Hence, SQLCHECK does not recognize this CIAO as an attack. Similarly, an output program of the form `...WHERE flag=1000>GLOBAL` wouldn't be recognized as an attack, despite the injection of a greater-than operator (which may allow an attacker to efficiently extract the value of the `GLOBAL` variable, by performing a binary search over its range). Although SQLCHECK allows policy engineers to specify a set of terminal and nonterminal ancestors that inputs may derive from—so engineers could disallow inputs derived as function-call and comparison expressions—it's unclear how an engineer would know exactly which ancestors to allow derivations from. Moreover, engineers may wish to sometimes allow, and sometimes disallow, inputs to derive from particular terminals and nonterminals (as illustrated in Section 3.3), which is impossible in SQLCHECK.

Conversely, some of what SQLCHECK considers unintended (i.e., attack) structures are actually not attacks. For example, an application might input two strings, a file name `f` and a file extension `e`, and concatenate them to generate the program `SELECT * FROM properties WHERE filename='f.e'`. Although the user has injected no code, SQLCHECK flags this output as a CIAO because the user's inputs are not complete sequences of leaves for a single terminal or nonterminal ancestor. In this case, the immediate ancestor of the user's inputs would (assuming a typical grammar) be a string literal, but neither of the user's inputs form a complete string literal—they're missing the dot and single-quote symbols.

The CANDID papers describe other, lower-level problems with SQLCHECK's definitions [2, 3].

2.2 CIAOs in Candid

CANDID considers the intended syntactic structure of an output program, generated by running application A on input I, to be whatever syntactic structure is present in the output of A on input $VR(I)$. Here VR is a (valid representation) function that converts any input I into an input I' known to (1) be valid (i.e., non-CIAO-inducing) and (2) cause A to follow the same control-flow path as it would on input I. CANDID begins by assuming this VR function exists, while acknowledging that it does not; in this basic case,

[1] All major SQL implementations we are familiar with allow statements to call functions, including administrator-defined functions [19, 28, 29].

CANDID defines a CIAO to occur when A's output on input I has a different syntactic structure from A's output on input *VR*(I).

Besides the nonexistence of function *VR*, there are some problems with this definition of CIAOs. First, the definition is circular; CIAOs are defined in terms of *VR*, which itself is assumed to output non-CIAO-inducing inputs (i.e., the definition of CIAOs relies on the definition of *VR*, which relies on the definition of CIAOs). Second, the definition assumes that multiple valid syntactic structures cannot exist. For example, suppose *VR*(`','`)=aaa and application A on input `','` outputs `SELECT * FROM t WHERE name IN ('a','b')`, while A on input `aaa` executes in the same way to output `SELECT * FROM t WHERE name IN ('aaaab')`. Both of these outputs are valid SQL programs, yet the programs have different syntactic structures (a two-element list versus a single-element list), and neither exhibits a CIAO (in no case has *code* been injected; only values, which take no steps dynamically, have been injected). CANDID would classify the non-CIAO input of `','` as an attack in this case.

To deal with the nonexistence of function *VR*, CANDID attempts to approximate *VR* by defining *VR*(I) to be 1 when I is an integer and $a^{|I|}$ when I is a string (where $a^{|I|}$ is a sequence of a's having the same length as I). Supplying a concrete definition of *VR* resolves the circularity problem in CANDID's basic definition of CIAOs, but it doesn't resolve the second problem described in the previous paragraph (that multiple valid syntactic structures may exist).

Moreover, CANDID's approximation of *VR* creates new problems:

- The approximation incorrectly assumes a string of a's or a 1 could never be attack inputs. An application could inject an input a or 1 into an output program as part of a function call, field selection, or even keyword (e.g., and), all of which could be CIAOs. For example, suppose an application outputs a constant string, echoes its input, and then outputs parentheses; on input `exit` it outputs the program `...pin=exit()`. CANDID would not recognize this CIAO because the application outputs `...pin=aaaa()` on input `aaaa`, which has the same syntactic structure as the `...pin=exit()` output. The problem here is that `aaaa` is actually an attack input for this application.
- The approximation may also cause benign inputs to be detected as attacks. For example, suppose an application outputs `SELECT * FROM t WHERE flag=TRUE` on input `TRUE`, and follows the same control-flow path to output `SELECT * FROM t WHERE flag=aaaa` on input *VR*(TRUE)=aaaa. Because these two output programs have different syntactic structures (a boolean literal versus a variable identifier), CANDID would flag the input `TRUE` as an attack, even though the user has injected no code.
- The approximation can also break applications, as discussed in [3]. To illustrate this problem, let's consider the application `if(input<2) then restart() else output(1/(input-1))`. CANDID cannot in general operate on this application because it evaluates applications on both actual (I) and candidate (*VR*(I)) inputs, while following the control-flow path required to evaluate the actual input. In this case, whenever the application's actual input is greater than one, CANDID will try to evaluate `1/(input-1)` on the candidate input 1, which causes the application to halt with a divide-by-zero error, despite there being no errors in CANDID's absence.

It could be argued that the example applications in the bullets above would be uncommon in practice. But limiting the definition of CIAOs to common applications obligates us to define what makes an application common, so we can test whether a given application is "common" enough for the definition of CIAOs to apply. Even then, one couldn't say anything about CIAOs in uncommon applications.

Related-work Summary CIAOs cannot be said to occur when an application's output program has an altered syntactic structure.

- CIAOs can occur without altering the syntactic structure of output programs (e.g., by injecting `exit()` or `1000>GLOBAL` in SQLCHECK, or `exit` in CANDID).
- Non-CIAOs can occur while altering the syntactic structure of output programs (e.g., by injecting file name `f` and extension `e` in SQLCHECK, or `TRUE` in CANDID).

3. Partitioning Program Symbols into Code and Noncode

This section begins building a new definition of CIAOs. Because CIAOs occur when *code* symbols get injected into output programs, the question of which output-program symbols constitute code is key to defining CIAOs. This section addresses that question and defines how to separate code from noncode. (The discussion is limited to the context of CIAOs; in other contexts it makes sense to consider entire output programs as "code".)

3.1 Overview of Partitioning Technique

Let's begin by defining what is not code, rather than what is. This paper considers noncode to be the closed *values* in a programming language. Values are valid but operationally irreducible terms (i.e., normal forms) [16, 32]. Values can be thought of as the "fully evaluated" computations in a programming language, typically including standalone string and integer literals, pointers, objects, lists and tuples of other values, etc. Values are closed when they contain no free variables; open values have free variables (e.g., a tuple value like `(4,x)` and standalone variables are open values).

Closed values are fully evaluated, dynamically passive constructs, which by themselves cause no dynamic computation to occur. On the other hand, because nonvalues and open values are not part of these passive terms, they are used to help specify dynamically active computation and therefore constitute code (in the case of open values, the dynamic activity specified by a free variable is a substitution operation, which substitutes a term for the free variable at runtime). Injecting symbols that only form closed values into an output program therefore cannot be considered a CIAO—only irreducible, dynamically passive terms (i.e., "noncode") will have been introduced. CIAOs occur when untrusted inputs get used outside of closed values in output programs.

3.2 Formal Assumptions and Definitions

An application vulnerable to CIAOs outputs programs in some language L (e.g., SQL) having finite concrete-syntax alphabet Σ_L (e.g., the set of printable ASCII characters). An output program, which we call an L-program, is a finite sequence of Σ_L symbols that form an element of L.

Definition 1. *For all languages L with alphabet Σ_L (i.e., $L \subseteq \Sigma_L^*$), an L-*program *is an element of L.*

Additional definitions will rely on the following assumptions and notational conventions:

- The length of program p is denoted as $|p|$ (so when $p = \sigma_1\sigma_2..\sigma_n$, where each σ is a program symbol in Σ_L, we have $|p| = n$).
- The ith symbol in program p is denoted as $p[i]$.
- Well-defined functions exist for computing free variables in all output-program languages under consideration. Function

$FV_L(p, l, h)$ takes an L-program $p = \sigma_1\sigma_2..\sigma_n$, a low symbol number $l \in \{1..n\}$, and a high symbol number $h \in \{l..n\}$ and returns the set of variables that are free in the shortest term in p that contains all of the symbols $\sigma_l..\sigma_h$.

- Well-defined functions also exist for testing whether terms are values in all output-program languages under consideration. Predicate $Val_L(p, l, h)$ is true iff the shortest term that contains the lth to h^{th} symbols in L-program p is a value.

When the output language L is clear from context, we'll omit it as a subscript on FV_L and Val_L functions.

We now formalize Section 3.1's intuition of noncode program symbols. We use the predicate NCV to indicate whether symbols in an L-program form a *noncode value*. NCV is true for an L-program p and low and high program-symbol numbers l and h iff the shortest term containing the lth to h^{th} symbols in p is a closed value.

Definition 2. *For all languages L, predicate* $NCV(p, l, h)$ *over* $L \times \{1..|p|\} \times \{l..|p|\}$ *is true iff* $FV(p, l, h) = \emptyset$ *and* $Val(p, l, h)$.

Code symbols are those that cannot possibly be part of any noncode value. When $p[i]$ is code (where p is an output program), we write $Code(p, i)$.

Definition 3. *For all L-programs* $p = \sigma_1\sigma_2..\sigma_n$ *and position numbers* $i \in \{1..|p|\}$, $Code(p, i)$ *is true iff for all low and high symbol-position numbers* $l \in \{1..i\}$ *and* $h \in \{i..|p|\}$, $\neg NCV(p, l, h)$.

3.3 Example Separation of Code from Noncode

The remainder of this section illustrates Definition 3 in the context of SQL° (SQL Diminished), an idealized SQL-style language inspired by the MSDN SQL Minimum Grammar [18]. Figure 1 presents SQL°'s syntax, which makes several assumptions:

- Full SQL° programs are valid `statement`s.
- Operators in SQL° have standard precedence and associativity.
- A set of (administrator-defined and/or standard-library) paramterless functions exists, and SQL° expressions (i.e., `exprs`) can invoke these functions with the `ID()` syntax (where `ID` is an identifier, in this case a function name). Such function calls are possible in typical SQL implementations [14, 19, 28, 29].
- Similarly, a set of (administrator-defined and/or standard) variables exists, and variable identifiers are valid SQL° expressions.
- Comments in SQL° begin with `--` and continue to the first newline.
- String literals in SQL° have the same escape sequence as string literals in full SQL (i.e., a double apostrophe represents a single apostrophe). Also as in full SQL, apostrophe directions are irrelevant in SQL°, though we use directed apostrophes in this paper for clarity.

Values in SQL° are the last six terms listed in Figure 1 for category `expr` (i.e., from `INT_LITERAL` to `NULL`). Intuitively, the values in a typed programming language are normally all the fully evaluated terms of each type in the language. SQL° has types for integers (`INT`), strings having a given size (`CHAR(INT_LITERAL)`), booleans (`BOOL`), and floats having a given precision (`FLOAT(INT_LITERAL)`), so its values are the fully evaluated terms of each of these types—including integer literals, string literals, the true and false keywords, and floating-point literals. Finally, `NULL` is a fully evaluated term of any type, also a value.

Given that values in SQL° are exactly the last six terms listed as `exprs` in Figure 1, Definitions 2 and 3 imply that $Code(p, i)$ holds iff, after parsing program p, $p[i]$ is not part of a nonterminal categorized as one of these six kinds of `exprs`. Noncode symbols

```
statement     ::=  CREATE TABLE ID ( id_type_list )
                |  DELETE FROM ID w_option
                |  DROP TABLE ID
                |  INSERT INTO ID vals
                |  SELECT s_list FROM ID w_option

id_type_list  ::=  ID type | id_type_list , ID type

type          ::=  INT | CHAR ( INT_LITERAL ) | BOOL
                |  FLOAT ( INT_LITERAL )

w_option      ::=  ε | WHERE expr

expr          ::=  expr op expr | NOT expr | ( expr )
                |  expr IS NULL | ID | ID ( )
                |  INT_LITERAL | STR_LITERAL | TRUE
                |  FALSE | FLOAT_LITERAL | NULL

op            ::=  OR | AND | < | > | = | + | *

vals          ::=  VALUES ( e_list )
                |  SELECT s_list FROM ID w_option

e_list        ::=  expr | e_list , expr

s_list        ::=  * | i_list

i_list        ::=  ID | i_list , ID
```

Figure 1. Syntax of SQL°.

are those in closed values; all others are code. This definition also works when partitioning whitespace and comment symbols: no symbol involved in whitespace or comments can possibly be within a value (all values in SQL° are single tokens), so whitespace and comment symbols are code.[2]

A few observations about this definition of code in SQL°:

- Parsing is necessary to determine whether a symbol is code. For example, an integer literal is code when used in a `type` specification, but noncode when used as an expression.
- Conventional definitions of CIAOs are incompatible with the definition of code in SQL°. For example, there exists no set of terminals and nonterminals in Figure 1 that exactly derive noncode symbols (`exprs` may contain code, and even `INT_LITERAL`s may be code depending on the context); hence, our definition of code is inexpressible with SQLCHECK [34].
- Code and noncode can't be partitioned by considering noncode to be literals. Some literals are code (e.g., an integer in a `type`) and other are not (e.g., an integer expression). Although all nonliterals (e.g., a `CREATE` keyword) are code in SQL°, languages with more sophisticated values (e.g., lists) may have nonliteral, noncode symbols (e.g., commas between elements of a list value).
- Code and noncode also can't be partitioned by considering code to be keywords and operators. Some keywords are code (e.g., `CREATE`) and others are not (e.g., `TRUE`). Some symbols that are neither keywords nor operators are code (e.g., function-name `ID`s) and others are not (e.g., literals).

Next, let's consider several example output programs, beginning with the examples from Sections 2.1 and 2.2, to see how the new definitions partition injected symbols.

[2] It may also be reasonable to partition lexer-removed symbols (typically whitespace and comments) into code and noncode in other ways. For example, one might consider lexer-removed symbols code iff their existence affects the sequence of tokens in the output program.

	1	2	3	4	5	6	7	8	9	10	11
This paper	Yes	Yes	Yes	No	Yes	Yes	No	Yes	Yes	Yes	No
SQLCHECK [34]	Yes	No	No	Yes	No	No	No	No	No	No	No
CANDID [3]	Yes	Yes	Yes	No	No	No	Yes	No	No	No	Yes
WASP [8] and Nguyen-Tuong et. al. [25]	Yes	Yes	Yes	No	No	No	No	No	No	No	Yes
Xu et. al. [38]	Yes	Yes	Yes	No	No	No	No	No	No	No	No

Figure 2. A comparison of definitions for partitioning code and noncode. Column numbers refer to the example output programs enumerated in Section 3.3, row names indicate partitioning techniques, and cells specify whether any of the underlined symbols are considered code.

1. `SELECT balance FROM acct WHERE password='' OR 1=1 --'` The injected OR, =, and -- (and spaces) are code, so a CIAO has occurred.
2. `SELECT balance FROM acct WHERE pin= exit()` All the injected symbols are code, so a CIAO has occurred.
3. `...WHERE flag=1000>GLOBAL` The injected > is code, so a CIAO has occurred.
4. `SELECT * FROM properties WHERE filename='f.e'` No injected symbols are code, so a CIAO has not occurred.
5. `...pin=exit()` All the injected symbols are code, so a CIAO has occurred.
6. `...pin=aaaa()` Again, all the injected symbols are code, so a CIAO has occurred.
7. `SELECT * FROM t WHERE flag=TRUE` No injected symbols are code, so a CIAO has not occurred.
8. `SELECT * FROM t WHERE flag=aaaa` An open expression (which causes a substitution operation to be performed at runtime) was injected, so a CIAO has occurred.
9. `SELECT * FROM t WHERE password=password` Again, an open expression (which causes a substitution operation to be performed at runtime) was injected, so a CIAO has occurred.
10. `CREATE TABLE t (name CHAR(40))` All the injected symbols are code, so a CIAO has occurred.
11. `SELECT * FROM t WHERE name='x'` No injected symbols are code, so a CIAO has not occurred.

In all of these cases, the partitioning avoids the problems with conventional CIAO definitions described in Section 2 and matches our intuition about which program symbols are code (and consequently cause a CIAO if injected).

Figure 2 compares this paper's partitioning of the example output programs enumerated above with the partitionings used in previous work. The only scenarios in which we believe previous definitions would be favored over this paper's definitions are when the assumptions made by this paper's definitions cannot be satisfied easily, that is, when it's difficult to define the set of closed values in the output-program language.

4. Definition of CIAOs

Defining CIAOs requires subdefinitions of *code* and *injection*. At this point code has been defined; it is time to consider what it means for an attacker to inject symbols into an output program. Intuitively, injected symbols are the ones that propagate unmodified from an untrusted input source to the output program. A CIAO occurs when at least one untrusted input symbol propagates into, and gets used as code in, an output program.

To know when input symbols have propagated, possibly through copy operations, to output programs, one could taint all untrusted inputs to applications and have those applications transparently propagate taints through copy operations (Section 4.2 will consider propagating taints through other operations as well). Then output programs could be tested to determine whether any of their tainted symbols are used as code. Tracking taints to determine which output-program symbols derive from untrusted inputs is a well-studied technique (e.g., [6, 8, 25, 31, 38]).

4.1 Formal Assumptions and Definitions

As in earlier sections, underlines will represent tainted symbols (i.e., those injected from untrusted sources). As a technicality, if some element of Σ is already underlined then all underlines in this paper may need to be replaced with some other annotation not present on any Σ symbol. Then, for all languages L with alphabet Σ, let $\underline{L}$ denote the same language but with alphabet $\underline{\Sigma}$, where $\underline{\Sigma}$ contains tainted and untainted versions of every symbol in Σ. Thus, the *tainted output language* $\underline{L}$ contains exactly those programs in L, except that programs in $\underline{L}$ can have symbols tainted in any way. The following three definitions formalize these ideas.

Definition 4. *For all alphabets* Σ, *the* tainted-symbol alphabet $\underline{\Sigma}$ *is:* $\{\sigma \mid \sigma \in \Sigma \vee (\exists \sigma' \in \Sigma : \sigma = \underline{\sigma'})\}$.

Definition 5. *For all alphabets* Σ *and symbols* $\sigma \in \underline{\Sigma}$, *the predicate* $tainted(\sigma)$ *is true iff* $\sigma \notin \Sigma$.

Definition 6. *For all languages* L *with alphabet* Σ, *the* tainted output language $\underline{L}$ *with alphabet* $\underline{\Sigma}$ *is:*

$$\{\sigma_1..\sigma_n \mid \exists \sigma'_1..\sigma'_n \in L : \forall i \in \{1..n\} : (\sigma_i{=}\sigma'_i \vee \sigma_i{=}\underline{\sigma'_i})\}$$

Given a regular, non-taint-tracking application, which outputs L-programs, a *taint-tracking application*, which outputs $\underline{L}$-programs, is constructed by ensuring all the following.

1. All symbols input to the application from untrusted sources are marked tainted.
2. Taints propagate through all operations that copy or output symbols.
3. Besides inputting symbols from untrusted sources and copying and outputting already tainted symbols, there are no other ways to introduce tainted symbols.
4. Taints are invisible to the application; they have no effect on its execution.

The only assumption this paper makes of applications is that they can be reasoned about as taint-tracking applications obeying these four rules.

At last, CIAOs can be defined as occurring whenever an injected (i.e., tainted) symbol in an application's output is used as code.

Definition 7. *A* CIAO *occurs exactly when a taint-tracking application outputs* $\underline{L}$*-program* $p = \sigma_1..\sigma_n$ *such that* $\exists i \in \{1..n\}$: $(tainted(\sigma_i) \wedge Code(p, i))$.

4.2 Discussion of the CIAO Definition

There are several points of discussion related to Definition 7.

Syntactic versus Semantic Analysis Contrary to previous work [3, 34], Definition 7 does not limit CIAO detection to syntactic analysis. Although testing whether sequences of program symbols denote closed values typically requires only syntactic analysis (e.g., values are defined syntactically for SQL° in Section 3.3), such testing could conceivably require stronger-than-syntactic analysis. For example, semantic analysis may be required to determine whether the output programs `date:=1/1/11` and `balance:=1/1/11` exhibit CIAOs in output-program languages with slashes used in both date-literal and integer-division expressions.

Expected (Nonmalicious) CIAOs Although CIAOs often constitute malicious use of an application, some application programmers expect CIAOs to occur and don't consider them malicious. For example:

- A translator between programming languages may input an expression like `x+y` and output a program containing the same expression or some code like `r1:=r1+r2`, with the nonvalue `+` symbol having been injected. This is not a problem, and authors of programming-language translators would typically not consider CIAOs on their translators harmful.
- Tools like phpMyAdmin provide interfaces for remote users to enter MySQL programs and then have those programs output for other systems to execute [30].
- Applications may check inputs before injecting them as code in output programs, such as the application `if(input='safeFunction') then output(input+'()') else raise badNameExn`, or the application `if(input.matches('Math.*')) then output(input+'()') else raise badNameExn`. Programmers of these applications may not consider CIAOs of checked inputs to be malicious (though it may nonetheless be desirable to detect CIAOs in such programs, for example, to prevent the latter application from outputting `Math.pi+exit()`).

We believe that whether an act is "malicious" or an "attack" or against a programmer's "expectations" or "intentions" is subjective. The only artifact we can examine is the programmer's code, but that code may not capture the programmer's intentions. Definition 7 therefore does not depend on subjective factors like programmers' intentions; CIAOs are defined as occurring whenever an application injects untrusted input into the code of an output program, regardless of whether the application programmer would consider the CIAOs malicious.

To make an analogy to memory safety, there are mechanisms to prevent memory-safety violations, e.g., type checkers. However, some memory-safety violations are not harmful and may be fully intended by programmers. For example, a programmer with knowledge of how integers and floats are encoded may find that writing an arbitrary float value to integer-type memory does exactly what s/he wants very efficiently. As another example, one of the difficulties encountered by "Safe C" projects is that some memory-safety violations are actually intentional and clever optimizations [7, 11, 23].

Definitions of memory-safety violations don't (as far as we're aware) take into account programmer intentions; mechanisms for preventing memory-safety violations disregard programmer intentions and prevent all memory-safety violations, regardless of whether a programmer considers some particular violation malicious. Analogously, Definition 7, unlike the conventional definitions of CIAOs used by previous work, sidesteps the subjective questions of whether output programs are intended or malicious. Definition 7 just focuses on detecting whether code has been injected into output programs.

Non-CIAO injection attacks Some injection attacks on output programs are not *code*-injection attacks on output programs. For instance, consider the output program `SELECT balance FROM acct WHERE password = TRUE`. Here, a type error will occur (assuming that `password` is not of boolean type), potentially causing unexpected failures. Although this output program contains symbols that may have been injected with malicious intent, those symbols are part of a closed value and are therefore not used as code. Because code has not been injected, the output program does not exhibit a CIAO according to Definition 7.

Function values Functions are first-class values in many languages, and it may seem strange to allow arbitrary closed function values to be injected into output programs. However, a function value is dynamically passive; a function value only activates when operated upon, by applying the function. Hence, injecting a function value does not constitute a CIAO, but injecting a function application does (assuming the injected application is not within some other closed value, such as an outer lambda term).

Alternate-encoding and second-order attacks Definition 7 has no problem with "alternate-encoding attacks". Alternate encodings allow attackers to mask injected code, for example, by inputting `exec(char(0x73687574646f776e))` instead of a direct `SHUTDOWN` command [8]. Definition 7 detects such attacks because the injected function calls are recognized as code. Definition 7 also detects "second-order injection attacks" (where an attacker stores some code in a database that an application later retrieves and injects into its output [1, 26]), as long as the database input to the application is considered untrusted (or, as a more precise alternative, the database could store flags indicating which of its entries' symbols are tainted).

Defining "injection" Finally, Definition 7 interprets "injection" as meaning that symbols have been directly copied from input to output. For example, loading a tainted symbol from memory into a register would taint that register's value, but adding two tainted integers involves no direct copying and therefore produces an untainted result. Thus, Definition 7 does not consider CIAOs to occur when applications output programs whose code symbols are "massaged" versions of untrusted inputs—the massaging (i.e., noncopy manipulation) prevents the input symbols from being considered injected. Intuitively, an application like `output(input()+1)` may input a `1` from an untrusted user and then output the program `2`. In this case it seems inaccurate to say that the user "injected" the `2`, given that the user never entered a `2`, and the application produced the `2` by actively transforming its input. If anything, the application and user have collaborated to produce the `2` that got output. One could consider this example demonstrative of a more general class of attacks: data-dependency-based CIAOs.

4.2.1 Data-dependency-based CIAOs

Following this train of thought leads us to define *data-dependency-based CIAOs* in exactly the same way as regular CIAOs (which henceforth will also be called *copy-based CIAOs*), except that for data-dependency-based CIAOs we broaden taint propagation to occur on all data operations, not just copies and outputs. That is, for any data dependency in which the value of a symbol σ depends on the value of at least one tainted symbol, σ must also be tainted. In the example above, we would taint the `2` produced by adding a tainted `1` with an untainted `1`. As a better example, consider the application `output(toUpper(input())+'()')`, which outputs `EXIT()` after inputting `exit`. Definition 7 does not consider this `exit` input to be a copy-based CIAO because with copy-based tainting, the output is just `EXIT()`, with no symbols tainted/underlined. However, the `exit` input is a data-dependency-based CIAO because with data-dependency-based tainting, the output is EXIT(). Note that every copy-based CIAO is also a data-dependency-based CIAO.

In many cases, such as the all-caps-function-name application above, it may be helpful to detect and prevent data-dependency-based CIAOs. In other cases, data-dependency-based-CIAOs may be expected, so system administrators may not find it helpful for them to be caught and flagged (similar to expected copy-based CIAOs, discussed above). For example, an application for managing online courses might hash an input student number to obtain a discussion-group number g and then output a program like `SELECT numPosts FROM group_g where threadNum=4`. Assuming g is obtained through noncopy operations on the untrusted student-number input, this application exhibits a non-copy-based, data-dependency-based CIAO. But the application programmers and system administrators would likely not consider this data-dependency-based CIAO malicious.

4.2.2 Code-interference Attacks

Broadening taint propagation further, one might consider taints to propagate even through control dependencies. To illustrate, let's consider the following application, which is semantically equivalent to the input-echoing application `output(input())` and performs what [3] calls a "conditional copy".

```
while(there are more input symbols) {
  switch(next input symbol) {
    case 'a' : output('a'); break;
    case 'b' : output('b'); break;
    ...
  }
}
```

This switch-based application is *invulnerable* to (copy-based and data-dependency-based) CIAOs because there are no data dependencies between input and output symbols—every symbol output is a constant hardcoded into the application source code. On the other hand, the semantically equivalent input-echoing application *is* vulnerable to (copy-based and data-dependency-based) CIAOs because it directly copies input symbols into the output. These are reasonable consequences of only dealing with code-*injection* attacks; CIAOs only occur when code symbols in output programs directly depend on untrusted input.

Still, it may be desirable to prevent applications from behaving as the switch-based application above does, and more generally, to prevent untrusted inputs from interfering at all (even indirectly, through control dependencies) with the code symbols an application outputs. To do so, we propose studying *CIntAOs*—code-*interference* attacks on outputs. The switch-based application above *is* vulnerable to CIntAOs because its input can interfere with the code symbols that get output.

An application is vulnerable to CIntAOs whenever inputs differing in untrusted symbols can cause the application to output programs differing in code symbols. In other words, applications invulnerable to CIntAOs must, when given the same trusted inputs, always output programs containing the same code symbols.

Definition 8. *A CIntAO occurs exactly when:*

1. *Application A, on trusted and untrusted input sequences $T \in \Sigma^*$ and $U \in \Sigma^*$, outputs L-program p.*
2. *There exists another untrusted input sequence $U' \in \Sigma^*$ such that:*
   (a) *On T and U', A outputs L-program p'.*
   (b) *The subsequence of code symbols in p is not equal to the subsequence of code symbols in p'.*

The switch-based application above is invulnerable to CIAOs but vulnerable to CIntAOs. It also is possible for applications to be invulnerable to CIntAOs but vulnerable to CIAOs. For example, the application `if input='1+1' then output(input) else output('1+1')` exhibits a CIAO on input '1+1' but cannot exhibit a CIntAO because there is no way to change the subsequence of code symbols in the output program by changing the untrusted input.

Although it may sometimes be desirable to detect CIntAOs, the strictness with which they're defined causes many reasonable applications, which are free of CIAOs, to exhibit CIntAOs. For example, an application could accept some untrusted input indicating which currency to output an account balance in; if the desired currency is not the default, the application might output some code to multiply the fetched balance by a conversion rate. This application exhibits neither data-dependency-based nor copy-based CIAOs because the code symbols it outputs (e.g., the multiplication symbol) are not data-dependent on the input currency. However, this application does exhibit CIntAOs because the input currency affects (through a control dependency) the code that gets output (i.e., whether or not a multiplication gets included in the output program). Hence, this example application illustrates that CIntAOs, like copy- and data-dependency-based CIAOs, may be expected and not considered malicious for some applications.

5. Implications of the Definition of CIAOs

Analyzing the previous sections' definitions provides insight into the pervasiveness of CIAO and CIntAO vulnerabilities, as well as various mechanisms' effectiveness at mitigating CIAOs.

5.1 Pervasiveness of CIAO and CIntAO Vulnerabilities

We've been surprised to find that any application that always blindly copies some untrusted input verbatim into its SQL° output is vulnerable to a (copy-based) CIAO at runtime. Theorem 9 formalizes this result; it states that if an application always includes an untrusted input (i_m) verbatim in its output (without even inspecting that input), and the same application has some input ($v_1, .., v_n$) for which it outputs a valid SQL° program, then there exists a way to construct the untrusted input (a_m) such that the application's output will contain an injected code symbol. The proof is constructive; it shows how to inject code into any such application using a detailed case analysis of the kind of value the untrusted input (v_m) gets injected into. Although the proof is tailored to SQL°, the proof techniques are general.

Theorem 9. *For all n-ary functions A and (n-1)-ary functions A' and A'', if $\forall i_1, .., i_n \colon A(i_1, .., i_n) = A'(i_1, .., i_{m-1}, i_{m+1}, .., i_n)\underline{i_m}A''(i_1, .., i_{m-1}, i_{m+1}, .., i_n)$, where $1 \le m \le n$ and $\exists v_1, .., v_n \colon (v_m \in \Sigma^+_{SQL^\circ} \wedge A(v_1, .., v_n) \in SQL^\circ)$, then $\exists a_1, .., a_n \colon A(a_1, .., a_n) \in SQL^\circ$ and $A(a_1, .., a_n)$ exhibits a (copy-based) CIAO.*

Proof. By assumption, $\exists v_1, .., v_n \colon A(v_1, .., v_n) \in SQL^\circ$. First, if $A(v_1, .., v_n)$ exhibits a CIAO, then simply set $a_1, .., a_n$ to $v_1, .., v_n$. On the other hand, if $A(v_1, .., v_n)$ does not exhibit a CIAO, then, by the definition of CIAOs, v_m must be a substring of a value, because v_m is not empty and appears verbatim in the output of $A(v_1, .., v_n)$. Note that changing the untrusted v_m input to a_m, without changing any of the other $n-1$ inputs, will cause A to output $A'(v_1, .., v_{m-1}, v_{m+1}, .., v_n)\underline{a_m}A''(v_1, .., v_{m-1}, v_{m+1}, .., v_n)$, that is, the same output program but with a_m instead of v_m. We will show that no matter the type of the value that v_m is a substring of, there exists an a_m that will cause $A(v_1, .., v_{m-1}, a_m, v_{m+1}, .., v_n)$ to exhibit a (copy-based) CIAO but still remain valid.

- *Case* STR_LITERAL: a_m = if (the first character of v_m is not an apostrophe or is the first apostrophe of a double-apostrophe escape sequence) then ' + GLOBAL + 'v_m else ' ' + GLOBAL + v_m

Examples:

- 'fname' becomes 'f' + GLOBAL + 'name'.
- ' ' ' ' becomes ' ' + GLOBAL + ' ' ' '.
- 'fname' becomes ' ' + GLOBAL + 'fname'.

Let s_m denote the string literal that v_m is a substring of. If v_m does not start s_m (which could happen if v_m begins with the first apostrophe of a double-apostrophe escape sequence), then the string literal must have been started earlier, as $A(v_1, .., v_n) \in SQL^{\circ}$. In this case, our construction of a_m terminates the string literal that has been started, inserts a code symbol (the concatenation operator), a global variable, another code symbol, and then begins a second string literal. If v_m terminated s_m, then this new string literal will also be terminated by v_m. If v_m did not terminate s_m, then it must have been terminated later, again because $A(v_1, .., v_n) \in SQL^{\circ}$. As a result, this second string literal will also be terminated later. On the other hand, if v_m did start s_m (or is the second apostrophe of a double-apostrophe escape sequence), then our construction creates an empty string literal (or finishes the escape sequence and terminates the literal) and concatenates a global variable and then concatenates another second string literal started by v_m. Again, we know that this second string literal will be terminated, either by v_m or the characters following it, for the same reasons as earlier. Thus, our construction of a_m causes s_m, when a_m has been substituted for v_m, to be parsed as $s' + GLOBAL + s''$, where s' and s'' are both valid string literals. Note that `expr OP expr` is a valid `expr`, and as long as GLOBAL is of type string, $s' + GLOBAL + s''$ will be of the same type as s_m. As any `expr` can by replaced by another `expr` of the same type, the program will remain valid after the substitution of a_m for v_m. As a_m contains a code symbol (i.e. 2 concatenation operators, as well as whitespace), a CIAO is exhibited.

- *Case* `INT_LITERAL`, `FLOAT_LITERAL`: $a_m = v_m$1*exit()*2

  Examples:

  - -100 becomes -1 * exit() * 2100.
  - 11E34 becomes 11E1 * exit() *234.

  This construction works for similar reasons as the `STRING_LITERAL` case above; In addition to the 2 multiplication code symbols, this construction also has a function call.

- *Case* `TRUE`, `FALSE`, `NULL`: Let ID_m denote the keyword that v_m is a substring of; hence ID_m can be written as $ID_{m-}v_m ID_{m+}$ (where ID_{m-} and ID_{m+} are in $\Sigma^*_{SQL^{\circ}}$). If ID_m has a boolean type, then let OP be `OR` and let SUB be $1000 > GLOBAL$. Otherwise, let OP be `+`, and let SUB be $exit()$ if ID_m has an integer or float type, or $GLOBAL$ otherwise. Then let $a_m = v_m ID_{m+}\ OP\ SUB\ OP\ ID_{m-}v_m$.

  Examples:

  - FALSE becomes FALSE OR 1000> GLOBAL OR FALSE.
  - NULL + 3 becomes NULL + exit() + NULL + 3.

  By assumption, v_m is a substring of a keyword ID_m. We assumed earlier that $A(v_1, .., v_n) \in SQL^{\circ}$, so ID_m must be a valid keyword. We also know that in $A(v_1, .., v_n)$, v_m is preceded by ID_{m-} and followed by ID_{m+}. We construct a_m such that it finishes the identifier or keyword started by the existing ID_{m-}, inserts a code symbol depending on the type of ID_m, conducts an attack, then inserts another code symbol, and begins a new identifier or keyword to be finished by the existing ID_{m+}. As a result, where originally the program used ID_m as an `expr`, the modified program uses $ID_m\ OP\ SUB\ OP\ ID_m$. Furthermore, the type of the `expr` remains unchanged, as if ID_m has a boolean type, then OP will be `OR`, and a boolean OR'd with a boolean is a boolean. If ID_m has a float or integer type, then OP will be the arithmetic operator `+`, which will return either a float or an integer type. If ID_m has a string type, then the `+` operator denotes concatenation, and two stings concatenated with each other form a string. Note that the only keyword that is a value and can have a type of int, float, or string is `NULL`, as it can assume any type.

  Note that a CIAO has already occurred when `NULL` is used in `expr IS NULL`, because `NULL` is only a value when parsed as an entire `expr`. □

Furthermore, any application that verbatim copies untrusted input into the (SQL°) output program is either vulnerable to CIntAOs or can be made to output an invalid program. Again, the proof is constructive; it shows how to create an untrusted input that changes the sequence of code symbols in, or invalidates, the output program.

Theorem 10. *For all n-ary functions A and (n-1)-ary functions A' and A'', if $\forall i_1, .., i_n\colon A(i_1, .., i_n) = A'(i_1, .., i_{m-1}, i_{m+1}, .., i_n)i_m A''(i_1, .., i_{m-1}, i_{m+1}, .., i_n)$, where $1 \le m \le n$ and $\exists v_1, .., v_n\colon (v_m \in \Sigma^+_{SQL^{\circ}} \land A(v_1, .., v_n) \in SQL^{\circ})$, then A either exhibits a CIntAO or can be made to produce an invalid SQL° program.*

Proof. Observe that every symbol in an SQL° program is either part of a value or not. If v_m contains a symbol recognized as part of a value, then the input can be modified in the manner described in the proof of Theorem 9, and the sequence of code symbols will be modified; by definition, A exhibits a CIntAO. On the other hand, if v_m contains a code symbol, then a different symbol can be provided. If the SQL° program is still valid, then a CIntAO has occurred, as the sequence of code symbols has changed. If changing the code symbol made the program invalid then the second condition of the implication is satisfied. □

Given that (program-outputting) applications commonly copy some untrusted input verbatim into the output, Theorems 9–10 show that vulnerabilities to CIAOs and CIntAOs are pervasive.

5.2 Limitations of Static and Black-box Mechanisms to Detect CIAOs

Determining whether an application is vulnerable to CIAOs requires knowing which input symbols propagate to the output program. This makes it undecidable to precisely detect (both copy-based and data-dependency-based) CIAOs using static code analysis or black-box analysis.

Theorem 11. *There exists an application A, which inputs a string of symbols over alphabet Σ and outputs L-programs, such that it is undecidable, when given only an input string $s \in \Sigma^*$ and a (e.g., Turing-machine) encoding of A, to determine whether A exhibits a (copy-based or data-dependency-based) CIAO on s.*

Proof. Let A be an application that inputs a string s, executes subprogram p, and then outputs s if s equals "1+1" but otherwise outputs just "1". This A outputs programs in any language having integers and addition. Also, A exhibits a (copy-based and data-dependency-based) CIAO iff its subprogram p halts and its input s is "1+1". Statically determining whether A exhibits a CIAO on input "1+1" therefore reduces to the halting problem. □

Theorem 12. *There exists an application A, which inputs a string of symbols over alphabet Σ and outputs L-programs, such that it is impossible, when given only an input string $s \in \Sigma^*$ and the*

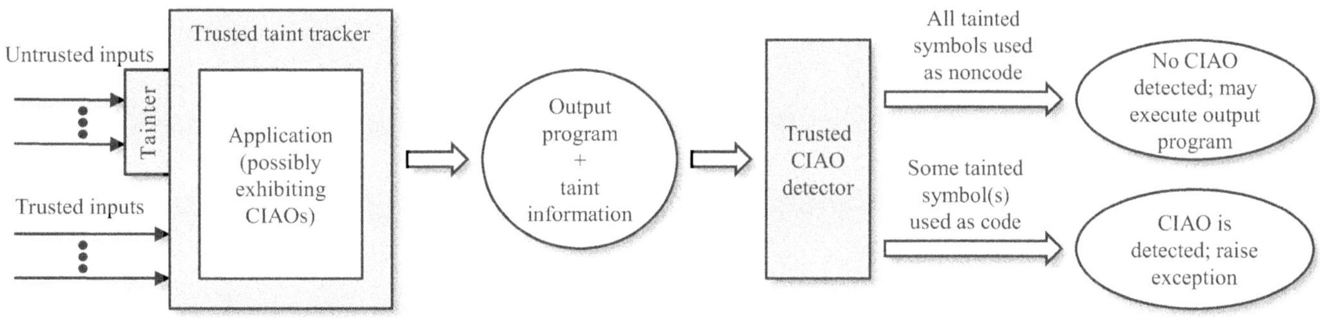

Figure 3. Overview of a CIAO-Preventing Mechanism. Trusted components are shaded.

ability (i.e., an oracle) to predict the output of A on any input, to determine whether A exhibits a (copy-based or data-dependency-based) CIAO on s. In other words, there exist observationally equivalent applications A and A' and a string s such that $A(s)$ exhibits a CIAO but $A'(s)$ does not exhibit a CIAO.

Proof. Let A be the input-echoing application `output(input)` and A' the conditional-copy application from Section 4.2.2. Recall from Section 4.2.2 that A and A' are observationally equivalent, A is vulnerable to CIAOs (e.g., on an input like `1+1`), and A' is invulnerable to CIAOs. □

Theorems 11–12 are interesting because they rule out certain classes of mechanisms from being able to precisely detect CIAOs. Some of the mechanisms ruled out were previously thought to precisely detect CIAOs; an example is SQLCHECK's black-box, "bracket"-based tainting mechanism (in which untrusted inputs get surrounded by special characters, and output symbols are considered tainted iff they're surrounded by those characters) [34]. Although previous work showed that SQLCHECK's tainting mechanism is flawed [3], Theorems 11–12 are more general, in that they rule out entire classes of mechanisms from being able to precisely detect CIAOs.

Of course, Theorems 11–12 don't rule out static analysis and black-box mechanisms as being useful for mitigating CIAOs. Although such mechanisms can't detect CIAOs precisely, they can detect CIAOs conservatively (i.e., soundly but not completely) with no/low runtime overhead, while avoiding the many practical obstacles to monitoring taints dynamically (some of which are described in Section 5.4).

However, sound static mechanisms for detecting CIAOs must be so conservative as to reject a large class of common applications, which may limit their appeal. Recall that Theorem 9 showed that all applications that copy some untrusted input verbatim into an output program can be made to exhibit a CIAO at runtime. Hence, sound static mechanisms for detecting CIAOs must reject all of this large class of common applications. (Similarly, Theorem 10 implies that sound CIntAO-detecting static mechanisms must reject all such applications as well.) Related work on static-analysis techniques for detecting CIAOs [12, 35, 40] appear to be consistent with this result; none seem to allow applications to copy untrusted input verbatim into output programs. Having a formal definition of CIAOs makes it possible to prove that this characteristic is mandatory for all sound, static, CIAO-detecting mechanisms.

5.3 Design of Mechanisms for Precisely Detecting and Preventing CIAOs

Theorems 11–12 prove that precisely detecting CIAOs requires a dynamic white-box mechanism. A high-level design of such a mechanism follows straightforwardly from the definitions in Sections 3–4.

A dynamic white-box mechanism can precisely detect and prevent CIAOs by:

- tainting all symbols input to an application A from untrusted sources,
- transparently tracking one taint bit per symbol,
- propagating taints through exactly A's copy and output operations (for copy-based CIAOs) or all data operations (for data-dependency-based CIAOs),
- intercepting A's output programs, and
- forbidding execution of output programs that contain at least one tainted symbol used outside a value (i.e., as code).

Figure 3 illustrates such a mechanism.

Theorem 13. *Assuming a mechanism M performs these operations on an application that outputs programs in a language with decidable free-variable (FV) and value (Val) functions, it is decidable for M to precisely detect and prevent CIAOs.*

Proof. Immediate by Definition 7 and the definitions of data-dependency CIAOs and mechanism M given above. □

Algorithm 1 directly implements this generic design of dynamic white-box mechanisms for preventing CIAOs. The algorithm relies on auxiliary functions for (1) adding taint tracking to applications, (2) signaling that untrusted inputs are tainted, (3) calculating the set of free variables in a sequence of program symbols, and (4) deciding whether program symbols constitute a value.

Each of the three nested *for* loops in Algorithm 1 executes $O(n)$ times, where n denotes the size of the output program. Hence, if we ignore the complexities of the FV and Val functions (which are dependent on the output-program language), the top-level *for* loop of Algorithm 1 runs in $O(n^3)$ time. Assuming that the FV and Val functions run in time linear in their input size, then, the top-level *for* loop of Algorithm 1 runs in $O(n^4)$ time.

The space required by the top-level *for* loop of Algorithm 1 consists of the i, low, and $high$ counters (each of size $O(\lg n)$), the $IsCiao$ flag (of size $O(1)$), and whatever space is required to invoke and execute the FV and Val functions. Assuming that invoking and executing the FV and Val functions uses space linear in their input size, then, the top-level *for* loop of Algorithm 1 uses $O(n)$ space.

Optimized CIAO-Preventing Mechanism Algorithm 1 can be optimized to run in $O(n)$ time and space, under the assumption that the output-program language has an LR(k) grammar in which every closed value matches some syntactic category (e.g., in SQL° every

Algorithm 1: Basic CIAO-Preventing Mechanism

```
Input: Application A and inputs T, U (trusted, untrusted)
Ensure: A's output is executed iff it doesn't exhibit a CIAO
  A' ← AddTaintTracking(A)
  Output ← A' (T, Taint(U))
  for i ← 1 to |Output| do
      if tainted(Output[i]) then
          IsCiao ← true
          for low ← 1 to i do
              for high ← i to |Output| do
                  if FV(Output, low, high) = ∅ and
                     Val(Output, low, high) then
                      IsCiao ← false
                  end if
              end for
          end for
          if IsCiao then
              throw CiaoException
          end if
      end if
  end for
  Execute(Output)
```

closed value matches the `expr` category). When output-program languages satisfy this assumption, Algorithm 1's top-level *for* loop can be replaced with a shift-reduce parse of the application's output program. When reducing a closed-value right-side R of a production to a nonterminal N, the parser sets an `isVal` attribute for N and erases taints on all output-program symbols represented by R (except for any symbols represented by nonterminals in R for which `isVal` has been set—such symbols have already had their taints erased). After running this taint-erasing parser, all output-program taints in closed values will have been erased, so a CIAO is detected if and only if some tainted symbol remains in the output program.

Algorithm 2 presents pseudocode for this optimized CIAO-preventing mechanism. The algorithm relies on auxiliary functions for (1) adding taint tracking to applications, (2) signaling that untrusted inputs are tainted, (3) tokenizing output programs, and (4) shift-reduce parsing output programs.

Algorithm 2: Optimized CIAO-Preventing Mechanism (for applications whose output-program language has an LR(k) grammar in which every closed value matches some syntactic category)

```
Input: Application A and inputs T, U (trusted, untrusted)
Ensure: A's output is executed iff it doesn't exhibit a CIAO
  A' ← AddTaintTracking(A)
  Output ← A' (T, Taint(U))
  let
      function clearTaints (p_1, ..., p_n) =
          for i ← 1 to n do
              Current ← dereference(p_i)
              if Current is a terminal then
                  for j ← Current.begin to Current.end do
                      Output[j].Tainted = false
                  end for
              else if Current.isVal=false then
                  clearTaints(Current.children)
              end if
              if i < n then // clear tainted whitespace, if any
                  Next ← dereference(p_{i+1})
                  for j ← Current.end to Next.begin do
                      Output[j].Tainted = false
                  end for
              end if
          end for
      end function
  end let
  in
      tokens ← run tokenize (Output)
          on recognition of token t do
              t.begin ← position of first symbol of t in Output
              t.end ← position of last symbol of t in Output
          end on
      end run
      run shift-reduce-parse (tokens)
          on reducing by production N ::= s_1 s_2 ... s_n, where
          s_1..s_n is a closed value do
              N.isVal ← true
              clearTaints(list of pointers to s_1, ..., s_n)
              N.begin ← s_1.begin
              N.end ← s_n.end
          end on
          on reducing by production N ::= s_1 s_2 ... s_n, where
          s_1..s_n is not a closed value do
              N.isVal ← false
              N.children ← list of pointers to s_1..s_n
              N.begin ← s_1.begin
              N.end ← s_n.end
          end on
      end run
      for i ← 1 to |Output| do
          if tainted(Output[i]) then
              throw CiaoException
          end if
      end for
  end in
  Execute(Output)
```

Theorem 14. *The* let-in *block of Algorithm 2 runs in $O(n)$ time and space.*

Proof. The tokenization portion of Algorithm 2 runs in $O(n)$ time and space (where again n is the size of the application's output program). A standard shift-reduce parse of the output program, without the additional actions performed on reductions, runs in $O(n)$ time and space; the total number of right-hand-side-production symbols reduced to nonterminals during the parse is $O(n)$ [15]. Because the total number of right-hand-side-production symbols reduced to nonterminals during the parse is $O(n)$, all the non-taint-clearing reduction actions in Algorithm 2 (i.e., N.isVal←`true`, N.begin ← s_1.begin, etc.) occur in $O(n)$ total time and space. The *for* loop in Algorithm 2's *in* block also runs in $O(n)$ time and space, so Algorithm 2's entire *in* block uses linear time and space, in addition to the time and space used to clear taints.

To determine the total time and space used by taint-clearing operations, observe that clearTaints is always initially invoked, in Algorithm 2's *in* block, on symbols matching a nonterminal N such that N.isVal=`true`. During execution, clearTaints may call itself recursively only on parse-tree-descendent nonterminals with `false` isVal attributes. Because parsing is bottom-up, then, pointers to the same syntax-tree symbol may never be passed as arguments to clearTaints more than once, and every output-program taint may be cleared at most once (technically this result also relies on the facts that isVal attributes are constant once set, taints can only be cleared by clearTaints, and clearTaints, when called on pointers to symbols $s_1..s_n$, can only clear taints at output-program positions s_1.begin to s_n.end). Also observe that, ignoring recursive clearTaints calls, each run of clearTaints executes in time proportional to the number of pointers to nonterminals passed as arguments plus the number of taints cleared. Then because (1) pointers to the same syntax-tree symbol may never be passed as arguments to clearTaints more than once, (2) the total number of nonterminals in the parse tree is $O(n)$ [15], (3) every output-program taint may be cleared at most once, and (4) each run of clearTaints executes in time proportional to the number of pointers to nonterminals passed as arguments plus the number of taints cleared, we have that the total time (and therefore space) used by all clearTaints operations is $O(n)$.

Hence, Algorithm 2's entire *let-in* block uses $O(n)$ time and space, as required. □

5.4 Obstacles to Monitoring Taints in Practice

Many taint-monitoring mechanisms and frameworks exist for mitigating CIAOs (e.g., [6, 8, 25, 31, 38]). None separate code from noncode the way this paper has, but one framework, Dytan [6], which has not yet been publicly released, implements (for x86 applications) the taint-tracking functionality our definitions require. Hence, it appears possible to use Dytan to precisely detect (copy-based and data-dependency-based) CIAOs in x86 applications (by ensuring that all operations in Section 5.3's bulleted list are performed).

Even with powerful taint-monitoring frameworks like Dytan, there are several obstacles to ensuring that taint-monitoring mechanisms obey the four tainting constraints listed in Section 4.1. This subsection briefly summarizes these obstacles, most of which are discussed in greater length elsewhere (e.g., [6, 8, 24, 31, 33]).

The first of the four tainting constraints in Section 4.1 requires all symbols input to the application from untrusted sources to be tainted. Untrusted inputs may come from many sources (e.g., HTTP GET and POST requests, cookies, server variables, or a database), and enumerating all these untrusted sources may be difficult and error prone. Hence, following Halfond, Orso, and Manolios, one might instead use *positive* tainting [8] (i.e., tracking which output-program symbols derive from *trusted* sources, often just the string literals hardcoded in an application). It would be straightforward to adjust this paper's definition of CIAOs to use positive (rather than negative) tainting: CIAOs would occur when some code symbol in an output program is not positively tainted.

The second and third of the four tainting constraints require that taints propagate through exactly copy and output operations (for copy-based CIAOs), or all data operations (for data-dependency-based CIAOs). Because a taint bit must be tracked for every input symbol, the tainting mechanism must operate with fine granularity, which previous work has found to induce high runtime overhead (e.g., many thousands of percent of overhead) [6, 24, 38]. In addition, monitoring taints typically requires executing applications in modified runtime environments, which limits portability [9]. And propagating taints through output operations, so output programs can be caught and checked prior to being executed, may be difficult; it may be hard to enumerate all the ways an application can output programs (e.g., to files, remote hosts, or standard output). If an application's outputs can circumvent a CIAO-mitigating mechanism, the mechanism is unsound. Applications might also circumvent taint-monitoring mechanisms by executing external (e.g., native) code [8].

The last of the four tainting constraints requires taints to be transparent. This transparency ensures that taint tracking does not affect application behaviors; CIAO-preventing mechanisms should only modify application behaviors when attacks are detected (in which case the behavior must be modified to prevent injected code from being output). To be transparent, tainting mechanisms have to isolate taints from applications. Hence, CIAO-mitigating mechanisms cannot use bracketing techniques to track taints (e.g., [34])—the brackets are visible to applications [3]. Another important obstacle to ensuring transparency in practice is that runtime mechanisms generally induce overhead on application performance, and this overhead may make time-sensitive applications behave differently. Perfect transparency may therefore be difficult or impossible to achieve for time-sensitive applications in practice.

6. Summary

This paper has defined code-injection attacks on outputs. The definition simply considers CIAOs to occur when untrusted inputs get used as nonvalues (or open values) in output programs. This definition avoids problems with conventional CIAO definitions, which sometimes consider CIAOs to be non-CIAOs and vice versa.

The new definition of CIAOs has been used to:

- Distinguish between copy-based CIAOs, data-dependency-based CIAOs, and CIntAOs based on whether taints propagate through copy, data, or all (data and control) dependencies.
- Prove that a large class of applications (i.e., those that always blindly copy some untrusted input to the output program) are inherently vulnerable to CIAOs and CIntAOs, so sound static mechanisms must disallow these applications from executing.
- Prove that precisely detecting CIAOs requires dynamic white-box mechanisms. The generic design of such mechanisms follows immediately from the definition of CIAOs. Under reasonable assumptions these mechanisms can be optimized to detect CIAOs in output programs in $O(n)$ time and space. Nonetheless, due to their reliance on taint tracking, many obstacles impede implementation of precise CIAO-mitigating mechanisms in practice.

Hence, the new definition of CIAOs has been used to analyze precisely when they occur, how they can be mitigated, and how efficiently they can be mitigated. We hope these results can serve as a foundation for improving the effectiveness of future CIAO-mitigating mechanisms.

Acknowledgments

We are grateful to the anonymous reviewers of this paper, who provided many valuable comments. This research was supported by NSF grants CNS-0716343 and CNS-0742736.

References

[1] C. Anley. Advanced SQL injection in SQL server applications. White paper, Next Generation Security Software, 2002.

[2] S. Bandhakavi, P. Bisht, P. Madhusudan, and V. N. Venkatakrishnan. Candid: preventing SQL injection attacks using dynamic candidate evaluations. In *Proceedings of the ACM Conference on Computer and Communications Security*, pages 12–24, 2007.

[3] P. Bisht, P. Madhusudan, and V. N. Venkatakrishnan. CANDID: Dynamic candidate evaluations for automatic prevention of SQL injection attacks. *ACM Trans. Inf. Syst. Secur.*, 13(2):1–39, Feb. 2010.

[4] M. Bravenboer, E. Dolstra, and E. Visser. Preventing injection attacks with syntax embeddings. *Science of Computer Programming*, 75(7): 473–495, July 2010.

[5] G. Buehrer, B. W. Weide, and P. A. G. Sivilotti. Using parse tree validation to prevent sql injection attacks. In *SEM '05: Proceedings of the 5th international workshop on software engineering and middleware*, pages 106–113, 2005.

[6] J. Clause, W. Li, and A. Orso. Dytan: a generic dynamic taint analysis framework. In *Proceedings of the ACM International Symposium on Software Testing and Analysis*, pages 196–206, 2007.

[7] J. Condit, M. Harren, S. McPeak, G. C. Necula, and W. Weimer. Ccured in the real world. *SIGPLAN Notices*, 38:232–244, May 2003.

[8] W. Halfond, A. Orso, and P. Manolios. Wasp: Protecting web applications using positive tainting and syntax-aware evaluation. *IEEE Trans. Softw. Eng.*, 34(1):65–81, 2008.

[9] W. G. Halfond, J. Viegas, and A. Orso. A Classification of SQL-Injection Attacks and Countermeasures. In *Proceedings of the IEEE International Symposium on Secure Software Engineering*, March 2006.

[10] R. Hansen and M. Patterson. *Stopping Injection Attacks with Computational Theory*, July 2005. In Black Hat USA.

[11] T. Jim, J. G. Morrisett, D. Grossman, M. W. Hicks, J. Cheney, and Y. Wang. Cyclone: A safe dialect of c. In *Proceedings of the General Track of the USENIX Annual Technical Conference*, pages 275–288, Berkeley, CA, USA, 2002. USENIX Association.

[12] N. Jovanovic, C. Kruegel, and E. Kirda. Pixy: A static analysis tool for detecting web application vulnerabilities (short paper). In *Proceedings of the IEEE Symposium on Security and Privacy*, pages 258–263, 2006.

[13] A. Kieżun, P. J. Guo, K. Jayaraman, and M. D. Ernst. Automatic creation of SQL injection and cross-site scripting attacks. In *Proceedings of the International Conference on Software Engineering*, May 2009.

[14] K. Kline and D. Kline. *SQL in a Nutshell*, chapter 4. O'Reilly, 2001.

[15] D. E. Knuth. On the translation of languages from left to right. *Information and Control*, 8(6):607–639, 1965.

[16] P. J. Landin. The mechanical evaluation of expressions. *Computer Journal*, 6(4):308–320, 1963.

[17] Z. Luo, T. Rezk, and M. Serrano. Automated code injection prevention for web applications. In *Proceedings of the Conference on Theory of Security and Applications*, 2011.

[18] Microsoft. *SQL Minimum Grammar*, 2011. `http://msdn.microsoft.com/en-us/library/ms711725(VS.85).aspx`.

[19] Microsoft. *CREATE FUNCTION (Transact-SQL)*, 2011. `http://msdn.microsoft.com/en-us/library/ms186755.aspx`.

[20] *CWE/SANS Top 25 Most Dangerous Software Errors*. The MITRE Corporation, 2009. Document version 1.4, `http://cwe.mitre.org/top25/archive/2009/2009_cwe_sans_top_25.pdf`.

[21] *CWE/SANS Top 25 Most Dangerous Software Errors*. The MITRE Corporation, 2010. Document version 1.08, `http://cwe.mitre.org/top25/archive/2010/2010_cwe_sans_top25.pdf`.

[22] *CWE/SANS Top 25 Most Dangerous Software Errors*. The MITRE Corporation, 2011. Document version 1.0.2, `http://cwe.mitre.org/top25/archive/2011/2011_cwe_sans_top25.pdf`.

[23] G. C. Necula, J. Condit, M. Harren, S. McPeak, and W. Weimer. Ccured: type-safe retrofitting of legacy software. *ACM Trans. Program. Lang. Syst.*, 27:477–526, May 2005.

[24] J. Newsome and D. X. Song. Dynamic taint analysis for automatic detection, analysis, and signature generation of exploits on commodity software. In *Proceedings of the Network and Distributed System Security Symposium*, Feb. 2005.

[25] A. Nguyen-tuong, S. Guarnieri, D. Greene, J. Shirley, and D. Evans. Automatically hardening web applications using precise tainting. In *Proceedings of the IFIP International Information Security Conference*, pages 372–382, 2005.

[26] G. Ollmann. Second order code injection attacks. Technical report, NGS Software, 2004.

[27] Oracle. How to write injection-proof PL/SQL. An Oracle White Paper, December 2008. URL `http://www.oracle.com/technetwork/database/features/plsql/overview/how-to-write-injection-proof-plsql-1-129572.pdf`. Page 11.

[28] Oracle. *CREATE FUNCTION Syntax for User-Defined Functions*, 2011. `http://dev.mysql.com/doc/refman/5.6/en/create-function-udf.html`.

[29] Oracle. *CREATE FUNCTION*, 2011. `http://download.oracle.com/docs/cd/E11882_01/server.112/e17118/statements_5011.htm`.

[30] php. *phpMyAdmin*. `http://www.phpmyadmin.net`.

[31] T. Pietraszek and C. V. Berghe. Defending against injection attacks through context-sensitive string evaluation. In *Proceedings of Recent Advances in Intrusion Detection (RAID)*, 2005.

[32] G. D. Plotkin. Call-by-name, call-by-value and the λ-calculus. *Theoretical Computer Science*, 1(2):125–159, 1975.

[33] E. J. Schwartz, T. Avgerinos, and D. Brumley. All you ever wanted to know about dynamic taint analysis and forward symbolic execution (but might have been afraid to ask). In *Proceedings of the IEEE Symposium on Security and Privacy*, May 2010.

[34] Z. Su and G. Wassermann. The essence of command injection attacks in web applications. In *Proceedings of the 33rd ACM SIGPLAN-SIGACT Symposium on Principles of Programming Languages*, pages 372–382, 2006.

[35] O. Tripp, M. Pistoia, S. J. Fink, M. Sridharan, and O. Weisman. TAJ: effective taint analysis of web applications. In *Proceedings of the ACM SIGPLAN Conference on Programming Language Design and Implementation*, pages 87–97, 2009.

[36] S. Tzu. The art of war. The Project Gutenberg eBook. Translated by Lionel Giles. `http://www.gutenberg.org/cache/epub/17405/pg17405.txt`.

[37] G. Wassermann and Z. Su. Sound and Precise Analysis of Web Applications for Injection Vulnerabilities. In *Proceedings of the ACM SIGPLAN Conference on Programming Language Design and Implementation*, June 2007.

[38] W. Xu, S. Bhatkar, and R. Sekar. Taint-enhanced policy enforcement: a practical approach to defeat a wide range of attacks. In *Proceedings of the 15th USENIX Security Symposium*, 2006.

[39] Y. Younan, P. Philippaerts, F. Piessens, W. Joosen, S. Lachmund, and T. Walter. Filter-resistant code injection on ARM. In *Proceedings of the ACM Conference on Computer and Communications Security*, pages 11–20, 2009.

[40] X. Zhang and Z. Wang. A static analysis tool for detecting web application injection vulnerabilities for ASP program. In *International Conference on e-Business and Information System Security (EBISS)*, pages 1 –5, May 2010.

Deciding Choreography Realizability

Samik Basu
Iowa State University
Email: sbasu@iastate.edu

Tevfik Bultan
University of California, Santa Barbara
Email: bultan@cs.ucsb.edu

Meriem Ouederni
University of Malaga
Email: meriem@lcc.uma.es

Abstract

Since software systems are becoming increasingly more concurrent and distributed, modeling and analysis of interactions among their components is a crucial problem. In several application domains, message-based communication is used as the interaction mechanism, and the communication contract among the components of the system is specified semantically as a state machine. In the service-oriented computing domain such communication contracts are called "choreography" specifications. A choreography specification identifies allowable ordering of message exchanges in a distributed system. A fundamental question about a choreography specification is determining its realizability, i.e., given a choreography specification, is it possible to build a distributed system that communicates exactly as the choreography specifies? Checking realizability of choreography specifications has been an open problem for several years and it was not known if this was a decidable problem. In this paper we give necessary and sufficient conditions for realizability of choreographies. We implemented the proposed realizability check and our experiments show that it can efficiently determine the realizability of 1) web service choreographies, 2) Singularity OS channel contracts, and 3) UML collaboration (communication) diagrams.

Categories and Subject Descriptors D.2.4 [*Software/Program Verification*]: [Formal Methods]

General Terms Verification

Keywords Message-based Interactions, Choreography, Realizability

1. Introduction

Most software systems nowadays involve concurrent or distributed behavior or both. They run concurrently on multi-core hardware, interact with each other over the network and access data and computational resources distributed over the compute cloud. An important concern in construction of concurrent and distributed software systems is the coordination of different components that form the whole system. In order to complete a task, components of a software system have to coordinate their executions by interacting with each other, and specification and analysis of such interactions is a challenging problem.

Message-based communication is a common interaction mechanism used in concurrent and distributed systems where components interact with each other by sending and receiving messages. Specification and analysis of message-based interactions has been an active research area studied in several application domains including coordination in service-oriented computing [9, 37], interactions in distributed programs [2] and process isolation at the OS level [12]. A crucial problem in all these domains is the choreography realizability problem. A choreography specification identifies the set of allowable message exchange sequences among the components (peers) of a distributed system. A choreography is realizable if there is a way to implement a set of components that conform to the choreography.

Many message-passing systems use asynchronous messaging [4, 23, 24, 28, 30] where components interact with each other by sending and receiving messages over unbounded FIFO channels. Even when the behavior of each component is modeled as a finite state machine, if asynchronous communication is used, the state space of the overall system is infinite. In fact, finite state systems communicating with unbounded FIFO communication channels are powerful enough to simulate Turing machines, and, hence, many verification and analysis problems for them are undecidable [6]. Determining realizability of choreography specifications for asynchronously communicating systems has been an open problem for several years and it was not known if it is decidable.

More precisely, the choreography realizability problem is, given a choreography specified as a finite state machine, is it possible to determine if there exists a set of asynchronously communicating (finite) state machines that generate precisely the set of message sequences specified by the choreography specification. Note that, given a set of asynchronously communicating (finite) state machines, it is not possible to automatically determine the set of message sequences generated by them. However, in this paper we show that the realizability of a choreography specification is decidable, and we give a necessary and sufficient condition for determining realizability. There have been earlier results in this area that provide sufficient conditions for choreography realizability (e.g., [14, 18, 25]). To the best of our knowledge this is the first paper that identifies a necessary and sufficient condition and demonstrates the decidability of the choreography realizability problem. We have also experimentally evaluated our approach by checking the realizability of Singularity channel contracts [12], web service choreographies [37] and collaboration diagrams [7].

Rest of the paper is organized as follows. In Section 2, to motivate our work, we discuss how the realizability problem arises in different domains. We also give a high level overview of the proposed approach. In Section 3 we formally define the realizability problem by formalizing the communication contracts as finite state conversation protocols and a distributed system as a set of finite state peers communicating via messages over FIFO message queues. In Section 4 we present our main results on realizability. In Section 5 we discuss our implementation using the CADP toolbox [17]. In Section 6 we discuss the related work and in Section 7 we conclude the paper.

POPL'12, January 25–27, 2012, Philadelphia, PA, USA.

```
...
<interaction name="SendOffer"
  operation="offer"
  channelVariable="tns:R1ToR2C">

  <participate
    relationshipType="tns:Hagglers"
    fromRoleTypeDef="tns:R1"
    toRoleType="tns:R2/>

    <exchange name=... action="sendOffer">
      <send var="cdl:getVar("offer")/>
    </exchange>
...
</interaction>
```

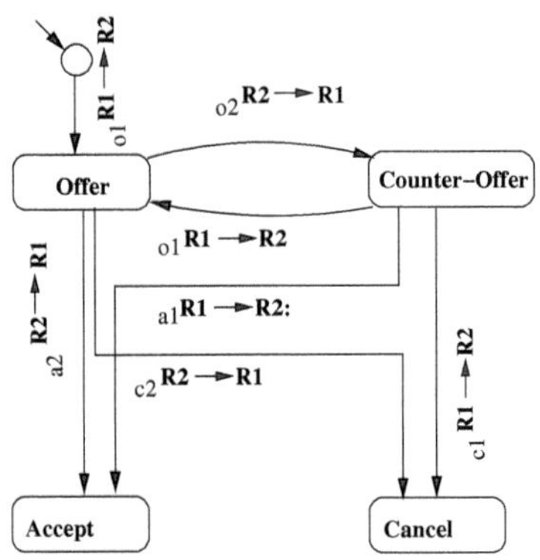

Figure 1. Part of the WS-CDL choreography specification for a bilateral negotiation protocol [22] and the corresponding state machine.

2. Motivation and Overview

In this section we motivate our work by describing four application domains where the choreography realizability problem appears and, therefore, the results from this paper are directly applicable.

2.1 Service Interactions: Choreography Specifications

Service oriented computing provides technologies that enable multiple organizations to integrate their businesses over the Internet [13, 31]. Typical execution behavior in such a distributed system involves a set of autonomous peers[1] interacting with each other through messages. For instance, consider a group of organizations that wish to integrate their online businesses. The front end that enables user interaction via web browsers may reside within one organization, however, in order to serve a user request, this front end may send and receive messages from software components that reside in other organizations. The goal of web services standards and technologies is to facilitate this type of business to business integration. Modeling and analysis of interactions is a crucial problem in this domain due to several distinguishing features of such systems.

First, organizations may not want to share the internal structures of their software components with other organizations they intend to do business with. This type of decoupling requires standardized and rich interface specifications that enable integration of software components that may be written using different languages and implementation platforms. In order to achieve such a decoupling among different components, it is necessary to specify the interactions among different components without referring to the details of their local implementations.

[1] We use "peer" to denote a process/component/program/service that interacts with other processes/components/programs/services.

Second, modeling and analyzing the global behavior of such distributed systems is challenging since no single party may know the full details of all the components in such a system. In the absence of detailed models for the distributed components that participate in such a system, the desired global behaviors have to be specified as constraints on the interactions among different components, since the messages exchanged among different components are the only observable global behavior. Moreover, for this type of distributed systems, it might be worthwhile to model the interactions among different software components before the components are written. This type of top-down design may help different organizations to better coordinate their development efforts.

Choreography specification languages target specification of this type of interactions. For example, Web Services Choreography Description Language (WS-CDL) [37] is an XML-based language for describing the interactions among the peers participating in a composite web service. A choreography specification in WS-CDL corresponds to a global ordering of the message-exchange events among the peers participating in a composite service, i.e., a choreography specification identifies the set of allowable message sequences for a composite web service. Figure 1 presents a snapshot of a WS-CDL specification for two services (behaving as `R1`, i.e., Role1 and `R2`, i.e., Role2) participating in a "haggling" process where each service continues sending offers to the other until one of them accepts the offer or cancels the process. The specification contains information regarding the roles, description of every action in terms of the sender, receiver and the message content and type, and the ordering (branching and sequencing) of actions.

2.2 Interactions Among Concurrent Processes: Singularity Channel Contracts

Singularity is a new, experimental, operating system developed by Microsoft Research to explore new approaches to OS design [21]. One of its main goals is to improve the dependability of software systems by rethinking some design decisions that have largely governed operating system architecture to date. Process isolation is a chief design principle of the Singularity operating system. To achieve this, certain constraints are enforced to ensure process independence. Among these is the rule that processes cannot share memory with each other or the kernel. All inter-process communication in Singularity, therefore, occurs via message-passing over bidirectional conduits, called channels.

Channels have two end points referred to as the client and the server. The client and the server processes use the channel to communicate with each other by sending and receiving messages. Communication through Singularity channels corresponds to asynchronous communication via FIFO queues.

In Singularity, each channel is governed by a *channel contract* [12, 33]. A channel contract is basically a state machine that specifies the allowable ordering of messages between the client and the server. Hence, channel contracts serve the same purpose that choreography specifications serve in service-oriented computing.

Singularity processes are written in an extension of C# called Sing#. It provides constructs for writing channel contracts and its compiler statically checks that the processes communicating over a channel conform to its contract. Figure 2 presents a simplified version of a Sing# contract governing a channel used by Singularity for interacting with a keyboard device. This contract defines three states (`Start`, `Ready`, and `Waiting`) and the evolution among states (`->`) correspond to message exchanges. Singularity contracts are written from the perspective of the server, where send actions by the server are appended with `!` to denote communication from the server to the client and receive actions by the server are appended with `?` to denote communication from the client to the server.

```
public contract KeyboardDeviceContract {
  state Start: {
    Success! -> Ready;
  }
  state Ready: {
    GetKey? -> Waiting;
    PollKey? -> (AckKey! or NakKey!) -> Ready;
  }
  state Waiting: {
    AckKey! -> Ready;
    NakKey! -> Ready;
  }
}
```

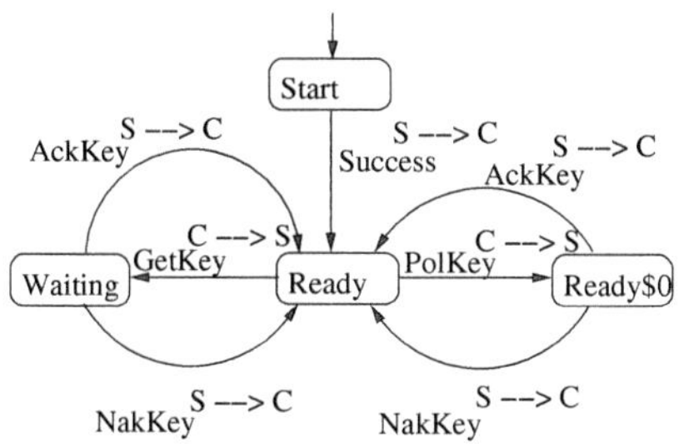

Figure 2. A simplified channel contract from the Singularity OS for keyboard interaction written in Sing# [33] and the corresponding state machine.

```
+NAME("IRC SERVER")
...
+STATE start
  logon()    => ok() & active
             | error() & stop
+STATE active
  ls()       => files() & active
  getFile()  => fileSent() & active
             | noFileErr() & stop
...
```

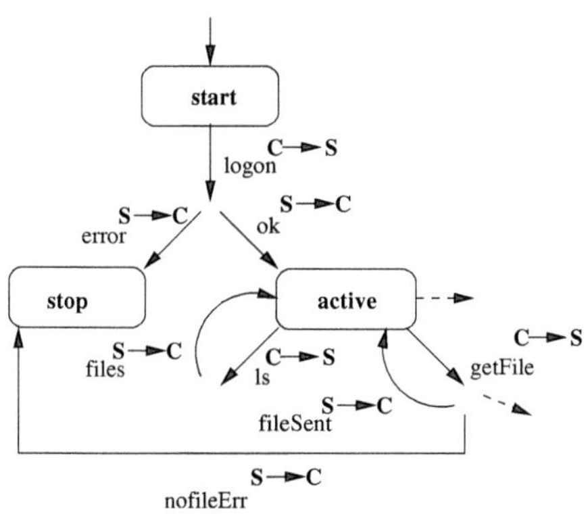

Figure 3. Part of a communication contract for a distributed Erlang program written in UBF(B) [2] and the corresponding state machine.

2.3 Interactions Among Distributed Components: UBF(B) Contracts

Erlang is a general purpose concurrent programming language that was developed initially at Ericsson for improving the dependability of telephony applications [3]. In Erlang, processes do not share memory and only interact with each other via exchanging messages asynchronously.

UBF(B) is a language for specifying *communication contracts* in distributed Erlang programs [2]. Figure 3 presents partial specification of a IRC server interface specification and describes the evolution of the server from one state (`start`, `active`, etc.) to another in response to external stimuli (`logon`, `ls`, etc.). UBF(B) contracts are based on finite state machines. Given a state (e.g., `start`), a transition from that state identifies a request-response sequence where, after receiving a message (e.g., `logon`), the process sends a response (e.g., `ok`) and moves to the destination state (e.g., `active`).

2.4 Visual Interaction Specifications: Collaboration Diagrams

Collaboration diagrams (called communication diagrams in [36]) provide a convenient visual formalism for specifying the interactions among the participants of a distributed system [7, 8]. A *collaboration diagram* is a visual representation of a set of peers, a set of communication links among them, and an ordering of the message exchanges among the peers. Unlike MSCs [29], collaboration diagrams specify the global ordering of send events rather than the local ordering of send and receive events. The semantics of collaboration diagrams can be formalized as a state machine characterizing all allowable ordering of message exchanges in a distributed system [8]. Hence, for example, collaboration diagrams can be used as a visual formalism for representing web service choreographies.

2.5 Overview of the Proposed Approach

Web service choreography specifications, Singularity channel contracts, UBF(B) contracts and collaboration diagrams are all different mechanisms for specifying ordering of messages exchanged among a set of concurrent or distributed processes. Analysis of message-based interactions is an essential problem for all these languages. And, although these languages target different application domains, the interaction analysis problem remains the same. In short (a) communication contract specifications cut across a wide range of application domains (service-oriented computing, new paradigms for OS, embedded systems); (b) communication contracts are used to specify message-based interactions among peers (services, client/servers, real-time software); and, finally, (c) one key problem for communication contracts used in each of these application domains is to check whether a given communication contract can be *realized*.

In this paper we present a necessary and sufficient condition for realizability and show how it can be applied to multiple domains. In our approach, we first translate communication contracts specified in different languages into a *conversation protocol* which is a finite state machine that specifies the allowable sequences of messages (i.e., conversations) among a set of peers. For instance, the state machine shown in Figure 1 (o_i: offer, a_i: acceptance and c_i: cancellation sent by R_i) is the conversation protocol for the corresponding WS-CDL choreography specification. We label the transitions of the conversation protocols with *Sender* → *Receiver*:*Msg*, denoting the sending of message *Msg* from the *Sender* peer to the *Receiver* peer. The state machines shown in Figures 2 and 3 are the conversation protocols for the corresponding Sing# channel contract and the UBF(B) communication contract specifications, respectively. In the following section we give a formal definition of conversation protocols.

In order to analyze realizability of conversation protocols, we also need a formal model of distributed systems that interact with messages. We model such systems as a set of peers, where the behavior of each peer is specified as a finite state machine. We assume that each peer has a FIFO message queue that stores messages sent to it by the other peers. When a peer executes a send transition, the sent message is appended to the message queue of the receiving peer. A peer can only execute a receive transition if the transition matches the message at the head of its receive queue. When a peer executes a receive transition, the message at the head of its receive queue is removed. The behavior of the overall system is defined by interleaving the executions of peers.

A conversation protocol is said to be realizable if and only if there exists a set of peers whose interactions conform to the contract. Note that, by interactions we mean send sequences (i.e., conversations); the receive actions occur locally when a peer consumes a message from its own message-queue. This is in contrast to the earlier work on realizability of MSCs (for example in [1, 35]) where both the send and receive actions are considered. The realizability problem MSC-graphs is undecidable. It is not immediately clear if ignoring the receive actions simplifies the realizability problem, since the basic formal model we are looking at involves peers that are interacting in an asynchronous fashion, and each peer is assumed to have a receive-queue of unbounded size. As a result, the state space of the global system consisting of multiple peers may be infinite.

The **main result** we present in this paper is that choreography realizability problem is decidable which has been an open problem for several years. We provide a necessary and sufficient condition for realizability which states that a choreography specification is realizable if and only if

- its behavior is language equivalent to the 1-bounded system of asynchronously communicating peers, where each peer behavior is obtained from the projection of the choreography (on each peer) and where each peer has a message queue of size 1 (equivalence condition); and
- the 1-bounded system satisfies a specific temporal property (well-formedness condition).

Since the choreography specification and the 1-bounded system both have finite state spaces, we were able to implement an automated choreography realizability checker using existing equivalence checking and model checking tools.

3. Conversations & Realizability

We formalize choreography specifications using conversations and conversation protocols (Section 3.1), define distributed systems with asynchronous communication (Section 3.2), and present different variations of choreography realizability (Section 3.3).

3.1 Conversations

We use state machines to characterize conversation protocols, peer behaviors and distributed systems that consist of asynchronously communicating peers [14].

DEFINITION 1 (Conversation Protocol). *A conversation protocol is represented by* $\mathcal{C} = (\mathcal{P}, S^C, s_0^C, L, \Delta^c)$ *where* $\mathcal{P}$ *is a finite set of peers,* S^C *is a finite set of states,* $s_0^C \in C$ *is the initial state,* L *is a finite set of message labels and, finally,* $\Delta^c \subseteq S^C \times \mathcal{P} \times L \times \mathcal{P} \times S^C$ *is the transition relation. A transition of the form* $(s_i^C, P, m, P', s_j^C) \in \Delta^c$ *represents the sending of message* m *from* P *to* P' $(P, P' \in \mathcal{P})$.

Figures 1, 2 and 3 present the communication contracts from three different domains and the corresponding conversation protocols. The start states are denoted by an incoming arrow without a source state. Each transition is labeled with a message along with the sender and the receiver of the message. We denote the transition labels as $m^{P \to P'}$, where m is the message being sent by P to P'.

3.2 Systems

DEFINITION 2 (Peer Behavior). *The behavior* $\mathcal{B}$ *of a peer* P *is a finite state machine* (M, T, t_0, δ) *where* M *is the union of input* (M^{in}) *and output* (M^{out}) *message sets,* T *is the finite set of states,* $t_0 \in T$ *is the initial state, and* $\delta \subseteq T \times (M \cup \{\epsilon\}) \times T$ *is the transition relation.*

A transition $\tau \in \delta$ *can be one of the following three types: (1) a send-transition of the form* $(t_1, !m_1, t_2)$ *which sends out a message* $m_1 \in M^{out}$*, (2) a receive-transition of the form* $(t_1, ?m_2, t_2)$ *which consumes a message* $m_2 \in M^{in}$ *from peer's input queue, and (3) an* ϵ*-transition of the form* (t_1, ϵ, t_2)*. We write* $t \xrightarrow{a} t'$ *to denote that* $(t, a, t') \in \delta$.

Figure 4 illustrates the behaviors of two communicating peers P_1 and P_2 with send and receive actions a, b and c.

DEFINITION 3 (System Behavior). *Given a set of peers* $\mathcal{P} = \{P_1, \ldots, P_n\}$ *with* $\mathcal{B}_i = (M_i, T_i, t_{0i}, \delta_i)$ *denoting the behavior of* P_i *and* $M_i = M_i^{in} \cup M_i^{out}$ *such that*

- $\forall i : M_i^{in} \cap M_i^{out} = \emptyset$,
- $\forall i, j : i \neq j \Rightarrow M_i^{in} \cap M_j^{in} = M_i^{out} \cap M_j^{out} = \emptyset$,

a system behavior or simply a system over $\mathcal{P}$ *is denoted by a state machine (possibly infinite state)* $\mathcal{I} = (\mathcal{P}, S, s_0, M, \Delta)$ *where*

1. $M = \cup_i M_i$
2. $S \subseteq \mathcal{Q}_1 \times T_1 \times \mathcal{Q}_2 \times T_2 \ldots \mathcal{Q}_n \times T_n$ *such that* $\forall i \in [1..n] : \mathcal{Q}_i \subseteq (M_i^{in})^*$
3. $s_0 \in S$ *such that* $s_0 = (\epsilon, t_{01}, \epsilon, t_{02} \ldots, \epsilon, t_{0n})$*; and*
4. $\Delta \subseteq S \times [(\mathcal{P} \times M \times \mathcal{P}) \cup \{\epsilon\}] \times S$*, and for* $s = (Q_1, t_1, Q_2, t_2, \ldots Q_n, t_n) \in S$ *and* $s' = (Q'_1, t'_1, Q'_2, t'_2, \ldots Q'_n, t'_n) \in S$
   - *(a)* $s \xrightarrow{m_{P_i \to P_j}} s' \in \Delta$ *if* $\exists i, j \in [1..n] : m \in M_i^{out} \cap M_j^{in}$, *(i)* $t_i \xrightarrow{!m} t'_i \in \delta_i$, *(ii)* $Q'_j = Q_j m$, *(iii)* $\forall k \in [1..n] : k \neq j \Rightarrow Q_k = Q'_k$ *and (iv)* $\forall k \in [1..n] : k \neq i \Rightarrow t'_k = t_k$ **[send action]**
   - *(b)* $s \xrightarrow{\epsilon} s' \in \Delta$ *if* $\exists i \in [1..n] : m \in M_i^{in}$ *(i)* $t_i \xrightarrow{?m} t'_i \in \delta_i$, *(ii)* $Q_i = mQ'_i$, *(iii)* $\forall k \in [1..n] : k \neq i \Rightarrow Q_k = Q'_k$ *and (iv)* $\forall k \in [1..n] : k \neq i \Rightarrow t'_k = t_k$ **[receive action]**
   - *(c)* $s \xrightarrow{\epsilon} s' \in \Delta$ *if (i)* $\exists i \in [1..n] : t_i \xrightarrow{\epsilon} t'_i \in \delta_i$, *(ii)* $\forall k \in [1..n] : Q_k = Q'_k$ *and (iii)* $\forall k \in [1..n] : k \neq i \Rightarrow t'_k = t_k$ **[internal action]**

The above definition states that peers in the system communicate in an asynchronous fashion. Each peer has an unbounded message queue (Q_i) and a message sent to a peer gets inserted to the tail of the queue, while a message consumed by a peer is consumed from the head of its message queue.

Note that, send actions involve two peers, the peer sending the message and the message queue of the receiver peer; on the other hand, the receive action is local and involves only the receiver peer. The behavior of the system depends on the order the send and receive actions as well as the size of the message queues associated with each peer participating in the system. In the following, we define k-bounded systems, where each participating peer has a message queue of size k. The send actions in such a system is blocked if the receiver peer's message queue is full (i.e., contains k pending messages to be consumed).

DEFINITION 4 (k-bounded System). *A* k*-bounded system (denoted by* $\mathcal{I}_k$*) is a system where the length of message queue for any peer is at most* k*. The description of* k*-bounded system behavior is, therefore, realized by augmenting condition 4(a) in Definition 3 to include the condition* $|Q_j| < k$*, where* $|Q_j|$ *denotes the length of the queue for peer* j.

Figure 4 illustrates the behavior of $\mathcal{I}_1$ obtained from the two peers P_1 and P_2 with asynchronous communication. For brevity, we only show the transitions that involve send actions.

We also define synchronous behavior of a system where every send action by a peer is consumed immediately by a receiver peer, i.e., the peers interact synchronously. This can be viewed as the case where the peers do not have any message queues.

DEFINITION 5 (Synchronous Behavior). *Given a set of peers $\mathcal{P} = \{P_1, \ldots, P_n\}$ with $\mathcal{B}_i = (M_i, T_i, t_{0i}, \delta_i)$ denoting the behavior of P_i and $M_i = M_i^{in} \cup M_i^{out}$, such that*

- $\forall i : M_i^{in} \cap M_i^{out} = \emptyset$,
- $\forall i, j : i \neq j \Rightarrow M_i^{in} \cap M_j^{in} = M_i^{out} \cap M_j^{out} = \emptyset$,

the synchronous system behavior containing the peers in $\mathcal{P}$ is denoted by a state machine $\mathcal{I}_0 = (\mathcal{P}, S, s_0, M, \Delta)$ where

1. $M = \cup_i M_i$
2. $S \subseteq T_1 \times T_2 \times \ldots \times T_n$
3. $s_0 \in S$ *such that* $s_0 = (t_{01}, t_{02} \ldots, t_{0n})$*; and*
4. $\Delta \subseteq S \times [(\mathcal{P} \times M \times \mathcal{P}) \cup \{\epsilon\}] \times S$ *and for* $s = (t_1, t_2, \ldots, t_n) \in S$ *and* $s' = (t'_1, t'_2, \ldots, t'_n) \in S$
   (a) $s \xrightarrow{m^{P_i \rightarrow P_j}} s' \in \Delta$ *if* $\exists i, j \in [1..n] : m \in M_i^{out} \cap M_j^{in}$*, (i)* $t_i \xrightarrow{!m} t'_i \in \delta_i$*, (ii)* $t_j \xrightarrow{?m} t'_j \in \delta_j$*, (iii)* $\forall k \in [1..n] : k \neq i \wedge k \neq j \Rightarrow t'_k = t_k$
   [synchronous send-receive action]
   (b) $s \xrightarrow{\epsilon} s' \in \Delta$ *if* $\exists i \in [1..n]$ *(i)* $t_i \xrightarrow{\epsilon} t'_i \in \delta_i$*, (ii)* $\forall k \in [1..n] : k \neq i \Rightarrow t'_k = t_k$
   [internal action]

The synchronous composition of behaviors $\mathcal{B}_1$ and $\mathcal{B}_2$ of peers P_1 and P_2, respectively, in Figure 4 would have a structure that is identical to $\mathcal{B}_2$, with one branch having transitions $a^{P_2 \rightarrow P_1}$, followed by $b^{P_1 \rightarrow P_2}$, followed by $c^{P_1 \rightarrow P_2}$; and the other branch having transitions $a^{P_2 \rightarrow P_1}$, followed by $c^{P_1 \rightarrow P_2}$, followed by $b^{P_1 \rightarrow P_2}$.

PROPOSITION 1. *The synchronous system behavior containing a set of peers $\mathcal{P} = \{P_1, \ldots, P_n\}$ with peer behaviors $\mathcal{B}_j$ $(1 \leq j \leq n)$ where each peer behavior $\mathcal{B}_j$ $(1 \leq j \leq n)$ is deterministic, is also deterministic, i.e., the labels on any pair of outgoing transitions from a state are distinct. Any peer behavior with finite state-space can be determinized and a system $\mathcal{I}$ (resp. $\mathcal{I}_k$, $k \geq 0$) obtained by determinizing the peer behaviors is denoted by* DETER$(\mathcal{I})$ *(resp.* DETER$(\mathcal{I}_k)$*).*

Finally, we define the concept of well-formed systems.

DEFINITION 6 (Well-formed System). *A system containing a set of peers $\mathcal{P} = \{P_1, P_2, \ldots, P_n\}$ with peer behaviors $\mathcal{B}_j$ $(1 \leq j \leq n)$ is said to be well-formed if and only if every message sent by any peer can be eventually consumed along some path in the system by the receiver of the message. This can be expressed precisely in temporal logic CTL [10] as*

$$AG(|Q_i| > 0 \Rightarrow EF(|Q_i| = 0)) \qquad (1)$$

The property states that whenever the size of the receive queue, Q_i, of the i-th peer is greater than 0 (i.e., Q_i is non-empty), the system can eventually *move to a state where Q_i is empty.*

All synchronous systems, $\mathcal{I}_0$, are well-formed by definition. For all k-bounded asynchronous systems, it can be automatically verified (via model checking) whether the system is well-formed or not. Any k-bounded system has finite state-space; one can model check such a system against the CTL property (Equation 1).

If a system $\mathcal{I}_k$ is well-formed, we say that WF$(\mathcal{I}_k)$. Note that, well-formedness checking for asynchronous systems (where message queues are unbounded) is undecidable in general.

3.3 Realizability

We consider two variations of realizability. We refer to these variations as Realizability$_\forall$ and Realizability$_\exists$.

DEFINITION 7 (Realizability). *A conversation protocol $\mathcal{C}$ defined over a set of peers $\mathcal{P} = \{P_1, P_2, \ldots, P_n\}$ is said to be realizable according to Realizability$_\forall$ or Realizability$_\exists$, if and only if there exists some peer behaviors $\mathcal{B}_j$ $(1 \leq j \leq n)$ and a system $\mathcal{I}$ defined using these behaviors, such that*

Realizability$_\forall$: for all $i \geq 0$, $\mathcal{C}$ is equivalent to $\mathcal{I}_i$ and WF$(\mathcal{I}_i)$*, or*
Realizability$_\exists$: $\mathcal{C}$ is equivalent to $\mathcal{I}$ and WF$(\mathcal{I})$

respectively.

Realizability$_\forall$ requires the existence of a system such that its behaviors *for all* possible receive queue sizes are equivalent to $\mathcal{C}$. Realizability$_\exists$ requires the existence of a system such that its behavior is equivalent to $\mathcal{C}$ when unbounded receive queues are used.

Note that, the above variations, Realizability$_\forall$ and Realizability$_\exists$, require the *equivalence* between the conversation $\mathcal{C}$, and the system(s) $\mathcal{I}_i$s and $\mathcal{I}$, respectively. We consider language equivalence, which ensures that any linear temporal logic property satisfied by the conversation protocol is also satisfied by the system that realizes the conversation. Earlier work [14, 18] on choreography realizability has focused on language equivalence and Realizability$_\exists$, where sufficient conditions for determining Realizability$_\exists$ have been provided.

It may appear that Realizability$_\forall$ is a stronger notion compared to Realizability$_\exists$ in the sense that if $\mathcal{C}$ is realizable according to Realizability$_\forall$ then it is also realizable according to Realizability$_\exists$. However, we show in this paper that Realizability$_\forall$ and Realizability$_\exists$ are equivalent.

3.3.1 Language Equivalence & Preorder

Language Equivalence. For a conversation protocol, the alphabet is $\Sigma = \cup\{m^{P \rightarrow P'}\}$, where P, P' are peers in the conversation and $m^{P \rightarrow P'}$ is a send action (Definition 1). We denote the language of a conversation $\mathcal{C}$ as $\mathcal{L}(\mathcal{C})$, which contains any sequence over Σ from the start state. For example, the language of the conversation in Figure 1 includes a sequence where $o_1^{R1 \rightarrow R2}$ is eventually followed by $a_2^{R2 \rightarrow R1}$ and in between there are finite number of subsequences of the form $o_2^{R2 \rightarrow R1} o_1^{R2 \rightarrow R1}$.

For a peer behavior, the alphabet is $\Sigma = M^{\text{in}} \cup M^{\text{out}}$, where M^{in} and M^{out} are receive and send actions of the peer respectively (Definition 2). We denote the language of a behavior $\mathcal{B}$ of a peer P as $\mathcal{L}(\mathcal{B})$. For example, in Figure 4, the behavior $\mathcal{B}_1$ of P_1 includes the sequence $?a!b!c$ in its language.

For a system, the alphabet is $\Sigma = \cup\{m^{P \rightarrow P'}\}$, where P, P' are peers participating in the system and $m^{P \rightarrow P'}$ is a send action in the behavior of peer P (Definition 3). We denote the language of a system $\mathcal{I}$ (resp. $\mathcal{I}_k$) as $\mathcal{L}(\mathcal{I})$ (resp. $\mathcal{L}(\mathcal{I}_k)$). For example, the language of the system $\mathcal{I}_1$ in Figure 4 includes the sequence $a^{P_2 \rightarrow P_1} b^{P_1 \rightarrow P_2} c^{P_1 \rightarrow P_2}$.

Based on the Definition 7, language realizability requires that $\mathcal{L}(\mathcal{C}) = \mathcal{L}(\mathcal{I}_i)$ for all $i \geq 0$ for Realizability$_\forall$ and $\mathcal{L}(\mathcal{C}) = \mathcal{L}(\mathcal{I})$ for Realizability$_\exists$.

Ordering. We also require the concept of an ordering between systems, conversations and peers in terms of their language. Ordering with respect to language can be easily obtained using the subset relation.

4. Deciding Realizability

In this section, we prove that determining realizability is decidable, present the necessary and sufficient condition for checking realizability of a given conversation protocol and show that this condition can be efficiently computed using existing techniques for equivalence checking and model checking. We prove that a conversation protocol $\mathcal{C}$ is realizable if and only if it is realized by a well-formed system obtained from peer projections of $\mathcal{C}$. We define the peer projection of a conversation protocol as follows.

DEFINITION 8 (Peer Projection). *The projection of a conversation protocol $\mathcal{C}$ on one of the peers P, participating in the conversation, is denoted by $\mathcal{C}_{\downarrow P}$ and is obtained from $\mathcal{C}$ by performing the following updates to the state machine describing $\mathcal{C}$.*

- *if a transition label is $m^{P \to P'}$ then replace it with $!m$,*
- *if a transition label is $m^{P' \to P}$ then replace it with $?m$,*
- *otherwise, replace transition label with ϵ.*

We denote the synchronous, k-bounded asynchronous and unbounded asynchronous systems obtained from the peer projections of $\mathcal{C}$ by $\mathcal{I}_0^{\mathcal{C}}$, $\mathcal{I}_k^{\mathcal{C}}$ and $\mathcal{I}^{\mathcal{C}}$, respectively. For example, Figure 5 presents a conversation protocol $\mathcal{C}$ and its projections to peers P_1 and P_2.

Next, we proceed by first considering Realizability$_\forall$ (Section 4.1) followed by Realizability$_\exists$ (Section 4.2), and finally summarize our findings in Section 4.3.

4.1 Deciding Realizability$_\forall$

In this section, by realizability, we mean Realizability$_\forall$, unless otherwise mentioned. The following outlines the steps of the proof establishing the decidability of realizability.

Outline.

1. *Behavioral Ordering.* We prove that if the conversation protocol $\mathcal{C}$ is equivalent to DETER($\mathcal{I}_0^{\mathcal{C}}$), then DETER($\mathcal{I}_0^{\mathcal{C}}$) is the "*smallest*" system with synchronously communicating peers that is language equivalent to $\mathcal{C}$. [Theorem 1].
2. *Synchronizability Checking.* The conversation protocol $\mathcal{C}$ is realizable according to Realizability$_\forall$ if and only if it is equivalent to $\mathcal{I}_i$ for all $i \geq 0$, and $\mathcal{I}_i$s are well-formed (see Definition 7). That is, $\mathcal{C}$ is equivalent to $\mathcal{I}_i$ irrespective of the size i of the receive queues. We use the concept of synchronizability of a system. A system is synchronizable if and only if the system behavior (over send actions) remains unaltered for any receive queue size. We show that $\forall i \geq 0$, $\mathcal{I}_i$s are equivalent to $\mathcal{I}$, i.e., $\mathcal{I}$ is synchronizable, if and only if $\mathcal{I}_0$ is equivalent to $\mathcal{I}_1$. [Theorem 2].
3. *Well-formedness Checking.* Realizability also requires that the system that realizes the conversation must be well-formed. We present the conditions when the synchronizable systems are well-formed; specifically, we prove that a synchronizable system $\mathcal{I}$ is well-formed if and only if $\mathcal{I}_1$ is well-formed [Theorem 3]. Finally, we show that deterministic synchronizable systems are always well-formed [Theorem 4].
4. *Realizability$_\forall$ Checking.* Finally, using the above theorems, we obtain that the conversation $\mathcal{C}$ is realizable if and only if DETER($\mathcal{I}^{\mathcal{C}}$) is synchronizable and well-formed, and $\mathcal{C}$ is equivalent to DETER($\mathcal{I}^{\mathcal{C}}$). This statement holds if and only if $\mathcal{C}$ is equivalent to DETER($\mathcal{I}_1^{\mathcal{C}}$). (Recall that DETER($\mathcal{I}^{\mathcal{C}}$) denotes the system over peer behaviors obtained by determinizing the projection of $\mathcal{C}$ over peers). As both, $\mathcal{C}$ and $\mathcal{I}_1^{\mathcal{C}}$ are finite state systems, verification of equivalence can be done effectively. [Theorem 5]

4.1.1 Language-based Ordering

For the step 1 noted above, we discuss certain ordering properties of the systems, conversations and peer behaviors, to qualify what we mean by the smallest system with synchronously communicating peers.

PROPOSITION 2.

$$\forall \mathcal{C} : \mathcal{L}(\mathcal{C}) \subseteq \mathcal{L}(\mathcal{I}_0^{\mathcal{C}}) \quad \textit{and} \quad \forall i \geq 0 : \mathcal{L}(\mathcal{I}_i) \subseteq \mathcal{L}(\mathcal{I}_{i+1})$$

Proof: The proof follows from the following observations. The peers in $\mathcal{I}_0^{\mathcal{C}}$ are obtained from projections of $\mathcal{C}$. Therefore, any path (in terms of send actions) from any state in $\mathcal{C}$ is also present in $\mathcal{I}_0^{\mathcal{C}}$. Any $\mathcal{I}_{i+1}$ can replicate the behavior (in terms of send actions) of $\mathcal{I}_i$ by avoiding the paths that occur due to the usage of message queues of length $i+1$. □

DEFINITION 9. *Let $\mathcal{P} = \{P_1, P_2, \ldots, P_n\}$ be a set of peers. Let $\mathcal{I}_0$ be a synchronous system obtained from the peer-behaviors $\mathcal{B}_i, 1 \leq i \leq n$; and $\mathcal{I}_0'$ be a synchronous system obtained from the peer-behaviors $\mathcal{B}_i', 1 \leq i \leq n$. We say that $\mathcal{I}_0 \leq_{\mathcal{L}} \mathcal{I}_0'$ if and only if $\forall i \geq 1, i \leq n : \mathcal{L}(\mathcal{B}_i) \subseteq \mathcal{L}(\mathcal{B}_i')$.*

In the above, we define the ordering relations $\leq_{\mathcal{L}}$ between systems based on the ordering between the behaviors of the corresponding peers that constitute the respective systems.

PROPOSITION 3. *Let $\mathcal{P} = \{P_1, P_2, \ldots, P_n\}$ be a set of peers. Let $\mathcal{I}_0$, $\mathcal{I}_k$, $\mathcal{I}$ denote the synchronous, k-bounded asynchronous and unbounded asynchronous systems, where the i-th peer-behavior is $\mathcal{B}_i$ for $1 \leq i \leq n$; and $\mathcal{I}_0'$, $\mathcal{I}_k'$, $\mathcal{I}'$ denote the corresponding systems, where the i-th peer-behavior is $\mathcal{B}_i'$ for $1 \leq i \leq n$.*

$$\mathcal{I}_0 \leq_{\mathcal{L}} \mathcal{I}_0' \Rightarrow [\mathcal{L}(\mathcal{I}_0) \subseteq \mathcal{L}(\mathcal{I}_0') \ \wedge \ \mathcal{L}(\mathcal{I}_k) \subseteq \mathcal{L}(\mathcal{I}_k') \ \wedge \ \mathcal{L}(\mathcal{I}) \subseteq \mathcal{L}(\mathcal{I}')]$$

Proof: The proof follows from the Definitions 3, 4, 5 and 9. $\mathcal{I}_0 \leq_{\mathcal{L}} \mathcal{I}_0'$ implies that the the language of any peer's behavior in $\mathcal{I}_0$ is a subset of the language of the corresponding peer's behavior in $\mathcal{I}_0'$ (Definition 9), i.e., any sequence of the i-th peer behavior in $\mathcal{I}_0$ is also present in the i-th peer behavior in $\mathcal{I}_0'$. As a result, from Definition 5, $\mathcal{L}(\mathcal{I}_0) \subseteq \mathcal{L}(\mathcal{I}_0')$. □

THEOREM 1. *Given a conversation protocol $\mathcal{C}$ over a set of peers $\mathcal{P}$, the following holds for all synchronous systems $\mathcal{I}_0$ defined over a set of peer behaviors for the peers in $\mathcal{P}$.*

$$\mathcal{L}(\mathcal{C}) = \mathcal{L}(\text{DETER}(\mathcal{I}_0^{\mathcal{C}})) \Rightarrow [\forall \mathcal{I}_0 : (\mathcal{L}(\mathcal{C}) = \mathcal{L}(\mathcal{I}_0) \Rightarrow \text{DETER}(\mathcal{I}_0^{\mathcal{C}}) \leq_{\mathcal{L}} \mathcal{I}_0)]$$

Proof: Assume that there exists an $\mathcal{I}_0$ such that $\mathcal{L}(\mathcal{C}) = \mathcal{L}(\text{DETER}(\mathcal{I}_0^{\mathcal{C}})) = \mathcal{L}(\mathcal{I}_0)$ and DETER($\mathcal{I}_0^{\mathcal{C}}$) $\not\leq_{\mathcal{L}} \mathcal{I}_0$. Let the behaviors of the i-th peer in DETER($\mathcal{I}_0^{\mathcal{C}}$) and $\mathcal{I}_0$ be $\mathcal{B}_i$ and B_i', respectively. Note that, $\mathcal{B}_i$'s are deterministic in DETER($\mathcal{I}_0^{\mathcal{C}}$).

Therefore, there exists an i such that $\mathcal{L}(\mathcal{B}_i) \not\subseteq \mathcal{L}(B_i')$ (Definition 9). That is, there exists at least one path in $\mathcal{B}_i$, which is not present in $\mathcal{B}_i'$. Recall that, $\mathcal{B}_i$ is $\mathcal{C}_{\downarrow P_i}$ and is determinized; each path in $\mathcal{B}_i$ corresponds to at least one path in $\mathcal{C}$ (Definition 8). Therefore, absence of a path in $\mathcal{B}_i'$ implies at least one of the paths in $\mathcal{C}$ is not realizable using $\mathcal{I}_0$. This results in contradiction. □

4.1.2 Synchronizability Checking

As mentioned in the outline (item 2), a conversation $\mathcal{C}$ is realizable according to Realizability$_\forall$ if and only if it is equivalent to systems $\mathcal{I}_i$, for all $i \geq 0$. The following theorem due to [5] establishes

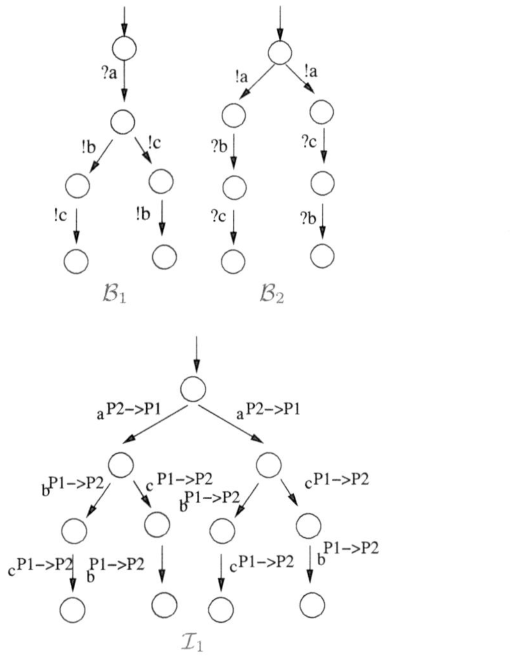

Figure 4. Two peer behaviors that are language synchronizable.

the necessary and sufficient condition under which the behaviors of $\forall i \geq 0 : \mathcal{I}_i$ are language equivalent. This is referred to as the synchronizability condition.

THEOREM 2. *$\mathcal{I}$ is language synchronizable (i.e., $\forall i \geq 0 : \mathcal{L}(\mathcal{I}_i) = \mathcal{L}(\mathcal{I}_{i+1})$) and only if $\mathcal{L}(\mathcal{I}_0) = \mathcal{L}(\mathcal{I}_1)$.*

Consider the behaviors $\mathcal{B}_1$ and $\mathcal{B}_2$ of peers P_1 and P_2, respectively, in Figure 4. The synchronous system $\mathcal{I}_0$ obtained from these peers has a behavioral structure similar to that of $\mathcal{B}_2$; there are two non-deterministic branches along which a is sent from P_2 to P_1. Along one branch, b is communicated before c and in the other branch, c is communicated before b. The 1-bounded asynchronous behavior, on the other hand, (see Figure 4) allows all possible ordering for communicating b and c along both the non-deterministic branches. The languages of $\mathcal{I}_0$ and $\mathcal{I}_1$ are identical. Therefore, the system obtained from P_1 and P_2 is language synchronizable.

4.1.3 Language Synchronizability & well-formedness

We present the condition under which a language synchronizable system is well-formed (see item 3 of outline of proof above for Realizability$_\forall$). We also use this result in the context of Realizability$_\exists$ (see Section 4.2).

THEOREM 3 (Synchronizability & well-formedness). *A synchronizable system $\mathcal{I}$ is well-formed if and only if $\mathcal{I}_1$ is well-formed.*

Proof: It is immediate that $\mathcal{I}$ is well-formed implies that $\forall i \geq 0 : \mathcal{I}_i$ is well-formed.

For proving the other direction, assume that $\mathcal{I}$ is synchronizable, $\textsc{wf}(\mathcal{I}_1)$ and $\neg\textsc{wf}(\mathcal{I})$. Therefore, there exists a $k > 1$ such that $\neg\textsc{wf}(\mathcal{I}_k)$, and there exists a path in $\mathcal{I}_k$ over a sequence of states $t_0, t_1, \ldots, t_l, t_{l+1}$, with $0 \leq i \leq l : t_i \stackrel{m_i^{P_i \to P_i'}}{\Longrightarrow} t_{i+1}$, and the message m_l is never consumed by peer P_l'. Recall that, as $\mathcal{I}$ is language synchronizable, any sequence of send actions in $\mathcal{I}_k$ is also present in $\mathcal{I}_1$. From these observations, we iteratively construct a path in $\mathcal{I}_1$.

1. We denote the sequence of send actions causing violation of well-formedness in $\mathcal{I}_k$ as $\omega\, m_l^{P_l \to P_l'}$. Consider the path in the behavior of peer P_l' over the sequence of local states identical to the local states of P_l' in the sequence $t_0, t_1, \ldots, t_l$ in $\mathcal{I}_k$.
2. As $\mathcal{I}$ is synchronizable, consider a path over a sequence of states $t_0', t_1', \ldots, t_l', t_{l+1}'$ in $\mathcal{I}_1$ that results in the same sequence of send actions $\omega\, m_l^{P_l \to P_l'}$, and where all send actions are immediately consumed by the receiver peer. Such a path is possible as $\mathcal{I}_0$, $\mathcal{I}_1$ and $\mathcal{I}_k$ contain identical sequences of send actions. Note that, this path in $\mathcal{I}_1$ is well-formed.

   Consider the path in the behaviors of all peers other than P_l' over the sequence of local states that are identical to their local states in the sequence $t_0', t_1', \ldots, t_l'$.
3. Construct a path in the system by considering the local states of P_l' (item 1 above), the local states of all other peers (item 2 above), and proceed by sequentially matching the send action sequence $\omega\, m_l^{P_l \to P_l'}$. In this path, if at any point a transition results in a message sent from a sender peer P_s to a receiver peer P_r whose receive queue contains one message (to be consumed), we delay this transition by moving ahead some transition that occurs after it (shuffle) and does not involve the peers P_s and P_r.
   (a) Given the sequence $\omega\, m_l^{P_l \to P_l'}$, if the above shuffle operation can be performed till the action $m_l^{P_l \to P_l'}$, then a new path is obtained along which none of the receive queues contain more than one pending message to be consumed, i.e., a path in $\mathcal{I}_1$ is obtained. Further note that, as we have considered the path of P_l', where it does not consume the last message m_l, $\mathcal{I}_1$ is not well-formeded. That is, when $\mathcal{I}$ is synchronizable, $\neg\textsc{wf}(\mathcal{I}) \Rightarrow \neg\textsc{wf}(\mathcal{I}_1)$.
   (b) Consider that such shuffling (item 3 above) can be performed on the prefix ω_1 (such that $\omega_1\, \omega_2\, b\, \omega_3\, m_l^{P_l \to P_l'} = \omega\, m_l^{P_l \to P_l'}$), after which the shuffle operation of moving b before ω_2 is not possible, without allowing at least one peer's receive queue to hold more than one message. In the above, ω_1, ω_2 and ω_3 are sequences of send actions. Let the shuffling of ω_1 resulted in a new sequence ω_1'. Observe that, $\omega_1'\, b\, \omega_2\, \omega_3\, m_l^{P_l \to P_l'}$ is a sequence in $\mathcal{I}_k$ and it not well-formeded. Repeat the above steps starting from item 2 with this new sequence $\omega_1'\, b\, \omega_2\, \omega_3\, m_l^{P_l \to P_l'}$. Note that in new iteration we are still considering the same path in peer P_l' (item 1 above); but considering new paths for all peers other than P_l'. The new paths will ensure that till ω_1', all send actions are immediately received making room for at least one more send action (i.e., b) to be performed without forcing any peer's receive queue to contain more than 1 message.

   As $\mathcal{I}$ is synchronizable, the above iteration will always terminate in Step $3a$, proving that when $\mathcal{I}$ is synchronizable, $\neg\textsc{wf}(\mathcal{I}) \Rightarrow \neg\textsc{wf}(\mathcal{I}_1)$. □

THEOREM 4 (Determinism, Synchronizability & well-formedness). *A synchronizable system $\mathcal{I}$ consisting of deterministic peers is well-formed.*

Proof: A system is synchronizable and consists of deterministic peers imply that $\mathcal{L}(\mathcal{I}_0) = \mathcal{L}(\mathcal{I}_1)$ and $\mathcal{I}_1$ is deterministic. Assume that, $\mathcal{I}_1$ is not well-formed.

There exists a sequence of send actions $\omega = m_0 m_1 \ldots m \ldots$ which leads to a state t from where a message m is never consumed. Due to synchronizability, the same sequence of send actions is also present in $\mathcal{I}_0$ where each message sent is immediately consumed. A similar path is present $\mathcal{I}_1$, where every send action is immediately followed by the corresponding receive action, resulting in the same sequence of send actions ω. Recall that, all peers are deterministic. Therefore, $\mathcal{I}_1$ cannot contain two different paths with the same send sequence ω; where one path leads to a state from where m is never consumed, and in the other all sent messages are consumed. In other words, a deterministic $\mathcal{I}_1$ containing deterministic peers is well-formed. From Theorem 3, the corresponding system $\mathcal{I}$ is well-formed, and therefore, $\forall i \geq 0 : \textsc{wf}(\mathcal{I}_i)$ also holds. □

4.1.4 Deciding Language Realizability$_\forall$

Based on the above theorems and propositions, we now proceed to present the necessary and sufficient conditions for language realizability according to Realizability$_\forall$.

THEOREM 5. *$\mathcal{C}$ is language realizable following Realizability$_\forall$* $\Leftrightarrow$ $[\mathcal{L}(\mathcal{C}) = \mathcal{L}(\textsc{Deter}(\mathcal{I}_1^{\mathcal{C}}))]$

Proof: To prove: $\mathcal{C}$ is language realizable according to Realizability$_\forall$ implies $\mathcal{L}(\mathcal{C}) = \mathcal{L}(\textsc{Deter}(\mathcal{I}_1^{\mathcal{C}}))$.
Assume that $\mathcal{C}$ is language realizable and

$$\mathcal{L}(\mathcal{C}) \neq \mathcal{L}(\textsc{Deter}(\mathcal{I}_1^{\mathcal{C}}))$$
$$\text{i.e., } \mathcal{L}(\mathcal{C}) \subset \mathcal{L}(\textsc{Deter}(\mathcal{I}_1^{\mathcal{C}})) \text{ (Proposition 2)}$$

As $\mathcal{C}$ is language realizable according to Realizability$_\forall$, there exists a $\mathcal{I}$ such that $\forall i \geq 0 : \mathcal{L}(\mathcal{C}) = \mathcal{L}(\mathcal{I}_i)$. Therefore, $\mathcal{I}$ is synchronizable, i.e., $\mathcal{L}(\mathcal{C}) = \mathcal{L}(\mathcal{I}_0) \wedge \mathcal{L}(\mathcal{C}) = \mathcal{L}(\mathcal{I}_1)$ (From Theorem 2).

We first establish that for $\mathcal{C}$ to be realizable, $\mathcal{L}(\mathcal{C})$ must be identical to $\mathcal{L}(\textsc{Deter}(\mathcal{I}_0^{\mathcal{C}}))$ (or $\mathcal{L}(\mathcal{I}_0^{\mathcal{C}})$; determinizing peers does not alter the language of the system).

Assuming $\mathcal{L}(\mathcal{C}) \neq \mathcal{L}(\mathcal{I}_0^{\mathcal{C}})$, from Proposition 2, we have $\mathcal{L}(\mathcal{C}) \subset \mathcal{L}(\mathcal{I}_0^{\mathcal{C}})$. This implies that there exists a specific ordering of send actions involving two independent pairs of peers. In other words, $\mathcal{C}$ has a state from where $a^{P_1 \rightarrow P_2}$ is followed by $b^{P_3 \rightarrow P_4}$, and P_i's are distinct and the reverse order $b^{P_3 \rightarrow P_4}$ followed by $a^{P_1 \rightarrow P_2}$ is not allowed from the same state in $\mathcal{C}$. Such a conversation $\mathcal{C}$ cannot be realized by any system as the send actions a and b are independent, and any specific ordering required by $\mathcal{C}$ cannot be obtained. Therefore, if $\mathcal{C}$ is realizable then $\mathcal{L}(\mathcal{C}) = \mathcal{L}(\mathcal{I}_0^{\mathcal{C}}) = \mathcal{L}(\textsc{Deter}(\mathcal{I}_0^{\mathcal{C}}))$.

From Theorem 1, it follows that $\textsc{Deter}(\mathcal{I}_0^{\mathcal{C}}) \leq_{\mathcal{L}} \mathcal{I}_0$. This implies that $\forall i : \mathcal{L}(\mathcal{B}_i) \subseteq \mathcal{L}(\mathcal{B}'_i)$, where $\mathcal{B}_i$ and $\mathcal{B}'_i$ denote the behavior of the i-th peer in $\textsc{Deter}(\mathcal{I}_0^{\mathcal{C}})$ and $\mathcal{I}_0$, respectively. (Recall that in $\textsc{Deter}(\mathcal{I}^{\mathcal{C}})$, the peer behaviors are determinized, i.e., $\mathcal{B}_i$ is deterministic.)

Proceeding further, from Proposition 3, we have $\mathcal{L}(\textsc{Deter}(\mathcal{I}_1^{\mathcal{C}})) \subseteq \mathcal{L}(\mathcal{I}_1)$. This leads to a contradiction as we have assumed $\mathcal{L}(\mathcal{C}) = \mathcal{L}(\mathcal{I}_1)$ and $\mathcal{L}(\mathcal{C}) \subset \mathcal{L}(\textsc{Deter}(\mathcal{I}_1^{\mathcal{C}}))$. Therefore, $\mathcal{C}$ is realizable according to Realizability$_\forall$ implies $\mathcal{L}(\mathcal{C}) = \mathcal{L}(\mathcal{I}_1) = \mathcal{L}(\textsc{Deter}(\mathcal{I}_1^{\mathcal{C}}))$, and note that, $\textsc{Deter}(\mathcal{I}_1^{\mathcal{C}})$ is well-formed (Theorem 4).

Next, $\mathcal{L}(\mathcal{C}) = \mathcal{L}(\textsc{Deter}(\mathcal{I}_1^{\mathcal{C}}))$

$$\Rightarrow \mathcal{L}(\mathcal{C}) = \mathcal{L}(\textsc{Deter}(\mathcal{I}_0^{\mathcal{C}})) = \mathcal{L}(\textsc{Deter}(\mathcal{I}_1^{\mathcal{C}})) \wedge \textsc{wf}(\textsc{Deter}(\mathcal{I}_1^{\mathcal{C}})) \quad \text{(Proposition 2)}$$
$$\Rightarrow \forall i \geq 0 : \mathcal{L}(\mathcal{C}) = \mathcal{L}(\textsc{Deter}(\mathcal{I}_i^{\mathcal{C}})) \wedge \textsc{wf}(\textsc{Deter}(\mathcal{I}_i^{\mathcal{C}})) \quad \text{(Theorems 2, 3, 4)}$$
$$\Rightarrow \mathcal{C} \text{ is language realizable according to Realizability}_\forall \quad \text{(Definition 7)}$$

□

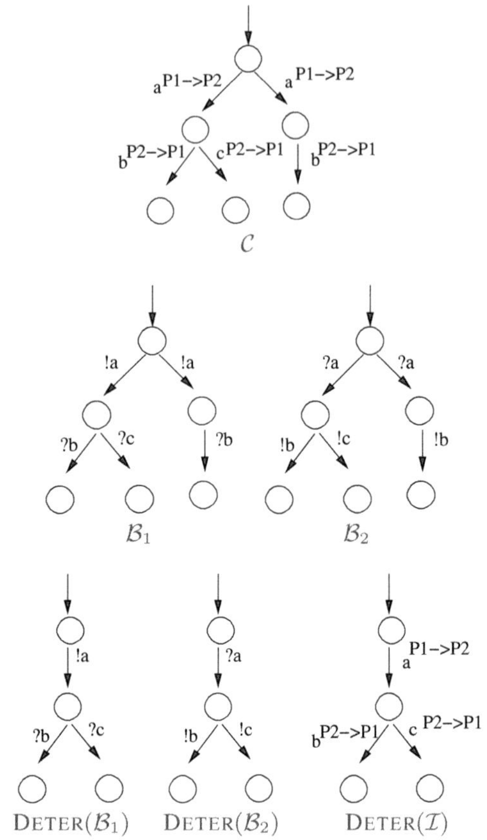

Figure 5. A conversation protocol that is language realizable according to Realizability$_\forall$.

Consider the conversation specification $\mathcal{C}$ in Figure 5. The system behavior $\textsc{Deter}(\mathcal{I})$ (irrespective of the receive queue size) based on peers determinized behaviors ($\textsc{Deter}(\mathcal{B}_1)$, $\textsc{Deter}(\mathcal{B}_2)$) is language equivalent to $\mathcal{C}$ and is $\textsc{wf}(\textsc{Deter}(\mathcal{I}))$. Therefore, $\mathcal{C}$ is language realizable according to Realizability$_\forall$.

4.2 Deciding Language Realizability$_\exists$

THEOREM 6. *$\mathcal{C}$ is language realizable following Realizability$_\exists$* $\Leftrightarrow$ $[\mathcal{L}(\mathcal{C}) = \mathcal{L}(\textsc{Deter}(\mathcal{I}_1^{\mathcal{C}}))]$.

Proof: The proof proceeds by showing the equivalence between Realizability$_\forall$ and Realizability$_\exists$.

$\mathcal{C}$ is language realizable following Realizability$_\forall$
$\Leftrightarrow \forall i \geq 0 : \mathcal{L}(\mathcal{C}) = \mathcal{L}(\mathcal{I}_i) \wedge \textsc{wf}(\mathcal{I}_i)$ (Definition 7)
$\Leftrightarrow \mathcal{L}(\mathcal{C}) = \mathcal{L}(\textsc{Deter}(\mathcal{I}_1^{\mathcal{C}}))$ (Theorem 5)
$\Leftrightarrow \mathcal{L}(\mathcal{C}) = \mathcal{L}(\textsc{Deter}(\mathcal{I}_1^{\mathcal{C}})) \wedge \textsc{wf}(\textsc{Deter}(\mathcal{I}^{\mathcal{C}}))$ (Theorem 4)
$\Leftrightarrow \mathcal{L}(\mathcal{C}) = \mathcal{L}(\textsc{Deter}(\mathcal{I}^{\mathcal{C}})) \wedge \textsc{wf}(\textsc{Deter}(\mathcal{I}^{\mathcal{C}}))$ (Theorem 2)
$\Leftrightarrow \exists \mathcal{I} : \mathcal{L}(\mathcal{C}) = \mathcal{L}(\mathcal{I}) \wedge \textsc{wf}(\mathcal{I})$
$\Leftrightarrow \mathcal{C}$ is language realizable following Realizability$_\exists$

Therefore, from Theorem 5, $\mathcal{C}$ is language realizable following Realizability$_\exists$ $\Leftrightarrow$ $[\mathcal{L}(\mathcal{C}) = \mathcal{L}(\textsc{Deter}(\mathcal{I}_1^{\mathcal{C}}))]$. □

The conversation in Figure 5 is realizable as per Realizability$_\exists$. The peer behaviors, obtained from projection of the conversation and determinization, results in a system that is well-formed and language equivalent to the conversation.

4.3 Summary of the Results

Theorems 5 and 6 lead to a methodology for automatically checking the realizability of a conversation specification $\mathcal{C}$ for Realizability$_\forall$ and Realizability$_\exists$.

Deciding realizability was an open problem. We have proved that realizability can be verified by checking the language equivalence between $\mathcal{C}$ and 1-bounded system over a set of peers obtained from projection of $\mathcal{C}$ on peers and verifying the satisfiability of a temporal property by the 1-bounded system (well-formedness verification). Both equivalence checking and well-formedness verification can be performed automatically (using existing tools) as the 1-bounded system and the conversation representing the choreography specification both have finite state-space. Furthermore, we have proved that Realizability$_\forall$ and Realizability$_\exists$ are equivalent when language equivalence between choreography and system is considered.

The complexity for well-formedness verification is linear to the size of the 1-bounded system and the size of the CTL formula specifying the well-formed property (complexity for CTL model checking [10]). The complexity for language equivalence checking is PSPACE-complete for language equivalence.

The conversation protocols shown in Figures 1, 2 and 3 are language realizable according to Realizability$_\forall$ and Realizability$_\exists$.

5. Experimental Evaluation

We have automated our approach for checking realizability of conversation protocols leveraging the CADP toolbox [17], which provides a wide range of constructs for representing communicating finite state machines and mechanisms for checking equivalences between such state machines.

We have implemented a translator, which takes a conversation protocol specification as input (specified in the conversation protocol format of the Web Service Analysis Tool [15]) and generates two LOTOS specifications (the specification language for CADP): (a) one that corresponds to the conversation protocol itself and (b) another one that corresponds to the 1-bounded-asynchronous projection of the protocol. We have developed SVL scripts [16] that automatically construct state machine representations from the LOTOS specifications, and check language realizability by deploying CADP's Reductor tool, which reduces the state machines and checks equivalence between them in an optimized fashion.

5.1 Conversation Protocol to LOTOS Translation

In LOTOS, processes are declared as `process proc[m1, m2, ...]: exit := behavior`, where `process` is a keyword, `proc` is the process name, `m1, m2, ...` are the messages that are sent and received by this process, and `behavior` describes the process behavior. The process behavior specifies the message exchange order using the LOTOS operators. The sequential ordering is specified using the operator ; where, *e.g.*, `m1;m2` means that message `m1` must precede message `m2`. Choices are specified using the operator `[]` where `m1[]m2` means that only one message can be executed. Looping behavior is encoded as a process with a recursive behavior. Lastly, the internal τ action and the system termination are described using the LOTOS messages `i` and `exit`, respectively.

Consider the `KeyboardDeviceContract` (Figure 2) which describes the interaction between a server and its client. Below we show a portion of the automatically generated LOTOS code for this contract. We use the suffix `_S_C` to denote the messages sent by the server to the client and we use the suffix `_C_S` to denote the messages sent by the client to the server. The process `KEYBOARDDEVICECONTRACT` starts with the message `Success_S_C` which is sent from the server to the client and then the contract makes a transition into a looping process which starts at the `Ready` state shown in Figure 2. This looping process describes all possible behaviors starting from the `Ready` state.

```
process KEYBOARDDEVICECONTRACT[Success_S_C,
 PollKey_C_S,AckKey_S_C,GetKey_C_S,NakKey_S_C]:
 exit :=
 Success_S_C ; LOOP_READY[...]
 where
 process LOOP_READY[...] : exit :=
  ((GetKey_C_S; ((AckKey_S_C ; LOOP_READY[...])
              [] (NakKey_S_C ; LOOP_READY[...])))
   [] (PollKey_C_S: ((AckKey_S_C ; LOOP_READY[...])
              [] (NakKey_S_C ; LOOP_READY[...]))))
 endproc
endproc
```

5.2 1-Bounded Asynchronous Projection in LOTOS

The LOTOS language does not support asynchronous communication directly. In order to generate the 1-bounded asynchronous model in LOTOS we create a bounded FIFO queue process (which can store at most one message) for each message queue. Given a conversation protocol, we need to create a message queue for each process generated from its projection. For instance, the projection of the `KeyboardDeviceContract` generates two processes, namely, `SERVER` and `CLIENT`. In order to generate the asynchronous version of the server process we compose the `SERVER` and the queue process using LOTOS composition operator `|[m1, m2, ...]|` where both processes synchronize on shared messages `m1, m2, ...`. This queue is responsible for storing the (at most one) messages to be consumed by the server.

```
process ASYNC_SERVER[...] : exit := ...
    ( SERVER[...]
      |[...]|
      SERVER_queue[...](queue(1,nil)) )
endproc
```

The queue associated with the server synchronizes with the client by receiving the actions sent by the client; it also synchronizes with the server by sending the actions that are consumed immediately by the server. The synchronized actions between the queue and the server are hidden during the composition and become τ (internal) transitions in LOTOS (i.e., ϵ-transition as per our notation). Similarly we generate the asynchronous version of the client process by composing the client's receive queue and the `CLIENT` process. Finally, the overall 1-bounded asynchronous model is obtained by composing the `ASYNC_SERVER` process with the `ASYNC_CLIENT` process using the LOTOS operator `|[...]|`. These two processes synchronize on the message send events.

5.3 Equivalence Checking

After generating the LOTOS specifications for the conversation protocol and 1-bounded asynchronous projection models, we generate the two corresponding LTSs using the state space generation tools in the CADP toolbox. We check the equivalence of the two LTSs to determine realizability of the protocol. During the equivalence checking, the receive actions are hidden (as internal action τ) and the send actions are left visible.

In order to check the language realizability in an optimized way, we first reduce the resulting LTSs modulo weak trace relation which reduces the transition systems without modifying their visible traces. Then we check the equivalence of reduced LTSs for the conversation protocol and its 1-bounded-asynchronous projection using the weak trace equivalence relation. If the two LTSs are equivalent this means that send-traces for the conversation protocol and its 1-bounded-asynchronous projection are identical and, hence, the conversation protocol is language-realizable. If the two LTSs are not equivalent, then we conclude that the conversation protocol is not language-realizable.

	Conversation Protocol Size		Async. Model Size		Analysis Time (seconds)	
	$\|C\|$	$\|\Delta\|$	$\|C\|$	$\|\Delta\|$	Reduction	Equivalence
Mean	6.70	9.74	3268.83	19133.72	11.53	2.18
Min	2	1	2	1	6.50	0.48
Max	31	68	302449	1791867	39.91	3.07
STDV	4.40	9.02	30713.29	181950.70	3.12	0.27

Table 1. Protocol and model sizes and analysis time for the experiments on the realizability of conversation protocols ($|C|$: the number of states; $|\Delta|$: the number of transitions).

	Conversation Protocols	Language Realizable
Singularity Channels	86	84
Choreographies	9	8
Collaboration Diagrams	9	8

Table 2. Results of the experiments on language realizability.

5.4 Experiments

We applied our approach to 104 conversation protocols which describe web service choreographies, Singularity OS channel contracts, and UML collaboration diagrams. All these specifications were first automatically translated to conversation protocols (in the conversation protocol format of the Web Service Analysis Tool) using the translators described in [15], [34], and [7], respectively. Then we used the conversation protocol to LOTOS translator we described above to generate the LOTOS specifications for the conversation protocol and the 1-bounded asynchronous projection.

We report the cumulative results of our analysis in Table 1 showing the sizes of the conversation protocol specifications, asynchronous models and the execution times for the reduction and the equivalence checking steps. The conversation protocol specifications are not very large, the biggest one has 31 states and 68 transitions. 1-bounded asynchronous model can be very large in some cases, however the reduction techniques we use reduces the sizes of the models significantly. The reductions take about 11 seconds on average and the equivalence check takes about 2 seconds on average. So realizability of a conversation protocol can be determined in about 13 seconds on average.

According to the results of our analysis (see Table 2) all conversation protocols in our base are language realizable except four. Two of the four that fail the realizability check are Singularity channel contracts which were confirmed by the Singularity developers to be faulty [34].

6. Related Work

The language-based choreography realizability problem for conversation protocols was first proposed in [14] where sufficient conditions for realizability were given. The work on session types [19, 20] is also related to the realizability of conversation protocols and has been used as a formal basis for modeling choreography languages [9]. The restrictions used in session types to guarantee that local implementations follow the global interaction protocol are similar to the sufficient conditions for realizability given in [14] and they are not necessary conditions, i.e., there are realizable choreography specifications which fail the conditions given in these earlier results. In particular, both of these earlier approaches do not allow a protocol containing a state with an *arbitrary initiator* [18], i.e., a state where more than one peer could send the next message and the protocol works fine for either case. Protocols which are of this type and are realizable appear in practice (for example, protocols where one of the peers can cancel the interaction at an arbitrary point) and cannot be shown to be realizable with these earlier approaches.

Choreography realizability problem for several different communication models have been investigated in [25], however, the presented techniques can only show realizability if the asynchronous projection of the protocol has a finite state space (which would not be the case if the protocol has a single self loop for example). More recently, [27] presented an approach that only allows specification of realizable choreographies but, like the approaches discussed above, this approach does not allow specification of realizable choreographies that have arbitrary initiator states. Finally, [18] proposed a new realizability check that correctly identifies the realizability of many arbitrary initiator protocols, however, like all the earlier results, it still provides a sufficient condition for realizability, and decidability of the realizability problem has remained open. In this paper we give a necessary and sufficient condition for realizability and show that it is a decidable problem. Interestingly, the similar realizability problem for the MSC-graphs (which is an extension of MSCs) is undecidable [1].

Realizability of collaboration diagrams has been studied [8] and it has been showed that language realizability for collaboration diagrams can be checked by checking the equivalence of the choreography model with the 1-bounded asynchronous model [32]. However, the collaboration diagram model used in [32] is not as expressive as the conversation protocols, and cannot model the Singularity contracts and the web service choreographies we analyzed in our experiments.

Realizability of Singularity channel contracts have been first studied in [34] using the realizability conditions from [14]. The realizability check we present in this paper can identify some Singularity channel contracts as realizable for which the realizability check used in [34] gives false positives.

Message patterns expressed with Petri nets using synchronous communication are "de-synchronized" in [11]—that is, one is interested in finding a specification that produces the same pattern of messages when communications become asynchronous. This work, however, already assumes that a conversation is realizable and does not provide realizability conditions.

The work presented in [26] checks choreography realizability using the controllability concept. Given a choreography description, a monitor service is computed from that choreography, and is used as a centralized orchestrator of the interaction to compute the distributed peers. The choreography is said to be realizable if the monitor service is controllable, that is, there exists a set of peers such that the composition of the monitor service and those peers is deadlock-free. Our approach is different since the distributed peers are computed without the centralized orchestrator, i.e., the realizability notion we study in this paper does not require a monitor service, and our techniques for checking realizability rely on equivalence checking rather than controllability checking.

7. Conclusion

In this paper, we prove that the choreography realizability problem is decidable for systems communicating with asynchronous messages using unbounded FIFO message queues. We provide a necessary and sufficient condition for realizability which states that, a choreography specification is realizable for systems with asynchronously communicating peers over unbounded message queues, if and only if, the choreography specification behavior is equivalent to the behavior of a well-formed 1-bounded system where each peer behavior is obtained from determinizing the projection of the choreography (on each peer) and where each peer has a message queue of size 1. As the choreography specification and the 1-bounded system both exhibit finite state-space, checking language realizability of the choreography specification can be automatically performed using existing equivalence checking and model checking tools. We have also implemented our technique for realizability checking in a prototype tool using CADP toolbox and verified the realizability of a wide range of choreography specifications that describe Web service interactions, Singularity OS contracts and UML collaboration diagrams.

Acknowledgment

The authors thank Gwen Salaün for fruitful discussions on the CADP implementation. This work has been partially supported by the US National Science Foundation grants CCF1117708, CCF1116836, CCF0702758, and project TIN2008-05932 funded by the Spanish Ministry of Innovation and Science and FEDER.

References

[1] R. Alur, K. Etessami, and M. Yannakakis. Realizability and verification of MSC graphs. In *Proc. 28th Int. Colloq. on Automata, Languages, and Programming*, pages 797–808, 2001.

[2] J. Armstrong. Getting Erlang to Talk to the Outside World. In *Proc. ACM SIGPLAN Work. on Erlang*, pages 64–72, 2002.

[3] J. Armstrong. *Programming Erlang, Software for a Concurrent World*. Pragmatic Bookshelf, 2007.

[4] G. Banavar, T. Deepak Chandra, R. E. Strom, and D. C. Sturman. A Case for Message Oriented Middleware. In *Proceedings of the 13th Int. Symp. Distributed Computing*, pages 1–18, 1999.

[5] S. Basu and T. Bultan. Choreography Conformance via Synchronizability. In *Proc. 20th Int. World Wide Web Conf.*, 2011.

[6] D. Brand and P. Zafiropulo. On communicating finite-state machines. *Journal of the ACM*, 30(2):323–342, 1983.

[7] T. Bultan, C. Ferguson, and X. Fu. A tool for choreography analysis using collaboration diagrams. In *Proc. 7th IEEE Int. Conf. Web Services*, 2009.

[8] T. Bultan and X. Fu. Specification of Realizable service conversations using collaboration diagrams. *Service Oriented Computing and Applications*, 2(1):27–39, 2008.

[9] M. Carbone, K. Honda, N. Yoshida, R. Milner, G. Brown, and S. Ross-Talbot. A Theoretical Basis of Communication-Centred Concurrent Programming, W3C Note, October 2006. http://www.w3.org/2002/-ws/chor/edcopies/theory/note.pdf.

[10] E.M. Clarke, O. Grumberg, and D. A. Peled. *Model Checking*. The MIT Press, Cambridge, Massachusetts, 1999.

[11] G. Decker, A. P. Barros, F. M. Kraft, and N. Lohmann. Non-desynchronizable Service Choreographies. In *Proc. ICSOC*, pages 331–346, 2008.

[12] M. Fähndrich, M. Aiken, C. Hawblitzel, O. Hodson, G. C. Hunt, J. R. Larus, and S. Levi. Language support for fast and reliable message-based communication in singularity os. In *Proc. 2006 EuroSys Conf.*, pages 177–190, 2006.

[13] C. Ferris and J. Farrell. What are web services? *Comm. of the ACM*, 46(6):31–31, June 2003.

[14] X. Fu, T. Bultan, and J. Su. Conversation protocols: A formalism for specification and analysis of reactive electronic services. *Theoretical Computer Science*, 328(1-2):19–37, November 2004.

[15] X. Fu, T. Bultan, and J. Su. WSAT: A tool for formal analysis of web services. In *Proc. 16th Int. Conf. on Computer Aided Verification*, pages 510–514, 2004.

[16] H. Garavel and Frédéric Lang. SVL: A Scripting Language for Compositional Verification. In *Proc. FORTE*, pages 377–394, 2001.

[17] H. Garavel, R. Mateescu, F. Lang, and W. Serwe. CADP 2006: A Toolbox for the Construction and Analysis of Distributed Processes. In *Proc. 18th Int. Conf. Computer Aided Verification*, 2006.

[18] S. Hallé and T. Bultan. Realizability Analysis for Message-Based Interactions using Shared-State Projections. In *Proc. 18th ACM SIGSOFT Int. Sym. Foundations of Software Engineering*, pages 27–36, 2010.

[19] K. Honda, V. T. Vasconcelos, and M. Kubo. Language primitives and type discipline for structured communication-based programming. In *Proc. 7th European Symp. on Programming Languages and Systems*, pages 122–138, 1998.

[20] K. Honda, N. Yoshida, and M. Carbone. Multiparty Asynchronous Session Types. In *Proc. 35th ACM SIGPLAN-SIGACT Sym. Principles of Programming Languages*, pages 273–284, 2008.

[21] G. C. Hunt and J. R. Larus. Singularity: rethinking the software stack. *Operating Systems Review*, 41(2):37–49, 2007.

[22] Conversation Support for agents, e-business, and component integration. http://www.research.ibm.com/convsupport.

[23] Java API for XML messaging (JAXM). http://java.sun.com/developer/earlyAccess/xml/jaxm/.

[24] Java Message Service. http://java.sun.com/products/jms/.

[25] R. Kazhamiakin and M. Pistore. Analysis of Realizability Conditions for Web Service Choreographies. In *Proc. FORTE*, pages 61–76, 2006.

[26] N. Lohmann and K. Wolf. Realizability is Controllability. In *Proc. 1st Central-European Work. on Services and Their Composition*, pages 61–67, 2009.

[27] A. McNeile. Protocol contracts with application to choreographed multiparty collaborations. *Service Oriented Computing and Applications*, 4:109–136, 2010.

[28] D. A. Menascé. Mom vs. rpc: Communication models for distributed applications. *IEEE Internet Computing*, 9(2):90–93, 2005.

[29] Message Sequence Chart (MSC). ITU-T, Geneva Recommendation Z.120, 1996.

[30] Microsoft Message Queuing Service. http://www.microsoft.com/windowsserver2003/technologies/msmq/default.mspx.

[31] E. Newcomer. *Understanding Web Services: XML, WSDL, SOAP, and UDDI*. Springer, 2004.

[32] G. Salaün and T. Bultan. Realizability of Choreographies Using Process Algebra Encodings. In *Proceedings of the 7th International Conference on Integrated Formal Methods*, pages 167–182, 2009.

[33] Singularity design note 5 : Channel contracts. singularity rdk documentation (v1.1). `http://www.codeplex.com/singularity`, 2004.

[34] Z. Stengel and T. Bultan. Analyzing Singularity Channel Contracts. In *Proceedings of the 18th International Symposium on Software Testing and Analysis*, pages 13–24, 2009.

[35] S. Uchitel, J. Kramer, and J. Magee. Incremental elaboration of scenario-based specifications and behavior models using implied scenarios. *ACM Transactions on Software Engineering and Methodology*, 13(1):37–85, 2004.

[36] OMG unified modeling language superstructure, version 2.1.2. `http://ww.uml.org/`, October 2007.

[37] Web Service Choreography Description Language (WS-CDL). http://www.w3.org/TR/ws-cdl-10/, 2005.

Analysis of Recursively Parallel Programs *

Ahmed Bouajjani
LIAFA, Université Paris Diderot, France
abou@liafa.jussieu.fr

Michael Emmi †
LIAFA, Université Paris Diderot, France
mje@liafa.jussieu.fr

Abstract

We propose a general formal model of isolated hierarchical parallel computations, and identify several fragments to match the concurrency constructs present in real-world programming languages such as Cilk and X10. By associating fundamental formal models (vector addition systems with recursive transitions) to each fragment, we provide a common platform for exposing the relative difficulties of algorithmic reasoning. For each case we measure the complexity of deciding state-reachability for finite-data recursive programs, and propose algorithms for the decidable cases. The complexities which include PTIME, NP, EXPSPACE, and 2EXPTIME contrast with undecidable state-reachability for recursive multi-threaded programs.

Categories and Subject Descriptors D.2.4 [*Software/Program Verification*]: Formal methods; F.3.1 [*Specifying and Verifying and Reasoning about Programs*]: Mechanical verification; D.3.2 [*Language Classifications*]: Concurrent, distributed, and parallel languages; F.1.2 [*Models of Computation*]: Parallelism and concurrency

General Terms Algorithms, Reliability, Verification

Keywords Concurrency, Parallelism, Verification

1. Introduction

Despite the ever-increasing importance of concurrent software (e.g., for designing reactive applications, or parallelizing computation across multiple processor cores), concurrent programming and concurrent program analysis remain challenging endeavors. The most widely available facility for designing concurrent applications is *multithreading*, where concurrently executing sequential threads nondeterministically interleave their accesses to shared memory. Such nondeterminism leads to rarely-occurring "Heisenbugs" which are notoriously difficult to reproduce and repair. To prevent such bugs programmers are faced with the difficult task of preventing undesirable interleavings, e.g., by employing lock-based synchronization, without preventing benign interleavings—otherwise the desired reactivity or parallelism is forfeited.

The complexity of multi-threaded program analysis seems to comply with the perceived difficulty of multi-threaded programming. The state-reachability problem for multi-threaded programs is PSPACE-complete [21] with a finite number of finite-state threads, and undecidable [29] with recursive threads. Current analysis approaches either explore an underapproximate concurrent semantics by considering relatively few interleavings [9, 22] or explore a coarse overapproximate semantics via abstraction [13, 18].

Explicitly-parallel programming languages have been advocated to avoid the intricate interleavings implicit in program syntax [24], and several such industrial-strength languages have been developed [2, 6, 7, 17, 25, 30, 32]. Such systems introduce various mechanisms for creating (e.g., **fork**, **spawn**, **post**) and consuming (e.g., **join**, **sync**) concurrent computations, and either encourage (through recommended programming practices) or ensure (through static analyses or runtime systems) that parallel computations execute in isolation without interference from others, through data-partitioning [7], data-replication [6], functional programming [17], message passing [27], or version-based memory access models [32], perhaps falling back on transactional mechanisms [23] when complete isolation is impractical. Although few of these systems behave deterministically, consuming one concurrent computation at a time, many are sensitive to the order in which multiple isolated computations are consumed. Furthermore, some allow computations creating an unbounded number of sub-computations, returning to their superiors an unbounded number of handles to unfinished computations. Even without multithreaded interleaving, nondeterminism in the order in which an unbounded number of computations are consumed has the potential to make program reasoning complex.

In this work we investigate key questions on the analysis of interleaving-free programming models. Specifically, we ask to what extent such models simplify program reasoning, how those models compare with each other, and how to design appropriate analysis algorithms. We attempt to answer these questions as follows:

- We introduce a general interleaving-free parallel programming model on which to express the features found in popular parallel programming languages (Section 2).
- We discover a surprisingly-complex feature of some existing languages: even simple classes of programs with the ability to pass unfinished computations both to and from subordinate computations have undecidable state-reachability problems (Section 2.4).
- We show that the concurrency features present in many real-world programming languages such as Cilk, X10, and Multilisp are captured precisely (modulo the possibility of interleaving) by various fragments of our model (Sections 4 and 6).
- For fragments corresponding to real-world language features, we measure the complexity of computing state-reachability for finite-data programs, and provide, in most cases, asymptotically optimal state-reachability algorithms (Sections 5 and 7).

* Partially supported by the project ANR-09-SEGI-016 Veridyc.

† Supported by a post-doctoral fellowship from the Fondation Sciences Mathématiques de Paris.

[0] Proofs to technical results are contained in an extended online report [3].

POPL'12, January 25–27, 2012, Philadelphia, PA, USA.

Our focus on finite-data programs without interleaving is a means to measuring complexity for the sake of comparison, required since state-reachability for infinite-data or multi-threaded programs is generally undecidable. Applying our algorithms in practice may rely on data abstraction [16], and separately ensuring isolation [23], or approximating possible interleavings [9, 13, 18, 22]; still, our handling of computation-order non-determinism is precise.

The major distinguishing language features are whether a single or an arbitrary number of subordinate computations are waited for at once, and whether the scope of subordinate computations is confined. Generally speaking, reasoning for the "single-wait" case of Section 4 is less difficult than for the "multi-wait" case of Section 6, and we demonstrate a range of complexities[1] from PTIME, NP, EXPSPACE, and 2EXPTIME for various scoping restrictions in Sections 5 and 7. Despite these worst-case complexities, a promising line of work has already demonstrated effective algorithms for practically-occurring EXPSPACE-complete state-reachability problem instances based on simultaneously computing iterative under- and over-approximations, and rapidly converging to a fixed point [15, 19].

We thus present a classification of concurrency constructs, connecting programming language features to fundamental formal models, which highlight the sources of concurrent complexity resulting from each feature, and provide a platform for comparing the difficulty of formal reasoning in each. We hope that these results may be used both to guide the design of impactful program analyses, as well as to guide the design and choice of languages appropriate for various programming problems.

2. Recursively Parallel Programs

We consider a simple concurrent programming model where computations are hierarchically divided into isolated parallely executing tasks. Each task executes sequentially while maintaining *regions* (i.e., containers) of *handles* to other tasks. The initial task begins without task handles. When a task t creates a subordinate (child) task u, t stores the handle to u in one of its regions, at which point t and u begin to execute in parallel. The task u may then recursively create additional parallel tasks, storing their handles in its own regions. At some later point when t requires the result computed by u, t must *await* the completion of u—i.e., blocking until u has finished—at which point t consumes its handle to u. When u does complete, the value it returns is combined with the current state of t via a programmer-supplied *return-value handler*. In addition to creating and consuming subordinate tasks, tasks can transfer ownership of their subordinate tasks to newly-created tasks—by initially passing to the child a subset of task handles—and to their superiors upon completion—by finally passing to the parent unconsumed tasks.

This model permits vastly concurrent executions. Each task along with all the tasks it has created execute completely in parallel. As tasks can create tasks recursively, the total number of concurrently executing tasks has no bound, even when the number of handles stored by each task is bounded.

2.1 Program Syntax

Let Procs be a set of procedure names, Vals a set of values, Exprs a set of expressions, Regs a finite set of region identifiers, and $\mathsf{Rets} \subseteq (\mathsf{Vals} \to \mathsf{Stmts})$ a set of return-value handlers. The grammar of Figure 1 describes our language of *recursively parallel programs*. We intentionally leave the syntax of expressions e unspecified, though we do insist Vals contains **true** and **false**, and Exprs contains Vals and the *(nullary) choice operator* $\star$. We

[1] In order to isolate concurrent complexity from the exponential factor in the number of program variables, we consider a fixed number of variables in each procedure frame; this allows us a PTIME point-of-reference for state-reachability in recursive sequential programs [31].

$$
\begin{array}{rcl}
P & ::= & (\ \textbf{proc}\ p\ (\texttt{var l:}\ T)\ s\ )^* \\
s & ::= & s;\ s \ \mid\ \texttt{l := } e \ \mid\ \textbf{skip} \ \mid\ \textbf{assume}\ e \\
& \mid & \textbf{if}\ e\ \textbf{then}\ s\ \textbf{else}\ s \ \mid\ \textbf{while}\ e\ \textbf{do}\ s \\
& \mid & \textbf{call}\ \texttt{l := } p\ e \ \mid\ \textbf{return}\ e \\
& \mid & \textbf{post}\ r \leftarrow p\ e\ \vec{r}\ d \ \mid\ \textbf{ewait}\ r \ \mid\ \textbf{await}\ r
\end{array}
$$

Figure 1. The grammar of recursively parallel programs. Here T is an unspecified type, p ranges over procedure names, e over expressions, r over regions, and d over return-value handlers.

refer to the class of programs restricted to a finite set of values as *finite-value* programs, and to the class of programs restricted to at most $n \in \mathbb{N}$ (resp., 1) region identifiers as *n-region* (resp., *single-region*) programs. A *sequential program* is a program without **post**, **ewait**, and **await** statements.

Each program P declares a sequence of procedures named $p_0 \dots p_i \in \mathsf{Procs}^*$, each p having single type-T parameter $\mathtt{l}$ and a top-level statement denoted s_p; as statements are built inductively by composition with control-flow statements, s_p describes the entire body of p. The set of program statements s is denoted Stmts. Intuitively, a **post** $r \leftarrow p\ e\ \vec{r}\ d$ statement stores the handle to a newly-created task executing procedure p in the region r; besides the procedure argument e, the newly-created task is passed a subset of the parent's task handles in regions $\vec{r}$, and a return-value handler d. The **ewait** r statement blocks execution until *some* task whose handle is stored in region r completes, at which point its return-value handler is executed. Similarly, the **await** r statement blocks execution until *all* tasks whose handles are stored in region r complete, at which point all of their return-value handlers are executed, in some order. We refer to the **call**, **return**, **post**, **ewait** and **await** as *inter-procedural statements*, and the others as *intra-procedural statements*, and insist that return-value handlers are comprised only of intra-procedural statements. The **assume** e statement proceeds only when e evaluates to **true**—we use this statement in subsequent sections to block undesired executions in our encodings of other parallel programming models.

Example 1. The Fibonacci function can be implemented as a single-region recursively parallel program as follows.

```
proc fib (var n: ℕ)
   var sum: ℕ
   if n < 2 then
      return 1
   else
      post r ← fib (n-1) ε (λv. sum := sum + v);
      post r ← fib (n-2) ε (λv. sum := sum + v);
      await r;
      return sum
```

Alternate implementations are possible, e.g., by replacing the **await** statement by two **ewait** statements, or storing the handles to the recursive calls in separate regions. Note that in this implementation task-handles are not passed to child tasks (ε specifies the empty region sequence) nor to parent tasks (all handles are consumed by the **await** statement before returning).

The programming language we consider is simple yet expressive, since the syntax of types and expressions is left free, and we lose no generality by considering only a single variable per procedure.

2.2 Parallel Semantics with Task-Passing

Unlike recursive sequential programs, whose semantics is defined over *stacks* of procedure frames, the semantics of recursively parallel programs is defined over *trees* of procedure frames. Intuitively, the frame of each posted task becomes a child of the posting task's frame. Each step of execution proceeds either by making a single intra-procedural step of some frame in the tree, creating a new frame by posting a task, or removing a frame by consuming a completed task; unconsumed sub-task frames of a completed task are added as children to the completed task's parent.

A *task* $\langle \ell, s, d\rangle$ is a valuation $\ell \in$ Vals to the procedure-local variable `l`, along with a statement s to be executed, and a return-value handler $d \in$ Rets. (Here s describes the entire body of a procedure p that remains to be executed, and is initially set to p's top-level statement s_p.) A *tree configuration* c is a finite unordered tree of task-labeled vertices and region-labeled edges, and the set of configurations is denoted Configs. Let $\mathbb{M}[\mathsf{Configs}]$ denote the set of configuration multisets. We represent configurations inductively, writing $\langle t, m\rangle$ for the tree with t-labeled root whose child subtrees are given by a *region valuation* m : Regs $\rightarrow \mathbb{M}[\mathsf{Configs}]$: for $r \in$ Regs, the multiset $m(r)$ specifies the collection of subtrees connected to the root of $\langle t, m\rangle$ by an r-edge. The *initial region valuation* $m_\emptyset$ is defined by $m_\emptyset(r) \stackrel{\text{def}}{=} \emptyset$ for all $r \in$ Regs. The singleton region valuation $(r \mapsto c)$ maps r to $\{c\}$, and $r' \in$ Regs $\setminus \{r\}$ to $\emptyset$, and the union $m_1 \cup m_2$ of region valuations is defined by the multiset union of each valuation: $(m_1 \cup m_2)(r) \stackrel{\text{def}}{=} m_1(r) \cup m_2(r)$ for all $r \in$ Regs. The projection $m \mid_{\vec{r}}$ of a region valuation m to a region sequence $\vec{r}$ is defined by $m \mid_{\vec{r}}(r') = m(r')$ when r' occurs in $\vec{r}$, and $m \mid_{\vec{r}}(r') = \emptyset$ otherwise.

For expressions without program variables, we assume the existence of an evaluation function $[\![\cdot]\!]_e$: Exprs $\rightarrow \wp(\mathsf{Vals})$ such that $[\![\star]\!]_e =$ Vals. For convenience, we define

$$e(\langle \ell, s, d\rangle) \stackrel{\text{def}}{=} e(\ell) \stackrel{\text{def}}{=} [\![e[\ell/\mathtt{l}]]\!]_e$$

—as `l` is the only variable, the expression $e[\ell/\mathtt{l}]$ has no free variables.

To reduce clutter and focus on the relevant parts of transition rules in the program semantics, we introduce a notion of contexts. A *configuration context* C is a tree with a single $\diamond$-labeled leaf, task-labeled vertices and leaves otherwise, and region-labeled edges. We write $C[c]$ for the configuration obtained by substituting a configuration c for the unique $\diamond$-labeled leaf of C. We use configuration contexts to isolate individual task transitions, writing, for instance $C[\langle t, m\rangle] \rightarrow C[\langle t', m\rangle]$ to indicate an intra-procedural transition of the task t. Similarly a *statement context* $S = \diamond;\ s_1;\ \ldots;\ s_i$ is a $\diamond$-led sequence of statements, and we write $S[s_0]$ for the statement obtained by substituting a statement s_0 for the unique occurrence of $\diamond$ as the first symbol of S, indicating that s_0 is the next-to-be-executed statement. A *task-statement context* $T = \langle \ell, S, d\rangle$ is a task with a statement context S in place of a statement, and we write $T[s]$ to indicate that s is the next statement to be executed in the task $\langle \ell, S[s], d\rangle$. Finally, we write $C[\langle T[s_1], m\rangle] \rightarrow C[\langle T[s_2], m'\rangle]$ to denote a transition of a task executing a statement s_1 and replacing s_1 by s_2—normally s_2 is the **skip** statement. Since the current statement s of a task $T[s]$ does not effect expression evaluation, we liberally write $e(T)$ to denote the evaluation $e(T[s])$.

We say a task $t = \langle \ell, S[s], d\rangle$ is *completed* when its next-to-be-executed statement s is **return** e, in which case we define $\mathsf{rvh}(t) \stackrel{\text{def}}{=} \{d(v) : v \in e(\ell)\}$ as the set of possible return-value handler statements for t; $\mathsf{rvh}(t)$ is undefined when t is not completed.

Figure 2 and Figure 3 define the transition relation $\rightarrow^{\text{rpp/p}}$ of recursively parallel programs as a set of operational steps on configurations. The intra-procedural transitions $\rightarrow^{\text{seq}}$ of individual tasks in Figure 2 are standard. More interesting are the inter-procedural transitions of Figure 3, which implicitly include a transition $C[\langle t_1, m\rangle] \rightarrow_P^{\text{rpp/p}} C[\langle t_2, m\rangle]$ whenever $t_1 \rightarrow_P^{\text{seq}} t_2$. The POST-T rule creates a procedure frame to execute in parallel, and links it to the current frame by the given region, passing ownership of tasks in the specified region sequence to the newly-created frame. The $\exists$WAIT-T rule consumes the result of a single child frame in the given region, and applies the return-value handler to update the parent frame's local valuation. Similarly, the $\forall$WAIT-NEXT-T and $\forall$WAIT-DONE-T rules consume the results of every child frame in the given region, applying their return handlers in the order they are consumed. The semantics of **call** statements reduces to that of **post** and **ewait**: supposing an unused region identifier $\mathtt{r}_{call}$, we translate each statement **call** `l :=` $p\ e$ into the sequence

post $\mathtt{r}_{call} \leftarrow p\ e\ \varepsilon\ \mathtt{d}_{call}$;
ewait $\mathtt{r}_{call}$,

where $\mathtt{d}_{call}(v) \stackrel{\text{def}}{=}$ `l :=` v is the return-value handler which simply writes the entire return value v into the local variable `l`, and ε denotes an empty sequence of region identifiers.

POST-T
$$\frac{v \in e(T) \qquad m' = m \setminus m\mid_{\vec{r}} \cup (r \mapsto \langle\langle v, s_p, d\rangle, m\mid_{\vec{r}}\rangle)}{C[\langle T[\mathbf{post}\ r \leftarrow p\ e\ \vec{r}\ d], m\rangle] \xrightarrow[P]{\text{rpp/p}} C[\langle T[\mathbf{skip}], m'\rangle]}$$

$\exists$WAIT-T
$$\frac{m_1 = (r \mapsto \langle t_2, m_2\rangle) \cup m_1' \qquad s \in \mathsf{rvh}(t_2)}{C[\langle T_1[\mathbf{ewait}\ r], m_1\rangle] \xrightarrow[P]{\text{rpp/p}} C[\langle T_1[s], m_1' \cup m_2\rangle]}$$

$\forall$WAIT-NEXT-T
$$\frac{m_1 = (r \mapsto \langle t_2, m_2\rangle) \cup m_1' \qquad s \in \mathsf{rvh}(t_2)}{C[\langle T_1[\mathbf{await}\ r], m_1\rangle] \xrightarrow[P]{\text{rpp/p}} C[\langle T_1[s;\ \mathbf{await}\ r], m_1' \cup m_2\rangle]}$$

$\forall$WAIT-DONE-T
$$\frac{m(r) = \emptyset}{C[\langle T[\mathbf{await}\ r], m\rangle] \xrightarrow[P]{\text{rpp/p}} C[\langle T[\mathbf{skip}], m\rangle]}$$

Figure 3. The tree-based transition relation for parallely-executing recursively parallel programs with task-passing.

A *parallel execution of a program* P *(from* c_0 *to* c_j*)* is a configuration sequence $c_0c_1 \ldots c_j$ where $c_i \rightarrow_P^{\text{rpp/p}} c_{i+1}$ for $0 \le i < j$. An initial condition $\iota = \langle p_0, \ell_0\rangle$ is a procedure $p_0 \in$ Procs along with a value $\ell_0 \in$ Vals. A configuration $\langle\langle \ell_0, s, d\rangle, m_\emptyset\rangle$ is called $\langle p_0, \ell_0\rangle$*-initial* when s is the top-level statement of p_0. A configuration c_f is called ℓ_f*-final* when there exists a context C such that $c_f = C[\langle t, m\rangle]$ and $\mathtt{l}(t) = \ell_f$. We say a valuation ℓ is *reachable in* P from ι when there exists an execution of P from some c_0 to c_f, where c_0 is ι-initial and c_f is ℓ-final.

Problem 1 (State-Reachability). *The* state-reachability problem *is to determine, given an initial condition* ι *of a program* P *and a valuation* ℓ*, whether* ℓ *is reachable in* P *from* ι.

2.3 Sequential Semantics with Task-Passing

Since tasks only exchange values at creation and completion-time, the order in which concurrently-executing tasks make execution steps does not affect computed program values. In this section we leverage this fact and focus on a particular execution order in which at any moment only a single task is enabled. When the currently enabled task encounters and **ewait**/**await** statement, suspending execution to wait for a subordinate task t, t becomes the currently-enabled task; when t completes, control returns to its waiting parent. At any moment only the tasks along one path ρ in the configuration tree have ever been enabled, and all but the last task in ρ are waiting for their child in ρ to complete. We encode this execution order into an equivalent stack-based operational semantics, which essentially transforms recursively parallel programs into sequential programs with an unbounded auxiliary storage device used to store subordinate tasks. We interpret the **ewait** and **await** statements as procedure calls which compute the values returned by previously-posted tasks.

$$\textsc{Skip}\quad \frac{}{T[\mathbf{skip};\ s] \xrightarrow[P]{\text{seq}} T[s]} \qquad \textsc{Assume}\quad \frac{\mathbf{true} \in e(T)}{T[\mathbf{assume}\ e] \xrightarrow[P]{\text{seq}} T[\mathbf{skip}]}$$

$$\textsc{If-Then}\quad \frac{\mathbf{true} \in e(T)}{T[\mathbf{if}\ e\ \mathbf{then}\ s_1\ \mathbf{else}\ s_2] \xrightarrow[P]{\text{seq}} T[s_1]} \qquad \textsc{If-Else}\quad \frac{\mathbf{false} \in e(T)}{T[\mathbf{if}\ e\ \mathbf{then}\ s_1\ \mathbf{else}\ s_2] \xrightarrow[P]{\text{seq}} T[s_2]}$$

$$\textsc{Assign}\quad \frac{\ell' \in e(\ell)}{\langle \ell, S[\mathtt{l}\ :=\ e], d\rangle \xrightarrow[P]{\text{seq}} \langle \ell', S[\mathbf{skip}], d\rangle} \qquad \textsc{Loop-Do}\quad \frac{\mathbf{true} \in e(T)}{T[\mathbf{while}\ e\ \mathbf{do}\ s] \xrightarrow[P]{\text{seq}} T[s; \mathbf{while}\ e\ \mathbf{do}\ s]}$$

$$\textsc{Loop-End}\quad \frac{\mathbf{false} \in e(T)}{T[\mathbf{while}\ e\ \mathbf{do}\ s] \xrightarrow[P]{\text{seq}} T[\mathbf{skip}]}$$

Figure 2. The intra-procedural transition relation for recursively parallel programs.

$$\textsc{Post-S}\quad \frac{v \in e(T) \qquad m' = m \setminus m\mid_{\vec{r}} \cup \left(r \mapsto \langle \langle v, s_p, d\rangle, m\mid_{\vec{r}}\rangle\right)}{\langle T[\mathbf{post}\ r \leftarrow p\ e\ \vec{r}\ d], m\rangle\, c \xrightarrow[P]{\text{rpp/s}} \langle T[\mathbf{skip}], m'\rangle\, c}$$

$$\exists\textsc{Wait-S}\quad \frac{m = (r \mapsto c_0) \cup m'}{\langle T[\mathbf{ewait}\ r], m\rangle\, c \xrightarrow[P]{\text{rpp/s}} c_0 \langle T[\mathbf{skip}], m'\rangle\, c}$$

$$\forall\textsc{Wait-Next-S}\quad \frac{m = (r \mapsto c_0) \cup m'}{\langle T[\mathbf{await}\ r], m\rangle\, c \xrightarrow[P]{\text{rpp/s}} c_0 \langle T[\mathbf{skip};\ \mathbf{await}\ r], m'\rangle\, c}$$

$$\forall\textsc{Wait-Done-S}\quad \frac{m(r) = \emptyset}{\langle T[\mathbf{await}\ r], m\rangle\, c \xrightarrow[P]{\text{rpp/s}} \langle T[\mathbf{skip}], m\rangle\, c}$$

$$\textsc{Return-S}\quad \frac{s \in \mathsf{rvh}(t_1)}{\langle t_1, m_1\rangle \langle T_2[\mathbf{skip}], m_2\rangle\, c \xrightarrow[P]{\text{rpp/s}} \langle T_2[s], m_1 \cup m_2\rangle\, c}$$

Figure 4. The stack-based transition relation for sequentially-executing recursively parallel programs with task-passing.

We define a *frame* to be a configuration in the sense of the tree-based semantics of Section 2.2, i.e., a finite unordered tree of task-labeled vertices and region-labeled edges. (Here all non-root nodes in the tree are posted tasks that have yet to take a single step of execution.) In our stack-based semantics, a *stack configuration c* is a sequence of frames, representing a procedure activation stack.

Figures 2 and 4 define the sequential transition relation $\rightarrow^{\text{rpp/s}}$ of recursively parallel programs as a set of operational steps on configurations. The inter-procedural transitions of Figure 4 implicitly include a transition $\langle t_1, m\rangle\, c \rightarrow_P^{\text{rpp/s}} \langle t_2, m\rangle\, c$ whenever $t_1 \rightarrow_P^{\text{seq}} t_2$. Interesting here are the rules for **ewait** and **await**. The $\exists$WAIT-S rule blocks the currently executing frame to obtain the result for a single, nondeterministically chosen, frame c_0 in the given region, by pushing c_0 onto the activation stack. Similarly, the $\forall$WAIT-NEXT-S and $\forall$WAIT-DONE-S rules block the currently executing frame to obtain the results for every task in the given region, in a nondeterministically-chosen order. Finally, the RETURN-S applies a completed task's return-value handler to update the parent frame's local valuation. The definitions of *sequential execution, initial,* and *reachable* are nearly identical to their parallel counterparts.

Lemma 1. *The parallel semantics and the sequential semantics are indistinguishable w.r.t. state reachability, i.e., for all initial conditions ι of a program P, the valuation ℓ is reachable in P from ι by a parallel execution if and only if ℓ is reachable in P from ι by a sequential execution.*

2.4 Undecidability of State-Reachability with Task-Passing

Recursively parallel programs allow pending tasks to be passed *bidirectionally*: both from completed tasks and to newly-created tasks. This capability makes the state-reachability problem undecidable—even for the very simple cases recursive programs with at least one region, and for non-recursive programs with at least two regions. Essentially, when pending tasks can be passed to newly-created tasks, it becomes possible to construct and manipulate unbounded task-chains by keeping a handle to most-recently created task, after having passed the handle of the previously-most-recently created task to the most-recently created task. We can then show that such unbounded chains of pending tasks can be used to simulate an arbitrary unbounded and ordered storage device.

Definition 1 (Task passing)**.** A program which contains a statement **post** $r \leftarrow p\ e\ \vec{r}\ d$, such that $|\vec{r}| > 0$ is called *task-passing*.

The *task-depth* of a program P is the maximum length of a sequence $p_1 \ldots p_i$ of procedures in P such that each p_j contains a statement **post** $r \leftarrow p_{i+j}\ e\ \vec{r}\ d$, for $0 < j < i$, and some $r \in \mathsf{Regs}$, $e \in \mathsf{Exprs}$, $\vec{r} \in \mathsf{Regs}^*$, and $d \in \mathsf{Rets}$. Programs with unbounded task-depth are *recursive*, and are otherwise *non-recrusive*.

Theorem 1. *The state-reachability problem for n-region finite-value task-passing parallel programs is undecidable for*

(a) non-recursive programs with $n > 1$, and
(b) recursive programs with $n > 0$.

The proof of Theorem 1 is given by two separate reductions from the emptiness problem for Turing machines to "single-wait" programs, i.e., those using **ewait** statements but not **await** statements. In essence, as each task-handle can point to an unbounded chain of task-handles, we can construct an unbounded Turing machine tape by using one task-chain to store the contents of cells to the left of the tape head, and another chain to store the contents of cells to the right of the tape head. If only one region is granted but recursion is allowed (i.e., as in (b)), we can still construct the tape using the task-chain for the cells right of the tape head, while using the (unbounded) procedure-stack to store the cells left of the head. When only one region is granted and recursion is not allowed, neither of these reductions work. Without recursion we can bound the procedure stack, and then we can show that single-stack machine suffices to encode the single unbounded chain of tasks.

3. Programs without Task Passing

Due to the undecidability result of Theorem 1 and our desire to compare the analysis complexities of parallel programming models, we consider, henceforth, unless otherwise specified, only non-task-passing programs, simplifying program syntax by writing **post** $r \leftarrow p\ e\ d$. When task-passing is not allowed, region valuations need not store an entire configuration for each newly-posted task, since the posted task's initial region valuation is empty. As this represents a significant simplification on which our subsequent analysis results rely, we redefine here a few key notions.

Post

$$\frac{v \in e(T) \qquad m' = m \cup (r \mapsto \langle v, s_p, d \rangle)}{\langle T[\mathbf{post}\ r \leftarrow p\ e\ d]\,, m\rangle\, c \xrightarrow[P]{\text{rpp}} \langle T[\mathbf{skip}]\,, m'\rangle\, c}$$

∃Wait

$$\frac{m = (r \mapsto t_2) \cup m'}{\langle T_1[\mathbf{ewait}\ r]\,, m\rangle\, c \xrightarrow[P]{\text{rpp}} \langle t_2, \emptyset\rangle \langle T_1[\mathbf{skip}]\,, m'\rangle\, c}$$

∀Wait-Next

$$\frac{m = (r \mapsto t_2) \cup m'}{\langle T_1[\mathbf{await}\ r]\,, m\rangle\, c \xrightarrow[P]{\text{rpp}} \langle t_2, \emptyset\rangle \langle T_1[\mathbf{skip};\ \mathbf{await}\ r]\,, m'\rangle\, c}$$

∀Wait-Done

$$\frac{m(r) = \emptyset}{\langle T[\mathbf{await}\ r]\,, m\rangle\, c \xrightarrow[P]{\text{rpp}} \langle T[\mathbf{skip}]\,, m\rangle\, c}$$

Return

$$\frac{s \in \mathsf{rvh}(t_1)}{\langle t_1, m_1\rangle \langle T_2[\mathbf{skip}]\,, m_2\rangle\, c \xrightarrow[P]{\text{rpp}} \langle T_2[s]\,, m_1 \cup m_2\rangle\, c}$$

Figure 5. The stack-based transition relation for sequentially-executing recursively parallel programs without task-passing.

3.1 Sequential Semantics without Task-Passing

A *region valuation* is a (non-nested) mapping $m : \mathsf{Regs} \to \mathbb{M}[\mathsf{Tasks}]$ from regions to multisets of tasks, a *frame* $\langle t, m\rangle$ is a task $t \in \mathsf{Tasks}$ paired with a region valuation m, and a *configuration* c is a sequence of frames representing a procedure activation stack. The transition relation $\to^{\text{rpp}}$ of Figures 2 and 5 implicitly include a transition $\langle t_1, m\rangle\, c \to_P^{\text{rpp}} \langle t_2, m\rangle\, c$ whenever $t_1 \to_P^{\text{seq}} t_2$. The definitions of *sequential execution*, *initial*, and *reachable* are nearly identical to their task-passing parallel and sequential counterparts. Since pending tasks need not store initial region-valuations in non-task-passing programs, this simpler semantics is equivalent to the previous stack-based semantics.

Lemma 2. *For all initial conditions ι non-task-passing programs P, the valuation ℓ is reachable in P from ι by a sequential execution with task-passing if and only if ℓ is reachable in P from ι by a sequential execution without task-passing.*

Even with this simplification, we do not presently know whether the state-reachability problem for (finite-value) recursively parallel programs is decidable in general. In the following sections, we identify several decidable, and in some cases tractable, restrictions to the program model which correspond to the concurrency mechanisms found in real-world parallel programming languages.

3.2 Recursive Vector Addition Systems with Zero-Test Edges

Fix $k \in \mathbb{N}$. A *recursive vector addition system (RVASS) $\mathcal{A} = \langle Q, \delta\rangle$ of dimension k* is a finite set Q of states, along with a finite set $\delta = \delta_1 \uplus \delta_2 \uplus \delta_3$ of transitions partitioned into *additive* transitions $\delta_1 \subset Q \times \mathbb{N}^k \times \mathbb{N}^k \times Q$, *recursive* transitions $\delta_2 \subseteq Q \times Q \times Q \times Q$, and *zero-test* transitions $\delta_3 \subseteq Q \times Q$. We write

$$q \overset{\vec{n}_1 \vec{n}_2}{\hookrightarrow} q' \quad \text{when } \langle q, \vec{n}_1, \vec{n}_2, q'\rangle \in \delta_1, \text{ and}$$

$$q \overset{q_1 q_2}{\hookrightarrow} q' \quad \text{when } \langle q, q_1, q_2, q'\rangle \in \delta_2.$$

$$q \hookrightarrow q' \quad \text{when } \langle q, q'\rangle \in \delta_3.$$

A *(non-recursive) vector addition system (with states) (VASS)* is a recursive vector addition system $\langle Q, \delta\rangle$ such that δ contains only additive transitions.

An *(RVASS) frame* $\langle q, \vec{n}\rangle$ is a state $q \in Q$ along with a vector $\vec{n} \in \mathbb{N}^k$, and an *(RVASS) configuration* $c \in (Q \times \mathbb{N}^k)^+$ is a non-empty sequence of frames representing a stack of non-recursive sub-computations. The transition relation $\to^{\text{rvas}}$ for recursive vector addition systems is defined in Figure 6. The Additive rule updates the top frame $\langle q, \vec{n}\rangle$ by subtracting the vector $\vec{n}_1$ from $\vec{n}$, adding the vector $\vec{n}_2$ to the result, and updating the control state to q'. The Call rule pushes on the frame-stack a new frame $\langle q_1, \mathbf{0}\rangle$ from which the Return rule will eventually pop at some point when the control state is q_2; when this happens, the vector $\vec{n}_1$ of the popped frame is added to the vector $\vec{n}_2$ of the frame below. We describe an application of the Call (resp., Return) rule as a *call (resp., return) transition*. Finally, the Zero rule proceeds only when the top-most frame's vector equals $\mathbf{0}$.

An *execution of a RVASS $\mathcal{A}$ (from c_0 to c_j)* is a configuration sequence $c_0 c_1 \dots c_j$ where $c_i \to^{\text{rvas}} c_{i+1}$ for $0 \leq i < j$. A configuration $\langle q, \vec{n}\rangle$ is called q_0*-initial* when $q = q_0$ and $\vec{n} = \mathbf{0}$, and a configuration c_f is called q_f*-final* when $c_f = \langle q_f, \vec{n}\rangle\, c$ for some configuration c and $\vec{n} \in \mathbb{N}^k$. We say a state q_f is *reachable in $\mathcal{A}$* from q_0 when there exists an execution of $\mathcal{A}$ from some q_0-initial configuration c_0 to some q_f-final configuration c_f. The *state-reachability problem* for recursive vector addition systems is to determine whether a given state q is reachable from some q_0.

Recently Demri et al. [8] have proved that state-reachability in branching vector addition systems (BVAS)—a very similar formal model to which RVASS reduces—is in 2EXPTIME. This immediately gives us an upper-bound on computing state-reachability in RVASS without zero-test edges. Though state-reachability in non-recursive systems is EXPSPACE-complete [26, 28], for the moment, we do not know matching upper and lower bounds for RVASS.

Lemma 3. *The state-reachability problem for recursive (resp., non-recursive) vector addition systems without zero-test edges is EXPSPACE-hard, and in 2EXPTIME (resp., EXPSPACE).*

3.3 Encoding Recursively Parallel Programs as RVASSs

When the value set Vals of a given program P is taken to be finite, the set Tasks also becomes finite since there are finitely many statements and return-value handlers occurring in P. As finite-domain multisets are equivalently encoded with a finite number of counters (i.e., one counter per element), we can encode each region valuation $m \in \mathsf{Regs} \to \mathbb{M}[\mathsf{Tasks}]$ by a vector $\vec{n} \in \mathbb{N}^k$ of counters, where $k = |\mathsf{Regs} \times \mathsf{Tasks}|$. To clarify the correspondence, we fix an enumeration $\mathsf{cn} : \mathsf{Regs} \times \mathsf{Tasks} \to \{1, \dots, k\}$, and associate each region valuation m with a vector $\vec{n}$ such that for all $r \in \mathsf{Regs}$ and $t \in \mathsf{Tasks}$, $m(r)(t) = \vec{n}(\mathsf{cn}(r,t))$. Let $\vec{n}_i$ denote the unit vector of dimension i, i.e., $\vec{n}_i(i) = 1$ and $\vec{n}_i(j) = 0$ for $j \neq i$.

Given a finite-data recursively parallel program P without task-passing, we associate a corresponding recursive vector addition system $\mathcal{A}_P = \langle Q, \delta\rangle$. We define $Q \stackrel{\text{def}}{=} \mathsf{Tasks} \cup \mathsf{Tasks}^3$, and define δ formally in Figure 7. Intra-procedural transitions translate directly to additive transitions. The **call** statements are handled by recursive transitions between entry and exit points t_0 and t_f of the called procedure. The **post** statements are handled by additive transitions that increment the counter corresponding to a region-task pair. The **ewait** statements are handled in two steps: first an additive transition decrements the counter corresponding to region-task pair $\langle r, t_0\rangle$, then a recursive transition between entry and exit points t_0 and t_f of the corresponding procedure is made, applying the return-value handler of t_f upon the return. (Here we use an intermediate state $\langle T[\mathbf{skip}]\,, t_0, t_f\rangle \in Q$ to connect the two transitions, in order to differentiate the intermediate steps of other **ewait** transitions.) The **await** statements are handled similarly, except the **await** statement must be repeated again upon the return. Finally, a zero-test transition allows $\mathcal{A}_P$ to eventually step past each **await** statement.

ADDITIVE
$$\frac{q \xhookrightarrow{\vec{n}_1 \vec{n}_2} q' \qquad \vec{n} \geq \vec{n}_1}{\langle q, \vec{n} \rangle\, c \xrightarrow{\text{rvas}} \langle q', \vec{n} \ominus \vec{n}_1 \oplus \vec{n}_2 \rangle\, c}$$

CALL
$$\frac{q \xhookrightarrow{q_1 q_2} q'}{\langle q, \vec{n} \rangle\, c \xrightarrow{\text{rvas}} \langle q_1, \mathbf{0} \rangle \langle q, \vec{n} \rangle\, c}$$

RETURN
$$\frac{q \xhookrightarrow{q_1 q_2} q'}{\langle q_2, \vec{n}_1 \rangle \langle q, \vec{n}_2 \rangle\, c \xrightarrow{\text{rvas}} \langle q', \vec{n}_1 \oplus \vec{n}_2 \rangle\, c}$$

ZERO
$$\frac{q \hookrightarrow q'}{\langle q, \mathbf{0} \rangle\, c \xrightarrow{\text{rvas}} \langle q', \mathbf{0} \rangle\, c}$$

Figure 6. The transition relation for recursive vector addition systems. To simplify presentation, we assume that there is at most one recursive transition originating from each state, i.e., for all $q \in Q$, $\left|\delta_2 \cap (\{q\} \times Q^3)\right| \leq 1$. We denote by $\mathbf{0}$ the vector $\langle 0, 0, \ldots, 0 \rangle$, and by $\oplus$ and $\ominus$ the usual vector addition and subtraction operators.

$$\frac{v_0 \in e(T) \qquad i = \mathsf{cn}(r, \langle v_0, s_p, d \rangle)}{T[\textbf{post}\ r \leftarrow p\ e\ d] \xhookrightarrow{\mathbf{0}\vec{n}_i} T[\textbf{skip}]} \qquad \frac{}{T[\textbf{await}\ r] \hookrightarrow T[\textbf{skip}]}$$

$$\frac{v_0 \in e(T) \qquad t_0 = \langle v_0, s_p, \mathtt{d}_{call} \rangle \qquad (\mathtt{l}\ \mathtt{:=}\ v_f) \in \mathsf{rvh}(t_f)}{T[\textbf{call}\ \mathtt{l}\ \mathtt{:=}\ p\ e] \xhookrightarrow{t_0 t_f} T[\mathtt{l}\ \mathtt{:=}\ v_f]}$$

$$\frac{t_1 \xrightarrow[P]{\text{seq}} t_2}{t_1 \xhookrightarrow{\mathbf{00}} t_2} \qquad \frac{i = \mathsf{cn}(r, t_0) \qquad s \in \mathsf{rvh}(t_f)}{T[\textbf{ewait}\ r] \xhookrightarrow{\vec{n}_i \mathbf{0}} \langle T[\textbf{skip}], t_0, t_f \rangle \xhookrightarrow{t_0 t_f} T[s]}$$

$$\frac{i = \mathsf{cn}(r, t_0) \qquad s \in \mathsf{rvh}(t_f)}{T[\textbf{await}\ r] \xhookrightarrow{\vec{n}_i \mathbf{0}} \langle T[\textbf{skip}], t_0, t_f \rangle \xhookrightarrow{t_0 t_f} T[s;\ \textbf{await}\ r]}$$

Figure 7. The transitions of the RVASS $\mathcal{A}_P$ encoding the behavior of a finite-data recursively parallel program P.

Notice that ignoring intermediate states $\langle t_1, t_2, t_3 \rangle \in Q$, the frames $\langle t, \vec{n} \rangle$ of $\mathcal{A}_P$ correspond directly to frames $\langle t, m \rangle$ of the given program P, given the correspondence between vectors and region valuations. This correspondence between frames indeed extends to configurations, and ultimately to the state-reachability problems between $\mathcal{A}_P$ and P.

Lemma 4. *For all programs P without task-passing, procedures $p_0 \in$ Procs, and values $\ell_0, \ell \in$ Vals, ℓ is reachable from $\langle \ell_0, p_0 \rangle$ in P if and only if there exist $s \in$ Stmts and $d_0, d \in$ Rets such that $\langle \ell, s, d \rangle$ is reachable from $\langle \ell_0, s_{p_0}, d_0 \rangle$ in $\mathcal{A}_P$.*

Our analysis algorithms in the following sections use Lemma 4 to compute state-reachability of a program P without task-passing by computing state-reachability on the corresponding RVASS $\mathcal{A}_P$. In general, our algorithms compute sets of region valuation vectors

$$\mathsf{sms}(t_0, t_f, P) \stackrel{\text{def}}{=} \{\vec{n} : \langle t_0, \mathbf{0} \rangle \xrightarrow[\mathcal{A}_P]{\text{rvas}} * \langle t_f, \vec{n} \rangle\},$$

summarizing the execution of a procedure between an entry point t_0 and exit point t_f, where we write $\rightarrow^{\text{rvas}}_{\mathcal{A}_P} *$ to denote zero or more applications of $\rightarrow^{\text{rvas}}_{\mathcal{A}_P}$. Given an effective way to compute such a function, we could systematically replace inter-procedural program steps (i.e., of the **call**, **ewait**, and **await** statements) with intra-procedural edges performing their net effect. Note however that even if the set of tasks is finite, the set $\mathsf{sms}(t_0, t_f, \mathcal{A}_P)$ of summaries between t_0 and t_f need not be finite; the ability to compute this set is thus the key to our summarization-based algorithms in the following sections.

4. Single-Wait Programs

Definition 2 (Single wait). A *single-wait program* is a program which does not contain the **await** statement.

Single-wait programs can wait only for a single pending task at any program point. Many parallel programming constructs can be modeled as single-wait programs.

4.1 Parallel Programming with Futures

The **future** annotation of Multilisp [17] has become a widely adopted parallel programming construct, included, for example, in X10 [7] and in Leijen et al. [25]'s task parallel library. Flanagan and Felleisen [12] provide a principled description of its semantics. The future construct leverages the procedural program structure for parallelism, essentially adding a "lazy" procedure call which immediately returns control to the caller with a placeholder for a value that may not yet have been computed, along with an operation for ensuring that a given placeholder has been filled in with a computed value. Syntactically, futures add two statements,

$$\textbf{future}\ x\ \mathtt{:=}\ p\ e \qquad \textbf{touch}\ x,$$

where x ranges over program variables, $p \in$ Procs, and $e \in$ Exprs. Though it is not necessarily present in the syntax of a source language with futures, we assume every use of a variable assigned by a **future** statement is explicitly preceded by a **touch** statement. Semantically, the **future** statement creates a new process in which to execute the given procedure, which proceeds to execute in parallel with the caller—and all other processes created in this way. The **touch** statement on a variable x blocks execution of the current procedure until the future procedure call which assigned to x completes, returning a value with which is copied into x. Even though each procedure can only spawn a bounded number of parallel processes—i.e., one per program variable—there is in general no bound on the total number of parallelly-executing processes, since procedure calls—even parallel ones—are recursive.

Example 2. The Fibonacci function can be implemented as a parallel algorithm using futures as follows.

```
proc fib (var n: ℕ)
    var x, y: ℕ
    if n < 2 then
        return 1
    else
        future x := fib (n-1);
        future y := fib (n-2);
        touch x;
        touch y;
        return x + y
```

As opposed to the usual (naïve) sequential implementation operating in time $\mathcal{O}(n^2)$, this parallel implementation runs in time $\mathcal{O}(n)$.

The semantics of futures is readily expressed with task-passing programs using the **post** and **ewait** statements. Assuming a region identifier $\mathtt{r}_x$ and return handler $\mathtt{d}_x$ for each program variable x, we encode

future x := p e	as	**post** $\mathtt{r}_x \leftarrow p\ e\ \vec{\mathtt{r}}\ \mathtt{d}_x$
touch x	as	**ewait** $\mathtt{r}_x$

where $\mathtt{d}_x(v) \stackrel{\text{def}}{=} x\ \mathtt{:=}\ v$ simply assigns the return value v to the variable x, and the vector $\vec{\mathtt{r}}$ contains each $\mathtt{r}_y$ such that the variable y appears in e.

4.2 Parallel Programming with Revisions

Burckhardt et al. [6]'s revisions model of concurrent programming proposes a mechanism analogous to (software) version control systems such as CVS and subversion, which promises to naturally and easily parallize sequential code in order to take advantage of multiple computing cores. There, each sequentially executing process is referred to as a *revision*. A revision can branch into two revisions, each continuing to execute in parallel on their own separate copies of data, or merge a previously-created revision, provided a programmer-defined *merge function* to mitigate the updates to data which each have performed. Syntactically, revisions add two statements,

$$x \texttt{ := } \mathbf{rfork}\ s \qquad \mathbf{join}\ x,$$

where x ranges over program variables, and $s \in \mathsf{Stmts}$. Semantically, the **rfork** statement creates a new process to execute the given statement, which proceeds to execute in parallel with the invoker—and all other processes created in this way. The assignment stores a *handle* to the newly-created revision in a *revision variable* x. The **join** statement on a revision variable x blocks execution of the current revision until the revision whose handle is stored in x completes; at that point the current revision's data is updated according to a programmer-supplied merge function $m : (\mathsf{Vals} \times \mathsf{Vals} \times \mathsf{Vals}) \rightarrow \mathsf{Vals}$: when v_0, v_1 are, resp., the initial and final data values of the merged revision, and v_2 is the current data value of the current revision, the current revisions data value is updated to $m(v_0, v_1, v_2)$.

The semantics of revisions is readily expressed with task-passing programs using the **post** and **ewait** statements. Assuming a region identifier $\mathtt{r}_x$ for each program variable x, and a programmer-supplied merge function m, we encode

$$x \texttt{ := } \mathbf{rfork}\ s \quad \text{as} \quad \mathbf{post}\ \mathtt{r}_x \leftarrow p_s\ \mathtt{l}\ \vec{\mathtt{r}}\ \mathtt{d}$$

$$\mathbf{join}\ x \quad \text{as} \quad \mathbf{ewait}\ \mathtt{r}_x$$

where p_s is a procedure declared as

```
proc p_s (var l: T)
    var l_0 := l
    s;
    return (l_0,l)
```

and $\mathtt{d}(\langle v_0, v_1\rangle) \stackrel{\text{def}}{=} \mathtt{l} \texttt{ := } m(v_0\texttt{,l,}v_1)$ updates the current local valuation based on the joined revision's initial and final valuations $v_0, v_1 \in \mathsf{Vals}$, and the joining revision's current local valuation stored in $\mathtt{l}$. The vector $\vec{\mathtt{r}}$ contains each $\mathtt{r}_y$ for which the revision variable y is accessed in s.[2]

4.3 Programming with Asynchronous Procedures

Asynchronous programs [14, 19, 33] are becoming widely-used to build reactive systems, such as device drivers, web servers, and graphical user interfaces, with low-latency requirements. Essentially, a program is made up of a collection of short-lived tasks running one-by-one and accessing a global store, which post other tasks to be run at some later time. Tasks are initially posted by an initial procedure, and may also be generated by external system events. An *event loop* repeatedly chooses a pending task from its collection to execute to completion, adding the tasks it posts back to the task collection. Syntactically, asynchronous programs add two statements,

$$\mathbf{async}\ p\ e \qquad \mathbf{eventloop}$$

such that **eventloop** is invoked only once as the last statement of the initial procedure. Semantically, the **async** statement initializes a procedure call and returns control immediately, without waiting for the call to return. The **eventloop** statement repeatedly dispatches pending—i.e., called but not yet returned—procedures, and executing them to completion; each procedure executes atomically making both synchronous calls, as well as an unbounded number of additional asynchronous procedure calls. The order in which procedure calls are dispatched is chosen non-deterministically.

We encode asynchronous programs as (non-deterministic) recursively parallel programs using the **post** and **ewait** statements. Assuming a single region identifier $\mathtt{r}_0$, we encode

$$\mathbf{async}\ p\ e \quad \text{as} \quad \mathbf{post}\ \mathtt{r}_0 \leftarrow p'\ e\ \mathtt{d}$$

$$\mathbf{eventloop} \quad \text{as} \quad \mathbf{while}\ \mathtt{true}\ \mathbf{do}\ \mathbf{ewait}\ \mathtt{r}_0.$$

Supposing p has top-level statement s accessing a shared global variable $\mathtt{g}$ (besides the procedure parameter $\mathtt{l}$), we declare p' as

```
proc p' (var l: T)
    var g_0 := *
    var g := g_0
    s; return (g_0,g).
```

Finally $\mathtt{d}(\langle v_0, v_1\rangle) \stackrel{\text{def}}{=} \mathbf{assume}\ \mathtt{l} = v_0\texttt{; l := } v_1$ models the atomic update p performs from an initial (guessed) shared global valuation v_0. Guessing allows us to simulate the communication of a shared global state $\mathtt{g}$, which is later ensured to have begun with v_0, which the previously-executed asynchronous task had written.

5. Single-Wait Analysis

The absence of **await** edges in a program P implies the absence of zero-test transitions in the corresponding recursive vector addition system $\mathcal{A}_P$. To compute state-reachability in P via procedure summarization, we must summarize the recursive transitions of $\mathcal{A}_P$ by additive transitions (in a non-recursive system) accounting for the left-over pending tasks returned by reach procedure. This is not trivial in general, since the space of possibly returned region valuations is infinite. In increasing difficulty, we isolate three special cases of single-wait programs, whose analysis problems are simpler than the general case. In the simplest "non-aliasing" case where the number of tasks stored in each region of a procedure frame is limited to one, the execution of **ewait** statements are deterministic. When the number of tasks stored in each region is not limited to one, non-determinism arises from the choice of which completed task to pick at each **ewait** statement (see the ∃WAIT rule of Figure 5). This added power makes the state-reachability problem at least as hard as state-reachability in vector addition systems—i.e., EXPSPACE-hard, though the precise complexity depends on the scope of pending tasks. After examining the PTIME-complete non-aliasing case, we examine two EXPSPACE-complete cases by restricting the scope of task handles, before moving to the general case.

5.1 Single-Wait Analysis without Aliasing

Many parallel programming languages consume only the computations of precisely-addressed tasks. In futures, for example, the **touch** x statement applies to the return value of a particular procedure—the last one whose future result was assigned to x. Similarly, in revisions, the **join** x statement applies to the last revision whose handle was stored in x. Indeed in the single-wait program semantics of each case, we are guaranteed that the corresponding region, $\mathtt{r}_x$, contains at most one task handle. Thus the non-determinism arising (from choosing between tasks in a given region) in the ∃WAIT rule of Figure 3 disappears. Though both futures and revisions allow task-passing, the following results apply to futures- and revisions-based programs which only pass pending tasks from child to parent.

[2] Actually $\vec{\mathtt{r}}$ must in general be chosen non-deterministically, as each revision handle may be joined either by the parent revision or its branch.

Definition 3 (Non aliasing)**.** We say a region $r \in \mathsf{Regs}$ is *aliased* in a region valuation $m : \mathsf{Regs} \rightarrow \mathbb{M}[\mathsf{Tasks}]$ when $|m(r)| > 1$. We say r is *aliasing* in a program P if there exists a reachable configuration $C[\langle t, m \rangle]$ of P in which r is aliased in m. A *non-aliasing program* is a program in which no region is aliasing.

Note that the set of non-aliasing region valuations is finite when the number of program values is. The non-aliasing restriction thus allow us immediately to reduce the state-reachability problem for single-wait programs to reachability in a recursive finite-data sequential program. To compute state-reachability we consider a sequence $\mathcal{A}_0\mathcal{A}_1 \ldots$ of finite-state systems iteratively under-approximating the recursive system $\mathcal{A}_P$ given from a single-wait program P. Initially, $\mathcal{A}_0$ has only the transitions of $\mathcal{A}_P$ corresponding to intra-procedural and **post** transitions of P. At each step $i > 0$, we add to $\mathcal{A}_i$ an additive edge summarizing an **ewait** transition

$$T[\mathbf{ewait}\ r] \xhookrightarrow{\vec{n}_j\vec{n}} T[s] ,$$

for some $t_0, t_f \in \mathsf{Tasks}$ such that $j = \mathsf{cn}(r, t_0)$, $s \in \mathsf{rvh}(t_f)$, and $\vec{n}$ is reachable at t_f from t_0 in $\mathcal{A}_{i-1}$, i.e., $\vec{n} \in \mathsf{sms}(t_0, t_f, \mathcal{A}_{i-1})$. This $\mathcal{A}_0\mathcal{A}_1 \ldots$ sequence is guaranteed to reach a fixed-point $\mathcal{A}_k$, since the set of non-aliasing region valuation vectors, and thus the number of possibly added edges, is finite. Furthermore, as each $\mathcal{A}_i$ is finite-state, only finite-state reachability queries are needed to determine the reachable states of $\mathcal{A}_k$, which are precisely the same reachable states of $\mathcal{A}_P$. Note that the number of region valuations grows exponentially in the number of regions.

Theorem 2. *The state-reachability problem for non-aliasing single-wait finite-value programs is PTIME-complete for a fixed number of regions, and EXPTIME-complete in the number of regions.*

5.2 Local-Scope Single-Wait Analysis

Definition 4 (Local scope)**.** A *local-scope program* is a program in which tasks only return with empty region valuations; i.e., for all reachable configurations $C[\langle t[\mathbf{return}\ e], m \rangle]$ we have $m = m_\emptyset$.

To solve state-reachability in local-scope single-wait programs, we compute a sequence $\mathcal{A}_0\mathcal{A}_1 \ldots$ of non-recursive vector addition systems iteratively under-approximating the recursive system $\mathcal{A}_P$ arising from a program P. The initial system $\mathcal{A}_0$ has only the transitions of $\mathcal{A}_P$ corresponding to intra-procedural and **post** transitions of P. At each step $i > 0$, we add to $\mathcal{A}_i$ an additive edge summarizing an **ewait** transition

$$T[\mathbf{ewait}\ r] \xhookrightarrow{\vec{n}_j\mathbf{0}} T[s]$$

for some $t_0, t_f \in \mathsf{Tasks}$ such that $j = \mathsf{cn}(r, t_0)$, $s \in \mathsf{rvh}(t_f)$, and $\vec{n} \in \mathsf{sms}(t_0, t_f, \mathcal{A}_{i-1})$; since P is local-scope, every such $\vec{n}$ must equal $\mathbf{0}$. Since the number of possibly added edges is polynomial in P, the $\mathcal{A}_0\mathcal{A}_1$ sequence is guaranteed to reach in a polynomial number of steps a fixed-point $\mathcal{A}_k$ whose reachable states are exactly those of $\mathcal{A}_P$. The entire procedure is EXPSPACE-complete, since each procedure-summarization reachability query is equivalent to computing state-reachability in vector addition systems.

Theorem 3. *The state-reachability problem for local-scope single-wait finite-value programs is EXPSPACE-complete.*

5.3 Global-Scope Single-Wait Analysis

Another relatively simple case of interest is when pending tasks are allowed to leave the scope in which they are posted, but can only be consumed by a particular, statically declared, task in an enclosing scope. This is the case, for example, in asynchronous programs [33], though here we allow for slightly more generality, since tasks can be posted to multiple regions, and arbitrary control in the initial procedure frame is allowed.

Definition 5 (Global scope)**.** A *global-scope programs* is a program in which the **ewait** (and **await**) statements are used only in the initial procedure frame.

Since each non-initial procedure p of a global-scope program cannot consume tasks, the set of tasks posted by p and recursively-called procedures along any execution from t_0 to t_f is a semi-linear set, described by the Parikh-image[3] of a context-free language. Following Ganty and Majumdar [14]'s approach, for each $t_0, t_f \in \mathsf{Tasks}$ we construct a polynomial-sized vector addition system $\mathcal{A}(t_0, t_f)$ characterizing this semi-linear set of tasks (recursively) posted between t_0 and t_f. Then, we use each $\mathcal{A}(t_0, t_f)$ as a component of a non-recursive vector addition system $\mathcal{A}'_P$ representing execution of the initial frame. In particular, $\mathcal{A}'_P$ contains transitions to and from the component $\mathcal{A}(t_0, t_f)$ for each $t_0, t_f \in \mathsf{Tasks}$,

$$T[\mathbf{ewait}\ r] \xhookrightarrow{\vec{n}_j\mathbf{0}} \langle q_0, T[\mathbf{skip}] \rangle \quad \langle q_f, T[\mathbf{skip}] \rangle \xhookrightarrow{\mathbf{00}} T[s] ,$$

for all $r \in \mathsf{Regs}$ such that $j = \mathsf{cn}(r, t_0)$, $s \in \mathsf{rvh}(t_f)$, and q_0 and q_f are the initial and final states of $\mathcal{A}(t_0, t_f)$. We assume each $\mathcal{A}(t_0, t_f)$ has unique initial and final states, distinct from the states of other components $\mathcal{A}(t'_0, t'_f)$. In order to transition to the correct state $T[s]$ upon completion, $\mathcal{A}(t_0, t_f)$ carries an auxiliary state-component $T[\mathbf{skip}]$. In this way, for each task t' posted to region r' in an execution between t_0 and t_f, the component $\mathcal{A}(t_0, t_f)$ does the incrementing of the $\mathsf{cn}(r', t')$-component of the region-valuation vector. As each of the polynomially-many components $\mathcal{A}(t_0, t_f)$ are constructed in polynomial time [14], this method constructs $\mathcal{A}'_P$ in polynomial time. Thus state-reachability in P is computed by state-reachability in the non-recursive vector addition system $\mathcal{A}'_P$, in exponential space. The complexity is asymptotically optimal since global-scope single-wait programs are powerful enough to capture state-reachability in vector addition systems.

Theorem 4. *The state-reachability problem for global-scope single-wait finite-value programs is EXPSPACE-complete.*

5.4 The General Case of Single-Wait Analysis

In general, the state-reachability problem for finite-value single-wait programs is as hard as state-reachability in recursive vector addition systems without zero-test edges.

Theorem 5. *The state-reachability problem for single-wait finite-value programs is EXPSPACE-hard, and in 2EXPTIME.*

Demri et al. [8]'s proof of membership in 2EXPTIME relies on a non-deterministically chosen reachability witness without materializing a practical algorithm for the search of said witness. Here we give a summarization-based algorithm.

To compute state-reachability we consider again a sequence $\mathcal{A}_0\mathcal{A}_1 \ldots$ of non-recursive vector addition systems successively under-approximating the recursive system $\mathcal{A}_P$ of a single-wait program P. Initially $\mathcal{A}_0$ has only the transitions of $\mathcal{A}_P$ corresponding to intra-procedural and **post** transitions of P. At each step $i > 0$, we add to $\mathcal{A}_i$ an additive edge summarizing an **ewait** transition

$$T[\mathbf{ewait}\ r] \xhookrightarrow{\vec{n}_j\vec{n}} T[s] ,$$

for some $t_0, t_f \in \mathsf{Tasks}$ such that $j = \mathsf{cn}(r, t_0)$, $s \in \mathsf{rvh}(t_f)$, and $\vec{n} \in \mathsf{sms}(t_0, t_f, \mathcal{A}_{i-1})$. Even though the set of possible added additive edges summarizing recursive transitions is infinite, with careful analysis we can show that this very simple algorithm terminates, provided we can bound the edge-labels $\vec{n}$ needed to compute state-reachability in $\mathcal{A}_P$. It turns out we can bound these

[3] The Parikh-image of a word w over an alphabet Σ is the $|\Sigma|$-dimension vector of integers counting the number of occurrences of each symbol of Σ in w. The image of a language is the set of images of its elements.

edge labels, by realizing that the minimal vectors required to reach a target state from any given program location are bounded.

We adopt an approach based on iteratively applying backward reachability analyses in order to determine for each task t the set of vectors $\eta(t)$ needed to reach the target state in $\mathcal{A}_P$. Let us first recall some useful basic facts. Vector addition systems are monotonic w.r.t. the natural ordering on vectors of integers, i.e., if a transition is possible from a vector v, it is also possible from any u greater than v. The ordering on vectors of integers is a well quasi-ordering (WQO), i.e., in every sequence of vectors $v_0, v_1, \ldots$, there are two indices $i < j$ such that v_i is less or equal than v_j. Thus, every infinite set of vectors has a finite number of minimals. A set of vectors is upward closed if whenever it contains v it also contains all vectors greater than v. Such a set can be characterized by its minimals. Moreover, the set of all predecessors in a vector addition system of an upward closed set of vectors is also upward closed; and therefore backward reachability analysis in these systems always terminates starting from an upward closed set [1, 11].

We observe that for every task t, the set $\eta(t)$ is upward closed (by monotonicity), and therefore we need only determine its minimals. However, since our model is *recursive* vector addition systems, we must solve several state-reachability queries on a sequence of vector addition systems with increasingly more transitions, which necessarily stabilizes. We elaborate below.

First, in order to reason backward about executions to the target state, consider the non-recursive system $\mathcal{A}'_i$ obtained by adding "return" transitions $t_f \overset{00}{\hookrightarrow} T[s]$ from every procedure exit point $t_f = T_f[\mathbf{return}\ e]$ and procedure return point $T[\mathbf{ewait}\ e]$ occurring in P such that $s \in \mathsf{rvh}(t_f)$. These extra transitions in $\mathcal{A}'_i$ simulate a return from t_f to t, transferring all of the pending tasks from a frame at t_f to a frame at $T[s]$, without any contribution from the $T[s]$'s intra-procedural predecessor $T[\mathbf{ewait}\ e]$.

Then define a sequence of functions $\eta_0, \eta_1, \ldots$: $\mathsf{Tasks} \to \wp(\mathbb{N}^k)$, each η_i mapping each $t \in \mathsf{Tasks}$ to the (possibly empty, upward-closed) set of vectors $\eta_i(t)$ such that for any $\vec{n} \in \eta_i(t)$, a configuration $\langle t, \vec{n} \rangle$ is guaranteed to reach the target reachable state in $\mathcal{A}'_i$—and thus $\langle t, \vec{n} \rangle\, c$ is guaranteed to reach the target reachable state in $\mathcal{A}_P$ for any c; each η_i can be computed in by backward reachability in the non-recursive vector addition system as explained above. Since each $\mathcal{A}_i$ contains at least the transitions of $\mathcal{A}_{i-1}$, the η_i-sequence is non-decreasing w.r.t. set inclusion; i.e., more and more configurations can reach the target state; i.e., for all $t \in \mathsf{Tasks}$ we have $\eta_{i-1}(t) \subseteq \eta_i(t)$. Since there can be no ever-increasing sequence of upward-closed sets of vectors over natural numbers (by the fact that the ordering on vectors of natural numbers if a WQO), the η_i sequence must stabilize after a finite number of steps.

Furthermore, since any $\vec{n} \in \eta_i(t)$ is guaranteed to reach the target state, it suffices to consider only vectors $\vec{n}'$ bounded by the minimals of the upward-closed set $\eta_i(t)$. To see why, notice that if some $\vec{n} \in \eta_i(t)$ labels an edge between t_0 and t, then *every* configuration at t_0 is guaranteed to reach the target state, since this edge adds the vector guaranteed to reach the target from t. Additionally, any vector greater than a minimal of $\eta_i(t)$ is already guaranteed to be present in $\eta_i(t)$, since $\eta_i(t)$ is upward closed. Thus we need only consider edge-labels bounded by the decreasing $\eta_0\eta_1 \ldots$ sequence, which shows that the $\mathcal{A}_0\mathcal{A}_1 \ldots$ sequence stabilizes after a finite number of steps.

6. Multi-Wait Programs

Though single-wait programs capture many parallel programming constructs, they can not express waiting for each and every of an unbounded number of tasks to complete. Some programming languages require this dual notion, expressed here with **await**.

Definition 6 (Multi wait). A *multi-wait program* is a program which does not contain the **ewait** statement.

Thus, multi-wait programs can wait only on every pending task (in a given region) at any program point. Many parallel programming constructs can be modeled as multi-wait programs.

6.1 Parallel Programming in Cilk

The Cilk parallel programming language [30] is an industrial-strength language with an accompanying runtime system which is used in a spectrum of environments, from modest multi-core computations to massively parallel computations with supercomputers. Similarly to futures (see Section 4.1), Cilk adds a form of procedure call which immediately returns control to the caller. Instead of an operation to synchronize with a *particular* previously-called procedure, Cilk only provides an operation to synchronize with *every* previously-called procedure. At such a point, the previously-called procedures communicate their results back to the caller one-by-one with atomically-executing procedure in-lined in scope of the caller. Syntactically, Cilk adds two statements

$$\mathbf{spawn}\ p\ e\ p' \qquad \mathbf{sync},$$

where p ranges over procedures, e over expressions, and p' over procedures declared by

$$\mathbf{inlet}\ p'\ (\mathbf{var}\ \mathtt{rv}\text{: } T)\ s.$$

Here s ranges over intra-procedural program statements containing two variables: `rv`, corresponding to the value returned from a spawned procedure, and `l`, corresponding to the local variable of the spawning procedure. Semantically, the **spawn** statement creates a new process in which to execute the given procedure, which proceeds to execute in parallel with the caller—and all other processes created in this way. The **sync** statement blocks execution of the current procedure until each spawned procedure completes, and executes its associated inlet. The inlets of each procedure execute atomically. Each procedure can spawn an unbounded number of parallel processes, and the order in which the inlets of procedures execute is chosen non-deterministically.

Example 3. The Fibonacci function can be implemented as a parallel algorithm using Cilk as follows.

```
proc fib (var n: ℕ)
   var sum: ℕ
   if n < 2 then
      return 1
   else
      spawn fib (n-1) summer;
      spawn fib (n-2) summer;
      sync;
      return sum

inlet summer (var i: ℕ)
   sum := sum + i
```

As opposed to the usual (naïve) sequential implementation operating in time $\mathcal{O}(n^2)$, this parallel implementation runs in time $\mathcal{O}(n)$.

The semantics of Cilk is ready expressed with recursively parallel programs using the **post** and **await** statements. Assuming a region identifier $\mathtt{r}_0$, we encode

$\mathbf{spawn}\ p\ e\ p'$	as	$\mathbf{post}\ \mathtt{r}_0 \leftarrow p\ e\ \mathtt{d}_{p'}$
$\mathbf{sync}$	as	$\mathbf{await}\ \mathtt{r}_0$

where $\mathtt{d}_{p'}(v) \overset{\text{def}}{=} s_{p'}[v/\mathtt{rv}]$ executes the top-level statement of the inlet p' with input parameter v.

6.2 Parallel Programming with Asynchronous Statements

The async/finish pair of constructs in X10 [7] introduces parallelism through asynchronously executing statements and synchronization blocks. Essentially, an asynchronous statement immediately passes control to a following statement, executing itself in parallel. A synchronization block executes as any other program block, but does not pass control to the following statements/block until every asynchronous statement within has completed. Syntactically, this mechanism is expressed with two statements,

$$\textbf{async } s \qquad \textbf{finish } s$$

where s ranges over program statements. Semantically, the **async** statement creates a new process to execute the given statement, which proceeds to execute in parallel with the invoker—and all other processes created in this way. The **finish** statement executes the given statement s, then blocks execution until every process created within s has completed.

Example 4. The Fibonacci function can be implemented as a parallel algorithm using asynchronous statements as follows.

```
proc fib (var n: ℕ)
    var x, y: ℕ
    if n < 2 then
        return 1
    else
        finish
            async call x := fib (n-1);
            async call y := fib (n-2);
        return x + y
```

As opposed to the usual (naïve) sequential implementation operating in time $\mathcal{O}(n^2)$, this parallel implementation runs in time $\mathcal{O}(n)$.

Asynchronous statements are readily expressed with (non-deterministic) recursively parallel programs using the **post** and **await** statements. Let N be the maximum depth of nested **finish** statements. Assuming region identifiers $\mathtt{r}_1, \ldots, \mathtt{r}_N$, we encode

$$\textbf{async } s \quad \text{as} \quad \textbf{post } \mathtt{r}_i \leftarrow p_s \star \mathtt{d}$$

$$\textbf{finish } s \quad \text{as} \quad \textbf{await } \mathtt{r}_i$$

where $i-1$ is number of enclosing **finish** statements, and p_s is a procedure declared as

```
proc p_s (var l: T)
    var l_0 := l
    s;
    return (l_0,l)
```

and $\mathtt{d}(\langle v_0, v_1\rangle) \stackrel{\text{def}}{=} \textbf{assume } \mathtt{l} = v_0\mathtt{;}\ \mathtt{l} := v_1$ models the update p performs from an initial (guessed) local valuation v_0. Using the same trick we have used to model asynchronous programs in Section 4.3, we model the sequencing of asynchronous tasks by initially guessing the value v_0 which the previously-executed asynchronous tasks had written, and validating that value when the return-value handler of a given task is finally run. Note that although X10 allows, in general, asynchronous tasks to interleave their memory accesses, our model captures only non-interfering tasks, by assuming either data-parallelism (i.e., disjoint accesses to data), or by assuming tasks are properly synchronized to ensure atomicity.

7. Multi-Wait Analysis

The presence of **await** edges implies the presence of zero-test transitions in the recursive vector addition system $\mathcal{A}_P$ corresponding to a multi-wait program P. As we have done for single-wait programs, we first examine the easier sub-case of local-scope programs, which in the multi-wait setting corresponds concurrency in the Cilk [30] language (modulo task interleaving), as well as structured parallel programming constructs such as the **foreach** parallel loop in X10 [7] and in Leijen et al. [25]'s task parallel library (see our extended online report [3]). The concurrent behavior of the asynchronous statements (Section 6.2) in X10 [7] does not satisfy the local-scope restriction, since **async** statements can include recursive procedure calls which are nested without interpolating **finish** statements. There computing state-reachability is equivalent to determining whether a particular vector is reachable in a non-recursive vector addition system—a decidable problem which is known to be EXPSPACE-hard, but for which the only known algorithms are non-primitive recursive. Since all multi-wait parallel languages we have encountered use only a single-region, we restrict our attention at present to single-region multi-wait programs.

7.1 Local-Scope Single-Region Multi-Wait Analysis

With the local-scoping restriction, executions of each procedure $p \in \mathsf{Procs}$ between entry point $t_0 \in \mathsf{Tasks}$ and exit point $t_f \in \mathsf{Tasks}$ are completely summarized by a Boolean indicating whether or not t_f is reachable from t_0. However, as executions of p may encounter **await** statements, modeled by zero-test edges in the recursive vector addition system $\mathcal{A}_P$, computing this Boolean requires determining the reachable program valuations between each pair of consecutive "synchronization points" (i.e., occurrences of the **await** statement), which in principle requires deciding whether the vector $\mathbf{0}$ is reachable in a vector addition system describing execution from the program point just after the first **await** statement to the point just after the second; i.e., when $T_1[\textbf{await } r]$ and $T_2[\textbf{await } r]$ are consecutively-occurring synchronization points, we must determine whether $\langle T_1[\textbf{skip}], \mathbf{0}\rangle$ can reach $\langle T_2[\textbf{skip}], \mathbf{0}\rangle$.

A careful analysis of our reachability problem reveals it does not have the EXPSPACE-hard complexity of determining vector-reachability in general, due to the special structure of our reachability query. We notice that between two synchronization points t_1 and t_2 of p, execution proceeds in two phases. In the first, **post** statements made by p only increment the vector valuations. In the second phase, starting when the second **await** statement is encountered, the **await** statement repeatedly consumes tasks, only decrementing the vector valuations—the vector valuations can not be re-incremented again because of the local-scope restriction: each consumed task is forbidden from returning addition tasks. Due to this special structure, deciding reachability between t_1 and t_2 reduces to deciding if a particular integer linear program $I(t_1, t_2)$ has a solution.

Since consuming tasks in the **await**-loop requires using the summaries computed for other procedures, we consider a sequence $\mathcal{A}_0\mathcal{A}_1 \ldots$ of non-recursive vector addition systems iteratively under-approximating the recursive system $\mathcal{A}_P$. Initially $\mathcal{A}_0$ has only the transitions of $\mathcal{A}_P$ corresponding to intra-procedural and **post** transitions of P. At each step $i > 0$, we add to $\mathcal{A}_i$ one of two edges types. One type is an additive procedure-summary edge, used to describe a single task-consumption step of an **await** transition,

$$T[\textbf{await } r] \xhookrightarrow{\vec{n}_j \mathbf{0}} T[s;\ \textbf{await } r],$$

for some $t_0, t_f \in \mathsf{Tasks}$ such that $j = \mathsf{cn}(r, t_0)$, $s \in \mathsf{rvh}(t_f)$, and $\mathsf{sms}(t_0, t_f, \mathcal{A}_{i-1}) \neq \emptyset$. The second possibility is an additive synchronization-point summary edge, summarizing an entire of sequence of program transitions between two synchronization points,

$$T_1[\textbf{skip}] \xhookrightarrow{\mathbf{00}} T_2[\textbf{skip}],$$

where $T_1[\textbf{await } r], T_2[\textbf{await } r] \in \mathsf{Tasks}$ are consecutive synchronization points occurring P, and $\mathbf{0} \in \mathsf{sms}(T_1[\textbf{skip}], T_2[\textbf{skip}], \mathcal{A}_P)$. The procedure-summary edges are computed using only finite-state reachability between program states, using the synchronization-point summary edges, while the synchronization-point summary edges are computed by reduction to integer linear programming. As the number of possible edges is bounded polynomially in the program size, the $\mathcal{A}_0\mathcal{A}_1$ sequence is guaranteed to reach a fixed-point $\mathcal{A}_k$ in a polynomial number of steps, though each step may take nondeterministic-polynomial time, in the worst case, to compute solutions to integer linear programs. The reachable states of $\mathcal{A}_k$ are precisely the same reachable states of $\mathcal{A}_P$.

Theorem 6. *The state-reachability problem for local-scope multi-wait single-region finite-value programs is NP-complete.*

7.2 Single-Region Multi-Wait Analysis

Without the local-scoping restriction, each execution of each procedure $p \in \mathsf{Procs}$ between entry point $t_0 \in \mathsf{Tasks}$ and exit point $t_f \in \mathsf{Tasks}$ is summarized by the tasks posted between the last-encountered **await** statement, at a "synchronization point" $t_s \in \mathsf{Tasks}$ (note that $t_s = t_0$ if no **await** statements are encountered), and a **return** statement, at the exit point t_f. Since p can make recursive procedure calls between t_s and t_f, and each called procedure can again return pending tasks, the possible sets of pending tasks upon p's return at t_f is described by the Parikh-image[3] of a context-free language $L(t_0, t_f)$. It turns out we can describe this image as the set of vectors computed by a polynomially-sized vector addition system $\mathcal{A}^L(t_0, t_f)$ without recursion and zero-test edges [14]. We use thus computations of $\mathcal{A}^L(t_0, t_f)$ to summarize the set of possible region-valuations reached in an execution from t_0 to t_f. However, computing $\mathcal{A}^L(t_0, t_f)$ is not immediate, since between t_0 and the last-encountered synchronization point t_s, execution of the given procedure p may encounter **await** statements (necessarily so when $t_0 \neq t_s$). Since we use zero-test edges to express **await** statements, we also need to summarize execution between synchronization points (i.e., between the procedure entry point and among **await** statements) using only additive edges. To further complicate matters, each such summarization requires, in turn, the summaries $\mathcal{A}^L(t_0', t_f')$ computed for other procedures!

We break the circular dependence between procedure summaries and synchronization-point summaries by iteratively computing both. In particular, we compute a sequence $\mathcal{A}_0^L\mathcal{A}_1^L \ldots$ of procedure summary vector addition systems along with a sequence $\mathcal{A}_0\mathcal{A}_1 \ldots$ of vector addition systems such that each $\mathcal{A}_i^L$, for $i > 0$, is computed using the transitions of $\mathcal{A}_{i-1}$, and $\mathcal{A}_i$, for $i \geq 0$ is computed using the procedure summaries of $\mathcal{A}_i^L$. Initially $\mathcal{A}_0^L$ contains only the pending-task sets reachable without taking **await** transitions, and $\mathcal{A}_0$ contains only the transitions of $\mathcal{A}_P$ corresponding to intra-procedural and **post** transitions of P, along with transitions to components $\mathcal{A}_0^L$. For $i \geq 0$, $\mathcal{A}_i$ contains transitions to and from the components $\mathcal{A}_i^L(t_0, t_f)$

$$T[\textbf{await } r] \xrightarrow{\vec{n}_j \mathbf{0}} \langle q_0, T[\textbf{skip}] \rangle \quad \langle q_f, T[\textbf{skip}] \rangle \xrightarrow{\mathbf{00}} T[s;\ \textbf{await } r]$$

for each $t_0, t_f \in \mathsf{Tasks}$ such that $j = \mathsf{cn}(r, t_0)$, $s \in \mathsf{rvh}(t_f)$, and q_0 and q_f are the unique initial and final states of $\mathcal{A}_i^L(t_0, t_f)$. (We assume each component $\mathcal{A}_i^L(t_0, t_f)$ has unique initial and final states, distinct from the states of other components. Additionally, we equip each $\mathcal{A}^L(t_0, t_f)$ with auxiliary state to carry the identity $T[\textbf{skip}]$ of the invoking task to ensure the proper return of control when $\mathcal{A}^L(t_0, t_f)$ completes.)

At each step $i > 0$, we add to $\mathcal{A}_i$ an additive edge summarizing the execution between two synchronization points $T_1[\textbf{await } r]$ and $T_2[\textbf{await } r]$ occurring in P:

$$T_1[\textbf{skip}] \xrightarrow{\mathbf{00}} T_2[\textbf{skip}]$$

such that $T_2[\textbf{skip}]$ is reachable in $\mathcal{A}_{i-1}$ from $T_1[\textbf{skip}]$, i.e., $\mathbf{0} \in \mathsf{sms}(T_1[\textbf{skip}], T_2[\textbf{skip}], \mathcal{A}_{i-1})$. Note that when $T[\textbf{await } r]$ is a synchronization point occurring in P, $T[\textbf{skip}]$ refers to the program point immediately after the **await** statement. Since there are only polynomially-many such edges that can possibly be added, we are guaranteed to reach a fixed-point $\mathcal{A}_k$ of $\mathcal{A}_0\mathcal{A}_1 \ldots$ in a polynomial number of steps. Furthermore, the reachable states of $\mathcal{A}_k$ are precisely the same reachable states of $\mathcal{A}_P$. However, computing $\mathbf{0} \in \mathsf{sms}(t_1, t_2, \mathcal{A}_{i-1})$ at each step is difficult due to the zero-test edge in the **await** statement immediately preceding t_2; this is computationally equivalent to computing reachability of a particular vector in non-recursive vector addition systems.

State-Reachability in Recursively Parallel Programs

	result	complexity	language/feature
Task-Passing			
general	Thm. 1	undecidable	futures, revisions
Single-Wait			
non-aliasing	Thm. 2	PTIME	futures†, revisions†
local scope	Thm. 3	EXPSPACE	—
global scope	Thm. 4	EXPSPACE	asynchronous programs
general	Thm. 5	2EXPTIME	—
† For programs without task-passing.			
Multi-Wait (single region)			
local scope	Thm. 6	NP	Cilk
general	Thm. 7	decidable	async (X10)

Figure 8. Summary of results for computing state-reachability for finite-value recursively parallel programs.

Theorem 7. *The state-reachability problem for multi-wait single-region finite-value programs is decidable.*

Since practical algorithms to compute vector-reachability is a difficult open problem, we remark that it is possible to obtain algorithms to approximate our state-reachability problem. Consider, for instance, the over-approximate semantics given by transforming each **await** r statement into **while** $\star$ **do ewait** r. Though many more behaviors are present in the resulting program, since not every task is necessarily consumed during the **while** loop, practical algorithmic solutions are more probable (see Section 5.4).

8. Related Work

Formal modeling and verification of multi-threaded programs has been heavily studied, including but not limited to identifying decidable sub-classes [20], and effective over-approximate [13, 18] and under-approximate [9, 22] analyses.

To our knowledge little work has been done in formal modeling and verification of programs written in explicitly-parallel languages which are free of thread interleaving. Sen and Viswanathan [33]'s asynchronous programs, which falls out as a special case of our single-wait programs, is perhaps most similar to our work in this regard. Practical verification algorithms by combining iterative over- and under-approximation [19], and in-depth complexity analysis [14] of asynchronous programs have been studied.

Though decidability results of abstract parallel models have been reported [5, 10] (Bouajjani and Esparza [4] survey of this line of work), these works target abstract computation models, and do not identify precise complexities and optimal algorithms for real-world parallel programming languages, nor do they handle the case where procedures can return unbounded sets of unfinished computations to their callers.

9. Conclusion

We have proposed a general model of recursively parallel programs which captures the concurrency constructs in a variety of popular programming languages. By isolating the fragments corresponding to various language features, we are able to associate corresponding formal models, measure the complexity of state-reachability, and provide precise analysis algorithms. We hope our complexity measurements may be used to guide the design and choice of concurrent programming languages and program analyses. Figure 8 summarizes our results.

Acknowledgments

We greatly appreciate formative discussions with Arnaud Sangnier and Peter Habermehl, and the feedback of Pierre Ganty, Giorgio Delzanno, Rupak Majumdar, Tom Ball, Sebastian Burckhardt, and the anonymous POPL reviewers.

References

[1] P. A. Abdulla, K. Cerans, B. Jonsson, and Y.-K. Tsay. General decidability theorems for infinite-state systems. In *LICS '96: Proc. 11th IEEE Symposium on Logic in Computer Science*, pages 313–321. IEEE Computer Society, 1996.

[2] E. Allen, D. Chase, V. Luchangco, J.-W. Maessen, S. Ryu, G. L. S. Jr., and S. Tobin-Hochstadt. The Fortress language specification. Technical report, Sun Microsystems, Inc., 2006.

[3] A. Bouajjani and M. Emmi. Analysis of recursively parallel programs. 2011. `http://hal.archives-ouvertes.fr/hal-00639351/en`.

[4] A. Bouajjani and J. Esparza. Rewriting models of boolean programs. In *RTA '06: Proc. 17th International Conference on Term Rewriting and Applications*, volume 4098 of *LNCS*, pages 136–150. Springer, 2006.

[5] A. Bouajjani, M. Müller-Olm, and T. Touili. Regular symbolic analysis of dynamic networks of pushdown systems. In *CONCUR '05: Proc. 16th International Conference on Concurrency Theory*, volume 3653 of *LNCS*, pages 473–487. Springer, 2005.

[6] S. Burckhardt, A. Baldassin, and D. Leijen. Concurrent programming with revisions and isolation types. In *OOPSLA '10: Proc. 25th Annual ACM SIGPLAN Conference on Object-Oriented Programming, Systems, Languages, and Applications*, pages 691–707. ACM, 2010.

[7] P. Charles, C. Grothoff, V. A. Saraswat, C. Donawa, A. Kielstra, K. Ebcioglu, C. von Praun, and V. Sarkar. X10: an object-oriented approach to non-uniform cluster computing. In *OOPSLA '05: Proc. 20th Annual ACM SIGPLAN Conference on Object-Oriented Programming, Systems, Languages, and Applications*, pages 519–538. ACM, 2005.

[8] S. Demri, M. Jurdzinski, O. Lachish, and R. Lazic. The covering and boundedness problems for branching vector addition systems. In *FSTTCS '09: IARCS Annual Conference on Foundations of Software Technology and Theoretical Computer Science*, pages 181–192, 2009.

[9] J. Esparza and P. Ganty. Complexity of pattern-based verification for multithreaded programs. In *POPL '11: Proc. 38th ACM SIGPLAN-SIGACT Symposium on Principles of Programming Languages*, pages 499–510. ACM, 2011.

[10] J. Esparza and A. Podelski. Efficient algorithms for pre* and post* on interprocedural parallel flow graphs. In *POPL '00: Proc. 27th ACM SIGPLAN-SIGACT Symposium on Principles of Programming Languages*, pages 1–11. ACM, 2000.

[11] A. Finkel and P. Schnoebelen. Well-structured transition systems everywhere! *Theor. Comput. Sci.*, 256(1-2):63–92, 2001.

[12] C. Flanagan and M. Felleisen. The semantics of future and an application. *J. Funct. Program.*, 9(1):1–31, 1999.

[13] C. Flanagan and S. Qadeer. Thread-modular model checking. In *SPIN '03: Proc. 10th International Workshop on Model Checking Software*, volume 2648 of *LNCS*, pages 213–224. Springer, 2003.

[14] P. Ganty and R. Majumdar. Algorithmic verification of asynchronous programs. *CoRR*, abs/1011.0551, 2010. `http://arxiv.org/abs/1011.0551`.

[15] G. Geeraerts, J.-F. Raskin, and L. V. Begin. Expand, enlarge and check: New algorithms for the coverability problem of wsts. *J. Comput. Syst. Sci.*, 72(1):180–203, 2006.

[16] S. Graf and H. Saïdi. Construction of abstract state graphs with PVS. In *CAV '97: Proc. 9th International Conference on Computer Aided Verification*, volume 1254 of *LNCS*, pages 72–83. Springer, 1997.

[17] R. H. Halstead Jr. Multilisp: A language for concurrent symbolic computation. *ACM Trans. Program. Lang. Syst.*, 7(4):501–538, 1985.

[18] T. A. Henzinger, R. Jhala, R. Majumdar, and S. Qadeer. Thread-modular abstraction refinement. In *CAV '03: Proc. 15th International Conference on Computer Aided Verification*, volume 2725 of *LNCS*, pages 262–274. Springer, 2003.

[19] R. Jhala and R. Majumdar. Interprocedural analysis of asynchronous programs. In *POPL '07: Proc. 34th ACM SIGPLAN-SIGACT Symposium on Principles of Programming Languages*, pages 339–350. ACM, 2007.

[20] V. Kahlon. Boundedness vs. unboundedness of lock chains: Characterizing decidability of pairwise CFL-reachability for threads communicating via locks. In *LICS '09: Proc. 24th Annual IEEE Symposium on Logic in Computer Science*, pages 27–36. IEEE Computer Society, 2009.

[21] D. Kozen. Lower bounds for natural proof systems. In *FOCS '77: Proc. 18th Annual Symposium on Foundations of Computer Science*, pages 254–266. IEEE Computer Society, 1977.

[22] A. Lal and T. W. Reps. Reducing concurrent analysis under a context bound to sequential analysis. *Formal Methods in System Design*, 35(1): 73–97, 2009.

[23] J. R. Larus and R. Rajwar. *Transactional Memory*. Morgan & Claypool, 2006. `http://www.morganclaypool.com/doi/abs/10.2200/S00070ED1V01Y200611CAC002`.

[24] E. A. Lee. The problem with threads. *IEEE Computer*, 39(5):33–42, 2006.

[25] D. Leijen, W. Schulte, and S. Burckhardt. The design of a task parallel library. In *OOPSLA '09: Proc. 24th Annual ACM SIGPLAN Conference on Object-Oriented Programming, Systems, Languages, and Applications*, pages 227–242. ACM, 2009.

[26] R. J. Lipton. The reachability problem requires exponential space. Technical Report 62, Yale University, 1976.

[27] P. Pratikakis, H. Vandierendonck, S. Lyberis, and D. S. Nikolopoulos. A programming model for deterministic task parallelism. In *MSPC '11: Proc. 2011 ACM SIGPLAN Workshop on Memory Systems Performance and Correctness*, pages 7–12. ACM, 2011.

[28] C. Rackoff. The covering and boundedness problems for vector addition systems. *Theor. Comput. Sci.*, 6:223–231, 1978.

[29] G. Ramalingam. Context-sensitive synchronization-sensitive analysis is undecidable. *ACM Trans. Program. Lang. Syst.*, 22(2):416–430, 2000.

[30] K. H. Randall. *Cilk: Efficient Multithreaded Computing*. PhD thesis, Department of Electrical Engineering and Computer Science, Massachusetts Institute of Technology, May 1998.

[31] T. W. Reps, S. Horwitz, and S. Sagiv. Precise interprocedural dataflow analysis via graph reachability. In *POPL '95: Proc. 22th ACM SIGPLAN-SIGACT Symposium on Principles of Programming Languages*, pages 49–61. ACM, 1995.

[32] C. Segulja and T. S. Abdelrahman. Synchronization-free and deterministic coarse-grain parallelism: Architectural support and programming model. In *FASPP '11: Proc. First International Workshop on Future Architectural Support for Parallel Programming*, 2011.

[33] K. Sen and M. Viswanathan. Model checking multithreaded programs with asynchronous atomic methods. In *CAV '06: Proc. 18th International Conference on Computer Aided Verification*, volume 4144 of *LNCS*, pages 300–314. Springer, 2006.

Programming Languages for Programmable Networks

Jennifer Rexford
Princeton University
jrex@cs.princeton.edu

Abstract

Today's computer networks perform a bewildering array of tasks, from routing and access control, to traffic monitoring and load balancing. To support wireless users accessing services hosted in the cloud, enterprise and data-center networks are under increasing pressure to support client mobility, virtual-machine migration, resource isolation between cloud services, and energy-efficient operation. Yet, network administrators must configure the network through closed and proprietary interfaces to heterogeneous devices, such as routers, switches, firewalls, load balancers, network address translators, and intrusion detection systems. Not surprisingly, configuring these complex networks is expensive and error-prone, and innovation in network management proceeds at a snail's pace.

During the past several years, the networking industry and research community have pushed for greater openness in networking software, and a clearer separation between networking devices and the software that controls them. This broad trend is known as *Software Defined Networking* (SDN). A hallmark of SDN is having an open interface for controller software running on a commodity computer to install packet-processing rules in the underlying switches. In particular, the *OpenFlow* protocol (see `www.openflow.org`) has significant momentum. Many commercial switches support OpenFlow, and a number of campus, data-center, and backbone networks have deployed the new technology.

With the emergence of open interfaces to network devices, the time is ripe to rethink the design of network software, to put networking on a stronger foundation and foster innovation in networked services. The programming languages community can play a vital role in this transformation, by creating languages, compilers, run-time systems, and testing and verification techniques that raise the level of abstraction for programming the network. In this talk, we give an overview of Software Defined Networking, and survey the early programming-languages research in this area. We also outline exciting opportunities for interdisciplinary research at the intersection of programming languages and computer networks.

Categories and Subject Descriptors C.2.1 [*Computer-Communication Networks*]: Network Architecture and Design; D.3.0 [*Programming Languages*]: General

General Terms Design, Languages

Keywords Software Defined Networking, OpenFlow, network protocols

POPL'12, January 25–27, 2012, Philadelphia, PA, USA.
ACM 978-1-4503-1083-3/12/01.

A Compiler and Run-time System for Network Programming Languages

Christopher Monsanto
Princeton University

Nate Foster
Cornell University

Rob Harrison *
US Military Academy

David Walker
Princeton University

Abstract

Software-defined networks (SDNs) are a new kind of network architecture in which a controller machine manages a distributed collection of switches by instructing them to install or uninstall packet-forwarding rules and report traffic statistics. The recently formed Open Networking Consortium, whose members include Google, Facebook, Microsoft, Verizon, and others, hopes to use this architecture to transform the way that enterprise and data center networks are implemented.

In this paper, we define a high-level, declarative language, called *NetCore*, for expressing packet-forwarding policies on SDNs. NetCore is expressive, compositional, and has a formal semantics. To ensure that a majority of packets are processed efficiently on switches—instead of on the controller—we present new compilation algorithms for NetCore and couple them with a new run-time system that issues rule installation commands and traffic-statistics queries to switches. Together, the compiler and run-time system generate efficient rules whenever possible and outperform the simple, manual techniques commonly used to program SDNs today. In addition, the algorithms we develop are generic, assuming only that the packet-matching capabilities available on switches satisfy some basic algebraic laws.

Overall, this paper delivers a new design for a high-level network programming language; an improved set of compiler algorithms; a new run-time system for SDN architectures; the first formal semantics and proofs of correctness in this domain; and an implementation and evaluation that demonstrates the performance benefits over traditional manual techniques.

Categories and Subject Descriptors D.3.2 [*Programming Languages*]: Language Classifications—Specialized application languages

General Terms Languages, Design

Keywords Software-defined Networking, OpenFlow, Frenetic, Network programming languages, Domain specific languages

* The views expressed in this paper are those of the authors and do not reflect the official policy or position of the US Military Academy, the Department of the Army, the Department of Defense, or the US Government.

POPL'12, January 25–27, 2012, Philadelphia, PA, USA.

1. Introduction

A network is a collection of connected devices that route traffic from one place to another. Networks are pervasive: they connect students and faculty on university campuses, they send packets between a variety of mobile devices in modern households, they route search requests and shopping orders through data centers, they tunnel between corporate networks in San Francisco and Helsinki, and they connect the steering wheel to the drive train in your car. Naturally, these networks have different purposes, properties, and requirements. To service these requirements, companies like Cisco, Juniper, and others manufacture a variety of devices including routers (which forward packets based on IP addresses), switches (which forward packets based on MAC addresses), NAT boxes (which translate addresses within a network), firewalls (which squelch forbidden or unwanted traffic), and load balancers (which distribute work among servers), to name a few.

While each of these devices behaves differently, internally they are all built on top of a *data plane* that buffers, forwards, drops, tags, rate limits, and collects statistics about packets at high speed. More complicated devices like routers also have a *control plane* that run algorithms for tracking the topology of the network and computing routes through it. Using statistics gathered from the data plane and the results computed using the device's specialized algorithms, the control plane installs or uninstalls forwarding rules in the data plane. The data plane is built out of fast, special-purpose hardware, capable of forwarding packets at the rate at which they arrive, while the control plane is typically implemented in software.

Remarkably, however, traditional networks appear to be on the verge of a major upheaval. On March 11th, 2011, Deutsche Telekom, Facebook, Google, Microsoft, Verizon, and Yahoo!, owners of some of the largest networks in the world, announced the formation of the Open Networking Foundation [19]. The foundation's proposal is extraordinarily simple: *eliminate the control plane from network devices*. Instead of baking specific control software into each device, the foundation proposes a standard protocol that a separate, general-purpose machine called a *controller* can use to program and query the data planes of many cooperating devices. By moving the control plane from special-purpose devices onto stock machines, companies like Google will be able to buy cheap, commodity switches, and write controller programs to customize and optimize their networks however they choose.

Networks built on this new architecture, which arose from earlier work on Ethane [4] and 4D [10], are now commonly referred to as *Software-Defined Networks* (SDNs). Already, several commercial switch vendors support OpenFlow [17], a concrete realization of the switch-controller protocol required for implementing SDNs, and researchers have used OpenFlow to develop new network-wide algorithms for server load-balancing, data center routing, energy-efficient network management, virtualization, fine-grained access control, traffic monitoring, fault tolerance, denial of service detection, host mobility, and many others [8, 12–14, 18, 26].

Now the obvious question is: Why should programming language researchers, and the POPL community in particular, care about these developments? The answer is clear: Some of our most important infrastructure—our networks—will soon be running *an entirely new kind of program*. Using our experience, principles, tools, and algorithms, our community has a unique opportunity to define the languages these programs will be written in and the infrastructure used to implement them. We can have major impact, and help make future networks easier to program, more secure, more reliable, and more efficient.

As a step toward carrying out this agenda, we propose a high-level language called NetCore, the *Network Core Programming Language*, for expressing packet-forwarding policies. NetCore has an intuitive syntax based on familiar set-theoretic operations that allows programmers to construct (and reason about!) rich policies in a natural way. NetCore's primitives for classifying packets include exact-match bit patterns and arbitrary wildcard patterns. It also supports using arbitrary functions to analyze packets and historical traffic patterns. This feature makes it possible to describe complicated, dynamic policies such as authentication and load balancing in a natural way, using ordinary functional programs.

Unfortunately, compiling these rich policies is challenging. On the one hand, the controller machine has the computational power to evaluate arbitrary policies, but the switches do not: they can only implement simple kinds of bit matching rules. On the other hand, directing a packet to the controller for processing incurs orders of magnitude more latency than processing it on a switch. Hence, despite the limited computational power of the switches, it is critical to find ways for them to perform most packet processing.

The NetCore compiler and run-time system surmounts this challenge by analyzing programs and automatically dividing them into two pieces: one that runs on the switches and another that runs on the controller. Moreover, this division of labour does not occur once at compile time; it occurs dynamically and repeatedly. Intuitively, when a packet cannot be handled by a switch, it is redirected to the controller. The controller partially evaluates the packet with respect to the current network policy and dynamically generates new switch-level rules that handle said packet as well as others like it. The new rules are subsequently sent to the switches so similar packets arriving in the future are handled in the network fast path. Over time, more and more rules are added to the switches and less and less traffic is diverted to the controller. We call this iterative strategy *reactive specialization*.

Our strategy is inspired by the idiom commonly used for SDN applications today [12, 13, 27], in which an event-driven program manually installs a rule to handle future traffic every time a packet is diverted to the controller. However, many programs written manually in this style use inefficient exact-match rules rather than wildcard rules, because reasoning about the semantics of overlapping wildcards quickly becomes very complicated—too complicated to do by hand. Hence, our strategy improves on past work by (1) providing high-level abstractions that obviate the need for programmers to deal with the low-level details of individual switches, (2) synthesizing efficient forwarding rules that exploit the capabilities of modern switches including wildcard rules implemented by ternary content-addressable memories (TCAMs), (3) automating the process of dynamically unfolding packet-processing rules on to switches instead of requiring that programmers craft tricky, low-level, event-based programs manually.

To summarize: the central contribution of this paper is a framework for implementing a canonical, high-level network programming language correctly and efficiently. More specifically:

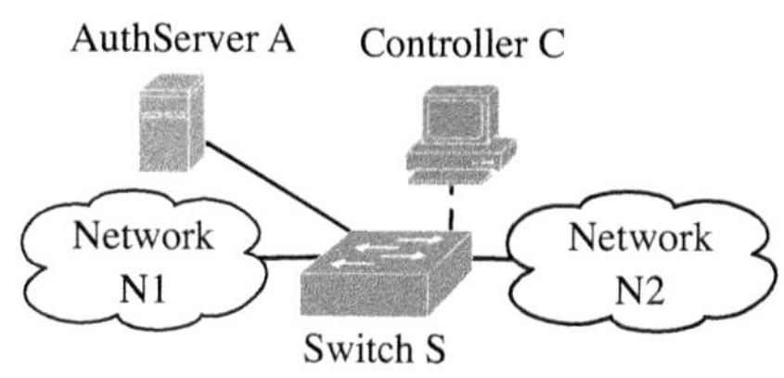

Figure 1. Example topology.

- We define the syntax and semantics for NetCore (Section 3) and model the interaction between the NetCore run-time system and the network in a process calculus style (Section 4). This is the first formal analysis of how a controller platform interacts with switches.
- We develop novel algorithms for compiling network programs and managing controller-switch interactions at run time, including *classifier generation* and *reactive specialization* (Section 5).
- We prove key correctness theorems (Section 6), establishing simulation relations between our low-level, distributed implementation strategy and our high-level NetCore semantics. We also prove an important *quiescence* theorem showing that our implementation successfully relocates computation from the controller onto switches.
- We describe a prototype implementation and an evaluation on some simple benchmarks demonstrating the practical utility of our framework (Section 7).

NetCore arose out of our previous work on Frenetic [9], another high-level network programming language. Frenetic has three main pieces: (1) an SQL-like query language for reading network state, (2) a language for specifying packet-forwarding policies and, (3) a functional reactive "glue" language that processes the results of queries and generates streams of forwarding policies for the network. NetCore replaces Frenetic's language for expressing forwarding policies with a significantly more powerful language that supports processing packets using *arbitrary functions*. In addition, NetCore also contains a minimalist "query language," as its predicates can analyze traffic history.

The main contribution of this paper relative to earlier work on Frenetic is the design of new algorithms for compiling these rich policies and for managing the controller-switch interactions that arise as compiled policies are executed in a network. These algorithms handle NetCore's new policy language, and the core elements of Frenetic's old policy language even better. In particular, the NetCore compiler generates efficient switch classifiers by (1) using *wildcard rules* that process more packets on switches instead of simple *exact-match rules*, and (2) generating rules *proactively* (*i.e.*, in advance of when they are needed), again to process more packets on switches, instead of strictly *reactively* (*i.e.*, on demand). Finally, NetCore has a formal semantics and correctness proofs for its core algorithms, whereas Frenetic had none.

2. NetCore Overview

This section presents additional background on SDNs and NetCore, using examples to illustrate the main ideas. For concreteness, we focus on the OpenFlow SDN architecture [20], but we elide and take liberty with certain inessential details. Our compiler does not assume the specifics of the current OpenFlow platform.

OpenFlow overview. OpenFlow is based on a two-tiered architecture in which a controller manages a collection of subordinate switches. Figure 1 depicts a simple topology with a controller C

managing a single switch S. Packets may either be processed on switches or on the controller, but processing a packet on the controller increases its latency by several orders of magnitude. Hence, to ensure good performance, the controller typically installs a *classifier* consisting of a set of packet-forwarding *rules* on each switch.

Each forwarding rule has a *pattern* that identifies a set of packets, an *action* that specifies how packets matching the pattern should be processed, *counters* that keep track of the number and size of all packets processed using the rule, and an integer *priority*. When a packet arrives at a switch, it is processed in three steps: First, the switch selects a rule whose pattern matches the packet. If it has no matching rules, then it drops the packet, and if it has multiple matching rules, then it picks the one with the highest priority. Second, the switch updates the counters associated with the rule. Finally, the switch applies the action listed in the rule to the packet. In this paper, we are concerned with two kinds of actions: (1) a forwarding action $\{l_1, \ldots, l_k\}$, which forwards the packet to a set of (usually one, sometimes zero, rarely more than one) adjacent network locations l_i, where each l_i may be the name of another switch, network, or host,[1] and (2) a controller action Ω, which forwards the packet to the controller for processing.

NetCore: A simple static forwarding policy. NetCore is a declarative language for specifying high-level packet-forwarding policies. The NetCore compiler and run-time system handle the details of translating these policies to switch-level rules and issuing commands to install the generated rules on switches.

The simplest NetCore policies are specified using a *predicate* e that matches some set of packets and a set S of locations to which those packets should be forwarded. We write these policies $e \rightarrow S$. The simplest predicates match bits in a particular packet header field. For example, the predicate `SrcAddr:10.0.0.0/8` specifies that the first octet of the packet's source address must be `10` (using the standard notation for expressing IP prefix patterns). More complex predicates are built by taking the union ($\cup$), intersection ($\cap$), negation ($\neg$), or difference ($\setminus$) of simpler predicates. Analogous set-theoretic operations may be used to compose more complex policies from simpler policies. As an example, consider the following policy.

```
SrcAddr:10.0.0.0/8 ∖ (SrcAddr:10.0.0.1 ∪ DstPort:80)
  → {Switch 1}
```

It states that packets from sources in subnet `10.0.0.0/8` should be forwarded to switch `1`, except for packets coming from `10.0.0.1` or going to a destination on port `80`.

The first challenge in compiling a high-level language such as NetCore to a low-level SDN framework such as OpenFlow arises from the relative lack of expressiveness in the switch packet-matching primitives. For instance, because switches cannot express the difference of two patterns in a single rule, this policy needs to be implemented using three rules installed in a particular prioritized order: one that drops packets from `10.0.0.1`, another that drops all packets going to port `80`, and a final rule that forwards all remaining packets from `10.0.0.0/8` to `Switch 1`. The following switch-level classifier implements this policy. We write these classifiers with the highest priority rule first. Switch-level patterns are on the left, actions are on the right, and a colon separates the two.

```
SrcAddr:10.0.0.1   : {}
DstPort:80         : {}
SrcAddr:10.0.0.0/8 : {Switch 1}
```

Next consider a similar high-level policy to the first:

```
SrcAddr:10.2.0.0/16 ∖ (SrcAddr:10.2.0.1 ∪ DstPort:22)
  → {Switch 2}
```

We can generate a classifier for this policy in the same way:

```
SrcAddr:10.2.0.1    : {}
DstPort:22          : {}
SrcAddr:10.2.0.0/16 : {Switch 2}
```

Now suppose that we want to generate a classifier that implements the union of the two policies. We cannot combine the classifiers in a simple way (*e.g.*, by concatenating or interleaving them) because the rules interact with each other. For example, if we were to simply concatenate the two lists of rules, the rule that drops packets to port 80 would incorrectly shadow the forwarding rule for traffic from `10.2.0.0/16`. Instead, we need to perform a much more complicated translation that produces the following classifier:

```
SrcAddr:10.2.0.1,    DstPort:80 : {},
SrcAddr:10.2.0.0/16, DstPort:80 : {Switch 2}
SrcAddr:10.2.0.1                : {Switch 1}
SrcAddr:10.2.0.0/16, DstPort:22 : {Switch 1}
SrcAddr:10.2.0.0/16             : {Switch 1,Switch 2}
SrcAddr:10.0.0.1                : {}
SrcAddr:10.0.0.0/8,  DstPort:80 : {}
SrcAddr:10.0.0.0/8              : {Switch 1}
```

Dealing with these complexities often leads SDN programmers to use *exact-match* rules—*i.e.*, rules that fully specify every bit in every single header field. Exact-match rules, for instance, do not use wildcard patterns that match many values for a single header field, such as `10.0.0.0/8`, nor do they leave certain header fields completely unconstrained. Our first implementation of Frenetic [9] used exact-match rules exclusively because such rules were far easier for its run-time system to reason about, particularly when it came to composing multiple user policies.

This paper presents new, general-purpose algorithms for synthesizing low-level switch classifiers that use wildcard rules to the extent possible. These new algorithms result in far more efficient system than the one we built in earlier work: in Frenetic's original exact-match architecture, many more packets wound up being sent to the controller (suffering orders of magnitude increase in latency) and many more rules had to be sent to switches. The results of our experiments, presented in Section 7, highlight the magnitude of these differences.

NetCore: Richer predicates and dynamic policies. The policies presented in the previous section were relatively simple—they did nothing besides match bits in header fields and forward packets accordingly. Such static policies can be expressed in Frenetic's simple policy language, though they are not be implemented nearly as efficiently as in the NetCore system. However, many applications demand dynamic policies whose forwarding behavior depends on complex functions of traffic history and other information. And these richer policies cannot be implemented by simply analyzing bits in header fields.

As an example, suppose we want to build a security application that implements in-network authentication for the topology shown in Figure 1. The network N_1 contains a collection of internal hosts, N_2 represents the upstream connection to the Internet, A is the server that handles authentication for hosts in N_1, and all three elements are connected to each other by the switch S. Informally, we want the network to perform routing and access control according to the following policy: Forward packets from unauthenticated hosts in N_1 to A, from authenticated hosts in N_1 to their intended destination in N_2, and from A and N_2 back to N_1 (although not from N_2 to A). This policy can be described succinctly in NetCore as follows.

[1] On real OpenFlow switches, locations are actually integers corresponding to physical ports on the switch; in this paper we model them symbolically.

```
  (InPort:Network 1 ∩ inspect ps auth → {Network 2})
∪ (InPort:Network 1 ∩ ¬(inspect ps auth) → {Server A})
∪ (InPort:Server  A ∪ InPort:Network 2 → {Network 1})
```

where

```
ps             = InPort:Server A
auth (Σ,s,p)   = any (isAddr p) Σ
isAddr p (_,p') = p.SrcAddr == p'.DstAddr
```

This policy uses an *inspector predicate* to classify traffic from N_1 as authenticated or unauthenticated. An inspector predicate `inspect` e f has two arguments: a filter predicate e over the network traffic history and an (almost) arbitrary boolean-valued function f. The filter predicate generates a *controller state* Σ, which is a collection of traffic statistics, represented abstractly as a multiset of switch-packet pairs (the switch being the place where the packet was processed). The boolean-valued function f receives the controller state as one its arguments and may analyze it as part of its decision-making process.

In the example above, the filter predicate `ps` selects all traffic coming from the authentication server. In this idealized example, we will treat an entity sending a packet `p` as authenticated if the authentication server has ever sent it a packet at any point in the past. The function `auth` takes three arguments: the controller state Σ, the switch `s` that should be handling the packet, and the packet `p` to which the policy applies. Here, the `auth` function tests whether the `SrcAddr` field of the packet `p` being processed is equal to the `DstAddr` of `any` other packet `p'` in the filtered traffic history (and because there is only one switch in this example, `auth` ignores its `s` argument). In other words, it tests whether the authentication server has sent a packet to that sender in the past. If it has, the inspector predicate is satisfied; if not, it is not satisfied. The `auth` function performs these tests using the auxiliary functions `any`, a built-in function that tests whether a boolean function is true of any element of a multiset, and `isAddr`, a user-defined function that tests whether one packet's `DstAddr` is equal to another packet's `SrcAddr`. This inspector is combined with the other set-theoretic operators to implement the overall packet-forwarding policy.

Policies that use inspectors are easy to write because forwarding decisions can be expressed using arbitrary functional programs. These programs can query past traffic history or look up facts they need such as authentication status in a database. On the other hand, these programs never have to manage the low-level details of generating or installing switch-level rules—the run-time system does that tedious, error-prone work for the programmer. Of course, this expressiveness presents an extreme challenge for the compiler and run-time system. While it would be easy to evaluate the results of such policies by sending all packets to the controller, doing so would be totally impractical. We must find a way to implement the policy while processing the majority of traffic on switches.

Our implementation strategy for such policies proceeds as follows. First, we compile the parts of the policy that do not involve inspectors as effectively as we can: The system generates normal forwarding rules when it can, and rules that send packets to the controller otherwise. Next, whenever a packet that cannot be handled by a switch arrives at the controller, the run-time system evaluates the packet against the current policy, which includes inspectors, producing a set of forwarding actions. There are two possibilities:

1. The policy with respect to this packet (and similar ones) is *invariant*. In other words, every subsequent time the system evaluates the policy against this packet, it will return the same set of forwarding actions.
2. The policy with respect to this packet (and similar ones) is *volatile*. In other words, the set of forwarding actions to be applied to this policy may change in the future.

In the first case, the system can install rules on the switch that associate packets similar to the one just processed with the set of forwarding actions just computed. Because the set of computed actions will never change, installing such rules on switches preserves the semantics of the policy. In the second case, the system can not install rules on the switch—the next packet might be forwarded differently, so the system will have to reevaluate it on the controller. In our example, once a host has been authenticated, it stays authenticated—once the `auth` function evaluates to true it will continue to do so, and is therefore *invariant*. Since inferring invariance automatically from an arbitrary program is a difficult problem, we currently ask NetCore programmers to supply invariance information to the compiler in the form of an auxiliary hand-written function. In this simple case, writing the invariance function `auth_inv` is trivial— it is true whenever `auth` is true:

```
auth_inv (Σ,s,p) = auth (Σ,s,p)
```

To effectively generate rules, even in the presence of inspector predicates, the run-time system must be able to determine when inspector returns the same results on one packet as it does on another—*i.e.*, it must be able to calculate the *similar packets* referred to above. Observe that an inspector always returns the same results on two different packets if those packets agree on all header fields that the inspector function examines. Conversely, if the inspector does not examine a particular header field, the value of that field does not affect its result. Hence, when generating a policy after evaluating it against a single packet, the run-time can substitute wildcards for all header fields that the policy does not inspect. Though it is likely possible to infer the set of headers any inspector function examines (at least conservatively), our current implementation assumes that programmers supply this information explicitly.

Overall, these techniques—(1) run-time evaluation of policies against particular packets on the controller, (2) invariance, and (3) specification of header information—collaborate to turn the difficult problem of evaluating policies containing arbitrary functions back in to the simpler problem of compiling static forwarding policies efficiently. We call these techniques *reactive specialization*.

3. A Core Calculus for Network Programming

This section defines the syntax and semantics of NetCore, a core calculus for high-level network programming. The calculus has two major components: *predicates*, which describe sets of packets, and *policies*, which specify where to forward those packets. Figure 2 presents the syntax of these constructs as well as various network values such as headers and packets.

Notation. Throughout this paper, whenever we define syntax, as in the grammar for packets, we will use the grammar non-terminal (p) as a metavariable ranging over the objects being defined, the capitalized version of the non-terminal (P) as a metavariable ranging over sets or multisets of such objects, and vector notation ($\vec{p}$) for sequences of objects.

We describe finite sets using the notation $\{x_1, \ldots, x_k\}$ and combine sets using operations $\cup$, $\cap$, $\neg$, and $\setminus$ (union, intersection, complement, and difference respectively). Typically, we give definitions for intersection and complement and leave union ($S_1 \cup S_2 = \neg(\neg S_1 \cap \neg S_2)$) and difference ($S_1 \setminus S_2 = S_1 \cap \neg S_2$) as derived forms. We also overload $\neg$ and use it to negate booleans; its meaning will be clear from context. We write multisets using the notation $\{\!|x_1, \ldots, x_n|\!\}$ and combine multisets using multiset union $M_1 \uplus M_2$. We write finite maps using the notation $\{x_1 \mapsto y_1, \ldots, x_n \mapsto y_n\}$ and lookup elements of a finite map m using function application $m(x_i)$.

Network values. For simplicity, we only model a single kind of network entity to forward to, switches s. Packets p are the basic

Network Values

Switch	s		
Header	h		
Switch Set	S	::=	$\{s_1, \ldots, s_n\}$
Header Set	H	::=	$\{h_1, \ldots, h_n\}$
Bit	b	::=	$1 \mid 0$
Packet	p	::=	$\{h_1 \mapsto \vec{b}_1, \ldots, h_n \mapsto \vec{b}_n\}$
State	Σ	::=	$\{\!\vert (s_1, p_1), \ldots, (s_n, p_n) \vert\!\}$

Language

Snapshot	x	::=	(Σ, s, p)
Wildcard	w	::=	$1 \mid 0 \mid ?$
Inspector	f	$\in$	$\text{State}[H_1] \times \text{Switch} \times \text{Packet}[H_2] \to \text{Bool}$
Predicate	e	::=	$h : \vec{w} \mid \text{switch } s \mid \text{inspect } e\ f \mid e_1 \cap e_2 \mid \neg e$
Policy	τ	::=	$e \to S \mid \tau_1 \cap \tau_2 \mid \neg\tau$

Figure 2. NetCore syntax.

$$[\![e]\!] = \{x_1, \ldots, x_k\}$$

$$[\![h : \vec{w}]\!] = \{(\Sigma, s, p) \mid p(h) \text{ matches } \vec{w}\}$$

$$[\![\text{switch } s']\!] = \{(\Sigma, s, p) \mid s' = s\}$$

$$[\![\text{inspect } e\ f]\!] = \{(\Sigma, s, p) \mid f(\Sigma', s, p)\}$$

$$\text{where } \Sigma' = \{\!\vert (s', p') \mid (s', p') \in \Sigma \text{ and } (\Sigma, s', p') \in [\![e]\!] \vert\!\}$$

$$[\![e_1 \cap e_2]\!] = [\![e_1]\!] \cap [\![e_2]\!]$$

$$[\![\neg e]\!] = \neg [\![e]\!]$$

$$[\![\tau]\!](x) = S$$

$$[\![e \to S]\!](x) = \begin{cases} S & \text{if } x \in [\![e]\!] \\ \varnothing & \text{otherwise} \end{cases}$$

$$[\![\tau_1 \cap \tau_2]\!](x) = [\![\tau_1]\!](x) \cap [\![\tau_2]\!](x)$$

$$[\![\neg\tau]\!](x) = \neg [\![\tau]\!](x)$$

Figure 3. NetCore semantics.

values processed by programs, which we represent as a finite map from headers h to bitstrings $\vec{b}$. We write $p(h)$ for the bitstring associated with the header h in p. We assume all fields have fixed, finite length and therefore the set of complete packets is finite. The *controller state* (Σ) accumulates information about packets that arrive at each switch. We represent controller state as a multiset of switch-packet pairs.

Predicates. Informally, predicates select sets of packets that are of interest in some forwarding policy. Formally, a predicate e denotes a set of *snapshots* x comprising a controller state Σ, a switch s, and a packet p located at s. The state component is essential for modeling predicates that depend upon historical traffic patterns, such as the past load on particular links or packets sent and received from various locations. Figure 3 defines the semantics of predicates. We say that a snapshot x *matches* a predicate e when it belongs to the denotation of e. We sometimes say that a packet p *matches* e, leaving the state and the switch implicit because they are irrelevant or uninteresting. We also say that a bitstring $\vec{b}$ *matches* a wildcard $\vec{w}$ whenever the corresponding bits match. For example, 1111 and 0011 both match the wildcard ??11.

Basic predicates have the form $h : \vec{w}$. A packet p matches $h : \vec{w}$ if $p(h)$, (*i.e.*, the h header of p) matches $\vec{w}$. For example, the predicate `DstPort:1010000` matches all packets with `DstPort` header field equal to 80 (as `1010000` is 80 in binary). Another basic predicate, `switch` s, matches all packets (in any state) sent to s. More complex predicates are built up from simpler ones using the intersection and complement operators. Additional building blocks such as True, False, $e_1 \cup e_2$, or $e_1 \setminus e_2$ can be implemented as derived forms.

The most interesting component of the language is the *inspector* predicate, `inspect` e f. The first component of an inspector is a filter predicate e that selects switch-packet pairs matching e from the current state Σ, creating a refined state Σ'. In other words, e acts as a query over the network traffic history. The second component, f, is an (almost) arbitrary Boolean-valued function over Σ' and the switch-packet pair (s and p) in question. The authentication example defined in the previous section used an inspector. Another example is (`inspect filterWeb cond`) where

```
filterWeb     = DstPort:1010000
cond (Σ,s,p) = cardinality Σ < 10000 ||
                p.SrcAddr == 10.0.0.1
```

Here, `cardinality` is a function that counts the number of elements in a multiset. This inspector extracts all web traffic (`DstPort` is `1010000`) from the current state. The inspector is satisfied if the total number web packets sent is less than `10000` or the packet p comes from a particular sender (`SrcAddr` is `10.0.0.1`).

To make compilation tractable, two additional pieces of information are associated with inspector functions f. The first piece of information comes from the sets of headers mentioned in its indexed type,

$$\text{State}[H_1] \times \text{Switch} \times \text{Packet}[H_2] \to \text{Bool}\,.$$

Such a type restricts f to only examine headers H_1 of packets in the state and headers H_2 in the packet. For instance, the function `cond` above may be assigned a type wherein H_1 is the empty set (as summing packet counts requires looking at no headers) and H_2 is {SrcAddr} (as `cond` only examines the SrcAddr field of its packet argument). The second piece of information associated with f comes from its *invariance oracle.* A function f is *invariant on* (Σ, s, p), written invariant$((\Sigma, s, p), f)$, if for all Σ', we have

$$f(\Sigma \uplus \Sigma', s, p) = f(\Sigma, s, p)\,.$$

Intuitively, a function is invariant on a state when its result does not change, no matter what additional information is added to it. Again, as an example, the `cond` function above is invariant on all snapshots involving packets from `10.0.0.1` as well as all snapshots where `cardinality` $\Sigma \geq$ `10000`—once the total volume of web traffic has crossed the threshold, the function always returns true. In our implementation, the programmer writes invariance oracles by hand as simple Haskell functions.

Together, the header sets in the inspector types, and the invariance oracle, allow the compiler to generate effective switch-level rules even though the inspector function itself cannot be analyzed. However, the language of predicates does have one significant limitation: it depends upon *permanent* invariance of predicates. There are predicates that are invariant for a long time, and hence could have rules installed on switches for that time, but are not permanently invariant. We believe our framework can be extended to handle such semi-permanent invariance properties, having the compiler uninstall rules at the end of a time period, or in response to a network event, but defer an investigation of this topic to future work.

Synchronous Machine $M_{\text{sync}} ::= (\tau, \Sigma, T)$
Asynchronous Machine $M_{\text{async}} ::= (\tau, \Sigma, T_1, T_2)$

$\boxed{M_{\text{sync}} \xrightarrow{o} M'_{\text{sync}}}$

$$\frac{[\![\tau]\!]\,(\Sigma, s, p) = S \qquad \mathsf{forward}(S,p) = T'}{(\tau, \Sigma, T \uplus \{\!|\,\mathbb{T}\,(s \mid p)\,|\!\}) \xrightarrow{s,p} (\tau, \Sigma \uplus \{\!|(s,p)|\!\}, T \uplus T')}$$

$\boxed{M_{\text{async}} \xrightarrow{o} M'_{\text{async}}}$

$$\frac{\begin{array}{c}[\![\tau]\!]\,(\Sigma, s, p) = S \qquad \mathsf{forward}(S,p) = T' \\ T_1' = T_1 \uplus T' \qquad T_2' = T_2 \uplus \{\!|\,\mathbb{T}\,(s \mid p)\,|\!\}\end{array}}{(\tau, \Sigma, T_1 \uplus \{\!|\,\mathbb{T}\,(s \mid p)\,|\!\}, T_2) \xrightarrow{s,p} (\tau, \Sigma, T_1', T_2')}$$

$$\frac{}{(\tau, \Sigma, T_1, T_2 \uplus \{\!|\,\mathbb{T}\,(s \mid p)\,|\!\}) \rightarrow (\tau, \Sigma \uplus \{\!|(s,p)|\!\}, T_1, T_2)}$$

Figure 4. Reference machines.

Policies. Policies τ specify how packets should be forwarded through the network. Basic policies, written $e \rightarrow S$, say that packets matching e should be forwarded to the switches in S. As with predicates, we build complex policies by combining simple policies using intersection and negation. Figure 3 defines the semantics of policies as a function from snapshots x to sets of switches S. Although the policy language is syntactically simple, it is remarkably expressive. In particular, inspectors are a powerful tool that can be used to express a wide range of behaviors including load balancing, fine-grained access control, and many standard routing policies.

Machines. To understand how the network behaves over time, we define two abstract machines. Both machines forward packets according to τ but they differ in how often the switches synchronize traffic statistics with the controller. The *synchronous machine* defines an idealized implementation that, at all times, has perfect information about the traffic sent over the network. Of course, it would be impractical to implement this machine in a real network because, in general, it would require sending every packet to the controller—if any packet were forwarded by a switch there would be a delay between when the packet was forwarded and when the controller state was augmented with information about that packet. The *asynchronous machine* defines a looser, more practical, implementation. Like the first machine, it is *policy-compliant*—it forwards packets according to the policy—but it updates its state asynchronously instead of in lockstep with each packet processed. Hence, it makes no guarantees about what it knows about the network's traffic. While the synchronous machine can be thought of as the best possible policy-compliant machine, the asynchronous machine can be thought of as the worst policy-compliant machine. Any reasonable implementation will sit between the two. In other words, implementations should be policy compliant, but users should not expect perfect synchrony—the cost of implementing it would be prohibitive. In practice, synchronization with switches typically happens at periodic, timed intervals (modulo variances in the latency of communication) but for simplicity, we do not model time explicitly.

Figure 4 defines both reference machines. They use the function $\mathsf{forward}(S,p)$, which generates a multiset of transmissions,

$$\mathsf{forward}(S,p) = \{\!|\,\mathbb{T}\,(s \mid p) \mid s \in S\,|\!\}\,.$$

The state of the synchronous machine (M_{sync}) includes the NetCore policy τ, the state Σ, and a multiset T of pending transmissions. At each step, the machine removes a transmission from T, processes it using the policy, updates the machine state, and adds the new transmissions generated by the policy to the multiset of pending transmissions. The state of the asynchronous machine (M_{async}) includes the program τ, state Σ, and two multisets of transmissions: T_1, which represents transmissions waiting to be processed by the policy, and T_2, which represents transmissions that have been processed by the policy but have not yet been added to the state. The first inference rule for the second machine takes a transmission from T_1, processes it using the policy, and places it in T_2, the set of transmissions waiting to be incorporated into Σ; the second rule takes a transmission from T_2 and adds it to Σ.

4. The Run-time System

In this section we discuss how to implement NetCore's semantics on a software-defined network by giving an operational semantics to the NetCore run-time system and the underlying network devices. This operational semantics explains the basic interactions between the controller and the switches.

Switch classifiers. Before we can present the run-time system, we need a concrete representation of the rules that switches use to process packets. A *classifier* $\vec{r}$ is a sequence of rules r, each containing a switch-level pattern z and an action α. While our high-level semantics uses sets, classifiers are represented as sequences to model rule priority: within a classifier, rules on the left have higher priority than rules on the right.

The *pattern* (z) component of a rule recognizes a set of packets, and hence is similar to (but less general than) a predicate in NetCore. We write $p \sqsubseteq z$ when packet m matches pattern z. We hold patterns abstract to model the variety of different matching capabilities in today's switches. For example, OpenFlow switches support prefix pattern matching on source and destination IP addresses (*i.e.*, patterns like `0110*`) but only exact or full unconstrained matching on most other headers. Some switches support various other extended patterns, such as ranges of the form $[n_1, n_2]$.

An action α is either a set of switches S, which forwards packets to each switch in the set, or Ω, which forwards packets to the controller. Most switches support other actions such as modifying header fields, but for simplicity we only model forwarding.

Given a packet p and a classifier $\vec{r}$, we match the packet against the classifier by finding the first rule whose pattern matches the packet. We write $\vec{r} \leadsto^{p} z : \alpha$ for the matching judgment. More formally, we define classifier matching as follows; note that it selects the highest priority (leftmost) matching rule:

$$\frac{p \not\sqsubseteq z_1 \qquad \cdots \qquad p \not\sqsubseteq z_{i-1} \qquad p \sqsubseteq z_i}{(z_1 : \alpha_1, \ldots, z_{i-1} : \alpha_{i-1}, z_i : \alpha_i, \ldots, z_n : \alpha_n) \leadsto^{p} z_i : \alpha_i}$$

Molecular machine. We formalize the operational semantics of the run-time system as a *molecular machine*, in the style of the chemical abstract machine [2]. The machine's components, called *molecules*, are given on the left side of Figure 5. For simplicity, we assume that packets arriving at a switch may be processed in any order and do not model failures that cause packets to be dropped.

The molecule $\mathbb{C}\,(\tau \mid \Sigma)$ represents the controller machine running the NetCore policy τ in state Σ. The molecule $\mathbb{S}\,(s \mid \vec{r} \mid Z)$ represents switch s with packet classifier $\vec{r}$ and local switch state Z. The switch state records the patterns of rules that have been used to match packets but not yet queried and processed by the controller. Real switches use integer counters as state; for simplicity, we represent these counters in unary using a multiset of patterns. A transmission molecule $\mathbb{T}\,(s \mid p)$ represents a packet p en route to switch

Pattern	z		
Switch Action	α	::=	$S \mid \Omega$
Rule	r	::=	$z : \alpha$
Classifier	$\vec{r}$	::=	$(r_1, \ldots, r_n)$
Switch State	Z	::=	$\{\!\mid z_1, \ldots, z_n \mid\!\}$
Molecule	m	::=	$\mathbb{C}(\tau \mid \Sigma) \mid \mathbb{S}(s \mid \vec{r} \mid Z) \mid \mathbb{T}(s \mid p) \mid \mathbb{H}(s \mid p)$
Machine	M	::=	$\{\!\mid m_1, \ldots, m_n \mid\!\}$
Observation	o	::=	$\cdot \mid s, p$

$\boxed{M \xrightarrow{o} M'}$

E-SWITCHPROCESS

$$\frac{\vec{r} \rightsquigarrow^p z : S \qquad \mathsf{forward}(S, p) = T'}{\mathbb{S}(s \mid \vec{r} \mid Z), \mathbb{T}(s \mid p) \xrightarrow{s,p} \mathbb{S}(s \mid \vec{r} \mid Z \uplus \{\!\mid z \mid\!\}), T'}$$

E-SWITCHHELP

$$\frac{\vec{r} \rightsquigarrow^p z : \Omega}{\mathbb{S}(s \mid \vec{r} \mid Z), \mathbb{T}(s \mid p) \rightarrow \mathbb{S}(s \mid \vec{r} \mid Z), \mathbb{H}(s \mid p)}$$

E-CONTROLLER

$$\frac{[\![\tau]\!](\Sigma, s, p) = S \qquad \mathsf{forward}(S, p) = T' \qquad \mathsf{Specialize}((\Sigma, s, p), \tau) = \vec{r}'}{\mathbb{C}(\tau \mid \Sigma), \mathbb{S}(s \mid \vec{r} \mid Z), \mathbb{H}(s \mid p) \xrightarrow{s,p} \mathbb{C}(\tau \mid \Sigma \uplus \{\!\mid (s,p) \mid\!\}), \mathbb{S}(s \mid (\vec{r}', \vec{r}) \mid Z), T'}$$

E-COLLECT

$$\frac{\vec{r} \rightsquigarrow^p z : \alpha}{\mathbb{C}(\tau \mid \Sigma), \mathbb{S}(s \mid \vec{r} \mid Z \uplus \{\!\mid z \mid\!\}) \rightarrow \mathbb{C}(\tau \mid \Sigma \uplus \{\!\mid (s,p) \mid\!\}), \mathbb{S}(s \mid \vec{r} \mid Z)}$$

E-STEP

$$\frac{M \xrightarrow{o} M'}{(M \uplus M'') \xrightarrow{o} (M' \uplus M'')}$$

Figure 5. The run-time system.

s. Finally, a help molecule $\mathbb{H}(s \mid p)$ represents a request issued by switch s to the controller for assistance in processing packet p.

The operational semantics of the molecular machine is defined by the inference rules on the right side of Figure 5. To lighten the notation in this figure, we drop the multiset braces when writing a collection of molecules. In other words, we write $m_1, m_2, \ldots$ instead of $\{\!\mid m_1, m_2, \ldots \mid\!\}$. Each operational rule may optionally be labelled with an *observation* o, which records when transmissions are processed. We use observations in Section 6 where we establish equivalences between the molecular machine and the reference machines defined in the last section.

The rules E-SWITCHPROCESS and E-SWITCHHELP model the work done by switches to process packets. The former rule is invoked when a packet matches a rule with a non-controller action (a set of switches to forward to). In this case, the switch forwards the packet accordingly and records the rule pattern in its state. The latter rule is invoked when a packet matches a rule with a controller action. In this case, the switch generates a help molecule.

The rule E-CONTROLLER models the work done by the controller to process help molecules. The controller interprets the packet using its NetCore policy, generating new transmissions T' to be sent into the network, and adds the packet to its state. In addition, the controller uses the NetCore compiler to generate new rules to process future, similar packets on switches, instead of on the controller. The compiler is accessed through the call to the Specialize function, which generates the new rules for the switch in question. We hold the definition of this function abstract for now; it is defined precisely in the next section.

The rule E-COLLECT models the work done by the controller to transfer information about the packets that matched a particular switch-level rule from the switch to the controller state. More precisely, it chooses a pattern z from a switch state and then uses the lookup judgement $\vec{r} \rightsquigarrow^p z : \alpha$ to synthesize a packet p that might have matched the corresponding rule in the switch classifier. The pair of the packet and the switch are then stored in the controller state as a past transmission that might have occurred.

The interesting part of this transfer is that the controller stores *full* packets whereas switches only store sets of patterns and a pattern only specifies *part* of a packet—perhaps its IP address or VLAN tag, but not the packet itself. Hence the transfer operation must fabricate those parts of the packets that are not specified in the switch pattern, and the system as a whole must be correct no matter how the under-specified parts of a packet are fabricated. This places an important constraint on the compiler: If the rules and their patterns are not specific enough then although one packet may have matched a rule on a switch, a completely different packet may be fabricated and passed back to the controller. Consequently, the controller state will not model past network traffic sufficiently accurately and forwarding policies that depend upon past network traffic will not be implemented correctly.

A second subtle issue with the E-COLLECT rule is that the patterns of higher-priority rules partially overlap and take precedence over patterns from lower-priority rules. Hence, examining the pattern of a low-priority rule in isolation does not provide sufficient information to synthesize a packet that might have matched that rule. One must take all of the rules of the classifier, and their priority order, in to account when synthesizing a packet that may have matched a pattern. The E-COLLECT rule does this through the use of the full classifier matching judgement.

Finally, note that the implementation does not actually fabricate all of these packets—in practice, the switch passes integer counters associated with patterns back to the controller. Still, this non-deterministic rule effectively captures a key correctness criterion for the system: The controller program cannot distinguish between any of the packets that might be synthesized by the E-COLLECT rule and must be correct no matter which one is fabricated. Of course, this is also where the compiler's use of header information comes in to play: the fabricated packets are only different in fields that inspector functions (and other predicates) do not analyze.

5. The NetCore Algorithms

The NetCore system performs two distinct tasks:

- *Classifier Generation:* given a NetCore policy, construct a set of classifiers, one for each switch in the network.

Primitive intermediate form	u	$::=$	$(h_1 : \vec{w}_1) \wedge \ldots \wedge (h_n : \vec{w}_n)$
Three-valued boolean	b	$::=$	$\mathsf{True} \mid \mathsf{Maybe} \mid \mathsf{False}$
Pattern intermediate form	π	$::=$	$\langle u : z : b : H \rangle$
Policy intermediate form	ρ	$::=$	$\langle u : z : S_1, S_2 : H \rangle$

$\boxed{\mathcal{I}(s, e) = \vec{\pi}}$

$$\mathcal{I}(s, h : \vec{w}) = \langle (h : \vec{w}) : \mathcal{O}(h : \vec{w}) : \mathsf{True} : \varnothing \rangle, \langle \star : \top : \mathsf{False} : \varnothing \rangle$$

$$\mathcal{I}(s, \mathsf{switch}\ s') = \begin{cases} \langle \star : \top : \mathsf{True} : \varnothing \rangle & \text{if } s = s' \\ \langle \star : \top : \mathsf{False} : \varnothing \rangle & \text{if } s \neq s' \end{cases}$$

$$\mathcal{I}(s, \mathsf{inspect}\ e\ f) = \prod_i \langle u_i : z_i : \mathsf{Maybe} : (H_i \cup H) \rangle$$
$$\text{where } f : \mathsf{State}[H] \times \mathsf{Switch} \times \mathsf{Packet}[H'] \to \mathsf{Bool}$$
$$\text{and } (\mathcal{I}(s, e))_i = \langle u_i : z_i : b_i : H_i \rangle$$

$$\mathcal{I}(s, e \cap e') = \prod_i \prod_j \langle u_i \wedge u'_j : z_i \sqcap z'_j : b_i \wedge b'_j : H_i \cup H'_j \rangle$$
$$\text{where } (\mathcal{I}(s, e))_i = \langle u_i : z_i : b_i : H_i \rangle$$
$$\text{and } (\mathcal{I}(s, e'))_j = \langle u'_j : z'_j : b'_j : H'_j \rangle$$

$$\mathcal{I}(s, \neg e) = \prod_i \langle u_i : z_i : \neg b_i : H_i \rangle$$
$$\text{where } (\mathcal{I}(s, e))_i = \langle u_i : z_i : b_i : H_i \rangle$$

$\boxed{\mathcal{I}(s, \tau) = \vec{\rho}}$

$$\mathcal{I}(s, e \to S) = \prod_i \begin{cases} \langle u_i : z_i : S, S : H_i \rangle & \text{if } b_i = \mathsf{True} \\ \langle u_i : z_i : \varnothing, S : H_i \rangle & \text{if } b_i = \mathsf{Maybe} \\ \langle u_i : z_i : \varnothing, \varnothing : H_i \rangle & \text{if } b_i = \mathsf{False} \end{cases}$$
$$\text{where } (\mathcal{I}(s, e))_i = \langle u_i : z_i : b_i : H_i \rangle$$

$$\mathcal{I}(s, \tau \cap \tau') = \prod_i \prod_j \langle u_i \wedge u'_j : z_i \sqcap z'_j : S'_1, S'_2 : H_i \cup H'_j \rangle$$
$$\text{where } (\mathcal{I}(s, \tau))_i = \langle u_i : z_i : S_{1i}, S_{2i} : H_i \rangle$$
$$\text{and } (\mathcal{I}(s, \tau'))_j = \langle u'_j : z'_j : S'_{1j}, S'_{2j} : H'_j \rangle$$
$$\text{and } S'_1 = S_{1i} \cap S'_{1j}$$
$$\text{and } S'_2 = S_{2i} \cap S'_{2j}$$

$$\mathcal{I}(s, \neg\tau) = \prod_i \langle u_i : z_i : \neg S_{2i}, \neg S_{1i} : H_i \rangle$$
$$\text{where } (\mathcal{I}(s, \tau))_i = \langle u_i : z_i : S_{1i}, S_{2i} : H_i \rangle$$

$\boxed{\mathcal{C}(s, \tau) = \vec{r}}$

$$\mathcal{C}(s, \tau) = \prod_i \begin{cases} z_i : S_{1i} & \text{if } S_{1i} = S_{2i} \text{ and } H_i \subseteq \mathsf{headers}(z_i) \\ & \text{and } \mathsf{consistent}(\vec{\rho}, i) \\ z_i : \Omega & \text{otherwise} \end{cases}$$
$$\text{where } \mathcal{I}(s, \tau) = \vec{\rho}$$
$$\text{and } (\vec{\rho})_i = \langle u_i : z_i : S_{1i}, S_{2i} : H_i \rangle$$
$$\text{and } \mathsf{consistent}(\vec{\rho}, i) =$$
$$\forall p. \exists j. \vec{\rho} \leadsto^p_z \langle u_i : z_i : S_{1i}, S_{2i} : H_i \rangle \Rightarrow \vec{\rho} \leadsto^p_u \langle u_j : z_j : S_{1i}, S_{2i} : H_j \rangle$$
$$\text{and } \mathsf{headers}(z) = \{ h \mid p_1 \sqsubseteq z \wedge p_2 \sqsubseteq z \Rightarrow p_1(h) = p_2(h) \}$$

Figure 6. NetCore classifier generation.

- *Reactive Specialization:* given a packet not handled by the current classifier installed on a switch, generate additional rules that allow the switch to handle future packets with similar header fields without consulting the controller.

This section presents the key algorithms that implement these tasks.

5.1 Parameters

The NetCore system is parameterized on several structures: a lattice of switch patterns, and two oracles that map primitive predicates onto switch-level and wildcard patterns respectively. Abstracting some of the low-level details of compilation makes it possible to execute NetCore policies on many diverse kinds of hardware and even use switches with different capabilities in the same network. Formally, we assume that switch patterns form a bounded lattice. A pattern z_1 sits lower than (or equal to) another pattern z_2, written $z_1 \sqsubseteq z_2$, when z_1 matches a subset of the packets matched by z_2. The $\top$ element matches every packet and the $\bot$ element matches none. Abusing notation slightly, we write $p \sqsubseteq z$ to indicate that packet p matches pattern z. To ensure that intersections are compiled correctly, we require that meets be *exact*, in the sense that $p \sqsubseteq z \sqcap z'$ if and only if $p \sqsubseteq z$ and $p \sqsubseteq z'$.

The first oracle, called the *compilation oracle* $\mathcal{O}$, maps primitives $h : \vec{w}$ into the pattern lattice. In many cases, the pattern generated by $\mathcal{O}(h : \vec{w})$ will match the set of packets described by $h : \vec{w}$ exactly, but sometimes this is not possible. For example, OpenFlow switches only support prefix wildcards for IP addresses, so the best approximation of the non-prefix pattern $\mathsf{SrcAddr} : 1?1?$ is $\mathsf{SrcAddr} : 1???$. We give the oracle some flexibility in selecting patterns and only require it to satisfy two conditions: (1) it must return an overapproximation of the primitive and (2) it must be monotonic, in the sense it translates (semantically) larger primitives to larger patterns. Formally, the requirements on compilation oracles are as follows: (1) $(\Sigma, s, p) \in [\![h : w]\!]$ implies $p \sqsubseteq \mathcal{O}(h : w)$ and (2) $[\![h : w]\!] \subseteq [\![h' : w']\!]$ implies $\mathcal{O}(h : w) \sqsubseteq \mathcal{O}(h' : w')$.

The second oracle, called the *refinement oracle* $\mathcal{U}$, takes a primitive $h : \vec{w}$ and a packet p as arguments and produces a pattern $h : \vec{w}'$. Unlike the compilation oracle, which overapproximates predicates, the refinement oracle underapproximates predicates, allowing the compilation infrastructure to generate effective switch-level rules for a subset of the pattern of interest. While there is generally one best overapproximation, there often exist many useful underapproximations; in such cases, we disambiguate by selecting the best underapproximation that matches p. For example, if we were to refine $\mathsf{SrcAddr} : 1?1?$ (which can't be compiled exactly on OpenFlow) with a packet with source address 1111, we would generate the underapproximation $\mathsf{SrcAddr} : 111?$, yet if we refined the same predicate with a packet with source address 1010, we would instead generate $\mathsf{SrcAddr} : 101?$.

5.2 Classifier Generation

Ideally, given a policy, the NetCore compiler would generate a classifier with the same semantics—*i.e.*, one that denotes the same function on packets. But certain NetCore features, such as inspectors and wildcard patterns (when not supported by the underlying hardware), cannot be implemented on switches. So in general, the generated classifier will only approximate the policy, and certain packets will have to be processed on the controller.

The classifier generator works in two phases. In the first phase, it translates high-level policies to an intermediate form containing switch-level patterns and actions, as well as precise semantic information about the policy being compiled. In the second phase, it builds a classifier by attaching actions to patterns, using the semantic information produced in the first phase to determine whether it is safe to attach forwarding actions to a pattern, or whether the special controller action Ω must be used instead.

The grammars at the top of Figure 6 define the syntax for the intermediate forms used in classifier generation. The intermediate form for predicates $\langle u : z : b : H \rangle$ contains four values: an "ideal" pattern u; a switch pattern z; a three-valued boolean b; and a set of headers H. The ideal pattern u represents the pattern we would generate if the pattern lattice supported arbitrary wildcards. Ideal patterns are represented as a conjunction of header and wildcard pairs. We write $\star$ for the unconstrained ideal pattern—*i.e.*, an empty conjunction. The switch pattern z represents the actual pattern generated by the compiler, which is an overapproximation of the ideal pattern in general. The three-valued boolean b indicates whether packets matching the predicate should definitely be accepted (True), rejected (False), or whether there is insufficient information and a definitive answer must be made by the controller (Maybe). To combine three-valued booleans, we extend the standard boolean operators as follows:

$$\mathsf{Maybe} \wedge \mathsf{False} = \mathsf{False} \qquad \mathsf{Maybe} \wedge \mathsf{True} = \mathsf{Maybe}$$
$$\mathsf{Maybe} \wedge \mathsf{Maybe} = \mathsf{Maybe} \qquad \neg\mathsf{Maybe} = \mathsf{Maybe}$$

The set of headers H keeps track of the header fields (within packets in the controller state) that inspector functions may examine. This header information is used to ensure the compiler generates sufficiently fine-grained switch rules so that when information is transferred from the switch to the controller (using the E-COLLECT rule discussed in the previous section), the information is precise enough to guarantee the correctness of the inspectors.

The intermediate form for policies $\langle u : z : S_1, S_2 : H \rangle$ is similar to the form for predicates, but instead of a three-valued boolean, it records lower and upper bounds (S_1 and S_2) on the sets of switches to which a packet might be forwarded. Intuitively, a proper forwarding rule can only be generated when we know exactly which switches to forward packets to (*i.e.*, when S_1 and S_2 are equal). In other cases, the compiler will generate a rule that sends packets to the controller.

Predicate translation. The heart of classifier generation is the function $\mathcal{I}(s, e)$, presented in Figure 6, which takes a predicate e and switch s as arguments and produces a sequence of intermediate predicates that approximate e on s. One of the invariants of the algorithm is that it always generates a *complete* sequence—*i.e.*, intermediate predicates whose patterns collectively match every packet. In addition, the algorithm attempts to produce a sequence whose patterns separate packets into two sets—one with packets that match the predicate being compiled and another with those that do not. However, it does not always succeed in doing so, for two fundamental reasons: (1) the algorithm cannot analyze the decisions made by inspectors—as far as the analysis is concerned, inspectors are black boxes, and (2) certain primitive predicates cannot be expressed precisely using switch patterns. The intermediate predicates contain sufficient information for the compiler to reason about the precision of the rules it generates. We write $(\mathcal{I}(s,e))_i = \langle u_i : z_i : b_i : H_i \rangle$ to indicate that compiling e returns a sequence of intermediate predicates whose i^{th} element is $\langle u_i : z_i : b_i : H_i \rangle$, and

$$\prod_i \langle u_i : z_i : b_i : H_i \rangle$$

to denote the sequence of intermediate predicates out of components $\langle u_i : z_i : b_i : H_i \rangle$ indexed by i.

The first equation at the top of Figure 6 states that the compiler translates primitive predicates $h : \vec{w}$ into two intermediate predicates: $\langle (h : \vec{w}) : \mathcal{O}(h : \vec{w}) : \mathsf{True} : \varnothing \rangle$, which contains the switch pattern produced by the compilation oracle, and $\langle \star : \top : \mathsf{False} : \varnothing \rangle$, which, by using the $\top$ pattern, ensures that the sequence is complete. Like classifiers, these sequences should be interpreted as a prioritized series of rules. Hence the second quadruple only rejects things the first does not match.

The case for switch predicates switch s' has two possible outcomes: If the switch s whose classifier is being compiled is the same as s', then the compiler generates an intermediate form that associates every packet with True. Otherwise, the compiler generates an intermediate form that associates every packet with False.

Intuitively, the classifier generated for inspect e f must satisfy three conditions. First, it should approximate the semantics of f. Because the behavior of f is unknown at compile time, the approximation cannot be exact. Hence, the intermediate predicates generated for the inspector should contain Maybe, indicating that matching packets should be sent to the controller for processing. Second, it should be structured so that it can identify packets matched by the traffic filter predicate e—*i.e.*, the packets that must be present in the controller state to evaluate f. Third, it should also be sufficiently fine-grained to provide information about the set of headers H mentioned in the type of f, which represent the headers of packets in the state that f examines.[2] Hence, the compiler recursively generates a sequence of intermediate predicates from e, and then iterates through it, replacing the three-valued boolean b_i with Maybe and adding H to the set of headers H_i in each $\langle u_i : b_i : z_i : H_i \rangle$.

To generate intermediate forms for an intersection $(e_1 \cap e_2)$, the compiler combines each pair of intermediate predicates generated for e_1 and e_2. The resulting classifier captures intersection in the following sense: if a packet matches z_i in the first intermediate form and matches z'_j in the second intermediate form, it matches the form with pattern $z_i \sqcap z'_j$ in the result, and likewise for u_i and u'_j. Performing this construction naively would result in a combinatorial blowup. However, it is often possible to exploit algebraic properties of patterns to reduce the size of the sequence in practice—see the examples below and also Section 7.

Finally, the case for negated predicates: $\neg e$ iterates through the sequence generated by the compiler for e and negates the three-valued boolean in each intermediate predicate.

Predicate translation examples. To illustrate some of the details of predicate compilation, consider the translation of the inspector-free predicate $(e_1 \cap e_2)$ where e_1 is $(h_1 : 0?)$ and e_2 is $(h_2 : 11)$ and h_1 and h_2 are distinct headers. Assume that switch patterns support wildcards such as $0?$ on h_1. The left and right sides of the intersection generate the following intermediate predicates:

$$\mathcal{I}(s, e_1) = \langle (h_1 : 0?) : (h_1 : 0?) : \mathsf{True} : \varnothing \rangle, \langle \star : \top : \mathsf{False} : \varnothing \rangle$$
$$\mathcal{I}(s, e_2) = \langle (h_2 : 11) : (h_2 : 11) : \mathsf{False} : \varnothing \rangle, \langle \star : \top : \mathsf{True} : \varnothing \rangle$$

Note that the negation in e_2 flips the parts of the intermediate forms designated as True—*i.e.*, it inverts the parts of the sequence that match and do not match the predicate.

Next, consider compilation of the intersection, and note that we simplify the results slightly using identities such as $z \sqcap \top = z$ and $u \wedge \star = u$ and $b \wedge \mathsf{True} = b$.

$$\begin{aligned}
&\langle (h_1 : 0? \wedge h_2 : 11) : (h_1 : 0? \sqcap h_2 : 11) : \mathsf{True} : \varnothing \rangle,\\
&\langle (h_1 : 0?) : (h_1 : 0?) : \mathsf{False} : \varnothing \rangle,\\
&\langle (h_2 : 11) : (h_2 : 11) : \mathsf{False} : \varnothing \rangle,\\
&\langle \star : \top : \mathsf{False} : \varnothing \rangle
\end{aligned}$$

This classifier can then be simplified further, as the last three rules overlap and are associated with the same three-valued boolean:

$$\begin{aligned}
&\langle (h_1 : 0? \wedge h_2 : 11) : (h_1 : 0? \sqcap h_2 : 11) : \mathsf{True} : \varnothing \rangle,\\
&\langle \star : \top : \mathsf{False} : \varnothing \rangle
\end{aligned}$$

Now suppose instead that the switch only has limited support for wildcards and cannot represent $h_1 : 0?$. In this case, the compilation

[2] Note that the compiler does not add the set H' mentioned in the type of f to H_i. This set is used during specialization to determine "similar" packets.

oracle provides an overapproximation of the pattern, say, $\top$. Hence, the intermediate predicate for e_1 above would be as follows:

$$\mathcal{I}(s, e_1) = \langle (h_1 : 0?) : \top : \mathsf{True} : \varnothing \rangle, \langle \star : \top : \mathsf{False} : \varnothing \rangle$$

For another example, consider compiling a predicate that includes an inspector such as $(\mathsf{inspect}\ (h_1 : 00)\ f) \sqcap (h_2 : 11)$. In this case, $(h_1 : 00)$ compiles similarly to the simple clauses above:

$$\langle (h_1 : 00) : (h_1 : 00) : \mathsf{True} : \varnothing \rangle, \langle \star : \top : \mathsf{False} : \varnothing \rangle$$

If the set of headers f examines on the state is H, the inspector $\mathsf{inspect}\ (h_1 : 00)\ f$ compiles to the following:

$$\langle (h_1 : 00) : (h_1 : 00) : \mathsf{Maybe} : H \rangle, \langle \star : \top : \mathsf{Maybe} : H \rangle$$

Note that the definitive booleans above have been replaced with Maybe, indicating that the controller will need to determine whether packets match the predicate. However, when we intersect the results of compiling $h_2 : 11$ with the results of compiling the inspector, we obtain the following:

$$\begin{array}{l} \langle (h_1 : 00 \wedge h_2 : 11) : (h_1 : 00 \sqcap h_2 : 11) : \mathsf{Maybe} : H \rangle, \\ \langle (h_2 : 11) : (h_2 : 11) : \mathsf{Maybe} : H \rangle, \\ \langle (h_1 : 00) : (h_1 : 00) : \mathsf{False} : H \rangle, \\ \langle \star : \top : \mathsf{False} : H \rangle \end{array}$$

Importantly, even though the inspector is uncertain (*i.e.*, it has Maybe in each intermediate predicate), the result is not entirely uncertain. Because $b \wedge \mathsf{False}$ is False even when b is Maybe, intersecting inspectors with definitive predicates can resolve uncertainty. Likewise, as $b \vee \mathsf{True}$ is True, compiling the union of a definitive clause with an inspector also eliminates uncertainty. And although the calculus does not represent unions explicitly, its encoding operates as expected—a fact we exploit in reactive specialization.

Policy translation. The function $\mathcal{I}(s, \tau)$, which translates a policy into intermediate form, is similar to the translation for predicates. Figure 6 gives the formal definition of the translation. To translate a basic policy $e \to S$, the compiler first generates a sequence from e, and then attaches a pair of actions representing lower and upper bounds for each rule. There are three cases: If the three-valued boolean b_i is true, it uses S as both the upper and lower bounds. If b_i is false, it uses $\varnothing$ as the bounds. If b_i is Maybe, it uses $\varnothing$ as the lower bound and S as the upper bound, which represents the range of possible actions. The translations of intersected and negated policies are analogous to the cases for predicates.

Classifier construction. The second phase of classifier generation analyzes the intermediate form of the policy and produces a bona fide switch classifier. The $\mathcal{C}(s, \tau)$ function that implements this phase is defined in Figure 6. It first uses $\mathcal{I}(s, \tau)$ to generate a sequence of intermediate policies, and then analyzes each $\langle u_i : S_{1i}, S_{2i} : z_i : H_i \rangle$ to generate a rule. There are two possible outcomes for each intermediate policy in the sequence. First, if (1) the bounds S_{1i} and S_{2i} are tight, (2) z_i is sufficiently fine grained to collect information about all headers in H_i, and (3) we get the same switch bounds (S_{1i}, S_{2i}) regardless of whether we match packets using the ideal primitives or the switch-level patterns, then it is safe for the compiler to throw away the high-level semantic information (bounds and ideal primitives) and emit an effective rule $z_i : S_{1i}$. Otherwise, it generates a rule with the controller action Ω. The formal conditions needed for this analysis are captured by $\mathsf{consistent}(\vec{\rho}, i)$ and $\mathsf{headers}(z)$. The predicate $\mathsf{consistent}(\vec{\rho}, i)$ is satisfied if looking up an arbitrary packet matching the ith switch pattern yields the same switch bounds as looking it up using the ideal pattern (where we extend classifier lookup to sequences of intermediate policies in the obvious way). The function $\mathsf{headers}(z)$ calculates the set of headers constrained fully by z.

Formal properties. For a classifier to be sound, it must satisfy two properties: it must forward packets according to the policy, and its rules must encode enough information about the packets that match them to implement inspectors. The correctness of classifier generation is captured in the following definition and lemma.

Definition 1 (Classifier Soundness). A classifier $\vec{r}$ is sound on switch s with respect to τ if the following two criteria hold:

- *Routing soundness:* for all snapshots (Σ, s, p), if $\vec{r} \rightsquigarrow^{p} S$ then $[\![\tau]\!]\,(\Sigma, s, p) = S$, and
- *Collection soundness:* for all packets p_1 and p_2, if $\vec{r} \rightsquigarrow^{p_1} z : S$ and $\vec{r} \rightsquigarrow^{p_2} z : S$, then for all snapshots (Σ, s', p'),

$$[\![\tau]\!]\,(\Sigma \uplus \{\!|(s, p_1)|\!\}, s', p') = [\![\tau]\!]\,(\Sigma \uplus \{\!|(s, p_2)|\!\}, s', p').$$

Lemma 1 (Classifier Generation Soundness). Classifier $\mathcal{C}(s, \tau)$ is sound on switch s with respect to τ.

Intuitively, routing soundness ensures that the actions computed by looking up rules in the classifier $\vec{r}$ are consistent with τ. Formally, the condition states that if looking up a packet p in $\vec{r}$ on switch s produces a set of switches S, then evaluating τ on snapshots containing s and p also produces S. Note that this condition does not impose any requirements if looking up p in $\vec{r}$ yields Ω, as the packet will be sent to the controller, which will evaluate τ on p directly. Collection soundness ensures that the rules in $\vec{r}$ are sufficiently fine grained so that when the controller collects traffic statistics from switches, the rule patterns contain enough information to implement the policy's inspectors. This is seen in the E-COLLECT rule in the molecular machine (Figure 5), which fabricates packets that match the rule being collected. Collection soundness ensures that fabricated packets are correct. Formally, it requires that τ behave the same on all snapshots in which the state Σ has been extended with arbitrary packets p_1 and p_2 matching a given rule $z : S$. Lemma 1 states that the classifiers generated by the NetCore compiler are sound.

5.3 Reactive Specialization

The algorithm described in the preceding section generates classifiers that can be installed on switches. But as we saw, it has some substantial limitations. Dynamic policies that use inspectors cannot be analyzed. And even for purely static policies, if the switch has poor support for wildcards, the classifier needed to implement the policy may be large—much larger than would be practical to generate. To deal with these situations, we define *reactive specialization*, a powerful generalization of the simple, reactive, strategy implemented manually by OpenFlow programmers. We define reactive specialization using two operations: *program refinement*, which expands the policy relative to a new snapshot witnessed at the controller, and *pruning*, which extracts new, effective rules from the classifier generated from the expanded policy.

Program refinement. When the controller receives a new packet that a switch could not handle, it interprets the policy with respect to the packet, switch, and its current state. The idea in program refinement is to augment the program with additional information gleaned from this packet that can be used to build a specialized classifier that handles similar packets on the switch in the future. Figure 7 defines the refinement function. The key invariant of this program transformation is that the semantics of the old and new policies are identical. However, syntactically, the new program will typically have a different structure, as the transformation uses the packet to unfold primitives and inspectors. This makes compilation more precise and the recompiled program more effective.

The rules for refining a predicate appear at the top of Figure 7. The first rule uses the refinement oracle $\mathcal{U}$ to refine basic predicates. Unlike the compilation oracle, which may *overapproximate*

$$\boxed{\mathcal{R}(x,e) = e'}$$

$$\mathcal{R}((\Sigma,s,p),h:\vec{w}) = (h:\vec{w}) \cup \mathcal{U}(h:\vec{w},p)$$
$$\mathcal{R}(x,\textsf{switch } s) = \textsf{switch } s$$
$$\mathcal{R}((\Sigma,s,p),\textsf{inspect } e\ f) =$$
$$\begin{cases} (\textsf{inspect } e'\ f) \cup e'' & \text{if invariant}(x,f) \wedge f(x) \\ (\textsf{inspect } e'\ f) \setminus e'' & \text{if invariant}(x,f) \wedge \neg f(x) \\ \textsf{inspect } e'\ f & \text{if} \neg \text{invariant}(x,f) \end{cases}$$
$$\text{where } f : \textsf{State}[H] \times \textsf{Switch} \times \textsf{Packet}[H'] \to \textsf{Bool}$$
$$\text{and } x = (\Sigma,s,p)$$
$$\text{and } e' = \mathcal{R}(x,e) \cup (\mathcal{R}(x,e) \cap \textsf{similar}(s,p,H))$$
$$\text{and } e'' = \textsf{similar}(s,p,H')$$
$$\mathcal{R}(x,e_1 \cap e_2) = \mathcal{R}(x,e_1) \cap \mathcal{R}(x,e_2)$$
$$\mathcal{R}(x,\neg e) = \neg\mathcal{R}(x,e)$$

$$\boxed{\mathcal{R}(x,\tau) = \tau'}$$

$$\mathcal{R}(x,e \to S) = \mathcal{R}(x,e) \to S$$
$$\mathcal{R}(x,\tau_1 \cap \tau_2) = \mathcal{R}(x,\tau_1) \cap \mathcal{R}(x,\tau_2)$$
$$\mathcal{R}(x,\neg\tau) = \neg\mathcal{R}(x,\tau)$$

$$\boxed{\textsf{Specialize}(x,\tau) = \vec{r}}$$

$$\textsf{Specialize}((\Sigma,s,p),\tau) = \textsf{prune}(\vec{r},p)$$
$$\text{where } \vec{r} = \mathcal{C}(s,\mathcal{R}((\Sigma,s,p),\tau))$$

Figure 7. NetCore refinement.

the predicate, the refinement oracle *underapproximates* it, so that the rest of the compilation infrastructure will be able to generate an effective switch-level rule that matches the given packet. Because the new predicate is the union of the old predicate and an underapproximation, the overall semantics is unchanged. In some cases, especially if the switch-supported patterns are weak, the best underapproximation the refinement oracle can generate is an exact-match predicate. In many other cases, however, if the switch supports prefix matching or wildcards, the refinement oracle will produce a predicate that matches many more packets.

The second rule refines switch predicates switch s. Because the switch predicate already reveals the maximum amount of information, it cannot be refined further.

The rule for inspectors is the most interesting. It uses a similarity predicate that describes the set of packets sent to the same switch that agree on a set of headers H:

$$\textsf{similar}(s,p,H) = \textsf{switch } s \cap \bigcap_{h \in H} (h : p(h)) .$$

We first refine the traffic filter predicate e to add additional structure for traffic collection. To ensure that the refined classifier has sufficiently fine-grained rules to collect the packets in the controller state examined by f, we form the union of the refined traffic filter and the similarity predicate $\textsf{similar}(s,p,H)$, restricted to the refined traffic filter. Next, we add additional information about the inspector's decision on the packet p to the policy. Recall that if f is invariant with respect to a snapshot x (which includes the controller state, switch, and packet) then it will return the same decision on all similar packets in the future. In the first case, if the inspector is invariant and evaluates to true on the current snapshot (Σ,s,p), then we refine it by taking the union of the inspector and the similarity predicate $\textsf{similar}(s,p,H')$. The second case is similar, except that the inspector does *not* evaluate to true, and hence we refine the inspector by subtracting the similarity predicate. Finally, in the third case, the inspector is not invariant so no sound refinement exists—the decision returned by the inspector may change in the future if the controller state changes. Hence, packets must continue being diverted to the controller until the inspector becomes invariant.

The rules for refining intersection $(e_1 \cap e_2)$ and negation $\neg e$ predicates and policies are all straightforward.

Pruning. In general, after a policy has been refined and recompiled, some of the new rules will be useless—they will not process additional packets on the switch. We prune away these useless rules using a function $\textsf{prune}(\vec{r},p)$ that removes rules from $\vec{r}$ that (1) send packets to the controller (adding such rules does not improve the efficiency of the switch), (2) have nothing to do with the packet p (meaning they are irrelevant to specialization with respect to p), or (3) overlap with a rule we removed earlier (to preserve the semantics of the rules).

Putting it all together. We define reactive specialization (the function Specialize at the bottom of Figure 7), by composing refinement, recompilation, and pruning to generate a specialized classifier from a snapshot x and policy τ.

Formal properties. We first establish that specialization, and therefore reactive rule generation, is sound.

Lemma 2 (Specialization Soundness). If $\vec{r}$ is sound on switch s with respect to τ and $\vec{r}' = \textsf{Specialize}((\Sigma,s,p),\tau)$, then $(\vec{r}',\vec{r})$ is sound on s with respect to τ.

To establish the other properties, we need a way of characterizing the packets that go to the controller. We define the *controller set* of a classifier $\vec{r}$ as follows:

$$\Omega(\vec{r}) = \{p \mid \vec{r} \rightsquigarrow^p \Omega\} .$$

The second property we establish is that refinement is *monotonic*. That is, if we append reactive rules to a switch's classifier, the resulting classifier does not send more packets to the controller that the original one. Formally,

Lemma 3 (Specialization Monotonicity). For all policies τ and classifiers $\vec{r}$ and $\vec{r}'$ such that $\vec{r}' = \textsf{Specialize}((\Sigma,s,p),\tau)$ we have $\Omega((\vec{r}',\vec{r})) \subseteq \Omega(\vec{r})$.

The final property we establish is that under certain assumptions, appending reactive rules to a classifier results in strictly fewer packets going to the controller. To make such a guarantee, we need two conditions: First, the policy τ must be *realizable*—intuitively, it must only use features that can be implemented on switches (*e.g.*, on an OpenFlow switch, the policy must not match on payloads).

Definition 2 (Realizable). A policy τ is *realizable* if, for every subterm $h : \vec{w}$ of τ and $p \in [\![h : w]\!]$, we have $(\Sigma,s,p) \in [\![\mathcal{U}(h : w,p)]\!]$ if and only if $p \sqsubseteq \mathcal{O}(\mathcal{U}(h : w,p))$.

Realizability states that compiling an underapproximation of a high-level predicate with respect to a packet matching the predicate yields a switch-level rule that exactly corresponds to the predicate. Second, all inspectors in the policy must be determinate. We formalize this by extending the notion of invariance to *full invariance*:

Definition 3 (Fully Invariant). A policy τ is *fully invariant* on Σ if for every subterm of τ of the form inspect e f and we have invariant$((\Sigma,s,p),f)$ for all switches s and packets p.

For policies satisfying these conditions, we can guarantee that the packet used to refine and recompile the policy will never be sent to the controller again.

Lemma 4 (Specialization Progress)**.** If τ is realizable and fully invariant on Σ, and $\vec{r}' = \mathsf{Specialize}((\Sigma, s, p), \tau)$, then for any classifier $\vec{r}$, we have $p \notin \Omega((\vec{r}', \vec{r}))$.

6. System-wide Correctness Properties

This section uses the tools developed in the previous section to deliver our two central theoretical results: (1) a proof of *functional correctness* for NetCore, and (2) a proof of *quiescence*, another fundamental theorem which establishes that, when inspectors are invariant, the network eventually reaches a state in which all processing occurs efficiently on its switches.

Functional correctness. Recall in Section 3 we defined two idealized reference machines: the synchronous reference machine, which at all times knows (and has recorded) information about every packet processed in the network, and the asynchronous reference machine, which nondeterministically learns about packets processed in the network. To demonstrate the correctness of the NetCore compiler, we show that it inhabits the space between the asynchronous and synchronous reference machines. More formally, we prove that the asynchronous reference machine simulates the NetCore molecular machine and the molecular machine simulates the synchronous reference machine.

Given a set of switches S and a policy τ, we initialize the molecular machine as follows:

$$\mathsf{Init}(S, \tau) = \{\!|\, \mathbb{C}\,(\tau \mid \varnothing) \,|\!\} \uplus \{\!|\, \mathbb{S}\,(s \mid \mathcal{C}\,(s, \tau) \mid \varnothing) \mid s \in S \,|\!\} \,.$$

The next theorem establishes the relationship between the reference and molecular machines.

Theorem 1 (Functional Correctness)**.** Given a set of switches S, an initial set of transmissions T such that $\mathbb{T}\,(s \mid p) \in T$ implies $s \in S$, and a molecular machine $M = \mathsf{Init}(S, \tau) \uplus T$, we have:

- The asynchronous machine $(\tau, \varnothing, T, \varnothing)$ weakly simulates M.
- M weakly simulates the synchronous machine $(\tau, \varnothing, T)$.

Proof sketch. We describe the first simulation only; the second is similar. The simulation relation between the asynchronous machine and the molecular machine satisfies the following: (1) each switch's classifier on the molecular machine is sound with respect to τ, (2) there exists an observation-preserving bijection between pending transmissions in the asynchronous machine and transmissions and help molecules in the molecular machine, and (3) there exists an observation–preserving bijection between the processed transmissions in the asynchronous machine and the switch states in the molecular machine. The initial state satisfies these criteria by classifier generation soundness. Now, consider taking a transition. If it forwards a packet, the first bijection is preserved by routing correctness; if it collects a pattern, the second bijection is preserved by collection soundness; finally, if it generates reactive rules, they are sound by specialization soundness. □

Quiescence. The quiescence theorem demonstrates that the NetCore compiler effectively moves work off of the controller and onto switches, even when the program is expressed in terms of patterns the switch cannot implement precisely and inspector functions the compiler cannot analyze. Formally, quiescence states that if all of the inspectors in the program are invariant, then the NetCore compiler will eventually install rules on switches that handle all future traffic—*i.e.*, eventually, the system can reach a configuration where no additional packets need to be sent to the controller.

Before we can state the quiescence theorem precisely, we need a few definitions and supporting lemmas. First, we say that M is derived from policy τ if $(\mathsf{Init}(S, \tau) \uplus T) \rightarrow^* M$, where $\rightarrow^*$ is the reflexive, transitive closure of the single step judgement, ignoring observations. Second, we lift the notion of full invariance to machines M; M is fully invariant if the controller's policy is fully invariant with respect to the controller's state. We also lift the notion of *controller set* on classifiers to machines M:

$$\Omega(M) = \{(s, p) \mid \mathbb{S}\,(s \mid \vec{r} \mid Z) \in M \text{ and } p \in \Omega(\vec{r})\} \,.$$

The first lemma, *controller set monotonicity*, states that the set of packets that require processing on the controller never increases:

Lemma 5 (Controller Set Monotonicity)**.** If M is derived from τ and $M \xrightarrow{o} M'$, then $\Omega(M') \subseteq \Omega(M)$.

Proof. Follows from specialization monotonicity. □

Now we are ready to prove the key lemma needed for quiescence. The *controller set progress* lemma states that if the controller program is realizable and has become fully invariant, then every time the controller processes a help molecule, the controller set becomes strictly smaller. In other words, every help molecule contains enough information (and the compiler is powerful enough to exploit it) for the E-CONTROLLER rule to generate useful new classifier rules.

Lemma 6 (Controller Set Progress)**.** For every realizable policy τ and fully invariant M derived from τ, if $M \xrightarrow{o} M'$ is an instance of E-CONTROLLER then $\Omega(M') \subset \Omega(M)$.

Proof. Follows from specialization progress. □

Quiescence follows from these lemmas, as the total number of possible packets is finite. The precise statement of quiescence says that the run-time system *may* (as opposed to *does*) quiesce, because the machine may non-deterministically choose to continue forwarding packets using the switches instead of processing the remaining help molecules. Formally, a machine configuration M *may quiesce* if there exists a configuration M' such that $M \rightarrow^* M'$ and the rule E-CONTROLLER is not used in any derivation in the operational semantics starting from M'. With this definition in hand, we can state quiescence.

Theorem 2 (Quiescence)**.** For every realizable policy τ and fully invariant M derived from τ, we have that M may quiesce.

7. Implementation and Evaluation

We have implemented a prototype NetCore compiler in Haskell using the ideas presented in this paper. The core algorithms are formulated in terms of abstract type classes (*e.g.*, lattices for switch patterns) and oracles. This makes it easy to instantiate the compiler for different switch architectures—one simply has to define instances for a few type classes and provide the appropriate oracles. We have built two back-ends, both targeting OpenFlow switches. The first generates coarse-grained wildcard rules. The other back-end, used for comparison, generates the kind of exact-match rules used in our earlier work on Frenetic [9] and most hand-written NOX applications [11].

Optimizations. The implementation uses a number of heuristic optimizations to avoid the combinatorial blowup that would result from compiling classifiers naively. For example, it applies algebraic rewritings on-the-fly to remove useless patterns and rules and reduce the size of the intermediate patterns and classifiers it needs to manipulate. The compilation algorithms identify and remove patterns completely "shadowed" by other patterns and patterns whose

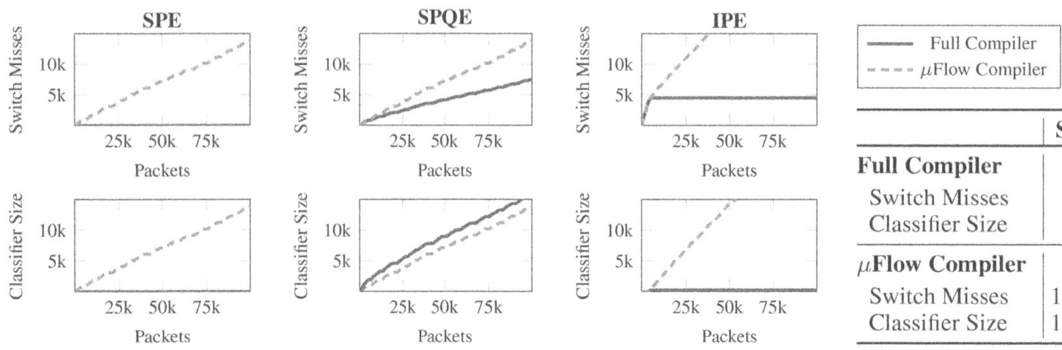

	SPE	SPQE	IPE
Full Compiler			
Switch Misses	0	7.5k	4.5k
Classifier Size	8	15.9k	0.3k
μFlow Compiler			
Switch Misses	13.7k	13.7k	33.4k
Classifier Size	13.7k	13.7k	29.2k

Figure 8. Experimental results.

effect is "covered" by a larger pattern with lower priority but the same actions. Although these heuristics are simple, they go a long way toward ensuring reasonable performance in our experience.

Evaluation. To evaluate our implementation, we built an instrumented version of the run-time system that collects statistics about the sizes of the classifiers generated by the compiler and the amount of traffic handled on switches (as opposed to the controller). Because space for classifiers is a limited resource on switches, and because the cost of diverting a packet to the controller slows down its processing by orders of magnitude, these metrics quantify some of the most critical performance aspects of the system.

We compared the performance of the "full" (which makes use of all OpenFlow rules, including wildcards) and "μflow" (which only generates exact-match rules, also known as *micro*flow rules) compilers on the following programs:

- **Static Policy Experiment (SPE)**: implements the simple static policy described at the beginning of Section 2. This benchmark measures the (in)efficiency of compilation strategies based on generating exact-match rules.
- **Static Policy with Query Experiment (SPQE)**: forwards packets using the same policy as in SPE but also collects traffic statistics for each host. Due to this collection, this program cannot be directly compiled to a switch classifier—at least, not without expanding all 4.3 billion possible hosts! Thus, this benchmark measures the efficiency of reactive specialization.
- **Inspector Policy Experiment (IPE)**: forwards packets and collects traffic statistics using the authentication application presented in Section 2. This benchmark measures the performance of a more realistic application implemented using inspectors.

To drive these experiments, we generated packets using *fs* [22], a tool that synthesizes realistic packet traces from several statistical parameters. We ran each experiment on 100K packets in total. For the SPE and SPQE benchmarks, we generated traffic with 1024 active hosts sending packets to an external network for 30 seconds each. For the IPE benchmark, we generated traffic with 254 hosts (a class C network) sending traffic to the authentication server and an external network for 30 seconds each. The results of the experiments are shown in Figure 8. The graphs on the top row show the number of packets that "missed" and had to be sent to the controller against the total number of packets processed. Likewise, the graphs on the bottom row show the size of the compiled classifier, in terms of number of rules, versus total packets. The table at the right gives the final results after all 100K packets were processed.

In terms of the proportion of packets processed on switches, the full OpenFlow compiler outperforms the microflow-based compiler on nearly all of the benchmarks. On the SPE benchmark, the full compiler generates a classifier that completely handles the policy, so no packets are sent to the controller. (The line for the full compiler overlaps with the x-axis.) The microflow compiler, of course, diverts a packet to the controller for each distinct microflow, generating 13.7k rules in total. On the SPQE benchmark, the full compiler generates wildcard rules (using reactive specialization) that handle all future traffic from each unique host after seeing a packet from it. These rules handle many more packets than the exact-match rule produced by the microflow compiler. On this benchmark, it is worth noting that the classifiers produced by the full compiler are larger than the ones produced by the microflow compiler, especially initially. This is due to the fact that the full compiler generates multiple rules in response to a single controller packet, attempting to cover a broad space of future similar packets, whereas the microflow compiler predictably generates a single microflow for each controller packet. One can see that the work done by the full compiler pays off in terms of the number of packets that must be diverted to the controller. Moreover, over time, the size of the microflow compiler-generated classifier approaches that of the full compiler. Lastly, the IPE benchmark demonstrates that the full compiler generates more effective classifiers than the microflow compiler, even in the presence of inspector functions that it cannot analyze directly. Note that a large number of packets must be diverted to the controller in any correct implementation—until they authenticate, the inspector is not invariant for any host. However, the full compiler quickly converges to a classifier that processes all traffic directly on the switch.

8. Related Work

Building on ideas first proposed in Ethane [4] and 4D [10], NOX [11] was the first concrete system to popularize what is currently known as software-defined networking. It provides an event-driven interface to OpenFlow [17] and requires that programmers write reactive programs using callbacks and explicit, switch-level packet-processing rules. There are numerous examples of network applications built on top of NOX using microflows [12, 13, 27], but relatively few that use wildcard rules (though Wang's load balancer [26] is a nice example of the latter).

Networking researchers are now actively developing next-generation controller platforms. Some of them, such as Beacon [1] (designed for Java) and Nettle [25] (designed for Haskell) provide elegant OpenFlow interfaces for new programming languages. Others, such as Onix [15], and Maestro [3] improve scalability and fault tolerance through parallelization and distribution. None of these systems automatically generate reactive protocols or provide formal semantics or correctness guarantees like NetCore does.

Both NetCore and NDLog [16] use high-level languages to program networking infrastructure, but the similarities end there. NDLog programs are written in an explicitly distributed style whereas high-level NetCore programs are written as if the program has an omniscient, centralized view of the entire network. The NetCore implementation automatically partitions work onto a distributed set of switches and synthesizes a reactive communication protocol that simulates the semantics of the high-level language.

Part of the job of the NetCore compiler is to generate efficient packet classifiers. Most previous research in this area (see Taylor [24] for a survey) focuses on static compilation. The NetCore compiler generates classifiers in the face of non-static policies, with unknown inspector functions, and synthesizes a distributed switch-controller implementation. Bro [21], Snortran [7], Shangri-La [5] and FPL-3E [6] compile rich packet-filtering and monitoring programs, designed to secure networks and detect intrusions, down to special packet-processing hardware and FPGAs. The main difference between NetCore and all of these systems is that they are limited to a single device. They do not address the issue of how to program complex, dynamic policies for a collection of interconnected switches and they do not synthesize the distributed communication patterns between the switches and controller.

Active Networking, as in the SwitchWare project [23], shares many high-level goals with Software-Defined Networking, but the implementation strategy is entirely different. The former uses smart switches to interpret programs encapsulated in packets, while the latter uses dumb switches controlled by a remote host.

Acknowledgments

We wish to thank Ken Birman, Mike Freedman, Sharad Malik, Jen Rexford, Cole Schlesinger, and Alec Story and the anonymous POPL reviewers for discussions about this research and comments on drafts of this paper. Our work is supported in part by ONR grants N00014-09-1-0770 and N00014-09-1-0652 and NSF grants CNS-1111698 and CNS-1111520. Any opinions, findings, and recommendations are those of the authors and do not necessarily reflect the views of the ONR or NSF.

References

[1] Beacon: A java-based OpenFlow control platform., Nov 2010. See `http://www.beaconcontroller.net`.

[2] G. Berry and G. Boudol. The chemical abstract machine. In *POPL*, pages 81–94, 1990.

[3] Z. Cai, A. Cox, and T. Ng. Maestro: A system for scalable OpenFlow control. Technical Report TR10-08, Rice University, Dec 2010.

[4] M. Casado, M. Freedman, J. Pettit, J. Luo, N. Gude, N. McKeown, and S. Shenker. Rethinking enterprise network control. *Trans. on Networking.*, 17(4), Aug 2009.

[5] M. Chen, X. Li, R. Lian, J. Lin, L. Liu, T. Liu, and R. Ju. Shangri-la: Achieving high performance from compiled network applications while enabling ease of programming. In *PLDI*, Jun 2005.

[6] M. Cristea, C. Zissulescu, E. Deprettere, and H. Bos. FPL-3E: Towards language support for reconfigurable packet processing. In *SAMOS*, pages 201–212, Jul 2005.

[7] S. Egorov and G. Savchuk. *SNORTRAN: An Optimizing Compiler for Snort Rules*. Fidelis Security Systems, 2002.

[8] D. Erickson et al. A demonstration of virtual machine mobility in an OpenFlow network, Aug 2008. Demo at *ACM SIGCOMM*.

[9] N. Foster, R. Harrison, M. Freedman, C. Monsanto, J. Rexford, A. Story, and D. Walker. Frenetic: A network programming language. In *ICFP*, Sep 2011.

[10] A. Greenberg, G. Hjalmtysson, D. Maltz, A. Myers, J. Rexford, G. Xie, H. Yan, J. Zhan, and H. Zhang. A clean slate 4D approach to network control and management. *SIGCOMM CCR*, 35:41–54, October 2005.

[11] N. Gude, T. Koponen, J. Pettit, B. Pfaff, M. Casado, N. McKeown, and S. Shenker. NOX: Towards an operating system for networks. *SIGCOMM CCR*, 38(3), 2008.

[12] N. Handigol, S. Seetharaman, M. Flajslik, N. McKeown, and R. Johari. Plug-n-Serve: Load-balancing web traffic using OpenFlow, Aug 2009. Demo at *ACM SIGCOMM*.

[13] B. Heller, S. Seetharaman, P. Mahadevan, Y. Yiakoumis, P. Sharma, S. Banerjee, and N. McKeown. ElasticTree: Saving energy in data center networks. In *NSDI*, Apr 2010.

[14] L. Jose, M. Yu, and J. Rexford. Online measurement of large traffic aggregates on commodity switches. In *Hot-ICE*, Mar 2011.

[15] T. Koponen, M. Casado, N. Gude, J. Stribling, L. Poutievski, M. Zhu, R. Ramanathan, Y. Iwata, H. Inoue, T. Hama, and S. Shenker. Onix: A distributed control platform for large-scale production networks. In *OSDI*, Oct 2010.

[16] B. Loo, J. Hellerstein, I. Stoica, and R. Ramakrishnan. Declarative routing: Extensible routing with declarative queries. In *SIGCOMM*, pages 289–300, 2005.

[17] N. McKeown, T. Anderson, H. Balakrishnan, G. Parulkar, L. Peterson, J. Rexford, S. Shenker, and J. Turner. Openflow: Enabling innovation in campus networks. *SIGCOMM CCR*, 38(2):69–74, 2008.

[18] A. Nayak, A. Reimers, N. Feamster, and R. Clark. Resonance: Dynamic access control in enterprise networks. In *WREN*, Aug 2009.

[19] The Open Networking Foundation, Mar 2011. See `http://www.opennetworkingfoundation.org/`.

[20] OpenFlow, Nov 2010. See `http://www.openflowswitch.org`.

[21] Vern Paxson. Bro: A system for detecting network intruders in real-time. *Computer Networks*, 31(23–24):2435–2463, Dec 1999.

[22] J. Sommers, R. Bowden, B. Eriksson, P. Barford, M. Roughan, and N. Duffield. Efficient network-wide flow record generation. In *INFOCOM*, pages 2363–2371, 2011.

[23] SwitchWare. `http://www.cis.upenn.edu/~switchware`, 1997.

[24] D. Taylor. Survey and taxonomy of packet classification techniques. *ACM Comput. Surv.*, 37:238–275, September 2005.

[25] A. Voellmy and P. Hudak. Nettle: Functional reactive programming of OpenFlow networks. In *PADL*, Jan 2011.

[26] R. Wang, D. Butnariu, and J. Rexford. OpenFlow-based server load balancing gone wild. In *Hot-ICE*, Mar 2011.

[27] K. Yap, M. Kobayashi, R. Sherwood, T. Huang, M. Chan, N. Handigol, and N. McKeown. OpenRoads: Empowering research in mobile networks. *SIGCOMM CCR*, 40(1):125–126, 2010.

Nested Refinements: A Logic for Duck Typing *

Ravi Chugh Patrick M. Rondon Ranjit Jhala
University of California, San Diego
{rchugh, prondon, jhala}@cs.ucsd.edu

Abstract

Programs written in dynamic languages make heavy use of features — run-time type tests, value-indexed dictionaries, polymorphism, and higher-order functions — that are beyond the reach of type systems that employ either purely syntactic or purely semantic reasoning. We present a core calculus, System D, that merges these two modes of reasoning into a single powerful mechanism of *nested refinement types* wherein the typing relation is itself a predicate in the refinement logic. System D coordinates SMT-based logical implication and syntactic subtyping to automatically typecheck sophisticated dynamic language programs. By coupling nested refinements with McCarthy's theory of finite maps, System D can precisely reason about the interaction of higher-order functions, polymorphism, and dictionaries. The addition of type predicates to the refinement logic creates a circularity that leads to unique technical challenges in the metatheory, which we solve with a novel stratification approach that we use to prove the soundness of System D.

Categories and Subject Descriptors F.3.1 [*Logics and Meanings of Programs*]: Specifying and Verifying and Reasoning about Programs – Logics of Programs

General Terms Languages, Verification

Keywords Refinement Types, Dynamic Languages

1. Introduction

So-called dynamic languages like JavaScript, Python, Racket, and Ruby are popular as they allow developers to quickly put together scripts without having to appease a static type system. However, these scripts quickly grow into substantial code bases that would be much easier to maintain, refactor, evolve and compile, if only they could be corralled within a suitable static type system.

The convenience of dynamic languages comes from their support of features like run-time type testing, value-indexed finite maps (*i.e.* dictionaries), and duck typing, a form of polymorphism where functions operate over any dictionary with the appropriate keys. As the empirical study in [18] shows, programs written in dynamic languages make heavy use of these features, and their safety relies on invariants which can only be established by sophisticated reasoning about the flow of control, the run-time types of values, and the contents of data structures like dictionaries.

The following code snippet, adapted from the popular Dojo Javascript framework [36], illustrates common dynamic features:

```
let onto callbacks f obj =
  if f = null then
    new List(obj, callbacks)
  else
    let cb = if tag f = "Str" then obj[f] else f in
    new List(fun () -> cb obj, callbacks)
```

The function `onto` is used to register callback functions to be called after the DOM and required library modules have finished loading. The author of `onto` went to great pains to make it extremely flexible in the kinds of arguments it takes. If the `obj` parameter is provided but `f` is not, then `obj` is the function to be called after loading. Otherwise, both `f` and `obj` are provided, and either: (a) `f` is a string, `obj` is a dictionary, and the (function) value corresponding to key `f` in `obj` is called with `obj` as a parameter after loading; or (b) `f` is a function which is called with `obj` as a parameter after loading. To verify the safety of this program, and dynamic code in general, a type system must reason about dynamic type tests, control flow, higher-order functions, and heterogeneous, value-indexed dictionaries.

Current automatic type systems are not expressive enough to support the full spectrum of reasoning required for dynamic languages.[1] *Syntactic* systems use advanced type-theoretic constructs like structural types [3], row types [38], intersection types [17], and union types [18, 39] to track invariants of individual values. Unfortunately, such techniques cannot reason about value-dependent relationships *between* program variables, as is required, for example, to determine the specific types of the variables `f` and `obj` in `onto`. *Semantic* systems like [4, 6, 14, 23, 31, 35] support such reasoning by using logical predicates to describe invariants over program variables. Unfortunately, such systems require a clear (syntactic) distinction between *complex* values that are typed with arrows, type variables, *etc.*, and *base* values that are typed with predicates. Hence, they cannot support the interaction of complex values and value-indexed dictionaries that is ubiquitous in dynamic code, for example in `onto`, which can take as a parameter a dictionary containing a function value.

Our Approach. We present System D, a core calculus that supports fully automatic checking of dynamic idioms. In System D *all* values are described uniformly by formulas drawn from a decidable, quantifier-free refinement logic. Our first key insight is that to reason precisely about complex values (*e.g.* higher-order functions) nested deeply inside structures (*e.g.* dictionaries), we require

* This work was supported by NSF Grants CCF-0644361, CNS-0964702, and generous gifts from Microsoft Research.

[1] Full dependent type systems like Coq [5] can support the necessary reasoning, but are not automatic as the programmer must provide explicit proofs to discharge type checking obligations.

a single new mechanism called *nested refinements* wherein syntactic types (resp. the typing relation) may be nested as special *type terms* (resp. *type predicates*) inside the refinement logic. Formally, the refinement logic is extended with atomic formulas of the form $x :: U$ where U is a type term, "::" (read "has type") is a binary, *uninterpreted* predicate in the refinement logic, and where the formula states that the value x "has the type" described by the term U. This unifying insight allows to us to express the invariants in idiomatic dynamic code like `onto` — including the interaction between higher-order functions and dictionaries — while staying within the boundaries of decidability.

Expressiveness. The nested refinement logic underlying System D can express complex invariants between base values and richer values. For example, we may disjoin two tag-equality predicates

$$\{\nu \mid tag(\nu) = \text{"}\mathtt{Int}\text{"} \vee tag(\nu) = \text{"}\mathtt{Str}\text{"}\}$$

to type a value ν that is either an integer or a string; we can then track control flow involving the dynamic type tag-lookup function `tag` to ensure that the value is safely used at either more specific type. To describe values like the argument `f` of the `onto` function we can combine tag-equality predicates with the type predicate. We can give `f` the type

$$\{\nu \mid \nu = \mathtt{null} \vee tag(\nu) = \text{"}\mathtt{Str}\text{"} \vee \nu :: Top \rightarrow Top\}$$

where Top is an abbreviation for $\{\nu \mid true\}$, which is a type that describes all values. Notice the uniformity — the types *nested* within this refinement formula are themselves refinement types.

Our second key insight is that dictionaries are finite maps, and so we can precisely type dictionaries with refinement formulas drawn from the (decidable) theory of finite maps [25]. In particular, McCarthy's two operators — $sel(x, a)$, which corresponds to the contents of the map x at the address a, and $upd(x, a, v)$, which corresponds to the new map obtained by updating x at the address a with the value v — are precisely what we need to describe reads from and updates to dictionaries. For example, we can write

$$\{\nu \mid tag(\nu) = \text{"}\mathtt{Dict}\text{"} \wedge tag(sel(\nu, \mathtt{y})) = \text{"}\mathtt{Int}\text{"}\}$$

to type dictionaries ν that have (at least) an integer field `y`, where `y` is a program variable that dynamically stores the key with which to index the dictionary. Even better, since we have nested function types into the refinement logic, we can precisely specify, for the first time, combinations of dictionaries and functions. For example, we can write the following type for `obj`

$$\{\nu \mid tag(\mathtt{f}) = \text{"}\mathtt{Str}\text{"} \Rightarrow sel(\nu, \mathtt{f}) :: Top \rightarrow Top\}$$

to describe the second portion of the `onto` specification, all while staying within a decidable refinement logic. In a similar manner, we show how nested refinements support polymorphism, datatypes, and even a form of bounded quantification.

Subtyping. The huge leap in expressiveness yielded by nesting types inside refinements is accompanied by some unique technical challenges. The first challenge is that because we nest complex types (*e.g.* arrows) as uninterpreted terms in the logic, subtyping (*e.g.* between arrows) cannot be carried out solely via the usual syntactic decomposition into SMT queries [6, 16, 31]. (A higher-order logic (*e.g.* [5]) would solve this problem, but that would preclude algorithmic checking; we choose the uninterpreted route precisely to relieve the SMT solver of higher-order reasoning!) We surmount this challenge with a novel decomposition mechanism where subtyping between types, syntactic type terms, and refinement formulas are defined *inter-dependently*, thereby using the logical structure of the refinement formulas to divide the labor of subtyping between the SMT solver for ground predicates (*e.g.* equality, uninterpreted functions, arithmetic, maps, *etc.*) and classical syntactic rules for type terms (*e.g.* arrows, type variables, datatypes).

Soundness. The second challenge is that the inter-dependency between the refinement logic and the type system renders the standard proof techniques for (refinement) type soundness inapplicable. In particular, we illustrate how uninterpreted type predicates break the usual substitution property and how nesting makes it difficult to define a type system that is well-defined and enjoys this property. We meet this challenge with a new proof technique: we define an infinite family of *increasingly precise* systems and prove soundness of the family, of which System D is a member, thus establishing the soundness of System D.

Contributions. To sum up, we make the following contributions:

- We show how nested refinements over the theory of finite maps encode function, polymorphic, dictionary and constructed data types within refinements and permit dependent structural subtyping and a form of bounded quantification.
- We develop a novel algorithmic subtyping mechanism that uses the structure of the refinement formulas to decompose subtyping into a collection of SMT and syntactic checks.
- We illustrate the technical challenges that nesting poses to the metatheory of System D and present a novel stratification-based proof technique to establish soundness.
- We define an algorithmic version of the type system with local type inference that we implement in a prototype checker.

Thus, by carefully orchestrating the interplay between syntactic- and SMT-based subtyping, the nested refinement types of System D enable, for the first time, the automatic static checking of features found in idiomatic dynamic code.

2. Overview

We start with a series of examples that give an overview of our approach. First, we show how by encoding types using logical refinements, System D can reason about control flow and relationships between program variables. Next, we demonstrate how nested refinements enable precise reasoning about values of complex types. After that, we illustrate how System D uses refinements over the theory of finite maps to analyze value-indexed dictionaries. We conclude by showing how these features combine to analyze the sophisticated invariants in idiomatic dynamic code.

Notation. We use the following abbreviations for brevity.

$$\begin{aligned}
Top(x) &\doteq true \\
Int(x) &\doteq tag(x) = \text{"}\mathtt{Int}\text{"} \\
Bool(x) &\doteq tag(x) = \text{"}\mathtt{Bool}\text{"} \\
Str(x) &\doteq tag(x) = \text{"}\mathtt{Str}\text{"} \\
Dict(x) &\doteq tag(x) = \text{"}\mathtt{Dict}\text{"} \\
IorB(x) &\doteq Int(x) \vee Bool(x)
\end{aligned}$$

We abuse notation to use the above as abbreviations for refinement types; for each of the unary abbreviations T defined above, an occurrence *without* the parameter denotes the refinement type $\{\nu \mid T(\nu)\}$. For example, we write Int as an abbreviation for $\{\nu \mid tag(\nu) = \text{"}\mathtt{Int}\text{"}\}$. Recall that function values are also described by refinement formulas (containing type predicates). We often write arrows outside refinements to abbreviate the following:

$$x{:}T_1 \rightarrow T_2 \quad \doteq \quad \{\nu \mid \nu :: x{:}T_1 \rightarrow T_2\}$$

We write $T_1 \rightarrow T_2$ when the return type T_2 does not refer to x.

2.1 Simple Refinements

To warm up, we show how System D describes all types through refinement formulas, and how, by using an SMT solver to discharge the subtyping (implication) queries, System D makes short work of value- and control flow-sensitive reasoning [18, 39].

Ad-Hoc Unions. Our first example illustrates the simplest dynamic idiom: programs which operate on *ad-hoc* unions. The function `negate` takes an integer or boolean and returns its negation:

```
let negate x =
  if tag x = "Int" then 0 - x else not x
```

In System D we can ascribe to this function the type

$$\texttt{negate} :: \mathit{IorB} \to \mathit{IorB}$$

which states that the function accepts an integer or boolean argument and returns either an integer or boolean result.

To establish this, System D uses the standard means of reasoning about control flow in refinement-based systems [31], namely strengthening the environment with the guard predicate when processing the then-branch of an if-expression and the negation of the guard predicate for the else-branch. Thus, in the then-branch, the environment contains the assumption that $tag(\texttt{x}) = \text{``}\texttt{Int}\text{''}$, which allows System D to verify that the expression $0 - \texttt{x}$ is well-typed. The return value has the type $\{\nu \mid tag(\nu) = \text{``}\texttt{Int}\text{''} \wedge \nu = 0 - \texttt{x}\}$. This type is a subtype of IorB as the SMT solver can prove that $tag(\nu) = \text{``}\texttt{Int}\text{''}$ and $\nu = 0 - \texttt{x}$ implies $tag(\nu) = \text{``}\texttt{Int}\text{''} \vee tag(\nu) = \text{``}\texttt{Bool}\text{''}$. Thus, the return value of the then-branch is deduced to have type IorB.

On the other hand, in the else-branch, the environment contains the assumption $\neg(tag(\texttt{x}) = \text{``}\texttt{Int}\text{''})$. By combining this with the assumption about the type of `negate`'s input, $tag(\texttt{x}) = \text{``}\texttt{Int}\text{''} \vee tag(\texttt{x}) = \text{``}\texttt{Bool}\text{''}$, the SMT solver can determine that $tag(\texttt{x}) = \text{``}\texttt{Bool}\text{''}$. This allows our system to type check the call to

$$\texttt{not} :: \mathit{Bool} \to \mathit{Bool},$$

which establishes that the value returned in the else branch has type IorB. Thus, our system determines that both branches return a value of type IorB, and thus that `negate` meets its specification.

Dependent Unions. System D's use of refinements and SMT solvers enable expressive *relational* specifications that go beyond previous techniques [18, 39]. While `negate` takes and returns ad-hoc unions, there is a relationship between its input and output: the output is an integer (resp. boolean) iff the input is an integer (resp. boolean). We represent this in System D as

$$\texttt{negate} :: x{:}\mathit{IorB} \to \{\nu \mid tag(\nu) = tag(x)\}$$

That is, the refinement for the output states that its tag is *the same as* the tag of the input. This function is checked through exactly the same analysis as before; the tag test ensures that the environment in the then- (resp. else-) branch implies that `x` and the returned value are both *Int* (resp. *Bool*). That is, in both cases, the output value has the same tag as the input.

2.2 Nested Refinements

So far, we have seen how old-fashioned refinement types (where the predicates refine base values [6, 23, 27, 31]) can be used to check ad-hoc unions over base values. However, a type system for dynamic languages must be able to express invariants about values of base and function types with equal ease. We accomplish this in System D by adding types (resp. the typing relation) to the refinement logic as nested *type terms* (resp. *type predicates*).

However, nesting raises a rather tricky problem: with the typing relation included in the refinement logic, subtyping can no longer be carried out entirely via SMT implication queries [6]. We solve this problem with a new subtyping rule that *extracts* type terms from refinements to enable syntactic subtyping for nested types.

Consider the function `maybeApply` which takes an integer `x` and a value `f` which is either `null` or a function over integers:

```
let maybeApply x f =
  if f = null then x else f x
```

In System D, we can use a refinement formula that combines a base predicate and a type predicate to assign `maybeApply` the type

$$\texttt{maybeApply} :: \mathit{Int} \to \{\nu \mid \nu = \texttt{null} \vee \nu :: \mathit{Int}{\to}\mathit{Int}\} \to \mathit{Int}$$

Note that we have *nested* a function type as a term in the refinement logic, along with an assertion that a value has this particular function type. However, to keep checking algorithmic, we use a simple first-order logic in which type terms and predicates are completely *uninterpreted*; that is, the types can be thought of as constant terms in the logic. Therefore, we need new machinery to check that `maybeApply` actually enjoys the above type, *i.e.* to check that (a) `f` is indeed a function when it is applied, (b) it can accept the input `x`, and (c) it will return an integer.

Type Extraction. To accomplish the above goals, we *extract* the nested function type for `f` stored in the type environment as follows. Let Γ be the type environment at the callsite `(f x)`. For each type term U occurring in Γ, we query the SMT solver to determine whether $[\![\Gamma]\!] \Rightarrow \texttt{f} :: U$ holds, where $[\![\Gamma]\!]$ is the embedding of Γ into the refinement logic where type terms and predicates are treated in a purely uninterpreted way. If so, we say that U *must flow to* (or just, flows to) the caller expression `f`. Once we have found the type terms that flow to the caller expression, we map the uninterpreted type terms to their corresponding type definitions to check the call.

Let us see how this works for `maybeApply`. The then-branch is trivial: the assumption that `x` is an integer in the environment allows us to deduce that the expression `x` is well-typed and has type *Int*. Next, consider the else-branch. Let U_1 be the type term $\mathit{Int} \to \mathit{Int}$. Due to the bindings for `x` and `f` and the else-condition, the environment Γ is embedded as

$$[\![\Gamma]\!] \doteq tag(\texttt{x}) = \text{``}\texttt{Int}\text{''} \wedge (\texttt{f} = \texttt{null} \vee \texttt{f} :: U_1) \wedge \neg(\texttt{f} = \texttt{null})$$

Hence, the SMT solver is able to prove that $\Gamma \Rightarrow \texttt{f} :: U_1$. This establishes that `f` is a function on integers and, since `x` is known to be an integer, we can verify that the else-branch has type *Int* and hence check that `maybeApply` meets its specification.

Nested Subtyping. Next, consider a client of `maybeApply`:

```
let _ = maybeApply 42 negate
```

At the call to `maybeApply` we must show that the actuals are subtypes of the formals, *i.e.* that the two subtyping relationships

$$\Gamma_1 \vdash \{\nu \mid \nu = 42\} \sqsubseteq \mathit{Int}$$
$$\Gamma_1 \vdash \{\nu \mid \nu = \texttt{negate}\} \sqsubseteq \{\nu \mid \nu = \texttt{null} \vee \nu :: U_1\} \qquad (1)$$

hold, where $\Gamma_1 \doteq \texttt{negate}{:}\{\nu \mid \nu :: U_0\}, \texttt{maybeApply}{:}\cdots$ and $U_0 = x{:}\mathit{IorB} \to \{\nu \mid tag(\nu) = tag(x)\}$. Alas, while the SMT solver can make short work of the first obligation, it cannot be used to discharge the second via implication; the "real" types that must be checked for subsumption, namely, U_0 and U_1, are embedded as totally unrelated terms in the refinement logic!

Once again, extraction rides to the rescue. We show that all subtyping checks of the form $\Gamma \vdash \{\nu \mid p\} \sqsubseteq \{\nu \mid q\}$ can be reduced to a finite number of sub-goals of the form:

$$(\text{``type predicate-free''}) \quad [\![\Gamma']\!] \Rightarrow p'$$
$$\text{or } (\text{``type predicate''}) \quad [\![\Gamma']\!] \Rightarrow x :: U$$

The former kind of goal has no type predicates and can be directly discharged via SMT. For the latter, we use extraction to find the finitely many type terms U_i that *flow to* x. (If there are none, the check fails.) For each U_i we use *syntactic* subtyping to verify that the corresponding type is subsumed by (the type corresponding to) U under Γ'.

In our example, the goal 1 reduces to proving either

$$[\![\Gamma_1']\!] \Rightarrow \nu = \texttt{null} \quad \text{or} \quad [\![\Gamma_1']\!] \Rightarrow \nu :: U_1$$

where $\Gamma_1' \doteq \Gamma_1, \nu = \texttt{negate}$. The former implication contains no type predicates, so we attempt to prove it by querying the SMT solver. The solver tells us that the query is not valid, so we turn to the latter implication. The extraction procedure uses the SMT solver to deduce that, under Γ_1' the type term U_0 flows into ν. Thus, all that remains is to retrieve the definition of U_0 and U_1 and check

$$\Gamma_1' \vdash x{:}\mathit{IorB} \rightarrow \{\nu \mid \mathit{tag}(\nu) = \mathit{tag}(x)\} \sqsubseteq \mathit{Int} \rightarrow \mathit{Int}$$

which follows via standard syntactic refinement subtyping [16], thereby checking the client's call. Thus, by carefully interleaving SMT implication and syntactic subtyping, System D enables, for the first time, the nesting of rich types *within* refinements.

2.3 Dictionaries

Next, we show how nested refinements allow System D to precisely check programs that manipulate dynamic dictionaries. In essence, we demonstrate how structural subtyping can be done via nested refinement formulas over the theory of finite maps [13, 25]. We introduce two abbreviations for dictionaries.

$$\mathit{Fld}(x, y, \mathit{Int}) \doteq \mathit{Dict}(x) \wedge \mathit{Str}(y) \wedge \mathit{Int}(\mathit{sel}(x, y))$$
$$\mathit{Fld}(x, y, U) \doteq \mathit{Dict}(x) \wedge \mathit{Str}(y) \wedge \mathit{sel}(x, y) :: U$$

The second abbreviation states that the type of a field is a syntactic type term U (*e.g.* an arrow).

Dynamic Lookup. SMT-based structural subtyping allows System D to support the common idiom of dynamic field lookup and update, where the field name is a value computed at run-time. Consider the following function:

```
let getCount t c =
  if has t c then toInt (t[c]) else 0
```

The function `getCount` uses the primitive operation

$$\texttt{has} :: d{:}\mathit{Dict} \rightarrow k{:}\mathit{Str} \rightarrow \{\nu \mid \mathit{Bool}(\nu) \wedge \nu = \texttt{true} \Leftrightarrow \mathit{has}(d, k)\}$$

to check whether the key `c` exists in `t`. The refinement for the input d expresses the precondition that d is a dictionary, while the refinement for the key k expresses the precondition that k is a string. The refinement of the output expresses the postcondition that the result is a boolean value which is true if and only if d has a binding for the key k, expressed in our refinements using $\mathit{has}(d, k)$, a predicate in the theory of maps that is true if and only if there is a binding for key k in the map d [13, 25].

The *dictionary lookup* `t[c]` is desugared to `get t c` where the primitive operation `get` has the type

$$\texttt{get} :: d{:}\mathit{Dict} {\rightarrow} k{:}\{\nu \mid \mathit{Str}(\nu) \;\wedge\; \mathit{has}(d, k)\} {\rightarrow} \{\nu \mid \nu = \mathit{sel}(d, k)\}$$

and $\mathit{sel}(d, k)$ is an operator in the theory of maps that returns the binding for key k in the map d. The refinement for the key k expresses the precondition that it is a string value in the domain of the dictionary d. Similarly, the refinement for the output asserts the postcondition that the value is the same as the contents of the map at the given key.

The function `getCount` first tests that the dictionary `t` has a binding for the key `c`; if so, it is read and its contents are converted to an integer using the function `toInt`, of type $\mathit{Top} {\rightarrow} \mathit{Int}$. Note that the if-guard strengthens the environment under which the lookup appears with the fact $\mathit{has}(\texttt{t}, \texttt{c})$, ensuring the safety of the lookup. If `t` does not contain the key `c`, the default value 0 is returned. Both branches are thus verified to have type Int, so System D verifies that `getCount` has the type `getCount` $:: \mathit{Dict} \rightarrow \mathit{Str} \rightarrow \mathit{Int}$.

Dynamic Update. Dually, to allow dynamic updates, System D includes a primitive

$$\texttt{set} :: d{:}\mathit{Dict} \rightarrow k{:}\mathit{Str} \rightarrow x{:}\mathit{Top} {\rightarrow} \{\nu \mid \nu = \mathit{upd}(d, k, x)\}$$

that produces a new dictionary, where $\mathit{upd}(d, k, x)$ is an operator in the theory of maps that denotes d updated (or extended) with a binding from k to x. The following illustrates how the `set` primitive can be used:

```
let incCount t c =
  let newcount = 1 + getCount t c in
  let res      = set t c newcount in res
```

We give the function `incCount` the type

$$d{:}\mathit{Dict} \rightarrow c{:}\mathit{Str} \rightarrow \{\nu \mid \mathit{EqMod}(\nu, d, \{c\}) \wedge \mathit{Fld}(\nu, c, \mathit{Int})\}$$

where $\mathit{EqMod}(d_1, d_2, K)$ abbreviates a predicate that stipulates that d_1 is identical to d_2 at all keys *except* for those in K. The output type of `getCount` allows System D to conclude that `newcount` $:: \mathit{Int}$. From the type of `set`, System D deduces

$$\texttt{res} :: \{\nu \mid \mathit{EqMod}(\nu, \texttt{t}, \{\texttt{c}\}) \wedge \mathit{sel}(\nu, \texttt{c}) = \texttt{newcount}\}$$

which is a subtype of the output type of `incCount`. Next, consider

```
let d0 = {"files" = 42 }
let d1 = incCount d0 "dirs"
let _  = d1["files"] + d1["dirs"]
```

System D verifies that

$$\texttt{d0} :: \{\nu \mid \mathit{Fld}(\nu, \text{“}\texttt{files}\text{”}, \mathit{Int})\}$$
$$\texttt{d1} :: \{\nu \mid \mathit{Fld}(\nu, \text{“}\texttt{files}\text{”}, \mathit{Int}) \wedge \mathit{Fld}(\nu, \text{“}\texttt{dirs}\text{”}, \mathit{Int})\}$$

and, hence, the field lookups return Ints that can be safely added.

2.4 Type Constructors

Next, we use nesting and extraction to enrich System D with data structures, thereby allowing for very expressive specifications. In general, System D supports arbitrary user-defined datatypes, but to keep the current discussion simple, let us consider a single type constructor $\mathit{List}[T]$ for representing unbounded sequences of T-values. Informally, an expression of type $\mathit{List}[T]$ is either a special `null` value or a dictionary with a “`hd`” key of type T and a “`tl`” key of type $\mathit{List}[T]$. As for arrows, we use the following notation to write list types outside of refinements:

$$\mathit{List}[T] \doteq \{\nu \mid \nu :: \mathit{List}[T]\}$$

Recursive Traversal. Consider a textbook recursive function that takes a list of arbitrary values and concatenates the strings:

```
let rec concat sep xs =
  if xs = null then "" else
    let hd = xs["hd"] in
    let tl = xs["tl"] in
    if tag hd != "Str" then concat sep tl
    else if tl != null then hd ^ sep ^ concat sep tl
    else hd
```

We ascribe the function the type `concat` $:: \mathit{Str} \rightarrow \mathit{List}[\mathit{Top}] \rightarrow \mathit{Str}$. The null test ensures the safety of the “`hd`” and “`tl`” accesses and the tag test ensures the safety of the string concatenation using the techniques described above.

Nested Ad-Hoc Unions. We can now define ad-hoc unions over constructed types by simply nesting $List[\cdot]$ as a type term in the refinement logic. The following illustrates a common Python idiom when an argument is either a single value or a list of values:

```
let runTest cmd fail_codes =
  let status = syscall cmd in
  if tag fail_codes = "Int" then
    not (status = fail_codes)
  else
    not (listMem status fail_codes)
```

Here, `listMem` :: $Top \to List[Top] \to Bool$ and `syscall` :: $Str \to Int$. The input `cmd` is a string, and `fail_codes` is either a single integer or a list of integer failure codes. Because we nest $List[\cdot]$ as a type term in our logic, we can use the same kind of type extraction reasoning as we did for `maybeApply` to ascribe `runTest` the type

$$\texttt{runTest} :: Str \to \{\nu \mid Int(\nu) \vee \nu :: List[Int]\} \to Bool$$

2.5 Parametric Polymorphism

Similarly, we can add parametric polymorphism to System D by simply treating type variables $A, B, etc.$ as (uninterpreted) type terms in the logic. As before, we use the following notation to write type variables outside of refinements.

$$A \doteq \{\nu \mid \nu :: A\}$$

Generic Containers. We can compose the type constructors in the ways we all know and love. Here is list `map` in System D:

```
let rec map f xs =
  if xs = null then null
  else new List(f xs["hd"], map f xs["tl"])
```

(Of course, pattern matching would improve matters, but we are merely trying to demonstrate how much can be — and is! — achieved with dictionaries.) By combining extraction with the reasoning used for `concat`, it is easy to check that

$$\texttt{map} :: \forall A, B.\ (A \to B) \to List[A] \to List[B]$$

Note that type abstractions are automatically inserted where a function is ascribed a polymorphic type.

Predicate Functions. Consider the list filter function:

```
let rec filter f xs =
  if xs = null then null
  else if not (f xs["hd"]) then filter f (xs["tl"])
  else new List(xs["hd"], filter f xs["tl"])
```

In System D, we can ascribe `filter` the type

$$\forall A, B.\ (x{:}A \to \{\nu \mid \nu = \texttt{true} \Rightarrow x :: B\}) \to List[A] \to List[B],$$

Note that the return type of the predicate, `f`, tells us what type is satisfied by values `x` for which `f` returns `true`, and the return type of `filter` states that the items `filter` returns all have the type implied by the predicate `f`. Thus, the general mechanism of nested refinements subsumes the kind of reasoning performed by specialized techniques like latent predicates [39].

Bounded Quantification. Nested refinements enable a form of bounded quantification. Consider the function

```
let dispatch d f = d[f] d
```

The function `dispatch` works for any dictionary `d` of type A that has a key `f` bound to a function that maps values of type A to values of type B. We can specify this via the dependent signature

$$\forall A, B.\ d{:}\{\nu \mid Dict(\nu) \wedge \nu :: A\} \to \{\nu \mid Fld(d, \nu, A \to B)\} \to B$$

Note that there is no need for explicit type bounds; all that is required is the conjunction of the appropriate nested refinements.

2.6 All Together Now

With the tools we've developed in this section, System D is now capable of type checking sophisticated code from the wild. The original source code for the following can be found in a technical report [8].

Unions, Generic Dispatch, and Polymorphism. We now have everything we need to type the motivating example from the introduction, `onto`, which combined multiple dynamic idioms: dynamic fields, tag-tests, and the dependency between nested dictionary functions and their arguments. Nested refinements let us formalize the flexible interface for `onto` given in the introduction:

$$\begin{aligned}
&\forall A.\ callbacks{:}List[Top \to Top] \\
&\quad \to f{:}\{\nu \mid \nu = \texttt{null} \vee Str(\nu) \vee \nu :: A \to Top\} \\
&\quad \to obj{:}\{\nu \mid \nu :: A \wedge (f = \texttt{null} \Rightarrow \nu :: Top \to Top) \\
&\qquad\qquad \wedge (Str(f) \Rightarrow Fld(\nu, f, A \to Top))\} \\
&\quad \to List[Top \to Top]
\end{aligned}$$

Using reasoning similar to that used in the previous examples, System D checks that `onto` enjoys the above type, where the specification for obj is enabled by the kind of bounded quantification described earlier.

Reflection. Finally, to round off the overview, we present one last example that shows how all the features presented combine to allow System D to statically type programs that introspect on the contents of dictionaries. The function `toXML` shown below is adapted from the Python 3.2 standard library's `plistlib.py` [37]:

```
let rec toXML x =
  if tag x = "Bool" then
    if x then element "true" null
    else      element "false" null
  else if tag x = "Int" then
    element "integer" (intToStr x)
  else if tag x = "Str" then
    element "string" x
  else if tag x = "Dict" then
    let ks = keys x in
    let vs = map {v| Str(v) and has(x,v)} Str
      (fun k -> element "key" k ^ toXML x[k]) ks in
    "<data>" ^ concat "\n" vs ^ "</data>"
  else element "function" null
```

The function takes an arbitrary value and renders it as an XML string, and illustrates several idiomatic uses of dynamic features. If we give the auxiliary function `intToStr` the type $Int \to Str$ and `element` the type $Str \to \{\nu \mid \nu = \texttt{null} \vee Str(\nu)\} \to Str$, we can verify that

$$\texttt{toXML} :: Top \to Str$$

Of especial interest is the dynamic field lookup `x[k]` used in the function passed to `map` to recursively convert each binding of the dictionary to XML. The primitive operation `keys` has the type

$$\texttt{keys} :: d{:}Dict \to List[\{\nu \mid Str(\nu) \wedge has(d, \nu)\}]$$

that is, it returns a list of string keys that belong to the input dictionary. Thus, `ks` has type $List[\{\nu \mid Str(\nu) \wedge has(\texttt{x}, \nu)\}]$, which enables the call to `map` to typecheck, since the body of the argument is checked in an environment where `k` :: $\{\nu \mid Str(\nu) \wedge has(\texttt{x}, \nu)\}$, which is the type that A is instantiated with. This binding suffices to prove the safety of the dynamic field access. The control flow reasoning described previously uses the tag tests guarding the other cases to prove each of them safe.

w	$::=$		**Values**
	$\mid$	x	variable
	$\mid$	c	constant
	$\mid$	$w_1 \mathbin{++} \{w_2 \mapsto w_3\}$	dictionary extension
	$\mid$	$\lambda x.\, e$	function
	$\mid$	$\lambda A.\, e$	type function
	$\mid$	$C(\overline{w})$	constructed data
e	$::=$		**Expressions**
	$\mid$	w	value
	$\mid$	$w_1\ w_2$	function application
	$\mid$	$w\ [T]$	type function application
	$\mid$	if w then e_1 else e_2	if-then-else
	$\mid$	let $x = e_1$ in e_2	let-binding
td	$::=$	type $C[\overline{\theta A}]\{\overline{f:T}\}$	**Datatype Definitions**
prg	$::=$	$\overline{td}; e$	**Programs**
lw	$::=$		**Logical Values**
	$\mid$	w	value
	$\mid$	$F(\overline{lw})$	logical function application
p, q, r	$::=$		**Refinement Formulas**
	$\mid$	$P(\overline{lw})$	predicate
	$\mid$	$lw :: U$	type predicate
	$\mid$	$p \wedge q \mid p \vee q \mid \neg p$	logical connective
T	$::=$	$\{\nu \mid p\}$	**Refinement Types**
U	$::=$		**Type Terms**
	$\mid$	$x{:}T_1 \to T_2$	arrow
	$\mid$	A	type variable
	$\mid$	$C[\overline{T}]$	constructed type
	$\mid$	$Null$	null
S	$::=$	$T \mid \forall A.\, S$	**Type Schemes**

Figure 1. Syntax of System D

3. Syntax and Semantics

We begin with the syntax and evaluation semantics of System D. Figure 1 shows the syntax of values, expressions, and types.

Values. Values w include variables constants, functions, type functions, dictionaries, and records created by type constructors. The set of constants c includes base values like integer, boolean, and string constants, the empty dictionary $\{\}$, and `null`. Logical values lw are all values and applications of primitive function symbols F, such as addition $+$ and dictionary selection sel, to logical values. The constant `tag` allows introspection on the type tag of a value at run-time. For example,

$$\begin{array}{rclrcl} \texttt{tag}(3) & \doteq & \text{"Int"} & \texttt{tag}(\texttt{true}) & \doteq & \text{"Bool"} \\ \texttt{tag}(\text{"john"}) & \doteq & \text{"Str"} & \texttt{tag}(\lambda x.\, e) & \doteq & \text{"Fun"} \\ \texttt{tag}(\{\}) & \doteq & \text{"Dict"} & \texttt{tag}(\lambda A.\, e) & \doteq & \text{"TFun"} \end{array}$$

Dictionaries. A dictionary $w_1 \mathbin{++} \{w_2 \mapsto w_3\}$ extends the dictionary w_1 with the binding from string w_2 to value w_3. For example, the dictionary mapping "x" to 3 and "y" to `true` is written

$$\{\} \mathbin{++} \{\text{"x"} \mapsto 3\} \mathbin{++} \{\text{"y"} \mapsto \texttt{true}\}.$$

The set of constants also includes operations for extending dictionaries and accessing their fields. The function `get` is used to access dictionary fields and is defined

$$\begin{array}{l} \texttt{get}\ (w \mathbin{++} \{\text{"x"} \mapsto w_x\})\ \text{"x"} \doteq w_x \\ \texttt{get}\ (w \mathbin{++} \{\text{"y"} \mapsto w_y\})\ \text{"x"} \doteq \texttt{get}\ w\ \text{"x"} \end{array}$$

The function `has` tests for the presence of a field and is defined

$$\begin{array}{r} \texttt{has}\ (w \mathbin{++} \{\text{"y"} \mapsto w_y\})\ \text{"x"} \doteq \texttt{has}\ w\ \text{"x"} \\ \texttt{has}\ (w \mathbin{++} \{\text{"x"} \mapsto w_x\})\ \text{"x"} \doteq \texttt{true} \\ \texttt{has}\ \{\}\ \text{"x"} \doteq \texttt{false} \end{array}$$

The function `set` updates the value bound to a key and is defined

$$\texttt{set}\ d\ k\ w \doteq d \mathbin{++} \{k \mapsto w\}$$

Expressions. The set of expressions e consists of values, function applications, type instantiations, if-then-else expressions, and let-bindings. We use an A-normal presentation so that we need only define substitution of values (not arbitrary expressions) into types.

Types. We stratify types into monomorphic types T and polymorphic type schemes $\forall A.\ S$. In System D, a type T is a *refinement type* of the form $\{\nu \mid p\}$, where p is a *refinement formula*, and is read "ν such that p." The values of this type are all values w such that the formula $p[w/\nu]$ "is true." What this means, formally, is core to our approach and will be considered in detail in section 5.

Refinement Formulas. The language of *refinement formulas* includes predicates P, such as the equality predicate and dictionary predicates has and sel, and the usual logical connectives. For example, the type of integers is $\{\nu \mid tag(\nu) = \text{"Int"}\}$, which we abbreviate to Int. The type of positive integers is

$$\{\nu \mid tag(\nu) = \text{"Int"} \wedge \nu > 0\}$$

and the type of dictionaries with an integer field "f" is

$$\{\nu \mid tag(\nu) = \text{"Dict"} \wedge tag(sel(\nu, \text{"f"})) = \text{"Int"}\}.$$

We refer to the binder ν in refinement types as "the value variable."

Nesting: Type Predicates and Terms. To express the types of values like functions and dictionaries containing functions, System D permits types to be nested within refinement formulas. Formally, the language of refinement formulas includes a form, $lw :: U$, called a *type predicate*, where U is a *type term*. The type term $x{:}T_1 \to T_2$ describes values that have a dependent function type, *i.e.* functions that accept arguments w of type T_1 and return values of type $T_2[w/x]$, where x is bound in T_2. We write $T_1 \to T_2$ when x does not appear in T_2. Type terms $A, B, etc.$ correspond to type parameters to polymorphic functions. The type term $Null$ corresponds to the type of the constant value `null`. The type term $C[\overline{T}]$ corresponds to records constructed with the C type constructor instantiated with the sequence of type arguments $\overline{T}$. For example, the type of the (integer) successor function is

$$\{\nu \mid \nu :: x{:}Int \to \{\nu \mid tag(\nu) = \text{"Int"} \wedge \nu = x + 1\}\},$$

dictionaries where the value at key "f" maps Int to Int have type

$$\{\nu \mid tag(\nu) = \text{"Dict"} \wedge sel(\nu, \text{"f"}) :: Int \to Int\},$$

and the constructed record $List(1, \texttt{null})$ can be assigned the type $\{\nu \mid \nu :: List[Int]\}$.

Datatype Definitions. A datatype definition of C defines a named, possibly recursive type. A datatype definition includes a sequence $\overline{\theta A}$ of type parameters A paired with *variance annotations* θ. A variance annotation is either `+` (covariant), `-` (contravariant), or `=` (invariant). The rest of the definition specifies a sequence $\overline{f:T}$ of field names and their types. The types of the fields may refer to the type parameters of the declaration. A well-formedness check,

Operational Semantics $\boxed{e \hookrightarrow e'}$

$$\frac{\text{if } \delta(c, w) \text{ is defined}}{c\ w \hookrightarrow \delta(c, w)}\ \text{[E-DELTA]}$$

$$(\lambda x.\ e)\ w \hookrightarrow e[w/x]\ \text{[E-APP]}$$

$$\text{let } x = w \text{ in } e \hookrightarrow e[w/x]\ \text{[E-LET]}$$

$$(\Lambda A.\ e)\ [T] \hookrightarrow e\ \text{[E-TAPP]}$$

$$\text{if } \mathtt{true} \text{ then } e_1 \text{ else } e_2 \hookrightarrow e_1\ \text{[E-IFTRUE]}$$

$$\text{if } \mathtt{false} \text{ then } e_1 \text{ else } e_2 \hookrightarrow e_2\ \text{[E-IFFALSE]}$$

$$\frac{e_1 \hookrightarrow e_1'}{\text{let } x = e_1 \text{ in } e_2 \hookrightarrow \text{let } x = e_1' \text{ in } e_2}\ \text{[E-COMPAT]}$$

Figure 2. Evaluation semantics of System D

which will be described in section 4, ensures that occurrences of type parameters in the field types respect their declared variance annotations. By convention, we will use the subscript i to index into the sequence $\overline{\theta A}$ and j for $\overline{f : T}$. For example, θ_i refers to the variance annotation of the ith type parameter, and f_j refers to the name of the jth field.

Programs. A program is a sequence of datatype definitions $\overline{td}$ followed by an expression e. Requiring all datatype definitions to appear first simplifies the subsequent presentation.

Semantics. The small-step operational semantics of System D is standard for a call-by-value, polymorphic lambda calculus, and is shown in Figure 2. Following standard practice, the semantics is parameterized by a function δ that assigns meaning to primitive functions c, including dictionary operations like `has`, `get`, and `set`. Because expressions are A-normalized, there is a single congruence rule, E-COMPAT. Our implementation desugars more palatable syntax into A-normal form.

4. Type Checking

In this section, we present the System D type system, comprising several well-formedness relations, an expression typing relation, and, at the heart of our approach, a novel subtyping relation which discharges obligations involving nested refinements through a combination of syntactic and semantic, SMT-based reasoning. We first define environments for type checking.

Environments. Type environments Γ are of the form

$$\Gamma \quad ::= \quad \emptyset \mid \Gamma, x : S \mid \Gamma, A \mid \Gamma, p$$

where bindings either record the derived type S for a variable x, a type variable A introduced in the scope of a type function, or a formula p that is recorded to track the control flow along branches of an if-expression. A type definition environment Ψ records the definition of each constructor type C. As type definitions appear at the beginning of a program, we assume for clarity that Ψ is fixed and globally visible, and elide it from the judgments. In the sequel, we assume that Ψ contains at least the definition

$$\text{type } List[+A]\{\text{“}\mathtt{hd}\text{”} : \{\nu \mid \nu :: A\};\ \text{“}\mathtt{tl}\text{”} : \{\nu \mid \nu :: List[A]\}\}.$$

4.1 Well-formedness

Figure 3 defines the well-formedness relations.

Well-Formed Type Schemes $\boxed{\Gamma \vdash S}$

$$\frac{x \text{ fresh} \qquad \Gamma, x : Top \vdash p[x/\nu]}{\Gamma \vdash \{\nu \mid p\}} \qquad \frac{\Gamma, A \vdash S}{\Gamma \vdash \forall A.\ S}$$

Well-Formed Formulas $\boxed{\Gamma \vdash p}$

$$\frac{\Gamma \vdash lw \qquad \Gamma \vdash U}{\Gamma \vdash lw :: U} \qquad \frac{\forall i.\ \Gamma \vdash lw_i}{\Gamma \vdash P(\overline{lw})} \qquad \frac{\Gamma \vdash p \qquad \Gamma \vdash q}{\Gamma \vdash p \wedge q}$$

Well-Formed Type Terms $\boxed{\Gamma \vdash U}$

$$\frac{\begin{array}{c}\Gamma \vdash T_1 \\ \Gamma, x : T_1 \vdash T_2\end{array}}{\Gamma \vdash x : T_1 \to T_2} \qquad \frac{A \in \Gamma}{\Gamma \vdash A} \qquad \frac{}{\Gamma \vdash Null} \qquad \frac{\begin{array}{c}C \in Dom(\Psi) \\ \forall i.\ \Gamma \vdash T_i\end{array}}{\Gamma \vdash C[\overline{T}]}$$

Well-Formed Type Environments $\boxed{\vdash \Gamma}$

$$\frac{}{\vdash \emptyset} \qquad \frac{\begin{array}{c}x \notin Dom(\Gamma) \\ \vdash \Gamma \qquad \Gamma \vdash S\end{array}}{\vdash \Gamma, x : S} \qquad \frac{\begin{array}{c}\vdash \Gamma \\ A \notin \Gamma\end{array}}{\vdash \Gamma, A} \qquad \frac{\vdash \Gamma \qquad \Gamma \vdash p}{\vdash \Gamma, p}$$

Well-Formed Type Definitions $\boxed{\vdash td}$

$$\frac{\forall j.\ \overline{A} \vdash T_j \qquad \forall i.\ \mathsf{VarianceOk}(A_i, \theta_i, \overline{T})}{\vdash \text{type } C[\overline{\theta A}]\{\overline{f : T}\}}$$

Figure 3. Well-formedness for System D

Formulas, Types and Environments. We require that types be *well-formed* within the current type environment, which means that formulas used in types are boolean propositions and mention only variables that are currently in scope. By convention, we assume that variables used as binders throughout the program are distinct and different from the special value variable ν, which is reserved for types. Therefore, ν is never bound in Γ. When checking the well-formedness of a refinement formula p, we substitute a fresh variable x for ν and check that $p[x/\nu]$ is well-formed in the environment extended with $x : Top$, to the environment, where $Top = \{\nu \mid true\}$. We use fresh variables to prevent duplicate bindings of ν.

Note that the well-formedness of formulas does *not* depend on type checking; all that is needed is the ability to syntactically distinguish between terms and propositions. Checking that values are well-formed is straightforward; the important point is that a variable x may be used only if it is bound in Γ.

Datatype Definitions. To check that a datatype definition is well-formed, we first check that the types of the fields are well-formed in an environment containing the declared type parameters. Then, to enable a sound subtyping rule for constructed types in the sequel, we check that the declared variance annotations are respected within the type definition. For this, we use a procedure $\mathsf{VarianceOk}$ (defined in a technical report [8]) that recursively walks formulas to record whether type variables occur in positive or negative positions within the types of the fields.

4.2 Expression Typing

The expression typing judgment $\Gamma \vdash e :: S$, defined in Figure 4, verifies that expression e has type scheme S in environment Γ. We highlight the important aspects of the typing rules.

Constants. Each primitive constant c has a type, denoted by $ty(c)$, that is used by T-CONST. Basic values like integers, booleans, *etc.* are given singleton types stating that their value equals the corresponding constant in the refinement logic. For example:

$$\begin{array}{llll} \texttt{1} :: & \{\nu \mid \nu = 1\} & \texttt{true} :: & \{\nu \mid \nu = \texttt{true}\} \\ \text{“john”} :: & \{\nu \mid \nu = \text{“john”}\} & \texttt{false} :: & \{\nu \mid \nu = \texttt{false}\} \end{array}$$

Arithmetic and boolean operations have types that reflect their semantics. Equality on base values is defined in the standard way, while equality on function values is physical equality.

$$\begin{aligned} \texttt{+} &:: x{:}Int \to y{:}Int \to \{\nu \mid Int(\nu) \wedge \nu = x + y\} \\ \texttt{not} &:: x{:}Bool \to \{\nu \mid Bool(\nu) \wedge x = \texttt{true} \Leftrightarrow \nu = \texttt{false}\} \\ \texttt{=} &:: x{:}Top \to y{:}Top \to \{\nu \mid Bool(\nu) \wedge \nu = \texttt{true} \Leftrightarrow x = y\} \\ \texttt{fix} &:: \forall A.\, (A \to A) \to A \\ \texttt{tag} &:: x{:}Top \to \{\nu \mid \nu = tag(x)\} \end{aligned}$$

The constant `fix` is used to encode recursion, and the type for the tag-test operation uses an axiomatized function in the logic.

The operations on dictionaries are given refinement types over McCarthy's theory of arrays extended with a default element, which we write as *bot*, that is different from all program values. The extended theory is shown to be decidable in [13].

$$\begin{aligned} \{\} &:: \{\nu \mid \nu = empty\} \\ \texttt{has} &:: d{:}Dict \to k{:}Str \to \{\nu \mid Bool(\nu) \wedge \nu = \texttt{true} \Leftrightarrow has(d,k)\} \\ \texttt{get} &:: d{:}Dict \to k{:}\{\nu \mid Str(\nu) \wedge has(d,\nu)\} \to \{\nu \mid \nu = sel(d,k)\} \\ \texttt{set} &:: d{:}Dict \to k{:}Str \to x{:}Top \to \{\nu \mid \nu = upd(d,k,x)\} \\ \texttt{keys} &:: d{:}Dict \to List[\{\nu \mid Str(\nu) \wedge has(d,\nu)\}] \end{aligned}$$

The types above use the constant $empty$ to denote the empty dictionary, and the predicate $has(d,k)$ to abbreviate $sel(d,k) \neq bot$. To relate two dictionaries, we use $EqMod(d_1, d_2, K)$ to abbreviate

$$\forall k'.\, (\wedge_{k \in K}\ k \neq k') \Rightarrow sel(d_1, k') = sel(d_2, k')$$

which states that the dictionaries d_1 and d_2 are identical *except* at the keys in K. This expansion falls into the array property fragment, shown to be decidable in [7] by reduction to an equisatisfiable quantifier-free formula. The $EqMod$ abbreviation is particularly useful for dictionary updates where we do not know the *exact* value being stored, but do know some abstraction thereof, *e.g.* its type. For example, in `incCounter` (from section 2) we do not know what value is stored in the count field `c`, only that it is an integer. Thus, we say that the new dictionary is the same as the old except at `c`, where the binding is an integer. A more direct approach would be to use an existentially quantified variable to represent the stored value and say that the resulting dictionary is the original dictionary updated to contain this quantified value. Unfortunately, that would take the formulas outside the decidable fragment of the logic, thereby precluding SMT-based logical subtyping.

Standard Rules. We briefly identify several typing rules that are standard for lambda calculi with dependent refinements. T-VAR and T-VARPOLY assign types to variable expressions x. If x is bound to a (monomorphic) refinement type in Γ, then T-VAR assigns x the singleton type that says that the expression x evaluates to the same value as the variable x. T-IF assigns the type scheme S to an if-expression if the condition w is a boolean-valued expression, the then-branch expression e_1 has type scheme S under the assumption that w evaluates to `true`, and the else-branch expression e_2 has type scheme S under the assumption that w evaluates to `false`. The T-APP rule is standard, but notice that the arrow type of w_1 is nested inside a refinement type. In T-LET, the type scheme S_2 must be well-formed in Γ, which prevents the variable x from escaping its scope. T-SUB allows expression e to be used with type S if e has type S' and S' is a subtype of S.

Type Checking $\boxed{\Gamma \vdash e :: S}$

$$\frac{}{\Gamma \vdash c :: ty(c)}\ [\text{T-CONST}]$$

$$\frac{\Gamma(x) = T}{\Gamma \vdash x :: \{\nu \mid \nu = x\}}\ [\text{T-VAR}] \qquad \frac{\Gamma(x) = \forall A.\, S}{\Gamma \vdash x :: \forall A.\, S}\ [\text{T-VARPOLY}]$$

$$\frac{\Gamma \vdash w_1 :: Dict \quad \Gamma \vdash w_2 :: Str \quad \Gamma \vdash w_3 :: S}{\Gamma \vdash w_1 \mathbin{++} \{w_2 \mapsto w_3\} :: \{\nu \mid \nu = w_1 \mathbin{++} \{w_2 \mapsto w_3\}\}}\ [\text{T-EXTEND}]$$

$$\frac{\begin{array}{c}\Gamma \vdash w :: Bool \\ \Gamma, w = \texttt{true} \vdash e_1 :: S \quad \Gamma, w = \texttt{false} \vdash e_2 :: S\end{array}}{\Gamma \vdash \text{if } w \text{ then } e_1 \text{ else } e_2 :: S}\ [\text{T-IF}]$$

$$\frac{\Gamma \vdash T_1 \quad \Gamma, x{:}T_1 \vdash e :: T_2}{\Gamma \vdash \lambda x.\, e :: \{\nu \mid \nu = \lambda x.\, e \wedge \nu :: x{:}T_1 \to T_2\}}\ [\text{T-FUN}]$$

$$\frac{\Gamma \vdash w_1 :: \{\nu \mid \nu :: x{:}T_{11} \to T_{12}\} \quad \Gamma \vdash w_2 :: T_{11}}{\Gamma \vdash w_1\, w_2 :: T_{12}[w_2/x]}\ [\text{T-APP}]$$

$$\frac{A \notin \Gamma \quad \Gamma, A \vdash e :: S}{\Gamma \vdash \lambda A.\, e :: \forall A.\, S}\ [\text{T-TFUN}]$$

$$\frac{\Gamma \vdash T \quad \Gamma \vdash w :: \forall A.\, S}{\Gamma \vdash w\, [T] :: \mathsf{Inst}(S, A, T)}\ [\text{T-TAPP}]$$

$$\frac{\begin{array}{c}\forall i.\, \Gamma \vdash T_i \quad \Psi(C) = [\theta \overline{A}]\{\overline{f{:}T'}\} \\ \forall j.\, \Gamma \vdash w_j :: \mathsf{Inst}(T'_j, \overline{A}, \overline{T})\end{array}}{\Gamma \vdash C(\overline{w}) :: \{\nu \mid \mathsf{Fold}(C, \overline{T}, \overline{w})\}}\ [\text{T-FOLD}]$$

$$\frac{\Gamma \vdash e :: \{\nu \mid \nu :: C[\overline{T}]\}}{\Gamma \vdash e :: \{\nu \mid \mathsf{Unfold}(C, \overline{T})\}}\ [\text{T-UNFOLD}]$$

$$\frac{\Gamma \vdash S_1 \quad \Gamma \vdash e_1 :: S_1 \quad \Gamma, x{:}S_1 \vdash e_2 :: S_2 \quad \Gamma \vdash S_2}{\Gamma \vdash \text{let } x = e_1 \text{ in } e_2 :: S_2}\ [\text{T-LET}]$$

$$\frac{\Gamma \vdash e :: S' \quad \Gamma \vdash S' \sqsubseteq S \quad \Gamma \vdash S}{\Gamma \vdash e :: S}\ [\text{T-SUB}]$$

Figure 4. Type checking for System D

Type Instantiation. The T-TAPP rules uses the procedure Inst to instantiate a type variable with a (monomorphic) type. Inst is defined recursively on formulas, type terms, and types, where the only non-trivial case involves type predicates with type variables:

$$\begin{aligned} \mathsf{Inst}(lw :: A, A, \{\nu \mid p\}) &= p[lw/\nu] \\ \mathsf{Inst}(lw :: B, A, T) &= lw :: B \end{aligned}$$

We write $\mathsf{Inst}(S, \overline{A}, \overline{T})$ to mean the result of applying Inst to S with the type variables and type arguments in succession.

Fold and Unfold. The T-FOLD rule is used for records of data created with the datatype constructor C and type arguments $\overline{T}$. The rule succeeds if the argument w_j provided for each field f_j has the required type T'_j after instantiating all type parameters $\overline{A}$ with the type arguments $\overline{T}$. If these conditions are satisfied, the formula

Subtyping $\boxed{\Gamma \vdash S_1 \sqsubseteq S_2}$

$$\frac{x \text{ fresh} \quad p_1' = p_1[x/\nu] \quad p_2' = p_2[x/\nu] \quad \mathsf{Normalize}(p_2') = \wedge_i(q_i \Rrightarrow r_i) \quad \forall i.\ \Gamma, p_1' \vdash q_i \Rrightarrow r_i}{\Gamma \vdash \{\nu \,|\, p_1\} \sqsubseteq \{\nu \,|\, p_2\}} \text{ [S-MONO]}$$

$$\frac{\Gamma \vdash S_1 \sqsubseteq S_2}{\Gamma \vdash \forall A.\ S_1 \sqsubseteq \forall A.\ S_2} \text{ [S-POLY]}$$

Clause Implication $\boxed{\Gamma \vdash q \Rrightarrow r}$

$$\frac{\mathsf{Valid}(\llbracket \Gamma \rrbracket \wedge q \Rightarrow r)}{\Gamma \vdash q \Rrightarrow r} \text{ [C-VALID]}$$

$$\frac{\exists j. \quad \mathsf{Valid}(\llbracket \Gamma \rrbracket \wedge q \Rightarrow lw_j :: U) \quad \Gamma, q \vdash U <: U_j}{\Gamma \vdash q \Rrightarrow \vee_i\, lw_i :: U_i} \text{ [C-IMPSYN]}$$

Syntactic Subtyping $\boxed{\Gamma \vdash U_1 <: U_2}$

$$\frac{\Gamma \vdash T_{21} \sqsubseteq T_{11} \quad \Gamma, x{:}T_{21} \vdash T_{12} \sqsubseteq T_{22}}{\Gamma \vdash x{:}T_{11} \rightarrow T_{12} <: x{:}T_{21} \rightarrow T_{22}} \text{ [U-ARROW]}$$

$$\frac{}{\Gamma \vdash A <: A} \text{ [U-VAR]} \qquad \frac{}{\Gamma \vdash \mathit{Null} <: C[\overline{T}]} \text{ [U-NULL]}$$

$$\frac{\Psi(C) = [\overline{\theta A}]\{\cdots\} \quad \forall i.\ \text{if } \theta_i \in \{\texttt{+},\texttt{=}\} \text{ then } \Gamma \vdash T_{1i} \sqsubseteq T_{2i} \quad \forall i.\ \text{if } \theta_i \in \{\texttt{-},\texttt{=}\} \text{ then } \Gamma \vdash T_{2i} \sqsubseteq T_{1i}}{\Gamma \vdash C[\overline{T_1}] <: C[\overline{T_2}]} \text{ [U-DATATYPE]}$$

Figure 5. Subtyping for System D

returned by $\mathsf{Fold}(C, \overline{T}, \overline{w})$, defined as

$$\nu \neq \texttt{null} \wedge \mathit{tag}(\nu) = \text{"}\texttt{Dict}\text{"} \wedge \nu :: C[\overline{T}] \wedge (\wedge_j\, \mathit{sel}(\nu, f_j) = w_j)$$

records that the value is non-null, that the values stored in the fields are precisely the values used to construct the record, and that the value has a type corresponding to the specific constructor used to create the value. T-UNFOLD exposes the fields of non-null constructed data as a dictionary, using $\mathsf{Unfold}(C, \overline{T})$, defined as

$$\nu \neq \texttt{null} \Rightarrow (\mathit{tag}(\nu) = \text{"}\texttt{Dict}\text{"} \wedge (\wedge_j \llbracket T_j'' \rrbracket(\mathit{sel}(\nu, f_j))))$$

where $\Psi(C) = [\overline{\theta A}]\{\overline{f{:}T'}\}$, $\llbracket\{\nu \,|\, p\}\rrbracket(lw) \doteq p[lw/\nu]$, and for all $j, T_j'' = \mathsf{Inst}(T_j', \overline{A}, \overline{T})$. For example, $\mathsf{Unfold}(\mathit{List}, \mathit{Int})$ is

$$\nu \neq \texttt{null} \Rightarrow (\mathit{tag}(\nu) = \text{"}\texttt{Dict}\text{"} \wedge \mathit{tag}(\mathit{sel}(\nu, \text{"hd"})) = \text{"}\texttt{Int}\text{"} \wedge \mathit{sel}(\nu, \text{"}\texttt{tl}\text{"}) :: \mathit{List}[\mathit{Int}])$$

4.3 Subtyping

In traditional refinement type systems, there is a two-level hierarchy between types and refinements that allows a syntax-directed reduction of subtyping obligations to SMT implications [16, 23, 31]. In contrast, System D's refinements include uninterpreted type predicates that are beyond the scope of (first-order) SMT solvers.

Let us consider the problem of establishing the subtyping judgment $\Gamma \vdash \{\nu \,|\, p_1\} \sqsubseteq \{\nu \,|\, p_2\}$. We cannot use the SMT query

$$\llbracket \Gamma \rrbracket \wedge p_1 \Rightarrow p_2 \qquad (2)$$

as the presence of (uninterpreted) type-predicates may conservatively render the implication invalid. Instead, our strategy is to massage the refinements into a normal form that makes it easy to factor the implication in (2) into a collection of subgoals whose consequents are either simple (non-type) predicates or type predicates. The former can be established via SMT and the latter by recursively invoking syntactic subtyping. Next, we show how this strategy is realized by the rules in Figure 5.

Step 1: Split query into subgoals. We start by converting p_2 into a *normalized conjunction* $\wedge_i(q_i \Rrightarrow r_i)$. Each conjunct, or *clause*, $q_i \Rrightarrow r_i$ is normalized such that its consequent is a *disjunction* of type predicates. We use the symbol $\Rrightarrow$ instead of the usual implication arrow $\Rightarrow$ to emphasize the normal structure of each clause. By splitting p_2 into its normalized clauses, rule S-MONO reduces the goal (2) to the equivalent collection of subgoals

$$\forall i.\ \Gamma, p_1 \vdash q_i \Rrightarrow r_i$$

Step 2: Discharge subgoals. The normalization ensures that the consequent of each subgoal above is a disjunction of type predicates. When the disjunction of a clause is *empty*, the subgoal is

$$(\textit{"type predicate-free"}) \qquad \Gamma, p_1 \vdash q_i \Rrightarrow \mathit{false}$$

which rule C-VALID handles by SMT. Otherwise, the subgoal is

$$(\textit{"type predicate"}) \qquad \Gamma, p_1 \vdash q_i \Rrightarrow lw_j :: U_j$$

which rule C-IMPSYN handles via type extraction followed by a use of of syntactic subtyping. In particular, the rule tries to establish *one of* the disjuncts $lw_j :: U_j$, by searching for a type term U that occurs in Γ that 1) *flows to* lw_j, *i.e.* for which we can deduce via SMT that

$$\llbracket \Gamma \rrbracket \wedge p_1 \wedge q_i \Rightarrow lw_j :: U$$

is valid and, 2) is a syntactic subtype of U_j in an appropriately strengthened environment (written $\Gamma, p_1, q_i \vdash U <: U_j$). The rules U-DATATYPE and U-ARROW establish syntactic (refinement) subtyping, by (recursively) establishing that subtyping holds for the matching components [6, 16, 31]. Because syntactic subtyping recursively refers to subtyping, the S-MONO rule uses fresh variables to avoid duplicate bindings of ν in the environment.

Formula Normalization. Procedure Normalize converts a formula p into a conjunction of clauses $\wedge_i(q_i \Rrightarrow r_i)$ as described above. The conversion is carried out by translating p to conjunctive normal form (CNF), and then for each CNF clause, rearranging literals and adding negations as necessary. For example,

$$\mathsf{Normalize}(\nu = \texttt{null}) \doteq \neg(\nu = \texttt{null}) \Rrightarrow \mathit{false}$$
$$\mathsf{Normalize}(\nu = \texttt{null} \vee \nu :: U) \doteq \neg(\nu = \texttt{null}) \Rrightarrow \nu :: U$$

Formula Implication. In each SMT implication query $\llbracket \Gamma \rrbracket \wedge p \Rightarrow q$, the operator $\llbracket\cdot\rrbracket$ describes the embedding of environments and types into the logic as follows:

$$\begin{array}{rclrcl} \llbracket\{\nu \,|\, p\}\rrbracket & \doteq & p & \llbracket \Gamma, x{:}T \rrbracket & \doteq & \llbracket \Gamma \rrbracket \wedge \llbracket T \rrbracket[x/\nu] \\ \llbracket \emptyset \rrbracket & \doteq & \mathit{true} & \llbracket \Gamma, x{:}\forall A.\ S \rrbracket & \doteq & \llbracket \Gamma \rrbracket \\ \llbracket \Gamma, p \rrbracket & \doteq & \llbracket \Gamma \rrbracket \wedge p & \llbracket \Gamma, A \rrbracket & \doteq & \llbracket \Gamma \rrbracket \end{array}$$

When embedding values into the logic, we represent each lambda by a distinct uninterpreted constant. Thus, function equality is "physical equality," so there is no concern about the equivalence of expressions. (Note that lambdas never need to appear inside refinement formulas in source programs, and are included in the grammar of formulas just for the metatheory.)

Ensuring Termination. An important concern remains: as we extract type terms from the environment and recursively invoke the subtyping relation on them, we do not have the usual guarantee that subtyping is recursively invoked on strictly syntactically smaller terms. Thus, it is not clear whether subtyping checks will terminate.

Indeed, if we are not careful, they may not! Consider the environment

$$\Gamma \doteq y : Top,\ x : \{\nu \mid \nu = y \wedge \nu :: U\}$$
$$\text{where } U \doteq a : \{\nu \mid \nu :: b : \{\nu \mid \nu = y\} \to Top\} \to Top$$

and suppose we wish to check that

$$\Gamma \vdash true \Rrightarrow y :: x : \{\nu \mid \nu = y\} \to Top. \qquad (3)$$

C-VALID cannot derive this judgment, since the implication

$$[\![\Gamma]\!] \wedge true \Rightarrow y :: x : \{\nu \mid \nu = y\} \to Top$$

is not valid. Thus, we must derive Equation 3 by C-IMPSYN. Type extraction derives that $y :: U$ in Γ, so the remaining obligation is

$$\Gamma \vdash U <: x : \{\nu \mid \nu = y\} \to Top.$$

Because of the contravariance of function subtyping on the left-hand side of the arrow, the following judgment must be derivable:

$$\Gamma \vdash \{\nu \mid \nu = y\} \sqsubseteq \{\nu \mid \nu :: b : \{\nu \mid \nu = y\} \to Top\}.$$

After SA-MONO substitutes a fresh variable, say ν', for ν in both types, this reduces to the clause implication obligation

$$\Gamma, \nu' = y \vdash true \Rrightarrow \nu' :: b : \{\nu \mid \nu = y\} \to Top.$$

Alas, this is essentially Equation 3, so we are stuck in an infinite loop! We will again extract the type U for y (aliased to ν' here) and repeat the process *ad inifinitum*.

This situation arises only if we are allowed to invoke the rule C-IMPSYN infinitely many times. In this case, C-IMPSYN extracts a single type term from the environment infinitely often, since there are only finitely many in the environment. We cut the loop with a modest restriction: along any branch of a subtyping derivation, we allow a type term to be extracted at most once. Since there are only finitely many type terms in the environment, this is enough to ensure termination. To implement this strategy, we augment the subtyping relations to take a set of "already-used" type terms as an additional parameter, which cannot be extracted by the rule C-IMPSYN. To keep the presentation in this paper simpler, we elide this restriction from the subtyping rules in Figure 5; the full definition can be found in a technical report [8]. The versions with and without this restriction may or may not coincide, but we are not particularly concerned with the outcome of this question because in our experience the kind of problematic subtyping obligation discussed in this section is a pathological corner case that does not arise in practice.

Recap. Recall that our goal is to typecheck programs which use value-indexed dictionaries which may contain functions as values. On the one hand, the theory of finite maps allows us to use logical refinements to express and verify complex invariants about the contents of dictionaries. On the other, without resorting to higher-order logic, such theories cannot express that a dictionary maps a key to a value of function type.

To resolve this tension, we introduced the novel concept of *nested refinements*, where types are nested into the logic as uninterpreted terms and the typing relation is nested as an uninterpreted predicate. The logical validity queries arising in typechecking are discharged by rearranging the formula in question into an implication between a purely logical formula and a disjunction of type predicates. This implication is discharged using a novel combination of logical queries, discharged by an SMT solver, and syntactic subtyping. This approach enables the efficient, automatic type checking of sophisticated dynamic language programs that manipulate complex data, including dictionaries which map keys to function values.

5. Soundness

At this point in the proceedings, it is customary to make a claim about the soundness of the type system by asserting that it enjoys the standard preservation and progress properties. Unfortunately, the presence of nested refinements means this route is unavailable to us, as the usual substitution property does not hold! Next, we describe why substitution is problematic and define a *stratified* system System D* for which we establish the preservation and progress properties. The soundness of System D follows, as it is a special case of the stratified System D*.

5.1 The Problems

The key insight in System D is that we can use uninterpreted functions to nest types inside refinements, thereby unlocking the door to expressive SMT-based reasoning for dynamic languages. However, this very strength precludes the usual substitution lemma upon which preservation proofs rest.

Substitution. The standard substitution property requires that if $x : S, \Gamma \vdash e :: S'$ and $\vdash w :: S$, then $\Gamma[w/x] \vdash e[w/x] :: S'[w/x]$. The following snippet shows why System D lacks this property:

```
let foo f = 0 in foo (fun x -> x + 1)
```

Suppose that we ascribe to `foo` the type

$$\texttt{foo} :: f : (Int \to Int) \to \{\nu \mid f :: Int \to Int\}.$$

The return type of the function states that its argument f is a function from integers to integers and does not impose any constraints on the return value itself. To check that `foo` does indeed have this type, by T-FUN, the following judgment must be derivable:

$$f : Int \to Int \vdash \texttt{0} :: \{\nu \mid f :: Int \to Int\} \qquad (4)$$

By T-CONST, T-SUB, S-MONO and C-VALID the judgment reduces to the implication

$$true \wedge f :: Int \to Int \wedge [\![ty(\texttt{0})]\!][\texttt{0}/\nu] \Rightarrow f :: Int \to Int.$$

which is trivially valid, thereby deriving (4), and showing that `foo` does indeed have the ascribed type.

Next, consider the call to `foo`. By T-APP, the result has type

$$\{\nu \mid \texttt{(fun x -> x + 1)} :: Int \to Int\}.$$

The expression `foo (fun x -> x + 1)` evaluates in one step to `0`. Thus, if the substitution property is to hold, `0` should also have the above type. In other words, System D must be able to derive

$$\vdash \texttt{0} :: \{\nu \mid \texttt{(fun x -> x + 1)} :: Int \to Int\}.$$

By T-CONST, T-SUB, S-MONO, and C-VALID, the judgment reduces to the implication

$$true \wedge [\![ty(\texttt{0})]\!][\texttt{0}/\nu] \Rightarrow \texttt{(fun x -> x + 1)} :: Int \to Int \qquad (5)$$

which is *invalid* as type predicates are *uninterpreted* in our refinement logic! Thus, the call to `foo` and the reduced value do not have the same type in System D, which illustrates the crux of the problem: the C-VALID rule is not closed under substitution.

Circularity. Thus, it is clear that the substitution lemma will require that we define an interpretation for type predicates. As a first attempt, we can define an interpretation $\mathcal{I}$ that interprets type predicates involving arrows as:

$$\mathcal{I} \models \lambda x.\, e :: x : T_1 \to T_2 \quad \textit{iff} \quad x : T_1 \vdash e :: T_2.$$

Next, let us replace C-VALID with the following rule that restricts the antecedent to the above interpretation:

$$\frac{\mathcal{I} \models [\![\Gamma]\!] \wedge p \Rightarrow q}{\Gamma \vdash p \Rrightarrow q}\ \text{[C-VALID-INTERPRETED]}$$

Notice that the new rule requires the implication be valid in the particular interpretation $\mathcal{I}$ instead of in all interpretations. This allows the logic to "hook back" into the type system to derive types for closed lambda expressions, thereby discharging the problematic implication query in (5). While the rule solves the problem with substitution, it does not take us safely to the shore — it introduces a circular dependence between the typing judgments and the interpretation $\mathcal{I}$. Since our refinement logic includes negation, the type system corresponding to the set of rules outlined earlier combined with C-VALID-INTERPRETED is not necessarily well-defined.

5.2 The Solution: Stratified System D*

Thus, to prove soundness, we require a well-founded means of interpreting type predicates. We achieve this by *stratifying* the interpretations and type derivations, requiring that type derivations at each level refer to interpretations at the same level, and that interpretations at each level refer to derivations at strictly lower levels. Next, we formalize this intuition and state the important lemmas and theorems. The full proofs may be found in a technical report [8].

Formally, we make the following changes. First, we index typing judgments ($\vdash_n$) and interpretations ($\mathcal{I}_n$) with a natural number n. We call these the level-n judgments and interpretations, respectively. Second, we allow level-n judgments to use the rule

$$\frac{\mathcal{I}_n \models [\![\Gamma]\!] \wedge p \Rightarrow q}{\Gamma \vdash_n p \Rrightarrow q} \text{[C-VALID-N]}$$

and the level-n interpretations to use lower-level type derivations:

$$\mathcal{I}_n \models \lambda x.\, e :: x{:}T_1 \rightarrow T_2 \quad \textit{iff} \quad x{:}T_1 \vdash_{n-1} e :: T_2.$$

Finally, we write

$$\Gamma \vdash_* e :: S \quad \textit{iff} \quad \exists n.\, \Gamma \vdash_n e :: S.$$

The derivations in System D* consist of the derivations at all levels. The following "lifting" lemma states that the derivations at each level include the derivations at all lower levels:

Lemma (Lifting Derivations).

1. *If* $\Gamma \vdash e :: S$, *then* $\Gamma \vdash_* e :: S$.
2. *If* $\Gamma \vdash_n e :: S$, *then* $\Gamma \vdash_{n+1} e :: S$.

The first clause holds since the original System D derivations cannot use the C-VALID-N rule, *i.e.* $\Gamma \vdash e :: S$ exactly when $\Gamma \vdash_0 e :: S$. The second clause follows from the definitions of $\vdash_n$ and $\mathcal{I}_n$. Stratification snaps the circularity knot and enables the proof of the following stratified substitution lemma:

Lemma (Stratified Substitution).
If $x{:}S, \Gamma \vdash_n e :: S'$ *and* $\vdash_n w :: S$,
then $\Gamma[w/x] \vdash_{n+1} e[w/x] :: S'[w/x]$.

The proof of the above depends on the following lemma, which captures the connection between our typing rules and the logical interpretation of formulas in our refinement logic:

Lemma (Satisfiable Typing).
If $\vdash_n w :: T$, *then* $\mathcal{I}_{n+1} \models [\![T]\!][w/x]$.

Stratified substitution enables the following preservation result:

Theorem (Stratified Preservation).
If $\vdash_n e :: S$, *and* $e \hookrightarrow e'$ *then* $\vdash_{n+1} e' :: S$.

From this, and a separate progress result, we establish the type soundness of System D*:

Theorem (System D* Type Soundness).
If $\vdash_* e :: S$, *then either* e *is a value or* $e \hookrightarrow e'$ *and* $\vdash_* e' :: S$.

By coupling this with Lifting, we obtain the soundness of System D as a corollary.

6. Algorithmic Typing

Having established the expressiveness and soundness of System D, we establish its practicality by implementing a type checker and applying it to several interesting examples. The declarative rules for type checking System D programs, shown in section 4, are not syntax-directed and thus unsuitable for implementation. We highlight the problematic rules and sketch an *algorithmic* version of the type system that also performs local type inference [29]. Our prototype implementation [8] verifies all of the examples in this paper and in [39], using Z3 [12] to discharge SMT obligations. A more detailed discussion of the algorithmic system may be found in a technical report [8].

6.1 Algorithmic Subtyping

Nearly all the declarative subtyping rules presented in Figure 5 are non-overlapping and directed by the structure of the judgment being derived. The sole exception is C-IMPSYN, whose first premise requires us to synthesize a type term U such that the SMT solver can prove $lw_j :: U$ for some j, where U is used in the second premise. We note that, since type predicates are uninterpreted, the only type terms U that can satisfy this criterion must come from the environment Γ. Thus, we define a procedure $\mathsf{MustFlow}(\Gamma, T)$ that uses the SMT solver to compute the set of type terms U', out of *all* possible type terms mentioned in Γ, such that for all values x, $x{:}T$ implies that $x :: U'$. To implement C-IMPSYN, we call $\mathsf{MustFlow}(\Gamma, \{\nu \mid \nu = lw_j\})$ to compute the set $\mathcal{U}$ of type terms that might be needed by the second premise. Since the declarative rule cannot possibly refer to a type term U not in Γ, this strategy guarantees that $U \in \mathcal{U}$ and, thus, does not forfeit precision.

6.2 Bidirectional Type Checking

We extend the syntax of System D with optional type annotations for binding constructs and constructed data, and, following work on local type inference [29], we define a *bidirectional* type checking algorithm. In the remainder of this section, we highlight the novel aspects of our bidirectional type system.

Function Applications. To typecheck an application $w_1\ w_2$, we must synthesize a type T_1 for the function w_1 and use type extraction to convert T_1 to a syntactic arrow. Since the procedure MustFlow can return an arbitrary number of type terms, we must decide how to proceed in the event that T_1 can be extracted to multiple different arrow types. To avoid the need for backtracking in the type checker, and to provide a semantics that is simple for the programmer, we synthesize a type for w_1 only if there is *exactly one* syntactic arrow that is applicable to the given argument w_2.

Remaining Rules. We will now briefly summarize some of the other algorithmic rules presented in a technical report [8]. Uses of T-SUB can be factored into other typing rules. However, uses of T-UNFOLD cannot, since we cannot syntactically predict where it is needed. Since we do not have pattern matching to determine exactly when to unfold type definitions, as in languages like ML, we eagerly unfold type definitions to anticipate all situations in which unfolding might be required. For let-expressions, to handle the fact that synthesized types might refer to variables that are about to go out of scope, making them ill-formed, we use several simple heuristics to eliminate occurrences of local variables. In all of the examples we have tested, the annotations provided on top-level let-bindings are sufficient to allow synthesizing well-formed types for all unannotated inner let-expressions. Precise types are synthesized for if-expressions by synthesizing the types of both branches, guarding them by the appropriate branch conditions, and conjoining them. For constructed data expressions, we allow the programmer to provide hints in type definitions that help the type checker decide how to infer type parameters that are omitted. For example, suppose the $List$ definition is updated as follows:

$$\text{type } List[+A]\{\text{"hd"}: \{\nu \mid \nu :: A\}; \text{"tl"}: \{\nu \mid \nu :: List[*A]\}\}$$

Due to the presence of the marker $*$ in the type of the "tl" field, local type inference will use the type of w_2 to infer the omitted type parameter in $List(w_1, w_2)$. Finally, although the techniques in [29] would allow us to, for simplicity we do not attempt to synthesize parameters to type functions.

Soundness. We write $\Gamma \vdash e \lhd S$ for the algorithmic type checking judgment, which verifies e against the given type S, and $\Gamma \vdash e \rhd S$ for the algorithmic type synthesis judgment, which produces a type S for expression e. Each of the techniques employed in this section are sound with respect to the declarative system, so we can show the following property, where we use a procedure erase to remove type annotations from functions, let-bindings, and constructed data because the syntax of the declarative system does not permit them:

Proposition (Sound Algorithmic Typing).
If $\Gamma \vdash e \rhd S$ *or* $\Gamma \vdash e \lhd S$, *then* $\Gamma \vdash \mathsf{erase}(e) :: S$.

7. Related Work

In this section, we highlight related approaches to statically verifying features of dynamic languages. For a thorough introduction to contract-based and other hybrid approaches, see [15, 23, 34].

Dynamic Unions and Control Flow. Among the earliest attempts at mixing static and dynamic typing was adding the special type `dynamic` to a statically-typed language like ML [1]. In this approach, an arbitrary value can be injected into `dynamic`, and a typecase construct allows inspecting its precise type at run-time. However, one cannot guarantee that a particular `dynamic` value is of one of a subset of types (cf. `negate` from section 2). Several researchers have used union types and tag-test sensitive control-flow analyses to support such idioms. Most recently, λ_{TR} [39] and λ_S [18] feature values of (untagged) union types that can be used at more precise types based on control flow. In the former, each expression is assigned two propositional formulas that hold when the expression evaluates to either true or false; these propositions are strengthened by recording the guard of an if-expression in the typing environment when typing its branches. Typechecking proceeds by solving propositional constraints to compute, for each value at each program point, the set of tags it may correspond to. The latter shows how a similar strategy can be developed in an imperative setting, by coupling a type system with a data flow analysis. However, both systems are limited to ad-hoc unions over basic and function values. In contrast, System D shows how, by pushing all the information about the value (resp. reasoning about flow) into expressive, but decidable refinement predicates (resp. into SMT solvers), one can statically reason about significantly richer idioms (related tags, dynamic dictionaries, polymorphism, *etc.*).

Records and Objects. There is a large body of work on type systems for objects [22, 28]. Several early advances incorporate records into ML [30], but the use of records in these systems is unfortunately unlikely to be flexible enough for dynamic dictionaries. In particular, record types cannot be joined when they disagree on the type of a common field, which is crucially enabled by the use of the theory of finite maps in our setting. Recent work includes type systems for JavaScript and Ruby. [3] presents a rich type system and inference algorithm for JavaScript, which uses row-types and width subtyping to model dictionaries (objects). The system does not support unions, and uses fixed field names. This issue is addressed in [38], which models dictionaries using row types labeled by singletons indexed by string constants, and depth subtyping. A recent proposal [41] incorporates an initialization phase during which object types can be updated. However, these systems preclude truly dynamic dictionaries, which require dependent types, and moreover lack the control flow analysis required to support ad-hoc unions. DRuby [17] is a powerful type system designed to support Ruby code that mixes intersections, unions, classes, and parametric polymorphism. DRuby supports "duck typing," by converting from nominal to structural types appropriately. However, it does not support ad-hoc unions or dynamic dictionary accesses.

Dependent Types for First-Order Programs. The observation that ad-hoc unions can be checked via dependent types is not new. [24] develops a dependent type system called guarded types that is used to describe records and ad-hoc unions in legacy Cobol programs that make extensive use of tag-tests, where the "tag" is simply the first few bytes of a structure. [21] presents an SMT-based system for statically inferring dependent types that verify the safety of ad-hoc unions in legacy C programs. [10] describes how type-checking and property verification are two sides of the same coin for C (which is essentially uni-typed.) It develops a precise logic-based type system for C and shows how SMT solvers can be used for type-checking. This system contains a `hastype(x,T)` which is similar to ours except that `T` ranges over a fixed set of type constants as opposed to arbitrary types. Thus, one cannot use their `hastype` to talk about complex values (*e.g.* dependent functions, duck-typed records with only some fields) nested within dictionaries in their system. Finally, the system supports function pointers but does not fully support higher-order functions. Dminor [6] uses refinement types to formalize similar ideas in a first-order functional data description language with fixed-key records and run-time tag-tests. The authors show how unions and intersections can be expressed in refinements (and even collections, via recursive functions), and hence how SMT solvers can wholly discharge all subtyping obligations. However, the above techniques apply only to first-order languages, with static keys and dictionaries over base values.

Refinement Types for Higher-Order Programs. The key novelty of System D is the introduction of *nested* refinement types, which are a generalization of the refinement types introduced by the long line of work pioneered by Xi and Pfenning [40] and further studied in [4, 11, 14, 23, 31, 35]. The main difficulty in applying these classical refinement type systems to dynamic languages is that they require a distinction between base values that are typed with refinement predicates and complex values that are typed with syntactic constructors. In particular, dynamic languages contain dependent dictionaries, which require refinements (over the theory of arrays) to describe keys but syntactic types to describe the values bound to keys. This combination is impossible with earlier refinement types systems but is enabled by nesting types within refinements.

Combining Decision Procedures. Our approach of combining logical reasoning by SMT solvers and syntactic reasoning by subtyping is reminiscent of work on combining decision procedures [26, 33]. However, such techniques require the theories being combined to be disjoint; since our logic includes type terms which themselves contain arbitrary terms, our theory of syntactic types cannot be separated from the other theories in our system, so these techniques cannot be directly applied.

8. Conclusions and Future Work

We have shown how, by nesting type predicates within refinement formulas and carefully interleaving syntactic- and SMT-based subtyping, System D can statically type check dynamic programs that manipulate dictionaries, polymorphic higher-order functions and containers. Thus, we believe that System D can be a foundation for two distinct avenues of research: the addition of heterogeneous dictionaries to static languages like C#, Java, OCaml and Haskell, or dually, the addition of expressive static typing to dynamic languages like Clojure, JavaScript, Racket, and Ruby.

We anticipate several concrete lines of work that are needed to realize the above goals. First, we need to add support for references and imperative update, features common to most popular dynamic languages. Since every dictionary operation in an imperative language goes through a reference, we will need to extend the type system with flow-sensitive analyses, as in [32] and [18], to precisely track the values stored in reference cells at each program point. Furthermore, to precisely track updates to dictionaries in the imperative setting, we will likely need to introduce some flow-sensitivity to the type system itself, adopting strong update techniques as in [19] and [41]. Second, our system treats strings as atomic constants. Instead, it should be possible to incorporate modern decision procedures for strings [20] to support logical operations on keys, which would give even more precise support for reflective metaprogramming. Third, we plan to extend our local inference techniques to automatically derive polymorphic instantiations [29] and use Liquid Types [31] to globally infer refinement types. Finally, for dynamic languages, it would be useful to incorporate some form of staged analysis to support dynamic code generation [2, 9].

Acknowledgements. The authors wish to thank Jeff Foster, Ming Kawaguchi, Sorin Lerner, Todd Millstein, Zachary Tatlock, David Walker, and the anonymous reviewers for their detailed feedback on drafts of this paper.

References

[1] M. Abadi, L. Cardelli, B. C. Pierce, and G. Plotkin. Dynamic typing in a statically-typed language. In *POPL*, 1989.

[2] J.-h. D. An, A. Chaudhuri, J. S. Foster, and M. Hicks. Dynamic inference of static types for ruby. In *POPL*, 2011.

[3] C. Anderson, S. Drossopoulou, and P. Giannini. Towards Type Inference for JavaScript. In *ECOOP*, pages 428–452, June 2005.

[4] J. Bengtson, K. Bhargavan, C. Fournet, A. Gordon, and S. Maffeis. Refinement types for secure implementations. In *CSF*, 2008.

[5] Y. Bertot and P. Castéran. Interactive theorem proving and program development. coq'art: The calculus of inductive constructions, 2004.

[6] G. M. Bierman, A. D. Gordon, C. Hritcu, and D. E. Langworthy. Semantic subtyping with an smt solver. In *ICFP*, 2010.

[7] A. R. Bradley, Z. Manna, and H. B. Sipma. What's decidable about arrays? In *VMCAI*, pages 427–442, 2006.

[8] R. Chugh, P. M. Rondon, and R. Jhala. Nested refinements: A logic for duck typing. `http://arxiv.org/abs/1103.5055v2`.

[9] R. Chugh, J. A. Meister, R. Jhala, and S. Lerner. Staged information flow for javascript. In *Proceedings of PLDI 2009*, pages 50–62, 2009.

[10] J. Condit, B. Hackett, S. K. Lahiri, and S. Qadeer. Unifying type checking and property checking for low-level code. In *POPL*, 2009.

[11] R. Davies. *Practical Refinement-Type Checking*. PhD thesis, Carnegie Mellon University, Pittsburgh, PA, USA, 2005.

[12] L. de Moura and N. Bjørner. Z3: An efficient SMT solver. In *TACAS*, 2008.

[13] L. de Moura and N. Bjørner. Generalized, efficient array decision procedures. In *FMCAD*, pages 45–52, 2009.

[14] J. Dunfield. *A Unified System of Type Refinements*. PhD thesis, Carnegie Mellon University, Pittsburgh, PA, USA, 2007.

[15] R. B. Findler and M. Felleisen. Contracts for higher-order functions. In *ICFP*, pages 48–59, 2002.

[16] C. Flanagan. Hybrid type checking. In *POPL*. ACM, 2006.

[17] M. Furr, J. hoon (David) An, J. S. Foster, and M. W. Hicks. Static type inference for ruby. In *SAC*, pages 1859–1866, 2009.

[18] A. Guha, C. Softoiu, and S. Krishnamurthi. Typing local control and state using flow analysis. In *ESOP*, 2011.

[19] P. Heidegger and P. Thiemann. Recency types for analyzing scripting languages. In *ECOOP*, pages 200–224, 2010.

[20] P. Hooimeijer and M. Veanes. An evaluation of automata algorithms for string analysis. In *VMCAI*, pages 248–262, 2011.

[21] R. Jhala, R. Majumdar, and R.-G. Xu. State of the union: Type inference via craig interpolation. In *TACAS*, 2007.

[22] A. J. Kennedy and B. C. Pierce. On decidability of nominal subtyping with variance. In *FOOL-WOOD*, 2007.

[23] K. Knowles and C. Flanagan. Hybrid type checking. *ACM TOPLAS*, 32(2), 2010.

[24] R. Komondoor, G. Ramalingam, S. Chandra, and J. Field. Dependent types for program understanding. In *TACAS*, pages 157–173, 2005.

[25] J. McCarthy. Towards a mathematical science of computation. In *In IFIP Congress*, pages 21–28. North-Holland, 1962.

[26] G. Nelson and D. C. Oppen. Simplification by cooperating decision procedures. *TOPLAS*, 1979.

[27] X. Ou, G. Tan, Y. Mandelbaum, and D. Walker. Dynamic typing with dependent types. In *IFIP TCS*, pages 437–450, 2004.

[28] J. Palsberg and M. I. Schwartzbach. *OO Type Systems*. Wiley, 1994.

[29] B. C. Pierce and D. N. Turner. Local type inference. In *POPL*, pages 252–265, 1998.

[30] D. Rémy. Type checking records and variants in a natural extension of ml. In *POPL*, 1989.

[31] P. Rondon, M. Kawaguchi, and R. Jhala. Liquid types. In *PLDI*, 2008.

[32] P. Rondon, M. Kawaguchi, and R. Jhala. Low-level liquid types. In *POPL*, pages 131–144, 2010.

[33] R. Shostak. Deciding combinations of theories. *Journal of the ACM*, 31(1):1–12, 1984.

[34] J. Siek and W. Taha. Gradual typing for functional languages. In *Scheme and Functional Programming Workshop*, 2006.

[35] N. Swamy, J. Chen, and R. Chugh. Enforcing stateful authorization and information flow policies in fine. In *ESOP*, 2010.

[36] The Dojo Foundation. Dojo toolkit. `http://dojotoolkit.org/`.

[37] The Python Software Foundation. Python 3.2 standard library. `http://python.org/`.

[38] P. Thiemann. Towards a type system for analyzing javascript programs. In *ESOP*, 2005.

[39] S. Tobin-Hochstadt and M. Felleisen. Logical types for untyped languages. In *ICFP*, pages 117–128, 2010.

[40] H. Xi and F. Pfenning. Dependent types in practical programming. In *POPL*, 1999.

[41] T. Zhao. Type inference for scripting languages with implicit extension. In *FOOL*, 2010.

An Abstract Interpretation Framework for Termination

Patrick Cousot
CNRS, École Normale Supérieure, and INRIA, France
Courant Institute*, NYU, USA
cousot@ens.fr, pcousot@cims.nyu.edu

Radhia Cousot
CNRS, École Normale Supérieure, and INRIA, France
rcousot@ens.fr

Abstract

Proof, verification and analysis methods for termination all rely on two induction principles: (1) a variant function or induction on data ensuring progress towards the end and (2) some form of induction on the program structure.

The abstract interpretation design principle is first illustrated for the design of new forward and backward proof, verification and analysis methods for *safety*. The safety collecting semantics defining the strongest safety property of programs is first expressed in a constructive fixpoint form. Safety proof and checking/verification methods then immediately follow by fixpoint induction. Static analysis of abstract safety properties such as invariance are constructively designed by fixpoint abstraction (or approximation) to (automatically) infer safety properties. So far, no such clear design principle did exist for termination so that the existing approaches are scattered and largely not comparable with each other.

For (1), we show that this design principle applies equally well to *potential and definite termination*. The trace-based termination collecting semantics is given a fixpoint definition. Its abstraction yields a fixpoint definition of the best variant function. By further abstraction of this best variant function, we derive the Floyd/Turing termination proof method as well as new static analysis methods to effectively compute approximations of this best variant function.

For (2), we introduce a generalization of the syntactic notion of structural induction (as found in Hoare logic) into a *semantic structural induction* based on the new semantic concept of *inductive trace cover* covering execution traces by *segments*, a new basis for formulating program properties. Its abstractions allow for generalized recursive proof, verification and static analysis methods by induction on both program structure, control, and data. Examples of particular instances include Floyd's handling of loop cut-points as well as nested loops, Burstall's intermittent assertion total correctness proof method, and Podelski-Rybalchenko transition invariants.

Categories and Subject Descriptors D.2.4 [*Software/Program Verification*]; D.3.1 [*Formal Definitions and Theory*]; F.3.1 [*Specifying and Verifying and Reasoning about Programs*].

General Terms Languages, Reliability, Security, Theory, Verification.

Keywords Abstract Interpretation, Induction, Proof, Safety, Static analysis, Variant function, Verification, Termination.

1. Introduction

Floyd/Turing program proof methods for invariance and termination [24, 40, 59] have inspired most sound static analysis methods.

For static *invariance* analysis by abstract interpretation [19, 21], a key step is to express the strongest invariant as a fixpoint and next to approximate this strongest invariant to automatically infer an abstract inductive invariant using the constructive fixpoint approximation methods.

For static *termination* analysis, the discovery of variant functions is either decidable in limited cases [54] or else is based on the Floyd/Turing idea of variant functions into well-founded sets obtained by observing quantities that strictly decrease within loops while remaining lower-bounded, or dually. So most termination analysis methods indirectly reduce to a relational invariance analysis hence can reuse classical static analysis methods.

The abstract interpretation design principle is instantiated with suitable abstractions for *safety* and *termination* analysis, proof, and checking/verification (either potential termination or definite termination for nondeterministic systems).

The first main idea for termination is that there exists a most precise variant function that can be expressed in fixpoint form by abstract interpretation of a termination collecting semantics itself abstracting the program operational trace semantics. This yields new static analysis methods automatically inferring abstractions of that variant function by the constructive fixpoint approximation methods of abstract interpretation.

The second main idea introduced in this paper both for safety and termination is that of *semantic structural induction*, including termination proofs, over *trace segment covers* and their abstractions. Trace segments are more powerful than binary relations between states which have been used traditionally in program termination proofs (for example, the transition invariants used in [53] are binary relation abstractions of the set of trace segments). Examples include structural induction on the program syntax (including loop invariants à la Floyd [40]), induction on data, à la Burstall [3], the covering of the transition relation closure by well-founded relations, à la Podelski-Rybalchenko [53], their combinations and generalizations.

2. Fixpoints, fixpoint induction, abstraction, and approximation

We express semantics as *fixpoints* of maps $f \in A \mapsto A$ i.e. elements $x \in A$ such that $x = f(x)$. We let $\mathsf{lfp}_a^{\sqsubseteq} f$ be the *least fixpoint* of $f \in A \mapsto A$ on the poset $\langle A, \sqsubseteq\rangle$ greater than or equal to $a \in A$, if any. The dual notion is that of *greatest fixpoint* $\mathsf{gfp}_a^{\sqsubseteq} f$. We write $\mathsf{lfp}^{\sqsubseteq} f$ if a is the infimum of A, and $\mathsf{lfp}\, f$ if the partial order $\sqsubseteq$ is clear from the context. By Tarski/Pataria's fixpoint theorem [50, 58], $\mathsf{lfp}_a^{\sqsubseteq} f = \bigsqcap\{P \in A \mid a \sqsubseteq P \wedge f(P) \sqsubseteq P\}$ exists for f increasing[1] on a complete lattice $\langle A, \sqsubseteq, a, \top, \sqcup, \sqcap\rangle$[2] or on a cpo $\langle A, \sqsubseteq, a, \sqcup\rangle$[3]. The *fixpoint iterates* are $f^0 \triangleq a$, $\forall n \in \mathbb{N} : f^{n+1} = f(f^n)$, $f^\omega \triangleq \bigsqcup_{n\in\mathbb{N}} f^n$ which is $\mathsf{lfp}_a^{\sqsubseteq} f$ when $a \sqsubseteq f(a)$ is a pre-fixpoint and f is continuous[4,5,6]. If f is increasing but not continuous, transfinite iterations may have to be used [22].

[1] $f \in A \mapsto A$ is *increasing* (also *monotone*, *isotone*, ...) on a poset $\langle A, \sqsubseteq\rangle$ if and only if $\forall x, y \in A : (x \sqsubseteq y) \implies (f(x) \sqsubseteq f(y))$ [36].

[2] A *complete lattice* $\langle A, \sqsubseteq, \bot, \top, \sqcup, \sqcap\rangle$ is a poset s. t. any subset has a least upper bound (lub) $\sqcup$, hence a greatest lower bound (glb) $\sqcap$, $\bot = \sqcup\emptyset$, $\top = \sqcap\emptyset$.

[3] A *complete partial order* (cpo) $\langle A, \sqsubseteq, \bot, \sqcup\rangle$ is a poset $\langle A, \sqsubseteq\rangle$ such that any increasing chain $C \subseteq A$ such that $\forall x, y \in C : x \sqsubseteq y \vee y \sqsubseteq x$ has a least upper bound (lub) $\sqcup C$, hence has an infimum $\bot = \sqcup\emptyset$ for the empty chain.

[4] $f \in A \mapsto A$ is *continuous* on a poset $\langle A, \sqsubseteq, \sqcup\rangle$ if and only if for all increasing chains $C \in \wp(A)$ such that its lub $\sqcup C$ does exist then the lub $\sqcup f[C]$ exists and is such that $\sqcup f[C] = f(\sqcup C)$.

[5] $\wp(X)$ or 2^X is the powerset of X i.e. the set of all subsets of a set X.

[6] The *post-image* (or *image*) of $X \in \wp(A)$ by a map $f \in A \mapsto B$ is $f[X] \triangleq \{f(x) \mid x \in X\} \in \wp(B)$.

* Work supported in part by the CMACS NSF Expeditions in Computing award 0926166.

POPL'12, January 25–27, 2012, Philadelphia, PA, USA.

Fixpoint induction follows immediately as a sound ($\Longleftarrow$) and complete ($\Longrightarrow$) proof method since for all $S \in A$,

$$\mathsf{lfp}^{\sqsubseteq}_{a} f \sqsubseteq S \quad\Longleftrightarrow\quad \exists P \in A : a \sqsubseteq P \wedge f(P) \sqsubseteq P \wedge P \sqsubseteq S\ .$$

S is called a *specification* or *invariant* and P is an *inductive invariant*. The idea is that to prove an invariant S, one has to check (in checking/verification methods), to guess (in proof methods) or to compute (in analysis methods) a stronger inductive invariant P.

Following [19, 21], abstraction is formalized by *Galois connections*[7] $\langle A, \sqsubseteq\rangle \underset{\alpha}{\overset{\gamma}{\leftrightarrows}} \langle B, \preceq\rangle$ between posets $\langle A, \sqsubseteq\rangle$ and $\langle B, \preceq\rangle$ meaning that $\alpha \in A \mapsto B$, $\gamma \in B \mapsto A$ and $\forall x \in A : \forall y \in B : \alpha(x) \preceq y \iff x \sqsubseteq \gamma(y)$. We write $\langle A, \sqsubseteq\rangle \underset{\alpha}{\overset{\gamma}{\leftarrows\!\!\twoheadrightarrow}} \langle B, \preceq\rangle$ when the *abstraction* α is surjective (hence the *concretization* γ is injective), $\langle A, \sqsubseteq\rangle \underset{\alpha}{\overset{\gamma}{\twoheadleftarrow\!\!\rightarrows}} \langle B, \preceq\rangle$ when α is injective (hence γ is surjective), and $\langle A, \sqsubseteq\rangle \underset{\alpha}{\overset{\gamma}{\twoheadleftarrow\!\!\twoheadrightarrow}} \langle B, \preceq\rangle$ when α is bijective.

Given a concrete fixpoint characterization $\mathsf{lfp}^{\sqsubseteq}_{a} f$ of program properties on complete lattices or cpos $\langle A, \sqsubseteq\rangle$ with $a \sqsubseteq f(a)$ and an abstraction $\langle A, \sqsubseteq\rangle \underset{\alpha}{\overset{\gamma}{\leftrightarrows}} \langle B, \preceq\rangle$, the sufficient *commutation condition* $\alpha \circ f = \overline{f} \circ \alpha$ (respectively *semi-commutation condition* $\alpha \circ f \mathrel{\dot\preceq} \overline{f} \circ \alpha$)[8] implies the *fixpoint abstraction* $\alpha(\mathsf{lfp}^{\sqsubseteq}_{a} f) = \mathsf{lfp}^{\preceq}_{\alpha(a)} \overline{f}$ (resp. *fixpoint approximation* $\alpha(\mathsf{lfp}^{\sqsubseteq}_{a} f) \preceq \mathsf{lfp}^{\preceq}_{\alpha(a)} \overline{f}$) [21]. The [semi-]commutation condition can be restricted to the iterates of f from a or to the elements of A which are $\sqsubseteq$-less that or equal to $\mathsf{lfp}^{\sqsubseteq}_{a} f$. The result also holds when α is continuous [13]. In absence of existence of a best abstraction, similar results can be obtained using only one of the abstraction or concretization functions [26].

3. Transition semantics

We consider a *programming language* with nondeterministic *programs* P. The set of all *states* of P is $\Sigma\llbracket \mathrm{P}\rrbracket$. The *transition relation* $\tau\llbracket \mathrm{P}\rrbracket \in \wp(\Sigma\llbracket \mathrm{P}\rrbracket \times \Sigma\llbracket \mathrm{P}\rrbracket)$ describes the possible transitions between a state and its immediate successor states during program execution [11, 21]. The program small-step operational semantics is the *transition system* $\langle \Sigma\llbracket \mathrm{P}\rrbracket, \tau\llbracket \mathrm{P}\rrbracket\rangle$. When restricting to *initial states* $\mathsf{I}\llbracket \mathrm{P}\rrbracket \in \wp(\Sigma\llbracket \mathrm{P}\rrbracket)$, we write $\langle \Sigma\llbracket \mathrm{P}\rrbracket, \mathsf{I}\llbracket \mathrm{P}\rrbracket, \tau\llbracket \mathrm{P}\rrbracket\rangle$. The *termination/blocking states* are $\beta_\tau\llbracket \mathrm{P}\rrbracket \triangleq \{s \in \Sigma\llbracket \mathrm{P}\rrbracket \mid \forall s' \in \Sigma\llbracket \mathrm{P}\rrbracket : \langle s, s'\rangle \notin \tau\llbracket \mathrm{P}\rrbracket\}$. For brevity we write X for $X\llbracket \mathrm{P}\rrbracket$ e.g. $\langle \Sigma, \tau\rangle$, $\langle \Sigma, \mathsf{I}, \tau\rangle$, or β_τ.

4. Trace semantics

4.1 Traces

We let Σ^n ($\Sigma^0 \triangleq \emptyset$), $\Sigma^+ = \bigcup_{n\in\mathbb{N}} \Sigma^n$, $\Sigma^* \triangleq \Sigma^+ \cup \{\varepsilon\}$, Σ^∞, $\Sigma^{+\infty} \triangleq \Sigma^+ \cup \Sigma^\infty$, and $\Sigma^{*\infty} \triangleq \Sigma^* \cup \Sigma^\infty$ be the set of all *finite traces of length* $n \in \mathbb{N}$, *non-empty finite*, *finite*, *infinite*, *non-empty finite or infinite*, and *finite or infinite traces* over the states Σ where ε is the *empty trace*.

We define the following operations on traces, writing $|\sigma|$ for the length of the trace $\sigma \in \Sigma^{+\infty}$, $\sigma[n, m]$, $0 \leqslant n \leqslant m$ for the *subtrace* $\sigma_n, \sigma_{n+1}, \ldots, \sigma_{\min(m,|\sigma|-1)}$ of σ, and $\sigma\sigma'$ for the *concatenation* of $\sigma, \sigma' \in \Sigma^{*\infty}$ (with $\sigma\varepsilon = \varepsilon\sigma = \sigma$ and $\sigma\sigma' = \sigma$ when $\sigma \in \Sigma^\infty$).

We define the following operations on sets of traces writing S for the set of traces $\{\sigma \in \Sigma^1 \mid \sigma_0 \in S\}$ made of one state of $S \in \wp(\Sigma)$ (for example, the termination states $\beta_\tau \triangleq \{s \in \Sigma \mid \forall s' \in \Sigma : \langle s, s'\rangle \notin \tau\}$ can also be understood as traces of length one $\{\sigma \in \Sigma^1 \mid \forall s \in \Sigma : \langle \sigma_0, s\rangle \notin \tau\}$), t for the set of traces $\{\sigma \in \Sigma^2 \mid \langle \sigma_0, \sigma_1\rangle \in t\}$ made of two consecutive states of the relation $t \in \wp(\Sigma \times \Sigma)$, $T^+ \triangleq T \cap \Sigma^+$ for the *selection of the non-empty finite traces* of $T \in \wp(\Sigma^{*\infty})$, $T^\infty \triangleq T \cap \Sigma^\infty$ for the *selection of the infinite traces* of $T, TT' \triangleq \{\sigma\sigma' \mid \sigma \in T \wedge \sigma' \in T'\}$ for the *concatenation* of sets of traces, and $T \fatsemi T' \triangleq \{\sigma s\sigma' \mid s \in \Sigma \wedge \sigma s \in T \wedge s\sigma' \in T'\}$ for the *sequencing* of sets of traces $T, T' \in \wp(\Sigma^{*\infty})$.

4.2 Partial and complete / maximal trace semantics

The *partial trace semantics* $\Theta^{+\infty}\llbracket \mathrm{P}\rrbracket \in \wp(\Sigma^{+\infty}\llbracket \mathrm{P}\rrbracket)$ of a program P is a set of non-empty execution traces. In particular, the *partial trace semantics generated by a transition system* $\langle \Sigma, \tau\rangle$ is $\tau^{\ddot{+}\infty}\llbracket \mathrm{P}\rrbracket$ such that[9]

$$\begin{aligned}
\tau^{\ddot{n}}\llbracket \mathrm{P}\rrbracket &\triangleq \left\{\sigma \in \Sigma^n \;\middle|\; \forall i \in [0, n-1) : \langle \sigma_i, \sigma_{i+1}\rangle \in \tau\llbracket \mathrm{P}\rrbracket\right\}, \quad n \geqslant 0\\
\tau^{\infty}\llbracket \mathrm{P}\rrbracket &\triangleq \left\{\sigma \in \Sigma^\infty \;\middle|\; \forall i \in \mathbb{N} : \langle \sigma_i, \sigma_{i+1}\rangle \in \tau\llbracket \mathrm{P}\rrbracket\right\}\\
\tau^{\ddot{+}}\llbracket \mathrm{P}\rrbracket &\triangleq \bigcup_{n>0} \tau^{\ddot{n}}\llbracket \mathrm{P}\rrbracket, \qquad \tau^{\ddot{+}\infty}\llbracket \mathrm{P}\rrbracket \triangleq \tau^{\ddot{+}}\llbracket \mathrm{P}\rrbracket \cup \tau^{\infty}\llbracket \mathrm{P}\rrbracket\ .
\end{aligned}$$

The *complete* or *maximal trace semantics* $\tau^{n}\llbracket \mathrm{P}\rrbracket \triangleq \alpha_M(\tau^{\ddot{n}}\llbracket \mathrm{P}\rrbracket)$, $\tau^{+}\llbracket \mathrm{P}\rrbracket = \alpha_M(\tau^{\ddot{+}}\llbracket \mathrm{P}\rrbracket)$ and $\tau^{+\infty}\llbracket \mathrm{P}\rrbracket \triangleq \alpha_M(\tau^{\ddot{+}\infty}\llbracket \mathrm{P}\rrbracket)$ are obtained by the abstraction $\langle \wp(\Sigma^{+\infty}), \subseteq\rangle \underset{\alpha_M}{\overset{\gamma_M}{\leftarrows\!\!\twoheadrightarrow}} \langle \wp(\Sigma^{+\infty}), \subseteq\rangle$ where

$$\alpha_M(T) \triangleq \bigcup_{n\in\mathbb{N}} \left\{\sigma \in T \cap \Sigma^n \;\middle|\; \sigma_{n-1} \in \beta_\tau\llbracket \mathrm{P}\rrbracket\right\} \cup T^\infty$$

eliminates those finite partial computations that are not terminated.

4.3 Fixpoint trace semantics

The partial trace semantics of a program P can be given in fixpoint form [28].

$$\begin{aligned}
\tau^{\ddot{+}}\llbracket \mathrm{P}\rrbracket &= \mathsf{lfp}^{\subseteq}_{\emptyset}\, \overleftarrow{\phi}^{\ddot{+}}_{\tau}\llbracket \mathrm{P}\rrbracket = \mathsf{lfp}^{\subseteq}_{\emptyset}\, \overrightarrow{\phi}^{\ddot{+}}_{\tau}\llbracket \mathrm{P}\rrbracket, \qquad \tau^{\infty}\llbracket \mathrm{P}\rrbracket = \mathsf{gfp}^{\subseteq}_{\Sigma^\infty}\, \overleftarrow{\phi}^{\infty}_{\tau}\llbracket \mathrm{P}\rrbracket\\
\tau^{\ddot{+}\infty}\llbracket \mathrm{P}\rrbracket &= \mathsf{lfp}^{\subseteq}_{\emptyset}\, \overleftarrow{\phi}^{\ddot{+}}_{\tau}\llbracket \mathrm{P}\rrbracket \cup \mathsf{gfp}^{\subseteq}_{\Sigma^\infty}\, \overleftarrow{\phi}^{\infty}_{\tau}\llbracket \mathrm{P}\rrbracket = \mathsf{lfp}^{\sqsubseteq}_{\Sigma^\infty}\, \overleftarrow{\phi}^{\ddot{+}\infty}_{\tau}\llbracket \mathrm{P}\rrbracket
\end{aligned}$$

$$\overleftarrow{\phi}^{\ddot{+}}_{\tau}\llbracket \mathrm{P}\rrbracket T \triangleq \Sigma^1 \cup \tau\llbracket \mathrm{P}\rrbracket \fatsemi T \qquad \overrightarrow{\phi}^{\ddot{+}}_{\tau}\llbracket \mathrm{P}\rrbracket T \triangleq \Sigma^1 \cup T \fatsemi \tau\llbracket \mathrm{P}\rrbracket$$

$$\overleftarrow{\phi}^{\infty}_{\tau}\llbracket \mathrm{P}\rrbracket T \triangleq \tau\llbracket \mathrm{P}\rrbracket \fatsemi T \qquad \overleftarrow{\phi}^{\ddot{+}\infty}_{\tau}\llbracket \mathrm{P}\rrbracket T \triangleq \Sigma^1 \sqcup \tau\llbracket \mathrm{P}\rrbracket \fatsemi T$$

where $\langle \wp(\Sigma^{*\infty}), \sqsubseteq, \Sigma^\infty, \Sigma^*, \sqcup, \sqcap\rangle$ is a complete lattice for the *computational order* $(T_1 \sqsubseteq T_2) \triangleq (T_1^+ \subseteq T_2^+) \wedge (T_1^\infty \supseteq T_2^\infty)$ and $(T_1 \sqcup T_2) \triangleq (T_1^+ \cup T_2^+) \cup (T_1^\infty \cap T_2^\infty)$. The fixpoint complete trace semantics of a program P is calculated by abstraction with α_M.

$\tau^{+\infty}\llbracket \mathrm{P}\rrbracket = \mathsf{lfp}^{\subseteq}_{\emptyset}\, \overleftarrow{\phi}^{+}_{\tau}\llbracket \mathrm{P}\rrbracket \cup \mathsf{gfp}^{\subseteq}_{\Sigma^\infty}\, \overleftarrow{\phi}^{\infty}_{\tau}\llbracket \mathrm{P}\rrbracket = \mathsf{lfp}^{\sqsubseteq}_{\Sigma^\infty}\, \overleftarrow{\phi}^{+\infty}_{\tau}\llbracket \mathrm{P}\rrbracket$ where $\overleftarrow{\phi}^{+}_{\tau}\llbracket \mathrm{P}\rrbracket T \triangleq \beta_\tau\llbracket \mathrm{P}\rrbracket \cup \tau\llbracket \mathrm{P}\rrbracket \fatsemi T$, and $\overleftarrow{\phi}^{+\infty}_{\tau}\llbracket \mathrm{P}\rrbracket T \triangleq \beta_\tau\llbracket \mathrm{P}\rrbracket \sqcup \tau\llbracket \mathrm{P}\rrbracket \fatsemi T$.

5. Properties

Following [19, 21], properties are represented by the set of elements which have these properties. So the properties of programs which semantics are sets of traces in $\wp(\Sigma^{+\infty})$ are sets of sets of traces in $\wp(\wp(\Sigma^{+\infty}))$.

The *collecting semantics* $\{\Theta^{+\infty}\llbracket \mathrm{P}\rrbracket\} \in \wp(\wp(\Sigma^{+\infty}))$ is the strongest program property[10] of a program with trace semantics $\Theta^{+\infty}\llbracket \mathrm{P}\rrbracket$.

The *trace property abstraction* of program properties is $\langle \wp(\wp(\Sigma^{+\infty})), \subseteq\rangle \underset{\alpha_\Theta}{\overset{\gamma_\Theta}{\leftrightarrows}} \langle \wp(\Sigma^{+\infty}), \subseteq\rangle$ such that

$$\alpha_\Theta(P) \triangleq \bigcup P \quad\text{and}\quad \gamma_\Theta(Q) \triangleq \wp(Q)\ .$$

The traditional safety/liveness program properties are relative to the trace property abstraction of the collecting semantics $\alpha_\Theta(\{\Theta^{+\infty}\llbracket \mathrm{P}\rrbracket\}) = \Theta^{+\infty}\llbracket \mathrm{P}\rrbracket \in \wp(\Sigma^{+\infty})$.

Some program properties are not trace properties [5]. An example is "all program executions are deterministic" which is $\{\{\sigma\} \mid$

---

[7] [21] also introduced formalizations of abstraction using closure operators, ideals, congruences, etc. and showed all of them to be equivalent to Galois connections.

[8] $\dot\sqsubseteq$ is the pointwise extension of a partial order $\sqsubseteq$ to maps $f \mathrel{\dot\sqsubseteq} g \triangleq \forall x : f(x) \sqsubseteq g(x)$.

[9] $[n, m] \triangleq \{n, n+1, \ldots, m\}$ is the closed interval, $\emptyset$ when $m < n$, while $[n, m) \triangleq \{n, n+1, \ldots, m-1\}$ is left closed and right opened, $\emptyset$ when $m \leqslant n$.

[10] *strongest* in that the collecting semantics implies all other program properties (where logical implication $A \Longrightarrow B$ is interpreted as $A \subseteq B$).

$\sigma \in \Sigma^{+\infty}\} \in \wp(\wp(\Sigma^{+\infty}))$ [11]. The corresponding trace property abstraction is $\alpha_\Theta(\{\{\sigma\} \mid \sigma \in \Sigma^{+\infty}\}) = \Sigma^{+\infty} \in \wp(\Sigma^{+\infty})$ which would allow any non-deterministic behavior so that determinism in the concrete domain $\wp(\wp(\Sigma^{+\infty}))$ is completely lost in the abstract domain $\wp(\Sigma^{+\infty})$.

For safety and termination and from now on, we only have to consider trace properties, which form a complete Boolean lattice $\langle \wp(\Sigma^{+\infty}), \subseteq, \emptyset, \Sigma^{+\infty}, \cup, \cap, \neg\rangle$ where the partial order $\subseteq$ is logical implication and the complement is $\neg X \triangleq \Sigma^{+\infty} \setminus X$ [12].

6. Safety trace semantics

We now illustrate the classical abstract interpretation framework by generalizing invariance verification and static analysis to arbitrary safety properties. Safety properties are abstractions of program trace properties (essentially forgetting about liveness properties).

6.1 Safety abstraction

The *prefix abstraction* of a set T of traces is the topological closure[13]

$$\mathsf{pf}(\sigma) \triangleq \{\sigma' \in \Sigma^{+\infty} \mid \exists \sigma'' \in \Sigma^{*\infty} : \sigma = \sigma'\sigma''\}$$
$$\mathsf{pf}(T) \triangleq \bigcup\{\mathsf{pf}(\sigma) \mid \sigma \in T\} .$$

The prefix abstraction expresses the fact that program executions can only be observed for a finite period of time ($\forall T : \varepsilon \notin \mathsf{pf}(T)$).

The *limit abstraction* of a set of traces is the topological closure

$$\mathsf{lm}(T) \triangleq T \cup \{\sigma \in \Sigma^{\infty} \mid \forall n \in \mathbb{N} : \sigma[0,n] \in T\} .$$

The limit abstraction expresses the fact that when observing program executions for finite periods of time it is impossible to distinguish between non-terminating and unbounded finite executions.

The *safety abstraction* of a set of traces is the topological closure

$$\mathsf{sf} \triangleq \mathsf{lm} \circ \mathsf{pf} = \mathsf{pf} \circ \mathsf{lm} \circ \mathsf{pf} .$$

The safety abstraction provides the strongest program property resulting from finite observations of program executions (excluding the observation of infinite executions).

(Topological) closures $\rho \in A \mapsto A$ on a poset $\langle A, \leqslant\rangle$ are abstractions[14] $\langle A, \leqslant\rangle \xrightleftharpoons[\rho]{1_A} \langle \rho[A], \leqslant\rangle$.

6.2 Safety trace properties

The *safety trace properties* are

$$\mathsf{SF} \triangleq \mathsf{sf}[\wp(\Sigma^{+\infty})] = \{\mathsf{sf}(P) \mid P \in \wp(\Sigma^{+\infty})\} = \{P \in \wp(\Sigma^{+\infty}) \mid \mathsf{sf}(P) = P\} .$$

We have the Galois isomorphism

$$\langle \mathsf{SF}, \subseteq\rangle \xrightleftharpoons[\mathsf{pf}^+]{\mathsf{lm}} \langle \mathsf{pf}^+[\wp(\Sigma^+)], \subseteq\rangle$$

where $\mathsf{pf}^+(T) = \mathsf{pf}(T)^+$ and so safety trace properties can equivalently be represented by their finite prefixes in Sect. 6.4 and 6.5.

6.3 Safety semantics

The *safety semantics* of a program P is its strongest safety property

$$\tau^{\mathsf{sf}}[\![\mathrm{P}]\!] \triangleq \mathsf{sf}(\tau^{\ddot{+}\infty}[\![\mathrm{P}]\!]) \simeq \mathsf{pf}^+ \circ \mathsf{sf}(\tau^{\ddot{+}\infty}[\![\mathrm{P}]\!]) .$$

6.4 Fixpoint safety semantics

It follows, by fixpoint abstraction, that the safety semantics of a program P with operational semantics $\langle\Sigma, \tau\rangle$ is

$$\tau^{\mathsf{sf}}[\![\mathrm{P}]\!] = \mathsf{lfp}^{\subseteq}_{\emptyset}\, \overrightarrow{\phi}^{\mathsf{sf}}_{\tau}[\![\mathrm{P}]\!] = \mathsf{lfp}^{\subseteq}_{\emptyset}\, \overleftarrow{\phi}^{\mathsf{sf}}_{\tau}[\![\mathrm{P}]\!] \quad \text{where}$$
$$\overrightarrow{\phi}^{\mathsf{sf}}_{\tau}[\![\mathrm{P}]\!]T \triangleq \Sigma^1 \cup T \,\mathring{,}\, \tau[\![\mathrm{P}]\!] \quad \text{forward trace transformer}$$
$$\overleftarrow{\phi}^{\mathsf{sf}}_{\tau}[\![\mathrm{P}]\!]T \triangleq \Sigma^1 \cup \tau[\![\mathrm{P}]\!] \,\mathring{,}\, T \quad \text{backward trace transformer.}$$

6.5 Proofs in the safety trace domain

By fixpoint induction, one immediately gets new forward and backward sound and complete safety proof methods[15] generalizing invariance [37, 40, 48, 49]. For all safety specifications $S \in \mathsf{SF}$,

$$\tau^{\mathsf{sf}}[\![\mathrm{P}]\!] \subseteq S \iff \exists P \in \mathsf{SF} : \Sigma^1 \subseteq P \wedge \tau[\![\mathrm{P}]\!] \,\mathring{,}\, P \subseteq P \wedge P \subseteq S$$
$$\iff \exists P \in \mathsf{SF} : \Sigma^1 \subseteq P \wedge P \,\mathring{,}\, \tau[\![\mathrm{P}]\!] \subseteq P \wedge P \subseteq S .$$

Observe that forward and backward safety semantics and proof methods are respectively equivalent. This property is preserved by relational abstractions in next Sect. 7, but this is not the general case (e.g. with abstractions of Sect. 7.6). [42] is an example of static analysis in the safety trace domain.

7. Invariance / reachability semantics

Invariance/reachability is an abstraction of safety and so invariance proof methods are abstractions of safety proof methods.

7.1 Relational abstraction

The *relational abstraction* $\langle \mathsf{SF}, \subseteq\rangle \xrightleftharpoons[\alpha^{\mathsf{R}}]{\gamma^{\mathsf{R}}} \langle \wp(\Sigma \times \Sigma), \subseteq\rangle$ such that

$$\alpha^{\mathsf{R}}(T) \triangleq \{\langle \sigma_0, \sigma_{n-1}\rangle \mid n > 0 \wedge \sigma \in \Sigma^n \cap T\} \quad (1)$$
$$\gamma^{\mathsf{R}}(R) \triangleq \{\sigma \in \Sigma^n \mid n > 0 \wedge \langle \sigma_0, \sigma_{n-1}\rangle \in R\}$$

abstracts traces by a relation between their initial and final states (so that intermediate computations are lost in that abstraction).

7.2 Relational invariance / reachability abstraction

Applied to a safety semantics which is prefix-closed, the relational abstraction provides a relation between initial and current states (where, in particular, "initial" can be any state).

The abstraction $\alpha^{\mathsf{R}} \circ \mathsf{sf}$ is therefore equal to the *relational reachability abstraction* $\langle \wp(\Sigma^{+\infty}), \subseteq\rangle \xrightleftharpoons[\alpha^{\mathsf{R}^*}]{\gamma^{\mathsf{R}^*}} \langle \wp(\Sigma \times \Sigma), \subseteq\rangle$ such that

$$\alpha^{\mathsf{R}^*}(T) \triangleq \{\langle \sigma_0, \sigma_i\rangle \mid \exists n : 0 \leqslant i < n \wedge \sigma \in \Sigma^n \cap T\}$$
$$\gamma^{\mathsf{R}^*}(R) \triangleq \{\sigma \in \Sigma^n \mid n > 0 \wedge \forall i \in [0,n) : \langle \sigma_0, \sigma_i\rangle \in R\}$$

abstract traces by a relation between their initial and current states.

7.3 Relational invariance / reachability semantics

The relational invariance/reachability semantics of a program P is its strongest relational reachability property

$$\tau^{\mathsf{R}}[\![\mathrm{P}]\!] \triangleq \alpha^{\mathsf{R}}(\tau^{+\infty}[\![\mathrm{P}]\!])$$
$$\tau^{\mathsf{R}^*}[\![\mathrm{P}]\!] \triangleq \alpha^{\mathsf{R}}(\tau^{\ddot{+}\infty}[\![\mathrm{P}]\!]) = \alpha^{\mathsf{R}^*}(\tau^{+\infty}[\![\mathrm{P}]\!]) = \alpha^{\mathsf{R}}(\tau^{\mathsf{sf}}[\![\mathrm{P}]\!]) = \alpha^{\mathsf{R}^*}(\tau^{\mathsf{sf}}[\![\mathrm{P}]\!]) .$$

7.4 Fixpoint relational invariance / reachability semantics

The commutation condition applied to the transformer of the safety semantics $\tau^{\mathsf{sf}}[\![\mathrm{P}]\!]$ yields the fixpoint characterization of the relational reachability semantics of a program P with operational semantics $\langle\Sigma, \tau\rangle$

$$\tau^{\mathsf{R}^*}[\![\mathrm{P}]\!] = \mathsf{lfp}^{\subseteq}_{\emptyset}\, \overrightarrow{\phi}^{\mathsf{R}^*}_{\tau}[\![\mathrm{P}]\!] = \mathsf{lfp}^{\subseteq}_{\emptyset}\, \overleftarrow{\phi}^{\mathsf{R}^*}_{\tau}[\![\mathrm{P}]\!]$$

where[16]

---

[11] Assuming inputs, if any, to be part of the states.

[12] $X \setminus Y \triangleq \{x \in X \mid x \notin Y\}$ is the *set difference*.

[13] A *topological closure* on a poset $\langle A, \leqslant, \vee\rangle$ with partial-order $\leqslant$ and lub $\vee$, if any, is a map $\rho \in A \mapsto A$ which is *extensive* $\forall x \in A : x \leqslant \rho(x)$, *idempotent* $\forall x \in A : \rho(\rho(x)) = \rho(x)$, and finite *lub-preserving* $\forall x, y \in A : \rho(x \vee y) = \rho(x) \vee \rho(y)$. This implies that ρ is *increasing*. A *closure* is extensive, idempotent, and increasing.

[14] 1_A is the *identity* map (respectively relation) on the set A mapping any element $x \in A$ to itself $1_A(x) = x$ (resp. $1_A \triangleq \{\langle x, x\rangle \mid x \in A\}$).

[15] In case a temporal logic is used for expressing the inductive safety invariant, this is *relative completeness* subject to an *expressivity* hypothesis of the temporal logic ensuring $P \in \mathsf{SF}$ to be expressible in the logic, see e.g. [10].

[16] The *post-image* (or *right-image*) of $X \in \wp(A)$ by a relation $r \in \wp(A \times B)$ is $r[X] \triangleq \{y \mid \exists x \in X : \langle x, y\rangle \in r\}$ also written $\mathbf{post}[r]X$.

$$\overrightarrow{\phi}^{\mathsf{R}^*}_{\tau}[\![\mathrm{P}]\!](R) \triangleq 1_\Sigma \cup R \circ \tau[\![\mathrm{P}]\!] \qquad \text{forward transformer}$$
$$\overleftarrow{\phi}^{\mathsf{R}^*}_{\tau}[\![\mathrm{P}]\!](R) \triangleq 1_\Sigma \cup \tau[\![\mathrm{P}]\!] \circ R \qquad \text{backward transformer.}$$

7.5 Relational invariance / reachability proof methods

Applying fixpoint induction to the fixpoint relational reachability semantics, we get sound and complete forward and backward proof methods for a specification $S \in \wp(\Sigma \times \Sigma)$ [23], respectively generalizing [40, 49] and [37, 48].

$$\begin{aligned}\tau^{\mathsf{R}^*}[\![\mathrm{P}]\!] \subseteq S &\iff \exists R \in \wp(\Sigma \times \Sigma) : 1_\Sigma \subseteq R \wedge R \circ \tau[\![\mathrm{P}]\!] \subseteq R \wedge R \subseteq S \\ &\iff \exists R \in \wp(\Sigma \times \Sigma) : 1_\Sigma \subseteq R \wedge \tau[\![\mathrm{P}]\!] \circ R \subseteq R \wedge R \subseteq S\,.\end{aligned}$$

7.6 Variations on invariance / reachability proof methods

Further abstractions yield other classical proof methods. It is possible to restrict to the *initial states* $\mathsf{I} \in \wp(\Sigma)$, $\langle \wp(\Sigma \times \Sigma), \subseteq\rangle \underset{\alpha_\mathsf{I}}{\overset{\gamma_\mathsf{I}}{\leftrightarrows}} \langle \wp(\Sigma \times \Sigma), \subseteq\rangle$ where

$$\alpha_\mathsf{I}(R) \triangleq \{\langle s, s'\rangle \mid s \in \mathsf{I} \wedge \langle s, s'\rangle \in R\} \tag{2}$$

and the *final states* $\mathsf{F} \in \wp(\Sigma)$, $\langle \wp(\Sigma \times \Sigma), \subseteq\rangle \underset{\alpha^\mathsf{F}}{\overset{\gamma^\mathsf{F}}{\leftrightarrows}} \langle \wp(\Sigma \times \Sigma), \subseteq\rangle$ where

$$\alpha^\mathsf{F}(R) \triangleq \{\langle s, s'\rangle \mid \langle s, s'\rangle \in R \wedge s \in \mathsf{F}\}\,. \tag{3}$$

It is also possible to use an invariant so as to restrict to the reachable states $\langle \wp(\Sigma \times \Sigma), \subseteq\rangle \underset{\alpha^r}{\overset{\gamma^r}{\leftrightarrows}} \langle \wp(\Sigma), \subseteq\rangle$ where

$$\alpha^r(R) \triangleq \{s' \mid \langle s, s'\rangle \in R\}\,. \tag{4}$$

Combining (2) and (4) we get forward invariance [40, 49] while (3) and the inverse of (4) yield backward invariance (called "subgoal induction" in [48]).

Proofs by reductio ad absurdum [23, 35] are obtained by $\langle \wp(\Sigma \times \Sigma), \subseteq\rangle \underset{\widetilde{\alpha}}{\overset{\widetilde{\gamma}}{\leftrightarrows}} \langle \wp(\Sigma \times \Sigma), \supseteq\rangle$ where $\widetilde{\alpha}(R) \triangleq \neg R$.

8. Termination trace collecting semantics

Our objective is now to apply the abstract interpretation methodology of Sect. 2, as illustrated in Sect. 6—7 for the safety properties and their invariance abstractions, to termination.

Starting from a collecting trace semantics, we define termination properties by abstraction, derive fixpoint charaterizations by fixpoint abstraction, conceive proof and verification methods by fixpoint induction, and design static analysis methods by fixpoint approximation using widening [19].

8.1 Termination property

The *termination property* states either that all executions in the trace semantics $\Theta^{+\infty}[\![\mathrm{P}]\!]$ of a program P must always be finite

$$\Theta^{+\infty}[\![\mathrm{P}]\!] \subseteq \Sigma^+[\![\mathrm{P}]\!] \qquad \textit{definite termination}$$

or that the trace semantics $\Theta^{+\infty}[\![\mathrm{P}]\!]$ may be finite (hence must not always be infinite)

$$\Theta^{+\infty}[\![\mathrm{P}]\!] \cap \Sigma^+[\![\mathrm{P}]\!] \neq \emptyset \qquad \textit{potential termination.}$$

The *infinite extension abstraction*

$$\begin{aligned}\alpha^\omega(T) \triangleq T \cup \{\sigma_1\sigma_2 \in \Sigma^\infty \mid \sigma_1 \in \Sigma^+ \wedge (\exists \sigma_2' \in \Sigma^\infty : \sigma_1\sigma_2' \in T \vee \\ \forall \sigma_2' \in \Sigma^* : \sigma_1\sigma_2' \notin T)\}\end{aligned}$$

is a topological closure and so $\langle \wp(\Sigma^{+\infty}), \subseteq\rangle \underset{\alpha^\omega}{\overset{\gamma^\omega}{\leftrightarrows}} \langle \alpha^\omega[\wp(\Sigma^{+\infty})], \subseteq\rangle$ where γ^ω is the identity. We have

$$\begin{aligned}\tau^{+\infty}[\![\mathrm{P}]\!] \subseteq \Sigma^+[\![\mathrm{P}]\!] &\iff \alpha^\omega(\tau^{+\infty}[\![\mathrm{P}]\!]) \subseteq \Sigma^+[\![\mathrm{P}]\!], \\ \tau^{+\infty}[\![\mathrm{P}]\!] \cap \Sigma^+[\![\mathrm{P}]\!] \neq \emptyset &\iff \alpha^\omega(\tau^{+\infty}[\![\mathrm{P}]\!]) \cap \Sigma^+[\![\mathrm{P}]\!] \neq \emptyset\end{aligned}$$

and so, if necessary, we only need to consider semantics closed by α^ω.

8.2 Termination trace abstraction

The termination trace abstraction eliminates the program execution traces not starting by a state from which execution may/must terminate.

Example 1. Consider the example of the non-deterministic program `b:[ 1:loop [] e:skip ]` with states $\{b, l, e\}$, transitions $\{\langle b, l\rangle, \langle b, e\rangle, \langle l, l\rangle\}$ and complete trace semantics $\{be, e, bllll\ldots, llll\ldots\}$. □

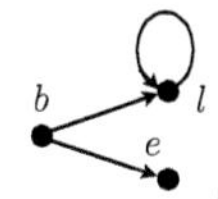

8.2.1 Potential termination trace abstraction

The *potential termination* or *may-terminate trace semantics* eliminates infinite traces.

Example 2. The potential termination trace semantics of program `b:[ 1:loop [] e:skip ]` in Ex. **1** is $\{be, e\}$ since an execution starting in state b *may* terminate (by choosing a transition to state e). □

The corresponding *potential termination abstraction* is $\langle \wp(\Sigma^{+\infty}), \subseteq\rangle \underset{\alpha^{\mathsf{mt}}}{\overset{\gamma^{\mathsf{mt}}}{\leftrightarrows}} \langle \wp(\Sigma^+), \subseteq\rangle$ and $\langle \wp(\Sigma^{+\infty}), \sqsubseteq\rangle \underset{\alpha^{\mathsf{mt}}}{\overset{\gamma'^{\mathsf{mt}}}{\leftrightarrows}} \langle \wp(\Sigma^+), \subseteq\rangle$ where

$$\alpha^{\mathsf{mt}}(T) \triangleq T \cap \Sigma^+, \quad \gamma^{\mathsf{mt}}(S) \triangleq S \cup \Sigma^\infty \quad \text{and} \quad \gamma'^{\mathsf{mt}}(S) \triangleq S\,.$$

The abstraction forgets about non-terminating executions. This abstraction corresponds to Dijkstra's weakest liberal/angelic precondition [37]. It is considered in [11] (together with backward reachability) to automatically compute *necessary* conditions for termination (in example **1**, this analysis would yield the potential termination states $\{b, e\}$ proving definite non-termination in state l).

8.2.2 Definite termination trace abstraction

The *definite termination* or *must-terminate trace semantics* eliminates all traces potentially branching, through local non-determinism, to non-termination.

Example 3. The definite termination trace semantics of program `b:[ 1:loop [] e:skip ]` in Ex. **1** is $\{e\}$ since in state b there is a possibility of non-termination (by choosing a transition to state l). □

A trace is in the definite termination semantics if and only if it is finite, independently of the potential non-deterministic choices along that trace. The corresponding *definite termination abstraction* is

$$\alpha^{\mathsf{Mt}}(T) \triangleq \{\sigma \in T^+ \mid \mathsf{pf}(\sigma) \cap \mathsf{pf}(T^\infty) = \emptyset\}$$

$\alpha^{\mathsf{Mt}} \in \langle \wp(\Sigma^{+\infty}), \sqsubseteq\rangle \hookrightarrow\!\!\!\!\rightarrow \langle \wp(\Sigma^+), \subseteq\rangle$ is a *retract*[17] and onto but not continuous[18]. However, on the following we consider only *transition closed* semantics [35] i.e. generated by a transition system (see counter example 5).

Example 4. If $T = \{ab, aba, ba, bb, ba^\omega\}$ then $\alpha^{\mathsf{mt}}(T) = \{ab, aba, ba, bb\}$ and $\alpha^{\mathsf{Mt}}(T) = \{ab, aba\}$ since $\mathsf{pf}(\sigma) \cap \mathsf{pf}(ba^\omega) = \emptyset$ for $\sigma = ab, aba$. □

This abstraction corresponds to Dijkstra's weakest/demonic precondition that is to the *definite termination analysis* we are mostly interested in for transition systems.

8.3 Termination trace semantics

The *potential termination collecting semantics* of a program P is therefore defined as

[17] A *retract* $r \in \langle A, \sqsubseteq\rangle \hookrightarrow \langle B, \leqslant\rangle$ where $B \subseteq A$ is increasing and idempotent. We write $r \in \langle A, \sqsubseteq\rangle \hookrightarrow\!\!\!\!\rightarrow \langle B, \leqslant\rangle$ when it is onto.

[18] Consider the $\sqsubseteq$-increasing chain $T_n \triangleq \{0\} \cup \{0i^\omega \mid i \geqslant n\}$, $n \geqslant 0$. We have $\bigsqcup_{n\geqslant 0} \alpha^{\mathsf{Mt}}(T_n) = \emptyset$ while $\bigcap_{n\geqslant 0}\{0i^\omega \mid i \geqslant n\} = \emptyset$ so that $\alpha^{\mathsf{Mt}}(\bigsqcup_{n\geqslant 0} T_n) = \alpha^{\mathsf{Mt}}(\{a\}) = \{a\}$.

$$\tau^{\mathsf{mt}}[\![\mathsf{P}]\!] \triangleq \alpha^{\mathsf{mt}}(\tau^{+\infty}[\![\mathsf{P}]\!]) \quad \text{potential termination semantics}$$

while the *definite termination collecting semantics* of a program P is defined as

$$\tau^{\mathsf{Mt}}[\![\mathsf{P}]\!] \triangleq \alpha^{\mathsf{Mt}}(\tau^{+\infty}[\![\mathsf{P}]\!]) \quad \text{definite termination semantics.}$$

8.4 Fixpoint termination trace semantics

By abstraction of the fixpoint trace semantics of Sect. 4.3, the strongest termination property of a program P with operational semantics $\langle\Sigma[\![\mathsf{P}]\!],\ \tau[\![\mathsf{P}]\!]\rangle$ and termination states $\beta_\tau[\![\mathsf{P}]\!]$ is

$$\begin{aligned}
\tau^{\mathsf{mt}}[\![\mathsf{P}]\!] &= \mathsf{lfp}_{\emptyset}^{\subseteq}\ \overleftarrow{\phi}_{\tau}^{\mathsf{mt}}[\![\mathsf{P}]\!] && \text{potential termination}\\
\overleftarrow{\phi}_{\tau}^{\mathsf{mt}}[\![\mathsf{P}]\!]T &\triangleq \beta_\tau[\![\mathsf{P}]\!] \cup \tau[\![\mathsf{P}]\!] \fatsemi T\\
\tau^{\mathsf{Mt}}[\![\mathsf{P}]\!] &= \mathsf{lfp}_{\emptyset}^{\subseteq}\ \overleftarrow{\phi}_{\tau}^{\mathsf{Mt}}[\![\mathsf{P}]\!] && \text{definite termination}\\
\overleftarrow{\phi}_{\tau}^{\mathsf{Mt}}[\![\mathsf{P}]\!]T &\triangleq \beta_\tau[\![\mathsf{P}]\!] \cup (\tau[\![\mathsf{P}]\!] \fatsemi T \cap \neg(\tau[\![\mathsf{P}]\!] \fatsemi \neg T))
\end{aligned}$$

where the term $\neg(\tau[\![\mathsf{P}]\!] \fatsemi \neg T)$ eliminates potential transitions towards non-terminating executions.

8.5 Proofs in the termination trace domain

Fixpoint induction provides formal methods to check fixpoint over-approximations, either $\tau^{\mathsf{mt}}[\![\mathsf{P}]\!] \subseteq S$ or $\tau^{\mathsf{Mt}}[\![\mathsf{P}]\!] \subseteq S$. Over-approximations yield necessary but not sufficient termination conditions which may introduce spurious infinite traces for which the proof cannot be done. The proof method is therefore useful to prove invariance under termination assumptions[19] but not for may/must termination.

On the contrary, termination proofs require fixpoint under-approximations $S \subseteq \tau^{\mathsf{mt}}[\![\mathsf{P}]\!]$ or $S \subseteq \tau^{\mathsf{Mt}}[\![\mathsf{P}]\!]$. Under-approximations yield sufficient but not necessary termination conditions and so may eliminate some termination cases for which the termination proof could have been done automatically. Fixpoint under-approximation proof methods have been proposed e.g. by [15, Sect. 11] and would yield the requested termination proof methods. More classically, we will favor over-approximations for static analysis.

9. Termination domain

Programs may not always potentially/definitely terminate in all states. So one problem is to determine for which states $\mathsf{I} \in \wp(\Sigma)$ do executions starting from these states may/must terminate.

9.1 Termination domain abstraction

This potential/definite termination domain semantics is provided by the *weakest precondition abstraction* $\langle\wp(\Sigma^{+\infty}),\ \subseteq\rangle \xleftrightarrow[\alpha^{\mathsf{w}}]{\gamma^{\mathsf{w}}} \langle\wp(\Sigma),\ \subseteq\rangle$ of the termination trace semantics, such that

$$\alpha^{\mathsf{w}}(T) \triangleq \{\sigma_0 \mid \sigma \in T\} \quad \text{precondition abstraction.}$$

9.2 Termination domain semantics

$$\begin{aligned}
\tau^{\mathsf{wmt}}[\![\mathsf{P}]\!] &\triangleq \alpha^{\mathsf{w}}(\tau^{\mathsf{mt}}[\![\mathsf{P}]\!]) && \text{potential termination}\\
\tau^{\mathsf{wMt}}[\![\mathsf{P}]\!] &\triangleq \alpha^{\mathsf{w}}(\tau^{\mathsf{Mt}}[\![\mathsf{P}]\!]) && \text{definite termination.}
\end{aligned}$$

Using Dijkstra's notations [37], $\tau^{\mathsf{wmt}}[\![\mathsf{P}]\!] = \mathsf{wlp}[\![\mathsf{P}]\!]\mathbf{true}$ and $\tau^{\mathsf{wMt}}[\![\mathsf{P}]\!] = \mathsf{wp}[\![\mathsf{P}]\!]\mathbf{true}$.

9.3 Fixpoint termination domain semantics

By fixpoint abstraction of the termination trace semantics in Sect. 8.4 using transformer commutation, we get Dijkstra's fixpoint weakest (liberal) termination precondition semantics [38][20]

$$\begin{aligned}
\tau^{\mathsf{wmt}}[\![\mathsf{P}]\!] &= \mathsf{lfp}_{\emptyset}^{\subseteq}\ \overrightarrow{\phi}_{\tau}^{\mathsf{wmt}}[\![\mathsf{P}]\!] && \text{weakest liberal termin. precond.}\\
\overrightarrow{\phi}_{\tau}^{\mathsf{wmt}}[\![\mathsf{P}]\!](R) &\triangleq \beta_\tau[\![\mathsf{P}]\!] \cup \tau[\![\mathsf{P}]\!]^{-1}[R]\\
\tau^{\mathsf{wMt}}[\![\mathsf{P}]\!] &= \mathsf{lfp}_{\emptyset}^{\subseteq}\ \overrightarrow{\phi}_{\tau}^{\mathsf{wMt}}[\![\mathsf{P}]\!] && \text{weakest termination precondition}\\
\overrightarrow{\phi}_{\tau}^{\mathsf{wMt}}[\![\mathsf{P}]\!](R) &\triangleq \beta_\tau[\![\mathsf{P}]\!] \cup (\tau[\![\mathsf{P}]\!]^{-1}[R] \cap \neg\tau[\![\mathsf{P}]\!]^{-1}[\neg R])\,.
\end{aligned}$$

9.4 Proof and static analysis in the termination domain

As was the case in Sect. 8.5, fixpoint induction is useful for over-approximations, which can be automatically inferred by static analysis [11, 12]. On the contrary, termination proofs require under-approximations [15, Sect. 11] proof methods. Although static under-approximation analysis is possible (e.g. [34]), this is not the termination proof technique which is used in practice [38].

10. Termination proofs for the trace semantics generated by a transition system

In practice a termination proof is decomposed in two parts. First a necessary termination condition is found by over-approximating $\tau^{\mathsf{wmt}}[\![\mathsf{P}]\!]$ or $\tau^{\mathsf{wMt}}[\![\mathsf{P}]\!]$. Then this necessary termination condition is shown to be sufficient by Floyd/Turing variant function method (e.g. [17]) or inversely (e.g. [8]). This corresponds to different abstractions, specific to the trace semantics generated by a transition system, that we now elaborate.

10.1 Transition-based termination proofs

A program which trace semantics is generated by a transition system $\langle\Sigma,\ \tau\rangle$ definitely terminates if and only if the program transition relation is well-founded[21].

$$\tau^{+\infty}[\![\mathsf{P}]\!] \subseteq \Sigma^{+}[\![\mathsf{P}]\!] \iff \langle\Sigma,\ \tau\rangle \text{ is well-founded.}$$

In practice one considers traces starting from initial states $\mathsf{I} \in \wp(\Sigma)$, e.g. I is the termination domain of Sect. 9. In that case a program which trace semantics is generated by a transition system $\langle\Sigma,\ \tau\rangle$ definitely terminates for traces starting from initial states $\mathsf{I} \in \wp(\Sigma)$ if and only if the program transition relation restricted to reachable states is well-founded.

$$\alpha^{\mathsf{i}}(\mathsf{I})(\tau^{+\infty}[\![\mathsf{P}]\!]) \subseteq \Sigma^{+}[\![\mathsf{P}]\!] \iff \langle\alpha^{\mathsf{r}}(\alpha^{\mathsf{i}}(\mathsf{I})(\tau^{+\infty}[\![\mathsf{P}]\!])),\ \tau\rangle \text{ is well-founded}$$

where the *initialization abstraction* $\langle\wp(\Sigma^{+\infty}),\ \subseteq\rangle \xleftrightarrow[\alpha^{\mathsf{i}}(\mathsf{I})]{\gamma^{\mathsf{i}}(\mathsf{I})} \langle\wp(\Sigma^{+\infty}),\ \subseteq\rangle$ is

$$\begin{aligned}
\alpha^{\mathsf{i}} &\in \wp(\Sigma) \mapsto (\Sigma^{+\infty} \mapsto \Sigma^{+\infty}) && \text{initialization abstraction}\\
\alpha^{\mathsf{i}}(\mathsf{I})T &\triangleq \{\sigma \in T \mid \sigma_0 \in \mathsf{I}\}
\end{aligned}$$

and the *reachable states abstraction* $\langle\wp(\Sigma^{+\infty}),\ \subseteq\rangle \xleftrightarrow[\alpha^{\mathsf{r}}]{\gamma^{\mathsf{r}}} \langle\wp(\Sigma),\ \subseteq\rangle$ is

$$\alpha^{\mathsf{r}}(T) \triangleq \{s \mid \exists\sigma \in \Sigma^{*}, \sigma' \in \Sigma^{*\infty} : \sigma s \sigma' \in T\} \quad \text{reachability abstraction.}$$

The transition-based termination proof method is sound and complete. As noticed in Sect. 9, the precondition I can be inferred automatically by static analysis. Moreover, an over-approximation $R \supseteq \alpha^{\mathsf{r}}(\alpha^{\mathsf{i}}(\mathsf{I})(\tau^{+\infty}[\![\mathsf{P}]\!])) = \tau[\![\mathsf{P}]\!]^{*}[\mathsf{I}]$[22] of the reachable states can be computed by classical abstract interpretation algorithms [19].

[19] e.g. for Ex. **1**, $\{b, e, l\}$ is invariant, $\{b, e\}$ is invariant under potential termination hypothesis, and $\{e\}$ is invariant under definite termination hypothesis.

[20] The pre-image of $Y \in \wp(A)$ by a relation $r \in \wp(A \times B)$ is $r^{-1}[Y] \triangleq \{x \mid \exists y \in Y : \langle x,\ y\rangle \in r\}$ also written $\mathbf{pre}[r]Y$ while $\neg r^{-1}[\neg Y] \triangleq \{x \mid \forall y : y \in Y \Longrightarrow \langle x,\ y\rangle \in r\}$ is $\widetilde{\mathbf{pre}}[r]Y$.

[21] A relation $\prec \in \wp(\mathbb{W} \times \mathbb{W})$ on a set $\mathbb{W}$ is *well-founded* if and only if there is no strictly decreasing infinite chain $x_0 \succ x_1 \succ \ldots \succ x_n \succ x_{n+1} \succ \ldots$ of elements $x_0, x_1, \ldots, x_n, x_{n+1}, \ldots$ of $\mathbb{W}$. $\langle\mathbb{W},\ \prec\rangle$ is called a *well-founded set*. A *(total) well-order* is well-founded (total) strict order relation $\prec$. The set of all well-founded relations in $\wp(\mathbb{W} \times \mathbb{W})$ is written $\mathcal{W}\!f(\mathbb{W} \times \mathbb{W})$.

[22] t^{*} is the reflexive transitive closure of a binary relation t.

10.2 Transition abstraction

If the program semantics $\Theta^{+\infty}[\![\mathsf{P}]\!]$ is not generated by a transition system we might consider the transition abstraction $\langle\Sigma, \overrightarrow{\alpha}(\Theta^{+\infty}[\![\mathsf{P}]\!])\rangle$ where the *transition abstraction* $\langle\wp(\Sigma^{+\infty}), \subseteq\rangle \xleftarrow[\overrightarrow{\alpha}]{\overrightarrow{\gamma}} \langle\wp(\Sigma\times\Sigma), \subseteq\rangle$ is

$$\overrightarrow{\alpha}(T) \triangleq \{\langle s, s'\rangle \mid \exists\sigma,\sigma' : \sigma s s'\sigma' \in T\} \qquad \text{transition abstraction}$$

but the following counter-example shows that the condition is sufficient but not necessary.

Counter-example 5. Let $T \triangleq \{ab, ba\}$ be a trace semantics. The corresponding transition relation $\tau \triangleq \overrightarrow{\alpha}(T) = \{\langle a, b\rangle, \langle b, a\rangle\}$ generates the infinite trace *ababab*a... and so the transition relation τ restricted to the reachable states $\{a, b\}$ is not well-founded. □

Another counter-example is fairness [35]. In the following, we consider complete/maximal trace semantics T that are *transition closed* (also *generated by a transition system*) that is $\overrightarrow{\alpha}(T) = T$ or equivalently T is closed by elimination of strict prefixes, closed by extension by fusion, and closed by limits [35, Th. 2.6.8].

11. Variant semantics

It remains to design verification and static analysis methods to show that $\langle R, \tau\rangle$ is well-founded where

$$R \supseteq \alpha^{r}(\alpha^{\downarrow}(I)(\tau^{+\infty}[\![\mathsf{P}]\!])) = \tau[\![\mathsf{P}]\!]^{*}[I]$$

over-approximates the reachable states. There are two important remarks.

1. If $\tau \subseteq r$ and $\langle R, r\rangle$ is well-founded then $\langle R, \tau\rangle$ is well-founded.
2. $\langle R, \tau\rangle$ is well-founded if and only if there exists a variant function $v \in \Sigma \not\mapsto \mathbb{W}$[23] into a well-founded set $\langle\mathbb{W}, <\rangle$ which domain is R[24].

So for the traces generated by a transition system, termination can be proved by mapping invariant states to a well-founded relation which is the principle of Floyd/Turing variant function method.

11.1 Variant function

A *variant function* $v \in \Sigma \not\mapsto \mathbb{W}$ is a partial function from the set of states into a well-founded set $\langle\mathbb{W}, <\rangle$ where $<$ is a well-founded relation on the set $\mathbb{W}$ (and $\preccurlyeq$ is its non-strict version). With appropriate hypotheses on states and the transition relation, the co-domain of the variant function can be fixed a priori and the variant function can be found by constraint solving e.g. [17, 54]. However, these methods are not as general as Floyd/Turing's method.

In mathematics, the ordinals provide a standard well-founded set thanks to ranking functions mapping each element of a well-founded set to its ordinal rank. So, up to a ranking function, the well-founded set $\langle\mathbb{W}, <\rangle$ can always be chosen as the class $\langle\mathbb{O}, <\rangle$ of ordinals. The intuition is that any execution σ starting in a state $\sigma_0 \in \mathsf{dom}(v)$ must terminate in "at most" $v(\sigma_0)$ execution steps while an execution σ starting in a state $\sigma_0 \notin \mathsf{dom}(v)$ might not terminate. We have $\tau \subseteq \{\langle s, s'\rangle \in \Sigma^2 \mid s \in \mathsf{dom}(v) \wedge v(s) > v(s')\}$ and this relation is well-founded on states, proving termination.

11.2 Variant abstraction

A variant function is an abstraction of a set of finite traces. It is a partial function which domain is the set of terminating states. Its value is an upper bound of the remaining number of "steps" to termination. It may be transfinite for unbounded non-determinism with unbounded execution trace lengths. Let us define

$$\begin{array}{rcll} \alpha^{\mathsf{rk}} & \in & \wp(\Sigma\times\Sigma) \mapsto (\Sigma \not\mapsto \mathbb{O}) & \text{ranking abstraction} \\ \alpha^{\mathsf{rk}}(r)s & \triangleq & 0 \quad \text{when} \quad \forall s' \in \Sigma : \langle s, s'\rangle \notin r & \\ \alpha^{\mathsf{rk}}(r)s & \triangleq & \mathsf{sup}\left\{\alpha^{\mathsf{rk}}(r)s' + 1 \;\middle|\; s' \in \mathsf{dom}(\alpha^{\mathsf{rk}}(r)) \wedge \langle s, s'\rangle \in r\right\}^{25} . & \end{array}$$

$\alpha^{\mathsf{rk}}(r)s$ extracts the well-founded part of relation r and provides the rank of the elements s of its domain. $\alpha^{\mathsf{v}}(T)$ does the same for the transition relation by abstracting the set T of finite traces

$$\begin{array}{rcll} \alpha^{\mathsf{v}} & \in & \wp(\Sigma^{+}) \mapsto (\Sigma \not\mapsto \mathbb{W}) & \text{variant abstraction} \\ \alpha^{\mathsf{v}}(T) & \triangleq & \lambda s \bullet \alpha^{\mathsf{rk}}(\overrightarrow{\alpha}(T))s . & \end{array}$$

It follows that the abstraction $\langle\wp(\Sigma^{+\infty}), \sqsubseteq\rangle \xleftarrow[\alpha^{\mathsf{v}}\circ\alpha^{\mathsf{mt}}]{\gamma'^{\mathsf{mt}}\circ\gamma^{\mathsf{v}}} \langle\Sigma \not\mapsto \mathbb{W}, \sqsubseteq^{\mathsf{v}}\rangle$ holds for potential termination and $\langle\wp(\Sigma^{+\infty}), \sqsubseteq\rangle \to \langle\Sigma \not\mapsto \mathbb{W}, \sqsubseteq^{\mathsf{v}}\rangle$ for definite termination. These abstractions state, by def. of $\sqsubseteq$, that adding finite execution traces or suppressing infinite traces can only, by def. of $\sqsubseteq^{\mathsf{v}}$, augment the termination domain and, maybe, increase execution times. It follows that the *computational variant order* is

$$v \sqsubseteq^{\mathsf{v}} v' \triangleq \mathsf{dom}(v) \subseteq \mathsf{dom}(v') \wedge \forall x \in \mathsf{dom}(v) : v(x) \preccurlyeq v'(x) .$$

11.3 Variant semantics

A variant function can always be found by abstraction of the termination semantics into a *variant semantics*

$$\begin{array}{rcll} \tau^{\mathsf{mv}}[\![\mathsf{P}]\!] & \triangleq & \alpha^{\mathsf{v}}(\tau^{\mathsf{mt}}[\![\mathsf{P}]\!]) & \text{potential termination variant} \\ \tau^{\mathsf{Mv}}[\![\mathsf{P}]\!] & \triangleq & \alpha^{\mathsf{v}}(\tau^{\mathsf{Mt}}[\![\mathsf{P}]\!]) & \text{definite termination variant.} \end{array}$$

This yields new termination proof methods and static analysis methods by abstraction of this fixpoint definition.

11.4 Fixpoint variant semantics

By fixpoint abstraction of the fixpoint termination trace semantics of Sect. 8.4, we get the fixpoint characterization of the variant semantics[26,27]

$$\begin{array}{rcll} \tau^{\mathsf{mv}}[\![\mathsf{P}]\!] & = & \mathsf{lfp}_{\dot\emptyset}^{\sqsubseteq^{\mathsf{v}}} \overleftarrow{\phi}_{\tau}^{\mathsf{mv}}[\![\mathsf{P}]\!] & \text{potential termination} \\ \overleftarrow{\phi}_{\tau}^{\mathsf{mv}}[\![\mathsf{P}]\!](v)s & \triangleq & \llparenthesis\, s \in \beta_\tau[\![\mathsf{P}]\!] \;?\; 0 \;\text{:}\; \mathsf{sup}\left\{v(s') + 1 \;\middle|\; s' \in \mathsf{dom}(v) \wedge \langle s, s'\rangle \in \tau[\![\mathsf{P}]\!]\right\} \rrparenthesis & \\ \tau^{\mathsf{Mv}}[\![\mathsf{P}]\!] & = & \mathsf{lfp}_{\dot\emptyset}^{\sqsubseteq^{\mathsf{v}}} \overleftarrow{\phi}_{\tau}^{\mathsf{Mv}}[\![\mathsf{P}]\!] & \text{definite termination} \\ \overleftarrow{\phi}_{\tau}^{\mathsf{Mv}}[\![\mathsf{P}]\!](v)s & \triangleq & \llparenthesis\, s \in \beta_\tau[\![\mathsf{P}]\!] \;?\; 0 \;\text{:}\; \mathsf{sup}\left\{v(s') + 1 \;\middle|\; s' \in \mathsf{dom}(v) \wedge \langle s, s'\rangle \in \tau[\![\mathsf{P}]\!] \wedge \forall s'' : \langle s, s''\rangle \in \tau[\![\mathsf{P}]\!] \Longrightarrow s'' \in \mathsf{dom}(v)\right\} \rrparenthesis . & \end{array}$$

Example 6. Consider the trace semantics as represented on the right. We have represented below the fixpoint iterates for the corresponding potential and definite variant functions. Unlabelled states are outside the variant function domain.

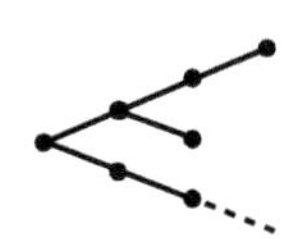

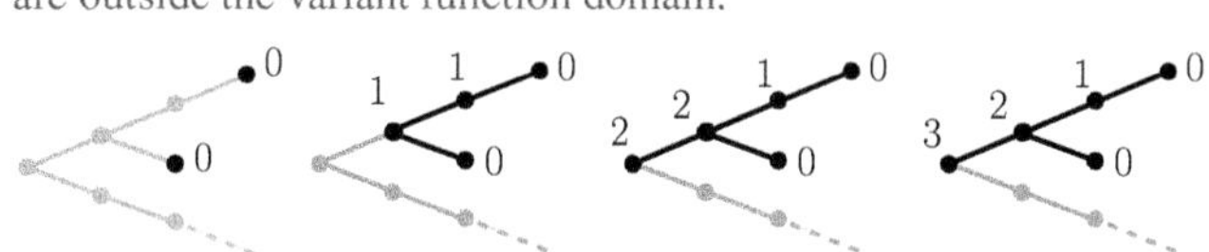

Potential termination

[23] $A \not\mapsto B$ (resp. $A \mapsto B$) is the set of *partial* (resp. *total*) *maps* from set A into set B. We write $\mathsf{dom}(f)$ for the domain of a partial function $f \in A \not\mapsto B$ and $\mathsf{codom}(f)$ for its co-domain. If $f \in A \mapsto B$ then $\mathsf{dom}(f) = A$.

[24] For a proof, take $\langle\mathbb{W}, <\rangle$ to be the ordinals $\langle\mathbb{O}, <\rangle$ and v to be the ordinal rank of elements of R for the well-founded relation τ.

[25] This can be generalized from $\langle\mathbb{O}, <\rangle$ to well-orders $\langle\mathbb{W}, <\rangle$ using $\mathsf{succ}(x) \triangleq \{y \in \mathbb{W} \mid x < y \wedge \nexists z \in \mathbb{W} : x < z < y\}$ and sup is an upper-bound. For ordinals $\mathsf{succ}(x) = \{x + 1\}$ is the successor ordinal and sup is the lub.

[26] The partial map $\dot\emptyset \in \Sigma \not\mapsto \mathbb{O}$ is totally undefined and has $\mathsf{dom}(\dot\emptyset) \triangleq \emptyset$.

[27] The conditional is $\llparenthesis\, \mathsf{true} \;?\; a \;\text{:}\; b \,\rrparenthesis \triangleq a$ and $\llparenthesis\, \mathsf{false} \;?\; a \;\text{:}\; b \,\rrparenthesis \triangleq b$.

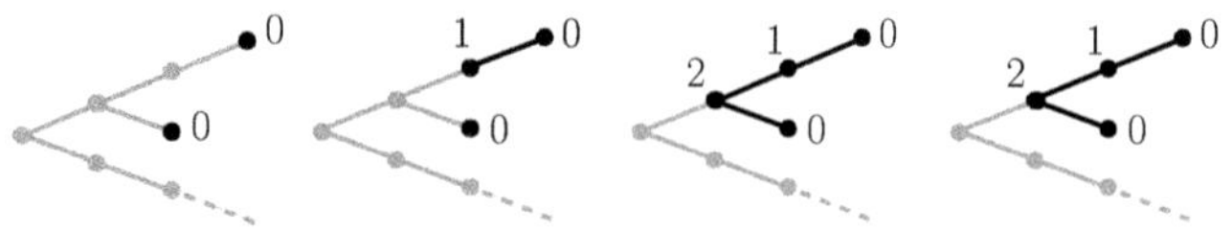

Definite termination

The potential variant can be used as a run-time check of definite non-termination (since beyond 4 execution steps termination is inevitable). This general observation is not in contradiction with the fact that termination is not checkable at runtime since here it relies on a prior static analysis considering all possible executions. □

Example 7. The definite termination variant semantics $\mathsf{lfp}^{\sqsubseteq^{\mathsf{v}}}_{\dot\emptyset}\, \overleftarrow{\phi}^{\mathsf{Mv}}_{\tau}[\![\mathsf{P}]\!]$ of the following program P

```
int main () { int x; while (x > 0) { x = x - 2; }}
```

is the limit v^{ω} of the iterates v^n, $n \in \mathbb{N}$ of $\overleftarrow{\phi}^{\mathsf{Mv}}_{\tau}[\![\mathsf{P}]\!]$ from $\dot\emptyset$. Considering only one loop head control point so that the state can be reduced to the value x of x, we have

$$\overleftarrow{\phi}^{\mathsf{Mv}}_{\tau}[\![\mathsf{P}]\!](v)x \triangleq \big(\!\!\big|\, x \leqslant 0 \;?\; 0 \;\text{\textbf{:}}\; \sup\{\, v(x-2)+1 \mid x-2 \in \mathsf{dom}(v)\}\,\big|\!\!\big) .$$

The program being deterministic, the potential termination equation $v = \overleftarrow{\phi}^{\mathsf{mv}}_{\tau}[\![\mathsf{P}]\!](v)$ is similar. The fixpoint iterates are[28,29]

$$\begin{aligned}
v^0 &= \dot\emptyset\\
v^1 &= \lambda\, x \in [-\infty, 0] \bullet 0\\
v^2 &= \lambda\, x \in [-\infty, 0] \bullet 0 \,\dot\cup\, \lambda\, x \in [1, 2] \bullet 1\\
v^3 &= \lambda\, x \in [-\infty, 0] \bullet 0 \,\dot\cup\, \lambda\, x \in [1, 2] \bullet 1 \,\dot\cup\, \lambda\, x \in [3, 4] \bullet 2\\
&\dots\\
v^n &= \lambda\, x \in [-\infty, 0] \bullet 0 \,\dot\cup\, \lambda\, x \in [1, 2 \times (n-1)] \bullet (x+1) \div 2\\
&\dots\\
v^{\omega} &= \lambda\, x \in [-\infty, 0] \bullet 0 \,\dot\cup\, \lambda\, x \in [1, +\infty] \bullet (x+1) \div 2 .
\end{aligned}$$
□

11.5 Termination proof method

The variant semantics is sound and complete to prove termination of a program P for initial states I since

$$\begin{aligned}
\alpha^{\mathsf{i}}(\mathsf{I})(\tau^{+\infty}[\![\mathsf{P}]\!]) \subseteq \Sigma^{+}[\![\mathsf{P}]\!] &\iff \mathsf{I} \subseteq \mathsf{dom}(\tau^{\mathsf{Mv}}[\![\mathsf{P}]\!])\\
&\iff \exists v \in \Sigma \not\mapsto \mathbb{O} : \mathsf{lfp}^{\sqsubseteq^{\mathsf{v}}}_{\dot\emptyset}\, \overleftarrow{\phi}^{\mathsf{Mv}}_{\tau}[\![\mathsf{P}]\!] \sqsubseteq^{\mathsf{v}} v \wedge \mathsf{I} \subseteq \mathsf{dom}(v)\\
\alpha^{\mathsf{i}}(\mathsf{I})(\tau^{+\infty}[\![\mathsf{P}]\!]) \cap \Sigma^{+}[\![\mathsf{P}]\!] \neq \emptyset &\iff \mathsf{I} \subseteq \mathsf{dom}(\tau^{\mathsf{mv}}[\![\mathsf{P}]\!])\\
&\iff \exists v \in \Sigma \not\mapsto \mathbb{O} : \mathsf{lfp}^{\sqsubseteq^{\mathsf{v}}}_{\dot\emptyset}\, \overleftarrow{\phi}^{\mathsf{mv}}_{\tau}[\![\mathsf{P}]\!] \sqsubseteq^{\mathsf{v}} v \wedge \mathsf{I} \subseteq \mathsf{dom}(v)
\end{aligned}$$

Applying fixpoint induction to check for the least fixpoint over-approximation, we get a termination proof method. We have

$\exists v \in \Sigma \not\mapsto \mathbb{O} : \tau^{\mathsf{Mv}}[\![\mathsf{P}]\!] \sqsubseteq^{\mathsf{v}} v$

$\Leftrightarrow \exists v : \mathsf{lfp}^{\sqsubseteq^{\mathsf{v}}}_{\dot\emptyset}\, \overleftarrow{\phi}^{\mathsf{Mv}}_{\tau}[\![\mathsf{P}]\!] \sqsubseteq^{\mathsf{v}} v$ ⟅fixpoint semantics of Sect. 11.4⟆

$\Leftrightarrow \exists v : \exists v' : \dot\emptyset \sqsubseteq^{\mathsf{v}} v' \wedge \overleftarrow{\phi}^{\mathsf{Mv}}_{\tau}[\![\mathsf{P}]\!]v' \sqsubseteq^{\mathsf{v}} v' \wedge v' \sqsubseteq^{\mathsf{v}} v$ ⟅fixpoint ind.⟆

$\Leftrightarrow \exists v' : \overleftarrow{\phi}^{\mathsf{Mv}}_{\tau}[\![\mathsf{P}]\!]v' \sqsubseteq^{\mathsf{v}} v'$ ⟅def. $\sqsubseteq^{\mathsf{v}}$ and choosing $v = v'$⟆

$\Leftrightarrow \exists v : \lambda\, s \bullet \big(\!\!\big|\, s \in \beta_{\tau}[\![\mathsf{P}]\!] \;?\; 0 \;\text{\textbf{:}}\; \sup\{v(s')+1 \mid \exists s' : \langle s,\, s'\rangle \in \tau[\![\mathsf{P}]\!] \wedge s' \in \mathsf{dom}(v) \wedge \forall s' : \langle s,\, s'\rangle \in \tau[\![\mathsf{P}]\!] \Longrightarrow s' \in \mathsf{dom}(v)\}\,\big|\!\!\big) \sqsubseteq^{\mathsf{v}} v$ ⟅def. $\overleftarrow{\phi}^{\mathsf{Mv}}_{\tau}[\![\mathsf{P}]\!]$⟆

$\Leftrightarrow \exists v : \lambda\, s \bullet \sup\{v(s')+1 \mid \exists s' : \langle s,\, s'\rangle \in \tau[\![\mathsf{P}]\!] \wedge s' \in \mathsf{dom}(v) \wedge \forall s' : \langle s,\, s'\rangle \in \tau[\![\mathsf{P}]\!] \Longrightarrow s' \in \mathsf{dom}(v)\} \sqsubseteq^{\mathsf{v}} v$
⟅since $\forall s : v(s') \geqslant 0$ and $\exists s' : \langle s,\, s'\rangle \in \tau[\![\mathsf{P}]\!]$ implies $s \notin \beta_{\tau}[\![\mathsf{P}]\!]$⟆

$\Leftrightarrow \exists v : \mathsf{dom}(\lambda\, s \bullet \sup\{v(s')+1 \mid \exists s' : \langle s,\, s'\rangle \in \tau[\![\mathsf{P}]\!] \wedge s' \in \mathsf{dom}(v) \wedge \forall s' : \langle s,\, s'\rangle \in \tau[\![\mathsf{P}]\!] \Longrightarrow s' \in \mathsf{dom}(v)\}) \subseteq \mathsf{dom}(v) \wedge \forall s \in \mathsf{dom}(v) : \sup\{v(s')+1 \mid \exists s' : \langle s,\, s'\rangle \in \tau[\![\mathsf{P}]\!] \wedge s' \in \mathsf{dom}(v) \wedge \forall s' : \langle s,\, s'\rangle \in \tau[\![\mathsf{P}]\!] \Longrightarrow s' \in \mathsf{dom}(v)\} \leqslant v(s)$

⟅def. $\sqsubseteq^{\mathsf{v}}$ for ordinals⟆

$\Leftrightarrow \exists v : \forall s \in \mathsf{dom}(v) : \big(\exists s' \in \mathsf{dom}(v) : \langle s,\, s'\rangle \in \tau[\![\mathsf{P}]\!]\big) \Longrightarrow \big(\forall s' : \langle s,\, s'\rangle \in \tau[\![\mathsf{P}]\!] \Longrightarrow s' \in \mathsf{dom}(v) \wedge v(s') < v(s)\big)$ ⟅def. sup⟆

$\Leftrightarrow \exists \langle \mathbb{W},\, <\rangle : \exists v \in \Sigma \not\mapsto \mathbb{W} : \forall s \in \mathsf{dom}(v) : \big(\exists s' \in \mathsf{dom}(v) : \langle s,\, s'\rangle \in \tau[\![\mathsf{P}]\!]\big) \Longrightarrow \big(\forall s' : \langle s,\, s'\rangle \in \tau[\![\mathsf{P}]\!] \Longrightarrow s' \in \mathsf{dom}(v) \wedge v(s') < v(s)\big)$ ⟅since an ordinal is the order type of a well-founded set⟆

$\Leftrightarrow \exists I \in \wp(\Sigma) : \exists \langle \mathbb{W},\, <\rangle : \exists v \in \Sigma \not\mapsto \mathbb{W} : \forall s \in I : \big(\exists s' \in I : \langle s,\, s'\rangle \in \tau[\![\mathsf{P}]\!]\big) \Longrightarrow \big(\forall s' : \langle s,\, s'\rangle \in \tau[\![\mathsf{P}]\!] \Longrightarrow s' \in I \wedge v(s') < v(s)\big)$
⟅choosing $I = \mathsf{dom}(v)$.⟆

This calculational design yields the following *definite termination induction principle*

$$\begin{aligned}
&\alpha^{\mathsf{i}}(\mathsf{I})(\tau^{+\infty}[\![\mathsf{P}]\!]) \subseteq \Sigma^{+}[\![\mathsf{P}]\!] \qquad \text{definite termination proof}\\
\iff\;& \exists I \in \wp(\Sigma) : \exists \langle \mathbb{W},\, <\rangle : \exists v \in \Sigma \not\mapsto \mathbb{W} : \mathsf{I} \subseteq \mathsf{dom}(v) \wedge \forall s \in I :\\
&\big(\exists s' \in I : \langle s,\, s'\rangle \in \tau[\![\mathsf{P}]\!]\big) \Longrightarrow\\
&\qquad \big(\forall s' : \langle s,\, s'\rangle \in \tau[\![\mathsf{P}]\!] \Longrightarrow s' \in I \wedge v(s') < v(s)\big) .
\end{aligned}$$

A similar calculational design, yields the *potential termination induction principle*

$$\begin{aligned}
&\alpha^{\mathsf{i}}(\mathsf{I})(\tau^{+\infty}[\![\mathsf{P}]\!]) \cap \Sigma^{+}[\![\mathsf{P}]\!] \neq \emptyset \qquad \text{potential termination proof}\\
\iff\;& \exists I \in \wp(\Sigma) : \exists \langle \mathbb{W},\, <\rangle : \exists v \in \Sigma \not\mapsto \mathbb{W} : \mathsf{I} \subseteq \mathsf{dom}(v) \wedge \forall s \in I :\\
&(\exists s' \in I : \langle s,\, s'\rangle \in \tau[\![\mathsf{P}]\!]) \Longrightarrow\\
&\qquad (\exists s'' \in I : \langle s,\, s''\rangle \in \tau[\![\mathsf{P}]\!] \wedge s'' \in I \wedge v(s'') < v(s)) .
\end{aligned}$$

Observe that the fixpoint variant semantics of Sect. 11.4 is calculated backwards (the variant function increases on previous steps) but that the termination induction principles proceed forward (the variant function decreases on next steps).

Example 8. A similar induction principle is proposed in [35, Ch. 5.2.3] for relational inevitability proofs (a state must be reached that relates to the initial state as given by a specification relation Ψ). The following example is used in [35, Ch. 5.2.5] to show that, the invariant and variant function must also be relational, that is relate the current and initial state: $\Sigma \triangleq \{1, 2, 3\}$, $\mathsf{I} \triangleq \{1, 2\}$, $\tau \triangleq \{\langle x,\, x+1\rangle \mid x, x+1 \in \Sigma\}$, $\Psi \triangleq \tau$. We can prove termination with assertions, no relational invariants being needed. For the above example, choose $I = \Sigma$, $\langle \mathbb{W},\, <\rangle = \langle \Sigma,\, <\rangle$, $v(1) = 2$, $v(2) = 1$, $v(3) = 0$. This example shows that termination proofs are simpler than inevitability proofs. □

Example 9. For the program of Ex. 7, the definite termination proof for the simplified transition system

$$\tau[\![\mathsf{P}]\!] \;\triangleq\; \{\langle x,\, x'\rangle \mid x > 0 \wedge x' = x + 1\}$$

requires guessing $I = \mathbb{Z}$, $\langle \mathbb{W},\, <\rangle = \langle \mathbb{N},\, <\rangle$, $v = \lambda\, x \bullet \big(\!\!\big|\, x \leqslant 0 \;?\; 0 \;\text{\textbf{:}}\; (x+1) \div 2\,\big|\!\!\big)$ and proving $\forall x, x' \in \mathbb{Z} : (x > 0 \wedge x' = x + 1) \Longrightarrow (\forall x'' : x'' = x + 1 \Longrightarrow v(x'') < v(x))$. □

Because Turing/Floyd method uses the reachability abstraction α^{r} of (4), it is not possible to directly relate states occurring at different times during computations. This is why the program is transformed by using auxiliary variables to relate the current values of the variables to their past values. This induces a transformed transition system, which under the reachability abstraction α^{r} is equivalent to the relational abstraction of the original transition system by the relational abstraction (1).

Example 10. Continuing Ex. 9, the program is transformed into

```
int main () { int x, x0;
    while (x > 0) { x0 = x; x = x - 2; }}
```

which consists in reasoning on the transformed transition system

[28] $\dot\cup$ joins partial functions with disjoint domains $f_1 \,\dot\cup\, f_2(x) \triangleq f_1(x)$ if $x \in \mathsf{dom}(f_1)$ and $f_1 \,\dot\cup\, f_2(x) \triangleq f_2(x)$ if $x \in \mathsf{dom}(f_2)$ where $\mathsf{dom}(f_1) \cap \mathsf{dom}(f_2) = \emptyset$.

[29] $\div$ is the integer division.

$$\tau_0[\![\mathrm{P}]\!] \triangleq \{\langle\langle x_0,\, x\rangle,\, \langle x_0',\, x'\rangle\rangle \mid x_0' = x \wedge \langle x,\, x'\rangle \in \tau[\![\mathrm{P}]\!]\}\,. \quad \square$$

This is an abstraction $\langle \wp(\Sigma\times\Sigma),\, \subseteq\rangle \xleftrightarrow[\alpha^0]{\gamma^0} \langle\wp(\Sigma^2\times\Sigma^2),\, \subseteq\rangle$ such that

$$\alpha^0(\tau) \triangleq \{\langle\langle x_0,\, x\rangle,\, \langle x_0',\, x'\rangle\rangle \mid x_0' = x \wedge \langle x,\, x'\rangle \in \tau\}\,.$$

The benefit is that a relational abstraction α^{R} used with τ is equivalent to a non-relational reachability abstraction α^r for $\alpha^0(\tau)$. However, in both cases, a limitation is that, for a given control point, it is only possible to refer to one past instant of time when control is at that program point, which is a limitation when compared to the more flexible reasoning by induction on traces (see Sect. 15.3).

12. Variant abstraction analysis

We get a termination static analysis by abstracting the variant semantics. We need an abstraction $\langle\Sigma \not\mapsto \mathbb{O},\, \sqsubseteq^{\mathsf{v}}\rangle \xleftrightarrow[\alpha]{\gamma} \langle A,\, \sqsubseteq\rangle$ of functions. Many abstractions of functions have been proposed e.g. [20, 30] that can be reused for termination static analysis. As a simple example, we consider a piecewise linear variant abstraction. The purpose of this new abstract domain is to illustrate the abstraction of fixpoint definitions of variant functions with widening, many more abstractions being necessary to cover all practical cases.

12.1 Piecewise linear variant abstraction

Let us consider a program with integer variables $\mathbb{X} = \mathtt{x}_1, \ldots, \mathtt{x}_n$, $n > 0$. We first apply an abstraction of states extracting the numerical variables in the form of an environment $\alpha_{\mathbb{X}} \in \Sigma \mapsto (\mathbb{X} \mapsto \mathbb{Z})$ so that, by composition, we are left with an abstraction $\langle(\mathbb{X} \mapsto \mathbb{Z}) \not\mapsto \mathbb{O},\, \sqsubseteq^{\mathsf{v}}\rangle \xleftrightarrow[\alpha]{\gamma} \langle A,\, \sqsubseteq\rangle$. Encoding the partial map by a total map (using "$\perp$" for "undefined/not in the domain" and abstracting higher-order ordinals by "$\top$" ("unknown/infinite", e.g. in case of non-termination or unbounded nondeterminism), we can choose $(\mathbb{X} \mapsto \mathbb{Z}) \mapsto \mathbb{N} \cup \{\perp, \top\}$. There is no loss of information for bounded determinism and unbounded executions are still allowed but disregarded by the abstraction. We can now further abstract by piecewise linear functions.

The values x_i of each variable $\mathtt{x}_i \in \mathbb{X}$, $i \in [1, n]$ are segmented into $\ell_i^1 = -\infty < \cdots < \ell_i^{j_i} < \cdots < \ell_i^{m_i} = +\infty$. This provides a partition of the space $\mathbb{Z}^n$ of values $x_1, \ldots, x_n$ of the variables $\mathtt{x}_1, \ldots, \mathtt{x}_n$. The blocks of the partition are therefore $[\ell_i^{j_i}, \ell_i^{j_i+1})$, $i \in [1, n]$, $j_i \in [1, m_i)$. In practice machine integers are bounded, in which case $-\infty$ and $+\infty$ are the smallest and largest machine integers. The number of blocks in the partitions can also be limited by widening thus favoring efficiency of the abstract domain to the detriment of precision.

12.1.1 The abstract domain of piecewise linear variants

The positive value of the variant function for elements $\vec{x} = x_1, \ldots, x_n$ of each block $[\ell_i^{j_i}, \ell_i^{j_i+1})$ of the partition is a linear expression $\vec{a}^{\,\ell_1^{j_1}\ldots\ell_i^{j_i}\ldots\ell_n^{j_n}}.\vec{x}$ of the form [30]

$$a_1^{\ell_1^{j_1}\ldots\ell_i^{j_i}\ldots\ell_n^{j_n}}\, x_1 + \ldots + a_i^{\ell_1^{j_1}\ldots\ell_i^{j_i}\ldots\ell_n^{j_n}}\, x_i + \ldots + a_n^{\ell_1^{j_1}\ldots\ell_i^{j_i}\ldots\ell_n^{j_n}}\, x_n + a_{n+1}^{\ell_1^{j_1}\ldots\ell_i^{j_i}\ldots\ell_n^{j_n}}$$

where the coefficients $a_k^{\ell_1^{j_1}\ldots\ell_i^{j_i}\ldots\ell_n^{j_n}} \in \mathbb{Q}$, $k \in [1, n+1]$ are rationals (or $\perp/\top$). For example, in two dimensions

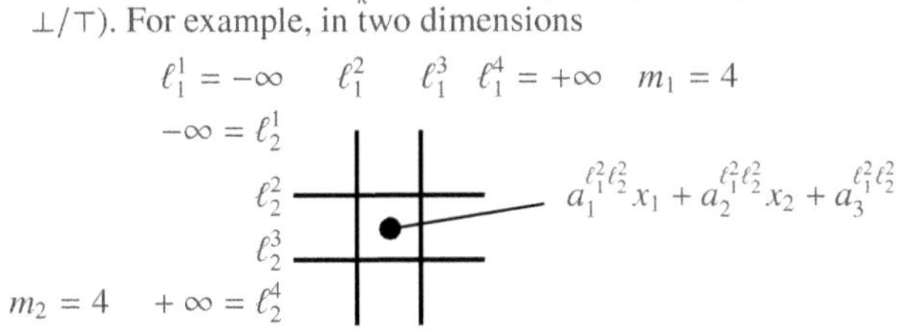

[30] More rigorously, we should write the dot product $\vec{a}^{\,\ell_1^{j_1}\ldots\ell_i^{j_i}\ldots\ell_n^{j_n}} \cdot (\vec{x}, 1)$.

The abstract domain is therefore (omitting the case of blocks with $\perp$ for "not in the domain" and $\top$ for "unknown")

$$A \triangleq \Big\{\lambda\vec{x}\in\mathbb{Z}^n \bullet \prod_{\substack{i\in[1,n],\\ j_i\in[1,m_i)}} (\!| \ell_i^{j_i} \leqslant x_i < \ell_i^{j_i+1} \,?\, \vec{a}_1^{\,\ell_1^{j_1}\ldots\ell_i^{j_i}\ldots\ell_n^{j_n}}.\vec{x} \,:\, \perp |\!)$$
$$\Big|\ \forall i \in [1, n] : \ell_i^1 = -\infty < \cdots < \ell_i^{j_i} < \cdots < \ell_i^{m_i} = +\infty \,\wedge$$
$$\vec{a}^{\,\ell_1^{j_1}\ldots\ell_i^{j_i}\ldots\ell_n^{j_n}} \in \mathbb{Q}^{n+1} \,\wedge$$
$$\forall j_i \in [1, m_i), x_i \in [\ell_i^{j_i}, \ell_i^{j_i+1}) : \vec{a}_1^{\,\ell_1^{j_1}\ldots\ell_i^{j_i}\ldots\ell_n^{j_n}}.\vec{x} \geqslant 0\Big\}\ .$$

When the $\ell_i^{j_i} \in \mathbb{Q}$, $i \in [1, n]$, $j_i \in [1, m_i)$ are rationals, this abstraction essentially reuses the classical abstractions of intervals [18, 19], linear inequalities [31] and segmentation [33]. An immediate generalization consists in using consecutive segments with symbolic bounds as done in [33] for array content analysis. A further generalization consists in using decision trees [32] instead of a segmentation of the domain of the abstract variant function.

12.1.2 Piecewise linear variant abstract transformers

The abstract transformer $\overleftarrow{\phi}^{\sharp\,\mathsf{mv}}_{\tau}[\![\mathrm{P}]\!]$ abstracting the concrete transformer $\overleftarrow{\phi}^{\,\mathsf{mv}}_{\tau}[\![\mathrm{P}]\!]$ of Sect. 11.4 is applied blockwise by computing the abstract pre-image of each block by assignments or tests. The condition in tests may split the block into sub-blocks for which the condition is true or false.

Example 11. Here is an example of first iteration of the backward termination analysis of an exit preceded by a test. The initialization of the fixpoint iterates by $\lambda x \in [-\infty, +\infty] \bullet \perp$ indicates potential non-termination. The exit enforces termination in 0 steps. The test splits the block $[-\infty, +\infty]$ into $[-\infty, 0]$ and $[1, +\infty]$.

```
/* λx•(| x∈[-∞,0] ? 0 : x∈[1,+∞] ? ⊥ |) */
if (x <= 0) { /* λx∈[-∞,+∞]•0 */
    exit; /* λx∈[-∞,+∞]•⊥ */ }
else { /* λx∈[-∞,+∞]•⊥ */ ... }
```
$\square$

An assignment backward propagates the linear variant functions by blocks which are incremented by 1 step, but for those corresponding to non-termination.

Example 12. Assuming $-\infty - 2 = -\infty$ and $+\infty + 2 = +\infty$, the backward termination analysis of the following assignment is

```
/* λx•(| x∈[-∞,2] ? 1 : x∈[3,+∞] ? ⊥ |) */
x = x - 2;
/* λx•(| x∈[-∞,0] ? 0 : x∈[1,+∞] ? ⊥ |) */
```
$\square$

12.1.3 Piecewise linear variant abstract order

The abstract order $\sqsubseteq^{\mathsf{v}}$ first unifies segments of the domain into a common refined partition by segmentation of each variable (as in [33, Sect. 11.4: Segmentation unification]) and then compares the linear expressions blockwise, assuming $\perp$ is the infimum and $\top$ is the supremum (so that the domain comparison of Sect. 9 is done implicitly by the fact that the "undefined" $\perp$ is used outside this domain).

Example 13.

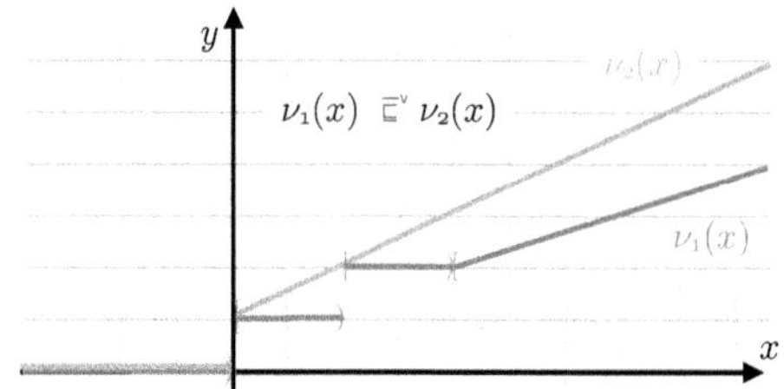

$\square$

12.1.4 Piecewise linear variant abstract join

Similarly, the join $\nu_1 \mathbin{\dot{\sqcup}^{\mathsf{v}}} \nu_2$ first unifies blocks of the partitioned domains of ν_1 and ν_2 into a common refined partition. Then the linear expressions are joined blockwise. This blockwise join $\overline{\sqcup}^{\mathsf{v}}$ is $\vec{a}.\vec{x}$ defined for each block $\ell_1^{j_1} \ldots \ell_i^{j_i} \ldots \ell_n^{j_n}$, $i \in [1, n]$, $j_i \in [1, m_i]$ of the partition such that $\forall i \in [1, n], \forall x_i \in [\ell_i^{j_i}, \ell_i^{j_i+1}], \forall \vec{a}\,' \in \mathbb{Q}^{n+1}$,

- $\vec{a}^{\,\ell_1^{j_1} \ldots \ell_i^{j_i} \ldots \ell_n^{j_n}}.\vec{x} \leqslant \vec{a}.\vec{x}$
- $\vec{a}^{\,\ell_1^{j_1} \ldots \ell_i^{j_i} \ldots \ell_n^{j_n}}.\vec{x} \leqslant \vec{a}\,'.\vec{x} \implies \vec{a}.\vec{x} \leqslant \vec{a}\,'.\vec{x}$.

Example 14.

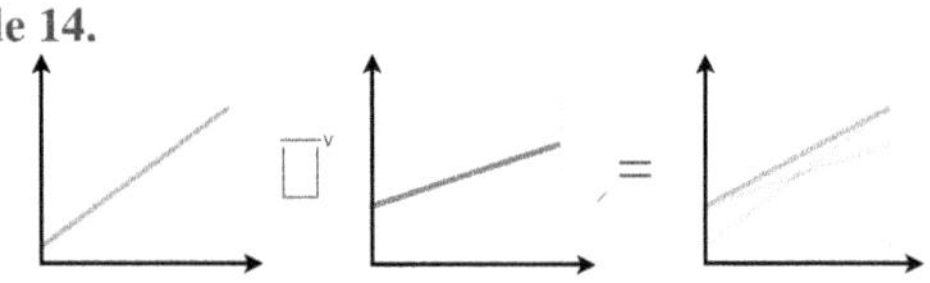

□

A coarser partition can also be used in the join (as in [33, Sect. 11.4: Segmentation unification]) which is less precise but enforces faster convergence.

12.1.5 Piecewise linear variant abstract widening

Finally, the widening $\nu_1 \mathbin{\dot{\overline{\nabla}}^{\mathsf{v}}} \nu_2$ follows the idea introduced in [20] of widening functions by widening the domain of their parameters with a domain widening $\dot{\overline{\nabla}}_{\mathsf{d}}^{\mathsf{v}}$ and then their results with a range widening $\dot{\overline{\nabla}}_{\mathsf{r}}^{\mathsf{v}}$. So the blocks of the partitioned domains of ν_1 and ν_2 are first widened using e.g. interval widening $\dot{\overline{\nabla}}_{\mathsf{d}}^{\mathsf{v}}$ (possibly with thresholds) of the blocks with respect to their neighbors in all directions.

Example 15. An interval widening for a two-dimensional domain $\langle x, y\rangle \in \mathbb{Z}^2$ yields

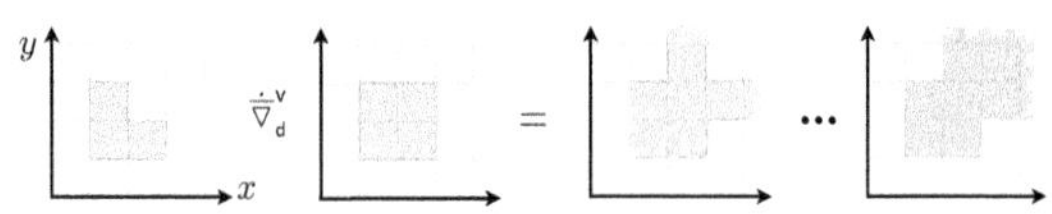

□

Then the range-widening $\dot{\overline{\nabla}}_{\mathsf{r}}^{\mathsf{v}}$ increases the gradient (i.e. slope in two dimensions) of the variant function of each block in the directions of its domain-widened neighbors to over-approximate their respective variants functions (extended to the widened domains).

Example 16.

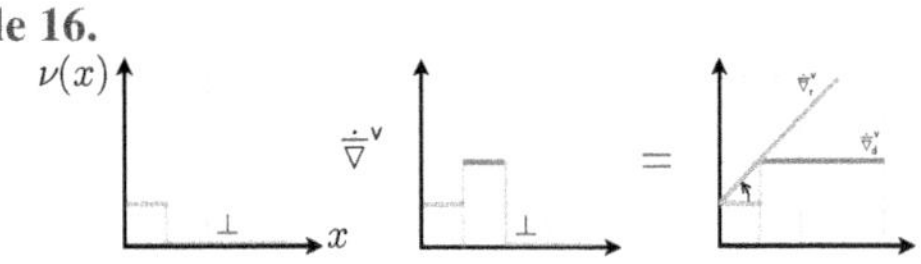

□

To enforce convergence, the widening may have to skip to finitely many given thresholds of gradients before abandoning the constraint to $\top$.

Example 17. We use two loop unrollings to stabilize iterations before widening [56].

$$\begin{aligned}
\nu_A^0 &= \lambda x \in [-\infty, +\infty] \bullet \bot \\
\nu_A^1 &= \lambda x \bullet \llparenthesis\, x \in [-\infty, 0] \mathrel{?} 0 \mathrel{:} x \in [1, +\infty] \mathrel{?} \bot \,\rrparenthesis \\
\nu_A^2 &= \lambda x \in [-\infty, 0] \bullet 0 \mathbin{\dot\cup} \lambda x \in [1, 2] \bullet 1 \mathbin{\dot\cup} \lambda x \in [3, +\infty] \bullet \bot \\
\nu'^3_A &= \lambda x \bullet \llparenthesis\, x \in [-\infty, 0] \mathrel{?} 0 \mathrel{:} x \in [1, 2] \mathrel{?} 1 \mathrel{:} x \in [3, 4] \mathrel{?} 2 \\
&\qquad\qquad \mathrel{:} x \in [5, +\infty] \mathrel{?} \bot \,\rrparenthesis \\
\nu_A^3 &= \nu_A^2 \mathbin{\dot{\overline{\nabla}}^{\mathsf{v}}} \nu'^3_A \\
\nu'^4_A &= \lambda x \bullet \llparenthesis\, x \in [-\infty, 0] \mathrel{?} 0 \mathrel{:} x \in [1, 2] \mathrel{?} 1 \mathrel{:} x \in [3, +\infty] \mathrel{?} \frac{x}{2} + 1 \,\rrparenthesis \\
\nu_A^4 &= \nu_A^3 .
\end{aligned}$$

The over-approximation of ν in Ex. 7, by ν_A is as follows

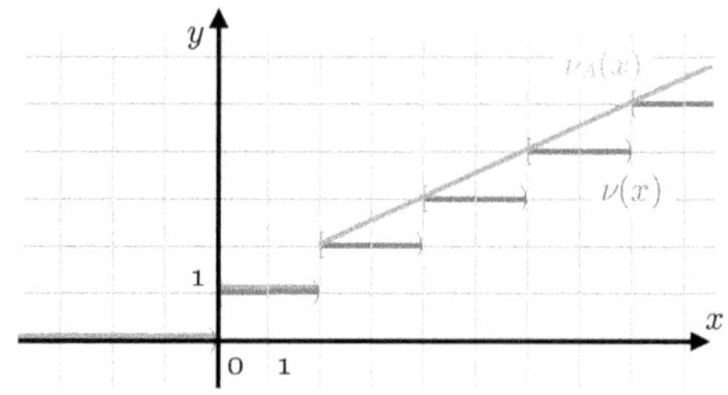

□

Notice that the domain of termination is widened which is an over-approximation which might include non-termination cases. However, the iterates with widening stop at a post-fixpoint ν_A

$$\overleftarrow{\phi}^{\sharp\mathsf{mv}}_{\tau}[\![\mathsf{P}]\!](\nu_A) \mathrel{\overline{\sqsubseteq}^{\mathsf{v}}} \nu_A$$

which, by definition of the abstract partial order $\overline{\sqsubseteq}^{\mathsf{v}}$ ensures that ν_A is decreasing on blocks for which it is defined. Termination is therefore proven for blocks with either 0 or a strictly decreasing variant. By undecidability, there might be blocks which variant value is $\top$ indicating insufficient precision to conclude.

12.2 Non-linear variant abstraction

Besides classical linear relational abstractions (e.g. octagons [46], polyhedra [31], etc.) which can be used pointwise as in Sect. 12.1, the variant function in each block of the partition can also be non-linear (e.g. polynomials [47], exponentials [39], etc.).

13. Relational variant semantics

To use relational abstractions for static termination analysis, we can further abstract variant functions into relations.

13.1 Relational variant abstraction

A variant function ν can be abstracted as the pair of an abstraction of its domain $\mathsf{dom}(\nu)$ by a set abstraction (such as e.g. intervals) and an abstraction of its value by (a relational abstraction of) the down-closed relation r which over-approximates the variant function on its domain that is $\forall s \in \mathsf{dom}(\nu), w \in \Sigma : \langle s, w\rangle \in r \implies w \preccurlyeq \nu(s)$. The abstraction is therefore (the first component is redundant but useful for static analysis)

$$\alpha^{\mathsf{rv}}(\nu) \triangleq \langle \mathsf{dom}(\nu),\ \alpha^{\downarrow}(\{\langle s, \nu(s)\rangle \mid s \in \mathsf{dom}(\nu)\})\rangle$$

where the *down-closure* of a relation $r \in \wp(\Sigma \times \mathbb{W})$ is

$$\alpha^{\downarrow}(r) \triangleq \{\langle s, w'\rangle \mid \exists w : w' \preccurlyeq w \wedge \langle s, w\rangle \in r\} .$$

Observe that the effect of the down-closure is to replace equalities by inequalities for which numerous abstract domains are available. Moreover, an over-approximation of the first component is known by Sect. 9 but for correction we either need an under-approximation or prove termination for this over-approximation, which is the usual option. For the second component, an over-approximation is correct (this over-estimates the termination time). We have[31]

$$\langle \Sigma \not\mapsto \mathbb{W}, \sqsubseteq^{\mathsf{v}}\rangle \xrightleftharpoons[\alpha^{\mathsf{v}}]{\gamma^{\mathsf{v}}} \langle \wp(\Sigma) \times \alpha^{\downarrow}[\wp(\Sigma \times \mathbb{W})], \subseteq \times \subseteq\rangle .$$

13.2 Relational variant semantics

The *relational variant semantics* of a program P is

$$\begin{aligned}
\tau^{\mathsf{mrv}}[\![\mathsf{P}]\!] &\triangleq \alpha^{\mathsf{rv}}(\tau^{\mathsf{mv}}[\![\mathsf{P}]\!]) && \text{potential termination relational variant} \\
\tau^{\mathsf{Mrv}}[\![\mathsf{P}]\!] &\triangleq \alpha^{\mathsf{rv}}(\tau^{\mathsf{Mt}}[\![\mathsf{P}]\!]) && \text{definite termination relational variant.}
\end{aligned}$$

[31] $\leqslant \times \sqsubseteq$ is the componentwise partial order $\langle x, y\rangle \leqslant \times \sqsubseteq \langle x', y'\rangle \iff x \leqslant x' \wedge y \sqsubseteq y'$.

13.3 Fixpoint relational variant semantics

By fixpoint abstraction of the fixpoint variant semantics of Sect. 11.4, we get, by calculational design, the fixpoint definite and potential relational variant semantics[32].

$$\tau^{\mathsf{mrv}}[\![\mathtt{P}]\!] \;=\; \mathsf{lfp}_{\dot{\emptyset}}^{\subseteq\times\subseteq}\; \overleftarrow{\phi}_{\tau}^{\mathsf{mrv}}[\![\mathtt{P}]\!] \qquad \text{potential termination}$$

$$\begin{aligned}\overleftarrow{\phi}_{\tau}^{\mathsf{mrv}}[\![\mathtt{P}]\!]\langle D,\, r\rangle \;\triangleq\;& \text{let } D' = D \cup \beta_\tau[\![\mathtt{P}]\!] \cup \tau[\![\mathtt{P}]\!]^{-1}[D] \text{ in}\\ & \langle D',\, \{\langle s,\, 0\rangle \mid s \in \beta_\tau[\![\mathtt{P}]\!]\} \cup \alpha^{\downarrow}(\{\langle s,\, \rho+1\rangle \mid\\ & \quad \wedge\, \exists s' : \langle s,\, s'\rangle \in \tau[\![\mathtt{P}]\!] \wedge s' \in D \wedge \langle s',\, \rho\rangle \in r\})\rangle\end{aligned}$$

$$\tau^{\mathsf{Mrv}}[\![\mathtt{P}]\!] \;=\; \mathsf{lfp}_{\dot{\emptyset}}^{\subseteq\times\subseteq}\; \overleftarrow{\phi}_{\tau}^{\mathsf{Mrv}}[\![\mathtt{P}]\!] \qquad \text{definite termination}$$

$$\begin{aligned}\overleftarrow{\phi}_{\tau}^{\mathsf{Mrv}}[\![\mathtt{P}]\!](\langle D,\, r\rangle)s \;\triangleq\;& \text{let } D' = D \cup \beta_\tau[\![\mathtt{P}]\!] \cup (\tau[\![\mathtt{P}]\!]^{-1}[D] \cap \tau[\![\mathtt{P}]\!]^{\widetilde{-1}}[D])\\ & \text{in } \langle D',\, \{\langle s,\, 0\rangle \mid s \in \beta_\tau[\![\mathtt{P}]\!]\} \cup \{\langle s,\, \rho+1\rangle \mid\\ & \quad \wedge\, \exists s' : \langle s,\, s'\rangle \in \tau[\![\mathtt{P}]\!] \wedge s' \in D \wedge \langle s',\, \rho\rangle \in r\\ & \quad \wedge\, \forall s' : \langle s,\, s'\rangle \in \tau[\![\mathtt{P}]\!] \Longrightarrow s' \in D \wedge \exists \rho' : \langle s',\, \rho'\rangle \in r\}\rangle\,.\end{aligned}$$

The over-approximation of D is classical in static analysis [19, 21] so we concentrate on the over-approximation of the relational variant r.

14. Transition-based termination analysis

We consider the case when states $s \in \Sigma$ consist of a pair $\langle \xi,\, \mu\rangle$ of a control state ξ (used for state or trace partitioning) and a memory state μ. The memory state maps variables $\mathtt{x} \in \mathbb{X}$ to numerical values $\mu(\mathtt{x}) \in \mathbb{Z}$ (for simplicity all other types are ignored in the examples). We consider a relational abstraction $\langle \alpha^{\downarrow}[\wp(\Sigma \times \mathbb{W})],\, \subseteq\rangle \underset{\alpha}{\overset{\gamma}{\leftrightarrows}} \langle A,\, \sqsubseteq\rangle$ of the fixpoint relational variant semantics of Sect. 13.2. In practice, we choose $\mathbb{W} = \mathbb{N}$ and adjoint an extra variable # to contain the value of ρ.

We can use octagons [46], polyhedra [31], polynomials [47], exponentials [39], their numerous variants, possibly partitioned on states [12], traces [56], or conditions of decision trees [32].

Example 18. Consider the program of Ex. 7, where a forward interval analysis has determined the invariants given as comments.

```
int main () { int x;
    /* x:[-2147483648, 2147483647] */
    while (x > 0) {
        /* x:[1, 2147483647] */
        x = x - 2;
        /* x:[-1, 2147483645] */
    }
    /* x:[-2147483648, 0] */
}
```

The abstraction of the fixpoint equations of Sect. 13.3 is given below in logical form (representing a set by its characteristic predicate) with restriction to the reachable states over-approximated by the interval analysis.

$$\begin{aligned} r(x, \#) \Longleftarrow\;& (-2147483648 \leqslant x \leqslant \# = 0) \vee (\exists x', \#' :\\ & x \in [1, 2147483647] \wedge x' = x - 2 \wedge \# \leqslant \#' + 1 \wedge r(x', \#'))\,.\end{aligned}$$

Inverting the assignment yields the classical simplification

$$\begin{aligned} r(x, \#) \Longleftarrow\;& (-2147483648 \leqslant x \leqslant \# = 0) \vee (\exists \#' :\\ & x \in [1, 2147483647] \wedge \# \leqslant \#' + 1 \wedge r(x-2, \#'))\,.\end{aligned}$$

Partitioning into $r_1(x, \#) = r(x, \#) \wedge x \leqslant 0$ and $r_2(x, \#) = r(x, \#) \wedge x > 0$, the iterates for $r_1(x, \#)$ immediately converge while the iterates for $r_2(x, \#)$ abstracted with octagons [46] are

$$\begin{aligned}
r_2^0(x, \#) &= \mathsf{false}\\
r_2^1(x, \#) &= \exists \#' : x \in [1, 2147483647] \wedge \# \leqslant \#' + 1 \wedge r_1(x-2, \#')\\
&= x = 1 \wedge \# \leqslant 1\\
r_2^2(x, \#) &= \exists \#' : x \in [1, 2147483647] \wedge \# \leqslant \#' + 1 \wedge\\
&\qquad (r_1(x-2, \#') \vee r_2^1(x-2, \#'))\\
&= (x = 1 \wedge \# \leqslant 1) \vee (x = 3 \wedge \# \leqslant 2)\\
&= 1 \leqslant x \leqslant \# \leqslant 2 \qquad \text{octagon abstraction of } \vee\\
r_2^3(x, \#) &= \exists \#' : x \in [1, 2147483647] \wedge \# \leqslant \#' + 1 \wedge\\
&\qquad (r_1(x-2, \#') \vee r_2^2(x-2, \#'))\\
&= (x = 1 \wedge \# \leqslant 1) \vee (2 \leqslant x \leqslant \# + 1 \wedge \# \leqslant 3)\\
&= 1 \leqslant x \leqslant \# \leqslant 3 \qquad \text{octagon abstraction of } \vee\\
&= 1 \leqslant x \leqslant \# \wedge x \leqslant 2147483647 \quad \text{widening with } r_2^2(x, \#)\\
r_2^4(x, \#) &= r_2^3(x, \#)
\end{aligned}$$

proving termination since # strictly decreases around the loop and remains positive. Of course direct resolution methods [17, 54] would find the same result. However tests are excluded within loops in [54] while the presence of tests is not impairing the above octagon abstraction or the piecewise linear variant abstraction of Sect. 12.1. For example, the loop body `if (odd (x)) { x = x - 1; } else { x = x - 2 }` with state partitioning on the conditional branches yields the same results. □

15. Semantic structural induction

Semantic structural induction is by induction on the structure of computations as opposed to transitional verification based on an induction on the program steps as in Floyd/Turing method [40, 59]. This point of view generalizes syntactic structural induction on program syntax as in Hoare logic [43], replacing the syntactic by a semantic point of view using the concept of structural inductive cover. We start by the simple case of structuring states in next Sect. 15.1 before generalizing to the more concrete trace computations in Sect. 15.3 and their abstractions in Sect. 16.

15.1 Inductive state cover

Many inductive formal definitions and verification methods can be formalized in a language-independent way by an inductive cover of the set Σ of states (examples are given in next Sect. 15.2).

Definition 1. An *inductive state cover* of a non-empty set $\chi \in \wp(\Sigma)$ of states is tree encoded as a set $C \in \mathfrak{C}(\chi)$ of (finite) sequences S of non-empty members $B \in \wp(\chi) \setminus \{\emptyset\}$ such that

1. if $S S' \in C$ then $S \in C$ (prefix-closure)
2. if $S \in C$ then $\exists S' : S = \chi S'$ (root)
3. if $S B B' \in C$ then $B \supset B'$ (well-foundedness)
4. if $S B B' \in C$ then $B \subseteq \bigcup_{S B B' \in C} B'$ (cover). □

By the prefix-closure condition Def. 1.1, the inductive cover is a tree (so that proofs based on the cover C are by case analysis on the tree width and induction on the tree depth). By the root condition Def. 1.2, the tree is rooted at χ (which ensures that inductive proofs based on the cover C are valid for χ). By the strictly-decreasing condition Def. 1.3, the sequences S are necessarily finite so the immediate component relation between a node of the tree and its sons is well-founded. It follows that proofs on states can be done by induction on this well-founded relation. And, by the covering condition Def. 1.4, the states in a node are covered by the join of the states in its sons (which ensures that proofs based on the cover C do not forget any possible case). Inductive state covers are abstractions of inductive trace covers introduced in forthcoming Sect. 15.3 but are introduced first for simplicity. An example is [45].

[32] The dual pre-image of $Y \in \wp(A)$ by a relation $r \in \wp(A \times B)$ is $r^{\widetilde{-1}}[Y] \triangleq \neg r^{-1}[\neg Y]$ also written $\widetilde{\mathbf{pre}}[r]Y$.

15.2 Examples of semantic structural induction

15.2.1 Loop invariants and variants

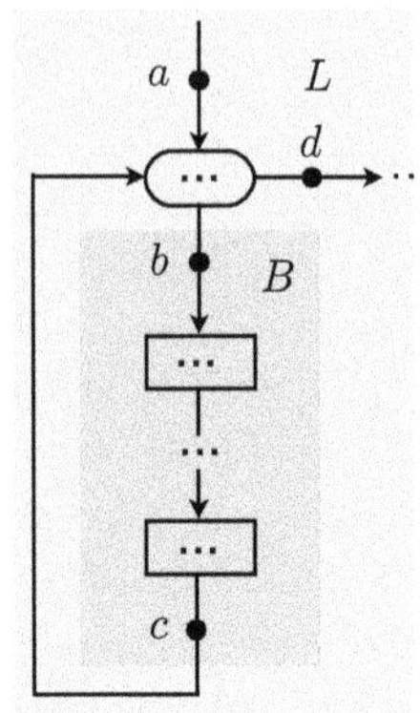

In Floyd's total correctness proof method, one typically provides a loop invariant and a loop variant function for termination. It is not necessary for the variant function to strictly decrease at each program step but only once around each loop iterate. This corresponds to a cover of the states of the loop according to their control component which induces a decomposition of executions into trace segments for the loop containing trace segments for the loop body considered as one step in the inductive reasoning on loop iterations.

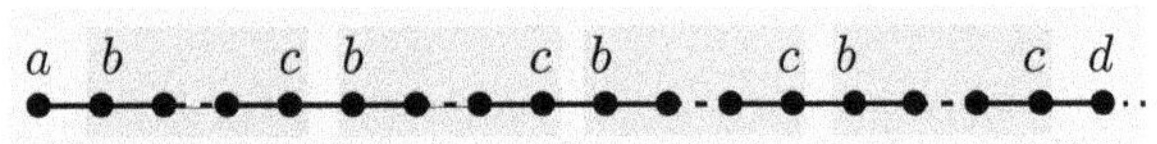

Moreover a different variant function is used for each loop so that this decomposition is applied recursively for nested loops.

15.2.2 Hoare logic

Inductive definition/verification in the form of structural induction on the program syntax originates from axiomatic semantics [43], denotational semantics [57], and operational semantics [51].

Hoare logic for a structured imperative language [43], and its extension to total correctness [44], can be understood as the inductive state cover based on the control states of a command (ignoring its memory states). For example, a while loop can be covered by the states which control is in the condition and the states which control is in the loop body. The states of the loop body can themselves be covered recursively, by structural induction on the program syntax. This structural induction on the program syntax can be understood as induction on a state cover which itself induces a cover of the execution traces by segments which states are in a block of the state cover. A termination proof by structural induction on the program syntax [44] has the advantage, a.o., to be able to handle unbounded non-determinism without requiring transfinite ordinals (equivalent to a lexicographic ordering on nested loops).

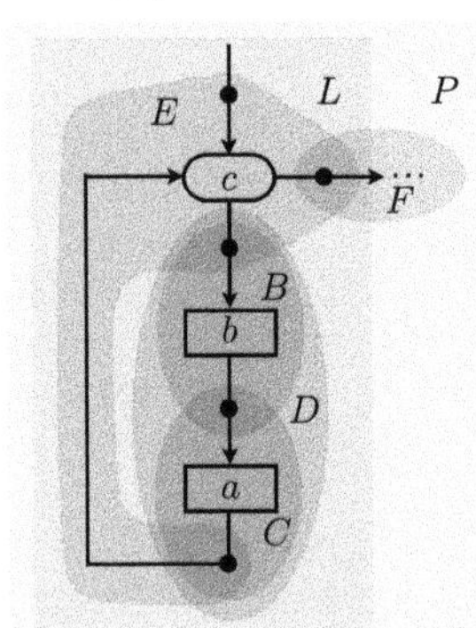

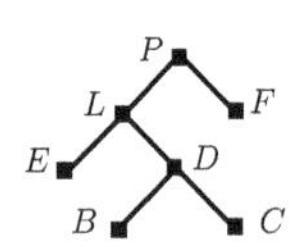

$\{P, PF, PL, PLE, PLD, PLDB, PLDC\}$

15.2.3 Burstall intermittent assertion proof method

Burstall's total correctness proof method [3, 29] can be understood as an inductive reasoning by recurrence on data (as well as control as in Floyd/Turing and Hoare's methods). Although Burstall's proof method [3] is equivalent in power to Floyd/Turing's method [25], it is much easier to use in practice. The formalization of Burstall's total correctness proof method [3] in [25] can be understood as a tree cover on both control and data. The example below shows how hand-simulation/symbolic execution (HS) and lemmas (L_1, L_2) apply to a particular execution trace.

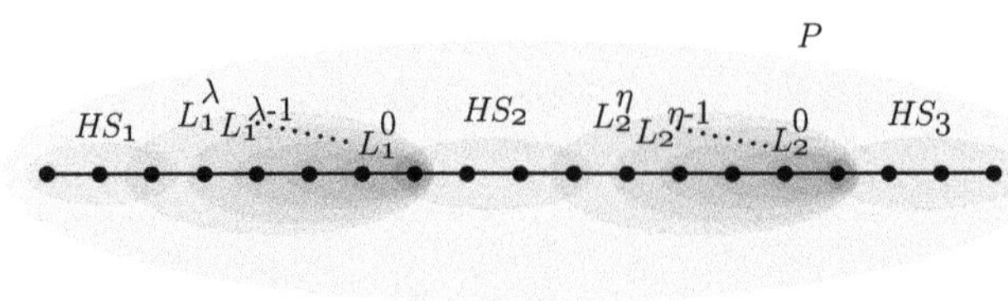

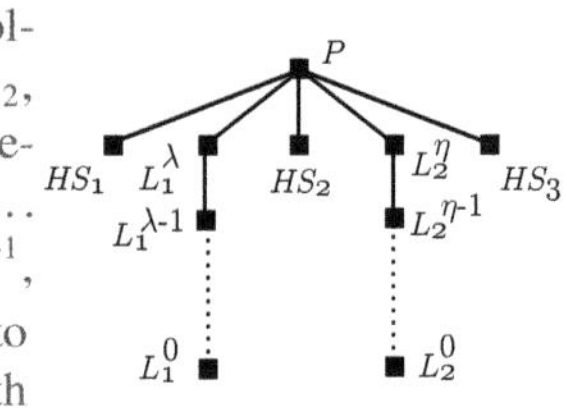

The inductive cover contains the program P, the hand-simulation/symbolic execution blocks $P\ HS_1$, $P\ HS_2$, $P\ HS_3$, and two lemmas with respective blocks $P\ L_1^\lambda$, $P\ L_1^\lambda\ L_1^{\lambda-1}$, ..., $P\ L_1^\lambda\ L_1^{\lambda-1} \cdots L_1^0$ and $P\ L_2^\eta$, $P\ L_2^\eta\ L_2^{\eta-1}$, ..., $P\ L_2^\eta\ L_2^{\eta-1} \cdots L_2^0$ corresponding to proofs by recurrence on the data with respective ranks λ and η.

Observe that the termination analysis method of [9] can be seen as implicitly relying on Burstall's proof method.

15.3 Trace-based semantic structural induction

The previous examples of Sect. 15.2 show the need to go beyond purely syntactic, language-dependent induction and that induction on states can be generalized to induction on trace segments. Consequently, we introduce a general form of inductive reasoning on the semantic structure of computations, first starting by induction on blocks of trace segments and then their abstractions in Sect. 16.

15.3.1 Trace segment abstraction

We first observe that considering segments of traces is an abstraction. The *segment abstraction* $\langle\wp(\Sigma^{+\infty}), \subseteq\rangle \xrightleftharpoons[\alpha^+]{\gamma^+} \langle\wp(\Sigma^{+\infty}), \subseteq\rangle$

$$\alpha^+(T) \triangleq \{\sigma \in \Sigma^{+\infty} \mid \exists\sigma' \in \Sigma^*, \sigma'' \in \Sigma^{*\infty} : \sigma'\sigma\sigma'' \in T\}$$

is the set of segments of traces of T. If $T, T' \in \wp(\Sigma^{+\infty})$, we define

$$T \Subset T' \triangleq T \subseteq \alpha^+(T') = \forall\sigma \in T : \exists\sigma', \sigma'' : \sigma'\sigma\sigma'' \in T'$$

to mean that all traces of T are segments of the traces of T'. We define the join

$$\biguplus_{i\in\Delta} T_i \triangleq \gamma^+\Big(\bigcup_{i\in\Delta} T_i\Big) = \{\sigma_{i_1} \ldots \sigma_{i_n} \mid \forall k \in [1, n] : \sigma_{i_k} \in T_{i_k}\}$$

to be the set of all the traces made out of segments in the T_i, $i \in \Delta$.

15.3.2 Inductive trace segment cover

Definition 2. An *inductive trace segment cover* of a non-empty set $\chi \in \wp(\Sigma^{+\infty})$ of traces is a set $C \in \mathfrak{C}(\chi)$ of sequences S of members B of $\wp(\alpha^+(\chi))$ such that

1. if $S S' \in C$ then $S \in C$ (prefix-closure)
2. if $S \in C$ then $\exists S' : S = \chi S'$ (root)
3. if $S B B' \in C$ then $B \supsetneq B'$ (well-foundedness)
4. if $S B B' \in C$ then $B \subseteq \biguplus_{S B B' \in C} B'$ (cover). □

Example 19. An example of inductive trace segment cover is trace partitioning [56]. □

Example 20. A variant function $\nu \in \Sigma \not\mapsto \mathbb{N}$ defines a trivial inductive trace cover. Each value $v \in \mathsf{codom}(\nu)$ defines segments starting with states σ such that $\nu(\sigma) = v$ of length at most v. □

The following definitions are classical for trees $C \in \mathfrak{C}(\chi)$.

$$\begin{aligned}
\mathsf{root}(C) &\triangleq \chi \\
\mathsf{leaves}(C) &\triangleq \{B \in \wp(\chi) \mid \exists S : S B \in C \wedge \forall S' : S B S' \notin C\} \\
\mathsf{inner}(C) &\triangleq \{B \in \wp(\chi) \mid \exists S, B', S' : S B B' S' \in C\} \\
\mathsf{nodes}(C) &\triangleq \mathsf{leaves}(C) \cup \mathsf{inner}(C) \\
\mathsf{sons}_C(B) &\triangleq \{B' \in \mathsf{nodes}(C) \mid \exists S, S' : S B B' S' \in C\} .
\end{aligned}$$

The *immediate component relation* $B' \rtimes_C B \triangleq B' \in \mathsf{sons}_C(B) = \exists S : S B B' \in C$ is well-founded, so that proofs on segments can be done by induction on this well-founded relation. The *component relation* $\rtimes_C^*$ is its reflexive transitive closure. The blocks of a cover C are $\mathsf{nodes}(C) \triangleq \{B \in \wp(\Sigma) \mid B \rtimes_C^* \Sigma\}$.

15.4 State cover induced by an inductive trace cover

Given an inductive trace cover $C \in \mathfrak{C}(\chi)$, $\chi \in \wp(\Sigma^{+\infty})$ of Def. 2, define the abstractions

$$\begin{array}{rcll} \alpha^{\mathsf{ts}}(C) & \triangleq & \{\alpha^{\mathsf{ts}}(S) \mid S \in C\} & C \in \wp((\wp(\alpha^+(\chi)))^+) \\ \alpha^{\mathsf{ts}}(S\,S') & \triangleq & \alpha^{\mathsf{ts}}(S)\alpha^{\mathsf{ts}}(S') & S, S' \in (\wp(\alpha^+(\chi)))^+ \\ \alpha^{\mathsf{ts}}(B) & \triangleq & \{\alpha^{\mathsf{ts}}(\sigma) \mid \sigma \in B\} & B \in \wp(\alpha^+(\chi)) \\ \alpha^{\mathsf{ts}}(\sigma) & \triangleq & \{\sigma_i \mid i \in [0, |\sigma| - 1]\} & \sigma \in \alpha^+(\chi)\,. \end{array}$$

Then $\alpha^{\mathsf{ts}}(C)$ is an inductive state cover in the sense of Def. 1.

15.5 Trace cover induced by a inductive state cover

Inversely, given an inductive state cover $C \in \mathfrak{C}(\chi)$, $\chi \in \wp(\Sigma)$ of Def. 1, define

$$\begin{array}{rcll} \gamma^{\mathsf{st}}(C) & \triangleq & \{\gamma^{\mathsf{st}}(S) \mid S \in C\} & C \in \wp((\wp(\chi))^+) \\ \gamma^{\mathsf{st}}(S\,S') & \triangleq & \gamma^{\mathsf{st}}(S)\gamma^{\mathsf{st}}(S') & S, S' \in (\wp(\chi))^+ \\ \gamma^{\mathsf{st}}(B) & \triangleq & B^+ & B \in \wp(\chi) \end{array}$$

We have $\langle \wp((\wp(\Sigma^+))^+), \subseteq\rangle \underset{\alpha^{\mathsf{ts}}}{\overset{\gamma^{\mathsf{st}}}{\leftrightarrows}} \langle \wp((\wp(\Sigma))^+), \subseteq\rangle$ and $\gamma^{\mathsf{ts}}(C)$ is an inductive trace cover of χ^+.

15.6 Syntactic trace cover

Similarly one can define the inductive state cover induced by the syntax of commands of a programming language by considering the states which control is in a given command. This in turns induces a trace cover which is the basis for e.g. Hoare logic or structural static analysis by induction on program commands, as opposed to induction on program transitions as in dataflow analysis.

15.6.1 Inductive proof method

We have a sound and complete *inductive proof method* of a semantic property $\Theta^{+\infty}[\![\mathrm{P}]\!] \cap \chi \in \mathcal{P}$ for an inductive trace cover $C \in \mathfrak{C}(\chi)$

$$\Theta^{+\infty}[\![\mathrm{P}]\!] \cap B \in \mathcal{P}, \quad B \in \mathsf{leaves}(C) \qquad \text{basis}$$

$$\frac{\forall B' \in \mathsf{sons}_C(B) : \Theta^{+\infty}[\![\mathrm{P}]\!] \cap B' \in \mathcal{P}}{\Theta^{+\infty}[\![\mathrm{P}]\!] \cap B \in \mathcal{P}}, \quad B \in \mathsf{inner}(C) \qquad \text{induction}$$

In particular, for termination $\tau^{+\infty}[\![\mathrm{P}]\!] \subseteq \Sigma^+[\![\mathrm{P}]\!]$ with a trace cover $C \in \mathfrak{C}(\Sigma^{+\infty}[\![\mathrm{P}]\!])$, we get

$$\Theta^{+\infty}[\![\mathrm{P}]\!] \subseteq B \subseteq \Sigma^+, \quad B \in \mathsf{leaves}(C) \qquad \text{basis}$$

$$\frac{\forall B' \in \mathsf{sons}_C(B) : \Theta^{+\infty}[\![\mathrm{P}]\!] \subseteq B' \subseteq \Sigma^+}{\Theta^{+\infty}[\![\mathrm{P}]\!] \subseteq B \subseteq \Sigma^+}, \quad B \in \mathsf{inner}(C) \qquad \text{induction}$$

Example 21. Another form of decomposition of reasonings on termination is proposed by the transition invariants proof method of Podelski-Rybalchenko [53] based on a relational semantics [15].

The transition invariants proof method of [53] can be seen as the α^{R} abstraction of the above inductive proof method based on an inductive trace cover of height 1 with root $\Sigma^+[\![\mathrm{P}]\!]$ and sons $\alpha^+(T_1)$, $\ldots, \alpha^+(T_n)$ where $T_1, \ldots, T_n \in \wp(\Sigma^+[\![\mathrm{P}]\!])$ such that

$$\Theta^{+\infty}[\![\mathrm{P}]\!] \subseteq \Sigma^+[\![\mathrm{P}]\!] \iff \forall i \in [1, n] : \Theta^{+\infty}[\![\mathrm{P}]\!] \cap T_i \subseteq \Sigma^+\,.$$

The generalization by inductive trace covers is both on the use of trace segments (instead of their relational abstraction of Sect. 7.1), and the possibility of recursive application of the method by induction, including on data, à la Burstall [3]. □

16. Abstract semantic structural induction

Assume that we can prove a program trace property in the concrete using an inductive trace cover. Can we prove an abstract program property using the abstraction of the inductive trace cover? We have seen an example in Sect. 15.5. The question is whether this observation is general.

16.1 Abstract inductive cover

Definition 3. An *inductive abstract cover* of a trace semantics $\chi \in \wp(\Sigma^{+\infty})$ is an element $C \in A_C$ of an abstract domain A_C such that

$$\langle \wp((\wp(\Sigma^+))^+), \subseteq\rangle \underset{\alpha^{\mathsf{ta}}}{\overset{\gamma^{\mathsf{at}}}{\leftrightarrows}} \langle A_C, \sqsubseteq_C\rangle$$

and $\gamma^{\mathsf{ts}}(C)$ is an inductive trace cover of χ. □

A standard way to define such inductive abstract covers is to follow the example of Sect. 15.5 generalized to a block abstraction $\langle \wp(\Sigma^+), \subseteq\rangle \underset{\alpha^{\mathsf{ta}}}{\overset{\gamma^{\mathsf{at}}}{\leftrightarrows}} \langle A_B, \sqsubseteq_B\rangle$. We get the cover abstraction $\langle \wp((\wp(\Sigma^+))^+), \subseteq\rangle \underset{\alpha^{\mathsf{ta}}}{\overset{\gamma^{\mathsf{at}}}{\leftrightarrows}} \langle \wp((A_B)^+), \subseteq\rangle$ by generalizing α^{ta} to sequences of abstract blocks and sets of such abstract sequences as follows

$$\begin{array}{rcll} \gamma^{\mathsf{at}}(S\,S') & \triangleq & \gamma^{\mathsf{at}}(S)\gamma^{\mathsf{at}}(S') & S, S' \in (A_B)^+ \\ \gamma^{\mathsf{at}}(C) & \triangleq & \{\gamma^{\mathsf{at}}(S) \mid S \in C\} & C \in \wp((A_B)^+)\,. \end{array}$$

Then A_C is chosen to be the set of elements $C \in \wp((A_B)^+)$ of sequences S of members B of A_B such that

1. if $S\,S' \in C$ then $S \in C$ (prefix-closure)
2. if $S \in C$ then $\exists S' : S = \alpha^{\mathsf{at}}(\chi)S'$ (root)
3. if $S\,B B' \in C$ then $\gamma^{\mathsf{at}}(B) \supsetneq \gamma^{\mathsf{at}}(B')$ (well-foundedness)
4. if $S\,B B' \in C$ then $\gamma^{\mathsf{at}}(B) \subseteq \biguplus_{S\,B B' \in C} \gamma^{\mathsf{at}}(B')$ (cover).

It follows that any $C \in A_C$ is an inductive abstract cover of the trace semantics $\chi \in \wp(\Sigma^{+\infty})$ in the sense of Def. 3.

Example 22. The transition invariant proof method of [53] follows from the relational abstraction $\langle \wp(\Sigma^+), \subseteq\rangle \underset{\alpha^{\mathsf{ta}}}{\overset{\gamma^{\mathsf{at}}}{\leftrightarrows}} \langle \wp(\Sigma \times \Sigma), \subseteq\rangle$ [15] where $\alpha^{\mathsf{ta}}(B) \triangleq \{\langle \sigma_0, \sigma_n - 1\rangle \mid n > 0 \wedge \sigma \in B \cap \Sigma^n\}$ is limited to the trace covers of the form given in Ex. 21. □

16.2 Abstract inductive proof

The inductive proof method of Sect. 15.6.1 can be abstracted as follows.

$$\alpha^{\mathsf{at}}(\Theta^{+\infty}[\![\mathrm{P}]\!]) \sqsubseteq_C B, \quad B \in \mathsf{leaves}(C) \qquad \text{basis}$$

$$\frac{\forall B' \in \mathsf{sons}_C(B) : \alpha^{\mathsf{at}}(\Theta^{+\infty}[\![\mathrm{P}]\!]) \sqsubseteq_C B'}{\alpha^{\mathsf{at}}(\Theta^{+\infty}[\![\mathrm{P}]\!]) \sqsubseteq_C B^+}, \quad B \in \mathsf{inner}(C) \qquad \text{induction}$$

The proofs $\alpha^{\mathsf{at}}(\Theta^{+\infty}[\![\mathrm{P}]\!]) \sqsubseteq_C B$ can be done in the abstract by fixpoint induction using a fixpoint abstraction of the fixpoint definition of the trace semantics $\Theta^{+\infty}[\![\mathrm{P}]\!]$.

17. Related work

Most directly relevant work has been cited in the text. For programs with unbounded executions, any finite homomorphic abstraction must introduce a loop so that finite model-checking [4] or bounded model-checking [2] are unapplicable (or unsound) to prove termination (or non-termination). Nevertheless, predicate abstraction [41] remains applicable since it is a finite encoding of an infinite abstract interpretation [16]. With predicate abstraction the end-user is left with the hard problem of providing candidate variant functions [14], as in [1]. Moreover [27] shows that infinitary abstractions with widening/narrowing, as considered in this paper, are definitely strictly more powerful than finite abstractions. The computation of variant functions by abstraction is new, and different from the counter-example guided ways to find disjunctive ranking functions, used in tools like Terminator [7] and derivatives.

18. Conclusion

Abstract interpretation has established constructive principles for reasoning about semantics. A semantics is a fixpoint so proving a semantic property at some level of abstraction consists in verifying properties of abstract fixpoints which have to be checked (in checking/verification methods), guessed (in proof methods), or automatically inferred or approximated (in static analysis methods).

This principle was mainly applied in the past to invariance and indirectly to termination by reduction to invariance. We have shown that the abstract interpretation principle directly applies to both safety (generalizing invariance) and termination.

Moreover we have generalized the classical syntactic structural induction into the language-independent semantic concept of *semantic structural induction* based on (abstractions of) inductive trace covers which includes induction on syntax, control states, memory states, and execution trace segments and thus generalizes all verification and static analysis methods.

This methodology allowed us to establish new *principles* for proving termination by abstract interpretation of a termination semantics. It remains to design a suitable collection of abstract domains beyond the examples proposed in this paper and the corresponding implementations.

The present abstract interpretation termination framework has to be extended to liveness [6, 53] and more generally to inevitability under fairness hypotheses [35, 52, 55].

References

[1] I. Balaban, A. Pnueli, and L. Zuck. Modular ranking abstraction. *Int. J. Found. Comput. Sci.*, 18(1):5–44, 2007.

[2] A. Biere, A. Cimatti, E. Clarke, O. Strichman, and Y. Zhu. Bounded model checking. *Advances in Computers*, 58:118–149, 2003.

[3] R. Burstall. Program proving as hand simulation with a little induction. *Information Processing*, 308–312. North-Holland, 1974.

[4] E. Clarke, O. Grumberg, and D. Peled. *Model Checking*. MIT Press, 1999.

[5] M. Clarkson and F. Schneider. Hyperproperties. *Journal of Computer Security*, 18(6):1157–1210, 2010.

[6] B. Cook and E. Koskinen. Making prophecies with decision predicates. *POPL*, 399–410, 2011.

[7] B. Cook, A. Gotsman, A. Podelski, A. Rybalchenko, and M. Vardi. Proving that programs eventually do something good. *POPL*, 265–276, 2007.

[8] B. Cook, S. Gulwani, T. Lev-Ami, A. Rybalchenko, and M. Sagiv. Proving conditional termination. *CAV*, LNCS *5123*, 328–340, 2008.

[9] B. Cook, A. Podelski, and A. Rybalchenko. Summarization for termination: no return! *Form. Methods Syst. Des.*, 35:369–387, 2009.

[10] S. Cook. Soundness and completeness of an axiom system for program verification. *SIAM J. Comput.*, 7:70–80, 1978.

[11] P. Cousot. *Méthodes itératives de construction et d'approximation de points fixes d'opérateurs monotones sur un treillis, analyse sémantique de programmes.* Thèse d'État ès sciences math., USMG, Grenoble, 1978.

[12] P. Cousot. Semantic foundations of program analysis. *Program Flow Analysis: Theory and Applications*, ch. 10, 303–342. Prentice-Hall, 1981.

[13] P. Cousot. The calculational design of a generic abstract interpreter. M. Broy and R. Steinbrüggen, eds., *Calculational System Design*. NATO ASI Series F. IOS Press, Amsterdam, 1999.

[14] P. Cousot. Partial completeness of abstract fixpoint checking. *SARA*, LNCS *1864*, 1–25, 2000.

[15] P. Cousot. Constructive design of a hierarchy of semantics of a transition system by abstract interpretation. *TCS*, 277(1–2):47–103, 2002.

[16] P. Cousot. Verification by abstract interpretation. *Proc. Int. Symp. on Verification – Theory & Practice*, LNCS 2772, 243–268, 2003.

[17] P. Cousot. Proving program invariance and termination by parametric abstraction, Lagrangian relaxation and semidefinite programming. *VMCAI*, LNCS *3385*, 1–24, 2005.

[18] P. Cousot and R. Cousot. Static determination of dynamic properties of programs. *Proc. 2nd Int. Symp. on Programming*, 106–130. Dunod, Paris, 1976.

[19] P. Cousot and R. Cousot. Abstract interpretation: a unified lattice model for static analysis of programs by construction or approximation of fixpoints. *POPL*, 238–252, 1977.

[20] P. Cousot and R. Cousot. Static determination of dynamic properties of recursive procedures. *Formal Description of Programming Concepts*, 237–277. North-Holland, 1977.

[21] P. Cousot and R. Cousot. Systematic design of program analysis frameworks. *POPL*, 269–282, 1979.

[22] P. Cousot and R. Cousot. Constructive versions of Tarski's fixed point theorems. *P. J. of Math.*, 82(1):43–57, 1979.

[23] P. Cousot and R. Cousot. Induction principles for proving invariance properties of programs. *Tools & Notions for Program Construction: an Advanced Course*, 75–119. Cambridge University Press, Cambridge, UK, 1982.

[24] P. Cousot and R. Cousot. "À la Floyd" induction principles for proving inevitability properties of programs. *Algebraic methods in semantics*, 277–312. Cambridge University Press, Cambridge, UK, 1985.

[25] P. Cousot and R. Cousot. Sometime = always + recursion ≡ always, on the equivalence of the intermittent and invariant assertions methods for proving inevitability properties of programs. *Acta Informatica*, 24:1–31, 1987.

[26] P. Cousot and R. Cousot. Abstract interpretation frameworks. *JLC*, 2(4):511–547, 1992.

[27] P. Cousot and R. Cousot. Comparing the Galois connection and widening/narrowing approaches to abstract interpretation. *PLILP*, LNCS *631*, 269–295, 1992.

[28] P. Cousot and R. Cousot. Inductive definitions, semantics and abstract interpretation. *POPL*, 83–94, 1992.

[29] P. Cousot and R. Cousot. "À la Burstall" intermittent assertions induction principles for proving inevitable ability properties of programs. *TCS*, 120(1): 123–155, 1993.

[30] P. Cousot and R. Cousot. Higher-order abstract interpretation (and application to comportment analysis generalizing strictness, termination, projection and PER analysis of functional languages). *Int. Conf. on Comp. Lang.*, 95–112, 1994.

[31] P. Cousot and N. Halbwachs. Automatic discovery of linear restraints among variables of a program. *POPL*, 84–97, 1978.

[32] P. Cousot, R. Cousot, and L. Mauborgne. A scalable segmented decision tree abstract domain. *Time for Verification, Essays in Memory of A. Pnueli*, LNCS *6200*, 72–95, 2010.

[33] P. Cousot, R. Cousot, and F. Logozzo. A parametric segmentation functor for fully automatic and scalable array content analysis. *POPL*, 105–118, 2011.

[34] P. Cousot, R. Cousot, and F. Logozzo. Precondition inference from intermittent assertions and application to contracts on collections. *VMCAI*, LNCS *6538*, 150–168, 2011.

[35] R. Cousot. *Fondements des méthodes de preuve d'invariance et de fatalité de programmes parallèles.* Thèse d'État ès sciences math. INPL, Nancy, 1985.

[36] B. Davey and H. Priestley. *Introduction to Lattices and Order, 2nd Edition.* Cambridge University Press, 2002.

[37] E. Dijkstra. Guarded commands, nondeterminacy and formal derivation of programs. *CACM*, 18(8):453–457, 1975.

[38] E. Dijkstra. *A Discipline of Programming*. Prentice-Hall, 1976.

[39] J. Feret. The arithmetic-geometric progression abstract domain. *VMCAI*, LNCS *3385*, 42–58, 2005.

[40] R. Floyd. Assigning meaning to programs. *Proc. Symp. in Applied Math.*, Vol. 19, 19–32. Amer. Math. Soc., 1967.

[41] S. Graf and H. Saïdi. Construction of abstract state graphs with PVS. *CAV*, LNCS *1254*, 72–83, 1997.

[42] M. Heizmann, J. Hoenicke, and A. Podelski. Refinement of trace abstraction. *SAS*, LNCS *5673*, 69–85, 2009.

[43] C. Hoare. An axiomatic basis for computer programming. *Communications of the Association for Computing Machinery*, 12(10):576–580, 1969.

[44] Z. Manna and A. Pnueli. Axiomatic approach to total correctness of programs. *Acta Inf.*, 3:243–263, 1974.

[45] K. McMillan and L. Zuck. Invisible invariants and abstract interpretation. *SAS*, LNCS *6887*, 249–262, 2011.

[46] A. Miné. The octagon abstract domain. *HOSC*, 19:31–100, 2006.

[47] D. Monniaux. Automatic modular abstractions for template numerical constraints. *Logical Methods in Comp. Sci.*, 6(3), 2010.

[48] J. Morris and B. Wegbreit. Subgoal induction. *CACM*, 20(4):209–222, 1977.

[49] P. Naur. Proofs of algorithms by general snapshots. *BIT*, 6:310–316, 1966.

[50] D. Pataria. A constructive proof of Tarski's fixed-point theorem for DCPO's. *Reported by M.H. Escardó in "Joins in the frame of nuclei"*, Applied Categorical Structures *11 (2) 117–124*, 2003.

[51] G. Plotkin. A structural approach to operational semantics. Technical Report DAIMI FN-19, Aarhus University, 1981.

[52] A. Pnueli, A. Podelski, and A. Rybalchenko. Separating fairness and well-foundedness for the analysis of fair discrete systems. *TACAS*, LNCS *3440*, 124–139, 2005.

[53] A. Podelski and A. Rybalchenko. Transition invariants. *LICS*, 32–41, 2004.

[54] A. Podelski and A. Rybalchenko. A complete method for the synthesis of linear ranking functions. *VMCAI*, LNCS *2937*, 239–251, 2004.

[55] A. Podelski and A. Rybalchenko. Transition predicate abstraction and fair termination. *POPL*, 132–144, 2005.

[56] X. Rival and L. Mauborgne. The trace partitioning abstract domain. *TOPLAS*, 29(5), 2007.

[57] D. Scott and C. Strachey. Towards a mathematical semantics for computer languages. Tech. rep. PRG-6, Oxford Univ. Comp. Lab., 1971.

[58] A. Tarski. A lattice theoretical fixpoint theorem and its applications. *P. J. of Math.*, 5:285–310, 1955.

[59] R. Turing. Checking a large routine. *Con. on High Speed Automatic Calculating Machines, Math. Lab., Cambridge, UK*, 67–69, 1949.

Playing in the Grey Area of Proofs

Kryštof Hoder
University of Manchester
krystof.hoder@gmail.com

Laura Kovács
TU Vienna
lkovacs@complang.tuwien.ac.at

Andrei Voronkov
University of Manchester
andrei@voronkov.com

Abstract

Interpolation is an important technique in verification and static analysis of programs. In particular, interpolants extracted from proofs of various properties are used in invariant generation and bounded model checking. A number of recent papers studies interpolation in various theories and also extraction of smaller interpolants from proofs. In particular, there are several algorithms for extracting of interpolants from so-called local proofs. The main contribution of this paper is a technique of minimising interpolants based on transformations of what we call the "grey area" of local proofs. Another contribution is a technique of transforming, under certain common conditions, arbitrary proofs into local ones.

Unlike many other interpolation techniques, our technique is very general and applies to *arbitrary* theories. Our approach is implemented in the theorem prover Vampire and evaluated on a large number of benchmarks coming from first-order theorem proving and bounded model checking using logic with equality, uninterpreted functions and linear integer arithmetic. Our experiments demonstrate the power of the new techniques: for example, it is not unusual that our proof transformation gives more than a tenfold reduction in the size of interpolants.

Categories and Subject Descriptors D.2.4 [*Software Engineering*]: Formal Methods; F.3.1 [*Logic and Meanings of Programs*]: Assertions; I.2.3 [*Artificial Intelligence*]: Deduction, inference engines, resolution

General Terms Theory, Verification, Experimentation

Keywords Program verification, theorem proving, interpolation

1. Introduction

Interpolants extracted from proofs have several applications in verification and static analysis, see e.g. [3, 6, 12, 15, 21]. Although interpolants are guaranteed to exist in some theories (for example, those having quantifier elimination), interpolants extracted from proofs turn out to be smaller and more useful than those obtained by general interpolation algorithms, see, e.g. [16]. For this reason, recent papers [5, 9, 11, 14, 18, 19, 21] consider the problem of obtaining small interpolants for various theories.

In this paper we consider two related problems: extracting interpolants from proofs and minimising such interpolants. Papers [18, 20] define algorithms for extracting interpolants from so-called *local proofs*. Roughly, in local proofs some symbols are colored in the red or blue colors and others are uncolored. Uncolored symbols are said to be grey. A local proof cannot contain an inference that uses both red and blue symbols. In other words, colors cannot be mixed within the same inference.

However, building local proofs may require substantial changes to a first-order theorem prover or an SMT solver. In addition, local proofs do not necessarily exist. One of the contributions of this paper is a technique for changing proofs into local ones under some conditions. The ideas of this technique can be traced to an observation made in [17, 18] that existential quantification of constants results in an interpolant. We prove a simple result showing that this technique is correct and can be applied to translate non-local proofs with colored constants into local proofs.

When we already have a local proof, one can extract an interpolant from it. This interpolant is a boolean combination of (some) formulas occurring in the proof, if one uses the algorithm of [18]. More exactly, the interpolant is obtained as a boolean combination of conclusions of some *symbol-eliminating inferences*: an inference having at least one colored premise and a grey conclusion. The interpolation extraction theorem of [18] is not restricted to any particular theory. Essentially the only condition on proofs is *inference soundness*, that is, the conclusion of any inference is a logical consequence of its premises. This generality gives one a lot of freedom since one does not have to follow rules of any specific calculus (such as resolution and superposition) in building local proofs.

In this paper, we exploit the generality of [18] by considering proof transformations that preserve both inference soundness and locality. It is interesting that such transformations can drastically change the shape and the size of the extracted interpolant. The transformations we consider are always applied to grey formulas in the proof, which inspired the title of this paper.

While the class transformations we consider (cutting off a grey formula) obviously preserve inference soundness, they can violate locality. To preserve locality, we create a SAT problem whose solutions encode all local proofs obtained by a sequence of cut-offs. Further, we create a linear expression over the variables of the SAT problem that expresses some numeric characteristics of the interpolant, for example, the number of different atoms in it. Thus, we are interested in the solutions of the problem that minimise the linear expression: any such solution can be used to build a proof giving a smaller (in some sense) interpolant. These solutions can be found using an SMT solver or a pseudo-boolean optimisation tool.

The main contributions of our paper are summarised below.

- ▷ We present a new method of producing smaller interpolants from local proofs. The methods is based on transformation of the "grey area" of proofs. It uses the idea that proof locality can be expressed by a set of propositional formulas whose models represent all local proofs obtained by such transformations (Sections 5.1-5.2).

POPL'12, January 25–27, 2012, Philadelphia, PA, USA.

- ▷ We present a method for changing proofs into local ones. This method is applicable to all proofs in which all colored symbols are uninterpreted constants (Section 4).
- ▷ We define a transformation of interpolant minimisation problems into the problem of solving pseudo-boolean constraints (Section 5.4). Minimality is defined with respect to various measures of the size of interpolants.
- ▷ We implemented our minimisation algorithm in the Vampire theorem prover [24]. It uses the Yices SMT solver [10] for solving pseudo-boolean constraints (Section 6.1). As Vampire cannot yet efficiently handle the combination of various theories, we generate proofs over SMT problems using Z3 [8].
- ▷ We show experimentally that our method improves [18] by generating considerably better/smaller interpolants in the size, the total weight and the number of quantifiers (Section 6).

The rest of this paper is structured as follows. Section 2 overviews relevant definitions and properties of first-order logic and interpolation. In Section 3 the notion of colored and local proofs are introduced. Our result on translating non-local proofs into local ones is formulated in Section 4. Section 5 details our approach to minimising interpolants. We present experimental results in Section 6 and overview related work in Section 7. Section 8 concludes the paper.

2. Interpolation

We consider the standard first-order predicate logic with equality. We allow all standard boolean connectives and quantifiers in the language. We assume that the language contains the logical constants $\top$ for always true and $\perp$ for always false formulas.

Throughout this paper, we denote formulas by A, B, C, D, G, R, terms by r, s, t, variables by x, y, z, constants by a, b, c and function symbols by f, g, possibly with indices. Let A be a formula with free variables $\bar{x}$, then $\forall A$ (respectively, $\exists A$) denotes the formula $(\forall \bar{x})A$ (respectively, $(\exists \bar{x})A$). A formula is called *closed*, or a *sentence*, if it has no free variables. We call a *symbol* a predicate symbol, a function symbol or a constant. Thus, variables are not symbols. We consider equality $=$ part of the language, that is, equality is not a symbol. A formula or a term is called *ground* if it has no occurrences of variables. A formula is called *universal* (respectively, *existential)* if it has the form $(\forall \bar{x})A$ (respectively, $(\exists \bar{x})A$), where A is quantifier-free. We write $C_1, \ldots, C_n \vdash C$ to denote that the formula $C_1 \wedge \ldots \wedge C_n \rightarrow C$ is a tautology. Note that $C_1, \ldots, C_n, C$ may contain free variables.

A *signature* is any finite set of symbols. The *signature of a formula* A is the set of all symbols occurring in this formula. For example, the signature of $b = g(z)$ is $\{g, b\}$. The *language of a formula* A, denoted by $\mathcal{L}_A$, is the set of all formulas built from the symbols occurring in A, that is formulas whose signatures are subsets of the signature of A.

We recall the following theorem from [7].

THEOREM 2.1 (Craig's Interpolation Theorem). *Let A, B be closed formulas and let $A \vdash B$. Then there exists a closed formula $I \in \mathcal{L}_A \cap \mathcal{L}_B$ such that $A \vdash I$ and $I \vdash B$.*

In other words, every symbol occurring in I also occurs in both A and B. Every formula I satisfying this theorem will be called an *interpolant* of A and B.

We call a *theory* any set of closed formulas. If T is a theory, we write $C_1, \ldots, C_n \vdash_T C$ to denote that the formula $C_1 \wedge \ldots \wedge C_1 \rightarrow C$ holds in all models of T. In fact, our notion of theory corresponds to the notion of *axiomatisable theory* in logic. When we work with a theory T, we call symbols occurring in T *interpreted* while all other symbols *uninterpreted*.

As proved in [18], Craig's interpolation also holds for theories in the following sense:

THEOREM 2.2. *Let A, B be formulas and let $A \vdash_T B$. Then there exists a formula I such that*

1. *$A \vdash_T I$ and $I \vdash B$;*
2. *every uninterpreted symbol of I occurs both in A and B;*
3. *every interpreted symbol of I occurs in B.*

Likewise, there exists a formula I such that

1. *$A \vdash I$ and $I \vdash_T B$;*
2. *every uninterpreted symbol of I occurs both in A and B;*
3. *every interpreted symbol of I occurs in A.*

The proof of this theorem in [18] uses compactness, which is guaranteed when T is axiomatisable.

In the sequel we will sometimes be interested in the interpolation property with respect to a given theory T. We will use $\vdash_T$ instead of $\vdash$ and relativise all definitions to T. To be precise, we call an *interpolant* of A and B any formula I such that $A \vdash_T I$, $I \vdash_T B$, and every uninterpreted symbol of I occurs both in A and B.

If E is a set of expressions (for example, formulas) and constants $c_1, \ldots, c_n$ do not occur in E, then we say that $c_1, \ldots, c_n$ are *fresh* for E. We will less formally simply say *fresh constants* when E is the set of all expressions considered in the current context.

We call a *reverse interpolant* of A and B any formula I such that $A \vdash_T I$, $I, B \vdash_T \perp$, and every uninterpreted symbol of I occurs both in A and B.

Reverse interpolants for A and B are exactly interpolants of A and $\neg B$. Moreover, when B is closed, reverse interpolants are exactly interpolants in the sense of [20, 21]. Reverse interpolants are convenient when we use a refutation-based inference system, such as resolution, for finding a proof of $A \rightarrow B$ that can give us an interpolant: in this case one can search for a refutation from the set of formulas $A, \neg B$ instead.

3. Local Proofs

In this section we recall some terminology related to inference systems. Inference systems are commonly used in the theory of resolution and superposition [1, 22]; however we do not restrict ourselves to the superposition calculus. The material of this section is based on [18], adapting the terminology of [18] to our setting.

We also introduce the notion of *local proofs* and recall results on extracting interpolants from local proofs as proved in [18].

DEFINITION 3.1. An *inference rule* is an n-ary relation on formulas, where $n \geq 0$. The elements of such a relation are called *inferences* and usually written as

$$\frac{A_1 \quad \ldots \quad A_n}{A} .$$

The formulas $A_1, \ldots, A_n$ are called the *premises* of this inference, whereas the formula A is the *conclusion* of the inference.

An *inference system* $\mathfrak{I}$ is a set of inference rules. An *axiom* of an inference system is any conclusion of an inference with 0 premises. Any inferences with 0 premises and a conclusion A will be written without the bar line, simply as A.

A *derivation* in an inference system $\mathfrak{I}$ is a tree built from inferences in $\mathfrak{I}$. If the root of this derivation is A, then we say it is a *derivation of* A. A derivation of A is called a *proof* of A if it is finite and all leaves in the derivation are axioms. A formula A is called *provable* in $\mathfrak{I}$ if it has a proof. We say that a derivation of A is *from assumptions* $A_1, \ldots, A_m$ if the derivation is finite and every leaf in it is either an axiom or one of the formulas $A_1, \ldots, A_m$. A formula A is said to be *derivable from* assumptions $A_1, \ldots, A_m$ if there exists a derivation of A from $A_1, \ldots, A_m$. A *refutation* is a derivation of $\perp$. □

Note that a proof is a derivation from the empty set of assumptions. Any derivation from a set of assumptions S can be considered as a derivation from any larger set of assumptions $S' \supseteq S$.

Let us now fix two sentences R (red) and B (blue). In the sequel we assume R and B to be fixed and give all definitions relative to R and B. Denote by $\mathcal{L}$ the intersection of the languages of R and B, that is the set $\mathcal{L}_R \cap \mathcal{L}_B$. We call signature symbols occurring both in R and B *grey*, symbols occurring only in R *red* and symbols occurring only in B *blue*. A symbol that is either red or blue is also called *colored*. For a formula C, we say that C is *grey* if $C \in \mathcal{L}$, otherwise we say that C is *colored*. In other words, grey formulas contain only grey symbols and every colored formula contains at least one red or blue symbol. A colored formula that only contains red and grey symbols, is called a *red* formula. Similarly, a *blue* formula is a colored formula containing only blue and grey symbols. In the rest of this paper, red formulas will be denoted by R, blue formulas by B, and grey formulas by G, possibly with indices.

DEFINITION 3.2 (RB-derivation). Let us call an *RB-derivation* any derivation Π satisfying the following conditions.

(RB1) For every leaf C of Π one of the following conditions holds:
1. $R \vdash_T \forall C$ and $C \in \mathcal{L}_R$ or
2. $B \vdash_T \forall C$ and $C \in \mathcal{L}_B$.

(RB2) For every inference

$$\frac{C_1 \quad \ldots \quad C_n}{C}$$

of Π we have $\forall C_1, \ldots, \forall C_n \vdash_T \forall C$.

We will refer to property (RB2) as *soundness*. □

We will be interested in finding reverse interpolants of R and B. The case $\mathcal{L}_R \subseteq \mathcal{L}_B$ is obvious, since in this case R is a reverse interpolant of R and B. Likewise, if $\mathcal{L}_B \subseteq \mathcal{L}_R$, then $\neg B$ is a reverse interpolant of R and B. For this reason, in the sequel we assume that $\mathcal{L}_R \not\subseteq \mathcal{L}_B$ and $\mathcal{L}_B \not\subseteq \mathcal{L}_R$, that is, *both R and B contain at least one colored symbol.*

We are mostly interested in a special kind of derivation introduced in [14] and called *local* (or sometimes called *split-proofs*). The definition of a local derivation is relative to formulas R and B.

DEFINITION 3.3 (Local RB-derivation). An inference

$$\frac{C_1 \quad \ldots \quad C_n}{C}$$

in an RB-derivation is called *local* if the following two conditions hold.

(L1) Either $\{C_1, \ldots, C_n, C\} \subseteq \mathcal{L}_R$ or $\{C_1, \ldots, C_n, C\} \subseteq \mathcal{L}_B$.

(L2) If all of the formulas $C_1, \ldots, C_n$ are grey, then C is grey, too.

A derivation is called *local* if so is every inference of this derivation. □

In other words, (L1) says that inferences cannot mix colors: no inference contains both red and blue symbols. Condition (L2) is natural (inferences should not introduce irrelevant symbols) but it is absent in other works. Condition (L2) is however essential for us since without it the proof of Theorem 3.4 does not go through [18]. Note that standard derivations produced by theorem provers often contain inferences violating (L2), especially, in instantiation rules:

$$\frac{(\forall x)A(x)}{A(r)} \ ,$$

where r is a red term. However, such inferences can be removed from derivations without violating (L1).

We will now formulate one of the main theorems of [18] on the extraction of interpolants from local proofs and explain the structure of interpolants obtained by the algorithm of [18].

Consider any RB-derivation Π. Note that by the soundness condition (RB2) we can replace every formula C occurring in this derivation by its universal closure $\forall C$ and obtain an RB-derivation Π' where inferences are only performed on closed formulas. We will call such derivations Π' *closed* and assume, for simplicity, that we are dealing only with closed derivations.

We call a *symbol-eliminating inference* any inference that is

1. either a grey leaf G of Π such that $R \vdash_T G$.
2. or has the form

$$\frac{A_1 \quad \cdots \quad A_n}{G} \ ,$$

such that G is grey and and at least one of the formulas $A_1, \ldots, A_n$ is colored.

Any such inference "eliminates" at least one colored symbol. One could also call such inferences *color-eliminating*. The following theorem is proved in [18]:

THEOREM 3.4. *Let Π be a closed local RB-refutation. Then one can extract from Π a reverse interpolant I of R and B. This reverse interpolant is a boolean combination of conclusions of symbol-eliminating inferences of* Π. □

The proof of Theorem 3.4 in [18] gives an algorithm for extracting an interpolant from a refutation.

By a close inspection of the algorithm of [18], we noted that not all conclusions of symbol-eliminating inferences occur in the extracted interpolant. To characterise the set of all formulas occurring in the interpolant, in this paper we introduce a new notion, called the *digest* of a refutation, as given below.

DEFINITION 3.5 (Digest). Consider any conclusion G of a symbol-eliminating inference.

If the inference eliminates a red symbol, then it has the form:

$$\frac{\cdots \quad R_0 \quad \cdots}{G}$$

Consider the path from G to the bottom formula of the refutation:

$$\begin{array}{c}\dfrac{\cdots \quad R_0 \quad \cdots}{G} \\ \vdots \\ \perp\end{array}$$

We say that G belongs to the *digest* of the refutation if either all formulas on the path are grey *or* the first (closest to G) colored formula on the path is blue.

Likewise, for a blue symbol eliminating inference:

$$\begin{array}{c}\dfrac{\cdots \quad B_0 \quad \cdots}{G} \\ \vdots \\ \perp\end{array}$$

G belongs to the *digest* of the refutation if at least one formula on the path is colored *and* the first (closest to G) colored formula on the path is red. □

Note the slight asymmetry in Definition 3.5 between red and blue symbol eliminating inferences, which is due to the interpolant generation algorithm of [18]. Using the notion of digest, we can now refine Theorem 3.4 as follows:

THEOREM 3.6. *Let Π be a closed local RB-refutation. Then one can extract from Π a reverse interpolant I of R and B. This reverse interpolant is a boolean combination of the formulas in the digest of Π.* □

In what follows we will refer to the interpolant obtained from a refutation as described in Theorem 3.6 as the *interpolant extracted from* Π.

4. Proof Localisation

Extracting interpolants from proof requires a special interpolating prover, or a prover producing local proofs. While, as reported in [13], the theorem prover Vampire can search for local proofs only and hence the algorithm of [18] can be used in first-order resolution proofs, most provers and SMT solvers do not necessarily generate local proofs.

One of the main motivations of this paper was to check how our minimisation technique works on real-life examples taken from static analysis of software. Although such benchmarks exist, they can only be solved using an SMT solver, which in general produces non-local proofs.

In is interesting that in real-life examples, especially those taken from bounded model checking, all the colored symbols are normally uninterpreted constants representing state variables from intermediate states. In this section we show that for such examples one can transform arbitrary proofs into local ones, at the cost of quantifying some formulas in the proof. This idea has already appeared in [17, 18], see Lemma 4.1 below.

The downside of this approach is that a ground refutation can become a non-ground one, thus, the extracted interpolant may contain quantifiers. Once we have a local proof, the number of such quantifiers can be reduced using the technique of Section 5 (line 18 of Algorithm 1).

LEMMA 4.1. *[17, 18] Consider two formulas $A_1(a)$ and A_2 such that $A_1(a) \vdash_T A_2$ and a is an uninterpreted constant not occurring in A_2. Then, $A_1(a) \vdash (\exists x)A_1(x)$ and $(\exists x)A_1(x) \vdash A_2$.*

This lemma can be used to localise non-local derivations by quantifying away colored constants that result in mixing colors.

THEOREM 4.2. *Given two formulas R and B such that $R \rightarrow B$ and all the colored symbols of R and B are uninterpreted constant symbols. Then any proof Π of $R \rightarrow B$ can be translated into a local proof Π_l.*

PROOF. Let us take a non-local refutation Π of $R \rightarrow B$. This means, that Π contains at least one inference that violates conditions (L1)-(L2) of Definition 3.3. The proof is by induction on Π. We will eliminate all color conflicts one by one, starting from the bottom of the proof. Thus, for every conflicting inference, we can assume that the derivation below it is already local. In particular, the conclusion of the violating inference cannot mix colors. Consider the case when the conclusion is blue (other cases are similar). Then the violating inference has the form

$$\frac{R_1 \quad \cdots \quad R_n \quad A_1 \quad \cdots \quad A_m}{A},$$

where $A, A_1, \ldots, A_m$ are either grey or blue and $R_1, \ldots, R_n$ are red. Let $r_1, \ldots, r_k$ be all the red constants occurring in this inference and formulas R'_i are obtained from R_i by replacing $r_1, \ldots, r_k$ by fresh variables $x_1, \ldots, x_k$. Note that all of the R'_i are either grey or blue. The above non-local inference can then be replaced by:

$$\frac{(\exists x_1 \ldots x_k)(R'_1 \wedge \ldots \wedge R'_n) \quad A_1 \quad \cdots \quad A_m}{A},$$

This inference does not contain the red color, and we are done. Note that the premises of the formula $(\exists x_1 \ldots x_k)(R'_1 \wedge \ldots \wedge R'_n)$ are given by the union of the premises of $R_1, \ldots, R_n$. The correctness of the transformation is guaranteed by Lemma 4.1.

The above transformation can also be applied on inferences where a premise contains both a red and a blue symbol. The non-local inference is replaced by a local inference at the cost of using existential quantifiers over the premise with colored symbols. □

This theorem gives us an algorithm for changing any non-local refutation to a local one, provided that the condition on colored symbols is satisfied.

Figure 1 illustrates how the non-local proof given in Figure 1(a) is translated into the local proof listed in Figure 1(b).

5. Playing in the Grey Area

This section presents the main idea of this paper. It is based on the following observation. One can change, sometimes considerably, the grey areas (that is, areas consisting of grey formulas) of the proof without violating locality. In addition, such proof transformations can change the extracted interpolant.

We will only consider one kind of proof transformations, called here *grey slicing*. Other proof transformations can be proposed as well, but are beyond the scope of this paper.

DEFINITION 5.1 (Grey slicing). Consider any derivation Π containing a subderivation Δ of the form

$$\frac{A_1 \quad \cdots \quad A_n \quad \dfrac{A_{n+1} \quad \cdots \quad A_m}{A}}{A_0}, \tag{1}$$

where $n \geq 0$.

We say that a derivation Π' is obtained from Π by *slicing off A in Δ* (or simply, *slicing off A*) if Π' is obtained from Π by replacing the subderivation Δ by

$$\frac{A_1 \quad \cdots \quad A_n \quad A_{n+1} \quad \cdots \quad A_m}{A_0} \tag{2}$$

When A is a grey formula, we will refer to this transformation as *grey slicing*. □

Apparently, grey slicing preserves properties (RB1)-(RB2) of Definition 3.2, so it transforms an RB-derivation into an RB-derivation. It is also easy to see that grey slicing can violate the locality conditions (L1) of Definition 3.3. For example, slicing off G_1 in

$$\frac{B_0 \quad \dfrac{R_0}{G_1}}{G_0}$$

yields a non-local derivation

$$\frac{B_0 \quad R_0}{G_0}.$$

Consider now an example showing that grey slicing transformations can change the digest, and hence the extracted interpolant.

$$\dfrac{\dfrac{(\forall x_1)(p(x_1) \lor q(x_1, r_1)) \quad \neg p(b_1)}{q(b_1, r_1)} \quad \dfrac{(\forall x_2)(s(x_2) \lor \neg q(x_2, r_1)) \quad \neg s(b_1)}{\neg q(b_1, r_1)}}{\bot}$$

(a)

$$\dfrac{\dfrac{\dfrac{\dfrac{(\forall x_1)(p(x_1) \lor q(x_1, r_1)) \quad (\forall x_2)s(x_2) \lor \neg q(x_2, r_1)}{(\exists y)\big((\forall x_1)(p(x_1) \lor q(x_1, y)) \land (\forall x_2)(s(x_2) \lor \neg q(x_2, y))\big)} \quad \neg p(b_1)}{(\exists y)\big(q(b_1, y) \land (\forall x_2)(s(x_2) \lor \neg q(x_2, y))\big)} \quad \neg s(b_1)}{(\exists y)\big(q(b_1, y) \land \neg q(b_1, y)\big)}}{\bot}$$

(b)

Figure 1. Proof localisation of proof (a) into proof (b).

EXAMPLE 5.2. *Take the following refutation* Π*:*

$$\dfrac{\dfrac{\dfrac{R_3 \quad \dfrac{\dfrac{\dfrac{R_1 \quad G_1}{G_3} \quad \dfrac{B_1 \quad G_2}{G_4}}{G_5}}{G_6}}{R_4}}{G_7}}{\bot}$$

The digest of this refutation is $\{G_4, G_7\}$ *and the extracted reverse interpolant is* $G_4 \to G_7$. *Slicing off* G_4 *in* Π *results in the refutation* Π_1*:*

$$\dfrac{\dfrac{\dfrac{R_3 \quad \dfrac{\dfrac{\dfrac{R_1 \quad G_1}{G_3} \quad B_1 \quad G_2}{G_5}}{G_6}}{R_4}}{G_7}}{\bot}$$

with the digest $\{G_5, G_7\}$ *and the extracted reverse interpolant* $G_5 \to G_7$. *Slicing off now* G_5 *in* Π_1 *results in* Π_2*:*

$$\dfrac{\dfrac{\dfrac{R_3 \quad \dfrac{\dfrac{R_1 \quad G_1}{G_3} \quad B_1 \quad G_2}{G_6}}{R_4}}{G_7}}{\bot}$$

with the digest $\{G_6, G_7\}$ *and the extracted reverse interpolant* $G_6 \to G_7$. *We can slice off* G_7 *in* Π_2 *and obtain the refutation:*

$$\dfrac{\dfrac{R_3 \quad \dfrac{\dfrac{R_1 \quad G_1}{G_3} \quad B_1 \quad G_2}{G_6}}{R_4}}{\bot}$$

with the digest $\{G_6\}$*, and the reverse interpolant* $\neg G_6$.

However, if we slice off G_3 *in the original derivation* Π*, we obtain the refutation:*

$$\dfrac{\dfrac{\dfrac{R_3 \quad \dfrac{\dfrac{R_1 \quad G_1 \quad \dfrac{B_1 \quad G_2}{G_4}}{G_5}}{G_6}}{R_4}}{G_7}}{\bot}$$

in which slicing off G_4 *would violate the locality of the resulting refutation.*

Example 5.2 gives us the following observations:

1. grey slicing can change the extracted interpolant, and sometimes considerably (compare $G_4 \to G_7$ and $\neg G_6$).
2. a grey slicing step can prevent other grey slicing steps, thus preventing previously possible interpolants.

The main question we are going to answer in this section is how to use grey slicing to obtain smaller, and even minimal, in some sense, interpolants. To this end we will use the following ideas. First, we will introduce a set V_Π of propositional variables expressing some properties of refutations obtained by grey slicing from a given proof Π. Next, we will define propositional formulas P_Π of the variables V_Π that express locality. Thus, every refutation obtained from Π by grey slicing is local if and only if it satisfies P_Π. This means we can use a SAT solver to "compute" all local refutations that can be obtained from Π by grey slicing. Finally, we introduce propositional formulas expressing the digest of refutations. This set of propositional formulas allows us to use an SMT solver or a pseudo-boolean optimisation tool to find refutations minimising the digest in various ways.

Let us now formalise this idea. In the rest of this section, when we speak about a formula from a derivation, we will normally mean a concrete node in the derivation containing this formula (note that a tree-like derivation may contain more than one node with the same formula). Later we will also discuss derivations in the dag form. Nonetheless, for simplicity, for the moment we prefer to deal with trees instead of dags.

The first thing to note is that every derivation is also a set of nodes occurring in it and slicing off simply removes one node from this set. This means that a sequence of slicing off transformations removes a subset of nodes. Every removed node G, at the point of removal, is replaced by a set of other nodes occurring in the derivation (namely, the premises of G at that point). Each of the nodes in this set can in turn be removed (and replaced by other nodes) etc., so eventually the place of any removed node will be taken by a set of nodes occurring in the final derivation. We will call this set a *trace* of F and define it formally below.

DEFINITION 5.3 (Trace). Let $S = \Pi_0, \ldots, \Pi_k$ be a sequence of derivations such that each member in the sequence except Π_0 is obtained by slicing off a single grey node from the previous one. For every grey node G in Π_0 we define a set of formulas, call *trace of* G (with respect to S), as follows:

1. If G was never sliced off, that is, it occurs in Π_k, then $trace(G) \stackrel{\text{def}}{=} \{G\}$.
2. Suppose G was sliced off at some point, that is, G is the formula A as in Definition 5.1. Then $trace(G) \stackrel{\text{def}}{=} trace(A_{n+1}) \cup \ldots \cup trace(A_m)$. □

Denote any sequence S of slicing off transformations with the initial derivation Π and final derivation Π' by $\Pi \dashrightarrow \Pi'$. It is not hard to argue that the following lemma holds.

LEMMA 5.4. *The trace of a node does not depend on the sequence of transformations* S *but only depends on the initial and the final* *derivation in S. That is, for every two derivations of the form $\Pi \dashrightarrow \Pi'$ with the same initial derivation Π and final derivation Π', and for every grey node G in Π, the trace of G is the same in both derivations.* □

In the rest of this section we will normally assume a fixed initial derivation Π and various sequences $\Pi \dashrightarrow \Pi'$. In view of this lemma we will simply speak about the *trace of G in Π'*.

Suppose $\Pi \dashrightarrow \Pi'$ is a sequence of transformations. Let us introduce some propositions characterising the behaviour of grey nodes in Π on this sequence.

- ▷ $s(G)$: G was sliced off;
- ▷ $r(G)$: the trace of G contains a red formula;
- ▷ $b(G)$: the trace of G contains a blue formula;
- ▷ $g(G)$: the trace of G contains only grey formulas;
- ▷ $d(G)$: G belongs to the digest of Π'.

We define the set V_Π of propositional variables as consisting of all the variables $s(G), r(G), b(G), g(G), d(G)$ denoting these propositions. Later we will add to V_Π more variables.

Then, for every sequence of transformations $\Pi \dashrightarrow \Pi'$ and every grey node G in Π, each of the above propositions is either true or false on this sequence. Therefore, if we take any propositional formula built from these propositions, it is also either true or false on this sequence.

5.1 Expressing the Digest

Our next aims are to write down a propositional formula that expresses that Π' is local, and also represent the digest of any local refutation. To this end we will first introduce propositional variables and formulas over grey nodes, then write down further formulas of these propositions that are satisfied when Π' is local, and finally show that satisfiability of these propositions implies locality of Π'.

Propositions rc and bc. Take a local derivation Π with $\Pi \dashrightarrow \Pi'$. For each grey node G in Π we first introduce the *propositions $rc(G)$ and $bc(G)$* expressing that G is not sliced off and is a conclusion of a symbol-eliminating inference in Π with at least one red (respectively, blue) premise. The propositional variables $rc(G)$ and $bc(G)$ are added to V_Π.

We will only define $rc(G)$, since the case of bc is symmetric.

Consider the following cases depending on the inference introducing G in Π.

1. G is introduced by an inference with only grey premises:
$$\frac{G_1 \quad \cdots \quad G_m}{G},$$
We then write:
$$rc(G) \leftrightarrow (\neg s(G) \wedge (r(G_1) \vee \ldots \vee r(G_m))). \qquad (3)$$
The conditions on the traces of $G_1, \ldots, G_m$ ensure that G can be written as the conclusion of a symbol eliminating inference with at least one red premise. Namely, if $r(G_i)$ holds, then by slicing off G_i and some of the grey nodes from its derivation, G becomes the conclusion of a symbol eliminating inference with at least one red premise.
2. G is introduced by an inference with at least one red premise:
$$\frac{R_1 \quad \cdots \quad R_n \quad G_1 \quad \cdots \quad G_m}{G}.$$
We then have:
$$rc(G) \leftrightarrow \neg s(G). \qquad (4)$$
3. G is introduced by an inference with at least one blue premise
$$\frac{B_1 \quad \cdots \quad B_n \quad G_1 \quad \cdots \quad G_m}{G}.$$
Due to the locality of derivations, we write:
$$\neg rc(G). \qquad (5)$$

Equations (3)-(5) are added to the set of propositional formulas P_Π over V_Π.

Propositions rf and bf. We introduce the propositions $rf(G)$ and $bf(G)$ for every grey node G, and add the corresponding variables to V_Π. These propositions are closely related to the definition of digest. The proposition $rf(G)$ holds iff on the path from G to the root of Π either (i) all nodes are grey, or (ii) the first colored node is a blue one. Likewise, the proposition $bf(G)$ expresses that on the path from G to the root of Π, there exists a colored node and the first colored node is a red one.

We will only write down properties of rf, the case of bf is similar. We define rf "inductively", starting from the root (the bottom formula) of the derivation Π.

1. If the successor of G in Π is a red formula, then we write
$$\neg rf(G). \qquad (6)$$
2. If the successor of G in Π is a blue formula, then we write
$$rf(G). \qquad (7)$$
3. Finally, if the successor of G in Π is a grey node G_1, then we write
$$rf(G) \leftrightarrow (rf(G_1) \vee bc(G_1)) \wedge \neg rc(G_1). \qquad (8)$$

Equations (6)-(8) are added to P_Π.

Proposition d. By straightforward inspection of the definition of digest, it is not hard to argue that $d(G)$ can be expressed as follows:
$$d(G) \leftrightarrow (rc(G) \wedge rf(G)) \vee (bc(G) \wedge bf(G)). \qquad (9)$$
We add (9) to P_Π.

5.2 Expressing Locality

Take a local derivation Π and a grey node G in it. Depending on the inference introducing G, there are four possible cases:

1. G is a leaf of Π;
2. G is introduced by an inference with grey premises;
3. G is introduced by an inference with at least one red premise;
4. G is introduced by an inference with at least one blue premise. In this case, due to the locality of Π, all premises in the derivation tree of G are either blue or grey.

For each of these cases, we will show how to write down formulas expressing that $\Pi \dashrightarrow \Pi'$ results in a local derivation, that is, Π' is local. Each below listed propositional formulas is added to P_Π.

General properties of grey nodes. Note that, if a node G is not sliced off, then its trace is $\{G\}$, so we have $g(G)$:
$$\neg s(G) \rightarrow g(G). \qquad (10)$$
We also know that a node which is sliced off cannot belong to the digest:
$$s(G) \rightarrow \neg d(G). \qquad (11)$$

Observe that equations (10)-(11) do not make use of the assumptions that Π is local. That is, (10)-(11) hold for *arbitrary* derivations.

Further, note that for local derivations the properties b, r and g are mutually exclusive. Therefore, for every grey node node G we add the following properties expressing mutual exclusion:

$$\begin{array}{rcl} color(G) & \stackrel{\text{def}}{=} & (b(G) \vee r(G) \vee g(G)) \wedge \\ & & (b(G) \rightarrow \neg r(G) \wedge \neg g(G)) \wedge \\ & & (r(G) \rightarrow \neg b(G) \wedge \neg g(G)) \wedge \\ & & (g(G) \rightarrow \neg r(G) \wedge \neg b(G)). \end{array} \tag{12}$$

G is a leaf. In this case, G cannot be sliced off and we have:

$$leaf(G) \stackrel{\text{def}}{=} \neg s(G) \wedge g(G) \tag{13}$$

G is introduced by an inference with grey premises:

$$\frac{G_1 \quad \cdots \quad G_m}{G}\ .$$

The locality of $\Pi \dashrightarrow \Pi'$ implies that if the trace of any $G_1, \ldots, G_m$ contains a red (respectively, blue) formula, then the traces of $G_1, \ldots, G_m$ cannot contain a blue (respectively, red) formula. To further reason about the trace of G, consider the following cases.

(i) If G is never sliced off in $\Pi \dashrightarrow \Pi'$, then the trace of G is clearly grey. Whether G is a conclusion of a symbol eliminating inference only depends on whether the trace of some of the $G_1, \ldots, G_m$ contains either a blue or a red formula.

(ii) If G is sliced off, then the color of the formulas in the trace of G depend on the color of the formulas from the traces of $G_1, \ldots, G_m$.

Based on the above reasoning, we introduce the following formula capturing the properties of the trace of G:

$$\begin{array}{rl} grey(G) \stackrel{\text{def}}{=} & (r(G_1) \vee \ldots \vee r(G_m) \rightarrow \neg b(G_1) \wedge \ldots \wedge \neg b(G_m)) \wedge \\ & (b(G_1) \vee \ldots \vee b(G_m) \rightarrow \neg r(G_1) \wedge \ldots \wedge \neg r(G_m)) \wedge \\ & (s(G) \wedge (r(G_1) \vee \ldots \vee r(G_m)) \rightarrow r(G)) \wedge \\ & (s(G) \wedge (b(G_1) \vee \ldots \vee b(G_m)) \rightarrow b(G)) \wedge \\ & (s(G) \wedge g(G_1) \wedge \ldots \wedge g(G_m) \rightarrow g(G)) \wedge \\ & (\neg s(G) \rightarrow g(G)). \end{array} \tag{14}$$

G is introduced by an inference with at least one red premise:

$$\frac{R_1 \quad \cdots \quad R_n \quad G_1 \quad \cdots \quad G_m}{G}\ .$$

In this case the locality of Π implies that the trace of G can contain only red and grey formulas. Moreover, the color of the formulas from the trace of G only depends on whether G is sliced off, as follows.

(i) If G is sliced off, then the trace of G depends on the traces of $R_1, \ldots, R_n$, $G_1, \ldots, G_m$, and hence the trace of G contains at least one red formula. Also note, that if G is sliced off, then G cannot belong to the digest of Π'.

(ii) If G is not sliced off, then $trace(G) = \{G\}$. Hence, the trace of G only contains grey formulas. Moreover, note that G is the conclusion of symbol eliminating inference. Thus, G also belongs to the digest of Π'.

We therefore introduce the below formula for G, capturing the properties of the trace of G:

$$\begin{array}{rcl} red(G) & \stackrel{\text{def}}{=} & \neg b(G_1) \wedge \ldots \wedge \neg b(G_m) \wedge \\ & & (s(G) \rightarrow r(G)) \wedge \\ & & (\neg s(G) \rightarrow g(G)). \end{array} \tag{15}$$

G is introduced by an inference with at least one blue premise:

$$\frac{B_1 \quad \cdots \quad B_n \quad G_1 \quad \cdots \quad G_m}{G}\ .$$

Similarly to the previous case, we introduce the following formula:

$$\begin{array}{rcl} blue(G) & \stackrel{\text{def}}{=} & \neg r(G_1) \wedge \ldots \wedge \neg r(G_m) \wedge \\ & & (s(G) \rightarrow b(G)) \wedge \\ & & (\neg s(G) \rightarrow g(G)). \end{array} \tag{16}$$

This completes our construction of the propositional variables and formulas explained in the beginning of this section. Namely, the set of variables V_Π consists of all variable $s(G)$, $r(G)$, $b(G)$, $g(G)$, $rc(G)$, $bc(G)$, $rf(G)$, $bf(G)$ and $d(G)$, and the set P_Π of formulas are all formulas (3)–(16).

Our construction clearly implies the following result.

THEOREM 5.5. *Let Π be a local derivation. Then a sequence $\Pi \dashrightarrow \Pi'$ satisfies all formulas (8)-(16) from P_Π if and only if Π' is local. Moreover, the propositions $r(G)$, $b(G)$, $g(G)$, $rc(G)$, $bc(G)$, $rf(G)$, $bf(G)$ and $d(G)$ have their intended meaning, in particular, in every model Π' of these formulas G belongs to the digest of Π' if and only if $d(G)$ holds on Π'.*

5.3 Derivations as Dags

Refutations found by theorem provers are normally dags. Transforming a dag to a tree can result in an exponential growth in size. Therefore, it is desirable to change our technique to deal with dags. The modification is quite simple: we allow a formula in a dag to be sliced off only if *all* the tree derivations corresponding to the resulting dag are local. Note that this may result in a smaller choice of grey slicing transformations as compared to refutations as trees and hence larger interpolants. Nonetheless, expanding dags to trees may turn to be unfeasible. Therefore, our implementation uses dags.

To build propositional formulas expressing locality on dags, one should only modify the propositions $rf(G)$ and $bf(G)$.

Propositions rf and bf for dags. The proposition $rf(G)$ holds iff on *all paths* from G to the root of Π either (i) all nodes are grey, or (ii) the first colored node is a blue one. Likewise, the proposition $bf(G)$ expresses that on *all paths* from G to the root of Π, the first colored node is a red one. The axiomatisation of these propositions is given below, and (6)-(8) are replaced by the below formulas in P_Π.

We will only define rf, since the axiomatisation of bf is similar. It is defined "inductively" starting from the root (the bottom formula) of the derivation Π.

1. Suppose at least one of the successors of G is a red formula. In this case we write:

$$\neg rf(G). \tag{17}$$

2. Otherwise, all the successors of G are either grey or blue:

$$\frac{G}{G_1 \quad \cdots \quad G_m \quad B_1 \quad \cdots \quad B_k}\ .$$

In this case we write

$$\begin{array}{l} rf(G) \leftrightarrow ((rf(G_1) \vee bc(G_1)) \wedge \ldots \wedge (rf(G_m) \vee bc(G_m)) \wedge \\ \quad \neg rc(G_1) \wedge \ldots \wedge \neg rc(G_m)). \end{array} \tag{18}$$

5.4 Minimising Interpolants in Local Proofs

Theorem 5.5 shows how one expresses locality and digest using the propositional formulas P_Π. This allows us to introduce various measures of "quality" of interpolants and use these measures, together with an SMT solver, to find local proofs giving interpolants that are better in these measures.

As usual, we define a clause to be a disjunction, possibly empty, of literals, that is, atomic formulas and their negations. Since most theorem provers and SMT solvers present proofs as dags of clauses, apart from some preprocessing deriving a set of clauses from R, B and the theory, we assume that the digest of a proof is a set of clauses. If such a clause contains free variables, it is assumed to be implicitly universally quantified. We know that the interpolant extracted from a proof is a propositional combination of clauses occurring in this proof. If a particular clause is a propositional combination of smaller formulas, then the interpolant can be considered a propositional combination of these smaller formulas. The smallest formulas of this form are well-studied in the automated deduction community and called *components*. We will take a slightly modified definition of components from [23].

DEFINITION 5.6 (Component). A *component* of a clause C is either

- ▷ a ground atomic formula occurring in C, or
- ▷ a non-ground clause C_1 such that C has the form $C_1 \vee C_2$, both C_1 and C_2 are non-empty, and the only component of C_1 is C_1 itself.

A clause C is said to be a *g-atom* if C is the only component of itself.

For example, the clause $p(x) \vee a \neq 2 \vee q(x)$ has two components: $p(x) \vee q(x)$ and $a = 2$. Note that we have the following equivalence:

$$\forall x(p(x) \vee a \neq 2 \vee q(x)) \equiv \forall x(p(x) \vee q(x)) \vee \neg(a = 2).$$

In general, the universal closure of every clause is a boolean combination of the universal closures of its components. Therefore, the extracted interpolant is a boolean combinations of g-atoms, which are components of the formulas in the digest.

The problem of generating minimal interpolants can be thus reduced to the problem of minimising, in some sense, the set of g-atoms used in the interpolant. As minimality of interpolants is not well-understood, we introduce various measures for minimising the size of interpolants. Namely, we are interested in minimising interpolants with respect to (i) the number of g-atoms and (ii) the total weight of g-atoms, counted as a number of symbols. One can also argue that ground interpolants are more useful than those containing quantifiers, so in addition, when the refutation is non-ground, we can also minimise (iii) the number of quantifiers in the g-atoms.

For doing so, we use the fact that the digest of a derivation can be expressed using propositional variables $d(G)$ over grey nodes G and transform the minimisation problem to solving a pseudo-boolean optimisation problem over V_Π as explained below.

We consider a local refutation Π. For every component g of a grey clause G of Π, we introduce a distinct propositional variable $v(g)$. Intuitively, this variable will denote that g occurs in the digest of the transformed proof Π'. For every grey node G in Π, let $g_1, \ldots, g_k$ be all g-atoms of G. We then introduce the following axiom:

$$d(G) \rightarrow v(g_1) \wedge \ldots \wedge v(g_k). \tag{19}$$

In what follows, let $g_1, \ldots, g_m$ be all g-atoms occurring in all grey nodes of Π. Let $w_1, \ldots, w_m$ be the total weights of these atoms, respectively. We denote by $q_1, \ldots, q_m$ the number of quantifiers used, respectively, in $g_1, \ldots, g_m$.

The problem of minimising interpolants is then reduced to the problem of minimising (one of) the following sums:

$$\text{atom}_{\text{cost}} \stackrel{\text{def}}{=} v(g_1) + \ldots + v(g_m). \tag{20}$$

$$\text{weight}_{\text{cost}} \stackrel{\text{def}}{=} w_1 v(g_1) + \ldots + w_m v(g_m). \tag{21}$$

$$\text{quantifier}_{\text{cost}} \stackrel{\text{def}}{=} q_1 v(g_1) + \ldots + q_m v(g_m). \tag{22}$$

Each of these sums is expressed as a pseudo-boolean constraint over the g-atoms $g_1, \ldots, g_m$. A solution to the minimisation problem of the left-hand side of (20)-(22) gives us a subset of $\{g_1, \ldots, g_m\}$, such that the interpolant constructed from the boolean combinations of the formulas in this subset is a smallest interpolant among all interpolants that can be extracted from the various local Π' resulting from grey slicing.

Minimisation of $\text{atom}_{\text{cost}}$ gives the smallest interpolant in the number of distinct g-atoms. Likewise, the minimal values of $\text{weight}_{\text{cost}}$ and $\text{quantifier}_{\text{cost}}$ correspond to the interpolant with the smallest total weight and the smallest number of quantifiers, respectively. Algorithm 1 puts together the algorithm for minimising interpolants.

ALGORITHM 1. ***Minimising Interpolants***
Input: *Closed formulas R and B such that $R \rightarrow \neg B$, and a refutation Π from R, B.*
Output: *Minimised interpolants I_{atom}, I_{weight}, I_{quant} of R and $\neg B$*
Assumption: *All colored symbols of R and B are uninterpreted constants*

begin

I. Proof Localisation.

Compute local proof Π_l from Π, using Theorem 4.2.

II. Expressing locality.

$\mathcal{G} := \{\}$, $P_\Pi := \{\}$
for *each grey node G in Π_l* **do**
  Express $d(G)$. Let $P_\Pi := P_\Pi \cup \{(3), (4), (5), (17), (18), (9)\}$.
  Express general properties. Let $P_\Pi := P_\Pi \cup \{(10), (11), (12)\}$.
  If G is a leaf, $P_\Pi := P_\Pi \cup \{(13)\}$.
  If G is introduced by an inference with only grey premises,
    $P_\Pi := P_\Pi \cup \{(14)\}$.
  If G is introduced by an inference with a red premise,
    $P_\Pi := P_\Pi \cup \{(15)\}$.
  If G is introduced by an inference with a blue premise,
    $P_\Pi := P_\Pi \cup \{(16)\}$.
  Compute $G = g_1 \vee \cdots \vee g_k$, where g_i are g-atoms.
  $\mathcal{G} = \mathcal{G} \cup \{g_1, \ldots, g_k\}$
  endfor
  $P_\Pi := P_\Pi \cup \{(19)\}$
endfor

III. Minimising Interpolants.

min_atom$_{cost}$ $:= \{g_{i_1}, \ldots, g_{i_n}\}$

$$:= min_{\{g_{i_1}, \ldots, g_{i_n}\}} \Big(\sum_{g_i \in \mathcal{G}} v(g_i) \ \wedge \ P_\Pi \Big)$$

min_weight$_{cost}$ $:= \{g_{i_1}, \ldots, g_{i_n}\}$

$$:= min_{\{g_{i_1}, \ldots, g_{i_n}\}} \Big(\sum_{g_i \in \mathcal{G}} w_i v(g_i) \ \wedge \ P_\Pi \Big)$$

where w_i denotes the weight of g_i

18 $\mathit{min\_quant}_{cost} := \{g_{i_1}, \ldots, g_{i_n}\}$

$$:= min_{\{g_{i_1},\ldots,g_{i_n}\}}\left(\sum_{g_i \in \mathcal{G}} q_i v(g_i) \wedge P_\Pi\right)$$

where q_i denotes the number of quantifiers uses in g_i

19 $I_{atom} = \mathit{Interpolant}_{R,B}(\mathit{min\_atom}_{cost})$
20 $I_{weight} = \mathit{Interpolant}_{R,B}(\mathit{min\_weight}_{cost})$
21 $I_{quant} = \mathit{Interpolant}_{R,B}(\mathit{min\_quant}_{cost})$
22 **return** $\{I_{atom}, I_{weight}, I_{quant}\}$.
23 **end**

Algorithm 1 uses the result of Theorem 4.2 and starts with translating the input refutation Π of R, B into a local one Π_l (line 2). Note that this step is only applied when Π is non-local, more precisely, when the non-local steps of Π contain colored constants. Further, the set $\mathcal{G}$ of g-atoms from Π_l and the set P_Π of (pseudo-boolean) constraints expressing locality of Π_l are initialised (line 3). Next, for each grey node G in Π_l the constraints expressing locality conditions over the digest and inferences of Π_l are constructed, (lines 5-10). Note that the propositional formulas $rf(G)$ and $bf(G)$ are expressed based on the dag-representation of proofs. The set of g-atoms of G is extracted and added to $\mathcal{G}$ (lines 11-12). Then, the property whether G is in the digest of Π_l is expressed in terms of g-atoms and added to the constraint set P_Π (line 14). As a result of these steps, at the end of line 15 of Algorithm 1, the constraint set P_Π is expressed as a set of clauses ensuring the locality of Π_l (Theorem 5.5). Next, minimal interpolants wrt to the number of g-atoms (line 16), the total weight of g-atoms (line 17), and the number of quantifiers in the g-atoms (line 18) are derived by solving a pseudo-boolean optimisation problem over g-atoms. To this end, the interpolation procedure $\texttt{Interpolant}_{R,B}(\ldots)$ of [18] is called to generate interpolants as boolean combinations of the derived minimal set of g-atoms (lines 19-21).

THEOREM 5.7. *Algorithm 1 is correct. That is, given two formulas R and B and a refutation Π, Algorithm 1 returns the minimal interpolants of R and $\neg B$ wrt the imposed measures* (20)-(22) *among all interpolants extracted from proofs obtained by grey slicing of* Π.

We next show that finding minimal interpolants by Algorithm 1 is NP-hard.

THEOREM 5.8. *Given two formulas R and B and a refutation Π of $R, B \rightarrow \bot$. Extracting a minimal reversed interpolant from Π by grey slicing is an NP-hard optimisation problem.*

PROOF. We use a reduction from finding a maximal independent set of a graph $G(V, E)$ with a set of vertices $V = \{v_1, \ldots, v_m\}$ and a set of edges $E = \{(u_1, w_1), \ldots, (u_n, w_n)\}$, which is known to be NP-hard.

To fulfil conditions of Theorem 2.2, we first fix a background theory T. For each vertex $v \in V$ we introduce a propositional grey variable, also denoted by v, of weight 1. Further, for each edge $(u, v) \in E$ we add $u \rightarrow v$ to the theory T.

Introduce also a blue propositional variable b and a red propositional variable r. Define B to be the blue formula $v_1 \wedge \cdots \wedge v_m \wedge b$ and R to be the red formula $\neg v_1 \wedge \cdots \wedge \neg v_m \wedge r$.

Further, for each edge $(u, w) \in E$ we introduce the following derivation $\Pi_{u,w}$:

$$\cfrac{\cfrac{B}{u}}{w}$$

Note that this derivation is sound in the underlying theory T. We next construct the proof tree Π to be:

$$\cfrac{\cfrac{\cfrac{B}{u_1}}{w_1} \quad \ldots \quad \cfrac{\cfrac{B}{u_n}}{w_n} \quad R}{\bot}$$

where the weight of $\bot$ is considered to be zero. Observe that Π is a valid refutation of R, B. Also note that building a minimal interpolant from Π reduces to finding a derivation Π' obtained from Π by grey slicing with a minimal number of g-atoms.

Let Π' be any derivation obtained from Π by grey slicing. Denote by D' the digest of Π'. For every edge $(u, w) \in E$, the subderivation $\Pi_{u,w}$ either remains a subderivation of Π', or u gets sliced off. In the first case we have $u \in D'$, in the second case $w \in D'$. Therefore, either $u \notin V - D'$, or $w \notin V - D'$, which implies that $V - D'$ is an independent set.

Using similar arguments, one can prove that every independent set S of vertices is a subset of $V - D'$ for some digest D' of a derivation obtained from Π by grey slicing. As each set $V - D'$ is an independent set as well, for every maximal independent set S there exists a digest D' such that S is equal to $V - D'$. Therefore finding a digest of the minimal size is equivalent to finding a maximal independent set. □

Let us finally note that our method can be extended with other proof transformations and optimisation criteria (e.g., [9, 16]), to improve the quality of interpolants. For example, many approaches use templates to identify predicates desirable to be used in invariants or interpolants. Algorithm 1, thanks to its generality, can easily be modified to give preference to predicates matching predefined templates. We therefore believe that our method is of an independent value, since one can first minimise the interpolant and then try to make it semantically better using other methods. Another important feature of our algorithm is that it optimises the proof globally: that is, the optimal solution is not necessarily a sum of optimal solutions given by local proof transformations. We believe this a very essential property of the algorithm not shared by other known approaches to minimising interpolants.

	Interpolant size decrease					
	some	$2-4$	$4-6$	$6-8$	>8	to 0
Symbols	1369	369	55	24	20	386
g-atoms	912	248	37	16	7	386

Table 1. Minimisation results on 6577 TPTP problems with non-trivial interpolants.

6. Experimental Results

6.1 Implementation

We implemented our interpolant minimisation method in C++ and integrated it in version 1.8 of the Vampire theorem prover [24]. For minimising the set of pseudo-boolean constraints we used version 1.0.29 of the SMT solver Yices [10].

Due to the lack of realistic verification benchmarks, that is examples coming from some industrial project, we evaluated our method on the following two classes of problems. First, we took a collection of examples over first-order logic with equality from the TPTP library [25]. We minimised interpolants in the first-order proofs generated by Vampire. Second, we considered SMT benchmarks from the SMT-Lib library [2] that come from bounded model checking. We analysed proofs generated by the Z3 SMT solver [8]. We used version 2.19 of Z3 without any modification. However, for minimising interpolants from Z3 proofs, we implemented a parser for processing and translating Z3 proofs into local proofs. To this end, we used our algorithm for proof localisation (see proof of Theorem 4.2).

	0	< 5	$5 - 9$	$10 - 19$	$20 - 49$	$50 - 99$	$100 - 199$	≥ 200
Before	3055	530	1099	1578	2035	991	260	84
After	3441	522	1225	1557	1882	766	166	73

Table 2. Number of symbols in TPTP benchmark interpolants, before and after minimisation.

	0	<5	5-9	10-19	20-49	50-99	100-199	≥200
$\text{Symbols}_{\text{pre}}$	112	3	149	150	82	90	321	1216
$\text{Symbols}_{\text{post}}$	112	5	168	158	56	87	323	1214
g-atoms	112	1558	303	114	9	0	0	0
Quantifiers	464	279	291	367	394	157	123	48

Table 3. Minimisation results on 2123 SMT benchmarks.

All experiments reported in this paper were carried out using a 64-bit 2.33 GHz quad core Dell server with 12 GB RAM.

6.2 First-Order Problems

For this part of the experiments, we took a collection of first-order problems from the TPTP library. We started with annotating these problems with coloring information, using the following coloring strategies.

(1) We order symbols by the number of their occurrences in the problem, and starting with the symbols occurring the least number of times, we attempt to assign colors to them. A color can be assigned to a symbol if the symbol does not occur in a formula with a symbol that was already assigned with the opposite color. The colors are being assigned in an alternating manner. If the last assigned color was red, we first attempt assigning blue to the next symbol, and try to assign red only if this the blue color ended in an unsuccessful assignment (i.e. an input formula with two different colored symbols is obtained). We stop when we have attempted to assign a color to all the symbols.

(2) The previous assignment strategy is more or less random. To use interpolants in a more logical way, we used the following idea. Typically, TPTP problems come with annotations classifying formulas from a problem into axioms, conjectures and hypotheses. We have to prove the conjecture from the axioms and hypotheses. It is commonly the case that axioms axiomatise some theory, so we have to prove that the hypotheses imply the conjecture in the theory given by the axioms. This gives us the following way of coloring the problem symbols. We assign blue color to symbols appearing only in the formulas of the conjecture (i.e. formula B), and red color to symbols occurring only in hypothesis (i.e. formula R). The symbols shared by the conjecture and the hypotheses are considered grey, as well as the symbols occurring only in the axioms.

Local proofs for the colored TPTP problems were generated using the interpolation mode of Vampire [13]. Altogether, we evaluated our minimisation method on 9632 colored TPTP examples. Out of the 9632 problem instances, 3055 problems had trivial interpolants, that is the interpolant was either $\top$ or $\bot$. This left us with 6577 problems with non-trivial interpolants. We were interested to see how our minimisation algorithm performs on these problems. To this end, for each of the 6577 problems, our minimisation method took the corresponding local proof generated by Vampire and derived the smallest interpolants by minimising (i) the number of symbols (i.e total weight) and (ii) the number of g-atoms in the interpolant. Table 1 gives a summary on how the size of the interpolant decreases after minimisation, as compared to the interpolant extracted from the original proof. Rows 1 and 2 of Table 1 show respectively the changes in the interpolant size after minimising the number of symbols, respectively the number of g-atoms in the interpolant. For each imposed measure, column 1 of Table 1 lists the number of examples where the size of the interpolants has decreased only by a small amount. The numbers shown in column 2 (resp. in column 3, column 4, and column 5) correspond to the number of those examples whose interpolants became 2-4 (resp. 4-6, 6-8, and more than 8) times smaller after minimisation. Column 6 gives the number of examples whose interpolants became trivial after minimisation, even though the non-minimised interpolants were non-trivial.

In Table 2 we report on the number of symbols in the interpolants before (row 1) and after (row 2) minimisation. Each column of Table 2 gives the number of interpolants whose number of symbols satisfy the numeric constraint given in the first cell of the column. That is, column 1 gives the number of trivial interpolants (the number of symbols is 0), column 2 shows the number of interpolants with less than 5 symbols, column 3 reports shows the number of interpolants that contain between 5 and 9 symbols etc.

By analysing the results of Table 1, we note that for 854 (respectively 694) examples the number of symbols (respectively, the number of g-atoms) of the interpolant decreased by at least a factor of 2. However, we also note that for 4354 (respectively 4971) problems out of the 6577 examples we tried minimisation did not improve the size: these examples are omitted in Table 1. As the qualitative studies of interpolants is a challenging topic, we believe that the experimental results reported in Table 1 show the potential of our method in generating better interpolants.

In Figures 2 and 3 we show a colored proof of a TPTP problem before and after minimization. Formulas appearing in the interpolant are given in bold, while other consequences of symbol eliminating inferences in italic. Red symbols in the proof are underlined, whereas blue symbols are underbraced. Figures 4 and 5 show the proof before and after minimisation in a tree form. As mentioned, formulas denoted by R (resp. by B or G) refer to red (resp. blue or grey formulas). The formulas G_{814} and G_{41} appear in the original interpolant, but when G_{815}, G_{45} and G_{41} are sliced off by the minimisation algorithm, the new interpolant formulas are G_{853} and G_{86}. This is because the formula G_{853} is eliminating red symbols from the premises it received as a result of the slicing. The formula G_{86} now appears in the interpolant because it is an ancestor of a red symbol eliminating formula. Even though we still have two formulas in the interpolant, its size decreased because G_{853} is a trivial formula $\bot$. When compared to Figure 4, note that the number of grey formulas in Figure 5 has decreased due to grey slicing.

6.3 Experiments with SMT Problems

We used a set of SMT-Lib benchmarks coming from bounded model checking. Variables in these problems correspond to state variables representing various unrolling steps of loops. These variables are typically indexed by integer constants, where the integer index expresses the unrolling step to which the state variable belongs to.

Translating and localising Z3 proofs. We generated proofs of SMT problems by using Z3. Z3 proofs are expressed in the sequent calculus, while our proof localisation and minimisation algorithms work with resolution-style proofs. We therefore parsed and translated Z3 proofs into our framework by using a simple Lisp parser. To this end, we replaced conditionalised Z3 formulas of the form $A_1, \ldots, A_n \vdash F$ by implications $(A_1 \vee \ldots \vee A_n) \to F$.

The coloring strategy we used for the SMT benchmarks was as follows. Except the state variables, all other symbols were colored grey. We divided the set of state variables into three parts. State variables corresponding to the middle loop unrolling step were left grey, variables from earlier states were marked red and those from later states were colored blue. In our experiment this coloring strategy turned out to be successful, in 95% of all examples we

853. $\bot$ [815,86]
815. $\neg\, \mathrm{udl}(sK_0,\mathrm{rl}(sK_0))$ [814,45]
814. $\neg\, \mathbf{udl}(x_0,\mathbf{rl}(x_1)) \vee \neg\, \mathbf{udl}(x_0,x_1)$ **[813,17]**
813. $\neg\, \mathrm{udl}(x_0,x_1) \vee lcl(x_0,x_1) \vee \neg\, \mathrm{udl}(x_0,\mathrm{rl}(x_1))$ [15,17]
86. $udl(x_0,rl(x_0))$ *[79,49]*
79. $\mathrm{udl}(x_9,x_7) \vee \neg\, \mathrm{udl}(\underbrace{ptp}(x_7,x_8),x_9)$ [61,42]
61. $\mathrm{udl}(x_7,\underbrace{ptp}(x_6,x_8)) \vee \neg\, \mathrm{udl}(x_7,x_5) \vee \mathrm{udl}(x_5,x_6)$ [57,33]
57. $\neg\, \mathrm{udl}(x_5,\underbrace{ptp}(x_6,x_7)) \vee \mathrm{udl}(x_5,x_6)$ [33,43]
49. $\mathrm{udl}(\underbrace{ptp}(\mathrm{rl}(x_3),x_4),x_3)$ [38,43]
45. $\mathrm{udl}(sK_0,\mathrm{rl}(\mathrm{rl}(sK_0)))$ [30,41]
43. $\neg\, \mathrm{udl}(\underbrace{ptp}(x_1,x_2),x_1)$ [25,24]
42. $\neg\, \mathrm{udl}(x_0,x_0)$ [25,27]
41. $\mathbf{udol}(sK_0,\mathbf{rl}(sK_0))$ **[6,7]**
38. $\mathrm{udl}(x_0,\mathrm{rl}(x_1)) \vee \mathrm{udl}(x_0,x_1)$ [input]
33. $\mathrm{udl}(x_1,x_2) \vee \neg\, \mathrm{udl}(x_0,x_1) \vee \mathrm{udl}(x_0,x_2)$ [input]
30. $\neg\, \mathrm{udol}(x_0,x_1) \vee \mathrm{udl}(x_0,\mathrm{rl}(x_1))$ [input]
27. $\mathrm{eld}(x_0,x_0)$ [input]
25. $\neg\, \mathrm{udl}(x_0,x_1) \vee \neg\, \mathrm{eld}(x_0,x_1)$ [input]
24. $\mathrm{eld}(\underbrace{ptp}(x_1,x_0),x_1)$ [input]
17. $\neg\, lcl(x_0,x_1)$ [input]
15. $\neg\, \mathrm{udl}(x_0,x_1) \vee lcl(x_0,x_1) \vee \neg\, \mathrm{udl}(x_0,\mathrm{rl}(x_1)) \vee lcl(x_0,\mathrm{rl}(x_1))$ [input]
7. $\neg\, edol(sK_0,\mathrm{rl}(sK_0))$ [input]
6. $\mathrm{udol}(x_0,x_1) \vee edol(x_0,x_1)$ [input]

Figure 2. Proof of the GEO269+3 problem from the TPTP library.

853. $\bot$ **[814,86,30,6,7]**
814. $\neg\, udl(x_0,rl(x_1)) \vee \neg\, udl(x_0,x_1)$ *[813,17]*
813. $\neg\, \mathrm{udl}(x_0,x_1) \vee lcl(x_0,x_1) \vee \neg\, \mathrm{udl}(x_0,\mathrm{rl}(x_1))$ [15,17]
86. $\mathbf{udl}(x_0,\mathbf{rl}(x_0))$ **[79,49]**
79. $\mathrm{udl}(x_9,x_7) \vee \neg\, \mathrm{udl}(\underbrace{ptp}(x_7,x_8),x_9)$ [61,42]
61. $\mathrm{udl}(x_7,\underbrace{ptp}(x_6,x_8)) \vee \neg\, \mathrm{udl}(x_7,x_5) \vee \mathrm{udl}(x_5,x_6)$ [57,33]
57. $\neg\, \mathrm{udl}(x_5,\underbrace{ptp}(x_6,x_7)) \vee \mathrm{udl}(x_5,x_6)$ [33,43]
49. $\mathrm{udl}(\underbrace{ptp}(\mathrm{rl}(x_3),x_4),x_3)$ [38,43]
43. $\neg\, \mathrm{udl}(\underbrace{ptp}(x_1,x_2),x_1)$ [25,24]
42. $\neg\, \mathrm{udl}(x_0,x_0)$ [25,27]
38. $\mathrm{udl}(x_0,\mathrm{rl}(x_1)) \vee \mathrm{udl}(x_0,x_1)$ [input]
33. $\mathrm{udl}(x_1,x_2) \vee \neg\, \mathrm{udl}(x_0,x_1) \vee \mathrm{udl}(x_0,x_2)$ [input]
30. $\neg\, \mathrm{udol}(x_0,x_1) \vee \mathrm{udl}(x_0,\mathrm{rl}(x_1))$ [input]
27. $\mathrm{eld}(x_0,x_0)$ [input]
25. $\neg\, \mathrm{udl}(x_0,x_1) \vee \neg\, \mathrm{eld}(x_0,x_1)$ [input]
24. $\mathrm{eld}(\underbrace{ptp}(x_1,x_0),x_1)$ [input]
17. $\neg\, lcl(x_0,x_1)$ [input]
15. $\neg\, \mathrm{udl}(x_0,x_1) \vee lcl(x_0,x_1) \vee \neg\, \mathrm{udl}(x_0,\mathrm{rl}(x_1)) \vee lcl(x_0,\mathrm{rl}(x_1))$ [input]
7. $\neg\, edol(sK_0,\mathrm{rl}(sK_0))$ [input]
6. $\mathrm{udol}(x_0,x_1) \vee edol(x_0,x_1)$ [input]

Figure 3. Transformed proof of Figure 2 by slicing off formulas using weight minimization.

tried input formulas have been translated into formulas colored by at most one color.

However, the usage of colors yielded non-local Z3 proofs in more than 90% of all examples we tried. We translated non-local Z3 proofs into local ones by applying our proof localisation algorithm. To this end, we always used existential quantification to eliminate red symbols from non-local inferences. As the size of generated interpolants depends on the introduced quantified formulas, we believe that a dynamic analysis over the colored symbols to be eliminated, for example eliminate blue symbol instead of a red one, is an interesting topic for further examination.

The result of proof localisation was further used to minimise interpolants.

Minimising local SMT proofs. Altogether, we used 4347 SMT benchmarks. Out of these 4347 examples, we generated interpolants for 2123 problems. We analyse these interpolants below and summarize our results in Table 3.

The remaining 2224 SMT problems we could not fully process. This was due to a 60s time limit which we imposed as the processing time of one problem, including proof translation, coloring and localisation. In 102 cases the run was terminated by reaching the time limit in translating and coloring Z3 proofs, in 1580 cases the timeout was reached in the proof localisation phase, and for 542 benchmarks the time limit was reached during the minimization phase (in constructing and minimising the set of propositional formulas).

Among the 2123 interpolants, 112 interpolants were trivial, and 1659 contained existential quantifiers introduced by proof localisation. The number of symbols in the interpolants was decreased by our minimisation algorithm for 331 interpolants, out of which 14 interpolants had a decrease by more than two times. The number of g-atoms in the interpolant decreased for 83 interpolants, whereas the number of quantified variables was minimised for 7 interpolants. Table 3 shows the distribution of the number of symbol occurring in interpolants before (row 1) and after minimization (row 2). The distribution of the number of g-atoms (row 3) and quantifiers (row 4) in interpolants is shown only before minimization, because the effect of minimisation on these values was not significant. Each column of Table 3 gives the number of interpolants whose number of size/g-atoms/quantifiers are bounded by the numeric value given in the first cell of the column. That is, for examples, the number of symbols in 168 (row 2, column 3) interpolants is between 5-9 after minimisation. The numbers given in column 1 of Table 3 correspond to the number of trivial interpolants.

The experiments show that our minimisation algorithm is not very efficient on this benchmark suite compared to the first-order benchmarks. We believe that the problem is not in the method but in the way Z3 produces proofs (since the produced proofs were not intended for interpolation). It was often the case that the proofs contained very large formulas, sometimes mixing colors in these formulas. The formulas are then quantified by other algorithm and cannot further be removed from the proof, thus spoiling the minimisation statistics. These formulas are normally large conjunctions or if-then-else expressions, which can also be represented as conjunctions and could have been split into smaller ones. This would not only replace large formulas by smaller one, but also improve coloring of proofs and reduce (or eliminate) the necessity to quantify formulas in them. We believe that our technique will work very well if SMT solvers are modified to obtain proofs of a better quality. Moreover, once a proof is found, post processing can also be done and one may try to change non-local parts of the proof again by theorem proving.

7. Related Work

Interpolation has a number of application in formal verification, ranging from approximating the set of reachable sets in predicate abstraction [14, 16] to invariant generation of loops [21]. Formal verification thus crucially depends to which extent "good" interpolants can be automatically generated.

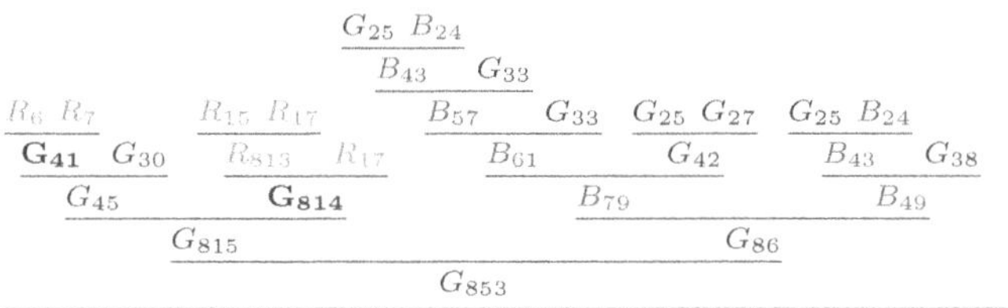

Figure 4. Proof tree for Figure 2.

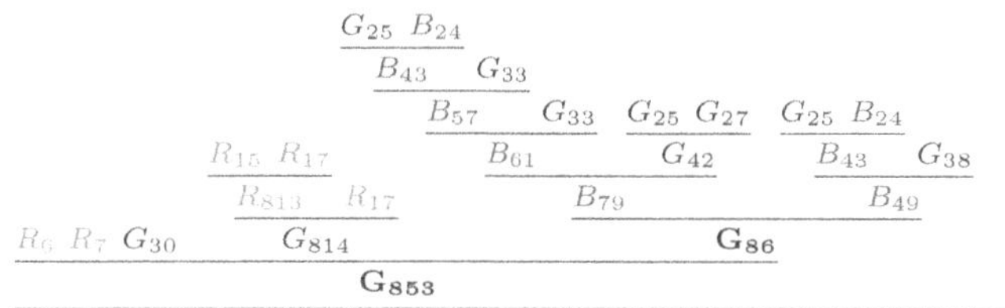

Figure 5. Proof tree for the minimized proof of Figure 3.

General criteria for comparing interpolants can be defined by the logical strength of the interpolant, see e.g. [9, 16]. The approach described in [16] reorders the sequence of resolution steps in a proof to strengthen the derived interpolants. The main heuristic used for proof transformation is to make resolution steps on red/blue variables before those on grey variables. The work of [9] extends [16] and gives a theoretical investigation on the logical strength of propositional interpolants extracted from resolution proofs. The approach uses the notion of labeling functions, which essentially label literals by red, blue or grey labels. The differences among the labeling functions come from how grey literals are labeled (red, blue, or grey). The strength of the various labeling functions is compared, and weaker or stronger interpolants are derived by changing the deployed labeling functions and swapping some nodes in the derivation.

Examples of [9] emphasise that weaker interpolants might lead to better performance, whereas experimental results of [16] show that stronger interpolants can speed up the convergence of a software model checker based on predicate abstraction. Optimising interpolants by only using the logical strength of the interpolant as a selection criteria is thus not always the best way to go in designing efficient interpolation algorithms.

The logical strength of the interpolant is also evaluated in [14, 21], in the context of verification of programs with loops. Although one can derive various program properties by unwinding loop iteration, the resulting set of program properties is a diverging sequence of non-inductive formulas. In [14] interpolants are generated by searching the proof space and avoiding divergence by deeper unwindings of loop iterations. The method is further extended in [21] to infer quantified interpolants. It is shown that by bounding the behavior of the interpolating prover (e.g. delaying inferences over colored or grey symbols), divergence is prevented and an inductive invariant is eventually produced from quantified interpolants. A somehow related approach is presented in [13, 18], where quantified interpolants are extracted from first-order local proof. These techniques generate interpolants by taking the boolean combinations of the grey conclusions of the largest colored subderivations.

The works of [4, 5, 11, 19] evaluate the quality of interpolants by using, in some sense, a different selection criteria. These methods are motivated to generate interpolants that are small in the number of their components, and describe interpolation procedures for the theory of linear integer arithmetic w/o uninterpreted function and predicate symbols. The approach of [4] computes ground interpolants that are exponential in the size of the proofs. The method is improved in [19] by restricting the logical power of the interpolating prover, and is further extended in [5] by handling uninterpreted function and predicate symbols. To this end, [5] shows that quantified interpolants are needed. However, by using guarded quantifiers and divisibility predicates, the quantified interpolants can be translated into equivalent quantifier-free formulas. A similar problem is addressed and solved in [11], where ceiling functions are used to avoid quantified interpolants and generate quantifier-free interpolants of quantifier-free formulas in linear integer arithmetic. Ceiling functions are handled in the interpolating prover by replacing every non-variable ceiling term by a fresh integer variable. Inequality constraints over the newly introduced integer variables are added to capture the semantics of ceiling terms. Whereas [4, 5, 11, 19] show good performance on experiments, due to the lack of realistic benchmarks, it is hard to draw broad conclusions whether the interpolants generated by these works are the "best" in size and expressiveness.

Contrary to all aforementioned works, we define a set of pseudo-boolean constraints over the grey formulas of the proof. Any solution to this set of constraints gives a different interpolant, and any interpolant can be expressed as a solution of the constraint set. The proof transformations carried out in our approach use only slicing off formulas that are logical consequences of other formulas. Furthermore, we evaluate the logical strength of interpolants by minimising the size, the total weight and the number of quantifiers. Unlike [4, 5, 9, 11, 14, 16, 19], our method can generate and minimise interpolants of quantified formulas. When compared to [13], our experiments show that we get better interpolants then the ones of [13] extracted from the largest colored subderivations. More generally spoken, our minimisation algorithm can be applied to any input proof, provided that the input proof can be translated into an equivalent local proof. A special case of such proofs are those whose only colored symbols are uninterpreted constants. Although such a condition might sound severe, it turns out that in practice a large class of examples satisfy this imposed restriction: interpolation benchmarks in the combined theory of uninterpreted functions, predicates and linear integer arithmetic coming from the SMT community satisfy this coloring constraint [4, 5, 11, 19].

8. Conclusion

We described how interpolants extracted from arbitrary proofs can be obtained and minimised in various ways giving smaller interpolants. Our method (1) takes an arbitrary refutation proof, (2) translates it into a local one, provided that all colored symbols are uninterpreted constants, (3) applies minimisation based on analysis of grey areas in the refutation, and (4) computes a minimal interpolant by using pseudo-boolean optimisation.

Our method is very general and can be used with any theory and in conjunction with any theorem prover that outputs refutation proofs of interpolation problems. The evaluation of our method on first-order and SMT bounded model checking benchmarks shows that, in many cases, minimisation considerably decreases the interpolant size.

We intend to integrate our method into concrete verification tools and evaluate our approach on more realistic verification benchmarks. An interesting question we plan to address in the future is how the quality of minimised interpolants effects the efficiency of interpolation-based verification methods. Using a highly optimised pseudo-boolean solver instead an SMT solver is left for further experiments.

We believe that our method opens a new avenue on research in interpolation-based methods. Indeed, other proof transformation methods can be used as well. For example, we can quantify away not only red, but sometimes also blue symbols or slice off colored formulas. In addition, as we pointed out in Section 6 better proofs can considerably improve the quality of interpolants.

Acknowledgments

We acknowledge funding from the University of Manchester and an EPSRC Pathfinder grant (Hoder), the FWF Hertha Firnberg Research grant T425-N23 and the FWF National Research Network RiSE S11410-N23 (Kovács), and an EPSRC grant (Voronkov).

References

[1] L. Bachmair and H. Ganzinger. Resolution theorem proving. In A. Robinson and A. Voronkov, editors, *Handbook of Automated Reasoning*, volume I, chapter 2, pages 19–99. Elsevier Science, 2001.

[2] C. Barrett, A. Stump, and C. Tinelli. The Satisfiability Modulo Theories Library (SMT-LIB). `www.SMT-LIB.org`, 2010.

[3] D. Beyer, T. A. Henzinger, and G. Théoduloz. Lazy Shape Analysis. In *Proc. of CAV*, pages 532–546, 2006.

[4] A. Brillout, D. Kroening, P. Rümmer, and T. Wahl. An Interpolating Sequent Calculus for Quantifier-Free Presburger Arithmetic. In *Proc. of IJCAR*, pages 384–399, 2010.

[5] A. Brillout, D. Kroening, P. Rümmer, and T. Wahl. Beyond Quantifier-Free Interpolation in Extensions of Presburger Arithmetic. In *Proc. of VMCAI*, pages 88–102, 2011.

[6] A. Cimatti, A. Griggio, A. Micheli, I. Narasamdya, and M. Roveri. Kratos - A Software Model Checker for SystemC. In *Proc. of CAV*, pages 310–316, 2011.

[7] W. Craig. Three uses of the Herbrand-Gentzen Theorem in Relating Model Theory and Proof Theory. *Journal of Symbolic Logic*, 22(3):269–285, 1957.

[8] L. de Moura and N. Bjorner. Z3: An Efficient SMT Solver. In *Proc. of TACAS*, pages 337–340, 2008.

[9] V. D'Silva, D. Kroening, M. Purandare, and G. Weissenbacher. Interpolant strength. In *Proc. of VMCAI*, pages 129–145, 2010.

[10] B. Dutertre and L. de Moura. A Fast Linear-Arithmetic Solver for DPLL(T). In *Proc. of CAV*, pages 81–94, 2006.

[11] A. Griggio, T. T. H. Le, and R. Sebastiani. Efficient Interpolant Generation in Satisfiability Modulo Linear Integer Arithmetic. In *Proc. of TACAS*, pages 143–157, 2011.

[12] T. A. Henzinger, R. Jhala, R. Majumdar, and K. L. McMillan. Abstractions from Proofs. In *Proc. of POPL*, pages 232–244, 2004.

[13] K. Hoder, L. Kovacs, and A. Voronkov. Interpolation and Symbol Elimination in Vampire. In *Proc. of IJCAR*, pages 188–195, 2010.

[14] R. Jhala and K. L. McMillan. A practical and complete approach to predicate refinement. In *Proc. of TACAS*, pages 459–473, 2006.

[15] R. Jhala and K. L. McMillan. Array Abstractions from Proofs. In *Proc. of CAV*, pages 193–206, 2007.

[16] R. Jhala and K. L. McMillan. Interpolant-Based Transition Relation Approximation. *Logical Methods in Computer Science*, 3(4), 2007.

[17] D. Kapur, R. Majumdar, and C. G. Zarba. Interpolation for Data Structures. In *SIGSOFT FSE*, pages 105–116, 2006.

[18] L. Kovacs and A. Voronkov. Interpolation and Symbol Elimination. In *Proc. of CADE*, pages 199–213, 2009.

[19] D. Kroening, J. Leroux, and P. Rümmer. Interpolating Quantifier-Free Presburger Arithmetic. In *Proc. of LPAR-17*, pages 489–503, 2010.

[20] K. L. McMillan. An Interpolating Theorem Prover. *Theor. Comput. Sci.*, 345(1):101–121, 2005.

[21] K. L. McMillan. Quantified Invariant Generation Using an Interpolating Saturation Prover. In *Proc. of TACAS*, pages 413–427, 2008.

[22] R. Nieuwenhuis and A. Rubio. Paramodulation-based theorem proving. In *Handbook of Automated Reasoning*, volume I, chapter 7, pages 371–443. 2001.

[23] A. Riazanov and A. Voronkov. Splitting without Backtracking. In *Proc. of IJCAI*, pages 611–617, 2001.

[24] A. Riazanov and A. Voronkov. The Design and Implementation of Vampire. *AI Communications*, 15(2-3):91–110, 2002.

[25] G. Sutcliffe. The TPTP Problem Library and Associated Infrastructure. *J. Autom. Reasoning*, 43(4):337–362, 2009.

Static and User-Extensible Proof Checking

Antonis Stampoulis Zhong Shao

Department of Computer Science
Yale University
New Haven, CT 06520, USA
{antonis.stampoulis,zhong.shao}@yale.edu

Abstract

Despite recent successes, large-scale proof development within proof assistants remains an arcane art that is extremely time-consuming. We argue that this can be attributed to two profound shortcomings in the architecture of modern proof assistants. The first is that proofs need to include a large amount of minute detail; this is due to the rigidity of the proof checking process, which cannot be extended with domain-specific knowledge. In order to avoid these details, we rely on developing and using tactics, specialized procedures that produce proofs. Unfortunately, tactics are both hard to write and hard to use, revealing the second shortcoming of modern proof assistants. This is because there is no static knowledge about their expected use and behavior.

As has recently been demonstrated, languages that allow type-safe manipulation of proofs, like Beluga, Delphin and VeriML, can be used to partly mitigate this second issue, by assigning rich types to tactics. Still, the architectural issues remain. In this paper, we build on this existing work, and demonstrate two novel ideas: an *extensible conversion rule* and support for *static proof scripts*. Together, these ideas enable us to support both user-extensible proof checking, and sophisticated static checking of tactics, leading to a new point in the design space of future proof assistants. Both ideas are based on the interplay between a light-weight staging construct and the rich type information available.

Categories and Subject Descriptors D.3.1 [*Programming Languages*]: Formal Definitions and Theory

General Terms Languages, Verification

1. Introduction

There have been various recent successes in using proof assistants to construct foundational proofs of large software, like a C compiler [Leroy 2009] and an OS microkernel [Klein et al. 2009], as well as complicated mathematical proofs [Gonthier 2008]. Despite this success, the process of large-scale proof development using the foundational approach remains a complicated endeavor that requires significant manual effort and is plagued by various architectural issues.

The big benefit of using a foundational proof assistant is that the proofs involved can be checked for validity using a very small proof checking procedure. The downside is that these proofs are very large, since proof checking is fixed. There is no way to add domain-specific knowledge to the proof checker, which would enable proofs that spell out less details. There is good reason for this, too: if we allowed arbitrary extensions of the proof checker, we could very easily permit it to accept invalid proofs.

Because of this lack of extensibility in the proof checker, users rely on tactics: procedures that produce proofs. Users are free to write their own tactics, that can create domain-specific proofs. In fact, developing domain-specific tactics is considered to be good engineering when doing large developments, leading to significantly decreased overall effort – as shown, e.g. in Chlipala [2011]. Still, using and developing tactics is error-prone. Tactics are essentially untyped functions that manipulate logical terms, and thus tactic programming is untyped. This means that common errors, like passing the wrong argument, or expecting the wrong result, are not caught statically. Exacerbating this, proofs contained within tactics are not checked statically, when the tactic is defined. Therefore, even if the tactic is used correctly, it could contain serious bugs that manifest only under some conditions.

With the recent advent of programming languages that support strongly typed manipulation of logical terms, such as Beluga [Pientka and Dunfield 2008], Delphin [Poswolsky and Schürmann 2008] and VeriML [Stampoulis and Shao 2010], this situation can be somewhat mitigated. It has been shown in Stampoulis and Shao [2010] that we can specify what kinds of arguments a tactic expects and what kind of proof it produces, leading to a type-safe programming style. Still, this does not address the fundamental problem of proof checking being fixed – users still have to rely on using tactics. Furthermore, the proofs contained within the type-safe tactics are in fact proof-producing programs, which need to be evaluated upon invocation of the tactic. Therefore proofs within tactics are not checked statically, and they can still cause the tactics to fail upon invocation.

In this paper, we build on the past work on these languages, aiming to solve both of these issues regarding the architecture of modern proof assistants. We introduce two novel ideas: support for an **extensible conversion rule** and **static proof scripts** inside tactics. The former technique enables proof checking to become user-extensible, while maintaining the guarantee that only logically sound proofs are admitted. The latter technique allows for statically checking the proofs contained within tactics, leading to increased guarantees about their runtime behavior. Both techniques are based on the same mechanism, which consists of a light-weight staging construct. There is also a deep synergy between them, allowing us to use the one to the benefit of the other.

Our main contributions are the following:

- First, we present what we believe is the first technique for having an extensible conversion rule, which combines the following characteristics: it is safe, meaning that it preserves logical soundness; it is user-extensible, using a familiar, generic pro-

POPL'12, January 25–27, 2012, Philadelphia, PA, USA.

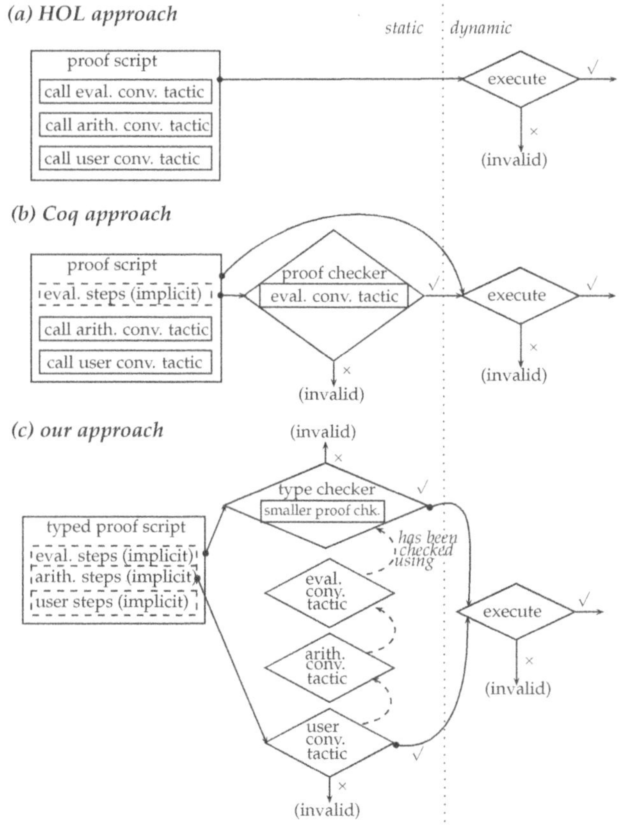

Figure 1. Checking proof scripts in various proof assistants

gramming model; and, it does not require metatheoretic additions to the logic, but can be used to simplify the logic instead.

- Second, building on existing work for typed tactic development, we introduce static checking of the proof scripts contained within tactics. This significantly reduces the development effort required, allowing us to write tactics that benefit from existing tactics and from the rich type information available.
- Third, we show how typed proof scripts can be seen as an alternative form of proof witness, which falls between a proof object and a proof script. Receivers of the certificate are able to decide on the tradeoff between the level of trust they show and the amount of resources needed to check its validity.

In terms of technical contributions, we present a number of technical advances in the metatheory of the aforementioned programming languages. These include a simple staging construct that is crucial to our development and a new technique for variable representation. We also show a condition under which static checking of proof scripts inside tactics is possible. Last, we have extended an existing prototype implementation with a significant number of features, enabling it to support our claims, while also rendering its use as a proof assistant more practical.

2. Informal presentation

Glossary of terms. We will start off by introducing some concepts that will be used throughout the paper. The first fundamental concept we will consider is the notion of a *proof object*: given a derivation of a proposition inside a formal logic, a proof object is a term representation of this derivation. A *proof checker* is a program that can decide whether a given proof object is a valid derivation of a specific proposition or not. Proof objects are extremely verbose and are thus hard to write by hand. For this reason, we use *tactics*: functions that produce proof objects. By combining tactics together, we create proof-producing programs, which we call *proof scripts*. If a proof script is evaluated, and the evaluation completes successfully, the resulting proof object can be checked using the original proof checker. In this way, the trusted base of the system is kept at the absolute minimum. The language environment where proof scripts and tactics are written and evaluated is called a *proof assistant*; evidently, it needs to include a proof checker.

Checking proof objects. In order to keep the size of proof objects manageable, many of the logics used for mechanized proof checking include a *conversion rule*. This rule is used implicitly by the proof checker to decide whether any two propositions are equivalent; if it determines that they are indeed so, the proof of their equivalence can be omitted. We can thus think of it as a special tactic that is embedded within the proof checker, and used implicitly.

The more sophisticated the relation supported by the conversion rule is, the simpler are proof objects to write, since more details can be omitted. On the other hand, the proof checker becomes more complicated, as does the metatheory proof showing the soundness of the associated logic. The choice in Coq [Barras et al. 2010], one of the most widely used proof assistants, with respect to this trade-off, is to have a conversion rule that identifies propositions up to evaluation. Nevertheless, extended notions of conversion are desirable, leading to proposals like CoqMT [Strub 2010], where equivalence up to first-order theories is supported. In both cases, the conversion rule is fixed, and extending it requires significant amounts of work. It is thus not possible for users to extend it using their own, domain-specific tactics, and proof objects are thus bound to get large. This is why we have to resort to writing proof scripts.

Checking proof scripts. As mentioned earlier, in order to validate a proof script we need to evaluate it (see Fig. 1a); this is the modus operandi in proof assistants of the HOL family [Harrison 1996; Slind and Norrish 2008]. Therefore, it is easy to extend the checking procedure for proof scripts by writing a new tactic, and calling it as part of a script. The price that this comes to is that there is no way to have any sort of static guarantee about the validity of the script, as proof scripts are completely untyped. This can be somewhat mitigated in Coq by utilizing the static checking that it already supports: the proof checker, and especially, the conversion rule it contains (see Fig. 1b). We can employ proof objects in our scripts; this is especially useful when the proof objects are trivial to write but trigger complex conversion checks. This is the essential idea behind techniques like proof-by-reflection [Boutin 1997], which lead to more robust proof scripts.

In previous work [Stampoulis and Shao 2010] we introduced VeriML, a language that enables programming tactics and proof scripts in a typeful manner using a general-purpose, side-effectful programming model. Combining typed tactics leads to *typed proof scripts*. These are still programs producing proof objects, but the proposition they prove is carried within their type. Information about the current proof state (the set of hypotheses and goals) is also available statically at every intermediate point of the proof script. In this way, the static assurances about proof scripts are significantly increased and many potential sources of type errors are removed. On the other hand, the proof objects contained within the scripts are still checked using a fixed proof checker; this ultimately means that the set of possible static guarantees is still fixed.

Extensible conversion rule. In this paper, we build on our earlier work on VeriML. In order to further increase the amount of static checking of proof scripts that is possible within this language, we propose the notion of an extensible conversion rule (see Fig. 1c). It enables users to write their own domain-specific conversion checks

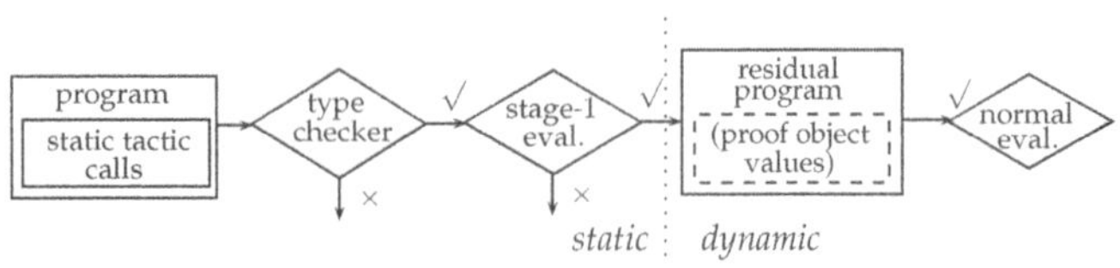

Figure 2. Staging in VeriML

$t ::=$ *proof object constructors* | *propositions*
| *natural numbers, lists, etc.* | *sorts and types* | X/σ

$\Phi ::= \bullet \mid \Phi,\ x : t \qquad T ::= [\Phi]\,t$

$\Psi ::= \bullet \mid \Psi,\ X : T \qquad \sigma ::= \bullet \mid \sigma,\ x \mapsto t$

main judgement: $\Psi;\ \Phi \vdash t : t'$ *(type of a logical term)*

Figure 3. Assumptions about the logic language

that get included in the conversion rule. This leads to simpler proof scripts, as more parts of the proof can be inferred by the conversion rule and can therefore be omitted. Also, it leads to increased static guarantees for proof scripts, since the conversion checks happen before the rest of the proof script is evaluated.

The way we achieve this is by programming the conversion checks as type-safe tactics within VeriML, and then evaluating them statically using a simple staging mechanism (see Fig. 2). The type of the conversion tactics requires that they produce a proof object which proves the claimed equivalence of the propositions. In this way, type safety of VeriML guarantees that soundness is maintained. At the same time, users are free to extend the conversion rule with their own conversion tactics written in a familiar programming model, without requiring any metatheoretic additions or termination proofs. Such proofs are only necessary if decidability of the extra conversion checks is desired. Furthermore, this approach allows for metatheoretic reductions as the original conversion rule can be programmed within the language. Thus it can be removed from the logic, and replaced by the simpler notion of explicit equalities, leading to both simpler metatheory and a smaller trusted base.

Checking tactics. The above approach addresses the issue of being able to extend the amount of static checking possible for proof scripts. But what about tactics? Our existing work on VeriML shows how the increased type information addresses some of the issues of tactic development using current proof assistants, where tactics are programmed in a completely untyped manner.

Still, if we consider the case of tactics more closely, we will see that there is a limitation to the amount of checking that is done statically, even using this language. When programming a new tactic, we would like to reuse existing tactics to produce the required proofs. Therefore, rather than writing proof objects by hand inside the code of a tactic, we would rather use proof scripts. The issue is that in order to check whether the contained proof scripts are valid, they need to be evaluated – but this only happens when an invocation of the tactic reaches the point where the proof script is used. Therefore, the static guarantees that this approach provides are severely limited by the fact that the proof scripts inside the tactics cannot be checked statically, when the tactic is defined.

Static proof scripts. This is the second fundamental issue we address in this paper. We show that the same staging construct utilized for introducing the extensible conversion rule, can be leveraged to perform *static proof checking for tactics*. The crucial point of our approach is the proof of existence of a transformation between proof objects, which suggests that under reasonable conditions, a proof script contained within a tactic can be transformed into a static proof script. This static script can then be evaluated at tactic definition time, to be checked for validity.

Last, we will show that this approach lends itself well to writing extensions of the conversion rule. We show that we can create a layering of conversion rules: using a basic conversion rule as a starting point, we can utilize it inside static proof scripts to implicitly prove the required obligations of a more advanced version, and so on. This minimizes the required user effort for writing new conversion rules, and enables truly modular proof checking.

3. Our toolbox

In this section, we will present the essential ingredients that are needed for the rest of our development. The main requirement is a language that supports type-safe manipulation of terms of a particular logic, as well as a general-purpose programming model that includes general recursion and other side-effectful operations. Two recently proposed languages for manipulating LF terms, Beluga [Pientka and Dunfield 2008] and Delphin [Poswolsky and Schürmann 2008], fit this requirement, as does VeriML [Stampoulis and Shao 2010], which is a language used to write type-safe tactics. Our discussion is focused on the latter, as it supports a richer ML-style calculus compared to the others, something useful for our purposes. Still, our results apply to all three.

We will now briefly describe the constructs that these languages support, as well as some new extensions that we propose. The interested reader can read more about these constructs in Sec. 6 and in our technical report [Stampoulis and Shao 2012].

A formal logic. The computational language we are presenting is centered around manipulation of terms of a specific formal logic. We will see more details about this logic in Sec. 4. For the time being, it will suffice to present a set of assumptions about the syntactic classes and typing judgements of this logic, shown in Fig. 3. Logical terms are represented by the syntactic class t, and include proof objects, propositions, terms corresponding to the domain of discourse (e.g. natural numbers), and the needed sorts and type constructors to classify such terms. Their variables are assigned types through an ordered context Φ. A package of a logical term t together with the variables context it inhabits Φ is called a contextual term and denoted as $T = [\Phi]\,t$. Our computational language works over contextual terms for reasons that will be evident later. The logic incorporates such terms by allowing them to get substituted for *meta-variables* X, using the constructor X/σ. When a term $T = [\Phi']\,t$ gets substituted for X, we go from the Φ' context to the current context Φ using the substitution σ.

Logical terms are classified using other logical terms, based on the normal variables environment Φ, and also an environment Ψ that types meta-variables, thus leading to the $\Psi;\ \Phi \vdash t : t'$ judgement. For example, a term t representing a closed proposition will be typed as $\bullet;\ \bullet \vdash t : \mathsf{Prop}$, while a proof object t_{pf} proving that proposition will satisfy the judgement $\bullet;\ \bullet \vdash t_{\mathrm{pf}} : t$.

ML-style functional programming. We move on to the computational language. As its main core, we assume an ML-style functional language, supporting general recursion, algebraic data types and mutable references (see Fig. 4). Terms of this fragment are typed under a computational variables environment Γ and a store typing environment Σ, mapping mutable locations to types. Typing judgements are entirely standard, leading to a $\Sigma;\ \Gamma \vdash e : \tau$ judgement for typing expressions.

Dependently-typed programming over logical terms. As shown in Fig. 5, the first important additions to the ML computational core are constructs for dependent functions and products over contextual terms T. Abstraction over contextual terms is denoted as $\lambda X : T.e$. It has the dependent function type $(X : T) \to \tau$. The type is dependent since the introduced logical term might be used as the type of

$$k ::= * \mid k_1 \to k_2$$
$$\tau ::= \mathsf{unit} \mid \mathsf{int} \mid \mathsf{bool} \mid \tau_1 \to \tau_2 \mid \tau_1 + \tau_2 \mid \tau_1 \times \tau_2 \mid \mu\alpha : k.\tau$$
$$\mid \forall \alpha : k.\tau \mid \alpha \mid \mathsf{array}\ \tau \mid \lambda\alpha : k.\tau \mid \tau_1\ \tau_2 \mid \cdots$$
$$e ::= () \mid n \mid e_1 + e_2 \mid e_1 \leq e_2 \mid \mathsf{true} \mid \mathsf{false} \mid \mathsf{if}\ e\ \mathsf{then}\ e_1\ \mathsf{else} e_2$$
$$\mid \lambda \mathbf{x} : \tau.e \mid e_1\ e_2 \mid (e_1,\ e_2) \mid \mathsf{proj}_i\ e \mid \mathsf{inj}_i\ e$$
$$\mid \mathsf{case}(e, \mathbf{x}_1.e_1, \mathbf{x}_2.e_2) \mid \mathsf{fold}\ e \mid \mathsf{unfold}\ e \mid \Lambda\alpha : k.e \mid e\ \tau$$
$$\mid \mathsf{fix}\ \mathbf{x} : \tau.e \mid \mathsf{mkarray}(e, e') \mid e[e'] \mid e[e'] := e'' \mid l \mid \mathsf{error} \mid \cdots$$
$$\Gamma ::= \bullet \mid \Gamma,\ \mathbf{x} : \tau \mid \Gamma,\ \alpha : k \qquad \Sigma ::= \bullet \mid \Sigma,\ l : \mathsf{array}\ \tau$$

Figure 4. Syntax for the computational language (ML fragment)

$$\tau ::= \cdots \mid (X : T) \to \tau \mid (X : T) \times \tau \mid (\phi : \mathsf{ctx}) \to \tau$$
$$e ::= \cdots \mid \lambda X : T.e \mid e\ T \mid \lambda\phi : \mathsf{ctx}.e \mid e\ \Phi \mid \langle T,\ e \rangle$$
$$\mid \mathsf{let}\ \langle X,\ \mathbf{x} \rangle = e\ \mathsf{in}\ e'$$
$$\mid \mathsf{holcase}\ T\ \mathsf{return}\ \tau\ \mathsf{of}\ (T_1 \mapsto e_1) \cdots (T_n \mapsto e_n)$$
$$\mid \mathsf{ctxcase}\ \Phi\ \mathsf{return}\ \tau\ \mathsf{of}\ (\Phi_1 \mapsto e_1) \cdots (\Phi_n \mapsto e_n)$$

Figure 5. Syntax for the computational language (logical term constructs)

another term. An example would be a function that receives a proposition plus a proof object for that proposition, with type: $(P : \mathsf{Prop}) \to (X : P) \to \tau$. Dependent products that package a contextual logical term with an expression are introduced through the $\langle T,\ e \rangle$ construct and eliminated using $\mathsf{let}\ \langle X,\ \mathbf{x} \rangle = e\ \mathsf{in}\ e'$; their type is denoted as $(X : T) \times \tau$. Especially for packages of proof objects with the unit type, we introduce the syntax $\mathsf{LT}(T)$.

Last, in order to be able to support functions that work over terms in any context, we introduce context polymorphism, through a similarly dependent function type over contexts. With these in mind, we can define a simple tactic that gets a packaged proof of a universally quantified formula, and an instantiation term, and returns a proof of the instantiated formula as follows:

$$\mathsf{instantiate} : \ (\phi : \mathsf{ctx},\ T : [\phi]\,\mathsf{Type},\ P : [\phi,\ x : T]\,\mathsf{Prop},\ a : [\phi]\,T) \to$$
$$\mathsf{LT}([\phi]\,\forall x : T, P) \to \mathsf{LT}([\phi]\,P/[\mathsf{id}_\phi,\ a])$$
$$\mathsf{instantiate}\ \phi\ T\ P\ a\ \mathsf{pf} = \mathsf{let}\ \langle H \rangle = \mathsf{pf}\ \mathsf{in}\ \langle H\ a \rangle$$

From here on, we will omit details about contexts and substitutions in the interest of presentation.

Pattern matching over terms. The most important new construct that VeriML supports is a pattern matching construct over logical terms denoted as holcase. This construct is used for dependent matching of a logical term against a set of patterns. The return clause specifies its return type; we omit it when it is easy to infer. Patterns are normal terms that include unification variables, which can be present under binders. This is the essential reason why contextual terms are needed.

Pattern matching over environments. For the purposes of our development, it is very useful to support one more pattern matching construct: matching over logical variable contexts. When trying to construct a certain proof, the logical environment represents what the current proof context is: what the current logical hypotheses at hand are, what types of terms have been quantified over, etc. By being able to pattern match over the environment, we can "look up" things in our current set of hypotheses, in order to prove further propositions. We can thus view the current environment as representing a simple form of the current *proof state*; the pattern matching construct enables us to manipulate it in a type-safe manner.

One example is an "assumption" tactic, that tries to prove a proposition by searching for a matching hypotheses in the context:

$$\mathsf{assumption} : \ (\phi : \mathsf{ctx}, P : \mathsf{Prop}) \to \mathsf{option}\ \mathsf{LT}(P)$$
$$\mathsf{assumption}\ \phi\ P =$$
$$\mathsf{ctxcase}\ \phi\ \mathsf{of}$$
$$\phi',\ H : P \mapsto \mathsf{return}\ \langle H \rangle$$
$$\mid \phi',\ \_ \qquad \mapsto \mathsf{assumption}\ \phi'\ P$$

Proof object erasure semantics (new feature). The only construct that can influence the evaluation of a program based on the structure of a logical term is the pattern matching construct. For our purposes, pattern matching on proof objects is not necessary – we never look into the structure of a completed proof. Thus we can have the typing rules of the pattern matching construct specifically disallow matching on proof objects.

In that case, we can define an alternate operational semantics for our language where all proof objects are *erased* before using the original small-step reduction rules. Because of type safety, these proof-erasure semantics are guaranteed to yield equivalent results: even if no proof objects are generated, they are still bound to exist.

Implicit arguments. Let us consider again the *instantiate* function defined earlier. This function expects five arguments. From its type alone, it is evident that only the last two arguments are strictly necessary. The last argument, corresponding to a proof expression for the proposition $\forall x : T, P$, can be used to reconstruct exactly the arguments ϕ, T and P. Furthermore, if we know what the resulting type of a call to the function needs to be, we can choose even the instantiation argument a appropriately. We employ a simple inferrence mechanism so that such arguments are omitted from our programs. This feature is also crucial in our development in order to implicitly maintain and utilize the current proof state within our proof scripts.

Minimal staging support (new feature). Using the language we have seen so far we are able to write powerful tactics using a general-purpose programming model. But what if, inside our programs, we have calls to tactics where all of their arguments are constant? Presumably, those tactic calls could be evaluated to proof objects prior to tactic invocation. We could think of this as a form of generalized constant folding, which has one intriguing benefit: we can tell statically whether the tactic calls succeed or not.

This paper is exactly about exploring this possibility. Towards this effect, we introduce a rudimentary staging construct in our computational language. This takes the form of a letstatic construct, which binds a static expression to a variable. The static expression is evaluated during stage one (see Fig. 2), and can only depend on other static expressions. Details of this construct are presented in Fig. 11d and also in Sec. 6. After this addition, expressions in our language have a three-phase lifetime, that are also shown in Fig. 2.

- type-checking, where the well-formedness of expressions according to the rules of the language is checked, and inference of implicit arguments is performed
- static evaluation, where expressions inside letstatic are reduced to values, yielding a residual expression
- run-time, where the residual expression is evaluated

4. Extensible conversion rule

With these tools at hand, let us now return to the first issue that motivates us: the fact that proof checking is rigid and cannot be extended with user-defined procedures. As we have said in our introduction, many modern proof assistants are based on logics that include a *conversion rule*. This rule essentially identifies proposi-

$$
\begin{array}{rrcl}
\text{(sorts)} & s & ::= & \mathsf{Type} \mid \mathsf{Type}' \\
\text{(kinds)} & \mathcal{K} & ::= & \mathsf{Prop} \mid \mathsf{Nat} \mid \mathcal{K}_1 \to \mathcal{K}_2 \\
\text{(props.)} & P & ::= & P_1 \to P_2 \mid \forall x : \mathcal{K}.P \mid x \mid \mathsf{True} \\
 & & & \mid \mathsf{False} \mid P_1 \wedge P_2 \mid \cdots \\
\text{(dom.obj.)} & d & ::= & \mathsf{Zero} \mid \mathsf{Succ}\, d \mid P \mid \cdots \\
\text{(proof objects)} & \pi & ::= & x \mid \lambda x : P.\pi \mid \pi_1\, \pi_2 \mid \lambda x : \mathcal{K}.\pi \\
 & & & \mid \pi\, d \mid \cdots \\
\text{(HOL terms)} & t & ::= & s \mid \mathcal{K} \mid P \mid d \mid \pi
\end{array}
$$

Selected rules:

$$
\to\text{INTRO}\quad \frac{\Psi;\ \Phi, x : P \vdash \pi : P'}{\Psi;\ \Phi \vdash \lambda x : P.\pi : P \to P'}
\qquad
\to\text{ELIM}\quad \frac{\Psi;\ \Phi \vdash \pi : P \to P' \qquad \Psi;\ \Phi \vdash \pi' : P}{\Psi;\ \Phi \vdash \pi\, \pi' : P'}
$$

Figure 6. Syntax and selected rules of the logic language λHOL

$$
\text{CONVERSION}\quad \frac{\Psi;\ \Phi \vdash_c \pi : P \qquad P =_{\beta\mathbb{N}} P'}{\Psi;\ \Phi \vdash_c \pi : P'}
$$

$d \to_{\beta\mathbb{N}} d'$:

$$
\begin{array}{l}
(\lambda x : \mathcal{K}.d)\, d' \to_{\beta\mathbb{N}} d[d'/x] \\
\mathsf{natElim}_{\mathcal{K}}\ d_z\ d_s\ \mathsf{zero} \to_{\beta\mathbb{N}} d_z \\
\mathsf{natElim}_{\mathcal{K}}\ d_z\ d_s\ (\mathsf{succ}\ d) \to_{\beta\mathbb{N}} d_s\ d\ (\mathsf{natElim}_{\mathcal{K}}\ d_z\ d_s\ d)
\end{array}
$$

$d =_{\beta\mathbb{N}} d'$ is the compatible, reflexive, symmetric and transitive closure of $d \to_{\beta\mathbb{N}} d'$

Figure 7. Extending λHOL with the conversion rule (λHOL$_c$)

tions up to some equivalence relation: usually this is equivalence up to partial evaluation of the functions contained within propositions.

The supported relation is decided when the logic is designed. Any extension to this relation requires a significant amount of work, both in terms of implementation, and in terms of metatheoretic proof required. This is evidenced by projects that extend the conversion rule in Coq, such as Blanqui et al. [1999] and Strub [2010]. Even if user extensions are supported, those only take the form of first-order theories. Can we do better than this, enabling arbitrarily complex user extensions, written with the full power of ML, yet maintaining soundness?

It turns out that we can: this is the subject of this section. The key idea is to recognize that the conversion rule is essentially a tactic, embedded within the type checker of the logic. Calls to this tactic are made implicitly as part of checking a given proof object for validity. So how can we support a flexible, extensible alternative? Instead of hardcoding a conversion tactic within the logic type checker, we can program a type-safe version of the same tactic within VeriML, with the requirement that it provides proof of the claimed equivalence. Instead of calling the conversion tactic as part of proof checking, we use staging to call the tactic statically – after (VeriML) type checking, but before runtime execution. This can be viewed as a second, potentially non-terminating proof checking stage. Users are now free to write their own conversion tactics, extending the static checking available for proof objects and proof scripts. Still, soundness is maintained, since full proof objects in the original logic can always be constructed. As an example, we have extended the conversion rule that we use by a congruence closure procedure, which makes use of mutable data structures, and by an arithmetic simplification procedure.

4.1 Introducing: the conversion rule

First, let us present what the conversion rule really is in more detail. We will base our discussion on a simple type-theoretic higher-order

$$
\frac{\Psi;\ \Phi \vdash_e d_1 : \mathcal{K} \qquad \Psi;\ \Phi \vdash_c d_2 : \mathcal{K}}{\Psi;\ \Phi \vdash_e d_1 = d_2 : \mathsf{Prop}}
\qquad
\frac{\Psi;\ \Phi \vdash_e d : \mathcal{K}}{\Psi;\ \Phi \vdash_e \mathsf{refl}\ d : d = d}
$$

$$
\frac{\Psi;\ \Phi,\ x : \mathcal{K} \vdash_e P : \mathsf{Prop} \qquad \Psi;\ \Phi \vdash_e d_1 : \mathcal{K} \qquad \Psi;\ \Phi \vdash_e \pi : P[d_1/x] \qquad \Psi;\ \Phi \vdash_e \pi' : d_1 = d_2}{\Psi;\ \Phi \vdash_e \mathsf{leibniz}\ (\lambda x : \mathcal{K}.P)\ \pi\ \pi' : P[d_2/x]}
$$

$$
\frac{\Psi;\ \Phi,\ x : \mathcal{K} \vdash_e \pi : d_1 = d_2}{\Psi;\ \Phi \vdash_e \mathsf{lamEq}\ (\lambda x : \mathcal{K}.\pi) : (\lambda x : \mathcal{K}.d_1) = (\lambda x : \mathcal{K}.d_2)}
$$

$$
\frac{\Psi;\ \Phi,\ x : \mathcal{K} \vdash_e \pi : d_1 = d_2 \qquad \Psi;\ \Phi \vdash_e d_1 : \mathsf{Prop}}{\Psi;\ \Phi \vdash_e \mathsf{forallEq}\ (\lambda x : \mathcal{K}.\pi) : (\forall x : \mathcal{K}.d_1) = (\forall x : \mathcal{K}.d_2)}
$$

$$
\frac{\Psi;\ \Phi,\ x : \mathcal{K} \vdash_e d : \mathcal{K}' \qquad \Psi;\ \Phi \vdash_e d' : \mathcal{K}}{\Psi;\ \Phi \vdash_e \mathsf{betaEq}\ (\lambda x : \mathcal{K}.d)\ d' : (\lambda x : \mathcal{K}.d)\ d' = d[d'/x]}
$$

Axioms assumed:

$$
\begin{array}{lcl}
\mathsf{natElimBase}_{\mathcal{K}} & : & \forall f_z.\forall f_s.\mathsf{natElim}_{\mathcal{K}}\ f_z\ f_s\ \mathsf{zero} = f_z \\
\mathsf{natElimStep}_{\mathcal{K}} & : & \forall f_z.\forall f_s.\forall n.\ \mathsf{natElim}_{\mathcal{K}}\ f_z\ f_s\ (\mathsf{succ}\ n) = \\
 & & \quad f_s\ n\ (\mathsf{natElim}_{\mathcal{K}}\ f_z\ f_s\ n)
\end{array}
$$

Figure 8. Extending λHOL with explicit equality (λHOL$_e$)

logic, based on the λHOL logic as described in Barendregt and Geuvers [1999], and used in our original work on VeriML [Stampoulis and Shao 2010]. We can think of such a logic composed by the following broad classes: the objects of the domain of discourse d, which are the objects that the logic reasons about, such as natural numbers and lists; their classifiers, the kinds $\mathcal{K}$ (classified in turn by sorts s); the propositions P; and the derivations, which prove that a certain proposition is true. We can represent derivations in a linear form as terms π in a typed lambda-calculus; we call such terms proof objects, and their types represent propositions in the logic. Checking whether a derivation is a valid proof of a certain proposition amounts to type-checking its corresponding proof object. Some details of this logic are presented in Fig. 6; the interested reader can find more information about it in the above references and in our technical report [Stampoulis and Shao 2012].

In Fig. 6, we show what the conversion rule looks like for this logic: it is a typing judgement that effectively identifies propositions up to an equivalence relation, with respect to checking proof objects. We call this version of the logic λHOL$_c$ and use $\vdash_c$ to denote its entailment relation. The equivalence relation we consider in the conversion rule is evaluation up to β-reductions and uses of primitive recursion of natural numbers, denoted as natElim. In this way, trivial arguments based on this notion of computation alone need not be witnessed, as for example is the fact that $(\mathsf{Succ}\,x) + y = \mathsf{Succ}\,(x+y)$ – when the addition function is defined by primitive recursion on the first argument. Of course, this is only a very basic use of the conversion rule. It is possible to omit larger proofs through much more sophisticated uses. This leads to simpler proofs and smaller proof objects.

Still, when using this approach, the choice of what relation is supported by the conversion rule needs to be made during the definition of the logic. This choice permeates all aspects of the metatheory of the logic. It is easy to see why, even with the tiny fragment of logic we have introduced. Most typing rules for proof objects in the logic are similar to the rules →INTRO and →ELIM: they are syntax-directed. This means that upon seeing the associated proof object constructor, like $\lambda x : P.\pi$ in the case of →INTRO, we can directly tell that it applies. If all rules were syntax directed, it would

$$
\begin{array}{l}
\beta\mathbb{N}\mathsf{equal} : (\phi : \mathsf{ctx}, T : \mathsf{Type}, t_1 : T, t_2 : T) \to \mathsf{option}\ \mathsf{LT}(t_1 = t_2) \\
\beta\mathbb{N}\mathsf{equal}\ \phi\ T\ t_1\ t_2 = \\
\quad \mathsf{holcase\ whnf}\ \phi\ T\ t_1,\ \mathsf{whnf}\ \phi\ T\ t_2\ \mathsf{of} \\
\qquad ((t_a : T' \to T)\ t_b), (t_c\ t_d) \mapsto \\
\qquad\quad \mathsf{do}\ \langle \mathsf{pf}_1 \rangle \leftarrow \beta\mathbb{N}\mathsf{equal}\ \phi\ (T' \to T)\ t_a\ t_c \\
\qquad\quad\quad\ \ \langle \mathsf{pf}_1 \rangle \leftarrow \beta\mathbb{N}\mathsf{equal}\ \phi\ T'\ t_b\ t_d \\
\qquad\quad\quad\ \ \mathsf{return}\ \langle \cdots\ \textit{proof of}\ t_a\, t_b = t_c\, t_d \cdots \rangle \\
\qquad |\ (t_a \to t_b), (t_c \to t_d) \mapsto \\
\qquad\quad \mathsf{do}\ \langle \mathsf{pf}_1 \rangle \leftarrow \beta\mathbb{N}\mathsf{equal}\ \phi\ \mathsf{Prop}\ t_a\ t_c \\
\qquad\quad\quad\ \ \langle \mathsf{pf}_1 \rangle \leftarrow \beta\mathbb{N}\mathsf{equal}\ \phi\ \mathsf{Prop}\ t_b\ t_d \\
\qquad\quad\quad\ \ \mathsf{return}\ \langle \cdots\ \textit{proof of}\ t_a \to t_b = t_c \to t_d \cdots \rangle \\
\qquad |\ (\lambda x : T.t_1), (\lambda x : T.t_2) \mapsto \\
\qquad\quad \mathsf{do}\ \langle \mathsf{pf} \rangle \leftarrow \beta\mathbb{N}\mathsf{equal}\ [\phi,\ x : T]\ \mathsf{Prop}\ t_1\ t_2 \\
\qquad\quad\quad\ \ \mathsf{return}\ \langle \cdots\ \textit{proof of}\ \lambda x : T.t_1 = \lambda x : T.t_2 \cdots \rangle \\
\qquad |\ t_1, t_1 \mapsto \mathsf{do\ return}\ \langle \cdots\ \textit{proof of}\ t_1 = t_1 \cdots \rangle \\
\qquad |\ t_1, t_2 \mapsto \mathsf{None}
\end{array}
$$

$$
\begin{array}{l}
\mathsf{requireEqual} : (\phi : \mathsf{ctx}, T : \mathsf{Type}, t_1 : T, t_2 : T).\mathsf{LT}(t_1 = t_2) \\
\mathsf{requireEqual}\ \phi\ T\ t_1\ t_2 = \\
\quad \mathsf{match}\ \beta\mathbb{N}\mathsf{equal}\ \phi\ T\ t_1\ t_2\ \mathsf{with\ Some}\ x \mapsto x \mid \mathsf{None} \mapsto \mathsf{error}
\end{array}
$$

Figure 9. VeriML tactic for checking equality up to β-conversion

be entirely simple to prove that the logic is sound by an inductive argument: essentially, since no proof constructor for False exists, there is no valid derivation for False.

In this logic, the only rule that is not syntax directed is exactly the conversion rule. Therefore, in order to prove the soundness of the logic, we have to show that the conversion rule does not somehow introduce a proof of False. This means that proving the soundness of the logic passes essentially through the specific relation we have chosen for the conversion rule. Therefore, this approach is foundationally limited from supporting user extensions, since any new extension would require a new metatheoretic result in order to make sure that it does not violate logical soundness.

4.2 Throwing conversion away

Since having a fixed conversion rule is bound to fail if we want it to be extensible, what choice are we left with, but to throw it away? This radical sounding approach is what we will do here. We can replace the conversion rule by an explicit notion of equality, and provide explicit proof witnesses for rewriting based on that equality. Essentially, all the points where the conversion rule was alluded to and proofs were omitted, need now be replaced by proof objects witnessing the equivalence. Some details for the additions required to the base λHOL logic are shown in Fig. 8, yielding the λHOL_e logic. There are good reasons for choosing this version: first, the proof checker is as simple as possible, and does not need to include the conversion checking routine. We could view this routine as performing proof search over the replacement rules, so it necessarily is more complicated, especially since it needs to be relatively efficient. Also, the metatheory of the logic itself can be simplified. Even when the conversion rule is supported, the metatheory for the associated logic is proved through the explicit equality approach; this is because model construction for a logic benefits from using explicit equality [Siles and Herbelin 2010].

Still, this approach has a big disadvantage: the proof objects soon become extremely large, since they include painstakingly detailed proofs for even the simplest of equivalences. This precludes their use as independently checkable proof certificates that can be sent to a third party. It is possible that this is one of the reasons why systems based on logics with explicit equalities, such as HOL4

$$
\begin{array}{l}
\mathsf{whnf} : (\phi : \mathsf{ctx}, T : \mathsf{Type}, t : T) \to (t' : T) \times \mathsf{LT}(t = t') \\
\mathsf{whnf}\ \phi\ T\ t = \mathsf{holcase}\ t\ \mathsf{of} \\
\quad (t_1 : T' \to T)(t_2 : T') \mapsto \\
\qquad \mathsf{let}\ \langle t_1',\ pf_1 \rangle = \mathsf{whnf}\ \phi\ (T' \to T)\ t_1\ \mathsf{in} \\
\qquad \mathsf{holcase}\ t_1'\ \mathsf{of} \\
\qquad\quad \lambda x : T'.t_f \mapsto \langle [\phi]\, t_f / [\mathsf{id}_\phi, t_2], \cdots \rangle \\
\qquad\quad |\ t_1' \mapsto \langle [\phi]\, t_1'\ t_2, \cdots \rangle \\
\quad |\ \mathsf{natElim}_{\mathcal{K}}\ f_z\ f_s\ n \mapsto \\
\qquad \mathsf{let}\ \langle n',\ pf_1 \rangle = \mathsf{whnf}\ \phi\ \mathsf{Nat}\ n\ \mathsf{in\ holcase}\ n'\ \mathsf{of} \\
\qquad\quad \mathsf{zero} \mapsto \langle [\phi]\, f_z, \cdots \rangle \\
\qquad\quad |\ \mathsf{succ}\ n' \mapsto \langle [\phi]\, f_s\ n'\ (\mathsf{natElim}_{\mathcal{K}}\ f_z\ f_s\ n'), \cdots \rangle \\
\qquad\quad |\ n' \mapsto \langle [\phi]\, \mathsf{natElim}_{\mathcal{K}}\ f_z\ f_s\ n', \cdots \rangle \\
\quad |\ t \mapsto \langle t, \cdots \rangle
\end{array}
$$

Figure 10. VeriML tactic for rewriting to weak head-normal form

[Slind and Norrish 2008] and Isabelle/HOL [Nipkow et al. 2002], do not generate proof objects by default.

4.3 Getting conversion back

We will now see how it is possible to reconcile the explicit equality based approach with the conversion rule: we will gain the conversion rule back, albeit it will remain completely outside the logic. Therefore we will be free to extend it, all the while without risking introducing unsoundness in the logic, since the logic remains fixed (λHOL_e as presented above).

We do this by revisiting the view of the conversion rule as a special "trusted" tactic, through the tools presented in the previous section. First, instead of hardcoding a conversion tactic in the type checker, we program a *type-safe conversion tactic*, utilizing the features of VeriML. Based on typing alone we require that it returns a valid proof of the claimed equivalences:

$$\beta\mathbb{N}\mathsf{equal} : (\phi : \mathsf{ctx},\ T : \mathsf{Type},\ t : T,\ t' : T) \to \mathsf{option}\ \mathsf{LT}(t = t')$$

Second, we evaluate this tactic under *proof erasure semantics*. This means that no proof objects are produced, leading to the same space gains as the original conversion rule. Third, we use the staging construct in order to *check conversion statically*.

Details. We now present our approach in more detail. First, in Fig. 9, we show a sketch of the code behind the type-safe conversion check tactic. It works by first rewriting its input terms into weak head-normal form, via the whnf function in Fig. 10, and then recursively checking their subterms for equality. In the equivalence checking function, more cases are needed to deal with quantification; while in the rewriting procedure, a recursive call is missing, which would complicate our presentation here. We also define a version of the tactic that raises an error instead of returning an option type if we fail to prove the terms equal, which we call requireEqual. The full details can be found in our implementation.

The code of the βℕequal tactic is in fact entirely similar to the code one would write for the conversion check routine inside a logic type checker, save for the extra types and proof objects. It therefore follows trivially that everything that holds for the standard implementation of the conversion check also holds for this code: e.g. it corresponds exactly to the $=_{\beta\mathbb{N}}$ relation as defined in the logic; it is bound to terminate because of the strong normalization theorem for this relation; and its proof-erased version is at least as trustworthy as the standard implementation.

Furthermore, given this code, we can produce a form of *typed proof scripts* inside VeriML that correspond exactly to proof objects in the logic with the conversion rule, both in terms of their actual code, and in terms of the steps required to validate them. This is done by constructing a proof script in VeriML by induction on the derivation of the proof object in λHOL_c, replacing each proof object constructor by an equivalent VeriML tactic as follows:

constructor	to tactic	of type
$\lambda x : P.\pi$	Assume e	$\mathsf{LT}([\phi, H : P] P') \to \mathsf{LT}(P \to P')$
$\pi_1\ \pi_2$	Apply $e_1\ e_2$	$\mathsf{LT}(P \to P') \to \mathsf{LT}(P) \to \mathsf{LT}(P')$
$\lambda x : \mathcal{K}.\pi$	Intro e	$\mathsf{LT}([\phi, x : T] P') \to \mathsf{LT}(\forall x : T, P')$
$\pi\ d$	Inst $e\ a$	$\mathsf{LT}(\forall x : T, P) \to (a : T) \to \mathsf{LT}(P/[\mathsf{id},\ a])$
c	Lift c	$(H : P) \to \mathsf{LT}(P)$
(conversion)	Conversion	$\mathsf{LT}(P) \to \mathsf{LT}(P = P') \to \mathsf{LT}(P')$

Here we have omitted the current logical environment ϕ; it is maintained through syntactic means as discussed in Sec. 7 and through type inference. The only subtle case is conversion. Given the transformed proof e for the proof object π contained within a use of the conversion rule, we call the conversion tactic as follows:

$$\text{letstatic pf} = \text{requireEqual}\ P\ P'\ \text{in Conversion e pf}$$

The arguments to requireEqual can be easily inferred, making crucial use of the rich type information available. Conversion could also be used implicitly in the other tactics. Thus the resulting expression looks entirely identical to the original proof object.

Correspondence with original proof object. In order to elucidate the correspondence between the resulting proof script expression and the original proof object, it is fruitful to view the proof script as a proof certificate, sent to a third party. The steps required to check whether it constitutes a valid proof are the following. First, the whole expression is checked using the type checker of the computational language. Then, the calls to the requireEqual function are evaluated during stage one, using proof erasure semantics. We expect them to be successful, just as we would expect the conversion rule to be applicable when it is used. Last, the rest of the tactics are evaluated; by a simple argument, based on the fact that they do not use pattern matching or side-effects, they are guaranteed to terminate and produce a proof object in λHOL_e. This validity check is entirely equivalent to the behavior of type-checking the λHOL_c proof object, save for pushing all conversion checks towards the end.

4.4 Extending conversion at will

In our treatment of the conversion rule we have so far focused on regaining the $\beta\mathbb{N}$ conversion in our framework. Still, there is nothing confining us to supporting this conversion check only. As long as we can program a conversion tactic in VeriML that has the right type, it can safely be made part of our conversion rule.

For example, we have written an eufEqual function, which checks terms for equivalence based on the equality with uninterpreted functions decision procedure. It is adapted from our previous work on VeriML [Stampoulis and Shao 2010]. This equivalence checking tactic isolates hypotheses of the form $d_1 = d_2$ from the current context, using the newly-introduced context matching support. Then, it constructs a union-find data structure in order to form equivalence classes of terms. Based on this structure, and using code similar to $\beta\mathbb{N}$equal (recursive calls on subterms), we can decide whether two terms are equal up to simple uses of the equality hypotheses at hand. We have combined this tactic with the original $\beta\mathbb{N}$equal tactic, making the implicit equivalence supported similar to the one in the Calculus of Congruent Constructions [Blanqui et al. 2005]. This demonstrates the flexibility of this approach: equivalence checking is extended with a sophisticated decision procedure, which is programmed using its original, imperative formulation. We have programmed both the rewriting procedure and the equality checking procedure in an extensible manner, so that we can globally register further extensions.

4.5 Typed proof scripts as certificates

Earlier we discussed how we can validate the proof scripts resulting from turning the conversion rule into explicit tactic calls. This discussion shows an interesting aspect of typed proof scripts: they can be viewed as a proof witness that is a flexible compromise between untyped proof scripts and proof objects. When a typed proof script consists only of static calls to conversion tactics and uses of total tactics, it can be thought of as a proof object in a logic with the corresponding conversion rule. When it also contains other tactics, that perform potentially expensive proof search, it corresponds more closely to an untyped proof script, since it needs to be fully evaluated. Still, we are allowed to validate parts of it statically. This is especially useful when developing the proof script, because we can avoid the evaluation of expensive tactic calls while we focus on getting the skeleton of the proof correct.

Using proof erasure for evaluating requireEqual is only one of the choices the receiver of such a proof certificate can make. Another choice would be to have the function return an actual proof object, which we can check using the λHOL_e type checker. In that case, the VeriML interpreter does not need to become part of the trusted base of the system. Last, the 'safest possible' choice would be to avoid doing any evaluation of the function, and ask the proof certificate provider to do the evaluation of requireEqual themselves. In that case, no evaluation of computational code would need to happen at the proof certificate receiver's side. This mitigates any concerns one might have for code execution as part of proof validity checking, and guarantees that the small λHOL_e type checker is the trusted base in its entirety. Also, the receiver can decide on the above choices selectively for different conversion tactics – e.g. use proof erasure for $\beta\mathbb{N}$equal but not for eufEqual, leading to a trusted base identical to the λHOL_c case. This means that the choice of the conversion rule rests with the proof certificate receiver and not with the designer of the logic. Thus the proof certificate receiver can choose the level of trust they require at will.

5. Static proof scripts

In the previous section, we have demonstrated how proof checking for typed proof scripts can be made user-extensible, through a new treatment of the conversion rule. It makes use of user-defined, type-safe tactics, which are evaluated statically. The question that remains is what happens with respect to proofs within tactics. If a proof script is found within a tactic, must we wait until that evaluation point is reached to know whether the proof script is correct or not? Or is there a way to check this statically, as soon as the tactic is defined?

In this section we show how this is possible to do in VeriML using the staging construct we have introduced. Still, in this case matters are not as simple as evaluating certain expressions statically rather than dynamically. The reason is that proof scripts contained within tactics mention uninstantiated meta-variables, and thus cannot be evaluated through staging. We resolve this by showing the existence of a transformation, which "collapses" logical terms from an arbitrary meta-variables context into the empty one.

We will focus on the case of developing conversion routines, similar to the ones we saw earlier. The ideas we present are generally applicable when writing other types of tactics as well; we focus on conversion routines in order to demonstrate that the two main ideas we present in this paper can work in tandem.

A rewriter for plus. We will consider the case of writing a rewriter –similar to whnf– for simplifying expressions of the form $x+y$, depending on the second argument. The addition function is defined by induction on the first argument, as follows:

$$(+) = \lambda x.\lambda y.\mathsf{natElim}_{\mathsf{Nat}}\ y\ (\lambda p.\lambda r.\mathsf{Succ}\ r)\ x$$

In order for rewriters to be able to use existing as well as future rewriters to perform their recursive calls, we write them in the open recursion style – they receive a function of the same type that corresponds to the "current" rewriter. The code looks as follows:

$$\begin{array}{l}
\mathsf{rewriterType} = (\phi : \mathsf{ctx}, T : \mathsf{Type}, t : T) \to (t' : T) \times \mathsf{LT}(t = t') \\
\mathsf{plusRewriter1} : \mathsf{rewriterType} \to \mathsf{rewriterType} \\
\mathsf{plusRewriter1\ recursive}\ \phi\ T\ t = \mathsf{holcase}\ t\ \mathsf{with} \\
\quad x + y \mapsto \\
\quad\quad \mathsf{let}\ \langle y', \langle \mathsf{pfy}' \rangle \rangle = \mathsf{recursive}\ \phi\ y\ \mathsf{in} \\
\quad\quad \mathsf{let}\ \langle t', \langle \mathsf{pft}' \rangle \rangle = \\
\quad\quad\quad \mathsf{holcase}\ y'\ \mathsf{return}\ \Sigma t' : [\phi]\,\mathsf{Nat}.\mathsf{LT}([\phi]\, x + y' = t')\ \mathsf{of} \\
\quad\quad\quad\quad 0 \quad\quad \mapsto \langle x, \cdots \mathit{proof\ of}\ x + 0 = x \cdots \rangle \\
\quad\quad\quad \mid \mathsf{Succ}\ y' \mapsto \Big\langle \mathsf{Succ}(x + y'), \\
\quad\quad\quad\quad\quad \cdots \mathit{proof\ of}\ x + \mathsf{Succ}\ y' = \mathsf{Succ}\ (x + y') \cdots \Big\rangle \\
\quad\quad\quad \mid y' \quad\quad \mapsto \langle x + y', \cdots \mathit{proof\ of}\ x + y' = x + y' \cdots \rangle \\
\quad\quad \mathsf{in}\ \langle t', \langle \cdots \mathit{proof\ of}\ x + y = t' \cdots \rangle \rangle \\
\quad \mid t \quad\quad \mapsto \langle t, \cdots \mathit{proof\ of}\ t = t \cdots \rangle
\end{array}$$

While developing such a tactic, we can leverage the VeriML type checker to know the types of missing proofs. But how do we fill them in? For the interesting cases of $x + 0 = x$ and $x + \mathsf{Succ}\ y' = \mathsf{Succ}\ (x + y')$, we would certainly need to prove the corresponding lemmas. But for the rest of the cases, the corresponding lemmas would be uninteresting and tedious to state, such as the following for the $x + y = t'$ case:

$$\mathsf{lemma1} : \forall x, y, y', t', y = y' \to (x + y' = t') \to x + y = t$$

Stating and proving such lemmas soon becomes a hindrance when writing tactics. An alternative is to use the congruence closure conversion rule to solve this trivial obligation for us directly at the point where it is required. Our first attempt would be:

$$\begin{array}{l}
\text{proof of } x + y = t' \equiv \\
\quad \mathsf{let}\ \langle \mathsf{pf} \rangle = \mathsf{requireEqual}\ [\phi, H_1 : y = y', H_2 : x + y' = t']\ (x + y)\ t' \\
\quad \mathsf{in}\ \big\langle [\phi]\, \mathsf{pf}/[\mathsf{id}_\phi, \mathsf{pfy}', \mathsf{pft}'] \big\rangle
\end{array}$$

The benefit of this approach is evident when utilizing implicit arguments, since most of the details can be inferred and therefore omitted. Here we had to alter the environment passed to requireEqual, which includes several extra hypotheses. Once the resulting proof has been computed, the hypotheses are substituted by the actual proofs that we have.

The problem with this approach is two-fold: first, the call to the requireEqual tactic is recomputed every time we reach that point of our function. For such a simple tactic call, this does not impact the runtime significantly; still, if we could avoid it, we would be able use more sophisticated and expensive tactics. The second problem is that if for some reason the requireEqual is not able to prove what it is supposed to, we will not know until we actually reach that point in the function.

Moving to static proofs. This is where using the letstatic construct becomes essential. We can evaluate the call to requireEqual statically, during stage one interpretation. Thus we will know at the time that plusRewriter1 is defined whether the call succeeded; also, it will be replaced by a concrete value, so it will not affect the runtime behavior of each invocation of plusRewriter1 anymore. To do that, we need to avoid mentioning any of the metavariables that are bound during runtime, like x, y, and t'. This is done by specifying an appropriate environment in the call to requireEqual, similarly to the way we incorporated the extra knowledge above and substituted it later. Using this approach, we have:

$$\begin{array}{l}
\text{proof of } x + y = t' \equiv \\
\quad \mathsf{letstatic}\ \langle \mathsf{pf} \rangle = \\
\quad\quad \mathsf{let}\ \phi' = [x, y, y', t' : \mathsf{Nat}, H_1 : y = y', H_2 : x + y' = t']\ \mathsf{in} \\
\quad\quad \mathsf{requireEqual}\ \phi'\ (x + y)\ t' \\
\quad \mathsf{in}\ \big\langle [\phi]\, \mathsf{pf}/[x/\mathsf{id}_\phi, y/\mathsf{id}_\phi, y'/\mathsf{id}_\phi, t'/\mathsf{id}_\phi, \mathsf{pfy}'/\mathsf{id}_\phi, \mathsf{pft}'/\mathsf{id}_\phi] \big\rangle
\end{array}$$

What we are essentially doing here is replacing the meta-variables by normal logical variables, which our tactics can deal with. The meta-variable context is "collapsed" into a normal context; proofs are constructed using tactics in this environment; last, the resulting proofs are transported back into the desired context by substituting meta-variables for variables. We have explicitly stated the substitutions in order to distinguish between normal logical variables and meta-variables.

The reason why this transformation needs to be done is that functions in our computational language can only manipulate logical terms that are open with respect to a normal variables context; not logical terms that are open with respect to the meta-variables context too. A much more complicated, but also more flexible alternative to using this "collapsing" trick would be to support meta-n-variables within our computational language directly.

Overall, this approach is entirely similar to proving the auxiliary lemma mentioned above, prior to the tactic definition. The benefit is that by leveraging the type information together with type inference, we can avoid stating such lemmas explicitly, while retaining the same runtime behavior. We thus end up with very concise proof expressions that are statically validated. We introduce syntactic sugar for binding a static proof script to a variable, and then performing a substitution to bring it into the current context, since this is a common operation.

$$\langle e \rangle_{\mathsf{static}} \equiv \mathsf{letstatic}\ \langle \mathsf{pf} \rangle = e\ \mathsf{in}\ \langle [\phi]\, \mathsf{pf}/\cdots \rangle$$

Based on these, the trivial proofs in the above tactic can be filled in using a simple $\langle \mathsf{requireEqual} \rangle_{\mathsf{static}}$ call; for the other two we use $\langle \mathsf{Instantiate}\ (\mathsf{NatInduction}\ \mathsf{requireEqual}\ \mathsf{requireEqual})\ x \rangle_{\mathsf{static}}$.

After we define plusRewriter1, we can register it with the global equivalence checking procedure. Thus, all later calls to requireEqual will benefit from this simplification. It is then simple to prove commutativity for addition:

$$\begin{array}{lcl}
\mathsf{plusComm} & : & \mathsf{LT}(\forall x, y. x + y = y + x) \\
\mathsf{plusComm} & = & \mathsf{NatInduction}\ \mathsf{requireEqual}\ \mathsf{requireEqual}
\end{array}$$

Based on this proof, we can write a rewriter that takes commutativity into account and uses the hash values of logical terms to avoid infinite loops. We have worked on an arithmetic simplification rewriter that is built by layering such rewriters together, using previous ones to aid us in constructing the proofs required in later ones. It works by converting expressions into a list of monomials, sorting the list based on the hash values of the variables, and then factoring monomials on the same variable. Also, the eufEqual procedure mentioned earlier has all of its associated proofs automated through static proof scripts, using a naive, potentially non-terminating, equality rewriter.

Is collapsing always possible? A natural question to ask is whether collapsing the metavariables context into a normal context is always possible. In order to cast this as a more formal question, we notice that the essential step is replacing a proof object π of type $[\Phi]\, t$, typed under the meta-variables environment Ψ, by a proof object π' of type $[\Phi']\, t'$ typed under the empty meta-variables environment. There needs to be a substitution so that π' gets transported back to the Φ, Ψ environment, and has the appropriate type.

Syntax of the logic — $(\textit{terms})\ t ::= s \mid c \mid f_i \mid b_i \mid \lambda(t_1).t_2 \mid t_1\ t_2 \mid \Pi(t_1).t_2 \mid t_1 = t_2 \mid \mathsf{refl}\ t \mid \mathsf{leibniz}\ t_1\ t_2 \mid \mathsf{lamEq}\ t \mid \mathsf{forallEq}\ t_1\ t_2 \mid \mathsf{betaEq}\ t_1\ t_2$

$(\textit{sorts})\ s ::= \mathsf{Prop} \mid \mathsf{Type} \mid \mathsf{Type}' \qquad (\textit{var. context})\quad \Phi ::= \bullet \mid \Phi,\ t \qquad (\textit{substitutions})\quad \sigma ::= \bullet \mid \sigma,\ t$

Example of representation: $a : \mathsf{Nat} \vdash \lambda x : \mathsf{Nat}.(\lambda y : \mathsf{Nat}.\mathsf{refl}\ (\mathsf{plus}\ a\ y))(\mathsf{plus}\ a\ x) \ \mapsto\ \mathsf{Nat} \vdash \lambda(\mathsf{Nat}).(\lambda(\mathsf{Nat}).\mathsf{refl}\ (\mathsf{plus}\ f_0\ b_0))\ (\mathsf{plus}\ f_0\ b_0)$

Freshen: $\lceil t \rceil^n_m$

$$\begin{aligned}
\lceil f_i \rceil &= f_i \\
\lceil b_n \rceil^n_m &= f_m \\
\lceil b_i \rceil^n &= b_i \text{ when } i < n \\
\lceil (\lambda(t_1).t_2) \rceil^n &= \lambda(\lceil t_1 \rceil^n).\lceil t_2 \rceil^{n+1} \\
\lceil t_1\ t_2 \rceil &= \lceil t_1 \rceil\ \lceil t_2 \rceil
\end{aligned}$$

Bind: $\lfloor t \rfloor^n_m$

$$\begin{aligned}
\lfloor f_{m-1} \rfloor^n_m &= b_n \\
\lfloor f_i \rfloor^n_m &= f_i \text{ when } i < m-1 \\
\lfloor b_i \rfloor &= b_{i+1} \\
\lfloor (\lambda(t_1).t_2) \rfloor &= \lambda(\lfloor t_1 \rfloor^n).\lfloor t_2 \rfloor^{n+1} \\
\lfloor t_1\ t_2 \rfloor &= \lfloor t_1 \rfloor\ \lfloor t_2 \rfloor
\end{aligned}$$

(a) Hybrid deBruijn levels-deBruijn indices representation technique

---

Syntax — $t ::= \cdots \mid f_{\mathbf{I}} \mid X_i/\sigma \quad \Phi ::= \bullet \mid \Phi,\ t \mid \Phi,\ \phi_i \quad \sigma ::= \bullet \mid \sigma,\ t \mid \sigma,\ \mathbf{id}(\phi_i) \quad (\textit{indices})\ \mathbf{I} ::= n \mid \mathbf{I} + |\phi_i| \quad (\textit{ctx.terms})\ T ::= [\Phi]t \mid [\Phi]\Phi'$

$(\textit{ctx.kinds})\ K ::= [\Phi]t \mid [\Phi]\mathsf{ctx} \quad (\textit{extension context})\ \Psi ::= \bullet \mid \Psi,\ K \quad (\textit{ext. subst.})\ \sigma_\Psi ::= \bullet \mid \sigma_\Psi,\ T$

$\Psi;\ \Phi \vdash t : t'$ (sample)

$$\frac{\Phi.\mathbf{I} = t}{\Psi;\ \Phi \vdash f_{\mathbf{I}} : t} \qquad \frac{\Psi;\ \Phi \vdash t_1 : \Pi(t).t' \qquad \Psi;\ \Phi \vdash t_2 : t}{\Psi;\ \Phi \vdash t_1\ t_2 : \lceil t' \rceil \cdot (\mathsf{id}_\Phi.t_2)} \qquad \frac{\Psi.i = [\Phi']t' \qquad \Psi;\ \Phi \vdash \sigma : \Phi'}{\Psi;\ \Phi \vdash X_i/\sigma : t' \cdot \sigma}$$

$\Psi \vdash T : K$

$$\frac{\Psi;\ \Phi \vdash t : t'}{\Psi \vdash [\Phi]t : [\Phi]t'} \qquad \frac{\Psi \vdash \Phi,\ \Phi' \text{ wf}}{\Psi \vdash [\Phi]\Phi' : [\Phi]\mathsf{ctx}}$$

$\Psi \vdash \Phi$ wf (sample)

$$\frac{\Psi \vdash \Phi \text{ wf} \qquad \Psi.i = [\Phi]\mathsf{ctx}}{\Psi \vdash (\Phi,\ \phi_i) \text{ wf}}$$

(b) Extension variables: meta-variables and context variables

---

Subst. application: $t \cdot \sigma$ — $c \cdot \sigma = c \quad f_{\mathbf{I}} \cdot \sigma = \sigma.\mathbf{I} \quad b_i \cdot \sigma = b_i \quad (\lambda(t_1).t_2) \cdot \sigma = \lambda(t_1 \cdot \sigma).(t_2 \cdot \sigma) \quad (t_1\ t_2) \cdot \sigma = (t_1 \cdot \sigma)\ (t_2 \cdot \sigma)$

Ext. subst. application (sample)

$(\mathbf{I},\ |\phi_i|) \cdot \sigma_\Psi = (\mathbf{I} \cdot \sigma_\Psi),\ |\Phi'| \text{ when } \sigma_\Psi.i = [\_]\Phi' \qquad (X_i/\sigma) \cdot \sigma_\Psi = t \cdot (\sigma \cdot \sigma_\Psi) \text{ when } \sigma_\Psi.i = [\_]t$

$(\sigma,\ \mathbf{id}(\phi_i)) \cdot \sigma_\Psi = \sigma \cdot \sigma_\Psi,\ \mathsf{id}_{\sigma_\Psi.i} \qquad (\Phi,\ \phi_i) \cdot \sigma_\Psi = \Phi \cdot \sigma_\Psi,\ \Phi' \text{ when } \sigma_\Psi.i = [\_]\Phi'$

$\Psi;\ \Phi \vdash \sigma : \Phi'$

$$\frac{}{\Psi;\ \Phi \vdash \bullet : \bullet} \qquad \frac{\Psi;\ \Phi \vdash \sigma : \Phi' \qquad \Psi;\ \Phi \vdash t : t' \cdot \sigma}{\Psi;\ \Phi \vdash (\sigma,\ t) : (\Phi',\ t')} \qquad \frac{\Psi;\ \Phi \vdash \sigma : \Phi' \qquad \Psi.i = [\Phi']\mathsf{ctx} \qquad \Phi',\ \phi_i \subseteq \Phi}{\Psi;\ \Phi \vdash (\sigma,\ \mathbf{id}(\phi_i)) : (\Phi',\ \phi_i)}$$

$\Psi \vdash \sigma_\Psi : \Psi'$ (selected)

$$\frac{\Psi \vdash \sigma_\Psi : \Psi' \qquad \Psi \vdash T : K \cdot \sigma_\Psi}{\Psi \vdash (\sigma_\Psi,\ T) : (\Psi',\ K)}$$

Subst. lemmas:

$$\frac{\Psi;\ \Phi \vdash t : t' \qquad \Psi;\ \Phi' \vdash \sigma : \Phi}{\Psi;\ \Phi' \vdash t \cdot \sigma : t' \cdot \sigma} \qquad \frac{\Psi;\ \Phi' \vdash \sigma : \Phi \qquad \Psi;\ \Phi'' \vdash \sigma' : \Phi'}{\Psi;\ \Phi'' \vdash \sigma \cdot \sigma' : \Phi} \qquad \frac{\Psi \vdash T : K \qquad \Psi' \vdash \sigma_\Psi : \Psi}{\Psi' \vdash T \cdot \sigma_\Psi : K \cdot \sigma_\Psi}$$

(c) Substitutions over logical variables and extension variables

---

Syntax: $\Gamma ::= \bullet \mid \Gamma,\ x : \tau \mid \Gamma,\ x :_s \tau \mid \Gamma,\ \alpha : k \qquad e ::= \cdots \mid \mathsf{letstatic}\ x\ =\ e\ \mathsf{in}\ e'$

Limit ctx:

$$\begin{aligned}
\bullet|_{\text{static}} &= \bullet \\
(\Gamma,\ x :_s t)|_{\text{static}} &= \Gamma|_{\text{static}},\ x : t \\
(\Gamma,\ x : t)|_{\text{static}} &= \Gamma|_{\text{static}} \\
(\Gamma,\ \alpha : k)|_{\text{static}} &= \Gamma|_{\text{static}}
\end{aligned}$$

$\Psi;\ \Sigma;\ \Gamma \vdash e : \tau$ (part)

$$\frac{\bullet;\ \Sigma;\ \Gamma|_{\text{static}} \vdash e : \tau \qquad \Psi;\ \Sigma;\ \Gamma.x :_s \tau \vdash e' : \tau}{\Psi;\ \Sigma;\ \Gamma \vdash \mathsf{letstatic}\ x\ =\ e\ \mathsf{in}\ e' : \tau} \qquad \frac{x :_s \tau \in \Gamma}{\Psi;\ \Sigma;\ \Gamma \vdash x : \tau}$$

Evaluation:

$v ::= \Lambda(K).e_d \mid \mathsf{pack}\ T\ \mathsf{return}\ (.\tau)\ \mathsf{with}\ v \mid () \mid \lambda x : \tau.e_d \mid (v,\ v') \mid \mathsf{inj}_i\ v \mid \mathsf{fold}\ v \mid l \mid \Lambda\alpha : k.e_d$

$\mathcal{S} ::= \mathsf{letstatic}\ x\ =\ \bullet\ \mathsf{in}\ e' \mid \mathsf{letstatic}\ x\ =\ \mathcal{S}\ \mathsf{in}\ e' \mid \Lambda(K).\mathcal{S} \mid \lambda x : \tau.\mathcal{S} \mid \mathsf{unpack}\ e_d\ (.)x.(\mathcal{S}) \mid \mathsf{case}(e_d,\ x.\mathcal{S},\ x.e_2)$

$\quad \mid \mathsf{case}(e_d,\ x.e_d,\ x.\mathcal{S}) \mid \Lambda\alpha : k.\mathcal{S} \mid \mathsf{fix}\ x : \tau.\mathcal{S} \mid \mathsf{unify}\ T\ \mathsf{return}\ (.\tau)\ \mathsf{with}\ (\Psi.T' \mapsto \mathcal{S}) \mid \mathcal{E}_s[\mathcal{S}]$

$\mathcal{E}_s ::= \mathcal{E}_s\ T \mid \mathsf{pack}\ T\ \mathsf{return}\ (.\tau)\ \mathsf{with}\ \mathcal{E}_s \mid \mathsf{unpack}\ \mathcal{E}_s\ (.)x.(e') \mid \mathcal{E}_s\ e' \mid e_d\ \mathcal{E}_s \mid (\mathcal{E}_s,\ e) \mid (e_d,\ \mathcal{E}_s) \mid \mathsf{proj}_i\ \mathcal{E}_s \mid \mathsf{inj}_i\ \mathcal{E}_s$

$\quad \mid \mathsf{case}(\mathcal{E}_s,\ x.e_1,\ x.e_2) \mid \mathsf{fold}\ \mathcal{E}_s \mid \mathsf{unfold}\ \mathcal{E}_s \mid \mathsf{ref}\ \mathcal{E}_s \mid \mathcal{E}_s := e' \mid e_d := \mathcal{E}_s \mid !\mathcal{E}_s \mid \mathcal{E}_s\ \tau$

$e_d ::= \text{all of } e \text{ except } \mathsf{letstatic}\ x\ =\ e\ \mathsf{in}\ e' \qquad \mathcal{E} ::= \text{exactly as } \mathcal{E}_s \text{ with } \mathcal{E}_s \to \mathcal{E} \text{ and } e \to e_d$

Stage 1 op.sem.:

$$\frac{(\,\mu\,,\ e_d\,) \longrightarrow (\,\mu'\,,\ e'_d\,)}{(\,\mu\,,\ \mathcal{S}[e_d]\,) \longrightarrow_s (\,\mu'\,,\ \mathcal{S}[e'_d]\,)} \qquad (\,\mu\,,\ \mathcal{S}[\mathsf{letstatic}\ x\ =\ v\ \mathsf{in}\ e]\,) \longrightarrow_s (\,\mu\,,\ \mathcal{S}[e[v/x]]\,)$$

$$(\,\mu\,,\ \mathsf{letstatic}\ x\ =\ v\ \mathsf{in}\ e\,) \longrightarrow_s (\,\mu\,,\ e[v/x]\,)$$

(d) Computational language: staging support

Figure 11. Main definitions in metatheory

We have proved that this is possible under certain restrictions: the types of the metavariables in the current context need to depend on the same free variables context Φ_{max}, or prefixes of that context. Also the substitutions they are used with need to be prefixes of the identity substitution for Φ_{max}. Such terms are characterized as collapsible. We have proved that collapsible terms can be replaced using terms that do not make use of metavariables; more details can be found in Sec. 6 and in the accompanying technical report [Stampoulis and Shao 2012].

This restriction corresponds very well to the treatment of variable contexts in the Delphin language. This language assumes an ambient context of logical variables, instead of full, contextual modal terms. Constructs to extend this context and substitute a specific variable exist. If this last feature is not used, the ambient context grows monotonically and the mentioned restriction holds trivially. In our tests, this restriction has not turned out to be limiting.

6. Metatheory

We have completed an extensive reworking of the metatheory of VeriML, in order to incorporate the features that we have presented in this paper. Our new metatheory includes a number of technical advances compared to our earlier work [Stampoulis and Shao 2010]. We will present a technical overview of our metatheory in this section; full details can be found in our technical report [Stampoulis and Shao 2012].

Variable representation technique. Though our metatheory is done on paper, we have found that using a concrete variable representation technique elucidates some aspects of how different kinds of substitutions work in our language, compared to having normal named variables. For example, instantiating a context variable with a concrete context triggers a set of potentially complicated α-renamings, which a concrete representation makes explicit. We use a hybrid technique representing bound variables as deBruijn indices, and free variables as deBruijn levels. Our technique is a small departure from the named approach, requiring fewer extra annotations and lemmas than normal deBruijn indices. Also it identifies terms not only up to α-equivalence, but also up to extension of the context with new variables; this is why it is also used within the VeriML implementation.The two fundamental operations of this technique are freshening and binding, which are shown in Fig. 11a.

Extension variables. We extend the logic with support for meta-variables and context variables – we refer to both these sorts of variables as extension variables. A meta-variable X_i stands for a contextual term $T = [\Phi]t$, which packages a term together with the context it inhabits. Context variables ϕ_i stand for a context Φ, and are used to "weaken" parametric contexts in specific positions. Both kinds of variables are needed to support manipulation of open logical terms. Details of their definition and typing are shown in Fig. 11b. We use the same hybrid approach as above for representing these variables. A somewhat subtle aspect of this extension is that we generalize the deBruijn levels $\mathbf{I}$ used to index free variables, in order to deal effectively with parametric contexts.

Substitutions. The hybrid representation technique we use for variables renders simultaneous substitutions for all variables in scope as the most natural choice. In Fig. 11c, we show some example rules of how to apply a full simultaneous substitution σ to a term t, denoted as $t \cdot \sigma$. Similarly, we define full simultaneous substitutions σ_Ψ for extension contexts; defining their application has a very natural description, because of our variable representation technique. We prove a number of substitution lemmas which have simple statements, as shown in Fig. 11c. The proofs of these lemmas comprise the main effort required in proving the type-safety of a computational language such as the one we support, as they represent the point where computation specific to logical term manipulation takes place.

Computational language. We define an ML-style computational language that supports dependent functions and dependent pairs over contextual terms T, as well as pattern matching over them. Lack of space precludes us from including details here; full details can be found in the accompanying technical report [Stampoulis and Shao 2012]. A fairly complete ML calculus is supported, with mutable references and recursive types. Type safety is proved using standard techniques; its central point is extending the logic substitution lemmas to expressions and using them to prove progress and preservation of dependent functions and dependent pairs. This proof is modular with respect to the logic and other logics can easily be supported.

Pattern matching. Our metatheory includes many extensions in the pattern matching that is supported, as well as a new approach for dealing with typing patterns. We include support for pattern matching over contexts (e.g. to pick out hypotheses from the context) and for non-linear patterns. The allowed patterns are checked through a restriction of the usual typing rules $\Psi \vdash_p T : K$.

The essential idea behind our approach to pattern matching is to identify what the relevant variables in a typing derivation are. Since contexts are ordered, "removing" non-relevant variables amounts to replacing their definitions in the context with holes, which leads us to partial contexts $\widehat{\Psi}$. The corresponding notion of partial substitutions is denoted as $\widehat{\sigma_\Psi}$. Our main theorem about pattern matching can then be stated as:

Theorem 6.1 (Decidability of pattern matching) *If $\Psi \vdash_p T : K$, $\bullet \vdash_p T' : K$ and $\mathsf{relevant}(\Psi;\ \Phi \vdash T : K) = \widehat{\Psi}$, then either there exists a unique partial substitution $\widehat{\sigma_\Psi}$ such that $\bullet \vdash \widehat{\sigma_\Psi} : \widehat{\Psi}$ and $T \cdot \widehat{\sigma_\Psi} = T'$, or no such substitution exists.*

Staging. Our development in this paper critically depends on the letstatic construct we presented earlier. It can be seen as a dual of the traditional box construct of Davies and Pfenning [1996]. Details of its typing and semantics are shown in Fig. 11d. We define a notion of "static evaluation contexts" $\mathcal{S}$, which enclose a hole of the form $\mathsf{letstatic}\ x = \bullet\ \mathsf{in}\ e$. They include normal evaluation contexts, as well as evaluation contexts under binding structures. We evaluate expressions e that include staging constructs using the $\longrightarrow_s$ relation; internally, this uses the normal evaluation rules, that are used in the second stage as well, for evaluating expressions which do not include other staging constructs. If stage-one evaluation is successful, we are left with a residual dynamic configuration $(\mu',\ e_d)$ which is then evaluated normally. We prove type-safety for stage-one evaluation; its statement follows.

Theorem 6.2 (Stage-one Type Safety) *If $\bullet; \Sigma; \bullet \vdash e : \tau$ then: either e is a dynamic expression e_d; or, for every store μ such that $\vdash \mu : \Sigma$, we have: either $\mu, e \longrightarrow_s$ error, or, there exists an e', a new store typing $\Sigma' \supseteq \Sigma$ and a new store μ' such that: $(\mu, e) \longrightarrow (\mu', e')$; $\vdash \mu' : \Sigma'$; and $\bullet; \Sigma'; \bullet \vdash e' : \tau$.*

Collapsing extension variables. Last, we have proved the fact that under the conditions described in Sec. 5, it is possible to collapse a term t into a term t' which is typed under the empty extension variables context; a substitution σ with which we can regain the original term t exists. This suggests that whenever a proof object t for a specific proposition is required, an equivalent proof object that does not mention uninstantiated extension variables exists. Therefore, we can write an equivalent proof script producing the collapsed proof object instead, and evaluate that script statically. The statement of this theorem is the following:

Theorem 6.3 *If $\Psi \vdash [\Phi]t : [\Phi]t_T$ and $\mathsf{collapsible}(\Psi \vdash [\Phi]t : [\Phi]t_T)$, then there exist Φ', t', t'_T and σ such that $\bullet \vdash \Phi'$ wf, $\bullet \vdash [\Phi']t' : [\Phi']t'_T$, $\Psi; \Phi \vdash \sigma : \Phi'$, $t' \cdot \sigma = t$ and $t'_T \cdot \sigma = t_T$.*

The main idea behind the proof is to maintain a number of substitutions and their inverses: one to go from a general Ψ extension context into an "equivalent" Ψ' context, which includes only definitions of the form $[\Phi]\,t$, for a constant Φ context that uses no extension variables. Then, another substitution and its inverse are maintained to go from that extension variables context into the empty one; this is simpler, since terms typed under Ψ' are already essentially free of metavariables. The computational content within the proof amounts to a procedure for transforming proof scripts inside tactics into static proof scripts.

7. Implementation

We have completed a prototype implementation of the VeriML language, as described in this paper, that supports all of our claims. We have built on our existing prototype [Stampoulis and Shao 2010] and have added an extensive set of new features and improvements. The prototype is written in OCaml and is about 6k lines of code. Using the prototype we have implemented a number of examples, that are about 1.5k lines of code. Readers are encouraged to download and try the prototype from `http://flint.cs.yale.edu/publications/supc.html`.

New features. We have implemented the new features we have described so far: context matching, non-linear patterns, proof-erasure semantics, staging, and inferencing for logical and computational terms. Proof-erasure semantics are utilized only if requested by a per-function flag, enabling us to selectively "trust" tactics. The staging construct we support is more akin to the $\langle\cdot\rangle_{\text{static}}$ form described as syntactic sugar in Sec. 5, and it is able to infer the collapsing substitutions that are needed, following the approach used in our metatheory.

Changes. We have also changed quite a number of things in the prototype and improved many of its aspects. A central change, mediated by our new treatment of the conversion rule, was to modify the used logic in order to use the explicit equality approach; the existing prototype used the λHOL_c logic. We also switched the variable representation to the hybrid deBruijn levels-deBruijn indices technique we described, which enabled us to implement subtyping based on context subsumption. Also, we have adapted the typing rules of the pattern matching construct in order to support refining the environment based on the current branch.

Examples implemented. We have implemented a number of examples to support our claims. First, we have written the type-safe conversion check routine for $\beta\mathbb{N}$, and extended it to support congruence closure based on equalities in the context. Proofs of this latter tactic are constructed automatically through static proof scripts, using a naive rewriter that is non-terminating in the general case. We have also completed proofs for theorems of arithmetic for the properties of addition and multiplication, and used them to write an arithmetic simplification tactic. All of the theorems are proved by making essential use of existing conversion rules, and are immediately added into new conversion rules, leading to a compact and clean development style. The resulting code does not need to make use of translation validation or proof by reflection, which are typically used to implement similar tactics in existing proof assistants.

Towards a practical proof assistant. In order to facilitate practical proof and program construction in VeriML, we introduced some features to support surface syntax, enabling users to omit most details about the environments of contextual terms and the substitutions used with meta-variables. This syntax follows the style of Delphin, assuming an ambient logical variable environment which is extended through a construct denoted as $\nu x : t.e$. Still, the full power of contextual modal type theory is available, which is crucial in order to change what the current ambient environment is, used, as we saw earlier, for static calls to tactics. In general the surface syntax leads to much more concise and readable code.

Last, we introduced syntax support for calls to tactics, enabling users to write proof expressions that look very similar to proof scripts in current proof assistants. We developed a rudimentary ProofGeneral mode for VeriML, that enables us to call the VeriML type-checker and interpreter for parts of source files. By adding holes to our sources, we can be informed by the type inference mechanism about their expected types. Those types correspond to what the current "proof state" is at that point. Therefore, a possible workflow for developing tactics or proofs, is writing the known parts, inserting holes in missing points to know what remains to be proved, and calling the typechecker to get the proof state information. This workflow corresponds closely to the interactive proof development support in proof assistants like Coq and Isabelle, but generalizes it to the case of tactics as well.

8. Related work

There is a large body of work that is related to the ideas we have presented here.

Techniques for robust proof development. There have been multiple proposals for making proof development inside existing proof assistants more robust. A well-known technique is *proof-by-reflection* [Boutin 1997]: writing total and certified decision procedures within the functional language contained in a logic like CIC. A recently introduced technique is *automation through canonical structures* [Gonthier et al. 2011]: the resolution mechanism for finding instances of canonical structures (a generalization of type classes) is cleverly utilized in order to program automation procedures for specific classes of propositions. We view both approaches as somewhat similar, as both are based in cleverly exploiting static "interpreters" that are available in a modern proof assistant: the partial evaluator within the conversion rule in the former case; the unification algorithm within instance discovery in the latter case.

Our approach can thus be seen as similar, but also as a generalization of these approaches, since a general-purpose programming model is supported. Therefore, users do not have to adapt to a specific programming style for writing automation code, but can rather use a familiar functional language. Proof-by-reflection could perhaps be used to support the same kind of extensions to the conversion rule; still, this would require reflecting a large part of the logic in itself, through a prohibitively complicated encoding. Both techniques are applicable to our setting as well and could be used to provide benefits to large developments within our language.

The style advocated in Chlipala [2011] (and elsewhere) suggests that proper proof engineering entails developing sophisticated automation tactics in a modular style, and extending their power by adding proved lemmas as hints. We are largely inspired by this approach, and believe that our introduction of the extensible conversion rule and static checking of tactics can significantly benefit it. We demonstrate similar ideas in layering conversion tactics.

Traditional proof assistants. There are many parallels of our work with the *LCF family of proof assistants*, like HOL4 [Slind and Norrish 2008] and HOL-Light [Harrison 1996], which have served as inspiration. First, the foundational logic that we use is similar. Also, our use of a dedicated ML-like programming language to program tactics and proof scripts is similar to the approach taken by HOL4 and HOL-Light. Last, the fact that no proof objects need to be generated is shared. Still, checking a proof script in HOL requires evaluating it fully. Using our approach, we can selectively evaluate parts of proof scripts; we focus on conversion-like tactics, but we are not limited inherrently to those. This is only possible because our proof scripts carry proof state information within their types. Similarly, proof scripts contained within LCF tactics cannot be evaluated statically, so it is impossible to establish their validity upon tactic definition. It is possible to do a transformation similar to ours manually (lifting proof scripts into auxiliary lemmas that are proved prior to the tactic), but the lack of type information means that many more details need to be provided.

The Coq proof assistant [Barras et al. 2010] is another obvious point of reference for our work. We will focus on the conversion rule that CIC, its accompanying logic, supports – the same problems with respect to proof scripts and tactics that we described in the LCF case also apply for Coq. The conversion rule, which identifies computationally equivalent propositions, coupled with the rich type universe available, opens up many possibilities for constructing small and efficiently checkable proof objects. The implementation of the conversion rule needs to be part of the trusted base of the proof assistant. Also, the fact that the conversion check is built-in to the proof assistant makes the supported equivalence rigid and non-extensible by frequently used decision procedures.

There is a large body of work that aims to extend the conversion rule to arbitrary confluent rewrite systems (e.g. Blanqui et al. [1999]) and to include decision procedures [Strub 2010]. These approaches assume some small or larger addition to the trusted base, and extend the already complex metatheory of Coq. Furthermore, the NuPRL proof assistant [Constable et al. 1986] is based on extensional type theory which includes an extensional conversion rule. This enables complex decision procedures to be part of conversion; but it results in a very large trusted base. We show how, for a subset of these type theories, the conversion check can be recovered outside the trusted base. It can be extended with arbitrarily complex new tactics, written in a familiar programming style, without any metatheoretic additions and without hurting the soundness of the logic. The question of whether these type theories can be supported in full remains as future work, but as far as we know, there is no inherrent limitation to our approach.

Dependently-typed programming. The large body of work on dependently-typed languages has close parallels to our work. Out of the multitude of proposals, we consider the Russell framework [Sozeau 2006] as the current state-of-the-art, because of its high expressivity and automation in discharging proof obligations. In our setting, we can view dependently-typed programming as a specific case of tactics producing complex data types that include proof objects. Static proof scripts can be leveraged to support expressivity similar to the Russell framework. Furthermore, our approach opens up a new intriguing possibility: dependently-typed programs whose obligations are discharged statically and automatically, through code written within the same language.

Last, we have been largely inspired by the work on languages like Beluga [Pientka and Dunfield 2008] and Delphin [Poswolsky and Schürmann 2008], and build on our previous work on VeriML [Stampoulis and Shao 2010]. We investigate how to leverage type-safe tactics, as well as a number of new constructs we introduce, so as to offer an extensible notion of proof checking. Also, we address the issue of statically checking the proof scripts contained within tactics written in VeriML. As far as we know, our development is the first time languages such as these have been demonstrated to provide a workflow similar to interactive proof assistants.

Acknowledgments

We thank anonymous referees for their suggestions and comments on an earlier version of this paper. This research is based on work supported in part by DARPA CRASH grant FA8750-10-2-0254 and NSF grants CCF-0811665, CNS-0910670, and CNS 1065451. Any opinions, findings, and conclusions contained in this document are those of the authors and do not reflect the views of these agencies.

References

H.P. Barendregt and H. Geuvers. Proof-assistants using dependent type systems. In A. Robinson and A. Voronkov, editors, *Handbook of Automated Reasoning*. Elsevier Sci. Pub. B.V., 1999.

B. Barras, S. Boutin, C. Cornes, J. Courant, Y. Coscoy, D. Delahaye, D. de Rauglaudre, J.C. Filliâtre, E. Giménez, H. Herbelin, et al. The Coq proof assistant reference manual (version 8.3), 2010.

F. Blanqui, J.P. Jouannaud, and M. Okada. The calculus of algebraic constructions. In *Rewriting Techniques and Applications*, pages 671–671. Springer, 1999.

F. Blanqui, J.P. Jouannaud, and P.Y. Strub. A calculus of congruent constructions. *Unpublished draft*, 2005.

S. Boutin. Using reflection to build efficient and certified decision procedures. *Lecture Notes in Computer Science*, 1281:515–529, 1997.

A. Chlipala. Mostly-automated verification of low-level programs in computational separation logic. In *Proceedings of the 2011 ACM SIGPLAN conference on Programming Language Design and Implementation*. ACM, 2011.

R.L. Constable, S.F. Allen, H.M. Bromley, W.R. Cleaveland, J.F. Cremer, R.W. Harper, D.J. Howe, T.B. Knoblock, N.P. Mendler, P. Panangaden, et al. *Implementing Mathematics with the Nuprl Proof Development System*. Prentice-Hall, NJ, 1986.

R. Davies and F. Pfenning. A modal analysis of staged computation. In *Proceedings of the 23rd ACM SIGPLAN-SIGACT symposium on Principles of programming languages*, pages 258–270. ACM, 1996.

G. Gonthier. Formal proof–the four-color theorem. *Notices of the AMS*, 55 (11):1382–1393, 2008.

G. Gonthier, B. Ziliani, A. Nanevski, and D. Dreyer. How to make ad hoc proof automation less ad hoc. In *Proceeding of the 16th ACM SIGPLAN International Conference on Functional Programming*, pages 163–175. ACM, 2011.

J. Harrison. HOL Light: A tutorial introduction. *Lecture Notes in Computer Science*, pages 265–269, 1996.

G. Klein, K. Elphinstone, G. Heiser, J. Andronick, D. Cock, P. Derrin, D. Elkaduwe, K. Engelhardt, R. Kolanski, M. Norrish, et al. seL4: Formal verification of an OS kernel. In *Proceedings of the ACM SIGOPS 22nd Symposium on Operating Systems Principles*, pages 207–220. ACM, 2009.

X. Leroy. Formal verification of a realistic compiler. *Communications of the ACM*, 52(7):107–115, 2009.

T. Nipkow, L.C. Paulson, and M. Wenzel. Isabelle/HOL : A Proof Assistant for Higher-Order Logic, volume 2283 of LNCS, 2002.

B. Pientka and J. Dunfield. Programming with proofs and explicit contexts. In *Proceedings of the 10th international ACM SIGPLAN conference on Principles and Practice of Declarative Programming*, pages 163–173. ACM New York, NY, USA, 2008.

A. Poswolsky and C. Schürmann. Practical programming with higher-order encodings and dependent types. *Lecture Notes in Computer Science*, 4960:93, 2008.

V. Siles and H. Herbelin. Equality is typable in semi-full pure type systems. In *2010 25th Annual IEEE Symposium on Logic in Computer Science*, pages 21–30. IEEE, 2010.

K. Slind and M. Norrish. A brief overview of HOL4. *Theorem Proving in Higher Order Logics*, pages 28–32, 2008.

M. Sozeau. Subset coercions in coq. In *Proceedings of the 2006 International Conference on Types for Proofs and Programs*, pages 237–252. Springer-Verlag, 2006.

A. Stampoulis and Z. Shao. VeriML: Typed computation of logical terms inside a language with effects. In *Proceedings of the 15th ACM SIGPLAN International Conference on Functional Programming*, pages 333–344. ACM, 2010.

A. Stampoulis and Z. Shao. Static and user-extensible proof checking (extended version). Available in the ACM Digital Library, 2012.

P.Y. Strub. Coq modulo theory. In *Proceedings of the 24th International Conference on Computer Science Logic*, pages 529–543. Springer-Verlag, 2010.

Run Your Research

On the Effectiveness of Lightweight Mechanization

Casey Klein[1] John Clements[2] Christos Dimoulas[3] Carl Eastlund[3] Matthias Felleisen[3]
Matthew Flatt[4] Jay A. McCarthy[5] Jon Rafkind[4] Sam Tobin-Hochstadt[3] Robert Bruce Findler[1]

PLT

[1]Northwestern University, Evanston, IL [2]California Polytechnic State University, San Luis Obispo, CA
[3]Northeastern University, Boston, MA [4]University of Utah, Salt Lake City, UT [5]Brigham Young University, Provo, UT

Abstract

Formal models serve in many roles in the programming language community. In its primary role, a model communicates the idea of a language design; the architecture of a language tool; or the essence of a program analysis. No matter which role it plays, however, a faulty model doesn't serve its purpose.

One way to eliminate flaws from a model is to write it down in a mechanized formal language. It is then possible to state theorems about the model, to prove them, and to check the proofs. Over the past nine years, PLT has developed and explored a lightweight version of this approach, dubbed Redex. In a nutshell, Redex is a domain-specific language for semantic models that is embedded in the Racket programming language. The effort of creating a model in Redex is often no more burdensome than typesetting it with LaTeX; the difference is that Redex comes with tools for the semantics engineering life cycle.

In this paper we report on a validation of this form of lightweight mechanization. The largest part of this validation concerns the formalization and exploration of nine ICFP 2009 papers in Redex, an effort that uncovered mistakes in all nine papers. The results suggest that Redex-based lightweight modeling is effective and easy to integrate into the work flow of a semantics engineer. This experience also suggests lessons for the developers of other mechanization tools.

Categories and Subject Descriptors D.3.1 [*Programming Languages*]: Formal Definitions and Theory—Semantics

General Terms Design, Reliability, Theory

Keywords Lightweight Semantics Engineering

1. The Role of Language Models

Programming language researchers use formal models to communicate ideas in a concise manner. Many of their models explain a small piece of language design, perhaps a new linguistic construct or a new type system. Other models express the essence of a compiler transformation, the software architecture of an IDE tool, or the workings of a program analysis. For decades researchers have used paper and pencil to develop these models. Paper-and-pencil models come with flaws, however. Since flawed models can lead to miscommunications, researchers state and prove theorems about models, which forces them to "debug" the model.

Some flaws nevertheless survive this paper-only validation step, and others are introduced during typesetting. These mistakes become obstacles to communication. For example, Martin Henz from National University of Singapore recently shared with one of this paper's authors his frustration with a historic paper (Plotkin 1975):

> *The readability is not helped by the fact that there are lots of typos, e.g. page 134, Rule II 1: M = N should be M = M. The rule II 3 on page 136 is missing the subscript 1 above the bar. [personal communication, 6/4/2011]*

Once the reader understands a model, fixing such typos is straightforward. But during the initial struggle with the paper, flawed rules may pose seemingly insurmountable obstacles to the reader. In contrast, authors who have spent months or years exploring the intricacies of their model are prone to discount the significance of typos and small mistakes even if readers report extreme frustration.

Over the past decade, mechanized theorem proving has come into its own as one alternative to the paper-and-pencil approach (Aydemir et al. 2005). In this world, researchers "program" their models in formal languages, state theorems, and create machine-checked proofs. We consider this kind of theorem proving heavyweight, because it requires more explicit details than programming.

An alternative is to program models in functional languages such as Haskell: creating interpreters, typecheckers, etc. This approach provides important mechanical scrutiny, but the gap between the program and what appears in a paper's figures tends to make the task laborious and reduces the strength of the validation.

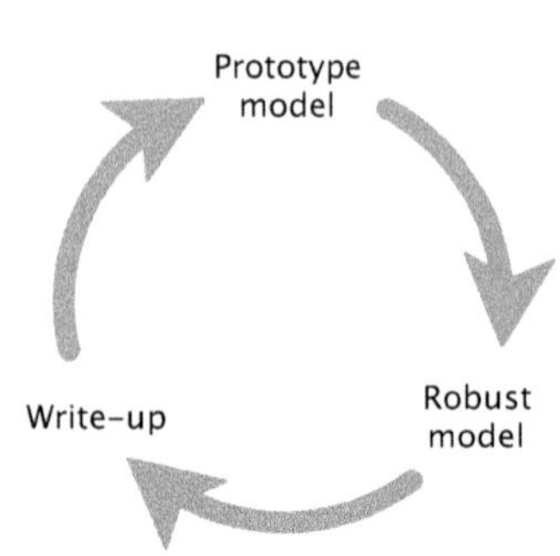

With these considerations in mind, PLT has developed Redex (Matthews et al. 2004; Felleisen et al. 2010), an executable domain-specific language for mechanizing semantic models. The philosophy of Redex is to treat semantic models as software artifacts just like plain software systems. As such, semantic models have a life cycle, and the life cycle idea for semantic models is similar to the one of software systems. Using Redex a semantics engineer formulates the syntax and semantics of the model; creates test suites;

POPL'12, January 25–27, 2012, Philadelphia, PA, USA.

$e ::= (e\ e\ ...)$
$\mid x$
$\mid (\lambda\ (x\ ...)\ e)$
$\mid$ call/cc
$\mid +$
$\mid number$

```
(define-language Λc
  (e (e e ...)
     x
     (λ (x ...) e)
     call/cc
     +
     number)
  (x variable-not-otherwise-mentioned))
```

$e ::= ....\mid (\mathsf{A}\ e)$
$v ::= (\lambda\ (x\ ...)\ e)$
$\mid$ call/cc
$\mid +$
$\mid number$
$E ::= (v\ ...\ E\ e\ ...)$
$\mid []$

```
(define-extended-language
  Λc/red Λc
  (e .... (A e))
  (v (λ (x ...) e)
     call/cc
     +
     number)
  (E (v ... E e ...)
     hole))
```

Figure 1: λ-calculus plus `call/cc`

$$E[(\mathsf{A}\ e)] \longrightarrow e \quad \text{[abort]}$$

$$E[(\text{call/cc}\ v)] \longrightarrow E[(v\ (\lambda\ (x)\ (\mathsf{A}\ E[x])))] \quad \text{[call/cc]}$$
where x fresh

$$E[((\lambda\ (x\ ..._1)\ e)\ v\ ..._1)] \longrightarrow E[e\{x{:=}v, ...\}] \quad [\beta v]$$

$$E[(+\ number\ ...)] \longrightarrow E[\Sigma[[number, ...]]] \quad [+]$$

```
(define red
  (reduction-relation
   Λc/red #:domain e
   (--> (in-hole E (A e))
        e
        "abort")
   (--> (in-hole E (call/cc v))
        (in-hole E (v (λ (x) (A (in-hole E x)))))
        (fresh x)
        "call/cc")
   (--> (in-hole E ((λ (x ..._1) e) v ..._1))
        (in-hole E (subst e (x v) ...))
        "βv")
   (--> (in-hole E (+ number ...))
        (in-hole E (Σ number ...))
        "+")))
```

Figure 2: The Λc reductions

runs random tests on conjectures; uses graphical tools for visualizing examples and debugging; and automatically renders the model as a PDF snippet.

It is our hypothesis that *small Redex efforts quickly pay off for the working semantics engineer.* To validate our hypothesis, we conducted two case studies, and this paper presents the results of these studies. The first shows how Redex helps test a language implementation with a language model. The second shows that the Redex methodology applies to a broad spectrum of contemporary research papers. Specifically, the authors encoded nine ICFP 2009 papers in Redex; equipped the models with unit tests; translated formal and informal claims into testable conjectures; and checked their validity. In the process, we found mistakes in all of the papers, including one whose essential result had been verified in Coq.

The next section reviews the Redex modeling language and tool suite. From there, the paper covers ten case studies. Our experience suggests lessons for the authors of semantic models as well as the designers of validation tools; we discuss these lessons in the paper's final sections, along with related work.

2. Welcome to Redex

Semantics engineers use the Redex language to write down the grammar, reductions, and metafunctions for calculi or transition systems. The language is a domain-specific language embedded in Racket. Redex programmers inherit the DrRacket IDE, a large standard library, and a large set of user-contributed libraries. The Redex toolkit covers a variety of tasks related to executing semantics definitions: a stepper for small-step operational semantics; inspectors for reduction graphs; a unit testing framework; a tool for randomized testing à la QuickCheck (Claessen and Hughes 2000); and automatic typesetting support.

From a linguistic perspective, Redex is a strict functional language with a powerful pattern matcher and domain-specific constructs supporting operational semantics. This section illustrates Redex with a model of the λ-calculus, extended with `call/cc`.

2.1 Grammars

The left-hand side of figure 1 shows the grammar of the language and the corresponding Redex code. The latter binds the Racket-level variable `Λc` to a Redex language, a series of non-terminals and alternatives. In this case, there are two non-terminals, ***e*** and ***x***. The ***e*** non-terminal has six alternatives. The first, application expressions, uses an ellipsis to indicate repetition. In this case, the ellipsis amounts to insisting that each application expression consist of at least one sub-expression. Similarly, the third alternative uses an ellipsis to indicate that λ expressions can bind an arbitrary number of variables. The fourth and fifth alternatives are constants, **call/cc** and **+**, leaving ***x*** and ***number***, two other non-terminals. The ***number*** non-terminal is built-in and matches arbitrary Racket numbers. The production for ***x*** uses the special keyword `variable-not-otherwise-mentioned`. It matches any symbol except **call/cc**, **+**, and **λ** because they are used as terminal symbols elsewhere in the grammar.

To give a reduction semantics to Λc, we add an alternative to ***e*** and define two extra non-terminals. The right-hand side of figure 1 shows both the mathematical extension and the Redex code.

The first position in a `define-extended-language` form names the new language and the second names to the to-be-extended language. Non-terminals appearing in the body of `define-extended-language` replace those of the same name in the old language, unless a `....` appears, in which case the non-terminal is extended. In this case, we extend ***e*** with the expression form (**A** ***e***), which we use to give a reduction semantics for continuations.

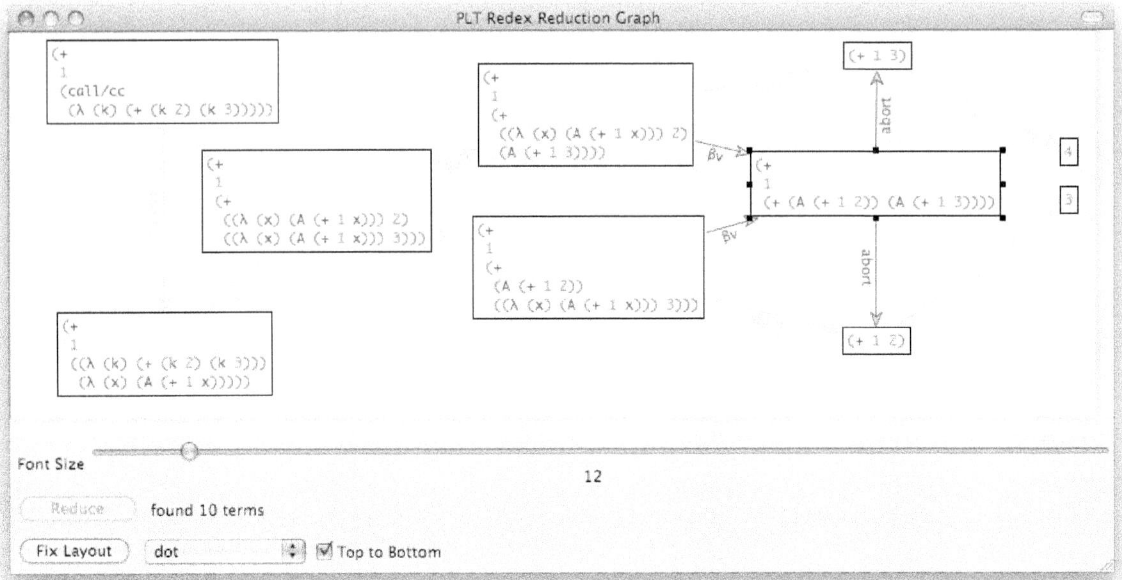

Figure 3: A screenshot of Redex's reduction visualizer

The other non-terminals, v and E, for values and evaluation contexts, respectively, are used to formulate standard reduction rules. The definition of E uses `hole`, a pattern matching construct that represents the hole in a context. Our running example uses two alternatives for evaluation contexts: the first mandates a left-to-right order of evaluation by insisting that evaluation can only take place to the right of values; the second says that a context can be a hole.

2.2 Reduction Relations and Metafunctions

Figure 2 contains the reductions for Λc on the left and the corresponding Redex source code on the right. A reduction relation is defined as a series of rules of the form

```
(--> pat_1 pat_2)
```

where any expression matching `pat_1` is transformed into `pat_2`. The `#:domain` keyword specifies a contract, in this case declaring that `red` relates terms matching the pattern e.

With `(in-hole E e)` a Redex programmer specifies a context decomposition, $E[e]$, meaning the first rule aborts the computation by dropping the context around **A** expressions.

The second rule of `red` rewrites (**call/cc** v) into an application of v to a function that behaves like a continuation. The `(fresh x)` annotation in the rule demands that the parameter of the new function does not appear anywhere else in the rewritten expression.

The left-hand side of the third rule uses ellipses with subscripts (`..._1`) to specify that the lengths of the two sequences must match, thus restricting the rule to applications without arity errors. The rule's right-hand side appeals to the metafunction `subst`, which Redex requires to be defined explicitly.

The `define-metafunction` keyword defines a metafunction; the first two positions specify a language and a contract, followed by the cases of the function, each enclosed in a pair of square brackets. The `subst` function recurs on a list of bindings, repeatedly applying a single-variable substitution function:

```
(define-metafunction Λc/red
  subst : e (x v) ... -> e
  [(subst e (x_1 v_1) (x_2 v_2) ...)
   (subst-1 x_1 v_1 (subst e (x_2 v_2) ...))]
  [(subst e) e])
```

The single-variable substitution function is defined as usual.[1]

The final rule appeals to a Σ metafunction. This metafunction exploits Redex's embedding in Racket:

```
(define-metafunction Λc/red
  Σ : number ... -> number
  [(Σ number ...)
   ,(foldr + 0 (term (number ...)))])
```

The right-hand side begins with an `unquote` (written as a comma), meaning that it is evaluated in Racket, and the Racket expression is expected to return a term that is the result of the metafunction. In this case, the function exploits the representation of Λc's numbers as Racket numbers to compute their sum. The expression `(term (number ...))` produces a list of the numbers supplied as arguments to Σ. In general, `term` behaves like `quote`, but also picks up the bindings of pattern variables (`number` in this case) and supports ellipses to indicate repetition.

Finally, Redex provides `apply-reduction-relation` to experiment with reduction relations. It accepts a relation and a term and returns a list of all contractions of the term:

```
> (apply-reduction-relation
   red (term (+ 1 (A (+ 2 3)))))
'((+ 2 3))
```

2.3 Exploring Examples

Redex provides visualization tools for exploring the behavior of examples. The `traces` function accepts a reduction relation and a term and shows the entire reduction graph of the term. To demonstrate the value of these tools, we adjust our reduction system to model an unspecified order of evaluation in the spirit of C:[2]

[1] In this case, it is an exact copy of the example model's substitution function from the Redex website: `http://redex.racket-lang.org/`.

[2] Scheme's unspecified order of evaluation is more sophisticated than C's, but Redex is up to the task (Matthews and Findler 2005; Sperber et al. 2007).

```
(define-extended-language
  any-which-way-Λc Λc/red
  (E (e ... E e ...)
     hole))
```

This extension replaces the *E* non-terminal entirely, allowing reductions to occur in any position inside an application expression.

Next, we use `extend-reduction-relation` to replace the language of the reduction relation (without adding any reductions):

```
(define any-which-way-red
  (extend-reduction-relation
   red any-which-way-Λc))
```

That is, this extension merely re-interprets the existing rules with the new definition of *E*.

This extended language does not satisfy the Church-Rosser property, as a quick experiment with `traces` shows:

```
> (traces any-which-way-red
          (term (+ 1 (call/cc
                      (λ (k)
                        (+ (k 2) (k 3)))))))
```

Figure 3 displays a screenshot of the resulting window. Each box contains a term that the original reduces to and the arrows are labeled with the reduction rule's name that connects the two terms. The arrows connected to the term underneath the mouse cursor are darkened to make them easier to pick out.

2.4 Randomized Testing

Redex's randomized testing support follows QuickCheck. A programmer writes down a property with `redex-check` (Klein and Findler 2009) and Redex generates instances of the property in an attempt to falsify it. Specifically,

```
(redex-check G n e)
```

tests the boolean-valued expression *e*, interpreted as a predicate universally quantified over *n*, by evaluating it at random terms generated from the non-terminal *n* of the grammar *G*.

For example, we can test the property that every expression in Λc is a value or reduces to another expression. To check whether an expression is a value, we use `redex-match`, which tests whether a particular term matches a given pattern; to check whether an expression reduces, we check whether `apply-reduction-relation`'s result is non-empty:

```
> (redex-check
   Λc/red e
   (or (redex-match Λc/red v (term e))
       (cons?
        (apply-reduction-relation
         red (term e)))))
counterexample found after 9 attempts:
S
```

Of course, there are a number of stuck states and Redex quickly finds a simple one, namely a free variable. If we add an explicit reduction to `error` as a way to signal an error for a free variable:

```
(--> (in-hole E x) error "free variable")
```

and then iteratively run the test above, fixing errors as they are discovered, `redex-check` eventually finds all of the (known) stuck states in the model.

2.5 Typesetting

Redex provides automatic typesetting support which transforms a language, reduction relation, metafunction, or a term into PostScript or PDF to be included in a paper. Indeed, all of the typeset versions of elements of the Λc model shown in this paper are generated automatically using Redex.

This example shows Redex's vanilla support for rendering a reduction relation:

```
> (render-reduction-relation red)
```

E[(A e)] $\longrightarrow$ [abort]
e

E[(call/cc v)] $\longrightarrow$ [call/cc]
E[(v (λ (x) (A E[x])))]
where x fresh

E[((λ (x $..._1$) e) v $..._1$)] $\longrightarrow$ [βv]
E[subst[[e, (x v), ...]]]

E[(+ *number* ...)] $\longrightarrow$ [+]
E[Σ[[*number*, ...]]]

The main difference between this rendering of the reduction relation and the one shown on the left in figure 2 is that the rules are oriented vertically instead of horizontally. Adjusting the orientation is a matter of passing a flag to control the basic layout option. In addition, the substitution function is shown here using Redex's default typesetting for metafunctions, **subst**[[e, (x v), ...]]. Redex also provides hooks for tuning the rendering of calls to metafunction, which may be used to render substitution in the conventional style, $e\{x:=v, ...\}$.

When a reduction relation or a metafunction escapes to Racket, Redex renders the Racket code in a monospaced font but with a pink background so it stands out:

```
> (render-metafunction Σ)
```

Σ[[*number*, ...]] = `(foldr + 0` (*number* ...))

Redex programmers can then set hooks to adjust how such fragments are typeset.

3. Redex Models for Production Systems

Redex can help language designers validate their implementations against their specifications with low cost. To demonstrate this thesis, we conducted a case study using the model of delimited control by Flatt et al. (2007). Figure 4 shows the model's complete internal syntax, including forms left out of the original paper's presentation. At the time of the publication of that paper, the model's authors had implemented a Redex model,[3] built a thorough test suite, and mechanically generated their paper's figures from the Redex definitions. They did not, however, employ randomized testing; Redex had no built-in support for it at the time. This section explains how we revisited that model to see if randomized testing could find more issues in a well-tested model. It did: we found mistakes in both the implementation and specification of delimited control.

3.1 Randomized Testing in Redex

The obvious use of randomized testing is to check a paper's claims. Flatt et al. do not explicitly state any theorems, but all is not lost—they do imply that the model is a faithful abstraction of the production Racket implementation. We can therefore test the claim that the implementation produces the result predicted by the model:

```
(redex-check
 delim-cont-grammar e
 (equal? (model-eval (term e))
         (racket-eval (term e))))
```

In this claim, `model-eval` uses Redex to reduce its argument to a value and `racket-eval` evaluates the term via Racket.

[3] Available online: `http://www.cs.utah.edu/plt/delim-cont/`

```
e ::= m | (wcm w m)
m ::= x | v | (e e ...) | (begin e e) | (% e e e) | (dw x e e e)
    | (if e e e) | (set! x e)
v ::= (list v ...) | (λ (x ...) e) | (cont v E) | (comp E)
    | dynamic-wind | abort | current-marks
    | cons | u | n | #f | #t
    | zero? | print | + | first | rest
n ::= number
u ::= call/cc | call/comp | call/cm
w ::= ((v v) ...)
E ::= W | W[(dw x e E e)]
W ::= M | (wcm w M)
M ::= [] | (v ... W e ...) | (begin W e) | (% v W v)
    | (set! x W) | (if W e e)
D ::= [] | E[(dw x e [] e)]
```

Figure 4: The syntax of the delimited control model.

Unlike in QuickCheck, where users specify test generators for the data types they define, Redex derives naive test generators automatically from the language's grammar. In this case, the derived generator has two immediate problems. First, Redex's grammar specifications do not address variable binding. As a result, the generator often produces expressions with free variables, which Racket statically rejects. Second, the *e* non-terminal in figure 4 includes non-surface syntax such as (comp *E*) that Racket programmers cannot write directly. Since our goal is not to prove a proposition but to falsify it, we begin with simple solutions to these problems.

3.2 A Weak Attempt

One possibility is to discard test expressions that contain free variables and to avoid non-surface forms entirely:

```
(redex-check
 delim-cont-grammar e
 (with-handlers ([free-var-exn? (λ (_) #t)])
   (equal? (model-eval (term e))
           (racket-eval (term e))))
 #:prepare drop-non-surface)

; drop-non-surface : expr -> expr
(define (drop-non-surface e) --)
```

This revision discards open expressions by catching unbound identifier errors with an exception handler that reports the test as a success. It eliminates uses of non-surface forms in the generated expression by rewriting them using `drop-non-surface`, which replaces non-surface expressions with one of their sub-expressions or a random constant if there are no sub-expressions.

This approach is naive, but it reveals three previously unknown errors, one in the portion of the semantics shown in the published paper and two in elided definitions:

1. The error visible in the paper's figures[4] is in the definition of evaluation contexts ***M***, reproduced in figure 4. A prompt expression (% ***e e e***) has three sub-expression: a tag used by the other control operators to identify the prompt, a body, and a handler expression that receives values thrown by abort expressions within the dynamic extent of the body. The expressions should be evaluated from left to right, but the definition of ***M*** lacks evaluation contexts corresponding to the first and third sub-expressions. For example, this omission causes evaluation of the following expression to get stuck:

   ```
   > (model-eval (% (+ 1 2) 3 (λ (x) x)))
   'stuck
   ```

2. The model defines function application with a rule like this one:

   ```
   (--> ((λ (x ...) e) v ...)
        (subst* (x ...) (v ...) e)
        "beta")
   ```

   Unlike the corresponding rule in section 2.2, the ellipses have no subscripts. Thus, the rule also applies to expressions with arity mismatches, e.g., ((λ () 1) 2). Reducing this expression with Redex raises a meta-level error because the formal parameters and actual arguments cannot be paired.

3. The reduction rule for zero? expressions may also raise a meta-level exception. The model's Redex encoding, which represents numbers as Racket numbers and primitive operators like + as Racket symbols, appeals to Racket's `zero?` function to reduce (zero? *v*) redexes. But the `zero?` function carries a contract that restricts its application to numbers, making reduction of the expression (zero? +), for example, raise a meta-error instead of producing #f.

[4] See p. 174 of the 2007 ICFP proceedings.

3.3 Refining the Test Generator

Despite our initial success, there is good reason to explore more sophisticated test generation strategies. To start, in one sample of 10,000 expressions produced by Redex's naive generator, only 1,220 contain no free variables, and only 599 of those are not values. We can avoid discarding so many tests by supplying a function `close` that replaces unbound variables with random bound ones or constants when none are bound:

```
(redex-check
 delim-cont-grammar e
 (equal? (model-eval (term e))
         (racket-eval (term e)))
 #:prepare (compose close drop-non-surface))

; close : expr -> closed-expr
(define (close e) --)
```

For this particular model, though, we do not discover any new errors this way.

Redex's test coverage tool suggests another improvement, however. Executing one round of 10,000 random tests fails to exercise 20 of the 30 reduction rules even once. Three more rules, including the β_v rule shown in section 3.2, fire only a few times each.

To exercise these rules, the test generator must make several fortuitous choices. In the case of the β_v rule, the generator must first choose to place an application expression in a position that will ultimately be evaluated. Second, in the application's operator position, the generator must construct an expression that evaluates to a function. Third, in the operand positions, the generator must construct expressions that do not result in runtime errors or discard the continuation containing the application. Fourth, the generator must choose to construct the right number of operands.

We can encourage these choices by providing `redex-check` the hint that it should occasionally use the rules' left-hand sides instead of the more general pattern e as its basis for test generation. The left-hand side of the β_v rule, for example, directly addresses the second and fourth choices above.

Many of the patterns in the rules' left-hand sides, however, refer to non-surface forms, and so we must first replace the pass that removes non-surface expressions with one that transforms them into equivalent surface expressions. For example, expressions equivalent to **comp** values can be constructed from **%** (prompt), **call/comp**, and **abort**. We implement this transformation, as well as ones for the other non-surface forms for which it is possible (see section 3.4), using a function `transform-non-surface` and supply it to `redex-check`, along with the hint to use the `delim-cont-rules` reduction relation.

```
(redex-check
 delim-cont-grammar e
 (equal? (model-eval (term e))
         (racket-eval (term e)))
 #:prepare (compose close transform-non-surface)
 #:source delim-cont-rules)

; transform-non-surface : expr -> expr
(define (transform-non-surface e) --)
```

This technique finds six more previously unknown errors.

Two of these six are mistakes in the model made available with the paper, though they did not appear in the publication:

1. The model includes a semantics for continuation marks, a feature for associating name-value pairs with continuation frames (Clements et al. 2001). The expression (**call/cm** e_k e_v e_t) marks the active continuation frame with key e_k and value e_v then applies the thunk e_t. The expression (**current-marks** e_k e_p) collects all marks for key e_k on frames up to the nearest enclosing prompt tagged with e_p.

   The model's reduction rule for **current-marks** appeals to a metafunction that traverses the delimited context to construct a list of its mark values. This metafunction, however, lacks a case for contexts of the form (**if** E e e), making mark collection undefined within the dynamic extent of the test position of **if** expressions. For example, evaluation of the following expression raises a meta-level error:

```
(% 0
   (call/cm 1 #t
     (λ ()
       (if (first (current-marks 1 0))
           2
           3)))
   (λ (x) x))
```

2. The model's definition of capture-avoiding substitution is wrong. To perform the substitution **subst**[[x_1, e_1, (**λ** (x_2) e_2)]], the model takes care to rename x_2 to a variable not free in e_1, but it fails to avoid choosing x_1 or the free variables of e_2.

The remaining four errors are in the implementation of Racket (version 5.0.2). These errors eluded a hand-crafted test suite and years of production use, but randomized testing finds them quickly:

3. Continuation marks are not represented directly on continuation frames. Instead, a stack of marks is kept in parallel with the stack that represents the continuation. Delimited continuations therefore capture parts of the mark stack, and different slices of the stack involve different base offsets. While restoring part of a continuation to execute a **dynamic-wind** pre-/post-thunk, one of the offsets is installed incorrectly. The resulting crash would only happen for a pre-/post-thunk that is captured in a continuation that is itself captured as an extension of a composed continuation, possibly with a few more ingredients we have yet to identify.
4. This error is similar to the previous one. Like continuation marks, **dynamic-wind** frames are kept in a separate stack that is synchronized with the continuation stack. An offset connecting the two stacks is forced to an incorrect value when composing continuations in certain cases. The mistake produces a crash only after one more round of continuation capture and invocation.
5. Non-composable continuations store a prompt tag and, when they are invoked, the implementation checks that the current continuation includes a prompt with the same tag. Composable continuations come without a tag. The two kinds of continuations share much of the implementation infrastructure, however, and this shared implementation incorrectly stores and checks prompt tags for composable continuations.
6. This error is similar to the previous one. The implementation also performs a prompt-tag check after each the application of each **dynamic-wind** pre-thunk during the process of applying a non-composable continuation. For composable continuations, the implementations should not perform such prompt-tag checks, but once again, the shared implementation performs these checks for both kinds of continuations.

At the time of writing, we still do not fully understand the behavior of the test that discovered the first of these four errors, making the prospect of manually devising a test like it appear dismal. Fortunately, the repair was clear from the resulting core dump.

The implementation's hand-crafted test suite contains tests that get close to finding these errors, but the suite's author did not have the patience to construct tests of the necessary complexity. Patience aside, finding these errors seems to require a degree of uninhibited creativity that is difficult to achieve. Hanford (1970), one of the first to apply randomized testing to the implementation of programming languages, observes about his test generator for PL/1—dubbed "syntax machine"—that

> *[a]lthough as a writer of test cases, the syntax machine is certainly unintelligent, it is also uninhibited. It can test a [language] processor with many combinations that would not be thought of by a human test case writer.*

3.4 Unwelcome Errors

In addition to these nine errors, we found many more which we would have preferred to avoid—errors in the specification relating the model to its implementation and errors in the post-generation passes. We mention their discovery not as successes of randomized testing but as a reminder of its cost.

Formalizing the relationship between the model and its implementation with enough precision to test it is a non-trivial task. The primary challenge is to decide which non-surface expressions from figure 4 are well-formed. For example, the grammar includes continuation frames that contain two marks at a single key, but such configurations should not occur. Developing a specification that includes these invariants takes some effort. We used randomized testing to find expressions where violations of unknown invariants yield different behaviors in the model and implementation. There is no guarantee that this sort of randomized test-driven development results in a complete specification, but we are satisfied as long as the working draft avoids false positives in our tests.

The source of most unwelcome errors was our implementation of the passes that enforce well-formedness of non-surface expressions, transform well-formed ones into surface expressions, and remove free variables. Together, these passes comprise 259 non-comment, non-whitespace lines of code.

4. An Empirical Study of ICFP Papers

To improve our understanding of how lightweight metatheory mechanization can help authors with their papers, we used Redex to explore nine papers from the ICFP 2009 proceedings. The papers were chosen because we considered them suitable for mechanization in Redex, but some turned out to be challenges.

The nine papers include two which had already been mechanized. We chose two such papers not really expecting to find errors, but to see if we would learn something about Redex when implementing papers that already had a significant mechanized metatheory effort put into them.

We found mistakes in all nine papers, with less effort in each case than exhibited in section 3. We explain most of the errors we found below, in the order in which the papers appear in the 2009 proceedings. We omit some uninteresting errors common to multiple systems (e.g., confusing the particular object-language variable `x` with the meta-variable V that ranges over object-language variables). The authors of the papers we studied have confirmed the errors described here. The Redex models are available online: `www.eecs.northwestern.edu/~robby/lightweight-metatheory/`

4.1 *Safe functional reactive programming through dependent types* by Neil Sculthorpe and Henrik Nilsson

Sculthorpe and Nilsson (2009) define a functional reactive programming language embedded in Agda (Norell 2007). The embedded language's dependent type system rules out domain-specific errors such as loops with immediate feedback and uses of uninitialized signals. Its operational semantics, given as an Agda function defining discrete evaluation steps, carries a machine-checked proof of type safety since Agda accepts the function as total.

The paper does not show the Agda definition; it instead presents the semantics in the usual inference rules notation for big-step semantics. Encoding the paper's formulation in Redex revealed one error, introduced in the manual translation of the Agda code to nearly three full pages of figures. Specifically, the conclusion of the ϕ_1-DSW-EV rule in the paper's figure 6 applies to *switch* expressions; it should apply to *dswitch* expressions.

This paper has since been revised (Sculthorpe 2011).

4.2 *Causal commutative arrows and their optimization* by Hai Liu, Eric Cheng, and Paul Hudak

Liu et al. (2009) define a class of recursive arrows that they call *causal commutative arrows* (CCA) and show how they can be compiled into a single imperative loop. Our focus was the portion of the transformation that they describe formally, a procedure for computing an efficient normal form they call *causal commutative normal form* (CCNF).

The procedure takes the form of a normalization relation $\Downarrow$ that reduces expressions bottom-up using a relation $\mapsto$ based on the standard arrow axioms (Hughes 2000). For example, the normalization rule for sequential compositions $e_1 \ggg e_2$ normalizes the sub-expressions, reduces the result, then normalizes the contractum.

$$\frac{e_1 \Downarrow e_1' \qquad e_2 \Downarrow e_2' \qquad (e_1' \ggg e_2') \mapsto e \qquad e \Downarrow e'}{e_1 \ggg e_2 \Downarrow e'}$$

Using randomized testing to check whether $\Downarrow$ is indeed a function with the claimed domain and codomain found two problems:

1. In addition to arrow constructors, the language on which $\Downarrow$ is defined includes functions and pairs; consequently, some arrow-typed expression do not have arrow constructors at their roots. The proof in the paper's appendix mentions that such expressions must first be β-reduced, but there are no corresponding steps in the $\Downarrow$ definition.
2. Reduction via the $\mapsto$ relation creates arrows built from the *loopB* combinator, defined in terms of the primitive CCA constructors. To account for *loopB* expressions, the $\Downarrow$ relation includes the following rule:

$$\frac{f \Downarrow f' \qquad loopB\ i\ f' \mapsto e \qquad e \Downarrow e'}{loopB\ i\ f \Downarrow e'}$$

   For some f, $loopB\ i\ f'$ is already in normal form. In these cases there is no e such that $loopB\ i\ f' \mapsto e$, leaving the rule's second premise unsatisfiable (and the implied procedure stuck).

This paper has since been revised (Liu et al. 2011).

4.3 *Partial memoization of concurrency and communication* by Lukasz Ziarek, KC Sivaramakrishnan, and Suresh Jagannathan

Ziarek et al. (2009) show how memoization can be applied in a concurrent language with synchronous message-passing primitives. To show that memoization preserves meaning, they define two evaluators for a concurrent language, one that uses memoization and one that does not. Encoding these systems in Redex exposed two mistakes:

1. The paper's theoretical result is a safety theorem guaranteeing that when memoized evaluation takes a state P to a state P', then non-memoized evaluation takes $\mathcal{T}[\![P]\!]$ to $\mathcal{T}[\![P']\!]$, where the meta-function $\mathcal{T}$ erases the extra structure used for memoization. As randomized testing quickly discovers, this theorem is false. It fails to exclude states in which the memo table incorrectly predicts the behavior of some function. The correspondence appears to hold for executions beginning with the empty table (the important case), but the proof's inductive structure requires a generalized claim about states with non-empty but well-formed tables. A proof typically gives this generalization explicitly, since well-formedness conditions for such accumulated data structures tend to be complex.
2. The non-memoizing evaluator operates on program states P taken from the following grammar, in which t ranges over thread identifiers and e ranges over expressions:

$$P ::= P \parallel P \mid t[e]$$

   Because a state P contain sat least one thread, the following communication rule cannot apply in the absence of a third thread:

$$\frac{P = P' \parallel t[E[send(l,v)]] \parallel t'[E'[recv(l)]]}{P \longmapsto P' \parallel t[E[unit]] \parallel t'[E'[v]]}$$

   The same problem exists with the memoizing evaluator.

4.4 *A concurrent ML library in Concurrent Haskell* by Avik Chaudhuri

Chaudhuri (2009) describes a way to implement the Concurrent ML primitives (Reppy 1999) in a language that supports only first-order message passing, such as Concurrent Haskell (Jones et al. 1996). He builds an abstract machine that abstracts the message-passing model common to Concurrent Haskell and other concurrent systems and then shows how programs using the Concurrent ML primitives may be compiled into terms in his abstract machine, while preserving safety, progress, and fairness.

We encoded this abstract machine, source language, and compiler in Redex. In addition to writing test cases by hand, we used randomized testing to check a weak variant of the paper's correctness theorem. Randomized testing did not produce any counterexamples to the theorem, but it did lead us to programs for which the abstract machine consumes unbounded resources where proper Concurrent ML implementations would not.

For example, consider the following source expression, in which `c` is a fresh channel:

```
select(in c, out c)
```

This expression permanently blocks any thread that evaluates it because `select` cannot perform either communication. In Concurrent ML, garbage collection reclaims this thread because no other thread can reach the channel; the abstract machine, on the other hand, performs infinitely many steps for this expression—effectively busy waiting for an event that cannot occur. This error also shows up in the released implementation of the Concurrent ML library for Concurrent Haskell based on the abstract machine.

4.5 *Automatically RESTful web applications: marking modular serializable continuations* by Jay McCarthy

McCarthy (2009) extends a technique for implementing first-class continuations via continuation marks (Pettyjohn et al. 2005), adding support for source programs that themselves use continuation marks. Despite a pencil-and-paper proof of correctness, a combination of manual and randomized testing found five errors in the translation's specification, as well as three errors in the semantics of its source and target languages:

1. The translation consists of four mutually recursive functions: one for translating values and expressions that would be values if not for a variable in some component, one for redexes, one for evaluation contexts, and a driver function that either defers to the values translation or decomposes the input and applies the translations for redexes and evaluation contexts. This schema relies on a unique decomposition lemma that turns out not to hold, due to four mistakes in the grammars for redexes and evaluation contexts.
2. The source and target languages are variants of A-normal form (Flanagan et al. 1993), but the translation of evaluation contexts inserts applications in a position that does not allow them. Adapting translation to preserve A-normal form seems to require abandoning the invariant that evaluation contexts translate to evaluation contexts rather than more general contexts, which the translation for continuation values assumes. In practice, there is no need to translate such values anyway, since they do not appear in the source text of realistic programs.
3. In translated programs, `call/cc` produces a procedure that discards the current continuation using `abort` then calls a function `resume` for rebuilding the captured continuation from a data representation of its frames. A mistake in the definition of `resume`, however, causes it to leave some frames out of the rebuilt continuation.
4. The translation's handling of continuation marks in the original program involves installing an additional mark on each frame. This mark holds a data structure that records all of the other marks on the associated frame. To maintain this cumulative mark, the translated program first fetches its current value using `c-w-i-c-m` ("call with immediate continuation mark"), which has the following signature:

   $$\texttt{c-w-i-c-m: key } (\alpha \texttt{ -> } \beta)\ \alpha \texttt{ -> } \beta$$

   This function examines the active frame's marks and calls the provided function with the value associated with the given key or the provided default value if there is no such mark. The translation's `c-w-i-c-m` call forgets the mandatory third argument.
5. The translation lacks recursive calls for two of the three positions inside the `(w-c-m e e e)` form, used for installing continuation marks.
6. Instead of including an explicit form for dereferencing store pointers, the source language semantics has two rules for each form that demands its operand. For example, in addition to the usual β_v rule, there is a rule that applies when the function position holds a pointer σ:

   $$\Sigma / E[(\sigma\ \overline{v})] \quad \longrightarrow_{SL} \quad \Sigma / E[e[\overline{x \mapsto v}]] \quad \text{where} \quad \Sigma(\sigma) = (\lambda\ (\overline{x})\ e)$$

   But with the usual definition of store-lookup (the author's intention), this strategy does not handle pointers to pointers to functions.
7. The source language semantics lacks a rule like the following, for indirect continuation application.

   $$\Sigma / E[(\sigma\ v)] \quad \longrightarrow_{SL} \quad \Sigma / E'[v] \quad \text{where} \quad \Sigma(\sigma) = \kappa.E'$$

8. The source and target languages provide a form `(c-c-m e ...)` for collecting continuation marks. This form is similar to the `current-marks` operator explained in section 3.3, but there are two differences. First, `c-c-m` has no prompt-tag operand, since the source and target languages do not provide delimited control. Second, `c-c-m` collects the marks for several keys at once. Its result should be a list of lists, in which the inner lists contain the marks on each continuation frame; as defined in the semantics, however, the marks for the final frame become the list's tail instead of its last element.

4.6 *Control-flow analysis of function calls and returns by abstract interpretation* by Jan Midtgaard and Thomas P. Jensen

Midtgaard and Jensen (2009) systematically derive a tail-call sensitive control-flow analysis using abstract interpretation and then prove that their analysis is equivalent to a CPS-based one from earlier work. We discovered two problems with the paper:

1. The CPS transformation's domain contains expressions with constants, but there is no case in the transformation functions to deal with the constants. This leads to a problem in lemma 5.1, which states that transforming a program to CPS and then transforming it back results in the original program. As stated, this lemma is only true for programs that contain no constants.
2. The paper defines $\equiv$ to be the least equivalence relation on expressions satisfying these two equations:

   `let x = t in s` $\equiv$ `s`   `let x = t0 t1 in s` $\equiv$ `s`

   and the analysis result includes a mapping from representative elements of this equivalence class to the values that the corresponding expressions have at runtime. This definition of $\equiv$ breaks the equivalence of the direct-style and CPS analysis (theorem 5.1). Specifically, the direct-style analysis imprecisely predicts that `id2` might be returned by the term

   ```
   let W = fn N. (N N) in
     let id1 = fn x1. x1 in
       let id2 = fn x2. x2 in
         let J = (fn t. id2) id1
           let d = (W W) in id2
   ```

   but the CPS analysis correctly predicts that it never returns. The problem is, the equivalence relation equates the two occurrences of `id2` in the above program but should not.

This paper has since been revised (Midtgaard and Jensen 2012).

4.7 *Implementing first-class polymorphic delimited continuations by a type-directed selective CPS-transform* by Tiark Rompf, Ingo Maier, and Martin Odersky

Rompf et al. (2009) describe an implementation of delimited continuations for Scala. They define a type system that distinguishes expressions with control effects, allowing continuations to be implemented by a selective CPS transformation that leaves expressions in direct style when they do not reify their continuations.

As we discovered while encoding the system in Redex, the paper merely sketches the typing and transformation rules. A modest Redex model can close the gap between a sketch and a consistent description, and our model uncovered a significant omission in the paper's explanation. The definition of the transformation function $[\![.]\!]$ neglects necessary recursive calls on sub-expressions (e.g., on the operand of `shift`).

We did discover one inaccuracy not arising from the rules' informal nature. The transformation, which operates on expressions in A-normal form, distinguishes two classes of non-tail calls that reify their continuations—those where the expression *e* following the call also reifies its continuation (a behavior indicated in *e*'s type) and those where *e* does not. In the latter case, the transformation has an optimization opportunity. In an attempt to exploit the opportunity, the definition of $[\![.]\!]$ mistakenly dispatches on the type of $[\![e]\!]$ instead of the type of *e*, causing it to apply the optimization even when it is unsound.[5]

4.8 *A Theory of typed coercions and its applications* by Nikhil Swamy, Michael Hicks, and Gavin M. Bierman

Swamy et al. (2009) define a proof system for validating particular program rewritings and give conditions under which various program-rewriting systems operate unambiguously. For all results except the ones on rewriting using polymorphic coercions, they provide Coq proof scripts.[6]

We discovered two problems with an example in the section explaining polymorphic coercions. First, one instantiation of a polymorphic coercion is missing. Second, the example is based on the assumption that the rewriting process will leave one particular expression alone when, in fact, it might be rewritten.

4.9 *Complete and decidable type inference for GADTs* by Tom Schrijvers, Simon Peyton Jones, Martin Sulzmann, and Dimitrios Vytiniotis

Schrijvers et al. (2009) define a type system for generalized algebraic datatypes (GADTs), giving both a declarative specification and a sound and complete inference algorithm. Encoding the algorithm in Redex uncovered three flaws in the paper's definition:

1. The type system that Schrijvers et al. consider most natural for GADTs is undecidable. Their key insight is that decidability can be recovered by designating sets of unification variables called *untouchables* that may not be unified to solve certain constraints. The rules for `let` expressions, typed-annotated `let` expressions, and individual `case` clauses introduce these variables, which stand for unknown types. The third of these three rules, however, designates the wrong variables as untouchable.
2. The rule for entire `case` expressions correctly insists that all of its clauses produce a result of the same type β. But instead of assigning the entire `case` the type β, the rule gives it the type α, a meta-variable that does not appear anywhere else in the rule though the notation $\overline{\alpha}$ does appear.
3. The constraint solving algorithm lacks a rule for arrow types.

[5] In an email exchange (Feb. 2, 2011 – Mar. 3, 2011), the paper's lead author stated that they did not intend their model as a precise description. He also explained that they meant for the $[\![.]\!]$ function to be applied by a driver function whose operation accounts for the absent recursive calls. The paper does not mention this driver. This author also reported that the Scala implementation does not make the same optimization mistake as the transformation sketch.

[6] Available online: `http://research.microsoft.com/~nswamy/papers/coercion-proofs.tgz`

4.10 Our Effort

§	Tests	LOC	Props
4.1	24	1196	1
4.2	10	849	5
4.3	32	1197	5
4.4	55	1445	4
4.5	105	1548	3
4.6	148	1159	8
4.7	97	1223	5
4.8	57	1335	3
4.9	67	1143	1
Mean	66	1233	3.88

Our case studies required two kinds of efforts. First, each investigator had to understand his assigned paper to a sufficient degree so that he could formulate a paper-and-pencil model. Second, the investigator had to implement the model in Redex. The adjacent table quantifies the second kind of effort. Each row shows the number of lines of code, the number of test cases, and the number of properties tested for each of the models in the above subsections. On the average, a model consists of 1,200 lines of code, including 66 tests and three or four claims.

5. Lessons Learned

Our experience suggests lessons for the authors of programming languages papers, for us as the developers of Redex, and for the developers of other validation tools.

5.1 Lessons for Authors

Redex supports mechanization in a form that accommodates time-pressed semantics engineers and still uncovers common errors. Although we do not have precise effort logs for the case study of section 4, we estimate that encoding and testing each model required less time than understanding the content of the paper. As our case studies show, lightweight mechanization reduces the number of mistakes in a model and thus increases its value as a communication vehicle.

Flaws aside, we would not have managed to understand these papers without their models. Prose is too imprecise and frequently too brief to build more than a superficial understanding. For example, one of the authors of the present paper would have rated himself an expert reviewer for the paper in section 4.5, having seen the semantics for continuation marks many times and having worked with continuation-based web servers. Despite this preparation, he failed to understand the paper's intuitive explanation of the system until he studied its formal model. In such cases, where the reader primarily relies on the model for explanation, typos—even ones obvious to experts in hindsight—can become significant barriers to communication.

Lightweight mechanization enables interactive exploration, expanding the means with which authors and readers communicate. In the case of every paper, we found that executing examples improved our understanding—even after we had already understood enough of the system to encode at least part of it in Redex. When we were unsure if we understood a definition or if its implications appeared problematic, we ran examples. Often the ones we choose would have been too tedious or too error-prone to work out by hand. Sometimes the experiment confirmed our hypothesis; other times it revealed a mistake in our reasoning. Either way, the exercise improved our understanding of the system.

5.2 Lessons for Redex

Our experience suggests that Redex is a mature technology but also highlights gaps in its ecosystem.

Redex offers little support for handling binding constructs in object languages. It provides a generic function for obtaining a fresh variable but no help in defining capture-avoiding substitution or α-equivalence. Three of the nine papers in section 4 require definitions of one these concepts, and definitions of these concepts facilitate testing in two other papers and the model of section 3. In one case (section 4.4), managing binding in Redex constituted a significant portion of the overall time spent studying the paper. Redex should benefit from a mechanism for dealing with binding, starting from the recently studied approaches (Gabbay and Pitts 2002; Lakin 2010; Pottier 2005; Sewell et al. 2010).

Next, Redex lacks direct support for non-algorithmic relations such as the coercion-insertion theory of Swamy et al. and the declarative typing rules of Schrijvers et al. When we modeled these systems, we were forced to escape to Redex's host language or to adopt an elaborate encoding, which we would not expect a casual Redex user to be comfortable with. Extending Redex with support for logic programming, as in Typol (Despeyroux 1984), Twelf (Pfenning and Schürmann 1999), αProlog (Cheney and Urban 2004), or αML (Lakin 2010) should solve this problem.

At present, Redex also provides no mechanism for specifying structural congruence. This gap complicates the encoding of transition rules such as those Ziarek et al. and Chaudhuri define on concurrent programs. We hope to adapt Maude's (Clavel et al. 2003) associative-commutative matching to Redex's notion of patterns.

Finally, while is often a boon that Redex's random test case generators require little programmer intervention, sometimes they are not as effective as they could be. The generator derived from the grammar in section 3, for example, requires substantial massaging to achieve high test coverage. This deficiency is especially pressing in the case of typed object languages, where the massaging code almost duplicates the specification of the type system.[7] The dynamic-monitoring technique behind Korat (Boyapati et al. 2002) may be effective in automatically constructing tests from the original specification. Alternatively, αProlog's counterexample-search strategies (Cheney and Momigliano 2007) are possibilities with the addition of more declarative support for binding specifications and inference rules.

5.3 Lessons for Developers of Other Tools

Last but not least, our case study suggests several lessons that should apply to all validation tools, regardless of how much they differ from Redex.

First, the lessons for authors concern developers too, since authors require tool support to apply the lessons. In particular, support for execution enables interactive exploration, benefiting authors and readers alike.

Second, tests complement proofs. We encountered five papers in which explicitly claimed theorems are false as stated. In three cases (section 4.2, section 4.6, and section 4.9), we could fix the problems; in the others (section 4.3 and section 4.5), we were unable to find and verify a fix in a modest time frame. In every case, though, rudimentary testing discovered errors missed with pencil-and-paper proofs.

Indeed, we claim that tests complement even machine-checked proofs. As one example, two of the POPLmark solutions that contain proofs of type soundness use call-by-name beta in violation of the specification (Crary and Gacek, personal communication). We believe unit testing would quickly reveal this error.

[7] See Klein et al. (2010, section 7) for another example.

	αML	αProlog	K	Ott	Redex	Ruler
Execution	✓	✓	✓	✓	✓	✓
Unit Tests			✓		✓	
Automated Tests		✓	✓		✓	
Typesetting			✓	✓	✓	✓
Binding	✓	✓	✓	✓		
Visualization			✓		✓	

Figure 5: A comparison of lightweight semantics engineering tools

Even better, one can sometimes test propositions that cannot be validated via proof. Our experience with the model of Racket's delimited control operators provides one example, as no formalization currently exists of the more than 230,000 lines of C and assembly in the Racket implementation. Testing also removes another obstacle to proof, the requirement that we first state the proposition of interest. Due to its exploratory nature, testing can inadvertently falsify unstated but desired propositions, e.g., that threads block without busy waiting (section 4.4). This is especially true for system-level and randomized testing. To some degree, the same is true of proving, but testing seems to be more effective at covering a broad space of system behaviors. Many other validation tools provide some level of support for executing examples without requiring an algorithm to be specified separately; αProlog and Isabelle go so far as to provide tools for automatically falsifying conjectures.

Third, mechanized typesetting avoids many transcription errors. Given the apparent frequency with which we observed typos in ICFP papers and their potential impact on communication, mechanically generating figures from a source subjected to *some* form of mechanical scrutiny seems justified. Ott (Sewell et al. 2010) and Isabelle (Nipkow et al. 2011) already support this workflow.

Fourth, example visualization aids debugging. We relied extensively on Redex's visualization features while investigating the flaws described in section 4, as well as the many more introduced by the manual process of translating figures to Redex. The features have been similarly useful in other efforts, e.g., the formalization of Typed Racket (Tobin-Hochstadt and Felleisen 2008, section 3.4). We conjecture that all validation tools would benefit from visualization components.

6. Related Work

The closest form of related work would be other studies that attempt to validate semantics engineering tools on published formal models, but we are unaware of any such studies. Accordingly, this section focuses on tools that could be used for such studies, large formal models that have been subjected to lightweight forms of validation, and studies of the validity of research results in general.

Other tools. The development of Redex draws inspiration from Alloy (Jackson 2002), a system designed to provide software engineers with a lightweight alternative to theorem proving. With Alloy, software engineers build models of software systems and explore them with mechanical support. Redex seeks to provide a similar experience to semantics engineers.

The Typol system for natural semantics supports a range of tools, providing execution by compilation to Prolog (Despeyroux 1984), a debugger and mechanized typesetting (Despeyroux 1988), and a bridge from lightweight to heavyweight validation (Terrasse 1995). These features and more survive in Redex and other contemporary tools.

Figure 5 provides a comparison between Redex and other modern lightweight semantics engineering tools. All of αML (Lakin 2010), αProlog (Cheney and Urban 2004), K (Rosu and Serbanuta

2010), Ott (Sewell et al. 2010), Redex, and Ruler (Dijkstra and Swierstra 2006) provide support for executing definitions, though in the case of Ott, the precise level of support depends on the particular proof assistant chosen as the backend. αProlog features an automated testing tool similar to `redex-check` but based on bounded-exhaustive search rather than randomized testing. Similarly, K can exploit's Maude's model checker to check predicates. K, Ott, Redex, and Ruler all support mechanized typesetting, but Redex's approach to fine-tuning the output differs—users write Racket code to transform Redex parse trees instead of annotating definitions with LaTeX snippets. αML, αProlog, K, and Ott provide the sort of binding support Redex lacks. Only Redex provides a library of domain-specific constructs for unit-testing and interactive visualization, but K users can write jUnit tests.

Thanks in part to the impetus of the POPLmark Challenge (Aydemir et al. 2005), semantics engineers increasingly use proof assistants (Nipkow et al. 2011; Norell 2007; Pfenning and Schürmann 1999; Slind and Norrish 2008; The Coq Development Team 2010) to validate semantic models. These tools have various levels of support for executing examples, but none share Redex's beginning-to-end support for the semantics engineering life cycle—yet.

Testing Language Definitions. Several groups report success with testing techniques where proof systems fail. For example, Fox (2003), Hardin et al. (2006), Sarkar et al. (2009), and Fox and Myreen (2010) check that they have defined correct models of various assembly and machine languages by comparing their models' answers to the answers produced by actual hardware or by off-the-shelf compilers. Ellison and Rosu (2011) employ similar techniques for C using K. Some of their efforts exploit randomized testing. Klein et al. (2010) also use a randomized technique to compare a model of the Racket virtual machine to the production implementation. The formal model of the R6RS (Sperber et al. 2007) helped catch bugs in the informal, prose specification.

Research Validity. This paper reveals mistakes in our own work and the work of our colleagues. While we did not discover any flaws that invalidate the essential contributions of any of the papers we studied, others have done so. Dwyer et al. (2006) examine several bug-finding systems and invalidate a number of published claims on lowering the search cost; their basic insight is that factors outside the control of an investigator—e.g., the search order for path-sensitive bug-finding tools—may heavily influence the performance of such tools. Similarly, Arcuri and Briand (2011) conduct "a systematic review of the use of randomized algorithms in selected software engineering venues in 2009 [and] show that randomized algorithms are used in a significant percentage of papers but that, in most cases, randomness is not properly accounted for. This casts doubts on the validity of most empirical results assessing randomized algorithms". Further afield, studies concerning the quality of research results are common in the biomedical community. Young et al. (2008), for example, write that "an empirical evaluation of the 49 most-cited papers on the effectiveness of medical interventions, published in highly visible journals in 1990–2004, showed that a quarter of the randomised trials and five of six non-randomised studies had already been contradicted or found to have been exaggerated by 2005."

7. Conclusion

Our validation project confirms the "lightweight mechanization" conjecture. Specifically it establishes Redex as an effective tool that can uncover mistakes in mathematical models of programming languages. The two case studies contribute two different insights.

With the survey of nine ICFP papers we validate the folklore claim that all mathematical papers contain mistakes. Our conclusion is *not* to blame the ICFP authors or reviewers for these mistakes but to suggest the routine use of lightweight tools to write such papers. Every mistake in a published model narrows the communication channel between authors and readers; conversely, we can widen this channel when we equip papers with executable lightweight models that readers can easily explore interactively.

With the case study of delimited continuations in production systems we illustrate how an implementor can benefit from the designers' lightweight model. Redex can help expose errors in an implementation, even a heavily-tested one, merely by testing the correspondence between it and a model. This aspect of semantics engineering is overlooked and deserves more attention, especially for large languages that evolve over many years.

Acknowledgments Thanks to Gavin Bierman, Avik Chaudhuri, Michael Hicks, Suresh Jagannathan, Thomas Jensen, Hai Liu, Jan Midtgaard, Tiark Rompf, Neil Sculthorpe, and Dimitrios Vytiniotis for patient and candid discussions of their work. Thanks also to Henrik Nilsson for helpful comments on a draft of this paper.

The authors gratefully acknowledge support for this research from the NSF, DARPA, and AFOSR.

Bibliography

Andrea Arcuri and Lionel C. Briand. A practical guide for using statistical tests to assess randomized algorithms in software engineering. In *Proc. Intl. Conf. Soft. Eng.* , pp. 1–10, 2011.

Brian E. Aydemir, Aaron Bohannon, Matthew Fairbairn, J. Nathan Foster, Benjamin C. Pierce, Peter Sewell, Dimitrios Vytiniotis, Geoffrey Washburn, Stephanie Weirich, and Steve Zdancewic. Mechanized metatheory for the masses: the POPLMark Challenge. In *Proc. Intl. Conf. Theorem Proving in Higher Order Logics*, Lecture Notes in Computer Science volume 3603, pp. 50–65, 2005.

Chandrasekhar Boyapati, Sarfraz Khurshid, and Darko Marinov. Korat: automated testing based on Java predicates. In *Proc. Intl. Symp. Soft. Testing and Analysis*, pp. 123–133, 2002.

Avik Chaudhuri. A concurrent ML library in Concurrent Haskell. In *Proc. ACM Intl. Conf. Functional Programming*, pp. 269–280, 2009.

James Cheney and Alberto Momigliano. Mechanized metatheory model-checking. In *Proc. Intl. Conf. Principles and Practice of Declarative Programming*, pp. 75–86, 2007.

James Cheney and Christian Urban. αProlog: a logic programming language with names, binding, and α-equivalence. In *Proc. Intl. Conf. Logic Programming*, Lecture Notes in Computer Science volume 3132, pp. 269–283, 2004.

Koen Claessen and John Hughes. QuickCheck: a lightweight tool for random testing of Haskell programs. In *Proc. ACM Intl. Conf. Functional Programming*, pp. 268–279, 2000.

Manuel Clavel, Francisco Durán, Steven Eker, Patrick Lincoln, Narciso Martí-Oliet, José Meseguer, and Carolyn Talcott. Maude 2.0 system. In *Proc. Intl. Conf. Rewriting Techniques and Applications*, Lecture Notes in Computer Science volume 2706, pp. 76–87, 2003.

John Clements, Matthew Flatt, and Matthias Felleisen. Modeling an algebraic stepper. In *Proc. Euro. Symp. Programming*, pp. 320–334, 2001.

Thierry Despeyroux. Executable specification of static semantics. In *Proc. Intl. Symp. Semantics of Data Types*, Lecture Notes in Computer Science volume 173, pp. 215–233, 1984.

Thierry Despeyroux. Typol: a formalism to implement natural semantics. INRIA, Research Report No. 94, 1988.

Atze Dijkstra and S. Doaitse Swierstra. Ruler: programming Type rules. In *Proc. Intl. Symp. Functional and Logic Programming*, Lecture Notes in Computer Science volume 3945, pp. 30–46, 2006.

Matthew B. Dwyer, Suzette Person, and Sebastian G. Elbaum. Controlling factors in evaluating path-sensitive error detection techniques. In *Proc. ACM Symp. Foundations of Soft. Eng.* , pp. 92–104, 2006.

Chucky Ellison and Grigore Rosu. An Executable Formal Semantics of C with Applications. University of Illinois, http://hdl.handle.net/2142/25816, 2011.

Matthias Felleisen, Robert Bruce Findler, and Matthew Flatt. *Semantics Engineering with PLT Redex*. MIT Press, 2010.

Cormac Flanagan, Amr Sabry, Bruce F. Duba, and Matthias Felleisen. The essence of compiling with continuations. In *Proc. ACM Intl. Conf. Functional Programming*, pp. 237–247, 1993.

Matthew Flatt, Gang Yu, Robert Bruce Findler, and Matthias Felleisen. Adding delimited and composable control to a production programming environment. In *Proc. ACM Intl. Conf. Functional Programming*, pp. 165–176, 2007.

Anthony Fox. Formal specification and verification of ARM6. In *Proc. Intl. Conf. Theorem Proving in Higher Order Logics*, Lecture Notes in Computer Science volume 2758, pp. 25–40, 2003.

Anthony Fox and Magnus O. Myreen. A trustworthy monadic formalization of the ARMv7 instruction set architecture . In *Proc. Intl. Conf. Interactive Theorem Proving*, Lecture Notes in Computer Science volume 6172, pp. 243–258, 2010.

Murdoch J. Gabbay and Andrew M. Pitts. A new approach to abstract syntax with variable binding. *Formal Aspects of Computing* 13(3–5), pp. 341–363, 2002.

Kenneth V. Hanford. Automatic generation of test cases. *IBM Systems Journal* 9(4), pp. 244–257, 1970.

David S. Hardin, Eric W. Smith, and William D. Young. A robust machine code proof framework for highly secure applications. In *Proc. Intl. Wksp. ACL2 Theorem Prover and its Applications*, pp. 11–20, 2006.

John Hughes. Generalizing monads to arrows. *Science of Computer Programming* 37(1–3), pp. 67–111, 2000.

Daniel Jackson. Alloy: a lightweight object modelling notation. *ACM Trans. Software Engineering and Methodology* 11(2), pp. 256–290, 2002.

Simon Peyton Jones, Andrew Gordon, and Sigbjorn Finne. Concurrent Haskell. In *Proc. ACM Symp. Principles of Programming Languages*, pp. 295–308, 1996.

Casey Klein and Robert Bruce Findler. Randomized testing in PLT Redex. In *Proc. Scheme and Functional Programming*, pp. 26–36, 2009.

Casey Klein, Matthew Flatt, and Robert Bruce Findler. The Racket virtual machine and randomized testing. 2010. `http://plt.eecs.northwestern.edu/racket-machine/`

Matthew R. Lakin. An Executable Meta-Language for Inductive Definitions with Binders. PhD dissertation, University of Cambridge, 2010.

Hai Liu, Eric Cheng, and Paul Hudak. Causal commutative arrows and their optimization. In *Proc. ACM Intl. Conf. Functional Programming*, pp. 35–46, 2009.

Hai Liu, Eric Cheng, and Paul Hudak. Causal commutative arrows. *J. Functional Programming* 21(4-5), pp. 467–496, 2011.

Jacob Matthews and Robert Bruce Findler. An operational semantics for R5RS Scheme. In *Proc. Scheme and Functional Programming*, pp. 157–165, 2005.

Jacob Matthews, Robert Bruce Findler, Matthew Flatt, and Matthias Felleisen. A visual environment for developing context-sensitive term rewriting systems. In *Proc. Intl. Conf. Rewriting Techniques and Applications*, Lecture Notes in Computer Science volume 3091, pp. 301–311, 2004.

Jay McCarthy. Automatically RESTful web applications: marking modular serializable continuations. In *Proc. ACM Intl. Conf. Functional Programming*, pp. 299–309, 2009.

Jan Midtgaard and Thomas P. Jensen. Control-flow analysis of function calls and returns by abstract interpretation. In *Proc. ACM Intl. Conf. Functional Programming*, pp. 287–298, 2009.

Jan Midtgaard and Thomas P. Jensen. Control-flow analysis of function calls and returns by abstract interpretation. *Information and Computation*, 2012. `http://www.cs.au.dk/~jmi/ANF-CFA`

Tobias Nipkow, Lawrence C. Paulson, and Markus Wenzel. Isabelle/HOL—A Proof Assistant for Higher-Order Logic. Springer Verlag, 2011.

Ulf Norell. Towards a Practical Programming Language Based on Dependent Type Theory. PhD dissertation, Chalmers University of Technology, 2007.

Greg Pettyjohn, John Clements, Joe Marshall, Shriram Krishnamurthi, and Matthias Felleisen. Continuations from generalized stack inspection. In *Proc. ACM Intl. Conf. Functional Programming*, pp. 216–227, 2005.

Frank Pfenning and Carsten Schürmann. System description: Twelf—a meta-logical framework for deductive systems. In *Proc. Intl. Conf. Automated Deduction*, pp. 202–206, 1999.

Gordon D. Plotkin. Call-by-name, call-by-value, and the λ-calculus. *Theoretical Computer Science* 1(2), pp. 125–159, 1975.

François Pottier. An overview of Cαml. In *Proc. ACM SIGPLAN ML Wksp.* , Electronic Notes in Theoretical Computer Science volume 148, pp. 27–52, 2005.

John H. Reppy. *Concurrent Programming in ML*. Cambridge University Press, 1999.

Tiark Rompf, Ingo Maier, and Martin Odersky. Implementing first-class polymorphic delimited continuations by a type-directed selective CPS-transform. In *Proc. ACM Intl. Conf. Functional Programming*, pp. 317–328, 2009.

Grigore Rosu and Traian Florin Serbanuta. An Overview of the K Semantic Framework. *J. Logic and Algebraic Programming* 79(6), pp. 397–434, 2010.

Susmit Sarkar, Peter Sewell, Francesco Zappa Nardelli, Scott Owens, Tom Ridge, Thomas Braibant, Magnus O. Myreen, and Jade Alglave. The semantics of x86-CC multiprocessor machine code. In *Proc. ACM Symp. Principles of Programming Languages*, pp. 379–391, 2009.

Tom Schrijvers, Simon Peyton Jones, Martin Sulzmann, and Dimitrios Vytiniotis. Complete and decidable type inference for GADTs. In *Proc. ACM Intl. Conf. Functional Programming*, pp. 341–352, 2009.

Neil Sculthorpe. Towards Safe and Efficient Functional Reactive Programming. Ph.D. dissertation, University of Nottingham, 2011.

Neil Sculthorpe and Henrik Nilsson. Safe functional reactive programming through dependent types. In *Proc. ACM Intl. Conf. Functional Programming*, pp. 23–34, 2009.

Peter Sewell, Francesco Zappa Nardelli, Scott Owens, Gilles Peskine, Thomas Ridge, Susmit Sarkar, and Rok Strniša. Ott: effective tool support for the working semanticist. *J. Functional Programming* 20(1), pp. 71–122, 2010.

Konrad Slind and Michael Norrish. A brief overview of HOL4. In *Proc. Intl. Conf. Theorem Proving in Higher Order Logics*, Lecture Notes in Computer Science volume 5170, pp. 28–32, 2008.

Michael Sperber, R. Kent Dybvig, Matthew Flatt, Anton van Straaten, Richard Kelsey, William Clinger, Jonathan Rees, Robert Bruce Findler, and Jacob Matthews. Revised [6] report on the algorithmic language Scheme. Cambridge University Press, 2007.

Nikhil Swamy, Michael Hicks, and Gavin M. Bierman. A Theory of typed coercions and its applications. In *Proc. ACM Intl. Conf. Functional Programming*, pp. 329–340, 2009.

Delphine Terrasse. Encoding natural semantics in Coq. In *Proc. Intl. Conf. Algebraic Methodology and Software Technology*, Lecture Notes in Computer Science volume 936, pp. 230–244, 1995.

The Coq Development Team. The Coq Proof Assistant Reference Manual. Version 8.3, 2010. `http://coq.inria.fr/`

Sam Tobin-Hochstadt and Matthias Felleisen. The design and implementation of Typed Scheme. In *Proc. ACM Symp. Principles of Programming Languages*, pp. 395–406, 2008.

Neal S. Young, John P.A. Ioannidis, and Omar Al-Ubaydli. Why Current Publication Practices May Distort Science. *PLoS Med* 5(10), pp. 1418–1422, 2008.

Lukasz Ziarek, KC Sivaramakrishnan, and Suresh Jagannathan. Partial memoization of concurrency and communication. In *Proc. ACM Intl. Conf. Functional Programming*, pp. 161–172, 2009.

Verification of Parameterized Concurrent Programs By Modular Reasoning about Data and Control

Azadeh Farzan Zachary Kincaid

University of Toronto *

azadeh,zkincaid@cs.toronto.edu

Abstract

In this paper, we consider the problem of verifying thread-state properties of multithreaded programs in which the number of active threads cannot be statically bounded. Our approach is based on decomposing the task into two modules, where one reasons about data and the other reasons about control. The data module computes thread-state invariants (e.g., linear constraints over global variables and local variables of one thread) using the thread interference information computed by the control module. The control module computes a representation of thread interference, as an incrementally constructed *data flow graph*, using the data invariants provided by the data module. These invariants are used to rule out patterns of thread interference that can not occur in a real program execution. The two modules are incorporated into a feedback loop, so that the abstractions of data and interference are iteratively coarsened as the algorithm progresses (that is, they become weaker) until a fixed point is reached. Our approach is sound and terminating, and applicable to programs with infinite state (e.g., unbounded integers) and unboundedly many threads. The verification method presented in this paper has been implemented into a tool, called DUET. We demonstrate the effectiveness of our technique by verifying properties of a selection of Linux device drivers using DUET, and also compare DUET with previous work on verification of parameterized Boolean program using the Boolean abstractions of these drivers.

Categories and Subject Descriptors D.2.4 [*Software Engineering*]: Software/Program Verification—Assertion Checkers, Correctness Proofs; F.3.1 [*Logics and Meanings of Programs*]: Specifying and Verifying and Reasoning about Programs—Invariants, Assertions; D.3.1 [*Programming Languages*]: Formal Definitions and Theory—Semantics; D.4.6 [*Operating Systems*]: Security and Protection—Verification

General Terms Verification, Algorithms, Reliability

Keywords Concurrency, Abstract Interpretation, Compositional Reasoning, Data Flow Graphs, Parameterized Programs, Thread Invariants

* Both authors were partially supported by an National Science and Engineering Research Council (NSERC) Discovery Grant for this work.

1. Introduction

Concurrent programs are notoriously hard to verify. Verification of concurrent systems has been a very active area of research in the past few years. There has been significant progress with testing and bug finding techniques, but due to a huge number of possible schedules (even with a fixed input), it is hard to provide useful coverage guarantees. Standard model checking techniques provide coverage, but suffer from the state explosion problem. Static analysis techniques [7, 14, 26, 27, 31, 32] have been successful in checking simple generic properties such as race and deadlock freedom.

There is a large class of concurrent programs that are designed to be executed by an arbitrary number of clients (for example, device drivers, concurrent data structure libraries, and file systems). This class of programs, commonly called *parameterized concurrent programs*, are more difficult to verify than concurrent programs with a fixed number of threads. The verification problem for parameterized systems has been studied extensively [2, 3, 6, 10, 12, 13, 16, 20, 21, 23, 29, 30]; however, the focus has mostly been on verifying *protocols*. These protocols (for example, Lamport's Bakery protocol [24] and Peterson's mutual exclusion algorithm) are often *small* programs, but the reasoning behind their correctness is usually complicated (see Section 7 for a more detailed discussion), specially when functional correctness is the goal (e.g. mutual exclusion). In contrast, we are interested in *large* programs such as device drivers and file systems, where the reasoning behind their correctness is more straightforward. In these programs, undesired inter-thread interference is usually prevented by simple synchronization mechanisms, and the majority of the verification effort is spent in reasoning about the sequential behaviour of each thread. Moreover, we are interested in proving *program assertions*, which is easier to handle than proving functional correctness of protocols. Program assertions are boolean combinations of program expressions that relate shared variables to local variables of a specific thread at a location in that thread. They are expressive enough to include interesting properties of concurrent programs such as the absence of null pointer dereferences or out of bounds array accesses. We believe that this combination of programs and properties is a good candidate for automated verification in the parameterized setting, and is the target of the work presented in this paper.

We propose a static analysis technique that separates the verification task into a data module and a control module. This separation achieves both *precision* and *scalability* for proving assertions correct in concurrent programs with unboundedly many threads. The data module, using an abstract interpreter, computes data invariants for each program location. These invariants are guaranteed to be consistent with the most recent information about inter-thread interference, provided by the control module. The control module, using a deduction system, determines the pattern of inter-thread interference by using the most recent information from the data module about data invariants. The two modules are combined into a feedback loop to collaboratively compute a solution to the verification problem. This strategy can be used to generate *thread-state invariants* for program locations, i.e. invariants that do not refer to the local variables of more than one thread. These invariants can be used for proving the absence of program assertion failures.

One of the enabling ideas of our modular approach is to use a data flow graph as a program representation for performing abstract interpretation. In data flow graphs, only the flow of data is modelled; control constructs (which are irrelevant to a data analysis) are abstracted away. Data flow graphs offer a convenient way to represent the interference between threads: for example, if one thread writes to a global variable at some location u which is subsequently read by another thread at location v, then u and v are connected by a data flow edge. Also, since each program location (regardless of the number of threads in the system) is represented by one vertex in the data flow graph (i.e. there is no explicit representation for threads), it is possible to use them to analyze data in parameterized systems. Computing data invariants over a data flow graph is mostly as straightforward as abstract interpretation for sequential programs; the idea is that the structure of a data flow graph captures the interference among threads, and therefore, one only needs to focus on how data flows through this structure.

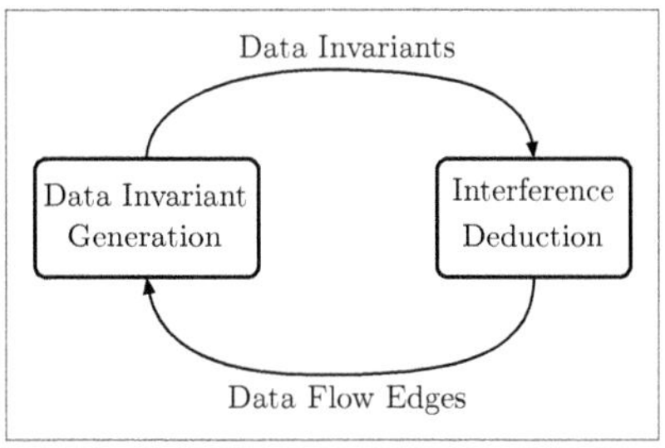

The figure on the right illustrates the idea behind our approach. We start by assuming no interference among threads (as if threads are running sequentially), and through abstract interpretation compute the first set of *data invariants* (per program location). At this stage, the data flow graph only contains data flow edges that correspond to the sequential executions of program threads. Then, the data invariants are passed to a deduction system, which uses them to compute a new set of data flow edges. The deduction system uses the data invariants to reason about what patterns of inter-thread interference are feasible, and adds the corresponding data flow edges, which capture these new interference patterns, to the data flow graph. These new data flow edges may result in computing weaker data invariants in the next round. These weaker invariants may trigger the addition of more data flow edges (*coarsening* the data flow graph). This loop continues until a fixed point is reached.

The analysis we use for computing data flow edges is *semi-compositional*. Inter-thread data flow is a property that intuitively involves two threads: one that writes to a global variable, and one that reads from it. Ideally, one would like to reason about the existence of data flow edges by considering only two threads at a time. However, it is not generally sound to reason using only two threads, since a program path (e.g. from a write to a read) may involve many threads synchronizing with each other. We overcome this problem by using data invariants (from the data invariant generation module) to soundly approximate the effects of other threads that may contribute to a data flow path being realizable. An invariant associated with a program location corresponds to an overapproximation of the values of the program variables when at least one thread is at that location. Therefore, we may reason about data flow paths that may require the participation of arbitrarily many threads while considering only two threads at a time. We call our approach *semi-compositional* (in contrast to fully compositional) because our reasoning method over two threads is non-compositional (all pairs of locations are considered), while every other thread in the system is accounted for in a compositional manner.

We implemented our approach in a tool called DUET and evaluated it on a set of 15 Linux device drivers. DUET can prove a total of 1312 (out of 1597) of array bounds and integer over/underflow assertions safe in 13 minutes. We also compared DUET against two recent tools that deal with parameterized concurrent Boolean programs, namely Getafix [22], and the dynamic cutoff detection (DCD) algorithm of [19], which are both based on model checking. We compared against DCD [19] and Getafix [22] on the set of benchmarks provided by the authors, which are Boolean abstractions (generated by the SatAbs [9] tool) of the aforementioned Linux device drivers. DUET has the clear advantage of being directly applicable to the drivers (as opposed to their Boolean abstractions), but we performed these experiments to show that it does outperform these tools even at the level of Boolean programs. Our experiments shows that DUET substantially outperforms Getafix, by proving 2505 (compared to 1382 for Getafix) Boolean programs correct. DUET also outperforms DCD by proving 58 programs safe in contrast to only 19 programs that DCD can prove safe.

1.1 Motivating example

In concurrent programs, threads communicate using many different methods. They may communicate through synchronization primitives such as locks or wait/notify, which can be viewed as *control* type primitives that only affect the feasible control paths in a thread, and not the data. Threads may also communicate via reading from and writing to shared memory, which are *data* type primitives. In the presence of both patterns of communication among threads, precise reasoning about the program often involves reasoning about both *data* and *control* simultaneously. But, doing so can be very expensive, specially for a programs with an unbounded number of threads. In this paper, we present a scalable approach to reason about *data* and *control* in separate but collaborating modules. In this section, we use an example that includes both modes of communication among threads (through both data variables and locks) to provide a high level understanding of our approach.

Figure 1 illustrates a simplified concurrent producer-consumer example. Let us assume that each statement is executed atomically, and that initially no thread holds any locks, and `counter` is 0. The producer can produce items one-by-one or in batch mode, and keeps track of the number of produced items waiting to be consumed using the global variable `counter`. Two producers cannot produce items simultaneously, but a consumer can run in parallel with a producer in batch mode. The consumer, if there are items to process, consumes them one-by-one, by decrementing `counter`. The assertion at v_6 states a correctness property for the consumer: the number of items waiting to be consumed must be nonnegative. At position u_{10} in the producer, the value of `counter` is always zero, so the assignment at u_{10} does not add any behaviour, but it helps us demonstrate an interesting point.

This program demonstrates the use of both synchronization primitives (locks in this case), and conditional statements to rule out undesired interference from other threads. For example, if the goal is to prove that the assertion at v_6 holds, then one must prove that the zero value assigned to `counter` at u_{10} cannot reach the decrement at v_5, and consequently falsify the assertion. In other words, we need to rule out a pattern of thread interference in order to prove the desired invariant at v_5 and v_6. The interesting aspect of this example is that the reverse is also true: since the locations u_{10} and v_5 are not protected by a common lock, in order to rule out the undesired interference, one needs to rely on the fact that at v_5, the value of `counter` is always strictly positive. In this scenario, if one starts from a weak invariant at v_5, one cannot rule out interference from u_{10}, and (reversely), if one starts by assuming the interference from u_{10} may occur, one cannot prove the data invariant needed to rule out this interference.

Here, we explain how our algorithm operates on the program in Figure 1 at a high level. In Section 5 (in Example 5.1), we will revisit this example and explain it in more detail. First, we assume that `Producer` and `Consumer` are executed sequentially with no interaction, and compute a sequential data flow graph $P_1^\sharp$. Next, a set of data invariants is generated from $P_1^\sharp$. This analysis determines that the `Consumer` threads cannot reach location v_5 and that in `Producer` threads, location u_4 is unreachable. Using the previously computed data invariants, the interference deduction unit computes new data flows, and adds the appropriate edges to $P_1^\sharp$ to get a data flow graph $P_2^\sharp$. For example, this analysis determines that the value of `counter` from u_{12} may reach the beginning of the `Producer` and `Consumer` threads, and so adds the edges $u_{12} \to v_4$ and $u_{12} \to u_3$. The interference deduction unit uses the fact that `counter=0` is an invariant at u_{10} to infer that the value of `counter` from u_{10} cannot flow to v_5 without passing through v_4, and therefore, does *not* add an edge from u_{10} to v_5. Data invariants are then generated for the data flow graph $P_2^\sharp$, which determines that u_4 and v_5 are now reachable, and that `counter` $\in [0, \infty)$ at u_1. The subsequent interference analysis computes new data flow edges, for example $u_4 \to u_1$, which is possible as the result of u_1's new (weaker) invariant. The invariants are still strong enough to prove that there is no data flow from u_{10} to v_5. These edges are added to $P_2^\sharp$ to get a new data flow graph $P_3^\sharp$. The data analysis runs on $P_3^\sharp$, but does not produce weaker invariants, and consequently, the subsequent interference analysis does not produce any new data flow edges. The algorithm then terminates, having computed a set of invariants that soundly approximate the dynamic behaviours of the program. These invariants are strong enough to prove that the assertion at v_6 never fails.

The rest of this paper is organized as follows. In Section 2, we define our program model. We define the data flow graphs in Section 3, and discuss how data invariants can be computed by abstract interpretation of data flow graphs; this constitutes the *data* portion of our analysis. We then discuss construction of the data flow graphs in Section 4 where we explain how data invariants are used to infer new data flow edges. The complete algorithm as an iterative framework is presented in Section 5. Section 6 presents our experiments, Section 7 discusses related work, and Section 8 concludes.

```
     int Producer(int batch)
     {
u1:    acquire(lock2)
u2:    acquire(lock1)
       if (*) {
u3:      assume(counter>0)
u4:      counter++
u5:      unlock(lock1)
u6:      unlock(lock2)
u7:      return 1
       } else {
u8:      assume(counter<=0)
u9:      unlock(lock1)
u10:     counter = 0
         while(*) {
u11:       assume(batch>0)
u12:       counter++
u13:       batch--
         }
u14:     assume(batch<=0)
u15:     unlock(lock2)
u16:     return batch
       }
     }
```

```
     void Consumer()
     {
v1:    lock(lock1)
       while(*) {
v2:      unlock(lock1)
v3:      lock(lock1)
       }
v4:    assume(counter>0)
v5:    counter--
v6:    assert(counter>=0)
v7:    unlock(lock1)
     }
```

Figure 1. Producer-Consumer Example.

2. Notation and the program model

We define a program to be a 4-tuple $P = \langle H, GV, LV, \mathcal{L}[\![\cdot]\!]\rangle$, where $H = \langle Loc, CF\rangle$ is a finite control flow graph (CFG) whose vertices we call *locations*, GV is a finite set of global variables, LV is a finite set of local variables, and $\mathcal{L}[\![\cdot]\!]$ assigns to each control location a transition relation. For the rest of this section, we will formalize this program model and introduce notation to be used in the rest of the paper.

We will identify threads with natural numbers, where the behaviour of an individual thread is given by the control flow graph $H = \langle Loc, CF\rangle$ together with the semantic function $\mathcal{L}[\![\cdot]\!]$. The initial vertex of H, which is assumed to have no control flow predecessors, is denoted by $init_{loc}$. The behaviour of the program P is defined to be that of the infinite parallel composition of all threads $n \in \mathbb{N}$. Since we are interested in thread invariants, we can restrict ourselves to finite executions, in which only finitely many threads can participate. Thus, for proving thread invariants, our program model is equivalent to the parameterized model in which P is taken to be the finite parallel composition of all threads up to some $k \in \mathbb{N}$, where k is a parameter. We also note that we lose no generality in assuming that every thread $n \in \mathbb{N}$ executes the same code, since several code segments can be simply combined into one.

We will assume that GV, LV, and $\mathbb{N} \times LV$ are pairwise disjoint (a pair $\langle n, x\rangle \in \mathbb{N} \times LV$ is conceptually thread n's copy of the local variable x) and define the set of variables $Var = GV \cup LV$. For simplicity, we will assume that all variables are of type integer.

A *global state* is a pair $s = \langle s_{env}, s_{loc}\rangle$ consisting of a global environment $s_{env} \in GEnv = (GV \cup \mathbb{N} \times LV) \to \mathbb{Z}$ and an assignment of a control location to each thread $s_{loc} : \mathbb{N} \to Loc$. A *thread state* is a mapping $e \in TEnv = Var \to \mathbb{Z}$ from variables to values. For a given thread $n \in \mathbb{N}$ and global state s, the *thread state of n in s*, which we denote by $s[n]$, and which is defined by

$$s[n](x) = \begin{cases} s_{env}(x) & \text{if } x \in GV \\ s_{env}(\langle n, x\rangle) & \text{otherwise} \end{cases}$$

The function $\mathcal{L}[\![\cdot]\!] : Loc \to TEnv \times TEnv$ associates a transition relation on thread states to every location. We call a pair $a = \langle n, \langle v, v'\rangle\rangle$ consisting of a thread $n \in \mathbb{N}$ and a control flow edge $\langle v, v'\rangle \in CF$ an *action*. If the target v' of the control flow edge $\langle v, v'\rangle$ is understood from the context or irrelevant, we simply write $\langle n, v\rangle$. We use $\mathcal{A}[\![a]\!]$ to denote the (global state) transition relation associated with the action a, which is obtained by lifting $\mathcal{L}[\![v]\!]$ from thread states to global states as follows: $\langle s, s'\rangle \in \mathcal{A}[\![\langle n, \langle v, v'\rangle\rangle]\!] \iff \exists\langle e, e'\rangle \in \mathcal{L}[\![v]\!]$ such that

- $s[n] = e$ and $s'[n] = e'$
- $s_{loc}(n) = v$ and $s'_{loc}(n) = v'$
- $\forall n' \in \mathbb{N} \setminus \{n\}.\ s_{loc}(n') = s'_{loc}(n')$
- $\forall n' \in \mathbb{N} \setminus \{n\}, \forall x \in LV.\ s_{env}(\langle n', x\rangle) = s'_{env}(\langle n', x\rangle)$.

Given a sequence of actions ρ and a subset $N \subseteq \mathbb{N}$, the *projection* of ρ onto N, denoted $\rho|_N$, is the subsequence of ρ consisting of all actions whose thread identifiers belong to N. A *trace* σ is a finite sequence of actions such that, when projected onto a single thread, corresponds to a path in the CFG H beginning at the initial location $init_{loc}$. For a trace σ, the *post states of σ* (denoted $\sigma^\bullet$) is the set of final states of that execution. A trace τ is *feasible* if $\tau^\bullet$ is nonempty. For a trace σ and a thread $n \in \mathbb{N}$, we use $endloc(\sigma, n)$ to denote the end location of the CFG path

$\sigma|_{\{n\}}$. Note that *endloc* has the property that $\forall s \in \sigma^\bullet$, $\forall n \in \mathbb{N}$, $s_{loc}(n) = endloc(\sigma, n)$.

A thread-state property is an assertion φ with free variables in *Var*. We will denote the set of such formulae by $\mathcal{F}(Var)$ (and more generally, $\mathcal{F}(V)$ will denote first-order formulae with free variables in V). For a thread state e, we write $e \models \varphi$ to denote that e satisfies φ.

To provide some intuition on our program model, we will describe how to represent locking. A lock is represented by a global variable $lock \in GV$. Let *acq* be a location where *lock* is to be acquired, and let *rel* be a location where it is to be released. Then we can define

$$\mathcal{L}[\![acq]\!] = \{\langle e, e[lock \leftarrow 1]\rangle : e(lock) = 0\}$$

$$\mathcal{L}[\![rel]\!] = \{\langle e, e[lock \leftarrow 0]\rangle : e(lock) = 1\}$$

Note that, given a feasible trace τ, the fact that $\tau^\bullet$ is nonempty implies that there is no point along τ in which two threads hold the same lock.

Our program model does not support conditional branching, but this can be simulated with nondeterministic branching and `assume` actions, where $\mathcal{L}[\![\texttt{assume}(c)]\!] = \{\langle e, e\rangle : e \models c\}$. Programs that depend on the initial state satisfying some property φ can be simulated by defining $\mathcal{L}[\![init_{loc}]\!]$ as $\mathcal{L}[\![\texttt{assume}(\varphi)]\!]$. Although our algorithm (and our implementation) handles dynamic thread creation, we omit it from this presentation for the sake of simplicity.

3. Data flow graphs

Data flow graphs (DFGs) are a program representation that explicitly represents the flow of data in a program, rather than the flow of control as in a control flow graph. Our analysis uses DFGs to compute program invariants by interpreting each edge of the DFG as a constraint and then computing an overapproximation of the least solution to this constraint system via abstract interpretation.[1]

A DFG for a program P is a directed graph $P^\sharp = \langle Loc, DF\rangle$, where $DF \subseteq Loc \times Var \times Loc$ is a set of directed edges labeled by program variables, and where we assume that *Loc* contains an additional location `uninit` (with no incoming or outgoing edges in the control flow graph of P). We will use $u \to^x v$ to denote the triple $\langle u, x, v\rangle \in Loc \times Var \times Loc$.

We define the collecting semantics of a DFG $P^\sharp = \langle Loc, DF\rangle$ to be the least solution to the following set of equations:

$$\text{VAL}(u, x) = \{e(x) : e \in \text{OUT}(u)\}$$

$$\text{IN}(v) = \bigcap_{x \in Var} \{e \in TEnv : \exists u \to^x v \in DF . e(x) \in \text{VAL}(u, x)\}$$

$$\text{OUT}(v) = \begin{cases} TEnv & \text{if } v = \texttt{uninit} \\ \{e' : \exists e \in \text{IN}(v). \langle e, e'\rangle \in \mathcal{L}[\![v]\!]\} & \text{otherwise} \end{cases}$$

Consider the example in Figure 2. This figure depicts a program with two code segments, each of which may be executed by arbitrarily many threads. Variable `c` is global, and variable `incr` is local. Each vertex (except the special vertex `uninit`) has at least one incoming edge for each variable. Each of these incoming edges provides a value for a particular variable. For example, the edge $u_2 \to^{\texttt{c}} v_2$ represents the constraint that any value for `c` *after* executing u_2 is a possible value for `c` *before* excuting v_2 (that is, $\{e(\texttt{c}) : e \in \text{IN}(v_2)\} \subseteq \{e(\texttt{c}) : e \in \text{OUT}(u_2)\}$). The two edges from `uninit` to $init_{loc}$ indicate that any value is possible for `incr` and `c` at $init_{loc}$, the location at which both threads begin execution. The vertex $init_{loc}$ sets the initial condition of the program, acting as $\texttt{assume}(\texttt{c} = 0 \wedge \texttt{incr} = 0)$. Thus, edges originating at $init_{loc}$ indicate that a particular variable may get its value from the initial state. The fact that $v_1 \to^{\texttt{incr}} u_2$ does *not* belong to this graph indicates that the value of `incr` at v_1 is not observable at u_2.

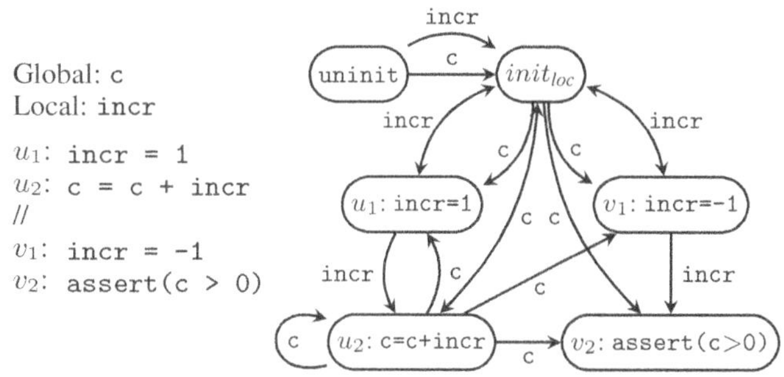

Figure 2. A program and a data flow graph representing it.

Intuitively, a DFG for a program P represents a trace σ if it has "enough" edges to ensure that any thread state reached by σ belongs to $\text{IN}(v)$ for some v. The remainder of this section formalizes this notion.

We will assume the existence of a function $mod : Loc \to \mathcal{P}(Var)$ that maps every control location to the set of variables modified at that location. We require that *mod* satisfies the following: for any $x \in Var$, if there exists some $\langle e, e'\rangle \in \mathcal{L}[\![v]\!]$ with $e(x) \neq e'(x)$, then $x \in mod(v)$. A notable feature of the *mod* we use in practice is that a location of the form $\texttt{assume}(\varphi)$ is considered to be a modification of every variable occuring in φ. This allows us to take advantage of information at conditional branches that otherwise would not be possible in a data flow graph.

For a trace σ, variable x, and thread n, we define $latest(\sigma, x, n)$ to be the location of the last action to write to the variable x along σ (or thread n's copy of x, if x is local). More formally, if x is a global variable, $latest(\sigma, x, n)$ is the unique location v such that $\sigma = \pi\langle m, v\rangle\rho$ (for some $m \in \mathbb{N}$) and where no action (of any thread) along ρ modifies x if such a v exists, and `uninit` otherwise. Similarly, if x is a local variable, $latest(\sigma, x, n)$ is the unique location v such that $\sigma = \pi\langle n, v\rangle\rho$ and no action of thread n along ρ modifies x if such a v exists, and `uninit` otherwise.

DEFINITION 3.1 (Witness). *Let u, v be locations, x be a variable, and σ be a trace. We say that σ is a* witness *for the data flow edge $u \to^x v$ if there exists some thread $n \in \mathbb{N}$ such that $latest(\sigma, x, n) = u$ and $endloc(\sigma, n) = v$.*

Conceptually, σ is a witness for $u \to^x v$ if, on σ, u sets a value for x which is not changed until the end of the trace, where some thread is at v. We are now ready to define a representation condition for traces and program.

DEFINITION 3.2 (Representation). *A DFG $P^\sharp = \langle Loc, DF\rangle$* represents *a trace σ iff for every $u, v \in Loc$ and $x \in Var$, if some subtrace (not necessarily proper) σ' of σ is a witness for $u \to^x v$, then $u \to^x v \in DF$. $P^\sharp$* represents *a program P if it represents τ for every feasible trace τ of P.*

The relationship between the collecting semantics of a DFG and the traces it represents is given by the following:

THEOREM 3.3 (DFG Soundness). *Let σ be a trace and let $P^\sharp$ be a DFG such that $P^\sharp$ represents σ. Then the collecting semantics of $P^\sharp$ overapproximates the set of thread states reached by σ. Formally, for all $s \in \sigma^\bullet$, for all $n \in \mathbb{N}$, we have that $s[n] \in IN(s_{loc}(n))$.*

[1] For a similar use of data-flow graphs, see for example [17].

Proof sketch Let $P^\sharp = \langle Loc, DF \rangle$ be a DFG and let σ be a trace represented by $P^\sharp$. We proceed by induction on σ.

Base case: follows from the fact that for all x, $\texttt{uninit} \rightarrow^x init_{loc} \in DF$ (since $P^\sharp$ represents ϵ) and the fact that for all x, $\text{VAL}(\texttt{uninit}, x) = \mathbb{Z}$.

Inductive step: suppose σ is a trace such that $P^\sharp$ represents σ, let $n \in \mathbb{N}$, and let $v = endloc(\sigma, n)$. We need to show that $s[n] \in \text{IN}(s_{loc}(n))$. To prove this, it is sufficient to show that $\forall x \in Var$, $\exists u \in Loc$ such that $u \rightarrow^x v \in DF$ and $s[n](x) \in \text{VAL}(u, x)$.

Let x be a variable, and take u to be $latest(\sigma, x, n)$. Then $u \rightarrow^x v \in DF$ because σ witnesses this data flow and $P^\sharp$ represents σ. If $u = \texttt{uninit}$, we are done since $\text{VAL}(\texttt{uninit}, x) = \mathbb{Z}$. If $u \neq \texttt{uninit}$, it follows that $\sigma = \pi\langle m, u\rangle\rho$ for some thread $m \in \mathbb{N}$, trace π, and sequence of actions ρ such that x is not modified along ρ (by the definition of $latest(\sigma, x, n)$). Moreover, we must have that there is some $s' \in \pi^\bullet$ such that $\exists s''$ with $\langle s', s''\rangle \in \mathcal{A}[\![\langle m, u\rangle]\!]$ and $s''[n](x) = s[n](x)$. By the induction hypothesis, $s'[m] \in \text{IN}(u)$, so $s''[m] \in \text{OUT}(u)$ and $s[n](x) = s''[n](x) = s''[m](x) \in \text{VAL}(u, x)$. □

We also note that, unlike typical definitions of data flow graphs, we require that each location has inputs for every variable, rather than just the variables read by that location. This is a technical convenience that simplifies the presentation of our algorithm.

3.1 Abstract interpretation of data flow graphs

In this section, we discuss how invariants are computed over a data flow graph. For clarity of this presentation, we will assume a concrete representation of an abstract domain as a subset of $\mathcal{F}(Var)$. The semantics of program locations is given by an abstract transition relation $\mathcal{L}[\![\cdot]\!]^\sharp : Loc \rightarrow \mathcal{F}(Var) \rightarrow \mathcal{F}(Var)$ that overapproximates the strongest postcondition (i.e., $\langle e, e'\rangle \in \mathcal{L}[\![v]\!]$ implies $e' \models \mathcal{L}[\![v]\!]^\sharp(e)$). An *annotation* for a DFG $P^\sharp$ is a map $\iota : Loc \rightarrow \mathcal{F}(Var)$ that assigns each location $v \in Loc$ a thread-state formula $\iota(v)$. We define an inductiveness condition for annotations that follows the structure of the collecting semantics, and which holds when the annotation overapproximates the collecting semantics of the DFG.

DEFINITION 3.4. *An annotation ι is* inductive *for a data flow graph $\langle Loc, DF\rangle$ if:*

- $\iota(\texttt{uninit}) = true$
- *For all $v \in Loc$,*

$$\Big[\bigwedge_{x \in Var}\Big(\bigvee_{u \rightarrow^x v \in DF} \overline{\mathcal{L}[\![u]\!]^\sharp(\iota(u))}^{x}\Big)\Big] \Rightarrow \iota(v)$$

where $\overline{\mathcal{L}[\![u]\!]^\sharp(\iota(u))}^{x}$ denotes the formula obtained from the formula $\mathcal{L}[\![u]\!]^\sharp(\iota(u))$ by existentially quantifying every variable except x.

Standard techniques can be used to compute inductive annotations from a DFG (inductive annotations correspond to post-fixpoint solutions in the terminology of abstract interpretation). For example, in our implementation, we use a variation of the well-known worklist algorithm. The following is a consequence of Theorem 3.3 and the fact that inductive annotations overapproximate the collecting semantics:

COROLLARY 3.5. *Let σ be a trace, let $P^\sharp$ be a dataflow graph that represents σ (Definition 3.2), and let ι be an inductive annotation for $P^\sharp$ (Definition 3.4). Then for all states $s \in \sigma^\bullet$, and all threads $n \in \mathbb{N}$, $s[n] \models \iota(s_{loc}(n))$ (i.e., the thread state of thread n in the global state s is overapproximated by the annotation at the location of thread n).*

Note that in the collecting semantics, and therefore in inductive annotations, the values of different variables cannot be correlated. For example, if v is a location, x and y are variables, and $e, e' \in \text{IN}(v)$ are reachable thread states such that $e(x) = e(y) = 0$ and $e'(x) = e'(y) = 1$, then there exists an $e'' \in \text{IN}(v)$ in which $e''(x) = 0 \neq 1 = e''(y)$. This suggests that DFGs are most appropriate for analyses based on *non-relational* abstract domains, such as intervals, signs, or the even/odd domain, which are also incapable of representing relationships between variables. In Section 5.1, we will discuss a variation of DFGs which are more appropriate for relational abstract domains.

4. Interference analysis

We now address the problem of how to compute a DFG that represents a program. We start by defining a subset of traces, called ι-feasible traces (where ι is a given annotation), and then develop an interference analysis that computes the set of data flow edges that are witnessed by ι-feasible traces. The definition of ι-feasibility is such that if ι is a "weak enough" annotation, then every feasible trace is ι-feasible. With such an annotation ι, every edge which is witnessed by a feasible trace will also be witnessed by an ι-feasible trace, and thus will be found by our interference analysis.

Our interference analysis relies on a finite domain of data invariants, which is defined using finite set of observable conditions.[2] An *observable condition* is a predicate c with free variables in GV. In the remainder of this section, we assume a fixed finite set of observable conditions, which we denote by $\mathcal{C}$. We define the set of observable formulae $\mathcal{F}^\sharp(GV) \subseteq \mathcal{F}(GV)$ to be the set of formulae φ that can be expressed as a conjunction $\bigwedge_i \varphi_i$, where for each i, $\varphi_i \in \mathcal{C}$ or $\neg\varphi_i \in \mathcal{C}$.

An annotation $\iota : Loc \rightarrow \mathcal{F}(Var)$ (along with the set of observable conditions $\mathcal{C}$) determines an *abstract annotation* $\iota^\sharp : Loc \rightarrow \mathcal{F}^\sharp(GV)$ that assigns to each location $u \in Loc$ an observable formula φ that is implied by $\iota(u)$ and which is at least as strong as any other observable formula with this property. Thus, going from concrete to abstract (and using $\subseteq$ to denote "is more precise than"), we have $\text{IN}(v) \subseteq \iota(v) \subseteq \iota^\sharp(v)$ for any location v.

The set of observable conditions $\mathcal{C}$ determines an *enabling condition enabled* : $Loc \rightarrow \mathcal{F}^\sharp(GV)$ where $\exists e'.\langle e, e'\rangle \in \mathcal{A}[\![v]\!] \Rightarrow \langle e, v\rangle \models enabled(v)$ and $enabled(v)$ is at least as strong as any other observable formula with this property.

We are now ready to state our definition of ι-feasibility:

DEFINITION 4.1. *Let σ be a trace and ι be an annotation. Then σ is ι-*feasible *if:*

- $\sigma = \epsilon$, *or*
- $\sigma = \sigma'\langle n, v\rangle$, *where σ' is an ι-feasible trace, and for all $m \in \mathbb{N}$, $\iota^\sharp(endloc(\sigma', m)) \wedge enabled(v)$ is satisfiable.*

Note that the condition for extending an ι-feasible path σ by an action $\langle n, v\rangle$ depends only on the annotations at the end locations of each thread, rather than on the states in $\sigma^\bullet$.

EXAMPLE 4.2. *Consider the trace $\sigma = \langle 0, u_1\rangle\langle 0, u_2\rangle\langle 0, u_3\rangle$ of the program in Figure 1. This trace is not feasible, because every state in $(\langle 0, u_1\rangle\langle 0, u_2\rangle)^\bullet$ has* `counter` *= 0, so $\langle 0, u_3\rangle$ is not enabled. However, assuming that $\iota(u_2) = \texttt{counter} \geq 0 \wedge \texttt{lock1} = 1$, $\iota(u_1) = \texttt{counter} \geq 0$, and $\mathcal{C} = \{\texttt{counter} > 0, \texttt{lock1} = 0, \texttt{lock2} = 0\}$ (which implies $\iota^\sharp(u_1) = true$, $\iota^\sharp(u_1) = \neg(\texttt{lock1} = 0)$, and $enabled(u_3) = \texttt{counter} > 0$), this trace is ι-feasible. To illustrate how ι-feasibility depends on ι, consider the infeasible trace $\langle 0, u_1\rangle\langle 0, u_2\rangle\langle 1, v_1\rangle$. This trace is*

[2] This finiteness condition is not strictly necessary, but makes for a more efficient analysis.

$$\text{INIT-COREACH}\quad \frac{}{\mathit{coreachable}(\mathit{init}_{loc}, \mathit{init}_{loc})} \qquad \text{COREACH-SYM}\quad \frac{\mathit{coreachable}(u, v)}{\mathit{coreachable}(v, u)} \qquad \text{COREACH-STEP}\quad \frac{\mathit{coreachable}(u_0, v) \quad \mathit{enabled}(u_0, \iota^\sharp(v)) \quad \langle u_0, u_1\rangle \in \mathit{CF}}{\mathit{coreachable}(u_1, v)}$$

$$\text{MAYREACH-BASE}\quad \frac{\mathit{coreachable}(u_0, v) \quad x \in \mathit{mod}(u_0) \quad \mathit{enabled}(u_0, \iota^\sharp(v)) \quad \langle u_0, u_1\rangle \in \mathit{CF}}{\mathit{mayReach}(u, x, u_0, v)}$$

$$\text{MAYREACH-STEPL}\quad \frac{\mathit{mayReach}(u_0, x, u_1, v) \quad x \notin \mathit{mod}(u_1) \quad \mathit{enabled}(u_1, \iota^\sharp(v)) \quad \langle u_1, u_2\rangle \in \mathit{CF}}{\mathit{mayReach}(u_0, x, u_2, v)}$$

$$\text{MAYREACH-STEPR}\quad \frac{\mathit{mayReach}(u_0, x, u_1, v_0) \quad x \notin \mathit{mod}(v_0) \quad \mathit{enabled}(v_0, \iota^\sharp(u_1)) \quad \langle v_0, v_1\rangle \in \mathit{CF}}{\mathit{mayReach}(u_0, x, u_1, v_1)} \qquad \text{MAYREACH}\quad \frac{\mathit{mayReach}_0(u_0, x, u_1, v)}{u_0 \rightsquigarrow^x v}$$

Figure 3. Interference analysis.

ι-feasible if $\iota(u_3) =$ `counter` $\geq 0 \wedge$ `lock1` $= 1$, and ι-infeasible if $\iota(u_3) = \iota(u_8) =$ `counter` $\geq 0 \wedge$ `lock1` $= 1 \wedge$ `lock2` $= 1$.

By combining the definition of ι-feasibility with the definition of a witness of a data flow edge, we arrive at the following:

DEFINITION 4.3. *Let σ be a trace, ι be an annotation, u and v be locations, and x be a variable. Then σ is an ι-feasible witness of the data flow $u \rightarrow^x v$ if σ is ι-feasible and witnesses the data flow $u \rightarrow^x v$ (that is, σ simultaneously satisfies definitions 3.1 and 4.1).*

A key property of our notion of ι-feasibility is that it is preserved under projections; that is, for any ι, if σ is an ι-feasible trace, then for any sets of threads $N \subseteq \mathbb{N}$, $\sigma|_N$ is also ι-feasible. The following lemma states a projection result that forms the basis of our semi-compositional algorithm for interference analysis. It implies that, in order to compute the set of data flow edges that are witnessed by ι-feasible traces, it is sufficient to consider only traces that involve two threads.

LEMMA 4.4 (Projection). *Let ι be an annotation, u, v be locations, and x be a variable. Let σ be an ι-feasible witness for the data flow $u \rightarrow^x v$. Then there exists $m, n \in \mathbb{N}$ such that $\sigma|_{\{m,n\}}$ is an ι-feasible witness for $u \rightarrow^x v$.*

Proof sketch We will first prove that for any $N \subseteq \mathbb{N}$ and any ι-feasible trace σ, $\sigma|_N$ is an ι-feasible trace, by induction on σ.

The base case is obvious. For the inductive step, let $\sigma\langle n, v\rangle$ be an ι-feasible trace, and assume that $\sigma|_N$ is ι-feasible. If $n \notin N$, then $\sigma\langle n, v\rangle|_N = \sigma|_N$, and the result is immediate from the induction hypothesis.

If $n \in N$, then $\sigma\langle n, v\rangle|_N = \sigma|_N\langle n, v\rangle$. In this case, we need to show that for all $m \in \mathbb{N}$, $\iota^\sharp(\mathit{endloc}(\sigma|_N, m)) \wedge \mathit{enabled}(v)$ is satisfiable. Let $m \in \mathbb{N}$ and distinguish two cases:

- $m \in N$: then $\mathit{endloc}(\sigma|_N, m) = \mathit{endloc}(\sigma, m)$, and the fact that $\iota^\sharp(\mathit{endloc}(\sigma|_N, m)) \wedge \mathit{enabled}(v)$ is satisfiable follows from the fact that $\sigma\langle n, v\rangle$ is ι-feasible.
- $m \notin N$: then $\mathit{endloc}(\sigma|_N, n) = \mathit{init}_{loc}$. Since σ is finite, only finitely many threads execute actions in σ, so there exists a thread $i \in \mathbb{N}$ that does not execute actions in σ. Since $\sigma\langle n, v\rangle$ is ι-feasible, $\iota^\sharp(\mathit{endloc}(\sigma, i)) \wedge \mathit{enabled}(v)$ is satisfiable. Since $\mathit{endloc}(\sigma, i) = \mathit{init}_{loc} = \mathit{endloc}(\sigma|_N, m)$, we are done.

Now, we must prove that the property of being a witness is preserved by projections. Let u, v be locations and x be a variable, and let σ by a witness of the data flow $u \rightarrow^x v$. We assume that x is a global variable – the case of local variables is similar. It follows from Definition 3.1 that there exists some $m, n \in \mathbb{N}$, a trace π, and a sequence of actions ρ such that $\sigma = \pi\langle n, u\rangle\rho$ such that $x \in \mathit{mod}(u)$, x is not modified by any action along ρ, and $v = \mathit{endloc}(\sigma, m)$. It is easy to check that $\sigma|_{\{m,n\}}$ witnesses $u \rightarrow^x v$. □

4.1 Inferring data flow edges

Our algorithm for inferring data flow edges is stated declaratively in Figure 3 as a set of deduction rules for ι-feasible witnesses. For $u, v \in \mathit{Loc}$ and $x \in \mathit{Var}$, we write $u \rightsquigarrow^x_\iota v$ iff an ι-feasible witness for the data flow $u \rightarrow^x v$ exists. These proof rules are sound and complete for determining whether a witness for an inter-thread data flow edge exists – intra-thread data flows can be computed independently using a standard sequential reaching definitions analysis.

The rules use an input relation $\mathit{enabled}(u, \varphi)$ which holds iff $\varphi \wedge \mathit{enabled}(u)$ is satisfiable. Additionally, two auxiliary relations are used:

- $\mathit{coreachable}(u, v)$ holds iff there is some ι-feasible trace σ such that $u = \mathit{endloc}(\sigma, 0)$ and $v = \mathit{endloc}(\sigma, 1)$.
- $\mathit{mayReach}(u, x, v, w)$ holds iff there is some ι-feasible trace σ such that $u = \mathit{latest}(\sigma, x, 0)$, $v = \mathit{endloc}(\sigma, 0)$ and $u = \mathit{endloc}(\sigma, 1)$.

Since the set of locations and the set of variables are finite, $\mathit{coreachable}$, $\mathit{mayReach}$, and $\rightsquigarrow_\iota$ all must be finite. As a result, we may compute all members of $\rightsquigarrow_\iota$ in finite time by iteratively applying these rules until no new members of any relation are deduced (i.e., until a fixed point is reached). Moreover, the fact that these relations are all finite allows us to leverage efficient propositional techniques, for example representing relations by binary decision diagrams.

LEMMA 4.5 (Interference analysis soundness & completeness). *Let $u, v \in \mathit{Loc}$ and $x \in \mathit{Var}$. There exists an ι-feasible trace that witnesses data flow the $u \rightarrow^x v$ iff there exists a single-threaded witness, or if $u \rightsquigarrow^x_\iota v$ belongs to the least fixpoint solution of the system of interference rules in Figure 3.*

Note that this lemma implies that, although we lose information in our interference analysis by going from feasible traces to ι-feasible traces, we do *not* lose information by going from n-thread ι-feasible traces to 2-thread ι-feasible traces.

The rules in Figure 3 are a simplified version of the ones we implement in DUET. DUET handles some additional language features (thread creation and atomic blocks) and has several optimizations

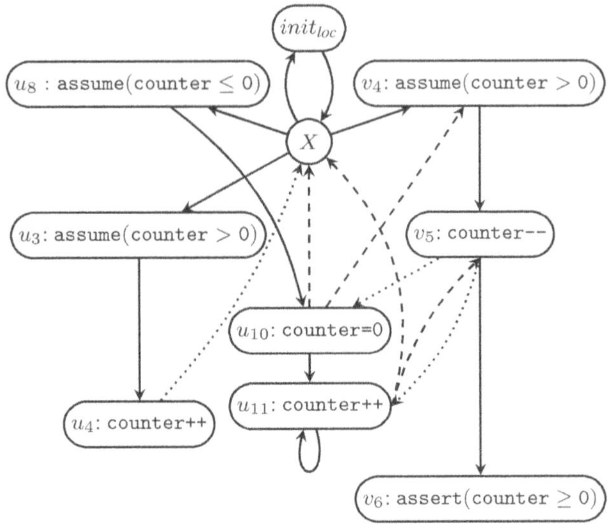

	ι_1	ι_2	ι_3
$init_{loc}$	true	true	true
u_3	counter=0	counter≥0	counter≥0
u_4	counter=0	counter≥0	counter≥0
u_8	counter=0	counter≥0	counter≥0
u_{10}	counter=0	counter=0	counter=0
u_{11}	counter≥0	counter≥0	counter≥0
v_4	counter=0	counter≥0	counter≥0
v_5	false	counter>0	counter>0
v_6	false	counter≥0	counter≥0

Figure 4. COARSEN computation on the program in Figure 1.

to make it more efficient. However, all the essential ideas of the analysis are present in the rules of Figure 3.

5. Iterative coarsening

In Section 3, we gave a method for computing an annotation for a data flow graph; in Section 4, we gave a method for computing data flow edges given an annotation. By incorporating both components into a feedback loop, we obtain our main algorithm, COARSEN (Algorithm 1). Given a parameterized multi-threaded program, COARSEN computes a DFG that represents that program as well as an annotation that is inductive for that DFG.

Given a program P, COARSEN begins by computing a data flow graph $P_1^\sharp$ with only intra-thread (sequential) data flow edges. It then computes an inductive annotation ι_1 for $P_1^\sharp$ as discussed in Section 3. This annotation ι_1 is used as input to the interference analysis of Section 4, which computes the set of ι_1-feasible data flow edges and adds them to $P_1^\sharp$ to obtain a DFG $P_2^\sharp$. After adding these edges, a new (possibly weaker) annotation is computed that is inductive for $P_2^\sharp$. This process continues until a fixed point is reached; that is, until we reach some k such that $P_k^\sharp = P_{k+1}^\sharp$. At this point, $P_k^\sharp$ represents the program P and ι_k is inductive for $P_k^\sharp$, and therefore ι_k overapproximates the reachable thread states of P by Theorem 3.3.

This algorithm makes use of several auxiliary functions, which are defined below.

- SequentialDFG(P) computes a sequential data flow graph for P. This computation is a standard sequential reaching definitions analysis. This graph contains all intra-thread data flow edges, including all those for local variables, and all those originating from `uninit`.
- ExtractCond(P) computes a set of observable conditions for P by mining the program for locks and predicates q such that q only uses global variables and `assume`(q) occurs in P.
- Invariants($\langle Loc, DF\rangle$) computes an annotation that is inductive for the DFG $\langle Loc, DF\rangle$ using a modification of the standard worklist algorithm, as discussed in Section 3.
- AbstractAnnotation(ι, C) computes an observable formula $\iota^\sharp(v)$ for every location v that is implied by $\iota(v)$ and is at least as strong as any other observable formula with that property.
- FeasibleDataflows($P, \iota^\sharp$) computes the relation $\rightsquigarrow_\iota$ through a bottom-up evaluation of the logic program given in Figure 3.

EXAMPLE 5.1. *Consider the program in Figure 1. Figure 4 depicts how the DFG and annotation computed by* COARSEN *evolve on this program. For simplicity, we show only information that is relevant to the* `counter` *variable. In particular, the DFG contains only vertices that modify or block on* `counter` *and all the* `counter`*-labeled edges between them, and the annotation is restricted to refer only to the variable* `counter`.

A special vertex X appears in the DFG to improve readability by "factoring" edges; it does not represent a real DFG vertex. An edge $u \to X$ from some arbitrary vertex u to X represents four edges: $u \to init_{loc}$, $u \to u_8$, $u \to u_3$ and $u \to v_4$. The vertex $init_{loc}$ is the initial location of the program where every thread begins its execution, and which has u_1 and v_1 as its control flow successors. Its action is to assume the condition of the initial state, as in:

$$\texttt{assume(counter} = 0 \wedge \texttt{lock1} = 0 \wedge \texttt{lock2} = 0 \wedge \texttt{batch} \geq 0)$$

The solid edges in Figure 4 are added in the first round, the dashed edges are added in the second round, and the dotted edges are added in the third round. The columns labeled ι_1, ι_2, and ι_3 represent the annotation of the corresponding location in the first, second, and third rounds. Note that there is no edge from $u_1 0$ to v_5. This is very important for proving the assertion at v_6. Since the invariant at $u_1 0$ always remains `counter=0`, *the interference analysis can infer that there is no feasible path of the program witnessing this edge. Any feasible path of the program that visits $u_1 0$ has to go through a counter increment ($u_1 1$) or an assume statement (v_4) before it can reach v_5, and since each of those paths contains a location modifying counter in the segment from $u_1 0$ to v_5, they cannot be witnesses for a data flow edge from $u_1 0$ to v_5.*

Finally, the correctness condition of Algorithm 1 is stated in the following theorem:

THEOREM 5.2 (Soundness). *For any program P,* COARSEN *computes an annotation ι and a DFG $P^\sharp$ such that $P^\sharp$ represents P, and for every reachable state s of P and thread n, $s[n] \models \iota(s_{loc}(n))$.*

Proof sketch Let ι and $P^\sharp$ be the be the annotation and data flow graph computed by COARSEN. The termination condition

Algorithm 1 COARSEN

Input: A program $P = \langle\langle Loc, CF\rangle, GV, LV, \mathcal{L}[\![\cdot]\!]\rangle$
Output: A sound annotation for P
  $\langle Loc, DF\rangle \leftarrow$ SequentialDFG(P)
  $\mathcal{C} \leftarrow$ ExtractCond(P)
  $DF' \leftarrow \emptyset$
  repeat
    $DF \leftarrow DF \cup DF'$
    $\iota \leftarrow$ Invariants($\langle Loc, DF\rangle$)
    $\iota^\sharp \leftarrow$ AbstractAnnotation($\iota, \mathcal{C}$)
    $DF' \leftarrow$ FeasibleDataflows($P, \iota^\sharp$)
  until $DF' \subseteq DF$
  return ι

of COARSEN implies that ι is inductive for $P^\sharp$ and every ι-feasible trace of P is represented in $P^\sharp$. We first prove that every feasible trace τ of P is ι-feasible by induction on τ.

The base case is trivial, since ϵ is ι-feasible for any ι. For the induction step, assume that $\tau\langle n, v\rangle$ is a feasible trace and τ is ι-feasible; we must prove that $\tau\langle n, v\rangle$ is ι-feasible.

Since $\tau\langle n, v\rangle$ is feasible, there must exist some $s \in \tau^\bullet$ and $s' \in State$ such that $\langle s, s'\rangle \in \mathcal{A}[\![\langle n, v\rangle]\!]$. By the definition of $enabled(v)$, we have that $s \models enabled(v)$. We note that for a formula φ with free variables in GV, the meaning of $s \models \varphi$ is unambigious since s_{env} assigns a single value to each global variable $x \in GV$; moreover, we note that if φ's free variables are in GV then $s[n] \models \varphi$ iff $s \models \varphi$, since $s[n]$ and s agree on the values of all global variables.

Let $m \in \mathbb{N}$ be an arbitrary thread. Since τ is ι-feasible, τ is represented by the DFG $\langle Loc, DF\rangle$. Since ι is inductive for $\langle Loc, DF\rangle$ and $s \in \tau^\bullet$, we have that $s[m] \models \iota(s_{loc}(m))$ by Corollary 3.5. It follows from the definition of $\iota^\sharp$ that $s \models \iota^\sharp(s_{loc}(m))$, and thus $s \models \iota^\sharp(s_{loc}(m)) \wedge enabled(v)$. Since this holds for all m, $\tau\langle n, v\rangle$ is ι-feasible (noting that $s_{loc}(m) = endloc(\tau, m)$).

Since every feasible trace is an ι-feasible trace, and every ι-feasible trace is represented by $P^\sharp$, every feasible trace is represented by $P^\sharp$, and so P is represented by $P^\sharp$. Finally, let s be a reachable thread state and let $n \in \mathbb{N}$ be a thread. Then there exists some feasible trace τ such that $s \in \tau^\bullet$. Since τ is ι-feasible (by the above argument), it follows that τ is represented by $P^\sharp$. Finally, since τ is represented by $P^\sharp$ and ι is inductive for $P^\sharp$, we have that $s[n] \models \iota(s_{loc}(n))$ by Corollary 3.5. □

5.1 Relational abstract domains

We have discussed only the use of non-relational (also known as independent attribute) abstract domains up to this point. Although such domains are typically very efficient, the fact that they cannot encode relationships between variables limits their expressive power. In our framework, it is possible to use relational domains, such as octagons and polyhedra, by modifying the data flow graph. Instead having data flow graph edges labeled with a single variable, we allow *sets* of variables as labels, indicating that the value of every variable in this set flows from the source to the target. Since a value for each $x \in X$ flows along such an edge $u \rightarrow^X v$, relationships between variables in X can be maintained.

A particularly simple instance of this idea is to create a partition $\mathbb{P}$ of the set of variables *Var* into semantically related sets. Intuitively, we can think of each cell $X \in \mathbb{P}$ as a record-typed variable, with one field for each $x \in X$. For a given partition $\mathbb{P}$ of *Var*, the collecting semantics for a relational DFG $\langle Loc, DF\rangle$ with $\mathbb{P}$-labeled edges is given by the following:

$$\text{VAL}(u, X) = \{e' : \exists e \in \text{OUT}(u).\forall x \in X.e(x) = e'(x)\}$$

$$\text{IN}(v) = \bigcap_{X \in \mathbb{P}} \{e \in TEnv : \exists u \rightarrow^X v \in DF.e \in \text{VAL}(u, X)\}$$

$$\text{OUT}(v) = \begin{cases} TEnv & \text{if } v = \texttt{uninit} \\ \{e' : \exists e \in \text{IN}(v).\langle e, e'\rangle \in \mathcal{L}[\![v]\!]\} & \text{otherwise} \end{cases}$$

Using the collecting semantics as a guideline, it is straightforward to define inductive invariants for relational DFGs. The interference analysis of Section 4 must then be adapted to infer relational data flow edges. Towards this end, we redefine mod to act on cells rather than variables as follows:

$$mod_{\mathbb{P}}(v) = \{X \in \mathbb{P} : mod(v) \cap X \neq \emptyset\}$$

By re-instantiating the interference analysis in Figure 3 with $mod_{\mathbb{P}}$ in place of mod, we obtain our algorithm for calculating data flows in a relational DFG.

Since nonrelational analyses and relational analyses operate on different data flow graphs, it is not generally true (as in the case of sequential analyses) that a relational analysis is necessarily more accurate than a non-relational analysis. There is a positive side and a negative side to grouping variables when it comes to concurrent program analysis. On the positive side, grouping variables together makes it possible to infer relationships between variables, which results in a more precise analysis. On the negative side, grouping variables together may create additional interference edges (resulting in a less precise analysis), as $mod_{\mathbb{P}}(v)$ is generally larger than $mod(v)$ (for $v \in Loc$). For example, if `batch` and `counter` are grouped together in the relational DFG construction for Figure 1, then the interference analysis will infer the {`batch`, `counter`}-labeled edges $v_5 \rightarrow u_{13}$ and $u_{13} \rightarrow v_5$. With these edges present, the invariant that `counter` ≥ 0 at v_5 can no longer be proved, because the inductiveness condition for annotations implies that there is no lower bound for `counter` at v_5. In our experiments in Section 6, there are cases when interval analysis succeeds in proving a property correct when octagon analysis fails, and vice versa.

In Section 6.1, we briefly discuss the simple algorithm that we use to partition variables into semantically related sets. While simple, this algorithm performs fairly well on our benchmarks. However, we believe that there is considerable room for improvement with a better variable grouping algorithm.

6. Experiments

The approach presented in this paper is implemented into a tool called DUET.[3] We used a benchmark suite of 15 Linux device drivers to evaluate DUET. Additionally, we ran DUET on the set of Boolean programs generated by SatAbs [9] from these Linux drivers to compare DUET with two recent techniques on verification of parameterized Boolean programs.

6.1 Implementation

DUET is written in OCaml, and makes use of the CIL front-end for the C language [28] and the goto program front-end distributed with CBMC [8]. Our abstract interpreter uses the APRON library [5] for its numerical abstract domains. We use the BDD-based Datalog implementation bddbddb[33] to perform the interference analysis described in Section 4. Currently, DUET accepts three types of inputs: (1) C programs using *pthreads* library for thread operations, (2) Boolean programs in the input language of *Boom* [19] as an input, or (3) goto programs, as produced by the goto-cc C/C++ frontend (part of the CPROVER project [1].

[3] For more information on this tool, see `http://duet.cs.toronto.edu`

Device Drivers	#assertions	DUET: Interval Analysis		DUET: Octagon Analysis	
		safe	time	safe	time
i8xx_tco	90	75	1m51s	71	1m25s
ib700wdt	75	64	30s	64	20s
machzwd	87	73	39s	67	14m44s
mixcomwd	91	72	22s	74	25
pcwd	240	147	2m43s	145	23m48s
pcwd_pci	204	187	2m18s	188	2m59s
sbc60xxwdt	91	77	28s	69	11m27s
sc520_wdt	85	71	28s	65	13m20s
sc1200wdt	77	66	34s	66	33s
smsc37b787_wdt	93	80	47s	80	47s
w83877f_wdt	92	78	29s	72	13m24s
w83977f_wdt	101	90	34s	82	34s
wdt	99	88	25s	86	25s
wdt977	88	77	27s	75	28s
wdt_pci	84	67	33s	66	5m33s
total	1597	1312	13m9s	1277	90m21s

Table 1. DUET's Performance on Parameterized Integer Programs, run on an 3.16GHz Intel(R) Core 2(TM) machine with 4GB of RAM.

Our implementation currently inlines all function calls and then performs an intraprocedural analysis.

Alias Analysis. We use a type-based alias analysis to handle pointers. For each variable whose address is not taken, we assign a memory location which receives strong updates. For every type in the program, we assign a memory location which receives weak updates, and each access path of that type (other than variables whose address is not taken) is considered to be a reference to that memory location. The interference analysis implemented in DUET operates on these memory locations rather than variables. This scheme is sound under the assumption that pointer-typed expressions are never cast. For the benchmark suite used in Section 6.2, aliasing is not particularly important for proving array bounds and integer overflow properties. Therefore, we expect the consequences of our unsound and imprecise alias analysis to be negligible.

We use Algorithm 2 to partition variables into semantically related sets for our implementation of octagon analysis. While simple, it seems to be effective in practice when performing an octagon analysis on Boolean abstractions of Linux device drivers.

Algorithm 2 Variable partitioning algorithm

Input: A set of program locations *Loc*, a set of local variables *LV* and global variables *GV*
Output: A partition of *Var*
  //$\mathbb{P}$ is a disjoint set data structure
  $\mathbb{P} \leftarrow \{\{x\} : x \in Var\}$
  for $v \in Loc$ **do**
    if v is an assignment statement **then**
      $vs \leftarrow mod(v) \cup ref(v)$
      if $|vs| = 2 \wedge (vs \subseteq LV \vee vs \subseteq GV)$ **then**
        Merge the partitions of each $x \in vs$
      end if
    else if $v =$ `assume(p)` **then**
      if $vars(v) \subseteq LV \vee vars(v) \subseteq GV$ **then**
        Merge the partitions of each $x \in vars(v)$
      end if
    end if
  end for
  return $\mathbb{P}$

6.2 Evaluation

Below, we provide the results of experimenting with DUET on a collection of Linux device drivers and on Boolean abstractions of those drivers. Since a driver may have arbitrary many clients, it is important to verify these drivers in a parameterized setting.

Parameterized Integer Programs. Table 1 presents the result of running DUET on a collection of 15 Linux device drivers. These drivers are all written in C, and include infinite data (such as integer types). We know of no other tool that can verify numerical properties of such large programs with arbitrarily many threads,[4] and therefore we present the result of running DUET on these integer benchmarks without comparison with other tools.

DDVerify and goto-cc are used to (automatically) process each driver into a fully-inlined goto program annotated with assertions checking array bounds and integer overflows/underflows. With an inverval analysis, DUET manages to prove most of the assertions correct (1312 out of a total 1597), and does so in 13 minutes. DUET's performance using an octagon analysis is slightly worse, proving 1277 assertions correct in 90 minutes.

Most false positives for DUET appear to be caused by one of two reasons: imprecision in the abstract domain, and imprecision in how DUET handles the treatment of spinlocks in goto programs. In particular, many drivers use traverse zero-terminated arrays as in the snippet below:

```
for (i=0; array[i]; i++) { ... }
```

Since our abstraction of arrays has no special representation for zero-terminated arrays, DUET flags this as an array bound error (since no upper bound for i can be inferred). Our handling of spinlocks is imprecise because goto programs model them as pointers to integers (which take value either 0 or 1, depending on whether the lock is acquired), access to which is protected by atomic blocks. Due to our imprecise alias analysis, lock acquisitions can only *weakly* update this integer field, which means that two threads can

[4] It is possible to run Boom on the integer benchmarks by first extracting Boolean programs with SatAbs. However, SatAbs is designed for sequential programs rather than concurrent ones, and the Boolean programs extracted by the version of SatAbs that was available at the time we ran our experiments produced poor results: the combined SatAbs+Boom procedure took 2 days and did not prove any assertions correct.

Device Drivers	#programs	LI				Duet: Octagon Analysis			Duet: Interval Analysis		
		safe	unsafe	unknown	timeout	safe	unsafe	timeout	safe	unsafe	timeout
`i8xx_tco`	338	214	14	0	110	259	79	0	198	140	0
`ib700wdt`	181	109	13	0	59	124	56	1	91	90	0
`machzwd`	255	56	24	94	81	182	70	3	148	105	2
`mixcomwd`	178	103	24	0	51	117	59	2	81	95	2
`pcwd`	100	81	1	0	18	74	16	10	44	50	6
`sbc60xxwdt`	174	92	23	0	59	113	60	1	79	94	1
`sc1200wdt`	247	138	13	0	96	178	67	2	138	107	2
`sc520_wdt`	186	15	23	97	51	123	61	2	89	95	2
`smsc37b787_wdt`	340	154	13	0	173	272	65	3	151	187	2
`w83877f_wdt`	230	15	23	97	95	150	77	3	98	128	4
`w83977f_wdt`	389	147	13	0	229	322	65	2	144	243	2
`wdt`	230	109	17	0	104	161	59	10	108	114	8
`wdt977`	351	139	13	0	199	282	67	2	132	218	1
`wdt_pci`	217	10	34	4	169	146	69	2	146	69	2
total	3416	1382	248	292	1494	2503	870	43	1647	1735	34

Table 2. Comparison with linear interfaces [22] for Parameterized Boolean Programs. Average time per benchmark was 16.9s for LI and 3.4s for Duet. Benchmarks were run on an 3.16GHz Intel(R) Core 2(TM) machine with 4GB of RAM.

acquire the same lock. Neither of these sources of imprecision is due to a fundamental limitation of the analysis technique proposed in this paper (or related to concurrency), and we expect that our false positive rate to drop considerably with the core algorithm unchanged.

Parameterized Boolean Programs. Although Boolean programs are not the target of this work, we experimented with them for two reasons: (1) two recent approaches [19, 22] for verification of *parameterized* concurrent programs only accept Boolean programs as their input, and (2) there is no aliasing present in Boolean programs, which limits the scope of implementation-related imprecisions for a better evaluation of the core method.

Duet does not require a predicate abstraction phase to handle Linux device drivers, but to present a more fair comparison with the existing tools [19, 22], we also ran Duet on the Boolean abstractions. We compare Duet against two recent algorithms that handle parameterized Boolean programs: dynamic cutoff detection (DCD) from [19], as implemented in Boom, and linear interfaces (LI) from [22], as implemented in Getafix. We compared these tools against our own on the benchmarks used in the papers (as provided by the authors). The programs were generated by SatAbs from a set of Linux device drivers. The input formats of Boom and Getafix are slightly different, so we report the results separately. The `ib700wdt` and `mixcomwd` benchmarks were generated from the same device drivers, but refer to a different set of Boolean programs in Tables 2 and 3. Each LI benchmark consists of a server and a client thread template, where the client template is replicated arbitrarily many times. The client thread template is the device driver code, and the server thread template simulates the OS interacting with the drivers. In the DCD benchmarks, there is a single thread template that is replicated. All benchmarks were run with a timeout of 5 minutes.

Table 2 presents the results of comparison with the LI algorithm on the set of Boolean programs used in [22]. In the LI algorithm, the system is tested under 4 rounds of scheduling to look for a counter example, and if one is not found then an adequacy checker is executed that *may* succeed in proving the program safe for arbitrarily many threads and rounds of scheduling. The *safe* columns refer to the number of instances that were proved safe (for each analysis). The *unsafe* column for LI refers to the instances for which LI found a counterexample (a confirmed bug), while in Duet, it refers to the instances where assertions could not be proved safe.[5] The *timeout* column for LI refers to instances where LI cannot finish checking the program under 4 rounds, or cannot find a counterexample under 4 rounds and the adequacy checker times out while trying to prove the program safe. The *timeout* column for Duet refers to all the instances that Duet cannot prove safe within the timeout limit. The *unknown* column for LI refers to the instances that no counterexample is found, and the adequacy checker finishes but fails to prove the program safe for arbitrary number of threads.

In almost all benchmarks (other than `pcwd`), Duet can prove many more instances safe (and for `pcwd`, it is close: 74 vs. 81). Duet can prove many of the *unknown* and *timeout* instances of LI safe. The small table below presents a different view of the same results (not distinguishing among individual drivers).

		LI			
		safe	unsafe	timeout	unknown
OCT	safe	1320	0	267	916
	unsafe	60	247	25	538
	timeout	2	1	0	40

The above table compares the results of the octagon analysis in Duet with LI. Duet can prove an additional 1183 (267+916) programs correct compared to LI. There are 60 instances that Duet reports a *confirmed false positive* (a program that is known to be safe, but Duet fails to prove safe). There are a total of 2503 (1320+267+916) programs that are proved safe by Duet, and 247 programs that are correctly declared unsafe, and therefore Duet generates a total of 2750 correct answers. This puts the percentage of incorrect answers out of the total number of *confirmed* correct and incorrect answers for Duet at 2.1% (60/(2750+60)).

Table 3 presents the results of comparison with the DCD algorithm on the set of Boolean programs used in [19]. In the DCD algorithm, there is only one thread template which is increasingly replicated until a counterexample or a cutoff point is found (a cutoff point is a number of threads n such every thread state that is reachable with $m \geq n$ threads is also reachable with n threads). For the subset of these benchmarks where DCD does not time out, the cutoff is at most 3 threads. Duet's interval and octagon analysis substantially outperforms DCD in proving programs correct. In

[5] Note that since our approach is not complete, failure to prove an assertion does not imply that the assertion is necessarily false.

Device Drivers	#programs	DCD			DUET: Octagon Analysis			DUET: Interval Analysis		
		safe	unsafe	timeout	safe	unsafe	timeout	safe	unsafe	timeout
`ib700wdt`	132	10	102	20	16	113	3	28	101	3
`mixcomwd`	138	9	108	21	16	118	4	27	107	4

Table 3. Comparison with dynamic cutoff detection (DCD) [19] for parameterized Boolean programs. Average time per benchmark was 24.9s for DCD and 8.2s for DUET. Benchmarks were run on an 800MHz AMD Opteron(tm) machine with 32 GB of RAM.

particular, DUET can prove a total 58 programs correct (with interval and octagon analysis combined) in contrast to 19 for DCD, and there are no programs which DCD proves safe and which DUET cannot.

7. Related Work

Verification and analysis of concurrent programs has been vastly studied. Here, we focus on verification of parameterized concurrent programs and systems which is more relevant to our work.

Extensive research has been done in the area verification of parameterized protocols. These include (but are not limited to) *split invariants* [10], regular model checking [6, 20], parameterized model checking [12], network invariants [16, 21], and exploiting symmetry [13] in the Murϕ tool [16]. *Counter abstraction* [3, 30] has been a useful technique in verifying replicated components, although bounded. As discussed in Section 1, we believe that proving functional correctness of a protocol is much more involved compared to proving program assertions correct in program such as a device driver (the focus of our work). For example, the correctness of Lamport's Bakery protocol [24] requires complex global invariant with quantifiers. In contrast, we expect driver code to use significantly simpler invariants to enforce synchronization, such as a flag being set or a lock being held. Moreover, *global* program properties (such as mutual exclusion) are part of the correctness of a protocol (such as Bakery), whereas we focus on program assertions, which are not expressive enough to relate the states of different threads to each other.

To the best of our knowledge, the body of work on verification of parameterized protocols (some of it mentioned above) does not contain a single tool that can, for example, effectively verify numerical properties of Linux device drivers with unboundedly many threads. Recently, two new approaches [19, 22] have been proposed for verification of parameterized Boolean programs that target Boolean abstractions of Linux device drivers, and are more closely related to our work. In [19], a *cutoff detection* algorithm is proposed to determine a bound on the number of threads needed to explore all thread states. In [22], an under approximation method based on limiting the number of scheduler rounds (as opposed to context-switches) and the use of *linear interfaces* to summarize interference in a round is proposed. We compare against both these algorithms in our experiments in Section 6. The most important advantage of our framework is that we handle unbounded data domains such as integers, whereas these other techniques are limited to Boolean programs. Based on our experiments, it is a significant advantage to be able to apply directly to integer programs, since predicate abstraction does not make any considerations for threads (a very recent work [11] takes a first step towards closing this gap by making predicate abstraction *symmetry-aware*).

In [4], an abstract domain construction was presented which can represent invariants of the form $\forall t.\varphi(t)$, where t is a variable representing a thread $\varphi(t)$ is an abstract value in some base domain. Since such an invariant is an assertion about *all* threads rather than some fixed set, this technique is applicable to parameterized programs. The authors apply their construction to a shape domain and successfully verify linearizability for a number of concurrent data structures, a property that is more complex than the type we consider in this paper. However, computation of abstract transformers for quantified domains is potentially very expensive. Moreover, our computation of thread interference using traces is potentially more accurate than their method, which is state-based.

There are a few recent approaches in concurrent program verification [15, 18, 25] which assume a *fixed* number of threads (and therefore not applicable to parameterized programs and not directly comparable to our work), but are worth mentioning here. The work in [15] uses predicate abstraction to automatically generate environment abstractions for threads in a rely-guarantee based proof method. They attempt to find a modular proof (where the environment of every thread refers only to global variables) if one exists, and generate a non-modular one (local variables can occur everywhere) otherwise. They can prove more sophisticated properties (such as correctness of Bakery algorithm) than DUET, but only for a small fixed number of threads (2-4); therefore, it is hard to draw any fair comparison between the two tools. The work in [18] is based on abstract interpretation, where they *refine* the *transaction graphs* which model interference among threads, using abstract interpretation. At a high level, our work is similar to the approach in [25]; however, there are significant differences (besides the fact that our approach deals with parameterized programs). Our notion of interference is quite different, and our need to iterate our analysis until convergence is for a different reason. In particular, in [25], the notion of interference is *static* in the sense that the structure of the dataflow equations do not change from one round to the next; only the abstract values involved change.

8. Conclusion and future work

We propose a solution to the problem of verifyinbg thread invariants for parameterized multithreaded programs. Our approach is based on an iterative framework consisting of a feedback loop between two components: one that computes data invariants using a data flow graph representation of the program and another that uses the data invariants to infer new data flow edges and update the data flow graph. Our algorithm is sound and terminating, and is applicable to programs with infinite state (e.g., unbounded integers) and unboundedly many threads. We have implemented our approach into a tool, called DUET, and applied it to a selection of Linux device drivers and a large suite of Boolean programs. Our experiments demonstrate the effectiveness of the approach in proving properties of parameterized concurrent programs in terms of both speed and precision.

Aliasing is a big obstacle for any program verification method, and more specifically for concurrency verification. In our framework, distinguishing two global variables as non-aliases can potentially have a huge impact on the patterns of interference among threads, and make or break a proof of correctness. Also, naturally, information about data invariants and thread interferences can result in a more precise alias analysis for concurrent programs. We believe that combining alias analysis inside the feedback loop in our framework is an interesting research question for future work. As discussed in Section 5.1, a more intelligent algorithm for computing variable groups for relational analyses will also definitely improve the precision and scalability of our analysis.

Acknowledgments

We wish to thank Andreas Podelski for his significant role in improving the presentation of this paper. We would also like to thank Patrick and Radhia Cousot for their comments on an earlier version of this paper. Finally, we thank Alexander Kaiser and Gennaro Parlato for providing the Boolean programs and for their help with running Boom and Getafix.

References

[1] J. Alglave, D. Kroening, N. He, A. Ranjan, N. Seghir, and M. Tautschnig. CPROVER project, Nov. 2011. URL http://www.cprover.org/.

[2] T. Arons, A. Pnueli, S. Ruah, J. Xu, and L. D. Zuck. Parameterized verification with automatically computed inductive assertions. In *CAV*, pages 221–234, 2001.

[3] G. Basler, M. Mazzucchi, T. Wahl, and D. Kroening. Symbolic counter abstraction for concurrent software. In *CAV*, pages 64–78, 2009.

[4] J. Berdine, T. Lev-Ami, R. Manevich, G. Ramalingam, and M. Sagiv. Thread quantification for concurrent shape analysis. In *CAV*, volume 5123 of *LNCS*, pages 399–413. 2008.

[5] J. Bertrand and A. Miné. Apron: A library of numerical abstract domains for static analysis. In *CAV*, pages 661–667, 2009.

[6] A. Bouajjani, B. Jonsson, M. Nilsson, and T. Touili. Regular model checking. In *CAV*, pages 403–418, 2000.

[7] J. Choi, K. Lee, A. Loginov, R. O'Callahan, V. Sarkar, and M. Sridharan. Efficient and precise datarace detection for multithreaded object-oriented programs. *SIGPLAN Not.*, 37:258–269, 2002.

[8] E. Clarke, D. Kroening, and F. Lerda. A tool for checking ANSI-C programs. In K. Jensen and A. Podelski, editors, *Tools and Algorithms for the Construction and Analysis of Systems (TACAS 2004)*, volume 2988 of *Lecture Notes in Computer Science*, pages 168–176. Springer, 2004. ISBN 3-540-21299-X.

[9] E. M. Clarke, D. Kroening, N. Sharygina, and K. Yorav. Satabs: Sat-based predicate abstraction for ansi-c. In *TACAS*, pages 570–574, 2005.

[10] A. Cohen and K. S. Namjoshi. Local proofs for linear-time properties of concurrent programs. In *CAV*, pages 149–161, 2008.

[11] A. F. Donaldson, A. Kaiser, D. Kroening, and T. Wahl. Symmetry-aware predicate abstraction for shared-variable concurrent programs. In *CAV*, pages 356–371, 2011.

[12] E. A. Emerson and V. Kahlon. Model checking large-scale and parameterized resource allocation systems. In *TACAS*, pages 251–265, 2002.

[13] E. A. Emerson and A. P. Sistla. Symmetry and model checking. *Form. Methods Syst. Des.*, 9:105–131, 1996.

[14] D. Engler and K. Ashcraft. Racerx: effective, static detection of race conditions and deadlocks. *SIGOPS Oper. Syst. Rev.*, 37:237–252, 2003.

[15] A. Gupta, C. Popeea, and A. Rybalchenko. Predicate abstraction and refinement for verifying multi-threaded programs. In *POPL*, pages 331–344, 2011.

[16] C. N. Ip and D. L. Dill. Verifying systems with replicated components in murϕ;, 1997.

[17] R. Johnson and K. Pingali. Dependence-based program analysis. In *PLDI*, pages 78–89, 1993.

[18] V. Kahlon, S. Sankaranarayanan, and A. Gupta. Semantic reduction of thread interleavings in concurrent programs. In *TACAS*, pages 124–138, 2009.

[19] A. Kaiser, D. Kroening, and T. Wahl. Dynamic cutoff detection in parameterized concurrent programs. In *CAV*, pages 645–659. 2010.

[20] Y. Kesten, O. Maler, M. Marcus, A. Pnueli, and E. Shahar. Symbolic model checking with rich assertional languages. In *CAV*, pages 424–435, 1997.

[21] Y. Kesten, A. Pnueli, E. Shahar, and L. D. Zuck. Network invariants in action. In *CONCUR*, pages 101–115, 2002.

[22] S. La Torre, P. Madhusudan, and G. Parlato. Model-checking parameterized concurrent programs using linear interfaces. In *CAV*, pages 629–644. 2010.

[23] S. K. Lahiri and R. E. Bryant. Predicate abstraction with indexed predicates. *ACM Trans. Comput. Logic*, 9, 2007.

[24] L. Lamport. A new solution of dijkstra's concurrent programming problem. *Commun. ACM*, 17(8):453–455, 1974.

[25] A. Miné. Static analysis of run-time errors in embedded critical parallel c programs. In *ESOP*, pages 398–418, Berlin, Heidelberg, 2011. Springer-Verlag. ISBN 978-3-642-19717-8.

[26] M. Naik and A. Aiken. Conditional must not aliasing for static race detection. *SIGPLAN Not.*, 42:327–338, 2007.

[27] M. Naik, A. Aiken, and J. Whaley. Effective static race detection for Java. *SIGPLAN Not.*, 41:308–319, 2006.

[28] G. C. Necula, S. McPeak, S. P. Rahul, and W. Weimer. Cil: Intermediate language and tools for analysis and transformation of c programs. In *CC*, pages 213–228, 2002.

[29] A. Pnueli, S. Ruah, and L. D. Zuck. Automatic deductive verification with invisible invariants. In *TACAS*, pages 82–97, 2001.

[30] A. Pnueli, J. Xu, and L. D. Zuck. Liveness with $(0, 1, \infty)$-counter abstraction. In *CAV*, pages 107–122, 2002. ISBN 3-540-43997-8.

[31] P. Pratikakis, J. S. Foster, and M. Hicks. Locksmith: context-sensitive correlation analysis for race detection. *SIGPLAN Not.*, 41:320–331, 2006.

[32] N. Sterling. Warlock - a static data race analysis tool. In *USENIX Winter*, pages 97–106, 1993.

[33] J. Whaley and M. S. Lam. Cloning-based context-sensitive pointer alias analysis using binary decision diagrams. *SIGPLAN Not.*, 39:131–144, June 2004. ISSN 0362-1340.

Resource-Sensitive Synchronization Inference by Abduction

Matko Botinčan
University of Cambridge
matko.botincan@cl.cam.ac.uk

Mike Dodds
University of Cambridge
mike.dodds@cl.cam.ac.uk

Suresh Jagannathan
Purdue University
suresh@cs.purdue.edu

Abstract

We present an analysis which takes as its input a sequential program, augmented with annotations indicating potential parallelization opportunities, and a sequential proof, written in separation logic, and produces a correctly-synchronized parallelized program and proof of that program. Unlike previous work, ours is not an independence analysis; we insert synchronization constructs to preserve relevant dependencies found in the sequential program that may otherwise be violated by a naïve translation. Separation logic allows us to parallelize fine-grained patterns of resource-usage, moving beyond straightforward points-to analysis.

Our analysis works by using the sequential proof to discover dependencies between different parts of the program. It leverages these discovered dependencies to guide the insertion of synchronization primitives into the parallelized program, and to ensure that the resulting parallelized program satisfies the same specification as the original sequential program, and exhibits the same sequential behaviour. Our analysis is built using frame inference and abduction, two techniques supported by an increasing number of separation logic tools.

Categories and Subject Descriptors D.2.4 [*Software Engineering*]: Program Verification—Correctness proofs; D.3.3 [*Programming Languages*]: Language Constructs and Features—Concurrent programming structures

General Terms Languages, Theory, Verification

Keywords Separation Logic, Abduction, Frame Inference, Deterministic Parallelism

1. Introduction

Automatically verifying the safety properties of shared-memory concurrent programs remains a challenging problem. To be useful in practice, proof tools must (a) explore a potentially large number of interleavings, and (b) construct precise flow- and path-sensitive abstractions of a shared heap.

Just as significantly, verification complexity is often at odds with the straightforward intentions of the programmer. Low-level concurrency control abstractions such as locks obfuscate higher-level notions such as atomicity and linearizability, likely to be exploited by the programmer when writing programs. While attempts to incorporate these notions directly into programs have met with some success—for example, in software transactional memory [21], there remains a substantial burden on the programmer to ensure programs can be partitioned into easily-understood atomic and thread-local sections. Automated proof engines used to verify program correctness must also assimilate this knowledge to ensure proof-search focusses on relevant behaviour (e.g., serializability), and eschews irrelevant details (e.g., thread-local state) [18]; the alternative, expressing such distinctions in programmer-supplied specifications, is too often onerous to be acceptable in practice. In any case, the inherent complexity of dealing with concurrency, both for the programmer and for the verifier, unfortunately remains.

In many cases concurrency is an optimization, rather than intrinsic to the behaviour of the program. That is, a concurrent programs is often intended to achieve the same effect of a simpler sequential counterpart. Consequently, an attractive alternative to *constructing* a concurrent programming is to automatically *synthesise* one. In this approach, the programmer writes a sequential program; the program is automatically transformed into a concurrent one exhibiting the same behaviour [3–5, 17][1]. In this context, the verification problem becomes significantly more tractable. Understanding and verifying the concurrent program reduces to first verifying the sequential program, and second, verifying the parallelising transformation.

We propose a program analysis and transformation that yields a parallelized program, guided by a safety proof of the original sequential program. To guide the transformation, we assume that the programmer annotates points in the sequential program where concurrency can be profitably exploited, *without* supplying any additional concurrency control or synchronization. The result of the transformation is a concurrent program with corresponding behaviour, and a safety proof for the concurrent program; in this sense, parallelized programs are *verified by construction*. While our analysis is driven by a safety proof, parallelization protects all behaviours, not just those specified in the proof. Thus we can apply our approach to complex algorithms without needing to verify total functional correctness.

Our transformation ensures that behaviour is preserved by requiring that the concurrent program respects sequential data-dependencies. In other words, the way threads access and modify shared resources never results in behaviour that would not be possible under sequential evaluation. To enforce these dependencies, the transformation injects *barriers*, signalling operations that regulate when threads are allowed to read or write shared state. These barriers can be viewed as resource transfer operations which acquire and relinquish access to shared resources such as shared-memory data structures and regions when necessary.

Our analysis is built on separation logic [32]. By tracking how resources are demanded and consumed within a separation logic

[1] This approach is commonly known as *deterministic parallelism*, although our approach does not, in fact, require that the input sequential program is deterministic.

POPL'12, January 25–27, 2012, Philadelphia, PA, USA.

proof, we can synthesize barriers to precisely control access to these resources. Our approach critically relies on frame inference and abduction [11], two techniques that generate fine-grained information on when resources are necessary and when they are redundant. This information enables optimizations that depend on deep structural properties of the resource—for example, we can split a linked list into dynamically-sized segments and transmit portions between threads piece-by-piece.

Our analysis thus enforces sequential order over visible behaviours, while allowing parallelization where it has no effect on behaviour. Insofar as our technique safely transforms a sequential program into a concurrent one, it can also be viewed as a kind of proof-directed compiler optimization. Notably, our transformation is *not* based on an independence analysis—our focus is not to identify when two potentially concurrent code regions do not interfere; instead, our analysis injects sufficient synchronization to ensure relevant sequential dependencies are preserved, even when regions share state and thus potentially interfere.

Contributions.

1. We present an automated technique to synthesize a parallel program given a partially-specified sequential program augmented with annotations indicating computations that are candidates for parallelization. The provided specifications are used to define relevant loop invariants.
2. We leverage abduction and frame inference to define a path- and context-sensitive program analysis capable of identifying per program-point resources that are both *redundant*—these are resources that would no longer be used by the thread executing this computation; and, *needed*—these are resources that would be required by any thread that executes this computation, but which is not known to have been released at this point.
3. We use information from the above analysis to inject *grant* and *allowed* barriers into the original program; their semantics enable resource transfer from redundant to needed resource points. The analysis also constructs a safety proof in separation logic which validates the correctness of the barrier injections.
4. We prove that our transformation is specification-preserving: the parallelized program is guaranteed to satisfy the same specification as the sequential program. Moreover, for terminating programs that do not dispose memory, we also show that the transformed program preserves the *behaviour* of the original. Complete proofs and other supporting material can be found in an associated technical report [8].

Paper structure. An overview of the approach and motivating examples are given in §2. Issues that arise in dealing with loops and recursive datatypes (such as lists) are discussed in §3. The analysis and transformation are formalized in §4 and §5. Behaviour preservation results are discussed in §6. Observations about the interplay between analysis precision and the predicates available in defining specifications are given in §7. §8 discusses related work.

2. Overview

The objective of our analysis is to take a sequential program (with annotations indicating where concurrency may be exploited), and to produce a *parallelized* program that conforms to the same specification. To do this, we insert *synchronization barriers* enforcing those sequential dependencies that can affect the observable behaviour of the program.

Our analysis uses *separation logic* to capture and manipulate these dependencies. The programmer must provide a proof of safety for the sequential program. This proof is used to drive the parallelization process, allowing our analysis to calculate precisely

```
global *x, *y;
void main() {                void f(i){              void g(*p, v){
  local i, n;                  local v=*x;             *p = v;
  n = nondet();                if (v>=i) {          }
  x = alloc();                   g(y, v);
  y = alloc();                 }
  pfor(i=1;i++;i<n){           else {
    f(i);                        g(x, 0);
  }                            }
}                            }
```

Figure 1. A simple parallel program that operates over shared locations `x` and `y`. The number of concurrent iterations performed is chosen nondeterministically to represent the act of receiving values from some unknown process or user interaction.

which resources can be accessed in parallel, and which must be accessed sequentially, in order to preserve salient sequential dependencies.

2.1 Parallelization and Parallel-for

We assume that the portions of a program that can be parallelized will be written as *parallel-for* loops, **pfor**. The intended semantics of a parallel-for loop is that every iteration will run in parallel, but that the behaviour will be identical to running them in sequence; this semantics provides a simple but useful form of data parallelism in which concurrently executing computations may nonetheless have access to shared state.

For example, consider the program shown in Fig. 1. How can we parallelize this program without introducing any unwanted new behaviours, *i.e.*, behaviours not possible under sequential execution? Naïvely, we might simply run every iteration of the **pfor** in parallel, without synchronization. That is:

```
f(1) || f(2) || ...
```

In some cases, this parallelization is good, and introduces no new observable behaviours (e.g., if `v` is greater than `n`). But, under others, the second call to `f()` may write to a memory location that is subsequently read by the first call to `f()`, violating intended sequential ordering. For example, consider the case when `v` is initially `1` and `n` is 2; sequential execution would produce a final result in which the locations pointed to by `x` and `y` resp. are 0 and 1, while executing the second iteration before the first would yield a result in which the location pointed to by `y` remains undefined.

To be sure that no new observable behaviour is introduced, we must ensure that:

- no iteration can read from a location that was already written to by a later iteration.
- no iteration can write to a location that was already read from or written to by a later iteration.

In order to enforce this behaviour, we must introduce a mechanism to force later iterations to wait for earlier ones.

Note, crucially, that later iterations *need not always* wait for earlier ones—synchronization is only needed when reads and writes to a particular memory location could result in out-of-order behaviour. We want to enforce *salient* dependencies, while allowing beneficial race-free concurrency.

2.2 Dependency-Enforcing Barriers

Our analysis inserts barriers into the parallelized program requiring logically later iterations to wait for earlier ones. We introduce **grant()**, a barrier that signals to subsequent iterations that a resource can safely be accessed, and **wait()**, a barrier that blocks until the associated resource becomes available from preceding iterations [17].

```
f1(i){                ga1(*p, v){      | f2(i){              ga2(*p, v){
 local v=*x;           *p=v;           |  wait(wx);           wait(wy);
 if (v>=i) {           grant(wy);      |  local v=*x;         *p=v;
   grant(wx);         }                |  if (v>=i) {        }
   ga1(y, v);                          |    ga2(y, v);
 }                                     |  }
 else {               gb1(*p, v){      |  else {             gb2(*p, v){
   grant(wy);          *p=v;           |    gb2(x, 0);        *p=v;
   gb1(x, 0)           grant(wx);      |    wait(wy);        }
 }                    }                |  }
}                                      | }
```

Figure 2. Parallelization of `f()`. Only synchronization barriers between the first and second iterations are shown.

How can we use these barriers to enforce sequential dependencies in the example program? The exact pattern of parallelization depends on the granularity of our parallelization analysis. In the best case, there are no dependencies between iterations (e.g., each iteration operates on a different portion of a data structure). In this case, we need no barriers, and all iterations run independently. However, our example program shares the locations `x` and `y`, meaning barriers are required. In the worst case, each iteration of the `pfor` begins with a call to `wait()` and ends with a call to `grant()`—this would enforce sequential ordering on the iterations.

A better (although still relatively simple) parallelization is shown in Fig. 2. To simplify the presentation, we only show the synchronization barriers between the first and second iterations of `pfor`. We write $\mathtt{f}_1$ for the first iteration, and $\mathtt{f}_2$ for the second. (Our full analysis generates a single version of `f()` with sufficient barriers to run an arbitrary number of iterations in parallel. See §2.6 for a description.)

Two channels, `wx` and `wy`, are used to signal between $\mathtt{f}_1$ and $\mathtt{f}_2$—`wx` (resp. `wy`) is used to signal that the later thread can read and write to the heap location referred to by `x` (resp. `y`). The function `g()` has different resource requirements depending on its calling context. Consequently, we have specialized it to embed appropriate barriers depending on its context.

Our analysis inserts barriers so that an iteration of the parallel-for only calls `grant()` on a signal when the associated resource will no longer be accessed. Similarly, it ensures that an iteration calls `wait()` to acquire the resource before the resource is accessed.

How does our analysis generate these synchronization barriers? The example we have given here is simple, but in general our analysis must cope with complex dynamically-allocated resources such as linked lists. It must deal with the partial ownership (for example, read-access), and with manipulating portions of a dynamic structure (for example, just the head of a linked list). We therefore need a means to express complex (dynamic) patterns of resource management and transfer.

To achieve this, our analysis assumes a sequential *proof*, written in separation logic, rather than just an undecorated program. This proof need not capture full functional correctness—it is sufficient just to prove memory-safety. We exploit the dependencies expressed within this proof to determine the resources that are needed at a program point, and when they can be released. Our analysis inserts barriers to enforce the sequential dependancies represented in this proof. As our proof system is sound, these dependencies faithfully represent those in the original sequential program.

2.3 Resources, Separation and Dependency

At the heart of our analysis is automated reasoning using concurrent separation logic [28, 32]. Separation logic is a Hoare-style program logic for reasoning about mutable, allocatable resources. A separation logic proof of a program C establishes a specification

$$\{P\}\ C\ \{Q\}$$

This can be be read as saying: "*the program C, if run in a resource satisfying P, will not fault, and will give a resource satisfying Q if it terminates*". In general, a *resource* can be anything for which ownership can be partitioned ('separated') between different threads [10]. In practice, resources are most often heap-allocated structures such as lists, trees, locks, etc, where separation corresponds to disjointness between underlying heap addresses.

An essential feature of separation logic is that specifications are *tight*. This means that all of the resources accessed by a program C must be described in its precondition P, or acquired through explicit resource transfer. No other resources will be accessed or affected by C when executed from a resource satisfying P. The tight interpretation is essential for our analysis. Suppose we prove a specification for a program (or portion thereof); resources outside of the precondition cannot affect the program's behaviour, and consequently can be safely transferred to other threads.

One result of this tight interpretation is the *frame rule*, which allows a small specification to be embedded into a larger context.

$$\frac{\{P\}\ C\ \{Q\}}{\{P * F\}\ C\ \{Q * F\}}\ \textsc{Frame}$$

Here $*$ is the *separating conjunction*. An assertion $P * F$ is satisfied if P and F hold, and the portions of the state they denote do not overlap.

The concurrent counterpart of the frame rule is the *parallel rule*. This allows two threads that access non-overlapping resources to run in parallel, without affecting each other's behaviour.

$$\frac{\{P_1\}\ C_1\ \{Q_1\} \qquad \{P_2\}\ C_2\ \{Q_2\}}{\{P_1 * P_2\}\ C_1 \| C_2\ \{Q_1 * Q_2\}}\ \textsc{Parallel}$$

The parallel rule enforces the absence of data-races between C_1 and C_2. The two threads can consequently only affect each other's behaviour by communicating through race-free synchronization mechanisms, such as locks or barriers.

Automatic inference. Automated reasoning in separation logic revolves around two kinds of inference questions. The first, *frame inference*, calculates the portion of a formula S which is 'left over', once another formula P has been satisfied. We call this remainder $F_?$ the *frame*, and write the inference question as follows:

$$S \vdash P * [F_?]$$

(Throughout the paper, we use square brackets to indicate the portion of the entailment that is to be computed.)

The second kind of inference question, *abduction*, calculates the 'missing' formula that must be combined with a formula S in order to satisfy some other formula P. We call this formula $A_?$ the *antiframe*, and write the inference question as follows:

$$S * [A_?] \vdash P$$

Frame inference and abduction form the basis of symbolic execution in separation logic [2, 11]. Intuitively, frame inference lets us reason forwards, while abduction lets us reason backwards. Frame inference can work out which portions of the state will (and will not) be affected by the command, while abduction can work out what extra resources are necessary to execute the command safely.

Suppose we have a symbolic state represented by an assertion S, and a command c with specification $\{P\}\,c\,\{Q\}$. If we calculate the frame in $S \vdash P * [F_?]$, the symbolic state after executing c must be $Q * F_?$. The tight interpretation of triples is necessary for this kind of reasoning. Because a specification must describe all the resources affected by a thread, any resources in the frame must be unaffected. Conversely, if we calculate the antiframe $S * [A_?] \vdash P$, it must be the case that before executing c, we must first acquire the additional resource $A_?$ (as well as S).

Redundant and needed resources. The tight interpretation means that a proof in separation logic expresses all resources modified by each individual command. Because separation logic ensures race-free behaviour, a proof also expresses all the resources that can affect the observable behaviour of each individual command in the program. Our parallelization analysis uses this to calculate resources that are redundant and those that are needed during the execution of the program.

We use frame inference to determine *redundant resources*—resources that will not be accessed in a particular portion of the program, and which can thus be safely transferred to other threads. Conversely, we use abduction to determine *needed resources*—resources that must be held for a particular portion of the program to complete, and which must thus be acquired before the program can proceed safely.

In our analysis, we generally calculate the redundant resource from the current program point to the start of the subsequent iteration. This resource can be transferred to the subsequent iteration using a `grant()` barrier. We generally calculate the needed resource from the end of the previous iteration to the current program point. This resource must be acquired from the previous iteration using a `wait()` barrier before execution can proceed further.

Note that these two resources need not be disjoint. A resource may be used early in an iteration, in which case it will be both needed from the previous iteration to the current point, and redundant from the current point up to the next iteration. Note also that redundant and needed resources need not cover the entire state—some resource described in the proof may never be accessed or modified by the program.

2.4 Algorithm Overview

The user supplies a sequential program which makes use of the `pfor` parallel-for construct, as well as a sequential proof written in separation logic establishing the memory-safety of the program. The high-level structure of our algorithm is then as follows:

1. The *resource usage analysis* phase uses abduction and frame inference to discover redundant and needed resources for different portions of the program.
2. The *parallelising transformation* phase consists of two parts:
   (a) The *resource matching* phase matches redundant resources in one iteration of the parallel-`for` with needed resources in the subsequent iteration.
   (b) The *barrier insertion* phase converts the sequential program into a concurrent program and inserts `grant()` and `wait()` barriers consistent with the discovered resource-transfer.

The result is a parallelized program, and its separation logic proof.

2.5 Resource Usage Analysis

The resource usage analysis takes as its input the program, and a separation logic proof for the program for some specification. Consider once again the functions `f()` and `g()`, which we introduced at the start of this section. Let us assume the programmer proves the following specification:

$$\{\mathtt{x} \mapsto x * \mathtt{y} \mapsto y\}$$
`f(i)`
$$\{(x \geq \mathtt{i} \wedge \mathtt{x} \mapsto x * \mathtt{y} \mapsto x) \vee (\mathtt{x} \mapsto 0 * \mathtt{y} \mapsto y)\}$$

Fig. 3 shows an outline proof of this specification.

For each program point, the resource usage analysis computes a pair of assertions: the *needed* resource and the *redundant* resource

```
{x ↦ x * y ↦ y}
void f(i) {
  {x ↦ x * y ↦ y}
  local v = *x;
  {v = x ∧ x ↦ x * y ↦ y}
  if (v >= i) {
    {v = x ∧ v ≥ i ∧ x ↦ x * y ↦ y}
    g(y, v);
  }
  else {
    {v = x ∧ v < i ∧ x ↦ x * y ↦ y}
    g(x, 0);
  }
}
{(x ≥ i ∧ x ↦ x * y ↦ x) ∨ (x ↦ 0 * y ↦ y)}
```

```
{p ↦ _ ∧ v = v}
void g(*p, v) {
  {p ↦ _ ∧ v = v}
  *p = v;
}
{p ↦ v}
```

Figure 3. Proofs of functions `f()` and `g()`.

(see Fig. 4). The needed resource is the portion of the sequential precondition required to reach the program point without faulting; the redundant resource is the portion of the resource held in the sequential proof that is unnecessary for reaching the end of the function. In other words, needed assertions at program point p denote resources that are needed from the beginning of the function up to (but not including) p; redundant assertions denote resources that are not required from p to the end of the function.

For example, the redundant resource established within the false branch of the conditional in `f` asserts that a thread executing this function will no longer require access to `y` at this point whenever `v < i`. The needed resource here asserts that the thread reaching this point still requires access to `x`, provided `v < i`.

2.6 Generalizing to n Threads

Our analysis can handle an unbounded number of loop iterations running in parallel. Fig. 5 shows the final parallelization of our example, generalized to deal with an arbitrary number of iterations.

A `pfor` is translated to a sequential `for` loop, in which each iteration forks a new copy of the parallelized loop body. Resources are transferred between the threads in order of thread-creation. That is, the nth iteration of the `pfor` acquires resources from the logically-preceding $(n-1)$th iteration, and releases resources to the logically $(n+1)$th iteration. This ordering is implemented through shared channels—a thread shares with its predecessor a set of channels for receiving resources, and with its successor a set of channels for sending resources.

The number of threads—and so, the required number of channels—is potentially decided at run-time. Consequently, channels are dynamically allocated in the main `for`-loop using the `newchan()` operation [17]. Each iteration creates a set of new channels, and passes the prior and new set to the forked thread. The parallelized version of `f` (Fig. 5) now takes four channel arguments, a pair of each for `x` and `y`. The prior channels are used for resource transfer with the logically-preceding thread (here `wx`, `wy`), and the new channels are used to communicate resource transfer with the logically-following thread (here, `wx'`, `wy'`).

Our analysis generates two versions of function `g`, specialized to the two contexts in which it is invoked. Function `ga` executes when `v >= i`. Here, the executing thread needs write access to `y`, which it acquires by calling `wait(wyp)`. Function `gb` needs write access to `x`, but it runs in a context where the resource `x` has already been acquired. Consequently, it need not call `wait`. Both versions release a resource to the following thread using `grant` before returning.

```
void f(i) {
 n:{emp}
 r:{x < i ∧ y ↦ y}
  local v = *x;
 n:{x ↦ x}
 r:{x ≥ i ∧ x ↦ x) ∨ (x < i ∧ y ↦ y)}
  if (v >= i) {
   n:{x ≥ i ∧ x ↦ x}
   r:{x ≥ i ∧ x ↦ x}
    g(y, v); ⟶ void g(*p, v) {
                   n:{x ≥ i ∧ x ↦ x}
                   r:{x ≥ i ∧ x ↦ x}
                    *p = v;
                   n:{x ≥ i ∧ x ↦ x * y ↦ y}
                   r:{x ↦ x * y ↦ y}
                  }
  }
  else {
   n:{x < i ∧ x ↦ x}
   r:{x < i ∧ y ↦ y}
    g(x, 0); ⟶ void g(*p, v) {
                   n:{x < i ∧ x ↦ x}
                   r:{x < i ∧ y ↦ y}
                    *p = v;
                   n:{x < i ∧ x ↦ x}
                   r:{x ↦ x * y ↦ y}
                  }
  }
 n:{(x ≥ i ∧ x ↦ x * y ↦ y) ∨ (x < i ∧ x ↦ x)}
 r:{x ↦ x * y ↦ y}
}
```

Figure 4. Redundant and needed resources in the function `f()`. Function `g()` is inlined, as its resource usage depends on the calling context.

3. Loops and Recursive Data Structures

Up to this point, we have dealt with channels transferring single heap locations injected into straight-line code. Our analysis can in fact handle more complicated heap-allocated data-structures such as linked lists, and control-flow constructs such as loops. To illustrate, consider the example program `sum_head(n)` shown (and verified) in Fig. 6. `sum_head(n)` sums the values stored in the first `n` elements of the list, then zeros the rest of the list.

An important feature of our approach is that the input safety proof need not specify all the relevant sequential properties; all sequential dependencies are enforced. Thus we can see `sum_head` as representative of the class of algorithms that traverse the head of a list, then mutate the tail. With minor modifications, the same proof pattern would cover insertion of a node into a list, or sorting the tail of the list.

Consider two calls to this function within a parallel-`for`:

```
void main(){ pfor(i=1;i++;i<3){ n=nondet(); sum_head(n) }
```

As above, for the sake of exposition we specialize the first and second iterations of the `pfor` loop, calling them $\texttt{sum\_head}_1$ and $\texttt{sum\_head}_2$. Our analysis generalizes to n iterations exactly as described in §2.6. The barriers injected into `sum_head` must enforce the following properties:

- $\texttt{sum\_head}_2$ must not write to a list node until $\texttt{sum\_head}_1$ has finished both writing to and reading from it. Consequently, if `n2` < `n1`, $\texttt{sum\_head}_2$ must wait for $\texttt{sum\_head}_1$ to finish summing the values stored in the first `n1` nodes before writing to them.
- $\texttt{sum\_head}_2$ must not read from a list node until $\texttt{sum\_head}_1$ has finished writing to them. Consequently, $\texttt{sum\_head}_2$ must wait for $\texttt{sum\_head}_1$ to finish zeroing the value stored in a node before reading from the node.

```
void main() {
  local i, n = nondet();
  x = alloc(); y = alloc();
  chan wx', wy';
  chan wx = newchan(); chan wy = newchan();
  grant(wx); grant(wy);
  for (i = 0; i++; i < n) {
    wx' = newchan(); wy' = newchan();
    fork(f(i, wx, wy, wx', wy'));
    wx = wx'; wy = wy';
  }
  wait(wx); wait(wy);
}

f(i, wxp, wyp, wx, wy){           ga(*p, v, wyp, wy){
  wait(wxp);                        wait(wyp);
  local v = *x;                     *p = v;
  if (v >= i) {                     grant(wy);
    grant(wx);                    }
    ga(y, v, wy);
  }
  else {                          gb(*p, v, wx){
    wait(wyp);                      *p = v;
    grant(wy);                      grant(wx);
    gb(x, 0, wx);                 }
} }
```

Figure 5. Parallelization of our running example generalized to deal with n threads. Channels are used to signal availability of resources from one thread to another.

This example is substantially more subtle than our earlier one, requiring more than a simple points-to analysis, because the list is not divided into statically-apparent reachable segments. In the worst case, a `wait()` at the start of $\texttt{sum\_head}_2$`()` and a `grant()` at the end of $\texttt{sum\_head}_1$`()` enforces sequential order. However, by reasoning about the structure of the manipulated list using the safety proof given in Fig. 6, our approach can do considerably better.

The parallelization synthesized by our analysis is shown in Fig. 7 (the general n-thread version is given in the technical report [8]). This parallelization divides the list into two segments, consisting of the portions read and written to by $\texttt{sum\_head}_1$`()`. A shared heap-location `xpr` stores the starting address of the portion written by $\texttt{sum\_head}_1$`()`. The thread $\texttt{sum\_head}_2$ uses `xpr` to control when to access the second segment of the list[2]. We discuss how the analysis materializes `xpr` below.

Handling dynamic structures means dealing with allocation and disposal. Fortunately, separation logic handles both straightforwardly. Updates to the data-structure and object allocation are by assumption reflected in the invariants of the original sequential proof. Thus updates and allocations are also reflected in the invariants which our analysis constructs to represent the contents of channels. However, introducing allocation and disposal affects the behaviour-preservation result discussed in §6; this result ensures

[2] For simplicity, here we write $\texttt{sum\_head}_2$ with `wait` controlled by conditionals. The actual transformation performs syntactic loop-splitting to avoid the need to modify the loop invariant. Details are given in §5.2.

```
lnode *hd;
{hd ↦ h * lseg(h, nil)}
sum_head(n) {
  local i, sum, x;
  int i = 1;
  int sum = 0;
  x = *hd;
  {hd ↦ x * lseg(x, nil)}
  // entailment on lseg predicate
  {hd ↦ h * lseg(h, x) * lseg(x, nil)}
  while(x!=nil && i!=n) {
    {hd ↦ h * lseg(h, x) * ∃v, y. x.val ↦ v * x.nxt ↦ y * lseg(y, nil)}
    sum += x.val;
    i++;
    x = x.nxt;
  }
  {hd ↦ h * lseg(h, x) * lseg(x, nil)}
  while(x!=nil) {
    {hd ↦ h * lseg(h, x) * ∃v, y. x.val ↦ v * x.nxt ↦ y * lseg(y, nil)}
    x.val = 0;
    x = x.nxt;
  }
}
{hd ↦ h * lseg(h, nil)}
```

Figure 6. Separation logic proof of `sum_head`, a list-manipulating program whose automated parallelization requires reasoning over complex assertions and predicates.

```
sum_head1(n){                   sum_head2(n){
  i = 1;                          i = 1;
  sum = 0;                        sum = 0;
  x = *hd;                        wait(i1);
  while(x!=nil && i!=n){          x = *hd;
    sum+=x.val;                   while(x!=nil && i!=n){
    i++;                            if(x==*xpr) wait(i2);
    x = x.nxt;                      sum +=x.val;
  }                                 i++;
  *xpr = x;                         x = x.nxt;
  grant(i1);                      }
  while(x!=nil){                  while(x!=nil){
    x.val = 0;                      if(x==*xpr) wait(i2);
    x = x.nxt;                      x.val = 0;
  }                                 x = x.nxt;
  grant(i2);                      }
}                               }
```

Figure 7. Parallelization of `sum_head` for two threads.

the program behaviour is unaffected by the translation (i.e. the translation enforces deterministic parallelism).

Reasoning about list segments. We assume that our separation logic domain includes the predicate $\mathsf{lseg}(x, t)$, which asserts that a segment of a linked list exists with head x and tail-pointer t. We define lseg as the least separation logic predicate satisfying the following recursive equation[3]:

$$\mathsf{lseg}(x,t) \triangleq x = t \wedge \mathsf{emp} \vee \exists v, y.\, x.\mathrm{val} \mapsto v * x.\mathrm{nxt} \mapsto y * \mathsf{lseg}(y, t)$$

We assume that the programmer proves the following specification for the sequential version of `sum_head`:

$$\{\mathtt{hd} \mapsto h * \mathsf{lseg}(h, \mathsf{nil})\} \quad \mathtt{sum\_head(n)} \quad \{\mathtt{hd} \mapsto h * \mathsf{lseg}(h, \mathsf{nil})\}$$

[3] Our analysis depends strongly on the choice of these basic predicates. See §7 for a discussion of alternatives to lseg.

This specification is trivial: all it says is that executing `sum_head` beginning with a list segment, results in a list segment. Fig. 6 shows a proof of this specification.

We run our resource-usage analysis over the program to determine redundant and needed resources. Consider the following loop from the end of $\mathtt{sum\_head}_1$:

```
...
while(x!=nil) {
  x.val = 0; x = x.nxt;
}
```

Our analysis reveals that only the resource defined by $\mathsf{lseg}(\mathtt{x}, \mathsf{nil})$ is needed from the start of this loop to the end of the iteration. Comparing this resource to the corresponding invariant in the sequential proof reveals that the resource $\exists h.\, \mathtt{hd} \mapsto h * \mathsf{lseg}(h, \mathtt{x})$ is redundant at this point. This assertion represents the segment of the list that has already been traversed, from the head of the list to `x`.

Materialization and barrier injection. Notice that the assertions generated by our analysis are partly expressed in terms of the local variable `x`, which may change during execution. In order to safely transfer these assertions to subsequent iterations of the `pfor`, we need them to be *globally accessible* and *invariant*. To satisfy this goal, we could simply existentially quantify the offending variable, `x`, giving a redundant invariant

$$\exists h, y.\, \mathtt{hd} \mapsto h * \mathsf{lseg}(h, y)$$

However, such a weakening loses important information, in particular the relationship between the necessary resource, the list segment from `x` and the tail of the list. To retain such dependency relationships, our analysis *materializes* the current value of `x` into a location `xpr` shared between $\mathtt{sum\_head}_1$ and $\mathtt{sum\_head}_2$. An assignment is injected into $\mathtt{sum\_head}_1$ at the start of the second loop:

```
...
*xpr = x;
while(x!=nil) {
...
```

After the assignment to `xpr`, the redundant state can now be described as follows:

$$\exists h, y.\, \mathtt{hd} \mapsto h * \mathsf{lseg}(h, y) * \mathtt{xpr} \overset{1/2}{\longmapsto} y$$

Here we use fractional permissions in the style of [6] to allow a location to be shared between threads. The assertion $\mathtt{xpr} \overset{1/2}{\longmapsto} y$ represents fractional, read-only permission on the shared location `xpr`. This helps in binding together the head of the list and the remainder of the list when they are recombined.

When traversing the list, $\mathtt{sum\_head}_2$ compares its current position with `xpr`. If it reaches the pointer stored in `xpr`, it must wait to receive the second, remainder segment of the list from $\mathtt{sum\_head}_1$.

4. Technical Background

4.1 Programming Language and Representation

We assume the following heap-manipulating language[4]:

e	$::=$	$\mathtt{x} \mid \mathtt{nil} \mid t(\bar{e}) \mid \ldots$	*(expressions)*
b	$::=$	$\mathtt{true} \mid \mathtt{false} \mid e = e \mid e \neq e \mid \ldots$	*(booleans)*
a	$::=$	$\ldots$	*(atomic commands)*
C	$::=$	$C; C \mid \ell\colon \mathtt{skip} \mid \ell\colon a \mid \ell\colon \mathtt{x} := \mathtt{f}(\bar{e}) \mid \ell\colon \mathtt{return}\ e$	
	$\mid$	$\ell\colon \mathtt{if}(b)\,\{\,C\,\}\,\mathtt{else}\,\{\,C\,\} \mid \ell\colon \mathtt{while}(b)\,\{\,C\,\}$	
$\mathbb{P}$	$::=$	$\mathtt{global}\ \bar{\mathtt{r}};\ (\mathtt{f}(\bar{\mathtt{x}})\ \{\mathtt{local}\ \bar{\mathtt{y}};\ C\,\})^{+}$	

[4] To avoid introducing an extra construct, we define $\mathtt{for}(C_1; C_2; b)\{C_3\}$ as $C_1; \mathtt{while}(b)\{C_2; C_3\}$.

```
void f(int i){          | f_s: x ↦ x * y ↦ y
ℓ1: int v = *x;         | ℓ1: x ↦ x * y ↦ y
ℓ2: if (v >= i){        | ℓ2: v = x ∧ x ↦ x * y ↦ y
ℓ3: g(y, v);            | ℓ3: v = x ∧ v ≥ i ∧ x ↦ x * y ↦ y
    }                   | ℓ4: v = x ∧ v < i ∧ x ↦ x * y ↦ y
    else{               | f_e: (x ≥ i ∧ x ↦ x * y ↦ x) ∨
ℓ4: g(x, 0);            |        (x < i ∧ x ↦ 0 * y ↦ y)
    }                   | g_s: p ↦ _ ∧ v = v
}                       | ℓ5: p ↦ _ ∧ v = v
                        | g_e: p ↦ v
void g(int* p,          |
       int v){          |
ℓ5: *p = v;             |
}                       |
```

Figure 8. Left: labels for commands in `f` and `g`. Right: associated assertions in the sequential proof.

To simplify the exposition slightly, we assume a fixed input program $\mathbb{P}$ of the following form:

$$\texttt{main}_{\mathbb{P}}()\,\{\,\texttt{pfor}(C_1; C_2; b)\,\{\,\texttt{work}();\,\}\,\}$$

Our parallelization approach generates a new program $\mathbb{P}_{par}$ that allows safe execution of (a transformed version of) `work` in separate threads. We denote by $\mathsf{Func} \ni \{\texttt{main}, \texttt{work}\}$ the set of functions declared in a program $\mathbb{P}$.

Labelling of commands. Every command $C \in \mathsf{Cmd}$ in the program is indexed by a unique label $\ell \in \mathsf{Label}$; function identifiers are also treated as labels. We identify a particular command by its label, and when needed denote by $\mathsf{cmd}(\ell)$ the command at the label ℓ. The set of all labels occurring in C is given by $\mathsf{Lbs}(C)$. The left-hand side of Fig. 8 shows a labelling of the functions `f` and `g`.

Commands within a block (function, `if-else` or `while`) form a sequence identified by the sequence of the corresponding labels. Functions $\mathsf{pred}, \mathsf{succ} \colon \mathsf{Label} \rightharpoonup \mathsf{Label}$ return the label of the previous (the next, resp.) command in the sequence. For ℓ corresponding to a function name, a function call or a `while` loop, the predecessor of the first command and successor of the last command in the block are denoted by ℓ_{s} and ℓ_{e}, respectively. For ℓ corresponding to `if-else`, $\ell^{\mathsf{t}}_{\mathsf{s}}$ ($\ell^{\mathsf{t}}_{\mathsf{e}}$) and $\ell^{\mathsf{f}}_{\mathsf{s}}$ ($\ell^{\mathsf{f}}_{\mathsf{e}}$) are labels of the predecessor of the first (the successor of the last) commands in the `if` and `else` branches, respectively.

Given labels ℓ and ℓ' within the same block, we say that $\ell < \ell'$ if $\exists n \geq 1$ such that $\ell' = \mathsf{succ}^n(\ell)$. Let $\ell_\uparrow$ and $\ell_\downarrow$ denote the smallest (resp. largest) label in the block containing ℓ. Let $[\ell, \ell')$ denote the sequence of labels between ℓ inclusively and ℓ' exclusively, and let $\mathbb{P}_{[\ell,\ell')}$ stand for the corresponding program fragment. Analogously, we define $\langle \ell, \ell' \rangle$ and $\mathbb{P}_{\langle \ell, \ell' \rangle}$.

Program representation. A program is represented via a control-flow graph with Label as the set of nodes and as the set of edges all (ℓ, ℓ') such that ℓ corresponds to a label of a function call and $\ell' \in \langle \ell_{\mathsf{s}}, \ell_{\mathsf{e}} \rangle$, or ℓ corresponds to `if-else` and $\ell' \in \langle \ell^{\mathsf{t}}_{\mathsf{s}}, \ell^{\mathsf{t}}_{\mathsf{e}} \rangle \cup \langle \ell^{\mathsf{f}}_{\mathsf{s}}, \ell^{\mathsf{f}}_{\mathsf{e}} \rangle$. A *path delimiter* is a finite sequence of nodes in the control-flow graph. Intuitively, a path delimiter represents the sequence of function calls and conditionals that need to be traversed in order to reach a particular assertion. Due to the structure of our analysis, we are only interested in the set of path delimiters in the function `work`, denoted by AP.

We often want to manipulate and compare path delimiters. For $\gamma = \ell_1 \ldots \ell_n \in \mathsf{AP}$, we write $\gamma[i]$ to denote ℓ_i, $\gamma[i..j]$ to denote $\ell_i \ldots \ell_j$ and $|\gamma|$ to denote the length n. For path delimiters γ and γ', $\gamma \curlywedge \gamma'$ denotes their longest common prefix, i.e., for $k = |\gamma \curlywedge \gamma'|$ we have $\forall j \leq k, \gamma \curlywedge \gamma' = \gamma[j] = \gamma'[j]$ and if $|\gamma|, |\gamma'| > k$ then $\gamma[k+1] \neq \gamma'[k+1]$. We define a partial order $\prec$ on AP as follows. We say that $\gamma \prec \gamma'$ iff $\gamma \curlywedge \gamma' = \gamma$ and $|\gamma| < |\gamma'|$, or for $k = |\gamma \curlywedge \gamma'|$ we have $|\gamma|, |\gamma'| > k$ and $\gamma[k+1] < \gamma'[k+1]$. We say that $\gamma \preceq \gamma'$ iff $\gamma \prec \gamma'$ or $\gamma = \gamma'$.

Lemma 1. $(\mathsf{AP}, \preceq)$ *is a lattice with the least element* $\texttt{work}_{\mathsf{s}}$ *and the greatest element* $\texttt{work}_{\mathsf{e}}$.

For $\Gamma \subseteq_{fin} \mathsf{AP}$ we define $\max(\Gamma)$ as $\max(\Gamma) := \{\gamma \in \Gamma \mid \neg\exists\gamma' \in \Gamma \,.\, \gamma \prec \gamma'\}$. We define $\min(\Gamma)$ analogously.

4.2 Assertion Language and Theorem Prover

Assertions in our approach are expressed using a class of separation logic formulae called *symbolic heaps*. A symbolic heap Δ is a formula of the form $\exists \bar{x} \,.\, \Pi \wedge \Sigma$ where Π (the pure part) and Σ (the spatial part) are defined by:

$$\begin{aligned} \Pi &::= \mathsf{true} \mid e = e \mid e \neq e \mid p(\bar{e}) \mid \Pi \wedge \Pi \\ \Sigma &::= \mathsf{emp} \mid x \mapsto e \mid \mathsf{lseg}(e, e) \mid s(\bar{e}) \mid \Sigma * \Sigma \end{aligned}$$

Here $\bar{x}$ are logical variables, e ranges over expressions, $p(\bar{e})$ is a family of pure (first-order) predicates (such as e.g., arithmetic inequalities, etc), and $s(\bar{e})$ a family of other spatial predicates (such as e.g., doubly-linked lists, trees, etc) besides points-to and linked-list predicates previously discussed. We refer to the pure and the spatial part of Δ as Δ^Π and Δ^Σ. We denote set of all quantifier-free first-order formulae built in the same way as Π but also allowing the $\vee$ connective by $\Pi_\vee$.

During our analysis, we often need to substitute variables, for example when recasting an assertion into a different calling context. If $\varrho = \bar{x} \mapsto \bar{e}$ is a mapping from variables in $\bar{x}$ to $\bar{e}$ then by $\Delta[\varrho]$ we denote the formula obtained by simultaneously substituting every occurrence of x_i in Δ with the corresponding e_i. We denote by δ^{-1} the inverse variable mapping, if δ is injective[5].

The set of all symbolic heaps is denoted by SH. We represent a disjunction of symbolic heaps as a set and interchangeably use the $\cup$ and $\vee$ operators. The set of all disjunctive symbolic heaps is $\mathcal{P}(\mathsf{SH})$. We overload the $\wedge$ and $*$ operators in a natural way: for $\Delta_i = \Pi_i \wedge \Sigma_i, i = 1, 2$, we define $\Delta_1 * \Delta_2 = (\Pi_1 \wedge \Pi_2) \wedge (\Sigma_1 * \Sigma_2)$, $\Pi \wedge \Delta_i = (\Pi \wedge \Pi_i) \wedge \Sigma_i$ and $\Sigma * \Delta_i = \Pi_i \wedge (\Sigma * \Sigma_i)$. Operators $\wedge$ and $*$ distribute over $\vee$, thus we allow these operations on disjunctive heaps just as if they were on symbolic heaps and furthermore use the same notation Δ to refer to both symbolic and disjunctive symbolic heaps.

We assume a sufficiently powerful (automated) prover for separation logic that can deal with three types of inference queries:

- $\Delta_1 \vdash \Delta_2 * [\Delta_F]$ (frame inference): given Δ_1 and Δ_2 find the frame Δ_F such that $\Delta_1 \vdash \Delta_2 * \Delta_F$ holds;
- $\Delta_1 * [\Delta_A] \vdash \Delta_2$ (abduction): given Δ_1 and Δ_2 find the "missing" assumption Δ_A such that $\Delta_1 * \Delta_A \vdash \Delta_2$ holds;
- $\Delta_1 * [\Delta_A] \vdash \Delta_2 * [\Delta_F]$ (bi-abduction): given Δ_1 and Δ_2 find Δ_A and Δ_F such that $\Delta_1 * \Delta_A \vdash \Delta_2 * \Delta_F$ holds.

As before, square brackets denote the portion of the entailment that should be computed. We sometimes write $[\_]$ for a computed assertion that is existentially quantified and will not be reused.

None of these queries has a unique answer in general. However, for our analysis any answer is acceptable (though some will give rise to a better parallelization than the others). Existing separation logic tools generally provide only one answer.

[5] In our framework, substitutions are always guaranteed to be injective because the variables being substituted correspond to heap locations and channel resources whose denotations are guaranteed to be distinct; if the substitution involves values, then they must be implicitly existentially quantified, and can therefore be assumed to be distinct.

4.3 Sequential Proof

We assume a separation logic proof of the program $\mathbb{P}$, represented as a map $\mathfrak{P}\colon \mathsf{Label} \to \mathcal{P}(\mathsf{SH})$. Intuitively, assertions in the proof have the property that for any label ℓ executing the program from a state satisfying $\mathfrak{P}(\ell)$ up to some subsequent label ℓ' will result in a state satisfying $\mathfrak{P}(\ell')$, and will not fault.

More formally, we assume functions $\mathsf{Pre}, \mathsf{Post}\colon \mathsf{Label} \rightharpoonup \mathcal{P}(\mathsf{SH})$ associating labels of atomic commands and function calls with their pre- and post-condition, respectively, and a function $\mathsf{Inv}\colon \mathsf{Label} \rightharpoonup \mathcal{P}(\mathsf{SH})$ associating `while` labels with loop invariants. We also assume Ω, a mapping from labels to variable substitutions such that $\Omega(l) = \bar{x} \mapsto \bar{x'}$ maps formal variables $\bar{x}$ in the specification assertion to actual variables $\bar{x'}$ in the proof assertion. Finally, we assume a function $\mathfrak{F}\colon \mathsf{Label} \rightharpoonup \mathcal{P}(\mathsf{SH})$ giving the framed portion of the state. We write $\Delta[\Omega(l)]$ to represent the heap constructed by applying the substitutions defined by $\Omega(l)$ to the assertion Δ.

Then at each label ℓ we have $\mathfrak{P}(\ell) \vdash \mathsf{Pre}(\ell)[\Omega(\ell)] * \mathfrak{F}(\ell)$ and $\mathsf{Post}(\ell)[\Omega(\ell)] * \mathfrak{F}(\ell) \vdash \mathfrak{P}(\mathsf{succ}(\ell))$. If ℓ is a `while` label then $\mathsf{Pre}(\ell)$ and $\mathsf{Post}(\ell)$ are replaced by $\mathsf{Inv}(\ell)$.

This structure means that the proof is *modular*, i.e., each atomic command, function and loop is given a specification "in isolation", without a reference to the particular context in which the specification is being used. The right-hand side of Fig. 8 shows a proof for the functions `f` and `g` which is in this form. Our approach is agnostic to the method by which the proof $\mathfrak{P}$ is created: it can be discovered automatically (e.g., by a tool such as Abductor [11]), prepared by a proof assistant, or written manually.

Proof assertions inlining. The proof $\mathfrak{P}$ assumes use of a modular specification for each function. However, our analysis needs to refer to the assertions in the local function with respect to the variables of the caller, all the way up to the top-most `work` function. We therefore define a process for lifting local assertions with respect to their global contexts.

For $\gamma \in \mathsf{AP}$ such that $|\gamma| = m$ and $\ell_1, \ldots, \ell_n$ are the labels corresponding to the function calls (in the order of occurrence as in γ) we define the lifted ("inlined") proof assertion $\mathfrak{P}(\gamma)$ as

$$\mathfrak{F}(\ell_1) * (\mathfrak{F}(\ell_2) * \ldots (\mathfrak{F}(\ell_n) * \mathfrak{P}(\gamma[m])[\Omega(\ell_n)])[\Omega(\ell_{n-1})] \ldots)[\Omega(\ell_1)]$$

Intuitively, the assertion $\mathfrak{P}(\gamma)$ represents the "global" proof state at γ (including the framed portions) in terms of `work`'s variables.

Finally, let $\mathsf{pc}\colon \mathsf{AP} \rightharpoonup \Pi_\vee$ represent the path constraint associated with each path delimiter. The path constraint at γ comprises the pure part of $\mathfrak{P}(\gamma)$ corresponding to the assumptions from the conditionals encountered on the way from $\mathtt{work_s}$ to γ. The path constraint may be extracted directly from the proof or computed by some other means.

5. Parallelization Algorithm

We now formally define our parallelization algorithm. The goal of our approach is to construct a parallelized version of the input program $\mathbb{P}$. In particular, our approach generates a new function `work'` in $\mathbb{P}_{par}$ (invoking possibly transformed callees) such that

```
main_Ppar() {
  // initial channel creation.
  for(C1; C2; b) {
    // channel creation.
    fork(work', ...);
  }
  // channel finalization.
}
```

has the same behaviour as the original $\mathtt{main}_{\mathbb{P}}$.

Algorithm 1 Computing locally needed resources using backward symbolic execution.

> **function** NEEDED-LOC$((\ell', \ell'')\colon \mathsf{Label} \times \mathsf{Label}, \Delta\colon \mathcal{P}(\mathsf{SH}))$
> $\quad \ell := \ell''$
> $\quad$**while** $\ell \neq \ell'$ **do**
> $\quad\quad \ell := \mathsf{pred}(\ell)$
> $\quad\quad$**if** $\mathsf{cmd}(\ell)$ matches $\mathtt{if}(b)\,\{\,C\,\}\,\mathtt{else}\,\{\,C'\,\}$ **then**
> $\quad\quad\quad \Delta := \mathfrak{P}(\ell)^{\Pi} \wedge \begin{pmatrix}\text{NEEDED-LOC}((\ell^{\mathsf{t}}_{\mathsf{s}}, \ell^{\mathsf{t}}_{\mathsf{e}}), \Delta) \cup \\ \text{NEEDED-LOC}((\ell^{\mathsf{f}}_{\mathsf{s}}, \ell^{\mathsf{f}}_{\mathsf{e}}), \Delta)\end{pmatrix}$
> $\quad\quad$**if** $\mathsf{cmd}(\ell)$ matches $\mathtt{while}(b)\,\{\,C\,\}$ **then**
> $\quad\quad\quad \mathsf{Inv}(\ell)[\Omega(\ell)] * [\Delta_A] \vdash \Delta * [\_]$
> $\quad\quad\quad \Delta := \mathfrak{P}(\ell)^{\Pi} \wedge (\mathsf{Inv}(\ell)[\Omega(\ell)] * \Delta_A)$
> $\quad\quad$**else**
> $\quad\quad\quad \mathsf{Post}(\ell)[\Omega(\ell)] * [\Delta_A] \vdash \Delta * [\_]$
> $\quad\quad\quad \Delta := \mathfrak{P}(\ell)^{\Pi} \wedge (\mathsf{Pre}(\ell)[\Omega(\ell)] * \Delta_A)$
> $\quad$**return** Δ

5.1 Resource Usage Analysis

Our approach to parallelization traverses the program by referring to a finite prefix- and $<$-closed subset of path delimiters $\mathsf{P} \subseteq_{fin} \mathsf{AP}$. This subset reflects the portions of the program that are path- and context-sensitive targets of parallelization. The set P provides precise control over which functions the analysis should address, but how this set is chosen is not considered here. Function invocations whose successors are not in P are treated as a single operation with effects defined by their specification.

The goal of resource usage analysis is to compute the maps:

$$\mathsf{redundant}\colon \mathsf{P} \times \mathsf{P} \rightharpoonup \mathcal{P}(\mathsf{SH})$$
$$\mathsf{needed}\colon \mathsf{P} \times \mathsf{P} \rightharpoonup \mathcal{P}(\mathsf{SH})$$

For $p, q \in \mathsf{P}$ such that $p \prec q$, $\mathsf{redundant}(p, q)$ gives the resources that are guaranteed to not be accessed by the program between p and q. In parallelization, these are resources that can safely be transferred to other parallel threads. For $p \prec q$, $\mathsf{needed}(p, q)$ gives the resources that might be accessed during execution from p to q. In parallelization, these are the resources that must be acquired before execution of the current thread can proceed.

The function NEEDED-LOC (Alg. 1) uses backward symbolic execution to compute needed resources between pairs of path delimiters (ℓ', ℓ'') in the same function block. It uses the pure parts of the sequential proof to guide the abductive inference. Since we already have function summaries and loop invariants in the sequential proof, NEEDED-LOC gives a symbolic heap sufficient to execute the fragment $\mathbb{P}_{[\ell', \ell'')}$.

Lemma 2. NEEDED-LOC(ℓ', ℓ'') *is a sufficient precondition for* $\mathbb{P}_{[\ell', \ell'')}$.

Proof. Follows from the disjunctive version of the frame rule:

$$\frac{\{P\}\, C\, \{\bigvee_{i \in \mathcal{I}} Q_i\} \qquad \Delta * \bigvee_{j \in \mathcal{J}} \Delta^A_j \vdash P * \bigvee_{k \in \mathcal{K}} \Delta^F_k}{\{\bigvee_{j \in \mathcal{J}} (\Delta * \Delta^A_j)\}\, C\, \{\bigvee_{i \in \mathcal{I}, k \in \mathcal{K}} (Q_i * \Delta^F_k)\}}$$

and Hoare's rule of composition. □

The function NEEDED(γ_e, γ_s) (Alg. 2) lifts NEEDED-LOC to the context-sensitive interprocedural level. Given two assertion points represented as path delimiters γ_s and γ_e, NEEDED(γ_e, γ_s) works by successively pushing backwards an assertion Δ from γ_e to γ_s. The algorithm operates in two phases. In phase A, it steps backwards from γ_e towards the outermost calling context in the function-invocation hierarchy. This context, represented as the longest common prefix of γ_s and γ_e, is the dominator of the two

Algorithm 2 Computing needed resources.

function NEEDED(γ_s : P, γ_e : P)
  $k := |\gamma_e|$
  $\Delta := \mathfrak{P}(\gamma_e)$
  while $k > |\gamma_s \curlywedge \gamma_e| + 1$ **do** } A
    $\varrho := \Omega(\gamma_e[1..k])$
    $\Delta :=$ NEEDED-LOC$((\gamma_e[k]_\uparrow, \gamma_e[k]), \Delta[\varrho^{-1}])[\varrho]$
    $k := k - 1$
    if $\mathsf{cmd}(\gamma_e[k])$ is function call **then**
      $\Delta := \Delta[\Omega(\gamma_e[k])^{-1}]$
  $\varrho := \Omega(\gamma_s[1..k])$
  $\Delta :=$ NEEDED-LOC$((\gamma_e[k], \gamma_s[k]), \Delta[\varrho^{-1}])[\varrho]$
  while $k < |\gamma_s|$ **do** } B
    if $\mathsf{cmd}(\gamma_s[k])$ is function call **then**
      $\Delta := \Delta[\Omega(\gamma_s[k])]$
    $k := k + 1$
    $\varrho := \Omega(\gamma_s[1..k])$
    $\Delta :=$ NEEDED-LOC$((\gamma_s[k], \gamma_s[k]_\downarrow), \Delta[\varrho^{-1}])[\varrho]$
  return Δ

Algorithm 3 Computing redundant resources

function REDUNDANT(γ_s : P, γ_e : P)
  $\mathfrak{P}(\gamma_s) \vdash$ NEEDED$(\gamma_s, \gamma_e) * [\Delta_R]$
  return Δ_R

functions in which γ_s and γ_e are found in the function call graph. Phase B of the algorithm keeps stepping backwards, but proceeds inwards into the function-invocation hierarchy towards γ_s. Both phases of the algorithm use Alg. 1 to compute the needed resources in-between function call boundaries: in phase A we establish the needed assertions from the dominating point to γ_e, and in phase B from γ_s to the dominating point.

Since the invariants of the input proof are written in terms of the outermost calling context, comparing locally-computed specifications with these invariants requires the local specifications to be recast in terms of the outer context. In the first line of phase A we construct a variable substitution ϱ that recasts the assertion in terms of the calling context at the start of γ_e. The second line constructs $\Delta[\varrho^{-1}]$—the running state recast in terms of γ_e's starting context; this is typically the context defined by the `work()` function used in a `pfor` command. NEEDED-LOC constructs a new needed state up to the start of the current block. Finally, ϱ recasts the resulting state back into the current context. When a function call is reached, we unwind the variable substitution by one call since we now have moved from the callee's context to a caller's. Operations in phase B are similar.

The results computed by NEEDED are tabulated as follows. If $\mathfrak{P}(\gamma_s) \vdash$ NEEDED$(\gamma_s, \gamma_e) * [_]$, then $\mathsf{needed}(\gamma_s, \gamma_e) := \mathfrak{P}(\gamma_s)^{\Pi} \wedge$ NEEDED(γ_s, γ_e); otherwise, $\mathsf{needed}(\gamma_s, \gamma_e) := \mathfrak{P}(\gamma_s)$.

Lemma 3. $\mathsf{needed}(\gamma_s, \gamma_e)$ *is a sufficient precondition to execute* $\mathbb{P}$ *from* γ_s *to* γ_e.

In order to be able to use the needed map further in the algorithm we must ensure that it grows monotonically, i.e., that $\forall \gamma, \gamma', \gamma'' \in \mathsf{P}$ such that $\gamma \prec \gamma' \prec \gamma''$ we have $\mathsf{needed}(\gamma, \gamma'') \vdash \mathsf{needed}(\gamma, \gamma') * [\_]$. If the underlying theorem prover behaves consistently with respect to failing and precision this property always holds. However, we can also make an additional check and insert assertions from the sequential proof as needed.

The redundant resource between two path delimiters is the portion of the inlined proof-state in $\mathfrak{P}$ that is not required by the needed map. In Alg. 3 we calculate this by frame inference.

	$\mathtt{f_e}$
ℓ_1	$x < \mathtt{i} \wedge \mathtt{y} \mapsto y$
ℓ_2	$(\mathtt{v} = x \wedge \mathtt{v} \geq \mathtt{i} \wedge \mathtt{x} \mapsto x)$ $\vee (\mathtt{v} = x \wedge \mathtt{v} < \mathtt{i} \wedge \mathtt{y} \mapsto y)$
$\ell_2\ell_3$	$\mathtt{v} = x \wedge \mathtt{v} \geq \mathtt{i} \wedge \mathtt{x} \mapsto x$
$\ell_2\ell_3\mathtt{g_e}$	$\mathtt{v} = x \wedge \mathtt{v} \geq \mathtt{i} \wedge \mathtt{x} \mapsto x * \mathtt{y} \mapsto y$
$\ell_2\ell_4$	$\mathtt{v} = x \wedge \mathtt{v} < \mathtt{i} \wedge \mathtt{y} \mapsto y$
$\ell_2\ell_4\mathtt{g_e}$	$\mathtt{v} = x \wedge \mathtt{v} < \mathtt{i} \wedge \mathtt{x} \mapsto x * \mathtt{y} \mapsto y$

Figure 10. redundant map with respect to $\mathtt{f_e}$.

Lemma 4. *If* $\mathfrak{P}(\gamma_s) \vdash \mathsf{redundant}(\gamma_s, \gamma_e) * [\Delta]$ *then* Δ *is a sufficient precondition to execute* $\mathbb{P}$ *from* γ_s *to* γ_e.

Consider the functions `f` and `g` from §2. Fig. 8 shows the labels and sequential proof for these functions. The map obtained by NEEDED is shown in Fig. 9. Fig. 10 shows the map computed by REDUNDANT with respect to path delimiter $\mathtt{f_e}$.

5.2 Parallelising Transformation

We now describe a parallelising transformation based on our resource-usage analysis. The construction proceeds in two phases. First, we compute an idealized resource transfer between threads. Then we inject `grant` and `wait` barriers to realise this resource transfer. The resource transfer mechanism transfers a resource from one invocation of the `work` function to another.

This parallelising transformation can be viewed as just one application of the resource-usage analysis; more optimized proof-preserving parallelising transformations are certainly possible. Our overall goal is to describe a framework for a resource-sensitive dependency-preserving analysis.

Conditions on released and acquired resources. In the first phase we determine resources that should be released and acquired at particular points in the parallelized program. Released resources cannot be revoked, i.e., each released resource should be included in the redundant map from the point of the release to the end of the `work` function—this way we know the resource will not be needed further. Acquired resources are held by the executing thread until released. Resources that are acquired along a sequence of path delimiters should contain what is prescribed by the needed map between each of the path delimiters.

We represent the result of this phase of the algorithm via the following maps:

- $\mathsf{resource}$: $\mathsf{ResId} \rightarrow \mathcal{P}(\mathsf{SH})$, denoting resource identifiers that identify released and acquired resources;
- $\mathsf{released}$: $\mathsf{P} \rightharpoonup \mathsf{ResId} \times \mathsf{Subst}$, representing resources that are going to be released at a path delimiter together with the variable substitution applied at that point;
- $\mathsf{acquired}$: $\mathsf{P} \rightharpoonup \mathsf{ResId}$, representing resources that are going to be acquired at a path delimiter.

We require the following well-formedness properties:

1. $\forall \gamma \in \mathrm{dom}(\mathsf{released}) \,.\, \forall \gamma' \succ \gamma \,.\, \mathsf{released}(\gamma) = (r, \rho) \rightarrow (\mathsf{redundant}(\gamma, \gamma') \vdash \mathsf{resource}(r)[\rho] * [\_])$;
2. $\forall \gamma \in \mathsf{P} \,.\, \circledast_{r \in \mathrm{dom}(\mathsf{resource})} \{\mathsf{resource}(r) \mid \exists \gamma' \prec \gamma \wedge \mathsf{acquired}(\gamma') = r\} \vdash \mathsf{needed}(\gamma, \mathtt{work_e}) * [\_]$;
3. $\forall \gamma \in \mathrm{dom}(\mathsf{released}) \,.\, \circledast_{r \in \mathrm{dom}(\mathsf{resource})} \{\mathsf{resource}(r) \mid \exists \gamma' \prec \gamma \wedge \mathsf{acquired}(\gamma') = r\} \vdash \mathsf{released}(\gamma) * [\_]$.

The first property states we can release only resources that are not needed between the given path delimiter and any subsequent one. The second property states that the resources needed at a

	ℓ_2	$\ell_2\ell_3$	$\ell_2\ell_3\mathtt{g_e}$	$\ell_2\ell_4$	$\ell_2\ell_4\mathtt{g_e}$	$\mathtt{f_e}$
ℓ_1	$\mathtt{x} \mapsto x$	$x \geq \mathtt{i} \wedge \mathtt{x} \mapsto x$	$x \geq \mathtt{i} \wedge \mathtt{x} \mapsto x * \mathtt{y} \mapsto y$	$x < \mathtt{i} \wedge \mathtt{x} \mapsto x$	$x < \mathtt{i} \wedge \mathtt{x} \mapsto x$	$(x \geq \mathtt{i} \wedge \mathtt{x} \mapsto x * \mathtt{y} \mapsto y)$ $\vee (x < \mathtt{i} \wedge \mathtt{x} \mapsto x)$
ℓ_2		$\mathtt{v} = x \wedge \mathtt{v} \geq \mathtt{i}$	$\mathtt{v} = x \wedge \mathtt{v} \geq \mathtt{i} * \mathtt{y} \mapsto y$	$\mathtt{v} = x \wedge \mathtt{v} < \mathtt{i}$	$\mathtt{v} = x \wedge \mathtt{v} < \mathtt{i} \wedge \mathtt{x} \mapsto x$	$(\mathtt{v} = x \wedge \mathtt{v} \geq \mathtt{i} * \mathtt{y} \mapsto y)$ $\vee (\mathtt{v} = x \wedge \mathtt{v} < \mathtt{i} \wedge \mathtt{x} \mapsto x)$
$\ell_2\ell_3$			$\mathtt{v} = x \wedge \mathtt{v} \geq \mathtt{i} * \mathtt{y} \mapsto y$			$\mathtt{v} = x \wedge \mathtt{v} \geq \mathtt{i} * \mathtt{y} \mapsto y$
$\ell_2\ell_3\mathtt{g_e}$						$\mathtt{v} = x \wedge \mathtt{v} \geq \mathtt{i}$
$\ell_2\ell_4$					$\mathtt{v} = x \wedge \mathtt{v} < \mathtt{i} * \mathtt{x} \mapsto x$	$\mathtt{v} = x \wedge \mathtt{v} < \mathtt{i} * \mathtt{x} \mapsto x$
$\ell_2\ell_4\mathtt{g_e}$						$\mathtt{v} = x \wedge \mathtt{v} < \mathtt{i}$

Figure 9. needed map (some entries omitted).

Algorithm 4 Computing released and acquired resources.

1: $\mathcal{N}$:= needed; $\mathcal{R}$:= redundant
2: $\mathcal{C} := \max\{\gamma \in \mathsf{P} \mid \mathcal{N}(\mathtt{work_s}, \gamma) = \mathsf{emp}\}$
3: **while** $\mathcal{C} \neq \{\mathtt{work_e}\}$ **do**
4: $\quad \Sigma_R := \mathcal{N}(\mathit{choose}(\{(\gamma, \gamma') \mid \gamma \in \mathcal{C}, \gamma' \in \mathsf{P}\}))^{\Sigma}$
5: $\quad \varrho := \bar{\mathtt{x}} \mapsto \bar{\mathtt{x}}'$, where $\bar{\mathtt{x}}'$ fresh
6: $\quad \Sigma_R' := \Sigma_R[\varrho]$
7: $\quad \mathcal{C}_r := \min\left\{\gamma \in \mathsf{P} \,\middle|\, \begin{array}{l}\mathcal{R}(\gamma, \mathtt{work_e})^{\Sigma} \vdash \Sigma_R' * [\_] \\ \wedge \exists \gamma' \in \mathcal{C}. \gamma' \preceq \gamma\end{array}\right\}$
8: $\quad$ **if** $\bigvee_{\gamma \in \mathcal{C}_r} \mathsf{pc}(\gamma) \Leftrightarrow \mathsf{true}$ **then**
9: $\quad\quad r$:= fresh resource id
10: $\quad\quad \mathsf{resource}(r) := \Sigma_R'$
11: $\quad\quad$ **for all** $\gamma \in \mathcal{C}_r$ **do**
12: $\quad\quad\quad \mathsf{released}(\gamma) := (r, \varrho)$
13: $\quad\quad\quad$ **for all** γ' s.t. $\gamma \preceq \gamma'$ **do**
14: $\quad\quad\quad\quad \mathcal{R}(\gamma', \mathtt{work_e})^{\Sigma} \vdash \Sigma_R * [\Delta]$
15: $\quad\quad\quad\quad \mathcal{R}(\gamma', \mathtt{work_e}) := \Delta$
16: $\quad\quad$ **for all** $\gamma \in \mathcal{C}$ **do**
17: $\quad\quad\quad \mathsf{acquired}(\gamma) := r$
18: $\quad\quad\quad$ **for all** γ', γ'' s.t. $\gamma \preceq \gamma' \preceq \gamma''$ **do**
19: $\quad\quad\quad\quad \mathcal{N}(\gamma', \gamma'') * [\_] \vdash \Sigma_R' * [\Delta]$
20: $\quad\quad\quad\quad \mathcal{N}(\gamma', \gamma'') := \Delta$
21: $\quad\quad \mathcal{C} := \max\{\gamma' \mid \exists \gamma \in \mathcal{C}. \mathcal{N}(\gamma, \gamma') = \mathsf{emp}\}$

path delimiter must have already been acquired. The third property states that only the resources that have been previously acquired can be released.[6]

In general, there are many solutions satisfying properties 1–3. For instance, there is always a trivial solution that acquires needed($\mathtt{work_s}, \mathtt{work_e}$) before the first command and releases it after the last, causing each invocation of `work` to be blocked until the preceding invocation finishes the last command. Of course, some solutions are better than others.

Computing released and acquired maps. Algorithm 4 constructs released, acquired and resource maps satisfying properties 1–3. Each iteration of the algorithm heuristically picks a needed resource, and then iteratively searches for matching redundant resource along all paths. The algorithm maintains a set $\mathcal{C}$ of all path delimiters up to which no more resources are needed. It terminates once no unsatisfied needed resources remain (line 3).

At the start of the main loop (line 4) the algorithm picks a still-needed resource between a path delimiter in $\mathcal{C}$ and some further path delimiter. The picking of the needed resource is governed by a heuristic function *choose*, for which we make no assumption. The *choose* function serves as a proxy for external knowledge about likely points for parallelization.

The key step of the algorithm is performed on line 7:

$$\mathcal{C}_r := \min\{\gamma \in \mathsf{P} \mid \mathcal{R}(\gamma, \mathtt{work_e})^{\Sigma} \vdash \Sigma_R' * [\_] \wedge \exists \gamma' \in \mathcal{C}. \gamma' \preceq \gamma\}$$

Here $\mathcal{R}(\gamma, \mathtt{work_e})$ is the redundant resource from γ to the end of the `work` function and Σ_R' is the candidate resource that we want to acquire. The constructed set $\mathcal{C}_r$ is a set of path delimiters along which we can satisfy the candidate needed resource. In line 8, the algorithm checks that $\mathcal{C}_r$ covers all paths by checking the conjunction of path constraints is tautologous.

Resources stored in needed contain path constraints (and other conditions on local variables) embedded in the pure part of the symbolic heap. Since we can transfer resources between different path delimiters, we only take the spatial part of the resource into consideration when asking entailment questions; this is denoted by a superscript Σ. Moreover, since the acquired resource is being sent to a different function invocation, we substitute a fresh set of variables (line 5).

The remainder of the algorithm is devoted to constructing the new resource (line 10), and with updating released (lines 11–15), acquired (lines 16–20), and $\mathcal{C}$ (line 21).

Lemma 5. *Maps* resource, released *and* acquired *computed by Algorithm 4 satisfy properties 1–3.*

Consider our running example. If *choose* picks (ℓ_1, ℓ_2) in the first iteration and $(\ell_2\ell_3, \ell_2\ell_3\mathtt{g_e})$ in the second iteration, then the end result of Alg. 4 is resource $= \{r_1 \mapsto (\mathtt{x} \mapsto x), r_2 \mapsto (\mathtt{y} \mapsto y)\}$, released $= \{\ell_2\ell_3 \mapsto (r_1, \emptyset), \ell_2\ell_4\mathtt{g_e} \mapsto (r_1, \emptyset), \ell_2\ell_3\mathtt{g_e} \mapsto (r_2, \emptyset), \ell_2\ell_4 \mapsto (r_2, \emptyset)\}$ and acquired $= \{\ell_1 \mapsto r_1, \ell_2\ell_3\ell_5 \mapsto r_2, \ell_2\ell_4 \mapsto r_2\}$.

Inserting grant and wait barriers. In this phase we transform the sequential program $\mathbb{P}$ into a parallel program $\mathbb{P}_{par}$ by inserting `grant` and `wait` barriers. The inserted barriers realise resource transfer defined by the maps released and acquired.

We generate the parallel function $\mathtt{work}'(\bar{\mathtt{i}}_r^{(p)}, \bar{\mathtt{i}}_r, \mathtt{env}^{(p)}, \mathtt{env})$ in $\mathbb{P}_{par}$ as follows:

1. To each $r \in$ ResId we assign a unique channel name $\mathtt{i}_r$. Denote by $\mathtt{i}_r^{(p)}$ the corresponding channel of the previous thread in the sequence.
2. Let `env` be an associative array that for each channel maps (escaped) local variable names to values. Let $\mathtt{env}^{(p)}$ be such map from the previous thread in the sequence. `env` and $\mathtt{env}^{(p)}$ are used for *materialization*.
3. For each $\gamma = \ell_1 \ldots \ell_n \in \mathrm{dom}(\mathsf{released}) \cup \mathrm{dom}(\mathsf{acquired})$ let $\ell_{k_1}, \ldots \ell_{k_m}$ be the labels in γ corresponding to function calls. Then for each $\gamma_j := \ell_1 \ldots \ell_{k_j}$ we create in $\mathbb{P}_{par}$ an identical copy $\mathtt{f}'$ of the function $\mathtt{f}$ called at ℓ_{k_j} and replace the call to $\mathtt{f}$ with the call to $\mathtt{f}'$. Let us denote by $\mathtt{tr}(\gamma')$ the path delimiter

[6] We could relax the third requirement if we extended our barriers to support *renunciation* [17], the ability to release a resource without first acquiring it. Renunciation allows a resource to 'skip' iterations, giving limited out-of-order signalling. We believe it would be straightforward to fold such techniques into the analysis, although such extensions are outside the focus of this paper.

in $\mathbb{P}_{par}$ corresponding to γ' after this transformation has been applied for all $\gamma \in \mathrm{dom}(\mathsf{released}) \cup \mathrm{dom}(\mathsf{acquired})$.

4. For each $\gamma \in \mathrm{dom}(\mathsf{acquired})$ such that $\mathsf{acquired}(\gamma) = r$ we insert a wait barrier $\mathtt{wait}(\mathtt{i}_r^{(p)})$ between path delimiters $\mathsf{tr}(\mathsf{pred}(\gamma))$ and $\mathsf{tr}(\gamma)$.
5. For each $\gamma \in \mathrm{dom}(\mathsf{released})$ such that $\mathsf{released}(\gamma) = (r, \_)$, between path delimiters $\mathsf{tr}(\mathsf{pred}(\gamma))$ and $\mathsf{tr}(\gamma)$ we insert a sequence of assignments of the form $\mathtt{env}(\mathtt{i}_r)[\text{"y"}] := \mathtt{y}$ for every local variable y, followed by a grant barrier $\mathtt{grant}(\mathtt{i}_r)$.

Each invocation of `work` creates a fresh set of local variables that are bound to the scope of the function. However, some resources must be expressed in terms of function-local variables. Parallelization must take account of this. If the structure of a resource depends on local variables from a previous invocation, this must be encoded explicitly by *materialising* the variables of the previous invocation.

The main function $\mathtt{main}_{\mathbb{P}_{par}}$ in $\mathbb{P}_{par}$ first creates the set of "dummy" channels; then in the `while` loop repeatedly creates a set of new channels for the current iteration, forks a new thread with `work'` taking the channels from the previous iteration as $\bar{\mathtt{i}}_r^{(p)}$ and from the current iteration as $\bar{\mathtt{i}}_r$, and at the end of the loop body assigns the new channels to the previous channels; and, after the `while` loop completes waits on the channels in the last set.

We generate the parallel proof $\mathfrak{P}_{par}$ from the sequential proof $\mathfrak{P}$ using the following specifications from [17]:

$$\begin{array}{rcl} \{\mathsf{emp}\} & \mathtt{i} := \mathtt{newchan}() & \{\mathsf{req}(\mathtt{i}, R) * \mathsf{fut}(\mathtt{i}, R)\} \\ \{\mathsf{req}(\mathtt{i}, R) * R\} & \mathtt{grant}(\mathtt{i}) & \{\mathsf{emp}\} \\ \{\mathsf{fut}(\mathtt{i}, R)\} & \mathtt{wait}(\mathtt{i}) & \{R\} \end{array}$$

Each variable R in $\mathfrak{P}_{par}$ associated with channel $\mathtt{i}_r$ is instantiated with the corresponding resource $\mathsf{resource}(r)$. The predicates req and fut track the ownership of the input and output ends of the channel. To reason about threads, we use the standard separation logic rules for fork-join disjoint concurrency (e.g., as in [19]).

Theorem 6. *$\mathfrak{P}_{par}$ is a proof of the parallel program $\mathbb{P}_{par}$, and defines the same specification for $\mathtt{main}_{\mathbb{P}_{par}}$ as $\mathfrak{P}$ does for $\mathtt{main}_{\mathbb{P}}$.*

Loop-splitting. The approach presented so far treats a loop as a single command with a specification derived from its invariant. Acquiring or releasing resources within a loop is subtle, as it changes the sequential loop invariant. It is not clear how to handle this in full generality, so we take a pragmatic approach that performs heuristic loop-splitting.

The example in §3 uses two channels to transfer the segment of the list traversed after the first and the second `while` loop, respectively. The resource released via channel `i1` in Fig. 7 is $\mathtt{hd} \mapsto h * \mathsf{lseg}(h, \mathtt{xpr})$. In the following iteration, the needed resource for the whole loop is $\mathtt{hd} \mapsto h * \mathsf{lseg}(h, \mathtt{x})$. If we try to match released against needed, the entailment $\mathcal{R}(\gamma, \mathtt{work_e})^{\Sigma} \vdash \Sigma'_R * [\_]$ in Algorithm 4 will fail. This is because the value of x is unknown at the start of the loop, meaning we cannot establish whether the released resource will cover the needed resource.

One way to resolve this would be to acquire the entire list before the first loop, but this would result in a very poor parallelization. Instead, we modify the structure of the loop to expose the point at which the second list segment becomes necessary:

1. We split the spatial portion of the resource needed by the whole loop into a "dead" (already traversed) and a "live" (still to be traversed) part. In our example, $\mathtt{hd} \mapsto h * \mathsf{lseg}(h, \mathtt{x})$ would be the "dead" and $\mathsf{lseg}(\mathtt{x}, \mathsf{nil})$ the live part. This kind of splitting is specific to some classes of programs, e.g., linked list programs that do not traverse a node twice.
2. We match the resource against the "dead" part of the loop invariant and infer the condition under which the two resources are the same. In our example, the entailment between the two resources holds if $\mathtt{x} = \mathtt{xpr}$. This condition can be inferred by asking a bi-abduction question $\mathcal{R}(\gamma, \mathtt{work_e})^{\Sigma} \wedge [c] \vdash \Sigma'_R * [\_]$ with the pure abducted fact c.

```
...
xpr:=envp(i1)["x"];
while(x!=nil&&i!=n&&x!=xpr){
  sum+=x.val;
  i++;
  x:=x.nxt;
}
if(x!=nil&&i!=n&&x==xpr){
  sum+=x.val;
  i++;
```

```
  x:=x.nxt;
  while(x!=nil&&i!=n){
    sum+=x.val;
    i++;
    x:=x.nxt;
  }
  // remainder skipped.
  ...
else{
...
```

Figure 11. Loop splitting for the `sum_head` example.

Now we can syntactically split the loop against the inferred condition $c = (\mathtt{x} = \mathtt{xpr})$ and obtain a transformed version that ensures that after entering the true branch of the `if` statement the condition c holds. The transformation of our example is shown in Fig 11.

Formally, we define splitting of a command (comprising possibly multiple loops) against a condition c as follows (to simplify, we assume here that every command ends with `skip`):

function $\textsc{Split}(C\colon \mathsf{Cmd}, c\colon \Pi_\vee)$
  match C **with**
  | $\mathtt{while}(b)\,\{\,C'\,\};\, C'' \rightarrow$
    $\mathtt{while}(b \wedge \neg c')\,\{\,C'\,\};$
    $\mathtt{if}(b \wedge c')\,\{\,C';\, \mathtt{while}(b)\,\{\,C'\,\};\, C''\,\}$
    $\mathtt{else}\,\{\,\textsc{Split}(C'', c)\,\}$
  | $C';\, C'' \rightarrow C';\, \textsc{Split}(C'', c)$
  | $\mathtt{skip} \rightarrow \mathtt{skip}$

The condition c' is obtained from c by replacing a reference to every primed variable $\mathtt{y}'$ by a reference to $\mathtt{env}^{(p)}(\mathtt{i}_r^{(p)})[\text{"y"}]$, where $\mathtt{i}_r$ is the channel name associated to the resource. It is not difficult to see that the accompanying proof of C can be split in a proof preserving way against c. This transformation can either be applied to $\mathbb{P}$ between the resource-usage analysis and parallelization, or embedded within Alg. 4.

5.3 Implementation

We have validated our parallelization algorithm by crafting a prototype implementation on top of the existing separation logic tool, coreStar [7]. While our implementation is not intended to provide full end-to-end automated translation, it is capable of validating the algorithms on the examples given in the paper, and automatically answering the underlying theorem proving queries.

Our parallelization algorithm does not assume a shape invariant generator, except possibly to help construct the sequential proof. Soundness is independent of the "cleanliness" of the invariants (the analysis will always give a correct result, in the worst case defaulting to sequential behaviour). Our examples in coreStar [7] have been validated using automatically-generated invariants. Other efforts [11] indicate that bi-abduction works well with automatically-generated invariants produced by shape analysis, even over very large code bases.

6. Behaviour Preservation

A distinctive property of our parallelization analysis is that it enforces sequential data-dependencies in the parallelized program even if the safety proof does not explicitly reason about such dependencies. The result is that our analysis preserves the sequential behaviour of the program: any behaviour exhibited by the parallelized program is also a behaviour that could have occurred in the original sequential program. However, there are important caveats relating to *termination* and *allocation*.

Termination. If the original sequential program does not terminate, our analysis may introduce new behaviours simply by virtue of running segments of the program that would be unreachable under a sequential schedule. To see this, suppose we have a `pfor` such that the first iteration of the loop will never terminate. Sequentially, the second iteration of the loop will never execute. However, our parallelization analysis will execute all iterations of the loop in parallel. This permits witnessing behaviours from the second (and subsequent) iterations. These behaviours were latent in the original program, and become visible only as a result of parallelization.

Allocation and disposal. If the program both allocates and disposes memory, the parallelized program may exhibit aliasing that could not occur in the original program. To see this, consider the following sequential program:

```
x=alloc(); y=alloc(); dispose(x).
```

For simplicity, we have avoided re-structuring the program to use data parallelism via `pfor`—this example could easily be encoded as such, however. Parallelization might give us the following program:

```
(x=alloc(); grant(wx); y=alloc())
        || (wait(wx); dispose(x))
```

This parallelized version of the program is race-free and obeys the required sequential ordering on data. Depending upon the implementation of the underlying memory allocator, however, `x` and `y` may be aliased if the `dispose` operation was interleaved between the two allocations. Such aliasing could not happen in the original non-parallelized version.

Either kind of new behaviour might result in further new behaviours—for example, we might have an if-statement conditional on `x==y` in the second example above. These caveats are common to our analysis and others based on separation logic—for example, see the similar discussion in [13].

Proving behaviour preservation. We now sketch a behaviour preservation result (a detailed proof is given in [8]). The theorem defines preservation in terms of an interleaved operational semantics for a core language, similar to the one described in §4.1, additionally equipped with threads, and operations on channels (such as `grant` and `wait`). Data-races are interpreted as faults in this semantics. We prove our result for a sequential thread t possibly executing concurrently with other sequential threads—this degenerates into the purely sequential case when there are no other runnable threads. Because t is sequential, it does not call `fork`; we also assume that it is guaranteed to terminate, and that it never disposes memory based on the caveats discussed above.

Theorem 7. *Let t be a sequential thread, and let t_{par} a corresponding parallelized version, equipped with thread creation operations, and synchronization actions that enforce sequential dependencies among the child threads it creates. Let $\mathcal{K}_{\mathrm{par}}$ be a terminating non-faulting (i.e., data-race free) trace of an execution of t_{par}. There exists a corresponding trace $\mathcal{K}$ derived by substituting corresponding operations in t for t_{par} such that: (1) $\mathcal{K}$ and $\mathcal{K}_{\mathrm{par}}$ begin in the same state; (2) for every thread $t' \neq t$ in $\mathcal{K}$, $\mathcal{K}$ and $\mathcal{K}_{\mathrm{par}}$ exhibit identical thread-local behaviour; and (3) the terminal state of thread t in $\mathcal{K}_{\mathrm{par}}$ is a substate of the corresponding state in $\mathcal{K}$.*

Proof sketch. We show that, under the assumption that forked child threads never wait for channels granted by their parent or later-forked child threads, any terminating non-faulting trace $\mathcal{K}_{\mathrm{par}}$ can be reordered into a sequentialized trace $\mathcal{K}_{\mathrm{seq}}$ with the same thread-local behaviour. By *sequentialized*, we mean that forked children must execute to completion before their parents can be scheduled.

We establish a simulation invariant between executions of t_{par} decorated with arbitrary calls to `newch`, `wait`, `grant` and `fork`, and executions of $t_{\mathrm{par}}^{\downarrow}$ identical to t_{par} except with all such constructs erased. The invariant establishes that every non-faulting sequentialized trace $\mathcal{K}_{\mathrm{seq}}$ of t_{par} simulates some trace $\mathcal{K}$ of $t_{\mathrm{par}}^{\downarrow}$.

We tie this result to our analysis by observing that parallelization only inserts the four constructs `newch`, `wait`, `grant` and `fork` (leaving aside issues of loop-splitting and materialization). As a result, $t_{\mathrm{par}}^{\downarrow} = t$. We also show that the way we insert signals ensures that they are ordered with respect to thread creation, as assumed in the previous step.

This establishes a behaviour-preservation result for non-faulting traces, but parallelization might introduce faults. However, parallelized programs are verified using separation logic, meaning we can assume that they do not fault when executed in a state satisfying the precondition. This completes the proof. □

One attractive property is that this proof does not place any explicit requirements on the positioning of barriers—it is sufficient that we can provide a separation-logic proof for t_{par}. The caveat on memory disposition manifests in the way we establish our simulation invariant, which necessarily assumes newly allocated data is always "fresh" and thus does not alias with any accessible heap-allocated structure. The caveat on termination is necessary to ensure we can suitably reorder forked threads to yield a sequentialized trace.

In addition to inserting barriers, our analysis mutates the program by materialising thread-local variables and splitting loops. Both of these can be performed as mutations on the initial sequential program, and neither affect visible behaviour. Loop-splitting is straightforwardly semantics-preserving, while materialized variables are only used to control barrier calls.

Theorem 7 guarantees that parallelisation does not introduce deadlocks; otherwise the simulation relation would not exist. The ordering on barriers ensures that termination in the sequential program is preserved in the resulting parallel program.

7. Refining the Predicate Domain

The structure of the sequential proof affects the success of parallelization in two ways. First, the loop invariants may allow the analysis to verify a parallelized program when it would otherwise have failed. Second, the choice of predicate domain controls how much information about resource-usage is available to the analysis. Intuitively, enriching the domain may permit a finer-grained splitting of resources, allowing redundant resources to be identified earlier or missing resources later.

To see how the choice of abstract domain influences precision and effectiveness of the analysis, consider the example discussed in §3; there, we parallelized `sum_head` using the list segment predicate lseg. An alternative predicate is $\mathsf{lsegni}(h, t, n, i)$, which extends lseg with a parameter $n \in \mathbb{Z}$ recording the *length* of the list segment, and with a parameter $i \in (0, 1]$ recording the *permission* on the list segment. If $i = 1$ the thread has read-write access; otherwise it has read access only. We define lsegni as the least predicate satisfying the following equation:

$$\mathsf{lsegni}(x, t, n, i) \triangleq (x = t \wedge n = 0 \wedge \mathsf{emp}) \vee \left(\begin{array}{r}\exists v, y.\, x.\mathrm{val} \overset{i}{\mapsto} v * x.\mathrm{nxt} \overset{i}{\mapsto} y \\ * \,\mathsf{lsegni}(y, t, n-1, i)\end{array}\right)$$

The equivalence $\mathsf{lseg}(h, t) \iff \exists n.\, \mathsf{lsegni}(h, t, n, 1)$ would allow the analysis to exploit this finer-grained predicate even if the sequential proof is written using the coarse-grained lseg predicate.

```
sum_head1(n){
  *npr = n;
  grant(i1);
  i = 1;
  sum = 0;
  x = *hd;
  while(x!=nil && i!=n){
    sum += x.val;
    i++;
    x = x.nxt;
  }
  *xpr = x;
  grant(i2);
  while(x!=nil){
    x.val = 0;
    x = x.nxt;
  }
  grant(i3);
}
```

```
sum_head2(n){
  i = 1;
  sum = 0;
  wait(i1);
  x = *hd;
  while(x!=nil && i!=n){
    if(n==*npr) wait(i2);
    sum += x.val;
    i++;
    x = x.nxt;
  }
  wait(i2);
  while(x!=nil){
    if(x==*xpr) wait(i3);
    x.val = 0;
    x = x.nxt;
  }
}
```

Figure 12. Improved parallelization of `sum_head`.

Function `sum_head` only writes to the list after traversing `n` nodes. Consequently, it needs only non-exclusive, read-only access to the first `n` nodes. (Or the entire list, if the list is shorter than `n` nodes long.) We can extend our resource usage analysis to deal with this richer predicate such that it identifies the following as a sufficient precondition for the *entire* `sum_head` function:

$$\mathsf{hd} \overset{j}{\mapsto} h * \begin{pmatrix} (\exists t.\, \mathsf{lsegni}(h, t, \mathtt{n}, i) * \mathsf{lseg}(t, \mathsf{nil})) \vee \\ (\exists n'.\, \mathsf{lsegni}(h, \mathsf{nil}, n', i) \wedge n' < \mathtt{n}) \end{pmatrix}$$

Without the lsegni predicate, this precondition could not be expressed. The availability of lsegni would also allow the analysis to discover that this resource is redundant at the start of `sum_head`:

$$\exists h, i, j.\, \mathsf{hd} \overset{j}{\mapsto} h * \\ \mathsf{lsegni}(h, t, \mathtt{n}, i) \vee (\exists n'.\, \mathsf{lsegni}(h, \mathsf{nil}, n', i) \wedge n' < \mathtt{n})$$

When `sum_head(n)` is called in a parallel-`for`, the subsequent call to `sum_head` can *immediately* read from the first `n` nodes of the list. Applying our analysis using the lsegni predicate yields the the two-thread parallelization shown in Fig. 12. `i1` signals that the first `n` nodes can be read by the subsequent iteration of `sum_head`. Similar to the transformation discussed in §3, `grant` calls can be inserted on `i2` to signal that the subsequent iteration can write to the first `n` nodes; and on `i3` to signal that the entire list can be written to. Because this parallelization calls `grant` earlier than the parallelization discussed earlier, it can consequently extract more parallelism from the original sequential program.

As this discussion reveals, our analysis is generic in the choice of abstract domain; any separation logic predicate could be used in place of lseg, for example. However, the success of *automated* parallelization is highly dependent on the power of the entailment prover in the chosen domain. The lseg domain is one of the best-developed in separation logic, and consequently automated parallelization is feasible using tools such as coreStar [7]. Other domains (such as trees) are far less developed.

8. Related Work

Resource-usage inference by abduction. We have defined an interprocedural, control-flow-sensitive analysis capable of determining the resource that will (and will not) be accessed between particular points in the program. At its core, our analysis uses abductive reasoning [11] to discover *redundancies*—that is, state used earlier in the program that will not be accessed subsequent to the current program point. Using abduction in this way was first proposed in [15], where it is used to discover memory leaks, albeit without conditionals, procedures, loops, or code specialization.

In [12], abduction is used to infer resource invariants for synchronization, using a process of counterexample-driven refinement. Our approach similarly infers resource invariants, but using a very different technique: invariants are derived from a sequential proof, and we also infer synchronization points and specialise the program to reveal synchronization opportunities.

Behaviour-preserving parallelization. We expect our resource-usage analysis can be used in other synchronization-related optimizations, but in this paper, we have used it as the basis for a parallelising transformation. This transformation is in the style of *deterministic parallelism* [3–5, 9]—although our approach does not, in fact, require determinacy of the source program. In this vein, our transformation ensures that every behaviour of the parallelized program is a behaviour of the source sequential program (modulo the caveats about allocation and termination discussed in §6).

Previous approaches to deterministic parallelism operate without the benefit of a high-level specification. This places a substantial burden on the analysis and runtime to safely extract information on resource usage and transfer—information that is readily available in a proof. As a result, these analyses tend to be much more conservative in their treatment of mutable data. Our proof-based technique gives us a general approach to splitting mutable resources; for example, by allowing the analysis to perform ad-hoc list splitting, as we do with `sum_head`.

Our approach transforms a sequential `for`-loop by running all the iterations in parallel and signalling between them. This idea has been proposed previously, for example in numerical computation [33]. The novelty in our approach lies in inferring synchronization over (portions of) complex mutable data-structures. Alternatively, we could have used a more irregular concurrency annotation, for example safe futures [27], or an unordered parallel-`for`, as in the Galois system [30]. In the former case, our resource-usage analysis would be mostly unchanged, but our parallelized program would construct a set of syntactically-distinct threads, rather than a pipeline of identical threads. Removing ordering between iterations, as in the latter case, would mean replacing ordered `grant`-`wait` pairs with conventional locks, and would introduce an obligation to show that locks were always acquired together, as a set.

Proof-driven parallelization. A insight central to our approach is that a separation logic proof expresses data dependencies for *parts* of a program, as well as for the whole program. These internal dependencies can be used to inject safe parallelism. This insight is due to [13, 31] and [24], both of which propose parallelization analyses based on separation logic. The analyses proposed in these papers are much more conservative than ours, in that they discover independence which already exists between commands of the program. They do not insert synchronization constructs, and consequently cannot enforce sequential dependencies among concurrent computations that share and modify state. Indeed, [31] does not consider any program transformations, since the goal of that work is to identify memory separation of different commands, while [24] expresses optimizations as reordering rewrites on proof trees.

Bell *et. al* [1] construct a proof of an *already-transformed* multithreaded program parallelized by the DSWP transformation [29]. This approach assumes a specific pattern of (linear) dependencies in the while-loop consistent with DSWP, a specific pattern of sequential proof, and a fixed number of threads. In our `sum_head` example, the outermost (parallelising) loop contains two successive inner loops, while the example in Fig. 2 illustrates how the technique can deal with interprocedural and control-flow sensitive dependencies. In both cases, the resulting parallelization is specialized to inject synchronization primitives to enforce sequential dependencies. We believe examples like these do not fall within the scope of either DSWP or the proof techniques supported by [1].

Outside separation logic, Deshmukh *et. al* [14] propose an analysis which augments a sequential library with synchronization. This approach takes as input a sequential proof expressing the correctness criteria for the library, and generates synchronization ensuring this proof is preserved if methods run concurrently. A basic assumption is that the sequential proof represents all the properties that must be preserved. In contrast, we also preserve sequential order on access to resources. Consequently, Deshmukh et al. permit parallelizations that we would prohibit, and can introduce new behaviours into the parallelized program. Another difference is that [14] derives a linearizable implementation given a sequential specification in the form of input-output assertions; because they do not consider *specialization* of multiple instances of the library running concurrently, it is unclear how their approach would deal with transformations of the kind we use for `sum_head`.

Separation logic and concurrency. Separation logic is essential to our approach. It allows us to localise the behaviour of a program fragment to precisely the resources it accesses. Our proofs are written using concurrent separation logic [28]. CSL has been extended to deal with dynamically-allocated locks [19, 23, 25], re-entrant locks [20], and primitive channels [1, 22, 26, 34]. Sequential tools for separation logic have achieved impressive scalability—for example [11] has verified a large proportion of the Linux kernel. Our work can be seen as an attempt to leverage the success of such sequential tools. Our experiments are built on coreStar [7, 16], a language-independent proof tool for separation logic.

The parallelization phase of our analysis makes use of the specifications for parallelization barriers proposed in [17]. That paper defined high-level specifications representing the abstract behaviour of barriers, and verified those specifications against the barriers' low-level implementations. However, it assumed that barriers were already placed in the program, and made no attempt to infer barrier positions. In contrast, we assume the high-level specification, and define an analysis to insert barriers. The semantics of barriers used in that paper and here was initially proposed in [27].

Acknowledgments

This work was supported by the Gates trust, by EPSRC grant EP/H010815/1, and by NSF grant CCF-0811631. Thanks to Dino Distefano, Matthew Parkinson, Mohammad Raza, John Wickerson and the anonymous reviewers for comments and suggestions.

References

[1] C. J. Bell, A. Appel, and D. Walker. Concurrent Separation Logic for Pipelined Parallelization. In *SAS*, pages 151–166, 2009.

[2] J. Berdine, C. Calcagno, and P. W. O'Hearn. Smallfoot: Modular automatic assertion checking with separation logic. In *FMCO*, pages 115–137, 2005.

[3] T. Bergan, O. Anderson, J. Devietti, L. Ceze, and D. Grossman. CoreDet: A Compiler and Runtime System for Deterministic Multithreaded Execution. *SIGPLAN Not.*, 45(3):53–64, 2010.

[4] E. D. Berger, T. Yang, T. Liu, and G. Novark. Grace: Safe multithreaded programming for C/C++. In *OOPSLA*, pages 81–96, 2010.

[5] R. L. Bocchino, Jr., V. S. Adve, D. Dig, S. V. Adve, S. Heumann, R. Komuravelli, J. Overbey, P. Simmons, H. Sung, and M. Vakilian. A Type and Effect System for Deterministic Parallel Java. In *OOPSLA*, pages 91–116, 2009.

[6] R. Bornat, C. Calcagno, P. O'Hearn, and M. Parkinson. Permission Accounting in Separation Logic. In *POPL*, pages 259–270, 2005.

[7] M. Botinčan, D. Distefano, M. Dodds, R. Griore, Naudžiūnienė, and M. Parkinson. coreStar: The Core of jStar. In *Boogie*, pages 65–77, 2011.

[8] M. Botinčan, M. Dodds, and S. Jagannathan. Resource-Sensitive Synchronization Inference by Abduction. Technical Report 808, University of Cambridge Computer Laboratory, 2011.

[9] J. Burnim and K. Sen. Asserting and Checking Determinism for Multithreaded Programs. *Commun. ACM*, 53:97–105, June 2010.

[10] C. Calcagno, P. W. O'Hearn, and H. Yang. Local Action and Abstract Separation Logic. In *LICS*, pages 366–378, 2007.

[11] C. Calcagno, D. Distefano, P. O'Hearn, and H. Yang. Compositional Shape Analysis by Means of Bi-Abduction. In *POPL*, pages 289–300, 2009.

[12] C. Calcagno, D. Distefano, and V. Vafeiadis. Bi-abductive Resource Invariant Synthesis. In *APLAS*, pages 259–274, 2009.

[13] B. Cook, S. Magill, M. Raza, J. Simsa, and S. Singh. Making Fast Hardware with Separation Logic, 2010. Unpublished, `http://cs.cmu.edu/~smagill/papers/fast-hardware.pdf`.

[14] J. V. Deshmukh, G. Ramalingam, V. P. Ranganath, and K. Vaswani. Logical Concurrency Control from Sequential Proofs. In *ESOP*, pages 226–245, 2010.

[15] D. Distefano and I. Filipović. Memory Leaks Detection in Java by Bi-abductive Inference. In *FASE*, pages 278–292, 2010.

[16] D. Distefano and M. J. Parkinson J. jStar: Towards Practical Verification for Java. In *OOPSLA*, pages 213–226, 2008.

[17] M. Dodds, S. Jagannathan, and M. J. Parkinson. Modular Reasoning for Deterministic Parallelism. In *POPL*, pages 259–270, 2011.

[18] T. Elmas, S. Qadeer, and S. Tasiran. A Calculus of Atomic Actions. In *POPL*, pages 2–15, 2009.

[19] A. Gotsman, J. Berdine, B. Cook, N. Rinetzky, and M. Sagiv. Local Reasoning for Storable Locks and Threads. In *APLAS*, pages 19–37, 2007.

[20] C. Haack, M. Huisman, and C. Hurlin. Reasoning about Java's Reentrant Locks. In *APLAS*, pages 171–187, 2008.

[21] T. Harris, J. Larus, and R. Rajwar. *Transactional Memory, 2nd edition*. Morgan-Claypool, 2010.

[22] C. A. R. Hoare and P. W. O'Hearn. Separation Logic Semantics for Communicating Processes. *ENTCS*, 212:3–25, 2008.

[23] A. Hobor, A. W. Appel, and F. Zappa Nardelli. Oracle semantics for concurrent separation logic. In *ESOP*, 2008.

[24] C. Hurlin. Automatic Parallelization and Optimization of Programs by Proof Rewriting. In *SAS*, pages 52–68, 2009.

[25] B. Jacobs and F. Piessens. Modular full functional specification and verification of lock-free data structures. Technical Report CW 551, Katholieke Universiteit Leuven, Dept. of Computer Science, 2009.

[26] K. R. M. Leino, P. Müller, and J. Smans. Deadlock-free Channels and Locks. In *ESOP*, pages 407–426, 2010.

[27] A. Navabi, X. Zhang, and S. Jagannathan. Quasi-static Scheduling for Safe Futures. In *PPoPP*, pages 23–32. ACM, 2008.

[28] P. W. O'Hearn. Resources, Concurrency and Local Reasoning. *TCS*, 375:271–307, 2007.

[29] G. Ottoni, R. Rangan, A. Stoler, and D. I. August. Automatic Thread Extraction with Decoupled Software Pipelining. In *MICRO*, pages 105–118, 2005.

[30] K. Pingali, D. Nguyen, M. Kulkarni, M. Burtscher, M. A. Hassaan, R. Kaleem, T.-H. Lee, A. Lenharth, R. Manevich, M. Méndez-Lojo, D. Prountzos, and X. Sui. The Tao of Parallelism in Algorithms. In *PLDI*, pages 12–25, 2011.

[31] M. Raza, C. Calcagno, and P. Gardner. Automatic Parallelization with Separation Logic. In *ESOP*, pages 348–362, 2009.

[32] J. C. Reynolds. Separation Logic: A Logic for Shared Mutable Data Structures. In *LICS*, pages 55–74, 2002.

[33] P. Tang, P. Tang, J. N. Zigman, and J. N. Zigman. Reducing Data Communication Overhead for DOACROSS Loop Nests. In *International Conference on Supercomputing*, pages 44–53, 1993.

[34] J. Villard, É. Lozes, and C. Calcagno. Tracking Heaps That Hop with Heap-Hop. In *TACAS*, pages 275–279, 2010.

Syntactic Control of Interference for Separation Logic

Uday S. Reddy
University of Birmingham
u.s.reddy@cs.bham.ac.uk

John C. Reynolds
Carnegie-Mellon University
jcr@cs.cmu.edu

Abstract

Separation Logic has witnessed tremendous success in recent years in reasoning about programs that deal with heap storage. Its success owes to the fundamental principle that one should keep separate areas of the heap storage separate in program reasoning. However, the way Separation Logic deals with program variables continues to be based on traditional Hoare Logic without taking any benefit of the separation principle. This has led to unwieldy proof rules suffering from lack of clarity as well as questions surrounding their soundness. In this paper, we extend the separation idea to the treatment of variables in Separation Logic, especially Concurrent Separation Logic, using the system of Syntactic Control of Interference proposed by Reynolds in 1978. We extend the original system with permission algebras, making it more powerful and able to deal with the issues of concurrent programs. The result is a streamined presentation of Concurrent Separation Logic, whose rules are memorable and soundness obvious. We also include a discussion of how the new rules impact the semantics and devise static analysis techniques to infer the required permissions automatically.

Categories and Subject Descriptors D.3.1 [*Programming Languages*]: Formal Definitions and Theory—Syntax; F.1.2 [*Theory of Computation*]: Computation by Abstract Devices—Models of Computation - Parallelism and concurrency; F.3.1 [*Logics and Meanings of Programs*]: Specifying and Verifying and Reasoning about Programs—Logics of programs; F.3.2 [*Logics and Meanings of Programs*]: Semantics of Programming Languages—Denotational semantics

General Terms Program Logic, Concurrency, Denotational Semantics, Type Systems

Keywords Separation Logic, Syntactic Control of Interference, Conditional Critical Regions, Fractional Permissions, Static Analysis

1. Introduction

In reasoning about programs that alter the state, one often encounters stylized side conditions that have to do with how variable symbols are used. For example, the "invariance" rule of Hoare Logic [3] (or the "constancy" rule in Specification Logic [37]), written as

$$\frac{\{P\}\, C\, \{Q\}}{\{P \wedge R\}\, C\, \{Q \wedge R\}}$$

has a side condition that states that "C should not modify any variables occurring free in R." This rule becomes the all-important "frame rule" in Separation Logic [30] but the same side condition is retained. Similar conditions also occur in the rules for procedures [3, 37]. In fact, such conditions are not only employed in the proof rules for procedures, but it has also been argued that intelligible programming requires adherence to them even if no efforts are made at formal reasoning. A procedure call $P(A)$ is regarded as intelligible only if the procedure P does not modify any of the variables occurring free in the argument A and, likewise, the argument A does not cause state changes via the variables occurring free in P. (This is more commonly called "aliasing" control. Consider call-by-name or call-by-reference parameter passing methods or higher-order arguments to see the full effect of this observation.)

These observations are also made with additional force in concurrent programming. Hoare [17, 18] and Brinch Hansen [10] have argued convincingly that parallel processes should not interfere with each other. A process should not modify variables that are concurrently used by other processes unless the variables are under the control of resources enforcing mutual exclusion. Program logic proof rules similarly employ these conditions in their proof rules [17, 25, 31].

Noticing that essentially the same side condition arises in all such contexts, Reynolds [36] formulated it as a uniform principle of *non-interference*. Two program phrases P_1 and P_2 are considered non-interfering if the variables used in one of them for state-modification do not occur free in the other phrase. This work presents a system of rules called "syntactic control of interference" (SCI) which bring structure to the conditions employed in intelligible programming as well as the formal rules of programming logics. These rules incorporate, at syntactic level, what we now regard as the "separation principle," the same principle that is responsible for the success of Separation Logic in reasoning about heap storage. The SCI system has been studied quite extensively since this early work. O'Hearn [26] reformulated Reynolds's rules in the notation of type systems (or proof theory) and noted its overriding similarity to Girard's Linear Logic [15]. Reddy [33] formulated a novel semantic model for programs in the SCI framework, exploiting the non-interference property of the programs in a crucial way, which turns out to be the first fully abstract model ever discovered for a higher-order imperative programming language [22]. (The games models of Abramsky et al. [1, 2] generalize Reddy's model to deal with interference and represent fully abstract models as well.) Generalizing the SCI framework, O'Hearn and Pym formulated bunched type systems and the logic of Bunched Implications [27], the latter of which forms the foundation for Separation Logic [30, 34]. In retrospect, it is fair to say that SCI has proved to

POPL '12 January 25–27, 2012, Philadelphia, PA, USA.

be a deep foundational principle of imperative programs leading to numerous developments in our understanding of their structure.

Curiously, despite all the historical background, SCI has not been used in formulating Separation Logic itself. We believe that this has led to unwieldy proof rules fraught with side conditions. The problems become critical in the formulation of Concurrent Separation Logic [25]. Brookes's attempt to formalize such rules [11] turned out to be faulty, with known counterexamples to their soundness [4].

In this paper, we reformulate the rules of sequential as well as concurrent Separation Logic using the principles of SCI to bring structure to their side conditions. It turns out that the traditional SCI is not quite adequate to the task. It incorporates a limited treatment of "passive" or "read-only" uses of variables which is unable to deal with the more advanced usage of variables in concurrent programs. We enrich the traditional SCI with the idea of fractional permissions, borrowed from Boyland [8] and Bornat et al [6], to devise a more powerful variant. This system is then used to create a streamlined formulation of Separation Logic.

While fractional permissions for variables allow a streamlined presentation of the proof rules and clarify their semantics, they would be an overkill to use in practice. A programmer should not have to explicitly annotate all the variable uses in processes and shared resources with fractional annotations. To address the issue, we devise a *permission inference system*, which can take a Separation Logic proof outline without any permissions specified with shared resources and fills them in if at all possible according to the rules of the logic. The effect is similar to that of Hindley-Milner type inference in programming languages like ML [14, 23].

Related Work

Hoare [17] and Brinch Hansen [9] have formulated conventions for controlling variable aliasing in concurrent programs. Hoare also proposed proof rules for reasoning with conditional critical regions. Owicki and Gries [31] generalized Hoare's conventions as well as the proof rules. O'Hearn [25] extended the Owicki-Gries system to deal with heap storage, formulating a *Concurrent Separation Logic*, which is currently a subject of active study [11, 13, 16, 20, 32, 38]. We refer to this logic as the "Owicki-Gries-O'Hearn system."

The main issue of our concern is how the variable usage is controlled across parallel processes and the interplay between such control and the proof rules of the programming logic. The original logic formulated by Owicki and Gries employed informal statements of the form "variable not modified by any other process". Such a statement is ambiguous (e.g., does it include modification inside critical regions?). It is also non-compositional. Checking if a proof is correctly constructed involves examining the entire program. (For instance, the Smallfoot verification tool implements such global analysis [19].) It is also problematic in defining semantics of the programming logic and verifying its soundness.

Two previous attempts have been made to formalise the variable usage rules of Concurrent Separation Logic. Brookes [11] formulated a compositional set of rules in his effort to prove the soundness of the logic. However, the rules generalize the original Owicki-Gries rules in new ways and their soundness is not obvious. In fact, subsequently, Ian Wehrman has found counterexamples to their soundness in one particular case [4]. The second attempt was that of Bornat *et al.* [7, 32], where they treat variables as "resources" similar to heap locations, whose access is controlled via programming logic proof rules. Their rules do address the non-compositionality issue mentioned above and the soundness of their rules is more immediate. However the rules are clumsy to use in practice because the normal pun of variable symbols as mutable variable and logical variables is not retained. For instance, a formula such as $x = x$ is true if x is a logical variable, but not necessarily so when x is a program variable.

Although we arrived at our formulation via a different route, using the ideas of syntactic control of interference to formalize the original Owicki-Gries-O'Hearn system, our system can also be seen as a syntactic variant of the Parkinson-Bornat-Calcagno logic described in [32]. The benefits of using the syntactic approach are:

- The normal conventions of variable usage in Hoare-style logics are respected. So pitfalls in reasoning from improper treatment of variable symbols can be avoided.
- We are able to devise a compositional (or "modular") static analysis system to automatically infer permissions required for variable usage.
- The system should be extensible to higher-order languages with procedures and objects. For instance, the methods of objects can be categorized as active or passive. (Even though we do not discuss the higher-order aspects in this paper, the traditional principles of syntactic control of interference for higher-order procedures apply. These principles however do not generalize to storable procedures as in ML. So, further work is needed to address such issues.)

In recent work, Brookes [12] has independently devised a revised set of proof rules for Concurrent Separation Logic using ideas resembling ours. His rules do not employ fractional permissions as ours do and the relationship to SCI is less clear cut. We do not know at present the precise relationship between his formulation and ours, but we anticipate that the two are very close.

Inference of fractional permissions has been studied by Yasuoka and Terauchi [40] and Bierhoff [5]. Both these pieces of work address the permissions needed for heap cells (which is a harder problem than that for variables). However, they do not deal with concurrency, which is our main concern. Yasuoka et al. use a region-based analysis to make the heap permission problem tractable, which may be seen as a reduction to the corresponding problem for variable names. The techniques employed in their work rely on sophisticated constraint-solving methods. In contrast, our permission inference algorithm a two-pass algorithm on the syntax tree, similar to regular compiler analysis methods, with only rudimentary constraint solving issues.

The rest of this paper is organized as follows. In Section 2, we informally motivate the issues addressed by our formulation of Separation Logic. The logical system itself is described in Sections 3 and 4. We also include a detailed comparison with the proof systems of O'Hearn [25] Parkinson et al. [32]. A comparison with Brookes's original system [11] is include in Appendix B. In Section 5, we describe the denotational semantic framework of the proof system and indicate how the soundness is proved. Finally, in Section 6, we describe an algorithm to automatically infer variable permissions needed in the proof system.

2. Motivation

As mentioned in the Introduction, Hoare and Brinch Hansen advocated the avoidance of interference between concurrent processes as a good practice of intelligible programming. That requires that, in forming a parallel composition of commands $C_1 \parallel C_2$, one must ensure that C_1 does not modify any variable that occurs free in C_2 and *vice versa.* We use the terminology *"actively used"* for variables that are used for state-modification. Any variables that are used *only* for reading the state are said to be *"passively used."*

We first consider how to treat active free variables of phrases using Syntactic Control of Interference using the notations of [26, 29]. If a command C is formed using a set of active free variables Σ, it is described using a judgement of the form $\Sigma \vdash C\ \mathbf{Comm}$.

```
x := 0; a := 0; b := 0;
{x = a + b ⋆ a = 0 ⋆ b = 0}
resource r(x, a, b) {x = a + b} in
begin
  {a = 0}                        {b = 0}
  with r do                      with r do
    {a = 0 ⋆ x = a + b}            {b = 0 ⋆ x = a + b}
    x := x+1;              ||      x := x+1;
    a := 1                         b := 1
    {a = 1 ⋆ x = a + b}            {b = 1 ⋆ x = a + b}
  od                             od
  {a = 1}                        {b = 1}
end
{x = a + b ⋆ a = 1 ⋆ b = 1}
{x = 2}
```

Table 1. Example proof outline in Concurrent Separation Logic

Now, the well-formedness of an intelligible parallel composition in the sense of Hoare and Brinch Hansen can be described by the rule:

$$\frac{\Sigma_1 \vdash C_1\ \textbf{Comm} \quad \Sigma_2 \vdash C_2\ \textbf{Comm}}{\Sigma_1, \Sigma_2 \vdash (C_1 \parallel C_2)\ \textbf{Comm}}$$

Notice that the active free variables of C_1 and C_2 are combined "multiplicatively," requiring them to be separate or disjoint. Thus, the non-interference conditions of Hoare and Brinch Hansen can be described in a pleasingly symmetric fashion without employing side conditions.

The judgements used above describe the *well-formedness* of commands. Rules of program logic can be stated in essentially the same way. The Separation Logic proof rule for parallel composition becomes:

$$\frac{\Sigma_1 \vdash \{P_1\}\, C_1\, \{Q_1\} \quad \Sigma_2 \vdash \{P_2\}\, C_2\, \{Q_2\}}{\Sigma_1, \Sigma_2 \vdash \{P_1 \star P_2\}\, C_1 \parallel C_2\, \{Q_1 \star Q_2\}}$$

Each judgement in this rule asserts the well-formedness of a Hoare triple specification *as well as* the truth of the specification. Once again, *no side conditions are required* to describe a sound inference.

While Reynolds [36] only considered independent parallel composition, it is possible to add shared resources, e.g., Hoare-style resources and conditional critical regions, in the same way. A resource declaration command

$$\textbf{resource}\ r(\Sigma_0)\ \textbf{in}\ C$$

should split the available active variable context into two separate parts, Σ_0 for the variables encapsulated in the resource and the remainder of the context for the body C. A critical region command:

$$\textbf{with}\ r\ \textbf{when}\ B\ \textbf{do}\ C\ \textbf{od}$$

should add the encapsulated context of the resource r to the current context for the scope C. All this seems essentially straightforward. However, it turns out to be *inadequate* in practice.

To see the problem, consider the example proof outline shown in Table 1, discussed by Owicki and Gries [31]. Even though we use separating conjunction $\star$ in assertions, $\star$ has the same force as the ordinary conjunction $\wedge$ here because the formulas involved are pure. The purpose of the proof outline is to argue that running $x := x + 1$ in parallel with itself increments x by 2. The variable x is placed in a resource r, allowing it to be safely shared across the parallel branches. Notice that placing it in the resource precludes it from being mentioned in the parallel branches outside any critical regions. So, it is not possible to write assertions that show that each critical region increments x.

To solve the problem, Owicki and Gries recommend adding auxiliary variables a and b and using them to record control information about the increment actions performed in the two processes. The auxiliary variables are also included in the shared resource. So, a and b can only be modified inside critical regions.[1] The resource invariant $x = a + b$ captures the control information recorded by a and b. However, notice that a and b need to be mentioned in assertions *outside* the critical regions. Owicki and Gries tailor their proof rules to allow such usage. Evidently, we are entering tricky territory here. The variable x cannot be used outside critical regions whereas the variables a and b are allowed to be used. The difference is that x is modified in *both* the processes. Making assertions about it in one of the processes would not be sound because the other process can invalidate the assertions. On the other hand, the variable a is only modified in the left process. So, assertions mentioning a remain true independent of the progress of the other process. Thus, Owicki-Gries as well as O'Hearn's proof systems use a critical region proof rule *which allows the variables owned by a resource to appear in local assertions of a process, as long as they are not modified in "other processes."*

Note that the notion of a variable being "modified in other processes" is quite subtle. One might expect that neither x nor a should be regarded as being modified in the "other process" because the other process does not have direct access to them. Any modification happens only inside critical regions. So, the modification actions cannot be attributed to the process. Rather they should be charged to the resource, with the understanding that entering critical sections adds the access rights of the resource to the process. The putative Syntactic Control of Interference framework we alluded to above would treat the variables in that way.

To handle these issues, we generalize the active versus passive free variable distinction inherited from [29, 36] to *total* versus *partial* ownership of the free variables [6, 8]. (It has become conventional to call such ownership constraints "permissions." We continue to use that terminology even though we regard it as misleading.) A total permission for a variable allows writing to the variable (in other words, an *active* use) and a partial permission allows only reading (a *passive* use). In the algebra of *fractional permissions*, a total permission is denoted by 1 and a partial permission by some non-zero fraction. The use of permissions gives us more powerful control over variable usage because fractional permissions can be combined, possibly leading to a total permission, which then allows writing.

Returning to our example in Table 1, we can define the the resource r to contain the permissions x^1, $a^{\frac{1}{2}}$, $b^{\frac{1}{2}}$. The entire program is specified in the context x^1, a^1, b^1. The remaining permissions $a^{\frac{1}{2}}$ and $b^{\frac{1}{2}}$ are distributed to the two processes: $a^{\frac{1}{2}}$ to the left process and $b^{\frac{1}{2}}$ to the right process. This allows the two processes to use a and b in their local assertions because such usage is passive. When the left process enters its critical region, its local permissions are combined with those owned by the resource, leading to the set of permissions x^1, a^1, $b^{\frac{1}{2}}$. This allows the critical region to modify x and a, while only reading is permitted for b. The right process is similar. This provides a *compositional description* of the variable usage in the example, eliding the references to "other processes."

In the following sections, we formalize the system of Syntactic Control of Interference with permissions and use it to formulate the rules of sequential as well as concurrent Separation Logic.

[1] In Brookes's variant of the Owicki-Gries-O'Hearn system [11], a and b need not be included among the owned variables of the resource. Thus, Brookes's logic is subtly more general than the original Concurrent Separation Logic.

3. Sequential Separation Logic

Our form of syntactic control is a modified version of Reynolds SCI, using the ideas of permissions for read-only access [6, 8].

We assume a permission algebra $(\mathcal{P}, \oplus, \top)$, i.e., a partial commutative semigroup that is cancellative, has a distinguished element $\top$ denoting full permission and satisfies the following axioms [32]:

(non-zero)	$\forall p, p' \in \mathcal{P}.\, p \oplus p' \neq p$
(top)	$\forall p \in \mathcal{P}.\, \top \oplus p$ is undefined
(divisibility)	$\forall p \in \mathcal{P}.\, \exists p_1, p_2 \in \mathcal{P}.\, p = p_1 \oplus p_2$

A significant case of permission algebras is that of *fractional permissions*: the real interval $(0, 1]$ with $\oplus$ being the partial operation of addition and $\top = 1$. The idea is that a full permission (1 in the fractional permission algebra) allows an "active" usage, i.e., both reading and writing, whereas a partial permission (represented by fractional values in the fractional algebra) allows a read-only or "passive" usage.

A *variable context* Σ is an unordered list of the form

$$x_1^{p_1}, \ldots, x_n^{p_n}$$

where $x_1, \ldots, x_n$ are variable symbols and $p_1, \ldots, p_n$ are permissions, subject to the following condition:[2]

- *if the same variable symbol x occurs in Σ multiple times with permissions $p_{i_1}, \ldots, p_{i_k}$ respectively then $p_{i_1} \oplus \cdots \oplus p_{i_k}$ is defined.*

We call a putative variable context *well-defined* when it satisfies this condition. If the variables $x_1, \ldots, x_n$ are pairwise distinct, then we say that the variable context is in *normal form*. A non-normal form variable context can be *normalized* by replacing the multiple copies of each variable by a single copy and associating with it the permission $p_{i_1} \oplus \cdots \oplus p_{i_k}$ as above. We denote the normalized version of variable context Σ by $norm(\Sigma)$. Whenever two variable contexts are combined, as in "Σ_1, Σ_2", one needs to ensure that the combination is well-defined. We say that Σ_1 and Σ_2 are compatible, and denote this fact by $\Sigma_1 \sharp \Sigma_2$.

We assume that all the variable contexts appearing in legal inferences are well-defined, i.e., any inference that leads to an ill-defined variable context is illegal. (Formally, our system of rules is a *natural deduction system*, where the variable contexts are used as assumptions of the deductions. Even though we use the notation of sequents for presenting the deduction rules, it is *not* a sequent calculus.)

The syntactic well-formedness of program phrases is expressed using a variety of judgements:

$$\Sigma \vdash x\ \mathbf{Var} \quad \Sigma \vdash E\ \mathbf{Exp} \quad \Sigma \vdash P\ \mathbf{Assert} \quad \Sigma \vdash C\ \mathbf{Comm}$$

These say, respectively, that the displayed phrase is a well-formed variable, expression, assertion or command in the variable context Σ. All these forms of judgements have a structural rule:

$$\textit{Contraction}\ \frac{\Sigma, x^p, x^q \vdash \mathcal{S}}{\Sigma, x^{p \oplus q} \vdash \mathcal{S}}$$

This allows two copies of a variable x to be combined into a single copy or to split a single copy into two, while keeping account of the permissions.

[2] It is more conventional to require that all the variable symbols listed in a context are distinct. It would be possible to formulate variants of our rules using such a convention. But we feel that our approach is more intuitive.

The following rules will be *admissible rules* in our proof systems (if the premises are derivable then so is the conclusion):

$$\textit{Weakening}\ \frac{\Sigma \vdash \mathcal{S}}{\Sigma, \Sigma' \vdash \mathcal{S}}$$

$$\textit{Subst}_A\ \frac{\Sigma \vdash E\ \mathbf{Exp} \quad \Sigma, x^{\top} \vdash P\ \mathbf{Assert}}{\Sigma \vdash P[E/x]\ \mathbf{Assert}}$$

The substitution rules allow a variable with a *full* permission to be substituted by an expression.

To use a variable symbol x as a variable phrase in a program (thereby allowing assignments to it), one needs the full permission for the variable. On the other hand, to use a variable as an expression, any permission will do.

$$\frac{}{\Sigma, x^{\top} \vdash x\ \mathbf{Var}} \qquad \frac{}{\Sigma, x^{p} \vdash x\ \mathbf{Exp}}$$

More generally, for all expressions and assertions, the requirement is that all their free variables must have some permission in Σ. We omit the formal rules for brevity.

We can write down well-formedness rules for commands as well, but we will save a bit of work by combining the well-formedness of commands with program logic, which we look at next. (For completeness, we include the well-formedness rules in Appendix A.)

A judgement of sequential Separation Logic is of the form

$$\Sigma \vdash \{P\}\, C\, \{Q\} \tag{1}$$

which means that:

1. P, C and Q are well-formed phrases in the context Σ, and
2. the failure-avoiding specification $\{P\}\, C\, \{Q\}$ holds assuming a variable context Σ.

The variables that are modified in the command C would be required to have $\top$ permission in Σ. Other variables, which might be employed in C in a read-only fashion or employed only in assertions, can have non-$\top$ permissions.

The rules for commands are shown in Table 2. Since we incorporate the well-formedness of assertions and commands in specifications, most rules have premises to do with well-formedness of assertions, commands or components of commands. In the rule for assignment, we depend on the admissible rule $\textit{Subst}_A$ which allows us to substitute for a variable symbol with the $\top$ permission. The rule for heap cell lookup illustrates the use of side conditions for specifying genuine logical conditions about the occurrence of free variables (as opposed to the conditions that are purely to do with well-formedness issues). Contrast this with the rule for local variable declaration, where we require that E, P and Q should be well-formed in the *outer* variable context. So, they cannot have x occurring free. This seems to be a reasonable choice, because most programmers understand the scope of x to be command C. So, its free occurrence in other places would be considered odd.

The frame rule of Separation Logic gives us the first application of the syntactic control of interference:

$$\textit{FRAME}\ \frac{\Sigma \vdash \{P\}\, C\, \{Q\} \quad \Sigma' \vdash R\ \mathbf{Assert}}{\Sigma, \Sigma' \vdash \{P \star R\}\, C\, \{Q \star R\}}$$

(Note that there is an implicit side condition for the rule that says that Σ, Σ' is a well-formed variable context.) Since the variable contexts of $\{P\}\, C\, \{Q\}$ and R are required to be separate, it is not possible for C to modify any free variables of R. If C modifies a variable x then Σ needs to include $x^{\top}$. But then x^p cannot occur in Σ', for any permission p, because $\top \oplus p$ is undefined. Thus the splitting of the variable context into Σ and Σ' has exactly the

$$\frac{\Sigma \vdash P', Q' \ \mathbf{Assert} \quad \Sigma \vdash \{P\}\, C\, \{Q\}}{\Sigma \vdash \{P'\}\, C\, \{Q'\}} \ \text{if } P' \supset P \text{ and } Q \supset Q'$$

$$\frac{\Sigma \vdash P \ \mathbf{Assert}}{\Sigma \vdash \{P\}\, \mathbf{skip}\, \{P\}} \qquad \frac{\Sigma \vdash x \ \mathbf{Var} \quad \Sigma \vdash E \ \mathbf{Exp} \quad \Sigma \vdash P \ \mathbf{Assert}}{\Sigma \vdash \{P[E/x]\}\, x := E\, \{P\}}$$

$$\frac{\Sigma \vdash x \ \mathbf{Var} \quad \Sigma \vdash E \ \mathbf{Exp} \quad \Sigma \vdash E' \ \mathbf{Exp}}{\Sigma \vdash \{P[E'/x] \wedge E \mapsto E'\}\, x := [E]\, \{P \wedge E \mapsto E'\}} \ (\text{if } x \notin FV(E, E')) \qquad \frac{\Sigma \vdash E \ \mathbf{Exp} \quad \Sigma \vdash E' \ \mathbf{Exp}}{\Sigma \vdash \{E \mapsto -\}\, [E] := E'\, \{E \mapsto E'\}}$$

$$\frac{\Sigma \vdash \{P \wedge B\}\, C_1\, \{Q\} \quad \Sigma \vdash \{P \wedge \neg B\}\, C_2\, \{Q\}}{\Sigma \vdash \{P\}\, \mathbf{if}\ B\ \mathbf{then}\ C_1\ \mathbf{else}\ C_2\, \{Q\}} \qquad \frac{\Sigma \vdash P, Q \ \mathbf{Assert} \quad \Sigma, x^{\top} \vdash \{P\}\, C\, \{Q\}}{\Sigma \vdash \{P\}\, \mathbf{local}\ x\ \mathbf{in}\ C\, \{Q\}}$$

Table 2. Proof rules of sequential Separation Logic

$$\mathit{ASSIGN}\ \frac{\Sigma \vdash x \ \mathbf{Var} \quad \Sigma \vdash E \ \mathbf{Exp} \quad \Sigma \vdash P \ \mathbf{Assert}}{\Sigma \mid \Gamma \vdash \{P[E/x]\}\, x := E\, \{P\}} \qquad \mathit{COND}\ \frac{\Sigma \mid \Gamma \vdash \{P \wedge B\}\, C_1\, \{Q\} \quad \Sigma \mid \Gamma \vdash \{P \wedge \neg B\}\, C_2\, \{Q\}}{\Sigma \mid \Gamma \vdash \{P\}\, \mathbf{if}\ B\ \mathbf{then}\ C_1\ \mathbf{else}\ C_2\, \{Q\}}$$

$$\mathit{PAR}\ \frac{\Sigma_1 \mid \Gamma \vdash \{P_1\}\, C_1\, \{Q_1\} \quad \Sigma_2 \mid \Gamma \vdash \{P_2\}\, C_2\, \{Q_2\}}{\Sigma_1, \Sigma_2 \mid \Gamma \vdash \{P_1 \star P_2\}\, C_1 \parallel C_2\, \{Q_1 \star Q_2\}}$$

$$\mathit{CRIT}\ \frac{\Sigma \vdash P, Q \ \mathbf{Assert} \quad \Sigma, \Sigma_0 \mid \Gamma \vdash \{P \star R \wedge B\}\, C\, \{Q \star R\}}{\Sigma \mid \Gamma,\, r(\Sigma_0)\colon R \vdash \{P\}\, \mathbf{with}\ r\ \mathbf{when}\ B\ \mathbf{do}\ C\ \mathbf{od}\, \{Q\}}$$

$$\mathit{RESOURCE}\ \frac{\Sigma_0 \vdash R \ \mathbf{Assert} \quad \Sigma \mid \Gamma,\, r(\Sigma_0)\colon R \vdash \{P\}\, C\, \{Q\}}{\Sigma, \Sigma_0 \mid \Gamma \vdash \{P \star R\}\, \mathbf{resource}\ r(\Sigma_0)\ \mathbf{in}\ C\, \{Q \star R\}} \ (R \text{ precise})$$

$$\mathit{AUXILIARY}\ \frac{\Sigma \vdash P, Q \ \mathbf{Assert} \quad \Sigma, X^{\top} \mid \Gamma \vdash \{P\}\, C\, \{Q\}}{\Sigma \mid \Gamma \vdash \{P\}\, C \setminus X\, \{Q\}} \ \text{if } X \text{ is auxiliary for } C$$

Table 3. Proof rules of Concurrent Separation Logic

same force as the usual side condition "C does not modify any free variables of R" in the conventional formulation of Separation Logic.

As an example, using the fractional permission algebra, we can derive the inference using *FRAME*:

$$\frac{x^1, y^{\frac{1}{2}} \vdash \{y = 0\}\, x := y\, \{x = 0\} \quad y^{\frac{1}{2}}, z^{\frac{1}{2}} \vdash y = z \ \mathbf{Assert}}{x^1, y^1, z^{\frac{1}{2}} \vdash \{y = 0 * y = z\}\, x := y\, \{x = 0 * y = z\}}$$

4. Concurrent Separation Logic

In this section, we formalize the rules of O'Hearn's Concurrent Separation Logic, treating Hoare-style resources and conditional critical regions. The context-free syntax of the commands is:

$$\begin{aligned} C \ ::= \ & x := E \mid x := [E] \mid [E] := E' \mid \mathbf{skip} \\ & \mid C_1; C_2 \mid \mathbf{if}\ B\ \mathbf{then}\ C_1\ \mathbf{else}\ C_2 \\ & \mid C_1 \parallel C_2 \mid \mathbf{with}\ r\ \mathbf{when}\ B\ \mathbf{do}\ C\ \mathbf{od} \\ & \mid \mathbf{resource}\ r(\Sigma)\ \mathbf{in}\ C \end{aligned}$$

Note that the resource declarations include permission contexts Σ for the variables associated with them. The notation enhances that of Owicki and Gries [31] and O'Hearn [25], who list only variable names with resource declarations. In Section 6, we present an inference algorithm that allows the resource declarations to be written simply in the form **resource** r **in** C and finds the appropriate permission contexts Σ to be used with them, avoiding the annotation burden for the programmer.

The well-formedness of commands is defined using judgements of the form

$$\Sigma \mid \Gamma \vdash C \ \mathbf{Comm}$$

Here, Σ is a variable context and Γ is a *resource context* of the form $r_1(\Sigma_1), \ldots, r_n(\Sigma_n)$ where r_i are resource names, Σ_i are variable contexts owned by the resources, subject to the following conditions:

- *The resource names r_i are distinct from each other.*
- *The variable context $\Sigma, \Sigma_1, \ldots, \Sigma_n$ is well-defined.*

A putative syntactic context satisfying these conditions is said to be *well-defined*. Note that only commands require resource contexts (which get used in checking the well-formedness of critical regions). Variables, expressions, and assertions only need variable contexts.

Just as in the sequential case, our rules of the programming logic incorporate the well-formedness of commands. So, no special attention needs to be paid to their well-formedness.

The programming logic is formulated using judgements of the form

$$\Sigma \mid \Gamma \vdash \{P\}\, C\, \{Q\}$$

Here, Σ is a variable context and Γ is an *annotated resource context* where each resource $r_i(\Sigma_i)$ is annotated with a "resource invariant" formula R_i which is a *precise* assertion [25] and satisfies $\Sigma_i \vdash R_i$ **Assert**. This means that a resource invariant for a resource can only employ the variables available in its variable context.

All the rules of the sequential Separation Logic can be lifted to Concurrent Separation Logic by simply adding " $\mid \Gamma$" to all the specification judgements. For example, see the rules for assignment and conditional commands in Table 3. The resource contexts do not play any rule in the sequential fragment of the programming language.

The proof rule for parallel composition is the rule *PAR*. As one would expect, the variable context of the composite command, Σ_1, Σ_2, needs to be split into separate portions Σ_1 and Σ_2, for the two processes. The resource context, on the other hand, is shared. The rule allows C_1 and C_2 to share read-only variables, via separate copies with partial permissions. However, it is not possible for one process to modify a variable employed in the other process or *its proof*.

A resource's variables can be imported when a critical region is entered (the *CRIT* rule). The body of the critical region, C, can use the combined variable contexts of the process and the resource, Σ and Σ_0 respectively. However, the pre-condition and the post-condition can only employ the variables available in the process's context. This captures the Owicki-Gries requirement that they should only employ variables not modified by "other processes".

The rule for the resource declaration is *RESOURCE*. The variable context Σ_0 is sliced out of the current context, and transferred to the resource r. The resource invariant is based on these variables. The body of the resource declaration, C, can only use the remaining context Σ outside any critical regions.

Finally, the rule *AUXILIARY*, which is similar to the rule for local variable declaration in its form, allows a set of variables $X = \{x_1, \ldots, x_n\}$ to be deleted from a command C along with all assignments to them, provided they are "auxiliary", i.e., each free occurrence in C of a variable from X is in an assignment whose left hand side also belongs to X. The notation $C \setminus X$ denotes the command obtained by deleting all the assignments to variables in X. Note that all the variables in X are assigned the $\top$ permission in the second premise. This guarantees that the variables do not occur in Σ or the permission contexts in Γ.

4.1 Comparison with Owicki-Gries-O'Hearn system

O'Hearn's version of Concurrent Separation Logic [25] is based on the Owicki-Gries system [31] as its underlying framework for variable usage. In this system, the free variables of the resource invariant must be listed in the resource, similar to our *RESOURCE* rule. The rules governing the variables of a resources are as follows:

1. If a variable x belongs to a resource r, it cannot appear in a parallel process except in a critical region for r.
2. If a variable x is changed in process S_i, it cannot appear in S_j $(i \neq j)$ unless it belongs to a resource.

The rule 1 is relaxed in our proof rules. Recall that our resources encapsulate not merely variables but variables with permissions. So, if x belongs to a resource with permission $\top$ then the restrictions on its usage in our rules are exactly the same as in the Owicki-Gries system. However, if x belongs to the resource with a partial permission, then one or more processes can possibly use x in a read-only fashion using the remaining partial permission.

The rule 2 is represented exactly the same way in our proof rules.

The rule 1 is somewhat misleading. While it requires that a variable x belonging to a resource cannot appear in the *code* of a parallel process except in a critical region, it nevertheless permits it to appear in the *assertions* of the process outside critical regions.

$\{57 \mapsto -\}$
resource $r_1(p^{\frac{1}{2}})$ **in**
  resource $r_2(p^{\frac{1}{2}})$ **in begin**
    with r_1 **do** (**with** r_2 **do** p := 0 **od**); [57] := 3 **od**
    $\|$ **with** r_2 **do** (**with** r_1 **do** p := 1 **od**); [57] := 4 **od**
  end
$\{57 \mapsto -\}$

Table 4. "Problematic program" due to Berdine and Reynolds

Thus, the proof outline of Table 1 is legal in the Owicki-Gries-O'Hearn system. However, there is a rider to this allowance in the Owicki-Gries proof rule for critical regions. A variable occurring free in the assertions surrounding a critical region should not be changed in "another process". The allowance as well as its rider are already covered in our relaxation of the rule 1 above. We treat the free occurrences of variables in assertions as well as read-only occurrences in code in exactly the same way. A variable that is not modified in "another process," is available to the current process with a partial permission. So, it can use it in a read-only fashion in both code and assertions. Our relaxation of the Owicki-Gries rule 1 leads to a simpler formulation.

Thus all valid proof outlines of the Owicki-Gries-O'Hearn system remain valid proof outlines in our logic with syntactic control of interference. It is quite straightforward to come up with an assignment of permissions to the variables listed in a resource.

- If a variable appears in multiple processes, either in code or assertions, and modified in at least one of them, then the resource should contain the $\top$ permission for the variable.
- If a variable has read-only occurrences in one or more processes, then then resource may contain any permission p for the variable and the complement of p should be distributed to all processes that use it outside critical sections.
- If a variable is used in only one process (but possibly in assertions outside critical regions), then the resource may contain any permission p for the variable and the complement of p is given to the process.

For the example in Table 1, the variable x appears in multiple processes. So, it gets the permission 1 in the resource. The variable a (respectively, b) is used only in the left process (respectively, the right process). So, the resource is given $\frac{1}{2}$ permission and the process is given the remaining $\frac{1}{2}$.

However, our version of the Concurrent Separation Logic is more expressive. By associating permission contexts with resources, we make it possible for the permission to be combined in nested critical regions. For example, consider the program fragment shown in Table 4 due to Berdine and Reynolds [35]. The purpose of the two resources r_1 and r_2 is to achieve mutual exclusion to a shared data structure, in this case just the location 57. If the specification has a proof in Concurrent Separation Logic, the race-freedom property of the logic guaruantees that only one process can potentially access the memory location 57 at any given time. A proof can be given in our version of the logic using the following resource invariants:

$$\begin{array}{rcl} R_1 & = & (p = 0 \wedge 57 \mapsto -) \vee (p \neq 0 \wedge \mathbf{emp}) \\ R_2 & = & (p = 0 \wedge \mathbf{emp}) \vee (p \neq 0 \wedge 57 \mapsto -) \end{array}$$

Note that $R_1 \star R_2$ is equivalent to $57 \mapsto -$. So, both the pre-condition and the post-condition can be rewritten to $R_1 \star R_2$.

What makes the proof work is the idea that the permissions for the variable p are split across the two resources. So, a process can modify it only by entering critical regions for both the resources. This form of split-permissions for variables is not available in the Owicki-Gries-O'Hearn system.

Brookes [11], in his effort to prove the soundness of Concurrent Separation Logic, defined a variant of the original system which is subtly more general. Unfortunately, the generalization proved to be unsound. However, all the valid proofs that can be carried out in Brookes's system can be represented in our system. A detailed comparison with Brookes's system, along with soundness issues, appears in Appendix B.

4.2 Comparison with "Variables as Resource" systems

Parkinson et al. [32] and Brookes [13] define a general scheme of treating variables as resources with permissions. In contrast to our approach of syntactic control, the variable resources are included in program assertions, through ownership formulas of the form $\mathbf{own}_p(x)$ and used with all the normal logical connectives. So, this approach can be termed "logical control of interference" for variables.

It is easy to see that the syntactic control system can be translated to the logical control system. For every variable context $\Sigma = (x_1^{p_1}, \ldots, x_n^{p_n})$, there is an ownership formula $O_\Sigma \equiv \mathbf{own}_{p_1}(x_1) \star \cdots \star \mathbf{own}_{p_n}(x_n)$. A judgement $\Sigma \mid \Gamma \vdash \{P\}\, C\, \{Q\}$ of our system can be translated to a judgement $\Gamma \vdash \{O_\Sigma \wedge P\}\, C\, \{O_\Sigma \wedge Q\}$ in the "Variables as resource" system. In fact, Parkinson et al [32] give translations of this form for Hoare logics.

It is not possible to go in the reverse direction. The "Variables as resource" system uses logical formulas to express ownership of variables. So, it can express a much richer set of ownership constraints than possible in the syntactic control system. For example, the formula

$$(x = 0 \wedge \mathbf{own}_\top(y)) \vee (x \neq 0 \wedge \mathbf{own}_\top(z))$$

does not correspond to any syntactic variable context.

Thus, the "Variables as Resource" logic is more expressive than the syntactic control system. However, we argue that the syntactic control system offers considerable simplicity and convenience. In particular,

- There are no issues of undefinedness in expressions and formulas. So, one does not need to write formulas of the form $E = E$ just to ensure that E is defined in the current context.
- Substitution is a valid operation in expressions and assertions.
- The system has no logical anomalies, e.g., the equivalence $\neg(E_1 = E_2) \iff E_1 \neq E_2$ holds in our system, whereas the two formulas have different interpretations in the Variables as Resource logic.
- We need no special treatment of logical variables. The "pun" of program variables as logical variables, characteristic of Hoare logics, continues to work in our system.

5. Semantics and soundness

The standard proof of soundness for sequential Separation Logic is due to Yang and O'Hearn [39]. Bornat et al. [6] have extended it to deal with permissions. The soundness proof of the original Concurrent Separation Logic was provided by Brookes [11] using novel denotational methods. Brookes [13] has also used these methods to prove the soundness of the "variables as resource" system. Since then, other proofs of soundness have appeared. See [38] for an overview. We regard Brookes's semantics as the canonical one since it is denotationally based and allows easy extensions and adaptations.

In this section, we discuss how the presentation of Separation Logic using the SCI principles impacts the semantics. We regard the SCI judgements for phrases and specifications as a form of type system, and use the approach of "Church typing" to define the semantics, i.e., we regard well-formedness judgement $\Sigma \vdash C\ \mathbf{Comm}$ and $\Sigma \mid \Gamma \vdash C\ \mathbf{Comm}$ as a form of typing for C and interpret C using denotations that are *appropriate* for the specified context $\Sigma \mid \Gamma$. It is also possible to conceive of a "Curry typing" semantics where the commands are interpreted without regard to their contexts of well-formedness, and the well-formed judgements are given a logical meaning as properties of the untyped denotations. However, we follow the Church typing approach here because it seems more natural.

5.1 Sequential Separation Logic

A *state* is modelled as a pair (s, h) of a "store" and a "heap," which are finite partial functions from, respectively, variables and addresses. To keep track of permissions, we define them to map their arguments to *pairs of values and permissions*:

$$\begin{array}{rcl} \text{Store} & = & \text{Vars} \rightharpoonup \text{Val} \times \mathcal{P} \\ \text{Heap} & = & \text{Addr} \rightharpoonup \text{Val} \times \mathcal{P} \end{array}$$

We refer to such maps as *permissive store* and *permissive heap* respectively, and both kinds of maps generically as *permissive maps*. Two permissive maps ϕ_1 and ϕ_2 are said to be *compatible*, denoted $\phi_1 \sharp \phi_2$, if, for all arguments common to both of their domains, they agree on values and provide compatible permissions. More formally, $\phi_1 \sharp \phi_2$ iff:

$$\phi_1(x) = (v, p) \wedge \phi_2(x) = (v', p') \Longrightarrow v = v' \wedge p \oplus p' \text{ is defined}$$

If ϕ_1 and ϕ_2 are compatible, their joining operation is denoted $\phi_1 \cdot \phi_2$ (which combines permissions whenever both ϕ_1 and ϕ_2 are defined). It is extended to states by defining $(s_1, h_1) \cdot (s_2, h_2) = (s_1 \cdot s_2,\ h_1 \cdot h_2)$.

Given a variable context Σ with $norm(\Sigma) = (x_1^{p_1}, \ldots, x_n^{p_n})$, a store s is said to be *of type* Σ if dom $s = \{x_1, \ldots, x_n\}$ and the permission component of $s(x_i)$ is p_i for every i. It is easy to see that, whenever $\Sigma_1 \sharp \Sigma_2$, any stores s_1 of type Σ_1 and s_2 of type Σ_2 are compatible, and $s_1 \cdot s_2$ is of type Σ_1, Σ_2.

A state $\sigma = (s, h)$ is said to be *of type* Σ just if s is of type Σ. The heap component of the state is unconstrained. If (s_1, h_1) and (s_2, h_2) are states of of type Σ_1 and Σ_2 respectively, $\Sigma_1 \sharp \Sigma_2$ and $h_1 \sharp h_2$, then $(s_1, h_1) \cdot (s_2, h_2)$ is of type Σ_1, Σ_2.

The meaning of a command in the sequential programming language is defined in [39] as a *local state transformer*, i.e., a binary relation $[\![C]\!] \subseteq \text{State} \times \text{State} \uplus \{\mathsf{fault}\}$ satisfying safety monotonicity, termination monotonicity and the frame property. It was extended to permissive states in [6]. While it is not stated there, it is also easy to see that $[\![C]\!]$ always preserves the domain and permission structure of the store. This allows us to define a typed semantics for commands. If $\Sigma \vdash C\ \mathbf{Comm}$ is a well-formedness judgement then its meaning is a relation $[\![C]\!]_\Sigma$ consisting of just the pairs (σ, σ') where both σ and σ' are of type Σ.

DEFINITION 1. *A judgement of the sequential Separation Logic* $\Sigma \vdash \{P\}\, C\, \{Q\}$ *is valid iff, for all states* σ *of type* Σ *satisfying* P*:*

- $(\sigma, \mathsf{fault}) \notin [\![C]\!]_\Sigma$, *and*
- *if* $(\sigma, \sigma') \in [\![C]\!]_\Sigma$ *then* σ' *is of type* Σ *and satisfies* Q.

THEOREM 2 (Soundness). *Every derivable judgement of sequential Separation Logic is valid.*

The proof is by induction on the derivation of the judgement. Consider the FRAME rule as a significant example. Let σ be a state of type Σ, Σ' satisfying $P \star R$. Then σ can be written as $\sigma_1 \cdot \sigma_0$ where σ_1 is of type Σ and satisfies P and σ_0 is of type Σ' and satisfies R. Then by inductive hypothesis, $\Sigma \vdash \{P\}\, C\, \{Q\}$ is valid. Hence $[\![C]\!]_\Sigma$ is safe for σ_1 and, whenever $(\sigma_1, \sigma_1') \in [\![C]\!]_\Sigma$, σ_1' is of type Σ and satisfies Q. So, by the safety monotonicity and frame properties, $[\![C]\!]_{\Sigma,\Sigma'}$ is safe for σ, and $(\sigma, \sigma') \in [\![C]\!]_{\Sigma,\Sigma'}$ implies σ' is of type Σ, Σ' and σ' satisfies $Q \star R$.

5.2 Concurrent Separation Logic

The denotational semantics of commands in the concurrent programming language is given in two stages. First, commands are interpreted as *traces*, i.e., stylized sequences of actions. Second, these traces are described by their effect on states as state transitions. It is not possible to interpret the commands directly as state transitions, because such transitions only relate initial and final states whereas parallel composition makes intermediate states visible.

Trace semantics

A *pre-action* (or an untyped action) is a syntactic token given by the syntax:

$$\begin{array}{rcl} \lambda & ::= & \delta \mid x = v \mid x := v \mid [l] = v \mid [l] := v \\ & & \mid \mathit{try}(r) \mid \mathit{acq}(r) \mid \mathit{rel}(r) \mid \mathit{abort} \end{array}$$

As in [11], δ is a do-nothing or idle action, $x = v$ denotes the action of reading the variable x, $x := v$ denotes the action of writing to the variable x. The actions $[l] = v$ and $[l] := v$ denote similar actions for heap locations. The tokens $\mathit{try}(r)$, $\mathit{acq}(r)$ and $\mathit{rel}(r)$ denote the actions of attempting to acquire a resource, acquiring a resource and releasing a resource respectively. The token abort denotes the action of aborting a computation in case of an error.

A *pretrace* is a possibly infinite sequence of actions subject to the identifications $\alpha \cdot \delta \cdot \beta = \alpha \cdot \beta$, and $\alpha \cdot \mathit{abort} \cdot \beta = \alpha \cdot \mathit{abort}$.

We model the actions and action traces "appropriate" for a syntactic context $\Sigma \mid \Gamma$ as a form of typing. First of all, the contexts enable certain actions and prohibit others. A variable action $x = v$ or $x := v$ would only be possible in a context that contains x with requisite permissions. The resource actions $\mathit{try}(r)$ and $\mathit{acq}(r)$ would only be possible in a context that contains a resource named r. Secondly, as a result of an action, the context available for the rest of a trace might change. For instance, $\mathit{acq}(r)$ has the effect of removing the resource $r(\Sigma_0)$ from the resource context and adding its variables Σ_0 to the variable context. A $\mathit{rel}(r)$ action has the opposite effect. We represent these effects by a transition relation $\xrightarrow{\lambda}$ on contexts. Finally, when a resource is acquired by a process, it is not available for another acquisition until it is released. At the same time, the type information of the resource should continue to be retained in the context. Therefore, we work with a form of extended contexts where the resources acquired by a trace are marked "busy," by enclosing them in square brackets as $[r(\Sigma)]$.

An *extended context* is a context of the form

$$\Sigma \mid r_1(\Sigma_1), \ldots, r_n(\Sigma_n), [r'_1(\Sigma'_1)], \ldots, [r'_m(\Sigma'_m)]$$

such that

- the resource names $r_1, \ldots, r_n, r'_1, \ldots, r'_m$ are all distinct, and
- the variable context $\Sigma, \Sigma_1, \ldots, \Sigma_n$ is well-defined.

A putative extended context satisfying these conditions is said to be *well-defined*. We use the letter $\widetilde{\Gamma}$ to range over extended resource contexts where some of the resources are marked busy. The notation $(\widetilde{\Gamma})^\circ$ denotes the underlying resource context of $\widetilde{\Gamma}$ where all the busy markers are erased.

An *action* is a triple $\langle \Sigma|\widetilde{\Gamma},\ \Sigma'|\widetilde{\Gamma}',\ \lambda \rangle$ consisting of the initial and final contexts and a pre-action that leads from the former to the latter. We write it using the notation $\Sigma|\widetilde{\Gamma} \xrightarrow{\lambda} \Sigma'|\widetilde{\Gamma}'$. The list of actions used in the semantics of the programming language are shown in Table 6. There are no constraints on the actions for reading and writing heap locations because the access to heap locations is controlled in the programming logic rather than the syntax.

$$\begin{array}{l}
\Sigma \mid \widetilde{\Gamma} \xrightarrow{\delta} \Sigma \mid \widetilde{\Gamma} \\
\Sigma \mid \widetilde{\Gamma} \xrightarrow{x=v} \Sigma \mid \widetilde{\Gamma} \text{ where } x^p \in \Sigma \text{ for some } p \\
\Sigma \mid \widetilde{\Gamma} \xrightarrow{x:=v} \Sigma \mid \widetilde{\Gamma} \text{ where } x^\top \in \mathit{norm}(\Sigma) \\
\Sigma \mid \widetilde{\Gamma} \xrightarrow{[l]=v} \Sigma \mid \widetilde{\Gamma} \\
\Sigma \mid \widetilde{\Gamma} \xrightarrow{[l]:=v} \Sigma \mid \widetilde{\Gamma} \\
\Sigma \mid \widetilde{\Gamma}, r(\Sigma_0) \xrightarrow{\mathit{try}(r)} \Sigma \mid \widetilde{\Gamma}, r(\Sigma_0) \\
\Sigma \mid \widetilde{\Gamma}, r(\Sigma_0) \xrightarrow{\mathit{acq}(r)} \Sigma, \Sigma_0 \mid \widetilde{\Gamma}, [r(\Sigma_0)] \\
\Sigma, \Sigma_0 \mid \widetilde{\Gamma}, [r(\Sigma_0)] \xrightarrow{\mathit{rel}(r)} \Sigma \mid \widetilde{\Gamma}, r(\Sigma_0)
\end{array}$$

Table 6. Actions used in traces

A trace is a finite or infinite sequence of the form

$$\Sigma_0|\widetilde{\Gamma}_0 \xrightarrow{\lambda_1} \Sigma_1|\widetilde{\Gamma}_1 \xrightarrow{\lambda_2} \Sigma_2|\widetilde{\Gamma}_2 \xrightarrow{\lambda_3} \cdots$$

If the sequence $\alpha = \lambda_1\lambda_2\cdots$ is finite, we use the notation $\Sigma_0|\widetilde{\Gamma}_0 \xrightarrow{\alpha} \Sigma_n|\widetilde{\Gamma}_n$ to denote the corresponding trace. If it is infinite, we use the notation $\Sigma_0|\widetilde{\Gamma}_0 \xrightarrow{\alpha} \infty$. We also use the notation $\Sigma_0|\widetilde{\Gamma}_0 \xrightarrow{\alpha} \cdot$ for both finite and infinite traces, and say that the pretrace α is *enabled* in the context $\Sigma_0|\widetilde{\Gamma}_0$.

For defining the meaning of parallel composition, we define an operation of *interleaving* two traces. Suppose α_1 and α_2 are two traces with α_1 enabled in a context $\Sigma_1|\widetilde{\Gamma}_1$ and α_2 enabled in a context $\Sigma_2|\widetilde{\Gamma}_2$. Then $\widetilde{\Gamma}_1$ and $\widetilde{\Gamma}_2$ should have the same underlying resource contexts, i.e., $(\widetilde{\Gamma}_1)^\circ = (\widetilde{\Gamma}_2)^\circ$, and they should mark disjoint sets of resources as busy. Then the resource context obtained by marking the busy resources of both $\widetilde{\Gamma}_1$ and $\widetilde{\Gamma}_2$ is denoted $\widetilde{\Gamma}_1 \wedge \widetilde{\Gamma}_2$. Interleaving is only possible for traces α_1 and α_2 such that $\widetilde{\Gamma}_1$ and $\widetilde{\Gamma}_2$ are in this form and $\Sigma_1, \Sigma_2 \mid \widetilde{\Gamma}_1 \wedge \widetilde{\Gamma}_2$ is well-defined.

Two actions λ_1 and λ_2 are said to *interfere*, written $\lambda_1 \not\parallel \lambda_2$, if λ_1 writes to a heap location l and λ_2 reads or writes the same location l, or *vice versa*. The set of *mutex fairmerges* of $\Sigma_1|\widetilde{\Gamma}_1 \xrightarrow{\alpha_1} \cdot$ and $\Sigma_2|\widetilde{\Gamma}_2 \xrightarrow{\alpha_2} \cdot$ is a set of traces of type $\Sigma_1, \Sigma_2|\widetilde{\Gamma}_1 \wedge \widetilde{\Gamma}_2 \longrightarrow \cdot$ given by induction on the lengths of α_1 and α_2:

$$\begin{array}{l}
\alpha_1 \parallel \epsilon = \{\alpha_1\} \\
\epsilon \parallel \alpha_2 = \{\alpha_2\} \\
(\lambda_1\alpha_1) \parallel (\lambda_2\alpha_2) = \\
\quad \{\, \mathit{abort} \mid \lambda_1 \not\parallel \lambda_2 \} \cup \\
\quad \{\, \Sigma_1, \Sigma_2 \mid \widetilde{\Gamma}_1 \wedge \widetilde{\Gamma}_2 \xrightarrow{\lambda_1} \Sigma'_1, \Sigma_2 \mid \widetilde{\Gamma}'_1 \wedge \widetilde{\Gamma}_2 \xrightarrow{\beta} \cdot \\
\qquad \text{such that } \beta \in \alpha_1 \parallel (\lambda_2\alpha_2) \,\} \cup \\
\quad \{\, \Sigma_1, \Sigma_2 \mid \widetilde{\Gamma}_1 \wedge \widetilde{\Gamma}_2 \xrightarrow{\lambda_2} \Sigma_1, \Sigma'_2 \mid \widetilde{\Gamma}_1 \wedge \widetilde{\Gamma}'_2 \xrightarrow{\beta} \cdot \\
\qquad \text{such that } \beta \in (\lambda_1\alpha_1) \parallel \alpha_2 \,\}
\end{array}$$

This definition is a typed version of the notion of mutex fairmerges in Brookes [11]. Note that the typing information of traces obviates the need to consider possible interference via variable usage.

The definition is extended to *sets* of traces in the natural way. If T_1 and T_2 are trace sets enabled in contexts $\Sigma_1|\widetilde{\Gamma}_1$ and $\Sigma_2|\widetilde{\Gamma}_2$ then the trace set $T_1 \parallel T_2$, obtained as the union of all $\alpha_1 \parallel \alpha_2$ for all $\alpha_1 \in T_1$ and $\alpha_2 \in T_2$ is enabled in the context $\Sigma_1, \Sigma_2 \mid \widetilde{\Gamma}_1 \wedge \widetilde{\Gamma}_2$.

A *(well-bracketed) trace for an extended context* $\Sigma \mid \widetilde{\Gamma}$ is either abort, a finite trace α such that $\Sigma \mid \widetilde{\Gamma} \xrightarrow{\alpha} \Sigma \mid \widetilde{\Gamma}$, or an infinite trace whose every finite prefix can be extended to a well-bracketed finite trace. The terminology is motivated by thinking of the $\mathit{acq}(r)$ and $\mathit{rel}(r)$ actions as brackets. A trace set T is a *(well-bracketed)*

$$\begin{array}{l}
[\![x]\!]_\Sigma = \{\, (x = v, v) \mid v \text{ Value} \,\} \\
[\![E_1 + E_2]\!]_\Sigma = \{\, (\rho_1\rho_2, v_1 + v_2) \mid (\rho_1, v_1) \in [\![E_1]\!]_\Sigma \wedge (\rho_2, v_2) \in [\![E_2]\!]_\Sigma \,\}
\end{array}$$

$$\begin{array}{l}
[\![\mathbf{skip}]\!]_{\Sigma|\Gamma} = \{\delta\} \\
[\![x := E]\!]_{\Sigma|\Gamma} = \{\, \rho(x := v) \mid (\rho, v) \in [\![E]\!]_\Sigma \,\} \\
[\![x := [E]]\!]_{\Sigma|\Gamma} = \{\, \rho([v] = v')(x := v') \mid (\rho, v) \in [\![E]\!]_\Sigma \,\} \\
[\![[E] := E']\!]_{\Sigma|\Gamma} = \{\, \rho\rho'([v] := v') \mid (\rho, v) \in [\![E]\!]_\Sigma \wedge (\rho', v') \in [\![E']\!]_\Sigma \,\} \\
[\![\mathbf{if}\ B\ \mathbf{then}\ C_1\ \mathbf{else}\ C_2]\!]_{\Sigma|\Gamma} = ([\![B]\!]_\Sigma \restriction \mathbf{true})\, [\![C_1]\!]_{\Sigma|\Gamma} \cup ([\![B]\!]_\Sigma \restriction \mathbf{false})\, [\![C_2]\!]_{\Sigma|\Gamma} \\
[\![\mathbf{local}\ x\ \mathbf{in}\ C]\!]_{\Sigma|\Gamma} = \{\, (\rho \setminus x) \mid \rho \in [\![C]\!]_{\Sigma, x^\top|\Gamma} \,\} \\
[\![C_1 \parallel C_2]\!]_{\Sigma_1, \Sigma_2|\Gamma} = [\![C_1]\!]_{\Sigma_1|\Gamma} \parallel [\![C_2]\!]_{\Sigma_2|\Gamma} \\
[\![\mathbf{with}\ r\ \mathbf{when}\ B\ \mathbf{do}\ C\ \mathbf{od}]\!]_{\Sigma|\Gamma, r(\Sigma_0)} = \mathit{wait}^*\, \mathit{enter} \cup \mathit{wait}^\omega \\
\qquad\qquad \text{where } \mathit{wait} = \mathit{acq}(r)\, ([\![B]\!]_{\Sigma,\Sigma_0} \restriction \mathbf{false})\, \mathit{rel}(r) \cup \{\mathit{try}(r)\} \\
\qquad\qquad\qquad\quad \mathit{enter} = \mathit{acq}(r)\, ([\![B]\!]_{\Sigma,\Sigma_0} \restriction \mathbf{true})\, [\![C]\!]_{\Sigma,\Sigma_0|\Gamma}\, \mathit{rel}(r) \\
[\![\mathbf{resource}\ r(\Sigma_0)\ \mathbf{in}\ C]\!]_{\Sigma,\Sigma_0|\Gamma} = \{\, \rho \setminus r \mid \rho \in [\![C]\!]_{\Sigma|\Gamma, r(\Sigma_0)} \,\}
\end{array}$$

Table 5. Trace semantics of phrases

trace set for context $\Sigma \mid \tilde{\Gamma}$ if each trace in T is a well-bracketed trace for the context.

LEMMA 3 (Weakening of contexts). *If α is a trace for an extended context $\Sigma|\tilde{\Gamma}$, and $\Sigma, \Sigma'|\tilde{\Gamma}, \tilde{\Gamma}'$ is a longer well-defined extended context, then α is a trace for $\Sigma, \Sigma'|\tilde{\Gamma}, \tilde{\Gamma}'$.*

LEMMA 4 (Parallel composition preserves contexts). *If α_1 and α_2 are traces for extended contexts $\Sigma_1|\tilde{\Gamma}$ and $\Sigma_2|\tilde{\Gamma}$ respectively, and $\Sigma_1, \Sigma_2|\tilde{\Gamma}$ is a well-defined extended context then $\alpha_1 \parallel \alpha_2$ is a trace set for the context $\Sigma_1, \Sigma_2|\tilde{\Gamma}$.*

All expressions and commands can be given a compositional semantics in terms of trace sets.

- The meaning of an expression $\Sigma \vdash E$ **Exp** is a set of pairs (ρ, v) where ρ is an action trace of type $\Sigma| \xrightarrow{\rho} \Sigma|$ (i.e., a context with no resources, because expressions do not access resources), and v is a value (obtained as the result of evaluating E). We denote it by $[\![E]\!]_\Sigma$.
- The meaning of a command $\Sigma \mid \Gamma \vdash C$ **Comm** is a set of traces ρ for the context $\Sigma|\Gamma$. We denote it by $[\![C]\!]_{\Sigma|\Gamma}$.

The semantics is defined in the standard fashion [11]. However, it is defined by induction on the *derivations* of well-formedness judgements $\Sigma \vdash E$ **Exp** and $\Sigma \mid \Gamma \vdash C$ **Comm**, instead of induction on the structure of terms. We show the meanings of sample phrases in Table 5. The notation $[\![E]\!]_\Sigma \restriction v$ denotes the set of traces $\{\, \rho \mid (\rho, v) \in [\![E]\!]_\Sigma \,\}$. The notations $\rho \setminus x$ and $\rho \setminus r$ remove the actions mentioning x and r respectively from ρ.

THEOREM 5 (Type soundness of trace semantics). *The meaning of command $\Sigma \mid \Gamma \vdash C$ **Comm** is a (well-bracketed) trace set for the context $\Sigma \mid \Gamma$. Likewise, for every (ρ, v) in the meaning of an expression $\Sigma \vdash E$ **Exp**, ρ is a (well-bracketed) trace for the context $\Sigma \mid$.*

Local state semantics

A *state* for a concurrent program is a triple (s, h, A) where s is a permissive store, h is a permissive heap and A is a set of resource names (deemed to have been acquired by the process). We also use an error state **abort**. The types for states will be annotated extended contexts of the form $\Sigma \mid \tilde{\Gamma}$ where the resources are *annotated* with resource invariants as in $r(\Sigma_0) : R$. It is a characteristic of Brookes's semantics for Concurrent Separation Logic that the resource invariants play a central role in the state transition semantics.

A *state of type* $\Sigma \mid \tilde{\Gamma}$ is either **abort** or a normal state (s, h, A) where s is a store of type Σ, h is a heap, and A is a subset of the resources marked busy in $\tilde{\Gamma}$.

We can interpret actions (and action traces) of type $\Sigma \mid \tilde{\Gamma} \longrightarrow \Sigma' \mid \tilde{\Gamma}'$ as state transformations that transform states of type $\Sigma \mid \tilde{\Gamma}$ to states of type $\Sigma' \mid \tilde{\Gamma}'$. For actions of type $\Sigma \mid \tilde{\Gamma} \longrightarrow \Sigma \mid \tilde{\Gamma}$ (where the state type is unchanged), the state transformations are as follows:

$$\begin{array}{l}
(s,h,A) \xrightarrow{\delta} (s,h,A) \\
(s,h,A) \xrightarrow{abort} \mathbf{abort} \\
(s,h,A) \xrightarrow{x=v} (s,h,A) \quad \text{iff} \quad \exists p.\, s(x) = (v,p) \\
(s,h,A) \xrightarrow{x:=v} (s[x \mapsto (v,\top)], h, A) \quad \text{iff} \quad \exists v_0.\, s(x) = (v_0, \top) \\
(s,h,A) \xrightarrow{[l]=v} (s,h,A) \quad \text{iff} \quad \exists p.\, h(l) = (v,p) \\
(s,h,A) \xrightarrow{[l]=v} \mathbf{abort} \quad \text{iff} \quad l \notin \mathrm{dom}(h) \\
(s,h,A) \xrightarrow{[l]:=v} (s, h[l \mapsto (v,\top)], A) \quad \text{iff} \quad \exists v_0.\, h(l) = (v_0, \top) \\
(s,h,A) \xrightarrow{[l]:=v} \mathbf{abort} \quad \text{iff} \quad l \notin \mathrm{dom}(h) \\
(s,h,A) \xrightarrow{try(r)} (s,h,A)
\end{array}$$

For an acq action of type

$$\Sigma \mid \tilde{\Gamma}, r(\Sigma_0) \colon R \xrightarrow{acq(r)} \Sigma, \Sigma_0 \mid \tilde{\Gamma}, [r(\Sigma_0) \colon R]$$

the transformations are given by:

$$\begin{array}{l}
(s,h,A) \xrightarrow{acq(r)} (s \cdot s_0,\ h \cdot h_0,\ A \cup \{r\}) \\
\qquad \text{iff} \quad (s_0, h_0) \models R,\ s \sharp s_0,\ h \sharp h_0
\end{array}$$

For a rel action of type

$$\Sigma, \Sigma_0 \mid \tilde{\Gamma}, [r(\Sigma_0) \colon R] \xrightarrow{rel(r)} \Sigma \mid \tilde{\Gamma}, r(\Sigma_0) \colon R$$

the transformations are:

$$\begin{array}{l}
(s \cdot s_0,\ h \cdot h_0,\ A \uplus \{r\}) \xrightarrow{rel(r)} (s,h,A) \quad \text{iff} \quad (s_0, h_0) \models R \\
(s,h,A) \xrightarrow{rel(r)} \mathbf{abort} \quad \text{iff} \quad \forall h_0 \subseteq h.\, \neg(s, h_0) \models R
\end{array}$$

The key property of these transformations, inherited from Brookes [11], is that the transitions for $acq(r)$ *extend* the current state with an *arbitrary* state of the resource satisfying the resource invariant R. The condition $s \sharp s_0$ ensures that the values of any common variables agree. The transitions for $rel(r)$ do the opposite: they remove the state of the resource from the current state. If and when the resource is reacquired in a future action, the state of the resource obtained may bear no relationship to the state previously released.

In fact, since other processes can intervene in the interim, nothing more can be assumed about the reacquired state of the resource.

LEMMA 6 (Type soundness of traces). *Given a trace* α *of type* $\Sigma \mid \widetilde{\Gamma} \xrightarrow{\alpha} \Sigma' \mid \widetilde{\Gamma}'$ *and a state* (s, h, A) *of type* $\Sigma \mid \widetilde{\Gamma}$, *if* $(s, h, A) \xrightarrow{\alpha} (s', h', A')$ *then* (s', h', A') *is of type* $\Sigma' \mid \widetilde{\Gamma}'$.

Soundness

DEFINITION 7 (Validity). *A judgement* $\Sigma \mid \Gamma \vdash \{P\}\, C\, \{Q\}$ *is valid iff, for all well-bracketed traces* α *for the context* $\Sigma|\Gamma$ *in* $[\![C]\!]_{\Sigma|\Gamma}$, *all local states* $(s, h, \emptyset)$ *and* σ' *of type* $\Sigma|\Gamma$,

$$(s, h) \models P \;\wedge\; (s, h, \emptyset) \xrightarrow{\alpha} \sigma' \implies \exists s', h'.\, \sigma' = (s', h', \emptyset) \wedge \sigma' \models Q$$

THEOREM 8 (Soundness). *Every provable judgement of concurrent SCI Separation Logic is valid.*

Standard semantics

In addition to the semantics defined above, which is with respect to a program proof, traces can be interpreted as actions on global states. The relation is denoted $(s, h, A) \overset{\alpha}{\Longrightarrow} (s', h', A')$ and is similar to an untyped version of the local state transition semantics, except that the rules for *acq* and *rel* actions are modified as follows:

$$(s, h, A) \overset{acq(r)}{\Longrightarrow} (s,\, h,\, A \cup \{r\}) \qquad \text{if } r \notin A$$
$$(s, h, A \uplus \{r\}) \overset{rel(r)}{\Longrightarrow} (s, h, A \setminus \{r\}) \qquad \text{if } r \in A$$

This relation corresponds to running a process on the global state without any interference from any other processes.

The following result says that the standard semantics obtained by executing traces on the global state corresponds to the local state semantics defined above. The notation $\mathsf{inv}(\Gamma)$ stands for the conjunction of all the resource invariants in Γ.

THEOREM 9. *Let* $(s, h, \emptyset)$ *be a global state and* $\Sigma \mid \Gamma$ *a context. Suppose the state* (s, h) *can be split as* $(s_1, h_1) \cdot (s_2, h_2)$ *where* $(s_1, h_1, \emptyset)$ *is of type* $\Sigma \mid \Gamma$ *and* $(s_2, h_2) \models \mathsf{inv}(\Gamma)$.

- *If* $(s, h, \emptyset) \overset{\alpha}{\Longrightarrow}$ **abort** *then* $(s_1, h_1, \emptyset) \xrightarrow{\alpha}$ **abort**.
- *If* $(s, h, \emptyset) \overset{\lambda}{\Longrightarrow} (s', h', \emptyset)$ *then either*
  - $(s_1, h_1, \emptyset) \xrightarrow{\lambda}$ **abort**, *or*
  - (s', h') *can be split as* $(s_1', h_1') \cdot (s_2', h_2')$ *such that* $(s_1', h_1', \emptyset)$ *is of some type* $\Sigma' \mid \Gamma'$, $(s_1, h_1, \emptyset) \xrightarrow{\lambda} (s_1', h_1', \emptyset)$ *and* $(s_2', h_2') \models \mathsf{inv}(\Gamma')$.

6. Permission inference

In this section, we investigate the problem of permission inference. We construct an algorithm which, given a program and a proof outline with no variable contexts listed with resources, fills them in if at all possible in accordance with the rules of SCI Separation Logic.

We restrict our attention to the permission algebra of fractional permissions, the real interval $(0, 1]$ with addition as the partial binary operation. For theoretical simplicity, we extend the algebra to include 0 as an abnormal permission value, indicating that the resource or the process possesses no permission for the variable, and extend addition to 0 in the standard way. An element of $[0, 1]$ is referred to as an "extended permission."

A normal form context with n variables and m resources is of the form

$$x_1^{p_{01}}, \ldots, x_n^{p_{0n}} \mid$$
$$r_1(x_1^{p_{11}}, \ldots, x_n^{p_{1n}}) : R_1,\; \ldots,\; r_m(x_1^{p_{m1}}, \ldots, x_n^{p_{mn}}) : R_m \vdash$$

where each p_{ij} is an extended permission, with the index i corresponding to the owner of the permission (0 for the process or "**self**," $1, \ldots, n$ for the shared resources), and the index j corresponding to the variable. We represent all the data in the context by two finite functions:

$$\Delta : \text{Vars} \to \text{Owners} \to [0, 1] \qquad \Upsilon : \text{Resources} \to \text{Invariant}$$

where $\text{Owners} = \{\mathbf{self}\} \uplus \text{Resources}$, and Δ satisfies

$$\Sigma_{o \in \text{Owners}} (\Delta\, v\, o) \leq 1$$

The sets Vars and Resources include all the variable and resource names appearing in the program fragment being analyzed.

Using these notations, the proof system of SCI Separation Logic can be rewritten using judgements of the form:

$$\Delta|\Upsilon \vdash E\ \mathbf{Exp} \quad \Delta|\Upsilon \vdash P\ \mathbf{Assert} \qquad \text{(Passive)}$$
$$\Delta|\Upsilon \vdash x\ \mathbf{Var} \quad \Delta|\Upsilon \vdash \{P\}\, C\, \{Q\} \qquad \text{(Active)}$$

(where the first three forms have the resource context Υ added for uniformity in discussion). For example, the parallel composition rule is rewritten as:

$$\frac{\Delta_1 \mid \Upsilon \vdash \{P_1\}\, C_1\, \{Q_1\} \quad \Delta_2 \mid \Upsilon \vdash \{P_2\}\, C_2\, \{Q_2\}}{\Delta \mid \Upsilon \vdash \{P_1 \star P_2\}\, C_1 \parallel C_2\, \{Q_1 \star Q_2\}}$$
$$\text{if } \Delta_1\, v\, o = \Delta_2\, v\, o = \Delta\, v\, o \text{ for all } o \neq \mathbf{self}$$
$$\Delta\, v\, \mathbf{self} = \Delta_1\, v\, \mathbf{self} + \Delta_2\, v\, \mathbf{self} \leq 1$$

We also use abbreviated rules for the passive judgements:

$$\frac{}{\Delta \mid \Upsilon \vdash E\ \mathbf{Exp}} \quad \text{if } \forall v \in FV(E), \Delta\, v\, \mathbf{self} > 0$$

$$\frac{}{\Delta \mid \Upsilon \vdash P\ \mathbf{Assert}} \quad \text{if } \forall v \in FV(P), \Delta\, v\, \mathbf{self} > 0$$

Define a *write-proof* as a proof where the side conditions of passive judgements are ignored. Since the passive judgements involve variable reading, this means that the permissions needed for variable reading are not checked. However, the permissions needed for variable writing are still checked, hence the name.

Define a "pre-judgement" as a judgement with variable contexts Δ erased, i.e., a judgement of one of the forms:

$$\Upsilon \vdash E\ \mathbf{Exp} \quad \Upsilon \vdash P\ \mathbf{Assert} \qquad \text{(Passive)}$$
$$\Upsilon \vdash x\ \mathbf{Var} \quad \Upsilon \vdash \{P\}\, C\, \{Q\} \qquad \text{(Active)}$$

A "pre-rule" is an SCI Separation Logic rule with variable contexts erased. A "pre-inference" is an instance of a pre-rule and a "pre-proof" is a derivation made up of pre-inferences. The *erasure* of a judgement, rule, inference or proof X is a pre-judgement, pre-rule, pre-inference or pre-proof (respectively) denoted X^0, obtained by erasing all the variable contexts. In that case, we say that X "erases" to X^0 or X "extends" X^0.

The problem of permission inference is now stated formally as follows:

Given a pre-proof P^0, *is there a proof* P *whose erasure is* P^0*?*

The algorithm described below answers the question. Moreover, if the answer is yes, it produces a maximally permissive proof $P^{\max}$ that extends P^0.

We regard proof trees as *formal trees*, i.e., graphs satisfying the tree conditions, labelled by judgements. P^0 and P are different labellings of the *same* formal tree. We use the notation $(P^0)_N$ and $(P)_N$, respectively, to refer to the judgements labeling a node N of the formal tree.

We use a few auxiliary concepts:

- A *permission restriction* Φ is an assignment

  $$[v_1 : O_1,\; \ldots,\; v_k : O_k]$$

  where $v_i \in \text{Vars}$ and $O_i \subseteq \text{Owners}$. We also feel free to treat Φ as a partial function of type $\text{Vars} \rightharpoonup \mathcal{P}(\text{Owners})$. Such a

$\{57 \mapsto -\}$
resource r_1 **in**
  resource r_2 **in begin**
    with r_1 **do** (**with** r_2 **do** p := 0 **od**); [57] := 3 **od**
  || **with** r_2 **do** (**with** r_1 **do** p := 1 **od**); [57] := 4 **od**
  end
$\{57 \mapsto -\}$

Table 7. "Problematic program" due to Berdine and Reynolds

Φ represents the condition that, for each of the variables v_i, the owners in O_i share the full permission for v_i. A variable v_i will occur in a permission restriction exactly when the program phrase being described contains an assignment to v_i. The corresponding O_i lists all the owners that can contribute permissions required for that assignment to be legal. Formally, the satisfaction of a permission restriction by a variable context is defined as:

$$\Delta \models \Phi \iff \forall (v_i : O_i) \in \Phi.\ \Sigma_{o \in O_i} (\Delta\ v_i\ o) = 1$$

Note that $\Delta\ v_i\ o$ must be 0 for all owners outside O_i. There are *no* constraints on Δ for the other variables not mentioned in Φ.

- We define a *permission ordering* on variable contexts $\Delta \preceq \Delta'$ by the rule:

$$\Delta\ v\ o > 0 \Longrightarrow \Delta'\ v\ o > 0$$

We say that Δ' is "more permissive" than Δ. The intuition is that Δ' has non-zero permissions for at least as many combinations as Δ.

A permission restriction $\Phi = [v_1 : O_1, \ldots, v_k : O_k]$ is satisfiable only if every O_i is nonempty. In that case, a maximally permissive variable context satisfying Φ can be defined as follows:

$$\Delta^{\max}\ v\ o = \begin{cases} 1/\#O, & \text{if } (v:O) \in \Phi \wedge o \in O \\ 0, & \text{if } (v:O) \in \Phi \wedge o \notin O \\ 1/(\#\text{Owners}+1), & \text{if } v \notin \text{dom}\,\Phi \end{cases}$$

where $\#S$ denotes the size of the set S. In other words, a full permission is apportioned among all the owners permitted by Φ or, if Φ imposes no restriction, then a partial permission is apportioned among all owners.

Our algorithm for permission inference is a two-phase algorithm. The first phase traverses a pre-proof leaves to root ("bottom-up" in the syntax tree), and computes, at each inference step, the permission restriction that must be satisfied by any write-proof. If any permission restriction computed in this phase is unsatisfiable then there is no proof corresponding to the pre-proof. The second phase traverses the pre-proof from the root to leaves ("top-down" in the syntax tree), computing variable contexts that extend the pre-proof to a *maximally permissive write-proof* in the sense of the pre-order $\preceq$. The maximally permissive write-proof is then checked to verify that it contains non-zero permissions for all the passive uses of variables.

We illustrate the algorithm using the "problematic program" of Berdine and Reynolds [35], reproduced in Table 7 for ease of reference: Let Υ stand for the resource context $r_1 : R_1,\ r_2 : R_2$.

The first phase of the algorithm traverses the pre-proof leaves to root and computes, at each inference step, the permission restrictions needed to extend the pre-proof to a write proof. Since the inference steps correspond to program terms, we just show the terms involved in each case.

1. For the variable p, i.e., the inference step concluding $\Upsilon \vdash p$ **Var**, the permission restriction is $\Phi_1 = [p : \{\mathbf{self}\}]$. The total permission must be owned by **self** at this point in order to allow assignments to p.
2. For the command $p := 0$, the permission restriction is the same, $\Phi_2 = [p : \{\mathbf{self}\}]$.
3. For the critical section $\mathbf{with}\ r_2\ \mathbf{do}\ p := 0\ \mathbf{od}$, the permission restriction is $\Phi_3 = [p : \{\mathbf{self}, r_2\}]$. This means that both the process and the resource r_2 could have non-zero permission for p. Since the critical section combines the permissions from **self** and r_2 to execute the body, this is well-justified.
4. The command $[57] := 3$ does not write to any variables. So, its permission restriction is empty: $\Phi_4 = [\,]$.
5. For the outer critical section

   $$P_1 \equiv \mathbf{with}\ r_1\ \mathbf{do}\ (\mathbf{with}\ r_2\ \mathbf{do}\ p := 0\ \mathbf{od});\ [57] := 3\ \mathbf{od}$$

   r_1 is added to the restriction: $\Phi_5 = [p : \{\mathbf{self}, r_1, r_2\}]$.
6. The second process P_2 similarly has the permission restriction $\Phi_6 = [p : \{\mathbf{self}, r_1, r_2\}]$.
7. For the parallel composition $P_1 \parallel P_2$, the permission restriction is $\Phi_7 = [p : \{r_1, r_2\}]$, i.e., **self** is *removed* from the permission restrictions obtained from the component processes.

   Why? In this phase of the algorithm, we are only considering what permissions are needed for writing variables. Since both the processes have permission restrictions for p, that means that they are both writing to p, which is only possible if each of them has 0 as the **self** permission for p. (If the first process has non-zero permission for p then, since the second process has the sum of all its permissions for p summing to 1, the total sum of the permissions for p in the parallel composition would exceed 1, which is forbidden.) All the permissions for writing to p in both the processes must be obtained by entering critical regions for the resources.
8. **resource** r_2 **in** $P_1 \parallel P_2$ has the permission context $\Phi_8 = [p : \{r_1, \mathbf{self}\}]$, which is obtained by replacing r_2 in Φ_7 by **self**. This is justified by noting that the resource declaration allows the process to shift some portion of the permission for p from **self** to r_2. Since Φ_7 potentially requires a non-zero permission for p in r_2, Φ_8 must require it in **self**.
9. **resource** r_1 **in resource** r_2 **in** $P_1 \parallel P_2$ has the permission restriction $\Phi_9 = [p : \{\mathbf{self}\}]$, using the same reasoning as in the previous step.

The key observation is the fact that permission restriction Φ_7 for $P_1 \parallel P_2$ does not contain **self**. This requires us to divide the full permission for p among only the two resources r_1 and r_2.

Since all the permission restrictions computed in phase 1 are satisfiable, we proceed to phase 2 of the algorithm. This phase moves *top-down*, from the root to the leaves, using the permission restrictions computed in the previous phase.

1. For the overall program, the permission restriction is $\Phi_9 = [p : \{\mathbf{self}\}]$. The maximally permissive variable context satisfying Φ_9 is given by $\Delta\ p = [\mathbf{self} : 1]$.
2. The last inference step is of the form:

$$\frac{\Delta_1 \mid\ \vdash R_1\ \mathbf{Assert} \quad [\,] \qquad \Delta_2 \mid r_1 : R_1 \vdash \{R_2\}\ \mathbf{resource}\ r_2\ \mathbf{in}\ P_1 \parallel P_2\ \{R_2\} \quad [\Phi_8]}{\Delta \mid\ \vdash \{R_1 \star R_2\} \begin{pmatrix} \mathbf{resource}\ r_1\ \mathbf{in} \\ \mathbf{resource}\ r_2\ \mathbf{in} \\ P_1 \parallel P_2 \end{pmatrix} \{R_1 \star R_2\}\ [\Phi_9]}$$

   (where the Δ's need to satisfy various side conditions detailed in the formal rules given below). Note that the permission restriction for the first premise is empty because it is a passive judgement. We calculate maximally permissive variable contexts Δ_1 and Δ_2 using Δ (obtained in the previous step) and the permission restrictions for the premises $[\,]$ and Φ_8 calculated in the first phase. Recall that $\Phi_8 = [p : \{r_1, \mathbf{self}\}]$. This implies that $\Delta_2\ p$ should be of the form $[r_1 : \pi_1,\ \mathbf{self} : \pi_s]$ for some non-zero fractions π_1 and π_s such that $\pi_1 + \pi_s = 1$. The precise fractions do not matter, just that they should be non-zero. For instance, we can pick $\pi_1 = \pi_s = \frac{1}{2}$. Δ_1 should be of the form $[p : [\mathbf{self} : \pi_1]]$ because the permission allocated to **self** in the resource invariant should be the permission allocated to r_1 in Δ_2.

3. Moving top-down in the pre-proof, we need to construct the inference:

$$\frac{\Delta'_1 \mid\ \vdash R_2\ \mathbf{Assert}\ [\,] \qquad \Delta'_2 \mid r_1 : R_1, r_2 : R_2 \vdash \{\mathbf{emp}\}\, P_1 \parallel P_2\, \{\mathbf{emp}\}\ [\Phi_7]}{\Delta_2 \mid r_1 : R_1 \vdash \{R_2\}\ \mathbf{resource}\ r_2\ \mathbf{in}\ P_1 \parallel P_2\ \{R_2\}\ [\Phi_8]}$$

where $\Delta_2 = [p : [r_1 : \pi_1,\ \mathbf{self} : \pi_s]]$ is the variable context from the previous step. Proceeding similarly to the previous step, we can calculate that the variable context Δ'_2 in the judgement should be of the form $[r_1 : \pi'_1,\ r_2 : \pi'_2,\ \mathbf{self} : \pi'_s]$ such that $\pi'_1 = \pi_1$ and $\pi'_2 + \pi'_s = \pi_s$. However, the permission restriction Φ_7 only lists r_1 and r_2 for p. Hence, π_s should be 0, and $\pi'_2 = \pi_s$. If $\pi_1 = \pi_s = \frac{1}{2}$ was chosen in the previous step, then we obtain $\pi'_1 = \pi'_2 = \frac{1}{2}$.

We omit the remaining steps, which are straightforward. Note that the main task of the algorithm is now accomplished. The permissions for p in the two resources r_1 and r_2 have been inferred. They are $\frac{1}{2}$ each.

The algorithm for permission inference takes as input a pre-proof P^0, regarded as a labeling function $(P^0)_N$ of a formal tree of nodes. In phase 1, it traverses the tree leaf-to-root and constructs a permission restriction Φ_N for each node N. If the pre-inference for $(P^0)_N$ is of the form

$$X^0 : \frac{\Upsilon_{N_1} \vdash S_{N_1} \quad \cdots \quad \Upsilon_{N_k} \vdash S_{N_k}}{\Upsilon_N \vdash S_N} \qquad (2)$$

then the algorithm computes the permission restriction Φ_N for node N as a partial function $\mathcal{F}_R(\Phi_{N_1}, \ldots, \Phi_{N_k})$ of the permission restrictions of its children (antecedents of the pre-inference), satisfying:

Property L0: If each $\mathrm{dom}\,\Phi_{N_i}$ contains exactly the modified free variables of S_{N_i} (i.e., varaibles that occur on the left hand sides of assignments) then $\mathrm{dom}\,\Phi_N$ likewise contains exactly the modified free variables of S_N.

Property L1: For every inference X that extends X^0:

$$X : \frac{\Delta_1 \mid \Upsilon_{N_1} \vdash S_{N_1} \quad \cdots \quad \Delta_k \mid \Upsilon_{N_k} \vdash S_{N_k}}{\Delta \mid \Upsilon_N \vdash S_N}$$

we have $(\bigwedge_{i=1}^{k} \Delta_i \models \Phi_{N_i}) \implies \Delta \models \Phi_N$ where $\Phi_N = \mathcal{F}_R(\Phi_{N_1}, \ldots, \Phi_{N_k})$.

If, on the other hand, $\mathcal{F}_R(\Phi_{N_1}, \ldots, \Phi_{N_k})$ is undefined then there exists no inference X extending X^0. This case arises only for the variable declaration rule.

LEMMA 10. *Given a pre-proof P^0, if Φ_N is a family of of permission restrictions for the nodes of P^0 produced in phase 1, then, for every write-proof P^w that extends P^0, the variable context Δ_N of $(P^w)_N$ satisfies Φ_N.*

The proof is by induction on the structure of the underlying tree of P^0. Thus, the result holds for all sub-proofs of P^0 as well.

In phase 2, we construct a maximally permissive write-proof that extends P^0 by calculating $\Delta_N^{\max}$ for every node N. For the root node, we choose a maximally permissive Δ satisfying Φ_{root}. Then phase 2 proceeds from the root to leaves, constructing $\Delta_N^{\max}$ for each node using the $\Delta^{\max}$ of the the parent (consequent of the pre-inference) and the permission restrictions computed in phase 1. Specifically, given a pre-inference X^0

$$X^0 : \frac{\Upsilon_{N_1} \vdash S_{N_1} \quad \cdots \quad \Upsilon_{N_k} \vdash S_{N_k}}{\Upsilon_N \vdash S_N}$$

and $\Delta_N^{\max}$ satisfying Φ_N, it computes $\Delta_{N_1}^{\max}, \ldots, \Delta_{N_k}^{\max}$ for the child nodes of N (antecedents of the pre-inference) as a function $\mathcal{G}_R(\Phi_{N_1}, \ldots, \Phi_{N_k}, \Delta_N^{\max})$ of the given $\Delta_N^{\max}$ and the permission restrictions $\Phi_{N_1}, \ldots, \Phi_{N_k}$ of the child nodes, satisfying:

Property L2: $\Delta_{N_1}^{\max} \models \Phi_{N_1}, \ldots, \Delta_{N_k}^{\max} \models \Phi_{N_k}$, and the following is a legal inference that extends X^0:

$$X^{\max} : \frac{\Delta_{N_1}^{\max} \mid \Upsilon_{N_1} \vdash S_{N_1} \quad \cdots \quad \Delta_{N_k}^{\max} \mid \Upsilon_{N_k} \vdash S_{N_k}}{\Delta_N^{\max} \mid \Upsilon_N \vdash S_N}$$

Moreover, for any other legal inference X that extends X^0:

$$X : \frac{\Delta_1 \mid \Upsilon_{N_1} \vdash S_{N_1} \quad \cdots \quad \Delta_k \mid \Upsilon_{N_k} \vdash S_{N_k}}{\Delta \mid \Upsilon_N \vdash S_N}$$

such that $\forall i.\ \Delta_i \models \Phi_{N_i}$ and $\Delta \models \Phi_N$, we have $\Delta \preceq \Delta_N^{\max} \implies \forall i. \Delta_i \preceq \Delta_{N_i}^{\max}$.

LEMMA 11. *Given a pre-proof P^0, a family of permission restrictions Φ_N produced in phase 1, and a variable context $\Delta_{\mathrm{root}}^{\max}$ satisfying Φ_{root}, let $P^{\max}$ be the write-proof on the same underlying tree of nodes obtained by using the given $\Delta_{\mathrm{root}}^{\max}$ and contexts $\Delta_N^{\max}$ satisfying the Property L2. Then*

1. *$P^{\max}$ is a legal write-proof extending P^0.*
2. *if P is any other write-proof extending P^0 using variable contexts Δ_N, and $\Delta_{\mathrm{root}} \preceq \Delta_{\mathrm{root}}^{\max}$, then $\Delta_N \preceq \Delta_N^{\max}$ for all nodes N.*

The proof is by induction on the depth of the nodes in the underlying tree of P^0.

We describe all these aspects compactly by writing down the rules of SCI Separation Logic using the notations of this section, and displaying the computations of both the phases of the algorithm. We decorate the judgements with schematic permission restrictions Φ:

$$\Delta \mid \Upsilon \vdash S\ [\Phi]$$

in order to refer to the permission restrictions computed in phase 1 and used in phase 2. The side conditions of passive rules are ignored in phase 1, but used in phase 2.

Some of rules are as follows (the others are similar):

Expressions:

$$\frac{}{\Delta \mid \Upsilon \vdash E\ \mathbf{Exp}\ [\,]} \quad \text{where } \forall v \in FV(E).\ \Delta\ v\ \mathbf{self} > 0$$

Phase 1 is trivial: $\Phi = [\,]$.
Phase 2 checks to verify that $\Delta^{\max}$ satisfies the side condition. If and only if the side condition is satisfied, the write-proof that extends P^0 with $\Delta^{\max}$ for this node will be a proof.

The rule for Assertions is similar.

Assignable Variable:

$$\frac{}{\Delta \mid \Upsilon \vdash x\ \mathbf{Var}\ [\Phi]} \quad \text{where } \Delta\ x\ o = \begin{cases} 1, & \text{if } o = \mathbf{self} \\ 0, & \text{otherwise} \end{cases}$$

Phase 1: $\Phi = [x : \{\textbf{self}\}]$
Phase 2 computation is trivial because there are no premises.

Sequencing:

$$\frac{\Delta_1 \mid \Upsilon \vdash \{P\}\, C_1\, \{Q\}\, [\Phi_1] \quad \Delta_2 \mid \Upsilon \vdash \{Q\}\, C_2\, \{R\}\, [\Phi_2]}{\Delta \mid \Upsilon \vdash \{P\}\, C_1; C_2\, \{R\}\, [\Phi]}$$

where $\Delta_1 = \Delta_2 = \Delta$

Phase 1:

$$\text{dom}\ \Phi = \text{dom}\ \Phi_1 \cup \text{dom}\ \Phi_2$$
$$\Phi\ v = \begin{cases} \Phi_1\ v & \text{if } v \in \text{dom}\ \Phi_1 \setminus \text{dom}\ \Phi_2 \\ \Phi_2\ v & \text{if } v \in \text{dom}\ \Phi_2 \setminus \text{dom}\ \Phi_1 \\ (\Phi_1 v \cap \Phi_2 v) & \text{if } v \in \text{dom}\ \Phi_1 \cap \text{dom}\ \Phi_2 \end{cases}$$

Phase 2: $\Delta_1^{\max} = \Delta_2^{\max} = \Delta^{\max}$.

All other rules such as conditionals, assignment, lookup and mutation are similar to Sequencing in that Δ remains unchanged in the premises. Their Phase 1 and Phase 2 computations are exactly the same as for Sequencing.

Parallel composition:

$$\frac{\Delta_1 \mid \Upsilon \vdash \{P_1\}\, C_1\, \{Q_1\}\, [\Phi_1] \quad \Delta_2 \mid \Upsilon \vdash \{P_2\}\, C_2\, \{Q_2\}\, [\Phi_2]}{\Delta \mid \Upsilon \vdash \{P_1 \star P_2\}\, C_1 \parallel C_2\, \{Q_1 \star Q_2\}\, [\Phi]}$$

where $\Delta_1\ v\ o = \Delta_2\ v\ o = \Delta\ v\ o$ for all $o \neq \textbf{self}$
$\Delta\ v\ \textbf{self} = \Delta_1\ v\ \textbf{self} + \Delta_2\ v\ \textbf{self} \leq 1$

Phase 1:

$$\text{dom}\ \Phi = \text{dom}\ \Phi_1 \cup \text{dom}\ \Phi_2$$
$$\Phi\ v = \begin{cases} \Phi_1\ v & \text{if } v \in \text{dom}\ \Phi_1 \setminus \text{dom}\ \Phi_2 \\ \Phi_2\ v & \text{if } v \in \text{dom}\ \Phi_2 \setminus \text{dom}\ \Phi_1 \\ (\Phi_1 v \cap \Phi_2 v) \setminus \{\textbf{self}\} & \text{if } v \in \text{dom}\ \Phi_1 \cap \text{dom}\ \Phi_2 \end{cases}$$

Phase 2: The pair $(\Delta_1^{\max}\ v\ o,\ \Delta_2^{\max}\ v\ o)$ is as follows:

- If $o \neq \textbf{self}$, it is $(\Delta^{\max}\ v\ o,\ \Delta^{\max}\ v\ o)$.
- If $o = \textbf{self}$ and $v \in \text{dom}\ \Phi_1 \setminus \text{dom}\ \Phi_2$, it is $(\Delta^{\max}\ v\ \textbf{self},\ 0)$
- If $o = \textbf{self}$ and $v \in \text{dom}\ \Phi_2 \setminus \text{dom}\ \Phi_1$, it is $(0,\ \Delta^{\max}\ v\ \textbf{self})$.
- If $o = \textbf{self}$ and $v \in \text{dom}\ \Phi_1 \cap \text{dom}\ \Phi_2$, it is $(\frac{1}{2}\Delta^{\max}\ v\ \textbf{self},\ \frac{1}{2}\Delta^{\max}\ v\ \textbf{self})$.
- If $o = \textbf{self}$ and $v \notin \text{dom}\ \Phi_1 \cup \text{dom}\ \Phi_2$, it is $(\frac{1}{2}\Delta^{\max}\ v\ \textbf{self},\ \frac{1}{2}\Delta^{\max}\ v\ \textbf{self})$.

The Frame rule is similar to parallel composition.

Critical regions:

$$\frac{\begin{array}{ll}\Delta_1 \mid \Upsilon, r \colon R \vdash P, Q\ \textbf{Assert} & [\,] \\ \Delta_2 \mid \Upsilon \vdash \{(P \star R) \wedge B\}\, C\, \{Q \star R\} & [\Phi_2]\end{array}}{\Delta \mid \Upsilon, r \colon R \vdash \{P\}\ \textbf{with}\ r\ \textbf{when}\ B\ \textbf{do}\ C\ \textbf{od}\ \{Q\}\ [\Phi]}$$

where $\Delta_2\ v\ o = \Delta\ v\ o$ for all $o \notin \{\textbf{self}, r\}$
$\Delta_2\ v\ \textbf{self} = \Delta\ v\ \textbf{self} + \Delta\ v\ r \leq 1$
$\Delta_2\ v\ r = 0$
$\Delta_1 = \Delta$

Phase 1: $\text{dom}\ \Phi = \text{dom}\ \Phi_2$
$\Phi\ v = \{\, o \in \Phi_2\, v \mid o \neq \textbf{self},\, o \neq r \,\} \cup \{\, \textbf{self} \mid \textbf{self} \in \Phi_2\, v \,\} \cup \{\, r \mid \textbf{self} \in \Phi_2\, v \,\}$

Phase 2:

- For $o \notin \{\textbf{self}, r\}$, $\Delta_2^{\max}\ v\ o = \Delta^{\max}\ v\ o$.
- $\Delta_2^{\max}\ v\ \textbf{self} = \Delta^{\max}\ v\ \textbf{self} + \Delta^{\max}\ v\ r$.
- $\Delta_1^{\max} = \Delta^{\max}$ and $\Delta_2^{\max}\ v\ r = 0$.

Resource declaration:

$$\frac{\Delta_1 \mid \Upsilon \vdash R\ \textbf{Assert}\ [\,] \quad \Delta_2 \mid \Upsilon, r : R \vdash \{P\}\, C\, \{Q\}\ [\Phi_2]}{\Delta \mid \Upsilon \vdash \{P \star R\}\ \textbf{resource}\ r\ \textbf{in}\ C\ \{Q \star R\}\ [\Phi]}$$

where R is precise
$\Delta_2\ v\ o = \Delta\ v\ o$ for all $o \notin \{\textbf{self}, r\}$
$\Delta\ v\ \textbf{self} = \Delta_2\ v\ \textbf{self} + \Delta_2\ v\ r \leq 1$
$\Delta_1\ v\ o = \begin{cases} \Delta_2\ v\ r, & \text{if } o = \textbf{self} \\ 0, & \text{otherwise} \end{cases}$

Phase 1: $\text{dom}\ \Phi = \text{dom}\ \Phi_2$
$\Phi\ v = \{\, o \in \Phi_2\, v \mid o \neq \textbf{self}, o \neq r \,\} \cup \{\, \textbf{self} \mid \textbf{self} \in \Phi_2\, v \vee r \in \Phi_2\, v \,\}$
Phase 2: The context $\Delta_2^{\max}$ is defined as follows:

- For $o \notin \{\textbf{self}, r\}$, $\Delta_2^{\max}\ v\ o$ is $\Delta^{\max}\ v\ o$.
- The pair $(\Delta_2^{\max}\ v\textbf{self},\ \Delta_2^{\max}\ v r)$ is as follows: If $v \notin \text{dom}\Phi_2$ then it is $(\frac{1}{2}\Delta^{\max}\ v\ \textbf{self},\ \frac{1}{2}\Delta^{\max}\ v\ \textbf{self})$. If $v \in \text{dom}\ \Phi_2$:
  - If $\textbf{self} \in \Phi_2\ v$ and $r \in \Phi_2\ v$, it is $(\frac{1}{2}\Delta^{\max}\ v\ \textbf{self},\ \frac{1}{2}\Delta^{\max}\ v\ \textbf{self})$.
  - If $\textbf{self} \in \Phi_2\ v$ and $r \notin \Phi_2\ v$, it is $(\Delta^{\max}\ v\ \textbf{self},\ 0)$.
  - If $\textbf{self} \notin \Phi_2\ v$ and $r \in \Phi_2\ v$, it is $(0,\ \Delta^{\max}\ v\ \textbf{self})$.
  - If $\textbf{self} \notin \Phi_2\ v$ and $r \notin \Phi_2\ v$, it is $(0, 0)$.

$\Delta_1^{\max}\ v\ \textbf{self}$ is the same as $\Delta_2^{\max}\ v\ r$. For all $o \neq \textbf{self}$, $\Delta_1^{\max}\ v\ o$ is 0.

Variable declaration:

$$\frac{\Delta_1 \mid \Upsilon \vdash P, Q\ \textbf{Assert}\ [\,] \qquad \Delta_2 \mid \Upsilon \vdash \{P\}\, C\, \{Q\}\ [\Phi_2]}{\Delta \vdash \Upsilon \vdash \{P\}\ \textbf{local}\ x\ \textbf{in}\ C\ \{Q\}\ [\Phi]}$$

where $\Delta_2\ v\ o = \Delta\ v\ o$ for all $v \neq x$
$\Delta_2\ x\ o = \begin{cases} 1, & \text{if } o = \textbf{self} \\ 0, & \text{otherwise} \end{cases}$
$\Delta_1\ v\ o = \Delta\ v\ o$ for all $v \neq x$
$\Delta_1\ x\ o = 0$

Phase 1: If $\textbf{self} \in \Phi_2\ x$ or $x \notin \text{dom}\ \Phi_2$ then the computation is:

$$\text{dom}\ \Phi = (\text{dom}\ \Phi_2) \setminus \{x\}$$
$$\Phi\ v = \Phi_2\ v \text{ for all } v \neq x$$

If $x \in \text{dom}\ \Phi_2$ and $\textbf{self} \notin \Phi_2\ x$ then Phase 1 fails, i.e., there is no write-proof extending P^0.
Phase 2:

- $\Delta_2^{\max}\ x\ o$ is 1 when o is $\textbf{self}$, 0 otherwise. For all other v, $\Delta_2^{\max}\ v\ o = \Delta^{\max}\ v\ o$.
- $\Delta_1^{\max} = \Delta^{\max}$.

It may be verified that all the phase 1 and phase 2 computations listed above satisfy the properties L1 and L2 respectively, completing the proof of correctness.

7. Conclusion

We have provided a streamlined formulation of Sequential and Concurrent Separation Logic rules without awkward side conditions for variable usage. The rules are more expressive than the original Owicki-Gries-O'Hearn system. Yet, they retain the "syntactic" character of the variable conditions without adding proof burden in the programming logic itself. This syntactic character is exploited in devising an algorithm to automatically infer the annotations required in resource declarations. This should prove useful for Separation Logic-based verification tools like Smallfoot.

Our work is also a modest contribution to the theory of Syntactic Control of Interference, which dates back to 1978. While the system has been studied from a semantics point of view, it has not been previously applied to the formulation of programming logics, which is somewhat paradoxical given its natural fit with reasoning principles. We have extended the traditional framework with permission algebras, which should prove useful for further development.

Further work along this line would include the extension of Concurrent Separation Logic with higher-order features such as procedures and objects, for which Syntactic Control of Interference is well-suited.

Acknowledgments

We are grateful to Philippa Gardner and her group for the "yak" session at Imperial College where this work was first presented. Peter O'Hearn has provided much appreciated encouragement and inspiration throughout the development of this work. Special thanks go to Josh Berdine and Ian Wehrman for making us aware of the technical problems with the earlier proof systems. John Reynolds's work was partially supported by National Science Foundation Grant CCF-0916808.

References

[1] S. Abramsky and G. McCusker. Linearity, sharing and state. In *Algol-like Languages* O'Hearn and Tennent [28], chapter 20.

[2] S. Abramsky, K. Honda, and G. McCusker. A fully abstract game semantics for general references. In *LICS 1998*, pages 334–344, 1998.

[3] K. R. Apt. Ten years of Hoare's logic: A survey. *ACM Trans. Program. Lang. Syst.*, 3(4):431–483, Oct. 1981.

[4] J. Berdine and I. Wehrman. Variable conditions and CSL. Private communication, 4th April, 2011.

[5] K. Bierhoff. API protocol compliance in object-oriented software. Technical Report CMU-ISR-09-108, Carnegie-Mellon University, Apr 2009.

[6] R. Bornat, C. Calcagno, P. O'Hearn, and M. Parkinson. Permission accounting in Separation Logic. In *ACM Symp. on Princ. of Program. Lang.*, pages 59–70. ACM Press, 2005.

[7] R. Bornat, C. Calcagno, and H. Yang. Variables as resource in Separation Logic. In *Proc. 22nd Ann. Conf. on Math. Found. of Program. Semantics (MFPS XXII)* Main et al. [21], pages 247–276.

[8] J. Boyland. Checking interference with fractional permissions. In R. Cousot, editor, *Static Analysis: 10th Intern. Symp.*, volume 2694 of *LNCS*, pages 55–72. Springer, 2003.

[9] P. Brinch Hansen. *Operating System Principles*. Prentice-Hall, Englewood Cliffs, 1973.

[10] P. Brinch Hansen. Structured multiprogramming. *Comm. ACM*, 15: 574–577, July 1972.

[11] S. D. Brookes. A semantics for Concurrent Separation Logic. *Theoretical Comput. Sci.*, 375(1-3):227–270, Apr 2007.

[12] S. D. Brookes. A revisionist history of Concurrent Separation Logic. In Mislove and Ouaknine [24], pages 5–28.

[13] S. D. Brookes. Variables as resource for shared-memory programs: Semantics and soundness. In *Proc. 22nd Ann. Conf. on Math. Found. of Program. Semantics (MFPS XXII)* Main et al. [21], pages 123–150. doi: DOI: 10.1016/j.entcs.2006.04.008.

[14] L. Damas and R. Milner. Principal type-schemes for functional programs. In *ACM Symp. on Princ. of Program. Lang.*, pages 207–212, 1982.

[15] J.-Y. Girard. Linear logic. *Theoretical Comput. Sci.*, 50:1–102, 1987.

[16] A. Gotsman, J. Berdine, and B. Cook. Precision and the conjunction rule in Concurrent Separation Logic. In Mislove and Ouaknine [24].

[17] C. A. R. Hoare. Towards a theory of parallel programming. In C. A. R. Hoare and R. H. Perrott, editors, *Operating Systems Techniques*, pages 61–71. Academic Press, 1972.

[18] C. A. R. Hoare. Monitors: An operating system structuring concept. *Comm. ACM*, 17(10):549–558, Oct. 1974.

[19] B. J., C. Calcagno, and P. W. O'Hearn. Smallfoot: Modular automatic assertion checking with Separation Logic. In F. S. de Boer, editor, *Formal Methods for Components and Objects, 4th Intern. Symp.*, volume 4111 of *LNCS*, pages 115–137. Springer-Verlag, 2005.

[20] K. Kapoor, K. Lodaya, and U. S. Reddy. Fine grained concurrency with Separation Logic. *J. Philosophical Logic*, 40(5):583–632, Oct 2011. doi: 10.1007/s10992-011-9195-1.

[21] M. Main, A. Melton, and M. Mislove. *Proc. 22nd Ann. Conf. on Math. Found. of Program. Semantics (MFPS XXII)*, volume 158 of *Elect. Notes in Theor. Comput. Sci.* Elsevier, 2006.

[22] G. McCusker. A graph model for imperative computation. *Logical Methods in Comp. Sci.*, 6(1-2), Jan 2010.

[23] R. Milner. A theory of type polymorphism in programming. *J. Comput. Syst. Sci.*, 17:348–375, 1978.

[24] M. Mislove and J. Ouaknine, editors. *Proc. 27nd Ann. Conf. on Math. Found. of Program. Semantics (MFPS XXVII)*, volume 276 of *Elect. Notes in Theor. Comput. Sci.* Elsevier, 2011.

[25] P. W. O'Hearn. Resources, concurrency and local reasoning. *Theoretical Comput. Sci.*, 375(1-3):271–307, May 2007.

[26] P. W. O'Hearn. Linear logic and interference control. In *Category Theory and Computer Science*, volume 350 of *LNCS*, pages 74–93. Springer-Verlag, 1991.

[27] P. W. O'Hearn and D. J. Pym. The logic of bunched implications. *Bulletin Symbolic Logic*, 5(2):215–244, June 1999.

[28] P. W. O'Hearn and R. D. Tennent. *Algol-like Languages (Two volumes)*. Birkhäuser, Boston, 1997.

[29] P. W. O'Hearn, A. J. Power, M. Takeyama, and R. D. Tennent. Syntactic control of interference revisited. In S. D. Brookes, M. Main, A. Melton, and M. Mislove, editors, *Math. Found. of Program. Semantics: Eleventh Ann. Conference*, volume 1 of *Elect. Notes in Theor. Comput. Sci.* Elsevier, 1995. (Reprinted as Chapter 18 of [28]).

[30] P. W. O'Hearn, J. C. Reynolds, and H. Yang. Local reasoning about programs that alter data structures. In L. Fribourg, editor, *CSL 2001*, volume 2142 of *LNCS*, pages 1–19, Berlin, 2001. Springer-Verlag.

[31] S. Owicki and D. Gries. Verifying properties of parallel programs: An axiomatic approach. *Comm. ACM*, 19(5):279–285, May 1976.

[32] M. Parkinson, R. Bornat, and Calcagno. Variables as resource in Hoare Logics. In *Symp. on Logic in Comput. Sci.*, pages 137–146. IEEE, 2006.

[33] U. S. Reddy. Global state considered unnecessary: An introduction to object-based semantics. *J. Lisp and Symbolic Computation*, 9:7–76, 1996. (Reprinted as Chapter 19 of [28]).

[34] J. Reynolds. Separation Logic: A logic for shared mutable data structures. In *LICS*, pages 55–74, 2002.

[35] J. C. Reynolds. A problematic program (joint work with Josh Berdine). Presentation at the Dagstuhl workshop on Types, Logics and Semantics for State, 2008.

[36] J. C. Reynolds. Syntactic control of interference. In *ACM Symp. on Princ. of Program. Lang.*, pages 39–46. ACM, 1978. (Reprinted as Chapter 10 of [28]).

[37] J. C. Reynolds. Idealized Algol and its specification logic. In D. Neel, editor, *Tools and Notions for Program Construction*, pages 121–161. Cambridge Univ. Press, 1982. (Reprinted as Chapter 6 of [28]).

[38] V. Vafeiadis. Concurrent Separation Logic and operational semantics. In Mislove and Ouaknine [24].

[39] H. Yang and P. W. O'Hearn. A semantics basis for local reasoning. In *FOSSACS*, pages 402–416, Berlin, 2002. Springer-Verlag.

[40] H. Yasuoka and T. Terauchi. Polymorphic fractional capabilities. In *Static Analysis Symposium/Workshop on Static Analysis*, pages 36–51, 2009. doi: 10.1007/978-3-642-03237-0_5.

Canonicity for 2-Dimensional Type Theory

Daniel R. Licata* Robert Harper*
Carnegie Mellon University
{drl,rwh}@cs.cmu.edu

Abstract

Higher-dimensional dependent type theory enriches conventional one-dimensional dependent type theory with additional structure expressing equivalence of elements of a type. This structure may be employed in a variety of ways to capture rather coarse identifications of elements, such as a universe of sets considered modulo isomorphism. Equivalence must be respected by all families of types and terms, as witnessed computationally by a type-generic program. Higher-dimensional type theory has applications to code reuse for dependently typed programming, and to the formalization of mathematics. In this paper, we develop a novel judgemental formulation of a two-dimensional type theory, which enjoys a canonicity property: a closed term of boolean type is definitionally equal to true or false. Canonicity is a necessary condition for a computational interpretation of type theory as a programming language, and does not hold for existing axiomatic presentations of higher-dimensional type theory. The method of proof is a generalization of the NuPRL semantics, interpreting types as syntactic groupoids rather than equivalence relations.

Categories and Subject Descriptors D.3.1 [*Programming Languages*]: Formal Definitions and Theory; F.3.2 [*Logics and Meanings of Programs*]: Semantics of Programming Languages

General Terms Languages, Theory

1. Introduction

A growing body of work [4, 8, 9, 12, 14, 15, 22–24] on intensional dependent type theory [11, 16, 18] elucidates the latent higher-dimensional structure given by the Martin-Löf intensional identity type. The identity type, $\mathsf{Id}_A\ M\ N$, is the type of evidence for equivalence of the objects M and N of type A. The elimination rule for the identity type ensures that type families indexed by A respect equivalence at A: if F is an A-indexed family of types, and $\alpha : \mathsf{Id}_A\ M\ N$, then $F[M]$ and $F[N]$ are isomorphic types. Similarly, families of objects indexed by A must respect equivalence at A: mappings are functional in their domain, in that application to equivalent elements yields equivalent results. Objects of identity type are themselves subject to higher equivalences inhabiting the iterated identity type $\mathsf{Id}_{\mathsf{Id}_A\ M\ N}\ \alpha\ \beta$, and so on, indefinitely. This higher-dimensional structure is the key to establishing surprisingly close connections between type theory, category theory (interpreting types as higher-dimensional groupoids, and equivalences as morphisms), and homotopy theory (interpreting types as topological spaces, and equivalences as paths). The interplay between these viewpoints is a source of much current investigation.

However, experience with intensional type theory, both as a programming formalism and as a language for formalizing mathematics, suggests that the general principles of equivalence originally proposed by Martin-Löf are too restrictive. For example, equivalence at function types amounts to definitional equality, whereas in mathematical practice one tends to identify functions extensionally—two functions are equal iff they take equal arguments to equal results. Equivalence of types themselves is similarly restrictive. Formally, this is typically considered as equivalence for members of a *universe*, which is a type whose elements themselves determine types. The standard account of equivalence for universes amounts to equivalence of presentations: two types are equivalent if they are written the same way. However, it is common mathematical practice to identify *isomorphic* sets—to treat two sets as interchangable when there are functions back and forth that compose to the identity.

This motivates extensions of intensional type theory with coarser notions of equivalence: Altenkirch [2], Altenkirch et al. [3], Hofmann [10] investigate functional extensionality. Voevodsky's *univalence axiom* [23] goes further by treating elements of universes as equivalent whenever the spaces they determine are weakly equivalent in the sense of homotopy theory. A particular case of univalence, considered here, arises when considering the universe set of extensional sets: two sets are deemed equivalent iff they are isomorphic. This amounts to introducing a new canonical form, $\mathsf{iso}(f, g, \alpha, \beta)$, of the identity type $\mathsf{Id}_{\mathsf{set}}\ A\ B$, given by functions $f : A \to B$ and $g : B \to A$ and evidence α and β witnessing their inverse relationship to one another. However, this represents a more significant departure from the traditional view of equivalence than might at first be apparent. Since two sets can be isomorphic in many ways, isomorphism must be treated as a computationally relevant *structure* imposed on two sets, rather than as a computationally irrelevant *property* of them. For example, the set 2 of booleans is isomorphic to itself both by the identity function and by the negation function, which swaps the two booleans. Thus, the type $\mathsf{Id}_{\mathsf{set}}\ 2\ 2$ is not a proof-irrelevant proposition, but has real computational content. A *higher-dimensional type* is one, such as set, whose identity type has computational content.

Higher-dimensional type theory has several applications in programming and formal mathematics. In programming, postulating that equivalence of sets is isomorphism has the consequence that *all families of types respect isomorphism*. For example, consider

* This research was sponsored in part by the National Science Foundation under grant number CCF-0702381 and CCF-1116703 and by the Microsoft-Carnegie Mellon Center for Computational Thinking. The views and conclusions contained in this document are those of the author and should not be interpreted as representing the official policies, either expressed or implied, of any sponsoring institution, the U.S. government or any other entity.

POPL'12, January 25–27, 2012, Philadelphia, PA, USA.

the family of types $\mathsf{Mon}[A]$, where $A : \mathsf{set}$, representing monoids on A:

$$\begin{array}{l}\mathsf{Mon}[A] = \\ \quad \Sigma\, m : A \to A \to A. \\ \quad \Sigma\, u : A. \\ \quad \Sigma\, assoc : (\Pi x, y, z : A.\mathsf{Id}\ (m\ (m\ x\ y)\ z)\ (m\ x\ (m\ y\ z))). \\ \quad \Sigma\, unitl : (\Pi x : A.\mathsf{Id}\ (m\ u\ x)\ x). \\ \quad \Sigma\, unitr : (\Pi x : A.\mathsf{Id}\ (m\ x\ u)\ x).1\end{array}$$

A monoid consists of a multiplication operation m, a unit operation u, together with proofs that these satisfy the monoid laws. Monoid structures are useful for a parallel reduce operator, which schedules computation in an arbitrary way while producing a deterministic result. In current dependent type theories, a programmer must show that each individual type family, such as Mon, respects isomorphism—that $A \cong B$ entails $\mathsf{Mon}[A] \cong \mathsf{Mon}[B]$. This is particularly laborious for dependently typed programming, where isomorphisms arise frequently from type refinements; e.g. if the type $\mathsf{vec}[n : \mathbb{N}]$ classifies vectors of length n, then $\Sigma\, n{:}\mathbb{N}.\, \mathsf{vec}[n]$ is isomorphic to the unrefined type list. Moreover, it is unnecessary, as there is in fact no way to define a family that does *not* respect isomorphism. In contrast, in higher-dimensional type theory, the elimination rule for the identity type induces a monoid structure on B from a monoid structure on A, and shows that these structures are isomorphic: using substitutivity of Id-types $\mathsf{subst}_C : \mathsf{Id}_A\ M\ N \to C[M] \to C[N]$, given any $\mathsf{iso}(f, g, \alpha, \beta) : \mathsf{Id}_{\mathsf{set}}\ A\ B$, the term

$$\mathsf{subst}_{\mathsf{Mon}}(\mathsf{iso}(f, g, \alpha, \beta)) : \mathsf{Mon}[A] \to \mathsf{Mon}[B]$$

induces an isomorphism between monoid structures.

The same idea also has applications to the formalization of mathematics: a proof assistant based on higher-dimensional type theory supports the common informal mathematical practice of identifying isomorphic sets. Another application is to the formalization of homotopy theory in type theory [1] in which types are interpreted as topological spaces, and equivalences as paths in the space [4]. Under this correspondence a space may be inductively defined by giving generators for its points and for its paths. For example, the interval, I, may be specified by the endpoints $0, 1 : I$ and the path *seg* : $\mathsf{Id}_I\ 0\ 1$ between them. Similarly, the circle S^1 may be specified as having, say, two points, $0, 1 : S^1$, and two paths $a : \mathsf{Id}_{S^1}\ 0\ 1$ and $b : \mathsf{Id}_{S^1}\ 1\ 0$. The higher-dimensional structure of type theory ensures, for example, that a family of types indexed by a space induces an action that transports objects along paths in the space. These definitions have already been used to formalize some basic results in algebraic topology [1]—all higher homotopy groups are abelian; the fundamental group of the circle is isomorphic to $\mathbb{Z}$—and suggest a new, type-theoretic approach towards more sophisticated problems, like determining the homotopy groups of the spheres.

A fundamental question that arises in higher-dimensional type theory concerns the computational behavior of identity elimination. For example, when we use $\mathsf{subst}_{\mathsf{Mon}}(\mathsf{iso}(f, g, \alpha, \beta))$ to construct a function $\mathsf{Mon}[A] \to \mathsf{Mon}[B]$, what function does it construct? The answer lies in the functorial action of the dependent type constructors, as expressed by Hofmann and Streicher [12]. In this example, the action of Mon sends the unit to to its image under f, wraps multiplication with f and g to transfer back and forth between the two algebras, and uses the cancellation of inverses to validate the laws. Thus, from a programming standpoint, the main benefit of higher-dimensional type theory is to equip every type and term in the language with their functorial actions, as a generic program. This allows programmers to work up to isomorphism and other such structures, facilitating code reuse for dependently typed programs. Topologically, these programs witness the process of transporting points along paths in spaces.

However, this computational behavior is latent in current presentations of higher-dimensional type theory, which extend the canonical members of the identity type, without extending the computation rules for its elimination form. The standard computation rule for subst says that $\mathsf{subst}_C(\mathsf{refl})$ reduces to the identity function. Higher dimensional types add new canonical forms of equivalence, such as $\mathsf{iso}(f, g, \alpha, \beta)$, but, in current presentations, no new computation rules. This runs afoul of the computational interpretation of type theory, which demands that the elimination forms for a type be post-inverse to the introductory forms. For example, the term $\mathsf{subst}_{\mathsf{Mon}}(\mathsf{iso}(f, g, \alpha, \beta))$ "gets stuck", even though it is well-typed! In logical terms, the property of *canonicity* [10] of observable types fails: there are closed terms of, say, boolean type that are neither equal to true nor equal to false. A weaker notion of canonicity-up-to-equivalence has been conjectured, but not yet proved [23].

In this paper, we define a *two*-dimensional univalent type theory (2TT), and prove that it does enjoy canonicity. 2TT is based on a *judgemental*, rather than *propositional*, account of its higher-dimensional structure. The key innovation is to consider a judgement of the form $\Gamma \vdash \alpha : M \simeq_A N$ stating that α is evidence for the equivalence of M and N as objects of type A. The computational content of such equivalences is made explicit by judgemental operations that ensure that families of types and objects respect equivalence. Function extensionality and univalence are naturally accommodated as rules of equivalence, and the induced action accounts for the computational content of the equivalence proofs. As we show in Section 4, the identity type is reformulated simply as an internalization of the equivalence judgement (that is, as a hom-type). The Martin-Löf elimination rule is derivable from this interpretation using the judgemental apparatus for equivalence.

The judgemental formulation, described in Section 2, is adapted from earlier work [14] on the directed (non-symmetric) case. We require that the forms of evidence include identity ($\mathsf{refl}_M : M \simeq_A M$), composition (if $\alpha : M \simeq_A N$ and $\beta : N \simeq_A P$ then $\beta \circ \alpha : M \simeq_A P$), and inverse (if $\alpha : M \simeq_A N$ then $\alpha^{-1} : N \simeq_A M$), corresponding to the reflexivity, symmetry, and transitivity properties of an equivalence relation. Moreover, these operations must satisfy the unit, associativity, and inverse laws (on the nose, in the two-dimensional case) for a *groupoid* [12], a category in which all maps are invertible. Preservation of equivalence amounts to the requirement that families of types be *functorial* in their indices: if $\alpha : M \simeq_A N$, and F is an A-indexed family of types, then $\mathsf{map}_{x:A.F}\ \alpha : F[M] \to F[N]$ is the *action* of F on evidence for the equivalence of indices. This action must preserve identities (the null action) and composition (the composite action), and hence inverses (the reverse action).

2TT has a simple interpretation in the category of groupoids: each type is interpreted as a groupoid, with objects modeling terms, and maps modeling equivalences—in essence, 2TT constructs a type-theoretic syntax out of the groupoid interpretation of type theory [12]. To justify that 2TT solves the aforementioned problems with the computational interpretation of higher-dimensional type theory, we prove canonicity in Section 3, showing that a closed term of boolean type is definitionally equal to either true or false. The proof may be seen as a generalization of the semantics of the NuPRL type theory [5] (in turn based on Tait's reducibility method): in our proof, types are interpreted as groupoids [12], rather than as equivalence relations.

2. Syntax

Judgemental Framework As discussed above, we achieve canonicity in 2TT using a judgemental presentation of equivalence. First, this means that, starting from the usual judgement forms of contexts Γ ctx, dependent types $\Gamma \vdash A$ type (where Γ ctx), and terms

Identity and composition for $\Gamma \vdash \theta : \Delta$

$$\frac{\Gamma \supseteq \Delta}{\Gamma \vdash \mathsf{id}^{\Gamma}_{\Delta} : \Delta} \qquad \frac{\Gamma_2 \vdash \theta_2 : \Gamma_3 \quad \Gamma_1 \vdash \theta_1 : \Gamma_2}{\Gamma_1 \vdash \theta_2[\theta_1] : \Gamma_3} \qquad \frac{\Gamma \vdash \theta : \Delta \quad \Gamma_0 \vdash \delta : \theta_1 \simeq_{\Gamma} \theta_2}{\Gamma_0 \vdash \theta[\delta] : \theta[\theta_1] \simeq_{\Delta} \theta[\theta_2]}$$

$\theta_0[\theta[\theta']]$	$\equiv$	$\theta_0[\theta][\theta']$	*1-subst assoc/unit*
$\theta_0[\mathsf{id}_{\Gamma}]$	$\equiv$	θ_0	
$\mathsf{id}^{\Gamma}_{\Gamma}[\theta]$	$\equiv$	θ	
$\theta[\delta[\delta']]$	$\equiv$	$\theta[\delta][\delta']$	*1-resp assoc*
$\theta[\mathsf{refl}_{\theta'}]$	$\equiv$	$\mathsf{refl}_{\theta[\theta']}$	*1-resp preserves refl.*
$\theta[\theta'][\delta]$	$\equiv$	$\theta[\theta'[\delta]]$	*1-resp for 1-subst*

Identity, Inverses, and Composition for $\Gamma \vdash \delta : \theta \simeq_{\Delta} \theta'$

$$\frac{}{\Gamma \vdash \mathsf{refl}^{\Delta}_{\theta} : \theta \simeq_{\Delta} \theta} \qquad \frac{\Gamma \vdash \delta : \theta_1 \simeq_{\Delta} \theta_2}{\Gamma \vdash \delta^{-1} : \theta_2 \simeq_{\Delta} \theta_1} \qquad \frac{\Gamma \vdash \delta_1 : \theta_1 \simeq_{\Delta} \theta_2 \quad \Gamma \vdash \delta_2 : \theta_2 \simeq_{\Delta} \theta_3}{\Gamma \vdash \delta_2 \circ \delta_1 : \theta_1 \simeq_{\Delta} \theta_3} \qquad \frac{\Gamma \vdash \delta : \theta \simeq_{\Delta} \theta' \quad \Gamma_0 \vdash \delta_0 : \theta_0 \simeq_{\Gamma} \theta'_0}{\Gamma_0 \vdash \delta[\delta_0] : \theta[\theta_0] \simeq_{\Delta} \theta'[\theta'_0]}$$

$(\delta_3 \circ \delta_2) \circ \delta_1$	$\equiv$	$\delta_3 \circ (\delta_2 \circ \delta_1)$	*trans assoc/unit*
$(\delta \circ \mathsf{refl})$	$\equiv$	δ	
$(\mathsf{refl} \circ \delta)$	$\equiv$	δ	
$(\delta \circ \delta^{-1})$	$\equiv$	refl	*inverse*
$(\delta^{-1} \circ \delta)$	$\equiv$	refl	

$\delta_0[\delta[\delta']]$	$\equiv$	$\delta_0[\delta][\delta']$	*2-resp assoc/unit*
$\delta_0[\mathsf{refl}_{\mathsf{id}}]$	$\equiv$	δ_0	
$\mathsf{refl}_{\mathsf{id}^{\Gamma}_{\Gamma}}[\delta]$	$\equiv$	δ	
$(\delta_1 \circ \delta_2)[\delta_3 \circ \delta_4]$	$\equiv$	$\delta_1[\delta_3] \circ \delta_2[\delta_4]$	*interchange*
$\mathsf{refl}_{\theta}[\delta]$	$\equiv$	$\theta[\delta]$	*delegate*

Composition for $\Gamma \vdash A$ type

$$\frac{\Gamma \vdash \theta : \Delta \quad \Delta \vdash A\ \mathsf{type}}{\Gamma \vdash A[\theta]\ \mathsf{type}} \qquad \frac{\Delta\ \mathsf{ctx} \quad \Delta \vdash C\ \mathsf{type} \quad \Gamma \vdash \delta : \theta_1 \simeq_{\Delta} \theta_2 \quad \Gamma \vdash M : C[\theta_1]}{\Gamma \vdash \mathsf{map}_{\Delta.C}\ \delta\ M : C[\theta_2]}$$

$A[\theta[\theta']]$	$\equiv$	$A[\theta][\theta']$	*0-subst assoc/unit*
$A[\mathsf{id}_{\Gamma}]$	$\equiv$	A	
$\mathsf{map}_{\Delta.C}\ \mathsf{refl}_{\theta}\ M$	$\equiv$	M	*0-resp functoriality*
$\mathsf{map}_{\Delta.C}\ (\delta_2 \circ \delta_1)\ M$	$\equiv$	$\mathsf{map}_{\Delta.C}\ \delta_2\ (\mathsf{map}_{\Delta.C}\ \delta_1\ M)$	
$(\mathsf{map}_{\Delta.C}\ \delta\ M)[\theta_0]$	$\equiv$	$\mathsf{map}_{\Delta.C}\ \delta[\mathsf{refl}_{\theta_0}]\ M[\theta_0]$	*1-subst for* map
$(\mathsf{map}_{C}\ (\delta : \theta_1 \simeq \theta_2)\ M)[\delta' : \theta'_1 \simeq \theta'_2]$	$\equiv$	$\mathsf{resp}\ (x.\mathsf{map}_{C}\ (\delta[\mathsf{refl}_{\theta'_2}])\ x)\ (M[\delta'])$	*1-resp for* map
$\mathsf{map}_{\Delta.C[\theta : \Delta']}\ \delta\ M$	$\equiv$	$\mathsf{map}_{\Delta'.C}\ \mathsf{refl}_{\theta}[\delta]\ M$	*def.* map *for* $A[\theta]$

Composition for $\Gamma \vdash M : A$

$$\frac{\Gamma \vdash \theta : \Delta \quad \Delta \vdash M : A}{\Gamma \vdash M[\theta] : A[\theta]} \qquad \frac{\Delta \vdash M : A \quad \Gamma \vdash \delta : \theta_1 \simeq_{\Delta} \theta_2}{\Gamma \vdash M[\delta] : (\mathsf{map}_{\Delta.A}\ \delta\ (M[\theta_1])) \simeq_{A[\theta_2]} M[\theta_2]}$$

$M[\theta[\theta']]$	$\equiv$	$M[\theta][\theta']$	*1-subst assoc/unit*
$M[\mathsf{id}_{\Gamma}]$	$\equiv$	M	
$M[\delta[\delta']]$	$\equiv$	$M[\delta][\delta']$	*1-resp assoc/unit*
$M[\mathsf{refl}_{\theta}]$	$\equiv$	$\mathsf{refl}_{M[\theta]}$	*1-resp preserves refl.*
$M[\theta][\delta]$	$\equiv$	$M[\theta[\delta]]$	*1-resp for 1-subst*

Identity, Inverses, and Composition for $\Gamma \vdash \alpha : M \simeq_A N$

$$\frac{}{\Gamma \vdash \mathsf{refl}^{A}_{M} : M \simeq_A M} \qquad \frac{\Gamma \vdash \alpha : M_1 \simeq_A M_2}{\Gamma \vdash \alpha^{-1} : M_2 \simeq_A M_1} \qquad \frac{\Gamma \vdash \alpha_1 : M_1 \simeq_A M_2 \quad \Gamma \vdash \alpha_2 : M_2 \simeq_A M_3}{\Gamma \vdash \alpha_2 \circ \alpha_1 : M_1 \simeq_A M_3} \qquad \frac{\Gamma_0 \vdash \delta_0 : \theta_0 \simeq_{\Gamma} \theta'_0 \quad \Gamma \vdash \alpha : M \simeq_A N}{\Gamma_0 \vdash \alpha[\delta_0] : (\mathsf{map}_{\Gamma.A}\ \delta_0\ (M[\theta_0])) \simeq_{A[\theta'_0]} N[\theta'_0]}$$

$(\alpha_3 \circ \alpha_2) \circ \alpha_1$	$\equiv$	$\alpha_3 \circ (\alpha_2 \circ \alpha_1)$	*trans assoc/unit*
$(\alpha \circ \mathsf{refl})$	$\equiv$	α	
$(\mathsf{refl} \circ \alpha)$	$\equiv$	α	
$(\alpha \circ \alpha^{-1})$	$\equiv$	refl	*inverse*
$(\alpha^{-1} \circ \alpha)$	$\equiv$	refl	
$\alpha[\delta[\delta']]$	$\equiv$	$\alpha[\delta][\delta']$	*2-resp assoc/unit*
$\alpha[\mathsf{refl}_{\mathsf{id}}]$	$\equiv$	α	
$(\alpha_1 \circ \alpha_2)[\delta_3 \circ \delta_4]$	$\equiv$	$\alpha_1[\delta_3] \circ \mathsf{resp}\ (x.\mathsf{map}\ \delta_3\ x)\ (\alpha_2[\delta_4])$	*interchange*
$\mathsf{refl}_M[\delta]$	$\equiv$	$M[\delta]$	*delegate*

Omitted Rules: All judgements respect equality; all equality judgements are congruences.

Derived forms:

$\mathsf{resp}\ (x.F)\ \alpha$	means	$(x.F)[\mathsf{refl}_{\mathsf{id}}, \alpha/x]$
$\mathsf{map}^1_{x:A.B}\ \alpha\ M$	means	$\mathsf{map}_{\Gamma,x:A.B}\ (\mathsf{refl}_{\mathsf{id}}, \alpha/x)\ M$

Figure 1. Judgemental Presentation of Equivalence

Empty context:

$$\frac{}{\cdot\ \mathsf{ctx}} \quad \text{(id. is the only canonical substitution)} \quad (\mathsf{refl}_{\mathsf{id.}} \text{ is the only canonical equivalence}) \quad \begin{array}{lcll} \theta : \cdot & \equiv & \mathsf{id.} & \textit{1-}\eta \\ \delta : \theta \simeq_{\cdot} \theta' & \equiv & \mathsf{refl.} & \textit{2-}\eta \end{array}$$

Term variables:

$$\frac{\Gamma\ \mathsf{ctx} \quad \Gamma \vdash A\ \mathsf{type}}{\Gamma\,,\, x{:}A\ \mathsf{ctx}} \qquad \frac{x{:}A \in \Gamma}{\Gamma \vdash x : A} \qquad \frac{\Gamma \vdash \theta : \Delta \quad \Gamma \vdash M : A[\theta]}{\Gamma \vdash \theta, M/x : \Delta, x : A} \qquad \frac{\Gamma \vdash \delta : \theta \simeq_\Delta \theta' \quad \Gamma \vdash \alpha : (\mathsf{map}_{\Delta.A}\ \delta\ M) \simeq_{A[\theta']} N}{\Gamma \vdash (\delta, \alpha/x) : (\theta, M/x) \simeq_{\Delta, x:A} (\theta', N/x)}$$

$$\begin{array}{rcll}
\mathsf{id}_\Gamma^{\Gamma, x:A}[\theta, M/x] & \equiv & \theta & \textit{1-}\beta \\
x[\theta, M/x] & \equiv & M & \textit{1-}\beta \\
\theta : (\Gamma\,,\, x{:}A) & \equiv & \mathsf{id}_\Gamma[\theta], x[\theta]/x & \textit{1-}\eta \\
\mathsf{id}_\Gamma^{\Gamma, x:A}[\delta, \alpha/x] & \equiv & \delta & \textit{2-}\beta \\
x[\delta, \alpha/x] & \equiv & \alpha & \textit{2-}\beta \\
\delta : \theta \simeq_{(\Gamma, x:A)} \theta' & \equiv & \mathsf{id}_\Gamma[\delta], x[\delta]/x & \textit{2-}\eta
\end{array}
\qquad
\begin{array}{rcll}
\mathsf{id}_{\Gamma, x:A} & \equiv & \mathsf{id}_\Gamma, x/x & \textit{1-id} \\
(\theta, M/x)[\theta_0] & \equiv & \theta[\theta_0], M[\theta_0]/x & \textit{1-subst} \\
(\theta, M/x)[\delta_0] & \equiv & \theta[\delta_0], M[\delta_0]/x & \textit{1-resp} \\
\mathsf{refl}_{\theta, M/x} & \equiv & \mathsf{refl}_\theta, \mathsf{refl}_M/x & \textit{refl} \\
(\delta, \alpha/x)^{-1} & \equiv & (\delta^{-1}, (\mathsf{resp}\ (x.\mathsf{map}_{\Delta.A}\ \delta^{-1}\ x)\ \alpha^{-1})/x) & \textit{sym} \\
(\delta_2, \alpha_2/x) \circ (\delta_1, \alpha_1/x) & \equiv & (\delta_2 \circ \delta_1), (\alpha_2 \circ \mathsf{resp}\ (x.\mathsf{map}_{\Delta.A}\ \delta_2\ x)\ \alpha_1)/x & \textit{trans} \\
(\delta, \alpha/x)[\delta_0] & \equiv & \delta[\delta_0], \alpha[\delta_0]/x & \textit{2-resp}
\end{array}$$

Figure 2. Contexts

$$\frac{\Gamma \vdash A\ \mathsf{type} \quad \Gamma\,,\, x{:}A \vdash B\ \mathsf{type}}{\Gamma \vdash \Pi\, x{:}A.\, B\ \mathsf{type}} \qquad \frac{\Gamma\,,\, x{:}A \vdash M : B}{\Gamma \vdash \lambda\, x.\, M : \Pi\, x{:}A.\, B} \qquad \frac{\Gamma \vdash M_1 : \Pi\, x{:}A.\, B \quad \Gamma \vdash M_2 : A}{\Gamma \vdash M_1\ M_2 : B[M_2/x]} \qquad \frac{\Gamma\,,\, x{:}A \vdash \alpha : (M\ x) \simeq_B (N\ x)}{\Gamma \vdash \lambda\, x.\, \alpha : M \simeq_{\Pi\, x:A.\, B} N} \qquad \frac{\Gamma \vdash \alpha : M \simeq_{\Pi\, x:A.\, B} N \quad \Gamma \vdash \beta : M_1 \simeq_A N_1}{\Gamma \vdash \alpha\, \beta : \mathsf{map}^1_B\ \beta\ (M M_1) \simeq_{B[N_1/x]} (N N_1)}$$

$$\begin{array}{rcll}
(\lambda\, x.\, M)\ N & \equiv & M[N/x] & \textit{1-}\beta \\
M : \Pi\, x{:}A.\, B & \equiv & \lambda\, x.\, M\ x & \textit{1-}\eta \\
(\lambda\, x.\, \alpha_1)\ \alpha_2 & \equiv & \alpha_1[\mathsf{refl}, \alpha_2/x] & \textit{2-}\beta \\
\alpha : M \simeq_{\Pi\, x:A.\, B} N & \equiv & \lambda\, x.\, \alpha\ (\mathsf{refl}_x) & \textit{2-}\eta \\
 & & & \\
(\Pi\, x{:}A.\, B)[\theta_0] & \equiv & \Pi\, x{:}A[\theta_0].\, B[\theta_0, x/x] & \textit{0-subst} \\
\mathsf{map}_{\Delta.\Pi\, x:A.\, B}\ \delta\ M & \equiv & & \textit{0-resp} \\
\multicolumn{4}{r}{\lambda\, x.\, \mathsf{map}_{\Delta, x:A.B}\ (\delta, \mathsf{refl}/x)\ (M\ (\mathsf{map}_{\Delta.A}\ \delta^{-1}\ x))}
\end{array}
\qquad
\begin{array}{lcll}
(\lambda\, x.\, M)[\theta_0] & \equiv & \lambda\, x.\, M[(\theta_0, x/x)] & \textit{1-subst} \\
(M_1\ M_2)[\theta_0] & \equiv & (M_1[\theta_0])\ (M_2[\theta_0]) & \textit{1-subst} \\
(\lambda\, x.\, M)[\delta] & \equiv & \lambda\, x.\, M[\delta, \mathsf{refl}/x] & \textit{1-resp} \\
(M\ N)[\delta] & \equiv & M[\delta]\ N[\delta] & \textit{1-resp} \\
 & & & \\
\mathsf{refl}_M & \equiv & \lambda\, x.\, \mathsf{refl}_{M\ x} & \textit{refl} \\
(\lambda\, x.\, \alpha)^{-1} & \equiv & \lambda\, x.\, \alpha^{-1} & \textit{sym} \\
(\lambda\, x.\, \alpha_2) \circ (\lambda\, x.\, \alpha_1) & \equiv & \lambda\, x.\, \alpha_2 \circ \alpha_1 & \textit{trans} \\
(\lambda\, x{:}A.\, \alpha)[\delta_0] & \equiv & \lambda\, x{:}A[\theta'_0].\, \alpha[\delta_0, \mathsf{refl}/x] & \textit{2-resp} \\
(\alpha_1\ \alpha_2)[\delta_0] & \equiv & (\alpha_1[\delta_0])\ (\alpha_2[\delta_0]) & \textit{2-resp}
\end{array}$$

Figure 3. Π-Types

$$\frac{}{\Gamma \vdash 2\ \mathsf{type}} \qquad \frac{}{\Gamma \vdash \mathsf{true} : 2} \qquad \frac{}{\Gamma \vdash \mathsf{false} : 2} \qquad \frac{\Gamma \vdash M : 2 \quad \Gamma\,,\, x{:}2 \vdash C\ \mathsf{type} \quad \Gamma \vdash M_1 : C[\mathsf{true}/x] \quad \Gamma \vdash M_2 : C[\mathsf{false}/x]}{\Gamma \vdash \mathsf{if}_{x.C}(M, M_1, M_2) : C[M/x]} \qquad \frac{\Gamma \vdash M : 2 \quad \Gamma\,,\, x{:}2 \vdash C\ \mathsf{type} \quad \Gamma\,,\, x{:}2 \vdash M_1, M_2 : C \quad \Gamma \vdash \alpha_1 : M_1[\mathsf{true}/x] \simeq_{C[\mathsf{true}/x]} M_2[\mathsf{true}/x] \quad \Gamma \vdash \alpha_2 : M_1[\mathsf{false}/x] \simeq_{C[\mathsf{false}/x]} M_2[\mathsf{false}/x]}{\Gamma \vdash \mathsf{if}_{x.C}(M, \alpha_1, \alpha_2) : M_1[M/x] \simeq_{C[M/x]} M_2[M/x]}$$

$$(\mathsf{refl}_{\mathsf{true}} \text{ and } \mathsf{refl}_{\mathsf{false}} \text{ are canonical}) \qquad \frac{\Gamma \vdash \alpha : M \simeq_2 N}{\Gamma \vdash M \equiv N}\ \textit{reflection} \qquad \frac{\Gamma \vdash \alpha : M \simeq_2 N}{\Gamma \vdash \alpha \equiv \mathsf{refl}_M}\ \textit{uip} \qquad \frac{\Gamma \vdash \alpha : \mathsf{true} \simeq_2 \mathsf{false}}{\Gamma \vdash \mathcal{J}} \quad \text{(where } \mathcal{J} \text{ is any judgement)}$$

$$\begin{array}{rcll}
\mathsf{if}(\mathsf{true}, M_1, M_2) & \equiv & M_1 & \textit{1-}\beta \\
\mathsf{if}(\mathsf{false}, M_1, M_2) & \equiv & M_2 & \textit{1-}\beta \\
M[(N : El(2))/x] & \equiv & \mathsf{if}(N, M[\mathsf{true}/x], M[\mathsf{false}/x]) & \textit{1-}\eta \\
\mathsf{if}_{x.C}(\mathsf{true}, \alpha_1, \alpha_2) & \equiv & \alpha_1 & \textit{12-}\beta \\
\mathsf{if}_{x.C}(\mathsf{false}, \alpha_1, \alpha_2) & \equiv & \alpha_2 & \textit{12-}\beta \\
\alpha[(\mathsf{refl}_{M\,:\,2})/x] & \equiv & \mathsf{if}(M, \alpha[\mathsf{refl}_{\mathsf{true}}/x], \alpha[\mathsf{refl}_{\mathsf{false}}/x]) & \textit{12-}\eta \\
 & & & \\
2[\theta] & \equiv & 2 & \textit{0-subst} \\
\mathsf{map}_{\Delta.2}\ \delta\ M & \equiv & M & \textit{0-resp}
\end{array}
\qquad
\begin{array}{rcll}
\mathsf{true}[\theta] & \equiv & \mathsf{true} & \textit{1-subst} \\
\mathsf{false}[\theta] & \equiv & \mathsf{false} & \textit{1-subst} \\
\mathsf{if}_{x\,:\,2.C}(M, M_1, M_2)[\theta] & \equiv & & \textit{1-subst} \\
\multicolumn{4}{l}{\quad \mathsf{if}_{x\,:\,2.C[\theta, x/x]}(M[\theta], M_1[\theta], M_2[\theta])} \\
 & & & \\
\mathsf{true}[\delta] & \equiv & \mathsf{refl}_{\mathsf{true}} & \textit{1-resp} \\
\mathsf{false}[\delta] & \equiv & \mathsf{refl}_{\mathsf{false}} & \textit{1-resp} \\
\mathsf{if}_{x\,:\,2.C}(M, M_1, M_2)[\delta : \theta_1 \simeq \theta_2] & \equiv & & \textit{1-resp} \\
\multicolumn{4}{l}{\quad \mathsf{if}_{x\,:\,2.C[\theta_2, x/x]}(M[\theta_2], M_1[\delta], M_2[\delta])} \\
 & & & \\
\mathsf{refl} & & \text{is canonical} & \\
_^{-1}, _ \circ _ & & \text{trivial by } \textit{uip} & \\
\mathsf{if}(M, \alpha_1, \alpha_2)[\delta : \theta_1 \simeq \theta_2] & \equiv & \mathsf{if}(M[\theta_2], \alpha_1[\delta], \alpha_2[\delta]) & \textit{2-resp}
\end{array}$$

Figure 4. Booleans (as an Extensional Set)

$$\frac{}{\Gamma \vdash \mathsf{set\ type}} \quad \frac{\Gamma \vdash S : \mathsf{set}}{\Gamma \vdash \mathit{El}(S)\ \mathsf{type}}$$

$$\frac{\Gamma \vdash \alpha : M \simeq_{\mathit{El}(S)} N}{\Gamma \vdash M \equiv N} \quad \frac{\Gamma \vdash \alpha : M \simeq_{\mathit{El}(S)} N}{\Gamma \vdash \alpha \equiv \mathsf{refl}_M}$$

$$\begin{array}{rcll} \mathsf{set}[\theta_0] & \equiv & \mathsf{set} & \textit{0-subst} \\ (\mathit{El}(S))[\theta_0] & \equiv & \mathit{El}(S[\theta_0]) & \\ \mathsf{map}_{\Delta.\mathsf{set}}\ \delta\ M & \equiv & M & \textit{0-resp} \\ -^{-1}, - \circ - \text{ for set} & & \text{groupoid laws plus below} & \\ \mathsf{refl}_{M\,:\,\mathit{El}(S)} & & \text{is canonical} & \\ -^{-1}, - \circ -, \text{2-resp for } \mathit{El}(S) & & \text{trivial by } \textit{uip} & \end{array}$$

$$\frac{}{\Gamma \vdash \mathsf{bool} : \mathsf{set}} \ (\mathsf{refl}_{\mathsf{bool}} \text{ is canonical}) \quad \frac{}{\Gamma \vdash \mathsf{not} : \mathsf{bool} \simeq_{\mathsf{set}} \mathsf{bool}} \quad \frac{\Gamma \vdash M : 2}{\Gamma \vdash \mathsf{in}\ M : \mathit{El}(\mathsf{bool})} \quad \frac{\Gamma \vdash M : \mathit{El}(\mathsf{bool})}{\Gamma \vdash \mathsf{out}\ M : 2}$$

$$\begin{array}{rclll} \mathsf{out}\,(\mathsf{in}\ M) & \equiv & M & & \textit{1-}\beta \\ \mathsf{in}\,(\mathsf{out}\ M) & \equiv & M & & \textit{1-}\eta \\ \mathsf{map}_{\Delta.\mathit{El}(S)}\ \delta\ \mathsf{true} & \equiv & \mathsf{false} & \text{if } S[\delta] \equiv \mathsf{not} & \textit{0-resp} \\ \mathsf{map}_{\Delta.\mathit{El}(S)}\ \delta\ \mathsf{false} & \equiv & \mathsf{true} & \text{if } S[\delta] \equiv \mathsf{not} & \textit{0-resp} \end{array}$$

$$\begin{array}{rcll} \mathsf{bool}[\theta] & \equiv & \mathsf{bool} & \textit{1-subst} \\ (\mathsf{in}\ M)[\theta] & \equiv & \mathsf{in}\ M[\theta] & \textit{1-subst} \\ (\mathsf{out}\ M)[\theta] & \equiv & \mathsf{out}\ M[\theta] & \textit{1-subst} \\ \mathsf{bool}[\delta] & \equiv & \mathsf{refl}_{\mathsf{bool}} & \textit{1-resp} \\ \mathsf{not}^{-1} & \equiv & \mathsf{not} & \textit{sym} \\ \mathsf{not}[\delta] & \equiv & \mathsf{not} & \textit{2-resp} \end{array}$$

Figure 5. Universe

$\Gamma \vdash M : A$ (where Γ ctx and $\Gamma \vdash A$ type), we add a judgement of term equivalences $\Gamma \vdash \alpha : M \simeq_A M'$ (where Γ ctx and $\Gamma \vdash A$ type and $\Gamma \vdash M, M' : A$). Second, this equivalence judgement is defined by rules specific to each type A, including equations explaining the meaning of identity (refl), inverses (α^{-1}), and composition ($\alpha_2 \circ \alpha_1$) at each type. Third, all families of types and terms respect equivalence, as expressed by the following operations:

$$\frac{\Gamma, x{:}A \vdash B\ \mathsf{type} \quad \Gamma \vdash \alpha : M_1 \simeq_A M_2 \quad \Gamma \vdash M : B[M_1/x]}{\Gamma \vdash \mathsf{map}^{1}_{x:A.B}\ \alpha\ M : B[M_2/x]}$$

$$\frac{\Gamma \vdash \alpha : M \simeq_A N \quad \Gamma, x{:}A \vdash F : B}{\Gamma \vdash \mathsf{resp}\ (x.F)\ \alpha : F[M/x] \simeq_B F[N/x]}$$

map expresses that a family of types indexed by A respects equivalence at A: Given equivalent terms M_1 and M_2, map determines a function from $B[M_1/x]$ to $B[M_2/x]$. As we discuss below, this function has an inverse given by $\mathsf{map}^1_{x:A.B}\ \alpha^{-1}$, so $B[M_1/x]$ and $B[M_2/x]$ are isomorphic. Similarly, resp $(x.F)\ \alpha$ expresses that a family of terms of type B (where x is not free in B) with a free variable $x{:}A$ respects equivalence at A. $\mathsf{map}^1_{x:A.B}\ \alpha\ M$ computes on the structure of the family B, while resp $(x.F)\ \alpha$ computes on the structure of the family F. There is an additional resp-like operation which expresses that equivalences themselves respect equivalence.

To define these operations, it is helpful to consider n-ary families such as $x_1{:}A_1, x_2{:}A_2, \ldots, x_n{:}A_n.B$. To this end, we present 2TT as an explicit substitution calculus, with additional judgements for substitutions $\Gamma \vdash \theta : \Delta$ (where Γ ctx and Δ ctx) and equivalences between them $\Gamma \vdash \delta : \theta \simeq_\Delta \theta'$ (where Γ ctx and Δ ctx and $\Gamma \vdash \theta, \theta' : \Delta$). The treatment of dependent types in Pitts [20]'s survey article provides an introduction to this style of syntax, with an explicit substitution judgement and internalized composition principles. In full generality, map and resp express respect for equivalence between substitutions for a whole context, and are written $\mathsf{map}_{\Delta.C}\ \delta\ M$ and $M[\delta]$ respectively. An analogous operation $\alpha[\delta]$ expresses that equivalence itself respects equivalence, while $\theta[\delta]$ and $\delta[\delta']$ extend these resp-principles to substitutions for an entire context, and equivalences between them.

The rules for this judgemental framework are presented in Figure 1. We present the definitional equality rules as equations (e.g. $\theta \equiv \theta'$), as a notational shorthand for inference rules defining typed equality judgements (e.g. $\Gamma \vdash \theta \equiv \theta' : \Delta$). By convention, each equation implicitly has premises asserting that each of the metavariables occuring in the equation are well-typed, and maintains the invariant that the subjects of the equation are well-typed given these assumptions. Showing that the two sides of the equation have the same type sometimes involves definitional equality reasoning, but the equation being defined is never necessary for showing that its subjects have the same type.

The first three rules define identity and composition for substitutions. To improve readability, we make weakening admissible (rather than using de Bruijn form), so the identity substitution id is really the composition of the identity substitution with projections that forget any number of variables. We write $\Gamma \supseteq \Delta$ to mean that Δ is obtained from Γ by dropping some number of variables. All judgements of the form $\Gamma \vdash J$ are weakenable: If $\Gamma \vdash J$ and $\Gamma' \supseteq \Gamma$ then $\Gamma' \vdash J$. Composition of substitutions $\theta_2[\theta_2]$, which we refer to as 1-substitution, is standard in explicit substitution calculi. The additional composition operation, $\theta[\delta]$, forces substitutions to respect equivalence, analogously to resp for terms above: substitution instances by equivalent substitutions are equivalent. For this reason, we refer to it as *1-resp*. The first three equations say that 1-substitution is associative and unital. In the second equation, id_Γ can in fact be a weakening, in which case θ is tacitly weakened in the right-hand side. The third equation only makes sense when $\Gamma \vdash \mathsf{id} : \Gamma$, which we notate by $\mathsf{id}^\Gamma_\Gamma$. The next two rules say that *1-resp* associates with *2-resp* ($\delta[\delta']$), which is the analogous operation for equivalences (defined below), and preserves identities refl(defined below).

The next four rules define identity, inverses, and composition for equivalences. Equivalences are always reflexive (refl), symmetric (δ^{-1}), and transitive ($\delta_2 \circ \delta_1$). Additionally, equivalences themselves respect equivalence ($\delta[\delta_0]$), which we call *2-resp*. The equations say that: Transitivity is associative, with unit refl, and inverses given by $-^{-1}$. *2-resp* is also associative and unital, with unit $\Gamma \vdash \mathsf{refl}_{\mathsf{id}^\Gamma_\Gamma} : \mathsf{id}_\Gamma \simeq_\Gamma \mathsf{id}_\Gamma$ (by above, $\theta[\mathsf{id}_\Gamma]$ equals θ). The *interchange law* relates *2-resp* and transitivity: transitivity followed by *2-resp* is the same as *2-resp* followed by transitivity. This is a coherence requirement between the two forms of composition in a 2-category; we discuss some special cases in the extended version of this article [13].

The rule *delegate* delegates *2-resp* at reflexivity to *1-resp*. We do not define *2-subst*, $\delta[\theta]$, directly, as this composition is definable as $\delta[\mathsf{refl}_\theta]$.

Next, we define the corresponding operations for dependent types, terms, and term equivalences. A dependent type A can be pre-composed with a substitution, written $A[\theta]$; and has a functorial action $\mathsf{map}_{\Delta.A}\ \delta\ M$, which expresses that families of types respect equivalence. We refer to these as *0-subst* and *0-resp*. The equations say: Substitution into types (*0-subst*) is associative with unit refl. map is functorial, preserving reflexivity and transitivity. The next two rules define *1-subst* and *1-resp* for map, which reassociate the

1-subst/*1-resp* with the *0-resp*. The next rule defines map for a composition, again by reassociating.

Like all contextual judgements, terms are closed under substitution ($M[\theta]$) and respect equivalence ($M[\delta]$). Because terms are dependent on the context, the latter requires "adjusting" $M[\theta_1]$ by δ so that it lives in the same type as $M[\theta_2]$. The equality rules are analogous to those for substitutions: *1-subst* is associative and unital, and *1-resp* is associative and preserves reflexivities.

The rules for term equivalences are analogous to the rules for equivalences, specifying reflexivity, transitivity, and *2-resp*. The equations say that transitivity is associative, invertible, and unital, that *2-resp* is associative and unital, and that the order of trans and *2-resp* can be interchanged. The interchange rule uses the derived form resp, described above.

Contexts The general methodology for defining a context is to specify (1) A formation rule for Γ. (2) A substitution rule $\theta : \Gamma$, and a hypothesis rule for one of the other judgements (e.g. the term rule for x for the context former $\Gamma\ ,\ x{:}A$). These function as the introduction and elimination rules for the context, which are products of some sort, eliminated by first projections (which are implicit in id) and variables (representing projections). (3) An equivalence rule for $\delta : \theta \simeq_\Gamma \theta'$ (4) Equations defining *1-βη* (*βη* for θ), *2-βη* (*βη* for δ), *identity* id_Γ, *1-subst* $\theta[\theta']$, *1-resp* $\theta[\delta']$, *reflexivity* refl_θ, *symmetry* δ^{-1}, *transitivity* $\delta \circ \delta'$, and *2-resp* $\delta[\delta']$. In general, refl and δ^{-1} and $\delta \circ \delta'$ are defined in a type-directed manner, while the *subst/resp* principles are defined in a syntax-directed manner, giving one rule for each syntactic construct.

In Figure 2 we carry out this methodology for the basic contexts: The empty context has a trivial substitution into it, and a trivial equivalence from this substitution to itself. For the equations, it suffices to stipulate that these are unique.

For context extension, if A is a type well-formed in Γ, then Γ can be extended with a variable of type A. A variable can be used as a term; the typing rule checks that the variable is in the context. The substitution into an extended context $\Delta\ ,x{:}A$ is a pair of a substitution θ into Δ and a term of type A, adjusted by θ (this is analogous to the usual introduction rule for a Σ-type). An equivalence between such substitutions is a pair of equivalences, one between the substitutions, and the other between the terms (adjusted by the first component). As these substitutions and equivalences are pairs, the first set of rules gives the expected $\beta\eta$ rules, for the projections given by id and variables. The next rules define the identity, composition, and inverse operations componentwise.

Π-types In general, a type is specified by (1) A formation rule for A. (2) Introduction and elimination rules for terms, defining $M : A$. (3) Introduction and elimination rules for equivalences, defining $\alpha : M \simeq_A M'$. (4) Equations defining *1-βη* (*βη* for M), *2-βη* (*βη* for α), *0-substitution* $A[\theta]$, *0-resp* $\mathsf{map}_A\ \delta\ M$, *1-substitution* $M[\theta]$, *1-resp* $M[\delta]$, *reflexivity* refl_M, *transitivity* $\alpha \circ \alpha'$, and *2-resp* $\alpha[\delta]$.

In Figure 3, we give the rules for dependent function types. The formation and term rules are standard. The equivalence introduction rule says that an equivalence at Π can be introduced by giving a family of equivalences that work for each element—the function extensionality rule. An equivalence is eliminated by applying to equivalent arguments, yielding an equivalence between the results. These rules have been considered in categorically-motivated accounts of functionally extensional propositional equality [9].

The $\beta\eta$-rules are the expected rules for functions, both at the term and equivalence levels. We write $M[N/x]$ to abbreviate $M[\mathsf{id}, N/x]$. Substitution into a Π-type proceeds compositionally. $\mathsf{map}_{\Pi\ x:A.\ B}$ is given by pre- and post-composition. *1-subst* and *1-resp* are both defined compositionally, as is *2-resp*. The rule for refl defines the identity at function type in terms of the componentwise identity.

The rules for dependent pairs, which are analogous to the rules for $\Gamma\ ,\ x{:}A$, are presented in the extended version [13].

Booleans In Figure 4, we give rules for a base type of booleans, including the usual true, false, and if-then-else constructs. We additionally include an if-then-else that eliminates towards equivalences, permitting equivalences to be defined by case distinction. For simplicity, we specify booleans as an *extensional set*, corresponding semantically to the discrete groupoid with two objects. This means that (1) equivalent booleans are definitionally equal (*reflection*) and (2) any equivalence is equal to reflexivity (*uip*). Finally, we include a rule stipulating that true and false are not equivalent, which would otherwise require large eliminations to prove. These rules illustrate that 2TT is compatible with treating discrete types as in extensional type theory, though a more intensional treatment of booleans is also possible. The $\beta\eta$-rules are standard for sum types; *0-resp* is trivial because 2 is a constant family; the *0/1-subst* rules are standard. The *1-resp* rule for if uses the equivalence-level if-then-else, and is well-typed because of *reflection*; the *2-resp* rule for if-then-else is analogous. No specific equations need to be given for $-^{-1}$ and $- \circ -$ because of *uip*.

Sets and elements Finally, we need to seed the type theory with a base type with non-trivial equivalences, and a family of types dependent on it, to ensure that we have an example where map really has computational content. A simple example is to consider a universe set that contains discrete types. That is, each term S : set will determine a type $El(S)$ whose elements have no non-identity equivalences between them. However, set itself is *not* a discrete type, because equivalence between sets S and T may be given by an isomorphism between $El(S)$ and $El(T)$:

$$\frac{f : S \to T \qquad \alpha : \lambda x.\, f(g(x)) \simeq \lambda x.\, x \qquad g : T \to S \qquad \beta : \lambda x.\, g(f(x)) \simeq \lambda x.\, x}{\mathsf{iso}(f, g, \alpha, \beta) : S \simeq_{\mathsf{set}} T}$$

Then $\mathsf{map}^1_{a:\mathsf{set}.C}\ (\mathsf{iso}(f, g, \alpha, \beta))$ asserts that all families of types respect isomorphism of sets.

In Figure 5, we define a simple universe of sets. We make two simplifications: first, the universe contains a code for exactly one set, booleans; second, equivalences are given explicitly by the two automorphisms on 2, refl (the identity function) and not. The approach readily scales to a richer universe closed under Π and Σ, following our previous work [14], and to programmer-defined isomorphisms given by $\mathsf{iso}(f, g, \alpha, \beta)$, as we show in the extended version of this article [13]. The first four rules define the type set and the family $El(-)$, and give *reflection* and *uip* for $El(-)$, expressing discreteness of sets in the universe. The equations for *0-subst* are compositional; *0-resp* for set is trivial because it is a constant family. For $M : El(S)$, *1-resp* generates an equation $\mathsf{map}_{El(S)}\ \delta\ M[\theta_1] \equiv M[\theta_2]$ by *reflection*, so no equations for $M[\delta]$ are necessary.

The next four inference rules specify the type 2: $El(\mathsf{bool})$ is isomorphic to 2 by in and out and their $\beta\eta$ rules. The two equivalences bool $\simeq_{\mathsf{set}}$ bool are $\mathsf{refl}_{\mathsf{bool}}$ (identity) and not (negation); map not *is* computationally relevant, as it interchanges true and false. The symmetry rule says that not is involutive.

3. Properties

3.1 Consistency

To show that the calculus is consistent, we can adapt Hofmann and Streicher's groupoid interpretation [12] to our formulation of 2TT. We have given a proof for a similar formalism for directed type theory in previous work [14]. We interpret each judgement as follows:

$[\![\Gamma]\!]$ is a category. $[\![\Gamma \vdash \theta : \Delta]\!]$ is a functor $[\![\theta]\!] : [\![\Gamma]\!] \longrightarrow [\![\Delta]\!]$. $[\![\Gamma \vdash \delta : \theta_1 \simeq_\Delta \theta_2]\!]$ is a natural transformation $[\![\delta]\!] : [\![\theta_1]\!] \simeq [\![\theta_2]\!] : [\![\Gamma]\!] \longrightarrow [\![\Delta]\!]$. $[\![A]\!]$ is a functor $[\![A]\!] : [\![\Gamma]\!] \longrightarrow GPD$, where *GPD* is the (large) category of groupoids and functors. Terms and term equivalences are interpreted as "dependent" functors and natural transformations. Because the details of this proof have been covered in previous work, we do not review them here. As a corollary of the interpretation, we get various consistency results: $[\![2]\!]$ is the discrete category on two objects, so the interpretation shows that it is not the case that $\cdot \vdash \mathsf{true} \equiv \mathsf{false} : 2$, or that $\cdot \vdash \alpha : \mathsf{true} \simeq_2 \mathsf{false}$. Moreover, if the calculus is extended with an empty type 0 interpreted as the empty category, the interpretation implies that not all types are inhabited. We do not attempt a proof-theoretic proof of consistency of definitional equality, e.g. using reduction or normalization-by-evaluation [7]. Proving consistency using these approaches typically involves giving a decision procedure for definitional equality, and equality for 2-dimensional type theory is not decidable, due to the equality reflection rules for identity types discussed in in Section 4. Given this, we also exploit equality reflection for 2 and $El(S)$, though these types could be treated in a more intensional way instead.

3.2 Canonicity

Our main new result in this paper is to check a kind of completeness, verifying that we have not omitted any necessary definitional equations for map, resp, etc. Specifically, we show that the equations of 2TT are sufficient to equate a closed term of type 2 to a value:

THEOREM 3.1: CANONICITY. *If* $\cdot \vdash M : 2$ *then either* $\cdot \vdash M \equiv \mathsf{true} : 2$ *or* $\cdot \vdash M \equiv \mathsf{false} : 2$.

This result fails for higher-dimensional type theory based on the univalence axiom [23], due to stuck applications of Id-elimination, as illustrated in the introduction—though it is currently conjectured that every closed term of boolean type may be *equivalent* to a value. In our setting, we prove the stronger result that canonicity holds for definitional equality.

The proof is organized as follows: First, we define the semantic domains into which we interpret, which consist of *syntactically presented groupoids and functors*. Using the usual terminology of logical relations, we say that an expression is "reducible" iff it is a member of these semantic domains. In a simple logical relations argument, open terms are reducible iff they take reducible arguments to reducible results. For 2-dimensional type theory, this generalizes to both (1) taking reducible terms to reducible terms and (2) taking reducible equivalences to reducible equivalences—i.e. functoriality. Analogous definitions are necessary for dependent types, dependently typed terms, and equivalences. Next, we show that the semantic domains are closed under the type formers, and prove the fundamental theorem, which says that all well-typed expressions are reducible. Finally, we obtain canonicity as a corollary.

3.2.1 Theorem Statement

Syntactically presented groupoids and functors

DEFINITION 3.2. *A groupoid G is presented by Γ (where Γ ctx) iff*

1. *The set of objects of G, written $Ob\ G$, is a subset of the equivalence classes of substitutions $\cdot \vdash \theta : \Gamma$ modulo definitional equality. Due to the preponderance of brackets in the syntax of 2TT, we write «θ» for the equivalence class of θ.*
2. *The set of morphisms «θ_1» $\longrightarrow_G$ «θ_2» is a subset of the equivalence classes of equivalences $\cdot \vdash \delta : \theta_1 \simeq_\Gamma \theta_2$ modulo definitional equality.*
3. *identity at «θ» is given by «refl_θ», composition of «δ_2» and «δ_1» is given by «$\delta_2 \circ \delta_1$», and the inverse of «δ» is given by «δ^{-1}».*

Note that we choose representatives of equivalence classes at various points in this definition; these uses are well-defined by the congruence laws for definitional equality. We write $\langle\Gamma\rangle$ to mean some groupoid that is presented by Γ, and use the analogous notation for the other syntactic presentations defined below.

Analogously, we define what it means for a groupoid to be presented by a closed type:

DEFINITION 3.3. *A groupoid G is presented by A (where $\cdot \vdash A$ type) iff*

1. *$Ob\ G$ is a subset of the equivalence classes of terms $\cdot \vdash M : A$ modulo definitional equality.*
2. *The set of morphisms «M_1» $\longrightarrow_G$ «M_2» is a subset of the equivalence classes of equivalences $\cdot \vdash \alpha : M_1 \simeq_\Gamma M_2$ modulo definitional equality.*
3. *identity at «M» is given by «refl_M», composition of «α_2» and «α_1» is given by «$\alpha_2 \circ \alpha_1$», and the inverse of «α» is given by «α^{-1}».*

A functor may be presented by a term with one free variable:

DEFINITION 3.4. *A functor $F : \langle A\rangle \longrightarrow \langle B\rangle$ is presented by M (where $x : A \vdash M : B$) iff*

1. *For all «N» $\in Ob\ \langle A\rangle$, $F($«N»$) =$ «$M[N/x]$».*
2. *For all «α» : «N_1» $\longrightarrow_{\langle A\rangle}$ «N_2», $F($«α»$) =$ «$M[\alpha/x]$».*

Let *GPD* be the category of groupoids and functors between them. A functor into *GPD* may be presented by a type:

DEFINITION 3.5. *A functor $F : \langle\Gamma\rangle \longrightarrow GPD$ is presented by A, where $\Gamma \vdash A$ type iff*

1. *For all «θ_1» $\in Ob\ \langle\Gamma\rangle$, $F($«θ_1»$)$ is presented by $A[\theta_1]$.*
2. *For all «δ» : «θ_1» $\longrightarrow_{\langle\Gamma\rangle}$ «θ_2», $F($«δ»$)$ is presented by $x : A[\theta_1].\mathsf{map}_A\ \delta\ x$.*

We write $\langle A\rangle$ for a functor presented by A.

Observe that all of these definitions respect definitional equality. For example, if G is presented by Γ, and $\Gamma \equiv \Gamma'$, then G is also presented by Γ'.

Reducible expressions Given these definitions, we can define the invariants about each syntactic category that are demanded by the proof:

DEFINITION 3.6. *Given groupoids $\langle\Gamma\rangle$ and $\langle\Delta\rangle$, define the set $RedSubst\ \langle\Gamma\rangle\ \langle\Delta\rangle$ (reducible substitutions) to be those substitutions $\Gamma \vdash \theta : \Delta$ such that*

1. *For all «θ_1» $\in Ob\ \langle\Gamma\rangle$, «$\theta[\theta_1]$» $\in Ob\ \langle\Delta\rangle$*
2. *For all «δ» : «θ_1» $\longrightarrow_{\langle\Gamma\rangle}$ «θ_2», «$\theta[\delta]$» : «$\theta[\theta_1]$» $\longrightarrow_{\langle\Delta\rangle}$ «$\theta[\theta_2]$»*

θ necessarily preserves identity and composition, by the corresponding rules of definitional equality. Thus, if $\theta \in RedSubst\langle\Gamma\rangle\langle\Delta\rangle$, then we can define a functor $\theta^* : \langle\Gamma\rangle \longrightarrow \langle\Delta\rangle$ using the given actions on objects and arrows.

DEFINITION 3.7. *Given $\langle\Gamma\rangle$ and $\langle\Delta\rangle$ and $\theta_1, \theta_2 \in RedSubst\langle\Gamma\rangle\langle\Delta\rangle$, define the set $RedEquiv^{\langle\Gamma\rangle}_{\langle\Delta\rangle}\ \theta_1\ \theta_2$ (reducible equivalences) to contain those $\Gamma \vdash \delta : \theta_1 \simeq_\Delta \theta_2$ such that for all «δ'» : «θ_1'» $\longrightarrow_{\langle\Gamma\rangle}$ «θ_2'», «$\delta[\delta']$» : «$\theta_1[\theta_1']$» $\longrightarrow_{\langle\Delta\rangle}$ «$\theta_2[\theta_2']$»*

As a special case, this means that for any $\theta \in Ob\ \langle\Gamma\rangle$, «$\delta[\mathsf{refl}_\theta]$» : «$\theta_1[\theta]$» $\longrightarrow_{\langle\Delta\rangle}$ «$\theta_2[\theta]$». This family of morphisms is natural (a consequence of the interchange law rule of definitional equality). Consequently, if δ is reducible, then it determines a natural isomorphism $\delta^* : \langle\theta_1\rangle \simeq \langle\theta_2\rangle : \langle\Gamma\rangle \longrightarrow \langle\Delta\rangle$. We write $RedEquiv\ \theta_1\ \theta_2$ for $RedEquiv^{\langle\Gamma\rangle}_{\langle\Delta\rangle}\ \theta_1\ \theta_2$ when the contexts are unambiguous.

DEFINITION 3.8. *Given a groupoid* $\langle\Gamma\rangle$ *and a functor* $\langle A\rangle$: $\langle\Gamma\rangle \longrightarrow$ *GPD, define the set* $RedTm^{\langle\Gamma\rangle}\ \langle A\rangle$ *(reducible terms) to be those terms* $\Gamma \vdash M : A$ *such that*

1. *For all* $«\theta_1» \in Ob\ \langle\Gamma\rangle$, $«M[\theta_1]» \in Ob\ \langle A\rangle(«\theta_1»)$
2. *For all* $«\delta» : «\theta_1» \longrightarrow_{\langle\Gamma\rangle} «\theta_2»$,
   $«M[\delta]» : «\mathsf{map}_A\ \delta\ M[\theta_1]» \longrightarrow_{\langle A\rangle(«\theta_2»)} «M[\theta_2]»$

We write $RedTm\ \langle A\rangle$ for $RedTm^{\langle\Gamma\rangle}\ \langle A\rangle$ when the context is unambiguous.

DEFINITION 3.9. *Given* $M, N \in RedTm^{\langle\Gamma\rangle}\ \langle A\rangle$, *define the set RedEquiv M N (reducible equivalences) to contain those* $\Gamma \vdash \alpha : M \simeq_A N$ *such that for all* $«\delta» : «\theta_1» \longrightarrow_{\langle\Gamma\rangle} «\theta_2»$, $«\alpha[\delta]» : «\mathsf{map}_A\ \delta\ M[\theta_1]» \longrightarrow_{\langle A\rangle(«\theta_2»)} «N[\theta_2]»$

Theorem Statement Using these definitions, we are in a position to state the fundamental theorem.

In the remainder of this section, we will define partial functions $[\![\Gamma]\!]$ and $[\![A]\!]$ such that:

THEOREM 3.10: FUNDAMENTAL THEOREM.

1. *If* Γ ctx *then* $[\![\Gamma]\!]$ *is a groupoid presented by* Γ.
2. *If* $\Gamma \equiv \Gamma'$ *then* $[\![\Gamma]\!] = [\![\Gamma']\!]$.
3. *If* $\Gamma \vdash \theta : \Delta$ *then* $\theta \in RedSubst\ [\![\Gamma]\!]\ [\![\Delta]\!]$
4. *If* $\Gamma \vdash \delta : \theta_1 \simeq_\Delta \theta_2$ *then* $\delta \in RedEquiv^{[\![\Gamma]\!]}_{[\![\Delta]\!]}\ \theta_1\ \theta_2$.
5. *If* $\Gamma \vdash A$ type *then* $[\![A]\!]$ *is a functor* $[\![\Gamma]\!] \longrightarrow$ *GPD presented by A.*
6. *If* $\Gamma \vdash A \equiv A'$ type *then* $[\![A]\!] = [\![A']\!]$.
7. *If* $\Gamma \vdash M : A$ *then* $M \in RedTm^{[\![\Gamma]\!]}\ [\![A]\!]$
8. *If* $\Gamma \vdash \alpha : M \simeq_A N$ *then* $\alpha \in RedEquiv^{[\![\Gamma]\!]}_{[\![A]\!]}\ M\ N$

The proof is by mutual induction on the given derivations.

As usual, the interpretation is defined compositionally, in terms of semantic counterparts of each type constructor:

$$\begin{aligned}
[\![\cdot]\!] &= \cdot \\
[\![\Gamma, x : A]\!] &= \textstyle\int_{[\![\Gamma]\!]} [\![A]\!] \\
[\![\Pi\, x{:}A.\, B]\!] &= \mathbf{\Pi}_{[\![A]\!]}\ [\![B]\!] \\
[\![2]\!] &= \mathbf{const}(\mathbf{2}) \\
[\![\mathsf{set}]\!] &= \mathbf{const}(\mathbf{set}) \\
[\![El(M)]\!] &= \mathbf{El}[M^*] \\
[\![A[\theta]]\!] &= [\![A]\!][\theta^*]
\end{aligned}$$

These should be understood as partial functions, due to the typing constraints on the semantic type formers, as described below. The fundamental theorem states that they are defined on all well-typed expressions.

3.2.2 Definitions of Semantic Contexts and Types

First, we give the inductive steps of the interpretation of contexts and types, describing the semantic analogue of each context and type constructor. For each context, we define a groupoid, and for each type, we define a functor $\langle\Gamma\rangle \longrightarrow$ *GPD*. Moreover, we prove that these constructions are presented by the appropriate contexts and types. The type-directed definitional equalities for refl, $-^{-1}$, and $- \circ -$, as well as the equations defining map_A , are used in these verifications.

Contexts Corresponding to the empty context, let $\cdot$ be the groupoid with one object, «id.», and one identity arrow, «$\mathsf{refl}_{\mathsf{id.}}$», and all compositions and inverses defined to be «$\mathsf{refl}_{\mathsf{id.}}$». Observe that this is presented by $\cdot$: the objects are classes of closed substitutions; the morphisms of closed equivalences; identity is «refl»; $«\delta»^{-1}$ is $«\delta^{-1}»$ = «refl» by 2η; and similarly for composition.

For context extension, given $\langle\Gamma\rangle$ and $\langle A\rangle : \langle\Gamma\rangle \longrightarrow$ *GPD*, the Grothendieck construction constructs a fibration from the total category $\int_{\langle\Gamma\rangle}\langle A\rangle$ to $\langle\Gamma\rangle$ given by a projection functor p. Concretely, we define $\int_{\langle\Gamma\rangle}\langle A\rangle$ so that it is presented by $\Gamma, x : A$:

1. An object $«(\theta, M/x)»$ is the equivalence class of a pair, where $«\theta» \in Ob\ \langle\Gamma\rangle$ and $«M» \in Ob\ \langle A\rangle(«\theta»)$.
2. A morphism $«(\delta, \alpha/x)» : «(\theta_1, M_1/x)» \longrightarrow_{\int_{\langle\Gamma\rangle}\langle A\rangle} «(\theta_2, M_2/x)»$ is the equivalence class of a pair, where $«\delta» : «\theta_1» \longrightarrow_{\langle\Gamma\rangle} «\theta_2»$ and $«\alpha» : «\mathsf{map}_A\ \delta\ M_1» \longrightarrow_{\langle A\rangle(«\theta_2»)} «M_2»$
3. Identity is defined to be

   $$«\mathsf{refl}_{(\theta,M/x)}» : «(\theta, M/x)» \longrightarrow_{\int_{\langle\Gamma\rangle}\langle A\rangle} «(\theta, M/x)»$$

   To verify that this is a morphism, we must show that it is the equivalence class of a pair of morphisms, each in the appropriate category. By definitional equality, $«\mathsf{refl}_{(\theta,M/x)}» = «(\mathsf{refl}_\theta, \mathsf{refl}_M/x)»$, so it remains to show that

   $$\begin{aligned}
   &«\mathsf{refl}_\theta» : «\theta» \longrightarrow_{\langle\Gamma\rangle} «\theta» \\
   &«\mathsf{refl}_M» : «\mathsf{map}_A\ \mathsf{refl}_\theta\ M» \longrightarrow_{\langle A\rangle(«\theta»)} «M».
   \end{aligned}$$

   For the first, because $\langle\Gamma\rangle$ is presented, «refl_θ» is a morphism in $\langle\Gamma\rangle$ (and is in fact the identity). For the second, «$\mathsf{map}_A\ \mathsf{refl}_\theta\ M$» = «$M$» by definitional equality, and because $\langle A\rangle$ is presented, $\langle A\rangle(\theta)$ is presented by $A[\theta]$, and therefore «refl_M» is a morphism (and moreover is the identity).

   The verification of the definition of symmetry by $«\delta»^{-1}$ = $«\delta^{-1}»$ and composition by $«\delta_1» \circ «\delta_1»$ = $«\delta_2 \circ \delta_1»$ is similar. The groupoid equations hold because they hold for definitional equality.

Observe that $\int_{\langle\Gamma\rangle}\langle A\rangle$ is presented by $\Gamma, x : A$. Because $\int_{\langle\Gamma\rangle}\langle A\rangle$ is only defined when the base is presented by a context Γ, and $\langle A\rangle : \langle\Gamma\rangle \longrightarrow$ *GPD*, the equation for $[\![\Gamma\ ,\ x{:}A]\!]$ has tacit side conditions that $[\![\Gamma]\!]$ is presented by Γ, and that $[\![A]\!] : [\![\Gamma]\!] \longrightarrow$ *GPD*. In the proof of the fundamental theorem, we show that these are satisfied for well-formed syntax.

Types We define $[\![2]\!]$ to be the constant functor returning the groupoid **2**, the discrete groupoid with two objects, «true» and «false», and only identity arrows «$\mathsf{refl}_{\mathsf{true}}$» and «$\mathsf{refl}_{\mathsf{false}}$». A priori, it is not necessarily the case that all terms of type 2 are objects of this groupoid—only the ones that are equal to true or false—but the fundamental theorem will show that, in fact, they all are. To see that this is presented by 2, we must show: (1) that for any θ, **2** is presented by $2[\theta]$. Because "presented by" respects definitional equality, and $2[\theta] \equiv 2$, it suffices to show that it is presented by 2, which it is—the conditions on inverses and composition follow from *uip*. (2) That for any δ, the identity functor (which is the action of a constant functor) is presented by $x.\mathsf{map}_2\ \delta\ x$. Again using respect for equality, by the definition of map for 2, it suffices to show that the identity functor is presented by $x.x$—which it is, using the β rules for $x[\theta]$ and $x[\delta]$.

Similarly, we define $[\![\mathsf{set}]\!]$ to be the constant functor delivering the groupoid **set** with one object, «bool», and two arrows, «$\mathsf{refl}_{\mathsf{bool}}$» and «not», such that «$\mathsf{refl}_{\mathsf{bool}}$» is the identity and $«\mathsf{not}»^{-1}$ = «not» (the definitions of the remaining compositions are forced by the groupoid laws). The verification that it is presented by set is analogous to the above for 2.

For **El**, first observe that because $\mathbf{const}(\mathbf{set})$ is a constant functor, an $M \in RedTm^{\langle\Gamma\rangle}\ \mathbf{const}(\mathbf{set})$ determines a functor $M^* : \langle\Gamma\rangle \longrightarrow \mathbf{set}$. Thus, it suffices to define a functor $\mathbf{El} : \mathbf{set} \longrightarrow$ *GPD* and interpret $El(M)$ by composition. For our simple universe, **El** is defined as follows: On objects, take **El**(«bool») to be the discrete groupoid with two objects, «in true» and «in false». For a richer universe, with more type constructors, this definition would be extended to analyze the other possible codes for types. A functor between discrete groupoids is determined by a function between their sets of objects, so for morphisms, take $\mathbf{El}(«\mathsf{refl}_{\mathsf{bool}}»)$ to be the identity function, and $\mathbf{El}(\mathsf{not})$ to be the function that interchanges «in true» and «in false». This is well-defined because, by the semantic consistency argument, $\mathsf{true} \not\equiv \mathsf{false}$ and $\mathsf{refl}_{\mathsf{bool}} \not\equiv \mathsf{not}$, so we can map these equivalence classes to different results. It is simple to verify that this obeys the functor laws. It remains to check that $\mathbf{El}[«M»]$ is presented by $El(M)$. We have two obligations:

1. For all $«\theta» \in Ob\,\langle\Gamma\rangle$, $\mathbf{El}[«M»](\theta)$ is presented by $El(M)[\theta]$. Because M is reducible, $«M[\theta]»$ is an object of **set**, and therefore equals «bool». This means that $M[\theta] \equiv \mathsf{bool}$, so in the syntax we can derive that $El(M)[\theta] \equiv El(\mathsf{bool})$ by pushing the substitution inside, and then using congruence and transitivity. The verification that $\mathbf{El}(«\mathsf{bool}»)$ is presented by $El(\mathsf{bool})$ is analogous to the above.
2. For all $«\delta» : «\theta_1» \longrightarrow «\theta_2»$, $\mathbf{El}[«M»](«\delta»)$ is presented by $x.\mathsf{map}_{El(M)}\ \delta\ x$. Due to discreteness/*uip*, the morphism part is trivial, so we show the objects, which amounts to: assuming $«N» \in Ob\ \mathbf{El}[«M»](\theta_1)$, we must show that $«\mathsf{map}_{El(M)}\ \delta\ N» \in Ob\,\mathbf{El}[«M»](\theta_2)$. As in the first part, we know that $\mathbf{El}[«M»](\theta_1)$ and $\mathbf{El}[«M»](\theta_2)$ are both $\mathbf{El}(«\mathsf{bool}»)$, and that $El(M)[\theta_1] \equiv El(M)[\theta_2] \equiv El(\mathsf{bool})$. Moreover, because M is reducible, $«M[\delta]»$ is a morphism in **set**, which means that it is either $«\mathsf{refl}_{\mathsf{bool}}»$ or «not». In the first case, $(x.\mathsf{map}_{El(M)}\ \delta\ x) \equiv (x.\mathsf{map}_{El(M)}\ \mathsf{refl}\ x) \equiv x.x$ by *0-resp functoriality*. In the second, $(x.\mathsf{map}_{El(M)}\ \ /x)$ agrees with the semantic negation function on «in true» and «in false» by *0-resp* for $El(-)$.

To interpret $A[\theta]$, we overload $F[G]$ to mean functor composition. We verify that, when $\langle A\rangle : \langle\Delta\rangle \longrightarrow GPD$ and $\theta \in RedSubst\ \langle\Gamma\rangle\ \langle\Delta\rangle$, $\langle A\rangle[\theta^*]$ is presented by $A[\theta]$.

1. First, for an object $«\theta'» \in \langle\Gamma\rangle$, we must show that $\langle A\rangle(\theta^*(«\theta'»))$ is presented by $(A[\theta])[\theta']$. By respect for equality, it suffices to show presentation by $A[\theta[\theta']]$. By definition of θ^*, $\theta^*(«\theta'») = «\theta[\theta']» \in Ob\ \langle\Delta\rangle$. Thus, by definition of $\langle A\rangle$, $\langle A\rangle(«\theta[\theta']»)$ is presented by $A[(\theta[\theta'])]$, as we needed to show.
2. Second, for a morphism $«\delta» : «\theta_1» \longrightarrow_{\langle\Gamma\rangle} «\theta_2»$, we must show that $\langle A\rangle[\theta^*](«\delta»)$ is presented by $x.\mathsf{map}_{A[\theta]}\ \delta\ x$. This follows from the equation for map for composition, equating it to $x.\mathsf{map}_A\ (\mathsf{refl}_\theta[\delta])\ x$.

Finally, we come to $\mathbf{\Pi}_A\ B$. First we interpret closed Π-types: given a groupoid $\langle A\rangle$ and a functor $\langle B\rangle : \langle x:A\rangle \longrightarrow GPD$, we construct a groupoid $\pi_{\langle A\rangle}\ \langle B\rangle$, which is the dependent analogue of the functor category $\langle B\rangle^{\langle A\rangle}$:

1. An object is an equivalence class $«\lambda\,x.\,M»$, where $M \in RedTm\ \langle x:A\rangle\langle B\rangle$.
2. A morphism $«\lambda\,x.\,M» \longrightarrow_{(\pi_{\langle A\rangle}\ \langle B\rangle)} «\lambda\,x.\,N»$ is $«\lambda\,x.\,\alpha»$, where $\alpha \in RedEquiv\ M\ N$.
3. Identity at $«\lambda\,x.\,M»$ is $«\mathsf{refl}_{\lambda\,x.\,M}»$. To see that this is a morphism, we have to show that it is the equivalence class of a function, whose body is reducible. But $«\mathsf{refl}_{\lambda\,x.\,M}» = «\lambda\,x.\,\mathsf{refl}_M»$, so it suffices to show that $\mathsf{refl}_M \in RedEquiv\ M\ M$. By definition, this means that for any $\delta : \theta_1 \longrightarrow_{\langle x:A\rangle} \theta_2$, $«M[\delta]» : «\mathsf{map}_B\ \delta\ M[\theta_1]» \longrightarrow «M[\theta_2]»$. But this follows immediately from $M \in RedTm\ B$, which is necessary for $«\lambda\,x.\,M»$ to be an object. The definitions of inverse and composition are analogous; the groupoid equations hold because they hold for definitional equality.

Observe that $\pi_{\langle A\rangle}\ \langle B\rangle$ is presented by $\Pi\,x{:}A.\,B$.

Next, for a functor $\langle B\rangle : \langle\Gamma\ ,\, x{:}A\rangle \longrightarrow GPD$, its restriction to $«\theta» \in Ob\,\Gamma$, is the functor $\langle B\rangle|_{«\theta»} : \langle x : A(«\theta»)\rangle \longrightarrow GPD$ defined by

$$\langle B\rangle|_{«\theta»}«(M/x)» = \langle B\rangle«(\theta, M/x)»$$
$$\langle B\rangle|_{«\theta»}«(\alpha/x)» = \langle B\rangle«(\mathsf{refl}_\theta, \alpha/x)»$$

Observe that $\langle B\rangle|_{«\theta»}$ is presented by $B[\theta, x/x]$. The restriction thus corresponds to holding the Γ part of the functor fixed at a particular object.

Now we can define the functor $\mathbf{\Pi}_{\langle A\rangle}\ \langle B\rangle : \langle\Gamma\rangle \longrightarrow GPD$, given $\langle A\rangle : \langle\Gamma\rangle \longrightarrow GPD$ and $\langle B\rangle : \langle\Gamma\ ,\, x{:}A\rangle \longrightarrow GPD$:

$$\begin{array}{rcl}\mathbf{\Pi}_{\langle A\rangle}\ \langle B\rangle(«\theta») & = & \pi_{\langle A\rangle(«\theta»)}\ \langle B\rangle|_{«\theta»}\\ \mathbf{\Pi}_{\langle A\rangle}\ \langle B\rangle(«\delta» : «\theta_1» \longrightarrow_{\langle\Gamma\rangle} «\theta_2») & = & \langle x.\mathsf{map}_{\Pi\,x:A.\,B}\ \delta\ x\rangle\end{array}$$

First, observe that for each $«\theta»$, $\mathbf{\Pi}_A\ B(«\theta»)$ is presented by $\Pi\,x{:}A.\,B[\theta] \equiv \Pi\,x{:}A[\theta].\,B[\theta, x/x]$. Second, we must verify that $x.\mathsf{map}_{\Pi\,x:A.\,B}\ \delta\ x$ is reducible for any δ, so that it extends to a functor. Observe that the converse holds: If the action on morphisms of a functor $\langle C\rangle$ is presented by map_C , then for any δ, $x.\mathsf{map}_C\ \delta\ x$ is reducible. Thus, by the assumptions about $\langle A\rangle$ and $\langle B\rangle$, map_A and map_B are reducible for any δ. By the definition of map for Π, we have that

$$\mathsf{map}_{\Gamma.\Pi\,x:A.\,B}\ \delta\ f \equiv \lambda\,x.\ \mathsf{map}_{\Gamma,x:A.B}\ (\delta, \mathsf{refl})\ (f\ (\mathsf{map}_{\Gamma.A}\ \delta^{-1}\ x))$$

By respect for equality, it suffices to show that the RHS is reducible. This follows from the definition of π and the reducibility of map_A and map_B .

Using these definitions, it is simple to check the cases of the fundamental theorem for parts 1, 2, 5, and 6. For parts 1 and 5, in each case the inductive hypotheses satisfy the pre-conditions of the designated semantic construction, and we have already verified that these constructions define groupoids that are appropriately syntactically presented. For parts 2 and 6: the congruence rules hold because the interpretation is defined compositionally; the equivalence relation rules hold because equality in the meta-language is an equivalence relation. The only non-trivial equations between types are the rules that commute substitution with type formers (e.g. $\Pi\,x{:}A.\,B[\theta] \equiv \Pi\,x{:}A[\theta].\,B[\theta, x/x]$), which are simple to verify for the above definitions. Observe that the proof does not descend into equations between terms, because the only source of dependency is $El(M)$, where $[\![El(M)]\!] \equiv \mathbf{El}[M^*]$, and M^* automatically respects equality in M.

3.2.3 Reducibility of Substitutions/Terms and Equivalences

Finally, we must show that each θ, M, δ and α is reducible. In general: To show that an introduction forms is reducible, we will argue that $[\![-]\!]$ is defined to be "intro forms whose subterms are reducible", and that the subterms will be reducible by the inductive hypotheses. To show that an elimination form is reducible, we will argue that $[\![-]\!]$ tells you that it suffices to check the β-redices, that the result of reduction is reducible by induction, and that the elim. form is reducible because definitional equality contains reduction. To show that the judgemental operations are reducible, we will observe that syntactic presentation of $[\![-]\!]$ ensures that all closed instances of these operations exist, and that, using associativity laws, the definition of reducibility reduces to checking closed instances. We show some representative cases for δ, M, and α; the other cases, including those for θ, are available in the extended version [13].

Equivalences between Substitutions The case for refl follows from $\theta \in RedSubst\ [\![\Gamma]\!]\ [\![\Delta]\!]$ and *delegate*. The case for δ^{-1} reduces to symmetry of morphisms of $[\![\Gamma]\!]$ and $[\![\Delta]\!]$ using the equation $\delta^{-1}[\delta'] \equiv \delta[\delta'^{-1}]^{-1}$, which is derivable from interchange. The case for $\delta \circ \delta'$ is similar, using interchange to push the compositions inward. The case for $\theta[\delta]$ uses *1-resp assoc* to associate, while the case for $\delta[\delta']$ uses *2-resp assoc* to associate. The case for $(\delta, \alpha/x)$ uses the definition of *2-resp* for such pairs.

Terms Case for $\mathsf{map}_A\ \delta\ M$: On objects, we must show that «$(\mathsf{map}_A\ \delta\ M)[\theta]$» $\in$ *Ob* $[\![A[\theta_2]]\!](«\theta»)$ $=$ *Ob* $[\![A[\theta_2[\theta]]]\!]$. By *1-subst for* map, it suffices to show that «$\mathsf{map}_A\ \delta[\mathsf{refl}_\theta]\ M[\theta]$» is. This follows from the inductive hypotheses for M and δ, which show that their instances by θ are a morphism and object of the appropriate categories, and from syntactic presentation of $[\![A]\!]$, which shows that map_A is functorial, and therefore reducible. The argument for morphisms is similar, using *1-resp for* map.

Case for $\lambda\,x.\,M$: On objects, we must show that «$\lambda\,x.\,M[\theta]$» $\in$ *Ob* $[\![\Pi\,x{:}A.\,B]\!](«\theta»)$ $=$ *Ob* $\pi_{[\![A[\theta]]\!]}\ [\![B[\theta, x/x]]\!]$. By def. *subst*, this equals «$\lambda\,x.\,M[\theta, x/x]$». So it suffices to show that $x.M \in RedTm^{[\![x\,:\,A[\theta]]\!]}\ [\![B[\theta, x/x]]\!]$. The obligations for both objects and morphisms follow from the IH $M \in RedTm^{[\![\Gamma, x\,:\,A]\!]}\ [\![B]\!]$, holding the Γ part fixed at θ. The action on morphisms is similar, using «$(\lambda\,x.\,M)[\delta]$» = «$\lambda\,x.\,M[\delta, \mathsf{refl}_x/x]$».

Case for $M_1\ M_2$: On objects, we must show that «$M_1\ M_2[\theta]$» = «$M_1[\theta]\ M_2[\theta]$» $\in$ *Ob* $[\![B[M_2/x]]\!](«\theta»)$ $=$ *Ob* $[\![B[\theta, M_2[\theta/x]]]\!]$. By the inductive hypothesis, we know that «$M_1[\theta]$» = «$\lambda\,x.\,M_1'$» where M_1' is reducible, and that «$M_2[\theta]$» is an appropriate object. Thus, «$M_1'[M_2[\theta]/x]$» = «$(\lambda\,x.\,M_1')\ M_2[\theta]$» = «$M_1[\theta]\ M_2[\theta]$» is an object of the result. The morphism part is analogous, because $M_1\ M_2[\delta] = M_1[\delta]\ M_2[\delta]$.

We omit the cases for $M[\theta]$, x, bool, true, false, if, in, and out.

Equivalences between Terms The cases for the judgemental framework operations (refl, α^{-1}, $\alpha \circ \alpha'$, $M[\delta]$, $\alpha[\delta]$) are analogous to those for substitutions above.

Case for $\lambda\,x.\alpha$: Given δ, «$(\lambda\,x.\,\alpha)[\delta]$» = «$\lambda\,x.\,\alpha[\delta, \mathsf{refl}_x/x]$», so it suffices to show that $\alpha[\delta, \mathsf{refl}_x/x]$ is reducible. Picking a substitution «β/x», the obligation is to show that «$\alpha[\delta, \mathsf{refl}_x/x][\beta/x]$» is a morphism. This holds by reassociating the substitution, and then using the IH that α is reducible.

Case for $\alpha\ \beta$: Pick «δ» : «θ_1» $\longrightarrow_{[\![\Gamma]\!]}$ «θ_2». To show:

$$«\alpha\ \beta[\delta]» : \mathsf{map}_{B[M_2/x]}\ \delta\ (M_1\ M_2)[\theta_1] \longrightarrow_{[\![B[N_1/x][\theta_2]]\!]} (N\ N_1)[\theta_2]$$

By equality, this is«$(\alpha[\delta])\ (\beta[\delta])$». The IH gives that α,β are reducible, so

$$\alpha[\delta] : «\mathsf{map}_{\Pi\,x:A.\,B}\ \delta\ M[\theta_1]» \longrightarrow_{[\![\Pi\,x:A.\,B]\!](«\theta'»)} «N[\theta_2]»$$
$$\beta[\delta] : «\mathsf{map}_A\ \delta\ M_1[\theta_1]» \longrightarrow_{[\![A]\!]} «N_1[\theta_2]»$$

To complete the case, we (1) show that if «α'» is a morphism of $\pi_{\langle X\rangle}\ \langle Y\rangle$ and «β'» is a morphism of $\langle X\rangle$, then «$\alpha'\ \beta'$» is a morphism of $\langle Y\rangle$—the argument uses *2-β-expansion*, analogously to the case for application above. (2) deduce that

$$(\mathsf{map}_{\Pi\,x:A.\,B}\ \delta\ (M[\theta_1]))\ (\mathsf{map}_A\ \delta\ (M_1[\theta_1]))$$
$$\equiv \mathsf{map}_{B[M_2/x]}\ \delta\ (M_1\ M_2)[\theta_1]$$

—the proof uses the definition of map for Π, functoriality of map, cancellation of inverses, and the *def.* map *for* $A[\theta]$. This shows that «$(\alpha[\delta])\ (\beta[\delta])$» is a morphism of the appropriate type.

We omit the cases for if and not.

3.2.4 Canonicity

Here, we check that Theorem 3.1 is a corollary of the fundamental theorem. Assume $\cdot\ \vdash M : 2$. Then $M \in RedTm^{[\![\cdot]\!]}\ [\![2]\!]$, so $M \in RedTm^{\cdot}\ \mathbf{const}(\mathbf{2})$. By definition, «id.» $\in$ *Ob* $\cdot$, so «M[id.]» $\in$ *Ob* $(\mathbf{const}(\mathbf{2})(«\text{id.}»))$. But $M[\text{id.}] \equiv M$ and $\mathbf{const}(\mathbf{2})(«\text{id.}») = \mathbf{2}$, so «$M$» $\in$ *Ob* $\mathbf{2}$. By definition of $\mathbf{2}$, this means «M» = «true» or «M» = «false», which means that $M \equiv$ true or $M \equiv$ false.

4. Identity Types

In this section, we show how to internalize the judgemental notion of equivalence as an identity type $\mathsf{Id}_A\ M\ N$, satisfying the usual rules. The rules for the identity type are presented in Figure 6. in, out, and the $\beta\eta$ rules for them state that the inhabitants of the identity type $\mathsf{Id}_A\ M\ N$ are exactly the equivalences $M \simeq_A N$. The *reflection* and *uip* rules express two-dimensionality: equivalences themselves are equivalent only if they are equal, and all equivalences between equivalences are the identity. These rules express *strict* 2-dimensionality, and are an inherent source of undecidability for a strictly 2-dimensional theory; Garner [9] discusses this point further. The *0-resp* rule expresses the action of the *Hom*-functor, given by pre- and post-composition. out M determines a 2-cell from a one-cell, and is the first mechanism in our calculus for introducing variable equivalences. Because *2-resp* is determined by the structure of the equivalence being substituted into, (out M)$[\delta]$ is stuck until M is determined. Canonicity remains true in the presence of the identity type, interpreting $[\![\mathsf{Id}_A\ M\ N]\!]$ as the *Hom*-functor.

Surprisingly, we can derive the standard J elimination rule for the identity type. In traditional presentations of MLTT, map (which is usually called subst) does not entail J. In 2TT, it does, because of the following properties of the judgemental presentation of equivalence:

1. It axiomatizes the 2-cell structure of types using the operations refl, $-^{-1}$, $- \circ -$ $M[\delta]$, and map_C . Our derivation of J uses unit law equations for these operations:

$$\mathsf{refl}^{-1} \equiv \mathsf{refl}$$
$$M[\mathsf{refl}_\theta] \equiv \mathsf{refl}_{M[\theta]}$$
$$\mathsf{refl} \circ \alpha \equiv \alpha$$
$$\mathsf{map}_C\ \mathsf{refl}\ M \equiv M$$

2. It interprets the identity type as the Hom-functor. Our derivation of J exploits the Hom-functor's action, which defines $\mathsf{map}_{\Gamma.\mathsf{Id}_A\ M\ N}$ in terms of pre- and post-composition.
3. It axiomatizes the 2-cell structure of Σ-types as context extension Γ , $x{:}A$. The derivation of J uses the pairing introduction rule for $\simeq_{\Gamma,x:A}$, and the definition of $\mathsf{refl}_{\theta,M/x} \equiv (\mathsf{refl}_\theta, \mathsf{refl}_M/x)$.

In traditional type theory, this 2-cell structure is instead derived from the identity type, which requires taking J as a primitive rule.

We state J in the Paulin-Mohring form [19]:

$$\frac{\begin{array}{l}\Gamma \vdash A\ \mathsf{type} \quad \Gamma \vdash M : A \\ \Gamma, x : A, p : \mathsf{Id}_A\ M\ x \vdash C\ \mathsf{type} \\ \Gamma \vdash b : C[\mathsf{id}_\Gamma, M/x, \mathsf{refl}_M/p] \\ \Gamma \vdash N : A \quad \Gamma \vdash P : \mathsf{Id}_A\ M\ N\end{array}}{\Gamma \vdash \mathsf{J}_C(b, P) : C[\mathsf{id}_\Gamma, N/x, P/p]} \qquad \mathsf{J}_C(b, \mathsf{in}\ \mathsf{refl}_M) \equiv b$$

and define it by

$$\mathsf{J}_C(b, \mathsf{in}\ \mathsf{refl}_M) := \mathsf{map}_{\Gamma,x:A,p:\mathsf{Id}_A\ M\ x.C}\ (\mathsf{refl}_{\mathsf{id}_\Gamma}, \mathsf{out}\ P/x, \mathsf{in}\ (\mathsf{refl}_P)/p)\ b$$

As Awodey has observed,[1] J can be defined in terms of map, given, for any A, M, N, P as in the premises of J, an equivalence

$$(M/x, \mathsf{refl}_M/p) \simeq_{(x\,:\,A, p\,:\,\mathsf{Id}_A\ M\ x)} (N/x, P/p)$$

Homotopically, this says that any path from M with a free endpoint, represented by the pair (N, P), is homotopic to the pair (M, refl) of M itself and the trivial path. Geometrically, (M, refl) can be expanded to (N, P) by dragging M along P.

Here, we observe that this equivalence is in fact provable, by $(\mathsf{out}\ P/x, \mathsf{in}\ (\mathsf{refl}_P)/p)$, using the rules described above. Because we work with total substitutions, we show that

$$(\mathsf{refl}_{\mathsf{id}_\Gamma}, \mathsf{out}\ P/x, \mathsf{in}\ (\mathsf{refl}_P)/p) :$$
$$(\mathsf{id}_\Gamma, M/x, \mathsf{refl}_M/p) \simeq_{(\Gamma, x\,:\,A, p\,:\,\mathsf{Id}_A\ M\ x)} (\mathsf{id}_\Gamma, N/x, P/p)$$

so that map_C coerces the b to the appropriate type. Unpacking the pairing introduction rule for equivalence at Γ , $x{:}A$, our first goal

[1] Personal communication.

$$\frac{\Gamma \vdash A\ \mathsf{type} \quad \Gamma \vdash \{M, N\} : A}{\Gamma \vdash \mathsf{Id}_A\ M\ N\ \mathsf{type}} \qquad \frac{\Gamma \vdash \alpha : M \simeq_A N}{\Gamma \vdash \mathsf{in}\,\alpha : \mathsf{Id}_A\ M\ N} \qquad \frac{\Gamma \vdash M : \mathsf{Id}_A\ M\ N}{\Gamma \vdash \mathsf{out}\,M : M \simeq_A N} \qquad (\mathsf{refl}_{\mathsf{in}\,\alpha} \text{ is canonical if } \alpha \text{ is}) \qquad \frac{\Gamma \vdash \alpha : P \simeq_{\mathsf{Id}_A\ M\ N} Q}{\Gamma \vdash P \equiv Q} \qquad \frac{\Gamma \vdash \alpha : P \simeq_{\mathsf{Id}_A\ M\ N} Q}{\Gamma \vdash \alpha \equiv \mathsf{refl}_P}$$

$\mathsf{out}\,(\mathsf{in}\,\alpha)$	$\equiv$	α	*1-β*	$(\mathsf{in}\,\alpha)[\theta]$	$\equiv$	$\mathsf{in}\,(\alpha[\mathsf{refl}_\theta])$	*1-subst*
$\mathsf{in}\,(\mathsf{out}\,M)$	$\equiv$	M	*1-η*	$(\mathsf{in}\,\alpha)[\delta]$	$\equiv$	$\mathsf{in}\,(\alpha[\delta])$	*1-resp*
$(\mathsf{Id}_A\ M\ N)[\theta]$	$\equiv$	$\mathsf{Id}_{A[\theta]}\ M[\theta]\ N[\theta]$	*0-subst*	refl		is canonical	
$\mathsf{map}_{\Delta.\mathsf{Id}_A\ M\ N}\ \delta\ P$	$\equiv$		*0-resp*	$-^{-1}, - \circ -$		trivial by extensionality	
$\mathsf{in}\,(N[\delta] \circ (\mathsf{resp}\,(x.\mathsf{map}_A\ \delta\ x)\ (\mathsf{out}\,P)) \circ M[\delta]^{-1})$				$(\mathsf{out}\,M)[\delta]$		stuck until M reduces (neutral)	*2-resp*

Figure 6. Identity Types

is to show that $\mathsf{refl}_{\mathsf{id}_\Gamma} : \mathsf{id}_\Gamma \simeq_\Gamma \mathsf{id}_\Gamma$, which it clearly does. Next, the second component of the pair must have type $M \simeq_A N$ (the "adjustment" $\mathsf{map}_{\Gamma.A}\ \mathsf{refl}_{\mathsf{id}_\Gamma}\ M$ cancels by the unit law for map), which $\mathsf{out}\,P$ does. Our final goal is to prove

$$\mathsf{map}_{\Gamma,x:A.\mathsf{Id}_A\ M\ x}\ (\mathsf{refl}_{\mathsf{id}_\Gamma}, \mathsf{out}\,P/x)\ (\mathsf{in}\,\mathsf{refl}) \simeq P$$

In fact, the left-hand-side is definitionally equal to the right-hand, so refl_P gives the result. This follows from the fact that

$$\mathsf{map}_{\Gamma,x:A.\mathsf{Id}_A\ M\ x}\ (\mathsf{refl}_{\mathsf{id}_\Gamma}, \alpha/x)\ Q \equiv \mathsf{in}\,(\alpha \circ \mathsf{out}\,(Q))$$

I.e. map at this type is post-composition with α (the derivation is in the extended version [13]).

The computation rule holds because

$$\mathsf{J}_C(b, \mathsf{refl}) := \mathsf{map}_C\ (\mathsf{refl}_{\mathsf{id}_\Gamma}, \mathsf{out}\,(\mathsf{in}\,\mathsf{refl})/x, \mathsf{in}\,(\mathsf{refl}_P)/p)\ b$$

which, by *1-β* for Id and the definition of refl for $\Gamma\ ,\ x{:}A$, is $\mathsf{map}_C\ \mathsf{refl}\ b$, which is b by the unit law for map.

Conversely, the type-generic operations on equivalence that we have taken as primitive here (map, $M[\delta]$, refl, $-^{-1}$ $- \circ -$, $\alpha[\delta]$) can be defined in traditional Martin-Löf type theory using the identity type $\mathsf{Id}_A\ M\ N$ in place of the equivalence judgement $M \simeq_A N$, as consequences of J. However, many of the equations on these operations hold only as higher-dimensional equivalences, rather than as definitional equalities, which breaks definitional canonicity. A resolution of the conjecture that univalent intensional type theory satisfies canonicity up to equivalence [23] is an important area of future work.

5. Related Work

Higher-dimensional type theory is based on a type-directed definition of equivalence, including extensional equality for functions and universes. The idea of defining *equality* in a type directed manner is central to Martin-Löf type theory Martin-Löf [17], especially as presented in NuPRL [5]. Relative to NuPRL, the main benefit of a 2-dimensional theory is that all types respect computationally-relevant notions of equivalence, such as isomorphism of sets; this generalizes NuPRL, where equality is computationally irrelevant.

A similar contrast applies to OTT [3]: In OTT, equality is a computationally irrelevant proposition, so all types are sets—OTT is 1-dimensional. In contrast, 2TT accounts for computationally relevant notions of equivalence—2-dimensional structure. For example, in OTT, coercing any term by any equality proof gives a result that is equal to the original term. This is not true in 2TT, because, for example, not exchanges true and false, which are not equal.

Hofmann and Streicher [12] give intensional type theory a semantics in groupoids. 2TT can be seen as an effort to read this semantics back into the syntax, enriching the type theory with a number of new equations, such as the computation rules for map and resp and the type-directed rules for equivalences. They use the groupoid interpretation to justify an axiomatic account of a universe of types modulo isomorphism, but this extension does not seem to enjoy canonicity.

Hofmann [10] justifies various extensional concepts, such as functional extensionality and quotient types, by a semantics constructed in intensional type theory; Altenkirch [2] adapts this construction to coexist better with other type-theoretic features, such as large eliminations. Canonicity is achieved by defining definitional equality as equality of denotations. Hofmann [10] does not take this approach for the groupoid model, because the groupoid model cannot be defined in intensional type theory without functional extensionality. An alternative to our current work would be to parallel this approach, and define a groupoid interpretation into *extensional* type theory, and thereby inherit equality from the meta-language. The benefit of the approach we take here is that it provides a more direct description of the equational theory, presenting it directly in terms of the source language.

Garner [9] studies a two-dimensional theory ML_2, and shows it sound and complete for a class of 2-categories. ML_2 introduced the two-dimensional identity types, with *reflection* and *uip* for identity types only, which we adopted in Section 4. It additionally included some new computation rules for Π-types, which in our notation would be written $\mathsf{refl}_{M\,:\,\Pi\,x:A.\,B} \equiv \lambda\,x.\,\mathsf{refl}_{M\ x}$ and $(\lambda\,x.\,\alpha : M \simeq_{\Pi\,x:A.\,B} N)\ \mathsf{refl}_{M_0} \equiv \alpha[M_0/x]$. However, it did not include, e.g., the type-directed rules for map and thus would not enjoy canonicity in the presence of something like univalence. In future work, we may consider identifying a class of two-categories that is sound and complete for 2TT.

Voevodsky's univalence axiom [23] equips intensional type theory with full homotopy equivalence, which includes isomorphism for sets, equivalence for categories, and so on. However, the axiomatic account does not satisfy canonicity for definitional equality. Voevodsky conjectures that every closed term of type nat is *equivalent* (using univalence) to one that does not use the univalence axiom (and therefore to a numeral, by canonicity for the base theory). However, this conjecture has not yet been proved, and our work suggests an approach to it, as we discuss below. Moreover, Voevodsky conjectures that this numeral can be computed, which is not something we have yet established here.

Our presentation here is based on our previous work on 2DTT [14], a 2-dimensional directed type theory, which generalizes equivalence to an asymmetric notion of transformation. Our presentation here avoids some of the complexities of 2DTT, like the need to account for variances of type constructors, but on the other hand shows that the presentational style can account for symmetry. The proof of canonicity and the derivation of identity types are novel to the present work; we conjecture that our proof of canonicity could be applied to 2DTT as well.

In concurrent work, de Queiroz and de Oliveira [6] have also developed a type theory with a judgemental notion of equivalence, which has explicit evidence with a groupoid structure, and which is internalized by the identity type. Their type theory is weaker (in the category-theoretic sense), in that every equation is part of equivalence—including $\beta\eta$-like rules, which we treat as equalities. However, there is no account of a higher-dimensional base type, nor a claim of canonicity. A number of equations on equivalences are oriented as rewrite rules, which are proved terminating and confluent, but it is unclear what equational theory this decides.

Interestingly, F_C [21], the calculus used as an intermediate language in the Haskell compiler GHC, has some similarities to 2TT. While there are no higher-dimensional types in F_C, type equalities are witnessed by explicit coercions, written in programs using a construct similar to map, and the class of coercions is closed under the 2-category operations considered here, such as refl, $- \circ -$, $-^{-1}$, and $-[-]$. Moreover, GHC includes a coercion simplification algorithm, whose purpose is to reduce the size of coercion terms, which exploits many of the equations on these 2-category operations. An interesting application of 2TT would be to analyze this coercion simplification algorithm by translating its reductions into 2TT equations, which might suggest some additional coercion reductions,

Other related work concerns categorical or homotopy-theoretic semantics of pure intensional type theory. On the homotopy-theoretic side, Awodey and Warren [4], Warren [24] show how to interpret intensional type theory into abstract homotopy theory (i.e. Quillen model categories). Lumsdaine [15] and van den Berg and Garner [22] show that the syntax of intensional type theory forms a weak ω-category, and Gambino and Garner [8] shows that identity types admit a weak factorization system.

6. Conclusion

We have presented a novel formulation of 2-dimensional type theory, 2TT, based on a judgemental account of higher-dimensional structure. This judgemental account reifies the groupoid structure of types and the functorial actions of families. 2TT enjoys a canonicity property for closed terms of observable type, which we have proved by a logical-relations style argument in which types are interpreted as groupoids rather than as equivalence relations. The identity type can be defined by internalizing this judgemental notion of equivalence, and the judgemental apparatus suffices to derive its standard elimination rule.

One direction for future work is to sharpen the canonicity theorem to state that $\cdot \vdash M : \mathsf{bool}$ evaluates to true or to false using a deterministic operational semantics. The result given here leaves open the possibility that the derivation of $M \equiv \mathsf{true}$ or $M \equiv \mathsf{false}$ proceeds by a non-operational rule, such as the various η principles, or an instance of equality reflection. The consistency of the equational theory suggests that such a maneuver cannot be essential, and hence only the β-like rules, including those for map and resp, are relevant to canonicity. A possible route to this result would be to define the groupoid interpretation in *extensional* type theory, and then prove a Plotkin-style computational adequacy theorem for this interpretation to obtain the sharper result.

Another direction for future work is to investigate canonicity for the many possible variations on 2TT: For example, we may extend 2TT with standard features in current proof assistants, such as inductive types. Another possible extension is an impredicative universe. A third possibility is to consider directed type theory [14], which has applications to generic programming with abstract syntax and directed homotopy theory. More ambitiously, we may consider an extension to a fully higher-dimensional univalent dependent type theory, for which canonicity remains an open problem. By analogy with our judgemental formulation, which reifies the groupoid structure of a type, we would present the syntax in such a way that it reifies the weak ω-groupoid structure of a type. However, an obstacle to this generalization is the complexity of the proposed definitions of "weak ω-groupoid" and their adaptation to the type-theoretic setting.

Acknowledgments We thank Thorsten Altenkirch, Jeremy Avigad, Steve Awodey, Caylee Hogg, Chris Kapulkin, Peter Lumsdaine, Gordon Plotkin, Mike Shulman, Kristina Sojakova, and the anonymous reviewers for helpful conversations about this work and feedback on this article.

References

[1] Homotopy type theory Web site. `www.homotopytypetheory.org`, 2011.

[2] T. Altenkirch. Extensional equality in intensional type theory. In *IEEE Symposium on Logic in Computer Science*, 1999.

[3] T. Altenkirch, C. McBride, and W. Swierstra. Observational equality, now! In *Programming Languages meets Program Verification Workshop*, 2007.

[4] S. Awodey and M. Warren. Homotopy theoretic models of identity types. *Mathematical Proceedings of the Cambridge Philosophical Society*, 2009.

[5] R. L. Constable, S. F. Allen, H. M. Bromley, W. R. Cleaveland, J. F. Cremer, R. W. Harper, D. J. Howe, T. B. Knoblock, N. P. Mendler, P. Panangaden, J. T. Sasaki, and S. F. Smith. *Implementing Mathematics with the NuPRL Proof Development System*. Prentice Hall, 1986.

[6] R. J. G. B. de Queiroz and A. G. de Oliveira. Propositional equality, identity types, and direct computational paths. *ArXiv e-prints*, July 2011.

[7] P. Dybjer and A. Filinski. Normalization and partial evaluation. In *Applied Semantics: International Summer School, APPSEM 2000*, volume 2395 of *Lecture Notes in Computer Science*, pages 137–192. Springer-Verlag, September 2000.

[8] N. Gambino and R. Garner. The identity type weak factorisation system. *Theoretical Computer Science*, 409(3):94–109, 2008.

[9] R. Garner. Two-dimensional models of type theory. *Mathematical. Structures in Computer Science*, 19(4):687–736, 2009.

[10] M. Hofmann. *Extensional Concepts in Intensional Type Theory*. PhD thesis, University of Edinburgh, 1995.

[11] M. Hofmann. Syntax and semantics of dependent types. In *Semantics and Logics of Computation*, pages 79–130. Cambridge University Press, 1997.

[12] M. Hofmann and T. Streicher. The groupoid interpretation of type theory. In *Twenty-five years of constructive type theory*. Oxford University Press, 1998.

[13] D. R. Licata and R. Haprer. Canonicity for 2-dimensional type theory (extended version). Technical Report CMU-CS-11-143, Carnegie Mellon University, 2011.

[14] D. R. Licata and R. Harper. 2-dimensional directed type theory. In *Mathematical Foundations of Programming Semantics (MFPS)*, 2011.

[15] P. L. Lumsdaine. Weak ω-categories from intensional type theory. In *International Conference on Typed Lambda Calculi and Applications*, 2009.

[16] P. Martin-Löf. An intuitionistic theory of types: Predicative part. In H. Rose and J. Shepherdson, editors, *Logic Colloquium '73, Proceedings of the Logic Colloquium*, volume 80 of *Studies in Logic and the Foundations of Mathematics*, pages 73 – 118. Elsevier, 1975.

[17] P. Martin-Löf. Constructive mathematics and computer programming. *Philosophical Transactions of the Royal Society of London. Series A, Mathematical and Physical Sciences*, 312(1522):501–518, 1984.

[18] B. Nordström, K. Peterson, and J. Smith. *Programming in Martin-Löf's Type Theory, an Introduction*. Clarendon Press, 1990.

[19] C. Paulin-Mohring. *Extraction de programmes dans le Calcul des Constructions*. PhD thesis, Université Paris 7, 1989.

[20] A. M. Pitts. Categorical logic. In S. Abramsky, D. M. Gabbay, and T. S. E. Maibaum, editors, *Handbook of Logic in Computer Science, Volume 5. Algebraic and Logical Structures*, chapter 2, pages 39–128. Oxford University Press, 2000.

[21] M. Sulzmann, M. M. T. Chakravarty, S. P. Jones, and K. Donnell. System f with type equality coercions. In *ACM Workshop on Types in Language Design and Implementaion*, 2007. Appendix at `http://research.microsoft.com/ simonpj/papers/ext-f/`.

[22] B. van den Berg and R. Garner. Types are weak ω-groupoids. Available from `http://www.dpmms.cam.ac.uk/ rhgg2/Typesom/Typesom.html`, 2010.

[23] V. Voevodsky. Univalent foundations of mathematics. Invited talk at WoLLIC 2011 18th Workshop on Logic, Language, Information and Computation, 2011.

[24] M. A. Warren. *Homotopy theoretic aspects of constructive type theory*. PhD thesis, Carnegie Mellon University, 2008.

Algebraic Foundations for Effect-Dependent Optimisations

Ohad Kammar Gordon D. Plotkin

Laboratory for Foundations of Computer Science
School of Informatics, University of Edinburgh, Scotland
ohad.kammar@ed.ac.uk gdp@ed.ac.uk

Abstract

We present a general theory of Gifford-style type and effect annotations, where effect annotations are sets of effects. Generality is achieved by recourse to the theory of algebraic effects, a development of Moggi's monadic theory of computational effects that emphasises the operations causing the effects at hand and their equational theory. The key observation is that annotation effects can be identified with operation symbols.

We develop an annotated version of Levy's Call-by-Push-Value language with a kind of computations for every effect set; it can be thought of as a sequential, annotated intermediate language. We develop a range of validated optimisations (i.e., equivalences), generalising many existing ones and adding new ones. We classify these optimisations as structural, algebraic, or abstract: structural optimisations always hold; algebraic ones depend on the effect theory at hand; and abstract ones depend on the global nature of that theory (we give modularly-checkable sufficient conditions for their validity).

Categories and Subject Descriptors D.3.4 [*Processors*]: Compilers; Optimization; F.3.1 [*Specifying and Verifying and Reasoning about Programs*]: Logics of programs; F.3.2 [*Semantics of Programming Languages*]: Algebraic approaches to semantics; Denotational semantics; Program analysis; F.3.3 [*Studies of Program Constructs*]: Type structure

General Terms Languages, Theory.

Keywords Call-by-Push-Value, algebraic theory of effects, code transformations, compiler optimisations, computational effects, denotational semantics, domain theory, inequational logic, relevant and affine monads, sum and tensor, type and effect systems, universal algebra.

1. Introduction

In Gifford-style type and effect analysis [27], each term of a programming language is assigned a type and an effect set. The type describes the values the term may evaluate to; the effect set describes the effects the term may cause during its computation, such as memory assignment, exception raising, or I/O.

For example, consider the following term M:

$$\mathbf{if\ true\ then}\ \mathtt{x} := \mathtt{1}\ \mathbf{else}\ \mathtt{x} := \mathbf{deref}(\mathtt{y})$$

It has unit type $\mathbf{1}$ as its sole purpose is to cause side effects; it has effect set $\{\mathtt{update}, \mathtt{lookup}\}$, as it might cause memory updates or look-ups. Type and effect systems commonly convey this information via a type and effect judgement:

$$\mathtt{x} : \mathbf{Loc}, \mathtt{y} : \mathbf{Loc} \vdash M : \mathbf{1} \ ! \ \{\mathtt{update}, \mathtt{lookup}\}$$

The information gathered by such effect analyses can be used to guarantee implementation correctness[1], to prove authenticity properties [15], to aid resource management [44], or to optimise code using transformations. We focus on the last of these. As an example, purely functional code can be executed out of order:

$$\mathtt{x} \leftarrow M_1;\ \mathtt{y} \leftarrow M_2;\ N \quad = \quad \mathtt{y} \leftarrow M_2;\ \mathtt{x} \leftarrow M_1;\ N$$

This reordering holds more generally, if the terms M_1 and M_2 have non-interfering effects. Such transformations are commonly used in optimising compilers. They are traditionally called *optimisations*, even if neither side is always the more optimal.

In a sequence of papers, Benton et al. [4–8] prove soundness of such optimisations for increasingly complex sets of effects. However, any change in the language requires a complete reformulation of its semantics and so of the soundness proofs, even though the essential reasons for the validity of the optimisations remain the same. Thus, this approach is not robust, as small language changes cause global theory changes.

A possible way to obtain robustness is to study effect systems in general. One would hope for a modular approach, seeking to isolate those parts of the theory that change under small language changes, and then recombining them with the unchanging parts. Such a theory may not only be important for compiler optimisations in big, stable languages. It can also be used for effect-dependent equational reasoning. This use may be especially helpful in the case of small, domain-specific languages, as optimising compilers are hardly ever designed for them and their diversity necessitates proceeding modularly.

The only available general work on effect systems seems to be that of Marino and Millstein [28]. They devise a methodology to derive type and effect frameworks which they apply to a call-by-value language with recursion and references; however, their methodology does not account for effect-dependent optimisations.

Fortunately, Wadler and Thiemann [46, 47] had previously made an important connection with the monadic approach to computational effects. They translated judgements of the form $\Gamma \vdash M : A \ ! \ \varepsilon$ in a region analysis calculus to judgements of the form $\Gamma' \vdash M' : T_\varepsilon A$ in a multi-monadic calculus. They gave the latter calculus an operational semantics, and conjectured the existence of a corresponding general monadic denotational semantics in which T_ε would denote a monad corresponding to the effects in ε, and in which the partial order of effect sets and inclusions would

[1] E. Cooper, S. Lindley, P. Wadler, and J. Yallop. Links 0.5, 2009. `http://groups.inf.ed.ac.uk/links`.

POPL'12, January 25–27, 2012, Philadelphia, PA, USA.

induce a hierarchy of monads and monad morphisms, as follows:

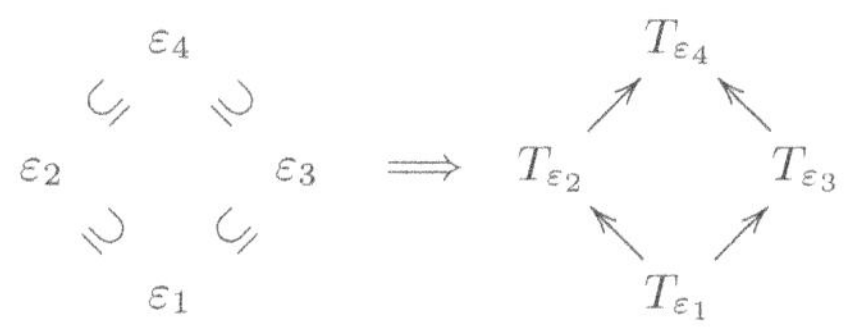

Hierarchies of monads in this spirit were identified by both Tolmach [45] and Kieburtz [23]. However, neither hierarchy corresponded fully to their effect set partial order.

Plotkin and Power's algebraic theory of effects [34, 35] provides a semantic foundation for computational effects that focuses on the operations causing the effects. These operations form a single-sorted signature with a natural equational theory. Using tools from universal algebra and category theory, one obtains the standard monadic semantics for such computational effects. The shift in focus from monads to effect operations and their equational theories allows a modular treatment: Hyland et al. [19] show that the theories of combinations of effects can often be built up from those for individual effects by simple operations such as disjoint sum. To model recursion, the algebraic theory of effects turns to domain theory, replacing equational theories by inequational theories.

We argue that the algebraic view of effects provides the missing link needed to develop a general theory of type and effect systems. With the right choice of signature, effects (i.e., the elements of effect sets ε) can be *identified* with the operations. This suggests the way to a full and general account of Gifford-style type and effect systems: effect systems and effect reconstruction arise out of the effect signature; denotational semantics arises out of the (in)equations; and effect-dependent program logic, including optimisations, arises from this semantics.

We concentrate on denotational semantics and optimisations. We present a language, MAIL (Multi-Adjunctive Intermediate Language), which can be thought of as the intermediate language of a compiler. Its terms have both type and effect annotations; these can be thought of as having arisen from a source code syntactic analysis. The denotational semantics of MAIL provides a foundation for optimisations. An optimisation is simply an equation between MAIL terms, and it is *valid* in a MAIL model if both terms have the same denotation.

We see optimisations as falling into three classes: *structural*, *algebraic*, and *abstract*. Structural optimisations arise out of the structure of MAIL models, hence hold in all models; η, β and sequencing laws provide typical examples. Algebraic optimisations arise from equations for individual effects in the inequational theories underlying the semantics; a typical example is

$$(\mathtt{x} := 1; \mathtt{x} := 0) = (\mathtt{x} := 0)$$

These are the bread and butter of effectful program optimisation.

Finally, abstract optimisations arise from global properties of effects. The *Discard* optimisation $x \leftarrow M;\ N = N$ is one such example. There is a strong connection to Führmann's work [13]. He had previously considered properties of arrows in Kleisli categories and their dependence on the nature of the monad, and it turns out that these give rise to several abstract optimisations. In particular, as we see below, Discard holds if, and only if, the underlying monad is affine.

Viewing abstract optimisations algebraically reveals a connection to algebraic laws. For example, the underlying monad is affine if, and only if, the *absorption law* $f(\mathtt{x}, \ldots, \mathtt{x}) = \mathtt{x}$ holds generally, i.e., for every operation f. Making use of [19], one can then establish the validity of abstract optimisations modularly. For example, if the absorption law holds generally for each of two theories, then it also holds for their disjoint sum.

Our language arose from a category-theoretic formulation of the semantics, specifically as presheaves of adjunctions over partial orders of sets of effects. In order to maintain an accessible account, we use a minimum of category theory. We hope this will allow informed readers to recognise the inherent categorical structure without excluding readers who are not familiar with category theory.

The syntax and denotational semantics of MAIL are given in Sections 2 and 3. Two classes of semantic models for MAIL are given (Theorems 9 and 12), both based on standard algebraic semantics, settling Wadler and Thiemann's conjecture (while we write in terms of theories and their translations, rather than monads and their morphisms, their relationship is well-known, see, e.g., [18]). The two classes of models are related to the semantics of Alg-CBPV, an algebraic variant of Call-by-Push-Value, justifying the validity of effect dependent optimisations (Theorems 9 and 12).

Next, Section 4 validates, unifies, generalises, and classifies effect dependent optimisations, including new ones (Figure 7). Algebraic conditions for validating these optimisations are presented (Figure 7), and algebraic techniques are given to recognise and modularly combine validity of optimisations (Theorem 13–Proposition 17).

Section 5 considers an example effectful language with recursion, memory regions, exceptions (normal and rollback), terminal I/O and non-determinism, and applies our theory to validate effect dependent optimisations for it. Our modular methodology enables us to significantly cut down on the amount of work involved. We conclude, and discuss related and further work, in Sections 6 and 7.

2. Multi-Adjunctive Intermediate Language

MAIL is based on Levy's Call-by-Push-Value (CBPV) [26] and inspired by Filinski's M^{3}L (MultiMonadic MetaLanguage) [11], whose latest version draws heavily on CBPV [12]. The CBPV paradigm subsumes call-by-name and call-by-value, both syntactically and semantically, and hence is appealing for a general account. Also, in CBPV evaluation order is explicit, as in intermediate languages. Moreover, expressing our optimisations in CBPV decomposes more complicated optimisations into orthogonal ones (see Section 4). Thus the CBPV paradigm seems well-suited for use in intermediate languages for effect-dependent optimisation. We reuse as much of Levy's work as possible, in order to focus on the issues inherent to effect systems.

MAIL is parameterised by *signatures*. An auxiliary notion of pre-signatures makes the definition of signatures more manageable:

Definition 1. *A* MAIL pre-signature σ *is a tuple* $\langle \mathbf{Bsc}, |\sigma|, \Omega, \mathcal{E}, \kappa \rangle$, *where:* $\mathbf{Bsc}$ *is a set of* basic types, *ranged over by* K*;* $|\sigma|$ *is a set of* effect operation symbols, *ranged over by* op *with a distinguished element* Ω*;* $\mathcal{E} \subseteq \mathcal{P}(|\sigma|)$ *is a subset of the powerset of* $|\sigma|$, *the set of* effect sets, *ranged over by* ε*; and* κ *is a set of* built-in constants, *ranged over by* c.

For example, $\mathbf{Bsc}$ may include the types: $\mathbf{Word}$ for 64-bit words, $\mathbf{Loc}$ for memory locations, $\mathbf{Str}$ for strings, $\mathbf{Char}$ for characters, or $\mathbf{Exc}$ for exceptions. The effect operation symbol set $|\sigma|$ may be finite:

$$\{\Omega, \mathtt{lookup}, \mathtt{update}, \mathtt{input}, \mathtt{output}, \mathtt{throw}, \mathtt{choose}\}$$

or even countably infinite: $\{\Omega, \mathtt{throw}^n \mid n \in \mathbb{N}\}$. In the latter case, we may want to restrict $\mathcal{E}$ to be a countable set, such as that of all finite subsets $\mathcal{P}_{\mathrm{fin}}(|\sigma|)$, guaranteeing a countable syntax. The distinguished symbol Ω represents non-termination. The set κ typically includes primitives to manipulate basic values, such as: number constants 0, 1, 2; arithmetic operators $+$, $*$, $\mathtt{div}$; boolean operations $=$, $>=$, $<$; string manipulation primitives $''\mathtt{abcd123}''$, $+\!\!+$; and predefined exceptions $\mathtt{ArithmeticOverflow}$, $\mathtt{DivideByZero}$.

Kinds:	$\mathcal{K} ::=$	$\mathsf{Val} \mid \mathsf{Comp}(\varepsilon)$
Value Types:	$A, B, \ldots ::=$	$K \mid \mathbf{1} \mid A_1 \times A_2 \mid \mathbf{0} \mid A_1 + A_2 \mid \mathbf{U}_\varepsilon \underline{B}$
Computation Types:	$\underline{A}, \underline{B}, \ldots ::=$	$\mathbf{F}_\varepsilon A \mid \underline{B}_1 \times \underline{B}_2 \mid A \to \underline{B}$
Ground Value Types:	$G ::=$	$K \mid \mathbf{1} \mid G_1 \times G_2 \mid \mathbf{0} \mid G_1 + G_2$
Value Terms:	$V ::=$	$c \mid x \mid \star \mid (V_1, V_2) \mid \mathbf{inj}_\mathbf{1}^{A_1+A_2} V \mid \mathbf{inj}_\mathbf{2}^{A_1+A_2} V \mid \mathbf{thunk}\, M$
Computation Terms:	$M, N, \ldots ::=$	$\mathbf{coerce}_{\varepsilon_1 \subseteq \varepsilon_2} M \mid \mathbf{return}_\varepsilon V \mid M \;\mathbf{to}\; x : A.\, N$
		$\mid \lambda\{\mathbf{1} \mapsto M_1, \mathbf{2} \mapsto M_2\} \mid \mathbf{1}`M \mid \mathbf{2}`M \mid \lambda x : A.\, M$
		$\mid V`M \mid \mathbf{match}\; V \;\mathbf{as}\; (x_1 : A_1, x_2 : A_2).\, M$
		$\mid \mathbf{match}\; V : \mathbf{0} \;\mathbf{as}\; \{\}^{\underline{B}}$
		$\mid \mathbf{match}\; V \;\mathbf{as}\; \{\mathbf{inj}_\mathbf{1} x_1 : A_1.\, M_1, \mathbf{inj}_\mathbf{2} x_2 : A_2.\, M_2\}$
		$\mid \mathbf{force}\; V \mid \mu x : \mathbf{U}_\varepsilon \underline{B}.\, M \mid \mathrm{op}_V^{\underline{B}} M$

Figure 1. MAIL Syntax

$$\vdash_{\mathrm{k}} K : \mathsf{Val} \qquad \vdash_{\mathrm{k}} \mathbf{1} : \mathsf{Val} \qquad \frac{\vdash_{\mathrm{k}} A_1 : \mathsf{Val} \quad \vdash_{\mathrm{k}} A_2 : \mathsf{Val}}{\vdash_{\mathrm{k}} A_1 \times A_2 : \mathsf{Val}}$$

$$\vdash_{\mathrm{k}} \mathbf{0} : \mathsf{Val} \qquad \frac{\vdash_{\mathrm{k}} A_1 : \mathsf{Val} \quad \vdash_{\mathrm{k}} A_2 : \mathsf{Val}}{\vdash_{\mathrm{k}} A_1 + A_2 : \mathsf{Val}} \qquad \frac{\vdash_{\mathrm{k}} \underline{B} : \mathsf{Comp}(\varepsilon)}{\vdash_{\mathrm{k}} \mathbf{U}_\varepsilon \underline{B} : \mathsf{Val}}$$

$$\frac{\vdash_{\mathrm{k}} A : \mathsf{Val}}{\vdash_{\mathrm{k}} \mathbf{F}_\varepsilon A : \mathsf{Comp}(\varepsilon)} \qquad \frac{\vdash_{\mathrm{k}} \underline{B}_1 : \mathsf{Comp}(\varepsilon) \quad \vdash_{\mathrm{k}} \underline{B}_2 : \mathsf{Comp}(\varepsilon)}{\vdash_{\mathrm{k}} \underline{B}_1 \times \underline{B}_2 : \mathsf{Comp}(\varepsilon)}$$

$$\frac{\vdash_{\mathrm{k}} A : \mathsf{Val} \quad \vdash_{\mathrm{k}} \underline{B} : \mathsf{Comp}(\varepsilon)}{\vdash_{\mathrm{k}} A \to \underline{B} : \mathsf{Comp}(\varepsilon)}$$

Figure 2. MAIL Kind System

The syntax of MAIL, for a given pre-signature σ, is displayed in Figure 1. It refines the CBPV dichotomy between values and computations. Instead of one kind of computation, for each effect set $\varepsilon \in \mathcal{E}$, we have ε-computations $\mathsf{Comp}(\varepsilon)$ that can cause effects in ε. We view MAIL as multiple copies of CBPV, one for each ε, sharing the same values. One can translate between these different CBPVs by means of coercion (see below).

Our types are a slight variation on CBPV types. Note that basic types are always value types. The unit, product, zero, and sum value types are standard. We have modified the CBPV thunk type to thunks $\mathbf{U}_\varepsilon \underline{B}$ of ε-computations of type $\underline{B}$. For each $\varepsilon \in \mathcal{E}$, the *returner type* $\mathbf{F}_\varepsilon A$ is the type of ε-computations that return a value of type A. It plays a similar rôle to that of the monadic type TA (where T is a monad) in Haskell. Levy's CBPV also has products of computations, which we include, and functions are computations that depend on a value. The *ground value types* $G \in \mathbf{Gnd}$ are those value types which do not include thunks. We call types of the form $\mathbf{F}_\varepsilon G$ *ground returner types*.

All of the built-in constants of σ-MAIL are value terms. The variables, unit value, and pairing construct are standard. Injections are annotated with their sum type. Computations M are thunked into values $\mathbf{thunk}\, M$, just as in ordinary CBPV.

Many type and effect systems contain a sub-effecting rule: if M is an ε_1-computation and $\varepsilon_1 \subseteq \varepsilon_2$ then M is an ε_2-computation. One implication of such a rule is that well-typed terms can have multiple types, and even multiple type derivations. As a consequence, the denotational semantics can no longer be defined directly on terms. Instead, it needs to be defined on the proofs that these terms are well-typed, and then *coherence* results are needed to show that the different semantics are compatible with each other.

This issue is familiar from languages that support *subtyping*. One standard way to circumvent it, followed here, is to use explicit coercion between a subtype and its supertype [43]. The terms $\mathbf{coerce}_{\varepsilon_1 \subseteq \varepsilon_2} M$ explicitly coerce ε_1-computations to ε_2-computations.

As usual in CBPV, we can turn any value into an ε-computation by returning it. The $M \;\mathbf{to}\; x : A.\, N$ construct sequences computations; it is analogous to $x \leftarrow M; N$ in Haskell. Note the intrinsic typing (a.k.a. Church-style typing).

The standard operational semantics of CBPV uses a stack machine. The two λ terms pop from the stack while the application terms $-`M$ push onto it. Thus, $\lambda\{\mathbf{1} \mapsto M_1, \mathbf{2} \mapsto M_2\}$ pops a *tag* off the stack and executes $M_1$ or $M_2$ accordingly. In turn, $\mathbf{1}`M$ pushes the tag $\mathbf{1}$ onto the stack and continues to execute M. Similarly, $\lambda x : A.\, M$ pops a value of type A and binds x to it, while $V`M$ pushes V onto the stack.

The pattern-matching terms eliminating products, zero and sum values are standard. Thunked computations are eliminated by forcing. Recursion is expressed by least fixed-points, as usual.

Importantly, computational effects are caused by the $\mathrm{op}_V^{\underline{B}} M$ terms. As an example, the following computation consists of a memory lookup operation, dereferencing memory location ℓ, followed by returning the memory word $\mathtt{w}$ stored there:

$$\mathtt{deref}^\varepsilon(\ell) \stackrel{\text{def}}{=} \mathtt{lookup}_\ell^{\mathbf{F}_\varepsilon \mathbf{Word}}(\lambda \mathtt{w} : \mathbf{Word}.\, \mathbf{return}_\varepsilon \mathtt{w})$$

The *effect operation symbol* `lookup` takes as a *parameter* the location ℓ to be dereferenced, and requires as *argument* a computation depending on the dereferenced memory word.

As another example, consider a non-deterministic choice operator `choose`, and a computation for non-deterministic coin tossing:

$$\mathtt{toss}^\varepsilon \stackrel{\text{def}}{=} \mathtt{choose}_\star^{\mathbf{F}_\varepsilon \mathbf{1}+\mathbf{1}}(\lambda \mathtt{v} : \mathbf{1}+\mathbf{1}.\, \mathbf{return}_\varepsilon \mathtt{v})$$

In this case the parameter is the unit value $\star$.

In general, $\mathrm{op}_V^{\underline{B}} M$ is an effect operation term with parameter V and argument M. Terms of the form

$$\mathrm{gen}_{\mathrm{op}}^\varepsilon(V) \stackrel{\text{def}}{=} \mathrm{op}_V^{\mathbf{F}_\varepsilon A}(\lambda x : A.\, \mathbf{return}_\varepsilon x)$$

are called *generic effects*. Thus $\mathtt{deref}^\varepsilon$ and $\mathtt{toss}^\varepsilon$ are the generic effects corresponding to `lookup` and `choose` respectively.

Our combination of CBPV syntax, intrinsic typing and explicit coercion leads to a verbose and cumbersome syntax. However, considering our setting as an *intermediate representation* used by an optimising compiler, this issue becomes irrelevant, as the syntax is generated automatically, being seen only by the compiler.

The kind system for MAIL, given a pre-signature σ, is displayed in Figure 2; it consists of a kind judgement relation $\vdash_{\mathrm{k}}$ between types and kinds. We denote by $\mathbf{Val}$ the set of well-kinded value types $\{V \mid \vdash_{\mathrm{k}} V : \mathsf{Val}\}$. Similarly, we write $\mathbf{Comp}(\varepsilon)$ for the set of well-kinded ε-computation types. A *well-kinded context* $\Gamma : \mathrm{Dom}(\Gamma) \to \mathbf{Val}$ is a function from a *finite* set of variables to $\mathbf{Val}$. We write $\Gamma, x : A$ for the extension $\Gamma[x \mapsto A]$.

Given a pre-signature σ, an *arity assignment* $\mathrm{ar} : |\sigma| \to \mathbf{Gnd}^2$ sends elements of $|\sigma|$ to pairs of ground types such that $\mathrm{ar}(\Omega) = \langle \mathbf{0}, \mathbf{1} \rangle$. When $\mathrm{ar}(\mathrm{op}) = \langle A, P \rangle$ we write instead $\mathrm{op} : A \to P$. The first component A is called the *arity type* and the second component P is called the *parameter type*. When the parameter type is $P = \mathbf{1}$ we simply write $\mathrm{op} : A$. When $\mathrm{op} : \mathbf{0}$ we call op an *(effect) constant symbol*. Thus, Ω is a constant symbol.

For example, one would have $\mathtt{lookup} : \mathbf{Word} \to \mathbf{Loc}$ as `lookup` has a location parameter and its argument expects the cor-

$$\Gamma \vdash_{\mathrm{v}} c : A_c \qquad \frac{\Gamma(x) = A}{\Gamma \vdash_{\mathrm{v}} x : A} \qquad \Gamma \vdash_{\mathrm{v}} \star : \mathbf{1} \qquad \frac{\Gamma \vdash_{\mathrm{v}} V_1 : A_1 \quad \Gamma \vdash_{\mathrm{v}} V_2 : A_2}{\Gamma \vdash_{\mathrm{v}} (V_1, V_2) : A_1 \times A_2}$$

$$\frac{\Gamma \vdash_{\mathrm{v}} V : A_i}{\Gamma \vdash_{\mathrm{v}} \mathbf{inj_i}^{A_1+A_2} V : A_1 + A_2} \qquad \frac{\Gamma \vdash_{\varepsilon} M : \underline{B}}{\Gamma \vdash_{\mathrm{v}} \mathbf{thunk}\, M : \mathbf{U}_{\varepsilon}\underline{B}}$$

$$\frac{\Gamma \vdash_{\varepsilon_1} M : \mathbf{F}_{\varepsilon_1} A}{\Gamma \vdash_{\varepsilon_2} \mathbf{coerce}_{\varepsilon_1 \subseteq \varepsilon_2} M : \mathbf{F}_{\varepsilon_2} A} \qquad \frac{\Gamma \vdash_{\mathrm{v}} V : A}{\Gamma \vdash_{\varepsilon} \mathbf{return}_{\varepsilon} V : \mathbf{F}_{\varepsilon} A}$$

$$\frac{\Gamma \vdash_{\varepsilon} M : \mathbf{F}_{\varepsilon} A \quad \Gamma, x : A \vdash_{\varepsilon} N : \underline{B}}{\Gamma \vdash_{\varepsilon} M \,\mathbf{to}\, x : A.\, N : \underline{B}}$$

$$\frac{\Gamma \vdash_{\varepsilon} M_1 : \underline{B}_1 \quad \Gamma \vdash_{\varepsilon} M_2 : \underline{B}_2}{\Gamma \vdash_{\varepsilon} \lambda\{\mathbf{1} \mapsto M_1, \mathbf{2} \mapsto M_2\} : \underline{B}_1 \times \underline{B}_2} \qquad \frac{\Gamma \vdash_{\varepsilon} M : \underline{B}_1 \times \underline{B}_2}{\Gamma \vdash_{\varepsilon} \mathbf{i}`M : \underline{B}_i}$$

$$\frac{\Gamma, x : A \vdash_{\varepsilon} M : \underline{B}}{\Gamma \vdash_{\varepsilon} \lambda x : A.\, M : A \to \underline{B}} \qquad \frac{\Gamma \vdash_{\mathrm{v}} V : A \quad \Gamma \vdash_{\varepsilon} M : A \to \underline{B}}{\Gamma \vdash_{\varepsilon} V`M : \underline{B}}$$

$$\frac{\Gamma \vdash_{\mathrm{v}} V : A_1 \times A_2 \quad \Gamma, x_1 : A_2, y : A_2 \vdash_{\varepsilon} M : \underline{B}}{\Gamma \vdash_{\varepsilon} \mathbf{match}\, V \,\mathbf{as}\, (x_1 : A_1, x_2 : A_2) .\, M : \underline{B}}$$

$$\frac{\Gamma \vdash_{\mathrm{v}} V : \mathbf{0}}{\Gamma \vdash_{\varepsilon} \mathbf{match}\, V : \mathbf{0} \,\mathbf{as}\, \{\}^{\underline{B}} : \underline{B}}$$

$$\frac{\Gamma \vdash_{\mathrm{v}} V : A_1 + A_2 \quad \Gamma, x_1 : A_1 \vdash_{\varepsilon} M_1 : \underline{B} \quad \Gamma, x_2 : A_2 \vdash_{\varepsilon} M_2 : \underline{B}}{\Gamma \vdash_{\varepsilon} \mathbf{match}\, V \,\mathbf{as}\, \{\mathbf{inj_1} x_1 : A_1.\, M_1, \mathbf{inj_2} x_2 : A_2.\, M_2\} : \underline{B}}$$

$$\frac{\Gamma \vdash_{\mathrm{v}} V : \mathbf{U}_{\varepsilon}\underline{B}}{\Gamma \vdash_{\varepsilon} \mathbf{force}\, V : \underline{B}} \qquad \frac{\Gamma, x : \mathbf{U}_{\varepsilon}\underline{B} \vdash_{\varepsilon} M : \underline{B}}{\Gamma \vdash_{\varepsilon} \mu x : \mathbf{U}_{\varepsilon}\underline{B}.\, M : \underline{B}}\,(\Omega \in \varepsilon)$$

$$\frac{\Gamma \vdash_{\varepsilon} V : P \quad \Gamma \vdash_{\varepsilon} M : A \to \underline{B}}{\Gamma \vdash_{\varepsilon} \mathrm{op}_V^{\underline{B}} M : \underline{B}}\,(\mathrm{op} : A \to P, \mathrm{op} \in \varepsilon)$$

Figure 3. MAIL Type System

responding memory word. Similarly, one would have `choose` : $\mathbf{2}$ where, $\mathbf{2} = \mathbf{1} + \mathbf{1}$, as `choose` has a trivial parameter. We say that `choose` is a *binary* operation symbol. Example constant type assignments are: $'\mathtt{a}' : \mathbf{Char}$, $+\!\!+ : \mathbf{U}_{\emptyset}((\mathbf{Str} \times \mathbf{Str}) \to \mathbf{F}_{\emptyset}\mathbf{Str})$, and, for $\varepsilon \stackrel{\text{def}}{=} \{\mathtt{ArithmeticOverflow}\}$:

$$+ : \mathbf{U}_{\varepsilon}(\mathbf{Word} \times \mathbf{Word} \to \mathbf{F}_{\varepsilon}\mathbf{Word})$$

Definition 2. *A* MAIL signature *is a triple* $\Sigma = \langle \sigma, \mathrm{ar}, A_{-} \rangle$ *where:* σ *is a pre-signature;* ar *is an arity assignment; and* $A_{-} : \kappa \to \mathbf{Val}$ *is a* type assignment *for the built-in constant symbols.*

The type system of MAIL, given a signature Σ, is displayed in Figure 3; it is given by type judgement relations $\Gamma \vdash_{\mathrm{v}} V : A$ and $\Gamma \vdash_{\varepsilon} M : \underline{B}$, where Γ, A, $\underline{B}$ are well-kinded contexts, value types and ε-computation kinds, respectively, and where V, M are value and computation terms, respectively. Signatures Σ determine the language of MAIL, meaning its syntax and kind and typing relations; when we need to mention this dependence we write Σ-MAIL. We call closed ground returners $\vdash_{\varepsilon} P : \mathbf{F}_{\varepsilon} G$ *programs.*

The type system is straightforward, apart from the rules for coercion, recursion and effect operation symbols. The coercion rule may seem surprising — we only allow coercion of returners. However this restriction, which is semantically natural, allows sufficient generality. For if $\varepsilon \subseteq \varepsilon'$, then for any $\underline{B} : \mathsf{Comp}(\varepsilon)$ one can inductively define a type $\underline{B}' : \mathsf{Comp}(\varepsilon')$ by: $(\mathbf{F}_{\varepsilon} A)' = \mathbf{F}_{\varepsilon'} A$, $(\underline{B}_1 \times \underline{B}_2)' = (\underline{B}_1)' \times (\underline{B}_2)'$, and $(A \to \underline{B})' = A \to \underline{B}'$; there is then an evident coercion from $\underline{B}$ to $\underline{B}'$.

We note too that, from a CBPV perspective, call-by-value types are always translated into returners [26], hence the coercion rule immediately suffices to subsume existing effect systems. We do not know of any call-by-name effect systems (see also Section 7).

Next, the recursion rule only allows recursive calls when the effect set includes possible divergence. Finally, the effect operation rule formalises the informal explanation given earlier. Another way to view this rule is via continuation passing — we pass a continuation M that, depending on the effect's result, proceeds after the effect has been caused. For example, the rules for the I/O effects `input` : $\mathbf{Char}$ and `output` : $\mathbf{1} \to \mathbf{Char}$ are, for suitable ε's:

$$\frac{\Gamma \vdash_{\varepsilon} M : \mathbf{Char} \to \underline{B}}{\Gamma \vdash_{\varepsilon} \mathtt{input}^{\underline{B}} M : \underline{B}} \qquad \frac{\Gamma \vdash_{\mathrm{v}} V : \mathbf{Char} \quad \Gamma \vdash_{\varepsilon} M : \mathbf{1} \to \underline{B}}{\Gamma \vdash_{\varepsilon} \mathtt{output}_V^{\underline{B}} M : \underline{B}}$$

The latter is analogous to Levy's `print` statement [26]. For the corresponding generic effects we derive the familiar $\mathtt{get}^{\varepsilon}$, $\mathtt{put}^{\varepsilon}$:

$$\Gamma \vdash_{\varepsilon} \mathtt{get}^{\varepsilon} : \mathbf{F}_{\varepsilon}\mathbf{Char} \qquad \frac{\Gamma \vdash_{\mathrm{v}} V : \mathbf{Char}}{\Gamma \vdash_{\varepsilon} \mathtt{put}^{\varepsilon} : \mathbf{F}_{\varepsilon}\mathbf{1}}$$

3. Semantics

We begin with some preliminary material on domain theory in Section 3.1 concerning ω-cpos, and then consider inequational theories and their models in ω-cpos in Section 3.2. We can then define models of MAIL and its denotational semantics in Section 3.3. In Section 3.4 we consider the validity of optimisations and construct our two main MAIL models — the conservative and axiomatic restriction models.

3.1 ω-cpos

Domain theory provides the mathematical machinery needed to model recursion; here we review terminology and relevant notation. The simplest type of domains sufficient for our needs are *ω-complete partial orders (ω-cpos)*, i.e., partial orders $W = \langle |W|, \leq \rangle$ closed under suprema $\bigvee a_n$ of increasing ω-chains $\langle a_n \rangle$. A *(Scott) continuous function* $f : W_1 \to W_2$ between ω-cpos is a monotone function preserving such suprema (i.e., $f(\bigvee a_n) = \bigvee f(a_n)$ for any increasing ω-chain $\langle a_n \rangle$).

A *discrete* ω-cpo is a set ordered by equality $\langle A, = \rangle$. The *empty ω-cpo* $\mathbb{0}$ is $\langle \emptyset, = \rangle$; we write $?_W : \emptyset \to |W|$ for the empty map. The singleton ω-cpo $\mathbb{1}$ is $\langle \{\star\}, = \rangle$; we write $!_W : |W| \to \{\star\}$ for the constantly-$\star$ map.

The *sum* $W_1 + W_2$ of two ω-cpos is the evident ω-cpo over their disjoint union $|W_1| + |W_2|$. We write $\iota_i : W_i \to W_1 + W_2$ for the evident injections. Given two continuous functions $f_i : W_i \to W'$, $i = 1, 2$, the map $[f_1, f_2] : W_1 + W_2 \to W'$, where:

$$[f_1, f_2]\,(w) \stackrel{\text{def}}{=} \begin{cases} f_1(w_1) & w = \iota_1 w_1 \\ f_2(w_2) & w = \iota_2 w_2 \end{cases}$$

is continuous. We write $\mathbb{n}$ for the discrete domain over n elements, namely $\mathbb{1} + \ldots + \mathbb{1}$.

The *product* $W_1 \times W_2$ of two ω-cpos is the componentwise partial order over their Cartesian product $|W_1| \times |W_2|$. We write $\pi_i : W_1 \times W_2 \to W_i$ for the evident projections. Given two continuous functions $f_i : W' \to W_i$, $i = 1, 2$, the map $\langle f_1, f_2 \rangle : W' \to W_1 \times W_2$, where:

$$\langle f_1, f_2 \rangle\,(w) \stackrel{\text{def}}{=} \langle f_1(w), f_2(w) \rangle$$

is continuous. The product $\prod_{i=1}^{n} W_i$ of any finite number of ω-cpos is defined similarly.

The *function space* $W_2^{W_1}$ of two ω-cpos consists of all continuous functions from W_1 to W_2, ordered pointwise: $f \leq g$ iff for all $w \in W_1$, $f(w) \leq g(w)$; its lubs are also given pointwise. We write $\mathrm{eval} : W_2^{W_1} \times W_1 \to W_2$ for the evaluation map given by $\langle f, d \rangle \mapsto f(w)$. If $f : \prod_i W_i \to W$ is continuous then *currying* the j-th component $\langle d_i \rangle_{i \neq j} \mapsto (w_j \mapsto f \langle d_i \rangle)$ yields a continuous map $\text{curry}_j f : \left(\prod_{i \neq j} W_i\right) \to W^{W_j}$.

An ω-cpo W is *pointed* if it has a least element $\bot$. Continuous functions over pointed ω-cpos have *least* fixed-points and the least fixed-point operation $\mu : W^W \to W$ is continuous.

3.2 Inequational Theories

A full account of Plotkin and Power's algebraic theory of effects requires the notion of (discrete) countable $\omega\mathbf{CPO}$-enriched Lawvere theories [17]. Here we restrict to the simpler, and more elementary, *(finitary) inequational theories.*

An *(equational) signature* is a pair $\Sigma = \langle |\Sigma|, \text{ar}_\Sigma \rangle$ where $|\Sigma|$ is a set of *operation symbols* and the *arity function* ar_Σ assigns to each operation $f \in \Sigma$ a finite set $\text{ar}_\Sigma(f)$ called its *arity*. We adopt the notation $f : A$ for $A = \text{ar}(f)$. When $f : \mathbb{n}$ we say that f is *n-ary*. Nullary operations are also called *constants*. We will write $\{f_1 : \text{ar}(f_1), \ldots, f_n : \text{ar}(f_n)\}$ for the signature $\langle \{f_1, \ldots, f_n\}, \text{ar} \rangle$.

For example, the *non-determinism* signature, Σ_{ND}, is $\{\vee : \mathbb{2}\}$. It consists of exactly one binary operation $\vee : \mathbb{2}$. Again, given a finite set $\mathbb{V}$ of *storable values*, the global $\mathbb{V}$-state signature, $\Sigma_{\text{GS}(\mathbb{V})}$ is given by a look-up operation $\texttt{lookup} : \mathbb{V}$ and $\mathbb{V}$-many unary operations for updating the state $\texttt{update}_v : \mathbb{1}$ $(v \in \mathbb{V})$.

Fix a countable set of *variables* $\mathbf{Var}$ ranged over by $\mathbf{x}$, $\mathbf{y}$, etc. Given a signature Σ, we define the set Terms^Σ of Σ-terms inductively: a term is either a variable $\mathbf{x}$, or of the form $f(\tau)$ where $f : A$ and $\tau : A \to \text{Terms}^\Sigma$. When f is n-ary we may use the usual positional notation $f(t_1, \ldots, t_n)$ to write such terms, and, in the binary case, we may use infix notation. It is routine to define substitutions $\theta : \mathbf{Var} \to \text{Terms}$, and their applications $t\theta$ to terms.

Recall that a preorder is a reflexive, transitive binary relation. An *inequational theory* $\mathcal{T}$ is a pair $\langle \Sigma, \leq \rangle$ where Σ is a signature and $\leq$ is a preorder over terms, which is a *substitutive congruence*, meaning that it satisfies the following two properties:

Congruence For all substitutions θ_1, θ_2 satisfying, for all $\mathbf{x}$ in $\mathbf{Var}$, $\theta_1(\mathbf{x}) \leq \theta_2(\mathbf{x})$, and for all terms t, we have $t\theta_1 \leq t\theta_2$.

Substitution For all terms t_1,t_2 for which $t_1 \leq t_2$, and for all substitutions θ, we have $t_1\theta \leq t_2\theta$.

We write $t = s$ iff $t \leq s$ and $s \leq t$.

Let Σ be a signature. The *free* or *empty* theory for Σ is given by syntactic equality, $\langle \Sigma, \equiv \rangle$. The *inconsistent* theory for Σ is given by the full relation $\langle \Sigma, \text{Terms}^2 \rangle$. Note that all theories $\langle \Sigma, \leq \rangle$ lie between these two theories, i.e., $\equiv \subseteq \leq \subseteq \text{Terms}^2$.

Let $\text{Ax} \subseteq \text{Terms} \times \text{Terms}$ be any set of *axioms*. The *theory generated from* Ax is $\text{Th}^\Sigma \text{Ax} = \langle \Sigma, \leq \rangle$ where $\leq$ is the least preorder over terms that contains Ax and which is a substitutive congruence. Note that the empty theory is $\text{Th}^\Sigma \emptyset$ and the inconsistent theory is $\text{Th}^\Sigma \{\mathbf{x} \leq \mathbf{y}\} = \text{Th}^\Sigma \{\mathbf{x} = \mathbf{y}\}$. The *lifting* theory $\mathcal{T}_\bot$ is given by $\text{Th}^{\{\bot : \mathbb{0}\}} \{\bot \leq \mathbf{x}\}$. A more interesting example is the theory of *semilattices*, which consists of commutativity, associativity and absorption equations for the non-determinism signature Σ_{ND}:

$$\mathbf{x} \vee \mathbf{y} = \mathbf{y} \vee \mathbf{x}, \quad (\mathbf{x} \vee \mathbf{y}) \vee \mathbf{z} = \mathbf{x} \vee (\mathbf{y} \vee \mathbf{z}), \quad \mathbf{x} \vee \mathbf{x} = \mathbf{x}$$

The theory of *lower* semilattices is obtained by adding the axiom $\mathbf{x} \leq \mathbf{x} \vee \mathbf{y}$; the theory of *upper* semilattices is obtained by instead adding $\mathbf{x} \geq \mathbf{x} \vee \mathbf{y}$. As a final example, let $\mathbb{V}$ be a finite set of storable values. The corresponding theory of global state arises out of the following three equations [29, 34] over the global state signature $\Sigma_{\text{GS}(\mathbb{V})}$:

$$\texttt{lookup}\,(\lambda v : \mathbb{V}.\texttt{update}_v(\mathbf{x})) = \mathbf{x}$$
$$\texttt{update}_{v_0}(\texttt{lookup}\,(\lambda v : \mathbb{V}.\mathbf{x}_v)) = \texttt{update}_{v_0}(\mathbf{x}_{v_0})$$
$$\texttt{update}_{v_1}(\texttt{update}_{v_2}(\mathbf{x})) = \texttt{update}_{v_2}(\mathbf{x})$$

Given a signature Σ, an *ω-cpo Σ-algebra* $\mathcal{A}$ consists of a pair $\langle |\mathcal{A}|, [\![-]\!]_\mathcal{A} \rangle$ where $|\mathcal{A}|$ is an ω-cpo and $[\![-]\!]_\mathcal{A}$ assigns to each operation $f : A$ a continuous function $[\![f]\!] : |\mathcal{A}|^A \to |\mathcal{A}|$. Every ω-cpo Σ-algebra $\mathcal{A}$ induces an *interpretation function* $\mathcal{I}_\mathcal{A}[\![-]\!]_- : \text{Terms} \times |\mathcal{A}|^{\mathbf{Var}} \to |\mathcal{A}|$, given for every variable assignment $\delta \in |\mathcal{A}|^{\mathbf{Var}}$ inductively over terms t by:

$$\mathcal{I}_\mathcal{A}[\![t]\!]_\delta \stackrel{\text{def}}{=} \begin{cases} \delta(\mathbf{x}) & t = \mathbf{x} \\ ([\![f]\!]_\mathcal{A}(\lambda a : A.[\![\tau(a)]\!]_\delta)) & t = f(\tau), f : A \end{cases}$$

Let $\mathcal{A}_1, \mathcal{A}_2$ be two such Σ-algebras. Their *product* $\mathcal{A}_1 \times \mathcal{A}_2$ is given by $\langle |\mathcal{A}|_1 \times |\mathcal{A}|_2, [\![-]\!]_\times \rangle$, where, for all $f : A$, $[\![f]\!]_\times (\tau)$ is given pointwise by $\left\langle [\![f]\!]_{\mathcal{A}_1}(\pi_1 \circ \tau), [\![f]\!]_{\mathcal{A}_2}(\pi_2 \circ \tau) \right\rangle$. Let $\mathcal{A}$ be a Σ-algebra and W an ω-cpo. The *power algebra* $\mathcal{A}^W$ is given by $\left\langle |\mathcal{A}|^W, [\![-]\!] \right\rangle$, where, for all $f : A$, $[\![f]\!](\tau)$ is given pointwise by $\lambda w.[\![f]\!]_\mathcal{A}(\lambda a.\tau(a)(w))$.

Given an inequational theory $\mathcal{T} = \langle \Sigma, \leq \rangle$, an *$\omega$-cpo $\mathcal{T}$-model* is a Σ-algebra $\mathcal{A}$ such that, for all $t_1 \leq t_2$, and for all $\delta \in |\mathcal{A}|^{\mathbf{Var}}$, we have $[\![t_1]\!]_\delta \leq [\![t_2]\!]_\delta$. For example, the discretely-ordered collection of all non-empty finite subsets of a set with the union operation is a model of the theory of semilattices. As another example, let $\mathbb{V}$ be a finite discrete ω-cpo of storable values and let W be any ω-cpo. Then $(\mathbb{V} \times W)^\mathbb{V}$ is the carrier set for a $\Sigma_{\text{GS}(\mathbb{V})}$-algebra with the obvious operations. The product of two $\mathcal{T}$-models is again a $\mathcal{T}$-model. If $\mathcal{A}$ is a $\mathcal{T}$ model and W an ω-cpo, then $\mathcal{A}^W$ is also a $\mathcal{T}$-model.

Given two Σ-algebras $\mathcal{A}_1$, $\mathcal{A}_2$, a *Σ-algebra homomorphism* $h : \mathcal{A}_1 \to \mathcal{A}_2$ is a continuous function $h : |\mathcal{A}_1| \to |\mathcal{A}_2|$ that satisfies, for all $f : A$ and $\tau \in |\mathcal{A}_1|^A$:

$$h\left([\![f]\!]_1(\tau)\right) = [\![f]\!]_2(h \circ \tau)$$

Homomorphisms between two *$\mathcal{T}$-models* are Σ-algebra homomorphisms between them as algebras. For example, the projections $\pi_i : |\mathcal{A}_1| \times |\mathcal{A}_2| \to |\mathcal{A}_i|$ are Σ-algebra homomorphisms from the product $\mathcal{A}_1 \times \mathcal{A}_2$, for all Σ-algebras $\mathcal{A}_1$, $\mathcal{A}_2$.

Let $\mathcal{T}$ be a theory and W an ω-cpo. The *free $\mathcal{T}$-model over* W is a $\mathcal{T}$-model $F_\mathcal{T} W$ for which exists a continuous function $\eta^\mathcal{T}_W : W \to |F_\mathcal{T} W|$, called the *unit* of the free model, such that for all $\mathcal{T}$-models $\mathcal{A}$ and continuous functions $f : W \to |\mathcal{A}|$ there exists a unique $\mathcal{T}$-algebra homomorphism $f^\dagger_\mathcal{T} : F_\mathcal{T} W \to \mathcal{A}$ satisfying $f = f^\dagger \circ \eta$.

For example, the free model of the *lifting theory*, defined by $\text{Th}^{\{\bot : \mathbb{0}\}}\{\Omega \leq \mathbf{x}\}$, over an ω-cpo W is given by $|W| + \{\bot\}$ with $w \leq v$ iff $w = \bot$ or $w \leq_W v$. As another example, the $\mathcal{T}_{\text{GS}(\mathbb{V})}$-algebra on $(\mathbb{V} \times W)^\mathbb{V}$ described above is the free model over W [19, 34]. The free model for any theory over any ω-cpo always exists, by appeal to Freyd's adjoint functor theorem, cf. Abramsky and Jung [1]. However, its structure may be non-trivial [16, 31].

Let Σ_1, Σ_2 be signatures. A *translation* $\mathfrak{T} : \Sigma_1 \to \Sigma_2$ is a pair $\langle \mathbf{x}^-_-, \mathfrak{T}(-) \rangle$ where $\mathbf{x}^f_- : A \hookrightarrow \mathbf{Var}$ is an injection, for each Σ_1-operation $f : A$, and $\mathfrak{T}(-) : \Sigma_1 \to \text{Terms}^{\Sigma_2}$ such that, for each Σ_1-operation f, all the variables in $\mathfrak{T}(f)$ are in the image of $\mathbf{x}^f_-$. I.e., for each a in A there is a distinct variable $\mathbf{x}^f_a$, and the variables in $\mathfrak{T}(f)$ may only involve these variables. Each translation $\mathfrak{T} : \Sigma_1 \to \Sigma_2$ induces a *translation function* $\mathfrak{T} : \text{Terms}^{\Sigma_1} \to \text{Terms}^{\Sigma_2}$ where $\mathfrak{T}(\mathbf{x}) = \mathbf{x}$ and where $\mathfrak{T}(f(\tau))$ is given by substituting $\mathfrak{T}(\tau a)$ for $\mathbf{x}^f_a$ in $\mathfrak{T}(f)$ simultaneously for all $a \in A$, i.e., $\mathfrak{T}(f(\tau)) = \mathfrak{T}(f)\left[\mathfrak{T}(\tau a)/\mathbf{x}^f_a\right]_{a \in A}$.

Let $\mathcal{T}_1$, $\mathcal{T}_2$ be theories. A *translation* $\mathfrak{T} : \mathcal{T}_1 \to \mathcal{T}_2$ is a translation $\mathfrak{T} : \Sigma_1 \to \Sigma_2$ that respects the inequalities:

$$t_1 \leq_1 t_2 \implies \mathfrak{T}(t_1) \leq_2 \mathfrak{T}(t_2)$$

For example, given a finite set $\mathbb{V}$, consider the overwrite theory $\mathcal{T}_{\mathrm{OW}(\mathbb{V})}$ given by the signature $\{\mathtt{update}_v : \mathbb{1} \mid v \in \mathbb{V}\}$ and the axioms $\{\mathtt{update}_{v_1}(\mathtt{update}_{v_2}\mathbf{x}) = \mathtt{update}_{v_2}\mathbf{x} \mid v_1, v_2 \in \mathbb{V}\}$. The map $\mathtt{update}_v \mapsto \mathtt{update}_v\mathbf{x}_\star$ induces a translation from $\mathcal{T}_{\mathrm{OW}(\mathbb{V})}$ to $\mathcal{T}_{\mathrm{GS}(\mathbb{V})}$. We will only use such trivial translations, which have the form $\langle\langle f, a\rangle \mapsto \mathbf{x}_a, f \mapsto f(\lambda a.\mathbf{x}_a)\rangle$, i.e., they translate operation symbols to themselves. They are translations from $\mathcal{T}_1$ to $\mathcal{T}_2$ iff $\Sigma_1 \subseteq \Sigma_2$ and $\leq_1 \subseteq \leq_2$.

Let $\mathfrak{T} : \mathcal{T}_1 \to \mathcal{T}_2$ be a translation. Every $\mathcal{T}_2$-model $\mathcal{A}$ induces a $\mathcal{T}_1$-model $\mathfrak{T}^*(\mathcal{A})$ as follows. The carrier ω-cpo $|\mathfrak{T}^*(\mathcal{A})|$ is $|\mathcal{A}|$. For each operation $f : A$ in Σ_1, we have a term $\mathfrak{T}(f) \in \mathrm{Terms}^{\Sigma_2}$. Recall the interpretation function $\mathcal{I}_{\mathcal{A}}[\![-]\!]_-$, and set, for all δ in $|\mathcal{A}|^{\mathbf{Var}}$:

$$[\![f]\!]_{\mathfrak{T}^*(\mathcal{A})}(\delta) \stackrel{\mathrm{def}}{=} \mathcal{I}_{\mathcal{A}}[\![\mathfrak{T}(f)]\!]_\delta$$

We obtain a continuous function $|\mathfrak{T}^*(\mathcal{A})|^A \to |\mathfrak{T}^*(\mathcal{A})|$. Thus $\mathfrak{T}^*(\mathcal{A})$ is a Σ_1-algebra, and because $\mathfrak{T}$ preserves $\mathcal{T}_1$-inequalities and $\mathcal{A}$ is a $\mathcal{T}_2$-model, $\mathfrak{T}^*(\mathcal{A})$ is a $\mathcal{T}_1$-model. Given an ω-cpo W, the $\mathcal{T}_2$ unit over W is a map $\eta_W^{\mathcal{T}_2} : W \to |\mathfrak{T}^*(F_{\mathcal{T}_2}W)|$. Therefore, by the free $\mathcal{T}_1$-model definition, there exists a (unique) homomorphism

$$m_W^{\mathfrak{T}} \stackrel{\mathrm{def}}{=} \left(\eta_W^{\mathcal{T}_2}\right)^{\dagger}_{\mathcal{T}_1} : F_{\mathcal{T}_1}W \to \mathfrak{T}^*(F_{\mathcal{T}_2}W)$$

such that $\eta_W^{\mathcal{T}_2} = m_W^{\mathfrak{T}} \circ \eta_W^{\mathcal{T}_1}$. Following Filinski's *layered monads* [10], we call the function $m_W^{\mathfrak{T}} : |F_{\mathcal{T}_1}W| \to |F_{\mathcal{T}_2}W|$ the *layering of $F_{\mathcal{T}_1}W$ over $F_{\mathcal{T}_2}W$ along $\mathfrak{T}$*.

Finally, we introduce two common methods to combine theories [19]. Let Σ_1, Σ_2 be signatures. Their *sum* $\Sigma_1 + \Sigma_2$ is given by $|\Sigma_1 + \Sigma_2| \stackrel{\mathrm{def}}{=} |\Sigma_1| + |\Sigma_2|$ and $\mathrm{ar}_{\Sigma_1+\Sigma_2}(\iota_i f) \stackrel{\mathrm{def}}{=} \mathrm{ar}_i(f)$. Given a term t in $\mathrm{Terms}^{\Sigma_i}$, relabelling the operations in t according to the injection $\iota_i : |\Sigma_i| \to |\Sigma_1 + \Sigma_2|$ yields a term $\iota_i t$ in $\mathrm{Terms}^{\Sigma_1+\Sigma_2}$. We can apply this relabelling to binary relations over Σ_i in the obvious manner. Let $\mathcal{T}_1$, $\mathcal{T}_2$ be two theories. Their *sum* $\mathcal{T}_1 + \mathcal{T}_2$ is given by $\mathrm{Th}^{\Sigma_1+\Sigma_2}((\iota_1 \leq_1) \cup (\iota_2 \leq_2))$. Their *tensor* $\mathcal{T}_1 \otimes \mathcal{T}_2$ is given by $\mathrm{Th}^{\Sigma_1+\Sigma_2}((\iota_1 \leq_1) \cup (\iota_2 \leq_2) \cup (\mathrm{Ax}_{\Sigma_1 \otimes \Sigma_2}))$, where $\mathrm{Ax}_{\Sigma_1 \otimes \Sigma_2}$ contains all equations of the form:

$$f^1(\lambda a_1.f^2(\lambda a_2.\mathbf{x}_{a_1,a_2})) = f^2(\lambda a_2.f^1(\lambda a_1.\mathbf{x}_{a_1,a_2}))$$

where $f^i : A_i$ in $\iota_i\Sigma_i$, and $a_i \in A_i$.

3.3 Semantics

Given a MAIL signature Σ, a Σ-MAIL *model* consists of a quadruple $\langle \mathcal{B}[\![-]\!], \mathcal{T}_-, \mathfrak{T}_-, \mathcal{K}[\![-]\!]\rangle$ which we describe presently.

To each basic type $K \in \mathbf{Bsc}$, we assign an ω-cpo $\mathcal{B}[\![K]\!]$. This assignment allows us to interpret ground value types $G \in \mathbf{Gnd}$:

$$\mathcal{G}[\![K]\!] \stackrel{\mathrm{def}}{=} \mathcal{B}[\![K]\!]$$
$$\mathcal{G}[\![\mathbf{1}]\!] \stackrel{\mathrm{def}}{=} \mathbb{1} \quad \mathcal{G}[\![G_1 \times G_2]\!] \stackrel{\mathrm{def}}{=} \mathcal{G}[\![G_1]\!] \times \mathcal{G}[\![G_2]\!]$$
$$\mathcal{G}[\![\mathbf{0}]\!] \stackrel{\mathrm{def}}{=} \mathbb{0} \quad \mathcal{G}[\![G_1 + G_2]\!] \stackrel{\mathrm{def}}{=} \mathcal{G}[\![G_1]\!] + \mathcal{G}[\![G_2]\!]$$

We impose on $\mathcal{B}[\![-]\!]$ that, for all $\mathrm{op} : A \to P$, $\mathcal{G}[\![A]\!]$ is a finite discrete ω-cpo and $\mathcal{G}[\![P]\!]$ is discrete. For example, we may choose $\mathcal{B}[\![\mathbf{Word}]\!]$ and $\mathcal{B}[\![\mathbf{Loc}]\!]$ to be 2^{64} in a 64-bit setting, and $\mathcal{B}[\![\mathbf{Char}]\!]$ to be 2^7 for ASCII characters. As these interpretations are finite discrete domains, every ground type involving them will denote a finite discrete ω-cpo.

The signature Σ and this assignment induce an equational signature:

$$\mathcal{S}[\![|\sigma|]\!] \stackrel{\mathrm{def}}{=} \{\mathrm{op}_p : \mathcal{G}[\![A]\!] \mid \mathrm{op} : A \to P \in |\sigma|, p \in \mathcal{G}[\![P]\!]\}$$

which, in turn, induces an equational sub-signature, for each $\varepsilon \in \mathcal{E}$:

$$|\mathcal{SUB}[\![\varepsilon]\!]| \stackrel{\mathrm{def}}{=} \{\mathrm{op}_p \in \mathcal{S}[\![|\sigma|]\!] \mid \mathrm{op} \in \varepsilon\}$$

$$\mathcal{V}[\![K]\!] \stackrel{\mathrm{def}}{=} \mathcal{B}[\![K]\!] \qquad \mathcal{CXT}[\![\Gamma]\!] \stackrel{\mathrm{def}}{=} \prod_{x \in \mathrm{Dom}(\Gamma)}[\![\Gamma(x)]\!]$$
$$\mathcal{V}[\![\mathbf{1}]\!] \stackrel{\mathrm{def}}{=} \mathbb{1}$$
$$\mathcal{V}[\![A_1 \times A_2]\!] \stackrel{\mathrm{def}}{=} [\![A_1]\!] \times [\![A_2]\!]$$
$$\mathcal{V}[\![\mathbf{0}]\!] \stackrel{\mathrm{def}}{=} \mathbb{0} \qquad \mathcal{C}_\varepsilon[\![\mathbf{F}_\varepsilon A]\!] \stackrel{\mathrm{def}}{=} F_\varepsilon[\![A]\!]$$
$$\mathcal{V}[\![A_1 + A_2]\!] \stackrel{\mathrm{def}}{=} [\![A_1]\!] + [\![A_2]\!] \qquad \mathcal{C}_\varepsilon[\![\underline{B}_1 \times \underline{B}_2]\!] \stackrel{\mathrm{def}}{=} [\![\underline{B}_1]\!] \times [\![\underline{B}_2]\!]$$
$$\mathcal{V}[\![\mathbf{U}_\varepsilon \underline{B}]\!] \stackrel{\mathrm{def}}{=} |[\![\underline{B}]\!]| \qquad \mathcal{C}_\varepsilon[\![A \to \underline{B}]\!] \stackrel{\mathrm{def}}{=} [\![\underline{B}]\!]^{[\![A]\!]}$$

Figure 4. Type Interpretation

The next component, $\mathcal{T}_-$, assigns to each $\varepsilon \in \mathcal{E}$ an inequational theory $\mathcal{T}_\varepsilon = \langle \Sigma_\varepsilon, \leq_\varepsilon\rangle$, such that $\mathcal{SUB}[\![\varepsilon]\!] \subseteq \Sigma_\varepsilon$ as a sub-signature, and such that if $\Omega \in \varepsilon$ then $\Omega \leq_\varepsilon \mathbf{x}$. Thus we get, for each $\varepsilon \in \mathcal{E}$ and ω-cpo W, the free ω-cpo $\mathcal{T}_\varepsilon$-algebra, $F_\varepsilon W$ and its corresponding unit η^ε and bijection $-^\dagger_\varepsilon$. The side condition guarantees that if $\Omega \in \varepsilon$ then all $\mathcal{T}_\varepsilon$-models are pointed ω-cpos. This assignment allows us to interpret the Σ-MAIL type system (see Figure 4): value types are interpreted as ω-cpos via $\mathcal{V}[\![-]\!]$; ε-computations as $\mathcal{T}_\varepsilon$-algebras via $\mathcal{C}_\varepsilon[\![-]\!]$; and contexts Γ as products via $\mathcal{CXT}[\![-]\!]$. For example, take $\mathcal{T}_\emptyset$ to be $\mathrm{Th}^\emptyset\emptyset$ the empty theory over the empty signature. In this case, $\mathcal{T}_\emptyset$-models are just ω-cpos, and $F_\emptyset W = W$.

The third component, $\mathfrak{T}_-$, assigns to each pair of subsets $\varepsilon_1 \subseteq \varepsilon_2$ in $\mathcal{E}$ a translation $\mathfrak{T}_{\varepsilon_1 \subseteq \varepsilon_2} : \mathcal{T}_{\varepsilon_1} \to \mathcal{T}_{\varepsilon_2}$. We require this translation to be *operation-compatible*, $\mathfrak{T}_{\varepsilon_1 \subseteq \varepsilon_2}(\mathrm{op}) = \mathrm{op}(\lambda a.\mathbf{x}_a^{\mathrm{op}})$, for all $\mathrm{op} \in \varepsilon_1$, and *inclusion-compatible (functorial)*:

$$\mathfrak{T}_{\varepsilon' \subseteq \varepsilon''}(\mathfrak{T}_{\varepsilon \subseteq \varepsilon'}(\mathrm{op})) = \mathfrak{T}_{\varepsilon \subseteq \varepsilon''}(\mathrm{op}) \qquad \mathfrak{T}_{\varepsilon \subseteq \varepsilon}(\mathrm{op}) = \mathrm{op}(\lambda a.\mathbf{x}_a^{\mathrm{op}})$$

for every triple $\varepsilon \subseteq \varepsilon' \subseteq \varepsilon''$ in $\mathcal{E}$ and $\mathrm{op} : A \to P$ in ε. For example, if $\mathcal{T}_\emptyset = \mathrm{Th}^\emptyset\emptyset$, we can choose $\mathfrak{T}_{\emptyset \subseteq \varepsilon}$ to be the empty translation. These translations induce an inclusion-compatible layering $m^{\varepsilon_1 \subseteq \varepsilon_2}$.

The final component, $\mathcal{K}[\![-]\!]$, assigns to each built-in constant $c \in \kappa$ an element $\mathcal{K}[\![c]\!] \in \mathcal{V}[\![A_c]\!]$. It is instructive to interpret the arithmetic constants on 64-bit integers that can cause exceptions as an example.

We summarise the definition of a Σ-MAIL model:

Definition 3. *Let Σ be a MAIL signature. A Σ-MAIL* model *is a quadruple $\mathcal{M} = \langle \mathcal{B}[\![-]\!], \mathcal{T}_-, \mathfrak{T}_-, \mathcal{K}[\![-]\!]\rangle$, where: $\mathcal{B}[\![-]\!]$ assigns to each basic type K an ω-cpo such that all $|\sigma|$-arities are interpreted as finite discrete domains; $\mathcal{T}_-$ assigns to each effect set a theory whose signature includes $\mathcal{SUB}[\![\varepsilon]\!]$, such that if $\Omega \in \varepsilon$ then $\Omega \leq \mathbf{x}$; $\mathfrak{T}_-$ assigns to each inclusion $\varepsilon_1 \subseteq \varepsilon_2$ a translation $\mathfrak{T}_{\varepsilon_1 \subseteq \varepsilon_2} : \mathcal{T}_{\varepsilon_1} \to \mathcal{T}_{\varepsilon_2}$ in a compatible manner; and $\mathcal{K}[\![-]\!]$ assigns to each built-in constant c an element $\mathcal{K}[\![c]\!] \in \mathcal{V}[\![A_c]\!]$.*

Given a Σ-MAIL model $\mathcal{M}$, we interpret Σ-MAIL terms as follows (see Figure 5): value terms $\Gamma \vdash_{\mathrm{v}} V : A$ are interpreted as continuous functions $\mathcal{VT}[\![V]\!] : \mathcal{CXT}[\![\Gamma]\!] \to \mathcal{V}[\![A]\!]$; and ε-computation terms $\Gamma \vdash_\varepsilon M : \underline{B}$ are interpreted as continuous functions $\mathcal{CT}_\varepsilon[\![M]\!] : \mathcal{CXT}[\![\Gamma]\!] \to |\mathcal{C}_\varepsilon[\![\underline{B}]\!]|$. The semantic functions have straightforward definitions. The only exception is coercion from ε_1-returners to ε_2-returners via the layering $m^{\varepsilon_1 \subseteq \varepsilon_2}$. Also note how the type system and the side condition over $\mathcal{T}_\varepsilon$ ensures these semantic functions are well-defined.

3.4 Validity and Models

First, we define the validity of optimisations in MAIL:

Definition 4. *Let $\mathcal{M}$ be a Σ-MAIL model, and $\Gamma \vdash P_i : X$, $i = 1, 2$ be two well-typed Σ-MAIL terms. We say that the optimisation $\Gamma \vdash P_1 = P_2 : X$ is* valid *in $\mathcal{M}$ if $\mathcal{M}[\![P_1]\!] = \mathcal{M}[\![P_2]\!]$. In this case we write $\mathcal{M} \models \Gamma \vdash P_1 = P_2 : X$. When Γ and X are clear, we simply write $\mathcal{M} \models P_1 = P_2$.*

$$\mathcal{VT}[\![c]\!](\gamma) \stackrel{\text{def}}{=} [\![c]\!] \quad \mathcal{VT}[\![x]\!](\gamma) \stackrel{\text{def}}{=} \pi_x(\gamma) \quad \mathcal{VT}[\![\star]\!](\gamma) \stackrel{\text{def}}{=} \star$$

$$\mathcal{VT}[\![(V_1, V_2)]\!](\gamma) \stackrel{\text{def}}{=} \langle [\![V_1]\!](\gamma), [\![V_2]\!](\gamma)\rangle$$

$$\mathcal{VT}\left[\!\!\left[\mathbf{inj_i}^{A_1+A_2} V\right]\!\!\right](\gamma) \stackrel{\text{def}}{=} \iota_i([\![V]\!](\gamma))$$

$$\mathcal{CT}_{\varepsilon_2}[\![\mathbf{coerce}_{\varepsilon_1 \subseteq \varepsilon_2} M]\!](\gamma) \stackrel{\text{def}}{=} m^{\varepsilon_1 \subseteq \varepsilon_2}([\![M]\!](\gamma))$$

$$\mathcal{CT}_\varepsilon[\![\mathbf{return}_\varepsilon V]\!](\gamma) \stackrel{\text{def}}{=} \eta^\varepsilon([\![V]\!](\gamma))$$

$$\mathcal{CT}_\varepsilon[\![M \text{ to } x : A.\, N]\!](\gamma) \stackrel{\text{def}}{=} (\lambda a.[\![N]\!](\gamma[x \mapsto a]))^\dagger_\varepsilon([\![M]\!](\gamma))$$

$$\mathcal{CT}_\varepsilon[\![\mathbf{i}`M]\!](\gamma) \stackrel{\text{def}}{=} \pi_i([\![M]\!](\gamma))$$

$$\mathcal{CT}_\varepsilon[\![V`M]\!](\gamma) \stackrel{\text{def}}{=} ([\![M]\!](\gamma))([\![V]\!](\gamma))$$

$$\mathcal{CT}_\varepsilon\left[\!\!\left[\text{ match } V : \mathbf{0} \text{ as } \{\}^{\underline{B}}\right]\!\!\right] \stackrel{\text{def}}{=} ?_{[\![\underline{B}]\!]}$$

$$\mathcal{CT}_\varepsilon[\![\text{ match } V \text{ as } \{\mathbf{inj_1} x_1 : A_1.\, M_1, \mathbf{inj_2} x_2 : A_2.\, M_2\}]\!](\gamma)$$

$$\stackrel{\text{def}}{=} \begin{cases} [\![M_1]\!](\gamma[x_1 \mapsto a_1]) & [\![V]\!](\gamma) = \iota_1 a_1 \\ [\![M_2]\!](\gamma[x_2 \mapsto a_2]) & [\![V]\!](\gamma) = \iota_2 a_2 \end{cases}$$

$$\mathcal{CT}_\varepsilon[\![\mu x : \mathbf{U}_\varepsilon \underline{B}.\, M]\!](\gamma) \stackrel{\text{def}}{=} \mu\lambda f \in |[\![\underline{B}]\!]|.[\![M]\!](\gamma[x \mapsto f])$$

$$\mathcal{CT}_\varepsilon\left[\!\!\left[\mathrm{op}_V^{\underline{B}} M\right]\!\!\right](\gamma) \stackrel{\text{def}}{=} [\![\mathrm{op}_{[\![V]\!](\gamma)}]\!]_{[\![\underline{B}]\!]}([\![M]\!](\gamma))$$

Figure 5. Term Interpretation

However, we are actually interested in the validity of optimisations with the effect annotations erased, as that will correspond to the validity of optimisations in the source language. So we need a suitable "algebraic" version of CBPV. We obtain such a language, Σ-Alg-CBPV, by specialising MAIL to signatures with $\mathcal{E} \stackrel{\text{def}}{=} \{|\sigma|\}$. Models of Σ-Alg-CBPV consist of interpretations for basic types, a *single* inequational theory $\mathcal{T}_{|\sigma|}$, and interpretations for the built-in constants. Thus we obtain a syntax and semantics for CBPV with recursion and algebraic effects.

Definition 5. *A* simple MAIL signature *is a* MAIL *signature* Σ *such that* $|\sigma| \in \mathcal{E}$, *and for each built-in constant c, the only effect set appearing in* A_c *is* $|\sigma|$.

Let Σ be a simple signature. Then, by replacing $\mathcal{E}$ with $\{|\sigma|\}$ and ε's with $|\sigma|$ one obtains an Alg-CBPV signature $\Sigma^\natural$. There is an obvious erasure operation $(-)^\natural$ that yields, for each syntactic Σ-MAIL entity, such as type X or term P, a corresponding $\Sigma^\natural$-Alg-CBPV entity, such as $X^\natural$ or $P^\natural$ respectively. This erasure operation preserves well-kindedness and well-typedness.

Models for Algebraic CBPV with common combinations of effects, and means to combine and construct them, are readily available in the literature [19, 20, 34]. Given a simple signature Σ and one such $\Sigma^\natural$-Alg-CBPV model, we now give three corresponding Σ-MAIL models that can be used for reasoning about $\Sigma^\natural$-Alg-CBPV programs.

Lemma 6. *Let* Σ *be a simple* MAIL *signature. For each* $\Sigma^\natural$-*Alg-*CBPV *model* $\mathcal{M}$ *there exists a* Σ-MAIL *model* $\mathcal{M}^\flat$ *such that* $\mathcal{T}_\varepsilon = \mathcal{T}$, *and* $\mathfrak{T}_{\varepsilon_1 \subseteq \varepsilon_2}$ *is the identity translation.*

Further, for all well-typed terms $\Gamma \vdash P : X$ *we have* $\mathcal{M}^\flat[\![X]\!] = \mathcal{M}[\![X^\natural]\!]$ *and* $\mathcal{M}^\flat[\![P]\!] = \mathcal{M}[\![P^\natural]\!]$.

The proof is straightforward, where the notion of a *simple* signature guarantees our ability to choose interpretations for Σ-MAIL's constants. (It would be useful to extend our results to non-simple signatures.) We call $\mathcal{M}^\flat$ the *benchmark model.* Lemma 6 immediately yields a connection between Σ-MAIL and $\Sigma^\natural$-Alg-CBPV validity:

Theorem 7. *Let* $\mathcal{M}$ *be a* $\Sigma^\natural$-*Alg-*CBPV *model. For any two well-typed* Σ-MAIL *programs* $\vdash P_i : \mathbf{F}_\varepsilon G$, $i = 1, 2$, *we have:*

$$\mathcal{M} \models P_1^\natural = P_2^\natural \iff \mathcal{M}^\flat \models P_1 = P_2$$

This theorem then allows us to compare other Σ-MAIL models to a given $\Sigma^\natural$-Alg-CBPV model via logical relations arguments [11, 30, 41] comparing Σ-MAIL models with the benchmark model.

The benchmark model completely ignores the effect annotations. We next introduce a model that takes them into account:

Definition 8. *Let* $\mathcal{T} = \langle \Sigma, \leq \rangle$ *be an inequational theory. For any* $\varepsilon \subseteq \Sigma$, *the* conservative restriction of $\mathcal{T}$ to ε, $\mathcal{T}|_\varepsilon$, *is the inequational theory* $\langle \varepsilon, \leq \cap \mathrm{Terms}^\varepsilon \times \mathrm{Terms}^\varepsilon \rangle$.

Theorem 9. *Let* $\mathcal{M}$ *be an* $\Sigma^\natural$-*Alg-*CBPV *model. There exists a* Σ-MAIL *model* $\mathcal{M}^\sharp$ *such that* $\mathcal{T}_\varepsilon$ *is* $\mathcal{T}|_{[\![\varepsilon]\!]}$, *and* $\mathfrak{T}_{\varepsilon_1 \subseteq \varepsilon_2}$ *is the trivial translation.*

Further, for any two well-typed Σ-MAIL *programs* $\vdash P_i : \mathbf{F}_\varepsilon G$, $i = 1, 2$, *we have:*

$$\mathcal{M} \models P_1^\natural = P_2^\natural \iff \mathcal{M}^\sharp \models P_1 = P_2$$

We call $\mathcal{M}^\sharp$ the *conservative restriction model.*

Validating optimisations in $\mathcal{M}^\sharp$ depends on finding $\mathcal{T}_\varepsilon$ explicitly. This is non-trivial, but is easier with simpler theories. One might hope to express restrictions of a combination of theories in terms of the restrictions of their components. This hope leads to the following (incomplete) conjecture:

Conjecture 10. *Let* $\mathcal{T}_1, \mathcal{T}_2$ *be inequational theories, and let* $\varepsilon_1 + \varepsilon_2 \subseteq \Sigma_1 + \Sigma_2$ *be any subset. Under some conditions, the restriction* $(\mathcal{T}_1 + \mathcal{T}_2)|_{\varepsilon_1+\varepsilon_2}$ *is identical to the sum of restrictions* $\mathcal{T}_1|_{\varepsilon_1} + \mathcal{T}_2|_{\varepsilon_2}$. *Similarly, under some conditions,* $(\mathcal{T}_1 \otimes \mathcal{T}_2)|_{\varepsilon_1+\varepsilon_2}$ *is identical to* $\mathcal{T}_1|_{\varepsilon_1} \otimes \mathcal{T}_2|_{\varepsilon_2}$.

To see that the conjecture is not trivial, consider the theory for monoids. The signature is $\{\cdot : \mathbb{2}, e : \mathbb{0}\}$ and the axioms are:

$$(\mathbf{x} \cdot \mathbf{y}) \cdot \mathbf{z} = \mathbf{x} \cdot (\mathbf{y} \cdot \mathbf{z}) \quad \mathbf{x} \cdot e = \mathbf{x} = e \cdot \mathbf{x}$$

The non-intuitive, yet elementary, Eckmann-Hilton argument [9] shows that the two theories $(\mathrm{Monoids} \otimes \mathrm{Monoids})|_{\{\cdot,e\}+\emptyset}$ and $\mathrm{Monoids}|_{\{\cdot,e\}} \otimes \mathrm{Monoids}|_\emptyset$ are different: multiplication is commutative in the former, but not the latter.

As an intermediate solution, we give a model based on the presentation of a theory as a collection of axioms.

Definition 11. *Let* Σ *be a signature and* Ax *a set of axioms over it. For any* $\varepsilon \subseteq \Sigma$, *the* axiomatic restriction of Ax to ε, $\mathrm{Th}|_\varepsilon \langle \Sigma, \mathrm{Ax}\rangle$, *is the inequational theory* $\mathrm{Th}^\varepsilon(\mathrm{Ax} \cap (\mathrm{Terms}^\varepsilon \times \mathrm{Terms}^\varepsilon))$.

We then have an analogue of Theorem 9:

Theorem 12. *Let* Ax *be a set of axioms over* Σ, *and* $\mathcal{M}$ *a* $\Sigma^\natural$-*Alg-*CBPV *model such that* $\mathcal{T} = \mathrm{Th}^\Sigma \mathrm{Ax}$. *There exists a* Σ-MAIL *model* $\mathcal{M}_\sharp$ *such that* $\mathcal{T}_\varepsilon$ *is* $\mathrm{Th}|_{[\![\varepsilon]\!]} \langle [\![\Sigma]\!], \mathrm{Ax}\rangle$, *and* $\mathfrak{T}_{\varepsilon_1 \subseteq \varepsilon_2}$ *is the trivial translation.*

Further, for any two well-typed programs $\vdash P_i : X$, $i = 1, 2$, *we have:*

$$\mathcal{M} \models P_1{}^\natural = P_2{}^\natural \impliedby \mathcal{M}_\sharp \models P_1 = P_2$$

We call $\mathcal{M}_\sharp$ the *axiomatic restriction model.* Note that by construction $\mathcal{M}_\sharp$ has an explicit axiomatisation of $\mathcal{T}_\varepsilon$. Moreover, if $\mathcal{T} = \mathcal{T}_1 + \mathcal{T}_2$ and $\mathcal{T}_i = \mathrm{Th}^{[\![\Sigma_i]\!]}\mathrm{Ax}_i$, then $\mathcal{T} = \mathrm{Th}(\mathrm{Ax}_1 + \mathrm{Ax}_2)$ and the axiomatic restriction model resulting for $\mathrm{Ax}_1 + \mathrm{Ax}_2$ satisfies for all $\varepsilon_i \subseteq \Sigma_i$, $i = 1, 2$:

$$\begin{aligned} \mathcal{T}_{\varepsilon_1+\varepsilon_2} &= \mathrm{Th}|_{[\![\varepsilon_1+\varepsilon_2]\!]} \langle [\![\Sigma_1 + \Sigma_2]\!], (\mathrm{Ax}_1 + \mathrm{Ax}_2)\rangle \\ &= \mathrm{Th}^{[\![\Sigma_1]\!]}\mathrm{Ax}_1 + \mathrm{Th}^{[\![\Sigma_2]\!]}\mathrm{Ax}_2 = \mathcal{T}_{\varepsilon_1} + \mathcal{T}_{\varepsilon_2} \end{aligned}$$

β laws: $\mathbf{match}\ (V, V')\ \mathbf{as}\ (x : A, y : A') .\ M = M\,[V/x, V'/y]$

$$\mathbf{match}\ \mathbf{inj}_{\mathbf{i}}^{A_1+A_2} V\ \mathbf{as}\ \{\mathbf{inj}_{\mathbf{1}} x_1 : A_1 .\ M_1, \mathbf{inj}_{\mathbf{2}} x_2 : A_2 .\ M_2\} = M_i\,[V/x_i]$$

$$\mathbf{force}\ (\ \mathbf{thunk}\ M) = M \qquad (\mathbf{return}_\varepsilon V)\ \mathbf{to}\ x : A.\ M = M\,[V/x]$$

$$\mathbf{i}`\lambda\,\{\mathbf{1} \mapsto M_1, \mathbf{2} \mapsto M_2\} = M_i \qquad V`\lambda x : A.\ M = M\,[V/x]$$

η laws: $\qquad V = \star$

$$M\,[V/z] = \mathbf{match}\ V\ \mathbf{as}\ (x : A, y : A') .\ M\,[(x,y)/z] \quad x, y \text{ fresh in } M$$

$$M = \mathbf{match}\ V : \mathbf{0}\ \mathbf{as}\ \{\}^{\underline{B}}$$

$$M\,[V/z] = \mathbf{match}\ V\ \mathbf{as} \begin{cases} \mathbf{inj}_{\mathbf{1}} x : A\ .\ M\,[\mathbf{inj}_1 x/z], \\ \mathbf{inj}_{\mathbf{2}} y : A' .\ M\,[\mathbf{inj}_2 y/z] \end{cases} \quad x, y \text{ fresh in } M$$

$$V = \mathbf{thunk}\ (\ \mathbf{force}\ V) \qquad M = M\ \mathbf{to}\ x : A.\ \mathbf{return}_\varepsilon x$$

$$M = \lambda\,\{\mathbf{1} \mapsto \mathbf{1}`M, \mathbf{2} \mapsto \mathbf{2}`M\} \qquad N = \lambda x : A.\ x`N \qquad x \text{ fresh in } N$$

Sequencing:

$$M\ \mathbf{to}\ x : A.\ (N\ \mathbf{to}\ y : A'.\ N') = (M\ \mathbf{to}\ x : A.\ N)\ \mathbf{to}\ y : A'.\ N' \quad x \text{ fresh in } N'$$

$$M\ \mathbf{to}\ x : A.\ \lambda\,\{\mathbf{1} \mapsto N_1, \mathbf{2} \mapsto N_2\} = \lambda \begin{cases} \mathbf{1} \mapsto M\ \mathbf{to}\ x : A.\ N_1, \\ \mathbf{2} \mapsto M\ \mathbf{to}\ x : A.\ N_2 \end{cases}$$

$$M\ \mathbf{to}\ x : A.\ \lambda y : A'.\ N = \lambda y : A'.\ (M\ \mathbf{to}\ x : A.\ N) \quad y \text{ fresh in } M$$

Effects:

$$\mathrm{op}_V^{\underline{B}} \lambda x : A.\ (M\ \mathbf{to}\ y : A'.\ N) = \left(\mathrm{op}_V^{\mathbf{F}_\varepsilon A'} \lambda x : A.\ M\right) \mathbf{to}\ y : A'.\ N \quad x \text{ fresh in } N$$

$$\mathrm{op}_V^{\underline{B}_1 \times \underline{B}_2} \lambda x : A.\ \lambda \begin{cases} \mathbf{1} \mapsto M_1, \\ \mathbf{2} \mapsto M_2 \end{cases} = \lambda \begin{cases} \mathbf{1} \mapsto \mathrm{op}_V^{\underline{B}_1} \lambda x : A.\ M_1, \\ \mathbf{2} \mapsto \mathrm{op}_V^{\underline{B}_2} \lambda x : A.\ M_2 \end{cases}$$

$$\mathrm{op}_V^{A' \to \underline{B}} \lambda x : A.\ \lambda y : A'.\ M = \lambda y : A'.\ \mathrm{op}_V^{\underline{B}} \lambda x : A.\ M \quad x \neq y$$

Recursion: $\mu x : \mathbf{U}_\varepsilon \underline{B}.\ M = M\,[\ \mathbf{thunk}\ \mu x : \mathbf{U}_\varepsilon \underline{B}.\ M/x]$

Coercion: $\mathbf{coerce}_{\varepsilon_2 \subseteq \varepsilon_3} (\mathbf{coerce}_{\varepsilon_1 \subseteq \varepsilon_2} M) = \mathbf{coerce}_{\varepsilon_1 \subseteq \varepsilon_3} M$

$$\mathbf{coerce}_{\varepsilon_1 \subseteq \varepsilon_2} (\mathbf{return}_{\varepsilon_1} M) = \mathbf{return}_{\varepsilon_2} M$$

$$\mathbf{coerce}_{\varepsilon \subseteq \varepsilon'} (M\ \mathbf{to}\ x : A.\ N) = \left(\mathbf{coerce}_{\varepsilon \subseteq \varepsilon'} M\right) \mathbf{to}\ x : A.\ \mathbf{coerce}_{\varepsilon \subseteq \varepsilon'} N$$

$$\mathbf{coerce}_{\varepsilon_1 \subseteq \varepsilon_2} \left(\mathrm{op}_V^{\mathbf{F}_{\varepsilon_1} A'} \lambda x : A.\ M\right) = \mathrm{op}_V^{\mathbf{F}_{\varepsilon_2} A'} \lambda x : A.\ \mathbf{coerce}_{\varepsilon_1 \subseteq \varepsilon_2} M$$

Figure 6. Structural Optimisations

Similarly, if $\mathcal{T} = \mathcal{T}_1 \otimes \mathcal{T}_2$, then $\mathcal{T}_{\varepsilon_1+\varepsilon_2} = \mathcal{T}_{\varepsilon_1} \otimes \mathcal{T}_{\varepsilon_2}$ in the axiomatic restriction model resulting for $\mathrm{Ax}_1 + \mathrm{Ax}_2 + (\mathrm{Ax}_{\Sigma_1 \otimes \Sigma_2})$. Thus the analogue of Conjecture 10 holds by construction for $\mathcal{M}_\sharp$.

Also note that for our purposes, this theorem implies that validation of optimisations in the modular approximation model is *sound*. However, it may not be *complete* — some sound optimisations may not be valid in this model.

4. Optimisations

We turn to validating effect-dependent optimisations, formulated as MAIL equations. This is done semantically, using Theorems 9 or 12 (either one can be used in all cases considered below). We divide optimisations into *structural*, *algebraic*, and *abstract* groups. We validate versions of almost all the optimisations in Benton et al. [4–8], and also some others, not previously considered in the semantics literature. The only optimisations considered by Benton et al. [4–8] that we do not treat deal with exception handlers (see Section 7).

Structural optimisations reflect the general structure of our models. Let Σ be a MAIL signature. Then a Σ-MAIL structural optimisation is one that is valid in all Σ-MAIL models. Figure 6 shows example schemes for such optimisations. They are all variants of the standard β, η, sequencing and similar laws found in the CBPV literature [26, 36], together with ones concerning effect coercion.

Algebraic optimisations originate locally in the inequational theories $\mathcal{T}_\varepsilon$ associated to a given model of Σ-MAIL. Each equation yields such an optimisation. To derive these optimisations from the equations, one follows [36]. We just give an example here. The global state theory includes the axiom

$$\mathtt{update}_{v_0}(\mathtt{lookup}(\lambda v.\mathbf{x}_v)) = \mathtt{update}_{v_0}(\mathbf{x}_{v_0})$$

The corresponding algebraic optimisation is

$$\mathtt{update}_V^{\underline{B}}(\mathtt{lookup}\,M) = \mathtt{update}_V^{\underline{B}}(V`M)$$

Abstract optimisations follow from overall, global properties of the theories. Each appears in two forms, which we call *utilitarian* and *pristine*. The utilitarian form readily applies to program optimisation; the pristine form is shorter and easier to validate, but perhaps less useful. For example, the utilitarian form of Discard is

$$\frac{\Gamma \vdash_\varepsilon M : \mathbf{F}_\varepsilon A \qquad \Gamma \vdash_{\varepsilon'} N : \underline{B}}{\mathcal{M} \models \mathbf{coerce}_{\varepsilon \subseteq \varepsilon'} M\ \mathbf{to}\ x : A.\ N = N}\ (\varepsilon \subseteq \varepsilon')$$

and its pristine form is

$$\frac{\Gamma \vdash_\varepsilon M : \mathbf{F}_\varepsilon A}{\mathcal{M} \models M\ \mathbf{to}\ x : A.\ \mathbf{return}_\varepsilon \star = \mathbf{return}_\varepsilon \star}$$

The two forms can always be shown equivalent using structural optimisations. Instances of both appear in the work of Benton et al.

This optimisation is valid if, for example, $\mathcal{T}_\varepsilon$ is the environment theory $\mathcal{T}_{\mathrm{Env}(\mathbb{V})}$, whose signature is $\{\mathtt{lookup} : \mathbb{V}\}$ and axioms are:

$$\mathbf{x} = \mathtt{lookup}(\lambda v.x)$$

$$\mathtt{lookup}(\lambda v_1.\mathtt{lookup}(\lambda v_2.\mathbf{x}_{v_1,v_2})) = \mathtt{lookup}(\lambda v.\mathbf{x}_{v,v})$$

Note that the optimisation obtained by erasure, $M\ \mathbf{to}\ x : A.\ N = N$ is in general not valid.

Let $\vdash P : \mathbf{F}_\varepsilon G$ be a well-typed Σ-MAIL program. Let P' be a well-typed Σ-MAIL program obtained by applying the Discard optimisation to P. If Discard is valid in the conservative (axiomatic) restriction model, then Theorem 9 (respectively, Theorem 12) guarantees that $P^\natural = P'^\natural$ is valid. This equation is valid, even if the erased Discard used is invalid. Thus Theorems 9 and 12 formalise the justification for effect dependent optimisation.

Discard also supplies a non-example. Taking M to be a thunk in the pristine form of the optimisation yields on the right hand side the term $\lambda \mathtt{m} : \mathbf{U}_\varepsilon \mathbf{F}_\varepsilon A.\ \mathbf{force}\ \mathtt{m}\ \mathbf{to}\ x : A.\ \mathbf{return}_\varepsilon \star$, and on the left the term $\lambda \mathtt{m} : \mathbf{U}_\varepsilon \mathbf{F}_\varepsilon A.\ \mathbf{return}_\varepsilon \star$. When Discard is valid, these two terms are equal. When the erased Discard is invalid, the erased terms are not equal. Note that these are closed term of the *non-ground* type $\mathbf{U}_\varepsilon \mathbf{F}_\varepsilon A \to \mathbf{F}_\varepsilon \mathbf{1}$. This non-example demonstrates why it is important to restrict to *ground* returners in Theorems 9 and 12.

Validating abstract optimisations denotationally reveals an intimate connection[2] to Führmann's work on the structure of call-by-value [13, 14]: each has a characterisation in semantic terms. For example, the Discard optimisation holds iff $\mathcal{T}_\varepsilon$ is an *affine* theory [13, 21, 24], that is, iff $\eta_{\mathbb{1}}^{\varepsilon} : \mathbb{1} \to |F_\varepsilon \mathbb{1}|$ is an isomorphism.

There are also *algebraic* characterisations of these semantic properties. For example, a theory $\mathcal{T}$ is affine iff for every term t, $t(\mathbf{x}, \ldots, \mathbf{x}) = \mathbf{x}$, that is, iff a *global absorption law* holds. (Here, and below, we are displaying *all* the variables of the terms at hand.) Such algebraic properties can be investigated using the equational presentation of the theory. As an example, the theory for environments $\mathcal{T}_{\mathrm{Env}(\mathbb{V})}$ and the various semilattice theories are affine.

A summary of the results appears in Figure 7; in any row, all the conditions are equivalent in any model of MAIL, taking the condition in the first column as universally quantified over all ε' such that $\varepsilon' \supseteq \varepsilon$. Benton et al. [4–8] (Führmann [13, 14]) considered call-by-value analogues of the optimisations labelled by **B** (respectively **F**) in Figure 7, albeit for particular combinations of effects (respectively for a fixed monad); Führmann also showed the

[2] Alex Simpson, private communication.

name	utilitarian form	pristine form	abstract side condition	algebraic equivalent	example basic theories
Discard	B F $\dfrac{\Gamma \vdash_\varepsilon M : \mathbf{F}_\varepsilon A \quad \Gamma \vdash_{\varepsilon'} N : \underline{B}}{(\mathbf{coerce}\, M)\ \mathbf{to}\ x : A.\, N = N}$	B F $\dfrac{\Gamma \vdash_\varepsilon M : \mathbf{F}_\varepsilon A}{M\ \mathbf{to}\ x : A.\, \mathbf{return}_\varepsilon \star = \mathbf{return}_\varepsilon \star}$	$\mathcal{T}_\varepsilon$ affine: F $\eta^\varepsilon_{\mathbb{1}} : \mathbb{1} \to \lvert F_\varepsilon \mathbb{1} \rvert$ has a continuous inverse	For all ε-terms t: $t(\mathbf{x}, \dots, \mathbf{x}) = \mathbf{x}$	read-only state, convex, upper and lower semilattices
Copy	B F $\dfrac{\Gamma \vdash_\varepsilon M : \mathbf{F}_\varepsilon A \quad \Gamma, x : A, y : A \vdash_{\varepsilon'} N : \underline{B}}{\begin{array}{l}\mathbf{coerce}\, M\ \mathbf{to}\ x : A.\\ \mathbf{coerce}\, M\ \mathbf{to}\ y : A.\, N =\\ \mathbf{coerce}\, M\ \mathbf{to}\ x : A.\, N\,[x/y]\end{array}}$	B F $\dfrac{\Gamma \vdash_\varepsilon M : \mathbf{F}_\varepsilon A}{\begin{array}{c} M\ \mathbf{to}\ x : A.\, M\ \mathbf{to}\ y : A.\, \mathbf{return}_\varepsilon (x, y)\\ =\\ M\ \mathbf{to}\ x : A.\, \mathbf{return}_\varepsilon (x, x)\end{array}}$	$\mathcal{T}_\varepsilon$ relevant: F $\psi_\varepsilon \circ \delta = L^\varepsilon \delta$	For all ε-terms t: $t(t(\mathbf{x}_{11}, \dots, \mathbf{x}_{1n}), \dots,$ $t(\mathbf{x}_{n1}, \dots, \mathbf{x}_{nn}))$ $= t(\mathbf{x}_{11}, \dots, \mathbf{x}_{nn})$	exceptions, lifting, read-only state, write-only state
Weak Copy	$\dfrac{\Gamma \vdash_\varepsilon M : \mathbf{F}_\varepsilon A \quad \Gamma, x : A \vdash_{\varepsilon'} N : \underline{B}}{\begin{array}{l}\mathbf{coerce}\, M\ \mathbf{to}\ x : A.\\ \mathbf{coerce}\, M\ \mathbf{to}\ y : A.\, N =\\ \mathbf{coerce}\, M\ \mathbf{to}\ x : A.\, N\end{array}}$	$\dfrac{\Gamma \vdash_\varepsilon M : \mathbf{F}_\varepsilon A}{M\ \mathbf{to}\ x : A.\, M = M}$	$\mu^\varepsilon \circ \mathrm{str}^\varepsilon \circ \delta = \mathrm{id}$	For all ε-terms t: $t(t(\mathbf{x}_1, \dots, \mathbf{x}_n), \dots,$ $t(\mathbf{x}_1, \dots, \mathbf{x}_n))$ $= t(\mathbf{x}_1, \dots, \mathbf{x}_n)$	any affine or relevant theory: lifting, exceptions, read-only and write-only state, all three semilattice theories
Swap	B F $\dfrac{\Gamma \vdash_{\varepsilon_1} M_1 : \mathbf{F}_{\varepsilon_1} A_1 \quad \Gamma \vdash_{\varepsilon_2} M_2 : \mathbf{F}_{\varepsilon_2} A_2 \quad \Gamma, x_1 : A_1, x_2 : A_2 \vdash_{\varepsilon'} N}{\begin{array}{l}\mathbf{coerce}\, M_1\ \mathbf{to}\ x_1 : A_1.\\ \mathbf{coerce}\, M_2\ \mathbf{to}\ x_2 : A_2.\, N =\\ \mathbf{coerce}\, M_2\ \mathbf{to}\ x_2 : A_2.\\ \mathbf{coerce}\, M_1\ \mathbf{to}\ x_1 : A_1.\, N\end{array}}$	B F $\dfrac{\Gamma \vdash_{\varepsilon_1} M_1 : \mathbf{F}_{\varepsilon_1} A_1 \quad \Gamma \vdash_{\varepsilon_2} M_2 : \mathbf{F}_{\varepsilon_2} A_2}{\begin{array}{l}\mathbf{coerce}\, M_1\ \mathbf{to}\ x_1 : A_1.\\ \mathbf{coerce}\, M_2\ \mathbf{to}\ x_2 : A_2.\, \mathbf{return}_\varepsilon (x_1, x_2) =\\ \mathbf{coerce}\, M_2\ \mathbf{to}\ x_2 : A_2.\\ \mathbf{coerce}\, M_1\ \mathbf{to}\ x_1 : A_1.\, \mathbf{return}_\varepsilon (x_1, x_2)\end{array}}$	$\mathfrak{T}_{\varepsilon_1 \subseteq \varepsilon}, \mathfrak{T}_{\varepsilon_2 \subseteq \varepsilon}$ commute: F $\psi_\varepsilon \circ (m^{\varepsilon_1 \subseteq \varepsilon} \times m^{\varepsilon_2 \subseteq \varepsilon})$ $=$ $\tilde{\psi}_\varepsilon \circ (m^{\varepsilon_1 \subseteq \varepsilon} \times m^{\varepsilon_2 \subseteq \varepsilon})$	$\mathfrak{T}_{\varepsilon_1 \subseteq \varepsilon}$ translations commute with $\mathfrak{T}_{\varepsilon_2 \subseteq \varepsilon}$ translations (see tensor equations)	$\mathcal{T}_1 \to \mathcal{T}_1 \otimes \mathcal{T}_2 \leftarrow \mathcal{T}_2$, e.g., distinct global memory cells
Weak Swap	$\dfrac{\Gamma \vdash_{\varepsilon_1} M_1 : \mathbf{F}_{\varepsilon_1} A_1 \quad \Gamma \vdash_{\varepsilon_2} M_2 : \mathbf{F}_{\varepsilon_2} A_2 \quad \Gamma, x_1 : A_1 \vdash_{\varepsilon'} N}{\text{(same as Swap)}}$	$\dfrac{\Gamma \vdash_{\varepsilon_1} M_1 : \mathbf{F}_{\varepsilon_1} A_1 \quad \Gamma \vdash_{\varepsilon_2} M_2 : \mathbf{F}_{\varepsilon_2} A_2}{\begin{array}{l}\mathbf{coerce}\, M_1\ \mathbf{to}\ x_1 : A_1.\\ \mathbf{coerce}\, M_2\ \mathbf{to}\ x_2 : A_2.\, \mathbf{return}_\varepsilon x_1 =\\ \mathbf{coerce}\, M_2\ \mathbf{to}\ x_2 : A_2.\\ \mathbf{coerce}\, M_1\ \mathbf{to}\ x_1 : A_1.\, \mathbf{return}_\varepsilon x_1\end{array}}$	$\psi_\varepsilon \circ (m^{\varepsilon_1} \times m^{\varepsilon_2})$ $\circ\, (\mathrm{id} \times \eta^{\varepsilon_2}_{\mathbb{1}}) =$ $\tilde{\psi}_\varepsilon \circ (m^{\varepsilon_1} \times m^{\varepsilon_2})$ $\circ\, (\mathrm{id} \times \eta^{\varepsilon_2}_{\mathbb{1}})$	For all ε-terms $t = \mathfrak{T}_1(t')$, $s = \mathfrak{T}_2(s')$: $t(s(\mathbf{x}_1, \dots, \mathbf{x}_1), \dots,$ $s(\mathbf{x}_n, \dots, \mathbf{x}_n)) =$ $s(t(\mathbf{x}_1, \dots, \mathbf{x}_n), \dots,$ $t(\mathbf{x}_1, \dots, \mathbf{x}_n))$	when $\mathcal{T}_{\varepsilon_2}$ is affine, e.g.: read-only state and convex, upper and lower semilattices.
Isolated Swap	$\dfrac{\Gamma \vdash_{\varepsilon_1} M_1 : \mathbf{F}_{\varepsilon_1} A_1 \quad \Gamma \vdash_{\varepsilon_2} M_2 : \mathbf{F}_{\varepsilon_2} A_2 \quad \Gamma \vdash_{\varepsilon'} N}{\text{(same as Swap)}}$	$\dfrac{\Gamma \vdash_{\varepsilon_1} M_1 : \mathbf{F}_{\varepsilon_1} A_1 \quad \Gamma \vdash_{\varepsilon_2} M_2 : \mathbf{F}_{\varepsilon_2} A_2}{\begin{array}{l}\mathbf{coerce}\, M_1\ \mathbf{to}\ x_1 : A_1.\\ \mathbf{coerce}\, M_2\ \mathbf{to}\ x_2 : A_2.\, \mathbf{return}_\varepsilon \star =\\ \mathbf{coerce}\, M_2\ \mathbf{to}\ x_2 : A_2.\\ \mathbf{coerce}\, M_1\ \mathbf{to}\ x_1 : A_1.\, \mathbf{return}_\varepsilon \star\end{array}}$	$\psi_\varepsilon \circ (m^{\varepsilon_1} \times m^{\varepsilon_2})$ $\circ\, (\eta^{\varepsilon_1}_{\mathbb{1}} \times \eta^{\varepsilon_2}_{\mathbb{1}}) =$ $\tilde{\psi}_\varepsilon \circ (m^{\varepsilon_1} \times m^{\varepsilon_2})$ $\circ\, (\eta^{\varepsilon_1}_{\mathbb{1}} \times \eta^{\varepsilon_2}_{\mathbb{1}})$	For all ε-terms $t = \mathfrak{T}_1(t')$, $s = \mathfrak{T}_2(s')$: $t(s(\mathbf{x}, \dots, \mathbf{x}), \dots,$ $s(\mathbf{x}, \dots, \mathbf{x})) =$ $s(t(\mathbf{x}, \dots, \mathbf{x}), \dots,$ $t(\mathbf{x}, \dots, \mathbf{x}))$	when $\mathcal{T}_{\varepsilon_1}$ is affine: read-only state and convex, upper and lower semilattices.
Unique	B $\dfrac{\Gamma \vdash_\varepsilon M_i : \mathbf{F}_\varepsilon \mathbf{0}, i = 1, 2}{M_1 = M_2}$	(same as utilitarian form)	$F_\varepsilon \mathbb{0} = \mathbb{0}, \mathbb{1}$	$\mathcal{T}_\varepsilon$ equates all ε-constants	all three state theories, all three semilattice theories, a single unparameterised exception, lifting
Pure Hoist	B F $\dfrac{\Gamma \vdash_\varepsilon M : \mathbf{F}_\varepsilon A \quad \Gamma, x : A \vdash_{\varepsilon'} N : \underline{B}}{\begin{array}{c}\mathbf{return}_\varepsilon\ \mathbf{thunk}\ (\mathbf{coerce}\, M\ \mathbf{to}\ x : A.\, N)\\ = M\ \mathbf{to}\ x : A.\, \mathbf{return}_\varepsilon\ \mathbf{thunk}\ N\end{array}}$	B F $\dfrac{\Gamma \vdash_\varepsilon M : \mathbf{F}_\varepsilon A}{\begin{array}{l}\mathbf{return}_\varepsilon\ \mathbf{thunk}\ M =\\ M\ \mathbf{to}\ x : A.\, \mathbf{return}_\varepsilon\ \mathbf{thunk}\ \mathbf{return}_\varepsilon x\end{array}}$	F $L^\varepsilon \eta^\varepsilon_W = \eta^\varepsilon_{\lvert F_\varepsilon W \rvert}$	all ε-terms are equal to variables in $\mathcal{T}_\varepsilon$	the empty theory, inconsistent theories
Hoist	B F $\dfrac{\Gamma \vdash_\varepsilon M : \mathbf{F}_\varepsilon A \quad \Gamma, x : A \vdash_{\varepsilon'} N : \underline{B}}{\begin{array}{l}M\ \mathbf{to}\ x : A.\\ \mathbf{return}_\varepsilon\ \mathbf{thunk}\ (\mathbf{coerce}\, M\ \mathbf{to}\ x : A.\, N)\\ = M\ \mathbf{to}\ x : A.\, \mathbf{return}_\varepsilon\ \mathbf{thunk}\ N\end{array}}$	B F $\dfrac{\Gamma \vdash_\varepsilon M : \mathbf{F}_\varepsilon A}{\begin{array}{l}M\ \mathbf{to}\ x : A.\\ \quad \mathbf{thunk}\ \mathbf{return}_\varepsilon (x,\ \mathbf{thunk}\ M) =\\ M\ \mathbf{to}\ x : A.\\ \quad \mathbf{thunk}\ \mathbf{return}_\varepsilon (x,\ \mathbf{thunk}\ \mathbf{return}_\varepsilon x)\end{array}}$	F $L^\varepsilon \langle \eta^\varepsilon, \mathrm{id} \rangle = \mathrm{str}^\varepsilon \circ \delta$	all ε-terms are either a variable or independent of their variables via $\mathcal{T}_\varepsilon$	all theories containing only constants: lifting and exceptions

Figure 7. Abstract Optimisations

equivalence of the two forms and the abstract side condition in his setting.

The abstract conditions in Figure 7 use the following standard categorical notions. The diagonal function $\delta_W : W \to W \times W$ is given by $\delta(w) \stackrel{\text{def}}{=} \langle w, w \rangle$. Let $\mathcal{T}$ be an inequational theory. Given a continuous function $f : V \to W$, we can *lift* it to a homomorphism $(\eta \circ f)^\dagger : FV \to FW$. We denote the underlying map by $Lf : |FV| \to |FW|$. The *multiplication* $\mu : |F|FW|| \to |FW|$ is the underlying map of the homomorphism $\mathrm{id}^\dagger : F|FW| \to FW$. The *(left) strength*, $\mathrm{str} : V \times |FW| \to |F(V \times W)|$, is given by $\lambda \langle v, w \rangle.(\mathrm{curry}\ \eta)^\dagger(w)(v)$. Similarly we define the *right strength*, $\mathrm{str}' : |FV| \times W \to |F(V \times W)|$. The two *double strength* functions $\psi, \tilde{\psi}; |FV| \times |FW| \to |F(V \times W)|$ are defined by $\psi = \theta \circ L\,\mathrm{str}' \circ \mathrm{str}$ and by $\tilde{\psi} = \theta \circ L\,\mathrm{str} \circ \mathrm{str}'$.

Note how Copy corresponds to a global *idempotency* law, and how Swap corresponds to *commutativity*. Slight variations on these two laws yield the Weak Copy[3], and Weak and Isolated Swap optimisations, which are new in the formal methods optimisation literature. Also note the algebraic condition for Pure Hoist. It means that $\mathcal{T}_\varepsilon$ is either inconsistent, or the operations project one of their arguments without effect.

Note too the two hoisting optimisations and compare them to the structural optimisations dealing with effect operations (Figure 6). The simplicity of the latter over the former suggests that the complications arise from the process of *thunking* rather than abstracting over variables. This clean separation between thunks and abstraction supports our use of CBPV.

Most (but, unfortunately, not all) of the optimisations can be validated *operation-wise*:

Theorem 13. *For each of the optimisations Discard, Pure Hoist, and Hoist, the algebraic condition holds for a theory $\mathcal{T}$ iff for all operations $f : A$ it holds for the term $t = f(\lambda a.\mathbf{x}_a)$.*

Analogously, for each of the various Swap optimisations, the algebraic condition holds for $\mathcal{T}_1 \xrightarrow{\mathfrak{T}_1} \mathcal{T} \xleftarrow{\mathfrak{T}_2} \mathcal{T}_2$ iff for each $f^i :_{\Sigma_i} A_i$, $i = 1, 2$, it holds for the terms $t = f^1(\lambda a_1.\mathbf{x}_{a_1})$ and $s = f^2(\lambda a_2.\mathbf{x}_{a_2})$.

The theorem is proved by a straightforward induction over ε-terms, demonstrating the benefits of the algebraic characterisation. The theorem was used to obtain most of the examples column in Figure 7. We can also use this it to deduce optimisation validity modularly:

Corollary 14. *For each algebraic condition for Discard, Pure Hoist, and Hoist, if $\mathcal{T}^1, \mathcal{T}^2$ satisfy it, then so does $\mathcal{T}^1 + \mathcal{T}^2$.*

Analogously, for each algebraic condition for the various Swap optimisations, if $\mathcal{T}_1^i \xrightarrow{\mathfrak{T}_1^i} \mathcal{T} \xleftarrow{\mathfrak{T}_2^j} \mathcal{T}_2^j$, for all $i, j = 1, 2$, satisfy it, then so does $\mathcal{T}_1^1 + \mathcal{T}_1^2 \to \mathcal{T} \leftarrow \mathcal{T}_2^1 + \mathcal{T}_2^2$.

Optimisation validity is inherited by super-theories:

Proposition 15. *If $\mathcal{T}$ satisfies any of the algebraic conditions in Figure 7, and if $\mathcal{T}'$ is any theory with $\Sigma = \Sigma'$ and $(\le) \subseteq (\le')$, then $\mathcal{T}'$ satisfies the same condition.*

Analogously, if $\mathcal{T}_1 \xrightarrow{\mathfrak{T}_1} \mathcal{T}_3 \xleftarrow{\mathfrak{T}_2} \mathcal{T}_2$ satisfy the algebraic condition for any of the various Swap optimisations, and if, further, $\mathcal{T}_1' \xrightarrow{\mathfrak{T}_1'} \mathcal{T}_3' \xleftarrow{\mathfrak{T}_2'} \mathcal{T}_2'$ are such that $\Sigma_i = \Sigma_i'$, $\mathcal{T}_i \subseteq \mathcal{T}_i'$ and for each $f \in \Sigma_i$, $\mathfrak{T}_i(f) = \mathfrak{T}_i'(f)$, then $\mathcal{T}_1' \xrightarrow{\mathfrak{T}_1'} \mathcal{T}_3' \xleftarrow{\mathfrak{T}_2'} \mathcal{T}_2'$ satisfy the same algebraic condition.

For example, the semilattice theories are *commutative* — the identity translations commute. Thus given two locations ℓ, ℓ' in memory with associated operations $\mathtt{lookup}^\ell$ and $\mathtt{update}_v^{\ell'}$, the trivial translations of $\mathcal{T}_{\mathrm{Env}(\mathbb{V})} \otimes \mathcal{T}_{\mathrm{ND}}$, $\mathcal{T}_{\mathrm{ND}} \otimes \mathcal{T}_{\mathrm{OW}(\mathbb{V})}$ into the theory with two distinct memory cells and non-determinism, $\mathcal{T}_{\mathrm{GS}(\mathbb{V})} \otimes \mathcal{T}_{\mathrm{ND}} \otimes \mathcal{T}_{\mathrm{GS}(\mathbb{V})}$, commute.

Note that each algebraic condition for Discard and Copy implies that of Weak Copy. Similarly, the algebraic condition for Swap implies that of Weak Swap, which implies that of Isolated Swap.

The notable exceptions to Theorem 13 are the Copy, Weak Copy and Unique optimisations. For example, in the global state theory $\mathcal{T}_{\mathrm{GS}(2)}$ both $\mathtt{lookup}$ and $\mathtt{update}$ are idempotent, but the term $\mathtt{lookup}(\lambda a.\mathtt{update}_0\mathbf{x}_a)$ is not idempotent. However, in practice, we can use equational reasoning to establish them. For example, the write-only state theory is relevant, because any term can be rewritten to a single operation $\mathtt{update}_v\mathbf{x}$. As these *are* idempotent, all terms satisfy the idempotency law.

We can use similar equational arguments to establish these idempotency laws for theory combinations:

Theorem 16. *Let $\mathcal{T}$, $\mathcal{T}'$ be two relevant algebraic theories.*

- *If all Σ operations have arity $\mathbb{0}$, then $\mathcal{T} + \mathcal{T}'$ is relevant.*
- *If all Σ operations have arity $\mathbb{1}$, then $\mathcal{T} \otimes \mathcal{T}'$ is relevant.*
- *If $\mathcal{T}$ is also affine, then $\mathcal{T} \otimes \mathcal{T}'$ is relevant.*

The same is true replacing "relevant" by the Weak Copy characterisation.

In practice, the relevant theories with which one usually tensors are the lifting theory or with the read-only and write-only state theories, and they all satisfy the conditions of this theorem.

Similarly, we can deduce the condition for the unique optimisation in the following case:

Proposition 17. *Let $\mathcal{T}$ be an inequational theory. If every nullary operation in Σ commutes with every Σ-operation, then $\mathcal{T}$ satisfies the algebraic condition for the* Unique *optimisation.*

5. Example Language

To demonstrate our results, we consider a non-trivial language. Assume the memory has been partitioned into a finite set of disjoint regions [27] $\mathbf{Reg}$. The set $\mathbf{Reg}$ is partitioned into three subsets: read-only regions $\mathbf{Reg}_{\mathbf{RO}}$; write-only regions $\mathbf{Reg}_{\mathbf{WO}}$; and read-write regions $\mathbf{Reg}_{\mathbf{RW}}$. We denote by $\mathbf{Reg}_{\mathbf{R}}$ the read-able regions $\mathbf{Reg}_{\mathbf{RO}} \cup \mathbf{Reg}_{\mathbf{RW}}$, and by $\mathbf{Reg}_{\mathbf{W}}$ the write-able regions $\mathbf{Reg}_{\mathbf{WO}} \cup \mathbf{Reg}_{\mathbf{RW}}$.

The MAIL signature in question Σ is given as follows. The basic types $\mathbf{Bsc}$ are $\mathbf{Char}$, $\mathbf{Word}$, $\mathbf{Str}$ and $\mathbf{Loc}$. The effect operations $|\sigma|$ and their arities are: $\Omega : \mathbf{0}$, as required; $\mathtt{input} : \mathbf{Char}$ for terminal input; $\mathtt{output} : \mathbf{1} \to \mathbf{Char}$ for terminal output; $\mathtt{raise} : \mathbf{0}$ for causing an exception; $\mathtt{throw} : \mathbf{0} \to \mathbf{Str}$ for causing an exception with an error message; $\mathtt{rollback} : \mathbf{0}$ for causing a rollback exception; $\mathtt{abort} : \mathbf{0} \to \mathbf{Str}$ for causing a rollback exception with an error message; for all write-able regions $\rho \in \mathbf{Reg}_{\mathbf{R}}$, $\mathtt{lookup}^\rho : \mathbf{Word} \to \mathbf{Loc}$, note that each region consists of $\mathbf{Loc}$-many locations; for all read-able regions ρ in $\mathbf{Reg}_{\mathbf{W}}$, $\mathtt{update}^\rho : \mathbf{1} \to \mathbf{Loc} \times \mathbf{Word}$; and finally, $\vee : \mathbf{2}$ for non-deterministic choice. The effect sets $\mathcal{E}$ are given by all (finite) effect subsets $\mathcal{P}(|\sigma|)$. Finally, the built-in constants κ we choose are: $\mathtt{'c'} : \mathbf{Char}$ for each ASCII character c; $\mathtt{n}$ for each 64-bit number n; $\mathtt{"s"}$ for each character string s; $\mathtt{l}$ for each 64-bit memory address ℓ. The resulting Σ is indeed simple.

The Alg-CBPV signature $\Sigma^\natural$ is $\langle \langle \mathbf{Bsc}, |\sigma|, \Omega, \kappa \rangle, \mathrm{ar}, A_- \rangle$. The chosen $\Sigma^\natural$-Alg-CBPV model $\mathcal{M}$ interprets the basic types as follows: $[\![\mathbf{Char}]\!]$ is 2^8, the usual ASCII encoding; $[\![\mathbf{Word}]\!]$ is 2^{64}, which we also denote by $\mathbb{V}$; $[\![\mathbf{Str}]\!]$ is $[\![\mathbf{Char}]\!]^*$, the set of finite $[\![\mathbf{Char}]\!]$ sequences; and $[\![\mathbf{Loc}]\!]$ is 2^{64}. The theory $\mathcal{T}$ is given

[3] Paul B. Levy, private communication.

by [19]:

$$\begin{aligned}&\mathrm{Th}^{\{\mathtt{raise},\mathtt{throw}\}}\emptyset + (\\ &\quad \mathcal{T}_{\mathrm{Env}(\mathbb{V})}^{\bigotimes_{\rho\in\mathbf{Reg}_{\mathbf{RO}}},\ell} \otimes \mathcal{T}_{\mathrm{OW}(\mathbb{V})}^{\bigotimes_{\rho\in\mathbf{Reg}_{\mathbf{WO}}},\ell} \otimes \mathcal{T}_{\mathrm{GS}(\mathbb{V})}^{\bigotimes_{\rho\in\mathbf{Reg}_{\mathbf{RW}}},\ell} \otimes \\ &\qquad (\mathrm{Th}^{\{\mathtt{rollback},\mathtt{abort}\}}\emptyset + \mathrm{Th}^{\{\mathtt{input}\}}\emptyset + \\ &\qquad\qquad \mathrm{Th}^{\{\mathtt{output}\}}\emptyset + (\mathcal{T}_{\mathrm{ND}} \otimes \mathcal{T}_{\Omega})))\end{aligned}$$

where the `lookup` operations in the signature in the $\langle\rho,\ell\rangle$-th component of the folded tensor $\mathcal{T}_{\mathrm{Env}(\mathbb{V})}^{\bigotimes_{\rho\in\mathbf{Reg}_{\mathbf{RO}}}}$ are tagged with ρ and ℓ, i.e. $\mathtt{lookup}_{\ell}^{\rho}$, and similarly for the other folded tensors. Finally, the constants are given the obvious interpretations.

By Theorem 12, we have an axiomatic restriction model $\mathcal{M}_{\sharp}$ for the natural modular axiomatisation of $\mathcal{T}$. Validating optimisations in this model yields valid optimisations for $\Sigma^{\natural}$-Alg-CBPV.

For each optimisation o in {Discard, Pure Hoist, Hoist}, we define a set $\zeta^{o} \subseteq |\sigma|$ of the operations that satisfy its algebraic condition:

$$\zeta^{\text{Discard}} \stackrel{\text{def}}{=} \{\mathbb{V}, \mathtt{lookup}^{\rho} \mid \rho \in \mathbf{Reg}_{\mathbf{R}}\} \qquad \zeta^{\text{Pure Hoist}} \stackrel{\text{def}}{=} \emptyset$$

$$\zeta^{\text{Hoist}} \stackrel{\text{def}}{=} \{\mathtt{raise}, \mathtt{throw}, \mathtt{abort}, \mathtt{rollback}, \Omega\}$$

By Theorem 13 we obtain the following condition:

Proposition 18. *For each optimisation o in {Discard, Pure Hoist, Hoist}, if $\varepsilon \subseteq \zeta^{o}$ then o is valid in the theory $\mathcal{T}_{\varepsilon}$ of $\mathcal{M}_{\sharp}$.*

Analogously, for each o in {Swap, Weak Swap (WSwap), isolated swap (ISwap)} and for each op $\in |\sigma|$ define the set $\zeta^{o}(\mathrm{op})$ of effect operations that o-commute with op. For Weak Swap, op replaces t in the algebraic condition. Note that because Swap implies Weak Swap, which implies Isolated Swap, we have $\zeta^{\text{Swap}}(\mathrm{op}) \subseteq \zeta^{\text{WSwap}}(\mathrm{op}) \subseteq \zeta^{\text{ISwap}}(\mathrm{op})$. These sets are given in Figure 8.

From Theorem 13 we can deduce the validity of swapping:

Proposition 19. *Let o be one of the various Swap optimisations. Let ε_1, ε_2 be two effect sets. If $\varepsilon_2 \subseteq \bigcap_{\mathrm{op}\in\varepsilon_1} \zeta^{o}(\mathrm{op})$ then the optimisation o is valid for $\mathcal{T}_{\varepsilon_1} \to \mathcal{T}_{\varepsilon_1\cup\varepsilon_2} \leftarrow \mathcal{T}_{\varepsilon_2}$.*

We should note that despite our brute force method of examining 200 pairs of effect operations, we are still exponentially better off than trying to exhaust the space of 2^{20} possible pairs $\varepsilon_1, \varepsilon_2$. It is worthwhile to wonder whether mechanised assistance is possible. It would also be good to be able to decide exactly which of the 2^{20} possible optimisations is valid in the benchmark model.

Theorem 20. *Let $\varepsilon \subseteq |\sigma|$. If $\mathtt{input}, \mathtt{update}, \mathbb{V} \notin \varepsilon$ and for all ρ in $\mathbf{Reg}_{\mathbf{RW}}$, $\{\mathtt{lookup}^{\rho}, \mathtt{update}^{\rho}\} \not\subseteq \varepsilon$, then $\mathcal{T}_{\varepsilon}$ validates the Copy optimisation.*

Note that the premise of the theorem and the structure of the axiomatic restriction model guarantees that $\mathcal{T}_{\varepsilon}$ is of the form:

$$\mathrm{Th}^{\{\mathtt{raise},\mathtt{throw}\}}\emptyset + (\mathcal{T}_{\mathrm{Env}(\mathbb{V})}^{\otimes} \otimes \mathcal{T}_{\mathrm{OW}(\mathbb{V})}^{\otimes} \otimes (\mathrm{Th}^{\{\mathtt{rollback},\mathtt{abort}\}}\emptyset + \mathcal{T}_{\Omega}))$$

where each of the theories may be omitted. Note that all of them are relevant. Repeated application of Theorem 16 shows the combination's relevance.

The optimisation Weak Copy is treated similarly:

Theorem 21. *Let $\varepsilon \subseteq |\sigma|$. If $\mathtt{input}, \mathtt{output} \notin \varepsilon$ and for all ρ in $\mathbf{Reg}_{\mathbf{RW}}$, $\{\mathtt{lookup}^{\rho}, \mathtt{update}^{\rho}\} \not\subseteq \varepsilon$, then $\mathcal{T}_{\varepsilon}$ validates the Weak Copy optimisation.*

To conclude our example, we treat the Unique optimisation using Proposition 17:

Theorem 22. *Let $\varepsilon \subseteq |\sigma|$. If $\varepsilon \cap \{\Omega, \mathtt{raise}, \mathtt{rollback}\} = \{\mathrm{op}\}$ and $\varepsilon \subseteq \zeta^{\mathit{Swap}}(\mathrm{op})$, or if the intersection is empty, then $\mathcal{T}_{\varepsilon}$ validates the Unique optimisation.*

6. Related Work

Filinski used $\mathrm{M^3L}$ [10, 11] to investigate *effect reification* [12]. Its earlier call-by-value versions had a denotational semantics and inspired our CBPV MAIL. Marino and Millstein [28] developed a technique to derive type and effect frameworks based on the notions of *redexes* and *contexts* [48]. These frameworks are parameterised by two functions `check` and `adjust`. They applied their technique to a fixed ML-like, call-by-value language with recursion, exceptions and higher-order dynamic allocation, capturing many existing effect systems, mostly more general than the Gifford-style. They gave a mechanically checked soundness proof of their effect system, with respect to a suitable operational semantics.

Atkey applied *permission-parameterised monads* to the semantics of type and effect systems [2, 3] more general than Gifford-style ones. His parameterised monads can be generated by a notion of equational theory in which the signature assigns input and output permissions to operations, thereby connecting operations and effects (qua permissions). He also established relations to standard monadic semantics analogous to Theorems 9 and 12.

7. Conclusions and Further Work

We have given a theory of Gifford-style effect systems, generalising and unifying existing work. The algebraic approach provides a valuable general point of view, resulting in: the connection between effect operations and effect sets; the conservative and the axiomatic restriction models; the relation between effect-annotated semantics and standard algebraic semantics; optimisation classification and discovery of new optimisations; criteria for the validity of abstract optimisations; and methods to derive the validity of optimisations for combinations of effects modularly. Rather than having to proceed from case to case by analogy, we hope that the generality of our approach will provide a first step on the way to obtaining a scientifically-based engineering methodology.

The use of CBPV enabled a systematic account that highlights the interplay between programming constructs and effects. Categorical language greatly helped the organisation of this work. It was also crucial in seeing the connection with Führmann's work, and unifying it with Benton et al.'s. Finally, the example language demonstrated the ease of application of the theory to a language equipped with an algebraic semantics. Note too that model constructions are not ad hoc: they come for *free* given only the algebraic theory of the effects at hand.

Further work abounds. It would be good to resolve Conjecture 10, and to establish means to decide the validity of optimisations in the benchmark model. It is also important to include *effect handlers* [37, 40] such as exception handlers and rollback in the language. Pretnar and Plotkin describe a β rule for handlers, and a rule for the interaction of algebraic operations and handlers. These rules have many consequences in their logic, and will surely be valid in our setting. There may also be useful abstract optimisations involving handlers, possibly unifying existing accounts [4].

Effect reconstruction is of immediate importance. It should be possible to derive general algorithms for type and effect annotation. Our semantics can then be used to give semantics to such programs. Levy's translations of call-by-value and call-by-name into CBPV could then be used to deduce general effect systems for these paradigms, generalising and unifying existing work.

Notions of locality, particularly local state, are very important. It may be possible to make use of work on the algebraic treatment of locality, e.g., [29, 34, 42], to obtain a more general optimisation theory. This should enable the work of Benton et al. on dynamic allocation [8] to be incorporated. (Incorporating higher-order store [6] would require solving recursive domain equations [1, 25].)

op	$\varsigma^{\mathrm{Swap}}$	$\varsigma^{\mathrm{WSwap}} \setminus \varsigma^{\mathrm{Swap}}$	$\varsigma^{\mathrm{ISwap}} \setminus \varsigma^{\mathrm{WSwap}}$	$\lvert\sigma\rvert \setminus \varsigma^{\mathrm{ISwap}}$
Ω	Ω, lookup$^{\rho}$, update$^{\rho}$, $\vee$	$\emptyset$	$\emptyset$	input, output, raise, throw, rollback, abort
input	lookup$^{\rho}$, update$^{\rho}$	$\vee$	input	Ω, output, raise, throw, rollback, abort
output	lookup$^{\rho}$, update$^{\rho}$	$\vee$	output	Ω, input, raise, throw, rollback, abort
raise	lookup$^{\rho}$, raise, $\vee$	$\emptyset$	$\emptyset$	Ω, input, output, throw, rollback, abort, update$^{\rho}$
throw	lookup$^{\rho}$	$\vee$	$\emptyset$	Ω, input, output, raise, throw, rollback, abort, update$^{\rho}$
rollback	lookup$^{\rho}$, update$^{\rho}$, rollback, $\vee$	$\emptyset$	$\emptyset$	Ω, input, output, raise, throw, abort
abort	lookup$^{\rho}$, update$^{\rho}$	$\vee$	$\emptyset$	Ω, input, output, raise, throw, rollback, abort
lookup$^{\rho_0}$	Ω, input, output, raise, throw, abort, rollback, abort, lookup$^{\rho}$, update$^{\rho \neq \rho_0}$, $\vee$	$\emptyset$	update$^{\rho_0}$	$\emptyset$
update$^{\rho_0}$	Ω, input, output, rollback, abort, lookup$^{\rho \neq \rho_0}$, update$^{\rho \neq \rho_0}$, $\vee$	lookup$^{\rho_0}$	$\emptyset$	raise, throw, update$^{\rho_0}$
$\vee$	Ω, raise, throw, rollback, abort, lookup$^{\rho}$, update$^{\rho}$, $\vee$	$\emptyset$	input, output	$\emptyset$

Figure 8. Swap Sets

In a different direction, the distributive combination of theories [17] (used for combining ordinary and probabilistic computation) should be investigated. Also, our theory should be extended to include non-algebraic effects, such as continuations [20].

Our arities are required to be *ground*, *finite* and *discrete*. The finiteness and discreteness conditions can be relaxed by using, respectively, *infinitary (in)equational theories* [39]; and *enriched Lawvere theories* [38]. Our treatment of the finite discrete case exploited inequational logic; in the infinitary, enriched case, corresponding proof theories are needed [32]. Generalising arities to non-ground types may involve recursive domain equations, as in the hypothesised treatment of higher-order store.

The logic we used for our optimisations is a simple equational logic — we have only considered equations between terms. It seems straightforward to devise a richer effect-dependent counterpart to Plotkin and Pretnar's logic [36, 40].

Additional work is needed to distill the general account into methodologies. In particular, it is desirable to reproduce the exponential improvement in operation-wise validation for the other optimisations. Also, machine assistance and model-checking tools could alleviate the repetitive burden of operation-wise validation.

We conjecture that Benton et al.'s logical relations method can be related to the conservative restriction model. Our approach is denotational; it would be interesting to devise an operational account [22, 33]. A precise relationship between our theory and Atkey's is in order, particularly with his parameterised monads. Finally it would be good to go beyond Gifford-style, e.g., allowing effect traces, and to account for parallelism, as in Gifford's work [27].

Acknowledgments

We thank Robert Atkey, Andrej Bauer, Nick Benton, Jeff Egger, Ben Kavanagh, Neelakantan Krishnaswami, Paul Levy, Sam Lindley, Matija Pretnar, Alex Simpson, Ross Tate, Phil Wadler, and the anonymous reviewers for helpful discussions and comments. This research was supported by a Scottish Informatics and Computer Science Alliance studentship and a Royal Society Wolfson Award.

References

[1] S. Abramsky and A. Jung. *Hand. of Log. in CS*, 3:1–168, 1994.
[2] R. Atkey. *Proc. 3rd CALCO*, 3–17, 2009.
[3] R. Atkey. *JFP*, 19:335–376, 2009.
[4] N. Benton and P. Buchlovsky. *Proc. 3rd TLDI*, 15–26, 2007.
[5] N. Benton and A. Kennedy. *ENTCS*, 26:3–20, 1999.
[6] N. Benton et al. *Proc. 11th PPDP*, 301–312, 2009.
[7] N. Benton et al. *Proc. 4th APLAS*, 114–130, 2006.
[8] N. Benton et al. *Proc. 9th PPDP*, 87–96, 2007.
[9] B. Eckmann and P. J. Hilton. *Math. Ann.*, 145(3):227–255, 1962.
[10] A. Filinski. *Proc. 26th POPL*, 175–188, 1999.
[11] A. Filinski. *TCS*, 375(1-3):41–75, 2007.
[12] A. Filinski. *Proc. 37th POPL*, 483–494, 2010.
[13] C. Führmann. PhD thesis, University of Edinburgh, 2000.
[14] C. Führmann. *Proc. 5th FoSSaCS*, 144–158, 2002.
[15] A. D. Gordon and A. Jeffrey. *J. Comput. Secur.*, 12:435–483, 2004.
[16] M. Hennessy and G. D. Plotkin. *Proc. 8th MFCS*, 108–120, 1979.
[17] M. Hyland and J. Power. *TCS*, 366(1-2):144–162, 2006.
[18] M. Hyland and J. Power. *ENTCS*, 172:437–458, 2007.
[19] M. Hyland, G. D. Plotkin, and J. Power. *TCS*, 357(1-3):70–99, 2006.
[20] M. Hyland et al. *TCS*, 375(1-3):20–40, 2007.
[21] B. Jacobs. *Annals of Pure and Applied Logic*, 69(1):73–106, 1994.
[22] P. Johann et al. *Proc. 25th LICS*, 209–218, 2010.
[23] R. B. Kieburtz. *Proc. 3rd ICFP*, 51–62, 1998.
[24] A. Kock. *Mathematica Scandinavia*, 29:161–174, 1971.
[25] P. B. Levy. *Proc. 16th CSL*, 232–246, 2002.
[26] P. B. Levy. *Call-by-Push-Value*, Springer, 2004.
[27] J. M. Lucassen and D. K. Gifford. *Proc. 15th POPL*, 47–57, 1988.
[28] D. Marino and T. Millstein. *Proc. 4th TLDI*, 39–50, 2009.
[29] P.-A. Melliès. *Proc. 25th LICS*, 150–159, 2010.
[30] J. C. Mitchell. *Hand. of TCS*, B:365–458, 1990.
[31] G. D. Plotkin. *SIAM J. of Computing*, 5:452–487, 1976.
[32] G. D. Plotkin. *LNCS*, 4060:150–156, 2006.
[33] G. D. Plotkin and J. Power. *Proc. 4th FoSSaCS*, 1–24, 2001.
[34] G. D. Plotkin and J. Power. *LNCS*, 2303:342–356, 2002.
[35] G. D. Plotkin and J. Power. *ENTCS*, 73:149–163, 2004.
[36] G. D. Plotkin and M. Pretnar. *Proc. 23rd LICS*, 118–129, 2008.
[37] G. D. Plotkin and M. Pretnar. *Proc. 19th ESOP*, 80–94, 2009.
[38] J. Power. *Theory and Applications of Categories*, 6:83–93, 2000.
[39] J. Power. *ENTCS*, 161:59–71, 2006.
[40] M. Pretnar. PhD thesis, University of Edinburgh, 2009.
[41] J. Reynolds. *Proc. 2nd ICALP*, 141–156, 1974.
[42] S. Staton. *ENTCS*, 249:471–490, 2009.
[43] T. Coquand et al. *Inf. Comp.*, 93(1):172–221, 1991.
[44] M. Tofte and J.-P. Talpin. *Inf. Comp.*, 132(2):109–176, 1997.
[45] A. P. Tolmach. *Proc. 2nd TIC*, 97–115, 1998.
[46] P. Wadler. *Proc. 3rd ICFP*, 63–74, 1998.
[47] P. Wadler and P. Thiemann. *ACM Trans. Comp. Log.*, 4(1):1–32, 2003.
[48] A. K. Wright and M. Felleisen. *Inf. Comp.*, 115(1):38–94, 1994.

On the Power of Coercion Abstraction

Julien Cretin Didier Rémy

INRIA

{julien.cretin,didier.remy}@inria.fr

Abstract

Erasable coercions in System F_η, also known as retyping functions, are well-typed η-expansions of the identity. They may change the type of terms without changing their behavior and can thus be erased before reduction. Coercions in F_η can model subtyping of known types and some displacement of quantifiers, but not subtyping assumptions nor certain forms of delayed type instantiation. We generalize F_η by allowing abstraction over retyping functions. We follow a general approach where computing with coercions can be seen as computing in the λ-calculus but keeping track of which parts of terms are coercions. We obtain a language where coercions do not contribute to the reduction but may block it and are thus not erasable. We recover erasable coercions by choosing a weak reduction strategy and restricting coercion abstraction to value-forms or by restricting abstraction to coercions that are polymorphic in their domain or codomain. The latter variant subsumes F_η, $\mathsf{F}_{<:}$, and MLF in a unified framework.

Categories and Subject Descriptors D.3.1 [*Programming Languages*]: Formal Definitions and Theory

General Terms Design, Languages, Theory

Keywords Type, System F, F-eta, Polymorphism, Coercion, Conversion, Retyping functions, Type containment, Subtyping, Bounded Polymorphism.

1. Introduction

Parametric polymorphism and subtyping polymorphism are the two most popular means of increasing expressiveness of type systems: although first studied independently, they can be advantageously combined together. Each mechanism alone is relatively simple to understand and has a more or less canonical presentation. However, their combination is more complex. The most popular combination is the language $\mathsf{F}_{<:}$ [Cardelli 1993]. However, this is just one (relatively easy) spot in the design space. In fact, much work in the 90's has been devoted to improving the combination of parametric and subtyping polymorphism, motivated by its application to the typechecking of object-oriented features.

Contravariance, the key ingredient of subtyping polymorphism, is already modeled in the language F_η proposed by Mitchell [1988]. One way to define F_η is as the closure of Curry-style System F by η-conversion. We write $\mathcal{C}[\mathcal{M}]$ for filling a context $\mathcal{C}$ with a term $\mathcal{M}$. A *retyping context* from τ to σ is a closed one-hole context $\mathcal{C}$ such that $\lambda x.\mathcal{C}\langle x\rangle$ is an η-expansion of the identity, also called a retyping function, and has type $\tau \to \sigma$ in System F. If $\mathcal{C}$ is a retyping context from τ to σ and $\mathcal{M}$ is a term of type τ, then $\mathcal{C}[\mathcal{M}]$ is a term of type σ in System F. In System F_η, the type-containment rule allows $\mathcal{M}$ itself to be claimed of type σ. Moving to Church-style System F, we may keep type-containment, *i.e.* filling of retyping contexts explicit. We write $G\langle M\rangle$ for the application of retyping context (*i.e.* a coercion) G to the term M. We write $\Diamond^\tau$ for the empty (retyping) context of type τ. Contravariance is induced by η-expansion as follows: if G_1 and G_2 are retyping contexts from τ_1 to τ_1' and from τ_2 to τ_2', then $\lambda(x:\tau_1)\; G_2\langle \Diamond^{\tau_1'\to\tau_2}\; (G_1\langle x\rangle)\rangle$ is a retyping context from type $\tau_1' \to \tau_2$ to $\tau_1 \to \tau_2'$.

Besides contravariance, η-expansion also introduces opportunities for inserting type abstractions and type applications, which may change polymorphism a posteriori. For instance, from the type $\forall\alpha.\,\tau \to \sigma$, we can find a retyping context to any type of the form $(\forall\alpha.\,\tau) \to (\forall\bar\beta.\,\sigma[\alpha \leftarrow \rho])$ provided $\bar\beta$ does not appear free in $\forall\alpha.\,\sigma$; this context is $\lambda(x:\forall\alpha.\,\tau)\;\Lambda\bar\beta\;\Diamond^{\forall\alpha.\,\tau\to\sigma}\;\rho\;(x\;\rho)$. Such retypings are not supported in $\mathsf{F}_{<:}$ where polymorphism can only be introduced and eliminated explicitly at the topmost part of terms.

Conversely, $\mathsf{F}_{<:}$ allows reasoning under subtyping assumptions, which F_η does not support. Indeed, bounded quantification $\Lambda(\alpha <: \tau)\,M$ of $\mathsf{F}_{<:}$ introduces a type variable α that stands for any subtype of τ inside M. In particular, a *covariant occurrence* of α in M can be converted to type τ by subtyping.

Therefore F_η and $\mathsf{F}_{<:}$ are incomparable: is there a language that supersedes both? Before we tackle this question, let us first consider another form of retyping assumptions that have been introduced in MLF [Le Botlan and Rémy 2009]: instance-bounded polymorphism $\Lambda(\alpha \geq \tau)\,M$ introduces a type variable α that stands for any instance of τ inside M. That is, an occurrence of type α within M in an *instantiable position* can be converted to any instance of τ. Instance-bounded quantification delays the choice of whether a polymorphic expression should be instantiated immediately or kept polymorphic. This mechanism enables expressions to have more general types and has been introduced in MLF to enable partial type inference in the presence of first-class second-order polymorphism and some type annotations.

Notice that bounded type instantiation allows for deep type instantiation of binders, as F_η does, but using a quite different mechanism. Bounded type instantiation has similarities with bounded quantification of $\mathsf{F}_{<:}$, but the two also differ significantly, since for instance, type conversion is not congruent on arrow types in MLF.

Surprisingly, among the three languages F_η, $\mathsf{F}_{<:}$, and MLF, any combination of two have features in common that the other one lacks! Hence, the challenge becomes whether all their features can be combined together. This question has in fact already been raised in previous work on MLF [Rémy and Yakobowski 2010].

Our contributions We answer positively by introducing a language F_ι^p that extends F_η with abstraction over retyping functions,

POPL'12, January 25–27, 2012, Philadelphia, PA, USA.

combining all features simultaneously in a unified framework (§5). The language F_ι^p subsumes F_η, $\mathsf{F}_{<:}$, and MLF (§6); it also fixes and extends a previous language of coercions designed for modeling MLF alone [Manzonetto and Tranquilli 2010]. Our subset of F_ι^p that coincides with MLF is *well-behaved*: it satisfies the subject reduction and progress lemmas and strongly normalizes. It also has an untyped semantics.

Actually, the extension of F_η with abstraction over coercion functions leads to a larger language F_ι of which F_ι^p is a restriction (§2). The language F_ι is well-behaved. We show that F_ι can be simulated into System F. Hence, reduction rules in F_ι are just particular instances of β-reduction (§4). F_ι can also be simulated into the untyped λ-calculus, by dropping coercions, which shows that coercions do not contribute to the computation. Unfortunately, they may block it, and are thus not erasable (§3). Erasability can be recovered by choosing a weak reduction strategy (§7), but this is not entirely satisfactory. So, other restrictions or extensions of F_ι with erasable coercions are still to be found. Nevertheless, we believe that F_ι is a solid ground for understanding erasable coercions (§9).

System F All languages we consider are second order calculi whose origin is System F. System F comes in two flavors: in Curry-style, terms do not carry type information and are thus a subset of the untyped λ-calculus, while in Church-style, terms carry explicit type information, namely type abstractions, type applications, and annotations of function parameters.

Of course, both presentations are closely related, since there is a bisimulation between the reduction of terms in Church-style and terms in Curry-style via type erasure, where the reduction of type application between terms in Church-style is reflected as an equality on terms in Curry-style. That is, calling ι the reduction of type applications and β the reduction of term applications, the type erasures of two explicitly-typed terms related by β-reduction (*resp.* ι-reduction) are related by β-reduction (*resp.* equality); conversely, if the erasure of a term M β-reduces to a term $\mathcal{M}'$, then M also reduces by a sequence of ι-reductions followed by a single β-reduction to a term whose erasure is $\mathcal{M}'$.

Both views are equally useful: we prefer source expressions to be explicitly typed, so that type checking is a trivial process and types can be easily maintained during program transformations; we also wish types to be erasable after compilation for efficiency of program execution. Moreover, a source language with an untyped semantics is generally simpler to understand, reason about, and use. We may argue that even if the source language has intentional polymorphism, it should first be compiled in a type-dependent way to an intermediate language with an untyped semantics [Crary et al. 2002].

From types to type conversions Our approach to coercions is similar to polymorphism in System F because we focus here on retyping functions that are *erasable*. In some circumstances, one may use *other* forms of coercions that may have some computational content, *e.g.* change the representation of values, and thus not be erasable. Then, we should compile source expressions into an intermediate language where remaining coercions, if any, are erasable; this is then the language we wish to study here.

Erasability also means that the dynamic semantics of our language is ultimately that of the underlying λ-calculus—possibly enriched with more constructs. Therefore the semantics only depends on the reduction strategy we choose and not on the typechecking details nor on the coercions we may use. Types are useful for programmers to understand their programs. It is also useful for programmers that types do not determine the semantics of their programs. At least, we should provide an intermediate representation in which this is true.

Coercions may also be introduced a posteriori to make type conversions explicit inside source terms. Coercions usually simplify the meta-theoretical study of the language by providing a concrete syntax to manipulate typing derivations. Proofs such as subject reduction become *computation* on concrete terms instead of *reasoning* on derivations.

While in practice programming languages use weak evaluation strategies, strong evaluation strategies provide more insight into the calculus by also modeling reduction of open terms. Since our focus is on *understanding* the essence of coercions, and the meta-theoretical properties, we prefer strong reduction strategies. Imposing a weak reduction strategy on a well-behaved strong calculus afterward is usually easy—even if all properties do not automatically transfer. Conversely, properties for weak reduction strategies do not say much about strong reduction strategies.

The two faces of F_η Let us first return to the definition of F_η, which in Mitchell's original presentation is given in Curry-style. It is defined by adding to System F a *type containment* rule that allows to convert a term $\mathcal{M}$ of type τ to one of type σ whenever there exists a retyping context from type τ to σ, which we write $\vdash \tau \triangleright \sigma$. This judgment, called type containment, is equivalent to the existence of a (closed) retyping function $\mathcal{M}'$ of System F such that $\vdash \mathcal{M}' : \tau \to \sigma$, *i.e.* a function that is an η-expansion of the identity.

Interestingly, Mitchell gave another characterization of type containment, exhibiting a proof system for the judgment $\vdash \tau \triangleright \sigma$, which can be read back as the introduction of a language of coercions whose expressions G witness type containment derivations. Then, we write $\vdash G : \tau \triangleright \sigma$ where G fully determines the typing derivation—much as a Church-style System-F term M fully determines its typing derivation. For example, $G_1 \to G_2$ is a coercion that, given a function M, returns a function that coerces its argument with G_1, passes it to M, and coerces the result with G_2—hence the contravariance of type containment. (A full presentation of coercions appears in §2 where F_η is described as a subset of F_ι.)

The interpretation of coercions as λ-terms is more intuitive than coercions as proof witnesses. Unfortunately, its formal presentation F_ι^λ, which is equivalent to F_ι, is technically more involved for reasons explained in §4. Hence, we prefer to present F_ι first in §2 and only introduce F_ι^λ informally in §4. Interestingly, the reification of F_ι into System F given in §3.3 already reveals this intuitive interpretation of coercions—without the technicalities—and we refer to it when describing the typing rules and reduction rules of F_ι.

In Church-style System F, the use of a coercion G around a term M is witnessed explicitly as $G\langle M\rangle$. (We may continue seeing a coercion G as a retyping context and reading this as filling the hole of G or, equivalently, see G as a retyping function and read this as an application of a coercion to a term.) Reduction rules are added to reduce such applications when both G and M have been sufficiently evaluated—in a way depending on the form of both—so that a coercion G is never stuck in the middle of a (well-typed) redex as in $(G\langle\lambda(x : \tau)\ M\rangle)\ N$. The type system ensures that G is of a certain shape for which a reduction exists. In the above example, G may be $G_1 \overset{\sigma}{\to} G_2$ and then $G\langle\lambda(x : \tau)\ M\rangle$ can be reduced to $\lambda(x : \sigma)\ G_2\langle M[x \leftarrow G_1\langle x\rangle]\rangle$.

The genesis of F_ι To abstract over coercion functions, we introduce a new form $\lambda(c : \tau \triangleright \sigma)\ M$ in F_ι, where the parameter c stands for a coercion function that can be used inside M to convert an expression of type τ to one of type σ. This abstraction can be typed as $(\tau \triangleright \sigma) \Rightarrow \rho$ where ρ is the type of M. Correspondingly, we need a new application form $M\{G\}$ to pass a coercion G to a coercion abstraction, *i.e.* a term M of type $(\tau \triangleright \sigma) \Rightarrow \rho$.

By typing constraints, coercion abstractions can only be instantiated with coercions, which by construction are erasable. Thus,

$$
\begin{array}{lll}
x, y & & \text{variables} \\
\mathcal{M} & ::= x \mid \lambda x.\mathcal{M} \mid \mathcal{M}\,\mathcal{M} & \text{terms} \\
\mathcal{C} & ::= \lambda x.[] \mid []\,\mathcal{M} \mid \mathcal{M}\,[] & \text{reduction contexts}
\end{array}
$$

$$
\text{RedContext}\ \frac{\mathcal{M} \rightsquigarrow \mathcal{M}'}{\mathcal{C}[\mathcal{M}] \rightsquigarrow \mathcal{C}[\mathcal{M}']} \qquad \text{RedBeta}\ (\lambda x.\mathcal{M})\,\mathcal{M}' \rightsquigarrow \mathcal{M}[x \leftarrow \mathcal{M}']
$$

Figure 1. λ-calculus: syntax and semantics

intuitively, coercions do not really contribute to the computation. Is this enough to erase them? Formally, we can exhibit a forward simulation between reduction of terms in F_ι and of their erasure in the untyped λ-calculus. Moreover, F_ι has the subject reduction property and is strongly normalizing. Still, coercions cannot be erased in F_ι, since although they do not create new evaluation paths, they may block existing evaluation paths: a subterm may be stuck while its erasure could proceed. Since coercions are erasable in F_η, this can only be due to the use of a coercion variable. Indeed, a coercion variable c may appear in the middle of a β-redex as in $(c\langle\lambda(x : \tau)\ M\rangle)\ N$. This is irreducible because reduction of coercion applications $G\langle M\rangle$ depends simultaneously on the shapes of G and M so that no rule fires when G is unknown. More generally, we call a wedge an irreducible term of the form $(G\langle\lambda(x : \tau)\ M\rangle)\ N$. Notice that the erasure of a wedge $(\lambda(x : \tau)\ \lfloor M\rfloor)\ \lfloor N\rfloor$ can be reduced, immediately. Hence, the existence of wedges in reduction contexts prevents erasability.

Taming coercions in F_ι^p An obvious solution to recover erasability is to make wedge configurations ill-typed—so that they never appear during the reduction of well-typed programs. One interesting restriction, called F_ι^p (read Parametric F_ι), is to request that coercion parameters be polymorphic in either their domain or their codomain. This allows coercion variables to appear either applied to a function or inside an application, but not both simultaneously.

Another solution is to change the semantics: choosing a weak reduction strategy for coercion abstractions and restricting them to appear only in front of value forms, coercion variables, hence wedges, cannot occur in a reduction context any more. This variant is called F_ι^w (read Weak F_ι).

Although our main goal—combining F_η, $\mathsf{F}_{<:}$, and MLF in a same language—is reached, both F_ι^p and F_ι^w are restrictions of F_ι. We may thus wonder whether other yet more interesting solutions exist. We further discuss some of the issues in §9, argue about some of the difficulties in the general case, and suggest other restrictions worth exploring. We defer a discussion of related works to §8.

2. The language F_ι

The language F_ι generalizes F_η with abstraction over coercions. We recall the definition of the (untyped) λ-calculus on Figure 1. We normally include pairs and projections both to have non trivial errors (otherwise, even untyped terms cannot be stuck) and to have more interesting forms of subtyping. However, we omit them in this summary for conciseness of exposition. We occasionally refer to them informally to explain how the definitions generalize to pairs. We assume an enumerable collection of term variables, ranged over by letters x and y. Untyped terms, written $\mathcal{M}$, include variables, abstractions $\lambda x.\mathcal{M}$, and applications $\mathcal{M}\,\mathcal{M}'$. The semantics of untyped λ-terms is given by a small-step strong reduction relation. Reduction contexts of the λ-calculus are all one-hole contexts, written $\mathcal{C}$. We now write $\mathcal{C}[\mathcal{M}]$ for the term obtained by filling the hole of $\mathcal{C}$ with $\mathcal{M}$ and $\mathcal{M}[x \leftarrow \mathcal{M}']$ for the capture avoiding substitution of $\mathcal{M}'$ for x in $\mathcal{M}$. Expressions are considered equal up to the renaming of bound variables, which are defined in the usual way. This convention applies to the λ-calculus, as well as to all typed languages presented below.

$$
\begin{array}{lll}
\tau, \sigma & ::= \alpha \mid \tau \to \tau \mid \forall\alpha.\tau \mid \top & \text{Types} \\
& \mid \varphi \Rightarrow \tau & \textit{coercion abstraction} \\
\varphi & ::= \tau \rhd \tau & \text{coercion type} \\
M, N & ::= x \mid \lambda(x : \tau)\ M \mid M\ M & \text{Terms} \\
& \mid \lambda\alpha\ M \mid M\ \tau & \textit{type abs \& app} \\
& \mid G\langle M\rangle & \textit{term coercion} \\
& \mid \lambda(c : \varphi)\ M \mid M\{G\} & \textit{coercion abs \& app} \\
G & ::= c \mid \mathsf{Top}^\tau \mid \Diamond^\tau \mid G \xrightarrow{\tau} G & \text{Coercions} \\
& \mid \mathsf{Dist}^{\forall\alpha.}_{\tau\to\tau} \mid \mathsf{Dist}^{\varphi\Rightarrow}_{\tau\to\tau} & \textit{distributivity} \\
& \mid \lambda\alpha\ G \mid G\ \tau & \textit{type abs \& app} \\
& \mid G\langle G\rangle & \textit{coercion coercion} \\
& \mid \lambda(c : \varphi)\ G \mid G\{G\} & \textit{coercion abs \& app} \\
\Gamma & ::= \emptyset \mid \Gamma, \alpha \mid \Gamma, x : \tau \mid \Gamma, c : \varphi & \text{Typing environments}
\end{array}
$$

Figure 2. Syntax of F_ι.

2.1 Syntax of F_ι

The language F_ι is explicitly typed. Types are described on Figure 2. We assume given an enumerable set of type variables, ranged over by α and β. Types are type variables, arrow types $\tau \to \tau$, polymorphic types $\forall\alpha.\,\tau$, the top type $\top$, or coercion abstractions $\varphi \Rightarrow \tau$ where the coercion type φ is of the form $\tau \rhd \tau$. Coercions are not first class, hence a coercion type φ is not itself a type.

The language of expressions is split into *terms* and *coercions*. We reuse the term variables of the λ-calculus. In addition, we assume an enumerable set of coercion variables written c. Terms are an extension of Church-style System F. Hence, they include type variables x, abstractions $\lambda(x : \tau)\ M$, applications $M M$, type abstractions $\lambda\alpha\ M$, and type applications $M\ \tau$. A construct already present in F_η is the use of the application $G\langle M\rangle$ of a coercion G to a term M. There are two new constructs specific to F_ι and not present in F_η: coercion abstraction $\lambda(c : \varphi)\ M$ which is annotated with the coercion type φ; and coercion application $M\{G\}$ that passes a coercion G to a term M—and should not be confused with the earlier construct $G\langle M\rangle$ of F_η that places a coercion G around a term M.

Since the main purpose of coercions is to change types, we could postpone the description of coercion constructs together with their typing rules—and their associated reduction rules that justify the typing rules. Still, each coercion expression can be understood as a one-hole retyping context witnessing some type-containment rule. So we introduce each construct with the retyping context it stands for, also preparing for the reification of coercions as System-F terms given in §3.3.

A coercion variable c stands for the coercion it will be bound to. The opaque coercion Top^τ is a downgraded version of existential types (we currently do not handle existential types for reasons explained in §9): it turns a term of any type into an opaque term of type $\top$ that can only be used abstractly. The empty coercion $\Diamond^\tau$ stands for the empty retyping context and witnesses reflexivity of type containment. The arrow coercion $G_1 \xrightarrow{\tau} G_2$ stands for $\lambda(x : \tau)\ G_2\langle[]\ (G_1\langle x\rangle)\rangle$ and witnesses contravariance of the arrow type constructor. The distributivity coercion $\mathsf{Dist}^{\forall\alpha.}_{\tau\to\sigma}$ stands for $\lambda(x : \tau)\ \lambda\alpha\ []\ \alpha\ x$ and permutes a type abstraction with a term abstraction: assuming the hole has type $\forall\alpha.\,\tau \to \sigma$ where α does not appear free in τ, it returns a term of type $\tau \to \forall\alpha.\,\sigma$. For instance, the coercion of a polymorphic function $\lambda\alpha\ \lambda(y : \tau)\ N$

$$
\begin{array}{rlrl}
\lfloor x \rfloor &= x & \lfloor \lambda\alpha\ M \rfloor = \lfloor M\ \tau \rfloor &= \lfloor M \rfloor \\
\lfloor \lambda(x:\tau)\ M \rfloor &= \lambda x.\lfloor M \rfloor & \lfloor G\langle M\rangle \rfloor &= \lfloor M \rfloor \\
\lfloor M\ N \rfloor &= \lfloor M \rfloor \lfloor N \rfloor & \lfloor \lambda(c:\varphi)\ M \rfloor = \lfloor M\{G\} \rfloor &= \lfloor M \rfloor
\end{array}
$$

Figure 3. Coercion erasure

makes it appear as if it had been defined as $\lambda(y : \tau)\ \lambda\alpha\ N$—which is actually what it will reduce to once coerced. The other distributivity coercion $\mathsf{Dist}^{\varphi\Rightarrow}_{\tau\to\sigma}$, which stands for $\lambda(x : \tau)\ \lambda(c : \varphi)\ ([]\{c\}\ x)$, is similar but permutes a coercion abstraction with a term abstraction.

We may need more distributivity coercions when extending the language of terms. Hence, the notation $\mathsf{Dist}^{a}_{b\to c}$ uses the following mnemonic: the superscript a and the subscript $b \to c$ indicate the kind of the first and second type constructs, respectively. They can be combined into $a(b \to c)$ to form the type of the hole, or recombined into $b \to ac$ to form the type of the coerced term. For example, $\mathsf{Dist}^{\forall\alpha.}_{\tau\to\sigma}$ is a coercion from $\forall\alpha.\,(\tau \to \sigma)$ to $\tau \to (\forall\alpha.\,\sigma)$, while $\mathsf{Dist}^{\varphi\Rightarrow}_{\tau\to\sigma}$ is a coercion from $\varphi \Rightarrow (\tau \to \sigma)$ to $\tau \to (\varphi \Rightarrow \sigma)$.

The remaining coercions are the lifting of all term constructs without computational content to coercions: type abstraction $\lambda\alpha\ G$ and type application $G\ \tau$; coercion of a coercion $G'\langle G\rangle$ which intuitively stands for $G'\langle G\langle[]\rangle\rangle$ and witnesses transitivity of coercions: it has type $\rho \triangleright \sigma$ if G' and G have coercion types $\tau \triangleright \sigma$ and $\rho \triangleright \tau$, respectively; finally, coercion abstraction $\lambda(c : \varphi)\ G$ and coercion application $G'\{G\}$. All these coercions are of the form $P[G]$ where P is one of the contexts $\lambda\alpha\ []$, $[]\ \tau$, $G'\langle[]\rangle$, $\lambda(c : \varphi)\ []$, or $[]\{G'\}$, where the hole is filled with G. It is convenient to overload the notation P when the hole holds a term instead of a coercion, although this is formally another syntactic node.

We recover the syntax of System F_η by removing coercion types from types and coercion variables, coercion abstractions and applications from both terms and coercions. We recover the syntax of System F by further removing the top type, term coercions, and all coercion forms, which become vacuous.

The coercion erasure, written $\lfloor\cdot\rfloor$, defined on Figure 3, is as expected: type annotations on function parameters and coercions are erased, while other constructs are projected on their equivalent constructs in the untyped λ-calculus.

2.2 Typing rules

Typing environments, written Γ, are lists of bindings where bindings are either type variables α, coercion variables along with their coercion type $c : \varphi$, or term variables along with their type $x : \tau$ (Figure 2). We write $\Gamma \vdash M : \tau$ if term M has type τ under Γ and $\Gamma \vdash G : \varphi$ if coercion G has coercion type φ under Γ.

The two typing judgments are recursively defined on figures 4 and 5. They use auxiliary well-formedness judgments for types and typing contexts: we write $\Gamma \vdash ok$ to mean that typing environment Γ is well-formed and $\Gamma \vdash \tau$ or $\Gamma \vdash \varphi$ to mean that type τ or coercion type φ is well-formed in Γ.

As usual, we require that typing contexts do not bind twice the same variable, which is not restrictive as all expressions are considered equal up to renaming of bound variables (details can be found in the extended version).

Typing rules for terms are described in Figure 4. Rules TermVar, TermTermLam, TermTermApp, TermTypeLam, and TermTypeApp are exactly the typing rules of System F. Rule TermCoer is similar to rule TermTermApp, except that a coercion G of coercion type $\tau \triangleright \sigma$ is used instead of a function M of type $\tau \to \sigma$. Rule TermCoerLam is similar to TermTermLam, except that the parameter c stands for a coercion of coercion type φ instead of a term of type σ: the result is a coercion abstraction of type $\varphi \Rightarrow \tau$.

$$
\begin{array}{rcll}
p & ::= & x \mid p\ v \mid p\,\tau \mid p\{G\} \mid c\langle v\rangle & \text{Prevalues} \\
 & \mid & \mathsf{Dist}^{\forall\alpha.}_{\tau\to\tau}\langle p\rangle \mid \mathsf{Dist}^{\forall\alpha.}_{\tau\to\tau}\langle\lambda\alpha\ p\rangle \mid (G \xrightarrow{\tau} G)\langle p\rangle & \\
 & \mid & \mathsf{Dist}^{\varphi\Rightarrow}_{\tau\to\tau}\langle p\rangle \mid \mathsf{Dist}^{\varphi\Rightarrow}_{\tau\to\tau}\langle\lambda(c:\varphi)\ p\rangle & \\
v & ::= & p \mid \lambda(x:\tau)\ v \mid \lambda\alpha\ v \mid \lambda(c:\varphi)\ v \mid \mathtt{Top}^{\tau}\langle v\rangle & \text{Values} \\
C & ::= & \lambda(x:\tau)\ [] \mid []\ M \mid M\ [] \mid P & \text{Reduction contexts} \\
P & ::= & \lambda\alpha\ [] \mid []\ \tau \mid G\langle[]\rangle \mid \lambda(c:\varphi)\ [] \mid []\{G\} & \text{Retyping contexts}
\end{array}
$$

Figure 6. System F_ι: values and reduction contexts

Consistently, TermCoerApp applies a term that is a coercion abstraction of type $\varphi \Rightarrow \tau$ to a coercion G of coercion type φ.

Typing rules for coercions are described in Figure 5. They are all straightforward when read with the retyping context that the coercion stands for in mind. Rule CoerVar reads the coercion type of a coercion variable from its typing context. The empty coercion has type $\tau \triangleright \tau$ provided τ is well-formed in the current context. As all basic coercions, it contains just enough type information so that its typing rule is syntax-directed. The top coercion $\mathtt{Top}^{\tau}$ converts an expression of type τ to the top type, provided τ is well-formed. The arrow coercion $G_1 \xrightarrow{\tau_1} G_2$ turns an arrow type $\tau_1' \to \tau_2$ into an arrow type $\tau_1 \to \tau_2'$, provided G_i coerces type τ_i into τ_i' for i in $\{1, 2\}$. The distributivity coercion $\mathsf{Dist}^{\forall\alpha.}_{\tau\to\sigma}$ turns an expression of type $\forall\alpha.\,\tau \to \sigma$ into one of type $\tau \to \forall\alpha.\,\sigma$ provided τ is well-formed in the current environment, which prevents α from appearing free in τ, and σ is well-formed in the current environment extended with α. Finally, Rule CoerDistCoerArrow is similar to CoerDistTypeArrow, but swaps a coercion abstraction and a term abstraction.

The remaining rules CoerTypeLam, CoerTypeApp, CoerCoer, CoerCoerLam, and CoerCoerApp are similar to their counterpart for terms, but where the term M of type τ has been replaced by a coercion (*i.e.* a one-hole context) G of coercion type $\tau_1 \triangleright \tau_2$, where τ_1 is the type of the hole and τ_2 the type of the body. Rule CoerTypeLam for typing $\lambda\alpha\ G$ introduces a variable α that is bound in G and can be used in the type of the body of G but not in the type of its hole, which is enforced by the first premise. In particular, $\lambda\alpha\ G$ builds a coercion to a polymorphic type $\tau \triangleright \forall\alpha.\,\sigma$ and not a polymorphic coercion $\forall\alpha.\,\tau \triangleright \sigma$. Accordingly, only the codomain of the type of the conclusion is polymorphic. Rule CoerCoerLam is typed in a similar way: $\lambda(c : \varphi)\ G$ has type $\tau_1 \triangleright (\varphi \Rightarrow \tau_2)$ and not $\varphi \Rightarrow (\tau_1 \triangleright \tau_2)$ as one could naively expect—which would be ill-formed. Type and coercion applications are typed accordingly (CoerTypeApp and CoerCoerApp).

The typing rules for F_η are obtained by removing TermCoerLam and TermCoerApp for terms and their counter parts CoerCoerLam and CoerCoerApp for coercions as well as Rule CoerVar for coercion variables and Rule CoerDistCoerArrow for distributivity of coercion abstraction.

The type superscripts that appear in reflexivity, distributivity, and top coercions make type checking syntax directed. The type superscript in arrow coercions is not needed for typechecking but to keep reduction a local rewriting rule. (We may leave superscripts implicit when they are unimportant or can be unambiguously reconstructed from the context.)

Our presentation of F_ι is in Church-style. Curry-style F_ι is the image of F_ι by coercion erasure. That is, it is the subset of terms of the untyped λ-calculus that are the erasure of a term of Church-style System F_ι. We write $\Gamma \vdash \mathcal{M} : \tau$ to mean that there exists M such that $\Gamma \vdash M : \tau$ and $\lfloor M \rfloor$ is $\mathcal{M}$.

TermVar
$$\frac{\Gamma \vdash ok \qquad x : \tau \in \Gamma}{\Gamma \vdash x : \tau}$$

TermTermLam
$$\frac{\Gamma, x : \tau \vdash M : \sigma}{\Gamma \vdash \lambda(x : \tau)\ M : \tau \to \sigma}$$

TermTermApp
$$\frac{\Gamma \vdash M : \tau \to \sigma \qquad \Gamma \vdash N : \tau}{\Gamma \vdash M\ N : \sigma}$$

TermTypeLam
$$\frac{\Gamma, \alpha \vdash M : \tau}{\Gamma \vdash \lambda\alpha\ M : \forall\alpha.\tau}$$

TermTypeApp
$$\frac{\Gamma \vdash M : \forall\alpha.\tau \qquad \Gamma \vdash \sigma}{\Gamma \vdash M\,\sigma : \tau[\alpha \leftarrow \sigma]}$$

TermCoer
$$\frac{\Gamma \vdash G : \tau \triangleright \sigma \qquad \Gamma \vdash M : \tau}{\Gamma \vdash G\langle M\rangle : \sigma}$$

TermCoerLam
$$\frac{\Gamma, c : \varphi \vdash M : \tau}{\Gamma \vdash \lambda(c : \varphi)\ M : \varphi \Rightarrow \tau}$$

TermCoerApp
$$\frac{\Gamma \vdash M : \varphi \Rightarrow \tau \qquad \Gamma \vdash G : \varphi}{\Gamma \vdash M\{G\} : \tau}$$

Figure 4. System F_ι: term typings

CoerDot
$$\frac{\Gamma \vdash \tau}{\Gamma \vdash \Diamond^\tau : \tau \triangleright \tau}$$

CoerForget
$$\frac{\Gamma \vdash \tau}{\Gamma \vdash \mathsf{Top}^\tau : \tau \triangleright \top}$$

CoerArrow
$$\frac{\Gamma \vdash G_1 : \tau_1 \triangleright \tau_1' \qquad \Gamma \vdash G_2 : \tau_2 \triangleright \tau_2'}{\Gamma \vdash G_1 \xrightarrow{\tau_1} G_2 : (\tau_1' \to \tau_2) \triangleright (\tau_1 \to \tau_2')}$$

CoerDistTypeArrow
$$\frac{\Gamma \vdash \tau \qquad \Gamma, \alpha \vdash \sigma}{\Gamma \vdash \mathsf{Dist}^{\forall\alpha.}_{\tau\to\sigma} : \forall\alpha.(\tau \to \sigma) \triangleright \tau \to \forall\alpha.\sigma}$$

CoerDistCoerArrow
$$\frac{\Gamma \vdash \tau \qquad \Gamma \vdash \varphi \qquad \Gamma \vdash \sigma}{\Gamma \vdash \mathsf{Dist}^{\varphi\Rightarrow}_{\tau\to\sigma} : (\varphi \Rightarrow (\tau \to \sigma)) \triangleright (\tau \to (\varphi \Rightarrow \sigma))}$$

CoerTypeLam
$$\frac{\Gamma \vdash \tau \qquad \Gamma, \alpha \vdash G : \tau \triangleright \sigma}{\Gamma \vdash \lambda\alpha\ G : \tau \triangleright \forall\alpha.\sigma}$$

CoerTypeApp
$$\frac{\Gamma \vdash G : \tau' \triangleright \forall\alpha.\sigma \qquad \Gamma \vdash \tau}{\Gamma \vdash G\,\tau : \tau' \triangleright \sigma[\alpha \leftarrow \tau]}$$

CoerCoer
$$\frac{\Gamma \vdash G : \tau \triangleright \sigma \qquad \Gamma \vdash G' : \rho \triangleright \tau}{\Gamma \vdash G\langle G'\rangle : \rho \triangleright \sigma}$$

CoerCoerLam
$$\frac{\Gamma, c : \varphi \vdash G : \tau \triangleright \sigma}{\Gamma \vdash \lambda(c : \varphi)\ G : \tau \triangleright (\varphi \Rightarrow \sigma)}$$

CoerCoerApp
$$\frac{\Gamma \vdash G' : \tau \triangleright (\varphi \Rightarrow \sigma) \qquad \Gamma \vdash G : \varphi}{\Gamma \vdash G'\{G\} : \tau \triangleright \sigma}$$

CoerVar
$$\frac{\Gamma \vdash ok \quad c : \varphi \in \Gamma}{\Gamma \vdash c : \varphi}$$

Figure 5. System F_ι: coercion typings

RedContextBeta
$$\frac{M \rightsquigarrow_\beta N}{C[M] \rightsquigarrow_\beta C[N]}$$

RedContextIota
$$\frac{M \rightsquigarrow_\iota N}{C[M] \rightsquigarrow_\iota C[N]}$$

RedTerm
$$(\lambda(x : \tau)\ M)\ N \rightsquigarrow_\beta M[x \leftarrow N]$$

RedType
$$(\lambda\alpha\ M)\,\tau \rightsquigarrow_\iota M[\alpha \leftarrow \tau]$$

RedCoer
$$(\lambda(c : \varphi)\ M)\{G\} \rightsquigarrow_\iota M[c \leftarrow G]$$

RedCoerArrow
$$(G_1 \xrightarrow{\tau} G_2)\langle\lambda(x : \sigma)\ M\rangle \rightsquigarrow_\iota \lambda(x : \tau)\ G_2\langle M[x \leftarrow G_1\langle x\rangle]\rangle$$

RedCoerDistTypeArrow
$$\mathsf{Dist}^{\forall\alpha.}_{\tau'\to\sigma'}\langle\lambda\alpha\ \lambda(x : \tau)\ M\rangle \rightsquigarrow_\iota \lambda(x : \tau)\ \lambda\alpha\ M$$

RedCoerDistCoerArrow
$$\mathsf{Dist}^{\varphi'\Rightarrow}_{\tau'\to\sigma'}\langle\lambda(c : \varphi)\ \lambda(x : \tau)\ M\rangle \rightsquigarrow_\iota \lambda(x : \tau)\ \lambda(c : \varphi)\ M$$

RedCoerDot
$$\Diamond^\tau\langle M\rangle \rightsquigarrow_\iota M$$

RedCoerFill
$$(P[G])\langle M\rangle \rightsquigarrow_\iota P[G\langle M\rangle]$$

Figure 7. Reduction rules for F_ι

2.3 Dynamic semantics

The dynamic semantics of System F_ι is given by a standard small-step strong reduction relation. The syntax of values and reduction contexts is recalled on Figure 6.

A value is an abstraction of a value, an opaque value $\mathsf{Top}^\tau\langle v\rangle$, or a prevalue. A prevalue is a variable, a prevalue applied to a value, type, or coercion, a value coerced by a coercion variable, or a partial application of a distributivity coercion. Reduction contexts C are all one-hole term contexts. For convenience, we have distinguished a subset of reduction contexts P, called *retyping reduction contexts*: a term M placed in a retyping reduction context is just a retyping of M, *i.e.* a term that behaves as M but possibly with another type.

Reduction rules are defined on Figure 7. We have indexed the reduction rules so as to distinguish between β-steps with computational content (RedTerm), that are preserved after erasure, and ι-steps (RedType) that become equalities after erasure. We write $\rightsquigarrow_{\beta\iota}$ for the union of $\rightsquigarrow_\beta$ and $\rightsquigarrow_\iota$.

Hence, Rule RedContext is split into two rules, so as to preserve the index of the premise. The only β-redex is RedTerm; all other reductions are ι-reductions. Rule RedType is type reduction (a ι-reduction). The first four rules cover System F. Notice that RedContext allows all possible contexts. Hence, there is no particular reduction strategy and a call-by-value evaluation would be a particular case of reduction.

Rule RedCoer is the counterpart of β-reduction for coercion application $M\{G\}$. It only reduces a term applied to a coercion; a coercion applied to a coercion is a coercion and is not reduced directly, but only when it is applied to a term so that rule RedCoerCoerApp eventually applies.

All other rules reduce the application $G\langle M\rangle$ of a coercion G to a term M, which plays the role of a destructor: both G and M must be sufficiently evaluated before it reduces—except when G is the opaque coercion or a variable since $\mathsf{Top}^\tau\langle v\rangle$ and $c\langle v\rangle$ are values.

Other coercion nodes are all constructors. We thus have one rule for each possible shape of G. The most interesting rules are:

- When G is an arrow coercion $G_1 \xrightarrow{\tau} G_2$ and M is a function $\lambda(x : \sigma)\ M$, Rule RedCoerArrow reduces the application by pushing G_1 on all occurrences of x in M and G_2 outside of M. This changes the type of the parameter x from σ to τ, hence the need for the annotation τ on arrow coercions.
- When G is a distributivity coercion $\mathsf{Dist}^{\forall\alpha.}_{\tau'\to\sigma'}$ and M is a polymorphic function $\lambda\alpha\ \lambda(x : \tau)\ M$, Rule RedCoerDistTypeArrow reduces the application to $\lambda(x : \tau)\ \lambda\alpha\ M$ by exchanging the type and value parameters; this is sound since α cannot be free in τ.
- When G is a distributivity coercion $\mathsf{Dist}^{\varphi'\Rightarrow}_{\tau'\to\sigma'}$ and M is a coercion abstraction followed by a value abstraction $\lambda(c : \varphi)\ \lambda(x : \tau)\ M$, Rule RedCoerDistCoerArrow reduces the application to $\lambda(x : \tau)\ \lambda(c : \varphi)\ M$ by exchanging the parameters.

The remaining cases for G can be factored as $P[G']$. Rule RedCoerFill fills G' with M, transforming $P[G']\langle M\rangle$ into $P[G'\langle M\rangle]$. Notice that the two occurrences of P are different abstract nodes on each side of the rule—a coercion on the left-hand side and a term on the right-hand side. Rule RedCoerFill is actually a meta-rule that could be expanded into, and should be understood as, the following five different rules:

$$(\lambda\alpha\ G)\langle M\rangle \rightsquigarrow_\iota \lambda\alpha\ (G\langle M\rangle) \quad \text{RedCoerTypeLam}$$
$$(G\ \tau)\langle M\rangle \rightsquigarrow_\iota (G\langle M\rangle)\ \tau \quad \text{RedCoerTypeApp}$$
$$(G_2\langle G_1\rangle)\langle M\rangle \rightsquigarrow_\iota G_2\langle G_1\langle M\rangle\rangle \quad \text{RedCoerCoer}$$
$$(\lambda(c:\varphi)\ G)\langle M\rangle \rightsquigarrow_\iota \lambda(c:\varphi)\ (G\langle M\rangle) \quad \text{RedCoerCoerLam}$$
$$(G_1\{G_2\})\langle M\rangle \rightsquigarrow_\iota (G_1\langle M\rangle)\{G_2\} \quad \text{RedCoerCoerApp}$$

The use of the meta-rule emphasizes the similarity between all five cases; it is also more concise.

For example, the application $G_1\{G_2\}$ of a coercion abstraction G_1 to a coercion G_2 is only reduced when it is further applied to a term M (as other complex coercions), by first wrapping elements of G around M (two first steps below) so that Rule RedCoer can finally fire (last step):

$$\begin{aligned}((\lambda(c:\tau\triangleright\sigma)\ G)\{G'\})\langle M\rangle &\rightsquigarrow_\iota ((\lambda(c:\tau\triangleright\sigma)\ G)\langle M\rangle)\{G'\}\\ &\rightsquigarrow_\iota (\lambda(c:\tau\triangleright\sigma)\ (G\langle M\rangle))\{G'\}\\ &\rightsquigarrow_\iota (G\langle M\rangle)[c\leftarrow G']\end{aligned}$$

The reduction rules for System F_η are obtained by removing rules RedCoer, RedCoerCoerLam, RedCoerCoerApp, and RedCoerDistCoerArrow.

Optional reduction rules Our presentation of F_ι could be extended with additional reduction rules for arrow and distributivity coercions such as $((G_1 \xrightarrow{\tau} G_2)\langle M\rangle)\ N \rightsquigarrow_\iota G_2\langle M\ (G_1\langle N\rangle)\rangle$. However, this narrows the set of values and reestablishing progress would require *binding coercions*, as for F_ι^λ described in §4, which are technically more involved. For sake of simplicity, the current presentation has fewer, but sufficiently many, reduction paths.

2.4 Examples

Let us first see examples in the F_η subset. Retyping functions in F_η allow for the commutation of quantifiers and removal of useless quantifiers. They also let terms have more principal types. For example, in System F, the S-combinator $\lambda x.\lambda y.\lambda z.x\ z\ (y\ z)$ can be given the two incomparable types:

$$\forall\alpha.\forall\beta.\forall\gamma.\,(\alpha\to\beta\to\gamma)\to(\alpha\to\beta)\to\alpha\to\gamma$$
$$(\forall\alpha.\,\alpha\to\alpha)\to(\forall\alpha.\,\alpha\to\alpha)\to(\forall\alpha.\,\alpha\to\alpha)\to(\forall\alpha.\,\alpha\to\alpha)$$

However, the former type is more general as it can be coerced to the latter (already in F_η), using three η-expansions. This example does not use distributivity, but the following example, still in F_η, does. (In the examples, we use type constructors List and D, which we assume to be covariant.) The map function has type:

$$\forall\alpha.\forall\beta.\,(\alpha\to\beta)\to\mathsf{List}\ \alpha\to\mathsf{List}\ \beta \qquad (1)$$

It can also be given the type

$$(\forall\alpha.\,\alpha\to D\,\alpha)\to\forall\alpha.\,\mathsf{List}\ (D\,\alpha)\to\mathsf{List}\ (D(D\,\alpha)) \qquad (2)$$

for some type constructor D, using the following coercion, which is already typable in F_η:

$$((\Diamond\to\lambda\alpha\ \Diamond\ (D\,\alpha))\langle\mathsf{Dist}^\forall\rangle)\langle\lambda\alpha\ (\Diamond\ \alpha\to\Diamond)\langle\Diamond\ \alpha\ (D\,\alpha)\rangle\rangle$$

Indeed, applying the coercion $\lambda\alpha\ (\Diamond\ \alpha\to\Diamond)\langle\Diamond\ \alpha\ (D\,\alpha)\rangle$ turns a term of type (1) into one of type:

$$\forall\alpha.\,(\forall\alpha.\,\alpha\to D\,\alpha)\to\mathsf{List}\ (\alpha)\to\mathsf{List}\ (D\,\alpha) \qquad (3)$$

which in turn $(\Diamond\ \to\ \lambda\alpha\ \ \Diamond\ (D\,\alpha))\langle\mathsf{Dist}^\forall\rangle$ coerces to type (2). This example also illustrates the low-level nature of the language of coercions, to which we will come back in §4.

The last two examples illustrate coercion abstraction. We define a function first, inspired from $\mathsf{F}_{<:}$, that implements the first projection for non-empty tuples of arbitrary length. Tuples are encoded as chained pairs ending with $\top$. (We assume pairs have been added to F_ι and write proj_1 and proj_2 for the projections.) The function first

$$\lambda\beta\ \lambda\alpha\ \lambda(c:\alpha\triangleright(\beta*\top))\ \lambda(x:\alpha)\ \mathsf{proj}_1\ (c\langle x\rangle)$$

of type $\forall\beta.\forall\alpha.\,(\alpha\triangleright(\beta*\top))\Rightarrow\alpha\to\beta$ abstracts over a coercion c from arbitrary tuples to the singleton tuple. It can be applied to any non-zero tuple by passing the appropriate coercion. (In this example, subtyping could be encoded with just polymorphism instead of coercion abstration, but this is not true in general.)

The other example of coercion abstraction, inspired from MLF, delays the instantiation of a call to the polymorphic function choose of type $\forall\gamma.\,\gamma\to\gamma\to\gamma$, say σ_{ch}, when given itself as an argument. Let chch be $\lambda\gamma\ \lambda(c:\sigma_{ch}\triangleright\gamma)$ choose $\gamma\ (c\langle\mathsf{choose}\rangle)$ of type $\forall\gamma.\,(\sigma_{ch}\triangleright\gamma)\Rightarrow\gamma\to\gamma$. We may then pass chch the function plus of type int $\to$ int $\to$ int, say σ_{plus}. This application is written $(\mathsf{chch}\ \ \sigma_{plus})\{\Diamond^{\sigma_{ch}}\ \mathsf{int}\}$ plus and has type σ_{plus}.

3. Properties of F_ι

In this section, we show that F_ι is well-behaved; moreover, there is a forward simulation between terms of F_ι and their coercion erasure. Hence, coercions do not really contribute to the reduction. However, coercions are not erasable as they may sometimes appear in wedges and block the reduction.

3.1 Soundness

Type soundness of F_ι follows as usual from the subject reduction and progress lemmas. The proof of subject reduction uses substitution lemmas for terms, types, and coercions, which in turn use weakening. The proof is easy because coercions are explicit. So the reduction rules actually *are* the proof.

Proposition 1 (Subject Reduction). *If $\Gamma\vdash M:\tau$ and $M\rightsquigarrow_{\beta\iota}N$ hold, then $\Gamma\vdash N:\tau$ holds.*

Proposition 2 (Progress). *If $\Gamma\vdash M:\tau$ holds, then either M is a value or M reduces.*

3.2 Termination of reduction

The termination of reduction for F_ι can be piggybacked on the termination of reduction in System F: following Manzonetto and Tranquilli [2010], we show a forward simulation between F_ι and System F, by translating F_ι into System F so that every reduction step in F_ι is simulated by at least one reduction step in System F.

3.3 Reification of F_ι in System F

There is indeed a natural translation of F_ι into System F obtained by reifying coercions as actual computation steps: even though we ultimately erase ι-steps, we do not actually need to do so, and on the contrary, we may see them as computation steps in System F.

Reification is described on Figure 8. We write $\lceil M\rceil$ for the reification of M. Coercions of coercion type $\tau\triangleright\sigma$ are reified as functions of type $\tau\ \to\ \sigma$. Hence, a coercion abstraction $\lambda(c\ :\ \tau\triangleright\sigma)\ M$ is reified as a higher-order function $\lambda(x_c\ :\ \lceil\tau\rceil\ \to\ \lceil\sigma\rceil)\ \lceil M\rceil$. A coercion variable c is reified as a term variable x_c (we assume an injective mapping of coercion variables to reserved term variables). Thus, the type $(\tau\triangleright\sigma)\ \Rightarrow\ \rho$ of a term abstracted over a coercion is translated into the type $(\lceil\tau\rceil\ \to\ \lceil\sigma\rceil)\ \to\ \lceil\rho\rceil$ of a higher-order function. Other type expressions are reified homomorphically. The application of a coercion to a term and the application of a term to a coercion are both reified as applications.

The remaining cases are the translation of coercions G, which are all done in two steps: we first translate G into some F_ι-term performing η-expansions to transform a coercion from τ to σ into a function from τ to σ. For atomic coercions (variables, identity, or distributivity), the result of this step is in the System-F subset

$$
\begin{aligned}
\lceil \alpha \rceil &= \alpha \\
\lceil \tau \to \sigma \rceil &= \lceil \tau \rceil \to \lceil \sigma \rceil \\
\lceil \forall \alpha.\, \tau \rceil &= \forall \alpha.\, \lceil \tau \rceil \\
\lceil \varphi \Rightarrow \tau \rceil &= \lceil \varphi \rceil \to \lceil \tau \rceil \\
\lceil \top \rceil &= \forall \alpha.\, (\forall \beta.\, \beta \to \alpha) \to \alpha \\
\lceil \tau \rhd \sigma \rceil &= \lceil \tau \rceil \to \lceil \sigma \rceil
\end{aligned}
\qquad
\begin{aligned}
\lceil x \rceil &= x \\
\lceil \lambda(x:\tau)\, M \rceil &= \lambda(x:\lceil \tau \rceil)\, \lceil M \rceil \\
\lceil M\, N \rceil &= \lceil M \rceil\, \lceil N \rceil
\end{aligned}
\qquad
\begin{aligned}
\lceil \lambda\alpha\, M \rceil &= \lambda\alpha\, \lceil M \rceil \\
\lceil M\, \tau \rceil &= \lceil M \rceil\, \lceil \tau \rceil \\
\lceil G\langle M \rangle \rceil &= \lceil G \rceil\, \lceil M \rceil \\
\lceil \lambda(c:\varphi)\, M \rceil &= \lambda(x_c : \lceil \varphi \rceil)\, \lceil M \rceil \\
\lceil M\{G\} \rceil &= \lceil M \rceil\, \lceil G \rceil
\end{aligned}
\qquad
\begin{aligned}
\lceil \emptyset \rceil &= \emptyset \\
\lceil \Gamma, B \rceil &= \lceil \Gamma \rceil, \lceil B \rceil \\
\lceil \alpha \rceil &= \alpha \\
\lceil (x:\tau) \rceil &= (x : \lceil \tau \rceil) \\
\lceil (c:\varphi) \rceil &= (x_c : \lceil \varphi \rceil)
\end{aligned}
$$

$$
\begin{aligned}
\lceil c \rceil &= \lceil x_c \rceil \\
\lceil \Diamond^{\tau} \rceil &= \lceil \lambda(x:\tau)\, x \rceil \\
\lceil \mathsf{Top}^{\tau} \rceil &= \lceil \lambda(y:\tau)\, \lambda\alpha\, \lambda(x : \forall\beta.\, \beta \to \alpha)\, x\, \tau\, y \rceil
\end{aligned}
\qquad
\begin{aligned}
\lceil G_1 \xrightarrow{\tau} G_2 \rceil &= \lceil \lambda(y : \mathsf{dom}(G_1 \xrightarrow{\tau} G_2))\, \lambda(x:\tau)\, G_2\langle y\, (G_1\langle x \rangle)\rangle \rceil \\
\lceil \mathsf{Dist}^{\forall\alpha.}_{\tau\to\sigma} \rceil &= \lceil \lambda(y : \mathsf{dom}(\mathsf{Dist}^{\forall\alpha.}_{\tau\to\sigma}))\, \lambda(x:\tau)\, \lambda\alpha\, y\, \alpha\, x \rceil \\
\lceil \mathsf{Dist}^{\varphi\Rightarrow}_{\tau\to\sigma} \rceil &= \lceil \lambda(y : \mathsf{dom}(\mathsf{Dist}^{\varphi\Rightarrow}_{\tau\to\sigma}))\, \lambda(x:\tau)\, \lambda(c:\varphi)\, y\{c\}\, x \rceil \\
\lceil P[G] \rceil &= \lceil \lambda(x : \mathsf{dom}(G))\, P[G\langle x \rangle] \rceil
\end{aligned}
$$

Figure 8. Reification of F_ι into System F

of F_ι. However, for complex coercions, the result still contains inner coercions. Hence, in the second step, we recursively translate the result of the first step. This translates types and residual coercions. Notice that the first step may introduce applications of coercions to terms, which are then turned into applications of terms to terms.

The translation of $P[G]$ covers five subcases, one for each form of P. Here as in the reduction rules, the two occurrences of P are different abstract nodes since P is a coercion on the left-hand side and a term on the right-hand side.

The translation uses an auxiliary predicate dom that computes the domain of a coercion: the domain of a coercion G in environment Γ is the unique type τ such that $\Gamma \vdash G : \tau \rhd \sigma$ for some type σ. This cannot be computed locally. Hence, we assume that terms of F_ι have been previously typechecked and all coercions have been annotated with their domain type. Alternatively, we can define the reification as a translation of typing derivations. We actually use such a translation to show that reification preserves well-typedness (easy but lengthy details can be found in the extended version).

Proposition 3 (Well-typedness of reification). *If $\Gamma \vdash M : \tau$ then $\lceil M \rceil$ is well-defined and $\lceil \Gamma \rceil \vdash \lceil M \rceil : \lceil \tau \rceil$.*

It is easy to verify that reduction in F_ι can be simulated in the translation, which implies the termination of reduction in F_ι.

Lemma 4 (Forward simulation). *If $\Gamma \vdash M : \tau$ holds, then:*

1. *If $M \leadsto_\beta N$, then $\lceil M \rceil \leadsto \lceil N \rceil$;*
2. *If $M \leadsto_\iota N$, then $\lceil M \rceil \leadsto^{+} \lceil N \rceil$.*

Corollary 5 (Termination). *Reduction in F_ι is terminating.*

3.4 Confluence

Reduction in F_ι is allowed in any term-context. Since coercions do not contain terms and coercions are never reduced alone, we may equivalently allow reduction in all coercion contexts, since no rule will ever apply. Hence, reduction in F_ι is a rewriting system.

An analysis of reduction rules in F_ι shows that there are no critical pairs. Hence, the reduction is weakly confluent. Since reduction is also terminating, it is confluent. In fact, the relation $\leadsto_\iota$ alone is confluent. Moreover, the reduction $\leadsto_\beta$ and $\leadsto_\iota^\star$ commute.

Corollary 6 (Confluence). *Reduction in F_ι is confluent.*

Lemma 7. *If $M \leadsto_\beta M_1$ and $M \leadsto_\iota M_2$ hold, then there is a term N such that $M_1 \leadsto_\iota^\star N$ and $M_2 \leadsto_\beta N$.*

3.5 Forward simulation

Coercion erasure sends terms of F_ι into the (untyped) λ-calculus. It also induces a simulation from the reduction in F_ι by the reduction in the λ-calculus, where ι-steps becomes equalities.

Lemma 8 (Forward simulation). *If $\Gamma \vdash M : \tau$ holds, then:*

1. *If $M \leadsto_\beta N$, then $\lfloor M \rfloor \leadsto \lfloor N \rfloor$.*
2. *If $M \leadsto_\iota N$, then $\lfloor M \rfloor = \lfloor N \rfloor$.*

Unfortunately, the backward simulation fails. The wedge $\lambda(c : \tau \to \tau \rhd \tau \to \tau)\, \lambda(y:\tau)\, c\langle \lambda(x:\tau)\ x\rangle\ y$ is a well-typed closed value in F_ι while its erasure $\lambda y.(\lambda x.x)\, y$ β-reduces to $\lambda y.y$.

To recover bisimulation, the definition of the language must be adjusted so that wedge configurations cannot appear in a reduction context. This observation leads to two opposite solutions, which we present in §5 and §7.

4. Coercions as retyping functions: F_ι^λ

While the reification of F_ι into System F carries good intuitions about what coercions really are, it lacks the ability to distinguish coercions from expressions with computational content. There is an alternative presentation of F_ι, called F_ι^λ and described in the extended version, that maintains the distinction between coercions and expressions while remaining closer to the reified form of coercions: F_ι^λ is mainly a coercion decoration of System F. In this sense, it can be seen as an explicit version (with coercion abstraction) of Mitchell's presentation of F_η as System F with retyping functions.

The reification of F_ι into System F can be redefined as the composition of a translation from F_ι to F_ι^λ that keeps the distinction between coercions and terms and the final erasing of this difference. The first part, along with its inverse, define translations between F_ι and F_ι^λ that preserves well-typedness and coercion erasure. Although we have not proved it, F_ι and F_ι^λ should be the same up to their representation of coercions.

Unfortunately, typechecking in F_ι^λ is more involved than in F_ι, as we need to typecheck coercions as *binding* expressions.

The reason is that coercions are not *exactly* λ-expressions. Having coercions as λ-expressions would require an even more elaborated type system, as it would have to ensure that coercions are η-expansions, which means maintaining a stack of the currently η-expanded variables to remember closing them. For example, consider typechecking the retyping context $\lambda(x : \tau)\ \lambda\alpha\ []\ \alpha\ x$ that permutes term abstraction and type abstraction (known as distributivity): when typechecking the subterm $\lambda\alpha\ []\ \alpha\ x$, we must verify that it is the body of an η-expansion with the variable x. We initially followed this approach and it was cumbersome; moreover, it did not scale to products as the type system must also ensure that two sub-derivation trees have the same coercion erasure.

Instead, we make the η-expansion of a term M an atomic construct, namely $\lambda(\phi_1 : \tau)\, G_2\, \{\phi_2 \leftarrow M\, G_1\}$ where ϕ's stand for *hole* variables. This can be interpreted as $\lambda(x:\tau)\ G_2'[M\ G_1'[x]]$ which is the η-expansion of M (*i.e.* $\lambda x.M\,x$) using coercion G_1 (interpreted as G_1') around the argument and coercion G_2 (interpreted as G_2') around the result. Here G_2 may bind coercion or hole variables that are used inside M and G_1. Hence, the type system must keep track of those variables with their types when type-

$$
\begin{array}{rcll}
\lhd\!\rhd & ::= & \lhd \mid \rhd & \text{bounds} \\
\tau & ::= & \ldots \not\mid\ \varphi \Rightarrow \tau \mid \forall(\alpha \lhd\!\rhd \tau) \Rightarrow \tau & \text{types} \\
M & ::= & \ldots \not\mid\ \lambda(c:\varphi)\ M \mid \lambda(\alpha \lhd\!\rhd c:\tau)\ M & \text{expressions} \\
 & & \not\mid\ M\{G\} \mid M\{\tau \lhd\!\rhd G\} & \\
G & ::= & \ldots \not\mid\ \mathsf{Dist}^{\varphi\Rightarrow}_{\tau\to\tau} \mid \mathsf{Dist}^{\forall\alpha\lhd\!\rhd\tau\Rightarrow}_{\tau\to\tau} & \text{coercions} \\
 & & \not\mid\ \lambda(c:\varphi)\ G \mid \lambda(\alpha \lhd\!\rhd c:\tau)\ G & \\
 & & \not\mid\ G\{G\} \mid G\{\tau \lhd\!\rhd G\} & \\
\Gamma & ::= & \ldots \not\mid\ \Gamma, c:\varphi \mid \Gamma, \alpha \lhd\!\rhd c:\tau & \text{environments}
\end{array}
$$

Figure 9. Parametric F_ι: syntax restriction *wrt* F_ι

checking G_2 and extend the typing environment accordingly when typechecking M and G_1.

We presented F_ι rather than its more intuitive version F_ι^λ to avoid the additional complexity in the type system; moreover, it is not obvious how to extend F_ι^λ with projectors, as discussed in §9.

5. Parametric F_ι

Parametric F_ι, written F_ι^p, restricts the language so as to rule out wedge configurations by means of typechecking. The restriction is on the type φ of coercion abstractions $\lambda(c:\varphi)\ M$, *i.e.* on the type of coercion variables. Observe that a coercion variable appearing in a wedge position $c\langle\lambda(x:\tau)\ M\rangle\ N$ has a coercion type $\sigma \rhd \rho$ where σ and ρ are both arrow types. To prevent this situation from happening in F_ι^p, we require that either the domain or the codomain of the type of a coercion parameter be a variable. Hence, we only allow $\lambda(c:\alpha \rhd \rho)\ M$ or $\lambda(c:\sigma \rhd \alpha)\ M$.

In order to preserve this invariant by reduction, we must request the type variable to be introduced simultaneously. So, we may write $\lambda\alpha\ \lambda(c:\alpha \rhd \tau)\ M$ but not $\lambda(c:\alpha \rhd \tau)\ M$ alone. This is a form of parametricity since either the domain or the codomain of c must be treated abstractly (and thus not as an arrow type) in M. To enforce this restriction we stick a type abstraction to every coercion abstraction and see $\lambda\alpha\ \lambda(c:\alpha \rhd \tau)\ M$ as a single syntactic node, which we write $\lambda(\alpha \rhd c:\tau)\ M$ to avoid confusion. Although, we modify the syntax of source terms, F_ι^p can still be understood as a syntactic restriction of F_ι.

5.1 Syntax changes

The syntax of Parametric F_ι is defined on Figure 9 as a patch to the syntax of F_ι (we write $\not\mid$ for removal of a previous grammar form). We replace coercion abstraction $\lambda(c:\tau \rhd \sigma)\ M$ of F_ι by two new constructs $\lambda(\alpha \rhd c:\tau)\ M$ and $\lambda(\alpha \lhd c:\tau)\ M$ to mean $\lambda\alpha\ \lambda(c:\alpha \rhd \tau)\ M$ and $\lambda\alpha\ \lambda(c:\tau \rhd \alpha)\ M$ but atomically. For conciseness, we introduce a mode $\lhd\!\rhd$ that ranges over $\rhd$ and $\lhd$. Hence, we write $\lambda(\alpha \lhd\!\rhd c:\tau)\ M$ for either $\lambda(\alpha \rhd c:\tau)\ M$ or $\lambda(\alpha \lhd c:\tau)\ M$. Note that the type variable α is bounded in both τ and M. As a mnemonic device, we can read the type of the coercion variable by moving "c :" in front, *i.e.* $\alpha \rhd c:\tau$ becomes $c:\alpha \rhd \tau$ while $\alpha \lhd c:\tau$ becomes $c:\alpha \lhd \tau$ which can also be read $c:\tau \rhd \alpha$. The reason to keep the type variable α before the coercion variable is to preserve the order of the abstractions in F_ι.

We say that $\lambda(\alpha \rhd c:\tau)\ M$ and $\lambda(\alpha \lhd c:\tau)\ M$ are *negative* and *positive* coercion abstractions, respectively. The positive form is parametric on the codomain of the coercion and implements a lower bounded quantification $\tau \rhd \alpha$, as in xMLF. The negative form is parametric on the domain of the coercion and implements an upper bounded quantification $\alpha \rhd \tau$, as in $\mathsf{F}_{<:}$.

Continuing with the definition of F_ι^p, we replace coercion application $M\{G\}$ by $M\{\tau \lhd\!\rhd G\}$ to perform type and coercion applications $(M\ \tau)\{G\}$ atomically. Both positive and negative versions

$$
\begin{array}{rcll}
p & ::= & \ldots \not\mid\ p\{G\} \mid p\{\tau \lhd\!\rhd G\} & \text{prevalues} \\
 & & \not\mid\ \mathsf{Dist}^{\varphi\Rightarrow}_{\tau\to\tau}\langle p\rangle \mid \mathsf{Dist}^{\forall\alpha\lhd\!\rhd\tau\Rightarrow}_{\tau\to\tau}\langle p\rangle & \\
 & & \not\mid\ \mathsf{Dist}^{\varphi\Rightarrow}_{\tau\to\tau}\langle\lambda(c:\varphi)\ p\rangle \mid \mathsf{Dist}^{\forall\alpha\lhd\!\rhd\tau\Rightarrow}_{\tau\to\tau}\langle\lambda(\alpha \lhd\!\rhd c:\tau)\ p\rangle & \\
v & ::= & \ldots \not\mid\ \lambda(c:\varphi)\ v \mid \lambda(\alpha \lhd\!\rhd c:\tau)\ v & \text{values} \\
P & ::= & \ldots \not\mid\ \lambda(c:\varphi)\ [] \mid \lambda(\alpha \lhd\!\rhd c:\tau)\ [] & \text{retyping contexts} \\
 & & \not\mid\ []\{G\} \mid []\{\tau \lhd\!\rhd G\} &
\end{array}
$$

Figure 11. Parametric F_ι: changes in values *wrt* F_ι

have the same meaning, but different typing rules. Type τ appears before G to remind that the type application is performed before the coercion application in the expanded form. As a mnemonic device, the $\lhd\!\rhd$ is oriented towards the side of the variable it instantiates in the coercion type of M. Hence, if M is $\lambda(\alpha \rhd c:\sigma)\ N$, we must write $M\{\tau \rhd G\}$.

We must change types accordingly, replacing coercion types $\varphi \Rightarrow \tau$ by $\forall(\alpha \lhd\!\rhd \tau) \Rightarrow \sigma$, which factors the two forms $\forall(\alpha \rhd \tau) \Rightarrow \sigma$ and $\forall(\alpha \lhd \tau) \Rightarrow \sigma$ whose expansions in F_ι are $\forall\alpha.\,(\alpha \rhd \tau) \Rightarrow \sigma$ and $\forall\alpha.\,(\tau \rhd \alpha) \Rightarrow \sigma$, respectively. Typing environments are modified accordingly. Notice that $\Gamma, \alpha \lhd\!\rhd c:\tau$ stands for $\Gamma, \alpha, c : \alpha \lhd\!\rhd \tau$ ($c : \alpha \lhd \tau$ should be read as $c : \tau \rhd \alpha$) and therefore α may appear free in τ—as for coercion abstractions: this allows the encoding of "recursively defined bounds" discussed below.

In the syntax of coercions, we replace coercion abstractions and coercion applications as we did for expressions. We also change the distributivity coercion that exchanges term abstraction with coercion abstraction to reflect the change in coercion types: it must simultaneously permute the term abstraction with the type abstraction and coercion abstraction that are stuck together.

5.2 Adjustments to the semantics

The syntactic changes imply corresponding adjustments to the semantics of the language. Notice that all restrictions are captured syntactically, so no further restriction of typing rules is necessary.

Typing rules Consistently with the change of syntax, we replace the typing rules TermCoerLam and TermCoerApp by rules TermTCoerLam and TermTCoerApp given on Figure 10. The corresponding typing rules CoerCoerLam and CoerCoerApp for coercions are changed similarly. We also replace CoerVar by TCoerVar. Finally, the modified distributivity coercion is typed as described by Rule CoerDistTCoerArrow. Notice that $\lhd\!\rhd$ is a meta-variable as M or τ and different occurrences of the same meta-variable can only be instantiated simultaneously all by $\rhd$ or all by $\lhd$. (We use different meta-variables $\lhd\!\rhd_1$ and $\lhd\!\rhd_2$ when we mean to instantiate them independently.)

The new typing rules for F_ι^p are derived from the typing rules of the corresponding nodes in F_ι. For example, TermTCoerLam is the combination of rules TermCoerLam and TermTypeLam in F_ι.

Well-formedness judgments are adjusted in the obvious way (details can be found in the extended version).

Operational semantics The operational semantics is modified in the obvious way. The syntax of values for F_ι^p is defined on Figure 11 as a modification of the syntax of F_ι. The adjustments in the reduction rules are the replacement of RedCoer by RedTCoer, RedCoerDistCoerArrow by RedCoerDistTCoerArrow, and the change of retyping contexts that induces a change in RedCoerFill as described in Figure 11.

5.3 Properties

Since F_ι^p can be seen as a restriction of F_ι where coercion abstraction is always preceded by a type abstraction, some properties of

$$\textsc{TermTCoerLam}\quad \frac{\Gamma, \alpha \diamond c : \tau \vdash M : \sigma}{\Gamma \vdash \lambda(\alpha \diamond c : \tau)\, M : \forall(\alpha \diamond \tau) \Rightarrow \sigma}$$

$$\textsc{TermTCoerApp}\quad \frac{\Gamma \vdash M : \forall(\alpha \diamond \tau) \Rightarrow \tau' \qquad \Gamma \vdash G : \sigma \diamond \tau[\alpha \leftarrow \sigma]}{\Gamma \vdash M\{\sigma \diamond G\} : \tau'[\alpha \leftarrow \sigma]}$$

$$\textsc{TCoerVar}\quad \frac{\Gamma \vdash ok \qquad \alpha \diamond c : \tau \in \Gamma}{\Gamma \vdash c : \alpha \diamond \tau}$$

$$\textsc{CoerTCoerLam}\quad \frac{\Gamma, \alpha \diamond c : \tau \vdash G : \sigma \triangleright \sigma' \qquad \Gamma \vdash \sigma}{\Gamma \vdash \lambda(\alpha \diamond c : \tau)\, G : \sigma \triangleright \forall(\alpha \diamond \tau) \Rightarrow \sigma'}$$

$$\textsc{CoerTCoerApp}\quad \frac{\Gamma \vdash G' : \rho \triangleright \forall(\alpha \diamond \tau) \Rightarrow \tau' \qquad \Gamma \vdash G : \sigma \diamond \tau[\alpha \leftarrow \sigma]}{\Gamma \vdash G'\{\sigma \diamond G\} : \rho \triangleright \tau'[\alpha \leftarrow \sigma]}$$

$$\textsc{CoerDistTCoerArrow}\quad \frac{\Gamma \vdash \tau \qquad \Gamma, \alpha \vdash \rho \qquad \Gamma, \alpha \vdash \sigma}{\Gamma \vdash \mathsf{Dist}_{\tau \to \sigma}^{\forall \alpha \diamond \rho \Rightarrow} : (\forall(\alpha \diamond \rho) \Rightarrow \tau \to \sigma) \triangleright (\tau \to \forall(\alpha \diamond \rho) \Rightarrow \sigma)}$$

Figure 10. Parametric F_ι: typing rules *wrt* F_ι

$$\textsc{RedTCoer}\quad (\lambda(\alpha \diamond c : \tau)\, M)\{\sigma \diamond G\} \rightsquigarrow_\iota M[\alpha \leftarrow \sigma][c \leftarrow G]$$

$$\textsc{RedCoerDistTCoerArrow}\quad \mathsf{Dist}_{\sigma_2 \to \sigma_3}^{\forall \alpha \diamond \sigma_1 \Rightarrow} \langle \lambda(\alpha \diamond c : \tau)\, \lambda(x : \sigma)\ M \rangle \rightsquigarrow_\iota \lambda(x : \sigma)\ \lambda(\alpha \diamond c : \tau)\, M$$

Figure 12. Parametric F_ι: new reduction rules *wrt* F_ι

F_ι^p can be derived from those of F_ι. In particular, normalization and subject reduction properties are preserved, just by observing that F_ι^p is syntactically closed by reduction.

Proposition 9 (Preservation). *If* $\Gamma \vdash M : \tau$ *and* $M \rightsquigarrow_{\beta\iota} N$ *hold, then* $\Gamma \vdash N : \tau$ *holds.*

Confluence and progress must still be verified. For confluence, we observe that there are still no critical pairs (although this does not follow from the absence of critical pairs in F_ι), so weak confluence is still preserved and confluence comes as a corollary.

Progress is a proof on its own, but it is similar to the one in F_ι.

Proposition 10 (Progress). *If* $\Gamma \vdash M : \tau$ *holds, then either* M *is a value or* M *reduces.*

As expected, coercions are erasable in F_ι^p. Because the new reduction rules are a combination of two ι-rules, and are themselves ι-rules, the forward simulation follows from forward simulation in F_ι. It remains to check the backward simulation.

Proposition 11 (Backward simulation). *If* $\Gamma \vdash M : \tau$ *and* $\lfloor M \rfloor \rightsquigarrow \mathcal{M}$, *then* $M \rightsquigarrow_\iota^\star \rightsquigarrow_\beta N$ *such that* $\lfloor N \rfloor = \mathcal{M}$.

The proof schema is not original [Manzonetto and Tranquilli 2010]. We assume that $\lfloor M \rfloor$ reduces to $\mathcal{M}$ and show that the ι-normal-form of M β-reduces to N with $\lfloor N \rfloor$ equal to $\mathcal{M}$. Since F_ι strongly normalizes, we may assume, without lost of generality, that M is already in ι-normal form. Because $\lfloor M \rfloor$ reduces, we can use the reduction derivation to show that it must be of the form $\mathcal{C}[(\lambda x.\mathcal{M}_1)\, \mathcal{M}_2]$. By inversion of the coercion-erasure function, we show that M is of the form $C[Q[\lambda(x : \tau)\ M_1]\ M_2]$ where C is a reduction context and Q a retyping context of arbitrary depth, such that C, M_1, and M_2 erase to $\mathcal{C}$, $\mathcal{M}_1$, and $\mathcal{M}_2$, respectively. We show that if a ι-normal term of the form $Q[\lambda(x : \tau)\ M]$ has an arrow type, then Q is empty. Hence, M is of the form $C[(\lambda(x : \tau)\ M_1)\ M_2]$ and β-reduces to $C[M_1[x \leftarrow M_2]]$ whose erasure is $\mathcal{C}[\mathcal{M}_1[x \leftarrow \mathcal{M}_2]]$.

6. Expressiveness of Parametric F_ι

Although it is bridled by-design, F_ι^p is already an interesting spot in the design space, as it subsumes in a unified framework three known languages: F_η, xMLF, and $\mathsf{F}_{<:}$ (in fact, its more expressive version with F-bounded polymorphism [Canning et al. 1989]).

By construction, F_η is included (and simulated) in Parametric F_ι. In the rest of this section, we show that xMLF and $\mathsf{F}_{<:}$ are also subsumed by F_ι^p. In each case, we exhibit a translation of typing judgments from the source language to typing judgments of F_ι^p so that the coercion erasure of the translation of a source term is equal to the type erasure of this term, and therefore the translation is semantics preserving.

To avoid confusion between source and target terms, we write T or S for terms, A or B for types, and Σ for typing environments in the source language. Formally, we exhibit a translation of judgments $\Sigma \vdash T : A \rightsquigarrow \Gamma \vdash M : \tau$ that is well-defined, type preserving, and semantics preserving. That is, if $\Sigma \vdash T : A$ then $\Sigma \vdash T : A \rightsquigarrow \Gamma \vdash M : \tau$ holds for some Γ, M, and τ such that $\Gamma \vdash M : \tau$ and $\lfloor T \rfloor = \lfloor M \rfloor$. As a consequence, reduction in the source language terminates, since it is simulated in F_ι^p.

Bounded polymorphism. $\mathsf{F}_{<:}$ is a well-known extension of System F with subtyping. There are several variations on $\mathsf{F}_{<:}$, all sharing the same features, but with different expressiveness due to the way they deal with subtyping of bounded quantification. Bounded quantification $\forall(\alpha <: A)\ B$ restricts types A' that α ranges over to be subtypes of the bound A. The differences lie in when the subtyping judgment $\Sigma \vdash \forall(\alpha <: A)\ B <: \forall(\alpha <: A')\ B'$ holds. Different versions of the corresponding subtyping rule are given on Figure 13. In Kernel $\mathsf{F}_{<:}$, the bounds A and A' must be equal, whereas Full $\mathsf{F}_{<:}$ only requires the bound A' to be a subtype of the bound A. Moreover, α cannot appear free in the bounds A or A' in Kernel or Full $\mathsf{F}_{<:}$, while $\mathsf{F}_{\mu<:}$ allows this form of recursion, called F-bounded polymorphism. The most general assumption, $\Sigma, \alpha <: A' \vdash \alpha <: A$, is that of $\mathsf{F}_{\mu<:}$. Perhaps surprisingly, this is a slightly more general rule [Baldan et al. 1999] than the more intuitive one $\Sigma, \alpha <: A' \vdash A' <: A$. In summary, we have Kernel $\mathsf{F}_{<:} \subset$ Full $\mathsf{F}_{<:} \subset \mathsf{F}_{\mu<:}$ where all inclusions are strict.

We show that the most expressive version $\mathsf{F}_{\mu<:}$ is included into F_ι^p. The translation of typing judgments uses auxiliary translations of subtyping judgments $\Sigma \vdash A <: B \rightsquigarrow \Gamma \vdash G : \tau \triangleright \sigma$ and well-formedness judgments. Bounded polymorphism $\forall(\alpha <: A)\ B$ is translated into a negative coercion abstraction $\forall(\alpha \triangleright \tau) \Rightarrow \sigma$ which encodes upper bounds. (Positive coercion abstraction $\forall(\alpha \triangleleft \tau) \Rightarrow \sigma$ encodes lower bounds and are never needed in the translation of $\mathsf{F}_{\mu<:}$.)

Translation of expressions is easy. For example, the translation of a type application is a coercion application, as follows:

$$\frac{\Sigma \vdash T : \forall(\alpha <: B)\ B' \rightsquigarrow \Gamma \vdash M : \forall(\alpha \triangleright \sigma) \Rightarrow \sigma' \qquad \Sigma \vdash A <: B[\alpha \leftarrow A] \rightsquigarrow \Gamma \vdash G : \tau \triangleright \sigma[\alpha \leftarrow \tau]}{\Sigma \vdash T\,A : B'[\alpha \leftarrow A] \rightsquigarrow \Gamma \vdash M\{\tau \triangleright G\} : \sigma'[\alpha \leftarrow \tau]}$$

The most involved part in the translation is for subtyping judgments—in particular, for the bounded-quantification case:

$$\frac{\Sigma, \alpha <: A' \vdash \alpha <: A \rightsquigarrow \Gamma, \alpha \triangleright c : \tau' \vdash G : \alpha \triangleright \tau \quad \textbf{(1)} \qquad \Sigma, \alpha <: A' \vdash B <: B' \rightsquigarrow \Gamma, \alpha \triangleright c : \tau' \vdash G' : \sigma \triangleright \sigma' \quad \textbf{(2)}}{\Sigma \vdash \forall(\alpha <: A)\ B <: \forall(\alpha <: A')\ B' \rightsquigarrow \Gamma \vdash \lambda(\alpha \triangleright c : \tau')\, G'\langle \Diamond\{\alpha \triangleright G\}\rangle : \forall(\alpha \triangleright \tau) \Rightarrow \sigma \triangleright \forall(\alpha \triangleright \tau') \Rightarrow \sigma'}$$

Let us check that the judgment returned by the conclusion holds under the assumptions returned by the premises (1) and (2). The

$$\frac{\Sigma, \alpha <: A \vdash B <: B'}{\Sigma \vdash \forall(\alpha <: A)\ B <: \forall(\alpha <: A)\ B'}\ \textsc{Kernel-Fsub} \qquad \frac{\Sigma \vdash A' <: A \quad \Sigma, \alpha <: A' \vdash B <: B'}{\Sigma \vdash \forall(\alpha <: A)\ B <: \forall(\alpha <: A')\ B'}\ \textsc{Full-Fsub}$$

$$\frac{\Sigma, \alpha <: A' \vdash \alpha <: A \quad \Sigma, \alpha <: A' \vdash B <: B'}{\Sigma \vdash \forall(\alpha <: A)\ B <: \forall(\alpha <: A')\ B'}\ \textsc{F-Bounded}$$

Figure 13. Bounded polymorphism: variants on the subtyping rule

implicit superscript of the hole in the conclusion is the domain of the coercion $\forall(\alpha \triangleright \tau) \Rightarrow \sigma$, say ρ. In environment $\Gamma, \alpha \triangleright c : \tau'$, the coercion $\Diamond\{\alpha \triangleright G\}$ has type $\rho \triangleright \sigma$ by rule CoerTCoerApp and, since G' coerces σ to σ', the coercion $G'\langle\Diamond\{\alpha \triangleright G\}\rangle$ has type $\rho \triangleright \sigma'$. Hence, by rule CoerTCoerLam, the coercion of the conclusion has type $\rho \triangleright \forall(\alpha \triangleright \tau') \Rightarrow \sigma'$, as expected.

Notice that $\mathsf{F}_{\mu<:}$ is missing type abstraction and type application in coercions, as well as distributivity of the universal on the arrow as in F_η. Indeed, $\mathsf{F}_{\mu<:}$ only allows instantiation of quantifiers at the root of types, as in System F and contrary to F_η. Hence, the inclusion $\mathsf{F}_{\mu<:} \subset \mathsf{F}_\iota^p$ is strict.

It is remarkable that F_ι^p naturally matches the most expressive version $\mathsf{F}_{\mu<:}$. This encourages following a systematic approach and viewing type conversions as erasable coercions as in F_ι^p rather then a limited subtyping relation. Additionally, F_ι^p may simplify the proof of type soundness for $\mathsf{F}_{\mu<:}$, as coercions are explicit.

Instance-bounded polymorphism. The language xMLF [Rémy and Yakobowski 2010] is the internal language of MLF which is itself an extension of System F with *instance-bounded polymorphism*. Instance-bounded polymorphism is a mechanism to delay type instantiation of System F; it is a key to performing type inference in MLF and keeping principal types—given optional type annotations of function parameters. As our current concern is not type inference but expressiveness, we use xMLF rather than MLF for comparison with F_ι^p. By lack of space, we cannot formally present xMLF. Instead, we identify a subset F_ι^x of F_ι^p and explains how it closely relates to xMLF without giving all the details of xMLF, which can be found in the extended version.

We first define the subset $\mathsf{F}_\iota^{\mu x}$ of F_ι^p by removing negative coercion abstractions (in types, terms, and coercions), arrow coercions $G \xrightarrow{\tau} G$, and distributivity coercions from the syntax of terms. Of course, we remove typing rules and reduction rules for these constructs, accordingly.

We then define F_ι^x as the restriction of $\mathsf{F}_\iota^{\mu x}$ where a type variable cannot appear in its instance bound, *i.e.* α is not free in τ in $\forall(\alpha \triangleleft \tau) \Rightarrow \sigma$. Both restrictions are closed by reduction, so they preserve the properties of F_ι^p.

We claim that xMLF is equivalent to F_ι^x. Unsurprisingly, the translation of instance-bounded polymorphism $\forall(\alpha \geq A).B$ is a positive coercion abstraction $\forall(\alpha \triangleleft \tau) \Rightarrow \sigma$ where τ and σ are the translation of A and B. The translation of expressions and type instantiations is then routine (see the extended version). The proof for the direct inclusion is similar to one by Manzonetto and Tranquilli [2010]. The proof for the reverse inclusion is new but not much more difficult.

In summary, we have $x\mathsf{MLF} \approx \mathsf{F}_\iota^x \subset \mathsf{F}_\iota^{\mu x} \subset \mathsf{F}_\iota^p$. It is interesting that the natural restriction of F_ι that resembles xMLF allows variables to appear in their instance bounds, much as with F-bounded polymorphism. This suggests an extension to xMLF with recursively defined bounds. However, we do not know whether this extension could still permit partial type inference in MLF.

Moreover, reduction in xMLF is simulated in F_ι^x. This implies termination of reduction in xMLF (a result already proved by Manzonetto and Tranquilli [2010]).

Summary Features of F_ι^p and its variants are summed up on Figure 14. The expressiveness of F_η, xMLF, and $\mathsf{F}_{<:}$ can be compared by checking which feature is present in one language and not in the others. Deep instantiation corresponds to the $\lambda\alpha\ G$ and $G\ \tau$ constructs, allowed in F_η and xMLF, but not in $\mathsf{F}_{<:}$. Upper bounds are used in $\mathsf{F}_{<:}$ and lower bounds are used xMLF. They correspond to coercion abstraction $\lambda(\alpha \triangleleft\!\triangleright c : \tau)\ G$ and $G\{\tau \triangleleft\!\triangleright G\}$ when $\triangleleft\!\triangleright$ is $\triangleright$ or $\triangleleft$, respectively. F_η allows neither. Arrow congruence is the $G \xrightarrow{\tau} G$ construct, allowed in F_η and $\mathsf{F}_{<:}$. Distributivity $\mathsf{Dist}_{\tau\to\sigma}^{\forall\alpha.}$ is used in F_η. The other form $\mathsf{Dist}_{\tau\to\sigma}^{\forall\alpha\triangleleft\!\triangleright\rho\Rightarrow}$ is only used in F_ι^p since it involves coercion abstraction.

Extension of System F	F_η	$\mathsf{F}_{<:}$	xMLF	F_ι^p
Deep instantiation	√	-	√	√
Arrow congruence	√	√	-	√
Permutation of $\forall$ and $\rightarrow$	√	-	-	√
Upper bounds	-	√	-	√
Lower bounds	-	-	√	√

Figure 14. Language and feature comparison

Notice that xMLF and $\mathsf{F}_{<:}$ only have coercion abstraction in common, but with opposite polarities. Each of them share a different feature with F_η. None of them uses distributivity as it only makes sense when deep instantiation and arrow congruence are available simultaneously.

All examples of §2.4 are actually typable in F_ι^p—with some syntactic adjustment of course. For instance, the last example becomes $\lambda(\gamma \triangleleft c : \sigma_{ch})\ \mathsf{choose}\ \{\gamma \triangleleft (c\{\mathsf{choose}\})\}$ of type $\forall(\gamma \triangleleft \sigma_{ch}) \Rightarrow \gamma \rightarrow \gamma$. For instance, it can be coerced to the type $\forall(\gamma \triangleleft \sigma_{plus}) \Rightarrow \gamma \rightarrow \gamma$. This uses the coercion $\lambda(\gamma \triangleleft c : \sigma_{plus})\ \Diamond\{\gamma \triangleleft c\langle\Diamond^{\sigma_{ch}}\ \mathsf{int}\rangle\}$.

7. Weak F_ι

Another solution to recover erasability is to prevent wedges from appearing in a reduction context.

At first, it seems to suffice to use weak reduction on coercion abstraction. Indeed, if a coercion variable cannot appear under a reduction context, it cannot appear in a wedging configuration. However, since $\lambda(c : \varphi)\ M$ is irreducible, its erasure $\lfloor M \rfloor$ should also be irreducible, *i.e.* a value. If we choose strong reduction for term abstraction, we must also choose strong reduction in the λ-calculus used as the target, hence $\lfloor M \rfloor$ must be a value for strong reduction. That is, $\lambda(c : \varphi)\ M$ would only be allowed when M is fully evaluated, which would considerably limit the interest of abstracting over c. Therefore, we choose a weak strategy for both coercions and terms. Keeping strong reduction on types is optional and independent.

The syntax of Weak F_ι, written F_ι^w, is defined on Figure 15 as a restriction of the syntax of F_ι. We replace $\lambda(c : \varphi)\ M$ in terms by $\lambda(c : \varphi)\ u$ where u is a value form. A *value form* is a term that erases to a value, *i.e.* a value or an application of a coercion G to a value form. A value is any form of abstraction whose subterm is an arbitrary term for a term abstraction, a value for a type abstraction (because we may evaluate under type abstractions), or a value form for a coercion abstraction.

The static semantics of F_ι^w and F_ι are the same. The reduction relation of F_ι^w is a subrelation of the reduction relation of F_ι that prevents evaluation under term and coercion abstractions and preserves the value restriction. Reduction contexts are modified accordingly: $\lambda(x : \tau)\ []$ and $\lambda(c : \varphi)\ []$ are removed. Rule RedCoerCoerLam (the coercion abstraction part of RedCoerFill) is

$$
\begin{array}{rcll}
M & ::= & \ldots \not| \; \lambda(c:\varphi)\, M \mid \lambda(c:\varphi)\, u & \text{expressions} \\
G & ::= & \ldots \not| \; \mathsf{Dist}^{\varphi \Rightarrow}_{\tau \to \sigma} & \text{coercions} \\
v & ::= & \lambda(x:\tau)\, M \mid \lambda\alpha\, v \mid \lambda(c:\varphi)\, u \mid \mathtt{Top}^{\tau}\langle v \rangle & \text{values} \\
u & ::= & v \mid G\langle u \rangle & \text{value forms} \\
C & ::= & [] \, M \mid M \, [] \mid \lambda\alpha \, [] \mid [] \, \tau \mid G\langle [] \rangle \mid []\{G\} & \text{reduction ctx}
\end{array}
$$

$$
\textsc{RedCoerCoerLam}^{w} \quad (\lambda(c:\varphi)\, G)\langle u \rangle \leadsto_{\iota} \lambda(c:\varphi)\, G\langle u \rangle
$$

Figure 15. Weak F_ι: syntax and semantics *wrt* F_ι

restricted to make it call-by-value. Indeed, keeping the F_ι rule:

$$(\lambda(c:\varphi)\, G)\langle M \rangle \leadsto_{\iota} \lambda(c:\varphi)\, G\langle M \rangle$$

would place the arbitrary term M under a coercion abstraction.

It is routine to check that F_ι^w is well-behaved and that coercions are erasable. We refer the reader to the extended version.

8. Related work

Although many type systems could be explained using coercions, since for instance they use a form of subtyping, very few have followed this path and made the connection with coercions explicit.

We have already widely discussed F_η, $\mathsf{F}_{<:}$, and $x\mathsf{MLF}$. Parts of F_ι^x is closely related to the work of Manzonetto and Tranquilli [2010] who proposed the first encoding of $x\mathsf{MLF}$ in a calculus of coercions, but for the main purpose of proving the termination of $x\mathsf{MLF}$. They exhibit a type and semantics preserving encoding of $x\mathsf{MLF}$ into (their version of) F_ι^x and show a simulation of computation between their F_ι^x and System F. Unfortunately, subject reduction and other properties that depend on it do not hold in their system. Our version of F_ι^x can be seen as a fix to their definition. Hence, there are many resemblances between their development of F_ι^x and our development of F_ι—but the typing rules differ. We omitted the proof of inclusion from $x\mathsf{MLF}$ into F_ι^x by lack of space, but also because it resembles theirs. In fact, their translation of $x\mathsf{MLF}$ into F_ι^x has itself been inspired by the translation of MLF into System F by Leijen and Löh [2005] and Leijen [2007]. However, Manzonetto and Tranquilli restrict their study to the termination of $x\mathsf{MLF}$ without any interest in F_η or $\mathsf{F}_{<:}$, while our main interest is not in F_ι^x, but in F_ι^p and F_ι, *i.e.* a general treatment of abstraction over coercion functions that extends F_η, and as a side result a possible enhancement of $x\mathsf{MLF}$.

Although F_ι subsumes core $\mathsf{F}_{<:}$, we have not included records in F_ι, which are often the first application of $\mathsf{F}_{<:}$. Our formalization in the extended version includes tuples, and therefore models tuple inclusion. We claim that F_ι can model record subtyping as well. However, our treatment of records in F_ι would be similar to their treatment in $\mathsf{F}_{<:}$ and require an expressive runtime system so that subtyping is erasable.

Record subtyping in $\mathsf{F}_{<:}$ may also be compiled away into records without subtyping in plain System F by inserting coercions with computational content [Breazu-Tannen et al. 1991] that change the representation of records whenever subtyping is used. Since these coercions are not erasable and can be inserted in different ways, the soundness of the approach depends on a coherence result to show that the semantics of the translation does not actually depend on the places where coercions are inserted.

Another method for eliminating subtyping has been used by Crary [2000]: bounded polymorphism $\forall(\alpha \le \tau).\, \sigma$ is compiled away into an intersection type $\forall\alpha.\, \sigma[\alpha \leftarrow \alpha \cap \tau]$ while intersection types are themselves encoded with explicit erasable coercions. This directly relates to our work by their canonization, which is similar to our ι-reduction, and their use of bisimulation up to canonization to show erasability of coercions. Of course, the languages are different, as we do not consider intersection types while they do have neither coercion abstraction nor distributivity and only consider call-by-value reduction. Their work could serve as a reference to extend F_ι with recursive types.

Languages with dependent types often split terms with and without computational content using kinds so that parts of terms that contribute only to the static semantics can be dropped at runtime. This is more powerful than our notion of coercions; for instance, it could allow to build coercions by computation—a feature that we would like to have. However, we do not know whether this approach could be applied and benefit to our extension of F_η.

Coercions introduced in FC_2 [Weirich et al. 2011], the internal language of Haskell, are interesting because they use coercion projections and cannot be expressed in F_ι^λ. Although FC_2 uses a weak evaluation strategy, it can declare abstract coercions at the toplevel, which amount to a form of coercion abstraction—hence they need coercion projections to regain erasability. However, coercions in FC_2 are non-oriented, do not have distributivity nor deep instantiation of quantifiers and are thus *structural*, which allows for an easier setting and a simple criteria to be used for consistency checking. A new version of FC_2 [Vytiniotis and Jones 2011] makes coercions first-class values in an otherwise comparable setting. Coercions can be abstracted over as in F_ι and also stored in data-structures. However, as a result of being first-class, coercions may change the termination (hence the semantics) of programs and are not erasable in our terminology. The two languages F_ι and FC_2 follow orthogonal approaches and are thus not easily comparable; combining the features of both would be an interesting challenge.

Adding coercion projections to F_ι and taking distributivity away, we could obtain a version much closer to FC_2 but where coercions are oriented. Surprisingly few works have consider distributivity and include the power of F_η, apart from theoretical papers on F_η itself.

Retyping functions can also be seen as a way of rearranging typing derivations. Abstraction over coercions is then abstraction over type derivation transformations. There might be interesting connections to establish with expansion variables for $\forall$-quantifiers introduced by Lenglet and Wells [2010].

9. Discussion and future work

The language F_ι extends F_η with abstraction over coercion functions in a general way where coercions are retyping functions, *i.e.* certain terms of the λ-calculus that do not contribute but may block the evaluation. In order to solve this problem and make coercions erasable, we have proposed two restrictions of F_ι.

Weak F_ι restricts the reduction relation by choosing a weak evaluation strategy for both coercions and terms and restrict coercion abstraction to value forms. The main advantage of this solution is its simplicity and its generality. Still, the restriction of coercion abstractions to value forms, which is analogous to value-only polymorphism in languages with side effects, is significant. Moreover, it allows the abstraction over coercions of uninhabited coercion types, which are never applicable, thus leaving the possibility of non-sensible code hidden under coercion abstraction undetected—or at least delaying its detection.

Instead, F_ι^p restricts the types of coercion parameters and forces them to be polymorphic in either their domain or codomain. The advantage of F_ι^p is to retain a strong reduction relation, which shows that the calculus is really well-behaved. Although restrictive, it already subsumes F_η, $x\mathsf{MLF}$, and $\mathsf{F}_{<:}$. We believe it is an interesting point in the design space. It also shows that an extension of $x\mathsf{MLF}$ with subtyping would be possible and beneficial, even if the question of designing the surface language to make type inference possible remains open.

Still, as both solutions are significant and orthogonal restrictions to F_ι, we may explore other possibilities.

Relaxing F_ι^p Relaxing F_ι^p so that it could type more expressions but still prevent wedges from being typable is probably the easiest extension to this work. An obvious but minor generalization is to let $\lambda(\alpha \diamond \bar{c} : \bar{\tau})\ M$ abstract over several coercions simultaneously, but all with the same polarity. Allowing multiple polarities cannot come without further restrictions, as transitivity could then be used to build an abstract coercion between arrow types.

A more ambitious generalization is to replace the local constraint on the type of coercions by a global constraint defined by some auxiliary consistency judgment. We could allow abstractions of the form $\lambda(\bar{\alpha}, \bar{c} : \bar{\tau} \triangleright \bar{\sigma})\ M$ using a side condition on the typing rule to ensure that the combination of coercions in context still prevents the creation of wedges. However, finding a suitable notion of consistency in the presence of distributivity is challenging.

Beyond F_ι So far, we have explored restrictions of F_ι to prevent wedges from appearing in a reduction context. Instead, we could perhaps extend the calculus to allow breaking them apart. Observe that when a coercion variable appears in a wedge, it is always a coercion between arrow types and that any actual coercion that will be passed at runtime will start with an arrow coercion $G_1 \xrightarrow{\tau} G_2$ that can be decomposed into G_1 and G_2 and pushed out of the way. So, we could decompose the abstract coercion as well, by introducing coercion projections $\mathsf{Left}\,G$ and $\mathsf{Right}\,G$ that behaves as G_1 and G_2 whenever G is $G_1 \xrightarrow{\tau} G_2$.

While this idea is intuitively simple, it is actually quite involved as new difficulties appear one after the other when solving them, due to the presence of distributivity. Projectors require both binding coercions as in F_ι^λ and, independently, a notion of structural equivalence to treat coercions up to some rearrangements; unfortunately, the combination of both breaks confluence; a fix to confluence is to reduce coercions themselves, which introduces further problems! (See the extended version for more details.) Moreover, even assuming that such a calculus can be set up, there will remain to solve a typechecking problem quite similar to (although more flexible than) the one for relaxing F_ι^p with non-local consistency. Indeed, decomposing nonsensical coercions cannot ensure erasability, ι-reduction may either get stuck, being unsound, or loop forever. We leave this exploration for future work.

Leaving F_η and freezing quantifiers We have added coercion abstraction to the language F_η as it is the reference in the absence of abstraction. However, many of the difficulties in F_ι come from the distributivity rules, which allow coercions to move quantifiers inside types, or more precisely, from the combination of distributivity with contravariance of the arrow constructor—which is already the source of difficulties in F_η, including undecidability of type-containment. This suggests exploring a restriction of F_ι that does not have distributivity, nor type abstraction and type application of coercions, that would not extend F_η, but have a much simpler metatheory.

Language extensions Several features of programming languages have also been left out of F_ι. Although products are not included in this short presentation, we have already verified that they can easily be added. Labeled products should work as well.

We do not expect difficulties with tagged unions or iso-recursive types, *e.g.* following Crary [2000] although details are subtle and still need to be checked. We don't foresee any difficulties for adding fix points to the source language.

Some care is needed for existential types, which already raise a problem in System F as they do not have an erasing semantics with a strong evaluation strategy. Therefore, we left them out of F_ι and replaced them by a top type. This is, however, an orthogonal issue.

An interesting extension is to make coercion first-class objects which raises another challenge for erasability: since coercions can then be built by computation, should a computation that just builds coercions be erasable as well? Coercion types are monomorphic in F_ι but between possibly polymorphic types. We do not expect difficulties to have polymorphic coercion types. First-class coercions would naturally bring polymorphic coercion types.

We have studied coercions for second-order polymorphism. We should not expect difficulties with higher-order polymorphism. However, adding coercions to a language with dependent types may be more challenging.

References

P. Baldan, G. Ghelli, and A. Raffaetà. Basic theory of F-bounded quantification. *Inf. Comput.*, 153:173–237, September 1999. URL `http://portal.acm.org/citation.cfm?id=320278.320285`.

V. Breazu-Tannen, T. Coquand, C. Gunter, and A. Scedrov. Inheritance as implicit coercion. *Information and Computation*, 93:172–221, 1991.

P. Canning, W. Cook, W. Hill, W. Olthoff, and J. C. Mitchell. F-bounded polymorphism for object-oriented programming. In *FPCA*, 1989. URL `http://doi.acm.org/10.1145/99370.99392`.

L. Cardelli. An implementation of FSub. Research Report 97, Digital Equipment Corporation Systems Research Center, 1993. URL `http://research.microsoft.com/Users/luca/Papers/SRC-097.pdf`.

K. Crary. Typed compilation of inclusive subtyping. In *ICFP*, 2000. URL `http://doi.acm.org/10.1145/351240.351247`.

K. Crary, S. Weirich, and J. G. Morrisett. Intensional polymorphism in type-erasure semantics. *Journal of Functional Programming*, 12(6):567–600, 2002. URL `http://dx.doi.org/10.1017/S0956796801004282`.

D. Le Botlan and D. Rémy. Recasting MLF. *Information and Computation*, 207(6), 2009. URL `http://dx.doi.org/10.1016/j.ic.2008.12.006`.

D. Leijen. A type directed translation of MLF to System F. In *ICFP*, Oct. 2007. URL `http://research.microsoft.com/users/daan/download/papers/mlftof.pdf`.

D. Leijen and A. Löh. Qualified types for MLF. In *ICFP*, Sept. 2005. URL `http://murl.microsoft.com/users/daan/download/papers/qmlf.pdf`.

S. Lenglet and J. B. Wells. Expansion for forall-quantifiers. Available electronically, 2010. URL `http://sardes.inrialpes.fr/~slenglet/papers/systemFs.pdf`.

G. Manzonetto and P. Tranquilli. Harnessing MLF with the Power of System F. In *MFCS*, volume 6281, 2010. doi: http://dx.doi.org/10.1007/978-3-642-15155-2_46.

J. C. Mitchell. Polymorphic type inference and containment. *Information and Computation*, 2/3(76), 1988.

D. Rémy and B. Yakobowski. A Church-Style Intermediate Language for MLF. In *FLOPS*, volume 6009, pages 24–39. 2010. URL `http://dx.doi.org/10.1007/978-3-642-12251-4_4`.

D. Vytiniotis and S. P. Jones. Practical aspects of evidence-based compilation in system FC. Available electronically, 2011. URL `http://research.microsoft.com/en-us/um/people/simonpj/papers/ext-f/`.

S. Weirich, D. Vytiniotis, S. Peyton Jones, and S. Zdancewic. Generative type abstraction and type-level computation. In *POPL*, 2011. URL `http://doi.acm.org/10.1145/1926385.1926411`.

Abstractions from Tests

Mayur Naik
Georgia Institute of Technology, USA
naik@cc.gatech.edu

Hongseok Yang
University of Oxford, UK
hongseok.yang@cs.ox.ac.uk

Ghila Castelnuovo
Tel-Aviv University, Israel
ghila.castelnuovo@gmail.com

Mooly Sagiv
Tel-Aviv University, Israel
mooly.sagiv@gmail.com

Abstract

We present a framework for leveraging dynamic analysis to find good abstractions for static analysis. A static analysis in our framework is parametrised. Our main insight is to directly and efficiently compute from a concrete trace, a necessary condition on the parameter configurations to prove a given query, and thereby prune the space of parameter configurations that the static analysis must consider. We provide constructive algorithms for two instance analyses in our framework: a flow- and context-sensitive thread-escape analysis and a flow- and context-insensitive points-to analysis. We show the efficacy of these analyses, and our approach, on six Java programs comprising two million bytecodes: the thread-escape analysis resolves 80% of queries on average, disproving 28% and proving 52%; the points-to analysis resolves 99% of queries on average, disproving 29% and proving 70%.

Categories and Subject Descriptors D.2.4 [*SOFTWARE ENGINEERING*]: Software/Program Verification; F.3.2 [*LOGICS AND MEANINGS OF PROGRAMS*]: Semantics of Programming Languages—Program analysis

General Terms Languages, Verification

Keywords Parametrised Static Analysis, Testing, Thread-Escape Analysis, Points-to Analysis, Necessary-Condition Problem

1. Introduction

Static analyses based on the Abstract Interpretation technique [6] are guaranteed to be sound: if such an analysis reports that a given query holds for a given program, it must indeed hold. In practice, however, the analysis may not be cheap enough to apply to the program, or it may not be precise enough to prove the query. This problem is inherent with the undecidability of static analysis.

One of the most interesting questions in static analysis concerns how to *specialise* a given static analysis to prove a given query. The idea is to make the analysis cheap yet precise by tailoring it to prove a specific query. Counterexample-guided abstraction refinement (CEGAR) [1, 5, 13, 19] aims to solve this problem. The idea is to gradually refine the abstraction until either a concrete counterexample is found or the query is proven. Despite many advances, the CEGAR approach includes many limitations which hinder its practicality: it is costly and may fail due to limitations of the theorem prover, the inability to appropriately refine the abstraction, the huge size of the counterexample, and the cost of the static analysis to compute the intermediate abstractions.

This paper takes a radically different approach: it uses dynamic analysis to compute good abstractions for static analysis. The static analysis is parametrised, and the space of parameter configurations is typically large, e.g., exponential in program size or even infinite. Given a query, a set of parameter configurations, and a concrete trace, our dynamic analysis computes a *necessary condition* on the parameter configurations for proving the query. Our limited experience shows that this condition can be used to choose, from among the remaining parameter configurations, one that yields an abstraction that is cheap enough to drastically cut the cost of the static analysis yet precise enough to prove the query.

One advantage of our approach is that the necessary condition is inferred efficiently and directly from the concrete trace without the need to run the static analysis on the whole program, which may be infeasible. Additionally, our method can be seen as an auditing procedure for static analysis: when an abstraction fails to satisfy our condition, it can neither prove nor disprove the query, independently of the existence of the counterexample. This means that some abstractions are pruned even before they are computed, which is in contrast to the CEGAR approach.

We do not provide a general algorithm to compute the necessary condition from a given trace. Instead, we provide a formal, non-constructive definition of the *necessary-condition problem*, and algorithms that compute the condition directly from the trace for two instance analyses: a flow- and context-sensitive thread-escape analysis, and a flow- and context-insensitive points-to analysis.

We have evaluated our approach on six real-world Java programs comprising two million bytecodes in total, the largest being 500K bytecodes. For thread-escape analysis, our approach resolves 80% of queries on average, disproving 28% and proving 52%. For points-to analysis, it resolves 99% of queries on average, disproving 29% and proving 70%. The fact that the vast majority of queries are resolved—and, more significantly, proven—shows that our approach is precise in practice. It is also scalable: despite being top-down, inter-procedural, and fully flow- and context-sensitive, our thread-escape analysis takes only 7 seconds on average over 1,750 invocations, with a maximum of 20 seconds.

To summarise, the key contributions of this paper are as follows:

POPL'12, January 25–27, 2012, Philadelphia, PA, USA.

1. We present a novel approach for using concrete traces in order to obtain good abstractions in certain cases for static analysis.
2. We present a formulation of a necessary condition for an abstraction to be precise enough for a given concrete trace.
3. We provide constructive algorithms to compute the necessary condition from a concrete trace for two static analyses (thread-escape analysis and points-to analysis).
4. We provide empirical evidence that our approach can be efficiently implemented and that the resulting static analysis is both precise and scalable.

2. Example

In this section, we provide the reader a flavour of our approach using thread-escape analysis.

2.1 The thread-escape analysis problem

We introduce the thread-escape analysis problem using the example Java program in Figure 1. Object allocation sites have unique labels `h1`, `h2`, and so on, and we elide all types. Variables `u`, `v`, and `w` are locals and `g` is a global (i.e., static field). The program is multi-threaded: in each iteration of the loop, the main thread executes the statement `u.start()`, which calls the `start()` method of class `java.lang.Thread`, which asynchronously starts a new thread corresponding to the object pointed to by `u`. Thus, after the call, the main thread proceeds to the next loop iteration while the freshly started child thread runs code not shown in the figure.

The graph at the top of Figures 1(a)–(c) (ignoring the dotted boxes) shows the concrete data structure created just before program position `pc` in any iteration $\mathtt{i} \geq 1$ of the loop. For convenience, each object is labeled with the site at which it was created (`h1`, `h2`, etc.). The clear nodes denote *thread-local* objects and the shaded nodes denote *thread-escaping* objects. An object is thread-local if it is reachable from at most one thread, and thread-escaping otherwise. An object becomes reachable from multiple threads if it is assigned to a global or if the `start()` method of class `java.lang.Thread` is invoked on it: in the former case, the object becomes reachable from all threads in the program, while in the latter case, the object becomes reachable from at least the parent thread and the freshly started child thread. Moreover, any object reachable in the heap from a thread-escaping object is also thread-escaping. Finally, once an object thread-escapes, it remains thread-escaping for the rest of the execution. In our example, the statement `g = new h3` which writes to global `g` causes the freshly created object to thread-escape (depicted by the shaded object labeled `h3`). Likewise, the call `u.start()` causes the object pointed to by `u` to thread-escape (depicted by the shaded object labeled `h1` from an earlier iteration). Moreover, the object pointed to by `w` is reachable from this object in the heap via field `f2`; hence, that object also thread-escapes (depicted by the shaded object labeled `h4` from an earlier iteration).

We formulate the thread-escape analysis problem in the form of program queries. The query we focus on in our example is $q_{\mathsf{local}}(\mathtt{pc}, \mathtt{w})$, which is true if, whenever any thread reaches program position `pc`, the object pointed to by local variable `w` in that thread's environment is thread-local. It is easy to see that this query is true in our example: the only thread that reaches `pc` is the main thread, and whenever it does, `w` points to the object most recently created at site `h4`, which is thread-local (note that this object thread-escapes only after the following statement `u.start()` is executed). Many clients in verification, testing, optimisation, and program understanding for multi-threaded programs can benefit from answering such queries. For instance, proving our example query enables a static race detector to prove that field `id` is race-free.

2.2 Parametrised thread-escape analysis

A key challenge in proving thread-escape analysis queries lies in choosing a heap abstraction that separates thread-local objects from thread-escaping objects. One class of heap abstractions involves partitioning all objects based on some static program property. A natural way is to use a separate partition for all objects created at the same allocation site. But even this simple heap abstraction can be too costly when applied to a large program with procedures. Our goal is to derive cheaper heap abstractions that in most cases are still precise enough to prove the given query.

The first step in our approach is to parameterise the static analysis in a manner that admits a large (possibly infinite) family of abstractions, and cast the problem as a search for a good parameter configuration to use for proving a given query. Examples of such analyses abound: a safety model checker can be viewed as parametrised by a set of program predicates that dictates the *predicate abstraction* it computes, *shape analysis* is parametric in which predicates to use as *abstraction predicates*, and cloning-based points-to analyses (k-CFA, etc.) are parametrised by a vector of integers that dictate the degree of context- and object-sensitivity the analysis must use for each call site and each allocation site.

Our thread-escape analysis uses heap abstractions with two partitions, denoted L and E, that summarise "definitely thread-local" objects and "possibly thread-escaping" objects, respectively. The analysis is parametrised by the partition to be used for summarising objects created at each allocation site. A parameter configuration η thus maps each allocation site in the program to either L or E. Each object created at a particular site starts in the partition dictated by η for that site, and may subsequently migrate from L to E but not vice versa. The analysis succeeds in proving a query $q_{\mathsf{local}}(pc, x)$ if variable x does not point to an object summarised by the E partition in any abstract state at program position pc.

Our goal in the parametrised analysis setting is to efficiently find a parameter configuration that is cheap yet precise enough to prove a given query. In practice, most configurations yield abstractions that are not cheap enough to apply to the given program, or not precise enough to prove the given query. Moreover, proving different queries can require different configurations. We next illustrate the difficulty in efficiently finding good configurations. We begin by noting that enumerating and testing configurations is infeasible due to the large space from which they can be chosen.

Consider the trivial η_1 in Figure 1(a), which maps each site to L. The analysis using η_1 computes at position `pc` the abstract state shown at the bottom of the figure, with the corresponding concrete state shown above it. This analysis fails to prove our query because variable `w` points to partition E in the abstract state at position `pc`, despite *all* objects starting in partition L. This is because statement `g = new h3` "pollutes" the L partition since η_1 maps `h3` to L (recall that objects can migrate from partition L to partition E).

This leads us to η_2 in Figure 1(b), which is similar to η_1 but maps `h3` to E. The analysis using η_2 proves our query, but it is not the cheapest configuration. Our analysis reasons about reads from objects that are summarised by the L partition and so it tracks outgoing fields from such objects. Being fully flow- and context-sensitive, the analysis is exponential in the number of such fields. Hence, it is cheapest to map as few sites as possible in η to L, and thereby limit the number of such fields. In particular, it is not necessary to map `h2` to L, which causes field `f` to be tracked.

This leads us to η_3 in Figure 1(c) which is the cheapest configuration that proves our query. Note that further coarsening it fails to prove the query: mapping `h4` to E clearly fails because query variable `w` is allocated at site `h4`, but mapping `h1` to E also fails because variable `u` is allocated at site `h1` and statement `u.f2 = w` will "pollute" the L partition.

```
// u, v, w are local variables
// g is a global variable
// start() spawns a new thread

for (i = 0; i < *; i++) {
    u = new h1;
    v = new h2;
    g = new h3;
    v.f = g;
    w = new h4;
    u.f2 = w;
pc: w.id = i;
    u.start();
}
```

thread-escape query: $q_{\text{local}}(\texttt{pc}, \texttt{w})$

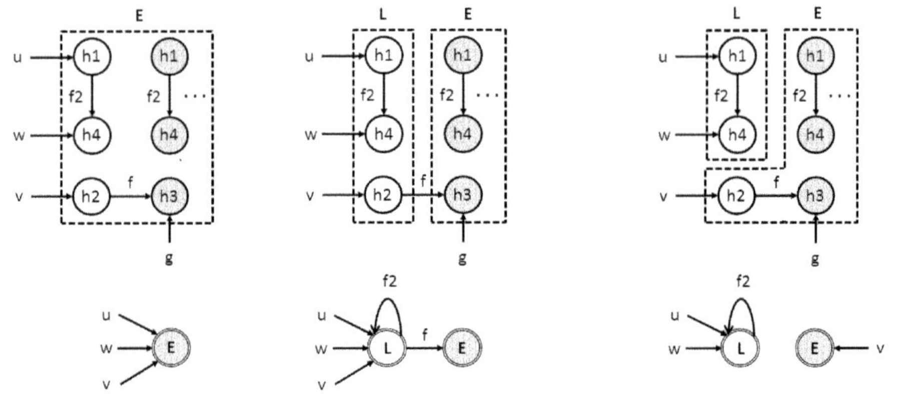

$\eta_1 = [\texttt{h1} \mapsto \text{L}, \texttt{h2} \mapsto \text{L}, \texttt{h3} \mapsto \text{L}, \texttt{h4} \mapsto \text{L}]$

(a) fails to prove query

$\eta_2 = [\texttt{h1} \mapsto \text{L}, \texttt{h2} \mapsto \text{L}, \texttt{h3} \mapsto \text{E}, \texttt{h4} \mapsto \text{L}]$

(b) proves query but not cheapest

$\eta_3 = [\texttt{h1} \mapsto \text{L}, \texttt{h2} \mapsto \text{E}, \texttt{h3} \mapsto \text{E}, \texttt{h4} \mapsto \text{L}]$

(c) proves query and cheapest

Figure 1. Example Java program and abstract states computed by our thread-escape analysis at pc using different parameter configurations.

2.3 Parameter configurations from tests

We have seen that choosing a good parameter configuration for a given query requires striking a delicate balance between precision and scalability. The key insight in our work is to directly and efficiently infer from a concrete program trace a *necessary condition* on the parameter configurations for proving the query. Our work does not provide a general algorithm for computing the necessary condition but it serves as a principle for designing good abstractions. We provide constructive algorithms using the principle for two instance analyses: a thread-escape analysis and a points-to analysis. We also prove that these algorithms indeed compute a necessary condition: any parameter configuration not satisfying the condition will fail to prove the query.

In the case of our thread-escape analysis, the necessary condition is computed using an algorithm we call **backward pointer reachability**: Given a query $q_{\text{local}}(pc, x)$ and a concrete program state (ρ, π, σ) at location pc, where ρ and π are the environments providing the values of local and global variables respectively and σ is the heap, this algorithm dictates that any parameter configuration that can prove this query must map the allocation site of each object from which the object $\rho(x)$ is reachable in σ to L. For our example query, this algorithm outputs $[\texttt{h1} \mapsto \text{L}, \texttt{h4} \mapsto \text{L}]$. This is because, whenever program position pc is reached, variable w points to an object allocated at site h4, and the only other object from which that object is reachable in the heap is the one pointed to by variable u, which is allocated at site h1.

Note that the configuration output by the algorithm does not constrain the values of h2 and h3. Moreover, many allocation sites in the program may not even be visited in the trace. Since it is cheaper to summarise objects using the E partition instead of the L partition (recall that the analysis tracks outgoing fields of only objects in the L partition), we simply map all unconstrained sites to E. Thus, our approach yields configuration η_3 shown in Figure 1(c), which is the cheapest configuration that proves the query.

Our backward pointer reachability algorithm is not the only algorithm that satisfies our necessary condition principle. In the extreme, one could envision an algorithm that also infers a condition that is *sufficient* for the given trace. Such an algorithm, for instance, would map h3 to E (recall from Figure 1(a) that any configuration that maps h3 to L fails to prove the query). However, there is a trade-off between the amount of computation that the dynamic analysis does and the quality of the configuration it infers, and the motivation underlying our backward pointer reachability algorithm is to strike a good balance.

3. Necessary-condition problem

In this section, we explain the formal setting of our result. In particular, we define the necessary-condition problem, whose solution plays a crucial role in our approach.

Definition 1. *A* **transition system** *is a triple* $(\mathcal{S}, T, I)$ *where* $T \subseteq \mathcal{S} \times \mathcal{S}$ *and* $I \subseteq \mathcal{S}$. *A* **query** q *on a transition system* $(\mathcal{S}, T, I)$ *is a function from* $\mathcal{S}$ *to* $\{\text{true}, \text{false}\}$.

Intuitively, $\mathcal{S}$ defines the state space of the transition system, T all the possible state changes, and I the set of initial states. A query q specifies a particular safety property of the transition system.

We assume that a transition system $(\mathcal{S}, T, I)$ and a query q are given as input to a static analysis. The goal is to prove that the query is true in all reachable states: $\forall s \in T^*(I).\ q(s) = \text{true}$.

We solve this problem by using a dynamic analysis together with a parametrised static analysis. A dynamic analysis here is simply a run of the given transition system from some initial state. In our combination, this dynamic analysis is run first, and it either disproves the query or discovers a condition on the parameters of the static analysis, which should hold in order for the analysis to prove the query at all. In the latter case, this condition is converted to a particular parameter setting, and the static analysis is run with this setting to attempt to prove the query.

The transition system used by the dynamic analysis is often instrumented to track extra information about program execution in its states. One example is to record in each object the timestamp of its creation. Then, just looking at a single state provides the order of creation of objects in the state. Note that finding such an order in a standard semantics requires looking at a concrete trace. The instrumentation transforms such trace properties to state properties, which can be better exploited by our dynamic analyses.

In the following subsections, we describe our parametrised static analysis and how we combine dynamic and static analyses in detail. We fix a transition system $(\mathcal{S}_c, T_c, I_c)$ and a query q_c, and call this transition system the **concrete program**.

3.1 Parameterised static analysis

We remind the reader of a standard definition of a sound static analysis and a well-known consequence of the soundness condition:

DEFINITION 2. *A* **static analysis** *is a tuple* $(\mathcal{D}, T^\sharp, I^\sharp, \gamma)$ *of a complete lattice* $\mathcal{D}$*, a monotone function* $T^\sharp : \mathcal{D} \to \mathcal{D}$*, an element* $I^\sharp \in \mathcal{D}$ *representing the set of initial states, and a monotone function* $\gamma : \mathcal{D} \to \mathcal{P}(\mathcal{S}_c)$*. We call the function* γ **concretisation map**, *and it gives the meaning of elements in* $\mathcal{D}$ *as sets of states in the concrete program. A static analysis is* **sound** *iff*

$$I_c \subseteq \gamma(I^\sharp) \ \wedge \ \forall d \in \mathcal{D}.\ T_c(\gamma(d)) \subseteq \gamma(T^\sharp(d)).$$

LEMMA 3. *If a static analysis* $(\mathcal{D}, T^\sharp, I^\sharp, \gamma)$ *is sound, every prefixpoint of* $\lambda d.\, I^\sharp \sqcup T^\sharp(d)$ *overapproximates the set* $T_c^*(I_c)$ *of reachable states in the concrete program:*

$$\forall d \in \mathcal{D}.\ (I^\sharp \sqcup T^\sharp(d)) \sqsubseteq d \implies T_c^*(I_c) \subseteq \gamma(d).$$

We consider static analyses with multiple parameters. We formalise the domain of parameter settings as follows:

DEFINITION 4. *A domain* PConfig *of* **parameter configurations** *is a set of functions from a set* Param *of parameters to a set* PVal *of parameter values. The domain does not necessarily contain all such functions, and it is ranged over using symbol* η.

Intuitively, parameters p in Param decide parts of the analysis to be controlled, such as the abstract semantics of a particular memory allocation in the given program. A parameter configuration η maps such p's to elements in PVal, which determine an abstraction strategy to employ for the p part of the analysis. We allow the possibility that multiple parameter configurations essentially express the same abstraction strategy, and we make this duplication explicit assuming an equivalence relation $\sim$ on PConfig.

DEFINITION 5. *A* **parametrised static analysis** *is a family of static analyses* $\{(\mathcal{D}_\eta, T_\eta^\sharp, I_\eta^\sharp, \gamma_\eta)\}_{\eta \in \mathsf{PConfig}}$ *indexed by parameter configurations in some* $(\mathsf{PConfig}, \sim)$*. We require that equivalent components of the analysis satisfy the condition:*

$$\eta \sim \eta' \implies \{\gamma_\eta(d) \mid d \in \mathcal{D}_\eta\} = \{\gamma_{\eta'}(d) \mid d \in \mathcal{D}_{\eta'}\}.$$

A parametrised static analysis is **sound** *if all of its component analyses are sound.*

3.2 Problem description

Assume that we are given a sound parametrised static analysis $\{(\mathcal{D}_\eta, T_\eta^\sharp, I_\eta^\sharp, \gamma_\eta)\}_{\eta \in \mathsf{PConfig}}$. We now formulate the necessary-condition problem for this parametrised static analysis. A solution extracts useful information for a parametrised static analysis from results of a dynamic analysis, and it forms the main component of our combination of dynamic and static analyses.

We say that a finite subset S_d of $\mathcal{S}_c$ **validates the query** q_c when $q_c(s) = \mathsf{true}$ for every $s \in S_d$. In our setting, such a validating set S_d of states is obtained from multiple runs performed during dynamic analysis, and it carries information potentially useful for the following static analysis. One example of such information is formalised by our predicate $\mathsf{cannotProve}(\eta, S_d)$ on parameter configurations $\eta \in \mathsf{PConfig}$:[1]

$$\mathsf{cannotProve}(\eta, S_d) \iff$$
$$(\forall d \in \mathcal{D}_\eta.\ S_d \subseteq \gamma_\eta(d) \implies \exists s' \in \gamma_\eta(d).\ q_c(s') = \mathsf{false}).$$

Intuitively, the predicate holds for η, when the η-component analysis cannot separate S_d from states violating the query q_c. As a result, $\mathsf{cannotProve}(\eta, S_d)$ implies that the η component cannot prove that the query holds for all the states in S_d. Using this predicate, we describe our necessary-condition problem:

> **Necessary-condition problem (in short, NC problem).** Find an algorithm that takes a finite set S_d validating the query q_c and returns a set $N \subseteq \mathsf{Param} \times \mathsf{PVal}$ satisfying the conditions below: for all $\eta \in \mathsf{PConfig}$,
>
> $$\neg(\exists \eta' \in \mathsf{PConfig}.\ \eta \sim \eta' \wedge \forall (p, v) \in N.\ \eta'(p) = v) \iff \mathsf{cannotProve}(\eta, S_d) \quad (1)$$

The left-to-right implication implies that if η is not equivalent to any parameter configuration that realises all the parameter bindings (p, v) in N, we can skip the option of setting parameters to η, because the resulting η analysis cannot prove the query. Hence, to have any hope for proving the query with the static analysis, we should ensure that some parameter configuration equivalent to our setting η respects all the bindings (p, v) in N. The phrase "necessary condition" mirrors this property of N. The other right-to-left direction is a completeness requirement, and it asks the algorithm to discover all the binding pairs that can be used to detect the satisfaction of $\mathsf{cannotProve}(-, S_d)$.

We make two further remarks on the NC problem. First, if every parameter configuration $\eta \in \mathsf{PConfig}$ satisfies $\mathsf{cannotProve}(\eta, S_d)$ so that no parameter settings can make the static analysis prove the query, the problem requires that the algorithm should return an unsatisfiable set N up to the equivalence $\sim$: for every η, no η' equivalent to η follows all the bindings in N. This usually happens when N contains two different bindings (p, v) and (p, v') for the same parameter p. Second, even if some parameter configuration equivalent to η respects all the bindings in N, the analysis with η can fail to prove the query. According to the equivalence, such η satisfies $\neg\mathsf{cannotProve}(\eta, S_d)$, but this just means that the η-component analysis has an abstract element in $\mathcal{D}_\eta$ that can overapproximate S_d without including bad states (i.e., those violating the given query). In practice, however, we found that $\neg\mathsf{cannotProve}(\eta, S_d)$ is a good indicator of the success of the analysis with η, especially when states S_d are instrumented and carry additional information about concrete traces.

A solution to the NC problem enables an interesting combination of a dynamic analysis and a parametrised static analysis. In this combination, a dynamic analysis is first run, and it gives a set of states $s_1, \ldots, s_n$ that are reachable from some initial states in I_c. If the given query q_c does not hold for some s_i, we have found a counterexample, and the combined analysis terminates with this counterexample s_i. Otherwise, the solution to the NC problem is run for $s_1, \ldots, s_n$, and then it computes a set N. The combined analysis then checks the unsatisfiability of N as follows:

$$\exists p \in \mathsf{Param}.\ \exists v, v' \in \mathsf{PVal}.\ (p, v) \in N \wedge (p, v') \in N \wedge v \neq v'.$$

If the check goes through, the analysis stops and returns "impossible to prove". Otherwise, it picks one element v_0 from PVal (which normally makes the static analysis run fast), and constructs a parameter configuration η_N as follows:

$$\eta_N(p) = \mathsf{if}\ ((p, v) \in N \text{ for some } v)\ \mathsf{then}\ v\ \mathsf{else}\ v_0. \quad (2)$$

The element v_0 is chosen carefully so that η_N belongs to PConfig. Finally, the analysis with the parameter setting η_N is run on the given program. In what follows, we explain how to solve the NC problem for instance analyses.

4. Generic solution

We have developed solutions to the NC problem for two instance analyses. This section is a prelude of the description of these solutions, where we explain their commonalities. In particular, we clar-

[1] The cannotProve predicate is related to so called supervaluation of abstract elements. The formula $\neg\mathsf{cannotProve}(\eta, S_d)$ holds iff there is an abstract element d in $\mathcal{D}_\eta$ overapproximating S_d and containing only those concrete states where q_c evaluates to true. The latter property of d is the definition of q_c having the super-truth at d.

ify an assumption made by both solutions on parametrised static analyses and queries, and describe a recipe for developing an algorithm for the NC problem, called **generic solution**, from which the solutions can be derived. This recipe can also be used for other instance analyses. As in the previous section, we assume a fixed concrete program $(\mathcal{S}_c, T_c, I_c)$ and a fixed query q_c on $\mathcal{S}_c$.

Our generic solution requires that a parametrised static analysis $\{(\mathcal{D}_\eta, T^\sharp_\eta, I^\sharp_\eta, \gamma_\eta)\}_{\eta \in \mathsf{PConfig}}$ should **have coupled components**, which means that the following three conditions hold:

1. The component static analyses use the same abstract domain. That is, $\mathcal{D}_{\eta_0} = \mathcal{D}_{\eta_1}$ for all $\eta_0, \eta_1 \in \mathsf{PConfig}$. We let $\mathcal{D}$ be this common abstract domain. Note that we do not impose a similar requirement on γ_η and component analyses can, therefore, use different concretisation maps. This means that although the components share the same set $\mathcal{D}$ of abstract representations, they can still have different abstract domains, because they might interpret these representations differently.
2. For all $\eta_0, \eta_1 \in \mathsf{PConfig}$ and all $d \in \mathcal{D}$,

   $$(\forall s \in \gamma_{\eta_0}(d).\, q_c(s) = \mathsf{true}) \iff (\forall s \in \gamma_{\eta_1}(d).\, q_c(s) = \mathsf{true}).$$

   Note that both sides of the equivalence are the same except the subscripts η_0 and η_1. The common part

   $$\forall s \in \gamma_{-}(d).\, q_c(s) = \mathsf{true} \quad (3)$$

   means that query q_c holds for all states abstracted by d. Hence, if the static analysis with a certain parameter configuration returns such d, it can prove that query q_c holds for all the reachable states of the given concrete program. For this reason, we call d satisfying formula (3) a **good abstract element**. Because of the equivalence above, the identification of such good abstract elements does not depend on the choice of a parameter configuration η, and we use some $\eta \in \mathsf{PConfig}$ and define the set of good elements D_g as follows:

   $$D_g = \{d \mid \forall s \in \gamma_\eta(d).\, q_c(s) = \mathsf{true}\}$$

3. There are a finite lattice Aux_s, and monotone functions $F_s : \mathsf{Aux}_s \to \mathsf{Aux}_s$ and $G_s : \mathsf{Aux}_s \to \mathcal{P}(\mathsf{Param} \times \mathsf{PVal})$ for each $s \in \mathcal{S}_c$, such that the equivalence below holds for all finite subsets $S_d \subseteq \mathcal{S}_c$:

   $$\begin{aligned}(\exists d \in D_g.\, S_d \subseteq \gamma_\eta(d)) \iff \\ \exists \eta'.\, \eta \sim \eta' \wedge (\forall s \in S_d.\, \exists a \in \mathsf{Aux}_s.\, (F_s(a) \sqsubseteq a) \\ \wedge \forall (p, v) \in G_s(a).\, \eta'(p) = v).\end{aligned}$$

   The left side of the equivalence means that the static analysis with η can use a good abstract element $d \in D_g$ to abstract a given set of states S_d. Hence, it can at least separate S_d from bad states where query q_c gets evaluated to false. According to the equivalence, this property on η can be checked using F and G. That is, we iterate over all parameter configurations η' equivalent to η, and do the following. For every state $s \in S_d$, we compute some pre-fixpoint of F_s over Aux_s, map this pre-fixpoint to a subset N_0 of $\mathsf{Param} \times \mathsf{PVal}$ using G_s, and check whether η' respects all the bindings in N_0. If the check succeeds, we stop the iteration, and return "yes". If the iteration finishes without any successful check, we return "no".

Assume that we are given a sound parametrised analysis that has coupled components. Our generic algorithm for solving the NC problem is given in Figure 2. Given a finite set S_d validating query q_c, the algorithm iterates over every element $s \in S_d$, and computes the least fixpoint $\mathsf{leastFix}\ F_s$, which is mapped to a subset N_s of $\mathsf{Param} \times \mathsf{PVal}$ by G_s. The resulting subsets N_s from iterations are combined, and become the result $N = \bigcup_{s \in S_d} N_s$.

Input: a finite subset $S_d \subseteq \mathcal{S}_c$ such that $\forall s \in S_d.\, q_c(s) = \mathsf{true}$
Output: the finite subset $N \subseteq \mathsf{Param} \times \mathsf{PVal}$ computed by

$$N = \bigcup \{G_s(a) \mid s \in S_d \wedge a = \mathsf{leastFix}\, F_s\}$$

Figure 2. Generic algorithm for solving the NC problem.

Note that the least fixpoint of F_s exists and can be computed by the standard method (which generates $\bot, F_s(\bot), F_s(F_s(\bot)), \ldots$ until the fixpoint is reached), because Aux_s is a finite lattice (hence complete) and F_s is monotone.

THEOREM 6. *Our generic algorithm solves the NC problem.*

Proof: Let N be the result of our algorithm when it is given a set S_d of states as the input. We need to prove that for every parameter configuration $\eta \in \mathsf{PConfig}$, $\mathsf{cannotProve}(\eta, S_d)$ holds if and only if we cannot find η' equivalent to η such that $\eta'(p) = v$ for all $(p, v) \in N$. We will discharge this proof obligation by showing:

$$\neg\mathsf{cannotProve}(\eta, S_d) \iff \exists \eta'.\, \eta \sim \eta' \wedge \forall (p, v) \in N.\, \eta'(p) = v.$$

We first transform the left side of the equivalence by unrolling the definition of $\mathsf{cannotProve}$ and using the first condition of having coupled components, which says that $\mathcal{D}_\eta = \mathcal{D}$ for all η:

$$\begin{aligned}&\neg\mathsf{cannotProve}(\eta, S_d) \\ &\iff \neg(\forall d \in \mathcal{D}.\, S_d \subseteq \gamma_\eta(d) \implies \exists s' \in \gamma_\eta(d).\, q_c(s') = \mathsf{false}) \\ &\iff \exists d \in \mathcal{D}.\, S_d \subseteq \gamma_\eta(d) \wedge \forall s' \in \gamma_\eta(d).\, q_c(s') = \mathsf{true}.\end{aligned}$$

In the first equivalence, we unroll the definition of $\mathsf{cannotProve}$ and replace $\mathcal{D}_\eta$ by $\mathcal{D}$ in the result of unrolling. The second equivalence is the standard one from classical logic.

Next, we use the second condition of having coupled components, which allows us to define the set D_g of good abstract elements independently of a parameter configuration η:

$$\begin{aligned}&\exists d \in \mathcal{D}.\, S_d \subseteq \gamma_\eta(d) \wedge \forall s' \in \gamma_\eta(d).\, q_c(s') = \mathsf{true} \\ &\iff \exists d \in \mathcal{D}.\, S_d \subseteq \gamma_\eta(d) \wedge d \in D_g \\ &\iff \exists d \in D_g.\, S_d \subseteq \gamma_\eta(d) \\ &\iff \exists \eta'.\, \eta \sim \eta' \wedge \exists d \in D_g.\, S_d \subseteq \gamma_{\eta'}(d) \quad (4)\end{aligned}$$

The first equivalence uses the definition of D_g, and the second equivalence and the left-to-right implication of the third follow from standard reasoning in classical logic. The remaining right-to-left implication in the last equivalence relies on the following condition on $\sim$:

$$\eta \sim \eta' \implies \{\gamma_\eta(d) \mid d \in \mathcal{D}\} = \{\gamma_{\eta'}(d) \mid d \in \mathcal{D}\}$$

as well as the fact that if $\gamma_\eta(d) = \gamma_{\eta'}(d')$, then both d and d' belong to D_g, or neither does so.

Finally, we use the last condition of having coupled components to reach the property on the result N of our generic algorithm. By the third condition of having coupled components, the property in (4) is equivalent to

$$\begin{aligned}\exists \eta', \eta''.\, \eta \sim \eta' \wedge \eta' \sim \eta'' \wedge (\forall s \in S_d.\exists a \in \mathsf{Aux}_s.\, F_s(a) \sqsubseteq a \\ \wedge \forall (p, v) \in G_s(a).\, \eta''(p) = v).\end{aligned}$$

Since $\sim$ is an equivalence relation, the property above means the same as the following condition:

$$\exists \eta'.\, \eta \sim \eta' \wedge \forall s \in S_d.\exists a.\, F_s(a) \sqsubseteq a \wedge \forall (p, v) \in G_s(a).\, \eta'(p) = v.$$

In what follows, we transform the second conjunct of the condition until we reach our target property for N:

$$(\forall s \in S_d.\, \exists a.\, F_s(a) \sqsubseteq a \wedge \forall (p,v) \in G_s(a).\, \eta'(p) = v)$$
$$\iff \forall s \in S_d.\, \forall (p,v) \in G_s(\mathsf{leastFix}\ F_s).\, \eta'(p) = v$$
$$\iff \forall (p,v) \in \{G_s(\mathsf{leastFix}\ F_s) \mid s \in S_d\}.\, \eta'(p) = v$$
$$\iff \forall (p,v) \in N.\, \eta'(p) = v.$$

The last two equivalences are standard equivalence-preserving steps from logic. The right-to-left direction of the first equivalence holds, because $F_s(\mathsf{leastFix}\, F_s) \sqsubseteq \mathsf{leastFix}\, F_s$. Now, it remains to show the left-to-right direction of the same equivalence. To do so, we pick $s \in S_d$, and assume that for some $a_0 \in \mathsf{Aux}_s$,

$$F_s(a_0) \sqsubseteq a_0 \wedge \forall (p,v) \in G_s(a_0).\, \eta(p) = v. \tag{5}$$

Since F_s is monotone on a complete lattice, $\mathsf{leastFix}\ F_s$ is the least element in Aux_s satisfying $F_s(a) \sqsubseteq a$. Hence,

$$\mathsf{leastFix}\ F_s \sqsubseteq a. \tag{6}$$

Furthermore, since G_s is monotone, $G_s(\mathsf{leastFix}\ F_s)$ is a subset of $G_s(a)$. This subset relationship and the second conjunct of the property (5) for a_0 imply that

$$\forall (p,v) \in G_s(\mathsf{leastFix}\ F_s).\, \eta(p) = v \tag{7}$$

We get the right side of the second equivalence from (6) and (7). □

5. Instance analyses

Following our general recipe for solving the NC problem, we have developed algorithms for solving the problem for two instance analyses. In this section, we describe these algorithms. We start with a model of concrete program states. This storage model is used by both instance analyses, as it is or in a slightly adjusted form.

Our storage model defines a set of concrete states of a given heap-manipulating program. It assumes the nonempty set PC of program positions in the given program. Also, the model assumes five nonempty disjoint sets: a finite set LVar for local variables, another finite set GVar for global variables, yet another finite set Fld for fields, and two countable sets, Loc for objects and $\mathsf{AllocSite}$ for allocation sites[2]. The formal definition of our model is given by these equations:

$$\mathsf{ILoc} = \mathsf{AllocSite} \times \mathsf{Loc} \qquad \mathsf{Val} = \mathsf{ILoc} \cup \{\mathsf{nil}\}$$
$$\mathsf{Local} = \mathsf{LVar} \to \mathsf{Val} \qquad \mathsf{Global} = \mathsf{GVar} \to \mathsf{Val}$$
$$\mathsf{Heap} = \mathsf{ILoc} \times \mathsf{Fld} \rightharpoonup_{fin} \mathsf{Val}$$
$$\mathcal{S}_{\mathsf{base}} = \{(pc, \rho, \pi, \sigma) \in \mathsf{PC} \times \mathsf{Local} \times \mathsf{Global} \times \mathsf{Heap} \mid \text{there are no dangling pointers in } \rho, \pi \text{ and } \sigma\}$$

Intuitively, $(h, o) \in \mathsf{ILoc}$ means an object o instrumented with its allocation site h. Such instrumented objects and nil form the set of values. The storage model defines states as tuples of four components. [3] The first is the current program position pc, and the other two, denoted ρ and π, hold the values of local variables and global variables, respectively. The last component is the heap σ with finitely many allocated objects. Note that we treat local and global variables separately. This separation helps formulate one of our instance analyses below.

We consider two analyses over the storage model:

[2] Although there are infinitely many values for denoting allocation sites, only a finite subset of them are used in a given program, because the program includes only finitely many instructions for memory allocations

[3] The formal statement of the absence of dangling pointers is: $\mathsf{range}(\rho) \cup \mathsf{range}(\pi) \cup \mathsf{range}(\sigma) \subseteq \{l \mid \exists f.\, (l, f) \in \mathsf{dom}(\sigma)\} \cup \{\mathsf{nil}\}$.

1. **Thread-escape analysis:** It attempts to prove that at a given program position pc, a particular *local* variable x never stores an object that is reachable from any *global* variable. Note the use of our separation of local variables from global variables.
2. **Points-to analysis:** This analysis tries to show that program variables x and y always point to different heap objects at all program positions.

The objectives of both analyses have the same format, and demand the proof that a certain query should hold for all reachable program states. We denote these queries by $q_{\mathsf{local}}(pc_q, x_q)$ and $q_{\mathsf{noalias}}(x_q, y_q)$.

5.1 Thread-escape analysis

Our first instance analysis is a fully flow- and context-sensitive thread-escape analysis. It answers the query $q_{\mathsf{local}}(pc_q, x_q)$, which asks whether, at program position pc_q, local variable x_q never points to an object that is reachable from global variables.

The thread-escape analysis summarises objects in a program state using two abstract locations L and E, such that L abstracts nil and a set of objects that are not reachable from global variables, and E abstracts the set of all remaining objects in the state. Thus, E includes all objects reachable from any global variable, and possibly more. The abstract domain tracks outgoing fields from objects summarised by L, and it is defined as follows:

$$\mathsf{Val}^\sharp = \{\mathrm{L}, \mathrm{E}\} \qquad \mathsf{Local}^\sharp = \mathsf{LVar} \to \mathcal{P}(\mathsf{Val}^\sharp)$$
$$\mathsf{Heap}^\sharp = \mathsf{Fld} \to \mathcal{P}(\mathsf{Val}^\sharp) \qquad \mathcal{D} = \mathsf{PC} \to \mathsf{Local}^\sharp \times \mathsf{Heap}^\sharp$$

An abstract heap is a map from fields to sets of abstract locations. This map concerns only the objects summarised by L, and overapproximates the values stored in the fields of these objects. Note that we do not track values stored in global variables or objects summarised by E. This is our intentional choice based on the following observation: if an object is reachable from a global variable, it usually remains so, and as a result, tracking what are stored in such escaping objects does not normally help improve precision of the analysis.

The thread-escape analysis is an instance of our parametrised static analysis that has coupled components. Its parameters are defined as follows:

$$\mathsf{Param} = \mathsf{AllocSite} \qquad \mathsf{PVal} = \{\mathrm{L}, \mathrm{E}\}$$
$$\mathsf{PConfig} = \mathsf{Param} \to \mathsf{PVal} \qquad \eta \sim \eta' \iff \eta = \eta'$$

Parameters are allocation sites, and parameter configurations η map them to one of the abstract locations L and E. Setting an allocation site h to $v \in \mathsf{PVal}$ entails that objects allocated at h are summarised initially by v. This initial membership of a newly created object can change, but only in a limited manner: an object can move from L to E but not vice versa. In this way, a parameter configuration controls how objects are abstracted using L and E, and it affects the precision and scalability of the analysis, because the analysis generally tracks information about L more precisely but at a higher cost. Finally, the thread-escape analysis does not have symmetry among component analyses, so that the equivalence relation on parameter configurations is simply the equality.

The intuition described so far on the analysis is formalised by our concretisation map γ_η, which we will now explain. For a set $L \in \mathcal{P}(\mathsf{ILoc})$ of objects, let $\mathsf{abs}_L : \mathsf{Val} \to \mathsf{Val}^\sharp$ be the following function, which abstracts concrete values in Val:

$$\mathsf{abs}_L(v) = \text{if } (v \in L \cup \{\mathsf{nil}\}) \text{ then L else E}.$$

The subscript L here provides the meaning of the abstract location L, which our abstraction function abs exploits in a standard way to abstract concrete values. Using this value abstraction, we define concretisation maps $\gamma_\eta : \mathcal{D} \to \mathcal{P}(\mathcal{S}_{\mathsf{base}})$ as follows:

$$\begin{aligned}
(pc, \rho, \pi, \sigma) \in \gamma_\eta(d) \iff & \exists \rho^\sharp, \sigma^\sharp.\ d(pc) = (\rho^\sharp, \sigma^\sharp) \wedge \\
& (\exists L \in \mathcal{P}(\mathsf{ILoc}).\ (\forall x \in \mathsf{LVar}.\ \mathsf{abs}_L(\rho(x)) \in \rho^\sharp(x)) \\
& \wedge (\forall (l, f) \in (L \times \mathsf{Fld}) \cap \mathsf{dom}(\sigma).\ \mathsf{abs}_L(\sigma(l, f)) \in \sigma^\sharp(f)) \\
& \wedge (\forall (l, f) \in (\mathsf{ILoc} \times \mathsf{Fld}) \cap \mathsf{dom}(\sigma).\ \sigma(l, f) \in L \implies l \in L) \\
& \wedge (\forall g \in \mathsf{GVar}.\ \pi(g) \notin L) \wedge (\forall (h, a) \in L.\ \eta(h) = \mathrm{L})).
\end{aligned}$$

This definition requires that the abstract location L should have an appropriate interpretation as a set L of objects, with respect to the abstract stack $\rho^\sharp$ and heap $\sigma^\sharp$ at pc. By the word "appropriate", we mean that L should satisfy the five conjuncts given above. The first two of these conjuncts express that $\rho^\sharp$ and $\sigma^\sharp$ overapproximate values that are stored in local variables and in fields of objects in L. The next two are concerned with L containing only objects that are unreachable from global variables. They say that L is closed under backward pointer reachability and it does not contain any object stored in any global variable. Hence, when these conjuncts hold, no object in L can be reached from global variables. Finally, the last conjunct says that all objects in L are allocated at sites mapped by η to L. Equivalently, it says that L never contains objects from sites mapped by η to E. This is the place where the concretisation depends on the parameter configuration η, and the conjunct describes a unique property of the η-component analysis, which holds because objects from sites mapped to E are abstracted using E and this membership in E never changes during the analysis.

We order $\mathcal{P}(\mathsf{Val}^\sharp)$ using the subset relation, and $\mathsf{Local}^\sharp$ and $\mathsf{Heap}^\sharp$ by the pointwise extension of this subset order. Then, from these order relations of $\mathsf{Local}^\sharp$ and $\mathsf{Heap}^\sharp$, we construct the order on our abstract domain $\mathcal{D}$, again using a standard pointwise extension for the product and function spaces.

LEMMA 7. *The abstract domain $\mathcal{D}$ is a complete lattice. Furthermore, γ_η is monotone for every $\eta \in \mathsf{PConfig}$.*

5.1.1 NC algorithm

Assume that we are given a query $q_{\mathsf{local}}(pc_q, x_q)$ for some program position pc_q and a local variable x_q. Our NC algorithm for this query takes a finite set $S_d \subseteq \mathcal{S}_{\mathsf{base}}$ such that every state $s \in S_d$ satisfies the query. Then, the algorithm computes a subset N of $\mathsf{Param} \times \mathsf{PVal}$, which describes a necessary condition for proving the query, as formulated by the equivalence (1) in Section 3.

Our algorithm works as follows. Given an input S_d, it iterates over every state $s = (pc, \rho, \pi, \sigma) \in S_d$ with $pc = pc_q$, and calculates **backward pointer reachability**, starting from the queried object $\rho(x_q)$. Concretely, the backward reachability first looks up the object stored in variable x_q in the state s, then it computes all the objects that reach object $\rho(x_q)$ via fields in the state, and finally it takes the allocation sites A_s of the resulting objects and builds the set of parameter binding $N_s = \{(h, \mathrm{L}) \mid h \in A_s\}$. Once all the iterations are completed, the algorithm gathers the N_s's and returns their union $N = \bigcup_{s \in S_d} N_s$ as a result.

Formally, the NC algorithm is an instantiation of the generic solution in Figure 2, with the following data specific to the thread-escape analysis:

1. The first datum is the sub-domain $D_g \subseteq \mathcal{D}$ of good abstract elements, whose concretisations do not contain bad states violating $q_{\mathsf{local}}(pc_q, x_q)$. This property of abstract elements should hold regardless of what parameter configuration η is chosen to do the concretisation. Such a sub-domain D_g exists for the thread-escape analysis, and it has the definition: $D_g = \{d \mid \forall \rho^\sharp, \sigma^\sharp.\ (d(pc_q) = (\rho^\sharp, \sigma^\sharp) \wedge \forall x.\ \rho^\sharp(x) \neq \emptyset) \implies \rho^\sharp(x_q) = \{\mathrm{L}\}\}$.
2. The second datum is a finite lattice Aux_s for each state $s = (pc, \rho, \pi, \sigma) \in \mathcal{S}_{\mathsf{base}}$. In the case of the thread-escape analysis, $\mathsf{Aux}_s = \mathcal{P}(\{l \mid \exists f \in \mathsf{Fld}.\ (l, f) \in \mathsf{dom}(\sigma)\} \cup \{\mathsf{nil}\})$.
3. The remaining data are monotone functions $F_s : \mathsf{Aux}_s \to \mathsf{Aux}_s$ and $G_s : \mathsf{Aux}_s \to \mathcal{P}(\mathsf{Param} \times \mathsf{PVal})$ for all $s \in \mathcal{S}_{\mathsf{base}}$:

$$\begin{aligned}
F_{(pc,\rho,\pi,\sigma)}(L) &= \{\rho(x_q) \mid pc = pc_q\} \cup L \\
&\quad \cup \{l \mid \exists f \in \mathsf{Fld}.\ (l, f) \in \mathsf{dom}(\sigma) \wedge \sigma(l, f) \in L\} \\
G_{(pc,\rho,\pi,\sigma)}(L) &= \{(h, \mathrm{L}) \mid \exists o.\ (h, o) \in L\} \\
&\quad \cup \{(h, \mathrm{E}) \mid \exists o, g.\ (h, o) \in L \wedge (h, o) = \pi(g)\}
\end{aligned}$$

The first function F_s comes from the query $q_{\mathsf{local}}(x_q, pc_q)$ and a condition on L in the concretisation γ_η, which says that L should be closed under backward pointer reachability. The function computes one-step backward closure of the set L, and extends the result with the object $\rho(x_q)$ stored in x_q. The second function $G_s(L)$ collects all the allocation sites appearing in L, and turns them to conditions that those sites should be mapped to L. When L contains an object (h, o) stored in some global variable (so the object $\rho(x_q)$ is escaping), $G_s(L)$ adds both (h, L) and (h, E), so that no parameter configurations can satisfy all the bindings in $G_s(L)$. The computation of the fixpoint of F_s and its conversion via G_s are the formal implementation of the backward reachability calculation alluded to in our informal explanation of the algorithm above.

LEMMA 8. *The data $D_g, \mathsf{Aux}_s, F_s, G_s$ satisfy the conditions in Section 4. Hence, our parametrised thread-escape analysis has coupled components. Also, the induced NC algorithm solves the NC problem for the thread-escape analysis.*

5.1.2 Construction of a parameter configuration

The result N of our NC algorithm needs to be converted to a specific parameter configuration, so that our parametrised thread-escape analysis can be instantiated with that configuration. We use a simple conversion described at the end of Section 3. If N contains two different bindings for a single allocation site, we return "impossible to prove." Otherwise, we construct a parameter configuration $\eta(h) = (\text{if } (h, v) \in N \text{ then } v \text{ else } \mathrm{E})$. Note that in the construction, we chose E as a default value. Usually, setting an allocation site to L makes the analysis more precise, but slower as well. Hence, our choice of E corresponds to using the most abstract and also cheapest component of the analysis, which can still separate good states S_d obtained by the dynamic analysis from bad states violating the query $q_{\mathsf{local}}(pc_q, x_q)$.[4]

5.2 Points-to analysis

Our second instance analysis is a flow- and context-insensitive points-to analysis. It answers the query $q_{\mathsf{noalias}}(x_q, y_q)$, which asks whether program variables x_q and y_q point to different objects at all program positions.

Our version of the points-to analysis uses parameter configurations to optimise an existing flow- and context-insensitive points-to analysis. The purpose of looking for such optimisation is not to improve the existing analysis. It is well-known that the existing analysis scales. Rather, our purpose is to test whether our approach of combining dynamic and static analyses can produce a cheap abstraction that is still good enough for proving a given query.

[4] Our thread-escape analysis finds a minimal abstraction for proving a given query in the following sense. Consider a partial order L, E defined by $\mathrm{L} \sqsubseteq \mathrm{E}$, and extend this order to parameter configurations pointwise. A successful run of our analysis computes a minimal parameter configuration according to this extended order. If one accepts that this order correctly compares the degree of abstractions of parameter configurations, she or he can see that the computed parameter configuration is also a minimal abstraction.

Our points-to analysis abstracts objects using three abstract locations P1, P2 and P3. These abstract locations form a partition of all objects, and they are used to describe aliasing relationships among program variables and fields that arise during program execution. Based on this intuition on abstract locations, we define the abstract domain of our points-to analysis:

$$\mathsf{Loc}^\sharp = \{\text{P1}, \text{P2}, \text{P3}\} \qquad \mathsf{Var} = \mathsf{LVar} \cup \mathsf{GVar}$$
$$\mathsf{Stack}^\sharp = \mathsf{Var} \to \mathcal{P}(\mathsf{Loc}^\sharp) \quad \mathsf{Heap}^\sharp = \mathsf{Loc}^\sharp \times \mathsf{Fld} \to \mathcal{P}(\mathsf{Loc}^\sharp)$$
$$\mathcal{D} = \mathsf{Stack}^\sharp \times \mathsf{Heap}^\sharp$$

An abstract state $(\pi^\sharp, \sigma^\sharp)$ conservatively describes all objects stored in program variables and fields. Note that a program position is not a part of an abstract state. This omission implies that our abstract state $(\pi^\sharp, \sigma^\sharp)$ specifies a flow-insensitive property of a given program, as expected for any flow-insensitive static analyses.

Our points-to analysis is parametrised by maps from allocation sites to abstract locations:

$$\mathsf{Param} = \mathsf{AllocSite} \qquad \mathsf{PVal} = \mathsf{Loc}^\sharp$$
$$\mathsf{PConfig} = \{\eta : \mathsf{Param} \to \mathsf{PVal} \mid \forall l^\sharp \in \mathsf{Loc}^\sharp.\, \exists h.\, \eta(h) = l^\sharp\}$$
$$\eta \sim \eta' \iff (k \circ \eta = \eta' \text{ for some bijection } k \text{ on } \mathsf{PVal})$$

A parameter configuration $\eta \in \mathsf{PConfig}$ decides, at each allocation site, which abstract location to use to summarise objects created at the site. Since there are only three abstract locations, all sites are partitioned into three groups, each of which is summarised using one abstract location. Unlike the thread-escape analysis, once an object is summarised by an abstract location, say P1, this summary relationship never changes during the analysis, so the object never becomes summarised by P2 or P3 later. For each parameter configuration $\eta \in \mathsf{PConfig}$, we care only about how η partition allocation sites into three groups, not about the names of these groups. Whether groups are named (P1, P2, P3) or (P2, P3, P1) does not matter for the behavior of the analysis. This independence on names is made explicit by our equivalence relation $\sim$ on parameter configurations above.

The way that parameter configurations control the analysis here can be seen in our concretisation map γ_η, which we present next. For sets of objects $L_1, L_2 \subseteq \mathsf{ILoc}$ with $L_1 \cap L_2 = \emptyset$, let $\mathsf{abs}_{L_1,L_2} : \mathsf{Val} \to \mathcal{P}(\mathsf{Loc}^\sharp)$ be the following function that abstracts concrete values:

$$\mathsf{abs}_{L_1,L_2}(v) = \text{if } (v = \mathsf{nil}) \text{ then } \{\} \text{ else}$$
$$\quad (\text{if } v \in L_1 \text{ then } \{\text{P1}\} \text{ else } (\text{if } v \in L_2 \text{ then } \{\text{P2}\} \text{ else } \{\text{P3}\}))$$

Note the role of subscripts L_1 and L_2. They give the meaning of P1 and P2, and guide the function to abstract concrete objects according to this meaning. These subscripts are usually constructed by taking the inverse image from a parameter configuration:

$$(L_1^\eta, L_2^\eta) = (\{(h,a) \mid \eta(h) = \text{P1}\}, \{(h,a) \mid \eta(h) = \text{P2}\}).$$

Another thing to notice is that the concrete value nil gets abstracted to the empty set. Hence, every abstract value $v \in \mathcal{P}(\mathsf{Loc}^\sharp)$ represents a non-empty set of concrete values, which contains nil. Using both the value abstraction and the subscript generation explained so far, we define the concretisation map γ_η as follows:

$$(pc, \rho, \pi, \sigma) \in \gamma_\eta(\pi^\sharp, \sigma^\sharp) \iff$$
$$(\forall x \in \mathsf{LVar}.\, \mathsf{abs}(\rho(x)) \subseteq \pi^\sharp(x)) \wedge (\forall g \in \mathsf{GVar}.\, \mathsf{abs}(\pi(g)) \subseteq \pi^\sharp(g))$$
$$\wedge\, (\forall (l,f) \in (L_1^\eta \times \mathsf{Fld}) \cap \mathsf{dom}(\sigma).\, \mathsf{abs}(\sigma(l,f)) \subseteq \sigma^\sharp(\text{P1}, f))$$
$$\wedge\, (\forall (l,f) \in (L_2^\eta \times \mathsf{Fld}) \cap \mathsf{dom}(\sigma).\, \mathsf{abs}(\sigma(l,f)) \subseteq \sigma^\sharp(\text{P2}, f))$$
$$\wedge\, (\forall (l,f) \in ((\mathsf{ILoc} - L_1^\eta - L_2^\eta) \times \mathsf{Fld}) \cap \mathsf{dom}(\sigma).$$
$$\mathsf{abs}(\sigma(l,f)) \subseteq \sigma^\sharp(\text{P3}, f))$$

We omit the subscripts L_1^η, L_2^η from $\mathsf{abs}_{L_1^\eta,L_2^\eta}$ to avoid clutter. The first two conjuncts ensure the sound abstraction of objects stored in local and global variables. The remaining ones guarantee that $\sigma^\sharp$ overapproximates the concrete heap σ, according to the partitioning scheme dictated by the parameter configuration η.

We order elements in $\mathcal{D}$ in a standard way, by extending the subset order for $\mathcal{P}(\mathsf{Loc}^\sharp)$ pointwise over the function space first and the product space next.

LEMMA 9. *The abstract domain $\mathcal{D}$ is a complete lattice. Furthermore, for all $\eta \in \mathsf{PConfig}$, their concretisation maps γ_η are monotone, and satisfy the following condition:*

$$\eta \sim \eta' \implies \{\gamma_\eta(d) \mid d \in \mathcal{D}_\eta\} = \{\gamma_{\eta'}(d) \mid d \in \mathcal{D}_{\eta'}\}.$$

5.2.1 NC algorithm

Given a set S_d of states from the dynamic analysis, our NC algorithm for the points-to analysis first computes the following sets H_x and H_y:

$$H_x = \{h \mid \exists (pc, \rho, \pi, \sigma) \in S_d.\, \exists o.\, (\rho \uplus \pi)(x_q) = (h, o)\},$$
$$H_y = \{h \mid \exists (pc, \rho, \pi, \sigma) \in S_d.\, \exists o.\, (\rho \uplus \pi)(y_q) = (h, o)\}.$$

The first set H_x consists of allocation sites of x_q-pointed objects that appear in some states of S_d. Similarly, the second H_y is made from allocation sites of y_q-pointed objects appearing in some $s \in S_d$. Next, our algorithm converts H_x, H_y to a set N of parameter bindings: $N = \{(h, \text{P1}) \mid h \in H_x\} \cup \{(h, \text{P2}) \mid h \in H_y\}$, which is returned as a result of the algorithm.

Our algorithm is a solution to the NC problem for the points-to analysis. This is because it is an instance of the generic solution in Section 4 with the following data:

1. The η-independent set D_g of good elements exists, and it is: $D_g = \{(\pi^\sharp, \sigma^\sharp) \mid \pi^\sharp(x_q) \cap \pi^\sharp(y_q) = \emptyset\}$.
2. For each state s, we let $X_s = \mathcal{P}(\{l \mid \exists f.\, (l,f) \in \mathsf{dom}(\sigma)\} \cup \{\mathsf{nil}\})$, and define $\mathsf{Aux}_s = X_s \times X_s$. Hence, Aux_s consists of pairs (L_1, L_2), where L_i is a set of allocated locations in s or nil.
3. The remaining data are the following functions F_s and G_s for every $s = (pc, \rho, \pi, \sigma) \in \mathcal{S}_{\mathsf{base}}$:

   $$F_{(pc,\rho,\pi,\sigma)}(L_1, L_2) = (L_1 \cup \{(\rho \uplus \pi)(x_q)\}, L_2 \cup \{(\rho \uplus \pi)(y_q)\})$$
   $$G_{(pc,\rho,\pi,\sigma)}(L_1, L_2) =$$
   $$\{(h, \text{P1}) \mid \exists o.\, (h,o) \in L_1\} \cup \{(h, \text{P2}) \mid \exists o.\, (h,o) \in L_2\}$$

   The function F_s simply adds the value of x_q to the first set, and that of y_q to the second. Hence, the fixpoint of F_s is just $(\{(\rho \uplus \pi)(x_q)\}, \{(\rho \uplus \pi)(y_q)\})$, which will be computed by one fixpoint iteration. From this fixpoint, the function G_s gets the bindings of allocation sites to P1 or P2.

LEMMA 10. *The data $D_g, \mathsf{Aux}_s, F_s, G_s$ satisfy the conditions in Section 4. Hence, our parametrised points-to analysis has coupled components. Also, the induced NC algorithm solves the NC problem for the points-to analysis.*

5.2.2 Construction of a parameter configuration

From the result N of the NC algorithm, we construct a parameter configuration $\eta \in \mathsf{PConfig}$ to be used by our static points-to analysis. Our construction follows the method described at the end of Section 3 with only a minor adjustment. As before, if the same allocation site is bound to P1 and P2 at the same time by N, our combined dynamic and static analysis stops and returns "impossible to prove." Otherwise, it chooses mutually distinct $h_1, h_2, h_3 \in \mathsf{AllocSite}$ that do not appear in a given program nor

N, and defines $N' = N \cup \{(h_1, \text{P1}), (h_2, \text{P2}), (h_3, \text{P3})\}$. Choosing such h_i's is possible since AllocSite is an infinite set and the given program uses only finitely many allocation sites in AllocSite. Then, our analysis uses P3 as a default parameter value, and constructs a configuration $\eta_{N'}(h) = (\text{if } (h, v) \in N' \text{ then } v \text{ else P3})$. Using P3 as a default value is our decision choice based on the observation: whatever parameter configuration η is used, the resulting η-component points-to analysis is very cheap, hence it is wise to go for the option that maximises precision, which is precisely to use P3 as a default value. We point out that $\eta_{N'}$ belongs to PConfig since N' includes the bindings $(h_1, \text{P1})$, $(h_2, \text{P2})$ and $(h_3, \text{P3})$.

6. Experimental evaluation

In this section, we evaluate the effectiveness of the two instance analyses of our framework: the thread-escape analysis and the points-to analysis. We implemented these analyses and applied them to the six multi-threaded Java programs described in Table 1, including four from the DaCapo benchmark suite [4].[5] All experiments were done using IBM J9 VM 1.6.0 on a Linux machine with two Intel Xeon 2.9 GHz six-core processors and 32GB RAM (though the experiments were run in a single thread and the JVM was limited to use up to 4GB RAM). We next evaluate the precision of these analyses (Section 6.1), their scalability (Section 6.2), and the quality of the computed abstractions (Section 6.3).

6.1 Precision

In this section, we evaluate the precision of our thread-escape and points-to analyses. Figure 3 shows the precision of our thread-escape analysis. Each query to this analysis is a pair (pc, x) where pc is the program position of a statement that accesses an instance field or an array element of an object denoted by local variable x:

$$\text{pc} : \text{y} = \text{x.f}; \quad \text{pc} : \text{y} = \text{x[i]}; \quad \text{pc} : \text{x.f} = \text{y}; \quad \text{pc} : \text{x[i]} = \text{y};$$

Such queries may arise from any analysis of multi-threaded programs that desires to reason only about instructions that possibly access thread-shared memory, such as a static race detection tool or a software transactional memory runtime.

The top of each column shows how many queries were considered for each benchmark, that is, queries where program position pc was reached at least once in a concrete trace of the benchmark on a single supplied input. It shows both the absolute number of considered queries and what fraction they constitute of the queries reachable in a static 0-CFA call graph. The latter provides a measure of the coverage achieved by each trace (29–60%). The considered queries are classified into three categories: those disproven by our dynamic analysis of the trace ("Escaping"), those proven by our static analysis using the parameter configuration inferred by the dynamic analysis ("Local"), and those neither disproven nor proven ("Unknown"). On average, 80% of the queries in each benchmark are either disproven (28%) or proven (52%), highlighting the effectiveness of our approach using only a single trace. Also, note that our approach does not preclude the use of multiple traces, which would only further improve both coverage and precision.

Figure 4 shows the precision of our points-to analysis. Each query to this analysis is a tuple (pc_1, x, pc_2, y) where (pc_1, x) and (pc_2, y) are identical to the queries described above for our thread-escape analysis, with the additional constraint that they both

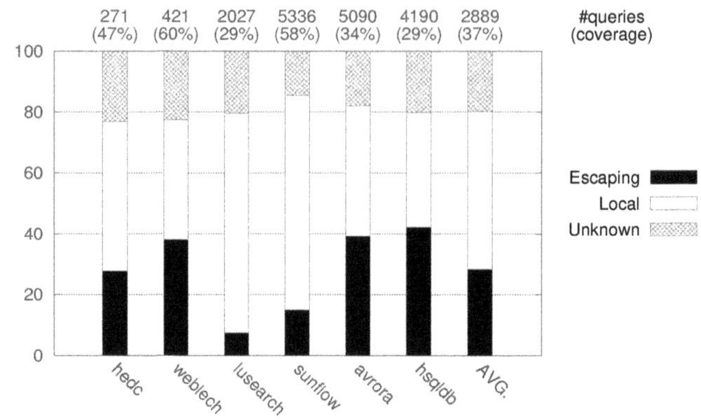

Figure 3. Precision results for our thread-escape analysis.

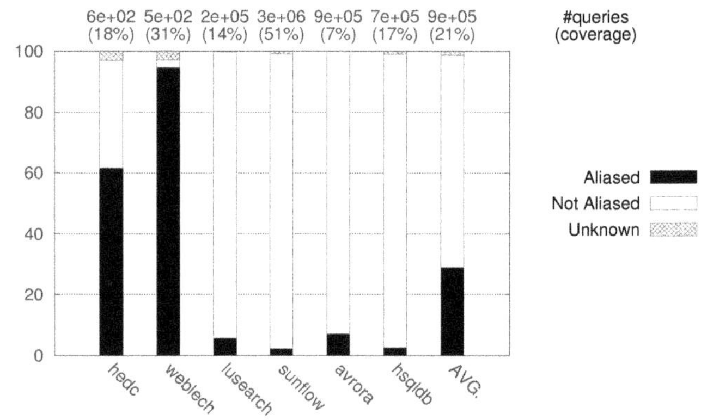

Figure 4. Precision results for our points-to analysis.

access array elements or they both access the same instance field, and at least one of them is a write. Such queries may be posed by, for instance, a static race detection client to determine whether the statements at pc_1 and pc_2 can be involved in a race.

The top of each column shows how many queries were considered for each benchmark, that is, queries where both program positions pc_1 and pc_2 were reached at least once in the single trace. The traces cover 7–51% of all statically reachable queries. The average coverage is lower for queries of this analysis compared to that of our thread-escape analysis (21% vs. 37%). This is because the points-to analysis requires *both* pc_1 and pc_2 to be reached for a query to be considered whereas the thread-escape analysis requires a single program position pc to be reached.

The considered queries are classified into three categories: (1) those disproven by our dynamic analysis of the trace ("Aliased"), namely, those where x and y pointed to objects created at the same allocation site at least once; (2) those proven by our static analysis using the parameter configuration inferred by the dynamic analysis ("Not Aliased"); and (3) those neither disproven nor proven ("Unknown"). Note that category (1) includes not only queries that are false concretely but also queries that might be true concretely but are impossible to prove using an object allocation site abstraction. Almost all queries (99% on average) are either disproven or proven. This result suggests that, in practice, a flow- and context-insensitive points-to analysis based on object allocation site abstraction for Java does not require representing objects allocated at each site using a separate abstract location; merely three abstract locations (albeit specialised to the query) suffice.

[5] Among all benchmarks in dacapo-2006-10-MR2, dacapo-9.10-beta0, and dacapo-9.12, we excluded single-threaded benchmarks (`bloat`, `chart`, `antlr`, `fop`, etc.), and multi-threaded benchmarks with little concurrency (`batik`, `pmd`, etc.), because one of our instance analyses is thread-escape analysis. We also excluded `luindex` because it is too similar to `lusearch`, which we include (both are built atop Apache Lucene). We tried the remaining four benchmarks in our experiments.

	description	# classes		# methods		# bytecodes (KB)		# alloc.
		app	total	app	total	app	total	sites
hedc	web crawler from ETH	44	355	234	2,062	16	161	1,587
weblech	website download/mirror tool (version 0.0.3)	57	579	311	3,295	20	237	2,636
lusearch	text indexing and search tool (dacapo-9.12)	229	648	1,510	3,893	100	273	2,879
sunflow	photo-realistic rendering system (dacapo-9.12)	164	1,018	1,327	6,652	117	480	5,170
avrora	microcontroller simulation/analysis tool (dacapo-9.12)	1,159	1,525	4,245	5,980	223	316	4,860
hsqldb	relational database engine (dacapo-2006-10-MR2)	199	837	2,815	6,752	221	491	4,564

Table 1. Benchmark characteristics. The "# classes" column is the number of classes containing reachable methods. The "# methods" column is the number of reachable methods computed by a static 0-CFA call-graph analysis. The "# bytecodes" column is the number of bytecodes of reachable methods. The "total" columns report numbers for *all* reachable code whereas the "app" columns report numbers for only application code (excluding JDK library code). The "# alloc. sites" column is the number of object allocation sites in reachable methods.

	pre-process time	dynamic analysis		static analysis time (serial)
		time	# events	
hedc	18s	6s	0.6M	38s
weblech	33s	8s	1.5M	74s
lusearch	27s	31s	11M	8m
sunflow	46s	8m	375M	74m
avrora	36s	32s	11M	41m
hsqldb	44s	35s	25M	86m

Table 2. Running time of our thread-escape analysis.

6.2 Scalability

In this section, we evaluate the scalability of our thread-escape analysis. Table 2 provides the running time of the analysis. The "pre-process time" column reports the time to prepare the benchmark for analysis (resolving reflection, computing a call graph, etc.). The "dynamic analysis" column reports the running time of our dynamic analysis, which includes the time to instrument the benchmark and run it on a single supplied input. It also reports the length of the trace that was analyzed. The trace includes a separate event for each execution of each object allocation instruction, each instance field or array element access, and each thread-escaping instruction (i.e., a write to a static field or a call to the `start()` method of class `java.lang.Thread`). We tried multiple different inputs for each benchmark but found only marginal improvements in coverage and precision. This suggests that the truthhood of most queries, and the abstractions for proving them, are not sensitive to program inputs, which in turn plays into our approach's favour.[6]

For each reachable query, the dynamic analysis either disproves the query or provides a parameter configuration that is used by the subsequent static analysis. The "static analysis" column reports the serial running time of all invocations of the static analysis, one per set of queries for which the same parameter configuration is inferred by the dynamic analysis. Note that these invocations do not share anything and could be run in an embarrassingly parallel manner on a multi-core machine or a cluster; hence, we next study the running time of each invocation.

Figure 5 provides the cumulative distribution function (CDF) of the running times of individual invocations of the static analysis for each of our four large benchmarks (all from the DaCapo suite). The blue curve (–○–) shows the CDF of an optimised version of the static analysis while the red curve (–×–) shows the CDF of the naive version (we explain the difference between the two versions shortly). The CDFs have a separate point for each different running time; the x-intercept of the point denotes that time while the y-intercept of the point denotes the number of invocations that took at most that time. The optimised version of the analysis takes almost constant time across different invocations for each benchmark, suggesting that our approach is effective at tailoring the abstraction to each query (Section 6.3 provides more statistics about the computed abstractions). Specifically, it takes an average of 7 seconds per invocation and a maximum of 20 seconds over all 1,743 invocations for all benchmarks. The naive version, on the other hand, takes an average of 30 seconds per invocation and runs out of memory for the 18 invocations (14 for `hsqldb` and 4 for `sunflow`) that are denoted by the points taking 300 seconds—the timeout we used for those invocations.

The optimised and naive versions of our static thread-escape analysis differ only in how they compute method summaries, which we explain next. Let $(pc^\sharp, \rho^\sharp, \sigma^\sharp)$ denote the incoming abstract state for a method. Recall that $\rho^\sharp$ provides the incoming abstract value of each formal argument of the method, and $\sigma^\sharp$ is the incoming abstract heap. If the incoming abstract value of none of the formal arguments contains abstract location L (i.e., $\forall x.\ \mathrm{L} \notin \rho^\sharp(x)$), then the analysis of that method will *never* read the incoming abstract heap $\sigma^\sharp$. The optimised version of our analysis exploits this observation and analyzes the method in context $(\rho^\sharp, \emptyset)$ (i.e., using an empty incoming abstract heap), whereas the naive version still analyzes it in context $(\rho^\sharp, \sigma^\sharp)$. In practice, we observed that our top-down inter-procedural analysis repeatedly visits methods with the same incoming abstract environment satisfying the above condition, but with different incoming abstract heaps. Thus, the naive version results in significantly lesser reuse of summary edges than the optimised version, evident from the CDFs plotted in Figure 6. These CDFs have a separate point for each different number of summary edges that was computed for any method in the benchmark in any invocation of the analysis; the x-intercept of the point provides that number while the y-intercept of the point provides the fraction of methods for which at most that many summary edges were computed in any invocation. Note that while in both versions, only under a handful of summary edges is computed for the vast majority of methods, there are outliers in the naive version for which vastly more summary edges are computed than in the optimised version, for all four benchmarks. These outliers cause the 18 invocations described above to run out of memory.

It is worth emphasizing that sophisticated optimizations have been proposed to efficiently compute and concisely represent method summaries over abstract heaps (e.g., [20]). While those optimizations are hard to understand and implement, ours is relatively simple yet highly effective in practice. Notice that the only reason why our optimization is enabled is due to the unique capability of our dynamic analysis to map only a few necessary allocation sites to L and the vast majority of allocation sites to E in the parameter configurations with which the static analysis is invoked (see Section 6.3); without this capability, many methods would be analyzed with incoming abstract environments containing L in the abstract

[6] We conjecture that the input insensitivity happens, because thread-escape analysis and pointer analysis concern heap structure and pointer connectivity, which is less sensitive to the specific data values in different program inputs (e.g., different keywords to be searched by `lusearch`, different SQL queries to be answered by `hsqldb`, etc.).

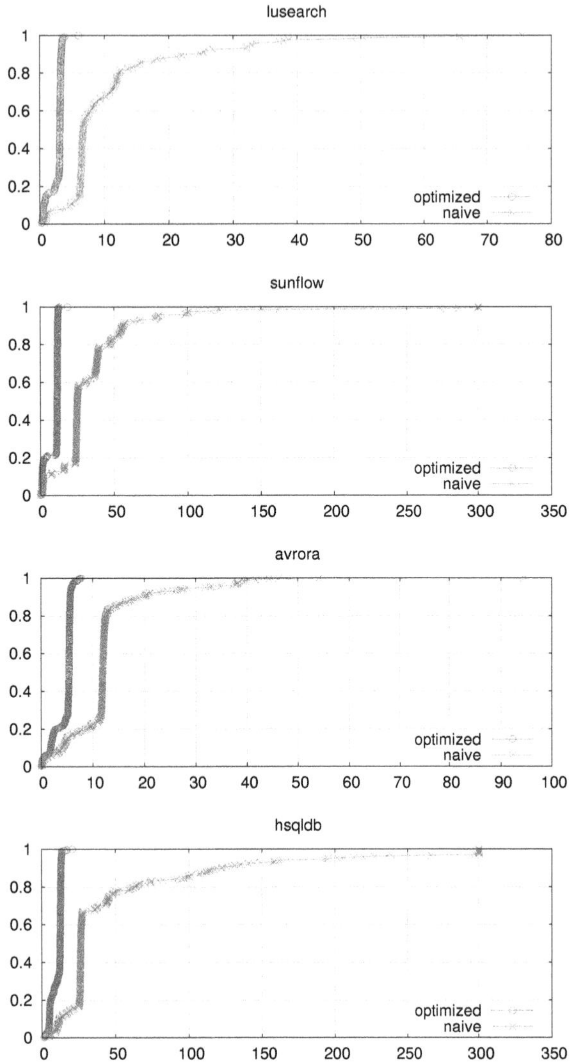

Figure 5. CDF of the running time (secs.) of invocations of the optimised and naive versions of our static thread-escape analysis.

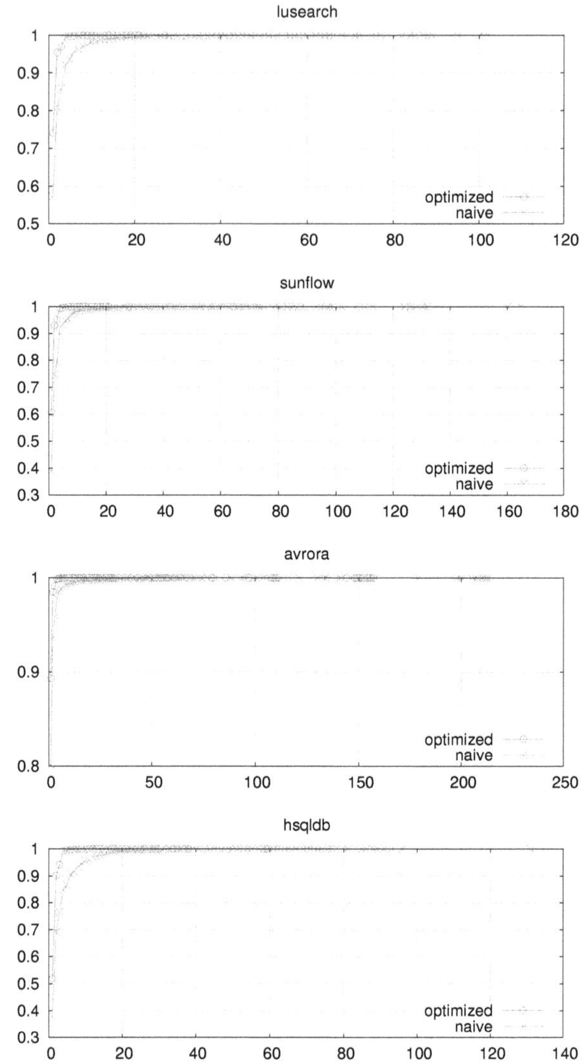

Figure 6. CDF of summary sizes of methods in invocations of the optimised and naive versions of our static thread-escape analysis.

values of formal arguments, which in turn would prevent the optimised version of our analysis from ignoring the incoming abstract heap and drastically hurt summary reuse.

6.3 Abstraction quality

This section evaluates the quality of the abstractions computed by our thread-escape analysis. The key question we want to answer is: how hard is the thread-escape analysis problem to justify using query specialisation and dynamic analysis?

We experimented with various purely static strawman approaches and found that they were not precise or scalable enough. Below, we describe two such approaches.

Strawman 1. The goal of this strawman was to determine how much flow and/or context sensitivity matters for precision. We implemented a flow- and context-insensitive analysis based on object allocation site abstraction, and found that it proved only 13-34% of the queries for our benchmarks, with an average of 27.5%. In contrast, the combined dynamic-static approach presented in this paper, which is flow- and context-sensitive, proves 38-72% of the queries, with an average of 52%. This shows that flow and/or context sensitivity is likely important for precision.

Strawman 2. The goal of this strawman was to determine whether a trivial parameter configuration is precise and scalable enough. We used the static thread-escape analysis presented in this paper, but invoked it with a parameter configuration that simply sets each allocation site in the program to L, instead of using our dynamic analysis to obtain parameter configurations tailored to individual queries. We found the resulting analysis to be highly unscalable—it ran out of memory on all our six benchmarks—but highly precise on much smaller benchmarks (not shown) that it was able to successfully analyze. This shows that: (1) even though the above trivial parameter configuration is not the most precise in principle, it is likely very precise in practice; and (2) the ability of our dynamic analysis to avoid unnecessarily mapping sites to L is critical in practice for scalability.

Lastly, we would like to answer the question: if a few allocation sites must be mapped to L for scalability, how small is that number to justify an approach as sophisticated as backward pointer reachability, and how different are the allocation sites for different queries to justify query specialisation? We next answer these questions.

Figure 7 shows the CDF of the number of allocation sites that were mapped to L for each query by the dynamic analysis. Recall

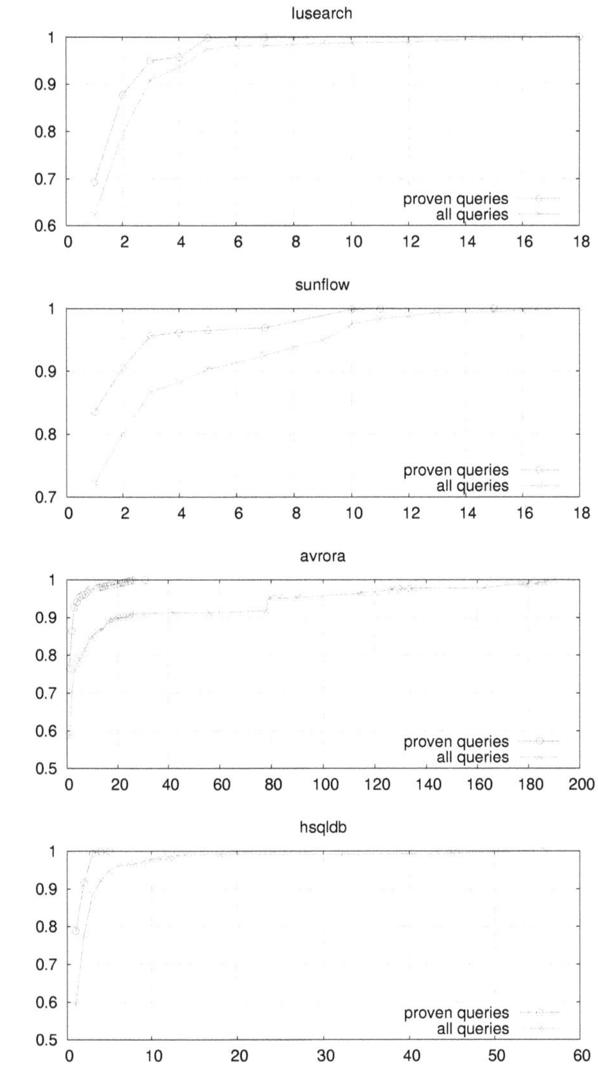

Figure 7. CDFs of the number of allocation sites mapped to L in each parameter configuration, for all queries considered by our static thread-escape analysis and for just those that were proven.

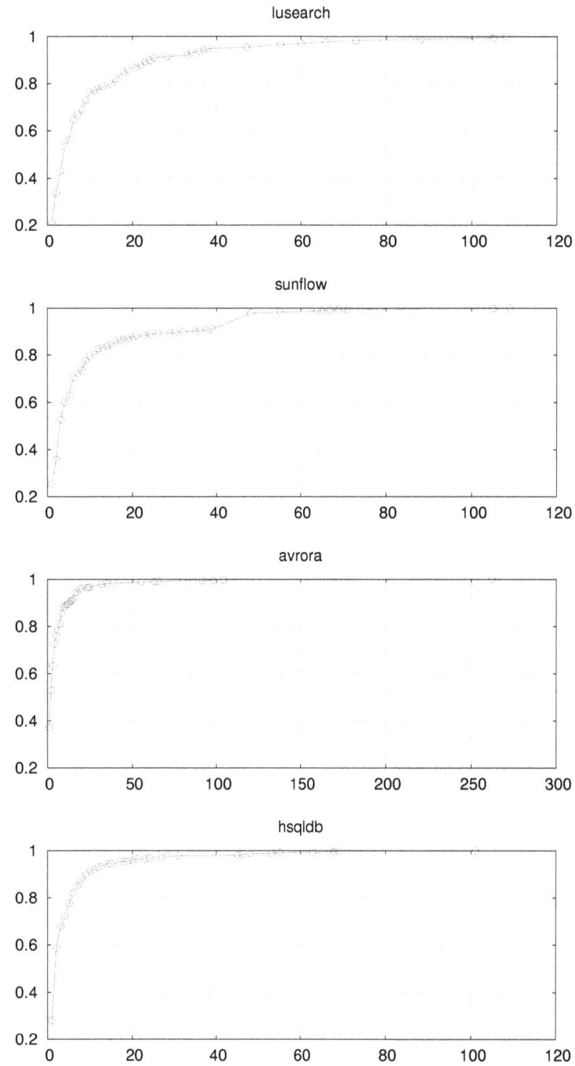

Figure 8. CDF of the number of queries in each invocation of our static thread-escape analysis.

that these are the sites the dynamic analysis has determined must be mapped to L: mapping any of them to E is guaranteed to make the static analysis fail to prove the query. The red curve (-✱-) shows the CDF for all queries that were considered by the static analysis whereas the blue curve (-○-) shows the CDF for only queries that it ended up proving. For each point shown, the x-intercept denotes the number of sites that were mapped to L for some query, and the y-intercept denotes the fraction of queries that needed at most those many sites. The relative shapes of the two curves are expected: as the number of sites needed to be mapped to L by a query grows, the chance that our dynamic analysis will miss some needed site due to lack of coverage and thereby cause our static analysis to fail to prove the query increases. The CDFs show that, while just 1-2 sites are needed to prove around 50% of the queries for each benchmark, at least a handful of sites are needed to prove another 40%, and tens of sites are needed to prove the remaining 10%. On average, 4.8 sites are needed for all queries that the static analysis attempts to prove, with the highest being 195 sites for `avrora`.

Figure 8 shows the CDF of the number of queries in each invocation of our static thread-escape analysis for which the same parameter configuration is inferred by the dynamic analysis. For each point shown, the x-intercept denotes the size of at least one such query set, and the y-intercept denotes the fraction of query sets of at most that size. On average, an invocation of the static analysis considers 14 queries, with some outliers considering over hundred queries each. This shows that the abstraction needed for proving each query is neither too unique nor too generic.

7. Related work

Our approach is related to techniques for client-driven abstraction specialisation and to techniques for combining dynamic and static analyses. We next survey each of these kinds of techniques.

Client-driven abstraction specialisation. In the client-driven specialisation problem, a program and a query (assertion) are given and the goal is to find either a counterexample program trace showing a violation of the query, or an abstraction which is cheap yet precise enough for the analysis to efficiently prove the query on the program. There are two natural solutions to this problem: *abstraction refinement*, which starts with a coarse abstraction and refines it, and *abstraction coarsening*, which starts with a precise abstraction and coarsens it. The CEGAR approach (e.g., [1, 3, 5, 13, 19]) falls in the first category, and refines the abstraction guided by false counterexample traces. Besides the CEGAR approach, there are other approaches to refine abstractions that are based on a dependence analysis that relates unproven queries to sources of imprecision such as flow-, context-, or object insensitivity in the abstraction [12, 14, 18]. In more recent work, Liang et al. [15] present randomised algorithms to find a *minimal abstraction* that are based on both abstraction refinement and coarsening.

A fundamental difference between our approach and all the above techniques is that we utilise the concrete trace in order to avoid performing the static analysis at all. This can be handy in cases where the static analysis is exploring too many paths and considering too many configurations. Interestingly, our method could be combined with abstraction refinement, e.g. by computing an initial abstraction which respects the necessary condition and then applying refinement if necessary.

Combining static and dynamic analyses. Recent work combines static and dynamic analyses in interesting ways. The Yogi project [2, 9, 10, 17] exploits a dynamic analysis to improve the performance of the abstraction-refinement step of a static analysis. A form of concolic testing is used to reduce the number of theorem prover calls and case splits due to pointer aliasing, which a static analysis considers during refinement.

Gupta et al. [11] uses a dynamic analysis to simplify non-linear constraints generated during inference of program invariants. Yorsh et al. [22] uses a static analysis to construct a concrete trace that is then used by an automated theorem prover to check if it covers all executions. It proves safety properties if the check passes on the concrete trace and produces a counterexample that can be used to generate new traces if the check fails.

One of the interesting questions for a program analysis is how to infer the right invariants to prove a query. One potential idea which is similar to ours is to start from a given concrete trace and then generalise it. McMillan [16] uses interpolants to perform generalisation. This approach is interesting but it requires computing interpolants which is not yet feasible for many programming language features. Also, like CEGAR this approach fails to generalise from multiple paths. In contrast we simplify the problem by assuming that the abstract domains already provide generalisation, and use the concrete trace to trim inadequate abstractions.

Techniques combining random test generation and concrete execution with symbolic execution and model generation have been explored [7, 8, 21]. They use symbolic methods to direct tests towards unexplored paths to find errors faster. But they do not use abstraction and in general cannot find proofs in the presence of loops.

To our knowledge, our technique is unique in that it uses a dynamic analysis for computing necessary conditions on abstractions, and also for directly providing a static analysis with an abstraction that is specialised to a given query and which in most cases succeeds in proving the query.

8. Conclusion

Efficiently finding good abstractions is a long-standing problem in static analysis. Parametrised static analyses offer the flexibility to specialise the abstraction to a given query but also pose a hard search for a suitable parameter configuration. We have presented a novel solution to this problem: using a dynamic analysis to compute a necessary condition on the parameter configurations for proving a given query. We have given constructive algorithms for two instance analyses: thread-escape analysis and points-to analysis. We have proven that these algorithms indeed compute necessary conditions and shown that, in practice, these algorithms are efficient and the resulting static analyses are both precise and scalable.

Acknowledgments We thank Percy Liang for technical discussions on thread-escape analysis and the necessary-condition problem, and Peter O'Hearn and the anonymous referees for helpful comments on the paper. Yang acknowledges support from EPSRC.

References

[1] T. Ball and S. Rajamani. The slam project: Debugging system software via static analysis. In *POPL*, pages 1–3, 2002.

[2] N. E. Beckman, A. V. Nori, S. K. Rajamani, and R. J. Simmons. Proofs from tests. In *ISSTA*, pages 3–14, 2008.

[3] D. Beyer, T. A. Henzinger, R. Majumdar, and A. Rybalchenko. Path invariants. In *PLDI*, pages 300–309, 2007.

[4] S. M. Blackburn, R. Garner, C. Hoffman, A. M. Khan, K. S. McKinley, R. Bentzur, A. Diwan, D. Feinberg, D. Frampton, S. Z. Guyer, M. Hirzel, A. Hosking, M. Jump, H. Lee, J. E. B. Moss, A. Phansalkar, D. Stefanović, T. VanDrunen, D. von Dincklage, and B. Wiedermann. The DaCapo benchmarks: Java benchmarking development and analysis. In *OOPSLA*, pages 169–190, 2006.

[5] E. M. Clarke, O. Grumberg, S. Jha, Y. Lu, and H. Veith. Counterexample-guided abstraction refinement for symbolic model checking. *JACM*, 50(5), 2003.

[6] P. Cousot and R. Cousot. Abstract interpretation: A unified lattice model for static analysis of programs by construction of approximation of fixed points. In *POPL*, pages 238–252, 1977.

[7] C. Csallner and Y. Smaragdakis. Check 'n' Crash: combining static checking and testing. In *ICSE*, pages 422–431, 2005.

[8] P. Godefroid, N. Klarlund, and K. Sen. Dart: directed automated random testing. In *PLDI*, pages 213–223, 2005.

[9] P. Godefroid, A. Nori, S. Rajamani, and S. Tetali. Compositional may-must program analysis: unleashing the power of alternation. In *POPL*, pages 43–56, 2010.

[10] B. S. Gulavani, T. A. Henzinger, Y. Kannan, A. V. Nori, and S. K. Rajamani. Synergy: a new algorithm for property checking. In *SIGSOFT FSE*, pages 117–127, 2006.

[11] A. Gupta, R. Majumdar, and A. Rybalchenko. From tests to proofs. In *TACAS*, pages 262–276, 2009.

[12] S. Guyer and C. Lin. Client-driven pointer analysis. In *SAS*, pages 214–236, 2003.

[13] T. Henzinger, R. Jhala, R. Majumdar, and K. McMillan. Abstractions from proofs. In *POPL*, pages 232–244, 2004.

[14] P. Liang and M. Naik. Scaling abstraction refinement via pruning. In *PLDI*, pages 590–601, 2011.

[15] P. Liang, O. Tripp, and M. Naik. Learning minimal abstractions. In *POPL*, pages 31–42, 2011.

[16] K. McMillan. Relevance heuristics for program analysis. In *POPL*, pages 145–146, 2008.

[17] A. V. Nori, S. K. Rajamani, S. Tetali, and A. V. Thakur. The yogi project: Software property checking via static analysis and testing. In *TACAS*, pages 178–181, 2009.

[18] J. Plevyak and A. Chien. Precise concrete type inference for object-oriented languages. In *OOPSLA*, pages 324–340, 1994.

[19] J. P. Quielle and J. Sifakis. Specification and verification of concurrent systems in cesar. In *Proceedings of the 5th International Symposium on Programming*, pages 337–350, 1982.

[20] N. Rinetzky, J. Bauer, T. Reps, M. Sagiv, and R. Wilhelm. A semantics for procedure local heaps and its abstractions. In *POPL*, pages 296–309, 2005.

[21] K. Sen, D. Marinov, and G. Agha. Cute: a concolic unit testing engine for c. In *FSE*, pages 263–272, 2005.

[22] G. Yorsh, T. Ball, and M. Sagiv. Testing, abstraction, theorem proving: Better together! In *ISSTA*, pages 145–156, 2006.

Sound Predictive Race Detection in Polynomial Time

Yannis Smaragdakis
University of Athens and
University of Massachusetts, Amherst
smaragd@di.uoa.gr

Jacob M. Evans
University of Massachusetts, Amherst
jmevans@cs.umass.edu

Caitlin Sadowski Jaeheon Yi
Cormac Flanagan
University of California at Santa Cruz
{supertri,jaeheon,cormac}@cs.ucsc.edu

Abstract

Data races are among the most reliable indicators of programming errors in concurrent software. For at least two decades, Lamport's happens-before (HB) relation has served as the standard test for detecting races—other techniques, such as lockset-based approaches, fail to be sound, as they may falsely warn of races. This work introduces a new relation, causally-precedes (CP), which generalizes happens-before to observe more races without sacrificing soundness. Intuitively, CP tries to capture the concept of happens-before ordered events that must occur in the observed order for the program to observe the same values. What distinguishes CP from past predictive race detection approaches (which also generalize an observed execution to detect races in other plausible executions) is that CP-based race detection is both sound and of polynomial complexity.

We demonstrate that the unique aspects of CP result in practical benefit. Applying CP to real-world programs, we successfully analyze server-level applications (e.g., Apache FtpServer) and show that traces longer than in past predictive race analyses can be analyzed in mere seconds to a few minutes. For these programs, CP race detection uncovers races that are hard to detect by repeated execution and HB race detection: a single run of CP race detection produces several races not discovered by 10 separate rounds of happens-before race detection.

Categories and Subject Descriptors D.1.3 [*Concurrent Programming*]; D.2.4 [*Software/Program Verification*]

General Terms Languages, Reliability, Verification

1. Introduction

Data races are the most common symptom of a programming error in the increasingly central field of concurrent programming. Two memory accesses are "conflicting" if they are performed by different threads, they access the same memory location, and at least one of them is a write. A data race is then typically defined as two *concurrent* (or *unordered* or *not happens-before-ordered*) conflicting accesses [7, 21, 26, 36].

Typical modern high-performance dynamic race detectors are based on one of two principles: *happens-before* (HB) ordering or *lockset* computation. Lockset-based race detectors follow an idea popularized by Eraser [42] and attempt to detect inconsistent use of locks for access to the same memory location by different threads. This approach has the advantage of detecting many races, even if these are not observed in the execution being monitored. For instance, if the detector records two write accesses by different threads to the same memory word without holding a common lock, it will report a possible race. The drawback of lockset-based race detectors is that they are *unsound*. The reported races are often spurious since the two suspicious events may be well-ordered via other thread communication (e.g., the prior reading of a well-synchronized flag indicating that the thread can now freely read shared data without synchronization). Consider, for instance, the example execution in Figure 1. (Our visual convention is that events occur top-to-bottom in the total order of the observed execution. We use the standard syntax `acq(l)`/`rel(l)` for the acquisition/release of lock `l`, and `w(x)`/`r(x)` for the write/read of variable `x`.)

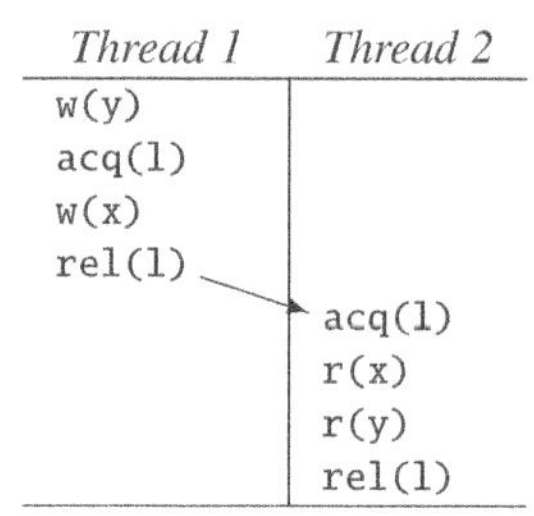

Figure 1. Example of no race on variable y.

Although the two accesses to shared variable y do not occur with the same lock held, they are well-ordered—the second access only occurs after Thread 2 has observed a value written by Thread 1. It is quite possible that, if the two critical sections over lock l had been swapped, Thread 2 would not have attempted to read y since its read of x would have yielded a different value.

In our work, we focus on sound race detection: races are extremely hard to debug and reporting false positives to the user severely reduces the usability of a race detection tool. Sound race detection is a hallmark feature of happens-before based approaches. HB race detectors attempt to discern when there has been inter-thread communication that effectively orders the two conflicting events. Unordered events are reported as a race, since there is no reason why they could not have occurred at exactly the same instance. In its simplest form, happens-before is a partial order that generalizes the observed total order of a multithreaded program's execution by:

- ordering all events by a single thread in the order they were actually observed
- ordering lock releases and subsequent acquisitions of the same lock in the order they were observed.

POPL'12, January 25–27, 2012, Philadelphia, PA, USA.

All events unordered by happens-before are then considered to be potentially performed simultaneously. Under the assumption that threads can only communicate via mechanisms represented in the HB order[1] this approach is sound. Consider again the above execution trace. The inter-thread HB edge shown as an arrow, together with the transitivity of the HB partial order, ensure that the two writes to y are HB-ordered, thus no HB race is reported.

The problem with plain happens-before race detection is that it can miss many races due to accidental HB edges. The original definition of happens-before by Lamport [30] was in the context of distributed systems, with an HB edge introduced for explicit inter-process communication. Lock synchronization does not induce the same hard ordering as explicit communication, however. A lock-based critical section can often be reordered with others, as long as lock semantics (mutual exclusion) is preserved. Consider the code example shown in Figure 2. In this example, the `PolarCoord` class has two fields, `radius` and `angle`, protected by the object lock `this`. The `count` field tallies the number of accesses to `radius` and `angle`, and the `main` method forks two concurrent threads. This program has a race condition on `count`; unfortunately, precise race detectors such as FASTTRACK [21] or DJIT^{+} [38] fail to detect this race condition on 94% of test runs.

Figure 3(A) illustrates the essence of the problem by showing the trace that the HotSpot JVM typically generates for the program of Figure 2, with no overlap between the executions of the two threads. For this trace, a happens-before race detector would not find a race on `count`, since the lock release by Thread 1 *happens-before* the lock acquire of Thread 2, thereby masking the lack of synchronization between the accesses to `count`. In contrast, trace B presents a different scheduling where there is clearly a race on `count`. By inspection, we are able to predict from trace A that a race condition *could* occur as in trace B; we say that trace A has a *predictable* race.

Our work consists of defining a new relation, *causally-precedes* (CP), by analogy to happens-before, to detect such races. A race occurs if two conflicting actions are not CP-ordered. Unlike prior precise race detectors, a CP-based race detector can detect predictable race conditions as in Figure 3. The essence of detecting this predictable race is that the critical section of Thread 2 has received no information that can reveal whether the critical section of Thread 1 has already executed or not. More precisely, reordering events as in trace B (thus exposing an HB race) maintains the property that *all read operations return exactly the same values as in the original execution*—we call this a *correct reordering* of the observed behavior. A correctly reordered execution is just as feasible as the observed one.

Some previous work has addressed the problem of latent races in the context of happens-before race detection [10, 11, 45, 47]. This work typically comes under the label of *predictive* race analysis, and is a subset of the general area of predictive and generalizing concurrency analysis [18, 20, 28, 29, 48, 49, 57–59]. The main idea of this body of work is to consider which of the correct reorderings of critical sections would have triggered a race in an HB detector. The problem with a reorderings-based approach is that it requires exploring all reorderings of critical sections to determine which ones are correct and produce a race. This exploration is an expensive process: the space of possible reorderings is exponential and executions with races are often hard to discover. When applied to dynamic (i.e., run-time) race detection "[the] predictive runtime analysis technique can be understood as a hybrid of testing and model checking" [9].

[1] Although this simplistic definition only covers locks, other inter-thread communication can be captured as happens-before edges.

Figure 2: Example Program PolarCoord

```
class PolarCoord {
  int radius, angle;
  int count; // counts accesses

  static PolarCoord pc = new PolarCoord();

  void setRadius(int r) {
    count++;
    synchronized(this) { radius = r; }
  }

  int getAngle() {
    int t;
    synchronized(this) { t = angle; }
    count++;
    return t;
  }

  public static void main(String[] args){
    fork { pc.setRadius(10); }
    fork { pc.getAngle(); }
  }
}
```

Figure 3: Example Traces for the PolarCoord Program.

Thread 1	Thread 2
r(count)	
w(count)	
acq(this)	
w(radius)	
rel(this)	
	acq(this)
	r(angle)
	rel(this)
	r(count)
	w(count)

Tool	Report
Happens-Before:	"no race"
Causally-Precedes:	"race"

(A) predictable race condition

Thread 1	Thread 2
	acq(this)
	r(angle)
	rel(this)
r(count)	
w(count)	
	r(count)
	w(count)
acq(this)	
w(radius)	
rel(this)	

Tool	Report
Happens-Before:	"race"
Causally-Precedes:	"race"

(B) happens-before race

In contrast, our work offers the first sound yet scalable technique for predictive race detection. Specifically, CP weakens the HB order while still maintaining soundness. CP is guaranteed to have a polynomial cost of evaluation, and our efficient implementation allows turning this into a linear cost, by limiting the size of the reordering window. CP race detection results are not complete: examining all correct reorderings of the original trace would necessitate an exponential search. Consequently, our detector may miss some races. Nevertheless, it is guaranteed to detect a superset of the observed happens-before races and to only give warnings for true races. (More accurately, the soundness theorem we prove is more subtle: if our detector issues a warning, there is either a correct reordering of the observed execution that exhibits an HB race, or a reordering that exhibits a deadlock. Thus, our race soundness guarantee only applies to deadlock-free programs, yet in practice our sound warning of a possible deadlock is just as valuable as a warning of a race.)

Specifically our work makes the following contributions:

- We present causally-precedes, a weaker relation than happens-before, yet offering the same desirable features: CP leads to sound race detection, and can be evaluated efficiently (in polynomial time). It is worth emphasizing that multiple researchers have fruitlessly pursued such a weakening of HB in the past. We demonstrate with numerous examples why it is not easy to weaken HB while remaining sound. (Both the definition of CP and our proof of soundness are results of multi-year collaborative work, with several intermediate failed attempts.)
- We present an efficient implementation of CP. Although the relation is polynomial, practical race detection can hardly afford even quadratic complexity: an $\Omega(n^2)$ algorithm (with n being the number of observed events) is unscalable in practice, with event counts in the millions. We implement our algorithm in Datalog, for declarative logical reasoning, and apply successive optimizations, first to make the algorithm's complexity depend only on synchronization events, and then to derive a family of linear algorithms by allowing finite reordering windows.
- Our experiments showcase the advantages of CP and our implementation. The extra races detected are among the hardest to discover with plain HB analysis. A single CP-based race detection run discovers several new races, unexposed by 10 independent runs of plain HB race detection. Our implementation avoids past scalability pitfalls. If we examine races appearing within a finite reordering window (e.g., 1,000 non-redundant shared memory events) we can achieve linear runtime costs for our analysis, even for real-world programs and workloads.

The rest of the paper introduces our causally-precedes relation (Section 2), illustrates the kind of reasoning it supports and its soundness properties (Section 3), describes our implementation (Section 4), presents experimental results (Section 5), and discusses related work (Section 6) before concluding (Section 7).

2. Causally-Precedes

We next introduce our new relation, causally-precedes, and subsequently illustrate it via examples.

2.1 Definitions

We consider a standard single-observer model for assigning semantics to a concurrent execution. That is, all events are observed in a total order and we define our concepts relative to the observed order. Events have the form $[t : a]_i$, where t is the thread performing the event, and i is the event's index in the total order. The action, a performed by an event is of the form $w(x)$, $r(x)$, $acq(l)$ and $rel(l)$. Thread creation and joining can be added straightforwardly, as explicit causally-precedes edges; for simplicity, we do not discuss these events in the examples.

Definition 1 (Happens-before). In this framework the happens-before ($\ll_{HB}$) relation is defined simply as the smallest relation that satisfies the following (we use underscores as a "don't care" value):

- Events by the same thread are ordered as they appear. This partial order of events in a trace is also called Program Order (PO).
  $([t : \_]_{i_1} \ll_{HB} [t : \_]_{i_2}$ if $i_1 \leq i_2)$
- Releases and acquisitions of the same lock are ordered as they appear.
  $([t_1 : rel(l)]_{i_{rel}} \ll_{HB} [t_2 : acq(l)]_{i_{acq}}$ if $i_{rel} < i_{acq})$
- $\ll_{HB}$ is closed under composition with itself.
  $(\ll_{HB} = (\ll_{HB} \circ \ll_{HB}))$

We also assume two helper relations:

- the binary relation $\asymp$ (read *conflicts*). Two events by different threads conflict if they both access the same variable and one of the actions is a write.
- the function $RL(e)$ that maps a lock acquisition event to the corresponding lock release. (I.e., $RL([t_1 : acq(l)]_{i_{acq}}) = [t_1 : rel(l)]_{i_{rel}}$ if there is no $[t_1 : rel(l)]_{i'_{rel}}$ with $i_{acq} < i'_{rel} < i_{rel}$.) In this case, we say that $[t_1 : acq(l)]_{i_{acq}}$ *is paired with* $[t_1 : rel(l)]_{i_{rel}}$. $RL(e)$ is a one-to-one function for a well-formed execution, so we also consider its inverse, $RL^{-1}(e)$.[2]

Definition 2 (Causally Precedes). Causally precedes ($\ll_{CP}$) is then the smallest relation such that:

a) $\ll_{CP}$ has a release-acquire edge between critical sections over the same lock that contain conflicting events.
$([t_1 : rel(l)]_{i_{rel}} \ll_{CP} [t_2 : acq(l)]_{j_{acq}}$ if there are
$[t_1 : \_]_{k_1} \asymp [t_2 : \_]_{k_2}$ such that
$i_{acq} < k_1 < i_{rel} < j_{acq} < k_2 < j_{rel}$, where
$RL^{-1}([t_1 : rel(l)]_{i_{rel}}) = [t_1 : acq(l)]_{i_{acq}}$ and
$RL([t_2 : acq(l)]_{j_{acq}}) = [t_2 : rel(l)]_{j_{rel}})$

b) $\ll_{CP}$ has a release-acquire edge between critical sections over the same lock that contain CP-ordered events. (These events can be lock acquisition or release events, and not necessarily internal events in the critical section.)
Because of Rule (c), below, this condition turns out to be equivalent to the seemingly weaker "releases and acquisitions of the same lock are ordered if the beginning of one critical section is CP-ordered with the end of the other"—since there is an HB order between the start of a critical section and every internal event, as well as all internal events and the end of a critical section. $([t_1 : rel(l)]_{i_{rel}} \ll_{CP} [t_2 : acq(l)]_{j_{acq}}$, if
$RL^{-1}([t_1 : rel(l)]_{i_{rel}}) \ll_{CP} RL([t_2 : acq(l)]_{j_{acq}}))$

c) CP is closed under left and right composition with HB.
$(\ll_{CP} = (\ll_{HB} \circ \ll_{CP}) = (\ll_{CP} \circ \ll_{HB}))$

Note that $\ll_{CP}$ is a subset of the happens-before relation. Inspecting the three cases of the $\ll_{CP}$ definition, we see that all $\ll_{CP}$ edges produced by the first two rules are release-acquire edges on the same lock and so are also $\ll_{HB}$ edges. The third rule then states that CP is closed under composition with HB, which still produces a subset of the HB edges, since HB is transitively closed. It is similarly easy to see that CP is transitive.

Definition 3 (CP-Race). We define a *race* (or *CP-race* when we need to distinguish from happens-before races) to be a pair of conflicting events that are not CP-ordered in either direction.

2.2 Illustration

There are a few aspects of the definition of CP that should be emphasized for clarity. Probably most important among them is that CP is not a reflexive relation. (If it were, Rule (c) would make CP equal to HB.) Consequently, CP is also not a partial order.

Recall that we want CP to retain only some of the HB edges (i.e., ordering dependencies) in a way that captures which conflicting events could have happened simultaneously in a reordered but certain-to-be-feasible execution. Consider again the example of Figure 3 from Section 1 and observe that the shown HB edge is not a CP edge. None of the events shown are CP-ordered—i.e., they constitute a CP-race (and a predictable race). The same occurs in the execution of Figure 4.

[2] In this section we try to strike a balance between precise presentation and avoiding tedious definitions for pre-existing, well-understood concepts. We thus try to be more formal when defining elements unique to our approach and otherwise rely on intuition—e.g., the preconditions for a well-formed trace (such as pairing of lock acquisitions and releases, well-nesting of critical sections) are omitted here but stated fully in our proof of soundness.

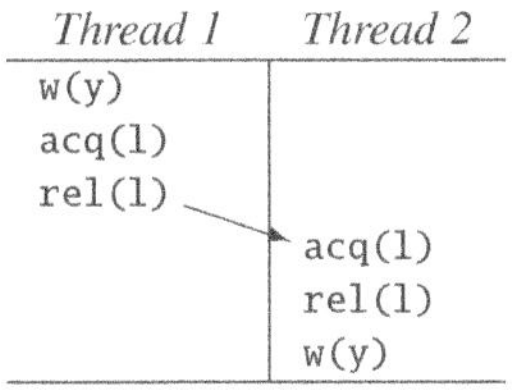

Figure 4. Another example of a certain race not reported by HB.

In both cases, the critical sections do not contain conflicting events, which would order them per Rule (a) of the CP definition. In contrast, Figure 1 in Section 1 incurs no CP race report: the HB release-acquire edge is also a CP edge (per Rule (a)) and Rule (c) can then be used to CP-order the two operations on variable y.

Indeed, Rule (a) of the CP definition is almost inevitable. To see this consider what constitutes a feasible execution.

Definition 4 (Correctly Reorders). We say that an execution ex' correctly reorders (CR) another execution ex (also written $ex' =_{CR} ex$) iff ex' is a total order over a subset of the events of ex that:

- contains a prefix of the events of every thread in ex and respects program order, i.e., if an event e in ex appears in ex' then all events by the same thread that precede e in ex also appear in ex' and precede e.
- for every read event that appears in ex', the most recent write event of the same variable in ex' is the same as the most recent write event of the same variable in ex.

The definition of CR matches the intuition for feasible alternative executions: if every value read is the same as in the observed execution, then the alternative is certainly also feasible.[3]

In this light, Rule (a) from the definition of CP is intuitively clear: as far as later events are concerned, two conflicting events have to occur in the same order in every correctly-reordered execution. Thus, conflicting events induce a hard ordering dependency, if it is certain that they do not constitute a race (in this case, because they are protected by a common lock). Since two critical sections over the same lock have to be ordered in their entirety (i.e., all events of one have to precede all events of the other) the ordering constraint on conflicting events becomes an ordering constraint on the entire critical section containing them. The same reasoning applies to Rule (b) of the CP definition: if two events internal to respective critical sections are CP-ordered, then the entire critical sections are also CP-ordered.

Rule (c) is the most interesting aspect of the CP definition. The rule is both very conservative and surprisingly weak, in different ways. Intuitively, Rule (c) is directly responsible for the soundness of CP: once some evidence of inevitable event ordering is found, all earlier and later events in an HB order automatically maintain their relative order. This conservative aspect of the Rule is necessary for ensuring that a CP race truly indicates that the events could have been concurrent. At the same time, Rule (c) is quite weak. Consider three events e_1, e_2, e_3. It could be that $e_1 \ll_{CP} e_2$, $e_2 \ll_{HB} e_3$, and consequently $e_1 \ll_{CP} e_3$. This still does *not* mean that $e_2 \ll_{CP} e_3$, even though the HB order between e_2 and e_3 is what allows e_1 to CP e_3. This aspect is what prevents CP from missing the possibility of predictable races (as in e_2-does-not-CP-e_3) even when it assumes conservatively that certain reorderings are not possible, in order to maintain soundness.

[3] This pairing of a read with the most recent write event implicitly introduces sequential consistency as an assumption. Nevertheless, this is not a constraint: Every HB race is a CP race. In case no HB races are observed for an execution, a relaxed memory model yields sequentially consistent behavior, thus our assumption is valid.

3. Complications and Soundness

We discuss the subtleties of CP through examples of hard-to-reason-about executions. Such examples naturally lead to the statement of our soundness theorem and its proof.

3.1 Example Reasoning

For each example, it is interesting for the reader to consider independently whether there is a predictable race or not. Reasoning about concurrent executions is quite hard: even concise examples require exhaustive examination of a large number of possible schedulings or complex formal reasoning to establish ordering properties. In the following examples, we expressed the constraints as symbolic inequalities with disjunctions (e.g. "this event is either before that or after the other") and proved manually they were unsatisfiable.

Figure 5 contains a first example that suggests why sound predictive race detection is hard in the presence of many threads and nested locks. We use the shorthand sync(*lock*) for a sequence of events that induces an inevitable ordering with other identical sync sequences. (E.g., sync(n) can be short for acq(n) r(nVar) w(nVar) rel(n).) For ease of reference, CP edges produced by Rule (a) of the CP definition are shown in the figure, as twin arrows.

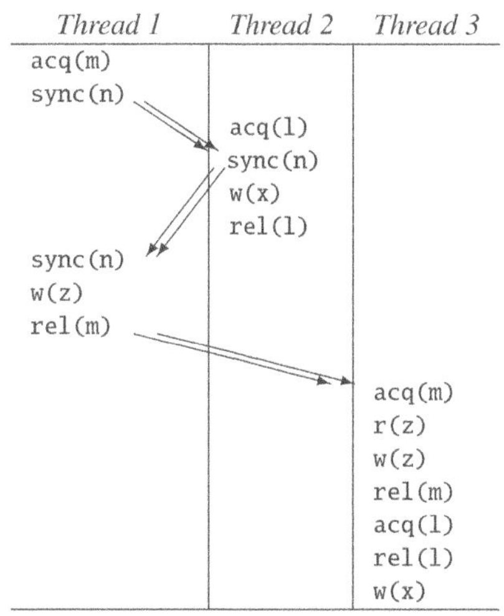

Figure 5. No race between the two writes to x in any correctly reordered execution. Twin arrows show the "hard" CP constraints, i.e., CP order because of Rule (a) of the CP definition. sync(n) can be thought of as acq(n) r(nVar) w(nVar) rel(n).

There is no predictable race between the two writes to x in the above example: any correct reordering of the execution will have the three sync sequences and the critical sections over lock m ordered in the way they were observed, resulting in an ordering of the two writes. (Interestingly, *the empty critical section over* l *in Thread 3 is necessary*, or there would be a predictable race.) The CP definition captures this reasoning accurately. Rule (b) is essential in establishing that the two critical sections over lock l are CP-ordered: because of rule (b), the end of the critical section over l in Thread 2 is CP-ordered relative to the (empty) critical section over l in Thread 3. (Since CP composes with HB to yield CP, the sync(n) event in Thread 2 is CP-ordered with acq(l) in Thread 3, thus triggering rule (b).)

For another interesting example, consider Figure 6.
There is no predictable race on x in this example, but establishing this fact requires case-based reasoning involving both the hard ordering constraints induced by sync sequences and the semantics

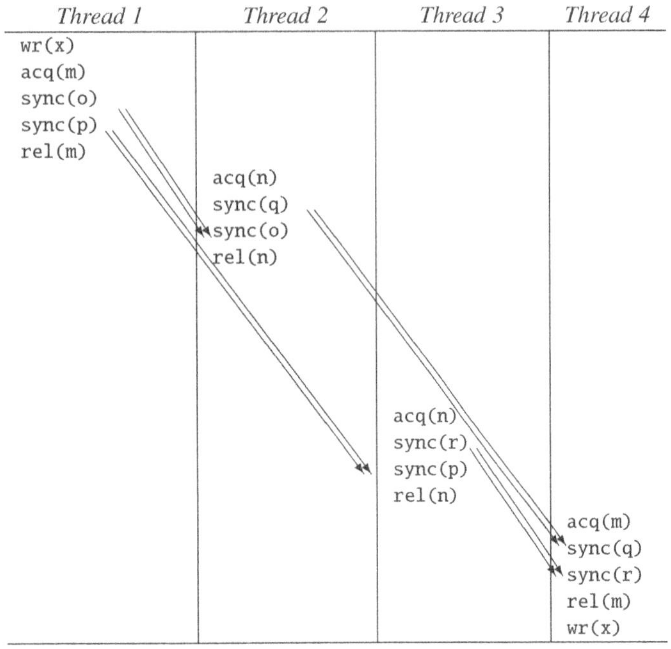

Figure 6. Trace with no predictable HB-race on x.

and identity of locks (e.g., the fact that the critical sections on n cannot overlap). CP avoids such reasoning but gives an accurate result. The two critical sections on n are not CP-ordered, and also do not necessarily occur in the order shown in a correctly reordered execution. The two critical sections on m, however, are CP-ordered and also necessarily in the order observed. Again, we see the interesting aspects of Rule (c) of the CP definition: even though the HB order between the critical sections on n is what enables the CP order between the critical section on m, the former does not get upgraded to a CP order.

Figure 7 presents another hard-to-reason-about example.

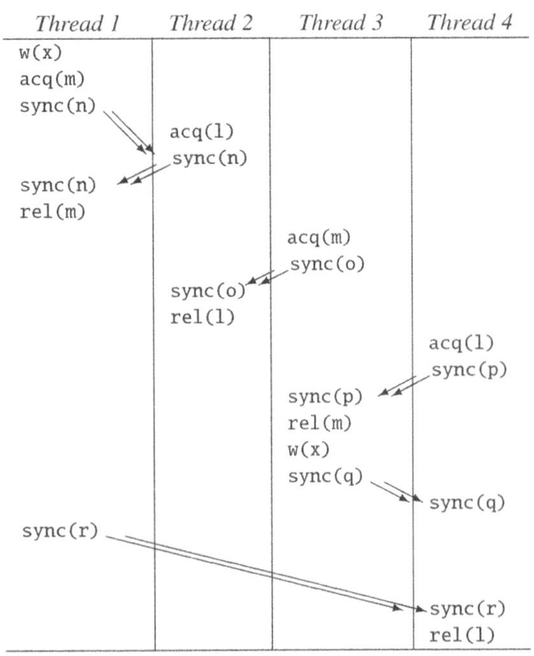

Figure 7. No predictable race between the two writes to x.

This execution does not have a predictable race on variable x. Nevertheless, the reasoning required to establish this fact can be quite complex. Removing events can easily result in a racy execution. For instance, removing the sync(r) edge allows a race by moving the entire set of actions by Thread 3 and Thread 4 before those of Thread 1 and Thread 2.

Detecting predictable races can often require complex reorderings of events. The value of a polynomial but sound predictive race detector is that it avoids exploring all such reorderings. Consider the case of Figure 8. There is a CP-race between the two writes

Thread 1	*Thread 2*
acq(m)	
sync(o)	
w(x)	
acq(n)	
rel(n)	
rel(m)	
	acq(n)
	acq(m)
	rel(m)
	w(x)
	sync(o)
	rel(n)

Thread 1	*Thread 2*
	acq(n)
	acq(m)
	rel(m)
acq(m)	
sync(o)	
w(x)	
	w(x)
	sync(o)
	rel(n)
acq(n)	
rel(n)	
rel(m)	

Figure 8. Exposing the HB race on x (execution on the left) requires a complex reordering of events (shown on the right).

to variable x. There is also a predictable race. It is not possible to expose this, however, without thread scheduling that breaks up the outer critical sections, as shown on the right part of the figure. CP does not need to reproduce the schedule in order to warn of a possible race.

At the same time, however, CP often avoids complex nested lock reasoning by not distinguishing between a predictable race and a deadlock. Our soundness theorem has an interesting form: a CP-race is a sound indication of either a race or a deadlock in a correctly reordered execution. The deadlock is immediately apparent: there is a cycle in the lock-blocking graph. To see this consider the example of Figure 9.

Thread 1	*Thread 2*
acq(m)	
acq(l)	
rel(l)	
w(x)	
rel(m)	
	acq(l)
	acq(m)
	rel(m)
	w(x)
	rel(l)

Thread 1	*Thread 2*
acq(m)	
	acq(l)
acq(l)	
	acq(m)

Figure 9. The observed execution (left) has a CP-race between the two writes to x. There is no predictable race, however! Instead, it is easy to reorder events to expose a deadlock (see right).

There is a CP-race between the accesses to variable x in this example. Yet there is no predictable HB race: no correctly reordered execution can have the two write events without synchronization between them. The CP soundness theorem states that this is only possible when a reordering can expose a deadlock due to threads acquiring locks in a way that introduces a cycle in the acquisition dependencies.

The above examples offer the reader a glimpse of the complexities of defining CP and proving its soundness. The difficulty of reasoning about event order highlights the challenge of defining a relation that weakens the observed ordering much more than happens-before, yet at the same time is guaranteed to be sound. A race analysis has to either perform heavy reasoning or to conservatively assume ordering every time events *may* be ordered. Rule (c) of the CP definition plays this role but it is still hard to prove that it is conservative enough. The ultimate conservative ordering is of course HB: all critical sections are assumed to always be precisely in the order they were observed.

3.2 Soundness

We now state more fully our assumptions on the execution form, as well as our soundness theorem. Our assumptions include the well-nesting of locks, as well as standard lock semantics.

Definition 5 (Trace). A *trace* is a total order of events such that

1. Acquisition of a lock is not followed by another acquisition of the same lock without an intervening paired lock release.
2. Critical sections are well-nested. More explicitly, if an acquisition of lock l_2 is performed after an acquisition of lock l_1 by the same thread and before l_1's paired release then the paired release of l_1 cannot appear before the paired release of l_2 does.

Our main soundness theorem has a simple statement:

Theorem 1 (CP is Sound). Given a trace *tr* with a CP-race, we can produce a $tr'' =_{CR} tr$ with either an HB-race or a deadlock.

The full proof can be found in the Appendix.

Note that the statement of the theorem applies only to one CP race. (And, since $\ll_{CP}$ is a subset of $\ll_{HB}$, every HB-race is also a CP-race.) That is, the theorem proof establishes that either the "first" CP-race of a trace is an HB-race in some correct reordering of the trace or we can produce a correct reordering with a deadlock. (The idea of stating the soundness guarantee so that it applies to the first error reported is standard [21, 23].) The first race is the one that *finishes* earliest in the total order of the trace, i.e., a CP-race between events $e_1 = [t_1 : u_1]_i$ and $e_2 = [t_2 : u_2]_j$, with $i < j$, such that that there is no CP-race between two events both of which appear before e_2, as well as no race between events e_3-e_2, with e_3 appearing after e_1 and before e_2.

Although the theorem's guarantee applies to only one race, we can conservatively maintain soundness when reporting multiple races, at the cost of potentially missing some. Specifically, once a CP-race (which may be merely an HB-race) is discovered (and reported), the rest of the trace can be treated as if the CP-race were a CP edge, thus hard-ordering the two racy events. This means that the soundness guarantee of the theorem then applies to the *next* CP-race reported: any correct reordering of a restricted trace (i.e., one with extra CP edges) is a correct reordering of the original trace. The drawback is that some CP-race nearby another CP race may not be reported due to our conservative treatment.

The form of the soundness theorem is quite interesting. Although a CP race implies a predictable race only in deadlock-free programs, this is hardly a disadvantage. Pointing out a potential deadlock is at least as important as pointing out races. Furthermore, deadlocks are arguably an easier problem to dynamically detect, or statically eliminate. Therefore we expect CP warnings to be almost always (correct) race warnings.

4. Implementation

CP reasoning, based on definition 2, is highly recursive. Notably, Rule (c) can feed into Rule (b), which can feed back into Rule (c). As a result, we have not implemented CP using techniques such as vector clocks, nor have we yet discovered a full CP implementation that only does online reasoning (i.e., never needs to "look back" in the execution trace); these remain challenging questions for future work. However, CP has an easy polynomial algorithm, derived directly from the definition. We express this algorithm in the Datalog language. (Datalog programs have guaranteed polynomial complexity, and Datalog can express any polynomial algorithm.) Consider a trace of execution expressed via the input relations of Figure 10. We report errors of the form "instruction X accessed memory location Y in a way that races with instruction Z".

```
TraceNext[e1] = e2.          // what is the next event after e1
ThreadForEvent[e] = t.  // what is the thread performing e
AcqEvent[e] = m.             // e is a lock acquire for mutex m
RelEvent[e] = m.             // e is a lock release for mutex m
WriteEvent[e] = x.           // e is a write for variable x
ReadEvent[e] = x.            // e is a read for variable x
```

Figure 10. Input relations for our Datalog algorithm.

(Datalog code notation: A relation in the form "`Relation[arg] = value`" is a function; the left arrow symbol, <-, is the implication used for inference, i.e., if the right hand side is true, the left hand side fact is inferred; ; is the logical "or" operator.)

We can then straightforwardly define concepts such as "critical sections", "matching lock/unlock" operations, etc. These are captured by relations "`InSameCriticalSec(e,eAcq)`" (*event* `e` *is in the critical section starting at* `eAcq`) and "`MatchingCriticalSecBoundary[eRel] = eAcq`" (*event* `eRel` *is the lock release paired with lock acquisition* `eAcq`). This allows defining HB and eventually CP as in Figure 11.

```
CP(e1Rel,e2Acq) <-
      MatchingCriticalSecBoundary[e1Rel] = e1Acq,
      RelEvent[e1Rel] = AcqEvent[e2Acq],
      InSameCriticalSec(e1,e1Acq),
      InSameCriticalSec(e2,e2Acq),
      (WriteEvent[e1] = WriteEvent[e2];
       WriteEvent[e1] = ReadEvent[e2];
       ReadEvent[e1] = WriteEvent[e2]).

CP(e1Rel,e2Acq) <-
      MatchingCriticalSecBoundary[e1Rel] = e1Acq,
      RelEvent[e1Rel] = AcqEvent[e2Acq],
      InSameCriticalSec(e1,e1Acq),
      InSameCriticalSec(e2,e2Acq),
      CP(e1,e2).

CP(e1,e2) <- CP(e1,e3), HB(e3,e2).
CP(e1,e2) <- HB(e1,e3), CP(e3,e2).
```

Figure 11. Straightforward CP logic in Datalog.

Having a polynomial algorithm is not sufficient for scalability, however. Realistic executions can have millions of "significant" shared memory events. (Significant events are those remaining after elimination of events that will not affect the reporting of a race—e.g., repeat accesses to the same shared memory variable by the same thread without intervening synchronization operations.) Defining relations such as HB or CP on a cross-product of events is prohibitive. In our implementation we address this challenge in two ways:

- We compute quadratic relations, such as HB or CP, only on lock acquisition and release events. The HB and CP order on regular memory events is then computed on-demand based on the HB and CP order of preceding/following synchronization events. This is already shown in the code of Figure 11.

- We do not fully compute HB or CP, but instead maintain a finite window K of allowed distance for event reorderings (typically 500 or 1000 significant shared memory events). `HB(e1,e2)` and `CP(e1,e2)` are guaranteed to be conservatively computed for endpoints `e1` and `e2` less than K significant events apart. This windowing strategy effectively makes our race detection often be of practically linear complexity: we only relate every event with at most K others.[4] (Our implementation does have some remaining $\Omega(n^2)$ or higher asymptotic complexity parts, but for relations that are expected to be small. A notable exception in practice is long critical sections, for which we have to relate all events to all others, thus suffering quadratic complexity.) The windowing strategy also means that our algorithm will only detect and report races between events less than K significant events apart.

Our computation of CP for only a finite window is implemented by computing a relation `FollowingNearbyEvent` and various specializations of it (for nearby events by the same thread, nearby synchronization actions, etc.). These relations are then threaded throughout the implementation to restrict computations that require examination of every pair of events. Importantly, this means that our main implementation logic differs from the simple form of Figure 11. In particular, all rules need to both have a filter (so that they trigger accurate computation only when events are within a distance of K) as well as a conservative closure (so that a sound overapproximation of CP is computed when there is a possibility of missing an ordering due to the finite window). This is well illustrated by looking at the form of the second rule of the CP definition, which is also the second rule in Figure 11. In the implementation the rule is broken up in two:

```
// the version for when CP is accurate
CP(e1Rel,e2Acq) <-
        MatchingCriticalSecBoundary[e1Rel] = e1Acq,
        RelEvent[e1Rel] = AcqEvent[e2Acq],
        InSameCriticalSec(e1,e1Acq),
        InSameCriticalSec(e2,e2Acq),
        CP(e1,e2),
        FollowingNearbySynchronizationEvent(e1,e2).

// the version for conservative CP when the
// base CP information may be inaccurate
CP(e1Rel,e2Acq) <-
        MatchingCriticalSecBoundary[e1Rel] = e1Acq,
        NearbyCriticalSecOnSameLock(e2Acq,e1Rel),
        InSameCriticalSec(e1,e1Acq),
        InSameCriticalSec(e2,e2Acq),
        SynchronizationEvent(e1),
        SynchronizationEvent(e2),
        !FollowingNearbySynchronizationEvent(e1,e2).
```

This approach allows us to maintain soundness while achieving scalability. Additional optimizations in our implementation include manual indexing for efficient relational joins, as well as join order optimizations.

5. Experiments

We evaluated the performance and prediction capability of our CP race detector on a collection of multithreaded Java benchmarks, mostly from previous studies [12, 17, 54]).

[4] One may argue that even an exponential search algorithm can become linear by limiting its search space to a finite window, but the constants (space and time overhead) would be prohibitive in that case. Our limiting the accurate-CP-computation window is practically feasible exactly because computing CP has a reasonable asymptotic complexity in the first place.

The most substantial of our benchmarks are:

- Jigsaw, W3C's web server [53], coupled with a stress test harness.
- FtpServer, a high-performance FTP server implementation from The Apache Foundation [51], coupled with a JMeter workload [52].
- StaticBucketMap, a part of the Apache Commons project, offering a thread-safe implementation of the Java Map interface. The code size of this benchmark is small, but its driver exercises it thoroughly, resulting in a long trace.

To perform the CP analysis on the benchmarks, we used the RoadRunner framework [22] to dynamically instrument the bytecode of each benchmark at load time. The instrumentation code creates a stream of events for field and array accesses, synchronization operations, thread fork/joins, etc.

We used this infrastructure to perform an inexpensive happens-before race analysis and to also produce a trace subsequently used for the CP analysis. The CP analysis was thus explicitly coded to report races if they were not also HB races (since the latter were discovered and reported already). We conservatively translate accesses to volatile variables and thread creation/join events into pseudo-lock accesses. The traces produced are quite sizable even though stack-variable references are filtered out. The traces are then reduced to only maintain events concerning shared memory locations, and to eliminate re-accesses to the same variable by the same thread without intervening synchronization. The reduced trace is then imported into a database and analyzed using our Datalog implementation.

The first columns of Table 1 show the main metrics for our benchmarks. The benchmark size in LoC is not entirely representative of its complexity for our analysis: much of the code in a program's directory is library code, not exercised at all. Conversely, much of the code actually exercised is Java library code, never shown in the benchmark size. (Library code is still valuable to analyze: the code may not contain races, but may be used in an unsafe way, exposing a race in client code.) StaticBucketMap is the most extreme example: if we were to report its code size uniformly with the other benchmarks, it would come to 110KLoC. The directory contains the entire Apache Commons Collections project, however. The main StaticBucketMap class and test driver file are just 807 LoC. Neither of the two sizes is representative of the code actually exercised, though the second is closer. Similar caveats apply to the report of thread counts. This metric lists the total number of thread created, which can be higher than the number of threads active simultaneously.

Table 1 collects the results of our experiments. We use a high-performance commercial Datalog engine by LogicBlox Inc., on academic license. All analysis was done on a machine with a Dual Six Core Intel Xeon X5650, 2.66GHz Processor and 24GB of RAM. (The CP analysis implementation is single-threaded, hence only one core was active at a time.) We performed CP analysis with the reordering window $K = 500$ significant events, as described in Section 4. We report the races found in a single HB run, in 10 HB runs, as well as the races found by CP in its single run but never found in the 10 HB detector runs. Races are reported per-variable (i.e., dynamic race instances are collapsed based on which data words they occur on). Still, multiple races may have the same underlying cause (e.g., a single missing lock/unlock may fix more than one race). Furthermore, recall that our soundness guarantee only applies to the first race and ensuring that all race reports are sound requires post-processing (which we currently perform manually and requires multiple re-runs of our analysis). For these reasons, the number of races and running times should be viewed

Programs	Size (LoC)	Trace Size (#events) Original	Reduced	Thread Count	Race Conditions Detected HB (1 run)	HB (10 runs)	CP	Time
banking	145	762	522	10	1	1	+0	10s
elevator	1.4k	25k	16k	5	0	0	+0	38s
FtpServer	39k	992k	543k	11	21	27	+7	20m 06s
hedc	25k	102k	1.4k	6	5	5	+0	9s
Jigsaw	49k	1,992k	42k	77	18	33	+3	17s
philo	86	669	382	6	0	0	+0	10s
pool1.2	8.4k	692	526	8	0	0	+0	10s
pool1.3	24k	841	683	8	0	0	+0	12s
StaticBucketMap	see text	265k	133k	5	7	7	+0	1m 35s
stringBuffer	1.4k	223	178	8	0	0	+0	9s
tsp	706	328k	381	4	0	0	+0	9s
vector	26k	325	270	15	1	1	+0	9s

Table 1. Benchmark metrics and number of races detected by our CP analysis but not found in 10 HB runs, as well as time taken for CP analysis. Running times of 9sec are effectively zero: this is the overhead of initializing the Datalog engine and importing data from text files.

only as an imperfect proxy of the utility of our approach. A likely way our analysis would be used by a programmer in practice would be not to report all races, but by analyzing a trace, fixing the first race in the code, then re-analyzing.

The results are representative of the position of our approach relative to others. As can be seen in Table 1, 8 of these benchmarks (i.e., two-out-of-three) produce tiny reduced traces (fewer than 2,000 events, with 7 of them having fewer than 1,000). These brief executions offer little opportunity to detect HB races and virtually no opportunity to correctly reorder events: For all of the tiny traces, CP does not discover any races that are not HB races. Nevertheless, a lockset-based approach would report races even for these executions, since it is easy to observe when a shared variable is accessed by a different thread with a disjoint set of locks held. This illustrates quite well how unsound, lockset-based race detectors tackle a fundamentally different problem. Unsound predictive analyses highlight *possible* race conditions, whereas our work focuses on *proving the presence* of race conditions.

Elevator is another benchmark that is mostly uninteresting. Although its trace is longer than the tiny ones, it is still fairly short (16k events), and has neither HB nor CP races. The jPredictor study [12] and the Said et al. work [40] showed no races on elevator either, despite using an unsound lockset-based analysis and an SMT solver that explores all valid trace reorderings, respectively.

The real benchmarks for our approach are the three longer traces: FtpServer, Jigsaw, and StaticBucketMap. It is instructive to compare results with HB. Clearly HB race detection and CP race detection are different in nature. The cost of our current CP analysis is at least one-to-two orders of magnitude higher than the cost of HB race detection. Nevertheless, the goal of CP is to perform a deep analysis, implicitly considering event reorderings, and to find "hard" races, which a plain HB analysis would not normally detect. For both FtpServer and Jigsaw, CP-based race detection uncovers several races that were not exposed by any of the 10 happens-before race detector runs. This ranges from 3 to 7, or an average of 17% new races for these two benchmarks, confirming that CP race detection can target deeper races than typical HB detectors. Examining the intermediate results of our analysis indicates that CP is a much weaker relation than HB: the number of CP edges computed by our analysis (among synchronization operations) is typically as low as 10% to 20% of the number of HB edges for these benchmarks. Thus, happens-before race detection often considers events to be ordered when there is no semantic reason why they should be.

StaticBucketMap is our final benchmark. It has a long execution, covering very little code, thus CP only reports races also detected by HB. This is the inverse problem from that of the tiny traces: CP does not win over HB not because of insufficient coverage but because of too-thorough coverage of the possible executions. It would be interesting in the future to perform a sensitivity analysis and create runs of several sizes, both for StaticBufferMap, as well as for the 9 programs with smaller traces, to see at what point CP starts detecting more races than HB and when HB catches up. This requires extensive knowledge of the benchmark programs, however.

The table also shows that the time required for CP analysis is quite low, although there is certainly room for further improvement of our CP implementation. For small traces, CP analysis is almost instantaneous. For traces with long critical sections, many threads, and deep lock nesting, the analysis time grows. Still, the overall scalability of CP analysis far exceeds reported numbers for past sound predictive concurrency analyses in the literature. For instance, Said et al.'s SMT-solver-based technique [40] takes 57sec to analyze a 1.4k event hedc trace. (The longest trace analyzed by Said et al. is much smaller than ours, at 45k events long. Yet even this size may be misleading, since the trace is for tsp, which performs a tiny number of thread-shared events relative to the original trace length.) We are not aware of a sound predictive analysis that can scale to executions at the level of our reactive applications Jigsaw and FtpServer with a running time in the low minutes.

6. Related Work

Our approach is distinguished from other related work by (1) maintaining precision while generalizing beyond an observed trace and (2) guaranteeing polynomial complexity and achieving scalability. We discuss other precise predictive and other dynamic approaches in some depth, and briefly overview other race detection techniques.

6.1 Predictive Approaches

The most relevant work to our precise race prediction technique [10–12, 40, 46] was briefly discussed in Section 1 and Section 5. Such work is typically a hybrid of testing and model checking and does not achieve the polynomial complexity and scalability of causally-precedes race detection. For instance, in the recent work by Said et al. [40] scalability relies on a modern SMT solver and an efficient encoding of the problem. Another interesting idea that past work [10, 11] has explored is *sliced causality*, which makes use of *a priori* control- and data-flow dependence information to obtain a reduced slice of the happens-before partial ordering for a particular observed trace. Race conditions are predicted with sliced causality by logging only the relevant operations in a program trace and model-checking all feasible trace permutations in a post-mortem analysis phase. These permutations are sound because one may infer and ignore irrelevant operations via static dependence information; the soundness of the predictions follow from the soundness of the trace permutations generated. Sliced causality requires two static analysis phases for prediction. This approach can detect races that our approach does not: recall that our correctly-reordered execution always respects intra-thread event order. However, our definition of causality is explicitly geared towards mechanisms that do not perform static program analysis, and, thus, cannot tell whether a value read by a thread influences subsequent values produced by the same thread. Adapting our causally-precedes order to also take such dependences into account (instead of assuming that every value read by a thread affects all subsequent thread actions) is orthogonal to the core properties of the definition.

Among this work, the jPredictor tool [12] is distinguished by explicitly producing a polynomial algorithm for race detection. Nevertheless, in order to do so, jPredictor abandons the general soundness guarantees of the theory that underlies it. The main soundness theorem of the jPredictor work (which applies to more than race detection) states that every produced "consistent permutation" corresponds to a possible program execution. Nevertheless, "generating all the consistent permutations of a partial order is a #P-complete problem" [12]. To avoid an exponential search, jPredictor employs two shortcuts for the case of race detection. The first is avoiding a search of permutations: events are processed following the order of the original execution. For predictive power, jPredictor relies on an unsound definition of what constitutes a race (Def. 5 of [12]). The definition adapts (to sliced causality) the lockset criterion for race detection: two conflicting, sliced causality-unordered accesses that occur without holding a common lock are considered to race. The examples of Section 3 (assuming a program text that causes the events in the order shown, under the sliced causality criterion) result in false race reports under this definition. The second shortcut is in the implementation, which performs a single slicing traversal of the trace, also resulting in unsoundness.

Another interesting predictive approach consists of reordering models that are more permissive than our correctly-reorders relation on executions. Past work [20, 27] assumes that threads only communicate via holding locks, and not by writing to shared memory locations. Any trace that holds the same locks in the same order of nesting is considered an appropriate generalization of the observed behavior in that predictive model. The Penelope [49] system then adds soundness back by trying to reproduce the predicted atomicity violation through changes to the scheduling of a real execution. The published experiment numbers imply that their approach does not scale at or near the level of CP race detection and can suffer from high costs in small yet complex executions. Nevertheless, there cannot be a valid comparison since Penelope is an atomicity violation detector and not a race detector (thus addressing an inherently harder problem). Combinations of approaches along these lines should be interesting future work.

6.2 Dynamic Analysis

Happens-Before Approaches Numerous tools are based on Lamport's happens-before relation [14, 21, 37, 43]. These tools are more precise than lockset-based race detectors, but are often less efficient. TRaDE [14] uses accordion clocks along with dynamic escape analysis to boost performance. Banerjee et al. [5] provide an alternative algorithm to the simple happens-before analysis that uses a linear amount of storage. Happens-before race detectors have also been applied to nested fork-join parallelism [32]. The DJIT+ [37] algorithm is an efficient happens-before vector clock algorithm that uses the epoch optimization for a 2-3x performance improvement. FASTTRACK [21] improves upon DJIT+ by using an adaptive lightweight representation for the happens-before relation and by introducing optimized constant-time fast paths that account for approximately 96% of operations encountered in a trace, and provides a 2.3x performance improvement over DJIT+. Pacer [7] improves on the performance further by employing sampling techniques.

Lockset Approaches A *lockset* for a shared variable is the set of locks that protect access to that variable. Locksets were introduced [15] as an alternative representation to the happens-before analysis. Later, locksets were used alone as an efficient technique for data race detection in Eraser [42].

Every CP race (and hence every HB race) is also a lockset race, since the absence of a CP edge between conflicting accesses to a location means that there is no consistently held protecting lock for that location. Consequently, a lockset-based race detector would detect all races detected by CP,[5] and may also report many additional warnings. In practice, many of these extra warnings are false alarms that do not correspond to actual races.

Various refinements and extensions for Eraser have been proposed. Static escape analysis can improve performance [35, 55]. Reasoning about races at the object level instead of the memory word level [55] improves performance but leads to more false alarms. The lockset technique was also extended with timing *thread segments* [25] to reduce false positives caused by data not being protected by a lock during an initialization phase. Further performance enhancements use whole-program static analysis to reduce the amount of instrumentation necessary [13] or involve type inference [2]. Eraser's algorithm has also been extended for the Java Memory Model [31] and implemented with AspectJ [6].

Hybrid Techniques Recent work on dynamic data race detection focuses on combining locksets and happens-before analysis. O'Callahan and Choi [36] developed a two-phase localization scheme; a first pass lockset analysis filters out problematic fields for a second pass hybrid analysis. RaceTrack [61] uses a happens-before analysis to estimate whether threads can concurrently access a memory location so as to reduce false positives caused by empty locksets. MultiRace [38] presents improved versions of happens-before and lockset algorithms. Locksets enable happens-before approaches to report additional warnings and reduce the number of vector clock comparisons needed in the happens-before analysis. Goldilocks [17] combines locksets and happens-before in an unusual way by using locksets to efficiently track the happens-before relation. This precise, complicated analysis is embedded in a Java virtual machine to enable continuous monitoring of race conditions.

6.3 Other Approaches

Several *static* approaches exist to deal with data races. Type systems [1, 8, 24, 41] and languages [4] have been proposed to prevent races in programs. Other static approaches include Warlock [50] and Locksmith [39] for ANSI C programs, scalable whole-program analyses [34, 56] and dataflow-analysis-based approaches [16, 19]. Aiken and Gay [3] also investigate static race detection focusing on SPMD programs.

Scheduler-driven approaches, such as model checking [33], involve running the target program with many different thread schedules, either concretely or symbolically. RaceFuzzer [44] takes potentially racing access pairs and uses a randomized scheduler to

[5] Note that the Eraser algorithm, which incorporates lockset-based reasoning, is also slightly incomplete in how it reasons about thread-local data, and so may miss some real HB or CP races.

drive the execution to exhibit an actual race condition. It would be interesting to try to combine such techniques with our approach, which is explicitly geared towards discovering "hard" races without exploring many complex interleavings.

7. Conclusions

Precise race detectors are important tools for developing reliable multithreaded programs, while avoiding the costs associated with false alarms. We showed how to extend the traditional notion of race detection to also support *race prediction*, without sacrificing scalability or soundness. Our work introduces the novel concept of the causally-precedes relation, which significantly weakens HB. We prove that CP race detection is sound and demonstrate its practical value. Defining and proving the soundness of CP was far from trivial: both tasks became possible only after several failed attempts and significant collaborative work.

We believe that our research can open several avenues for further work. First, it is quite possible that a more efficient implementation of CP can be derived, to push performance further by at least an order of magnitude and even bring it to levels comparable to HB. Such a development may, for instance, be based on a novel summarization of CP information using vector clocks, or on the use of Binary Decision Diagrams to represent Datalog relations. (We could try the bddbddb engine [60] for this purpose.) A second possibility is that of defining other relations that weaken HB in a sound yet efficient way. Finally, we suspect the underlying notion of trace prediction, based on the causally-precedes relation, may also provide benefits when checking properties such as deadlock-freedom, atomicity, and determinism.

Acknowledgments

We would like to thank Aarti Gupta and the anonymous reviewers for their valuable comments that helped strengthen the paper. This work was funded by the National Science Foundation under grants CCF-0917774, CCF-0934631, and CCF-1116883. We thank LogicBlox Inc. for providing the platform used for our implementation and for continuous support.

References

[1] M. Abadi, C. Flanagan, and S. N. Freund. Types for safe locking: Static race detection for Java. *Transactions on Programming Languages and Systems (TOPLAS)*, 28(2):207–255, 2006.

[2] R. Agarwal, A. Sasturkar, L. Wang, and S. D. Stoller. Optimized runtime race detection and atomicity checking using partial discovered types. In *International Conference on Automated Software Engineering (ASE)*, 2005.

[3] A. Aiken and D. Gay. Barrier inference. In *Symposium on Principles of Programming Languages (POPL)*, 1998.

[4] D. F. Bacon, R. E. Strom, and A. Tarafdar. Guava: a dialect of Java without data races. In *Object-Oriented Programming, Systems, Languages, and Applications (OOPSLA)*, 2000.

[5] U. Banerjee, B. Bliss, Z. Ma, and P. Petersen. A theory of data race detection. In *Workshop on Parallel and Distributed Systems: Testing, Analysis, and Debugging (PADTAD)*, 2006.

[6] E. Bodden and K. Havelund. Racer: effective race detection using AspectJ. In *International Symposium on Software Testing and Analysis (ISSTA)*, 2008.

[7] M. D. Bond, K. E. Coons, and K. S. McKinley. PACER: proportional detection of data races. In *Conference on Programming Language Design and Implementation (PLDI)*, 2010.

[8] C. Boyapati, R. Lee, and M. Rinard. A type system for preventing data races and deadlocks in Java programs. In *Object-Oriented Programming, Systems, Languages, and Applications (OOPSLA)*, 2002.

[9] F. Chen and G. Roşu. Predicting concurrency errors at runtime using sliced causality. Technical Report UIUCDCS-R-2006-2965, Department of Computer Science, University of Illinois at Urbana-Champaign, 2006.

[10] F. Chen and G. Roşu. Parametric and Sliced Causality. In *Computer Aided Verification (CAV)*, 2007.

[11] F. Chen, T. F. Şerbănuţă, and G. Roşu. Effective predictive runtime analysis using sliced causality and atomicity. Technical Report UIUCDCS-R-2007-2905, University of Illinois at Urbana-Champaign, Department of Computer Science, October 2007.

[12] F. Chen, T. F. Şerbănuţă, and G. Roşu. jPredictor: a predictive runtime analysis tool for Java. In *International Conference on Software Engineering (ICSE)*, 2008.

[13] J.-D. Choi, K. Lee, A. Loginov, R. O'Callahan, V. Sarkar, and M. Sridhara. Efficient and precise datarace detection for multithreaded object-oriented programs. In *Conference on Programming Language Design and Implementation (PLDI)*, 2002.

[14] M. Christiaens and K. D. Bosschere. TRaDe: Data Race Detection for Java. In *International Conference on Computational Science*, 2001.

[15] A. Dinning and E. Schonberg. Detecting access anomalies in programs with critical sections. *SIGPLAN Notices*, 26(12):85–96, 1991.

[16] M. B. Dwyer and L. A. Clarke. Data flow analysis for verifying properties of concurrent programs. In *International Symposium on Foundations of Software Engineering (FSE)*, 1994.

[17] T. Elmas, S. Qadeer, and S. Tasiran. Goldilocks: a race and transaction-aware Java runtime. In *Conference on Programming Language Design and Implementation (PLDI)*, 2007.

[18] M. Emmi, S. Qadeer, and Z. Rakamarić. Delay-bounded scheduling. In *Symposium on Principles of Programming Languages (POPL)*, 2011.

[19] D. R. Engler and K. Ashcraft. RacerX: Effective, static detection of race conditions and deadlocks. In *ACM Symposium on Operating Systems Principles (SOSP)*, 2003.

[20] A. Farzan, P. Madhusudan, and F. Sorrentino. Meta-analysis for atomicity violations under nested locking. In *Computer Aided Verification (CAV)*, 2009.

[21] C. Flanagan and S. N. Freund. FastTrack: efficient and precise dynamic race detection. In *Conference on Programming Language Design and Implementation (PLDI)*, 2009.

[22] C. Flanagan and S. N. Freund. The roadrunner dynamic analysis framework for concurrent programs. In *PASTE*, pages 1–8, 2010.

[23] C. Flanagan, S. N. Freund, and J. Yi. Velodrome: A sound and complete dynamic atomicity checker for multithreaded programs. In *Conference on Programming Language Design and Implementation (PLDI)*, 2008.

[24] D. Grossman. Type-safe multithreading in Cyclone. In *Workshop on Types in Language Design and Implementation (TLDI)*, 2003.

[25] J. J. Harrow. Runtime checking of multithreaded applications with visual threads. In *International SPIN Workshop on Model Checking of Software*, 2000.

[26] D. P. Helmbold, C. E. McDowell, and J. zhong Wang. Detecting data races by analyzing sequential traces. In *HICCS-24, Hawaii Intl. Conference on System Sciences (HICCS-24)*, 1990.

[27] V. Kahlon, F. Ivančić, and A. Gupta. Reasoning about threads communicating via locks. In *Computer Aided Verification (CAV)*, 2005.

[28] V. Kahlon and C. Wang. Universal causality graphs: A precise happens-before model for detecting bugs in concurrent programs. In *Computer Aided Verification (CAV)*, 2010.

[29] S. K. Lahiri, S. Qadeer, and Z. Rakamarić. Static and precise detection of concurrency errors in systems code using smt solvers. In *Computer Aided Verification (CAV)*, 2009.

[30] L. Lamport. Time, clocks, and the ordering of events in a distributed system. *Communications of the ACM*, 21:558–565, July 1978.

[31] J. Manson, W. Pugh, and S. V. Adve. The Java memory model. In *Conference on Programming Language Design and Implementation (PLDI)*, 2005.

[32] J. M. Mellor-Crummey. On-the-fly detection of data races for programs with nested fork-join parallelism. In *Supercomputing*, 1991.

[33] M. Musuvathi, S. Qadeer, T. Ball, G. Basler, P. A. Nainar, and I. Neamtiu. Finding and reproducing heisenbugs in concurrent pro-

grams. In *Operating Systems Design and Implementation (OSDI)*, 2008.

[34] M. Naik, A. Aiken, and J. Whaley. Effective static race detection for Java. In *Conference on Programming Language Design and Implementation (PLDI)*, 2006.

[35] H. Nishiyama. Detecting data races using dynamic escape analysis based on read barrier. In *Virtual Machine Research and Technology Symposium (VM)*, 2004.

[36] R. O'Callahan and J.-D. Choi. Hybrid dynamic data race detection. In *Symposium on Principles and Practice of Parallel Programming (PPoPP)*, 2003.

[37] E. Pozniansky and A. Schuster. Efficient on-the-fly data race detection in multihreaded C++ programs. In *Symposium on Principles and Practice of Parallel Programming (PPoPP)*, 2003.

[38] E. Pozniansky and A. Schuster. Multirace: efficient on-the-fly data race detection in multithreaded C++ programs. *Concurrency and Computation: Practice and Experience*, 19(3):327–340, 2007.

[39] P. Pratikakis, J. S. Foster, and M. Hicks. Context-sensitive correlation analysis for detecting races. In *Conference on Programming Language Design and Implementation (PLDI)*, 2006.

[40] M. Said, C. Wang, Z. Yang, and K. Sakallah. Generating data race witnesses by an smt-based analysis. In *NASA Formal Methods Symposium*, pages 313–327. Springer, 2011.

[41] A. Sasturkar, R. Agarwal, L. Wang, and S. D. Stoller. Automated type-based analysis of data races and atomicity. In *Symposium on Principles and Practice of Parallel Programming (PPoPP)*, 2005.

[42] S. Savage, M. Burrows, G. Nelson, P. Sobalvarro, and T. Anderson. Eraser: a dynamic data race detector for multi-threaded programs. In *ACM Symposium on Operating Systems Principles (SOSP)*, 1997.

[43] E. Schonberg. On-the-fly detection of access anomalies. In *Conference on Programming Language Design and Implementation (PLDI)*, 1989.

[44] K. Sen. Race directed random testing of concurrent programs. In *Conference on Programming Language Design and Implementation (PLDI)*, 2008.

[45] K. Sen and G. Agha. Detecting errors in multithreaded programs by generalized predictive analysis of executions. In *IIFIP International Conference on Formal Methods for Open Object-Based Distributed Systems (FMOODS)*, 2005.

[46] K. Sen, G. Rosu, and G. Agha. Online efficient predictive safety analysis of multithreaded programs. *International Journal on Software Technology and Tools Transfer (STTT)*, 8(3):248–260, 2006.

[47] T. F. Şerbănuţă, F. Chen, and G. Roşu. Maximal causal models for multithreaded systems. Technical Report UIUCDCS-R-2008-3017, University of Illinois at Urbana-Champaign, Department of Computer Science, December 2008.

[48] N. Sinha and C. Wang. On interference abstractions. In *Symposium on Principles of Programming Languages (POPL)*, 2011.

[49] F. Sorrentino, A. Farzan, and P. Madhusudan. PENELOPE: weaving threads to expose atomicity violations. In *International Symposium on Foundations of Software Engineering (FSE)*, 2010.

[50] N. Sterling. Warlock: A static data race analysis tool. In *USENIX Winter Technical Conference*, 1993.

[51] The Apache Software Foundation. Apache FtpServer. Available at `http://mina.apache.org/ftpserver/`, 2009.

[52] The Apache Software Foundation. Apache JMeter. Available at `http://jakarta.apache.org/jmeter/`, 2009.

[53] The World Wide Web Consortium. Jigsaw Web Server. Available from `http://www.w3.org/Jigsaw/`, 2009.

[54] C. von Praun and T. Gross. Static conflict analysis for multi-threaded object-oriented programs. In *Conference on Programming Language Design and Implementation (PLDI)*, 2003.

[55] C. von Praun and T. R. Gross. Object race detection. In *Object-Oriented Programming, Systems, Languages, and Applications (OOPSLA)*, 2001.

[56] J. W. Voung, R. Jhala, and S. Lerner. Relay: static race detection on millions of lines of code. In *International Symposium on Foundations of Software Engineering (FSE)*, 2007.

[57] C. Wang, S. Kundu, M. Ganai, and A. Gupta. Symbolic predictive analysis for concurrent programs. In *World Congress on Formal Methods (FM)*, 2009.

[58] C. Wang, R. Limaye, M. Ganai, and A. Gupta. Trace-based symbolic analysis for atomicity violations. In *Tools and Algorithms for the Construction and Analysis of Systems (TACAS)*, 2010.

[59] L. Wang and S. D. Stoller. Accurate and efficient runtime detection of atomicity errors in concurrent programs. In *Symposium on Principles and Practice of Parallel Programming (PPoPP)*, 2006.

[60] J. Whaley. *Context-Sensitive Pointer Analysis using Binary Decision Diagrams*. PhD thesis, Stanford University, Mar. 2007.

[61] Y. Yu. RaceTrack: Efficient detection of data race conditions via adaptive tracking. In *ACM Symposium on Operating Systems Principles (SOSP)*, 2005.

Appendix: Soundness Proof

Theorem (CP is Sound). Given a trace tr with a CP-race, we can produce a $tr'' =_{CR} tr$ with either an HB-race or a deadlock.

Proof. Let the first race of trace tr be between events e_1 and e_2, with e_1 appearing before e_2 in the trace. Being the first race means that there is no CP-race between two events both of which appear before e_2, as well as no race between events e_3-e_2, with e_3 appearing after e_1 and before e_2.

Consider a trace tr' such that:

- $tr' =_{CR} tr$ and tr' has the same first CP-race as tr, i.e., between events $e_1 = [t_1 : u_1]_i$ and $e_2 = [t_2 : u_2]_j$, with $i < j$. (With i and j the indices of the events in trace tr'.)
- Among traces satisfying the above property, tr' has minimal distance $j - i$ between events e_1 and e_2 of the first CP-race. (Intuitively, this means that all irrelevant events between e_1 and e_2 are correctly-reordered out of the e_1-e_2 segment in trace tr'.)
- Among traces that satisfy the above properties, tr' is one that also minimizes the distance between e_2 and every beginning of a critical section containing e_1, from innermost to outermost. That is, among traces that have the same (minimal) distance between e_2 and the innermost acquisition event k_1 for a critical section containing e_1, tr' minimizes the distance between e_2 and the second such lock acquire, among those satisfying all the above tr' minimizes the distance between e_2 and the third such lock acquire, k_3, and so on, all the way to the outermost critical section containing e_1.

We will refer to the last two requirements as *the minimality property*. For such a trace tr', we get important lemmas:

Lemma 1. All events e between e_1 and e_2 are such that

(a) $e_1 \ll_{HB} e$ and $e \ll_{HB} e_2$
(b) $e_1 \not\ll_{CP} e$ and $e \not\ll_{CP} e_2$.

Proof. We prove each case separately.

(a) • Assume $e \not\ll_{HB} e_2$. Then we can move e and all events e' that occur between e and e_2 such that $e \ll_{HB} e'$ to the point right after e_2. The result of the move maintains program order. (Note that thread t_2 is not affected by the move at all, since we have already assumed that $e \not\ll_{HB} e_2$, therefore e cannot happen-before any previous event in t_2.) If this move (or any move in later proofs) is not possible it is because of one of two reasons:

- It causes the result to not be a trace because the pairing of lock acquisition/releases becomes invalid (i.e., a lock is acquired while held).

- The result is a valid trace t but $t \neq_{CR} tr'$ because a read now sees a different written value.

The former means that the moved events have a common lock with some non-moved event (say, f) that occurs before e_2—an impossibility since in this case $e \ll_{HB} f$, hence f would be a moved event. The latter reason is also an impossibility since then a moved event would conflict with a non-moved event, f. If the two events were CP-ordered, then they would also be HB ordered, hence f would have moved. If the events were not CP-ordered then e_1-e_2 would not have been the first race of tr'. Hence the move is possible, which violates the first minimality property, therefore our assumption was false and $e \ll_{HB} e_2$.

- If $e_1 \not\ll_{HB} e$, then we can move e and all events e' that occur between e_1 and e such that $e' \ll_{HB} e$ to right before e_1. Again, with similar reasoning as above (or as in Lemma 2, below) we get a contradiction.

(b) If either $e_1 \ll_{CP} e$ or $e \ll_{CP} e_2$, then we would have had $e_1 \ll_{CP} e_2$, per part (a) and the definition of CP: a contradiction. □

Lemma 2. Consider any lock acquire event a_1 for a critical section containing e_1. All events e between a_1 (inclusive) and e_1 have $a_1 \ll_{HB} e$ and if $e1 \ll_{HB} e2$ then $e \ll_{HB} e_2$.

Proof. Assume $a_1 \not\ll_{HB} e$. Let E be the set of operations made up of e and all e' that occur between a_1 and e such that $e' \ll_{HB} e$. Note that set E cannot contain any events from thread t_1, or else $a_1 \ll_{HB} e$. Try to move all operations in E to right before a_1. If the move is not possible, it is either because these moved events have a common lock with some non-moved event, f (a contradiction, since then $f \ll_{HB} e$, and f would be moved) or that the moved events conflict with a non-moved event (also a contradiction since it would imply a race before e_1-e_2 or a CP relation, which violates the assumption of no-HB between a_1 and the moved events). Therefore, moving E before a_1 is possible, and the result of the move maintains intra-thread order. However, moving E violates the minimality property of tr'.

The fact that ($e \ll_{HB} e_2$) follows from similar reasoning as in Lemma 1, but uses the assumption that $e1 \ll_{HB} e2$ to establish that $e1$ is not among the moved events. □

Lemma 3. Any conflicting events that both occur before e_2, or with one being e_2 and the other occurring after e_1 and before e_2, have to be CP-ordered.

Proof. Otherwise we trivially have a CP-race earlier than e_1-e_2. □

Lemma 4. Consider any lock acquire event a_1 for a critical section containing e_1. If a critical section $c...c'$ starts before event a_1 and ends after a_1 and before e_1 then $a_1 \ll_{CP} c'$.

Proof. By induction.

Base case: Consider the $c...c'$ that ends the soonest after a_1 (among all such $c...c'$ that satisfy the stated conditions). Assume that $a_1 \not\ll_{CP} c'$. By the well-nesting of lock operations, such a critical section $c...c'$ cannot be performed by thread t_1.
Let d be the first event after a_1 in this critical section. We will try to move $d...c'$ to the point right before a_1, respecting intra-thread order. If the move is successful it violates the minimality of tr', hence the move must be illegal because it violates some property of CR or of the definition of a trace. Therefore, the move must be illegal for either of the usual two reasons:

1. It causes the result to not be a trace because the pairing of lock acquisition/releases becomes invalid (i.e., a lock is acquired while held).
2. The result is a valid trace t but $t \neq_{CR} tr'$ because a read now sees a different written value.

For case (1), the moved events cannot be acquiring a lock held by thread t_1 at position a_1, since that lock would not be released before e_1. If the lock were held by a thread other than t_1, we have a critical section with the stated properties for $c...c'$ that ends before the currently considered $c...c'$, which is impossible. Case (2) means that the moved events conflict with some non-moved event that occurs after a_1. This non-moved event e'' has to CP the moved event it conflicts with (by Lemma 3). But from Lemma 2 we have $a_1 \ll_{HB} e''$ and therefore $a_1 \ll_{CP} c'$.

Inductive case: the argument is identical to the base case, except in case (1) when we consider the possibility that a lock that needs to be acquired by the moved events is held by a thread other than t_1. In this case, we have an earlier critical section $g...g'$ with the stated properties, and therefore $a_1 \ll_{CP} g'$, by the inductive assumption. But since our $c...c'$ acquires the same lock, we get the desired $a_1 \ll_{CP} c'$. □

Lemma 5. There cannot be a critical section by a thread other than t_2 that starts after event e_1 and before e_2, and ends after event e_2.

Proof. Assume that such critical sections exist. Among them pick the $c...c'$ that starts last, i.e., closest to e_2. Let d be the last event before e_2 of this critical section. We have two cases:

1. If $c...d$ does not contains nested critical sections inside it, we can move all events $c...d$ to the point right after e_2. The proof is similar to that of Lemma 4. The move respects intra-thread ordering. Also the moved events cannot be acquiring a lock held at point e_2. (There are no nested critical sections in the moved events, and the lock acquired by event c is still held at e_2.) Furthermore, the resulting trace is a correct reordering of the original because if it were not we would then have a conflict between events whose relative position changes, i.e., between the moved events and non-moved events. But in that case there would be a CP edge originating in $c...d$ to an event before e_2 (by Lemma 3) and since c is between e_1 and e_2 we would get (using Lemma 1) $e_1 \ll_{CP} e_2$ (a contradiction).
2. If $c...d$ does contain critical sections, let $g...g'$ be the one ending last before e_2. Consider an event sequence produced as follows:
   - we drop all events starting from (and including) g of that thread
   - we drop all events after e_2 by all other threads.

   Clearly the result is a prefix of tr'. If it is a legal trace that correctly reorders tr' then we are violating the minimality of tr'. In the resulting event sequence there cannot be an event acquiring a lock already held: the only dropped lock release events are either after e_2 (in which case subsequent lock acquisitions are also dropped), or are dropped together with their lock acquisition event (in the case of $g...g'$ events). Note that if there is a critical section inside $c...c'$ that starts before $g...g'$, it has to also end before g, or it would violate the definition of either $g...g'$ or $c...c'$. Also, no read can see a different write, or this would imply a conflict between a dropped event after g and another before e_2. In such a case we would have a CP ordering, per Lemma 3 and $e_1 \ll_{CP} e_2$, as before. We conclude that the resulting trace correctly reorders tr' and violates its minimality assumption: a contradiction.

□

Armed with these lemmas about trace tr' we can now attempt to prove the soundness theorem. We will show that tr' either has an HB race (in fact, e_1 and e_2 have to be adjacent in this minimal trace) or, if not, the trace exposes a deadlock which can be caused by a slightly reordered trace.

Clearly, if e_1-e_2 is an HB race in tr' then we are done. Assume it is not. We will try to CR-reorder tr' so that one of the minimality properties is violated (which is a contradiction). Consider the first event f such that:

- f is performed by a thread other than t_1
- f occurs after e_1 and before e_2.

Such an event needs to exist if e_1-e_2 are HB-ordered. Furthermore, by Lemma 1, $e_1 \ll_{HB} f$, and since f is the first such event in any thread other than t_1, it needs to be a lock acquire. Consider then the critical section $f...f'$. There are two cases:

1. f' occurs before e_2. Let $f...f'$ be over lock l. We get two subcases:
   (a) l is not held by t_1 during e_1.
   Since $e_1 \ll_{HB} f$ and f is the first such event outside t_1, there must be a critical section over l after e_1 and before f. Let g be the lock acquire event of that critical section. g has to be an event by thread t_1, otherwise the definition of f would be violated (there would be another "first" event). Also, g has to be after e_1, by our assumption that l is not held during e_1. Consider a move of $f...f'$ to right before point g. The move respects intra-thread order. Also, if a read sees a different write then a moved event must conflict with one of the non-moved events after g, hence (Lemma 3) we have some e'' such that $e'' \ll_{CP} f'$. But we have $e_1 \ll_{HB} e''$ (by Lemma 1), $e'' \ll_{CP} f'$, and $f' \ll_{HB} e_2$ (by Lemma 1), hence $e_1 \ll_{CP} e_2$: a contradiction.
   Finally, the move may cause a lock, m, to be acquired while being held: this means a critical section acquiring and releasing that lock is inside $f...f'$. (Assume w.l.o.g. that m is the first such lock.) If m is held at point g by a thread t_3, other than t_1, then it has to be released before f, violating the definition of f (since there is a different first event after e_1 by a thread other than t_1).
   A more interesting case is when lock m is held at point g by thread t_1. In that case, lock l is nested inside lock m in thread t_1 (because l is acquired at position g with m held) and lock m is nested inside lock l in thread t_2. We can cause a deadlock by moving a prefix of the $f...f'$ critical section (up until the lock m acquisition) to point g. Therefore the move of $f...f'$ to point g either produces a legal trace t such that $t =_{CR} tr'$, or exposes a deadlock. The move can be repeated until there are no more critical sections over lock l between e_1 and $f...f'$. At that point, we can just move event f to right before e_1. This would produce a correctly reordered trace that violates the minimality of tr': a contradiction.
   We conclude that if Case 1(a) occurs, there is always a deadlock in a correct reordering of trace tr'.
   (b) l is held by t_1 during e_1.

   Let a_2 be the last lock acquisition event of lock l before e_1. Consider a move of $f...f'$ and all previous events by the same thread after a_2 to right before point a_2. Let a_2' be the lock release paired with a_2. The move respects intra-thread order. Also, if a read sees a different write then a moved event must conflict with one of the non-moved events after a_2, hence (by Lemma 3) we have some e'' such that $e'' \ll_{CP} e'$, where e' is a moved event, and therefore $e'' \ll_{CP} f'$ (since all the moved events precede f' and are by the same thread). But (by Lemma 2) we have $a_2 \ll_{HB} e''$ and therefore $a_2 \ll_{CP} f'$. Since, however, the critical sections starting at a_2 and ending at f' are over the same lock l, we get that $a_2' \ll_{CP} f'$, because of the second rule in the CP definition. This implies $e_1 \ll_{CP} e_2$ (since e_1 is before a_2', by assumption of case 1(b), and $f' \ll_{HB} e_2$, by Lemma 1): a contradiction.
   Finally, we consider the case of the move being illegal because it causes a lock, m, to be acquired while being held. If such an m is held by a thread t_3, other than t_1, at point a_2, then it has to be released before e_1 (otherwise the release event would violate the definition of f, since it would come before it, after e_1 and by a thread other than t_1). This means that Lemma 4 applies to the critical section of that thread. Hence, we have that $a_2 \ll_{CP} h'$, where h' is m's release event in t_3. But since h' happens-before some moved event (since the moved events acquire lock m), we get $e_1 \ll_{CP} f'$ (again, all moved events are program-ordered with f') and consequently (via Lemma 1) $e_1 \ll_{CP} e_2$: a contradiction.
   If lock m is held at position a_2 by thread t_1, then l is nested inside m in thread t_1, while m is nested inside l in the thread performing $f...f'$. (The lock acquisition of m by that thread cannot be before f since the lock is released after e_1 and f is the first event after e_1 by a thread other than t_1. Therefore m is acquired and released inside critical section $f...f'$.) As before, we can cause a deadlock by moving a prefix of the $f...f'$ critical section (and any earlier events after a_2 by the same thread) to a_2.
   Therefore, this case again implies a deadlock in a reordering of trace tr'.
2. f' occurs after e_2.
   We then have by Lemma 5 that $f...f'$ has to be performed by thread t_2. Let $f...f'$ be over lock l. Lock l cannot be held by t_1 during event e_1, or $e_1 \ll_{CP} e_2$. Therefore, there must be some critical section $g...g'$ over l, performed by thread t_1 after e_1, such that $g' \ll_{HB} f$. (Recall that f is the first event after e_1 by a thread other than t_1.) Assume w.l.o.g. that $g...g'$ is the last such critical section.
   Consider an event sequence produced as follows:
   - we drop g and all events e' after g by a thread other than t_2.
   - we drop all events after e_2 by all threads.

   Clearly the result is a prefix of tr'. If it is a legal trace that correctly reorders tr' then we are violating the minimality of tr'. Therefore the result of this event drop has to be illegal. The drop respects intra-thread order. Also, if a read sees a different write then a dropped event must conflict with one of the non-dropped events before e_2. By Lemma 3 we get a CP edge between events after e_1 and before e_2 in tr', and by Lemma 1 and CP properties we have $e_1 \ll_{CP} e_2$: a contradiction.
   Thus, the event sequence cannot be a trace: a lock has to be acquired while held. Such a lock, m, has to be acquired before one of the dropped events, with its release among the dropped events. The lock is then re-acquired by one of the non-dropped events, i.e., by thread t_2. The acquisition of m has to be in thread t_1 (otherwise f would not be the first event between e_1 and e_2 by a thread other than t_1). In thread t_1, for trace tr', lock l has to be nested inside m (since dropping every event after g, which is an acquisition of l, caused the drop of the release but not the acquisition of m). However, lock m is nested inside l in thread t_2, since it is acquired after l's acquisition (point f) and before l's release (which occurs after e_2). We can again cause a deadlock with an event move (of a prefix of $f...e_2$).

This concludes the proof of the theorem: any CP race implies either an HB race in the minimal trace tr', or a deadlock in a reordered trace. □

Towards Nominal Computation

Mikołaj Bojańczyk * Laurent Braud † Bartek Klin Sławomir Lasota ‡

University of Warsaw

{bojan,klin,sl}@mimuw.edu.pl, laurent.braud@labri.fr

Abstract

Nominal sets are a different kind of set theory, with a more relaxed notion of finiteness. They offer an elegant formalism for describing λ-terms modulo α-conversion, or automata on data words.

This paper is an attempt at defining computation in nominal sets. We present a rudimentary programming language, called Nλ. The key idea is that it includes a native type for finite sets in the nominal sense. To illustrate the power of our language, we write short programs that process automata on data words.

Categories and Subject Descriptors D.3.3 [*Programming Languages*]: Language Constructs and Features; F.3.2 [*Logic and Meanings of Programs*]: Semantics of Programming Languages

General Terms Theory

Keywords λ-calculus, nominal sets, automata on data words

1. Introduction

The theory of nominal sets originates from the work of Fraenkel in 1922, further developed by Mostowski in the 1930s. At that time, nominal sets were used to prove independence of the axiom of choice and other axioms. In Computer Science, they have been rediscovered by Gabbay and Pitts in [11], as an elegant formalism for modeling name binding. Since then, nominal sets have become a lively topic in semantics. They were also independently rediscovered by the concurrency community, as a basis for syntax-free models of name-passing process calculi, see [14, 16]; and used in automata theory as a framework for describing automata on data words, see [3].

From the point of view of this paper, the most appealing feature of nominal sets is that their natural notion of finiteness, called *orbit-finiteness*, is more relaxed than in classical set theory. For instance, in one variant of nominal sets (the notion of variant is formalized later in the paper as a *data symmetry*), the set of rational numbers is orbit-finite.

Using orbit-finiteness, one can define more powerful variants of automata or other computing devices. As an example, take the standard definition of a nondeterministic finite automaton: it consists of finite sets Q and A for the states and alphabet, as well as three relations $\delta \subseteq Q \times A \times Q$ and $I, F \subseteq Q$. Suppose that we read this definition using orbit-finite sets instead. As proved in [3], the resulting objects have the same expressive power as well-known automata for data words, namely Finite Memory Automata of Francez and Kaminski [10]. The same idea can be applied to other computation models such as monoids [2], deterministic automata [3], two-way automata, pebble automata, or pushdown automata. Each time, the nominal model corresponds to a natural device for data words.

The examples above concerned restricted machine models, with the most expressive being pushdown automata. In this paper, we are interested in general nominal computation, and we attempt to understand it by defining a basic programming language called Nλ, designed so that it can directly process orbit-finite nominal sets. The key idea is that it includes a native type $\mathsf{F_n}\alpha$, which represents orbit-finite sets of elements of type α.

Structure of the paper. The paper has three parts. In Part I, we discuss our design objectives and related work, and show some example problems that our language can help solve. In Part II, we define the syntax and operational semantics of Nλ. The language is parametrized by a data symmetry subject to some conditions. We also show how to represent programs of Nλ so that they can be interpreted on a normal machine. Finally, in Part III, we present a substantial case study: the emptiness problem for alternating automata on data words.

Acknowledgment. We are grateful to Andrew Pitts, Dan Ghica, Paweł Urzyczyn and the anonymous referees, whose constructive comments lead to a great improvement of the presentation of this paper.

Part I: Motivation

2. Design objective for Nλ: avoid coding

Suppose, informally, that we want to design an algorithm that processes possibly infinite, but orbit-finite data structures. As a typical example, let I be the set of nondeterministic finite automata in the nominal sense. In such an automaton all components (states, alphabet, transitions, initial and final states) are orbit-finite, but perhaps infinite in the classical sense. Then consider the function $f : I \to \{\top, \bot\}$ that checks if an automaton accepts some word.

* Partially supported by ERC Starting Grant Sosna.

† Partially supported by the ESF *Games for Design and Verification* exchange grant nr 3070, and by the FET grant FOX, number FP7-ICT-233599.

‡ Partially supported by the Polish Ministry of Science grant nr N N206 567840.

POPL'12, January 25–27, 2012, Philadelphia, PA, USA.

One way to compute such a function is to encode orbit-finite sets as finite data structures (and, implicitly, bit strings). In [3, 16], one can essentially find such representations. Applying such a coding to the problem domain, one can reduce a nominal computational problem to a classical one. The resulting notion of computability depends on the coding scheme, but the schemes implicit in the literature are essentially the same, and the small differences can be corrected by Turing machines.

This approach has been implicitly used in the literature when giving decidability results for decision problems in nominal sets. One example is an algorithm [7] for deciding bisimulation equivalence of orbit-finite transitions systems. Some algorithms for problems from automata theory can be found in [3], including the above example of nondeterministic automata. Another example is the algorithm from [2] for deciding if the language recognized by a given data monoid is first-order definable.

An advantage of this approach is that it does not introduce any new concepts; it just treats nominal sets as syntactic sugar for normal sets. In particular, there is no new "Nominal Church-Turing Thesis". The very same thing can be seen as a disadvantage: it is a clumsy way of doing computation, and it defeats the purpose of using nominal sets as an attractive syntax.

Nλ is a rudimentary functional programming language that abstracts away from the clumsy details. The design goal for Nλ can be summed up in two words: *avoid coding*. The abstract semantics of the language is defined in terms of nominal sets, and does not refer to any coding scheme. In particular, this means that correctness proofs for programs in Nλ are simpler and more convincing. The language comes with a more concrete semantics which implements a coding, therefore any function expressed in Nλ is effectively computable. However, the coding has to be done only once, as it is done in this paper. Once it has been implemented and proved correct, the programmer can simply use the language without thinking about how nominal objects are represented.

Related work. A closely related language is Fresh O'Caml [17, 18], a functional programming language based on nominal sets, aimed at defining and manipulating data structures with binding, such as λ-terms up to α-conversion. It is similar to Nλ in that both can be seen as typed λ-calculi with some additional type and term constructors. However, these extensions are substantially different.

A crucial ingredient of Fresh O'Caml is a binary type constructor <<α>>β, whose values, intuitively, are values of type β with values of type α (typically basic data values, called names in this context) "abstracted", or bound. These abstraction types, together with a few other primitives, allow a particularly elegant treatment of α-conversion and capture-avoiding substitution in data structures.

Nλ does not have abstraction types; instead, it has a type constructor F_n to represent finitary collections. In Section 15, we show that Nλ also offers a way to treat binding in data structures, albeit in a slightly less direct and appealing way than Fresh O'Caml. However, binding in data structures is just one of the many things that we can do using our language. Also, our language works not just in standard nominal sets, but also in the more general setting of Fraïssé nominal sets [3].

Another difference with Fresh O'Caml is that the latter is a fully grown programming language, with a working compiler and extensive documentation. On the other hand, Nλ is a rudimentary core language, and a work in progress. We have tried to keep the primitives as simple as possible, while still covering a wide range of examples. We make no claim on universality of the language, and it is likely to evolve. However, it seems that our current version of Nλ is a rather expressive formalism. In Section 4, we survey some functions that can be expressed in it. First, however, we formally define nominal sets and related notions.

3. Nominal sets

We now recall the basics of nominal sets as studied by Gabbay and Pitts [11]. Then, in Section 3.1, we generalize the definitions along the lines of [3].

Data values. Fix a countably infinite set $\mathbb{D}$ of *data values*. In the examples below, we assume $\mathbb{D} = \mathbb{N}$, and write $1, 2, 3$ for elements of $\mathbb{D}$. However, no structure of the data values is used except for equality[1]. A *permutation* of $\mathbb{D}$ is any bijection $\mathbb{D} \to \mathbb{D}$. The group of all permutations will be denoted by G.

Nominal sets. A *right action* of G on a set X is a function $\cdot : X \times G \to X$ subject to the following associativity axioms (we use infix notation, writing $x \cdot \pi$ instead of $\cdot(x, \pi)$):

$$x \cdot (\pi\sigma) = (x \cdot \pi) \cdot \sigma \qquad x \cdot 1 = x,$$

where $\pi\sigma$ refers to multiplication in G and 1 is the unit of G, which is the identity function on $\mathbb{D}$.

Every subset of data values $C \subseteq \mathbb{D}$ defines a subgroup of G,

$$G_C = \{\pi \in G : \pi|_C = id_C\}.$$

A *nominal set* is a set X equipped with a right action of G, such that for every $x \in X$, there is a finite set $C \subseteq \mathbb{D}$ such that

$$x = x \cdot \pi \qquad \text{for every } \pi \in G_C.$$

The set C is then called a *support* of x. In words, every element of a nominal set has a finite support.

For example, consider the set $\mathbb{D}^\omega$ of infinite words over the alphabet of data values. Under the coordinatewise action

$$(d_1, d_2, \ldots) \cdot \pi = (\pi(d_1), \pi(d_2), \ldots).$$

every word w is supported by the set C of all letters that appear in w. The set $\mathbb{D}^\omega$ is not nominal, but the subset of words that contain only finitely many different data values is. Also the smaller set $\mathbb{D}^*$ of finite words is nominal.

Orbit-finite sets. The *orbit* of an element x is the set $x \cdot G \stackrel{\text{def}}{=} \{x \cdot \pi : \pi \in G\}$. A nominal set is called *orbit-finite* if it is a finite union of orbits, i.e. it has a decomposition

$$X = \bigcup_{i=1}^{n} x_i \cdot G \qquad \text{for some } x_1, \ldots, x_n \in X.$$

For example, the set $\mathbb{D}$ is orbit-finite (with one orbit). The set $\mathbb{D}^2$ has two orbits, namely the diagonal $\{(d, d) : d \in \mathbb{D}\}$ and the rest.

Nominal subsets. A subset Y of a nominal set X is called a *nominal subset of* X if it has a finite support as an element of the powerset of X. Formally, a finite set $C \subseteq \mathbb{D}$ is a support of Y if

$$Y = Y \cdot \pi \stackrel{\text{def}}{=} \{y \cdot \pi : y \in Y\} \qquad \text{for every } \pi \in G_C.$$

For example, nominal subsets of $\mathbb{D}$ are its finite or cofinite subsets.

Example 1 For a fixed $d \in \mathbb{D}$, the set $\{(d, e) : e \in \mathbb{D}\}$ is a nominal subset of $\mathbb{D}^2$.

Finitary subsets. A nominal subset Y of X is called *finitary* if it intersects finitely many orbits of X. In particular, if X is orbit-finite (for instance $\mathbb{D}$ or $\mathbb{D}^2$) then all its nominal subsets are finitary. As another example, the set of words of length at most 7 where the data value 6 appears at least twice is a finitary subset of $\mathbb{D}^*$.

Finitary subsets are the foundation of our programming language. We write $\mathsf{F}_n X$ for the family of finitary subsets of a nominal set X. In a nutshell, Nλ is simply typed λ-calculus with a type constructor for finitary subsets.

[1] We will add structure to data values in Section 3.1.

3.1 Generalized nominal sets

The centerpiece example of our paper is an algorithm for deciding emptiness of alternating automata in the nominal world. In its full generality, this example may exploit some nontrivial structure (e.g. an order relation) on the set $\mathbb{D}$. This motivates us to work in the framework of *generalized nominal sets*, introduced in [3]. The idea there was to add more structure to the data values $\mathbb{D}$, such as a total or partial order. For automata, this corresponds to more expressive tests on input letters.

To define generalized nominal sets, one begins with a *data symmetry* (called nominal signature in [3]), i.e., a set $\mathbb{D}$ of data values together with a group G of permutations of $\mathbb{D}$. It is important that G need not contain all permutations. Some examples of data symmetries include:

- The *classical symmetry*, where $\mathbb{D}$ is empty, and G contains only the empty bijection. This symmetry yields classical sets.
- The *equality symmetry*, where $\mathbb{D}$ is a countably infinite set, and G contains all bijections. This symmetry yields nominal sets as studied by Gabbay and Pitts.
- The *total order symmetry*, where $\mathbb{D}$ is the set of rational numbers, and G contains all order-preserving bijections of rational numbers.

Later on we will define further data symmetries. Importantly, all examples in this paper are so-called Fraïssé symmetries; this notion follows [3] and will be explained in Section 7.

Given a data symmetry $(\mathbb{D}, G)$, one defines $(\mathbb{D}, G)$*-nominal sets* exactly as in Section 3, except with the group G and the data values $\mathbb{D}$ substituted in place of the equality symmetry. Similarly one defines the related notions, like nominal and finitary subsets. From now on, the notion of a nominal set will always be parametrized by a data symmetry.

3.2 Example: subsets of $\mathbb{D}^2$

We now show examples of finitary subsets in the total order symmetry. All examples given here will be subsets of $\mathbb{D}^2$, which is shown in the following picture, with the first coordinate on the horizontal axis and the second coordinate on the vertical axis[2].

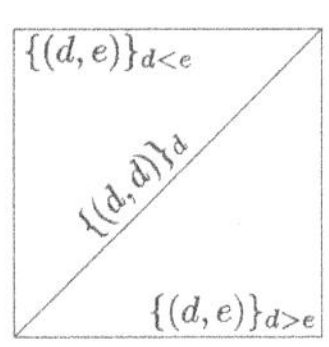

The picture also shows the three orbits of $\mathbb{D}^2$ under the action of G: above the diagonal, the diagonal, and below the diagonal. Because $\mathbb{D}^2$ is orbit-finite, any nominal subset will be finitary. Consider a support $C = \{0.3\}$. Under the action of G_C, the set $\mathbb{D}^2$ breaks up into thirteen orbits. A subset $X \subseteq \mathbb{D}^2$ has support C if and only if it is a union of some of these orbits. The partition of $\mathbb{D}^2$ into orbits under G_C and a subset X are illustrated below.

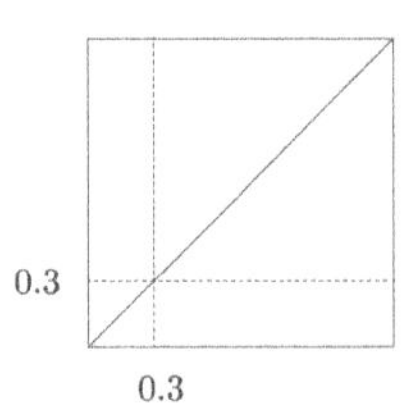

$X =$

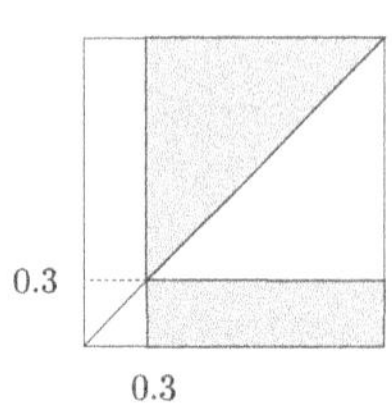

[2] The reader might recognize some similarity to the region construction from timed automata.

Consider now a bigger support than C, say $D = \{0.3, 27.6\}$. The partition of $\mathbb{D}^2$ into orbits under G_D is more refined (there are thirty one orbits), as G_D is a subgroup of G_C. In particular, there are more subsets with support D. The partition and an example subset Y are illustrated below.

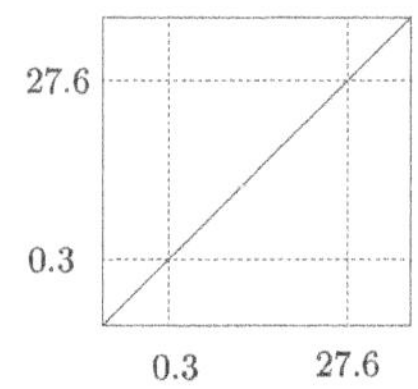

$Y =$

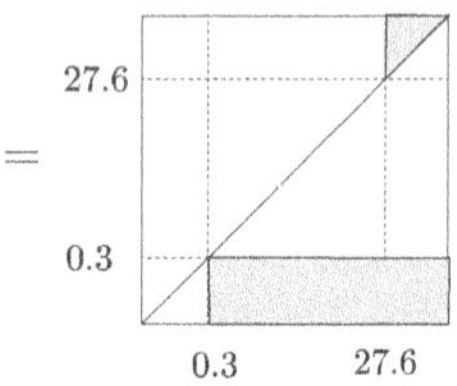

The reader can easily see that as the support grows, so does the number of subsets with the support. Also observe that it does not make sense to count the number of "elements" in a finitary set, because the number of elements depends on the choice of support. Even if we choose the least support when counting the number of elements, there is still some room for confusion. Observe that the example set Y has least support D, but it can be decomposed into one orbit under G_C and one orbit under G_D.

4. Nλ as an algorithmic toolkit

Equipped with the basic notions of nominal sets, we discuss some functions that can be programmed in Nλ. In all examples except Section 4.3, we work with the equality symmetry only.

4.1 Transitive closure of a binary relation.

Consider the following binary relation on $\mathbb{D}$

$$R = \{(5,2)\} \cup \{(2,d) : d \neq 5\} \subseteq \mathbb{D}^2.$$

The set R has support $\{2,5\}$. The set $\mathbb{D}^2$ has two orbits, namely the diagonal and the rest. It follows that R, like any nominal subset of $\mathbb{D}^2$, is a finitary subset of $\mathbb{D}^2$, and therefore can be input and processed by programs of Nλ.

A typical thing one might want to do with a binary relation is compute its transitive closure. In this particular example, the transitive closure is

$$R^* = \{(c,d) : c \in \{2,5\},\ d \neq 5\}.$$

Note that R^* is a finitary subset of $\mathbb{D}^2$; one can prove that this holds whenever R is finitary. Also, we may write a recursive program in Nλ that inputs a finitary binary relation R over some type α and outputs its transitive closure. In our example the type α is $\mathbb{D}$, but the program works also for types that are not orbit-finite, such as lists of $\mathbb{D}$. The only condition is that α is an equality type, admitting an equality predicate eq_α.

4.2 Data monoids.

A *data monoid*, as defined in [2], is a monoid where the carrier is a nominal set, and the monoid operation is equivariant. The main result of [2] was a theorem that related first-order logic with aperiodic data monoids. However, nowhere in the paper was it said how one can represent a data monoid in a computer, or test if it is aperiodic. Nλ can help with this.

For example, consider the data monoid M where the carrier is $\{\epsilon\} \cup \mathbb{D}^2$, the identity is ϵ, and the monoid operation is defined by

$$\begin{aligned} \epsilon \cdot m = m \cdot \epsilon = m \qquad & \text{for all } m \in M \text{ and} \\ (d,e) \cdot (d',e') = (d,e') \qquad & \text{for all } d,e,d',e' \in \mathbb{D} \end{aligned}$$

This is the syntactic monoid of the language

$$\{d_1 \cdots d_n \in \mathbb{D}^+ : d_1 = d_n\}.$$

The carrier of this monoid can be seen as the finitary subset of $\mathbb{D}$ `list` that contains lists of sizes zero or two. This set can be represented in Nλ by a short piece of code. The identity of the monoid M is the empty list, while the monoid operation can be easily implemented, using pattern matching, as a function

$$\mathtt{f} : \mathbb{D}\,\mathtt{list} \times \mathbb{D}\,\mathtt{list} \to \mathbb{D}\,\mathtt{list}.$$

(As far as the example monoid is concerned, it is not important what `f` does for lists of lengths other than zero or two.)

Using Nλ we can test some properties of monoids represented in this fashion. For instance, we can write a polymorphic function that inputs a finitary set M of values of type α and a binary operation `f` on α, and checks whether `f` is idempotent when restricted to M (in our example, $\alpha = \mathbb{D}\,\mathtt{list}$). In the same spirit, we can write functions that test if a data monoid is aperiodic, commutative, etc.

4.3 Alternating automata with one register

In the literature on data words, there are many automata models, often of incomparable expressive power. One of the maximally expressive automaton models that still has decidable emptiness is an alternating automaton with one register. Roughly speaking, this is an alternating automaton which can store a single data value in a register. Emptiness is decidable for this automaton model, with a proof based on well quasi-orders [6].

In Part III of this paper, we encode the emptiness test for alternating automata with one register into Nλ. To do this, we provide an abstract definition of alternating automata with one register, a definition that only uses the concepts of nominal sets. Then we write a program in Nλ which tests a given automaton for emptiness.

An important advantage of our abstract definition of automata is that it is meaningful for any data symmetry. If the definition is interpreted in the equality symmetry (the usual symmetry for nominal sets), the resulting model is equivalent to the automata from [6, 10]. However, the definition can also be interpreted in the classical symmetry, in which case we get standard alternating automata without data values [4, 5]. Finally, the definition can also be interpreted in the total order symmetry, in which case we get alternating automata on ordered data values, a model that has been studied in [8] and closely related to one-clock timed automata [12, 13, 15]. In all these cases (equality, classical, total order), *the same program* in Nλ decides emptiness for alternating automata with one register; the program only needs to be fed into different interpreters (each symmetry defines a different interpreter).

The proof that the emptiness-testing program terminates depends on the chosen data symmetry. We give an example where the termination proof fails, and indeed the emptiness problem is undecidable.

4.4 Terms of λ-calculus modulo α-conversion.

Nominal sets were originally motivated [11] as an elegant algebraic approach to name binding in syntax, and in particular as a way to represent λ-terms up to α-conversion in a way that admits natural inductive reasoning, using the so-called abstraction types that have α-equivalence classes of terms as values. This idea has been implemented in the nominal programming language Fresh O'Caml [17, 18].

Although Nλ does not have abstraction types, one may represent in it α-equivalence classes of λ-terms directly, as finitary sets of terms. Such a representation is less appealing than the one used in Fresh O'Caml, as it contains many values that do not correspond to α-equivalence classes. However, it still lets us write functions that manipulate terms (such as capture-avoiding substitution). We can also write a Nλ program that tests whether a set of terms is an α-equivalence class.

We elaborate a little on this example in Section 15.

Part II: Nλ

In this part of the paper we introduce Nλ, a rudimentary language for programming in nominal sets over an arbitrary data symmetry of a certain form. The essential idea is to extend simply typed λ-calculus with a collection type that represents finitary sets of values.

We present Nλ in three stages. First, in Section 5, we present a version for the classical symmetry, where no data values or group actions are involved. This is to accustom the reader to our syntax in a familiar setting. Notably, to store intermediate values during a computation according to our operational semantics, we introduce a syntactic construct that collects a finite set of terms. In a practical implementation, these sets would be represented as lists of terms.

Then, after some semantic considerations in Sections 6-7, we generalize the language to arbitrary data symmetries in Sections 8-9. The main conceptual difference, apart from a few new primitives, is that now *finitary*, but potentially infinite, families of terms are considered in intermediate values. This may be seen as problematic, and indeed one may wonder if our semantics is really "operational", given that it directly manipulates infinite structures.

Therefore, in Section 10, we replace infinite collections of terms with a finitary syntactic construct, in a step analogous to replacing finite sets of terms with lists. The result is an entirely finitely presentable language, with a clearly computable reduction semantics, amenable to direct implementation.

The semantics of Sections 8 and 10 are equivalent (formally, bisimilar). The latter may be seen as a reference definition for implementation purposes. The former is more abstract, better suited for reasoning, and more closely related to the simple language of Section 5.

5. A simply typed calculus with finite subsets

In this section, we show how Nλ works in the classical symmetry, where nominal sets are simply sets, and where orbit-finite sets are simply finite sets. The core language is presented in Fig. 1.

The types are as in a simply typed λ-calculus (where b comes from some set of base types), extended with a type constructor F to represent finite collections. The idea is that $\mathbf{1}$ represents a singleton set, and Fα represents finite sets of elements from α. In terms, c comes from some set of term constants with fixed types. In particular, we assume (polymorphic families of) special constants; note that F1 takes the role of a boolean type. The typing rules of basic terms are standard and omitted from Fig. 1.

To simplify the operational semantics, we extend the language with an additional construct $\mathtt{set}(X)$ of a more semantic flavor, with an intuitive typing rule. With these as intermediate values, the reduction relation $\to_\beta$ on closed terms is defined as expected. We do not commit to any particular evaluation strategy, admitting reduction of arbitrary subterms.

We refrain from showing a formal denotational semantics for the language, but our intention should be clear: types are interpreted as sets, with $\mathbf{1}$ as a singleton type, $\to$ as function space, and F as the finite powerset monad, with the obvious interpretation of constants from Fig 1.

We may now define other typical constants (operations), such as the Haskell bind (written infix as usual):

$$\mathtt{>>=} : \mathsf{F}\alpha \to (\alpha \to \mathsf{F}\beta) \to \mathsf{F}\beta \qquad \mathtt{a >>= f} = \mathtt{sum(map\ f\ a)},$$

singleton and set union:

$$\mathtt{just} : \alpha \to \mathsf{F}\alpha \qquad \mathtt{just\ a} = \mathtt{add}\ \varnothing\ \mathtt{a}$$
$$\mathtt{union} : \mathsf{F}\alpha \to \mathsf{F}\alpha \to \mathsf{F}\alpha \qquad \mathtt{union\ a\ b} = \mathtt{a >>= (add\ b)}.$$

Types:

$$\alpha ::= b \mid \mathbf{1} \mid \alpha \to \alpha \mid \mathsf{F}\alpha$$

Basic terms:

$$M ::= c \mid x \mid \lambda x.M \mid MM$$

Intermediate terms: (X ranges over finite sets of terms)

$$M ::= \cdots \mid \mathtt{set}(X) \qquad \frac{\Gamma \vdash M : \alpha \quad \text{for all } M \in X}{\Gamma \vdash \mathtt{set}(X) : \mathsf{F}\alpha}$$

Special constants:

$$* : \mathbf{1} \qquad \varnothing : \mathsf{F}\alpha \qquad \mathtt{add} : \mathsf{F}\alpha \to \alpha \to \mathsf{F}\alpha$$

$$\mathtt{map} : (\alpha \to \beta) \to \mathsf{F}\alpha \to \mathsf{F}\beta \qquad \mathtt{sum} : \mathsf{FF}\alpha \to \mathsf{F}\alpha$$

$$\mathtt{if} : \mathsf{F1} \to \alpha \to \alpha \to \alpha$$

Redexes:

$$(\lambda x.M)N \to_\beta M[N/x] \qquad \varnothing \to_\beta \mathtt{set}(\emptyset)$$

$$\mathtt{add}\ \mathtt{set}(X)\ M \to_\beta \mathtt{set}(X \cup \{M\})$$

$$\mathtt{map}\ M\ \mathtt{set}(X) \to_\beta \mathtt{set}(\{MN \mid N \in X\})$$

$$\mathtt{sum}\ \mathtt{set}(\{\mathtt{set}(X_i) \mid i \in I\}) \to_\beta \mathtt{set}(\textstyle\bigcup_{i \in I} X_i)$$

$$\mathtt{if}\ \mathtt{set}(X)\ M\ N \to_\beta M \qquad \text{if } X \neq \emptyset$$

$$\mathtt{if}\ \mathtt{set}(\emptyset)\ M\ N \to_\beta N$$

Set reduction:

$$\frac{M \in X \quad M \to_\beta N}{\mathtt{set}(X) \to_\beta \mathtt{set}(X \setminus \{M\} \cup \{N\})}$$

Figure 1. Nλ without data

Writing `bool` instead of $\mathsf{F1}$ we define boolean constants and operations:

$$\begin{array}{ll} \mathtt{true} : \mathtt{bool} & \mathtt{true} = \mathtt{just}\ * \\ \mathtt{false} : \mathtt{bool} & \mathtt{false} = \varnothing \\ \mathtt{or} : \mathtt{bool} \to \mathtt{bool} \to \mathtt{bool} & \mathtt{or} = \mathtt{union} \\ \mathtt{not} : \mathtt{bool} \to \mathtt{bool} & \mathtt{not\ a} = \mathtt{if\ a\ false\ true}, \end{array}$$

quantifiers and predicate filtering:

$$\mathtt{exists}, \mathtt{forall} : \mathsf{F}\alpha \to (\alpha \to \mathtt{bool}) \to \mathtt{bool}$$

$$\mathtt{filter} : \mathsf{F}\alpha \to (\alpha \to \mathtt{bool}) \to \mathsf{F}\alpha$$

$$\mathtt{exists} = \mathtt{>>=}$$

$$\mathtt{forall\ X\ f} = \mathtt{not(exists\ X\ \lambda x.not(f\ x))}$$

$$\mathtt{filter\ X\ f} = \mathtt{X\ >>=\ \lambda x.if\ (f\ x)(just\ x)}\varnothing.$$

If a type α comes equipped with an equality predicate:

$$\mathtt{eq}_\alpha : \alpha \to \alpha \to \mathtt{bool}$$

we may lift it to an equality predicate for $\mathsf{F}\alpha$ by defining membership and subset predicates:

$$\mathtt{member} : \mathsf{F}\alpha \to \alpha \to \mathtt{bool}$$

$$\mathtt{subset} : \mathsf{F}\alpha \to \mathsf{F}\alpha \to \mathtt{bool}$$

$$\mathtt{member\ X\ x} = \mathtt{exists\ X\ (eq}_\alpha\ \mathtt{x)}$$

$$\mathtt{subset\ X\ Y} = \mathtt{forall\ X\ (member\ Y)}$$

Finally, equality $\mathtt{eq}_{\mathsf{F}\alpha}$ is defined as subset in both directions.

This core language can be routinely extended with further standard features, e.g. product types:

$$\alpha ::= \cdots \mid \alpha \times \alpha \qquad M ::= \cdots \mid (M, M) \mid \pi_1 M \mid \pi_2 M$$

$$\pi_1(M, N) \to_\beta M \qquad \pi_2(M, N) \to_\beta N$$

Then one can write programs such as binary relation composition `comp`, using an auxiliary function `comp0`:

$$\mathtt{comp0} : (\alpha \times \beta) \to (\beta \times \gamma) \to \mathsf{F}(\alpha \times \gamma)$$

$$\mathtt{comp} : \mathsf{F}(\alpha \times \beta) \to \mathsf{F}(\beta \times \gamma) \to \mathsf{F}(\alpha \times \gamma)$$

$$\mathtt{comp0\ p\ q} = \mathtt{if\ (eq}_\beta(\pi_2\mathtt{p})(\pi_1\mathtt{q}))\ \mathtt{just}(\pi_1\mathtt{p},\pi_2\mathtt{q})\ \varnothing$$

$$\mathtt{comp\ R\ S} = \mathtt{R\ >>=\ \lambda p.(S\ >>=\ comp0\ p)}$$

where β is assumed to be an equality type. Similarly we could add recursive types such as lists (that we used in Section 4.2), etc.

Note that in a typical programming language finite collections are modeled by lists. In presence of recursive types, one could view the constants $\varnothing$ and `add` as constructors and define other operations by pattern matching and recursion; with this in mind, our `set()` construct might look like an unnecessary complication. However, in the world of nominal sets the simple list representation fails, and finding a good representation of finitary subsets of nominal sets is one of the technical challenges we shall face. Our "semantic" term construct `set()` is introduced in anticipation of a world where it is easier to say what a finitary collection is than how to write it down.

6. Nominal types: semantic considerations

We now wish to extend the calculus of Section 5 to deal with nominal sets for a data symmetry $(\mathbb{D}, G)$. The general idea is clear: given $(\mathbb{D}, G)$, we interpret types as nominal sets.

Function type. Categories of nominal sets are Cartesian closed, and it is natural to interpret function types as nominal function spaces. There, for nominal sets X and Y, the action of G on a function $f : X \to Y$ is defined by

$$(f \cdot \pi)(x) = (f(x \cdot \pi^{-1})) \cdot \pi.$$

The *nominal function space* $X \to_{\mathrm{fs}} Y$ is the set of functions from X to Y, equipped with the action above, restricted to those functions that have finite support; we call such functions *nominal*. Note that not all nominal functions are equivariant [11]; in fact, a function is equivariant if and only if it has empty support. Write $f : X \to_{\mathrm{fs}} Y$ to say that $f : X \to Y$ is nominal.

Example 2 Consider the equality symmetry. A function $f : \mathbb{D} \to \mathbb{D}$ is nominal if and only if there is a cofinite set $Z \subseteq \mathbb{D}$ such that $f|_Z$ is either the identity or a constant function.

Collection type. It remains to interpret the collection type constructor in the nominal world. This will be of use already in the definition of syntax: we intend to view finitary nominal collections of terms as terms, so we need to define what they are.

The *powerset* of a nominal set X is easy to define:

$$\mathsf{P}(X) = X \to_{\mathrm{fs}} 2$$

where 2 is a two-element set with a trivial G-action. Equivalently, $\mathsf{P}(X)$ is the set of subsets $Y \subseteq X$ with an action defined by

$$Y \cdot \pi = \{y \cdot \pi \mid y \in Y\}$$

restricted to those subsets that have finite support; these are the *nominal subsets* as defined in Section 3.

Example 3 The powerset of an orbit-finite set need not be orbit-finite. For instance, for every data symmetry $(\mathbb{D}, G)$, the powerset of $\mathbb{D}$ contains all finite subsets of $\mathbb{D}$, because every finite subset has a finite support (itself). Two finite subsets of $\mathbb{D}$ cannot be in the same orbit if they have different cardinalities. Therefore, there are infinitely many orbits in $\mathsf{P}(\mathbb{D})$ if $\mathbb{D}$ is infinite.

Observe that a nominal subset Y of a nominal set X is not a $(\mathbb{D}, G)$-nominal set in general, as Y need not be preserved by all permutations from G. However, if $C \subseteq \mathbb{D}$ supports Y then Y is a $(\mathbb{D}, G_C)$-nominal set.

We now introduce our intended nominal interpretation of the collection type: the *finitary powerset*. Recall from Section 3 that a nominal subset $Y \in \mathsf{P}(X)$ is called *finitary* if Y intersects finitely many orbits of X. If C supports Y then Y is finitary if and only if Y is orbit-finite as a $(\mathbb{D}, G_C)$-nominal set. By $\mathsf{F}_{\mathsf{n}}X$ we denote the set of all finitary subsets of X. If X is orbit-finite then all nominal subsets are finitary, i.e. $\mathsf{P}(X) = \mathsf{F}_{\mathsf{n}}X$. It follows that $\mathsf{F}_{\mathsf{n}}X$ need not be orbit-finite even if X is. Actually, the only case when $\mathsf{F}_{\mathsf{n}}X$ is orbit-finite is when X is finite.

Note that our $\mathsf{F}_{\mathsf{n}}X$ is not the free semi-lattice over X; the latter contains only finite subsets of X. Although we do not yet have a clear categorical understanding of $\mathsf{F}_{\mathsf{n}}X$, we choose it for pragmatic reasons: it is a rich collection of subsets of X that we are able to represent in a finite way (see Section 10).

7. Fraïssé symmetries

From now on we restrict attention to a special case of data symmetries, called *Fraïssé symmetries*, defined in [3] (and called Fraïssé signature there). A Fraïssé symmetry is induced by a class $\mathcal{K}$ of finite relational structures, which needs to be closed under isomorphism, substructures and amalgamation. Given such a class, the construction from [3] uses the Fraïssé limit [9] to produce a data symmetry $(\mathbb{D}, G)$, which is well behaved. All three examples listed in Section 3.1 are Fraïssé symmetries:

- The classical symmetry arises from the empty class $\mathcal{K}$.
- The equality symmetry arises from the class $\mathcal{K}$ of finite sets, i.e. finite structures over the empty vocabulary.
- The total order symmetry arises from the class $\mathcal{K}$ of all finite total orders, over a vocabulary with a binary relation.

Other examples include the class $\mathcal{K}$ of finite partial orders or finite graphs. We will see other Fraïssé symmetries in Section 14.

From now on we consider a fixed data symmetry $(\mathbb{D}, G)$ and assume that it satisfies the following conditions:

- *Fraïssé symmetry*: the symmetry is induced by a class $\mathcal{K}$.
- *Least supports*: any element x of a nominal set has the least support with respect to inclusion, which we will denote $supp(x)$.

Under these assumptions, the following basic results hold that will be extensively used in the following:

Lemma 1 $\mathbb{D}$ is orbit-finite under the action of G.

Lemma 2 Orbit-finite sets are closed under Cartesian products.

Lemma 3 (orbit refinement) Let $x \in X$ for some nominal set X. For any finite sets $C \subseteq D$ of data values, there exists a finite subset $\{z_1, \ldots, z_n\} \subseteq X$ such that

$$x \cdot G_C = \bigcup_{i=1}^{n} z_i \cdot G_D.$$

8. A calculus with finitary nominal subsets

An extension of the language of Section 5 to nominal sets over a Fraïssé symmetry $(\mathbb{D}, G)$, is summarized in Fig. 2. We write $supp(X)$ for the least support of X.

Types:

$$\alpha ::= b \mid \mathbf{1} \mid \alpha \to \alpha \mid \mathbb{D} \mid \mathsf{F}\alpha \mid \mathsf{F}_{\mathsf{n}}\alpha$$

Basic terms: as in Fig. 1,

Intermediate terms: as in Fig. 1, but X ranges over finitary sets in

$$\mathtt{set}(X) : \mathsf{F}_{\mathsf{n}}\alpha$$

Special constants: to Fig. 1, add:

$$d : \mathbb{D} \qquad \text{(for each } d \in \mathbb{D})$$

$$\mathtt{eq}_{\mathbb{D}} : \mathbb{D} \to \mathbb{D} \to \mathtt{bool} \qquad \mathtt{hull} : \mathsf{F}\mathbb{D} \to \mathsf{F}_{\mathsf{n}}\alpha \to \mathsf{F}_{\mathsf{n}}\alpha$$

Redexes: to Fig. 1, add:

$$\mathtt{eq}_{\mathbb{D}}\; d\; d \to_\beta \mathtt{set}(\{*\})$$

$$\mathtt{eq}_{\mathbb{D}}\; d\; e \to_\beta \mathtt{set}(\emptyset) \qquad (\text{if } d \neq e)$$

$$\mathtt{hull}\; \mathtt{set}(C)\; \mathtt{set}(X) \to_\beta \mathtt{set}(\textstyle\bigcup_{x\in X} x \cdot G_C) \qquad (C \subseteq_{\text{fin}} \mathbb{D})$$

Set reduction:

$$\frac{M \in X \quad M \to_\beta N \quad supp(X) = C}{\mathtt{set}(X) \to_\beta \mathtt{set}(X \setminus (M \cdot G_C) \cup (N \cdot G_C))}$$

Figure 2. Nλ with data: abstract terms

First, a new type $\mathbb{D}$ of data values is introduced, together with a constant for each data value and an equality predicate on $\mathbb{D}$.

Second, instead of one type constructor F we now have two, written F and F_{n}. The type $\mathsf{F}\alpha$ represents all *finite subsets* of α, as in Section 5, while $\mathsf{F}_{\mathsf{n}}\alpha$ represents all *finitary nominal subsets* of α. Both type constructors are equipped with constants listed in Fig. 1, and further operations for F_{n} (such as `forall`, $\mathtt{eq}_{\mathsf{F}_{\mathsf{n}}\alpha}$ etc.) are defined as in Section 5 for F. The name clash between constants should not lead to confusion and will always be resolved by context. In particular, the are two constructs $\mathtt{set}(X) : \mathsf{F}\alpha$ and $\mathtt{set}(X) : \mathsf{F}_{\mathsf{n}}\alpha$, where in the latter case X ranges over finitary and not finite sets of terms (we explain below how to regard the set of all terms as a nominal set). To avoid confusion, the latter `set()` construct we call *nominal*.

Finally, the new constant `hull` can be used to construct finitary nominal sets, just as `add` could be used to construct finite sets in Section 5. It inputs a finite set C of data values and a finitary set X, and closes X under the action of G_C. For instance in the equality symmetry, the following piece of code

```
hull ∅ {2}
```

represents the whole set $\mathbb{D}$, and the following two calls:

```
hull ∅ {(2,2)}        hull ∅ {(2,3)}
```

create the two orbits of $\mathbb{D}^2$. The relation R from Section 4.1 can be generated by

```
R = hull {2,5} {(5,2), (2,2), (2,3)}.
```

(We use some syntactic sugar here; for example, `{2,5}` would have to be written as `'add 2 (add 5 ∅)'` in our core language.)

Terms of Nλ remain as in Fig. 1, but in the nominal $\mathtt{set}(X)$ construct, X ranges over *finitary*, rather than finite sets of terms. Here we must proceed with care to avoid a circular definition where the existence of a term $\mathtt{set}(X)$ depends on all terms understood as a nominal set. Formally, this can be done by introducing an explicit rank to terms, where the rank of a term is the maximal degree of nesting of `set()` in it. Then the group action of G on terms of rank n is defined by induction, and every term of rank n has a finite support. In other words, the set of terms of each rank n is a nominal set and we may meaningfully speak of its finitary subsets used in the `set()` construct.

Example 4 In the total order symmetry, we have a term that represents the set of all data values bigger than 7:

$$\texttt{set}(\{d \mid d > 7\}).$$

This term has rank 1 and type $\mathsf{F}_n\mathbb{D}$. We also have a term that represents a set of constant functions:

$$\texttt{set}(\{\lambda x.d \mid d > 7\}).$$

We could also write a term for the union of the two sets above, but this would not have a type.We cannot, however, write a term for all data values that are integers, as $\mathbb{Z}$ is not a nominal subset of $\mathbb{D}$:

$$\texttt{set}(\{i : i \in \mathbb{Z}\}) \text{ is not a valid term.}$$

The β-reduction relation $\to_\beta$ is defined as in Section 5, with new redexes for $\texttt{eq}_{\mathbb{D}}$ and `hull`. Note that for the reduction of `hull` to happen, C must be fully evaluated to a finite set of data value constants.

Finally, the set reduction rule given in Fig. 1 is unsatisfactory for the nominal $\texttt{set}(X)$ construct, as X may have infinitely many elements, causing potentially infinite reductions. We fix this problem by insisting that all elements of X that are in the same orbit of G_C (where C is the least support of X) reduce in parallel and in a uniform way. In other words, the last rule in Fig. 1 is replaced with the last rule of Fig. 2.

Our semantics satisfies the basic properties expected from a typed λ-calculus:

Proposition 4 The β-reduction is well-defined, i.e., if $M \to_\beta N$ then N is a valid term. In addition, types are preserved and so are supports: if C supports M then it also supports N.

Proof
For the first part, we must check that the reduct N only contains finitary sets of terms under the $\texttt{set}()$ construct. The proof goes by induction on the structure of terms. In some cases we make use of the fact that in Fraïssé symmetries, Cartesian products of orbit-finite sets are orbit-finite. □

Proofs of other desirable properties are routine using standard methods:

Proposition 5 The reduction relation $\to_\beta$ has the Church-Rosser property and is weakly normalising.

9. Recursion and examples

The treatment of recursion is standard: we extend the language with a new constant `fix` for any type α, with the type

$$\texttt{fix} : (\alpha \to \alpha) \to \alpha$$

and the reduction rule

$$\texttt{fix}\, M \to_\beta M\, (\texttt{fix}\, M).$$

Using this we may define recursive functions, via the following syntactic sugar:

$$\texttt{F x = M} \quad \stackrel{\text{def}}{=} \quad \texttt{fix}\, \lambda\texttt{F.}(\lambda\texttt{x.M})$$

where F may appear in M.

As usual with recursion, one can write nonterminating programs, so weak normalisation fails. However, the Church-Rosser property holds, and types and supports are still preserved by $\to_\beta$.

We now show some simple examples of recursive programs.

Example 5 Recall Section 4.1 and the problem of computing the transitive closure of a finitary relation. W may write a function

$$\texttt{trans} : \mathsf{F}_n(\alpha \times \alpha) \to \mathsf{F}_n(\alpha \times \alpha)$$

that inputs a finitary binary relation over some equality type α and outputs its transitive closure:

$$\texttt{step} : \mathsf{F}_n(\alpha \times \alpha) \to \mathsf{F}_n(\alpha \times \alpha)$$

```
step R = union R (comp R R)
trans R = if (eq_{F_n(α×α)} (step R) R) R (trans(step R))
```

where `union` and `comp` calculate the union and composition of given relations, as defined in Section 5.

Example 6 Recall Section 4.2 and the problem of checking properties of monoids. Carriers of data monoids can be represented in Nλ as finitary subsets of some equality type α, with the monoid structure given by an element of α (the unit) and a function of the type $\alpha \times \alpha \to \alpha$ (the multiplication).

Assuming the presence of list types, the carrier of the monoid of Section 4.2 can be represented by taking $\alpha = \mathbb{D}\,\texttt{list}$ and (again, with some syntactic sugar):

```
M = hull ∅ {[],[1,1],[1,2]},
```

and the monoid operation

$$\texttt{f} : \mathbb{D}\,\texttt{list} \times \mathbb{D}\,\texttt{list} \to \mathbb{D}\,\texttt{list}.$$

is easily defined by pattern matching.

Suppose that we want to know if a monoid is idempotent. This can be accomplished by a polymorphic function

$$\texttt{idempotent} : \mathsf{F}_n\alpha \to (\alpha \times \alpha \to \alpha) \to \texttt{bool}$$

which inputs a set of arguments and a binary operation on any equality type α. The code of the function is:

```
idempotent M f = forall M (λx.eq_α (f x x) x).
```

If we execute the `idempotent` function on our example monoid, the expression:

```
idempotent M f
```

will evaluate to `true` in finite time.

The above two examples do not involve data values directly, and the polymorphic programs `trans` and `idempotent` could be just as well interpreted in the simple language of Section 5. The next example uses data explicitly.

Example 7 One could wonder why there is no primitive in the language that returns a support of a given argument. Somewhat surprisingly, with primitives listed so far we can define a function that computes the least support for equality types. The function will simply exhaustively enumerate all candidates (infinitely many of them!). We stress, however, that this search can be implemented by a finite computation, as we explain in Section 10.

We start by writing a function

$$\texttt{supports} : \alpha \to \mathsf{F}\mathbb{D} \to \texttt{bool}$$

that checks if an element x of an equality type α is supported by a finite set of data values C. It returns true if the orbit of x with respect to G_C is a singleton:

```
supports x C =   singleton (hull C (just x))
 singleton X =   exists X λx.(forall X (eq_α x))
```

Having the function `supports` we define

$$\texttt{supp} : \alpha \to \mathsf{F}_n\mathsf{F}\mathbb{D}$$

$$\texttt{search} : \alpha \to \mathsf{F}_n\mathsf{F}\mathbb{D} \to \mathsf{F}_n\mathsf{F}\mathbb{D}.$$

The result type of `supp` is $\mathsf{F}_n\mathsf{F}\mathbb{D}$ and not just $\mathsf{F}\mathbb{D}$, but the function will always return just a single support. It is implemented by an exhaustive search:

```
supp x =    search x (just ∅)
search x X =    if (exists X (supports x))
                    (filter X (supports x))
                    (search x (enlarge X))
```

The search starts with the family X containing just one set of data values: the empty one. If this set is not a support, in the first recursive call the family X contains all singletons. In general, at recursive depth n, X contains all nonempty subsets of data of cardinality at most n. An auxiliary function enlarge : $\mathsf{F_n F}D \to \mathsf{F_n F}D$ increases this cardinality bound by one:

```
enlarge X =    X >>= λx.(𝔻 >>= λd.just(add x d))
```

Observe that the search surely terminates, as every element of type α has a finite support, and always computes the least support with respect to inclusion. Finally note that we allow ourselves to use the set of data values $\mathbb{D}$ as an object of type $\mathsf{F_n}\mathbb{D}$, since $\mathbb{D}$ can be easily represented as discussed in Section 8.

10. Term representation

The language defined so far is a bit abstract in that is uses a "semantic" construct set() in its terms. For practical use, we need to represent the terms in a finite way, so that they can be input by users and manipulated by algorithms, for example by an interpreter that chooses a specific evaluation strategy. Such a representation is possible under the assumption that we work in a Fraïssé symmetry.

The cornerstone of our approach is Lemma 3 from Section 7, which provides a finite representation of finitary subsets:

Lemma 6 For every finitary subset Y of X there are elements $y_1, \ldots, y_k$ and a finite set $D \subseteq \mathbb{D}$ such that

$$Y = \bigcup_{i=1}^{k} y_i \cdot G_D.$$

Proof
Take as D any support of Y, and as $x_1, \ldots x_k$ any representatives of those G-orbits of X that are intersected by Y. Apply Lemma 3 to each x_i with $C = \emptyset$; take the union of the results and choose as y_i those z's that are elements of Y. □

Note that the representation is not unique. Consider, for instance, the total order symmetry, where $\mathbb{D}$ is the rational numbers. Let Y be the finitary subset of $\mathbb{D}$ that contains data values in the open interval $(1; 7)$. Here are some representations of Y:

$$2{\cdot}G_{\{1,7\}};\quad 6{\cdot}G_{\{1,7\}};\quad 2{\cdot}G_{\{1,3,7\}} \cup 3{\cdot}G_{\{1,3,7\}} \cup 6{\cdot}G_{\{1,3,7\}}.$$

As the last one suggests, one can make the set D of data values grow, which entails a growing set of representatives $\{y_1, \ldots, y_k\}$.

Thanks to Lemma 6, for a finitely presented language we may replace the nominal set() construct from Fig. 2 with a construct

$$\langle M_1, \ldots, M_k \rangle^{\{d_1 \ldots d_n\}}$$

of finite arity (cf. Fig. 3). Intuitively, its purpose is to mimic

$$\mathtt{hull}\ \{d_1 \ldots d_n\}\ \{M_1, \ldots, M_k\};$$

we prefer however a separate construct for technical convenience. We shall call terms built with the new construct *concrete*, as opposed to *abstract* terms built using the nominal set() construct.

To define a reduction relation on concrete terms, a few notions and results are needed. First, there is an obvious function $M \mapsto [M]$ from concrete to abstract terms, defined by induction with the only nontrivial case:

$$[\langle M_1, \ldots, M_k \rangle^C] = \mathtt{set}(\bigcup_{i=1}^{k} [M_i] \cdot G_C).$$

Types: as in Fig. 2.
Basic terms: as in Fig. 1-2.
Intermediate terms: (C ranges over finite subsets of $\mathbb{D}$)

$$M ::= \cdots \mid \langle M_1, \ldots, M_k \rangle^C \qquad \frac{\Gamma \vdash M_i : \alpha \quad \text{for } i = 1..k}{\Gamma \vdash \langle M_1, \ldots, M_k \rangle^C : \mathsf{F_n}\alpha}$$

Special constants: as in Fig. 2.
Redexes:

$$(\lambda x.M)N \to_{\hat\beta} M[N/x] \qquad \varnothing \to_{\hat\beta} \langle\rangle^{\emptyset} \qquad \mathtt{fix}\, M \to_{\hat\beta} M\,(\mathtt{fix}\, M)$$

$$\frac{D = supp([M]) \quad \langle K_1, \ldots, K_n \rangle = ref^{C \cup D}(\langle M_1, \ldots, M_k \rangle^C)}{\mathtt{add}\ \langle M_1, \ldots, M_k \rangle^C\ M \to_{\hat\beta} \langle M, K_1, \ldots, K_n \rangle^{C \cup D}}$$

$$\frac{D = supp([M]) \quad \langle K_1, \ldots, K_n \rangle = ref^{C \cup D}(\langle M_1, \ldots, M_k \rangle^C)}{\mathtt{map}\ M\ \langle M_1, \ldots, M_k \rangle^C \to_{\hat\beta} \langle MK_1, \ldots, MK_n \rangle^{C \cup D}}$$

$$\frac{\begin{array}{c} M_i = \langle M_{i1}, \ldots, M_{in_i} \rangle^{C_i} \text{ for } i = 1 \ldots k \\ E = C_1 \cup \cdots \cup C_k \\ \langle K_{i1}, \ldots, K_{il_i} \rangle = ref^E(\langle M_{i1}, \ldots, M_{in_i} \rangle^{C_i}) \text{ for } i = 1 \ldots k \end{array}}{\mathtt{sum}\langle M_1, \ldots, M_k \rangle^C \to_{\hat\beta} \langle K_{11}, \ldots, K_{1l_1}, \ldots, K_{k1}, \ldots, K_{kl_k} \rangle^E}$$

$$\mathtt{if}\ \langle M_1, \ldots, M_k \rangle^C\ M\ N \to_{\hat\beta} M \qquad \mathtt{if}\ \langle\rangle^C\ M\ N \to_{\hat\beta} N$$

$$\frac{\langle K_1, \ldots, K_n \rangle = ref^{C \cup D}(\langle M_1, \ldots, M_k \rangle^C)}{\mathtt{hull}\ \mathtt{set}(D)\ \langle M_1, \ldots, M_k \rangle^C \to_{\hat\beta} \langle K_1, \ldots, K_n \rangle^{C \cup D}}$$

Set reduction:

$$\frac{\begin{array}{c} \langle N_1, \ldots, N_n \rangle^D \text{ is a short form of } \langle M_1, \ldots, M_k \rangle^C \\ N_i \to_{\hat\beta} K \end{array}}{\langle M_1, \ldots, M_k \rangle^C \to_{\hat\beta} \langle N_1, \ldots, N_{i-1}, K, N_{i+1}, \ldots, N_n \rangle^D,}$$

Figure 3. Nλ with data: concrete terms

Lemma 6 implies that the mapping $M \mapsto [M]$ is surjective (although, as we explained above, not injective). It also obviously preserves types.

Lemma 7 The following operations can be computed:

1. Given concrete terms M, N, decide if $[M] = [N]$;
2. Given a concrete term M, find $supp([M])$;
3. Given concrete terms M, N, and a finite set C of data values, decide if $[M] \cdot G_C = [N] \cdot G_C$.

Proof
By simultaneous induction on the size of terms. □

The following is a computational version of the orbit refinement lemma (Lemma 3):

Lemma 8 Given concrete terms $M_1, \ldots, M_k$ and $C \subseteq E$, one can compute concrete terms $K_1, \ldots, K_n$ such that

$$[\langle M_1, \ldots, M_k \rangle^C] = [\langle K_1, \ldots, K_n \rangle^E].$$

We then denote

$$ref^E(\langle M_1, \ldots, M_k \rangle^C) = \langle K_1, \ldots, K_n \rangle.$$

We may now formulate reduction rules for basic redexes of the language as in Fig. 3. For instance, to reduce a concrete term

$$\mathtt{add}\ \langle M_1, \ldots, M_k \rangle^C\ M,$$

one first computes the least support of M using Lemma 7(2), then uses Lemma 8 to refine $\langle M_1, \ldots, M_k \rangle^C$, and finally adds M to the resulting list of terms. Other redexes are similar.

For the set reduction rule, it is tempting to write simply:

$$\frac{M_i \to_{\hat\beta} N}{\langle M_1, \dots, M_n \rangle^C \to_{\hat\beta} \langle M_1, \dots, M_{i-1}, N, M_{i+1}, \dots, M_n \rangle^C}.$$

However, this leads into problems: note that if $[M_1] \cdot G_C = [M_2] \cdot G_C$ then $[\langle M_1, M_2 \rangle^C] = [\langle M_1 \rangle^C]$, but the above rule may let $\langle M_1, M_2 \rangle^C$ and $\langle M_1 \rangle^C$ reduce differently. To avoid this, we convert concrete terms to a canonical form before they can reduce.

Specifically, we say that a concrete term $M = \langle M_1, \dots, M_k \rangle^C$ is in *short form* if:

- $C = supp([M])$, and
- $[M_i] \cdot G_C \neq [M_j] \cdot G_C$ for $i \neq j$.

An arbitrary concrete term is in short form if all its subterms $\langle M_1, \dots, M_k \rangle^C$ are in short form.

Lemma 9 For each concrete term M, a concrete term N in short form such that $[M] = [N]$ exists and can be computed. (N is then called a short form of M).

Proof
By induction on M, using Lemma 7. □

Using short forms, the set reduction rule is defined as in Fig. 3.

All these complications are rewarded by a close correspondence of reduction semantics of concrete and abstract terms:

Proposition 10 The reduction $\to_{\hat\beta}$ is bisimilar to $\to_\beta$, i.e.:

- if $M \to_{\hat\beta} N$ then $[M] \to_\beta [N]$, and
- if $[M] \to_\beta K$ then there exists a concrete term N such that $M \to_{\hat\beta} N$ and $K = [N]$.

Proof
By structural induction on concrete terms. □

Part III: Case studies

In this part, we demonstrate the potential of Nλ as a basis of an expressive programming language.

So far we have ignored many useful features typically found in functional languages, such as recursive datatypes (e.g. lists) and pattern matching, the `let` construct etc. We believe that adding this kind of features to Nλ is an issue orthogonal to our concerns and may be done along standard lines. In the examples to follow we feel free to use recursive types and `let` as if they were in the language.

11. Alternating automata

As a non-trivial example of nominal programming, in the remaining sections we consider the emptiness problem for alternating automata. We deliberately choose a borderline problem: it is decidable only under some restrictions on the state space of the automaton, and only for certain data symmetries. Moreover, even in known decidable cases the problem is extremely complex (non-primitive recursive, except for the classical symmetry, where it is PSPACE-complete).

Definition of alternating automaton Given a data symmetry $(\mathbb{D}, G)$, an alternating automaton is given by:

1. An input alphabet A, an orbit-finite nominal set.
2. A set of states Q, an orbit-finite nominal set.
3. A partition of states $Q = Q_\exists \cup Q_\forall$ into two nominal subsets.
4. A transition function, that is a nominal function

$$\delta : Q \times A \to_{\mathrm{fs}} \mathsf{F}Q.$$

5. An initial state $q_I \in Q$.
6. The final states F, a nominal subset of Q.

An alternating automaton is used to accept or reject a word $w \in A^*$. The semantics is defined as follows. A *configuration* of the automaton is a finite set of states. We write X, Y, Z for configurations. The initial configuration is $\{q_I\}$. A configuration is called *final* if it is a subset of F.

We now define a one step transition relation which says how to go from one configuration to another by reading an input letter. Suppose that X, Y are configurations and $a \in A$ is an input letter. Then we write $X \overset{a}{\rightsquigarrow} Y$ if the following hold for every $q \in X$:

- If $q \in Q_\exists$, then Y contains some state from $\delta(q, a)$.
- If $q \in Q_\forall$, then Y contains all states from $\delta(q, a)$.

We say the automaton *accepts* an input word $a_1 \cdots a_n \in A^*$ if there are configurations $X_0, \dots, X_n$ such that X_0 is the initial configuration, X_n is final, and

$$X_0 \overset{a_1}{\rightsquigarrow} X_1 \overset{a_2}{\rightsquigarrow} X_2 \overset{a_3}{\rightsquigarrow} \cdots \overset{a_n}{\rightsquigarrow} X_n. \quad (1)$$

We say X can reach Y in one step if $X \overset{a}{\rightsquigarrow} Y$ holds for some $a \in A$, and we write this $X \rightsquigarrow Y$. We denote the reflexive transitive closure of $\rightsquigarrow$ by $\rightsquigarrow_*$. When $X \rightsquigarrow_* Y$ holds, we say that X can reach Y. The automaton accepts some word if and only if the initial configuration can reach some final configuration.

From now on, we are interested in the *emptiness problem*: given an alternating automaton, decide if it accepts some word.

Example 8 Consider the equality symmetry. We construct an automaton that recognizes the language

$$\{d_1 \cdots d_n : n \in \mathbb{N} \text{ and } d_i \neq d_j \text{ for all } i \neq j\}.$$

The state space is $Q = \mathbb{D} \cup \{\top, \bot\}$, where the states $\top$ and $\bot$ are in their own orbits. The initial state is $\top$, and all states except $\bot$ are final. All states belong to $Q_\forall$ and $Q_\exists$ is empty.

The automaton scans the word in state $\top$, and every time it sees a data value d, it spawns a new thread with state d. This corresponds to the transition

$$\delta(\top, d) = \{\top, d\} \qquad \text{for } d \in \mathbb{D}.$$

When a thread with state d sees a letter e, then it ignores it and keeps on scanning the word if $e \neq d$, otherwise it enters the error state, because d has appeared twice:

$$\delta(d, e) = \begin{cases} \{d\} & \text{if } d \neq e \\ \{\bot\} & \text{otherwise} \end{cases} \qquad \text{for } d, e \in \mathbb{D}$$

Finally, it is impossible to recover from the error:

$$\delta(\bot, d) = \{\bot\} \qquad \text{for } d \in \mathbb{D}.$$

One-dimensional alternating automata Let $k \in \mathbb{N}$. A nominal set is called *k-dimensional* if every element is supported by a set $C \subseteq \mathbb{D}$ of cardinality k. Clearly, an orbit-finite set is k-dimensional iff each of its orbits is so.

Example 9 Up to isomorphism, there is only one zero-dimensional one-orbit set. Examples of one-dimensional sets are $\mathbb{D}$ and the set $\{d\} \times \mathbb{D}$ for any $d \in \mathbb{D}$ (with the action of G not changing the first coordinate). Examples of two-dimensional sets are $\mathbb{D}^2$ or the set of all two-element subsets of $\mathbb{D}$. Every k-dimensional set is also l-dimensional for $l > k$.

In most data symmetries, with the exception of the classical symmetry, the set $\mathbb{D}^2$ is not one-dimensional.

An alternating automaton is k-dimensional if its state space is (the alphabet is not taken into account). For instance, the automaton in Example 8 is one-dimensional. From now on we consider only one-dimensional automata.

Fact 11 A single-orbit set is k-dimensional if and only if it is an image, under some equivariant function, of an orbit of the set $\mathbb{D}^k$.

Our definition of alternating automaton can be instantiated to various data symmetries.

- In the classical symmetry, the notion of dimension is irrelevant, since every nominal set is already zero-dimensional. When instantiated to the classical symmetry, our definition is equivalent to ordinary alternating automata.
- When instantiated to the equality symmetry, our k-dimensional alternating automata are equivalent to alternating k-register automata of Demri and Lazić [6]. Emptiness is known to be undecidable for $k \geq 2$, and decidable for $k = 1$. In the latter case, the complexity of the problem is very high: it is not bounded by any primitive recursive function [1, 12].
- When instantiated to the total order symmetry, k-dimensional alternating automata are equivalent to the model of k-register automata studied by Figueira, Hofman and Lasota in [8]. These automata are very closely related (some details have to be adjusted) to alternating k-clock timed automata. Emptiness of those is known to be undecidable for $k \geq 2$, and decidable for $k = 1$ (with a similar lower complexity bound as above). The decidability result was obtained independently by Lasota and Walukiewicz [12, 13], as well as Ouaknine and Worrell [15].

In the remaining sections we will prove the following result:

Theorem 12 *There exists a single program in Nλ, which decides emptiness of alternating one-dimensional automata for:*

- *the classical symmetry,*
- *the equality symmetry, and*
- *the total order symmetry.*

12. Well-quasi order

Well-quasi orders (WQOs) are the key technical tool in the algorithm and its proof of correctness. According to a classical definition, a quasi order $(X, \leq)$ is a WQO, if for every infinite sequence

$$x_1, x_2, \ldots \in X$$

there exist indexes $i < j$ such that $x_i \leq x_j$. It is well known that $\leq$ is a WQO iff it is well-founded and every antichain is finite.

We extend this definition to the nominal setting. A *nominal quasi order* is a nominal set X together with a quasi order $\leq$ which is a nominal subset of $X \times X$. Let C be the least support of $\leq$. A nominal quasi order is called a *nominal WQO* if for every infinite sequence

$$x_1, x_2, \ldots \in X$$

there exist indexes $i < j$ and a permutation $\pi \in G_C$ such that $x_i \cdot \pi \leq x_j$. (As C supports the order $\leq$ relation, one could equivalently require $x_i \leq x_j \cdot \pi$ for some $\pi \in G_C$.) The following lemma gives an equivalent and maybe cleaner definition.

Lemma 13 A nominal quasi order X is a nominal WQO iff it is well founded and every antichain is a finitary subset of X.

For example, any orbit-finite set X, with the discrete partial order (all different elements are incomparable) is a nominal WQO.

Theorem 14 *For all data symmetries mentioned in Theorem 12, if Q is an orbit-finite one-dimensional nominal set then* $\mathsf{F}Q$*, ordered by inclusion, is a nominal WQO.*

Proof
The proof depends heavily on the data symmetry involved and used deep combinatoric results such as Dickson's Lemma (for the equality symmetry) or Higman's Lemma (for the total order symmetry). □

Example 10 The assumption on Q being one-dimensional is important. As an illustrating example consider the equality symmetry and the two-dimensional set $Q = \mathbb{D}^2$. The family of finite sets, for all $n \in \mathbb{N}$, of the following form

$$X_n = \{\langle d_1, d_2\rangle, \langle d_2, d_3\rangle, \ldots, \langle d_n, d_1\rangle\},$$

where $d_1, \ldots, d_n$ are distinct data values, forms an orbit-infinite antichain in $\mathsf{F}Q$. Indeed, if $n \neq m$ then there is no bijection π such that $X_n \cdot \pi \subseteq X_m$. Thus Q is not a nominal WQO.

13. Decision procedure for emptiness

We now use the results of the previous section to give an emptiness algorithm for one-dimensional alternating automata. The algorithm works in the total order symmetry and in the equality symmetry, thus reproving the results of [6, 8]. The algorithm also works in the classical symmetry, but in this case it has suboptimal complexity. One of our contributions is that we make the similarities between [6, 8] explicit: we produce one piece of code in Nλ, which solves the emptiness problem for one-dimensional alternating automata for all these data symmetries[3]. Also, because the code is generic, it only focusses on the essence of the problem, and needs not to talk about technical details.

In addition, the same code solves the emptiness problem for any data symmetry which satisfies the condition of Theorem 14:

> If Q is an orbit-finite one-dimensional nominal set then $\mathsf{F}Q$, ordered by inclusion, is a nominal WQO. (2)

As an illustrating example, in Section 14 we describe a new data symmetry, called the forest symmetry, that has property (2). We also show that the partial order symmetry does not have property (2), so the code does not work (i.e. may not terminate) for that symmetry. In fact, the emptiness of one-dimensional alternating automata is undecidable there.

In short, although our program works in many Fraïssé symmetries, the decidability (and also complexity) landscape depends on the choice of symmetry.

13.1 High-level overview of the algorithm

The algorithm for checking emptiness of alternating automata runs two semidecision procedures in parallel. The first procedure terminates if and only if the automaton is nonempty, the second procedure terminates if and only if the automaton is empty[4].

[3] Our code makes syntactic sense for two- and higher dimensional automata as well. When executed for such inputs, the program may not terminate.

[4] Formally speaking, our language does not allow running two procedures in parallel. However, it is not difficult to combine the two procedures into a single one.

The nonemptiness semidecision procedure. This procedure simply does a breadth-first search through all reachable configurations. Define $\mathcal{X}_n$ to be the set of configurations that can be reached from the initial configuration in n steps,

$$\mathcal{X}_0 \stackrel{\text{def}}{=} \{\{q_I\}\} \qquad \mathcal{X}_{n+1} \stackrel{\text{def}}{=} \{X' : X \rightsquigarrow X' \text{ for some } X \in \mathcal{X}_n\}.$$

The algorithm calculates the sets $\mathcal{X}_0, \mathcal{X}_1, \mathcal{X}_2, \ldots$ and searches each one for a final configuration. The procedure terminates if and only if the automaton is non-empty. The only question is: how can we represent $\mathcal{X}_n$? The following fact implies that each $\mathcal{X}_n$ can be stored by a program of Nλ.

Fact 15 If $\mathcal{X}_n$ is finitary, then so is $\mathcal{X}_{n+1}$.

The nonemptiness semidecision procedure is very straightforward, and it requires almost no assumptions to work. In particular, it works for all Fraïssé symmetries, not just those satisfying (2), and it works also for automata of arbitrary dimension, not just one.

The emptiness semidecision procedure. The whole weight of the algorithm is in the emptiness semidecision procedure, which searches for a finitary witness of emptiness. Unlike the nonemptiness semidecision procedure, its proof of termination requires the automaton to be one-dimensional and the data symmetry to satisfy (2).

For a set $\mathcal{X}$ of configurations, define

$$\mathcal{X}\!\uparrow \;=\; \{X' : X' \text{ is a configuration that includes some } X \in \mathcal{X}\}.$$

Proposition 16 The automaton is empty if and only if there is a finitary subset $\mathcal{X}$ of configurations such that:

- $\mathcal{X}\!\uparrow$ contains the initial configuration.
- $\mathcal{X}\!\uparrow$ contains no final configurations.
- Whenever $X \in \mathcal{X}$ and $X \rightsquigarrow X'$ then $X' \in \mathcal{X}\!\uparrow$.

The emptiness semidecision procedure searches through all finitary subsets of configurations, and terminates if it finds one that satisfies the conditions in Proposition 16.

13.2 Implementing the algorithm in Nλ

We begin by typing the program. The input to the program is an alternating automaton. Its alphabet is thus a parameter of type $\mathsf{F_n}\alpha$ for some type α. Similarly, the set of states of the automaton is of type $\mathsf{F_n}\beta$, for some type β. We assume that α and β are equality types. An automaton is thus given by a tuple of type:

$$\mathsf{F_n}\alpha \times \mathsf{F_n}\beta \times \mathsf{F_n}\beta \times (\beta \times \alpha \to \mathsf{F}\beta) \times \beta \times \mathsf{F_n}\beta,$$

where the six coordinates correspond to A, $Q_\exists$, $Q_\forall$, δ, q_I and F, respectively. Call the type above $\mathtt{aut}(\alpha,\beta)$. Therefore, our emptiness algorithm will have the following type

$$\mathtt{aut}(\alpha,\beta) \to \mathtt{bool}. \tag{3}$$

We now code the algorithm described in Section 13.1. The program consists of two semidecision procedures, `nonempty` and `empty`, both of type (3). The simpler nonemptiness procedure is described below; the more complex emptiness procedure is omitted due to lack of space.

We start with a wrong solution to `nonempty`, to motivate the correct one. At first sight, the problem could be solved by computing the transitive closure of the $\rightsquigarrow$ relation, for instance using the program `trans` defined in Example 5. However, we cannot apply `trans` to $\rightsquigarrow$, as $\rightsquigarrow$ is not finitary!

Instead, we systematically compute configurations reachable from $\{q_I\}$ in k steps, for $k = 0, 1, \ldots$. We focus only on the nominal aspects of the program and skip those fragments that do not process infinite nominal sets. For instance, we assume for simplicity that we have a function

$$\mathtt{conf\text{-}input\text{-}succ} : \mathsf{F}\beta \to \alpha \to \mathsf{F_n}(\mathsf{F}\beta)$$

that computes, for a given configuration X and an input letter a, the finite set of all successor configurations of X via a. This function uses functions `add` and δ. Then we may easily define $\mathtt{conf\text{-}succ} : \mathsf{F}\beta \to \mathsf{F_n}(\mathsf{F}\beta)$ that computes, for a given configuration X, the finitary set $\{X' : X \rightsquigarrow X'\}$:

```
conf-succ x = A >>= (conf-input-succ x)
```

Similarly, `conf-succ` may be lifted to finitary sets of configurations:

```
X >>= conf-succ
```

The above term inputs a finitary set `X` of configurations, and outputs the set of its successors. Therefore, this term realizes the mapping $\mathcal{X}_n \mapsto \mathcal{X}_{n+1}$ discussed in Section 13.1. The last two auxiliary functions needed to define `nonempty` are:

$$\mathtt{final} : \mathsf{F}\beta \to \mathtt{bool}$$
$$\mathtt{final\text{-}reach} : \mathsf{F_n}(\mathsf{F}\beta) \to \mathtt{bool}$$

```
      final x =  forall x (member F)
final-reach X =  if (exists X final) true
                 (final-reach (X >>= conf-succ))
```

For a set `X` of configurations, the function `final-reach` checks if a configuration containing only final states is reachable from any configuration in `X`, by recursively computing successors. Finally:

```
nonempty A Q∃ Q∀ δ qI F = final-reach (just [qI])
```

Note that all auxiliary functions above must be defined in an environment that contains all ingredients of an automaton, that is A, $Q_\exists$, $Q_\forall$, δ, q_I and F.

14. Decidability border

In this section we discuss what happens to our program for data symmetries other than those mentioned in Theorem 12. We provide a negative example and a positive one. This demonstrates that decidability of the emptiness problem in dimension 1 is a delicate issue and it strongly depends on a data symmetry.

Positive example: forest orders. Consider a *forest symmetry*, which corresponds to the Fraïssé class of forests. A partial order is called a forest if for every element x, the elements smaller than x are linearly ordered. The class of finite forests has amalgamation, so there is a universal structure, and we can study Nλ in the resulting data symmetry.

One can show that the forest symmetry satisfies condition (2) from Section 13. The proof is the same as in Theorem 14, except that we use Kruskal's Tree Theorem instead of Dickson's or Higman's Lemma. Because condition (2) is satisfied, our emptiness algorithm works, and therefore emptiness is decidable for one-dimensional alternating automata for the forest symmetry. This is a new decidability result, unknown in the automata literature.

Negative example: partial orders. Consider the partial order symmetry, arising from the Fraïssé class of finite partial orders.

Fact 17 Condition (2) fails in the partial order symmetry.

In fact, emptiness is undecidable for one-dimensional alternating automata in the partial order symmetry.

15. Name binding

As another case study, we use Nλ to capture name binding on the example of untyped lambda calculus, up to α-conversion. Our objective is to define a datatype to implement lambda terms, such that two α-equivalent terms are represented by the same object of that datatype. In this section we work with the equality symmetry.

Our basic idea is that a term, in particular a lambda abstraction modulo α-conversion, is represented as a finitary set of terms. For instance, the following two terms:

$$m_1 = \lambda d.d\,d \qquad m_2 = \lambda d.\lambda e.d,$$

will be represented, intuitively, by the following two sets:

$$\{\lambda d.d\,d\}_{d\in\mathbb{D}} \qquad \{\lambda d.\{\lambda e.d\}_{e\in\mathbb{D}\setminus\{d\}}\}_{d\in\mathbb{D}}.$$

The lambda terms that we want to implement are built out of variables using application and lambda abstraction. To store them, we use a recursive datatype `term`:

$$\texttt{term} = \text{VAR}(\mathbb{D}) \mid \text{APP}(\texttt{term} \times \texttt{term}) \mid \text{ABS}(\mathsf{F}_n(\mathbb{D} \times \texttt{term}))$$

In particular, we use data values to stand for variables. We will explain the idea using m_1 and m_2. The term m_1 is represented by

```
t1 = ABS(hull ∅ (just (d, APP(VAR(d), VAR(d)))))
```

Thus binding of a variable, say d above, in a term t, is obtained by considering the orbit of (d, t). The term $m_2' = \lambda e.d$ will be represented by

```
t2' = ABS(hull (just d) (just (e, VAR(d))))
```

that is by the orbit of `(e, VAR(d))` with respect to $G_{\{d\}}$. Intuitively, a difference between free and bound variables is that a free variable of a term is an element of its least support while the bound variable is not. Finally m_2 is represented by:

```
t2 = ABS(hull ∅ (just (d, t2')))
```

The set of free variables of a term can be computed as the least support of that term, cf. Section 9.

We have decided to model lambda abstraction as a suitable one-orbit set of type $\mathsf{F}_n(\mathbb{D}\times\texttt{term})$. Note that this type contains elements that do not correspond to well-formed terms. However, one can define a function $\texttt{abstr} : \mathbb{D} \times \texttt{term} \to \texttt{term}$, that constructs a well-formed lambda abstraction up to α-conversion:

```
abstr d t =   ABS( (supp t) >>= λ fvars.
                let C = minus fvars (just d)
                in hull C (just (d, t)) )
```

where $\texttt{supp} : \texttt{term} \to \mathsf{F}_n(\mathsf{F}\mathbb{D})$ is defined as in Section 9. For instance, the terms t_1 and t_2 could be defined as:

```
t1 =  abstr d APP(VAR(d), VAR(d))
t2 =  abstr d (abstr e VAR(d))
```

for arbitrary $\texttt{d} \neq \texttt{e}$. For simplicity we assume from now on that all terms are well-formed, i.e., defined using only VAR(), APP() and `abstr` as exemplified above (in fact, a well-formedness check may be easily programmed).

Now we will write a capture-avoiding substitution function:

$$\texttt{subst} : \texttt{term} \to \mathbb{D} \to \texttt{term} \to \texttt{term}$$

with the meaning that `subst t d u` substitutes the term `t` for every free occurrence of `d` in term `u`. It can be defined recursively:

```
subst t d VAR(e) = if (eq_D e d) t VAR(e)
subst t d APP(t1, t2) =
    APP((subst t d t1), (subst t d t2))
subst t d ABS(X) =
    let C = fvars t in
    let X' = filter (λ(e, u).not(member C e)) X in
    ABS(map (λ(e, u).(e, subst t d u)) X')
```

Before term `t` is substituted inside a lambda abstraction `ABS(X)`, we filter out from `X` all pairs `(e, u)` such that `e` occurs free in `t`. Thus the free variables of `t` are not captured and remain free.

We should note that the code of the basic programs above is rather unpleasant, especially when compared to the neat treatment of α-conversion in Fresh O'Caml [17, 18]. Also the fact that the property of being a well-formed lambda term is not captured by the type system of Nλ, is a deficiency. We see this case study as evidence of the limitations of Nλ, just as the automata-theoretic examples of the preceding sections are evidence of its strength. A detailed study of relations between Nλ and Fresh O'Caml, as well as an attempt to combine their strong points, is left for future work.

References

[1] P. Aziz Abdulla, J. Deneux, J. Ouaknine, and J. Worrell. Decidability and complexity results for timed automata via channel machines. In *ICALP*, pages 1089–1101, 2005.

[2] M. Bojańczyk. Data monoids. In *STACS*, 2011.

[3] M. Bojańczyk, B. Klin, and S. Lasota. Languages with group actions. In *LICS*, 2011.

[4] J. A. Brzozowski and E. L. Leiss. On equations for regular languages, finite automata, and sequential networks. *Theor. Comput. Sci.*, 10:19–35, 1980.

[5] A. K. Chandra, D. Kozen, and L. J. Stockmeyer. Alternation. *J. ACM*, 28(1):114–133, 1981.

[6] S. Demri and R. Lazic. LTL with the freeze quantifier and register automata. *ACM Trans. Comput. Log.*, 10(3), 2009.

[7] G. L. Ferrari, U. Montanari, and M. Pistore. Minimizing transition systems for name passing calculi: A co-algebraic formulation. In *FoSSaCS*, volume 2303 of *LNCS*, pages 129–158, 2002.

[8] D. Figueira, P. Hofman, and S. Lasota. Relating timed and register automata. In *Proc. EXPRESS'10*, volume 41 of *EPTCS*, pages 61–75, 2010.

[9] R. Fraïssé. *Theory of relations*. North-Holland, 1953.

[10] N. Francez and M. Kaminski. Finite-memory automata. *Theor. Comput. Sci.*, 134(2):329–363, 1994.

[11] M. Gabbay and A. M. Pitts. A new approach to abstract syntax with variable binding. *Formal Asp. Comput.*, 13(3-5):341–363, 2002.

[12] S. Lasota and I. Walukiewicz. Alternating timed automata. In *FoSSaCS*, pages 250–265, 2005.

[13] S. Lasota and I. Walukiewicz. Alternating timed automata. *ACM Trans. Comput. Log.*, 9(2), 2008.

[14] U. Montanari and M. Pistore. History-dependent automata: An introduction. In *SFM*, pages 1–28, 2005.

[15] J. Ouaknine and J. Worrell. On the decidability of metric temporal logic. In *LICS*, pages 188–197, 2005.

[16] M. Pistore. *History Dependent Automata*. PhD thesis, University of Pisa, 1999.

[17] M. R. Shinwell. The Fresh Approach: functional programming with names and binders. Technical Report UCAM-CL-TR-618, University of Cambridge, Computer Laboratory, February 2005.

[18] M. R. Shinwell and A. M. Pitts. Fresh Objective Caml user manual. Technical Report UCAM-CL-TR-621, University of Cambridge Computer Laboratory, February 2005.

Programming with Binders and Indexed Data-Types

Andrew Cave   Brigitte Pientka
McGill University
{acave1,bpientka}@cs.mcgill.ca

Abstract

We show how to combine a general purpose type system for an existing language with support for programming with binders and contexts by refining the type system of ML with a restricted form of dependent types where index objects are drawn from contextual LF. This allows the user to specify formal systems within the logical framework LF and index ML types with contextual LF objects. Our language design keeps the index language generic only requiring decidability of equality of the index language providing a modular design. To illustrate the elegance and effectiveness of our language, we give programs for closure conversion and normalization by evaluation.

Our three key technical contribution are: 1) We give a bi-directional type system for our core language which is centered around refinement substitutions instead of constraint solving. As a consequence, type checking is decidable and easy to trust, although constraint solving may be undecidable. 2) We give a big-step environment based operational semantics with environments which lends itself to efficient implementation. 3) We prove our language to be type safe and have mechanized our theoretical development in the proof assistant Coq using the fresh approach to binding.

Categories and Subject Descriptors D.3.3 [*Programming Languages*]: Language Constructs and Features—Data types and structures

General Terms Design, Languages

Keywords Logical frameworks, higher-order abstract syntax, dependent types, recursive types

1. Introduction

To reason about the runtime behavior of software, we routinely design and use formal systems, given by axioms and inference rules, such as logics to reason about access control [Abadi et al. 1993, 1999; Garg and Pfenning 2006] and information flow [Miyamoto and Igarashi 2004], logics to reason about memory access [Nanevski et al. 2008a] or simply the scope of names [Pottier 2007]. Over the last decade we have come closer to narrowing the gap between programming software systems and reasoning about them [Chen and Xi 2005; Sheard 2004; Westbrook et al. 2005]. The general mantra is to design rich type systems which allow programmers to specify and enforce statically powerful invariants about their programs. Yet, existing approaches lack rich abstractions that allow users to describe formal systems and proofs on a high-level, factor out common and recurring issues, make it easy to use, and at the same time have a small trusted kernel.

In this paper, we extend a general purpose language to support programming with formal systems and ultimately proofs. This is achieved by indexing types with contextual LF objects [Pientka 2008]. Contextual LF extends the logical framework LF [Harper et al. 1993] with the power of contextual objects $\hat{\Psi}.M$ of type $A[\Psi]$. M denotes an object which may refer to the bound variables listed in $\hat{\Psi}$ and has type A in the context Ψ (see also [Nanevski et al. 2008b]). It also supports first-class contexts and allows us to abstract over contexts. This allows the user to specify formal systems within the logical framework LF and obtaining support for representing and managing binders, renaming, fresh name generation, and capture-avoiding substitutions. Contextual LF allows programmers to pack "open" LF objects together with the context in which they are meaningful thereby obtaining closed objects which can be passed and manipulated. In particular, contextual LF objects can be used to index types and track rich formal properties. We demonstrate the advantages of combining contextual LF with data-types by discussing implementations of closure conversion and normalization by evaluation. These examples have been a good benchmark in comparing systems and demonstrate the benefits and elegance of our approach.

Fundamentally, our approach follows the tradition of indexed types (see Xi and Pfenning [1999]; Zenger [1997]) choosing as an index domain contextual LF which allows us to express properties about open objects, the scope of variables and contexts which previous systems such as ATS/LF [Xi 2004] lack. Instead of generating and propagating constraints which is common in indexed type systems, we will associate patterns with refinements substitution and work only with constraints in solved form. This leads to a small trusted kernel.

Compared to languages such as Beluga [Pientka and Dunfield 2010] or Delphin [Poswolsky and Schürmann 2009, 2008] which support programming with binders already, the language we propose in this paper supports recursive types which the former languages lack; this extension is key to tackle important problems such as normalization by evaluation which are typically out of reach for these languages. Having the ability to define data-types is convenient; it is also more efficient than supporting data-types via a Church-encoding which is in principle already possible.

In contrast to Licata and Harper [2009] which supports mixing binding and computation, we keep the separation of data and computations. This has several advantages: Because our index language remains pure, it is straightforward to establish adequacy of the formal system and its encoding using standard techniques (see for example Harper and Licata [2007]). This allows us to maintain all the good properties of contextual objects, namely strong normalization and decidable equality. Moreover, our computation language remains close to traditional ML-like languages and is designed to

POPL'12, January 25–27, 2012, Philadelphia, PA, USA.

be modular in the index domain. As a consequence, one can easily replace contextual LF with for example a higher-order logic with inductive types without affecting the computations. Compared to other systems with a uniform language for computations and types such as the Calculus of Construction or Martin Löf type theory, our computation language can easily be combined with imperative features, allows non-terminating computation, and requires fewer annotations to make type checking decidable.

The main technical contributions of this paper are:

- We present a core language with dependent types where we separate the types from computations. One can think of this core language as the target of elaborating a surface language where we may omit implicit indices via type reconstruction. Our language is a conservative extension of a general purpose language where types are indexed by contextual LF objects and contexts and at the same time supports pattern matching on its index objects. Because it may be viewed as an extension of Beluga with recursive types, we call our language Beluga$^{\mu}$. However, we emphasize that our design of the computation language is generic and we can replace the index language which in our case is contextual LF with any other language where equality between two index objects is decidable.
- We present a bi-directional type system for our core language. Theoretically, we model dependently typed recursive types as fixpoints with explicit equality constraints on contextual objects. This is similar to Xi et al. [2003] and Sulzmann et al. [2007] where recursive types are endowed with equalities between types to model GADTs. However, instead of accumulating and solving constraints during type checking, our approach relies on refinement substitutions in branches. Although constraint solving may be undecidable in our setting, type checking based on refinements remains decidable. Type checking is hence easier to trust.
- We give a big-step environment-based operational semantics. Because we allow matching on computation-level expressions and index objects, we distinguish between the environment for computation-level values and index objects and show that types are preserved. By extending our operational semantics to also track diverging computations following Cousot and Cousot [1992]; Leroy and Grall [2009], we prove progress.
- We have mechanized the typing rules, the operational semantics and the type safety proof (preservation and progress) in the proof assistant Coq. We use the fresh approach to binding by Pouillard and Pottier [2010] to model variables in our language.

The proposed programming language with support for contextual objects and data-types is a prime candidate for programming code transformations and certified programming. More generally, it provides a foundation for programming with domain-specific logics and demonstrates how to endow a general purpose programming language with direct support for programming with logics and proofs.

The remainder of the paper is organized as follows. To illustrate the main idea of defining types indexed with contextual objects, we discuss in detail three examples (Section 2): closure-based evaluator, closure conversion and normalization by evaluation. We then introduce Beluga$^{\mu}$, a language which supports contextual objects and computation-level data-types in Section 3. We begin by introducing our index domain in Section 3.1 which in our case is contextual LF [Pientka 2008]. This will review and summarize previous work in this area. We then present the computation language in Section 4 which includes indexed types, recursive types, variants and general pattern matching. We will leave out polymorphism and imperative features which are orthogonal issues and which are straightforward to add. The typing rules for Beluga$^{\mu}$ and an environment-based big-step semantics together with the type safety proof are presented in Section 4.4. We explain our mechanization of the type safety proof in Section 5. The rest of the paper is concerned with some related work, current status and future research directions.

2. Motivating Examples

In this section, we discuss three examples which illustrate the utility of a language combining contextual types with indexed recursive types. We use an informal surface syntax inspired by both Beluga and Agda [Norell 2007]. This surface syntax is intended to elaborate to the core language presented in Section 4.

2.1 Closure-based evaluator for the lambda-calculus

We begin with a demonstration of a closure-based evaluator for the untyped lambda-calculus which is directly comparable to that of Licata and Harper [2009]. This allows us to explain contextual objects in a simple setting. We first represent the untyped lambda calculus in LF with higher order abstract syntax (HOAS).

```
lam: (tm → tm) → tm.
app: tm → tm → tm.
```

To implement an evaluator, we must analyze and pattern match on lambda-terms and consequently we must be able to handle open objects. Hence, the evaluator will be parameterized with a context ψ which keeps track of variables of type `tm` and manipulates contextual objects of type `tm[ψ]`. To type contexts we define a *context schema* `ctx` as follows: **schema** `ctx = tm;` To express that ψ contains only variables of type `tm` we write `ψ:ctx`.

The highlight of this example, when compared to Beluga or Delphin, is that we can write the closure of a term under an environment of bindings as a computation-level data-type with a single constructor `cl` as follows:

```
datatype  clos : ctype =
  cl : {ψ:ctx} → tm[ψ,x:tm] → (#tm[ψ] → clos) → clos
type  envr ψ = #tm[ψ] → clos
```

We write `tm[ψ]` for the type of terms whose free variables come only from the context ψ. We write `#tm[ψ]` for the type of variables of type `tm` in context ψ – i.e. elements of ψ. We overload → using it for LF types and also computation-level types; since **datatype** is part of the *computation* language, the arrow in `#tm[ψ] → clos` does not indicate the LF function space, but rather the usual computational function space. Hence this datatype represents the bodies of lambda abstractions in some context together with a binding for each of the free variables minus one. Note that we wrap arguments in {} to indicate that they are passed *implicitly*.

We can now proceed to evaluate a term in a context ψ and in an environment which provides bindings for the variables in ψ.

```
rec  eval : {ψ:ctx} tm[ψ] → envr ψ  → clos =
fn  e ⇒ fn  env ⇒ case  e of
| ψ. #p .. ⇒ env (ψ. #p ..)
| ψ. lam (λx. E .. x) ⇒ cl (ψ,x:exp . E .. x) env
| ψ. app (E1 ..) (E2 ..) ⇒
 let  cl (ϕ,x:tm . E .. x) env' = eval (ψ. E1 ..) env
 let  v = eval (ψ. E2 ..) env in
 in  eval  (ϕ,x:tm . E .. x)  (fn  var ⇒ case  var of
                 | ϕ,x:tm . x ⇒ v
                 | ϕ,x:tm . #p .. ⇒ env' (ϕ. #p .. ))
```

When we pattern match on a contextual object `e : tm[ψ]`, we might obtain a variable in ψ, which we write as `ψ. #p ..` . The item `#p` is a *parameter variable*, standing for a position in ψ. Its association with the identity substitution for ψ (written `..`) turns it from a position into a genuine `tm[ψ]`. In this case, we look it up in the environment. A lambda abstraction simply evaluates to a closure. We think of the ψ in `ψ. lam (λx. E .. x)` as binding all the free variables of `lam (λx. E .. x)`. We explicitly apply ψ's identity substitution `..` to `E` in the pattern to indicate that the variables in ψ *are* permitted to occur in `E`. Conversely, writing the pattern as `ψ. lam (λx. E x)` attempts to strengthen the variables of ψ out of `E`, which is not the intention.

An application evaluates the function position to obtain a body `E` in the *possibly different* context ϕ with an associated `env'` providing bindings for the variables in ϕ. We now evaluate the body `E` in the environment `env'` extended with the appropriate binding for `x`.

This implementation is quite close to that of Licata and Harper [2009]. One noticeable difference is that contexts appear explicitly in our definition of `clos`, which is arguably more readable.

2.2 Relating Contexts: Closure Conversion

When implementing a transformation between languages, as is common in compilers, we often need the resulting terms to be in a different but related context. In systems such as Twelf [Pfenning and Schürmann 1999] and Beluga, the solution is somewhat unsatisfactory. The programmer states results in a combined context, and relies on sophisticated subordination and subsumption mechanisms. However, by encoding this relation on contexts as an inductive predicate, we can express this directly and do away with world subsumption.

We demonstrate this idea with an implementation of closure conversion. Guillemette and Monnier [2007] provide a good overview of closure conversion. Our implementation resembles theirs, although we use HOAS for our term representations. The particulars of closure conversion are not tremendously important here. We wish primarily to demonstrate how data-types complement contextual types.

The source language is the language of Section 2.1. The target language is augmented with constructs for explicit closures, shown in part below:

```
clam : (envr → ctm) → ctm.     proj : envr → nat → ctm.
close : ctm → envr → ctm.      nil : envr.
create : envr → ctm.           snoc : envr → ctm → envr
```

An `envr` is an arbitrary length tuple of terms. Closure conversion will turn contexts into explicit `ctm` objects such that the bodies of lambda abstractions will only refer to their `envr` and no other variables. The reason is that we want to be able to hoist them to the top level. `close` constructs an explicit closure which binds all but the last argument. `proj E N` projects out the `N`th component of the environment `E`.

We must now do as we promised and turn the *open* bodies of lambdas into *closed* terms which instead project from their environment. To characterize the free variables in the open bodies we define the context `cctx`. We depart from Guillemette and Monnier [2007] by performing substitutions instead of let-bindings, which is easy thanks to HOAS.

```
schema cctx = ctm;

rec addProjs : (φ:cctx) (N:nat[]) (M:cexp[φ,e:envr])
  → cexp[e:envr] =
λ φ ⇒ λ N ⇒ λ M ⇒ case φ of
| [] ⇒ [e:envr]. M e
| φ,x:ctm ⇒ addProjs φ (s N) (φ,e. M .. (proj e N) e)
```

We write `[]` for the empty context and `[e:envr]` for a singleton context containing a single variable of type `envr`.

Of course if we insist that contexts be passed explicitly as environments, we had better be able to turn contexts into environments:

```
rec ctxToEnv : (φ:cctx) envr[φ] =
λ φ ⇒ case φ of
| [] ⇒ []. nil
| φ,x:ctm ⇒ let φ. env .. = ctxToEnv φ in
  φ,x:ctm. snoc (env ..) x
```

So far this is more or less standard Beluga code. The *raison d'être* for this example is the recursive relation on contexts:

```
datatype ctx_rel : ctx → cctx → ctype
| rnil : ctx_rel [] []
| rsnoc : {ψ φ} → ctx_rel ψ φ
  → ctx_rel (ψ,x:tm) (φ,x:ctm)
```

We freely omit types where they might reasonably be inferred. `ctx_rel ψ φ` states only that ψ and ϕ are the same length. We illustrate more sophisticated relations later.

The closure conversion function takes vanilla terms in a context ψ into target language terms in a related context ϕ. We only explain the cases for variables and lambda-abstraction. The full implementation can be found in the appendix.

```
rec conv : {ψ:ctx} (φ:cctx) → ctx_rel ψ φ → tm[ψ]
  → ctm[φ] = λ φ ⇒ fn cr ⇒ fn m ⇒ case m of
```

Variables are taken to corresponding variables. When we learn that ψ is non-empty, we learn by inspecting `cr` that so too is ϕ. The $\{\phi = ...\}$ syntax passes the implicit argument ϕ explicitly.

```
| ψ',x:tm. x ⇒ let rsnoc {φ=φ',x:ctm} _ = cr in φ',x. x
| ψ',x:tm. #p .. ⇒ let rsnoc {φ=φ',x:ctm} cr' = cr in
 let φ'. M .. = conv _ cr' (ψ'. #p ..) in φ',x. M ..
```

To closure convert a lambda, we closure convert the body in the extended context `ψ,x` using an extended context relation `rsnoc cr`. We *close* it and return an explicit closure. For simplicity, we cheat and do not compute the set of variables occuring in the body: we instead close over the entire context.

```
| ψ. lam (λx. M .. x) ⇒
 let φ, x:ctm. M' .. x =
   conv _ (rsnoc cr) (ψ,x. M .. x) in
 let [ev:envr]. M'' ev =
   addProjs _ 0 (φ, x:ctm, ev:envr. M' .. x) in
 let φ. Env .. = ctxToEnv φ in
 φ. close (clam (λev. M'' ev)) (Env ..)
```

We omit here the case for applications which is straightforward.

A more sophisticated example of a context relation appears if we wish to express that a transformation is type preserving. In type-preserving closure conversion (see Minamide et al. [1996] and Guillemette and Monnier [2007]), there is also a non-trivial relation between source language types and target language types. Assuming now that we use *intrinsically-typed* terms, we might wish to use a relation such as the following:

```
datatype ctx_rel : ctx → cctx → ctype =
| rnil : ctx_rel [] []
| rsnoc : {ψ φ} {T:tp[]} {S:ctp[]} → ctx_rel ψ φ
  → tp_rel T S → ctx_rel (ψ, x:tm T) (φ, x:ctm S)
```

2.3 Logical Relations: Normalization by Evaluation

Implementing normalization proofs or normalization by evaluation (NbE) in a system such Beluga has been difficult to do directly. Here we demonstrate an implementation of typed normalization by evaluation [Berger and Schwichtenberg 1991] in our language which supports both contextual types and indexed data-types.

The essence of normalization by evaluation is to normalize object level terms by reusing the evaluation of the computation level. There are therefore two levels of terms: object language terms using the LF function space, and computation level (semantic) terms using the computation level function space. Normalization proceeds by interpreting object level terms as semantic terms and reifying the result.

The source language is `tm`: a standard (intrinsically) simply-typed family of LF-level terms with `lam` and `app` as constructors.

We have an open type `atomic_tp` of atomic (base) types which our implementation is essentially parametric over. The target is simply-typed terms in β-normal η-long form:

```
nlam : (neut T → norm S) → norm (arr T S).
rapp : neut (arr T S) → norm T → neut S.
embed : neut (atomic P) → norm (atomic P).
```

To characterize the free variable context of the source language, we define **schema** `ctx` = **some** `[T:tp] tm T`. The context of the target language is described by **schema** `tctx` = **some** `[T:tp] neut T`.

Semantic terms must be defined as a datatype, because we must use the computation-level function space:

```
type sub ψ φ = {T:tp[]} → #(neut T)[ψ] → #(neut T)[φ]

datatype sem : ctx → tp[] → ctype =
| syn : {ψ} {P:atomic_tp[]}
   → (neut (atomic P))[ψ] → sem ψ (atomic P)
| slam : {ψ A B} ({φ} → sub ψ φ → sem φ A → sem φ B)
   → sem ψ (arr A B)
```

The type `{T:tp[]} → #(neut T)[ψ] → #(neut T)[φ]` is read as the type of (type preserving) substitutions of variables in ψ for variables in ϕ. The need for this will become clear in our implementations of substitution and reification. Observe that we restrict the embedding of `neut` into `sem` to atomic types. This enforces η-longness.

We must manually implement substitution of variables for variables in `sem`, since we do not provide substitution for free for datatypes. In fact, it is substantially different from LF substitution. Licata [2011] explains this difference in depth.

The interesting case is `slam`. It makes essential use of the quantification over substitutions in `slam`. Similar mechanisms appear in both Licata and Harper [2009] and Pouillard and Pottier [2010].

```
rec subst:{ψ φ S} → sub ψ φ → sem ψ S → sem φ S =
fn σ ⇒ fn e ⇒ case e of
| syn (ψ. R ..) ⇒ nsubst σ (ψ. R ..)
| slam f ⇒ slam (fn σ' ⇒ fn s ⇒ f (σ' ∘ σ) s)

rec nsubst : {ψ φ S} → sub ψ φ → (neut S)[ψ]
 → (neut S)[φ] = ...
```

Where `nsubst` performs substitution on syntactic neutral terms. We show the full code for this example in the appendix.

Embedding `neut` into `sem` is only possible at atomic types, so we must η-expand in the general case:

```
rec reflect : (ψ A) (R:(neut A)[ψ]) → sem ψ A =
λ ψ ⇒ λ A ⇒ λ R ⇒ case []. A of
| []. atomic P ⇒ syn (ψ. R ..)
| []. arr T S ⇒ slam (λ {φ} ⇒ fn σ ⇒ fn s ⇒
 let φ. R' .. = nsubst σ (ψ. R ..) in
 let φ. N .. = reify _ T s in
  reflect _ S (φ. rapp (R' ..) (N ..)))
```

We can then reify semantic terms as object level terms by calling the computation level functions on fresh variables:

```
rec reify : (ψ A) → sem ψ A → (norm A)[ψ] =
λ ψ ⇒ λ A ⇒ fn s ⇒ case [] . A of
| []. atomic P ⇒ let syn (ψ. R ..) = s
 in ψ. embed (R ..)
| []. arr T S ⇒ let slam f = s in
 let ψ,x:tm T. E .. x =
   reify (f weaken (reflect _ T (ψ,x:neut T. x)))
 in ψ. nlam (λx. E .. x)
```

Where `weaken` is the weakening substitution of type:

```
{ψ:ctx} {S:tp[]} → sub ψ (ψ,x:tm S)
```

We can now implement evaluation with the help of an environment of bindings. The `lam` case evaluates in the extended environment. In the application case, the evaluation of `E1` must produce an `slam` since `syn` is only applicable to atomic types.

```
rec eval : {ψ φ S} →
  → ({T} #(tm T)[ψ] → sem φ T)
  → (tm S)[ψ] → sem φ S =
fn r ⇒ fn σ ⇒ fn e ⇒ case e of
| ψ. #p .. ⇒ σ (ψ . #p .. )
| ψ. lam (λx. E .. x) ⇒ slam (fn σ' ⇒ fn s ⇒
   eval (extend ((subst σ') ∘ σ) s) (ψ,x. E .. x)
| ψ. app (E1 ..) (E2 ..) ⇒
  let slam f = eval σ (ψ. E1 ..) in
  f id (eval σ (ψ. E2 ..))
```

We have used `extend` to extend the domain of the environment in the `lam` case. Its type is shown below.

```
rec extend : {ψ:tctx} {φ:ctx} {S}
  → ({T} → #(tm T)[ψ] → sem φ T) → sem φ S
  → ({T} → #(tm T)[ψ,x:tm S] → sem φ T)
```

Normalization is then simply evaluation followed by reification:

```
rec nbe : {A} → (tm A)[ ] → (norm A)[ ] =
fn e ⇒ reify [] A (eval (fn y ⇒ impossible y) e)
```

Notably, this implementation cleanly enforces η-longness and type preservation by employing dependent types. Expressing these invariants together with a clean approach to variable binding in NbE is rarely found in other work. Licata and Harper [2009] and Shinwell et al. [2003] lack dependent types. Pouillard and Pottier [2010] have this ability, although their implementation is untyped NbE, and hence does not employ it. Further, this illustrates that arbitrary mixing of computation and LF function spaces is not crucial to NbE, as suggested by Licata and Harper [2009]. Their framework, however, obtains weakening for free for `sem` while we have to do a modicum of work to implement it.

From a logic perspective, this can be seen as a (partial) completeness and consistency proof for a natural deduction system by the method of *logical relations*. We say *partial* because we postpone the issues of totality checking to future work. We anticipate that this can be scaled to normalization proofs for the simply-typed lambda calculus without any difficulty. The addition of indexed data-types hence brings substantial benefit to programming and proof systems such as Beluga, since it makes such systems capable of proofs by logical relations.

3. A Review of Contextual LF

Here we describe the index domain, which in our case is contextual LF [Pientka 2008, 2011] which builds on contextual types which were first introduced in Nanevski et al. [2008b].

3.1 Contextual LF

Contextual LF extends the logical framework LF [Harper et al. 1993] with the power of contextual objects $\hat{\Psi}.M$ of type $A[\Psi]$. M denotes an object which may refer to the bound variables listed in $\hat{\Psi}$ and has type A in the context Ψ (see also [Nanevski et al. 2008b]). $\hat{\Psi}$ can be obtained from the context Ψ by simply dropping the type annotations and keeping only the declared variable names. We characterize only objects in $\beta\eta$ normal form, since these are the only meaningful objects in LF. Furthermore, we concentrate here on characterizing well-typed terms, but defining kinds and kinding rules for types is straightforward and omitted.

Atomic types	P, Q	$::=$	$\mathbf{a}\,\vec{M}$
Types	A, B	$::=$	$P \mid \Pi x{:}A.B$
Heads	H	$::=$	$x \mid \mathbf{c} \mid p[\sigma]$
Neutral Terms	R	$::=$	$H \mid R\,N \mid u[\sigma]$
Normal Terms	M, N	$::=$	$R \mid \lambda x.M$
Substitutions	σ	$::=$	$\cdot \mid \mathsf{id}_\psi \mid \sigma, M \mid \sigma; H$
Contexts	Ψ	$::=$	$\cdot \mid \psi \mid \Psi, x{:}A$

Normal objects may contain *ordinary bound variables* which are used to represent object-level binders and are bound by λ-abstraction or in a context Ψ. They may also contain meta-variables $u[\sigma]$ and parameter variables $p[\sigma]$ which we call *contextual variables*. Contextual variables are associated with a post-poned substitution σ. The meta-variable u stands for a contextual object $\hat{\Psi}.R$ where $\hat{\Psi}$ describes the ordinary bound variables which may occur in R. This allows us to rename the free variables occurring in R when necessary. The parameter variable p stands for a contextual object $\hat{\Psi}.R$ where R must be either an ordinary bound variable from $\hat{\Psi}$ or another parameter variable.

In the simultaneous substitutions σ, we do not make its domain explicit. Rather we think of a substitution together with its domain Ψ and the i-th element in σ corresponds to the i-th declaration in Ψ. We have two different ways of building a substitution: either by using a normal term M or a variable x. Note that a variable x is only a normal term M if it is of base type. However, as we push a substitution σ through a λ-abstraction $\lambda x.M$, we need to extend σ with x. The resulting substitution σ, x may not be well-typed, since x may not be of base type and in fact we do not know its type. Hence, we allow substitutions not only to be extended with normal terms M but also with variables x. Without loss of generality we require that meta-variables have base type.

A bound variable context Ψ contains bound variable declarations in addition to context variables. A context may only contain at most one context variable and it must occur at the left. This will make it easier to ensure bound variable dependencies are satisfied in the dependently typed setting.

Following Pientka [2008] we use a bi-directional type system where we check normal terms against a type and synthesize a type for neutral terms. LF objects may depend on variables declared in the context Ψ and the meta-context Δ which contains contextual variables such as meta-variables u, parameter variables p and context variables ψ. We introduce Δ more formally in the next section. All typing judgments have access to both contexts and a well-typed signature Σ where we store constants together with their types and kinds.

$\Delta; \Psi \vdash M \Leftarrow A$	Normal term M checks against type A
$\Delta; \Psi \vdash R \Rightarrow A$	Neutral term R synthesizes type A
$\Delta; \Psi \vdash \sigma \Leftarrow \Psi'$	Substitution σ has domain Ψ' and range Ψ.

The bi-directional typing rules are mostly straightforward and are presented in Figure 1. We will tacitly rename bound variables, and maintain that contexts and substitutions declare no variable more than once. Note that substitutions σ are defined only on ordinary variables x and not contextual variables. Moreover, we require the usual conditions on bound variables. For example in the rule for λ-abstraction the bound variable x must be new and cannot already occur in the context Ψ. This can be always achieved via α-renaming. Similarly, in meta-terms we tacitly apply α-renaming.

As is common, we rely on hereditary substitutions, written as $[N/x]_A(B)$ (or $[\sigma]_\Psi(B)$) to guarantee that when we substitute a term N which has type A for the variable x in the type B, we obtain a type B' which is in normal form. Hereditary substitutions continue to substitute, if a redex is created; for example, when replacing naively x by $\lambda y.c\ y$ in the object $x\ z$, we would obtain $(\lambda y.c\ y)\ z$ which is not in normal form and hence not a valid term in our grammar. Hereditary substitutions continue to substitute z for y in $c\ y$ to obtain $c\ z$ as a final result. For a more detailed description of hereditary substitution, we refer the reader to for example Nanevski et al. [2008b].

Finally, we remark on equality checking. When checking $A = B$ we must take into account η-contraction, because we have two

Neutral Terms $\boxed{\Delta; \Psi \vdash R \Rightarrow A}$

$$\frac{\Psi(x) = A}{\Delta; \Psi \vdash x \Rightarrow A} \qquad \frac{\Delta(p) = \#A[\Phi] \quad \Delta; \Psi \vdash \sigma \Leftarrow \Phi}{\Delta; \Psi \vdash p[\sigma] \Rightarrow [\sigma]_\Phi A}$$

$$\frac{\Sigma(\mathbf{c}) = A}{\Delta; \Psi \vdash \mathbf{c} \Rightarrow A} \qquad \frac{\Delta(u) = P[\Phi] \quad \Delta; \Psi \vdash \sigma \Leftarrow \Phi}{\Delta; \Psi \vdash u[\sigma] \Rightarrow [\sigma]_\Phi P}$$

$$\frac{\Delta; \Psi \vdash R \Rightarrow \Pi x{:}A.B \quad \Delta; \Psi \vdash M \Leftarrow A}{\Delta; \Psi \vdash R\, M \Rightarrow [M/x]_A B}$$

Normal Terms $\boxed{\Delta; \Psi \vdash M \Leftarrow A}$

$$\frac{\Delta; \Psi \vdash R \Rightarrow P \quad P = Q}{\Delta; \Psi \vdash R \Leftarrow Q} \qquad \frac{\Delta; \Psi, x{:}A \vdash M \Leftarrow B}{\Delta; \Psi \vdash \lambda x.M \Leftarrow \Pi x{:}A.B}$$

Substitutions $\boxed{\Delta; \Psi \vdash \sigma \Leftarrow \Psi'}$

$$\frac{}{\Delta; \Psi \vdash \cdot \Leftarrow \cdot} \qquad \frac{\Delta; \Psi \vdash \sigma \Leftarrow \Phi \quad \Delta; \Psi \vdash H \Rightarrow B \quad B = [\sigma]_\Phi A}{\Delta; \Psi \vdash \sigma ; H \Leftarrow \Phi, x{:}A}$$

$$\frac{}{\Delta; \psi, \Psi \vdash \mathsf{id}_\psi \Leftarrow \psi} \qquad \frac{\Delta; \Psi \vdash \sigma \Leftarrow \Phi \quad \Delta; \Psi \vdash M \Leftarrow [\sigma]_\Phi A}{\Delta; \Psi \vdash \sigma, M \Leftarrow \Phi, x{:}A}$$

Figure 1. Typing for contextual LF

ways to build substitutions. If x has type $\Pi y{:}A.B$ then we may have written $\sigma; x$ or $\sigma, \lambda y.x\ y$.

3.2 Meta-Objects and Meta-types

We lift contextual LF objects to meta-types and meta-objects to treat abstraction over meta-objects uniformly. Meta-objects are either contextual objects written as $\hat{\Psi}.R$ or contexts Ψ. These are the index objects which can be used to index computation-level types. There are three different meta-types: $P[\Psi]$ denotes the type of a meta-variable u and stands for a general contextual object $\hat{\Psi}.R$. $\#A[\Psi]$ denotes the type of a parameter variable p and it stands for a variable object, i.e. either $\hat{\Psi}.x$ or $\hat{\Psi}.p[\pi]$ where π is a variable substitution. A variable substitution π is a special case for general substitutions σ; however unlike $p[\sigma]$ which can produce a general LF object, $p[\pi]$ guarantees we are producing a variable. G describes the schema (i.e. type) of a context. The tag $\#$ on the type of parameter variables is a simple syntactic device to distinguish between the type of meta-variables and parameter variables. It does not introduce a subtyping relationship between the type $\#A[\Psi]$ and the type $A[\Psi]$. The meta-context in which an LF object appears uniquely determines if X denotes a meta-variable, parameter variable or context variable. We use the following convention: if X denotes a meta-variable we usually write u or v; if it stands for a parameter-variable, we write p and for context variables we use ψ.

Context schemas	G	$::=$	$\exists\overrightarrow{(x{:}A)}.B \mid G + \exists\overrightarrow{(x{:}A)}.B$
Meta Objects	C	$::=$	$\hat{\Psi}.R \mid \Psi$
Meta Types	U	$::=$	$P[\Psi] \mid \#A[\Psi] \mid G$
Meta substitutions	θ	$::=$	$\cdot \mid \theta, C/X$
Meta-context	Δ	$::=$	$\cdot \mid \Delta, X{:}U$

Context schemas consist of different schema elements $\exists\overrightarrow{(x{:}A)}.B$ which are built using $+$. Intuitively, this means a concrete declaration in a context must be an instance of one of the elements specified in the schema. For example, a context $x{:}\mathsf{exp\ nat}, y{:}\mathsf{exp\ bool}$ will check against the schema $\exists T{:}\mathsf{tp}.\mathsf{exp}\ T$.

Meta Terms $\boxed{\Delta \vdash C \Leftarrow U}$

$$\frac{}{\Delta \vdash \cdot \Leftarrow G} \quad \frac{\Delta(\psi) = G}{\Delta \vdash \psi \Leftarrow G}$$

$$\frac{\begin{array}{l}\Delta \vdash \Psi \Leftarrow G \\ \exists\overrightarrow{(x : B')}.B \in G \quad \Delta; \Psi \vdash \sigma \Leftarrow \overrightarrow{(x{:}B')} \quad A = [\sigma]_{\overrightarrow{(x:B')}} B\end{array}}{\Delta \vdash \Psi, x{:}A \Leftarrow G}$$

$$\frac{\Delta; \Psi \vdash \sigma \Leftarrow \Phi}{\Delta \vdash \hat{\Psi}.\sigma \Leftarrow \Phi[\Psi]} \quad \frac{\Delta; \Psi \vdash R \Leftarrow P}{\Delta \vdash \hat{\Psi}.R \Leftarrow P[\Psi]} \quad \frac{\Psi(x) = A}{\Delta \vdash \hat{\Psi}.x \Leftarrow \#A[\Psi]}$$

$$\frac{\Delta(p) = \#A[\Phi] \qquad \Delta; \Psi \vdash \pi \Leftarrow \Phi \quad [\pi]_\Phi(A) = B}{\Delta \vdash \hat{\Psi}.p[\pi] \Leftarrow \#B[\Psi]}$$

Meta-Substitutions $\boxed{\Delta \vdash \theta \Leftarrow \Delta'}$

$$\frac{}{\Delta \vdash \cdot \Leftarrow \cdot} \quad \frac{\Delta \vdash \theta \Leftarrow \Delta' \quad \Delta \vdash C \Leftarrow [\![\theta]\!]_{\Delta'}(U)}{\Delta \vdash \theta, C/X \Leftarrow \Delta', X{:}U}$$

Figure 2. Typing for meta-terms

The uniform treatment of meta-terms, called C, and meta-types, called U, allows us to give a compact definition of meta-substitutions θ and meta-contexts Δ.

We omit here the rules stating when meta-types and meta-contexts are well-formed and show only the typing rules for meta-terms and meta-substitutions in Figure 2.

A consequence of the uniform treatment of meta-terms is that the design of the computation language is modular and parameterized over meta-terms and meta-types. This has two main advantages: First, we can in principle easily extend meta-terms and meta-types without affecting the computation language; in particular, it is straightforward to add substitution variables which were present in Pientka [2008] or allow for richer context schemas. Second, it will be key to a modular, clean design of computations.

The single meta-substitution, written as $[\![C/X]\!]_U(*)$ where $*$ stands for A, M, R, σ, Ψ, is defined inductively on the structure of the given object. (see for example Pientka [2011] or the appendix). We only discuss briefly here some of the fundamental ideas. Let us first consider the case where X stands for a meta-variable u and C is a meta-object $\hat{\Psi}.R$. We note that there are no capture issues when we push $[\![\hat{\Psi}.R/u]\!]$ through a lambda-expression and the only interesting issue arises when we encounter an object $u[\sigma]$. In this case, we apply $[\![\hat{\Psi}.R/u]\!]$ to σ to obtain σ'. Subsequently, we apply σ' to R to obtain the final result.

Next, we consider the case where X stands for a parameter variable p and C is a meta-object $\hat{\Psi}.x$ or $\hat{\Psi}.q[\pi]$. The only interesting case is when we encounter $p[\sigma]$. Similar to the case for meta-variables, we apply the meta-substitution to σ to obtain σ' and subsequently apply σ' to x or $q[\pi]$. There is however a small caveat: since σ' is an arbitrary substitution, applying it to x, may yield a normal object M. Hence, simply returning M may produce a non-normal term which is not meaningful in our grammar. The solution to this problem is to define meta-substitutions hereditarily; hence we index the meta-substitution with its domain.

Finally, the case where X stands for a context variable ψ and C is a meta-object Ψ. There are two interesting cases: 1) when we encounter the identity substitution id_ψ, we unroll Ψ and create at the same time a concrete identity substitution which maps all variables from Ψ to themselves. 2) when we encounter a context variable ψ in a context, then we simply replace it with the concrete context Ψ. The full definition of meta-substitutions is given in the appendix and has been previously described in [Nanevski et al. 2008b; Pientka 2008, 2011].

The simultaneous meta-substitution, written as $[\![\theta]\!]$, is a straightforward extension of the single substitution.

Theorem 3.1 (Meta-substitution property).
If $\Delta' \vdash \theta \Leftarrow \Delta$ *and* $\Delta; \Psi \vdash J$ *then* $\Delta'; [\![\theta]\!]_\Delta \Psi \vdash [\![\theta]\!]_\Delta J$.

4. Beluga$^\mu$: a language with binding support and recursive types

We present in this section a dependently typed programming language Beluga$^\mu$ along the lines of Mini-ML, including recursive types, variants and general pattern matching which is critical in practice and whose theory in this setting is non-trivial. Polymorphism, on the other hand, is largely orthogonal and therefore postponed. The type index objects are drawn from the domain of meta-objects presented in the previous section, but we emphasize that this language is parametric over the index domain, requiring only decidable equality.

4.1 Types and Kinds

Our type language supports function types (written as $T_1 \rightarrow T_2$), products (written as $T_1 \times T_2$), labelled sums (written as $\langle\overrightarrow{l{:}T}\rangle$), dependent function types (written as $\Pi X{:}U.T$) and dependent product types (written as $\Sigma X{:}U.T$). We only allow dependencies on meta-terms not on arbitrary computation-level expressions. The novel part in our type language is our definition of recursive types together with the equality constraint which may be associated with a given type. The recursive type is written as $\mu Z.\lambda\vec{X}.T$; while Z denotes a type variable, $\lambda\vec{X}.T$ describes a type-level function which expects meta-terms.

$$\begin{array}{lll}
\text{Kinds} & K ::= & \mathsf{ctype} \mid \Pi X{:}U.K \\
\text{Types} & T ::= & \mathsf{Unit} \mid Z \mid T_1 \rightarrow T_2 \mid T_1 \times T_2 \mid \langle\overrightarrow{l : T}\rangle \\
 & & \mid \Pi X{:}U.T \mid \Sigma X{:}U.T \mid C_1 = C_2 \wedge T \\
 & & \mid \mu Z.\lambda\vec{X}.T \mid T\,\vec{C} \mid U \\
\text{Context} & \Gamma ::= & \cdot \mid \Gamma, Z : K \mid \Gamma, x : T
\end{array}$$

We note that we can directly refer to meta-types and embed them in our computation-level types. Hence meta-objects can be directly analyzed and manipulated by our computation language. This is convenient in our setting, however, it also prevents a naive erasure of all the meta-objects.

We also note that equalities cannot occur just by themselves in our grammar. The reason is that equalities are treated silently during type checking and equality proofs which establish $C_1 = C_2$ do not pollute our computation-level expressions. In fact, equalities typically occur inside a recursive type and they are trivially true once we have chosen the correct instantiation for the existentially quantified variable. We illustrate this idea shortly.

To illustrate, we give here three examples.

Example 1 The type of a vector of booleans which keeps track of their length can be defined as follows. We assume an LF signature which declares `nat:type` together with two constants, `0:nat` and `s: nat → nat`. Because all index objects to the recursive type V are closed, we omit writing the empty context and simply write nat for $\mathsf{nat}[]$ and Y for $\cdot.Y$.

$$\begin{array}{ll}
\mathsf{Vec} = \mu\mathsf{Vec}.\lambda X.\ \langle\ \mathsf{nil} & :\ X = 0 \wedge \mathsf{Unit}\ , \\
\qquad\qquad\qquad\quad \mathsf{cons} & :\ \Sigma Y{:}\mathsf{nat}.X = \mathsf{s}\ Y \wedge \mathsf{bool} \times \mathsf{Vec}\ Y\ \rangle
\end{array}$$

Example 2 The relation between contexts from Section 2.2 can be written as follows:

$$\begin{array}{l}\mu\mathrm{Ctx\_rel}.\lambda\psi\lambda\phi.\ \langle\ \mathsf{rnil}\ \ :\psi=\cdot\wedge\phi=\cdot\wedge\mathsf{Unit}\ ,\\ \qquad\qquad\quad \mathsf{rsnoc}\!:\Sigma\psi'\!:\!\mathsf{ctx}.\Sigma\phi'\!:\!\mathsf{cctx}.\\ \qquad\qquad\qquad \psi=\psi',x{:}\mathsf{tm}\ \wedge\ \phi=\phi',y{:}\mathsf{ctm}\\ \qquad\qquad\qquad \wedge\ \mathrm{Ctx\_rel}\ \psi'\ \phi'\ \rangle\end{array}$$

Our treatment of recursive types with equalities is similar to Xi et al. [2003] and Sulzmann et al. [2007] where recursive types are endowed with equalities between types to model GADTs. Recently fixed points with equalities between terms have appeared in Licata [2011] and in Baelde et al. [2010] for example. In our setting, we treat equality between contextual objects. Next, we give the kinding rules for computation-level types.

Well-kinded computation-level types $\boxed{\Delta;\Gamma\vdash T:K}$

$$\frac{\Delta,\overrightarrow{X{:}U}\ ;\ \Gamma,Z:\Pi\overrightarrow{X{:}U}.K\vdash T:K}{\Delta;\Gamma\vdash\mu Z.\lambda\vec{X}.T:\Pi\overrightarrow{X{:}U}.K}$$

$$\frac{\Delta;\Gamma\vdash T_1:\mathsf{ctype}\quad \Delta;\Gamma\vdash T_2:\mathsf{ctype}\quad *\in\{\rightarrow,\times\}}{\Delta;\Gamma\vdash T_1*T_2:\mathsf{ctype}}$$

$$\frac{\Delta\,;\,\Gamma\vdash U\Leftarrow\mathsf{mtype}\quad \Delta,X{:}U\,;\,\Gamma\vdash T:\mathsf{ctype}}{\Delta;\Gamma\vdash\Pi X{:}U.T:\mathsf{ctype}}$$

$$\frac{\Delta\,;\,\Gamma\vdash U\Leftarrow\mathsf{mtype}\quad \Delta,X{:}U\,;\,\Gamma\vdash T:\mathsf{ctype}}{\Delta;\Gamma\vdash\Sigma X{:}U.T:\mathsf{ctype}}$$

$$\frac{\Delta\vdash C_1\Leftarrow U\quad \Delta\vdash C_2\Leftarrow U\quad \Delta;\Gamma\vdash T:\mathsf{ctype}}{\Delta;\Gamma\vdash C_1=C_2\wedge T:\mathsf{ctype}}$$

$$\frac{\Delta\vdash U\Leftarrow\mathsf{mtype}}{\Delta;\Gamma\vdash U:\mathsf{ctype}}\qquad\frac{}{\Delta;\Gamma\vdash\mathsf{Unit}:\mathsf{ctype}}$$

$$\frac{\Gamma(Z)=K}{\Delta;\Gamma\vdash Z:K}\qquad\frac{\Delta;\Gamma\vdash T:\Pi X{:}U.K\quad \Delta\vdash C:U}{\Delta;\Gamma\vdash T\ C:[\![C/X]\!]K}$$

4.2 Computations

Our language of computations includes recursion (written as rec $f.E$), nameless functions (written as fn $x.E$) and dependent functions (written as $\lambda X.\,E$). We also include pairs (written as (E_1,E_2)) and dependent pairs (written as pack $(C,\ E)$). Finally, we include labeled variants (written as $\langle l\ =\ E\rangle$) and a fold constructor for recursive types.

$$\begin{array}{lll}\text{Expressions (synth.)} & I ::= y\mid I\ E\mid I\ C\mid(E:T)\\ \text{Expressions (checked)} & E ::= I\mid C\mid \mathsf{fn}\ y.E\mid\lambda X.\,E\mid\mathsf{rec}\ f.E\mid\mathsf{unit}\\ & \quad\mid\mathsf{fold}\ E\mid\langle l=E\rangle\mid\mathsf{pack}\ (C,E)\\ & \quad\mid(E_1,E_2)\mid\mathsf{case}\ I\ \mathsf{of}\ \vec{B}\\ \text{Pattern} & pat ::= x\mid C\mid\mathsf{unit}\mid\mathsf{fold}\ pat\mid\langle l=pat\rangle\\ & \quad\mid\mathsf{pack}\ (C,pat)\mid(pat_1,pat_2)\\ \text{Branch} & B ::= \Delta;\Gamma\ .\ pat:\theta\mapsto E\\ \text{Contexts} & \Gamma ::= \cdot\mid\Gamma,y{:}T\end{array}$$

Our language is split into expressions for which we synthesize types and expressions which are checked against a type. This minimizes the necessary type annotations and provides a syntax directed recipe for a type checker. Intuitively, the expressions which introduce a type are expressions which are checked and expressions which eliminate a type are in the synthesis category. We have two different kinds of function applications, one for applying computation-level functions to an expression and the other to apply a dependent function to a meta-object C. Pairs and dependent pairs are analyzed by pattern matching.

$\boxed{\Delta;\Gamma\vdash I\Rightarrow T}$ Expression I synthesizes type T

$$\frac{y{:}T\in\Gamma}{\Delta;\Gamma\vdash y\Rightarrow T}\qquad\frac{\Delta;\Gamma\vdash I\Rightarrow C=C\wedge T}{\Delta;\Gamma\vdash I\Rightarrow T}$$

$$\frac{\Delta;\Gamma\vdash I\Rightarrow T_2\rightarrow T\quad \Delta;\Gamma\vdash E\Leftarrow T_2}{\Delta;\Gamma\vdash I\ E\Rightarrow T}$$

$$\frac{\Delta;\Gamma\vdash I\Rightarrow\Pi X{:}U.T\quad \Delta\vdash C\Leftarrow U}{\Delta;\Gamma\vdash I\ C\Rightarrow[\![C/X]\!]T}\qquad\frac{\Delta;\Gamma\vdash E\Leftarrow T}{\Delta;\Gamma\vdash(E:T)\Rightarrow T}$$

$\boxed{\Delta;\Gamma\vdash E\Leftarrow T}$ Expression E checks against type T

$$\frac{\Delta;\Gamma\vdash E_i\Leftarrow T_i\quad\text{where } l_i:T_i\in\overrightarrow{l:T}}{\Delta;\Gamma\vdash\langle l_i=E_i\rangle\Leftarrow\langle\overrightarrow{l:T}\rangle}\qquad\frac{\Delta;\Gamma,\ f:T\vdash E\Leftarrow T}{\Delta;\Gamma\vdash\mathsf{rec}\ f.E\Leftarrow T}$$

$$\frac{\Delta;\Gamma,y{:}T_1\vdash E\Leftarrow T_2}{\Delta;\Gamma\vdash\mathsf{fn}\ y.E\Leftarrow T_1\rightarrow T_2}\qquad\frac{\Delta,X{:}U;\Gamma\vdash E\Leftarrow T}{\Delta;\Gamma\vdash\lambda X.\,E\Leftarrow\Pi X{:}U.T}$$

$$\frac{\Delta;\Gamma\vdash E_1\Leftarrow T_1\quad \Delta;\Gamma\vdash E_2\Leftarrow T_2}{\Delta;\Gamma\vdash(E_1,E_2)\Leftarrow T_1\times T_2}\qquad\frac{\Delta;\Gamma\vdash I\Rightarrow T\quad T=T'}{\Delta;\Gamma\vdash I\Leftarrow T'}$$

$$\frac{\Delta\vdash C\Leftarrow U\quad \Delta;\Gamma\vdash E\Leftarrow[\![C/X]\!]T}{\Delta;\Gamma\vdash\mathsf{pack}\ (C,E)\Leftarrow\Sigma X{:}U.T}\qquad\frac{\Delta\vdash C\Leftarrow U}{\Delta;\Gamma\vdash C\Leftarrow U}$$

$$\frac{\Delta;\Gamma\vdash E\Leftarrow[\mu Z.\lambda\vec{X}.\,S/Z][\![\vec{C}/\vec{X}]\!]S}{\Delta;\Gamma\vdash\mathsf{fold}\ E\Leftarrow(\mu Z.\lambda\vec{X}.\,S)\ \vec{C}}\qquad\frac{\Delta;\Gamma\vdash E\Leftarrow T}{\Delta;\Gamma\vdash E\Leftarrow C=C\wedge T}$$

$$\frac{\Delta;\Gamma\vdash I\Rightarrow S\quad\text{for all } i\ \Delta;\Gamma\vdash B_i\Leftarrow S\rightarrow T}{\Delta;\Gamma\vdash\mathsf{case}\ I\ \mathsf{of}\ \vec{B}\Leftarrow T}$$

$\boxed{\Delta;\Gamma\vdash B\Leftarrow S\rightarrow T}$ Branch B with pattern of S checks against T

$$\frac{\Delta_i\vdash\theta_i\Leftarrow\Delta\quad \Delta_i;\Gamma_i\vdash pat\Leftarrow[\![\theta_i]\!]S\quad \Delta_i;[\![\theta_i]\!]\Gamma,\Gamma_i\vdash E\Leftarrow[\![\theta_i]\!]T}{\Delta;\Gamma\vdash\Delta_i;\Gamma_i\,.\,pat:\theta_i\mapsto E\Leftarrow S\rightarrow T}$$

Figure 3. Typing for computations

Branches are modelled by $\Delta;\Gamma\ .\ pat\ :\ \theta\ \mapsto\ E$ where Δ describes the meta-variables occurring in the pattern which are often left implicit in the surface language, while Γ corresponds to the explicit arguments. The refinement substitution θ describes how the type of the scrutinee is instantiated so the given branch is applicable.

Example 3 We show next the elaboration of a simple program to compute the tail of a vector and its elaboration:

```
rec tail : {N:nat[]} → vec (s N) → vec N =
fn l ⇒ case l of cons h t ⇒ t
```

Which can be elaborated into:

$$\begin{array}{l}\mathsf{rec\ tail}.\lambda N.\,\mathsf{fn}\ l.\ \mathsf{case}\ \ l\ \ \mathsf{of}\\ \mid M:\mathsf{nat}\ ;\ h:\mathsf{bool},\ t{:}\mathsf{Vec}\ M\ .\\ \quad\mathsf{fold}\ \langle\ \mathsf{cons}=\mathsf{pack}\ (M,\ (h,t)\ )\ \rangle\quad:\quad M/N\quad\mapsto\quad t\end{array}$$

We insert the length argument to `cons` which was left implicit in the source-level program and the refinement `M/N` which guarantees that the type of the pattern is compatible with the type of the scrutinee. We also list explicitly the type of the index variable `M` as well as the type of the arguments `h` and `t`.

4.3 Typing rules

Next, we give the typing rules for computations in Figure 3. We present bi-directional typing rules for computations which will minimize the amount of typing annotations. We distinguish between typing of expressions and branches. In the typing judgment, we will distinguish between the context Δ for contextual variables from our index domain and the context Γ which includes declarations of computation-level variables. Contextual variables will be introduced via λ-abstraction. The contextual variables in Δ are also introduced in the branch of a case-expression. Computation-level variables in Γ are introduced by recursion or functions and in addition in branches. We use the following judgments:

$\Delta; \Gamma \vdash E \Leftarrow T$	Expression E checks against type T
$\Delta; \Gamma \vdash I \Rightarrow T$	Expression I synthesizes type T
$\Delta; \Gamma \vdash B \Leftarrow S \rightarrow T$	Branch B with pattern of type S checks against T

The typing rules are given in Figure 3. We will tacitly rename bound variables, and maintain that contexts declare no variable more than once. Moreover, we require the usual conditions on bound variables. For example in the rule for λ-abstraction the contextual variable X must be new and cannot already occur in the context Δ. This can be always achieved via α-renaming. Similarly, in the rule for recursion and function abstraction, the variable x must be new and cannot already occur in Γ.

The rules which synthesize and check are mostly standard and we only point out a few rules. We have two rules for applications: to synthesize the type S of a non-dependent application $(I\ \ E)$, we synthesize the type for I to be $T \rightarrow S$ and check E against T. For the dependent application $I\ \ C$, we synthesize the type $\Pi X{:}U.T$ for I and check that C is a well-typed meta-object of type U. Note that we drop the computation context Γ when we transition to type check a meta-object, since meta-objects cannot refer to computations. The final type for $I\ \ C$ is $[\![C/X]\!]T$. If we have synthesized a type T together with a trivial equality constraint, we simply drop the constraint and return T.

To check a λ-abstraction against $\Pi X{:}U.T$, we add $X{:}U$ to the meta-context Δ and continue to check that the body of the abstraction has type T. To check that a function $\mathsf{fn}\ y.E$ has type $T_1 \rightarrow T_2$, we add the assumption $y{:}T_1$ to the computation context Γ and continue to check the body E against T_2. For checking a non-dependent pair $(E_1,\ E_2)$ against the type $T_1 \times T_2$, we check each part of the pair against their respective type. For checking a dependent pair $\mathsf{pack}\ (C,\ E)$ against $\Sigma X{:}U.T$, we check that C is a well-typed meta-object of type U switching to the typing rules for the meta-level and dropping the context Γ. In addition, we check that E has type $[\![C/X]\!]T$.

When we check a contextual meta-object C against a type U, we simply convert to the type checking rules for meta-objects and forget about the computation-level context Γ. Our typing rules will ensure that meta-objects are pure objects and do not contain any computation-level expressions. When checking an expression against $C = C \wedge T$, we can simply drop the constraint $C = C$, since it is trivially true. We check $(\mathsf{fold}\ \ E)$ against the recursive type $(\mu Z.\lambda\vec{X}.\,S)\ \vec{C}$ by unrolling the fixed point definition and checking E against $[\mu Z.\lambda\vec{X}\,.\,S/Z][\![\vec{C}/\vec{X}]\!]S$. The difference to simply-typed recursive types is that dependently typed recursive types are applied to index objects $\vec{C}$.

To illustrate that our data carries enough information to ensure that the equality constraints are trivially true, if the term is well-typed, we show the typing derivation for `cons (true,nil)` in Figure 4.

In the rule for case expressions, we first infer the type S of the scrutinee and then proceed to check that each branch B_i has a pattern compatible with S and its body has a type compatible with T. To check a branch $\Delta_i; \Gamma_i \vdash pat_i : \theta_i \mapsto E_i$, we check that the refinement substitution θ_i provides instantiations from the outer meta-context Δ to the current meta-context Δ_i. Moreover, the pattern has type $[\![\theta_i]\!]S$, i.e. it is compatible with the type of the scrutinee, and only refers to the local variables Δ_i and Γ_i. We then proceed to check the body E_i against $[\![\theta_i]\!]T$. Because the pattern may refine the types, we must make sure to apply θ_i to the appropriate parts and extend the computation context $[\![\theta_i]\!]\Gamma$ with the bindings Γ_i introduced in the branch.

The typing rules for patterns are given in Fig. 5. They duplicate some of the type checking rules for tuples, dependent pairs, meta-objects, recursive types, and variants. We ensure that the computation variables occurring in patterns occur uniquely and we split the computation context in the rule for tuples. The meta-context on the other hand remains. As a consequence, contextual variables may occur more than once, which is also often necessary to obtain well-typed expressions, but we enforce linearity for computation variables occurring in patterns.

Theorem 4.1 (Decidability of Type Checking).
Type-checking computation-level expressions is decidable.

Proof. The typing judgments are syntax-directed and therefore clearly decidable. □

4.4 Big-step operational semantics

Next, we define the operational semantics for computations in Fig. 7. We adopt an environment-based approach where we do not eagerly propagate values. Recall that we distinguish between meta-variables in Δ and program variables in Γ. To work elegantly with refinement substitutions in branches, we hence define two environments: θ denotes the instantiation for meta-variables in Δ; ρ provides instantiations for program variables in Γ.

Values	V	$::=$	$F\,[\theta\,;\,\rho] \mid \mathsf{unit} \mid \mathsf{fold}\ V \mid \langle l = V\rangle \mid \mathsf{pack}\ (C, V) \mid (V_1, V_2)$
Function Values	F	$::=$	$\mathsf{fn}\ y.E \mid \lambda X.\,E$
Extended Values	W	$::=$	$V \mid (\mathsf{rec}\ f.E)\ [\theta\,;\,\rho]$
Closures	L	$::=$	$E\,[\theta\,;\,\rho]$
Environments	ρ	$::=$	$\cdot \mid \rho, W/y$

Values are either meta-terms C, unit, pairs (V_1, V_2), dependent pairs $\mathsf{pack}\ (C,\ V)$, variants $\langle l = V\rangle$, $\mathsf{fold}\ V$, or functions as closures. Since we have non-dependent and dependent functions, we have two corresponding closures. Closures are snapshots of computation inside an environment. The environment is represented by the two suspended substitutions θ and ρ for each of the two contexts Δ and Γ respectively. We write $E[\theta; \rho]$ for a closure consisting of the expression E and the suspended meta-substitution θ and the program environment ρ. The intended meaning is that first meta-substitution θ is applied to E and then ordinary substitution ρ to the result. For clarification, we show the typing for environments and values in Figure 6.

We give a big-step semantics for computations in Figure 7. To evaluate a variable y in the environment θ and ρ, we simply look up its binding in the computation environment ρ. Since ρ contains extended values, in particular y may be bound to a recursive function which in itself is not a valid result, we continue to evaluate the extended value we retrieve from ρ to a proper value. When we encounter a meta-object C in the environment θ and ρ, we apply θ to C to compute a closed meta-object. unit simply evaluates to itself regardless of the environment. Evaluating a function $\mathsf{fn}\ y.E$ in the environment θ and ρ simply returns the closure $\mathsf{fn}\ y.E\ [\theta\,;\,\rho]$. When evaluating a recursive function $\mathsf{rec}\ f.E$ in an environment θ and ρ, we evaluate the body E and extend the computation environment ρ binding f to itself.

Evaluating a tuple $(E_1,\ E_2)$ in the environment θ and ρ is straightforward: we evaluate E_1 in the environment θ and ρ and we proceed similarly to evaluate E_2. The evaluation rules for fold and variants are straightforward.

$$
\dfrac{\dfrac{\vdash 0 \Leftarrow \mathsf{nat} \qquad \dfrac{\dfrac{\vdash \mathsf{true} \Leftarrow \mathsf{bool} \qquad \dfrac{\dfrac{\dfrac{\dfrac{}{() \Leftarrow \mathsf{Unit}}}{() \Leftarrow 0 = 0 \wedge \mathsf{Unit}}}{\vdash \langle\, \mathsf{nil} = () \rangle \Leftarrow \langle \mathsf{nil} : 0 = 0 \wedge \mathsf{Unit}\ ,\ \mathsf{cons} : \Sigma Y{:}\mathsf{nat}.0 = \mathsf{s}\ Y \wedge \mathsf{bool} \times \mathsf{Vec}\ Y\ \rangle}}{\vdash \mathsf{fold}\ \langle\ \mathsf{nil} = () \rangle \Leftarrow \mathsf{Vec}\ 0}}{\vdash (\mathsf{true}, \mathsf{fold}\ \langle\ \mathsf{nil} = ()\ \rangle\ ) \Leftarrow \mathsf{bool} \times \mathsf{Vec}\ 0}}{\vdash (\mathsf{true}, \mathsf{fold}\ \langle\ \mathsf{nil} = ()\ \rangle\ ) \Leftarrow \mathsf{s}\ 0 = \mathsf{s}\ 0 \wedge \mathsf{bool} \times \mathsf{Vec}\ 0}}{\vdash \mathsf{pack}\ (0,\ (\mathsf{true},\ \mathsf{fold}\ \langle\ \mathsf{nil} = ()\ \rangle\ )) \Leftarrow \Sigma Y{:}\mathsf{nat}.\mathsf{s}\ 0 = \mathsf{s}\ Y \wedge \mathsf{bool} \times \mathsf{Vec}\ Y}}{\dfrac{\vdash \langle\ \mathsf{cons} = \mathsf{pack}\ (0,\ (\mathsf{true}, \mathsf{fold}\ \langle\ \mathsf{nil} = ()\ \rangle\ ))\ \rangle \Leftarrow \langle \mathsf{nil} : \mathsf{s}\ 0 = 0 \wedge \mathsf{Unit}\ ,\ \mathsf{cons} : \Sigma Y{:}\mathsf{nat}.\mathsf{s}\ 0 = \mathsf{s}\ Y \wedge \mathsf{bool} \times \mathsf{Vec}\ Y\ \rangle}{\vdash \mathsf{fold}\ \langle\ \mathsf{cons} = \mathsf{pack}\ (0,\ (\mathsf{true},\ \mathsf{fold}\ \langle\ \mathsf{nil} = ()\ \rangle\ ))\ \rangle \Leftarrow \mathsf{Vec}\ (\mathsf{s}\ 0)}}
$$

Figure 4. Typing derivation for vector `cons (true, nil)` $:=$ $\mathsf{fold}\ \langle\ \mathsf{cons} = \mathsf{pack}\ (0,\ (\mathsf{true}, \mathsf{fold}\ \langle\ \mathsf{nil} = ()\ \rangle\ ))\ \rangle$

$\boxed{\Delta; \Gamma \vdash pat \Leftarrow T}$ Pattern checks against type T

$$
\dfrac{\Gamma(x) = T}{\Delta; \Gamma \vdash x \Leftarrow T} \qquad \dfrac{\Delta \vdash C \Leftarrow U}{\Delta; \Gamma \vdash C \Leftarrow U} \qquad \dfrac{}{\Delta; \Gamma \vdash \mathsf{unit} \Leftarrow \mathsf{Unit}} \qquad \dfrac{T = \mu Z.\lambda \vec{X}.\, S \quad \Delta; \Gamma \vdash pat \Leftarrow [T/Z][\![\vec{C}/\vec{X}]\!]S}{\Delta; \Gamma \vdash \mathsf{fold}\ pat \Leftarrow T\ \vec{C}} \qquad \dfrac{\Delta; \Gamma \vdash pat \Leftarrow T}{\Delta; \Gamma \vdash pat \Leftarrow C = C \wedge T}
$$

$$
\dfrac{\Delta; \Gamma \vdash pat_i \Leftarrow T_i \quad \text{where } l_i : T_i \in \overrightarrow{l : T}}{\Delta; \Gamma \vdash \langle l_i = pat_i \rangle \Leftarrow \langle \overrightarrow{l : T} \rangle} \qquad \dfrac{\Delta \vdash C \Leftarrow U \quad \Delta; \Gamma \vdash pat \Leftarrow [\![C/X]\!]T}{\Delta; \Gamma \vdash \mathsf{pack}\ (C, pat) \Leftarrow \Sigma X{:}U.T} \qquad \dfrac{\Delta; \Gamma_1 \vdash pat_1 \Leftarrow T_1 \quad \Delta; \Gamma_2 \vdash pat_2 \Leftarrow T_2}{\Delta; \Gamma_1, \Gamma_2 \vdash (pat_1, pat_2) \Leftarrow T_1 \times T_2}
$$

Figure 5. Typing rules for patterns

$\boxed{E\ [\theta\ ;\ \rho] \Downarrow V}$ Expression E in environment $[\theta; \rho]$ evaluates to value V

$$
\dfrac{I_1\ [\theta\ ;\ \rho] \Downarrow (\mathsf{fn}\ y.E)\ [\theta_1\ ;\ \rho_1] \quad E_2\ [\theta\ ;\ \rho] \Downarrow V_2 \quad E\ [\theta_1\ ;\ \rho_1, V_2/y] \Downarrow V}{(I_1\ E_2)\ [\theta\ ;\ \rho] \Downarrow V} \qquad \dfrac{I\ [\theta\ ;\ \rho] \Downarrow (\lambda X.\, E)\ [\theta_1\ ;\ \rho_1] \quad E\ [\theta_1, [\![\theta]\!]C/X\ ;\ \rho_1] \Downarrow V}{(I\ \ C)\ [\theta\ ;\ \rho] \Downarrow V}
$$

$$
\dfrac{}{C\ [\theta\ ;\ \rho] \Downarrow [\![\theta]\!]C} \qquad \dfrac{}{\mathsf{unit}\ [\theta\ ;\ \rho] \Downarrow \mathsf{unit}} \qquad \dfrac{\rho(y) = V}{y\ [\theta\ ;\ \rho] \Downarrow V} \qquad \dfrac{\rho(y) = (\mathsf{rec}\ f.E)\ [\theta_1\ ;\ \rho_1] \quad \rho(y) \Downarrow V}{y\ [\theta\ ;\ \rho] \Downarrow V} \qquad \dfrac{E\ [\theta\ ;\ \rho] \Downarrow V}{(E : T)\ [\theta\ ;\ \rho] \Downarrow V} \qquad \dfrac{E\ [\theta\ ;\ \rho] \Downarrow V}{(\mathsf{fold}\ E)\ [\theta\ ;\ \rho] \Downarrow \mathsf{fold}\ V}
$$

$$
\dfrac{E\ [\theta\ ;\ \rho] \Downarrow V}{\langle l = E \rangle\ [\theta\ ;\ \rho] \Downarrow \langle l = V \rangle} \qquad \dfrac{}{(\mathsf{fn}\ y.E)\ [\theta\ ;\ \rho] \Downarrow (\mathsf{fn}\ y.E)\ [\theta\ ;\ \rho]} \qquad \dfrac{}{(\lambda X.\, E)\ [\theta\ ;\ \rho] \Downarrow (\lambda X.\, E)\ [\theta\ ;\ \rho]} \qquad \dfrac{E\ [\theta\ ;\ \rho, (\mathsf{rec}\ f.E)\ [\theta\ ;\ \rho]/f] \Downarrow V}{(\mathsf{rec}\ f.E)\ [\theta\ ;\ \rho] \Downarrow V}
$$

$$
\dfrac{E\ [\theta\ ;\ \rho] \Downarrow V}{\mathsf{pack}\ (C, E)\ [\theta\ ;\ \rho] \Downarrow \mathsf{pack}\ ([\![\theta]\!]C, V)} \qquad \dfrac{E_1\ [\theta\ ;\ \rho] \Downarrow V_1 \quad E_2\ [\theta\ ;\ \rho] \Downarrow V_2}{(E_1, E_2)\ [\theta\ ;\ \rho] \Downarrow (V_1, V_2)} \qquad \dfrac{\Delta_i \vdash \theta \not\doteq \theta_i \quad \mathsf{case}\ I\ \mathsf{of}\ \vec{B}\ [\theta\ ;\ \rho] \Downarrow V}{\mathsf{case}\ I\ \mathsf{of}\ (\Delta_i; \Gamma_i\, .\, pat : \theta_i \mapsto E_i \mid \vec{B})\ [\theta\ ;\ \rho] \Downarrow V}
$$

$$
\dfrac{\begin{array}{cc} \Delta_i \vdash \theta \doteq \theta_i/(\theta'; \Delta_i') & \Delta_i'; [\![\theta']\!]\Gamma_i \vdash V_1 \not\doteq [\![\theta']\!]pat \\ I\ [\theta\ ;\ \rho] \Downarrow V_1 & \mathsf{case}\ I\ \mathsf{of}\ \vec{B}\ [\theta\ ;\ \rho] \Downarrow V \end{array}}{\mathsf{case}\ I\ \mathsf{of}\ (\Delta_i; \Gamma_i\, .\, pat : \theta_i \mapsto E_i \mid \vec{B})\ [\theta\ ;\ \rho] \Downarrow V} \qquad \dfrac{\begin{array}{cc} \Delta_i \vdash \theta \doteq \theta_i/(\theta'; \Delta_i') & \Delta_i'; [\![\theta']\!]\Gamma_i \vdash V_1 \doteq [\![\theta']\!]pat/(\theta''; \rho') \\ I\ [\theta\ ;\ \rho] \Downarrow V_1 & E_i\ [[\![\theta'']\!]\theta'\ ;\ \rho, \rho'] \Downarrow V \end{array}}{\mathsf{case}\ I\ \mathsf{of}\ (\Delta_i; \Gamma_i\, .\, pat : \theta_i \mapsto E_i \mid \vec{B})\ [\theta\ ;\ \rho] \Downarrow V}
$$

Figure 7. Big-step semantics

We have two rules for evaluating applications: the first is for a non-dependent application $I_1\ \ E_2$ in an environment $[\theta; \rho]$. We first evaluate I_1 in the given environment obtaining a closure $(\mathsf{fn}\ y.E)\ [\theta_1\ ;\ \rho_1]$. Then we evaluate E_2 to a value V_2 and finally proceed to evaluate E in the extended environment $[\theta_1\ ; \rho_1, V_2/y]$ where the meta-substitution θ_1 remains unchanged. On the other hand, when evaluating a dependent application $I\ C$ in an environment $[\theta\ ;\ \rho]$, we evaluate I to a closure $(\lambda X.\, E)\ [\theta_1\ ;\ \rho_1]$. We now extend the meta-substitution θ with the binding $[\![\theta]\!]C/X$ and evaluate E in the extended environment $[\theta_1, [\![\theta]\!]C/X\ ;\ \rho_1]$ where the computation environment ρ_1 remains unchanged.

The most interesting cases are those for case-expressions. A branch may be skipped if either the type of the scrutinee and the type of the pattern are not compatible, i.e. the current meta-substitution and the refinement substitution in the given branch do not unify, or if the types are compatible then the scrutinee itself may still be incompatible with the pattern of the current branch. Evaluating a case expression, we first evaluate the scrutinee I in the current environment $[\theta\ ;\ \rho]$ to some value V_1. Next, we check that the current meta-substitution θ is unifiable with the refinement substitution θ_i of the given branch. This is written as $\Delta_i\ \vdash \theta \doteq \theta_i/(\theta'\ ;\ \Delta_i')$ and θ' is the result of unifying θ with θ_i s.t. $\theta = [\![\theta']\!]\theta_i$ and θ' is a substitution which maps contextual variables from Δ_i to Δ_i'. Unifying the contextual substitutions ensures that the type of the scrutinee and the type of the pattern are compatible. Next, we check that the pattern is compatible with the

$\boxed{V : T}$ Value V has type T

$$\frac{\cdot \vdash \theta \Leftarrow \Delta \quad \rho : [\![\theta]\!]\Gamma \quad \Delta ; \Gamma \vdash F \Leftarrow T}{F\ [\theta\ ;\ \rho] : [\![\theta]\!]T} \qquad \frac{\cdot \vdash C \Leftarrow U}{C : U} \qquad \frac{}{\mathsf{unit} : \mathsf{Unit}}$$

$$\frac{V : T_i \quad \text{where } l_i : T_i \in \overrightarrow{l : T}}{\langle l_i = V \rangle : \langle \overrightarrow{l : T} \rangle} \qquad \frac{T = \mu Z.\lambda \vec{X}.\, S \quad V : [T/Z][\![\vec{C}/\vec{X}]\!]S}{\mathsf{fold}\ V : T\ \vec{C}}$$

$$\frac{V : T}{V : C = C \wedge T} \qquad \frac{\cdot \vdash C \Leftarrow U \quad V : [\![C/X]\!]T}{\mathsf{pack}\ (C, V) : \Sigma X{:}U.T} \qquad \frac{V_1 : T_1 \quad V_2 : T_2}{(V_1, V_2) : T_1 \times T_2}$$

$\boxed{L : T}$ Closure L has type T

$$\frac{\cdot \vdash \theta \Leftarrow \Delta \qquad \rho : [\![\theta]\!]\Gamma \qquad \Delta ; \Gamma \vdash E \Leftarrow T \text{ or } \Delta ; \Gamma \vdash E \Rightarrow T}{E\ [\theta\ ;\ \rho] : [\![\theta]\!]T}$$

$\boxed{\rho : \Gamma}$ Environment ρ has domain Γ

$$\frac{}{\cdot : \cdot} \qquad \frac{\rho : \Gamma \qquad W : T}{(\rho, W/y) : \Gamma, y{:}T}$$

Figure 6. Value and closure typing

value of the scrutinee. Before matching the value of the scrutinee against the the pattern, we apply the contextual substitution θ' to the pattern *pat* and also to the variables listed Γ_i which occur in the pattern. The result will be a contextual substitution θ'' for the meta-context Δ_i' and a substitution ρ' for actual pattern variables from $[\![\theta']\!]\Gamma_i$. Finally, the body of the branch E_i is evaluated. Recall that if the overall case-expression has type T in a meta-context Δ and computation context Γ, then E_i has type $[\![\theta_i]\!]T$ in a meta-context Δ_i and computation context $[\![\theta_i]\!]\Gamma, \Gamma_i$. Therefore, we will now evaluate E_i in the contextual environment $[\![\theta'']\!]\theta'$ and extend the computation environment ρ with the new bindings in ρ'.

We now proceed to prove subject reduction which guarantees that types are preserved during evaluation.

Theorem 4.2 (Subject reduction). *Let $L : T$. If $L \Downarrow V$ then $V : T$.*

Proof. Structural induction on $L \Downarrow V$. □

To prove progress, we follow Cousot and Cousot [1992] and Leroy and Grall [2009] and extend our big-step operational semantics to allow for non-terminating computations. In addition to the judgment $E\ [\theta\ ;\ \rho] \Downarrow V$ we also allow for diverging computation using the judgment $E\ [\theta\ ;\ \rho] \Downarrow^\infty$. For example, the diverging evaluation rules for products are shown below:

$$\frac{E_1\ [\theta\ ;\ \rho] \Downarrow^\infty}{(E_1, E_2)\ [\theta\ ;\ \rho] \Downarrow^\infty} \qquad \frac{E_1\ [\theta\ ;\ \rho] \Downarrow V_1 \quad E_2\ [\theta\ ;\ \rho] \Downarrow^\infty}{(E_1, E_2)\ [\theta\ ;\ \rho] \Downarrow^\infty}$$

These rules should be read coinductively. We note that matching described by $\doteq$ and the substitution operation do not lead to non-termination in our operational semantics.

Lemma 4.3 (Canonical Forms).

1. *If $V : T \to S$ then V is of the form:* $(\mathsf{fn}\ y.E)\ [\theta\ ;\ \rho]$
2. *If $V : \Pi X{:}U.T$ then V is of the form:* $(\lambda X.\ E)\ [\theta\ ;\ \rho]$

Proof. By inversion on value typing. □

Assuming that patterns cover all cases, we finally can state and prove progress.

Theorem 4.4.
If $L : T$ and for all values V, $\neg L \Downarrow V$ then $L \Downarrow^\infty$

Proof. (Classical) By coinduction and case analysis on the typing derivation, appealing to canonical forms. □

Corollary 4.5 (Progress).
If $L : T$ then either $L \Downarrow V$ or $L \Downarrow^\infty$.

5. Mechanization

We have mechanized the proofs of the subject reduction and progress theorems presented in Section 4.4 in the Coq proof assistant. The development is approximately 800 lines of specification and under 500 lines of proof. We refer the interested reader to the supplementary material for this paper for the Coq proofs.

We do not formalize contextual LF. Rather, the proofs are abstract over the domain of meta-terms C and meta-types U. We need only assume that they behave well with meta-substitution and that pattern matching for C is decidable. This demonstrates our point that the computation language forms a general core for dependently typed languages parametric over the domain C.

We use the fresh look approach to binding due to Pouillard and Pottier [2010], which is an abstract interface to well-scoped de Brujin indices. Informally we found that the additional abstraction pushed us towards a more high-level algebraic approach relying heavily on simultaneous substitutions in place of low level de Bruijn shifting.

A natural question to ask is why we did not choose to formalize the language in a system with built-in support for binding and substitution such as Beluga. One answer is that Beluga is currently lacking the recursive types we propose here. We would argue that the computation language is best represented as a recursive type, since the syntax contains meta-substitutions θ, which are conveniently represented as computational functions `#tm[ψ] -> tm[φ]` which cannot be written in LF. In fact we never perform substitutions on computation level expressions, hence the lack of substitution for free is moot.

6. Related Work

Over the past two decades, programming language researchers have been investigating language-based approaches to design safe and reliable software. Our work draws on and combines two domains: programming with binders and programming with indexed types.

Our work follows the tradition of indexed types [Xi and Pfenning 1999; Zenger 1997] where we separate the index domain of types from the computation-language. This has several known advantages: it is easy to allow state, exceptions, and polymorphism. Moreover, we are not restricted to total functions as in full dependently-typed languages such as Coq [Bertot and Castéran 2004] or Agda [Norell 2007]. However, since we can pattern match on index objects, we cannot naively erase them.

Most closely related to our work is the work by Chen and Xi [2005]; Xi [2004] and Sarkar [2009]. The ATS system designed by Xi and collaborators [Xi 2004] allows programmers to specify formal systems within the logical framework LF and embed LF objects as indices in computation-level types (see [Donnelly and Xi 2005]). The programmer can then supply her own proofs witnessing the equality between two objects when automatic constraint solving in ATS fails. However, the major challenge when manipulating and traversing LF objects is that we will encounter open LF objects, i.e. LF objects which may contain "free" variables. Unfortunately, ATS does not provide support for manipulating such open LF objects. To support certified programming, Sarkar [2009] proposed ML/LF which extended an ML-like language with LF as an index domain. To allow programming with open LF objects, he proposes to reify the dynamic assumptions which arise when traversing a binder and manipulate their representatives explicitly. This requires an extension of LF with Sigma-types and unit to model contexts and their dependencies. In contrast, our work builds on contextual LF [Pientka 2008] and explicitly supports contexts and parameter variables and types for them. This allows us to express strong invariants by for example stating that we map variables from a context to variables in another context which seems difficult in Sarkar's approach, since there is no guarantee by the underlying type system that we are only storing and manipulating variables in the reified context.

Westbrook et al. [2005] also suggests to index types with LF objects in a type-safe functional language to support programming with proofs in the presence of unrestricted recursion and imperative features while retaining decidable type checking. However their work restricts LF to the first-order fragment and explicitly forbids λ-abstractions. As a consequence, encodings based on higher-order abstract syntax are not supported.

In recent years, we have also made substantial advances in programming with binders. We build on the idea of contextual types which is central to Beluga [Pientka 2008]; however so far, Beluga and similar systems such as Delphin [Poswolsky and Schürmann 2008] are limited to only manipulating contextual LF objects. We take it in this paper one step further of allowing contextual objects and contexts as indices to computation-level types. Recently, Licata and Harper [2009] have proposed a system where one can mix computation functions and binding abstractions; this builds on their earlier ideas in Licata et al. [2008]. A prototype based on these ideas is implemented as a library within Agda and has been used to for example implement normalization by evaluation. Structural properties such as weakening or substitution do however not hold in general, but they can be implemented generically. While Licata and Harper [2009] demonstrate convincingly that their library within Agda elegantly supports programming with binders, it is less clear whether their prototype will scale to support dependent types and meta-reasoning. It is also remarkable that we do not need to fully mix LF function space with the function space for computations to implement normalization-by-evaluation.

Taking a broader view on programming with binders, our work also seems superficially similar to Pouillard and Pottier [2010] where the authors describe an Agda library to support safe programming with names. The fundamental idea is to index terms with a world which names inhabit. When traversing a binding construct, we build up a chain of worlds which is similar to our context. However, it is unclear whether their work scales to support dependent types and hence encoding proofs and meta-reasoning. We hope that the presented work will enable us to shed further light on the relationship between nominal systems and LF-style encodings.

An interesting application of the presented work is its use as a tactic language for an interactive theorem prover. Stampoulis and Shao [2010] for example propose a language VeriML where we write computations about λHOL^{ind}, a higher-order logic with inductive definitions. At this point, VeriML only allows direct pattern matching on λHOL^{ind} objects, but does not allow in general computation-level types to be indexed with λHOL^{ind} objects. As a consequence, recursive types in VeriML cannot be dependently typed. Our approach of adding dependently-typed inductive types to the computation language is directly applicable to their work and would add additional flexibility to their language.

Our work takes inspiration from the work on inductive definitions in proof theory, in particular the work by McDowell and Miller [2002] and more recently Baelde et al. [2010]; Gacek et al. [2008] which targets reasoning about higher-order abstract syntax representations. Our addition of recursive types in Beluga$^{\mu}$ gives us effectively the same power as fixpoint definitions in their work. To facilitate reasoning about HOAS representations, Miller and his collaborators have extended the logic itself with the ∇-quantifier which allows generic quantification. Contexts must be modelled and reasoned about explicitly. In contrast, our work allows us to remain in first-order logic by generalizing the term language to allow for contextual meta-objects and contexts. This allows us to parameterize our recursive types over contexts and provide explicit support for reasoning about contexts. We believe the described work is an important step of understanding the differences and similarities between the approaches based on proof theory on the one hand and the approaches grounded in type theory on the other hand.

7. Conclusion and future work

We presented a type-theoretic foundation for programming with binders and indexed data-types. In particular, we have shown how to add indexed recursive types to the Beluga language and proven the extension to be type safe. We have also mechanized the type safety proof in Coq.

There are however more general lessons: we have streamlined earlier presentations of Beluga by separating meta-objects from computations. This has two important consequence: first, our computation language becomes modular; we can in fact easily replace contextual objects by another decidable index domain. Second, our modular approach lays the groundwork for adding contextual objects to other languages richer than the ML-like computation language we used in this paper, such as Agda.

In this paper, we have concentrated on programming with binders and indexed data-types, however frameworks such as Beluga are also proof development environments. To use the presented language as a core language for a proof assistant, we need to guarantee that the implemented functions are total, i.e. all cases are covered and the functions themselves are terminating. We believe coverage checking can be solved by extending prior work on coverage checking contextual objects [Dunfield and Pientka 2009; Schürmann and Pfenning 2003]. Termination checking requires us to identity a suitable notion of acceptable inductive datatypes, e.g. based on strict positivity as in Coq [Paulin-Mohring 1993], and we plan to adapt sized types as for example in Abel [2007, 2008] in the future.

References

Martín Abadi, Michael Burrows, Butler W. Lampson, and Gordon D. Plotkin. A calculus for access control in distributed systems. *ACM Transaction on Programming Language Systems*, 15(4):706–734, 1993.

Martin Abadi, Anindya Banerjee, Nevin Heintze, and Jon G. Riecke. A core calculus of dependency. In *26th ACM SIGPLAN-SIGACT Symposium on Principles of Programming Languages (POPL '99)*, pages 147–160. ACM Press, 1999.

Andreas Abel. Mixed inductive/coinductive types and strong normalization. In Zhong Shao, editor, *5th ASIAN Symposium on Programming Languages and Systems (APLAS'07)*, volume 4807 of *Lecture Notes in Computer Science*, pages 286–301. Springer, 2007.

Andreas Abel. Polarized subtyping for sized types. *Mathematical Structures in Computer Science*, 18(5):797–822, 2008. Special issue on subtyping, edited by Healfdene Goguen and Adriana Compagnoni.

David Baelde, Zach Snow, and Dale Miller. Focused inductive theorem proving. In Jürgen Giesl and Reiner Haehnle, editors, *5th International Joint Conference on Automated Reasoning (IJCAR'10)*, Lecture Notes in Artificial Intelligence (LNAI 6173), pages 278–292. Springer, 2010.

Ulrich Berger and Helmut Schwichtenberg. An inverse of the evaluation functional for typed lambda-calculus. In *Logic in Computer Science*, pages 203–211, 1991.

Yves Bertot and Pierre Castéran. *Interactive Theorem Proving and Program Development. Coq'Art: The Calculus of Inductive Constructions*. Springer, 2004.

Chiyan Chen and Hongwei Xi. Combining programming with theorem proving. In Olivier Danvy and Benjamin C. Pierce, editors, *10th International Conference on Functional Programming*, pages 66–77, 2005.

Patrick Cousot and Radhia Cousot. Inductive definitions, semantics and abstract interpretations. In *19th ACM SIGPLAN-SIGACT Symposium on Principles of Programming Languages (POPL'92)*, pages 83–94. ACM, 1992.

Kevin Donnelly and Hongwei Xi. Combining higher-order abstract syntax with first-order abstract syntax in ats. In Randy Pollack, editor, *Workshop on Mechanized Reasoning about Languages with Variable Binding (MERLIN'05)*, pages 58–63. ACM, 2005.

Joshua Dunfield and Brigitte Pientka. Case analysis of higher-order data. In *International Workshop on Logical Frameworks and Meta-Languages: Theory and Practice (LFMTP'08)*, volume 228 of *Electronic Notes in Theoretical Computer Science (ENTCS)*, pages 69–84. Elsevier, June 2009.

Andrew Gacek, Dale Miller, and Gopalan Nadathur. Combining generic judgments with recursive definitions. In F. Pfenning, editor, *23rd Symposium on Logic in Computer Science*. IEEE Computer Society Press, 2008.

D. Garg and F. Pfenning. Non-interference in constructive authorization logic. In *Proceedings of the 19th IEEE Computer Security Foundations Workshop (CSFW 19)*. IEEE Computer Society Press, 2006.

Louis-Julien Guillemette and Stefan Monnier. A type-preserving closure conversion in Haskell. In *Proceedings of the ACM SIGPLAN Workshop on Haskell*, Haskell '07, pages 83–92, 2007.

Robert Harper and Daniel R. Licata. Mechanizing Metatheory in a Logical Framework. *Journal of Functional Programming*, 17(4-5):613–673, 2007.

Robert Harper, Furio Honsell, and Gordon Plotkin. A framework for defining logics. *Journal of the ACM*, 40(1):143–184, January 1993.

Xavier Leroy and Herv Grall. Coinductive big-step operational semantics. *Information and Computation*, pages 284–304, 2009.

Daniel R. Licata. *Dependently Typed Programming with Domain-Specific Logics*. PhD thesis, Carnegie Mellon University, 2011.

Daniel R. Licata and Robert Harper. A universe of binding and computation. In Graham Hutton and Andrew P. Tolmach, editors, *14th ACM SIGPLAN International Conference on Functional Programming*, pages 123–134. ACM Press, 2009.

Daniel R. Licata, Noam Zeilberger, and Robert Harper. Focusing on binding and computation. In F. Pfenning, editor, *23rd Symposium on Logic in Computer Science*, pages 241–252. IEEE Computer Society Press, 2008.

Raymond C. McDowell and Dale A. Miller. Reasoning with higher-order abstract syntax in a logical framework. *ACM Transactions on Computational Logic*, 3(1):80–136, 2002. ISSN 1529-3785.

Yasuhiko Minamide, Greg Morrisett, and Robert Harper. Typed closure conversion. In *In Twenty-Third ACM Symposium on Principles of Programming Languages*, pages 271–283. ACM Press, 1996.

Kenji Miyamoto and Atsushi Igarashi. A modal foundation for secure information flow. In A. Sabelfeld, editor, *Workshop on Foundations of Computer Security (FCS'04)*, pages 187–203, 2004.

Aleksandar Nanevski, J. Gregory Morrisett, and Lars Birkedal. Hoare type theory, polymorphism and separation. *Journal of Functional Programming*, 18(5-6):865–911, 2008a.

Aleksandar Nanevski, Frank Pfenning, and Brigitte Pientka. Contextual modal type theory. *ACM Transactions on Computational Logic*, 9(3): 1–49, 2008b.

Ulf Norell. *Towards a practical programming language based on dependent type theory*. PhD thesis, Department of Computer Science and Engineering, Chalmers University of Technology, September 2007. Technical Report 33D.

Christine Paulin-Mohring. Inductive definitions in the system coq - rules and properties. In Marc Bezem and Jan Friso Groote, editors, *International Conference on Typed Lambda Calculi and Applications(TLCA '93)*, volume 664 of *Lecture Notes in Computer Science*, pages 328–345. Springer, 1993.

Frank Pfenning and Carsten Schürmann. System description: Twelf — a meta-logical framework for deductive systems. In H. Ganzinger, editor, *16th International Conference on Automated Deduction (CADE-16)*, volume 1632 of *Lecture Notes in Artificial Intelligence*, pages 202–206. Springer, 1999.

Brigitte Pientka. A type-theoretic foundation for programming with higher-order abstract syntax and first-class substitutions. In *35th Annual ACM SIGPLAN-SIGACT Symposium on Principles of Programming Languages (POPL'08)*, pages 371–382. ACM Press, 2008.

Brigitte Pientka. Programming proofs: A novel approach based on contextual types. *submitted*, 2011.

Brigitte Pientka and Joshua Dunfield. Beluga: a framework for programming and reasoning with deductive systems (System Description). In Jürgen Giesl and Reiner Haehnle, editors, *5th International Joint Conference on Automated Reasoning (IJCAR'10)*, Lecture Notes in Artificial Intelligence (LNAI 6173), pages 15–21. Springer-Verlag, 2010.

Adam Poswolsky and Carsten Schürmann. System description: Delphin— a functional programming language for deductive systems. In *International Workshop on Logical Frameworks and Meta-Languages: Theory and Practice (LFMTP'08)*, volume 228 of *Electronic Notes in Theoretical Computer Science (ENTCS)*, pages 135–141. Elsevier, 2009.

Adam B. Poswolsky and Carsten Schürmann. Practical programming with higher-order encodings and dependent types. In *17th European Symposium on Programming (ESOP '08)*, volume 4960, pages 93–107. Springer, 2008.

François Pottier. Static name control for FreshML. In *22nd IEEE Symposium on Logic in Computer Science (LICS'07)*, pages 356–365. IEEE Computer Society, July 2007.

Nicolas Pouillard and Franois Pottier. A fresh look at programming with names and binders. In *15th ACM SIGPLAN International Conference on Functional Programming (ICFP 2010)*, pages 217–228, 2010.

Susmit Sarkar. *A Dependently Typed Programming Language, with applications to Foundational Certified Code Systems*. PhD thesis, Carnegie Mellon University, 2009. CMU-CS-09-128.

Carsten Schürmann and Frank Pfenning. A coverage checking algorithm for LF. In D. Basin and B. Wolff, editors, *Proceedings of the 16th International Conference on Theorem Proving in Higher Order Logics (TPHOLs'03)*, pages 120–135. Springer, 2003.

Tim Sheard. Languages of the future. *SIGPLAN Notices*, 39(12):119–132, 2004.

Mark R. Shinwell, Andrew M. Pitts, and Murdoch J. Gabbay. FreshML: programming with binders made simple. In *8th International Conference on Functional Programming (ICFP'03)*, pages 263–274. ACM Press, 2003.

Antonis Stampoulis and Zhong Shao. VeriML: typed computation of logical terms inside a language with effects. In Paul Hudak and Stephanie Weirich, editors, *15th ACM SIGPLAN International Conference on Functional Programming (ICFP'10)*, pages 333–344. ACM, 2010.

Martin Sulzmann, Manuel M. T. Chakravarty, Simon Peyton Jones, and Kevin Donnelly. System f with type equality coercions. In *ACM SIGPLAN International Workshop on Types in Languages Design and Implementation (TLDI'07)*, pages 53–66. ACM, 2007.

E. Westbrook, A. Stump, and I. Wehrman. A Language-based Approach to Functionally Correct Imperative Programming. In Olivier Danvy and Benjamin C. Pierce, editors, *10th International Conference on Functional Programming (ICFP05)*, pages 268–279. ACM, 2005.

Hongwei Xi. Applied type system. In *TYPES 2003*, volume 3085 of *Lecture Notes in Computer Science*, pages 394–408. Springer, 2004.

Hongwei Xi and Frank Pfenning. Dependent types in practical programming. In *26th ACM SIGPLAN-SIGACT Symposium on Principles of Programming Languages (POPL'99)*, pages 214–227. ACM Press, 1999.

Hongwei Xi, Chiyan Chen, and Gang Chen. Guarded recursive datatype constructors. In *30th ACM SIGPLAN-SIGACT Symposium on Principles of Programming Languages (POPL '03)*, pages 224–235. ACM Press, 2003.

Christoph Zenger. Indexed types. *Theoretical Computer Science*, 187(1-2): 147–165, 1997.

Meta-Level Features in an Industrial-Strength Theorem Prover

J Strother Moore

Department of Computer Sciences
University of Texas at Austin
moore@cs.utexas.edu

Categories and Subject Descriptors F.3.1 [*Specifying and Verifying and Reasoning about Programs*]: Mechanical verification

General Terms Verification

Keywords ACL2

Abstract

The ACL2 theorem prover—the current incarnation of "the" Boyer-Moore theorem prover—is a theorem prover for an extension of a first-order, applicative subset of Common Lisp. ACL2 is in use at several major microprocessor manufacturers to verify functional correctness of important components of commercial designs. Among the applications of ACL2 are the following:

- All elementary floating point operations on all desktop AMD microprocessors fabricated since 1997 have been verified with ACL2 to satisfy the IEEE 754 floating point standard.
- The Rockwell Collins AAMP7 cryptoprocessor was verified with ACL2 as specified by the EAL-7 level of the Common Criteria and was certified capable of simultaneously processing unclassified through Top Secret Codeword classified data.
- The media unit of the Centaur (VIA) Nano 64-bit x86 CPU has been verified to be functionally correct with ACL2. In addition, important properties of the clock tree for the entire x86 design have been verified.

These and other industrial applications establish that the ACL2 system provides a useful specification and modeling language as well as a useful mechanical theorem proving environment.

Surprising to many in the programming languages community is the fact the ACL2 language is remarkably primitive: it is untyped, all functions are total, there are no quantifiers, and there are no functional objects (it is a first-order language). These compromises can make ACL2 models more verbose and cumbersome than comparable models in other languages would be, but also make it easier to build a powerful proof engine for the language. Such a powerful theorem prover can in turn be exploited to produce very efficient runtime code.

The ACL2 theorem prover is a program written in the same language supported by the theorem prover. All of the data structures used in the theorem prover are objects in that language. Users of the proof assistant must understand the language since it is their specification and modeling language. Furthermore, users are permitted to write "programs" (i.e., to define functions) in the language and to run those programs on the theorem prover's data because those programs are side-effect-free. Thus, the prover can be opened up to much user-specialization.

Among other things, the ACL2 user can

1. build and efficiently run models of complex computing artifacts like microprocessors or floating point units, while experimenting with specifications, theorems, and proofs;
2. build new theorem prover components, use ACL2 to prove that those components meet the specifications required by ACL2, and then cause the system to use the user-defined components in place of the primitives provided by the ACL2 implementors;
3. define functions that inspect the goal being proved and the ACL2 data base and context and then compute goal-specific hints at runtime.

Perhaps surprisingly, such sophisticated meta-level facilities were implemented primarily at the request of the ACL2 user community and find routine use in the industrial projects mentioned above. ACL2 is thus exploiting the programming prowess of the engineers and scientists who use it to produce industrial-scale proofs.

Short Biography

J Strother Moore holds the Admiral B.R. Inman Centennial Chair in Computing Theory in the Department of Computer Science at the University of Texas at Austin. He was chair of the Computer Science Department for 8 years, 2001-09, and led the $120M drive to build the Bill & Melinda Gates Center for Computer Science and the Michael & Susan Dell Computer Science Hall, upon which ground was broken in October, 2010. He is the author of many books and papers on automated theorem proving and mechanical verification of computing systems. Along with Boyer he is a co-author of the Boyer-Moorve theorem prover and the Boyer-Moore fast string searching algorithm. With Matt Kaufmann he is the co-author of the ACL2 theorem prover. Moore got his S.B. in mathematics from MIT in 1970 and his Ph.D. in computational logic from the University of Edinburgh in 1973. Moore was a co-founder of Computational Logic, Inc., and served as its Chief Scientist for ten years. He and Bob Boyer were awarded the 1991 Current Prize in Automatic Theorem Proving by the American Mathematical Society. In 1999 they were awarded the Herbrand Award for their work in automatic theorem proving. Moore is a Fellow of the American Association for Artificial Intelligence, an ACM Fellow, and a member of the National Academy of Engineering (NAE). Boyer, Moore, and Kaufmann won the 2005 ACM Software System Award "For pioneering and engineering a most effective theorem prover (named the Boyer-Moore Theorem Prover) as a formal methods tool for verifying safety-critical hardware and software."

POPL'12, January 25–27, 2012, Philadelphia, PA, USA.
ACM 978-1-4503-1083-3/12/01.

Formalizing the LLVM Intermediate Representation for Verified Program Transformations *

Jianzhou Zhao Santosh Nagarakatte Milo M. K. Martin Steve Zdancewic

Computer and Information Science Department, University of Pennsylvania

jianzhou@cis.upenn.edu santoshn@cis.upenn.edu milom@cis.upenn.edu stevez@cis.upenn.edu

Abstract

This paper presents Vellvm (*verified LLVM*), a framework for reasoning about programs expressed in LLVM's intermediate representation and transformations that operate on it. Vellvm provides a mechanized formal semantics of LLVM's intermediate representation, its type system, and properties of its SSA form. The framework is built using the Coq interactive theorem prover. It includes multiple operational semantics and proves relations among them to facilitate different reasoning styles and proof techniques.

To validate Vellvm's design, we extract an interpreter from the Coq formal semantics that can execute programs from LLVM test suite and thus be compared against LLVM reference implementations. To demonstrate Vellvm's practicality, we formalize and verify a previously proposed transformation that hardens C programs against spatial memory safety violations. Vellvm's tools allow us to extract a new, verified implementation of the transformation pass that plugs into the real LLVM infrastructure; its performance is competitive with the non-verified, ad-hoc original.

Categories and Subject Descriptors D.2.4 [*Software Engineering*]: Software/Program Verification - Correctness Proofs; F.3.1 [*Logics and Meanings of Programs*]: Speficying and Verifying and Reasoning about Programs - Mechanical verification; F.3.2 [*Logics and Meanings of Programs*]: Semantics of Programming Languages - Operational semantics

General Terms Languages, Verification, Reliability

Keywords LLVM, Coq, memory safety

1. Introduction

Compilers perform their optimizations and transformations over an *intermediate representation* (IR) that hides details about the target execution platform. Rigorously proving properties about these IR transformations requires that the IR itself have a well-defined formal semantics. Unfortunately, the IRs used in main-stream production compilers generally do not. To address this deficiency, this paper formalizes both the static and dynamic semantics of the IR that forms the heart of the LLVM compiler infrastructure.

* This research was funded in part by the U.S. Government. The views and conclusions contained in this document are those of the authors and should not be interpreted as representing the official policies, either expressed or implied, of the U.S. Government.

POPL'12, January 25–27, 2012, Philadelphia, PA, USA.

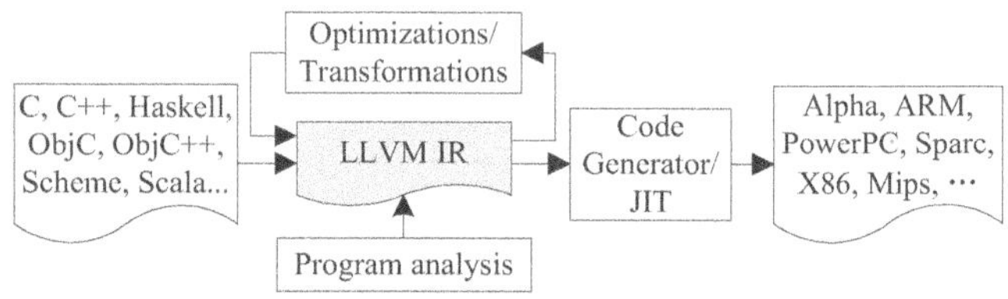

Figure 1. The LLVM compiler infrastructure

LLVM [19] (*Low-Level Virtual Machine*) uses a platform-independent SSA-based IR originally developed as a research tool for studying optimizations and modern compilation techniques [16]. The LLVM project has since blossomed into a robust, industrial-strength, and open-source compilation platform that competes with GCC in terms of compilation speed and performance of the generated code [16]. As a consequence, it has been widely used in both academia and industry.

An LLVM-based compiler is structured as a translation from a high-level source language to the LLVM IR (see Figure 1). The LLVM tools provide a suite of IR to IR translations, which provide optimizations, program transformations, and static analyses. The resulting LLVM IR code can then be lowered to a variety of target architectures, including x86, PowerPC, and ARM (either by static compilation or dynamic JIT-compilation). The LLVM project focuses on C and C++ front-ends, but many source languages, including Haskell, Scheme, Scala, Objective C and others have been ported to target the LLVM IR.

This paper introduces Vellvm—for *verified* LLVM—a framework that includes a formal semantics and associated tools for mechanized verification of LLVM IR code, IR to IR transformations, and analyses. The description of this framework in this paper is organized into two parts.

The first part formalizes the LLVM IR. It presents the LLVM syntax and static properties (Section 2), including a variety of well-formedness and structural properties about LLVM's static single assignment (SSA) representation that are useful in proofs about LLVM code and transformation passes. Vellvm's memory model (Section 3) is based on CompCert's [18], extended to handle LLVM's arbitrary bit-width integers, padding, and alignment issues. In developing the operational semantics (Section 4), a significant challenge is adequately capturing the nondeterminism that arises due to LLVM's explicit **undef** value and its intentional underspecification of certain erroneous behaviors such as reading from uninitialized memory; this underspecification is needed to justify the correctness of aggressive optimizations. Vellvm therefore implements several related operational semantics, including a nondeterministic semantics and several deterministic refinements to facilitate different proof techniques and reasoning styles.

The second part of the paper focuses on the utility of formalizing the LLVM IR. We describe Vellvm's implementation in Coq [10] and validate its LLVM IR semantics by extracting an executable interpreter and comparing its behavior to that of the LLVM reference interpreter and compiled code (Section 5). The Vellvm framework provides support for moving code between LLVM's IR representation and its Coq representation. This infrastructure, along with Coq's facility for extracting executable code from constructive proofs, enables Vellvm users to manipulate LLVM IR code with high confidence in the results. For example, using this framework, we can extract verified LLVM transformations that plug directly into the LLVM compiler. We demonstrate the effectiveness of this technique by using Vellvm to implement a verified instance of SoftBound [21], an LLVM-pass that hardens C programs against buffer overflows and other memory safety violations (Section 6).

To summarize, this paper and the Vellvm framework provide:

- A formalization of the LLVM IR, its static semantics, memory model, and several operational semantics;
- Metatheoretic results (preservation and progress theorems) relating the static and dynamic semantics;
- Coq infrastructure implementing the above, along with tools for interacting with the LLVM compiler;
- Validation of the semantics in the form of an extracted LLVM interpreter; and
- Demonstration of applying this framework to extract a verified transformation pass for enforcing spatial memory-safety.

2. Static Properties of the LLVM IR

The LLVM IR is a typed, static single assignment (SSA) [13] language that is a suitable representation for expressing many compiler transformations and optimizations. This section describes the syntax and basic static properties, emphasizing those features that are either unique to the LLVM or have non-trivial implications for the formalization. Vellvm's formalization is based on the LLVM release version 2.6, and the syntax and semantics are intended to model the behavior as described in the LLVM Language Reference,[1] although we also used the LLVM IR reference interpreter and the x86 backend to inform our design.

2.1 Language syntax

Figure 3 shows (a fragment of) the abstract syntax for the subset of the LLVM IR formalized in Vellvm. The metavariable *id* ranges over LLVM identifiers, written `%X`, `%T`, `%a`, `%b`, *etc.*, which are used to name local types and temporary variables, and `@a`, `@b`, `@main`, *etc.*, which name global values and functions.

Each source file is a module *mod* that includes data layout information *layout* (which defines sizes and alignments for types; see below), named types, and a list of *prods* that can be function declarations, function definitions, and global variables. Figure 2 shows a small example of LLVM syntax (its meaning is described in more detail in Section 3).

Every LLVM expression has a type, which can easily be determined from type annotations that provide sufficient information to check an LLVM program for type compatibility. The LLVM IR is not a type-safe language, however, because its type system allows arbitrary casts, calling functions with incorrect signatures, accessing invalid memory, *etc.* The LLVM type system ensures only that the size of a runtime value in a well-formed program is compatible with the type of the value—a well-formed program can still be stuck (see Section 4.3).

[1] See `http://llvm.org/releases/2.6/docs/LangRef.html`

```
%ST = type { i10 , [10 x i8*] }

define %ST* @foo(i8* %ptr) {
entry:
  %p = malloc %ST, i32 1
  %r = getelementptr %ST* %p, i32 0, i32 0
  store i10 648, %r         ; decomposes as 136, 2
  %s = getelementptr %ST* %p, i32 0, i32 1, i32 0
  store i8* %ptr, %s
  ret %ST* %p
}
```

Figure 2. An example use of LLVM's memory operations. Here, `%p` is a pointer to a single-element array of structures of type `%ST`. Pointer `%r` indexes into the first component of the first element in the array, and has type `i10*`, as used by the subsequent **store**, which writes the 10-bit value 648. Pointer `%s` has type `i8**` and points to the first element of the nested array in the same structure.

Types *typ* include arbitrary bit-width integers **i**8, **i**16, **i**32, *etc.*, or, more generally, $\mathbf{i}sz$ where sz is a natural number. Types also include **float**, **void**, pointers $typ*$, arrays $[\,sz \times typ\,]$ that have a statically-known size sz. Anonymous structure types $\{\,\overline{typ_j}^{\,j}\,\}$ contain a list of types. Functions $typ\;\overline{typ_j}^{\,j}$ have a return type, and a list of argument types. Here, $\overline{typ_j}^{\,j}$ denotes a list of typ components; we use similar notation for other lists throughout the paper. Finally, types can be named by identifiers id which is useful to define recursive types.

The sizes and alignments for types, and endianness are defined in $layout$. For example. **int** $sz\ align_0\ align_1$ dictates that values with type $\mathbf{i}sz$ are $align_0$-byte aligned when they are within an aggregate and when used as an argument, and $align_1$-byte aligned when emitted as a global.

Operations in the LLVM IR compute with values val, which are either identifiers id naming temporaries, or constants $cnst$ computed from statically-known data, using the compile-time analogs of the commands described below. Constants include base values (*i.e.,* integers or floats of a given bit width), and zero-values of a given type, as well as structures and arrays built from other constants.

To account for uninitialized variables and to allow for various program optimizations, the LLVM IR also supports a type-indexed **undef** constant. Semantically, **undef** stands for a *set* of possible bit patterns, and LLVM compilers are free to pick convenient values for each occurrence of **undef** to enable aggressive optimizations or program transformations. As described in Section 4, the presence of **undef** makes the LLVM operational semantics inherently nondeterministic.

All code in the LLVM IR resides in top-level functions, whose bodies are composed of block *bs*. As in classic compiler representations, a basic block consists of a labeled entry point l, a series of ϕ nodes, a list of commands, and a terminator instruction. As is usual in SSA representations, the ϕ nodes join together values from a list of predecessor blocks of the control-flow graph—each ϕ node takes a list of (value, label) pairs that indicates the value chosen when control transfers from a predecessor block with the associated label. Block terminators (**br** and **ret**) branch to another block or return (possibly with a value) from the current function. Terminators also include the **unreachable** marker, indicating that control should never reach that point in the program.

The core of the LLVM instruction set is its *commands* (c), which include the usual suite of binary arithmetic operations (*bop*—e.g., **add**, **lshr**, etc.), memory accessors (**load**, **store**), heap operations (**malloc** and **free**), stack allocation (**alloca**), conversion operations among integers, floats and pointers (*eop*, *trop*, and *cop*), comparison over integers (**icmp** and **select**), and calls (**call**).

Modules	mod, P	$::=$	$\overline{layout}\ \overline{namedt}\ \overline{prod}$
Layouts	$layout$	$::=$	$\mathbf{bigendian} \mid \mathbf{littleendian} \mid \mathbf{ptr}\ sz\ align_0\ align_1 \mid \mathbf{int}\ sz\ align_0\ align_1$
		$\mid$	$\mathbf{float}\ sz\ align_0\ align_1 \mid \mathbf{aggr}\ sz\ align_0\ align_1 \mid \mathbf{stack}\ sz\ align_0\ align_1$
Products	$prod$	$::=$	$id = \mathbf{global}\ typ\ const\ align \mid \mathbf{define}\ typ\ id(\overline{arg})\{\overline{b}\} \mid \mathbf{declare}\ typ\ id(\overline{arg})$
Floats	fp	$::=$	$\mathbf{float} \mid \mathbf{double}$
Types	typ	$::=$	$\mathbf{i}sz \mid fp \mid \mathbf{void} \mid typ* \mid [\,sz \times typ\,] \mid \{\,\overline{typ_j}^{\,j}\,\} \mid typ\,\overline{typ_j}^{\,j} \mid id$
Values	val	$::=$	$id \mid cnst$
Binops	bop	$::=$	$\mathbf{add} \mid \mathbf{sub} \mid \mathbf{mul} \mid \mathbf{udiv} \mid \mathbf{sdiv} \mid \mathbf{urem} \mid \mathbf{srem} \mid \mathbf{shl} \mid \mathbf{lshr} \mid \mathbf{ashr} \mid \mathbf{and} \mid \mathbf{or} \mid \mathbf{xor}$
Float ops	$fbop$	$::=$	$\mathbf{fadd} \mid \mathbf{fsub} \mid \mathbf{fmul} \mid \mathbf{fdiv} \mid \mathbf{frem}$
Extension	eop	$::=$	$\mathbf{zext} \mid \mathbf{sext} \mid \mathbf{fpext}$
Cast op	cop	$::=$	$\mathbf{fptoui} \mid \mathbf{ptrtoint} \mid \mathbf{inttoptr} \mid \mathbf{bitcast}$
Trunc op	$trop$	$::=$	$\mathbf{trunc}_{int} \mid \mathbf{trunc}_{fp}$
Constants	$cnst$	$::=$	$\mathbf{i}sz\ Int \mid fp\ Float \mid typ * id \mid (typ*)\,\mathbf{null} \mid typ\,\mathbf{zeroinitializer} \mid typ[\,\overline{cnst_j}^{\,j}\,] \mid \{\,\overline{cnst_j}^{\,j}\,\}$
		$\mid$	$typ\,\mathbf{undef} \mid bop\ cnst_1\ cnst_2 \mid fbop\ cnst_1\ cnst_2 \mid trop\ cnst\ \mathbf{to}\ typ \mid eop\ cnst\ \mathbf{to}\ typ$
		$\mid$	$cop\ cnst\ \mathbf{to}\ typ \mid \mathbf{getelementptr}\ cnst\ \overline{cst_j}^{\,j} \mid \mathbf{select}\ cnst_0\ cnst_1\ cnst_2 \mid \mathbf{icmp}\ cond\ cnst_1\ cnst_2$
		$\mid$	$\mathbf{fcmp}\ fcond\ cnst_1\ cnst_2$
Blocks	b	$::=$	$l\ \overline{\phi}\ \overline{c}\ tmn$
ϕ nodes	ϕ	$::=$	$id = \mathbf{phi}\ typ\ \overline{[val_j, l_j]}^{\,j}$
Tmns	tmn	$::=$	$\mathbf{br}\ val\ l_1\ l_2 \mid \mathbf{br}\ l \mid \mathbf{ret}\ typ\ val \mid \mathbf{ret\ void} \mid \mathbf{unreachable}$
Commands	c	$::=$	$id = bop(\,\mathbf{int}\ sz)val_1\ val_2 \mid id = fbop\ fp\ val_1\ val_2 \mid id = \mathbf{load}\ (typ*)val_1\ align$
		$\mid$	$\mathbf{store}\ typ\ val_1\ val_2\ align \mid id = \mathbf{malloc}\ typ\ val\ align \mid \mathbf{free}\,(\,typ*\,)\ val$
		$\mid$	$id = \mathbf{alloca}\ typ\ val\ align \mid id = trop\ typ_1\ val\ \mathbf{to}\ typ_2 \mid id = eop\ typ_1\ val\ \mathbf{to}\ typ_2$
		$\mid$	$id = cop\ typ_1\ val\ \mathbf{to}\ typ_2 \mid id = \mathbf{icmp}\ cond\ typ\ val_1\ val_2 \mid id = \mathbf{select}\ val_0\ typ\ val_1\ val_2$
		$\mid$	$id = \mathbf{fcmp}\ fcond\ fp\ val_1\ val_2 \mid option\ id = \mathbf{call}\ typ_0\ val_0\ \overline{param}$
		$\mid$	$id = \mathbf{getelementptr}\,(\,typ*\,)\ val\ \overline{val_j}^{\,j}$

Figure 3. Syntax for LLVM. Note that this figure omits some syntax definitions (*e.g.*, *cond*—the comparison operators) for the sake of space; they are, of course, present in Vellvm's implementation. Some other parts of the LLVM have been omitted from the Vellvm development; these are discussed in Section 5.

Note that a call site is allowed to ignore the return value of a function call. Finally, **getelementptr** computes pointer offsets into structured datatypes based on their types; it provides a platform- and layout-independent way of performing array indexing, struct field access, and pointer arithmetic.

2.2 Static semantics

Following the LLVM IR specification, Vellvm requires that every LLVM program satisfy certain invariants to be considered well formed: every variable in a function is well-typed, well-scoped, and assigned exactly once. At a minimum, any reasonable LLVM transformation must preserve these invariants; together they imply that the program is in SSA form [13].

All the components in the LLVM IR are annotated with types, so the typechecking algorithm is straightforward and determined only by local information.The only subtlety is that types themselves must be well formed. All *typ*s except **void** and function types are considered to be *first class*, meaning that values of these types can be passed as arguments to functions. A set of first-class type definitions is well formed if there are no degenerate cycles in their definitions (*i.e.*, every cycle through the definitions is broken by a pointer type). This ensures that the physical sizes of such *typ*s are positive, finite, and known statically.

The LLVM IR has two syntactic scopes—a global scope and a function scope—and does not have nested local scopes. In the global scope, all named types, global variables and functions have different names, and are defined mutually. In the scope of a function *fid* in module *mod*, all the global identifiers in *mod*, the names of arguments, locally defined variables and block labels in the function *fid* must be unique, which enforces the single-assignment part of the SSA property.

The set of blocks making up a function constitute a control-flow graph with a well-defined entry point. All instructions in the function must satisfy the SSA scoping invariant with respect to the control-flow graph: the instruction defining an identifier must *dominate* all the instructions that use it. Within a block $insn_1$ dominates $insn_2$ if $insn_1$ appears before $insn_2$ in a program order. A block labeled l_1 dominates a block labeled l_2 if every execution path from the program entry to l_2 must go through l_1.

The Vellvm formalization provides an implementation of this dominator analysis using a standard dataflow fixpoint computation [14]. It also proves that the implementation is correct, as stated in the following lemma, which is needed to establish preservation of the well-formedness invariants by the operational semantics (see Section 4).

LEMMA 1 (Dominator Analysis Correctness).

- *The entry block of a function dominates itself.*
- *Given a block b_2 that is an immediate successor of b_1, all the strict dominators of b_2 also dominate b_1*

These well-formedness constraints must hold only of blocks that are *reachable* from a function's entry point—unreachable code may contain ill-typed and ill-scoped instructions.

3. A Memory Model for Vellvm

3.1 Rationale

Understanding the semantics of LLVM's memory operations is crucial for reasoning about LLVM programs. LLVM developers make many assumptions about the "legal" behaviors of such LLVM code, and they informally use those assumptions to justify the correctness of program transformations.

There are many properties expected of a reasonable implementation of the LLVM memory operations (especially in the absence of errors). For example, we can reasonably assume that the **load** instruction does not affect which memory addresses are allocated, or that different calls to **malloc** do not inappropriately reuse memory locations. Unfortunately, the LLVM Language Reference Manual does not enumerate all such properties, which should hold of *any* "reasonable" memory implementation.

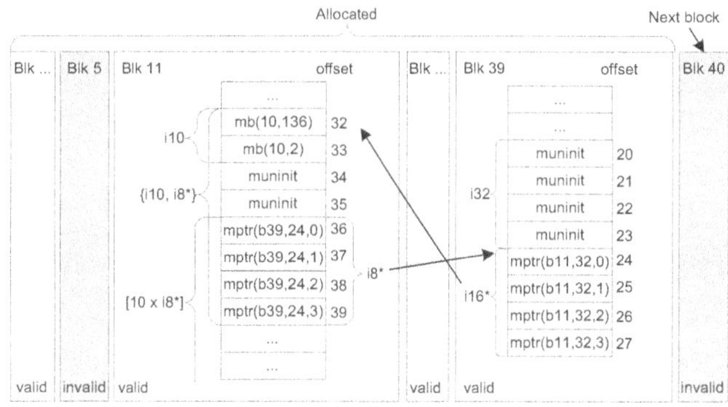

Figure 4. Vellvm's byte-oriented memory model. This figure shows (part of) a memory state that might be reached by calling the function `foo` from Figure 2. Blocks less than 40 were allocated; the next fresh block to allocate is 40. Block 5 is deallocated, and thus marked invalid to access; fresh blocks (≥ 40) are also invalid. Invalid memory blocks are gray, and valid memory blocks that are accessible are white. Block 11 contains data with structure type `{i10, [10 x i8*]}` but it might be read (due to physical subtyping) at the type `{i10, i8*}`. This type is flattened into two byte-sized memory cells for the i10 field, two uninitialized padding cells to adjust alignment, and four pointer memory cells for the first element of the array of 32-bit `i8*` pointers. Here, that pointer points to the 24th memory cell of block 39. Block 39 contains an uninitialized i32 integer represented by four muninit cells followed by a pointer that points to the 32nd memory cell of block 11.

On the other hand, details about the particular memory management implementation *can* be observed in the behavior of LLVM programs (*e.g.,* you can print a pointer after casting it to an integer). For this reason, and also to address error conditions, the LLVM specification intentionally leaves some behaviors undefined. Examples include: loading from an unallocated address; loading with improper alignment; loading from properly allocated but uninitialized memory; and loading from properly initialized memory but with an incompatible type.

Because of the dependence on a concrete implementation of memory operations, which can be platform specific, there are *many* possible memory models for the LLVM. One of the challenges we encountered in formalizing the LLVM was finding a point in the design space that accurately reflects the intent of the LLVM documentation while still providing a useful basis for reasoning about LLVM programs.

In this paper we adopt a memory model that is based on the one implemented for CompCert [18]. This model allows Vellvm to accurately implement the LLVM IR and, in particular, detect the kind of errors mentioned above while simultaneously justifying many of the "reasonable" assumptions that LLVM programmers make. The nondeterministic operational semantics presented in Section 4 takes advantage of this precision to account for much of the LLVM's under-specification.

Although Vellvm's design is intended to faithfully capture the LLVM specification, it is also partly motivated by pragmatism: building on CompCert's existing memory model allowed us to reuse a significant amount of their Coq infrastructure. A benefit of this choice is that our memory model is compatible with CompCert's memory model (*i.e.,* our memory model implements the CompCert `Memory` signature).

This Vellvm memory model inherits some features from the CompCert implementation: it is single threaded (in this paper we consider only single-threaded programs); it assumes that pointers are 32-bits wide, and 4-byte aligned; and it assumes that the memory is infinite. Unlike CompCert, Vellvm's model must also deal with arbitrary bit-width integers, padding, and alignment constraints that are given by layout annotations in the LLVM program, as described next.

3.2 LLVM memory commands

The LLVM supports several commands for working with heap-allocated data structures:

- **malloc** and **alloca** allocate array-structured regions of memory. They take a type parameter, which determines layout and padding of the elements of the region, and an integral size that specifies the number of elements; they return a pointer to the newly allocated region.
- **free** deallocates the memory region associated with a given pointer (which should have been created by **malloc**). Memory allocated by **alloca** is implicitly freed upon return from the function in which **alloca** was invoked.
- **load** and **store** respectively read and write LLVM values to memory. They take type parameters that govern the expected layout of the data being read/written.
- **getelementptr** indexes into a structured data type by computing an offset pointer from another given pointer based on its type and a list of indices that describe a path into the datatype.

Figure 2 gives a small example program that uses these operations. Importantly, the type annotations on these operations can be any first-class type, which includes arbitrary bit-width integers, floating point values, pointers, and aggregated types—arrays and structures. The LLVM IR semantics treats memory as though it is dynamically typed: the sizes, layout, and alignment, of a value read via a **load** instruction must be consistent with that of the data that was **stored** at that address, otherwise the result is undefined.

This approach leads to a memory model structured in two parts: (1) a low-level byte-oriented representation that stores values of basic (non-aggregated) types along with enough information to indicate physical size, alignment, and whether or not the data is a pointer, and (2) an encoding that flattens LLVM-level structured data with first-class types into a sequence of basic values, computing appropriate padding and alignment from the type. The next two subsections describe these two parts in turn.

3.3 The byte-oriented representation

The byte-oriented representation is composed of blocks of memory cells. Each cell is a byte-sized quantity that describes the smallest chunk of contents that a memory operation can access. Cells come in several flavors:

$$\text{Memory cells } mc \ ::= \ \mathsf{mb}(sz, byte) \mid \mathsf{mptr}(blk, ofs, idx) \mid \mathsf{muninit}$$

The memory cell $\mathsf{mb}(sz, byte)$ represents a byte-sized chunk of numeric data, where the LLVM-level bit-width of the integer is given by sz and whose contents is $byte$. For example, an integer with bit-width 32 is represented by four mb cells, each with size parameter 32. An integer with bit-width that is not divisible by 8 is encoded by the minimal number of bytes that can store the integer, *i.e.,* an integer with bit-width 10 is encoded by two bytes, each with size parameter 10 (see Figure 4). Floating point values are encoded similarly.

Memory addresses are represented as a block identifier blk and an offset ofs within that block; the cell $\mathsf{mptr}(blk, ofs, idx)$

is a byte-sized chunk of such a pointer where idx is an index identifying which byte the chunk corresponds to. Because Vellvm's implementation assumes 32-bit pointers, four such cells are needed to encode one LLVM-pointer, as shown in Figure 4. Loading a pointer succeeds only if the 4 bytes loaded are sequentially indexed from 0 to 3.

The last kind of cell is muninit, which represents uninitialized memory, layout padding, and bogus values that result from undefined computations (such as might arise from an arithmetic overflow).

Given this definition of memory cells, a memory state $M = (N, B, C)$ includes the following components: N is the next fresh block to allocate, B maps a valid block identifier to the size of the block; C maps a block identifier and an offset within the block to a memory cell (if the location is valid). Initially, N is 1; B and C are empty. Figure 4 gives a concrete example of such a memory state for the program in Figure 2.

There are four basic operations over this byte-oriented memory state: **alloc**, **mfree**, **mload**, and **mstore**. **alloc** allocates a fresh memory block N with a given size, increments N, fills the newly allocated memory cells with muninit. **mfree** simply removes the deallocated block from B, and its contents from C. Note that the memory model does not recycle block identifiers deallocated by a **mfree** operation, because this model assumes that a memory is of infinite size.

The **mstore** operation is responsible for breaking non-byte sized *basic values* into chunks and updating the appropriate memory locations. Basic values are integers (with their bit-widths), floats, addresses, and padding.

$$\begin{array}{lll} \text{Basic values} \; bv & ::= & Int\ sz \mid Float \mid blk.ofs \mid \mathbf{pad}\ sz \\ \text{Basic types} \; btyp & ::= & \mathbf{i}sz \mid fp \mid typ* \end{array}$$

mload is a partial function that attempts to read a value from a memory location. It is annotated by a basic type, and ensures compatibility between memory cells at the address it reads from and the given type. For example, memory cells for an integer with bit-width sz cannot be accessed as an integer type with a different bit-width; a sequence of bytes can be accessed as floating point values if they can be decoded as a floating point value; pointers stored in memory can only be accessed by pointer types. If an access is type incompatible, **mload** returns **pad** sz, which is an "error" value representing an arbitrary bit pattern with the bitwidth sz of the type being loaded. **mload** is undefined in the case that the memory address is not part of a valid allocation block.

3.4 The LLVM flattened values and memory accesses

LLVM's structured data is flattened to lists of basic values that indicate its physical representation:

$$\text{Flattened Values}\ v \quad ::= \quad bv \mid bv, v$$

A constant $cnst$ is flattened into a list of basic values according to it annotated type. If the $cnst$ is already of basic type, it flattens into the singleton list. Values of array type $[sz \times typ]$ are first flattened element-wise according to the representation given by typ and then padded by uninitialized values to match typ's alignment requirements as determined by the module's $layout$ descriptor. The resulting list is then concatenated to obtain the appropriate flattened value. The case when a $cnst$ is a structure type is similar.

The LLVM **load** instruction works by first flattening its type annotation typ into a list of basic types, and mapping **mload** across the list; it then merges the returned basic values into the final LLVM value. Storing an LLVM value to memory works by first flattening to a list of basic values and mapping **mstore** over the result.

$$\begin{array}{ccccccc} & & \mathrm{LLVM}_{ND} & & & & \\ & & \Cup & & & & \\ \mathrm{LLVM}_{Interp} & \approx & \mathrm{LLVM}_{D} & \gtrsim & \mathrm{LLVM}^{*}_{DFn} & \gtrsim & \mathrm{LLVM}^{*}_{DB} \end{array}$$

Figure 5. Relations between different operational semantics. Each equivalence or inclusion is justified by a proof in Vellvm.

This scheme induces a notion of dynamically-checked *physical subtyping*: it is permitted to read a structured value at a different type from the one at which it was written, so long as the basic types they flatten into agree. For non-structured data types such as integers, Vellvm's implementation is conservative—for example, reading an integer with bit width two from the second byte of a 10-bit wide integer yields `undef` because the results are, in general, platform specific. Because of this dynamically-checked, physical subtyping, pointer-to-pointer casts can be treated as the identity. Similar ideas arise in other formalizations of low-level language semantics [24, 25].

The LLVM **malloc** and **free** operations are defined by **alloc** and **mfree** in a straightforward manner. As the LLVM IR does not explicitly distinguish the heap and stack and function calls are implementation-specific, the memory model defines the same semantics for stack allocation (**alloca**) and heap allocation (**malloc**) — both of them allocate memory blocks in memory. However, the operational semantics (described next) maintains a list of blocks allocated by **alloca** for each function, and it deallocates them on return.

4. Operational Semantics

Vellvm provides several related operational semantics for the LLVM IR, as summarized in Figure 5. The most general is LLVM_{ND}, a small-step, nondeterministic evaluation relation given by rules of the form $config \vdash S \twoheadrightarrow S'$ (see Figure 6). This section first motivates the need for nondeterminism in understanding the LLVM semantics and then illustrates LLVM_{ND} by explaining some of its rules. Next, we introduce several equivalent deterministic refinements of LLVM_{ND}—LLVM_{D}, LLVM^{*}_{DB}, and LLVM^{*}_{DFn}—each of which has different uses, as described in Section 4.4. All of these operational semantics must handle various error conditions, which manifest as partiality in the rules. Section 4.3 describes these error conditions, and relates them to the static semantics of Section 2.

Vellvm's operational rules are specified as transitions between *machine states* S of the form $M, \overline{\Sigma}$, where M is the memory and $\overline{\Sigma}$ is a stack of *frames*. A frame keeps track of the current function fid and block label l, as well as the "continuation" sequence of commands $\overline{c}$ to execute next ending with the block terminator tmn. The map Δ tracks bindings for the local variables (which are not stored in M), and the list α keeps track of which memory blocks were created by the **alloca** instruction so that they can be marked as invalid when the function call returns.

4.1 Nondeterminism in the LLVM operational semantics

There are several sources of nondeterminism in the LLVM semantics: the **undef** value, which stands for an arbitrary (and ephemeral) bit pattern of a given type, various memory errors, such as reading from an uninitialized location. Unlike the "fatal" errors, which are modeled by stuck states (see Section 4.3), we choose to model these behaviors nondeterministically because they correspond to choices that would be resolved by running the program with a concrete memory implementation. Moreover, the LLVM optimization passes use the flexibility granted by this underspecificity to justify aggressive optimizations.

Configurations:

$$\text{Fun tables } \theta \ ::= \ v \mapsto id \qquad \text{Globals } g \ ::= \ id \mapsto v \qquad \text{Configurations } \mathit{config} \ ::= \ mod, g, \theta$$

Nondeterministic Machine States:

$$\begin{array}{llllllll} \text{Value sets } V & ::= & \{v \mid \Phi(v)\} & \text{Locals } \Delta & ::= & id \mapsto V & \text{Allocas } \alpha & ::= \ [] \mid blk, \alpha \\ \text{Frames } \Sigma & ::= & fid, l, \overline{c}, tmn, \Delta, \alpha & \text{Call stacks } \overline{\Sigma} & ::= & [] \mid \Sigma, \overline{\Sigma} & \text{Program states } S & ::= \ M, \overline{\Sigma} \end{array}$$

$\boxed{\mathit{config} \vdash S \twoheadrightarrow S'}$

$$\frac{\begin{array}{c}\mathbf{eval}_{ND}(g, \Delta, val) = \lfloor V \rfloor \quad \mathbf{findfdef}\,(mod, \theta, v) = \lfloor \mathbf{define}\ typ\ fid'\ (\overline{arg})\{(l'[]\overline{c}'tmn'), \overline{b}\} \rfloor \\ v \in V \quad \mathbf{initlocals}\,(g, \Delta, \overline{arg}, \overline{param}) = \lfloor \Delta' \rfloor \quad c_0 = (option\ id\ =\ \mathbf{call}\ typ\ val\ \overline{param})\end{array}}{mod, g, \theta \vdash M, ((fid, l, (c_0, \overline{c}), tmn, \Delta, \alpha), \overline{\Sigma}) \twoheadrightarrow M, ((fid', l', \overline{c}', tmn', \Delta', []), (fid, l, (c_0, \overline{c}), tmn, \Delta, \alpha), \overline{\Sigma})} \ \text{NDS\_CALL}$$

$$\frac{\mathbf{eval}_{ND}(g, \Delta, val) = \lfloor V \rfloor \quad c_0 = (option\ id\ =\ \mathbf{call}\ typ\ val\ \overline{param}) \quad \mathbf{freeallocas}\,(M, \alpha') = \lfloor M' \rfloor}{mod, g, \theta \vdash M, ((fid', l', [], \mathbf{ret}\ typ\ val, \Delta', \alpha'), (fid, l, (c_0, \overline{c}), tmn, \Delta, \alpha), \overline{\Sigma}) \twoheadrightarrow M', ((fid, l, \overline{c}, tmn, \Delta\{id \leftarrow V\}, \alpha), \overline{\Sigma})} \ \text{NDS\_RET}$$

$$\frac{\begin{array}{l}\mathbf{eval}_{ND}(g, \Delta, val) = \lfloor V \rfloor \quad \mathbf{true} \in V \\ \mathbf{findblock}\,(mod, fid, l_1) = (l_1 \overline{\phi}_1 \overline{c}_1 tmn_1) \quad \mathbf{computephinodes}_{ND}(g, \Delta, l, l_1, \overline{\phi}_1) = \lfloor \Delta' \rfloor\end{array}}{mod, g, \theta \vdash M, ((fid, l, [], \mathbf{br}\ val\ l_1\ l_2, \Delta, \alpha), \overline{\Sigma}) \twoheadrightarrow M, ((fid, l_1, \overline{c}_1, tmn_1, \Delta', \alpha), \overline{\Sigma})} \ \text{NDS\_BR\_TRUE}$$

$$\frac{\mathbf{eval}_{ND}(g, \Delta, val) = \lfloor V \rfloor \quad v \in V \quad c_0 = (id = \mathbf{malloc}\ typ\ val\ align) \quad \mathbf{malloc}\,(M, typ, v, align) = \lfloor M', blk \rfloor}{mod, g, \theta \vdash M, ((fid, l, (c_0, \overline{c}), tmn, \Delta, \alpha), \overline{\Sigma}) \twoheadrightarrow M', ((fid, l, \overline{c}, tmn, \Delta\{id \leftarrow \{blk.0\}\}, \alpha), \overline{\Sigma})} \ \text{NDS\_MALLOC}$$

$$\frac{\mathbf{eval}_{ND}(g, \Delta, val) = \lfloor V \rfloor \quad v \in V \quad c_0 = (id = \mathbf{alloca}\ typ\ val\ align) \quad \mathbf{malloc}\,(M, typ, v, align) = \lfloor M, blk \rfloor}{mod, g, \theta \vdash M, ((fid, l, (c_0, \overline{c}), tmn, \Delta, \alpha), \overline{\Sigma}) \twoheadrightarrow M', ((fid, l, \overline{c}, tmn, \Delta\{id \leftarrow \{blk.0\}\}, (blk, \alpha)), \overline{\Sigma})} \ \text{NDS\_ALLOCA}$$

$$\frac{\mathbf{eval}_{ND}(g, \Delta, val_1) = \lfloor V_1 \rfloor \quad \mathbf{eval}_{ND}(g, \Delta, val_2) = \lfloor V_2 \rfloor \quad \mathbf{evalbop}_{ND}(bop, sz, V_1, V_2) = V_3}{mod, g, \theta \vdash M, ((fid, l, (id = bop(\,\mathbf{int}\ sz)val_1\ val_2, \overline{c}), tmn, \Delta, \alpha), \overline{\Sigma}) \twoheadrightarrow M, ((fid, l, \overline{c}, tmn, \Delta\{id \leftarrow V_3\}, \alpha), \overline{\Sigma})} \ \text{NDS\_BOP}$$

Figure 6. LLVM_{ND}: Small-step, nondeterministic semantics of the LLVM IR (selected rules).

Nondeterminism shows up in two ways in the LLVM_{ND} semantics. First, stack frames bind local variables to sets of values V; second, the $\twoheadrightarrow$ relation itself may relate one state to many possible successors. The semantics teases apart these two kinds of nondeterminism because of the way that the **undef** value interacts with memory operations, as illustrated by the examples below.

From the LLVM Language Reference Manual: "Undefined values indicate to the compiler that the program is well defined no matter what value is used, giving the compiler more freedom to optimize." Semantically, LLVM_{ND} treats **undef** as the set of *all* values of a given type. For some motivating examples, consider the following code fragments:

```
(a)  %z = xor i8 undef undef

(b)  %x = add i8 0 undef
     %z = xor i8 %x %x

(c)  %z = or i8 undef 1

(d)  br undef %l1 %l2
```

The value computed for `%z` in example (a) is the set of all 8-bit integers: because each occurrence of **undef** could take on any bit pattern, the set of possible results obtained by `xor`ing them still includes all 8-bit integers. Perhaps surprisingly, example (b) computes the *same* set of values for `%z`: one might reason that no matter which value is chosen for **undef**, the result of `xor`ing `%x` with itself would always be `0`, and therefore `%z` should always be `0`. However, while that answer is *compatible* with the LLVM language reference (and hence allowed by the nondeterministic semantics), it is also safe to replace code fragment (b) with `%z = undef`. The reason is that the LLVM IR adopts a liberal substitution principle: because `%x = undef` would be a legitimate replacement for first assignment in (b), it is allowed to *substitute* **undef** for `%x` throughout, which reduces the assignment to `%z` to the same code as in (a).

Example (c) shows why the semantics needs arbitrary sets of values. Here, `%z` evaluates to the set of odd 8-bit integers, which is the result of `or`ing 1 with each element of the set $\{0, \ldots, 255\}$. This code snippet could therefore *not* safely be replaced by `%z = undef`; however it could be optimized to `%z = 1` (or any other odd 8-bit integer).

Example (d) illustrates the interaction between the set-semantics for local values and the nondeterminism of the $\twoheadrightarrow$ relation. The control state of the machine holds *definite* information, so when a branch occurs, there may be multiple successor states. Similarly, we choose to model memory cells as holding definite values, so when writing a set to memory, there is one successor state for each possible value that could be written. As an example of that interaction, consider the following example program, which was posted to the LLVMdev mailing list, that reads from an uninitialized memory location:

```
%buf = alloca i32
%val = load i32* %buf
store i32 10, i32* %buf
ret %val
```

The LLVM mem2reg pass optimizes this program to program (a) below; though according to the LLVM semantics, it would also be admissible to replace this program with option (b) (perhaps to expose yet more optimizations):

```
(a)  ret i32 10          (b)  ret i32 undef
```

4.2 Nondeterministic operational semantics of the SSA form

The LLVM_{ND} semantics we have developed for Vellvm (and the others described below) is parameterized by a *configuration*, which is a triple of a module containing the code, a (partial) map g that gives the values of global constants, and a function pointer table θ that is a (partial) map from values to function identifiers (see the top of Figure 6). The globals and function pointer maps are initialized from the module definition when the machine is started.

The LLVM_{ND} rules relate machine states to machine states, where a machine state takes the form of a memory M (from Section 3) and a stack of evaluation frames. The frames keep track of the (sets of) values bound to locally-allocated temporaries and which instructions are currently being evaluated. Figure 6 shows a selection of evaluation rules from the development.

Most of the commands of the LLVM have straight-forward interpretation: the arithmetic, logic, and data manipulation instructions are all unsurprising—the $\mathbf{eval}_{ND}$ function computes a set of flattened values from the global state, the local state, and an LLVM val, looking up the meanings of variables in the local state as needed; similarly, $\mathbf{evalbop}_{ND}$ implements binary operations, computing the result set by combining all possible pairs drawn from its input sets. LLVM_{ND}'s **malloc** behaves as described in Section 3, while **load** uses the memory model's ability to detect ill-typed and uninitialized reads and, in the case of such errors, yields **undef** as the result. Function calls push a new stack frame whose initial local bindings are computed from the function parameters. The α component of the stack frame keeps track of which blocks of memory are created by the **alloca** instruction (see rule NDS_ALLOCA); these are freed when the function returns (rule NDS_RET).

There is one other wrinkle in specifying the operational semantics when compared to a standard environment-passing call-by-value language. All of the ϕ instructions for a block must be executed atomically and with respect to the "old" local value mapping due to possibility of self loops and dependencies among the ϕ nodes. For example the well-formed code fragment below has a circular dependency between `%x` and `%z`

```
blk:
  %x = phi i32 [ %z, %blk ], [ 0, %pred ]
  %z = phi i32 [ %x, %blk ], [ 1, %pred ]
  %b = icmp leq %x %z
  br %b %blk %succ
```

If control enters this block from `%pred`, `%x` will map to `0` and `%z` to `1`, which causes the conditional branch to succeed, jumping back to the label `%blk`. The new values of `%x` and `%z` should be `1` and `0`, and not, `1` and `1` as might be computed if they were handled sequentially. This update of the local state is handled by the $\mathbf{computephinodes}_{ND}$ function in the operational semantics, as shown, for example, in rule NDS_BR_TRUE.

4.3 Partiality, preservation, and progress

Throughout the rules the "lift" notation $f(x) = \lfloor v \rfloor$ indicates that a partial function f is defined on x with value v. As seen by the frequent uses of lifting, both the nondeterministic and deterministic semantics are *partial*—the program may get stuck.

Some of this partiality is related to well-formedness of the SSA program. For example, $\mathbf{eval}_{ND}(g, \Delta, \text{\%x})$ is undefined if `%x` is not bound in Δ. These kinds of errors are ruled out by the static well-formedness constraints imposed by the LLVM IR (Section 2).

In other cases, we have chosen to use partiality in the operational semantics to model certain failure modes for which the LLVM specification says that the behavior of the program is undefined. These include: (1) attempting to **free** memory via a pointer not returned from **malloc** or that has already been deallocated, (2) allocating a negative amount of memory, (3) calling **load** or **store** on a pointer with bad alignment or a deallocated address, (4) trying to call a non-function pointer, or (5) trying to execute the **unreachable** command. We model these events by stuck states because they correspond to fatal errors that will occur in *any* reasonable realization of the LLVM IR by translation to a target platform. Each of these errors is precisely characterized by a predicate over the machine state (*e.g.,* $\text{BadFree}(\mathit{config}, S)$), and the "allowed" stuck states are defined to be the disjunction of these predicates:

$$\begin{array}{rcl}\text{Stuck}(\mathit{config}, S) & = & \text{BadFree}(\mathit{config}, S)\\ & \vee & \text{BadLoad}(\mathit{config}, S)\\ & \vee & \ldots\\ & \vee & \text{Unreachable}(\mathit{config}, S)\end{array}$$

To see that the well-formedness properties of the static semantics rule out all but these known error configurations, we prove the usual *preservation* and *progress* theorems for the LLVM_{ND} semantics.

THEOREM 2 (Preservation for LLVM_{ND}). *If (config, S) is well formed and* $\mathit{config} \vdash S \twoheadrightarrow S'$, *then* (config, S') *is well formed.*

Here, well-formedness includes the static scoping, typing properties, and SSA invariants from Section 2 for the LLVM code, but also requires that the local mappings Δ present in all frames of the call stack must be inhabited—each binding contains at least one value v—and that each defined variable that dominates the current continuation is in Δ's domain.

To show that the Δ bindings are inhabited after the step, we prove that (1) non-**undef** values V are singletons; (2) undefined values from constants typ **undef** contain all possible values of first class types typ; (3) undefined values from loading uninitialized memory or incompatible physical data contain at least paddings indicating errors; (4) evaluation of non-deterministic values by $\mathbf{evalbop}_{ND}$ returns non-empty sets of values given non-empty inputs.

The difficult part of showing that defined variables dominate their uses in the current continuation is proving that control-transfers maintain the dominance property [20]. If a program branches from a block b_1 to b_2, the first command in b_2 can use either the falling-through variables from b_1, which must be defined in Δ by Lemma 1, or the variables updated by the ϕs at the beginning of b_2. This latter property requires a lemma showing that $\mathbf{computephinode}_{ND}$ behaves as expected.

THEOREM 3 (Progress for LLVM_{ND}). *If the pair (config, S) is well formed, then either S has terminated successfully or* $\text{Stuck}(\mathit{config}, S)$ *or there exists S' such that* $\mathit{config} \vdash S \twoheadrightarrow S'$.

This theorem holds because in a well-formed machine state, $\mathbf{eval}_{ND}$ always returns a non-empty value set V; moreover jump targets and internal functions are always present.

4.4 Deterministic refinements

Although the LLVM_{ND} semantics is useful for reasoning about the validity of LLVM program transformations, Vellvm provides a LLVM_{D}, a deterministic, small-step refinement, along with two large-step operational semantics LLVM^{*}_{DFn} and LLVM^{*}_{DB}.

These different deterministic semantics are useful for several reasons: (1) they provide the basis for testing LLVM programs with a concrete implementation of memory (see the discussion about Vellvm's extracted interpreter in the next Section), (2) proving that LLVM_{D} is an instance of the LLVM_{ND} and relating the small-step rules to the large-step ones provides validation of *all* of the semantics (*i.e.,* we found bugs in Vellvm by formalizing multiple semantics and trying to prove that they are related), and (3) the small- and large-step semantics have different applications when reasoning about LLVM program transformations.

Unlike LLVM_{ND}, the frames for these semantics map identifiers to single values, not sets, and the operational rules call deterministic variants of the nondeterministic counterparts (*e.g.,* **eval** instead of $\textbf{eval}_{ND}$). To resolve the nondeterminism from **undef** and faulty memory operations, these semantics fix a concrete interpretation as follows:

- **undef** is treated as a **zeroinitializer**
- Reading uninitialized memory returns **zeroinitializer**

These choices yield unrealistic behaviors compared to what one might expect from running a LLVM program against a C-style runtime system, but the cases where this semantics differs correspond to *unsafe* programs. There are still many programs, namely those compiled to LLVM from type-safe languages, whose behaviors under this semantics should agree with their realizations on target platforms. Despite these differences from LLVM_{ND}, LLVM_{D} also has the preservation and progress properties.

Big-step semantics Vellvm also provides big-step operational semantics LLVM^*_{DFn}, which evaluates a function call as one large step, and LLVM^*_{DB}, which evaluates each sub-block—*i.e.,* the code between two function calls—as one large step. Big-step semantics are useful because compiler optimizations often transform multiple instructions or blocks within a function in one pass. Such transformations do not preserve the small-step semantics, making it hard to create simulations that establish correctness properties.

As a simple application of the large-step semantics, consider trying to prove the correctness of a transformation that re-orders program statements that do not depend on one another. For example, the following two programs result in the same states if we consider their execution as one big-step, although their intermediate states do not match in terms of the small-step semantics.

```
(a) %x = add i32 %a, %b    (b) %y = load i32* %p
    %y = load i32* %p          %x = add i32 %a, %b
```

The proof of this claim in Vellvm uses the LLVM^*_{DB} rules to hide the details about the intermediate states. To handle memory effects, we use a simulation relation that uses *symbolic evaluation* [22] to define the equivalence of two memory states. The memory contents are defined abstractly in terms of the program operations by recording the sequence of writes. Using this technique, we defined a simple translation validator to check whether the semantics of two programs are equivalent with respect to such re-orderings execution. For each pair of functions, the validator ensures that their control-flow graphs match, and that all corresponding sub-blocks are equivalent in terms of their symbolic evaluation. This approach is similar to the translation validation used in prior work for verifying instruction scheduling optimizations [32].

Although this is a simple application of Vellvm's large-step semantics, proving correctness of other program transformations such as dead expression elimination and constant propagation follow a similar pattern—the difference is that, rather than checking that two memories are syntactically equivalent according to the symbolic evaluation, we must check them with respect to a more semantic notion of equivalence [22].

Relationships among the semantics Figure 5 illustrates how these various operational semantics relate to one another. Vellvm provides proofs that LLVM^*_{DB} simulates LLVM^*_{DFn} and that LLVM^*_{DFn} simulates LLVM_{D}. In these proofs, simulation is taken to mean that the machine states are syntactically identical at corresponding points during evaluation. For example, the state at a function call of a program running on the LLVM^*_{DFn} semantics matches the corresponding state at the function call reached in LLVM_{D}. Note that in the deterministic setting, one-direction simulation implies bisimulation [18]. Moreover, LLVM_{D} is a refinement instance of the nondeterministic LLVM_{ND} semantics.

These relations are useful because the large-step semantics induce different proof styles than the small-step semantics: in particular, the induction principles obtained from the large step semantics allow one to gloss over insignificant details of the small step semantics.

5. Vellvm Infrastructure and Validation

This section briefly describes the Coq implementation of Vellvm and its related tools for interacting with the LLVM infrastructure. It also describes how we validate the Vellvm semantics by extracting an executable interpreter and comparing its behavior to the LLVM reference interpreter.

5.1 The Coq development

Vellvm encodes the abstract syntax from Section 2 in an entirely straightforward way using Coq's inductive datatypes (generated in a preprocessing step via the Ott [27] tool). The implementation uses Penn's Metatheory library [4], which was originally designed for the locally nameless representation, to represent identifiers of the LLVM, and to reason about their freshness.

The Coq representation deviates from the full LLVM language in only a few (mostly minor) ways. In particular, the Coq representation requires that some type annotations be in normal form (*e.g.,* the type annotation on **load** must be a pointer), which simplifies type checking at the IR level. The Vellvm tool that imports LLVM bitcode into Coq provides such normalization, which simply expands definitions to reach the normal form. In total, the syntax and static semantics constitute about 2500 lines of Coq definitions and proof scripts.

Vellvm's memory model implementation extends CompCert's with approximately 5000 lines of code to support integers with arbitrary precision, padding, and an experimental treatment of casts that has not yet been needed for any of our proofs. On top of this extended memory model, all of the operational semantics and their metatheory have been proved in Coq. In total, the development represents approximately 32,000 lines of Coq code. Checking the entire Vellvm implementation using `coqc` takes about 13.5 minutes on a 1.73 GHz Intel Core i7 processor with 8 GB RAM. We expect that this codebase could be significantly reduced in size by refactoring the proof structure and making it more modular.

The LLVM distribution includes primitive OCaml bindings that are sufficient to generate LLVM IR code ('bitcode" in LLVM jargon) from OCaml. To convert between the LLVM bitcode representation and the extracted OCaml representation, we implemented a library consisting of about 5200 lines of OCaml-LLVM bindings. This library also supports pretty-printing of the AST's; this code was also useful in the extracted the interpreter.

Omitted details This paper does not discuss all of the LLVM IR features that the Vellvm Coq development supports. Most of these features are uninteresting technically but necessary to support real LLVM code: (1) The LLVM IR provides aggregate data operations (**extractvalue** and **insertvalue**) for projecting and updating the elements of structures and arrays; (2) the operational semantics supports external function calls by assuming that their behavior is specified by axioms; the implementation applies these axioms to transition program states upon calling external functions; (3) the LLVM **switch** instruction, which is used to compile jump tables, is lowered to the normal branch instructions that Vellvm supports by a LLVM-supported pre-processing step.

Unsupported features Some features of LLVM are not supported by Vellvm. First, the LLVM provides *intrinsic* functions for extending LLVM or to represent functions that have well known names and semantics and are required to follow certain restrictions—for example, functions from standard C libraries, handling variable argument functions, *etc.* Second, the LLVM functions, global variables, and parameters can be decorated with attributes that denote linkage type, calling conventions, data representation, *etc.* which provide more information to compiler transformations than what the LLVM type system provides. Vellvm does not statically check the well-formedness of these attributes, though they should be obeyed by any valid program transformation. Third, Vellvm does not support the *invoke* and *unwind* instructions, which are used to implement exception handling, nor does it support variable argument functions. Forth, Vellvm does not support vector types, which allow for multiple primitive data values to be computed in parallel using a single instruction.

5.2 Extracting an interpreter

To test Vellvm's operational semantics for the LLVM IR, we used Coq's code extraction facilities to obtain an interpreter for executing the LLVM distribution's regression test suite. Extracting such an interpreter is one of the main motivations for developing a deterministic semantics, because the evaluation under the nondeterministic semantics cannot be directly compared against actual runs of LLVM IR programs.

Unfortunately, the small-step deterministic semantics LLVM_D is defined relationally in the logical fragment of Coq, which is convenient for proofs, but can not be used to extract code. Therefore, Vellvm provides yet another operational semantics, LLVM_{Interp}, which is a deterministic functional interpreter implemented in the computational fragment of Coq. LLVM_{Interp} is proved to be bisimilar to LLVM_D, so we can port results between the two semantics.

Although one could run this extracted interpreter directly, doing so is not efficient. First, integers with arbitrary bit-width are inductively defined in Coq. This yields easy proof principles, but does not give an efficient runtime representation; floating point operations are defined axiomatically. To remedy these problems, at extraction, we realize Vellvm's integer and floating point values by efficient C++ libraries that are a standard part of the LLVM distribution. Second, the memory model implementation of Vellvm maintains memory blocks and their associated metadata as functional lists, and it converts between byte-list and value representations at each memory access. Using the extracted data-structures directly incurs tremendous performance overhead, so we replaced the memory operations of the memory model with native implementations from the C standard library. A value v in local mappings δ is boxed, and it is represented by a reference to memory that stores its content.

Our implementation faithfully runs 134 out of the 145 tests from the LLVM regression suite that `lli`, the LLVM distribution interpreter, can run. The missing tests cover instructions (like variable arguments) that are not yet implemented in Vellvm.

Although replacing the Coq data-structures by native ones invalidates the absolute correctness guarantees one would expect from an extracted interpreter, this exercise is still valuable. In the course of carrying out this experiment, we found one severe bug in the semantics: the **br** instruction inadvertently swapped the true and false branches.

6. Verified SoftBound

SoftBound [21] is a previously proposed program transformation that hardens C programs against spatial memory safety violations (*e.g.,* buffer overflows, array indexing errors, and pointer arithmetic errors). SoftBound works by first compiling C programs into the LLVM IR, and then instrumenting the program with instructions that propagate and check per-pointer metadata. SoftBound maintains base and bound metadata with each pointer, shadowing loads and stores of pointer with parallel loads and stores of their associated metadata. This instrumentation ensures that each pointer dereferenced is within bounds and aborts the program otherwise.

The original SoftBound paper includes a mechanized proof that validates the correctness of this idea, but it is not complete. In particular, the proof is based on a subset of a C-like language with only straight-line commands and non-aggregate types, while a real SoftBound implementation needs to consider all of the LLVM IR shown in Figure 3, the memory model, and the operational semantics of the LLVM. Also the original proof ensures the correctness only with respect to a specification that the SoftBound instrumentation must implement, but does not prove the correctness of the instrumentation pass itself. Moreover, the specification requires that every temporary must contain metadata, not just pointer temporaries.

Using Vellvm to verify SoftBound This section describes how we use Vellvm to formally verify the correctness of the SoftBound instrumentation pass with respect to the LLVM semantics, demonstrating that the promised spatial memory safety property is achieved. Moreover, Vellvm allows us to extract a verified OCaml implementation of the transformation from Coq. The end result is a compiler pass that is formally verified to transform a program in the LLVM IR into a program augmented with sufficient checking code such that it will dynamically detect and prevent all spatial memory safety violations.

SoftBound is a good test case for the Vellvm framework. It is a non-trivial translation pass that nevertheless only inserts code, thereby making it easier to prove correct. SoftBound's intended use is to prevent security vulnerabilities, so bugs in its implementation can potentially have severe consequences. Also, the existing SoftBound implementation already uses the LLVM.

Modifications to SoftBound since the original paper As described in the original paper, SoftBound modifies function signatures to pass metadata associated with the pointer parameters or returned pointers. To improve the robustness of the tool, we transitioned to an implementation that instead passes all pointer metadata on a shadow stack. This has two primary advantages. The first is that this design simplifies the implementation while simultaneously better supporting indirect function calls (via function pointers) and more robustly handling improperly declared function prototypes. The second is that it also simplifies the proofs.

6.1 Formalizing SoftBound for the LLVM IR

The SoftBound correctness proof has the following high-level structure:

1. We define a *nonstandard* operational semantics SBspec for the LLVM IR. This semantics "builds in" the safety properties that should be enforced by a correct implementation of SoftBound. It uses meta-level datastructures to implement the metadata and meta-level functions to define the semantics of the bounds checks.
2. We prove that an LLVM program P, when run on the SBspec semantics, has no spatial safety violations.
3. We define a translation pass $\mathrm{SBtrans}(-)$ that instruments the LLVM code to propagate metadata.
4. We prove that a program if $\mathrm{SBtrans}(P) = \lfloor P' \rfloor$ then P', when run on the LLVM_D, simulates P running on SBspec.

The SoftBound specification Figure 7 gives the program configurations and representative rules for the SBspec semantics. SBspec behaves the same as the standard semantics except that it creates, propagates, and checks metadata of pointers in the appropriate instructions.

Nondeterministic rules:

Metadata	md	$::=$	$[v_1, v_2)$	Memory metadata	MM	$::=$	$blk.ofs \mapsto md$	Frames	$\hat{\Sigma}$	$::=$	$fid, l, \overline{c}, tmn, \Delta, \mu, \alpha$
Call stacks	$\overline{\hat{\Sigma}}$	$::=$	$[] \mid \hat{\Sigma}, \overline{\hat{\Sigma}}$	Local metadata	μ	$::=$	$id \mapsto md$	Program states	$\hat{S}$	$::=$	$M, MM, \overline{\hat{\Sigma}}$

$$\frac{\begin{array}{l}\mathbf{eval}_{ND}(g, \Delta, val) = \lfloor V \rfloor \quad v \in V \quad c_0 = (id = \mathbf{malloc}\ typ\ val\ align) \\ \mathbf{malloc}\,(M, typ, v, align) = \lfloor M', blk \rfloor \quad \mu' = \mu\{id \leftarrow [blk.0, blk.(sizeof\ typ \times v))\}\end{array}}{mod, g, \theta \vdash M, MM, ((fid, l, (c_0, \overline{c}), tmn, \Delta, \mu, \alpha), \overline{\hat{\Sigma}}) \twoheadrightarrow M', MM, ((fid, l, \overline{c}, tmn, \Delta\{id \leftarrow \{blk.0\}\}, \mu', \alpha), \overline{\hat{\Sigma}})}\ \text{SB\_MALLOC}$$

$$\frac{\begin{array}{l}\mathbf{eval}_{ND}(g, \Delta, val) = \lfloor V \rfloor \quad v \in V \quad c_0 = (id = \mathbf{load}\,(typ*)val\ align) \\ \mathbf{findbounds}(g, \mu, val) = \lfloor md \rfloor \quad \mathbf{checkbounds}(typ, v, md) \quad \mathbf{load}\,(M, typ, v, align) = \lfloor v' \rfloor \\ \text{if } \mathbf{isPtrTyp}\ typ \text{ then } \mu' = \mu\{id \leftarrow \mathbf{findbounds}\,(MM, v)\} \text{ else } \mu' = \mu\end{array}}{mod, g, \theta \vdash M, MM, ((fid, l, (c_0, \overline{c}), tmn, \Delta, \mu, \alpha), \overline{\hat{\Sigma}}) \twoheadrightarrow M, MM, ((fid, l, \overline{c}, tmn, \Delta\{id \leftarrow \{|v'|\}\}, \mu', \alpha), \overline{\hat{\Sigma}})}\ \text{SB\_LOAD}$$

$$\frac{\begin{array}{l}\mathbf{eval}_{ND}(g, \Delta, val_1) = \lfloor V_1 \rfloor \quad v_1 \in V_1 \quad \mathbf{eval}_{ND}(g, \Delta, val_2) = \lfloor V_2 \rfloor \quad v_2 \in V_2 \\ c_0 = (\mathbf{store}\ typ\ val_1\ val_2\ align) \quad \mathbf{findbounds}(g, \mu, val_2) = \lfloor md \rfloor \quad \mathbf{checkbounds}(typ, v_2, md) \\ \mathbf{store}\,(M, typ, v_1, v_2, align) = \lfloor M' \rfloor \quad \text{if } \mathbf{isPtrTyp}\ typ \text{ then } MM' = MM\{v_2 \leftarrow md\} \text{ else } MM' = MM\end{array}}{mod, g, \theta \vdash M, MM, ((fid, l, (c_0, \overline{c}), tmn, \Delta, \mu, \alpha), \overline{\hat{\Sigma}}) \twoheadrightarrow M', MM', ((fid, l, \overline{c}, tmn, \Delta, \mu, \alpha), \overline{\hat{\Sigma}})}\ \text{SB\_STORE}$$

Deterministic configurations:

Frames $\hat{\sigma} ::= fid, l, \overline{c}, tmn, \delta, \mu, \alpha$ Call stacks $\overline{\hat{\sigma}} ::= [] \mid \hat{\sigma}, \overline{\hat{\sigma}}$ Program states $\hat{s} ::= M, MM, \overline{\hat{\sigma}}$

Figure 7. SBspec: The specification semantics for SoftBound. Differences from the LLVM_{ND} rules are highlighted.

A program state $\hat{S}$ is an extension of the standard program state S for maintaining metadata md, which is a pair defining the start and end address for a pointers: μ in each function frame $\hat{\Sigma}$ maps temporaries of pointer type to their metadata; MM is the shadow heap that stores metadata for pointers in memory. Note that although the specification is nondeterministic, the metadata is deterministic. Therefore, a pointer loaded from uninitialized memory space can be **undef**, but it cannot have arbitrary md (which might not be valid).

SBspec is correct if a program P must either abort on detecting a spatial memory violation with respect to the SBspec, or preserve the LLVM semantics of the original program P; and, moreover, P is not stuck by any spatial memory violation in the SBspec (*i.e.*, SBspec must catch *all* spatial violations).

DEFINITION 1 (Spatial safety). *Accessing a memory location at the offset ofs of a block blk is spatially safe if blk is less than the next fresh block N, and ofs is within the bounds of blk:*

$$blk < N \wedge (B(blk) = \lfloor size \rfloor \rightarrow 0 \leq ofs < size)$$

The legal stuck states of SoftBound—$\text{Stuck}_{SB}(config, \hat{S})$ include all legal stuck states of LLVM_{ND} (recall Section 4.3) *except* the states that violate spatial safety. The case when B does not map blk to some size indicates that blk is not valid, and pointers into the blk are dangling—this indicates a temporal safety error that is not prevented by SoftBound and therefore it is included in the set of legal stuck states.

Because the program states of a program in the LLVM_{ND} semantics are identical to the corresponding parts in the SBspec, it is easy to relate them: let $\hat{S} \supseteq^\circ S$ mean that common parts of the SoftBound state $\hat{S}$ and S are identical. Because memory instructions in the SBspec may abort without accessing memory, the first part of correctness is by a straightforward simulation relation between states of the two semantics.

THEOREM 4 (SBspec simulates LLVM_{ND}). *If the state $\hat{S} \supseteq^\circ S$, and $config \vdash \hat{S} \twoheadrightarrow \hat{S}'$, then there exists a state S', such that $config \vdash S \twoheadrightarrow S'$, and $\hat{S}' \supseteq^\circ S'$.*

The second part of the correctness is proved by the following *preservation* and *progress* theorems.

THEOREM 5 (Preservation for SBspec). *If $(config, \hat{S})$ is well formed, and $config \vdash \hat{S} \twoheadrightarrow \hat{S}'$, then $(config, \hat{S}')$ is well formed.*

Here, SBspec well-formedness strengthens the invariants for LLVM_{ND} by requiring that if any id defined in Δ is of pointer type, then μ contains its metadata and a *spatial safety invariant*: all bounds in μs of function frames and MM must be memory ranges within which all memory addresses are spatially safe.

The interesting part is proving that the spatial safety invariant is preserved. It holds initially, because a program's initial frame stack is empty, and we assume that MM is also empty. The other cases depend on the rules in Figure 7.

The rule SB_MALLOC, which allocates the number v of elements with typ at a memory block blk, updates the metadata of id with the start address that is the beginning of blk, and the end address that is at the offset $blk.(sizeof\ typ \times v)$ in the same block. LLVM's memory model ensures that the range of memory is valid.

The rule SB_LOAD reads from a pointer val with runtime data v, finds the md of the pointer, and ensures that v is within the md via **checkbounds**. If the val is an identifier, **findbounds** simply returns the identifier's metadata from μ, which must be a spatial safe memory range. If val is a constant of pointer type, **findbounds** returns bounds as the following. For global pointers, **findbounds** returns bounds derived from their types because globals must be allocated before a program starts. For pointers converted from some constant integers by **inttoptr**, it conservatively returns the bounds $[\mathbf{null}, \mathbf{null})$ to indicate a potentially invalid memory range. For a pointer $cnst_1$ derived from an other constant pointer $cnst_2$ by **bitcase** or **getelementptr**, **findbounds** returns the same bound of $cnst_2$ for $cnst_1$. Note that $\{|v'|\}$ denotes conversion from a deterministic value to a nondeterministic value.

If the load reads a pointer-typed value v from memory, the rule finds its metadata in MM and updates the local metadata mapping μ. If MM does not contain any metadata indexed by

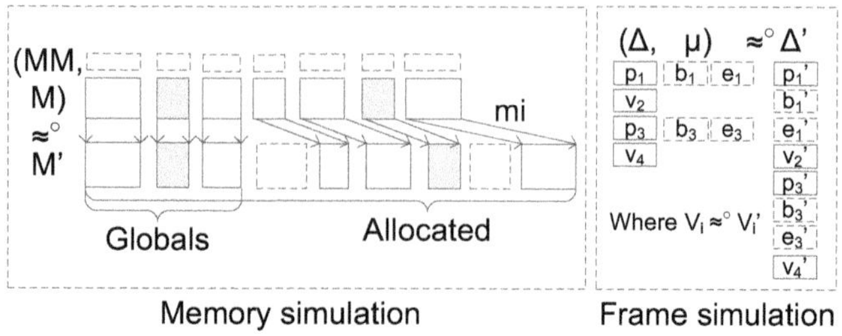

Figure 8. Simulation relations of the SoftBound pass

v, that means the pointer being loaded was not stored with valid bounds, so **findbounds** returns $[\textbf{null}, \textbf{null})$ to ensure the spatial safety invariant. Similarly, the rule SB_STORE checks whether the address to be stored to is in bounds and, if storing a pointer, updates MM accordingly. SoftBound disallows dereferencing a pointer that was converted from an interger, even if that integer was originally obtained from a valid pointer. Following the same design choice, **findbounds** returns $[\textbf{null}, \textbf{null})$ for pointers cast from integers. **checkbounds** fails when a program accesses such pointers.

THEOREM 6 (Progress for SBspec). *If $\hat{S}_1$ is well-formed, then either $\hat{S}_1$ is a final state, or $\hat{S}_1$ is a legal stuck state, or there exists a $\hat{S}_2$ such that config $\vdash \hat{S}_1 \twoheadrightarrow \hat{S}_2$.*

This theorem holds because all the bounds in a well-formed SBspec state give memory ranges that are spatially safe, if **checkbounds** succeeds, the memory access must be spatially safe.

The correctness of the SoftBound instrumentation Given SBspec, we designed an instrumentation pass in Coq. For each function of an original program, the pass implements μ by generating two fresh temporaries for every temporary of pointer type to record its bounds. For manipulating metadata stored in MM, the pass axiomatizes a set of interfaces that manage a disjoint metadata space with specifications for their behaviors.

Figure 8 pictorially shows the simulation relations $\simeq^\circ$ between an original program P in the semantics of SBspec and its transformed program P' in the LLVM semantics. First, because P' needs additional memory space to store metadata, we need a mapping mi that maps each allocated memory block in M to a memory block in M' without overlap, but allows M' to have additional blocks for metadata, as shown in dashed boxes. Note that we assume the two programs initialize globals identically. Second, basic values are related in terms of the mapping between blocks: pointers are related if they refer to corresponding memory locations; other basic values are related if they are same. Two values are related if they are of the same length and the corresponding basic values are related.

Using the value simulations, $\simeq^\circ$ defines a simulation for memory and stack frames. Given two related memory locations $blk.ofs$ and $blk'.ofs'$, their contents in M and M' must be related; if MM maps $blk.ofs$ to the bound $[v_1, v_2)$, then the additional metadata space in M' must store v_1' and v_2' that relate to v_1 and v_2 for the location $blk'.ofs'$. For each pair of corresponding frames in the two stacks, Δ and Δ' must store related values for the same temporary; if μ maps a temporary id to the bound $[v_1, v_2)$, then Δ' must store the related bound in the fresh temporaries for the id.

THEOREM 7. *Given a state $\hat{s}_1$ of P with configuration config and a state s_1' of P' with configuration config', if $\hat{s}_1 \simeq^\circ s_1'$, and config $\vdash \hat{s}_1 \longrightarrow \hat{s}_2$, then there exists a state s_2', such that config' $\vdash s_1' \longrightarrow^* s_2'$, $\hat{s}_2 \simeq^\circ s_2'$.*

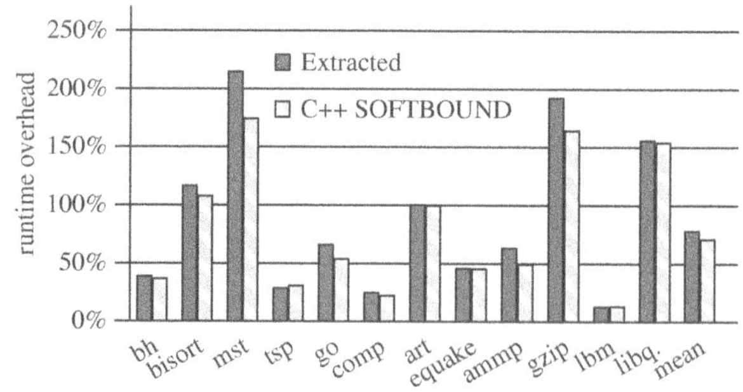

Figure 9. Execution time overhead of the extracted and the C++ version of SoftBound

Here, config $\vdash \hat{s}_1 \longrightarrow \hat{s}_2$ is a deterministic SBspec that, as in Section 4, is an instance of the non-deterministic SBspec.

The correctness of SoftBound

THEOREM 8 (SoftBound is correct). *Let* $\text{SBtrans}(P) = \lfloor P' \rfloor$ *denote that the SoftBound pass instruments a well-formed program P to be P'. A SoftBound instrumented program P' either aborts on detecting spatial memory violations or preserves the LLVM semantics of the original program P. P' is not stuck by any spatial memory violation.*

6.2 Extracted verified implemention of SoftBound

The above formalism not only shows that the SoftBound transformation enforces the promised safety properties, but the Vellvm framework allows us to extract a translator directly from the Coq code, resulting in a verified implementation of the SoftBound transformation. The extracted implementation uses the same underlying shadowspace implementation and wrapped external functions as the non-extracted SoftBound transformation written in C++. The only aspect not handled by the extracted transformation is initializing the metadata for pointers in the global segment that are non-NULL initialized (*i.e.*, they point to another variable in the global segment). Without initialization, valid programs can be incorrectly rejected as erroneous. Thus, we reuse the code from the C++ implementation of the SoftBound to properly initialize these variables.

Effectiveness To measure the effectiveness of the extracted implementation of SoftBound versus the C++ implementation, we tested both implementations on the same programs. To test whether the implementations detect spatial memory safety violations, we used 1809 test cases from the NIST Juliet test suite of C/C++ codes [23]. We chose the test cases which exercised the buffer overflows on both the heap and stack. Both implementations of SoftBound correctly detected *all* the buffer overflows without any false violations. We also confirmed that both implementations properly detected the buffer overflow in the `go` SPEC95 benchmark. Finally, the extracted implementation is robust enough to successfully transform and execute (without false violations) several applications selected from the SPEC95, SPEC2000, and SPEC2006 suites (around 110K lines of C code in total).

Performance overheads Unlike the C++ implementation of SoftBound that removes some obviously redundant checks, the extracted implementation of SoftBound performs no SoftBound-specific optimizations. In both cases, the same suite of standard LLVM optimizations are applied post-transformation to optimize the code to reduce the overhead of the instrumentation. To determine the performance impact on the resulting program, Figure 9 reports the execution time overheads (lower is better) of extracted SoftBound (leftmost bar of each benchmark) and the C++ implementation (rightmost bar of each benchmark) for various benchmarks from SPEC95, SPEC2000 and SPEC2006. Because of the check elimination optimization performed by the C++ implementation, the code is slightly faster, but overall the extracted implementation provides similar performance.

Bugs found in the original SoftBound implementation In the course of formalizing the SoftBound transformation, we discovered two implementation bugs in the original C++ implementation of SoftBound. First, when one of the incoming values of a ϕ node with pointer type is an **undef**, **undef** was propagated as its base and bound. Subsequent compiler transformations may instantiate the undefined base and bound with defined values that allow the **checkbounds** to succeed, which would lead to memory violation. Second, the base and bound of constant pointer $(typ*)$ **null** was set to be $(typ*)$ **null** and $(typ*)$ **null** $+$ $sizeof(typ)$, allowing dereferences of **null** or pointers pointing to an offset from **null**. Either of these bugs could have resulted in faulty checking and thus expose the program to the spatial violations that SoftBound was designed to prevent. These bugs underscore the importance of a formally verified and extracted implementation to avoid such bugs.

7. Related Work

Mechanized language semantics There is a large literature on formalizing language semantics and reasoning about the correctness of language implementations. Prominent examples include: Foundational Proof Carrying Code [2], Foundational Typed Assembly Language [11], Standard ML [12, 30], and (a substantial subset of) Java [15].

Verified compilers Compiler verification has a considerable history; see the bibliography [18] for a comprehensive overview. Other research has also used Coq for compiler verification tasks, including much recent work on compiling functional source languages to assembly [5, 8, 9].

Vellvm is closer in spirit to CompCert [18], which was the first fully-verified compiler to generate compact and efficient assembly code for a large fragment of the C language. CompCert also uses Coq. It formalizes the operational semantics of CompCert C, several intermediate languages used in the compilation, and assembly languages including PowerPC, ARM and x86. The latest version of CompCert also provides an executable reference interpreter for the semantics of CompCert C. Based on the formalized semantics, the CompCert project fully proves that all compiler phases produce programs that preserve the semantics of the original program. Optimization passes include local value numbering, constant propagation, coalescing graph coloring register allocation [6], and other back-end transformations. CompCert has also certified some advanced compiler optimizations [32–34] using translation validation [22, 26]. The XCERT project [29, 31] extends the CompCert compiler by a generic translation validator based on SMT solvers.

Other mechanization efforts The verified software tool-chain project [3] assures that the machine-checked proofs claimed at the top of the tool-chain hold in the machine language program. Typed assembly languages [7] provide a platform for proving back-end optimizations. Similarly, The Verisoft project [1] also attempts to mathematically prove the correct functionality of systems in automotive engineering and security technology. ARMor [37] guarantees control flow integrity for application code running on embedded processors. The Rhodium project [17] uses a domain specific language to express optimizations via local rewrite rules and provides a soundness checker for optimizations

Validating LLVM optimizations The CoVac project [36] develops a methodology that adapts existing program analysis techniques to the setting of translation validation, and reports on a prototype tool that applies their methodology to verification of the LLVM compiler. The LLVM-MD project [35] validates LLVM optimizations by symbolic evaluation. The Peggy tool performs translation validation for the LLVM compiler using a technique called equality saturation [28]. These applications are not fully certified.

8. Conclusion

Although we do not consider it in this paper, our intention is that the Vellvm framework will serve as a first step toward a fully-verified LLVM compiler, similar to that of Leroy *et al.*'s CompCert [18]. Our Coq development extends some of CompCert's libraries and our LLVM memory model is based on CompCert's memory model. The focus of this paper is the LLVM IR semantics itself, the formalization of which is a necessary step toward a fully-verified LLVM compiler. Because much of the complexity of an LLVM-based compiler lies in the IR to IR transformation passes, formalizing correctness properties at this level stands to yield a significant payoff, as demonstrated by our SoftBound case study, even without fully verifying a compiler.

Acknowledgments

This research was funded in part by the U.S. Government. The views and conclusions contained in this document are those of the authors and should not be interpreted as representing the official policies, either expressed or implied, of the U.S. Government. This research was funded in part by DARPA contract HR0011-10-9-0008 and ONR award N000141110596.

This material is based upon work supported by the National Science Foundation under Grant No. CNS-1116682, CCF-1065166, and CCF-0810947. Any opinions, findings, and conclusions or recommendations expressed in this material are those of the author(s) and do not necessarily reflect the views of the National Science Foundation.

References

[1] E. Alkassar and M. A. Hillebrand. Formal functional verification of device drivers. In *VSTTE '08: Proceedings of the 2nd International Conference on Verified Software: Theories, Tools, Experiments*, 2008.

[2] A. W. Appel. Foundational proof-carrying code. In *LICS '01: Proceedings of the 16th Annual IEEE Symposium on Logic in Computer Science*, 2001.

[3] A. W. Appel. Verified software toolchain. In *ESOP '11: Proceedings of the 20th European Conference on Programming Languages and Systems*, 2011.

[4] B. Aydemir, A. Charguéraud, B. C. Pierce, R. Pollack, and S. Weirich. Engineering formal metatheory. In *POPL '08: Proceedings of the 35th Annual ACM SIGPLAN-SIGACT Symposium on Principles of Programming Languages*, 2008.

[5] N. Benton and N. Tabareau. Compiling functional types to relational specifications for low level imperative code. In *TLDI '09: Proceedings of the 4th International Workshop on Types in Language design and Implementation*, 2009.

[6] S. Blazy, B. Robillard, and A. W. Appel. Formal verification of coalescing graph-coloring register allocation. In *ESOP '10: Proceedings of the 19th European Conference on Programming Languages and Systems*, 2010.

[7] J. Chen, D. Wu, A. W. Appel, and H. Fang. A provably sound TAL for back-end optimization. In *PLDI '03: Proceedings of the ACM SIGPLAN 2003 Conference on Programming Language Design and Implementation*, 2003.

[8] A. Chlipala. A verified compiler for an impure functional language. In *POPL '10: Proceedings of the 37th Annual ACM SIGPLAN-SIGACT Symposium on Principles of Programming Languages*, 2010.

[9] A. Chlipala. A certified type-preserving compiler from lambda calculus to assembly language. In *PLDI '07: Proceedings of the ACM SIGPLAN 2007 Conference on Programming Language Design and Implementation*, 2007.

[10] *The Coq Proof Assistant Reference Manual (Version 8.3pl1)*. The Coq Development Team, 2011.

[11] K. Crary. Toward a foundational typed assembly language. In *POPL '03: Proceedings of the 30th ACM SIGPLAN-SIGACT Symposium on Principles of Programming Languages*, 2003.

[12] K. Crary and R. Harper. Mechanized definition of standard ml (alpha release), 2009. `http://www.cs.cmu.edu/~crary/papers/2009/mldef-alpha.tar.gz`.

[13] R. Cytron, J. Ferrante, B. K. Rosen, M. N. Wegman, and F. K. Zadeck. Efficiently computing static single assignment form and the control dependence graph. *ACM Trans. Program. Lang. Syst.*, 13:451–490, 1991.

[14] G. A. Kildall. A unified approach to global program optimization. In *POPL '73: Proceedings of the 1st Annual ACM SIGACT-SIGPLAN Symposium on Principles of Programming Languages*, 1973.

[15] G. Klein, T. Nipkow, and T. U. München. A machine-checked model for a Java-like language, virtual machine and compiler. *ACM Trans. Program. Lang. Syst.*, 28:619–695, 2006.

[16] C. Lattner and V. Adve. LLVM: A Compilation Framework for Lifelong Program Analysis & Transformation. In *CGO '04: Proceedings of the International Symposium on Code Generation and Optimization: Feedback-directed and Runtime Optimization*, 2004.

[17] S. Lerner, T. Millstein, E. Rice, and C. Chambers. Automated soundness proofs for dataflow analyses and transformations via local rules. In *POPL '05: Proceedings of the 32th ACM SIGPLAN-SIGACT Symposium on Principles of Programming Languages*, 2005.

[18] X. Leroy. A formally verified compiler back-end. *Journal of Automated Reasoning*, 43(4):363–446, 2009.

[19] *The LLVM Reference Manual (Version 2.6)*. The LLVM Development Team, 2010. http://llvm.org/releases/2.6/docs/LangRef.html.

[20] V. S. Menon, N. Glew, B. R. Murphy, A. McCreight, T. Shpeisman, A.-R. Adl-Tabatabai, and L. Petersen. A verifiable SSA program representation for aggressive compiler optimization. In *POPL '06: Proceedings of the 33th ACM SIGPLAN-SIGACT Symposium on Principles of Programming Languages*, 2006.

[21] S. Nagarakatte, J. Zhao, M. M. K. Martin, and S. Zdancewic. SoftBound: Highly compatible and complete spatial memory safety for C. In *PLDI '09: Proceedings of the ACM SIGPLAN 2009 Conference on Programming Language Design and Implementation*, 2009.

[22] G. C. Necula. Translation validation for an optimizing compiler. In *PLDI '00: Proceedings of the ACM SIGPLAN 2000 Conference on Programming Language Design and Implementation*, 2000.

[23] *NIST Juliet Test Suite for C/C++*. NIST, 2010. http://samate.nist.gov/SRD/testCases/suites/Juliet-2010-12.c.cpp.zip.

[24] M. Nita and D. Grossman. Automatic transformation of bit-level C code to support multiple equivalent data layouts. In *CC'08: Proceedings of the 17th International Conference on Compiler Construction*, 2008.

[25] M. Nita, D. Grossman, and C. Chambers. A theory of platform-dependent low-level software. In *POPL '08: Proceedings of the 35th Annual ACM SIGPLAN-SIGACT Symposium on Principles of Programming Languages*, 2008.

[26] A. Pnueli, M. Siegel, and E. Singerman. Translation validation. In *TACAS '98: Proceedings of the 4th International Conference on Tools and Algorithms for Construction and Analysis of Systems*, 1998.

[27] P. Sewell, F. Zappa Nardelli, S. Owens, G. Peskine, T. Ridge, S. Sarkar, and R. Strniša. Ott: Effective tool support for the working semanticist. In *ICFP '07: Proceedings of the 9th ACM SIGPLAN International Conference on Functional Programming*, 2007.

[28] M. Stepp, R. Tate, and S. Lerner. Equality-Based translation validator for LLVM. In *CAV '11: Proceedings of the 23rd International Conference on Computer Aided Verification*, 2011.

[29] Z. T. Sudipta Kundu and S. Lerner. Proving optimizations correct using parameterized program equivalence. In *PLDI '09: Proceedings of the ACM SIGPLAN 2009 Conference on Programming Language Design and Implementation*, 2009.

[30] D. Syme. Reasoning with the formal definition of Standard ML in HOL. In *Sixth International Workshop on Higher Order Logic Theorem Proving and its Applications*, 1993.

[31] Z. Tatlock and S. Lerner. Bringing extensibility to verified compilers. In *PLDI '10: Proceedings of the ACM SIGPLAN 2010 Conference on Programming Language Design and Implementation*, 2010.

[32] J.-B. Tristan and X. Leroy. Formal verification of translation validators: a case study on instruction scheduling optimizations. In *POPL '08: Proceedings of the 35th Annual ACM SIGPLAN-SIGACT Symposium on Principles of Programming Languages*, 2008.

[33] J.-B. Tristan and X. Leroy. Verified validation of lazy code motion. In *PLDI '09: Proceedings of the ACM SIGPLAN 2009 Conference on Programming Language Design and Implementation*, 2009.

[34] J. B. Tristan and X. Leroy. A simple, verified validator for software pipelining. In *POPL '10: Proceedings of the 37th Annual ACM SIGPLAN-SIGACT Symposium on Principles of Programming Languages*, 2010.

[35] J.-B. Tristan, P. Govereau, and G. Morrisett. Evaluating value-graph translation validation for llvm. In *PLDI '11: Proceedings of the ACM SIGPLAN 2011 Conference on Programming Language Design and Implementation*, 2011.

[36] A. Zaks and A. Pnueli. Program analysis for compiler validation. In *PASTE '08: Proceedings of the 8th ACM SIGPLAN-SIGSOFT Workshop on Program Analysis for Software Tools and Engineering*, 2008.

[37] L. Zhao, G. Li, B. De Sutter, and J. Regehr. ARMor: Fully verified software fault isolation. In *EMSOFT '11: Proceedings of the 9th ACM International Conference on Embedded Software*, 2011.

Randomized Accuracy-Aware Program Transformations For Efficient Approximate Computations

Zeyuan Allen Zhu Sasa Misailovic Jonathan A. Kelner Martin Rinard

MIT CSAIL

zeyuan@csail.mit.edu misailo@mit.edu kelner@mit.edu rinard@mit.edu

Abstract

Despite the fact that approximate computations have come to dominate many areas of computer science, the field of program transformations has focused almost exclusively on traditional semantics-preserving transformations that do not attempt to exploit the opportunity, available in many computations, to acceptably trade off accuracy for benefits such as increased performance and reduced resource consumption.

We present a model of computation for approximate computations and an algorithm for optimizing these computations. The algorithm works with two classes of transformations: *substitution transformations* (which select one of a number of available implementations for a given function, with each implementation offering a different combination of accuracy and resource consumption) and *sampling transformations* (which randomly discard some of the inputs to a given reduction). The algorithm produces a $(1+\varepsilon)$ randomized approximation to the optimal randomized computation (which minimizes resource consumption subject to a probabilistic accuracy specification in the form of a maximum expected error or maximum error variance).

Categories and Subject Descriptors D.3.4 [*Programming Languages*]: Processors—*optimization*; G.3 [*Probability and Statistics*]: Probabilistic Algorithms; F.2.1 [*Analysis of Algorithms and Problem Complexity*]: Numerical Algorithms and Problems

General Terms Algorithms, Design, Performance, Theory

Keywords Optimization, Error-Time Tradeoff, Discretization, Probabilistic

1. Introduction

Computer science was founded on *exact computations* with discrete logical correctness requirements (examples include compilers and traditional relational databases). But over the last decade, *approximate computations* have come to dominate many fields. In contrast to exact computations, approximate computations aspire only to produce an acceptably accurate approximation to an exact (but in many cases inherently unrealizable) output. Examples include machine learning, unstructured information analysis and retrieval, and lossy video, audio and image processing.

POPL'12, January 25–27, 2012, Philadelphia, PA, USA.

Despite the prominence of approximate computations, the field of program transformations has remained focused on techniques that are guaranteed not to change the output (and therefore do not affect the accuracy of the approximation). This situation leaves the developer solely responsible for managing the approximation. The result is inflexible computations with hard-coded approximation choices directly embedded in the implementation.

1.1 Accuracy-Aware Transformations

We investigate a new class of transformations, *accuracy-aware transformations*, for approximate computations. Given a computation and a probabilistic accuracy specification, our transformations change the computation so that it operates more efficiently while satisfying the specification. Because accuracy-aware transformations have the freedom to change the output (within the bounds of the accuracy specification), they have a much broader scope and are therefore able to deliver a much broader range of benefits.

The field of accuracy-aware transformations is today in its infancy. Only very recently have researchers developed general transformations that are designed to manipulate the accuracy of the computation. Examples include task skipping [27, 28], loop perforation [14, 23, 24, 31], approximate function memoization [6], and substitution of multiple alternate implementations [2, 3, 12, 33]. When successful, these transformations deliver programs that can operate at multiple points in an underlying accuracy-resource consumption tradeoff space. Users may select points that minimize resource consumption while satisfying the specified accuracy constraints, maximize accuracy while satisfying specified resource consumption constraints, or dynamically change the computation to adapt to changes (such as load or clock rate) in the underlying computational platform [12, 14].

Standard approaches to understanding the structure of the tradeoff spaces that accuracy-aware transformations induce use training executions to derive empirical models [2, 3, 14, 24, 27, 28, 31, 33]. Potential pitfalls include models that may not accurately capture the characteristics of the transformed computation, poor correlations between the behaviors of the computation on training and production inputs, a resulting inability to find optimal points in the tradeoff space for production inputs, and an absence of guaranteed bounds on the magnitude of potential accuracy losses.

1.2 Our Result

We present a novel analysis and optimization algorithm for a class of approximate computations. These computations are expressed as a tree of *computation nodes* and *reduction nodes*. Each computation node is a directed acyclic graph of nested *function nodes*, each of which applies an arbitrary function to its inputs. A reduction node applies an aggregation function (such as min, max, or mean) to its inputs.

We consider two classes of accuracy-aware transformations. *Substitution transformations* replace one implementation of a function node with another implementation. Each function has a *propagation* specification that characterizes the sensitivity of the function to perturbations in its inputs. Each implementation has *resource consumption* and *accuracy* specifications. Resource consumption specifications characterize the resources (such as time, energy, or cost) each implementation consumes to compute the function. Accuracy specifications characterize the error that the implementation introduces.

Sampling transformations cause the transformed reduction node to operate on a randomly selected subset of its inputs, simultaneously eliminating the computations that produce the discarded inputs. Each sampling transformation has a *sampling rate*, which is the ratio between the size of the selected subset of its inputs and the original number of inputs.

Together, these transformations induce a space of *program configurations*. Each configuration identifies an implementation for every function node and a sampling rate for every reduction node. In this paper we work with randomized transformations that specify a probabilistic choice over configurations. Our approach focuses on understanding the following technical question:

> What is the optimal accuracy-resource consumption tradeoff curve available via our randomized transformations?

Understanding this question makes it possible to realize a variety of optimization goals, for example minimizing resource consumption subject to an accuracy specification or maximizing accuracy subject to a resource consumption specification. The primary technical result in this paper is an optimization algorithm that produces a $(1 + \varepsilon)$-approximation to the optimal randomized computation (which minimizes resource consumption subject to a probabilistic accuracy specification in the form of a maximum expected error or maximum error variance). We also discuss how to realize a variety of other optimization goals.

1.3 Challenges and Solutions

Finding optimal program configurations presents several algorithmic challenges. In particular:

- **Exponential Configurations:** The number of program configurations is exponential in the size of the computation graph, so a brute-force search for the best configuration is computationally intractable.
- **Randomized Combinations of Configurations:** A transformed program that randomizes over multiple configurations may substantially outperform one that chooses any single fixed configuration. We thus optimize over an even larger space—the space of probability distributions over the configuration space.
- **Global Error Propagation Effects:** Local error allocation decisions propagate globally throughout the program. The optimization algorithm must therefore work with global accuracy effects and interactions between errors introduced at the nodes of the computation graph.
- **Nonlinear, Nonconvex Optimization Problem:** The running time and accuracy of the program depend nonlinearly on the optimization variables. The resulting optimization problem is nonlinear and nonconvex.

We show that, in the absence of reduction nodes, one can formulate the optimization problem as a linear program, which allows us to obtain an exact optimization over the space of probability distributions of configurations in polynomial time.

The question becomes much more involved when reduction nodes come to the picture. In this case, we approximate the optimal tradeoff curve, but to a $(1 + \varepsilon)$ precision for an arbitrarily small constant $\varepsilon > 0$. Our algorithm has a running time that is polynomially dependent on $\frac{1}{\varepsilon}$. It is therefore a fully polynomial-time approximation scheme (FPTAS).

Our algorithm tackles reduction nodes one by one. For each reduction node, it discretizes the tradeoff curve achieved by the subprogram that generates the inputs to the reduction node. This discretization uses a special *bi-dimensional discretization* technique that is specifically designed for such tradeoff problems. We next show how to extend this discretization to obtain a corresponding discretized tradeoff curve that includes the reduction node. The final step is to recursively combine the discretizations to obtain a dynamic programming algorithm that approximates the optimal tradeoff curve for the entire program.

We note that the optimization algorithm produces a weighted combination of program configurations. We call such a weighted combination a *randomized configuration*. Each execution of the final randomized program chooses one of these configurations with probability proportional to its weight.

Randomizing the transformed program provides several benefits. In comparison with a deterministic program, the randomized program may be able to deliver substantially reduced resource consumption for the same accuracy specification. Furthermore, randomization also simplifies the optimization problem by replacing the discrete search space with a continuous search space. We can therefore use linear programs (which can be solved efficiently) to model regions of the optimization space instead of integer programs (which are, in general, intractable).

1.4 Potential Applications

A precise understanding of the consequences of accuracy-aware transformations will enable the field to mature beyond its current focus on transformations that do not change the output. This increased scope will enable researchers in the field to attack a much broader range of problems. Some potential examples include:

- **Sublinear Computations On Big Data:** Sampling transformations enable the optimization algorithm to automatically find *sublinear computations* that process only a subset of the inputs to provide an acceptably accurate output. Over the past decade, researchers have developed many sublinear algorithms [29]. Accuracy-aware transformations hold out the promise of automating the development of many of these algorithms.
- **Incrementalized and Online Computations:** Many algorithms can be viewed as converging towards an optimal exact solution as they process more inputs. Because our model of computation supports such computations, our techniques make it possible to characterize the accuracy of the current result as the computation incrementally processes inputs. This capability opens the door to the automatic development of *incrementalized* computations (which incrementally sample available inputs until the computation produces an acceptably accurate result) and *online* computations (which characterize the accuracy of the current result as the computation incrementally processes dynamically arriving inputs).
- **Sensor Selection:** Sensor networks require low power, low cost sensors [32]. Accuracy-aware transformations may allow developers to specify a sensor network computation with idealized lossless sensors as the initial function nodes in the computation. An optimization algorithm can then select sensors that minimize power consumption or cost while still providing acceptable accuracy.
- **Data Representation Choices:** Data representation choices can have dramatic consequences on the amount of resources (time, silicon area, power) required to manipulate that data [10]. Giving an optimization algorithm the freedom to adjust the ac-

curacy (within specified bounds) may enable an informed automatic selection of less accurate but more appropriate data representations. For example, a compiler may automatically replace an expensive floating point representation with a more efficient but less accurate fixed point representation. We anticipate the application of this technology in both standard compilers for microprocessors as well as hardware synthesis systems.

- **Dynamic Adaptation In Large Data Centers:** The amount of computing power that a large data center is able to deliver to individual hosted computations can vary dynamically depending on factors such as load, available power, and the operating temperature within the data center (a rise in temperature may force reductions in power consumption via clock rate drops). By delivering computations that can operate at multiple points in the underlying accuracy-resource consumption tradeoff space, accuracy-aware transformations open up new strategies for adapting to fluctuations. For example, a data center may respond to load or temperature spikes by running applications at less accurate but more efficient operating points [12].
- **Successful Use of Mostly Correct Components:** Many faulty components operate correctly for almost all inputs. By perturbing inputs and computations with small amounts of random noise, it is possible to ensure that, with very high probability, no two executions of the computation operate on the same values. Given a way to check if a fault occurred during the execution, it is possible to rerun the computation until all components happen to operate on values that elicit no faults. Understanding the accuracy consequences of these perturbations can make it possible to employ this approach successfully.[1]

The scope of traditional program transformations has been largely confined to standard compiler optimizations. As the above examples illustrate, appropriately ambitious accuracy-aware transformations that exploit the opportunity to manipulate accuracy within specified bounds can dramatically increase the impact and relevance of the field of program analysis and transformation.

1.5 Contributions

This paper makes the following contributions:

- **Model of Computation:** We present a model of computation for approximate computations. This model supports arbitrary compositions of individual function nodes into computation nodes and computation nodes and reduction nodes into computation trees. This model exposes enough computational structure to enable approximate optimization via our two transformations.
- **Accuracy-Aware Transformations:** We consider two classes of accuracy-aware transformations: function substitutions and reduction sampling. Together, these transformations induce a space of transformed programs that provide different combinations of accuracy and resource consumption.
- **Tradeoff Curves:** It shows how to use linear programming, dynamic programming, and a special bi-dimensional discretization technique to obtain a $(1+\epsilon)$-approximation to the underlying optimal accuracy-resource consumption tradeoff curve available via the accuracy-aware transformations. If the program contains no reduction nodes, the tradeoff curve is exact.
- **Optimization Algorithm:** It presents an optimization algorithm that uses the tradeoff curve to produce randomized programs that satisfy specified probabilistic accuracy and resource consumption constraints. In comparison with approaches that attempt to deliver a deterministic program, randomization enables our optimization algorithm to 1) deliver programs with better combinations of accuracy and resource consumption, and 2) avoid a variety of intractability issues.
- **Accuracy Bounds:** We show how to obtain statically guaranteed probabilistic accuracy bounds for a general class of approximate computations. The only previous static accuracy bounds for accuracy-aware transformations exploited the structure present in a set of computational patterns [6, 22, 23].

[1] The last author would like to thank Pat Lincoln for an interesting discussion on this topic.

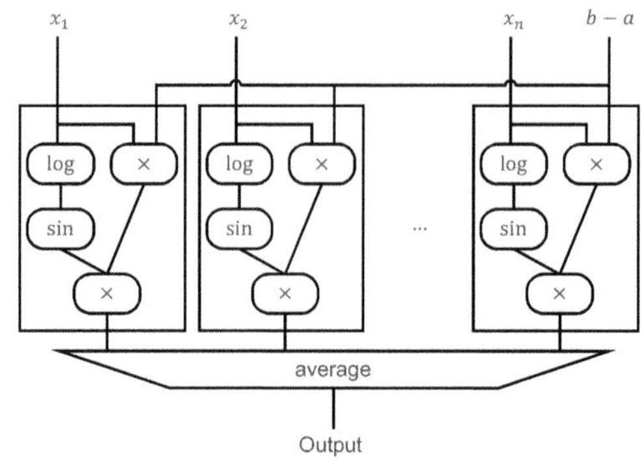

Figure 1: A numerical integration program.

2. Example

We next present an example computation that numerically integrates a univariate function $f(x)$ over a fixed interval $[a, b]$. The computation divides $[a, b]$ into n equal-sized subintervals, each of length $\Delta x = \frac{b-a}{n}$. Let $\boldsymbol{x} = (x_1, \ldots x_n)$, where $x_i = a + i \cdot \frac{\Delta x}{2}$. The value of the numerical integral I is equal to

$$I = \Delta x \cdot \sum_{i=1}^{n} f(x_i) = \frac{1}{n} \sum_{i=1}^{n} (b-a) \cdot f(x_i) \ .$$

Say, for instance, $f(x) = x \cdot \sin\bigl(\log(x)\bigr)$ is the function that we want to integrate and $[a, b] = [1, 11]$.

Our Model of Computation. As illustrated in Figure 1, in our model of computation, we have n input edges that carry the values of x_i's into the computation and an additional edge that carries the value of $b-a$. For each x_i, a computation node calculates the value of $(b-a) \cdot f(x_i)$. The output edges of these nodes are connected to a reduction node that computes the average of these values (we call such a node an averaging node), as the final integral I.

Program Transformations. The above numerical integration program presents multiple opportunities to trade end-to-end accuracy of the result I in return for increased performance. Specifically, we identify the following two transformations that may improve the performance:

- **Substitution.** It is possible to substitute the original implementations of the $\sin(\cdot)$ and $\log(\cdot)$ functions that comprise $f(x)$ with alternate implementations that may compute a less accurate output in less time.
- **Sampling.** It is possible to discard some of the n inputs of the averaging node (and the computations that produce these inputs) by taking a random sample of $s \leq n$ inputs (here we call s the reduction factor). Roughly speaking, this transformation introduces an error proportional to $\frac{1}{\sqrt{s}}$, but decreases the running time of the program proportionally to $\frac{s}{n}$.

Tradeoff Space. In this numerical integration problem, a *program configuration* specifies which implementation to pick for each of the functions $\sin(\cdot)$, $\log(\cdot)$, and (in principle, although we do not

Configuration.	Weight	$x_{\log,0}$	$x_{\log,1}$	$x_{\log,2}$	$x_{\sin,0}$	$x_{\sin,1}$	$x_{\sin,2}$	s/n	Error	Speedup
C_1	0.608	0	0	1	0	0	1	100%	0.024	1.39
C_2	0.392	0	1	0	0	1	0	47.5%	0.090	2.63

Table 1: The $(1+\varepsilon)$-optimal randomized program configuration for $\Delta = 0.05$ and $\varepsilon = 0.01$.

do so in this example) $\times$. The configuration also specifies the reduction factor s for the averaging node. If we assume that we have two alternate implementations of $\sin(\cdot)$ and $\log(\cdot)$, each program configuration provides the following information: 1) $x_{u,i} \in \{0,1\}$ indicating whether we choose the i-th implementation of the function $u \in \{\log, \sin\}$, and $i \in \{0,1,2\}$, and 2) s indicating the reduction factor for the averaging node we choose. A *randomized* program configuration is a probabilistic choice over program configurations.

Function Specifications. We impose two basic requirements on the implementations of all functions that comprise $f(x)$.

The first requirement is that we have an error bound and time complexity specification for each implementation of each function. In this example we will use the following model: the original implementation of $\log(\cdot)$ executes in time $T_{\log,0}$ with error $E_{\log,0} = 0$; the original implementation of $\sin(\cdot)$ executes in time $T_{\sin,0}$ with error $E_{\sin,0} = 0$. We have two alternate implementations of $\log(\cdot)$ and $\sin(\cdot)$, where the i-th implementation of a given function $u \in \{\log(\cdot), \sin(\cdot)\}$ runs in time $T_{u,i} = (1 - \frac{\sqrt{i}}{5})T_{u,0}$ with error $E_{\log,i} = i \cdot 0.008$, and $E_{\sin,i} = i \cdot 0.004$ ($i \in \{1,2\}$).

The second requirement is that the error propagation of the entire computation is bounded by a linear function. This requirement is satisfied if the functions that comprise the computation are *Lipschitz continuous*[2]. In our example, the function $\sin(\cdot)$ is 1-Lipschitz continuous, since its derivative is bounded by 1. The function $\log(x)$ is also Lipschitz continuous, when $x \geq 1$. Finally, the product function $\times$ is Lipschitz continuous, when the two inputs are bounded. We remark here that this second requirement ensures that an error introduced by an approximate implementation propagates to cause at most a linear change in the final output.

Finding the $(1+\varepsilon)$-Optimal Program Configuration. Given performance and accuracy specifications for each function, we can run our optimization algorithm to $(1+\varepsilon)$-approximately calculate the optimal accuracy-performance tradeoff curve. For each point on the curve our algorithm can also produce a randomized program configuration that achieves this tradeoff.

Given a target expected error bound Δ, we use the tradeoff curve to find a randomized program configuration that executes in expected time τ. The $(1+\varepsilon)$-approximation ensures that this expected running time τ is at most $(1+\varepsilon)$ times the optimal expected running time for the expected error bound Δ. In this example we use $\varepsilon = 0.01$ so that our optimized program will produce a 1.01-approximation. In addition, we define:

- the number of inputs $n = 10000$,
- the overall expected error tolerance $\Delta = 0.05$, and
- the running times $T_{\sin,0} = 0.08\ \mu$s and $T_{\log,0} = 0.07\ \mu$s.

For this example our optimization algorithm identifies the point $(\Delta, T_0/1.71)$ on the tradeoff curve, where T_0 is the running time of the original program. This indicates that the optimized program achieves a speedup of 1.71 over the original program while keeping the expected value below the bound Δ. Table 1 presents the randomized program configuration that achieves this tradeoff. This randomized program configuration consists of two program configurations C_1 and C_2. Each configuration has an associated weight which is the probability with which the randomized program will execute that configuration. The table also presents the error and speedup that each configuration produces.

The configuration C_1 selects the less accurate approximate versions of the functions $\log(\cdot)$ and $\sin(\cdot)$, and uses all inputs to the averaging reduction node. The configuration C_2, on the other hand, selects more accurate approximate versions of the functions $\log(\cdot)$ and $\sin(\cdot)$, and at the same time samples 4750 of the 10,000 original inputs.

Note that individually neither C_1 nor C_2 can achieve the desired tradeoff. The configuration C_1 produces a more accurate output but also executes significantly slower than the optimal program. The configuration C_2 executes much faster than the optimal program, but with expected error greater than the desired bound Δ. The randomized program selects configuration C_1 with probability 60.8% and C_2 with probability 39.2%. The randomized program has expected error Δ and expected running time $T_0/1.71$.

We can use the same tradeoff curve to obtain a randomized program that minimizes the expected error Δ' subject to the execution time constraint τ'. In our example, if the time bound $\tau' = T_0/1.71$ the optimization algorithm will produce the program configuration from Table 1 with expected error $\Delta' = \Delta$.

More generally, our optimization algorithm will produce an efficient representation of a probability distribution over program configurations along with an efficient procedure to sample this distribution to obtain a program configuration for each execution.

3. Model of Approximate Computation

We next define the graph model of computation, including the error-propagation constraints for function nodes, and present the accuracy-aware substitution and sampling transformations.

3.1 Definitions

Programs. In our model of computation, programs consist of a directed tree of *computation nodes* and *reduction nodes*. Each edge in the tree transmits a stream of values. The *size* of each edge indicates the number of transmitted values. The multiple values transmitted along an edge can often be understood as a stream of numbers with the same purpose — for example, a million pixels from an image or a thousand samples from a sensor. Figure 2 presents an example of a program under our definition.

Reduction Nodes. Each reduction node has a single input edge and a single output edge. It reduces the size of its input by some multiplicative factor, which we call its *reduction factor*. A node with reduction factor S has an input edge of size $R \cdot S$ and an output edge of size R. The node divides the $R \cdot S$ inputs into blocks of size S. It produces R outputs by applying an S-to-1 aggregation function (such as min, max, or mean) to each of the R blocks.

For clarity of exposition and to avoid a proliferation of notation, we primarily focus on one specific type of reduction node, which we call an *averaging node*. An averaging node with reduction factor S will output the average of the first S values as the first output, the average of the next S values as the second output, and so on.

The techniques that we present are quite general and apply to any reduction operation that can be approximated well by sampling. Section 8 describes how to extend our algorithm to work with other reduction operations.

[2] A univariate function is α-Lipschitz continuous if for any $\delta > 0$, it follows that $|f(x) - f(x+\delta)| < \alpha\delta$. As a special case, a differentiable function is Lipschitz continuous if $|f'(x)| \leq \alpha$. This definition extends to multivariate functions.

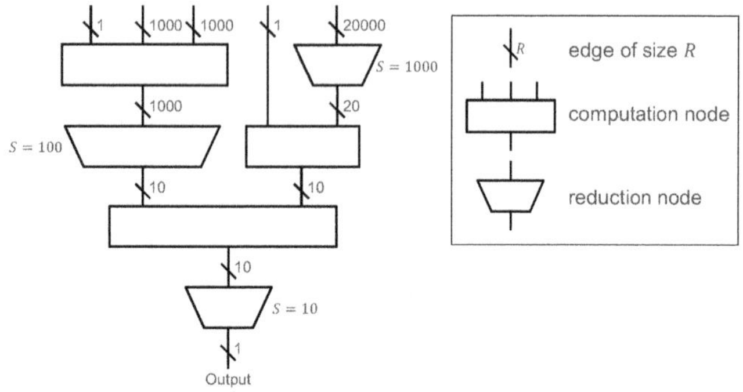

Figure 2: An example program in our model of computation.

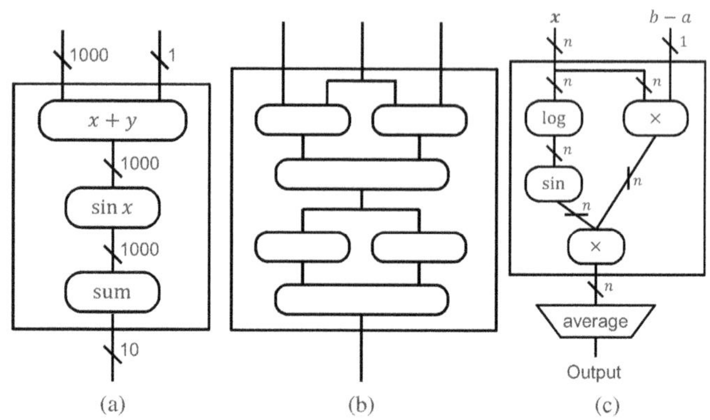

Figure 3: (a)(b): A closer look at two computation nodes, and (c): Numerical integration example, revisited.

Computation Nodes. A computation node has potentially multiple input edges and a single output edge. A computation node of size R has:

- a single output edge of size R;
- a non-negative number of input edges, each of size
  - either 1 (which we call a *control-input* edge),
  - or some multiple tR of R (which we call a *data-input* edge).

Each control-input edge carries a single *global constant*. Data-input edges carry a stream of values which the computation node partitions into R chunks. The computation node executes R times to produce R outputs, with each execution processing the value from each control-input edge and a block of t values from each data-input edge. The executions are independent.

For example, consider a computation node of size 10 with two input edges: one data-input edge of size 1000, denoted by $(a_1, a_2, \dots, a_{1000})$, and one control-input edge of size 1, denoted by b. Then, the function that outputs the vector

$$\Big(\sum_{i=1}^{100} \sin(a_i, b), \sum_{i=101}^{200} \sin(a_i, b), \dots, \sum_{i=901}^{1000} \sin(a_i, b)\Big) \quad (1)$$

is a computation node.

We remark here that a reduction node is a special kind of computation node. We treat computation and reduction nodes separately because we optimize computation nodes with substitution transformations and reduction nodes with sampling transformations (see Section 3.2).

Inner Structure of Computation Nodes. A computation node can be further decomposed into one or more *function nodes*, connected via a directed acyclic graph (DAG). Like computation nodes, each function node has potentially multiple input edges and a single output edge. The size of each input edge is either 1 or a multiple of the size of the output edge. The functions can be of arbitrary complexity and can contain language constructs such as conditional statements and loops.

For example, the computation node in Eq.(1) can be further decomposed as shown in Figure 3a. Although we require the computation nodes and edges in each program to form a tree, the function nodes and edges in each computation node can form a DAG (see, for example, Figure 3b).

In principle, any computation node can be represented as a single function node, but its decomposition into multiple function nodes allows for finer granularity and more transformation choices when optimizing entire program.

Example. Section 2 presented a numerical integration program example. Figure 3c presents this example in our model of computation (compare with Figure 1). Note that the multiplicity of computation nodes in Figure 1 corresponds to the edge sizes in Figure 3c. The log function node with input and output edges of size n runs n times. Each run consumes a single input and produces a single output. The $\times$ function node with input edges of size n and 1 runs n times. Each execution produces as output the product of an x_i with the common value $b - a$ from the control edge.

3.2 Transformations

In a *program configuration*, we specify the following two kinds of transformations at function and reduction nodes.

- **Substitution.** For each function node f_u of size R, we have a polynomial number of implementations $f_{u,1}, \dots, f_{u,k}$. The function runs R times. We require each implementation to have the following properties:
  - each run of $f_{u,i}$ is in expected time $T_{u,i}$, giving a total expected running time of $R \cdot T_{u,i}$, and
  - each run of $f_{u,i}$ produces an expected absolute additive error of at most $E_{u,i}$, i.e., $\forall \boldsymbol{x}, \mathbb{E}[|f_u(\boldsymbol{x}) - f_{u,i}(\boldsymbol{x})|] \le E_{u,i}$. (The expectation is over the the randomness of $f_{u,i}$ and f_u.)

  We assume that all $(T_{u,i}, E_{u,i})$ pairs are known in advance (they are constants or depend only on control inputs).
- **Sampling.** For each reduction node r with reduction factor S_r, we can decrease this factor S_r to a smaller factor $s_r \in \{1, \dots, S_r\}$ at the expense of introducing some additive sampling error $E_r(s_r)$. For example, for an averaging node, instead of averaging all S_r inputs, we would randomly select s_r inputs (without replacement) and output the average of the chosen samples. For convenience, we denote the sampling rate of node r as $\eta_r = \frac{s_r}{S_r}$.

  If the output edge is of size R, the computation selects $s_r \cdot R$ inputs, instead of all $S_r \cdot R$ inputs. The values for the reduction node inputs which are not selected need not be computed. Discarding the computations that would otherwise produce these discarded inputs produces a speed-up factor of $\eta_r = \frac{s_r}{S_r}$ for all nodes above r in the computation tree.

The following lemma provides a bound on the sampling error $E_r(s_r) = (B - A)\sqrt{\frac{S_r - s_r}{s_r(S_r - 1)}}$ for an averaging node. The proof is available in the full version of the paper.

Lemma 3.1. *Given m numbers $x_1, x_2, \ldots, x_m \in [A, B]$, randomly sampling s of the numbers $x_{i_1}, \ldots, x_{i_s}$ (without replacement) and computing the sample average gives an approximation to $\frac{x_1+\cdots+x_m}{m}$ with the following expected error guarantee:*

$$\mathbb{E}_{i_1,\ldots,i_s}\Big[\Big|\frac{x_{i_1}+\cdots+x_{i_s}}{s} - \frac{x_1+\cdots+x_m}{m}\Big|\Big] \le (B-A)\sqrt{\frac{m-s}{s(m-1)}}\ .$$

3.3 Error Propagation

The errors that the transformations induce in one part of the computation propagate through the rest of the computation and can be amplified or attenuated in the process. We next provide constraints on the form of functions that characterize this error propagation. These constraints hold for all functions in our model of computation (regardless of whether they have alternate implementations or not).

We assume that for each function node $f_u(x_1, \ldots, x_m)$ with m inputs, if each input x_j is replaced by some approximate input $\hat{x}_j$ such that $\mathbb{E}[|x_j - \hat{x}_j|] \le \delta_j$, the propagation error is bounded by a linear *error propagation function* $\mathcal{E}_u$:

$$\mathbb{E}\big[|f_u(x_1,\ldots,x_m) - f_u(\hat{x}_1,\ldots,\hat{x}_m)|\big] \le \mathcal{E}_u(\delta_1,\ldots,\delta_m). \quad (2)$$

We assume that all of the error propagation functions $\mathcal{E}_u$ for the functions f_u are known a priori:

$$\mathbb{E}\big[|f_u(x_1,\ldots,x_m) - f_u(\hat{x}_1,\ldots,\hat{x}_m)|\big] \le \big(\sum_j \alpha_j\delta_j\big). \quad (3)$$

This condition is satisfied if all functions f_u are *Lipschitz-continuous* with parameters $\boldsymbol{\alpha}$. Furthermore, if $f_u(x_1, \ldots, x_m)$ is differentiable, we can let $\alpha_i = \max_{\boldsymbol{x}} \big|\frac{\partial f_u(x_1,\ldots,x_m)}{\partial x_i}\big|$. If f_u is itself probabilistic, we can take the expected value of such α_i's.

Substitute Implementations. For functions with multiple implementations, the overall error when we choose the i-th implementation $f_{u,i}$ is bounded by an error propagation function $\mathcal{E}_u$ and the local error induced by the i-th implementation $E_{u,i}$ (defined in the previous subsection):

$$\mathbb{E}\big[|f_u(x_1,\ldots,x_m) - f_{u,i}(\hat{x}_1,\ldots,\hat{x}_m)|\big] \le \mathcal{E}_u(\delta_1,\ldots,\delta_m) + E_{u,i}. \quad (4)$$

This bound follows immediately from the triangle inequality.

We remark here that the randomness for the expectation in Eq.(4) comes from 1) the randomness of its input $\hat{x}_1, \ldots, \hat{x}_m$ (caused by errors from previous parts of the computation) and 2) random choices in the possibly probabilistic implementation $f_{u,i}$. These two sources of randomness are mutually independent.

Averaging Reduction Node. The averaging function is a Lipschitz-continuous function with all $\alpha_i = \frac{1}{m}$, so in addition to Lemma 3.1 we have:

Corollary 3.2. *Consider an averaging node that selects s random samples from its m inputs, where each input $\hat{x}_j$ has bounded error $\mathbb{E}[|\hat{x}_j - x_j|] \le \delta_j$. Then:*

$$\mathbb{E}_{i_1,\ldots,i_s,\hat{x}_1,\ldots,\hat{x}_m}\Big[\Big|\frac{\hat{x}_{i_1}+\cdots+\hat{x}_{i_s}}{s} - \frac{x_1+\cdots+x_m}{m}\Big|\Big] \le \frac{1}{m}\big(\sum_{j=1}^{m}\delta_j\big) + (B-A)\sqrt{\frac{m-s}{s(m-1)}}\ .$$

If all input values have the same error bound $\mathbb{E}[|\hat{x}_j - x_j|] \le \delta$, then $\frac{1}{m}\big(\sum_{j=1}^{m}\delta_j\big) = \delta$.

4. Approximation Questions

We focus on the following question:

Question 1. *Given a program P in our model of computation and using randomized configurations, what is the optimal error-time tradeoff curve that our approximate computations induce?*

Here the time and error refer to the expected running time and error of the program. We say that the expected error of program P' is Δ, if for all input x, $\mathbb{E}[|P(x) - P'(x)|] \le \Delta$. The error-time tradeoff curve is a pair of functions $(E(\cdot), T(\cdot))$, such that $E(t)$ is the optimal expected error of the program if the expected running time is no more than t, and $T(e)$ is the optimal expected running time of the program if the expected error is no more than e.

The substitution and sampling transformations give rise to an exponentially large space of possible program configurations. We optimize over *arbitrary probability distributions* of such configurations. A naive optimization algorithm would therefore run in time at least exponential in the size of the program. We present an algorithm that approximately solves Question 1 within a factor of $(1+\varepsilon)$ in time:[3] 1) polynomial in the size of the computation graph, and 2) polynomial in $\frac{1}{\varepsilon}$. The algorithm uses linear programming and a novel technique called *bi-dimensional discretization*, which we present in Section 5.

A successful answer to the above question leads directly to the following additional consequences:

Consequence 1: Optimizing Time Subject to Error

Question 2. *Given a program P in our model, and an overall error tolerance Δ, what is the optimal (possibly randomized) program P' available within our space of transformations, with expected error no more than Δ?*

We can answer this question approximately using the optimization algorithm for Question 1. This algorithm will produce a randomized program with expected running time no more than $(1+\varepsilon)$ times the optimal running time and expected error no more than Δ. The algorithm can also answer the symmetric question to find a $(1+\varepsilon)$-approximation of the optimal program that minimizes the expected error given a bound on the expected running time.

Consequence 2: From Error to Variance

We say that the overall variance (i.e., expected squared error) of a randomized program P' is Δ^2, if for all input x, $\mathbb{E}[|P(x) - P'(x)|^2] \le \Delta^2$. A variant of our algorithm for Question 1 $(1+\varepsilon)$-approximately answers the following questions:

Question 3. *Given a program P in our model of computation, what is the optimal error-variance tradeoff curve that our approximate computations induce?*

Question 4. *Given a program P in our model, and an overall variance tolerance Δ^2, what is the optimal (possibly randomized) program P' available within our space of transformations, with variance no more than Δ^2?*

Section 7 presents the algorithm for these questions.

Consequence 3: Probabilities of Large Errors

A bound on the expected error or variance also provides a bound on the probability of observing large errors. In particular, an execution

[3] We say that we approximately obtain the curve within a factor of $(1+\varepsilon)$, if for any given running time t, the difference between the optimal error $E(t)$ and our $\hat{E}(t)$ is at most $\varepsilon E(t)$, and similarly for the time function $T(e)$. Our algorithm is a fully polynomial-time approximation scheme (FPTAS). Section 5 presents a more precise definition in which the error function $\hat{E}(t)$ is also subject to an additive error of some arbitrarily small constant.

of a program with expected error Δ will produce an absolute error greater than $t\Delta$ with probability at most $\frac{1}{t}$ (this bound follows immediately from Markov's inequality). Similarly, an execution of a program with variance Δ^2 will produce an absolute error greater than $t\Delta$ with probability at most $\frac{1}{t^2}$.

5. Optimization Algorithm for Question 1

We next describe a recursive, dynamic programming optimization algorithm which exploits the tree structure of the program. To compute the approximate optimal tradeoff curve for the entire program, the algorithm computes and combines the approximate optimal tradeoff curves for the subprograms. We stage the presentation as follows:

- **Computation Nodes Only:** In Section 5.1, we show how to compute the optimal tradeoff curve exactly when the computation consists only of computation nodes and has no reduction nodes. We reduce the optimization problem to a linear program (which is efficiently solvable).
- **Bi-dimensional Discretization:** In Section 5.2, we introduce our *bi-dimensional discretization* technique, which constructs a piecewise-linear discretization of any tradeoff curve $(E(\cdot), T(\cdot))$, such that 1) there are only $O(\frac{1}{\varepsilon})$ segments on the discretized curve, and 2) at the same time the discretization approximates $(E(\cdot), T(\cdot))$ to within a multiplicative factor of $(1+\varepsilon)$.
- **A Single Reduction Node:** In Section 5.3, we show how to compute the approximate tradeoff curve when the given program consists of computation nodes that produce the input for a *single* reduction node r (see Figure 6).
  We first work with the curve when the reduction factor s at the reduction node r is constrained to be a single integer value. Given an expected error tolerance e for the entire computation, each randomized configuration in the optimal randomized program allocates part of the expected error $E_r(s)$ to the sampling transformation on the reduction node and the remaining expected error $e_{\text{sub}} = e - E_r(s)$ to the substitution transformations on the subprogram with only computation nodes.
  One inefficient way to find the optimal randomized configuration for a given expected error e is to simply search all possible integer values of s to find the optimal allocation that minimizes the running time. This approach is inefficient because the number of choices of s may be large. We therefore discretize the tradeoff curve for the input to the reduction node into a small set of linear pieces. It is straightforward to compute the optimal integer value of s within each linear piece. In this way we obtain an *approximate* optimal tradeoff curve for the output of the reduction node when the reduction factor s is constrained to be a single integer.
  We next use this curve to derive an approximate optimal tradeoff curve when the reduction factor s can be determined by a *probabilistic* choice among multiple integer values. Ideally, we would use the convex envelope of the original curve to obtain this new curve. But because the original curve has an infinite number of points, it is infeasible to work with this convex envelope directly. We therefore perform another discretization to obtain a piecewise-linear curve that we can represent with a small number of points. We work with the convex envelope of this new discretized curve to obtain the final approximation to the optimal tradeoff curve for the output of the reduction node r. This curve incorporates the effect of both the substitution transformations on the computation nodes and the sampling transformation on the reduction node.

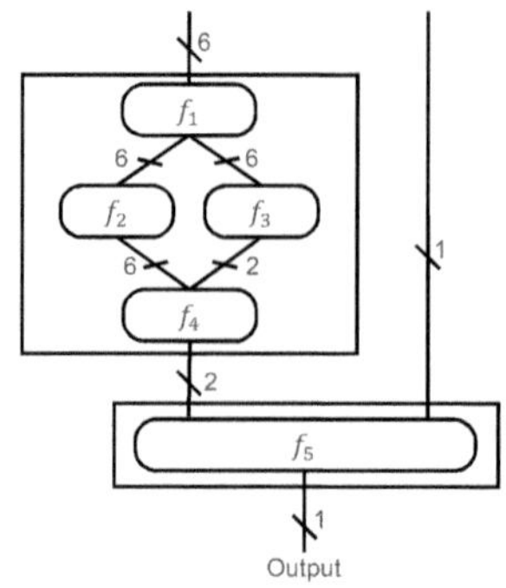

Figure 4: Example to illustrate the computation of time and error.

- **The Final Dynamic Programming Algorithm:** In Section 5.4, we provide an algorithm that computes an approximate error-time tradeoff curve for an *arbitrary* program in our model of computation. Each step uses the algorithm from Section 5.3 to compute the approximate discretized tradeoff curve for a subtree rooted at a topmost reduction node (this subtree includes the computation nodes that produce the input to the reduction node). It then uses this tradeoff curve to replace this subtree with a single function node. It then recursively applies the algorithm to the new program, terminating when it computes the approximate discretized tradeoff curve for the output of the final node in the program.

5.1 Stage 1: Computation Nodes Only

We start with a base case in which the program consists only of computation nodes with no reduction nodes. We show how to use linear programming to compute the optimal error-time tradeoff curve for this case.

Variables $\boldsymbol{x}$. For each function node f_u, the variable $x_{u,i} \in [0,1]$ indicates the probability of running the i-th implementation $f_{u,i}$. We also have the constraint that $\sum_i x_{u,i} = 1$.

Running Time $\text{TIME}(\boldsymbol{x})$. Since there are no reduction nodes in the program, each function node f_u will run R_u times (recall that R_u is the number of values carried on the output edge of f_u). The running time is simply the weighted sum of the running times of the function nodes (where each weight is the probability of selecting each corresponding implementation):

$$\text{TIME}(\boldsymbol{x}) = \sum_u \sum_i (x_{u,i} \cdot T_{u,i} \cdot R_u) \ . \tag{5}$$

Here the summation u is over all function nodes and i is over all implementations of f_u.

Total Error $\text{ERROR}(\boldsymbol{x})$. The total error of the program also admits a linear form. For each function node f_u, the i-th implementation $f_{u,i}$ incurs a local error $E_{u,i}$ on each output value. By the linear error propagation assumption, this $E_{u,i}$ is amplified by a constant factor β_u which depends on the program structure. It is possible to compute the β_u with a traversal of the program backward against the flow of values.

Consider, for example, β_1 for function node f_1 in the program in Figure 4. Let α_2 be the linear error propagation factor for the univariate function $f_2(\cdot)$. The function $f_3(\cdot,\cdot,\cdot)$ is trivariate with 3 propagation factors $(\alpha_{3,1}, \alpha_{3,2}, \alpha_{3,3})$. We similarly define $(\alpha_{4,1}, \ldots, \alpha_{4,4})$ for the quadvariate function f_4, and $(\alpha_{5,1}, \alpha_{5,2}, \alpha_{5,3})$ for f_5. Any error in an output value of f_1 will be amplified by a factor β_1:

$$\beta_1 = (\alpha_2(\alpha_{4,1}+\alpha_{4,2}+\alpha_{4,3})+(\alpha_{3,1}+\alpha_{3,2}+\alpha_{3,3})\alpha_{4,4})(\alpha_{5,1}+\alpha_{5,2}).$$

The total expected error of the program is:

$$\text{ERROR}(\boldsymbol{x}) = \sum_u \sum_i (x_{u,i} \cdot E_{u,i} \cdot \beta_u) \quad . \tag{6}$$

Optimization Given a fixed overall error tolerance Δ, the following *linear program* defines the minimum expected running time:

$$\begin{array}{lll} \text{Variables:} & \boldsymbol{x} & \\ \text{Constraints:} & 0 \le x_{u,i} \le 1, & \forall u, i \\ & \sum_i x_{u,i} = 1 & \forall u \\ & \text{ERROR}(\boldsymbol{x}) \le \Delta & \\ \text{Minimize:} & \text{TIME}(\boldsymbol{x}) & \end{array} \tag{7}$$

By swapping the roles of $\text{ERROR}(\boldsymbol{x})$ and $\text{TIME}(\boldsymbol{x})$, it is possible to obtain a linear program that defines the minimum expected error tolerance for a given expected maximum running time.

5.2 Error-Time Tradeoff Curves

In the previous section, we use linear programming to obtain the optimal *error-time tradeoff curve*. Since there are an infinite number of points on this curve, we define the curve in terms of functions. To avoid unnecessary complication when doing inversions, we define the curve using two related functions $E(\cdot)$ and $T(\cdot)$:

Definition 5.1. *The* **(error-time) tradeoff curve** *of a program is a pair of functions $(E(\cdot), T(\cdot))$ such that $E(t)$ is the optimal expected error of the program if the expected running time is no more than t and $T(e)$ is the optimal expected running time of the program if the expected error is no more than e.*

We say that a tradeoff curve is *efficiently computable* if both functions E and T are efficiently computable.[4] The following property is important to keep in mind:

Lemma 5.2. *In a tradeoff curve (E, T), both E and T are non-increasing convex functions.*

Proof. T is always non-increasing because when the allowed error increases the minimum running time does not increase, and similarly for E.

We prove convexity by contradiction: assume $\alpha E(t_1) + (1 - \alpha)E(t_2) < E(\alpha t_1 + (1-\alpha)t_2)$ for some $\alpha \in (0, 1)$. Then choose the optimal program for $E(t_1)$ with probability α, and the optimal program for $E(t_2)$ with probability $1 - \alpha$. The result is a new program P' in our probabilistic transformation space. This new program P' has an expected running time less than the "optimal" running time $E(\alpha t_1 + (1 - \alpha)t_2)$, contradicting the optimality of E. A similar proof establishes the convexity of T. □

We remark here that, given a running time t, one can compute E and be sure that $(E(t), t)$ is on the curve; but one cannot write down all of the infinite number of points on the curve concisely. We therefore introduce a *bi-dimensional discretization* technique that allows us to approximate (E, T) within a factor of $(1 + \varepsilon)$. This technique uses a piecewise linear function with roughly $O(\frac{1}{\varepsilon})$ segments to approximate the curve.

Our bi-dimensional discretization technique (see Figure 5) approximates E in the bounded range $[0, E_{\max}]$, where $E_{\max}$ is an upper bound on the expected error, and approximates T in the bounded range $[T(E_{\max}), T(0)]$. We assume that we are given the maximum acceptable error $E_{\max}$ (for example, by a user of the program). It is also possible to conservatively compute an $E_{\max}$ by analyzing the least-accurate possible execution of the program.

[4] In the remainder of the paper we refer to the function $E(\cdot)$ simply as E and to the function $T(\cdot)$ as T.

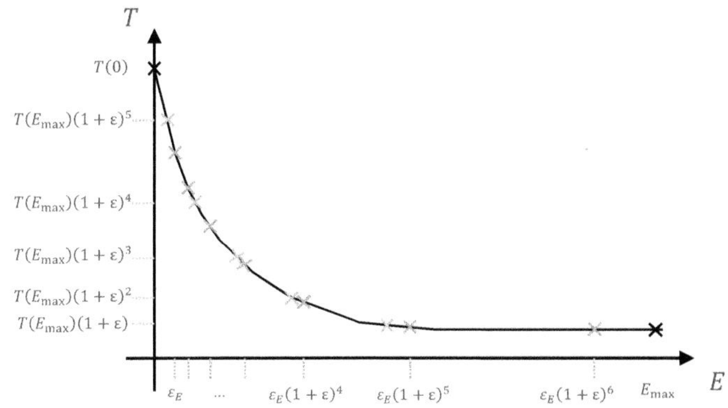

Figure 5: An example of bi-dimensional discretization.

Definition 5.3. *Given a tradeoff curve (E, T) where E and T are both non-increasing, along with constants $\varepsilon \in (0, 1)$ and $\varepsilon_E > 0$, we define the* **$(\varepsilon, \varepsilon_E)$-discretization curve of** *(E, T) to be the piecewise-linear curve defined by the following set of endpoints (see Figure 5):*

- *the two black points $(0, T(0))$, $(E_{\max}, T(E_{\max}))$,*
- *the red points $(e_i, T(e_i))$ where $e_i = \varepsilon_E(1+\varepsilon)^i$ for some $i \ge 0$ and $\varepsilon_E(1 + \varepsilon)^i < E_{\max}$, and*
- *the blue points $(E(t_i), t_i)$ where $t_i = T(E_{\max})(1 + \varepsilon)^i$ for some $i \ge 1$ and $T(E_{\max})(1 + \varepsilon)^i < T(0)$.*

Note that there is some asymmetry in the discretization of the two axes. For the vertical time axis we know that the minimum running time of a program is $T(E_{\max}) > 0$, which is always greater than zero since a program always runs in a positive amount of time. However, we discretize the horizontal error axis proportional to powers of $(1 + \varepsilon)^i$ for values above ε_E. This is because the error of a program can indeed reach zero, and we cannot discretize forever.[5]

The following claim follows immediately from the definition:

Claim 5.4. *If the original curve (E, T) is non-increasing and convex, the discretized curve $(\hat{E}, \hat{T})$ is also non-increasing and convex.*

5.2.1 Accuracy of bi-dimensional discretization

We next define notation for the bi-dimensional tradeoff curve discretization:

Definition 5.5. *A curve $(\hat{E}, \hat{T})$ is an* **$(\varepsilon, \varepsilon_E)$-approximation to** *$(E, T)$ if for any error $0 \le e \le E_{\max}$,*

$$0 \le \hat{T}(e) - T(e) \le \varepsilon T(e) \ ,$$

and for any running time $T(E_{\max}) \le t \le T(0)$,

$$0 \le \hat{E}(t) - E(t) \le \varepsilon E(t) + \varepsilon_E \ .$$

We say that such an approximation has a multiplicative error *of ε and an* additive error *of ε_E.*

Lemma 5.6. *If $(\hat{E}, \hat{T})$ is an $(\varepsilon, \varepsilon_E)$-discretization of (E, T), then it is an $(\varepsilon, \varepsilon_E)$-approximation of (E, T).*

Proof Sketch. The idea of the proof is that, since we have discretized the vertical time axis in an exponential manner, if we compute $\hat{T}(e)$ for any value e, the result does not differ from $T(e)$ by

[5] If instead we know that the minimum expected error is greater than zero (i.e., $E(T_{\max}) > 0$) for some maximum possible running time $T_{\max}$, then we can define $\varepsilon_E = E(T_{\max})$ just like our horizontal axis.

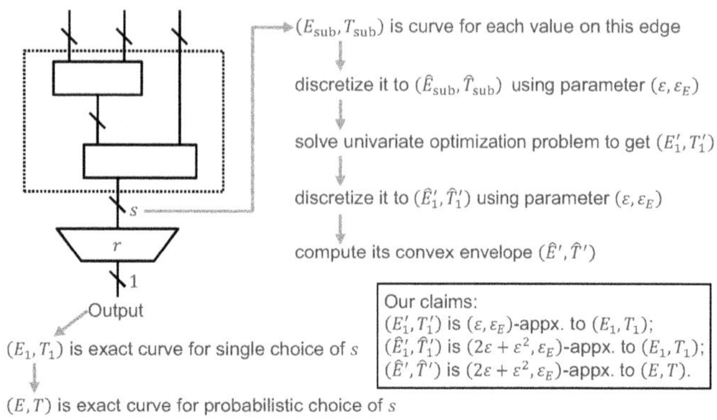

Figure 6: Algorithm for Stage 2.

more than a factor of $(1 + \varepsilon)$. Similarly, since we have discretized the horizontal axis in an exponential manner, if we compute $\hat{E}(t)$ for any value t, the result does not differ by more than a factor of $(1 + \varepsilon)$, except when $E(t)$ is smaller than ε_E (when we stop the discretization). But even in that case the value $\hat{E}(t) - E(t)$ remains smaller than ε_E.

Because every point on the new piecewise-linear curve $(\hat{E}, \hat{T})$ is a linear combination of some points on the original curve (E, T), $0 \le \hat{T}(e) - T(e)$ and $0 \le \hat{E}(t) - E(t)$, Because (E, T) is convex (recall Lemma 5.2), the approximation will always lie "above" the original curve. □

5.2.2 Complexity of bi-dimensional discretization

The number of segments that the approximate tradeoff curve has in an $(\varepsilon, \varepsilon_E)$-discretization is at most

$$n_p \stackrel{\text{def}}{=} 2 + \frac{\log \frac{E_{\max}}{\varepsilon_E}}{\log(1+\varepsilon)} + \frac{\log \frac{T(0)}{T(E_{\max})}}{\log(1+\varepsilon)}$$
$$\le O\Big(\frac{1}{\varepsilon}\big(\log E_{\max} + \log \frac{1}{\varepsilon_E} + \log T_{\max} + \log \frac{1}{T_{\min}}\big)\Big) \ , \quad (8)$$

where $T_{\min}$ is a lower bound on the expected execution time and $T_{\max}$ is an upper bound on the expected execution time. Our discretization algorithm only needs to know $E_{\max}$ in advance, while $T_{\max}$ and $T_{\min}$ are values that we will need later in the complexity analysis.

5.2.3 Discretization on an approximate curve

The above analysis does not rely on the fact that the original tradeoff curve (E, T) is exact. In fact, if the original curve (E, T) is only an $(\varepsilon, \varepsilon_E)$-approximation to the exact error-time tradeoff curve, and if $(\hat{E}, \hat{T})$ is the $(\varepsilon', \varepsilon'_E)$-discretization of (E, T), then one can verify by the triangle inequality that $(\hat{E}, \hat{T})$ is a piecewise linear curve that is an $(\varepsilon + \varepsilon' + \varepsilon\varepsilon', \varepsilon_E + \varepsilon'_E)$ approximation of the exact error-time tradeoff curve.

5.3 Stage 2: A Single Reduction Node

We now consider a program with exactly one reduction node r, with original reduction factor S, at the end of the computation. The example in Figure 3c is such a program. We describe our optimization algorithm for this case step by step as illustrated in Figure 6.

We first define the error-time tradeoff curve for the subprogram without the reduction node r to be (E_{sub}, T_{sub}) (Section 5.1 describes how to compute this curve; Lemma 5.2 ensures that it is non-increasing and convex). In other words, for *every input value* to the reduction node r, if the allowed running time for computing this value is t, then the optimal expected error is $E_{sub}(t)$ and similarly for $T_{sub}(e)$. Note that when computing (E_{sub}, T_{sub}) as described in Section 5.1, the size of the output edge R_i for each node i must be divided by S, as the curve (E_{sub}, T_{sub}) characterizes each single input value to the reduction node r.

If at reduction node r we choose an actual reduction factor $s \in \{1, 2, \ldots, S\}$, the total running time and error of this entire program is:[6]

$$\begin{array}{rcl} \text{TIME} & = & T_{sub} \times s \\ \text{ERROR} & = & E_{sub} + E_r(s) \ . \end{array} \quad (9)$$

This is because, to obtain s values on the input to r, we need to run the subprogram s times with a total time $T_{sub} \times s$; and by Corollary 3.2, the total error of the output of an averaging reduction node is simply the sum of its input error E_{sub}, and a local error $E_r(s)$ incurred by the sampling.[7]

Let (E_1, T_1) be the exact tradeoff curve (E_1, T_1) of the *entire* program, assuming that we can choose only a single value of s. We start by describing how to compute this (E_1, T_1) approximately.

5.3.1 Approximating (E_1, T_1): single choice of s

By definition, we can write (E_1, T_1) in terms of the following *two* optimization problems:

$$T_1(e) = \min_{\substack{s \in \{1,\ldots,S\} \\ e_{sub} + E_r(s) = e}} \{T_{sub}(e_{sub}) \times s\}$$
$$\text{and} \quad E_1(t) = \min_{\substack{s \in \{1,\ldots,S\} \\ t_{sub} \times s = t}} \{E_{sub}(t_{sub}) + E_r(s)\} \ ,$$

where the first optimization is over variables s and e_{sub}, and the second optimization is over variables s and t_{sub}. We emphasize here that this curve (E_1, T_1) is by definition non-increasing (because (E_{sub}, T_{sub}) is non-increasing), but may not be convex.

Because these optimization problems may not be convex, they may be difficult to solve in general. But thanks to the piecewise-linear discretization defined in Section 5.2, we can approximately solve these optimization problems efficiently. Specifically, we produce a bi-dimensional discretization $(\hat{E}_{sub}, \hat{T}_{sub})$ that $(\varepsilon, \varepsilon_E)$-approximates (E_{sub}, T_{sub}) (as illustrated in Figure 6). We then solve the following two optimization problems:

$$T'_1(e) = \min_{\substack{s \in \{1,\ldots,S\} \\ e_{sub} + E_r(s) = e}} \{\hat{T}_{sub}(e_{sub}) \times s\}$$
$$\text{and} \quad E'_1(t) = \min_{\substack{s \in \{1,\ldots,S\} \\ t_{sub} \times s = t}} \{\hat{E}_{sub}(t_{sub}) + E_r(s)\} \ . \quad (10)$$

We remark here that E'_1 and T'_1 are both non-increasing since $\hat{E}_{sub}$ and $\hat{T}_{sub}$ are non-increasing using Claim 5.4.

Each of these two problems can be solved by 1) computing the optimal value within each linear segment defined by $(\hat{E}_{sub,k}, \hat{T}_{sub,k})$ and $(\hat{E}_{sub,k+1}, \hat{T}_{sub,k+1})$, and 2) returning the smallest optimal value across all linear segments.

Suppose that we are computing $T'_1(e)$ given an error e. In the linear piece of $\hat{T}_{sub} = a e_{sub} + b$ (here a and b are the slope and intercept of the linear segment), we have $e_{sub} = e - E_r(s)$. The objective that we are minimizing therefore becomes univariate with respect to s:

$$\hat{T}_{sub} \times s = (a e_{sub} + b) \times s = (a(e - E_r(s)) + b) \times s \ . \quad (11)$$

[6] Here we have ignored the running time for the sampling procedure in the reduction node, as it is often negligible in comparison to other computations in the program. It is possible to add this sampling time to the formula for TIME in a straightforward manner.

[7] We extend this analysis to other types of reduction nodes in Section 8.

The calculation of s is a simple univariate optimization problem that we can solve quickly using our expression for $E_r(s)$.[8] Comparing the optimal answers from all of the linear pieces gives us an efficient algorithm to determine $T'_1(e)$, and similarly for $E'_1(t)$. This algorithm runs in time linear in the number of pieces n_p (recall Eq.(8)) in our bi-dimensional discretization. This finishes the computation of (E'_1, T'_1) in Figure 6. We next show that (E'_1, T'_1) accurately approximates (E, T):

Claim 5.7. *(E'_1, T'_1) is an $(\varepsilon, \varepsilon_E)$-approximation to (E_1, T_1).*

Proof. Because $\hat{T}_{\text{sub}}$ approximates T_{sub}, we know that for any e_{sub}, $0 \le \hat{T}_{\text{sub}}(e_{\text{sub}}) - T_{\text{sub}}(e_{\text{sub}}) \le \varepsilon T_{\text{sub}}(e_{\text{sub}})$, and this gives:

$$\begin{aligned} T'_1(e) &= \min_{\substack{s\in\{1,\ldots,S\}\\ e_{\text{sub}}+E_r(s)=e}} \{\hat{T}_{\text{sub}}(e_{\text{sub}}) \times s\} \\ &\le \min_{\substack{s\in\{1,\ldots,S\}\\ e_{\text{sub}}+E_r(s)=e}} \{(1+\varepsilon)T_{\text{sub}}(e_{\text{sub}}) \times s\} = (1+\varepsilon)T_1(e). \end{aligned}$$

Similarly, this also gives that $T'_1(e) \ge T_1(e)$ using $0 \le \hat{T}_{\text{sub}}(e_{\text{sub}}) - T_{\text{sub}}(e_{\text{sub}})$.

Using a similar technique, we can also prove that $E'_1(t) \ge E_1(t)$ and $E'_1(t) \le (1+\varepsilon)E_1(t) + \varepsilon_E$. Therefore, the (E'_1, T'_1) curve $(\varepsilon, \varepsilon_E)$-approximates the exact tradeoff curve (E_1, T_1). □

We next further bi-dimensionally discretize the curve (E'_1, T'_1) that we obtained into $(\hat{E}'_1, \hat{T}'_1)$ using the same discretization parameter $(\varepsilon, \varepsilon_E)$. A discretization of an approximate curve is still approximate (see Section Section 5.2.3). We therefore conclude that

Claim 5.8. *$(\hat{E}'_1, \hat{T}'_1)$ is a $(2\varepsilon+\varepsilon^2, 2\varepsilon_E)$-approximation to (E_1, T_1).*

5.3.2 Approximating (E, T): probabilistic choice of s

Now, we define (E, T) to be the exact tradeoff curve (E_1, T_1) of the *entire* program, assuming that we can choose s probabilistically. We claim:

Claim 5.9. *(E, T) is the* convex envelope *of (E_1, T_1).*

Proof. We first prove the claim that T is the convex envelope of T_1. The proof for E is similar. One side of the proof is straightforward: every weighted combination of points on T_1 should lie on or above T, because this weighted combination is one candidate randomized configuration that chooses s probabilistically, and T is defined to be the optimal curve that takes into account all such randomized configurations.

For the other side of the proof, we need to show that every point on T is a weighted combination of points on T_1. Let us take an arbitrary point $(e, T(e))$. Suppose that $T(e)$ is achieved when the optimal probabilistic choice of s is $\{(s_i, p_i)\}_{i\ge1}$ at reduction node r, where we choose s_i with probability p_i and when s_i is chosen, the overall error-time incurred is (e_i, t_i). Therefore, we have $e = \sum_i p_i e_i$ and $T(e) = \sum_i p_i t_i$.

Because $T(e)$ is the exact optimal tradeoff curve, each t_i is also minimized with respect to e_i and the fixed choice of s_i. This is equivalent to saying that (e_i, t_i) lies on the curve (E_1, T_1), i.e., $T_1(e_i) = t_i$. This implies that T is the convex envelope of T_1. □

In general, computing the convex envelope of an arbitrary function (E_1, T_1) may be hard, but thanks to our piecewise-linear discretization, we can compute the convex envelope of $(\hat{E}'_1, \hat{T}'_1)$ easily. Let us denote the convex envelope of $(\hat{E}'_1, \hat{T}'_1)$ by $(\hat{E}', \hat{T}')$. In fact, $(\hat{E}', \hat{T}')$ can be computed in time $O(n_p \log n_p)$ because $(\hat{E}'_1, \hat{T}'_1)$ contains only n_p endpoints.

[8] Note that for each different type of reduction code, the optimization procedure for this univariate optimization can be hardcoded.

Since $(\hat{E}'_1, \hat{T}'_1)$ is a $(2\varepsilon + \varepsilon^2, \varepsilon_E)$-approximation to (E_1, T_1) by Claim 5.8, we should expect the same property to hold for their convex envelopes:

Claim 5.10. *$(\hat{E}', \hat{T}')$ is a $(2\varepsilon+\varepsilon^2, 2\varepsilon_E)$-approximation to (E, T).*

Proof. By the definition of convex envelope, for all time t, there exists some $\alpha \in [0, 1]$ such that $E(t) = \alpha E_1(t_1) + (1-\alpha)E_1(t_2)$ and $\alpha t_1 + (1-\alpha)t_2 = t$. Then,

$$\begin{aligned} \hat{E}'(t) &\le \alpha\hat{E}'_1(t_1) + (1-\alpha)\hat{E}'_1(t_2) \\ &\le 2\varepsilon_E + (1+2\varepsilon+\varepsilon^2)(\alpha E_1(t_1) + (1-\alpha)E_1(t_2)) \\ &= 2\varepsilon_E + (1+2\varepsilon+\varepsilon^2)E(t) \ , \end{aligned}$$

where the first inequality uses the fact that $\hat{E}'$ is the convex envelope of $\hat{E}'_1$, and the second uses the fact that $\hat{E}'_1$ approximates E_1.

At the same time, there exists some $\beta \in [0, 1]$ such that $\hat{E}'(t) = \beta\hat{E}'_1(t_3) + (1-\beta)\hat{E}'_1(t_4)$ and $\beta t_3 + (1-\beta)t_4 = t$. Then,

$$\begin{aligned} \hat{E}'(t) &= \beta\hat{E}'_1(t_3) + (1-\beta)\hat{E}'_1(t_4) \\ &\ge \beta E_1(t_3) + (1-\beta)E_1(t_4) \ge E(t) \ , \end{aligned}$$

where the first inequality uses the fact that $\hat{E}'_1$ approximates E_1, and the second uses the fact that E is the convex envelope of E_1.

We can derive the two similar inequalities for the time function $\hat{T}'$ and conclude that $(\hat{E}', \hat{T}')$ is a $(2\varepsilon + \varepsilon^2, 2\varepsilon_E)$-approximation to (E, T). □

So far, we have finished all steps described in Figure 6. We have ended with a piecewise-linear tradeoff curve $(\hat{E}', \hat{T}')$ that $(2\varepsilon + \varepsilon^2, 2\varepsilon_E)$-approximates the exact tradeoff curve (E, T), taking into account the probabilistic choices at this reduction node as well.

5.4 The Final Dynamic Programming Algorithm

We next show how to compute the approximate error-time tradeoff curve for *any* program in our model of computation. We first present the algorithm, then we discuss how to choose the discretization parameters ε and ε_E and how the discretization errors compose.

If the program has no reduction nodes, we can simply apply the analysis from Section 5.1. Otherwise, there must exist at least one topmost reduction node r whose input is computed from computation nodes only. Assume (E, T) is the exact error-time tradeoff curve for the output of r. Applying Stage 2 (Section 5.3) to the subprogram rooted at r, we can efficiently find some piecewise-linear curve $(\hat{E}', \hat{T}')$ that accurately approximates (E, T).

Recall that this piecewise-linear curve $(\hat{E}', \hat{T}')$ is convex (since it is a convex envelope). If we pick all of its at most n_p endpoints on the curve $\mathcal{P} = \{(E_{r,i}, T_{r,i})\}_{i=1}^{n_p}$, then 1) every point on the curve can be spanned by at most two points in $\mathcal{P}$ because the function is piecewise linear, and 2) all points that can be spanned by $\mathcal{P}$ lie above the curve because the function is convex.

The two observations 1) and 2) above indicate that we can *replace* this reduction node r along with all computation nodes above it, by a single function node f_r such that its i-th substitute implementation $f_{r,i}$ gives an error of $E_{r,i}$ and a running time of $T_{r,i}$. Observation 1) indicates that every error-time tradeoff point on $(\hat{E}', \hat{T}')$ can be implemented by a probabilistic mixture of $\{f_{r,i}\}_{i=1}^{n_p}$, and observation 2) indicates that every error-time tradeoff point that can be implemented, is no better than the original curve $(\hat{E}', \hat{T}')$. In sum, this function node achieves the same error-time tradeoff as the piecewise-linear curve $(\hat{E}', \hat{T}')$.

This completes the description of the algorithm. We can recursively choose a reduction node with only computation nodes above it, replace the subtree rooted at the reduction node with a function node, continue until we have no reduction nodes left, and compute the final error-time tradeoff curve. We next consider the accuracy and running time of this recursive algorithm.

Maximum Error Propagation Factor (MEPF). We use a value MEPF to bound the cumulative additive error of the optimized program. Specifically, we choose MEPF so that a local additive error e at some node in the computation will produce at most a $e \times \text{MEPF}$ additive error at the final output. Specifically, we set MEPF to be the maximum β_u over all function nodes f_u in the program.

Accuracy. Our algorithm repeatedly approximates error-time curves with their discretizations. This typically occurs twice during the analysis of each reduction node. If the inputs of a reduction node come from some computation node, the first discretization approximates the tradeoff curve for that computation node (we do not need this step if inputs come from some other reduction node.) The second discretization approximates the tradeoff curve for the outputs of the reduction node. By bounding the total error introduced by all of these approximations, we show that our algorithm produces a good approximation to the exact error-time curve.

We remark that there are two very different types of errors being discussed here: errors that we trade off against time in our approximate computation and errors that our optimization algorithm incurs in computing the optimal error-time tradeoff curve for the approximate computation. For clarity, we shall refer to the former as *computation error* and to the latter as *optimization error*.

If we choose parameters $(\varepsilon, \varepsilon_E)$ for both discretizations of a single reduction node r, the argument in Section 5.2.3 shows that we obtain a $(2\varepsilon+\varepsilon^2, 2\varepsilon_E)$-approximation to its error-time tradeoff curve.

A computation node may amplify the computation error, which will result in a corresponding increase in the optimization error of our approximation to it. However, we can bound the total effect of all computation nodes on our optimization error using our linear error propagation assumption. In particular, we can study the effect of a single reduction node's $(2\varepsilon+\varepsilon^2, 2\varepsilon_E)$-approximation on the program's overall additive and multiplicative optimization error:

- The additive error $2\varepsilon_E$ is multiplied by the computation nodes' Lipschitz parameters. The result is an overall additive optimization error of at most $2\varepsilon_E\text{MEPF}$.
- The multiplicative error is not affected, since both the actual computation error and our approximation to it are multiplied by the same factors. The overall multiplicative optimization error introduced is thus at most $2\varepsilon+\varepsilon^2$.

This bounds the optimization errors introduced by the discretization in our analysis of a single reduction node. We can add these up to bound the total optimization error.

We fix parameters $\varepsilon = \frac{\varepsilon'}{\Omega(n)}$ and $\varepsilon_E = \frac{\varepsilon'_E}{\Omega(n)\times\text{MEPF}}$ for all of the discretizations, where n is the number of nodes in the original program. Since we have at most n reduction nodes, this sums up to a total multiplicative error of ε' and additive error of ε'_E (both of these errors are optimization errors) in the final approximation of the exact error-time tradeoff curve of the whole program. Our overall optimization algorithm thus produces a piecewise-linear curve $(\hat{E}, \hat{T})$, that $(\varepsilon', \varepsilon'_E)$-approximates the exact error-time tradeoff curve.[9]

[9] If we choose ε'_E to be the smallest unit of error that we care about, then this essentially becomes an ε' multiplicative approximation to the actual error-time tradeoff curve.

Time Complexity. The most expensive operation in our optimization algorithm is solving the multiple linear programs that the algorithm generates. We next bound the number of linear programs that the algorithm generates.

Recall by Eq.(8) that n_p is the number of pieces in our bi-dimensional discretizations. By our choices of ε and ε_E:

$$\begin{aligned} n_p &= O\Big(\frac{1}{\varepsilon}\big(\log E_{\max} + \log\frac{1}{\varepsilon_E} + \log T_{\max} + \log\frac{1}{T_{\min}}\big)\Big) \\ &= O\Big(\frac{n}{\varepsilon'}\big(\log E_{\max} + \log\frac{n\text{MEPF}}{\varepsilon'_E} + \log T_{\max} + \log\frac{1}{T_{\min}}\big)\Big) \ . \end{aligned}$$

For each reduction node, we solve a linear program for each of the n_p points in its discretization. We therefore run the LP solver $O(n \times n_p)$ number of times. The number of variables in these linear program is $O(n \times n_p)$, since each node may have n_p implementations (which occurs when we replace a reduction node with its bi-dimensional discretization). This yields:

Theorem 5.11. *Our proposed recursive algorithm calls the LP solver $O(n \times n_p)$ times, each time with $O(n \times n_p)$ variables. The algorithm produces a $(1+\varepsilon')$-approximation to the exact error-time tradeoff curve, and thus approximately solves Question 1.*

Note that in practice we can find constants that appropriately bound $T_{\min}$, $T_{\max}$, $E_{\max}$, MEPF and ε_E.[10] In addition, all those numbers stay *within log functions*. We can therefore assume that in practice:

$$n_p \approx O\big(\frac{n\log n}{\varepsilon'}\big) \ .$$

We also note that 1) the worst-case time complexity of linear programming is polynomial, and 2) efficient linear programming algorithms exist in practice.

6. Optimization Algorithm for Question 2

At this point, we have approximately solved the error-time tradeoff curve problem in Question 1. Given an overall error tolerance Δ, we have an efficient algorithm that approximates the optimal running time $T(\Delta)$ up to a multiplicative factor $(1+\varepsilon)$.

We next show that our algorithm is constructive: it uses substitution and sampling transformations to obtain a randomized program P' with expected error bound Δ that runs in expected time no more than $(1+\varepsilon)T(\Delta)$. The algorithm therefore answers Question 2 approximately. Our proof first considers the two simpler cases that we introduced in Section 5.

Stage 1: Computation Nodes Only. If the program has no reduction nodes, then the solution $\boldsymbol{x}$ to the linear program gives explicitly the probability of choosing each implementation at each function node, which in turn gives us a randomized configuration for the randomized program P'.

Stage 2: A Single Reduction Node. If the program consists of computation nodes that generate the input for a single reduction node (this reduction node is therefore the root of the program), recall that we have perform two discretizations as illustrated in Figure 6.

Specifically, let (E, T) be the exact error-time tradeoff curve of the final output, which we have approximated by a piecewise-linear curve $(\hat{E}', \hat{T}')$ in the last step of Figure 6. We want to obtain a program P' whose error-time pair is $(\Delta, \hat{T}'(\Delta))$, because $\hat{T}'$ is guaranteed to be a $(1+\varepsilon)$-approximation to T.

[10] For example, we may lower bound $T_{\min}$ with the clock cycle time of the machine running the computation, ε_E with the smallest unit of error we care about, upper bound $T_{\max}$ with the estimated lifetime of the machine running the computation, $E_{\max}$ with the largest value representable on the machine running the computation, and MEPF with the ratio between the largest and smallest value representable on the machine running the computation.

By piecewise linearity, the point $(\Delta, \hat{T}'(\Delta))$ lies on some linear segment of $(\hat{E}', \hat{T}')$:

$$\hat{T}'(\Delta) = \lambda \hat{T}'(e_1) + (1-\lambda)\hat{T}'(e_2)$$
$$\Delta = \lambda e_1 + (1-\lambda) e_2 \ ,$$

where $[e_1, e_2]$ are the two endpoints of that segment. To achieve an error-time pair $(\Delta, \hat{T}'(\Delta))$, we can let the final program P' run 1) with probability λ some randomized program P_1' whose error-time pair is $(e_1, \hat{T}'(e_1))$, and 2) with probability $1-\lambda$ some other randomized program P_2' whose error-time pair is $(e_2, \hat{T}'(e_2))$. We next verify that both P_1' and P_2' can be constructed explicitly. We focus on the construction of P_1.

The goal is to construct P_1' with error-time pair $p = (e_1, \hat{T}'(e_1))$. Note that p is an endpoint of $(\hat{E}', \hat{T}')$, and thus is also an endpoint of $(\hat{E}_1', \hat{T}_1')$. Since $(\hat{E}_1', \hat{T}_1')$ is a discretization of (E_1', T_1'), p is also a point on the curve (E_1', T_1'). We can therefore write $p = (e_1, T_1'(e_1))$.

Recall that we obtained $T_1'(e_1)$ by exactly solving the univariate optimization problem defined in Eq.(11). Because this solution is constructive, it provides us with the optimal reduction factor s to use at the reduction node. Substituting this optimal value s into Eq.(10), we obtain the error-time pair $(e_{\text{sub}}, \hat{T}_{\text{sub}}(e_{\text{sub}}))$ that we should allocate to the subprogram (without the reduction node). We therefore only need to construct a program for the subprogram whose error-time pair is $(e_{\text{sub}}, \hat{T}_{\text{sub}}(e_{\text{sub}}))$.

Because $\hat{T}_{\text{sub}}$ is a piecewise-linear discretization of T_{sub}, we can obtain a program whose error-time pair is $(e_{\text{sub}}, \hat{T}_{\text{sub}}(e_{\text{sub}}))$ by combining at most two points on the $(E_{\text{sub}}, T_{\text{sub}})$ curve. The linear program described above implements this $(E_{\text{sub}}, T_{\text{sub}})$ curve. This completes the construction of P'.

We have therefore shown that as part of the algorithm for Stage 2 (see Section 5.3), we can indeed construct a program P' with the desired error and time bounds $(\Delta, \hat{T}'(\Delta))$.

Putting It All Together. We prove, by induction, that for a program with an arbitrary number of reduction nodes, we can obtain a randomized program P' with expected error bound Δ and expected running time no more than $(1+\varepsilon)T(\Delta)$. We are done if there is no reduction node (by Stage 1). Otherwise, suppose that we have n_r reduction nodes.

We will substitute one of the reduction nodes r, along with all computations above it, by a function node f_r with piecewise-linear tradeoff $(\hat{E}', \hat{T}')$. This function node has a set of implementations $\{f_{r,i}\}_{i=1}^{n_p}$, and in our Stage 2, we have actually shown that each $f_{r,i}$, being a point on the $(\hat{E}', \hat{T}')$ curve, is achievable by some explicit randomized program P_i.

In other words, this new function node f_r is a "real" function node: every approximate implementation $f_{r,i}$ has a corresponding randomized program P_i that can be constructed by our algorithm. This reduces the problem into a case with $n_r - 1$ reduction nodes. Using our induction hypothesis, we conclude that for any Δ, we can construct a program P' that runs in expected time no more than $(1+\varepsilon)T(\Delta)$.

7. Optimization Algorithm for Question 3

We next describe how to modify our algorithm if one instead is interested in the time-variance tradeoff.

7.1 Changes to Function Nodes

For each function node f_u, the algorithm for Question 1 works with an error-time pair $(T_{u,i}, E_{u,i})$ for each implementation $f_{u,i}$. Now we instead work with a pair $(T_{u,i}, V_{u,i})$, where $V_{u,i}$ is the variance (i.e., the expected squared error):

$$\forall \boldsymbol{x}, \quad \mathbb{E}[|f_u(\boldsymbol{x}) - f_{u,i}(\boldsymbol{x})|^2] \le V_{u,i} \ , \tag{12}$$

where the expectation is over the the randomness of $f_{u,i}$ and f_u.

We also assume that the variance propagation function is linear with coefficients $\alpha_1, \ldots, \alpha_m$. In other words, if f_u has an arity of m, and each input x_i is approximated by some input $\hat{x}_i$ such that $\mathbb{E}[|x_i - \hat{x}_i|^2] \le v_i$, then the final variance:

$$\mathbb{E}\big[|f_u(x_1,\ldots,x_m) - f_{u,i}(\hat{x}_1,\ldots,\hat{x}_m)|^2\big] \le \big(\sum_j \alpha_j v_j\big) + 2V_{u,i} \ . \tag{13}$$

We next check that a large class of meaningful functions satisfies the above definition. Note that if f_u is a deterministic Lipschitz-continuous function (with respect to vector $\boldsymbol{L} = (L_1, \ldots, L_m)$):

$$\begin{aligned}
&\mathbb{E}\big[|f_u(\boldsymbol{x}) - f_{u,i}(\hat{\boldsymbol{x}})|^2\big] \\
&= \mathbb{E}\big[|(f_u(\boldsymbol{x}) - f_u(\hat{\boldsymbol{x}})) + (f_u(\hat{\boldsymbol{x}}) - f_{u,i}(\hat{\boldsymbol{x}}))|^2\big] \\
&\le 2\mathbb{E}\big[|f_u(\boldsymbol{x}) - f_u(\hat{\boldsymbol{x}})|^2 + |f_u(\hat{\boldsymbol{x}}) - f_{u,i}(\hat{\boldsymbol{x}})|^2\big] \\
&\le 2\mathbb{E}\big[|f_u(\boldsymbol{x}) - f_u(\hat{\boldsymbol{x}})|^2\big] + 2V_{u,i} \\
&\le 2\mathbb{E}\big[(\textstyle\sum_i L_i|x_i - \hat{x}_i|)^2\big] + 2V_{u,i} \\
&\le 2m\mathbb{E}\big[\textstyle\sum_i L_i^2(x_i - \hat{x})^2\big] + 2V_{u,i} \\
&\le 2m \textstyle\sum_i L_i^2 v_i + 2V_{u,i} \ .
\end{aligned} \tag{14}$$

So let $\alpha_i = 2mL_i^2$ in Eq.(13). If f_u is probabilistic and each deterministic function in its support is Lipschitz-continuous (perhaps for different $\boldsymbol{L}$'s), then we can similarly set the final $\alpha_i = 2m\mathbb{E}[L_i^2]$ using the expectation.[11]

7.2 Changes to Reduction Nodes

Recall that for a reduction node r with reduction factor S_r, we can decrease this factor to a smaller value $s_r \in \{1, \ldots, S_r\}$ at the expense of introducing some additive sampling error $E_r(s_r)$. In our Question 3, we have a different variance bound $V_r(s_r) = (B-A)^2 \frac{S_r - s_r}{s_r(S_r - 1)}$, whose proof can be found in the full version of this paper.

Lemma 7.1. *Given m numbers $x_1, x_2, \ldots, x_m \in [A, B]$, randomly sampling s of the numbers $x_{i_1}, \ldots, x_{i_s}$ (without replacement) and computing the sample average gives an approximation to $\frac{x_1 + \cdots + x_m}{m}$ with the following variance guarantee:*

$$\mathbb{E}_{i_1,\ldots,i_s}\Big[\Big|\frac{x_{i_1} + \cdots + x_{i_s}}{s} - \frac{x_1 + \cdots + x_m}{m}\Big|^2\Big] \le (B-A)^2 \frac{m-s}{s(m-1)} \ .$$

Similar to Corollary 3.2, we also verify that an averaging node satisfies our linear variance propagation assumption, due to its Lipschitz continuity We defer the proof to the full version of this paper.

Corollary 7.2. *Consider an averaging node that will pick s random samples among all m inputs where each input $\hat{x}_j$ has bounded variance $\mathbb{E}[|\hat{x}_j - x_j|^2] \le v_j$. Then:*

$$\mathbb{E}_{i_1,\ldots,i_s,\hat{x}_1,\ldots,\hat{x}_m}\Big[\Big|\frac{\hat{x}_{i_1} + \cdots + \hat{x}_{i_s}}{s} - \frac{x_1 + \cdots + x_m}{m}\Big|^2\Big] \le 2(B-A)^2 \frac{m-s}{s(m-1)} + \frac{2}{m}\sum_{i=1}^{m} v_i \ .$$

[11] Because the randomness within f_u is independent of the randomness for input error $\hat{x}_i - x_i$, we have $\mathbb{E}[L_i^2(x_i - \hat{x}_i)^2] = \mathbb{E}[L_i^2]\mathbb{E}[(x_i - \hat{x}_i)^2]$.

7.3 Putting Things Together

As before, if there is no reduction node, we can write the variance in the following linear form:

$$\text{ERROR2}(\boldsymbol{x}) = \sum_u \sum_i (x_{u,i} \cdot V_{u,i} \cdot \beta_u) \ .$$

The amplification factors β_u can be pre-computed using the linear variance propagation factors α_i.

The expressions for the reduction node are slightly changed. Instead of Eq.(9), we now have

$$\text{TIME} = T_{\text{sub}} \times s$$
$$\text{ERROR2} = 2V_{\text{sub}} + 2V_r(s) \ .$$

One can use almost the same arguments as in Section 5 to show that the optimization problem with respect to one reduction node can be reduced to optimizing a univariate function. This yields a fully polynomial-time approximation scheme (FPTAS) that solves Question 3. The solution for Question 4 can be derived similarly if one follows the arguments in Section 6.

8. Other Reduction Nodes

We have stated our main theorems for programs that contain only averaging reduction nodes. More generally, our algorithm supports any reduction node that can be approximated using sampling. This includes, for example, variances, ℓ^p norms, and order statistics functions. In this section we discuss the analysis of some additional reduction nodes.

Summation Reduction Nodes. For a summation node with reduction factor S_r (i.e., S_r numbers to sum up), the sampling procedure randomly selects s_r numbers, then outputs the partial sum multiplied by $\frac{S_r}{s_r}$. The output is therefore an unbiased estimator of the exact sum. The derivation of the expressions for the expected error and the variance of the error closely follows the derivation for averaging nodes. The final expressions are the corresponding averaging expressions multiplied by S_r.

Minimization and Maximization Reduction Nodes. Note that all reasonable sampling techniques may, with some non-negligible probability, discard the smallest input value. We therefore consider *percentile minimization nodes*, which have two parameters $q \in (0, 1)$ and B. If the output is any of the smallest $\lfloor qm \rfloor$ numbers in the input (here m is the number of inputs), the error is 0. Otherwise, the error is B. We also define $m' = \lceil (1-q)m \rceil$.

Lemma 8.1. *For a percentile minimization (or maximization) node r with parameters $q \in (0, 1)$ and B, sampling s_r of m input elements gives an expected error of*

$$E_r(s_r) = \begin{cases} \dfrac{\binom{m'}{s_r}}{\binom{m}{s_r}} B & \text{if } s_r \le m' \\ 0 & \text{if } s_r > m', \end{cases}$$

which is a convex function. It is also possible to define a simpler approximate bound if m is large or sampling is done without replacement: $E_r(s_r) \approx (1-q)^{s_r} B$.

Proof. There are a total of $\binom{m}{s_r}$ ways to take samples of size s_r. $\binom{m'}{s_r}$ of these samples will contain no element in the smallest q fraction of the original S_r inputs. The probability that a sample contains no element that lies in this smallest q fraction is therefore $\frac{\binom{m'}{s_r}}{\binom{m}{s_r}}$. The expected error is this probability multiplied by B. One can verify that this is a convex function by taking the second-order discrete derivative. When m is large, the probability can be approximated by $(1-q)^{s_r}$, which is obviously convex. □

Also, the error propagates linearly (with a constant factor of 1) for such nodes. In other words, if all inputs to a minimization (or maximization) node are subject to an error of $\mathbb{E}[|x_i - \hat{x}_i|] \le \delta$, the output will have error $\delta + E'_r(s_r)$. Now, if we replace $E_r(s_r)$ in Eq.(9) with this function we just derived, all of the analysis in Section 5 goes through unchanged.

It is also straightforward to verify that if one uses the variance of the error, $V_r(s_r) = E_r(s_r)B$.

Argmin and Argmax Reduction Nodes. We can similarly define percentile argmin and argmax nodes, where the output value is a pair (i, v) in which i is the index for the smallest/largest element and v is the actual minimum or maximum value. The error depends exclusively on the element v. We can output the index i, but it can not be used as a value in arithmetic expressions.

9. Related Work

Empirical Accuracy-Performance Tradeoffs. Profitably trading accuracy for performance is a well known practice, often done at an algorithmic or system level. For many computationally expensive problems, researchers have developed approximation, randomized, or iterative algorithms which produce an approximate solution with guaranteed error bounds [25]. Researchers have also proposed a number of system-level techniques that specifically aim to trade accuracy for performance, energy, or fault tolerance. The proposed techniques operate at the level of hardware [4, 17, 34], system software [9, 13, 17, 20, 21], and user applications [2, 3, 6, 14, 24, 27, 28, 30, 31, 33].

Previous research has explored the tradeoff space by running and comparing the results of the original and transformed programs on either training inputs [12, 27, 28, 31] or online for chosen production inputs [2, 3, 13, 33]. The result of this exploration is often an empirical approximation of the accuracy-performance tradeoff curve. This approximation may be valid only for inputs similar to those used to construct the empirical curve. In some cases the approximation comes with empirical statistical accuracy bounds [27, 28]. In other cases there are no accuracy bounds at all. This paper, in contrast, statically analyzes the computation to produce a $(1+\epsilon)$-approximation to the exact tradeoff curve. This approximation provides guaranteed probabilistic accuracy bounds that are valid for all legal inputs.

Probabilistic Accuracy Bounds For Single Loops. Researchers have recently developed static analysis techniques for characterizing the accuracy effects of loop perforation (which transforms loops to execute only a subset of their iterations) [22, 23] or loops with approximate function memoization (which transforms functions to return a previously computed value) [6]. These techniques analyze single loops and do not characterize how the accuracy effects propagate through the remaining computation to affect the output. This paper, in contrast, presents a technique that characterizes and exploits the accuracy-performance curve available via substitution and sampling transformations applied to complete computations. Unlike previous research, the techniques presented in this paper capture how global interactions between multiple approximate transformations propagate through the entire computation (instead of just a single loop) and does not require specification of probability distributions of the inputs.

Analytic Properties of Programs. Researchers have developed techniques to identify continuous or Lipschitz-continuous programs [5, 6, 18, 19, 26]. Identified applications include differential privacy [5, 6, 26] and robust functions for embedded systems [6, 18, 19]. This paper, in contrast, presents techniques that apply accuracy-aware transformations to obtain new computations that occupy more desirable points on the underlying accuracy-performance tradeoff curve that the transformations induce.

Smooth interpretation [7, 8] uses a gradient descent based method to synthesize control parameters for imperative computer programs. The analysis returns a set of parameters that minimize the difference between the expected and computed control values for programs that control cyberphysical interactions.

Approximate Queries in Database Systems. Modern databases often enable users to define queries that operate on some subset of the records in a given table. Such queries come with no accuracy or performance guarantees. Researchers have explored multiple directions for supporting approximate queries with probabilistic guarantees. Approximate aggregate queries let a user specify a desired accuracy bound or execution time of a query [1, 15, 16]. The database then generates a sampling strategy that satisfies the specification [15, 16] or uses a cached sample, when applicable [1]. Online queries compute the exact answer for the entire data-set, but provide intermediate results and confidence bounds [11]. Probabilistic databases [35] operate on inherently uncertain data. The accuracy bounds of all queries (including aggregation) depend on the uncertainty of data.

These systems work with specific classes of queries defined in a relational model. They sample data but do not consider multiple function implementations. They also do not provide general mechanisms to achieve optimal accuracy-performance tradeoffs for sampling when processing complex nested queries.

10. Conclusion

Despite the central role that approximate computations play in many areas of computer science, there has been little research into program optimizations that can trade off accuracy in return for other benefits such as reduced resource consumption. We present a model of computation for approximate computations and an algorithm for applying accuracy-aware transformations to optimize these approximate computations. The algorithm produces a randomized program, which randomly selects one of multiple weighted alternative program configurations to maximize performance subject to a specified expected error bound.

Given the growing importance of approximation in computation, we expect to see more approximate optimization algorithms in the future. We anticipate that these algorithms may share many of the key characteristics of the computations and optimizations that we present in this paper: program transformations that trade off accuracy in return for performance, the ability to optimize programs in the presence of errors that propagate globally across multiple composed programming constructs, and randomization to improve performance and tractability.

Acknowledgements

We thank Michael Carbin, Stelios Sidiroglou, Jean Yang, and the anonymous reviewers for useful feedback on previous versions of this paper.

This research was supported in part by the National Science Foundation (Grants CCF-0811397, CCF-0843915, CCF-0905244, CCF-1036241 and IIS-0835652), the United States Department of Energy (Grant DE-SC0005288), and a Sloan Fellowship.

References

[1] S. Acharya, P. Gibbons, V. Poosala, and S. Ramaswamy. Join synopses for approximate query answering. In *SIGMOD*, 1999.

[2] J. Ansel, C. Chan, Y. Wong, M. Olszewski, Q. Zhao, A. Edelman, and S. Amarasinghe. Petabricks: A language and compiler for algorithmic choice. In *PLDI*, 2009.

[3] W. Baek and T. Chilimbi. Green: A framework for supporting energy-conscious programming using controlled approximation. In *PLDI '10*.

[4] L. Chakrapani, K. Muntimadugu, A. Lingamneni, J. George, and K. Palem. Highly energy and performance efficient embedded computing through approximately correct arithmetic: A mathematical foundation and preliminary experimental validation. In *CASES*, 2008.

[5] S. Chaudhuri, S. Gulwani, and R. Lublinerman. Continuity analysis of programs. In *POPL*, 2010.

[6] S. Chaudhuri, S. Gulwani, R. Lublinerman, and S. Navidpour. Proving Programs Robust. In *FSE*, 2011.

[7] S. Chaudhuri and A. Solar-Lezama. Smooth interpretation. In *PLDI*, 2010.

[8] S. Chaudhuri and A. Solar-Lezama. Smoothing a program soundly and robustly. In *CAV*, 2011.

[9] J. Flinn and M. Satyanarayanan. Energy-aware adaptation for mobile applications. In *SOSP*, 1999.

[10] R. Hameed, W. Qadeer, M. Wachs, O. Azizi, A. Solomatnikov, B. Lee, S. Richardson, C. Kozyrakis, and M. Horowitz. Understanding sources of inefficiency in general-purpose chips. In *ISCA*, 2010.

[11] J. Hellerstein, P. Haas, and H. Wang. Online aggregation. In *SIGMOD/PODS*, 1997.

[12] H. Hoffman, S. Sidiroglou, M. Carbin, S. Misailovic, A. Agarwal, and M. Rinard. Dynamic knobs for power-aware computing. In *ASPLOS*, 2011.

[13] H. Hoffmann, M. Maggio, M. D. Santambrogio, A. Leva, and A. Agarwal. Seec: A general and extensible framework for self-aware computing. Technical Report MIT-CSAIL-TR-2011-046, 2011.

[14] H. Hoffmann, S. Misailovic, S. Sidiroglou, A. Agarwal, and M. Rinard. Using Code Perforation to Improve Performance, Reduce Energy Consumption, and Respond to Failures . Technical Report MIT-CSAIL-TR-2009-042, 2009.

[15] W.-C. Hou, G. Ozsoyoglu, and B. K. Taneja. Processing aggregate relational queries with hard time constraints. SIGMOD, 1989.

[16] Y. Hu, S. Sundara, and J. Srinivasan. Supporting time-constrained SQL queries in Oracle. VLDB, 2007.

[17] S. Liu, K. Pattabiraman, T. Moscibroda, and B. Zorn. Flikker: Saving dram refresh-power through critical data partitioning. ASPLOS, 2011.

[18] R. Majumdar and I. Saha. Symbolic robustness analysis. In *RTSS '09*.

[19] R. Majumdar, I. Saha, and Z. Wang. Systematic testing for control applications. In *MEMOCODE*, 2010.

[20] J. Meng, S. Chakradhar, and A. Raghunathan. Best-Effort Parallel Execution Framework for Recognition and Mining Applications. In *IPDPS*, 2009.

[21] J. Meng, A. Raghunathan, and S. B. S. Chakradhar. Exploiting the Forgiving Nature of Applications for Scalable Parallel Execution. In *IPDPS*, 2010.

[22] S. Misailovic, D. Roy, and M. Rinard. Probabilistic and statistical analysis of perforated patterns. Technical Report MIT-CSAIL-TR-2011-003, January 2011.

[23] S. Misailovic, D. Roy, and M. Rinard. Probabilistically Accurate Program Transformations. In *SAS*, 2011.

[24] S. Misailovic, S. Sidiroglou, H. Hoffmann, and M. Rinard. Quality of service profiling. In *ICSE*, 2010.

[25] R. Motwani and P. Raghavan. *Randomized algorithms*. Cambridge University Press, 1995.

[26] J. Reed and B. C. Pierce. Distance makes the types grow stronger: a calculus for differential privacy. In *ICFP*, 2010.

[27] M. Rinard. Probabilistic accuracy bounds for fault-tolerant computations that discard tasks. In *ICS*, 2006.

[28] M. Rinard. Using early phase termination to eliminate load imbalances at barrier synchronization points. In *OOPSLA*, 2007.

[29] R. Rubinfeld. Sublinear time algorithms. In *Intl. Congress of Mathematicians*, 2006.

[30] A. Sampson, W. Dietl, E. Fortuna, D. Gnanapragasam, L. Ceze, and D. Grossman. EnerJ: approximate data types for safe and general low-power computation. In *PLDI*, 2011.

[31] S. Sidiroglou, S. Misailovic, H. Hoffmann, and M. Rinard. Managing Performance vs. Accuracy Tradeoffs With Loop Perforation. In *FSE, 2011*.

[32] K. Sohraby, D. Minoli, and T. Znati. *Wireless sensor networks: technology, protocols, and applications*. Wiley-Blackwell, 2007.

[33] J. Sorber, A. Kostadinov, M. Garber, M. Brennan, M. D. Corner, and E. D. Berger. Eon: a language and runtime system for perpetual systems. In *SenSys*, 2007.

[34] P. Stanley-Marbell and D. Marculescu. Deviation-Tolerant Computation in Concurrent Failure-Prone Hardware. Technical Report ESR-2008-01, Eindhoven University of Technology, 2008.

[35] D. Suciu, D. Olteanu, C. Ré, and C. Koch. *Probabilistic Databases*. Morgan-Claypool, 2011.

A Rely-Guarantee-Based Simulation for Verifying Concurrent Program Transformations

Hongjin Liang Xinyu Feng Ming Fu

School of Computer Science and Technology, University of Science and Technology of China
Hefei, Anhui 230026, China

lhj1018@mail.ustc.edu.cn xyfeng@ustc.edu.cn fuming@ustc.edu.cn

Abstract

Verifying program transformations usually requires proving that the resulting program (the target) refines or is equivalent to the original one (the source). However, the refinement relation between individual sequential threads cannot be preserved in general with the presence of parallel compositions, due to instruction reordering and the different granularities of atomic operations at the source and the target. On the other hand, the refinement relation defined based on fully abstract semantics of concurrent programs assumes arbitrary parallel environments, which is too strong and cannot be satisfied by many well-known transformations.

In this paper, we propose a Rely-Guarantee-based Simulation (RGSim) to verify concurrent program transformations. The relation is parametrized with constraints of the environments that the source and the target programs may compose with. It considers the interference between threads and their environments, thus is less permissive than relations over sequential programs. It is compositional *w.r.t.* parallel compositions as long as the constraints are satisfied. Also, RGSim does not require semantics preservation under all environments, and can incorporate the assumptions about environments made by specific program transformations in the form of rely/guarantee conditions. We use RGSim to reason about optimizations and prove atomicity of concurrent objects. We also propose a general garbage collector verification framework based on RGSim, and verify the Boehm *et al.* concurrent mark-sweep GC.

Categories and Subject Descriptors D.2.4 [*Software Engineering*]: Software/Program Verification – Correctness proofs, Formal methods; F.3.1 [*Logics and Meanings of Programs*]: Specifying and Verifying and Reasoning about Programs

General Terms Theory, Verification

Keywords Concurrency, Program Transformation, Rely-Guarantee Reasoning, Simulation

1. Introduction

Many verification problems can be reduced to verifying program transformations, *i.e.*, proving the target program of the transformation has no more observable behaviors than the source. Below we give some typical examples in concurrent settings:

POPL'12, January 25–27, 2012, Philadelphia, PA, USA.

- *Correctness of compilation and optimizations of concurrent programs.* In this most natural program transformation verification problem, every compilation phase does a program transformation $\mathbf{T}$, which needs to preserve the semantics of the inputs.
- *Atomicity of concurrent objects.* A concurrent object or library provides a set of methods that allow clients to manipulate the shared data structure with abstract atomic behaviors [15]. Their correctness can be reduced to the correctness of the transformation from abstract atomic operations to concrete and executable programs in a concurrent context.
- *Verifying implementations of software transactional memory (STM).* Many languages supporting STM provide a high-level atomic block **atomic**$\{\mathbb{C}\}$, so that programmers can assume the atomicity of the execution of $\mathbb{C}$. Atomic blocks are implemented using some STM protocol (*e.g.*, TL2 [11]) that allows very fine-grained interleavings. Verifying that the fine-grained program respects the semantics of atomic blocks gives us the correctness of the STM implementation.
- *Correctness of concurrent garbage collectors (GCs).* High-level garbage-collected languages (*e.g.*, Java) allow programmers to work at an abstract level without knowledge of the underlying GC algorithm. However, the concrete and executable low-level program involves interactions between the mutators and the collector. If we view the GC implementation as a transformation from high-level mutators to low-level ones with a concrete GC thread, the GC safety can be reduced naturally to the semantics preservation of the transformation.

To verify the correctness of a program transformation $\mathbf{T}$, we follow Leroy's approach [19] and define a refinement relation $\sqsubseteq$ between the target and the source programs, which says the target has no more observable behaviors than the source. Then we can formalize the correctness of the transformation as follows:

$$\mathsf{Correct}(\mathbf{T}) \triangleq \forall C, \mathbb{C}.\ C = \mathbf{T}(\mathbb{C}) \implies C \sqsubseteq \mathbb{C}\,. \tag{1.1}$$

That is, for any source program $\mathbb{C}$ acceptable by $\mathbf{T}$, $\mathbf{T}(\mathbb{C})$ is a refinement of $\mathbb{C}$. When the source and the target are shared-state concurrent programs, the refinement $\sqsubseteq$ needs to satisfy the following requirements to support effective proof of $\mathsf{Correct}(\mathbf{T})$:

- Since the target $\mathbf{T}(\mathbb{C})$ may be in a different language from the source, the refinement should be general and independent of the language details.
- To verify fine-grained implementations of abstract operations, the refinement should support different views of program states and different granularities of state accesses at the source and the target levels.
- When $\mathbf{T}$ is syntax-directed (and it is usually the case for parallel compositions, *i.e.*, $\mathbf{T}(\mathbb{C} \parallel \mathbb{C}') = \mathbf{T}(\mathbb{C}) \parallel \mathbf{T}(\mathbb{C}'))$, a *com-*

positional refinement is of particular importance for modular verification of **T**.

However, existing refinement (or equivalence) relations cannot satisfy all these requirements at the same time. Contextual equivalence, the canonical notion for comparing program behaviors, fails to handle different languages since the contexts of the source and the target will be different. Simulations and logical relations have been used to verify compilation [4, 16, 19, 21], but they are usually designed for sequential programs (except [21, 25], which we will discuss in Section 8). Since the refinement or equivalence relation between sequential threads cannot be preserved in general with parallel compositions, we cannot simply adapt existing work on sequential programs to verify transformations of concurrent programs. Refinement relations based on fully abstract semantics of concurrent programs are compositional, but they assume arbitrary program contexts, which is too strong for many practical transformations. We will explain the challenges in detail in Section 2.

In this paper, we propose a Rely-Guarantee-based Simulation (RGSim) for compositional verification of concurrent transformations. By addressing the above problems, we make the following contributions:

- RGSim parametrizes the simulation between concurrent programs with rely/guarantee conditions [17], which specify the interactions between the programs and their environments. This makes the corresponding refinement relation compositional *w.r.t.* parallel compositions, allowing us to decompose refinement proofs for multi-threaded programs into proofs for individual threads. On the other hand, the rely/guarantee conditions can incorporate the assumptions about environments made by specific program transformations, so RGSim can be applied to verify many practical transformations.
- Based on the simulation technique, RGSim focuses on comparing externally observable behaviors (*e.g.*, I/O events) only, which gives us considerable leeway in the implementations of related programs. The relation is mostly independent of the language details. It can be used to relate programs in different languages with different views of program states and different granularities of atomic state accesses.
- RGSim makes relational reasoning about optimizations possible in parallel contexts. We present a set of relational reasoning rules to characterize and justify common optimizations in a concurrent setting, including hoisting loop invariants, strength reduction and induction variable elimination, dead code elimination, redundancy introduction, *etc.*.
- RGSim gives us a refinement-based proof method to verify fine-grained implementations of abstract algorithms and concurrent objects. We successfully apply RGSim to verify concurrent counters, the concurrent GCD algorithm, Treiber's non-blocking stack and the lock-coupling list.
- We reduce the problem of verifying concurrent garbage collectors to verifying transformations, and present a general GC verification framework, which combines unary Rely-Guarantee-based verification [17] with relational proofs based on RGSim.
- We verify the Boehm *et al.* concurrent garbage collection algorithm [7] using our framework. As far as we know, it is the first time to formally prove the correctness of this algorithm.

In the rest of this paper, we first analyze the challenges for compositional verification of concurrent program transformations, and explain our approach informally in Section 2. Then we give the basic technical settings in Section 3 and present the formal definition of RGSim in Section 4. We show the use of RGSim to reason about optimizations in Section 5, verify atomicity of concurrent objects in Section 6, and prove the correctness of concurrent GCs in Section 7. Finally we discuss related work and conclude in Section 8.

```
local r1;                  local r2;
x  := 1;                   y  := 1;
r1 := y;               ||  r2 := x;
if (r1 = 0) then           if (r2 = 0) then
  critical region            critical region
```

(a) Dekker's Mutual Exclusion Algorithm

```
x := x+1; || x := x+1;
```

vs.

```
local r1;          local r2;
r1 := x;       ||  r2 := x;
x  := r1 + 1;      x  := r2 + 1;
```

(b) Different Granularities of Atomic Operations

Figure 1. Equivalence Lost after Parallel Composition

2. Challenges and Our Approach

The major challenge we face is to have a compositional refinement relation $\sqsubseteq$ between concurrent programs, *i.e.*, we should be able to know $\mathbf{T}(\mathbb{C}_1) \parallel \mathbf{T}(\mathbb{C}_2) \sqsubseteq \mathbb{C}_1 \parallel \mathbb{C}_2$ if we have $\mathbf{T}(\mathbb{C}_1) \sqsubseteq \mathbb{C}_1$ and $\mathbf{T}(\mathbb{C}_2) \sqsubseteq \mathbb{C}_2$.

2.1 Sequential Refinement Loses Parallel Compositionality

Observable behaviors of sequential imperative programs usually refer to their control effects (*e.g.*, termination and exceptions) and final program states. However, refinement relations defined correspondingly cannot be preserved after parallel compositions. It has been a well-known fact in the compiler community that sound optimizations for sequential programs may change the behaviors of multi-threaded programs [5]. The Dekker's algorithm shown in Figure 1(a) has been widely used to demonstrate the problem. Reordering the first two statements of the thread on the left preserves its sequential behaviors, but the whole program can no longer ensure exclusive access to the critical region.

In addition to instruction reordering, the different granularities of atomic operations between the source and the target programs can also break the compositionality of program equivalence in a concurrent setting. In Figure 1(b), the target program at the bottom behaves differently from the source at the top (assuming each statement is executed atomically), although the individual threads at the target and the source have the same behaviors.

2.2 Assuming Arbitrary Environments is Too Strong

The problem with the refinement for sequential programs is that it does not consider the effects of threads' intermediate state accesses on their parallel environments. People have given fully abstract semantics to concurrent programs (*e.g.*, [1, 8]). The semantics of a program is modeled as a set of execution traces. Each trace is an interleaving of state transitions made by the program itself and *arbitrary* transitions made by the environment. Then the refinement between programs can be defined as the subset relation between the corresponding trace sets. Since it considers all possible environments, the refinement relation has very nice compositionality, but unfortunately is too strong to formulate the correctness of many well-known transformations, including the four classes of transformations mentioned before:

- Many concurrent languages (*e.g.*, C++ [6]) do not give semantics to programs with data races (like the examples shown in Figure 1). Therefore the compilers only need to guarantee the semantics preservation of data-race-free programs.
- When we prove that a fine-grained implementation of a concurrent object is a refinement of an abstract atomic operation, we can assume that all accesses to the object in the context of the target program use the same set of primitives.
- Usually the implementation of STM (*e.g.*, TL2 [11]) ensures the atomicity of a transaction $\textbf{atomic}\{\mathbb{C}\}$ only when there are no data races. Therefore, the correctness of the transformation from high-level atomic blocks to fine-grained concurrent code assumes data-race-freedom in the source.
- Many garbage-collected languages are type-safe and prohibit operations such as pointer arithmetics. Therefore the garbage collector could make corresponding assumptions about the mutators that run in parallel.

In all these cases, the transformations of individual threads are allowed to make various assumptions about the environments. They do not have to ensure semantics preservation within all contexts.

2.3 Languages at Source and Target May Be Different

The use of different languages at the source and the target levels makes the formulation of the transformation correctness more difficult. If the source and the target languages have different views of program states and different atomic primitives, we cannot directly compare the state transitions made by the source and the target programs. This is another reason that makes the aforementioned subset relation between sets of program traces in fully abstract semantics infeasible. For the same reason, many existing techniques for proving refinement or equivalence of programs in the same language cannot be applied either.

2.4 Different Observers Make Different Observations

Concurrency introduces tensions between two kinds of observers: human beings (as external observers) and the parallel program contexts. External observers do not care about the implementation details of the source and the target programs. For them, intermediate state accesses (such as memory reads and writes) are silent steps (unobservable), and only external events (such as I/O operations) are observable. On the other hand, state accesses have effects on the parallel program contexts, and are not silent to them.

If the refinement relation relates externally observable event traces only, it cannot have parallel compositionality, as we explained in Section 2.1. On the other hand, relating all state accesses of programs is too strong. Any reordering of state accesses or change of atomicity would fail the refinement.

2.5 Our Approach

In this paper we propose a Rely-Guarantee-based Simulation (RGSim) $\preceq$ between the target and the source programs. It establishes a weak simulation, ensuring that for every externally observable event made by the target program there is a corresponding one in the source. We choose to view intermediate state accesses as silent steps, thus we can relate programs with different implementation details. This also makes our simulation independent of language details.

To support parallel compositionality, our relation takes into account explicitly the expected interference between threads and their parallel environments. Inspired by the Rely-Guarantee (R-G) verification method [17], we specify the interference using rely/guarantee conditions. In Rely-Guarantee reasoning, the rely condition R of a thread specifies the permitted state transitions that its environment may have, and its guarantee G specifies the possible transitions made by the thread itself. To ensure parallel threads can collaborate, we need to check the interference constraint, *i.e.*, the guarantee of each thread is permitted in the rely of every others. Then we can verify their parallel composition by separately verifying each thread, showing its behaviors under the rely condition indeed satisfy its guarantee. After parallel composition, the threads should be executed under their common environment (*i.e.*, the intersection of their relies) and guarantee all the possible transitions made by them (*i.e.*, the union of their guarantees).

Parametrized with rely/guarantee conditions for the two levels, our relation $(C, \mathcal{R}, \mathcal{G}) \preceq (\mathbb{C}, \mathbb{R}, \mathbb{G})$ talks about not only the target C and the source $\mathbb{C}$, but also the interference $\mathcal{R}$ and $\mathcal{G}$ between C and its target-level environment, and $\mathbb{R}$ and $\mathbb{G}$ between $\mathbb{C}$ and its environment at the source level. Informally, $(C, \mathcal{R}, \mathcal{G}) \preceq (\mathbb{C}, \mathbb{R}, \mathbb{G})$ says the executions of C under the environment $\mathcal{R}$ do not exhibit more observable behaviors than the executions of $\mathbb{C}$ under the environment $\mathbb{R}$, and the state transitions of C and $\mathbb{C}$ satisfy $\mathcal{G}$ and $\mathbb{G}$ respectively. RGSim is now compositional, as long as the threads are composed with well-behaved environments only. The parallel compositionality lemma is in the following form. If we know $(C_1, \mathcal{R}_1, \mathcal{G}_1) \preceq (\mathbb{C}_1, \mathbb{R}_1, \mathbb{G}_1)$ and $(C_2, \mathcal{R}_2, \mathcal{G}_2) \preceq (\mathbb{C}_2, \mathbb{R}_2, \mathbb{G}_2)$, and also the interference constraints are satisfied, *i.e.*, $\mathcal{G}_2 \subseteq \mathcal{R}_1$, $\mathcal{G}_1 \subseteq \mathcal{R}_2$, $\mathbb{G}_2 \subseteq \mathbb{R}_1$ and $\mathbb{G}_1 \subseteq \mathbb{R}_2$, we could get

$$(C_1 \,\|\, C_2, \mathcal{R}_1 \cap \mathcal{R}_2, \mathcal{G}_1 \cup \mathcal{G}_2) \preceq (\mathbb{C}_1 \,\|\, \mathbb{C}_2, \mathbb{R}_1 \cap \mathbb{R}_2, \mathbb{G}_1 \cup \mathbb{G}_2)\,.$$

The compositionality of RGSim gives us a proof theory for concurrent program transformations.

Also different from fully abstract semantics for threads, which assumes arbitrary behaviors of environments, RGSim allows us to instantiate the interference $\mathcal{R}$, $\mathcal{G}$, $\mathbb{R}$ and $\mathbb{G}$ differently for different assumptions about environments, therefore it can be used to verify the aforementioned four classes of transformations. For instance, if we want to prove that a transformation preserves the behaviors of data-race-free programs, we can specify the data-race-freedom in $\mathbb{R}$ and $\mathbb{G}$. Then we are no longer concerned with the examples in Figure 1, both of which have data races.

3. Basic Technical Settings

In this section, we present the source and the target programming languages. Then we define a basic refinement $\sqsubseteq$, which naturally says the target has no more externally observable event traces than the source. We use $\sqsubseteq$ as an intuitive formulation of the correctness of transformations.

3.1 The Languages

Following standard simulation techniques, we model the semantics of target and source programs as labeled transition systems. Before showing the languages, we first define events and labels in Figure 2(a). We leave the set of events unspecified here. It can be instantiated by program verifiers, depending on their interest (*e.g.*, input/output events). A label that will be associated with a state transition is either an event or τ, which means the corresponding transition does not generate any event (*i.e.*, a silent step).

The target language, which we also call the low-level language, is shown in Figure 2(b). We abstract away the forms of states, expressions and primitive instructions in the language. An arithmetic expression E is modeled as a function from states to integers lifted with an undefined value $\perp$. Boolean expressions are modeled similarly. An instruction is a partial function from states to sets of label and state pairs, describing the state transitions and the events it generates. We use $\mathcal{P}(\_)$ to denote the power set. Unsafe executions

$(Events)\quad e ::= \ldots \qquad (Labels)\quad o ::= e \mid \tau$

(a) Events and Transition Labels

$$
\begin{array}{llll}
(LState) & \sigma & ::= & \ldots \\
(LExpr) & E & \in & LState \rightarrow Int_\bot \\
(LBExp) & B & \in & LState \rightarrow \{\textbf{true}, \textbf{false}\}_\bot \\
(LInstr) & c & \in & LState \rightharpoonup \mathcal{P}((Labels \times LState) \cup \{\textbf{abort}\}) \\
(LStmt) & C & ::= & \textbf{skip} \mid c \mid C_1; C_2 \mid \textbf{if}\ (B)\ C_1\ \textbf{else}\ C_2 \\
& & \mid & \textbf{while}\ (B)\ C \mid C_1 \,\|\, C_2 \\
(LStep) & \longrightarrow_L & \in & \mathcal{P}((LStmt/\{\textbf{skip}\} \times LState) \times Labels \\
& & & \times ((LStmt \times LState) \cup \{\textbf{abort}\}))
\end{array}
$$

(b) The Low-Level Language

$$
\begin{array}{llll}
(HState) & \Sigma & ::= & \ldots \\
(HExpr) & \mathbb{E} & \in & HState \rightarrow Int_\bot \\
(HBExp) & \mathbb{B} & \in & HState \rightarrow \{\textbf{true}, \textbf{false}\}_\bot \\
(HInstr) & \mathrm{c} & \in & HState \rightharpoonup \mathcal{P}((Labels \times HState) \cup \{\textbf{abort}\}) \\
(HStmt) & \mathbb{C} & ::= & \textit{skip} \mid \mathrm{c} \mid \mathbb{C}_1;;\mathbb{C}_2 \mid \textit{if}\ \mathbb{B}\ \textit{then}\ \mathbb{C}_1\ \textit{else}\ \mathbb{C}_2 \\
& & \mid & \textit{while}\ \mathbb{B}\ \textit{do}\ \mathbb{C} \mid \mathbb{C}_1 |\!|\!| \mathbb{C}_2 \\
(HStep) & \longrightarrow_L & \in & \mathcal{P}((HStmt/\{\textit{skip}\} \times HState) \times Labels \\
& & & \times ((HStmt \times HState) \cup \{\textbf{abort}\}))
\end{array}
$$

(c) The High-Level Language

Figure 2. Generic Languages at Target and Source Levels

lead to **abort**. Note that the semantics of an instruction could be non-deterministic. Moreover, it might be undefined on some states, making it possible to model blocking operations such as acquiring a lock.

Statements are either primitive instructions or compositions of them. **skip** is a special statement used as a flag to show the end of executions. A single-step execution of statements is modeled as a labeled transition $\_ \overset{-}{\longrightarrow}_L \_$, which is a triple of an initial program configuration (a pair of statement and state), a label and a resulting configuration. It is undefined when the initial statement is **skip**. The step aborts if an unsafe instruction is executed.

The high-level language (source language) is defined similarly in Figure 2(c), but it is important to note that its states and primitive instructions may be different from those in the low-level language. The compound statements are almost the same as their low-level counterparts. $\mathbb{C}_1;;\mathbb{C}_2$ and $\mathbb{C}_1|\!|\!|\mathbb{C}_2$ are sequential and parallel compositions of $\mathbb{C}_1$ and $\mathbb{C}_2$ respectively. Note that we choose to use the same set of compound statements in the two languages for simplicity only. This is not required by our simulation relation, although the analogous program constructs of the two languages (*e.g.*, parallel compositions $C_1 \,\|\, C_2$ and $\mathbb{C}_1|\!|\!|\mathbb{C}_2$) make it convenient for us to discuss the compositionality later.

Figure 3 shows part of the definition of $\_ \overset{-}{\longrightarrow}_H \_$, which gives the high-level operational semantics of statements. We often omit the subscript H (or L) in $\_ \overset{-}{\longrightarrow}_H \_$ (or $\_ \overset{-}{\longrightarrow}_L \_$) and the label on top of the arrow when it is τ. The semantics is mostly standard. We only show the rules for primitive instructions and parallel compositions here. Note that when a primitive instruction c is blocked at state Σ (*i.e.*, $\Sigma \notin dom(\mathrm{c})$), we let the program configuration reduce to itself. For example, the instruction `lock(l)` would be blocked when `l` is not 0, making it be repeated until `l` becomes 0; whereas `unlock(l)` simply sets `l` to 0 at any time and would never be blocked. Primitive instructions in the high-level and low-level languages are *atomic* in the interleaving semantics. Below we use $\_ \longrightarrow^* \_$ for zero or multiple-step transitions with no events generated, and $\_ \overset{e}{\longrightarrow}{}^* \_$ for multiple-step transitions with *only one* event e generated.

3.2 The Event Trace Refinement

Now we can formally define the refinement relation $\sqsubseteq$ that relates the set of externally observable event traces generated by the target and the source programs. A trace is a sequence of events e, and may end with a termination marker **done** or a fault marker **abort**.

$$(EvtTrace)\quad \mathcal{E} \ ::= \ \epsilon \mid \textbf{done} \mid \textbf{abort} \mid e::\mathcal{E}$$

Definition 1 (Event Trace Set). $ETrSet_n(C,\sigma)$ represents a set of external event traces produced by C in n steps from the state σ:

- $ETrSet_0(C,\sigma) \triangleq \{\epsilon\}$;
- $ETrSet_{n+1}(C,\sigma) \triangleq$
  $\{\mathcal{E} \mid (C,\sigma) \longrightarrow (C',\sigma') \wedge \mathcal{E} \in ETrSet_n(C',\sigma')$
  $\vee (C,\sigma) \overset{e}{\longrightarrow} (C',\sigma') \wedge \mathcal{E}' \in ETrSet_n(C',\sigma') \wedge \mathcal{E} = e::\mathcal{E}'$
  $\vee (C,\sigma) \longrightarrow \textbf{abort} \wedge \mathcal{E} = \textbf{abort}$
  $\vee C = \textbf{skip} \wedge \mathcal{E} = \textbf{done}\}$.

We define $ETrSet(C,\sigma)$ as $\bigcup_n ETrSet_n(C,\sigma)$.

We overload the notation and use $ETrSet(\mathbb{C},\Sigma)$ for the high-level language. Then we define an event trace refinement as the subset relation between event trace sets, which is similar to Leroy's refinement property [19].

Definition 2 (Event Trace Refinement). We say (C,σ) is an *e-trace refinement* of $(\mathbb{C},\Sigma)$, *i.e.*, $(C,\sigma) \sqsubseteq (\mathbb{C},\Sigma)$, if and only if

$$ETrSet(C,\sigma) \subseteq ETrSet(\mathbb{C},\Sigma).$$

The refinement is defined for program configurations instead of for code only because the initial states may affect the behaviors of programs. In this case, the transformation $\mathbf{T}$ should translate states as well as code. We overload the notation and use $\mathbf{T}(\Sigma)$ to represent the state transformation, and use $C \sqsubseteq_{\mathbf{T}} \mathbb{C}$ for

$$\forall \sigma, \Sigma.\ \sigma = \mathbf{T}(\Sigma) \Longrightarrow (C,\sigma) \sqsubseteq (\mathbb{C},\Sigma),$$

then $\mathsf{Correct}(\mathbf{T})$ defined in formula (1.1) can be reformulated as

$$\mathsf{Correct}(\mathbf{T}) \triangleq \forall C, \mathbb{C}.\ C = \mathbf{T}(\mathbb{C}) \Longrightarrow C \sqsubseteq_{\mathbf{T}} \mathbb{C}. \qquad (3.1)$$

4. The RGSim Relation

The e-trace refinement is defined directly over the externally observable behaviors of programs. It is intuitive, and also abstract in that it is independent of language details. However, as we explained before, it is *not* compositional *w.r.t.* parallel compositions. In this section we propose RGSim, which can be viewed as a compositional proof technique that allows us to derive the simple e-trace refinement and then verify the corresponding transformation $\mathbf{T}$.

4.1 The Definition

Our co-inductively defined RGSim relation is in the form of $(C,\sigma,\mathcal{R},\mathcal{G}) \preceq_{\alpha;\gamma} (\mathbb{C},\Sigma,\mathbb{R},\mathbb{G})$, which is a simulation between program configurations (C,σ) and $(\mathbb{C},\Sigma)$. It is parametrized with the rely and guarantee conditions at the low level and the high level, which are binary relations over states:

$$\mathcal{R},\mathcal{G} \in \mathcal{P}(LState \times LState), \quad \mathbb{R},\mathbb{G} \in \mathcal{P}(HState \times HState).$$

The simulation also takes two additional parameters: the *step invariant* α and the *postcondition* γ, which are both relations between the low-level and the high-level states.

$$\alpha, \gamma, \zeta \in \mathcal{P}(LState \times HState).$$

$$\frac{(\tau, \Sigma') \in \mathrm{c}\,\Sigma}{(\mathrm{c}, \Sigma) \longrightarrow (\textbf{\textit{skip}}, \Sigma')} \qquad \frac{(e, \Sigma') \in \mathrm{c}\,\Sigma}{(\mathrm{c}, \Sigma) \stackrel{e}{\longrightarrow} (\textbf{\textit{skip}}, \Sigma')} \qquad \frac{\textbf{abort} \in \mathrm{c}\,\Sigma}{(\mathrm{c}, \Sigma) \longrightarrow \textbf{abort}} \qquad \frac{\Sigma \notin dom(\mathrm{c})}{(\mathrm{c}, \Sigma) \longrightarrow (\mathrm{c}, \Sigma)}$$

$$\frac{}{(\textbf{\textit{skip}} \,|||\, \textbf{\textit{skip}}, \Sigma) \longrightarrow (\textbf{\textit{skip}}, \Sigma)} \qquad \frac{(\mathbb{C}_1, \Sigma) \longrightarrow (\mathbb{C}_1', \Sigma')}{(\mathbb{C}_1 \,|||\, \mathbb{C}_2, \Sigma) \longrightarrow (\mathbb{C}_1' \,|||\, \mathbb{C}_2, \Sigma')} \qquad \frac{(\mathbb{C}_2, \Sigma) \longrightarrow (\mathbb{C}_2', \Sigma')}{(\mathbb{C}_1 \,|||\, \mathbb{C}_2, \Sigma) \longrightarrow (\mathbb{C}_1 \,|||\, \mathbb{C}_2', \Sigma')}$$

$$\frac{(\mathbb{C}_1, \Sigma) \stackrel{e}{\longrightarrow} (\mathbb{C}_1', \Sigma')}{(\mathbb{C}_1 \,|||\, \mathbb{C}_2, \Sigma) \stackrel{e}{\longrightarrow} (\mathbb{C}_1' \,|||\, \mathbb{C}_2, \Sigma')} \qquad \frac{(\mathbb{C}_2, \Sigma) \stackrel{e}{\longrightarrow} (\mathbb{C}_2', \Sigma')}{(\mathbb{C}_1 \,|||\, \mathbb{C}_2, \Sigma) \stackrel{e}{\longrightarrow} (\mathbb{C}_1 \,|||\, \mathbb{C}_2', \Sigma')} \qquad \frac{(\mathbb{C}_1, \Sigma) \longrightarrow \textbf{abort} \quad \text{or} \quad (\mathbb{C}_2, \Sigma) \longrightarrow \textbf{abort}}{(\mathbb{C}_1 \,|||\, \mathbb{C}_2, \Sigma) \longrightarrow \textbf{abort}}$$

Figure 3. Operational Semantics of the High-Level Language

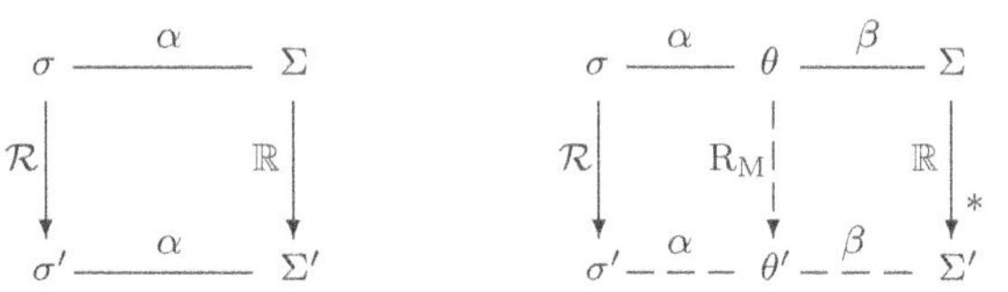

(a) α-Related Transitions (b) The Side Condition of TRANS

Figure 4. Related Transitions

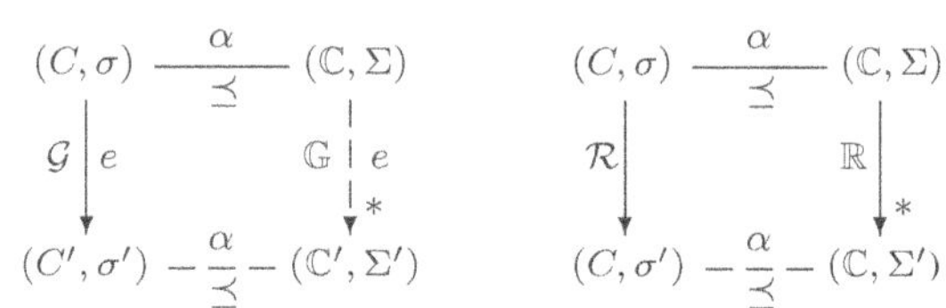

(a) Program Steps (b) Environment Steps

Figure 5. Simulation Diagrams of RGSim

Before we formally define RGSim in Definition 4, we first introduce the α-related transitions as follows.

Definition 3 (α-Related Transitions).

$$\langle \mathcal{R}, \mathbb{R} \rangle_\alpha \triangleq \{((\sigma, \sigma'), (\Sigma, \Sigma')) \mid (\sigma, \sigma') \in \mathcal{R} \wedge (\Sigma, \Sigma') \in \mathbb{R} \wedge (\sigma, \Sigma) \in \alpha \wedge (\sigma', \Sigma') \in \alpha\}.$$

$\langle \mathcal{R}, \mathbb{R} \rangle_\alpha$ represents a set of the α-related transitions in $\mathcal{R}$ and $\mathbb{R}$, putting together the corresponding transitions in $\mathcal{R}$ and $\mathbb{R}$ that can be related by α, as illustrated in Figure 4(a). $\langle \mathcal{G}, \mathbb{G} \rangle_\alpha$ is defined in the same way.

Definition 4 (RGSim). Whenever $(C, \sigma, \mathcal{R}, \mathcal{G}) \preceq_{\alpha;\gamma} (\mathbb{C}, \Sigma, \mathbb{R}, \mathbb{G})$, then $(\sigma, \Sigma) \in \alpha$ and the following are true:

1. if $(C, \sigma) \longrightarrow (C', \sigma')$, then there exist $\mathbb{C}'$ and Σ' such that $(\mathbb{C}, \Sigma) \longrightarrow^* (\mathbb{C}', \Sigma')$, $((\sigma, \sigma'), (\Sigma, \Sigma')) \in \langle \mathcal{G}, \mathbb{G}^* \rangle_\alpha$ and $(C', \sigma', \mathcal{R}, \mathcal{G}) \preceq_{\alpha;\gamma} (\mathbb{C}', \Sigma', \mathbb{R}, \mathbb{G})$;
2. if $(C, \sigma) \stackrel{e}{\longrightarrow} (C', \sigma')$, then there exist $\mathbb{C}'$ and Σ' such that $(\mathbb{C}, \Sigma) \stackrel{e}{\longrightarrow}{}^* (\mathbb{C}', \Sigma')$, $((\sigma, \sigma'), (\Sigma, \Sigma')) \in \langle \mathcal{G}, \mathbb{G}^* \rangle_\alpha$ and $(C', \sigma', \mathcal{R}, \mathcal{G}) \preceq_{\alpha;\gamma} (\mathbb{C}', \Sigma', \mathbb{R}, \mathbb{G})$;
3. if $C = \textbf{skip}$, then there exists Σ' such that $(\mathbb{C}, \Sigma) \longrightarrow^* (\textbf{\textit{skip}}, \Sigma')$, $((\sigma, \sigma), (\Sigma, \Sigma')) \in \langle \mathcal{G}, \mathbb{G}^* \rangle_\alpha$, $(\sigma, \Sigma') \in \gamma$ and $\gamma \subseteq \alpha$;
4. if $(C, \sigma) \longrightarrow \textbf{abort}$, then $(\mathbb{C}, \Sigma) \longrightarrow^* \textbf{abort}$;
5. if $((\sigma, \sigma'), (\Sigma, \Sigma')) \in \langle \mathcal{R}, \mathbb{R}^* \rangle_\alpha$, then $(C, \sigma', \mathcal{R}, \mathcal{G}) \preceq_{\alpha;\gamma} (\mathbb{C}, \Sigma', \mathbb{R}, \mathbb{G})$.

Then, $(C, \mathcal{R}, \mathcal{G}) \preceq_{\alpha;\zeta\ltimes\gamma} (\mathbb{C}, \mathbb{R}, \mathbb{G})$ iff for all σ and Σ, if $(\sigma, \Sigma) \in \zeta$, then $(C, \sigma, \mathcal{R}, \mathcal{G}) \preceq_{\alpha;\gamma} (\mathbb{C}, \Sigma, \mathbb{R}, \mathbb{G})$. Here the *precondition* ζ is used to relate the initial states σ and Σ.

Informally, $(C, \sigma, \mathcal{R}, \mathcal{G}) \preceq_{\alpha;\gamma} (\mathbb{C}, \Sigma, \mathbb{R}, \mathbb{G})$ says the low-level configuration (C, σ) is simulated by the high-level configuration $(\mathbb{C}, \Sigma)$ with behaviors $\mathcal{G}$ and $\mathbb{G}$ respectively, no matter how their environments $\mathcal{R}$ and $\mathbb{R}$ interfere with them. It requires the following hold for every execution of C:

- Starting from α-related states, each step of C corresponds to zero or multiple steps of $\mathbb{C}$, and the resulting states are α-related too. If an external event is produced in the step of C, the same event should be produced by $\mathbb{C}$. We show the simulation diagram with events generated by the program steps in Figure 5(a), where solid lines denote hypotheses and dashed lines denote conclusions, following Leroy's notations [19].
- The α relation reflects the abstractions from the low-level machine model to the high-level one, and is preserved by the related transitions at the two levels (so it is an *invariant*). For instance, when verifying a fine-grained implementation of sets, the α relation may relate a concrete representation in memory (*e.g.*, a linked-list) at the low level to the corresponding abstract mathematical set at the high level.
- The corresponding transitions of C and $\mathbb{C}$ need to be in $\langle \mathcal{G}, \mathbb{G}^* \rangle_\alpha$. That is, for each step of C, its state transition should satisfy the guarantee $\mathcal{G}$, and the corresponding transition made by the multiple steps of $\mathbb{C}$ should be in the transitive closure of $\mathbb{G}$. The guarantees are abstractions of the programs' behaviors. As we will show later in the PAR rule in Figure 7, they will serve as the rely conditions of the sibling threads at the time of parallel compositions. Note that we do not need each step of $\mathbb{C}$ to be in $\mathbb{G}$, although we could do so. This is because we only care about the coarse-grained behaviors (with mumbling) of the source that are used to simulate the target. We will explain more by the example (4.1) in Section 4.2.
- If C terminates, then $\mathbb{C}$ terminates as well, and the final states should be related by the postcondition γ. We require $\gamma \subseteq \alpha$, *i.e.*, the final state relation is not weaker than the step invariant.
- C is not safe only if $\mathbb{C}$ is not safe either. This means the transformation should not make a safe high-level program unsafe at the low level.
- Whatever the low-level environment $\mathcal{R}$ and the high-level one $\mathbb{R}$ do, as long as the state transitions are α-related, they should not affect the simulation between C and $\mathbb{C}$, as shown in Figure 5(b). Here a step in $\mathcal{R}$ may correspond to zero or multiple steps of $\mathbb{R}$. Note that different from the program steps, for the environment steps we do not require each step of $\mathcal{R}$ to correspond to zero or multiple steps of $\mathbb{R}$. On the other hand, only requiring that $\mathcal{R}$ be simulated by $\mathbb{R}$ is not sufficient for parallel compositionality, which we will explain later in Section 4.2.

$\mathsf{InitRel}_{\mathbf{T}}(\zeta) \triangleq \forall \sigma, \Sigma.\ \sigma = \mathbf{T}(\Sigma) \implies (\sigma, \Sigma) \in \zeta$

$B \Leftrightarrow \mathbb{B} \triangleq \{(\sigma, \Sigma) \mid B\,\sigma = \mathbb{B}\,\Sigma\} \qquad B \wedge\!\!\wedge \mathbb{B} \triangleq \{(\sigma, \Sigma) \mid B\,\sigma \wedge \mathbb{B}\,\Sigma\}$

$\mathsf{Intuit}(\alpha) \triangleq \forall \sigma, \Sigma, \sigma', \Sigma'.\ (\sigma, \Sigma) \in \alpha \wedge \sigma \subseteq \sigma' \wedge \Sigma \subseteq \Sigma' \implies (\sigma', \Sigma') \in \alpha$

$\eta \# \alpha \triangleq (\eta \cap \alpha) \subseteq (\eta \uplus \alpha)$

$\beta \circ \alpha \triangleq \{(\sigma, \Sigma) \mid \exists \theta.\ (\sigma, \theta) \in \alpha \wedge (\theta, \Sigma) \in \beta\}$

$\alpha \uplus \beta \triangleq \{(\sigma_1 \uplus \sigma_2, \Sigma_1 \uplus \Sigma_2) \mid (\sigma_1, \Sigma_1) \in \alpha \wedge (\sigma_2, \Sigma_2) \in \beta\}$

$\mathsf{Id} \triangleq \{(\sigma, \sigma) \mid \sigma \in \mathit{LState}\} \qquad \mathsf{True} \triangleq \{(\sigma, \sigma') \mid \sigma, \sigma' \in \mathit{LState}\}$

$\mathrm{R}_{\mathrm{M}}\ \mathsf{isMidOf}\ (\alpha, \beta; \mathcal{R}, \mathbb{R}) \triangleq \forall \sigma, \sigma', \Sigma, \Sigma'.\ ((\sigma, \sigma'), (\Sigma, \Sigma')) \in \langle \mathcal{R}, \mathbb{R} \rangle_{\beta \circ \alpha} \implies \forall \theta.\ (\sigma, \theta) \in \alpha \wedge (\theta, \Sigma) \in \beta \implies \exists \theta'.\ ((\sigma, \sigma'), (\theta, \theta')) \in \langle \mathcal{R}, \mathrm{R}_{\mathrm{M}} \rangle_\alpha \wedge ((\theta, \theta'), (\Sigma, \Sigma')) \in \langle \mathrm{R}_{\mathrm{M}}, \mathbb{R} \rangle_\beta$

Figure 6. Auxiliary Definitions for RGSim

Then based on the simulation, we hide the states by the precondition ζ and define the RGSim relation between programs only. By the definition we know $\zeta \subseteq \alpha$ if $(C, \mathcal{R}, \mathcal{G}) \preceq_{\alpha;\zeta \ltimes \gamma} (\mathbb{C}, \mathbb{R}, \mathbb{G})$, *i.e.*, the precondition needs to be no weaker than the step invariant.

RGSim is sound *w.r.t.* the e-trace refinement (Definition 2). That is, $(C, \sigma, \mathcal{R}, \mathcal{G}) \preceq_{\alpha;\gamma} (\mathbb{C}, \Sigma, \mathbb{R}, \mathbb{G})$ ensures that (C, σ) does not have more observable behaviors than $(\mathbb{C}, \Sigma)$.

Theorem 5 (Soundness). *If there exist $\mathcal{R}$, $\mathcal{G}$, $\mathbb{R}$, $\mathbb{G}$, α and γ such that $(C, \sigma, \mathcal{R}, \mathcal{G}) \preceq_{\alpha;\gamma} (\mathbb{C}, \Sigma, \mathbb{R}, \mathbb{G})$, then $(C, \sigma) \sqsubseteq (\mathbb{C}, \Sigma)$.*

The soundness theorem can be proved by first strengthening the relies to the identity transitions and weakening the guarantees to the universal relations. Then we prove that the resulting simulation under identity environments implies the e-trace refinement.

For program transformations, since the initial state for the target program is transformed from the initial state for the source, we use $\mathsf{InitRel}_{\mathbf{T}}(\zeta)$ (defined in Figure 6) to say the transformation $\mathbf{T}$ over states ensures the binary precondition ζ.

Corollary 6. *If there exist $\mathcal{R}$, $\mathcal{G}$, $\mathbb{R}$, $\mathbb{G}$, α, ζ and γ such that $\mathsf{InitRel}_{\mathbf{T}}(\zeta)$ and $(C, \mathcal{R}, \mathcal{G}) \preceq_{\alpha;\zeta \ltimes \gamma} (\mathbb{C}, \mathbb{R}, \mathbb{G})$, then $C \sqsubseteq_{\mathbf{T}} \mathbb{C}$.*

4.2 Compositionality Rules

RGSim is compositional *w.r.t.* various program constructs, including parallel compositions. We present the compositionality rules in Figure 7, which gives us a relational proof method for concurrent program transformations.

As in the R-G logic [17], we require that the pre- and post-conditions be *stable* under the interference from the environments. Here we introduce the concept of stability of a relation ζ *w.r.t.* a set of transition pairs $\Lambda \in \mathcal{P}((\mathit{LState} \times \mathit{LState}) \times (\mathit{HState} \times \mathit{HState}))$.

Definition 7 (Stability). $\mathsf{Sta}(\zeta, \Lambda)$ holds iff
for all σ, σ', Σ and Σ',
if $(\sigma, \Sigma) \in \zeta$ and $((\sigma, \sigma'), (\Sigma, \Sigma')) \in \Lambda$, then $(\sigma', \Sigma') \in \zeta$.

Usually we need $\mathsf{Sta}(\zeta, \langle \mathcal{R}, \mathbb{R}^* \rangle_\alpha)$, which says whenever ζ holds initially and $\mathcal{R}$ and $\mathbb{R}^*$ perform related actions, the resulting states still satisfy ζ. By unfolding $\langle \mathcal{R}, \mathbb{R}^* \rangle_\alpha$, we could see that α itself is stable *w.r.t.* any α-related transitions, *i.e.*, $\mathsf{Sta}(\alpha, \langle \mathcal{R}, \mathbb{R}^* \rangle_\alpha)$. Another simple example is given below, where both environments could increment $\mathtt{x}$ and the unary stable assertion $\{\mathtt{x} \geq 0\}$ is lifted to the relation ζ:

$$\zeta \triangleq \{(\sigma, \Sigma) \mid \sigma(\mathtt{x}) = \Sigma(\mathtt{x}) \geq 0\} \qquad \alpha \triangleq \{(\sigma, \Sigma) \mid \sigma(\mathtt{x}) = \Sigma(\mathtt{x})\}$$
$$\mathcal{R} \triangleq \{(\sigma, \sigma') \mid \sigma' = \sigma\{\mathtt{x} \rightsquigarrow \sigma(\mathtt{x}) + 1\}\}$$
$$\mathbb{R} \triangleq \{(\Sigma, \Sigma') \mid \Sigma' = \Sigma\{\mathtt{x} \rightsquigarrow \Sigma(\mathtt{x}) + 1\}\}$$

We can prove $\mathsf{Sta}(\zeta, \langle \mathcal{R}, \mathbb{R}^* \rangle_\alpha)$. Stability of the pre- and post-conditions under the environments' interference is assumed as an implicit side condition at every proof rule in Figure 7, *e.g.*, we assume $\mathsf{Sta}(\zeta, \langle \mathcal{R}, \mathbb{R}^* \rangle_\alpha)$ in the SKIP rule. We also require implicitly that the relies and guarantees are closed over identity transitions, since stuttering steps will not affect observable event traces.

In Figure 7, the rules SKIP, SEQ, IF and WHILE reveal a high degree of similarity to the corresponding inference rules in Hoare logic. In the SEQ rule, γ serves as the postcondition of C_1 and $\mathbb{C}_1$ and the precondition of C_2 and $\mathbb{C}_2$ at the same time. The IF rule requires the boolean conditions of both sides to be evaluated to the same value under the precondition ζ. We give the definitions of the sets $B \Leftrightarrow \mathbb{B}$ and $B \wedge\!\!\wedge \mathbb{B}$ in Figure 6. The rule also requires the precondition ζ to imply the step invariant α. In the WHILE rule, the γ relation is viewed as a loop invariant preserved at the loop entry point, and needs to ensure $B \Leftrightarrow \mathbb{B}$.

Parallel compositionality. The PAR rule shows parallel compositionality of RGSim. The interference constraints say that two threads can be composed in parallel if one thread's guarantee implies the rely of the other. After parallel composition, they are expected to run in the common environment and their guaranteed behaviors contain each single thread's behaviors.

Note that, although RGSim does not require every step of the high-level program to be in its guarantee (see the first two conditions in Definition 4), this relaxation does not affect the parallel compositionality. This is because the target could have less behaviors than the source. To let $\mathbb{C}_1 \| \mathbb{C}_2$ simulate $C_1 \| C_2$, we only need a subset of the interleavings of $\mathbb{C}_1$ and $\mathbb{C}_2$ to simulate those of C_1 and C_2. Thus the high-level relies and guarantees need to ensure the existence of those interleavings only. Below we give a simple example to explain this subtle issue. We can prove

$$(\mathtt{x:=x+2}, \mathcal{R}, \mathcal{G}) \preceq_{\alpha;\zeta \ltimes \gamma} (\mathtt{x:=x+1;x:=x+1}, \mathbb{R}, \mathbb{G}), \tag{4.1}$$

where the relies and the guarantees say $\mathtt{x}$ can be increased by 2 and α, ζ and γ relate $\mathtt{x}$ of the two sides:

$$\mathcal{R} = \mathcal{G} \triangleq \{(\sigma, \sigma') \mid \sigma' = \sigma \vee \sigma' = \sigma\{\mathtt{x} \rightsquigarrow \sigma(\mathtt{x}) + 2\}\};$$
$$\mathbb{R} = \mathbb{G} \triangleq \{(\Sigma, \Sigma') \mid \Sigma' = \Sigma \vee \Sigma' = \Sigma\{\mathtt{x} \rightsquigarrow \Sigma(\mathtt{x}) + 2\}\};$$
$$\alpha = \zeta = \gamma \triangleq \{(\sigma, \Sigma) \mid \sigma(\mathtt{x}) = \Sigma(\mathtt{x})\}.$$

Note that the high-level program is actually finer-grained than its guarantee, but to prove (4.1) we only need the execution in which it goes two steps to the end without interference from its environment. Also we can prove $(\mathtt{print(x)}, \mathcal{R}, \mathcal{G}) \preceq_{\alpha;\zeta \ltimes \gamma} (\mathtt{print(x)}, \mathbb{R}, \mathbb{G})$. Then by the PAR rule, we get

$$(\mathtt{x:=x+2} \| \mathtt{print(x)}, \mathcal{R}, \mathcal{G}) \preceq_{\alpha;\zeta \ltimes \gamma} ((\mathtt{x:=x+1;x:=x+1}) \| \mathtt{print(x)}, \mathbb{R}, \mathbb{G}),$$

which does not violate the natural meaning of refinements. That is, all the possible external events produced by the low-level side can also be produced by the high-level side, although the latter could have more external behaviors due to its finer granularity.

Another subtlety in the RGSim definition is with the fifth condition over the environments, which is crucial for parallel compositionality. One may think a more natural alternative to this condition is to require that $\mathcal{R}$ be simulated by $\mathbb{R}$:

$$\text{If } (\sigma, \sigma') \in \mathcal{R}, \text{then there exists } \Sigma' \text{ such that } (\Sigma, \Sigma') \in \mathbb{R}^* \text{ and } (C, \sigma', \mathcal{R}, \mathcal{G}) \preceq'_{\alpha;\zeta \ltimes \gamma} (\mathbb{C}, \Sigma', \mathbb{R}, \mathbb{G}). \tag{4.2}$$

We refer to this modified simulation definition as $\preceq'$. Unfortunately, $\preceq'$ does not have parallel compositionality. As a counter-example, if the invariant α says the left-side $\mathtt{x}$ is not greater than the right-side $\mathtt{x}$ and the precondition ζ requires $\mathtt{x}$ of the two sides are equal, *i.e.*,

$$\alpha \triangleq \{(\sigma, \Sigma) \mid \sigma(\mathtt{x}) \leq \Sigma(\mathtt{x})\} \qquad \zeta \triangleq \{(\sigma, \Sigma) \mid \sigma(\mathtt{x}) = \Sigma(\mathtt{x})\},$$

$$\frac{\zeta \subseteq \alpha}{(\textbf{skip}, \mathcal{R}, \mathsf{Id}) \preceq_{\alpha;\zeta\ltimes\zeta} (\textbf{\textit{skip}}, \mathbb{R}, \mathsf{Id})}\ (\text{SKIP}) \qquad \frac{(C_1, \mathcal{R}, \mathcal{G}) \preceq_{\alpha;\zeta\ltimes\gamma} (\mathbb{C}_1, \mathbb{R}, \mathbb{G}) \quad (C_2, \mathcal{R}, \mathcal{G}) \preceq_{\alpha;\gamma\ltimes\eta} (\mathbb{C}_2, \mathbb{R}, \mathbb{G})}{(C_1; C_2, \mathcal{R}, \mathcal{G}) \preceq_{\alpha;\zeta\ltimes\eta} (\mathbb{C}_1;; \mathbb{C}_2, \mathbb{R}, \mathbb{G})}\ (\text{SEQ})$$

$$\frac{\begin{array}{c}(C_1, \mathcal{R}, \mathcal{G}) \preceq_{\alpha;\zeta_1\ltimes\gamma} (\mathbb{C}_1, \mathbb{R}, \mathbb{G}) \quad (C_2, \mathcal{R}, \mathcal{G}) \preceq_{\alpha;\zeta_2\ltimes\gamma} (\mathbb{C}_2, \mathbb{R}, \mathbb{G}) \\ \zeta \subseteq (B \Leftrightarrow \mathbb{B}) \quad \zeta_1 = (\zeta \cap (B \wedge\!\!\wedge \mathbb{B})) \quad \zeta_2 = (\zeta \cap (\neg B \wedge\!\!\wedge \neg\mathbb{B})) \quad \zeta \subseteq \alpha\end{array}}{(\textbf{if}\ (B)\ C_1\ \textbf{else}\ C_2, \mathcal{R}, \mathcal{G}) \preceq_{\alpha;\zeta\ltimes\gamma} (\textbf{\textit{if}}\ \mathbb{B}\ \textbf{\textit{then}}\ \mathbb{C}_1\ \textbf{\textit{else}}\ \mathbb{C}_2, \mathbb{R}, \mathbb{G})}\ (\text{IF})$$

$$\frac{(C, \mathcal{R}, \mathcal{G}) \preceq_{\alpha;\gamma_1\ltimes\gamma} (\mathbb{C}, \mathbb{R}, \mathbb{G}) \quad \gamma \subseteq (B \Leftrightarrow \mathbb{B}) \quad \gamma_1 = (\gamma \cap (B \wedge\!\!\wedge \mathbb{B})) \quad \gamma_2 = (\gamma \cap (\neg B \wedge\!\!\wedge \neg\mathbb{B}))}{(\textbf{while}\ (B)\ C, \mathcal{R}, \mathcal{G}) \preceq_{\alpha;\gamma\ltimes\gamma_2} (\textbf{\textit{while}}\ \mathbb{B}\ \textbf{\textit{do}}\ \mathbb{C}, \mathbb{R}, \mathbb{G})}\ (\text{WHILE})$$

$$\frac{\begin{array}{c}(C_1, \mathcal{R}_1, \mathcal{G}_1) \preceq_{\alpha;\zeta\ltimes\gamma_1} (\mathbb{C}_1, \mathbb{R}_1, \mathbb{G}_1) \quad (C_2, \mathcal{R}_2, \mathcal{G}_2) \preceq_{\alpha;\zeta\ltimes\gamma_2} (\mathbb{C}_2, \mathbb{R}_2, \mathbb{G}_2) \\ \mathcal{G}_1 \subseteq \mathcal{R}_2 \quad \mathcal{G}_2 \subseteq \mathcal{R}_1 \quad \mathbb{G}_1 \subseteq \mathbb{R}_2 \quad \mathbb{G}_2 \subseteq \mathbb{R}_1\end{array}}{(C_1 \,\|\, C_2, \mathcal{R}_1 \cap \mathcal{R}_2, \mathcal{G}_1 \cup \mathcal{G}_2) \preceq_{\alpha;\zeta\ltimes(\gamma_1\cap\gamma_2)} (\mathbb{C}_1 \,|||\, \mathbb{C}_2, \mathbb{R}_1 \cap \mathbb{R}_2, \mathbb{G}_1 \cup \mathbb{G}_2)}\ (\text{PAR})$$

$$\frac{\begin{array}{c}(C, \mathcal{R}, \mathcal{G}) \preceq_{\alpha;\zeta\ltimes\gamma} (\mathbb{C}, \mathbb{R}, \mathbb{G}) \\ (\zeta \cup \gamma) \subseteq \alpha' \subseteq \alpha \quad \mathsf{Sta}(\alpha', \langle \mathcal{G}, \mathbb{G}^* \rangle_\alpha)\end{array}}{(C, \mathcal{R}, \mathcal{G}) \preceq_{\alpha';\zeta\ltimes\gamma} (\mathbb{C}, \mathbb{R}, \mathbb{G})}\ (\text{STREN-}\alpha) \qquad \frac{\begin{array}{c}(C, \mathcal{R}, \mathcal{G}) \preceq_{\alpha;\zeta\ltimes\gamma} (\mathbb{C}, \mathbb{R}, \mathbb{G}) \\ \alpha \subseteq \alpha' \quad \mathsf{Sta}(\alpha, \langle \mathcal{R}, \mathbb{R}^* \rangle_{\alpha'})\end{array}}{(C, \mathcal{R}, \mathcal{G}) \preceq_{\alpha';\zeta\ltimes\gamma} (\mathbb{C}, \mathbb{R}, \mathbb{G})}\ (\text{WEAKEN-}\alpha)$$

$$\frac{(C, \mathcal{R}, \mathcal{G}) \preceq_{\alpha;\zeta\ltimes\gamma} (\mathbb{C}, \mathbb{R}, \mathbb{G}) \quad \zeta' \subseteq \zeta \quad \gamma \subseteq \gamma' \subseteq \alpha \quad \mathcal{R}' \subseteq \mathcal{R} \quad \mathbb{R}' \subseteq \mathbb{R} \quad \mathcal{G} \subseteq \mathcal{G}' \quad \mathbb{G} \subseteq \mathbb{G}'}{(C, \mathcal{R}', \mathcal{G}') \preceq_{\alpha;\zeta'\ltimes\gamma'} (\mathbb{C}, \mathbb{R}', \mathbb{G}')}\ (\text{CONSEQ})$$

$$\frac{\begin{array}{c}(C, \mathcal{R}, \mathcal{G}) \preceq_{\alpha;\zeta\ltimes\gamma} (\mathbb{C}, \mathbb{R}, \mathbb{G}) \\ \eta \subseteq \beta \quad \mathsf{Intuit}(\{\alpha, \zeta, \gamma, \beta, \eta, \mathcal{R}, \mathbb{R}, \mathcal{R}_1, \mathbb{R}_1\}) \\ \eta \# \{\zeta, \gamma, \alpha\} \quad \mathsf{Sta}(\eta, \{\langle \mathcal{G}, \mathbb{G}^* \rangle_\alpha, \langle \mathcal{R}_1, \mathbb{R}_1^* \rangle_\beta\})\end{array}}{(C, \mathcal{R} \uplus \mathcal{R}_1, \mathcal{G} \uplus \mathcal{G}_1) \preceq_{\alpha\uplus\beta;(\zeta\uplus\eta)\ltimes(\gamma\uplus\eta)} (\mathbb{C}, \mathbb{R} \uplus \mathbb{R}_1, \mathbb{G} \uplus \mathbb{G}_1)}\ (\text{FRAME}) \qquad \frac{\begin{array}{c}(C, \mathcal{R}, \mathcal{G}) \preceq_{\alpha;\zeta\ltimes\gamma} (M, \mathrm{R_M}, \mathrm{G_M}) \\ (M, \mathrm{R_M}, \mathrm{G_M}) \preceq_{\beta;\delta\ltimes\eta} (\mathbb{C}, \mathbb{R}, \mathbb{G}) \\ \mathrm{R_M}\ \mathsf{isMidOf}\ (\alpha, \beta; \mathcal{R}, \mathbb{R}^*)\end{array}}{(C, \mathcal{R}, \mathcal{G}) \preceq_{\beta\circ\alpha;(\delta\circ\zeta)\ltimes(\eta\circ\gamma)} (\mathbb{C}, \mathbb{R}, \mathbb{G})}\ (\text{TRANS})$$

Figure 7. Compositionality Rules for RGSim

we could prove the following:

$$(\texttt{x:=x+1}, \mathsf{Id}, \mathsf{True}) \preceq'_{\alpha;\zeta\ltimes\alpha} (\texttt{x:=x+2}, \mathsf{Id}, \mathsf{True})\,;$$
$$(\texttt{print(x)}, \mathsf{True}, \mathsf{Id}) \preceq'_{\alpha;\zeta\ltimes\alpha} (\texttt{print(x)}, \mathsf{True}, \mathsf{Id})\,.$$

Here we use Id and True (defined in Figure 6) for the sets of identity transitions and arbitrary transitions respectively, and overload the notations at the low level to the high level. However, the following refinement does *not* hold after parallel composition:

$$(\texttt{x:=x+1} \,\|\, \texttt{print(x)}, \mathsf{Id}, \mathsf{True}) \preceq'_{\alpha;\zeta\ltimes\alpha}$$
$$(\texttt{x:=x+2} \,|||\, \texttt{print(x)}, \mathsf{Id}, \mathsf{True})\,.$$

This is because the rely $\mathcal{R}$ (or $\mathbb{R}$) is an abstraction of all the permitted behaviors in the environment of a thread. But a concrete sibling thread that runs in parallel may produce less transitions than $\mathcal{R}$ (or $\mathbb{R}$). To obtain parallel compositionality, we need to ensure that the simulation holds for all concrete sibling threads. With *our* definition $\preceq$, the refinement $(\texttt{print(x)}, \mathsf{True}, \mathsf{Id}) \preceq_{\alpha;\zeta\ltimes\alpha} (\texttt{print(x)}, \mathsf{True}, \mathsf{Id})$ is not provable because, after the environments' α-related transitions, the target may print a value smaller than the one printed by the source.

Other rules. We also develop some other useful rules about RGSim. For example, the STREN-α rule allows us to replace the invariant α by a stronger invariant α'. We need to check that α' is indeed an invariant preserved by the related program steps, *i.e.*, $\mathsf{Sta}(\alpha', \langle \mathcal{G}, \mathbb{G}^* \rangle_\alpha)$ holds. Symmetrically, the WEAKEN-α rule requires α to be preserved by environment steps related by the weaker invariant α'. As usual, the pre/post conditions, the relies and the guarantees can be strengthened or weakened by the CONSEQ rule.

The FRAME rule allows us to use local specifications. When verifying the simulation between C and $\mathbb{C}$, we need to only talk about the locally-used resource in α, ζ and γ, and the local relies and guarantees $\mathcal{R}$, $\mathcal{G}$, $\mathbb{R}$ and $\mathbb{G}$. Then the proof can be reused in contexts where some extra resource η is used, and the accesses of it respect the invariant β and $\mathcal{R}_1$, $\mathcal{G}_1$, $\mathbb{R}_1$ and $\mathbb{G}_1$. We give the auxiliary definitions in Figure 6. The disjoint union $\uplus$ between states is lifted to state pairs. An intuitionistic state relation is monotone *w.r.t.* the extension of states. The disjointness $\eta \# \alpha$ says that any state pair satisfying both η and α can be split into two disjoint state pairs satisfying η and α respectively. For example, let $\eta \triangleq \{(\sigma, \Sigma) \mid \sigma(\mathtt{y}) = \Sigma(\mathtt{y})\}$ and $\alpha \triangleq \{(\sigma, \Sigma) \mid \sigma(\mathtt{x}) = \Sigma(\mathtt{x})\}$, then both η and α are intuitionistic and $\eta \# \alpha$ holds. We also require η to be stable under interference from the programs (*i.e.*, the programs do not change the extra resource) and the extra environments. We use $\eta \# \{\zeta, \gamma, \alpha\}$ as a shorthand for $(\eta \# \zeta) \wedge (\eta \# \gamma) \wedge (\eta \# \alpha)$. Similar representations are used in this rule.

Finally, the transitivity rule TRANS allows us to verify a transformation by using an intermediate level as a bridge. The intermediate environment $\mathrm{R_M}$ should be chosen with caution so that the $(\beta \circ \alpha)$-related transitions can be decomposed into β-related and α-related transitions, as illustrated in Figure 4(b). Here $\circ$ defines the composition of two relations and $\mathsf{isMidOf}$ defines the side condition over the environments, as shown in Figure 6. We use θ for a middle-level state.

Soundness of all the rules in Figure 7 is proved in the technical report [20], showing that for each rule the premises imply the conclusion. The proofs are also mechanized in the Coq proof assistant [10].

Instantiations of relies and guarantees. We can derive the sequential refinement and the fully-abstract-semantics-based refinement by instantiating the rely conditions in RGSim. For example, the refinement (4.3) over closed programs assumes identity environments, making the interference constraints in the PAR rule unsatisfiable. This confirms the observation in Section 2.1 that the sequential refinement loses parallel compositionality.

$$(C, \mathsf{Id}, \mathsf{True}) \preceq_{\alpha;\zeta\ltimes\gamma} (\mathbb{C}, \mathsf{Id}, \mathsf{True}) \tag{4.3}$$

The refinement (4.4) assumes arbitrary environments, which makes the interference constraints in the PAR rule trivially true. But this assumption is too strong: usually (4.4) cannot be satisfied in practice.

$$(C, \mathsf{True}, \mathsf{True}) \preceq_{\alpha;\zeta\ltimes\gamma} (\mathbb{C}, \mathsf{True}, \mathsf{True}) \qquad (4.4)$$

4.3 A Simple Example

Below we give a simple example to illustrate the use of RGSim and its parallel compositionality in verifying concurrent program transformations. The high-level program $\mathbb{C}_1 \,|||\, \mathbb{C}_2$ is transformed to $C_1 \parallel C_2$, using a lock `l` to synchronize the accesses of the shared variable `x`. We aim to prove $C_1 \parallel C_2 \sqsubseteq_{\mathbf{T}} \mathbb{C}_1 |||\mathbb{C}_2$. That is, although `x:=x+2` is implemented by two steps of incrementing `x` in C_2, the parallel observer C_1 will not print unexpected values. Here we view output events as externally observable behaviors.

```
print(x);    |||  x := x + 2;

                ⇓
lock(l);          lock(l);
print(x);    ||   x := x+1; x := x+1;
unlock(l);        ⟨unlock(l); X := x; ⟩
```

To facilitate the proof, we introduce an auxiliary shared variable `X` at the low level to record the value of `x` at the time when releasing the lock. It specifies the value of `x` outside every critical section, thus should match the value of the high-level `x` after every corresponding action. Here $\langle C \rangle$ means C is executed atomically.

By the soundness and compositionality of RGSim, we only need to prove simulations over individual threads, providing appropriate relies and guarantees. We first define the invariant α, which only cares about the value of `x` when the lock is free.

$$\alpha \;\triangleq\; \{(\sigma, \Sigma) \mid \sigma(\mathtt{X}) = \Sigma(\mathtt{x}) \wedge (\sigma(\mathtt{l}){=}0 \Longrightarrow \sigma(\mathtt{x}) = \sigma(\mathtt{X}))\}\,.$$

We let the pre- and post-conditions be α as well.

The high-level threads can be executed in arbitrary environments with arbitrary guarantees: $\mathbb{R} = \mathbb{G} \triangleq \mathsf{True}$. The transformation uses the lock to protect every access of `x`, thus the low-level relies and guarantees are not arbitrary:

$$\begin{aligned}\mathcal{R} \triangleq\ & \{(\sigma, \sigma') \mid \sigma(\mathtt{l}){=}\mathtt{cid} \Longrightarrow \\ & \qquad \sigma(\mathtt{x}){=}\sigma'(\mathtt{x}) \wedge \sigma(\mathtt{X}){=}\sigma'(\mathtt{X}) \wedge \sigma(\mathtt{l}){=}\sigma'(\mathtt{l})\}\,; \\ \mathcal{G} \triangleq\ & \{(\sigma, \sigma') \mid \sigma'{=}\sigma \;\vee\; \sigma(\mathtt{l}){=}0 \wedge \sigma'{=}\sigma\{\mathtt{l} \leadsto \mathtt{cid}\} \\ & \quad \vee\, \sigma(\mathtt{l}){=}\mathtt{cid} \wedge \sigma'{=}\sigma\{\mathtt{x} \leadsto \_\} \\ & \quad \vee\, \sigma(\mathtt{l}){=}\mathtt{cid} \wedge \sigma'{=}\sigma\{\mathtt{l} \leadsto 0, \mathtt{X} \leadsto \_\}\}\,.\end{aligned}$$

Every low-level thread guarantees that it updates `x` only when the lock is acquired. Its environment cannot update `x` or `l` if the current thread holds the lock. Here `cid` is the identifier of the current thread. When acquired, the lock holds the id of the owner thread.

Following the definition, we can prove $(C_1, \mathcal{R}, \mathcal{G}) \preceq_{\alpha;\alpha\ltimes\alpha} (\mathbb{C}_1, \mathbb{R}, \mathbb{G})$ and $(C_2, \mathcal{R}, \mathcal{G}) \preceq_{\alpha;\alpha\ltimes\alpha} (\mathbb{C}_2, \mathbb{R}, \mathbb{G})$. By applying the PAR rule and from the soundness of RGSim (Corollary 6), we know $C_1 \parallel C_2 \sqsubseteq_{\mathbf{T}} \mathbb{C}_1 |||\mathbb{C}_2$ holds for any $\mathbf{T}$ that respects α.

Perhaps interestingly, if we omit the lock and unlock operations in C_1, then $C_1 \parallel C_2$ would have more externally observable behaviors than $\mathbb{C}_1 \,|||\, \mathbb{C}_2$. This does *not* indicate the unsoundness of our PAR rule (which is sound!). The reason is that `x` might have different values on the two levels after the environments' α-related transitions, so that we cannot have $(\mathtt{print(x)}, \mathcal{R}, \mathcal{G}) \preceq_{\alpha;\alpha\ltimes\alpha} (\mathtt{print(x)}, \mathbb{R}, \mathbb{G})$ with the current definitions of α, $\mathcal{R}$ and $\mathcal{G}$, even though the code of the two sides are syntactically identical.

More discussions. RGSim ensures that the target program preserves safety properties (including the partial correctness) of the source, but allows a terminating source program to be transformed to a target having infinite silent steps. In the above example, this allows the low-level programs to be blocked forever (*e.g.*, at the time when the lock is held but never released by some other thread). Proving the preservation of the termination behavior would require liveness proofs in a concurrent setting (*e.g.*, proving the absence of deadlock), which we leave as future work.

In the next three sections, we show more serious examples to demonstrate the applicability of RGSim.

5. Relational Reasoning about Optimizations

As a general correctness notion of concurrent program transformations, RGSim establishes a relational approach to justify compiler optimizations on concurrent programs. Below we adapt Benton's work [3] on sequential optimizations to the concurrent setting.

5.1 Optimization Rules

Usually optimizations depend on particular contexts, *e.g.*, the assignment $x := E$ can be eliminated only in the context that the value of x is never used after the assignment. In a shared-state concurrent setting, we should also consider the parallel context for an optimization. RGSim enables us to specify various sophisticated requirements for the parallel contexts by rely/guarantee conditions. Based on RGSim, we provide a set of inference rules to characterize and justify common optimizations (*e.g.*, dead code elimination) with information of both the sequential and the parallel contexts. Due to the space limit, we only present some interesting rules here and leave other rules in the technical report [20]. Note in this section the target and the source programs are in the same language.

Sequential* skip *Law

$$\frac{(C_1, \mathcal{R}_1, \mathcal{G}_1) \preceq_{\alpha;\zeta\ltimes\gamma} (C_2, \mathcal{R}_2, \mathcal{G}_2)}{(\mathbf{skip}; C_1, \mathcal{R}_1, \mathcal{G}_1) \preceq_{\alpha;\zeta\ltimes\gamma} (C_2, \mathcal{R}_2, \mathcal{G}_2)}$$

$$\frac{(C_1, \mathcal{R}_1, \mathcal{G}_1) \preceq_{\alpha;\zeta\ltimes\gamma} (C_2, \mathcal{R}_2, \mathcal{G}_2)}{(C_1, \mathcal{R}_1, \mathcal{G}_1) \preceq_{\alpha;\zeta\ltimes\gamma} (\mathbf{skip}; C_2, \mathcal{R}_2, \mathcal{G}_2)}$$

Plus the variants with **skip** after the code C_1 or C_2. That is, **skips** could be arbitrarily introduced and eliminated.

Common Branch

$$\frac{\begin{array}{c}\forall \sigma_1, \sigma_2.\, (\sigma_1, \sigma_2) \in \zeta \Longrightarrow B\,\sigma_2 \neq \bot \\ (C, \mathcal{R}, \mathcal{G}) \preceq_{\alpha;\zeta_1\ltimes\gamma} (C_1, \mathcal{R}', \mathcal{G}') \qquad \zeta_1 = (\zeta \cap (\mathbf{true} \mathbin{\underline{\wedge}} B)) \\ (C, \mathcal{R}, \mathcal{G}) \preceq_{\alpha;\zeta_2\ltimes\gamma} (C_2, \mathcal{R}', \mathcal{G}') \qquad \zeta_2 = (\zeta \cap (\mathbf{true} \mathbin{\underline{\wedge}} \neg B))\end{array}}{(C, \mathcal{R}, \mathcal{G}) \preceq_{\alpha;\zeta\ltimes\gamma} (\mathbf{if}\,(B)\; C_1 \;\mathbf{else}\; C_2, \mathcal{R}', \mathcal{G}')}$$

This rule says that, when the if-condition can be evaluated and both branches can be optimized to the same code C, we can transform the whole if-statement to C without introducing new behaviors.

Dead While

$$\frac{\zeta = (\zeta \cap (\mathbf{true} \mathbin{\underline{\wedge}} \neg B)) \qquad \zeta \subseteq \alpha \qquad \mathsf{Sta}(\zeta, \langle \mathcal{R}_1, \mathcal{R}_2^* \rangle_\alpha)}{(\mathbf{skip}, \mathcal{R}_1, \mathsf{Id}) \preceq_{\alpha;\zeta\ltimes\zeta} (\mathbf{while}\,(B)\{C\}, \mathcal{R}_2, \mathsf{Id})}$$

We can eliminate the loop, if the loop condition is **false** (no matter how the environments update the states) at the loop entry point.

Dead Code Elimination

$$\frac{(\mathbf{skip}, \mathsf{Id}, \mathsf{Id}) \preceq_{\alpha;\zeta\ltimes\gamma} (C, \mathsf{Id}, \mathcal{G}) \qquad \mathsf{Sta}(\{\zeta, \gamma\}, \langle \mathcal{R}_1, \mathcal{R}_2^* \rangle_\alpha)}{(\mathbf{skip}, \mathcal{R}_1, \mathsf{Id}) \preceq_{\alpha;\zeta\ltimes\gamma} (C, \mathcal{R}_2, \mathcal{G})}$$

Intuitively $(\mathbf{skip}, \mathsf{Id}, \mathsf{Id}) \preceq_{\alpha;\zeta\ltimes\gamma} (C, \mathsf{Id}, \mathcal{G})$ says that the code C can be eliminated in a sequential context where the initial and the final states satisfy ζ and γ respectively. If both ζ and γ are stable *w.r.t.* the interference from the environments $\mathcal{R}_1$ and $\mathcal{R}_2$, then the code C can be eliminated in such a parallel context as well.

Redundancy Introduction

$$\frac{(c, \mathsf{Id}, \mathcal{G}) \preceq_{\alpha;\zeta\ltimes\gamma} (\textbf{skip}, \mathsf{Id}, \mathsf{Id}) \qquad \mathsf{Sta}(\{\zeta,\gamma\}, \langle \mathcal{R}_1, \mathcal{R}_2^* \rangle_\alpha)}{(c, \mathcal{R}_1, \mathcal{G}) \preceq_{\alpha;\zeta\ltimes\gamma} (\textbf{skip}, \mathcal{R}_2, \mathsf{Id})}$$

As we lifted sequential dead code elimination, we can also lift sequential redundant code introduction to the concurrent setting, so long as the pre- and post-conditions are stable *w.r.t.* the environments. Note that here c is a single instruction, because we should consider the interference from the environments at every intermediate state when introducing a sequence of redundant instructions.

5.2 An Example of Invariant Hoisting

With these rules, we can prove the correctness of many traditional compiler optimizations performed on concurrent programs in appropriate contexts. Here we only give a small example of hoisting loop invariants. More examples (*e.g.*, strength reduction and induction variable elimination) can be found in the technical report [20].

Target Code (C_1)		Source Code (C)

`local t;`
`t := x + 1;`
`while(i < n) {`
`  i := i + t;`
`}`
	$\Leftarrow$	`local t;`
		`while(i < n) {`
		`  t := x + 1;`
		`  i := i + t;`
		`}`

When we do not care about the final value of `t`, it's not difficult to prove that the optimized code C_1 preserves the sequential behaviors of the source C [3]. But in a concurrent setting, safely hoisting the invariant code `t:=x+1` also requires that the environment should not update `x` nor `t`.

$$\mathcal{R} \triangleq \{(\sigma, \sigma') \mid \sigma(\mathtt{x}) = \sigma'(\mathtt{x}) \wedge \sigma(\mathtt{t}) = \sigma'(\mathtt{t})\}\,.$$

The guarantee of the program can be specified as arbitrary transitions. Since we only care about the values of `i`, `n` and `x`, the invariant relation α can be defined as:

$$\alpha \triangleq \{(\sigma_1, \sigma) \mid \sigma_1(\mathtt{i}) = \sigma(\mathtt{i}) \wedge \sigma_1(\mathtt{n}) = \sigma(\mathtt{n}) \wedge \sigma_1(\mathtt{x}) = \sigma(\mathtt{x})\}\,.$$

We do not need special pre- and post-conditions, thus the correctness of the optimization is formalized as follows:

$$(C_1, \mathcal{R}, \mathsf{True}) \preceq_{\alpha;\alpha\ltimes\alpha} (C, \mathcal{R}, \mathsf{True})\,. \tag{5.1}$$

We could prove (5.1) directly by the RGSim definition and the operational semantics of the code. But below we give a more convenient proof using the optimization rules and the compositionality rules instead. We first prove the following by the Dead-Code-Elimination and Redundancy-Introduction rules:

$$(\mathtt{t:=x+1}, \mathcal{R}, \mathsf{True}) \preceq_{\alpha;\alpha\ltimes\gamma} (\textbf{skip}, \mathcal{R}, \mathsf{True})\,;$$
$$(\textbf{skip}, \mathcal{R}, \mathsf{True}) \preceq_{\alpha;\gamma\ltimes\eta} (\mathtt{t:=x+1}, \mathcal{R}, \mathsf{True})\,,$$

where γ and η specify the states at the specific program points:

$$\gamma \triangleq \alpha \cap \{(\sigma_1, \sigma) \mid \sigma_1(\mathtt{t}) = \sigma_1(\mathtt{x}) + 1\}\,;$$
$$\eta \triangleq \gamma \cap \{(\sigma_1, \sigma) \mid \sigma(\mathtt{t}) = \sigma(\mathtt{x}) + 1\}\,.$$

After adding **skip**s to C_1 and C to make them the same "shape", we can prove the simulation by the compositionality rules SEQ and WHILE. Finally, we remove all the **skip**s and conclude (5.1), *i.e.*, the correctness of the optimization in appropriate contexts. Since the relies only prohibit updates of `x` and `t`, we can execute C_1 and C concurrently with other threads which update `i` and `n` or read `x`, still ensuring semantics preservation.

6. Proving Atomicity of Concurrent Objects

A concurrent object provides a set of methods, which can be called in parallel by clients as the only way to access the object. RGSim gives us a refinement-based proof method to verify the atomicity

```
ADD(e) :                      RMV(e) :
  atom {                        atom {
    S := S ∪ {e};                 S := S − {e};
  }                             }
```

(a) An Abstract Set

```
add(e) :                      rmv(e) :
  local x,y,z,u;                local x,y,z,v;
  <x := Head;>                  <x := Head;>
  lock(x);                      lock(x);
  <z := x.next;>                <y := x.next;>
  <u := z.data;>                <v := y.data;>
  while (u < e) {               while (v < e) {
    lock(z);                      lock(y);
    unlock(x);                    unlock(x);
    x := z;                       x := y;
    <z := x.next;>                <y := x.next;>
    <u := z.data;>                <v := y.data;>
  }                             }
  if (u != e) {                 if (v = e) {
    y := new();                   lock(y);
    y.lock := 0;                  <z := y.next;>
    y.data := e;                  <x.next := z;>
    y.next := z;                  unlock(x);
    <x.next := y;>                free(y);
  }                             } else {
  unlock(x);                      unlock(x);
                                }
```

(b) The Lock-Coupling List-Based Set

Figure 8. The Set Object

of implementations of the object: we can define abstract atomic operations in a high-level language as specifications, and prove the concrete fine-grained implementations refine the corresponding atomic operations when executed in appropriate environments. For instance, in Figure 8(a) we define two atomic set operations, `ADD(e)` and `RMV(e)`. Figure 8(b) gives a concrete implementation of the set object using a lock-coupling list. Partial correctness and atomicity of the algorithm has been verified before [28, 29]. Here we show that its atomicity can also be verified using our RGSim by proving the low-level methods refine the corresponding abstract operations. We will discuss the key difference between the previous proofs and ours in Section 8.

We first take the generic languages in Figure 2, and instantiate the high-level program states below.

(*HMem*)	M_s, M_l	$\in$	$(\mathit{Loc} \cup \mathit{PVar}) \rightharpoonup \mathit{HVal}$
(*HThrds*)	Π	$\in$	$\mathit{ThrdID} \to \mathit{HMem}$
(*HState*)	Σ	$\in$	$\mathit{HThrds} \times \mathit{HMem}$

The state consists of shared memory M_s (where the object resides) and a thread pool Π, which is a mapping from thread identifiers ($\mathtt{t} \in \mathit{ThrdID}$) to their memory M_l. The low-level state σ is defined similarly. We use m_s, m_l and π to represent the low-level shared memory, thread-local memory and the thread pool respectively.

To allow ownership transfer between the shared memory and thread-local memory, we use $\textbf{\textit{atom}}\{\mathbb{C}\}_{\mathbb{A}}$ (or $\langle C \rangle_{\mathcal{A}}$ at the low level) to convert the shared memory to local and then execute $\mathbb{C}$ (or C) atomically. Following RGSep [29], an abstract transition $\mathbb{A} \in \mathcal{P}(\mathit{HMem} \times \mathit{HMem})$ (or $\mathcal{A} \in \mathcal{P}(\mathit{LMem} \times \mathit{LMem})$) is used to specify the effects of the atomic operation over the shared memory, which allows us to split the resulting state back into shared and local when we exit the atomic block. The atomic blocks are instantiations of the generic primitive operations $\mathbb{c}$ (or c) in Figure 2. Their semantics is shown in the technical report [20]. We omit the annotations $\mathbb{A}$ and

$$
\begin{array}{lll}
m_s \models \mathsf{list}(x, A) & \triangleq & (m_s = \phi \wedge x = \mathbf{null} \wedge A = \epsilon) \vee (\exists m_s'.\exists v.\exists y.\exists A'.\ m_s = m_s' \uplus \{x \rightsquigarrow (\_, v, y)\} \wedge A = v :: A' \wedge m_s' \models \mathsf{list}(y, A')) \\
\mathsf{shared\_map}(m_s, M_s) & \triangleq & \exists m_s'.\exists A.\exists x.\ m_s = m_s' \uplus \{\mathtt{Head} \rightsquigarrow x\} \wedge (m_s' \models \mathsf{list}(x, \mathtt{MIN\_VAL} :: A :: \mathtt{MAX\_VAL})) \wedge \mathsf{sorted}(A) \wedge (\mathsf{elems}(A) = M_s(\mathtt{S})) \\
\mathsf{local\_map}(m_l, M_l) & \triangleq & m_l(\mathsf{e}) = M_l(\mathsf{e}) \wedge \exists m_l'.\ m_l = m_l' \uplus \{\mathtt{x} \rightsquigarrow \_, \mathtt{y} \rightsquigarrow \_, \mathtt{z} \rightsquigarrow \_, \mathtt{u} \rightsquigarrow \_, \mathtt{v} \rightsquigarrow \_\} \\
\alpha & \triangleq & \{((\pi, m_s), (\Pi, M_s)) \mid \mathsf{shared\_map}(m_s, M_s) \wedge \forall \mathsf{t} \in dom(\Pi).\ \mathsf{local\_map}(\pi(\mathsf{t}), \Pi(\mathsf{t}))\} \\
\\
\mathcal{G}_{\text{lock}}(\mathsf{t}) & \triangleq & \{((\pi, m_s), (\pi, m_s')) \mid \exists x, v, y.\ m_s(x) = (0, v, y) \wedge m_s' = m_s\{x \rightsquigarrow (\mathsf{t}, v, y)\}\} \\
\mathcal{G}_{\text{unlock}}(\mathsf{t}) & \triangleq & \{((\pi, m_s), (\pi, m_s')) \mid \exists x, v, y.\ m_s(x) = (\mathsf{t}, v, y) \wedge m_s' = m_s\{x \rightsquigarrow (0, v, y)\}\} \\
\mathcal{G}_{\text{add}}(\mathsf{t}) & \triangleq & \{((\pi \uplus \{\mathsf{t} \rightsquigarrow m_l\}, m_s), (\pi \uplus \{\mathsf{t} \rightsquigarrow m_l'\}, m_s')) \\
& & \mid \exists x, y, z, u, v, w.\ m_s(x) = (\mathsf{t}, u, z) \wedge m_s(z) = (\_, w, \_) \\
& & \quad \wedge m_s' = m_s\{x \rightsquigarrow (\mathsf{t}, u, y)\} \uplus \{y \rightsquigarrow (0, v, z)\} \wedge (m_l' \uplus \{y \rightsquigarrow (0, v, z)\} = m_l) \wedge u < v < w\} \\
\mathcal{G}_{\text{rmv}}(\mathsf{t}) & \triangleq & \{((\pi \uplus \{\mathsf{t} \rightsquigarrow m_l\}, m_s), (\pi \uplus \{\mathsf{t} \rightsquigarrow m_l'\}, m_s')) \\
& & \mid \exists x, y, z, u, v.\ m_s(x) = (\mathsf{t}, u, y) \wedge m_s(y) = (\mathsf{t}, v, z) \\
& & \quad \wedge m_s' \uplus \{y \rightsquigarrow (\mathsf{t}, v, z)\} = m_s\{x \rightsquigarrow (\mathsf{t}, u, z)\} \wedge m_l' = m_l \uplus \{y \rightsquigarrow (\mathsf{t}, v, z)\} \wedge v < \mathtt{MAX\_VAL}\} \\
\mathcal{G}_{\text{local}}(\mathsf{t}) & \triangleq & \{((\pi \uplus \{\mathsf{t} \rightsquigarrow m_l\}, m_s), (\pi \uplus \{\mathsf{t} \rightsquigarrow m_l'\}, m_s)) \mid \pi \in (\mathit{ThrdID} \rightarrow \mathit{LMem}) \wedge m_l, m_l', m_s \in \mathit{LMem}\} \\
\mathcal{G}(\mathsf{t}) & \triangleq & \mathcal{G}_{\text{lock}}(\mathsf{t}) \cup \mathcal{G}_{\text{unlock}}(\mathsf{t}) \cup \mathcal{G}_{\text{add}}(\mathsf{t}) \cup \mathcal{G}_{\text{rmv}}(\mathsf{t}) \cup \mathcal{G}_{\text{local}}(\mathsf{t}) \qquad \mathcal{R}(\mathsf{t}) \triangleq \bigcup_{\mathsf{t}' \neq \mathsf{t}} \mathcal{G}(\mathsf{t}') \\
\\
\mathbb{G}_{\text{add}}(\mathsf{t}) & \triangleq & \{((\Pi \uplus \{\mathsf{t} \rightsquigarrow M_l\}, M_s), (\Pi \uplus \{\mathsf{t} \rightsquigarrow M_l'\}, M_s')) \mid \exists e.\ M_s' = M_s\{\mathtt{S} \rightsquigarrow M_s(\mathtt{S}) \cup \{e\}\}\} \\
\mathbb{G}_{\text{rmv}}(\mathsf{t}) & \triangleq & \{((\Pi \uplus \{\mathsf{t} \rightsquigarrow M_l\}, M_s), (\Pi \uplus \{\mathsf{t} \rightsquigarrow M_l'\}, M_s')) \mid \exists e.\ M_s' = M_s\{\mathtt{S} \rightsquigarrow M_s(\mathtt{S}) - \{e\}\}\} \\
\mathbb{G}_{\text{local}}(\mathsf{t}) & \triangleq & \{((\Pi \uplus \{\mathsf{t} \rightsquigarrow M_l\}, M_s), (\Pi \uplus \{\mathsf{t} \rightsquigarrow M_l'\}, M_s)) \mid \Pi \in (\mathit{ThrdID} \rightarrow \mathit{HMem}) \wedge M_l, M_l', M_s \in \mathit{HMem}\} \\
\mathbb{G}(\mathsf{t}) & \triangleq & \mathbb{G}_{\text{add}}(\mathsf{t}) \cup \mathbb{G}_{\text{rmv}}(\mathsf{t}) \cup \mathbb{G}_{\text{local}}(\mathsf{t}) \qquad \mathbb{R}(\mathsf{t}) \triangleq \bigcup_{\mathsf{t}' \neq \mathsf{t}} \mathbb{G}(\mathsf{t}')
\end{array}
$$

Figure 9. Useful Definitions for the Lock-Coupling List

$\mathcal{A}$ in Figure 8, which are the same as the corresponding guarantees in Figure 9, as we will explain below.

In Figure 8, the abstract set is implemented by an ordered singly-linked list pointed to by a shared variable `Head`, with two sentinel nodes at the two ends of the list containing the values `MIN_VAL` and `MAX_VAL` respectively. Each list node is associated with a lock. Traversing the list uses "hand-over-hand" locking: the lock on one node is not released until its successor is locked. `add(e)` inserts a new node with value `e` in the appropriate position while holding the lock of its predecessor. `rmv(e)` redirects the predecessor's pointer while both the node to be removed and its predecessor are locked.

We define the α relation, the guarantees and the relies in Figure 9. The predicate $m_s \models \mathsf{list}(x, A)$ represents a singly-linked list in the shared memory m_s at the location x, whose values form the sequence A. Then the mapping shared_map between the low-level and the high-level shared memory is defined by only concerning about the value sequence on the list: the concrete list should be sorted and its elements constitute the abstract set. For a thread t's local memory of the two levels, we require that the values of `e` are the same and enough local space is provided for `add(e)` and `rmv(e)`, as defined in the mapping local_map. Then α relates the shared memory by shared_map and the local memory of each thread t by local_map.

The atomic actions of the algorithm are specified by $\mathcal{G}_{\text{lock}}$, $\mathcal{G}_{\text{unlock}}$, $\mathcal{G}_{\text{add}}$, $\mathcal{G}_{\text{rmv}}$ and $\mathcal{G}_{\text{local}}$ respectively, which are all parameterized with a thread identifier t. For example, $\mathcal{G}_{\text{rmv}}(\mathsf{t})$ says that when holding the locks of the node y and its predecessor x, we can transfer the node y from the shared memory to the thread's local memory. This corresponds to the action performed by the code of line `13` in `rmv(e)`. Every thread t is executed in the environment that any other thread t' can only perform those five actions, as defined in $\mathcal{R}(\mathsf{t})$. Similarly, the high-level $\mathbb{G}(\mathsf{t})$ and $\mathbb{R}(\mathsf{t})$ are defined according to the abstract `ADD(e)` and `RMV(e)`. The relies and guarantees are almost the same as those in the proofs in RGSep [28].

We can prove that for any thread t, the following hold:

$$
(\mathsf{t}.\mathtt{add(e)}, \mathcal{R}(\mathsf{t}), \mathcal{G}(\mathsf{t})) \preceq_{\alpha;\alpha\ltimes\alpha} (\mathsf{t}.\mathtt{ADD(e)}, \mathbb{R}(\mathsf{t}), \mathbb{G}(\mathsf{t}))\ ;
$$
$$
(\mathsf{t}.\mathtt{rmv(e)}, \mathcal{R}(\mathsf{t}), \mathcal{G}(\mathsf{t})) \preceq_{\alpha;\alpha\ltimes\alpha} (\mathsf{t}.\mathtt{RMV(e)}, \mathbb{R}(\mathsf{t}), \mathbb{G}(\mathsf{t}))\ .
$$

We give the detailed proofs in the technical report [20], which are done operationally based on the definition of RGSim.

By the compositionality and the soundness of RGSim, we know that the fine-grained operations (under the parallel environment $\mathcal{R}$) are simulated by the corresponding atomic operations (under the high-level environment $\mathbb{R}$), while $\mathcal{R}$ and $\mathbb{R}$ say all accesses to the set must be done through the add and remove operations. This gives us the atomicity of the concurrent implementation of the set object.

More examples. In the technical report [20], we also show the use of RGSim to prove the atomicity of other fine-grained algorithms, including the non-blocking concurrent counter [27], Treiber's stack algorithm [26], and a concurrent GCD algorithm (calculating greatest common divisors).

7. Verifying Concurrent Garbage Collectors

In this section, we explain in detail how to reduce the problem of verifying concurrent garbage collectors to transformation verification, and use RGSim to develop a general GC verification framework. We apply the framework to prove the correctness of the Boehm *et al.* concurrent GC algorithm [7].

7.1 Correctness of Concurrent GCs

A concurrent GC is executed by a dedicate thread and performs the collection work in parallel with user threads (mutators), which access the shared heap via read, write and allocation operations. To ensure that the GC and the mutators share a coherent view of the heap, the heap operations from mutators may be instrumented with extra operations, which provide an interaction mechanism to allow arbitrary mutators to cooperate with the GC. These instrumented heap operations are called barriers (*e.g.*, read barriers, write barriers and allocation barriers).

The GC thread and the barriers constitute a concurrent garbage collecting system, which provides a higher-level user-friendly programming model for garbage-collected languages (*e.g.*, Java). In this high-level model, programmers feel they access the heap using regular memory operations, and are freed from manually disposing objects that are no longer in use. They do not need to consider the implementation details of the GC and the existence of barriers.

We could verify the GC system by using a Hoare-style logic to prove that the GC thread and the barriers satisfy their specifications. However, we say this is an indirect approach because it is unclear if the specified correct behaviors would indeed make the mutators happy and generate the abstract view for high-level programmers. Usually this part is examined by experts and then trusted.

Here we propose a more direct approach. We view a concurrent garbage collecting system as a transformation $\mathbf{T}$ from a high-level garbage-collected language to a low-level language. A standard atomic memory operation at the source level is transformed into the corresponding barrier code at the target level. In the source level, we assume there is an *abstract GC thread* that magically turns unreachable objects into reusable memory. The abstract collector *AbsGC* is transformed into the concrete GC code C_{gc} running concurrently with the target mutators. That is,

$$\mathbf{T}(\mathsf{t}_{gc}.\mathit{AbsGC} \,|||\, \mathsf{t}_1.\mathbb{C}_1 \,|||\, \ldots \,|||\, \mathsf{t}_n.\mathbb{C}_n) \triangleq \mathsf{t}_{gc}.C_{gc} \,\|\, \mathsf{t}_1.\mathbf{T}(\mathbb{C}_1) \,\|\, \ldots \,\|\, \mathsf{t}_n.\mathbf{T}(\mathbb{C}_n)\,,$$

where $\mathbf{T}(\mathbb{C})$ simply translates some memory access instructions in $\mathbb{C}$ into the corresponding barriers, and leaves the rest unchanged.

Then we reduce the correctness of the concurrent garbage collecting system to $\mathsf{Correct}(\mathbf{T})$, saying that any mutator program will not have unexpected behaviors when executed using this system.

7.2 A General Framework

The compositionality of RGSim allows us to develop a general framework to prove $\mathsf{Correct}(\mathbf{T})$, which cannot be done by monolithic proof methods. By the parallel compositionality of RGSim (the PAR rule in Figure 7), we can decompose the refinement proofs into proofs for the GC thread and each mutator thread.

Verifying the GC. The semantics of the abstract GC thread can be defined by a binary state predicate $\mathsf{AbsGCStep}$:

$$\frac{(\Sigma, \Sigma') \in \mathsf{AbsGCStep}}{(\mathsf{t}_{gc}.\mathit{AbsGC}, \Sigma) \longrightarrow (\mathsf{t}_{gc}.\mathit{AbsGC}, \Sigma')}$$

That is, the abstract GC thread always makes $\mathsf{AbsGCStep}$ to change the high-level state. We can choose different $\mathsf{AbsGCStep}$ for different GCs, but usually $\mathsf{AbsGCStep}$ guarantees not modifying reachable objects in the heap.

Thus for the GC thread, we need to show that C_{gc} is simulated by *AbsGC* when executed in their environments. This can be reduced to unary Rely-Guarantee reasoning about C_{gc} by proving $\mathcal{R}_{gc}; \mathcal{G}_{gc} \vdash \{p_{gc}\}C_{gc}\{q_{gc}\}$ in a standard Rely-Guarantee logic with proper $\mathcal{R}_{gc}$, $\mathcal{G}_{gc}$, p_{gc} and q_{gc}, as long as $\mathcal{G}_{gc}$ is a concrete representation of $\mathsf{AbsGCStep}$. The judgment says given an initial state satisfying the precondition p_{gc}, if the environment's behaviors satisfy $\mathcal{R}_{gc}$, then each step of C_{gc} satisfies $\mathcal{G}_{gc}$, and the postcondition q_{gc} holds at the end if C_{gc} terminates. In general, the collector never terminates, thus we can let q_{gc} be **false**. $\mathcal{G}_{gc}$ and p_{gc} should be provided by the verifier, where p_{gc} needs to be general enough that can be satisfied by any possible low-level initial state. $\mathcal{R}_{gc}$ encodes the possible behaviors of mutators, which can be derived, as we will show below.

Verifying mutators. For the mutator thread, since $\mathbf{T}$ is syntax-directed on $\mathbb{C}$, we can reduce the refinement problem for arbitrary mutators to the refinement on each primitive instruction only, by the compositionality of RGSim. The proof needs proper rely/guarantee conditions. Let $\mathbb{G}(\mathsf{t.c})$ and $\mathcal{G}(\mathsf{t}.\mathbf{T}(\mathsf{c}))$ denote the guarantees of the source instruction c and the target code $\mathbf{T}(\mathsf{c})$ respectively. Then we can define the general guarantees for a mutator thread t:

$$\begin{array}{lcl} \mathbb{G}(\mathsf{t}) & \triangleq & \bigcup_{\mathsf{c}} \mathbb{G}(\mathsf{t.c})\,; \\ \mathcal{G}(\mathsf{t}) & \triangleq & \bigcup_{\mathsf{c}} \mathcal{G}(\mathsf{t}.\mathbf{T}(\mathsf{c}))\,. \end{array} \quad (7.1)$$

Its relies should include all the possible guarantees made by other threads, and the GC's abstract and concrete behaviors respectively:

$$\begin{array}{lcl} \mathbb{R}(\mathsf{t}) & \triangleq & \mathsf{AbsGCStep} \cup \bigcup_{\mathsf{t}' \neq \mathsf{t}} \mathbb{G}(\mathsf{t}')\,; \\ \mathcal{R}(\mathsf{t}) & \triangleq & \mathcal{G}_{gc} \cup \bigcup_{\mathsf{t}' \neq \mathsf{t}} \mathcal{G}(\mathsf{t}')\,. \end{array} \quad (7.2)$$

The $\mathcal{R}_{gc}$ used to verify the GC code can now be defined below:

$$\mathcal{R}_{gc} \triangleq \bigcup_{\mathsf{t}} \mathcal{G}(\mathsf{t})\,. \quad (7.3)$$

The refinement proof also needs definitions of binary α, ζ and γ relations. The invariant α relates the low-level and the high-level states and needs to be preserved by each low-level step. In general, a high-level state Σ can be mapped to a low-level state σ by giving a concrete local store for the GC thread, adding additional structures in the heap (to record information for collection), renaming heap cells (for copying GCs), *etc.*. For each mutator thread t, the relations $\zeta(\mathsf{t})$ and $\gamma(\mathsf{t})$ need to hold at the beginning and the end of each basic transformation unit (every high-level primitive instruction in this case) respectively. We let $\gamma(\mathsf{t})$ be the same as $\zeta(\mathsf{t})$ to support sequential compositions. We require $\mathsf{InitRel}_{\mathbf{T}}(\zeta(\mathsf{t}))$ (see Figure 6), *i.e.*, $\zeta(\mathsf{t})$ holds over the initial states. In addition, the target and the source boolean expressions should be evaluated to the same value under related states, as required in the IF and WHILE rules in Figure 7.

$$\mathsf{Good}_{\mathbf{T}}(\zeta(\mathsf{t})) \triangleq \mathsf{InitRel}_{\mathbf{T}}(\zeta(\mathsf{t})) \land \forall \mathbb{B}.\, \zeta(\mathsf{t}) \subseteq (\mathbf{T}(\mathbb{B}) \Leftrightarrow \mathbb{B}) \quad (7.4)$$

Theorem 8 (Verifying Concurrent Garbage Collecting Systems). *If there exist $\mathcal{R}_{gc}$, $\mathcal{G}_{gc}$, p_{gc}, $\mathcal{R}(\mathsf{t})$, $\mathbb{R}(\mathsf{t})$, $\zeta(\mathsf{t})$ and α such that (7.1), (7.2), (7.3), (7.4) and the following hold:*

1. *(Verification of the GC code)*
   $\mathcal{R}_{gc}; \mathcal{G}_{gc} \vdash \{p_{gc}\}C_{gc}\{\mathbf{false}\}$;
2. *(Correctness of $\mathbf{T}$ on mutator instructions)*
   $\forall \mathsf{c}.\ (\mathsf{t}.\mathbf{T}(\mathsf{c}), \mathcal{R}(\mathsf{t}), \mathcal{G}(\mathsf{t})) \preceq_{\alpha;\zeta(\mathsf{t})\ltimes\zeta(\mathsf{t})} (\mathsf{t.c}, \mathbb{R}(\mathsf{t}), \mathbb{G}(\mathsf{t}))$;
3. *(Side conditions)*
   $\mathcal{G}_{gc} \circ \alpha^{-1} \subseteq \alpha^{-1} \circ (\mathsf{AbsGCStep})^*$;
   $\forall \sigma, \Sigma.\ \sigma = \mathbf{T}(\Sigma) \implies p_{gc}\ \sigma$;

then $\mathsf{Correct}(\mathbf{T})$.

That is, to verify a concurrent garbage collecting system, we need to do the following:

- Define the α and $\zeta(\mathsf{t})$ relations, and prove the correctness of $\mathbf{T}$ on high-level primitive instructions. Since $\mathbf{T}$ preserves the syntax on most instructions, it's often immediate to prove the target instructions are simulated by their sources. But for instructions that are transformed to barriers, we need to verify the barriers that they implement both the source instructions (by RGSim) and the interaction mechanism (shown in their guarantees).
- Find some proper $\mathcal{G}_{gc}$ and p_{gc}, and verify the GC code by R-G reasoning. We require the GC's guarantee $\mathcal{G}_{gc}$ should not contain more behaviors than $\mathsf{AbsGCStep}$ (the first side condition), and C_{gc} can start its execution from any state σ transformed from a high-level one (the second side condition).

7.3 Application: Boehm *et al.* Concurrent GC Algorithm

We illustrate the applications of the framework (Theorem 8) by proving the correctness of a mostly-concurrent mark-sweep garbage collector proposed by Boehm *et al.* [7]. Variants of the algorithm have been used in practice (*e.g.*, by IBM [2]). Due to the space limit, we only describe the proof sketch here. Details are presented in the technical report [20].

Overview of the GC algorithm. The top-level code of the GC thread is shown in Figure 10. In each collection cycle, after an

```
  {wfstate}
0 Collection() {
1   local mstk: Seq(Int);
    Loop Invariant: {wfstate ∗ (own_np(mstk) ∧ mstk = ϵ)}
2   while (true) {
3     Initialize();
      {(wfstate ∧ reach_inv) ∗ (own_np(mstk) ∧ mstk = ϵ)}
4     Trace();
      {(wfstate ∧ reach_inv) ∗ (own_np(mstk) ∧ mstk = ϵ)}
5     CleanCard();
      {(wfstate ∧ reach_inv) ∗ (own_np(mstk) ∧ mstk = ϵ)}
      atomic{
6       ScanRoot();
        {∃X.(wfstate ∧ reach_rtnw_stk(X) ∧ stk_black(X))
          ∗(own_np(mstk) ∧ mstk = X)}
7       CleanCard();
      }
      {(wfstate ∧ reach_black) ∗ (own_np(mstk) ∧ mstk = ϵ)}
8     Sweep();
    }
  }
  {false}
```

Figure 10. Outline of the GC Code and Proof Sketch

```
update(x.id, E) { // id ∈ {pt1, ..., ptm}
  atomic{ x.id := E; aux := x; }
  atomic{ x.dirty := 1; aux := 0; }
}
```

Figure 11. The Write Barrier for Boehm *et al.* GC

initialization process, the GC enters the concurrent mark-phase (line 4) and traces the objects reachable from the *roots* (*i.e.*, the mutators' local pointer variables that may contain references to the heap objects). A *mark stack* (`mstk`) is used to do a depth-first tracing. During the tracing, the connectivity between objects might be changed by the mutators, thus a write barrier is required to notify the collector of those modified objects by dirtying the objects' tags (called cards). When the tracing is done, the GC suspends all the mutators and re-traces from the dirty objects that have been marked (called *card-cleaning*, line 6 and 7). The stop-the-world phase is implemented by **atomic**$\{C\}$. Finally, all the reachable objects are ensured marked and the GC performs the concurrent sweep-phase (line 8), in which unmarked objects are reclaimed. Usually in practice, there is also a concurrent card-cleaning phase (line 5) before the stop-the-world card-cleaning to reduce the pause time. The full GC code C_{gc} is given in the technical report [20].

The write barrier is shown in Figure 11, where the `dirty` field is set after modifying the object's pointer field. Here we use a write-only auxiliary variable `aux` for each mutator thread to record the current object that the mutator is updating. We add `aux` only for the purpose of verification, so that we can easily specify the fine-grained property of the write barrier in the guarantees that immediately after updating the pointer field, the thread would do nothing else except setting the corresponding `dirty` field. The GC does not use read barriers nor allocation barriers.

We first present the high-level and low-level program state models in Figure 12. The behaviors of the high-level abstract GC thread are defined as follows:

$$\mathsf{AbsGCStep} \triangleq \{((\Pi, \mathrm{H}), (\Pi, \mathrm{H}')) \mid \forall l.\ \mathsf{reachable}(l)(\Pi, \mathrm{H}) \Longrightarrow \mathrm{H}(l) = \mathrm{H}'(l)\},$$

saying that, the mutator stores and the reachable objects in the heap are remained unmodified. Here $\mathsf{reachable}(l)(\Pi, \mathrm{H})$ means the object at the location l is reachable in H from the roots in Π.

$(HStore)\ \mathrm{S} \in PVar \rightharpoonup HVal$	$(HHeap)\ \mathrm{H} \in Loc \rightharpoonup HObj$
$(HThrds)\ \Pi \in MutID \rightarrow HStore$	$(HState)\ \Sigma \in HThrds \times HHeap$
$(LStore)\ s \in PVar \rightharpoonup LVal \times \{0,1\}$	$(LHeap)\ h \in [1..M] \rightharpoonup LObj$
$(LThrds)\ \pi \in ThrdID \rightarrow LStore$	$(LState)\ \sigma \in LThrds \times LHeap$

Figure 12. High-Level and Low-Level State Models

The transformation. The transformation $\mathbf{T}$ is defined as follows. For *code*, the high-level abstract GC thread is transformed to the GC thread shown in Figure 10. Each instruction x.id $:= \mathbb{E}$ in mutators is transformed to the write barrier, where id is a pointer field of x. Other instructions and the program structures of mutators are unchanged.

The following transformations are made over initial states.

- First we require the high-level initial state to be *well-formed*:
  $\mathsf{wfstate}(\Pi, \mathrm{H}) \triangleq \forall l.\ \mathsf{reachable}(l)(\Pi, \mathrm{H}) \Longrightarrow l \in dom(\mathrm{H})$.
  That is, reachable locations cannot be dangling pointers.
- High-level locations are transformed to integers by a bijective function $\mathsf{Loc2Int} : Loc \leftrightarrow [0..M]$ satisfying $\mathsf{Loc2Int}(\mathbf{nil}) = 0$.
- Variables are transformed to the low level using an extra bit to preserve the high-level type information (0 for non-pointers and 1 for pointers).
- High-level objects are transformed to the low level by adding the `color` and `dirty` fields with initial values `WHITE` and 0 respectively. Other addresses in the low-level heap domain $[1..M]$ are filled out using unallocated objects whose `colors` are `BLUE` and all the other fields are initialized by 0. Here we use `BLACK` and `WHITE` for marked and unmarked objects respectively, and `BLUE` for unallocated memory.
- The concrete GC thread is given an initial store.

The formal definition of $\mathbf{T}$ is included in the technical report [20].

To prove $\mathsf{Correct}(\mathbf{T})$ in our framework, we apply Theorem 8, prove the refinement between low-level and high-level mutators, and verify the GC code using a unary Rely-Guarantee-based logic.

Refinement proofs for mutator instructions. We first define the α and $\zeta(\mathsf{t})$ relations.

$$\alpha \triangleq \{((\pi \uplus \{\mathsf{t}_{gc} \leadsto \_\}, h), (\Pi, \mathrm{H})) \mid \forall \mathsf{t} \in dom(\Pi).\ \mathsf{store\_map}(\pi(\mathsf{t}), \Pi(\mathsf{t})) \wedge \mathsf{heap\_map}(h, \mathrm{H}) \wedge \mathsf{wfstate}(\Pi, \mathrm{H})\}.$$

In α, the relation between low-level and high-level stores and heaps are enforced by $\mathsf{store\_map}$ and $\mathsf{heap\_map}$ respectively. Their definitions reflect the state transformations we describe above, ignoring the values of those high-level-invisible structures. It also requires the well-formedness of high-level states.

For each mutator thread t, the $\zeta(\mathsf{t})$ relation enforced at the beginning and the end of each transformation unit (each high-level instruction) is stronger than α. It requires that the value of the auxiliary variable `aux` (see Figure 11) be a null pointer (0^{p}):

$$\zeta(\mathsf{t}) \triangleq \alpha \cap \{((\pi, h), (\Pi, \mathrm{H})) \mid \pi(\mathsf{t})(\mathtt{aux}) = 0^{\mathsf{p}}\}.$$

The refinement between the write barrier at the low level and the pointer update instruction at the high level is formulated as:

$$(\mathsf{t}.\mathtt{update}(x.id, E), \mathcal{R}(\mathsf{t}), \mathcal{G}^{\mathsf{t}}_{\text{write\_barrier}}) \preceq_{\alpha;\zeta(\mathsf{t})\ltimes\zeta(\mathsf{t})} (\mathsf{t}.(x.\text{id} := \mathbb{E}), \mathbb{R}(\mathsf{t}), \mathbb{G}^{\mathsf{t}}_{\text{write\_pt}}),$$

where $\mathcal{G}^{\mathsf{t}}_{\text{write\_barrier}}$ and $\mathbb{G}^{\mathsf{t}}_{\text{write\_pt}}$ are the guarantees of the two-step write barrier and the high-level atomic write operation respectively.

Since the transformation of other high-level instructions is identity, the corresponding refinement proofs are simple.

Rely-Guarantee reasoning about the GC code. The unary program logic we use to verify the GC thread is a standard Rely-Guarantee logic adapted to the target language. We describe states using separation logic assertions, as shown below:

$$p, q ::= B \mid \mathsf{t.own_p}(x) \mid \mathsf{t.own_{np}}(x) \mid E_1.id \mapsto E_2 \mid p * q \mid \ldots$$

Following Parkinson *et al.* [23], we treat program variables as resource and use $\mathsf{t.own_p}(x)$ and $\mathsf{t.own_{np}}(x)$ for the thread t's ownerships of pointers and non-pointers respectively. We omit the thread identifiers if these predicates hold for the current thread.

We first give the precondition and the guarantee of the GC. The GC starts its executions from a low-level *well-formed* state, *i.e.*, $p_{gc} \triangleq \mathsf{wfstate}$. Just corresponding to the high-level wfstate definition, the low-level wfstate predicate says none of the reachable objects are BLUE. We define $\mathcal{G}_{gc}$ as follows:

$$\begin{array}{rl} \mathcal{G}_{gc} \triangleq & \{((\pi \uplus \{\mathsf{t_{gc}} \rightsquigarrow s\}, h), (\pi \uplus \{\mathsf{t_{gc}} \rightsquigarrow s'\}, h')) \\ & \mid \forall n.\ \mathsf{reachable}(n)(\pi, h) \\ & \quad \Longrightarrow \lfloor h(n) \rfloor = \lfloor h'(n) \rfloor \\ & \quad\quad \wedge\ h(n).\mathtt{color} \neq \mathtt{BLUE} \wedge h'(n).\mathtt{color} \neq \mathtt{BLUE}\}\,. \end{array}$$

The GC guarantees not modifying the mutator stores. For any mutator-reachable object, the GC does not update its fields coming from the high-level mutator, nor does it reclaim the object. Here $\lfloor \_ \rfloor$ lifts a low-level object to a new one that contains mutator data only.

The proof sketch is given in Figure 10. One of the key invariants used in the proof is reach_inv, which says any WHITE reachable object can either be traced from a root object in a path on which every object is WHITE, or be reachable from a BLACK object whose pointer field was updated and dirty bit was set to 1. Since the proof is done in the unary logic, the details here are orthogonal to our simulation-based proof (but it is RGSim that allows us to derive Theorem 8, which then links proofs in the unary logic with relational proofs). We give the complete proofs in the technical report [20].

8. Related Work and Conclusion

There is a large body of work on refinements and verification of program transformations. Here we only focus on the work most closely related to the typical applications discussed in this paper.

Verifying compilation and optimizations of concurrent programs. Compiler verification for concurrent programming languages can date back to work by Wand [31] and Gladstein *et al.* [14], which is about functional languages using message-passing mechanisms. Recently, Lochbihler [21] presents a verified compiler for Java threads and prove semantics preservation by a weak bisimulation. He views every heap update as an observable move, thus does not allow the target and the source to have different granularities of atomic updates. To achieve parallel compositionality, he requires the relation to be preserved by any transitions of shared states, *i.e.*, the environments are assumed arbitrary. As we explained in Section 2.2, this is a too strong requirement in general for many transformations, including the examples in this paper.

Burckhardt *et al.* [9] present a proof method for verifying concurrent program transformations on relaxed memory models. The method relies on a compositional trace-based denotational semantics, where the values of shared variables are always considered arbitrary at any program point. In other words, they also assume arbitrary environments.

Following Leroy's CompCert project [19], Ševčík *et al.* [25] verify compilation from a C-like concurrent language to x86 by simulations. They focus on correctness of a particular compiler, and there are two phases in their compiler whose proofs are not compositional. Here we provide a general, compiler-independent, compositional proof technique to verify concurrent transformations.

We apply RGSim to justify concurrent optimizations, following Benton [3] who presents a declarative set of rules for sequential optimizations. Also the proof rules of RGSim for sequential compositions, conditional statements and loops coincide with those in relational Hoare logic [3] and relational separation logic [32].

Proving linearizability or atomicity of concurrent objects. Filipović *et al.* [13] show linearizability can be characterized in terms of an observational refinement, where the latter is defined similarly to our Correct($\mathbf{T}$). There is no proof method given to verify the linearizability of fine-grained object implementations.

Turon and Wand [27] propose a refinement-based proof method to verify concurrent objects. They first propose a simple refinement based on Brookes' fully abstract trace semantics [8], which is compositional but cannot handle complex algorithms (as discussed in Section 2.2). Their fenced refinement then uses rely conditions to filter out illegal environment transitions. The basic idea is similar to ours, and the refinement can also be used to verify Treiber's stack algorithm. However, it is "not a congruence for parallel composition". In their settings, both the concrete (fine-grained) and the abstract (atomic) versions of object operations need to be expressed in the same language. They also require that the fine-grained implementation should have only one update action over the shared state to correspond to the high-level atomic operation. These requirements and the lack of parallel compositionality limit the applicability of their method. It is unclear if the method can be used for general verification of transformations, such as concurrent GCs.

Elmas *et al.* [12] prove linearizability by incrementally rewriting the fine-grained implementation to the atomic abstract specification. Their behavioral simulation used to characterize linearizability is an event-trace subset relation with requirements on the orders of method invocations and returns. Their rules heavily rely on movers (*i.e.*, operations that can commute over any operation of other threads) and always rewrite programs to instructions, thus are designed specifically for atomicity verification.

In his thesis [28], Vafeiadis proves linearizability of concurrent objects in RGSep logic by introducing abstract objects and abstract atomic operations as auxiliary variables and code. The refinement between the concrete implementation and the abstract operation is implicitly embodied in the unary verification process, but is not spelled out formally in the meta-theory (*e.g.*, the soundness).

Verifying concurrent GCs. Vechev *et al.* [30] define transformations to generate concurrent GCs from an abstract collector. Afterwards, Pavlovic *et al.* [24] present refinements to derive concrete concurrent GCs from specifications. These methods focus on describing the behaviors of variants (or instantiations) of a correct abstract collector (or a specification) in a single framework, assuming all the mutator operations are atomic. By comparison, we provide a general correctness notion and a proof method for verifying concurrent GCs and the interactions with mutators (where the barriers could be fine-grained). Furthermore, the correctness of their transformations or refinements is expressed in a GC-oriented way (*e.g.*, the target GC should mark no less objects than the source), which cannot be used to justify other transformations.

Kapoor *et al.* [18] verify Dijkstra's GC using concurrent separation logic. To validate the GC specifications, they also verify a representative mutator in the same system. In contrast, we reduce the problem of verifying a concurrent GC to verifying a transformation, ensuring semantics preservation for *all* mutators. Our GC verification framework is inspired by McCreight *et al.* [22], who propose a framework for separate verification of stop-the-world and incremental GCs and their mutators, but their framework does not handle concurrency.

Conclusion and future work. We propose RGSim to verify concurrent program transformations. By describing explicitly the interference with environments, RGSim is compositional, and can support many widely-used transformations. We have applied RGSim to reason about optimizations, prove atomicity of fine-grained concurrent algorithms and verify concurrent garbage collectors. In the future, we would like to further test its applicability with more applications, such as verifying STM implementations and compilers. It is also interesting to explore the possibility of building tools to automate the verification process.

Acknowledgments

We would like to thank Matthew Parkinson and anonymous referees for their suggestions and comments on earlier versions of this paper. This work is supported in part by grants from National Natural Science Foundation of China (NSFC) under Grant No. 60928004, 61073040 and 61103023. Xinyu Feng is also supported in part by NSFC under Grant No. 90818019, by Program for New Century Excellent Talents in Universities (NCET), and by the Fundamental Research Funds for the Central Universities.

References

[1] M. Abadi and G. Plotkin. A model of cooperative threads. In *Proc. 36th ACM Symp. on Principles of Prog. Lang. (POPL'09)*, pages 29–40. ACM Press, January 2009.

[2] K. Barabash, O. Ben-Yitzhak, I. Goft, E. K. Kolodner, V. Leikehman, Y. Ossia, A. Owshanko, and E. Petrank. A parallel, incremental, mostly concurrent garbage collector for servers. *ACM Trans. Program. Lang. Syst.*, 27(6):1097–1146, 2005.

[3] N. Benton. Simple relational correctness proofs for static analyses and program transformations. In *Proc. 31th ACM Symp. on Principles of Prog. Lang. (POPL'04)*, pages 14–25. ACM Press, January 2004.

[4] N. Benton and C.-K. Hur. Biorthogonality, step-indexing and compiler correctness. In *Proc. 14th ACM Int'l Conf. on Functional Prog. (ICFP'09)*, pages 97–108. ACM Press, September 2009.

[5] H.-J. Boehm. Threads cannot be implemented as a library. In *Proc. 2005 ACM Conf. on Prog. Lang. Design and Impl. (PLDI'05)*, pages 261–268. ACM Press, June 2005.

[6] H.-J. Boehm and S. V. Adve. Foundations of the C++ concurrency memory model. In *Proc. 2008 ACM Conf. on Prog. Lang. Design and Impl. (PLDI'08)*, pages 68–78. ACM Press, June 2008.

[7] H.-J. Boehm, A. J. Demers, and S. Shenker. Mostly parallel garbage collection. In *Proc. 1991 ACM Conf. on Prog. Lang. Design and Impl. (PLDI'91)*, pages 157–164. ACM Press, June 1991.

[8] S. D. Brookes. Full abstraction for a shared-variable parallel language. *Inf. Comput.*, 127(2):145–163, 1996.

[9] S. Burckhardt, M. Musuvathi, and V. Singh. Verifying local transformations on relaxed memory models. In *Proc. 19th Int'l Conf. on Compiler Construction (CC'10)*, volume 6011 of *Lecture Notes in Computer Science*, pages 104–123. Springer, March 2010.

[10] Coq Development Team. The Coq proof assistant reference manual. The Coq release v8.3, October 2010.

[11] D. Dice, O. Shalev, and N. Shavit. Transactional locking II. In *Proc. 20th Int'l Symp. on Distributed Computing (DISC'06)*, volume 4167 of *Lecture Notes in Computer Science*, pages 194–208. Springer, September 2006.

[12] T. Elmas, S. Qadeer, A. Sezgin, O. Subasi, and S. Tasiran. Simplifying linearizability proofs with reduction and abstraction. In *Proc. 16th Int'l Conf. on Tools and Algorithms for the Construction and Analysis of Systems (TACAS'10)*, volume 6015 of *Lecture Notes in Computer Science*, pages 296–311. Springer, March 2010.

[13] I. Filipović, P. O'Hearn, N. Rinetzky, and H. Yang. Abstraction for concurrent objects. In *Proc. 18th European Symp. on Prog. (ESOP'09)*, volume 5502 of *Lecture Notes in Computer Science*, pages 252–266. Springer, March 2009.

[14] D. S. Gladstein and M. Wand. Compiler correctness for concurrent languages. In *Proc. 1st Int'l Conf. on Coordination Languages and Models (COORDINATION'96)*, volume 1061 of *Lecture Notes in Computer Science*, pages 231–248. Springer, April 1996.

[15] M. Herlihy and N. Shavit. *The Art of Multiprocessor Programming*. Morgan Kaufmann, April 2008.

[16] C.-K. Hur and D. Dreyer. A Kripke logical relation between ML and assembly. In *Proc. 38th ACM Symp. on Principles of Prog. Lang. (POPL'11)*, pages 133–146. ACM Press, January 2011.

[17] C. B. Jones. Tentative steps toward a development method for interfering programs. *ACM Trans. Program. Lang. Syst.*, 5(4):596–619, 1983.

[18] K. Kapoor, K. Lodaya, and U. Reddy. Fine-grained concurrency with separation logic. *J. Philosophical Logic*, 40(5):583–632, 2011.

[19] X. Leroy. A formally verified compiler back-end. *J. Autom. Reason.*, 43(4):363–446, December 2009.

[20] H. Liang, X. Feng, and M. Fu. A rely-guarantee-based simulation for verifying concurrent program transformations. Technical report (with Coq implementation), University of Science and Technology of China, October 2011. `http://kyhcs.ustcsz.edu.cn/relconcur/rgsim`.

[21] A. Lochbihler. Verifying a compiler for java threads. In *Proc. 20th European Symp. on Prog. (ESOP'10)*, volume 6012 of *Lecture Notes in Computer Science*, pages 427–447. Springer, March 2010.

[22] A. McCreight, Z. Shao, C. Lin, and L. Li. A general framework for certifying garbage collectors and their mutators. In *Proc. 2007 ACM Conf. on Prog. Lang. Design and Impl. (PLDI'07)*, pages 468–479. ACM Press, June 2007.

[23] M. Parkinson, R. Bornat, and C. Calcagno. Variables as resource in Hoare logics. In *Proc. 21th IEEE Symp. on Logic In Computer Science (LICS'06)*, pages 137–146. IEEE Computer Society, August 2006.

[24] D. Pavlovic, P. Pepper, and D. R. Smith. Formal derivation of concurrent garbage collectors. In *Proc. 10th Int'l Conf. on Mathematics of Program Construction (MPC'10)*, volume 6120 of *Lecture Notes in Computer Science*, pages 353–376. Springer, June 2010.

[25] J. Ševčík, V. Vafeiadis, F. Z. Nardelli, S. Jagannathan, and P. Sewell. Relaxed-memory concurrency and verified compilation. In *Proc. 38th ACM Symp. on Principles of Prog. Lang. (POPL'11)*, pages 43–54. ACM Press, January 2011.

[26] R. K. Treiber. System programming: coping with parallelism. Technical Report RJ 5118, IBM Almaden Research Center, 1986.

[27] A. Turon and M. Wand. A separation logic for refining concurrent objects. In *Proc. 38th ACM Symp. on Principles of Prog. Lang. (POPL'11)*, pages 247–258. ACM Press, January 2011.

[28] V. Vafeiadis. Modular fine-grained concurrency verification. Technical Report UCAM-CL-TR-726, University of Cambridge, Computer Laboratory, July 2008.

[29] V. Vafeiadis and M. J. Parkinson. A marriage of rely/guarantee and separation logic. In *Proc. 18th Int'l Conf. on Concurrency Theory (CONCUR'07)*, volume 4703, pages 256–271. Springer, 2007.

[30] M. T. Vechev, E. Yahav, and D. F. Bacon. Correctness-preserving derivation of concurrent garbage collection algorithms. In *Proc. 2006 ACM Conf. on Prog. Lang. Design and Impl. (PLDI'06)*, pages 341–353. ACM Press, June 2006.

[31] M. Wand. Compiler correctness for parallel languages. In *Proc. Conf. on Functional Prog. Lang. and Computer Architecture (FPCA'95)*, pages 120–134. ACM Press, June 1995.

[32] H. Yang. Relational separation logic. *Theoretical Computer Science*, 375(1-3):308–334, 2007.

A Unified Approach to Fully Lazy Sharing

Thibaut Balabonski

Univ Paris Diderot, Sorbonne Paris Cité,
PPS, UMR 7126, CNRS,
F-75205 Paris, France
thibaut.balabonski@pps.jussieu.fr

Abstract

We give an axiomatic presentation of sharing-via-labelling for weak λ-calculi, that makes it possible to formally compare many different approaches to fully lazy sharing, and obtain two important results. We prove that the known implementations of full laziness are all equivalent in terms of the number of β-reductions performed, although they behave differently regarding the duplication of terms. We establish a link between the optimality theories of weak λ-calculi and first-order rewriting systems by expressing fully lazy λ-lifting in our framework, thus emphasizing the first-order essence of weak reduction.

Categories and Subject Descriptors I.1.3 [*Languages and Systems*]: Evaluation strategies

General Terms Theory, Languages

Keywords Sharing, Full laziness, Lambda-lifting, Rewriting, Lambda-calculus, Weak reduction, Optimality, Labelling.

1. Introduction

In the implementation of functional programming languages, a fundamental problem is the efficient evaluation of β-reduction. This problem has been studied for a long time. Its difficulty comes from the fact that one has to minimize the number of β-steps as well as control the actual (amortized) cost of single β-reduction steps. The minimization of the number of β-steps requires, in turn, to handle two different issues: avoiding non-needed computations, and minimizing duplications of unfinished work.

In λ-calculus, some reduction strategies [BKKS87] can completely avoid non-needed computations. However, it is also known that no reduction strategy can completely avoid duplications [Lam90]. Hence, in any case, one has to cope with duplications that still occur, and find some appropriate ways to deal with them.

This is exactly the point of sharing: building implementations in which the duplicated occurrences of a given original subterm keep a unique shared representation. This allows one to evaluate all the copies simultaneously, as if they were only one. The idea is to make sure that some parts of a program which are *logically* duplicated (in the term representation of the program) remain *physically* single pieces (in the memory of the evaluator).

Sharing cannot be achieved using only λ-terms: it requires the use of other technical tools, for instance graphs, closures, or program transformations. The various resulting formalisms may be hardly comparable.

This paper focuses on one particularly rich flavor of sharing called *fully lazy sharing* (described in section 1.2) and aims at formally relating its various implementations. This is done by defining a framework called *sharing-via-labelling systems* in which they can all be expressed and compared.

This unified approach provides compiler writers with increased knowledge on the wide panorama of full laziness. In particular, it replaces a series of sometimes informal justifications of equivalence by a central theorem ensuring that all the considered approaches are equivalent with respect to the number of shared β-steps. As a consequence, one can safely restrict any subsequent comparison of two fully lazy models to other parameters of interest such as their space consumption or the actual cost of maintaining sharing. Having a unified framework will also simplify the task of comparing full laziness to the other efficient implementation techniques, such as other degrees of laziness (up to optimality), or partial evaluation.

The rest of the introduction is organized as follows: Section 1.1 presents the various technical tools commonly used to specify sharing, Section 1.2 describes how these tools have been used and combined over the past 40 years to propose different definitions of fully lazy sharing, and Section 1.3 details our approach and the contributions of the paper.

1.1 Many tools for sharing

Graphs. The most intuitive way of expressing sharing might be by using graphs. In the pictures, the binary node @ represents application, and redexes[1] are marked with bold lines. For instance in the center of the following picture, an abstraction $\lambda x.t$ is applied to an argument a. The function body t contains two occurrences of the variable x: the argument a is thus logically duplicated (on the left).

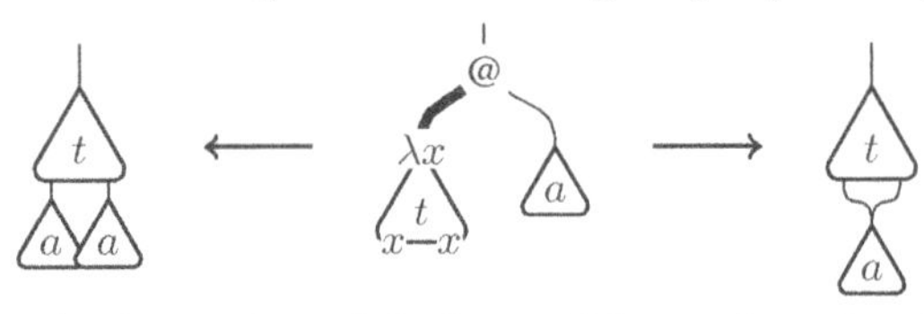

The simplest notion of sharing, which may be referred to as *lazy sharing*, or just *laziness*, prevents the previous duplication by keeping a physically unique, with two pointers to its location (right hand side part of the previous picture).

Here the term *laziness* is to be taken in literal sense: the duplications are postponed as long as it is possible, but some of them will

[1] a **red***ucible* **ex***pression*, or **redex**, designs a place where an evaluation step can take place

POPL'12, January 25–27, 2012, Philadelphia, PA, USA.

eventually happen. For instance, a shared function has to be copied prior to any instantiation, as shown in the picture below.

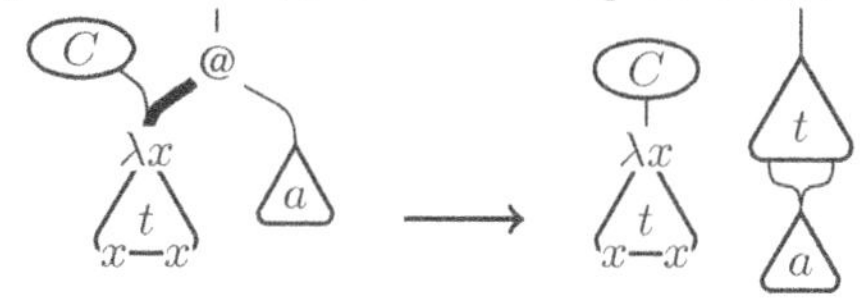

Extraction of free parameters. The previous pictures feature graphs built with λ-calculus constructs, and in particular with binders. This requires either to define variable renaming (α-conversion) or to add some special structure to represent binding. In any case the resulting graph formalism is quite complex. Graph reduction can be made easier by turning λ-terms (that are higher-order terms) to applicative expressions (that are first-order terms). This is the point when compiling the λ-calculus into combinators [Tur79] or supercombinators [Hug82], techniques that finally led to the λ-lifting program transformation [Joh85, Jon87].

This transformation extracts all the free variables from a function and replaces what remains of the function by a symbol called supercombinator. New reduction rules are added to deal with the new symbols.

Closures and memory heaps. While graphs are a simple and old way to describe lazy sharing, the reference system for the semantics of lazy evaluation is J. Launchbury's natural semantics [Lau93]. It introduces *let ... in ...* constructs to name the arguments of the applications, and then puts these arguments in a heap. Sharing then appears as memoization: when one needs to access the content of a variable, the corresponding expression found in the heap is evaluated, and the heap is updated with the obtained result.

In contrast to the previous big-step approach, a small-step description of lazy evaluation based on terms is the call-by-need λ-calculus of Z. Ariola et al. [AFM⁺95]. Here again, sharing is expressed thanks to additional *let ... in ...* constructs used as closures. Similar effects can also be achieved by expressing sharing using explicit substitutions [Yos94]. The big-step and small-step styles can be related by well-known transformations [DMMZ10].

Labels and weak reduction. Finally, laziness is seen in [Yos94, Mar91] as the optimal way of sharing in weak λ-calculi: variants of the λ-calculus where reduction under λ-abstractions is restricted. First, J.-J. Lévy [Lé80] described optimal sharing for the plain λ-calculus (unrestricted, untyped, usual λ-calculus) by means of labelled λ-terms. Then L. Maranget [Mar91] adapted these ideas for a weak λ-calculus and for first-order rewriting and got an additional result that is not valid for the plain λ-calculus: labelled terms represent graphs implementing optimal sharing.

In [Mar91] the link between labelled terms and graphs is made by interpreting the label of a term as its location in memory, or graphically by its coordinate:

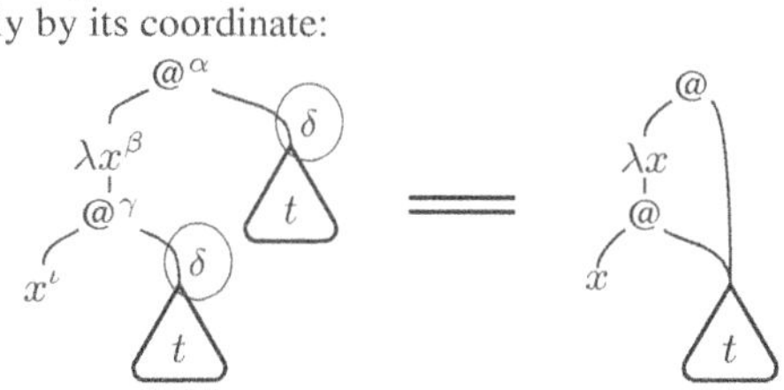

We call this principle *sharing-via-labelling*. The idea is also explored in [DLLL05]. In this setting the equality of labels corresponds to the physical equality of two terms, which should in turn imply their syntactic equality: two terms stored/drawn at the same place ought to be equal. The reduction of a graph-redex is simulated by the reduction of all the labelled term-redexes with a given label. One then needs to ensure that the *sharing property* (terms with equal labels are syntactically equal) is preserved by reduction.

1.2 Full laziness: State of the art

The main idea. Full laziness is based upon the following remark: the *constant parts* of a function body are not affected by the instantiation of the function, hence they need not be duplicated.

This can be formalized by means of the notion of free expression. We recall the definition given in [Jon87]. Say a subterm s of t is **free** in $\lambda x.t$ if all the free variables of s are free in $\lambda x.t$. A **maximal free expression** of $\lambda x.t$ is a free expression of $\lambda x.t$ which is not contained into any other free expression of $\lambda x.t$.

Fully lazy sharings. The various definitions of fully lazy sharing come from a combination of the previous idea with one or more of the technical tools described in section 1.1.

The first description of fully lazy sharing is in the *graph* evaluation technique presented by C.P. Wadsworth [Wad71]. This graph reduction performs only a partial copy of a duplicated function body, by avoiding the copy of its maximal free expressions (see Example 1a). O. Shivers and M. Wand [SW05] enrich the graph structure of [Wad71] to allow a simple and efficient implementation. For this they also use a different characterization of what has to be copied, which we detail in Section 3.1.

Two other approaches combine *graphs* with other tools. First S. Peyton-Jones [Jon87] reaches a simple graph formalism thanks to a fully-lazy version of λ-lifting. Following [Hug82], fully-lazy λ-lifting replaces the extraction of the free variables of a function by the *extraction* of its maximal free expressions. Second, T. Blanc, J.-J. Lévy and L. Maranget [BLM07] derive a graph implementation of fully lazy sharing through the sharing-via-labelling principle, using *labels* that characterize optimal sharing for a weak λ-calculus studied in [ÇH98]. This approach can copy *fewer* graph nodes of the duplicated abstractions (see Example 1b).

Finally, Z. Ariola and M. Felleisen [AF97] and P. Sestoft [Ses97] use the *extraction* of maximal free expressions to build fully lazy versions of (respectively) the call-by-need λ-calculus [AFM⁺95] and Launchbury's natural semantics for laziness [Lau93]. Both solutions are based on *closures* represented by *let ... in ...* constructs. The former solution [AF97] uses a more restrictive definition of free expressions and hence may in some cases copy *more* nodes than the others (see Example 1c).

Example 1.

Bold lines identify the parts of the function that are duplicated by the different models. See Section 3.1 for a formal statement.

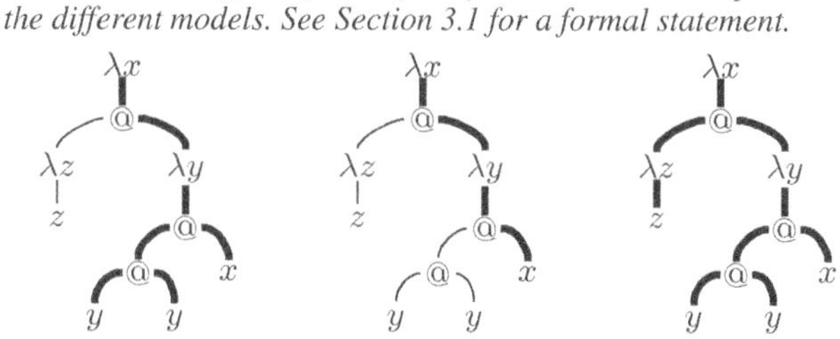

(a) [Wad71] (b) [BLM07] (c) [AF97]

Summary. The following table sums up how each of the previous works gives its own view on fully lazy sharing, with different interpretations of the same main idea and using various combinations of technical tools that are sometimes hardly comparable. We use the symbol = to mean "as many copied nodes as [Wad71]".

		Tools			
	Dupl.	Graphs	Extraction	Closures	Labels
[Wad71]	=	✓			
[Jon87]	=	✓	✓		
[AF97]	More		✓	✓	
[Ses97]	=		✓	✓	
[SW05]	=	✓			
[BLM07]	Fewer	✓			✓

This paper proposes a formal setting in which all the approaches mentioned above can be expressed. This allows us to formally compare them and leads us to the two following conclusions:

- The previous approaches correspond to at least three different graph implementations. This means that, strictly speaking, they do not all induce the same amount of sharing. Hence, despite the fact that all these approaches intend to implement the same idea their equivalence is not obvious.
- However, all these approaches have the same reduction space. This means that the different implementations of fully lazy sharing perform the same number of β-reductions. In other words, any further comparison of these approaches need not anymore take this parameter into account.

1.3 Content of the paper

An axiomatic framework for sharing-via-labelling. We build in Section 2 an axiomatic framework which generalizes the work of T. Blanc, J.-J. Lévy and L. Maranget [BLM07] and allows us to express all the previous approaches. We use labelled terms to describe the graphs realizing optimal sharing for a given notion of weak reduction. Various weak reduction notions are defined thanks to an axiomatic description of the parts of the program where reduction is forbidden. In any case the restrictions concern only evaluation in the body of a non-instantiated function, called partial evaluation. This implies that the call-by-value and call-by-name strategies are always valid. However, the different weak calculi may or may not be confluent (see [ÇH98] and Example 3).

This approach of sharing-via-labelling allows us in Section 3 to relate all the definitions of fully lazy sharing that do not rely on supercombinators and λ-lifting. In other words this axiomatic framework, which is designed in higher-order rewriting, covers the definitions of full laziness which directly operate in the higher-order world [Wad71, AF97, Ses97, SW05, BLM07]. The remaining approaches using a translation to first-order rewriting by λ-lifting [Hug82, Jon87] are studied separately in Section 4. The translation to first-order by means of combinators of D. Turner [Tur79] is out of the scope of the present paper, since these combinators simulate explicit substitutions and then introduce additional reduction steps.

Notably due to its axiomatic nature, our framework is not suitable for an immediate implementation. On the other hand, this approach teaches us something about full laziness in general and on its various concrete implementations. The novelty of our framework lies in the fact that it cannot be seen as a straightforward generalization of any of the aforementioned embodiments of full laziness taken in isolation: the axiomatization rather comes from an analysis of the similarities and the differences of all the concrete systems. This yields a new system whose specific properties may be understood as the *intersection* of the particular properties of the various concrete systems. In other words, our axiomatization tries to grasp the essence of full laziness.

A formal coding of higher order into first order by λ-lifting. The λ-lifting program transformation turns a λ-term into a first-order term. The main feature of λ-lifting is the transformation of λ-abstractions into function symbols, also called supercombinators, over which first-order reduction rules are defined. As emphasized in [LM09], this transformation unveils a tight relation between weak λ-calculus and first-order rewriting.

Usual definitions of λ-liftings [Joh85] proceed by first defining the transformation of λ-abstractions, and then iteratively applying the process to a λ-term until it contains no more λ-abstractions. Definitions differ in particular in the way in which a single λ-abstraction is transformed and on the order in which the iteration is applied. For instance, [Jon87] describes a bottom-up transformation, while [Ses97] iterates in an unspecified order. We ensure the consistence of these two views by giving a definition of fully-lazy λ-lifting in which the order of the iterative process is irrelevant.

Since λ-lifting is an iterative process that turns progressively a λ-term into a first-order term, none of the intermediate steps is in either of these worlds. Nevertheless, we would like to embody the source, the target, and all the intermediate steps of the transformation into a single formalism. To this aim we use Combinatory Reduction Systems (CRS), a higher-order rewriting framework introduced by J.W. Klop and reviewed in [KvOvR93] that mixes abstractions and symbols. The β-reduction as well as the target first-order reduction have a straightforward encoding into CRS rules. Moreover, fully lazy λ-lifting itself can then be seen as a rewriting process: it is expressed in Section 4 as a confluent and strongly normalizing CRS reduction relation.

We provide a new proof of correctness of fully lazy λ-lifting by showing that the transformation preserves reduction sequences: each single reduction step in the source (resp. target) system is simulated by exactly one single step in the target (resp. source) system. The proof is small-step: the reduction sequences are proved to be preserved in every intermediate step of the transformation. Moreover, we prove that the notion of optimal sharing is also preserved, which has two consequences:

- The direct [Wad71] and the λ-lifting based [Jon87] approaches of full laziness are reduction-wise equivalent.
- Fully-lazy λ-lifting establishes a link between optimal sharing in the weak λ-calculus [BLM07] and the better known optimality theory of first-order rewriting [Mar91, Ter03]. This emphasizes in a new way the "first-order" nature of weak reduction, without any de Bruijn indices or explicit substitutions (contrary to [Mar91]).

A final bonus remark is an incidental point which happens to have some theoretical significance: while β-reduction and λ-lifting considered separately can be seen as orthogonal systems[2], their combination cannot. As far as the author is aware, the system derived in this paper is the first successful optimality-oriented labelling of a non-orthogonal system.

Outline. The paper comprises three main parts: Section 2 presents the abstract notions of prefix, weak reduction, and sharing-via-labelling and gives a proof of the sharing property for the axiomatic framework. Section 3 restricts the axiomatics to enforce full laziness and proves a generic equivalence between several notions of fully lazy sharing. Section 4 focuses on the particular fully lazy system of [Wad71, SW05] whose properties allow a clean definition of fully lazy λ-lifting which establishes a strong link between weak β-reduction and first-order rewriting.

For lack of space most proofs are only sketched here. The full versions are in a companion technical report [Bal11].

2. Sharing and β-reduction

We define in this section an axiomatic framework in which the higher-order approaches [Wad71, AF97, Ses97, SW05, BLM07] to fully lazy sharing can be expressed. We propose an axiomatic notion of *weak β-reduction* in Subsection 2.1, whose optimal sharing is characterized by the *sharing-via-labelling systems* introduced in Section 2.2. Section 2.3 then shows that reduction of labelled terms in sharing-via-labelling systems represents *reduction of graphs*.

All this is expressed in Combinatory Reduction Systems (CRS). For lack of space, we only recall the basic syntax and mechanisms.

[2] in brief, a system is orthogonal when no two rules are applicable to overlapping sets of positions of a term, see for instance [Ter03, Bru03]

We refer the reader to [KvOvR93] for a comprehensive presentation. The grammar of **metaterms** in a CRS is:

$$t \quad ::= \quad x \mid [x]t \mid f(t_1, ..., t_n) \mid Z(t_1, ..., t_n)$$

where x is a **variable**, $[x]$ denotes the **binding** of a variable, f is an n-ary **function symbol** taken in a **signature** Σ, and Z is an n-ary **meta-variable**. A **term** is a metaterm without meta-variable, and a **reduction rule** is a pair $L \to R$ of closed metaterms satisfying the following conditions: the meta-variables in L appear as $Z(x_1, ..., x_n)$ with $x_1, ..., x_n$ distinct bound variables, and all the meta-variables of R also appear in L. A rule matches a term by application of a **valuation** σ that maps n-ary meta-variables to n-ary contexts avoiding variable capture. **Reduction** by a rule $L \to R$ with valuation σ in a context c is $c[L^\sigma] \to c[R^\sigma]$.

2.1 Weak β-reduction systems

This section gives an abstract definition of *weak reduction* in the λ-calculus and states one of its crucial properties: disjoint redexes remain disjoint along any reduction sequence (Lemma 1). This lemma serves in particular in the definition of graph reduction in Section 2.3.

Weak reduction forbids the reduction of so-called *frozen redexes*, which are identified by their belonging to the *prefix* of some λ-abstraction. Prefixes are parts of λ-abstractions defined by a *prefix function* satisfying the axioms of a *weak β-reduction system.*

Weak β-reduction systems are CRS over the signature Σ comprising:

- a binary symbol @ for application,
- a unary symbol λ for λ-abstraction,
- a unary dummy symbol ϵ,
- for all $n \in \mathbb{N}$, a countable set $\mathcal{F}_n$ of n-ary symbols.

From now on, by **term** we mean a CRS term over the signature Σ (notation t, u, v, w, a). We use the usual notion of **positions** of terms (notation q), contexts and free variables [KvOvR93]. We write $t^{\{x:=u\}}$ the substitution by u of all the free occurrences of the variable x in t.

Application and λ-abstraction symbols are used to embody λ-terms in this signature, which is made in the usual way: the λ-term $(\lambda x.x)y$ for instance is encoded in the CRS term $@(\lambda([x]x), y)$. We write $\lambda x.t$ as a shorthand for $\lambda([x]t)$. Hence the encoding of $(\lambda x.x)y$ is simply written $@(\lambda x.x, y)$, and the usual β-reduction is represented by the CRS rule $@(\lambda x.Z(x), Z') \to Z(Z')$.

The symbols in the sets $\mathcal{F}_n$ are used in Section 4 to represent supercombinators. Until then they play no role and may be ignored.

The dummy symbol ϵ has no meaning in itself. It is needed for labelling (Subsection 2.2), and serves in particular as a container for dynamically created labels. In the graphical interpretation of labelled terms, the occurrences of ϵ will represent indirections (see Subsection 3.1). As a consequence, occurrences of ϵ should not interfere with β-reduction. This leads to the following countable set of rules to simulate β-reduction by allowing any number of ϵ's between the application and the λ-abstraction:

$$\begin{array}{llll}\beta_0: & @(\lambda x.Z(x), Z') & \to_\beta & \epsilon(Z(\epsilon(Z'))) \\ \beta_1: & @(\epsilon(\lambda x.Z(x)), Z') & \to_\beta & \epsilon(Z(\epsilon(Z'))) \\ \beta_2: & @(\epsilon(\epsilon(\lambda x.Z(x))), Z') & \to_\beta & \epsilon(Z(\epsilon(Z'))) \\ \ldots & & & \end{array}$$

The two ϵ's in the right hand sides are used for the correct labelling of collapsing reductions (see Subsection 2.2). The use of the dummy symbol ϵ is inspired by the notion of *expansion* in term rewriting systems [Ter03, Chap. 8].

Write $\rho : t \to t'$ a reduction ρ of a term t to a term t'. The usual notions of **ancestors** and **descendants**, which track subterms along reduction in the λ-calculus are straightforwardly adapted, as illustrated in Example 2. A **residual** of a redex r is a descendant of r which is still a redex.

Example 2.

The term $t = @(\epsilon(\lambda x.@(x, x)), y)$ reduces by rule β_1 to $t' = \epsilon(@(\epsilon(y), \epsilon(y)))$. The two occurrences of y in t' are the descendants of the y in t, and the latter is the ancestor of the formers. The ϵ in t has no descendant and the ϵ's in t' have no ancestor.

We call **plain** λ-calculus the usual reduction relation where the previous rules can be applied in any context. Weak reduction consists in restricting this reduction relation. Particularly, it affects the reduction under λ-abstractions. Before introducing the formal definition, let us present two different well-known examples:

Example 3.

1. *The **naive weak reduction** simply forbids any reduction under λ-abstractions.*
2. *A more refined version, studied in particular in [ÇH98], allows no reduction between an occurrence of a bound variable and its binder. Formally, if r is a redex of contractum r', then the reduction $C[r] \to C[r']$ is allowed if and only if the context C binds no variable that appears free in r. We call this version **CH-weak reduction**.*

It is known that CH-weak reduction yields a confluent weak calculus while naive weak reduction does not [ÇH98].

To specify the previous notions, we introduce a notion of prefix: call a n-ary **closed prefix** of a term t a n-ary context p which does not contain any free variable and such that there are terms $t_1, ..., t_n$ satisfying $t = p[t_1, ..., t_n]$. Example 4 gives two closed prefixes of the same term. Call a **prefix function** a function that takes a term t as input and returns a closed prefix of t.

Example 4.

Let $t = \lambda x.@(@(z_1, z_2), \lambda y.@(@(y, z_3), x))$. The two contexts $\lambda x.@([], \lambda y.@([], x))$ and $\lambda x.@([], \lambda y.@(@(y, []), x))$ are two closed prefixes of t, called respectively spine *and* skeleton *(see Section 3.1). These two prefixes are marked with bold lines in the two following pictures.*

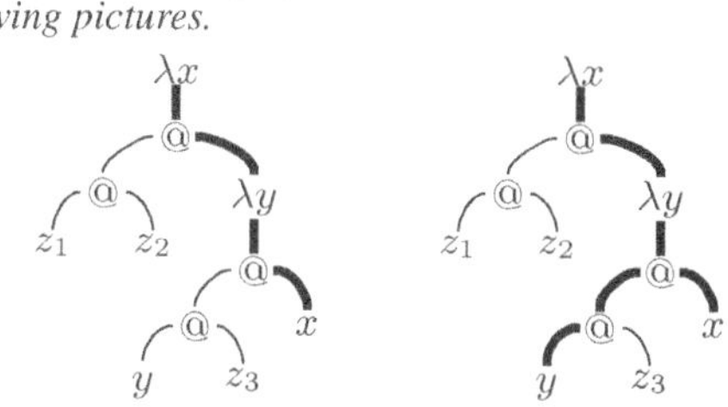

Spine *Skeleton*

A *weak β-reduction system* is defined below by a prefix function $\mathcal{P}$ satisfying some conditions. The first condition is a simple restriction linked to bound variables. The second condition controls the evolution of $\mathcal{P}(t)$ when free variables of t are substituted by terms. In particular, $\mathcal{P}(t^{\{x:=u\}})$ is required to contain $\mathcal{P}(t)$, and the extension from $\mathcal{P}(t)$ to $\mathcal{P}(t^{\{x:=u\}})$ has to be uniform. This uniformity is enforced by the use of an auxiliairy function $\mathcal{P}^\Box$.

Call a **weak β-reduction system** a prefix function $\mathcal{P}$ such that:

- For any term $\lambda x.t$ such that $\mathcal{P}(\lambda x.t) = p$ and $\lambda x.t = p[t_1, ..., t_n]$, the variable x does not appear free in any of the t_i's (which are called the **parameters** of $\lambda x.t$). In other words, $\mathcal{P}(\lambda x.t)$ contains all the occurrences of x that are free in t.
- There is an auxiliary prefix function $\mathcal{P}^\Box$ such that for any p in the codomain of $\mathcal{P}$ and for any terms $t_1, ..., t_n$ where no free

variable of a t_i is bound in p, the equation $\mathcal{P}(p[t_1, ..., t_n]) = p[\mathcal{P}^{\Box}(t_1), ..., \mathcal{P}^{\Box}(t_n)]$ holds.

A weak β-reduction system defines a notion of **weak reduction** as follows: β-reduction is forbidden in the prefix of any λ-abstraction. Call a **frozen position** of a term t a position that is in the prefix of some λ-abstraction of t. Call a **frozen β-redex** a redex whose main @ symbol occurs at a frozen position.

Example 5.

The two weak reductions of Example 3 can be captured by our axiomatic definition:

1. *Naive weak reduction is given by $\mathcal{P}_n$ such that $\mathcal{P}_n(t) = p$ where $t = p[x_1, ..., x_n]$ and $x_1, ..., x_n$ are all the free variable occurrences of t. The auxiliary function is $\mathcal{P}_n^{\Box} = \mathcal{P}_n$ (the whole substituted term is included into the prefix).*
2. *CH-weak reduction can be given by $\mathcal{P}_{ch}$ such that $\mathcal{P}_{ch}(t) = p$ where $t = p[t_1, ..., t_n]$ and $t_1, ..., t_n$ are all the* maximal *free expressions of t. The auxiliary function $\mathcal{P}_{ch}^{\Box}$ is the constant mapping returning the empty unary context $[]$ (the prefix is stable by substitution). We will see in Section 3.2 that $\mathcal{P}_{ch}$ is not the unique representation of CH-weak reduction.*

An important feature of weak reduction is that it cannot nest the residuals of disjoint redexes. This fact is formalized in Lemma 1, and will be useful in Section 2.3 to ground the notion of parallel reduction.

Lemma 1 (Disjoint residuals). *Let $\rho : t \to t'$ be a reduction and $r_1, ..., r_n$ (non frozen) redexes of t occurring at disjoint positions. Then the descendants of $r_1, ..., r_n$ also occur at disjoint positions.*

Example 6 shows why Lemma 1 is a feature of weak reduction which is not valid in the plain λ-calculus.

Example 6.

Suppose r_1 and r_2 are two redexes. In the left term r_1 is frozen for any weak β-reduction system.

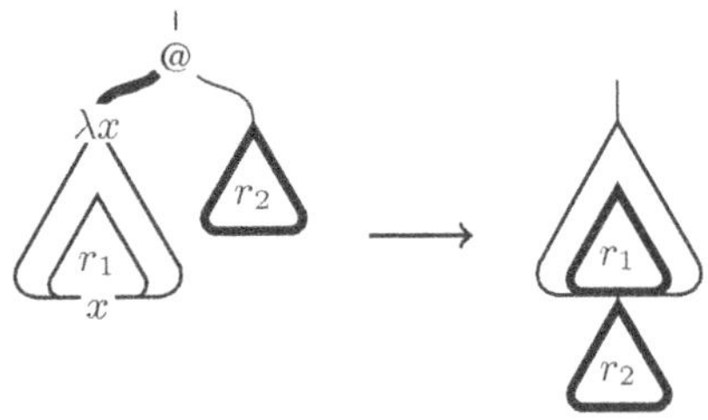

To prepare the implementation of optimal sharing for weak β-reduction systems in next section (2.2), we give a characterization of redex creation in these systems. Suppose $\rho : t \to_\beta t'$ in a weak β-reduction system. A redex of t' is **created** by ρ if it is not the descendant of a (non frozen) redex of t. The reduction can create redexes in t' at exactly three places:

1. At the root of the contractum, the body of the main λ-abstraction is connected to the context. This can create a new contact between an application and a λ-abstraction.
2. At the places where a substitution occurs, the argument is connected to the body of the main λ-abstraction, or to the context if the body is degenerated.
3. In the prefix of the main λ-abstraction, a previously frozen redex can be "unfrozen" by ρ, as r_1 in Example 6. In other words, a reduction forbidden by the weak restriction in t can be authorized in t'.

2.2 Sharing-via-labelling systems

We define in this section a *labelling* for weak β-reduction systems which characterizes optimal sharing and yields a graph implementation. As in [Lé80], the labels record the past history of a term. This is done in a distributed way since each label remembers only what is relevant to its position. The important point for optimality is that the labels of a redex r are characterized by the past reductions that contributed to the creation of r, which is ensured by the concluding lemmas 2 and 3. These two lemmas also play a key role in the proof of the preservation of the graph structure (so-called sharing property) in Section 2.3.

To embody this *contribution* relation into the labels, we build compound labels of the form $[\Omega, \alpha]$ where a pre-existing label α is *modified* by the *name* Ω of a contributing redex. The *labelled β-reduction* then modifies the labels of the positions where the reduction can contribute to something, following the characterization of redex creation given at the end of the previous subsection. Names and contribution are required to satisfy three axioms which ensure that the name of a redex correctly reflects its contributors.

The labelled terms are formalized as usual CRS terms over a *labelled signature*. Since the labels should not interfere with the normal reduction behaviour, the labelled β-reduction is defined for any possible labelling of the source.

For any countable set $\mathcal{L}$ whose elements are called labels (and written α, β, γ...), a **labelled signature** $\Sigma_{\mathcal{L}}$ is defined as the set $\{f^\alpha | f \in \Sigma, \alpha \in \mathcal{L}\}$. From now on, a **$\mathcal{L}$-labelled term** denotes a CRS term over $\Sigma_{\mathcal{L}}$. In other words, the labels are associated to the symbols, and never directly to the variables or the bindings. Remark that the labels are arbitrary objects: in a concrete definition they can be simple letters as well as richly structured objects.

We write $\lambda^\alpha x.t$ (resp. x^α) as a shorthand for $\lambda^\alpha([x]t)$ (resp. $\epsilon^\alpha(x)$). Write $\tau(t)$ for the label of the root symbol of the labelled term t. Write $\epsilon_k^{\alpha_1 \dots \alpha_k}(t)$ as a shorthand for $\epsilon^{\alpha_1}(...\epsilon^{\alpha_k}(t))$, where the case $k = 0$ represents t.

Write $|.|$ the (trivial) map from terms over $\Sigma_{\mathcal{L}}$ to terms over Σ that removes the labels of all symbols. By requiring the condition $|\mathcal{P}(t)| = \mathcal{P}(|t|)$, we get a straightforward extension to $\Sigma_{\mathcal{L}}$ of any weak β-reduction system $\mathcal{P}$ over Σ.

Since neither ϵ's nor labels shall interfere with β-reduction, labelled β-redexes allow any number of ϵ occurrences and can be decorated with any labels: for any $\mathcal{L}$, a **$\mathcal{L}$-labelled β-redex** is a $\mathcal{L}$-labelled term of the form $@^\alpha(\epsilon_k^{\beta_1 \dots \beta_k}(\lambda^\gamma x.t), a)$. Labelled β-reduction is defined later, since it requires an additional notion of sharing-via-labelling systems given below.

We consider sets of labels of the form $\mathcal{L} = \mathcal{V}^{\mathcal{N}}$, generated by the following grammar for any two countable sets $\mathcal{V}$ and $\mathcal{N}$:

$$\mathcal{V}^{\mathcal{N}} \quad ::= \quad \mathcal{V} \mid [\mathcal{N}, \mathcal{V}^{\mathcal{N}}]$$

The label $[\Omega, \alpha]$ denotes "the label α modified by Ω". Write $[\Omega_1 ... \Omega_n, \alpha]$ as a shorthand for $[\Omega_1, ...[\Omega_n, \alpha]]$. Any Ω_i is called a **modifier** of $[\Omega_1 ... \Omega_n, \alpha]$. The *virginal* labels (the labels in $\mathcal{V}$) denote positions that are free from any past history, they will be modified into labels of the form $[\Omega_1 ... \Omega_n, \alpha]$ along the reductions. Let $\mathcal{S}$ be a tuple $\langle \mathcal{P}, \mathcal{N}, \mathcal{V}, \eta, \hookrightarrow \rangle$ where:

- $\mathcal{P}$ is a weak β-reduction system.
- $\mathcal{N}$ is a countable set whose elements are called **(redex) names** (notation Ω).
- $\mathcal{V}$ is a countable set whose elements are called **virginal labels**, with two distinguished elements $\top$ and $\bot$.
- η is a function from $\mathcal{V}^{\mathcal{N}}$-labelled redexes to names.
- $\hookrightarrow$ is a transitive and irreflexive relation on $\mathcal{N}$ called **contribution relation**.

The **terms** considered in $\mathcal{S}$ are the $\mathcal{V}^{\mathcal{N}}$-labelled terms. Call **virginal term** a term whose labels are all virginal and different.

Write $\uparrow\Omega = \{\Omega' \mid \Omega' \hookrightarrow \Omega\}$ the set of all the contributors of the name Ω. Contribution is extended to labels: define $\uparrow\alpha = \emptyset$ if α is a virginal label, and $\uparrow[\Omega,\alpha] = \{\Omega\} \cup \uparrow\Omega \cup \uparrow\alpha$ otherwise. Write $\Omega \hookrightarrow \alpha$ when $\Omega \in \uparrow\alpha$.

$\mathcal{S}$ is a **sharing-via-labelling** system if the following axioms are satisfied:

- (*Redex contributors*)
$$\uparrow\eta(@^\alpha(\epsilon_k^{\beta_1\dots\beta_k}(\lambda^\gamma x.t),a)) = \uparrow\alpha \cup (\textstyle\bigcup_i \uparrow\beta_i) \cup \uparrow\gamma$$
- (*Name scope*) If $\lambda^\gamma x.p$ is in the codomain of $\mathcal{P}$, and a_t, a_u are any terms and $t_1,\dots,t_n,u_1,\dots,u_n$ are terms whose free variables are not bound in $\lambda^\gamma x.p$, then
$$\eta(@^\alpha(\epsilon_k^{\beta_1\dots\beta_k}(\lambda^\gamma x.p[t_1,\dots,t_n]),a_t)) = \eta(@^\alpha(\epsilon_k^{\beta_1\dots\beta_k}(\lambda^\gamma x.p[u_1,\dots,u_n]),a_u))$$
- (*Name equality*) If $\eta(r) = \eta(r')$ then $\tau(r) = \tau(r')$.

The axiom *Redex contributors* states that the name of a redex collects the contributors of the essential parts of the redex, that means its main application, its main λ-abstraction, and all that lays in between these two positions. The axiom *Name scope* states that the name of a redex does not depend of what is deeper than the smallest prefix of the main abstraction, while axiom *Name equality* states that the equality of the names of two redexes implies the equality of their respective root labels.

Example 7.

Let $\mathcal{V}$ be any countable set.

1. *The names in $\mathcal{N}_{seq}$ are sequences of labels. Since the names also take part into the definition of the labels, a mutually recursive definition of names and labels is required:*
$$\mathcal{N}_{seq} ::= \mathcal{L};\dots;\mathcal{L}$$
$$\mathcal{L} ::= \mathcal{V}^{\mathcal{N}_{seq}}$$
Define the name of a redex as
$$\eta_{seq}(@^\alpha(\epsilon_k^{\beta_1\dots\beta_k}(\lambda^\gamma x.t),a)) = \alpha;\beta_1;\dots;\beta_k;\gamma$$
The contribution relation is defined by: $\Omega \hookrightarrow_{seq} \alpha_1;\dots;\alpha_n$ if and only if there is at least one i such that $\Omega \hookrightarrow_{seq} \alpha_i$.
For $\mathcal{P} \in \{\mathcal{P}_n, \mathcal{P}_{ch}\}$, the system $\langle\mathcal{P}, \mathcal{N}_{seq}, \mathcal{V}, \eta_{seq}, \hookrightarrow_{seq}\rangle$ is a sharing-via-labelling system. The definitions of $\mathcal{N}_{seq}$, η_{seq}, and $\hookrightarrow_{seq}$ correspond to the system presented in [BLM07].
2. *The names in $\mathcal{N}_{ctx}$ are $\mathcal{L}$-labelled contexts, with once again a mutually recursive definition using $\mathcal{L} ::= \mathcal{V}^{\mathcal{N}_{ctx}}$. Define*
$$\eta_{ctx}(@^\alpha(\epsilon_k^{\beta_1\dots\beta_k}(\lambda^\gamma x.t),a)) = @^\alpha(\epsilon_k^{\beta_1\dots\beta_k}(\lambda^\gamma x.p),[])$$
where $\mathcal{P}(\lambda^\gamma x.t) = \lambda^\gamma x.p$.
Write $\Omega \hookrightarrow_{ctx} c$ if there is a label α in c such that $\Omega \hookrightarrow_{ctx} \alpha$.
For $\langle\mathcal{P}_{ch}, \mathcal{N}_{ctx}, \mathcal{V}, \eta_{ctx}, \hookrightarrow_{ctx}\rangle$ to be a sharing-via-labelling system, the axiom Redex contributors requires that the prefixes satisfy the following property: all the contributors of the labels of a prefix $\lambda^\gamma x.p$ contribute to γ. Fortunately, in this system this property is an invariant of labelled β-reduction (defined below).
The system $\langle\mathcal{P}_n, \mathcal{N}_{ctx}, \mathcal{V}, \eta_{ctx}, \hookrightarrow_{ctx}\rangle$ is not a sharing-via-labelling system since it breaks the axiom Name scope.

Labelled β-reduction is defined by a rule scheme which propagates the name of the reduced redex in the reduced term for recording of the contributions. For this, the constructor $[.,.]$ extends to a function on labelled terms: $[\Omega, t]$ is defined as the labelled term t in which all the labels are modified by the function $\alpha \mapsto [\Omega,\alpha]$.

Labelled β-reduction in a sharing-via-labelling system is defined by the rule scheme:

$$@^\alpha(\epsilon_k^{\beta_1\dots\beta_k}(\lambda^\gamma x.p[t_1,\dots,t_n]),a) \rightarrow_\beta \epsilon^{[\Omega,\top]}([\Omega,p])^{\{x:=\epsilon^{[\Omega,\bot]}(a)\}}[t_1,\dots,t_n]$$

where $\lambda^\gamma x.p = \mathcal{P}(\lambda^\gamma x.p[t_1,\dots,t_n])$ and
where $\Omega = \eta(@^\alpha(\epsilon_k^{\beta_1\dots\beta_k}(\lambda^\gamma x.p[t_1,\dots,t_n]),a))$.
The name Ω is added in three areas of the reduced term:

1. At the root of the contractum, with the new label $[\Omega,\top]$.
2. At the places where a substitution occurs, with the new label $[\Omega,\bot]$. Remark in Example 8 how $\top$ and $\bot$ work as parentheses in the syntactic tree of the term.
3. In the prefix of the main abstraction of the redex, as an additional modifier to pre-existing labels.

Remark that these three places follow the three cases of redex creation given in Section 2.1 and that removing the labels in this rule yields exactly the unlabelled β-reduction of Section 2.1.

Example 8.

Let $r = @^\alpha(\lambda^\gamma x.@^\delta(@^\iota(x^\mu,x^\nu),\lambda^\kappa y.y^\sigma),a)$ be a β-redex. We reduce r in two sharing-via-labelling systems of Example 7.

1. *In $\langle\mathcal{P}_n, \mathcal{N}_{seq}, \mathcal{V}, \eta_{seq}, \hookrightarrow_{seq}\rangle$ the name of r is the sequence $\Omega = \alpha;\gamma$, and the prefix of the λ-abstraction is its whole body. Then all the labels are modified in the contractum:*

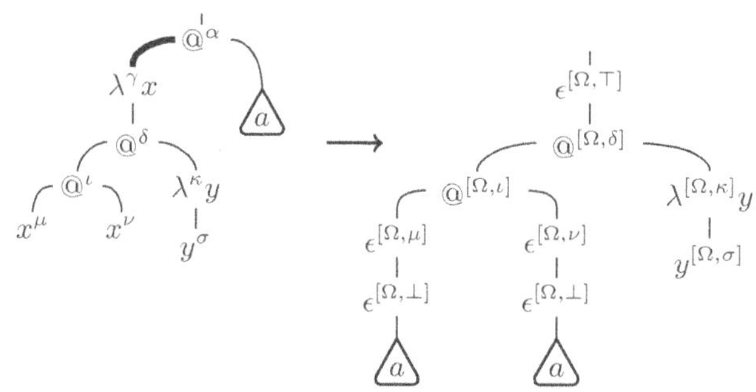

2. *In $\langle\mathcal{P}_{ch}, \mathcal{N}_{ctx}, \mathcal{V}, \eta_{ctx}, \hookrightarrow_{ctx}\rangle$, the name of r is the labelled context $\Omega = @^\alpha(\lambda^\gamma x.@^\delta(@^\iota(x^\mu,x^\nu),[]),[])$. The only modified labels are those of the prefix of the λ-abstraction, marked with bold lines below.*

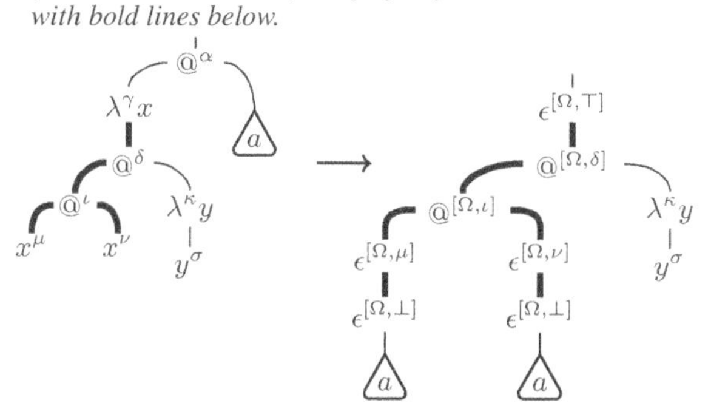

This section ends with the two lemmas 2 and 3, which show how the labels reflect the contribution relation between redexes. In particular, the name of a redex r characterizes the past reductions that led to the creation of r.

Lemma 2 (Redex stability). *Let r be a (non frozen) redex of a term t. If r_d is a descendant of r after a reduction $\rho : t \to_\beta t'$, then r_d is still a (possibly frozen) redex and $\eta(r_d) = \eta(r)$.*

Lemma 3 (Direct contribution). *If a redex of name Ω_c is created by the reduction of a redex of name Ω, then $\Omega \hookrightarrow \Omega_c$.*

2.3 Sharing

This section proves the main property of sharing-via-labelling systems: *parallel labelled reduction* simulates graph reduction (Theorem 1). As in [BLM07], the labelled terms are linked to graphs with the sharing-via-labelling principle seen in the introduction: labels are interpreted as memory locations. The proof of the simulation is then done by ensuring that the two following invariants are preserved by parallel labelled reduction:

1. A term t has the **sharing property**, written $\mathbb{S}(t)$, when any two subterms of t with same label are syntactically equal. This is the main property we want to preserve.
2. A term t has the **maximality property**, written $\mathbb{M}(t)$, when for any (non frozen) redex of name Ω and any subterm of label α in t it is not true that $\Omega \hookrightarrow \alpha$. This property is widely used in the subsequent proofs, it ensures in particular that all the occurrences of a given label are created at the same time (see Example 9). Lemmas 2 and 3 are the cornerstone of the preservation of the maximality property.

Parallel labelled reduction is defined for any term t satisfying the sharing property $\mathbb{S}(t)$: let α be the label of a (non frozen) redex of t. Since $\mathbb{S}(t)$ holds, all the redexes labelled by α are equal and have disjoint positions (however, some may be frozen). The parallel labelled reduction of α, written $t \overset{\alpha}{\Rightarrow}_\beta t'$, is then defined as the simultaneous replacement of all the (non frozen) redexes with label α by their contractum. By lemmas 1 and 2, parallel labelled reduction is well defined as a sequence of single steps, for instance any iterated reduction of the non frozen redexes with label α.

Theorem 1 (Preservation of sharing). *If $\mathbb{M}(t)$, $\mathbb{S}(t)$ and $t \overset{\alpha_\Omega}{\Longrightarrow}_\beta t'$, then $\mathbb{M}(t')$, and $\mathbb{S}(t')$.*

Proof. (Sketch) Verification of $\mathbb{M}(t')$. Suppose there is a redex r' with name Ω' and a subterm u' with label α' in t' such that $\Omega' \hookrightarrow \alpha'$. If r' is created by the reduction, then Lemma 3 contradicts $\mathbb{M}(t)$. Else, Lemma 2 and axiom *Redex contributors* contradict either $\mathbb{M}(t)$ or axiom *Name equality*.

Verification of $\mathbb{S}(t')$. Let u' and v' be two subterms of t' with same label α'. By case on the origin of both labels α': if one is created and the other is a descendant of a label α' of t, then by $\mathbb{M}(t)$ and Lemma 3 we reach a contradiction, else both have the same origin and evolution (using $\mathbb{S}(t)$). □

Example 9 shows why maximality $\mathbb{M}$ is necessary to the preservation of sharing $\mathbb{S}$.

Example 9.
Consider the system $\langle \mathcal{P}_{ch}, \mathcal{N}_{seq}, \mathcal{V}, \eta_{seq}, \hookrightarrow_{seq}\rangle$ defined in Example 7 and the labelled term $t = @^\alpha(x^{[\gamma;\delta,\iota]}, @^\gamma(\lambda^\delta z.z^\iota, y^\kappa))$. The property $\mathbb{S}(t)$ holds since all the labels of t are different. Remark that t contains a redex $@^\gamma(\lambda^\delta z.z^\iota, y^\kappa)$ of name $\gamma;\delta$. Hence $\mathbb{M}(t)$ does not hold since t contains a label $[\gamma;\delta,\iota]$.
Then $t \overset{\gamma}{\Rightarrow}_\beta @^\alpha(x^{[\gamma;\delta,\iota]}, \epsilon^{[\gamma;\delta,\iota]}(y^\kappa)) = t'$ where the two subterms of t' with label $[\gamma;\delta,\iota]$ are different: $\mathbb{S}(t')$ is falsified.

Finally, labelled terms represent graphs and parallel labelled reduction represents graph reduction.

3. Full laziness

This section shows how the various known implementations of full laziness correspond to several (at least three) different sharing-via-labelling systems (Section 3.1). Thus, they correspond to different graph reductions featuring different amounts of sharing. However, we are going to prove in Section 3.2 that these implementations are reduction-wise equivalent.

Along this section, the signature Σ is restricted to $\{@, \lambda, \epsilon\}$.

3.1 Encodings into sharing-via-labelling systems

The motto of sharing-via-labelling is "labels denote memory locations". What happens to the labels during reduction describes directly what happens to the nodes of the corresponding graph:

- A new label corresponds to a new node. There are two cases:
  - A label of the form $[\Omega, \top]$ or $[\Omega, \bot]$ appears only on ϵ. It represents a new indirection node that contains a pointer leading to the term.
  - Any other $[\Omega, \alpha]$ denotes a new copy of a node labelled α.
- An unchanged label is a node unaffected by the reduction.

The key of the encoding of graph reduction systems or closure-based systems into sharing-via-labelling systems is to modify exactly the labels of what is needed to be copied. Since the rules of a sharing-via-labelling system modify exactly the labels of the prefix of the main λ-abstraction, this amounts to take as prefix of a λ-abstraction exactly what has to be duplicated of its body.

Remark 1. *Our β-rule falsely suggests that an arbitrary number of indirections can be contracted in unit time. The techniques presented in [Jon87] can be used to avoid chains of indirections.*

To describe the encodings of the higher-order approaches to full laziness into sharing-via-labelling systems, we formally define two useful prefixes mentioned in Example 4.

- Call **spine** of a term $\lambda x.t$ the prefix $\lambda x.p$ where p is the prefix of t which contains exactly the positions that are above a free occurrence of x, including the free occurrences of x. Remark that in any weak β-reduction system $\mathcal{P}$, any prefix $\mathcal{P}(\lambda x.t)$ contains the spine of $\lambda x.t$.
- Call **skeleton** of a term $\lambda x.t$ the prefix $\lambda x.p$ where p is the prefix of t containing exactly the positions that are not in a free expression of $\lambda x.t$. As done in [SW05] the skeleton can also be seen as an iterated spine: to get the skeleton of $\lambda x.t$, start with the spine of $\lambda x.t$ and iteratively add to the obtained prefix the spines of all the λ-abstractions that are in the prefix built so far.

The two approaches by C.P. Wadsworth [Wad71] and O. Shivers and M. Wand [SW05] reach fully lazy sharing by two graph implementations in which the duplicated part of an instantiated function is its skeleton. The former uses the definition based on the maximal free expressions while the latter follows the characterization by iterated spine. They are both represented by the weak β-reduction system $\mathcal{P}_{ch}$ such that $\mathcal{P}_{ch}(\lambda x.t)$ is the skeleton of $\lambda x.t$.

In [Ses97], P. Sestoft revises Launchbury's lazy semantics [Lau93] and proposes a fully lazy variant using additional let-bindings: if $\lambda x.p$ is the skeleton of $\lambda x.t$ and $\lambda x.t = \lambda x.p[t_1, ..., t_n]$, then $\lambda x.t$ is replaced by *let* $x_1 = t_1, ..., x_n = t_n$ *in* $\lambda x.p[x_1, ..., x_n]$ with $x_1, ..., x_n$ fresh variables. After this extraction of the maximal free expressions $t_1, ..., t_n$ of $\lambda x.t$, a duplication of the λ-abstraction duplicates the subterm $\lambda x.p[x_1, ..., x_n]$ but does not duplicate the let-parameters $t_1, ..., t_n$. This is again represented by the weak reduction system $\mathcal{P}_{ch}$.

The work by T. Blanc, J.-J. Lévy and L. Maranget [BLM07] already uses a system isomorphic to a sharing-via-labelling system.

Their labelled β-reduction modifies only the labels of the spine of the main λ-abstraction. Thus it corresponds to a weak β-reduction system $\mathcal{P}_{blm}$ where $\mathcal{P}_{blm}(\lambda x.t)$ is the spine of $\lambda x.t$. Moreover their frozen redexes are the redexes containing a free occurrence of a variable bound above: they coincide with those given by $\mathcal{P}_{ch}$.

In their call-by-need λ-calculus [AF97], Z. Ariola and M. Felleisen allow the substitution, and thus the duplication, of values. Their fully lazy extension consists in restricting these allowed duplications to a set of fully lazy values: values that do not contain any "free expression". The difference with the previous cases lies in their non-standard definition of free expressions: they use the usual criterion given in Section 1.2 but they exclude the variables and the λ-abstractions. Hence their fully lazy values correspond to the prefixes of the weak β-reduction system $\mathcal{P}_{af}$ such that:

- If $\lambda x.p$ is the skeleton of $\lambda x.t$ and $\lambda x.t = \lambda x.p[t_1, ..., t_n]$ then $\mathcal{P}_{af}(\lambda x.t) = \lambda x.p[\mathcal{P}^{\square}_{af}(t_1), ..., \mathcal{P}^{\square}_{af}(t_n)]$.
- $\mathcal{P}^{\square}_{af}(\lambda x.t) = \mathcal{P}_{af}(\lambda x.t)$.
- $\mathcal{P}^{\square}_{af}(@(t_1, t_2)) = []$.
- If $\mathcal{P}^{\square}_{af}(t) = []$ then $\mathcal{P}^{\square}_{af}(\epsilon(t)) = []$ else $\mathcal{P}^{\square}_{af}(\epsilon(t)) = \epsilon(\mathcal{P}^{\square}_{af}(t))$.

Finally, the higher-order approaches [Wad71, AF97, Ses97, SW05, BLM07] to full laziness correspond to three different weak β-reduction systems $\mathcal{P}_{ch}$, $\mathcal{P}_{blm}$ and $\mathcal{P}_{af}$, which we are going to relate in the next section. Example 10 illustrates how the systems $\mathcal{P}_{blm}$ and $\mathcal{P}_{af}$ can yield the same parallel labelled reduction in spite of their differences.

Example 10.

Let $t = \lambda x.\lambda y.@(@(x, r_1), \lambda z.r_2)$ be a term such that r_1, r_2 are two redexes that do not contain any free occurrence of x. Hence a duplication of the spine $\mathcal{P}_{blm}(t)$ of t (marked with bold lines in the picture) do not duplicate these redexes.

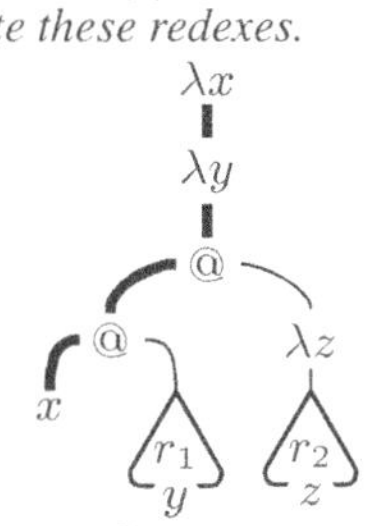

If r_1 (resp. r_2) contains a free occurrence of y (resp. z), then both redexes are at least partially contained in $\mathcal{P}_{af}(t)$, and thus duplicated in this system. However, in this case r_1 and r_2 are and remain frozen in both systems, and their label will change before they are unfrozen: the additional duplications are not harmful.

3.2 Equivalence of the parallel labelled reductions

In this section we define a family $\mathcal{W}$ of weak β-reduction systems that contains $\mathcal{P}_{ch}$, $\mathcal{P}_{blm}$ and $\mathcal{P}_{af}$ and we show that all the sharing-via-labelling systems based on the weak β-reduction systems of $\mathcal{W}$ are equivalent, in the sense that they can simulate one another using exactly the same number of shared reduction steps. For this we define a relation $\sim$ on labelled terms which is stable by reduction, and prove that any two terms in relation share the same non-frozen redexes. The relation $\sim$ relates two terms t_1 and t_2 of two different systems $\mathcal{S}_1$ and $\mathcal{S}_2$ whenever t_1 and t_2 can be reached from a common source by two equivalent reduction sequences in $\mathcal{S}_1$ and $\mathcal{S}_2$ (the whole being called a *mirror reduction sequence*).

The definition of $\mathcal{W}$ follows two ideas: the weak β-reduction systems in $\mathcal{W}$ shall enforce CH-weak reduction (for this the third point in particular prevents some applications to be included into a prefix), and all the prefixes are built from spines and skeletons (the first two points, which make the proofs tractable).

A weak β-reduction system $\mathcal{P}$ is in $\mathcal{W}$ if the following additional conditions are satisfied:

- For each abstraction $t = \lambda x.u$, either $\mathcal{P}(t)$ is the spine of t, or $\mathcal{P}(t) = p[\mathcal{P}^{\square}(t_1), ..., \mathcal{P}^{\square}(t_n)]$ where p is the skeleton of t and $t = p[t_1, ..., t_n]$.
- For any $\lambda x.t$, $\mathcal{P}^{\square}(\lambda x.t) = []$ or $\mathcal{P}^{\square}(\lambda x.t) = \mathcal{P}(\lambda x.t)$.
- $\mathcal{P}^{\square}(@(t_1, t_2)) = []$.
- If $\mathcal{P}^{\square}(t) = []$ then $\mathcal{P}^{\square}(\epsilon(t)) = []$ else $\mathcal{P}^{\square}(\epsilon(t)) = \epsilon(\mathcal{P}^{\square}(t))$.

Let $\mathcal{P}_1$ and $\mathcal{P}_2$ be two systems of $\mathcal{W}$. A **mirror reduction sequence** in the systems $\mathcal{P}_1$ and $\mathcal{P}_2$ is a pair (ϱ_1, ϱ_2) such that $\varrho_i = \rho_i^1 ... \rho_i^n$ is a reduction sequence in $\mathcal{P}_i$ and for any $j \in \{1...n\}$ the redexes reduced by the single steps ρ_1^j and ρ_2^j have the same position q_j in the respective source terms. The notion of mirror reduction sequence extends to parallel labelled reduction in two sharing-via-labelling systems based on two (possibly equal) weak β-reduction systems of $\mathcal{W}$.

Let t_1 (resp. t_2) be a term in a sharing-via-labelling system $\mathcal{S}_1$ (resp. $\mathcal{S}_2$). Write $t_1 \sim t_2$ when there is a virginal term t_0 in the intersection of $\mathcal{S}_1$ and $\mathcal{S}_2$ and a mirror reduction sequence (ϱ_1, ϱ_2) in the systems $\mathcal{S}_1$ and $\mathcal{S}_2$ such that ϱ_i is a parallel labelled reduction sequence from t_0 to t_i.

Remark 2. *If $t_1 \sim t_2$ then the two terms have the same set of positions. In particular they contain the same number of ϵ occurrences.*

For any labelled term t, the labels in t induce an equivalence relation on the subterms of t. Say that two subterms u_1 and u_2 of t are **label-equivalent** if and only if $\tau(u_1) = \tau(u_2)$.

Theorem 2 (Sharing equivalence). *If $t_1 \sim t_2$ then the labellings of t_1 and t_2 induce the same label-equivalence on their non frozen applications.*

Proof. (Sketch) We prove two invariants on the pair (t_1, t_2):

1. The equivalence classes of non frozen applications are equal.
2. In each spine, the equivalence classes of applications are equal.

By definition of $t_1 \sim t_2$ there is a parallel labelled mirror reduction sequence (ϱ_1, ϱ_2) leading from a virginal term t_0 to (t_1, t_2). The proof of both invariants is by induction on the number of parallel steps in (ϱ_1, ϱ_2). Remark by Theorem 1 that any intermediate term t in the mirror reduction sequence satisfies $\mathbb{M}(t)$ and $\mathbb{S}(t)$. $\square$

Theorem 2 proves in particular that $\sim$ is a bisimulation: any diagram $\begin{array}{ccc} t & \sim & u \\ {\scriptstyle\beta}\Downarrow & & \\ t' & & \end{array}$ or $\begin{array}{ccc} t & \sim & u \\ & & \Downarrow{\scriptstyle\beta} \\ & & u' \end{array}$ can be closed as $\begin{array}{ccc} t & \sim & u \\ {\scriptstyle\beta}\Downarrow & & \Downarrow{\scriptstyle\beta} \\ t' & \sim & u' \end{array}$

This means that in $\mathcal{W}$, two sharing-via-labelling systems generate the same notion of parallel labelled reduction. In other words, their (possibly different) sharings have the same impact on the reduction. This applies in particular to $\mathcal{P}_{ch}$, $\mathcal{P}_{blm}$ and $\mathcal{P}_{af}$, and thus it shows that all the notions of full laziness in [Wad71, AF97, Ses97, SW05, BLM07] define the same reduction spaces.

4. Fully lazy λ-lifting

The primary goal of the present section is to prove that the notion of full laziness defined by fully lazy λ-lifting in [Hug82, Jon87] is equivalent to the unified notion of the previous section. This study of λ-lifting also reveals a strong relationship between optimal sharing in weak λ-calculi [BLM07] and the optimality theory of first-order rewriting [Mar91, Ter03].

In this section fully lazy λ-lifting is ultimately seen as a morphism between two systems: the **source** is the set of the λ-terms equipped with weak β-reduction, whereas the **target** is the set of first-order terms built with supercombinators equipped with their associated first-order reduction rules. However, the source and the target system are mixed in the intermediate steps. Fully lazy λ-lifting is then defined as an endomorphism of an **object** system combining the source and the target.

Our object system is a CRS over a labelling of the signature Σ defined in Section 2.1. The weak β-reduction is as defined in Section 2. The supercombinators forming the target subsystem are represented by the symbols in $\mathcal{F} = \bigcup_n \mathcal{F}_n$ and their reduction rules are defined in Section 4.1. Fully lazy λ-lifting itself is represented by a set of CRS rules which is proved to be confluent (Lemma 4), to be strongly normalizing (Lemma 5), to preserve one-step reduction (Theorem 3) and to preserve shared reduction (Theorem 4). Since we aim for this last result on shared reduction and since shared reduction is formalized in this paper by the labels, our λ-lifting is defined on labelled terms.

Section 4.1 introduces an extension of sharing-via-labelling systems and defines fully lazy λ-lifting as a rewriting process. Section 4.2 proves that fully lazy λ-lifting is a bisimulation between the source system and the target system, and Section 4.3 proves that parallel labelled fully lazy λ-lifting preserves optimal sharing.

4.1 Fully lazy λ-lifting systems

This section introduces the fully lazy λ-lifting systems as an extension of the sharing-via-labelling systems. Then, λ-lifting is defined as a CRS reduction in a fully-lazy λ-lifting system. This reduction is confluent and strongly normalizing.

The basic mechanism of λ-lifting is the replacement of a whole prefix by a supercombinator, the prefix and the supercombinator being related by an abstract invertible function called *contractor*. In order to preserve sharing, this replacement has to preserve all the information contained in the labels. Our solution consists in labelling the supercombinator with a structured label containing all the labels of the contracted prefix. Hence the basic operations of λ-lifting are reversible, and we define two inverse transformations (*contraction* and *expansion*) which reversibly relate labelled prefixes and labelled supercombinators.

Fully lazy λ-lifting is related in this paper to the weak β-reduction system $\mathcal{P}_{ch}$ of Example 5, whose definition is reminded below. The ch subscript is omitted along this section.

- $\mathcal{P}(\lambda x.t)$ is the skeleton of $\lambda x.t$.
- $\mathcal{P}^{\Box}(t) = []$ for any term t.

The structured labels used for labelled λ-lifting are tree-shaped, similarly to terms (see Example 11). For any countable set $\mathcal{V}$ (whose elements are called **atomic labels**), the set $\widehat{\mathcal{V}}$ of **tree labels** over $\mathcal{V}$ is defined by the following grammar:

$$\widehat{\mathcal{V}} ::= \Box \mid \top \mid \bot \mid \mathcal{V} \mid \widehat{\mathcal{V}}(\widehat{\mathcal{V}}, ..., \widehat{\mathcal{V}})$$

The label $\Box$ is an "empty" label which is used to denote the lack of label of the empty context $[]$ (see Example 11). The labels in $\widehat{\mathcal{V}}$ are used as virginal labels along this section. A tree label is **well-formed** when no atomic label appears twice in it. For any $\Omega_1, ..., \Omega_n$, a label $[\Omega_1 ... \Omega_n, \alpha]$ with $\alpha \in \widehat{\mathcal{V}}$ is well-formed when α is well-formed.

The **clash** relation is defined on tree labels as: $\alpha \wr \beta$ when α and β have an atomic label in common. The notion is used in Section 4.3 to express invariants on labels. For any $\mathcal{V}$ and any $\mathcal{N}$, the clash extends to $\widehat{\mathcal{V}}^{\mathcal{N}}$ as follows: $\alpha \wr \beta$ if and only if $\alpha = [\Omega_1 ... \Omega_n, \alpha^*]$ and $\beta = [\Omega_1 ... \Omega_n, \beta^*]$ with $\alpha^*, \beta^* \in \widehat{\mathcal{V}}$ and $\alpha^* \wr \beta^*$.

A **contractor** is an injective partial function φ mapping unlabelled n-ary skeletons to unlabelled n-ary function symbols. For any set of atomic labels $\mathcal{V}$ and any set of names $\mathcal{N}$, a contractor φ is extended to $\widehat{\mathcal{V}}^{\mathcal{N}}$-labelled skeletons and $\widehat{\mathcal{V}}^{\mathcal{N}}$-labelled symbols by the following rules.

- If p is labelled with virginal labels, then $\varphi(p) = f^{\alpha}$ such that $f = \varphi(|p|)$ and $\alpha = \|p\|$, where

$$\begin{array}{rcl} \|[]\| & = & \Box \\ \|x^{\alpha}\| & = & \alpha \\ \|\epsilon^{\alpha}(t)\| & = & \alpha(\|t\|) \\ \|\lambda^{\alpha}x.t\| & = & \alpha(\|t\|) \\ \|@^{\alpha}(t_1, t_2)\| & = & \alpha(\|t_1\|, \|t_2\|) \\ \|f^{\alpha}(t_1, ..., t_n)\| & = & \alpha(\|t_1\|, ..., \|t_n\|) \end{array}$$

- If p can be decomposed as $p = [\Omega, p']$, then $\varphi(p) = [\Omega, \varphi(p')]$.
- Else, $\varphi(p)$ is undefined.

The extension of φ to labelled skeletons is still injective, hence the labelled φ admits an inverse.

Example 11.

1. *Consider the skeleton* $p = \lambda^{\alpha}x.@^{\beta}([], \lambda^{\gamma}y.@^{\delta}(@^{\kappa}(y^{\nu}, []), x^{\iota}))$. *The collected label is* $\|p\| = \alpha(\beta(\Box, \gamma(\delta(\kappa(\nu, \Box), \iota))))$. *It is interesting to compare the graphical representations of the prefix and the label:*

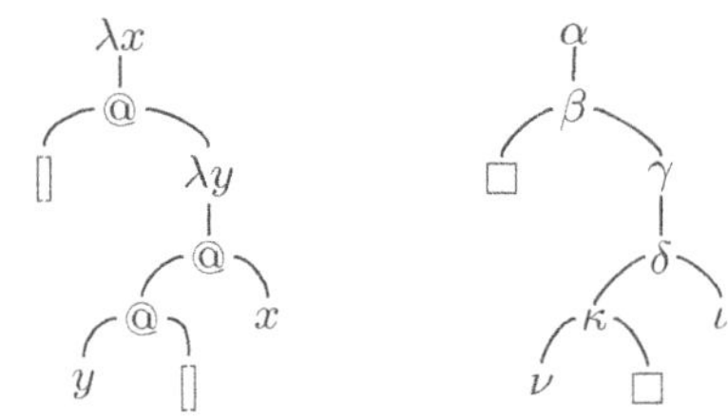

2. *Suppose* $\varphi(\lambda x.@([], x)) = g$. *Then*
   - $\varphi^{-1}(g^{\alpha(\beta(\Box, \gamma))}) = \lambda^{\alpha}x.@^{\beta}([], x^{\gamma})$
   - $\varphi^{-1}(g^{[\Omega, \alpha(\beta(\Box, \gamma))]}) = \lambda^{[\Omega, \alpha]}x.@^{[\Omega, \beta]}([], x^{[\Omega, \gamma]})$
   - $\varphi^{-1}(g^{\alpha(\beta(\delta(\iota), \gamma))})$ *is undefined because the label has not the same structure as* $\varphi^{-1}(g)$.
   - $\varphi(\lambda^{[\Omega_1, \alpha]}x.@^{[\Omega_2, \beta]}([], x^{[\Omega_2, \gamma]}))$ *is undefined because the labels have different modifiers* Ω_1 *and* Ω_2.

For any set of atomic labels $\mathcal{V}$, for any set of names $\mathcal{N}$ and for any contractor φ, φ-contraction and φ-expansion are two CRS rule schemes on $\widehat{\mathcal{V}}^{\mathcal{N}}$-labelled terms. For any skeleton $\lambda^{\alpha}x.p$ and symbol f^{β} such that $\varphi(\lambda^{\alpha}x.p) = f^{\beta}$ we have the two rules:

$$\begin{array}{lrcl} (\varphi\text{-contraction}) & \lambda^{\alpha}x.p[Z_1, ..., Z_n] & \to_c & f^{\beta}(Z_1, ..., Z_n) \\ (\varphi\text{-expansion}) & f^{\beta}(Z_1, ..., Z_n) & \to_e & \lambda^{\alpha}x.p[Z_1, ..., Z_n] \end{array}$$

Call an **object redex** a labelled term having one of the two following forms:

$$\begin{array}{ll} (\textbf{source redex}) & @^{\alpha}(\epsilon_k^{\beta_1 ... \beta_k}(\lambda^{\gamma}x.t), a) \\ (\textbf{target redex}) & @^{\alpha}(\epsilon_k^{\beta_1 ... \beta_k}(f^{\gamma}(t_1, ..., t_n)), a) \end{array}$$

Remark that the set of object redexes is stable by $\to_c$ and $\to_e$.

A **fully lazy λ-lifting system** is a tuple $\langle \varphi, \mathcal{N}, \mathcal{V}, \eta, \hookrightarrow \rangle$ such that:

- $\langle \mathcal{P}, \mathcal{N}, \widehat{\mathcal{V}}, \eta, \hookrightarrow \rangle$ is a sharing-via-labelling system.
- φ is a contractor.
- $\mathcal{P}$ commutes with φ-contraction and φ-expansion.
- η is a function from object redexes to names that is stable by φ-contraction and φ-expansion.

In a fully lazy λ-lifting system $\langle \varphi, \mathcal{N}, \mathcal{V}, \eta, \hookrightarrow \rangle$ we consider $\mathcal{L}$-labelled terms with $\mathcal{L} = \widehat{\mathcal{V}}^{\mathcal{N}}$.

Example 12 shows a straightforward extension of the function η_{seq} of Example 7 which is not stable by contraction. Example 13 then gives stable variants of the functions η_{seq} and η_{ctx}.

Example 12.

Consider the redex $r = @^{\alpha}(\lambda^{\gamma}x.@^{\delta}(x^{\iota}, y^{\kappa}), a)$, which can be φ-contracted to $r' = @^{\alpha}(f^{\gamma(\delta(\iota,\Box))}(y^{\kappa}), a)$ for some unary symbol f. Then $\eta_{seq}(r) = \alpha;\gamma$ and $\eta_{seq}(r') = \alpha;\gamma(\delta(\iota,\Box))$: the name is not stable.

Example 13.

1. *Define $\eta'_{seq}(@^{\alpha}(\epsilon_k^{\beta_1\ldots\beta_k}(\lambda^{\gamma}x.t), a)) = \alpha;\beta_1;...;\beta_k;\delta$ with $\gamma = [\Omega_1...\Omega_n, \gamma^*]$ and $\delta = [\Omega_1...\Omega_n, \delta^*]$ where γ^* is virginal and δ^* is the leftmost atomic label of γ^*. This name function is stable since the leftmost atomic label is stable by contraction and expansion.*
2. *If $\mathcal{P}(\lambda x.t) = p$, then define $\eta'_{ctx}(@^{\alpha}(\epsilon_k^{\beta_1\ldots\beta_k}(\lambda^{\gamma}x.t), a)) = @^{\alpha}(\epsilon_k^{\beta_1\ldots\beta_k}(f^{\delta}([], ..., [])), [])$ where f^{δ} is the unique normal form of $\lambda^{\gamma}x.p$ by λ-lifting (see definition of λ-lifting and lemmas 4 and 5 below). This name function is stable by normalization.*

We call **source reduction** the β-reduction, whose rule scheme can be simplified:

$$\begin{array}{c} @^{\alpha}(\epsilon_k^{\beta_1\ldots\beta_k}(\lambda^{\gamma}x.p[Z_1, ..., Z_n]), Z) \\ \to_{\beta} \\ \epsilon^{[\Omega,\top]}([\Omega, p])^{\{x:=\epsilon^{[\Omega,\bot]}(Z)\}}[Z_1, ..., Z_n] \end{array}$$

where $\lambda^{\gamma}x.p$ is a skeleton and
where $\Omega = \eta(@^{\alpha}(\epsilon_k^{\beta_1\ldots\beta_k}(\lambda^{\gamma}x.p[z_1, ..., z_n]), z))$.

We call **target reduction** the first-order reduction defined by the scheme:

$$\begin{array}{c} @^{\alpha}(\epsilon_k^{\beta_1\ldots\beta_k}(f^{\gamma}(Z_1, ..., Z_n)), Z) \\ \to_{t} \\ \epsilon^{[\Omega,\top]}([\Omega, p])^{\{x:=\epsilon^{[\Omega,\bot]}(Z)\}}[Z_1, ..., Z_n] \end{array}$$

where $\varphi^{-1}(f^{\gamma}) = \lambda^{\delta}x.p$ and
where $\Omega = \eta(@^{\alpha}(\epsilon_k^{\beta_1\ldots\beta_k}(f^{\gamma}(z_1, ..., z_n)), z))$.

Call **object reduction** the union of source reduction and target reduction: $\to_o = \to_{\beta} \cup \to_t$.

Remark 3. *Target reduction can be decomposed by φ-expanding the function symbol and then applying β-reduction.*

Remark 4. *Consider the system $\mathcal{S} = \langle \mathcal{P}_{ch}, \mathcal{N}_{ctx}, \mathcal{V}, \eta'_{ctx}, \hookrightarrow_{ctx}\rangle$ where $\mathcal{N}_{ctx}$ and $\hookrightarrow_{ctx}$ are defined in Example 7, η'_{ctx} is defined in Example 13, and $\mathcal{V}$ is any countable set. The target reduction of $\mathcal{S}$ is isomorphic to what is called Lévy-labelling in [Ter03, Chap. 8].*

For a clean definition of λ-lifting and for simple proofs of its basic properties we use an extended notion of positions of a term. The so-called *φ-positions* contain the usual syntactic positions but also the positions that are "hidden" in supercombinators: through the contractor φ each symbol represents a prefix, and the positions of these prefixes are taken into account in φ-positions.

The set $\mathcal{Q}(t)$ of φ-positions of t is defined by:

$$\begin{array}{rcl} \mathcal{Q}(x) & = & \{\varepsilon\} \\ \mathcal{Q}([]) & = & \{\varepsilon\} \\ \mathcal{Q}(\epsilon(t)) & = & \{\varepsilon\} \cup 1.\mathcal{Q}(t) \\ \mathcal{Q}(\lambda^{\alpha}x.t) & = & \{\varepsilon\} \cup 1.\mathcal{Q}(t) \\ \mathcal{Q}(@^{\alpha}(t_1, t_2)) & = & \{\varepsilon\} \cup 1.\mathcal{Q}(t_1) \cup 2.\mathcal{Q}(t_2) \\ \mathcal{Q}(f^{\alpha}(t_1, ..., t_n)) & = & \{\varepsilon\} \cup 0.\mathcal{Q}(\varphi^{-1}(f^{\alpha})) \cup (\bigcup_i i.\mathcal{Q}(t_i)) \end{array}$$

The following cases define λ-lifting as a CRS reduction:

- (Reify) If $\lambda^{\alpha}x.p$ is a skeleton such that $\varphi(\lambda^{\alpha}x.p) = f^{\beta}$, then
$$\lambda^{\alpha}x.p[Z_1, ..., Z_n] \quad \xrightarrow{\varepsilon}_{\mathit{lft}} \quad f^{\beta}(Z_1, ..., Z_n)$$
- (Inside) If $\varphi^{-1}(f^{\alpha})[x_1, ..., x_n] \xrightarrow{q}_{\mathit{lft}} \varphi^{-1}(g^{\beta})[x_1, ..., x_n]$ where $x_1, ..., x_n$ are fresh variables then
$$f^{\alpha}(Z_1, ..., Z_n) \quad \xrightarrow{0.q}_{\mathit{lft}} \quad g^{\beta}(Z_1, ..., Z_n)$$
- (Context) If $t \xrightarrow{q_1}_{\mathit{lft}} t'$ and c is a unary context with a hole at position q_2, then
$$c[t] \quad \xrightarrow{q_2 \cdot q_1}_{\mathit{lft}} \quad c[t']$$

While *Reify* is the main rule of λ-lifting, *Inside* allows us to close confluence diagrams (see Example 14) and to consider λ-lifting as an orthogonal rewriting system (in the sense of [GKK05]). An *Inside* reduction can be seen as a reduction *Reify* inside a symbol. An equivalent of *Inside* naturally appears in [AF97] or [Ses97] as a reduction in the context of a *let ... in ...* construct. Please note that in the rule *Context*, c is an arbitrary context. This means that there is no particular weak restriction here.

Example 14.

Let $t = \lambda^{\alpha}x.@^{\beta}(@(z_1, z_2), \lambda^{\gamma}y.@^{\delta}(@^{\kappa}(y^{\nu}, z_3), x^{\iota}))$ be a labelled term, where some labels are omitted. Write

$$\begin{array}{rcl} \varphi^{-1}(f) & = & \lambda x.@([], \lambda y.@(@(y, []), x)) \\ \mu & = & \alpha(\beta(\Box, \gamma(\delta(\kappa(\nu, \Box), \iota)))) \\ \varphi^{-1}(g) & = & \lambda y.@(@(y, []), []) \\ \sigma & = & \gamma(\delta(\kappa(\nu, \Box), \Box)) \\ \varphi^{-1}(f') & = & \lambda x.@([], g([], x)) \\ \mu' & = & \alpha(\beta(\Box, \sigma(\Box, \iota))) \end{array}$$

The dotted lines denote the skeleton of the abstraction $\lambda^{\gamma}y$, while the bold lines (solid or dotted) denote the skeleton of the abstraction $\lambda^{\alpha}x$.

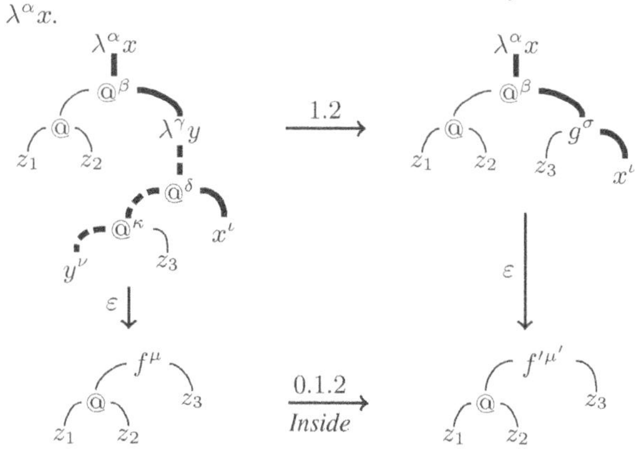

Remark 5. *The reduction Reify is a straightforward use of contraction $\to_c$, and the reduction Inside can be factorized using contraction $\to_c$ and expansion $\to_e$: if $t \to_{\mathit{lft}} t'$ by Inside, then there are u and u' such that $t \to_e u \to_c u' \to_c t'$.*

Lemma 4 (Diamond property). *If $t \to_{\mathit{lft}} u$ and $t \to_{\mathit{lft}} v$ with $u \neq v$ then there is w such that $u \to_{\mathit{lft}} w$ and $v \to_{\mathit{lft}} w$.*

Lemma 5 (Termination). *The system $\to_{\mathit{lft}}$ is strongly normalizing.*

Lemma 4 implies that $\to_{\mathit{lft}}$ is confluent, and that all the $\to_{\mathit{lft}}$-sequences between two given terms have the same length [Ter03]. An immediate corollary of lemmas 4 and 5 is that any term has a unique $\to_{\mathit{lft}}$-normal form.

4.2 Fully-lazy λ-lifting as a bisimulation

This section proves that $\rightarrow_{lft}$ does not only transform terms but also reduction sequences, and that the transformation operates forward as well as backward. Formally, the reflexive-transitive closure of the relation $\rightarrow_{lft}$ (written $\twoheadrightarrow_{lft}$) is a bisimulation between $\rightarrow_o$ and itself. Thanks to the CRS formalism which allows reasoning on the intermediate steps of the transformation, the proof can be reduced to a one-step simulation property (Lemma 6).

Lemma 6 (One-step simulation).

- *If* $t' \; {}_o\!\leftarrow t \rightarrow_{lft} u$ *then there is* u' *such that* $t' \twoheadrightarrow_{lft} u' \; {}_{lft}\!\leftarrow u$.
- *It* $t \rightarrow_{lft} u \rightarrow_o u'$ *then there is* t' *such that* $t \rightarrow_o t' \twoheadrightarrow_{lft} u'$.

Proof. (Sketch) By case on the relative positions of the two redexes. Most cases use the stability of η and the commutation of $\mathcal{P}$ with $\rightarrow_{lft}$. The diagram is closed by $t' \twoheadrightarrow_{lft} u'$ because a $\rightarrow_o$-reduction can destroy or duplicate the considered $\rightarrow_{lft}$-redex. □

Lemma 6 yields as immediate corollary:

Theorem 3 (Bisimulation). *The relation* $\twoheadrightarrow_{lft}$ *is a bisimulation between the reduction* $\rightarrow_o$ *and itself, which means that any diagram*

$$\begin{array}{ccc} t & \overset{lft}{\twoheadrightarrow} & u \\ {}_o\!\downarrow & & \\ t' & & \end{array} \quad \textit{or} \quad \begin{array}{ccc} t & \overset{lft}{\twoheadrightarrow} & u \\ & & \downarrow_o \\ & & u' \end{array} \quad \textit{can be closed as} \quad \begin{array}{ccc} t & \overset{lft}{\twoheadrightarrow} & u \\ {}_o\!\downarrow & & \downarrow_o \\ t' & \underset{lft}{\twoheadrightarrow} & u' \end{array}$$

This bisimulation is a strong property for λ-lifting: it associates a progressive transformation of reduction sequences to the progressive transformation of terms. Moreover, there is a bijection between the single steps of the image and the antecedent reduction sequences. In the next section, we show that this holds also for parallel labelled reduction.

4.3 Fully-lazy λ-lifting as a graph bisimulation

For $r \in \{\beta, t, o, c, e, lft\}$, write $\overset{\alpha}{\Rightarrow}_r$ the simultaneous reduction of all the $\rightarrow_r$-redexes of label α in a term satisfying the sharing property $\mathbb{S}$. This last section shows that $\Rightarrow_{lft}$ preserves sharing: the same subterms are shared in the source and in the target of this reduction. This allows us to conclude that the full lazinesses of [Wad71] and [Jon87] are bisimilar.

In this section we use again the invariants $\mathbb{S}$ and $\mathbb{M}$ introduced in Section 2.3. In our new setting we extend $\mathbb{M}$ to any object redex. We moreover use the following three invariants:

3. Say a term t has the **independent labelling property**, written $\mathbb{I}(t)$, when all the labels of t are well-formed and there is no pair of labels (α, β) of t such that $\alpha \neq \beta$ and $\alpha \wr \beta$. This property is useful to ensure that contraction and expansion do not break the sharing property.
4. Say a term t has the **tuned skeletons property**, written $\mathbb{T}(t)$, when every skeleton p in t is of the form $[\Omega_1...\Omega_n, p^*]$ where p^* has only virginal labels. This property allows applying a contractor φ to any prefix, and rules out the last case of Example 11.
5. Say a term t has the **harmonious binding property**, written $\mathbb{H}(t)$, when any two variables with the same label are either both free or both bound by abstractions bearing the same label. This property strengthens the sharing property: when both are present, two whole skeletons are shared whenever one of their nodes is shared.

Finally, say a term t has the $\mathbb{SMITH}$ property (written $\mathbb{SMITH}(t)$) when the five properties are satisfied by t as well as by $\varphi^{-1}(f^\alpha)$ for any f^α appearing in t (or recursively in the antecedent by φ of a symbol).

Lemma 7. *For any* $r \in \{\beta, t, o, c, e, lft\}$ *and any two terms* t, t', *if* $\mathbb{SMITH}(t)$ *and* $t \overset{\alpha_0}{\Rightarrow}_r t'$ *then* $\mathbb{SMITH}(t')$.

Proof. (Sketch) By remarks 3 and 5 we need only consider the cases where $r \in \{\beta, c, e\}$. As in Theorem 1 the proof is by case analysis on the origin of the considered labels. □

Theorem 4 (Preservation of optimal sharing). *Let* t *be a term such that* $\mathbb{SMITH}(t)$. *Suppose* $t \overset{\alpha_0}{\Rightarrow}_{lft} t'$. *Let* u' *(resp.* v'*) be a subterm of* t'*, with ancestor* u *(resp.* v*) in* t. *Then* $\tau(u') = \tau(v')$ *if and only if* $\tau(u) = \tau(v)$.

Proof. Suppose $\tau(u') = \tau(v') = \alpha'$. Case on the origin of α':

- If $\tau(u) = \tau(v) = \alpha'$, it's over.
- If $\tau(u) = \alpha'$ and $\tau(v) \neq \alpha'$, then $\tau(v) = \alpha_0$ such that $\alpha_0 = [\Omega_1...\Omega_n, \alpha_0^*]$ and $\alpha' = [\Omega_1...\Omega_n, \alpha^*]$ with α_0^* appearing into α^*, which implies $\alpha' \wr \alpha_0$ and contradicts $\mathbb{I}(t)$.
- If $\tau(u) \neq \alpha'$ and $\tau(v) \neq \alpha'$ then $\tau(u) = \tau(v) = \alpha_0$.

Suppose $\tau(u) = \tau(v) = \alpha$. If $\alpha \neq \alpha_0$, then $\tau(u') = \tau(u) = \tau(v) = \tau(v')$. Else $u = v$, $u \overset{\alpha_0}{\Rightarrow}_{lft} u'$, $v \overset{\alpha_0}{\Rightarrow}_{lft} v'$ and $u' = v'$. In particular $\tau(u') = \tau(v')$. □

Finally, write $t \approx t'$ is t and t' are $\Rightarrow_{lft}$-convertible. We deduce that

$$\text{any} \quad \begin{array}{ccc} t & \approx & u \\ {}_o\!\Downarrow & & \\ t' & & \end{array} \quad \text{or} \quad \begin{array}{ccc} t & \approx & u \\ & & \Downarrow_o \\ & & u' \end{array} \quad \text{can be closed as} \quad \begin{array}{ccc} t & \approx & u \\ {}_o\!\Downarrow & & \Downarrow_o \\ t' & \approx & u' \end{array}$$

This implies that the implementations of full laziness in [Wad71] and [Jon87] define the same reduction space, which also correspond to optimal sharing along [Mar91, Ter03] for the first-order system defined by the target reduction $\rightarrow_t$, and to optimal sharing along [BLM07] for the CH-weak reduction of the λ-calculus.

5. Conclusion

Sharing, and in particular fully lazy sharing, is described and implemented by different technical tools including graphs, closures, and program transformations. As a consequence, the many definitions of fully lazy sharing [Wad71, Jon87, Ses97, AF97, SW05, BLM07] are sometimes hardly comparable. Yet they all intend to implement the same basic ideas.

This paper unifies all these views of full laziness. To achieve this we define an axiomatic framework of sharing-via-labelling systems, in which the various approaches can be expressed. Then we prove that all the resulting systems are bisimilar, in the sense that they have isomorphic reduction spaces.

In particular, by linking [BLM07] to other definitions of full laziness, we confirm the intuition of its authors that fully lazy sharing gives an optimal sharing for the weak λ-calculus of [ÇH98].

Last but not least, we show that weak reduction in λ-calculus can be expressed in orthogonal first-order rewriting by means of fully lazy λ-lifting, with a one-to-one correspondence between their reduction steps. This remarkable last property makes our first-order formulation really different from the formulations that use de Bruijn indices or explicit substitutions [Tur79, Mar91]. Moreover, our transformation preserves optimal sharing and expresses fully lazy sharing as optimal sharing for the target first-order system.

5.1 Related work

Related approaches to the efficient implementation of functional programming languages include in particular the study of optimal reduction and the attempts to implement it. The study of optimal reduction [Lé80, Mar91, GK96, vO96, BLM07] traditionally uses three equivalent characterizations called labelling, extraction, and zig-zag. This paper extends the labelling-based characterization of optimality to weak β-reduction systems.

The possibility of a straightforward implementation in graphs of the label-based characterization of optimality has for long been known to be a feature of first-order rewriting [Mar91] that did not hold in the λ-calculus. However, more recently this feature has been observed in a weak restriction of the λ-calculus [BLM07]. The present paper confirms this observation by showing that it holds in any weak β-reduction system, and explains this first-order behaviour of weak reduction by expliciting a link between weak β-reduction systems and first-order rewriting.

Two kinds of implementations are known to perform less shared β-reduction steps than some fully lazy implementations. In particular partial evaluation [HG91] has been compared to [Jon87], and optimality [Lé80] is born as an idealization of [Wad71]. Hence this paper shows that partial evaluation [HG91] as well as any implementation of optimality [AG98, PQ07] is able to perform less shared β-reduction steps than any implementation of full laziness.

On the other hand, a global comparison between all these approaches is still missing. In particular, the following facts keep the question open for now: the number of shared β-reduction steps in a fully lazy system is polynomially related to the actual cost of performing the reduction on a Turing machine (simple extension of [LM09]), but this does not hold with optimal sharing [AM98].

5.2 Future work

Fully lazy λ-lifting is shown to be a powerful tool to give a faithful first-order account of higher-order systems. This phenomenon prompts us to carry on investigations in at least two directions.

- Generalization of λ-lifting to any weak β-reduction system satisfying our axioms. Two interesting and challenging examples would be the plain λ-lifting of [Joh85], in which the prefixes are not stable by reduction, and a new notion of λ-lifting based on $\mathcal{P}_{blm}$, which would turn the spines into supercombinators. Since the spines can bind variables in their holes, some function symbols would also bind some variables in their arguments.
- Generalization of sharing and λ-lifting to higher-order rewriting, which includes richer systems that rewrite functions, such as proof assistants and compilers. As far as the author is aware, general higher-order rewriting knows no notion of weak reduction, sharing-via-labelling, or λ-lifting. However, the present work seems to be abstract enough to be generalized to higher-order frameworks such as combinatory reduction systems.

Acknowledgments

The author would like to thank Delia Kesner for her continuous support, Vincent van Oostrom for several discussions and for a mysterious but insightful remark that triggered this investigation, and Roberto di Cosmo, Olivier Danvy, John Field and the anonymous reviewers for numerous helpful comments and suggestions.

References

[AF97] Z.M. Ariola and M. Felleisen. The call-by-need lambda calculus. *J. Funct. Program.*, 7(3):265–301, 1997.

[AFM+95] Z.M. Ariola, M. Felleisen, J. Maraist, M. Odersky, and P. Wadler. The call-by-need lambda calculus. In *POPL*, pages 233–246, 1995.

[AG98] A. Asperti and S. Guerrini. *The optimal implementation of functional programming languages*. Cambridge University Press, 1998.

[AM98] A. Asperti and H.G. Mairson. Parallel Beta Reduction is not Elementary Recursive. In *POPL*, pages 303-315, 1998.

[Bal11] T. Balabonski. A Unified Approach to Fully Lazy Sharing. `http://hal.archives-ouvertes.fr/hal-00637048/`. Rapport technique PPS, 2011.

[BKKS87] H.P. Barendregt, R. Kennaway, J-W. Klop, and M. Ronan Sleep. Needed reduction and spine strategies for the lambda calculus. *Inf. Comput.*, 75(3):191–231, 1987.

[BLM07] T. Blanc, J.-J. Lévy, and L. Maranget. Sharing in the Weak Lambda-Calculus Revisited. In *Reflections on Type Theory, Lambda Calculus and the Mind*, 2007.

[Bru03] H.J.S. Bruggink. Residuals in higher-order rewriting. In *RTA*, pages 123–137, 2003.

[ÇH98] N. Çağman and J. R. Hindley. Combinatory weak reduction in lambda calculus. *TCS*, 198(1-2):239–247, 1998.

[DMMZ10] O. Danvy, K. Millikin, J. Munk, and I. Zerny. Defunctionalized Interpreters for Call-by-Need Evaluation. In *FLOPS*, pages 240–256, 2010.

[DLLL05] D. Dougherty, P. Lescanne, L. Liquori, and F. Lang. Addressed Term Rewriting Systems: Syntax, Semantics, and Pragmatics: Extended Abstract. *ENTCS*, 127(5):57–82, 2005.

[GK96] J. Glauert and Z. Khasidashvili. Relative normalization in deterministic residual structures. In *CAAP*, pages 180–195, 1996.

[GKK05] J.R.W. Glauert, D. Kesner, and Z. Khasidashvili. Expression reduction systems and extensions: An overview. In *Processes, Terms and Cycles*, pages 496–553, 2005.

[HG91] C.K. Holst and D.K. Gomard. Partial evaluation is fuller laziness. In *PEPM*, pages 223–233, 1991.

[Hug82] R.J.M. Hughes. Super combinators: A new implementation method for applicative languages. In *LFP*, pages 1–10, 1982.

[Joh85] T. Johnsson. Lambda lifting: Transforming programs to recursive equations. In *FPCA*, pages 190–203, 1985.

[Jon87] S. Peyton Jones. *The Implementation of Functional Programming Languages*. Prentice-Hall, Inc., 1987.

[KvOvR93] J.W. Klop, V. van Oostrom, and F. van Raamsdonk. Combinatory reduction systems: Introduction and survey. *Theor. Comput. Sci.*, 121(1&2):279–308, 1993.

[Lam90] J. Lamping. An algorithm for optimal lambda calculus reduction. In *POPL*, pages 16–30, 1990.

[Lau93] J. Launchbury. A natural semantics for lazy evaluation. In *POPL*, pages 144–154, 1993.

[LM09] U. Dal Lago and S. Martini. On constructor rewrite systems and the lambda-calculus. In *ICALP (2)*, pages 163–174, 2009.

[Lé80] J.-J. Lévy. Optimal reductions in the lambda-calculus. In *To H.B. Curry: Essays on Combinatory Logic, Lambda Calculus and Formalisms*, pages 159–191, 1980.

[Mar91] L. Maranget. Optimal Derivations in Weak Lambda-calculi and in Orthogonal Terms Rewriting Systems. In *POPL*, pages 255–269, 1991.

[PQ07] M. Pedicini and F. Quaglia. Pelcr: Parallel environment for optimal lambda-calculus reduction. *ACM Trans. Comput. Logic*, 8, July 2007.

[Ses97] P. Sestoft. Deriving a lazy abstract machine. *J. Funct. Program.*, 7(3):231–264, 1997.

[SW05] O. Shivers and M. Wand. Bottom-up β-reduction: Uplinks and λ-DAGs. In *ESOP*, pages 217–232, 2005.

[Ter03] Terese. *Term Rewriting Systems*. Cambridge Univ.Press, 2003.

[Tur79] D.A. Turner. A new implementation technique for applicative languages. In *Softw., Pract. Exper.*, 9(1):31–49, 1979.

[vO96] V. van Oostrom. Higher-order families. In *RTA*, pages 392–407, 1996.

[Wad71] C. P. Wadsworth. *Semantics and Pragmatics of the Lambda Calculus*. Ph.D. thesis, 1971.

[Yos94] N. Yoshida. Optimal reduction in weak-λ-calculus with shared environments. *J. of Computer Software*, 11(5):2–20, 1994.

The Ins and Outs of Gradual Type Inference

Aseem Rastogi
Stony Brook University
arastogi@cs.stonybrook.edu

Avik Chaudhuri Basil Hosmer
Advanced Technology Labs, Adobe Systems
{achaudhu,bhosmer}@adobe.com

Abstract

Gradual typing lets programmers evolve their dynamically typed programs by gradually adding explicit type annotations, which confer benefits like improved performance and fewer run-time failures.

However, we argue that such evolution often requires a giant leap, and that type inference can offer a crucial missing step. If omitted type annotations are interpreted as *unknown* types, rather than the dynamic type, then static types can often be inferred, thereby removing unnecessary assumptions of the dynamic type. The remaining assumptions of the dynamic type may then be removed by either reasoning outside the static type system, or restructuring the code.

We present a type inference algorithm that can improve the performance of existing gradually typed programs without introducing any new run-time failures. To account for dynamic typing, types that flow in to an unknown type are treated in a fundamentally different manner than types that flow out. Furthermore, in the interests of backward-compatibility, an escape analysis is conducted to decide which types are safe to infer. We have implemented our algorithm for ActionScript, and evaluated it on the SunSpider and V8 benchmark suites. We demonstrate that our algorithm can improve the performance of unannotated programs as well as recover most of the type annotations in annotated programs.

Categories and Subject Descriptors D.3.4 [*Programming Languages*]: Processors—Optimization; F.3.2 [*Logics and Meaning of Programs*]: Semantics of Programming Languages—Program analysis; F.3.3 [*Logics and Meaning of Programs*]: Studies of Program Constructs—Type structure

General Terms Algorithms, Languages, Performance, Theory

Keywords Gradual typing, Type inference, ActionScript

1. Introduction

Gradual Typing and Evolutionary Programming Gradual typing [12, 17] aims to combine the benefits of static typing and dynamic typing in a language. In a gradually typed program, dynamically typed code can be mixed with statically typed code. While the dynamically typed fragments are not constrained to follow the structure enforced by a static type system, the statically typed fragments enjoy not only some static safety guarantees ("well-typed programs cannot be blamed"—the blame theorem [24]) but also admit performance optimizations that the dynamically typed fragments do not. Gradual typing envisions a style of programming where dynamically typed programs can be *evolved* into statically typed programs by gradually trading off liberties in code structure for assurances of safety and performance.

Although there has been much recent progress on mastering the recipe of gradual typing, a key ingredient has been largely missing—*type inference*. The only previous work on type inference for gradually typed languages is based on unification [18], which is unsuitable for use in object-oriented languages with subtyping. Unfortunately, as we argue below, the lack of type inference may be the most significant obstacle towards adopting the style of evolutionary programming envisioned by gradual typing.

The Key Missing Ingredient: Type Inference In a gradually typed language, a program may be partially annotated with types. Any missing types are uniformly assumed to be the dynamic type. This means that the fragments of the program that have missing type annotations do not enjoy any of the benefits of static typing. In particular, their performance is hindered by dynamic casts, even if they implicitly satisfy the constraints of static typing (i.e., even if the dynamic casts never fail). To improve performance, the missing types have to be declared.

However, in our experience with a mainstream gradually typed language, ActionScript [13], the task of evolving dynamically typed programs to statically typed programs by declaring missing types can be quite onerous. The annotation burden is often intimidating: in the limit, types must be declared for every variable in the evolving fragment, and the programmer may need to juggle several annotations to satisfy the constraints of the static type system.

Furthermore, the programmer may eventually be forced to declare dynamic types for some variables: it may not be possible to satisfy the constraints of the static type system without restructuring the code. This is because the programmer may be relying on an invariant that cannot be expressed via static types in the language, i.e., the proof of safety may rely on a form of reasoning (typically, path-sensitive) that is outside the scope of the static type system.

Unfortunately, due to these difficulties, gradually typed programs often continue to miss out on important benefits of static typing, such as performance optimizations. Consequently, evolutionary programming remains a fantasy.

The crux of the problem is that a missing type is misinterpreted as the dynamic type, whereas the intended interpretation is that of an *unknown* type. Often, an unknown type can be inferred to be a static type. In contrast, the dynamic type is a "fallback" to encode imprecision: a variable must be of the dynamic type when the set of values that the variable may denote cannot be expressed as a static type in the language, thereby forcing imprecision in the type abstraction.

Therefore, we envision an iterative process for evolution of dynamically typed programs to statically typed programs, that alternates between two states. In one state, type inference removes un-

POPL'12, January 25–27, 2012, Philadelphia, PA, USA.

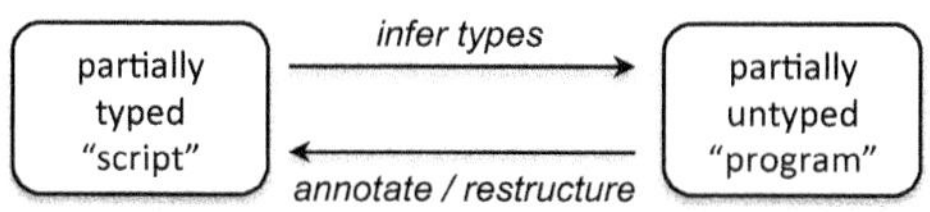

Figure 1. Iterative Evolution of Scripts to Programs

necessary assumptions of the dynamic type, so that elimination of any remaining dynamic types in the code requires either reasoning outside the static type system, or restructuring the code. In the other state, the programmer either introduces further type annotations or restructures parts of the program to conform to the static type discipline. Furthermore, at any state, the programmer may decide to pause the evolution process, deploy the program, and take advantage of the improved precision of static types that have already replaced dynamic types in the program. At a later point, the programmer should be free to resume the evolution process. This process is depicted in Figure 1.

Since the programmer may choose to evolve an existing, deployed program, type inference must ensure that the program remains backward-compatible: it should have exactly the same run-time behavior after type inference as it would have before type inference. In particular, if the program was safe (did not fail at run time) then it should continue to be safe, and any other programs that ran safely with the program should continue to run safely.

Retrofitting Type Inference on Gradually Typed Programs In this paper we study the problem of retrofitting type inference in an existing gradually typed language. The practical motivation for our work is to improve the performance of existing ActionScript programs "under the hood." Our aim is to let existing programs reap the benefits of type-directed performance optimizations as much as possible, while remaining backward-compatible.

On the other hand, our aim is not to eliminate run-time failures in existing programs: indeed, any run-time failures need to be preserved as well. Thus, the static types we infer may not satisfy some static safety guarantees, such as the blame theorem [24]. Nevertheless, the static types we infer can improve performance, since they soundly approximate precise sets of run-time values. Thus, we prefer to infer static types where possible rather than falling back on the (imprecise) dynamic type. Of course, it remains possible to recover static safety guarantees by forgoing some opportunities for optimization—we can fall back on the dynamic type whenever the inferred static type may be cast to an incompatible type.

Design Challenges The aim of our type inference algorithm is to reduce the imprecision associated with dynamic types, so that programs with missing type annotations can benefit from various performance optimizations. We try to infer, for each variable, a precise type abstraction of the set of values that flow into it. The setting of a gradually typed language and the requirement of backward-compatibility present several unique challenges, as outlined next.

In a purely static type system, the definitions of a variable determine a lower bound on its type, since the type must admit every value flowing into the variable; dually, the uses of a variable determine an upper bound on its type, since the type must admit only those values that are admitted by the type of every context to which the variable flows out. Thus, for a type that satisfies both sets of constraints, it is possible to prove statically that every use of the variable is safe for every definition of that variable. In contrast, in a gradual type system, every use of a variable need not be safe for every definition of that variable: instead, run-time failures may be avoided if each use is safe for *some* definition. Thus, the type of a variable must be inferred by considering only its definitions, deferring type checks on its uses until run time.

Furthermore, the type of a variable may only be inferred if it is *local*, i.e., if all of its definitions are visible during compilation. In the absence of this guarantee, we cannot exclude the possibility that values of an unexpected type may flow into the variable at run time: for example, consider a parameter of a global function, which can be defined by arbitrary arguments through calls that are not visible during compilation. In such cases, replacing the variable's assumed dynamic type with an inferred static type may break the program in some unknown run-time environment.

Based on these observations, we infer types of only those variables for which we can infer the types of all values flowing in, i.e., their *inflows*; and we derive the solutions by computing the least upper bounds of those types, without checking that the solutions satisfy the greatest lower bounds of the types of the contexts to which they flow out, i.e., their *outflows*.

Higher-order values, such as functions and objects, present some interesting subtleties. There is an immediate problem if we take the standard least upper bounds of their (higher-order) types, since we will then be taking the greatest lower bounds of the "input" (negative) parts of these types—which violates the principle we motivated above, giving us prescriptive "safe" types rather than descriptive "precise" types for the input parts of the higher-order solution. Another possibility might be to take the least upper bounds of both "input" and "output" parts, following naïve subtyping [24][1]. However this also is not quite right, since we are still neglecting to observe the types of the actual inputs, e.g., the types of arguments in calls to a function; rather, as with standard subtyping, we are still considering the types of values that such a function considers safe to input, i.e., the function's parameter types. The key insight is that if we are to obey the principle of solving based on inflows alone, we must *recursively deconstruct* higher-order types down to their first-order parts, solve for those based on inflows (e.g., the inflow of arguments to the parameter of a function-typed variable), and then reconstruct the higher-order parts in such a way as to preserve the desired asymmetry.

We devise an elegant way of inferring such higher-order solutions, via a notion of *kinds*; this requires us to treat higher-order inflows in a fundamentally different manner than higher-order outflows (Section 2.3).

Another complication arises when local functions and objects *escape*. In this case we cannot infer the parts of their types in negative ("input") positions, since values may then flow into them from some code that cannot be analyzed at compile time. Therefore, it seems that we need some kind of escape analysis to figure out if some local function or object escapes. Perhaps surprisingly, the escape analysis we require is carried out "for free" by our algorithm: it suffices to assume that in the enclosing program's type, the parts in negative positions are either explicitly annotated, or are the dynamic type (Section 2.5).

Guarantees Our main guarantee is that the type inference algorithm is sound: if a program fails at run time with our inferred types, it would have failed at exactly the same point with the dynamic type. The soundness guarantee is compositional, in the sense that it holds even when the program is placed in an arbitrary run-time environment. Furthermore, we show how to recover solutions from our inferred types that satisfy the blame theorem [24]. We also prove that the time complexity of our type inference algorithm is quadratic in the size of the input program.

Implementation and Evaluation We have implemented our type-inference algorithm for ActionScript, and evaluated it on the SunSpider [20] and V8 [23] benchmark suites. Overall, we are able to

[1] Naïve subtyping is covariant in both negative and positive positions, unlike standard subtyping (which is contravariant in negative positions).

achieve 1.6x performance improvement on average over partially typed benchmarks (with type annotations only on required parts of the interfaces), with a maximum performance improvement of 5.6x (Section 5).

Contributions To summarize, we make the following main contributions in this paper:

- We argue that the evolution of gradually typed programs is essentially an iterative process, with type inference being a key missing component.
- We design a type inference algorithm for gradually typed languages with the goal of improving the performance of programs as much as possible, while preserving the run-time behaviors of unannotated programs. Our design involves new ideas that are specific to the setting of a gradual type system and the requirement of backward-compatibility, such as the need to treat definitions and uses asymmetrically, and the need for escape analysis to decide what types are safe to infer.
- We formalize our type inference algorithm in a core calculus of functions and objects, and prove soundness and complexity theorems for the algorithm. Technical novelties in our algorithm include a notion of kinds to compute precise higher-order solutions, and the encoding of escape analysis as a syntactic condition on the program's type.
- We implement our algorithm for ActionScript, a mainstream gradually typed language, and evaluate its effectiveness, with encouraging results.

Overall, we believe that the techniques and insights developed in this paper will elucidate the intricacies of type inference for gradually typed languages, and spur further research in this area.

2. Overview

2.1 Algorithm

While existing compilers for gradually typed languages such as ActionScript [13] consider missing type annotations to be the dynamic type, our aim is to infer precise static types where possible, and fall back on the dynamic type only where necessary.

As usual, our type inference algorithm begins by replacing missing type annotations in the program with fresh *type variables*. Then we compile the program, using type annotations to generate *coercions* between types.

A coercion is of the form $S \rhd T$, where S and T are types; such a coercion witnesses the flow of a term of type S into a context of type T. In particular, coercions involving type variables are interpreted as *flows* for those type variables: for example, if X is a type variable, then $T \rhd X$ is an *inflow* for X, whereas $X \rhd T$—where T is not a type variable—is an *outflow* for X.

Starting from the original set of coercions collected during compilation, we now iterate, generating new coercions from existing ones using carefully designed rules which treat the implications of inflows and outflows differently. At each step, new coercions represent flows that are implied by, but are not directly expressed by, extant coercions.

Iteration continues until our rules can produce no new coercions, at which point we have a *closure* of the flows implied by the type annotations in the program. For each type variable X, we can now derive a solution, namely the least upper bound of all types T that can flow into X—via inflows expressed by coercions of the form $T \rhd X$. A formal treatment of the algorithm is presented in Section 3.

We now demonstrate the fine points of the algorithm, viz. the computation of closures and the derivation of solutions, using examples in ActionScript [13]; ActionScript is an extension of JavaScript with a gradual type system, and is the programming language underlying Flash applications.

We show type variables as part of programs below, although they are not part of ActionScript. In actual programs, these type variables are just missing annotations. We follow the convention that type variables (in italics) have similar names as corresponding unannotated variables, with the first letter capitalized. For example, the type variable for an unannotated variable `foo` in the program is written as *Foo*. If `foo` is an unannotated function, *Foo?* represents the type variable for the parameter type of `foo` and *Foo!* represents the type variable for the return type of `foo`. The dynamic type is denoted by $\star$. `Number` and `Boolean` are base types. We also use $\bot$ to denote the bottom type, although it is not part of ActionScript. For the purpose of our examples, operators are typed as follows:

```
+ : (Number, Number) -> Number
< : (Number, Number) -> Boolean
```

2.2 Local Variables having Base Types

We start with a simple example to show how our algorithm infers primitive types for local variables in a function, and how it improves performance.

```
1 function foo(n:Number):Foo! {
2     var index:Index = 0;
3     var sum:Sum = index;
4     while(index < n)
5         { index = index + 1; sum = sum + index }
6     return sum
7 }
```

In the absence of type inference, `index` and `sum` will be given type $\star$. Since the `+` operator has type `(Number, Number)` $\rightarrow$ `Number`, evaluation of `index + 1` and `sum + index` will cause in run-time conversions $\star \rhd$ `Number` for `index` and `sum`. To store the results back to `index` and `sum`, further run-time conversions `Number` $\rhd \star$ will happen. As we show later in our experiments, such run-time conversions can hurt the performance of programs.

We now show how our inference algorithm works. After adding type variables for missing types, as shown, we compile the program and collect coercions. The initializations of `index` and `sum` on lines 2 and 3 generate `Number` $\rhd$ *Index* and *Index* $\rhd$ *Sum*. The operations `index < n`, `index = index + 1`, and `sum = sum + index` on lines 4 and 5 generate *Index* $\rhd$ `Number`, `Number` $\rhd$ *Index*, *Sum* $\rhd$ `Number`, *Index* $\rhd$ `Number`, and `Number` $\rhd$ *Sum*.

To solve these flows, we note that the only type flowing into *Index* is `Number`. So, we infer *Index* = `Number`. Next, we see that types flowing into *Sum* are `Number` and *Index*. Therefore, the solution for *Sum* is the union of `Number` and *Index*, which is `Number`. And finally, the only type flowing into *Foo!* is *Sum*. So, *Foo!* = `Number` as well.

Annotating `index` and `sum` with `Number` rather than $\star$ improves run-time performance by eliminating unnecessary run-time conversions between `Number` and $\star$ in the loop body.

Note that we also generated *Sum* $\rhd$ `Number` and *Index* $\rhd$ `Number` but did not use them for inference. A typical type checker will check that the solutions of *Sum* and *Index* satisfy these outflows, but we skip this step. We say more about why we do so in Section 2.6.

2.3 Local Variables having Function Types

2.3.1 Unions of Function Types are Problematic

When a base type (like `Number` or `Boolean`) flows into a type variable, the solution of the type variable is simply that type; and if several base types flow in, the solution is the union of those base types. Unfortunately, the obvious ways of generalizing this approach to higher-order types (like function types) do not work.

For example, consider the following program:

```
8 var x:X = function(a:*):Number { ... };
9 x(1)
```

On line 8, we generate $\star \rightarrow$ `Number` $\rhd X$. Thus, we may infer the solution of X to be the type flowing into it, $\star \rightarrow$ `Number`. However, a more precise solution is `Number` $\rightarrow$ `Number`, based on the fact that the only values flowing into the parameter of the function stored in `x` are of type `Number` (line 9).

Furthermore, when several function types flow into a type variable, we cannot combine those inflows by taking the union of all such types. Consider the following example:

```
10 var x:X;
11 if(b) { x = function(y:Number):Number { ... }; x(1) }
12 else { x = function(y:Boolean):Number { ... }; x(true) }
```

We generate `Number` $\rightarrow$ `Number` $\rhd X$ from line 11 and `Boolean` $\rightarrow$ `Number` $\rhd X$ from line 12. Since the union of two function types is a type $S \rightarrow T$ where S is the intersection of their parameter types and T is the union of their return types, we would infer X to be $\perp \rightarrow$ `Number` using the standard approach. This would mean that in the running program, any application of `x` to a `Number` or a `Boolean` value would result in an error. This is clearly unsound as the programmer applies `x` to a `Number` at line 11, and to a `Boolean` at line 12, both of which are safe.

2.3.2 Kinds as Higher-Order Solutions

To deal with higher-order types, we introduce a notion of *kinds*. A kind can be thought of as a "view" of a type variable: it describes a structure, and introduces type variables for the types of parts within that structure. Coercions between type variables and kinds are generated during compilation and closure computation, in either direction: a coercion from a type variable T to a kind K witnesses the flow of T-typed values into a context whose higher-order type is exemplified by K; conversely, a coercion from K to T witnesses the flow of higher-order values of kind K into a T-typed context.

For example, on line 9, the function call `x(1)` induces a view of X as a function type. To realize this view, we generate the coercion $X \rhd X? \rightarrow X!$, where $X? \rightarrow X!$ is a kind for X corresponding to function types; this witnesses values of type X flowing to a context in which they are used as functions. We also generate `Number` $\rhd X?$, which witnesses the flow of arguments of type `Number` into the parameters of those functions.

Combining $\star \rightarrow$ `Number` $\rhd X$ and $X \rhd X? \rightarrow X!$, we get $\star \rightarrow$ `Number` $\rhd X? \rightarrow X!$. Deconstructing this flow using contravariance for the parameter type and covariance for the return type, we get $X? \rhd \star$ and `Number` $\rhd X!$. Intuitively, these coercions witness the flows into and out of the concrete function value assigned to `x` on line 8, resulting from the call to `x` on line 9.

Solving these flows, we obtain $X?$ = `Number`, and $X!$ = `Number`. But what should X's solution be? We claim it should be X's function kind, i.e. $X? \rightarrow X!$, which after substituting for $X?$ and $X!$, becomes `Number` $\rightarrow$ `Number`. Our closure rules introduce the necessary intermediate step, the coercion $X? \rightarrow X! \rhd X$, as a consequence of the assignment on line 8.

Thus, a kind not only gives a view of a type variable as a higher-order type, but also encodes the corresponding higher-order solution of the type variable.

In other programs, there may be no occasion to generate a coercion from a type variable X to a kind at all, due to an absence of contexts in which X-typed values are used in a syntactically higher-order way, such as the function application term `x(1)` in the previous example. Consider the following variation:

```
13 var x:X = function(a:*):Number { ... };
14 function f(y:Number -> Number):Number { y(1) }
15 f(x)
```

We generate $\star \rightarrow$ `Number` $\rhd X$ and $X \rhd$ `Number` $\rightarrow$ `Number` on lines 13 and 15 respectively. Here we don't need the view of X as a function type since `x` is not applied directly, but we still need to represent the solution for X. This is accomplished by the coercions introduced by our closure rules as a result of the assignment on line 13, namely $\star \rightarrow$ `Number` $\rhd X? \rightarrow X!$, and $X? \rightarrow X! \rhd X$. Combining $X? \rightarrow X! \rhd X$ and $X \rhd$ `Number` $\rightarrow$ `Number` gives us $X? \rightarrow X! \rhd$ `Number` $\rightarrow$ `Number`. Solving the flows gives us $X?$ = `Number` and $X!$ = `Number`. As before, since only function types flow into X, its solution is its function kind $X? \rightarrow X!$, which after substituting for $X?$ and $X!$ gives us `Number` $\rightarrow$ `Number`.

Finally, decomposition using kinds enables us to take unions of kinds, not types, giving us types inferred from inflows alone. For example, the decomposition of X into $X? \rightarrow X!$ lets us capture the flow of argument types to $X?$ in the calls to `x` on lines 11 and 12, yielding *Number* $\rhd X?$ and *Boolean* $\rhd X?$, respectively. These first-order flows may then be combined by taking the least upper bound in the usual way, after which reconstruction of X proceeds as described above.

2.4 Function Parameters

2.4.1 Functions Callable by Existing Code Are Problematic

Since we cannot assume that all existing ActionScript programs will be available for our analysis, a key goal of our algorithm is to ensure that our inferred types are backward-compatible—i.e., programs compiled using inferred types are able to interoperate with programs compiled under the assumption that missing type annotations are the dynamic type, without introducing any new run-time failures.

We now show an example in which we try to extend our algorithm to infer the parameter type of a function that can be called by other programs that are not available for analysis.

```
16 function foo(x:Foo?):Foo!
17     { if(b) { return x + 1 } else { return 0 } }
18 foo(1)
```

The function call `foo(1)` on line 18 generates `Number` $\rhd$ *Foo?*. Furthermore, as before we generate *Foo?* $\rhd$ `Number` and `Number` $\rhd$ *Foo!* on line 17. Solving for type variables, we get *Foo?* = `Number` and *Foo!* = `Number`. (As before, we do not use *Foo?* $\rhd$ `Number` for inference.)

Suppose that the function `foo` is part of the interface of some library, and clients of `foo` have been compiled under the assumption that *Foo?* and *Foo!* are $\star$. Then the solution for *Foo!* is sound, because it can be used in any context of type $\star$: in particular, it will not throw an error unless it flows to a context whose type is incompatible with `Number`, in which case it would already throw an error without type inference.

Unfortunately, the solution for *Foo?* is not sound. For example, suppose a caller sets the global variable `b = false` and then calls `foo` with `x = true`. In the absence of type inference, the `true` argument will be successfully converted at run time from type `Boolean` to type $\star$—after which it will go unused, since `b = false`, avoiding a run-time error. In contrast, if we add the annotation `x:Number` after type inference, this will have the effect of requiring a run-time conversion of the `true` argument from `Boolean` to `Number` at the point of the call to `foo`, and this conversion will always fail. Thus inferring *Foo?* = `Number` can break existing programs.

In general, we conclude that we cannot safely infer the parameter types of functions that are part of the interface of the program with existing code, because our analysis cannot be guaranteed to include every call to such functions.

2.4.2 Local Functions

On the other hand, it is safe to infer the parameter types of *local* functions—i.e., functions defined within other functions and objects—whenever all their calls are available for analysis.

Consider the local function `foo` in the following example:

```
19 function bar(y:Number):Bar! {
20     function foo(x:Foo?):Foo!
21         { if(b) { return x + 1 } else { return 0 } }
22     return foo(y)
23 }
```

As before, we get the solutions *Foo?* = `Number` and *Foo!* = `Number`. (Here, we also get *Bar!* = `Number`.) Since `foo` is a local function that does not *escape* `bar`, we know it cannot be called from outside `bar`, meaning that all calls to `foo` are available for analysis. In this case it is safe to infer *Foo?* = `Number`, even if the function `bar` is callable by existing code.

2.4.3 Local Functions that Escape Are Problematic

However, if a local function escapes—e.g. by being returned as a higher-order value from a function that is callable by existing code—then it becomes available to callers in the wild. This again makes it unsafe to infer the local function's parameter type, since not every call to the function is available for analysis.

```
24 function bar(y:Number):Bar! {
25     function foo(x:Foo?):Foo!
26         { if(b) { return x + 1 } else { return 0 } }
27     foo(y);
28     return foo
29 }
```

In this example, inferring *Foo?* = `Number` based on function call `foo(y)` on line 27 would again be unsound, assuming the function `bar` is callable by existing code. Since `foo` is returned by `bar`, clients can set `b = false` and call `foo` with any `x` value. Thus, as in Section 2.4.1, annotating `x` as `Number` could introduce run-time errors in existing programs.

2.5 What Types are Safe To Infer?

To summarize, the examples above illustrate that while it may be safe to infer the types of local variables in a function, the return types of functions, and the parameter types of local functions that do not escape, it is definitely not safe to infer parameter types of functions that are callable by existing code, and those of local functions that do escape. Furthermore, if values from such parameters flow into other variables, then inferring the types of those variables is clearly also unsafe.

So what is the principle that lets us decide which types are safe to infer?

2.5.1 Seeing All Inflows is Necessary

We observe that in a gradually typed language, we must see the types of all the values that may flow into a variable before we can infer the variable's type.

Suppose that at compile time we see only a proper subset of the types of values that may flow into a variable x—i.e., some of the types of values that may flow into x are unknown at compile time, because they flow into x from a run-time environment that cannot be analyzed during compilation.

Next, suppose that the compiled program is executed in such a run-time environment. In the absence of type inference, x has type $\star$, which means that the run-time environment could write any type of value into x.

Furthermore, the programmer could reason outside the type system to ensure that once such a value reaches x, it is then used correctly under appropriate conditions.

Thus, if the inferred type of x is based only on the subset of types that are seen, then we could end up breaking the program in this run-time environment, by causing a run-time error to be thrown upon the write to x: not only would this error not have occurred in the absence of type inference, but as described in the previous paragraph, it is quite possible that no error would have occurred at all.

2.5.2 Flows Encode Escape Analysis

For a function that is callable by existing code, we require the programmer to explicitly annotate the parts of the function's type that have negative polarity (in particular, the parameter type), if those parts have static types. In the absence of annotations, we must assume they have the dynamic type. For a local function, our ability to infer the parts of its type with negative polarity depends on whether the function escapes into an unknown run-time environment.

There are many ways a local function can escape: it can be returned as a value, it can be assigned to a global variable, it can be assigned to some object property and that object could be returned, and so on. At first glance, it seems that either we need a sophisticated escape analysis to figure out if a local function escapes, or we need the programmer to annotate parameter types for local functions as well.

Fortunately, we observe that the flows already encode an escape analysis. If we require that types with negative polarities in the interface of the program with existing code be explicitly annotated if static—i.e., if we assume that they are the dynamic type when unannotated—then our closure computation ensures that escape information is properly propagated to all type variables.

Let us consider the example from Section 2.4.3 with different possibilities for *Bar!*.

First, suppose that the programmer has annotated the return type of `bar` as `Number` $\to$ `Number`. In this case, the programmer has annotated the types with negative polarity in `bar` explicitly. Now, it's safe to infer *Foo?* = `Number`, since the programmer has told us that `foo` will always be called with `x` as `Number` (otherwise there will be a run-time error).

On the other hand, if the programmer had not explicitly annotated the return type of `bar`, we would have assumed it to be some type variable *Bar!*. As before, we generate *Foo?* $\to$ *Foo!* $\rhd$ *Bar!* from `return foo` on line 28. We introduce function kind (Section 2.3.2) for *Bar!* and add *Foo?* $\to$ *Foo!* $\rhd$ *Bar!?* $\to$ *Bar!!* and *Bar!?* $\to$ *Bar!!* $\rhd$ *Bar!*. Now, we observe that *Bar!?* has negative polarity. Since the function `bar` is callable by existing code, we assign *Bar!?* = $\star$. Thus, we have *Foo?* $\to$ *Foo!* $\rhd$ $\star$ $\to$ *Bar!!*. Deconstructing the flow, we get $\star$ $\rhd$ *Foo?*. And finally, we infer *Foo?* = $\star$, which is always safe.

In this way, escape analysis is manifested through our closure computation. Thus, we require explicit type annotations only for types that have negative polarities in the interface of the program with existing code; all the remaining types we can infer.

2.6 Outflows

So far we have maintained that we are looking at inflows, of the form $T \rhd X$, to solve for type variable X. But we have not said anything about outflows, of the form $X \rhd T$, where T is not a type variable. Such outflows correspond to dynamic consistency checks.

2.6.1 Outflows Need Not Contribute to Solutions

We observe that outflows, of the form $X \rhd T$, need not contribute to the solution for X—although in general, such outflows do play a role in propagating flows between parts of higher-order types, as we have seen in Section 2.3.2. If we can analyze all writes to X, we know precisely the types of all values that X will need to hold at run time and so, by just looking at inflows, of the form $T \rhd X$, we can infer a more precise solution for X.

2.6.2 Outflows Need Not be Validated Statically

We also do not need to validate the outflows at compile time, as the runtime does it anyway. As we show in the following example, if we try to validate outflows statically, we could end up being too conservative and infer less precise types than we could.

```
30 function foo(f:Foo?):Number {
31     if(b) { return f(true) } else { return 0 }
32 }
33 if(b) { foo(function (x:Boolean):Number { ... }) }
34 else { foo(function (x:Number):Number { ... }) }
```

First we note that this program is safe if *Foo?* = $\star$, which is the case when there is no type inference. When `b` is `false`, `foo` doesn't use its argument and returns `0`.

In our inference algorithm, we generate the flows: `Boolean` $\rightarrow$ `Number` $\rhd$ *Foo??* $\rightarrow$ *Foo?!* (line 33), `Number` $\rightarrow$ `Number` $\rhd$ *Foo??* $\rightarrow$ *Foo?!* (line 34), and `Boolean` $\rhd$ *Foo??* (from function call `g(true)` on line 31). Deconstructing the first two flows gives us *Foo??* $\rhd$ `Boolean`, *Foo??* $\rhd$ `Number`, and `Number` $\rhd$ *Foo?!*. Therefore, we infer *Foo??* = `Boolean` and *Foo?!* = `Number`, and our solution is *Foo?* = `Boolean` $\rightarrow$ `Number`. With these inferred types, the program is still safe. There is no change in the run-time semantics of the program.

But note that our solution *Foo??* = `Boolean` turns the outflow *Foo??* $\rhd$ `Number` to the dynamic consistency check `Boolean` $\rhd$ `Number`, which will fail, if executed at run time. So, if we were to validate outflows statically, we would have promoted *Foo??* to $\star$, which means we would have inferred a less precise type that we could.

In this example, the programmer encodes path sensitive reasoning about correctness of his program and ensures that the dynamic consistency check `Boolean` $\rhd$ `Number` never happens at run time (when the function in line 34 is passed to `foo`, `foo` doesn't invoke it). Since it is not possible to statically determine whether dynamic consistency checks will fire at run time, we do not validate outflows. But, we maintain that our inference doesn't introduce any new run-time errors. Our soundness theorem proves that if a program fails at run time with our inferred types, it would have failed even if those types were $\star$, and vice versa.

2.6.3 Validating Outflows for Blame Guarantees

Traditionally, type inference algorithms in statically typed languages ensure that the solution of X is a subtype of the greatest lower bound of all the types T that flow out of X. This implies that all dynamic consistency checks always succeed.

In our system we do not validate outflows because this may unnecessarily constrain our inferred types, as we saw in the previous example. But this comes with a trade-off. Type inference for statically typed languages guarantees that inferred types will not generate any run-time type errors. While we clearly cannot hope for such guarantees, gradually typed languages often provide weaker blame guarantees [24]—the statically typed parts of a program cannot be blamed for any run-time type errors. On the other hand, by default, we do not give any such guarantee: dynamic consistency checks may throw errors at run time. Instead, our inferred types can be thought of as directives to a runtime to optimize memory, run-time conversions, property lookups, and so on; we only guarantee that they do not introduce any new run-time errors in the program.

If, on the other hand, the programmer wants some blame guarantees from our system, we can run an additional step wherein we validate outflows. If some outflow may cause an error, we either promote the type variable that may cause the error to the $\star$ type, or if there is no type variable involved, fail the compilation. In the example of previous section, once we find that inferring *Foo??* = `Boolean` will fail the consistency check *Foo??* $\rhd$ `Number`, we can promote the type variable *Foo??* = $\star$, and recover blame guarantees for our system.

2.7 Objects

The treatment of objects in our system follows that of functions, in that we use polarities to model object properties with various access controls. For example, private properties of objects have no polarity, so we infer types of private properties. Read-only properties, like public functions, have positive polarity and so, we infer positive parts of the types of those functions and we require programmers to annotate the negative parts. On the other hand, public variables in an object are read-write, so they have both negative and positive polarities, and we require programmers to annotate the types of public variables. As before, we do not need escape analysis to figure out if some private function escapes the scope of an object, or if a private object escapes the scope of a function. Escape analysis is manifested in the closure computation. We show an example in ActionScript where object templates are defined using classes.

```
class A {
    private var b:B = true;
    private function foo(var x:Foo?):Foo!
        { if(b) { return x + 1; } else { return 0; } }
    public function bar():Bar! { return foo; }
}
```

In this example, our solution will be: B = `Boolean`, *Foo?* = $\star$, *Foo!* = `Number`, *Bar!* = $\star$ $\rightarrow$`Number`. Note that as before, we infer *Foo?* = $\star$ because it is returned from a public function `bar`.

Summary Our key observations can be summarized as follows.

1. Unlike type inference in statically typed languages, we treat inflows, which represent definitions, in a fundamentally different manner than outflows, which represent uses. The inflows for a type variable determine its solution. The outflows for a type variable represent dynamic consistency checks that happen at the runtime.
2. When the inflows for a type variable involve higher-order types, its solution is encoded by a kind, which deconstructs the the type variable into parts, recursively solves for those parts, and reconstructs the solutions to determine the solution of the type variable. In particular, the negative parts of such a solution are determined by the negative parts of higher-order types in the outflows for the type variable.
3. We need to see all the types of all values flowing into a variable before we can infer its type. This means that we can only infer positive parts of the type that serves as the program's interface with existing code. The negative parts of that interface can be defined by some unknown run-time environment, so we either need the programmer to annotate those parts explicitly, or we assume them to be the dynamic type.
4. We do not need a separate escape analysis to find which types escape their scope. Once we have put sufficient type annotations in the interface of the program with existing code, our flows encode the escape analysis.
5. Our framework extends naturally to objects (and classes). We use polarities to model object properties with various access controls: private, read-only, write-only, and public.

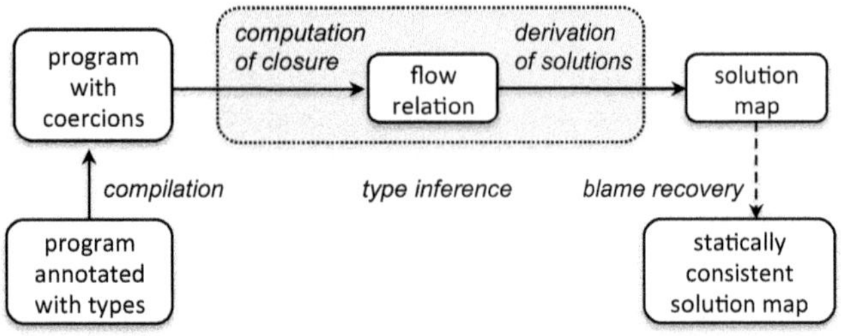

Figure 2. Overall Architecture for Type Inference

3. Formal Development

In this section, we formally develop our type inference algorithm for a core gradually typed calculus of functions and objects.

Unknown types are modeled as type variables in the language. We formalize the static semantics of the language by a compilation judgment that translates a program annotated with types to a program with coercions (Section 3.2). We then describe a type inference algorithm that analyzes the coercions to compute a flow relation over types, and derives a solution map for the type variables based on this flow relation (Section 3.3). We also describe how the solution map may be "weakened" to recover standard blame guarantees (Section 3.4). Figure 2 depicts the overall architecture for type inference.

We prove complexity theorems for the type inference algorithm (Section 3.5). Next, we formalize the dynamic semantics of the language by an evaluation judgment that, under a solution map for the type variables, reduces programs with coercions to values (Section 3.6). Based on this dynamic semantics, we prove soundness theorems for the type inference algorithm, by comparing the behaviors of programs under the solution map inferred by our algorithm with those under the "default" solution map that interprets every type variable as the dynamic type (Section 3.7).

3.1 Syntax

The syntax of the language is shown below. We model function parameters and object properties as variables x. In contrast to standard object calculi, we distinguish readability and writability of object properties: we model access capabilities κ for object properties as subsets of $\{+,-\}$, where $+$ denotes readability and $-$ denotes writability. We express objects and their types as indexed collections of object properties and their types; for any non-negative integer m the notation $[m]$ means the set of indices $\{1,\ldots,m\}$, and for any syntactic entity ϕ the notation $\{\phi_i\}^{i\in[m]}$ means the collection $\{\phi_1,\ldots,\phi_m\}$ indexed by $[m]$.

$$
\begin{array}{llcl}
\text{term} & t & ::= & \mathsf{null} \\
 & & | & \mathsf{fun}\ (x\!:\!T)\ t\!:\!T' \mid \{x_i^{\kappa_i}\!:\!T_i = t_i\}^{i\in[m]} \\
 & & | & x \mid x = t \\
 & & | & t(t') \mid t.x \mid t.x = t' \\
 & & | & \langle T \rhd T' \rangle\ t \mid \mathsf{if}\ t\ \mathsf{then}\ t'\ \mathsf{else}\ t'' \\
\text{type variable} & X & ::= & \alpha \mid X? \mid X! \mid X.x \\
\text{type} & T & ::= & \bot \\
 & & | & T \to T' \mid \{x_i^{\kappa_i} : T_i\}^{i\in[m]} \\
 & & | & \star \mid X
\end{array}
$$

Terms include functions (of the form $\mathsf{fun}\ (x : T)\ t : T'$), objects (of the form $\{x_i^{\kappa_i} : T_i = t_i\}^{i\in[m]}$), and the null value (null), as well as applications of functions (of the form $t(t')$), reads and writes of object properties (of the form $t.x$ and $t.x = t'$), and null checks (of the form if t then t' else t''). They also include reads and writes of variables (of the form x and $x = t$). Furthermore, they include coercions between types (of the form $T \rhd T'$). Coercions may be interpreted syntactically as flows, and semantically as representation-conversion operations. We assume that in source code, there are no coercions.

Types include function types (of the form $T \to T'$), objects types (of the form $\{x_i^{\kappa_i} : T_i\}^{i\in[m]}$), the null type ($\bot$), and the dynamic type ($\star$). Furthermore, they include type variables X. Some type variables may be derived by others: $X.x$ denotes the type of the property x of objects of type X, while $X?$ and $X!$ denote the type of the input and output of functions of type X. We assume that in source code, type variables are distinct and are of the form α.

Recursive functions, self references, and loops can be readily encoded in the language; so can blocks with "local" variables. Thus, we do not include those constructs in the language. Furthermore, we do not model classes: their treatment is similar to that of objects, and we discuss them further in Section 4.

3.2 Compilation

We now describe the compilation semantics of our language. The goal of compilation is to compute types and embed coercions in source programs, thereby preparing them for type inference (Section 3.3) and evaluation (Section 3.6).

Compilation proceeds under a type environment. A type environment Γ is a finite map from variables to types. Compilation judgments are of the form $\Gamma \vdash t \hookrightarrow t' :: T$, meaning that t compiles to t' of type T under Γ. Figure 3 lists the rules for deriving compilation judgments.

The compilation rules are fairly straightforward: the type of a term is computed in a syntax-directed manner, and whenever a term of type T appears in a context that is annotated with type T', the coercion $T \rhd T'$ is attached to the term. We elaborate on the rules for deconstructing functions and objects, namely (C-APP) for function applications and (C-PROPR) and (C-PROPW) for object property accesses: they rely on a partial relation $\multimap$ between types, defined below. Intuitively, this relation captures the condition under which a term of a certain type can be deconstructed, by viewing the type either as the type of a function that can be applied or as the type of an object for which a property can be read or written.

Definition 3.1 (View). *A type T can be viewed as a type T' if $T \multimap T'$ can be derived by any of the following rules.*

- $X \multimap X? \to X!$
- $\star \multimap \star \to \star$
- $T \to T' \multimap T \to T'$
- $X \multimap \{x^\kappa : X.x\}$ *for* $\kappa = \{+\}$ *or* $\kappa = \{-\}$
- $\star \multimap \{x^\kappa : \star\}$ *for* $\kappa = \{+\}$ *or* $\kappa = \{-\}$
- $\{x_i^{\kappa_i} : T_i\}^{i\in[m]} \multimap \{x_j^\kappa : T_j\}$ *such that* $j \in [m]$ *and* $\kappa \subseteq \kappa_j$, *for* $\kappa = \{+\}$ *or* $\kappa = \{-\}$

Compilation may fail due to the partiality of the view relation: essentially, whenever a term of some type is deconstructed in a context that is annotated with an "incompatible" type. In particular, a function cannot be viewed as an object, an object cannot be viewed as a function, and an object without a particular access capability for a property cannot be viewed as an object with that access capability for that property.

Further restrictions can be imposed statically. In particular, a standard gradual type system would detect other "unsafe" coercions, by interpreting all type variables as the dynamic type $\star$ and ensuring that coercions are between *statically consistent* types (cf. consistency and consistent-subtyping [16, 17]). Static consistency is defined in Section 3.4, where we discuss how to carry over "blame" guarantees offered by such systems to our setting. How-

Compilation judgment $\Gamma \vdash t \hookrightarrow t' :: T$

(C-NULL)

$$\frac{}{\Gamma \vdash \mathsf{null} \hookrightarrow \mathsf{null} :: \bot}$$

(C-FUN)

$$\frac{\Gamma[x \mapsto T_1] \vdash t_2 \hookrightarrow t_2' :: T_2' \qquad t_2'' = \langle T_2' \rhd T_2 \rangle\, t_2'}{\Gamma \vdash \mathsf{fun}\ (x\!:\!T_1)\ t_2\!:\!T_2 \hookrightarrow \mathsf{fun}\ (x\!:\!T_1)\ (t_2'')\!:\!T_2 :: T_1 \to T_2}$$

(C-OBJ)

$$\frac{\begin{array}{c}\Gamma' = \Gamma[x_1 \mapsto T_1, \ldots, x_m \mapsto T_m] \\ \forall i \in [m].\quad \Gamma' \vdash t_i \hookrightarrow t_i' :: T_i' \quad t_i'' = \langle T_i' \rhd T_i \rangle\, t_i'\end{array}}{\Gamma \vdash \{x_i^{\kappa_i}\!:\!T_i = t_i\}^{i \in [m]} \hookrightarrow \{x_i^{\kappa_i}\!:\!T_i = t_i''\}^{i \in [m]} :: \{x_i^{\kappa_i}\!:\!T_i\}^{i \in [m]}}$$

(C-PROPR)

$$\frac{\Gamma \vdash t \hookrightarrow t' :: T \qquad T \multimap \{x_j^{\{+\}} : T_j\}}{\Gamma \vdash t.x_j \hookrightarrow (\langle T \rhd \{x_j^{\{+\}} : T_j\}\rangle\, t').x_j :: T_j}$$

(C-PROPW)

$$\frac{\begin{array}{c}\Gamma \vdash t \hookrightarrow t' :: T \qquad T \multimap \{x_j^{\{-\}} : T_j\} \\ \Gamma \vdash t_j \hookrightarrow t_j' :: T_j' \qquad t_j'' = \langle T_j' \rhd T_j \rangle\, t_j'\end{array}}{\Gamma \vdash t.x_j = t_j \hookrightarrow (\langle T \rhd \{x_j^{\{-\}} : T_j\}\rangle\, t').x_j = t_j'' :: T_j}$$

(C-APP)

$$\frac{\begin{array}{c}\Gamma \vdash t \hookrightarrow t' :: T \qquad T \multimap T_1 \to T_2 \\ \Gamma \vdash t_1 \hookrightarrow t_1' :: T_1' \qquad t_1'' = \langle T_1' \rhd T_1 \rangle\, t_1'\end{array}}{\Gamma \vdash t\ (t_1) \hookrightarrow (\langle T \rhd T_1 \to T_2 \rangle\, t')\ (t_1'') :: T_2}$$

(C-VARR)

$$\frac{\Gamma(x) = T}{\Gamma \vdash x \hookrightarrow x :: T}$$

(C-VARW)

$$\frac{\Gamma(x) = T \qquad \Gamma \vdash t \hookrightarrow t' :: T'}{\Gamma \vdash x = t \hookrightarrow x = \langle T' \rhd T \rangle\, t' :: T}$$

(C-IF)

$$\frac{\begin{array}{c}\Gamma \vdash t \hookrightarrow t' :: T \\ \alpha \text{ fresh} \qquad \forall i \in \{1,2\}.\quad \Gamma \vdash t_i \hookrightarrow t_i' :: T_i \quad t_i'' = \langle T_i \rhd \alpha \rangle\, t_i'\end{array}}{\Gamma \vdash \mathsf{if}\ t\ \mathsf{then}\ t_1\ \mathsf{else}\ t_2 \hookrightarrow \mathsf{if}\ t'\ \mathsf{then}\ t_1''\ \mathsf{else}\ t_2'' :: \alpha}$$

Figure 3. Compilation

Flow judgment $T \rhd T'\ \checkmark$

(F-BASE)

$$\frac{T \rhd T' \text{ is a coercion in the compiled program}}{T \rhd T'\ \checkmark}$$

(F-COMP)

$$\frac{\begin{array}{c}T \text{ is the type of the compiled program} \\ C \in \{X \rhd \star \mid X \text{ is positive in } T\} \cup \{\star \rhd X \mid X \text{ is negative in } T\}\end{array}}{C\ \checkmark}$$

(F-PULL)

$$\frac{\mathbb{K}^X \rhd X\ \checkmark \qquad X \rhd Y\ \checkmark}{\mathbb{K}^X \rhd Y\ \checkmark}$$

(F-FACTOR)

$$\frac{T \rhd X\ \checkmark \qquad \|T\|_X = \mathbb{K}^X \qquad C \in \{T \rhd \mathbb{K}^X, \mathbb{K}^X \rhd X\}}{C\ \checkmark}$$

(F-TRAN)

$$\frac{\mathbb{K}^X \rhd X\ \checkmark \qquad X \rhd T\ \checkmark \qquad \mathbb{K}^X \preccurlyeq T}{\mathbb{K}^X \rhd T\ \checkmark}$$

(F-EXPFUNL)

$$\frac{\star \rhd T_1 \to T_2\ \checkmark}{\star \to \star \rhd T_1 \to T_2\ \checkmark}$$

(F-EXPOBJL)

$$\frac{\star \rhd \{x_i^{\kappa_i} : T_i\}^{i \in [m]}\ \checkmark}{\{x_i^{\kappa_i} : \star\}^{i \in [m]} \rhd \{x_i^{\kappa_i} : T_i\}^{i \in [m]}\ \checkmark}$$

(F-EXPFUNR)

$$\frac{T_1 \to T_2 \rhd \star\ \checkmark}{T_1 \to T_2 \rhd \star \to \star\ \checkmark}$$

(F-EXPOBJR)

$$\frac{\{x_i^{\kappa_i} : T_i\}^{i \in [m]} \rhd \star\ \checkmark}{\{x_i^{\kappa_i} : T_i\}^{i \in [m]} \rhd \{x_i^{\kappa_i} : \star\}^{i \in [m]}\ \checkmark}$$

(F-SPLITFUN)

$$\frac{T_1 \to T_2 \rhd T_1' \to T_2'\ \checkmark \qquad C \in \{T_1' \rhd T_1, T_2 \rhd T_2'\}}{C\ \checkmark}$$

(F-SPLITOBJ)

$$\frac{\begin{array}{c}\{x_i^{\kappa_i} : T_i\}^{i \in [m]} \rhd \{x_i^{\kappa_i'} : T_i'\}^{i \in [n]}\ \checkmark \\ n \le m \qquad \forall i \in [n] : \kappa_i' \subseteq \kappa_i \\ j \in [n] \qquad C \in \{T_j \rhd T_j' \mid + \in \kappa_j'\} \cup \{T_j' \rhd T_j \mid - \in \kappa_j'\}\end{array}}{C\ \checkmark}$$

Figure 4. Computation of Closure

ever, we emphasize that we do not require those restrictions for our soundness theorem: we can tolerate existing run-time failures as long as we do not introduce any new run-time failures.

3.3 Type Inference

Following compilation, the coercions embedded in a program say what types of terms appear in what types of contexts. Other coercions are implicit in the type of the compiled program, which serves as the interface with existing code: these are coercions between the dynamic type and type variables in the type of the compiled program (which continue to be interpreted as the dynamic type by existing code). Based on this set of coercions, we conduct type inference as follows:

1. We apply some carefully designed closure rules on this set of coercions, to compute a flow relation between types (Section 3.3.1). The flow relation overapproximates the set of all possible flows of terms to contexts at run time.
2. We then derive a solution map for type variables based on that flow relation (Section 3.3.2). In particular, if some context is annotated by a type variable, the solution for that type variable is an overapproximation of the types of terms that may flow to that context at run time.

3.3.1 Computation of Closure

Given a compiled program and its type, we compute a flow relation between types by initializing and growing a set of coercions until fixpoint. Flow judgments are of the form $T \rhd T'\ \checkmark$, meaning that "flows" from type T to type T' are possible, i.e., terms of type T may flow to contexts annotated with type T' at run time. Figure 4 lists the rules for deriving flow judgments. Those rules are explained below.

Unlike usual flow relations for statically typed languages with subtyping, our flow relation is not merely a transitive closure of the coercions in a compiled program, interpreted as subtyping constraints. Instead, it is designed carefully to account for gradual typing, and is tuned for efficiency.

Rules (F-BASE) and (F-COMP) generate the initial facts. In particular, (F-COMP) relies on a standard notion of polarity for type variables, defined below, to ensure that any type variable that appears in the type of the compiled program is (or becomes, by other rules) "tainted" with the dynamic type in the contravariant parts.

Definition 3.2 (Polarity of a type variable in a type). *The set of positive variables and the set of negative variables in a type T are $\mathbb{P}^+(T)$ and $\mathbb{P}^-(T)$, respectively, defined as follows. Let s range over $\{+,-\}$; let $\overline{s}$ be $-$ when s is $+$, and $+$ when s is $-$.*

- $\mathbb{P}^+(X) = \{X\}, \mathbb{P}^-(X) = \{\}$
- $\mathbb{P}^s(\star) = \mathbb{P}^s(\bot) = \{\}$
- $\mathbb{P}^s(T_1 \to T_2) = \mathbb{P}^{\overline{s}}(T_1) \cup \mathbb{P}^s(T_2)$
- $\mathbb{P}^s(\{x_i^{\kappa_i} : T_i\}^{i\in[m]}) = \bigcup\{\mathbb{P}^{\overline{s}}(T_i) \mid i \in [m], - \in \kappa_i\} \cup \bigcup\{\mathbb{P}^s(T_i) \mid i \in [m], + \in \kappa_i\}$

For example, if the interface of the compiled program with existing code is $X_1 \to X_2$, then (F-COMP) reflects the following assumptions:

- We assume that there is a flow from $\star$ to X_1.
- We also assume that there is a flow from X_2 to $\star$, so that if (say) there is a local function that escapes through X_2, then (by other rules) we can derive a flow from $\star$ to the parameter type of the escaping function.

Similar considerations apply if the interface is an object type: if a writable property is annotated with a type variable, there is a flow from $\star$ to that type variable, and if a readable property is annotated with a type variable, there is a flow from that type variable to $\star$. (If a property is both, we assume both flows; if a property is neither, we assume neither.)

Other rules, namely (F-PULL), (F-FACTOR), and (F-TRAN), rely on a notion of kinding for type variables, defined below. Intuitively, a type variable has, for every type constructor that may form a solution for the type variable, a kind that encodes that solution.

Definition 3.3 (Kinds for a type variable). *Kinds for a type variable X, ranged over by $\mathbb{K}^X$, are types of the form $\bot$, $X? \to X!$, $\{x_i^{\kappa_i} : X.x_i\}^{i\in[m]}$, or $\star$.*

Eventually, the solution of a type variable is derived by the kinds that flow into it, either directly or indirectly through other type variables. Thus, the rule (F-PULL) "pulls" any kind on the left of a type variable to any other type variable on its right.

The rule (F-FACTOR) factors a coercion from a type to a type variable into intermediate coercions through a corresponding kind for that type variable, computed as shown below. This factoring ensures that flows from types to a type variable are appropriately captured in solutions for that type variable.

Definition 3.4 (Kind of a type for a type variable). *The kind $\|T\|_X$ of a type T, where T is not a type variable, for a type variable X is defined as follows:*

- $\|\bot\|_X = \bot$
- $\|\star\|_X = \star$
- $\|T_1 \to T_2\|_X = X? \to X!$
- $\|\{x_i^{\kappa_i} : T_i\}^{i\in[m]}\|_X = \{x_i^{\kappa_i} : X.x_i\}^{i\in[m]}$

The rule (F-TRAN) limits transitive flows through a type variable in two ways: it only considers a kind on the left, and it only considers a type on the right such that the kind on the left is *dynamically consistent* with the type on its right. Dynamic consistency $\preccurlyeq$ is a partial relation between types that are not type variables, defined as follows; it models coercions that never fail at run time.

Definition 3.5 (Dynamic Consistency). *A type T is dynamically consistent with another type T' if T and T' are not type variables, and $T \preccurlyeq T'$ can be derived by any of the following rules.*

- $\bot \preccurlyeq T$
- $T \preccurlyeq \star, \star \preccurlyeq T$
- $T_1 \to T_2 \preccurlyeq T_1' \to T_2'$
- $\{x_i^{\kappa_i} : T_i\}^{i\in[m]} \preccurlyeq \{x_i^{\kappa_i'} : T_i'\}^{i\in[n]}$ *if $n \le m$, and for all $i \in [n]$, we have $\kappa_i' \subseteq \kappa_i$*

In combination with (F-FACTOR), the rule (F-TRAN) ensures that flows from types on the left of a type variable to types on the right of the type variable are taken into account, without computing a standard transitive closure. (In Section 4, we discuss why computing a standard transitive closure is undesirable.)

The remaining rules are fairly straightforward. (F-EXPFUNL), (F-EXPFUNR), (F-EXPOBJL), and (F-EXPOBJR) expand $\star$ on the left or right of a higher-order type to the appropriate shape. Finally, (F-SPLITFUN) and (F-SPLITOBJ) split flows between higher-order types into flows between their parts, respecting covariance and contravariance. Note that since we distinguish access capabilities for reading and writing object properties, the types of object properties are not necessarily invariant: they may be covariant (read-only), contravariant (write-only), invariant (read-write), or even abstract (no access).

3.3.2 Derivation of Solutions

Based on the flow judgment, we derive a solution map $\mathbb{I}$ that associates each type variable X to a type without type variables. We also extend $\mathbb{I}$ to a function $\widehat{\mathbb{I}}$ from types to types without type variables, such that $\widehat{\mathbb{I}}(T)$ is the type obtained by substituting each type variable X in type T by $\mathbb{I}(X)$.

To solve for X, let $\mathbb{T}^+(X)$ be the set of types T such that T is not a type variable, and $T \rhd X\ \checkmark$; we compute the least upper bound of the kinds of types for X in $\mathbb{T}^+(X)$, as defined below.

Definition 3.6 (Least upper bound of kinds). *The least upper bound $\mathbb{K}_1^X \sqcup \mathbb{K}_2^X$ of two kinds $\mathbb{K}_1^X$ and $\mathbb{K}_2^X$ for X is defined as follows:*

- $\bot \sqcup \mathbb{K}^X = \mathbb{K}^X, \mathbb{K}^X \sqcup \bot = \mathbb{K}^X$
- $\star \sqcup \mathbb{K}^X = \star, \mathbb{K}^X \sqcup \star = \star$
- $(X? \to X!) \sqcup (X? \to X!) = X? \to X!$
- $\{x_i^{\kappa_i} : X.x_i\}^{i\in[m]} \sqcup \{y_j^{\kappa_j} : X.y_j\}^{j\in[n]} = \{z_k^{\kappa_k} : X.z_k\}^{k\in[p]}$, *where $\{z_k\}^{k\in[p]} = \{x_i\}^{i\in[m]} \cap \{y_j\}^{j\in[n]}$ and for all $i \in [m]$, $j \in [n]$, and $k \in [p]$, if $x_i = y_j = z_k$ then $\kappa_k = \kappa_i \cap \kappa_j$.*
- $(X? \to X!) \sqcup \{x_i^{\kappa_i} : X.x_i\}^{i\in[m]} = \star$
- $\{x_i^{\kappa_i} : X.x_i\}^{i\in[m]} \sqcup (X? \to X!) = \star$

The solution $\mathbb{I}(X)$ for X is then defined as $\widehat{\mathbb{I}}(\sqcup_{T\in\mathbb{T}^+(X)}\|T\|_X)$. Such solutions are always well-founded, since kinds do not have cyclic dependencies.

3.4 Blame Recovery

Standard gradual type systems enforce that the coercions in a compiled program satisfy *static consistency*, which is a partial relation between types that are not type variables, defined as follows:

Definition 3.7 (Static Consistency). *A type T is statically consistent with another type T' if T and T' are not type variables, and $T \preceq T'$ can be derived by any of the following rules.*

- $\bot \preceq T$
- $T \preceq \star, \star \preceq T$
- $T_1 \to T_2 \preceq T_1' \to T_2'$ *if* $T_1' \preceq T_1$ *and* $T_2 \preceq T_2'$
- $\{x_i^{\kappa_i} : T_i\}^{i \in [m]} \preceq \{x_i^{\kappa_i'} : T_i'\}^{i \in [n]}$ *if* $n \leq m$, *and for all* $i \in [n]$, *we have* $\kappa_i' \subseteq \kappa_i$, *and if* $+ \in \kappa_i'$ *then* $T_i \preceq T_i'$, *if* $- \in \kappa_i'$ *then* $T_i' \preceq T_i$.

This static consistency relation extends similar relations defined separately for a gradually typed language of functions and for a gradually typed language of objects. We conjecture that programs in our language satisfy the blame theorem whenever they compile to programs whose coercions satisfy the static consistency relation, following similar type-safety results for existing languages.

However, the solution map $\mathbb{I}$ derived above does not guarantee static consistency. This means that blame guarantees offered by standard gradual type systems do not carry over with type inference. Fortunately, it is possible to "weaken" $\mathbb{I}$ to recover those blame guarantees, as follows. For any type variable X, let $\mathbb{T}^-(X)$ be the set of types T such that T is not a type variable and $X \rhd T \checkmark$. If there is any $T \in \mathbb{T}^-(X)$ such that $\mathbb{I}(X) \not\preceq T$, then $\mathbb{I}(X)$ is redefined to be $\star$. We can then prove the following theorem.

Theorem 3.8 (Blame recovery). *Suppose that for every coercion* $T \rhd T'$ *in the compiled program, we have* $\widehat{*}(T) \preceq \widehat{*}(T')$, *where* $\widehat{*}$ *is the solution map that associates every type variable with* $\star$. *Then for every flow judgment* $T \rhd T' \checkmark$, *we have* $\widehat{\mathbb{I}}(T) \preceq \widehat{\mathbb{I}}(T')$.

3.5 Algorithmic Complexity

Although computation of closure may be performed by applying the flow rules in arbitrary order until fixpoint, an effective algorithm would apply them systematically, as described below; we can then reason about its efficiency.

Definition 3.9 (Flow computation). *The computation of flow judgments proceeds in the following steps until fixpoint:*

(1) Initially, rules (F-BASE) *and* (F-COMP) *are applied until saturation.*
(2) Next, rules (F-PULL) *and* (F-FACTOR) *are applied until saturation.*
(3) Next, rules (F-TRAN), (F-EXPFUNL), (F-EXPOBJL), (F-EXPFUNR), (F-EXPOBJR) *are applied until saturation.*
(4) Next, rule (F-SPLITFUN) *and* (F-SPLITOBJ) *is applied until saturation.*
(5) Finally, control returns to step (2), where if no new flow judgments are derived, the algorithm terminates.

We prove that our algorithm terminates and is efficient.

Theorem 3.10 (Termination). *Flow computation terminates.*

Proof. Recall that all type variables in the system are distinct, so they have unique depths. Let d be the maximum depth of types in the system after step (1).

Steps (2) and (3) introduce types of depth $\leq d$ in the system. Step (4) introduces types of depth $\leq d-1$. Finally, in step (5), types of depth d and type variables of depth 1 can be thrown away. This means that maximum depth of types in the system after step (5) is $d-1$.

Thus, flow computation must terminate in $\leq d$ iterations. □

Theorem 3.11 (Time Complexity). *The time complexity of flow computation is quadratic in the size of the program.*

Proof. Let k be the number of type variables, n be the number of types other than type variables, and d be the maximum depth of types after step (1).

Step (2) takes $O(k^2)$ time. Step (3) takes $O(kn)$ time, and increases the number of types by some factor w that denotes the maximum width of types. Step (4) takes $O(n^2)$ time, and increases the number of types by the same factor w.

Thus, before step (5), the total time taken is $O((k+n)^2)$, and after step (5), we have wk variables and wn types other than type variables.

Since the algorithm terminates in $\leq d$ iterations, the total time complexity is $O(w^{2d}(k+n)^2)$. Typically, w and d are small constants, so the time complexity is almost quadratic in the number of types $k+n$. In general, if the size of the program is N, then $w^d(k+n) = O(N)$. Thus the total time complexity is $O(N^2)$. □

3.6 Evaluation

We now describe the evaluation semantics of our language, which enables us to prove that our type inference algorithm is sound.

Let ℓ range over locations. A stack S is a sequence of locations. The syntax of values is as follows.

$$\begin{array}{lrcl} \text{value} & v & ::= & \langle \bot \rhd \cdots \rhd T \rangle \ \mathsf{null} \\ & & | & \langle T_1 \to T_2 \rhd \cdots \rhd T \rangle \ \lambda^S x.\, t \\ & & | & \langle \{x_i^{\kappa_i} : T_i\}^{i \in [m]} \rhd \cdots \rhd T \rangle \ \ell \end{array}$$

A value of the form $\langle T \rhd T \rangle\ u$ is abbreviated as $u :: T$. Furthermore, we use the notation $\langle T' \rhd \cdots \rhd T'' \rangle\ \langle T \rhd \cdots \rhd T' \rangle\ u$ to denote $\langle T \rhd \cdots \rhd T' \rhd \cdots \rhd T'' \rangle\ u$. Unlike previous work that focuses on space-efficient implementations of gradually typed languages [19], our dynamic semantics admits unbounded chains of coercions to simplify the specification and proof of soundness: essentially, we keep coercions in symbolic form and check that they normalize "along the way."

A record is a map from variables to values. A heap H is a map from locations to records.

We rely on the following operations for querying/updating variables on the stack through the heap.

$$H[x \mapsto v]_{S,\ell} = \begin{cases} H[\ell \mapsto H(\ell)[x \mapsto v]] & \text{if } x \in \mathtt{dom}(H(\ell)) \\ H[x \mapsto v]_S & \text{if } x \notin \mathtt{dom}(H(\ell)) \end{cases}$$

$$H[x]_{S,\ell} = \begin{cases} H(\ell)(x) & \text{if } x \in \mathtt{dom}(H(\ell)) \\ H[x]_S & \text{if } x \notin \mathtt{dom}(H(\ell)) \end{cases}$$

The evaluation judgment is $S \vdash (H, t) \Downarrow_\sigma (H', v)$, where σ is a solution map, which associates type variables to types without type variables. Figure 5 lists the rules for deriving evaluation judgments.

The rules are fairly standard, except that the coercions on values are symbolic: the type variables in those coercions are not substituted by their solutions, but instead the solutions are looked up when normalizing the coercions. This is convenient for our soundness proof. Normalization is defined as follows.

Definition 3.12 (Normalization). *The chain of coercions* $T_0 \rhd \cdots \rhd T_{n+1}$ *normalizes under* σ *if for all* $j \in [n+1]$, $\sigma(T_0) \preccurlyeq \sigma(T_j)$.

Furthermore, a value v *normalizes under* σ, *written* $v \Downarrow_\sigma$, *if it is of the form* $\langle T_0 \rhd \cdots \rhd T_{n+1} \rangle\ u$ *and* $\langle T_0 \rhd \cdots \rhd T_{n+1} \rangle$ *normalizes under* σ.

The deconstruction rules for functions and objects, namely (E-APP), (E-PROPR), and (E-PROPW), rely on the following standard splitting rules for higher-order coercions.

$$\frac{\forall i \in [n+1].\quad T_i \multimap \{x_j^{\{+\}} : T_i'\}}{\langle T_0 \ldots T_{n+1} \rhd \{x_j^{\{+\}} : U_j\}\rangle \multimap\!\!\bullet\ \{x_j^{\{+\}} : \langle T_0' \ldots T_{n+1}' \rangle\}}$$

$$\frac{\forall i \in [n+1].\quad T_i \multimap \{x_j^{\{-\}} : T_i'\}}{\langle T_0 \ldots T_{n+1} \rhd \{x_j^{\{-\}} : U_j\}\rangle \multimap\!\!\bullet\ \{x_j^{\{-\}} : \langle T_{n+1}' \ldots T_0' \rangle\}}$$

Evaluation judgment $S \vdash (H, t) \Downarrow_\sigma (H', v)$

(E-NULL)

$$\frac{}{S \vdash (H, \mathsf{null}) \Downarrow_\sigma (H, \mathsf{null} :: \bot)}$$

(E-FUN)

$$S \vdash (H, \mathsf{fun}\ (x\!:\!T_1)\ t_2\!:\!T_2) \Downarrow_\sigma (H, \lambda^S x.\, t_2 :: T_1 \to T_2)$$

(E-OBJ)

$$\frac{\begin{array}{c}\ell \text{ is fresh} \qquad H_1 = H[\ell \mapsto [x_1 \mapsto \mathsf{null}, \ldots, x_n \mapsto \mathsf{null}]] \\ \forall i \in [m].\quad S, \ell \vdash (H_i, t_i) \Downarrow_\sigma (H'_i, v_i) \quad H'_i[x_i \Mapsto v_i]_{S,\ell} = H_{i+1}\end{array}}{S \vdash (H, \{x_i^{\kappa_i}\!:\!T_i = t_i\}^{i \in [m]}) \Downarrow_\sigma (H_{m+1}, \ell :: \{x_i^{\kappa_i}\!:\!T_i\}^{i \in [m]})}$$

(E-PROPR)

$$\frac{\begin{array}{c}S \vdash (H, t) \Downarrow_\sigma (H', \langle \mathcal{C} \rangle\, \ell) \qquad \mathcal{C} \multimap\!\bullet \{x_j^{\{+\}} : \langle \mathcal{C}_j \rangle\} \\ H'(\ell) = R \qquad v_j = R(x_j) \qquad \langle \mathcal{C}_j \rangle\, v_j \Downarrow_\sigma\end{array}}{S \vdash (H, t.x_j) \Downarrow_\sigma (H', \langle \mathcal{C}_j \rangle\, v_j)}$$

(E-PROPW)

$$\frac{\begin{array}{c}S \vdash (H, t) \Downarrow_\sigma (H', \langle \mathcal{C} \rangle\, \ell) \qquad \mathcal{C} \multimap\!\bullet \{x_j^{\{-\}} : \langle \mathcal{C}_j \rangle\} \\ S \vdash (H', t_j) \Downarrow_\sigma (H_j, v_j) \qquad \langle \mathcal{C}_j \rangle\, v_j \Downarrow_\sigma \\ H_j(\ell) = R \qquad H'' = H_j[\ell \mapsto R[x_j \mapsto \langle \mathcal{C}_j \rangle\, v_j]]\end{array}}{S \vdash (H, t.x_j = t_j) \Downarrow_\sigma (H'', \langle \mathcal{C}_j \rangle\, v_j)}$$

(E-APP)

$$\frac{\begin{array}{c}S \vdash (H, t) \Downarrow_\sigma (H', \langle \mathcal{C} \rangle\, \lambda^{S'} x.t_2) \qquad \mathcal{C} \multimap\!\bullet \mathcal{C}_1 \to \mathcal{C}_2 \\ S \vdash (H', t_1) \Downarrow_\sigma (H_1, v_1) \qquad \langle \mathcal{C}_1 \rangle\, v_1 \Downarrow_\sigma \\ \ell \text{ is fresh} \qquad H'' = H_1[\ell \mapsto [x \mapsto \langle \mathcal{C}_1 \rangle\, v_1]] \\ S', \ell \vdash (H'', t_2) \Downarrow_\sigma (H_2, v_2) \qquad \langle \mathcal{C}_2 \rangle\, v_2 \Downarrow_\sigma\end{array}}{S \vdash (H, t\ (t_1)) \Downarrow_\sigma (H_2, \langle \mathcal{C}_2 \rangle\, v_2)}$$

(E-VARR)

$$\frac{H[x]_S = v}{S \vdash (H, x) \Downarrow_\sigma (H, v)}$$

(E-VARW)

$$\frac{S \vdash (H, t) \Downarrow_\sigma (H', v) \qquad H'[x \Mapsto v]_S = H''}{S \vdash (H, x = t) \Downarrow_\sigma (H'', v)}$$

(E-CAST)

$$\frac{S \vdash (H, t_1) \Downarrow_\sigma (H', v_1) \qquad \langle T_1 \rhd T_2 \rangle\, v_1 \Downarrow_\sigma}{S \vdash (H, \langle T_1 \rhd T_2 \rangle\, t_1) \Downarrow_\sigma (H', \langle T_1 \rhd T_2 \rangle\, v_1)}$$

(E-IF)

$$\frac{\begin{array}{c}S \vdash (H, t) \Downarrow_\sigma (H', v) \\ v \neq \mathsf{null} \Rightarrow i = 1 \qquad v = \mathsf{null} \Rightarrow i = 2 \\ S \vdash (H', t_i) \Downarrow_\sigma (H'', v')\end{array}}{S \vdash (H, \mathsf{if}\ t\ \mathsf{then}\ t_1\ \mathsf{else}\ t_2) \Downarrow_\sigma (H'', v')}$$

Figure 5. Evaluation

$$\frac{\forall i \in [n+1].\quad T_i \multimap T'_i \to T''_i}{\langle T_0 \ldots T_{n+1} \rhd U_1 \to U_2 \rangle \multimap\!\bullet \langle T'_{n+1} \ldots T'_0 \rangle \to \langle T''_0 \ldots T''_{n+1} \rangle}$$

3.7 Soundness

Since we infer more precise types where there were less precise types ($\star$), the interesting direction for soundness is to establish, as above, that we do not introduce any run-time errors. The other direction is trivial, and can be established by reasoning about positive and negative blames [24] (see Section 6).

We prove the following soundness theorem for our type inference algorithm, which says that if a compiled program evaluates to a value with dynamic types for type variables, then it evaluates to the same value with inferred types for type variables. (Recall that the dynamic semantics is symbolic in type variables, but ensures that any coercions in values normalize.)

Theorem 3.13 (Soundness). *Let $\varnothing \vdash t \hookrightarrow t' :: T$. Let $\mathbb{I}$ be the inferred solution map for $t' :: T$, and let $*$ be the solution map that associates every type variable with $\star$. If $\varnothing \vdash (\varnothing, t') \Downarrow_* (H', v)$, then $\varnothing \vdash (\varnothing, t') \Downarrow_{\mathbb{I}} (H', v)$.*

Soundness follows as a corollary of our main lemma, Term Correspondence (Lemma 3.16, see below), which states not only (i) there a correspondence between reductions in the original program and reductions in the program with inferred types, but also (ii) any coercions that may be generated at run time have already been generated at compile time (via closure computation). Of course, (ii) is a crucial invariant to show (i), since it means that the solutions we compute at compile time behave as expected at run time.

Definition 3.14 (Knowledge of coercions). *The chain of coercions $T_0 \rhd \cdots \rhd T_{n+1}$ is known if for all $j \in [n+1]$, $T_{j-1} \rhd T_j \checkmark$.*

Definition 3.15 (Compatibility of type environment with stack and heap). *The type environment Γ is compatible with the stack S under heap H, written $\Gamma \sim_H S$, if whenever $\Gamma(x) = T_{n+1}$, we have $H[x]_S = \langle T_0 \rhd \cdots \rhd T_{n+1} \rangle\, v$ and $\langle T_0 \rhd \cdots \rhd T_{n+1} \rangle$ is known.*

Lemma 3.16 (Term Correspondence). *Let $\Gamma \vdash t \hookrightarrow t' :: T$ and $\Gamma \sim_H S$. If $S \vdash (H, t') \Downarrow_* (H', \langle T_0 \rhd \cdots \rhd T_{n+1} \rangle\, v)$ then:*

- *$S \vdash (H, t') \Downarrow_{\mathbb{I}} (H', \langle T_0 \rhd \cdots \rhd T_{n+1} \rangle\, v$*
- *$\langle T_0 \rhd \cdots \rhd T_{n+1} \rangle$ is known*

The proof of Term Correspondence requires Value Correspondence (Lemma 3.17, see below), and two other lemmas on knowledge of coercions, Function Flow and Object Flow, which are used in the cases of function application and object property access.

Lemma 3.17 (Value Correspondence). *If $T_0 \rhd \cdots \rhd T_{n+1}$ is known and normalizes under $*$, then it normalizes under $\mathbb{I}$.*

Lemma 3.18 (Function Flow). *If $T_0 \to T'_0 \rhd T''_1 \rhd \cdots \rhd T''_{n+1}$ is known and $T''_i \multimap T_i \to T'_i$ for all $i \in [n+1]$, then $T_n \ldots T_1 \rhd T_0$ is known and $T'_0 \rhd T'_1 \ldots T'_n$ is known.*

Lemma 3.19 (Object Flow). *If $\{x_{i-1}^{\kappa_{i-1}} : T_{i-1}\}^{i \in [m]} \rhd T''_1 \rhd \cdots \rhd T''_{n+1}$ is known and $T''_i \multimap \{x_0^{\kappa'_0} : T_i\}$ for all $i \in [n+1]$, then $T_n \ldots T_1 \rhd T_0$ is known if $\kappa'_0 = \{-\}$ and $T'_0 \rhd T'_1 \ldots T'_n$ is known if $\kappa'_0 = \{+\}$.*

The proofs of these lemmas in turn require the closure rules, and the following two basic lemmas on dynamic consistency.

Lemma 3.20 (Kind Ordering). *If $\sqcup_{T \in \mathcal{T}} T = T'$ then for all $T \in \mathcal{T}$, we have $T \preccurlyeq T'$.*

Lemma 3.21 (Monotonicity). *If $X \rhd Y \checkmark$ then $\mathbb{I}(X) \preccurlyeq \mathbb{I}(Y)$.*

Furthermore, we can prove the following soundness theorem that says that our type inference is compositional.

Theorem 3.22 (Compositional Soundness). *Suppose that $\varnothing \vdash t_1 \hookrightarrow t'_1 :: T_1$. Let $\mathbb{I}$ be the inferred solution map for $t'_1 :: T_1$, and $*$ be the solution map that associates every type variable with $\star$. Let t be a program without type variables, such that $\varnothing \vdash t \hookrightarrow t' :: \widehat{*}(T_1) \to T_2$. Let $t''_1 = \langle T_1 \rhd \widehat{*}(T_1) \rangle\, t'_1$. Then $\varnothing \vdash (\varnothing, t'\ (t''_1)) \Downarrow_* (H, v_2)$ implies $\varnothing \vdash (\varnothing, t'\ (t''_1)) \Downarrow_{\mathbb{I}} (H, v_2)$.*

Proof. The new coercion is $T_1 \rhd \widehat{*}(T_1)$. However, by (F-COMP) we already know coercions of the form $X \rhd \star$ for positive type variables X and $\star \rhd X'$ for negative type variables X' in T_1. So by Term Correspondence, the composition is sound. ☐

Finally, in Section 4.4 we discuss the adequacy of our inferred types, and conjecture that our algorithm is *relatively* complete (i.e., the solution maps it infers are optimal in a restricted family of possible solution maps). Unfortunately, we cannot compete with manual reasoning: we are working in a setting that admits reasoning outside the static type system via $\star$.

4. Discussion

4.1 Feature Extensions

Base Types Base types in our language can be modeled as kinds. Kinds correspond to type constructors, and the base types are type constructors of arity 0. By Definition 3.3, any base type is a kind for any X, and by Definition 3.4 the kind of a base type for a type variable as that base type itself. Finally, in Definition 3.6 the least upper bounds over base types takes into account partial subtyping relations between base types in the obvious manner.

Classes and Nominal Subtyping We do not model classes in our formal language, but could do so by closely following the treatment of objects. In particular, instance methods are modeled as read-only properties and instance fields are modeled as read-write properties; private properties are also modeled. Our algorithm and its guarantees carry over to a language with nominal subtyping, if the compiler ensures that nominal subtyping implies structural subtyping. For example, in ActionScript, nominal subtyping of objects is available via subclassing. The ActionScript compiler ensures that when class `B` is a subclass of class `A`, the structural type of `B`-objects is a subtype of the structural type of `A`-objects, by checking that the properties in `A` that are overridden in `B` are related by subtyping, taking into account read/write polarities.

4.2 Limited Transitivity

Previous type inference algorithms for object-oriented languages with subtyping [14, 15] involve taking full transitive closure of subtyping constraints, which makes them $O(n^3)$, where n is the size of the program. In contrast, we have designed our closure rules for flows so that transitivity is limited, which not only makes our algorithm $O(n^2)$, but also allows for more precise type inference. For example, consider this sequence of flows: `Number` $\rhd X \rhd Y \rhd$ `Boolean`. Our core algorithm infers $X =$ `Number` and $Y =$ `Number`. Now, if we want our solutions to satisfy the blame theorem, we fall back to $Y = \star$, since $Y =$ `Number` is inconsistent with $Y \rhd$ `Boolean`. However, we do not need to fall back to $X = \star$. In contrast, full transitivity would have lost the information that there is no immediate dynamic consistency check between X and `Boolean`.

4.3 Performance Optimizations

As we will see in our experiments, adding more precise types improves run-time performance in most cases. But more precise types can also *degrade* run-time performance by introducing new run-time conversions. It does not matter whether these precise types are added by type inference or manually—the effect is the same. For example, consider the following program:

```
function foo(x:*):Number { return x + 1 }
function bar(max:Number):Number {
    var sum:Number = 0;
    var y = 1;
    while(sum < max) { sum = sum + foo(y) }
    return sum
}
```

The function `foo` could be part of some external library which we cannot modify. Without any type annotation, variable `y` in `bar` will be assigned $\star$ type. So, the function call `foo(y)` will not involve any run-time conversions for `y`, since the parameter type for `foo` is also $\star$. But if we annotate `y` with `Number`, either using our type inference algorithm or manually, function call `foo(y)` will result in a run-time conversion from `Number` to $\star$ for `y`.

We observe that the fix for this problem lies in the runtime rather than our inference algorithm. Our type inference algorithm tries to infer more precise types for unannotated variables. The runtime should use these precise types to optimize the program. In particular, it can do type specialization [10] for `foo`: i.e., it can create a copy of `foo` which takes a `Number` argument, and patch the function call `foo(y)` in `bar` to this new copy. (Type specialization already happens in ActionScript for numeric operations.) The resulting program will be more optimized than the unannotated version.

4.4 Adequacy of Inferred Types

We now analyze how precise our inferred types are. Our closure algorithm ensures that if there exists some flow from a concrete type T to a type variable X via other type variables, we consider T when computing the solution for X. We do this to make sure that we do not introduce any new run-time errors by missing out some types that could flow into X. We promote the solution for X to $\star$ when two different kinds flow into X or $\star$ flows into X explicitly.

One could give more precise types than our algorithm by reasoning outside the type system. For example, consider the following program:

```
48 var x:X, y:Y;
49 if(b) { x = 1 } else { x = false };
50 if(b) { y = x } else { y = 1 }
```

We generate `Number` $\rhd X$ and `Boolean` $\rhd X$ on line 49, and $X \rhd Y$ and `Number` $\rhd Y$ on line 50. When we do closure, we add `Boolean` $\rhd Y$ also, and we infer $X = \star$ and $Y = \star$. Whereas, with path-sensitive reasoning (outside the type system), the programmer can argue that Y need not be $\star$, it can be `Number`.

Blame recovery may also reduce the precision of our solutions. For example, if the generated flows are `Number` $\rhd X$, $X \rhd Y$, and $Y \rhd$ `Boolean`, we infer $X =$ `Number` and $Y =$ `Number`. When we do blame recovery, we see that the coercion $Y \rhd$ `Boolean` is not satisfied, and so we promote Y to $\star$. Whereas, the programmer could get away by annotating Y as `Number` and making sure that $Y \rhd$ `Boolean` does not happen at run time, again by reasoning outside the type system.

However, we expect that if reasoning outside the type system is banned, then our algorithm indeed infers optimal solutions. Formally, we can define a subset of the static consistency relation that forces the use of purely static reasoning (standard subtyping) for inflows. We then conjecture that there are no other solutions that are naïve subtypes of the solutions we infer upon blame recovery, and that satisfy the above relation.

5. Experiments

We have implemented our type inference algorithm for ActionScript. Our implementation takes an existing ActionScript program as input, and returns the same program with inferred types added to the source as output. The output program can then be compiled and run using the compiler and VM, and compared with the input program.

5.1 Methodology

We use the SunSpider [20] and V8 [23] benchmarks to evaluate our type inference algorithm. These are standard benchmarks used to measure the performance of JavaScript implementations; we use the ActionScript version of these benchmarks, which are part of the test suite of the ActionScript VM.

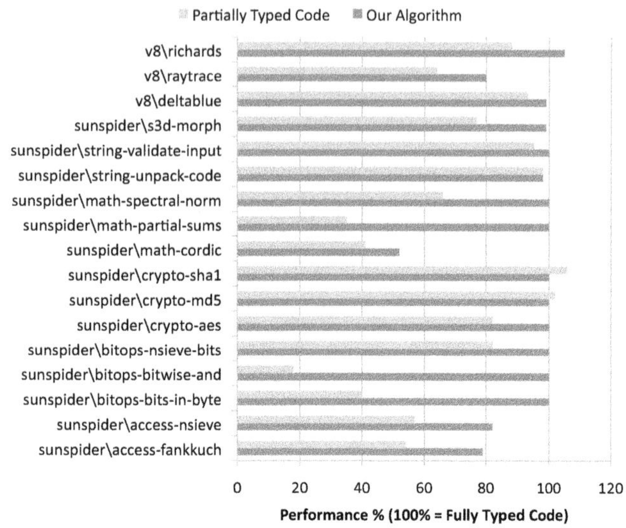

Figure 6. Comparison of our algorithm with partially typed code

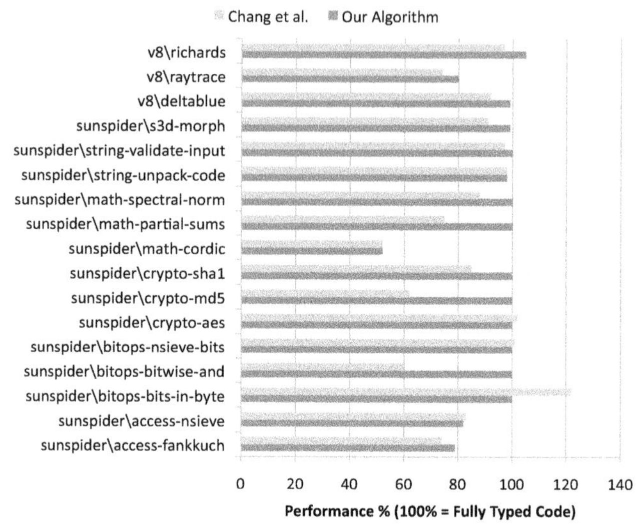

Figure 7. Comparison of our algorithm with Chang et al.

In their original form, these benchmarks are *fully typed*, i.e. their source code has complete type information. We remove all type annotations, except in those parts of the interface that are required by our algorithm to be explicitly annotated. We then run our algorithm on these *partially typed* benchmarks.

With performance of the fully typed benchmarks as the baseline, we compare the performance of partially typed benchmarks, with and without types added by our inference algorithm. We also compare the results of our algorithm on partially typed benchmarks with the results of Chang et al. [7], who have recently implemented a much simpler type inference algorithm (that only infers types for a subset of local variables) along with several other high-level optimizations for ActionScript at bytecode level, and report performance increases due to the added type information.

5.2 Results

5.2.1 Comparison with Partially Typed Code

Figure 6 compares the performance of partially typed benchmarks, with and without types added by our inference algorithm. Overall, our algorithm gives an average 1.6x performance improvement over partially typed benchmarks, with a maximum improvement of 5.6x.

We are able to recover $\sim$100% performance (i.e. the performance of fully typed benchmarks) in 13 out of the 17 benchmarks. For `v8\richards`, our performance is higher than the fully typed version. There are some private class variables in the benchmark which are typed as $\star$ in the fully typed version, whereas our algorithm is able to infer more precise types for them, resulting in an increased performance.

In the fully typed version of `sunspider\math-cordic`, an object is retrieved from an array and implicitly cast to an integer via an explicit `int` annotation. Since arrays are untyped in ActionScript, our inference algorithm infers the type of retrieved object as $\star$. This one annotation is the reason that we could reach only $\sim$50% performance as compared to the fully typed benchmark. Similar explicit type annotations for properties accessed from the type `Object`, which are also untyped in ActionScript, hurt our performance in `v8\raytrace`. For `sunspider\access-nsieve` and `sunspider\access-fankkuch`, we infer some variables as `Number`, whereas in the fully typed benchmarks, they are typed as `int`. In ActionScript, `int` represents 32 bit integers whereas `Number` has size 64 bits and can represent integers, unsigned integers, and floating-point numbers. At run time, operations involving `int` are much faster than those involving `Number`. Since we do not implement a range analysis, we conservatively infer all numeric types to be `Number`. This hurts the performance in the above benchmarks. Our algorithm can be augmented with a simple range analysis to mitigate this problem.

5.2.2 Comparison with Chang et al. [7]

Figure 7 compares the performance of partially typed benchmarks, with types added by our inference algorithm and with types added by inference algorithm of Chang et al. In 11 out of the 17 benchmarks, our numbers are better than them. In 5 out of the 17, the numbers are almost equal. For `bitops-bits-in-byte`, they report that the higher performance is because of a different intermediate code representation they implement in the ActionScript JIT compiler. This effect is independent of the type inference algorithm.

5.2.3 Performance Degradation after Type Inference

In Figure 6, we see that for `crypto-sha1`, the performance degrades after adding precise type information to the partially typed code. This general issue was also found by [7] (where the effect is even worse), and is already discussed in Section 4.3.

6. Related Work

Gradual Type Inference The only previous work on gradual type inference is the unification-based technique of [18], which is not suitable for an object-oriented language with subtyping.

Soft Typing Overall, our goal is the same as that of soft typing [6]: to improve run-time performance by eliminating run-time type checks where ever possible. However, to our knowledge, all the soft type inference systems proposed to date [2, 25] are based on unification, which is unsuitable for object-oriented languages with subtyping. Since we do not aim to infer polymorphic types in ActionScript, we are interested in algorithms with polynomial complexity. Furthermore, treating uses and definitions asymmetrically enables us to infer more precise types than soft type inference. Finally, existing soft type inference systems have not considered problems of soundness in the presence of partial compilation, whereas our algorithm retrofits type inference on existing programs under the assumption that complete source code may not be available for analysis. This restriction of preserving semantics of code outside the compilation unit implies that we must infer types for only those parts of the program that we can see all the writes to, i.e., those parts of the program that do not "escape" the compilation unit.

Blame Our algorithm seems to share deep connections with the blame calculus [19, 24] and other coercion calculi [11]; exploring these connections should be interesting future work. In particular, the blame calculus defines three new subtyping relations: $<:^+$ (positive subtyping), $<:^-$ (negative subtyping), and $<:_n$ (naïve subtyping), such that $S <:_n T$ denotes that S is more precise than T, and holds if and only if $S <:^+ T$ and $T <:^- S$. In particular, we have $S <:^+ \star$ and $\star <:^- T$. The main result in [24] is that if $S <:^+ T$ then a run-time cast error from S to T cannot be blamed on the term to which the cast is attached, and if $S <:^- T$ then a run-time cast error from S to T cannot be blamed on the context in which the cast appears.

The solutions of our algorithm are related to the default types by $<:_n$, so we can say that our solutions are more precise than the default types. In a context that previously expected the default type, we now effectively introduce a cast from a more precise type; this means that any blame for a run-time cast error must lie with the context, so there is nothing to prove about the program. On the other hand, wherever we infer a more precise type for a context, we effectively introduce a cast from the default type; this means that any blame for a run-time cast error must lie with the program, i.e., we must prove that a program that executed successfully before type inference continues to execute successfully after type inference—as we do in this paper.

Combining Static Typing and Dynamic Typing There has been a lot of interest in exploring ways to mix typed and untyped code, e.g., via occurrence typing [22], gradual typing [16, 17], hybrid typing [8], and like typing [26]. In these systems, types are supplied by the user. In contrast, our work focuses on type inference, which is complementary.

Static Type Inference Static type inference has been explored for dynamic languages, including Self [1], Ruby [9], Python [4], JavaScript [5, 21], and Scheme [25]. There is also a long history of work on type inference for languages with subtyping [14, 15].

Dynamic Type Inference Our type system gradually infers some static types, but is still bound by the limitations of static analysis on programs that use dynamic types. As such, we believe that dynamic type inference would be useful to improve the precision of those dynamic types which we cannot eliminate in a program. Recent work has explored dynamic techniques for type inference and type specialization [3, 10] for dynamic languages. As future work, we plan to explore such combinations in the just-in-time (JIT) compiler underlying the ActionScript VM.

7. Conclusion

In this paper, we design a type inference algorithm that can improve the performance of existing gradually typed programs, without introducing any new run-time failures. The distinguishing features of the algorithm lie in its asymmetric treatment of inflows and outflows, and its encoding of an escape analysis to preserve backward-compatibility. We prove that our algorithm is sound and efficient, and demonstrate its applicability on a mainstream gradually typed language, ActionScript.

Acknowledgments We would like to thank Bernd Mathiske, Dimitrios Vytiniotis, and several anonymous reviewers for their helpful comments and suggestions. This work was done while the first author was an intern at Advanced Technology Labs, Adobe Systems.

References

[1] O. Agesen, J. Palsberg, and M.I. Schwartzbach. Type Inference of SELF. *ECOOP*, 1993.

[2] A. Aiken, E. L. Wimmers, and T. K. Lakshman. Soft Typing with Conditional Types. In *POPL*, pages 163–173, 1994.

[3] J. D. An, A. Chaudhuri, J. S. Foster, and M. Hicks. Dynamic Inference of Static Types for Ruby. In *POPL*, pages 459–472. ACM, 2011.

[4] D. Ancona, M. Ancona, A. Cuni, and N. Matsakis. RPython: Reconciling Dynamically and Statically Typed OO Languages. In *DLS*. ACM, 2007.

[5] C. Anderson, P. Giannini, and S. Drossopoulou. Towards Type Inference for JavaScript. In *ECOOP*, 2005.

[6] R. Cartwright and M. Fagan. Soft typing. In *PLDI*, pages 278–292, 1991.

[7] M. Chang, B. Mathiske, E. Smith, A. Chaudhuri, A. Gal, M. Bebenita, C. Wimmer, and M. Franz. The Impact of Optional Type Information on JIT Compilation of Dynamically Typed Languages. In *DLS*. ACM, 2011.

[8] C. Flanagan. Hybrid Type Checking. In *POPL*, pages 245–256. ACM, 2006.

[9] M. Furr, J. D. An, J. S. Foster, and M. Hicks. Profile-Guided Static Typing for Dynamic Scripting Languages. In *OOPSLA*, 2009.

[10] A. Gal, B. Eich, M. Shaver, D. Anderson, D. Mandelin, M. R. Haghighat, B. Kaplan, G. Hoare, B. Zbarsky, J. Orendorff, J. Ruderman, E. W. Smith, R. Reitmaier, M. Bebenita, M. Chang, and M. Franz. Trace-based just-in-time type specialization for dynamic languages. In *PLDI*, pages 465–478. ACM, 2009.

[11] F. Henglein. Dynamic Typing: Syntax and Proof Theory. *Science of Computer Programming*, 22(3):197 – 230, 1994.

[12] D. Herman, A. Tomb, and C. Flanagan. Space-Efficient Gradual Typing. *Trends in Functional Programming*, 2007.

[13] C. Moock. *Essential ActionScript 3.0*. O'Reilly, 2007.

[14] J. Palsberg. Efficient Inference of Object Types. In *LICS*, pages 186–195. IEEE, 1994.

[15] F. Pottier. A Framework for Type Inference with Subtyping. In *ICFP*, pages 228–238. ACM, 1998.

[16] J. Siek and W. Taha. Gradual Typing for Objects. In *ECOOP*, pages 2–27. Springer-Verlag, 2007.

[17] J. G. Siek and W. Taha. Gradual Typing for Functional Languages. In *Scheme and Functional Programming Workshop*, 2006.

[18] J. G. Siek and M. Vachharajani. Gradual Typing with Unification-Based Inference. In *DLS*, pages 1–12. ACM, 2008.

[19] J. G. Siek and P. Wadler. Threesomes, With and Without blame. In *POPL*, pages 365–376. ACM, 2010.

[20] SunSpider Benchmarks, 2010. `http://www.webkit.org/perf/sunspider/sunspider.html`.

[21] P. Thiemann. Towards a Type System for Analyzing JavaScript Programs. In *ESOP*, 2005.

[22] S. Tobin-Hochstadt and M. Felleisen. The Design and Implementation of Typed Scheme. In *POPL*, 2008.

[23] V8 Benchmarks, 2011. `http://code.google.com/apis/v8/benchmarks.html`.

[24] P. Wadler and R. B. Findler. Well-Typed Programs Can't Be Blamed. In *ESOP*, pages 1–16. Springer-Verlag, 2009.

[25] A. K. Wright and R. Cartwright. A Practical Soft Type System for Scheme. *ACM TOPLAS*, 19(1), 1997.

[26] T. Wrigstad, F. Z. Nardelli, S. Lebresne, J. Östlund, and J. Vitek. Integrating Typed and Untyped Code in a Scripting Language. In *POPL*, pages 377–388. ACM, 2010.

Edit Lenses

Martin Hofmann
Ludwig-Maximilians-Universität

Benjamin Pierce
University of Pennsylvania

Daniel Wagner
University of Pennsylvania

Abstract

A *lens* is a bidirectional transformation between a pair of connected data structures, capable of translating an edit on one structure into an appropriate edit on the other. Many varieties of lenses have been studied, but none, to date, has offered a satisfactory treatment of how edits are *represented*. Many foundational accounts [5, 7] only consider edits of the form "overwrite the whole structure," leading to poor behavior in many situations by failing to track the associations between corresponding parts of the structures when elements are inserted and deleted in ordered lists, for example. Other theories of lenses do maintain these associations, either by annotating the structures themselves with change information [6, 15] or using auxiliary data structures [2, 4], but every extant theory assumes that the entire original source structure is part of the information passed to the lens.

We offer a general theory of *edit lenses*, which work with descriptions of changes to structures, rather than with the structures themselves. We identify a simple notion of "editable structure"—a set of states plus a monoid of edits with a partial monoid action on the states—and construct a semantic space of lenses between such structures, with natural laws governing their behavior. We show how a range of constructions from earlier papers on "state-based" lenses can be carried out in this space, including composition, products, sums, list operations, etc. Further, we show how to construct edit lenses for arbitrary *containers* in the sense of Abbott, Altenkirch, and Ghani [1]. Finally, we show that edit lenses refine a well-known formulation of state-based lenses [7], in the sense that every state-based lens gives rise to an edit lens over structures with a simple overwrite-only edit language, and conversely every edit lens on such structures gives rise to a state-based lens.

Categories and Subject Descriptors D.3.2 [*Programming Languages*]: Language Classifications—Specialized application languages

General Terms Design, Languages, Theory

Keywords algebra, bidirectional programming, edit, lens, symmetric

1. Introduction

Recent years have seen growing interest in *bidirectional programming languages*—domain-specific languages where a program describes how to maintain a connection between data structures of two different shapes, translating updates to one structure into appropriate updates to the other. The core concepts of bidirectional programming have roots in early work on the database view update problem (see [5] for a survey); more recently, they have been explored in diverse areas including model-driven software development [13], data synchronization [5], user interfaces [10], and Unix system configuration management [9].

The meaning of a bidirectional program connecting a set X to a set Y—often called a *lens* from X to Y—is intuitively a pair of transformations, one mapping X updates to Y updates and the other mapping Y updates to X updates, subject to some behavioral laws specifying how the two transformations fit together. Technically, this intuition can be realized in numerous ways. A naive definition is to say that a lens from X to Y is just a pair of functions, $f \in X \to Y$ (telling how to map an updated X state to an appropriate Y state) and $g \in Y \to X$. But this is too simple: if the lens laws impose the reasonable requirement that f and g should "round trip," then our bidirectional programs will only denote bijections—an important but limited special case. To allow for situations where each structure can contain a mixture of information that is shared with the other and information that is not, something more than just the updated structure must be given as input to the transformations.

Different variants of lenses differ as to what this "something more" should be. We might, for example, give the transformation from X to Y both a new X and an old Y—i.e., $f \in X \times Y \to Y$—with the intention that f should weave together the "shared" information from the new X with the "local" information from the old Y to produce a new Y. Or instead of a whole Y, we might pass f some smaller structure (a *complement*) representing just the information that is needed to build an updated Y out of an updated X. Or perhaps one of these plus some additional information about the *alignment* of the updated information (e.g., "a new element was inserted at the beginning of this list, so the second element in the new X corresponds to the first element in the old Y"), either in the form of an auxiliary data structure or perhaps somehow embedded as annotations in the updated X itself.

What all these variants have in common is that the inputs to a lens always include the *whole* updated state. This leaves an unfortunate gap between the theory and practical realizations, which generally represent updates in some simpler, more compact form that only describes what has changed in a possibly large structure.

In this paper, we offer the first foundational treatment of *edit lenses*—lenses that operate directly on edits, rather than on whole structures. Our theory of edit lenses is built from simple and familiar algebraic structures (§3). It supports a wide range of fundamental syntactic constructions—composition, products, sums, list operations, etc.—allowing us to construct lenses for complex data structures together with appropriate representations for edits in a compositional fashion (§4). Indeed, the theory includes a general account of how to construct "mapping" lenses for a wide class of *container* data structures [1] such as lists and trees (§5). This rich set of syntax constructors should form a suitable basis for the design of new

POPL'12, January 25–27, 2012, Philadelphia, PA, USA.

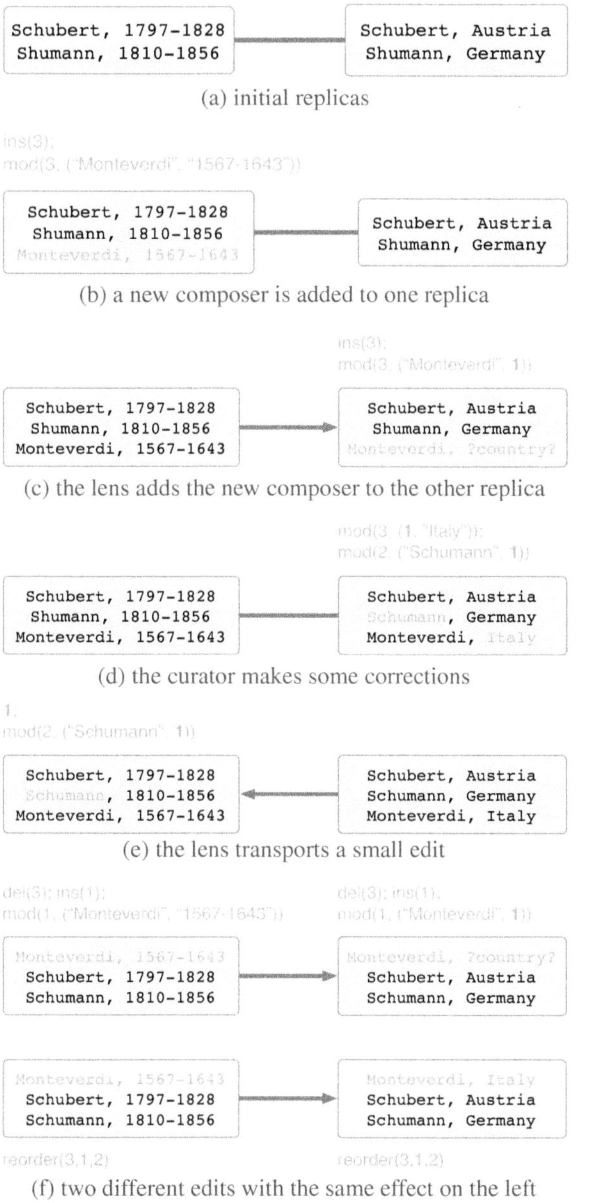

Figure 1. A simple (complement-less) edit lens in action.

bidirectional languages, for example in the style of Boomerang [2]. Our theory can support a wide variety of *edit languages*. We mostly concentrate on the simplest form, where compound edits are freely generated from some set of atomic edits; §6 considers the extension to richer languages with additional algebraic laws. Finally, our theory generalizes and refines the state-based *symmetric lenses* of Hofmann, Pierce, and Wagner [7] in a precise sense (§7). The paper ends with a discussion of related work (§8) and some remarks on future directions (§9).

2. Overview

Before diving into technicalities, let's take a brief tour of the main ideas via some examples. Figure 1 demonstrates a simple use of edit lenses to synchronize two replicas.[1] In part (a), we see the initial replicas, which are in a synchronized state. On the left, the replica is a list of records describing composers' birth and death years; on the right, a list of records describing the same composers' countries of origin. In part (b), the user interacting with the left-hand replica decides to add a new composer, Monteverdi, at the end of the list. This change is described by the edit script ins(3); mod(3, ("Monteverdi", "1567-1643")). The script says to first *insert* a dummy record at index three, then *modify* this record by replacing the left field with "Monteverdi" and replacing the right field with "1567-1643". (One could of course imagine other edit languages where the insertion would be done in one step. We represent it this way because this is closer to how our generic "container mapping" combinator in §5 will do things.) The lens connecting the two replicas now converts this edit script into a corresponding edit script that adds Monteverdi to the right-hand replica, shown in part (c): ins(3); mod(3, ("Monteverdi", **1**)). Note that the translated mod command overwrites the name component but leaves the country component with its default value, "?country?." This is the best it can do, since the edit was in the left-hand replica, which doesn't mention countries. Later, an eagle-eyed editor notices the missing country information and fills it in, at the same time correcting a spelling error in Schumann's name, as shown in (d). In part (e), we see that the lens discards the country information when translating the edit from right to left, but propagates the spelling correction.

Of course, a particular new replica state can potentially be achieved by many different edits, and these edits may be translated differently. Consider part (f) of Figure 1, where the left-hand replica ends up with a row for Monteverdi at the beginning of the list, instead of at the end. Two edit scripts that achieve this effect are shown. The upper script deletes the old Monteverdi record and inserts a brand new one (which happens to have the same data) at the top; the lower script rearranges the order of the list. The translation of the upper edit leaves Monteverdi with a default country, while the lower edit is translated to a rearrangement, preserving all the information associated with Monteverdi.

We do not address the question of where these edits come from or who decides, in cases like part (f), which of several possible edits is intended. As argued in [2], answers to these questions will tend to be intertwined with the specifics of particular editing and/or diffing tools and will tend to be messy, heuristic, and domain-specific—unpromising material for a foundational theory. Rather, our aim is to construct a theory that shows how edits, however generated, can be translated between replicas of different shapes.

Abstractly, the lens we are discussing maps between structures of the form $(X \times Y)^*$ and ones of the form $(X \times Z)^*$, where X is the set of composer names, Y the set of date strings, and Z the set of countries. We want to build it compositionally—that is, the whole lens should have the form ℓ^*, where $*$ is a "list mapping" lens combinator and ℓ is a lens for translating edits to a single record—i.e., ℓ is a lens from $X \times Y$ to $X \times Z$. Moreover, ℓ itself should be built as the product $\ell_1 \times \ell_2$ of a lens $\ell_1 \in X \to X$ that translates composer edits verbatim, while ℓ_2 is a "disconnect" lens that maps every edit on either side to a trivial identity edit on the other side.

In analogous fashion, the edit languages for the top-level structures will be constructed compositionally. The set of edits for structures of the form $(X \times Y)^*$, written $\partial((X \times Y)^*)$, will be defined together with the list constructor $*$. Its elements will have the form $\mathsf{ins}(i)$ where i is a position, $\mathsf{del}(i)$, $\mathsf{reorder}(i_1, \dots, i_n)$ where $i_1, \dots, i_n$ is a permutation on positions (compactly rep-

[1] We use the word "synchronize" informally to mean simply "maintain a correspondence between two replicas by propagating edits in both directions." A full-blown synchronization tool would also include, at a minimum, some mechanism for dealing with conflicts between disconnected edits to the two structures, which is outside the scope of this paper.

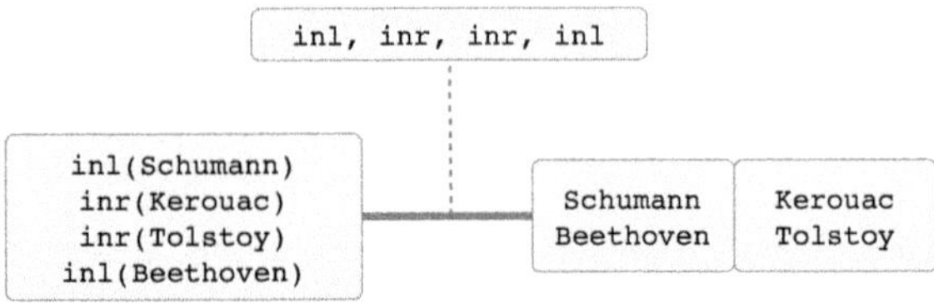

(a) the initial replicas: a tagged list of composers and authors on the left; a pair of lists on the right; a complement storing just the tags

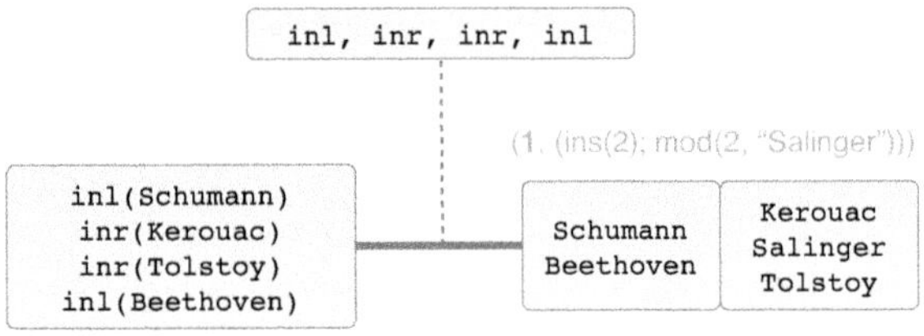

(b) an element is added to one of the partitions

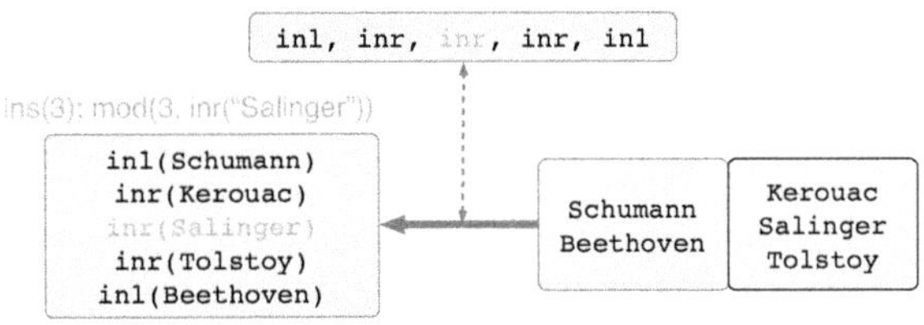

(c) the complement tells how to translate the index

Figure 2. A lens with complement.

resented, e.g. as a branching program), and $\mathsf{mod}(p, dv)$, where $dv \in \partial(X \times Y)$ is an edit for $X \times Y$ structures. Pair edits $dv \in \partial(X \times Y)$ have the form $\partial X \times \partial Y$, where ∂X is the set of edits to composers and ∂Y is the set of edits to dates. Finally, both ∂X and ∂Y are sets of primitive "overwrite edits" that completely replace one string with another, together with an identity edit $\mathbf{1}$ that does nothing at all; so ∂X can be just $\{()\} + X$ (with $\mathbf{1} = \mathsf{inl}(())$) and similarly for Y and Z.

Our lens ℓ^* will consist of two components—one for transporting edits from the left side to the right, written $(\ell^*).\!\Rrightarrow\ \in \partial(X \times Y)^* \to \partial(X \times Z)^*$,[2] and another for transporting edits from right to left, written $(\ell^*).\!\Lleftarrow\ \in \partial(X \times Z)^* \to \partial(X \times Y)^*$.

We sometimes need lenses to have a little more structure than this simple example suggests. To see why, consider defining a *partitioning* lens p between the sets $\partial((X+Y)^*)$ and $\partial(X^* \times Y^*)$. Figure 2 demonstrates the behavior of this lens. In part (a), we show the original replicas: on the left, a single list that intermingles authors and composers (with inl/inr tags showing which is which), and on the right a pair of homogeneous (untagged) lists, one for authors and one for composers. Now consider an edit, as in (b), that inserts a new element somewhere in the author list on the right. It is clear that we should transport this into an insertion on the left replica, but where, exactly, should we insert it? If the $\Lleftarrow$ function is given just an insertion edit for the homogeneous author list and nothing else, there is no way it can translate this edit into a sensible position in the combined list on the left, since it doesn't know how the lists of authors and composers are interleaved on the left.

[2] The symbol $\Rrightarrow$ is pronounced "put an edit through the lens from left to right," or just "put right." It is the edit-analog of the *putr* function of the state-based symmetric lenses in [7] and the *put* function of the state-based asymmetric lenses in [3, 5].

The solution is to store a small list, called a *complement*, off to the side, recording the *tags* (inl or inr) from the original, intermingled list, and pass this list as an extra argument to translation. We then enrich the types of the edit translation functions to accept a complement and return a new complement, so that $p.\!\Rrightarrow\ \in \partial((X+Y)^*) \times C \to \partial(X^* \times Y^*) \times C$ and $p.\!\Lleftarrow\ \in \partial(X^* \times Y^*) \times C \to \partial((X+Y)^*) \times C$. Part (c) demonstrates the use (and update) of the complement when translating the insertion.

Note that the complement stores just the inl/inr tags, not the actual names of the authors and composers in the left-hand list. In general, the information stored in C will be much smaller than the information in the replicas; indeed, our earlier example illustrates the common case in which C is the trivial single-element set $Unit$. The translation functions manipulate just the complements and the edits, which are also small compared to the size of the replicas.

3. Edit Lenses

A key design decision in our formulation of edit lenses is to separate the *description* of edits from the *action* of applying an edit to a state. This separation is captured by the standard mathematical notions of *monoid* and *monoid action*.

3.1 Definition: A *monoid* is a triple $\langle M, \cdot_M, \mathbf{1}_M \rangle$ of a set M, an associative binary operation $\cdot_M \in M \times M \to M$, and a unit element $\mathbf{1}_M \in M$ — that is, with $\cdot_M$ and $\mathbf{1}_M$ such that $x \cdot_M (y \cdot_M z) = (x \cdot_M y) \cdot_M z$ and $\mathbf{1}_M \cdot_M x = x = x \cdot_M \mathbf{1}_M$.

When no confusion results, we use M to denote both the set and the monoid, drop subscripts from $\cdot$ and $\mathbf{1}$, and write mn for $m \cdot n$.

The unit element represents a "change nothing" edit. Multiplication of edits corresponds to packaging up multiple edits into a single one representing their combined effects.

Modeling edits as monoid elements gives us great flexibility in concrete representations. The simplest edit language is a free monoid whose elements are just words over some set of primitive edits and whose multiplication is concatenation. However, it may be useful to put more structure on edits, either (a) to allow more compact representations or (b) to capture the intuition that edits to different parts of a structure do not interfere with each other and can thus be applied in any order. We will see an example of (b) in §6. For a simple example of (a), recall from §2 that, for every set X, we can form an *overwrite* monoid where the edits are just the elements of X together with a fresh unit element—i.e., edits can be represented as elements of the disjoint union $Unit + X$. Combining two edits in this monoid simply drops the second (unless the first is the unit): $\mathsf{inl}(()) \cdot e = e$ and $\mathsf{inr}(x) \cdot e = \mathsf{inr}(x)$. These equations allow this edit language to represent an arbitrarily long sequence of updates using a single element of X (and, *en passant*, to recover state-based lenses as a special case of edit lenses).The monoid framework can also accommodate more abstract notions of edit. For example, the set of all total functions from a set X to itself forms a monoid, where the multiplication operation is function composition. This is essentially the form of edits considered by Stevens [14]. We mostly focus on the simple case where edit languages are free monoids. §6 considers how additional laws can be added to the product and sum lens constructions.

3.2 Definition: Given a monoid M and a set X, a *monoid action* on M and X is a partial function $\odot \in M \times X \rightharpoonup X$ satisfying two laws: $\mathbf{1} \odot x = x$ and $(m \cdot n) \odot x = m \odot (n \odot x)$.

As with monoid multiplication, we often elide the monoid action symbol, writing mx for $m \odot x$. In standard mathematical terminology, a monoid action in our sense might instead be called a "partial monoid action," but since we always work with partial actions we find it convenient to drop the qualifier.

A bit of discussion of partiality is in order. Multiplication of edits is a total operation: given two descriptions of edits, we can always find a description of the composite actions of doing both in sequence. On the other hand, *applying* an edit to a particular state may sometimes fail. This means we need to work with expressions and equations involving partial operations. As usual, any term that contains an undefined application of an operation to operands is undefined—there is no way of "catching" undefinedness. An equation between possibly undefined terms (e.g., as in the definition above) means that if either side is defined then so is the other, and their values are equal (Kleene equality).

Why deal with failure explicitly, rather than keeping edit application total and simply defining our monoid actions so that applying an edit in a state where it is not appropriate yields the same state again (or perhaps some other state)? One reason is that it seems natural to directly address the fact that some edits are not applicable in some states, and to have a canonical outcome in all such cases. A more technical reason is that, when we work with monoids with nontrivial equations, making inapplicable edits behave like the identity is actually wrong.[3]

However, although the framework allows for the possibility of edits failing, we still want to know that the edits produced by our lenses will never actually fail when applied to replica states arising in practice. This requirement, corresponding to the *totality* property of previous presentations of lenses [5], is formalized in Theorem 3.7. In general, we adopt the design principle that partiality should be kept to a minimum; this simplifies the definitions.

It is convenient to bundle a particular choice of monoid and monoid action, plus an initial element, into a single structure:

3.3 Definition: A *module* is a tuple $\langle X, init_X, \partial X, \odot_X \rangle$ comprising a set X, an element $init_X \in X$, a monoid ∂X, and a monoid action $\odot_X$ of ∂X on X.

If X is a module, we refer to its first component by either $|X|$ or just X, and to its last component by $\odot$ or simple juxtaposition.

We will use modules to represent the structures connected by lenses. Before coming to the definition of lenses, however, we need one last ingredient: the notion of a *stateful homomorphism* between monoids. As we saw in §2, there are situations where the information in an edit may be insufficient to determine how it should be translated—we may need to know something more about how the two structures correspond. The exact nature of the extra information needed varies according to the lens. To give lenses a place to store such auxiliary information, we follow [7] and allow the edit-transforming components of a lens (the $\Rrightarrow$ and $\Lleftarrow$ functions) to take a *complement* as an extra input and return an updated complement as an extra output.

3.4 Definition: Given monoids M and N and a *complement set* C, a *stateful monoid homomorphism* from M to N over C is a function $h \in M \times C \to N \times C$ satisfying two laws:

$$\frac{}{h(\mathbf{1}_M, c) = (\mathbf{1}_N, c)}$$

$$\frac{h(m, c) = (n, c') \qquad h(m', c') = (n', c'')}{h(m' \cdot_M m, c) = (n' \cdot_N n, c'')}$$

These are basically just the standard monoid homomorphism laws, except that h is given access to some internal state $c \in C$ that it uses (and updates) when mapping from M to N; in the second law, we must thread the state c' produced by the first h into the second use of h, and we demand that both the result and the effect on the state should be the same whether we send a composite element $m' \cdot m$ through h all at once or in two pieces.

The intended usage of an edit lens is as follows. There are two users, one holding an element of X the other one an element of Y, both referred to hereafter as *replicas*. Initially, they hold $init_X$ and $init_Y$, respectively, and the lens is initialized with complement $\ell.init$. The users then perform actions and propagate them across the lens. An action consists of producing an edit $\mathrm{d}x$ (or $\mathrm{d}y$), applying it to one's current replica x (resp. y), putting the edit through the lens to obtain an edit $\mathrm{d}y$ (resp. $\mathrm{d}x$), and asking the user on the other side to apply $\mathrm{d}y$ ($\mathrm{d}x$) to their replica. In the process, the internal state c of the lens is updated to reflect the new correspondence between the two replicas. We further assume there is some *consistency* relation K between X, Y, and C, which describes the "synchronized states" of the replicas and complement. This gives us a natural way to state the totality requirement discussed above: if we start in a consistent state, make a successful edit (one that does not fail at the initiating side), and put it through the lens, the resulting edit is guaranteed (a) to be applicable on the receiving side and (b) to lead again to a consistent state. We make no guarantees about edits that fail at the initiating side: these should not be put through the lens.

3.5 Definition: A *symmetric edit lens* between modules X and Y consists of a complement set C, a distinguished element $init \in C$, two stateful monoid homomorphisms $\Rrightarrow \in \partial X \times C \to \partial Y \times C$ and $\Lleftarrow \in \partial Y \times C \to \partial X \times C$, and a ternary *consistency relation* $K \subseteq |X| \times C \times |Y|$ such that

- $(init_X, init, init_Y) \in K$;
- if $(x, c, y) \in K$ and $\mathrm{d}x\ x$ is defined and $\Rrightarrow(\mathrm{d}x, c) = (\mathrm{d}y, c')$, then $\mathrm{d}y\ y$ is also defined and $(\mathrm{d}x\ x, c', \mathrm{d}y\ y) \in K$;
- if $(x, c, y) \in K$ and $\mathrm{d}y\ y$ is defined and $\Lleftarrow(\mathrm{d}y, c) = (\mathrm{d}x, c')$, then $\mathrm{d}x\ x$ is also defined and $(\mathrm{d}x\ x, c', \mathrm{d}y\ y) \in K$.

Since symmetric edit lenses are the main topic of this paper, we will generally write "edit lens" or just "lens" for these, deploying additional adjectives to talk about other variants such as the state-based symmetric lenses of [7].

The intuition about K's role in guaranteeing totality can be formalized as follows.

3.6 Definition: Let $\ell \in X \leftrightarrow Y$ be a lens. A *dialogue* is a sequence of edits—a word in $(\partial X + \partial Y)^*$. The partial function $\ell.run \in (\partial X + \partial Y)^* \rightharpoonup X \times \ell.C \times Y$ is defined by:

$$\frac{}{\ell.run(\varepsilon) = (init_X, \ell.init, init_Y)}$$

$$\frac{\ell.run(w) = (x_0, c, y_0) \qquad \ell.\Rrightarrow(\mathrm{d}x_1, c) = (\mathrm{d}y_1, c_1)}{\ell.run(\mathsf{inl}(\mathrm{d}x_1)w) = (\mathrm{d}x_1\ x_0, c_1, \mathrm{d}y_1\ y_0)}$$

$$\frac{\ell.run(w) = (x_0, c, y_0) \qquad \ell.\Lleftarrow(\mathrm{d}y_1, c) = (\mathrm{d}x_1, c_1)}{\ell.run(\mathsf{inr}(\mathrm{d}y_1)w) = (\mathrm{d}x_1\ x_0, c_1, \mathrm{d}y_1\ y_0)}$$

3.7 Theorem: Let w be a dialogue and suppose that $\ell.run(w) = (x, c, y)$—in particular, all the edits in w succeed. Let $\mathrm{d}x \in \partial X$ be an edit with $\mathrm{d}x\ x$ defined. If $(\mathrm{d}y, c') = \ell.\Rrightarrow(\mathrm{d}x, c)$ then $\mathrm{d}y\ y$ is also defined. An analogous statement holds for $\Lleftarrow$.

[3] Here is a slightly contrived example. Suppose that the set of states is natural numbers and that edits have the form $(x \mapsto y)$, where the intended interpretation is that, if the current state is x, then the edit yields state y. It is reasonable to impose the equation $(y \mapsto z) \cdot (x \mapsto y) = (x \mapsto z)$, allowing us to represent sequences of edits in a compact form. But now consider what happens when we apply the edit $(5 \mapsto 7) \cdot (3 \mapsto 5)$ to the state 5. The second monoid action law demands that $((5 \mapsto 7) \cdot (3 \mapsto 5)) \odot 5 = (5 \mapsto 7) \odot ((3 \mapsto 5) \odot 5)$, which, by the equation we imposed, is the same as $(3 \mapsto 7) \odot 5 = (5 \mapsto 7) \odot ((3 \mapsto 5) \odot 5)$. But the left-hand side is equal to 5 (since the edit $(3 \mapsto 7)$ does not apply to the state 5), while the right-hand side is equal to 7 (since the first edit, $(3 \mapsto 5)$, is inapplicable to the state 5, so it behaves like the identity and returns 5 from which $(5 \mapsto 7)$ takes us to 7), so the action law is violated.

Beyond its role in guaranteeing totality, the consistency relation in a lens plays two important roles. First, it is a sanity check on the behavior of $\Rrightarrow$ and $\Lleftarrow$. Second, if we project away the middle component, we can present it to programmers as documentation of the synchronized states of the two replicas—i.e., as a partial *specification* of $\Rrightarrow$ and $\Lleftarrow$.

One technical issue arising from the definition of edit lenses is that the hidden complements cause many important laws—like associativity of composition—to hold only up to *behavioral equivalence*. This phenomenon was also observed in [7, §3] for the case of symmetric state-based lenses, and the appropriate behavioral equivalence for edit lenses is a natural refinement of the one used there (taking the consistency relations into account).

3.8 Definition [Lens equivalence]: Two lenses $k, \ell : X \leftrightarrow Y$ are *equivalent* (written $k \equiv \ell$) if, for all dialogues w,

- $k.run(w)$ is defined iff $\ell.run(w)$ is defined;
- if $k.run(w) = (x, c, y)$ and $\ell.run(w) = (x', d, y')$, then $x = x'$ and $y = y'$; and
- if $k.run(w) = (x, c, y)$ and $\ell.run(w) = (x', d, y')$ and $\mathrm{d}x\ x$ is defined and $\ell.\Rrightarrow(\mathrm{d}x, c) = (\mathrm{d}y, \_)$ and $k.\Rrightarrow(\mathrm{d}x, d) = (\mathrm{d}y', \_)$ then $\mathrm{d}y = \mathrm{d}y'$, and the analogous property for $\Lleftarrow$.

(Note that the second clause is actually implied by the third.)

Since the complements of the two lenses in question may not even have the same type, it does not make sense to require that they be equal. Instead, the equivalence hides the complements, relying on the observable effects of the lens actions. However, by finding a relationship between the complements, we can prove lens equivalence with a bisimulation-style proof principle:

3.9 Theorem: Lenses $k, \ell : X \leftrightarrow Y$ are equivalent iff there exists a relation $S \subseteq X \times k.C \times \ell.C \times Y$ such that (1) $(init_X, k.init, \ell.init, init_Y) \in S$; (2) if $(x, c, d, y) \in S$ and $\mathrm{d}x\ x$ is defined, then if $(\mathrm{d}y_1, c') = k.\Rrightarrow(\mathrm{d}x, c)$ and $(\mathrm{d}y_2, d') = \ell.\Rrightarrow(\mathrm{d}x, d)$, then $\mathrm{d}y_1 = \mathrm{d}y_2$ and $(\mathrm{d}x\ x, c', d', \mathrm{d}y_1\ y) \in S$; and (3) analogously for $\Lleftarrow$.

4. Edit Lens Combinators

We have proposed a semantic space of edit lenses and justified its design. But the proof of the pudding is in the syntax—in whether we can actually build primitive lenses and lens combinators that live in this semantic space and that do useful things.

Generic Constructions As a first baby step, here is an identity lens that connects identical structures and maps edits by passing them through unchanged.

$$id_X \in X \leftrightarrow X$$

$$\begin{array}{lcl} C & = & Unit \\ K & = & \{(x, (), x) \mid x \in X\} \\ \Rrightarrow(\mathrm{d}x, ()) & = & (\mathrm{d}x, ()) \\ \Lleftarrow(\mathrm{d}x, ()) & = & (\mathrm{d}x, ()) \end{array}$$

Here and below, we elide the definition of the $init$ component when $C = Unit = \{()\}$, since it can only be one thing.

In lens definitions like this one, the upper box serves both as a typing rule and as the implicit statement of a theorem saying that the functions in the box below it inhabit the appropriate types and satisfy the corresponding lens laws. For lens combinators, the definition also makes an implicit statement about compatibility with lens equivalence. For brevity, and because they are generally straightforward, we usually elide these theorems.

Now for a more interesting case: Given lenses k and ℓ connecting X to Y and Y to Z, we can build a composite lens $k;\ell$ that connects X directly to Z. Note how the complement of the composite lens includes a complement from each of the components, and how these complements are threaded through the $\Rrightarrow$ and $\Lleftarrow$ operations.

$$\frac{k \in X \leftrightarrow Y \qquad \ell \in Y \leftrightarrow Z}{k;\ell \in X \leftrightarrow Z}$$

$$\begin{array}{lcl} C & = & k.C \times \ell.C \\ init & = & (k.init, \ell.init) \\ K & = & \{(x, (c_k, c_\ell), z) \mid \\ & & \quad \exists y.\ (x, c_k, y) \in k.K \\ & & \quad\quad \wedge (y, c_\ell, z) \in \ell.K\ \} \\ \Rrightarrow(\mathrm{d}x, (c_k, c_\ell)) & = & \mathsf{let}\ (\mathrm{d}y, c_k') = k.\Rrightarrow(\mathrm{d}x, c_k)\ \mathsf{in} \\ & & \mathsf{let}\ (\mathrm{d}z, c_\ell') = \ell.\Rrightarrow(\mathrm{d}y, c_\ell)\ \mathsf{in} \\ & & (\mathrm{d}z, (c_k', c_\ell')) \\ \Lleftarrow(\mathrm{d}z, (c_k, c_\ell)) & = & \mathsf{let}\ (\mathrm{d}y, c_\ell') = \ell.\Lleftarrow(\mathrm{d}z, c_\ell)\ \mathsf{in} \\ & & \mathsf{let}\ (\mathrm{d}x, c_k') = k.\Lleftarrow(\mathrm{d}y, c_k)\ \mathsf{in} \\ & & (\mathrm{d}x, (c_k', c_\ell')) \end{array}$$

As might be expected, composition of lenses is associative, and the identity lens is a unit for composition. However, as mentioned above, we need to be a little careful: it is not quite the case that $(k;\ell);m = k;(\ell;m)$—in particular they have different complements. Instead, what we can show is that $(k;\ell);m \equiv k;(\ell;m)$.

Another simple lens combinator is dualization: for each lens $\ell \in X \leftrightarrow Y$, we can construct its dual, $\ell^{op} \in Y \leftrightarrow X$, by swapping $\Rrightarrow$ and $\Lleftarrow$.

For the next definition, observe that the set $Unit$ gives rise to a trivial monoid structure and, for any given set X and element $x \in X$, a trivial module with initial element x, which we write $Unit_{x \in X}$. When context clearly calls for a module, we will abbreviate $Unit_{() \in Unit}$ to simply $Unit$.

Now, for each module X, there is a *terminal lens* that connects X to the trivial $Unit$ module by throwing away all edits.

$$term_X \in X \leftrightarrow Unit$$

$$\begin{array}{lcl} C & = & Unit \\ K & = & X \times Unit \times Unit \\ \Rrightarrow(\mathrm{d}x, ()) & = & (\mathbf{1}, ()) \\ \Lleftarrow(\mathbf{1}, ()) & = & (\mathbf{1}, ()) \end{array}$$

The *disconnect* lens that we saw in §2 can be built from $term$. The $term$ lens is also unique (up to equivalence): the implementation of $\Rrightarrow$ is forced by the size of its range monoid $Unit$, and the implementation of $\Lleftarrow$ is forced by the homomorphism laws.

There is a trivial lens between any two isomorphic modules. Formally, a *module homomorphism* (f, h) between modules X and Y is a function $f \in X \to Y$ and a monoid homomorphism $h \in \partial X \to \partial Y$ such that $f(init_X) = init_Y$ and $f(\mathrm{d}x\, x) = h(\mathrm{d}x)\, f(x)$. There is an identity $(\lambda x. x, \lambda \mathrm{d}x. \mathrm{d}x)$ for every module, and the point-wise composition of module homomorphisms is also a homomorphism, so modules form a category. If module homomorphisms $(e, g) \in X \to Y$ and $(f, h) \in Y \to X$ satisfy $(e, g);(f, h) = id_X$ and $(f, h);(e, g) = id_Y$, then (e, g) is an *isomorphism* and (f, h) is *inverse* to (e, g). Now:

$$\frac{(f,h) \in X \to Y \qquad (f,h) \text{ is inverse to } (f^{-1},h^{-1})}{iso_{(f,h)} \in X \leftrightarrow Y}$$

$$\begin{array}{lcl} C & = & Unit \\ K & = & \{(x, (), f(x)) \mid x \in X\} \\ \Rrightarrow(\mathrm{d}x, ()) & = & (h(\mathrm{d}x), ()) \\ \Lleftarrow(\mathrm{d}y, ()) & = & (h^{-1}(\mathrm{d}y), ()) \end{array}$$

The fact that this always defines a lens, plus a couple of other easy facts, amounts to saying that there is a functor from the category of module isomorphisms to the category of edit lenses.

Generators for free monoids For writing practical lenses, we want not only generic combinators like the ones presented above, but also more specific lenses for structured data such as products, sums, and lists. We show in the rest of this section how to define simple versions of these constructors whose associated edit monoids are freely generated. §5 shows how to generalize the list mapping lens to other forms of containers, and §6 discusses edit languages with nontrivial laws.

Given a set G, we write G^* for the set of finite sequences of elements of G. We write ε for the empty sequence and g to denote both a generator element and the single-element sequence containing such an element. Sequence concatenation is denoted by juxtaposition; when discussing a sequence $g_1 \cdots g_n$, we also use g to refer to the entire sequence. The notation $|g|$ means the length of a sequence: $|g_1 \cdots g_n| = n$. It is easy to show that G^* together with sequence concatenation and ε forms a monoid.

It is often convenient to specify the behavior of a monoid homomorphism by giving its output on each generator. Given a function $f_g \in G \to M$ on generators, the monoid homomorphism $f \in G^* \to M$ is defined by $f(\varepsilon) = \mathbf{1}$ and $f(g_1 \cdots g_n) = f_g(g_1)f(g_2 \cdots g_n)$. Similarly, given a stateful function $f_g \in G \times C \to M \times C$, we can define a stateful monoid homomorphism $f \in G^* \times C \to M \times C$ by setting $f(\varepsilon, c) = (\mathbf{1}, c)$ and

$$\begin{array}{rl} f(g_1 \cdots g_n, c) = & \mathsf{let}\ (m', c') = f(g_2 \cdots g_n, c)\ \mathsf{in} \\ & \mathsf{let}\ (m'', c'') = f_g(g_1, c')\ \mathsf{in} \\ & (m''m', c''). \end{array}$$

Tensor Product Given modules X and Y, a primitive edit to a pair in $|X| \times |Y|$ is either an edit to the X part or an edit to the Y part.

$$G^{\otimes}_{X,Y} = \{\mathsf{left}(\mathrm{d}x) \mid \mathrm{d}x \in \partial X\} \cup \{\mathsf{right}(\mathrm{d}y) \mid \mathrm{d}y \in \partial Y\}$$

We can turn these generators into a module by giving specifying a monoid action for the free monoid $(G^{\otimes}_{X,Y})^*$:

$$\begin{array}{r} \mathsf{left}(\mathrm{d}x) \odot_g (x, y) = (\mathrm{d}x\ x, y) \\ \mathsf{right}(\mathrm{d}y) \odot_g (x, y) = (x, \mathrm{d}y\ y) \end{array}$$

The full module is then given by

$$X \otimes Y = \left\langle |X| \times |Y|, (init_X, init_Y), (G^{\otimes}_{X,Y})^*, \odot \right\rangle.$$

Now we can build a lens that "runs two sub-lenses in parallel" on the components of a product module. The $\Rrightarrow$ and $\Lleftarrow$ functions are defined via stateful monoid homomorphism specifications.

$$\frac{k \in X \leftrightarrow Z \qquad \ell \in Y \leftrightarrow W}{k \otimes \ell \in X \otimes Y \leftrightarrow Z \otimes W}$$

$$\begin{array}{lcl} C & = & k.C \times \ell.C \\ init & = & (k.init, \ell.init) \\ K & = & \{\ ((x,z),(c_k,c_\ell),(y,w)) \mid \\ & & \quad (x, c_k, y) \in k.K \\ & & \quad \wedge (z, c_\ell, w) \in \ell.K\ \} \\ \Rrightarrow_g(\mathsf{left}(\mathrm{d}x), (c_k, c_\ell)) & = & \mathsf{let}\ (\mathrm{d}z, c_k') = k.\Rrightarrow(\mathrm{d}x, c_k)\ \mathsf{in} \\ & & (\mathsf{left}(\mathrm{d}z), (c_k', c_\ell)) \\ \Rrightarrow_g(\mathsf{right}(\mathrm{d}y), (c_k, c_\ell)) & = & \mathsf{let}\ (\mathrm{d}w, c_\ell') = \ell.\Rrightarrow(\mathrm{d}y, c_\ell)\ \mathsf{in} \\ & & (\mathsf{right}(\mathrm{d}w), (c_k, c_\ell')) \\ \Lleftarrow_g\ \text{similarly} & & \end{array}$$

4.1 Theorem:

- $k \otimes \ell$ is indeed a lens.
- If $k \equiv k'$ and $\ell \equiv \ell'$, then $k \otimes \ell \equiv k' \otimes \ell'$.
- $id \otimes id \equiv id$.
- $(k \otimes \ell); (k' \otimes \ell') \equiv (k; k') \otimes (\ell; \ell')$.
- $((k \otimes \ell) \otimes m); iso_{assoc} \equiv \ell \otimes (k \otimes m)$, where $assoc$ is the isomorphism between $(X \otimes Y) \otimes Z$ and $X \otimes (Y \otimes Z)$ for all X, Y, Z.
- $(k \otimes \ell); iso_{swap} \equiv \ell \otimes k$, where $swap$ is the isomorphism between $X \times Y$ and $Y \times X$.

Proof: For the first statement (being a good lens), first note that preservation of monoid multiplication is immediate since $\partial(X \otimes Y)$ is free. It remains to show that the consistency relation of $k \otimes \ell$ is preserved and guarantees definedness. This is direct from the definition and the assumption that k and ℓ are lenses.

The remaining statements are direct consequences of the definitions, together with Theorem 3.9; for example, the third equivalence can be witnessed by the simulation relation

$$\begin{array}{l} \{((x,y),((c,d),(c',d')),((c,c'),(d,d')),(x'',y'')) \mid \\ \quad \exists (x',y').\ (x,c,x') \in k.K \wedge (x',c',x'') \in k'.K \\ \qquad \wedge (y,d,y') \in \ell.K \wedge (y',d',y'') \in \ell'.K\}. \qquad \square \end{array}$$

As in [7], the tensor construction is not quite a full categorical product, because duplicating information does not give rise to a well-behaved lens—there is no lens with type $X \leftrightarrow X \otimes X$ that satisfies all the equivalences a lens programmer would want.

However, tensor product does yield various symmetric monoidal categories of edit lenses; for lack of space we omit the details.

Sum We now present one way (not the only one—see footnote 4) of constructing a sum module and a sum lens. Given sets of edits ∂X and ∂Y, we can describe the generators for the free monoid of edits to a sum by:

$$\begin{array}{lcl} G^{\oplus}_{X,Y} & = & \{\mathsf{switch}_{iL}(\mathrm{d}x) \mid i \in \{L,R\}, \mathrm{d}x \in \partial X\} \\ & \cup & \{\mathsf{switch}_{iR}(\mathrm{d}y) \mid i \in \{L,R\}, \mathrm{d}y \in \partial Y\} \\ & \cup & \{\mathsf{stay}_L(\mathrm{d}x) \mid \mathrm{d}x \in \partial X\} \cup \{\mathsf{stay}_R(\mathrm{d}y) \mid \mathrm{d}y \in \partial Y\} \\ & \cup & \{\mathsf{fail}\} \end{array}$$

The idea is that edits to a sum can either change just the content or change the tag (and therefore necessarily also the content, which is superseded by the given new content). That is, we want the "atoms" of the edit language to express the operations of editing content and switching sides. This gives us the switch_{LR}, switch_{RL}, and stay edits. For present purposes, we could leave it at this and define the monoid of edits to be the free monoid over just these generators. However, in Section 6 we will introduce a more compact representation that allows multiple edits to be combined into one, and this

$$\frac{k \in X \leftrightarrow Y \qquad \ell \in Z \leftrightarrow W}{k \oplus \ell \in X \oplus Z \leftrightarrow Y \oplus W}$$

$$\begin{array}{lcl}
C & = & k.C + \ell.C \\
init & = & \mathsf{inl}(k.init) \\
K & = & \{(\mathsf{inl}(x), \mathsf{inl}(c), \mathsf{inl}(y)) \\
 & & \quad \mid (x, c, y) \in k.K\} \\
 & \cup & \{(\mathsf{inr}(z), \mathsf{inr}(c), \mathsf{inr}(w)) \\
 & & \quad \mid (z, c, w) \in \ell.K\} \\
c_k & = & k.init \\
c_\ell & = & \ell.init \\
\Rrightarrow_g(\mathsf{switch}_{LL}(dx), \mathsf{inl}(c)) & = & \mathsf{let}\ (dy, c') = k.\Rrightarrow(dx, c_k) \\
 & & \mathsf{in}\ (\mathsf{switch}_{LL}(dy), \mathsf{inl}(c')) \\
\Rrightarrow_g(\mathsf{switch}_{RL}(dx), \mathsf{inr}(c)) & = & \mathsf{let}\ (dy, c') = k.\Rrightarrow(dx, c_k) \\
 & & \mathsf{in}\ (\mathsf{switch}_{RL}(dy), \mathsf{inl}(c')) \\
\Rrightarrow_g(\mathsf{switch}_{LR}(dz), \mathsf{inl}(c)) & = & \mathsf{let}\ (dw, c') = \ell.\Rrightarrow(dz, c_\ell) \\
 & & \mathsf{in}\ (\mathsf{switch}_{LR}(dw), \mathsf{inr}(c')) \\
\Rrightarrow_g(\mathsf{switch}_{RR}(dz), \mathsf{inr}(c)) & = & \mathsf{let}\ (dw, c') = \ell.\Rrightarrow(dz, c_\ell) \\
 & & \mathsf{in}\ (\mathsf{switch}_{RR}(dw), \mathsf{inr}(c')) \\
\Rrightarrow_g(\mathsf{stay}_L(dx), \mathsf{inl}(c)) & = & \mathsf{let}\ (dy, c') = k.\Rrightarrow(dx, c) \\
 & & \mathsf{in}\ (\mathsf{stay}_L(dy), \mathsf{inl}(c')) \\
\Rrightarrow_g(\mathsf{stay}_R(dz), \mathsf{inr}(c)) & = & \mathsf{let}\ (dw, c') = \ell.\Rrightarrow(dz, c) \\
 & & \mathsf{in}\ (\mathsf{stay}_R(dw), \mathsf{inr}(c')) \\
\Rrightarrow_g(e, c) & = & (\mathsf{fail}, c)\ \text{in all other cases} \\
\Lleftarrow_g & & \text{is analogous}
\end{array}$$

Figure 3: The sum lens

representation will give rise to the other two switch operations; for example, switch_{LL} represents a switch_{LR} followed by a switch_{RL}. To avoid having two similar but subtly different definitions, we include these edits here in the basic generators as well. Finally, we introduce an always-failing edit to represent sequences of edits that are internally inconsistent—e.g., a switch to the left side followed by an attempt to apply an edit which stays on the right side. These intuitions are formalized in the application function:

$$\begin{array}{rcl}
\mathsf{switch}_{LL}(dx) \odot_g \mathsf{inl}(x) & = & \mathsf{inl}(dx\ init_X) \\
\mathsf{switch}_{LR}(dy) \odot_g \mathsf{inl}(x) & = & \mathsf{inr}(dy\ init_Y) \\
\mathsf{switch}_{RL}(dx) \odot_g \mathsf{inr}(y) & = & \mathsf{inl}(dx\ init_X) \\
\mathsf{switch}_{RR}(dy) \odot_g \mathsf{inr}(y) & = & \mathsf{inr}(dy\ init_Y) \\
\mathsf{stay}_L(dx) \odot_g \mathsf{inl}(x) & = & \mathsf{inl}(dx\ x) \\
\mathsf{stay}_R(dy) \odot_g \mathsf{inr}(y) & = & \mathsf{inr}(dy\ y) \\
e \odot_g v & & \text{undefined in all other cases}
\end{array}$$

We then define the sum of modules X and Y as

$$X \oplus Y = \langle |X| + |Y|, \mathsf{inl}(init_X), (G^{\oplus}_{X,Y})^*, \odot \rangle .$$

We now wish to give a lens combinator $k \oplus \ell$ that runs lens k on the parts of edits that apply to inl values and ℓ on the parts of edits that apply to inr values.[4] Figure 3 shows the full definition.

[4] In [7], there is some discussion regarding "forgetful" and "retentive" sum lenses, with the distinction revolving around what to do with the complement when an edit switches between sides of the sum. For state-based lenses, lenses on recursive structures like lists were given in terms of lenses on the non-recursive structure, and the retentive sum lens gave rise to a retentive list mapping lens whereas the forgetful sum lens gave rise to a forgetful list mapping lens. The poor alignment strategies given in that paper were mediated somewhat by the retentive map's ability to use complements from previous versions of a list, making retentive sums somewhat more attractive than forgetful ones. In this presentation, however, the mapping lens has much better alignment information, so we eschew the more complicated retentive lenses in favor of simpler forgetful versions.

$$\frac{\ell \in X \leftrightarrow Y}{\ell^* \in X^* \leftrightarrow Y^*}$$

$$\begin{array}{lcl}
C & = & \ell.C^* \\
init & = & \varepsilon \\
K & = & \{(x, c, y) \mid |x| = |c| = |y| \wedge \\
 & & \quad \forall 1 \le p \le |x|.\ (x_p, c_p, y_p) \in \ell.K\} \\
\Rrightarrow_g(\mathsf{mod}(p, dx), c) & = & \mathsf{let}\ (dy, c'_p) = \ell.\Rrightarrow(dx, c_p)\ \mathsf{in} \\
 & & (\mathsf{mod}(p, dy), c[p \mapsto c'_p])) \\
 & & \text{when } p \le n \\
\Rrightarrow_g(\mathsf{mod}(p, dx), c) & = & (\mathsf{fail}, c) \text{ when } p > n \\
\Rrightarrow_g(\mathsf{fail}, c) & = & (\mathsf{fail}, c) \\
\Rrightarrow_g(dx, c) & = & (dx, dx\ c) \text{ in all other cases} \\
\Lleftarrow & & \text{similar}
\end{array}$$

Figure 4: The list mapping lens

4.2 Theorem: When k and ℓ are lenses, so is $k \oplus \ell$.

Proof: The homomorphism laws are again trivial. We must show that the consistency relation K is maintained. We have

$$\begin{array}{cl}
 & (init_{X \oplus Z}, init, init_{Y \oplus W}) \\
= & (\mathsf{inl}(init_X), \mathsf{inl}(k.init), \mathsf{inl}(init_Y)) \in K,
\end{array}$$

since $(init_X, k.init, init_Y) \in k.K$. So it remains to show that that $\Rrightarrow$ and $\Lleftarrow$ preserve this relation. We need only consider the case where we begin with an arbitrary consistent triple $(\mathsf{inl}(x), \mathsf{inl}(c), \mathsf{inl}(y)) \in K$ and $dv \in X \oplus Z$ for which $dv\ \mathsf{inl}(x)$ is defined. (The cases where the triple is of the form $(\mathsf{inr}(x), \mathsf{inr}(c), \mathsf{inr}(y)) \in K$ are similar, swapping k and ℓ in some places; the cases where we are considering a $dv \in Y \oplus W$ are similar, but use $\Lleftarrow$ instead of $\Rrightarrow$ everywhere.) Since $dv\ \mathsf{inl}(x)$ is defined, there are three forms of dv to consider: $\mathsf{switch}_{LL}(dx)$, $\mathsf{switch}_{LR}(dz)$, and $\mathsf{stay}_L(dx)$. Here is the most interesting case:

Case $dv = \mathsf{switch}_{LL}(dx)$: We define $(dy, c') = k.putr(dx, k.init)$ and $(x', y') = (dx\ init_X, dy\ init_Y)$. Since k is a lens, we know $(init_X, k.init, init_Y) \in k.K$ and therefore that $(x', c', y') \in k.K$. This means $(\mathsf{inl}(x'), \mathsf{inl}(c'), \mathsf{inl}(y')) \in K$. Since $(k \oplus \ell).\Rrightarrow(dv, \mathsf{inl}(c)) = (\mathsf{switch}_{LL}(dy), \mathsf{inl}(c'))$ and $dv\ \mathsf{inl}(x) = \mathsf{inl}(x')$ and $\mathsf{switch}_{LL}(dy)\ \mathsf{inl}(y) = \mathsf{inl}(y')$, this shows that K is preserved in this case. □

Like the tensor product, this lens combinator is a bifunctor: $id \oplus id \equiv id$ and $(k \oplus \ell); (k' \oplus \ell') \equiv (k; k') \oplus (\ell; \ell')$.

List module Next, let us consider lists. Given a module X, we define the basic edits for lists over $|X|$ to include in-place modifications, insertions, deletions, and reorderings:

$$\begin{array}{rl}
G_X^{\text{list}} = & \{\mathsf{mod}(p, dx) \mid p \in \mathbb{N}^+, dx \in \partial X\} \\
\cup & \{\mathsf{ins}(i) \mid i \in \mathbb{N}\} \ \cup\ \{\mathsf{del}(i) \mid i \in \mathbb{N}\} \\
\cup & \{\mathsf{reorder}(f) \mid \forall i \in \mathbb{N}. f(i) \text{ permutes } \{1, \ldots, i\}\} \\
\cup & \{\mathsf{fail}\}
\end{array}$$

For compatibility with the generalization to arbitrary containers in §5, we slightly change the behavior of these operations from what we saw in §2. Insertions and deletions are now always performed at the end of the list; to insert in the middle of the list, you first insert at the end, then reorder the list. The argument i to $\mathsf{ins}(i)$ and $\mathsf{del}(i)$

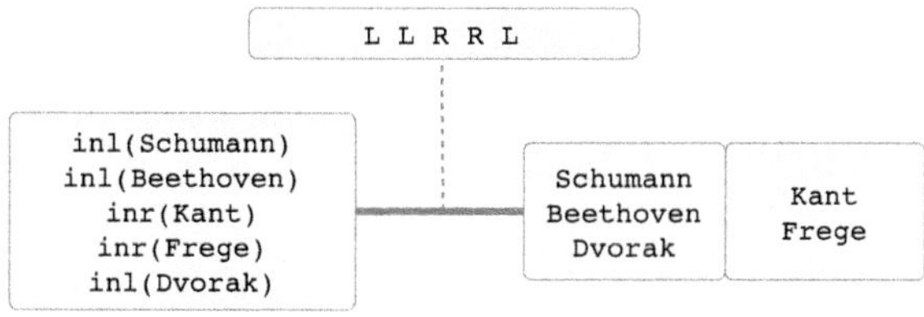

Figure 7. A consistent triple for the partition lens.

now specifies how *many* elements to insert or delete.

$$\begin{aligned}
\mathsf{mod}(p, \mathrm{d}x) \odot_g x_1 \cdots x_n &= x_1 \cdots x_{p-1}\ (\mathrm{d}x\ x_p)\ x_{p+1} \cdots x_n \\
\mathsf{ins}(i) \odot_g x_1 \cdots x_n &= x_1 \cdots x_n \underbrace{init_X \cdots init_X}_{i \text{ times}} \\
\mathsf{del}(i) \odot_g x_1 \cdots x_n &= x_1 \cdots x_{n-i} \\
\mathsf{reorder}(f) \odot_g x_1 \cdots x_n &= x_{f(n)(1)} \cdots x_{f(n)(n)} \\
\mathsf{fail} \odot_g x_1 \cdots x_n & \quad \text{undefined}
\end{aligned}$$

We take $\mathsf{mod}(p, \mathrm{d}x) \odot_g x$ to be undefined when $p > |x|$, and similarly take $\mathsf{del}(i) \odot_g x$ to be undefined when $i > |x|$. The list module is then $X^* = \langle |X|^*, \varepsilon, (G_X^{\text{list}})^*, \odot \rangle$.

Mapping lens The list mapping lens ℓ^* uses ℓ to translate mod edits from X to Y and vice versa (Figure 4). Other kinds of edits (ins, del, and reorder) are carried across unchanged. The notation $c[p \mapsto c'_p]$ in the rule for mod edits means "the list that is just like c except that the element in position p is replaced by c'_p." When translating non-modification edits, we update the complement in a way almost identical to the way the two replicas are updated; to reflect this similarity, we use edit application from the $Unit^*_{\ell.init \in \ell.C}$ module to define the new complement.

Partition lens Figures 5 and 6 give the definition of a list partitioning lens that (as we saw in §2) separates a list of tagged elements into those tagged inl and those tagged inr. We write fail to stand for left(fail)right(fail) when defining $\Rrightarrow_g$. Additionally, as with the mapping lens, we consider the complement to belong to a module; this time, to the module $Unit^*_{L \in \{L,R\}}$.

These figures may be a bit intimidating at first, but there is nothing very deep going on—just some everyday functional programming over lists. To illustrate how it all works, let's consider a few example invocations of the *partition* lens. Each of them begins with the consistent triple illustrated in Figure 7. Note that only the middle part—the complement—is actually available to the partition lens as it runs: its other input is just an edit.

As a warm-up, consider a simple edit: changing Dvorak's name to Dvořák (with correct diacritics) in the left repository. The edit describing this has the form $\mathsf{mod}(5, \mathsf{stay}_L(\mathrm{d}n))$, where $\mathrm{d}n$ describes the string edit to the name. To translate this edit, we first need to translate the index 5 to an index into the list of composers in the right-hand repository (line 5 in Figure 5). We can do this by simply counting how many composers appear up to and including Dvorak, that is, how many L values appear in the complement list up to index 5—in this case, 3. We then wrap this index up, along with the $\mathrm{d}n$ edit, in a new edit of the form $\mathsf{left}(\mathsf{mod}(3, \mathrm{d}n))$; the complement need not change because we have not changed the structure of the lists. This pattern—count to translate the index, then re-tag the edit appropriately—can be generalized to all modifications that stay on the same side of the sum; the count and tag functions defined in Figure 6 implement these two steps.

The left-to-right translation of other in-place modifications, insertions, and deletions and the right-to-left translation of in-place modifications, insertions, and deletions to either list are built from the same primitives, using count to translate indices and re-tagging edits with tag. In a few cases, we use some edit "macros": since insertions and deletions always happen at the end of a list, we write del′ and ins′ for edits that do some shuffling to ensure that the inserted or deleted element moves to the appropriate position.

Perhaps the most interesting of these is an in-place modification to the left repository that switches sides of a sum (line 4). For example, suppose we want to replace Beethoven with Plato. The edit to do this has the form $\mathsf{mod}(2, \mathsf{switch}_{LR}(\mathrm{d}n))$—that is, at position 2, switch from an inl to an inr. Here, the translated edit must do *four* things: delete Beethoven from the left list, insert a new element into the right list, re-tag $\mathrm{d}n$ so that it changes the new element to Plato, and finally fix up the complement to match the new interleaving. As before, we can use count to translate the position 2 in the interleaved list into a position in the left list in the right replica. But then we hit a minor snag: deletions only occur at the end of a list. The solution is to first reorder the list, so that Beethoven appears at the end, then delete one element. Figure 6 defines the cycle function, which constructs permutations to do this reordering. The function $\mathsf{cycle}_p(n)$ permutes lists of size n by moving position p to the end of the list, and shifting all the other elements after p down one to fill in the resulting hole. For example, $\mathsf{cycle}_2(5)$ looks like this:

p	1	2	3	4	5
$\mathsf{cycle}_2(5)(p)$	1	3	4	5	2

So, we can delete position p by first reordering with $\mathsf{reorder}(\mathsf{cycle}_p)$, then deleting one element with $\mathsf{del}(1)$. The $\mathsf{del}'(p)$ macro encapsulates this pattern; there is a similar pattern for inserting a new element at position p encapsulated by $\mathsf{ins}'(p)$. Finally, since position 2 in the interleaved list corresponds to positions 2 and 1 in the left and right non-interleaved lists, respectively, the final edit can be written as $\mathsf{right}(\mathsf{mod}(1, \mathrm{d}n))\ \mathsf{right}(\mathsf{ins}'(1))\ \mathsf{left}(\mathsf{del}'(2))$. To fix up the complement, we can simply set the flag at position p to match the new tag: in our case, position 2 is now an inr, so we should set $c_2 = R$.

The most delicate cases involve translating reorderings. Consider an edit to the right repository that swaps Schumann and Dvorak. One way to write this edit is in terms of a function that swaps indices one and three for lists of size at least three (and does nothing on lists of size smaller than three):

$$f(n)(p) = \begin{cases} 4 - p & n \geq 3 \wedge p \in \{1, 3\} \\ p & n < 3 \vee p \notin \{1, 3\} \end{cases}$$

The edit itself is then $\mathsf{left}(\mathsf{reorder}(f))$. Our job is now to compute some f' for which $\mathsf{reorder}(f')$ swaps inl(Schumann) and inl(Dvorak) in the left repository (line 14). There is one wrinkle: f and f' are parameterized by the length of the lists they permute. Translating f naively would therefore seem to require a way for f' to *guess* the number of composers in lists whose lengths do not match that of the complement. Fortunately, f' need only behave correctly for exactly those lists that are consistent with the current complement, for which our "guess" about how many composers there are is guaranteed to be accurate. So we need only construct a single permutation (and use, say, the identity permutation for all inconsistent list lengths). We use the count function to construct this permutation. It is convenient to derive an isomorphism between positions in the left repository and positions tagged by which list they are indexing into in the right repository; the iso function shows how to use count to do this. In our example, the resulting isomorphism looks like this:

left	1	2	3	4	5
right	inl(1)	inl(2)	inr(1)	inr(2)	inl(3)

We can use $f(3)$ as a permutation on the inl elements, defining $g(\mathsf{inl}(p)) = \mathsf{inl}(f(3)(p))$ and $g(\mathsf{inr}(p)) = \mathsf{inr}(p)$. Then, to find out

$$partition \in (X \oplus Y)^* \leftrightarrow X^* \otimes Y^*$$

$$
\begin{array}{lll}
C & = \{L, R\}^* & \\
init & = \varepsilon & \\
K & = \{(z, \mathsf{map}_{\mathsf{tagof}}(z), (\mathsf{lefts}(z), \mathsf{rights}(z))) \mid z \in (|X| + |Y|)^*\} & \\
\Rrightarrow_g(\mathsf{mod}(p, \mathrm{d}v), c) & = (\mathsf{fail}, c) \text{ when } p > |c| & (1)\\
\Rrightarrow_g(\mathsf{mod}(p, \varepsilon), c) & = (\varepsilon, c) \text{ when } 1 \le p \le |c| & (2)\\
\Rrightarrow_g(\mathsf{mod}(p, dvdvs), c) & = (d'\,d, c'') \text{ where } 1 < n \quad (d, c') = \Rrightarrow_g(\mathsf{mod}(p, dvs), c) & (3)\\
 & \qquad 1 \le p \le |c| \quad (d', c'') = \Rrightarrow_g(\mathsf{mod}(p, \mathrm{d}v), c') & \\
\Rrightarrow_g(\mathsf{mod}(p, \mathsf{switch}_{jk}(\mathrm{d}v)), c) & = (d_2 d_1 d_0, c[p \mapsto k]), \text{ where } (p_L, p_R) = \mathsf{count}(p, c) \quad d_0 = \mathsf{map}_{\lambda d.\, \mathsf{tag}(j,d)}(\mathsf{del}'(p_j)) & (4)\\
 & \qquad d_2 = \mathsf{tag}(k, \mathsf{mod}(p_k, \mathrm{d}v)) \quad d_1 = \mathsf{map}_{\lambda d.\, \mathsf{tag}(k,d)}(\mathsf{ins}'(p_k)) & \\
\Rrightarrow_g(\mathsf{mod}(p, \mathsf{stay}_j(\mathrm{d}v)), c) & = (\mathsf{tag}(j, \mathsf{mod}(p_j, \mathrm{d}v)), c), \text{ where } (p_L, p_R) = \mathsf{count}(p, c) & (5)\\
\Rrightarrow_g(\mathsf{mod}(p, \mathsf{fail}), c) & = (\mathsf{fail}, c) & (6)\\
\Rrightarrow_g(\mathsf{ins}(i), c) & = (\mathsf{left}(\mathsf{ins}(i)), \mathsf{ins}(i)\ c) & (7)\\
\Rrightarrow_g(\mathsf{del}(i), c) & = (d_1 d_0, \mathsf{del}(i)\ c), \text{ where } \quad c' = \mathsf{reverse}(c) \quad d_0 = \mathsf{left}(\mathsf{del}(n_L - 1)) & (8)\\
 & \qquad (n_L, n_R) = \mathsf{count}(i+1, c') \quad d_1 = \mathsf{right}(\mathsf{del}(n_R - 1)) & \\
\Rrightarrow_g(\mathsf{reorder}(f), c) & = (d_L d_R, c'), \text{ where } \quad h = \mathsf{iso}(c) \quad c' = \mathsf{reorder}(f)\ c & (9)\\
 & \qquad h' = \mathsf{iso}(c') \quad (n_L, n_R) = \mathsf{count}(|c|, c) & \\
 & \qquad h'' = h'^{-1}; f(|c|); h \quad f_k(n \ne n_k) = \lambda p.\, p & \\
 & \qquad d_L = \mathsf{left}(\mathsf{reorder}(f_L)) \quad f_L(n_L) = \mathsf{inl}; h''; \mathsf{out} & \\
 & \qquad d_R = \mathsf{right}(\mathsf{reorder}(f_R)) \quad f_R(n_R) = \mathsf{inr}; h''; \mathsf{out} & \\
\Rrightarrow_g(\mathsf{fail}, c) & = (\mathsf{fail}, c) & (10)\\
\Lleftarrow_g(\varepsilon, c) & = (\varepsilon, c) & (11)\\
\Lleftarrow_g(dvdvs, c) & = (d'd, c'') \text{ when } n > 1, \text{ where } (d, c') = \Lleftarrow_g(dvs, c) \quad (d', c'') = \Lleftarrow_g(\mathrm{d}v, c') & (12)\\
\Lleftarrow_g(\mathsf{left}(\mathsf{mod}(p, \mathrm{d}x)), c) & = (\mathsf{stay}_L(\mathsf{mod}(p', \mathrm{d}x)), c), \text{ where } p' = \mathsf{iso}(c)^{-1}(\mathsf{inl}(p)) & (13)\\
\Lleftarrow_g(\mathsf{left}(\mathsf{reorder}(f)), c) & = (\mathsf{reorder}(f'), c), \text{ where } g(\mathsf{inr}(p)) = \mathsf{inr}(p) \quad f'(n \ne |c|) = \lambda p.\, p & (14)\\
 & \qquad g(\mathsf{inl}(p)) = \mathsf{inl}(f(n_L)(p)) \quad f'(|c|) = h; g; h^{-1} & \\
 & \qquad (n_L, n_R) = \mathsf{count}(|c|, c) \quad h = \mathsf{iso}(c) & \\
\Lleftarrow_g(\mathsf{left}(\mathsf{ins}(i)), c) & = (\mathsf{ins}(i), \mathsf{ins}(i)\ c) & (15)\\
\Lleftarrow_g(\mathsf{left}(\mathsf{del}(0)), c) & = (\varepsilon, c) & (16)\\
\Lleftarrow_g(\mathsf{left}(\mathsf{del}(i)), c) & = (d''\ \mathsf{del}'(p), c''), \text{ where } h = \mathsf{iso}(c) \quad (n_L, n_R) = \mathsf{count}(|c|, c) & (17)\\
 & \qquad p = h^{-1}(\mathsf{inl}(n_L)) \quad (d'', c'') = \Lleftarrow_g(d', c') & \\
 & \qquad c' = \mathsf{del}'(p)\ c \quad d' = \mathsf{left}(\mathsf{del}(i-1)) & \\
 & \text{when } 0 < i \le n_L + 1 & \\
\Lleftarrow_g(\mathsf{left}(\mathsf{del}(i)), c) & = (\mathsf{fail}, c) \text{ otherwise} & (18)\\
\Lleftarrow_g(\mathsf{left}(\mathsf{fail}), c) & = (\mathsf{fail}, c) & (19)\\
\Lleftarrow_g(\mathsf{right}(\mathrm{d}y), c) & \quad \text{similar} &
\end{array}
$$

Figure 5: The *partition* lens

$$
\begin{array}{ll}
\mathsf{tagof}(\mathsf{inl}(x)) = L & \mathsf{map}_f(\varepsilon) = \varepsilon \\
\mathsf{tagof}(\mathsf{inr}(y)) = R & \mathsf{map}_f(cw) = f(c)\ \mathsf{map}_f(w) \\
\mathsf{lefts}(\varepsilon) = \varepsilon & \mathsf{rights}(\varepsilon) = \varepsilon \\
\mathsf{lefts}(\mathsf{inl}(x)w) = x\ \mathsf{lefts}(w) & \mathsf{rights}(\mathsf{inl}(x)w) = \mathsf{rights}(w) \\
\mathsf{lefts}(\mathsf{inr}(y)w) = \mathsf{lefts}(w) & \mathsf{rights}(\mathsf{inr}(y)w) = y\ \mathsf{rights}(w) \\
\mathsf{tag}(L, \mathrm{d}x) = \mathsf{left}(\mathrm{d}x) & \mathsf{out}(\mathsf{inl}(x)) = x \\
\mathsf{tag}(R, \mathrm{d}y) = \mathsf{right}(\mathrm{d}y) & \mathsf{out}(\mathsf{inr}(y)) = y \\
\mathsf{count}(p, \varepsilon) = (1, 1) & \mathsf{count}(1, c) = (1, 1)
\end{array}
$$

$$\mathsf{count}(p, c_1 \cdots c_n) = \mathsf{let}\ (n_L, n_R) = \mathsf{count}(p-1, c_2 \cdots c_n)\ \mathsf{in} \begin{cases} (n_L + 1, n_R) & c = L \\ (n_L, n_R + 1) & c = R \end{cases}$$

$$\mathsf{cycle}_p(n)(m) = \begin{cases} p & p < m = n \\ m + 1 & p \le m < n \\ m & \text{otherwise} \end{cases}$$

$$\mathsf{reverse}(c_1 \cdots c_n) = c_n c_{n-1} \cdots c_1$$

$$\mathsf{del}'(p) = \mathsf{del}(1)\ \mathsf{reorder}(\mathsf{cycle}_p)$$

$$\mathsf{ins}'(p) = \mathsf{reorder}(\lambda n.\ \mathsf{cycle}_p(n)^{-1})\ \mathsf{ins}(1)$$

$$\mathsf{iso}(c) = \lambda p.\ \mathsf{let}\ (n_L, n_R) = \mathsf{count}(p, c)\ \mathsf{in} \begin{cases} \mathsf{inl}(n_L) & c_p = L \\ \mathsf{inr}(n_R) & c_p = R \end{cases}$$

Figure 6: Supplementary functions for *partition*

where position p in the left repository should come from, we can simply translate p into an index into the right repository using iso, apply g to find out where that index came from, and translate back into the left repository using iso^{-1}. Expanding the table above with these translations yields:

left	1	2	3	4	5
iso(left)	inl(1)	inl(2)	inr(1)	inr(2)	inl(3)
g(iso(left))	inl(3)	inl(2)	inr(1)	inr(2)	inl(1)
$\mathsf{iso}^{-1}(g(\mathsf{iso}(\mathsf{left})))$	5	2	3	4	1

This swaps indices 1 and 5, so our final f' looks like:

$$f'(n)(p) = \begin{cases} 6-p & n=5 \wedge p \in \{1,5\} \\ p & n \neq 5 \vee p \notin \{1,5\} \end{cases}$$

Translating a reordering of the left repository follows a similar path (line 9): restrict the reordering to lists consistent with the current complement, then compose the permutation with isomorphisms between the indices in the two repositories. There is one subtlety here: a reordering of the list in the left repository may shuffle which positions are inl's and which are inr's. As a result, we must take care to construct *two* separate position isomorphisms: one for "before" the reordering, and one for "after."

5. Containers

The list mapping lens from the previous section can be generalized to a much larger set of structures, called *containers*, that also includes trees, labeled graphs, etc. We will also provide a general construction for "reorganization lenses" between *different* container types (over the same type of entries). Together with composition and tensor product, this will provide a set of building blocks for constructing many useful lenses. The reorganization lenses also furnish further examples of lenses with nontrivial complements. (Only a small part of §6 depends on this material; it can safely be skimmed on a first reading.)

Containers were first proposed by Abbott, Altenkirch, and Ghani [1]. The idea is that a container type specifies a set I of shapes and, for each shape i, a set of positions $P(i)$. A container with entries in X and belonging to such a container type comprises a shape i and a function $f : P(i) \to X$. For example, lists are containers whose shapes are the natural numbers and for which $P(i) = \{0, \ldots, i-1\}$, whereas binary trees are containers whose shapes are prefix-closed subsets of $\{0,1\}^*$ (access paths) and where $P(i) = i$ itself. Even labeled graphs can be modeled using unlabeled graphs as shapes. One can further generalize the framework to allow the types of entries to depend on their position, but for the sake of simplicity we will not do so here.

In the present context, containers are useful because they allow for the definition of a rich edit language, allowing the insertion and deletion of positions, modification of particular entries, and reorganizations such as tree rotations. We can then define lenses for containers that propagate these general edit operations.

In the case of state-based symmetric lenses [7], it has been observed that lens iterators akin to "fold left" for inductive data structures also permit the definition of powerful (state-based) lenses. In the edit-based framework iterators are less convenient because it is unclear how edits in an arbitrary module should be propagated to, say, list edits in such a way that the rich edit structure available for lists is meaningfully exploited. (Of course, it is possible to propagate everything to a "rebuild from scratch" edit, thus aping the state-based case.)

In the following we slightly deviate from the presentation of containers from [1, 7] in that we do not allow the set of positions to vary with the shapes. We rather have a universal set of positions P and a predicate live that delineates a subset of P for each shape i. We can then obtain a container type in the original sense by putting $P(i) = \{p \mid p \in \mathsf{live}(i)\}$. Conversely, given a container type in the sense of [1], we can define $P = \{(i,p) \mid p \in P(i)\}$ and $\mathsf{live}(i) = \{(i,p) \mid p \in P\}$. Furthermore, as we already did in [7], we require a *partially-ordered* set of shapes I and ask that live be monotone. Formulating this in the original setting would require a coherent family of transition functions $P(i) \to P(i')$ when $i \leq i'$, which is more cumbersome. Another advantage of the present formulation of container types is that it lends itself more easily to an implementation in a programming language without dependent types.

5.1 Definition: A *container type* is a triple $\langle I, P, \mathsf{live}\rangle$ comprising (1) a *module* I of *shapes* whose underlying set is partially ordered (but whose action need not be monotone); (2) a set P of *positions*; and (3) a *liveness predicate* in the form of a monotone function $\mathsf{live} \in I \to \mathcal{P}(P)$ which tells for each shape which positions belong to it.

If $T = \langle I, P, \mathsf{live}\rangle$ is a container type and X is a set, we can form the set $T(X)$ of containers of type T with entries from X by setting $T(X) = \sum_{i\in I} \mathsf{live}(i) \to X$. Thus a container of type T and entries from X comprises a shape i and, for every position that is live at i—i.e. every element of $\mathsf{live}(i)$—an entry taken from X.

Our aim is now to explain how the mapping $X \mapsto T(X)$ lifts to a functor on the category of lenses—i.e., for each module X, how to construct a module $T(X)$ whose underlying set of states is the set of containers $T(|X|)$, and for each lens $\ell \in X \leftrightarrow Y$, how to construct a "container mapping lens" $T(\ell) \in T(X) \leftrightarrow T(Y)$. We will see that this mapping is well defined on equivalence classes of lenses and respect identities and composition. We begin by defining a module structure on containers.

5.2 Definition: Let $T = \langle I, P, \mathsf{live}\rangle$ be a container type. An edit $\mathrm{d}i \in \partial I$ is an *insertion* if $\mathrm{d}i\ i \geq i$ whenever defined. It is a *deletion* if $\mathrm{d}i\ i \leq i$ whenever defined. It is a *rearrangement* if $|\mathsf{live}(\mathrm{d}i\ i)| = |\mathsf{live}(i)|$ (same cardinality) whenever defined. We only employ edits from these three categories as ingredients of container edits; any other edits in the module will remain unused. This division of container edits into "pure" insertions, deletions, and rearrangements facilitates the later definition of lenses operating on such edits.

5.3 Definition: If $\langle I, P, \mathsf{live}\rangle$ is a container type, $\mathrm{d}i \in \partial I$, and $f \in I \to P \to P$, then we say f is *consistent* with $\mathrm{d}i$ if, whenever $\mathrm{d}i\ i$ is defined, $f(i)$ restricted to $\mathsf{live}(i)$ is a bijection to $\mathsf{live}(\mathrm{d}i\ i)$.

A typical insertion could be the addition of a node to a binary tree, a typical deletion the removal of some node, and a typical rearrangement the rotation of a binary tree about some node.

5.4 Definition [Container edits]: Given container T and module X we define edits for $T(|X|)$ as follows (we give some intuition after Definition 5.5):

$$\begin{array}{ll} \{\mathsf{fail}\} & \\ \cup\,\{\mathsf{mod}(p,\mathrm{d}x) & \mid p \in P, \mathrm{d}x \in \partial X\} \\ \cup\,\{\mathsf{ins}(\mathrm{d}i) & \mid \mathrm{d}i \text{ an insertion}\} \\ \cup\,\{\mathsf{del}(\mathrm{d}i) & \mid \mathrm{d}i \text{ a deletion}\} \\ \cup\,\{\mathsf{rearr}(\mathrm{d}i, f) & \mid f \text{ consistent with } \mathrm{d}i\} \end{array}$$

In the last case, often either $\mathrm{d}i$ will only be defined for very few i or f will have a generic definition, so the representation of a rearrangement edit does not have to be large.

5.5 Definition [Edit application]: The application of an edit to a container (i, f) is defined as follows:

$$\begin{array}{l}
\mathsf{fail}\ (i,f) \text{ is always undefined}\\
\mathsf{mod}(p,\mathrm{d}x)\ (i,f) = (i, f[p \mapsto \mathrm{d}x\ f(p)]) \text{ when } p \in \mathsf{live}(i)\\
\mathsf{ins}(\mathrm{d}i)\ (i,f) = (\mathrm{d}i\ i, f')\\
\qquad \text{where } f'(p) = \text{if } p \in \mathsf{live}(i) \text{ then } f(p) \text{ else } init_X\\[4pt]
\mathsf{del}(\mathrm{d}i)\ (i,f) = (\mathrm{d}i\ i, f{\restriction}\mathsf{live}(\mathrm{d}i\ i))\\
\mathsf{rearr}(\mathrm{d}i,f)\ (i,g) = (\mathrm{d}i\ i, g')\\
\qquad \text{where } g'(p) = g(f(i)(p))
\end{array}$$

The $\mathsf{mod}(p, \mathrm{d}x)$ edit modifies the contents of position p according to $\mathrm{d}x$. If that position is absent the edit fails. The shape of the resulting container is unchanged. The $\mathsf{ins}(\mathrm{d}i)$ edit alters the shape by $\mathrm{d}i$, growing the set of positions in the process (since $\mathrm{d}i\ i \geq i$). The new positions are filled with $init_X$. The $\mathsf{del}(\mathrm{d}i)$ edit works similarly, but the set of positions may shrink; the contents of deleted positions are discarded. The fail edit never applies and will be returned *pro forma* by some container lenses if the input edit does not match the current complement.

The $\mathsf{rearr}(\mathrm{d}i, f)$ edit, finally, changes the shape of a container but neither adds nor removes entries. As already mentioned, a typical example is the left-rotation of a binary tree about the root. This rotation applies whenever the root has two grandchildren to the left and a child to the right. For this example, one may worry about the size of f, since it affects many positions; however, it can be serialized to a small, three line if-then-else. That we do not, at this point, provide edits that copy the contents of some position into other positions; their investigation is left for future work.

We define the monoid $\partial T(X)$ as the free monoid generated by the basic edits defined above. In Section 6 we discuss the possibility of imposing equational laws, in particular with a view to compact normal forms of container edits.

Setting $init_{T(X)} = (init_I, \lambda p.init_X)$ when $T = \langle I, P, \mathsf{live}\rangle$ completes the definition of the module $T(X)$.

5.6 Example: For any module X we can construe the list module X^* as a particular container type $\langle I, P, \mathsf{live}\rangle$ where $I = \mathbb{N}$ with ∂I generated by $i \in \mathbb{Z}$ with $i \odot n = \max(i+n, 0)$. Furthermore, $P = \mathbb{N}$ and $\mathsf{live}(n) = \{0, \ldots, n-1\}$.

Then all list edits arise as specific container edits, however, the generic formulation of container edits also includes some esoteric edits, such as $\mathsf{ins}(10 \cdot (-10))$ which brings a list to minimum length 10 by appending default elements if needed.

In Figure 8 we define the mapping lens turning $T(-)$ into an endofunctor on the category of lenses. We note that this is only the second lens to have a nontrivial complement (after $partition$).

Given that this definition looks complex at first we state and prove explicitly that it is indeed a lens.

5.7 Theorem: If $T = \langle I, P, \mathsf{live}\rangle$ is a container and ℓ is a lens so is $T(\ell)$. Moreover, $T(-)$ respects lens equivalence and preserves the identity lens and composition of lenses (up to equivalence), and thus defines a functor on the category of lenses.

We can also define a restructuring lens between containers of different container type but with the same type of entries, i.e. between $T(X)$ and $T'(X)$ where $T = \langle I, P, \mathsf{live}\rangle$ and $T' = \langle I', P', \mathsf{live}'\rangle$. For this to be possible, we need a lens ℓ between I and I' and for any triple $(i, c, i') \in \ell.K$ a bijection $f_{i,c,i'} \in \mathsf{live}'(i') \simeq \mathsf{live}(i)$. The complement of this lens consists of those triples (i, c, i'), and thus "knows" at any time which bijection links the positions at either end.

One typical instance of this kind of lens is list reversal; another is a lens between trees and lists which ensures that the list entries agree with the tree entries according to some fixed order, e.g. in-order or breadth first. Although the live positions of the containers to be synchronized are in bijective correspondence, there is—e.g. in the case of list reversal—no fixed edit that, say, a "modify the second position" edit is mapped to. Indeed, the restructuring lens we are about to construct can be seen as a kind of state-indexed isomorphism, but the full scaffolding of edit lenses is needed to make such a notion precise.

$$\frac{\ell \in X \leftrightarrow Y \qquad T = \langle I, P, \mathsf{live}\rangle \text{ a container type}}{T(\ell) \in T(X) \leftrightarrow T(Y)}$$

$$\begin{array}{lcl}
C & = & T(\ell.C)\\
init & = & (init_I, \lambda p.\ \ell.init)\\
\Rrightarrow_g(\mathsf{mod}(p,\mathrm{d}x),(i,f)) & = & (\mathsf{mod}(p,\mathrm{d}y),(i,f'))\\
\multicolumn{3}{c}{\text{when } p \in \mathsf{live}(i) \text{ and where}}\\
\multicolumn{3}{c}{f' = f[p{\mapsto}c'],\ (\mathrm{d}y, c') = \ell.{\Rrightarrow}(\mathrm{d}x, f(p))}\\
\Rrightarrow_g(\mathsf{mod}(p,\mathrm{d}x),(i,f)) & = & (\mathsf{fail},(i,f)) \text{ if } p \notin \mathsf{live}(i)\\
\Rrightarrow_g(\mathsf{ins}(\mathrm{d}i),(i,g)) & = & (\mathsf{ins}(\mathrm{d}i),\\
 & & (\mathrm{d}i\ i, g[p{\mapsto}\ell.init]))\\
 & & \text{when } \mathrm{d}i\ i \text{ is defined}\\
\Rrightarrow_g(\mathsf{del}(\mathrm{d}i),(i,g)) & = & (\mathsf{del}(\mathrm{d}i),(\mathrm{d}i\ i, g{\restriction}\mathsf{live}(\mathrm{d}i\ i)))\\
 & & \text{when } \mathrm{d}i\ i \text{ is defined}\\
\Rrightarrow_g(\mathsf{rearr}(\mathrm{d}i,h),(i,g)) & = & (\mathsf{rearr}(\mathrm{d}i,h),\\
 & & (\mathrm{d}i\ i, \lambda p.g(h(i)(p))))\\
 & & \text{when } \mathrm{d}i\ i \text{ is defined}\\
\Rrightarrow_g(\mathrm{d}z,c) & = & (\mathsf{fail},c) \text{ in all other cases}\\
\Lleftarrow_g(-,-) & = & \text{analogous}\\
K & = & \{((i,f),(i,g),(i,f')) \mid i \in I\\
 & & \wedge (f(p), g(p), f'(p)) \in \ell.K\}
\end{array}$$

Figure 8: Generic container-mapping lens

$$\frac{\begin{array}{c}T = \langle I, P, \mathsf{live}\rangle \text{ a container type}\\ T' = \langle I', P', \mathsf{live}'\rangle \text{ a container type}\\ \ell \in I \leftrightarrow I'\end{array}}{[T, T'](\ell) \in T(X) \leftrightarrow T'(X)}$$

$$\begin{array}{lcl}
C & = & \ell.K\\
init & = & (init_I, \ell.init, init_{I'})\\
\multicolumn{3}{l}{K = \{((i,f),(i,c,i'),(i',f'))}\\
\multicolumn{3}{l}{\quad \mid (i,c,i') \in \ell.K \wedge \forall p{\in}\mathsf{live}'(i').f(f_{i,c,i'}(p)) = f'(p)\}}\\
\Rrightarrow_g(\mathsf{fail},x) & = & (\mathsf{fail},x)\\
\Rrightarrow_g(\mathsf{mod}(p,\mathrm{d}x),(i,c,i')) & = & (\mathsf{mod}(f^{-1}_{i,c,i'}(p),\mathrm{d}x),(i,c,i')\\
 & & \text{when } p \in \mathsf{live}(i)\\
\Rrightarrow_g(\mathsf{ins}(\mathrm{d}i),(i,c,i')) & = & (\mathsf{rearr}(\mathbf{1},f_i)\mathsf{ins}(\mathrm{d}i'),\\
 & & (\mathrm{d}i\ i, c', \mathrm{d}i'\ i'))\\
\Rrightarrow_g(\mathsf{del}(\mathrm{d}i),(i,c,i')) & = & (\mathsf{rearr}(\mathbf{1},f_d)\mathsf{del}(\mathrm{d}i'),\\
 & & (\mathrm{d}i\ i, c', \mathrm{d}i'\ i'))\\
\Rrightarrow_g(\mathsf{rearr}(\mathrm{d}i,f),(i,c,i')) & = & (\mathsf{rearr}(\mathrm{d}i',f_r),\\
 & & (\mathrm{d}i\ i, c', \mathrm{d}i'\ i'))\\[6pt]
 & & \text{see below for } f_i, f_d, f_r\\
\text{in the last three clauses:} & & (\mathrm{d}i', c') = \ell.{\Rrightarrow}(\mathrm{d}i, c)\\
\Rrightarrow_g(\mathrm{d}c,(i,c,i')) & = & \text{fail in all other cases}\\
\Lleftarrow_g(-,-) & = & \text{analogous}
\end{array}$$

Figure 9: Container restructuring lens

We also require that ℓ maps insertions to insertions, deletions to deletions, and rearrangements to rearrangements. Note that this is well-defined on equivalence classes of lenses.

Given these data, we define the restructuring lens in Figure 9, with a few supplementary definitions below. The families of bijections f_i, f_d, f_r must be chosen in such a way that the container edits in which they appear are well-formed (this is possible since $\mathrm{d}i'$ is an insertion, deletion, or restructuring as appropriate) and such that the following three constraints are satisfied: in each case i, i', etc., refer to the current values from above and $p \in \mathsf{live}'(\mathrm{d}i'\ i')$ is an arbitrary position.

$$f_i(\mathrm{d}i'\ i')(p) = f^{-1}_{i,c,i'}(f_{\mathrm{d}i\ i,c',\mathrm{d}i'\ i'}(p)) \quad \text{when } f_{\mathrm{d}i\ i,c',\mathrm{d}i'\ i'}(p) \in \mathsf{live}(i)$$
$$f_d(\mathrm{d}i'\ i')(p) = f^{-1}_{i,c,i'}(f_{\mathrm{d}i\ i,c',\mathrm{d}i'\ i'}(p))$$
$$f_r(\mathrm{d}i'\ i')(p) = f^{-1}_{i,c,i'}(f(i)(f_{\mathrm{d}i\ i,c',\mathrm{d}i'\ i'}(p)))$$

The propagated edits are supposed to be applied to a container of the current shape i', so these arbitrary decisions do not really matter; nevertheless it would be nice if we could be a bit more uniform. This is indeed possible in the case where ℓ is an isomorphism lens, but we refrain from formulating details.

The bijection f_i contains a little more choice, namely the behavior on the T' positions in $f^{-1}_{\mathrm{d}i\ i,c',\mathrm{d}i'\ i'}(\mathsf{live}(\mathrm{d}i\ i) \setminus \mathsf{live}(i))$. Fortunately, they all contain $init_X$ so that the choice does not affect the resulting state after application of the edit.

We illustrate the propagation of an $\mathsf{ins}(\mathrm{d}i)$ edit in the particular case where we are synchronizing a tree with the list formed by its in-order traversal. Thus, $I = \mathbb{N}$; $P = \mathbb{N}$; $\mathsf{live}(i) = \{p \mid p < i\}$ and I' comprises prefix closed subsets of $\{0,1\}^*$; $P' = \{0,1\}^*$; $\mathsf{live}'(i') = i'$. The monoid ∂I has increment and decrement operations; the monoid $\partial I'$ has operations for adding and removing nodes in leaf positions and also for rotating tree shapes.

The lens $\ell \in I \leftrightarrow I'$ does not know anything about the intended application; it has a trivial complement $Unit$ and merely maintains the constraint that the list shape and the tree shape have the same number of positions. It has some freedom how it translates list edits; e.g., it might add and remove tree nodes at the left.

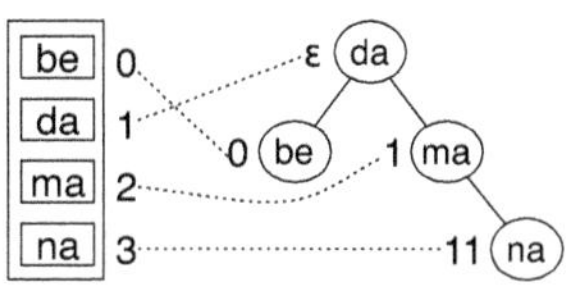

The family of bijections $f_{i,c,i'}$ models the in-order correspondence; thus, for example if $i = 4$ and $i' = \{\varepsilon, 0, 1, 11\}$ the bijection would be as shown above. (For illustration we also indicate possible X-contents of the positions.) Formally, we have $f_{i,c,i'} = \{(0,0),(1,\varepsilon),(2,1),(3,11)\}$.

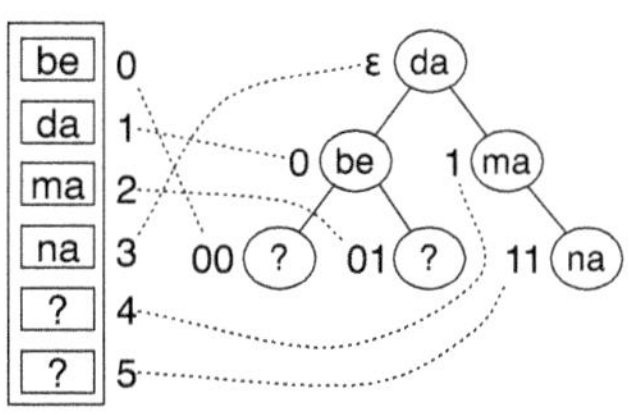

Now suppose that $\mathrm{d}i\ i = i+2$ and that $\mathrm{d}i'$ (the result of $\mathrm{d}i$ propagated through ℓ) installs two children at the leftmost node. In our in-order application we then have $f_{\mathrm{d}i\ i,c',\mathrm{d}i'\ i'} = \{(0,00),(1,0),(2,01),(3,\varepsilon),(4,1),(5,11)\}$ and after applying both $\mathsf{ins}(\mathrm{d}i)$ and $\mathsf{ins}(\mathrm{d}i')$ we are in the as-yet-inconsistent situation depicted above.

To restore consistency we also apply $\mathsf{rearr}(1, f_r)$ where $f_r(i') = \{(00,0),(0,\varepsilon),(01,1),(\varepsilon,11),(1,00),(11,01)\}$. We could also have chosen $f_r(i') = \{\ldots,(1,01),(11,01)\}$; this is precisely the additional freedom of choice. Of course $f_r(i'')$ for $i'' \neq i'$ is also completely unconstrained. After applying $\mathsf{rearr}(1, f_r)$ we end up with the desired consistent state.

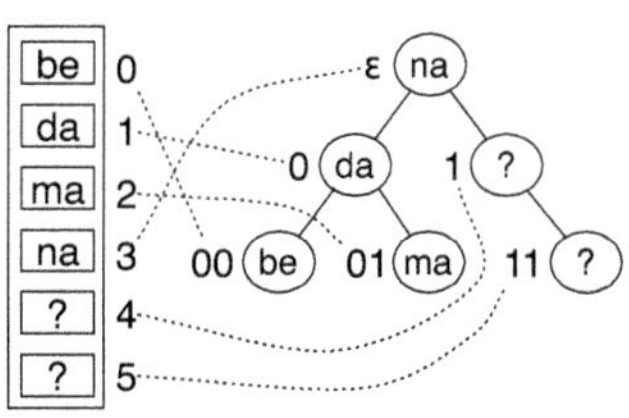

6. Adding Monoid Laws

The edit languages accompanying the constructions in the previous two sections were all freely generated. This was a good place to begin as it is relatively easy to understand, but, as discussed in §3, there are good reasons for investigating richer languages. This section takes a first step in this direction by showing how to equip the product and sum combinators with more interesting edits.

Given modules X and Y, there is a standard definition of *module product* motivated by the intuition that an edit to an $|X| \times |Y|$ value is a pair of an edit to the $|X|$ part and an edit to the $|Y|$ part. The monoid multiplication goes pointwise, and one can define an edit application that goes pointwise as well.

$$X \otimes Y = \langle |X| \times |Y|, (init_X, init_Y), \partial X \otimes \partial Y, \odot_{X \otimes Y} \rangle$$
$$\mathbf{1}_{M \otimes N} = (\mathbf{1}_M, \mathbf{1}_N)$$
$$(m,n) \cdot_{M \otimes N} (m',n') = (m\,m', n\,n')$$
$$(\mathrm{d}x, \mathrm{d}y) \odot_{X \otimes Y} (x,y) = (\mathrm{d}x\ x, \mathrm{d}y\ y)$$

One might wonder whether the standard definition has any connection to the definition we give earlier. One way to bridge the gap is to add equational laws to the free monoid.[5] The equations below demand that left and right be monoid homomorphisms, and that they commute:

$$\mathsf{left}(\mathbf{1}) = \varepsilon$$
$$\mathsf{left}(\mathrm{d}x)\mathsf{left}(\mathrm{d}x') = \mathsf{left}(\mathrm{d}x\mathrm{d}x')$$
$$\mathsf{right}(\mathbf{1}) = \varepsilon$$
$$\mathsf{right}(\mathrm{d}y)\mathsf{right}(\mathrm{d}y') = \mathsf{right}(\mathrm{d}y\mathrm{d}y')$$
$$\mathsf{left}(\mathrm{d}x)\mathsf{right}(\mathrm{d}y) = \mathsf{right}(\mathrm{d}y)\mathsf{left}(\mathrm{d}x)$$

It is not hard to show that the free monoid subject to the above equations is isomorphic to the natural monoid product.

However, it is not obvious that the definitions relying on the free monoid product remain well defined after imposing the above equations. In particular, we must check that any monoid homomorphisms we defined respect these laws. For homomorphisms f specified via specification of f_g, it is enough to prove that, for each equational law $g = g'$, the specification respects the law—i.e., $f(g) = f(g')$.

For example, to check that we can create a well-defined tensor product module that includes the above equations, we must show that $\odot_g$ respects the equations. For the commutativity equation, we must show

$$\mathsf{left}(\mathrm{d}x) \odot_g \mathsf{right}(\mathrm{d}y) \odot_g (x,y) = \mathsf{right}(\mathrm{d}y) \odot_g \mathsf{left}(\mathrm{d}x)_g \odot_g (x,y).$$

Simple calculation shows that both sides are equal to $(\mathrm{d}x\ x, \mathrm{d}y; y)$, so this law is respected; the rest follow similar lines.

Most importantly, we must check that the $\Rrightarrow$ and $\Lleftarrow$ functions are still monoid homomorphisms; indeed, this check makes these equations interesting as a *specification*: in addition to the usual round-tripping laws we expect of state-based lenses, each non-trivial equation in a monoid presentation represents a behavioral limitation on lenses operating on that monoid. Take again the commutativity law:

$$\mathsf{left}(\mathrm{d}x)\ \mathsf{right}(\mathrm{d}y) = \mathsf{right}(\mathrm{d}y)\ \mathsf{left}(\mathrm{d}x)$$

The force of this law is that lenses operating on a monoid including this equation must ignore the interleaving of left and right edits: those two edits are treated independently by the lens.

6.1 Lemma: If k and ℓ are lenses, then the $\Rrightarrow_g$ and $\Lleftarrow_g$ functions defined above for $k \otimes \ell$ respect all of the above equations.

Adding the first four equations lets us create a projection lens out of smaller parts by observing that there are some new isomorphisms available. Let f be the isomorphism between $X \otimes Unit$ and

[5] To make this formal, treat the equations as a relation between words in the free monoid; take the reflexive, symmetric, transitive, congruence closure of this relation; and quotient by the resulting equivalence relation.

X. Similarly, let g be the obvious isomorphism between $Unit \otimes Y$ and Y. We can then define $\pi_1 = (id_X \otimes term_Y); iso_f$ and $\pi_2 = (term_X \otimes id_Y); iso_g$. Thus, π_1 first throws away any information in the right-hand part of a tuple with $term_Y$, then collapses the (now degenerate) tuple with f.

We conjecture that these additional laws introduce enough isomorphisms that the tensor product gives rise to a symmetric monoidal category—that is, that tuples may be reordered and reassociated freely, provided the lens program acting on them is reordered and reassociated accordingly—but we have not explored this possibility fully.

We can perform a similar process for sum edits. We add the following equations:

$$
\begin{aligned}
\mathsf{switch}_{jk}(m)\ \mathsf{switch}_{ij}(m') &= \mathsf{switch}_{ik}(m)\\
\mathsf{switch}_{ij}(m)\ \mathsf{stay}_j(m') &= \mathsf{switch}_{ij}(m)\\
\mathsf{stay}_j(m)\ \mathsf{switch}_{ij}(m') &= \mathsf{switch}_{ij}(mm')\\
\mathsf{stay}_i(m)\ \mathsf{stay}_i(m') &= \mathsf{stay}_i(mm')\\
d\ d' &= \mathsf{fail} \qquad \text{in all other cases}
\end{aligned}
$$

This explains why we did not originally choose to have just two combinators, switch_L and switch_R, which would be interpreted as "switch to the left (respectively, right) side and reinitialize, no matter which side we are currently on." The idea of the above equations is that they allow us to collapse any sequence of edits down into a single one; if we only allowed ourselves switch_L and switch_R forms, this would not be possible. In particular, we need to represent the fact that a stay_L edit followed by a switch_i edit fails when applied to a value tagged with inr.

As with products, we must check that the remaining definitions are well-formed. In particular, it can be shown that, in the module defined above for sums, $\odot_g$ respects the above equations, and that, if k and ℓ are lenses, then $(k \oplus \ell).\Rrightarrow_g$ and $(k \oplus \ell).\Lleftarrow_g$ respect the above equations.

Unfortunately, the *partition* lens as given does *not* respect the above equations. It seems possible to enforce them by also imposing equations on list edits that coalesce adjacent $\mathsf{reorder}$ operations. We leave this to future work.

In a similar vein, we can impose equations on container edits—indeed, we need them, since we would like lists to form a special case of containers so that, possibly after *restructuring*, we can *partition* and reassemble containers, too. These equations would in particular allow us to coalesce adjacent reorderings and to reorder insertions and deletions with other edits so that insertions and deletions always come first. This would also give rise to a compact normal form of container edits. Again, we leave this to future work.

7. From State-Based to Edit Lenses and Back

In [7], we introduced a state-based framework for bidirectional transformations called *symmetric lenses*. We refer to them here as *state-based symmetric lenses*. Recall from [7] that a state-based symmetric lens ℓ between *sets* X and Y comprises a set of complements C, a distinguished element $missing \in C$, and two functions

$$
\begin{aligned}
putr &\in X \times C \to Y \times C\\
putl &\in Y \times C \to X \times C
\end{aligned}
$$

satisfying the following round-tripping laws:

$$\frac{putr(x,c) = (y,c')}{putl(y,c') = (x,c')} \qquad (\text{PUTRL})$$

$$\frac{putl(y,c) = (x,c')}{putr(x,c') = (y,c')} \qquad (\text{PUTLR})$$

Equivalence of state-based symmetric lenses is defined through the existence of a simulating relation between the respective complement sets that relates the *missing* elements and is preserved by *putl*, *putr*. A characterization in terms of "dialogues" is also given. State-based symmetric lenses modulo equivalence form a category (they compose) and support a variety of constructions, in particular tensor product, sum, lists, trees, and container types.

Now, for any set X we have the monoid ∂X whose elements (edits) are lists of elements of X modulo the equality $xx = x$. An action of ∂X on X is defined by $\varepsilon x = x$ and $(xw)y = x$ where $x \in X, w \in X^*$. Note that this is well defined as $x(xy) = x = xy$. If, in addition, we have a distinguished element $x \in X$, we thus obtain a module denoted X_x where $|X_x| = X$ and $init_X = x$ and $\partial X_x = \partial X$.

Let ℓ be a state-based symmetric lens between X and Y along with elements $x \in X$ and $y \in Y$ satisfying $\ell.putr(x, \ell.missing) = (y, \ell.missing)$. We then define a symmetric edit lens $\partial_{xy}\ell$ between the modules X_x and Y_y as follows: (1) $(\partial_{xy}\ell).C = \ell.C$; (2) $(\partial_{xy}\ell).init = \ell.missing$; (3) $(\partial_{xy}\ell).\Rrightarrow(\varepsilon, c) = (\varepsilon, c)$; (4) $(\partial_{xy}\ell).\Rrightarrow(xw, c) = (yv, c'')$ where $(\partial_{xy}\ell).\Rrightarrow(w, c) = (v, c')$ and $\ell.putr(x, c') = (y, c'')$; (5) analogous definitions for $\Lleftarrow$; and (6) $K = \{(x, c, y) \mid \ell.putr(x, c) = (y, c)\}$. $\partial_{xy}\ell$ is a symmetric edit lens and the passage from ℓ to $\partial\ell$ is compatible with the equivalences on symmetric lenses and symmetric edit lenses.

Let X be a module. A *differ* for X is a binary operation $dif \in X \times X \to \partial X$ satisfying $dif(x, x')x = x'$ and $dif(x, x) = \mathbf{1}$. Thus, a differ finds, for given states x, x', an edit operation $\mathrm{d}x$ such that $\mathrm{d}x\ x = x'$ and $\mathrm{d}x$ is "reasonable" at least in the sense that if $x = x'$ then the produced edit is minimal, namely $\mathbf{1}$. For example, the module X_x for set X and $x \in X$ admits the *canonical differ* given by $dif(x, x') = x'$ if $x \neq x'$ and $dif(x, x) = \varepsilon$, otherwise.

Given an edit lens ℓ between modules X and Y, both equipped with differs, we define a symmetric lens $|\ell|$ between $|X|$ and $|Y|$ by (1) $|\ell|.C = |X| \times \ell.C \times |Y|$; (2) $|\ell|.init = (init_X, \ell.init, init_Y)$; (3) $|\ell|.putr(x, (x_0, c, y_0)) = (\mathrm{d}y\ y_0, (x, c', \mathrm{d}y\ y_0))$ where $\mathrm{d}x = dif(x_0, x)$ and $(\mathrm{d}y, c') = \ell.\Rrightarrow(\mathrm{d}x, c)$; and (4) an analogous definition of $|\ell|.putl$ This defines a symmetric lens $|\ell|$ between $|X|$ and $|Y|$, and the passage $\ell \mapsto |\ell|$ is compatible with lens equivalence.

7.1 Theorem: Let X, Y be sets with distinguished elements x and y and equip the associated modules X_x and Y_y with their canonical differs. The constructions $|-|$ and ∂_{xy} then establish a one-to-one correspondence between equivalence classes of edit lenses between X_x and Y_y, on the one hand, and state-based lenses between X and Y, on the other.

We conjecture that this "isomorphism" between state-based and certain edit lenses is also compatible with various lens constructors, in particular tensor product and sum.

8. Related Work

The most closely related attempt at developing a theory of update propagation is [4] by Diskin et al. Their starting point is the observation (also discussed in [2]) that discovery of edits should be decoupled from their propagation. They thus propose a formalism, *sd-lenses*, for the propagation of edits across synchronized data structures, bearing some similarities with our edit lenses. The replicas, which we model as modules, are there modeled as categories (presented as reflexive graphs). Thus, for any two states x, x' there is a set of edits $X(x, x')$. An sd-lens then comprises two reflexive graphs X, Y and for any $x \in X$ and $y \in Y$ a set $C(x, y)$ of "correspondences" which roughly correspond to our complements. Forward and backward operations similar to our $\Lleftarrow$ and $\Rrightarrow$ then complete the picture. No concrete examples are given of sd-lenses, no composition, no notion of equivalence, and no combinators for constructing sd-lenses; the focus of the paper is rather on the discovery of suitable axioms, such as invertibility and undoability of edits, and a generalization of *hippocraticness* in the sense of Stevens [13]. They also develop a comparison with the state-based framework (cf. §7 above). In our opinion, the separation of edits and correspondences according to the states that they apply to or relate has two important disadvantages. First, in our examples, it is often the case that one and the same edit applies to more than one state and can be meaningfully propagated (and more compactly represented) as such. For example, while many of the container edits tend to only work for a particular shape, they are completely polymorphic in the contents of the container. Second, the fact that state sets are already categories suggests that a category of sd-lenses would be 2-categorical in flavor, entailing extra technical difficulties such as coherence conditions.

Meertens's seminal paper on *constraint maintainers* [10] discusses a form of containers for lists equipped with a notion of edits similar to our edit language for lists, but does not develop a general theory of edit-transforming constraint maintainers.

A long series of papers from the group at the University of Tokyo [6, 8, 11, 12, 15, etc.] deal with the alignment issue using an approach that might be characterized as a hybrid of state-based and edit-based. Lenses work with whole states, but these states are internally annotated with tags showing where edits have been applied—e.g., marking inserted or deleted elements of lists. Barbosa et al.'s *matching lenses* [2] offer another approach to dealing with issues of alignment in the framework of pure state-based lenses.

9. Conclusion

A prototype Haskell implementation of edit lenses is underway, as well as a demo showing how to construct GUIs connected by lenses. The main required extension to the theory presented here are extending the above constructions from algebraic data structures to strings, following Boomerang [3], and identifying good heuristics for converting unstructured string edits into structured edits of the form expected by the lenses above—a form of parsing and unparsing.

Containers offer a convenient abstraction on which to build generic lens combinators, as discussed in §5. To use these combinators in practice, we need to show how to instantiate the module of *shapes* for the kind of container we are interested in, as we did for lists. In the future, we would like to explore several other sorts of shapes; in particular, edit languages for graphs may be useful in model-driven development, while edits for relations are relevant to database applications.

Acknowledgments We are grateful to Nate Foster and Perdita Stevens for productive discussions of many points, to the members of the Penn PL Club for comments on an early draft, to the organizers and participants in the January 2011 Dagstuhl seminar on Bidirectional Transformations for creating a stimulating environment for work in this area, and to the POPL reviewers for their thoughtful suggestions. Our work has been supported by the National Science Foundation under grants 0534592, *Linguistic Foundations for XML View Update*, and 1017212, *Algebraic Foundations for Collaborative Data Sharing*.

References

[1] Michael Abbott, Thorsten Altenkirch, and Neil Ghani. Containers: constructing strictly positive types. *Theor. Comput. Sci.*, 342(1):3–27, 2005.

[2] Davi M. J. Barbosa, Julien Cretin, Nate Foster, Michael Greenberg, and Benjamin C. Pierce. Matching lenses: Alignment and view update. In *ACM SIGPLAN International Conference on Functional Programming (ICFP), Baltimore, Maryland*, September 2010.

[3] Aaron Bohannon, J. Nathan Foster, Benjamin C. Pierce, Alexandre Pilkiewicz, and Alan Schmitt. Boomerang: Resourceful lenses for string data. In *ACM SIGPLAN–SIGACT Symposium on Principles of Programming Languages (POPL), San Francisco, California*, January 2008.

[4] Zinovy Diskin, Yingfei Xiong, Krzysztof Czarnecki, Hartmut Ehrig, Frank Hermann, and Fernando Orejas. From state- to delta-based bidirectional model transformations: The symmetric case. Technical Report GSDLAB-TR 2011-05-03, University of Waterloo, May 2011.

[5] J. Nathan Foster, Michael B. Greenwald, Jonathan T. Moore, Benjamin C. Pierce, and Alan Schmitt. Combinators for bi-directional tree transformations: A linguistic approach to the view update problem. *ACM Transactions on Programming Languages and Systems*, 29 (3):17, 2007. ISSN 0164-0925. Extended abstract presented at *Principles of Programming Languages (POPL)*, 2005.

[6] S. Hidaka, Z. Hu, K. Inaba, H. Kato, K. Matsuda, and K. Nakano. Bidirectionalizing graph transformations. In *ACM SIGPLAN International Conference on Functional Programming (ICFP), Baltimore, Maryland*, September 2010.

[7] Martin Hofmann, Benjamin C. Pierce, and Daniel Wagner. Symmetric lenses. In *ACM SIGPLAN–SIGACT Symposium on Principles of Programming Languages (POPL), Austin, Texas*, January 2011.

[8] Zhenjiang Hu, Shin-Cheng Mu, and Masato Takeichi. A programmable editor for developing structured documents based on bidirectional transformations. In *Partial Evaluation and Program Manipulation (PEPM)*, pages 178–189, 2004. Extended version in *Higher Order and Symbolic Computation*, Volume 21, Issue 1-2, June 2008.

[9] David Lutterkort. Augeas: A Linux configuration API, February 2007. Available from `http://augeas.net/`.

[10] Lambert Meertens. Designing constraint maintainers for user interaction, 1998. Manuscript.

[11] Shin-Cheng Mu, Zhenjiang Hu, and Masato Takeichi. An injective language for reversible computation. In *Seventh International Conference on Mathematics of Program Construction (MPC)*, 2004.

[12] Shin-Cheng Mu, Zhenjiang Hu, and Masato Takeichi. An algebraic approach to bi-directional updating. In *ASIAN Symposium on Programming Languages and Systems (APLAS)*, pages 2–20, November 2004.

[13] Perdita Stevens. Bidirectional model transformations in QVT: Semantic issues and open questions. In *International Conference on Model Driven Engineering Languages and Systems (MoDELS), Nashville, TN*, volume 4735 of *Lecture Notes in Computer Science*, pages 1–15. Springer-Verlag, 2007. ISBN 978-3-540-75208-0.

[14] Perdita Stevens. Towards an algebraic theory of bidirectional transformations. In *Graph Transformations: 4th International Conference, Icgt 2008, Leicester, United Kingdom, September 7-13, 2008, Proceedings*, page 1. Springer, 2008.

[15] Yingfei Xiong, Dongxi Liu, Zhenjiang Hu, Haiyan Zhao, Masato Takeichi, and Hong Mei. Towards automatic model synchronization from model transformations. In *IEEE/ACM International Conference on Automated Software Engineering (ASE), Atlanta, GA*, pages 164–173, 2007.

Clarifying and Compiling C/C++ Concurrency: from C++11 to POWER

Mark Batty[1] Kayvan Memarian[1,2] Scott Owens[1] Susmit Sarkar[1] Peter Sewell[1]

[1]University of Cambridge [2]INRIA

{first.last}@cl.cam.ac.uk

Abstract

The upcoming C and C++ revised standards add concurrency to the languages, for the first time, in the form of a subtle *relaxed memory model* (the *C++11 model*). This aims to permit compiler optimisation and to accommodate the differing relaxed-memory behaviours of mainstream multiprocessors, combining simple semantics for most code with high-performance *low-level atomics* for concurrency libraries.

In this paper, we first establish two simpler but provably equivalent models for C++11, one for the full language and another for the subset without consume operations. Subsetting further to the fragment without low-level atomics, we identify a subtlety arising from atomic initialisation and prove that, under an additional condition, the model is equivalent to sequential consistency for race-free programs.

We then prove our main result, the correctness of two proposed compilation schemes for the C++11 load and store concurrency primitives to Power assembly, having noted that an earlier proposal was flawed. (The main ideas apply also to ARM, which has a similar relaxed memory architecture.)

This should inform the ongoing development of production compilers for C++11 and C1x, clarifies what properties of the machine architecture are required, and builds confidence in the C++11 and Power semantics.

Categories and Subject Descriptors C.1.2 [*Multiple Data Stream Architectures (Multiprocessors)*]: Parallel processors; D.1.3 [*Concurrent Programming*]: Parallel programming; F.3.1 [*Specifying and Verifying and Reasoning about Programs*]

General Terms Languages, Reliability, Standardization, Theory, Verification

Keywords Relaxed Memory Models, Semantics

1. Introduction

Most work on semantics and reasoning for shared-memory concurrency has assumed a sequentially consistent (SC) memory [Lam79], in which a single shared memory is acted upon by interleaved threads. In practice, however, mainstream multiprocessors (x86, Sparc, Power, ARM, Itanium) provide weaker and more subtle *relaxed* memory models, to permit various hardware optimisations. Mainstream concurrent programming languages (e.g. Java, C, C++) also provide relaxed memory models, although of rather different kinds, both to permit compiler optimisations and so that they can be compiled to those processors without excessive use of hardware memory barriers. Moreover, for several of those multiprocessors and languages, the actual memory model provided has long been poorly specified and not well understood.

In recent years that situation has improved. Of particular relevance here, the ISO C++ Standards Committee (JTC1/SC22/WG21) has introduced a memory model, as outlined by Boehm and Adve [BA08], into their revised standard (C++11) [Bec11], and it is expected that the upcoming revision of the C standard (informally, C1x) will adopt essentially the same model. This standard is written in prose, subject to the usual problems of ambiguity and not directly testable, but in previous work we produced a formal semantics for C++11 concurrency [BOS+11]. In discussion with members of the WG21 concurrency subgroup, we identified various issues with earlier drafts [BOS+10], proposing solutions that are now incorporated into the new ISO C++11 standard; the result has a close correspondence between the formal semantics and the standard prose.

The C++11 memory model is an axiomatic one: presuming a threadwise operational semantics that defines candidate executions consisting of the sets of memory read and write events for threads in isolation, it defines when such a candidate is *consistent* and whether it has a race of some kind; consistency is defined in terms of a happens-before relation. It is a data-race-free (DRF) model [AH90]: for a program that has no race in any consistent execution, the semantics is the set of all such, while other programs are undefined (and implementations are unconstrained). The design is stratified: there is a sublanguage with sequentially consistent atomic operations which is intended to have simple semantics for common use, then additional release/acquire and relaxed atomic operations (needing less hardware synchronisation to implement) for expert use in high-performance concurrency libraries and system code, and finally release/consume atomics, for maximum performance on architectures such as Power and ARM where dependencies provide useful ordering guarantees. The whole is relatively complex — for example, to accommodate release/consume atomics, it involves a happens-before relation that is, by design, not necessarily transitive.

The first contribution of this paper is to simplify the C++11 model, proving that it is equivalent to a simpler model M_1, without the technical concept of "visible sequences of side effects". Subsetting the language to remove release/consume atomics gives a further simplification, M_2, with a transitive happens-before relation. Subsetting still further, to the fragment without low-level atomics, one would like to know that that model is equivalent to a sequentially consistent model M_3. In Section 4 we show that this holds for

POPL'12, January 25–27, 2012, Philadelphia, PA, USA

programs that are race-free in M_2, but that the M_2 and M_3 notions of race can differ, with an example involving atomic initialisation; we give additional conditions under which the two do coincide.

Meanwhile, on the hardware side, Sarkar et al. [SSA$^+$11] have established a rigorous memory model for Power multiprocessors, based on extensive testing and discussion with IBM staff. Power has a more relaxed and more subtle model than Sparc TSO or x86-TSO, but it and ARM are similar in this respect, and preliminary testing and discussion with ARM staff suggests that the same model, with minor differences, applies there (Itanium is also quite relaxed but rather different). This model is of a very different kind to that for C++11: it deals with the Power dependencies and barriers (`sync`, `lwsync`, `isync`) rather than the C++11 atomic primitives; it gives semantics to all programs, not just race-free programs; and the presence of speculative execution is observable to the programmer on these machines. Accordingly, this model is in an abstract-machine style rather than an axiomatic style: it defines labelled transition systems for a thread semantics (with explicit speculation) and for a storage subsystem (abstracting from the cache hierarchy), with interactions between the two.

Between programming language and processor, how can one compile a programming language with the C++11 memory model to Power or ARM? There are three main parts to this question: one has to consider how each C++11 atomic operation is compiled to assembly code, perhaps with barriers and/or preserved dependencies; when conventional compiler optimisations are legal in this setting; and what new optimisations are needed, e.g. to remove redundant barriers. In the relaxed-memory-concurrency setting, all of these are sufficiently delicate that it is hard to have any confidence in correctness without proof. We focus here on the first.

A naive compilation scheme would be to insert the heavyweight Power `sync` barrier between every C++11 memory access. Even here, it is not at all obvious that this would be a correct implementation (indeed, on Itanium, inserting the `mf` barrier between every access is not sufficient to regain SC), and for a realistic implementation, with good performance, it is essential not to introduce unnecessary synchronisation. McKenney and Silvera have proposed a mapping of the core C++ atomic primitives to Power assembly [MS11]. For the different flavours of (nonatomic and atomic) loads and stores, this is:

C++11 Operation	Power Implementation
Non-atomic Load	`ld`
Load Relaxed	`ld`
Load Consume	`ld` (and preserve dependency)
Load Acquire	`ld; cmp; bc; isync`
Load Seq Cst	`sync; ld; cmp; bc; isync`
Non-atomic Store	`st`
Store Relaxed	`st`
Store Release	`lwsync; st`
Store Seq Cst	`sync; st`

This compiles some C++11 operations to normal Power loads and stores, some with a Power lightweight synchronisation barrier `lwsync` or heavier `sync`, and in some cases uses just a combination of an artificial control dependency (of a compare `cmp` and conditional branch `bc`) and an `isync`.

Our second contribution is to prove the above mapping correct. While the mapping involves only a few assembly instructions, its correctness involves much of the behavioural subtlety of the C++11 and Power relaxed memory models, and is far from obvious. Indeed, the mapping above has been updated in the light of our comments following Sarkar et al. [SSA$^+$11]: an earlier proposal included an optimisation that we observed is not sound w.r.t. the Power architectural intent (we give two counterexamples here). Our proof relies on the simplified general C++11 model M_1 from the first part. Along the way we obtain results about the Power architecture of independent interest, e.g. showing that (and why) inserting a `sync` between all accesses does restore SC. We also prove soundness of an alternative mapping, with the SC atomics implemented as below — the "trailing `sync`" convention, suggested (in the ARM context, with DMB in place of `sync` and `lwsync`) by Boehm [Boe11]:

C++11 Operation	Power Implementation
Load Seq Cst	`ld; sync`
Store Seq Cst	`lwsync; st; sync`

Depending on the relative frequencies of SC loads and store, and on the costs of the different hardware barriers (which may vary significantly from one architecture to another, and also between implementations), this may have better performance. Note that for code produced by different compilers to correctly interoperate, they must all make the same choice of mapping, which should be part of the ABI.

We also show that both these mapping are local optima: weakening any of the clauses (e.g. replacing a `sync` by a `lwsync`) yields an unsound scheme.

In the first contribution we covered the full C++11 primitives as in [BOS$^+$11], but for these correctness results we focus just on the load and store operations in the tables above, omitting dynamic thread creation, C++11 fences, read-modify-writes, and locks. The first two are minor simplifications, but the last two are substantial questions for future work, as their Power implementations involve the load-reserve/write-conditional instructions, for which we do not yet have a well-established relaxed-memory semantics.

To make this paper as self-contained as possible, we give a brief introduction to our source and target starting points, the C++11 [BOS$^+$11] and Power [SSA$^+$11] models, in Sections 2 and 6 respectively. Section 3 describes our simplifications of C++11 and Section 4 the atomic initialisation issue; Section 5 discusses the correctness of the above C++11-to-Power compilation schemes informally, looking at specific examples; and Section 7 discusses our correctness statement and proof that they are correct in general. We discuss related work and conclude in Sections 8 and 9.

We focus throughout on the key ideas, as it is not possible to include full details here (the model definitions alone for C++11 and Power are around 15 and 50 pages of typeset mathematics), but our definitions and proofs are available on-line [BMO$^+$]. Our definitions are expressed in Lem [OBZNS11], a lightweight language of machine-typechecked type, function, and relation definitions, from which one can generate LaTeX, prover definitions in HOL4, Isabelle/HOL, and (in progress) Coq, and executable OCaml code. Our proofs are a combination of machine-checked interactive HOL4 proof and rigorous hand proof (with auxiliary definitions and lemma statements in Lem).

This is a domain in which rigorously proved results are of direct interest to mainstream industrial software development, which typically relies almost entirely on testing for assurance. The nondeterminism of relaxed memory multiprocessors makes effective random testing challenging, and the fact that the programming language and processor architecture specifications are looser than current implementations makes it insufficient even in principle. Compiler groups are now implementing C++11 concurrency, and we are in ongoing discussion with members of the Red Hat GCC and ARM groups on how this should be done correctly, based in part on the work we present here (e.g., one early-draft implementation was found to put the SC store `sync` on the wrong side of the store).

2. Background: C++11 concurrency

This section gives a general introduction to the C++11 concurrency primitives and their semantics. We refer the reader to [BOS$^+$11,

Bec11, BA08] for a full discussion of many subtle points that we cannot cover here.

2.1 The Language: C++11 concurrency primitives

C++11 is a shared-memory-concurrency language with explicit thread creation and implicit sharing: any location might be read or written by any thread for which it is reachable from variables in scope. It is the programmer's responsibility to ensure that such accesses are *race-free*. For example, in the following program the spawned thread, executing `thread_body(&x)`, writes `x` while the `main` thread reads `x`, without any synchronisation between the two. These are *non-atomic* reads and writes, and this constitutes a *data race*; the fact that the program exhibits an execution containing a race makes the program *undefined* according to the standard: an implementation has freedom to behave arbitrarily (in particular, compilers can perform optimisations that are not sound for racy programs, which means that common thread-local optimisations can still be done without the compiler needing to determine which accesses might be shared).

```
#include <thread>
using namespace std;
void thread_body(int* p) {*p = 2;}
int main() {
  int x = 1;
  thread t1(thread_body, &x);
  int r = x;
  t1.join();
  return 0; }
```

The language provides several mechanisms for concurrent programming without races. First, accesses to shared state can be protected using mutex locks of various kinds, e.g. using `m.lock()` and `m.unlock()`. We then have various *sequentially consistent atomic* operations on objects of integral type (bytes, integer types, etc.): atomic loads, stores, and various read-modify-write operations. Atomic operations do not race with each other, by definition, so changing the above to use SC atomic operations for `x` gives a well-defined program, and the allowed behaviours are intended to be those one would naively expect in an SC semantics. The intention is that locks and SC atomics will suffice for most programmers. However, making all racy accesses sequentially consistent is not always required and can incur a significant performance cost, so C++11 also provides several *low-level* atomic operations (with different memory order parameters) for expert use, e.g. in concurrency libraries and other systems code. For message-passing idioms, in which one thread writes some (perhaps multi-word) data `x` and then a flag `y`, while another waits to see that flag write before reading the data, it suffices to make the flag write a *release* and the flag read an *acquire* atomic:

```
int x;
atomic<int> y(0);
-----------------------------------------
// sender thread T0
x=1;
y.store(1,memory_order_release);
-----------------------------------------
// receiver thread T1
while (0==y.load(memory_order_acquire)) {};
int r = x;
```

The synchronisation between the release and acquire ensures that the sender's write of `x` will be seen by the receiver, i.e., that the read of `x` must be from the write `x=1` rather than from some uninitialised value.

On multiprocessors with weak memory orders, notably Power and ARM, release/acquire pairs are cheaper to implement than SC atomics but still significantly more expensive than plain stores and loads (c.f. the preceding `lwsync` for the release and following `cmp; bc; isync` for the acquire in Section 1; we return later to how these act). However, these architectures do guarantee that certain dependencies in an assembly program are respected, and in many cases those suffice on the reader side. This motivates a *release/consume* variant of release/acquire atomics. For example, suppose one thread writes some data (again perhaps multi-word) then writes the address of that data to a shared atomic pointer, while the other thread reads the shared pointer, dereferences it and reads the data.

```
int x;
atomic<int *> p(0);
-----------------------------------------
// sender thread
x=1;
p.store(&x,memory_order_release);
-----------------------------------------
// receiver thread
int* xp = p.load(memory_order_consume);
int  r = *xp;
```

Here the combination of the release/consume pair and the dependency at the receiver from the read of `p` to the read of `x` suffices to ensure the intended behaviour.

Finally, in some cases one needs only very weak guarantees, and here `memory_order_relaxed` atomics can be used. The language also includes explicit fences, in acquire, release, acquire-release, and SC forms, to ease porting of older fence-based code.

2.2 Semantics: the C++11 axiomatic memory model

Traditional shared-memory operational semantics involves an explicit memory, with interleaved transitions by threads reading and writing that memory. That is intrinsically SC, and for a relaxed-memory language such as C++11 a quite different semantic style is needed.

We say a *candidate execution* ex of a C++ program comprises a set of memory actions together with various relations over them. The actions are of the form:

action ::=		
	$a{:}R_{na}\ x{=}v$	non-atomic read
|	$a{:}W_{na}\ x{=}v$	non-atomic write
|	$a{:}R_{mo}\ x{=}v$	atomic read
|	$a{:}W_{mo}\ x{=}v$	atomic write
|	$a{:}RMW_{mo}\ x{=}v1/v2$	atomic read-modify-write
|	$a{:}L\ x$	lock
|	$a{:}U\ x$	unlock
|	$a{:}F_{mo}$	fence

Here a is a unique id (including a thread id), x a location, and v a value. Memory orders mo range over those mentioned earlier, abbreviated thus: SC, RLX, REL, ACQ, CON, and A/R.

The relations include four binary relations determined by a threadwise operational semantics: *sequenced-before* (sb), *additional synchronises with* (asw), *data dependency* (dd), and *control dependency* (cd); together with three that determine an interrelationship between memory actions of different threads: *reads-from* (rf) relates a write to all the reads that read from it; the *sequential consistent order* (sc) is a total order over all SC actions; and *modification order* (mo) is the union of a per-location total order over writes to each atomic location.

Given a candidate execution, the semantics defines various derived relations: *release-sequence*, *hypothetical-release-sequence* (a variant of *release-sequence* used in the fence semantics), *synchronizes-with* (sw), *carries-a-dependency-to* (cad), *dependency-ordered-before* (dob), *inter-thread-happens-before* (ithb), *happens-before* (hb), *visible-side-effect*, and *visible-sequences-of-side-effects*. These are used to define when a candidate execution is *consistent* and whether it contains a *race* of some kind: a *data race*, *unsequenced race*, or *indeterminate read*, which we collect into a predicate *race* ex. A data race is a pair of accesses to the same address, at least one of which is a non-atomic write, which are not happens-before related. The *consistent_reads_from_mapping* check has subclauses as on the right below.

consistent_execution =
  well_formed_threads∧
  consistent_locks∧
  consistent_inter_thread_hb∧
  consistent_sc_order∧
  consistent_modification_order∧
  well_formed_reads_from_mapping∧
  consistent_reads_from_mapping

consistent_reads_from_mapping =
  consistent_non_atomic_read_values∧
  consistent_atomic_read_values∧
  coherent_memory_use ∧
  rmw_atomicity ∧
  sc_reads_restricted ∧
  sc_fences_heeded

For a program *c_prog* for which all its consistent executions are race-free with respect to all three kinds of race (which we write as drf *c_prog*), the semantics is the set of all those consistent executions; other programs are undefined. For example, the release-acquire program excerpted above is race-free, and one of its consistent executions is shown below (suppressing the initialisation write i:W_{na} y=0). To give some flavour of the semantics, we describe why this execution is indeed consistent, referring the reader to [BOS+11] for the detailed definitions. The *well_formed_threads* and *well_formed_reads_from_mapping* predicates are straightforward sanity conditions. For this simple example the inter-thread-happens-before (ithb) and happens-before relation (hb) coincide, and are just the transitive closure of the union of sequenced-before (sb) and the synchronised-with (sw) edge created by the release/acquire pair (b, c). The *consistent_inter_thread_happens_before* predicate checks that this is acyclic. The *consistent_locks* and *consistent_sc_order* checks are vacuous, as there are no lock or SC atomic operations in this example. The modification order (mo) is empty, as there is only one write to the atomic location, so *consistent_modification_order* is vacuous. For *consistent_reads_from_mapping*, the main subclause is *consistent_non_atomic_read_values*, which checks that the non-atomic read of `x` takes the value of a *visible side effect*, which in a race-free program is unique and is the most recent write in happens-before. Then *consistent_atomic_read_values* permits the atomic read of `y` to read from any element of a *visible sequence of side effects*, which is a set of writes of `y`, ordered by modification order, headed by a visible side effect and terminated before any write that happens-after the read. The *coherent_memory_use* does not contribute because the happens-before condition already enforces coherence here. The remaining three (*rmw_atomicity*, *sc_reads_restricted*, *sc_fences_heeded*) are vacuous, as there are no RMW operations or SC atomics.

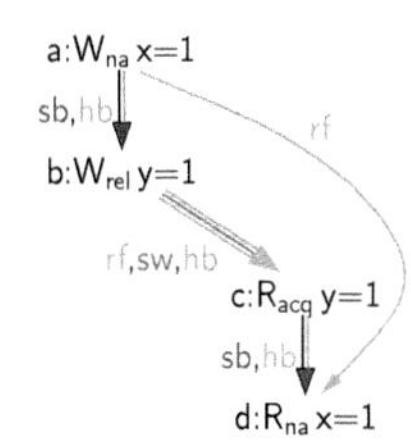

3. Simplifying the C++11 model

In this section, we establish two simplifications of the C++ model of [BOS+11]. The standard tries to give an intuitive definition of which values an atomic read might take using *visible sequences of side effects*. As Batty et al. [BOS+11, BOS+10] note, taken alone they are too weak, and additional coherence axioms (now incorporated into the ISO C++ Standard) are necessary to capture the intended semantics. Given those, we can prove that the concept of *visible sequences of side effects* is unnecessary, permitting a much simpler definition of *consistent_atomic_read_values* in a model M_1:

$consistent\_atomic\_read\_values_1$ =
  $\forall b \in actions.$
  (is_read b ∧ is_at_atomic_location lk b) ⇒
   (if ($\exists a\_vse \in actions.$ $(a\_vse, b) \in vse$)
    then ($\exists a \in actions.$ $((a, b) \in rf) \wedge \neg ((b, a) \in hb)$)
    else $\neg$ ($\exists a \in actions.$ $(a, b) \in rf$))

THEOREM 1. *A C++11 candidate execution is consistent in C++ iff it is consistent in M_1, and the races are identical.* [Proof: the happens-before relations coincide; mechanised in HOL4]

This has already been useful in automatic analysis [BWB+11], as it removes the only use of an existentially quantified set of sets of actions in the semantics.

Our second simplified model, M_2, removes the complications introduced by atomic consume operations (included only for expert programmers on Power and ARM) for the subset of the language without them. The original C++ model and M_1 have a complex, non-transitive definition of happens-before, from the standard:

$$ithb_1 = \text{let } r = sw \cup dob \cup (sw; sb) \text{ in } (r \cup (sb; r))^+$$
$$hb_1 = sb \cup ithb$$

If we subset the language to remove atomic consume operations, we can give an equivalent model M_2 with a much simpler

$$hb_2 = (sb \cup sw)^+$$

THEOREM 2. *A C++11 candidate execution without consume operations is consistent in M_1 iff it is consistent in M_2, and the races are identical.* [Proof: the two hb relations coincide; HOL4]

4. Atomic initialisation and SC semantics

Subsetting further to remove release/acquire and relaxed operations, leaving just nonatomics and SC atomics, one would like to prove a result along the lines of Boehm and Adve [BA08], showing that for such programs the M_2 semantics (and hence M_1 and Standard C++) and an SC-for-DRF-programs semantics are equivalent. Our third simplified model, M_3, has the obvious SC notion of consistent execution, with a total order over all operations, and requiring reads to read the most recent writes in that. For defining data races, it uses the same style of definition as C++11, using a happens-before relation, but calculates that from the total order. To prove the result, we would need to show that a program is race-free in M_2 iff it is race-free in M_3, and, for any race-free program, the sets of consistent executions are the same.

Unfortunately, this is not true in general. Given a program which is race-free in M_2, we can show that it is race-free in M_3 and that it has the same consistent executions in both:

THEOREM 3.
$drf_2\ c\_prog \Rightarrow drf_3 c\_prog \wedge$
  $\forall ex.\ opsem\ c\_prog\ ex \Rightarrow$
   $(consistent\_ex_2\ ex \Longleftrightarrow consistent\_ex_3\ ex)$

(Here we write $opsem\ c\_prog\ ex$ to mean that candidate execution ex is admitted by the threadwise operational semantics $opsem$ for C++11 program c_prog.) This is an easy corollary of the following lemma:

LEMMA 4.

1. $consistent\_ex_2\ ex \Rightarrow consistent\_ex_3\ ex \vee race_2\ ex$
2. $consistent\_ex_3\ ex \Rightarrow consistent\_ex_2\ ex \vee race_3\ ex$
3. $consistent\_ex_3\ ex \wedge opsem\ c\_prog\ ex \Rightarrow consistent\_ex_2\ ex \vee \exists ex'.\ consistent\_ex_2\ ex' \wedge race_2\ ex' \wedge opsem\ c\_prog\ ex'$

[Proof: the first two are straightforward; for the third, we can identify a minimal race in the M_3 total order and transfer that to a consistent execution in M_2.]

However, the other direction fails, as the program below shows. In the SC M_3 semantics, it is race-free, but in M_2 it has a consistent execution that has races. The example relies on the fact that in C++11 there can be non-atomic writes to atomic locations: the initialisation of atomic locations are non-atomic (so that they can be implemented without fences).

```
atomic<int> x(0);
atomic<int> y(0);
if (1==x.load(memory_order_seq_cst))
  atomic_init(&y,1);
if (1==y.load(memory_order_seq_cst))
  atomic_init(&x,1);
```

In the SC M_3 semantics, both loads must read 0 and so neither of the (non-atomic) **atomic_init** writes can take place; the program has no races and so has defined behaviour. But in M_2, there is a consistent execution in which both loads read 1. This execution has races, and so in M_2 the program's behaviour is undefined. (This execution also has dynamic re-initialisation; the program might also be considered undefined in M_2 for that reason.)

This issue can be eliminated by requiring atomics to be initialised when constructed, removing **atomic_init**, and requiring that atomics are accessed via a path through sequenced-before and reads-from corresponding to data-flow from their creation (i.e., not by forging pointers). Under these additional restrictions, we have proved the desired equivalence of M_2 and M_3, and hence that for this fragment C++11 has SC-for-DRF-programs semantics.

THEOREM 5. *A C++11 candidate execution that uses only nonatomic operations, SC-atomic operations, and locks, and that satisfies the conditions above, is consistent in C++11 iff it is consistent in M_3, and the races are identical.*

5. Correctness of the mapping, informally

We now instantiate the first mapping of §1 for some key examples, giving an introduction to the behaviour that Power does and does not guarantee for them, and hence explaining informally why the mapping is correct in these specific cases. We also show that both mappings are locally optimal.

In C++11, synchronisation effects are associated to atomic loads and stores with particular memory order parameters, but Power assembly language has just plain loads and stores; it provides the **sync**, **lwsync**, and **isync** instructions, together with certain dependencies, to constrain the otherwise highly relaxed memory model. We introduce these constraints and the model by example here, the key properties we depend on are summarised in §6. Applying the §1 mapping to the C++11 release-acquire example of §2.1 gives a Power assembly program as follows:

y=0			
T0		T1	
r1=1; r2=&x; r3=&y		r2=&x; r3=&y	
a: stw r1,0(r2)	write x=1	loop:	
b: lwsync	from write-rel	d: lwz r4,0(r3)	read y
c: stw r1,0(r3)	write y=1	e: cmpwi r4,0	
		f: beq loop	
		g: isync	from read-acq
		h: lwz r5,0(r2)	read x

Here **stw** is a store, **lwz** a load, **cmpwi** a compare-immediate, and **beq** a conditional branch. This is essentially the same as the MP+lwsync+ctrlisync example of [SSA$^+$11]: it has an **lwsync** between the two Thread 0 writes and an **isync** before the second Thread 1 read that follows a conditional branch that is data-dependent (via the compare) on the first Thread 1 read; we call the latter a *control-isync* relationship.

For this to be a correct implementation, that Power synchronisation must be strong enough to exclude any outcomes that the C++11 semantics forbids. In particular, it must prevent the Thread 1 read of x from reading the initial state instead of from the Thread 0 write of x=1. The **lwsync** and control-isync are both necessary and sufficient. The **lwsync** keeps the two Thread 0 writes in order as observed by any other thread (otherwise, as they are to different locations, they might be re-ordered in the storage hierarchy, or even committed out-of-order). Replacing the **lwsync** by an **isync** would still permit the former reordering, as is observable on Power 6 and 7 processors (MP+isync+ctrlisync), and just by typing it cannot be replaced by a control-isync, as one cannot have a dependency from a write. Meanwhile, the control-isync relationship ensures that the read of x cannot be satisfied until the **isync** is committed, which requires the program-order-previous branch to be committed, which requires the read of y=1 to be committed.

Without the **isync**, the Power architecture permits a processor to speculatively satisfy the read of x out-of-order, before satisfying the program-order-previous read(s) of y, despite the intervening conditional branch. It can thereby read from the initial state, and this is observable in practice, for a litmus test MP+lwsync+ctrl. (That test is also C++11-expressible: it is essentially the result of applying the mapping to the release-acquire example with the read-acquire replaced by a read-relaxed.) The **isync** alone, without the control dependency from the preceding read to a conditional branch, also would not suffice: in this case the **isync** could be committed first, enabling read h to be satisfied and committed before anything else occurs. We have not observed this outcome in practice on current Power 6 or Power 7 processors (for test MP+lwsync+isync), but it is architecturally permitted. For the analogous ARM test MP+dmb+isb, the outcome is observable.

Now consider the release-consume example of §2.1, mapped to:

p=0			
T0		T1	
r1=1; r2=&x; r3=&p		r3=&p	
a: stw r1,0(r2)	write x=1	d: lwz r4,0(r3)	read p
b: lwsync	from write-rel	e: lwz r5,0(r4)	read *xp
c: stw r2,0(r3)	write p=&x		

The writing side has an **lwsync** as before, but now the reading side has no control-isync. It is correct nonetheless, because the Power architecture respects *address dependencies* between loads: here the read e reads from an address in register **r4** which takes its value from the program-order-previous read d. In such a case the reads must be satisfied (and indeed also committed) in program order.

The above examples involve only two threads, which turns out to be a very special case. With three or more threads, one can observe that on Power a write does not necessarily become visible to the other threads atomically, and indeed can be propagated to them in different orders, or even never propagated to some threads. Any transitive reasoning across multiple threads relies on the *cumulativity* of the Power **sync** and **lwsync** barriers. Consider a three-thread version of the release-acquire example, with release-acquire synchronisation between the first pair of threads and between the second pair:

```
    int x;  atomic<int> y(0);  atomic<int> z(0);
T0  x=1;
    y.store(1,memory_order_release);
T1  while (0==y.load(memory_order_acquire)) {};
    z.store(1,memory_order_release);
T2  while (0==z.load(memory_order_acquire)) {};
    r = x;
```

The mapping introduces control-isyncs (from the load-acquires) and **lwsyncs** (from the store-releases) as in the candidate Power execution illustrated below:

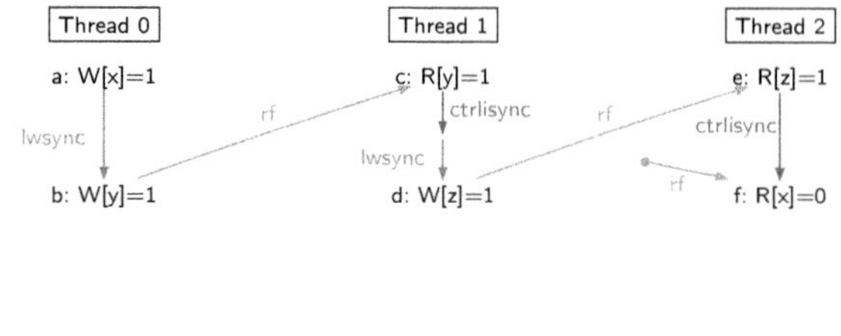

Here the effect of the Thread 1 control-isync is subsumed by the following `lwsync` (eliminating the former is likely to be an important compiler optimisation). That leaves the Thread 2 control-isync, which acts just as in the first release-acquire example, and the two `lwsyncs`. To rule out the C++11-forbidden execution shown, we need to know that the writes a and d, by different threads and to different locations, are propagated to Thread 2 in that order. By the thread-local property of `lwsync` used above, the Thread 1 `lwsync` ensures that a and b are propagated to Thread 1 in that order, so a must have been propagated to Thread 1 before c reads from b and hence before the Thread 1 `lwsync` is committed. This means that a is in the *Group A* of that `lwsync`, the set of writes that have been propagated to its thread already. In turn, the cumulativity of Power `lwsyncs` means that a must be propagated to any other thread, e.g. Thread 2, before the `lwsync` is, and hence before write d is.

Now consider the classic four-thread IRIW example (Independent Reads of Independent Writes). Here Threads 0 and 2 write to two different locations; the question is whether Threads 1 and 3 can see those writes in opposite orders, one reading `x=1` then `y=0` while the other reads `y=1` then `x=0`.

```
atomic<int> x(0);  atomic<int> y(0);
T0  x.store(1,memory_order_release);
T1  r1=x.load(memory_order_acquire);
    r2=y.load(memory_order_acquire);
T2  y.store(1,memory_order_release);
T3  r3=y.load(memory_order_acquire);
    r4=x.load(memory_order_acquire);
```

With release-acquire atomics, this is permitted in C++11 (this is clearly not a sequentially consistent outcome, and so release-acquire atomics do *not* guarantee SC), and indeed applying the mapping gives essentially the Power test IRIW+lwsyncs, which is architecturally permitted and observable in practice.

With SC atomics, on the other hand, this non-SC outcome is forbidden in C++11. To forbid it in the implementation requires a Power `sync` between both pairs of SC-atomic reads, not just an `lwsync`. The `sync` is stronger in that its Group A writes (or some coherence-successors thereof), including any program-order-previous writes, must be propagated to all threads before the `sync` completes and subsequent memory access instructions can begin.

A `sync` is also needed between the other three combinations of an SC atomic read or write, as shown by our SB+lwsyncs and R01 examples [SSA+11] for write-to-read and write-to-write, and by the WRW+WR+lwsync+sync example below for the read-to-write case, all of which are architecturally permitted. SB+lwsyncs is also observable on current implementations, whereas we have not observed the last two. Both of the latter can be explained by the fact that a Power coherence edge does not add writes into the Group A of a subsequent barrier (WRW+WR is similar to R01 but with the initial write pulled back along an rf edge). They are counterexamples to the correctness of a previous version of the mapping, which proposed an `lwsync` in place of the `sync` for SC stores in normal cacheable memory.

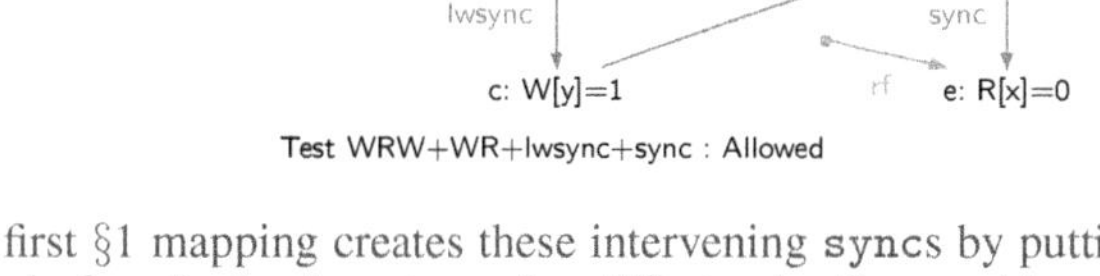

Test WRW+WR+lwsync+sync : Allowed

The first §1 mapping creates these intervening `syncs` by putting a `sync` before the load or store of an SC atomic. One could equally well put them after, as in the second mapping, though in C++11 SC atomics also have release/acquire semantics, so one then also needs a preceding `lwsync` for the SC atomic store (in the first mapping, the preceding `sync` does duty for both purposes).

Using the above examples, and some others, we can show:

THEOREM 6. *Both the §1 mappings are pointwise locally optimal.*

PROOF For each possible weakening there is a C++11 example with some forbidden behaviour which would map onto a Power program for which that behaviour is allowed, as checked by our `cppmem` [BOS+11] and `ppcmem` [SSA+11] tools using automatically generated executable versions of the models. All these examples are collected in the supplementary material [BMO+].

- The load-consume dependency cannot be removed (C++ message-passing with release/consume $\mapsto$ Power MP+lwsync+po).
- The load-acquire control-isync cannot be weakened to just a control dependency (MP+release/acquire $\mapsto$ MP+lwsync+ctrl), or to just an isync ($\mapsto$ MP+lwsync+isync).
- The load-seq-cst sync, whether before or after the load, cannot be weakened to an lwsync (IRIW+seq-csts $\mapsto$ IRIW+lwsyncs), or to an isync ($\mapsto$ IRIW+ctrlisyncs).
- The load-seq-cst control-isync in the original mapping cannot be weakened to just control (MP+seq-csts $\mapsto$ MP+sync+ctrl), or to just isync ($\mapsto$ MP+sync+isync).
- The store-release lwsync cannot be weakened to isync (MP+release/acquire $\mapsto$ MP+isync+ctrlisync).
- The store-seq-cst sync, whether before or after the store, cannot be weakened to lwsync (R01+seq-csts $\mapsto$ R01), or to an isync ($\mapsto$ R+isync+sync).

□

6. Background: the Power memory model

In preparation for the correctness proof in the next section, we recall the overall structure of the Power memory model [SSA+11], sketching how the concepts we used informally in §5, e.g. of a write being "propagated to" a thread, reflect the actual semantics.

As we saw there, the fact that reads can be satisfied speculatively, even program-order-after a conditional branch, is observable. This pushes us towards an operational abstract-machine semantics, expressed as a parallel composition of a thread model and a storage subsystem.

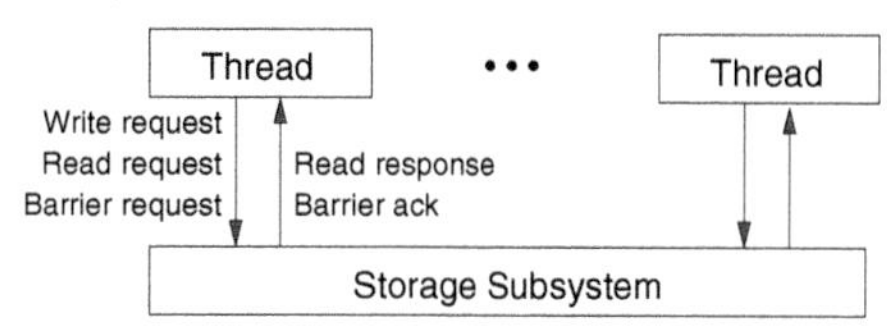

At any one time, a thread may have many in-flight (uncommitted) instructions; reads can be satisfied and instructions committed out-of-order, subject to constraints from barriers and dependencies, and uncommitted instructions are subject to restart or abort. The storage subsystem abstracts from the cache and store buffering hierarchy (and does not involve speculation). It does not have an explicit memory, but instead maintains the global accumulated constraints on the coherence order between writes to the same address that have been built up, together with a list for each thread of the writes and barriers that have been propagated to that thread.

The thread and storage subsystem models are each labelled transition systems (LTSs) synchronising on labels as in the diagram above; their composition gives another LTS with labels:

label ::=
| FETCH *tid ii*
| COMMIT_WRITE_INSTRUCTION *tid ii w*

| COMMIT_BARRIER_INSTRUCTION *tid ii barrier*
| COMMIT_READ_INSTRUCTION *tid ii rr*
| COMMIT_REG_OR_BRANCH_INSTRUCTION *tid ii*
| WRITE_PROPAGATE_TO_THREAD *w tid*
| BARRIER_PROPAGATE_TO_THREAD *barrier tid*
| SATISFY_READ_FROM_STORAGE_SUBSYSTEM *tid ii w*
| SATISFY_READ_BY_WRITE_FORWARDING *tid* ii_1 *w* ii_2
| ACKNOWLEDGE_SYNC *barrier*
| PARTIAL_COHERENCE_COMMIT w_1 w_2
| REGISTER_READ_PREV *tid* ii_1 *reg* ii_2
| REGISTER_READ_INITIAL *tid ii reg*
| PARTIAL_EVALUATE *tid ii*

Here *tid* ranges over thread ids, *ii* over instruction instances, *w* over write events, *rr* over read-response events, *barrier* over `sync` or `lwsync` events, and *reg* over Power register names.

A Power execution t is simply a trace of abstract-machine states and these labels; we write machine_executions *power_prog* for the set of all such for a Power program *power_prog* (Power programs, of type POWER_PROGRAM, are essentially maps from addresses to assembly instructions, together with the initial register state, including PC, for each thread.)

Key properties required for the proofs of §7 are derived from the preconditions and postconditions of the transitions. As an example, before a barrier (`sync` or `lwsync`) is propagated to a new thread by the BARRIER_PROPAGATE_TO_THREAD transition, any writes propagated before it to its original thread (the "Group A" writes) must first be propagated to that thread (by a WRITE_PROPAGATE_TO_THREAD transition). For a `sync`, the corresponding ACKNOWLEDGE_SYNC transition cannot fire until that `sync` is propagated to all threads (and this implies that all its Group A writes, or coherence successors thereof, must have been propagated to all threads before that in the trace). The combination of a conditional branch and an `isync` instruction ("ctrlisync") stops program-order-later reads being able to do their SATISFY_READ transitions before the branch is resolved and committed.

To isolate particular events of interest, we let the following metavariables range over transition labels from a trace as follows:

Metavariable	Transition labels ranged over
wc	COMMIT_WRITE_INSTRUCTION
rc	COMMIT_READ_INSTRUCTION
bc	COMMIT_BARRIER_INSTRUCTION
mc (memory)	COMMIT_WRITE_INSTRUCTION ∪ COMMIT_READ_INSTRUCTION
xc	COMMIT_WRITE_INSTRUCTION ∪ COMMIT_BARRIER_INSTRUCTION

7. Correct compilation from C++11 to Power

We now prove that the mappings of Section 1 are correct in general, focusing on the first mapping and then discussing the changes required for the second.

7.1 Correctness Statement

The usual form of whole-program correctness statement one might expect for a compiler is an inclusion between the observable behaviours of the compiled program and those of the source:

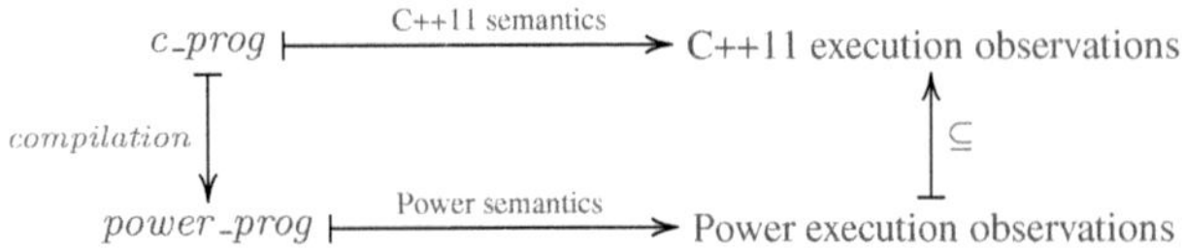

Here, however, we are proving correctness of compilation schemes for particular constructs (the C++11 atomic and nonatomic loads and stores), not correctness of a specific compiler. We therefore want to factor out as much as possible of the definition of the source language and of the rest of the compiler, both to remove extraneous complexity that is irrelevant to the relaxed-memory behaviour and to let us state a general result that should be re-usable in multiple later compiler correctness proofs. We do so by axiomatising the required threadwise properties of a C++11 operational semantics and a good compiler.

For the source language, we take a C++11 program, of type C_PROGRAM, to be a parallel composition of single-threaded programs from an abstract type C_PROGRAM_THREAD, with an arbitrary threadwise operational semantics for them that satisfies certain rather mild axioms. An operational semantics opsem is a relation between C_PROGRAMs and sets of C++11 actions $actions_c$ equipped with the three relevant operational-semantics relations of §2.2: sequenced-before sb_c, data-dependency dd_c, and control-dependency cd_c, packaged into a record op_c (additional-synchronises-with is empty in the absence of dynamic thread creation). Recall that this threadwise operational semantics should leave the values of memory reads unconstrained, as that is handled by the C++11 axiomatic memory model of §2.2. We return below to the axioms we need.

We take a strong intensional notion of observation: given a Power machine trace t we build read and write events $events_t$ from the COMMIT_READ_INSTRUCTION and COMMIT_WRITE_INSTRUCTION commit labels, together with a reads-from relation rf_t. The observation predicate obs_eq t $actions_c$ rf_c requires that there is an exact correspondence between these $events_t$ and the $actions_c$ of a C++11 execution, with isomorphic reads-from relations rf_t and rf_c.

Given a Power trace t, it is also straightforward to construct analogues of the threadwise C++11 relations over the constructed events, for program order po_t, data/address dependency dd_t, and control dependency cd_t; by analysing the trace, we can also identify the events from the same thread that are separated by control-isync, sync, or lwsync instructions in the trace, constructing relations $ctrlisync_t$, $sync_t$, and $lwsync_t$.

A compiler *comp* is a function from C_PROGRAM to POWER_PROGRAM; it satisfies threadwise_good_compiler if for any C++11 program *c_prog* and any Power trace of *comp c_prog*, there is a set of C++11 $actions_c$ with associated sb_c, dd_c, cd_c, and rf_c relations such that

1. the C++11 data has the same observations as the trace: obs_eq t $actions_c$ rf_c;
2. the C++11 data is allowed by the threadwise operational-semantics: opsem *c_prog* $actions_c$ op_c;
3. the C++11 relations sb_c, dd_c, and cd_c are subsets of the corresponding relations po_t, dd_t, and cd_t built from the trace (note that the C++11 sequenced-before relation may not be total within a thread, as evaluation order is sometimes unconstrained, but the Power program order is total within a thread); and
4. if one applies the mapping to the C++11 actions $actions_c$, the result is included in the $ctrlisync_t$, $sync_t$, and $lwsync_t$ relations constructed from the Power trace.

For example, a C++11 action a:W_{REL} x=1 can be presumed to arise from a source program instruction `x.store(e,memory_order_release)`, and so a threadwise good compiler following the mapping should have compiled it into a Power `lwsync` preceding a store, and any trace should contain a corresponding COMMIT_BARRIER_INSTRUCTION label followed (perhaps not immediately) by a COMMIT_WRITE_INSTRUCTION.

Finally, we express correctness on a per-execution basis and can assume that the source program is race-free, otherwise C++11 regards it as undefined and compilation is unconstrained. That leads us to the following statement of our main theorem:

THEOREM 7 (Correctness).

$\forall comp\ c\_prog.$
threadwise_good_compiler $comp \wedge$
drf c_prog
$\Rightarrow$
(let $power\_prog = comp\ c\_prog$ in
($\forall t \in$machine_executions $power\_prog$.
($\exists actions_c\ op_c\ rf_c\ mo_c\ sc_c$.
obs_eq $t\ actions_c\ rf_c \wedge$
opsem $c\_prog\ actions_c\ op_c \wedge$
consistent_ex $actions_c\ op_c\ rf_c\ mo_c\ sc_c$)))

Our proof follows this structure. Consider a Power trace t of a Power program $power\_prog$ produced by a threadwise-good compiler from a C++ program c_prog. The threadwise_good_compiler assumption tells us that there are some corresponding (up to obs_eq) C++11 $actions_c$, op_c, and rf_c for which the memory actions of each thread satisfy the threadwise operational semantics. We now construct a C++11 modification order mo_c and sequential consistent order sc_c, and then have to either prove that the C++11 execution comprising all this data is consistent, or to construct another consistent execution which contains a race, thereby contradicting the drf assumption.

The construction of a C++11 modification order mo_c is straightforward, as (like sb_c, dd_c, cd_c, and rf_c) there is a direct analogue in the Power trace: the coherence constraints in the storage subsystem state increase monotonically along a trace, so we can just take their union co_t, choose an arbitrary per-location linearisation thereof, and restrict to the atomic locations. Construction of a C++11 SC order sc_c is more involved, as we see below in §7.3.

Note that, in contrast to many compiler correctness proofs, this is not a simulation argument: the C++11 definition of consistent execution is a predicate on complete candidate executions; it is not generated by an operational semantics and does not involve any notions of a C++11 whole-program state or transition.

7.2 Analysis of a Power trace w.r.t. C++11 inter-thead-happens-before

The C++11 definition of consistent execution comprises seven conditions, as listed in §2.2, almost all of which rely heavily on the *happens-before* relation, which is the union of sequenced-before and a complex *inter-thread-happens-before* relation.

To establish those conditions, we need to analyse the Power trace with the shape of the *inter-thread-happens-before* relation in mind, making use of various ordering properties of the Power semantics and the fact that the Power program is obtained using the given mapping.

In broad terms, if there is a C++11 inter-thread-happens-before relation from a write to a read, we need to show that the write has propagated to the reading thread before the read is satisfied. For read-to-read pairs, we need to show that any write propagated to the thread of the first read, before it is satisfied, has propagated similarly. For write-to-write and read-to-write pairs, we need to ensure propagation before the commit of the final write.

In more detail, we must also allow coherence successors of writes to be propagated in their place, must consider propagation of barriers, must refer to the last satisfy label of any read that reads from a different thread, and must split the different-thread/same-thread cases. To capture all this, we define a *propBefore* relation over memory and barrier commit labels. For labels from different threads, we say:

- $bc \xrightarrow{propBefore} rc$ iff the barrier has propagated to the reading thread before the read is finally satisfied, i.e., if there is a BARRIER_PROPAGATE label for bc trace-order-before the last SATISFY_READ for rc;
- $wc \xrightarrow{propBefore} rc$ iff the write, or some coherence-successor write, has propagated to the reading thread before the read is finally satisfied; and
- $wc_1 \xrightarrow{propBefore} wc_2$ iff the write of wc_1, or some coherence-successor write, has propagated to the thread of wc_2 before the wc_2 commit.

For labels from the same thread, we say:

- $xc \xrightarrow{propBefore} rc$ iff xc is either a write commit label and is read by rc or it is trace-order-before rc is finally satisfied; and
- $xc \xrightarrow{propBefore} wc$ iff xc is trace-order-before wc.

Consider now the C++11 definition of happens-before (hb). Without relaxed or consume operations, it only crosses threads with a reads-from edge of a release/acquire pair that synchronise with each other. Under the mapping, this rf_t edge must be preceded by $sync_t$ or $lwsync_t$ and followed by a $ctrlisync_t$. With relaxed atomics, the acquire might read from something in the release sequence of the release it synchronises with. In Power terms, a release sequence is a series of same-thread co_t edges (if we covered read-modify-write operations, these would not necessarily be on the same thread). Adding consume atomics, release/consume synchronisation involves the dependency-ordered-before (dob) relation, which is similar to ithb except that on the right hand side it only reaches to dependent operations, not to all program-order successors of the read. In Power terms, in this case the $ctrlisync_t$ is replaced by $dd_t{}^*$. All this motivates the definition of a machine analogue of ithb, $machine\text{-}ithb_t$:

$$\left((sync_t \cup lwsync_t)^{\text{refl}};\ coi_t{}^*;\ rfe_t;\ (ctrlisync_t \cup dd_t{}^*)^{\text{refl}}\right)^+$$

where coi_t is the machine coherence order restricted to pairs of writes by the same thread, and rfe_t is the machine reads-from relation restricted to write/read pairs on distinct threads.

LEMMA 8. *Given two C++11 memory actions m_1 and m_2 and the corresponding Power commit events mc_1 and mc_2, if $m_1 \xrightarrow{ithb_c} m_2$ then $mc_1 \xrightarrow{machine\text{-}ithb_t} mc_2$.*

PROOF By a series of lemmas about the C++11 auxiliary relations, unfolding the definitions, with reasoning as above. □

To prove the required propagation property (Corollary 10 below), we first consider the left part of this relation:

LEMMA 9 (Propagation).

1. *If $wc \xrightarrow{((sync_t \cup lwsync_t)^{refl};coi_t{}^*;rfe_t)^+} rc$, then $wc \xrightarrow{propBefore} rc$.*
2. *If $rc_1 \xrightarrow{((sync_t \cup lwsync_t)^{refl};coi_t{}^*;rfe_t)^+} rc_2$, then for any write commit $wc \xrightarrow{propBefore} rc_1$, we have $wc \xrightarrow{propBefore} rc_2$.*

PROOF By induction on the transitive closure of the relation. In the base case, by decomposing the large relation, two intermediate write commit events appear (wc_1 and wc_2). In the case where $mc \xrightarrow{sync_t \cup lwsync_t} wc_1$, if mc is a write, then it falls into the Group A of the intervening barrier; if it is a read, then any write propagated to its thread before it is satisfied falls into the Group A of the barrier. The $coi_t{}^*$ relation is a subset of po_t, hence we also have $mc \xrightarrow{sync_t \cup lwsync_t} wc_2$. Hence, using the A-cumulativity property of the Power machine and since we know that wc_2 does propagate to the thread of rc before rc is last satisfied (because it is read from), the writes in the Group A of the barrier (or some coherence successors) must have previously been propagated to that thread. This establishes the desired $\xrightarrow{propBefore}$ relationship. In the other case, $mc = wc_1$, we just saw that wc_2 does propagate to the thread of rc in time and it is here a coherence-successor of mc. For the inductive case we use the same reasoning as for the first step to establish that the writes under consideration are first propagated to the thread of the intermediate read, and then the induction hypothesis. □

COROLLARY 10 (Propagation w.r.t. ithb).

1. *If* $rc \xrightarrow{machine\text{-}ithb_t} mc$ *then for any write commit* wc *with* $wc \xrightarrow{propBefore} rc$, *we have* $wc \xrightarrow{propBefore} mc$.
2. *If* $wc \xrightarrow{machine\text{-}ithb_t} mc$ *then* $wc \xrightarrow{propBefore} mc$.

PROOF $ctrlisync_t$ and dd_t are subsets of po so, without loss of generality, we can neglect all those edges except the last one:

$$wc \xrightarrow{((sync_t \cup lwsync_t)^{\text{refl}};coi_t{}^*;rfe_t)^+} rc \xrightarrow{(ctrlisync_t \cup dd_t{}^*)} mc$$

Lemma 9 establishes propagation to the thread of rc, then, using either the $ctrlisync_t$ or dd_t, if mc is a read then it is satisfied after rc is committed, and if mc is a write then it is committed after rc is committed. □

Several of the C++11 conditions are acyclicity properties (either explicitly so, e.g. the consistency of ithb, or requiring consistency between relations, e.g. rf_c and hb_c). To establish these, it is convenient to reduce them to the acyclicity of trace order, by the following lemma.

LEMMA 11 (Trace order respects $machine\text{-}ithb_t$).
If $mc_1 \xrightarrow{machine\text{-}ithb_t} mc_2$ *then* mc_1 *is before* mc_2 *in the trace.*

PROOF Along the same lines as the reasoning above, by induction on the transitive closure of $machine\text{-}ithb_t$. □

7.3 Analysis of a Power trace to construct a C++11 SC order

C++11 demands a single total order sc over all the SC atomic actions, subject to some consistency conditions. Broadly, this order must be consistent with the sequenced-before relation, with modification order, and for each SC read rc, if it reads from a SC write wc, then wc must be the last SC write to that location before rc in the SC order, while if it reads from a non-SC write wc', then wc' cannot be after (in happens-before) any SC write to the same location which is itself after rc in the SC order.

In Power terms, the first two conditions are straightforward to express: we need to construct a total order on SC actions which includes the subparts of po_t and co_t (po_t^{sc} and co_t^{sc} respectively) that are restricted to SC actions. However, there is no obvious corresponding total order visible in the trace. In particular, recall from §6 that for write commit labels trace order is not necessarily consistent with the coherence order co_t. It is also not sufficient to use an arbitrary linearisation of $(po_t^{sc} \cup co_t^{sc})^*$ (though po_t and co_t are individually acyclic), since that may introduce bad intervening writes to the same location in between a pair of a write and a read that reads-from it. Consider then an SC read rc, and the write wc (not necessarily SC) that it reads-from, and recall that we have a coherence order co_t for writes to that location. We define two new derived relations on SC reads and writes: from-reads (fr_t^{sc}) defined as $rc \xrightarrow{fr_t^{sc}} wc_1$ if $wc \xrightarrow{co_t} wc_1$, i.e. rc reads-from a coherence predecessor of the SC wc_1; and extended-reads-from (erf_t^{sc}) defined as $wc_1 \xrightarrow{erf_t^{sc}} rc$ if wc_1 is the last SC write in coherence order equal to or before the wc that rf_t reads from. From-reads relations have been used by various researchers [ABJ+93, AMSS10, Alg10], and the latter reference proves that if the union of program-order, coherence, reads-from, and from-reads is acyclic, then the execution is an SC execution by the traditional definition [Lam79] of a single global order over all events. We use this characterisation in Theorem 13 below.

We will use as the SC order an arbitrary linearisation of $(po_t^{sc} \cup co_t^{sc} \cup fr_t^{sc} \cup erf_t^{sc})^*$. We now show that this combination of relations is acyclic, and hence can be consistently extended to a total order. First note that if the above relation has a cycle, there must be at least one $mc_1 \xrightarrow{po_t^{sc}} mc_2$ edge in the cycle, as otherwise it is straightforward to deduce that the coherence relation implied by the machine trace is itself cyclic. Under the mapping, this means that mc_1 and mc_2 must be separated in the trace by a sync and its ACKNOWLEDGE_SYNC transition. Our main lemma for this (Lemma 12 below) says that for any mc with $mc \xrightarrow{(po_t^{sc} \cup co_t^{sc} \cup fr_t^{sc} \cup erf_t^{sc})^*} mc_1$, it must be in trace-order before that ACKNOWLEDGE_SYNC transition (call this the S transition), and this contradicts mc_2 being after that transition.

We will prove Lemma 12 by induction on the length of the relation, case analysing the relation in the first step. We have to strengthen the inductive hypothesis in two ways to make the proof go through. For example, consider the case where the first step is a $rc \xrightarrow{fr_t^{sc}} wc$ edge. We know inductively that wc is before S in the trace, but this does not immediately help us know that the read rc is also before S. What we need is the strong property of the sync (recall §6), that before the acknowledgement for a sync in the trace, preceding writes are not merely committed but also they (or some coherence successors) are propagated to all threads. This suffices, since if wc is propagated to the reading thread, and it is not read-from, the read must already have been done.

For the second strengthening, consider the case where the first step is a $wc \xrightarrow{rf_t} rc$ edge (one kind of an erf_t^{sc} edge is a rf_t edge). As above, we will have to inductively establish that the write wc have been propagated to all threads before the sync acknowledgement S. The Power machine guarantees this for any sync on the same thread as rc, but not necessarily for syncs on other threads. To make the induction work, we will find a new intermediate sync acknowledgement S_n, which is on the same thread as an event related to rc in the po_t^{sc}-free part of the relation. Since this involves only co_t^{sc}, fr_t^{sc} and erf_t^{sc} edges, these will be on the same location, and wc will then be correctly related by coherence to a write that is known to be propagated everywhere before S_n in the trace.

The final statement is then:

LEMMA 12 (Main Lemma for SC). *Suppose* $mc_1 \xrightarrow{po_t} mc_2$, *and there is a sync ack* S *between* mc_1 *and* mc_2 *in the trace. Suppose* $mc_n \xrightarrow{(po_t^{sc} \cup co_t^{sc} \cup fr_t^{sc} \cup erf_t^{sc})^*} mc_1$. *Then there is an* mc'_n *and a sync ack* S_n *such that:*

1. mc_n *is before* S_n *in the trace, and* S_n *is before or equal to* S *in the trace;*
2. *If* mc_n *is a write, then that write or a coherence successor has propagated to all threads before* S_n *in the trace;*
3. mc'_n *is before* S_n *in the trace;*
4. mc'_n *and* S_n *are from the same thread; and*
5. $mc_n \xrightarrow{(co_t^{sc} \cup fr_t^{sc} \cup erf_t^{sc})^*} mc'_n$ *(the subpart of the relation between* mc_n *and* mc'_n *is* po_t*-free).*

PROOF By induction on the length of the chain $mc_n \xrightarrow{(po_t^{sc} \cup co_t^{sc} \cup fr_t^{sc} \cup erf_t^{sc})^*} mc_1$. In the base case, $mc_n = mc_1$, and the required conditions are easily established by taking $mc'_n = mc_n$ and $S_n = S$.

In the inductive case, we case analyse on the kind of relation in the first step. For co_t^{sc}, fr_t^{sc} and erf_t^{sc}, we use the same intermediate event and sync acknowledgement as the inductive hypothesis, making $mc'_n = mc'_{n-1}$ and $S_n = S_{n-1}$. Then, for example, if the edge is $wc_1 \xrightarrow{co_t^{sc}} wc_2$, we have inductively that wc_2 is propagated to all threads as required before S_n, and thus a coherence successor of wc_1 is as well. We outlined the $rc \xrightarrow{fr_t^{sc}} wc$ and $wc \xrightarrow{erf_t^{sc}} rc$ cases in the description above.

In the remaining case, $mc_n \xrightarrow{po_t^{sc}} mc_{n-1}$, we have two SC events separated in program order. By the mapping, there must be a sync between them in program order. Let S_n be the acknowledgement transition for that sync, and $mc'_n = mc_n$. Then the required conditions are easy to check. □

Notice in the proof that we use the sync program-order between any two SC actions from the same thread. This is crucial for the induction to go through. Indeed, as shown in §5, for any pair of SC actions, if we weaken the sync to anything else (lwsync or weaker), we have a counterexample to show a program with only SC actions behaving in a non-sequentially consistent manner.

The proof is applicable in a wider setting than just for C++11. The key fact we used to create the SC order is that every pair of SC actions on the same thread is separated (in program order) by a sync. Looking at the proof for the case that every memory access is a SC atomic action (*i.e.* no other memory types, or non-atomic accesses) shows that such a program has only sequentially consistent behaviour, an interesting fact in its own right about Power assembly programs.

THEOREM 13 (Syncs between every pair of accesses restore SC). *Suppose we have a Power (assembly) program with every pair of memory accesses on the same thread separated in program order by a sync. Then the program has only sequential consistent behaviour.*

PROOF Given the premises, the proof of Lemma 12 shows that $(po_t \cup co_t \cup fr_t \cup rf_t)^*$ is acyclic, then by [Alg10, §4.2.1.3] the execution is Lamport-SC. □

7.4 Verification of consistent_execution

We now have the tools to verify the satisfaction of all the conjuncts of the *consistent_execution* predicate, as listed in §2.2 and simplified by Theorem 1 of §3. The two *well_formed* conjuncts hold by the obs_eq and assumptions on opsem, e.g. that the sequenced-before relation only relates actions of the same thread. The *consistent_locks* conjunct is vacuous in the sublanguage we consider in this section. For the others, we use the correspondences between C++11 actions and relations and Power trace events and relations we established in §7.1 and in §7.2, mostly using Corollary 10 and Lemma 11.

First, *consistent_inter_thread_happens_before* states the acyclicity of ithb. Using Lemma 11, we prove by contradiction that such a cycle implies a cycle in the trace order.

Next we have four coherence conditions for pairs of a read and a write (CoRR, CoRW, CoWR and CoWW), which are part of *consistent_modification_order* and *coherent_memory_use* (itself part of *consistent_reads_from_mapping*). These diagrams involve rf_c and hb_c edges relating two writes and some reads, all at the same atomic location; they require the writes to be correctly ordered in mo_c. For example:

LEMMA 14 (CoRW). *Given C++11 actions w_1, r, and w_2, all to the same location, and an rf_c and hb_c edge as below, the $w_1 \xrightarrow{mo_c} w_2$ edge exists.*

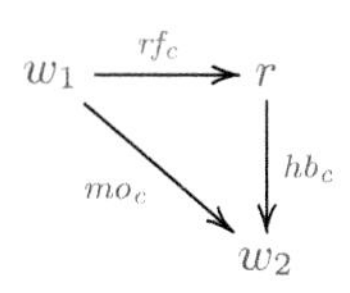

PROOF To establish this we first show that the Power write wc_1 corresponding to w_1 is propagated to the thread of the Power write wc_2 corresponding to w_2 before wc_2 is committed. In more detail: For the rf_c edge, the inclusion from §7.1 gives us a Power $wc_1 \xrightarrow{rf_t} rc$ relation between the corresponding commit events from the trace. For the hb_c edge, by the definition of C++11 happens-before, either (case 1) there is an sb_c edge, in which case we use the inclusion from §7.1 to show $rc \xrightarrow{po_t} wc_2$ (and they are on the same thread), or (case 2) an $ithb_c$ relationship, in which case there is an $rc \xrightarrow{machine\text{-}ithb_t} wc_2$ edge. We know (because of the Power rules involved in a reads-from relation, and with a case split on whether wc_1 and rc are on the same thread or not) that wc_1 propagates to the thread of rc before rc is finally satisfied. Hence wc_1 is propagated to the thread of wc_2 before the latter is committed, either (in case (1)) because the semantics of the commit transition guarantees that po_t is respected by the trace order for events at a same location, and using transitivity, or (in case (2)), by Corollary 10.

Finally, by the storage-subsystem semantics for COMMIT_WRITE_INSTRUCTION, when a write is committed, it automatically becomes coherence-after all the writes that have already been propagated to its thread, so $wc_1 \xrightarrow{co_t} wc_2$. And by the construction of mo_c, that gives $w_1 \xrightarrow{mo_c} w_2$. □

The other three coherence properties are similar, albeit administratively more complex. Two additionally use the fact that a Power read can only be satisfied from the last write (to the relevant address) that has been propagated to its thread.

The *consistent_sc_order* predicate checks that SC is a strict total order over the SC actions. The totality is by construction; strictness is by acyclicity. It also requires that hb_c and mo_c restricted to SC atomics are included in sc_c. The first is immediate from the construction of hb_c from subsets of the relations involved in the construction of sc_c. The second makes use of a lemma stating the inclusion in co_t of the relation from which we build the SC-order when restricted to pairs of writes at a same location, and the construction of mo_c.

The *consistent_modification_order* predicate consists of CoWW, dealt with above, a totality condition that is immediate from the construction of mo_c as a linearisation, and a check that it only relates writes at atomic locations, which is also by construction.

Now we have the subclauses of *consistent_reads_from_mapping*. Two, *rmw_atomicity* and *sc_fences_heeded*, are vacuous for the sublanguage we consider. We dealt with the coherence conditions of *coherent_memory_use* above.

The predicate *sc_reads_restricted* forces any SC read to read from the last sc_c-preceding write (wc) at the same location, or some non-SC write that is not hb_c-before wc. The proof is by constructing a SC-cycle for each forbidden situation, which contradicts the results of §7.3.

An interesting observation here is that, through the application of the acyclicity result of §7.3, we make use for the first time of the barriers placed by the mapping before the compilation of SC reads. And in fact, we do not rely anywhere else on these barriers as they play no part in the propagation property stated by Lemma 9.

Finally, we get to the constraints on read values. The *consistent_non_atomic_read_values* predicate says that a read r at a non-atomic location must read from a visible side-effect, i.e., a write w that happens-before r such that there is no write w' that happens-between w and r. Assuming the contrary, there are three possible situations:

1. r reads from a write that happens-after it;
2. r reads from an hb-hidden write: there exists a w' that happens-between w and r; or
3. r reads from an hb-unrelated write.

Cases 1 and 2 are lengthy but in the same style as the reasoning for CoRW and CoWR, showing that writes propagate appropriately.

Case 3 is quite different. Here we have a Power read rc that reads from a write wc for which neither $w \xrightarrow{hb_c} r$ nor $r \xrightarrow{hb_c} w$ hold. Intuitively, this is a race, but this is not a consistent execution: r cannot read from w in C++ unless $w \xrightarrow{hb_c} r$.

In the next section we show that in this case the original program has some other candidate execution that is consistent and that has a race (a data race or indeterminate read), contradicting the top-level assumption that the program was drf. A similar situation arises for the last subclause, *consistent_atomic_read_values*.

Formally, we case split at the top level on the following rf_in_hb predicate, capturing additional assumptions that ensure consistency:

$$
\begin{array}{l}
rf\_in\_hb = \forall w\ r. \\
\quad (w \xrightarrow{rf_c} r \wedge r \text{ is a non-atomic read } \Rightarrow w \xrightarrow{hb_c} r) \wedge \\
\quad (w \xrightarrow{rf_c} r \wedge r \text{ is an atomic read } \Rightarrow \\
\quad\quad (\exists w'.\ \text{is\_write } w' \wedge \text{same\_location } w\ w' \wedge w' \xrightarrow{hb_c} r))
\end{array}
$$

If rf_in_hb holds, case (3) is excluded and *consistent_non_atomic_read_values* and *consistent_atomic_read_values* can be established directly.

7.5 Construction of a racy consistent execution

In the situation where the rf_in_hb predicate of the previous section does not hold, our strategy is to 1) find a prefix of the trace for which rf_in_hb holds and build a consistent execution for it by applying the reasoning of Section 7.4 to that prefix; 2) add an indeterminate or data-race read to the consistent execution; 3) return any missing sequenced-before predecessor actions to the consistent execution; 4) extend the consistent execution until it is a complete execution of the original program.

For Step 1, we find the first read commit rc on the trace that causes a violation of rf_in_hb, and build a consistent execution for part of the trace that precedes it. Our ability to use Section 7.4 for this relies on the fact that the commit labels on the trace respect rf_t, dd_t, and cd_t, which are in turn consistent with rf_c, dd_c, and cd_c.

Steps 2–4 rely on the following receptiveness axiom about the C++ threadwise operational semantics, which we believe any reasonable operational semantics should satisfy.

$$
\begin{array}{l}
\forall c\_prog\ actions'_c\ actions_c\ op_c\ a\ new\_a. \\
\quad \text{opsem } c\_prog\ actions_c\ op_c \wedge \\
\quad a \in (actions_c \setminus actions'_c) \wedge new\_a \in \text{all\_values } a \wedge \\
\quad \text{is\_read } a \wedge actions'_c \subset actions_c \wedge \\
\quad (actions'_c \cup \{a\}) \text{ is downward closed under } (dd_c \cup cd_c)^+ \\
\quad \Rightarrow \\
\quad (\exists new\_act_c\ new\_op_c. \\
\quad\quad \text{let } stay\_act_c = actions'_c \cup \\
\quad\quad\quad \{b | b \in actions_c \setminus actions'_c \wedge b \neq a \wedge \neg\, a \xrightarrow{(dd_c \cup cd_c)^+} b\} \\
\quad\quad \text{in} \\
\quad\quad\quad stay\_act_c \cap new\_act_c = \emptyset \wedge \\
\quad\quad\quad ((op_c|_{(stay\_act_c \cup \{a\})})[new\_a/a] = \\
\quad\quad\quad new\_op_c|_{(stay\_act_c \cup \{new\_a\})}) \wedge \\
\quad\quad\quad (\forall x\ y.\ x \xrightarrow{(new\_dd_c \cup new\_cd_c)^+} y \wedge x \in new\_act_c \Rightarrow \\
\quad\quad\quad\quad y \notin stay\_act_c \cup \{new\_a\}) \wedge \\
\quad\quad\quad \text{opsem } c\_prog\ (stay\_act_c \cup \{new\_a\} \cup new\_act_c)\ new\_op_c)
\end{array}
$$

It states that if the operational semantics can perform a read at a certain point, it can instead perform any read that is of the same kind and from the same location, but that reads a (potentially) different value. This reflects the fact that the threadwise operational semantics relies on the memory model to determine how memory reads are satisfied. Furthermore, later actions that do not depend on the read via $(dd_c \cup cd_c)^+$ are unaffected by the change of value read. This reflects the fact that the threadwise operational semantics is required to correctly calculate the notions of control and data dependence. We now return to the construction of the racy execution. For Step 2, if there is a visible side effect w' of r (recall that r is the read that violated hb_in_rf), we create a new read r' according to the opsem axiom and have r' read from w'. This r' then races with the write w that r read from originally. If there is no visible side effect, we have r read from nothing, and the execution has an indeterminate read. We prove that this new execution is consistent by showing that the happens before relation is unchanged, except for switching r to r'.

Step 3 is necessary because the Power can speculatively execute reads out of program order, and so the prefix chosen in Step 1 might be missing actions that the C++ threadwise operational semantics requires. In other words, the trace ordering is not necessarily consistent with po_t, and hence the trace prefix might not be downward closed in sb_c. The addition of such a missing read r in Step 3 follows the same reasoning as in Step 2 with the added observation that r cannot be (atomic) sequentially consistent or acquire because the Power cannot speculate past the control+isync dependency that would follow such a read. The addition of missing writes is straightforward.

Step 4 is straightforward because there are no constraints on how the execution extended to completion; it already contains the race, and further application of opsem axiom will not disturb it.

This completes the proof of Theorem 7.

7.6 Alternate trailing-`sync` mapping

As mentioned in §1, a modified mapping has been proposed that has a `sync` barrier as the last instruction in the mapping for all SC actions. This keeps a `sync` barrier program-order between any pair of SC actions from the same thread, which ensures the results of §7.3 hold. The rest of the proof interacts with SC actions through the SC order, so it can be carried over unchanged. One additional subtlety is that SC stores are also release stores, and SC loads in C++ are also acquire loads. The first fact requires the `lwsync` before the store for SC stores, as for release stores. The second requires program-order-later loads to be stopped from being satisfied before the SC load is. The trailing `sync` suffices here.

8. Related Work

The most closely related work is our correctness proof of a compilation scheme from C++11 to x86 [BOS+11]. That covered RMWs in addition to loads and stores, but was nonetheless comparatively simple, as x86 has a strong TSO-based semantics [SSO+10]. For Section 3, Boehm and Adve gave a definition [BA08] of a memory model based on an earlier C++11 working paper, broadly in the same style as the eventual draft standard and [BOS+11], but differing in many details and with the semantics for low-level atomics only sketched. They give a hand proof that in that model DRF programs without low-level atomics have SC semantics.

Some previous work proves correctness of compilers for concurrent languages, rather than compilation schemes for particular primitives, in a relaxed-memory context. Ševčík et al. prove correctness of CompCert-TSO [SVZN+11], a compiler from a concurrent C-like language with TSO semantics to the x86 TSO model (building on Leroy's single-threaded CompCert [Ler09]). Here the source and target share the same relatively simple memory model, and the correctness proof is simulation-based, taking advantage of the fact that x86-TSO has a simple operational characterisation. Lochbihler proves correctness of compilation from a formalisation of multi-threaded Java to a JVM [Loc10], but this assumes SC and does no optimisation. Ševčík [Šev11] proves the correctness (or otherwise) for various optimisations for DRF languages, though not specifically for C++11. Burckhardt et al. [BMS10] consider the correctness of transformations in relaxed models. Vafeiadis and Zappa

Nardelli verify fence elimination optimisations in the context of the CompCert-TSO compiler [VZN11].

There is an extensive line of work inserting fences to restore SC, starting with Shasha and Snir [SS88]. Fang et al. [FLM03] do this in practice for sync on Power 3 machines, but they appear to implicitly assume that writes are atomic (discussing only thread-local reordering), which they are not on more recent Power implementations. Alglave et al. [AMSS10, Alg10, AM11] consider Power fence insertion with respect to an axiomatic memory model, the *CAV2010 model*. That model was a precursor to the abstract-machine model of Sarkar et al. [SSA+11] that we use in this paper. As described there, the CAV2010 model is stronger than the architectural intent for the R01 test (in this sense it is unsound w.r.t. the architecture, although not observed to be unsound w.r.t. current implementations), and it is weaker than the architecture (and current implementations) for cases such as MP+lwsync+addr. The latter might be generated by the mapping for a C++ release/consume example, so this model is too weak to prove the mapping correct.

Lea produced a guide to implementing the JSR-133 Java Memory Model on various multiprocessors [Lea]. Written when the Power architectural intent was less clear (considerably before [SSA+11]), its suggested uses of `isync` are not correct w.r.t. the architecture. It also focuses on the synchronisation required between pairs of operations on the same thread, without discussing the Power cumulativity properties that are essential for C++11 release/acquire, release/consume, and SC atomics.

9. Conclusion

We have proved the correctness of a realistic relaxed-memory compilation scheme, from the programming language memory model proposed for the mainstream C and C++ standards, to a realistic memory model for Power multiprocessors. The C++11 model was designed with implementation above the Power (and ARM) model in mind, among others, and this establishes that it is in fact implementable with what appears to be a reasonable mapping (using hardware synchronisation mechanisms commensurate with the C++11 semantics required). Moreover, our development explains why the mapping is correct and also what properties of the Power are actually required, increasing understanding and confidence in both models, and providing a good basis for compiler developers compiling C++11 and C1x to Power and ARM; we are discussing this with GCC and ARM compiler groups.

There are many interesting directions for future work. First, the development should be extended to cover other C++11 features: read-modify-write and locks operations require first a semantics for the Power load-reserve/store-conditional instructions, and one would also like to cover fences and dynamic thread creation.

Second, while a full compiler correctness proof for C++ (or even C) is still a long way off, we would like to instantiate our compilation-scheme proof to a concrete operational semantics and compiler for a small fragment.

Third, the proof suggests the construction of a more abstract axiomatic Power model, based on the derived properties we use in the proof. We can see there exactly which machine trace events are relevant, e.g. the last satisfy label for each committed read, and certain write propagation events; the more abstract model could deal just with those. This would give a simpler foundation for developing analysis and reasoning techniques for Power and ARM concurrent software.

Acknowledgements We thank Hans Boehm, Paul McKenney, Jaroslav Ševčík, and Francesco Zappa Nardelli for discussions on this work, and acknowledge funding from EPSRC grants EP/F036345, EP/H005633, and EP/H027351.

References

[ABJ+93] Mustaque Ahamad, Rida A. Bazzi, Ranjit John, Prince Kohli, and Gil Neiger. The power of processor consistency. In *Proc. SPAA*, 1993.

[AH90] S. V. Adve and M. D. Hill. Weak ordering — a new definition. In *Proc. ISCA*, 1990.

[Alg10] J. Alglave. *A Shared Memory Poetics*. PhD thesis, Université Paris 7 and INRIA, 2010.

[AM11] J. Alglave and L. Maranget. Stability in weak memory models. In *Proc. CAV*, 2011.

[AMSS10] J. Alglave, L. Maranget, S. Sarkar, and P. Sewell. Fences in weak memory models. In *Proc. CAV*, 2010.

[BA08] H.-J. Boehm and S.V. Adve. Foundations of the C++ concurrency memory model. In *Proc. PLDI*, 2008.

[Bec11] P. Becker, editor. *Programming Languages — C++*. 2011. ISO/IEC 14882:2011. A non-final but recent version is available at `http://www.open-std.org/jtc1/sc22/wg21/docs/papers/2011/n3242.pdf`.

[BMO+] M. Batty, K. Memarian, S. Owens, S. Sarkar, and P. Sewell. `http://www.cl.cam.ac.uk/users/pes20/cppppc`.

[BMS10] S. Burckhardt, M. Musuvathi, and V. Singh. Verifying local transformations on relaxed memory models. In *CC*, 2010.

[Boe11] Hans Boehm. Atomic synchronization sequences, 2011. Mailing list communication, July 18th.

[BOS+10] M. Batty, S. Owens, S. Sarkar, P. Sewell, and T. Weber. Mathematizing C++ concurrency: The post-Rapperswil model. Technical Report N3132, ISO IEC JTC1/SC22/WG21, August 2010. `http://www.open-std.org/jtc1/sc22/wg21/docs/papers/2010/n3132.pdf`.

[BOS+11] M. Batty, S. Owens, S. Sarkar, P. Sewell, and T. Weber. Mathematizing C++ concurrency. In *Proc. POPL*, 2011.

[BWB+11] J. C. Blanchette, T. Weber, M. Batty, S. Owens, and S. Sarkar. Nitpicking C++ concurrency. In *Proc. PPDP*, 2011.

[FLM03] X. Fang, J. Lee, and S. P. Midkiff. Automatic fence insertion for shared memory multiprocessing. In *Proc. ICS*, 2003.

[Lam79] L. Lamport. How to make a multiprocessor computer that correctly executes multiprocess programs. *IEEE Trans. Comput.*, C-28(9):690–691, 1979.

[Lea] D. Lea. The JSR-133 cookbook for compiler writers. `http://gee.cs.oswego.edu/dl/jmm/cookbook.html`.

[Ler09] X. Leroy. A formally verified compiler back-end. *Journal of Automated Reasoning*, 43(4):363–446, 2009.

[Loc10] A. Lochbihler. Verifying a compiler for Java threads. In *Proc. ESOP'10*, 2010.

[MS11] P. E. McKenney and R. Silvera. Example POWER implementation for C/C++ memory model. `http://www.rdrop.com/users/paulmck/scalability/paper/N2745r.2011.03.04a.html`, 2011.

[OBZNS11] S. Owens, P. Böhm, F. Zappa Nardelli, and P. Sewell. Lem: A lightweight tool for heavyweight semantics. In *Proc. ITP, LNCS 6898*, 2011. "Rough Diamond" section.

[Šev11] J. Ševčík. Safe optimisations for shared-memory concurrent programs. In *Proc. PLDI*, 2011.

[SS88] D. Shasha and M. Snir. Efficient and correct execution of parallel programs that share memory. *TOPLAS*, 10:282–312, 1988.

[SSA+11] S. Sarkar, P. Sewell, J. Alglave, L. Maranget, and D. Williams. Understanding POWER multiprocessors. In *PLDI*, 2011.

[SSO+10] P. Sewell, S. Sarkar, S. Owens, F. Zappa Nardelli, and M. O. Myreen. x86-TSO: A rigorous and usable programmer's model for x86 multiprocessors. *C. ACM*, 53(7):89–97, 2010.

[SVZN+11] J. Ševčík, V. Vafeiadis, F. Zappa Nardelli, S. Jagannathan, and P. Sewell. Relaxed-memory concurrency and verified compilation. In *Proc. POPL*, 2011.

[VZN11] V. Vafeiadis and F. Zappa Nardelli. Verifying fence elimination optimisations. In *Proc. SAS*, 2011.

A Mechanized Semantics for C++ Object Construction and Destruction, with Applications to Resource Management

Tahina Ramananandro
INRIA Paris-Rocquencourt
tahina.ramananandro@inria.fr

Gabriel Dos Reis *
Texas A&M University
gdr@cs.tamu.edu

Xavier Leroy †
INRIA Paris-Rocquencourt
xavier.leroy@inria.fr

Abstract

We present a formal operational semantics and its Coq mechanization for the C++ object model, featuring object construction and destruction, shared and repeated multiple inheritance, and virtual function call dispatch. These are key C++ language features for high-level system programming, in particular for predictable and reliable resource management. This paper is the first to present a formal mechanized account of the metatheory of construction and destruction in C++, and applications to popular programming techniques such as "resource acquisition is initialization." We also report on irregularities and apparent contradictions in the ISO C++03 and C++11 standards.

Categories and Subject Descriptors D.1.5 [*Programming techniques*]: Object-oriented Programming; D.2.0 [*Software Engineering*]: General—*Standards*; D.2.2 [*Software Engineering*]: Design Tools and Techniques—*Object-oriented design methods*; D.2.4 [*Software Engineering*]: Software/Program Verification—*Correctness proofs*; D.3.3 [*Programming Languages*]: Language Constructs and Features—*Classes and objects, Inheritance*; F.3.3 [*Logics and meanings of programs*]: Studies of program constructs—*Object-oriented constructs*

General Terms Languages, Verification

1. Introduction

One of the earliest decisions for C++ (in 1979) was to provide language support for the construction and destruction of objects [15]: programmer-supplied code fragments called *constructors* are automatically executed when a new object is created and before it is made available to the rest of the program; these constructors can execute arbitrary code sequences and are intended to establish the execution environment for operations by initializing fields and maintaining class-level invariants. Symmetrically, the language also supports *destructors*, which are executed before an object is destroyed at precisely-defined times. Such general constructors are now available in most programming languages supporting object-oriented programming. Many languages also provides some support for clean-up of objects at the end of their lifetime, e.g. finalizers executed asynchronously at loosely-specified times or `dispose` statements allowing a programmer to explicitly request clean-up.

Because it is enforced by the programming language itself and not by coding conventions, the object construction and destruction protocol provides strong guarantees that can be leveraged by good programming practices. This is the case for *Resource Acquisition Is Initialization* (RAII), a popular C++ programming idiom for safely managing system resources such as file descriptors. With RAII, resource acquisition is always performed in constructors, and resource release in the corresponding destructors. Since C++ guarantees that every execution of a constructor is eventually matched by an execution of a destructor, RAII minimizes the risk of leaking resources.

As practically useful as they are, constructors and destructors raise delicate issues for the programmers, for static analysis tools, and even for language designers. While an object is being constructed or destructed, it is not in a fully operational state. This raises the question of what operations constructor/destructor code should be allowed to perform on this object, and what semantics to give to these operations. A typical example of this dilemma is virtual method dispatch: in Java and C#, unrestricted virtual method calls are allowed in constructors, with the same semantics as on fully constructed objects; in contrast, C++ takes object construction states into account when resolving virtual function calls, in a way that provides stronger soundness guarantees but complicates semantics and compilation. Section 2 reviews the main features of C++ object construction and destruction.

This paper reports on a formal, mechanized semantics for construction and destruction in the C++ object model. This model is especially rich: it features multiple inheritance (both shared and repeated), fields of structure and structure array types, as well as subtle interactions between construction states, virtual function calls, and dynamic casts. Our semantics, fully mechanized in the Coq proof assistant, is, to the best of our knowledge, the first to capture faithfully these interactions as intended by the C++ standard. This semantics, described in section 3, is the first contribution of the paper.

The second contribution, in section 4, is the specification and formal verification of several expected properties of the construction/destruction protocol, ranging from common-sense properties such as "any subobject is constructed, or destroyed, at most once" to the first precise characterization of the properties that make the RAII programming idiom work in practice. We also study the evolutions of the dynamic types of objects throughout their life cycle and formally justify the program points where compilers must generate code to update dynamic types (v-tables).

As a third contribution, this work exposes some irregularities and apparent contradictions in the ISO C++03 and C++11 stan-

* Partially supported by NSF grants CCF-1035058 and OISE-1043084.

† Partially supported by ANR grants Arpège U3CAT and INS Verasco.

POPL'12, January 25–27, 2012, Philadelphia, PA, USA.

dards, summarized in section 5. These have been reported to the ISO C++ committee; some were resolved in C++11, others will be in future revisions. We finish the paper with a few words about verified compilation (§6), a discussion of related work (§7) and future work (§8), and concluding remarks (§9).

All results presented in this paper were mechanized using the Coq proof assistant [1]. The Coq development is available at `http://gallium.inria.fr/~tramanan/cxx/`. By lack of space, some aspects of the semantics are only sketched in this paper. A full description can be found in the first author's Ph.D. thesis [12, part 2].

2. Object construction and destruction in C++

A constructor is a special function that turns "raw memory" into an object. Its purpose is to create an environment where class invariants hold, and where the class's member functions will operate [2, 15, 16]. Conversely, at the end of the useful life of an object, another special function — called destructor — releases any acquired resources and turns the object back to mere raw memory. The time span between the completion of a constructor and the start of a destructor is the *lifetime* of the constructed object. The C++ language rules were designed to guarantee that class invariants set up by a constructor hold through the entire lifetime of an object. For example, a complete object's dynamic type does not change during its lifetime.

C++'s object construction and destruction mechanism is rooted in a few design principles:

I. Every object and each of its subobjects (if any) is constructed exactly once.
II. No object construction should rely on parts yet to be constructed, and no object destruction should rely on parts already destroyed.
III. Every object is destroyed in the exact reverse order it was constructed.

These principles, independently of implementation considerations, enable support for reliable, modular, large-scale software development.

Principle I supports the idea that a resource acquired by an object (say a file lock) is predictably acquired exactly once.

Principle II embodies a notion of locality and scoping. While the constructor is creating the computation environment for member functions, very few class guarantees can be made. It is desirable to localize the complexity and/or convolution needed to correctly call a function in a few specific places before an object begins its lifetime. Furthermore, the author of a class should not have to worry about which data members of possible derived classes are correctly initialized during the execution of a constructor. On the other hand, she should be able to rely on base-class invariants. Consider the following example:

```
struct Locus {
  Locus(int a, int b) : x(a), y(b) { show(); }
  virtual void show() const {
    cout << x << ' ' << y << endl;
  }
protected:
  int x;
  int y;
};

struct FeaturedLocus : Locus {
  FeaturedLocus(int a, int b, const vector& v)
    : Locus(a, b), features(v) { }
  void show() const {
    cout << x << ' ' << y
         << ' ' << features << endl;
  }
private:
  vector features;
};
```

Construction of a `FeaturedLocus` object entails constructing its `Locus` base-class subobject, followed by copy-initialization of its `features` field from the `v` parameter. If, in the `Locus` constructor, the call to the virtual function `show` resolved to the final overrider `FeaturedLocus::show` (as in Java or C#), it would access the yet-to-be-constructed field `FeaturedLocus::features` – an undesirable and unpleasant outcome. Consequently, Principle II argues for resolving the call (in the constructor) to an overrider not from a derived class; here it is `Locus::show`.

Finally, Principle III supports predictability and reliability. For instance, if an object acquires N resources through the construction of its subobjects, in general one would want to release them in the reverse order of acquisition, or else a deadlock might ensue.

Turning these general principles (and their implications) into executable specification in the face of object-oriented language features such as multiple inheritance (both repeated and shared), late binding function dispatch (virtual function calls), type queries, etc. is an interesting challenge. On the other hand, their fulfillment leads to interesting soundness results and, more importantly, reliable software development techniques for the programmer.

Initialization versus assignment There is a difference between initialization and "declaration followed by a first-time assignment". And it is not a stylistic distinction. Base-class subobjects and nonstatic data members are constructed before the proper body of the constructor is executed. Initializers for subobjects are specified in a comma-separated list before the opening brace of a constructor body (see the definition of the constructors for `Locus` and `FeaturedLocus` in the previous example.) In particular, there is *no other way* to initialize base-class subobjects, const or reference nonstatic data members. A base-class subobject, or a nonstatic data member, not mentioned in the member-initializer list is implicitly initialized with a default constructor, i.e. a constructor that can be called with no argument. Consequently, the language rules imply that all subobjects are constructed by the time the first statement of the constructor body (if not empty) is executed. The constructor for `FeaturedLocus` could have been written as

```
FeaturedLocus(int a, int b, const vector& v)
  : Locus(a,b) { features = v; }
```

In this variation, the `Locus` base-class subobject is initialized; the nonstatic data member `features` is default constructed, and finally the constructor body *assigns* the value of `v` to `features`. In C++, assignments of objects of class types are generally implemented by user-defined functions. These functions must assume that the left hand side of the assignment is an object *already constructed and in a valid state*. In particular, `vector`'s assignment function must carefully check for self-assignment to avoid premature memory release; it must properly release the resources the object was managing before taking hold on the new ones. By contrast, during copy-construction, the object being constructed has *not* acquired any resources yet; so the implementation code of the copy-constructor is usually far simpler than that for assignment.

Initialization order Principle III has an interesting implication on the construction order of the constituents of an object. Observe that there is exactly one destructor per class, and that there can be as many constructors (per class) as deemed necessary by the programmer. Therefore, for a given class, subobjects in all constructors must be initialized in the same order — for that order must be the reverse destruction order of the (unique) destructor. Any well-defined order can do. However, for simplicity, a natural choice is the declaration

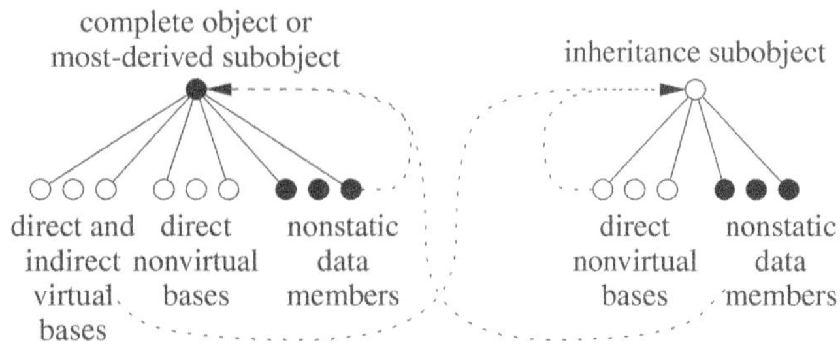

Figure 1. A recursive tree representation of the subobjects of a class, such that a depth-first left-to-right traversal yields the subobject construction order.

order: initialization of all base-class subobjects in the (left-to-right) order of declaration in the class definition; followed by initialization of all nonstatic data members in their order of declarations in the class definition.

This construction order is simple, predictable, and reflects the compositional aspect of "class growth". However, shared inheritance (virtual base classes) poses a problem for the principle of "base before derived" and "strict order of declaration construction". Indeed, consider the following hierarchy of IO stream classes:

```
struct istream : virtual basic_ios { ... };
struct ostream : virtual basic_ios { ... };
struct iostream : istream, ostream { ... };
```

where the class `basic_ios` maintains states and implements operations common to both input and output streams; the classes `istream` and `ostream` implement input and output stream functionalities. The class `iostream` combines both input and output facilities. If an `iostream` object was to be constructed according to the declaration order outlined above, the corresponding `basic_ios` base-class subobject would be constructed twice: once when the `istream` base-class subobject is constructed, and a second time when the `ostream` base-class subobject is constructed. This problem is resolved by executing constructors for virtual bases (in declaration order) before all other constructors. More generally, C++ retains the following *almost-declaration order* construction for a complete object, also depicted on Figure 1:

1. virtual base-class subobjects are constructed in a depth-first left-to-right traversal of the inheritance graph;
2. direct non-virtual base-class subobjects are constructed in declaration order;
3. nonstatic data members are constructed in declaration order.

Builtin object types The C++ programming language was designed with two competing ideals: a sound high-level object model with equal support for user-defined types and builtin types, and a near-total compatibility with C for system programming. The resulting tension has made the general model of object construction and destruction grow barnacles. Indeed, C lacks the notion of object construction so central to C++'s object model. But, in reality, both languages agree on the semantics of programs that read from uninitialized objects: undefined behavior, except in very limited cases where a read access is done as "raw memory". In C, object initialization is usually expressed in terms of storage acquisition followed by assignment; C++ distinguishes assignment from construction. To achieve the same ultimate semantics and to support generic programming, C++ extended the notion of constructor (and destructor) to builtin types. A builtin data member can be explicitly initialized with default value using the default construction syntax:

```
struct Locus { Locus() : x(), y() { } };
```

Here, the default constructor `Locus` explicitly constructs the data members `x` and `y` with a default value (zero) so that in the complete object declaration "`Locus origin;`", the `origin` object has its coordinates initialized to zero. Would the semantics be the same were `x` and `y` not explicitly listed in the member-initializer list? The answer is no: objects of builtin type with no explicit initializers are constructed but, left with indeterminate values. This irregularity was introduced as a way to satisfy the widespread practice in C where objects are given first-time values long after their declarations. This irregularity, and others related to destructors for builtin types, surely complicate the C++ semantics rules as well as formalization. However, they are not fundamental to the object model. In fact, the C++ standards committee is considering unifying initialization and lifetime rules in a post-C++11 standard. We hope this work will help in that endeavor.

3. Formal operational semantics

3.1 Syntax of the core language

We focus on a core language of objects that features the main aspects of the C++ object model: construction and destruction; multiple inheritance (both virtual and non-virtual), virtual functions, and nonstatic data members (a.k.a. "fields") of scalar, array or complete non-abstract object types. To simplify the presentation, we formalize only fields that are arrays of object types, viewing a field of object type T as a one-element array of type "$T[1]$".

The core language is a language of statements operating over variables in 3-address style. We assume that typechecking was performed, static overloading was resolved, and expressions were decomposed into elementary statements. The syntax of statements follows.

$op, \ldots$	$: Op$	Builtin operations
$var, \ldots$	$: Var$	Variables
$B, C, \ldots$	$: Class$	Classes
$fname$	$: Field$	Field names
$mname$	$: Method$	Method names
$Stmt$	$::=$ skip	Do nothing
	$\mid var' := op(var^*)$	Builtin operation
	$\mid var' := var\text{->}_C fname$	Field read
	$\mid var\text{->}_C fname := var'$	Scalar field write
	$\mid var' := \&var[var_{\mathsf{index}}]_C$	Array cell access
	$\mid var' :=$ $\mathtt{dynamic\_cast}\langle B\rangle_C(var)$	Dynamic cast
	$\mid var'\text{->}_C mname(var^*)$	Virtual function call
	$\mid Stmt_1; Stmt_2$	Statement sequence
	$\mid$ return	Function return
	$\mid \{C\ var[var_{\mathsf{count}}] = \{ObjInit^*\}; Stmt\}$	Block-scoped object

The Coq formalization also features simple control structures (if/then/else, infinite loops with early exits), as well as static casts. We leave these extra features out in this paper to concentrate on the essential features of the language: accesses to fields; virtual function calls; dynamic casts; and block-scoped objects. The statement $\{C\ x[N] = \{ObjInit^*\}; Stmt\}$ allocates an array of N objects of type C, constructs each of its elements according to the list of initializers $ObjInit^*$, binds the array to variable x, executes the block body $Stmt$, destructs each element of the array x, and finally deallocates the whole array.

Initializers are syntactically presented in C++ as constructor calls with expressions as arguments. Since our language lacks expressions, we model initializers as a statement (which evaluates the expression arguments into temporary variables) followed by an invocation of a constructor for object fields or the initialization of a scalar field.

$ObjInit ::= Stmt; C(var^*)$		Class object initializer
$FieldInit ::= (Stmt; fname(var))$		Scalar field initializer
$\mid fname\{ObjInit^*\}$		Structure field initializers (one for each array cell)
$Init ::= ObjInit \mid FieldInit$		

Arguments to functions and constructors can be scalar values, i.e. integers, or floating point data, or pointers to objects. We do not model passing objects by value: this raises delicate issues with the construction and destruction of *temporary objects*, discussed in §8.

$Constr$	$::= C(var^*) : Init^*\{Stmt\}$	Constructor
$Destr$	$::= \sim C()\{Stmt\}$	Destructor
$MethodDef$	$::=$ virtual void $mname(var^*)\{Stmt\}$	Virtual function (method)
$FieldDef$	$::=$ scalar $fname$; $\mid$ struct $C[size]\ fname$;	Data member (field)
$Base$	$::= B \mid$ virtual B	
$ClassDef$	$::=$ struct $C : Base^*$ $\{FieldDef^*\ MethodDef^*\ Constr^*\ Destr\}$	Class definition
$Program$	$::= ClassDef^*$; main$()\{Stmt\}$	Program

A complete program consists of a hierarchy of classes. Each class definition contains a list of virtual and non-virtual base classes, a list of data members (a.k.a. fields), definitions for virtual functions (a.k.a. methods), one or several constructors, and one destructor. Each constructor consists of a parameter list, a sequence of initializers (for direct non-virtual bases, fields, and direct or indirect virtual bases), and a constructor body (an arbitrary statement). Destructors take no parameters and consist only of a body.

3.2 Designating subobjects

A crucial issue in formalizing the C++ object model is to capture the fact that each object of a class C contains *subobjects*, one for each base and each field of C. Subobjects can be arbitrarily nested, but can also be shared along several inheritance paths, owing to virtual inheritance. For this reason, a subobject cannot be identified by a store locations ℓ; instead, it is described by a pair of the location ℓ of the array of complete objects containing it, and a *path* from this array to the desired subobject. Intuitively, a path is a sequence of selection operations of the form "select a base class" or "select a field" or "select an element of an array". This path-based approach was introduced by Rossie and Friedman [14], later mechanized in Isabelle/HOL by Wasserrab *et al.* [18], and further extended with structure array fields and mechanized in Coq by Ramananandro *et al.* [13]. We now briefly recall this path-based formalization, referring the reader to [13, 18] for full details.

An *inheritance path* σ is a pair (h, l) of an inheritance kind $h ::= \mathsf{Repeated} \mid \mathsf{Shared}$ and a list of class names l. Such a path designates a *base-class subobject* of some type A of an object of type C. If $h = \mathsf{Repeated}$, it is a path through the *repeated*, or *non-virtual*, inheritance graph. Each path from C to A corresponds to a distinct copy of A within C. If $h = \mathsf{Shared}$, it is a path from a virtual base B of C to A, regardless of how the virtual base B is reached.

Not all paths are valid with respect to the class hierarchy. The following inference rules define the relation $C \prec\!(h,l)\!\succ\!\xrightarrow{\mathcal{I}} A$, meaning that (h, l) is a valid inheritance path from C to a base-class subobject of C of static type A.

$$C \prec\!(\mathsf{Repeated}, C :: \epsilon)\!\succ\!\xrightarrow{\mathcal{I}} C$$

$$\frac{B \text{ direct non-virtual base of } C \qquad B \prec\!(\mathsf{Repeated}, l)\!\succ\!\xrightarrow{\mathcal{I}} A}{C \prec\!(\mathsf{Repeated}, C :: l)\!\succ\!\xrightarrow{\mathcal{I}} A}$$

$$\frac{B \text{ virtual base of } C \qquad B \prec\!(h,l)\!\succ\!\xrightarrow{\mathcal{I}} A}{C \prec\!(\mathsf{Shared}, l)\!\succ\!\xrightarrow{\mathcal{I}} A}$$

An object is said to be a *most-derived* object if, and only if, it is not a base-class subobject of any other object. A most-derived object of type C is designated by the trivial inheritance path $(\mathsf{Repeated}, C :: \epsilon)$.

Inheritance paths compose naturally: if $C \prec\!(h,l)\!\succ\!\xrightarrow{\mathcal{I}} B$ and $B \prec\!(h',l')\!\succ\!\xrightarrow{\mathcal{I}} A$, we have $C \prec\!(h,l)@(h',l')\!\succ\!\xrightarrow{\mathcal{I}} A$. Here, $@$ is the *cast to base* operator, defined as follows: for a cast through non-virtual inheritance, $(h,l)@(\mathsf{Repeated}, B :: l') = (h, l+\!\!+l')$; whereas through virtual inheritance, we have $(h,l)@(\mathsf{Shared}, l') = (\mathsf{Shared}, l')$. (We write $+\!\!+$ for list concatenation.)

In the presence of fields that are structures or arrays of structures, the notions of paths and subobjects must be extended to allow selecting elements of arrays of structures. Ramananandro *et al.* [13] define *array paths* as lists of (i, σ, F) triples, where i is an array index, σ an inheritance path, and F the name of a structure array field. An array path goes from an array of n structures of type C to an array of n' structures of type C', which we write $C[n] \prec\!\alpha\!\succ\!\xrightarrow{\mathcal{A}} C'[n']$ and define by the inference rules below. An auxiliary predicate $C[n] \prec\!i,\sigma\!\succ\!\xrightarrow{\mathcal{CI}} A$ captures the selection of the i-th element of an array followed by the extraction of a base-class subobject σ of type A.

$$\frac{0 \le i < n \qquad C \prec\!\sigma\!\succ\!\xrightarrow{\mathcal{I}} A}{C[n] \prec\!i,\sigma\!\succ\!\xrightarrow{\mathcal{CI}} A} \qquad \frac{0 \le n' \le n}{C[n] \prec\!\epsilon\!\succ\!\xrightarrow{\mathcal{A}} C[n']}$$

$$\frac{F = (f, D, m) \text{ is a structure field defined in } A \quad C[n] \prec\!i,\sigma\!\succ\!\xrightarrow{\mathcal{CI}} A \qquad D[m] \prec\!\alpha\!\succ\!\xrightarrow{\mathcal{A}} C'[n']}{C[n] \prec\!(i,\sigma,F) :: \alpha\!\succ\!\xrightarrow{\mathcal{A}} C'[n']}$$

In the core language of §3.1, a *complete* object (bound to a variable x by a block statement) is always an array of structures, with type $C[n]$. A *subobject* of type A of such a complete object is. therefore, a triple (α, i, σ) where α is an array path from $C[n]$ to some $C'[n']$ and $i \in [0, n')$ is an index in the array of type $C'[n']$ and σ is the inheritance path for a base-class subobject of C' of type A. We write $C[n] \prec\!(\alpha,i,\sigma)\!\succ\!\rightarrow A$ to mean that (α, i, σ) designates a valid subobject of type A of the array $C[n]$. This relation is defined by:

$$\frac{C[n] \prec\!\alpha\!\succ\!\xrightarrow{\mathcal{A}} C'[n'] \prec\!i,\sigma\!\succ\!\xrightarrow{\mathcal{CI}} A}{C[n] \prec\!(\alpha,i,\sigma)\!\succ\!\rightarrow A}$$

Then, a subobject of a complete C object is a most-derived C' object if, and only if, it can be written as $(\alpha, i, (\mathsf{Repeated}, C' :: \epsilon))$ where $C[n] \prec\!\alpha\!\succ\!\xrightarrow{\mathcal{I}} C'[n']$ and $0 \le i < n'$. In practice, this means that a most-derived object corresponds to a cell of a structure array, the array being either the complete C object itself ($\alpha = \epsilon$) or some structure field of a subobject of the complete object.

Our operational semantics uses these notions to unambiguously identify complete objects by locations ℓ in the store, subobjects by pairs $(\ell, (\alpha, i, \sigma))$ of a location and a subobject, and fields by triples $(\ell, (\alpha, i, \sigma), f)$ of a subobject of some type A and a name f of a field declared in A.

3.3 Construction states

In the C++ language, the behaviors of operations over objects depend on the *construction state* of these objects. For example, it is not possible to invoke a virtual function of a class C if the base classes of C have not been constructed yet, or are undergoing destruction. Likewise, as described in §2, virtual method dispatch behaves differently when a most-derived object is fully constructed and when it is undergoing construction or destruction.

Our operational semantics therefore associates a construction state to every subobject and every field, and updates these states during construction and destruction steps. A given subobject can be in one of 7 construction states, whose meanings differ slightly depending on whether the subobject is a most-derived subobject (e.g. an element of a structure array) or a base-class subobject. For a most-derived object, the construction states and their meanings are:

1. Unconstructed: Construction has not started yet.
2. StartedConstructing: The construction of base-class subobjects has started, but not the fields.
3. BasesConstructed: The base-class subobjects are completely constructed. Now constructing the fields or executing the constructor body.
4. Constructed: The constructor body has returned, and destruction has not started yet.
5. StartedDestructing: The body of the destructor is executing or the fields are undergoing destruction.
6. DestructingBases: The fields have been completely destructed. Bases are undergoing destruction.
7. Destructed: All bases and fields have been destructed.

For a base-class subobject, we need to exclude virtual bases from the meaning of its construction state. Indeed, as discussed in §2 and shown in Figure 1, virtual bases are morally attached to the enclosing most-derived object, not to the base-class subobject. Therefore, for those base class subobjects that are not most-derived objects, we reinterpret four of the construction states as follows:

1. Unconstructed: Construction of the *non-virtual part* has not started yet. However, virtual bases may have been already constructed.
2. StartedConstructing: The construction of *non-virtual* base-class subobjects has started, but not the fields
6. DestructingBases: The fields have been completely destructed. *Non-virtual bases* are undergoing destruction.
7. Destructed: All fields and *non-virtual bases* have been destructed.

Then, the *lifetime* of a subobject σ can be defined as the set of execution states where its construction state is exactly Constructed.

Construction states are naturally ordered by chronology. We write $c < c'$ to say that state c occurs earlier than state c' in the enumeration above, and $\mathsf{S}(c)$ to denote the state immediately following c, if it exists.

Finally, fields also carry a construction state: one among Unconstructed, StartedConstructing, Constructed, StartedDestructing, and Destructed, with similar meaning as for subobjects. As an example of use, writing to a scalar field is possible only if it is in state Constructed, therefore preventing accesses to an unconstructed or already destructed field.

3.4 Operational semantics

The semantics of the core language is stated in terms of evolutions of a global state $\mathcal{G}$, which contains four partial maps:

- LocType: maps locations ℓ of complete objects to pairs (C, n) representing the types $C[n]$ of the complete objects.
- FieldValue: associates values to pairs (π, f) of a subobject π and a scalar field f.
- ConstrState: associates construction states to subobjects π.
- ConstrState$^{\mathcal{F}}$: associates construction states to fields (π, f).

We write e.g. $\mathcal{G}.\mathsf{LocType}(\ell) = (C, n)$ to denote a lookup in a component of the state, and $\mathcal{G}[\mathsf{LocType}(\ell) \leftarrow (C, n)]$ to denote an update.

The main challenge in this semantics is to formalize the object construction and destruction protocol. (Other aspects of our language, such as accesses to fields, dynamic casts and virtual function dispatch, are semantically well understood from the work of Wasserrab *et al.* [18].) At a high level of abstraction, construction of a complete object corresponds to enumerating its subobjects according to a depth-first, left-to-right traversal of the construction tree depicted in Figure 1. The initializers encountered during this traversal are then executed to determine the arguments to the constructors, followed by invocations of the designated constructors (for bases and elements of structure array fields) or field assignments (for scalar fields). Construction states of subobjects and fields are updated along the way. Destruction is similar, but proceeds in the exact reverse order: depth-last, right-to-left traversal of the construction tree.

The description above strongly suggests a big-step operational semantics or, equivalently, a definitional interpreter, since the recursive structure of these semantics matches well the recursive nature of the construction tree. However, there are two reasons why we want a small-step transition semantics instead. First, statements, constructors and initializers may fail to terminate, and we would like to account both for terminating and diverging executions. Second and more importantly, we need our semantics to materialize the *context* in which a constructor or destructor executes, or in other terms the *continuation* of all pending constructor/destructor invocations which will be restarted when the current constructor/destructor finishes. Being able to reason on this explicit context/continuation is necessary in order to prove most of the high-level semantic properties of §4.

The operational semantics, therefore, is presented in small-step style as a transition relation $(\mathcal{P}, \mathcal{K}, \mathcal{G}) \to (\mathcal{P}', \mathcal{K}', \mathcal{G}')$ operating over triples of a control point $\mathcal{P}$, a continuation $\mathcal{K}$ and a global state $\mathcal{G}$. We distinguish 5 kinds of control points $\mathcal{P}$:

- Codepoint($Stmt_1, Stmt^*, Env, Block^*$): about to execute statement $Stmt_1$ followed by the list of statements $Stmt^*$, under variable environment Env. $Block^*$ is the list of all blocks enclosing the current statement, where a block is a pair $(\ell, Stmt^*)$ of a complete object ℓ to destruct at block exit and the remaining statements to execute after exiting from the block.
- Constr($\pi, ItemKind, \kappa, L, Env$): about to construct the list L of the bases or fields of the subobject π. Initializers are to be looked for using constructor κ, and they operate on the variable environment Env to pass arguments to their constructors. $ItemKind$ is one of Bases(DirectNonVirtual) or Bases(Virtual) or Fields, to request the construction of, respectively, direct non-virtual bases or virtual bases or fields of π.
- ConstrArray($\ell, \alpha, n, i, C, ObjInit^*, Env$): about to construct cells i to $n - 1$ of type C, of the array α from the complete object ℓ, using the initializers $ObjInit^*$ to initialize the cells, and Env as variable environment to execute the initializers.
- Destr($\pi, ItemKind, L$): about to destruct the list L of bases or fields of the subobject π.
- DestrArray(ℓ, α, i, C): about to destruct cells i down to 0 of type C, of the array α from the complete object ℓ.

We omit the grammar of continuations $\mathcal{K}$, which can be found in [12, chapter 9].

The operational semantics is composed of 56 inference rules defining the transition relation $(\mathcal{P}, \mathcal{K}, \mathcal{G}) \to (\mathcal{P}', \mathcal{K}', \mathcal{G}')$, for a total of about 900 lines of Coq definitions. We show some representative rules to give the general flavor, and refer the reader to the first author's thesis [12, chapter 9] for a full listing.

Field accesses Reading from a scalar field is modeled as follows:

$$\frac{\begin{array}{c} Env(var) = \pi \qquad \mathcal{G} \vdash \pi : C \qquad f = (\mathit{fid}, (\mathsf{Sc}, t)) \in \mathcal{F}(C) \\ \mathcal{G}.\mathsf{FieldValue}(\pi, f) = res \qquad Env' = Env[var' \leftarrow res] \end{array}}{\begin{array}{l} (\mathsf{Codepoint}(var' := var\text{->}_C f \ , L, Env, \mathcal{B}), \mathcal{K}, \mathcal{G}) \\ \to (\mathsf{Codepoint}(\mathsf{skip} \ , L, Env', \mathcal{B}), \mathcal{K}, \mathcal{G}) \end{array}}$$

Likewise, for an assignment to a scalar field, we have:

$$\frac{\begin{array}{c} Env(var) = \pi \qquad \mathcal{G} \vdash \pi : C \qquad f = (\mathit{fid}, (\mathsf{Sc}, t)) \in \mathcal{F}(C) \\ \mathcal{G}.\mathsf{ConstrState}^{\mathcal{F}}(\pi, f) = \mathsf{Constructed} \\ Env(var') = res \qquad \mathcal{G}' = \mathcal{G}[\mathsf{FieldValue}(\pi, f) \leftarrow res] \end{array}}{\begin{array}{l} (\mathsf{Codepoint}(var\text{->}_C f := var' \ , L, Env, \mathcal{B}), \mathcal{K}, \mathcal{G}) \\ \to (\mathsf{Codepoint}(\mathsf{skip} \ , L, Env, \mathcal{B}), \mathcal{K}, \mathcal{G}') \end{array}}$$

Note the side condition preventing assignment to a scalar field that is not Constructed. For reads, this conditions is not necessary: Theorem 4 below shows that if a field has a value, then it is Constructed.

Dynamic types Virtual function calls and dynamic casts both involve the notion of *dynamic type* of a subobject, which the C++ standard defines as its most-derived object during the lifetime of the latter. However, the standard also permits virtual function calls and dynamic casts during the execution of the constructor body, or field initializers, or destructor body corresponding to the subobject. To unify these two cases, we introduce the notion of *generalized dynamic type*. We define the predicate $\mathsf{gDynType}(\ell, \alpha, i, \sigma, B, \sigma', \sigma'')$, meaning that the base-class subobject σ' of static type B is the generalized dynamic type of the subobject $(\ell, (\alpha, i, \sigma))$ with $\sigma = \sigma' @ \sigma''$.

$$\frac{\begin{array}{c} \mathcal{G}.\mathsf{LocType}(\ell) = (D, n) \qquad D[n] \prec\!\langle \alpha \rangle\!\overset{\mathcal{A}}{\succ\!\!\to} C[m] \prec\!\langle (i, \sigma) \rangle\!\overset{\mathcal{CI}}{\succ\!\!\to} B \\ \mathcal{G}.\mathsf{ConstrState}(\ell, (\alpha, i, (\mathsf{Repeated}, C :: \epsilon))) = \mathsf{Constructed} \end{array}}{\mathcal{G} \vdash \mathsf{gDynType}(\ell, \alpha, i, \sigma, C, (\mathsf{Repeated}, C :: \epsilon), \sigma)}$$

$$\frac{\begin{array}{c} \mathcal{G}.\mathsf{LocType}(\ell) = (D, n) \\ D[n] \prec\!\langle \alpha \rangle\!\overset{\mathcal{A}}{\succ\!\!\to} C[m] \prec\!\langle (i, \sigma_\circ) \rangle\!\overset{\mathcal{CI}}{\succ\!\!\to} C_\circ \\ \mathcal{G}.\mathsf{ConstrState}(\ell, (\alpha, i, \sigma_\circ)) = c \\ c = \mathsf{BasesConstructed} \lor c = \mathsf{StartedDestructing} \\ C_\circ \prec\!\langle \sigma' \rangle\!\overset{\mathcal{I}}{\succ\!\!\to} B \qquad \sigma = \sigma_\circ @ \sigma' \end{array}}{\mathcal{G} \vdash \mathsf{gDynType}(\ell, \alpha, i, \sigma, C_\circ, \sigma_\circ, \sigma')}$$

The semantics of virtual function calls is similar to that given by Wasserrab *et al.* [18], except that we use the generalized dynamic type instead of the most-derived object. If $C_\circ$ is the generalized dynamic type of subobject σ', the predicate $\mathsf{VFDispatch}(C_\circ, \sigma', f, B'', \sigma'')$ determines the subobject $\sigma'' : B''$ of $C_\circ$ containing the definition of virtual function f that must be invoked, following the same algorithm as in [18]:

1. Determine the static resolving subobject σ_f declaring f.
2. Choose the *final overrider* for the method. The final overrider is the inheritance subobject σ'' between $C_\circ$ and σ_f, nearest to $C_\circ$, and declaring f.

The transition rule for a virtual function call is, then,

$$\frac{\begin{array}{c} Env(var) = (\ell, (\alpha, i, \sigma)) \\ \mathcal{G} \vdash \mathsf{gDynType}(\ell, \alpha, i, \sigma, C_\circ, \sigma_\circ, \sigma') \\ \mathsf{VFDispatch}(C_\circ, \sigma', f, B'', \sigma'') \\ B''.f = f(varg_1, \ldots, varg_n)\{body\} \qquad \forall j, Env(var_j) = v_j \\ Env' = \varnothing[varg_1 \leftarrow v_1] \ldots [varg_n \leftarrow v_n][\mathsf{this} \leftarrow (\ell, (\alpha, i, \sigma_\circ @ \sigma''))] \end{array}}{\begin{array}{l} (\mathsf{Codepoint}(var\text{->}_B f(var_1 \ldots var_n), L, Env, \mathcal{B}), \mathcal{K}, \mathcal{G}) \\ \to (\mathsf{Codepoint}(body, \epsilon, Env', \epsilon), \mathsf{Kretcall}(var, L, Env, \mathcal{B}) :: \mathcal{K}, \mathcal{G}) \end{array}}$$

Similarly, dynamic casts are handled as in Wasserrab *et al.* [18], using the generalized dynamic type instead of the most derived object. The transition rule is omitted for brevity, but can be found in [12, chapter 9].

Destruction We now give the flavor of the object construction and destruction protocol, starting with the simpler of the two, namely destruction. Destruction starts when the body of a block has reduced to skip or return:

$$\frac{(st = \mathsf{skip} \land L = \epsilon) \lor st = \mathsf{return} \qquad \mathcal{G}.\mathsf{LocType}(\ell) = (C, n)}{\begin{array}{l} (\mathsf{Codepoint}(st, L, Env, (\ell, L') :: \mathcal{B}), \mathcal{K}, \mathcal{G}) \\ \to (\mathsf{DestrArray}(\ell, L, n-1, C), \\ \quad \mathsf{Kcontinue}(st, Env, L', \mathcal{B}) :: \mathcal{K}, \mathcal{G}) \end{array}}$$

The DestrArray execution state requests the destruction of all elements of the structure array $C[n]$ at ℓ, starting with the last element $(n-1)$. Eventually, we reach a state where no more elements remain to be destructed, in which case we effectively exit from the block.

$$\frac{}{\begin{array}{l} (\mathsf{DestrArray}(\ell, \alpha, -1, C), \\ \quad \mathsf{Kcontinue}(st, Env, L, \mathcal{B}) :: \mathcal{K}, \mathcal{G}) \\ \to (\mathsf{Codepoint}(st, L, Env, \mathcal{B}), \mathcal{K}, \mathcal{G}) \end{array}}$$

When the destruction of a most-derived object (i.e. a structure array cell) is requested, we first enter the body of the associated destructor in a variable environment that binds this to the object.

$$\frac{\begin{array}{c} 0 \leq i \qquad \sim C()\{stmt\} \\ \pi = (\ell, (\alpha, i, (\mathsf{Repeated}, C :: \epsilon))) \qquad Env = \varnothing[\mathsf{this} \leftarrow \pi] \\ \mathcal{G}' = \mathcal{G}[\mathsf{ConstrState}(\pi) \leftarrow \mathsf{StartedDestructing}] \end{array}}{\begin{array}{l} (\mathsf{DestrArray}(\ell, \alpha, i, C), \mathcal{K}, \mathcal{G}) \\ \to (\mathsf{Codepoint}(stmt, \epsilon, Env, \epsilon), \\ \quad \mathsf{Kdestr}(\pi) :: \mathsf{Kdestrcell}(\ell, \alpha, i, C) :: \mathcal{K}, \mathcal{G}') \end{array}}$$

When the destructor body returns, the fields of the subobject have to be destructed, in reverse declaration order.

$$\frac{\pi = (\ell, (\alpha, i, (h, l))) \qquad \mathsf{last}(l) = C \qquad L = \mathsf{rev}(\mathcal{F}(C))}{\begin{array}{l} (\mathsf{Codepoint}(\mathsf{return}, Stmt^*, Env, \epsilon), \mathsf{Kdestr}(\pi) :: \mathcal{K}, \mathcal{G}) \\ \to (\mathsf{Destr}(\pi, \mathsf{Fields}, L), \mathcal{K}, \mathcal{G}) \end{array}}$$

Destructing a scalar field erases its value and changes its construction state to Destructed, before proceeding with the remaining fields.

$$\frac{\begin{array}{c} f = (\mathit{fid}, (\mathsf{Sc}, t)) \\ \mathcal{G}' = \mathcal{G}[\mathsf{FieldValue}(\pi, f) \leftarrow \bot][\mathsf{ConstrState}^{\mathcal{F}}(\pi, f) \leftarrow \mathsf{Destructed}] \end{array}}{\begin{array}{l} (\mathsf{Destr}(\pi, \mathsf{Fields}, f :: L), \mathcal{K}, \mathcal{G}) \\ \to (\mathsf{Destr}(\pi, \mathsf{Fields}, L), \mathcal{K}, \mathcal{G}') \end{array}}$$

Destructing a structure array field changes its construction state to StartedDestructing, then requests the destruction of the array, starting from its last cell, and remembering the remaining fields through Kdestrother in the continuation.

$$\frac{\begin{array}{c} \pi = (\ell, (\alpha, i, \sigma)) \\ f = (\mathit{fid}, (\mathsf{St}, (C, n))) \qquad \alpha' = \alpha +\!\!+ (i, \sigma, f) :: \epsilon \\ \mathcal{G}' = \mathcal{G}[\mathsf{ConstrState}^{\mathcal{F}}(\pi, f) \leftarrow \mathsf{StartedDestructing}] \end{array}}{\begin{array}{l} (\mathsf{Destr}(\pi, \mathsf{Fields}, f :: L), \mathcal{K}, \mathcal{G}) \\ \to (\mathsf{DestrArray}(\ell, \alpha', n-1, C), \\ \quad \mathsf{Kdestrother}(\pi, \mathsf{Fields}, f, L) :: \mathcal{K}, \mathcal{G}') \end{array}}$$

Then, once all cells have been destructed, the field enters the Destructed state, and we proceed with the destruction of the remaining fields.

$$\frac{\mathcal{G}' = \mathcal{G}[\mathsf{ConstrState}^{\mathcal{F}}(\pi, f) \leftarrow \mathsf{Destructed}]}{\begin{array}{l}(\mathsf{DestrArray}(\ell', \alpha', -1, C), \mathsf{Kdestrother}(\pi, \mathsf{Fields}, f, L) :: \mathcal{K}, \mathcal{G}) \\ \to (\mathsf{Destr}(\pi, \mathsf{Fields}, L), \mathcal{K}, \mathcal{G}')\end{array}}$$

Eventually, all fields have been destructed. The subobject then changes its construction state to DestructingBases. At this point, no virtual function call nor dynamic casts may be used on this subobject. The destruction of the direct non-virtual bases starts, in reverse declaration order.

$$\frac{\begin{array}{c}\pi = (\ell, (\alpha, i, (h, l))) \qquad \mathsf{last}(l) = C \qquad L = \mathsf{rev}(\mathcal{DNV}(C)) \\ \mathcal{G}' = \mathcal{G}[\mathsf{ConstrState}(\pi) \leftarrow \mathsf{DestructingBases}]\end{array}}{\begin{array}{l}(\mathsf{Destr}(\pi, \mathsf{Fields}, \epsilon), \mathcal{K}, \mathcal{G}) \\ \to (\mathsf{Destr}(\pi, \mathsf{Bases}(\mathsf{DirectNonVirtual}), L), \mathcal{K}, \mathcal{G}')\end{array}}$$

Destructing a (virtual or direct non-virtual) base B of π enters its destructor, remembering the other bases through Kdestrother.

$$\frac{\begin{array}{c}\sim B()\{stmt\} \\ \pi' = \mathsf{AddBase}(\pi, \beta, B) \qquad Env = \varnothing[\mathsf{this} \leftarrow \pi'] \\ \mathcal{G}' = \mathcal{G}[\mathsf{ConstrState}(\pi') \leftarrow \mathsf{StartedDestructing}]\end{array}}{\begin{array}{l}(\mathsf{Destr}(\pi, \mathsf{Bases}(\beta), B :: L), \mathcal{K}, \mathcal{G}) \\ \to (\mathsf{Codepoint}(stmt, \epsilon, Env, \epsilon), \\ \quad \mathsf{Kdestr}(\pi') :: \mathsf{Kdestrother}(\pi, \mathsf{Bases}(\beta), B, L) :: \mathcal{K}, \mathcal{G}')\end{array}}$$

Eventually, we reach a state where all direct non-virtual bases of π have been destructed. There are two cases to consider, depending on the top of the continuation stack. In the first case, the continuation stack starts with a $\mathsf{Kdestrother}(\pi', \mathsf{Bases}(\beta), B, L)$, indicating that π is not a most-derived object. In this case, there is no need to destruct the virtual part of π (this will be done later by the enclosing most-derived object) and we are done with the subobject π: its construction state becomes Destructed, and we proceed with the destruction of the remaining bases of π'.

$$\frac{\mathcal{G}' = \mathcal{G}[\mathsf{ConstrState}(\pi) \leftarrow \mathsf{Destructed}]}{\begin{array}{l}(\mathsf{Destr}(\pi, \mathsf{Bases}(\mathsf{DirectNonVirtual}), \epsilon), \\ \quad \mathsf{Kdestrother}(\pi', \mathsf{Bases}(\beta), B, L) :: \mathcal{K}, \mathcal{G}) \\ \to (\mathsf{Destr}(\pi', \mathsf{Bases}(\beta), L), \mathcal{K}, \mathcal{G}')\end{array}}$$

The second case is when the continuation stack starts with a Kdestrcell. Then, π must be a most-derived object, and its direct and indirect virtual bases need to be destructed. According to the C++ standard, virtual bases must be destructed in *reverse inheritance graph order*. Consider the following recursive function:

$$\begin{array}{rcl}\mathsf{list}(\{\mathsf{Repeated}, \mathsf{Shared}\} \times \mathcal{C}) & \overset{\mathcal{VO}}{\to} & \mathsf{list}(\mathcal{C}) \\ \mathcal{VO}(\epsilon) & = & \epsilon \\ \mathcal{VO}((\mathsf{Repeated}, B) :: q) & = & \mathcal{VO}(\mathcal{D}(B)) +\!\!+' \mathcal{VO}(q) \\ \mathcal{VO}((\mathsf{Shared}, B) :: q) & = & \mathcal{VO}(\mathcal{D}(B)) +\!\!+' (B :: \mathcal{VO}(q))\end{array}$$

where $\mathcal{D}(B)$ is the list of direct bases of B, in declaration order, tagged with Repeated(for non-virtual bases) or Shared(for virtual bases), and $+\!\!+'$ is list concatenation with elimination of duplicates ($l_1 +\!\!+' l_2 =_{\text{def}} l_1 +\!\!+ (l_2 \setminus l_1)$). It is easy to see that the list $L = \mathcal{VO}(\mathcal{D}(C))$ contains all the direct and indirect virtual bases of C, exactly once each, and contains no other classes. Moreover, the order in which virtual bases appear in list L is consistent with the inheritance graph order. In particular, if A and B are virtual bases of C such that A is a virtual base of B, then A appears before B in L.

$$\frac{L' = \mathsf{rev}(\mathcal{VO}(\mathcal{D}(C)))}{\begin{array}{l}(\mathsf{Destr}(\pi, \mathsf{Bases}(\mathsf{DirectNonVirtual}), \epsilon), \\ \quad \mathsf{Kdestrcell}(\ell, \alpha, i, C) :: \mathcal{K}, \mathcal{G}) \\ \to (\mathsf{Destr}(\pi, \mathsf{Bases}(\mathsf{Virtual}), L'), \mathcal{K}, \mathcal{G})\end{array}}$$

Finally, when all virtual bases have been destructed, the subobject under consideration (necessarily a most-derived object) becomes Destructed, and we proceed with the destruction of the preceding structure array cells.

$$\frac{\begin{array}{c}\pi = (\ell, (\alpha, i, (h, l))) \\ \mathsf{last}(l) = C \qquad \mathcal{G}' = \mathcal{G}[\mathsf{ConstrState}(\pi) \leftarrow \mathsf{Destructed}]\end{array}}{\begin{array}{l}(\mathsf{Destr}(\pi, \mathsf{Bases}(\mathsf{Virtual}), \epsilon), \mathcal{K}, \mathcal{G}) \\ \to (\mathsf{DestrArray}(\ell, \alpha, i - 1, C), \mathcal{K}, \mathcal{G}')\end{array}}$$

Construction To execute a block statement, we allocate memory for the structure array declared in the block, then start the construction protocol by requesting the construction of the first element of this array:

$$\frac{\begin{array}{c}\ell \notin \mathsf{dom}(\mathcal{G}.\mathsf{LocType}) \qquad \mathcal{G}' = \mathcal{G}[\mathsf{LocType}(\ell) \leftarrow (C, n)] \\ Env' = Env[c \leftarrow \mathsf{Ptr}(\ell, \epsilon, (\mathsf{Repeated}, C :: \epsilon))]\end{array}}{\begin{array}{l}(\mathsf{Codepoint}(\{C\ c[n] = \{\iota\}; st\}, St, Env, Bl), \mathcal{K}, \mathcal{G}) \\ \to (\mathsf{ConstrArray}(\ell, \epsilon, n, 0, C, \iota, Env'), \\ \quad \mathsf{Kcontinue}(st, Env', St, Bl) :: \mathcal{K}, \mathcal{G}')\end{array}}$$

The construction protocol implements the necessary traversal of all subobjects of c using the same "small-stepping" style, based on continuations, that was illustrated above in the case of destruction. There are two main differences. First, the construction order is the exact opposite of the destruction order: instead of enumerating array cells by decreasing indices, fields and non-virtual bases in reverse declaration order and virtual bases in reverse $\mathcal{VO}$ order, we enumerate array cells by increasing indices, fields and non-virtual bases in declaration order and virtual bases in $\mathcal{VO}$ order. Second and more importantly, we need to execute the initializers that compute initial values for scalar fields and the arguments to be passed to constructors, adding a number of transition rules. We refer the reader to [12, chapter 9] for full details.

4. Properties of construction and destruction

In this section, we state (and sometimes outline the proofs of) several semantic properties of interest for construction and destruction. Some are technical consequences of the definition of our semantics, but others capture higher-level properties that C++ programmers often rely on, such as the RAII principle.

4.1 Run-time invariant

Our transition rules and grammars for execution states are lax in that they put very few constraints on the general shapes of states. However, in transition sequences starting from the initial state, the reachable states are a small subset of all possible states and enjoy many low-level properties that are essential to prove the high-level theorems in this section. We gathered about 20 such properties in one invariant INV and proved that this invariant is satisfied by the initial state and preserved by the transition rules. This is the largest part of the Coq mechanization, totaling about 15000 lines of Coq and taking about 2 hours to re-check the proof.

A detailed explanation of the invariant is given in [12, section 10.1]. Here, we just show the two most interesting consequences of the invariant, which relate the construction states of certain subobjects.

Let p, p' be two subobjects of the same complete object. We say that p is a *direct subobject* of p' if, either, (1) p is a direct non-virtual base of p'; (2) or p' is a most-derived object and p is a virtual base of p'; (3) or p is a field subobject of p' (that is, p is a cell of a structure array field of p').

Lemma 1 (Vertical relations on construction states)**.** *Assume that p is a direct subobject of p'. The construction states of p and p' in any execution state satisfying INV are related as follows:*

If p' is...	*Then p is...*
Unconstructed	Unconstructed
StartedConstructing	Unconstructed *if p is field subobject of p'*
BasesConstructed	Constructed *if p is a base subobject of p'*
Constructed	Constructed
StartedDestructing	Constructed *if p is a base subobject of p'*
DestructingBases	Destructed *if p is a field subobject of p'*
Destructed	Destructed

Let p' be a subobject of static type C, and p_1, p_2 be two direct subobjects of p'. We say that p_1 *occurs before* p_2 if, either, (1) p' is a most-derived object and p_1, p_2 are two virtual bases of p' in inheritance graph order; (2) p_1 and p_2 are two direct non-virtual bases of p in declaration order; (3) p_1 and p_2 are two cells of the same array field, in the order of their indexes within the array; (4) p_1 and p_2 are two cells of two different fields in declaration order; (5) p' is a most-derived object and p_1 is a virtual base, and p_2 is a direct non-virtual base of p' or a cell of an array field; (6) p_1 is a direct non-virtual base of p' and p_2 is a cell of an array field.

Lemma 2 (Horizontal relations on construction states). *Assume that p_1 occurs before p_2. The construction states of p_1 and p_2 in any execution state satisfying INV are related as follows:*

If p_1 is...	*Then p_2 is...*
Unconstructed StartedConstructing BasesConstructed	Unconstructed
Constructed	*in an arbitrary state*
StartedDestructing DestructingBases Destructed	Destructed

In the remainder of this section, we only consider execution states that can be reached from the initial state and therefore satisfy the invariant INV.

4.2 Progress

To check that our transition rules make sense and that no rule is missing, we prove a "progress" property of construction and destruction: once construction of a complete object starts, it always eventually reaches a point where the object is fully constructed, without getting stuck in the middle; and likewise for destruction. This result is false in general: since constructors, initializers and destructors can perform arbitrary computation, they can get stuck on e.g. an attempt to assign an unconstructed scalar field. However, we can prove the expected result if we restrict ourselves to *nearly trivial* constructors and *trivial destructors*.

We say that a class C has a nearly trivial constructor if (1) C has a default constructor with no arguments and `return` as its body; (2) initializers for bases and fields just call the default constructors, without any other computations; (3) scalar fields are initialized with constants; (4) for each structure array field f of C, if f has type B, then B has a nearly trivial constructor. This notion extends the concept of *trivial constructor* from the C++ standard, e.g. by allowing virtual bases and virtual functions.

Theorem 3 (Construction progress). *Let $(\mathcal{P}, \mathcal{K}, \mathcal{G})$ be an execution state where $\mathcal{P} = \mathsf{Codepoint}(\{C\ c[n]; st\} = \iota, \ldots)$, i.e. we are about to execute a block statement. Assume that C is a class having a nearly trivial constructor and that the initializer list ι calls the default constructor for every array cell. Then, there exists a state $(\mathcal{P}', \mathcal{K}', \mathcal{G}')$ such that*

- $(\mathcal{P}, \mathcal{K}, \mathcal{G}) \xrightarrow{*} (\mathcal{P}', \mathcal{K}', \mathcal{G}')$
- $\mathcal{P}' = \mathsf{Codepoint}(st, \ldots)$*, i.e. construction has terminated and the block body is about to be executed;*
- *in state $\mathcal{G}'$, all cells of the array c are in the* Constructed *state.*

A similar theorem holds for destruction. Here, we use unchanged the notion of *trivial destructor* from the C++ standard: a class C has a trivial destructor if (1) its destructor is just `return`; (2) all virtual bases and direct non-virtual bases of C have trivial destructors; (3) for each structure array field f of C, if f has type B, then B has a trivial destructor.

4.3 Safety of field accesses and virtual function calls

The rule for reading the contents of a scalar field puts no precondition on the initialization state of the field. We can, however, show that this rule gets stuck whenever the field is not in the Constructed state.

Theorem 4. *A scalar field has a well-defined value only if it is* Constructed*.*

Proof. Follows from INV and the fact that setting the value of a scalar field only occurs in two cases: either on an ordinary scalar field, which is forbidden if the field is not Constructed, or on scalar field initialization, which turns the field construction state to Constructed. Moreover, our semantics erases the value of the scalar field when destructing it. □

Like C++ itself, our semantics allows fields to have no initializers and therefore remain without a defined value after construction. However, we also proved that if we remove the transition rule allowing fields without initializers to proceed, a scalar field has a well-defined value if and only if it is Constructed.

Virtual functions have no initialization state *per se*. However, the C++ semantics for virtual function calls provides a very useful guarantee concerning the construction state of the `this` subobject:

Theorem 5. *Whenever a virtual function is called, the subobject bound to its `this` parameter is in state* BasesConstructed *or* Constructed *or* StartedDestructing*, and all its base-class subobjects are in state* Constructed*.*

Proof. Consider a call to a virtual function f on a subobject (ℓ, p). Since this call does not go wrong, the generalized dynamic type p_o of this subobject is defined. By definition of generalized dynamic types, (ℓ, p_o) is in state BasesConstructed or Constructed or StartedDestructing. Invariant INV then guarantees that all base-class subobjects of (ℓ, p_o) are Constructed (from Lemma 1). The final overrider for function f being either (ℓ, p_o) or one of its base-class subobjects, the result follows. □

In other words, a virtual function can always safely assume that bases have been properly constructed. It cannot, however, assume that fields of its defining class are in the constructed state, since initializers for these fields can call the virtual function. As discussed in §2 and by Qi and Myers [11], Java does not provide a similar guarantee; through inheritance and method overriding, it is possible for a method to be invoked before its super classes have completed their initialization.

4.4 Evolution of construction states

Lemma 6. *If $s \to s'$ is a transition step of our small-step operational semantics, and if the construction state of the subobject (ℓ, p) is c in s and $c' \neq c$ in s', then $c' = \mathsf{S}(c)$ and any other subobject $(\ell', p') \neq (\ell, p)$ keeps its construction state unchanged.*

Proof. By case analysis on the transition rules, with the help of invariant INV. □

Corollary 7. *Any subobject is never constructed or destructed more than once.*

In particular, any virtual base subobject is constructed or destructed at most once, despite being potentially reachable through several inheritance paths. Also, if an object goes from one construction state to another, then it must go through all construction states in between:

Theorem 8 (Intermediate values theorem). *If $s \xrightarrow{*} s'$, then, for any subobject (ℓ, p) and for any construction state c such that:*

$$\mathsf{ConstrState}_s(\ell, p) \leq c < S(c) \leq \mathsf{ConstrState}_{s'}(\ell, p)$$

there exist "changing states" s_1, s_2 such that $s \xrightarrow{*} s_1 \to s_2 \xrightarrow{*} s'$ and $\mathsf{ConstrState}_{s_1}(\ell, p) = c$ and $\mathsf{ConstrState}_{s_2}(\ell, p) = S(c)$.

(Here, for a state $s = (\mathcal{P}, \mathcal{K}, \mathcal{G})$, we write $\mathsf{ConstrState}_s(\pi)$ for $\mathcal{G}.\mathsf{ConstrState}(\pi)$.)

4.5 Object lifetimes

An important design principle of C++ is that destruction is performed in the exact reverse order of construction. We now formalize and prove this property, along with more general properties about the relative lifetimes of two subobjects.

Two subobjects of the same complete object Let ℓ be a complete object of type $C[n]$.

Theorem 9. *If p_1 and p_2 are two subobjects of the complete object ℓ, either the lifetime of p_1 is included in that of p_2, or the lifetime of p_2 is included in that of p_1.*

To prove this theorem, we need to characterize the construction order between subobjects. We write $p_1 \preceq_{C[n]} p_2$ to say that p_1 occurs before p_2 in the depth-first, left-to-right traversal of the construction tree in Figure 1. (See [12, chapter 10] for a formal definition in terms of the "direct subobject" and "occurs before" relations of §4.1.) The two crucial properties of this construction order are the following:

Lemma 10 (The construction order is total). *If $C[n] \prec\!\!\langle p_1 \rangle\!\!\mapsto B_1$ and $C[n] \prec\!\!\langle p_2 \rangle\!\!\mapsto B_2$, then either $p_1 \preceq_{C[n]} p_2$ or $p_2 \preceq_{C[n]} p_1$.*

Lemma 11 (Construction order and lifetimes). *For any reachable execution state s and any complete object ℓ of type $C[n]$, if $p_1 \preceq_{C[n]} p_2$ and $\mathsf{ConstrState}_s(\ell, p_2) = \mathsf{Constructed}$, then $\mathsf{ConstrState}_s(\ell, p_1) = \mathsf{Constructed}$. In other words, if $p_1 \preceq_{C[n]} p_2$, then the lifetime of p_2 is included in the lifetime of p_1.*

Theorem 9 then follows directly from the two lemmas above. Using Lemma 11 and the definition of $\preceq_{C[n]}$, we have the following stronger special case:

Theorem 12. *If p_2 is a subobject of p_1, then the lifetime of p_1 is included in that of p_2.*

As a corollary of Theorem 9, it follows that if p_1 is constructed before p_2, then p_2 is destructed before p_1.

Theorem 13 (Destruction in reverse order of construction). *Let ℓ be a complete object of type $C[n]$ and p_1, p_2 be two subobjects of ℓ. Consider the reduction sequence below where p_1 is constructed before p_2, then later p_1 is destructed:*

$$\begin{array}{ccccccccccc} s_0 & \to & s_1 & \xrightarrow{*} & s_2 & \to & s_3 & \xrightarrow{*} & s_4 & \to & s_5 \\ (\neg c_1) & & (c_1) & & (\neg c_2) & & (c_2) & & (c_1) & & (\neg c_1) \end{array}$$

(We write c_i below a state s to denote that p_i is $\mathsf{Constructed}$ in state s, and $\neg c_i$ to mean that p_i is not $\mathsf{Constructed}$.) Then, there exist intermediate states s'_3, s'_4 such that p_2 stops being $\mathsf{Constructed}$ between these two states:

$$\begin{array}{ccccccccccccccc} s_0 & \to & s_1 & \xrightarrow{*} & s_2 & \to & s_3 & \xrightarrow{*} & s'_3 & \to & s'_4 & \xrightarrow{*} & s_4 & \to & s_5 \\ (\neg c_1) & & (c_1) & & (\neg c_2) & & (c_2) & & (c_2) & & (\neg c_2) & & (c_1) & & (\neg c_1) \end{array}$$

Proof. At state s_2, p_1 is $\mathsf{Constructed}$ but p_2 is not. Hence, the lifetime of p_1 cannot be included in that of p_2. By theorem 9, the lifetime of p_2 is therefore included in that of p_1. Since p_1 is no longer $\mathsf{Constructed}$ at state s_5, so is p_2 at state s_5. Since at most one subobject changes construction state during a given transition (Lemma 6), $p_1 \neq p_2$ and p_2 is no longer $\mathsf{Constructed}$ at state s_4. The result then follows from the the intermediate values theorem (Theorem 8). □

Subobjects of different complete objects In the full C++ language, including dynamic allocation, the lifetimes of two subobjects of different complete objects are, in general, unrelated: `new` and `delete` operations can be interleaved arbitrarily. In our core language, complete objects can only be created by block statements and therefore follow a stack discipline.

Theorem 14. *The lifetimes of two subobjects (ℓ_1, p_1) and (ℓ_2, p_2) of different complete objects $\ell_1 \neq \ell_2$ are either disjoint or included in one another.*

This result follows from Theorem 9 and the stronger property below, which shows that throughout the execution of a block, the construction states of subobjects of already-allocated complete objects do not change:

Lemma 15. *Let $s_1 \to s_2 \xrightarrow{*} s_3 \to s_4$ be the execution of a block: the transition $s_1 \to s_2$ enters the block and allocates a fresh complete object ℓ; the transition $s_3 \to s_4$ exits this block. For all complete objects ℓ' already allocated in state s_1, the allocation states of its subobjects (ℓ', p') are identical in s_1 and s_4.*

4.6 RAII: Resource Acquisition Is Initialization

RAII is a programming discipline where precious program resources (such as file descriptors) are systematically encapsulated in classes, all acquisitions of such resources are performed within constructors of the corresponding class, and all releases of such resources are performed within destructors of the corresponding class. We cannot prove a general result guaranteeing the proper encapsulation of resources in classes: this is a matter of program verification. We can, however, prove that in a terminating program every construction of a subobject is correctly matched by a destruction.

Theorem 16 (RAII). *Consider a partial program execution $s_{init} \xrightarrow{*} s_1 \to s_2$ where the transition $s_1 \to s_2$ marks the end of a block statement that allocated the complete object ℓ. Then, between the initial state s_{init} and s_1, the following events occurred, in this order:*

- *Every subobject of ℓ was constructed exactly once.*
- *Every subobject of ℓ was destructed exactly once, in reverse order of construction.*

Proof. The invariant INV implies that, at state s_1, all cells of the structure array ℓ are $\mathsf{Destructed}$, and so are all of their subobjects. Consider a subobject (ℓ, p). Its state is $\mathsf{Unconstructed}$ in the initial state and $\mathsf{Destructed}$ in s_1. Therefore, by the intermediate value theorem (Theorem 8), it must have entered state $\mathsf{Constructed}$ at some point, then left state $\mathsf{Constructed}$ at some later point, meaning that (ℓ, p) has been initialized once, then destructed once. The claim on construction and destruction order follows from Theorem 13. □

4.7 Generalized dynamic types

We finish this section with interesting properties of generalized dynamic types, which were introduced in §3.4 to give semantics to virtual function calls and dynamic casts.

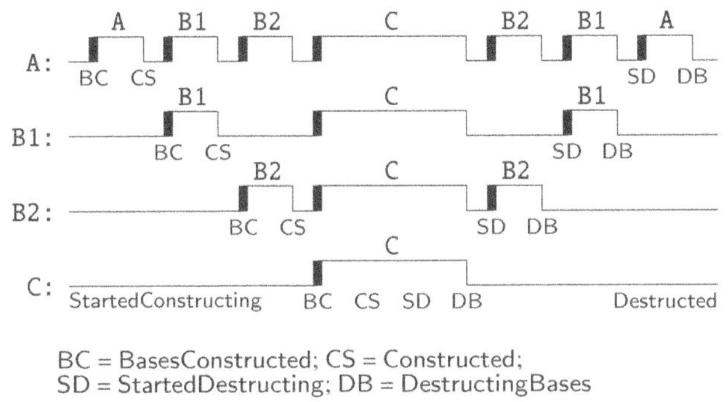

Figure 2. Evolution of the dynamic types of an instance of `C` and of its subobjects in the example of §4.7. Dynamic types are undefined at points where the "signal" is low, and defined and equal to the indicated type when the "signal" is high. Thick vertical transitions denote points where a compiled implementation must update pointers to v-tables.

Theorem 17. *The generalized dynamic type of a subobject, if defined, is unique.*

Proof. The result is trivial if the most-derived object is Constructed, since it is then equal to the generalized dynamic type. Otherwise, we observe that the most-derived object can have at most one base class subobject in state BasesConstructed or StartedDestructing (as a consequence of invariant INV), and conclude. □

A subtle aspect of generalized dynamic types is that they do not *continuously* exist: as the construction or destruction of a most-derived object proceeds, the generalized dynamic type of one of its base-class subobjects alternates between defined and undefined. Consider the following program:

```
struct A              {virtual void f ();};
struct B1: virtual A {};
struct B2: virtual A {virtual void f ();};
struct C: B1, B2 {}
```

Figure 2 shows the evolution of the dynamic type of an instance of `C` and of its subobjects while this instance undergoes construction then destruction. For example, during the construction of base `B2`, the subobject `B1` is already Constructed, but its generalized dynamic type is undefined (the constructor of `B1` has returned but `C` is not yet constructed), and calling `f` on `B1` has undefined behavior.

Theorem 18. *Let $(\ell, (\alpha, i, \sigma))$ be a subobject and $(\ell, (\alpha, i, \sigma_\circ))$ be its most derived object (i.e. $\sigma_\circ = (\mathsf{Repeated}, C :: \epsilon)$). Consider a transition $s \twoheadrightarrow s'$ where the construction state of $(\ell, (\alpha, i, \sigma))$ changes. Then, the generalized dynamic types for all subobjects in the program evolve as shown in Table 1.*

In a compiled implementation, dynamic types are materialized as extra fields in the in-memory representations of objects, these fields containing (in general) pointers to v-tables. When the generalized dynamic type of a subobject is undefined, its dynamic type field can contain any value. However, when the generalized dynamic type is defined, the dynamic type field must contain a pointer to the corresponding v-table. Theorem 18, therefore, pinpoints exactly the program points where the compiled code must update dynamic type fields: when all bases of a subobject are constructed, and just before the construction of fields begins, dynamic type fields must be updated for the subobject in question and all of its bases; likewise, when the subobject undergoes destruction, at the point where the destructor is entered.

5. Impact on the C++ language specification

The development of the formal semantics reported in this paper uncovered several issues with the C++03 standard. They were reported to the ISO C++ committee. Some of them were fixed in time for the C++11 standards; others will be addressed in future revisions.

Virtual functions calls during object construction and destruction The formulation of ISO C++03 [6] of the behavior of the abstract machine when a virtual function is called during construction (or destruction) was unclear and did not clearly support the original intent (correctly modeled in this paper). This was reported to the ISO C++ committee as CWG issue number 1202. The formulation was clarified in time for adoption in C++11.

Conflicting description of end of object lifetime Although the language formally defined in this paper does not allow explicit management of object lifetime, coming up with a simple, coherent, unified, and faithful description of object lifetime led us to discover conflicts and unintended semantics in the ISO C++ documents (both C++03 and C++11.) The C++11 standard [7] has a conflicting description of the effect of calling a destructor. Two paragraphs (3.8p1 and 3.8p4) claim that an object's lifetime ends when a call to a non-trivial destructor occurs or its storage is reused or released. However, another paragraph (14.2p4) claims that once a destructor is invoked (its triviality notwithstanding), "the object no longer exists". This issue will be resolved after C++11 is published. We expect that for consistency, the resolution will not consider "triviality" of the destructor to determine when an object's lifetime ends.

Effect of calling destructor for builtin types C++ allows an expression of the form `p->~T()` where `T` is a non-class type name and `p` is an expression that points to a `T` object. This form was introduced to support function templates explicitly managing object lifetime without forcing the author to distinguish between builtin types and class types. It was also intended to bring uniformity. However, the formulation of the behavior of the abstract machine *appears* to indicate that the following program fragment has a well-defined meaning, for any scalar type `T`.

```
T f(T x) {
  T t = x;
  t.~T();
  return t;
}
```

This is in a clear conflict with the case where `T` is a class type. Indeed, for every class type `T`, that function leads to an undefined behavior, as it attempts to destroy the local variable `t` twice: once explicitly through the call to the destructor and a second time implicitly when the function exits. Finally, it appears that the program is ill-formed (and a diagnostic is required) when `T` is an array type.

Lifetime of array objects The C++ standards explicitly indicate that the lifetime of an array object starts as soon as storage for it has been allocated, regardless of when the lifetime of its elements starts. In general, a complete object's lifetime starts after all its subobjects have been constructed. This irregularity appears to be a hand-over from C in its formulation. It will be reconsidered after publication of C++11 along with a more unified treatment of the lifetime of objects of builtin types.

6. Application to verified compilation

To strengthen confidence in the semantics presented here and stress its usability, the first author developed and proved correct a simple compiler that translates the core language presented in this paper

When the subobject	goes from	to	then the gen. dynamic type of	goes from	to
$(\ell, (\alpha, i, \sigma))$	Unconstructed	StartedConstructing	$(\ell, (\alpha, i, \sigma'))$	Undef.	Undef.
$(\ell, (\alpha, i, \sigma))$	StartedConstructing	BasesConstructed	$(\ell, (\alpha, i, \sigma@\sigma''))$	Undef.	σ
			$(\ell, (\alpha, i, \sigma'))$ not a base of σ	Undef.	Undef.
$(\ell, (\alpha, i, \sigma))$ with $\sigma \neq \sigma_\circ$	BasesConstructed	Constructed	$(\ell, (\alpha, i, \sigma@\sigma''))$	σ	Undef.
			$(\ell, (\alpha, i, \sigma'))$ not a base of σ	Undef.	Undef.
$(\ell, (\alpha, i, \sigma_\circ))$	BasesConstructed	Constructed	$(\ell, (\alpha, i, \sigma'))$	$\sigma_\circ$	$\sigma_\circ$
$(\ell, (\alpha, i, \sigma_\circ))$	Constructed	StartedDestructing	$(\ell, (\alpha, i, \sigma'))$	$\sigma_\circ$	$\sigma_\circ$
$(\ell, (\alpha, i, \sigma))$ with $\sigma \neq \sigma_\circ$	Constructed	StartedDestructing	$(\ell, (\alpha, i, \sigma@\sigma''))$	Undef.	σ
			$(\ell, (\alpha, i, \sigma'))$ not a base of σ	Undef.	Undef.
$(\ell, \alpha, i, \sigma)$	StartedDestructing	DestructingBases	$(\ell, (\alpha, i, \sigma@\sigma''))$	σ	Undef.
			$(\ell, (\alpha, i, \sigma'))$ not a base of σ	Undef.	Undef.
$(\ell, (\alpha, i, \sigma))$	DestructingBases	Destructed	$(\ell, (\alpha, i, \sigma'))$	Undef.	Undef.
$(\ell, (\alpha, i, \sigma))$	Any	Any	$(\ell', (\alpha', i', \sigma'))$ with $(\ell, \alpha, i) \neq (\ell', \alpha', i')$	Does not change	

Table 1. Evolutions of generalized dynamic types when the state of a subobject $(\ell, (\alpha, i, \sigma))$, of most-derived object $\sigma_\circ$, changes.

to a simple, non-object-oriented intermediate language similar to CompCert's Cminor [8]. This verification is described in [12, chapter 11]. The compiler proceeds in two passes, using as intermediate language the CoreC++ language of Wasserrab *et al.* [18] extended with a `setDynType` operation that explicitly modifies the dynamic type of an object.

The first translation pass is broadly similar to that outlined in Wasserrab's thesis [17], turning constructors, initializers and destructors into non-virtual function calls. However, `setDynType` operations are inserted at the program points characterized by Theorem 18 to implement the proper semantics for virtual function calls and dynamic casts. Following a popular optimization, two versions of every constructor are generated, one for the "most derived" case, the other for the "inheritance subobject" case. The second translation pass extends our earlier work on object layout [13].

The proofs of semantic preservation are standard arguments by forward simulation diagrams [8, §3.7]. The proofs are rather big (about 8000 lines of Coq for each pass) because there are many cases to consider, along with complex invariants relating execution states, but present no major conceptual difficulties.

7. Related work

Formal semantics for C++ Norrish [10] describes a formal semantics for C++ that was mechanized in HOL. His semantics describes a much larger subset of C++ than ours, including in particular expressions with side effects and partially-specified evaluation order, exceptions, free store (`new` and `delete`), and temporary objects. Construction and destruction are modeled by "dynamic translation": the reduction rule for the construction of an object produces "on the fly" a statement containing the necessary invocations of initializers and constructors for fields and bases; this statement is, then, reduced normally. As a way to state the semantics, Norrish's approach is arguably simpler than our "small-stepping" of the construction/destruction protocol. However, we suspect that Norrish's approach would make it more difficult to prove meta-properties about construction states and lifetimes, in the style of §4. Additionally, we suspect that Norrish's semantics does not correctly capture the interaction between construction, destruction, and virtual function calls. Consider:

```
struct B {
  B* b;
  virtual int f() { return 18; }
  B() : b(this) { }
};
struct D : B {
  virtual int f() { return 42; }
};
int main () { D d; return d.b->f(); };
```

In `B`'s constructor, the initialization `b(this)` saves in `b` a pointer whose dynamic type is `B` (correctly, at that time). However, after completion of `D`'s constructor, the dynamic type of `*b` is not updated to `D`, causing the wrong `f` virtual function to be dispatched in `main`.

The CoreC++ semantics of Wasserrab, Nipkow, Snelting and Tip [18] is a major starting point for our work. It does not cover object construction and destruction. Wasserrab's Ph.D. thesis [17] describes this semantics and its Isabelle/HOL formalization in greater details, as well as a static, unverified translation of construction and destruction into non-virtual function calls. This translation fails to correctly implement C++'s semantics for virtual function calls: in the translated program, the dynamic type of a subobject is always its most derived object, regardless of construction state.

We are not aware of any other formal semantics for C++ that addresses construction and destruction.

Type systems for safe object initialization Several research projects develop type systems for object-oriented languages that enforce safety guarantees about object initialization, such as the fact that well-typed programs never read fields of an uninitialized object. Fähndrich and Xia [3] introduce a type system to remove useless field initializations to `null` while still ensuring safe object initialization. Qi and Myers [11] introduce a more general type system to precisely and statically determine, at each program point, which fields may be read or not. Hubert *et al.* [5] formalize a type system for safe Java object initialization using the Coq proof assistant. Their type system shares with our operational semantics the use of construction states for objects, but in their case, construction states are lifted to the type level and maintained at compile-time. This enables their system to statically check contracts over methods that constrain the construction states of some of the arguments, for instance.

Our work makes no attempt at providing static typing safety properties beyond the few offered by C++. Instead, we aim at a precise description of the dynamic semantics of construction and destruction in the presence of multiple inheritance. The type systems mentioned above are based on the Java and C# single-inheritance object models. Moreover, they only deal with object initialization, without object destruction or finalization. Indeed, in Java, object finalization is weakly specified: although the Java language specification [4] requires objects to be finalized, it does not describe more precisely when object finalization should occur. C# offers a destruction mechanism, namely object disposal, but it must be called explicitly by the programmer.

8. Extending the semantics

Our semantics presents the core features of C++ object construction and destruction as faithfully as possible towards the Standard. However, it can be extended in a number of directions.

Manual memory management We anticipate no difficulties with supporting free store objects, i.e. the `new` and `delete` operators. Only slight modifications to the operational semantics appear necessary. Of course, Theorem 14 would be invalidated, since objects no longer follow a stack discipline. However, it appears very difficult to formalize more general manual memory management, allowing for instance explicit destructor calls and the use of placement operators such as "`new(p) C`" to construct an object at a given memory location.

Temporary objects of class types Expression evaluation, passing arguments by value to functions, or returning results by value entail construction and destruction of *temporary objects*. While the lifetime of these objects are well-defined by the C++ standard (and they follow a first-constructed-last-destroyed discipline), their storage durations are not specified. In fact, we found inconsistencies between the definitions of storage duration as specified by the C++11 standards and the C99 standards. Accounting for temporary objects beyond scalar values returned by functions or passed as arguments will require nontrivial extensions to our semantics.

Copy constructor elision More challenging is to give semantics to functions that return values of class types. They are objects constructed in the callee but destroyed in the caller at the end of the full expression containing the call. For decades, C++ has allowed elision of copy constructors (even if they have observable behavior) that would normally copy a local object to the (temporary) return value, provided certain non-aliasing conditions (easy to check) are met. These program transformations are necessary in practice to obtain good performance but are not semantics-preserving in the traditional sense. The same caveat applies for the C++11 notion of "move constructors".

Exceptions It is easy to capture a key aspect of C++ exceptions in our semantics: block-scoped objects are properly destroyed when an exception is thrown. Exception objects are temporary objects with lifetime dynamically controlled by exception handlers acting much like function invocations with the exception object as argument. C++ allows catching exceptions by value, so our observations for function call argument by value apply here. Furthermore, the semantics of constructors need to be altered to invoke destructors for completely constructed subobjects in presence of exception. Similarly, the semantics for destructors should be altered to include program abortion if a subobject destructor raises an exception. Finally, interaction between construction of dynamic objects and exceptions (both of which reflect related design decisions) should be investigated. These features are at the basis of generalized RAII techniques for dynamically controlled resources; popular examples include smart pointers such as `unique_ptr` and `smart_ptr`.

9. Concluding remarks

We hope that this work sheds light on the precise semantics of construction and destruction in C++ and what they actually guarantee to the working programmer. Several features remain to be addressed, but the subset that was formalized is already quite realistic and similar to recommended subsets for critical embedded systems [9]. The semantics implements a pattern for "small-stepping" a tree traversal which could perhaps be generalized and abstracted over. Finally, it would be interesting to exploit this semantics in the context of type systems and other static analyses that verify stronger safety properties about initialization.

References

[1] The Coq proof assistant, 1999–2012. URL `http://coq.inria.fr`.

[2] M. A. Ellis and B. Stroustrup. *The Annotated C++ Reference Manual*. Addison-Wesley, 1990.

[3] M. Fähndrich and S. Xia. Establishing object invariants with delayed types. In *22nd conf. on Object-Oriented Programming Systems and Applications (OOPSLA'07)*, pages 337–350. ACM, 2007.

[4] J. Gosling, B. Joy, G. Steele, and G. Bracha. *The Java Language Specification*. Addison Wesley, 3rd edition edition, 2005.

[5] L. Hubert, T. Jensen, V. Monfort, and D. Pichardie. Enforcing secure object initialization in Java. In *Computer Security – ESORICS 2010*, volume 6345 of *Lecture Notes in Computer Science*, pages 101–115. Springer, 2010.

[6] *International Standard ISO/IEC 14882:2003. Programming Languages — C++*. International Organization for Standards, 2003.

[7] *International Standard ISO/IEC 14882:2011. Programming Languages — C++*. International Organization for Standards, 2011.

[8] X. Leroy. A formally verified compiler back-end. *Journal of Automated Reasoning*, 43(4):363–446, 2009.

[9] Lockheed Martin. Joint Strike Fighter Air Vehicle C++ Coding Standards for the System Development and Demonstration Program, 2005. URL `http://www.research.att.com/~bs/JSF-AV-rules.pdf`.

[10] M. Norrish. A formal semantics for C++. Technical report, NICTA, 2008.

[11] X. Qi and A. C. Myers. Masked types for sound object initialization. In *36th symp. Principles of Programming Languages (POPL'09)*, pages 53–65. ACM, 2009.

[12] T. Ramananandro. *Mechanized Formal Semantics and Verified Compilation for C++ Objects*. PhD thesis, Université Paris Diderot, Jan. 2012.

[13] T. Ramananandro, G. Dos Reis, and X. Leroy. Formal verification of object layout for C++ multiple inheritance. In *38th symp. Principles of Programming Languages (POPL'11)*, pages 67–80. ACM, 2011.

[14] J. G. Rossie and D. P. Friedman. An algebraic semantics of subobjects. In *10th conf. on Object-Oriented Programming, Systems, Languages, and Applications (OOPSLA'95)*, pages 187–199. ACM, 1995.

[15] B. Stroustrup. Classes: An abstract data type facility for the C language. *SIGPLAN Not.*, 17:42–51, January 1982.

[16] B. Stroustrup. *The design and evolution of C++*. ACM Press/Addison-Wesley Publishing Co., New York, NY, USA, 1994.

[17] D. Wasserrab. *From Formal Semantics to Verified Slicing – A Modular Framework with Applications in Language Based Security*. PhD thesis, Karlsruher Institut für Technologie, Fakultät für Informatik, Oct. 2010.

[18] D. Wasserrab, T. Nipkow, G. Snelting, and F. Tip. An operational semantics and type safety proof for multiple inheritance in C++. In *21st conf. on Object-Oriented Programming, Systems, Languages, and Applications (OOPSLA'06)*, pages 345–362. ACM, 2006.

An Executable Formal Semantics of C with Applications *

Chucky Ellison Grigore Roșu
University of Illinois
{celliso2, grosu}@illinois.edu

Abstract

This paper describes an executable formal semantics of C. Being executable, the semantics has been thoroughly tested against the GCC torture test suite and successfully passes 99.2% of 776 test programs. It is the most complete and thoroughly tested formal definition of C to date. The semantics yields an interpreter, debugger, state space search tool, and model checker "for free". The semantics is shown capable of automatically finding program errors, both statically and at runtime. It is also used to enumerate nondeterministic behavior.

Categories and Subject Descriptors D.3.1 [*Programming Languages*]: Formal Definitions and Theory—Semantics

General Terms Languages, Standardization, Verification.

1. Introduction

C provides just enough abstraction above assembly language for programmers to get their work done without having to worry about the details of the machines on which the programs run. Despite this abstraction, C is also known for the ease in which it allows programmers to write buggy programs. With no runtime checks and little static checking, in C the programmer is to be trusted entirely. Despite the abstraction, the language is still low-level enough that programmers *can* take advantage of assumptions about the underlying architecture. Trust in the programmer and the ability to write *non*-portable code are actually two of the design principles under which the C standard was written [14]. These ideas often work in concert to yield intricate, platform-dependent bugs. The potential subtlety of C bugs makes it an excellent candidate for formalization, as subtle bugs can often be caught only by more rigorous means.

In this paper, we present a formal semantics of C that can be used for finding bugs. Rather than being an "on paper" semantics, it is executable, machine readable, and has been tested against the GCC torture tests (see Section 5). The semantics describes the features of the C99 standard [13], but we often cite the text from the proposed C1X standard [15]. We use the C1X text because it will eventually supersede the C99 standard, and because it offers clearer wording and more explicit descriptions of certain kinds of behavior.

Our semantics can be considered a *freestanding* implementation of C99. The standard defines a freestanding implementation as a version of C that includes every language feature except for `_Complex` and `_Imaginary` types, and that includes only a subset of the standard library. Our semantics is the first arguably complete dynamic semantics of C (see Section 2).

Above all else, our semantics has been motivated by the desire to develop formal, yet practical tools. Our semantics was developed in such a way that the single definition could be used immediately for interpreting, debugging, or analysis (described in Section 6). At the same time, this practicality does not mean that our definition is not formal. Being written in a subset of rewriting logic (RL), it comes with a complete proof system and initial model semantics [18]. Briefly, a rewrite system is a set of rules over terms constructed from a signature. The rewrite rules match and apply everywhere, making RL a simple, uniform, and general formal computational paradigm. This is explained in greater detail in Section 3.

Our C semantics defines 150 C syntactic operators. The definitions of these operators are given by 1,163 semantic rules spread over 5,884 source lines of code (SLOC). However, it takes only 77 of those rules (536 SLOC) to cover the behavior of statements, and another 163 for expressions (748 SLOC). There are 505 rules for dealing with declarations and types, 115 rules for memory, and 189 technical rules defining helper operators. Finally, there are 114 rules for the core of our standard library. The semantics itself is described in more detail in Section 4, and is available in its entirety at `http://c-semantics.googlecode.com/`.

Contributions The specific contributions of this paper include:

- a detailed comparison of other C formalizations;
- the most comprehensive formal semantics of C to date, which is executable and has been thoroughly tested;
- demonstrations as to its utility in discovering program flaws;
- constructive evidence that rewriting-based semantics scale.

Features Our semantics captures every feature required by the C99 standard. We include a partial list here to give an idea of the completeness, and explain any shortcomings in Section 7. All aspects related to the below features are included and are given a direct semantics (not by a translation to other features):

- Expressions: referencing and dereferencing, casts, array indexing (`a[i]`), structure members (`->` and `.`), arithmetic, bitwise, and logical operators, sizeof, increment and decrement, assignments, sequencing (`_,_`), ternary conditional (`_?_:_`);
- Statements: `for`, `do-while`, `while`, `if`, `if/else`, `switch`, `goto`, `break`, `continue`, `return`;
- Types and Declarations: `enums`, `structs`, `unions`, bitfields, initializers, static storage, `typedefs`, variable length arrays;
- Values: regular scalar values (signed/unsigned arithmetic and pointer types), `structs`, `unions`, compound literals;
- Standard Library: `malloc/free`, `set/longjmp`, basic I/O;
- Conversions: (implicit) argument and parameter promotions and arithmetic conversion, and (explicit) casts.

* Supported in part by NSA contract H98230-10-C-0294 and by (Romanian) SMIS-CSNR 602-12516 contract no. 161/15.06.2010.

POPL'12, January 25–27, 2012, Philadelphia, PA, USA.

2. Comparison with Existing Formal C Semantics

There have already been a number of formal semantics written for C. One might (rightfully) ask, "Why yet another?" We claim that the definitions so far have either made enough simplifying assumptions that for many purposes they are not C, or have lacked any way to use them other than on paper. While "paper semantics" are useful for teaching and understanding the language, we believe that without a mechanized definition, it is difficult to gain confidence in a definition's appropriateness for any other purpose. Below we highlight the most prominent definitions and explain their successes and shortcomings in comparison with our work.

Gurevich and Huggins (1993) One of the earliest formal descriptions of ANSI C is given by Gurevich and Huggins [11], using abstract state machines (ASMs) (then known as evolving algebras). Their semantics describes C using four increasingly precise layers, each formal and analyzable. Their semantics covers all the high-level constructs of the language, and uses external oracles to capture the underspecification inherent in the definition of C. Their semantics was written without access to a standard, and so is based on Kernighan and Ritchie [17]. However, many behavioral details of the lowest-level features of C are now partially standardized, including details of arithmetic, type representation, and evaluation strategies. The latter has been investigated in the context of ASMs [36], but none are present in the original definition. Based on our own experience, the details involving the lowest-level features of C are incredibly complex (see Section 3.2), but we see no reason why the ASM technique could not be used to specify them.

Their semantics was never converted into an executable tool, nor has it been used in applications. However, their purpose and context was different from ours. As pointed out elsewhere [22, p. 11], their semantics was constructed without the benefit of any mechanization. According to Gurevich,[1] their purpose was to "discover the structure of C," at a time when "C was far beyond the reach of denotational semantics, algebraic specifications, etc."

Cook, Cohen, and Redmond (1994) Soon after the previous definition, Cook et al. [5] describe a denotational semantics of C90 using a custom-made temporal logic for the express purpose of proving properties about C programs. Like us, they give semantics for particular implementation-defined behaviors in order to have a more concrete definition. These choices are then partitioned off so that one could, in theory, choose different implementation-defined values and behaviors.

They have given at least a basic semantics to most C constructs. We say "at least" without malicious intent—although their work was promising, they moved on to other projects before developing a testable version of their semantics and without doing any concrete evaluation.[1] Additionally, no proofs were done using this semantics.

Cook and Subramanian (1994) The related work of Cook and Subramanian [4, 33] is a semantics for a restricted subset of C, based loosely on the semantics above. This semantics is embedded in the theorem prover Nqthm [2] (a precursor to ACL2). They were successful in verifying at least two functions: one that takes two pointers and swaps the values at each, and one that computes the factorial. They were also able to prove properties about the C definition itself. For example, they prove that the execution of `p = &a[n]` puts the address of the nth element of the array `a` into `p` [4, p. 122]. Their semantics is, at its roots, an interpreter—it uses a similar technique to that described by Blazy and Leroy [1] to coax an interpreter from recursive functions—but there is no description in their work of any reference programs they were capable of executing. As above, it appears the work was terminated before it was able to blossom.

[1] Personal communication, 2010.

Norrish (1998) The next major semantics was provided by Norrish [22], who gives both static and dynamic formal semantics inside the HOL theorem proving system for the purpose of verifying C programs (later extended to C++ [23]). His semantics is in the Structural Operational Semantics (SOS) style, using small-step for expressions and big-step for statements. One of the focuses of his work is to present a precise description of the allowable evaluation orders of expressions. His semantics still stands as a precise representation of evaluation in C. In Section 6.3 we demonstrate how our definition captures the same behaviors.

Working inside HOL provides an elegant solution to the underspecification of the standard—Norrish can state facts given by the standard as axioms/theorems. To maintain executability, we chose instead to parameterize our definition for those implementation-defined choices. In that respect, our definitions conceptually complement each other—his is better for formal proofs about C, while ours is better for searching for behaviors in programs (see Section 6.3.1). Proofs of program correctness [31] as well as semantics-level proofs [8] have already been demonstrated in the framework used by our semantics, but we have not yet applied these techniques to C.

Norrish uses his definition to prove some properties about C itself, as well as to verify some strong properties of simple (≤ 5 line) programs, but was unable to apply his work to larger programs. His semantics is not executable, so it has not been tested against actual programs. However, the proofs done within the HOL system help lend confidence to the definition.

Papaspyrou (2001) A denotational semantics for C99 is described by Papaspyrou [24, 25] using a monadic approach to domain construction. The definition includes static, typing, and dynamic semantics, which enables him not only to represent the behavior of executing programs, but also check for errors like redefinition of an identifier in the same scope. Papaspyrou, Norrish, and Cook et al. each give a typing semantics in addition to the dynamic semantics, while we and Blazy and Leroy (below) give only dynamic semantics.

Papaspyrou represents his semantics in Haskell, yielding a tool capable of searching for program behaviors. This was the only semantics for which we were able to obtain a working interpreter, and we were able to run it on a few examples. Having modeled expression non-determinism, and being denotational, his semantics evaluates a program into a set of possible return values. However, we found his interpreter to be of limited capability in practice. For example, using his definition, we were unable to compute the factorial of six or the fourth Fibonacci number.

Blazy and Leroy (2009) A big-step operational semantics for a subset of C, called Clight, is given by Blazy and Leroy [1]. While they do not claim to have given semantics for the entirety of C, their semantics does cover most of the major features of the language and has been used in a number of proofs including the verification of the optimizing compiler CompCert.

To help validate their semantics, they have done manual reviews of the definition as well as proved properties of the semantics such as determinism of evaluation. They additionally have verified semantics-preserving transformations from their language into simpler languages, which are easier to develop confidence in. Their semantics is not directly executable, but they describe a mechanism by which they could create an equivalent recursive function that would act as an interpreter. This work has not yet been completed.

Clight does not handle non-determinism or sub-expressions with side effects. However, since publication, they have added a new front-end small-step definition called CompCert C that does handle these features, and is also being used to handle `goto`.[3]

[2] Personal communication, 2010.

[3] Personal communication, 2011.

Feature	Definition GH	CCR	CR	No	Pa	BL	ER
Bitfields	●	◐	○	○	◐	○	●
Enums	◐	●	○	○	●	○	●
Floats	○	○	○	○	●	●	●
String Literal	○	●	○	○	●	●	●
Struct as Value	○	○	○	●	○	○	●
Arithmetic	◐	●	●	○	●	●	●
Bitwise	○	●	○	○	●	●	●
Casts	◐	◐	○	◐	◐	●	●
Functions	●	●	◐	●	●	●	●
Exp. Side Effects	●	●	○	●	●	○	●
Break/Continue	◐	●	◐	●	●	●	●
Goto	◐	○	○	○	●	○	●
Switch	◐	●	○	○	●	◐	●
Longjmp	○	○	○	○	○	○	●
Malloc	○	○	○	○	○	○	●
Variadic Funcs.	○	○	○	○	○	○	●
Feature	GH	CCR	CR	No	Pa	BL	ER

●: Fully Described ◐: Partially Described ○: Not Described

GH represents Gurevich and Huggins [11], *CCR* is Cook et al. [5], *CR* is Cook and Subramanian [4], *No* is Norrish [22], *Pa* is Papaspyrou [25], *BL* is Blazy and Leroy [1], and *ER* is our work.

Figure 1. Dynamic Semantics Features

We condense our study of related works in Figure 1. For interested parties, this chart may be contentious. However, we believe that it is useful, both for developers of formal semantics of C and for users of them, to give a broad (though admittedly incomplete) overview of the state of the art of the formal semantics of C. Also, it may serve as an indication of the complexity involved in the C language, although not all features are equally difficult.

We did our best to give the authors the benefit of the doubt with features they explicitly mentioned, but the other features were based on our reading of their semantics. We have also discussed our views with the authors, where possible, to try and establish a consensus. Obviously the categories are broad, but our intention is to give an overview of some of the more difficult features of C. We purposefully left off any feature that all definitions had fully defined.

Finally, there are a number of other emergent features, such as multi-dimensional arrays, that are difficult to discern correctness through simple inspection of the formal semantics (i.e., without testing or verifying it). It is also difficult to determine if feature pairs work together—for example, does a definition allow bitfields inside of unions? We decided to leave most of these features out of the chart because they are simply too hard to determine if the semantics were complete enough for them to work properly.

3. Background

In this section we give a little background on the C standard, including some important definitions. We additionally explain the rewriting formalism we use to give our semantics of C.

3.1 C Standard Information

The C standard uses the idea of undefined and partially defined behaviors in order to avoid placing difficult requirements on implementations. It categorizes the particular behaviors of any C implementation that are not fully defined into four categories: unspecified, implementation-defined, undefined, and locale-specific behavior. For the purposes of this paper, we focus on three of these [15, §3.4]:

unspecified behavior Use of an unspecified value, or other behavior [with] two or more possibilities and [. . .] no further requirements on which is chosen in any instance.

implementation-defined Unspecified behavior where each implementation documents how the choice is made.

undefined behavior Behavior, upon use of a non-portable or erroneous program construct or [data, with] no requirements.

An example of unspecified behavior is the order in which the arguments to a function are evaluated. An example of implementation defined behavior is the size of an `int`. An example of undefined behavior is referring to an object outside of its lifetime.

To put these definitions in perspective, for a C program to be maximally portable, "it shall not produce output dependent on any unspecified, undefined, or implementation-defined behavior" [15, §4.5]. This is called "strictly conforming". However, programmers use C for many inherently non-portable tasks, such as writing device drivers. The standard offers another level of conformance (called "conforming") where the program may rely on implementation-defined or even unspecified (but never undefined) behavior. Based on this, our definition is parametric in implementation-defined behaviors, and uses symbolic computation to describe unspecified behaviors. As much as possible, this behavior is kept separate from the semantics underlying the high-level (defined for all implementations) aspects of the language. More details about our parameterization are described in Section 4.5, and about our use of symbolic values in Section 6.2.2.

3.2 Why Details Matter

It is tempting to gloss over the details of C's arithmetic and other low-level features when giving it a formal semantics. However, C is designed to be translatable to machine languages where arithmetic is handled by any number of machine instructions. The effects of this overloading are easily felt at the size boundaries of the types. It is a common source of confusion among programmers, and so a common source of bugs. Here we give a few examples that reveal even apparently simple C programs can involve complex semantics.

For the purposes of these examples, assume that `int`s are 2 bytes (capable of representing the values −32768 to 32767) and `long int`s are 4 bytes (−2147483648 to 2147483647). Also, unless specified, in C a type is assumed to be signed.[4] In the following program, what value does `c` receive [34, Q3.14]?

```
int a = 1000, b = 1000;
long int c = a * b;
```

One is tempted to say 1000000, but that misses an important C-specific detail. The two operands of the multiplication are `int`s, so the multiplication is done at the `int` level. It therefore overflows ($1000 * 1000 = 1000000 > 32767$), which, according to the C standard, makes the expression undefined.

What if we make the types of `a` and `b` unsigned (0 to 65535)?

```
unsigned int a = 1000, b = 1000;
long int c = a * b;
```

Here, the arithmetic is again performed at the level of the operands, but overflow on *unsigned* types is completely defined in C. The result is computed by simply reducing the value modulo one more than the max value [15, §6.3.1.3:2]. 1000000 mod 65536 gives us 16960.

One last variation—`signed char`s are one byte in C (−128 to 127).[5] What does `c` receive?

```
signed char a = 100, b = 100;
int c = a * b;
```

[4] Except `char`s and bitfields, whose signedness is implementation-defined.

[5] Bytes are only required to be at least 8 bits long.

Since the chars are signed, then based on the first example above the result would seem undefined ($100 * 100 = 10000 > 127$). However, this is not the case. In C, types smaller than `int`s are promoted to `int`s before doing arithmetic. There are essentially implicit casts on the two operands: `int c = (int)a * (int)b;`. Thus, the result is actually 10000.

While the above examples might seem like a game, the conclusion we draw is that it is critical when defining the semantics of C to handle *all* of the details. The semantics at the higher level of functions and statements is actually much easier than at the level of expressions and arithmetic. These issues are subtle enough that they are very difficult to catch just by manually inspecting the code, and so need to be represented in the semantics if one wants to find bugs in real programs. Even though errors related to the above details continue to be found in real compilers [35], previous semantics for C either did not give semantics at this level of detail, or were not suitable for identifying programs that misused these features. This is one of our primary reasons for wanting an executable semantics. We give some of the rules associated to binary arithmetic in Section 4.4.4.

3.3 Rewriting Logic and $\mathbb{K}$

To give our semantics, we use a rewriting-based semantic framework called $\mathbb{K}$ [28], inspired by RL [18]. In particular, our semantics is written using the K-Maude tool [32], which takes $\mathbb{K}$ rewrite rules and translates them into Maude [3]. Maude is a rewriting-logic engine that provides facilities for the execution and analysis of rewriting-logic theories.

RL organizes term rewriting *modulo equations* (namely associativity, commutativity, and identity) as a logic with a complete proof system and initial model semantics. The central idea behind using RL as a formalism for the semantics of languages is that the evolution of a program can be clearly described using rewrite rules. A rewriting theory consists essentially of a signature describing terms and a set of rewrite rules that describe steps of computation. Given some term allowed by signature (e.g., a program together with input), deduction consists of the application of the rules to that term. This yields a transition system for any program. A single path of rewrites describes the behavior of an interpreter, while searching all paths would yield all possible answers in a nondeterministic program.

For the purposes of this paper, the $\mathbb{K}$ formalism can be regarded as a front-end to RL designed specifically for defining languages. In $\mathbb{K}$, parts of the state are represented as labeled, nested multisets, as seen in Figure 2. These collections contain pieces of the program state like a computation stack or continuation (e.g., k), environments (e.g., env, types), stacks (e.g., callStack), etc. As this is all best understood through an example, let us consider a typical rule for a simple imperative language (see Section 4.4.2 for the equivalent rule in C) for finding the address of a variable:

$$\langle \frac{\&X}{L} \cdots \rangle_{\mathsf{k}} \ \langle \cdots X \mapsto L \cdots \rangle_{\mathsf{env}}$$

We see here two cells, k and env. The k cell represents a list (or stack) of computations waiting to be performed. The left-most (i.e., top) element of the stack is the next item to be computed. The env cell is simply a map of variables to their locations. The rule above says that if the next thing to be evaluated (which here we call a redex) is the application of the referencing operator (&) to a variable X, then one should match X in the environment to find its location L in memory. With this information, one should transform the redex into that location in memory, L.

This example exhibits a number of features of $\mathbb{K}$. First, rules only need to mention those cells (again, see Figure 2) relevant to the rule. The rest of the cell infrastructure can be inferred, making the rules robust under most extensions to the language. Second, to omit a part of a cell we write "$\cdots$". For example, in the above k cell, we are only interested in the current redex $\&X$, but not the rest of the context. Finally, we draw a line underneath parts of the state that we wish to change—in the above case, we only want to evaluate part of the computation, but neither the context nor the environment change.

This unconventional notation is actually quite useful. The above rule would be written out as a traditional rewrite rule like this:

$$\langle \&X \curvearrowright \kappa \rangle_{\mathsf{k}} \ \langle \rho_1, X \mapsto L, \rho_2 \rangle_{\mathsf{env}} \Rightarrow \langle L \curvearrowright \kappa \rangle_{\mathsf{k}} \ \langle \rho_1, X \mapsto L, \rho_2 \rangle_{\mathsf{env}}$$

Items in the k cell are separated with "$\curvearrowright$", which can now be seen. The κ and ρ_1, ρ_2 take the place of the "$\cdots$" above. The most important thing to notice is that nearly the entire rule is duplicated on the right-hand side (RHS). Duplication in a definition requires that changes be made in concert, in multiple places. If this duplication is not kept in sync, it leads to subtle semantic errors. In a complex language like C, the configuration structure is much more complicated, and would require actually including additional cells like control and local (Figure 2). These intervening cells are automatically inferred in $\mathbb{K}$, which keeps the rules more modular.

Going back to $\mathbb{K}$, we use "$\cdot$" to represent the unit element of any algebraic lists or sets (including the "$\curvearrowright$" list). We also use "—" to stand for a term that we do not care to name. Finally, in order to get the redexes to the top of the k cell (i.e., in order to identify which positions in the syntax tree can be reduced next), the grammar of C is annotated with additional "strictness" annotations. For example, for addition, we say that

$$Exp ::= Exp + Exp \ \text{[strict]}$$

meaning that either argument of the addition operator can be taken out for evaluation, nondeterministically. In contrast, the `if` construct looks like this:

$$Stmt ::= \texttt{if}\,(Exp)\ Stmt \ \text{[strict(1)]}$$

indicating that only the first argument can be taken out for evaluation. The two annotations above cause the following six rules to be automatically generated:

$$\langle \frac{E_1+E_2}{E_1 \curvearrowright \square+E_2} \cdots \rangle_{\mathsf{k}} \quad \Big| \quad \langle \frac{E_1+E_2}{E_2 \curvearrowright E_1+\square} \cdots \rangle_{\mathsf{k}} \quad \Big| \quad \langle \frac{\texttt{if}\,(E)\ S}{E \curvearrowright \texttt{if}\,(\square)\ S} \cdots \rangle_{\mathsf{k}}$$

$$\langle \frac{V \curvearrowright \square+E_2}{V+E_2} \cdots \rangle_{\mathsf{k}} \quad \Big| \quad \langle \frac{V \curvearrowright E_1+\square}{E_1+V} \cdots \rangle_{\mathsf{k}} \quad \Big| \quad \langle \frac{V \curvearrowright \texttt{if}\,(\square)\ S}{\texttt{if}\,(V)\ S} \cdots \rangle_{\mathsf{k}}$$

Here, E_1, E_2, and E represent unevaluated expressions and V represents an evaluated expression (i.e., a value). While these are the rules generated by K-Maude, in the theory of $\mathbb{K}$ they can apply anywhere (not just at the top of the k cell). There are additional annotations for specifying more particular evaluation strategies, and can be found in documentation on $\mathbb{K}$ [28]. We also give names to certain contexts that are evaluated differently. For example, the left-hand side (LHS) of an assignment is evaluated differently than the RHS. The use of this is described in Section 4.4.1.

4. The Semantics of C in $\mathbb{K}$

In this section, we describe the different components of our definition and give a number of example rules from the semantics.

4.1 Syntax

We use the FrontC parser, with additions made and included in CIL [19], an "off-the-shelf" C parser and transformation tool. FrontC itself parses only ANSI C (C90), but CIL extended it with syntax for C99. We use *only* the parser here, and none of the transformations of CIL; we give semantics directly to the abstract syntax tree generated by the parser. The FrontC parser (with C99 extensions) is used by a number of other tools, including CompCert [1] and Frama-C [6].

4.2 Configuration (Program + State)

The configuration of a running program is represented by nested multisets of labeled cells, and Figure 2 shows the most important cells used in our semantics. While this figure only shows 17 cells,

$$\left\langle \langle K\rangle_{\mathsf{k}} \left\langle \left\langle \langle Map\rangle_{\mathsf{env}} \langle Map\rangle_{\mathsf{types}} \langle Map\rangle_{\mathsf{structs}} \langle List\rangle_{\mathsf{loopStack}} \langle Bag\rangle_{\mathsf{locsWrittenTo}} \langle K\rangle_{\mathsf{currFunction}} \right\rangle_{\mathsf{control}} \langle List\rangle_{\mathsf{callStack}} \right\rangle_{\mathsf{local}} \langle Map\rangle_{\mathsf{genv}} \langle Map\rangle_{\mathsf{gtypes}} \langle Map\rangle_{\mathsf{gstructs}} \langle Map\rangle_{\mathsf{mem}} \langle Map\rangle_{\mathsf{malloced}} \langle Map\rangle_{\mathsf{gotoMap}} \right\rangle_{\mathsf{T}}$$

Figure 2. Subset of the C Configuration

we use over 60 in the full semantics. The outer T cell contains the cells used during program evaluation: at the top, a k cell contains the current computation itself and a local cell holds a number of cells related to control flow, and below, there are a number of cells dealing with global information.

In the local cell, there is a callstack used for calling and returning from functions, and a control cell which gets pushed onto the call stack. Inside the control cell, there is a local variable environment (env), a local type environment (types), local aggregate definitions (structs), a loop stack, a record of the locations that have been written to since the last sequence point (Section 4.6), and the name of the current function. The cells inside the control cell were separated in this manner because these are the cells that get pushed onto the call stack when making a function call.

Outside the local cell are a number of global mappings, such as the global variable environment (genv), the global type environment (gtypes), global aggregate definitions (gstructs), the heap (mem), the dynamic allocation map (malloced), and a map from function-name/label pairs to continuations (for use by `goto` and `switch`).

4.3 Memory Layout

Our memory is essentially a map from locations to blocks of bytes. It is based on the memory model of both Blazy and Leroy [1] and Roşu et al. [30] in the sense that the actual locations themselves are symbolic numbers. However, it is more like the former in that the actual blocks of bytes are really maps from offsets to bytes.

Below we see a snippet of a memory cell, holding four bytes:

$$\langle \cdots\ 32 \mapsto \mathrm{obj}(4,\ (0 \mapsto 7,\ 1 \mapsto 23,\ 2 \mapsto 140,\ 3 \mapsto 4))\ \cdots\rangle_{\mathsf{mem}}$$

This says that at symbolic location 32, there is an object whose size is 4 bytes; those bytes are 7, 23, 140, and 4. All objects are broken into individual bytes, including aggregate types like arrays or `structs`, as well as base types like integers.

Our pointers are actually base/offset pairs, which we write as $\mathrm{sym}(B) + O$, where B corresponds to the base address of an object itself, while the O represents the offset of a particular byte in the object. We wrap the base using "sym" because it is symbolic—despite representing a location, it is not appropriate to, e.g., directly compare $B < B'$ (Section 6.2.2). It is better to think of the 32 above as representing "object 32", as opposed to "location 32".

When looked up, the bytes are interpreted depending on the type of the construct used to give the address. The simplest example possible is dereferencing a pointer $\mathrm{sym}(32)+2$ of type `unsigned char*`, which would simply yield the value 140 of type `unsigned char`. Looking up data using different pointer types requires taking into account a number of implementation-defined details such as the use of signed magnitude, one's, or two's complement representation, or the order of bytes (endianness). These choices are made parametric in the semantics, and can be configured depending on which implementation a user is interested in working with (Section 4.5).

When new objects (`ints`, arrays, `structs`, etc.) get allocated, each is created as a new block and is mapped from a new symbolic number. The block is allowed to contain as many bytes as in the object, and accesses relative to that object must be contained in the block. We represent information smaller than the byte (i.e., bitfields) by using offsets within the bytes themselves. While it might seem that it would be more consistent to treat memory as mappings from bit locations to individual bits, bitfields themselves are not addressable in C, so we decided on this hybrid approach.

4.4 Semantics

We now give the flavor of our semantics by examining a few of the 1,163 rules. For the rules below, recall that in $\mathbb{K}$ what is above the line is considered the LHS of the rule, while what is below the line is considered the RHS. Parts of a rule without a line at all are considered to be on both sides of the rule.

4.4.1 Lookup and Assignment

We first consider one of the most basic expressions—the identifier. According to the standard, "An identifier is a primary expression, [...] designating an object (in which case it is an lvalue) or a function (in which case it is a function designator)" [15, §6.5.1:2]. Although in informal language an "lvalue" is an expression that appears on the LHS of an assignment, this is not the case according to the C standard. An lvalue can be more accurately thought of as any expression that designates a place in memory; a footnote in the standard suggests it might better be called a "locator value" [15, §6.3.2.1:1]. We denote lvalues with brackets; an lvalue that points to location L which is of type T is denoted by $[L]:T$. With this in mind, here then is our lookup rule:

$$\Big\langle \frac{X}{[L]:T} \cdots\Big\rangle_{\mathsf{k}}\ \langle \cdots X \mapsto L \cdots\rangle_{\mathsf{env}}\ \langle \cdots X \mapsto T \cdots\rangle_{\mathsf{type}}$$

This rule is actually very similar to the example address-of rule we gave in Section 3.3. It says that when the next thing to evaluate is the program variable X, both its location L and its type T should be looked up (in the env and type cells), and the variable should be replaced by an lvalue containing those two pieces of information. We distinguish between objects and functions based on type.

In almost all contexts, this lvalue will actually get converted to the value at that location:

> Except when it is the operand of the `sizeof` operator, the unary & operator, the ++ operator, the -- operator, or the left operand of the . operator or an assignment operator, an lvalue that does not have array type is converted to the value stored in the designated object (and is no longer an lvalue) [13, §6.3.2.1:2].

We call these contexts "reval", for "right" evaluation. Here is the rule for simplifying lvalues in the "right value" context:

$$\frac{\mathrm{reval}([L]:T)}{\mathrm{read}(L, T)} \qquad \text{where } \neg(\mathrm{isArrayType}(T) \vee \mathrm{isFunctionType}(T))$$

The rule for "read" then does the actual read from memory. Its evaluation involves a series of rules whose job is to determine the size of the type, pull the right bytes from memory, and to piece them together in the right order to reconstruct the value. There are over 10 highly technical rules defining "read", just for integer types alone. This process results in a normal value, instead of an lvalue, which we represent simply as $V:T$.

4.4.2 Reference and Dereference

We can now take a look at the rule for the & operator:

$$\Big\langle \frac{\&([L]:T)}{L:\mathrm{pointerType}(T)} \cdots\Big\rangle_{\mathsf{k}}$$

This rule says that when the next computation to be performed is taking the address of an lvalue, it should simply be converted into a "true value" holding the same address, but whose type is a pointer type to the original type. We can expect to find an lvalue as the argument because the "reval" context does not include the arguments of the address operator.

The rule for dereference is similarly simple:

$$\frac{\langle\ *(L:\text{pointerType}(T))\quad \cdots\rangle_{\mathsf{k}}}{\text{checkDerefLoc}(L) \curvearrowright [L]:T} \quad \text{where } T \neq \texttt{void}$$

This will first make sure that the location L is allowed to be dereferenced (e.g., it is valid memory), and will then evaluate to an lvalue of the same location. As with lookup, no memory is read by default. Notice that checkDerefLoc is "blocking" the top of the k cell. As long as it stays there, no rules that match other constructs on the top of k can apply. If checkDerefLoc succeeds, it will simply evaluate to the unit of the $\curvearrowright$ construct and disappear. This is called "dissolving". Our rule for checkDerefLoc is:

$$\frac{\langle\ \text{checkDerefLoc}(\text{sym}(B) + O)\ \cdots\rangle_{\mathsf{k}}}{\cdot}\ \langle\cdots B \mapsto \text{obj}(Len, \text{—})\cdots\rangle_{\mathsf{mem}} \quad \text{where } O < Len$$

Here we match the constituent parts of a location, B and O, or base and offset as explained in Section 4.3. We then match the base part of the pointer in the memory cell, giving us an object, and check that the offset is within the bounds of the object. If this is the case, we dissolve the checkDerefLoc task.

4.4.3 Structure Members

The standard says, "A postfix expression followed by the . operator and an identifier designates a member of a structure or union object. The value is that of the named member, and is an lvalue if the first expression is an lvalue" [15, §6.5.2.3:3].

Here is the rule for when the first expression is an lvalue:

$$\frac{\langle\ ([L]:\text{structType}(S)).F\ \cdots\rangle_{\mathsf{k}}}{[L + \mathit{Offset}]:T}\ \langle\cdots S \mapsto (F \mapsto (\mathit{Offset}, T)\ \text{—})\cdots\rangle_{\mathsf{structs}}$$

This rule finds the offset *Offset* and type T of the field F in struct S and simply adds the offset to the base address L of the struct to evaluate the expression. The result is another lvalue of the type of the field. In contrast, the rule for when the first expression is not an lvalue cannot simply work with pointers:

$$\frac{\langle\ (V:\text{structType}(S)).F\ \cdots\rangle_{\mathsf{k}}}{\text{extractField}(V, SD, S, F)}\ \langle\cdots S \mapsto (F \mapsto SD\ \text{—})\cdots\rangle_{\mathsf{structs}}$$

One situation in which this arises is when a function returns a struct, and the programmer uses the function call to access a particular field, as in the expression `fun().field`. The call to `fun()` will result in a struct value, represented in the rule above by $V:\text{structType}(S)$. The helper function extractField will look at the bytes of the struct (represented by V) and "read" a value of the appropriate type (SD contains the offset and type of the field). There are many rules shared by the extractField and read helpers, since both have to piece together bytes in implementation-defined orders to make new values.

The semantics for the arrow operator (`p->f`) is identical to that of the dot operator above after dereferencing the first subexpression:

$$E\ \texttt{->}\ F \Rightarrow (*E).F$$

There are similar rules as above for union, where all offsets of a union's fields are 0.

4.4.4 Multiplication (and Related Conversions)

As mentioned in Section 3.2, the rules for arithmetic in C are non-trivial. To show this in more detail, here we give many of the rules related to integer multiplication. Here is the core multiplication rule:

$$\frac{(I_1:T)\ *\ (I_2:T)}{\text{arithInterpret}(T, I_1 *_{Int} I_2)} \quad \text{where hasBeenPromoted}(T)$$

This rule matches when multiplying values with identical, promoted types (more on promotion shortly). It then uses a helper operator "arithInterpret" to convert the resulting product into a proper value:

$$\frac{\text{arithInterpret}(T, I)}{I:T} \quad \text{where } \min(T) \leq I \wedge \max(T) \geq I$$

$$\frac{\text{arithInterpret}(T, I)}{\text{arithInterpret}(T, I -_{Int} (\max(T) +_{Int} 1))} \quad \text{where } \begin{array}{l}\text{isUnsignedIntType}(T)\\ \wedge\ I > \max(T)\end{array}$$

$$\frac{\text{arithInterpret}(T, I)}{\text{arithInterpret}(T, I +_{Int} (\max(T) +_{Int} 1))} \quad \text{where } \begin{array}{l}\text{isUnsignedIntType}(T)\\ \wedge\ I < \min(T)\end{array}$$

The first rule creates a value as long as the product is the range of the type. The next two rules collapse out-of-range unsigned products into range [15, §6.3.1.3:2]. By not giving rules to out-of-range signed types, we catch signed overflow here.

With the above rules defined, the question becomes how to promote and convert the types of the operands so that the core multiplication rule can take effect. First, all arithmetic in C takes place at or above the size of `int`s. This means smaller types need to be coerced into `int` or `unsigned int`.

$$\langle(\text{—}:\frac{T}{\text{promote}(T)})\ *\ \text{—}\ \cdots\rangle_{\mathsf{k}} \quad \text{where } \neg\text{hasBeenPromoted}(T)$$

The above rule (and its commutative partner) cause unpromoted multiplication operands to be promoted. Of the actual promotion, the standard says, "If an `int` can represent all values of the original type [...], the value is converted to an `int`; otherwise, it is converted to an `unsigned int`" [15, §6.3.1.1:2]:

$$\frac{\text{promote}(T)}{\texttt{int}} \quad \text{where } \min(\texttt{int}) \leq \min(T) \wedge \max(\texttt{int}) \geq \max(T)$$

$$\frac{\text{promote}(T)}{\texttt{unsigned int}} \quad \text{where } \neg(\min(\texttt{int}) \leq \min(T) \wedge \max(\texttt{int}) \geq \max(T))$$

Finally, in order to perform the multiplication, the types of the operands have to be identical. If the types are not identical, an implicit conversion takes place to convert the different types to a common type. There are eight rules for this given in the standard. To give an idea of their flavor, we give a few of the rules for integer conversions here. First, the rule to enable conversion:

$$\langle\ \frac{I_1:T}{\text{cast}(\tau, I_1:T)}\ *\ \frac{I_2:T'}{\text{cast}(\tau, I_2:T')}\ \cdots\rangle_{\mathsf{k}} \quad \text{where } \begin{array}{l}T \neq T'\\ \wedge\ \tau = \text{arithConv}(T, T')\end{array}$$

The standard says, "if both operands have signed integer types or both have unsigned integer types, the operand with the type of lesser integer conversion rank is converted to the type of the operand with greater rank" [15, §6.3.1.8:1]:

$$\frac{\text{arithConv}(T, T')}{\text{maxType}(T, T')} \quad \text{where hasSameSignedness(T, T')}$$

Rank is a partial ordering on integer types based on their ranges and signedness, e.g., rank(`short int`) < rank(`int`). Additionally, the ranks of unsigned integer types equal the ranks of the corresponding signed integer types [15, §6.3.1.1:1]. Continuing with the conversion rules, "Otherwise, if the operand that has unsigned integer type has rank greater or equal to the rank of the type of the other operand, then the operand with signed integer type is converted to the type of the operand with unsigned integer type" [15, §6.3.1.8:1]:

$$\frac{\langle\ \text{arithConv}(T, T')\ \cdots\rangle_{\mathsf{k}}}{T} \quad \text{where } \begin{array}{l}\text{isUnsigned}(T)\\ \wedge\ \text{isSigned}(T')\\ \wedge\ \text{rank}(T) \geq \text{rank}(T')\end{array}$$

and similarly for the commutative case.

The above equations use a number of helper operators in the side conditions—the definitions for "min" and "max" are given in Section 4.5; the other operators are defined as expected.

4.4.5 Malloc and Free

Here we show our semantics of `malloc` and `free`. These are functions from the standard C library that perform dynamic memory allocation and deallocation. The declarations of these functions are:

```
void *malloc(size_t size);
void free(void *ptr);
```

where `size_t` is an unsigned integer type that is implementation defined. When a programmer calls `malloc()`, an implementation can return a new pointer pointing to a new block of memory the size specified by the programmer, or it can return `NULL` (e.g., if there is no memory available).

Here is the rule for a successful call to `malloc`:

$$\Big\langle \frac{\texttt{malloc}(N:\texttt{size\_t})}{\text{alloc}(L, N) \curvearrowright L:\text{pointerType(void)}} \cdots \Big\rangle_{\mathsf{k}} \Big\langle \cdots \frac{\cdot}{L \mapsto N} \cdots \Big\rangle_{\mathsf{malloced}}$$

where L is fresh

If the user requests N bytes, the semantics will schedule that many bytes to be allocated at a new location and record that this memory was dynamically allocated in the malloced cell. Here is the related rule for a failed called to `malloc`:

$$\Big\langle \frac{\texttt{malloc}(\text{—})}{\text{NullPointer}:\text{pointerType(void)}} \cdots \Big\rangle_{\mathsf{k}}$$

This rule is usually only useful when searching the state space.

A call to `free` is meant to deallocate space allocated by `malloc`. Its rule is also straightforward:

$$\Big\langle \frac{\texttt{free}(L:\text{—})}{\cdot} \cdots \Big\rangle_{\mathsf{k}} \Big\langle \cdots \frac{L \mapsto N}{\cdot} \cdots \Big\rangle_{\mathsf{malloced}} \Big\langle \cdots \frac{L \mapsto \text{obj}(N, \text{—})}{\cdot} \cdots \Big\rangle_{\mathsf{mem}}$$

When the user wants to free a pointer L, it is removed from both the malloced and mem cells. By matching these cells, the rule ensures that the pointer has not already been freed, and once applied, ensures no other rules that use that address can match into the memory.

4.4.6 Setjmp and Longjmp

Finally, we show our semantics of `setjmp` and `longjmp`. These are functions from the standard C library that perform complex control flow. They are reminiscent of `call/cc`, and are often used as a kind of exception handling mechanism in C. The declarations of these functions are:

```
int setjmp(jmp_buf env);
void longjmp(jmp_buf env, int val);
```

where `jmp_buf` is an array type "suitable for holding the information needed to restore a calling environment." A call to `setjmp` "saves its calling environment [...] for later use by the `longjmp` function." Additionally, the call to `setjmp` evaluates to zero [15, §7.13.1]. Here is our rule for `setjmp`:

$$\Big\langle \frac{\texttt{setjmp}(L:\texttt{jmp\_buf})}{\text{write}(L,\, C\,\langle\kappa\rangle_{\mathsf{k}}\,) \curvearrowright 0:\text{int}} \curvearrowright \kappa \Big\rangle_{\mathsf{k}} \langle C \rangle_{\mathsf{local}}$$

Because `jmp_buf` is an array type, it will evaluate to an address L. In the rule above, we match the remaining computation κ (similar to a continuation), as well as the local execution environment C. This includes cells like the call stack and the map from variables to locations (which we also call the environment). The rule then causes this information to be written at the location of the `jmp_buf`.

A call to `longjmp` "restores the environment saved by the most recent invocation of [`setjmp`] with the corresponding `jmp_buf` argument" [15, §7.13.2]. When the user calls `longjmp`, this address is read to find that previous context:

$$\Big\langle \frac{\texttt{longjmp}}{\text{longjmp-aux}} \Big(\frac{L:T}{\text{read}(L,T)}, \text{—}\Big) \cdots \Big\rangle_{\mathsf{k}}$$

and it is then restored:

$$\Big\langle \frac{\text{longjmp-aux}((C\,\langle\kappa\rangle_{\mathsf{k}}\,:\text{—}),\, I:\text{int})}{(\text{if } I = 0 \text{ then } 1 \text{ else } I \text{ fi}):\text{int}} \curvearrowright \frac{\text{—}}{\kappa} \Big\rangle_{\mathsf{k}} \Big\langle \frac{\text{—}}{C} \Big\rangle_{\mathsf{local}}$$

This function returns the `val` that the user passes, unless this is a 0, in which case it returns 1.

It should be clear that these rules operate on the configuration itself, treating it as a first-class term of the formalism. The fact that $\mathbb{K}$ allows one to grab the continuation κ as a term is what makes the semantics of these constructs so easy to define. This is in sharp opposition to semantic formalisms like SOS [27] where the context is a derivation tree and not directly accessible as an object inside a definition.

4.5 Parametric Behavior

We chose to make our definition parametric in the implementation-defined behaviors (and are not the first to do so [1, 5]). Thus, one can configure the definition based on the architecture or compiler one is interested in using, and then proceed to use the formalism to explore behaviors. This parameterization allows the definition to be "fleshed out" and made executable.

For a simple example of how the definition is parametric, our K-Maude module `C-SETTINGS` starts with:

numBytes(signed-char) $\Rightarrow$ 1	numBytes(short-int) $\Rightarrow$ 2
numBytes(int) $\Rightarrow$ 4	numBytes(long-int) $\Rightarrow$ 4
numBytes(long-long-int) $\Rightarrow$ 8	numBytes(float) $\Rightarrow$ 4
numBytes(double) $\Rightarrow$ 8	numBytes(long-double) $\Rightarrow$ 16

These settings are then used to define a number of operators:

$$\text{numBits}(T) \Rightarrow \text{numBytes}(T) * \text{bitsPerByte where } \neg\text{isBitfieldType}(T)$$
$$\min(\text{int}) \Rightarrow -_{Int}(2^{\text{numBits(int)}-_{Int}1})$$
$$\max(\text{int}) \Rightarrow 2^{\text{numBits(int)}-_{Int}1} -_{Int} 1$$

Here we use a side condition to check when a type is *not* a bitfield. Finally, the above rules are used to define how an integer I of type T is cast to an unsigned integer type T':

$$\text{cast}(T', I:T) \Rightarrow (I \,\%_{Int}\, (\max(T') +_{Int} 1))):T'$$
$$\text{where isIntegerType}(T) \wedge \text{isUnsignedIntType}(T') \wedge I > \max(T')$$

Here we use helper predicates in our side conditions to make sure this rule only applies when casting from integer types to unsigned integer types. There are similar equations used to define other cases.

4.6 Expression Evaluation Strategy and Undefined Behavior

The C standard allows compilers freedom in optimizing code, which includes allowing them to choose their own expression evaluation order. This includes allowing them to:

- delay side effects: e.g., allowing the write to memory required by `x=5` or `x++` to be made separately from its evaluation or use;
- interleave evaluation: e.g., `A + (B * C)` can be evaluated in the order B, A, C.

At the same time, the programmer must be able to write programs whose behaviors are reproducible, and only allow non-determinism in a controlled way. Therefore, the standard makes undefined certain situations where reordering creates a "race condition". The latest treatment of this restriction is given by the C1X standard:

> If a side effect on a scalar object is unsequenced relative to either a different side effect on the same scalar object or a value computation using the value of the same scalar object, the behavior is undefined. If there are multiple allowable orderings [...], the behavior is undefined if such an unsequenced side effect occurs in any of the orderings [15, §6.5:2].

This means that if there are two writes, or a write and a read to the same object that are unsequenced (i.e., either is allowed to happen before the other), then the expression is undefined. Examples of expressions made undefined by this clause include `(x=0)+(x=1)` and `(x=0)+x` and `x=x++` and `*p=x++`, for `int x` and `int* p=&x`. This relation is related to the concept of "sequence points", also defined by the standard. Sequence points cause the expressions they fall between to be sequenced. The most common example of a sequence point is the semicolon, i.e., the end of an expression-statement. All previous evaluations and side effects must be complete before crossing sequence points.

A hasty read of the standard may wrongly indicate that detecting this kind of undefined behavior is an easy problem that can be checked statically. In fact, it is undecidable statically; moreover, one needs to use the entire semantics in order to check it dynamically. Consider the following example:

```
int x, y, *p = &y;
int f(void){ if (guard) { p = &x; } return 0; }
int main(void){ return (x = 5) + (*p = 6) + f(); }
```

The undefinedness of this program is based on what happens in the call to `f()`. If `f` is called before the other subexpressions in `main` are evaluated, and if the `guard` expression (which could be arbitrarily complex) is true, then the remaining expression effectively becomes `(x = 5) + (x = 6)`, which is undefined. The possible complexity of the `guard` is a witness to the (static) undecidability of this problem. The evaluation of the `guard` may make arbitrary use of the entire C language, so the entire semantics is needed in order to determine whether this program is undefined.

Based on this, note that: when two expressions are unsequenced, it means that evaluation can happen in any order. Thus, it is natural to map unsequenced behavior into nondeterministic behavior. This way, we can use state space exploration as a single mechanism to find unsequenced behavior. To identify this kind of undefined behavior naively can be incredibly computationally expensive; some optimizations are necessary to make this feasible. We offer two such optimizations below.

First, with a little case analysis of the definition of the sequencing relation, it is clear that there can be no sequenced write before a read of the same object with no intervening sequence point. This means that if in searching the semantic state space, we find an execution in which the write of a scalar object happens before a write or read of the same object with no intervening sequence point, then we can conclude that this write/write or write/read pair is unsequenced. Whenever a write is made, its location is recorded in the locsWrittenTo cell, which is emptied whenever a sequence point is crossed. This cell is first checked whenever a read or write is made to ensure that there is no conflict. This strategy has the added benefit that some undefined behaviors of this kind can be detected even during interpretation (where only a single path through the state space is explored). It is similar to the strategy used by Norrish [22].

Second, it turns out that a large subset of allowed orderings do not need to be considered in order to detect undefined behavior or possible nondeterministic behaviors. Because we are looking for writes *before* other events, we can take the liberty of applying side effects immediately instead of delaying them.

What would it mean for there to exist an expression whose definedness relied on whether or not a side effect (a write) occurs later instead of earlier? There must be three parts to the expression: a subexpression E generating a side effect X, and, for generality's sake, further subexpressions E' and E''. The particular evaluation where we do side effects immediately would look like $E\ X\ E'\ E''$. Because this is always a possible execution, and we assume it does not show a problem, we can conclude neither E' nor E'' reads or writes to X. If there is a problem only when we delay the side effect, it can be seen in a path like $E\ E'\ X\ E''$. For this to be different than applying the changes to X immediately, it means there must be some use of X in the evaluation of E'. But this contradicts the previous assumption.

This shrinks the state space dramatically, while at the same time not missing any undefined behavior. Our semantics does capture the appropriate state space, as seen in Section 6.3.1.

4.7 KCC

Using a simple frontend that mimics the behavior of GCC [9], C programs are parsed and translated into a Maude term, then reduced using the rules of our formal semantics. For defined programs, this process produces indistinguishable behavior from the same C program run as native code. We call this interpreter, obtained automatically from our formal semantics, KCC. As we will show in Section 6, KCC is significantly more than an interpreter—in addition to simple interpretation, it is also capable of debugging, catching undefined behaviors, state space search, and model checking. Once KCC is installed on a system, compilation of C programs generates a single executable file (an "a.out") containing the semantics of C, together with a parsed representation of the program and a call to Maude. The output is captured by a script and presented so that for working programs the output and behavior is identical to that of a real C compiler. To emphasize the seamlessness, here is a simple transcript:

```
$ kcc helloworld.c
$ ./a.out
Hello world
```

While it may seem like a gimmick, it helped our testing and debugging tremendously. For example, we could run the definition using the same test harness GCC uses for its testing (see Section 5). It also means people with no formal background can get use out of our semantics simply by using it as they would a compiler.

5. Testing the Semantics

No matter what the intended use is for a formal semantics, its actual use is limited if one cannot generate confidence in its correctness. To this aim, we ensured that our formal semantics remained executable and computationally practical.

5.1 GCC Torture Tests

As discussed in the previous section, our semantics is encapsulated inside a drop-in replacement for GCC, which we call KCC. This enables us to test the semantics as one would test a compiler. We were then able to run our semantics against the GCC C-torture-test [10] and compare its behavior to that of GCC 4.1.2, as well as the Intel C++ Compiler (ICC) 11.1 and Clang 3.0 r132915 (C compiler for LLVM). We ran all compilers with optimizations turned off.

We use the torture test for GCC 4.4.2, specifically those tests inside the "testsuite/gcc.c-torture/execute" directory. We chose these tests because they focus particularly on portable (machine independent) executable tests. The README.gcc for the tests says, "The 'torture' tests are meant to be generic tests that can run on any target." We found that generally this is the case, although there are also tests that include GCC-specific features, which had to be excluded from our evaluation. There were originally 1093 tests, of which we excluded 267 tests because they used GCC-specific extensions or builtins, they used the `_Complex` data type or certain library functions (which are not required of a freestanding implementation of C), or they were machine dependent. This left us with 826 tests. Further manual inspection revealed an additional 50 tests that were non-conforming according to the standard (mostly signed overflow or reading from uninitialized memory), bringing us to a grand total of 776 viable tests.

In order to avoid "overfitting" our semantics to the tests, we randomly extracted about 30% of the conforming tests and developed our semantics using only this small subset (and other programs discussed in Section 5.2). After we were comfortable with the quality of our semantics when running this subset, we ran the remaining tests. Out of 541 previously untested programs, we successfully ran 514 (95%). After this initial test, we began to use all of the tests to help develop our semantics; we now pass 770 (99.2%) of the 776 compliant tests.

	Torture Tests Run (of 776)	
Compiler	Count	Percent
GCC	768	99.0
ICC	771	99.4
Clang	763	98.3
KCC	770	99.2

The 776 tests represent about 23,500 SLOC, or 30 SLOC/file.

Correctness Analysis Our executable formal semantics performed nearly as well as the best compiler we tested, and better than the others. We incorporated the passing tests into our regression suite that gets run every time we commit a change. This way, upon adding features or fixing mistakes, our accuracy can only increase.

Three of the six failed tests rely on floating point accuracy problems. Two more rely on evaluating expressions inside of function declarators, as in:

```
int fun(int i, int array[i++]) { return i; }
```

which we are not handling properly. The last is a problem with the lifetime of variable length arrays.

Coverage Analysis In order to have some measure of the effectiveness of our testing, we recorded the application of every semantic rule for all of the torture tests. Out of 887 core rules (non-library, non-helper operator), the GCC torture tests exercised 805 (91%).

In addition to getting a coverage measure, this process suggests an interesting application. For example, in the GCC tests looked at above, a rule that deals with casting large values to `unsigned int` was never applied. By looking at such rules, we can create new tests to trigger them. These tests would improve both confidence in the semantics as well as the test suite itself.

5.2 Exploratory Testing

We have also tested our semantics on programs gathered from around the web, including programs of our own design and from open source compilers. Not counting the GCC tests, we include over 17,000 SLOC in our regression tests that are run when making changes to the semantics. These tests include a number of programs from the LCC [12] and CompCert [1] compilers. We also execute the "C Reference Manual" tests (also known as cq.c),[6] which go through Kernighan and Ritchie [17] and test each feature described in about 5,000 SLOC. When these tests are added to the GCC tests described above, it brings our rule-coverage to 98% (867/887 rules).

We can successfully execute Duff's Device [7], an unstructured `switch` statement where the `case`s are inside of a loop inside of the `switch` statement itself, as well as quines (programs whose output are precisely their source code), and a number of programs from the Obfuscated C Code Contest [21]. All of these test programs, as well as our semantics, are available from our project webpage: `http://c-semantics.googlecode.com/`.

6. Applications—Formal Semantics is Useful!

Here we describe applications of our formal semantics, which are in addition to the interpreter already mentioned. These tools are automatically derived from the semantics—changes made to the semantics immediately affect the tools. We are permitted this luxury because we take advantage of general purpose tools available to RL theories, of which our semantics is one. Contrast this to the nearly universal strategy of writing analysis tools independently of semantics. Instead of developing a different model for each tool, a plethora of tools can be created around a single semantic definition. These tools are essentially wrappers, or views, of the semantics.

6.1 Debugging

By introducing a special function "`__debug`" that acts as a breakpoint, we can turn the Maude debugger into a simple debugger for C programs. This provides the ability to step through interesting parts of execution to find out what rules of semantics are invoked in giving meaning to a program.

In the semantics, we handle this function by giving a labeled rule that causes it to evaluate to a "void" value. It is essentially equivalent to `void __debug(int i) { }`. If this function is called during execution, it starts a debugger that allows the user to inspect the current state of the program. One can step through more rules individually from there, or simply note the information and proceed. If the `__debug` call is inside a loop, the user will see a snapshot each time it reaches the expression. For example:

```
int main(void){
  for (int i = 0; i < 10; i++){ __debug(i); }
  printf("done!\n");
}
```

We can run or debug the program above as follows:

```
$ kcc debug.c
$ ./a.out # run the program normally
done!
$ DEBUG=1 ./a.out # or run it in the debugger
Debug(1)> where .
          ⟨__debug(0 : int) ···⟩k ⟨··· i ↦ L ···⟩env ···
Debug(1)> resume .
          ⟨__debug(1 : int) ···⟩k ⟨··· i ↦ L ···⟩env ···
```

The user can use this to see what the value of the `__debug` argument is each time through the loop, as well as the entire state of the program when the breakpoint was reached. The state presented to the user includes all of the cells of the language (Figure 2). This elided state is represented by the ellipses above. In addition to the "where" and "resume" commands, there is also a "step" command to step through the application of a single semantic rule [3, §22.1].

6.2 Runtime Verification

There are two main avenues through which we can catch and identify runtime problems with a program: catching undefined behavior, and symbolic execution.

6.2.1 Undefined Behavior

The first mechanism is based around the idea that when something lacks semantics (i.e., when its behavior is undefined according to the standard) then the evaluation of the program will simply stop when it reaches that point in the program. We use this mechanism to catch errors like signed overflow or array out-of-bounds.

In this small program, the programmer forgot to leave space for a string terminator (`'\0'`). The call to `strcpy()` will read off the end of the array:

```
int main(void) {
  char dest[5], src[5] = "hello";
  strcpy(dest, src);
}
```

GCC will happily execute this, and depending on the state of memory, even do what one would expect. It is still undefined, and our semantics will detect trying to read past the end of the array. Because this program has no meaning, our semantics "gets stuck" when exploring its behavior. It is through this simple mechanism that we can identify undefined programs and report them to the user. By default, when a program gets stuck, we report the state of the configuration (a concrete instance of that shown in Figure 2) and what exactly the semantics was trying to do at the time of the problem. We have also begun to add explicit error messages for common problems—here is the output[7] from our tool for this code:

```
$ kcc buggy_strcpy.c ; ./a.out
ERROR encountered while executing this program.
Description: Reading outside the bounds of an object.
Function: strcpy
Line: 3
```

[6] We have been unable to determine the author or origin of this test suite. Please contact us with any information.

[7] Here and elsewhere in this section, we take the liberty to slightly simplify the output to make it fit in less vertical space.

6.2.2 Symbolic Execution

Through the use of symbolic execution, we can further enhance the above idea by expanding the behaviors that we consider undefined, while maintaining the good behaviors. Symbolic execution is straightforward to achieve using a rewriting-based semantics: whether a term is concrete or abstract makes no difference to the theory. Rules designed to work with concrete terms do not need to be changed in order to work with symbolic terms.

As we explained in Section 4.3, we treat pointers not as concrete integers, but as symbolic values. These values then have certain behavior defined on them, such as comparison, difference, etc. This technique is based on the idea of *strong memory safety*, which had previously been explored with a simple C-like language [30]. In this context, it takes advantage of the fact that addresses of local variables and memory returned from allocation functions like `malloc()` are unspecified [15, §7.20.3]. However, there are a number of restrictions on many addresses, such as the elements of an array being completely contiguous and the fields in a struct being ordered (though not necessarily contiguous).

For example, take the following program:

```
int main(void) {
  int a, b;
  if (&a < &b) { ... }
}
```

If we gave objects concrete, numerical addresses, then they would always be comparable. However, this piece of code is actually undefined according to the standard [15, §6.5.8:5]. Symbolic locations that are actually base/offset pairs allow us to detect this program as problematic. We only give semantics to relational pointer comparisons where the two addresses share a common base. Thus, evaluation gets stuck on the program above:

```
$ kcc bad_comparison.c ; ./a.out
ERROR encountered while executing this program.
Description: Cannot apply '<' to different base objects.
Function: main
Line: 3
```

Of course, sometimes locations are comparable. If we take the following code instead:

```
int main(void) {
  struct { int a; int b; } s;
  if (&s.a < &s.b) { ... }
}
```

the addresses of `a` and `b` are guaranteed to be in order [15, §6.5.8:5], and in fact our semantics finds the comparison to be true because the pointers share a common base.

Another example can be seen when copying a struct one byte at a time (as in a C implementation of `memcpy()`); every byte needs to be copied, even uninitialized fields (or padding), and no error should occur [15, §6.2.6.1:5–7]. Because of this, our semantics must give it meaning. Using concrete values here would mean missing some incorrect programs, so we use symbolic values that allow reading and copying to take place as long as the program never uses those uninitialized values in undefined ways.

6.3 State Space Search

We can also use our semantics to do both matching-based state search and explicit state model-checking with linear temporal logic (LTL). The basic examples below show how our semantics captures the appropriate expression evaluation semantics precisely.

6.3.1 Exploring Evaluation Order

To show our semantics captures the evaluation orders of C expressions allowed by the specification, we examine some examples from related works. The results given below are not just theoretical results from our semantics, but are actual results obtained from executing the tools provided by our semantic framework.

To start with a simple example from Papaspyrou and Maćoš [26], we take a look at `x+(x=1)` in an environment where `x` is 0. This expression is undefined because the read of `x` (the lone `x`) is unsequenced with respect to the write of `x` (the assignment). Using our semantics to do a search of the behaviors of this expression finds this unsequenced read/write pair, and reports an error.

Norrish [22] offers the deceptively simple addition expression `(x=0) + (x=0)`, which in many languages would be valid. However, in C it is again a technically undefined expression due to the unsequenced assignments to `x`. Our semantics reports an error for this expression as well.

Another example in the literature is given by Papaspyrou [25], which shows how C can exhibit nondeterministic behavior while staying conforming. The driving expression is the addition of two function calls. In C, function evaluation is not allowed to interleave [15, 6.5.2.2:10], so the behavior of this program is determined solely on which call happens last:

```
int r = 0;
int f (int x) { return (r = x); }
int main(void){ f(1) + f(2); return r; }
```

If `f()` is called with the argument 2 last, then the result will be 2, and similarly for 1. Searching with our semantics gives the behaviors `{r=1}` and `{r=2}`, which are indeed the two possible results.

As a last example, we look at a more complex expression of our own devising: `f()(a(b(), c(d())))`. Except for `f()`, each function call prints out its name and returns 0. The function `f()`, however, prints out its name and then returns a function pointer to a function that prints "e". The function represented by this function pointer will be passed results of `a()`. We elide the actual function bodies, because the behavior is more easily understood by this tree:

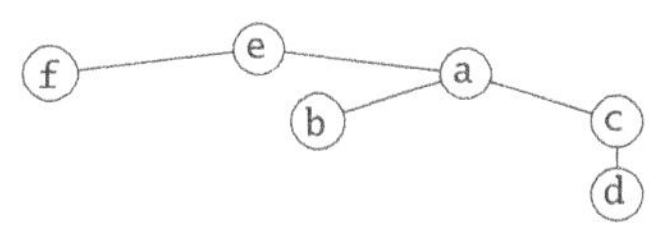

This tree (or Hasse diagram) describes the sequencing relation for this expression. That is, it must be the case that `d` happens before `c`, that `b` and `c` happen before `a`, and that `f` and `a` happen before `e`. Running this example through our search tool gives precisely the behaviors allowed by the standard:

```
$ kcc nondet.c ; SEARCH=1 ./a.out
15 solutions found
bdcafe bdcfae bdfcae bfdcae dbcafe dbcfae dbfcae dcbafe
dcbfae dcfbae dfbcae dfcbae fbdcae fdbcae fdcbae
```

6.3.2 Model Checking

In addition to the simple state search we showed above, one can also use our semantics for LTL model checking. For example, consider the following program:

```
typedef enum {green, yellow, red} state;
state lightNS = green; state lightEW = red;
int changeNS() {
  switch (lightNS) {
    case(green): lightNS = yellow; return 0;
    case(yellow): lightNS = red; return 0;
    case(red):
      if (lightEW == red) { lightNS = green; } return 0;
  }
}
...
int main(void) { while(1) { changeNS() + changeEW(); } }
```

This program is meant to represent two orthogonal traffic lights (`lightNS` and `lightEW`) at the same intersection. It provides an implementation of an algorithm to change the state of the lights from green to yellow to red and back. We elide the nearly identical `changeEW()` function. The program takes advantage of the unspecified order of evaluation of addition in the expression `changeNS() + changeEW()` to nondeterministically choose the order in which the lights are changed.

There are a number of properties one might like to prove about this program, including safety and liveness properties. One safety property is that it should always be the case that at least one of the lights is red, or $\Box$((`lightNS == red`) $\vee$ (`lightEW == red`)). We have added a special `#pragma`[8] allowing the programmer to write and name LTL formulae. If we call the above formula "safety", then we can invoke the model checker as follows:

```
$ kcc lights.c ; MODELCHECK=safety ./a.out
result Bool: true
```

Similarly, it is important that the lights always make progress, i.e., that it is always the case the lights will eventually become green. If we try to check $\Box\Diamond$(`lightNS == green`), we find that it does not hold of the above program:

```
$ kcc lights.c ; MODELCHECK=progress ./a.out
result ModelCheckResult: counterexample ...
```

The reason this property is not verified is that the algorithm is wrong! Because the calls to `changeNS()` and `changeEW()` can occur in any order, it is possible for either of the lights to get stuck on red. The program starts with `ns=gre, ew=red`. Consider the following execution:

```
changeNS, changeEW => ns=yel, ew=red
changeEW, changeNS => ns=red, ew=red
changeNS, changeEW => ns=gre, ew=red
```

By alternating evaluation orders, the program can change the N/S light without ever changing the E/W light. This evaluation order is highly implausable in most C compilers, but the semantics allows it. If we fix an evaluation order by changing `changeNS() + changeEW();` to `changeNS(); changeEW();`, then the property holds:

```
$ kcc lights.c ; MODELCHECK=progress ./a.out
result Bool: true
```

7. Limitations and Future Work

Here we delineate the limitations of our definition and explain their causes and effects.

There are two main ways in which semantics can be incomplete—under-definedness and over-definedness. Typically when one thinks of incompleteness, one thinks of failure to give meaning to correct programs. However, because we want to be able to identify incorrect or unportable programs, the semantics must be balanced appropriately between defining too much or too little. It is equally important not to give semantics to programs that should be undefined.

In the first case, we are not missing any features—we have given semantics to every feature required of a freestanding implementation of C. With this said, our semantics is not perfect. For example, we still are not passing 100% of our test cases (see Section 5). Also, our semantics of floating point numbers is particularly weak. During execution or analysis, we simply rely on an IEEE-754 implementation of floating point arithmetic provided to us by our definitional framework ($\mathbb{K}$). This is fine for interpretation and explicit state model checking, but not for deductive reasoning.

In the second case, although our semantics can catch many bad behaviors other tools cannot (e.g., we have not found any other tool that catches the undefined programs in Sections 6.2.2 or 6.3.1), there is still room for improvement. For one, our semantics aligns all types to one-byte boundaries. This means we cannot catch undefined behavior related to alignment restrictions. Note that others have worked on formalizing alignment requirements [20], but it has never been incorporated into a full semantics for C. We also do not handle type qualifiers (like `const` or `volatile`); we simply ignore them. This is safe to do when interpreting correct programs, but it means we are not detecting problems related to those features in incorrect programs. It also means that we are missing possible behaviors when searching programs that use `volatile`.

We have not yet used our C definition for doing language or program level proofs, even though the $\mathbb{K}$ Framework supports both program level [31] and semantics level proofs [8]. To do so, we need to extend our semantics with support for formal annotations (e.g., assume, assert, invariant) and connect it to a theorem prover. This is already being done for a subset of the C language [29], and we intend to apply those techniques to actual C in the future.

We still do not cover all of the standard library headers. So far, we have added library functions by need in order to run example programs, which is why we have semantics for library functions like `malloc()`, `longjmp()`, parts of `printf()`, variadic functions, and over 30 others. We intend on covering more libraries in the future, but for now, one could supplement what we provide by using implementations of libraries written in C.

In our current semantics, only some of the implementation-defined behaviors are available—the most common ones. By making the semantics parametric, we hope others can add or change implementation-defined rules to suit their needs.

Finally, we should mention the speed of our system. While it is not nearly as fast as C compiled natively, it is usable. Of the GCC torture test programs described listed in Section 5, our semantics ran over 93% of these programs in under 10 seconds (each). An additional 4% completed in 2 minutes, 2% in 5 hours, and 1% further in under 3 days. In comparison, it takes GCC about 0.05 s for each test. The reader should keep in mind that this is an interpreter obtained for free from a formal semantics. In addition, the search and model checking tools suffer the same state explosion problems inherent in all explicit-state model checking.

8. Conclusion

It is a shame that, despite the best efforts of over 40 years of research in formal programming languages, most language designers still consider the difficulties of defining formal semantics to outweigh the benefits. Formal semantics and practicality are not typically considered together. When C was being standardized, the standards committee explored using formal semantics, but in the end decided to use simple prose because, "Anything more ambitious was considered to be likely to delay the Standard, and to make it less accessible to its audience" [14, §6]. This is a common sentiment in the programming language community. Indeed, startlingly few "real" languages have ever been completely formalized, and even fewer were designed with formal specification in mind.

Based on our experience with our semantics, the development of a formal semantics for C could have taken place alongside the development of the standard. Within roughly 6 person-months, we had a working version of our semantics that covered more of the standard than any previous semantics. The version presented in this paper is the result of 18 person-months of work. To put this in perspective, one member of the standards committee estimated that it took roughly 62 person-*years* to produce the C99 standard [16]. We are *not* claiming that we have done the same job in a fraction of the time; obviously writing a semantics based on the standard is quite different than writing the standard itself. We are simply saying that the effort it takes to develop a rewriting-based semantics is quite small compared to the effort it took to develop the standard.

[8] A conforming way to add implementation-defined behavior to C.

The reluctance of the language community towards formal methods has not been without reason—it is not always clear that having a formal semantics earns the designer anything tangible for her effort. Commonly mentioned benefits like improving the understanding of the language or providing a model in which sound arguments about the language can be made are relatively intangible; to be accepted by the general language community, semantics needs to be shown to have concrete value beyond that of prose.

The time has come to start building analysis tools directly on formal models. Instead of building analysis tools for different languages and different versions of each language, the analysis infrastructure surrounding the semantics could be maintained independently so that one could derive tools for multiple languages simply by swapping out the semantic rules. We offer our work as one small step in this direction; we are not alone, and there are other tools including pluggable analysis architectures like Frama-C [6] and formal tools like CompCert [1] that share part of this vision.

Our semantics and its automatically generated tools have already found one serious application. Csmith [35] is a C program test generator that generates random conforming programs from a large, expressive subset of the C language. These tests are then used to perform differential testing among C compilers to find compilation bugs. To date, the Csmith team has found more than 325 bugs in common compilers like GCC and Clang. The programs Csmith generates are almost always too large (many between 1,000 and 10,000 SLOC) to submit as bug reports and need to be reduced. The reduction process is semi-automatic, but is riddled with the possibility of introducing undefined behavior. Until now, these tests would have to be carefully examined by hand for undefined behavior, because any such behavior would render the tests invalid. Our semantic tools are being used by the Csmith team to detect this undefined behavior and have allowed them to more completely automate the process and reduce the tests more aggressively.

References

[1] S. Blazy and X. Leroy. Mechanized semantics for the Clight subset of the C language. *J. Automated Reasoning*, 43(3):263–288, 2009.

[2] R. S. Boyer and J. S. Moore. *A Computational Logic Handbook*. Academic Press, second edition, 1998.

[3] M. Clavel, F. Durán, S. Eker, J. Meseguer, P. Lincoln, N. Martí-Oliet, and C. Talcott. *All About Maude, A High-Performance Logical Framework*, volume 4350 of *LNCS*. Springer, 2007.

[4] J. V. Cook and S. Subramanian. A formal semantics for C in Nqthm. Technical Report 517D, Trusted Information Systems, November 1994.

[5] J. V. Cook, E. L. Cohen, and T. S. Redmond. A formal denotational semantics for C. Technical Report 409D, Trusted Information Systems, September 1994.

[6] P. Cuoq, J. Signoles, P. Baudin, R. Bonichon, G. Canet, L. Correnson, B. Monate, V. Prevosto, and A. Puccetti. Experience report: OCaml for an industrial-strength static analysis framework. *SIGPLAN Not.*, 44: 281–286, August 2009.

[7] T. Duff. On Duff's device, 1988. URL `http://www.lysator.liu.se/c/duffs-device.html`. Msg. to the comp.lang.c Usenet group.

[8] C. Ellison, T. F. Şerbănuţă, and G. Roşu. A rewriting logic approach to type inference. In *19th Intl. Wkshp. on Algebraic Development Techniques (WADT'08)*, volume 5486 of *LNCS*, pages 135–151, 2009.

[9] FSF. GNU compiler collection, 2010. URL `http://gcc.gnu.org`.

[10] FSF. C language testsuites: "C-torture" version 4.4.2, 2010. URL `http://gcc.gnu.org/onlinedocs/gccint/C-Tests.html`.

[11] Y. Gurevich and J. K. Huggins. The semantics of the C programming language. In *Computer Science Logic*, volume 702 of *LNCS*, pages 274–308, 1993.

[12] D. R. Hanson and C. W. Fraser. *A Retargetable C Compiler: Design and Implementation*. Addison-Wesley, 1995.

[13] ISO/IEC JTC 1, SC 22, WG 14. ISO/IEC 9899:1999: Programming languages—C. Technical Report n1256, Intl. Organization for Standardization, December 1999.

[14] ISO/IEC JTC 1, SC 22, WG 14. Rationale for international standard—programming languages—C. Technical Report 5.10, Intl. Organization for Standardization, April 2003.

[15] ISO/IEC JTC 1, SC 22, WG 14. ISO/IEC 9899:201x: Programming languages—C. Technical Report n1570, Intl. Organization for Standardization, August 2011.

[16] D. M. Jones. *The New C Standard: An Economic and Cultural Commentary*. Self-published, December 2008. URL `http://www.knosof.co.uk/cbook/cbook.html`.

[17] B. W. Kernighan and D. M. Ritchie. *The C Programming Language*. Prentice Hall, second edition, 1988.

[18] J. Meseguer. Conditional rewriting logic as a unified model of concurrency. *Theoretical Computer Science*, 96(1):73–155, 1992.

[19] G. C. Necula, S. McPeak, S. P. Rahul, and W. Weimer. CIL: Intermediate language and tools for analysis and transformation of C programs. In *Intl. Conf. on Compiler Construction*, pages 213–228, 2002.

[20] M. Nita, D. Grossman, and C. Chambers. A theory of platform-dependent low-level software. In *35th ACM Symposium on Principles of Programming Languages (POPL'08)*, 2008.

[21] L. C. Noll, S. Cooper, P. Seebach, and L. A. Broukhis. The international obfuscated C code contest, 2010. URL `http://www.ioccc.org/`.

[22] M. Norrish. C formalised in HOL. Technical Report UCAM-CL-TR-453, University of Cambridge, December 1998.

[23] M. Norrish. A formal semantics for C++. Technical report, NICTA, 2008. URL `http://nicta.com.au/people/norrishm/attachments/bibliographies_and_papers/C-TR.pdf`.

[24] N. S. Papaspyrou. *A Formal Semantics for the C Programming Language*. PhD thesis, Natl. Technical University of Athens, 1998.

[25] N. S. Papaspyrou. Denotational semantics of ANSI C. *Computer Standards and Interfaces*, 23(3):169–185, 2001.

[26] N. S. Papaspyrou and D. Maćoš. A study of evaluation order semantics in expressions with side effects. *J. Functional Programming*, 10(3): 227–244, 2000.

[27] G. D. Plotkin. The origins of structural operational semantics. *J. Logic and Algebraic Programming*, 60:60–61, 2004.

[28] G. Roşu and T. F. Şerbănuţă. An overview of the K semantic framework. *J. Logic and Algebraic Programming*, 79(6):397–434, 2010.

[29] G. Roşu and A. Ştefănescu. Matching logic: A new program verification approach (NIER track). In *30th Intl. Conf. on Software Engineering (ICSE'11)*, pages 868–871, 2011.

[30] G. Roşu, W. Schulte, and T. F. Şerbănuţă. Runtime verification of C memory safety. In *Runtime Verification (RV'09)*, volume 5779 of *LNCS*, pages 132–152, 2009.

[31] G. Roşu, C. Ellison, and W. Schulte. Matching logic: An alternative to Hoare/Floyd logic. In *13th Intl. Conf. on Algebraic Methodology and Software Technology (AMAST'10)*, volume 6486 of *LNCS*, pages 142–162, 2010.

[32] T. F. Şerbănuţă and G. Roşu. K-Maude: A rewriting based tool for semantics of programming languages. In *8th Intl. Wkshp. on Rewriting Logic and its Applications (WRLA'09)*, volume 6381 of *LNCS*, pages 104–122, 2010.

[33] S. Subramanian and J. V. Cook. Mechanical verification of C programs. In *ACM SIGSOFT Wkshp. on Formal Methods in Software Practice*, January 1996.

[34] S. Summit. C programming FAQs: Frequently asked questions, 2005. URL `http://www.c-faq.com/`.

[35] X. Yang, Y. Chen, E. Eide, and J. Regehr. Finding and understanding bugs in C compilers. In *32nd Conf. on Programming Language Design and Implementation (PLDI'11)*, pages 283–294, 2011.

[36] W. Zimmermann and A. Dold. A framework for modeling the semantics of expression evaluation with abstract state machines. In *Abstract State Machines*, volume 2589 of *LNCS*, pages 391–406, 2003.

A Type Theory for Probability Density Functions

Sooraj Bhat
Georgia Institute of Technology
sooraj@gatech.edu

Ashish Agarwal
New York University
ashish.agarwal@nyu.edu

Richard Vuduc, Alexander Gray
Georgia Institute of Technology
{richie,agray}@cc.gatech.edu

Abstract

There has been great interest in creating probabilistic programming languages to simplify the coding of statistical tasks; however, there still does not exist a formal language that simultaneously provides (1) continuous probability distributions, (2) the ability to naturally express custom probabilistic models, and (3) probability density functions (PDFs). This collection of features is necessary for mechanizing fundamental statistical techniques. We formalize the first probabilistic language that exhibits these features, and it serves as a foundational framework for extending the ideas to more general languages. Particularly novel are our type system for *absolutely continuous* (AC) distributions (those which permit PDFs) and our PDF calculation procedure, which calculates PDFs for a large class of AC distributions. Our formalization paves the way toward the rigorous encoding of powerful statistical reformulations.

Categories and Subject Descriptors F.3.2 [*Logics and Meanings of Programs*]: Semantics of Programming Languages–Program analysis; F.3.1 [*Logics and Meanings of Programs*]: Specifying and Verifying and Reasoning about Programs–Mechanical verification; G.3 [*Probability and Statistics*]: Statistical computing

General Terms Theory, Languages

Keywords Continuous Probability, Probability Density Functions

1. Introduction

In the face of more complex data analysis needs, both the machine learning and programming languages communities have recognized the need to express probabilistic and statistical computations *declaratively*. This has led to a proliferation of probabilistic programming languages [7, 9, 12–14, 16, 18–22]. Program transformations on probabilistic programs are crucial: many techniques for converting statistical problems into efficient, executable algorithms are syntactic in nature. A rigorous language definition aids reasoning about the correctness of these program transformations.

However, several fundamental statistical techniques cannot currently be encoded as program transformations because current languages have weak support for probability distributions on continuous or hybrid discrete-continuous spaces. In particular, no existing language rigorously supports expressing the *probability density function* (PDF) of custom probability distributions. This is an impediment to mechanizing statistics; continuous distributions and their PDFs are ubiquitous in statistical theory and applications. Techniques such as maximum likelihood estimation (MLE), L_2 estimation (L2E), and nonparametric kernel methods are all formulated in terms of the PDF [3, 23, 24]. Specifically, we want the ability to naturally express a probabilistic model over a discrete, continuous or hybrid space and then mechanically obtain a usable form of its PDF. Usage of the PDF may entail direct numerical evaluation of the PDF or symbolic manipulation of the PDF and its derivatives. Continuous spaces pose some unique obstacles, however. First, the existence of the PDF is not guaranteed, unlike the discrete case. Second, stating the conditions for existence involves the language of measure theory, an area of mathematics renowned for nonconstructive results, suggesting that mechanization may not be straightforward. Notably, obtaining a PDF from its distribution is a non-computable operation in the general case [11]. In light of these issues, we make the following new contributions:

- We present a formal probability language with classical measure-theoretic semantics which allows naturally expressing a variety of useful probability distributions on discrete, continuous and hybrid discrete-continuous spaces, as well as their PDFs when they exist (Section 3). The language is a core calculus which omits functions and mutation.
- We define a type system for *absolutely continuous* probability distributions, *i.e.* those which permit a PDF. The type system does not require mechanizing σ-algebras, null sets, the Lebesgue measure, or other complex constructions from measure theory. The key insight is to analyze a distribution by how it transforms other distributions instead of using the "obvious" induction on the monadic structure of the distribution (Section 4).
- We define a procedure that calculates PDFs for a large class of distributions accepted by our type system. The design permits modularly adding knowledge about individual distributions with known PDFs (but which cannot be calculated from scratch), enabling the procedure to proceed with programs that use these distributions as subcomponents (Section 5).

We believe this is the first general treatment of PDFs in a language. We deliberately omit features that are not essential to the current investigation (*e.g.* expectation, sampling). Finally, we discuss the relation to existing and future work (Sections 6 and 7). In particular, we save a treatment of PDFs in the context of conditional probability for future work.

2. Background and motivation

We first introduce probability in the context of countable spaces to emphasize the complications that arise when moving to continuous spaces. We focus only on issues surrounding PDFs. We occasionally deviate from standard probability notation to circumvent imprecision in the standard notation and to create a harmonious notation throughout the paper. In this section we present a specialized ac-

POPL'12, January 25–27, 2012, Philadelphia, PA, USA.

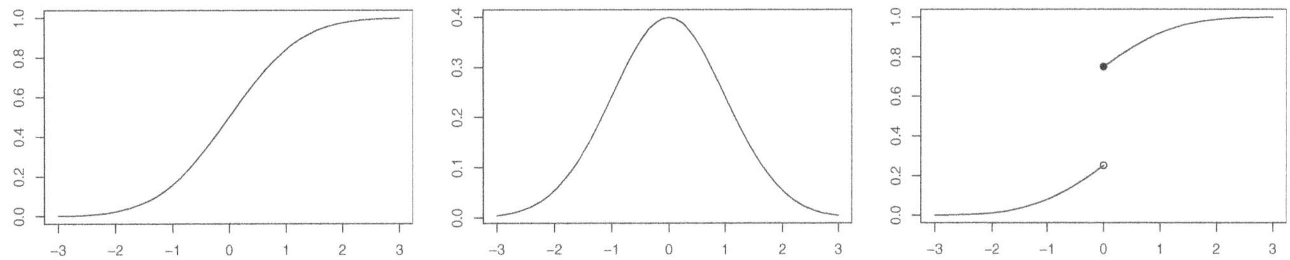

Figure 1. The CDF and PDF of a standard normal distribution and the CDF of a distribution that does not have a PDF.

count of probability for ease of exposition. We discuss the rigorous and generalized definitions in Section 3.3.

We use the term *discrete distribution* for distributions on discrete spaces (countable sets); *continuous distribution* for distributions on the continuous spaces $\mathbb{R}$ and $\mathbb{R}^n$; and *hybrid distribution* for distributions on products of discrete and continuous spaces that are themselves neither discrete nor continuous, such as $\mathbb{R} \times \mathbb{Z}$.

2.1 Probability on countable spaces

Consider a set of outcomes A. For now, let A be countable. It is meant to represent the possible states of the world we are modeling, such as the set of possible outcomes of an experiment or measurements of a quantity. An *event* is a subset of A, also understood as a predicate on elements of A. Events denote some occurrence of interest and partition the outcomes into those that exhibit the property and those that do not. A *probability distribution* $\mathbb{P}$ (or simply, *distribution*) on A is a function from events to $[0, 1]$ such that $\mathbb{P}(X) \geq 0$ for all events X, $\mathbb{P}(A) = 1$ and $\mathbb{P}(\bigcup_{i=0}^{\infty} X_i) = \sum_{i=0}^{\infty} \mathbb{P}(X_i)$ for countable sequences of mutually disjoint events X_i. Distributions tell us the probability that different events will occur. It is generally more convenient to work with a distribution's *probability mass function* (PMF) instead, defined $f(x) = \mathbb{P}(\{x\})$, which tells us how likely an individual outcome is. It satisfies

$$\mathbb{P}(X) = \sum_{x \in X} f(x)$$

for all events X on A. For example, if $\mathbb{P}$ is the distribution characterizing the outcome of rolling a fair die, its PMF is given by $f(x) = \frac{1}{6}$, where $x \in A$ and $A = \{1, 2, 3, 4, 5, 6\}$. The probability an even number is rolled is $\mathbb{P}(\{2, 4, 6\}) = \frac{1}{6} + \frac{1}{6} + \frac{1}{6} = \frac{1}{2}$.

2.2 Moving to continuous spaces

A *probability density function* (PDF) is the continuous analog of the PMF. Unfortunately, although every distribution on a countable set has a PMF, not every distribution on a continuous space has a PDF. Consider distributions on the real line. We say that a function f is a PDF of a distribution $\mathbb{P}$ on $\mathbb{R}$ if for all events X,

$$\mathbb{P}(X) = \int_X f(x)\, dx, \tag{1}$$

which states that the probability of X is the integral of f on X (in the simplest case, X is an interval). This idea can be extended to more general spaces. This equation does not determine f uniquely, but any two solutions f_1 and f_2 are equal "almost everywhere" (see Section 3.3) and give identical results under integration. Thus, we often refer to a PDF as *the* PDF.

For the spaces we consider in this paper, the property of having a PDF is equivalent to being *absolutely continuous* (AC). Roughly speaking, a distribution is AC if it never assigns positive probability to events that have "size zero" in the underlying space. For instance, the standard normal distribution is absolutely continuous and has the PDF $\phi(x) = \exp(-x^2/2)/\sqrt{2\pi}$. On the other hand, the distribution of y in the model

$$\begin{array}{l} z \sim \text{CoinFlip}(1/2) \\ x \sim \text{Normal}(0, 1) \end{array} \qquad y = \begin{cases} 0 & \text{if } z = \text{heads} \\ x & \text{if } z = \text{tails.} \end{cases}$$

does not have a PDF. We have used *random variables* to write the model; this is a commonly used informal notation that is shorthand for a more rigorous expression that defines the model. The model represents the following process: flip a fair coin; return 0 if it is heads, and sample from the standard normal distribution otherwise. We can see that it is not AC: the event $\{0\}$ occurs with probability $1/2$ (whenever the coin comes up heads), but has an interval length of zero. We use the *cumulative distribution function* (CDF) to visualize each distribution (Figure 1); the CDF F of a distribution $\mathbb{P}$ on $\mathbb{R}$ is $F(x) = \mathbb{P}(\ (-\infty, x]\ )$ and gives the probability that a sample from the distribution takes a value less than or equal to x. From Equation 1 we know that $\mathbb{P}$ has a PDF if and only if there exists a function f such that $F(x) = \int_{-\infty}^{x} f(t)\, dt$. Clearly, no such function exists for the CDF of y due to the jump discontinuity.

Mixing discrete and continuous types is not the only culprit. Consider the following process: sample a number u uniformly randomly from $[0, 1]$ and return the vector $x = (u, u) \in \mathbb{R}^2$. The distribution of x (a distribution on $\mathbb{R}^2$) is not AC: the event $X = \{(u, u) \mid u \in [0, 1]\}$ has probability 1, but X is a line segment and thus has zero area. Likewise, there is no PDF on $\mathbb{R}^2$ we could integrate to give positive mass on this zero area line segment.

2.3 Applications of the PDF

The PDF is often used to compute expectations (and probabilities, which are a special case of expectation). Expectation is a fundamental operation in probability and is used in defining quantities such as mean and variance. The expectation operation $\mathbb{E}$ of a distribution $\mathbb{P}$ on $\mathbb{R}$ is a higher-order function that satisfies

$$\mathbb{E}(g) = \int_{-\infty}^{\infty} g(x) \cdot f(x)\, dx$$

when $\mathbb{P}$ has a PDF, f, and the integral exists. Another application is *maximum likelihood estimation* (MLE), which addresses the problem of choosing the member of a family of distributions that "best explains" observed data. Let $\mathbb{P}(\,\cdot\,;\,\cdot\,)$ be a parameterized family of distributions, where $\mathbb{P}(\,\cdot\,;\theta)$ is the distribution for a given parameter θ. The MLE estimate θ^* of $\mathbb{P}$ for observed data x is given by

$$\theta^* = \arg\max_{\theta} f(x;\theta)$$

where $f(\,\cdot\,;\theta)$ is the PDF of $\mathbb{P}(\,\cdot\,;\theta)$. For example, x could be a set of points in $\mathbb{R}^n$ we wish to cluster, and θ^* could be the estimate of the locations of the cluster centroids. $\mathbb{P}$ would be the family of distributions we believe generated the clusters (a family parameterized by the positions of the cluster centroids), such as a mixture-of-Gaussians model. More details are available in [3].

2.4 Challenges for language design

Categorically, probability distributions form a monad [8, 20]. This structure forms the basis of many probabilistic languages because it is minimal, elegant, and presents many attractive features. First, it provides the look and feel of informal random variable notation, allowing us to express models as we normally would, while remaining mathematically rigorous. The monad structure affords formulating probability as an embedded domain specific language [7, 13, 18, 20] or as a mathematical theory in a proof assistant [2]. Additionally, many proofs about distributions expressed in the probability monad are greatly simplified by the monadic structure. We feel it is desirable to structure a language around the probability monad, and we investigate supporting PDFs specifically in such languages.

The probability monad consists of monadic return and monadic bind, as usual. Monadic return corresponds to the point mass distribution. We also provide the Uniform(0,1) distribution as a monadic value. These three combinators can be used to express a variety of distributions. The main issue when designing a type system for absolute continuity is that return creates non-AC distributions (on continuous types), yet—as a core member of the monadic calculus—it appears in the specification of nearly every distribution, even those that *are* AC. The "obvious" induction along the monadic structure is difficult to use to prove absolute continuity in the cases of interest. Consider for instance the joint distribution of two independent Uniform(0,1) random variables, written in our language as

$$\mathsf{var}\ x \sim \mathsf{random}\ \mathsf{in}\ \mathsf{var}\ y \sim \mathsf{random}\ \mathsf{in}\ \mathsf{return}\ (x, y). \qquad (2)$$

It is AC even though the subexpressions return (x, y) and var $y \sim$ random in return (x, y) are both *not* AC, where we treat x and y as real numbers, as dictated by the typing rule for bind. Also, as implementors we have found it difficult to "eyeball" the rules for absolute continuity. For example, only the first of these distributions is AC even though they are all nearly identical to Equation 2:

$$\mathsf{var}\ x \sim \mathsf{random}\ \mathsf{in}\ \mathsf{var}\ y \sim \mathsf{random}\ \mathsf{in}\ \mathsf{return}\ (x, x+y)$$
$$\mathsf{var}\ x \sim \mathsf{random}\ \mathsf{in}\ \mathsf{var}\ y \sim \mathsf{random}\ \mathsf{in}\ \mathsf{return}\ (x, y-y)$$
$$\mathsf{var}\ x \sim \mathsf{random}\ \mathsf{in}\ \mathsf{var}\ y \sim \mathsf{random}\ \mathsf{in}\ \mathsf{return}\ (x, y, x+y)$$

Clearly, what is needed is a principled analysis. We provide this in Section 4. A natural urge is wanting to remove return to create a language in which only AC distributions are expressible. We feel this is undesirable. Without return, we would not be able to express something as simple as adding two random variables (consider $(x + y)$ instead of (x, y) in Equation 2). Essentially, return allows us to express random variables as transformations of other random variables—a fundamental modeling tool we feel should be supported, allowing users to write down models that most naturally capture their domain. Without return we must extend the core calculus for each transformation we wish to use on random variables, and we must do so carefully if we want to ensure that non-AC distributions remain inexpressible. This extension of the core detracts from minimality and elegance, and it complicates developing the theory in a verification environment such as COQ, one of our eventual goals.

Finally, in addition to checking for existence, we would like to also calculate a usable form for the PDF. Many current probabilistic languages focus on distributions with only *finitely* many alternatives, which allows for implementing distributions as weighted lists of outcomes. The probability monad in this case is similar to the list monad, with some added logic describing how bind should propagate the weights. The weighted lists correspond directly to the PMF, but no such straightforward computational strategy exists for the PDF. We explore this further in Section 5.

Variables	x, y, z, u, v	Literals	l
Base types	$\tau ::= \mathsf{bool} \mid \mathsf{Z} \mid \mathsf{R} \mid \tau_1 \times \tau_2$		
Types	$t ::= \tau \mid \mathsf{dist}\ \tau$		
Expressions	$\varepsilon ::= x \mid l \mid op\ \varepsilon_1 ... \varepsilon_n \mid \mathsf{if}\ \varepsilon_1\ \mathsf{then}\ \varepsilon_2\ \mathsf{else}\ \varepsilon_3$		
Primops	$op ::= + \mid * \mid \mathsf{neg} \mid \mathsf{inv} \mid = \mid < \mid (\cdot,\cdot) \mid \mathsf{fst} \mid \mathsf{snd}$ $\mid \mathsf{exp} \mid \mathsf{log} \mid \mathsf{sin} \mid \mathsf{cos} \mid \mathsf{tan} \mid \mathsf{R\_of\_Z}$		
Distributions	$e ::= \mathsf{random} \mid \mathsf{return}\ \varepsilon \mid \mathsf{var}\ x \sim e_1\ \mathsf{in}\ e_2$		
Programs	$p ::= \mathsf{pdf}\ e$		
Contexts	$\Gamma ::= \emptyset \mid \Gamma, x : \tau$	$\Upsilon ::= \emptyset \mid \Upsilon, x : \tau \sim e$	
Substitution	$e[x := \varepsilon]$	Free variables	$FV(\cdot)$

Figure 2. The abstract syntax.

3. The language

In this section we present the abstract syntax, type system and semantics for our probabilistic language, except for the parts related to PDFs, which we cover in Section 4.

3.1 Abstract syntax

Figure 2 contains the syntax definitions. In addition to the standard letters for variables, we also use u and v when we want to emphasize that a random variable is distributed according to the Uniform(0,1) distribution. The syntactic category for literals includes Boolean (bool), integer (Z), and real number (R) literals. Types are stratified to ensure that distributions (dist τ) are only over base types. Integers are a distinct type from the reals; there is no subtyping in the language. We also stratify terms to simplify analysis. Expressions and primitive operations (primops) take their standard mathematical meaning, unless noted otherwise. For simplicity, we overload addition, multiplication, negation, and integer literals on the integers and reals, but fundamentally there is a $+$ for integers and a separate $+$ for reals, *etc.* Inversion inv denotes the reciprocal operation, and log is the natural logarithm. We give our semantics in terms of classical mathematics, so we do not concern ourselves with the issue of computation on the reals. Equality is defined on all base types in the usual way, and less-than is defined only on the numeric types. We write $(\varepsilon_1, \varepsilon_2, ..., \varepsilon_{n-1}, \varepsilon_n)$ as shorthand for $(\varepsilon_1, (\varepsilon_2, ...(\varepsilon_{n-1}, \varepsilon_n)...))$. The function R_of_Z injects an integer into the reals. The distribution random corresponds to the Uniform(0,1) distribution. The next two constructs correspond to monadic return and bind for the probability monad. The distribution return ε is the *point mass distribution*, which assigns probability 1 to the event $\{\varepsilon\}$. A random variable distributed according to return ε is in fact deterministic: there is no variation in the value it can take. The bind construct, var $x \sim e_1$ in e_2, is used to build complex distributions from simpler ones. It can be read: "introduce random variable x, distributed according to the distribution e_1, with scope in the distribution e_2". It is the only binding construct in the language. For simplicity, we have chosen to omit let-bindings and functions from our language, but we use both in our examples. We can use standard substitution rules to reduce such examples to the syntax of Figure 2. Examples include $\langle\varepsilon\rangle := \mathsf{if}\ \varepsilon\ \mathsf{then}\ 1\ \mathsf{else}\ 0$ (to inject Booleans into the reals), $\varepsilon_1 - \varepsilon_2 := \varepsilon_1 + \mathsf{neg}\ \varepsilon_2$, $\varepsilon_1 / \varepsilon_2 := \varepsilon_1 * \mathsf{inv}\ \varepsilon_2$, and $\varepsilon_1 < \varepsilon_2 < \varepsilon_3 := \mathsf{if}\ \varepsilon_1 < \varepsilon_2\ \mathsf{then}\ \varepsilon_2 < \varepsilon_3\ \mathsf{else}\ \mathsf{false}$. Finally, free variables, capture-avoiding substitution, and typing contexts (Γ) are defined in the usual way. The probability context Υ is used to additionally keep track of the distributions that random variables are bound to. When we use Υ in places Γ is expected, the understanding is that the extra information carried by Υ is ignored.

3.2 Examples of expressible distributions

With just random, return, and bind, we can already construct a wide variety of distributions we might care to use in practice. Though we do not have a formal proof of this expressivity, existing work on sampling suggests that this is the case. Non-uniform random variate generation is concerned with generating samples from arbitrary distributions using only samples from Uniform(0,1) [6]. We can see the connection with our language if we view the constructs by a sampling analogy, which emphasizes understanding a distribution by its generating process: the phrase var $x \sim e_1$ in e_2 samples a value x from the sampling function e_1, which is used to create a new sampling function e_2; random samples from the Uniform(0,1) distribution; return ε always returns ε as its sample. For instance, the *standard normal distribution* can be defined in our language using the Box-Muller sampling method:

$$\text{std\_normal} := \begin{array}{l}\text{var } u \sim \text{random in var } v \sim \text{random in} \\ \quad \text{return } (\text{sqrt}(-2 * \log u) * \cos(2 * \pi * v))\end{array}$$

where sqrt ε := exp $((1/2) * \log \varepsilon)$. In particular, our language is amenable to *inverse transform sampling*. Likewise, we can express other common continuous distributions:

```
uniform ε1 ε2 :=                     std_logistic :=
  var u ~ random in                    var u ~ random in
   return ((ε2 − ε1) * u + ε1)          return (log (1/u − 1))

normal ε1 ε2 :=                      std_exponential :=
  var x ~ std_normal in                var u ~ random in
   return (ε2 * x + ε1)                 return (−log u)
```

These are the Uniform(a,b), standard logistic, standard exponential, and Normal(μ, σ) distributions. We intentionally parameterize the normal distribution by its standard deviation instead of its variance, for simplicity. We define it as a transformation of a standard normal random variable and require $\varepsilon_2 > 0$. We can also express discrete distributions, such as the coin flip distribution,

$$\text{flip } \varepsilon := \text{var } u \sim \text{random in return } (u < \varepsilon),$$

which takes the value true with probability ε. This is equivalent to the Bernoulli distribution. In fact, we can express any distribution with finitely many outcomes:

```
var u ~ random in
   return (if u < 1/3 then 10 else if u < 2/3 then 20 else 30)
```

Admittedly, a more satisfying definition would be possible if we had lists in the language. The reason we do not is that, although others have addressed recursion and iteration in the context of defining probability distributions [14], we have not yet fully reconciled recursion with PDFs. The absence of recursion also means that we do not support distributions in the style of *rejection sampling* methods, which resample values until a stopping criterion is met. Furthermore, we do not elegantly support *infinite* discrete distributions in the core language, many of which are naturally described using recursion. However, in Section 5 we describe how to add special support for any distribution with a known PDF.

We also define some higher-order concepts. The following functions are used to create joint distributions and mixture models:

```
join e1 e2 :=                  mix ε e1 e2 :=
  var x1 ~ e1 in                 var z ~ flip ε in
   var x2 ~ e2 in                 var x1 ~ e1 in
    return (x1, x2)                var x2 ~ e2 in
                                    return (if z then x1 else x2).
```

The mixture model is created by flipping a coin with the specified probability to determine which component distribution to sample from. For instance, a simple mixture-of-Gaussians is given by mix $(1/2)$ std_normal std_normal. We have defined discrete and continuous distributions, and now we can use join to define nontrivial hybrid distributions as well, such as join (flip $(1/2)$) random, which has type dist (bool $\times$ R). Essentially, if-expressions enable mixture models and tuples enable joint models. These two concepts are special cases of *hierarchical models*, which are models that are defined in stages. Distributions defined using nested instances of bind correspond to hierarchical models.

These examples are all AC, but we can also express non-AC distributions, such as the example from Section 2, written jumpy := mix $(1/2)$ (return 0) std_normal. In our language, jumpy will successfully type check as a distribution, but the program pdf jumpy will be rejected—as it should be—because jumpy is not absolutely continuous. The ability to represent non-AC distributions, even though they cannot be used in programs, is in anticipation of future language features such as expectation and sampling, which *can* be used with non-AC distributions.

3.3 Measure theory preliminaries

Measure theory is the basis of modern probability theory and unifies the concepts of discrete and continuous probability distributions. It is a precise way of defining the notion of volume. We develop our formalization within this framework. We give only a brief overview of the necessary concepts; details are available in [17].

Basics Let A be a set we wish to measure. A *σ-algebra* $\mathcal{M}$ on A is a subset of the powerset $\mathcal{P}(A)$ that contains A and is closed under complement and countable union. The pair $(A, \mathcal{M})$ is a *measurable space*. A subset X of A is *$\mathcal{M}$-measurable* if $X \in \mathcal{M}$. In the context of probability, A is the set of outcomes and $\mathcal{M}$ is the set of events. For a function $f : A \to B$, the *f-image* of a subset X of A, written $f[X]$, denotes the set $\{f(x) \mid x \in A\}$, and the *f-preimage* of a subset Y of B, written $f^{-1}[Y]$, denotes the set $\{x \in A \mid f(x) \in Y\}$. When f is on measurable spaces, we say f is *$(\mathcal{M}_A, \mathcal{M}_B)$-measurable* when the f-preimage of any $\mathcal{M}_B$-measurable set is $\mathcal{M}_A$-measurable. Measurable functions are closed under composition. We drop the prefix and say *measurable* (for functions or sets) when it is clear what the σ-algebras are. The σ-algebra machinery is needed to ensure a consistent theory; there are spaces which contain pathological sets that violate intuition about volume, *e.g.* the Banach-Tarski "doubling ball" paradox. Measure theory sidesteps these issues by preferring measurable sets and functions as much as possible. When A is countable, no such problems arise, and we can always take $\mathcal{P}(A)$ for $\mathcal{M}$.

Measures A nonnegative function $\mu : \mathcal{M} \to \mathbb{R}^+ \cup \{\infty\}$ is a *measure* if $\mu(\emptyset) = 0$, $\mu(X) \geq 0$ for all X in $\mathcal{M}$, and $\mu(\bigcup_{i=1}^{\infty} X_i) = \sum_{i=1}^{\infty} \mu(X_i)$ for all sequences of mutually disjoint X_i (*countable additivity*). The triple $(A, \mathcal{M}, \mu)$ is a *measure space*. If additionally $\mu(A) = 1$ then μ is a *probability measure* (conventionally written $\mathbb{P}$), and the triple is a *probability space*. We use the terms *probability measure*, *probability distribution* and *distribution* interchangeably. We use $\mathfrak{C}$ to denote the counting measure, which uses the number of elements of a set as the set's measure. We use $\mathfrak{L}$ to denote the Lebesgue measure on $\mathbb{R}$, which assigns the length $|b - a|$ to an open interval (a, b); the sizes of other sets can be understood by complements and countable unions of intervals. The *product measure* $\mu_A \otimes \mu_B$ of two measures μ_A and μ_B on measurable spaces $(A, \mathcal{M}_A)$ and $(B, \mathcal{M}_B)$ is the measure μ, on $A \times B$ and the product σ-algebra $\mathcal{M}_A \otimes \mathcal{M}_B$, such that

$$\mu(X \times Y) = \mu_A(X) \cdot \mu_B(Y)$$

for $X \in \mathcal{M}_A$ and $Y \in \mathcal{M}_B$. The measure is unique when μ_A and μ_B are σ-finite. The σ-finiteness condition is a technical condition that is satisfied by all measures we will consider in this paper and requires that the space can be covered by a countable number of pieces of finite measure.

Null sets A measurable set X is *μ-null* if $\mu(X) = 0$; X is said to have μ-measure zero. The empty set is always null, the only $\mathfrak{C}$-null set is the empty set, and all countable subsets of $\mathbb{R}$ are $\mathfrak{L}$-null. A propositional function holds *μ-almost everywhere (μ-a.e.)* if the set of elements for which the proposition does not hold is μ-null. For instance, two functions of type $\mathbb{R} \to \mathbb{R}$ are equal $\mathfrak{L}$-almost everywhere if they differ at only a countable number of points. A measure space $(A, \mathcal{M}, \mu)$ is *complete* if all subsets of any μ-null set are $\mathcal{M}$-measurable. *Completion* is an operation that takes any measure space $(A, \mathcal{M}, \mu)$ and produces an "equivalent" complete measure space $(A, \mathcal{M}', \mu')$ such that $\mu'(X) = \mu(X)$ for $X \in \mathcal{M}$. Null sets are ubiquitous in measure theory, so it will be handy to work in spaces that support null sets as much as possible. Thus, completion makes measure spaces nicer to work with. The n-dimensional Lebesgue measure $\mathfrak{L}^n$ is the n-fold completed product of $\mathfrak{L}$. For measures μ and ν on a measurable space, ν is *absolutely continuous* with respect to μ if each μ-null set is also ν-null.

Integration A fundamental operation involving measures is the *abstract integral*, a generalization of the Riemann integral that avoids some of its deficiencies. The abstract integral of a measurable function $f : A \to \mathbb{R}$ w.r.t. a measure μ on A is written $\int f \, d\mu$. The integral is always defined for nonnegative f. The integral for arbitrary f is defined in terms of the positive and negative parts of f and may not exist; if it *does* we say f is μ-integrable. We write $\int_X f \, d\mu$ as shorthand for $\int \lambda x \,.\, \mathbf{1}_X(x) \cdot f(x) \, d\mu$, which restricts the integral to the subset X. We write $\mathbf{1}_X$ for the indicator function on X. *Expectation* refers to abstract integration w.r.t. a distribution. The abstract integral satisfies $\mu(X) = \int \mathbf{1}_X \, d\mu$ for all measurable X. In terms of probability, it says that the probability of X is the expectation of $\mathbf{1}_X$. Another consequence is that null sets cannot affect integration: two functions that are equal μ-a.e. give the same results under integration w.r.t. μ. Abstract integration w.r.t. $\mathfrak{C}$ and $\mathfrak{L}$ is ordinary (possibly infinite) summation and the ordinary Lebesgue integral, respectively. The Lebesgue integral agrees with the Riemann integral on Riemann-integrable functions.

Measurability Ordinarily, to conclude that a distribution such as $\mathsf{var}\ x \sim e\ \mathsf{in}\ \mathsf{return}\ (f\ x)$ is well-formed, we are obligated to verify that f is a measurable function. However, non-measurable sets and functions are actually quite pathological and constructing them requires the Axiom of Choice [25]. None of the constructs in our language are as powerful as the Axiom of Choice (though we do not have a formal proof of this), thus all constructible expressions represent measurable functions. This discharges the obligation, and we do not make any further mention of checking for measurability.

Stocked spaces For most applications, we often have a standard idea of how spaces are measured. We now formalize this practice. A space A is a *stocked space* if it comes equipped with a complete measure space $(A, \overline{\mathcal{M}}_A, \overline{\mu}_A)$, which is the *stock measure space* of A. We call $\overline{\mathcal{M}}_A$ the *stock σ-algebra* of A and $\overline{\mu}_A$ the *stock measure* of A. The abstract integral w.r.t. $\overline{\mu}_A$ is the *stock integral* of A. We define stock measure spaces for the spaces $\mathbb{B} = \{\text{true}, \text{false}\}$, $\mathbb{Z}$, $\mathbb{R}$, and product spaces between stocked spaces as follows:

$$(\overline{\mathcal{M}}_{\mathbb{B}}, \overline{\mu}_{\mathbb{B}}) = (\mathcal{P}(\mathbb{B}), \mathfrak{C})$$
$$(\overline{\mathcal{M}}_{\mathbb{Z}}, \overline{\mu}_{\mathbb{Z}}) = (\mathcal{P}(\mathbb{Z}), \mathfrak{C})$$
$$(\overline{\mathcal{M}}_{\mathbb{R}}, \overline{\mu}_{\mathbb{R}}) = (\text{the } \mathfrak{L}\text{-measurable sets}, \mathfrak{L})$$
$$(\overline{\mathcal{M}}_{A \times B}, \overline{\mu}_{A \times B}) = \text{completion}(\overline{\mathcal{M}}_A \otimes \overline{\mathcal{M}}_B, \overline{\mu}_A \otimes \overline{\mu}_B).$$

This definition matches what is used in practice: *e.g.* $\mathfrak{C}$ becomes the measure for countable spaces, and $\mathfrak{L}^n$ becomes the measure for $\mathbb{R}^n$. For the rest of the paper, we assume spaces are stocked, unless explicitly noted otherwise. We say that a distribution on A is AC if it is AC with respect to $\overline{\mu}_A$.

$$\frac{}{\Gamma \vdash \mathsf{random} : \mathsf{dist}\ \mathsf{R}}\ \text{T-RAND} \qquad \frac{\Gamma \vdash \varepsilon : \tau}{\Gamma \vdash \mathsf{return}\ \varepsilon : \mathsf{dist}\ \tau}\ \text{T-RET}$$

$$\frac{\Gamma \vdash e_1 : \mathsf{dist}\ \tau_1 \qquad \Gamma, x : \tau_1 \vdash e_2 : \mathsf{dist}\ \tau_2}{\Gamma \vdash \mathsf{var}\ x \sim e_1\ \mathsf{in}\ e_2 : \mathsf{dist}\ \tau_2}\ \text{T-BIND}$$

Figure 3. Standard monadic typing rules for distributions.

Densities A function f is a PDF of a distribution $\mathbb{P}$ on A if $\mathbb{P}(X) = \int_X f \, d\overline{\mu}_A$ for all measurable X. Expectation can be written using the PDF:

$$\int g \, d\mathbb{P} = \int \lambda x \,.\, g(x) \cdot f(x) \, d\overline{\mu}_A.$$

A *joint* PDF is the PDF of a *joint distribution*, which is simply a distribution on a product space. We later use the fact that the joint PDF f of a model such as $x_1 \sim \mathbb{P}_1, x_2 \sim \mathbb{P}_2(\cdot\,; x_1)$ can be written as the product of the individual (parameterized) PDFs: $f(x_1, x_2) = f_1(x_1) \cdot f_2(x_2; x_1)$.

3.4 Type system and semantics for distributions

We now discuss the type system and semantics for syntactic categories besides programs. The type system for expressions is ordinary. We assume an external mechanism for enforcing the preconditions necessary to ensure totality of functions, such as an automated theorem prover or the programmer themself. For instance, log must be applied to only positive real numbers. Distributions obey standard monadic typing rules (Figure 3). The "random variables" introduced by bind are really just normal variables and are typed as such; calling them random variables is a reminder about the role they play. The typing rules ensure that random variables are never used outside a probabilistic context.

We give our language a semantics based in classical mathematics with total functions. Base types have the usual meaning. The denotation of $\mathsf{dist}\ \tau$ is the set of distributions possible on τ:

$$\mathcal{T}[\![\mathsf{dist}\ \tau]\!] = \{\mathbb{P} \mid (\mathcal{T}[\![\tau]\!], \overline{\mathcal{M}}_\tau, \mathbb{P}) \text{ is a probability space}\}.$$

We overload stock measure space notation for types; thus, $\overline{\mathcal{M}}_\tau$ and $\overline{\mu}_\tau$ are shorthand for $\overline{\mathcal{M}}_{\mathcal{T}[\![\tau]\!]}$ and $\overline{\mu}_{\mathcal{T}[\![\tau]\!]}$. Let $\mathcal{E}[\![e]\!]\rho$ be the denotation of a distribution e under the environment ρ, also overloaded for expressions ε. Expressions have the semantics of their corresponding forms from classical mathematics. As stated before, random is the Uniform(0,1) distribution

$$\mathcal{E}[\![\mathsf{random}]\!]\rho = \lambda X \,.\, \mathfrak{L}(X \cap [0,1]),$$

which says that the probability of an event X is its "interval size" on [0,1]. Return is the point mass distribution

$$\mathcal{E}[\![\mathsf{return}\ \varepsilon]\!]\rho = \lambda X \,.\, \mathbf{1}_X(\mathcal{E}[\![\varepsilon]\!]\rho),$$

which gives an event X probability 1 as long as it includes the outcome ε. Bind expresses the Law of Total Probability,

$$\mathcal{E}[\![\mathsf{var}\ x \sim e_1\ \mathsf{in}\ e_2]\!]\rho = \lambda Y \,.\, \int \lambda x' \,.\, f(x')(Y) \, d\mathbb{P},$$

where $f(x') = \mathcal{E}[\![e_2]\!](\rho\{x \mapsto x'\})$ and $\mathbb{P} = \mathcal{E}[\![e_1]\!]\rho$. The family of distributions e_2 is parameterized by the variable x, in essence. The probability of an event Y is the "average opinion" (the $\mathbb{P}$-expectation) of what each member of the family thinks is the probability of Y. The integral exists because it is the expectation of a bounded function.

4. Type system and semantics for programs

The program pdf e is well-formed if the distribution e permits a PDF. The following theorem gives us a sufficient condition.

Theorem 4.1 (Radon-Nikodym). *For any two σ-finite measures μ and ν on the same measurable space such that ν is absolutely continuous w.r.t. μ, there is a function f such that $\nu(X) = \int_X f \, d\mu$.*

We call f a *Radon-Nikodym derivative* of ν with respect to μ, denoted $d\nu/d\mu$; pdf corresponds to the Radon-Nikodym operator. The condition is also necessary: given a satisfying f, ν is (trivially) AC. All stock measures we define and all distributions are σ-finite, so for our purposes absolute continuity is equivalent to possessing a PDF. Though not necessarily unique, Radon-Nikodym derivatives are equal μ-almost everywhere. When μ is the counting measure, the Radon-Nikodym derivative is a PMF. For hybrid spaces, it is a function which must be summed along one dimension and integrated along the other to obtain quantities interpretable as probabilities. Radon-Nikodym derivatives unify PMFs, PDFs and hybrids of the two. For this reason, we refer to all of these as PDFs. We use "PMF" when we want to emphasize its discrete nature.

Defining a type system for absolute continuity in terms of the straightforward induction on distribution terms proves unwieldy. Suppose we want to check if the distribution in Equation 2 is AC; we must verify that the probability of any $\mathfrak{L}^2$-null set Z is zero. A straightforward induction leads us to trying to show

$$\mathbb{P}(\{x \mid \left(\begin{array}{c} \mathsf{var}\ y \sim \mathsf{random\ in} \\ \mathsf{return}\ (x, y) \end{array} \right) (Z) \neq 0\}) = 0$$

where $\mathbb{P}$ is the Uniform(0,1) distribution, and we have abused notation slightly by mingling object language syntax with ordinary mathematics. This states that the body of the outermost bind assigns Z probability zero, $\mathbb{P}$-almost always. It is unclear how to proceed from here or how to remove concepts like null sets from the mechanization. We take an alternate approach based on the insight that we can reason about a distribution by examining how it transforms other distributions. Our approach, and outline of the following subsections, is as follows:

- We introduce the new notion of a *non-nullifying* function and prove a transformation theorem stating that when a random variable is transformed, the output distribution is AC if the input distribution is AC and the transformation is non-nullifying. We also prove some results about non-nullifying functions.
- We define the *random variables transform* of any distribution written in our language and show that for a large class of distributions the transformation theorem is applicable.
- We present a type system which defines absolute continuity of a distribution in terms of whether its RV transform is non-nullifying. As implementors, we have found it easier to come up with the rules for non-nullifying functions.

Measure-theoretic concepts like σ-algebras, null sets, and the Lebesgue measure, while present in the metatheory, do not need to be operationalized for implementing the type checker. Also, due to the measure-theoretic foundation, we correctly handle cases that are not typically explained, such as PDFs on hybrid spaces. We conclude the section with the semantics of programs.

4.1 Absolute continuity and non-nullifying functions

A function $h : A \to B$ is *non-nullifying* if the h-preimage of each $\overline{\mu}_B$-null set is $\overline{\mu}_A$-null; preimages of null sets are always null, and forward images of non-null sets are always non-null. A function that fails to be non-nullifying is called *nullifying*. The next theorem establishes the link between absolute continuity and non-nullity.

Theorem 4.2 (Transformation). *For a function $h : A \to B$ and an* AC *distribution $\mathbb{P}$ on A, the distribution*

$$\mathbb{Q}(Y) = \mathbb{P}(h^{-1}[Y]) \tag{3}$$

on B is AC *if h is non-nullifying.*

Proof. Let Y be a $\overline{\mu}_B$-null set. By the non-nullity of h, the set $h^{-1}[Y]$ is $\overline{\mu}_A$-null. By the absolute continuity of $\mathbb{P}$, we have $\mathbb{P}(h^{-1}[Y]) = 0$, implying that Y is also $\mathbb{Q}$-null. □

This style of defining $\mathbb{Q}$ may seem odd, but it actually underlies the use of random variables as a modeling language. For instance, the model $x \sim \mathbb{P}$, $y = h(x)$ exhibits the relationship $\mathbb{Q}(Y) = \mathbb{P}(h^{-1}[Y])$, where $\mathbb{Q}$ is the distribution of y. In general, the reverse direction does not hold; h can be nullifying even if $\mathbb{Q}$ is AC. This happens when h has nullifying behavior only in regions of the space where $\mathbb{P}$ is assigning zero probability. This will be a source of incompleteness in the type system.

Lemma 4.3 (Discrete domain). *A function $h : A \to \mathbb{R}$ is nullifying if A is non-empty and countable.*

Proof. Let x be an element of A. The set $\{x\}$ has positive counting measure while its h-image, which is a singleton set, is $\mathfrak{L}$-null. □

This implies R_of_Z is nullifying, meaning that when we view an integer random variable as a real random variable, it loses its ability to have a PDF. This is desirable behavior; different spaces have different ideas of what it means to be a PDF. We would not want to mark an integer random variable as AC and later attempt to integrate its PMF in a context expecting a real random variable.

Lemma 4.4 (Discrete codomain). *A function $h : A \to B$ is non-nullifying if B is countable.*

Proof. The h-preimage of the empty set (the only $\mathfrak{C}$-null set) is the empty set, which is always null. □

This reasoning corroborates the fact that distributions on countable spaces always have a PMF.

Lemma 4.5 (Interval). *A function $h : \mathbb{R} \to \mathbb{R}$ is nullifying if it is constant on any interval.*

Proof. Let h be constant on (a, b); (a, b) is not $\mathfrak{L}$-null, but its h-image (a singleton set) is $\mathfrak{L}$-null. □

One way to visualize how this leads to a non-AC distribution is to observe that the transformation h takes all the probability mass along (a, b) and non-smoothly concentrates it onto a single point in the target space.

Lemma 4.6 (Inverse). *An invertible function $h : \mathbb{R} \to \mathbb{R}$ is non-nullifying if its inverse h^{-1} is an* absolutely continuous function.

Proof. We have discussed absolute continuity of measures; the absolute continuity of functions is a related idea. It is a stronger notion than continuity and uniform continuity. Absolutely continuous functions are well behaved in many ways; in particular, the images of null sets are also null sets. Coupled with the fact that an h-preimage is an h^{-1}-image, this proves the claim. More details on absolutely continuous functions can be found in [17]. □

This result shows that log, exp, and non-constant linear functions are non-nullifying. We believe the idea can be extended without much difficulty to show that functions with a countable number of invertible pieces, such as the trigonometric functions and non-constant polynomials, are also non-nullifying.

Lemma 4.7 (Piecewise)**.** *For functions $c : A \to \mathbb{B}$ and $f, g, h : A \to B$, where $h(x) =$ if $c(x)$ then $f(x)$ else $g(x)$, h is non-nullifying if f and g are non-nullifying.*

Proof. Let Y be a $\overline{\mu}_B$-null set. The set $h^{-1}[Y]$ is a subset of $f^{-1}[Y] \cup g^{-1}[Y]$ and is thus $\overline{\mu}_A$-null, by non-nullity of f and g, and the countable additivity and completeness of $\overline{\mu}_A$. □

Lemma 4.8 (Composition)**.** *The set of non-nullifying functions is closed under function composition.*

Proof. Let $f : A \to B$ and $g : B \to C$ be non-nullifying functions and let $h = g \circ f$. The h-preimage of a $\overline{\mu}_C$-null set Z is given by $h^{-1}[Z] = f^{-1}[g^{-1}[Z]]$, and is thus $\overline{\mu}_A$-null, by the non-nullity of f and g. □

Lemma 4.9 (Projection)**.** *The function $h(x, y) = x$ of type $A \times B \to A$ is non-nullifying.*

Proof. Let X be a $\overline{\mu}_A$-null set. Its h-preimage is $X \times B$. By the properties of product measure, we have that

$$\overline{\mu}_{A\times B}(X \times B) = \overline{\mu}_A(X) \cdot \overline{\mu}_B(B) = 0 \cdot \overline{\mu}_B(B) = 0.$$

Even if $\overline{\mu}_B(B) = \infty$, the measure-theoretic definition of multiplication on extended nonnegative reals defines $0 \cdot \infty = 0$. □

Along these lines, we can show that returning a permutation of a subset of tuple components is also a non-nullifying function. The last two results permit us to ignore uninvolved arguments when reasoning about the non-nullity of the body of a function.

4.2 Distributions and RV transforms

A large class of distributions in our language can be understood by Equation 3. From the syntax we know that a distribution e must take the form of zero or more nested binds terminating in a body that is either random or $\mathsf{return}\ \varepsilon$. We focus on the latter, non-trivial case. The expression ε represents a transformation of the random variables x_i introduced by the binds. The function $\lambda(x_1, ..., x_n).\ \varepsilon$ is the *random variables transform (RV transform)* of the distribution e, where we use tuple pattern matching shorthand to name the components of a tuple argument. The correspondence between distributions in our language and Theorem 4.2 is as follows: let $\mathbb{Q}$ be the denotation of e, let h be the RV transform of e, and let $\mathbb{P}$ be the joint distribution of the random variables introduced on the spine of e. The class of distributions for which the theorem is applicable is given by the set of distributions for which each e_i is *parametrically* AC w.r.t. the random variables preceding it, where e_i is the distribution corresponding to x_i. In other words, the distribution for e_i must be AC while treating free occurrences of $x_1, ..., x_{i-1}$ as fixed, unknown constants. This ensures that the joint distribution is also AC; the joint PDF can be written as the product of the individual parameterized PDFs. This is a commonly used (implicit) assumption in practice. For example, the distribution

$$\mathsf{var}\ u \sim \mathsf{random}\ \mathsf{in}\ \mathsf{var}\ z \sim \mathsf{flip}\ u\ \mathsf{in}\ \mathsf{return}\ (u + \langle z \rangle)$$

has the RV transform $\lambda(u, z).\ u + \langle z \rangle$, which has type $\mathbb{R} \times \mathbb{B} \to \mathbb{R}$ and is transforming the joint distribution of random and $e_2 := \mathsf{flip}\ u$. The variable u appears free in e_2, making e_2 parametric in u; the restriction requires that e_2 is AC for all possible values of u, which is the case here. Two extensionally equivalent distributions may have different RV transforms and spines because of intensionally different representations. To show that this choice of $\mathbb{P}$, $\mathbb{Q}$, and h satisfies Equation 3, we appeal to the semantics of distributions (defined in Section 3.4). Consider the general case $e := \overline{\mathsf{var}\ x_i \sim e_i\ \mathsf{in}}\ \mathsf{return}\ \varepsilon$, where we have used the bar as shorthand for nested binds. The denotation $\mathbb{Q}$ of e under an environment ρ is given by

$$\mathbb{Q}(Y) = \overline{\int d\mathbb{P}_i\ \lambda x'_i.}\ \mathbf{1}_Y(\mathcal{E}[\![\varepsilon]\!]\rho\overline{\{x_i \mapsto x'_i\}})$$

where $\mathbb{P}_i$ is the denotation of e_i (extending ρ as necessary) and we have again used the bar notation, to denote iterated expectation and the repeated extension of the environment ρ with variable mappings. We can now rewrite the expectations to use their corresponding PDFs f_i and then replace the iterated integrals with a single product integral using their joint PDF f:

$$\begin{aligned}
\mathbb{Q}(Y) &= \overline{\int d\overline{\mu}_{\tau_i}\ \lambda x'_i.\ f_i(x'_i; x'_1, ..., x'_{i-1})} \cdot \mathbf{1}_Y(\mathcal{E}[\![\varepsilon]\!]\rho\overline{\{x_i \mapsto x'_i\}}) \\
&= \int d\overline{\mu}_\tau\ \lambda \mathbf{x}.\ f(\mathbf{x}) \cdot \mathbf{1}_Y(h(\mathbf{x})) \\
&= \int d\mathbb{P}\ \lambda \mathbf{x}.\ \mathbf{1}_Y(h(\mathbf{x})) \\
&= \mathbb{P}(\{\mathbf{x} \mid h(\mathbf{x}) \in Y\}) \ = \ \mathbb{P}(h^{-1}[Y])
\end{aligned}$$

where $\mathbf{x} = (x'_1, ..., x'_n)$, $h(\mathbf{x}) = \mathcal{E}[\![\varepsilon]\!]\rho\overline{\{x_i \mapsto \mathbf{x}_i\}}$, τ_i is the type of each x_i, and τ is their product. We have also used the fact that the expectation of the indicator function on a set is the probability of that set (the set here is $\{\mathbf{x} \mid h(\mathbf{x}) \in Y\}$, not Y). Replacing an iterated integral with a product integral is not always legal but is possible here because the integral is of a nonnegative function w.r.t. independent measures (see Tonelli's theorem, [17]).

$$\frac{}{\Upsilon; \Lambda \vdash \mathsf{random}\ \text{AC}}\ \text{AC-RAND} \qquad \frac{\Upsilon; \Lambda \vdash \varepsilon\ \text{NN}}{\Upsilon; \Lambda \vdash \mathsf{return}\ \varepsilon\ \text{AC}}\ \text{AC-RET}$$

$$\frac{\Upsilon; \emptyset \vdash e_1\ \text{AC} \qquad \Upsilon \vdash e_1 : \mathsf{dist}\ \tau \qquad \Upsilon, x : \tau \sim e_1; \Lambda, x \vdash e_2\ \text{AC}}{\Upsilon; \Lambda \vdash \mathsf{var}\ x \sim e_1\ \mathsf{in}\ e_2\ \text{AC}}\ \text{AC-BIND}$$

Figure 4. The absolute continuity judgment, $\Upsilon; \Lambda \vdash e$ AC.

4.3 Type system for programs

All judgments are defined modulo α-conversion. A program $\mathsf{pdf}\ e$ is well-formed if e is an AC distribution ($\emptyset \vdash e : \mathsf{dist}\ \tau$ holds for some τ and $\emptyset; \emptyset \vdash e$ AC holds). If the judgment $\Upsilon; \Lambda \vdash e$ AC (Figure 4) holds then e is an AC distribution under the probability context Υ and the active variable context Λ, where Λ is given by the grammar $\Lambda ::= \emptyset \mid \Lambda, x$. Variables in Λ are currently active and should be understood in a probabilistic sense, while those not in Λ are inactive and should be treated as fixed parameters. The contexts obey the following invariant: Λ is always the "prefix" of Υ, *i.e.* the variables in Λ correspond directly to the n most recent entries added to Υ, where n is the length of Λ. Rule AC-RAND asserts that the Uniform(0,1) distribution is AC. The main action of rules AC-BIND and AC-RETURN is to prepare a call to the non-nullity judgment. For Theorem 4.2 to be applicable, a distribution along the spine must be parametrically AC w.r.t. the random variables preceding it; thus, in AC-BIND we check that e_1 is AC without marking any current random variables as active. We reach the body of the RV transform in AC-RETURN. Roughly speaking, Λ (pointing into Υ) and ε correspond to $\mathbb{P}$ and h in Theorem 4.2.

Next is the non-nullity judgment (Figure 5). If $\Upsilon; \Lambda \vdash \varepsilon$ NN holds, then ε represents the body of a non-nullifying function under Υ and Λ. The variables in Λ are the arguments to the RV transform. Throughout this discussion, we implicitly use the composition and projection lemmas (Lemmas 4.8 and 4.9) to ignore uninvolved arguments during analysis. For example, in rule NN-VAR, we could

$$\frac{x \in \Lambda}{\Upsilon; \Lambda \vdash x \text{ NN}}\ \text{NN-VAR} \qquad \frac{\Upsilon \vdash \varepsilon : \tau \qquad \tau \text{ countable}}{\Upsilon; \Lambda \vdash \varepsilon \text{ NN}}\ \text{NN-COUNT}$$

$$\frac{\Upsilon; \Lambda \vdash \varepsilon \text{ NN} \qquad op \in \{\mathsf{neg}, \mathsf{inv}, \mathsf{log}, \mathsf{exp}, \mathsf{sin}, \mathsf{cos}, \mathsf{tan}\}}{\Upsilon; \Lambda \vdash op\ \varepsilon \text{ NN}}\ \text{NN-OP}$$

$$\frac{\Upsilon; \Lambda \vdash \varepsilon_1 \text{ NN} \qquad \Upsilon; \Lambda \vdash \varepsilon_2 \text{ NN}}{\Upsilon; \Lambda \vdash \mathsf{if}\ \varepsilon\ \mathsf{then}\ \varepsilon_1\ \mathsf{else}\ \varepsilon_2 \text{ NN}}\ \text{NN-IF}$$

$$\frac{\Upsilon; \Lambda \vdash \varepsilon \text{ NN} \qquad op \in \{\mathsf{fst}, \mathsf{snd}\}}{\Upsilon; \Lambda \vdash op\ \varepsilon \text{ NN}}\ \text{NN-PROJ}$$

$$\frac{\Upsilon; \Lambda \vdash \varepsilon_1 \perp \varepsilon_2 \qquad \Upsilon; \Lambda \vdash \varepsilon_1 \text{ NN} \qquad \Upsilon; \Lambda \vdash \varepsilon_2 \text{ NN}}{\Upsilon; \Lambda \vdash (\varepsilon_1, \varepsilon_2) \text{ NN}}\ \text{NN-PAIR}$$

$$\frac{x_i \in \Lambda \qquad x_1, ..., x_n \text{ are distinct}}{\Upsilon; \Lambda \vdash (x_1, ..., x_n) \text{ NN}}\ \text{NN-VARS}$$

$$\frac{\Upsilon; \Lambda \vdash (\varepsilon_1, \varepsilon_2) \text{ NN}}{\Upsilon; \Lambda \vdash \varepsilon_1 + \varepsilon_2 \text{ NN}}\ \text{NN-PLUS}$$

$$\frac{FV(\varepsilon_2) \cap \Lambda = \emptyset \qquad \Upsilon; \Lambda \vdash \varepsilon_1 \text{ NN}}{\Upsilon; \Lambda \vdash \varepsilon_1 + \varepsilon_2 \text{ NN}}\ \text{NN-LINEAR}$$

$$\frac{\Upsilon; \Lambda \vdash (\varepsilon_1, \varepsilon_2) \text{ NN}}{\Upsilon; \Lambda \vdash \varepsilon_1 * \varepsilon_2 \text{ NN}}\ \text{NN-MULT} \qquad \frac{l \neq 0 \qquad \Upsilon; \Lambda \vdash \varepsilon \text{ NN}}{\Upsilon; \Lambda \vdash l * \varepsilon \text{ NN}}\ \text{NN-SCALE}$$

Figure 5. The non-nullity judgment, $\Upsilon; \Lambda \vdash \varepsilon$ NN.

be analyzing a function with multiple inputs, but we can drop all of them but x, leaving us to analyze the function $\lambda x \,.\, x$, which is trivially non-nullifying. Under the hood, what we are actually doing is representing the original transform as the composition of a function that selects a single components of a tuple with the identity function $\lambda x \,.\, x$. The composition lemma is also the justification for being able to recurse into subexpressions. Rule NN-COUNT is merely an application of Lemma 4.4; the types bool, Z and products thereof define the countable types. Note that this covers the cases of $=$, $<$, integer neg, $+$ and $*$, and Boolean and integer literals. Rules NN-OP, NN-IF and NN-PROJ are direct translations of Lemmas 4.6, 4.7 and 4.9. The injection from integers into the reals is nullifying (Lemma 4.3), so there is no rule for R_of_Z. Rule NN-PAIR expresses the idea that the joint distribution of independent AC distributions is AC. If $\Upsilon; \Lambda \vdash \varepsilon_1 \perp \varepsilon_2$ holds then ε_1 and ε_2 represent independent distributions under Υ and Λ. Its definition is

$$\frac{\Lambda \cap \text{Anc}(\Upsilon, FV(\varepsilon_1)) \cap \text{Anc}(\Upsilon, FV(\varepsilon_2)) = \emptyset}{\Upsilon; \Lambda \vdash \varepsilon_1 \perp \varepsilon_2}\ \text{INDEP}$$

where $\text{Anc}(\Upsilon, X) = \bigcup_{x \in X} \text{anc}(\Upsilon, x)$. It states that ε_1 and ε_2 must not have any ancestors in common. The function $\text{anc}(\Upsilon, x)$ computes the ancestors of a random variable x. A random variable y is the parent of a random variable x if y appears free in the distribution that x is bound to. Rule NN-VARS corresponds to the corollary of Lemma 4.9 that states that you can drop and permute tuple components. The requirement that the variables are distinct is important; the distribution $\mathsf{var}\ u \sim \mathsf{random}\ \mathsf{in}\ \mathsf{return}\ (u, u)$ is not AC, as we saw in Section 2. We have multiple rules for addition because they each capture a different usage of plus. Rule NN-PLUS states that if the formation of the pair $(\varepsilon_1, \varepsilon_2)$ is non-nullifying, then $\varepsilon_1 + \varepsilon_2$ is also non-nullifying because it is the composition of tuple formation with $(+) : \mathbb{R} \times \mathbb{R} \to \mathbb{R}$, where the latter is non-nullifying by corollary to Lemma 4.6. Rule NN-LINEAR represents the idea of composing with the non-nullifying function $\lambda x \,.\, x + c$, where c is a constant w.r.t. the arguments of the RV transform. There is an analogous rule for when the constant appears as the left operand. Rules NN-MULT and NN-SCALE are analogous. Note that NN-SCALE is slightly weaker than its counterpart NN-LINEAR, only because it needs to prove that the scaling coefficient is nonzero.

Discussion We believe our type system is sound; the only remaining case to rigorously prove is NN-PAIR. The soundness of the reduction to non-nullity is given by Theorem 4.2, and the soundness of the other cases in the non-nullity judgment are covered by the lemmas in Section 4.1. Stating the needed lemma for NN-PAIR essentially requires formalizing the idea that the conditional distribution of the second component conditioned on the first component should be AC. In non-nullity terms, the second component should still have a degree of freedom even after fixing the first. Rigorously stating this involves conditional probability, putting it outside the scope of the current work.

There are few sources of incompleteness in our type system. For instance, NN-PAIR conservatively requires ε_1 and ε_2 to be independent. The distribution

$$\mathsf{var}\ x \sim \mathsf{random}\ \mathsf{in}\ \mathsf{var}\ y \sim \mathsf{random}\ \mathsf{in}\ \mathsf{return}\ (\mathsf{exp}\ x, x + y)$$

is AC despite the fact that the tuple components are not independent: even if we know the value of $\mathsf{exp}\ x$, the "residual" stochasticity in the quantity $x + y$ is still AC. The joint PDF is given by multiplying the marginal PDF of the first component by the conditional PDF of the second component conditioned on the first. This is a similar issue as the parametric AC requirement on spine distributions. Formulating this generalization of NN-PAIR is interesting future work. Likewise, NN-IF conservatively requires both branches of an if-expression to be non-nullifying. The distribution

$$\mathsf{var}\ x \sim \mathsf{std\_normal}\ \mathsf{in}\ \mathsf{return}(\mathsf{if}\ x < 0\ \mathsf{then}\ \mathsf{min}\ x\ 0\ \mathsf{else}\ \mathsf{max}\ x\ 0)$$

is not accepted as AC because both branches ($\lambda x \,.\, \mathsf{min}\ x\ 0$ and $\lambda x \,.\, \mathsf{max}\ x\ 0$) are nullifying, even though the distribution is extensionally equivalent to $\mathsf{var}\ x \sim \mathsf{std\_normal}\ \mathsf{in}\ \mathsf{return}\ x$, which is AC. We define min and max in the usual way, using if. Finally, non-nullity is sufficient but not necessary for absolute continuity to hold. For instance, the RV transform of

$$\mathsf{var}\ x \sim \mathsf{random}\ \mathsf{in}\ \mathsf{return}\ (\mathsf{if}\ x < 100\ \mathsf{then}\ x\ \mathsf{else}\ 100)$$

is $\lambda x \,.\, \mathsf{if}\ x < 100\ \mathsf{then}\ x\ \mathsf{else}\ 100$, which is nullifying due to the constant portion, thus our type system does not accept this distribution as AC. However, x only takes values on $(0, 1)$, so the second branch is never entered, and thus the distribution is extensionally equivalent to the AC distribution $\mathsf{var}\ x \sim \mathsf{random}\ \mathsf{in}\ \mathsf{return}\ x$.

4.4 Semantics of programs

The denotation of a program $\mathsf{pdf}\ e$ is that it is a member of the set of Radon-Nikodym derivatives of the distribution e:

$$[\![\mathsf{pdf}\ e]\!] \in \{f \mid \forall X, \mathbb{P}(X) = \int_X f\, d\overline{\mu}_\tau\}$$

where $\mathbb{P} = \mathcal{E}[\![e]\!]\{\}$ is the denotation of e under the empty environment and e has type $\mathsf{dist}\ \tau$. The procedure discussed in the next section calculates a member of this set.

5. Calculating density functions

The previous sections have defined a language in which it is possible to express PDFs. Our goal now is to mechanically obtain a usable form of the PDF for a given distribution. But what constitutes a usable form? We are motivated by applications of the PDF and the need to interface with existing software. For instance, we may want to use numerical optimization software to perform MLE, where the PDF appears in the objective function; we may also want to symbolically derive gradient information to improve the search. Or, we may want to use the PDF to calculate an expectation using a numerical integrator. Roughly speaking, we call a term "usable" if we can map it onto the capabilities of existing software in accordance with common practice. For example, the term $\lambda x \,.\, x + 5$ is

$$\text{Target types} \quad \sigma ::= \tau \mid \sigma_1 \to \sigma_2$$

$$\text{Target terms} \quad \delta ::= \varepsilon \mid \lambda x : \tau \,.\, \delta \mid \delta_1\, \delta_2 \mid \int \delta$$

$$\text{Typing} \quad \frac{\Gamma \vdash \delta : \tau \to \mathsf{R}}{\Gamma \vdash \int \delta : \mathsf{R}}\ \text{T-INT}$$

$$\text{Semantics} \quad \mathcal{E}[\![\int \delta]\!]\rho = \int \mathcal{E}[\![\delta]\!]\rho \; d\overline{\mu}_\tau$$

Figure 6. The target language.

$$\mathsf{random}\ \$\ \delta \mapsto \int \lambda x : \mathsf{R}\,.\, \langle 0 < x < 1 \rangle * \delta\, x$$

$$\mathsf{return}\ \varepsilon\ \$\ \delta \mapsto \delta\, \varepsilon$$

$$\frac{e_2\ \$\ \delta \mapsto \delta' \qquad e_1\ \$\ \lambda x \,.\, \delta' \mapsto \delta''}{\mathsf{var}\ x \sim e_1\ \mathsf{in}\ e_2\ \$\ \delta \mapsto \delta''}$$

Figure 7. The probability compiler, $e\ \$\ \delta \mapsto \delta'$.

$$\frac{}{\Upsilon; \Lambda \vdash \mathsf{random} \curvearrowright \lambda x : \mathsf{R}\,.\, \langle 0 < x < 1 \rangle}\ \text{P-RAND}$$

$$\frac{\Upsilon \vdash e_1 : \mathsf{dist}\ \tau \qquad \Upsilon, x : \tau \sim e_1; \Lambda, x \vdash e_2 \curvearrowright \delta}{\Upsilon; \Lambda \vdash \mathsf{var}\ x \sim e_1\ \mathsf{in}\ e_2 \curvearrowright \delta}\ \text{P-BIND}$$

$$\frac{\Upsilon; \Lambda \vdash \varepsilon \rightsquigarrow \delta}{\Upsilon; \Lambda \vdash \mathsf{return}\ \varepsilon \curvearrowright \delta}\ \text{P-RET}$$

Figure 8. The distribution-to-PDF converter, $\Upsilon; \Lambda \vdash e \curvearrowright \delta$.

usable; in practice, real addition is mapped to floating point addition. Likewise, $\int_0^5 x^2\, dx$ is usable; the integral is Riemannian and in a form accepted by computer algebra systems (CAS) and numerical integrators. On the other hand, terms like $\int g\ d\mathbb{P}$ and $d\mathbb{P}/d\mathfrak{L}$ make use of measure-theoretic operations such as abstract integration and the Radon-Nikodym derivative. Current software do not handle these operations (though, progress on mechanizing measure theory has been made [15]). Thus, the basic plan is to eliminate measure-theoretic concepts during PDF calculation. This means the constructs random, return, bind, and pdf should not appear in a PDF term because they involve measure theory, metatheoretically.

It will take some ingenuity to remove the Radon-Nikodym derivative (pdf). It has been shown that the Radon-Nikodym derivative is a non-computable operator: given a distribution, there is no general computable procedure for computing its PDF [11]. The discrete case at least enjoys the fact that the PMF has a straightforward definition in terms of its distribution; if $\mathbb{P}$ is an executable implementation of a discrete distribution, an executable implementation of its PMF $d\mathbb{P}/d\mathfrak{C}$ is given by $\lambda x \,.\, \mathbb{P}(\{x\})$. In general, however, we will need to tackle the calculation of PDFs with a collection of techniques. Our basic approach is as follows. First, we define a target language that defines what constitutes a usable form. Second, we provide a procedure that converts many distributions accepted as AC by our type system into PDFs expressed in the target language. Some RV transforms are mathematically inconvenient, so we will not be able to calculate certain PDFs from scratch; in particular, dependence between random variables makes the general case difficult. However, the design permits modularly adding knowledge about individual distributions with known PDFs, enabling the procedure to calculate PDFs for programs that use these distributions as subcomponents. This allows us to handle many useful cases.

5.1 The target language

The target language extends expressions with λ-abstraction, application, and the stock integral (Figure 6). We treat functions in a standard way. Notationally, we skip specifying τ in abstractions when the choice of τ is clear. Computing closed-form solutions for integrals is not always feasible or possible, so integrals cannot be completely eliminated from the target language. The integral is well-formed if its integrand is real-valued and summable (a function f is *μ-summable* if $\int f\ d\mu$ is finite). We require users of the target language (compiler writers) to manually ensure summability; this is reasonable for a back-end language. We have verified summability for each use of stock integration in the compilers presented in this section. Although a measure-theoretic concept, stock integration is close enough to the notion of integration used by numerical and symbolic solvers to be useful as a compilation target. Recall, stock integration over $\mathfrak{C}$ and $\mathfrak{L}$ is ordinary summation and Lebesgue integration, respectively. For most applications, Lebesgue integration will coincide with Riemann integration.

5.2 The probability compiler

We need to calculate probabilities as a subroutine of PDF calculation. We achieve this by translating distributions into Kozen-style terms [14]. The probability compiler $e\ \$\ \delta \mapsto \delta'$ performs this translation (Figure 7). It takes a distribution e of type $\mathsf{dist}\ \tau$ and a function δ from τ to $[0, 1]$ and returns the expectation of δ w.r.t. e. When δ is the indicator function on a set X, δ' is the e-probability of X. For instance, suppose we want to know the probability that a sample from flip (3/4) is true. We invoke the probability compiler with $e := \mathsf{flip}\ (3/4)$ and $\delta := \lambda z : \mathsf{bool}\,.\, \langle z \rangle$, producing

$$\int \lambda x : \mathsf{R}\,.\, \langle 0 < x < 1 \rangle * (\lambda u \,.\, (\lambda z \,.\, \langle z \rangle)\ (u < 3/4))\ x$$

for δ', which is equivalent to $\int_0^1 \langle x < 3/4 \rangle\, dx = 3/4$, as expected. Likewise, to derive the probability that a standard normal random variable stays within a standard deviation of its mean, we would invoke the probability compiler with $e := \mathsf{std\_normal}$ and $\delta := \lambda x \,.\, \langle -1 < x < 1 \rangle$. Details on how this computes probabilities are given by Kozen and can also be understood by the expectation monad [20]. We also need the judgment $\Upsilon \vdash \varepsilon\ \$\ \delta \mapsto \delta'$, which invokes the probability compiler on the distribution corresponding to the RV transform body ε in the context Υ.

5.3 The PDF calculation procedure

We structure the PDF calculation procedure as we did the type system: the judgment on distributions prepares a call to the judgment on RV transforms. The PDF of a well-formed program pdf e is given by the δ satisfying $\emptyset; \emptyset \vdash e \curvearrowright \delta$. The judgment $\Upsilon; \Lambda \vdash e \curvearrowright \delta$ calculates the PDF δ of the distribution e under Υ and Λ (Figure 8). Rule P-RAND gives the PDF of Uniform(0,1): the indicator function on $(0, 1)$. Rules P-RET and P-BIND build the contexts and invoke the next compiler. The real work begins in the judgment $\Upsilon; \Lambda \vdash \varepsilon \rightsquigarrow \delta$, which computes the PDF δ corresponding to the RV transform body ε under Υ and Λ. We present this judgment in two parts, one each for univariate and multivariate transforms. The multivariate transforms must deal with the issue of dependence between inputs or between outputs of the transform.

Univariate transforms We use *univariate* for RV transforms between spaces that are not product spaces. The correctness of rules P-LOG, P-EXP, P-LINEAR, and P-SCALE is given by the following lemma.

$$\frac{\Upsilon;\Lambda \vdash \varepsilon \rightsquigarrow \delta}{\Upsilon;\Lambda \vdash \mathsf{log}\ \varepsilon \rightsquigarrow \lambda x:\mathsf{R}\,.\ \delta\ (\mathsf{exp}\ x) * \mathsf{exp}\ x}\ \text{P-LOG}$$

$$\frac{\Upsilon;\Lambda \vdash \varepsilon \rightsquigarrow \delta}{\Upsilon;\Lambda \vdash \mathsf{exp}\ \varepsilon \rightsquigarrow \lambda x:\mathsf{R}\,.\ \delta\ (\mathsf{log}\ x) * (1/x)}\ \text{P-EXP}$$

$$\frac{FV(\varepsilon_2)\cap\Lambda=\emptyset \qquad \Upsilon;\Lambda \vdash \varepsilon_1 \rightsquigarrow \delta}{\Upsilon;\Lambda \vdash \varepsilon_1+\varepsilon_2 \rightsquigarrow \lambda x:\mathsf{R}\,.\ \delta\ (x-\varepsilon_2)}\ \text{P-LINEAR}$$

$$\frac{\Upsilon;\Lambda \vdash \varepsilon \rightsquigarrow \delta \qquad l>0}{\Upsilon;\Lambda \vdash l*\varepsilon \rightsquigarrow \lambda x:\mathsf{R}\,.\ \delta\ (x/l) * (1/l)}\ \text{P-SCALE}$$

$$\frac{\Upsilon;\Lambda \vdash \varepsilon \rightsquigarrow \delta}{\Upsilon;\Lambda \vdash \mathsf{neg}\ \varepsilon \rightsquigarrow \lambda x:\mathsf{R}\,.\ \delta\ (-x)}\ \text{P-NEG}$$

$$\frac{\Upsilon;\Lambda \vdash \varepsilon \rightsquigarrow \delta}{\Upsilon;\Lambda \vdash \mathsf{inv}\ \varepsilon \rightsquigarrow \lambda x:\mathsf{R}\,.\ \delta\ (1/x) * (1/(x*x))}\ \text{P-INV}$$

Figure 9. The transform-to-PDF converter, $\Upsilon;\Lambda \vdash \varepsilon \rightsquigarrow \delta$, univariate cases.

Lemma 5.1. *For absolutely continuous distributions* $\mathbb{P}$ *and* $\mathbb{Q}$ *on* $\mathbb{R}$ *and a function* $h:\mathbb{R}\to\mathbb{R}$ *such that* $\mathbb{Q}(Y)=\mathbb{P}(h^{-1}[Y])$, *if* h *is strictly increasing, differentiable and invertible, then the function*

$$g(y)=f(h^{-1}(y))\cdot\frac{d}{dy}h^{-1}(y).$$

is a PDF *of* $\mathbb{Q}$, *where* f *is the derivative of the* CDF F *of* $\mathbb{P}$.

Proof. The derivative of a CDF is a PDF. The CDF G of $\mathbb{Q}$ is

$$\begin{aligned} G(y)=\mathbb{Q}(\,(-\infty,y]\,) &= \mathbb{P}(h^{-1}[\,(-\infty,y]\,]) \\ =\mathbb{P}(\,(-\infty,h^{-1}(y)]\,) &= F(h^{-1}(y)), \end{aligned}$$

where we have used the fact that the h-preimage of $(-\infty,y]$ is $(-\infty,h^{-1}(y)]$ because h is strictly increasing and invertible. The claim follows from the fact that g is the derivative of G. □

The lemma is easily modified for P-NEG and also P-INV; an "extra" minus sign appears because they consist of strictly *decreasing* components. It is possible to define a version of P-SCALE for negative literals, as well as integer versions of P-NEG, P-LINEAR, and P-SCALE. With these rules (and P-VAR, discussed below) we can already compute some continuous PDFs. Consider the standard exponential from Section 3.2; we derive its PDF with $\emptyset;\emptyset \vdash \mathsf{std\_exponential} \curvearrowright \delta$, which builds the contexts $\Lambda := u$ and $\Upsilon := u:\mathsf{R}\sim\mathsf{random}$ and invokes the chain

$$\begin{array}{ll} \Upsilon;\Lambda\vdash -\mathsf{log}\ u \rightsquigarrow \delta & \delta'' := \lambda x''\,.\,\langle 0<x''<1\rangle \\ \Upsilon;\Lambda\vdash \mathsf{log}\ u \rightsquigarrow \delta' & \delta' := \lambda x'\,.\,\langle 0<\mathsf{exp}\ x'<1\rangle * \mathsf{exp}\ x' \\ \Upsilon;\Lambda\vdash u \rightsquigarrow \delta'' & \delta := \lambda x\,.\,\langle 0<\mathsf{exp}\ (-x)<1\rangle * \mathsf{exp}\ (-x). \end{array}$$

We β-reduce for clarity. The chain ends with P-VAR, which gives the PDF of Uniform(0,1) for δ''; then, P-LOG and P-NEG produce δ' and δ. The latter is equivalent to $\lambda x\,.\,\langle 0<x\rangle * \mathsf{exp}\ (-x)$, which is easily seen to be the PDF of the standard exponential. Likewise, the PDF of $\mathsf{uniform}\ \varepsilon_1\ \varepsilon_2$ is correctly calculated to be

$$\delta := \lambda x\,.\,\langle 0<(x-\varepsilon_1)/(\varepsilon_2-\varepsilon_1)<1\rangle * (1/(\varepsilon_2-\varepsilon_1)),$$

which is equivalent to $\lambda x\,.\,\langle \varepsilon_1<x<\varepsilon_2\rangle * (1/(\varepsilon_2-\varepsilon_1))$. We do not provide rules for sin, cos, and tan because we are unaware of any simple closed-form expression for the corresponding PDFs.

Multivariate transforms We use *multivariate* for RV transforms to or from a product space. The presence of multiple dimensions introduces the issue of dependence between the inputs or between the outputs of the transform, making it difficult to provide rules that work in the general case. As a result, some of the following rules introduce specific independence requirements.

$$\frac{\emptyset\vdash l:\tau \qquad \tau \text{ countable}}{\Upsilon;\Lambda\vdash l \rightsquigarrow \lambda x:\tau\,.\,\langle x=l\rangle}\ \text{P-LIT}$$

$$\frac{\Upsilon\vdash\varepsilon:\mathsf{bool} \qquad \Upsilon;\Lambda\vdash\varepsilon\ \$\ \lambda x:\mathsf{bool}\,.\,\langle x\rangle \mapsto \delta}{\Upsilon;\Lambda\vdash\varepsilon\rightsquigarrow\lambda x:\mathsf{bool}\,.\,\mathsf{if}\ x\ \mathsf{then}\ \delta\ \mathsf{else}\ 1-\delta}\ \text{P-BOOL}$$

$$\frac{\{\Upsilon;\Lambda\vdash\varepsilon_1\perp\varepsilon_i\}_{i=2,3} \qquad \{\Upsilon;\Lambda\vdash\varepsilon_i\rightsquigarrow\delta_i\}_{i=1,2,3}}{\begin{array}{l}\Upsilon;\Lambda\vdash \mathsf{if}\ \varepsilon_1\ \mathsf{then}\ \varepsilon_2\ \mathsf{else}\ \varepsilon_3 \rightsquigarrow \\ \qquad \lambda x\,.\,\delta_1\ \mathsf{true} * \delta_2\ x + \delta_1\ \mathsf{false} * \delta_3\ x\end{array}}\ \text{P-IF}$$

$$\frac{\Lambda=\{x\}\sqcup\{y_1,\ldots,y_m\} \qquad \mathcal{J}(\Upsilon;\Lambda)\mapsto\delta}{\Upsilon;\Lambda\vdash x\rightsquigarrow\lambda x\,.\,\textstyle\int\lambda(y_1,\ldots,y_m)\,.\,\delta}\ \text{P-VAR}$$

$$\frac{\Lambda=\{x_1,\ldots,x_n\}\sqcup\{y_1,\ldots,y_m\} \qquad \mathcal{J}(\Upsilon;\Lambda)\mapsto\delta}{\Upsilon;\Lambda\vdash (x_1,\ldots,x_n)\rightsquigarrow\lambda(x_1,\ldots,x_n)\,.\,\textstyle\int\lambda(y_1,\ldots,y_m)\,.\,\delta}\ \text{P-VARS}$$

$$\frac{\Upsilon;\Lambda\vdash\varepsilon\rightsquigarrow\delta}{\Upsilon;\Lambda\vdash\mathsf{fst}\ \varepsilon\rightsquigarrow\lambda x\,.\,\textstyle\int\lambda y\,.\,\delta\ (x,y)}\ \text{P-FST}$$

$$\frac{\Upsilon;\Lambda\vdash\varepsilon_1\perp\varepsilon_2 \qquad \{\Upsilon;\Lambda\vdash\varepsilon_i\rightsquigarrow\delta_i\}_{i=1,2}}{\Upsilon;\Lambda\vdash(\varepsilon_1,\varepsilon_2)\rightsquigarrow\lambda(x_1,x_2)\,.\,\delta_1\ x_1 * \delta_2\ x_2}\ \text{P-PAIR}$$

$$\frac{\Upsilon;\Lambda\vdash\varepsilon_1\perp\varepsilon_2 \qquad \{\Upsilon;\Lambda\vdash\varepsilon_i\rightsquigarrow\delta_i\}_{i=1,2}}{\Upsilon;\Lambda\vdash\varepsilon_1+\varepsilon_2\rightsquigarrow\lambda x:\mathsf{R}\,.\,\textstyle\int\lambda t:\mathsf{R}\,.\ \delta_1\ x*\delta_2\ (t-x)}\ \text{P-PLUS}$$

Figure 10. The transform-to-PDF converter, multivariate cases.

$$\frac{}{\mathcal{J}(\Upsilon;\emptyset)\mapsto 1}\ \text{J-NIL} \qquad \frac{\Upsilon;\emptyset\vdash e\curvearrowright\delta \qquad \mathcal{J}(\Upsilon;\Lambda)\mapsto\delta'}{\mathcal{J}(\Upsilon,x:\tau\sim e;\Lambda,x)\mapsto\delta\ x*\delta'}\ \text{J-CONS}$$

Figure 11. The joint PDF body constructor, $\mathcal{J}(\Upsilon;\Lambda)\mapsto\delta$.

Rule P-LIT states that the PMF of a point mass distribution on l is simply the indicator function on $\{l\}$. The transforms corresponding to the rules in this section tend to be less obvious; the transform in question for P-LIT is the constant function on l, whose argument may be a tuple. Rule P-BOOL calculates the PMF of a Boolean random variable, which is a simple expression of the probability that the random variable is true. We thus invoke the probability compiler in the current context to compute this probability δ. This rule covers the cases for $<$ and $=$. The ability to represent the PMF of a Boolean random variable allows us to encode arbitrary probability queries. Rule P-IF computes the PDF of a mixture, which is a weighted combination of the component PDFs, where the mixing probability is the probability the if-condition is true. For this to be valid, the if-condition must be independent of its branches, as required. For instance, the PDF of

$\mathsf{var}\ x \sim \mathsf{random}\ \mathsf{in}$
$\quad \mathsf{var}\ y \sim \mathsf{uniform}\ 2\ 3\ \mathsf{in}\ \mathsf{return}\ (\mathsf{if}\ x < 1/2\ \mathsf{then}\ x\ \mathsf{else}\ y).$

is *not* equivalent to $\lambda x\,.\,(1/2)*\langle 0<x<1\rangle + (1/2)*\langle 2<x<3\rangle$, as would be calculated without the restriction (there should be no probability mass on $[1/2,1]$).

Rule P-VAR is a special case of P-VARS. The transform corresponding to P-VARS is a function that returns a permutation of a subset of components of its tuple argument. We assume $x_1,\ldots,x_n$ and $y_1,\ldots,y_m$ are distinct, and we use $\sqcup$ to denote disjoint union. The resulting PDF is a marginal PDF. The *marginal* PDF of a joint PDF f on $A\times B$ is given by $g(x)=\int\lambda y\,.\,f(x,y)\ d\overline{\mu}_B$; g is a PDF on A whose density at x is given by adding up the contribution of the joint PDF along the other dimension, B. The corresponding process is one which generates tuples but then discards the second component, returning the first. We generalize to higher dimensions by integrating out random variables not appearing in the result tuple. When this set is empty ($m=0$), the integral reduces to δ. The resulting PDF may be computationally inefficient due to a large number of nested integrals. More efficient schemes that take advantage of the graphical structure of the probabilistic model, such as *variable elimination*, are possible [26]. The judgment $\mathcal{J}(\Upsilon;\Lambda) \mapsto \delta$ constructs the body of the joint PDF of the active random variables (Figure 11). Rule J-CONS first computes the PDF of e, parametric in all of the preceding random variables (thus, invoking the distribution-to-PDF converter with no active random variables). It then constructs the product with the PDFs of the remaining active variables; the product of these parametric PDFs is the joint PDF. The terms δ and δ' in J-CONS have type $\tau \to \mathsf{R}$ and R, respectively. The judgment returns an open term and relies on the fact that the free variables will be bound appropriately by the invoking judgment. Rule P-FST is analogous to P-VARS; we ask for a PDF and compute the marginal PDF of the first component. We define an analogous rule for snd. Rules P-PAIR and P-PLUS state the well known results that the joint PDF and the PDF of the sum of independent random variables is the product of and convolution of their individual PDFs, respectively.

On the face of it, these rules handle mixture models and joint models, but where they really shine is on general hierarchical models. For example, the PDF of

$$\mathsf{hier} := \mathsf{var}\ x \sim \mathsf{random\ in\ var}\ y \sim \mathsf{uniform}\ 0\ x\ \mathsf{in\ return}\ y$$

is not immediately obvious. The process is generated by sampling a value x uniformly from (0,1), and then sampling uniformly from $(0, x)$, discarding x. We calculate the PDF with $\emptyset;\emptyset \vdash \mathsf{hier} \curvearrowright \delta$, which builds $\Upsilon := y : \mathsf{R} \sim \mathsf{uniform}\ 0\ x, x : \mathsf{R} \sim \mathsf{random}$ and $\Lambda := y, x$ for $\Upsilon;\Lambda \vdash y \rightsquigarrow \delta$. Rule P-VAR then produces

$$\lambda y\,.\int \lambda x\,.(\langle 0<(y-0)/(x-0)<1\rangle*1/(x-0))*\langle 0<x<1\rangle*1$$

for δ, where we have β-reduced for clarity. The body of the inner λ-abstraction is generated by the joint PDF body constructor; the two non-trivial multiplicands are the parametric PDF of uniform $0\ x$ and the PDF of random, respectively. With some manipulation we can show δ corresponds to $f(y) = \int_y^1 1/x\, dx = -\log(y)$ for $y \in (0,1)$ and zero otherwise. The rules do not perform algebraic simplifications, but the benefit of automation can still be felt clearly.

Modularity Some RV transforms are inconvenient to work with, preventing us from calculating certain PDFs. For example, we cannot calculate the PDF of std_normal from scratch because its specification uses cos, which we do not handle. However, the design allows us to modularly address cases like this, where we want to specially handle the PDF for a specific distribution. We can add the rule $\Upsilon;\Lambda \vdash \mathsf{std\_normal} \curvearrowright \phi$, where $\phi := \lambda x.\mathsf{exp}(-x*x/2)/\mathsf{sqrt}(2*\pi)$ is the PDF of the standard normal. This new rule is used by the joint body constructor whenever std_normal appears on the spine of a distribution, enabling the calculation of PDFs for hierarchical models using std_normal that were previously not compilable. For example, the PDF of normal $\mu\ \sigma$ can now be calculated as

$$\begin{array}{ll}\Upsilon;\Lambda \vdash \sigma * x + \mu \rightsquigarrow \delta & \delta'' := \lambda x''\,.\,\phi\, x'' \\ \Upsilon;\Lambda \vdash \sigma * x \rightsquigarrow \delta' & \delta' := \lambda x'\,.\,\phi\,(x'/\sigma) * (1/\sigma) \\ \Upsilon;\Lambda \vdash x \rightsquigarrow \delta'' & \delta := \lambda x\,.\,\phi\,((x-\mu)/\sigma) * (1/\sigma)\end{array}$$

using the rules P-VAR, P-SCALE, and P-LINEAR, where $\Lambda := x$ and $\Upsilon := x : \mathsf{R} \sim \mathsf{std\_normal}$. We can see δ is equivalent to the classic formula for the normal PDF, $f(x) = \frac{1}{\sigma\sqrt{2\pi}}\exp(-\frac{1}{2\sigma^2}(x-\mu)^2)$. Likewise, we can now handle distributions like the log-normal and mixture-of-Gaussians. To support an infinite discrete distribution with a known PDF, such as the Poisson distribution, we can add a new primitive to the core calculus (poisson ε) and handle it specially in the distribution-to-PDF converter.

6. Related Work

Our work builds on a long tradition of probabilistic functional languages, most connected to the probability monad in some way. They work by incorporating distributional semantics into a functional language, so that one can express values which represent a *distribution* over possible outcomes. The distribution can either be manifest (available to the programmer) or implicit (existing only in the metatheory). An early incarnation of the latter was given by Kozen in [14], in which he provides the semantics for an imperative language endowed with a random number primitive supplying samples from Uniform(0,1). Values of type A in the object language are given semantics in functions of type $(A \to [0,1]) \to [0,1]$ in the metatheory. These functions represent distributions over A and satisfy the expected laws for measures. Kozen's work is far-reaching and will continue to inspire future languages: it can accommodate continuous and hybrid distributions; it handles unbounded iteration (general recursion), a traditionally thorny issue for probabilistic languages; and it even provides a treatment of distributions on function types. However, PDFs are not addressed at all.

Though not explicitly cast as functional or monadic, Kozen's approach forms the basis for Audebaud and Paulin-Mohring's monadic development for reasoning about randomized algorithms in COQ [2]. Their focus is on verification, and they define the probability monad from first principles (modulo an axiomatization of arithmetic on the [0,1] interval), whereas we provide it axiomatically. We hope to inspire a cross-fertilization of ideas between the efforts as we bring our theory of PDFs into COQ.

While suitable for semantics and verification, Kozen's representation is not ideal for direct use in computing certain operations. For instance, it is unclear how to sample or compute general expectations efficiently given a term of type $(A \to [0,1]) \to [0,1]$. More recent works explore alternate concrete embodiments of the probability monad; Ramsey and Pfeffer discuss some of the possibilities [20]. A popular choice is to represent distributions as weighted lists or trees. This has the drawback that only distributions with finitely many outcomes are expressible (ruling out essentially all commonly used continuous distributions), and PMFs are the only supported form of PDFs. On the other hand, distributions can occur on arbitrary types, expectation and computing the PMF is straightforward, and the approach works well as an embedded domain-specific language (PFP [7], HANSEI [13], probability monads in Haskell [20]). Dedicated languages like IBAL [19] or Church [9] offer more scope for program analysis, which is crucial for escaping the limitations of an embedded approach and mitigates some of the fundamental drawbacks of the representation. Ultimately, however, these languages do not support continuous or hybrid distributions (nor their PDFs) in a general sense. Sampling functions are a fun alternative representation. They are used by $\lambda_{\bigcirc}$ [18] to support continuous and hybrid distributions in a true sense and also allow distributions on arbitrary types. Distributions are represented by sampling functions that return a sample from the distribution when requested. Sampling and sampling-based routines are the only supported operations, thus PDFs are not accommodated.

Another recent work also rigorously supports continuous and hybrid distributions by providing a measure transformer semantics for a core functional calculus [4]. The work does not provide PDFs but is novel for its ability to support conditional probability in the presence of zero probability events in continuous spaces, a feature necessary in many machine learning applications. Their formalization is similar to ours, as both are based in standard measure theory. They have independently recognized the importance of analyzing distributions by their transformations, doing so in the context of conditional probability, whereas we have developed the idea for PDFs. This hints that reasoning via transforms may be a technique that is more broadly applicable to other program analyses for probabilistic languages.

The Hierarchical Bayes Compiler (HBC) is a toolkit for implementing hierarchical Bayesian models [5]. Its specification language represents a different point in the design space. Essentially, it removes `return` while adding a set of standard distributions (with PDFs) to the core calculus. This guarantees that all constructible models are AC. Many powerful models used in machine learning are expressible in HBC. However, something as basic as adding two random variables is not. Furthermore, if a distribution outside of the provided set is required, it must be added to the core. This is the fundamental tension surrounding `return`: with it, the core is minimal, expressivity is high, and PDFs are non-trivial; without it, PDFs are easily supported, but the core becomes large, and expressivity is crippled. HBC is not formally defined.

An entirely different tradition incorporates probabilistic semantics into logic programming languages (Markov Logic [21], BLOG [16], BLP [12], PRISM [22]). These languages are well suited for probabilistic knowledge engineering and statistical relational learning. In Markov Logic, for instance, programmers associate higher weights with logical clauses that are more strongly believed to hold. The semantics of a set of clauses is given by *undirected graphical models*, with the weights determining the potential functions (*e.g.* by Boltzmann weighting). Certain continuous distributions can be supported by manipulating the potential function calculation. Supporting PDFs in this context should not be problematic; the potential functions (essentially, unnormalized PDFs) always exist, by design. However, like HBC, it appears these languages are not quite as expressive as is possible in a probabilistic functional language.

The AutoBayes system [10] shares a key feature with our language in that PDFs are manifest in the object language. AutoBayes automates the derivation of maximum likelihood and Bayesian estimators for a significant class of statistical models, with a focus on code generation, and can express continuous distributions and PDFs. However, despite their focus on correctness-by-construction, the language is not formally defined. Furthermore, it is unclear how general the language actually is, *i.e.* how "custom" the models can be. Our work could serve as a formal basis for their system.

7. Conclusion

We have presented a formal language capable of expressing discrete, continuous and hybrid distributions and their PDFs. Our novel contributions include a type system for absolutely continuous distributions and a modular PDF calculation procedure. The type system uses the new ideas of RV transforms and non-nullifying functions. There are several interesting avenues for future work. The first is to address PDFs in the context of conditional probability, perhaps by incorporating our formalization of PDFs with the ideas presented in [4]. Secondly, to provide a complete account of continuous probability, one must support expectation. Generically supporting expectation requires a treatment of integrability or summability; reasoning via the RV transform may be a productive route. Finally, combining this work with a formal language for optimization such as [1] would create a true formal language for *statistics*, which would be able to express statistical problems in the object language itself. Current languages express *probability*; any notion of statistics is outside the language.

Acknowledgments

We thank Prof. Christopher Heil for valuable input on the idea of non-nullifying functions. We also thank the anonymous reviewers, whose thoughtful suggestions have greatly improved the paper.

References

[1] A. Agarwal, S. Bhat, A. Gray, and I. E. Grossmann. Automating Mathematical Program Transformations. In *Practical Aspects of Declarative Languages*, 2010.

[2] P. Audebaud and C. Paulin-Mohring. Proofs of Randomized Algorithms in Coq. In *Mathematics of Program Construction*, pages 49–68. Springer, 2006.

[3] C. Bishop. *Pattern Recognition and Machine Learning*. Springer, 2006.

[4] J. Borgstram, A. D. Gordon, M. Greenberg, J. Margetson, and J. V. Gael. Measure Transformer Semantics for Bayesian Machine Learning. In *European Symposium on Programming*, pages 77–96, 2011.

[5] H. Daumé III. HBC: Hierarchical Bayes Compiler, 2007. URL `http://hal3.name/HBC`.

[6] L. Devroye. Non-Uniform Random Variate Generation, 1986.

[7] M. Erwig and S. Kollmansberger. Functional Pearls: Probabilistic Functional Programming in Haskell. *Journal of Functional Programming*, 16(01):21–34, 2005.

[8] M. Giry. A Categorical Approach to Probability Theory. *Categorical Aspects of Topology and Analysis*, 915:68–85, 1981.

[9] N. Goodman, V. Mansinghka, D. Roy, K. Bonawitz, and J. Tenenbaum. Church: A Language for Generative Models. In *Uncertainty in Artificial Intelligence*, 2008.

[10] A. G. Gray, B. Fischer, J. Schumann, and W. Buntine. Automatic Derivation of Statistical Algorithms: The EM Family and Beyond. In *Advances in Neural Information Processing Systems*, 2003.

[11] M. Hoyrup, C. Rojas, and K. Weihrauch. The Radon-Nikodym operator is not computable. In *Computability & Complexity in Analysis*, 2011.

[12] K. Kersting and L. De Raedt. Bayesian Logic Programming: Theory and Tool. In *Introduction to Statistical Relational Learning*. 2007.

[13] O. Kiselyov and C. Shan. Embedded Probabilistic Programming. In *Working Conference on Domain Specific Languages*. Springer, 2009.

[14] D. Kozen. Semantics of Probabilistic Programs. *Journal of Computer and System Sciences*, 22(3):328–350, 1981.

[15] T. Mhamdi, O. Hasan, and S. Tahar. On the Formalization of the Lebesgue Integration Theory in HOL. *Interactive Theorem Proving*, pages 387–402, 2010.

[16] B. Milch, B. Marthi, S. Russell, D. Sontag, D. Ong, and A. Kolobov. BLOG: Probabilistic Models with Unknown Objects. In *International Joint Conference on Artificial Intelligence*, volume 19, 2005.

[17] O. Nielsen. *An Introduction to Integration and Measure Theory*. Wiley-Interscience, 1997.

[18] S. Park, F. Pfenning, and S. Thrun. A Probabilistic Language based upon Sampling Functions. In *Principles of Programming Languages*, pages 171–182. ACM New York, NY, USA, 2005.

[19] A. Pfeffer. IBAL: A Probabilistic Rational Programming Language. In *International Joint Conference on Artificial Intelligence*, 2001.

[20] N. Ramsey and A. Pfeffer. Stochastic Lambda Calculus and Monads of Probability Distributions. volume 37, pages 154–165. ACM, 2002.

[21] M. Richardson and P. Domingos. Markov Logic Networks. *Machine Learning*, 62(1):107–136, 2006.

[22] T. Sato and Y. Kameya. PRISM: A Symbolic-Statistical Modeling Language. In *International Joint Conference on Artificial Intelligence*, pages 1330–1339, 1997.

[23] D. Scott. Parametric Statistical Modeling by Minimum Integrated Square Error. *Technometrics*, 43(3):274–285, 2001.

[24] B. Silverman. *Density Estimation for Statistics and Data Analysis*. Chapman & Hall/CRC, 1986.

[25] R. Solovay. A Model of Set-Theory in Which Every Set of Reals is Lebesgue Measurable. *Annals of Mathematics*, pages 1–56, 1970.

[26] L. Wasserman. *All of Statistics: A Concise Course in Statistical Inference*. Springer, 2004.

A Type System for Borrowing Permissions

Karl Naden Robert Bocchino
Jonathan Aldrich
Carnegie Mellon University, Pittsburgh, PA, USA
{kbn,rbocchin,jonathan.aldrich}@cs.cmu.edu

Kevin Bierhoff
Two Sigma Investments, New York, NY, USA
kevin.bierhoff@cs.cmu.edu

Abstract

In object-oriented programming, unique permissions to object references are useful for checking correctness properties such as consistency of typestate and noninterference of concurrency. To be usable, unique permissions must be *borrowed* — for example, one must be able to read a unique reference out of a field, use it for something, and put it back. While one can null out the field and later reassign it, this paradigm is ungainly and requires unnecessary writes, potentially hurting cache performance. Therefore, in practice borrowing must occur in the type system, without requiring memory updates. Previous systems support borrowing with external alias analysis and/or explicit programmer management of *fractional permissions*. While these approaches are powerful, they are also awkward and difficult for programmers to understand. We present an integrated language and type system with unique, immutable, and shared permissions, together with new *local permissions* that say that a reference may not be stored to the heap. Our system also includes *change permissions* such as `unique>>unique` and `unique>>none` that describe how permissions flow in and out of method formal parameters. Together, these features support common patterns of borrowing, including borrowing multiple local permissions from a unique reference and recovering the unique reference when the local permissions go out of scope, without any explicit management of fractions in the source language. All accounting of fractional permissions is done by the type system "under the hood." We present the syntax and static and dynamic semantics of a formal core language and state soundness results. We also illustrate the utility and practicality of our design by using it to express several realistic examples.

Categories and Subject Descriptors D.3.1 [*Programming Languages*]: Formal Definitions and Theory—Borrowing; D.3.3 [*Programming Languages*]: Language Constructs and Features —Permissions

General Terms Design, Languages, Theory, Verification

Keywords Types, Permissions, Borrowing, Uniqueness, Immutability

1. Introduction

Permissions are annotations on pointer variables that specify how an object may be aliased, and which aliases may read or write to the object [9]. For example, `unique` [20] indicates an unaliased object, `immutable` [24] indicates an object that can be aliased but cannot be mutated, and `shared` [3] indicates an object that may be aliased and can be mutated. Permission systems have been proposed to address a diversity of software engineering concerns, including encapsulation [24], protocol checking [3, 13], safe concurrency [6, 8], security [5], and memory management [9, 15]. Recently, new programming languages have incorporated permissions [28] or related affine types [26] as fundamental parts of the type system.

In order to leverage permissions in practice, programmers must be able to manipulate them effectively. One form of manipulation is *permission splitting*: for example, converting a unique permission into multiple shared permissions, or alternatively into multiple immutable permissions. A shared (or immutable) permission can then be split further into more shared (respectively immutable) permissions. A second important form of manipulation is *borrowing*: extracting a permission from a variable field, using it temporarily, and then returning all or part of it to the source. For example, a method may require an immutable permission to the receiver; if we have a unique permission to an object, we'd like to call the method on that object, and provided the method does not allow an alias to the receiver to escape, we'd like to get our unique permission back at the end. Crucially, recovering the permission should not require reassigning the original variable (which may not even be assignable).

Borrowing was originally proposed by [19]; however, good support for this feature has remained an open and difficult problem. Prior type-based systems [1, 19, 22] provided a borrowed annotation, but they did not support the immutable references that are an essential part of many recent systems [3, 8, 28]. A number of systems supported borrowing via a program analysis [4, 7], but the program analysis relies on shape analysis, which is fragile and notoriously difficult for programmers to understand. Boyland proposed fractional permissions [8] to support splitting and recombining permissions, with borrowing as a special case, but its mathematical fraction abstraction is unnatural for programmers, to such an extent that the automated tools we know of once again hide the fractions behind an (inscrutable) analysis [3, 17].

A good borrowing facility should have a number of properties. It should support a natural programming style (e.g. avoid awkward constructs like replacing field write with a primitive swap operation [16], or a requirement to thread a reference explicitly from one call to the next by reassigning the reference each time [26]). Reasoning abstractions should likewise be natural (not fractions [8]). It should support borrowing from unique, immutable, and shared variables and fields. Rules should be local so the programmer can understand them and predict how they operate (vs. a non-local analysis [3, 7] or constraint-based inference).

The contribution of this paper is the first borrowing approach that meets all of the above properties. We provide a type system for a Java-like language with permissions that are tracked through local, predictable rules. Our technical approach includes a number of innovations, including change permissions that show the incoming

POPL'12, January 25–27, 2012, Philadelphia, PA, USA.

and outgoing permissions to a method parameter, local permissions that modify shared or immutable permissions to denote that they cannot escape, an expressive rule for handling borrowing across conditional branches, and a way to safely restore permissions to the variable or field from which they were borrowed. We formalize our type system, prove it sound, and demonstrate it via a series of examples which can be checked by our prototype implementation.[1]

We describe the features of the language in the next section. Section 3 formalizes our type system and gives soundness results. We cover additional related work in section 4, and section 5 concludes.

2. Language Features

In this section we informally explain the features of our language; the next section gives a more formal treatment. Our language is based on Plaid [28]. For our purposes, Plaid is similar to Java, except:

- Instead of classes, Plaid uses states. This is because Plaid has a first-class notion of *typestate*, which can be used to model object state and transitions between states. We don't use typestate in this work, but we adhere to the Plaid syntax.
- Plaid has a `match` construct that evaluates an argument and then uses its type to pick which of several cases to execute.
- Plaid has no `null` value in the surface syntax or programmer-visible semantics. Instead, every object field and variable is initialized to a non-null object.
- Plaid has a first-class notion of permissions. Supporting typestate is one important application of permissions, including the novel borrowing mechanisms discussed in this work.

In the rest of this section we first give an overview of the permissions in our language. Then we explain the mechanisms for creating aliases of variables and fields with consistent permissions. Then we explain the mechanism of change permissions, which allows modular checking of permission flow in and out of methods. Finally, we explain local permissions, which provide a way to split a unique permission into several permissions and later recombine them to unique, without explicit fractions.

2.1 Access Permissions

Permissions are a well-known way of controlling aliasing in applications such as typestate [3] and concurrency control [8]. Our permission system is adapted from the *access permissions* system of [3]. An access permission is a tag on an object reference that says how the reference may be used to access the fields of the object it refers to and how aliases of that reference may be created. In this work, we use the following permissions:

- A `unique` permission to object reference o says that this is the only usable copy of o: if any alias of o exists, then it has permission `none`. The reference may be used to read and write fields of the object O that it points to.
- A `none` permission says that the reference may not be used to read or write the object it points to.
- An `immutable` permission says that the reference o may be used only for reading, and not writing, the fields of the object O that it points to. Further, all other usable (non-`none`) references to O are guaranteed to be `immutable`, so no aliased reference can be used to write O either.
- A `shared` permission says that the reference o may be used for reading and writing, and there is no restriction on aliases of o (so `shared` is like an ordinary reference in Java).
- A `local immutable` or `local shared` permission is like an `immutable` (respectively `shared`) permission, except it can only be passed around in local variables, and can't be assigned to the heap. Local permissions are new with this work and are explained further in Section 2.4.

If any alias of a unique reference is created, then the `unique` permission must be consumed (but it can be transferred to the alias). A unique permission is therefore like a linear resource [14]. By contrast, `immutable` and `shared` references may be freely replicated.

While other access permissions are possible, these permissions suffice to illustrate the concepts in this paper. Further, these permissions can express a wide range of computation patterns. Other permissions could be added to the system without difficulty.

2.2 Aliasing Variables and Fields

In contrast to a language like Java with unrestricted aliasing, a language with access permissions must maintain careful control over how aliases are created. We now discuss how our language manages permissions for aliases of variables and object fields.

(a) Borrowing Unique from a Variable

```
unique x = new S1; // x:unique
{
  unique y = x;      // x:none,y:unique
}                    // x:unique
```

(b) Borrowing Unique from One of Two Variables

```
unique x = new S1; // x:unique
unique y = new S2; // x:unique,y:unique
{
  unique z = match(...) {
    S1=>x; S2=>y;    // x:none,y:none,z:unique
  }
}                    // x:unique,y:unique
```

(c) Taking Unique from a Variable

```
unique x = new S2; // x:unique
unique y = new S1; // x:unique,y:unique
{
  unique z = x;      // x:none,y:unique,z:unique
  y.f1 = z;          // x:none,y:unique,z:none
}                    // x:none,y:unique
```

Figure 1. Examples of variable aliasing.

Aliasing Variables: In our language the following rules govern aliasing of local variables:

1. Our local variables are single-assignment (i.e., they are assigned to only in their declaration) and are declared with explicit permissions, so the needed permission is always available on the left-hand side of a variable assignment.
2. In typing and assignment, we compute all variables and fields such that the value returned by the right-hand side of the assignment may be obtained by reading the variable or field. Because we can't statically resolve which `match` case will be taken, there may be more than one.
3. We maintain a typing environment, which we call a *context*, with the permission associated with each variable. For each possible source variable, we make sure there is enough permission in the context to extract the needed permission. We use permission splitting rules, given formally in the next section, to com-

[1] available at http://code.google.com/p/plaid-lang/

pute the permission remaining in the source variables after the extraction, and we update the context accordingly.

4. At the end of the scope of the assignee variable, we restore whatever permission is left in that variable to the source variables. For this operation we use permission joining rules, which are the reverse of the splitting rules.

Figure 1 shows examples, where the definitions of states `S1` and `S2` are as follows:

```
state S1 { unique S1 f1 = new S2; }
state S2 case of S1 { unique S1 f2 = new S3; }
state S3 case of S2 {}
```

Here `case of` is like `extends` in Java and denotes subclassing. In Figure 1(a), variable `x` is declared `unique` and initialized with a fresh object in line 1. In line 3, variable `y` is created and takes the unique permission out of `x`, leaving `none` in `x`. When `y` goes out of scope in line 4, its `unique` permission flows back into `x`. Figure 1(b) is similar, except that in line 5, we don't know which variable (`x` or `y`) will be read from at runtime, so we take permissions out of both, record both as source variables, and restore permissions to both at the end of `z`'s scope in line 7. The `match` statement in lines 4–5 says to evaluate the selector expression (represented as ellipses here) to an object reference *o*, then evaluate the whole expression to `x` if the type of *o* matches `S1`, to `y` if the type of *o* matches `S2`, and to halt if there is no match. While this example is simple, in general typing `match` in our language is subtle and requires *merging* the contexts generated by the different match cases; the details are given in Section 3.2. Figure 1(c) shows an example where the permission read out of `x` into `z` is stored into the heap, so it can't be returned to `x` at the end of `z`'s scope.

(a) Borrowing Unique from a Field

```
1 unique x = new S1; // x:unique
2 {
3   unique y = x.f1; // x:(unique,f1:none),y:unique
4 }                  // x:unique
```

(b) Borrowing Unique from a Variable or Field

```
1 unique x = new S1;    // x:unique
2 unique y = new S1;    // x:unique,y:unique
3 {
4   unique z = match(...) {
5     S1=>x; S2=>y.f1;
6     // x:none,y:(unique,f1:none),z:unique
7   }
8 }                     // x:unique,y:unique
```

(c) Taking Unique from a Field

```
1 unique x = new S1; // x:unique
2 unique y = new S1; // x:unique,y:unique
3 y.f1 = x.f1;       // x:(unique,f1:none),y:unique
```

Figure 2. Examples of field aliasing.

Aliasing Fields: The rules for aliasing of fields are similar to those for aliasing of local variables, with two exceptions. First, pulling a permission out of a field can cause the residual permission to violate the statically declared field permission. For example, pulling `unique` out of a field declared `unique` causes the field to have permission `none`. In this case, we say the field is *unpacked* [12]. If an object has any unpacked fields, then we say the object is unpacked. We must account for the actual permissions when accessing the fields of an unpacked object. Second, since fields can be assigned to, the reference in the field at the point of permission restore may not be the same reference that the permission came from. In this case, we must be careful not to restore permissions to the wrong reference, which would violate soundness.

Unpacking fields: To address the first issue, we store the current permission of each unpacked field of each object in the context. Figure 2 shows examples, where `S1` and `S2` are defined as before. In Figure 2(a), line 3 shows the context after taking a unique permission out of `x.f1`. The notation `x:(unique,f1:none)` means that `x` has unique permission and points to an unpacked object with `none` permission for field `f1`. Figure 2(b) shows how to use the same mechanism from Figure 1 to pull a permission out of either a variable or a field. Figure 2(c) shows an example of taking a unique permission from a field and assigning it to another field.

To ensure soundness, we place three restrictions on field unpacking. First, an object can be unpacked via a variable with unique permission, but not immutable or shared permission. This is so outstanding aliases to the object don't become inconsistent.[2] Our language also allows taking an immutable permission out of a unique field $v.f$ given immutable permission to v. In this case our type system does not report v as unpacked in the context; this is sound because once an object is seen with immutable permission it can never become unique again.

Second, once an object o stored in variable v is unpacked, permission to o may not be assigned to another variable or the heap until v is packed again; otherwise we would not be able to track the unpacked state of o through v's information in the context. For example, the following code is not allowed, because `x` is unpacked when it is assigned to `z`:

```
unique x = new S1; // x:unique
unique y = x.f1;   // x:(unique,f1:none),y:unique
unique z = x;      // Disallowed because x is not packed
```

Third, a variable v must be packed at the point where it goes out of scope; in particular method formal parameters must be packed at the end of a method body. That is because the permission stored in v could be flowing back to a different (packed) variable that gave its permission to v when v was declared.

In practice, the programmer can comply with the latter two requriements by carefully managing the scopes of variables that read permissions from unique fields and/or writing fresh objects into the fields to pack the fields at appropriate points. While in some cases these writes may not be strictly necessary, the requirements do not seem to be onerous in the examples we have studied. These restrictions could be relaxed at the cost of additional language complexity (for example, stating in method signatures which fields of an incoming parameter must be packed).

Consistent permission restore: As an example of the second issue identified above (erroneous permission restore), consider the following code:

```
1 unique x = new S2; // x:unique
2 {
3   unique y = x.f1; // x:(unique,f1:none),y:unique
4   x.f1 = new S2;   // x:unique,y:unique
5   x.f2 = x.f1;     // x:(unique,f1:none),y:unique
6 }                  // x:(unique,f1:none)
```

Restoring a permission to `x.f1` at the end of `y`'s scope in line 6 would create an alias between `x.f1` and `x.f2`, both with unique permission. The problem is that the reference in field `x.f1` in line 6 is not the same reference to which permission was taken in line 3, so restoring to it would be wrong.

To prevent this from happening, the static typing rules maintain an identifier that is updated every time a field goes from packed to unpacked. The permission restore occurs only if the identifier at the point of the field access matches the identifier at the point of restoration. For example, in the code shown above, at line 3 where

[2] Local permissions, discussed in Section 2.4, provide an additional way to unpack objects.

x.f1 is unpacked and its permission read into y, an identifier i is associated with x.f1 and with y. Then in line 5, when x.f1 is unpacked again, x.f1 gets a fresh identifier i'. In line 6, when y goes out of scope, its identifier i does not match the identifier i' of the source location x.f1, so permission is not restored from y into the location. Thus the identifier mechanism approximates object identity at runtime; the approximation is conservative because each assignment is assumed to assign a different object reference, even if the same one is actually assigned twice.

2.3 Modular Checking with Change Permissions

To support modular checking of permission flow across method scopes, we introduce a language feature called a *change permission*. Change permissions are inspired by, and similar to, change types in Plaid [28]. However, whereas a change type in Plaid says that an object may transition from one state to another (to support typestate), in our language change permissions specify only that a reference permission changes from a stronger to a weaker permission; the object type always persists. Further, while previous systems can distinguish borrowed and consumed permissions at method boundaries [7, 11], change permissions are more flexible, because they can record a change to any weaker permission (not just none).

Syntactically, a change permission looks like π>>π', where π and π' are permissions. Change permissions appear on method formal parameters, including the implicit parameter this. For example, a formal parameter can be declared π>>π' s x, where s is a state name. This declaration says the caller must ensure that on entry to the method permission π is available for the reference o stored in x, while the callee must ensure that on exit from the method permission π' is available for o. The bare permission π can also function as a change permission; it is shorthand for π>>π.

Change permissions naturally support both borrowing and non-borrowing uses of unique permissions. For example, a change permission unique>>unique says that the permission in the parameter value must be unique on entry to the method, and the unique permission will be restored at the end of the method; whereas unique>>none says that a unique permission is taken and not returned (for example, because it is stored on the heap).

```
1  state Cell {}
2  state Cons case of Cell {
3    immutable Data data;
4    unique Cell next;
5  }
6  state List {
7    unique Cell head = new Cell;
8    void prepend(immutable Data elt) unique {
9      unique Cons newHead = new Cons with {
10       this.data = elt;
11       this.next = this.head; // this:(unique,head:none)
12     }
13     this.head = newHead;     // this:unique
14   }
15 }
16
17 unique List list = new List; // list:unique
18 list.prepend(new Data);      // list:unique
```

Figure 3. List prepend example.

Figure 3 shows an example using unique>>unique (written in shorthand form as unique) to update a list with unique links. Line 1 defines a Cell state representing an empty list cell. Lines 2–5 define a Cons cell which is a substate of Cell; it has a data field with immutable permission and a next field with unique permission. Lines 6 and following define the actual list. It has a unique Cell for its head and a method prepend that (1) accepts an immutable permission in elt and a unique permission in this (unique in line 8 represents the change permission associated with this); (2) leaves a unique permission in this on exit; and (3) returns nothing. The comments in lines 11 and 13 show what happens when checking the method body. In line 11, this is unpacked when the unique permission is taken out of this.head and assigned into newHead. In line 14, this is packed back up when newHead is assigned into this.head.

Lines 17–18 show how things look from the point of view of a caller of prepend. In line 17, list gets a fresh reference with unique permission. This unique permission is passed into prepend in line 18. However, because of the change permission unique>>unique, the permission is restored on return from the method, and list still has unique permission at the end of line 18. Note that we could also have restored the permission by returning a reference from prepend and assigning it back into list but this is awkward and would require assignment into local variables.

```
1  state Data {
2    immutable Data publish() unique>>immutable {
3      // Add timestamp
4      this;
5    }
6    ...
7  }
8
9  unique List list = new List;
10 unique Data data = new Data; // data:unique
11 data.publish();              // data:immutable
12 list.prepend(data);          // data:immutable
```

Figure 4. Publication example.

Figure 4 shows another example, this time using a change permission unique>>immutable. In this example, the Data class has a publish method that (1) requires a unique permission to this; (2) uses the unique permission to write a time stamp to the object; then (3) "freezes" the object in an immutable state so it can only be read and never written by the rest of the program. Lines 9–12 show how this state might be used. Line 10 creates a fresh Data object with unique permission. Line 11 calls publish on Data, changing its permission to immutable. Line 12 puts the immutable permission into a list. Notice that since publish also returns an immutable permission to this, we could also have written list.prepend(data.publish()); but using the change permission on variable data makes clear in the client code that the same object is going into publish and into prepend.

2.4 Local Permissions

An important pattern for access permissions is to divide a unique permission up into several weaker permissions, use the weaker permissions for a while, and then put all the permissions back together to reform the original unique. Doing this requires careful accounting to ensure there are no outstanding permissions to the reference (other than none) at the point where the unique is recreated. One way to do this accounting is to use fractions [8]. However, while powerful, fractions are also difficult to use and suffer from modularity problems [17]. Instead, we observe the following:

- The complexity of fraction-based solutions arises in large part because they allow permissions to be stored into the heap, then taken out of the heap and recombined into unique.
- A common use of permissions split off from unique is to pass them into methods, where they are used in local variables and then returned, i.e., they never go into the heap.

Motivated by these observations, we introduce a new kind of permission called a *local permission*. A local permission is designated with the keyword `local`, which may modify a `shared` or `immutable` permission. A local permission annotates a local variable; it says that any aliases of the variable created during its lifetime exist only in local variables and are never stored to the heap. (Local permissions are not necessary for `unique` or `none`, because the permission itself already contains all the information about aliasing to the heap: a `unique` local variable says there is no alias on the heap or anywhere else, and a `none` local variable says it doesn't matter.) Since local permissions exist only in local variables, when all the variables that borrowed local permissions go out of scope, we can reform the original unique permission.

Borrowing Local Permissions from Variables: A local permission may be borrowed from a variable with `unique` permission, leaving a special *borrow permission* in the context. The borrow permission is used internally for accounting purposes, but never appears in the programmer-visible language syntax. For example, borrowing `local immutable` from a `unique` variable leaves `borrow(unique,immutable,1)` in the context for that variable. This entry says we are borrowing `local immutable` permissions from a `unique` permission, and one alias is outstanding. Borrowing again from the same variable increments the counter, while joining decrements the counter. Thus the counter tracks the number of outstanding local aliases to the original `unique` permission; when the counter is 1, joining the last local permission recreates `unique`. Note that we do this counting only when creating `local` permissions, because in this language `immutable` or `shared` permissions are never joined to `unique`.

(a) Rejoining Local Permissions to Unique

```
1  unique x = new S; // x:unique
2  {
3    local immutable y = x;
4    // x:borrow(unique,immutable,1),y:local immutable
5    {
6      local immutable z = x;
7      /* x:borrow(unique,immutable,2),
8            y:local immutable,z:local immutable */
9    }
10   // x:borrow(unique,immutable,1),y:local immutable
11 }
12 // x:unique
```

(b) This Example Does Not Type Check

```
1  local immutable S escape(unique S x) none {
2    // x:unique
3    local immutable y = x;
4    // x:borrow(unique,immutable,1),y:local immutable
5    y; // Local immutable permission taken here
6    /* x:borrow(unique,immutable,1),
7          y:borrow(local immutable,immutable,1) */
8  }
```

Figure 5. Borrowing local permissions from variables.

Figure 5(a) shows an example. The counter for x becomes 1 in line 4 when y borrows from it, and 2 in line 7 when z borrows from it. When z goes out of scope, the counter goes back down to 1, and when y goes out of scope, x becomes `unique` again. When the counter exceeds one (as in line 7), we don't rejoin to `unique` yet because there are still aliases outstanding. Notice how the counters in the borrow permissions effectively account for fractions of permissions, by counting outstanding aliases. However, these fractions are hidden in the typing and never seen or manipulated by the programmer.

We must carefully account for local permissions that might escape the current scope; otherwise we could not soundly reason that all local permissions are out of scope when the local variables holding them are out of scope. Figure 5(b) shows how we do this. In line 3, y takes a local immutable permission from x, and line 5 attempts to return the local immutable permission to the caller, while retaining the unique permission in x (as shown in the signature in line 1 — remember that `unique x` is shorthand for `unique>>unique x`). Of course this should not be allowed. This example doesn't type check, because when y goes out of scope at the end of the method, two borrow permissions would have to be joined, and our typing rules don't allow this. Only a local permission can be joined with a borrow permission. More generally, all aliases borrowed from a local permission must be rejoined before the local permission can be rejoined to unique. However, if the method signature in line 1 said `unique>>none S x`, then the example would type check, because now x wouldn't have to be rejoined to `unique` to satisfy the parameter's change permission.

```
1  state Cell { int size() none {0;} }
2  state Cons case of Cell {
3    immutable Data data;
4    unique Cell next;
5    int size() local immutable { 1 + this.next.size(); }
6  }
7  state List {
8    unique Cell head = new Cell;
9    int size() local immutable { this.head.size(); }
10   ...
11 }
12
13 unique List list = new List; // list:unique
14 list.prepend(new Data);      // list:unique
15 int size = list.size();      // list:unique
```

Figure 6. List size example.

Borrowing Local Permissions from Fields: Our language also allows borrowing local permissions from `unique` fields. This is particularly useful when the permission to the object is local. Otherwise, we would need unique permission to the object even to read a unique field of the object, and it is well known that this requirement is very restrictive (essentially, any access to a linear reference must be through a chain of linear references) [13].

Figure 6 shows how this works for a simple example that computes the size of a list with unique references, requiring read-only access to the list. In line 15, `size` requires `local immutable` permission to the list (line 11), so local immutable permission is borrowed from `list` as discussed above, then put back to reform `unique` at the end of the method call. Inside the `size` method of `List`, in line 9, `this` has local immutable permission at the start of the method. At the call of `this.head.size()`, local immutable permission is borrowed from `this.head`. At that point, the context entry for `this` is

```
this:(local immutable,head:borrow(unique,immutable,1))
```

saying that `this` has local immutable permission and points to an unpacked object with one local immutable reference borrowed from its `head` field. On return from `this.head.size()`, the permissions are put back together to repack the object. The same thing happens in `Cell.size` (line 5). Notice that the ability to borrow local permissions is very useful here: without it, we would either have to permanently convert the `unique` to `immutable`, thereby destroying the unique permission to the list to compute its size, or we would have to require unique permission to the list for the size computation, which is too restrictive.

One subtlety of this mechanism is that it allows multiple local variables that point to the same object to have different information about whether the object is packed. For example, consider an object O with a unique field f and two aliases of O, x and y, where y was created as an alias of x by pulling a `local` σ from the `unique` permission in x. This leaves x with the permission `local` σ as well, which allows us to pull a `local` σ from $x.f$, unpacking x. Since the type system does not explicitly track what variables are aliases y remains packed. This is fine because the splitting rules prevent anything other than a `local` σ from being pulled out through $y.f$. Furthermore, by the time y leaves scope and x becomes `unique` again, all `local` aliases to the field f of O must have been returned leaving it `unique` as well. Thus, it will be safe to pull a `unique` permission from $x.f$ as allowed by the static rules. At runtime, we will know that x and y are in fact aliases and do the proper accounting for the permission in field f even when permission are pulled from the field through different aliases. More details on this mechanism are given in Section 3.

3. Formal Language

In this section we formalize the ideas developed in the previous section. We give a syntax, static semantics, and dynamic semantics for a core language. Then we state the key soundness results, which are proved in our companion technical report [23].

3.1 Syntax

Figure 7 gives the syntax for the core language. A program consists of a number of state declarations S and an expression e to evaluate. A state consists of a state name s, a parent state s' (possibly itself), and field and method declarations. Fields F and methods M are declared in the usual way, except that field types specify permissions π, and method parameters specify change permissions π>>π'. Fields have initializer expressions. The change permission appearing in the method declaration before the method body is the change permission associated with the implicit parameter `this`.

The rest of the language features are standard for an expression-based object-oriented language. The `match` expression evaluates e to an object reference and compares its runtime state s' to the states s named in the cases. It executes the first case for which s' is a subtype of s, with a runtime error if there is no match. $v.f$=e updates the object in the field $v.f$ to the value of e, which it also returns as the result of the expression. `new` s creates an object of state s and initializes its fields by running the initializer expressions given in the state definition. The sequence expression evaluates each of its subexpressions in order and returns the result of the last one as the value of the whole expression.

Programs	P	$S^*\ e$
States	S	`state` s `case of` s `{` $F^*\ M^*$ `}`
Fields	F	$T\ f$=e;
Methods	M	$T\ m(\pi$>>$\pi\ s\ x)\ \pi$>>π `{` e `}`
Permissions	π	`unique` | `none` | σ | `local` σ
	σ	`immutable` | `shared`
Types	T	$\pi\ s$
Expressions	e	`let` $\pi\ x$=e `in` e | $e.m(e)$ | v | $v.f$ | $v.f$=e | `match`(e) $\{(s$=>$e;)^+\}$ | `new` s | $\{(e;)^+\}$
Variables	v	`this` | x

Figure 7. Core language syntax. s, f, m, and x are identifiers.

3.2 Static Semantics

We introduce our static semantics by formalizing the notions of states and permissions. We then define the ways that permissions are manipulated and show how the flow of permissions is integrated into the type system.

States: States take the place of standard types in our system. Figure 8 gives the judgments and rules relating to states. $P \vdash s$ says a state is valid if it is declared in P. $P \vdash s \leq s'$ says that s is a substate of s'. Substate relations are defined by the `case of` relation from the state definitions, reflexivity, and transitivity.

$\boxed{P \vdash s}$

TYPE-STATE
$$\frac{\texttt{state}\ s\ \texttt{case of}\ s'\ \{\ F^*\ M^*\ \} \in P}{P \vdash s}$$

$\boxed{P \vdash s \leq s'}$

SUBSTATE
$$\frac{\texttt{state}\ s\ \texttt{case of}\ s'\ \{\ F^*\ M^*\ \} \in P}{P \vdash s \leq s'}$$

SUBTYPE-REFLEXIVE
$$P \vdash s \leq s$$

SUBSTATE-TRANSITIVE
$$\frac{P \vdash s \leq s' \qquad P \vdash s' \leq s''}{P \vdash s \leq s''}$$

Figure 8. Valid states and substates.

$\boxed{\pi \Rrightarrow \pi' \otimes \pi''}$

SPLIT-UNIQUE-LOCAL
$$\texttt{unique} \Rrightarrow \texttt{local}\ \sigma \otimes \mathsf{borrow}(\texttt{unique}, \sigma, 1)$$

SPLIT-LOCAL
$$\texttt{local}\ \sigma \Rrightarrow \texttt{local}\ \sigma \otimes \mathsf{borrow}(\texttt{local}\ \sigma, \sigma, 0)$$

SPLIT-LOCAL-INCREMENT
$$\mathsf{borrow}(\pi, \sigma, n) \Rrightarrow \texttt{local}\ \sigma \otimes \mathsf{borrow}(\pi, \sigma, n+1)$$

SPLIT-NONE
$$\pi \Rrightarrow \texttt{none} \otimes \pi$$

SPLIT-UNIQUE-SYMMETRIC
$$\texttt{unique} \Rrightarrow \sigma \otimes \sigma$$

SPLIT-SYMMETRIC
$$\sigma \Rrightarrow \sigma \otimes \sigma$$

SPLIT-SYMMETRIC-LOCAL
$$\sigma \Rrightarrow \texttt{local}\ \sigma \otimes \sigma$$

SPLIT-UNIQUE
$$\texttt{unique} \Rrightarrow \texttt{unique} \otimes \texttt{none}$$

Figure 9. Splitting variable permissions.

Permissions: To the set of source permissions we add an additional form needed to track `local` permissions so they can be joined back to `unique`:

$$\pi ::= \ldots \mid \mathsf{borrow}(\pi, \sigma, n),$$

where n is a natural number. The borrow permission appears only in the context for a local variable or field that has had local permissions split from it. Inside borrow, π represents the original permission before the first split (`unique` or `local` σ), σ represents the kind of local permission borrowed (`immutable` or `shared`), and n counts the number of borrowings.

Splitting variable permissions: The judgment $\pi \Rrightarrow \pi' \otimes \pi''$ says that if variable v has permission π, then π' can be taken out of v leaving π'' in v. Figure 9 gives the rules for this judgment. Notice that SPLIT-UNIQUE-SYMMETRIC permanently splits `unique` into symmetric permissions, making it impossible to ever regain the `unique` permission. In contrast, the SPLIT-LOCAL-* rules pull a `local` permission and leave behind a borrow permission which will be turned back into the original permission when all the `local` permissions are returned. In these rules, the count is set to reflect the net gain in `local` permissions: splitting a `local` from a `unique` generates a new `local`, so the count starts at 1 (SPLIT-UNIQUE-LOCAL); pulling from an existing `local` replaces the original `local` with a borrow, resulting in no net gain in `local` permissions, so the count starts at 0 (SPLIT-LOCAL); taking a `local` from an existing borrow creates a new `local` and thus increments the count (SPLIT-LOCAL-INCREMENT). Also, SPLIT-SYMMETRIC-LOCAL says we may pull `local` σ out of σ. However, we can't get a non-`local` permission out of a `local`, so (in conjunction with the FIELD typing rule) we can't store local permissions to the heap.

$$\boxed{\pi_1 \,.\, \pi_2 \Rrightarrow \pi_3 \otimes \pi_4}$$

SPLIT-FIELD-UNIQUE
$$\frac{\pi \Rrightarrow \pi' \otimes \pi''}{\texttt{unique} \,.\, \pi \Rrightarrow \pi' \otimes \pi''}$$

SPLIT-FIELD-PRESERVE
$$\frac{\pi \neq \texttt{none} \qquad \pi' \Rrightarrow \pi'' \otimes \pi'}{\pi \,.\, \pi' \Rrightarrow \pi'' \otimes \pi'}$$

SPLIT-FIELD-UNIQUE-SYMMETRIC
$$\sigma \,.\, \texttt{unique} \Rrightarrow \sigma \otimes \texttt{unique}$$

SPLIT-FIELD-LOCAL
$$\frac{\pi \Rrightarrow \texttt{local}\ \sigma \otimes \pi'}{\texttt{local}\ \sigma \,.\, \pi \Rrightarrow \texttt{local}\ \sigma \otimes \pi'}$$

SPLIT-FIELD-BORROW
$$\frac{\pi' \Rrightarrow \texttt{local}\ \sigma \otimes \pi''}{\mathsf{borrow}(\pi, \sigma, n) \,.\, \pi' \Rrightarrow \texttt{local}\ \sigma \otimes \pi''}$$

Figure 10. Splitting field permissions.

$$\boxed{\pi \otimes \pi' \Rrightarrow \pi''}$$

JOIN-NOT-UNIQUE
$$\frac{\pi'' \neq \texttt{unique} \qquad \pi'' \Rrightarrow \pi \otimes \pi'}{\pi \otimes \pi' \Rrightarrow \pi''}$$

JOIN-NOT-SYMMETRIC
$$\frac{\neg\exists\sigma.(\pi = \sigma \wedge \pi' = \sigma) \qquad \pi'' \Rrightarrow \pi \otimes \pi'}{\pi \otimes \pi' \Rrightarrow \pi''}$$

Figure 11. Joining permissions.

Splitting field permissions: The judgment $\pi_1 \,.\, \pi_2 \Rrightarrow \pi_3 \otimes \pi_4$ says that if variable v has permission π_1, and field $v \,.\, f$ has permission π_2, then permission π_3 can be taken out of f, leaving π_4 behind. Figure 10 gives the rules. If the variable permission is `unique`, we can split permissions from the field as if it were a variable (SPLIT-FIELD-UNIQUE), possibly unpacking the field. Otherwise, we allow splitting in three cases. First, if the variable permission is not `none`, then we can do any splitting allowed for variables that preserves the original field permission (SPLIT-FIELD-PRESERVE). Second, if the variable permission is σ, then we can take permission σ out of a `unique` field $v \,.\, f$ without unpacking the object (SPLIT-FIELD-UNIQUE-SYMMETRIC). This is sound because all other references to the object must have permission σ for the remainder of program execution, and so all other accesses will consistently see the field with permission σ. Third, if the variable permission is `local` or borrow, then we can take a matching `local` permission out of a field with `unique` or borrow permission (SPLIT-FIELD-LOCAL, SPLIT-FIELD-BORROW). This is sound because all `local` permissions to the object and to the field must go out of scope before a `unique` permission to the object can be regained. In the mean time, all references to the object and to the field have compatible `local` or borrow permissions.

Joining permissions: The judgment $\pi \otimes \pi' \Rrightarrow \pi''$ says that permissions π and π' may be joined to form permission π''. The joining rules, given in Figure 11, are very simple: we just reverse all the variable splitting rules, except for SPLIT-UNIQUE-SYMMETRIC, which can't be undone.

Linear Context: To track permission flow, our typing rules use a *linear context*. It is similar to a standard typing environment, except that it maps variables to types that include a permission that may change over the course of typing. The linear context Δ is defined as follows, where i is chosen from an arbitrary set of identifiers:

$$\Delta ::= \varnothing \mid v : (T; \Pi), \Delta \qquad \Pi ::= \varnothing \mid f : (\pi, i), \Pi$$

For each variable v in scope, Δ stores a type $T = \pi\ s$ and a set Π containing the *unpacked state* $f : (\pi', i)$ of the fields f in the state s. A field $f : (\pi', i) \in \Pi$ records two pieces of information. First, π' indicates the current permission in the field. f will only appear in the unpacked state of v if π' is distinct from the declared permission of the field f in the state of v. Second, the object identifier i is used to prevent the restoration of permissions from one object to another object. For any $v : (T; \Pi) \in \Delta$ and field f declared in the state of v, if there exists $f : (\pi, i) \in \Pi$, then we say "the field f of v is unpacked"; otherwise we say "the field f of v is packed." By extension, if $\Pi = \varnothing$, then we say the object pointed to by v (or just v) is packed; otherwise it is unpacked.

$$\boxed{P; \Delta; \pi \vdash \ell^* : \Delta'}$$

RESTORE-EMPTY
$$P; \Delta; \pi \vdash\ : \Delta$$

RESTORE-VAR
$$\frac{\Delta = v : (\pi'\ s; \Pi), \Delta' \qquad \pi \otimes \pi' \Rrightarrow \pi'' \qquad P; v : (\pi''\ s; \Pi), \Delta'; \pi \vdash \ell^* : \Delta''}{P; \Delta; \pi \vdash \ell^*, v : \Delta''}$$

RESTORE-VAR-ABSENT
$$\frac{\neg\exists T, \Pi.(v : (T; \Pi) \in \Delta) \qquad P; \Delta; \pi \vdash \ell^* : \Delta'}{P; \Delta; \pi \vdash \ell^*, v : \Delta'}$$

RESTORE-FIELD-PACKED
$$\frac{v : (T; \Pi) \in \Delta \qquad \mathsf{packed}(f, \Pi) \qquad P; \Delta; \pi \vdash \ell^* : \Delta'}{P; \Delta; \pi \vdash \ell^*, (v \,.\, f, i) : \Delta'}$$

RESTORE-FIELD-STALE
$$\frac{v : (T; \Pi, f : (\pi'', j)) \in \Delta \qquad i \neq j \qquad P; \Delta; \pi \vdash \ell^* : \Delta'}{P; \Delta; \pi \vdash \ell^*, (v \,.\, f, i) : \Delta'}$$

RESTORE-FIELD-UNPACKED
$$\frac{\begin{array}{c}\Delta = v : (\pi\ s; \Pi, f : (\pi_2, i)), \Delta' \qquad \mathsf{field\text{-}type}(P, s, f) = \pi'\ s' \\ \pi_1 \otimes \pi_2 \Rrightarrow \pi_3 \qquad \pi_3 \neq \pi' \qquad P; v : (\pi\ s; \Pi, f : (\pi_3, i)), \Delta'; \pi_1 \vdash \ell^* : \Delta''\end{array}}{P; \Delta; \pi_1 \vdash \ell^*, (v \,.\, f, i) : \Delta''}$$

RESTORE-FIELD-PACK
$$\frac{\begin{array}{c}\Delta = v : (\pi\ s; \Pi, f : (\pi_2, i)), \Delta' \qquad \mathsf{field\text{-}type}(P, s, f) = \pi_3\ s' \\ \pi_1 \otimes \pi_2 \Rrightarrow \pi_3 \qquad P; v : (\pi\ s; \Pi), \Delta'; \pi_1 \vdash \ell^* : \Delta''\end{array}}{P; \Delta; \pi_1 \vdash \ell^*, (v \,.\, f, i) : \Delta''}$$

Figure 12. Restoring permissions. The predicate $\mathsf{packed}(f, \Pi)$ is true if no binding for f appears in Π. $\mathsf{field\text{-}type}(P, s, f) = T$ says that field f is defined in state s with type T in the program P.

Restoring Permissions: At certain points in the typing, permissions flow back into the linear context, such as when a let-bound variable goes out of scope. We restore permissions to a *source location list* consisting of zero or more elements ℓ:

$$\ell ::= v \mid (v \,.\, f, i).$$

Each element ℓ stores a location to restore to (either a variable v or a field $v \,.\, f$). For fields $v \,.\, f$, the identifiers i ensure that we restore permissions only to fields that have not been assigned to since the permission was taken out. We use a list because `match` expressions may report different source locations for each `case`. However, we do not allow duplicates in the list.

The judgment for restoring permissions is $P; \Delta; \pi \vdash \ell^* : \Delta'$. It says that if we start with context Δ and join permission π with the permission in each location in ℓ^*, then we get a new context Δ'. Figure 12 gives the rules for this judgment. If the next element in the source location list is a variable appearing in the context, then we restore the permission to it (RESTORE-VAR). Because we do not check that all of the locations in a source location list remain valid when passed outside of a let scope, it is possible that the variable may not be in the context to return to, in which case we do nothing (RESTORE-VAR-ABSENT).

When restoring to a field, there are several cases to consider. If the field is already packed, this means that pulling the permission did not unpack the field (left it unchanged) or the field was reassigned since the permission was pulled, so we do nothing (RESTORE-FIELD-PACKED). If the field is unpacked, and the

$$\boxed{\Delta_3 = \mathsf{merge}(\Delta_1, \Delta_2)}$$

MERGE-PACKED

$$\frac{\pi_1 \Rrightarrow \pi_3 \otimes \pi_2 \vee \pi_2 = \texttt{none}}{v : (\pi_2\ s; \varnothing) = \mathsf{merge}(v : (\pi_1\ s; \varnothing), v : (\pi_2\ s; \varnothing))}$$

MERGE-ONE-UNPACKED

$$\frac{\Pi \neq \varnothing \qquad \pi_1 \Rrightarrow \pi_3 \otimes \pi_2 \vee \pi_2 = \texttt{none}}{v : (\pi_2\ s, \Pi) = \mathsf{merge}(v : (\pi_1\ s; \varnothing), v : (\pi_2\ s; \Pi))}$$

MERGE-UNPACKED-EQUAL

$$\frac{v : (\pi_1\ s, \Pi_3) = \mathsf{merge}(v : (\pi_1\ s; \Pi_1), v : (\pi_1\ s; \Pi_2)) \qquad \pi_1 \,.\, \pi_2 \Rrightarrow \pi_4 \otimes \pi_3 \vee \pi_3 = \texttt{none}}{v : (\pi_1\ s; \Pi_3, f : (\pi_3, i)) = \mathsf{merge}(v : (\pi_1\ s; \Pi_1, f : (\pi_2, i)), v : (\pi_1\ s; \Pi_2, f : (\pi_3, i))}$$

MERGE-UNPACKED-UNEQUAL

$$\frac{v : (\pi_1\ s, \Pi_3) = \mathsf{merge}(v : (\pi_1\ s; \Pi_1), v : (\pi_1\ s; \Pi_2)) \qquad \pi_1 \,.\, \pi_2 \Rrightarrow \pi_4 \otimes \pi_3 \vee \pi_3 = \texttt{none} \qquad i_1 \neq i_2 \qquad \mathsf{fresh}(i_3)}{v : (\pi_1\ s; \Pi_3, f : (\pi_3, i_3)) = \mathsf{merge}(v : (\pi_1\ s; \Pi_1, f : (\pi_2, i_1)), v : (\pi_1\ s; \Pi_2, f : (\pi_3, i_2))}$$

Figure 13. Merging contexts in typing `match` (selected rules).

identifiers in the context and the source location don't match, then we also do nothing (RESTORE-FIELD-STALE). This occurs when an expression in an inner scope assigns to the field and then later unpacks it again, meaning the returned permission represents a permission to a different object than is in the field.

If f is unpacked, and the identifiers match, then there are two cases. First, if restoring the permission doesn't leave a permission equal to the declared permission for f, then we update the unpacked state (RESTORE-FIELD-UNPACKED). Otherwise we pack up the field (RESTORE-FIELD-PACK) by removing it from Π. Notice we don't consider the case where $v\,.\,f$ appears in the location list but v doesn't appear in the context. Why not? There are two ways this could happen: either $v\,.\,f$ is returned as the value of the `let` expression that declares v, or $v\,.\,f$ is returned as the value of a method body, where v is `this` or the method formal parameter. In either case v must be packed after the evaluation of $v\,.\,f$ (rules METHOD in Figure 15 and LET in Figure 14). Therefore, $v\,.\,f$ can not appear in the source location list (see rule FIELD-ACCESS-PACKED in Figure 14).

Merging Contexts: Each `case` in a `match` expression may update the permissions in the context in a different way. The merge judgment from Figure 13 defines how to combine two contexts into a more general context that can be soundly used to type subsequent expressions regardless of which `case` is actually executed. We provide only the important rules for merging contexts Δ_1 and Δ_2; the rest of the rules are about pulling apart the contexts and comparing elements. In summary we use the following rules for merging the two context entries for a variable v:

1. If v is packed in both Δ_1 and Δ_2 (MERGE-PACKED), then we choose the weaker permission. We define π_1 to be *weaker* than π_2 if π_1 is `none` or there exists $\hat{\pi}$ such that $\pi_2 \Rrightarrow \hat{\pi} \otimes \pi_1$. If neither permission is weaker than the other, then the contexts are inconsistent and typing fails.
2. If v is unpacked in both contexts, then we require it to have the same permission in both, and we use the field splitting rules to find the weaker of the two field permissions. If the identifier i associated with the unpacked field is the same in both contexts, then we pass it through (MERGE-UNPACKED-EQUAL), but if it is different we generate a fresh identifier (MERGE-UNPACKED-UNEQUAL). This is correct but conservative because it guarantees that no permission restore will occur to the location.
3. If v is unpacked in only one context (MERGE-ONE-UNPACKED), then we use the unpacked element, but we check that the unpacked permission for v is weaker than the packed one. Otherwise, we would have to pull a permission out of an unpacked object, which is not allowed in this language.

Expressions: Permissions are pulled out of the linear context by typing expressions. The judgment $P; \Delta; \pi \vdash e : s; \Delta'; \ell^*$ takes the starting context Δ, a needed permission π, and an expression e that specifies where π could be pulled from. It produces the state s of the expression, an updated context Δ', and a source location list ℓ^* that contains all the possible locations in the context that the permission π may have been pulled from. The exact location is not statically known because which branch of a `match` expression is executed is determined at runtime. Figure 14 gives the rules for typing expressions which we now summarize.

Let: We use the permission π' declared for x to type e, obtaining state s, a context Δ', and a source location list ℓ^*. Then we use the needed permission π of the whole expression to type e' in the context Δ' augmented by the type binding for x. This produces an updated context Δ'' where x is left with permission π'', and a source location list ℓ'^*. We require that x be packed because it is going out of scope. We restore π'' to ℓ^*, the locations that the permission for x may have been pulled from, which generates a final context Δ''' that is returned along with the state and source locations from the body.

Match: For a single-case `match`, we type e with a needed permission `none` yielding some state s and an updated context Δ'. We disregard the source location lists since returning `none` is a no-op. We ensure that the state s has a common superstate with the state s_c named in the `case`. This ensures that s_c is a potentially valid state of e. Using Δ' and the needed permission for the entire expression, we type e' to get the state s' and source location list ℓ^* which are reported as the result of the `case`. For a multiple-case `match`, we recursively check the `match` with all but the first `case`. Then we check the `match` with the remaining `case` in isolation using the original context. Finally, we return the the least upper bound of the resulting states, the merged contexts, and the union of the source location lists from the first `case` and the remaining cases.

Method invocation: We type e in the input context with needed permission π_1 yielding a state s_1 and a context Δ_2.[3] Next we look up the method named m in state s_1. This gives us the permission π_2 required for the argument. We use π_2 to type e' in the context Δ_2, which yields a state s'_2 and a context Δ_3. Now we check that s'_2 conforms to the method parameter state s_2. Then we check that needed permission π can be extracted from the permission π_3 returned by the method. We generate the output context Δ_5 by restoring the output permissions specified for the argument and receiver in the method signature to their respective source location lists. The outgoing source location list is empty because our system does not track what locations the permissions returned from method calls can come from.

Variables: We require that v is packed, because its value may be assigned to another variable or stored on the heap. We also check that the existing permission can be split to give the needed permis-

[3] π_1 is the needed permission for the receiver as determined by the signature of the method m in the state s_1 of the expression e. This permission can be determined by a pre-pass that ignores permissions and just gathers state information for all variables.

$$\boxed{P;\Delta;\pi \vdash e : s;\Delta';\ell^*}$$

LET
$$\frac{P;\Delta;\pi' \vdash e : s;\Delta';\ell^* \qquad P;\Delta',x:(\pi'\ s;\varnothing);\pi \vdash e' : s';\Delta'',x:(\pi''\ s;\varnothing);\ell'^* \qquad P;\Delta'';\pi'' \vdash \ell^* : \Delta'''}{P;\Delta;\pi \vdash \texttt{let}\ \pi'\ x\ \texttt{=}\ e\ \texttt{in}\ e' : s';\Delta''';\ell'^*}$$

MATCH-SINGLE
$$\frac{P;\Delta;\texttt{none} \vdash e : s;\Delta';\ell^* \qquad \exists s_l . P \vdash s_l = \mathsf{lub}(s,s_c) \qquad P;\Delta';\pi \vdash e' : s';\Delta'';\ell'^*}{P;\Delta;\pi \vdash \texttt{match}\,(e)\,\{s_c\texttt{=>}e'\texttt{;}\} : s';\Delta'';\ell'^*}$$

MATCH-MULTIPLE
$$\frac{\begin{array}{c}P;\Delta;\pi \vdash \texttt{match}\,(e)\,\{(s_c\texttt{=>}e_1\texttt{;})^+\} : s_1;\Delta_1;{\ell_1}^* \\ P;\Delta;\pi \vdash \texttt{match}\,(e)\,\{s'_c\texttt{=>}e_2\texttt{;}\} : s_2;\Delta_2;{\ell_2}^* \\ P \vdash s_3 = \mathsf{lub}(s_1,s_2) \qquad \Delta_3 = \mathsf{merge}(\Delta_1,\Delta_2) \qquad \ell_3^* = \ell_1^* \cup \ell_2^*\end{array}}{P;\Delta;\pi \vdash \texttt{match}\,(e)\,\{(s_c\texttt{=>}e_1\texttt{;})^+\ s'_c\texttt{=>}e_2\texttt{;}\} : s_3;\Delta_3;\ell_3^*}$$

INVOKE
$$\frac{\begin{array}{c}P;\Delta_1;\pi_1 \vdash e : s_1;\Delta_2;\ell^* \\ \mathsf{method}(P,s_1,m) = \pi_3\ s_3\ \ m\,(\pi_2\texttt{>>}\pi'_2\ s_2\ \ x)\ \ \pi_1\texttt{>>}\pi'_1\ \{\ e''\ \} \qquad P;\Delta_2;\pi_2 \vdash e' : s'_2;\Delta_3;\ell'^* \\ P \vdash s'_2 \le s_2 \qquad \pi_3 \Rrightarrow \pi \otimes \pi' \qquad P;\Delta_3;\pi'_2 \vdash \ell'^* : \Delta_4 \qquad P;\Delta_4;\pi'_1 \vdash \ell^* : \Delta_5\end{array}}{P;\Delta_1;\pi \vdash e.m\,(e')\ : s_3;\Delta_5;\varnothing}$$

VAR
$$\frac{\Delta = \Delta',v:(\pi'\ s;\varnothing) \qquad \pi' \Rrightarrow \pi \otimes \pi'' \qquad \Delta'' = \Delta',v:(\pi''\ s;\varnothing)}{P;\Delta;\pi \vdash v : s;\Delta'';v}$$

FIELD-ACCESS-PACKED
$$\frac{v:(\pi'\ s;\Pi) \in \Delta \qquad \mathsf{packed}(f,\Pi) \qquad \mathsf{field\text{-}type}(P,s,f) = \pi''\ s' \qquad \pi'.\pi'' \Rrightarrow \pi \otimes \pi''}{P;\Delta;\pi \vdash v.f : s';\Delta;\varnothing}$$

FIELD-ACCESS-UNPACK
$$\frac{\begin{array}{c}\Delta = \Delta',v:(\pi_1\ s;\Pi) \qquad \mathsf{packed}(f,\Pi) \qquad \mathsf{field\text{-}type}(P,s,f) = \pi_2\ s' \\ \pi_1.\pi_2 \Rrightarrow \pi_3 \otimes \pi_4 \qquad \pi_2 \ne \pi_4 \qquad \mathsf{fresh}(i) \qquad \Delta'' = \Delta',v:(\pi_1\ s;\Pi,f:(\pi_4,i))\end{array}}{P;\Delta;\pi_3 \vdash v.f : s';\Delta'';(v.f,i)}$$

FIELD-ACCESS-UNPACKED
$$\frac{\begin{array}{c}\Delta = \Delta',v:(\pi_1\ s;\Pi,f:(\pi_2,i)) \qquad \mathsf{field\text{-}type}(P,s,f) = \pi_3\ s' \\ \pi_1.\pi_2 \Rrightarrow \pi_4 \otimes \pi_5 \qquad \Delta'' = \Delta',v:(\pi_1\ s;\Pi,f:(\pi_5,i))\end{array}}{P;\Delta;\pi_4 \vdash v.f : s';\Delta'';(v.f,i)}$$

FIELD-ASSIGN-PACKED
$$\frac{\begin{array}{c}v:(\pi_1\ s_1;\Pi) \in \Delta \qquad \mathsf{field\text{-}type}(P,s_1,f) = \pi_2\ s_2 \\ P;\Delta;\pi_2 \vdash e : s_3;\Delta';\ell^* \qquad v:(\pi_3\ s_1;\Pi') \in \Delta' \qquad \mathsf{assignable}(\pi_3) \\ \mathsf{packed}(f,\Pi') \qquad P \vdash s_3 \le s_2 \qquad \pi_2 \Rrightarrow \pi \otimes \pi_2 \qquad \Delta''' = \Delta'',v:(\pi_3\ s_1;\Pi')\end{array}}{P;\Delta;\pi \vdash v.f\texttt{=}e : s_3;\Delta''';\varnothing}$$

FIELD-ASSIGN-UNPACKED
$$\frac{\begin{array}{c}v:(\pi_1\ s_1;\Pi) \in \Delta \qquad \mathsf{field\text{-}type}(P,s_1,f) = \pi_2\ s_2 \qquad P;\Delta;\pi_2 \vdash e : s_3;\Delta_1;\ell^* \\ \Delta_1 = \Delta_2,v:(\pi_3\ s_1;\Pi',f:(\pi_4,i)) \qquad \mathsf{assignable}(\pi_3) \qquad P \vdash s_3 \le s_2 \qquad \pi_2 \Rrightarrow \pi \otimes \pi_2 \qquad \Delta_3 = \Delta_2,v:(\pi_3\ s_1;\Pi')\end{array}}{P;\Delta;\pi \vdash v.f\texttt{=}e : s_3;\Delta_3;\varnothing}$$

NEW
$$\frac{P \vdash s}{P;\Delta;\pi \vdash \texttt{new}\ \ s : s;\Delta;\varnothing}$$

SEQUENCE-SINGLE
$$\frac{P;\Delta;\pi \vdash e : s;\Delta';\ell^*}{P;\Delta;\pi \vdash \{e\texttt{;}\} : s;\Delta';\ell^*}$$

SEQUENCE-MULTIPLE
$$\frac{P;\Delta;\texttt{none} \vdash \{(e\texttt{;})^+\} : s;\Delta';\ell^* \qquad P;\Delta';\pi \vdash \{e'\texttt{;}\} : s';\Delta'';\ell'^*}{P;\Delta;\pi \vdash \{(e\texttt{;})^+\ e'\texttt{;}\} : s';\Delta'';\ell'^*}$$

Figure 14. Typing expressions. $P \vdash s = \mathsf{lub}(s',s'')$ means s is the least state that is a superstate of both s' and s''. $\mathsf{method}(P,s,m) = M$ means that M is the method named m defined in state s for program P, and $\mathsf{field\text{-}type}(P,s,f) = T$ similarly produces the type T of field f from s in P. The predicate $\mathsf{assignable}(\pi)$ holds if π is not `none`, `immutable`, `local immutable`, or $\mathsf{borrow}(\texttt{local immutable},\texttt{immutable},n)$. $\mathsf{packed}(f,\Pi)$ means $\neg\exists(\pi,i).(f:(\pi,i) \in \Pi)$.

sion, and we leave the residue in the type reported in the outgoing context. The source expression list contains only the variable itself.
Field access: We start by finding the type of v in the context and then get the defined type of field f in its state s. Since we are only accessing the field of v, we do not update the permission of v. However, we may need to update the unpacked state of f in v. If f starts packed in v's type, then there are two cases to handle. First, if we can take the required permission out of the field and leave the same permission behind, then we leave the object packed (FIELD-ACCESS-PACKED). The source expression list is empty because no permission needs to be restored to a field that is packed. Second, if we need to leave a different residual permission, then we unpack the field, leaving the residual permission behind (FIELD-ACCESS-UNPACK). We also generate a fresh identifier i and report $(v.f,i)$ as the source location list. If f is already unpacked in v, then we split the needed permission from the current field permission, and replace the current permission in the unpacked field state with the residual permission (FIELD-ACCESS-UNPACKED). We report $(v.f,i)$ as the source location, using the existing identifier i.
Field assignment: If $v.f$ is packed, then to assign e to it we (1) look in the context to get the permission we need for the field; (2) type e; (3) check that we have writable permission to v in the resulting context; and (4) check that the states match (FIELD-ASSIGN-PACKED). We also ensure that the permission we need can be split off from the permission needed by the field, while retaining the field permission. If $v.f$ is unpacked, then we do the same thing, but we pack up f at the end (FIELD-ASSIGN-UNPACKED). In both cases, we do not need to return permissions to the source locations of e because what's left after assigning to $v.f$ must be `none` or symmetric and returning either is a no-op. For the same reason, the returned source location list is empty.
Object creation and expression sequence: These rules are straightforward. In SEQUENCE-MULTIPLE, notice that we pull the needed permission only for the last element in the sequence, whose value is returned by evaluating the expression; we pull `none` from the rest of the expressions in the sequence. For example, if `x` is `unique`, it is legal to request a `unique` permission from the expression `{x;x;x;}`, because `unique` is only pulled from the last `x`. Since returning a `none` permission is a no-op, we can safely discard the source location lists for these expressions.
Top-Level Program Structure: Figure 15 gives the rules for typing programs, states, fields, and methods. In rule PROGRAM we type the main expression with a needed permission `none`, because no permission to the result is needed after program execution is complete. In rule FIELD we type the initializer expression in the empty environment to ensure that `this` isn't stored to the heap by a `new` expression. Also, we require that user-declared field types cannot be declared with `local` permissions (borrow permissions are also excluded because they cannot appear in the source). This restriction ensures that a local permission is never assigned to the

$$\boxed{\vdash P}\qquad \textsc{Program}\ \frac{P = S^*\ e \qquad \forall S \in S^*.(P \vdash S) \qquad P;\varnothing;\mathtt{none} \vdash e : s;\varnothing;\ell^*}{\vdash P}$$

$$\boxed{P \vdash S}\qquad \textsc{State}\ \frac{\mathtt{state}\ s'\ \mathtt{case\ of}\ s''\ \{\ F'^*\ \ M'^*\ \} \in P \qquad \forall F \in F^*.(P \vdash F) \qquad \forall M \in M^*.(P, s \vdash M)}{P \vdash \mathtt{state}\ s\ \mathtt{case\ of}\ s'\ \{\ F^*\ \ M^*\ \}}$$

$$\boxed{P \vdash F}\qquad \textsc{Field}\ \frac{T = \pi\ s \qquad P \vdash s \qquad \neg\exists\sigma.(\pi = \mathtt{local}\ \ \sigma) \qquad P;\varnothing;\pi \vdash e : s';\varnothing;\ell^* \qquad P \vdash s' \le s}{P \vdash T\ \ f\mathtt{=}e\mathtt{;}}$$

$$\boxed{P, s \vdash M}\qquad \textsc{Method}\ \frac{P \vdash s \qquad P \vdash s_2 \qquad \Delta = \mathtt{this} : (\pi_1\ s_1;\varnothing), x : (\pi_2\ \ s_2;\varnothing) \qquad P;\Delta;\pi \vdash e : s', \Delta';\ell^* \qquad \mathtt{this} : (\pi_1'\ \ s_1;\varnothing), x : (\pi_2'\ \ s_2;\varnothing) \in \Delta' \qquad P \vdash s' \le s}{P, s_1 \vdash \pi\ s\ \ m\,\mathtt{(}\pi_2\mathtt{>>}\pi_2'\ \ s_2\ \ x\mathtt{)}\ \ \pi_1\mathtt{>>}\pi_1'\ \ \{\ e\ \}}$$

Figure 15. Programs, states, fields, and methods.

heap. In rule METHOD we check that the return type and parameters are valid. We check that the method body types in the context created by binding the method receiver and parameter to their types and that the resulting state is a substate of the return state. We require that the parameter and receiver be packed in the the output context Δ' and also that their permissions in Δ' agree with the output permissions given by their change types.

For simplicity, we implicitly disallow overriding, shadowing, and/or overloading of fields and methods. We also disallow cycles in the inheritance hierarchy and treat the set of states as a forest of trees, where a state s is a root if it has itself as a parent.

3.3 Dynamic Semantics

An execution state $H; e$ includes a heap H and an expression e.
Heap: Our model of the heap H is a partial function from object references to object identifiers and from object identifiers to objects. The addition of *object references* provide an additional level of indirection that allows us to explicitly track and reason about different aliases to a single object as in [28]. These serve a formal purpose only and are not necessary in an implementation. Consistent with this indirection, the fields of an object dF^* map field names to object references. Every object reference in $\mathsf{dom}(H)$ maps to an object identifier except the special reference null, which is used during object initialization.

$$\begin{array}{rcl} H & ::= & \mathsf{null} \mid o \mapsto O, H \mid O \mapsto s\{dF^*\}, H \\ dF & ::= & f \mapsto o \end{array}$$

Expressions: We enhance our expression language to support partially-executed programs. We add object references o as well as the new form `alias(`o`)` as expressions. `alias(`o`)` gives computational meaning to splitting a permission of o by creating a new alias to hold the split permission. As `alias` expressions will be substituted for bound variables in `let` bodies, we allow them to appear wherever variables can. Finally, we add a partial let form that keeps track of the scope in which an object reference o is bound.

$$\begin{array}{rcl} e & ::= & \ldots \mid o \mid \mathtt{alias(}o\mathtt{)} \mid \mathtt{alias(}o\mathtt{)}.f \mid \mathtt{alias(}o\mathtt{)}.f = e \mid \\ & & \mathtt{let}\ o\ \mathtt{in}\ e \end{array}$$

Reduction Rules: We formalize program execution using a small step operational semantics. Given a program P, the reduction rules shown in Figure 16 take one execution state to another.
Congruence: We specify reduction of subexpressions using an evaluation context E defined below:

$$\begin{array}{rcl} E & ::= & \square \mid \mathtt{let}\ \pi\ x\mathtt{=}E\ \mathtt{in}\ e \mid \mathtt{let}\ o\ \mathtt{in}\ E \mid \\ & & \mathtt{match(}E\mathtt{)}\ \{(s\mathtt{=>}e\mathtt{;})^+\} \mid E.m\mathtt{(}e\mathtt{)} \mid \\ & & o.m\mathtt{(}E\mathtt{)} \mid \mathtt{alias(}o\mathtt{)}.f\mathtt{=}E \mid \{E\mathtt{;}\ \ (e\mathtt{;})^*\} \end{array}$$

As usual, $\square$ is a "hole" that is filled in with the subexpression under evaluation to construct the entire expression being evaluated.

Alias: Reducing an `alias(`o`)` expression creates a fresh object reference that points to the same object identifier as the original object reference.
Let: Once the bound expression is reduced to an object reference o we substitute `alias(`o`)` for all occurrences of the bound variable x in the body. Thus, any use of x in the body must create a fresh alias. We also keep track of the scope of o by reducing to the partial let form. Once the body of a partial let has been evaluated to an object reference we remove the scoping annotation.
Match: Once the selector expression becomes an object reference o, we select the first match case, if any, that is a superstate of the state of o. If there is no match, then execution gets stuck.
Method invocation: Once we have object references for the receiver and argument of the method, we substitute the method body surrounded by let expressions binding the receiver and argument. This allows let reduction to handle the substitution and scoping.
Object creation: We create a new object identifier O and give its fields the reference null, which will be replaced by the proper values after running the initializer expressions. We reduce to a sequence expression which initializes each field of the object in turn through a fresh object reference o. The final expression in the sequence returns o.
Field access and assignment: A field access evaluates to a fresh alias to the object reference the heap associates with the field. Field assignment replaces the object reference in the field with object reference from evaluating the right-hand side. It returns a fresh alias of this same reference. Since we do not use the target of the field read or assignment except to access its field, we do not need a new alias to it, so we leave the `alias(`o`)` in the target unevaluated.
Sequence: Each expression in the sequence is evaluated in order until there are no further expressions at which point the sequence is reduced to the object reference resulting from the reduction of the final expression.

3.4 Soundness Results

In this section, we present the main soundness results and supporting definitions for our system. Our technical report [23] contains the full definitions and proofs.
Typing of Dynamic Expressions: We state and prove soundness in terms of a standard dynamic typing. To do this, we need rules for typing object references, `alias` expressions, and partial lets.

First, we enhance the definition of the linear context to map object references to types. We also add entries of the form $\ell \Leftarrow o$ to the context which indicate that o returns its permission to the source location ℓ when it leaves scope. We will also want to be able to return permissions to object references, so we extend the definition of source locations to include them.

$$\begin{array}{rcl} \Delta & ::= & \ldots \mid o : (\pi\ s, \Pi), \Delta \mid \ell \Leftarrow o, \Delta \\ \ell & ::= & \ldots \mid o \mid (o.f,i) \end{array}$$

$$\boxed{P \vdash H; e \to H'; e'}$$

E-CONGRUENCE
$$\frac{P \vdash H; e \to H'; e'}{P \vdash H; E[e] \to H'; E[e']}$$

E-ALIAS
$$\frac{H = H', o \mapsto O \qquad o' \notin \mathsf{dom}(H) \qquad H'' = H, o' \mapsto O}{P \vdash H; \texttt{alias}(o) \to H''; o'}$$

E-LET-BINDING
$$\frac{}{P \vdash H; \texttt{let}\ \pi\, x\ \texttt{=}\ o\ \texttt{in}\ e \to H; \texttt{let}\ o\ \texttt{in}\ e[x \leftarrow \texttt{alias}(o)]}$$

E-LET-BODY
$$\frac{H = H', o \mapsto O}{P \vdash H; \texttt{let}\ o\ \texttt{in}\ o' \to H'; o'}$$

E-MATCH
$$\frac{H = H', o \mapsto O \qquad O \mapsto s\{dF^*\} \in H' \qquad P \vdash s \le s_j \qquad \neg\exists k \in [1, j-1].(P \vdash s \le s_k)}{P \vdash H; \texttt{match}\ o\ \{(s_i \Rightarrow e_i)_{i \in [1,n]}\} \to H'; e_j}$$

E-INVOKE
$$\frac{H = H', o \mapsto O, O \to s\{dF^*\} \qquad \mathsf{method}(P, s, m) = \pi_3\ s\ m\,(\pi_2 \texttt{>>} \pi_2'\ s'\ x)\ \pi_1 \texttt{>>} \pi_1'\ \{\ e\ \}}{P \vdash H; o.m(o') \to H; \texttt{let}\ \pi_1\ \texttt{this=}o\ \texttt{in}\ \texttt{let}\ \pi_2\ x\texttt{=}o'\ \texttt{in}\ e}$$

E-FIELD
$$\frac{H = H', o \mapsto O, O \mapsto s\{dF, f \mapsto o'\}, o' \mapsto O' \qquad o'' \notin \mathsf{dom}(H) \qquad H'' = H, o'' \mapsto O'}{P \vdash H; \texttt{alias}(o)\texttt{.}f \to H''; o''}$$

E-ASSIGN
$$\frac{H; \texttt{alias}(o') \to H'; o'' \qquad H' = H'', o \mapsto O, O \mapsto s\{dF^*, f \mapsto o'''\} \qquad H''' = H'', o \mapsto O, O \mapsto s\{dF^*, f \mapsto o'\}}{P \vdash H; \texttt{alias}(o)\texttt{.}f\texttt{=}o' \to H'''; o''}$$

E-NEW
$$\frac{\texttt{state}\ s\ \texttt{case of}\ s'\ \{\ (\pi_i\ s_i\ f_i\texttt{=}e_i)_{i \in [1,n]}\ M^*\ \} \in P \qquad o, O \notin \mathsf{dom}(H) \qquad H' = H, o \to O, O \mapsto s\{(f_i \mapsto \mathsf{null})_{i \in [1,n]}\}}{P \vdash H; \texttt{new}\ s \to H'; \{(\texttt{alias}(o)\texttt{.}f_i = e_i\texttt{;})_{i \in [1,n]}\ o\texttt{;}\}}$$

E-SEQUENCE-SINGLE
$$\frac{}{P \vdash H; \{o\texttt{;}\} \to H; o}$$

E-SEQUENCE-MULTIPLE
$$\frac{H = H', o \mapsto O}{P \vdash H; \{o\texttt{;}\ (e\texttt{;})^+\} \to H'; \{(e\texttt{;})^+\}}$$

Figure 16. Reduction rules.

ALIAS
$$\frac{\Delta = \Delta', o : (\pi'\ s; \varnothing) \qquad \pi' \Rrightarrow \pi \otimes \pi'' \qquad \Delta'' = \Delta', o : (\pi''\ s; \varnothing)}{P; \Delta; \pi \vdash \texttt{alias}(o) : s; \Delta''; o}$$

OBJECT-REF
$$\frac{\Delta = \Delta', o : (\pi'\ s; \varnothing), \ell \Leftarrow o \qquad \pi' \Rrightarrow \pi \otimes \pi'' \qquad \Delta'' = \Delta', \ell \Leftarrow o}{P; \Delta; \pi \vdash o : s; \Delta''; \ell}$$

ALIAS-FIELD-ACCESS
$$\frac{x \notin \mathsf{dom}(\Delta) \qquad P; \Delta, x : (\pi'\ s', \Pi'); \pi \vdash x\texttt{.}f : s; \Delta, x : (\pi'\ s', \Pi''); \ell^*}{P; \Delta, o : (\pi'\ s', \Pi'); \pi \vdash \texttt{alias}(o)\texttt{.}f : s; \Delta, o : (\pi'\ s', \Pi''); \ell^*[x \leftarrow o]}$$

ALIAS-FIELD-ASSIGN
$$\frac{x \notin \mathsf{dom}(\Delta) \qquad P; \Delta, x : (\pi'\ s', \Pi'); \pi \vdash x\texttt{.}f = e : s; \Delta', x : (\pi''\ s', \Pi''); \varnothing}{P; \Delta, o : (\pi'\ s', \Pi'); \pi \vdash \texttt{alias}(o)\texttt{.}f = e : s; \Delta', o : (\pi''\ s', \Pi''); \varnothing}$$

LET-PARTIAL
$$\frac{\Delta = \Delta', o : (\pi'\ s', \Pi'), \ell \Leftarrow o \qquad P; \Delta; \pi \vdash e : \pi\ s; \Delta'', o : (\pi''\ s', \varnothing), \ell \Leftarrow o; \ell^* \qquad P; \Delta'', \pi'' \vdash \ell : \Delta'''}{P; \Delta; \pi \vdash \texttt{let}\ o\ \texttt{in}\ e : s; \Delta'''; \ell^*}$$

Figure 17. Intermediate typing rules.

The rules for typing partial expressions are found in Figure 17. The ALIAS rule says that typing `alias(o)` proceeds by typing o like a variable. In particular, the source location is o. A raw object reference o is typed using rule OBJECT-REF which is also similar to the VAR rule with two important exceptions. First, we look in the context to find the return location specified for o. This is because we need to maintain the typing after an `alias` expression steps to an object reference. In particular, after `alias(o)` steps to o', typing o' should still return o as the source location. Second, the binding for the type of o is removed from the outgoing context to ensure that o is not used later in the program which would break our model of execution where each variable and field is tracked as a separate object reference. To type a field read or assignment after an `alias` has been substituted for the target variable ALIAS-FIELD* undoes the substitution with a fresh variable x that replaces `alias(o)`. We give x the type of o from the context when typing the updated expression and then return the resulting outputs with o put back for x in the context and source location list. LET-PARTIAL assumes the scoped object reference o is already in the context along with a return location for it. After the body is typed, the remaining permission to o is restored to its return location.

Soundness Judgments: Figure 18 shows the soundness judgments for the system. $P; \Delta; \pi \vdash H; e : \pi\ s; \hat{\Delta}; \ell^*$ is the top-level judgment and says that the runtime environment $H; e$ is well-typed with respect to a a program P, a context Δ, and a permission π. The premises of this judgment are as follows. First, the context and the heap must map the same set of object references. Second, the incoming context must be able to be partitioned into two distinct parts: Δ_e to type the expression (which produces the outputs of the judgment), and Δ_f which contains all of the object references stored in fields f in H. Third, three invariants must hold for the context and the heap: (1) consistent object permissions, (2) consistent object references, and (3) distinct fields.

Consistent object permissions: The key soundness condition of our system is that for each O, the set of references o that point to it must have *consistent* permissions in Δ. This condition captures the meaning of the permissions in our system. Figure 19 defines this consistency condition. The judgment $\mathsf{perms}(\Delta, H, O) = [\pi^*]$ forms the list of all the permissions π given to object references o that point to O in H. The judgment $[\pi^*]$ **consistent** places three requirements on this list: (1) if `unique` appears in the list, then it appears only once, and all other permissions are `none`; (2) if a $\mathsf{borrow}(\texttt{unique}, \sigma, n)$ permission appears in the list, then the number of `local` σ permissions must match the sum of the counts of all borrow permissions in the list; and (3) no list may contain both `shared` and `immutable` permissions (including the `local` and borrow versions).

Consistent object references: Object references must also be internally consistent. We say that $P; \Delta; H \vdash o$ **ok** if the representation of the object reference o in H is consistent with the type of o in

$$P;\Delta;\pi \vdash H; e : \pi\ s; \hat{\Delta}; \ell^*$$

ENV-OK

$$\frac{\{o \mid o \in \mathsf{dom}(H)\} = \{o \mid o \in \mathsf{dom}(\Delta)\} \quad \Delta = \Delta_e, \Delta_f \quad P;\Delta_e;\pi \vdash e : \pi\ s; \hat{\Delta}; \ell^* \quad \Delta_f \vdash H\ \textbf{distinct fields} \quad \forall o \in \mathsf{dom}(H).\,(P;\Delta;H \vdash o\ \textbf{ok}) \quad \forall O \in \mathsf{dom}(H).\,(\mathsf{perms}(\Delta,H,O)\ \textbf{consistent})}{P;\Delta;\pi \vdash H; e : \pi\ s;\hat{\Delta};\ell^*}$$

$$P;\Delta;H \vdash o\ \textbf{ok}$$

OBJ-REF-OK

$$\frac{\begin{array}{c} o : (\pi\ s, \Pi) \in \Delta \quad o \mapsto O, O \mapsto s'\{dF^*\} \in H \quad P \vdash s' \le s \\ \forall f \in \mathsf{fields}(P,s).\left(\begin{array}{l} f\mapsto o_f \in dF^* \wedge \pi_f\ s_f = \mathsf{dyn\text{-}field\text{-}type}(P,s,f,\Pi) \wedge o_f : (\pi'_f\ s'_f, \Pi_f) \in \Delta \wedge \\ P\vdash s'_f \le s_f \wedge \pi_f, \pi'_f \in \mathsf{validFieldPerms} \wedge \pi'_f \rhd \pi.\pi_f\end{array}\right)\end{array}}{P;\Delta;H\vdash o\ \textbf{ok}}$$

$$\pi \rhd \pi_o.\pi_f$$

FIELD-FULFILLED

$$\frac{\forall \hat\pi \in \{\pi_s \mid \exists \pi_r.\ \pi_o.\pi_f \Rrightarrow \pi_s \otimes \pi_r\}.\ \exists\hat\pi'.\pi \Rrightarrow \hat\pi\otimes\hat\pi'}{\pi \rhd \pi_o.\pi_f}$$

$$\Delta \vdash H\ \textbf{distinct fields}$$

DISTINCT-FIELDS

$$\frac{O \mapsto s\{dF^*, f\mapsto o\} \in H \wedge O' \mapsto s'\{dF'^*, f'\mapsto o\}\in H \implies o\in\mathsf{dom}(\Delta) \wedge O = O' \wedge f = f'}{\Delta\vdash H\ \textbf{distinct fields}}$$

Figure 18. Soundness judgments. $\mathsf{dyn\text{-}field\text{-}type}(P, s, f, \Pi)$ reports the permission for f in Π if it is recorded there, otherwise the declared permission of f in state s. The set $\mathsf{validFieldPerms}$ excludes permissions of the form $\texttt{local}\ \sigma$ and $\mathsf{borrow}(\texttt{local}\ \sigma, \sigma, n)$.

$$\mathsf{perms}(\Delta, H, O) = [\pi^*]$$

PERMS-NO-MATCH

$$\frac{\neg\exists o \in \mathsf{dom}(H).\, o\mapsto O \in H}{\mathsf{perms}(\Delta,H,O) = [\,]}$$

PERMS-MATCH

$$\frac{H = o\mapsto O, H' \quad o:(\pi\ s,\Pi)\in\Delta \quad \mathsf{perms}(\Delta,H',O) = [\pi'^*]}{\mathsf{perms}(\Delta,H,O) = [\pi] +\!\!+ [\pi'^*]}$$

$$[\pi^*]\ \textbf{consistent}$$

C-UNIQUE

$$\frac{}{[(\texttt{none})^*] +\!\!+\ \texttt{unique}\ \textbf{consistent}}$$

C-BORROWUNIQUE

$$\frac{\begin{array}{c} L = [(\texttt{local}\ \sigma)^*] \\ B = [(\mathsf{borrow}(\texttt{local}\ \sigma,\sigma,n_i))_{i\in[1,m]}] \quad m\ge 0 \quad n' + \sum_{i=1}^{m} n_i = |L| \end{array}}{[(\texttt{none})^*] +\!\!+ L +\!\!+ B +\!\!+ [\mathsf{borrow}(\texttt{unique},\sigma,n')]\ \textbf{consistent}}$$

C-GENERAL

$$\frac{L = [(\texttt{local}\ \sigma)^*] \quad B = [(\mathsf{borrow}(\texttt{local}\ \sigma,\sigma,n))^*]}{[(\texttt{none})^*] +\!\!+ L +\!\!+ [(\sigma)^*] +\!\!+ B\ \textbf{consistent}}$$

Figure 19. Permission lists and consistent permissions. The notation $L = [\pi^*]$ means that L is a list of permissions (with duplicates allowed). The symbol $+\!\!+$ denotes list concatenation.

Δ. For the representation to be valid we first need the actual states of the object and its fields to be substates of the states given by the type of o. Second, we do not allow a permission $\texttt{local}\ \sigma$ or $\mathsf{borrow}(\texttt{local}\ \sigma, \sigma, n)$ to appear as the permission in a field or as the permission to an object reference that represents a field. This maintains our invariant that $\texttt{local}$ permissions never appear in the heap. Finally, we require that any permission that can be pulled from a field f of the state s through o can also be pulled from the permission of the object reference that represents the field in H. Given the field type $\pi_o.\pi_f$ of f in o, we say that π_r *fulfills* $\pi_o.\pi_f$ (represented by $\pi_r \rhd \pi_o.\pi_f$) if any permission that can be split from $\pi_o.\pi_f$ can also be split from π_r. Both judgments are formalized in Figure 18.

Distinct fields: In order to carry out the typing of a partially evaluated expression we must ensure that no object reference o ever appears (1) both in a field and in the expression being typed or (2) in two different fields in H. Otherwise, typing one location could

$$P \vdash \Delta_1 \downarrow \Delta_2$$

CTX-WEAKER

$$\frac{\forall p : (\pi\ s,\Pi)\in\Delta_2.\left(\begin{array}{l}P\vdash\Delta_1\downarrow\Delta_2@p\ \wedge\\ \forall f\in\mathsf{fields}(P,s).P\vdash\Delta_1\downarrow\Delta_2@p.f\end{array}\right)}{P\vdash\Delta_1\downarrow\Delta_2}$$

$$P\vdash\Delta_1\downarrow\Delta_2@p$$

CTX-WEAKER-VAR

$$\frac{\begin{array}{c} p:(\pi_1\ s_1;\Pi_1)\in\Delta_1 \quad p:(\pi_2\ s_2;\Pi_2)\in\Delta_2 \\ \pi_1\downarrow\pi_2 \quad P\vdash s_1\le s_2\end{array}}{P\vdash\Delta_1\downarrow\Delta_2@p}$$

$$P\vdash\Delta_1\downarrow\Delta_2@p.f$$

CTX-WEAKER-FIELD

$$\frac{\begin{array}{c} p:(\pi_1\ s_1;\Pi_1)\in\Delta_1 \quad p:(\pi_2\ s_2;\Pi_2)\in\Delta_2 \\ \mathsf{dyn\text{-}field\text{-}type}(P,s_1,f,\Pi_1) = \pi'_1\ s'_1 \quad \mathsf{dyn\text{-}field\text{-}type}(P,s_2,f,\Pi_2)=\pi'_2\ s'_2 \\ \pi'_1\downarrow\pi'_2 \quad P\vdash s'_1\le s'_2\end{array}}{P\vdash\Delta_1\downarrow\Delta_2@p.f}$$

$$\pi\downarrow\pi$$

PERM-WEAKER-NONE

$$\pi\downarrow\texttt{none}$$

PERM-WEAKER

$$\frac{\exists\hat\pi.\pi_1\Rrightarrow\hat\pi\otimes\pi_2}{\pi_1\downarrow\pi_2}$$

PERM-WEAKER-BORROW

$$\texttt{unique}\downarrow\mathsf{borrow}(\texttt{unique},\sigma,n)$$

Figure 20. Weaker contexts. Meta-variable p consists of v or o and $\mathsf{fields}(P, s)$ lists the names of the fields in state s.

have a non-local impact on the permission in the other location that would be difficult to track. This invariant is captured formally by the judgment $\Delta \vdash H$ **distinct fields** in Figure 18.

Weaker Contexts: As an expression is evaluated, specific paths of execution are chosen, reducing the number of possible future execution states. Consequently, the context produced by typing the updated expression gives a more precise view of the states and permissions of locations in the program when compared to the context produced by typing the original expression. For instance, if stepping from e to e' reduces away a $\texttt{match}$ expression, then there may be locations that have permissions pulled from them when typing e but not when typing e'. This leaves more permissions in the resulting context. We introduce the *weaker* relationship between contexts to account for this increase in permissions.

The judgment $P \vdash \Delta_1 \downarrow \Delta_2$ shown in Figure 20 states that Δ_2 is weaker than Δ_1. The judgment holds if we can transform Δ_1 into Δ_2 by making specific changes to the state and permission at each location (variable or field) appearing in both Δ_1 and Δ_2. We allow the type of a location in Δ_1 to be replaced in Δ_2 with a type containing a superstate and a weaker permission ($\pi \downarrow \pi$). `none` is weaker than any permission (PERM-WEAKER-NONE). Otherwise, for permission π_2 to be weaker than π_1, there must exist a single permission $\hat{\pi}$ that can be pulled from π_1 such that the residue is π_2 (PERM-WEAKER). We also admit the special case where π_1 is `unique` and π_2 is a borrow permission (PERM-WEAKER-BORROW). This can occur, for instance, if a field with a borrow permission is reassigned in the chosen brach of a `match`.

Progress and Preservation: We use these definitions to state the soundness of our system via standard progress and preservation theorems.

Theorem 3.1 (Progress). *If $P; \Delta; \pi \vdash H; e : s; \hat{\Delta}; \ell^*$, then either $e = o$ or $P \vdash H; e \to H'; e'$ or execution is stuck at a match statement where the matched expression has been evaluated to an object, but there is no matching case.*

Theorem 3.2 (Preservation). *If $P; \Delta; \pi \vdash H; e : s; \hat{\Delta}; \ell^*$, and $P \vdash H; e \to H'; e'$, then there exists Δ' such that*

1. *$P; \Delta'; \pi \vdash H'; e' : s'; \hat{\Delta}'; \ell'^*$ with $P \vdash \hat{\Delta}' \downarrow \hat{\Delta}$ and $P \vdash s' \leq s$*
2. *$P; \hat{\Delta}; \pi \vdash (\ell^* \setminus \ell'^*) : \hat{\Delta}_r$ where $P \vdash \hat{\Delta}' \downarrow \hat{\Delta}_r$*

The first condition of preservation requires that the new environment after reduction is still well-formed, with the extra restriction that the context $\hat{\Delta}$ generated by typing the old expression e must be weaker than the context $\hat{\Delta}'$ produced by typing the updated expression e'. However, this is not strong enough because it does not account for the permissions that were pulled out as a part of typechecking which may be returned to the context later. The second condition provides the extra power we need. Consider the source location list $\ell^* \setminus \ell'^*$ representing all the source locations from which the needed permission π was pulled when typing e but that were not used to get π when typing e'. There is potentially more permission at these locations in $\hat{\Delta}'$ than in $\hat{\Delta}$ because π was not split from them during the typing of e'. However, are we guaranteed that if we restore the pulled permission to these locations in $\hat{\Delta}$ using the judgment defined in Figure 12, the resulting context $\hat{\Delta}_r$ is still weaker than $\hat{\Delta}'$? The second condition of preservation says, "Yes." This fact is necessary to prove the weakening condition on $\hat{\Delta}'$ from the first condition in some cases such as when E-CONGRUENCE is used to reduce a `let` expression. This and other details of the proof of safety are discussed in our accompanying technical report [23].

4. Related Work

Wadler first introduced the concept of temporarily converting a linear (`unique`) reference into a non-linear reference using the `let!` construct [27]. Other early uniqueness type systems built on his work and added support for borrowing as a special annotation, such as "borrowed" or "lent" [1, 19, 22]. While convenient, these systems did not support borrowing immutable pointers, and generally provided weak guarantees: multiple borrowed pointers could co-exist and interfere with one another. Boyland devised alias burying to address this issue, using shape analysis to ensure that whenever a unique variable was read, all aliases to it were dead (or "buried") [7]. While this approach works well in an analysis tool, it is inappropriate for a type system: programmers would have to understand a shape analysis to comprehend and fix a type error message. The authors of Plural [3], which also uses analysis to support borrowing, have observed this to be a problem in practice. In contrast, our system provides a more natural abstraction for reasoning by modeling the flow of permissions through locations in the source.

Boyland proposed *fractional permissions* as a generalization of borrowing that does not require a stack discipline for creating and destroying borrowed aliases [8]. Although fractions have received a lot of attention in the verification community, we know of no practical tool support that leverages fractions—possibly because programmers find fractions an unintuitive abstraction. Instead, tools like Plural [3], Chalice [17], and VeriFast [21] provide abstractions (including borrowing) that hide fractions from users, but the use of program analysis and theorem provers makes these systems less predictable and more difficult to understand than the type system presented here. Boyland and Retert later developed a type system that allows borrowing unique permissions [10]. Like our system, their system tracks permissions taken out of individual fields using a technique they call "carving." However, where they use a substructural logic for tracking permissions, we use a more predictable linear context to type individual variables.

One of the authors previously observed the importance of borrowing for tracking permissions and presented the first fraction-free permission type system we are aware of that supports borrowing unique and immutable permissions [2]. While the technical details are somewhat different, the system presented in [2], similar to this system, avoids fractions by counting split-off permissions in variable types. We propose `local` permissions to distinguish borrowed permissions syntactically, as well as `none` permissions, both of which remain implicit in [2]. Our system additionally supports share permissions, match expressions and sequences, and our system tracks permissions taken out of individual fields. Unlike [2], we provide a dynamic semantics and prove our system sound.

Other programming languages have incorporated the ideas of uniqueness and borrowing into their type systems but use less flexible or more complicated mechanisms. The Clean programming language [25] is a functional language with support for unique references. However, since the language is functional, there is no concept of returning permissions to a location as in our system.

The Vault programming language [13] allows linear (`unique`) references to be split into guarded (`immutable`) types that are valid in the scope of a key. Their use of type-level keys adds notational and algorithmic complexity to the scoping of borrowed permissions that we avoid by using our simpler local permissions. On the other hand, Vault supports adoption whereby a linear permission stored in a field of a non-linear object can be treated linearly. Vault also includes annotations on methods that consume permissions similar to our change permissions. However ours are strictly more flexible because in our richer set of permissions we can specify a partial return of a permission (e.g. `unique>>immutable`).

The Cyclone language [18] has a feature similar to Vault's keys. Cyclone also includes explicit support for borrowing through reference counting that is similar to the mechanism that underlies our `local` permissions. However, unlike our approach, it is exposed to the programmer in the syntax. Also, Cyclone allows borrowing only for permissions stored in local variables; field accesses occur via swap, which is awkward. In contrast, we have designed a field unpacking mechanism that supports direct field access.

Other recent work on the Plaid type system [28] integrates permissions with typestate and uses change types, providing some of the expressiveness of our system. While this other work can express the publication example from Figure 4, it has very limited support for borrowing, and can only change field values with a swap operation, which is unnatural for programmers.

An alternative to borrowing is explicitly "threading" references from one call to another, as supported in Alms [26]. In this approach, the permission is tied to the reference; it is given up permanently when the reference is passed to a function, but the function may return the reference again along with a permission. This approach is very clear and explicit, but it is quite awkward and furthermore results in additional writes when the result reference is re-assigned to the reference variable.

Overall, the system presented in this paper is distinguished by supporting natural programming and reasoning abstractions together with a broad set of permissions including immutable, unique, and shared. As a type system defined by local rules, it is easy for programmers to follow, and separating permission flow from references makes it more succinct than systems in which references must be threaded explicitly. We hope it will serve as a robust foundation for making permission-based programming languages such as Plaid practical enough for widespread use.

5. Conclusion and Future Work

We have described a new type system for flexible borrowing of unique, shared, and immutable permissions without explicit fractions. As future work, we would like to integrate our borrowing mechanism with Plaid's typestate features, and gain experience using the type system on larger codebases.

Acknowledgements

This material is based upon work supported by the National Science Foundation under grant #CCF-1116907, "Foundations of Permission-Based Object-Oriented Languages," grant #CCF-0811592, "Practical Typestate Verification with Assume-Guarantee Reasoning," and grant #1019343 to the Computing Research Association for the CIFellows Project. We thank the anonymous reviewers for their helpful feedback.

References

[1] J. Aldrich, V. Kostadinov, and C. Chambers. Alias Annotations for Program Understanding. In *OOPSLA*, 2002.

[2] K. Bierhoff. Automated program verification made SYMPLAR: SYMbolic Permissions for Lightweight Automated Reasoning. In *Onward!*, 2011.

[3] K. Bierhoff and J. Aldrich. Modular typestate checking of aliased objects. In *OOPSLA*, 2007.

[4] K. Bierhoff, N. E. Beckman, and J. Aldrich. Practical API protocol checking with access permissions. In *OOPSLA*, 2009.

[5] B. Bokowski and J. Vitek. Confined types. In *OOPSLA*, 1999.

[6] C. Boyapati, R. Lee, and M. Rinard. Ownership types for safe programming: preventing data races and deadlocks. In *OOPSLA*, 2002.

[7] J. Boyland. Alias Burying: Unique Variables without Destructive Reads. *Software Practice and Experience*, 6(31):533–553, 2001.

[8] J. Boyland. Checking interference with fractional permissions. In *Static Analysis Symposium*, 2003.

[9] J. Boyland, J. Noble, and W. Retert. Capabilities for sharing: A generalisation of uniqueness and read-only. In *ECOOP*, 2001.

[10] J. T. Boyland and W. Retert. Connecting Effects and Uniqueness With Adoption. In *POPL*, 2005.

[11] R. DeLine and M. Fähndrich. Enforcing high-level protocols in low-level software. In *PLDI*, 2001.

[12] R. DeLine and M. Fähndrich. Typestates for objects. In *ECOOP*, 2004.

[13] M. Fähndrich and R. DeLine. Adoption and focus: Practical linear types for imperative programming. In *PLDI*, 2002.

[14] J.-Y. Girard. Linear logic. *Theoretical Comp. Sci.*, 50(1):1–102, 1987.

[15] D. Grossman, G. Morrisett, T. Jim, M. Hicks, Y. Wang, and J. Cheney. Region-based memory management in cyclone. In *PLDI*, 2002.

[16] D. Harms and B. Weide. Copying and Swapping: Influences on the design of reusable software components. *Trans. Software Engineering*, 17(5):424–435, May 1991.

[17] S. Heule, R. Leino, P. Müller, and A. Summers. Fractional permissions without the fractions. In *FTfJP*, 2011.

[18] M. Hicks, G. Morrisett, D. Grossman, and T. Jim. Experience with safe manual memory-management in cyclone. In *ISMM*, 2004.

[19] J. Hogg. Islands: Aliasing Protection in Object-Oriented Languages. In *OOPSLA*, 1991.

[20] R. C. Holt, P. A. Matthews, J. A. Rosselet, and J. R. Cordy. *The Turing Language: Design and Definition*. Prentice-Hall, 1988.

[21] B. Jacobs, J. Smans, P. Philippaerts, F. Vogels, W. Penninckx, and F. Piessens. VeriFast: A Powerful, Sound, Predictable, Fast Verifier for C and Java. In *NASA Formal Methods*, 2011.

[22] N. H. Minsky. Towards alias-free pointers. In *ECOOP*, 1996.

[23] K. Naden, R. Bocchino, J. Aldrich, and K. Bierhoff. A type system for borrowing permissions. Technical Report CMU-CS-11-142, Computer Science Department, Carnegie Mellon University, December 2011.

[24] J. Noble, J. Vitek, and J. Potter. Flexible alias protection. In *ECOOP*. Springer, 1998.

[25] S. Smetsers, E. Barendsen, M. van Eekelen, and R. Plasmeijer. Guaranteeing safe destructive updates through a type system with uniqueness information for graphs. In *Dagstuhl Seminar on Graph Transformations in Comp. Sci.*, volume 776 of *LNCS*. Springer, 1994.

[26] J. A. Tov and R. Pucella. Practical affine types. In *POPL*, 2011.

[27] P. Wadler. Linear types can change the world! In *Working Conf. on Programming Concepts and Methods*, 1990.

[28] R. Wolff, R. Garcia, Éric Tanter, and J. Aldrich. Gradual typestate. In *ECOOP*, 2011.

Self-Certification

Bootstrapping Certified Typecheckers in F* with Coq

Pierre-Yves Strub
MSR-INRIA
pierre-yves@strub.nu

Nikhil Swamy
Microsoft Research
nswamy@microsoft.com

Cédric Fournet
Microsoft Research
fournet@microsoft.com

Juan Chen
Microsoft Research
juanchen@microsoft.com

Abstract

Well-established dependently-typed languages like Agda and Coq provide reliable ways to build and check formal proofs. Several other dependently-typed languages such as Aura, ATS, Cayenne, Epigram, F*, F7, Fine, Guru, PCML5, and Ur also explore reliable ways to develop and verify programs. All these languages shine in their own regard, but their implementations do not themselves enjoy the degree of safety provided by machine-checked verification.

We propose a general technique called *self-certification* that allows a typechecker for a suitably expressive language to be certified for correctness. We have implemented this technique for F*, a dependently typed language on the .NET platform. Self-certification involves implementing a typechecker for F* in F*, while using all the conveniences F* provides for the compiler-writer (e.g., partiality, effects, implicit conversions, proof automation, libraries). This typechecker is given a specification (in F*) strong enough to ensure that it computes valid typing derivations. We obtain a typing derivation for the core typechecker by running it on itself, and we export it to Coq as a type-derivation certificate. By typechecking this derivation (in Coq) and applying the F* metatheory (also mechanized in Coq), we conclude that our type checker is correct. Once certified in this manner, the F* typechecker is emancipated from Coq.

Self-certification leads to an efficient certification scheme—we no longer depend on verifying certificates in Coq—as well as a more broadly applicable one. For instance, the self-certified F* checker is suitable for use in adversarial settings where Coq is not intended for use, such as run-time certification of mobile code.

Categories and Subject Descriptors D.3 [*Programming Languages*]: Formal Definitions and Theory; F.3.1 [*Specifying and Verifying and Reasoning about Programs*]: Specification techniques.

General Terms Verification, Languages.

Keywords Certification, Dependent Types, Refinement Types.

1. Introduction

Well-established dependently-typed languages like Agda (Norell 2007) and Coq (2011) provide highly reliable ways to build and check formal proofs. Researchers have also developed many other dependently-typed programming languages, with different design trade-offs, such as Cayenne (Augustsson 1998), ATS (Xi 2003), Epigram (McBride 2004), Aura (Jia et al. 2008), Fable (Swamy et al. 2008), F7 (Bengtson et al. 2008), Guru (Stump et al. 2008), Fine (Swamy et al. 2010), F* (Swamy et al. 2011), PCML5 (Avijit et al. 2010), Ur (Chlipala 2010b), etc., and more are in the works, such as Trellys (Casinghino et al. 2011).

All these languages shine in their own regard, but their implementations do not themselves enjoy the degree of formal safety their authors advocate. Even with full-fledged mechanized theories in Coq, for instance, new language implementations are often *ad hoc* and disconnected from the formalized systems. One may choose to write a core typechecker for one of these languages within Coq, and possibly extract it to another language with a similar semantics (Letouzey 2008), but this involves programming compiler internals in an impoverished language of pure total functions, and a correspondingly large interactive proof obligation. Besides, Coq is not a panacea for all automated verification tasks. For example, when dealing with hostile code at run-time, more specialized, defensive verifiers may be simpler and safer. They may, for instance, fit on a smartcard or address non-functional aspects of the Coq checker, such as parsing, formatting, and error handling.

We aspire to formal certification within general-purpose programming languages and systems. To this end, we propose a bootstrapping path that allows the implementation of a core typechecker (for such a language) to be mechanically certified for correctness using an external, independent tool such as Coq.

Traditionally, bootstrapping refers to the process of compiling a compiler with itself (Hart and Levin 1962) and, more usefully, of compiling a series of increasingly complex variants of a compiler with themselves, until a fixpoint is reached (see e.g. Appel 1994). The main benefit of bootstrapping is to reduce dependencies on external languages and tools, and thus provide flexibility as the compiler evolves. For instance, one may start with a core compiler for a subset of the language on a simple architecture, then gradually add language features, compiler optimizations, and target architectures. Another benefit is to provide reasonably complex sample code for testing, and thus gain confidence in the resulting compiler. At first sight, the benefits of bootstrapping for formal verification are limited, due to incompleteness results. Instead, a common architecture is to separate a trusted, minimal *core verifier* that just checks the proofs produced (and often already verified) by more complex, extensible, interactive tools.

The main contribution of this paper is a new, general method named *self-certification* (as opposed to self-validation; see e.g. Barras 2010 for Coq) that allows a typechecker for a suitably-expressive typed language to be certified for correctness. In combination with a mechanized theory that ensures type safety, self-certification guarantees that all programs accepted by the typechecker will be safe, without further use of external formal tools.

We implement this technique for F*, a dependently-typed programming language for the .NET platform primarily used to verify the security of distributed programs and protocols. Briefly, to self-certify F*, we carry out the following tasks:

POPL'12, January 25–27, 2012, Philadelphia, PA, USA.

(1) We program a core typechecker for F* in F*, while making use of all of the conveniences that F* provides for the compiler-writer (e.g., partiality, effects, implicit conversions, proof automation, libraries, etc.). Our typechecker takes a program and its candidate type and returns a detailed typing derivation—or reports an error.

(2) We equip it with a specification (using F* types) strong enough to ensure that it returns (at most) valid typing derivations. Thus, informally, our typechecker is correct by typing.

(3) We run our typechecker on itself: we thus produce a (large) certificate for its own typing, which we export to Coq.

(4) We import and typecheck this certificate within Coq and apply the F* metatheory (also mechanized in Coq) to formally deduce first that our typechecker is correct, and then that its termination implies the safety of any program it accepts.

(5) Once certified in this manner, the F* typechecker is emancipated from Coq. We can use it independently of Coq, with essentially the same formal guarantees for the programs it accepts. Going further, we can erase the production of typing-derivation certificates, treated as irrelevant proofs.

Self-certification leads to an efficient certification scheme—after bootstrapping, we no longer depend on verifying certificates in Coq—as well as a more broadly applicable one. The self-certified F* checker is suitable in adversarial settings where Coq is not intended for use, for instance to verify and then load mobile code at runtime. We plan to use F* to certify reference implementations of security-critical infrastructure, such as TLS (Dierks and Rescorla 2008). Meanwhile, we may already certify properties previously checked by typing for security protocols coded in F7 or F* for secure multiparty sessions (Bhargavan et al. 2009), identity management systems (Bhargavan et al. 2010), and data protection APIs (Acar et al. 2010) by running our self-certified typechecker on programs much larger than itself.

An F* primer We briefly review F*, a variant of ML with a similar syntax and dynamic semantics but with a more expressive type system. F* enables general-purpose programming with recursion and effects; it has libraries for concurrency, networking, cryptography, and interoperability with other .NET languages. After typechecking, F* is compiled to .NET bytecode, with runtime support for proof-carrying code. F* has been applied mostly to secure distributed programming; it subsumes F7 and Fine, two prior languages using types for security verification. It has been used to program and verify more than 30,000 lines of code, including security protocols, web browser extensions, and distributed applications. Its main typechecker, compiler, and runtime support are coded in F#.

The main technical novelty of F* is a kind system to keep track of different fragments of the language and control their interaction. By default, program terms (with kind $\star$) may have arbitrary effects. Within these programs, proof terms (with kind P) remain pure and terminating, and thereby provide a logically consistent core. Besides, affine resources (with kind A) may be used for modular reasoning on stateful properties. Finally, ghost terms (with kind E) may be used only in specifications, to selectively control the erasure of proof terms, when the proofs are irrelevant or unavailable (for instance, when calling legacy code or using cryptography).

F* is also parametric in the logic used to describe program properties and proofs. This provides support for custom logics (e.g., for expressing authorization policies) and enables integration with SMT solvers, which is important for proof automation when developing large programs. Thus, F* calls Z3 (de Moura and Bjørner 2008) during typechecking, to prove logical properties specified as type refinements and to decide type equivalences.

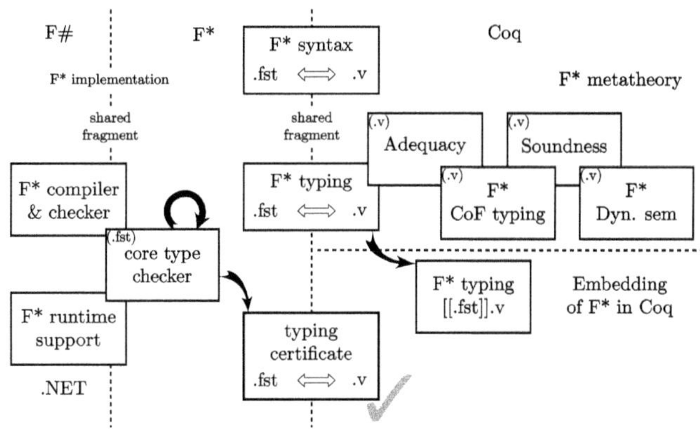

Figure 1. Self-Certification for an F* checker written in F*

The type system of F* has 4 main mutually-recursive judgments and 67 rules. Its theory has been formalized in Coq, showing substitutivity and subject reduction. (By design, F* provides only value dependencies and is inadequate for this sort of interactive theorem proving.)

Typechecking F* in F* Figure 1 outlines our method for self-certifying F*, which involves developments in F#, in F*, and in Coq. The rest of the paper provides a more precise, syntactic account of the developments in F* and Coq.

Its central component is our new core typechecker, programmed in F* using mutual recursion and exceptions for error-handling, state for name generation, as well as external .NET functions for I/O. Including the type definitions for the language and its type system, as well as basic library functions (mostly operations on lists and other functional data structures), our candidate certified program has 5,139 LOCs.

We adapt the F* compiler and main typechecker (in F#, on the left-hand-side) so that, after parsing and typing a given source program, it passes a typed abstract syntax tree for core typechecking certification, using a datatype shared between F# and F*. This F# code is significantly larger (35,000 LOCs). Thus, for a given F* program, we can call the F* compiler and obtain a typechecking certificate for (a desugared variant of) this program. In particular, we can call the core typechecker on itself and—after fixing any errors—produce its own typechecking certificate. Core typechecking is fast (a few minutes), but exporting the self-typechecking certificate in a format suitable for Coq verification then takes several hours, and still yields 7 GB of Coq source files.

Two theories of F* in Coq To relate the F* and Coq developments, we crucially rely on a well-identified fragment of F* (tracked by its P kind) that coincides with a fragment of the inductive types of Coq. To this end, we build tools that take F* types and values and emit them in the concrete syntax of Coq. In the picture, we label these definitions with both a '.fst' for F* and a '.v' for Coq. Thus, the definitions of the F* syntax, and (with some care) its core type system, are specified using value-dependent mutually-recursive inductive types in the shared fragment. This enables us, in particular, to emit a typing certificate in F* and typecheck it as a valid typing certificate in Coq. We intend to formally reason about our F* typechecker running on an F* program within Coq, so we emit surface definitions (for the typechecker and its type), embedded definitions (for its program parameter and its type, both typed as surface F* values), and embedding functions between the two. Conversely, we prove that, at least for the inductive types we use to represent typing derivations, the existence of an embedded value implies the existence of a surface value (Theorem 4).

Our shared definition of the F* type system is convenient for programming and typechecking, but not for developing its metatheory. Instead, we use another, cofinite definition of the type system (based on the same F* syntax), we prove subject-reduction for the cofinite system (Theorem 2), and we prove the adequacy of the shared system with regards to the cofinite system (Theorem 1).

With these results in hand, we can complete our bootstrapping within Coq. We load and typecheck the 7 GB self-typing certificate—despite many optimizations, this task still takes several machine-weeks—then we apply adequacy and subject reduction on complete runs of the typechecker applied to its own embedding as an F* term and its candidate type. This yields a valid embedded typing certificate for the embedded typechecker. Finally, we apply our Theorem 4 relating embedded and surface values and obtain a valid proof of its typing (Theorem 5).

Limitations Our path to certification depends on the correctness of the following components:

(1) The Coq kernel. We use a custom build of Coq with two extensions: a compact representation of strings for typechecking our typing certificates, and SSREFLECT for the metatheory and all interactive proofs.

(2) Some of our tools for parsing, translating, and embedding specifications between F* and Coq. Except for the concrete syntax, these are almost identities. The situation is similar to the use of notations within Coq—careful printing and manual inspection is required to interpret the formal theorem statements (Pollack 1998), although their proofs can be safely ignored.

(3) Z3. We see the certification of SMT deductions as an important, independent issue. We plan to adapt prior work on predecessors of F* (Chen et al. 2010) to extract valid F* proof terms from Z3 deductions. We may also rely on other verified SMT solvers (Armand et al. 2010; Moskal 2008).

(4) The F* back-end compiler and its .NET runtime with regards to our formal dynamic semantics. This trust assumption is rather large. On the other hand, we run our certified programs on the same platform, so we may as well trust it for typechecking. Still, in future work, it would be interesting to compile and run F* using a smaller TCB.

We should also note that we certify only the *partial* correctness of our typechecker. This is consistent with our usage of F*, which already relies on Z3, an incomplete prover. Pragmatically, bootstrapping and many other F* examples provide adequate coverage for completeness.

Related Work To our knowledge, our self-certification approach for bootstrapping verified typecheckers is new.

Self-verification Milawa/ACL2 (Davis 2009) provides an interesting example of verification bootstrapping for a first-order proof system, starting from a minimal checker (coded in Lisp) and gradually adding self-verified features, but does not formalize or certify its core checker. Jitawa (Myreen and Davis 2011) further provides a concrete x86 runtime for Milawa, verified using HOL4.

Coq implementation with extraction Several large developments of certified programs have been achieved using Gallina, the specification language of Coq, with or without extraction, notably for certified compilers (Chlipala 2010a; Leroy 2011). In comparison, our method does not rely on extraction.

Languages embedded in Coq Another method to obtain a reliable implementation is to embed a language within a trusted verifier. Hence, Nanevski et al. (2008) develop Ynot, a language for verified imperative programming, as a Coq library. While this method is arguably simpler than building a separate self-certified compiler from scratch, it also retains some of the limitations of its host language. For example, using Ynot to certify hostile code carries the same pitfalls as a direct deployment of Coq. Additionally, while Ynot, like F*, provides support for recursion and effects, it retains Coq's interactive proof style with explicit conversions.

Reflection Many recent works show how to efficiently verify large certificates in Coq using reflection (Armand et al. 2010; Keller and Werner 2010). We use reflection in our metatheory. However, as explained in §7, the soundness of self-certification limits the extent to which reflection can be used when checking certificates. Nevertheless, §7.2 describes how even our limited use of reflection yields significant reductions in the size of certificates.

Contents §2 introduces our method and main notations by certifying an F* typechecker for the simply-typed λ-calculus (STLC). §3 reviews the main features of F* and its type system. §4 presents our two theories of F* in Coq and discusses the sharing of inductive definitions and values between F* and Coq. §5 continues our example and shows how to certify an STLC typechecker in F*. §6 presents the main development of the paper, self-certifying the core typechecker for F*. §7 provides implementation details and experimental results. §8 concludes and discusses future work. A link to the latest core typechecker, its specification, and its meta-theory in Coq is available from the F* website at `http://research.microsoft.com/fstar`.

2. Warming up: a certifying typechecker for the simply-typed λ-calculus

We begin by introducing self-certification and illustrate its key elements in a simple setting: the problem of formally certifying the type safety of STLC programs. We describe three solutions with increasing degrees of emancipation:

- We may construct typing certificates for each λ-term in an *ad hoc* manner, for instance by programming a typechecker for STLC in ML, and then verify the typing certificates it produces using Coq. This approach is illustrated in Figure 2 and discussed in the remainder of this section.
- We may implement a similar STLC typechecker in F*, and give this program an F* specification that ensures it only constructs valid STLC typing derivations. We then build a single F* typing certificate for the typechecker program and check this certificate in Coq. We run Coq just once, rather than for each λ-term we wish to typecheck. We discuss this approach in §5.
- We may implement an F* core typechecker in F*, and give this program a specification that ensures it only constructs valid F* typing derivations. We then build a certificate for the core typechecker and check this certificate in Coq. This allows us to run Coq once for all F* programs. Once certified, we may run our core typechecker to certify any other program, including our STLC checker, without running Coq anymore. We discuss this approach in §6.

2.1 Formalizing STLC in Coq

A first step to certify the safety of STLC terms is to build a formal model of STLC in Coq. This model involves defining a specification of STLC syntax and typing judgments. We give below our sample Coq definitions for the syntax of STLC.

```
Definition Lbvar := string.
Inductive Ltyp : Type :=
| LTyp_unit : Ltyp
| LTyp_fun : Ltyp → Ltyp → Ltyp.
```

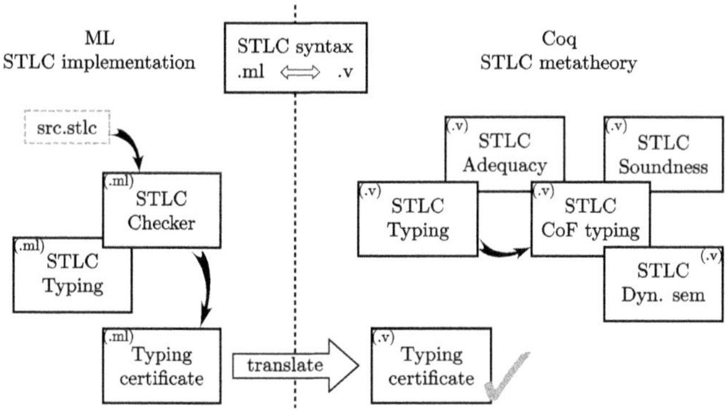

Figure 2. A traditional certifying typechecker for the STLC

```
Inductive Lexpr : Type :=
| LExpr_unit : Lexpr
| LExpr_var : Lbvar →Lexpr
| LExpr_fun : Lbvar →Ltyp →Lexpr →Lexpr
| LExpr_app : Lexpr →Lexpr →Lexpr.
Definition Lenv := seq (Lbvar * Ltyp).
```

These inductive types are just ML datatypes, so we can share our specification of the syntax between the formal development in Coq and our STLC implementation in ML. As such, these definitions are depicted in Figure 2 by the box labeled "STLC syntax[.ml|.v]". When sharing such definitions, we prove a theorem that for every value of the shared type in one language, there exists a corresponding value of the shared type in the other language.

Next, we define the typing judgments of the STLC as an inductive type in Coq—we give below the rule for functions ($\lambda x{:}t.e$).

```
Inductive LTyping : Lenv →Lexpr →Ltyp →Type := ...
| LTyping_fun : forall g x t e t',
      LTyping ((x,t)::g) e t'
   →LTyping g (LExpr_fun x t e) (LTyp_fun t t')
```

The inductive type `LTyping` is the reference specification of the type system, depicted by the box labeled "STLC typing.v". Our definitions are given in the style used in the rest of the paper (notably for the F* type system), which is convenient for use in the implementation of a typechecker in a real compiler. For instance, we use concrete strings to represent STLC variables.

Although natural for programming, the reference type system is not ideal for conducting metatheory. To this end, we give a second specification of the type system that uses cofinite quantification in a (named) locally nameless style to represent variables (Aydemir et al. 2008)—see also §4.2. This specification is depicted by the box labeled "STLC CoF typing.v". We also prove an adequacy result in Coq (the box "STLC Adequacy.v") that relates the two specifications. Adequacy states that, for every valid derivation in the reference system, there is a corresponding derivation in the cofinite system. We may then develop a standard cofinite theory for STLC, including a dynamic semantics and a type safety theorem.

2.2 Programming a certifying STLC typechecker in ML

Given a metatheory in Coq, a common approach to building a certified typechecker would be to implement it as a Coq function and to prove that it constructs valid typing derivations. The function can then be extracted to ML and run. This task is trivial for STLC, but for more complex languages (e.g., ML itself, or F*), implementing the typechecker within Coq can be quite challenging: Coq functions must be pure and total, whereas typechecking routinely uses general recursion; state for environments, unification, and symbol generation; and exceptions for error handling. Additionally, for this approach to work, one must prove the typechecking function correct in Coq, which involves interactive proofs on a large program.

To sidestep these difficulties, we implement the type checker in a general-purpose programming language with first-class support for features like effects that are hard to handle in Coq. As shown in the following sections, we can both use these features for programming our typechecker and formally ensure that it is correct.

To begin with, we program the typechecker in ML as a partial function stlc_typing given the signature below.

```
type LTypingML = ...
| LTyping_fun of Lenv * string * Ltyp * Lexpr * Ltyp * LTypingML
val stlc_typing: Lenv →Lexpr →Ltyp →LTypingML
```

The type LTypingML shown above is an ML data type for representing STLC typing derivations. This type is similar but much less precise than our reference specification `LTyping`—there exist values in LTypingML that do not correspond to valid reference typings. Using just this ML type as a specification, we have no way of showing that `stlc_typing` computes valid typing derivations. Still, whenever the ML term stlc_typing g e t computes a derivation d:LTypingML, we can attempt to translate d into a Coq value of type `LTyping`. Within Coq, if d typechecks, then from the rest of the metatheory we may conclude that the STLC program e is type safe.

We need not trust the programs that produce the derivation d and translate it from ML to Coq—all we care about is that the resulting certificate is a valid typing for the source term e. We do, however, care that the translated certificate is a valid typing for the program e, and not some other term. However, since the source term is a type Lexpr shared between ML and Coq, the translation from the abstract syntax of our ML implementation to Coq is simply the identity.

The method we have described so far is standard for a certifying compiler—many such instances exist in the literature (Colby et al. 2000; Morrisett et al. 1999). However, it requires running Coq on every compilation run. It is preferable to certify the STLC checker itself, that is, prove that any certificate it produces will always be typeable in Coq. Given such a proof, we would not have to run Coq on each compilation, and, furthermore, unless there were some other need for it, we need not produce the derivation value. To achieve this, §5 and §6 illustrate how to program the typechecker in F*, a call-by-value language (like ML) with higher-order functions, state, effects, and recursion, but with a verification system based on dependent typing that approaches Coq in expressive power.

3. A review of F*

Before proceeding towards self-certification, we briefly present the syntax and semantics of F*; we refer to Swamy et al. (2011) for a complete presentation and examples. The syntax is shown below.

Values, expressions, types, kinds, signatures, and environments

v	::=	$x \mid \lambda x{:}t.e \mid \Lambda\alpha{::}\kappa.e \mid D\,\bar{t}\,\bar{v} \mid v^{\ell}$	values
e	::=	$v \mid e\ v \mid e\ t \mid$ **assume** $\phi \mid$ **let** $x = e$ **in** $e' \mid$ **match** x **with** $D\ \bar{\alpha}\ \bar{x} \rightarrow e$ **else** e'	terms
ϕ, t	::=	$\alpha \mid T \mid x{:}t \rightarrow t' \mid \forall\alpha{::}\kappa.t \mid t\ v \mid t\ t' \mid \lambda x{:}t.t' \mid \Lambda\alpha{::}\kappa.t \mid x{:}t\{\phi\} \mid {¡}t$	types
c	::=	$\star \mid P \mid A$	concrete kinds
b	::=	$c \mid E$	base kinds
κ	::=	$b \mid x{:}t \Rightarrow \kappa \mid \alpha{::}\kappa \Rightarrow \kappa'$	kinds
S	::=	$\cdot \mid \overline{T{::}\kappa\{D{:}t\}} \mid S, S'$	signature
Γ	::=	$\cdot \mid x{:}t \mid \alpha{::}\kappa \mid v_1 = v_2 \mid t_1 = t_2 \mid \Gamma, \Gamma'$	type env.
$\mathscr{A}$	::=	$\cdot \mid \phi \mid \ell \mid \hat{\ell} \mid \mathscr{A}, \mathscr{A}'$	dynamic log

Values include variables, λ-abstractions over values and types, and fully applied n-ary data constructors. The value v^{ℓ} is a technical device used to prove the soundness of affine typing and can be ignored for our present purposes. The notation $\bar{a}$ stands for a finite sequence of elements $a_1, \ldots, a_n$ for arbitrary n. F* adopts a (partially) let-normalized view of the expression language e, in particular requiring function arguments to always be values—this is convenient when using value-dependent types, since it ensures that expressions never escape into the level of types. The only other non-standard expression form is **assume** ϕ, which is used in the semantics of ghost refinements and is not discussed further—we do not make use of it in our core typechecker.

Types are ranged over by meta-variables t and ϕ—we use ϕ for types that stand for logical formulas. Types include variables α, constants T, dependent functions ranging over values whose domain may be values ($x{:}t \to t'$) or types ($\forall\alpha{::}\kappa.t$), types applied to values ($t\ v$) and to types ($t\ t'$), type-level functions from values or types to types ($\lambda x{:}t.t'$ and $\Lambda\alpha{::}\kappa.t$), ghost refinements $x{:}t\{\phi\}$, and finally coercions to affine types $¡t$. This last modal operator serves to qualify the type of a closure that captures an affine assumption.

Kinds κ include the four base kinds $\star$, P, A, and E discussed previously—F* distinguishes the first three of these as *concrete kinds*, since E is used to characterize *erasable* specifications. As at the type level, F* has kinds for dependent function spaces whose range are types and whose domain may be either values ($x{:}t \Rightarrow \kappa$) or types ($\alpha{::}\kappa \Rightarrow \kappa'$). Stratifying the language into terms, types, and kinds allows F* to place key restrictions (discussed below) that facilitate automated verification, and to compile efficiently to .NET. However, stratification does come at a cost—several pieces of technical machinery are replicated across the levels.

Signatures S are finite lists of mutually recursive datatypes. Each definition $\overline{T{::}\kappa\{\overline{D{:}t}\}}$ introduces a set of type constants $T_1{::}\kappa_1, \ldots, T_n{::}\kappa_n$ and all their data constructors $D_1{:}t_1, \ldots, D_m{:}t_m$. We do not need a fixpoint form in the expression language since these types allow us to encode recursive functions. The addition of mutual recursion is an enhancement over our prior formalization of F*, where it was left out for simplicity. Here, we make heavy use of mutual recursion in the formalization of the type system of F* in F* and so include it in our core theory.

A characteristic feature of the F* type system is that the kind of a type indicates whether or not values of that type are pure. In particular, functions in the universe of P-kinded types are guaranteed to be total, whereas those in the $\star$-universe may diverge or have other effects. This allows us to embed a logically consistent sublanguage (namely the P-fragment) within F*. (The meaning of the other two kinds is beyond scope for this paper.) To ensure that terms given P-kinded types are strongly normalizing, a well-formedness condition on signatures imposes a positivity constraint on inductive definitions for P-kinded types. In addition, the kinding rules for function arrows are such that the kind of a function type is determined by the kind of its co-domain, i.e., the kind of $x{:}t \to t'$ is the kind of t'. Intuitively, since F* is a call-by-value language, the domain of a function consists of fully evaluated terms, and hence it is the co-domain that determines whether or not a function is total.

These and other restrictions (e.g., on cross-universe elimination) allow us to place the P-fragment of F* in close correspondence with Coq, where inductives are also positive. Specifically, P-kinded types in F* correspond to a fragment of the `Type` universe in Coq rather than `Prop`, i.e., P-terms in F* need not be computationally irrelevant. We exploit (a limited version of) this correspondence in an essential way in the main development of the paper, via our data embedding theorem (Theorem 4).

Typing judgments The F* type system has several mutually-recursive judgments. The judgments are given with respect to typing environments Γ that track in-scope value variables (x with type t), type variables (α with kind κ), and equivalences between values ($v_1 = v_2$) and types ($t_1 = t_2$) introduced when checking **match** expressions. These equalities enable implicit conversions, a distinctive feature of F* with regard to a system like Coq, where all type conversions must be performed by equality-witnessing coercions.

The four central judgments are as follows: (1) well-formedness of kinds: $S;\Gamma \vdash \kappa\ \mathrm{ok}(b)$, where the well-formedness is indexed by a base kind b; (2) kinding of types: $S;\Gamma \vdash t :: \kappa$; (3) typing for values: $S;\Gamma;X \vdash^m v : t$, and (4) typing for expressions $S;\Gamma;X \vdash^m e : t$. Note, unlike our presentation of the STLC, F* separates value and expression typing, which are the two most interesting judgments. They state that a value v (resp. expression e) has type t, under signature S, environment Γ, and an affine environment $X ::= \cdot \mid \ell \mid x \mid X,X'$, where X,X' denotes disjoint union of sets of names. The context X represents a set of available affine assumptions, and usual context splitting rules apply to X when typing the subterms of an expression. The index m on the turnstile represents two possible modes that distinguish the typing of terms that appear at the type level from those that appear at the term level—the former are subject to less stringent restrictions on affinity.

We give only two sample rules, for value-typing λ-abstractions and for expression-typing applications, which we also use for examples in the next sections.

$$\text{WFV-Fun}\ \frac{S;\Gamma \vdash t{::}c \qquad S;\Gamma,x{:}t;X,x \vdash^m e : t'}{S;\Gamma;X \vdash^m \lambda x{:}t.e : Q(X, x{:}t \to t')}$$

$$\text{WFE-App}\ \frac{S;\Gamma;X \vdash^m e : ?x{:}t \to t' \qquad S;\Gamma;X' \vdash^m v : t}{S;\Gamma;X,X' \vdash^m e\ v : t'[v/x]}$$

In WFV-Fun, the first premise requires that the argument type t have a concrete kind. The second premise types the body expression e in a context and an affine environment both extended with x (so that x may be used once if t is affine, e.g. c is A). Finally, the introduced function type is tagged with the affine modality (using $Q(X,t) = ¡t$, when X is non-empty, and t otherwise) if the function closure captures an affine assumption. In WFE-App, the two premises type e and v as a function and its argument, respectively, using disjoint parts X, X' of the affine environment. We write $?x{:}t \to t'$ to range over the types $x{:}t \to t'$ and $¡x{:}t \to t'$, thereby capturing the elimination of both standard and affine functions (respectively) in a single rule. Finally, the result type is obtained by substituting v for x in t'.

In addition to these four judgments, F* has several auxiliary judgments, including judgments for subkinding, subtyping, well-formedness of signatures and environments, and the like. We elide these here, since they do not play a central role in the remainder of our presentation. However, one judgment is worth mentioning: logic derivability.

The F* type system is parametrized by an external logic, where derivability in this logic is characterized by the judgment $S;\Gamma \models \phi$. The introduction of ghost refinements (as well as certain implicit conversions) are governed by this judgment. In effect, the value typing $S;\Gamma;X \vdash^m v : x{:}t\{\phi\}$ requires deriving $S;\Gamma \models \phi[v/x]$ in the external logic. As such, F* places various admissibility constraints on this judgment (e.g., that it be closed under substitution; that it be a congruence on equality etc.). The soundness of the F* type system is modulo the soundness of the logic meeting these conditions, and we rely on this for our embedding theorem in §4.3. This approach gives us the flexibility to use F* with an external theorem prover, like Z3, where we often instantiate the external logic in question to first-order logic with theories. However, instead of trusting the external logic, it is also possible to extract proof terms from a decision procedure from the logic and have them checked in pure F*. This is an approach followed by Chen et al. (2010) in the context of Fine, a predecessor of F*.

4. Formalizing F* in Coq

A prerequisite for self-certifying F*, and indeed certifying any F* program such as our STLC checker, is to formalize F* in Coq. There are three aspects to this formalism. First, we develop a reference specification of the F* type system. Next, we develop a cofinite version of the reference type system, prove an adequacy theorem relating the two, and prove the F* type system sound. The third and final aspect involves developing metatheory (currently by hand) that relates F* and Coq in a way that justifies sharing certain inductive types between the two systems. We consider each of these aspects in turn, returning (in §4.3) to the setting of our STLC checker for illustrative examples.

4.1 A reference specification of the F* type system in Coq

Our reference specification begins with a model of F* syntax. We show a fragment of this syntax below, starting with type definitions for the various kinds of names used in our formalization. We have `iname` for inductive type names; `cname` for data constructors; `vlname` for free value names; `tyname` for free type names; and `bvar` for bound (value or type) names. Each of these is represented using a string type with decidable equality, the same representation as in the F* implementation of the F* typechecker.

```
Definition iname := String.
Definition cname := String.
Definition vlname := String.
Definition tyname := String.
Definition bvar := String.
```

We have four mutually inductive types, for kinds, types, values and expressions. We list a representative fragment of these types below, starting with the variant type `gvar` that we use to distinguish bound names and free names in the syntax. We have the four base kinds, where `BK_Comp` corresponds to the ⋆-kind of §3.

```
Inductive gvar (T : Type) : Type :=
  GV_Bound : bvar → gvar T | GV_Free : T → gvar T.

Inductive basekind : Type :=
  BK_Comp | BK_Prop | BK_Erase | BK_Afn.

Inductive kind : Type :=
| K_Base : basekind → kind
| K_ProdK : bvar → kind → kind → kind
| K_ProdT : bvar → typ → kind → kind
with typ : Type := ...
| T_Var : gvar tyname → typ
| T_Ind : iname → typ
| T_VApp : typ → value → typ
| T_Prod : bvar → typ → typ → typ
| T_Ref : bvar → typ → typ → typ
| T_Ascribe : typ → kind → typ
with value : Type := ...
| V_Var : gvar vlname → value
| V_Fun : bvar → typ → expr → value
| V_Const : cname → seq typ → seq value → value
| V_Ascribe : value → typ → value
with expr : Type := ...
| E_Value : value → expr
| E_App : expr → value → expr
| E_Ascribe : expr → typ → expr.
```

The abstract syntax closely follows the informal syntax of §3. The one addition is the presence of type- and kind-ascription forms at each level, e.g., we use `T_Ascribe` to give a type a kind, which make (core) typechecking more syntax-directed.

The reference type system is formalized as a 4-way mutually recursive inductive type. We show the signatures of these types below: `wfK` is the judgment for well-formedness of kinds, `wfT` is the kinding judgment for types, `value_ty` is value typing, and `expr_ty` is expression typing.

```
Inductive wfK : icompartment → environment → bindings
    → kind → basekind → Type := ...
with wfT : icompartment → environment → bindings
    → typ → kind → Type := ...
with value_ty : icompartment → environment → bindings
    → seq bvar → mode → value → typ → Type := ...
with expr_ty : icompartment → environment → bindings
    → seq bvar → mode → expr → typ → Type := ....
```

Each judgment is given with respect to an environment that contains three compartments for binding various kind of names.

First, corresponding to signature S in §3, an `icompartment` is a sequence of records, one for each family of mutually recursive inductive types. Each record contains the names of the defined type constants, their kinds, and their constructors.

```
Record constructor : Type := mkConstructor
  { ct_name : cname; ct_type : typ }.
Record ikind : Type := mkIKind
  { it_name : iname; it_kind : kind }.
Record inductive : Type := mkIndType
  { it_ikind : seq ikind; it_constructors : seq constructor }.
Definition icompartment : Type := seq inductive.
```

Next, Γ is split into two parts. The `environment` compartment is a sequence recording free value and type names. The free names are kept separate from local `bindings` and equality assumptions induced by pattern matching. We show the definitions of both below. Separating these two compartments simplifies our adequacy proof, inasmuch as only the local names are subject to α-conversion and implicit type conversion. We include value and type equalities (`EB_VlName` and `EB_TyName`) in the environment as they become necessary in the cofinite system of §4.2—these constructors are not used in the reference system.

```
Inductive ebinding : Type :=
| EB_VlName : vlname → typ → ebinding
| EB_TyName : tyname → kind → ebinding.
| EB_VlEq : value → value → locbinding
| EB_TyEq : typ → typ → binding.
Definition environment : Type := seq ebinding.

Inductive locbinding :=
| LB_BvarTy : bvar → typ → locbinding
| LB_BvarKind : bvar → kind → locbinding
| LB_VlEq : value → value → locbinding
| LB_TyEq : typ → typ → binding.
Definition bindings := seq locbinding.
```

Value and expression typing judgments (`value_ty` and `expr_ty`) take two additional arguments, discussed in §3: a sequence of bound names that represents the affine compartment and a mode.

With these definitions in hand, we give a flavor of the `value_ty` and `expr_ty` judgments by showing the rules for λ-abstractions and applications, respectively. Note the intensional use of concrete names throughout the system.

```
| WFV_Fun : forall I G B X m t bt u x body Q,
    ConcreteKind bt → AQual X (T_Prod x t u) Q → wfT I G B t bt
  → expr_ty I G ((LB_BvarTy x t) :: B) (x :: X) m body u
  → value_ty I G B X m (V_Fun x t body) Q

| WFE_App : forall I G B X X1 X2 m e v x t u tv tres,
    Split X X1 X2 → StripQual tv (T_Prod x t u)
  → SubstTV u x v tres
  → expr_ty I G B X1 m e tv
  → value_ty I G B X2 m v t
  → expr_ty I G B X m e v tres
```

The rules use auxiliary predicates: `ConcreteKind` identifies the subclass c of kinds; `Split` specifies $X = X_1 \uplus X_2$; `Aqual` specifies $Q(X,t)$; `StripQual` specifies $?x{:}t \rightarrow t'$; and `SubstTV` specifies value substitutions in types. All of these predicates are defined as inductive types in Coq; for instance, `ConcreteKind` is defined as:

```
Inductive ConcreteKind : basekind → Type :=
| CK_Star : ConcreteKind BK_Comp
| CK_Aff : ConcreteKind BK_Afn
| CK_Prop : ConcreteKind BK_Prop.
```

One may wonder why we do not use functions to define `ConcreteKind`, `SubstTV`, etc. This is a key point related to the soundness of self-certification, discussed in detail in the coming sections. Keeping in mind that we aim to share these definitions between F* and Coq, one reason for using inductive predicates uniformly is that F*, being a value-indexed language, does not have function applications within types.

However, our reference type system is not entirely free of function applications. For example, in defining the well-formedness of typing environments, we use the following predicate for non-membership in a sequence.

```
Inductive NotMem : A → seq A → Prop :=
| NotMem_nil : forall x, NotMem x [::]
| NotMem_cons : forall x y ys,
        x != y → NotMem x ys → NotMem x (y::ys).
```

In writing `x != y` above, we make use of reflection and decidable equality on names: the type `x != y` is a function application that reduces in Coq to the type `true=true`. We permit such decidable (dis-)equalities in our reference specification and show in §4.3 how to model them in F* using ghost refinements.

4.2 F* metatheory in Coq

The reference specification of the type system conforms to the informal presentation of F* and to its compiler implementation. However, due to the usage of the *for-one locally nameless* representation of binders (Leroy 2007), this formulation is a poor one for conducting metatheory. As explained above, we provide a second specification of the F* type system, this time making use of the *for-all representation* of binders with the *co-finite quantification* optimization (Aydemir et al. 2008). We prove a correspondence between the two, and prove a subject reduction result for the second system.

We give a flavor of the cofinite system, still using the rule for λ-abstraction. As in the reference system, we have a 4-way mutually inductive type for the main judgments of the type system.

```
Inductive pname : Type :=
  TermName : vlname → pname | TypeName : tyname → pname.
Definition pnames := seq pname.
```

```
Inductive coF_wfK : ... := ...
with coF_value_ty:icompartment → environment → acontext
          → mode → value → typ → Type := | ...
| CoF_WFV_Fun :
  forall I G X m t bt u x body Q (L : pnames),
   concretekind bt → aqual X (T_Prod x t u) Q → coF_wfT I G t bt
  → (forall y, TermName y ∉ L →
      coF_expr_ty I ((EB_BvarTy y t)::G) ((ValueName y)::X) m
                    (subst_e body x y) (subst_t u x y))
  → coF_value_ty I G X m (V_Fun x t body) Q
```

The major difference between the two systems is in their treatment of binders. Rule `CoF_WFV_Fun` requires that the typing of `body` be insensitive to the particular choice of bound variable name. This is modeled by requiring the body to be typeable for a cofinite set of names, that is, those not in the set `L`. We type the body by substituting the bound name `x` for the chosen free name `y`. As such, in this formulation, there is no need for the local binding context—the free names in `environment` suffice. A relatively superficial difference is in the modeling of the affine environment, which in the cofinite system is a sequence of value names, whereas in the reference system, it is a sequence of bound variables.

A significant stylistic difference is that we make liberal use of functions and type-level reduction provided by Coq in the cofinite system. For example, `concretekind` is now a boolean function, given below. The cofinite system is not shared with F* and is thus not subject to the value-indexed restriction imposed on the reference system.

```
Definition concretekind (b : basekind) : bool :=
  match b with
  | BK_Comp | BK_Afn | BK_Prop ⇒ true
  | BK_Erase ⇒ false
  end.
```

Our first theorem is *adequacy* of the reference system with regards to the cofinite system. It is stated below for expression typing, but of course its proof requires a 4-way mutual induction on the main judgments.

THEOREM 1 (Adequacy).

```
forall I G X m e t,
    expr_ty I G [::] X m e t
 → coF_expr_ty I G X m e t.
```

Next, we give our main subject-reduction theorem. To simplify the presentation in this paper, we consider a specialization of our subject reduction theorem to programs that, first, make no use of affinity; and, second, have no dynamic assumptions for introducing ghost refinements. We consider `reduces: icompartment → expr → expr → Type`, an inductive definition specializing the general reduction relation for F*.

THEOREM 2 (Subject Reduction, specialized).

```
forall I G e e' t,
   coF_expr_ty I G [::] Term_level e t
 → reduces I e e'
 → coF_expr_ty I G [::] Term_level e' t.
```

In the rest of the paper, we only rely on the following corollary, obtained by composing the adequacy theorem with subject reduction and an induction on the sequence of reduction steps—`evaluates` is a transitive closure of `reduces` followed by matching on `E_Value`.

COROLLARY 3 (Subject Reduction to Values).

```
forall I G e v t,
   expr_ty I G [::] [::] Term_level e t
 → evaluates I e v
 → coF_value_ty I G [::] Term_level v t.
```

For convenience, we use abbreviations for typing closed terms, defined as follows:

```
Definition val_ty i v t := value_ty i [::] [::] [::] Term_level v t.
Definition exp_ty i e t := expr_ty i [::] [::] [::] Term_level e t.
Definition coF_val_ty i v t :=
  coF_value_ty i [::] [::] Term_level v t.
```

4.3 Sharing definitions and embeddings

Inductive types in F* are nearly as expressive as inductive types in Coq. In this section, we give an embedding result, Theorem 4, which allows us to soundly treat certain inductive types in Coq as if they were also inductive types in F*, and vice versa. We exploit this result to give strong specifications to typecheckers (and other programs) implemented in F*, ensuring, for example, that they only compute valid derivations. Theorem 4 then allows us to conclude that these derivations are also valid reference typings in Coq.

We illustrate this approach using the STLC reference specification as an example. In §2, we argued informally that the syntax of STLC terms can be shared between ML and Coq, whereas the inductive type specifying the typing judgment could not, since ML inductive types are not sufficiently precise—not so for F*. We can express both the syntax and the reference typing for STLC as inductives in F*, in a module STLC (outlined below) in close correspondence with our Coq definitions.

```
module STLC
type Ltyp :: P =
  | LTyp_unit : Ltyp | LTyp_fun : Ltyp → Ltyp → Ltyp
type Lexpr :: P =
  | LExpr_unit : Lexpr | LExpr_var : string → Lexpr
  | LExpr_fun : string → Ltyp → Lexpr → Lexpr
  | LExpr_app : Lexpr → Lexpr → Lexpr.
```

```
type Lenv = seq (string * Ltyp)
type LTyping :: Lenv ⇒ Lexpr ⇒ Ltyp ⇒ P= ...
  | LTyping_fun : g:Lenv →x:string →t:Ltyp →t':Ltyp →e:Lexpr
               →LTyping ((x,t)::g) e t'
               →LTyping g (LExpr_fun x t e) (LTyp_fun t t')
```

Formally, sharing between F* and Coq is justified by an embedding theorem (explained below). Pragmatically, resolving differences in concrete syntax is easily automated—we provide some basic support for this, although we often manually transcribe definitions from F* to Coq. Less superficially, we have implemented pretty printers that allow F* values and type definitions to be printed as values in the abstract syntax of F* in Coq. This is essential for importing large certificates and we use this tool extensively.

We describe the correspondence between inductive types in F* and Coq using examples from the STLC development. For every F* file, say `STLC.fst`, containing the type definitions in the STLC module, we have a Coq file, `STLC.v`, with the following elements.

Surface definitions We have Coq definitions such as `Inductive Lexpr : Type := ...` (listed in §2.1) that mirror STLC definitions such as LExpr. We apply this superficial translation only to the F* inductive types that can be viewed soundly as Coq inductives, namely those that meet the *P*-restriction formalized below. In addition to the basic inductive types we have seen so far, *P*-restricted types also include inductive types with ghost refinements, where the refinement formulas correspond to the use of reflection for computing decidable equalities. For example, the type in F* corresponding to the definition of `NotMem` from §4.1 is NotMem, shown below.

```
type tag = D:tag
type NEq v1 v2 = _:tag{v1 != v2}
type NotMem :: α⇒ seq α⇒ P=
  | NotMem_nil : x:α →NotMem x []
  | NotMem_cons : x:α →y:α →tl:seq α
      →NEq x y →NotMem x tl →NotMem x (y::tl)
```

Whereas in Coq we use the function application `x!=y`, in F* we use a type refined with the formula x!=y. In general, any F* ghost refinement formula can be embedded in Coq using reflection, provided we have a corresponding function in Coq that can decide the formula. In principle, we could use this embedding to specify the entire type system of F* using ghost refinements, but this would require having a function in Coq to decide typing—which, of course, renders moot building a certified typechecker for F* in the first place. As such, we restrict our use of reflection in the reference system to trivially decidable equalities. We show how to relate these formally below.

Embedded signatures We also embed the F* inductives as terms in our Coq formalization of F*. Specifically, we generate a Coq value of type `icompartment` that represents our formalization of these F* inductive definitions in Coq. All F* inductive types can be embedded in this manner, whether they meet the *P*-restricted condition or not. For instance, for the Lexpr inductive we generate:

```
Definition iLexpr: inductive := mkIndType
  [:: mkIKind "Lexpr" (K_Base BK_Prop)]
  [:: mkConstructor "LExpr_App"
      (T_Prod "" (T_Ind "Lexpr")
        (T_Prod "" (T_Ind "Lexpr") (T_Ind "Lexpr"))); ... ].
Definition iSTLC: icompartment := [:: expr ; ... ].
```

Type embedding functions For each *P*-restricted inductive type T of kind $\alpha_1::\kappa_1 \Rightarrow \ldots \Rightarrow \alpha_n::\kappa_n \Rightarrow x_1{:}t_1 \Rightarrow \ldots x_m{:}t_m \Rightarrow P$, we have a Coq function `tembed_T` of type `typ →... →typ →value →... → value →typ`, for n `typ`s and m `value`s. For instance, for the Lexpr and LTyping inductives of STLC, we generate:

```
Definition tembed_Lexpr := (T_Ind "Lexpr").
Definition tembed_LTyping (g e t:value) :=
  (T_VApp (T_VApp (T_VApp (T_Ind "LTyping") g) e) t).
```

Value embedding functions For values of shared inductive types, we have functions in Coq that produce terms in the `value` inductive that represents F* values in Coq. For instance, we have a function from surface to embedded STLC expressions:

```
Fixpoint embed_Lexpr (e: Lexpr) : value :=
  match e with ...
  | LExpr_App e0 e1 ⇒
    V_Const "LExpr_App" [::] [:: embed_Lexpr e0; embed_Lexpr e1 ].
```

Using these value embedding functions, we define analogs of the type embedding functions that allow us to combine the type and value embeddings. For example, we define the following wrapper around `tembed_LTyping`:

```
Definition tembed_LTyping' g e t :=
 tembed_LTyping (embed_Lenv g) (embed_Lexpr e) (embed_Ltyp t).
```

Finally, we have pretty-printers from F* values to Coq values representing F* abstract syntax. For instance, we print the F* value

```
LExpr_App (LExpr_var "x") (LExpr_Var "y"): Lexpr
```

as the Coq value

```
LExpr_App (LExpr_var "x") (LExpr_Var "y"): Lexpr
```

To this end, the F* code generator injects a ToString method into each .NET class that represents an F* data constructor. By calling ToString on any (first-order) F* value and printing the result, we get the representation of that value as a value of type `value`, the type of F* values, in Coq. This tool is in effect an (untrusted) F* primitive function, string_of_any : $\alpha \rightarrow$string.

Formal embedding Our theorem states that the existence of an embedded F* proof for a given inductive type implies the existence of a Coq proof for that type. We first define a restriction on inductive types such that our theorem applies. The purpose of the restriction is first to exclude non-*P*-fragment types: types that live in F*'s $\star$-universe, for instance, need not have any analog in Coq. Second, F* expressions, even in the *P*-fragment, employ constructs that do not translate directly to Coq—notably implicit conversions introduced by pattern matching, which must be made explicit in Coq. For this reason, the *P*-restriction also excludes types whose values may contain (non-value) sub-expressions, in particular λ-terms. We still allow some limited use of ghost refinements in *P*-restricted types, notably for types refined by formulas speaking about decidable, syntactic equality on F* values.

- A type t is *P*-restricted when it is a type variable whose kind is *P*-restricted; or NEq v_1 v_2; or $T\ \overline{\alpha}\ \overline{x}$ where T is *P*-restricted.
- A kind κ is *P*-restricted when it is of the form $\overline{\alpha::\kappa} \Rightarrow \overline{x{:}t} \Rightarrow P$ where each κ_i and each t_i is *P*-restricted.
- An inductive type T defined by $T{::}\kappa\{\overline{D{:}t}\}$ is *P*-restricted when the kind κ is *P*-restricted and each constructor $D{:}t$ has a type t of the form $\overline{\alpha::\kappa} \rightarrow \overline{x{:}t} \rightarrow T\ \overline{\alpha}\ \overline{x}$ where each κ_i and each t_i is *P*-restricted.

THEOREM 4 (Embedding). *Let S be a signature and* `i` *its embedding in Coq. Let* T *be a P-restricted inductive type of S with kind* $\overline{\alpha::\kappa} \Rightarrow \overline{x{:}t} \Rightarrow P$ *and let* `T` *be the Coq surface-level inductive type for* T. *We have*

$\forall\ \overline{(\alpha:\kappa)}\ \overline{(x:t)}$ `(v: value), coF_val_ty i v (tembed_T'` $\overline{\alpha}\ \overline{x}$`) →T` $\overline{\alpha}\ \overline{x}$.

The statement of this (meta) theorem is not expressible in Coq, since it involves quantifying over Coq inductive types, so we prove it by hand. However, we can easily express in Coq instances of the theorem for specific type constructors. We will later formally admit some of these instances for types such as `LTyping` for STLC. In future work, we anticipate mechanizing the proofs of specific instances of the data embedding theorem in Coq, rather than admitting them via the meta theorem.

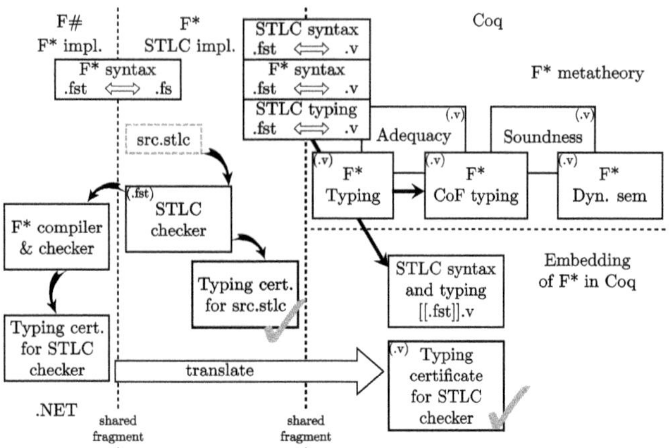

Figure 3. Certifying an STLC checker in F*

Our hand proof relies on a structurally inductive function that translates F* types and values to Coq. We show that this translation preserves types. This proof, in most cases, appeals to a more general lemma relating arbitrary *P*-fragment terms (including those with reducible expressions) to terms in the `Type` fragment of CiC (Swamy et al. 2011). The one case not handled by the general lemma is for embedding the F* type NEq v1 v2 = _:tag{v1 != v2}. For this case, we use the premise `coF_val_ty i v (T_Ref _ _ (embed v_1)!= (embed v_2)))`, which introduces a ghost refinement. As discussed in §3, the introduction of ghost refinements occurs via a judgment in an external logic, formally represented in the metatheory of F* as a predicate `LogicEntails`. We thus have `LogicEntails i [::] ((embed v_1)!= (embed v_2))`. One of several admissibility restriction on this judgment ensures that it soundly decides primitive (dis-)equalities, from which we conclude `v_1 != v_2`. In effect, this captures our assumption that the F* runtime system properly implements syntactic comparison of values, and that type-safety in F* is modulo the soundness of the external logic.

5. From certifying to certified: STLC in F*

We now return to the problem of certifying an STLC typechecker. Figure 3 illustrates the architecture we use, and §6 shows an instantiation of this architecture to certify a typechecker for F* itself.

The process begins at the top right of the figure, depicting our formalization of F* in Coq (in addition to the formalization of STLC). Next, in contrast to Figure 2, since we program in F*, we share *both* the definitions of the STLC syntax and its reference type system between F* and Coq. We also share the definitions of the F* syntax. We implement the STLC checker in F* and give it a strong specification, stating that it computes (at most) valid STLC typings. We let F* typecheck it and produce its typing certificate then, as in §2 for STLC typings, we translate the certificate to Coq and typecheck it there, against the reference specification of F* and the embedding as an `icompartment` of the STLC syntax and reference typing. We then complete the certification of our checker from its specification and the F* metatheory.

Programming and verifying the STLC checker Our STLC checker in F* is a partial function with the following signature:

```
stlc_checker: g:Lenv → e:Lexpr → t:Ltyp → Partial (LTyping g e t)
```

As discussed in §3, the F* kind system distinguishes partial and total functions. Since we intend stlc_checker to be partial (possibly throwing exceptions), we wrap its co-domain with a type constructor Partial, defined below, to lift the *P*-kinded LTyping g e t into the ⋆-universe of general computations.

```
type Partial :: P ⇒ ⋆ = P2S : ∀α::P. α → Partial α
```

We can run our checker to compute certificates for sample STLC programs, such as $\lambda x.x$, as follows:

```
let id: Lexpr = (LExpr_Fun "x" LTyp_unit (LExpr_Var "x"))
let t: typ = (LTyp_Fun LTyp_unit LTyp_unit)
let (P2S (pf : LTyping [] id t)) = stlc_checker [] id t
```

Now, instead of translating and checking each such pf using Coq, as in §2, we want to certify stlc_checker once and then run it repeatedly on STLC programs without further reliance on Coq. The process of certifying stlc_checker involves several steps, some of which we have already seen.

(1) We share the definitions in the F* module STLC with Coq to obtain a Coq module `STLC`. As we have seen in §2 and §4.3, this module contains the reference specification of the STLC type system in Coq, as well as various embeddings of STLC into F* abstract syntax within Coq.

```
Module STLC.
Inductive Ltyp : Type := ...
Inductive Lexpr : Type := ...
Definition Lenv := seq (Lbvar * Ltyp).
Inductive LTyping : Lenv → Lexpr → Ltyp → Type := ...
...
Definition iLexpr: inductive := ...
Definition iLTyping : inductive := ...
Definition iSTLC : icompartment := [:: iLexpr; iLTyping...].
...
Definition tembed_Ltyp : typ := (T_Ind "Ltyp").
Definition tembed_Lexpr : typ := (T_Ind "Lexpr").
Definition tembed_LTyping g e t : typ :=
  (T_VApp (T_VApp (T_VApp (T_Ind "LTyping") g) e) t).
...
Fixpoint embed_Ltyp (t: Ltyp) : value := ...
Fixpoint embed_Lexpr (e:Lexpr) : value := ...
Fixpoint embed_Lenv (e:Lenv) : value := ...
...
Definition tembed_LTyping' g e t := ...
```

(2) We print the abstract syntax of stlc_checker as an `expr` in Coq. The process of verifying stlc_checker involves trusting a parser and pretty printer (implemented in F#), since the main theorem will speak about the reduction to a value of this term. However, this degree of trust is no more that the trust one already places in Coq—to be confident that one has proved the theorem that one set out to prove, one must be careful to have Coq print the statement of the theorem that was proven, with notations and implicit coercions disabled, and to manually inspect that the theorem proven was what was intended—a recipe prescribed by Pollack (1998), among others.

```
Definition stlc_checker : expr := (E_Value (V_Fun ... )) .
```

(3) We verify stlc_checker by building a typing derivation for it with respect to the F* reference type system. The means by which this derivation is produced is irrelevant—any valid typing will do. We may, for example, run an (uncertified) F* typechecker implemented in F#, have it construct a derivation, print the resulting derivation, and check it in Coq using the embedded types listed below. (Eventually, using the self-certified F* typechecker of §6, we need not even check this certificate in Coq.)

```
Definition asVal (x:string) := V_Var (GV_Bound x).
Definition wf_iSTLC : wfEnv iSTLC [::] [::] := ... .
Definition stlc_checker_typing
: expr_ty iSTLC stlc_checker
 (T_Prod "g" tembed_Lenv
  (T_Prod "e" tembed_Lexpr
   (T_Prod "t" tembed_Ltyp
    (T_App (T_Ind "Partial")
     (tembed_LTyping (asVal "g") (asVal "e") (asVal "t"))))))
 := (* pretty-printed certificate *)
```

(4) Within Coq, we prove a lemma stating that the F* function `stlc_checker` applied to any F* values g of type `tembed_Lenv`, e of type `tembed_Lexpr`, and t of type `tembed_Ltyp` is an F* expression of type `embed_LTyping g e t`. The proof follows from three applications of the function-application rule (`WFE_App`) of the F* reference type system.

```
Definition embed_check g e t :=
  (E_App (E_App (E_App stlc_checker
    (embed_Lenv g)) (embed_Lexpr e)) (embed_Ltyp t)).
Lemma embed_check_ty : forall (g:Lenv) (e:Lexpr) (t:Ltyp),
  expr_ty iSTLC (embed_check g e t)
              (tembed_Partial (tembed_LTyping' g e t)).
```

(5) We admit an instance of Theorem 4 applied to `LTyping`. Rather than relying on this hand-proved theorem, we could, in principle, formally prove this instance by inversion of the embedded-typing assumption.

```
Axiom LTyping_data_embedding:
  forall (g:Lenv) (e:Lexpr) (t:Ltyp) (r:value),
     coF_val_ty iSTLC r (tembed_LTyping' g e t)
   → LTyping g e t.
```

(6) We also have a specific instance of a canonical forms lemma from the F* metatheory applied to the Partial type constructor. This provides us with a convenient inversion principle to reason about the result of stlc_checker.

```
Lemma Partial_inv: forall r t,
    coF_val_ty iSTLC r (T_App (T_Ind "Partial") t)
  →(exists v, coF_val_ty iSTLC v t).
```

(7) To complete the proof of certification for stlc_checker, we apply Corollary 3 (subject reduction to value) to `embed_check_ty`, followed by `Partial_inv` and `LTyping_data_embedding`.

```
Theorem partial_correctness_of_stlc_checker :
  forall (g:Lenv) (e:Lexpr) (t:Ltyp) (r:value),
     evaluates iSTLC (embed_check g e t) r
   → LTyping g e t.
```

Thus, we reach our stated goal—the F* program stlc_checker (partially) decides the type safety of STLC expressions. Going further, we may rely on the metatheory of STLC to replace `LTyping g e t` with runtime safety for `e`.

6. Emancipation through self-certification

The certification method of §5 is clearly not specific to STLC—the formal development generalizes naturally to F* itself. We apply this method to F*, as outlined in Figure 1, and obtain a certified F* core typechecker that can be used to check and certify all F* programs independently of Coq. We first explain the steps that lead to the main theorem of the paper. We then discuss some of the subtleties behind the proof, the impact of the *P*-restriction, and some aspects of our adequacy result.

6.1 Self-certifying F*: the main development

The first step in our development is to share the inductive types for the F* abstract syntax and reference type system between F* and Coq—this corresponds to step 1 in §5. All the definitions of §4.1 are expressed as F* inductive types in a CoreTyping module, and these definitions are also embedded in Coq within the F* theory. For example, we have mutually-recursive judgments in F*:

```
type wfK :: icompartment ⇒ environment ⇒ bindings
    ⇒ kind ⇒ basekind ⇒ P= ...
and wfT :: icompartment ⇒ environment ⇒ bindings
    ⇒ typ ⇒ kind ⇒ P= ...
and value_ty :: icompartment ⇒ environment ⇒ bindings
    ⇒ acontext ⇒ mode ⇒ value ⇒ typ ⇒ P= ...
and expr_ty :: icompartment ⇒ environment ⇒ bindings
    ⇒ acontext ⇒ mode ⇒ expr ⇒ typ ⇒ P= ...
```

embedded, e.g., as

```
Definition i_mutual_ty : inductive :=
  mkIndType [:: (mkIKind "wfK" ...); ... ;(mkIKind "expr_ty" ...)]
          [:: ...].
Definition iCoreTyping : icompartment := [:: ...; i_mutual_ty ].
```

In the rest of this section, we focus on expression typing and omit the details for the other mutually-recursive functions. We implement a core typechecking algorithm, an F* partial function with the following signature:

```
val etyping: i:icompartment → g:environment → b:bindings
  → a:acontext → m:mode → e:expr → t:typ
  → Partial (expr_ty i g b a m e t)
```

The definition of etyping relies on several other top-level let bindings defined in the CoreTyping module. We use an existing F# implementation of the F* typechecker to compile and verify CoreTyping. This F# typechecker is not certified, nor does it actually produce typing derivations that can be certified. Once built, we run the etyping function on (the abstract syntax of) the top-level let bindings in CoreTyping, each a value in the shared inductive type expr, including etyping itself. We print the abstract syntax of each let binding as a Coq value, corresponding to step 2 in §5. In the case of etyping, this is:

```
Definition etyping : expr := (E_Value (V_Fun ...)).
```

The function etyping applied to each let binding in CoreTyping produces a typing derivation d of type expr_ty, the reference specification of expression typing in the F* type system. Since this derivation is a value in a shared type, we print the derivation as a Coq value (step 3 of §5). For etyping, this is:

```
Definition etyping_cert :
  expr_ty iCoreTyping env [::] [::] Term_level
          etyping (T_Prod ...) := (* large certificate from F* *)
```

It is not strictly necessary to run etyping on CoreTyping to produce the certificates—any means of producing the certificate will do. However, by running a typechecked program on itself, we gain confidence that the resulting certificate will also typecheck in Coq. Indeed, once we had set up the infrastructure and typechecked a few certificates on small programs, the remaining 7 GB of certificates were typechecked in Coq slowly, but steadily. Running etyping on itself also provides a useful test of its completeness.

The certificate above provides a typing of `etyping` in a context `env`. The context includes assumptions for each top-level let binding that etyping depends on. After checking certificates for these let bindings, we compose them using a substitution lemma from the F* metatheory to obtain the following lemma, where `etyping'` is a closed term obtained by substituting each of the free variables in `etyping` with their corresponding value.

```
Lemma etyping_typing :
  coF_expr_ty iCoreTyping etyping' (T_Prod ...).
```

Next, we define an auxiliary function to abbreviate the application of `etyping'` to its embedded arguments and we show that it is well-typed by successive applications of `WFE_App`.

```
Definition embed_check_etyping i g b a m e t :=
E_App (E_App etyping' (embed_icompartment i) ...) (embed_typ t).
```

Then, we admit an instance of Theorem 4 for `expr_ty`, and use `Partial_inv` and Corollary 3 to conclude the formal proof for the main result of this paper: if the core typechecker applied to (embeddings of) the parameters of the `expr_ty` judgment returns any certificate `r`, then the judgment is valid.

THEOREM 5 (Self-certification).

```
Theorem partial_correctness_of_etyping:
  forall i g b a m e t r,
    evaluates iCoreTyping (embed_check_etyping i g b a m e t) r
  → expr_ty i g b a m e t.
```

With this theorem, the F* typechecker is emancipated from Coq. We may use etyping to check any F* source program—for instance our STLC checker—and, if it succeeds in constructing a derivation, we can be sure that this program is type-correct. We may also use it to bootstrap more sophisticated F* typecheckers. Of course, if the type system were to evolve, we would still have to conduct the metatheory of F*v2 in Coq, but, as long as the changes can still be expressed in F*, we can implement and certify F*v2 using our initial self-certified F* checker, without the need to generate and check large Coq certificates ever again.

6.2 Some technical aspects of the development

We discuss two technicalities in this section, starting with an analysis of the *P*-restriction of §4.3 and then considering the treatment of substitutions, α-conversion, and uniqueness of names.

Analyzing the *P*-restriction Using *P*-restricted types to define the F* type system gives us a convenient way (via Theorem 4) to reason about the adequacy of the specification of our core typechecker. However, the *P*-restriction also imposes some difficulties which require particular care. We have already seen in §4.2 that we cannot use function applications (like `concretekind`) in our reference system, since this falls outside the expressive power of F*'s value-dependent type system. There are also well-formed, potentially useful *P*-types in F* that are not *P*-restricted.

For example, while the basic idea of cofinite quantification can be easily expressed in value-dependent F*, an inductive type of the form shown below is not *P*-restricted, since its values contain function-typed subterms.

```
type value_ty :: _ = ...
  | WFV_Fun : x:bvar →t:typ →e:expr →L:seq pname
            →(y:vlname →NotMem (TermName y) L →expr_ty ... )
            →value_ty ... (V_Fun x t e)
```

Although such types are expressible in F*, we avoid them in our specifications for two reasons. Consider the shape of an F* typing certificate using the value above, say WFV_Fun ... (λy.e) .... To share this certificate with Coq, we must somehow translate the closure λy.e to a Coq lambda: this involves breaking the closure, inspecting its code, and printing it—in effect a form of higher-order marshalling. Further, the language of F* expressions does not correspond syntactically to the language of Coq terms: typing the body of the closure may require the use of implicit conversions and these have to translated to explicit equality-witnessing coercions in Coq, i.e., even after breaking closures, we need a type-directed translation to marshall them to Coq. The *P*-restriction conveniently sidesteps these problems. As pointed out earlier, implementing a compiler with cofinite quantification is undesirable anyway. For the few cases where we might use function types in our specification (e.g., when using negations), we rely on the correspondence between ghost refinements and reflection provided by Theorem 4.

Substitution, α-conversion, and adequacy In order to show its adequacy with regards to the cofinite system, we carefully restrict the (re-)use of names in the reference system: in particular, in any term, we require that any sequence of nested binders always bind distinct names. For instance, the value $\lambda x.\lambda x.x$ is not well-formed in our reference system.

Our core typechecker rejects such programs outright, since it relies on the F* front-end to introduce unique names. However, it must also maintain the invariant, notably as it applies substitutions. Consider typing the expression f λy:t.y in a context that binds f to the type x:(a:t →t) →y:t →t' x. All these terms meet our unique-binding requirement, but after the substitution (y:t →t' x) [(y:t →t / x)] the resulting type y:t →t' (y:t →t) binds y twice and would be rejected by the reference type system. (Such a type and substitution are usually considered well-formed, inasmuch as there is no name capture.) To prevent such instances, substitutions in our reference system are, essentially, partial functions that are undefined whenever they would produce a term that breaks our invariant. For this reason also, it is convenient to specify substitutions using inductive types (relations) rather than functions. To type the expression above, our typechecker first explicitly α-converts the type of f, renaming its bound variable y, then applies the substitution.

7. Programming and verifying the F* checker

The new self-certified typechecker, CoreTyping, is only a small part of the F* compiler. The concrete syntax of F* is parsed by modules implemented in F#, the parse tree is desugared into a minimal AST which is then typed by another, *ad hoc* source typechecker that implements various heuristics, including a form of bidirectional local type inference. This main typechecker makes calls to Z3 to prove refinement properties, and then builds a fully annotated core AST for the program, that is, a value in the shared inductive type expr. This AST is then passed to CoreTyping to build a reference typing. This section discusses the design of CoreTyping and presents several experimental aspects of the self-certification process.

7.1 The design of CoreTyping

The first difficulty in implementing CoreTyping is to make F* typing syntax-directed. We use the source typechecking pass for this: every use of subtyping and subkinding in the AST is annotated with an explicit type- or kind-ascription form, serving as an indicator to the core typechecker to apply the subtyping judgment. This simplifies core typing, but does not make it fully syntax-directed, for two reasons. First, the signature of etyping shown in the previous section is for a pure typechecking algorithm—it requires the context to provide the expected type of every subterm. Instead, we implement a function etyping_aux that computes and returns the type of an expression (relying on ascriptions etc.) with its certificate. The function etyping is simply a top-level wrapper of etyping_aux that checks that the computed type matches the type provided by the caller. A second difficulty in implementing etyping_aux is the splitting of affine contexts. The reference type system features non-deterministic context splits (as it should), but this is not directly implementable. Instead, etyping_aux implements a bottom-up computation of used affine names to provide a precise split of the affine context. The signature of etyping_aux follows:

```
val etyping_aux: i:icompartment →g:environment →b:bindings
  →a:seq bvar →m:mode →e:expr
  →(t:typ * used:seq bvar * unused:seq bvar *
     Split a used unused * expr_ty i g b used m e t)
```

This function returns a type t, a partition of the affine context a into two fragments used and unused, and a derivation for the typing of the expression e in the affine context used at the type t. Note that the default tuple constructor in F* (encoded using an inductive type of the kind $\alpha::\star \Rightarrow (\alpha \Rightarrow \star) \Rightarrow \star$) constructs types in the $\star$-universe. As such, the F* kinding rules treat etyping_aux as a partial function, without the need for an additional Partial wrapper.

Pattern matching and implicit conversions The most complex part of the typechecker deals with pattern matching. One distinctive feature of F* (as compared, say, to Coq) is its support of implicit type conversions and type refinements using equalities introduced in the context due to pattern matching. These conversions are particular convenient for programming in F*, and our core typechecker makes heavy use of them, with 196 conversions at various places. In contrast, Coq programmers must explictly apply conversions, although recent work alleviates some of this burden (Sozeau 2010).

Unification, state, and exceptions The implementation of pattern matching relies on an algorithm to find a substitution that unifies the type of the scrutinee with the type of the pattern. We implement this algorithm first in an *ad hoc* manner, by making use of recursion (without providing any termination proof), state, exceptions and the like, and in doing so compute a candidate substitution. We then implement a certification pass that builds a proof of validity for the candidate substitution. Programming in this style is convenient and is enabled by F*'s liberal support of recursion in its $\star$-fragment, but it is not particularly efficient. In the future, we hope to directly certify the substitution built by an efficient, stateful unification algorithm. We also use state and exceptions elsewhere in CoreTyping, for generating names, for performing I/O, and flagging errors; F*'s value-dependency makes it easy to cope with these features.

7.2 Engineering the certification process

As a first attempt, we simply printed the F* certificates into text files in the Coq syntax. Although the internal representation of certificates in F* is compact, their printing is rather verbose. For instance, fully printing a certificate for 6 lines of code generates a 480 MB Coq source file, which is too large to verify. Instead, we implement a fairly sophisticated, compact format that enables Coq to check all the certificates that we produce. Thankfully, we need not trust the code that prints the bulk of our certificates. As discussed in §5, we depend only on the statement of etyping_cert in Coq, but this part of the certificate is relatively small, so it can be printed verbatim and inspected manually.

Source-level splitting Our method lends itself naturally to incremental, modular verification: we generate separate certificates for each top-level let binding in the typechecker and compose these to obtain our certification result. This allows us to split our certification into 215 typing judgments. Formally, this approach is justified by the mechanized F* metatheory. Given a sequence of top-level bindings **let** $x_1 = e_1 \ldots$ **let** $x_n = e_n$, we typecheck each e_i in an environment that includes locbindings for each of $x_1 \ldots x_{i-1}$ at their certified types. Our adequacy and substitutivity theorems ensure that the closure of the final function etyping obtained by substituting each x_i with e_i is well-typed in the cofinite system.

Hash consing We share common sub-terms in certificates by hoisting them into sequences of Coq `Definitions`. (Coq also implements hash consing but does not do any memoization while type-checking, so hoisting still helps.) Aggressive hash consing may cause terms to be lifted out of their context, thereby breaking Coq inference for their implicit type arguments, so we implement a partial hash consing that keeps enough context around those terms.

Reflection A large portion of our certificates are devoted to trivial proofs of properties such as list membership and disjointness of lists. We print proofs of these properties by reflection, relying on Coq functions to show the existence of the corresponding proof terms. We rely on six such Coq functions. For example, an F* proof of NotMem x xs for some closed values substituted for x and xs may involve many nested constructors, but its Coq proof is just

```
notmemP x xs (refl_equal true)
```

relying on a simple reflection lemma:

```
Lemma notmemP :
  forall (A : eqType) (x : A) (xs : seq A),
    notmem x xs = true → NotMem x xs.
```

where `notmem x xs` is a Coq boolean function deciding if `x` is not a member of `xs`. When `x` is indeed not a member of `xs`, `notmem x xs` reduces to `true`, leading to `notmem x xs = true` being convertible to `true = true`. Hence, providing a trivial reflexivity proof (`refl_equal true`) is sufficient to have Coq check `NotMem x xs`.

Compact identifiers The default Coq representation of strings where each 8-bit character is coded as a sequence of eight booleans is inadequate for large certificates, especially as all our identifiers are coded as strings. Instead, we check certificates using a custom-built Coq version with native support for a compact representation of arrays (Armand et al. 2010).

Coq-level splitting and opacity Even after splitting, hash-consing and reflection, some certificates remain too large for Coq to handle. Our largest certificate is 214 MB. Thus, we perform another level of certificate splitting into sequences of definitions at most 10,000 lines a piece; this keeps the size of each resulting piece below 1 MB, faster for Coq to process. Coq checks one piece at a time, with all the previous pieces for the same certificate loaded as libraries. Such loading is very time- and memory-consuming, especially for large certificates. To optimize loading, subgoals of the previous parts are generated as opaque lemmas, allowing Coq to load just their types—and not their proofs—for checking the following pieces. However, all our definitions and lemmas are at the top-level. Thus, due to the transitive nature of the loading mechanism of Coq, it is not possible to load one specific subgoal of a previously checked part without loading the statements of the definitions and subgoals of all previous parts. Hence, checking a piece may spend several minutes just on loading.

7.3 Performance

CoreTyping consists of 5,139 lines of F* source code. We organize the checker into 11 modules. (Although F* has a module system that resembles F#'s, we make no essential use of it in CoreTyping, since this module system is outside the scope of our formalization.) For each module, the table below gives the number of lines of F* source code; the time taken to certify the module within F*; the number of Coq certificates generated; the time taken to print them; their total size; and, finally, the time taken to check them in Coq.

Module	LOC	tc(s)	# certs	pp(s)	size (MB)	Coq
Prims	57	4.7	16	8	5.4	3m
Util	131	0.7	9	10	9.8	6m
FiniteSet	344	3.7	30	90	71.8	1h
Terms	248	0.6	7	12	15.0	9m
Env	254	2.4	12	43	42.4	32m
FreeNames	417	14.3	12	204	197.0	3h
Binders	333	9.3	7	144	156.0	2h
Subst	482	21.1	11	232	246.0	3h
Unify	118	4.3	7	22	70.3	19m
Z3Interface	25	1.9	3	1	53.6	2m
Typing	2730	860.2	101	7641	6426.6	23d
Total	5139	15m 23s	215	2h 20m 7s	7.3GB	24d

The table begins with several smaller modules. Prims is the standard prelude for F*; Util provides auxiliary functions such as zip and map, typed with their precise specifications. FiniteSet provides sets and sequences with predicates for set membership, partition, and permutation. We use these to represent typechecking environments. Terms defines the core F* syntax, and corresponds to the inductive types for F* abstract syntax shared with Coq, i.e., kind, typ, value, expr etc. Env defines various types also shared with Coq, such as icompartment and environment. FreeNames provides functions to collect free term-level and type-level variables. Binders defines bindings of term-level and type-level variables. Subst provides both an axiomatization of type and value substitutions as an inductive predicate and functions that do the substitutions and build proofs of their predicates. Unify is used to compute the set of equalities when typing pattern matching.

Typing, the main module, contains the shared definitions of the reference type system, and implements functions that compute derivations for expression typing (etyping), value typing, subtyping, type conversion, and well-formedness checks on the environment. CoreTyping also includes a small module Z3Interface, which, for the moment, simply admits Z3 queries, since these have already been performed on the source AST. This last point is a significant limitation of our current implementation, although not a fundamental one. We plan to integrate CoreTyping with prior work on Fine and DCIL, a predecessor of F*, that extracts and type checks SMT proofs from Z3 (Chen et al. 2010), thus removing it from the TCB.

Overall, it takes the F* compiler over 15 minutes to internally produce a reference typing for the CoreTyping module. This includes the time taken by the source typechecker, the calls to Z3 that it makes, followed by the translation into the core AST, and finally the time taken for CoreTyping to typecheck itself. Compressing and printing the 7 GB of certificates takes longer—roughly 2 hours and 20 minutes. We ran this experiment on a 6 core 3.2GHz Intel Xeon workstation, with 16 GB of RAM, running Windows 7.

Checking the certificates in Coq takes much longer. To give an idea of the impact of our optimizations, we turn them off one at a time and report the checking time for a sample module (Env) on the workstation. Reflection greatly helps as we heavily rely on list properties; it also reduces certificate size by 65%. To our surprise, Coq is much faster on certificates split into smaller pieces. Opacity reduces the memory footprint but has less impact on time.

base time	−reflection	−strings	−splitting	−opacity
13m 27s	35m 4s	37m 54s	25m 23s	14m 14s

Overall, checking all certificates for CoreTyping took 24 machine-days, spread across 6 machines. Beside the workstation, we used five dual core 2.8 GHz Intel Xeon machines with 24GB of RAM running Windows 7. On all the machines we used a 64-bit build of Coq for Linux running under Oracle Virtual Box. Fortunately, with self-certification complete, we never have to export a certificate again. F* has been emancipated.

8. Conclusions

In summary, we have presented *self-certification*, a general method by which a certifying typechecker in a language of suitable expressive power can be bootstrapped into a certified typechecker. We have implemented this technique for F*, a dependently typed programming language for .NET, and relied on a formalization of the theory of F* in Coq to prove our methodology sound.

With an efficient certified typechecker in place, we aim to use it for a number of applications. Reflecting the security-oriented focus of prior work on F*, we hope to write applications that dynamically receive, load, core-typecheck, and run mobile code, possibly along the lines of code-carrying authorization (Maffeis et al. 2008). Also, in work currently underway, we use F* to build certified execution engines for various authorization logics.

We conclude with some perspective: mechanized metatheories for programming languages are gaining popularity, and rightly so. However, until now, these mechanization efforts have only served to increase the reliability of formal results, without much impact on the status of language implementations. Self-certification provides a path to build a certified core checker with an effort that compares favorably with mechanizing the metatheory in the first place. We hope other language designers will give it a try.

References

T. Acar, C. Fournet, and D. Shumow. Design and verification of a crypto-agile distributed key manager. Technical report, MSR, 2010.

A. W. Appel. Axiomatic bootstrapping: a guide for compiler hackers. *ACM TOPLAS*, 16, November 1994.

M. Armand, B. Grégoire, A. Spiwack, and L. Théry. Extending Coq with imperative features and its application to SAT verification. In *ITP*, 2010.

L. Augustsson. Cayenne: A language with dependent types. In *ICFP*, 1998.

K. Avijit, A. Datta, and R. Harper. Distributed programming with distributed authorization. In *TLDI*, 2010.

B. Aydemir, A. Charguéraud, B. C. Pierce, R. Pollack, and S. Weirich. Engineering formal metatheory. In *POPL*, 2008.

B. Barras. Sets in coq, coq in sets. *J. Formalized Reasoning*, 2010.

J. Bengtson, K. Bhargavan, C. Fournet, A. D. Gordon, and S. Maffeis. Refinement types for secure implementations. In *CSF*, 2008.

K. Bhargavan, R. Corin, P.-M. Dénielou, C. Fournet, and J. Leifer. Cryptographic protocol synthesis and verification for multiparty sessions. In *CSF*, 2009.

K. Bhargavan, C. Fournet, and A. D. Gordon. Modular verification of security protocol code by typing. In *POPL*, 2010.

C. Casinghino, H. D. Eades, G. Kimmell, V. Sjöberg, T. Sheard, A. Stump, and S. Weirich. The preliminary design of the Trellys core language. In *PLPV*, 2011.

J. Chen, R. Chugh, and N. Swamy. Type-preserving compilation of end-to-end verification of security enforcement. In *PLDI*, 2010.

A. Chlipala. A verified compiler for an impure functional language. In *POPL*, 2010a.

A. Chlipala. Ur: statically-typed metaprogramming with type-level record computation. PLDI, 2010b.

C. Colby, P. Lee, G. C. Necula, F. Blau, M. Plesko, and K. Cline. A certifying compiler for Java. In *PLDI*, 2000.

J. Davis. *A self-verifying theorem prover*. PhD thesis, U.T. Austin, 2009.

L. de Moura and N. Bjørner. Z3: An efficient SMT solver. In *TACAS*, 2008.

T. Dierks and E. Rescorla. The Transport Layer Security (TLS) Protocol Version 1.2, 2008.

T. Hart and M. Levin. The new compiler. AI Memo 39, MIT, 1962.

L. Jia, J. Vaughan, K. Mazurak, J. Zhao, L. Zarko, J. Schorr, and S. Zdancewic. Aura: A programming language for authorization and audit. In *ICFP*, 2008.

C. Keller and B. Werner. Importing HOL Light into Coq. In *ITP*, 2010.

X. Leroy. A locally nameless solution to the POPLmark challenge. Research report 6098, INRIA, Jan. 2007.

X. Leroy. The CompCert verified compiler, software and commented proof, Mar. 2011.

P. Letouzey. Coq extraction, an overview. In *LTA '08*, volume 5028 of *Lecture Notes in Computer Science*. Springer-Verlag, 2008.

S. Maffeis, M. Abadi, C. Fournet, and A. D. Gordon. Code-carrying authorization. In *ESORICS '08*, 2008.

C. McBride. Epigram: Practical programming with dependent types. In *Advanced Functional Programming School*, 2004.

G. Morrisett, D. Walker, K. Crary, and N. Glew. From System F to typed assembly language. *ACM Trans. Program. Lang. Syst.*, 21(3), 1999.

M. Moskal. Rocket-fast proof checking for SMT solvers. In *TACAS*, 2008.

M. O. Myreen and J. Davis. A verified runtime for a verified theorem prover. In *Interactive Theorem Proving*, Aug. 2011.

A. Nanevski, G. Morrisett, A. Shinnar, P. Govereau, and L. Birkedal. Ynot: dependent types for imperative programs. In *ICFP*, 2008.

U. Norell. *Towards a practical programming language based on dependent type theory.* PhD thesis, Chalmers Institute of Technology, 2007.

R. Pollack. How to believe a machine-checked proof. In G. Sambin and J. Smith, editors, *Twenty-Five Years of Constructive Type Theory*. 1998.

M. Sozeau. Equations: A dependent pattern-matching compiler. *LNCS*, 6172, 2010.

A. Stump, M. Deters, A. Petcher, T. Schiller, and T. Simpson. Verified programming in Guru. In *PLPV*, 2008.

N. Swamy, B. J. Corcoran, and M. Hicks. Fable: A language for enforcing user-defined security policies. In *S&P*, 2008.

N. Swamy, J. Chen, and R. Chugh. Enforcing stateful authorization and information flow policies in Fine. In *ESOP*, 2010.

N. Swamy, J. Chen, C. Fournet, P.-Y. Strub, K. Bhargavan, and J. Yang. Secure distributed programming with value-dependent types. In *ICFP*, Sept. 2011. See also the full paper at MSR-TR-2011-37.

The Coq Development Team. *The Coq Proof Assistant Reference Manual - Version 8.3*. INRIA, 2011. At URL `http://coq.inria.fr/`.

H. Xi. Applied type system: Extended abstract. In *Types for Proofs and Programs*, pages 394–408, 2003.